Jutta Vesper
Diplom-Dolmetscherin AIIC
Haffstrasse 12
5300 Bonn 3

D1667197

TECHNIK-WÖRTERBUCH
Geowissenschaften
Deutsch-Englisch

TECHNIK-WÖRTERBUCH

Geowissenschaften

Deutsch-Englisch

Herausgegeben von
Prof. Dr. rer. nat. Adolf Watznauer

Mit etwa 40 000 Wortstellen

3., bearbeitete Auflage

VEB VERLAG TECHNIK BERLIN

AUTOREN

Prof. Dr. *Werner Arnold*; Prof. Dr. *Horst Bachmann*; Dr. *Walter Bachmann*; Prof. Dr. *Hans-Jürgen Behr*; Ing. *Gerhard Bochmann*; Dr. *Peter Bormann*; Prof. Dr. *Klaus Dörter*; Prof. Dr. sc. *Klaus Fröhlich*; Dr. *G. Haas*; Dr. *Roland Hähne*; Prof. Dr. *Christian Hänsel*; Dr. *Christian Knothe*; Dr. sc. techn. *Hans-Jürgen Kretzschmar*; Dr. *Eberhard Künstner*; Dr. sc. *Manfred Kurze*; Dr. *Gerhard Mathé*; Prof. Dr. *Rudolf Meinhold*; Doz. Dr. *Christian Oelsner*; Dipl.-Ing. *Yadlapalli Venkateswara Rao*; Dr. sc. *Winfried Rasemann*; Geol.-Ing. *Wolfgang Reichel*; Prof. Dr. *Hans-Jürgen Rösler*; Dr. *Jörg Schneider*; Dr. *Karl-Armin Tröger*; Dr. *Richard Wäsch*

GUTACHTER

Prof. Dr. *Eberhard Kautzsch*, Dr. *Hans Prescher*, Dr. *Helmut Schmidt*

Eingetragene (registrierte) Warenzeichen sowie Gebrauchsmuster und Patente sind in diesem Wörterbuch nicht ausdrücklich gekennzeichnet. Daraus kann nicht geschlossen werden, daß die betreffenden Bezeichnungen frei sind oder frei verwendet werden können.

Geowissenschaften : dt.-engl. ; mit etwa 40000 Wortstellen / hrsg. von Adolf Watznauer. — 3., bearb. Auflage — Berlin : Verl. Technik, 1988. — 360 S. & 2 Beil.
ISBN 3-341-00538-2
NE: Watznauer, Adolf [Hrsg.]

ISBN 3-341-00538-2

3., bearbeitete Auflage
© VEB Verlag Technik, Berlin, 1988
Lizenz 201 · 370/122/88
Printed in the German Democratic Republic
Gesamtherstellung: Grafischer Großbetrieb Völkerfreundschaft Dresden
Lektor: Dipl. phil. *Gisela Rütz*
Schutzumschlag: *Kurt Beckert*
LSV 1407 · VT 4/4349-3
Bestellnummer: 553 934 1
03200

Vorwort zur dritten Auflage

Die günstige Aufnahme des Wörterbuchs für den Sektor Geowissenschaften in den angesprochenen Fachdisziplinen haben Verlag und Herausgeber bewogen, eine 3., bearbeitete Auflage vorzulegen.
Die Zahl der Wörter wurde um etwa 2000 auf 40000 erhöht. Die Erweiterung betrifft vor allem jene Wissenschaftsbereiche, deren Einfluß auf die Geowissenschaften nicht mehr übergangen werden kann. An einer Reihe von Wortstellen wurden darüber hinaus Korrekturen oder Präzisierungen vorgenommen. Die Begriffe für die Erweiterungen und Ergänzungen wurden wie bisher unmittelbar dem Schrifttum entnommen. Dem in einzelnen Fällen von der üblichen Form abweichenden Wortgebrauch durch bedeutende Autoren wurde dabei in manchen Fällen Rechnung getragen. Dies entspricht dem Charakter des Buches als dem eines „Wörter"-Buches. Eine Tendenz zur Entwicklung eines Thesaurus bzw. Begriffslexikons wurde damit nicht angestrebt. Ein solches Vorhaben ist für das Gesamtgebiet der Geowissenschaften undurchführbar.
Der Herausgeber dankt allen Fachkollegen, deren unmittelbare Mitarbeit bzw. mittelbare Hinweise zur Fertigstellung dieser Auflage wesentlich beigetragen haben. Dem Verlag gebührt vollste Anerkennung und Dank für die vertrauensvolle Zusammenarbeit.
Sachdienliche Hinweise für die weitere Verbesserung des Buches sollten wie bisher an den VEB Verlag Technik, Oranienburger Str. 13/14, Berlin, DDR-1020 gegeben werden.

Adolf Watznauer

Vorwort zur zweiten Auflage

In der vorliegenden zweiten Auflage ist der Wortschatz der ersten Auflage im wesentlichen erhalten geblieben. Die Entwicklung einzelner Untergebiete sowie die sich gegenwärtig vollziehende starke Verzahnung der Geowissenschaften mit anderen wissenschaftlichen und technischen Fachdisziplinen erforderten eine Überarbeitung und Erweiterung des erfaßten Wortschatzes. Es wurden etwa 3600 neue Stichwörter aufgenommen. Gleichzeitig wurden bei der Überarbeitung der vorhandenen Begriffe veraltete Termini herausgenommen, wobei jedoch in jenen Fällen, wo der alte Begriff noch gebräuchlich ist bzw. zum Verständnis der älteren Literatur als notwendig erscheint, dieser beibehalten wurde.
In einigen Spezialfächern sind die nomenklatorischen Diskussionen noch im Fluß. Dies betrifft vor allem die kohlenpetrografischen Begriffe. Hier wurde – insbesondere bei den Maceralen und Mikrolithotypen der Kohlen – auf das „Internationale Lexikon für Kohlenpetrologie" zurückgegriffen. Dabei wurden überwiegend die im System Stopes-Heerlen definierten Begriffe berücksichtigt. Die Schreibweise der stratigrafischen Einheiten im englischsprachigen Text bezieht sich auf die Vorschläge im „International Stratigraphic Guide (a Guide to Stratigraphic Classification, Terminology and Procedure)".
Der zweiten Auflage wurden zwei Tabellen beigefügt. Die stratigrafische Tabelle erleichtert dem Benutzer des Buches die Einordnung eines diesbezüglichen Terminus in das geologische Zeitschema. Die seismische Intensitätsskala, die Bezeichnungen der Umgangssprache verwendet, vermeidet die Hereinnahme solcher Begriffe in den Textteil bzw. deren umständliche begriffliche Definition als seismische Parameter. Von der Beigabe einer mineralogischen Tabelle wurde abgesehen, da das Mineral zweifellos im Stichwortverzeichnis unter seinem Namen gesucht wird; dagegen wurde die Schreibung des Mineralchemismus einheitlich gestaltet.
Die Ergänzungen und Veränderungen wären ohne die tätige Mithilfe zahlreicher Fachkollegen nicht möglich gewesen. Ihnen allen sei herzlichst für ihre mühevolle Arbeit gedankt, den Herren Dr. Kurze, Dr. Mathé und Dr. Schneider auch für ihre Hilfe beim Lesen der Korrekturen. Dank gebührt auch dem VEB Verlag Technik für sein verständnisvolles Eingehen auf die Wünsche des Herausgebers und der Bearbeiter.

Adolf Watznauer

Vorwort zur ersten Auflage

Mit diesem Buch liegt der deutsch-englische Teil des 1973 im gleichen Verlag erschienenen englisch-deutschen Fachwörterbuchs Geowissenschaften vor.
Aus der Notwendigkeit, ständig neue Rohstoff- und Energiequellen erschließen zu müssen, ergibt sich die steigende Bedeutung geowissenschaftlicher Forschungen. Durch die Einbeziehung des Meeresbodens z. B. oder durch die Flüge zum Mond erweitert sich das Aufgabengebiet für Geowissenschaftler ständig.
Zur Verbesserung der internationalen Kommunikation, besonders aber für Übersetzer, Dolmetscher und Dokumentalisten, soll dieser deutsch-englische Band als Hilfsmittel dienen.
Im Umfang enthält dieser Teil wiederum etwa 35000 Begriffe. Natürlich handelt es sich nicht nur um eine Umkehrung des englisch-deutschen Wortgutes, sondern die Begriffe wurden in ihrer Auswahl und in der sprachlichen Darstellung der deutsch-englischen Sprachrichtung angepaßt. So sind in den Fällen, in denen mehrere Übersetzungsmöglichkeiten vorliegen, möglichst Erklärungen gegeben worden, die dem Benutzer helfen sollen, das sinngemäß richtige Wort zu wählen. Prinzipiell verzichteten die Autoren auf Slangbegriffe in der Zielsprache. Die aus der amerikanischen Fachliteratur entnommenen Begriffe sind in der Regel nicht besonders gekennzeichnet.
Die inhaltliche Abgrenzung des Wortschatzes entspricht der des englisch-deutschen Teils. Im Mittelpunkt stehen die Kerngebiete der Geowissenschaften: Geologie im engeren Sinne, Mineralogie, Petrografie, Lagerstättenlehre sind im Umfang ihrer geologischen Aspekte berücksichtigt. Die Mineralnamen und ihre Formeln entsprechen in den meisten Fällen dem Standardwerk von *H. Strunz.* Für die Gesteinsnamen wurden die Lehrbücher von *H. Rosenbusch* herangezogen. Im Bereich der Paläontologie wurde auf die Aufführung von Gattungsnamen weitgehend verzichtet, da die Terminologie dort international ist. Die Perioden- und Stufenbezeichnungen aus der amerikanischen Systematik konnten entfallen. Randgebiete wie die physikalische Chemie, Geochemie, Geophysik, Gebirgsmechanik und Meteorologie erscheinen soweit, wie sie als Grundlage für die Hauptgebiete erforderlich sind. Das Prinzip, die praktische Anwendung der Geologie – z. B. in Verbindung mit der Lagerstättenlehre – zu betonen, wurde beibehalten. Deshalb sind eine ganze Reihe von Begriffen aus der technischen Praxis aufgenommen worden. Um den Entwicklungstendenzen gerecht zu werden, fanden auf die Geologie bezogene astronomische und astrophysikalische Termini sowie Begriffe aus der Raumfahrt Aufnahme in das Wörterbuch. Die in starker Entwicklung begriffene marine Geologie konnte nur in dem Rahmen berücksichtigt werden, in dem bereits eine exakte Begriffsbildung vorliegt. Bei späteren Nachauflagen können notwendige Ergänzungen eingearbeitet werden.
Es ist dem Herausgeber eine angenehme Pflicht, den Autoren, Herrn Dr. rer. nat. habil. *Hans-Jürgen Behr* und Herrn Dr. phil. *Walter Bachmann,* wärmstens zu danken, ebenso Prof. Dr. *Eberhard Kautzsch,* Berlin, der auf Grund einer gründlichen Durchsicht des gesamten deutsch-englischen Manuskriptes wertvolle Vorschläge zur endgültigen Fassung gegeben hat. Mein Dank gilt auch dem VEB Verlag Technik für die stets verständnisvolle Zusammenarbeit.
Hinweise, die zur Verbesserung weiterer Auflagen beitragen können, werden gern entgegengenommen und sind an den VEB Verlag Technik, DDR - 102 Berlin, Oranienburger Straße 13–14, zu richten.

Adolf Watznauer

Benutzungshinweise

1. Alphabetische Ordnung

Die Stichwörter sind alphabetisch geordnet.
Stichwörter können sein: Substantive im Nominativ, Verben im Infinitiv, Adjektive und Partizipien. Die alphabetischen Beispiele zeigen, in welcher Weise mit Zusätzen versehene Stichwörter zu „Nestern" zusammengefaßt wurden. Das Stichwort bzw. Nestwort wird innerhalb des Nestes mit einer Tilde wiedergegeben. Die natürliche Wortfolge bleibt im allgemeinen gewahrt. Haben Verb und Substantiv die gleiche Buchstabenfolge, stehen sie auch (mit dem dazugehörigen „Nest") in dieser Reihenfolge.

Einfall	Glutwolke	Lamprophyr
einfallen	~/absteigende	~/metamorpher
~/flach	~/überquellende	Lanarkit
~/steil	~/zurückfallende	Lance-Formation
Einfallen	Glyptogenese	Land
~ an Bohrkernen	Gmelinit	~/an
~ der Verwerfung	GM-Zählrohr	~/angeschwemmtes
~/entgegengesetztes	Gneis	~/bestelltes
~/flaches	~/gebänderter	~/verwehtes
einfallend	~/metatektischer	Landbedeckung
~/nach außen	~/pseudotachylitischer	Landbrücke
~/nach innen	gneisartig	landen/auf dem Mond
Einfallrichtung	Gneischarakter	Landenge

Anmerkung

Präpositionale Wendungen, d. h. Substantive mit davorstehender Präposition, stehen innerhalb des Substantivnestes. Die Umstellung der Wortfolge weist darauf hin, daß in diesem Fall das Substantiv nicht im Nominativ gebraucht wird. Mit Bindestrich gekoppelte Wörter werden wie ein zusammengeschriebenes Wort behandelt.

2. Bedeutung der Zeichen und Abkürzungen

/   gibt die Umstellung in der Wortfolge an:
      gabeln/sich = sich gabeln
      Integralgefüge/mit = mit Integralgefüge

( )   In ( ) stehende Wörter können für das unmittelbar vorhergehende Wort eingesetzt werden:
      abgeriebenes (abgerolltes) Fossil = abgeriebenes Fossil *oder* abgerolltes Fossil
      pyroclastic (tuff, ash) flow = pyroclastic flow *oder* tuff flow *oder* ash flow

[ ]   In [ ] stehende Wörter oder Wortteile können entfallen, ohne daß sich der Bedeutungsinhalt ändert:
      Prag[ium] = Prag *oder* Pragium
      Zubringer[fluß] = Zubringer *oder* Zubringerfluß
      Aalenian [Stage] = Aalenian *oder* Aalenian Stage
      hair[line] crack = hair crack *oder* hairline crack

( )   kursive Klammern enthalten Erklärungen.

s.	see/siehe verweist auf einen anderen Begriff mit gleicher Bedeutung. Wird auf einen Begriff im gleichen Nest verwiesen, so wird das Nestwort, wie üblich, abgekürzt.
s.a.	see also/siehe auch gibt einen Hinweis auf weitere Übersetzungsmöglichkeiten oder bei zusammengesetzten Begriffen darauf, daß die gesuchte Kombination unter dem Stichwort, auf das verwiesen wird, nachzuschlagen ist.
Am	Americanism/Amerikanismus

Anmerkung

Ausgenommen sind die in den mineralogischen Formeln auftretenden ( ) und [ ] Klammern.

3. Allgemeine Hinweise

In der Regel wurde bei unterschiedlicher englischer und amerikanischer Schreibung die englische Version gewählt. Wenn allerdings Fachbegriffe nur in der amerikanischen Literatur belegt sind, wurde auch die dort verwendete Schreibung übernommen.
Im Deutschen steht die f-Schreibung bei -foto- und -graf- und die i-Schreibung bei Oxid.
Kursiv gesetzt sind erklärende Hinweise (sie stehen in Klammern) und Umschreibungen des Bedeutungsinhaltes von deutschen Stichwörtern, für die keine einfache englische Entsprechung gefunden wurde.
Bedeutungsunterschiede werden wie folgt angegeben:

,	trennt inhaltsgleiche Begriffe
;	trennt Bedeutungsvarianten
1.; 2.	trennt Homonyme oder stark voneinander abweichende Bedeutungsvarianten.

A

a-Achse f a-axis
Aa-Lava f Aa lava
Aalen[ium] n Aalenian [Stage] *(lower Dogger)*
AAS s. Atomabsorptionsspektrometrie
Aasbydiabas m Aasby diabase
Aasfresser m carrion eater (feeder), scavenger, scavenging animal
abändern to alter
Abänderung f alteration
Abart f variety; varietal form
abätzen to corrode off
Abbau m 1. mining; exploitation, carrying; extracting, extraction; cutting, winning; 2. decay *(of radioactive substances)*; 3. decomposition *(of chemical and biological substances)*
~ **des Flözes in voller Mächtigkeit** full-seam extraction
~/**harmonischer** harmonic system of working
~ **im Ausbiß einer Lagerstätte** level-free workings
~ **in regelmäßigen Abständen** open stope with pillar
~ **mit Bergeversatz** mining with filling
~ **mit Druckwasser** hydraulic mining
~ **mit Schappe** auger mining
~ **mit Versatz** stowing exploitation
~/**stufenweiser** benching work[ing] *(above ground)*
~/**thermischer** thermal degradation
~/**unsystematischer** gouge
~ **unter Tage** underground stoping
~/**unterseeischer** undersea mining
~/**völliger** exhaustion
~/**vollständiger** complete extraction
~/**vom Ausstrich ansetzender** patching
~ **vom bloßgelegten Ausbiß** strip mining
~ **von Goldquarzgängen** reefing
Abbauablauf m mining sequence
Abbaubedingungen fpl mining conditions
Abbaubemusterung f mining sampling
Abbaubetrieb m working
Abbaudistrikt m mining district
Abbaudynamik f strata movement
abbauen to mine; to exploit, to work, to extract; to cut, to win, to break
~/**die Reicherzpartien** to gut
~/**einen Strossenstoß** to stope underhand
~/**im Firstenbau** to stope overhand
~/**planlos** to gopher
~/**völlig** to exhaust
Abbauen n s. Abbau
abbaufähig minable, workable, recoverable
Abbaufähigkeit f minability, workability
Abbaufeld n field, district, set
~/**unverritztes** maiden field
Abbauförderstrecke f haulage road
Abbaufortschritt m face advance, rate of advance, progress of mining
Abbaugebiet n mining region
Abbaugeschichte f *(Am)* pressure-production history

Abblätterung

Abbaugeschwindigkeitswert m index of mining intensity
Abbauhorizont m mining horizon
Abbaukante f pillar edge, rib
Abbaukosten pl cost of exploitation
Abbaumethode f exploitation method
Abbauort n stope
Abbauplan m mine layout
Abbauraum m face working space
Abbaurecht n mineral right
Abbaurichtung f direction of mining (advance)
Abbauriß m break
~ **im Hangenden** roof break
~ **im Liegenden** floor break
Abbauscheibe f/**obere** topmost slice
Abbauschwerpunkt m focal point of working
Abbausohle f horizon, [working] level, mining (working) floor
Abbaustoß m 1. face *(mining)*; 2. highwall *(open cut)*; 3. buttock *(buttock machine)*
Abbaustrecke f board, *(Am)* entry; gate road; driftway
~ **parallel zu den Schlechten** butt (side) entry
~ **senkrecht zu den Schlechten** face entry
Abbauteufe f depth of mining
~/**sichere** secure exploitation deepness (depth)
Abbautrichter m glory hole
abbauunwürdig inexploitable, unworkable, unprofitable
Abbauverfahren n mining method
Abbauverlauf m reservoir performance *(oil and gas)*
Abbauvorfeld n s. Vorfeld
Abbauvorgang m mining operation
abbauwürdig s. bauwürdig
Abbauwürdigkeit f s. Bauwürdigkeit
Abbauwürdigkeitsgrenze f s. Bauwürdigkeitsgrenze
abbiegen to warp down[ward]
Abbiegen n **eines Gebirgsrückens/scharfes** linkage
Abbiegung f deflection; downwarp, [downward] flexure, downward bowing
Abbild n image
Abbildungsantiklinale f/**sedimentäre** false anticline
Abbildungskristallisation f mimetic (facsimile) crystallization
Abbildungsmaßstab m image scale
Abbildungssystem n **aus Festkörperdetektoren** solid-state imaging system
Abbindebeschleuniger m accelerating agent, accelerator
Abbindeverzögerer m retarding agent, retarder
Abblasung f deflation[al erosion], wind corrasion
abblättern to exfoliate, to flake off, to peel off, to spall, to desquamate
Abblättern n s. Abblätterung
Abblätterung f exfoliation, flaking[-off], peeling[-off], scaling, desquamation

Abblätterung

~/zwiebelschalige onion-skin exfoliation
Abblätterungsdom m exfoliation dome
Abblätterungsfläche f exfoliation plane
Abblätterungsform f exfoliation form
abbohren to bore sound
Abbohren n/**dichtes** close boring
~ **einer ihrer Begrenzung nach bereits bekannten Erdöllagerstätte** inside pool drilling
abböschen to degrade, to scarp, to slant
~/**steil** to slope steeply
Abböschung f inclination; slanting, sloping, flattening
abbrechen to spall
~/**über sich** to stope (magma)
Abbrechen n 1. fall (of rock); 2. dismantling (of boring)
abbröckeln to peel off
Abbröckelung f **einer Böschung** slipping of a slope
Abbröckelungsglutwolke f avalanche of domal disintegration
Abbruch m 1. spalling; 2. broken-down bank (of a shore)
Abbruchfehler m truncation effect
Abbruchstufen fpl breakages
Abbruchzone f faulted zone
abdachen/sich to slant down
Abdachung f slope; ramp; scarp; shelvingness
~/**flache** glacis
~/**unterseeische** marine bench; seascarp
Abdachungstal n consequent valley
abdämmen to dam up (out, in)
Abdämmung f damming[-off]
Abdämmungssee m barrier lake
Abdampfen n boiling-down
Abdampfrückstand m residue on evaporation
abdecken to reveal
Abdeckung f revelation
Abdeckverfahren n/**seismisches** seismic stripping
Abdeichung f construction of levees
abdichten to seal [up]; to plug, to mud off, to clench; to make watertight, to coffer
Abdichten n packing
~ **eines Grundwasserleiters** aquifer packing
Abdichtung f 1. seal; sealing-up (of a hole); plugging; 2. damp-proofing
Abdichtungsgraben m cut-off trench
Abdichtungsschleier m grouted cut-off
Abdruck m impression, [im]print, [external] mould, external cast
ab-Ebene f ab-plane, displacement plane
Abenddämmerung f twilight
Abendröte f sunset colours
Aberration f 1. aberration; 2. aberration, malformation (palaeontology)
~/**tägliche** diurnal aberration
Abessinierbrunnen m Abyssinian well
Abessinierpumpe f Abyssinian pump
abfackeln to burn off
~/**Gas** to flare gas
Abfall m 1. waste, deads; scrap; 2. drop, fall, decline

~ **des Lagerstättendrucks/stetiger** steady pressure decline in the reservoir
~/**radioaktiver** radioactive waste
~/**steiler** steep fall
Abfallauge f waste brine
abfallen to slope [away]
abfallend sloping, shelving
~/**steil** steeply sloping
Abfallerz n tailings
Abfallhalde f waste heap
Abfallkohle f waste coal
Abfallprodukt n by-product
Abfallstücke npl bats
abfangen 1. to resist (the pressure); 2. to hold (a layer); 3. to capture
~/**eine ausbrechende Sonde durch Richtbohrung** to intercept a blowing well
Abfangen n 1. resistance (of pressure); 2. holding (of a layer); 3. admittance, capture, admission
Abfangkeil m power slip
abflachen to flatten
Abflachen n flattening
abfließen to flow off, to drain off
Abfluß m outflow, outlet, discharge, runoff; effluent
~/**direkter** direct runoff
~ **durch Aussickerung** seepage flow
~/**hypodermischer** interflow (flows directly from the unsaturated soil to the river)
~/**jahreszeitlicher** seasonal runoff
~/**jährlicher** annual runoff
~/**oberirdischer** surface runoff; overland flow
~/**regulierter** sustained runoff; regulated flow
~/**unterirdischer** subsurface runoff (discharge); underground flow
~/**veränderlicher** varied flow
Abflußbecken n drainage basin
Abflußbedingung f runoff factor
~/**morphologische** physiographic factor affecting runoff
Abflußbeiwert m coefficient of discharge (runoff); drainage ratio
Abflußbeobachtung f stream gauging
Abflußdefizit n flow deficit
Abflußfaktor m s. Abflußbeiwert
Abflußfläche f discharge area
Abflußgang m unit hydrograph (variability of river runoff)
Abflußganglinie f discharge-frequency curve, runoff hydrograph
Abflußgebiet n hydrographic[al] area; drainage area, catchment area (basin)
Abflußgeschehen n runoff phenomena; flow regime (summarized factors of runoff)
Abflußgeschwindigkeit f velocity of discharge
Abflußgesetz n outflow law
Abflußgraben m s. Abflußkanal
Abflußgröße f drainage large
Abflußhöhe f 1. depth of runoff; 2. amount of runoff
Abflußkanal m drain channel, catch drain; side channel; effluent channel

Abflußkerbe f outlet notch
Abflußkoeffizient m s. Abflußbeiwert
Abflußkurve f discharge curve
abflußlos without outlet
Abflußlosigkeit f internal drainage
Abflußmenge f flow, [rate of] discharge, delivery, runoff, efflux
~ **des Niederschlags** rainfall excess
~ **eines Wasserlaufs** stream (river) discharge
~/**jährliche** yearly discharge
Abflußmengenkurve f discharge hydrograph, hydrograph [curve of discharges]
Abflußmengenmessung f flow gauging; flow record
Abflußmesser m flow gauge
Abflußmeßstelle f gauging station
Abflußöffnung f overfall discharge
Abflußregulierung f stream-flow control
Abflußrinne f drainage channel (course, way), [drainage] furrow, runoff rill, scourway
Abflußschwankung f stream frequency
Abflußschwankungskoeffizient m factor of outflow variation
Abflußseparation f separation of flow (components of stream-flow), base-flow separation (separation of subsurface and surface runoff)
Abflußspende f yield factor, runoff modulus
Abflußverzögerung f durch Vegetation vegetal retardance (hydrology)
Abflußvorgang m runoff process
Abflußzone f zone of discharge
Abfolge f sequence, succession
~/**paragenetische** paragenetic succession
~/**zyklische** cyclic succession
Abformung f mould
abfrieren to freeze off
Abführkanal m outlet channel
Abgabe f **von Dämpfen** emission of steam (volcano)
Abgabeverlust m delivery loss (of an used aquifer)
Abgabevermögen n yield capacity (of an aquifer)
Abgänge mpl tailings, debris, discard
~ **bei hydraulischem Abbau** mining debris
Abgangspunkt m take-off point (of a seismic ray from the refractor)
abgebaut gotten, worked out
~/**nicht** unmined
abgebogen downflexed
abgeböscht scarped
ab-Gefügeebene f s. ab-Ebene
abgekantet subrounded
abgekehrt/dem Winde leeward
abgelagert/äolisch wind-deposited
~/**in Schmelzwasserseen** glaciolacustrine
~/**in schnellfließendem Wasser** torrent-laid
~/**unter Wasser** phenhydrous
abgeplattet oblate, flattened, flattish
abgerundet rounded
abgeschlossen/durch eine Nehrung bar-enclosed

abgeschmolzen melted away
abgeschrägt bevelled
abgeschwemmt truncated
abgesetzt dumped
Abgesiebtes n siftings
abgestuft/gut well graded
abgestumpft smooth[ed], truncated (crystals)
abgesunken/in Staffelbrüchen tangentially sliced
abgetragen graded; weathered; worn; truncated
abgewinnen/dem Meer Land to reclaim land from the sea
abgewittert weathered away
Abgleiten n downslide motion, slippage, decollement, decollation
~ **infolge Schwerkrafteinwirkung** gravitational sliding (slip)
~/**subaquatisches** subaqueous gliding (slumping)
Abgleitfläche f downslide level, surface of subsidence
Abgleitung f s. Abgleiten
Abgrenzung f delimitation
~ **von Gletscherverbreitungsräumen** glaposition
Abgrenzungsbohrloch n determining borehole
Abgrund m abyss, abysm, chasm, precipice
abgründig abyssal, abysmal
Abguß m cast, mould
~/**erhabener** cast-in relief, relief mould
Abhang m hillside, flank of hill; slope, decline, declivity, scarp, shelving, slant
~ **eines Gebirgszugs** versant
~ **eines Tiefseegrabens/kontinentseitiger** landward slope of trench
~/**stufenförmiger** stepped (steplike) profile
~/**unterseeischer** marine bench; seascarp
~/**windabseitiger** leeward slope
~/**windseitiger** windward slope
Abhängigkeitszone f domain of dependence
Abhangprofil n/**aufwärts gerichtetes** uphill sloping profile
abhauen to knock off
~/**splitterweise** to splinter
Abhauen n dip heading
Abhebung f ablation
abhobeln to plane [down]; to planate
Abhobelung f planing down; planation
abholzen to deforest
Abholzung f deforestation
Abioglyphe f abioglyph
abkanten to chamfer
Abkanten n chamfering
Abkehrfluß m obsequent river
abkippen to tip up
abklären to clarify
abklingen to fade
Abklingzeit f decay time
abklopfen to sound
Abkömmling m off-spring, descendant, branch

abkühlen

abkühlen to cool; to chill
Abkühlung f cooling[-down]; chilling
Abkühlungsfläche f cooling surface
Abkühlungsgeschwindigkeit f cooling rate
Abkühlungskluft f joint due to cooling
Abkühlungskonstante f cooling constant
Abkühlungsspalte f cooling crack (fissure)
Ablagerbecken n settling basin
ablagern to deposit, to sedimentate, to settle, to aggrade, to lay down
~/**sich** to lodge
~/**wieder** to redeposit
Ablagerung f deposition, laying-down, sedimentation, settling; deposit, sediment, alluviation (s.a. Sedimentation)
~/**allochthone** allochthonous deposit
~/**alluviale** geest, wash
~ **am Eisrand** ice-margin deposit
~ **am Kontinentalabhang** Aktian deposit
~/**äolische** aeolic deposit, wind[-laid] deposit
~/**äquivalente** homotaxial deposit
~ **arider Schuttwannen** red beds
~ **auf dem Schelf** topset
~/**autochthone** autochthonous deposit
~/**bathyale** bathyal (abyssal, deep-sea) deposit
~/**detritische** detrital deposit
~/**eisenhaltige** ochreous deposit
~/**eiszeitliche** cover of glacial till
~/**eupelagische** eupelagic (thalassic, oceanic) deposit
~/**fluvioglaziale** fluvioglacial deposit
~/**glaziale** glacial deposit
~/**gleichaltrige** synchronous deposit
~/**gleichzeitig entstandene** contemporaneous deposition
~/**gleichzeitige** cosedimentation
~/**goldhaltige** auriferous deposit
~/**grobe fluviatile** lag deposit
~/**hemipelagische** hemipelagic deposit
~/**heteromesische** heteromesical deposit
~/**heterotopische** heterotopic[al] deposit
~/**heutige** recent formation
~/**homotaxe** homotaxial deposit
~/**humitische** humic deposit
~/**interglaziale** interglacial deposit
~/**jahreszeitlich bedingte** seasonal deposit
~/**kieselige** siliceous deposit
~/**kontinentale** land sediment, terrestrial deposit
~/**küstenferne** offshore deposit
~/**küstennahe** near-shore deposit
~/**lakustroglaziale** glaciolacustrine deposit
~/**mächtige** thick deposit
~/**ozeanische** oceanic deposit
~/**paralische** paralic deposit
~/**pelagische** pelagic deposit
~/**rhythmische** rhythmic sedimentation
~/**salzige** saline lick
~/**strandnahe** near-shore sediment
~ **terrestrischer Herkunft** earthformed sediment
~/**terrigene** terrigenous deposit
~/**ungleichaltrige** asynchronous (heterotaxial) deposit
~/**verdeckte** shielded deposition
~ **von Material aus heißen Quellen** hot-spring deposit
~/**warmzeitliche** interglacial deposit
Ablagerungsart f kind of deposition
Ablagerungsbecken n depositional (decantation) basin, basin of deposition
Ablagerungsbedingungen fpl depositional factors
Ablagerungsfläche f deposition (bedding, stratification) plane
Ablagerungsgebiet n deposition area
Ablagerungsgeschwindigkeit f depositional rate
Ablagerungsgürtel m belt of deposition
Ablagerungsmedium n depositing medium
Ablagerungsmilieu n depositional environment
Ablagerungsmodell n depositional model
Ablagerungsmuster n depositional pattern
Ablagerungsplätze mpl depositories
Ablagerungsraum m s. Ablagerungsfläche
Ablagerungsstelle f deposition place, site of deposition
ablandig offshore
ablassen to discharge, to drain off
~/**Druck** to release pressure, to blow down pressure, to bleed [off] pressure
Ablation f ablation
~/**äolische** deflation
~/**geschiebeablagernde** wastage
Ablationsfläche f ablation area, dissipator
Ablationsform f ablation form
~/**pflugscharartige** ploughshare
Ablationsgebiet n ablation area
Ablationsrückstand m wastage
Ablationswärme f heat of ablation
Ablauf m discharge
Ablaufgraben m, **Ablaufkanal** m tailrace
Ablauge f waste brine
Ablaugung f subrosion
Ablaugungsebene f salt table
Ablaugungslösung f subrosion solution
Ablaugungssole f brine leachate
Ableitung f derivative (of a potential field)
~ **von unterirdischem Wasser** ground draining
Ableitungskanal m open channel; outlet
Ableitungsstollen m tail race tunnel
ablenken to deflect; to divert; to deviate; to side-track (a bore)
Ablenken n turn (s.a. Ablenkung)
Ablenkkeil m whipstock (at a bore)
Ablenkung f deflection; diversion (of a river); deviation; side-tracking (of a bore)
~ **des Bohrlochs** intentional deviation of the hole
Ablenkungsbohrgarnitur f bottom assembly for side-tracking operations
Ablenkungsknie n elbow of capture

Ablenkungswinkel *m* deflection angle; drift angle *(of the borehole)*; angle of setting *(of the whipstock)*
Ablenkwerkzeug *n* kick-off tool
Ablesefehler *m* observation error
Ablesegenauigkeit *f* reading accuracy, precision of reading
Ablesewert *m* reading
Ablesung *f* reading
Ablösefähigkeit *f* jointing
ablösen to detach
Ablösen *n* detachment (s.a. Ablösung); backcleat *(mining)*; hole sloughing *(borehole)*
Ablösung *f* detachment
~ **der Schichten** bed separation
~ **des Gebirges** slacking of the walls
~ **des Gebirges an der Firste** sluffing
~/**glatte, lettige** soapy back
~/**schalenförmige** scaling; flakes
Ablösungsfläche *f* cleat [plane]
abloten/den Grund to sound the ground
Ablykit *m* ablykite *(clay mineral)*
Abmessen *n* mensuration
abnehmen 1. to decrease, to drop; 2. to wane *(moon)*
Abnehmen *n* 1. decreasing, dropping; 2. waning *(of the moon)*
abnormal abnorm[al]
Abnormalität *f* abnormality
Abnutzung *f* wear; abrasion
Abnutzwiderstand *m* resistance to abrasion
aboral aboral
abplatten to flatten
Abplattung *f* flattening; flatness, oblateness
~ **an den Polen** polar flattening
~ **der Erde** flattening of the earth
Abplattungsindex *m* flattening index
Abplattungswulst *m*/**äquatorialer** equatorial bulge
abplatzen to peel off, to flake, to spall
Abplatzen *n* peeling-off, flaking
abpressen to squeeze out
Abpressen *n* squeezing-out
Abpressungsfiltration *f* filtration pressing
abquetschen to squeeze off
abradieren to abrade
abrammen to ram
Abrammen *n* ramming; beating
Abrasion *f* abrasion; attrition; degradation
~/**glaziale** glacial abrasion
Abrasionsbucht *f* corrosion embayment
Abrasionsebene *f*, **Abrasionsfläche** *f* abrasion plain, plain of abrasion (denudation), level of abrasion
~/**marine** plain of marine abrasion (denudation)
Abrasionsküste *f* shore line of retrogradation
Abrasions-pH-Wert *m* abrasion-pH
Abrasionsplatte *f*, **Abrasionsplattform** *f* abrasion (wave-cut) platform, wave-cut terrace
~/**gehobene** elevated wave-cut terrace
Abrasionsrate *f* attrition rate

Abrasionsterrasse *f* s. Abrasionsplatte
abrasiv abrasive
Abrasivität *f* abrasiveness; rock abrasive property
Abraum *m* earth roof, uncallow, overburden, globbing, barren rock, overlay shelf, stripping *(mining)*; waste, rubbish, rubble *(of an open cut)*; trash *(of ore dressing)*; spoil *(e.g. of a channel)*
~ **über einer Seife** leading
Abraumbagger *m* overburden dredger
Abraumbeseitigung *f* removal of debris (overburden)
abräumen to strip [away, off]; to discard; to clean *(in the quarry)*; to bar down *(off)*
Abräumen *n* **des Deckgebirges** overburden removing, baring
Abraumförderbrücke *f* conveying bridge for open cuts
Abraumgebirge *n* overburden
Abraumgestein *n* callow
Abraumhalde *f*, **Abraumkippe** *f* waste pile, overburden (mine, spoil) dump, spoil bank
Abraum-Kohle-Verhältnis *n* stripping ratio
Abraumsalz *n* waste salt, abraum [salt]; saline deposit
abreißen to break *(glacier)*; to detach *(current)*
Abreißen *n* break *(of a glacier)*; detachment *(of the current)*
Abrieb *m* abrasion; attrition; degradation
Abriebfestigkeit *f* abrasion strength
Abriß *m* 1. [roof] break; 2. time (shot) break *(seismics)*
Abrißgebiet *n* parent lodge *(rock slide)*
Abrißnische *f* scarf, landslide scar
Abrißpunkt *m*, **Abrißstelle** *f* bench mark, head *(of a landslide)*
Abrundungskoeffizient *m* roundness index
Abrutsch *m* slide
abrutschen/nach hinten to tailslide
~/**seitlich** to sideslip
Abrutschen *n* bedding slippage
~/**einseitiges** cant
absacken to sag [downward]
absanden to sand
Absanden *n*, **Absandung** *f* sanding, sand spreading *(dressing)*
Absarokit *m* absarokite *(alkali effusive rock)*
Absatz *m* 1. bench, terrace; nip; step; scarplet; 2. deposit[ion]
Absatzboden *m* colluvial (transported) soil
Absatzgestein *n* s. Sedimentgestein
absätzig intermittent; interrupted
Abschalung *f* sheeting
abscheiden to separate, to precipitate, to deposit
~/**sich** to separate out
Abscheidung *f* separation, precipitation, deposition; deposit
abscheren to shear
Abscherfestigkeit *f* s. Scherfestigkeit
Abscherkörper *m* dislodged slice

Abscherkraft

Abscherkraft f s. Scherfestigkeit
Abscherung f shear[ing]; detachment; decollement (of sediments)
~/verzögerte lag fault
Abscherungsdecke f shear (scission) thrust sheet, shearing (overthrust) nappe
Abscherungsstruktur f shear (decollement) structure
Abscherungstheorie f shearing theory (glacial theory)
Abscherungsüberschiebung f shear thrust
abscheuern to wear, to abrade, to chafe away; to scour [off]
Abscheuerung f wear, abrasion, chafing
Abschiebung f downthrown (tension, gravity, dip-slip) fault
Abschieferung f exfoliation
Abschießen n/stufenweises bending shooting
Abschirmelektrode f guard electrode
Abschirmung f/magnetische magnetic shielding (screening)
abschlämmen to elutriate, to clean
Abschlämmung f elutriation, levigation
~ des Bodens soil separation in layers
abschleifen to wear, to abrade, to corrade; to grind [down], to scour; to polish
Abschleifung f wearing, abrasion, attrition; grinding, scouring; polishing
Abschließung f closing (of an arm of the sea)
Abschlußdokument n über durchgeführte geologische Untersuchungsarbeiten deed of surrender of geological prospecting works
Abschlußfehler m closing error (surveying)
Abschlußfläche f end plane
Abschlußwiderstand m terminal resistance
abschmelzen to melt [away], to waste [away]
Abschmelzen n melting
Abschmelzgebiet n region of melting
abschneiden to cut off
Abschnitt m intercept (of crystals)
~/geradliniger straight-line portion (of pressure build-up curve)
abschrägen to bevel [off]; to chamfer; to slope
Abschrägen n bevel[ling]; chamfering
Abschrägung f slope
Abschrauben n/ungewolltes unintentional unscrewing (of the drill pipe or casing)
abschrecken to chill, to quench
Abschreckung f chilling, quenching
abschuppen to desquamate; to peel off
Abschuppung f desquamation; peeling[-off]
~/schalenförmige exfoliation
abschüssig declivate, decliv[it]ous, acclivous, sloping, sloped, aslope, slanting
Abschüssigkeit f declivity, steepness
Abschwächen n muting (of seismic signals)
Abschwächung f fade, fading; suppression
abschwelen to carbonize under vacuum at a low temperature
abschwemmen to wash away, to elutriate, to erode, to float off

Abschwemmung f durch Regen rainwash
absenken 1. to lower; 2. to settle (rock)
~/den Grundwasserspiegel to lower the water table
Absenken n s. Absenkung
Absenkung f 1. lowering; 2. settling (of a rock); downthrown fault; downwarp; subsidence; 3. drawdown component (hydrology)
~ der Firste swag
~ des Grundwasserspiegels lowering of the water table, drawdown
~ des Hangenden roof subsidence
~ durch Lösung solution subsidence
~/gleichmäßige regular subsidence
~/kapillare capillary depression
~/planmäßige planned subsidence
~/plötzliche sudden drawdown
Absenkungsbereich m range of depression (of a well)
Absenkungseffekt m lowering effect (ground water)
Absenkungsfaktor m subsidence factor, percentage subsidence
Absenkungsgeschwindigkeit f settling speed
Absenkungskurve f lowering (hydraulic gradient) curve (of ground water)
Absenkungsreichweite f radius of influence of depression (of a well)
Absenkungsschwerpunkt m focal point of subsidence
Absenkungsstadium n lowering stage (of ground water)
Absenkungstrichter m depression funnel, cone of depression
Absenkungszeit f lowering time
Absenkungszone f subsiding area
Absetzbecken n precipitation tank, decantation basin
~ für aussetzenden Betrieb, ~ mit ruhendem Abwasser absolute-rest precipitation tank (boring technique)
Absetzbehälter m mud settling trap pit (of a well boring)
absetzen 1. to settle, to deposit, to decant; 2. to abut against (layer)
~/Rohrfahrt to set casing
~/sich to settle, to deposit, to decant
~/Verrohrung to land casing
~/wieder to redeposit (by water)
Absetzen n abutment (of a layer)
~ von Schichten offset of beds (strata)
Absetzgeschwindigkeit f settling velocity
Absetzteich m settling pond
Absetzteufe f landing depth (of the casing)
absieben to sift
absinken 1. to sink down, to settle down[ward], to undergo subsidence (layer); 2. to suffer depression (meteorological)
Absinken n settling, [down]sinking, subsidence, downwedging, foundering
~/gravitatives gravity sinking
Absonderung f detachment; jointing; parting

~/bank[förm]ige sheet (bedded) jointing, slab (sheet) structure
~/brotlaibartige loaflike jointing
~/kissenförmige pillow structure
~/konzentrischschalige concentric[al] jointing
~/kugelige (kugelschalige) ball structure [parting], spheroidal jointing (parting)
~/parallelepipedische parallel-epipedal structure, mural jointing
~/plattenförmige slab jointing, platy parting
~/plattige tabular jointing, tabular structure
~/polyedrische polyhedric parting
~/prismatische prismatic jointing
~/quaderförmige mural jointing
~/säulenförmige columnar jointing; basaltic jointing (structure)
~/schalige peeling[-off]
~/unregelmäßige polyhedric parting
~/zwiebelschalige concentric[al] jointing
Absonderungsfläche f plane of division, parting, joint sheet
Absonderungsfuge f line of cleavage
Absonderungskluft f diaclase
Absonderungsklüftung f s. Absonderung
Absorbierbarkeit f absorbability
absorbieren to absorb
Absorption f absorption
~/atmosphärische atmospheric absorption
Absorptionsanlage f absorption plant (for crude oil)
Absorptionsfähigkeit f s. Absorptionsvermögen
Absorptionsfiguren fpl epoptic figures (optical)
Absorptionsflammenfotometrie f absorption flame photometry
Absorptionskoeffizient m absorption coefficient
Absorptionsmittel n absorbent
Absorptionsspektrum n absorption (dark-line) spectrum
Absorptionsturm m absorber
Absorptionsvermögen n absorptivity, absorptance, absorbency, absorbing power
Absorptionswasser n absorbed water
abspalten to wedge off; to spall (stone); to cleave (crystal)
Abspaltung f spalling (of stones); cleavage (of crystals)
Abspannseile npl guy lines
absperren/eine Förderbohrung to close (shut) a well
Absperren n einer Fördersonde close-in operation of a well
Absperrung f damming[-off]
Absperrventil n blow-out valve
Abspielung f playback (geophysics)
absprengen to spring, to burst, to strike off; to blow up (with powder); to blast (mine)
abspülen to wash [down]; to erode
Abspülung f downwash, washing-off; erosion
~/flächenhafte sheet flood

abstammen to descend
Abstammung f descent, descendance
Abstammungslehre f theory of descent
Abstand m distance, spacing, span; offset (seismics)
~ der Bohrlöcher well spacing
~ der Kristallebenen interplanar [crystal] spacing
~/lichter clear distance
~/seitlicher broadside offset
~ vom Schußpunkt shot point gap, [in-line, broadside] offset
~ zweier Trendflächen/taxonomischer taxonomic distance of trend-surfaces
abstandsgleich equidistant
Abstandsgleiche f isopleth
abstandstreu equidistant
Abstauchungsdecke f thrust plate
abstecken to stake out
Absteckpfahl m surveying rod
Absteckungslinie f alignment
absteigend descending; katabatic (current of air)
Abstellen n der Gestängezüge stacking of drill pipe stands
Abstelloch n für das Kelly rathole
abstoßen 1. to repel; 2. to abut against (a layer)
Abstoßlösung f barren solution
Abstoßungsexponent m/**Bornscher** Born's exponent of repulsion
abstreifen to strip
Abströmgeschwindigkeit f downwash velocity
abstrossen to mine by banks, to work by coffins
abstufen 1. to step; 2. to grade
Abstufung f 1. stepping; 2. gradation
~/diskontinuierliche gap grading (of grains)
Abstufungsschichtung f graded bedding
abstumpfen to truncate (crystals)
Abstumpfung f truncation (of crystals)
Absturz m precipice
~ im Krater intercrateral avalanche
Absturzhalde f dump[ing ground]
Abstützen n des Gesteins supporting of the rock
Abtastfunktion f sampling function
Abtastintervall n sample period
Abtastlinie f, **Abtastzeile** f scan line
Abtauchen n plunge, pitch (e.g. of folds)
~ mit inverser Schichtung inverted plunge
Abtauphase f thawing-off phase (of ice age)
Abteilung f s. Serie 1.; Hauptgruppe
Abteufarbeit f sinking work
abteufen to sink, to deepen, to carry down
~/eine Bohrung to sink a well
~/einen Schacht to sink a shaft
Abteufen n sinking, deepening
~ einer Bohrung drilling (deepening) of a well
~ von Gefrierschächten freezing shaft sinking
Abtorfen n cutting of peat
Abtrag m von Rutschungsmassen slide-correction excavation

abtragen

abtragen to remove; to abrade; to erode; to denude; to degrade; to wear [down, away]; to strip; to truncate; to work away *(by men)*
Abtragen *n* **des Abraums** encallowing
Abtraghöhe *f* digging height
Abtragsböschung *f* slope of embankment (cutting)
Abtragung *f* removal; abrasion; erosion *(s.a.* Erosion); denudation *(s.a.* Denudation); degradation; wearing away (down); stripping; truncation
~/flächenhafte areal degradation
~/glaziale glacial erosion
~/untermeerische submarine erosion
Abtragungsbetrag *m* amount of erosion
Abtragungsebene *f* plain of degradation (erosion)
Abtragungsform *f* erosional form
Abtragungsgebiet *n* region of denudation, area of truncation, oldland
Abtragungsgebirge *n* mountain of erosion
Abtragungskräfte *fpl* agents of denudation
Abtragungsküste *f* abrasion coast (embayment)
Abtragungsniveau *n* denudation level
Abtragungsoberfläche *f* erosion (gradational) surface
Abtragungsprozeß *m* process of erosion
Abtragungsstufe *f* cuesta
Abtragungsterrasse *f* erosional (denudation) terrace
Abtransport *m* removal
abtransportieren to remove
abtrennen to detach
Abtrennung *f* detachment
Abtreppen *n* benching
Abtrift *f* drift[ing]
Abukuma-Typ *m* Abukuma type *(metamorphism)*
Abundanz *f* abundance
abwandern to move
Abwärtsbewegung *f* downstroke
Abwärtsdruck *m* downward pressure
Abwasser *n* waste (residual, foul, used) water, sewage [water]
~/radioaktives radioactive water
Abwässer *npl* sewage, sullage
Abwasserbeseitigung *f* effluent disposal
Abwasserbohrung *f* water disposal well
Abwasserwesen *n* sewage engineering, sewerage and sewage disposal
Abwehung *f* deflation
Abwehungsbecken *n* deflation basin
Abwehungstal *n* deflation valley
Abweichung *f* aberration; deviation; departure; anomaly; variation
~ der Bohrung unintentional deviation of the hole; kick-out
~ der Magnetnadel aberration of the magnetic needle
~/magnetische magnetic declination
Abweichungseffekt *m* **vom Darcy-Gesetz** non-Darcy effect

Abweichungsmeßgerät *n* drift recorder (indicator)
Abweichungsmessung *f* hole deviation logging, directional log
Abweichungswinkel *m* angle of deflection; drift angle *(borehole)*
Abwerfen *n* shedding
Abwetter *pl* return air
abwickelbar developable
Abwölbung *f* downward bowing
abyssal *s.* abyssisch
Abyssal *n* abyssal zone
Abyssalregion *f* abyssal region
abyssisch abyssal, abysmal
abyssolithisch abyssolithic
abyssopelagisch abyssopelagic
abyssophil abyssophile
Abzapfbrunnen *m* **in artesisch gespanntem Grundwasser** bleeder well
Abziehstein *m* hone *(for grinding)*
Abzugsgraben *m* drainage ditch
Abzugskanal *m* off-take
abzweigen to bifurcate
Abzweigung *f* side branch; offset
~ eines Flusses binnacle
~ eines Ganges spur
~ von Arten filiation of species
Acadian *n s.* Albertan
ac-Ebene *f* ac-plane, deformation plane
acentrisch acentrous, without vertebral centre
Aceraten *mpl* acerates
ac-Gefügeebene *f s.* ac-Ebene
ac-Gürtel *m* ac-girdle
Achänodonten *mpl* achaenodonts
Achat *m* agate *(a fine-grained chalcedony)*
~/bleifarbener phassachate
achatähnlich agatiform, agatine, agatoid, agaty
achatartig agatine
Achatdruse *f* geode of agate
achathaltig agatiferous
Achatjaspis *m* agate jasper
Achatmandel *f* catalinite *(beach pebble)*
Achatschleiferei *f* agate mill
Achondrit *m* achondrite
Achroit *m* achroite *(variety of tourmaline)*
achromatisch achromatic
Achromatismus *m* achromatism
Achse *f* axis *(s.a.* Symmetrieachse)
~/dorsoventrale dorsoventral axis
~/eintauchende plunging (pitching) axis
~/erdmagnetische geomagnetic axis
~/kristallografische crystallographic axis
~/optische optic axis
~/parallaktische equatorial axis
Achsenabschnitt *m* intercept *(of crystals)*
Achsenaustritt *m* emergence of the axes
Achsendepression *f* axis depression
Achsendrehung *f* axial revolution *(of the earth)*
Achsenebene *f* axial (optic) plane
Achsenfläche *f* axial surface

Achsenflächenschieferung *f* axial plane foliation
Achsenkulmination *f* axis culmination (elevation)
Achsenmulde *f* sag
Achsenrichtung *f* axial direction
Achsensattel *m* bulge
achsensymmetrisch axially symmetric[al], symmetric[al] about axis, axisymmetric[al]
Achsensystem *n* axial system
Achsenverhältnis *n* axial ratio
Achsenverteilungsanalyse *f* topotropic analysis
Achsenwinkel *m* axial (optic) angle, optic axis angle
Achteck *n* octagon
achteckig octagonal
Achtflach *n* octahedron
achtflächig octahedral
Achtflächner *m* octahedron
Achtkant *n(m)* octagon
achtkantig octagonal
achtseitig octahedral, eight-sided
Achtundvierzigflächner *m* hexakisoctahedron
achtwertig octavalent
achtzählig eight-fold
Achtzehneck *n* octadecagon
achtzehnflächig octodecimal
Ackerbau *m* agriculture
Ackerboden *m* arable soil
Ackererde *f* arable earth, mould
ackerfähig arable
Ackerkrume *f* [agricultural] topsoil, solum, tilthtop (tilled) soil
Ackerland *n* tilth
Ackerwiese *f* arable meadow
ac-Kluft *f* ac-joint
Adamellit *m* adamellite *(quartz-monzonite)*
Adamin *m* adamine, adamite, $Zn_2[OH|AsO_4]$
Adaptivwert *m* *s.* Anpassungsfähigkeit
Adduktor *m* adductor
Adduktoreneindruck *m* adductor impression
Adelit *m* adelite, $CaMg[OH|AsO_4]$
adelomorph adelomorphic, indefinite in form
Ader *f* vein, leader *(s.a.* Gang 1.)
~/mächtige strong vein
~/reiche pay lead (streak)
Äderchen *n* veinlet, stringer *(in rocks)*
aderig veiny, veined, streaked, streaky
Adermarmor *m* veined marble
ädern to streak
Adertextur *f* phlebitic structure *(in migmatites)*
Äderung *f* veining
Adhäsion *f* adhesion
Adhäsionsvermögen *n* adhesiveness
Adhäsionswasser *n* cohesive (connate, attached) water
adiabatisch adiabatic
adiagnostisch adiagnostic
Adinol *m* adinole *(a dense rock, composed chiefly of quartz and albite)*
Adlerstein *m* eaglestone

Adorf[ium] *n* Adorfian [Stage] *(of Upper Devonian in Europe)*
adsorbieren to adsorb
Adsorption *f* adsorption
Adsorptionsisotherme *f* adsorption isotherm
Adsorptionspotential *n* adsorption potential
Adsorptionsvermögen *n* adsorption (adsorbing) capacity
Adsorptionswasser *n* adsorption water
adsorptiv adsorptive
Adular *m* adular[ia] *(variety of orthoclase)*
adult adult, wake-up
Advektion *f* advection
Adventivkegel *m* adventive (parasitic) cone
Adventivkrater *m* adventive (parasitic, lateral) crater
Adventivloben *mpl* adventive lobes *(ammonites)*
Adventivsattel *m* adventive saddle
Adventivschlot *m* adventive vent
Aegean *n* Aegean [Substage] *(of Middle Triassic, Tethys)*
Aegirin *m s.* Ägirin
Aenigmatit *m* aenigmatite, $Na_4Fe_{10}Ti_2[O_4|(Si_2O_6)_6]$
Aerationszone *f* aeration zone *(of soil)*
Aerenchym *n* aerenchym, aeration tissue *(palaeobotany)*
Aerodynamik *f* aerodynamics
Aerofotogrammetrie *f* aerophotogrammetry
Aerofototopografie *f* aerophototopography
Aerogeophysik *f* aerogeophysics
Aerogravimeter *n* aerogravimeter
Aerokartograf *m* aerocartograph
aeroklastisch anemoclastic
Aerolimnologie *f* aerolimnology
Aerolith *m* aerolite
Aerologe *m* aerologist
Aerologie *f* aerology
aerologisch aerologic
Aeromagnetik *f* aeromagnetics, airborne magnetics, aerial magnetometry
Aeromagnetometer *n* aeromagnetometer
Aerometer *n* aerometer
Aerometrie *f* aerometry
Aeronautik *f* aeronautics
aeronautisch aeronautic[al]
Aeronium *n* Aeronian *(stage of Llandovery)*
Aeroplankton *n* aeroplankton
Aeroradiometeorografie *f* aeroradiometeorography
Aerosiderit *m* aerosiderite *(meteorite composed mainly of iron)*
Aerosiderolit *m* aerosiderolite *(meteorite composed of both stone and iron)*
Aerosol *n* aerosol
Aerothermodynamik *f* aerothermodynamics
Aeschynit *m s.* Äschynit
Affenhaar *n* monkey hair
Affinität *f* affinity
AFMAG-Verfahren *n* AFMAG method *(magnetic audiofrequency method)*

Afterröhre

Afterröhre f anal tube
Afwillit m afwillite, $Ca_3[SiO_3OH]_2 \cdot 2H_2O$
Agalmatolith m agalmatolite, figured (Chinese figure) stone, pagodite
agam agamous *(palaeobotany)*
AGC-Verzerrungen fpl AGC distortions
AGC-Zeitkonstante f AGC time constant
Agens n agent
Agglomerat n agglomerate
Agglomeratlava f agglomeratic lava
Agglomeratstruktur f agglomerated structure
Agglomerattuff m agglomeratic tuff
agglomerieren to agglomerate, to nodulize
Agglomerierung f agglomeration, nodulizing
agglutinieren to agglutinate
Aggradation f aggradation
Aggregat n aggregate
~/parallelstengliges parallel acicular aggregate
~/parallelstrahliges parallel columnar aggregate
Aggregation f aggregation
Aggregatpolarisation f aggregate polarization
Aggregatprobenahme f cluster (nested) sampling
Aggregatzustand m state of aggregation *(of H_2O)*
Ägirin m aegirite, aegirine, acmite, $NaFe\cdots[Si_2O_6]$
Ägirintrachyt m aegirine trachyte, acmite-trachyte
Agmatit m agmatite *(a migmatite)*
Agnathen mpl jawless fishes
Agone f agonic line
Agpait m agpaite *(a migmatite)*
Agrargebiet n agricultural region
Agrarhydrologie f agricultural hydrology
Agrarklimatologie f agroclimatology
Agrarmeteorologie f agricultural meteorology, agrometeorology
Agricolit m agricolite, $Bi_4[SiO_4]_3$
Agrogeochemie f agrogeochemistry
Agrogeologie f agricultural geology
Aguilarit m aguilarite, $Ag_2(S,Se)$
ahermatyp ahermatypic
Ahnenform f ancestor
A-Horizont m A-horizon, eluvial (eluviated) horizon
Aikinit m aikinite, $2PbS \cdot Cu_2S \cdot Bi_2S_3$
Ajoit m ajoite, $Cu_2Al[OH|Si_3O_9] \cdot 2H_2O$
Akaganeit m akaganeite, β-FeOOH
Akanthit m acanthite, argentite, argyrose, argyrite, vitreous silver, Ag_2S
Akaustobiolith m acaustobiolith
Akenobeit m akenobeite *(dioritic dike rock)*
Akerit m akerite
Åkermanit m akermanite, $Ca_2Mg[Si_2O_7]$
Akkordanz f pseudoconformity
Akkumulate npl/**harte, verkittete** hardpan
Akkumulation f 1. accumulation; 2. cumulate *(of minerals)*
Akkumulationsgebiet n area of accumulation, surplus area
Akkumulationstheorie f theory of accumulation *(after Lyell)*
Akkumulationszone f eines Gletschers glacier reservoir
aklastisch aclastic
aklinal aclinal
Akmit m acmite, $NaFe[Si_2O_6]$
Akmolith m akmolith *(linguiform intrusive)*
Akratopege f cool spring
Akrochordit m akrochordite, $(Mn,Mg)_5[(OH)_2|AsO_4]_2 \cdot 5H_2O$
Aksait m aksaite, $Mg[B_3O_4(OH)_2]_2 \cdot 3H_2O$
Aktinolith m actino[li]te, $Ca_2(Mg,Fe)_5[(OH,F)|O_{11}]_2$
Aktinolithschiefer m actinolite schist
Aktinometer n actinometer
Aktinometrie f actinometry
aktinomorph actinomorphic
Aktionsherd m focus of activity *(of a volcano)*
aktiv active
aktivieren to activate
Aktivierung f activation
~ des Erkundungsaufwands von Lagerstätten activation of deposits
Aktivierungsanalyse f activation analysis
Aktivierungsenergie f energy of activation
Aktivierungslog n, **Aktivierungsmessung** f activation log[ging] *(radioactive)*
Aktivität f activity
~/bakterielle chemo-autotrophe chemical autotrophic bacterial activity
~/erdmagnetische geomagnetic activity
~/mikrobielle microbial activity
~/optische optical activity
Aktivitätsindex m activity index *(of water components)*
Aktualismus m actualism, uniformism, uniformitarianism
Aktualitätsprinzip n principle of actualism
Aktualitätstheorie f doctrine of uniformitarianism
Akustiklog n acoustic log[ging], sonic log[ging], acoustic velocity log[ging], continuous velocity log[ging]
akzessorisch accessory
Alabandin m alabandine, alabandite, MnS
Alabaster m alabaster *(variety of gypsum)*
Alabastergips m alabastrite, alum-soaked Keene's cement
Alait m alaite, VO_2OH
Alamosit m alamosite, $Pb[SiO_3]$
Alaskait m alaskaite, $Ag_2S \cdot 3Bi_2S_3$
Alaskit m alaskite *(rock of the granite clan)*
Alaun m alum
Alaun n Alaunian [Substage] *(of Late Triassic, Tethys)*
alaunartig aluminous
Alaunerde f alum earth
alaunerdehaltig alumy
Alaunerz n alum ore, alunite, $KAl_3[(OH)_6|(SO_4)_2]$
alaunhaltig aluminous

Alaunschiefer m alum schist (shale, slate)
Alaunsiederei f alum works
Alaunstein m alum ore, alunite, $KAl_3[(OH)_6|(SO_4)_2]$
Alb n Albian [Stage] (of Lower Cretaceous)
Albanit m albanite (leucitite)
Albedo f albedo
Albertan n Albertan [Series], Acadian [Series] (Middle Cambrian, North America)
Albertit m albertite, asphaltic coal, melanasphalt (bituminous mineral resembling asphaltum)
Albien n s. Alb
Albit m albite, white feldspar, $Na[AlSi_3O_8]$
albitisch albitic
albitisiert albitized
Albitisierung f albitization
Albitit m albitite (granular dike rock)
Albitophyr m albitophyre (albitic xenocryst containing porphyric rock)
Albitschiefer m albite (albitic) schist
Albitzwilling m albite twin
Alboranit m alboranite (hypersthene basalt)
Aleurit m aleurite
aleuritisch aleuritic
Aleurolith m aleurolite
aleurolitisch aleurolitic
Alexandrit m alexandrite (variety of chrysoberyl)
alferrisch alferric
Algen fpl algae
~/epilithische epilithic algae
~/inkrustierende incrusting algae
Algenabscheidung f algal secretion
Algenanhäufung f algous accumulation
Algenfäden mpl algae threads
Algenkalk m algal limestone
Algenkohle f algal (boghead) coal
Algenkohlenart f pelionite
Algenriff n algal reef
Algenstaub m algal dust
Algenwachstumsstruktur f algal growth structure
Alginat n alginate
Alginit m alginite (coal maceral); algal remains
Algit m algite (coal microlithotype); algal remains
Algodonit m algodonite, $Cu_{6-7}As$
Algonkium n Algonkian (Late Archaic and Proterozoic, North America)
Algovit m algovite (group of augite-plagioclase rocks)
Aliasing-Effekt m aliasing effect
a-Lineation f a-lineation
aliphatisch aliphatic
Alisonit m alisonite, $3Cu_2S \cdot PbS$
Alizarinkomplex m alizarin complex
Alkaleszenz f alkalinity
Alkaliamphibol m soda amphibole
Alkalibasalt m alkali basalt
Alkaliboden m alkali (alkaline) soil, alkaline podzol
~/ausgelaugter salt earth podzol, steppe-bleached earth

~/schwarzer black alkali soil
Alkaligestein n alkali rock
Alkaligranit m alkali granite
Alkalihornblende f s. Alkaliamphibol
Alkalikalkreihe f alkali-calcic series, alkali-calcareous suite
Alkalimetall n alkali metal, metalloid
Alkalimetallgruppe f alkaline group
alkalinisieren to alkalify
Alkalinität f alkalinity
Alkalireihe f alkali series
alkalisch alkaline, alkalinous
~/schwach alkalescent
alkalisieren to alkalize
Alkalisierung f alkalization
Alkalisilikat n alkali silicate
Alkaliverbindung f alkali compound
Allaktit m allactite, $Mn_7[(OH)_4|AsO_4]_2$
Allalinit m allalinite (rock of the gabbro clan)
Allanit m allanite, $(La,Ce)_2FeAl_2[O|OH|SiO_4|Si_2O_7]$
Allargentum n allargentum, ε-(Ag,Sb)
Alleghanyit m alleghanyite, $Mn_5[(OH)_2|(SiO_4)_2]$
Allemontit m allemontite, antimoniferous arsenic, $SbAs_3$
Alling-Skala f Alling scale (grain-size classification)
Allit m allite
allitisch allitic
allochemisch allochemical
allochroisch allochroic
Allochroit m s. Andradit
allochromatisch allochromatic
allochthon allochthonous, allochthonic, allochthon[al], exogenic, exogenous
Allodelphit m allodelphite (s.a. Synadelphit)
Allogamie f allogamy, cross-fertilization (palaeobotany)
allogen allogenous
Allomikrit m allomicrite
allomorph allomorphous, allomorphic, paramorphic
Allomorphismus m allomorphism, paramorphism
Allopalladium n allopalladium
Allophan m allophane, $Al_2Si_5 \cdot nH_2O$
allothigen allo[thi]gene, allothigenic, allothigenous, allothogenic
allotriomorph allotriomorphic, xenomorphic, anhedral
allotriomorph-körnig allotriomorphic-granular
allotrop allotropic
Allotropie f allotropy, allotropism
~/enantiomorphe enantiomorphic allotropy
allseitig directionless
alluvial alluvial, alluvious
Alluvialboden m alluvial soil (floor), erratic soil
~/grauer gray warp soil
Alluvialdecke f alluvial sheet
Alluvialebene f alluvial plain
Alluvialepoche f alluvium period

Alluvialfächer

Alluvialfächer *m* alluvial fan (apron)
Alluvialfächerschutt *m* alluvial fan accumulations
Alluvialgold *n* gulch gold
Alluvialkegel *m* cone of detritus (dejection)
Alluvialkies *m* alluvial gravel
Alluvialmoorboden *m* alluvial swamping soil
Alluvialschlamm *m* alluvial slime
Alluvialschotter *m* run gravel
Alluvialschutt *m* wash
Alluvialterrasse *f* alluvial bench
Alluvialton *m (Am)* adobe clay
Alluvionen *fpl* alluvial (valley) fill
~/goldführende auriferous gravels
Alluvium *n* 1. alluvial period (epoch, time) (*s.a.* Holozän); 2. alluvion, alluvium, alluvial deposit
alluviumbedeckt alluvium-covered
Allwetterfernerkundung *f* all-weather remote sensing
Almandin *m* almandine, almandite, $Fe_3Al_2[SiO_4]_3$
Almerait *m* almeraite, $KCl \cdot NaCl \cdot MgCl_2 \cdot H_2O$
Alnöit *m* alnoite *(melilite basalt)*
Alpen *pl* Alps
Alpenglühen *n* Alpine glow
Alpen-Karpaten-Bogen *m* Alpine-Carpathian arc
Alpentunnel *m* Alpine tunnel
Alpenvorland *n* Alpine piedmont (foothills)
Alphaaktivität *f* alpha radioactivity
Alphastrahler *m* alpha[-ray] emitter
Alphastrahlung *f* alpha radiation
Alphateilchen *n* alpha particle
Alphaumwandlung *f s.* Alphazerfall
Alphazähler *m* alpha meter
Alphazählrohr *n* alpha counter tube
Alphazerfall *m* alpha decay
Alphitit *m* alphitite *(powdered mineral)*
Alpiden *pl* Alpides, Mediterranean belt
alpidisch alpidic
alpin alpine
alpinotyp alpinotype
Alsbachit *m* alsbachite *(porphyritic aplite)*
Alstonit *m* alstonite (*s.a.* Bromellit)
alt old-aged
Altaiden *pl* Altaides
Altait *m* altaite, PbTe
Altarm *m* abandoned river course, old branch
Altbohrung *f* early boring
Alter *n* age
~/absolutes absolute age
~ des Weltalls age of the universe
~/geologisches geologic[al] age
~/konventionelles conventional age
~/radiometrisches radiometric age
~/scheinbares apparent age
~/stratigrafisches stratigraphic age
~/tatsächliches actual age
Alter Mann *m s.* Mann/Alter
Altersabhängigkeit *f* dependence of age

Altersbestimmung *f* age determination (assignment)
~/absolute *s.* ~/radioaktive
~/geologische geologic[al] age determination
~/physikalische physical time measurement
~/radioaktive (radiometrische) radioactive (isotopic) age determination, radioactive (isotopic) dating
Alterseinstufung *f* age dating
Altersfolge *f* order of age, age sequence
Alterskriterium *n* age characteristic
Altersstadium *n* stage of late maturity
Alterstrend *m* age-trend
Alterszeichen *n* indication of age
Alterung *f* ag[e]ing, age-hardening
Altgletschereis *n* blue ice
Altland *n* oldland, old landmass
Altmoräne *f* older moraine
Altpaläolithikum *n* Old Palaeolithic [Times]
Altpaläozoikum *n* Lower Palaeozoic *(Cambrian to Devonian)*
Altpräkambrium *n* Lower Precambrian
Altschnee *m* old snow
~/nasser wet firn
~/trockener dry firn
Altsteinzeit *f s.* Paläolithikum
Alttertiär *n* Palaeogene
altvulkanisch old volcanic, palaeovolcanic
Altwasser *n* stagnant water, dead waters, oxbow; abandoned [stream] channel; loop lake
~/halbmondförmiges oxbow (crescent) lake
Altwassersee *m* meander scrolls lake
Alumian *m* alumian, $NaAl_3[(OH)_6|(SO_4)_2]$
Aluminat *n* aluminate
Aluminit *m* aluminite, $Al_2[(OH)_4|SO_4] \cdot 7H_2O$
Aluminium *n* aluminium, *(Am)* aluminum, Al
Aluminiumerz *n* aluminium ore
aluminiumhaltig aluminiferous, aluminium-bearing
Alumogel *m* kliachite, $AlOOH + H_2O$
Alumohydrocalcit *m* alumohydrocalcite, $CaAl_2[(OH)_4|(CO_3)_2] \cdot 3H_2O$
Alumosilikat *n* aluminous silicate, aluminosilicate
Alunit *m* alunite, alumstone, $KAl_3[(OH)_6|(SO_4)_2]$
alunitisch alunitic
alunitisieren to alunitize
Alunitisierung *f* alunitization
Alunogen *n* alunogen, mountain butter, $Al_2(SO_4)_3 \cdot 18H_2O$
Alveolarverwitterung *f* alveolar weathering
Alveolinenkalk *m* Alveolina limestone
Amalgam *m* amalgam, (Ag,Hg)
Amarantit *m* amarantite, $Fe[OH|SO_4] \cdot 3H_2O$
Amazonasschild *m* Amazonian shield
Amazonenstein *m*, **Amazonit** *m* amazonite, Amazon stone, green feldspar
Ambatoarinit *m* ambatoarinite, $Sr(Ce,La,Nd) [O|(CO_3)_3]$
Amblygonit *m* amblygonite, hebronite, $LiAl[(F,OH)|PO_4]$

anbringen

Amblypoden *pl* amblypods
Ambonit *m* ambonite *(cordierite-bearing hornblende-biotite-andesite)*
Amboß *m* incus, anvil-shaped ear-ossicle
Ambulakralfeld *n* ambulacral area
Ambulakralfüße *mpl* ambulacral (tube) feet *(echinoderms)*
Ambursen-Staumauer *f* Ambursen-type dam
Amesit *m* amesite, $(Mg, Fe)_4Al_2[(OH)_8|Al_2Si_2O_{10}]$
Amethyst *m* amethyst *(variety of crystallized quartz)*
amethystartig, amethystfarben amethystine, amethyst-coloured
Amianth *m* amianthus, amiantine, mountain flax *(variety of asbestos)*
Aminoffit *m* aminoffite, $Ca_3Be[OH|Si_3O_{10}]$
Amman[ien] *n* Ammanian [Stage] *(Westphalian B and C, England)*
Ammiolith *m* ammiolite, $3CuO \cdot Sb_2O_3$
Ammonalaun *m s.* Tschermigit
Ammoniak *n* ammonia
Ammonifikation *f* ammonification
Ammonioborit *m* ammonioborite, $NH_4[B_5O_6(COH)_4] \cdot {}^2/_3H_2O$
Ammoniojarosit *m* ammoniojarosite, $NH_4Fe_3^{...}[(OH)_6|(SO_4)_2]$
Ammonit *m* ammonite
~/aufgerollter coiled ammonite
~/verkiester pyrite (pyritized) ammonite
amorph amorphous, uncrystalline, glasseous
Amorphismus *m* amorphism
Ampangabeit *m* ampangabeite *(a mineral consisting of a tantalo-niobate)*
Ampelit *m* ampelite *(black earth rich in pyrites)*
Amphibie *f* amphibian
amphibisch amphibious, amphibian, semiaquatic
Amphibol *m* amphibole
~/monokliner monoclinal amphibole
~/rhombischer rhombic amphibole
Amphibolfels *m* amphibolite
Amphibolgneis *m* amphibole-gneiss
amphibolisch amphibolic
Amphibolisierung *f* amphibolization
Amphibolit *m* amphibolite
Amphibolitfazies *f* amphibolite facies
Amphibolschiefer *m* amphibole schist
amphimorph amphimorphic
Amphiphyten *mpl* amphiphytes
Amphipoden *mpl* amphipod[e]s
amphoter amphoteric
Amplitude *f* amplitude
Amplitudencharakteristik *f* amplitude response
Amplituden-Frequenz-Verzerrung *f* amplitude-frequency distortion
Amplitudenmodulation *f* amplitude modulation
Amplitudenregelung *f* gain control
~/automatische automatic gain control, AGC

Amplitudenspektrum *n* amplitude spectrum
Amplitudenunterdrückung *f* fade, fading
Amputation *f* amputation *(of a nappe)*
Amstelien *n*, **Amstelium** *n* Amstelian *(preglacial complex at the Tertiary/Pleistocene boundary, West Europe)*
Amygdaloidbasalt *m* amygdaloidal basalt
amygdaloidisch amygdaloid[al], entoolitic
Amygdalophyr *m* amygdalophyre
Anabohitsit *m* anabohitsite *(an olivine-pyroxenite)*
Anadiagenese *f* anadiagenesis
anadiagenetisch anadiagenetic
anaerob anaerobic[al]
Anaerobiose *f* anaerobiosis
Anagenese *f* anagenesis
Anaklinaltal *n* anaclinal valley
Analbit *m* analbite, $Na[AlSi_3O_8]$
Analcim *m* analcime, analcite, analcidite, $Na[AlSi_2O_6] \cdot H_2O$
Analcimit *m* analcimite *(a nepheline-syenite)*
Analcitit *m* analcitite *(analcime basalt)*
Anale X *n* anal X *(echinoderms)*
Analogmodelluntersuchung *f* analogue model study
Analplatte X *f s.* Anale X
Analtubus *m* anal tube
Analysator *m* analyzer
Analysatornikol *n* analyzing Nicol
Analyse *f* analysis
~/chemische chemical analysis
~/densitometrische densitometric[al] analysis
~/massenspektrografische mass spectrographic analysis
~/megaskopische quantitative megascopic quantitative analysis
~/morphometrische morphometric[al] analysis
~/paläohydrogeologische palaeohydrogeological analysis
~/qualitative qualitative analysis
~/quantitative quantitative analysis
~/tektonische tectonic analysis
~/viskometrische viscometric analysis
~/volumetrische analysis by measure
Analysenprobe *f* analytical (analysis) sample
Anamorphose *f* anamorphism, anamorphosis
Anapait *m* anapaite, $Ca_2Fe[PO_4]_2 \cdot 4H_2O$
Anarcestes-Stufe *f s.* Couvin
anaseismisch anaseismic[al]
Anastomose *f* anastomosis *(palaeontology)*
Anatas *m* anatase, TiO_2
Anatexis *f* anatexis
Anatexit *m* anatexite
anätzen to etch, to corrode superficially
Anätzung *f* etching
Anauxit *m* anauxite, $(Al, H_3)_4[(OH)_8|Si_4O_{10}]$
anbauen to hold *(a layer)*
Anbauterrasse *f* field terrace
anbohren to drill into
Anbohrung *f* drilling-in, spud-in
anbringen/feine Schlitze in der Verrohrung to cut slots in the casing

Anchimetamorphose 22

Anchimetamorphose *f* anchimetamorphism, very low grade metamorphism
Anchroit *m* anchroite *(variety of diorite)*
Ancylussee *m* Ancylus lake
Ancyluszeit *f* Ancylus time
Andalusit *m* andalusite, crucite, cross stone, $Al^{[6]} Al^{[5]}[O|SiO_4]$
Andalusit-Biotit-Schiefer *m* andalusite biotite schist
Andalusit-Glimmerfels *m* andalusite mica rock
andersfarbig allochromatic
Andersonit *m* andersonite, $Na_2Ca[UO_2|(CO_3)_3] \cdot 6H_2O$
Änderung *f* **des Bohrfortschritts** drilling breaks
~ des magnetischen Erdfelds variation of the earth's magnetic field
~/periodische periodic change
~/tägliche daily variation
Andesin *m* andesine *(mixed crystal)*
Andesinit *m* andesinite
Andesit *m* andesite
Andesitgürtel *m s.* Andesitlinie
andesitisch andesitic
Andesitlinie *f,* **Andesitring** *m* andesite (Marshall) line
Andorit *m* andorite, $4PbS \cdot 2Ag_2S \cdot 6Sb_2S_3$
Andradit *m* andradite, $Ca_3Fe_2(SiO_4)_3$
aneinanderfügen/stumpf to abut
Aneinanderlagerung *f* juxtaposition; bond
anemogen anemogenic
Anemograf *m* anemograph
anemoklastisch anemoclastic
Anemometer *n* anemometer
Aneroidbarometer *n* aneroid barometer
anfahren to enter, to encounter
~/den Ölträger to drill in
~/einen Gang to cut a lode
Anfahren *n* **des Ölträgers** drilling-in
Anfangsaktivität *f* initial activity *(of a tracer)*
Anfangsbohrdurchmesser *m* initial diameter of drilling
Anfangsdämpfung *f* presuppression; initial suppression
Anfangsdruck *m* initial pressure
Anfangsdurchmesser *m* initial diameter of drilling
Anfangseinsatz *m* initial impulse, first arrival (impetus)
Anfangsfestigkeit *f* original strength
Anfangsintensität *f* source intensity *(of a tracer)*
Anfangskammer *f s.* Protoconch
Anfangskonzentration *f* initial concentration *(of a tracer or mineralized water)*
Anfangskraft *f* initial load-bearing capacity
Anfangsproduktion *f* initial production
Anfangsspannung *f* initial stress
Anfangsstadium *n* initial (incipient) stage
Anfangstemperaturverteilung *f* initial temperature distribution
Anfärbeprobe *f* staining test

Anfeuchten *n* moistening, wetting *(of a sample)*
Anflug *m* dash, touch, tinge, streak, tincture
anfressen to bite
Anfressung *f/***narbenartige** honeycomb corrosion
Angaralith *m* angaralite, $(Mg, Ca)_2(Al, Fe)_{10}[O_5|(SiO_4)_6]$
Angaraschild *m* Angara shield
Angaria *f* Angaria
angeboren innate; congenital
angelagert accretionary
angelaufen tarnished
angeordnet/linear-parallel streaked
~/radial radiating, radially arranged
~/strahlig *s.* ~/radial
~/zweireihig distichous, dichotomous
angeschwemmt alluvial, alluvian, alluvious
angeschwollen gibbous
angespült *s.* angeschwemmt
Angiospermen *npl* angiosperms, angiospermous plants
Anglesit *m* anglesite, lead vitriol, $PbSO_4$
Angliederungsinsel *f* attached (land-tied) island
Anglien *n* Anglian *(Pleistocene corresponding to Mindel Drift, Alps district)*
angrenzen to adjoin
angrenzend adjacent
Angriff *m/***chemischer** chemical attack
Angriffspunkt *m* bearing point, point of application *(of a force)*
Angrit *m* angrite *(meteorite)*
Angulare *n* angular *(palaeontology)*
anhäufen/sich to accumulate, to agglomerate
Anhäufung *f* accumulation, agglomeration, accretion, acervation
Anheftungslinie *f* line of junction
Anhöhe *f* height; mound; swell
~/felsige scar
anhydrisch anhydrous, anhydric
Anhydrit *m* anhydrite, anhydrous gypsum, $Ca[SO_4]$
~/durch Gipsdehydration entstandener regenerated anhydrite
~/massiger rock anhydrite
anhydrithaltig 1. anhydritic *(aggregal);* 2. anhydriceous *(integral)*
Anhydritknolle *f,* **Anhydritkonkretion** *f* anhydritic concretion, concretion of anhydrite
~/gewundene tripestone
Anhydritschnur *f* anhydrite band
Anhydrokainit *m* anhydrokainite, basaltkainite, $KMg[Cl|SO_4]$
Animikit *m* animikite, (Ag,Sb)
Anionenaustausch *m* anion exchange
Anionenpotential *n* anionic potential
Anis *n* Anisian [Stage], Anisic [Stage] *(of Triassic)*
Anisoklinalfalte *f* anisoclinal fold
anisomerisch anisomeric
anisometrisch anisometric

anisotrop anisotropic, anisotropous, aeolotropic
Anisotropie f anisotropy, anisotropism, aeolotropy
~ **des Untergrunds** anisotropy of the subsurface
~/**magnetische** magnetic anisotropy
Anisotropieparadoxon n paradox of anisotropy *(geoelectrics)*
Ankaramit m ankaramite *(melanocratic basaltic rock)*
Ankaratrit m ankaratrite *(nepheline basalt)*
Ankerausbau m roof (strata) bolting
Ankerbalken m anchor log
Ankerbolzen m roof bolt
Ankerit m ankerite, brown spar, iron dolomite, CaFe[CO$_3$]$_2$
Ankerkopf m roof-bolt head
Ankern n **der Sohlen** floor bolting
Ankerplatte f roof-bolt plate
Ankerpunkt m anchorage point
Ankerschraube f anchor bolt
Ankerseil n anchor line
Ankersitz m, **Ankerung** f anchorage *(of a roof bolt)*
Ankerwand f/**durchlaufende** anchor wall
Ankopplung f/**optimale** impedance matching
Ankunftszeit f arrival time *(e.g. of seismic waves)*
Ankylit m ancylite, Sr$_3$(Ce, La, Dy)$_4$[(OH)$_4$|(CO$_3$)$_7$] · 3H$_2$O
Anlagerung f accretion; juxtaposition, apposition
Anlagerungsgefüge n depositional (geopetal) fabric, superposition pattern
Anlagerungswasser n pellicular water
Anlandung f alluviation, alluvium, alluvial deposit; accretion; lateral spread
~ **an einem Ufer** accretion along a bank
Anlandungsstrand m feeder beach
Anlauf m [in-line] offset; end section *(of a stacked profile)*
Anlauffarbe f tempering colour, tarnish *(of minerals)*
Anlauflänge f lead-in section *(of a streamer)*
Anlegegoniometer n contact goniometer, protractor
anliegend adjacent
~/**satt** flush *(with the roof)*
Anmoor n turfy moulder
Annabergit m annabergite, nickel ochre, Ni$_3$[AsO$_4$]$_2$ · 8H$_2$O
Annäherungsgeschwindigkeit f closing rate
Annit m s. Lepidomelan
Annivit m annivite *(Bi-bearing tetrahedrite)*
Annulus m annulus, periphract *(cephalopods)*
anomal anomalous
Anomalie f anomaly
~/**allochthone geochemische** allochthonous geochemical anomaly
~/**autochthone** autochthonous anomaly
~/**Bouguersche** Bouguer anomaly
~/**erdmagnetische** geomagnetic anomaly
~/**geochemische** geochemical anomaly
~/**hydrochemische** hydrochemical anomaly
~/**isostatische** isostatic anomaly
~/**lokale** local anomaly
~/**lokale magnetische** local magnetic anomaly
~/**magnetische** magnetic anomaly
~/**mittlere** mean anomaly
~/**wahre** true anomaly
Anomit m anomite *(variety of biotite)*
Anordnung f arrangement, assembly; pattern; spread; array
~/**geradlinige** in-line system
~/**gleichartige** homotaxis
~/**lagenförmige** banded arrangement
~/**netzförmige** reticular arrangement *(of groups of wells)*
~/**regellose** random pattern
~/**rostförmige** trellised pattern
~/**staffelförmige** echelon arrangement
~/**ungeregelte** random pattern
~ **von Stempeln** system of supports
~/**zonale (zonenförmige)** zonal arrangement
anorganisch inorganic
anorganogen inorganogenic
anormal abnormal
anorogen anorogen[et]ic
Anorthit m anorthite, indianite, Ca[Al$_2$Si$_2$O$_8$]
Anorthitbasalt m anorthite-basalt
anorthitisch anorthitic
Anorthoklas m anorthoclase, anorthose, (Na, K)AlSi$_3$O$_8$
Anorthoklasit m anorthoclasite *(rock of the gabbro clan)*
Anorthosit m anorthosite
Anpassung f 1. fit; 2. adaption *(palaeobiology)*
~ **an die Speicherentwicklung** *(Am)* matching reservoir behavior
~ **nach dem Verfahren der kleinsten Quadratsumme** least squares fit
Anpassungselement n interface
Anpassungsfähigkeit f fitness
Anpassungsmodell n *(Am)* history match model *(reservoir mechanics)*
Anprall m impact
Anpreßarm m eccentering arm *(well logging)*
anregen to excite; to stimulate *(e.g. a well)*
Anreger m activator
Anregung f excitation; stimulation *(e.g. of a well)*
anreichern to enrich, to concentrate, to accumulate, to upgrade; to replenish *(ground water)*
~/**durch Versickerung** to recharge
Anreicherung f enrichment, concentration, accumulation; replenishment *(of ground water)*
~ **durch aszendente Lösungen** hypogene enrichment
~ **durch deszendente Lösungen** supergene enrichment
Anreicherungsanlage f concentration (concentrating) plant

Anreicherungsbedingungen 24

Anreicherungsbedingungen *fpl* conditions of enrichment
Anreicherungsboden *m* illuvial soil
Anreicherungsbrunnen *m* stock-water well; well for adding water
Anreicherungserz *n* concentrating ore
Anreicherungsfaktor *m* enrichment factor
Anreicherungsgrad *m* upgrading ratio
Anreicherungshorizont *m* B-horizon
Anreicherungsprodukt *n* concentrate
Anreicherungsverfahren *n* enrichment process
Anreicherungsverhältnis *n* ratio of enrichment
Anreicherungszone *f* enrichment zone *(of ore)*; accumulation zone *(of mineral water)*
Anriß *m* primary (initial) crack; slight break *(of a rock)*
ansammeln to accumulate
~/Druck to build up pressure
~/sich to aggregate
Ansammlung *f* accumulation
~/zementative cementative accumulation
Ansatzpunkt *m* location *(of a bore)*
Ansaughöhe *f* absorptive height
anschießen to blow down *(the roof)*
anschlagen to tighten *(prop wedges)*
Anschleppung *f* dragging
Anschliff *m/polierter* polished section
Anschluß *m* **der Förderleitung** flow-line connector
Anschlußpunkt *m* tie point
Anschmelzung *f/oberflächliche* vitrifaction
Anschnitt *m* cross bearing
~/schräger chamfer
Anschütte *f* alluvium, alluvial deposit
Anschüttung *f* embankment
anschwellen to tumefy
Anschwellen *n* swelling; swell
~ des Liegenden footwall swelling
Anschwellung *f* s. Anschwellen
Anschwemmland *n* alluvial fan; innings *(from the sea)*
Anschwemmschotter *m* outwash gravel
Anschwemmung *f* alluviation, aggradation, accretion [through alluvium], *(Am)* filling-up [with alluvium]; warp, silting[-up]
Anschwemmungsablagerung *f* aggradational deposit
Anschwemmungsebene *f* aggradation plain
Anschwemmungsküste *f* alluvial (accretion, prograded) coast
ansetzen/ein Bohrloch to start a borehole
~/eine Bohrung to locate a well
~/eine Strecke to start a drift
Ansetzen *n* **einer Bohrung** spud[ding]
anstauen s. aufstauen
Anstauung *f* stemming
anstehen to outcrop
anstehend solid *(coal, rock)*
Anstehendes *n* solid (native) bedrock, rock in place, ledge [rock]

ansteigend uphill
Anstieg *m* **des Grundgebirges** basement uplift
Anstoß *m* impetus
Antarktis *f* Antarctic
antarktisch antarctic, south-polar
Anteil *m/prozentualer* percentage distribution
Anteklise *f* anteclise *(tectonic structure of a platform)*
Antezedenztal *n* antecedent valley
ANT-Gesteine *npl* ANT-rocks *(anorthositic, noritic, troctolite rocks)*
Anthoinit *m* anthoinite, Al[OH|WO$_4$] · H$_2$O
Anthonyit *m* anthonyite, Cu(OH, Cl)$_2$ · 3H$_2$O
Anthophyllit *m* anthophyllite, (Mg, Fe)$_7$[OH|Si$_4$O$_{11}$]$_2$
Anthrakonit *m* anthraconite, anthracolite, swinestone, urinestone
Anthraxylon *m (Am)* [translucent] anthraxylon *(banded component ≙ vitrinite > 14 µm)*
Anthrazit *m* anthracite
~/feinkörniger flaxseed coal
anthrazitartig anthracitic, anthracitous
anthrazithaltig anthraciferous
anthrazitisch anthracitic, anthracitous
Anthrazitschiefer *m* anthracitic shale
anthropogen anthropogenic, anthropic[al]
Anthropogenese *f,* **Anthropogenie** *f* antropogeny, anthropogenesis
anthropoid anthropoid, man-like
Anthropologie *f* anthropology
anthropologisch anthropologic[al]
Anthroposphäre *f* anthroposphere
Antien *n* Antian *(basal Pleistocene, British Islands)*
Antiepizentrum *n* anti[epi]centre
Antiferromagnetismus *m* antiferromagnetism
Antigorit *m* antigorite, Mg$_6$[(OH)$_8$|Si$_4$O$_{10}$]
Antiklase *f* anticlase, tension[al] crack
antiklastisch anticlastic
antiklinal anticlinal
Antiklinalachse *f* anticlinal (saddle) axis
Antiklinale *f* anticline, upfold
~/abtauchende nose
~/aufgebrochene anticlinal valley
~/aufrechte symmetric[al] anticline
~/bloßgelegte exposed anticline
~/breite broad-crested anticline
~/durch eine Verwerfungsfläche abgeschnittene anticline cut off by a fault plane
~/enge narrow-crested anticline
~/gekappte scalped (bald-headed) anticline
~/geschlossene closed anticline
~/halbentwickelte nose
~/isoklinal gefaltete carinate anticline
~/liegende recumbent anticline
~/offene nose
~/überkippte overturned (recumbent) anticline
~/unsymmetrische asymmetric[al] anticline
~/zusammengesetzte composite anticline
Antiklinalfalte *f* s. Sattelfalte
Antiklinalflanke *f* anticlinal flank *(s.a. Antiklinalflügel)*

Antiklinalflügel *m* flank (slope) of anticline (*s.a.* Antiklinalflanke)
Antiklinalkamm *m* crest (apex) of anticline, anticlinal mountain (ridge)
Antiklinalkern *m* anticlinal (arch) core
Antiklinallinie *f* anticlinal [crest] line, ridge line
Antiklinalquelle *f* anticlinal spring
Antiklinalrücken *m*, **Antiklinalsattel** *m s.* Antiklinalkamm
Antiklinalscharnier *n* saddle (arch) bend
Antiklinalschenkel *m* anticlinal limb
Antiklinalspeicher *m* anticlinal reservoir
Antiklinalstruktur *f*/**geschlossene** closure
Antiklinaltal *n* anticlinal (saddle) valley
Antiklinaltheorie *f* anticlinal theory
Antikline *f s.* Antiklinale
Antiklinorium *n* anticlinorium, compound arch, composite fan structure
Antillia *f* Antillis
antimagnetisch non-magnetic
Antimon *n* antimony, Sb
~/fein verteiltes iron black
~/gediegenes native antimony
Antimonarsen *n* allemontite, antimoniferous arsenic, SbAs$_3$
antimonartig stibial
Antimonblende *f s.* Kermesit
Antimonblüte *f* antimony bloom, valentinite, Sb$_2$O$_3$
Antimonerz *n* antimony ore
Antimonfahlerz *n* tetrahedrite, gray copper ore, 3Cu$_2$S · Sb$_2$S$_3$
Antimonglanz *m s.* Antimonit
antimonhaltig antimonic, antimonial, antimon[i]ous
Antimonit *m* antimonite, antimony glance, gray antimony, stibnite, Sb$_2$S$_3$
Antimonkupferglanz *m* wheel ore
Antimonnickelglanz *m s.* Ullmannit
Antimonsilber *n s.* Dyskrasit
Antimonsilberblende *f s.* Pyrargyrit
Antipassat *m* antitrade [wind], counter trade
Antiperthit *m* antiperthite
Antiquuszeit *f* Antiquus time
Antistreßmineral *n* antistress mineral
antithetisch antithetic[al]
Antivergenz *f* antivergence
Antizentrum *n* anticentre *(seismics)*
Antizyklone *f* anticyclone
Antlerit *m* antlerite, Cu$_3$[(OH)$_4$|SO$_4$]
Antozonit *m* antozonite *(variety of fluorite)*
anvisieren to align the sights on, to take the bearings of
anwachsen to accrue
Anwachsküste *f* shore line of progradation
Anwachslinie *f*, **Anwachsstreifen** *m* growth line
Anwachsufer *n* deposition bluff
anzapfen to capture, to behead *(a river)*
Anzapfung *f* 1. tapping, bleeding, abstraction (e.g. of a bore); 2. capture, piracy, beheading (of a river)

aquatisch

~/unterirdische underground tapping
Anzapfungsknie *n* elbow of [stream] capture
Anzeichen *npl* signs, showings
Anziehung *f* attraction
~/magnetische magnetic attraction
Anziehungskraft *f* attractional force
äolisch [a]eolian, aerial, wind-blown
Äon *m* [a]eon *(greatest geochronologic unit)*
Äonothem *n* [a]eonothem *(greatest biostratigraphic unit)*
Apachit *m* apachite
Apatit *m* apatite, calcium phosphate, Ca$_5$[F|(PO$_4$)$_3$]
~/erdiger osteolite
Apatiteisenerz *n* apatite iron ore
Apatitgestein *n* phosphate rock
aperiodisch aperiodic[al]
Apertur *f* aperture *(palaeontology)*
~/numerische numerical aperture *(optical)*
Apex *m* apex
Aphanit *m* aphanite
aphanitisch aphani[ti]c
Aphel *n* aphelion
Aphelabstand *m* aphelion distance
Aphrosiderit *m* aphrosiderite *(variety of chlorite)*
Aphthitalit *m* aphthitalite, K$_3$Na[SO$_4$]$_2$
Apjohnit *m* apjohnite, MnAl$_2$[SO$_4$]$_4$ · 22H$_2$O
Aplazentalier *npl* aplacental mammals, aplacentals
Aplit *m* aplite
Aplitgang *m* aplite dike
aplitisch aplitic
Aplogranit *m* aplogranite
Aplom *m* aplome *(variety of andradite)*
Aplowit *m* aplowite, (Co, Mn, Ni) [SO$_4$] · 4H$_2$O
Apobsidian *m* apobsidian *(devitrified obsidian)*
apochromatisch apochromatic
Apogäum *n* apogee
apomagmatisch apomagmatic
apomorph apomorphic
Apomorphie *f* apomorphy
Apophyllit *m* apophyllite, KCa$_4$[F|(Si$_4$O$_{10}$)$_2$] · 8H$_2$O
Apophyse *f* apophyse, apophysis, dikelet, offshooting tongue, [off-]shoot, offset of the bed
Aporhyolith *m* aporhyolite
Appalachen-Provinz *f* Appalachian Province *(palaeobiogeography, Devonian)*
Appalachia *f* Appalachis, Appalachia
Appinit *m* appinite *(rock of the diorite clan)*
Apside *f* apsis
Apt[ien] *n*, **Aptium** *n* Aptian [Stage] *(of Lower Cretaceous)*
Aptychenmergel *m* Aptychus Marl *(Malm and Lower Cretaceous, pelagic facies)*
Aquädukt *m* aqueduct
Aqualunge *f* aqualung
Aquamarin *m* aquamarine *(variety of beryl)*
aquatisch aquatic

Äquator 26

Äquator *m* equator
~/erdmagnetischer [geo]magnetic equator, aclinic line
Äquatorebene *f* equatorial plane
äquatorial equatorial
Äquatorialkammern *fpl* median chambers *(foraminifers)*
Äquatorialstrom *m* equatorial current
Äquatorialwald *m* equatorial forest
Aquatorien *npl* **der Erde** water-covered areas of the earth
Äquatorleiste *f s.* Cingulum
Äquatorradius *m* equatorial radius
Äquatorströmung *f* equatorial drift
Äquatorumfang *m* equatorial circumference
Äquidensitendarstellung *f* density (level) slicing
Äquidensitometrie *f* equidensitometry
äquidensitometrisch equidensitometric
äquidistant equidistant
Äquidistanz *f* equidistance
Aquifer *m* aquifer [layer] *(s.a.* Grundwasserleiter)
Aquiferspeicher *m* aquifer store
Aquiferspeicherung *f* aquifer storage
Aquifertyp *m* aquifer type
äquinoktial equinoctial
Äquinoktiallinie *f* equinoctial line
Äquinoktialstürme *mpl* equinoctial gales (storms)
Äquinoktium *n* equinox
~/mittleres mean equinox
äquipotential equipotential
Äquipotentialfläche *f* equipotential surface
Äquipotentiallinie *f* contour (equipotential) line, piezometric contour
Aquitan[ien] *n,* **Aquitanium** *n* Aquitanian [Stage] *(of Miocene)*
äquivalent equivalent, homotaxial
Äquivalentgewicht *n* equivalent weight
Äquivalenz *f* equivalence
Ära *f* era *(geochronologic unit)*
Araeoxen *m* araeoxene *(variety of descloicite)*
Aragonit *m* aragonite, needle spar, $CaCO_3$
Arakawait *m s.* Veszelyit
Aramayoit *m* aramayoite, $Ag(Sb, Bi)S_2$
Arandisit *m* arandisite *(aggregate of hydrocassiterite and quartz)*
Aräometeranalyse *f* hydrometer analysis (test)
Arapahit *m* arapahite *(variety of basalt)*
Ärathem *n* erathem *(biostratigraphic unit)*
Arbeitsbarke *f* work barge
Arbeitsbühne *f* derrick floor
Arbeitshöhe *f* **im Flöz** working thickness of a seam
Arbeitsstoß *m* working face
~ senkrecht zu den Schlechten face on end
Arcanit *m* arcanite, α-$K_2[SO_4]$
Archäiden *pl* Archaides
Archaikum *n* Arch[a]ean [Era], Arch[a]eozoic [Era]
archäisch Arch[a]ean, Archaic, Arch[a]eozoic

Archäozoikum *n* Arch[a]eozoic [Era], Arch[a]ean [Era], Cryptozoic [Eon], Precambrian [Eon]
archäozoisch Arch[a]eozoic, Arch[a]ean
Archie-Gleichung *f* Archie's law
Archipel *m* archipelago
Ardennit *m* ardennite, $Mn_4MgAl_5[(OH)_2|(V, As)O_4|SiO_4)_5] \cdot 2H_2O$
Area *f* escutcheon
Areal *n/***disjunktes** discontinuous areal *(ecology)*
~/kontinuierliches continuous areal *(ecology)*
Arealeruption *f* areal eruption
Arenig *n* Arenigian [Stage] *(of Lower Ordovician)*
Arenit *m* arenite
~/äolischer anemosilicarenite, anemosilicarenyte
Arfvedsonit *m* arfvedsonite, $Na_3(Mg, Fe)_4(Fe,Al)[Si_4O_{11}]_2[OH,F]_2$
Argentit *m* argentite, acanthite, argyrose, argyrite, silver glance, vitreous silver, Ag_2S
Argentojarosit *m* argentojarosite, $AgFe_3[(OH)_6|(SO_4)_2]$
Argentopyrit *m* argentopyrite, $AgFe_2S_3$
Argillit *m* argillite, argillaceous slate
~/schwach metamorpher meta-argillite
argillitisch argillitic, shaly
Argon *n* argon, Ar
~/radiogenes radiogenic argon
Argonalter *n* argon age
Argonentgasung *f* argon degassing
Argov[ium] *n* Argovian [Substage] *(of Lusitanian)*
Argyrodit *m* argyrodite, $4Ag_2S \cdot GeS_2$
a-Richtung *f* a-direction *(tectonics)*
arid arid
Aridität *f* aridity, aridness
Ariégit *m* ariegite *(pyroxenite)*
Arietitenschichten *fpl* Arietites layers
Arikareean *n* Arikareean [Stage] *(mammalian stage, upper Oligocene including lower Miocene, North America)*
Arit *m* arite, $Ni(As,Sb)$
Arizonit *m* arizonite, $Fe_2O_3 \cdot 3TiO_2$
Arkit *m* arkite
Arkose *f* arkose, arcose
~ von granitartigem Habitus meta-arkose
arkosehaltig arkosic, arcosic
Arkosequarzit *m* arkose quartzite, arkosite
Arkosesandstein *m* arkosic grit, feldspathic sandstone
Arktis *f* Arctic region
arktisch arctic
arm lean, low-grade *(ore, gas)*
Arm *m/***toter** dead arm, dead (abandoned) channel
Armalkolith *m* armalcolite, $(Fe_{0,5} \cdot Mg_{0,5})Ti_2O_5$
Armangit *m* armangite, $Mn_3[AsO_3]_2$
Armerz *n* lean (low-grade) ore
Armfüßler *mpl* brachiopods
Armgas *n* lean gas
Armgerüst *n* brachidium, brachial (arm) supports *(brachiopods)*

Armklappe f brachial valve
Armorika f Armorica
Aromaten mpl aromatics *(hydrocarbons)*
Arrojadit m arrojadite, $Na_2(Fe^{..}, Mn^{..})_5[PO_4]_4$
Arroyo n arroyo
Arsen n arsenic, As
~/gediegenes native arsenic
Arsenblende f/**rote** ruby sulphur
Arsenblüte f arsenolite, pharmacolite *(partly As_2O_3, partly $CaH[AsO_4] \cdot 2H_2O$)*
Arseneisen n s. Löllingit
Arseneisensinter m pitticite, $Fe_{20}[(OH)_{24}|(AsO_4, SO_4)_{13}] \cdot 9H_2O$
Arsenerz n arsenic ore
Arsenfahlerz n s. Tennantit
arsenführend arseniferous, arsenical
arsenhaltig arsenical, arsenious
Arsenikalkies m s. Löllingit
Arsenikkobalt m s. Safflorit
Arseniopleit m arseniopleite *(variety of caryinite)*
Arseniosiderit m arseniosiderite, $Ca_3Fe_4[OH|AsO_4]_4 \cdot 4H_2O$
Arsenit n s. Arsenolith
Arsenkies m arsenopyrite, arsenical pyrite, FeAsS
Arsenkupfer n s. Domeykit
Arsennickel n s. Rotnickelkies
Arsenobismit m arsenobismite, $Bi_4[OH|AsO_4]_3 \cdot H_2O$
Arsenoferrit m s. Löllingit
Arsenoklasit m arsenoclasite, $Mn_5[(OH)_2|AsO_4]_2$
Arsenolamprit m arsenolamprite
Arsenolith m arsenolite, arsenite, white arsenic, As_2O_3
Arsenomelan m s. Sartorit
Arsenopalladinit m arsenopalladinite, Pd_3As
Arsenopolybasit m arsenpolybasite, pearceite, $8(Ag,Cu)_2S \cdot As_2S_3$
Arsenopyrit m arsenical pyrite, arsenopyrite, FeAsS
Arsensilberblende f s. Proustit
Arsensulvanit m arsensulvanite, $Cu_3(As,V)S_4$
Arsenuranylit m arsenuranylite, $Ca[(UO_2)_4|(OH)_4|(AsO_4)_2] \cdot 6H_2O$
Art f species
~/ausgestorbene extinct species
~/bodenständige endemic species
~/dominierende dominant species
~/eindringende invaders
~/überlebende survival species
~/vikarierende vicarious (representative) species
Artbildung f species formation, speciation
Artefakt n artifact, artefac[t]
artenreich varied
Artenreichtum m riches of species
Artentod m extinction of species
Artenverteilung f species distribution
Artenzahl f/**mittlere** average species number
Arterit m arterite *(migmatite)*

artesisch artesian
Artinit m artinite, $Mg_2[(OH)_2]CO_3 \cdot 3H_2O$
Artinsk n Artinskian [Stage] *(basal stage of Lower Permian)*
Arzrunit m arzrunite, $Pb_2Cu_4[O_2|Cl_6|SO_4] \cdot 4H_2O$
As[ar] m s. Os
Asbest m asbestos
~/kanadischer s. Chrysotil
~ mit Fasern senkrecht zum Salband cross fiber asbestos
~/verfilzter mass fiber asbestos
asbestartig asbestoid
asbestführend asbestine
Asbestschiefer m asbestos slate
Asbolan m asbolan[e] *(s.a. Kobaltmanganerz)*
Aschaffit m aschaffite *(lamprophyre)*
Ascharit m ascharite, camsellite, szaibelyite, $Mg_2[B_2O_5] \cdot H_2O$
Asche f ash
~/resurgente accessory ash
~/vulkanische volcanic ash
Aschebestandteile mpl/**syngenetische** extraneous ash *(of coal)*
Aschebildner m ash constituent, ashy component
Aschendecke f coating of ash
Aschenfall m ash fall
aschenfrei ashless
Aschengehalt m ash content
Aschengehaltsbestimmung f determination of the ash content
Aschenkegel m ash (cinder) cone
Aschenlawine f dry (dust) avalanche
Aschenregen m ash rain (shower)
Aschenschieferton m ashy shale, ash slate
Aschenstrom m ash flow (current), flow (current) of ashes
Aschentuff m cinerite
Aschen- und Schuttlawine f/**gemischte** mixed avalanche
Aschenwolke f ash cloud
~/elektrisch geladene electrified ash cloud
Aschenwurf m jet of ash
aschereich high-ash
Aschesediment n cinerite *(volcanic)*
aschig cinereous
aschist aschistic
Äschynit m [a]eschynite, (Ce, Th, Ca...) (Nb, Ti, Ta)$_2O_6$]
aseismisch aseismic[al], non-seismic[al]
Aseptaten npl aseptate corals, aseptates
Aser m s. Os
Ashcroftin m ashcroftine, $KNa(Ca, Mg, Mn) [Al_4Si_5O_{18}] \cdot 8H_2O$
Ashgill[ium] n, **Ashgill-Stufe** f Ashgillian (Stage) *(Upper Ordovician)*
Asowskit m asowskite, $Fe_3^{...}[(OH)_6|PO_4]$
Asphalt m asphalt[um], oil (stellar) coal, mineral pitch
~/mit Nebengestein verunreinigter land asphalt

Asphalt 28

~/reiner glance pitch
asphaltähnlich asphaltlike
Asphaltausbiß *m* asphalt seepage
Asphaltbeton *m* asphaltic concrete
Asphaltene *npl* asphaltenes
Asphaltgestein *n* asphalt[ic] rock, bituminous rock, asphalt stone, crude (rock) asphalt
Asphaltgrube *f* tar pit
asphalthaltig asphaltic, bituminiferous
asphaltisch asphaltic
Asphaltit *m* asphaltite, vein bitumen
Asphaltkalkstein *m* asphaltic (asphalt-impregnated) limestone
Asphaltlager *n* asphalt deposit
Asphaltöl *n* asphalt-base oil
Asphaltsand *m* asphaltic sand
Asphaltsandstein *m* bituminous sandstone
Asphaltteer *m* mineral tar
Asphaltvorkommen *n* asphalt deposit
Assel[ium] *n* Asselian [Stage] *(uppermost stage of Upper Carboniferous)*
Assimilation *f* assimilation
~/magmatische syntexis
Assoziation *f*/lithologische lithologic association
assyntisch assyntic
Ast *m* spur *(of a lode)*
~/rückläufiger reverse branch *(of a travel-time curve)*
astatisch astatic
Asterismus *m* asteriation, asterism
Asteroid *m* asteroid, planetoid, minor planet
Asteroidenbahn *f* planetoid orbit
Asteroidengürtel *m* asteroid belt
Asthenolit *m* asthenolith
Asthenosphäre *f* asthenosphere
Astit *m* astite *(variety of hornfels)*
Astrakanit *m* astrakanite, blödite, bloedite, $Na_2Mg(SO_4)_2 \cdot 4H_2O$
astral stellar
Astrobiologie *f* astrobiology
Astroblem *n* astrobleme
Astrobotanik *f* astrobotany
Astrochemie *f* astrochemistry
Astrodynamik *f* astrodynamics
Astrogeologie *f* astrogeology
Astrolith *m* astrolite, $(Na, K)_2Fe^-(Al,Fe^{...})_2Si_5O_{15} \cdot H_2O$
astrologisch astrological
Astrometrie *f* astrometry
astrometrisch astrometric
Astronomie *f* astronomy
~/aeronautische aeronautic[al] astronomy
astronomisch astronomic[al]
Astrophyllit *m* astrophyllite, $(K_2, Na_2, Ca) (Fe, Mn)_4(Ti, Zr) [OH|Si_2O_7]_2$
Astrophysik *f* astrophysics
astrophysikalisch astrophysical
Astrospektroskopie *f* astrospectroscopy
Ästuar *n* estuary, tidal river
ästuarin estuarine
Ästuarküste *f* estuary coast

Ästuartypus *m* estuarine type
Asymmetrie *f* 1. asymmetry, dissymmetry; 2. skewness
asymmetrisch 1. asymmetric[al], dissymmetric[al]; 2. enantiomorphic
aszendent ascendant, ascendent
Aszendenz *f* ascendancy, ascendency
Aszensionstheorie *f* ascension theory
Atakamit *m* atacamite, $Cu_2(OH)_3Cl$
Atatschit *m* atatschite *(variety of orthophyre)*
Atavismus *m* atavism *(palaeontology)*
Ataxit *m* ataxite *(iron meteorite)*
Atdaban[ium] *n* Atdabanian [Stage] *(upper part of Lower Cambrian, Siberia)*
atektonisch atectonic
Atelestit *m* atelestite, shagite, $Bi_2[O|OH|AsO_4]$
Äthan *n* ethane, C_2H_6
Äthylen *n* heavy-carburetted hydrogen, olefiant gas, C_2H_4
Atlantika *f* Atlantica
Atlas *m*/geologischer geologic[al] atlas
Atlasspat *m*, Atlasstein *m* satin spar (stone)
Atmogeochemie *f* atmogeochemistry
atmoklastisch atmoclastic
atmophil atmophilic, atmophil[e]
atmopyroklastisch atmopyroclastic
Atmosphäre *f* atmosphere
Atmosphärenforschungsprogramm *n*/globales global atmospheric research program, GARP
atmosphärisch atmospheric[al]
Atoll *n* atoll, lagoon island, circular reef, reef ring
~ mit vulkanischer Laguneninsel almost atoll
~ zweiter Ordnung faro
Atollon *n* faro
Atollriff *n* atoll reef
Atom *n* atom
Atomabsorptionsspektrometrie *f* atomic absorption spectrometry
Atombau *m* atomic structure
Atomgewicht *n* atomic weight
Atomgewichtstabelle *f* atomic chart
Atomgitter *n* atomic space lattice
Atomgruppe *f* atomic group
Atomhülle *f* shell of the atom
Atomkern *m* atomic nucleus (kernel)
Atomkernzerfall *m* nuclear disintegration
Atomkonzentration *f* atomic concentration
Atomkräfte *fpl* atomic forces
Atomlehre *f* atomic theory
Atommasse *f* atomic (isotopic) mass
Atommasseneinheit *f* atomic mass unit
Atommassenzahl *f* atomic mass number
Atomphysik *f* atomic physics
Atomspektrum *n* atomic spectrum
Atomstrahlung *f* atomic radiation
Atomsymbol *n* atomic symbol
Atomtheorie *f* atomic theory
Atomumwandlung *f* atomic transformation
Atomvolumen *n* atomic volume
Atomwärme *f* atomic heat

Atomzerfall *m* atomic disintegration (decay), degeneration of atoms
Atopit *m* atopite *(variety of romeite)*
Attrinit *m* attrinite *(maceral of brown coals and lignites)*
ätzen to etch; to corrode
ätzend corrosive
Ätzfigur *f* etch figure
Ätzgrübchen *n* etching pit
Ätzkalk *m* caustic (quick, live) lime
Ätzskulptur *f* etching figure
Ätzstruktur *f* etching structure
Ätzung *f* etching
Ätzungserscheinung *f* corrosional phenomenon
Ätzverhalten *n* behaviour of etching
Auboden *m s.* Auenboden
Aubrit *m* aubrite *(anachondrite containing enstatite)*
Aue *f* flood (bottom) land, callow
Auenablagerung *f* flood plain deposit
Auenboden *m* [alluvial] meadow soil, warp (flood-plain, riverside) soil
~/dunkler black meadow soil
~/schwarzerdeartiger *s.* Tschernosem
Auenlehm *m* meadow loam
Auensumpf *m* black swamp
Auenton *m* warp clay
Auerlith *m* auerlite, (Th,...) [(Si, P)O₄]
aufarbeiten to rework; to assort *(by water)*
Aufarbeitung *f* reworking; assorting *(by water)*
Aufbau *m* building-up; assembly; arrangement; constitution, structure; setting-up
~/atomarer atomic structure
~/innerer internal constitution *(of earth)*
aufbauen/Druck to build up pressure
Aufbauform *f* constructional form
Aufbauküste *f* constructional coast
aufbereitbar/naß washable
aufbereiten to prepare; to treat, to dress, to process; to separate; to concentrate, to beneficiate; to cleanse
Aufbereitung *f* preparation; treatment, dressing, processing; separation; concentration, beneficiation; cleansing; upgrading; milling
Aufbereitungsabgänge *mpl* feigh
Aufbereitungsanlage *f* preparation plant; dressing (upgrading) plant; concentrating (concentration) plant; cleansing plant; mill
Aufbereitungsherd *m* concentration table
Aufbereitungsindustrie *f* extractive industry
Aufbereitungskosten *pl* dressing expenses
Aufbereitungsprodukt *n* concentrate[s]
Aufbereitungsrückstand *m* feigh
Aufbereitungsschlämme *mpl* mill slurries
~/sandig-tonige garde
Aufbereitungstechnik *f* practice of dressing and preparation
Aufbereitungsverlust *m* loss in cleansing
Aufbeulung *f* bulging
aufblähen to inflate
~/sich to tumefy *(minerals)*

Aufblähung *f* intumescence *(of minerals)*
aufblättern to exfoliate
Aufblätterung *f* exfoliation, bed separation
Aufbrauch *m* consumptive use *(of water resources)*
aufbrausen to effervesce
Aufbrausen *n* effervescence
aufbrechen to break up
aufbrodeln to bubble
Aufbruch *m s.* Aufbrausen
aufbuckeln to buckle (hump) up
Aufdeckung *f* revelation, uncovering
Aufeinanderfolge *f* sequence, succession
~/geologische geological succession
~ von Schichten stratigraphic succession, stratigraphic sequence [of strata], succession of strata
Aufeis *n* fossil ice, pingo, ground-ice mound
Aufeishügel *m* frost mound, pingo
Aufenthaltsdauer *f* **im Boden** underground detention time *(of ground water)*
Auffächern *n* diffluence
auffahren to drive
Auffahrung *f* drive, drifting
~/bergmännische mining drive (working)
Auffaltung *f* upfolding, upthrust, arching; anticlinal fold, tectonic culmination
Auffaltungsfeld *n* area of tectonic culmination
Auffangfläche *f* catchment surface, catchment area
auffiedern to feather out, to finger out
auffinden to detect; to discover
Auffindung *f* detection; discovery
~ einer Struktur structure discovery
Auffingerung *f* **von Faltendeckenstirnen** digitation *(of the front of a fold nappe)*
aufforsten to reforest
Aufforstung *f* reforestation, afforestation
Auffrieren *n* frost lifting
auffrischen to freshen
auffüllen to infill
Auffüllung *f* 1. blocking-up; 2. made ground
Aufgabenstellung *f/***geologische** geological target
Aufgang *m* rise, uprising
aufgeben 1. to charge; to feed; 2. to abandon, to give up
~/eine Bohrung to abandon a well
~/eine Grube to abandon a mine
aufgehen to rise
Aufgehen *n* rise, rising
aufgerichtet upturned
~/steil steeply (sharply) upturned
aufgerissen eviscerated
aufgerollt coiled
~/nicht non-coiled
~/spiralig spirally coiled
aufgeschlickt silted-up
aufgesetzt superadded
aufgetaucht *s.* emers
aufgewölbt upbowed, arched-up
aufgleiten to slip over, to override

Aufgleiten 30

Aufgleiten *n* upslide motion
Aufgleitfläche *f* upslide surface; surface of discontinuity
Aufgleitregen *m* convectional rain
Aufgrabung *f* **für Fundamente** basement excavating
aufhacken to break up
aufhalden to bing
aufhauen to raise
Aufhauen *n* raise
aufholen to pull out, to withdraw
Aufholen *n* **des Bohrwerkzeugs** tool withdrawal
Aufkitten *n* cementing *(on glass slide)*
aufklaffen to gape
Aufklärungserkundung *f* reconnaissance survey
Aufklärungsflug *m* reconnaissance flight
Aufkochen *n* ebullition
Aufkrempen *n* dragging *(tectonics)*
Auflagefläche *f* bearing surface
Auflager *n* abutment
Auflagerdruck *m* bearing (supplementary) pressure
Auflagerung *f* superposition
~/übergreifende onlap
~/unterbrochene gleichförmige accordant unconformity
Auflandung *f* filling-up, silting-up, blocking-up, colmatage, aggradation, accretion; alluvium, alluvial deposit
auflassen to abandon; to disuse
~/eine Bohrung to shut in a well
Auflast *f* [super]imposed load, additional load; overlying weight; overburden pressure, loading, off-load
~ von Staubecken depressuring of reservoirs
Auflaufen *n* uprush *(of waves)*
aufleben/wieder to reappear
auflegen/sich to begin to bear on *(roof)*
Auflicht *n* reflected light
Auflichtbeleuchtung *f* episcopic illumination
Auflichtelektronenmikroskop *n* direct-light electron microscope
Auflichtmikroskop *n* mineragraphic microscope
Auflichtmikroskopie *f* **von Mineralen** mineralography
aufliegend superjacent
Auflockerung *f* loosening; breaking[-up], disaggregation
auflösen 1. to resolve *(optically)*; 2. to dissolve *(chemically)*
Auflösung *f* 1. resolution *(optically)*; 2. dissolution; resorption *(chemically, mineralogically)*
Auflösungselement *n* resolution element
~/effektives effective resolution element, ERE
~/effektives geometrisches spatial effective resolution element, SERE
~/effektives radiometrisches effective radiometric resolution element, ERRE

Auflösungsgrenze *f* limit of resolution
Auflösungsvermögen *n* resolving power, resolution
~/äquivalentes fotografisches equivalent photographic resolution
~/geometrisches spatial resolution
~/radiometrisches radiometric resolution
~/räumliches spatial resolution
Aufnahme *f* 1. uptake *(chemically)*; 2. survey *(of maps)*; 3. pick-up, logging *(of measuring data)*
~ eines Gebietes/geologische geological ground survey
~/elektronenmikroskopische electron micrograph
~/flächenhafte seismische three-D seismics
~/geologische geologic[al] survey
~/geophysikalische geophysic[al] survey[ing]
~/luftfotogrammetrische aerophotogrammetric survey
~/markscheiderische survey plan
~ radioaktiver Profile radiation logging
~/stereofotogrammetrische stereophotogrammetrical survey
~/topografische reconnaissance
Aufnahmebasis *f* air base
Aufnahmefähigkeit *f* absorptivity, absorbency
Aufnahmegeometrie *f* field layout *(seismics)*
Aufnahmegerät *n* surveying apparatus
Aufnahmekanal *m* receiving canal
Aufnahmen *fpl* **aus großer Flughöhe** high-altitude photography
~/großmaßstäbliche large-scale imagery
Aufnahmesystem *n/***nichtabbildendes** non-imaging sensor
aufnehmen 1. to take up; 2. to survey *(maps)*; 3. to pick up, to log *(measuring data)*; 4. to resist *(a force)*
~/eine Grube to survey a mine
~/mit dem Kompaß to dial
~/Profil to profile
Aufnehmer *m* detector; pick-up
Auf- oder Abschiebung *f/***schräge** diagonal slip fault
Aufprallmarke *f* bounce cast
Aufpressung *f* upturning, upwedging, upthrust, intumescence
Aufpressungsmoräne *f* push (shove) moraine
aufquellen to swell up; to bulge
Aufquellen *n* swelling-up; bulging
~ des Liegenden floor heave, creep, swelling
Aufragung *f* eminence
aufrecht upright
Aufreihung *f* arrangement in rows
aufreißen/wieder to tear (rip, break) up again
Aufreißen *n* fracturing
aufrichten to straighten up
~/sich to rear up
Aufrichtung *f* uplift
aufrollen to work out a whole district in one direction
~/sich to uncoil *(ammonites)*

Aufsandung *f* sanding
Aufsattelung *f* anticlinal (ridge) uplift
Aufsaugung *f* imbibition
Aufschiebung *f* 1. upfaulting, upthrust; 2. [up]thrust fault, upthrow (centrifugal, upcast) fault; ramp centrifugal fault, upcast fault; ramp
~/deckenartige nappelike overthrust
~ ins Hangende trap-up
aufschießen to flemish down
Aufschießen *n* shooting
Aufschlag *m* impact *(of a meteorite)*
aufschlagen to impinge *(meteorites)*
Aufschlagpunkt *m* point of impact *(of a meteorite)*
Aufschlagsbeiwert *m* impact coefficient
Aufschlagsloch *n* **von Tropfwasser** driphole
Aufschlagspur *f* impact mark *(of a meteorite)*
aufschlämmen to elutriate
Aufschlämmen *n* elutriation
Aufschlickung *f* silting; vertical accretion deposit *(from a river)*
aufschließbar capable of being opened
aufschließen to open [up], to develop, to expose; to win
Aufschluß *m* opening[-up], development, exposure; winning; [out]crop
~/flächenhafter extended exposure
~/künstlicher artificial opening
~/natürlicher natural outcrop
~/punktförmiger point-shaped exposure
~/verdeckter obscured exposure
Aufschlußarbeiten *fpl* exploratory work, carry[-on] explorations
Aufschlußbohrung *f* exploration (structure) drilling, exploratory (test) boring; exploratory hole (well), prospect well (hole)
~/geologische geologic[al] exploratory drill hole
Aufschlußdauer *f* time of exploration
Aufschlußdichte *f* density of exploration (exposure) *(of an exploration area)*
Aufschlußkonzession *f* exploration licence
Aufschlußkosten *pl* exploration expenses
Aufschlußpunkt *m* point of exposure
Aufschlußverhältnisse *npl* conditions of exposure
aufschmelzen to melt, to dissolve
Aufschmelzen *n* melting, dissolving
~/selektives selective fusion
Aufschmelzung *f* dissolution
~/partielle partial (fractional) melting *(anatexis)*
~/vollständige complete melting *(anatexis)*
Aufschmelzungstheorie *f* theory of dissolution
Aufschotterung *f* aggradation
Aufschotterungsgebiet *n* geest
Aufschotterungsterrasse *f* fill terrace
~/erodierte fillstrath terrace
~/vollständig erhaltene filltop terrace
Aufschüttung *f* accretion, upbuilding; aggradation

Aufschüttungsinsel *f* aggradation island
Aufschüttungskegel *m* alluvial cone
Aufschüttungsterrasse *f* aggradation[al] terrace, wave-built terrace
~/litorale wave-built terrace
~/marine marine-built terrace
Aufschüttungstheorie *f s.* Akkumulationstheorie
aufschwellen to swell up
Aufschwellung *f* upswelling
Aufschwemmung *f* accretion, aggradation, filling-up, silting-up, warp
~ des Bodens warping of land
~ von Erde colmatage
Aufsicht *f* top view
aufspalten to cleave, to split
Aufspaltung *f* cleavage, splitting
~ von Schiefern sculping
aufsprudeln to bubble
Aufsprudeln *n* ebullition
Aufspülbögen *mpl* wash-over crescents
Aufspülung *f* hydraulic fill
~ durch Sedimentanlagerung accretion
Aufspüren *n* **von Kohlenwasserstoffen** tracing of hydrocarbons
Aufstau *m* swell *(of water)*; storage, impoundage, backwater, raised water level
aufstauen to dam up, to impound, to pond back
aufsteigen to ascend
Aufsteigen *n* elevation; ascent
~ des Wassers ascent of water
aufsteigend ascending; anabatic
aufstellen 1. to set up; to plant *(e.g. geophones)*; 2. to advance *(a theory)*
Aufstellung *f* 1. spread *(seismics)*; 2. reading position, setting *(of a crystal)*
~/einseitige end-on spread, off-end spread
~/gestaffelte feathering [spread]
~ mit Richtungswirkung weighted array
Aufstellungslücke *f* **am Schußpunkt** shot point gap, offset
Aufstemmung *f* [overhead] stoping
~/magmatische magmatic stoping
Aufstemmungstheorie *f* overhead stoping hypothesis
Aufstiegsbahn *f* ascent path
Aufstiegsgeschwindigkeit *f* **der Spülung/optimale** optimum annular return velocity of mud
Aufstiegskanal *m* ascending channel
Aufstiegsmenge *f/kapillare* capillary yield
Aufstoßmarke *f* bounce cast
~/kammförmige ctenoid cast
Aufstülpung *f/gangartige* gangstock *(intrusion)*
Aufsturzhypothese *f* impact hypothesis
aufsuchen to explore
Aufsuchen *n* exploration
Auftauboden *m s.* Auftauschicht
auftauchen to emerge
Auftauchen *n* emersion, emergence

Auftauchen 32

~ der Küste emergence of coast
Auftauchküste f shore line of emergence
Auftauchungsinsel f emerged island
auftauen to thaw
Auftauen n thawing
Auftauschicht f thawing (involution) layer; active layer (in permafrost areas)
auftragen to plot (measuring data)
Auftragsarbeit f contract work (in geological exploration)
Auftragung f plotting (of measuring data)
~/punktweise point plotting
auftreten to appear; to occur
~/nesterförmig to occur in pockets
Auftreten n appearance; occurrence
~/linsenförmiges lenticularity
~/periodisches periodicity
~/schichtförmiges occurrence in strata
~ von Erdöl oil occurrence
~ von Frost incidence of frost
auftretend/im gleichen geografischen Gebiet sympatric
~/innerhalb einer Schichtlage intraformational
~/zwischen den Schichtlagen interformational
Auftrieb m buoyancy; uplift pressure
~/artesischer artesian uplift pressure
Auftriebsbeiwert m lift coefficient
Auftriebshöhe f head [of water], hydrostatic head
~/statische static head
Auftriebskoeffizient m lift coefficient
Auftriebwasser n upwell[ing] water
auftun/sich to thicken [up]
~/sich wieder to reappear
aufwallen to well up; to effervesce
Aufwallung f upwelling; effervescence
aufwältigen to clear up (a mine)
Aufwältigung f clearing-out, work-over (of a mine)
~ unter der See subsea work-over
Aufwältigungsarbeiten fpl work-over operations
Aufwärtsbohrung f raise boring
aufweckend awakening, strong (5th stage of the scale of seismic intensity)
Aufwind m upwind
Aufwirbeln n des Bodens bottom agitation
Aufwirbelung f raising
Aufwirbelungszone f whirl zone
aufwölben to arch up, to uparch, to dome up; to bow up; to warp up[ward], to upwarp; to buckle
Aufwölbung f [up]arching, upward arching, updoming, [upward] doming, [domal] uplift; upbowing, upward bowing, bowing-up; buckling; upbulge; tumescence
~ der Sohle flow-lift (in a mine); floor heave
~ im Torfmoor peat hillock
~/periklinale dome
~ von Schichten uparching of strata
~/weitspannige warping (tectonics)

Aufwuchs m overgrowth
Aufwulstung f des Lockerbodens durch Eis frost lifting
aufzeichnen to record; to plot (measuring data)
Aufzeichnung f recording; plotting (of measuring data)
~ der durchfahrenen Schichten record of the rocks penetrated
~ des Tidenhubs/grafische marigram
~/statistische statistical record
Aufzeit f uphole time
Aufzeitgeophon n uphole geophone
Aufzeitschießen n uphole shooting
Auganit m auganite (variety of andesite)
Auge n/bloßes unaided eye
Augelith m augelite, $Al_2[(OH)_3|PO_4]$
Augenblickspegel m actual level
Augengefüge n s. Augentextur
Augengneis m augen gneiss
Augenhöcker m eye tubercle
Augenhügel m palpebral lobe of the eye
Augenknoten m eye node
Augenkohle f eye (circular) coal (tectonical formation)
augenrein eye clean (precious stones)
Augentextur f eyed (ophthalmitic, orbicular, nodular) structure
Augit m augite, $(Ca,Mg,Fe,Ti,Al)_2[(Si,Al)_2O_6]$
Augitamphibolit m augite amphibolite
Augitandesit m augite andesite
Augitbasalt m augitic basalt
Augitgneis m augite gneiss
augithaltig augitic
Augitit m augitite
Augitporphyr m augitophyre
Augitschiefer m augite schist
Aulacoceras f aulacoceras
Aulakogen n aulacogene (tectonic structure of platform)
Aureole f aureole
~/geochemische geochemical aureole
Aurichalcit m aurichalcite, $(Zn,Cu)_5[(OH)_3|CO_3]_2$
Aurikel npl auricles (molluscans, echinoderms)
Auripigment n orpiment, yellow arsenic, As_2S_3
Aurostibit m aurostibite, $AuSb_2$
ausapern to become exposed
ausbaggern to dredge
Ausbau m lining, support, timbering
~ des Bohrstrangs pulling of the drilling string
~/endgültiger permanent support
~/verlorener abandoned support
~/vorläufiger temporary support
ausbaubar retrievable (e.g. track)
Ausbauchung f bulging (of the slope); widening (of a lode)
Ausbaueinheit f support unit
ausbauen 1. to line, to support, to timber; 2. to hoist; to pull out

Ausbaugeschwindigkeit f des Bohrstrangs pulling speed of the drill string
Ausbaukennlinie f characteristic curve *(prop)*
Ausbauschema n support pattern
Ausbauwiderstand m support resistance
Ausbauzeit f time of "coming out"
ausbeißen s. ausstreichen
Ausbeulung f buckling
Ausbeute f yield[ingness]; output; returns *(of a mine)*
~/sichere safe yield
~/wirtschaftliche economic[al] production
Ausbeutefaktor m recovery factor
Ausbeutegrube f productive (copious) mine
ausbeuten to exploit
Ausbeutezeche f s. Ausbeutegrube
Ausbeutung f exploitation
~ eines Feldes field exploitation
Ausbeutungsgemeinschaft f joint exploitation agreement
Ausbeutungskontrakt m lease
Ausbeutungsplatz m/ergiebiger payable place
Ausbeutungstantieme f lease
Ausbildung f/zyklische cyclic character
Ausbildungsform f external form *(e.g. of minerals)*
Ausbiß m s. Ausstrich
Ausbläser m blown-out shot, hole blow
Ausbleichung f bleaching [podzolization]
Ausblockung f division into blocks
ausblühen to effloresce; to come up to the grass
Aufblühung f efflorescence
ausbrechen to erupt, to break out *(volcano)*; to blow out *(well)*
Ausbrechen n flaking *(roof)*
Ausbreitung f propagation
Ausbreitungsbedingungen fpl propagation conditions
Ausbreitungsgeschwindigkeit f propagation velocity
Ausbreitungsrichtung f direction of propagation
Ausbreitungsvorgang m process of popagation
Ausbringen n output
Ausbruch m 1. eruption, breaking-forth, outburst *(of a volcano)*; 2. blow-out *(of a well)*; 3. backbreak *(quarrying mining)*; 4. explosion
~/phreatischer phreatic eruption
~/phreatomagmatischer phreatomagmatic eruption
~/plötzlicher sudden excavation *(of gas)*
~/subaerischer subaerial eruption
~/subglazialer subglacial eruption
~/subrezenter subrecent eruption
~/übermeerischer supramarine eruption
~/vulkanischer eruption
Ausbruchgestein n s. Ergußgestein
Ausbruchsherd m focus of eruption
Ausbruchskrater m eruption crater
Ausbruchsnische f in Hangunterschneidung conical wall niche

Ausbruchsöffnung f bocca *(volcanism)*
Ausbruchsquerschnitt m/lichter excavated [cross-]section ·
~/nutzbarer finished section
Ausbruchsspalte f fissure vent *(of eruption)*
Ausbruchsstelle f locus of the vent
Ausbruchstätigkeit f/einmalige ephemeral activity *(of a volcano)*
Ausbruchsverhütung f blow-out prevention
Ausbruchszentrum n centre of eruption
ausdauernd perennial
ausdehnen to expand; to extend; to dilate
Ausdehnung f expansion; extension; extent; dilatation
~ der Gaskappe expansion of the gas cap
~/horizontale horizontal extent
~/seitliche lateral extent
~/vertikale vertical extent
Ausdehnungskoeffizient m expansion coefficient
ausdünnen s. auskeilen
ausdünsten to exhale
Ausdünstung f exhalation
Auseinanderlaufen n diffluence
ausfahren to pull out
ausfällen to precipitate
Ausfallkörnung f discontinuously graded aggregate
Ausfällmittel n precipitant
Ausfallswinkel m angle of reflection
Ausfällung f precipitation
Ausfällungsbereich m range of precipitation
Ausfällungsgestein n rock of chemical precipitation
ausfließen to pour out, to flow out, to well out *(lava)*
~/eruptiv to gush
~/stoßweise frei to flow by heads
Ausfließen n welling-out, extravasation *(of lava)*
ausflocken to [de]flocculate, to coagulate [into lumps]
Ausflockung f [de]flocculation, coagulation
Ausfluß m effluent, efflux; outflow; outlet; discharge
~ aus Seen open-lake current
Ausflußgraben m bayou
Ausflußmenge f efflux
Ausflußstelle f point of issue
Ausführungsprojekt n executive program
Ausfüllung f filling-in, filling-up, replenishment
Ausfurchung f furrowing
Ausgangserz n protore
Ausgangsform f ancestor
Ausgangsgestein n source (parent) rock
Ausgangshorizont m base level
Ausgangslösung f initial solution *(of sedimentation water)*
Ausgangsmaterial n initial material
Ausgangsparameter m initial parameter
Ausgangsprodukt n initial product

Ausgangsschmelze

Ausgangsschmelze f initial melt
Ausgangsstoff m feed stock
Ausgasung f gas emission
ausgebaucht gibbous
ausgeflossen outpoured, poured-out
ausgehen s. ausstreichen
Ausgehendes n s. Ausstrich
ausgehöhlt hollowed out; kettled
ausgekolkt/vom Eis ice-scoured
ausgelaugt lixivial, lixiviated, leached
~/nicht unleached
ausgequetscht faulted-out *(in a fault)*
ausgeräumt/vom Eis glacially eroded
ausgesetzt/dem Wind windward
ausgestorben extinct
ausgetrocknet desiccated
ausgewaschen water-scoured
Ausgleich m/**isostatischer** isostatic adjustment
Ausgleichbecken n equalizing reservoir
Ausgleichsfläche f compensation level
~/isostatische isopiestic level, plane of isostatic compensation
Ausgleichsküste f simplified (simplification) coast; mature (graded) shore line
Ausgleichsküstenlinie f graded shore line
Ausgleichslager n buffer stock
Ausgleichsprofil n profile of equilibrium
Ausgleichsströmung f isostatic compensation current
~/subkrustale bathyrheal underflow
Ausgleichszahlung f compensation *(in geological investigations)*
ausgraben to excavate, to exhume, to disinter; to dig up, to unearth
Ausgrabung f excavation, exhumation, disinterment
Ausgrabungsfund m article of antiquity
Ausguß m 1. siphonal duct *(in fossils);* 2. s. Abguß
aushalten to extend *(e.g. a lode)*
Aushalten n **nach der Tiefe** vertical extent *(of a lode)*
Aushängebühne f quadruple platform, pipe-stabbing board; racking platform *(deep boring)*
aushauchen to exhale
Aushauchung f exhalation, volcanic emanation
aushöhlen to excavate, to hollow out
Aushöhlung f, **Aushub** m excavation
auskehlen to notch
Auskehlung f channelling
auskeilen to wedge out, to thin away, to thin out, to taper out, to edge away, to pinch out, to die away, to end off
~/linsenförmig to lens out
~/sich to dwindle
Auskeilen n thinning-out, wedging-out, tailing-out, balk, dwindling-away; lensing
auskeilend lensing-out
Auskesselung f wash-out; washed-out hole, cavity
ausklauben to pick out, to select *(the ore)*

auskleiden to case, to set casing *(e.g. the sides of a roadway in a mine)*
ausklingen s. abklingen
ausknicken to buckle
Ausknickung f buckling
auskohlen to work out, to extract
Auskohlen n getting-down of the coal
auskolken to excavate, to crater, to gouge out, to scour, to groove [out], to eddy out, to scoop [out]
Auskolkung f 1. excavation, cratering, gouging[-out], scour[ing]; subsurface erosion, evorsion; 2. flute, scour mark, pothole; current crescent
~ durch Eis glacial scour
auskragen to project, to jut out
Auskragung f cantilever
Auskristallisation f/**disperse** dissemination
auskristallisieren to crystallize out, to form into crystals
Auslage f layout *(seismics)*
Auslaßkörnung f omitted size fraction
Ausläufer m lead *(of a lode);* offset *(of a bed);* off-shoot[ing tongue] *(of ore);* spur *(of a mountain)*
Auslaufverlust m **auf dem offenen Meer** spillage in open sea
auslaugbar leachable
Auslaugbarkeit f leachability
auslaugen to leach, to lixiviate
Auslaugung f leaching, lixiviation, levigation, elution, eluviation
~ von Gestein dissolving of rocks
Auslaugungsbrekzie f evaporite-solution breccia
Auslaugungsdepression f/**flache** solution pan
auslaugungsfrei free from leaching
Auslaugungsgebiet n leaching area
Auslaugungshorizont m s. A-Horizont
Auslaugungsprodukt n leachate
Auslaugungsrückstand m leaching residue
Auslaugungsschicht f depletion layer
Auslaugungssenke f leaching depression
Auslaugungstasche f solution pocket
Auslaugungsvorgang m leaching process
Auslaugungswanne f mere
~/flache park
Auslaugungswässer npl leaching waters
Auslaugungszone f leached (barren) zone
auslegen to set up
Auslenkung f offset *(of a lode)*
Auslese f/**natürliche** natural selection
Auslesegerät n hand-picking apparatus
auslesen to select; to sort; to pick
Auslesen n selection; sorting; picking
Auslesenadel f hand-picking needle
auslöschend/schief diatonous *(crystals)*
Auslöschung f extinction
~/gerade straight extinction
~/parallele parallel extinction
~/schiefe inclined extinction
~/undulierende (undulöse) undulatory (undulous, wavy) extinction

Ausstrich

Auslöschungslage f extinction position
Auslöschungsrichtung f extinction direction
Auslöschungsschiefe f extinction angle
Auslöseimpuls m trigger pulse
auslösen to release *(stresses)*
Auslösung f release, relaxation *(of stresses)*; triggering *(of events)*
~/innerer Spannungen relaxation of internal stresses
ausloten to sound; to plumb
Ausnagung f erosion
Ausnahmelast f nominal gross capacity
Ausnutzungsfaktor m exploitation factor
ausplätten to flatten out
Auspressungsdifferentiation f filtration differentiation, filter pressing
auspumpen to pump out
Auspumpen n pumping-out
Ausräumungsbecken n/**glaziales** glacial trough
ausrichten 1. to align; 2. to develop, to explore
Ausrichtung f 1. alignment; orientation; 2. development, development work in store, opening[-up], dead work *(of a mine)*
~/bevorzugte prefered orientation
~ der Bohrung hole straightening
Ausrichtungsarbeit f prospecting work
Ausrollgrenze f plastic (rolling-out) limit *(after Atterberg)*
Aussagewert m usefulness *(of measurement)*
ausschachten to excavate
Ausschachtung f excavation
ausscheiden to separate [out]
Ausscheidung f separation; segregation; secretion
~/gleichzeitige simultaneous crystallization
Ausscheidungsfolge f precipitation order *(of minerals)*
Ausscheidungslagerstätte f precipitated deposit
Ausscheidungssedimente npl precipitated (secreted) sedimentaries
Ausscheidungssedimentgestein n chemically deposited sedimentary rock
Ausscheidungssedimentit m precipitated sedimentary rock
ausscheuern to scour out
Ausschlagwinkel m angle of deflection
ausschlämmen to wash out, to elutriate, to slough off
Ausschlämmethode f booming
Ausschlämmung f elutriation
ausschleudern to eject, to project, to expel, to eructate; to emit; to blow out
Ausschleudern n ejection, projection, expulsion, eructation; emission; blowing-out
Ausschnitt m section
Ausschöpfen n bailing
ausschrämen to hew trenches
ausschürfen to scour, to scoop [out]
Ausschürfung f scouring, scooping[-out]

Ausschwänzen n **eines Gangs** dying-out *(s.a. Auskeilen)*
Ausschwemmungsboden m eluvial (colluvial) soil
ausschwitzen to exud[at]e; to sweat
Ausschwitzung f exudation; sweating; exosmose, seep, oozing-out
~ von Erdöl oil exudation
Außenabdruck m, **Außenabguß** m exocast, external cast (mould), exterior cast (mould) *(of fossils)*
außenbürtig s. exogen
aussenden to emit
Außendruck m external pressure
Außendüne f exterior dune
Aussendung f emission
Außendurchmeser m **des gesteinszerstörenden Werkzeugs** outside diameter of the drilling tool
Außenküste f outer coast
Außenküstenlinie f outer shore line
Außenleiste f flange
Außenmolasse f external molasse
Außenschicht f outer layer
Außenskelett n external skeleton, exoskeleton
außerirdisch extraterrestrial; extramundane
aussetzend intermittent
aussickern to seep, to ooze out
Aussickerung f seepage, oozing
aussieben to sift [out]
Aussolen n **von Kavernen** cavern leaching process
aussondern to pick
Ausspeisedauer f feeding period
aussprengen to pry apart
ausspülen s. abspülen
Ausspülung f s. Abspülung
aussterben to suffer extinction, to die out, to become extinct *(species)*
Aussterben n disappearance *(of species)*
Ausstoß m belch *(of volcano)*
ausstoßen to eject, to extrude, to belch *(volcano)*
Ausstoßung f ejection
ausstrahlen to radiate; to emit; to emanate
ausstrahlend radiant; emissive
Ausstrahlung f radiation; emission; emanation
~/radioaktive radioactive emission
~/spezifische radiance, radiant emittance
ausstreichen to outcrop, to crop out, to basset, to be exposed at the surface, to pinch out
~/zu Tage to come out to the day, to come up to daylight
Ausstreichen n s. Ausstrich
ausstreuen to disseminate
Ausstrich m outcrop, cropping, basset edge, surface termination (edge), make-up, blossom, beat
~ eines Ganges outcrop (apex) of a vein
~ eines Kohlenflözes coal smut, blossom of coal
~ eines Quarzganges quartz boil

Ausstrich 36

~/submariner subcrop
~/verdeckter subterranean (buried) outcrop, subcrop
~/verdeckter fossiler incrop
~/verwitterter decomposed outcrop
Ausstrichbreite f width (breadth) of outcrop
Ausstrichlinie f line of outcrop (bearing)
~/durch Rutschung verbogene outcrop curvature
Ausstrichrichtung f course of outcrop
ausströmen 1. to extravasate, to well out *(lava);* to rush out; 2. to flow out, to release, to discharge *(ground water);* 3. to emanate, to exhale
~/heftig to gush [from]
Ausströmen n 1. extravasation *(of lava);* 2. emanation; exhalation
ausstrudeln to excavate
Ausstrudelung f excavation; evorsion
Ausstülpung f off-shoot
aussüßen to freshen
Aussüßung f freshening
Austausch m/**chemischer** chemical substitution
~ **von Ionen zwischen Wasser und fester Matrix** water-rock interaction
austauschbar interchangeable
austauschen to exchange; to interact *(ions between water and rock)*
Austauschkapazität f exchange capacity
Austauschreaktion f replacement (displacement) reaction; exchange reaction
Austauschvermögen n exchange capacity
Auster f oyster
Austernbank f oyster bed
Austin n Austin Chalk *(Coniacian and Santonian in North America, Gulf district)*
Austinit m austinite, $CaZn[OH|AsO_4]$
austragen to flush out
~/**das Bohrklein** to bring up the drillings
Australit m australite, obsidianite *(tektite)*
Austritt m/**natürlicher** seep *(oil, gas)*
Austrittsgefälle n exit gradient
Austrittskanal m volcanic vent
Austrittsstelle f outlet, exit, emergence point
Austrittsverlust m delivery loss *(of water)*
Austrittswinkel m angle of emergence
austrocknen to desiccate; to dry up; to dehumidify
austrocknend desiccative
Austrocknung f desiccation; exsiccation; drying-up; dehumidification
Austrocknungsform f desiccation form
Austrocknungsprozeß m drying-up process
Austrocknungsspalte f desiccation fissure
ausufern to overflow
Ausufern n spill
Ausuferungsgebiet n overbank area
Ausuferungs[wasser]stand m bank-full stage
Aus- und Vorrichtungsarbeiten fpl development work
auswalzen to squeeze out

auswandern to move
auswaschen to scour out; to erode
Auswaschung f scouring, washing-out, eluviation, gullying, wash, dilution
~ **des Flußbetts** stream bed erosion
~ **in Kohlenflözen/fossile** low
Auswaschungsrinne f channel
Auswaschungssand m outwash (scouring) sand
auswechseln to replace
Auswechslung f replacement
Ausweichungsschieferung f shear (false) cleavage, (strain-slip) cleavage
auswerfen to extrude; to eject, to project; to eructate; to expel; to emit; to discharge
Auswerfen n s. Auswurf 1.
Auswertbarkeit f interpretability
Auswertediagramm n target
auswerten to evaluate; to interprete; to plot
Auswerter m interpreter
Auswertetechnik f interpretation technique
Auswertung f evaluation; interpretation; plotting
~/**fehlerhafte** faulty interpretation
~/**fotogrammetrische** photogrammetric plotting
~/**multidisziplinäre** multidisciplinary analysis
~ **Spur für Spur** point plotting
~/**stratigrafische** stratigraphic interpretation
~/**visuelle** visual (eye-ball) interpretation
Auswertungsgenauigkeit f accuracy of evaluation
Auswertungsgerät n plotting apparatus
auswittern to weather
Auswitterung f weathering; efflorescence
Auswurf m 1. protrusion, extrusion, ejection, projection; eructation; expulsion; emission; discharge; 2. ejected material, ejecta; pyroclastic material; solid discharge
~/**oberflächenbedeckender** ejecta blanket *(by meteoritic impacts ejected material)*
Auswurfdruck m ejection pressure
Auswürflinge mpl ejecta[menta], ejected material, erupted blocks, fragmental products, fragmental ejecta (discharges)
~/**allothigene** allothigenic ejecta (discharges), accidental products (ejecta, discharges)
~/**glühende** incandescent detritus
~/**juvenil-authigene** authigenic (juvenile, essential) ejecta
~/**resurgent-authigene** accessory ejecta
Auswurfmaterial n s. Auswurf 2.
Auswurfprodukt n product of volcanic ejection
Auswurfsmassen fpl/**lose vulkanische** dejection rocks
Auszählineal n peripheral counter *(fabric diagram)*
Ausziehstrom m air return
authigen authigenic, authigene, authigenetic
autochthon autochthonous, in place, in situ
Autogamie f autogamy, self-pollination *(palaeobotany)*

autogen autogenous, autogenetic
Autogenese f autogenesis
Autogeosynklinale f autogeosyncline
Autohydration f autohydratation
autoklastisch autoclastic
Autökologie f autecology
Autolith m autolith, cognate inclusion (xenolith)
autometamorph autometamorphic, deuteric, paulopost, penecontemporaneous
Autometamorphose f auto[meta]morphism, self-alteration
Autometasomatose f autometasomatism
Automikrit m automicrite
Automolit m automolite *(variety of galmite)*
automorph automorphic, automorphous, idiomorphic, idiomorphous
Autopneumatolyse f autopneumatolysis
Autoradiografie f autoradiograph
Autothek f autotheca *(graptolites)*
autotroph autotrophic
Autun[ien] n Autunian *(uppermost Carboniferous, France)*
Autunit m autunite, lime uraninite, $Ca[UO_2|PO_4]_2 \cdot 10(12-10)H_2O$
Auxiliarlobus m auxiliary lobe
Aventurin m [gold] aventurine, goldstone, venturine quartz
Aventurinfeldspat m aventurine feldspar, sunstone
Aventuringlas n aventurine glass
Aventurinquarz m aventurine quartz *(subvariety of quartz)*
aventurisieren to aventurize, to schillerize
Aventurisieren n aventurism, schillerization
Avezakit m avezacite *(ultrabasic rock)*
Aviolith m aviolite *(variety of hornfels)*
Avogadrit m avogadrite, $K[BF_4]$
Avonium n Carboniferous Limestone, Avonian *(Lower Carboniferous in the South of Central England)*
Awaruit m awaruite, (Ni, Fe)
Axialrichtung f axial direction
Axialschub m end thrust
Axialspannung f axial stress
Axinit m axinite, tizenite, $Ca_2(Fe, Mn)\,Al\,Al[BO_3OH|Si_4O_{12}]$
axiolitisch axiolitic
Azetatfilm m, **Azetatfolie** f acetate peel
Azidität f acidity
Azimut m azimuth
~ des Bohrlochs azimuth of the hole
~/echter true azimuth
~/magnetischer magnetic bearing
Azimutabweichung f yaw *(of an airplane or a remote sensing platform relative to the flight direction)*
azimutal azimuthal
Azimutalprojektion f/**flächentreue** azimuthal equal area projection
Azimutwinkel m azimuth angle
Azoikum n azoic age (era)

azoisch azoic
azöl acoelous
Azurit m azurite, $Cu_3[OH|CO_3]_2$

B

Babingtonit m babingtonite, $Ca_2Fe_2[Si_5O_{14}OH]$
Babylonquarz m Babylonian quartz
Bach m brook, creek, rivulet, riveret
~/subglazialer subglacial streamlet
~/zeitweiliger blind creek
Bachbett n creek (brook) bed
Bachgeröll n rolled pebbles
Bächlein n brooklet, rivulet, runlet, streamlet, rillet
b-Achse f b axis
Bachwasser n brook water
Backeigenschaft f caking property *(of coal)*
backen to cake
Backen n caking
Backenbrecher m [reciprocating] jaw breaker
Backenknochen m s. Jugale
Backenpreventer m ram preventer
Backenzahn m cheek tooth
~/vorderer premolar
Backfähigkeit f caking capacity *(of coal)*
Backkohle f caking coal
Backsteinton m ball (potter's) clay
Bäckströmit m bäckströmite, baeckstroemite, $Mn(OH)_2$
Backung f paroptesis *(of rocks)*
Backvermögen n caking property *(of coal)*
Baculit m baculite *(fossil)*
Baculitenkalk m Baculites limestone
Baddeleyit m baddeleyite, ZrO_2
Badenit m badenite, $(Co,Ni,Fe)_3(As,Bi)_4$
Bafertisit m bafertisite, $BaFe_2Ti[O_2|Si_2O_7]$
Bagger m dredger *(under water);* excavator *(on land)*
Baggergut n dredgings
baggern to dredge; to excavate
Bahamit m bahamite *(carbonate rock)*
Bahiait m bahiaite *(variety of hypersthenite)*
Bahn f path, orbit *(astronomy)*
~/absteigende descendancy
~/aufsteigende ascendancy
Bahnbestimmung f determination of orbit
Bahnebene f orbital plane
Bahnelement n element of an orbit
Bahngeschwindigkeit f path speed, orbital velocity
Bahnmoment n orbital moment
Bahnschotter m ballast
Bahnumdrehung f orbital revolution
Bahnverlauf m course of orbit
Bai f bay; bight *(s. a. Bucht)*
~/kleine cove
Baikalit m baikalite *(variety of salite)*
Baikerinit m baikerinite *(a resin)*
Baikerit m baikerite *(a mineral wax)*
Baistörung f bay

Bajoc

Bajoc[ien] n, **Bajocium** n Bajocian [Stage] *(of Jurassic)*
Bakerit m bakerite *(variety of datolite)*
Bakterien fpl/**aerobische** aerobic[al] bacteria
~/anaerobische anaerobic[al] bacteria
~/denitrifizierende denitrifying bacteria
~/sulfatreduzierende sulphate-reducing bacteria
~/vererzte mineralized bacteria
Bakterientätigkeit f bacterial action (activity)
Balkaschit m balkhashite
Balken m lamella *(e.g. in meteorites)*
Ballas m ballas
Ballasrubin m balas[s ruby] *(a spinel)*
Ballast m ballast, inert material
Ballastelement n ballast element
Ballastmaterial n inert material, ballast
Ballclay m ball clay *(fire clay with few accessories)*
Ballenstruktur f ball-and-pillow structure
ballig lumpy; convex, dished
Ballon m/**verankerter** tethered balloon
Ballonsatellit m balloon satellite
Ballonsonde f balloon sonde, sounding balloon
Ballungsfähigkeit f spheroidizing property
Balme f overhang
Balneologie f balneology
Banakit m banakite *(variety of trachydolerite)*
Banalsit m banalsite, $BaNa_2[Al_2Si_2O_8]_2$
Banatit m banatite *(quartz diorite rich in orthoclase)*
Band n 1. belt; 2. tape
~/rechnerkompatibles computer compatible tape
Bandachat m banded (ribbon) agate
~/schwarz und weißer sardachate
Bandait m bandaite *(labrador dacite)*
Bandbreite f bandwidth
Bändererz n banded ore
Bändergabbro m flaser gabbro
Bändergneis m banded gneiss
Bänderschiefer m banded slate
Bänderschluff m banded silt
Bändertextur f ribbon structure
Bänderton m banded (ribbon, varved, bedded, leaf, laminated) clay
~/glazialer glacial clay (varve)
~ mit Jahresringen seasonly stratified (banded) clay
Bänderung f 1. lamination, banding, foliation, veining; 2. s. Blaublättertextur
~/jahreszeitliche seasonal bands
~/Liesegangsche Liesegang banding
Bandförderer m band conveyor
Bandjaspis m banded (ribbon) jasper, striped jasper [stone]
Bandpaß m bandpass
Bandpaßfilter n bandpass filter; passband filter
Bandsieb n conveyor sieve
Bandsperre f notch (band-reject) filter
bandstreifig streaked
Bandylith m bandylite, $Cu[Cl|B(OH)_4]$
Bank f 1. bank; massive bed (layer); measure; 2. shoal; bench
~/liegende bottom measure
~/verformte deformed layer
Bankett n berm, bench [surface]
bankförmig platy
bankig [thickly] bedded; stratified in thick beds
bankrecht normal (perpendicular) to the stratification
Bankschießarbeit f bank shooting
Bankschotter m bar gravels
bankschräg inclined (at an oblique angle) to the stratification
Bankung f banking structure, massive bedding
Bankungskluft f lift (bed) joint, stratification surface
Bankungsklüftung f/**engständige** mural jointing
~/engständige oberflächennahe shakes
Bankungsspalte f s. Bankungskluft
Bank-Zwischenmittel-Folgen fpl successions of layer and intercalation
Baotit m baotite, $Ba_4(Ti,Nb)_8[Cl|O_{16}|Si_4O_{12}]$
Bararit m bararite, $(NH_4)_2[SiF_6]$
Barbierit m barbierite, $NaAlSi_3O_8$
Barbosalith m barbosalite, $Fe\cdot Fe\cdot|(OH|PO_4)_2$
Barchan m barchan, crescent[-shaped] dune
Barium n barium, Ba
bariumhaltig barium-bearing
Barke f **zum Verlegen von Rohrleitungen** pipelaying barge
~ zur Gasabscheidung und -aufbereitung gas separating barge
Barkevikit m barkevikite *(variety of amphibole)*
bärlappähnlich lycopodiaceous
Bärlappsporen fpl lycopod spores
Barnesit m barnesite, $Na_2V_6O_{16} \cdot 3H_2O$
Barograf m barograph
Barometer n barometer
Barometersäule f barometric column
Barotropie f barotropy
Barrandit m barrandite, $(Al,Fe)PO_4 \cdot 2H_2O$
Barre f bar, barrier ridge
Barrem n, **Barrême** n, **Barrémien** n Barremian [Stage] *(of Lower Cretaceous)*
Barren m bullion
Barrenfalle f bar trap
Barrensande mpl bar sands
Barrentheorie f bar theory
Barriere f barrier, seal
~/geochemische geochemical barrier
~/hydraulische hydraulic barrier
~/unterirdische subsurface barrier
Barriereriff n barrier reef
Barroisit m barroisite *(Na-amphibole)*
Barrow-Typ m Barrovian type *(of metamorphism)*

Baugeologie

Barsanovit m barsanovite, $(Na,Ca,Sr,SE)_9(Fe,Mn)_2(Zr,Nb)_2[Cl|Si_{12}O_{36}]$
Barsowit m s. Anorthit
Barstovien n Barstovian [Stage] *(mammalian stage, Miocene in North America)*
Barthit m barthite *(variety of austinite)*
Barton[ien] n, **Bartonium** n Bartonian [Stage] *(of Eocene)*
Barylith m barylite, $BaBe_2[Si_2O_7]$
Barysilit m barysilite, $Pb_3[Si_2O_7]$
Barysphäre f barysphere
Baryt m baryte, barium sulphate, $BaSO_4$
~/unreiner cawk stone
barytartig barytic
Barytocalcit m barytocalcite, $BaCa[CO_3]_2$
Barytsalpeter m nitrobarite, $Ba[NO_3]_2$
basal basal
Basalamputation f base truncation
Basalbrekzie f basal breccia
Basalfauna f basal fauna
Basalfläche f basal face
Basalflora f basal flora
Basalkonglomerat n basal conglomerate, base[ment] conglomerate
Basalquarzit m basal quartzite
Basalscholle f overridden mass
Basalt m basalt
Basaltäfelchen npl basals *(palaeontology)*
basaltartig basaltic
Basaltdecke f basalt[ic] sheet
Basalteisenerz n basaltic iron ore
Basaltfluß m flow of basalt
Basaltgang m basaltic dike
Basaltglas n vitreous basalt
basaltisch basaltic, basaltine
Basaltkuppe f basaltic cupola (knob)
Basaltlava f basaltic lava
Basaltmagma n basaltic magma
Basaltmandelstein m amygdaloidal basalt
basaltoid basaltoid
Basalton m **im Flözliegenden** underclay, coal seat, root clay
Basaltrücken m basaltic ridge
Basaltsäule f basalt[ic] column
Basaltschicht f basaltic layer
Basaltschlacke f basaltic scoria
Basaltschutt m basaltic debris (scree)
Basaltton m basaltic clay
Basalttuff m basaltic tuff, whin-rock
Basaltwacke f basaltic wacke
Basalüberschürfung f base vubbing
Basalwulst m basalpib *(palaeontology)*
Basanit m basanite *(rock of the alkali gabbro clan)*
Baschkir n Baschkirian [Stage] *(of Middle Carboniferous, East Europe)*
Basenaustausch m base exchange
Basenaustauschkapazität f base exchange capacity
Basenbildner m basifier
Basengehalt m base content
Basensättigung f base saturation

Basifizierung f basification, depletion of SiO_2
Basis f 1. basis, base; 2. base line; 3. ground
~ befestigt/mit einer basifixed
~ der Langsamschicht base of weathering
~ einer regionalisierten Variablen/geometrische geometric base of a regionalized variable
Basisabfluß m base flow (runoff), basal flow
Basisbohrung f pilot hole; stratigraphic well
Basisbruch m toe failure
basisch basic
Basisebene f basal plane
Basiseinstellung f base adjustment
Basisfläche f basal face
basisflächenzentriert end-centered
Basisfolge f basal sequence
Basis-Höhen-Verhältnis n base-height ratio
Basisschicht f offshore clay, bottomset
Basisspaltbarkeit f basal cleavage
Basisstation f base (control) station
basiszentriert basis-centred
Basizität f basicity
Basobismutit m basobismutite, $2Bi_2O_3 \cdot CO_2 \cdot H_2O$
Basommatophoren pl Basommatophora
Bassanit m bassanite, $Ca[SO_4] \cdot {}^1/_2 H_2O$
Bassetit m bassetite, $Fe[UO_2|PO_4]_2 \cdot 10-12 H_2O$
Bassin n basin
~ mit natürlicher Dammschüttung barrier basin
Bastit m bastite (s. a. Enstatit)
Bastnäsit m bastnaesite, $Ce[F|CO_3]$
Bath n s. Bathonien
Batholith m batholite, batholith, bathylite, bathylith, abyssolith
batholithisch batholithic
Bathometer n bathometer, bathymeter
Bathonien n Bathonian [Stage] *(of Jurassic)*
Bathosphäre f bathosphere
Bathroklase f bathroclase
bathyal bathyal, abysmal, abyssal
Bathyalfazies f bathyal facies
bathygrafisch bathygraphic
bathymetrisch bathymetric
bathypelagisch bathypelagic
Bathythermograf m bathythermograph
Batukit m batukite *(variety of leucite)*
Bau m 1. structure; 2. support unit *(mining)*; 3. burrow *(of an animal)*
~/fazieller structure of the facies
~/geologischer geologic[al] structure
~/tafelförmiger tablelike (tabular) structure
~/tektonischer tectonic framework
~/variszischer Varisc[i]an tectonics
Bauchflosse f ventral fin
Bauchklappe f ventral (pedicle) valve *(brachiopodans)*
Baue mpl/**aufgegebene (verlassene)** abandoned workings
Baueinheit f/**geologisch-tektonische** geological-tectonic unit
bauen/Buhnen to groyne
Baugeologie f s. Ingenieurgeologie

Baugrube
40

Baugrube f open cut, excavation
Baugrund m building ground, foundation soil, subsoil
~/durchlässiger pervious subsoil
~/gewachsener substratum
Baugrundforschung f investigation of foundation
Baugrundkarte f soil (building ground) map
Baugrundmechanik f soil mechanics
Baugrunduntersuchung f soil investigation, subsoil (soil, site) exploration, foundation testing, field study
Baugrunduntersuchungsbohrung f foundation test boring
Baugrundverbesserung f artificial cementation
~/chemische artificial method of cementation by the injection of chemicals
~/elektroosmotische electroosmotic solidification
Baugrundverdichtung f/**natürliche** ground (subsoil) consolidation
Baugrundverfestigung f [artificial] cementation
Bauhöhe f panel, lift
~/flache projection of face length in the direction of full dip, inclined depth
~/seigere vertical projection of face length
Baulänge f/**streichende** life of face
Baumachat m tree (aborescent, dendritical) agate, dendrachate (s. a. Chalzedon)
Baumaterial n structural material
Baumfarn m tree (arborescent) fern
baumförmig dendriform, arborescent
Baumgrenze f tree line, limit of trees, timberline
Baumhauerit m baumhauerite, $Pb_5As_9S_{18}$
Bäumlerit m bäumlerite, $KCaCl_3$
baumlos treeless, devoid of trees, barren of timber
Baumstamm m tree trunk, log
~/versteinerter dendrolite
Baumsteppe f tree steppe
Baumstubben m tree stump, stool
Bausandstein m freestone
Bauschanalyse f bulk analysis
Bausohle f working level (horizon)
Baustein m building stone
Baustelle f project (building) site, site of works
Baustil m tectonic (structural) style
Baustoff m structural material
Baustoffindustrie f industry of building materials
Baute f burrow[ing]
Bauten mpl/**erdbebensichere** earthquake-proof constructions
Bauweise f/**erdbebensichere** earthquake engineering
Bauwerk n/**benachbartes** adjacent structure
bauwürdig minable, exploitable, workable, recoverable, payable, paying
~/bedingt marginal

~/nicht s. abbauunwürdig
Bauwürdigkeit f minability, workability, payability
Bauwürdigkeitsgrenze f payability limit, limit of pay
Bauxit m bauxite, alumina hydrate (Al-rich weathering product)
~/tonhaltiger argillaceous bauxite ($Al_2O > 50 \%$)
Bauxitisierung f bauxitization
Bauxitlagerstätte f bauxite deposit
Bavenit m bavenite, $Ca_4Al_2Be_2[(OH)_2|Si_9O_{26}]$
Baventien n Baventian (Pleistocene, British Islands)
Bayerit m bayerite, α-Al(OH)
Bayldonit m bayldonite, $PbCu_3[OH|AsO_4]_2$
beansprucht/äolisch wind-borne
Beanspruchung f/**gerichtete** directed stress
~/tektonische tectonic stress
~/zusammengesetzte combined stress
bearbeitbar workable
Bearbeitbarkeit f workability
bearbeiten to treat
Bearbeitung f treatment
~ des Gesteins sculpturing of rock
Bearsit m bearsite, $Be_2[OH|AsO_4] \cdot 4H_2O$
Beaverit m beaverite, $Pb(Cu,Fe)_3[(OH)_6|(SO_4)_2]$
beben to quake, to shake, to tremble
Beben n [earth]quake, shake, (Am) tremor (s. a. Erdbeben)
~/fossiles fossil earthquake
~/kontinentales inland earthquake
~/lineares linear earthquake
~/magmatisches cryptovolcanic earthquake, magmatic tremor
~/meteoritisches meteoritic seism
~ mit kontinentalem Herd inland earthquake
~ mit tiefliegendem Epizentrum bathyseism
~/tektonisches tectonic (dislocation) earthquake
~/verwüstendes disastrous earthquake
~/vulkanisches volcanic tremor
becherförmig cup-shaped, calicular
Bechilit m bechilite, $CaB_4O_7 \cdot 4H_2O$
Beckelith m beckelite, $Ca_3(Ce, La, Nd)_4[O|SiO_4]_3$
Becken n 1. basin; 2. s Pelvis
~/abflußloses undrained (closed, stagnant) basin
~/artesisches artesian basin
~/ausgehungertes starved basin
~/durch Blockkippung verursachtes tilt-block basin
~/durch Flachwasserzonen begrenztes marines restricted basin
~/epikontinentales epicontinental basin
~/geschlossenes s. **~/abflußloses**
~/intermontanes intermont[ane] basin
~/intrakontinentales interior basin, intracontinental basin, intracontinental trough
~/intramontanes intramontanous basin
~/tektonisches fault basin

41 **Belastungsriefen**

~/untermeerisch geschlossenes silled basin
~/versalzenes shott
Beckenbildung f basining
Beckenfazies f basin facies
beckenförmig basin-shaped
Beckenlandschaft f basin topography
Beckenwüste f basin desert
Becquerelit m becquerelite, $6[UO_2|(OH_2] \cdot Ca(OH)_2 \cdot 4H_2O$
bedeckt 1. overcast, cloudy, clouded; 2. coated
~/mit ewigem Schnee perpetually snow-capped
Bedecktsamer mpl Angiospermae
Bedenit m bedenite, $Ca_2(Mg,Fe^{...},Al)_5[OH|(Si,Al)_4O_{11}]_2$
bedeutend strong (lodes)
Bedienungspult n keybord
Bedingung f/Coulombsche Coulomb's condition
Bedoul n Bedoulian [Stage] (lower Aptian, Tethys)
Beegerit m beegerite, $6PbS \cdot Bi_2S_3$
Beeinflussung f/morphotropische morphotropic effect
~ von Sonden/gegenseitige well interference, interference of wells
Beeinflussungsbereich m zone of influence
Beekit m beekite (variety of quartz)
Beerbachit m beerbachite (variety of aplite)
Beestonien n Beestonian (Pleistocene, British Islands)
befahren/eine Grube to descend into a mine
befeuchten to wet, to moisten
Befeuchtung f wetting, moistening
befindlich/an der Luft subaerial
~/über der Erde superterrestrial, superterranean, superterrene
Beförderung f von gelösten Stoffen transport of solutes
Befund m/örtlicher field observation
beginnen/mit Bohren to start (commence) drilling
Begleitbruch m auxiliary fracture
begleitend concomitant
Begleiter m companion (of ores)
Begleitflöz n accompanying seam
~/kleines rider
Begleitgas n accompanying gas
Begleitgesteine npl associated rocks
Begleitkluft f auxiliary joint
Begleitmineral n associated (accessory, accompanying, subordinate) mineral
Begleitpegel m auxiliary gauge (of a well)
Begleitverwerfung f associated (auxiliary, minor, subsidiary) fault
begraben to bury; to overwhelm
Begräbnisbau m, Begräbnisstätte f entrapment burrow (of fossils)
begrenzt 1. limited; 2. exhaustible (provision)
~/von Verwerfung fault-bounded
Begriffsabgrenzung f/stratigrafische stratigraphic connotation

Begründung f/geologisch-ökonomische economic geological substantiation
Behandlung f/mathematische mathematical processing (of geochemical data)
Beharrungsvermögen n inertia
Beharrungszustand m state of inertia (during a pumping test)
Beherrschung f des Gebirges strata control
~ des Hangenden roof control
Behierit m behierite, $(Ta,Nb)[BO_4]$
Beidellit m beidellite, $Al_2[(OH)_2Si_4O_{10}] \cdot 4H_2O$
Beilstein m nephrite (compact tremolite or actinolite)
beimengen to add, to admix
Beimengung f addition, admixture, additive, additament, impurity
~/amorphe amorphous admixture
~/geringe minor constituent, dash
beimischen s. beimengen
Bein n leg (of a timber set); pillar (of coal)
Beitel m [hand] chisel
Beiwert m ratio
~ des Abflusses drainage ratio
beizen to bite
Bekinkinit m bekinkinite (volcanic alkaline rock)
beladen/mit Feuchtigkeit moisture-laden
Belag m incrustation; film
Belastbarkeit f load-carrying capacity
Belastung f load; loading, off-loading
~/außermittige eccentric (off-centre) loading
~/axiale axial loading
~/dynamische dynamic load
~ in Richtung der Achse axial loading
~/kritische critical load
~/mittige central loading
~/zulässige permissible load (stress)
Belastungsannahme f assumed (assumption of) load
Belastungsbereich m load range
Belastungsdruck m load (overburden) pressure
~/effektiver effective overburden pressure
Belastungseindruck m s. Belastungsmarke
Belastungsfahne f load wave (sedimentary structure)
Belastungsfalte f load fold
Belastungsfunktion f loading function
Belastungsgrenze f load limit
Belastungskurve f load diagram
Belastungslineation f load-cast lineation
Belastungsmarke f load cast (mould)
~/gerichtete directional load cast
~/schuppenförmige squamiform load cast
~/wulstige torose load cast
~/zusammengesetzte syndromous load cast
Belastungsmetamorphose f load (static, pressure) metamorphism
Belastungsplatte f loading plate
Belastungsprüfung f load test, bearing test
~/statische static load test
Belastungsriefen fpl load-cast lineation

Belastungssetzung

Belastungssetzung f sag structure
Belastungssetzungsdiagramm n load-settlement curve
Belastungstasche f load pocket
Belastungsverformungskurve f s. Lastdehnungskurve
Belastungsversuch m loading (bearing) test
Beldongrit m beldongrite *(variety of psilomelane)*
beleben to activate
~/eine Fördersonde wieder to rejuvenate a producer
Belegexemplar n proof copy, specimen
Belegungsdichte f packing (bit) density *(seismics)*
Belemnit m belemnite, thunderstone, thunder bolt, brontolith
Belemnitenmergel m belemnite marl
Beleuchtungskegel m cone of light
Belichtungszeit f exposure time
Bellerophonkalk m Bellerophon limestone
Bellingerit m bellingerite, $Cu_3(JO_3)_6 \cdot 2H_2O$
Bellit m bellite, $(Pb,Ag)_5[Cl\,|\,(CrO_4,AsO_4,SiO_4)_3]$
Belonit m s. Aikinit
Belovit m belovite, $Sr_5[OH\,|\,(PO_4)_3]$
Belt n Beltian *(Precambrian in North America)*
belteropor belteroporic
belüften to aerate
Belüftung f aeration
Belugit m belugite *(basis rock)*
Bementit m bementite, $Mn_8[(OH)_{10}\,|\,Si_6O_{15}]$
bemustern to take sample
Bemusterung f sampling
~/makroskopische macroscopic sampling
~/neue resampling
Bemusterungsablauf m process of sampling
Bemusterungsdaten pl sampling data
Bemusterungskonzeption f sampling conception
Bemusterungsmaterial n sampling material
Bemusterungsmethode f sampling method
benachbart adjacent
benetzbar wettable
Benetzbarkeit f wettability
~/gemischte mixed wettability
Benetzungseigenschaft f wetting (coating) property
Benetzungsfähigkeit f moistening power
Benetzungsfront f wetting front
Benetzungswiderstand m resistivity of wetting
Benetzungszone f splash zone
Benitoit m benitoite, $BaTi[Si_3O_9]$
Benjaminit m benjaminite *(variety of alaskaite)*
Benstonit m benstonite, $Ba_6Ca_7[CO_3]_{13}$
benthonisch benthonic, benthal, epibiont
benthopelagisch bentho-pelagic
Benthos n benthos, bottom-living life, epibiota, ground-living forms
~/sessiles sessile benthos
~/vagiles vagrant (mobile, free-moving) benthos
Bentonit m bentonite

~ mit kristallinem Detritus arkosic (arcosic) bentonite
Benzin n petrol, *(Am)* gasoline
~ aus Ölschiefer shale naphtha
beobachten/mit bloßem Auge to observe with the naked eye
Beobachter m observer
beobachtet/größtenteils largely observed *(4th stage of the scale of seismic intensity)*
~/nur teilweise partially observed only, weak *(3rd stage of the scale of seismic intensity)*
Beobachtung f observation
~ in unmittelbarer Objektnähe proximate sensing
Beobachtungsballon m observation balloon
Beobachtungsbasis f platform
Beobachtungsbohrung f observation well
Beobachtungsbrunnen m observation well
Beobachtungsdaten pl observed data
Beobachtungshöhe f observed altitude
Beobachtungsinstrument n observation instrument
Beobachtungsmaterial n observation material
Beobachtungsort m observational place
Beobachtungspunkt m/**seismischer** seismic observation point; seismic detector location
Beobachtungsreihe f series of observations
Beobachtungsrohr n observation pipe *(in an aquifer)*
Beobachtungsstation f observation station
Beobachtungsstrecke f inspection gallery
Beobachtungswinkel m observation angle
Bepflanzung f planting
beräumen to cheek off *(in a mine)*; to bar down (off) *(the side with pinching-bar)*; to clean *(in the quarry)*; to dress
Beraunit m beraunite, eleonorite, $Fe_3[(OH)_3\,|\,(PO_4)_2] \cdot 2^{1}/_{2}H_2O$
Berechnung f/**geochemische** geochemical calculation
~/mineralchemische mineralchemical calculation
~/petrochemische petrochemical calculation
Berechnungsverfahren n method of calculation
Beregnung f overhead irrigation
Beregnungswasser n irrigation water
Bereich m region, area; zone, field; range
~/küstennaher near-shore region
~/metamorpher metamorphic field (area, belt)
~/sichtbarer visible region *(of spectrum)*
bereißen s. beräumen
Beresit m beresite *(variety of aplite)*
Beresitisierung f beresitization
Berg m mountain; hill; mount *(in geographical names)*
~/submariner sea mountain
bergab downhill, downgrade, downslope; downdip
Bergabhang m mountain declivity
Bergakademie f Mining Academy
Bergalaun m stone alum

Bergalit *m* bergalite *(alkaline dike rock)*
Bergasphalt *m* asphalt (asphaltic, bituminous) rock, rock asphalt
bergauf uphill; updip
Bergbaugeophysik *f* mining geophysics
Bergbauschutzgebiet *n* mine claim
Bergbausenkungsgebiet *n* mine subsidence area
Bergbauwissenschaften *fpl* mining science
Bergbutter *f* impure iron alum (*s.a.* Halotrichit)
Berge *pl* dirt, deads, discard, rejects, tailings, refuse [rocks], waste rock
Bergeaustrag *m* refuse extractor
Bergedamm *m* pack
Bergehalde *f* dirt [refuse, rubbish, tip], heap, refuse (rubbish) dump
bergehaltig dirty
Bergekippe *f* tailing dam
Bergeklein *n* dirt
Bergemauer *f* pack
Bergemittel *n* dirt bed (band), [stone] band, parting, cleave, dividing slate
Bergenit *m* bergenite, Ba[(UO$_2$)$_4$|(OH)$_4$|(PO$_4$)$_2$] · 8H$_2$O
Bergepfeiler *m* rubbish pillar
Bergerippe *f* pack
Bergeschicht *f* dirt bed, attal
~/dünne mining ply
~/flözteilende middle band
Bergeteich *m* tailings pond
Bergeversatz *m* stowage, g[l]obbing, stope filling
Bergevollversatz *m* solid gob (packing)
Bergfeste *f* barren (boundary, rubbish) pillar
Bergfeuchte *f* inherent moisture
Bergfeuchtigkeit *f* water of imbibition, interstitial (quarry) water
Bergflachs *m* mountain flax (*s.a.* Aktinolith)
Bergfußebene *f* piedmont plain
Bergfußfläche *f* piedmont slope
Berggelb *n* [yellow, iron] ochre (*s.a.* Limonit)
Berggesetz *n* mining law
Berggipfel *m* mountain top (peak)
Berghang *m* mountain side (slope), hillside
~/steiler cleve
Bergharz *n* fossil resin
bergig mountainous; hilly
Bergingenieur *m* mining engineer
Bergkamm *m* mountain crest (ridge)
Bergkegel *m* cone
Bergkette *f* mountain chain (range)
~/untermeerische seamount chain
Bergkork *m* mountain (rock) cork *(an asbestos)*
Bergkristall *m* rock (mountain, berg) crystal (*s.a.* Quarz)
~/in Regenbogenfarben schillernder iris
Bergkupfer *n* native copper
Bergland *n* mountainous country, mountain[ous] region
Berglandschaft *f* mountain topography

Bergleder *n* leatherstone, mountain leather *(variety of palygorskite)*
Berglehne *f* mountain side, hillside
Bergmehl *n* rock meal
Bergmilch *f* rock milk, agaric mineral
Bergnase *f* mountain spur
Bergöl *n* rock oil
Bergordnung *f* mining regulations
Bergpech *n* mineral (earth) pitch
Bergrecht *n* mining law
Bergrücken *m s.* Bergkamm
Bergrutsch *m* fall of rock; earth slip
Bergschaden *m* surface damage (break, subsidence), mining damage
~ durch Bodensenkung damage due to subsidence (mining operations)
Bergschadengrenze *f* limit of mining damage
Bergschlag *m* bump; popping
Bergschlipf *m* rock slide
Bergschlucht *f* glen
~/steile griff
Bergschraffierung *f* [hill] hachure *(on maps)*
Bergschrund *m* marginal crevasse, bergschrund
Bergseife *f* rock (mountain) soap (*s.a.* Halloysit)
Bergseite *f* **der Talsperre** upstream facing of dam
~ des Wehrkörpers upstream facing of weir
bergseitig upstream
Bergspitze *f* hill top; peak; summit
Bergstrom *m* mountain stream (torrent)
Bergsturz *m* rock fall (avalanche); landslide, debris slide; mountain creep
Bergsturzmasse *f* rock stream, stone river (run)
Bergsturzsee *m* landslide lake
Bergteer *m* mineral (natural) tar, maltha; pissasphalt; bitumen
Bergtobel *m* mountain gulch
Bergufer *n* cliff bank
Berg- und Hüttenwesen *n* mining and metallurgical industries
Bergung *f* extrication *(of fossils)*
Bergvorsprung *m* headland
Bergwachs *n* earth (mineral, fossil, ader) wax, ozocerite
Bergwand *f* mountain wall (face)
Bergwerk *n* mine
~/aufgelassenes abandoned mine
Bergwerkseigentum *n* mining property
~ auf Erdöl oil property
Bergwerksspeicher *m* mine storage
Bergwind *m* downslope wind, mountain (downcast) breeze
Bergwolle *f* mountain wool *(type of asbestos)*
Bergzerreißung *f* mountain splitting
Bergzinn *n* mineral (vein) tin
berieseln to irrigate, to bedabble
Berieselung *f* irrigation
Berieselungsgraben *m* watering ditch
Berieselungsnetz *n* irrigation net

Berieselungsturm 44

Berieselungsturm *m* irrigation tower
Beringit *m* beringite *(alkaline trachyte)*
Berlinit *m* berlinite, $Al[PO_4]$ (Mn, Fe)$_8[(OH)_5|(PO_4)_4]_2 \cdot 15H_2O$
Berme *f* berm[e], bench [surface]; ledge
Bermudit *m* bermudite *(monchiquitic effusive rock)*
Bernstein *m* amber, succinite
~/wolkiger mineral amber
Bernsteineinschluß *m* amber inclusion
Bernsteinfichte *f* Pinus succinifera
Bernsteinwald *m* amber forest
Berondrit *m* berondrite *(variety of theralite)*
Berrias[ium] *n*, **Berrias-Stufe** *f* Berriasian [Stage] *(basal stage of Lower Cretaceous, Tethys)*
Berstdruck *m* bursting pressure
bersten to burst; to crack
Berthierit *m* berthierite, $FeS \cdot Sb_2S_3$
Berthonit *m* berthonite, $5PbS \cdot 9CU_2S \cdot 7Sb_2S_3$
Bertrandit *m* bertrandite, $Be_4[(OH)_2|Si_2O_7]$
Beruhigungsbecken *n* stilling basin (pool, well)
Berührungsebene *f* tangential plane
Berührungsfläche *f* [sur]face of junction
Berührungswinkel *m* angle of contact
Berührungszwillinge *mpl* juxtaposition (contact) twins
Beryll *m* beryl, $Al_2Be_3[Si_6O_{18}]$
Beryllerde *f* beryllia
Beryllium *n* beryllium, Be
Beryllonit *m* beryllonite, $NaBe[PO_4]$
Berzelianit *m* berzelianite, Cu_2Se
Berzeliit *m* berzeliite, $(Ca,Na)_3(Mg,Mn)_2[AsO_4]_3$
Beschaffenheit *f* condition, state; constitution; quality
~/basische basicity
~/felsige cragginess, craggedness
~/kiesige grittiness
~/körnige granularity
~/sumpfige marshiness, bogginess, swampiness
~/tauartige ropiness *(of lava)*
beschatten to shade
Beschlag *m* encrustation
beschlagen to encrust
Beschleunigermassenspektrometrie *f* accelerator mass spectrometry
Beschleunigungsmesser *m* accelerometer
beschneiden to taper *(a seismogram)*
beschotten to macadamize
Beschreibung *f* diagnosis *(e.g. of a species)*
Beschtanit *m* beschtanite *(quartz keratophyre)*
Beschwerungsmittel *n* weighting material
beseitigen to remove
Beseitigung *f* removal
~ radioaktiver Abfälle radioactive waste disposal
besenförmig scopiform
Besiedlung *f* colonization *(palaeontology)*
Besiedlungsgebiet *n* area occupied by settlements

beständig stable; continuous
Beständigkeit *f* stability; continuity; persistence
Bestandmineral *n* component mineral
Bestandsaufnahme *f*/**kluftstatistische** joint-statistical inventory
Bestandteil *m* component; constituent
~/authigener authigenic (authigenous) constituent
~/flüchtiger volatile constituent (substance)
~/leichtflüchtiger constituent of high volatility, easily volatilized constituent
~/unbrennbarer incombustible constituent
~/zufälliger incidental constituent
Bestandteile *mpl*/**atmosphärische** atmospheric constituents
~/flüchtige volatile matter, V.M. *(coal)*; volatile fluxes *(of magma)*
~/organische organic matter
Besteg *m* filling, weighboard
bestimmen to determine; to analyze
~/das Restfeld to residualize
Bestimmung *f* determination; analysis; assignment
~/adsorptive adsorptive determination
~ der Korngrößenanteile particle-size analysis
~ der primären Schichtorientierung facing of strata
~ der ursprünglichen Schichtoberkante facing
~ des Epizentrums determination of epicentre
~ von Spurenelementen determination of trace elements
Bestimmungsprobe *f* determinative test
bestirnt stelliferous
bestrahlen to irradiate
Bestrahlung *f* irradiation
Bestrahlungsalter *n* radiation age
betaaktiv beta-[radio]active
Betaaktivität *f* beta-[radio]activity
Betafit *m* betafite, samiresite, $(Ca,U)_2(Nb,Ti,Ta)_2O_6(O,OH,F)$
Betaquarz *m* beta quartz
Betastrahler *m* beta radiator (emitter)
Betastrahlung *f* beta-ray emission
Betateilchen *n* beta particle
Betazerfall *m* beta decay
Betechtinit *m* betechtinite, $Pb_2(Cu,Fe)_{21}S_{15}$
Betongerüst *n* einer permanent installierten **Betonbohr- und -förderinsel** marine concrete structure
Betonzuschlagstoffe *mpl* concrete aggregate
Betpakdalit *m* betpakdalite, $CaFe_2H_8[(MoO_4)_5|(AsO_4)_2] \cdot 10H_2O$
Betrachtungsgeräte *npl* viewing equipment
Betrag *m* amount
betreiben/Aufschlußarbeiten to reconnoitre, to carry exploration
~/Bergbau to mine
Betrieb *m*/**kontinuierlicher** continuous running
Betriebswasserstollen *m* pressure tunnel
Bett *n* base

betten to embed
Bettrauhigkeit f channel roughness *(of water)*
Bettungsziffer f coefficient of soil reaction, modulus of subgrade reaction
Bettverengung f constriction of the channel
Beudantit m beudantite, $PbFe_3[(OH)_6|SO_4 AsO_4]$
Beugung f diffraction; flexing
Beugungsaufnahme f, **Beugungsbild** n diffraction pattern (image)
Beugungsfarben fpl prismatic colours
Beugungsfigur f diffraction pattern
Beugungsgitter n diffraction grating
Beugungsspektrum n diffraction spectrum
Beugungswinkel m angle of diffraction
Beule f bending fold, upwarp[ing]
beulenförmig moundlike
Beulung f warping, arching
bewaldet wooded, forested
bewässern to irrigate, to bedabble
Bewässerung f irrigation, watering
~/geregelte check irrigation
~/unterirdische subsurface irrigation
Bewässerungsanlage f irrigation plant (works)
Bewässerungsgraben m irrigation channel
Bewässerungsnetz n irrigation net
Bewässerungsrinne f irrigation channel, feed ditch
Bewässerungssystem n irrigation system
Bewässerungstechnik f irrigation engineering
Bewässerungswirtschaft f irrigation agriculture
bewegen to move
~/sich abwärts to descend
~/sich auf einer Kreisbahn to orbit
Beweglichkeit f mobility *(geochemically)*
~/relative relative mobility
Bewegung f **an einer Störung/plötzliche** snapping dislocation
~/atektonische non-tectonic movement
~ entlang der Verwerfungsfläche fault movement
~/ep[e]irogene ep[e]irogen[et]ic movement
~/eustatische eustatic movement
~/lineamentäre lineagenic movement
~/mikroseismische microseismic movement
~/nachträgliche posthumous movement
~/postsedimentäre postdepositional movement
~/postume posthumous movement
~/scherende shearing displacement
~/senkrechte vertical movement
~/taphrogene taphrogenic movement
~/tektonische tectonic movement
Bewegungen fpl**/diastrophische** diastrophism
Bewegungsablauf m**/ep[e]irogener** ep[e]irogenetic sequence of movements
~/orogener orogenic sequence of movements
Bewegungsdifferentiation f flowage differentiation
Bewegungsebene f plane of motion
Bewegungsgleichung f equation of motion

Bewegungskomponente f component of movement
Bewegungsreibung f kinetic friction
Bewegungsrichtung f direction of motion (movement)
~/in directional
Bewegungsstreifen mpl fault striae
Bewegungswiderstand m kinetic resistance
Beweis m**/experimenteller** experimental verification
Bewertung f**/ökonomische** economic[al] valuation
Bewertungsgrad m degree of proof
bewettern to aerate
Bewetterung f aeration
~/gegenläufige antitropal ventilation
~/gleichlaufende homotropal ventilation
bewölkt cloudy, clouded, overcast
Bewölkung f cloudiness; cloud formation
Bewölkungsgrad m degree of cloudiness
Bewölkungskarte f cloud map
Bewölkungsmesser m neph[el]ometer
Beyerit m beyerite, $CaBi_2[O|CO_3]_2$
Beyrichienkalk m Beyrichia limestone
Bezahnung f dentation
Bezirk m district
~/metallogenetischer metallogenic district (region)
Bezugsfeld n reference field
Bezugsfläche f level of reference
Bezugshorizont m datum (key) horizon, datum level
Bezugskorngröße f basic mesh size
Bezugskornwichte f basic specific gravity
Bezugsniveau n level of reference, datum plane, reference datum
Bezugspunkt m reference point
Bezugssystem n system of reference
~/kartografisches cartographic reference system
B-Horizont m B-horizon, illuvial horizon
Bialith m bialite *(hydrous Mg, Ca, Al-phosphate)*
Bianchit m bianchite, $(Zn,Fe)[SO_4] \cdot 6H_2O$
Bieberit m bieberite, $Co[SO_4] \cdot 7H_2O$
Biegeachse f benching axis
Biegebeanspruchung f bending (transverse) stress
Biegefaltung f flexure folding
biegefest of high bending strength
Biegefestigkeit f bending strength
Biegefließen n bedding flow
Biegegleitfalte f flexure-slip fold
Biegegleitung f flexural gliding
Biegemoment n bending moment
biegen to plicate
Biegescherfaltung f bending shear folding
Biegespannung f bending (transverse) stress
biegesteif resistant to bending; rigid
Biegesteifigkeit f flexural rigidity
Biegeversuch m bending test
Biegewellen fpl bending waves

Biegezahl

Biegezahl f bending coefficient
biegsam flexible
Biegsamkeit f flexibility
Biegung f bend; flexing; flexure
Biegungsfläche f plane of flexure
Bienenwabenstruktur f honeycombed texture
Bifurkation f bifurcation, forking, partition
Bikarbonathärte f bicarbonate (temporary) hardness
Bikitait m bikitaite, $Li[AlSi_2O_6] \cdot H_2O$
Bilanz f/**geochemische** geochemical balance
Bilanzvorrat m balance resource *(of minerals)*
Bild n/**spannungsoptisches** fringe pattern
Bildaufnahmegerät n imaging system
Bildauswertung f image interpretation (analysis)
Bildbasis f photobase
~/**angepaßte** adjusted photobase
~/**mittlere** average photobase
Bildbearbeitung f image processing
~/**kohärente optische** coherent optical processing
bilden/Kristalle to form into crystals
~/**Zungen** to finger
Bilderkundung f photographic reconnaissance
Bildfeldwölbung f curvature of field
Bildhauerarbeit f carving
Bildhauermarmor m statue (statuary) marble
Bildkartierung f plotting from photographs
Bildkorrelation f image correlation
Bildmaßstab m scale of photo
~/**mittlerer** approximate scale
Bildmaterial n imagery
Bildmeßwesen n photogrammetry
Bildmittelpunkt m principal point
~/**übertragener** conjugate centre
Bildplan m mosaic *(of airphotos for geological uses)*
Bildradar n imaging (mapping) radar
Bildsamkeit f plasticity
Bildstein m agalmatolite *(compact variety of pyrophyllite)*
Bildung f 1. formation; 2. genesis
~ **der Fastebenen** base levelling
~/**kontinentale** continental formation
~/**limnische** limnetic formation
~/**marine** marine formation
~/**rezente** recent formation
~/**terrestrische** terrestrial formation
~ **von Kondensationskernen** nucleation
~ **von Spalten** crevassing, fissuring
Bildungsbedingungen fpl source aspects
Bildungsgeschichte f history of formation
Bildungsmilieu n environment, source aspects
Bildungsvorgang m formation process
Bildungswärme f heat of formation
Bildverzerrung f image distortion
Bildwiedergabegerät n image display
Bilibinit m bilibinite *(variety of coffinite)*
Bilinit m bilinite, $Fe \cdot Fe_2 \cdot [SO_4]_4 \cdot 22 H_2O$
Billietit m billietite, $6[UO_2|(OH)_2] \cdot Ba(OH)_2 \cdot 4 H_2O$

Billitonit m billitonite *(Indian tektite)*
Bilokulinenschlamm m Biloculina ooze
Bims m pumice
Bimsasche f pumice ash
Bimsbeton m pumice concrete
Bimsstein m pumice [stone], volcanic foam
~/**basaltischer** reticulite, thread-lace scoria
Bimssteinablagerung f/**nicht verschweißte** sillar
bimssteinartig pumiceous
Bimssteinbombe f pumiceous bomb
Bimssteingefüge n pumiceous structure
Bimssteinlava f pumice lava
Bimssteinschliff m pumicing
Bimssteintuff m pumice tuff
binär binary
Bindeerde f binder soil
Bindefähigkeit f cementing property
Bindemittel n binding agent (medium, material); binder; cement[ing material]
~ **aus Kalk** calcareous cement[ing material]
~/**eisenschüssiges** ferrugin[e]ous cementing material
~/**toniges** argillaceous [cementing] material
Bindeton m plastic (bond) clay
~/**feuerfester** plastic fire clay
Bindheimit m bindheimite, $Pb_{1-2}Sb_{2-1}(O,OH,H_2O)_{6-7}$
bindig cohesive
Bindigkeit f cohesion, cohesiveness
Bindung f/**chemische** chemical bond
~/**heteropolare** heteropolar (ionic) bond, ionic link[age], ion-dipole bond
~/**homöopolare** covalent (atomic) bond
~/**molekulare** molecular bond
~/**van der Waalssche** residual bond
Bindungsart f bond type
Bindungskraft f binding force
Binge f s. Pinge
Binnendelta n interior delta
Binnendüne f inland dune
Binneneis n inland ice
Binneneisdecke f continental ice sheet
Binnenentwässerung f interior (internal) drainage
Binnengewässer npl inland (interior) waters
Binnenklima n continental climate
Binnenland n inland
binnenländisch continental
Binnenmeer n inland (intercontinental, enclosed, land-locked) sea
Binnensee m [inland] lake
Binnenwanderdüne f inland-moving dune
Binokular n binocular microscope
Biocalcarenit m biocalcarenite
Biocalcirudit m biocalcirudite
Biochemie f biochemistry
biochemisch biochemical
Biochor n biochore
biochronologisch biochronological
Biodeformation f biodeformational structure *(ichnology)*

Bioerosion f bioerosion structure *(ichnology)*
biofaziell biofacial
Biofazies f biofacies
biogen biogenetic
Biogene *npl* biogens
biogenetisch biogenetic
Biogengehalt m biogenic composition
Biogeochemie f biogeochemistry
biogeochemisch biogeochemical
Biogeografie f biogeography
biogeografisch biogeographical
Bioglyphe f bioglyph
Bioherm n bioherm, knoll-reef, reef-knoll
Biohermbank f biohermal bed
Biohermriff n biohermal reef
Bioklasten *mpl* bioclasts
bioklastisch bioclastic, skeletal
Bioklimatologie f bioclimatology
Biolith m biolith, biolite, biolithite, biogenic rock
Biomasse f biomass
Biometeorologie f biometeorology
Biomikrit m biomicrite
bionomisch bionomic[al]
Biopelit m biopelite
biophil biophil[e], biophilous
Bios n biota
Biosparit m biosparite
Biosphäre f biosphere
Biostratigrafie f biostratigraphy
biostratigrafisch biostratigraphic[al]
Biostratonomie f biostratonomy
Biostrom n biostrome
biotisch biotic
Biotit m biotite, black mica, $K(Mg,Fe,Mn)_3[(OH,F)_2 | AlSi_3O_{10}]$
Biotitgneis m biotite gneiss
Biotitgranit m granitite
Biotitgruppe f biotite group
Biotitisierung f biotitization
Biotitschiefer m biotite schist
Biotitschüppchen n biotite flake
Biotop m biotope
Bioturbation f bioturbation *(ichnology)*
Biozönose f biocenose, biocenosis, biologic[al] association
Biprisma n biprism
Bipyramide f bipyramid
Bireflexion f bireflection
Biringuccit m biringuccite, $Na_2[B_5O_7(OH)_3] \cdot 1/2 H_2O$
Birkremit m bircremite *(variety of quartz syenite)*
Bisbeeit m bisbeeite, $CuSiO_3 \cdot H_2O$
Bischofit m bischofite, $MgCl_2 \cdot 6H_2O$
Bisektrix f bisectrix
Bismit m bismite, bismuth ochre, α-Bi_2O_3
Bismoclit m bismoclite, BiOCl
Bismuthin[it] m bismuthinite, bismuth glance, Bi_2S_3
Bismutit m bismut[h]ite, bismuth spar, $Bi_2[O_2 | CO_3]$

Bismutoferrit m bismutoferrite, $BiFe_2[OH | (SiO_4)_2]$
Bismutoplagionit m s. Galenobismutit
Bismutosphärit m bismutosphaerite, $Bi_2(CO_3)_3 \cdot 2Bi_2O_3$
Bismutotantalit m bismutotantalite, $Bi(Ta,Nb)O_4$
Bithek f bitheca *(graptolites)*
Bithyn[ium] n Bithynian [Substage] *(Middle Triassic, Tethys)*
Bittersalz n bitter (epsom) salt, epsomite, $Mg[SO_4] \cdot 7H_2O$
Bittersee m bitter lake
Bitterspat m magnesite, $MgCO_3$
Bitumen n bitumen, bituminous earth
Bitumendichtungshaut f asphaltic bitumen membrane, *(Am)* asphalt membrane
bitumenhaltig bituminiferous, bituminous
Bitumenkitt m bituminous mastic
Bitumenmethode f bituminological method
Bitumenvermörtelung f soil stabilization with asphaltic bitumen
bituminieren to bituminize
Bituminierung f bituminization
Bituminierungsbereich m bituminization range
Bituminit m bituminite *(coal maceral)*
bituminös bituminous
Bityit m bityite, $CaLiAl_2[(OH)_2 | AlBeSi_2O_{10}]$
Bixbyit m bixbyite, sitaparite, $(Mn, Fe)_2O_3$
Blackband n black band
Blackbox f blackbox
Blackriver[ien] n Blackriverian [Stage] *(Champlainian in North America)*
Blacksmoker m black smoker
Blähen n bloating
~ des Liegenden footwall swelling
blähend tumid
Blähgrad m swelling indice *(of coal)*
Blähpore f bubble hole
Blähton m foamclay, bloating (expanded, foam) clay
Blähvermögen n bloating property, swelling power *(of coal)*
Blähzahl f swelling indice *(of coal)*
Blairmorit m blairmorite *(alkaline volcanic rock)*
Blancan n Blancan [Stage] *(mammalian stage, Pliocene in North America)*
Blänke f bog pool
Blase f bubble; vesicle
Blasenlava f cellular (blister) lava
Blasenpunkt m bubble point
Blasenpunktdruck m bubble point pressure
Blasenröhre f spiracle
Blasensand m cavernous sand
Blasenströmung f/**turbulente** froth flow
Blasenstruktur f vesicular texture
Blasentang m bladder wrack, fucus vesiculosus
Blasenzüge *mpl* pipe vesicles (amygdules)
blasig bubbly; cavernous; vesicular
Blasloch n blow hole; gloup

Blassand

Blassand *m* abrasive sand
Blastese *f* blastesis
Blastitgefüge *n* blastic fabric
blastogranitisch blastogranitic
Blastoideen *fpl* blastoideans
Blastomylonit *m* blastomylonite
blastomylonitisch blastomylonitic
blastopelitisch blastopelitic
blastophitisch blastophitic
blastophyrisch blastophyric
blastoporphyrisch blastoporphyric
blastopsammitisch blastopsammitic
blastopsephitisch blastopsephitic
Blasversatz *m* pneumatic stowing
Blatt *n*/**gefiedertes** pinnate leaf
Blattabdruck *m* lithophyl, imprint of a leaf, leaf impression
Blattanlage *f* leaf primordium
Blättchen *n* scale; flake; lamella
blättchenförmig lamellar, lamelliform, lamellose
blätterartig lamelliferous
Blättergneis *m* leaf gneiss
Blätterkohle *f* laminated [brown] coal, foliated (slaty, paper) coal, leaf coal *(cutinite-rich; subaquatic coal)*
Blättersandstein *m* thin-laminated sandstone
Blätterschiefer *m* leaf (laminated) shale
Blätterserpentin *m* flaky serpentine (*s.a.* Antigorit)
Blättertellur *m* black telluride, nagyagite, $AuTe_2 \cdot 6Pb(S,Te)$
Blättertextur *f* foliated (foliaceous, micaceous, lepidoblastic) structure
Blätterton *m* foliated clay
Blätterung *f* foliation
blattförmig phylloid[al]
Blatt-für-Blatt-Injektion *f* parallel den s-Flächen leaf injection
Blattkohle *f s.* Blätterkohle
blattlos aphyllous
Blattmeißel *m* drag bit
Blattnarbe *f* leaf scar
blättrig leaflike, foliated, foliaceous laminated, lamellar; flaky
Blättrigkeit *f* foliation
Blattschichtung *f* lamellosity
Blattverschiebung *f* lateral (horizontal, wrench, transcurrent, strike-slip) fault, transverse thrust, flaw
Blattverschiebungssystem *n* transcurrent fault system
Blauasbest *m* blue asbestos
Blaublätter *npl* blue bands *(of a glacier)*
Blaublättertextur *f* stratification of the ice, dirt bed *(of a glacier)*
Blaueisenerz *n s.* Vivianit
Blaueisstück *n* glacier corn
Blauerde *f* blue ground *(in diamond pipes)*; killow *(black earth)*
blaugrün aquamarine
Blauquarz *m* amethystine quartz

Blauschieferfazies *f* blueschist (laucophane-lawsonite) facies
Blauschlick *m* blue mud
Blauspat *m s.* Lazulith
Blauton *m* blue clay
Blei *n* lead, plumbum, Pb
~/gediegenes native lead
Bleialter *n* lead age *(geochronology)*
Bleiaragonit *m* tarnowitzite *(mixed crystal)*
Bleiarsenglanz *m s.* Sartorit
bleiartig leady, leadlike, plumbeous
Bleibergwerk *n* lead mine
bleichen to bleach
Bleicherde *f* bleaching earth (clay), active earth, gray soil, podzol [soil]
~/saure acid clay
Bleichlorid *n s.* Chlorargyrit
Bleichschicht *f* bleached layer
Bleichton *m s.* Bleicherde
Bleichung *f* bleaching, weather stain
Bleichungsboden *m* bleached soil
Bleichungshof *m* reduction (deoxidation) sphere *(in red sediments)*
Bleichungszone *f* bleached zone
Bleierz *n* lead ore
~/bohnkorngroßes peasy
~/gewaschenes tails-common
~/hochwertiges bing ore
~/mulmiges friable lead ore
~/oxydiertes linnets
Bleierzformation *f* lead ore formation
Bleierzhaufwerk *n* chunck mineral
Bleierzstückchen *npl* nittings
Bleifahlerz *n* bournonite, $2PbS \cdot Cu_2S \cdot Sb_2S_3$
bleifarben plumbeous
bleiführend lead-bearing, plumbiferous
Bleiglanz *m* lead glance, galena, PbS
bleiglanzführend, bleiglanzhaltig galeniferous, galenical
Bleiglätte *f* massicot[ite], β-PbO
Bleigrube *f* lead mine
bleihaltig lead-bearing, plumbiferous
bleiig plumbeous
Bleiknottenerz *n* nodular galenite
Bleischweif *m* bleischweif, foliated galena *(variety of galenite)*
Bleispat *m* [black] lead spar, $PbCO_3$
Bleispiegel *m* specular galena
Blick *m* sight
Blickfeld *n* field of view
Blindbohrung *f* blind hole
Blindortversatz *m* airless end stowing
Blindschacht *m* blind (inside, staple) shaft, staple [pit]
Blitz *m* lightning
Blitzröhre *f*, **Blitzsinter** *m* lightning (sand) tube, fulgurite
Blitzstrahl *m* lightning flash
Block *m* block
~/erratischer erratic, erratic (perched) block, erratic (perched, drift) boulder
~/exotischer exotic block

~/glazial abgeschliffener soled cobble
~/großer boulder
Blockablagerung f/unverfestigte boulder gravel
Blockdiagramm n block diagram, perspective block
Blockeis n block ice
Blockgebirge n s. Schollengebirge
Blockgletscher m rock glacier
Blocklava f block lava
Blocklavafeld n clinker field
Blocklehm m boulder (drift) clay
~/fossiler tillite
Blockmeer n block (boulder) field
Blockmoräne f boulder moraine
Blockmoränenwall m boulder wall
Blockpackung f block packing, boulder masses (bed), bouldery deposit
blockreich bouldery
Blockriff n block reef
Blockschicht f boulder pavement
Blockstrom m boulder (rock, block) stream, boulder train
Blockstruktur f/eckig-kantige angular blocky structure
Blocktuff m lithic tuff
Blockverwerfung f block faulting
Blockwall m block rampart (embankment, levee)
Blockzerfall m block disintegration
Blödit m blödite, bloedite, astrakhanite, $Na_2Mg(SO_4)_2 \cdot 4H_2O$
Blomstrandin m blomstrandine, priorite, $(Y,Ce,Th,Ca,Na,U)[(Ti,Nb,Ta)_2O_6]$
bloßlegen to expose, to lay bare, to uncover, to strip, to denude
Bloßlegung f exposure, laying bare, uncovering, stripping, revelation
Blubber m bubble
Blumenkohlstruktur f cauliflower structure
Blutachat m h[a]emachate
blütenlos ananthous (palaeobotany)
Blütenpflanzen fpl phanerogams
Blütezeit f s. Klimax
Blutregen m blood rain
Blutstein m h[a]ematite
Bö f gust, squall, flaw, flurry, scud
Bobierrit m bobierrite, $Mg_3[PO_4]_2 \cdot 8H_2O$
Bocca f bocca
Bodden m bodden
Boddenküste f bodden-type of coast line
Boden m soil, ground; dirt
~/abfallender shelving bottom
~/alkalischer alkaline soil
~/allochthoner transported soil
~/angeschwemmter alluvial soil
~/anmooriger half bog soil, marsh border soil
~/anstehender site (in-situ) soil
~/armer low-productive soil
~/auftauender tabet soil
~/ausgelaugter leached (degraded) soil
~/bindiger harter tight soil

~/brauner s. ~/zimtfarbener
~/durchlässiger pervious ground
~/endodynamomorpher endodynamomorphic soil
~/entbaster s. ~/ausgelaugter
~/erschöpfter exhausted soil
~/eutropher active soil
~/fester compact soil
~/fester steiniger hard stony ground
~/fetter fat soil
~/fossiler buried soil, ancient soil bed
~/frostgefährdeter heaving soil
~/fruchtbarer fertile soil
~/gesättigter s. ~/wassergesättigter
~/gewachsener original soil, natural ground, bush mould
~/gewellter hogbacked bottom
~/goldführender pay dirt
~/halbsumpfiger semibog[gy] soil
~/humider podzol [soil]
~/jungfräulicher virgin earth material
~/kastanienfarbiger chestnut-brown soil
~/klebriger adhesive ground
~/klumpiger durable crumbling soil
~/kohäsionsloser cohesionless (non-cohesive, non-coherent) soil
~/krümeliger crumbly soil
~/kulturfähiger arable soil
~/magerer hungry soil (s. a. ~/verarmter)
~/mit verhärtetem Untergrund planosol
~/nackter bare ground
~/natriumhaltiger sodic soil
~/nichtbindiger s. ~/kohäsionsloser
~/nordischer podsoliger northern semipodzol
~ ohne Horizontbildung azonal soil
~/organischer organic soil
~/podsoliger podzolic soil
~/primärer embryonic soil
~/rutschender slippery soil, slipping earth-work
~/salziger solodized soil
~/saurer acid soil
~/schwellender heaving bottom
~/sekundärer transported soil
~/solodartiger solodic soil
~/stark farbiger chromosol
~/steiniger rubbly (cobbly) soil, rubble land
~/strukturloser loose grain soil
~/sumpfiger spewy soil, moss
~/takyrartiger takyrlike soil
~ über dem Pergelisol supragelisol
~/unbebauter bare soil
~/unfruchtbarer karoo land
~/unreifer interzonal soil
~/unverfestigter unfixed soil
~/urbarer arable soil
~/verarmter depleted (impoverished) soil
~/verfestigter consolidated ground
~/verschlämmter puddled soil
~/verschwemmter carried soil
~/versumpfter water-bogged soil
~/wassergesättigter waterlogged (saturated) soil

Boden

~/**weicher** weak soil
~/**windtransportierter** aeolian (windborne) soil
~/**zimtfarbener** cinnamonic (cinnamon-coloured) soil
Bodenabdichtung f soil (earth) waterproofing; soil sealing
Bodenablagerung f bottomset bed
Bodenabspülung f washing-away of soil
Bodenabtrag m, **Bodenabtragung** f soil erosion (denudation)
Bodenanalyse f soil analysis (test)
Bodenanschwellung f floor heaving
Bodenart f s. Bodentyp
Bodenassoziation f soil association
Bodenaufnahme f soil survey
Bodenaufschüttung f soil aggradation
Bodenausbruch m soil excavation
Bodenausdünstung f soil evaporation, evaporation from soil
Bodenauswaschung f soil washing (leaching)
Bodenazidität f soil acidity
Bodenbakterien fpl soil bacteria
Bodenbearbeitung f soil cultivation, land treatment
bodenbefestigend soil-stabilizing, soil-fixing
Bodenbefestigung f stabilization of earthwork
Bodenbeleg m ground verification *(confirmation of the conclusions drawn from remote sensing data by independent ground information, so-called "ground-truth")*
Bodenbenderit m bodenbenderite *(variety of spessartine)*
Bodenbeschaffenheit f quality (nature) of soil; composition of the ground; condition of the soil
Bodenbestandteil m soil constituent
Bodenbeton m soil cement
Bodenbewegung f earth (ground) movement, soil shifting
Bodenbewertung f land evaluation
bodenbildend soil-forming, soil-making
Bodenbildung f soil formation (development), pedogenesis
Bodenbildungsfaktor m soil-genetic factor
Bodenbonitierung f s. Bodenschätzung
Bodenchemie f soil chemistry, pedochemistry
Bodendampfwasser n vaporous water
Bodendaten pl ground data
Bodendecke f soil cover
~/**tote** dead litter
Bodendeckschicht f soil-cover complex
Bodendegradierung f soil degradation
Bodendichte f soil (ground) density
Bodendrift f bottom drift
Bodendruck m soil loading; earth pressure
~/**statischer** static bottom-hole pressure
Bodendruckmeßgerät n soil pressure bomb
Bodendruckpressung f compression of soil (ground)
Bodendünnschliff m soil thin section
Bodendurchlässigkeit f soil permeability
Bodendurchlüftung f soil aeration

50

Bodendynamik f soil dynamics
Bodeneigenschaft f soil property
Bodeneinschnitt m soil cut
Bodeneis n ground (anchor) ice; fossil ice
Bodenentsalzung f desalinization of soil
Bodenerhaltung f soil conservation
Bodenerhebung f uplift; upheaval; eminence
~/**wellenförmige** earth wave
Bodenerkundung f soil survey
Bodenermüdung f soil exhaustion
Bodenerosion f soil erosion
Bodenerschöpfung f soil exhaustion; sickness of soil
Bodenerschütterung f earth (ground) vibration, ground unrest
Bodenerschütterungswelle f earth wave
~/**künstlich erregte** artificially excited earth wave
Bodenfauna f benthonic fauna
Bodenfeuchte f soil (ground, surface) humidity, soil moisture (wetness)
~/**epigenetische** antecedent soil moisture
Bodenfeuchtedefizit n field-moisture deficiency
Bodenfeuchtigkeit f s. Bodenfeuchte
Bodenfeuchtigkeitsgradient m soil moisture gradient
Bodenfließen n solifluction, earth flow
~ **im Permafrostgebiet** congelifluction
~/**kleinlobiges** earth runs
Bodenfluktion f, **Bodenfluß** m s. Bodenfließen
Bodenform f land form
Bodenfracht f bed load
bodenfremd allochthonous
Bodenfrost m soil (ground) frost
Bodenfrostmesser m cryopedometer
Bodenfruchtbarkeit f soil fertility
Bodengare f [good] tilth, friable state
Bodengas n soil (ground) gas
Bodengefüge n soil structure
Bodengekriech n s. Bodenkriechen
Bodengenetik f soil genetics
Bodengeologe m agrogeologist
Bodengeologie f agrogeology
Bodengestaltung f configuration of soil
Bodengreifer m bottom catcher, box sampler
Bodenhebung f land upheaval (uplift)
Bodenhorizont m soil horizon
~/**fossiler** palaeosol
~ **mit Pflanzenresten/fossiler** dirt bed
~/**oberer** A-horizon
~ **unter dem Flöz/fossiler** seat earth
Bodenkarte f soil map
Bodenkartierung f soil mapping
Bodenkennzeichnung f identification of soils
Bodenklassifizierung f soil classification
Bodenklima n soil climate
Bodenkolloid n soil-colloid[al particle]
Bodenkorrosion f soil (underground) corrosion
Bodenkriechen n creeping of soil (ground)
Bodenkrume f surface soil, topsoil *(s.a. Mutterboden)*

Bodenkrümel *m* soil crumb
Bodenkruste *f*/**harte** duricrust
Bodenkunde *f* soil science, pedology
~/bautechnische soil mechanics
Bodenkundler *m* pedologist
bodenkundlich pedological
Bodenlast *f* bottom load, traction (bed) load
Bodenlebewelt *f s.* Bodenorganismen
Bodenlehre *f* soil science, pedology
Bodenlösung *f* soil solution
Bodenluft *f* soil (ground) air; ground gas
Bodenmächtigkeit *f* thickness of soil
Bodenmasse *f*/**abgerutschte** slipping mass
Bodenmechanik *f* soil mechanics
Bodenmechaniker *m* soil engineer
bodenmechanisch soil-mechanical
Bodenmelioration *f* land amelioration (improvement), land reclamation
Bodenmikroflora *f* soil microflora
Bodenmörtel *m* soil mortar
Bodenmüdigkeit *f* soil sickness
Bodennebel *m* ground fog
Bodennutzung *f* agriculture; land use
Bodennutzungsklassen *fpl* land-use capability classes
Bodenorganismen *mpl* soil organisms
Bodenpfropfen *m* bottom plug *(bore)*
Bodenphysik *f* soil physics
bodenphysikalisch soil-physical
Bodenplatte *f*/**vorläufige** temporary base plate
Bodenporosität *f* soil porosity
Bodenpressung *f* consolidation of the subsoil
Bodenprobe *f* soil sample (specimen), bottom-hole sample
~/ungestörte undisturbed soil sample
Bodenprobenehmer *m* bottom-hole sample taker
Bodenprobestück *n* bit of ground
Bodenprofil *n* soil profile
Bodenprüfung *f* soil test (analysis)
Bodenpufferung *f* buffering of soil
Bodenquellstoff *m* soil-colloid[al particle]
Bodenquellung *f* soil swelling
Bodenreaktion *f* pH-value of the soil
Bodenreibungsschicht *f* bottom frictional layer
Bodensatz *m* cumulate *(of a magma)*
Bodensaugvermögen *n* soil suction
Bodenschätze *mpl* natural (mineral) resources, mineral wealth
Bodenschätzung *f* soil taxation, evaluation of soil
Bodenschicht *f* soil bed (series, layer, stratum)
~/nicht verhärtete non-indurated pan
~/undurchlässige impermeable stratum
~/wasserführende aquifer [layer], water-bearing soil bed
Bodenschrumpfung *f* soil shrinkage
Bodenschutz *m* soil conservation
bodenschützend soil-protecting, soil-protective
Bodenschwelle *f* hummock

Bodensediment *n* bottomset
Bodensee *m* Lake Constance
Bodensenke *f* depression of ground, sink, swale
Bodensenkung *f* depression of ground, ground submergence (subsidence), sag[ging]
Bodensenkungskurve *f* development curve of subsidence
Bodensetzung *f* land subsidence; soil compaction
Bodenskelett *n* soil skeleton
Bodenspur *f* ground track *(e.g. of a satellite or airplane)*
Bodenstabilisator *m* soil stabilizer
Bodenstabilisierung *f* soil (ground, artificial) cementation
bodenständig autochthonous; indigenous
Bodensteinigkeit *f* stoniness of soils
Bodensterilisierung *f* soil sterilisation
Bodenstrom *m* bottom current
Bodenströmung *f* bottom current
Bodenstruktur *f* soil structure (array)
Bodensystematik *f* soil systematics
Bodentaxonomie *f* soil appraisal
Bodenteilchen *n* soil particle
Bodentemperatur *f* soil temperature
Bodentiefe *f* depth of soil
Bodentiere *npl*/**wühlende** burrowing animals
Bodentransport *m* soil transport[ation] *(in flowing waters)*
Bodentyp *m* soil type
~/aluminium- und eisenreicher pedalfer
~/anthropogener anthropogenic soil type
Bodenübersichtskarte *f* soil survey chart
Bodenumweltbedingungen *fpl* ground environment
Bodenundurchlässigkeit *f* impermeability (imperviousness) of the soil
Bodenunruhe *f* ground unrest
~/mikroseismische microseism, microseismic movement
Bodenuntersuchung *f* soil testing (exploration), subsurface investigation, site exploration, foundation testing
Bodenuntersuchungsbohrung *f* boring for soil investigation
Bodenuntersuchungsgeräte *npl* soil research equipment
Bodenvegetation *f* ground vegetation
bodenverbessernd soil-improving
Bodenverbesserung *f* soil improvement, amelioration
Bodenverdichtung *f* [/**künstliche**] soil consolidation (compaction, densification)
~/natürliche soil (earth) consolidation
Bodenverdunstung *f* soil evaporation; soil respiration
Bodenverdunstungsmesser *m* soil evaporation pan
Bodenverfestigung *f* soil stabilization, soil (earth) solidification
~/chemische chemical soil solidification

Bodenverfestigungswalze

Bodenverfestigungswalze f compactor, compaction roller
Bodenverhältnisse npl soil conditions
Bodenverkrustung f surface crusting
Bodenverlagerung f mass wasting, drifting of soil
Bodenvermörtelung f/**bituminöse** soil stabilization with asphaltic bitumen
~ **mit Stabilisatorbeigabe** additive soil stabilization
Bodenvernässung f waterlogging
Bodenversetzung f s.
Bodenversumpfung f soil swamping
Bodenverwehung f soil blowing
Bodenwärmefluß m ground heat flow
Bodenwasser n soil (bottom) water
Bodenwassergehalt m soil-moisture content
Bodenwasserspannung f soil-suction, soil-moisture tension, stress of soil moisture
Bodenwasserzone f soil-water belt
Bodenwelle f 1. ground (earth) wave; 2. s. Anhöhe
Bodenwert m land value
Bodenwind m surface wind
Bodenzähigkeit f plasticity of soil
Bodenzahl f soil characteristic
Bodenzement m soil cement
Bodenziffer f soil characteristic
Bodenzone f/**lufterfüllte** aerated soil zone
~/**mit Fe-Oxiden zementierte** ferricrete
Böenfront f squall[y] front
Böenmesser m gust meter
Böenschreiber m gust recorder
Bogen m/**Karibischer** Caribbean arc
Bogenanregung f arc excitation *(spectrum analysis)*
Bogendüne f crescentic (bow-shaped) dune
bogenförmig arcuate
Bogengewichtsmauer f, **Bogengewichtssperre** f arch-gravity dam
Bogenmoräne f crescentic moraine
Bogenscheitel m curve apex
Bogensperrmauer f, **Bogenstaumauer** f arch[ed] dam
Bogentrum n arcuate vein
Bogenwirkung f arching effect
Böggildit m boeggildite, $Na_2Sr_2Al_2[F_9|PO_4]$
Bogheadkohle f boghead coal; algal coal; parrot coal; torbanite *(Scotland)*
Bogheadkohlenflöz n boghead seam
Bogheadschiefer m boghead shale
bogig arching
Böhmit m boehmite, γ-AlOOH
Bohnerz n bean (pea) ore, pisiform (pisolitic) iron ore
Bohnerzboden m shot soil
Bohraggregat n drilling unit
Bohranlage f drilling rig
~/**bewegliche** mobile drilling rig
~/**fahrbare** travelling drilling rig
~/**ortsfeste** stationary drilling rig
~/**schwere** powerful drilling rig

52

~/**selbstfahrende** self-propelled drilling rig
~/**stationäre** stationary drilling rig
~/**tragbare** portable drilling rig
Bohranlagenleistung f drilling rig performance
Bohransatzpunkt m well location, drilling site, site (location) of well
~ **in Küstennähe** offshore location
Bohrarbeiten fpl drilling work (operations)
~ **auf dem Festland** land operations
Bohrarbeiter m driller; rig helper
Bohrarchiv n well file
Bohrausrüstung f drilling equipment (outfit)
Bohrbarkeit f drillability
~ **des Gesteins** rock drillability
Bohrbeginn m commencement of drilling
Bohrbelegschaft f drilling crew
Bohrbericht drilling (tour) report
Bohrbock m boring trestle
Bohrbrigade f drilling crew
Bohrbrücke f drilling bridge
Bohrbrunnen m bore[d] well, drilled (driven) well
Bohrbühne f drilling (derrick) platform
Bohrdauer f drilling time
Bohrdiamant m drilling (black, carbon) diamond, carbonado
Bohrdruck m bit weight, weight on bit
Bohrdruckmesser m [bit] weight indicator
Bohreinheit f boring unit
bohren to bore, to drill
~/**einen Kern** to core, to cut a core, to carry out coring
Bohren n drilling
~ **auf gut Glück** random drilling
~/**drehendes** drilling by rotation
~/**elektrohydraulisches** electrohydraulic drilling
~/**gerichtetes** directional drilling
~/**hydraulisches** hydraulic drilling
~ **im Gestein** rock drilling
~ **in der See** marine (offshore) drilling
~/**kernloses** full hole drilling
~/**kombiniertes** combination system of drilling
~ **mit der Sauerstofflanze** fire drilling
~ **mit Diamantkronen** diamond drilling
~ **mit Düsenmeißeln** jet drilling
~ **mit Gasspülung** gas drilling
~ **mit Luftspülung** air drilling
~ **mit mehrfacher Richtungsänderung** multidirectional (multibranched) drilling
~ **mit Sprengstoffen** drilling with explosives
~ **mit Umkehrspülung** counterflush (reverse circulation, reverse rotary) drilling
~ **mit Vorort-Antriebsmaschine** down-the-hole drilling
~ **mittels elektrischer Gesteinszertrümmerung** electrical disintegration drilling
~ **ohne geologische Vorarbeiten** blind drilling
~ **ohne Gestänge** drilling without a drill pipe
~/**schlagendes** percussion drilling
~/**thermisches** thermal drilling

53 Bohrlochlänge

~/übertiefes superdeep drilling *(more than 3000 m depth)*
~ unter Druck pressure drilling
~/untertägiges subsurface drilling
~ vor der Meeresküste offshore drilling
bohrend/im Sediment lithodomous *(organisms)*
Bohrer *m* bit
Bohrergebnisse *npl* drilling results
Bohrfläche *f* bore surface
Bohrflüssigkeit *f* drilling (borehole) fluid
Bohrfortschritt *m* drilling progress (rate), penetration rate (advance)
Bohrfortschrittslog *n* drilling-time log
Bohrfortschrittsmessung *f* mechanical logging
Bohrfortschrittsregistriereinrichtung *f* penetration rate recorder
Bohrfortschrittsschreiber *m* geograph
Bohrfortschrittswechsel *m* drilling-time break
Bohrgang *m* burrow *(by organisms)*
Bohrgarnitur *f* drilling assembly (string)
~/niedergebrachte downhole drilling assembly
Bohrgehilfe *m* assistant driller
Bohrgerät *n* boring tackle (implement)
~/auf schweren LKW montiertes truck rig
~/fahrbares rambler rig
~ für Tiefbohrungen deep boring tool
Bohrgerüst *n* derrick, boring trestle
~ mit senkbaren Stützen/schwimmendes platform on legs
Bohrgerüsthöhe *f* height of derrick
Bohrgeschwindigkeit *f* drilling speed (rate), penetration speed
Bohrgestänge *n* boring (drill) rod; drill pipe *(complete)*
Bohrgestängestrang *m* drill pipe string
Bohrgreifer *m* drilling grip
Bohrgut *n* drill (ditch) cuttings, drill chips, debris, returns
Bohrgutaustragsmessung *f* measurement of the amount of drilled material
Bohrhammer *m* hammer drill
Bohringenieur *m* drilling engineer
Bohrinsel *f* drilling island (platform), drill barge, floating derrick, offshore oil rig
~/zugseilverankerte tension-leg platform
Bohrjournal *n* drilling diary (journal)
Bohrkarte *f* base map for drilling work
Bohrkern *m* drill core, boring kernel
~/[erdöl]ausschwitzender weeping core
~/unberührter native-state core
Bohrkernuntersuchung *f* core analysis
Bohrklein *n* borings, drillings, [well] cuttings, drill dust, [rock] chips
Bohrkleinanalyse *f* cuttings analysis
Bohrkopf *m* boring head, bit
Bohrkosten *pl* cost of drilling
Bohrkrone *f* [drill] bit, crown, core bit
~/oberflächenbesetzte surface-set bit
Bohrlanze *f* drilling lance
Bohrleistung *f* penetration rate, boring (drilling) capacity; *s.a.* Bohrstrecke

Bohrloch *n* bore[hole], [drilled] hole, well; blasthole
~/gekrümmtes crooked hole
~/horizontales gopher (coyote) hole
~/in einer Ebene gekrümmtes hole with deviation in a plane
~ mit schiefer Richtung angling [drill]
~/räumlich gekrümmtes hole with deviation not in a plane
~/schräges slanting hole
~/unverrohrtes uncased (open) hole
~/verbohrtes crooked hole
~/verengtes undergauge hole
~/verrohrtes cased (lined) hole
Bohrlochabschluß *m* auf dem Meeresboden seafloor well head
~ auf dem Meeresboden/trockener dry seafloor well head
Bohrlochabsperrarmatur *f* blow-out preventer
Bohrlochabsperrvorrichtung *f* blow-out preventer assembly
Bohrlochabstand *m* borehole (well) spacing
Bohrlochabweichung *f* hole deviation, well dip
~ mit dem Schichtenfallen down structure deflection of the hole
~/zulässige allowable maximum of hole deviation
Bohrlochachse *f* well axis
Bohrlochanordnung *f* pattern of well spacing
Bohrlochanzahl *f* number of boreholes
Bohrlochauffüllung *f* well bore fill-up
Bohrlochaufnahme *f*/**magnetische** magnetic logging
Bohrlochauskesselung *f* well cavity
Bohrlochausrüstung *f* bottom-hole equipment
Bohrlochbehandlung *f* well treatment
~/chemische chemical well service
Bohrlochbergbau *m* auger mining *(of coal)*
Bohrlochdistanz *f s.* Bohrlochabstand
Bohrlochdurchmesser *m* diameter of drill hole, size of well, well diameter
Bohrlocherweiterung *f* underreaming [of a drill hole]
Bohrlochfilmkamera *f* moving picture borehole camera
Bohrlochgeochemie *f* well geochemistry
Bohrlochgeophon *n* uphole geophone
Bohrlochgeophysik *f* well logging
Bohrlochgravimeter *n* borehole gravimeter
Bohrlochkaliber *n* 1. hole calibre; 2. calipering device
Bohrlochkamera *f* borehole (downhole) camera
Bohrlochkonstruktion *f* casing program
Bohrlochkoordinaten *fpl* well coordinates
Bohrlochkopf *m* well-head
Bohrlochkopfausrüstung *f* well-head assembly
Bohrlochkopfgas *n* casing-head gas
Bohrlochkrümmung *f* curvature (deviation) of the hole
Bohrlochlänge *f s.* Bohrlochteufe

Bohrlochlängenkontrolle 54

Bohrlochlängenkontrolle *f* checking of borehole depth
Bohrlochlängsgeber *m* borehole axial strain transmitter
Bohrlochmeßapparatur *f* logging unit
Bohrlochmessung *f* borehole measurement (survey), drill-hole surveying, [well] logging
~/akustische acoustic logging
~/elektrische electrical logging (survey)
~/geochemische geochemical logging
~/geophysikalische geophysical logging
~/geothermische geothermal logging
~/kernphysikalische nuclear physical logging
~/magnetische magnetic logging
~/radiometrische radiometric logging
~/seismische seismic logging
Bohrlochmitte *f* centre of borehole
Bohrlochmund *m* well mouth, [hole] collar
Bohrlochneigungsmesser *m* bottom-hole inclinometer, direction indicator
Bohrlochnenndurchmesser *m* full-gauge hole
Bohrlochöffnung *f* heel
Bohrlochpfeife *f* blown-out hole
Bohrlochpfropfen *m* hole plug
Bohrlochprobe *f* borehole sample
Bohrlochprofil *n* profile of the hole
Bohrlochquergeber *m* borehole diametral strain indicator
Bohrlochquerschnittsmessung *f* caliper log
Bohrlochrichtung *f* drill-hole direction
Bohrlochschaber *m* well scraper
Bohrlochschädigung *f* well bore damage
Bohrlochschießen *n* borehole shooting *(e.g. in mines and quarries)*
Bohrlochseismik *f* well shooting
Bohrlochsohle *f* bottom hole, well face
Bohrlochsohlendruck *m* **bei geschlossenem Schieber** closed-in bottom-hole pressure
Bohrlochsohlenmotor *m* downhole motor
Bohrlochsohlenprobenehmer *m* bottom-hole sample taker
Bohrlochsohlentemperatur *f* bottom-hole temperature, BHT
Bohrlochsonde *f/***optische** introscope
Bohrlochspeicherung *f* well bore storage
Bohrlochstimulierung *f* well stimulation
Bohrlochstörungen *fpl* shot-hole noise *(geophysics)*
Bohrlochteufe *f,* **Bohrlochtiefe** *f* drill-hole depth, well depth [in plumb line]
Bohrlochtiefstes *n* hole bottom, back (toe) of the hole
Bohrlochtorpedierung *f* well shooting
Bohrlochuntersuchung *f s.* Bohrlochmessung
Bohrlochverformungsgeber *m* borehole deformation meter
Bohrlochverfüllung *f* borehole sealing
Bohrlochvermessung *f* drill log
Bohrlochverrohrung *f* string
Bohrlochverschluß *m* hole plug
Bohrlochverstopfung *f/***auflösbare** removable well damage

~/nicht zu beseitigende irreparable well damage
Bohrlochvorbereitung *f* well completion
Bohrlochwand *f* [bore]hole wall, wall of a well; sandface *(in the storage)*
Bohrlochwandung *f* bore surface
Bohrlochzementation *f* well cementing
Bohrlöffel *m* valve auger
Bohrmannschaft *f* drilling (rig) crew
Bohrmarke *f* foralite *(by organisms)*
Bohrmarsch *m* run, [round] trip
Bohrmast *m* drilling mast
~/ausziehbarer telescope mast
Bohrmehl *n* bore (drill) dust, drillings, drill (ditch) cuttings, borings, debris, returns
Bohrmeißel *m* boring tool, drill bit
Bohrmeister *m* toolpusher
Bohrmeisterlog *n* driller's log
Bohrmeterkosten *pl* cost per meter of hole
Bohrmeterleistung *f* drilling meterage
Bohrmuschel *f* boring mollusk, rock borer
Bohrnetz *n* drilling net[work]
Bohrpfahl *m* bored pile
Bohrplattform *f/***bewegliche** mobile barge (platform)
~/feststehende fixed platform
Bohrprobe *f* sampling of cuttings
Bohrprobenahme *f* prospect sampling
Bohrprobenanzeiger *m* sample logger
Bohrproduktivität *f* drilling efficiency
Bohrprofil *n* profile of a bore, drill (well) log, well section
~/elektrisches electric log
Bohrprogramm *n* drilling program
Bohrprotokoll *n* [boring, driller's] log, boring report (record sheet)
Bohrprozeß *m* drilling of the well
Bohrpunkt *m s.* Bohransatzpunkt
Bohrregime *n* drilling technique
Bohrrohr *n* drill (well) tube
Bohrsand *m s.* Bohrmehl
Bohrschappe *f* mud (valve, shell) auger
Bohrschiff *n* drilling ship, [floating] drilling vessel
~/verankertes anchored craft
Bohrschlamm *m* boring sludge, bore detritus, drilling mud (fluid), sludge (drill, ditch) cuttings, slime, silt
Bohrschlick *m,* **Bohrschmant** *m s.* Bohrschlamm
Bohrschrot *n* drilling shot
Bohrschwengel *m* walking beam *(cable drilling)*
Bohrseil *n* drilling cable
Bohrseiltrommel *f* hoisting drum
Bohrsonde *f* well
Bohrspindel *f* boring spindle
Bohrspülung *f s.* Bohrschlamm
Bohrspülungsleitung *f* mud line
Bohrspülungszusatzmittel *n* drilling mud additive
Bohrstange *f* drill rod

Bohrstangenlänge f length of tube (pipe)
Bohrstelle f s. Bohransatzpunkt
Bohrstock m drilling stock
Bohrstrang m drill string
Bohrstrangbruch m drill string break-off
Bohrstrecke f footage
Bohrtätigkeit f drilling activity
~ **in Küstennähe** offshore activity
Bohrtechnik f drilling engineering
Bohrtiefe f boring (drilling) depth
Bohrtrübe f s. Bohrschlamm
Bohrturm m boring tower (trestle), drill[ing] tower, derrick
~ **für Erdölbohrungen** oil-well derrick
~ **für höchste Beanspruchung** heavy-duty derrick
~/**ortsfester** stationary drill rig, fixed derrick
~/**schwimmender** floating derrick
~/**transportabler** mast
~/**verfahrbarer** self-propelled rig
~ **zum gleichzeitigen Bohren von mehreren Bohrungen** multiple-well derrick
Bohrturmfundament n derrick foundation
Bohrturmkeller m cellar
Bohrturmsockel m derrick foundation
Bohrturmunterbau m derrick substructure
Bohrung f 1. boring, drilling; 2. [bore]hole, drilled hole, well (s.a. Bohrloch)
~/**abgelenkte** deflected hole
~/**abgesetzte** stepped bore (hole)
~/**abgeteufte** put-down bore
~/**abgewichene** curved (deviated, crooked) hole
~ **auf dem Festland** onshore well
~/**eingestellte** abandoned (suspended) well
~/**ergebnislose** dry hole (well)
~/**erschöpfte** dead (exhausted, depleted) well
~/**flache** shallow boring
~/**fördernde** producing well
~/**frei ausfließende** well producing by flow; artesian well
~/**geheime** tight hole
~/**geneigte** slant hole
~/**geschlossene** shut-in well
~/**in Pumpbetrieb fördernde** pumping (beam) well, pumper
~ **mit starker Vertikalabweichung** high-drift-angle well
~ **mit unverrohrtem Ölträger** barefooted well
~ **mit unvollständigem Speicheraufschluß** partial penetrating well
~ **ohne Filterrohre** barefooted well
~/**ölführende** oil well
~/**produzierende** paying well
~/**schräg angesetzte** slant hole
~/**schräge** inclined (slope) boring
~/**selbstfließende** well producing by flow
~/**stoßweise erumpierende** belching well
~/**stratigrafische** stratigraphic well
~/**übertiefe** very deep hole drilling
~/**unergiebige** barren well
~/**unnötige** needless well
~/**unverrohrte** unlined hole
~/**verlassene** s. ~/eingestellte
~/**verrohrte** cased[-in] bore
~/**vertikale** vertical hole
~/**verwässerte** drowned well
~/**wasserfreie** water-free well
~/**wild erumpierende** wildcat well
~/**wirtschaftlich fördernde** commercial producer
Bohrungsintensivierung f well stimulation
Bohrungsproduktivität f well productivity
Bohrungsundichtheit f leakage of well
Bohrverfahren n drilling method
Bohrversuch m boring test
Bohrvorrichtung f drilling jig, drillstock
Bohrwagen m jumbo
Bohrwerkzeug n boring (drilling) tool
Bohrwerkzeugbelastung f bit weight
Bohrwerkzeugverschleiß m bit wear
Bohrzeit f drilling time
~ **auf Sohle** time on bottom
~/**reine** actual drilling time, rotating time
Bohrzeug n drilling string
böig gusty, squally
Böigkeit f gustiness
Bojit m bojite (hornblende gabbro)
Bol m bole
Boldyrevit m boldyrevite, $CaNaMg[AlF_5(F, H_2O]_3$
Boleit m boleite, $5PbCl_2 \cdot 4Cu(OH)_2 \cdot AgCl \cdot 1^1/_2 H_2O$
Bolid m bolide, fireball
~/**großer** great fireball
~/**heller** bright fireball
Bolivarit m bolivarite, $Al_2[(OH)_3|PO_4] \cdot 5H_2O$
Bölling-Interstadial n Bölling warmtime
Boltwoodit m boltwoodite, $K_2H_2[UO_2|SiO_4] \cdot 4H_2O$
Bolus m bole
~/**weißer** white bole, fuller's earth, malthacite
bolusartig bolar
Boluserde f bole
Bombe f bomb
~/**abgeflachte vulkanische** pancake-shaped bomb
~/**bipolare** spindle-shaped bomb
~/**gedrehte** twisted bomb
~/**geschwänzte** unipolar bomb
~/**kugelige** globular bomb
~/**vulkanische** [volcanic] bomb
Bombenloch n bomblike hole
Bonattit m bonattite, $Cu[SO_4] \cdot 3H_2O$
Bonchevit m bonchevite, $PbS \cdot 2Bi_2S_3$
Bonebed n bone bed
Boninit m boninite (vitreous andesite)
Boomer m boomer
Boothit m boothite, $Cu[SO_4] \cdot 7H_2O$
Bor n boron, B
Boracit m boracite, $Mg_3[Cl|B_7O_{13}]$
Borax m borax, $Na_2[B_4O_5(OH)_4] \cdot 8H_2O$
Boraxkalk m calcium borate
Boraxsee m borax lake

Bördelöß

Bördelöß m börde loess *(Magdeburg)*
Bordenschiefer m banded slate
Boreal n Boreal *(part of Flandrian, Holocene)*
Bořickyit m bořickyite, $CaFe_4[(OH)_8|(PO_4)_2] \cdot 3H_2O$
Borkenlehm m layer of shale chips
Bornhardtit m bornhardtite, Co_3Se_4
Bornit m bornite, peacock copper (ore), Cu_5FeS_4
Boronatrocalcit m boronatrocalcite, stiberite, raphite, ulexite, $NaCa[B_5O_6(OH)_6] \cdot 5H_2O$
Borosilikat n borosilicate
Bort m boart
böschen to chamfer
Böschung f slope; shelvingness; scarp [face]; acclivity; glint *(step, formed by different hard layers)*
~/abfallende downward slope
~ am Fuß des Kontinentalabhangs continental apron
~/meeresseitige offshore slope
~/obere head slope
~/sanft geneigte gentle-sloped talus
~/steile escarpment
Böschungsabsatz m berm[e]
Böschungsanstieg m acclivity
Böschungsausbruch m slope failure
Böschungsbruch m circular slip
Böschungsdruck m s. Versatzdruck
Böschungsfläche f surface of constant slope
Böschungsfließen n slope current
Böschungsfußentwässerung f drainage at the toe
Böschungsgrad m degree of slope
Böschungskante f coved edge
Böschungslinien fpl slope lines
Böschungsmauer f retaining wall
Böschungsneigung f batter *(of a dam)*
Böschungsprofil n profile of slope
Böschungsrutsch m, **Böschungsrutschung** f slope slip
Böschungsschnitt m cut of slope
Böschungsseite f slopeward side
Böschungsverhältnis n slope ratio
Böschungsverschneidung f slope cutting
Böschungswinkel m angle of slope (elevation)
~/natürlicher natural angle of slope, angle of repose (rest); critical angle
Bosjemanit m bosjemanite *(Mn-bearing pickeringite)*
bossieren to emboss, to scabble
Bossieren n embossing, scabbling
Bossierer m embosser
Bossierhammer m embossing (scabbling) hammer
Bostonit m bostonite *(alkaline syenite aplite)*
Botallackit m botallackite, $Cu_2(OH)_3Cl$
Botryogen m botryogen, quetenite, $MgFe[OH|(SO_4)_2] \cdot 7H_2O$
Boudinage f boudinage
boudinieren to boudiner
Bouguer-Anomalie f Bouguer anomaly

56

Bouguer-Reduktion f Bouguer correction
Boulangerit m boulangerite, $5PbS \cdot 2Sb_2S_3$
Bouma-Sequenz f Bouma sequence
Bournonit m bournonite, endellionite, $2PbS \cdot Cu_2S \cdot Sb_2S_3$
Boussingaultit m boussingaultite, $(NH_4)_2Mg[SO_4]_2 \cdot 6H_2O$
Bowralith m bowralite *(alkaline pegmatite)*
Braccianit m braccianite *(variety of leucite tephrite)*
Brache f layland, fallow land
Brachialklappe f brachial valve
Brachland n layland, fallow land
Brachyachse f brachyaxis
Brachyantiklinale f brachyanticline
Brachydoma n brachydome, side dome
Brachyfalte f brachyfold
brachyhalin brachyhaline
Brachypinakoid n brachypinacoid
Brachysynklinale f brachysyncline
Brackebuschit m brackebuschite, $Pb_2(Mn, Fe)[VO_4]_2 \cdot H_2O$
brackig brackish, saltish, fluviomarine, subsaline, mesohaline
Brackmarsch f salt (brackish) marsh
Brackwasser n brackish (estuarine) water
Brackwasserkalk m brackish water limestone
Brackwassermoor n brackish water swamp
Bradford[ien] n Bradfordian [Stage] *(upper Famennian in North America)*
Bradyseismus m bradyseism *(uplift or subsidence of land by volcanic activity)*
Brahman[ium] n Brahmanian [Stage] *(Lower Triassic, Tethys)*
Brammallit m brammallite, $(Na, H_2O)Al_2[(H_2O, OH)_2 | AlSi_3O_{10}]$
Brandbergit m brandbergite *(variety of aplite)*
brandend surfy
Brandfusit m charcoal
Brandschiefer m carbonaceous shale; bone coal
~/estnischer s. Kuckersit
Brandtit m brandtite, $CaMn[AsO_4]_2 \cdot 2H_2O$
Brandung f surf; breaker; breaking waves
Brandungsbrekzie f surf breccia
Brandungsebene f abrasion plain
Brandungserosion f marine erosion (abrasion)
Brandungshöhle f sea cave (cavern), wave-cut groove
Brandungs[hohl]kehle f, **Brandungskerbe** f wave-cut notch
Brandungskiesrücken mpl beach cusps
Brandungskluft f wave-cut chasm
Brandungsnische f cove
Brandungspfeiler m stack
Brandungsplatte f shore (wave-cut) platform, marine-cut terrace, plain of marine abrasion; marine (rock) bench
Brandungsrippeln fpl surf ripples
Brandungsrückströmung f rip current
Brandungssäule f stack
Brandungsschlag m surf beat

Brandungsschlucht f gully
Brandungsschutt m wave-worn material
Brandungsterrasse f s. Brandungsplatte
Brandungstopf m pothole
Brandungstor n marine (sea) arch
Brandungswoge f surf-surge
Brandungszone f surf zone
Brannerit m brannerite, $(U, Ca, Th, Y)[(Ti, Fe)_2O_6]$
Brasilia f Brasilia
Brasilianit m brasilianite, $NaAl_3[(OH)_2 | PO_4]_2$
Brauchwasser n industrial (service, process, tap) water
Braunbleierz n brown lead ore (s.a. Pyromorphit)
Brauneisenerz n brown h[a]ematite (iron ore), ochrey brown iron ore, limonite [ore], $FeOOH \cdot nH_2O$
~/**ockriges** ochreous iron ore
~/**stalaktitisches** brush ore
Brauneisenmulm m earthy brown h[a]ematite
Brauneisenstein m s. Brauneisenerz
Braunerde f braunerde
Braunerz n s. Brauneisenerz
Braunit m braunite, $Mn_7[O_8 | SiO_4]$
Braunkohle f brown coal; lignite
~/**erdige** attrital brown coal
~/**geringwertige bituminöse** black lignite
~/**ton- und pyritreiche** alum coal
~/**xylitische** xyloid brown coal
~/**zerreibliche** moor coal
braunkohleführend lignite-bearing, lignitiferous
braunkohlehaltig lignite-bearing, lignitiferous, lignitic
Braunkohlenasche f brown-coal ash
Braunkohlenbecken n brown-coal basin; lignite basin
Braunkohlenbergbau m brown-coal mining; lignite mining
Braunkohlenbergwerk n brown-coal mine; lignite mine
Braunkohlenbildung f brown-coal formation; lignite formation
Braunkohlenbrikett n brown-coal briquette
Braunkohlendolomit m coal ball (s.a. Torfdolomit); brown-coal dolomite; lignitic dolomite
Braunkohlenfazies f brown-coal facies
Braunkohlenfeld n brown-coal field; lignitic field
Braunkohlenflora f brown-coal flora; lignitic flora
Braunkohlenflöz n brown-coal seam; lignitic seam
Braunkohlenformation f s. Tertiär
Braunkohlengel n s. Gelinit
Braunkohlengrube f brown-coal mine; lignite mine
Braunkohlenhochtemperaturkoks m brown-coal high-temperature coke
Braunkohleninhaltsstoffe mpl substances contained in brown coal

Braunkohlenkalk m lignitiferous limestone
Braunkohlenlagerstätte f brown-coal deposit; lignite deposit
Braunkohlenquarzit m s. Tertiärquarzit
Braunkohlenrevier n brown-coal district
Braunkohlensand m brown-coal sand
Braunkohlensandstein m brown-coal grit
Braunkohlenschluff m brown-coal silt
Braunkohlenschwelkoks m brown-coal low-temperature coke
Braunkohlenstadium n brown-coal stage (rank); lignite stage
Braunkohlenstaub m powdered brown coal
Braunkohlentagebau m open-cast lignite mine; brown-coal open-cast mining
Braunkohlenteer m brown-coal tar; lignite coal tar, tar from lignite
Braunkohlenverschwelung f carbonization of brown coal
Braunkohlenvorkommen n brown-coal deposit; lignite deposit
Braunlehm m brown clay
Braunmoor n Hypnum moss bog
Braunocker m brown ochre
Braunplastosol m s. Braunlehm
Braunspat m brown spar, iron dolomite, ankerite, $CaFe[CO_3]_2$
Brauntorf n brown peat (turf)
Brausen n roar (volcanism)
Bravaisit m bravaisite, $(K, H_2O)Al_2[(H_2O, OH)_2 | AlSi_3O_{10}]$
Bravoit m bravoite, $(Fe, Ni)S_2$
Breccie f s. Brekzie
Brechanlage f breaking (crushing) plant
Brechbarkeit f breakability
brechen 1. to break; 2. to refract
~/**Steine** to quarry
Brechen n breaking
Brecher m 1. surf wave; 2. crusher (of stones)
~/**schwerer** roller
Brecherströmung f slug flow
Brechflüssigkeit f fracturing fluid
Brechgut n crushed material
Brechstange f dwang
Brechung f refraction
~/**atmosphärische** terrestrial refraction
~/**totale** total refraction
~/**übernormale** superstandard refraction
Brechungsebene f plane of refraction
Brechungsgesetz n law of refraction
Brechungsindex m refraction (refractive) index
Brechungskraft f refractivity, refrangibility
Brechungsspektrum n prismatic spectrum
Brechungsvermögen n s. Brechungskraft
Brechungswelle f refracted wave
Brechungswinkel m angle of refraction
Brecon[ium] n Breconian [Stage] (upper part of Lower Devonian, Old Red facies)
Bredigit m bredigite, $\gamma-Ca_2[SiO_4]$
Breitauffahren n shortwall working
Breitbandstapelung f wide-band stack (seismics)

Breite

Breite f width
~/astronomische astronomic[al] latitude
~ der Fahrrinne width of the channel
~/geografische [terrestrial] latitude
Breitengrad m latitude degree
Breitenkorrektur f latitude correction
Breitenkreis m latitude circle, parallel [of latitude]
Breitenunterschied m difference of latitude
Breithauptit m breithauptite, NiSb
Breitsattel m broad-crested anticline
Brekzie f breccia
~/autoklastische autoclastic (endolithic) breccia
~/eisenhaltige canga
~/tektonische tectonic (dynamic) breccia
~/vulkanische volcanic breccia
~/zementierte cenuglomerate
brekzienartig brecciated, brecciform[ous]
Brekzienbildung f brecciation
Brekziengang m brecciated vein
Brekzienporosität f breccia porosity
Brekziensandstein m brecciated sandstone
Brekzientextur f brecciated structure
Brekzientuff m breccia tuff
brekziös brecciated
Bremsberg m slope
brennbar combustible
~/leicht flammable
Brennbarkeit f combustibility
Brenngas n fuel gas
Brennpunkt m caustic, focus
Brennschiefer m pyroschist, pyroshale
Brennschwindigkeit f, **Brennschwindung** f fire shrinkage
Brennstoff m combustible, fuel
~/fossiler fossil fuel
Brennstoffgeologie f geology of fuels
Brennweite f focal length
Brennwert m calorific value
Breunnerit m s. Mesitinspat
Brewsterit m brewsterite
(Sr, Ba, Ca) [Al$_2$Si$_6$O$_{16}$] · 5H$_2$O
Brianit m brianite, Na$_2$MgCa(PO$_4$)$_2$
Bridgerien n Bridgerian [Stage] (mammalian stage, Middle Eocene in North America)
Brikett n briquette, coal-dust brick
Brikettabrieb m abrasion of briquette
Brikettieranlage f briquetting plant
brikettieren to briquette
Brikettierung f briquetting
Brikettierverfahren n briquetting process
Brikettpresse f briquetting press
Brillant m brilliant
Brillantschliff m brilliant cut[ting]
Brinellhärte f Brinell hardness [number]
Brinell[härte]prüfung f Brinell hardness test
Brise f breeze
~/frische fresh breeze
~/leichte flurry
~/schwache gentle breeze
~/steife stiff breeze, strong wind

Britholith m britholite, (Na, Ce, Ca)$_5$[F I SiO$_4$, PO$_4$)$_3$]
Brochantit m brochantite, Cu$_4$[(OH)$_6$ I SO$_4$]
bröckelig friable, fragile, shredded, crumbly
bröckelnd s. bröckelig
Bröckelschiefer m/roter red crumbly shale
Bröckeltuff m pozz[u]olana
Brockenfänger m junk basket (drilling engineering)
Brockenmergel m clastic marl
Brockit m brockite, CaTh[PO$_4$]$_2$ · H$_2$O
Brodelboden m patterned ground
Brodelstruktur f brodel (kneaded) texture, involution
Bröggerit m bröggerite (variety of uraninite)
Brom m bromine, Br
Bromargyrit m bromargyrite, bromyrite, AgBr
Bromchlorargyrit m, **Bromchlorsilber** n embolite, Ag(Br,Cl)
Bromellit m bromellite, BeO
Bromlit m bromlite, BaCa(CO$_3$)$_2$
Bromsilber n s. Bromargyrit
Bronzezeit f Bronze Age
Bronzit m bronzite, (Mg,Fe)$_2$[Si$_2$O$_6$]
Bronzitit m bronzitite (a hypoabyssal rock composed essentially of bronzite)
Brookit m brookite, TiO$_2$
brotlaibartig loaflike
Brownmillerit m brownmillerite, 2CaO · AlFeO$_3$
Bruce n Bruce (lower Huronian in North America)
Bruch m 1. rupture; fracture, failure, fall, fault (tectonics); 2. break, fracture, disturbance; 3. quarry; 4. s. Bruch n
~/am Fuße einer Rutschung base failure
~/blättriger lamellar fracture
~/bogiger crescentic fracture
~/ebener even fracture
~/faseriger fibrous fracture
~/fortschreitender progressive (successive) failure
~/frischer fresh cleavage
~/glatter smooth fracture, clean[-cut] fracture
~/intrakristalliner intracrystalline fracture
~ mit Verwerfung paraclase
~/muscheliger conchoidal (flinty, shell-like) fracture
~/nadelförmiger acicular fracture
~/normaler diaclase
~ ohne Verwerfung joint
~/progressiver s. ~/fortschreitender
~/splitteriger splintery (hackly) fracture
~/streifiger striated fracture
~/tektonischer tectonic fracture
~/unebener uneven fracture
~/vulkanotektonischer volcano-tectonic fracture (rent)
~/wiederbelebter recurrent (revived) faulting
Bruch n bog, fen, marsh, marshy ground, mire
Bruchabschirmung f flushing shield

Bruchanalyse f fracture analysis
Bruchaussehen n appearance of fracture
Bruchbau m roof-fall exploitation, caving
Bruchbeben n rift earthquake
Bruchbecken n fault basin
Bruchbedingung f/**Hubersche** Huber's fracture condition
Bruchbelastung f breaking load
Bruchberge pl s. Bruchmassen
Bruchbild n fracture pattern
Bruchbildung f faulting, fracturing, rupturing
~/wiederholte renewed (multiple) faulting
Bruchbrekzie f s. Kakirit
Bruchbündel n fault bundle
Bruchdeformation f breaking (rupture) deformation
Bruchdehnung f maximum (percentage) elongation
Bruchdokumentation f/**geologische** geological fracture documentation
Bruchebene f s. Bruchfläche
Bruchentstehung f fracture origin
Brucherscheinungen pl break phenomena
Bruchfalte f fault fold, disrupted (broken) fold, faulted overfold (anticline)
Bruchfaltenbau m fault-fold structure
Bruchfaltengebirge n mountain formed of disrupted folds
Bruchfeld n fracture[d] zone, fault mosaic, cavities, caved goaf
Bruchfestigkeit f breaking (fracture, rupture, ultimate) strength
Bruchfläche f 1. fracture plane (surface), 2. failure surface, breaking plane (mining); 3. cleavage plane (of minerals)
~/faserige fibrous fracture
~/frisch angeschlagene fresh fracture plane
~/grobkörnige granular-crystalline fracture
~/schieferige slaty fracture
Bruchflächenaussehen n appearance of fracture
Bruchflächenhäufigkeit f fracture frequency
Bruchfließen n breaking flow, flow by rupture, flow failure
Bruchfortpflanzung f fracture propagation
Bruchgebiet n faulted (fractured) area, fractured region
Bruchgebirge n fault[ed] mountains, faultblock mountains
Bruchgestein n quarry rocks, stones
Bruchgrenze f breaking (fracture) limit
brüchig fragile, brittle, cracky, frangible, friable
Brüchigkeit f fragility, brittleness, frangibility, friability
~/interkristalline intercrystalline (cleavage) brittleness
Bruchkante f breaking edge (of roof)
Bruchkegel m rupture cone
Bruchkessel m region of circular subsidence
Bruchkriterium n failure criterion
Bruchlandschaft f fault[ed] topography

Bruchlast f breaking (rupture) load
Bruchlinie f break (breaking, fracture, fault, caving) line, fault trace
Bruchlinienküste f fault-scarp coast
Bruchlinienstufe f, **Bruchlinienwand** f fault line scarp
Bruchmassen fpl rubbles, caved material, debris
Bruchmuster n fracture pattern
Bruchöffnung f fault vent (of a volcano)
Bruchortversatz m s. Blindortversatz
Bruchsattel m faulted anticline
Bruchschieferung f fracture cleavage
Bruchschleppung f fault drag
Bruchscholle f fault[ed] block
Bruchschollenbildung f block faulting
Bruchschollengebiet n block-faulted area
Bruchschollengebirge n [fault-]block mountains
Bruchsenke f fault basin, depression of downfaulting
Bruchsenkung f downward block faulting
Bruchsicherung f antiflushing measures
Bruchsohle f quarry floor
Bruchspalte f fault fissure (cleft)
Bruchspaltenbildung f rifting
Bruchspannung f breaking (fracture, failure) stress
Bruchspannungskreis m breaking limit circle
Bruchspannungsmodul m modulus of rupture
Bruchstein m quarrystone, quarry block, rubble [stone]
~/schiefriger ragged stone
Bruchstelle f diaclase (failure without sliding)
Bruchstück n fragment, clast
~/eckiges angular fragment, anguclast
~ vom Ausbiß eines Gangs shoad
bruchstückartig fragmental
Bruchstufe f fault scarp (cliff), kern but
Bruchstufenlandschaft f fault-scarp topography
Bruchsystem n system of faults
Bruchtal n fault [line] valley
Bruchtektonik f fracture (faulting) tectonics
Bruchterrasse f fault terrace
Bruchtheorie f/**Griffithsche** Griffith's [failure] theory
Bruchwaldtorf m forest-swamp peat
Bruchwand f fault scarp, bank, quarry face
Bruchwinkel m angle of break, fracture angle
Bruchzone f fault (ruptured, caving, fracture, crushing) zone, fault belt, rift zone
Brucit m brucite, $Mg(OH)_2$
Brückenkontinent m continental bridge
Brüggen-Kaltzeit f Brueggen-stadial
Brugnatellit m brugnatellite, $Mg_6Fe[(OH)_{13}|CO_3] \cdot 4H_2O$
Brumm m, **Brummen** n hum (electric noise)
Brunnen m well
~/artesischer artesian spring, artesian (flowing, blowing) well
~ mit freiem Grundwasserspiegel water table well

Brunnen

~ mit gespanntem Grundwasserspiegel artesian well
~/toter unused well
~/unvollkommener incomplete well
~/versiegender failing well
~/versiegter exhausted (depleted) well
~/vollkommener complete well
Brunnenabsenkung f well lowering
Brunnenalterung f aging of well
Brunnenaufnahmevermögen n inverted capacity of well
Brunnenausbau m well support
Brunnenbau m well construction
Brunnenbohranlage f well boring plant
Brunnenbohrer m well drill *(tool)*
Brunnenbohrung f well boring
Brunnenbohrwerkzeuge npl well drilling tools
Brunneneinsickerungsbereich m infiltration area of well
Brunneneinzugsgebiet n well collecting area
Brunnenergiebigkeit f well production; capacity (fertility, yieldingness) of a well; discharge of a well; output of a well
Brunnenfilter n well filter
Brunnenfördermenge f well output
Brunnenfunktion f well function *(mathematical function of discharge and capacity of well)*
Brunnengalerie f gang (battery) of wells; line of wells
Brunnengräber m well-digger, well-sinker, pit-man
Brunnengründung f well foundation
Brunnengruppe f multiple-well system
Brunneninterferenz f interference of wells
Brunnenmundloch n mouth of well, well orifice
Brunnenpfeife f well whistle *(measuring instrument for ground-water level)*
Brunnenradius m well radius
Brunnenregenerierung f regeneration of well
Brunnenschacht m well shaft
Brunnentest m well log
Brunnenverlust m well loss
Brunnenwasser n well water
Brunnenwirkungsbereich m influence zone of a well
Brunsvigit m brunsvigite, $(Fe,Al,Mg)_3[(OH)_2|AlSi_3O_{10}](Fe,Mg)_3(OH)_6$
Brushit m brushite, $HCaPO_4 \cdot 2H_2O$
Brustbein n s. Sternum
Brustflosse f pectoral fin
Brutkammer f, **Brutraum** m, **Bruttasche** f brood pouch *(palaeontology)*
Bruxellien n Bruxellian [Stage] *(of Eocene, Belgian basin)*
Bryozoenkalk m Bryozoa limestone
Bryozoenriff n bryozoan reef
B-Tektonit m B-tectonite
Bubnoff-Einheit f Bubnoff-unit
Buchit m buchite *(high-temperature contact rock)*
Bucht f bay; inlet, creek; bight, cove

~/fjordähnliche fiard
~/kleine schmale creek
Buchtende n bayhead
Buchtenküste f embayed coast
Buchtinneres n bayhead
Buckel m boss; hummock; hillock
buckelförmig knoblike
Buckelstruktur f/geschwänzte knob-and-trail [structure]
Buckley-Leverett-Theorie f Buckley-Leverett theory
Budnanium n Budnanian [Series, Epoch] *(upper Silurian)*
Bühl m neck
Buhne f groyne; mole, jetty
Buhnenbau m groyning
Buhnenkopf m groyne (dike) head
Buhnenpfahl m picket
Bulitien n Bulitian [Stage] *(mammalian stage, upper Palaeocene in North America)*
Bult m hummock; hillock
Bülten fpl earth hummocks
Bültenmoor n hillock bog
Bultfonteinit m bultfonteinite, $Ca_2[F|SiO_3OH] \cdot H_2O$
bündeln to group *(geophones)*
Bündelungskabelbaum m flyer
Bunsenit m bunsenite, NiO
bunt coloured; variegated
Buntbleierz n s. Pyromorphit
buntgestreift streaked with colours
Buntkupfererz n, **Buntkupferkies** m variegated copper ore, bornite, Cu_5FeS_4
Buntmetall n non-ferrous metal
Buntsandstein m 1. Lower Triassic [Period]; Bunter [Sandstone]; 2. variegated (mottled) sandstone
~/Mittlerer Middle Bunter *(Triassic, German basin)*
Buntton m mottled clay
Burbankit m burbankite, $Na_2(Ca,Sr,Ba,Ce,La)_4[CO_3]_5$
Burdigal[ien] n, **Burdigalium** n Burdigalian [Stage] *(of Miocene)*
Burkeit m burkeite, $Na_6(CO_3)(SO_4)_2$
Busch m shrub
Buschland n bushland, scrub
Buschsteppe f shrub steppe
Buschwerk n shrubbery
Bushveld-Komplex m Bushveld-Igneous-Complex
Büßerschnee m penitent ice (snow), snow of the penitents, sun spike
Bussole f dial
Bustamit m bustamite, $(Mn,Ca)_3[Si_3O_9]$
Bustit m bustite *(meteorite)*
Butlerit m butlerite, $Fe[OH|SO_4] \cdot 2H_2O$
Bütschliit m bütschliite, $K_6Ca_2[CO_3]_5 \cdot 6H_2O$
Buttgenbachit m buttgenbachite, $Cu_{19}[Cl_4|(OH)_{32}](NO_3)_2 + 2H_2O]$
Butze f, **Butzen** m pocket (bunch) of ore
Bysmalith m bysmalith *(intrusive body)*

Byssolith m byssolithe (s. a. Aktinolith)
Byssus m byssus (molluscans)
Byssusfurche f byssal notch (molluscans)
Bytownit m bytownite (plagioclase feldspar)

C

Cabrerit m cabrerite, $(Ni,Mg)_3As_2O_8 \cdot 8H_2O$
c-Achse f c axis
Cadmium n s. Kadmium
Cadmoselit m cadmoselite, β-CdSe
Cadwaladerit m cadwaladerite, $Al(OH)_2Cl \cdot 4H_2O$
Caesium n s. Zäsium
Ca-femisch Ca femic
Cafetit m cafetite, $(Ca,Mg)[Ti,Fe]_6O_{12}] \cdot 4H_2O$
Cahnit m cahnite, $Ca_2[AsO_4|B(OH)_4]$
Calamin m cadmia, calamine (a zinc ore)
Calamiten mpl calamites
Calamitenröhricht n calamitean reed
Calamitentorf m calamitean peat
Calaverit m calaverite, $(Au,Ag)Te_2$
Calcarenit m calcarenite, lime sandrock
Calciborit m calciborite, CaB_2O_4
Calcilutit m calcilutite
Calcioferrit m calcioferrite, $(Ca,Mg)_3(Fe,Al)_3[(OH)_3|(PO_4)_4] \cdot 8H_2O$
Calciovolborthit m s. Tangeit
Calcirudit m calcirudite, lime rubblerock
Calcisiltit m calcisiltite
Calcit m calcite, calcareous spar, calc-spar, $CaCO_3$ (s. a. Kalzit)
Calcium n s. Kalzium
Calciumbariummimetesit m hedyphane (variety of mimetesite)
Calclacit m calclacite, $Ca[Cl|(C_2H_3O_2)_2] \cdot 5H_2O$
Calclithit m calclithite
Calcurmolit m calcurmolite, $Ca[(UO_2)_3|(OH)_2|(MoO_4)_5] \cdot 9H_2O$
Caldera f caldera, inbreak crater
Caldera-Insel f caldera island
Calderit m calderite, $Mn_3Fe_2[SiO_4]_3$
Caledonit m caledonite, $Pb_5Cu_2[(OH)_6|CO_3|(SO_4)_3]$
Calichelagerstätte f calitreras
Calkinsit m calkinsite, $(Ce,La)_2[CO_3]_3 \cdot 4H_2O$
Callaghanit m callaghanite, $Cu_2Mg_2[(OH)_6|CO_3] \cdot 2H_2O$
Callainit m callainite, $Al[PO_4] \cdot 2^1/_2H_2O$
Callov[ien] n Callovian [Stage] (of Jurassic)
Callow-Methode f Callow method (graphical representation of screen analysis)
Calumetit m calumetite, $Cu(OH,Cl)_2 \cdot 2H_2O$
Calvarium n calvarium (skull without lower jaw)
Campan[ien] n Campanian [Stage] (of Upper Cretaceous)
Campanit m campanite (nepheline syenite)
Campanium n s. Campan
Camptonit m camptonite (alkali dike rock)
Camptospessartit m camptospessartite (alkali dike rock)

Camsellit m s. Ascharit
Canadien n Canadian [Series] (Tremadocian and Arenigian in North America)
Canadit m s. Kanadit
Canasit m canasite, $(Na,K)_5Ca_4[(OH,F)_3|Si_{10}O_{25}]$
Cancrinit m cancrinite, $Na_4Ca[CO_3|AlSiO_4]_6 \cdot 2H_2O$
Canfieldit m canfieldite, $4Ag_2S \cdot (Sn,Ge)S_2$
Cannizzarit m cannizzarite, $Pb_3Bi_5S_{11}$
Cañon m canyon, cañon, sinking creek
~/submariner submarine canyon
cañonartig canyon-shaped
Cañonbildung f canyoning, canyon cutting (formation)
Capitan[ium] n Capitanian [Stage] (of Middle Permian)
Cappelenit m cappelenite, $(Ba,Ca,Ce,Na)_3(Y,Ce,La)_6[(BO_3)_6|Si_3O_9]$
Caracolit m caracolite, $PbNa_2[OH|Cl|SO_4]$
Caradoc[ium] n Caradocian [Stage] (Middle Ordovician to lowest Upper Ordovician)
Carapax m carapace
Carbankerit m carbankerite (microlithotype, coal + 20–60 % by volume of carbonate minerals)
Carbargilit m carbargilite (microlithotype, coal +20–60 % by volume of clay minerals)
Carboborit m carboborite, $Ca_2Mg[CO_3|B_2O_5] \cdot 10H_2O$
Carbocernait m carbocernaite, $(Ca,Na,La,Ce)[CO_3]$
Carbominerit m carbominerite (microlithotype, collective name for coal-mineral association)
Carbo-Permian n s. Permokarbon
Carbopolyminerit m carbopolyminerite (microlithotype, coal + 20–60 % by volume of various minerals; the lower limit can be reduced to 5 %, depending on the content of pyrite)
Carbopyrit m carbopyrite (microlithotype, coal + 5–20 % by volume of sulphide minerals)
Carbosilicit m carbosilicite (microlithotype, coal + 20–60 % by volume of quartz)
Carix[ien] n, **Carixium** n Carix [Stage] (of Lower Lias)
Carlosit m carlosite, neptunite, $Na_2Fe(Ti(Si_4O_{12})$
Carmel-Formation f Carmel Formation, Gypsum Spring Formation (Dogger in North America)
Carnallit m s. Karnallit
Carnegieit m carnegieite, $NaAlSiO_4$
Carnivoren mpl carnivores, carnivorous animals
Carnotit m carnotite, $K_2[(UO_2)_2|V_2O_8] \cdot 3H_2O$
Carobbiit m carobbiite, KF
Carpalia npl carpalia, carpal bone
Carpus m carpus, wrist
Carraramarmor m Carrara [marble]
Carrollit m carrollite, $CuCo_2S_4$
Cascadit m cascadite (variety of lamprophyre)

Cassadaga

Cassadaga *m* Cassadagan [Stage] *(Famennian in North America)*
Cassidyit *m* cassidyite, $Ca_2(Ni,Mg)(PO_4)_2 \cdot 2H_2O$ *(in meteorites)*
Cassinien *n*, **Cassinium** *n* Cassinian [Stage] *(uppermost stage of Lower Ordovician in North America)*
Cassiterit *m* cassiterite, tin spar (ore, stone), SnO_2
Castanit *m* castanite *(variety of amarantite)*
Cattierit *m* cattierite, CoS_2
Cayugan *n* Cayugan [Series] *(Upper Silurian in North America)*
Cebollit *m* cebollite, $Ca_5Al_2[(OH)_4|(SiO_4)_3]$
Cedarit *m* cedarite *(an amber-like resin)*
Celsian *m* celsian, $BaAl_2Si_2O_8$
Cementit *m* cohenite, Fe_3C *(in meteorites)*
Cenoman *n* Cenomanian [Stage] *(of Upper Cretaceous)*
Centrallasit *m* centrallasite, $Ca_2[Si_4O_{10}] \cdot 4H_2O$
Cephalon *n* cephalon, headshield *(trilobites)*
Cephalopode *m* cephalopod
Cephalopodenfazies *f* cephalopod facies
Cer *n* cerium, Ce
Cerargyrit *m* chlorargyrite, AgCl
Ceratitenkalk *m* ceratite limestone
Ceratitenmergel *m* ceratite marl
ceratitisch ceratitic
Cerfluorit *m* cerfluorite, yttrocerite, $(Ca,Ce)F_2$
Cerianit *m* cerianite, $(Ce,Th)O_2$
Cerit *m* cerite, $(Ca,Fe)Ce_3H[(OH)_2|SiO_4]Si_2O_7]$
Cerussit *m s.* Zerussit
Cervantit *m s.* Stibiconit
Cervicalwirbel *m* cervical (neck) vertebra
Ceylongraphit *m* Ceylon plumbago
Ceylonit *m* pleonaste *(black spinel)*
Chabasit *m* chabasite, chabazite, $(Ca,Na_2)Al_2Si_4O_{12} \cdot 6H_2O$
Chadron[ien] *n* Chadronian [Stage] *(mamalian stage, Oligocene in North America)*
Chagrin *n* shagreen
chagrinieren to shagreen
Chalcedon *m s.* Chalzedon
Chalkanthit *m* chalcanthite, copper vitriol, $CuSO_4 \cdot 5H_2O$
Chalkoalumit *m* chalcoalumite, $CuAl_4[(OH)_{12}|SO_4] \cdot 3H_2O$
Chalkocyanit *m*, **Chalkokyanit** *m* chalcocyanite, $CuSO_4$
Chalkolamprit *m* chalcolamprite, $(Ca,Na)_2(Nb,Ta)_2O_6(O,OH,F)$
Chalkomenit *m* chalcomenite, $CuSeO_3 \cdot 2H_2O$
Chalkonatronit *m* chalconatronite, $Na_2Cu[CO_3]_2 \cdot 3H_2O$
Chalkophanit *m* chalcophanite, $ZnMn_3O_7 \cdot 3H_2O$
chalkophil chalcophilic, chalcophil[e]
Chalkophyllit *m* chalcophyllite, $(Cu,Al)_3[(OH)_4|(AsO_4,SO_4)] \cdot 6H_2O$
Chalkopyrit *m* chalcopyrite, $CuFeS_2$ *(s. a. Kupferkies)*
Chalkosiderit *m* chalcosiderite, $CuFe_6[(OH)_2|PO_4]_4 \cdot 4H_2O$

Chalkosin *m* chalcosine, chalcocite, glance (vitreous) copper, copper glance, Cu_2S
~/erdiger sooty chalcocite
Chalkostibit *m* chalcostibite, $Cu_2S \cdot Sb_2S$
Chalkotrichit *m* chalcotrichite *(variety of cuprite)*
Chalmersit *m s.* Kubanit
Chalypit *m* chalypite, Fe_2C *(in meteorites)*
Chalzedon c[h]alcedony, white agate, SiO_2
chalzedonisch chalcedonic
Chalzedonlagen *fpl*/**irisierende** rainbow chalcedony
Chambersit *m* chambersite, $Mn_3[Cl|B_7O_{13}]$
Chamosit *m* chamo[i]site, $(Fe,Mg)_6[O|(OH)_8|AlSi_3O_{10}]$
Champlainien *n* Champlainian [Series] *(Llanvirnian, Llandeilian and lower Caradocian in North America)*
changieren to iridize
Changieren *n* iridizing
changierend chatoyant
Chapmanit *m* chapmanite, $SbFe_2[OH|(SiO_4)_2]$
Charakter *m*/**geochemischer** geochemical character
~/historischer historical character *(of geochemical laws)*
Charmouth[ien] *n*, **Charmoutium** *n s.* Pliensbach
Charnockit *m* charnockite *(granulite facies rock)*
Chassignit *m* chassignite *(meteorite)*
Chathamit *m* chathamite, $(Fe,Co,Ni)As_3$
Catt[ium] *n s.* Katt
Chazy *n*, **Chazy-Kalk** *m* Chazyan [Stage] *(of Champlainian in North America)*
Chemie f der Atmosphäre atmochemistry
~ der Hydrosphäre hydrochemistry
Chemikalien *fpl* **zur Reduktion der Filtrationsverluste** fluid loss additives
Chemilumineszenz *f* chemiluminescence
Chemismus *m* chemism
Chenevixit *m* chenevixite, $Cu_2Fe_2[(OH)_2|AsO_4]_2 \cdot H_2O$
Cheralith *m* cheralithe, $(Ca,Ce,La,Th)[PO_4]$
Chervetit *m* chervetite, $Pb_2V_2O_7$
Chester *n* Chesterian [Stage] *(of Mississippian in North America)*
Chiastolith *m* chiastolite *(variety of andalusite)*
Chiastolithschiefer *m* chiastolite slate
Chibinit *m* chibinite
Chihsia *n* Chihsian [Stage] *(uppermost stage of Lower Permian)*
Childrenit *m* childrenite, $(Fe,Mn)Al[(OH)_2|PO_4] \cdot H_2O$
Chilenit *m* chilenite, (Ag,Bi)
Chilesalpeter *m* Chile nitre (saltpetre), caliche, soda nitre, $NaNO_3$
Chillagit *m* chillagite, $Pb[(Mo,W)O_4]$
Chinkolobwit *m s.* Sklodowskit
Chiolith *m* chiolite, $Na_5[Al_3F_{14}]$
Chi-Quadrat-Test *m* Chi-square test
Chitinhülle *f* chitinous integument

chitinös chitinous
Chitinzersetzung f **bei Fossilisation** distillation
Chiviatit m chiviatite, $Pb_2Bi_6S_{11}$
Chloanthit m chloanthite, nickel-skutterudite, white nickel, $NiAs_{3-2}$
Chlopinit m chlopinite *(variety of euxinite)*
Chlor n chlorine, Cl
Chlor-Apatit m chlorapatite, $Ca_5[Cl|(PO_4)_3]$
Chlorargyrit m cerargyrite, AgCl
Chlorit m chlorite *(s. a.* Chloritgruppe)
Chloritalbitschiefer m chlorite albite schist
Chloritbildung f chloritization
Chloritgestein n chloritic rock
Chloritglimmerschiefer m chlorite mica schist
Chloritgneis m chloritic gneiss
Chloritgruppe f chlorite group *(group of mica-like Fe,Mg,Al-SiO₂-minerals with H₂O)*
chloritisch chloritic
chloritisieren to chloritize
Chloritisierung f chloritization
Chloritmergel m chloritic marl
Chloritmuskovitschiefer m chlorite muscovite schist
Chloritoid m cloritoid, $Fe_2AlAl_3[(OH)_4|O_2|(SiO_4)_2]$
Chloritphyllit m chlorite phyllite
Chloritschiefer m chlorite schist (slate), chloritic schist
Chlorkalzium n calcium chloride, $CaCl_2$
Chlornatrium n sodium chloride, NaCl
Chlornatrokalit m chlornatrokalite, $6KCl + 1NaCl$
Chloroaluminit m chloroaluminite, $AlCl_3 \cdot 6H_2O$
Chloromagnesit m chloromagnesite, $MgCl_2$
Chloromanganokalit m chloromanganokalite, $K_4[MnCl_6]$
Chloropal m chloropal *(a clay mineral consisting of hydrous silicate of iron and aluminium)*
Chlorophoenicit m chlorophoenicite, $(Zn,Mn)_5[(OH)_7|AsO_4]$
Chlorophyllinit m chlorophyllinite *(maceral of brown coals and lignites)*
Chlorophyllit m chlorophyllite *(decomposed cordierite)*
Chlorospinell m chlorospinel *(green variety of spinel)*
Chlorotil m chlorotile, $(Cu,Fe)_2Cu_{12}[(OH,H_2O)_{12}|(AsO_4)_6] \cdot 6H_2O$
Chloroxiphit m chloroxiphite, $Pb_3O_2Cl_2 \cdot CuCl_2$
Chlorsilber n cerargyrite, AgCl
Chlorwasserstoffsäure f muriatic acid, HCl
Choana f choana, posterior naris
Chondrit m chondrite *(stone meteorite)*
~/kohlenstoffhaltiger carbonaceous chondrite
chondritisch chondritic
Chondrodit m chondrodite, $Mg_5[(OH),F]_2|(SiO_4)_2]$
Chondrostibian m chondrostibian *(complex Sb oxide)*
Chondrum n chondrule *(globular mineral aggregate of meteorites and lunar rocks)*

Chorismit m chorismite *(rock fabric)*
C-Horizont m C-horizon
Christbaum m Christmas tree
Chrom n chrome, chromium, Cr
Chromatit m chromatite, $Ca[CrO_4]$
Chromatografie f chromatography
Chromeisenerz n, **Chromeisenstein** m s. Chromit 1.
Chromepidot m s. Tawmawit
Chromerz n chrome ore
Chromglimmer m fuchsite *(s. a. Muskovit)*
chromhaltig chromiferous, chromic
Chromit m 1. chromite, chrome iron ore, chrome spinel, $FeCrO_4$; 2. chromitite *(crome spinel in form of massive ore)*
Chromosphäre f chromosphere
Chron n chron *(smallest chronostratigraphic unit)*
Chronolithologie f chronolithology
chronolithologisch chronolithologic
Chronologie f chronology
Chronometer n chronometer
Chronospezies f chronospecies
Chronostratigrafie f chronostratigraphy
Chrysoberyll m chrysoberyl, gold beryl, Al_2BeO_4
Chrysokoll m chrysocolla, $Cu_4H_4[(OH)_8|Si_4O_{10}]$
Chrysolith m chrysolite *(variety of olivine)*
Chrysopras m chrysoprase *(variety of chalcedony)*
Chrysotil m chrysotile *(fibrous silky serpentine)*
Chrysotilasbest m chrysotile-asbestos
Chuchrovit m chuchrovite, $(Ca,Y,Ce)_3[(AlF_6)_2|SO_4] \cdot 10H_2O$
Chudobait m chudobaite, $(Na,K)(Mg,Zn)_2H[AsO_4]_2 \cdot 4H_2O$
Churchit m churchite, $(Ce,Ca)(PO_4) \cdot 2H_2O$
Ciminit m ciminite *(olivine-bearing trachydolerite)*
Cimolit m cimolite *(a hydrous aluminium silicate)*
Cincinnatien n Cincinnatian [Series] *(upper Caradocian and Ashgillian in North America)*
Cingulum n cingulum, equatorial ridge *(palaeontology)*
Cinnabarit m cinnabar, HgS
Cirrostratus m stratocirrus
C-Isotop n/**instabiles** carbon 14
C-Isotopenverhältnis n carbon ratio
Citrin m citrine, false topaz, topaz quartz *(a semiprecious yellow stone)*
Claimmaß n mere
Clarain m clarain *(coal lithotype)*
Clarendon[ien] n Clarendonian [Stage] *(mammalian stage, middle Miocene in North America)*
Clarit m clarite *(coal microlithotype)*
Clarke m s. Clarkewert
Clarkeit m clarkeite, $Na_2U_2O_7$
Clarkewert m Clarke value
Clarkforkien n Clarkforkian [Stage] *(mammalian stage, Palaeocene in North America)*

Clarodurit

Clarodurit *m* clarodurite *(coal microlithotype)*
Claudetit *m* claudetite, As_2O_3
Clausthalit *m* clausthalite, PbSe
Cleavelandit *m* cleavelandite *(foliated albite)*
Clerici-Lösung *f* Clerici's solution
Cliftonit *m* cliftonite *(C in meteorites)*
Clinton-Erz *n* Clinton (flaxseed) ore
Clinton-Gruppe *f* Clinton Group *(Wenlockian in North America)*
Clintonit *m* clintonite, $Ca(Mg,Al)_{3-2}[(OH)_2|Al_2Si_2O_{10}]$
Cluster *m* cluster *(a set of similar objects obtained by a method of cluster analysis)*
Clusteranalyse *f* cluster analysis
Clymenienkalk *m* Clymenia limestone *(higher parts of Upper Devonian)*
Clymenienstufe *f* Clymenia Stage
¹⁴C-Methode *f s.* Radiokarbonmethode
Coahuila-Hauptgruppe *f* Coahuila Supergroup *(Valanginian to Barremian in North America, Gulf district)*
Cobalt *n s.* Kobalt
Cobaltin *m s.* Kobaltglanz
Cobaltomenit *m* cobaltomenite, $Co[SeO_3] \cdot 2H_2O$
Cobra-Meißel *m* chert bit *(drilling tool)*
Coccinit *m* coccinite, HgJ_2
Cocinerit *m* cocinerite, Cu_4AgS
Coda *f* tail *(of a seismogram)*
Codazzit *m* codazzite *(aggregate of ankerite and parisite)*
Coelenteraten *npl* Coelenterata
Coelestin *m* celestine, celestite, $SrSO_4$
Coenchym *n,* **Coenosteum** *n* coenosteum, coenchyme, vesicular tissue *(corals and bryozoans)*
Coeruleolaktit *m* coeruleolactite, $CaAl_6[(OH)_2|PO_4]_4 \cdot 4H_2O$
Coesit *m* coesite, SiO_2
Coffinit *m* coffinite, $USiO_4$
Cohenit *m* cohenite, Fe_3C
Cohocton[ien] *n* Cohoctonian [Stage] *(upper Frasnian in North America)*
Colemanit *m* colemanite, $Ca[B_3O_4(OH)_3] \cdot H_2O$
Collinit *m* collinite *(coal maceral)*
Collinsit *m* collinsite, $Ca_2(Mg,Fe)[PO_4]_2 \cdot 2H_2O$
Coloradoit *m* coloradoite, HgTe
Columbit *m* columbite, $(Fe,Mn)(Nb,Ta)_2O_6$
Colusit *m* colusite, $Cu_3(Fe,As,Sn)S_4$
Comanche-Hauptgruppe *f* Comanche Supergroup *(Aptian and Albian in North America)*
Combeit *m* combeite, $Na_4Ca_3[OH,F]_2|[Si_6O_{16}]$
Comendit *m* comendite *(alkaline rhyolithe)*
Compreignacit *m* compreignacite, $6[UO_2|(OH)_2] \cdot 2K(OH) \cdot 4H_2O$
Congelikontraktion *f,* **Congeliturbation** *f s.* Kryoturbation
Coniac[ien] *n,* **Coniacium** *n* Coniacian [Stage] *(of Upper Cretaceous)*
Coniferen *fpl* conifers
Connarit *m* con[n]arite *(variety of antigorite)*
Connellit *m* connellite, $Cu_{19}[Cl_4|(OH)_{32}|SO_4 + 4H_2O]$
Conrad-Diskontinuität *f,* **Conrad-Fläche** *f* Conrad discontinuity
Cookeit *m* cookeite, $LiAl_4[(OH)_8|AlSi_3O_{10}]$
Cooperit *m* cooperite, PtS
Coorongit *m* coorongite *(algal rock)*
Copiapit *m* copiapite, yellow copperas, $(Fe,Mg)Fe_4[OH|(SO_4)_3]_2 \cdot 20H_2O$
Coquimbit *m* coquimbite, white copperas, $Fe_2(SO_4)_3 \cdot 9H_2O$
Coquinit *m* coquinite
~/autochthoner coquinoid (biostromal) limestone
Cordatenschichten *fpl* Cordatus beds
Cordevol[ium] *n* Cordevolian [Substage] *(Upper Triassic, Tethys)*
Cordierit *m* cordierite, dichroite, $Mg_2Al_3[AlSi_5O_{18}]$
Cordieritgneis *m* cordierite gneiss
Coriolis-Kraft *f* Coriolis force
Corkit *m* corkite, $PbFe_3^{\cdot\cdot\cdot}[(OH)_6|SO_4PO_4]$
Cornetit *m* cornetite, $Cu_3[(OH)_3|PO_4]$
Cornubit *m* cornubite, $Cu_5[(OH)_2|AsO_4]_2$
Cornwallit *m* cornwallite, $Cu_5[(OH)_2|AsO_4]_2$
Coronadit *m* coronadite, $Pb_2Mn_8O_{16}$
Coronoid *n* coronoid, coronary bone, complementary
Corpocollinit *m* corpocollinite *(submaceral)*
Corpohuminit *m* corpohuminite *(maceral of brown coals and lignites)*
Cortlandit *m* cortlandite *(variety of peridodite)*
Corvusit *m* corvusite, $V_{14}O_{34} \cdot nH_2O$
Cosalit *m* cosalite, $2PbS \cdot Bi_2S_3$
Cotunnit *m* cotunnite, $PbCl_2$
Cotyp *m* cotype *(palaeontology)*
Coulometrie *f* coulometry *(electrochemical analysis)*
Coulsonit *m* coulsonite, FeV_2O_4
Couvin[ium] *n* Couvinian [Stage] *(lower Middle Devonian)*
Covellin *m* covellite, CuS
~/blaubleibender blue-remaining covellite
CO₂-Wetter *pl* white damp
Craelius-Bohren *n* Craelius drilling
Crandallit *m* crandallite, deltaite, $CaAl_3H[(OH)_6|(PO_4)_2]$
Cranium *n* cranium, skull
Crassidurit *m* crassidurite *(coal microlithotype)*
Crednerit *m* crednerite, $CuMnO_2$
Creedit *m* creedite, $Ca_3[(Al(F,OH,H_2O)_6)_2|SO_4]$
Crestmoreit *m* crestmoreite *(an aggregate of tobermorite and wilkeite)*
Crichtonit *m* crichtonite, $Fe_2(Ti,Fe)_5O_{12}$
Crinoidenfauna *f* crinoid fauna
Crinoidenkalk *m* crinoidal (encrinite) limestone
Crinoidenlumachelle *f* criquina
~/verfestigte criquinite
Crinoidenrasen *m* crinoid garden

Crinoidensand m crinoid sand
Crinoidenstengel m crinoid column (stalk)
Crinoidenstielglieder npl crinoid stem fragments
Cristobalit m christobalite, SiO_2
Croixien n Croixian, Potsdamian [Series] (Upper Cambrian in North America)
Cromer n Cromerian [Stage] (Pleistocene)
Cromer-Komplex m Cromerian (Pleistocene, British Islands corresponding to Günz-Mindel Interval of Alps district)
Cronstedtit m cronstedtite, $Fe_4\ddot{}Fe_2\ddot{}\ddot{}[(OH)_8|Fe_2\ddot{}\ddot{}Si_2O_{10}]$
Crookesit m crookesite, $(Cu,Tl,Ag)_2Se$
Crossit m crossite (Na-amphibole)
Crossopterygier mpl crossopterygians, crossopterygian ganoids, lobe-finned ganoids, fringe-finned ganoids
Csiklovait m csiklovait, $BiTe(S,Se)_2$
Ctenoidmarke f ctenoid cast
Ctenoidschuppe f ctenoid scale
Cuesta f cuesta
Cumengeit m cumeng[e]ite, $5PbCl_2 \cdot 5Cu(OH)_2 \cdot \frac{1}{2}H_2O$
Cummingtonit m cummingtonite, $(Mg,Fe)_7[OH|Si_4O_{11}]_2$
cumulusartig cumuliform
Cuprit m cuprite, Cu_2O
Cuprobismuthit m cuprobismuthite, $Cu_2S \cdot Bi_2S_3$
Cuprocopiapit m cuprocopiapite, $CuFe_4(SO_4)_6(OH)_2 \cdot 20H_2O$
Cupromagnesit m cupromagnesite (variety of boothite)
Cuprorivait m cuprorivaite, $CaCu[Si_4O_{10}]$
Cuprosklodowskit m cuprosklodowskite, $CuH_2[(UO_2|SiO_4]_2 \cdot 5H_2O$
Cuprotungstit m cuprotungstite, $Cu_2[(OH)_2|WO_2]$
Cuprouranit m s. Torbernit
Curie-Punkt m Curie point
Curit m curite, $3PbO \cdot 8UO_3 \cdot 4H_2O$
Curtisit m curtisite, $C_{24}H_{18}$
Cuselit m cuselite (augite porphyrite)
Cuticoclarit m cuticoclarite (coal microlithotype)
Cutinit m cutinite (coal maceral)
Cyanit m cyanite, kyanite, disthene, Al_2SiO_5
Cyanochroit m cyanochroite, $K_2Cu(SO_4)_2 \cdot 6H_2O$
Cyanotrichit m cyanotrichite, $Cu_4Al_2[(OH)_{12}|SO_4] \cdot 2H_2O$
Cyclowollastonit m cyclowollastonite, pseudowollastonite, $Ca_3[Si_3O_9]$
Cymrit m cymrite, $Ba[OH|AlSi_3O_8]$
Cypridenschlamm m cyprid ooze
Cypridinenschiefer m Cypridina Shale
Cyprin m s. Vesuvian
Cyprusit m cyprusite (s. a. Jarosit)
Cyrilovit m cyrilovite, $NaFe_3[(OH)_4|(PO_4)_2] \cdot 2H_2O$
Cystoideenkalk m cystoidean limestone

D

Dach n roof (s. a. Hangendes)
~/künstliches artificial roof
Dachaufstemmung f overhead stoping
Dachfläche f upper surface, superface [of stratum]
Dachgestein n overlying rock
Dachgesteinsscholle f/große roof pendant
Dachgranit m roof granite
D'Achiardit m dachiardite, $(K,Na,Ca_{0,5})_5[Al_5Si_{19}O_{48}] \cdot 12H_2O$
Dachplatte f roofing slab
Dachschichten fpl topset beds, roof strata, immediate roof
Dachschiefer m roof[ing] slate, table slate, shindle
Dachschieferplatten fpl roof slates
Dachschieferrevier n district of roofing slate
dachziegelartig tegular
Dachziegellagerung f imbricate structure
Dacien n Dacian [Stage] (of Pliocene)
Dahllit m dahllite (carbonate-apatite)
Dalyit m dalyite, $K_2Zr[Si_6O_{15}]$
Damm m 1. dam, levee, weir, bulkhead; 2. pack (in mines)
~/natürlicher natural levee (dike)
Dammböschung f slope of a dike
Dammbruch m dam break (failure)
Dammerde f topsoil, meat-earth
dämmerig twilit
Dammfuß m toe of the dam
Dammkernmauer f core wall, impervious diaphragm
Dammkörper m dam embankment
Dammkrone f crest of dam
Dammriff n encircling reef
Damourit m damourite (variety of muscovite)
Dampf m vapour, steam
~/geothermaler geothermal steam
Dampfdichte f vapour density
Dampfdruck m vapour tension (pressure), evaporation pressure
Dampffluten n steam flooding (secondary recovery)
Dampfflutverfahren n steam injection process
dampfförmig vaporous
Dampfhülle f vaporous (gas) envelope
Dampfsäule f vapour column, column of steam
Dampfspannung f vapour pressure (tension)
Dampfstrahl m jet of steam, steam blast
Dämpfung f damping, attenuation
~/aperiodische aperiodic[al] damping
~/kritische critical damping
Dämpfungseinrichtung f attenuator, damping arrangement (device)
Dämpfungslänge f stretch section (of a streamer)
Dämpfungsvorrichtung f s. Dämpfungseinrichtung
Dampfwolke f vapour (steam) cloud

Dan *n* Danian [Stage] *(basal stage of Tertiary System)*
Danait *m* danaite *(variety of arsenopyrite)*
Danalith *m* danalite, $Fe_8[S_2|(BeSiO_4)_6]$
Danburit *m* danburite, $Ca[B_2Si_2O_8]$
Danien *n*, **Danium** *n s.* Dan
Dannemorit *m* dannemorite *(Mn-bearing cummingtonite)*
Dano-Mont *n* Dano-Montian *(lowest part of Tertiary System)*
D'Ansit *m* dansite, $Na_{21}Mg[Cl_3|(SO_4)_{10}]$
Daphnit *m* daphnite, $(Fe,Al)_6[(OH)_8|AlSi_3O_{10}]$
Darapskit *m* darapskite, $Na_3[SO_4|NO_3] \cdot H_2O$
Darcy-Geschwindigkeit *f* Darcy (seepage) velocity
Darcy-Gesetz *n* Darcy-law (v = k · i)
Darcy-Strömung *f* Darcy flow
Darmkot *m*/**fossiler** fossil rejectamenta (droppings), fossilized excrements
Darstellung *f*/**multithematische** multithematic presentation *(e.g. of remote sensing results)*
darüberliegen to overlie
darüberliegend superincumbent
Dasberg *n*, **Dasberg-Stufe** *f* Dasbergian [Stage] *(Upper Devonian in Europe)*
Daten *pl*/**lithofazielle** lithofacies data
~/radiogeochronologische radiogeochronological data
Datenauswerter *m* data logger
Datenbus *m* bus
Datendirektempfang *m* data direct reception
Datenfernübertragung *f* telemetric data transfer
Datengewinnung *f* data acquisition
Datenrate *f* data rate
Datensammlung *f* **zu verschiedenen Zeitpunkten** multitime (multitemporal) sampling
Datenspeicherung *f* data storage
Datenübertragung *f* data transmission
Datenverarbeitung *f* data processing
Datenverdichtung *f* data compression
Datenverwaltung *f* data handling
Datenvorverarbeitung *f* data preprocessing
Datenwiederauffindung *f* data retrieval
Datierung *f*/**hydrologische** hydrological dating
~/pollenanalytische pollenanalytical dating
Datierungsmethode *f* dating method
Datolith *m* datolite, humboldtite, $CaB[OH|SiO_4]$
Datumsgrenze *f* [international] date line
Daubréeit *m* daubr[e]eite *(variety of bismoclite)*
Daubréelith *m* daubreelite, $FeCrS_4$
Dauer *f* **eines Bohrmarsches** time of a run
Dauerbeanspruchung *f* continuous stress
Dauerbewässerung *f* perennial irrigation
Dauerbiegefestigkeit *f* bending stress fatigue limit
Dauerbruch *m* fatigue break
Dauerbruchfläche *f* fatigue fracture
Dauerdruckfestigkeit *f* permanent compressive strength
Dauerfestigkeit *f* fatigue strength, durability
Dauerfestigkeitsversuch *m* fatigue test
Dauerfrost *m* eternal frost, ever-frost
Dauerfrostboden *m* ever frozen soil, permafrost [soil], pergelisol
Dauerfrostbodendeckschicht *f* suprapermafrost
Dauerfrostbodengrenze *f* permafrost line *(regional)*
Dauerfrostbodenoberfläche *f* permafrost table
Dauerfrostschicht *f* permafrost layer
Dauerfrostuntergrund *m* permafrost subsoil
Dauerlast *f* sustained load
Dauermagnet *m* permanent magnet
Dauerpumpversuch *m* 1. long-time pumping test; 2. production test *(ground water)*
Dauerquelle *f* perennial spring
Dauerschlagfestigkeit *f* impact fatigue limit
Dauersee *m* basinal lake
Dauerspende *f* perennial (sustained) yield *(of a spring)*
Dauerstandfestigkeit *f* limiting stress, creep strength
Dauerstandversuch *m* long-duration static test
Dauertyp *m* long-time type, perennial (permanent) type
Dauerzugfestigkeit *f* tensile fatigue strength
Dauphinézwilling *m* Dauphiné twin
Davidit *m* davidite, $(Fe,U,Ce,La)_2(Ti,Fe,Cr,V)_5O_{12}$
Daviesit *m* daviesite, $Zn_4[(OH)_2|SiO_7] \cdot H_2O$
Davisonit *m* davisonite *(s. a. Apatit)*
Davyn *m* davyne, $(Na,K)_6Ca_2[(SO_4)_2|(AlSiO_4)_6]$
Dawsonit *m* dawsonite, $NaAl[(OH)_2|CO_3]$
Dazit *m* dacite
dazitisch dacitic
Dazitporphyr *m* dacite porphyry
dazwischenliegend interjacent
Debye-Scherrer-Aufnahme *f*, **Debye-Scherrer-Diagramm** *n* Debyeogram, powder pattern
Debye-Scherrer-Methode *f* Debye-Scherrer method, powder method of analysis
Debye-Scherrer-Ring *m* Debye-Scherrer ring, Hull ring
Dechenit *m* dechenite, PbV_2O_6
Dechiffrieren *n* decoding
Deckbewegungsachse *f s.* Symmetrieachse
Deckblatt *n* overlay
Decke *f* 1. blanket, cover[ing], cap; 2. nappe, thrust-sheet *(tectonical)*; 3. mantle *(of sediments)*
~/autochthone autochthonous nappe
~/interkutane intercutaneous nappe
~/parautochthone parautochthonous nappe (klippe)
~/verkehrte inversion nappe
~/von helvetischem Typ Helvetic nappe
~/von penninischem Typ Pennine nappe
~/wurzellose rootless nappe
Deckenbasalt *m* plateau (blanket) basalt, cap[rock]
Deckenbasis *f* bottom of the nappe

Deckenbau *m* nappe structure
Deckenbildung *f* nappe formation
Deckenerguß *m* lava plain (plateau, field)
Deckenfalte *f* overthrust (recumbent) fold
Deckenfaltung *f* nappe tectonics, overthrust folding, thrust (sheet) structure
Deckenfenster *n* nappe inlier
Deckengebirge *n* overthrust mountains, thin-shelled mountains
Deckenhäufung *f s.* Deckenpaket
Deckenmulde *f* depression area of nappe
Deckenpaket *n* series of blanketing slices, pile of nappe
Deckenphänomen *n* nappe phenomenon
Deckenrücken *m* dorversal limb *(of the nappe)*
Deckenscholle *f* thrust outlier (*s. a.* Klippe 2.)
Deckensohle *f* bottom of the nappe
Deckensystem *n* nappe system
Deckentektonik *f* nappe tectonics
Deckentheorie *f* nappe (decken) theory
Deckenwurzel *f* root of a nappe
Deckfaltengebirge *n* mountains formed of overthrust (recumbent) folds
Deckformation *f* capping formation
Deckgebirge *n* superstructure, supracrustal formation *(tectonical);* surface rock, overlying rock (cover, strata), overburden (roof) rock *(in mines);* capping mass, cap of rock, caprock
~/loses caller
Deckgebirgseinschnitt *m* reef drive
Deckgestein *n s.* Deckgebirge
Deckpause *f* overlay
Decksand *m* cover (blanket) sand
Decksandstein *m (Am)* sheet sands
Deckschicht *f* overlying (covering) stratum, overburden, surface formation (stratum, layer), superficial (upper) layer, topset; caprock, capping
Deckschluff *m* cover silt
Deckscholle *f* [nappe, fault] outlier, parautochthonous nappe (klippe)
~/wurzellose floating fault block
Deckschutt *m* overlay, covering detritus, topspit
Decksteinsalz *n* cover rock salt
dedolomitisieren to dedolomitize
Dedolomitisierung *f* dedolomitization
Deduktores *mpl* deductors, divaricators, deductor muscles
Deerit *m* deerite, $MNFe_{12}\,Fe_7\,(OH)_{11}Si_{13}O_{44}$
Definitionsbereich *m* domain of definition
Deflation *f* deflation, wind abrasion
Deflationsbecken *n* deflation basin
Deflationsebene *f* deflation peneplain
Deflationskessel *m* deflation hole, blow-out
Deflationsrückstand *m* deflation residue, desert pavement (mosaic)
Deformation *f* deformation, strain
~/affine homogeneous deformation
~/ebene plane strain
~/elastische elastic deformation

~/infinitesimale infinitesimal strain
~/innere internal deformation
~/nichtaffine non-affine deformation
~/parakristalline paracrystalline deformation
~/plastische plastic deformation
~/postkristalline postcrystalline deformation
~/präkristalline precrystalline deformation
~/syndiagenetische syndiagenetic deformation
Deformationsabfall *m* strain drop
Deformationsarbeit *f* strain work
Deformationsart *f* mode of deformation
Deformationsbänder *npl* deformation bands
Deformationsbrekzie *f* tectonic breccia
Deformationsebene *f* deformation plane
~ senkrecht zur b-Achse ac-plane
Deformationsellipsoid *n* strain ellipsoid
Deformationsgefüge *n* deformation fabric
Deformationsgrad *m* degree of deformation
Deformationsprozesse *mpl/* krustengestaltende diastrophism
Deformationssprung *m* fissure due to deformation
Deformationszone *f* zone of deformation
Deformationszustand *m/* ebener plane strain
Deformationszwilling *m* deformation twin
Deformationszyklus *m/* krustengestaltender diastrophic cycle
deformierbar/in dünne Plättchen laminable
deformieren to deform
degasieren to degas[ify]
Degasierung *f* degasification, degasifying, degassing
degenerieren to degenerate
degeneriert degenerate
Degenerierung *f* degeneration, degeneracy
degradieren to degrade
Degradierung *f* degradation
Degradinit *m* degradinite *(coal maceral)*
Degradofusinit *m* degradofusinite *(submaceral)*
dehnbar ductile, extensible
Dehnbarkeit *f* ductility, extensibility
Dehnbarkeitsmesser *m* ductilimeter
Dehnung *f* extension, elongation, dilatation; stretch[ing]; strain
~/gleichförmige uniform dilatancy
Dehnungsbruch *m* tensile failure
Dehnungsfuge *f/* kleine mineralisierte gash vein
Dehnungskluft *f* extension joint
Dehnungsmarke *f* parting cast
Dehnungsmesser *m* extensometer, strainometer
Dehnungsmeßstreifen *m* expansion measuring strip, strain gauge
Dehnungsmessung *f* extension measurement
Dehnungsmeßverfahren *n* extensometric method
Dehnungsmodul *m* elasticity modulus
Dehnungsriß *m* tension fracture
Dehnungsschlechten *fpl* pin cracks

Dehnungsverlauf

Dehnungsverlauf m elongation curve
Dehnungsverwerfung f tension fault
Dehrnit m dehrnite *(variety of apatite)*
Dehydratation f dehydration
dehydrieren to dehydrate
Deich m dike, levee; sea wall
Deichböschung f slope of a dike
Deichbruch m dike burst, breaking (falling, failing) of a dike, breach in a dike
Deichland n dike land, innings
Deichsiel n overflow of dike
Deisterphase f Deister phase
Dekade f/**Internationale Hydrologische** International Hydrological Decade *(1965 to 1974)*
Dekaeder n decahedron
dekaedrisch decahedral
Dekantationstest m decantation test
dekantieren to decant; to levigate
Dekantieren n decantation; levigation
Dekantiergefäß n decanter
Deklination f declination *(of the magnetic needle)*
~/magnetische magnetic declination
Deklinationsparallele f parallel of declination
Deklinationstiden pl declination tides
Deklinationswinkel m angle of hade
Dekonvolution f deconvolution
Dekorationsstein m decoration stone
dekrepitieren to decrepitate
Dekrepitieren n decrepitation
Delafossit m delafossite, $CuFeO_2$
Delatynit m delatynite *(a resin)*
Delessit m delessite *(variety of chlorite)*
Delhayelith m delhayelithe, $(Na,K)_{10}Ca_5[(Cl_2F_2SO_4)_3|O_4|Al_6Si_{32}O_{76}] \cdot 18H_2O$
Dellenit m dellenite, quartz latite
Delmont[ien] n Delmontian [Stage] *(marine stage, upper Miocene to Pliocene in North America)*
Delorenzit m delorenzite *(a tanteuxinite)*
Delrioit m delrioite, $SrCaH_2[VO_4]_2 \cdot 2H_2O$
Delta n delta
~/ästuarines estuarine delta
~/fossiles fossil delta
~/verzweigtes anastomosing deltoid branch
~/vorgeschobenes protruding (thrust-out) delta, delta built into the sea
~/weit vorgeschobenes thrust far-out delta
Deltaabhang m prodelta slope
Deltaablagerungskegel m deltaic fan
Deltaarm m arm (branch) of a delta, distributary
Deltaaufschüttung f delta bedding (fill)
Deltabildung f deltafication, delta formation
Deltabucht f delta bay
Deltadamm m deltaic embankment
Deltaebene f delta plain
Deltaform f delta shape
deltaförmig deltaic
Deltafront-Flächensand m delta-front sheet sand
Deltafront-Inselsand m delta-margin island sand

Deltait m deltaite, $CaAl_3H[(OH)_6 | (PO_4)_2]$
Deltakiesablagerung f deltaic gravel deposit
Deltaniederung f delta flats
Deltarand m delta margin
Deltaschicht f topset
Deltaschichtung f delta bedding, deltaic stratification
Deltasediment n deltaic sediment
Deltasee m delta lake
Deltawachstum n delta growth
Deltoeder n deltohedron
Deltoiddodekaeder n deltoid dodecahedron
Deltoidikositetraeder n deltoid icositetrahedron
Deltoidplatten fpl deltoids *(palaeontology)*
Delvauxit m delvauxite, $Fe[(OH)_3 | PO_4] \cdot 5^1/_2H_2O$
Demantoid m demantoid *(green variety of garnet)*
Demineralisation f demineralization
Demingien Demingian [Stage] *(Lower Ordovician in North America)*
Demonstrationspumpversuch m demonstration pumping test
Demontage f dismantling *(of a boring)*
Demulgator m demulsifier
demulgieren to demulsify
Dendrit m dendrite, arborescent (treelike, pine, fir) crystal
Dendritenverästelung f branching dendrites
dendritisch dendritic[al], dendroid, arborescent
Dendrochronologie f dendrochronology
Dendrogramm n dendrogram
Dendrograph m dendrograph *(graphical representation of similarities within and between hierarchical ordered clusters)*
Dendroidae fpl dendroids
Dendrolith m dendrolite
Denitrifikation f denitrification
denitrifizieren to denitrify
Denitrifizieren n denitrifying
Denningit m denningite, $(Mn, Ca, Zn)Te_2O_5$
Dennisonit m s. Davisonit
Densinit m densinite *(maceral of brown coals and lignites)*
Dentale n dentary, tooth-bearing bone
Dentikel mpl denticles
Dentin n s. Zahnschmelz
Denudation f denudation *(s. a. Abtragung)*
~/tektonische tectonic denudation
Denudationsebene f denudation plain
Denudationsfläche f denudation surface, peneplain
Denudationsgebiet n area of denudation
Denudationsgebirge n mountain of denudation
Denudationsgrenze f denudation limit
Denudationsniveau n denudation (base) level
Denudationsrelikt n denudation remnant
Denudationsterrasse f denudation (rock, structural) terrace, rock bench

denudieren to denude
depolarisieren to depolarize
Deponie f disposal site, landfill, waste disposal
~/geordnete sanitary landfill
Depression f 1. depression; 2. depressed area, sag
~/verbindende pediment pass (between two pediment peneplains)
Depressionsfläche f surface of depression (of ground-water level)
Depressionskurve f water-table slope
Depressionswinkel m depression angle
Derberz n rough ore
derbstückig large-sized, lumpy
Derbylith m derbylite, $F_3Ti_3SbO_{11}OH$
Derivat n derivate
derivatografisch derivatographic
Dermalskelett n dermal skeleton, exoskeleton
Dermalspicula n dermal spicules, dermalia
Descloizit m s. Deskloizit
Desemulgator m emulsion breaker, demulsifying chemical
desilifizieren to desilicate
Desilifizierung f desilication
Deskloizit m descloizite, eusynchite, $Pb(Zn,Cu)[OH|VO_4]$
Desmocollinit m desmocollinite (submaceral)
Desmoines n, **Desmoines-Stufe** f Desmoinesian [Stage] (Pennsylvanian in North-America)
Desmosit m desmosite (contact rock)
Desorption f desorption
Desorptionseigenschaft f desorption characteristic
Desquamation f exfoliation (s.a. Abschuppung)
Destillation f/**fraktionierte** fractional distillation
Destinezit m destinezite, $Fe_4[(OH)_4|(PO_4,SO_4)_3] \cdot H_2O$
Destruktion f destruction
Destruktionsform f destructional form
Destruktionsgrad m degree of destruction
deszendent descending, descendant, supergene
Deszendenztheorie f doctrine of descent
Detailaufnahme f surveying of details
Detail-Filterverfahren n detailed filtering method
Detektor m pick-up
Detonation f detonation
detritisch detrital
Detritus m detritus
~/von Eisbergen verschleppter subaqueous (glaciomarine, marine) till
deuterisch deuteric, epimagmatic
Deuterium n deuterium
deuterogen deuterogenic, deuterogenous
deuteromorph deuteromorphic
Deutung f/**genetische** genetic interpretation
~/stratigrafische stratigraphic interpretation
Devensien n Devensian (Pleistocene of British Islands, corresponding to Würm Drift, Alps district)
Deviator m deviator
Devillin m devilline, herrengrundite, $CaCu_4[(OH)_3|SO_4]_2 \cdot 3H_2O$
Devon n Devonian [System] (chronostratigraphically); Devonian [Period] (geochronologically); Devonian [Age] (common sense)
devonisch Devonian
Devonperiode f Devonian [Period]
Devonprofil n Devonian profile
Devonsystem n Devonian [System]
Devonzeit f Devonian [Age]
Deweylit m deweylite (a mineral species of the serpentine group)
Dewindtit m dewindtite, $Pb[(UO_2)_4|(OH)_4|(PO_4|_2] \cdot 8H_2O$
DHI = Deutsches Hydrographisches Institut (BRD)
D-Horizont m D-horizon (of soil)
Diabantit m diabantite (chlorite mineral)
Diabas m diabase
diabasisch diabasic
Diabaslava f diabasic lava
Diabasmandelstein m amygdaloidal diabase
Diabasporphyr m diabase porphyry
Diabasstruktur f diabasic texture
Diabastuff m diabase tuff
Diablan-Orogenese f Diablan orogeny (at the Tithonian/Berriasian boundary in North America)
diablastisch diablastic
Diaboleit m diaboleite, $Pb_2[Cu(OH)_4Cl_2]$
Diabrochit m diabrochite (migmatite)
Diachronismus m diachronism
diadoch diadochic
Diadochie f diadochy, diadochism
Diadochit m diadochite, $Fe_4[(OH)_4|(PO_4,SO_4)_3] \cdot 13H_2O$
Diagenese f diagenesis, diagenism, lithification
Diagenesefazies f lapidofacies
Diagenesefrühstadium n syndiagenese
Diagenesehauptstadium n anadiagenese
Diagenesespätstadium n epidiagenese
diagenetisch diagenetic
diagonalgeschichtet false-bedded, cross-bedded
Diagonalgitter n diagonal lattice
Diagonalkluft f diagonal (oblique) joint
Diagonalschichtung f cross stratification (bedding, lamination), diagonal (oblique, false, inclined) bedding, planar (tubular) cross bedding
Diagonalstellung f diagonal position
Diagonalverwerfung f oblique fault
Diagramm n diagram, graph, grid, plot; log
~ einer Neigungsmessung inclinometer log
~ eines Kornteilgefüges selective (partial) diagram
~/synoptisches synoptic diagram
Diaklase f diaclase, diaclasis

Diaklinaltal 70

Diaklinaltal *n* diaclinal valley
diakritisch diacritical
Diallag *m* diallage *(monoclinic pyroxene)*
Dialyse *f* dialysis
diamagnetisch diamagnetic
Diamagnetismus *m* diamagnetism
Diamant *m* diamond
~/**einkarätiger** special round
~/**farbiger** fancy stone
~/**gelber** cape diamond
~/**gerundeter** rounded diamond
~/**hochwertiger** four-grainer
~/**minderwertiger** inferior stone
~ **mittlerer Qualität** regular
~/**rückgewonnener** recovered diamond
~/**schwarzer** carbon (black) diamond, carbonado
~/**trüber** cloudy diamond
~/**unechter** fake diamond
~/**ungeschliffener** dob
~ **von 1/4 Karat** grainer
~ **von 1/2 Karat** two-grainer
~ **von 3/4 Karat** three-grainer
~ **von reinstem Wasser** diamond of the purest water
Diamantbohren *n* diamond drilling
Diamantbohrer *m* diamond (adamantine) drill
Diamantbohrkrone *f* diamond-type cutter head
Diamantbohrmeißel *m* diamond drilling bit
Diamantbohrung *f* adamantine drill
diamantenartig adamantine
diamantenführend diamondiferous, diamantiferous, diamontiferous
Diamantglanz *m* diamond (adamantine) lustre
diamanthaltig diamondiferous, diamantiferous
Diamantkernbohrapparat *m* diamond core barrel
Diamantkernbohren *n* diamond core drilling
Diamantkernkrone *f* diamond core bit
Diamantkrone *m* diamond crown
Diamantstaub *m* diamond dust
Diamantvollbohrkrone *f* non-coring diamond bit
Diamiktit *m* diamictite
diamorph diamorphous
Diamorphismus *m* diamorphism
Diaphorit *m* diaphorite, ultrabasite, $4PbS \cdot 3Ag_2S \cdot Sb_2S_3$
Diaphthorese *f* diaphthoresis, retrogressive (retrograde) metamorphism
Diaphthorit *m* diaphthorite
diaphthoritisch diaphthoritic
Diaphthoritisierung *f* diaphthoritization
Diapir *m* diapir, acromorph
Diapirfalte *f* diapiric (piercement) fold
diapirisch diapiric
Diapirismus *m* diapirismus
Diapirkuppel *f* diapir dome
diaschist diaschistic
Diaspor *m* diaspore, α-AlOOH
diastatisch diastatic

Diastem *n* diastem
diastrophisch diastrophic
Diastrophismus *m* diastrophism
diatektisch diatectic
Diatexis *f* diatexis
Diatexit *m* diatexite *(migmatite)*
Diatomeen *fpl* diatoms
Diatomeenerde *f* diatomaceous (infusorial) earth, tellurine, molera, mountain flour, pulverulent silica, kieselgu[h]r
Diatomeenschale *f* diatom shell (frustule, case)
Diatomeenschlamm *m*, **Diatomeenschlick** *m* diatom[aceous] ooze
Diatomeenton *m* diatomaceous clay
Diatomit *m* diatomite, diatomaceous chert
Diatrema *n* diatreme, volcanic vent
dichotom dichotomous, bifurcate, two-forked
Dichotomie *f* dichotomous (forked) branching
Dichroismus *m* dichroism
Dichroit *m* dichroite, water sapphire (*s.a.* Cordierit)
dichroitisch dichro[it]ic
dicht dense, tight, compact; felty *(ground mass)*; close-grained *(crystals)*
Dichte *f* density, tightness, compactness
~ **der Spülung** mud density
Dichtelog *n* density log
Dichtemesser *m* densitometer
Dichtemessung *f* density logging
~/**radiometrische** radiographic density determination
Dichteprofil *n* density profile
Dichteunterschied *m* density difference (contrast)
Dichtewert *m* density value
Dichtheitsdruck *m* threshold pressure
Dichtheitskontrolle *f* control of leakage
Dichtheitsprüfung *f* leak proof
Dichtheitstest *m* leak-off test
Dichtigkeit *f* compactness
Dichtklüftungszone *f* shake
Dichtungsgürtel *m* grout curtain
Dichtungshaut *f* damp-proof membrane; watertight diaphragm (screen), waterproofing membrane
Dichtungskern *m* impervious core
Dichtungsmaterial *n* packing material
Dichtungsschicht *f* confining bed
Dichtungsschirm *m* grout curtain, diaphragm
Dichtungsschleier *m* watertight diaphragm (screen), sealing membrane
Dichtungsschürze *f* waterproof blanket; watertight facing, grout curtain
Dichtungsteppich *m*, **Dichtungsvorlage** *f* impervious blanket; waterproof blanket
Dichtungswand *f s.* Dichtungsschleier
dickbankig thick-layered, thick-bedded, heavy-bedded
Dicke *f* thickness
~ **der Filtrationskruste** thickness of the filter cake

~/optische optical thickness (e.g. of atmosphere)
dickflüssig viscous; viscid; glutinous
Dickinsonit m dickinsonite, $Na_2(Mn,Fe)_5[PO_4]_4$
Dickit m dickite, $Al_4[(OH)_8|Si_4O_{10}]$
dickplattig thick-shaly
dickschalig trachyostraceous
Dickschliff m thick section (slice)
Dickspülung f 1. drilling fluid (mud), mud [flush]; 2. circulation with mud (process)
dickwandig thick-walled
didekaedrisch didecahedral
Didymograptenschiefer m Didymograptus Shale (Ordovician)
Didymolith m didymolite, $(Ca, Mg, Fe) Al_2[Si_3O_{10}]$
dielektrisch dielectric[al]
Dielektrizitätseigenschaften fpl dielectric[al] properties
Dielektrizitätskonstante f dielectric constant
Dielektrizitätsmessung f dielectric logging
Dienerit m dienerite, Ni_3As
Dienst m/geologischer geological survey
~/meteorologischer weather service
Dietrichit m dietrichite, $ZnAl_2[SO_4]_4 \cdot 22H_2O$
Dietzeit m dietzeite, $Ca_2[CrO_4|(JO_3)_2]$
Differentialbewegung f differential movement
Differentialthermoanalyse f differential thermal analysis
Differentialverdampfung f differential liberation (gas-oil ratio)
Differentiat n differentiate
Differentiation f differentiation
~ durch Abpressung differentiation by pressing
~ durch Assimilation differentiation by assimilation
~ durch Diatexis differentiation by diatexis
~ durch Gastransport differentiation by gas transfer
~ durch Gravitation gravitative differentiation
~ durch Hybridisierung differentiation by hybridization
~ durch Metablastese differentiation by metablastesis
~ durch Metatexis differentiation by metatexis
~ durch Pneumatolyse pneumatolytic differentiation
~/gravitative gravity fractionation (of a magma)
~/magmatische magmatic differentiation
~/metamorphe metamorphic differentiation
Differentiationsprodukt n differentiation product
Differentiationsstadium n stage of differentiation
Differentiationsvorgang m differentiation process, diagnosis
Differenzdruck m differential pressure
Differenzierung f der Arten differentiation of species
differierend/im geologischen Alter diachronous

Diffluenz f diffluence
Diffraktion f diffraction
diffundieren to diffuse
diffus diffuse
Diffusion f diffusion
Diffusionsgeschwindigkeit f velocity (rapidity) of diffusion, diffusion rate
Diffusionsgleichung f diffusion equation
Diffusionskoeffizient m diffusivity coefficient
Diffusionsvermögen n diffusivity, diffusibility
Diffusionsvorgang m diffusion process
Digenit m digenite, Cu_9S_5
digital digital
digitalisieren to digitize
Digitalseismik f digital seismics
Digitation f digitation
dihexagonal dihexagonal
Dihydrit m dihydrite, $Cu_5[(OH)_2|PO_4]_2$
Diktyogenese f dictyogenesis
diktyogenetisch dictyogenetic
Diktyonit m diktyonite (migmatite)
Dilatanz f dilatancy
Dilatation f dila[ta]tion, rarefaction
Dilatometer n dilatometer
Diluvium n s. Pleistozän
Dimension f dimension (e.g. of sun, planets)
dimorph dimorphic, dimorphous
Dimorphin m dimorphine, As_4S_3
Dimorphismus m dimorphism
Dinant[ium] n Dinantian [Series, Epoch] (Lower Carboniferous)
Dinariden fpl Dinarids
Dinasstein m/tongebundener clay-bond silica brick
Dinit m dinite (hydrocarbon mineral)
Dinosauriereierschale f dinosaur egg shell
Dinosaurierfährte f dinosaur track
Dinotherium n dinothere
Diogenit m diogenite (meteorite)
Dioktaeder n dioctahedron
dioktaedrisch dioctahedral
Diopsid m diopside, $CaMg[Si_2O_6]$
Dioptas m dioptase, emerald copper, $Cu_6[Si_6O_{18}] \cdot 6H_2O$
Diorit m diorite
dioritartig dioritic
Dioritgang m dioritic dike
Dioritgestein n dioritic rock
Dioritgneis m diorite gneiss
Dioritmagma n diorite magma
diphycerk diphycercal (of caudal fin)
Diplograptiden fpl diplograptids
Diploporendolomit m diplopore dolomite
Dipnoer mpl dipnoans
Dipol m/magnetischer magnetic dipole
Dipolmeßsonde f dipole sonde
Dipolstrahlung f/magnetische magnetic dipole radiation
Dipyr m dipyre (solid solution of mejonite and marialite)
Direktaufzeichnung f direct recording

Direktnachweisverfahren 72

Direktnachweisverfahren *n* direction-finding method
Disjunktion *f* disjunction
Disjunktivbruch *m* tension (distensional) fault
diskontinuierlich dicontinuous, intermittent
Diskontinuität *f* discontinuity
Diskontinuitätsfläche *f* surface of discontinuity *(seismics)*
Diskontinuumlehre *f* discontinuum theory
diskordant discordant, disconformable, unconformable, non-conformable
Diskordanz *f* discordance, disconformity, unconformity, non-conformity
~/**maskierte** non-evident disconformity, paraconformity
~ **ohne scharfe Grenzfläche** graded unconformity
~/**stratigrafische** stratigraphic unconformity
~/**tektonische** tectonic unconformity, structural discordance (unconformity)
~/**topografische** topographic discordance
Diskordanzfalle *f* overlap seal, unconformity trap
Diskordanzfläche *f* surface of unconformity
Diskordanzquelle *f* non-conformity spring
Diskordanzwinkel *m* angle of unconformity
Diskriminanzanalyse *f* analysis of discrimination, discriminance analysis
Diskriminanzfunktion *f* discriminance (discriminant) function
Dislokation *f* dislocation, disturbance, displacement; leap
~/**disjunktive** tension fault
~/**kompressive** compression
Dislokationsbeben *n* dislocation (tectonic) earthquake
Dislokationsbrekzie *f* dislocation breccia
Dislokationsdiskordanz *f* structural discordance
Dislokationsfläche *f* dislocation plane
Dislokationsgebirge *n* dislocation mountains
Dislokationsmetamorphose *f* dislocation (cataclastic) metamorphism
Dislokationstal *n* dislocation (fault) valley
dislozieren to dislocate, to displace
dispergieren to disperse
Dispersion *f* dispersion
Dispersionshof *m* dispersion halo (train) *(by geochemical prospection)*
~/**primärer** primary halo *(by mineralization)*
~/**sekundärer** secondary halo *(by weathering)*
Dispersionskraft *f* dispersive power
Dispersionsmodell *n* dispersive model *(isotope hydrogeology)*
Dissemination *f* dissemination
Dissipation *f* **der Energie** energy dissipation
Dissoziation *f* dissociation
Dissoziationsgrad *m* coefficient of dissociation
Dissoziationskonstante *f* dissociation constant
Dissoziationswärme *f* heat of dissociation
dissoziieren to dissociate

distal distal
Distalende *n* distal end
Disthen *m* disthene, cyanite, kyanite, Al_2SiO_5
Distorsionswellen *fpl* distortional (shear) waves
Distraktion *f s.* Zerrung
ditetragonal ditetragonal
Dithizonmethode *f* dithizone method
ditrigonal ditrigonal
Ditroit *m* ditroite *(feldspathoidal syenite)*
Dittmarit *m* dittmarite, $(NH_4)Mg_3H_2[PO_4]_3 \cdot 8H_2O$
Ditton[ium] *n* Dittonian [Stage] *(lower part of Lower Devonian, Old Red facies)*
Divarikatores *mpl s.* Deduktores
divergent divergent
divergentstrahlig ophitic
Divergenz *f* divergence
~/**adaptive** adaptive divergence
~/**sphärische** spherical divergence
divergieren to diverge
Diversität *f* diversity
Dixenit *m* dixenite, $Mn_5As_2[O_6|SiO_4] \cdot H_2O$
Djalindit *m* djalindite, $In(OH)_3$
Djalmait *m* djalmaite *(variety of microlite)*
Djerfisherit *m* djerfisherite, $K_3CuFe_{12}S_{14}$ *(meteoritic mineral)*
Djurleit *m* djurleite, Cu_2S
Dodekaeder *n* dodecahedron
Dodekaedergleitung *f* dodecahedral slip
dodekaedrisch dodecahedral
Dogger *m* Dogger *(Series of Jurassic System)*
Dokumentation *f*/**geologische** geological record
~/**tabellarische** tabular documentation
Dolerit *m* dolerite, whin-rock *(rock of the gabbro clan)*
Dolerophanit *m* dolerophanite, $Cu_2[O|SO_4]$
Doline *f* doline, dell, dale, sinkhole
Dolinenkarst *m* cockpit landscape
Dolinensee *m* doline (sink) lake, sinkhole pond
Dolomit *m* 1. dolomite, bitter spar, $CaMg[CO_3]_2$; 2. *s.* Dolomitgestein
~/**arenitischer** dolarenite
~/**gebrannter** calcined dolomite
~/**gipsführender** gypsiferous dolomite
~/**kavernöser** cavernous dolomite
~/**primärer** orthodolomite
Dolomitasche *f* earthy dolomite
Dolomitbildung *f* dolomi[ti]zation
Dolomitfleckigkeit *f* dolomitic mottling
Dolomitgeschiebe *npl* dolomite boulders
Dolomitgestein *n* dolomite [rock], dolostone, magnesian limestone
dolomithaltig dolomitic
Dolomitindividuen *npl*/**klastische** clastic dolomitic individuals
Dolomitisation *f* dolomi[ti]zation
dolomitisch dolomitic
dolomitisieren to dolomitize
Dolomitisierung *f* dolomi[ti]zation
Dolomitkalk *m* magnesian limestone

Dolomitknolle f **im Kohlenflöz** coal ball (apple)
Dolomitmergelstein m dolomitic marl
Dolomitrückbildung f dedolomitization
Dolomitsandschicht f layer of dolomitic sand
Dolomitsandstein m dolomitic sandstone
Dolomitsiltstein m dolosiltite
Doloresit m doloresite, $V_3O_4(OH)_4$
Dom m dome
~/flacher parma
~/langgestreckter ridge fold
~/langgestreckter, flacher swell
domartig dome-shaped, domelike, domed, domal
Dombildung f doming
Domer[ium] n, **Domero** n Domerian [Stage] (upper Pliensbachian)
Domeykit m domeykite, arsenical copper, Cu_3As
Domstruktur f/**kreisförmige** quaquaversal dome
Donathit m donathite (variety of chromite)
Donbassit m donbassite, $(Na,Ca,Mg)Al_4[(OH)_8|AlSi_3O_{10}]$
Donezbecken n Donez basin
Donezphase f Donez phase of folding
Donner m thunder
donnern to thunder
Doppelbildung f gemination (of crystals)
Doppelbogenmauer f double arch[ed] dam
doppelbrechend double-refracting, birefringent
Doppelbrechung f double refraction, birefringence
~/optische optical double refraction
Doppelbrechungseffekt m/**Brewsterscher** Brewster effect of double refraction
Doppelfenster n double window (tectonics)
Doppelkeilanker m sliding wedge [roof-] bolt
Doppelkernrohr n double tube core barrel
Doppelkrater m double[-walled] crater
Doppelkristall m geminate crystal
Doppelnehrung f doule tombolo
Doppelquarzkeil m double quartz wedge
Doppelsägeblattanordnung f double sawtooth system
Doppelsalz n double salt
doppelschalig bivalve[d], bivalvular
doppelschichtig two-layered
Doppelsicherheitsschieber m double gate preventer
Doppelspat m [optical] calcite, doubly reflecting spar, Iceland spar, calcareous spar, calc-spar, $CaCO_3$
Doppelstern m double (twin, binary) star
Doppelvulkan m twin volcano, cone-in-crater structure
Dopplerit m dopplerite (ulmic acid gel)
Dorasham n Dorashamian [Stage] (uppermost stage of Upper Permian)
Dorn m spine
dorsal dorsal
Dorsalecke f dorsal corner

Dorsalflosse f dorsal (back) fin
Dorsalkapsel f dorsal cup
Dorsalklappe f dorsal (brachial) valve (of brachiopods)
Dorsalrand m dorsal margin
Dorsalstrang m marginal cord (foraminiferans)
Dorsalwinkel m dorsal angle
Dosenlibelle f cross level bubble, circular spirit level
Doublette f doublet
Douglasit m douglasite, $K_2[FeCl_4(H_2O)_2]$
Doverit m doverite, $CaY[Fl(CO_3)_2]$
Downton n, **Downtonstufe** f Downtonian [Stage] (of Silurian)
Drahtlotung f wire sounding
Drahtseil n wire line
Drahtsilber n wire silver
Dränage f drainage
~ in Rechteckform gridiron drainage
~ infolge Schwerkraft gravity drainage
Dränageradius m radius of drainage
Dränbewässerung f subterranean irrigation
dränen to drain
Drängraben m drainage ditch (trench)
~/natürlicher draught
dränieren to drain
Dränschicht f pervious shell (of a reservoir)
Dränung f s. Dränage
Draperiefalten fpl drape folds
Dravit m dravite (variety of tourmaline)
Dredge f dredge
Drehachse f rotation (pivotal) axis
Drehbelastung f torque loading
Drehbewegung f rotatory motion (movement)
Drehbewegungsachse f s. Symmetrieachse
Drehbohren n drilling by rotation, rotary drilling
~ mit Luftspülung gas drilling
Dreheinrichtung f swivel (spindle) head
Drehimpuls m angular momentum
Drehkristallmethode f rotating crystal method
Drehmeißel m drag bit
Drehmoment n torque
Drehmomentschlüssel m torque wrench
Drehpolarisation f optical rotation, rotatory polarization
Drehschlagbohren n rotary-percussive drilling
Drehsieb n rotational sieve
Drehsinn m sense of rotation
Drehspiegelung f ro[ta]tory reflection, combined rotation and reflection
Drehtisch m 1. turntable, rotary table (of a drilling rig); 2. revolving stage (of a microscope)
~/graduierter graded revolving stage
Drehtischantrieb m table drive
Drehtischeinsatz m drive bushing
Drehung f/**optische** optical rotation
Drehungskristall n twister [crystal]
Drehvermögen n/**optisches** optical rotatory power
Drehverwerfung f rotational (pivotal, rotatory, rotary) fault

Drehwaage 74

Drehwaage f torsion balance
~/Eötvössche Eötvös torsion balance
Drehwinkel m angle of rotation
Drehzahl f rotational speed
~ des gesteinszerstörenden Werkzeugs rotary speed, revolutions per minute
Drehzahlmesser m tachometer, revolution counter
dreiachsig triaxial *(stress)*
dreibankig composed of three banks
Dreieck n/**astronomisches** polar triangle
~/hydrologisches hydrological triangle
~/Osannsches Osann's triangle
Dreiecksanordnung f triangular (diagonal) system
Dreiecksüberfall m triangular overfall *(measuring of water volume)*
Dreielektrodenanordnung f infinite electrode [method]
Dreierkoordination f threefold coordination
dreiflächig trihedral
Dreiflächner m trihedron
Dreikanter m wind-cut pebble, wind-shaped pebble, wind-carved pebble, three-facetted stone, dreikanter, windkanter
dreilappig trilobate[d], trilobed, three-lobed
Dreiphasenpunkt m triple point
Dreiphasenströmung f three-phase flow
Dreipunktverfahren n three-point method
Dreirollenmeißel m tricone rock bit
Dreischichtstruktur f three-layer structure *(of clay minerals)*
Dreischichttonmineralwasser n second-to-last water interlayer
Dreissensienbänke fpl Dreissensia Beds
Dreistoffsystem n ternary system
dreistrahlig diradiate
Dresbach[ien] n Dresbachian [Stage] *(basal stage of Croixian)*
Driftblock m drift boulder
Driftgeschwindigkeit f drift mobility
Driftmarke f, **Driftspur** f drag mark, groove cast
Driftstreifung f striation cast (mark)
Driftströmung f drift current
Drifttheorie f drift theory
Drilling[skristall] m trilling, threeling, twister [crystal]
Drillometer n drillometer *(for measuring the drilling pressure)*
Drillung f torsion
Dropstein m dropstone
drosseln to choke
Druck m pressure
~/absoluter absolute pressure
~/allseitiger confining pressure, pressure acting in all directions, directionless pressure
~ am Bohrlochkopf casing-head pressure
~ an der Bohrlochsohle bottom-hole pressure
~/barometrischer barometric pressure
~ der hangenden Gesteinsschichten overburden pressure (load)

~/dynamischer dynamic[al] pressure
~/einseitiger directional (unilateral) pressure
~/hoher high (heavy) pressure
~/hydrostatischer hydrostatic (closed-in, confining) pressure, hydropressure
~/kritischer critical pressure
~/lithostatischer s. **~/petrostatischer**
~/mittiger axial compression
~/osmotischer osmotic force
~/petrostatischer rock (lithostatical) pressure
~/voreilender advancing pressure
Druckabfall m pressure decline (drop), drop in pressure
~ im Spülungssystem pressure drop in the circulation system
Druckabfallkurve f pressure drop curve
Druckabhängigkeit f pressure dependence
Druckänderung f pressure change (transient)
~/normierte dimensionless pressure drop
Druckanhäufung f bulb pressure
Druckanstieg m pressure rise
Druckaufbau m pressure build-up, pressure restoration
Druckaufbaumessung f build-up analysis
Druckausgleich m pressure balance
Druckbarriere f barrier of pressure
Druckbeanspruchung f compressive strain
Druckbedingungen fpl pressure conditions
Druckbeeinflussung f interference effect *(reservoir mechanics)*
Druckbeobachtungssonde f pressure observation well
Druckbereich m pressure range
Druckbestimmung f geobarometry
Druckblase f flat jack
Druckbombe f pressure bomb
Druckdifferenz f pressure difference; potential difference
Druckdose f s. **Druckmeßdose**
drückend sultry
Druckentlastung f pressure relief
Druckentwicklung f pressure behaviour
Druckerhaltung f pressure maintenance
~ durch Gasinjektion gas repressuring
Druckerhöhung f pressure increase
Druckerscheinungen fpl pressure phenomena
Druckfaltung f compressional folding
Druckfeld n pressure field
druckfest strong
Druckfestigkeit f 1. compressive strength *(mechanics)*; 2. crushing strength, resistance to crushing, pressure resistance *(of a rock)*
Druckfunktion f pressure function
Druckgefälle n pressure (hydraulic) gradient
Druckgewölbe n pressure arch
druckhaft subject to heavy pressure
Druckhöhe f [pressure] head, elevation (hydraulic) head, head of water
~/artesische artesian [pressure] head
~/kritische critical head
~/piezometrische piezometric head
~/potentielle pressure potential
~/statische static [pressure] head

Druckkristallisation f piezocrystallization
Drucklagen fpl pressure partings
Drucklagerschub m bearing thrust
Druckleitung f mud hose *(drilling engineering)*
Drucklöslichkeit f pressure solubility
Drucklösungserscheinungen fpl pressure-solution phenomena
Drucklösungsfläche f pressure-solution plane
Druckluftbohrer m air (pneumatic) drill
Druckluftpegel m pneumatic level gauge
Druckmarken fpl crescentic grooves
Druckmeßdose f load (pressure) cell, pressure capsule, sensator
Druckmesser m pressure gauge
Druckmeßgerät n pressure instrument
Druckmessung f pressure measurement
Druckmetamorphose f metamorphism by pressure; compressional deformation
Druckmittelpunkt m centre of pressure
Druckniveau n pressure level
Druckpotential n pressure potential
Druckprobe f compression-test specimen
Druckprofil n pressure log
Druckprüfung f compressive strength test
Druckquarzit m/**porenfreier** presolved quartzite
Druckregime n pressure regime
Druckrohrleitung f intake conduit
Druckschieferung f induced cleavage
Druckschlechten fpl thrust cleavage *(coal)*
Drucksenkungsschreiber m s. Lastsenkungsschreiber
Drucksonde f consistency gauge
Drucksondierung f pressure determination by acoustic (ultrasonic) means
Druckspalte f compression fissure, compression[al] joint, piezoclase
Druckspannung f compressive stress
Druckspiegel m piezometric level *(of ground water)*
Druckspielcharakteristik f *(Am)* pressure trace loop
Druckspitze f pressure peak
Druckstabilisierung f pressure level-off *(e.g. oil production)*
Druckstollen m pressure tunnel
Druckströmung f pressure flow
Drucksutur f styolitic structure (seam)
Drucküberwachung f pressure survey
Druckunterschied m pressure difference
Druckverlauf m development of pressure
~/**instationärer** transient pressure behaviour
Druckverlust m s. Druckabfall
Druckversuch m compression test
~/**dreiaxialer** triaxial [compression] test
Druckverteilung f pressure distribution
~/**hydrostatische** hydrostatic pressure distribution *(in aquifers)*
Druckverteilungsschicht f subbase
Druckwasserleitung f pressurized water conduit
Druckwasserstollen m pressure tunnel

Druckwelle f compression (blast) wave, pressure surge
Druckwiederaufbau m pressure replacement
Druckwirkung f pressure effect
Druck-Zeit-Regime n *(Am)* pound-day concept *(aquifer gas storage)*
Druckzelle f/**dreiaxiale** triaxial compression cell
Druckzementierung f squeeze cementation (cementing operation)
Druckzentrum n centre of pressure *(in aquifers)*
Druckzone f compression zone
Druckzwiebel f pressure bulb
Druckzwilling m compressive twin
Druckzwillingsbildung f pressure twinning, compressive twin formation
Druckzwillingslamellierung f twinning lamination due to pressure
Drum[lin] m drum[lin], whaleback
Druse f druse, v[o]ugh, vug[g], pocket, nodule corbond, loch
~/**große** loch hole, voog
~/**linsenförmige** lenticular vug
drusenartig drusy
Drusengang m hollow lode
Drusenhöhle f buddling hole
Drusenraum m drusy cavity, vuggy opening
drusenreich vuggy
drusig drusy, drused, pockety
Dschungel f(m,n) jungle
3-D-Seismik f 3-D-seismics
Dublette f doublet
Duchesnien n Duchesnian [Stage] *(mammalian stage, upper Eocene in North America)*
Dufrenit m dufrenite, kraurite, green iron ore, $Fe_3\cdot Fe_6\cdots[(OH)_3|PO_4]_4$
Dufrenoysit m dufrenoysite, $2PbS\cdot As_2S_3$
Duftit m duftite, $PbCu[OH|AsO_4]$
duktil ductile
Duktilometer n ductilometer
Dumontit m dumontite, $Pb[(UO_2)_3|(OH)_4|(PO_4)_2]\cdot 3H_2O$
Dumortierit m dumortierite, $(Al,Fe)_7[O_3|BO_3|(SiO_4)_3]$
Dumreicherit m dumreicherite, $Mg_4Al_2[SO_4]_7\cdot 36H_2O$
Dundasit m dundasite *(H_2O bearing PbAl carbonate)*
Düne f dune, drift hill
~/**befestigte** fixed dune
~/**ingenieurbiologisch befestigte** anchored dune
~/**kleine** dene
~/**ruhende** stationary dune
dünenbedeckt dune-covered
Dünenfeld n dune field
Dünengebiet n dune area
Dünengürtel m dune belt
Dünenkamm m crest of dune
~/**rauchender** smoking crest of dune
Dünenkette f s. Dünenzug
Dünenkliff n dune cliff

Dünenküste

Dünenküste f dune coast
Dünenreihe f, **Dünenrücken** m s. Dünenzug
Dünensand m dune (aeolian) sand, anemoarenyte
~/verfestigter aeolianite
Dünenschutzwerk n defence of dunes
Dünensee m dune lake
Dünensystem n dune system
Dünental n dune valley, interdune passage
Dünenwanderung f migration of dunes
Dünenzug m dune chain (ridge, range)
Düngekalk m agricultural limestone
Düngesalz n saline manure, manuring salt, (Am) fertilizing salt
Düngung f fertilization
Dunham-Klassifikation f Dunham classification
Dunit m dunite, olivine rock (rock of the ultramafic clan)
Dunkelfeld n dark field
Dunkelfeldabbildung f dark field image
Dunkelfeldbeleuchtung f dark field (ground) illumination
Dunkelfeldbeobachtung f dark field observation
Dunkelfeldblende f dark field stop
Dunkelglimmer m dark mica
Dunkelglimmergitter n dark-mica lattice
Dunkelmineral n mafic mineral, melane
Dunkelnebel m dark nebula
Dunkelstellung f dark position
Dunkelstrahlung f dark radiation
Dunlap-Orogenese f Dunlap orogeny (during the Pliensbachian in North America)
dünnbankig thin-stratified, in thin layers (banks)
dünnblättrig thin-foliated, thin-laminated
dünnflüssig highly fluid, free-flowing, non-viscous
dünngebändert thin-banded
dünngeschichtet thin-bedded
dünnplattig thin-shaly
dünnschalig thin-skinned
Dünnschichtchromatografie f thin-film chromatography
Dünnschliff m microsection, microscopic section (slide), thin section (slide), transparent cut
Dunst m[/trockener] haze
dunstig hazy
Dunstwolke f cloud of haze
Dünung f swell
Duplikatur f duplicature (palaeontology)
Dupuit-Brunnengleichung f Dupuit's well equation
Dupuit-Forchheimer-Näherung f Dupuit-Forchheimer assumption
Durain m durain (coal lithotype)
Durangit m durangite, NaAl[F|AsO₄]
Durbachit m durbachite (lamprophyric granite)

durchbauen to repair (e.g. an adit); to rerip (a roadway); to dint (the floor)
Durchbewegung f s. Deformation
~/scherende displacive shearing stress
Durchbiegung f deflection, bending
durchbohren 1. to drill through; 2. to penetrate
durchbrochen/von Granit intruded (invaded) by granite
Durchbruch m breakdown, break-through; breach (e.g. of a wall); cut-off (of a meander)
Durchbruchstal n transverse valley
~/durchflossenes water gap
~/trockenes wind gap
durchdringen to permeate, to penetrate; to pervade
~/sich to interpenetrate
durchdringend penetrative
Durchdringung f penetration
~/gegenseitige interpenetration
Durchdringungsvermögen n **der Wurzel** root penetrability (capability), capacity of root penetration
Durchdringungszwilling m penetrating (interpenetration) twin
durchfahren to pass; to hole, to cut across
Durchfeuchtung f moistening, wetting
Durchfluß m flow passage
Durchflußbedingung f flow condition
Durchflußbreite f width of flow
Durchflußfähigkeit f flow capacity
Durchflußgeschwindigkeit f flow velocity; percolation rate
Durchflußintensität f flow rate
Durchflußmenge f rate of flow
Durchflußmesser m, **Durchflußmeßgerät** n flowmeter, rate-of-flow meter
~ an der Bohrlochsohle bottom-hole flowmeter
Durchflußmessung f flow measurement
Durchflußprofil n flow profile
Durchflußquerschnitt m surface (cross section) of flow; flow section
Durchflußwiderstand m flow resistance
Durchflußzähler m volumetric flowmeter
Durchführbarkeitsstudie f feasibility study
~/vorläufige prefeasibility study
Durchgang m 1. duct; 2. pass (of a satellite)
Durchgangsgeschwindigkeit f s. Darcy-Geschwindigkeit
Durchgangsquerschnitt m cross section of passage
Durchgangszeit f transit time (astronomy)
Durchhalten n **einer Schicht** persistence of a bed, continuity of a bed (stratum)
Durchhieb m cut-through
durchklüftet penetrated (fissured) by joints
Durchklüftung f penetration by joints
durchkreuzend/sich wechselseitig mutually cross cutting
Durchkreuzung f decussation (of crystals)

Durchkreuzungsverzwillingung f fourling twinning
Durchkreuzungszwilling m cruciform twin
Durchlaß m passage; opening
~/schmaler senkrechter slot
Durchlaßcharakteristik f transmittance curve
durchlässig permeable, pervious, leaky
~/stark high-permeable
Durchlässigkeit f 1. permeability, perviousness; 2. transmissivity
~ des Gesteins rock permeability
~ für Wasser water permeability; coefficient of intrinsic permeability; hydraulic conductivity
~/relative relative permeability
~/vertikale vertical permeability
Durchlässigkeitsbeiwert m permeability coefficient; coefficient of hydraulic conductivity
Durchlässigkeitsgrenze f permeative boundary
Durchlässigkeitskoeffizient m s. Durchlässigkeitsbeiwert
Durchlässigkeitsmeßgerät n permeater (flow test)
~ mit fallender Druckhöhe falling-head permeameter
~ mit gleichbleibender Wasserhöhe constant head permeameter
Durchlässigkeitsvermögen n transmissibility
Durchlässigkeitsversuch m percolation test
~ mit gleichbleibender Wasserhöhe constant head permeability
Durchlaßwehr n sluice weir
Durchläufer m ubiquitous mineral
Durchlicht n transmitted light, T.L.
durchlüften to aerate
Durchlüftung f aeration (e.g. of water)
Durchmesser m diameter
Durchnässung f des Gebirges soakage of the rock
durchörtern to cut across, to work through
~/das Gebirge to cut across the ground, to intersect the ground
~/einen Gang to cross a lode
Durchörterung f intersection
durchscheinend transparent, translucent, diaphanous
Durchscherungsüberschiebung f scissions thrust
Durchschlag m s. Durchbruch
Durchschlagsloch n blow (puffing) hole
Durchschlagsröhre f pipe, diatreme
Durchschmelzung f des Daches deroofing (magmatism)
Durchschnitt m/annähernder rough average
Durchschnittsgehalt m average content
~ des Erzes average ore grade
Durchschnittshäufigkeit f average abundance
Durchschnittsmächtigkeit f average thickness
Durchschnittswert m mean value (of an element)
durchsenken to dint

durchsetzen 1. to interstratify; to interlaminate; 2. to intersect (lodes)
durchsetzt interstratified
~/mit Diamantstaub diamond impregnated
~/mit Drusen vuggulated
~/mit Schiefer ribbed
~/mit Spalten fissured
~/von Grubenbauen intermine
~/von Verwerfungen dissected by faults
Durchsetzung f intersection (of lodes)
durchsichtig transparent, translucent, diaphanous
~/völlig clear and slightly stained (quality of mica)
Durchsichtigkeit f transparency, translucence, diaphanousness
durchsickern to seep, to ooze [out], to percolate, to soak in[to], to leak downward
Durchsickerung f seepage, oozing, percolation, bleeding, sweating
~ des Wassers water percolation
durchspießen to pierce
Durchspießungsfalte f piercement (diapir) fold
Durchspießungsfaltung f piercement folding, diapir [folding]
Durchspießungsklippe f piercing klippe
Durchspießungssalzdom m piercement-type salt dome
durchsprenkelt sprinkled-through
Durchstechungskern m piercement core
Durchstich m cut
~ eines Tunnels tunnel driving
durchstoßen to pierce
Durchstoßpunkt m point of penetration
durchteufen to sink through
durchtränken to imbibe, to soak, to drench; to impregnate; to saturate
Durchtränkung f imbibition, soaking; impregnation, saturation
~/weitflächige large-area impregnation
Durchtrennungsgrad m degree of separation
durchtrümern to penetrate, to pervade
Durchtrümerung f stringer zone
durchwachsen to interpenetrate, to intermingle
Durchwachsung f intergrowth
~/symplektische symplectic intergrowth
Durchwachsungsstruktur f interlocked texture
Durchwachsungszwillinge mpl penetration twins
~/rechtwinklige plus-shaped twins
durchwatbar fordable
Durchwurzelung f rooting
durchzogen interstratified
~/von Eintrocknungsrissen desiccation-cracked
~/von Klüften jointed
~/von Schlammrissen mud-cracked
~/von Sprüngen ruptured
~/von Trockenrissen desiccation-cracked, sun-cracked
~/von Wasserläufen streamy

Durit *m* durite *(coal microlithotype);* black durain *(spore-rich);* grey durain *(spore-poor)*
Duroclarit *m* duroclarite *(coal microlithotype)*
dürr arid
Dürre *f* aridity, aridness, drought
Düse *f* jet
Düsenmeißel *m* jet bit
Düsenschrotbohren *n* pellet impact drilling
Dussertit *m* dussertite, $BaFeH[(OH)_6|(AsO_4)_2]$
Dütenmergel *m* stylolitic (cone-in-cone) limestone
Dütentextur *f* stylolitic structure
Duxit *m* duxite *(a resinite from the browncoal field of Dux in Bohemia)*
Dy *m* dy
Dyakisdodekaeder *n* didodecahedron
Dyakishexaeder *n* pentagonal dodecahedron
Dyas *n* Dyas
Dyktyonit *m* diktyonite, dyktyonite *(migmatite)*
Dynamik *f* dynamics
~/endogene endodynamics, internal dynamic processes
~/exogene exodynamics, external dynamic processes
~/glazigene glaciogenic dynamics
Dynamitsprengung *f* dynamiting
dynamometamorph dynamometamorphic
Dynamometamorphose *f* dynamometamorphism, dynamic (dislocation) metamorphism
Dynamometerstempel *m* dynamometer prop
dysaerobisch dysaerobic
Dysanalyt *m* dysanalyte, $(Ca,Na,Ce)(Ti,Nb,Fe)O_3$
Dyskrasit *m* dyscrasite, antimonsilver, Ag_3Sb
Dysodil *m* dysodile; paper coal *(sapropelite)*
Dysprosium *n* dysprosium *n*, Dy
Dzhulfa *n* Djulfian [Stage] *(of Upper Permian)*

E

Eagle Ford-Schiefer *m* Eagle Ford Shale *(Cenomanian and Turonian in North America)*
Eardleyit *m* eardleyite, $Ni_6Al_2[(OH)_{16}|CO_3] \cdot 4H_2O$
Earlandit *m* earlandite, $Ca_3(C_6H_5O_7)_2 \cdot 4H_2O$
Ebbe *f* ebb [tide], low tide (water), reflux
~ und Flut *f* tide, ebb and flow, flux and reflux
Ebbedelta *n* ebb delta
Ebbestrom *m* ebb tide (current), tidal outflow
Ebbetrichter *m* ebb channel
Ebbe- und Flut-Gebiet *n* tidal territory
Ebbewassermenge *f* volume of ebb (water discharging on ebb tide)
eben plane
Ebene *f* plane; plain, flat
~ der Teilbarkeit senkrecht zur Schieferung grain plane *(of metamorphic rocks)*
~/durch Zusammenfluß zweier Ströme gebildete confluence plain
~/durchkraterte cratered plain
~/gleichmäßige base-levelled plain
~/seewärts fallende panplain
~/submarine marginal platform *(continental slope)*
~/tischglatte dead level
ebenflächig evenly surfaced
Ebenflächigkeit *f* evenness
ebengeschichtet evenly laminated
Ebenheit *f* planeness, evenness, levelness, smoothness
ebnen to plane
Eburon-Eiszeit *f*, **Eburon-Kaltzeit** *f* Eburonian [Drift] *(Pleistocene in Northwest Europe)*
Echellit *m* echellite *(s.a. Natrolith)*
Echinodermen *mpl* echinoderms
Echinodermenkalk *m* echinoidal limestone
Echinoiden *fpl* echinoids
Echinosphaeritenkalk *m* Echinosphaerites Limestone *(Ordovician)*
Echo *n* echo
Echogramm *n* echogram
Echoimpulsempfänger *m* echo pulse receiver
Echolot *n* echo sounder (sounding device), sonic altimeter (depth finder), depth indicator (sounder)
Echolotmessung *f*, **Echolotung** *f* echo (sonic, reflection) sounding
Echtzeit *f* real time
Ecke *f* corner
eckig angular
Eckigkeit *f* angularity
edaphisch edaphic
Edaphon *n* edaphon
Edelerz *n* rich ore
Edelgas *n* rare (noble) gas
Edelgashülle *f* inert gas shell
Edelgaskonfiguration *f* inert gas configuration
Edelmetall *n* precious (noble) metal
Edelmetallgewicht *n* troy weight
Edelminerale *npl* gem minerals
Edelopal *m* precious (noble) opal
Edelsplitt *m* high-grade chippings
Edelstein *m* jewel, gem[stone], precious stone
~/fehlerloser flawless gem
~/synthetischer synthetic precious stone
Edelsteinkunde *f* gemmology
Edelsteinlupe *f* gem magnifier
Edelsteinschleifer *m* lapidary
Edelsteinschneider *m* gem cutter
Edelsteinseife *f* gem placer
Edelton *m* high-grade clay
Eden *n* Edenian [Stage] *(of Cincinnatian in North America)*
Edenit *m* edenite, $NaCa_2Mg_5[(OH,F)_2|AlSi_7O_{22}]$
Ediacara-Fauna *f* Ediacara fauna, Metazoan fauna of the Late Precambrian
Edingtonit *m* edingtonite, $BaAl_2Si_3O_{10} \cdot 3H_2O$
Edukt *n* original material, primary rock
Eem *n* Eemian [Stage] *(of Pleistocene)*
Eem-Interglazial *n*, **Eem-Warmzeit** *f* Eem [Interval], Eemian *(Pleistocene in Northwest Europe)*

Eindunstung

Effektivität *f* **geologischer Untersuchungsarbeiten** geological prospecting efficiency
Effloreszenz *f* efflorescence
effloreszieren to effloresce
Effosion *f* effosion
Effusion *f* effusion
Effusivgestein *n* effusive [rock]
Effusivkörper *m* effusive body
Effusivstrom *m* effusive stream
Egeran *m* egeran *(brown idocrase)*
Eglestonit *m* eglestonite, Hg_6Cl_4O
eichen to calibrate
Eichen-Hainbuchen-Phase *f* oak-hornbeam phase
Eichenmischwald *m* mixed oak forest
Eichkurve *f* calibration curve
~/für Isotope isotope calibration curve
Eichmaß *n* calibration standard, gauge
Eichpräparat *n* test pill
Eichprobe *f* calibrating sample
Eichung *f* calibration
Eifel *n*, **Eifel-Stufe** *f s*. Couvin
eiförmig ovoid, ooid
Eigenasche *f* inherent ash *(coal)*
eigenbürtig indignous
Eigenfarbe *f* particular colour
Eigenfrequenz *f* natural frequency
Eigengewicht *n* dead (self) weight *(s.a.* Eigenmasse)
Eigenimpulsverfahren *n* characteristic pulse method
Eigenmasse *f* dead load
Eigenmoment *n*/**magnetisches** intrinsic magnetic moment
Eigenpotential *n* spontaneous (self) potential
Eigenpotentialkurve *f* spontaneous potential curve
Eigenpotentialmessung *f* self-potential measurement, spontaneous potential logging
Eigenpotentialverfahren *n* spontaneous potential method, self-potential method
Eigenschaften *fpl*/**chemische** chemical properties
~/gesteinschemische rock-technical properties
~/rheologische rheological properties
Eigenschwingung *f* natural oscillation (vibration)
Eigensetzung *f* earth (soil) consolidation
Eigenspannung *f* initial (internal) stress; body stress
Eigenstabilität *f* inherent stability
Eigensymmetrie *f* specific symmetry
Eigenverfestigung *f* earth (soil) consolidation
Eigenversorgung *f* self-sufficiency *(proportion of home production of demand)*
Eigenwiderstand *m* internal resistance
~/elektrischer resistivity *(of a layer)*
Eiland *n* island
einachsig uniaxial
~/optisch optically uniaxial
Einbau *m* **des Bohrstrangs** running of the drilling string

~/diadocher diadochic incorporation *(of elements)*
~/einer geschlitzten Rohrtour screening
einbauen to install, to insert, to build in; to lower
~/eine Futterrohrtour to insert a string of casing
Einbauteufe *f*, **Einbautiefe** *f* setting (landing) depth *(of casing)*
einbetten to embed
Einbettung *f* embedding, interbedding
~ von Mineralkörnern briquetting of mineral grains
Einbettungsmedium *n* embedding material, mounting medium
Einbettungstiefe *f* depth of burial
Einbeulen *n* **der Verrohrung** collapse of [the] casing
Einbrechen *n* invasion, inrush, encroachment, inroad, ingress, advance *(of the sea)*
Einbruch *m* 1. collapse, breaking-down, cave-in *(s.a.* Einsturz); 2. *s.* Einbrechen
~/plötzlicher quake
~/vulkanotektonischer volcano-tectonic collapse
Einbruchs... *s.a.* Einsturz...
Einbruchsbecken *n* structural depression (basin), trough, cauldron subsidence
Einbruchskessel *m* caldera
Einbuchtung *f* embayment, indentation, reentrant
eindämmen 1. to embank; 2. to seal off *(a mine)*
eindampfen to evaporate
Eindampfen *n* evaporation
Eindampfpfanne *f* rine pan *(in a salt work)*
eindeichen to dam up (in), to dike [in], to embank, to bank in, to levee
Eindeichung *f* diking, embankment
eindicken to thicken, to inspissate
Eindicken *n* thickening, inspissation
eindringen to infiltrate, to ooze, to encroach, to ingress, to percolate, to intrude; to penetrate
Eindringen *n* infiltration, encroachment, ingress, percolation
~ des Meeres ingression of the sea
~ von Bohrspülung in die Formation mudding-off
Eindringkapazität *f* infiltrability
Eindringmeßgerät *n* penetrometer
Eindringtiefe *f* depth of penetration; skin depth *(electromagnetic method)*
~ der Spülung depth of mud invasion
Eindringung *f* penetration
Eindringungszone *f* **der Bohrlochspülung** zone of invasion of borehole fluid
Eindruck *m* impression, [im]print, [external] mould, external cast
Eindrücken *n* **der Verrohrung** collapse of [the] casing
Eindunstung *f* drying-up

Eindunstungslösung

Eindunstungslösung f solution of drying-up
einebnen to level, to flatten; to planate
Einebnung f flattening, applanation; planation
einfachbrechend singly refractive, monorefringent
Einfachkernrohr n single-core barrel
Einfachüberdeckung f hundred percent section
einfahren to enter, to descend into a mine
Einfahrt f 1. entrance; 2. pass
Einfall m s. Einfallen
einfallen 1. to fall down; 2. to dip, to slope, to hade
~/**flach** to dip gently (at low angles)
~/**steil** to dip steeply (at high angles)
Einfallen n 1. dip, hade, incline, fall; pitch, grade; 2. incidence (of rays)
~ **an Bohrkernen** core dip
~ **der Verwerfung** fault dip
~/**entgegengesetztes** reversal (reversed) dip
~/**flaches** low (gentle) dip, flat hade, dip at low angles
~/**mittleres** average hade
~/**periklinales** periclinal (centroclinal) dip
~/**scheinbares** apparent dip
~/**schwaches** slight dip, gentle grade (s.a. ~/flaches)
~/**stärkstes** s. ~/wahres
~/**steiles** steep (fast, sharp) dip, dip at high angles
~/**umlaufendes** partiversal (quaquaversal) dip
~/**wahres** true (full) dip
einfallend 1. dipping, hading; 2. incident (rays)
~/**nach außen** outward dipping
~/**nach innen** inward dipping
Einfallrichtung f direction of dip, inclination dip, line of dip (slope)
Einfallsebene f 1. plane of dip; 2. plane of incidence (of rays)
Einfallsfläche f entrance surface
Einfallswinkel m 1. dip angle, angle of dip[ping]; 2. angle of incidence, incidence angle (of rays)
Einfaltung f interfolding, backfolding
Einfaltungsfeld n area of tectonic depression
Einfang m capture; entrapment (of liquids, gases)
Einfanghypothese f accretion theory, capture hypothesis
Einfangquerschnitt m capture cross section
Einfangwinkel m acceptance angle
einfarbig monochromatic
Einfließen n inflow, influx
einfluchten to align
Einfluchtung f alignment
Einfluß m 1. influence; 2. inflow, influx
~ **der Umgebung** environmental influence
einfrieren to congeal
Einfrieren n **des Spannungszustands** stress freezing
einfüllen to fill in; to refill, to backfill

Einfüllung f refilling
eingebettet embedded, imbedded, interbedded, interjacent, interposed, buried
~ **im zentralen Teil eines Gletschers** intraglacial
eingeebnet planed (worn) down
eingelagert interstratified, intercalary, embedded, interbedded
~/**flözförmig** interleaved
eingeschaltet interposed, intercalary, interjacent
eingeschlossen/von Eis ice-bound
~/**von Felsen** rock-bound
eingeschnitten/tief deeply incised
eingeschnürt nipped (lode)
eingesprengt disseminated, ingrained, intermingled, spotty
eingestellt/vorübergehend temporarily abandoned (suspended)
eingesunken collapsed, downwarped
Eingliederung f classification
Einheit f/**aufgefingerte lithostratigrafische** lithosome
~/**biostratigrafische** biostratigraphic[al] unit
~/**chronostratigrafische** chronostratigraphic[al] unit
~/**fazielle** ecostratigraphic[al] unit
~/**geochronologische** geochronologic[al] unit
~/**lateral auffingernde stratigrafische** somal unit
~/**lithofazielle** isogeolith
~/**lithologische** lithologic[al] unit
~/**lithostratigrafische** lithostratigraphic[al] (rockstratigraphic) unit
~/**parachronologische** parachronologic[al] unit
~/**parallelschichtige lithostratigrafische** lithostrome
~/**pedostratigrafische** pedostratigraphic[al] unit
~/**stratigrafische** stratigraphic[al] unit
~/**verzahnte lithostratigrafische** lithosome
Einkieselung f silification (of river sands)
Einklemmung f s. Einschnürung, Verdrückung
einkneten to knead into, to mash
Einknetung f mashing
Einkristall m monocrystal, single crystal
Einlage f s. 1. Einlagerung; 2. Quetschholz
einlagern to interstratify, to intercalate, to interlay, to interlaminate
Einlagerung f interstratification, intercalation; tercalary bed; embedment, interbedding; insert; inclusion
~/**dünne** break
~/**linsenförmige** lenticular intercalation
Einlaßdruck m intake pressure
Einlaßsonde f input well
Einlaßventil n intake valve
Einlaufkanal m receiving canal
einlegen/Mutung to claim
Einlieger m inlier (1. a mass of rock whose outcrop is wholly surrounded by rock of younger

age; 2. a distinct area or formation that is completely surrounded by another)
Einmuldung f basining
Einmündung f embouchure
einordnen to range; to classify
Einordnung f ranging; classification
~/zeitliche chronological classification
einpeilen/Orte to shoot locations
Einphasenströmung f single-phase flow
Einpreßbohrloch n injection hole
Einpreßbohrung f input (inlet, intake, injection, pressure, index, key) well
Einpreßdruck m input (injection) pressure
einpressen 1. to grout under pressure; 2. to inject
Einpreßflüssigkeit f injection fluid
Einpreßgas n input gas
Einpreßindex m injectivity
Einpreßleitung f repressure line
Einpreßloch n grout hole
Einpreßprofil n injectivity profile
Einpreßsonde f s. Einpreßbohrung
Einpressung f injection
Einprismaspektrograf m single-prism spectrograph
Einpunktverankerungssystem n single point mooring system
einregeln to orient; to align, to orient strongly
Einregelung f orientation; alignment
Einregulierung f adjustment
einreihen to range; to sequence
Einreihenschießen n single-row shooting
einreihig uniserial *(palaeontologyl)*
einrollen/sich to enroll
Einrollvermögen n power of enrollment (coiling up)
einsägen to saw down *(river)*
Einsattelung f drowning
Einsatz m beginning, onset, event
~/deutlicher sudden (impulsive) beginning
~/erster first arrival (break, impetus)
~/scharfer s. ~/deutlicher
~/späterer later arrival
~ von Solen brine handling *(at drilling)*
Einsatzmaterial n feed stock
Einsatzmischung f charging blend *(coal)*
Einsatzzeit f arrival time, time of incidence (advent)
~ des Bohrgeräts rig time
Einsaugung f imbibition
Einschaler m univalve *(palaeontology)*
einschalig univalve
Einschaltung f s. Einlagerung
Einschlag m/**primärer** primary impact *(meteorite)*
~/sekundärer secondary impact *(caused by meteoritic impact)*
Einschlaggeschwindigkeit f impact velocity
Einschlaggrube f hole of impact *(e.g. of a meteorite)*
Einschlagmarke f impact cast *(sediment fabric)*

Einschlagschmelzen n impact melting *(by meteorites)*
Einschlagtrichter m bomb pit *(of volcanic bombs)*
einschließen to enclose, to occlude
Einschluß m inclusion, enclosure, pocket, occlusion
~/endogener cognate (endogenous) inclusion, homoeogene enclave
~/exogener exogenic inclusion, xenolith
~/federartiger flaw *(in jewels)*
~ in Magmatiten enclave
~/kohliger coaly inclusion
~/orientierter oriented inclusion
~/pneumatogener pneumatogene[tic] inclusion
~/pneumatolytisch überprägter pneumatogenous enclave
einschneiden to incise; to take cross bearings
Einschneiden n incision
Einschnitt m cut[ting], notch, trench
~ und Damm m cut and fill
Einschnittherstellung f breaking of ground
Einschnürung f [con]striction *(s.a. Verdrückung)*; tightening, pinch[ing]; narrow
einschrumpfen to shrink
Einschubwiderstand m resistance of yield
Einschwingvorgang m transient response
Einschwingwelle f transient wave
einseitig one-sided, unilateral
Einsenkung f depression, warping down, furrow
einsetzen/wieder to reappear
einsickern to seep, to ooze [out], to soak in (into), to percolate, to infiltrate
Einsickern n seepage, soaking-in, infiltration, percolation, weeping
~ von Wasser water seepage, descent of water
Einsickerungsfaktor m infiltration rate
Einsickerungskapazität f infiltration capacity
einsinken to cave in
Einsinken n **des Bodens** fall of ground
Einsinkweg m yield *(e.g. of props)*
Einsinkwiderstand m resistance to yield
Einspannlager n print of clamping
einsprengen to disseminate, to interstratify; to intersperse
Einsprengling m xenocryst; dissemination, phenocryst, megacryst
einsprenkeln to intersperse
einspritzen to inject
Einspritzung f injection
Einspülung f illuviation
Einstau m filling *(of a reservoir)*
einstellen 1. to adjust; 2. to abandon, to suspend
~/eine Bohrung to abandon a well
~/vorübergehend to shut down temporarily
Einstellung f 1. adjustment; 2. suspension
~ des Grubenbetriebs suspension of mine work

Einstellwinkel 82

Einstellwinkel *m* **des Ablenkelements** angle of setting of the whipstock
Einstoffsystem *n* one-phase system
Einstrich *m* bunton, barring, divider
einströmen to stream in, to flow in, to run in, to ingress
Einströmen *n* instreaming, incursion, inpouring, inrush
Einstufung *f* classification
Einsturz *m* cave[-in], falling-in, collapse, breaking-down, sinking, foundering
~ **der Bohrlochwandung** walls caving
~ **des Grubengebäudes** general collapse
Einsturzbeben *n* subsidence earthquake, earthquake due to collapse
Einsturzbecken *n* subsidence basin
Einsturzbrekzie *f* collapse (transformational) breccia
Einsturzdoline *f* collapse dolina (sink)
einstürzen to cave [in], to fall in, to collapse, to break down
Einsturzform *f*/**vulkanotektonische** volcano-tectonic subsidence structure
Einsturzkaldera *f* sunken (collapse) caldera, volcanic sink
Einsturzkessel *m* pit crater
~/**vulkanischer** caldera
Einsturzkrater *m* inbreak (pit) crater
Einsturzschlot *m* light hole
Einsturzsee *m* cave-in lake
Einsturzstruktur *f* gull
Einsturztal *n* collapse valley
Einsturztrichter *m* sink (leach) hole
Eintauchbeanspruchung *f* reentry stress
Eintauchen *n* dipping; submersion, immersion; reentry
~ **eines Erzkörpers** plunge of an ore body
~ **in die Atmosphäre** atmospheric entry
Eintauchtiefe *f* submergence
einteilen to classify, to assort
Einteilung *f* classification, assorting
~ **der Gesteine** classification of rocks
Einteilungsgrundlage *f* basis of classification
Eintiefung *f* deepening
Eintiefungsbecken *n*/**glaziales** glacial trough
eintragen to plot *(measuring data)*
~/**auf eine Karte** to chart
Eintragen *n* plotting *(of measuring data)*
Eintrittskorridor *m* entry corridor
Eintrittsverlust *m* entrance loss *(of ground water into a well)*
eintrocknen to dry up, to desiccate
Ein- und Ausbau *m* round trip *(of the track)*
Einvisieren *n* boning-in
Einwälzstruktur *f* convolute bedding
einwandern to immigrate
Einwanderung *f* immigration, entrainment
einwertig monovalent
Einwirkung *f* agency
Einwirkungsbereich *m* [zone of] affected overburden
Einwirkungsfläche *f* area of extraction; area of settlement

Einwirkungsschwerpunkt *m* focal point of subsidence
Einwirkungszeit *f* exposure time *(radiation)*
Einzelberg *m* island mount, outlier, butte
Einzelbohrung *f* individual borehole
Einzelgipfel *m* solitary peak
Einzelhorizont *m* individual horizon
Einzelinsel *f* solitary island
Einzelkoralle *f* solitary coral
Einzelkornstruktur *f* single-grain structure *(of the soil)*
Einzelkornverband/mit diskretem aggregal
~/**ohne diskreten** integral
Einzelkristall *m* individual crystal
Einzellast *f* concentrated (point) load
Einzeller *m* single-celled animal, protozoon
einzellig unicellular
Einzelprobe *f* random (change) sample, sample increment
Einzelrücken *mpl* incomplete (isolated) ripples
Einzelsonde *f* single well
Einzelvulkan *m* solitary volcano
Einziehschacht *m* intake shaft
Einzugsgebiet *n* drainage (catchment, recharge) area, river (drainage) basin; gathering (catchment, feeding) ground
~/**abflußloses** endorheic drainage area
~ **eines Grundwasserleiters** catchment area of an aquifer
~ **eines Sees** lake drainage area
~/**oberirdisches** topographical catchment area
~/**unterirdisches** subsurface catchment area
Einzugsgebietsprognose *f* river basin forecasting
Einzugsradius *m* radius of external boundary
Eis *n* ice
~/**aufgefaltetes** ridged ice
~/**fossiles** fossil (perennial, stone, dead) ice
~ **in Blöcken** block ice
~/**schneefreies** bare ice
~/**schwimmendes** floating ice
~/**verwittertes** weathered ice
Eisabscheuerung *f* ice (glacial) marking, ice (glacial) scouring, ice (glacial) wear
Eisanhäufung *f* ice accumulation
eisartig icy
Eisaufbruch *m* ice boom, debacle
Eisband *n* ice strip
Eisbank *f* patch
Eisbarr[ier]e *f* ice barrier (dam, gorge)
Eisberg *m* [ice]berg
~/**schwimmender** floe berg
Eisbergstück *n* bergy bit
Eisbewegung *f* motion of the ice
~ **im Gletscher** glacier (glacial) flow
Eisbildung *f* ice formation
Eisblumen *fpl* ice flowers (fern), window frost
Eisboden *m* frozen soil
Eisbrei *m* frazil [ice]
Eisdamm *m* *s.* Eisbarre
Eisdecke *f* ice cap (sheet); ice crust; ice cover *(of a lake)*

Eisdickenmessung f/**seismische** ice seismics
Eisdrift f ice (glacial) drift
Eisdruck m ice (glacial) push, ice (glacial) shove, ice (glacial) thrust, ice (glacial) crowding
Eisen n iron, ferrum, Fe
~/gediegenes native iron
Eisenalaun m s. Halotrichit
eisenartig ironlike
Eisenbakterien fpl iron[-depositing] bacteria
Eisenblauerde f earthy vivianite (s.a. Vivianit)
Eisenblüte f flower of iron, flos ferri (variety of aragonite)
Eisendihydroxid n ferrous hydroxide
Eisenerde f ferruginous earth
Eisenerz n iron ore
~/itabiritisches itabiritic iron ore
~/mulmiges friable iron ore
~/oolithisches oolitic iron ore
~/phosphorhaltiges phosphatic iron ore
~/stalaktitförmiges brush ore
Eisenerzgang m iron-ore lode
Eisenerzlager n iron-ore deposit
eisenfleckig iron-stained
Eisenformation f iron formation
Eisengestein n ferrolite
Eisenglanz m iron glance, specular iron [ore], [specular] haematite, specularite, Fe_2O_3
Eisenglimmer m iron mica, micaceous haematite (iron ore) (s.a. Haematit)
Eisenglimmerschiefer m ferruginous schist, itabirite, itabyryte
Eisengneis m iron gneiss
Eisengranat m/**brauner** allochroite, andradite, $Ca_3Fe_2[SiO_4]_3$
eisenhaltig 1. iron-bearing, irony, ferreous, ferriferous, ferrugin[e]ous; 2. ferrous (of bivalent iron); 3. ferric (of trivalent iron); 4. chalybeate (water)
Eisenhumusortstein m iron-humus ortstein (pan)
Eisenhut m capping of gossan
Eisenhydroxid n iron hydroxide
Eisen(II)-hydroxid n ferrous hydroxide
Eisen(III)-hydroxid n ferric hydroxide
Eisenhydroxidausfällungszone f ferreto zone (in drainage areas)
Eisenhydroxidkonkretion f/**hohle** aetite
Eisenhydroxidüberzug m iron hydroxide coating
Eisenjaspilit m ferruginous chert, banded ironstone
Eisenkalkstein m ferruginous limestone
Eisen(II)-karbonat n ferrous carbonate
Eisen(III)-karbonat n ferricarbonate
Eisenkarbonat n/**konkretionäres** ball iron-stone, ball mine
Eisenkies m [iron] pyrite, FeS_2
Eisenkiesel m ferriferous (ferruginous) quartz, ferruginous chert, sinople
Eisenkobaltkies m s. Safflorit
Eisenkonglomerat n ferruginous conglomerate

Eisenkonkretion f iron concretion
Eisenkruste f iron crust
Eisenlagerstätte f/**abbauwürdige** ferruginous deposit
Eisenlebererz n hepatic iron ore
eisen-magnesiumreich iron-magnesium rich
Eisenmagnesiumsilikat n ferromagnesian silicate
Eisenmangan n ferromanganese
Eisenmanganerz n iron manganese ore
Eisenmangankonkretion f iron and manganese concretion
Eisenmeteorit m iron meteorite, meteoric iron, [aero]siderite; holosiderite (without stony matter)
Eisenmohr m s. Eisenmulm
Eisenmonoxid n ferrous oxide
Eisenmulm m earthy [magnetic] iron ore, efflorescing clayey iron ore, earthy limonite
Eisennickelkern m iron nickel core (of earth)
Eisennickelkies m iron nickel pyrite, pentlandite, $(Fe,Ni)_9S_8$
Eisenniere f eaglestone
Eisenocker m iron ochre, ochreous iron ore
~/roter red ochre
Eisenoolith m iron oolite
Eisenoxidhaut f iron-oxide coat
Eisenpecherz n partly stilpnosiderite, partly triplite
Eisenphosphat n phosphate of iron
Eisenpisolit m pisiform (pisolitic) iron ore
Eisenquelle f ferruginous spring; chalybeate spring
Eisenrahm m porous haematite
Eisenrose f haematite rose
Eisen(II)-salz n ferrous salt
Eisen(III)-salz n ferric salt
Eisensandstein m iron (ferruginous) sandstone
Eisensäuerling m chalybeate spring
eisenschüssig ferrous, ferriferous, ferruginous, callen
Eisenschwärze f s. Eisenmulm
Eisensilikaterz n iron silicate ore
Eisensinter m iron dross
Eisenspat m siderite, steel ore, $FeCO_3$
Eisenstein n iron-stone (usual for post-Precambrian Fe-deposits)
Eisensteinbildung f ferruginization (in the soil)
Eisensulfat n ferrous sulphate
Eisentongranat m s. Almandin
Eisentrümmerlagerstätte f clastic iron-ore deposit
Eisenturmalin m black tourmaline, schorl, $NaFe_3Al_6[(OH)|(BO_3)_3|Si_6O_{18}]$
eisenummantelt iron-clad
Eisenverwitterungslagerstätte f iron deposit due to weathering
Eisenvitriol n green vitriol, [green] copperas, melanterite, $FeSO_4 \cdot 7H_2O$
Eisenwolframat n iron tungstate
Eisenzinkblende f marmatite
Eisenzinkspat m ferruginous calamine

Eiserosionssee 84

Eiserosionssee *m* ice-erosion lake
Eisfeld *n* ice field, ice (glacier) cap
~/schwimmendes [sea] floe
Eisfläche *f* ice veneer
eisfrei ice-free
Eisfront *f* ice front
Eisgang *m* ice motion (drift, boom), [spring] break of ice, embacle
eisgefältelt ice-crumpled
eisgeformt ice-shaped, crystic
eisgeglättet ice-smoothed
eisgeschrammt ice-scratched, ice-worn, scratched (channelled, abraded) by ice, glacially striated
eisgestaucht ice-crumpled
Eisgrenze *f* glacial limit
Eishöhle *f* ice cave
Eishügel *m* hummock
eisig icy
Eisisostasie *f* glacial isostasy
Eiskälte *f* frostiness
Eiskaskade *f* ice cascade
Eiskegel *m* ice cone
Eiskeil *m* ice wedge (vein), fissure caused by frost
Eiskeller *m* ice cave
Eiskern *m* ice core
Eiskliff *n* ice (glacier) cliff
Eisklüftigkeit *f* splitting by frost
Eiskrachen *n* ice quake
Eiskristall *m* ice crystal
Eiskristallmarken *fpl* ice crystal marks
Eiskruste *f* ice (glacial) crust
Eiskügelchen *n* pellet of ice
Eislakkolith *m* hydrolaccolith
Eislast *f* ice load
Eislawine *f* ice avalanche
Eislinie *f* ice line
Eislinse *f* ice lens
Eismeer *n* polar sea
~/Nördliches Arctic Ocean
~/Südliches Antarctic Ocean
Eismusterboden *m* patterned ground
Eisnadel *f* ice needle (spicule); ice crystal
Eisnebel *m* ice fog
Eisplateau *n* ice plateau
Eispressung *f* ice push (thrust, shove)
Eispunkt *m* freezing point
Eisrand *m* ice edge (margin, border)
Eisrandlagen *fpl* ice-marginal grounds
Eisrandtal *n* ice-marginal valley
Eisregen *m* ice rain
Eisrest *m* ice remnant
Eisrücken *m* ice ridge
Eisrückzug *m* ice recession (retreat)
Eisscheide *f* ice divide (shed)
Eisschicht *f* ice layer (cap, sheet), glacier cap
Eisschild *m*/**antarktischer** antarctic ice sheet
Eisscholle *f* block (sheet) of ice, ice cake (floe), pancake ice
Eisschollen *fpl*/**aufgetürmte** floeberg
Eisschrumpfung *f* glacial shrinkage

Eisschub *m* ice thrust (shove)
Eissee *m* lakelet
Eisspat *m* ice spar (*s.a.* Sanidin)
Eisstau *m* ice dam
Eisstausee *m* glacial (ice-dammed, ice-ponded, glacially impounded) lake
~/Baltischer Baltic ice-dammed lake
Eisstauung *f* ice jam
Eisstein *m* *s.* Kryolith
Eisstoß *m* ice push (jam)
Eisstrom *m* ice stream
Eisstück *n*/**in Wasser treibendes** growler
Eissturz *m* icefall
Eistätigkeit *f* ice action (agency)
Eistreiben *n* drift[ing] of ice
Eistrift *f* ice drift
eisüberzogen ice-coated, ice-glazed
Eisüberzug *m* ice sheathing
eisverfrachtet ice-carried, ice-transported, ice-floated, ice-rafted, glacial-borne, glacially transported, conveyed by ice
Eisvorstoß *m* ice advance
Eiswall *m* ice rampart
Eiswolke *f* ice cloud
Eiswüste *f* ice waste
Eiszapfen *m* ice needle, icicle
Eiszeit *f* diluvium, ice age, ice (diluvial, glacial, drift) period, glacial epoch (time)
Eiszeitalter *n* *s.* Eiszeit
eiszeitlich glacial, glacic
Eiszunge *f* glacial lobe, tongue of ice
eiweißhaltig albuminous
eiweißlos exalbuminous
Eiweißstoff *m* albuminoid
Ejektion *f* ejective fold
Ekdemit *m* ekdemite, ecdemite, $Pb_3AsO_{<4}Cl_{<2}$
Ekliptik *f* ecliptic
Ekliptikkoordinaten *fpl* ecliptic coordinates
ekliptisch ecliptic[al]
Eklogit *m* eclogite *(metamorphic rock)*
Eklogitfazies *f* eclogite facies
Eklogitschale *f* eclogite shell
Eläolith *m* el[a]eolite, nepheline, nephelite, $KNa_3[AlSiO_4]_4$
Eläolithsyenit *m* eleolite (nepheline) syenite
Elasmobranchier *mpl* elasmobranchs
Elasmosaurier *m* elasmosaur
elastisch elastic
Elastizität *f* elasticity
Elastizitätsgrenze *f* elastic limit
Elastizitätsmodul *m* Young's modulus [of elasticity], incompressibility modulus
Elastizitätstensor *m* tensor of elasticity
Elaterit *m* elaterite, mineral caoutchouc, elastic bitumen (mineral pitch)
Elbait *m* elbaite *(variety of tourmaline)*
Elbrussit *m* elbrussite *(variety of beidellite)*
Elektrobohren *n* electrodrilling
Elektrobohrer *m*, **Elektrobohrgerät** *n* electrodrill
Elektrode *f*/**unpolarisierbare** porous pot
~/versenkte buried electrode

Elektrodenanordnung f/**Wennersche** Wenner electrode array
elektromagnetisch electromagnetic
Elektronegativität f electronegativity
Elektronegativitätsdifferenz f electronegativity difference
Elektronenaffinität f electron affinity
Elektronendichte f electron density
Elektronengas n electron gas
Elektronenhülle f electron shell
Elektronenkonfiguration f electronic configuration
Elektronenleitfähigkeit f metallic conductivity
Elektronenmikroskopie f electron microscopy
Elektronenmikrosonde f electromicroprobe, electronic microprobe
Elektronenpaar n pair of electrons
Elektronensonde f electron probe
Elektronenspin-Resonanzspektren npl electron spin resonance spectra
Elektronenstrahlmagnetometer n electron beam magnetometer
Elektronenstrahlmikroanalyse f electromicroprobe analysis
Elektronenzahl f electron number
elektrovalent electrovalent
Elektrum n electrum *(Ag-bearing Au)*
Element n element
~/allgegenwärtiges ubiquitous element
~/atmophiles atmophilic element
~/chalkophiles chalcophilic element
~/chemisches chemical element
~/durchlaufendes ubiquitous element
~/gesondertes discrete element
~/giftiges toxic element
~/inkompatibles incompatible element
~/kompatibles compatible element
~/lithophiles lithophile element
~/radioaktives radioactive element
~/reflektierendes coverage
~/spaltbares fissile element
~/thalassophiles thalassophile element
~/thalassoxenes thalassoxene element
~/toxisches toxic element
Elementaranalyse f ultimate analysis
Elementarkristallzelle f elementary crystal cell
Elementarzelle f elementary cell; unit cell *(of a crystal structure)*
Elementbestimmung f/**quantitative** quantitative determination of elements
Elemententstehung f origin (genesis) of elements
Elementgeochemie f element geochemistry
Elementmigration f element migration
Elementparagenese f paragenesis of elements
Elementsonderung f sorting of elements
Elementverhältnis n element ratio
Elementverteilung f element distribution, partitioning [of elements]
~ im geochemischen Kreislauf dispersal pattern
Elevation f elevation

Elevationsachse f axis of elevation
Elevationstheorie f elevation theory
Elfenbein n/**fossiles** fossil ivory
Ellestadit m ellestadite, $Ca_5[OH|(SiO_4,SO_4)_3]$
Ellipse f/**parallaktische** parallactic ellipse
Ellipsoid n/**Fresnelsches** Fresnel's ellipsoid
ellipsoidisch ellipsoidal
elliptisch elliptic[al]
Ellsworthit m ellsworthite *(uranopyrochlore)*
Elmsfeuer n [Saint] Elmo's fire, brush discharge
Elpasolith m elpasolite, $K_2Na[AlF_6]$
Elpidit m elpidite, $Na_2Zr[Si_6O_{15}] \cdot 3H_2O$
Elster-Eiszeit f, **Elster-Kaltzeit** f Elsterian [Drift] *(Pleistocene in Northwest Europe)*
eluvial eluvial, residual, residuary
Eluvialboden m eluvium
Eluvialhorizont m eluvial horizon
Eluvium n eluvium
Emanation f emanation
Emanometrie f emanometry
Embolit m embolite, $Ag(Br,Cl)$
Embrechit m embrechite *(migmatic rock)*
Embryonalfalten fpl embryonic (incipient) folds
Embryonalfaltung f embryonic (incipient) folding
Embryonalform f incipient form *(of crystals)*
Embryonalkammer f initial shell, protoconch
Embryonaltyp m embryonic type
Emergenzwinkel m emergence angle
emers emersed *(parts of plants)*
Emersionsfläche f emersion plane, stratigraphic unconformity
Emission f emission
Emissionsspektralanalyse f emission spectrum analysis
Emissionsspektrum n emission (bright-line) spectrum
Emissionsvermögen n emissivity
~/spektrales spectral emissivity
emittieren to emit
emittierend emissive
Emmonsit m emmonsite, durderite, $Fe_2[TeO_3]_3 \cdot 2H_2O$
Empfänger m receiver, detector
Empfängereichung f receiver calibration
Empfangsanzeige f acknowledgement of receipt *(e.g. of seismical waves)*
Empfangsstation f/**bodengebundene** ground receiving station
Empfindlichkeit f sensitivity
Emplektit m emplectite, $Cu_2S \cdot Bi_2S_3$
emporheben to elevate
emporquellen to well up
Emporquellen n upwelling
Emportauchen n emergence *(of land)*
Empressit m empressite, AgTe
Ems n s. Emsien
Emscher n Emscherian *(Coniacian to Middle Santonian in Northwest Germany)*
Emsien n, **Emsium** n Emsian [Stage] *(of Devonian)*

Emulgierbarkeit

Emulgierbarkeit *f* emulsibility
emulgieren to emulsify
emulgierend emulsive
Emulgierung *f* emulsification
Emulsifrac *n* emulsifracturing *(drilling)*
Emulsion *f* emulsion
emulsionsbildend emulsive
Emulsionsbildner *m* emulsifier
Emulsionsbildung *f* emulsification
Emulsionskolloid *n* emulsoid
Emulsionsspülung *f* emulsion mud
Emulsionswasser *n* emulsified water
enantiomorph enantiomorphous, enantiomorphic, dissymmetric[al]
Enantiomorph *m* enantiomorph
Enantiomorphismus *m* enantiomorphism, dissymmetry
Enantiotropie *f* enantiotropy
enantiotropisch enantiotropic
Enargit *m* enargite, Cu_3AsS_4
Encrinit *m* encrinite *(limestone with more than 50% relicts of crinoids)*
Endablagerung *f* terminal deposit
Endabsenkung *f* final subsidence
Endbohrdurchmesser *m* final diameter of drilling
Endboje *f* tail buoy *(sea seismics)*
Enddruck *m* final (terminal) pressure
Enddurchmesser *m* final diameter of drilling
Endeffekt *m* 1. boundary effect *(reservoir technics)*; 2. end effect
Endellit *m s.* Halloysit
endemisch endemic
Enderbit *m* enderbite *(rock in granulitic facies)*
Endfläche *f* end face, pinacoid[al] plane, base *(of a crystal)*
Endform *f* final form
endigen/fingerförmig to finger out, to feather [out]
Endlauge *f* final brine
Endmoräne *f* end (terminal, border, stadial, submarginal) moraine
Endmoränengürtel *m* boulder belt
Endmoränenlandschaft *f* morainic-belt topography
Endoblastese *f* endoblastesis
endogen endogenous, endogen[et]ic, endogen, internal
endokinetisch endokinetic
endolithisch endolithic
endomorph endomorphic
Endomorphose *f* endomorphism
endostratisch endostratigraphic
endotherm endothermic, endoergic
Endphase *f* end portion, tail
Endproduktion *f* tail production
Endpunkt *m* terminal
Endschließdruck final shut-in pressure
Endsee *m* lake without outflow (outlet), desert lake
Endstadium *n* ultimate stage

endständig terminal
Endteufe *f* final (total) depth
Endwiderstand *m* terminal resistance
Energetik *f* **der Kristalle** energetics of crystals
Energie *f/* **kosmische** cosmic energy
Energieart *f* kind of energy
Energiegewinn *m* energy gain
Energiegewinnung *f/* **geothermische** geothermal recovery *(of energy)*
Energiehaushalt *m* energy budget
Energiehöhe *f* head
Energiekoeffizient *m* energy coefficient
Energielinie *f* energy grade line
Energiequelle *f* energy source
Energiespektrum *n* energy spectrum; power spectrum
Energieverlust *m* energy loss
engaufgerollt closely coiled, close-coiled *(palaeontology)*
Enge *f* narrow
Englishit *m* englishite, $K_2Ca_4Al_8[(OH)_{10}|(PO_4)_8] \cdot 9H_2O$
Engpaß *m* narrow pass, narrows, gorge, defile
Engständigkeit *f* **der Schichtung** narrowness of bedding
engverschlungen interlacing
Enhydros *m* enhydros
Enstatit *m* enstatite, $Mg_2[Si_2O_6]$
Entalkalisierung *f* dealkalization
entarten to degenerate
Entartung *f* degeneration, degeneracy
entblößen to lay bare
entblößt bare
entdecken to detect; to discover
~/eine Lagerstätte to discover a deposit
Entdeckung *f* detection; discovery
~ einer Struktur structure discovery
entdolomitisieren to dedolomitize
Entdolomitisierung *f* dedolomitization
Entemulgierungsmittel *n* demulsifying chemical
entfärben to decolourize
Entfärbung *f* decolourizing; bleaching; weather stain
entfernen to remove, to clear
~/Mutterboden to clear off surface soil
Entfernung *f* 1. removal; disposal; 2. distance
~ des Salzwassers disposal of brine
~ von der Erde distance from earth
Entfernungsmesser *m* range finder
Entfernungsmessung *f* distance measurement
Entfernungsunbestimmtheit *f* range ambiguity *(e.g. of a sidelooking radar in hilly or mountainous terrain)*
Entfestigung *f* destrengthening, deconsolidation, disintegration
entflocken to deflocculate
Entflockung *f* deflocculation
entgasen to degasify, to degas
Entgaser *m* degasifier
Entgasung *f* degasifying, degasification, degass-

ing, outgassing; gas escape (extraction); devolatilization *(coal-forming process);* gas emission, methane drainage
Entgasungsbeben *npl* degassing tremors
Entgasungsbeginn *m* bubble point
~ **von Erdöl in der Lagerstätte** bubble point of crude
Entgasungskanal *m* air heave structure *(in sediments)*
Entgasungskegel *m* blister cone
Entgasungsprozeß *m* degassing phenomenon
Entgasungsspur *f* air heave structure *(in sediments)*
entgiften to decontaminate
Entgiftung *f* decontamination
entglasen to devitrify
Entglasung *f* devitrification
entgletschert *(Am)* deglaciated
Entgletscherung *f* deglacierization, *(Am)* deglaciation
Enthalpie *f* enthalpy
enthärten to soften
Enthärtung *f* softening
Enthärtungsmittel *n* softener
enthaupten to capture, to behead, to decapitate
Enthauptung *f* capture, beheading, decapitation; piracy
entkalken to delime, to decalcify
Entkalken *n* deliming, decalcification
entkappen *s.* enthaupten
entkieseln to desilicify, to desilicate
Entkieselung *f* desilication
Entladung *f/elektrische* electrical discharge
entlasten to unload, to relieve of load; to lighten; to release; to relax
Entlastung *f* unloading, relief (reduction) of load; release; relaxation
Entlastungsbrunnen *m* relief (bleeder) well
Entlastungsgebiet *n* discharge area *(water)*
Entlastungskluft *f* release joint
Entlastungskoeffizient *m* coefficient of discharge
Entlastungsmethode *f* relaxation method
Entlastungsstollen *m* discharge tunnel (outlet)
entleeren to empty; to deplete; to evacuate
entlösen to come out of solution
Entlösung *f/plötzliche* flush eliberation *(e.g. gas from oil)*
Entlösungstrieb *m* dissolved-gas drive
entmagnetisieren to demagnetize
Entmagnetisierung *f* demagnetization, degaussing
~**/thermische** thermal demagnetization
entmischen to segregate, to differentiate; to unmix, to exsolve
Entmischung *f* segregation, differentiation; unmixing, exsolution
~**/liquide** liquation
~**/myrmekitische** myrmekitic exsolution
~**/orientierte** oriented exsolution
Entmischungslamellen *fpl* exsolution lamellae

Entmischungsminerale *npl* exsolution minerals
Entmischungssegregation *f* segregation due to unmixing
Entmischungsspindeln *fpl* clusters of exsolution
Entmischungsstruktur *f* unmixing texture
Entnahme *f* **von Erdöl (Gas)** product withdrawal *(from the deposit)*
~ **von Proben** sampling
Entnahmeboden *m* borrow soil
Entnahmegrube *f* borrow pit
Entnahmematerial *n* borrow excavation material
Entnahmemenge *f/zulässige* safe yield
Entnahmestelle *f* borrow source; point of withdrawal
Entnahmeteufe *f* sampling depth *(of the rock material)*
Entnahmetrichter *m* cone of depression
Entölung *f* oil recovery, sweep-out; drainage *(in hydrocarbon deposits)*
~ **infolge Schwerkraft** gravity drainage (depletion)
~**/tertiäre** tertiary oil recovery
~**/thermale** thermal oil recovery
Entölungsgrad *m* drainage-recovery factor *(in hydrocarbon deposits)*
Entpolderung *f* depoldering
entregeln to deorient
Entregelung *f* deorientation
entrohren to pull
Entropie *f* entropy
entsalzen to desalinify, to desalt, to desalinate; to freshen
Entsalzung *f* desalting, desalination, desalinization, desalinification, salt removal; freshening
Entsander *m* desander *(drilling engineering)*
entsäuern to deacidify
Entsäuerung *f* deacidification
Entschäumer *m* defoamer, antifoaming agent
entschlammen to desilt
entschlämmen to elutriate
Entschlammung *f* desilting
Entschlämmung *f* elutriation
Entschlüsseln *n* decoding
entschwefeln to desulphurate, to desulphurize
Entschwefelung *f* desulphur[iz]ation
Entschwefelungsanlage *f* desulphur[iz]ation unit
Entsilifizierung *f* desilification
entspannen to relieve, to relax, to unload
Entspannung *f* relief, relaxation, unloading
Entspannungskluft *f* relaxation joint, extension strain fracture
Entspannungssprengen *n* stress-relief blasting
Entstehung *f* origin; genesis; generation
~ **der Elemente** origin (genesis) of elements
~ **der Kontinente** continental origin
~ **der Landformen** glyptogenesis
~**/kosmische** cosmic origin

Entstehung

~/**polygene** polygenic origin
Entstehungsart f mode of origin
Entstehungsort m seat of generation
Entstehungszentrum n centre of origin
Entwaldung f deforestation
entwässern to dewater, to unwater, to drain, to sewer, to reclaim; to dehydrate
Entwässerung f dewatering, unwatering, draining, drainage, sewerage, reclamation; dehydration
~ **durch Elektroosmose** electrical drainage
~/**unterirdische** underground drainage, drainage by closed canals
Entwässerungsanlagen fpl drainage works (in open-cast-mines)
Entwässerungsgebiet n drain[age] district, drainage (catchment) area
Entwässerungsgraben m drainage ditch (trench), [catch] drain, culvert
Entwässerungshang m drainage slope
Entwässerungsnetz n drainage pattern (network, system); channel net (of a catchment area)
Entwässerungsrelief n drainage relief
Entwässerungsschacht m drainage shaft
Entwässerungsscheide f drainage divide
Entwässerungsschicht f pervious blanket
Entwässerungsstollen m culvert
Entwässerungsstreckennetz n dewatering roadway system
Entwässerungssystem n/**spalierartiges** trellised drainage
~/**unvollkommenes** aimless drainage
Entwässerungsteppich m drainage blanket
Entwässerungstrichter m drainage funnel
Entwässerungsverfahren n dewatering method, sewerage system
Entwässerungsweg m drainage path
Entwässerungszeit f drainage time
entweichen to escape
Entweichen n escape
~ **der flüchtigen Bestandteile** escape of the volatile constituents
Entweichgeschwindigkeit f escape velocity
entwickeln to develop (e.g. an oil field)
entwickelt/unvollkommen abortive, barren
Entwicklung f development (e.g. of an oil field); evolution (of species)
~/**epikontinentale** epicontinental development
~/**erdgeschichtliche** geological development
~/**kontinentale** continental development
~/**marin-geosynklinale** marine geosyncline development
~/**progressive** anagenesis
~/**regressive** katagenesis
Entwicklungsfortschritt m evolutionary progress
Entwicklungsgang m evolving (evolutionary) course, procedure of evolution
Entwicklungsgeschichte f evolutional (evolutionary, developmental) history, evolutional (evolutionary) record, chronogenesis
Entwicklungskurve f development curve

Entwicklungslehre f evolutionism, evolutionary doctrine
Entwicklungslinie f evolutional (genetic) line, line of evolution (development, ascent)
Entwicklungsreihe f evolutionary (developmental) series, lineage
Entwicklungsrichtung f evolutionary trend, trend of evolution
Entwicklungssprung m evolutionary spurt
Entwicklungsstadium n evolutionary (developmental) stage, stage of development (evolution)
~/**geosynklinales** geosynclinal stage of development
~/**orogenes** orogenic stage of development
Entwicklungsvorgang m evolutionary process
Entwicklungszyklus m cycle of development
entzerren to rectify; to reestablish (air photos)
Entzerrer m antidistortion device
Entzerrung f distortion correction
~/**fotogrammetrische** photogrammetric rectification
~/**kartografische** cartographic rectification
Entzerrungsgerät n rectifier, rectifying apparatus
entziehen 1. to extract; 2. to abstract (well)
~/**Feuchtigkeit** to dehumidify
Entziehung f 1. extraction; 2. abstraction
entzündbar inflammable, combustible
~/**leicht** easily catching (set on) fire
Entzündbarkeit f inflammability
Eobionten npl eobionts, dawn organisms
Eokambrium n Eocambrium [Period]
Eolith m eolith (primitive artefact)
Eosit m eosite (V-bearing wulfenite)
Eosphorit m eosphorite, (Mn, Fe)Al[(OH)$_2$|PO$_4$] · H$_2$O
Eötvös-Einheit f Eötvös unit (incoherent unit of the gradient of acceleration in geodesy; 1 E = 1 mGal/10km)
eozän Eocene
Eozän n Eocene [Series, Epoch] (Tertiary)
Eozoikum n s. Proterozoikum
eozoisch s. proterozoisch
Epeirogenese f ep[e]irogenesis, epirogeny
Epeirophorese f epeirophoresis (continental drift)
Ephemeride f ephemerid
Ephesit m ephesite, (Na, Ca)Al$_2$[(OH)$_2$|Al(Al, Si)Si$_2$O$_{10}$]
Epidermisstruktur f epidermal structure
Epididymit m epididymite, NaBe[OH|Si$_3$O$_7$]
Epidiorit m epidiorite (ortho-amphibolite)
Epidosit m epidosite (calc silicate rock)
Epidot m epidote, pistacite, Ca$_2$(Fe, Al)Al$_2$[O|OH|SiO$_4$|Si$_2$O$_7$]
Epidot-Amphibolit-Fazies f epidote-amphibolite facies
Epidotfels m s. Epidosit
epidotisieren to epidotize
Epidotisierung f epidotization
Epidot-Mandel-Metabasalt m epidotic amygdular metabasalt

Erdboden

Epieugeosynklinale f epieugeosyncline
Epifauna f epifauna
epigeantiklinal epigeanticlinal
Epigenese f epigenesis
epigenetisch epigenetic, xenogenous
Epigestein n epirock
Epiglyphe f epiglyph *(hieroglyph at the surface of stratum)*
Epiianthinit m epiianthinite, $[UO_2|(OH)_2] \cdot H_2O$
epiklastisch epiclastic
epikontinental epicontinental
Epikontinentalmeer n epicontinental (epeiric) sea
Epimagma n epimagma
epimagmatisch epimagmatic
epineritisch epineritic
epipaläozoisch epipalaeozoic
Epiphyse f epiphysis
epiphytisch epiphytic
epirogen ep[e]irogenic
Epirogenese f ep[e]irogeny
epirogenetisch ep[e]irogenic
Epirokratie f s. Geokratie
Epistilbit m epistilbite, $Ca[Al_2Si_6O_{16}] \cdot 5H_2O$
Epistolit m epistolite, (Na, Ca)(Nb, Ti, Mg, Fe, Mn)[OH|SiO_4]
Epitaxie f epitaxy
epithermal epithermal
epivariszisch epivarisc[i]an
Epizentralentfernung f epicentral distance, distance of epicentre
Epizentralgegend f epicentral area
Epizentrum n epicentre, seismic origin
Epizoen npl epizoa
epizonal epizonal
Epizone f epizone
Epoche f epoch *(geochronologic unit)*
~/metallogenetische metallogenic epoch
Epsomit m epsomite $Mg[SO_4] \cdot 7H_2O$
~/nadelförmiger hair salt
Equisetalen fpl Equisetales
erbeben to quake; to vibrate
Erbium n erbium, Er
erbsenförmig pisiform, pisolitic
Erbsenstein m pisiform limestone
Erdabplattung f earth's oblateness (flattening), flattening at the poles
Erdachse f earth's axis, axis of the earth
Erdalkali n alkaline earth
Erdalkalimetall n alkaline earth metal
erdalkalisch alkaline-earth
Erdaltertum n s. Paläozoikum
Erdanker m earth (guy) anchor
Erdanziehung f earth's attraction
Erdäquator m terrestrial (earth's) equator
Erdarbeiten fpl earthworks
Erdasphalt m native (rock) asphalt
Erdatmosphäre f terrestrial atmosphere
Erdaufbau m earth's structure
Erdaufwurf m mound
Erdbahn f terrestrial (earth's) orbit, earth's path, ecliptic

Erdball m mundane ball
Erdbau m earthwork[s]
Erdbaulabor[atorium] n soil testing (mechanics) laboratory, earth materials laboratory
Erdbeben n [earth]quake, shake, *(Am)* temblor (*s.a.* Beben)
~/künstliches artificial earthquake
~/leichtes microseism, earth tremor
~/regionales regional earthquake
~/vulkanisches volcanic earthquake
Erdbebenanzeiger m s. Erdbebenmesser
Erdbebenaufzeichnung f earthquake record
Erdbebenforscher m seismologist
Erdbebenforschung f earthquake research, seismic investigation
erdbebenfrei non-seismic, aseismic[al]
Erdbebengebiet n earthquake area (region), seismic area (district)
Erdbebengefahr f, **Erdbebengefährdung** f earthquake risk (hazard)
Erdbebenhäufigkeit f seismicity
Erdbebenherd m earthquake (seismic) focus, seismic centre, hypocentre
Erdbebenkunde f seismology, seismologic science
Erdbebenmesser m seismometer; seismograph
Erdbebenmessung f seismometry
Erdbebenriß m earthquake fissure
Erdbebenschreiber m seismograph
Erdbebenschwarm m earthquake series, swarm earthquakes
erdbebensicher earthquake-proof, earth-quake-resistant, aseismic[al]
Erdbebenspalte f earthquake rift
Erdbebenstärke f earthquake intensity
Erdbebenstärkeskala f scale of seismic intensity
Erdbebenstation f earthquake observatory, seismic station
Erdbebenstoß m earthquake (seismic) shock
Erdbebentätigkeit f seismic activity
Erdbebentrichter m craterlet
Erdbebenvorhersage f earthquake forecast (prediction)
Erdbebenvorläufer m earthquake precursor
Erdbebenwarte f seismic observatory, seismograph station
Erdbebenwelle f earthquake (earth, seismic) wave
Erdbebenzerstörung f earthquake damage
Erdbebenzone f seismic zone
Erdbeobachtung f geoscopy
Erdbeschleunigung f acceleration due to gravity, force of gravity
Erdbewegung f 1. earth's motion (movement); 2. earth movement, earthmoving
Erdbewegungsarbeiten fpl earthmoving
Erdbildmessung f terrestrial (ground) photogrammetry
Erdbildungslehre f geogony
Erdboden m earth, ground

Erdbodentemperatur 90

Erdbodentemperatur *f* grass temperature
Erdbohrer *m* auger, boring tube
Erdböschung *f* bank
Erdbrandgestein *n* combustion (burnt) rock, baked shale
Erdbrandmetamorphose *f* combustion metamorphism
Erddamm *m* earth[fill] dam
~/gespülter hydraulic fill dam
~/kleiner embankment
Erddrehung *f* earth's rotation
Erddruck *m* earth pressure, thrust of the ground, *(Am)* earth load
~/aktiver (angreifender) active [lateral] earth pressure
~/passiver passive earth pressure
Erddruckkoeffizient *m* coefficient of earth pressure
Erddrucktheorie *f*/**orthodoxe** classical earth pressure theory
Erde *f* 1. earth; 2. earth, ground
~/außerhalb der extraterrestrial
~/Blaue 1. blue ground *(in diamond pipes);* 2. blue earth *(view from the moon)*
~/lemnische Lemnian bole (earth)
~/seltene rare (noble) earth, rare-earth element
Erdelektrizität *f* terrestrial electricity
Erdellipsoid *n* earth ellipsoid
Erde-Mond-System *n* earth-moon system
Erdentstehung *f* earth's origin (genesis), genesis of the earth
Erdentwicklung *f* development of the earth
Erdfall *m* earth subsidence, landfall, collapse sink, sink[hole], deep digging
Erdfeld *n* earth's field
~/magnetisches magnetic field of the earth
Erdferne *f* apogee, distance from the earth
Erdfließen *n* earth flow, soil flow[age], solifluction, solifluxion
Erdfrühzeit *f s.* Proterozoikum
Erdgas *n* natural (rock) gas
~/feuchtes wet natural gas, combination (casing-head) gas
~/freies non-associated natural gas
~/im Öl gelöstes dissolved natural gas
~/saures *s.*~/**schwefelwasserstoffhaltiges**
~/schwefelwasserstofffreies sweet natural gas
~/schwefelwasserstoffhaltiges sour natural gas
~/süßes *s.*~/**schwefelwasserstofffreies**
~/trockenes dry [natural] gas
~/verflüssigtes liquefied natural gas, LNG
Erdgasakkumulation *f* gas pool
Erdgasausbiß *m* gas seepage
Erdgasaustritt *m* emanation (escape) of natural gas
Erdgasbenzin *n* natural gasoline
Erdgasexhalation *f* exhalation of natural gas
Erdgasfeld *n* gas field
Erdgasfund *m* gas discovery
Erdgasgewinnung *f* fluid recovery

Erdgashöffigkeit *f* gas prospectivity
Erdgaslagerstätte *f* gas pool
Erdgasprovinz *f* gas province
Erdgasquelle *f* natural gas well, gusher of natural gas
Erdgasressource *f* gas resource
Erdgasruß *m* carbon black
Erdgassättigung *f* gas saturation
Erdgassonde *f* natural gas well
Erdgasspeicher *m* reservoir of natural gas
Erdgasspuren *fpl* traces of natural gas
Erdgassuche *f* prospecting for gas
Erdgasverarbeitungsanlage *f* gas processing equipment
Erdgasverflüssigungsanlage *f* natural gas liquefaction plant
Erdgasvorkommen *n* deposit of natural gas
Erdgasvorrat *m*/**geologischer** initial gas in place
Erdgeruch *m* earthy smell
Erdgeschichte *f* geologic[al] history, history of the earth
erdgeschichtlich geologic[al]
Erdgestalt *f* shape of the earth
Erdgezeiten *pl* earth's [bodily] tides
Erdglobus *m* [terrestrial] globe
Erdhalbkugel *f* hemisphere
Erdharz *n* fossil resin
Erdhaufen *m* mound
Erdhügel *m* knoll
~/konischer conical mound
erdig earthy, terreous
Erdinduktionskompaß *m* earth-inductor compass, gyrosyne compass
Erdinneres *n* earth's interior
Erdkern *m* centrosphere, core of the earth, central core [of the earth], earth's nucleus (core)
Erdklumpen *m* clod
Erdkobalt *m*[/**schwarzer**] *s.* Kobaltmanganerz
Erdkörper *m* terrestrial body
Erdkrümel *m* soil crumb, topsoil
Erdkrümmung *f* earth's curvature, curvature (bulge) of the earth
Erdkruste *f* terrestrial crust, earth's shell (crust)
Erdkrustendeformation *f* crustal deformation
Erdkugel *f* terrestrial ball (globe, sphere)
Erdkunde *f* geography
Erdleisten *fpl* terracettes
Erdmagnetfeld *n* terrestrial magnetic field
erdmagnetisch geomagnetic, terrestrial-magnetic
Erdmagnetismus *m* geomagnetism, earth's (terrestrial) magnetism
Erdmantel *m* mantle [of the earth]
~/oberer upper mantle [of the earth]
Erdmaterie *f* terrestrial matter
Erdmittelalter *n s.* Mesozoikum
Erdmittelpunkt *m* earth's centre, geocentre
Erdnähe *f* perigee
Erdnaht *f* [earth] suture

Erdneuzeit f s. Känozoikum
Erdoberfläche f earth's surface, terrene
Erdoberflächenformen fpl topographic forms
Erdöl n crude naphtha (oil, petroleum), [mineral] oil; fossil (store, rock) oil
~/asphaltbasisches asphalt-base oil (petroleum)
~ aus Ölschiefer shale naphtha
~/entgastes stock tank oil
~/fließfähiges mobile oil
~ in Küstengewässern offshore oil
~ mit Asphaltbasis naphthene-base oil (petroleum)
~ mit Paraffinbasis paraffin-base oil (petroleum)
~ mit Paraffin- und Asphaltbasis paraffin-asphalt petroleum, mixed base oil (petroleum)
~/naphthenbasisches naphthene-base oil (petroleum)
~/paraffinöses paraffin-base oil (petroleum)
~/rohes crude (base) oil; gauged (piped) oil (after the separation from water)
~/schweres heavy oil, naphtha
~/schweres, rohes heavy (low-gravity) crude oil
~/teilweise emulgiertes cut oil (with gas or air)
Erdölabscheidung f oil separation
Erdölakkumulation f 1. oil accumulation; 2. oil pool (reservoir)
Erdölanreicherung f oil accumulation
Erdölanzeichen n oil indication
Erdölasche f petroleum ash
Erdölasphalt m oil asphalt, asphalt from petroleum oil
Erdölausbeute f recovery of oil
Erdölausbeutung f petroleum exploitation
Erdölausbeutungsrechte npl oil rights
Erdölausbruch m 1. oil-well blowing, wild[-cat] flowing; 2. blowing (wild) well gusher
Erdölaustritt m oil leakage (seepage, seep)
Erdölaustrittsstelle f oil seep
~/tätige active oil seep
Erdölbakterien fpl oil-well microorganisms
Erdölbank f oil bank
Erdölbecken n oil basin
Erdölbergbau m oil mining
Erdölbergwerk n oil mine
erdölbildend oil-forming
Erdölbildung f oleogenesis, formation of petroleum
Erdölbitumen n asphaltic bitumen
Erdölbohranlage f/schwimmende drill[ing] barge, floating derrick
Erdölbohrgerät n oil-well drill
Erdölbohrschiff n oil drilling vessel
Erdölbohrturm m oil derrick
Erdölbohrung f oil well; oil-well drilling
Erdölchemie f petrochemistry
Erdöldepot n tank farm
Erdölderivate npl petrochemicals
erdöldicht oil-proof

Erdölentnahme f oil withdrawal
Erdölentstehung f genesis of oil
Erdölerkundung f prospection for petroleum
Erdölerkundungsgeologie f exploratory geology of petroleum
Erdölexploration f oil finding
Erdölfalle f oil trap
Erdölfeld n oil (petroleum) field
~/küstennahes offshore oil field
~/produktives producing oil field
Erdölfeldgeologie f oil field geology
Erdölfeldleitungssystem n oil-field gathering system
Erdölfernleitung f [oil] pipe line
Erdölfleck m oil stain
erdölfleckig oil-stained
Erdölfluoreszenz f fluorescence of petroleum, bloom
Erdölfördersonde f producer, oil well
Erdölfördertechnik f petroleum production engineering (technology)
Erdölförderung f oil production
erdölfrei oilless
erdölführend petroliferous, oil-bearing, oil-containing
Erdölgas n oil (petroleum) gas
~/freies associated natural gas
Erdölgasteer m oil gas tar
Erdölgebiet n oil region (district); petroliferous area, oil [producing] area
Erdölgenese f petroleogenesis, petroleum genesis
Erdölgeochemie f oil geochemistry
Erdölgeologe m oil (petroleum) geologist
Erdölgeologie f oil (petroleum) geology
Erdölgerechtsame f oil lease (property)
erdölgesättigt oil-saturated
Erdölgewinnung f [mineral] oil extraction; oil (fluid) recovery; petroleum exploitation
~/gesteigerte enhanced oil recovery
Erdölgewinnungsanlage f oil production outfit
Erdölgrube f oil mine
Erdölgürtel m oil belt
erdölhaltig petroliferous, petroleum-bearing, oil-bearing, oily, oleaginous
Erdölhöffigkeit f oil prospectivity
Erdölhoffnungsgebiet n petroleum prospect
Erdölhorizont m petroliferous horizon
Erdölhydrogeologie f oil (petroleum) hydrogeology
Erdölkonzession f oil concession
Erdöllagerstätte f oil field, petroleum deposit; oil pool; oil sheet
~/eingetrocknete inspissated deposit
Erdöllagerstätteningenieur m petroleum reservoir engineer
Erdöllagerstättenwasser npl oil pool waters
Erdölmigration f migration of oil
Erdölmuttergestein n oil source rock (bed)
Erdölpech n petroleum pitch
Erdölprospektion f oil prospecting
Erdölprovinz f petroliferous province

Erdölquelle

Erdölquelle f oil spring (well)
Erdölraffinerie f oil plant
Erdölraffinerieanlage f petroleum refinery plant
Erdölrechte npl oil rights
Erdölreife f oil maturity
Erdölreifestadium n oil maturity stage
Erdölressource f oil resource
Erdölsand m *(Am)* oilsand
Erdölsättigung f oil saturation
Erdölsaum m thin oil column
Erdölschachtbau m oil mining
Erdölschicht f oil-bearing bed
Erdölschlamm m oil sludge
Erdölschrumpfung f oil shrinkage
Erdölsickerstelle f oil seep
Erdölsondenmeßgerät n oil-well surveying instrument
Erdölspeicher m oil reservoir
Erdölspeichergestein n oil reservoir rock
Erdölspuren fpl oil traces
Erdölsuche f oil research, prospecting for oil
Erdölteer m oil tar
erdölundurchlässig oil-proof
Erdölverarbeitung f mineral oil processing
Erdölverdrängung f displacement of oil
Erdölvergasung f oil gasification
Erdölverteilung f distribution of petroleum
Erdölvorkommen n oil occurrence
Erdölvorrat m oil in place
~/geologischer initial oil in place
Erdölvorräte mpl oil reserves
Erdölwasser n mineral oil water
Erdöl-Wasser-Grenze f oil-water surface; oil-water interface
Erdöl-Wasser-Kontakt m oil-water contact
Erdöl-Wasser-Zone f oil-water zone
Erdölwissenschaft f naphthology
Erdölzone f oil zone
Erdölzulauf m oil influx
Erdorgel f sand pipe (gall)
Erdpech n mineral pitch, natural asphalt
~/elastisches elaterite, elastic bitumen, mineral caoutchouc
erdpechhaltig asphaltic
Erdpfeife f s. Erdorgel
Erdpfeiler m earth pillar (column, pyramid), chimney rock
Erdplanum n earth (soil) subgrade, subgrade
~/aufgeschüttetes artificial subgrade
Erdpol m earth's (terrestrial) pole
~/magnetischer earth's (terrestrial) magnetic pole
Erdpyramide f s. Erdpfeiler
Erdradius m radius of the earth
Erdreich n/**durch Regen abgeschwemmtes** rainwash
Erdreservoir n sump hole
Erdrinde f s. Erdkruste
Erdrutsch m landslip, landslide, earth fall
~/kleiner shear slide, [earth] slip
Erdsatellit m earth satellite
~/künstlicher artificial earth satellite
Erdschatten m earth's shadow
Erdschein m earth-shine
Erdschlipf m s. Erdfließen
Erdschüttungsstaudamm m earthwork dam, earth fill dam
Erdschwerefeld n earth's gravitational field
Erdspalt m cleft
Erdsphäre f geosphere
Erdstoß m earth[quake] shock, seism
Erdstrahlungsmesser m pyrgeometer
Erdstreifen mpl soil stripes
Erdstrom m earth (terrestrial, telluric, natural) current
~/natürlicher natural earth current
~/vagabundierender stray earth current
Erdteer m mineral tar, maltha, sea wax
Erdtorf m earthy turf
Erdtrabant m earth satellite
Erdumdrehung f earth rotation
Erdumfang m earth's circumference
Erdumlauf m revolution of earth
Erdumlaufbahn f s. Erdbahn
Erd- und Grundbau m soil engineering
Erdung f grounding
Erdungspunkt m current electrode
Erdvermessung f geodesy; geodetic surveying, topographic survey
Erdvertiefung f bowl
Erdwachs n earth (mineral, ader, fossil) wax, ozocerite, ozokerite, [native] paraffin
Erdwall m mound
Erdwärme f heat (temperature) of the earth, terrestrial (ground) heat
Erdwärmemesser m geothermometer
Erdwiderstand m passive resistance
Erfassungsgrad m **einer Druckaufbaumessung** penetration effect on build-up analysis
erforschen to explore; to prospect
Erforschung f exploring, exploration; prospecting
Erforschungsgrad m stage of exploration
Erg f erg, dune desert *(Sahara)*
Ergänzbarkeit f complementarity *(of data)*
Ergänzungspunkt m fill-in station
Ergänzungszwillinge mpl supplementary twins
ergiebig payable, yielding, productive
Ergiebigkeit f payability, yield[ingness], productiveness
~ der Bohrung capacity of well, well production
~ einer Sonde open-flow delivery
~ eines artesischen Brunnens artesian discharge
~/spezifische specific capacity
Erguß m outflow, outpouring; outwelling; effusion; extrusion
Ergußgestein n effusive (extrusive, volcanic) rock, lava stone
erhalten conserved; preserved *(fossils)*
Erhaltung f conservation, maintenance; preserval, preservation *(of fossils)*

Erhaltungssatz *m* conservation principle
Erhaltungszustand *m* status (mode) of preservation *(of fossils)*
erhärten to harden; to become hardened; to solidify; to congeal
Erhärtung *f* hardening; solidifying; induration; congealing, congelation
Erhärtungsprozeß *m* hardening process; induration process
erheben/sich to upheave
Erhebung *f* 1. rise; elevation; 2. uphill
~/inselartige insular elevation
~/kleine colline
~/rundliche knoll *(of the sea bottom)*
Erhebungstheorie *f s.* Elevationstheorie
Erhöhung *f* elevation; increase
~ der Bodenfruchtbarkeit increase of soil fertility
Erholung *f* recreation *(of crystals)*
Eri *n* Erian *(Devonian series corresponding to Middle Devonian in Europe)*
Ericait *m* ericaite, $(Fe, MG, Mn)_3[Cl|B_7O_{13}]$
Erikit *m* erikite *(monacite pseudomorphous after eudialyte)*
Erinit *m* erinite, cornwallite, $Cu_5[(OH)_2|AsO_4]_2$
Erinnerungsvermögen *n* **von Deformation** memory function of strain
Eriochalcit *m* eriochalcite, $CuCl_2 \cdot 2H_2O$
Erionit *m* erionite, $(K_2, Na_2, Ca)[AlSi_3O_8]_2 \cdot 6H_2O$
Erkaltung *f* cooling-down
Erkennungsverfahren *n* identification method *(of reservoir properties)*
erkunden to explore
Erkunder *m* explorer
Erkundung *f* exploring, exploration; prospecting; reconnaissance; survey
~/biogeochemische biogeochemical exploration (prospecting)
~/eingehende detailed prospecting
~/elektromagnetische electromagnetic prospecting
~/geobotanische geobotanic[al] prospecting
~/geochemische geochemical exploration
~/geothermische geothermal prospecting
~/hydrodynamische hydrodynamic exploration
~/hydrogeochemische hydrogeochemical exploration (prospecting)
~/hydrogeologische hydrogeological exploration
~/luftfotografische aerophotographic reconnaissance
~/seismische seismic (seismograph) prospecting
~ vom Fahrzeug aus car-borne exploration
Erkundungsarbeiten *fpl* exploratory (exploration) work
~/bergmännische exploring mining
~/geologische geologic[al] reconnaissance work

Erkundungsbohren *n* exploratory drilling
Erkundungsbohrung *f* exploratory hole (well)
~ auf höheren Speicher shallower pool test
~ auf tieferen Speicher deeper pool test
~ im unbekannten Bereich wildcat
Erkundungsdaten *pl* exploratory data
Erkundungsergebnis *n* result of exploration
Erkundungsgeologe *m* exploration geologist
Erkundungsgeologie *f* exploration geology
Erkundungsgrad *m* degree of exploration
Erkundungsnetz *n* exploration net
Erkundungsobjekt *n* prospect
Erkundungspraxis *f* practical exploration
Erkundungsprogramm *n* program of exploration
Erkundungsprozeß *m* process of exploration
Erkundungsstadium *n* stage of exploration
Erkundungsstrecke *f* exploratory road
Erkundungswissenschaft *f* science of exploration
Erlan *m* erlane *(calc-silicate rock)*
Erläuterung *f* **eines Aufschlusses** annotation of an outcrop
erloschen extinct
erlöschen to become extinct
Erlöschen *n* extinction
Ermüdungsbruch *m* fatigue failure
Ermüdungsriß *m* fatigue crack
Ernährung *f* **des Gletschers** nourishment of the glacier
Ernährungsgebiet *n* recharge area *(water)*
erniedrigen to lower, to degrade
Erniedrigung *f* lowering
erodierbar erodible
erodieren to erode
erodierend erosive
erodiert/äolisch wind-carved
~/marin sea-worn
~/von den Wellen wave-cut
Erosion *f* erosion *(s.a.* Abtragung*)*
~/äolische wind corrasion
~ durch Regen splash erosion
~/fluviatile fluviatile erosion
~/fortschreitende headward erosion
~/kolkförmige scour and fill
~/marine marine erosin (abrasion)
~/nachträgliche sequential erosion
~/rinnenartige gully erosion, gullying
~/rückschreitende retrogressive (backward) erosion
~/schleichende sliding erosion
~/selektive differential erosion
~/spätere subsequent erosion
~/ungleichmäßige differential erosion
~/unterirdische tunnel erosion
~/untermeerische submarine erosion
~ unverfestigter Sedimente subelevation
~/verdeckte concealed erosion
~/von Porenräumen ausgehende internal erosion
~/wiederholte reerosion
Erosionsanzeichen *n* evidence of erosion

Erosionsbasis

Erosionsbasis *f* erosion [base] level
Erosionsbohren *n* erosion (jetted particle) drilling
Erosionsdiskordanz *f* erosion (stratigraphic, parallel, non-angular) unconformity, erosional disconformity (break)
~/mehrfache composite unconformity of erosion
Erosionsebene *f* erosion plane (plain), plane of denudation
~/tafelförmige panplane
erosionsempfindlich erodible
Erosionsempfindlichkeit *f* erodibility
Erosionsfähigkeit *f* erodibility, erosiveness
~ des Bodens soil erodibility
Erosionsfenster *n* erosional window (fenster)
erosionsfest non-erodible
Erosionsfläche *f* erosion surface
Erosionsfurche *f s.* Erosionsrinne
Erosionsgeschwindigkeit *f* erosional rate, rate of erosion
Erosionsgraben *m* erosion trench (gully)
Erosionsgrad *m* state of being eroded
Erosionshärtling *m/* **abgesunkener** letdown
~/karbonatischer klint
Erosionsintervall *n s.* Erosionslücke
Erosionskar *n* erosion car
Erosionsküste *f/* **ertrunkene glaziale** glacial trough coast
Erosionslücke *f* erosion interval (gap, break)
Erosionsmarke *f* scour mark
Erosionsmulde *f/* **gerippelte** ripple scour
Erosionsnische *f/* **schichtparallele** alcove
Erosionsprodukte *npl* float debris
Erosionsrest *m* erosional outlier (remnant)
~ eines Schuttfächers fan mesa
Erosionsrille *f* erosion groove
Erosionsrinne *f* erosional channel, wash-out, flute, gully; contact-erosion valley
~/kleindimensionale scour and fill
Erosionsrücken *m* denudation ridge
Erosionstal *n* erosion (denudation) valley
Erosionstätigkeit *f* erosional action (activity, work), erosive action (activity, work)
Erosionsterrasse *f* erosional (denudation) terrace
Erosionstopf *m* giant kettle
Erosionsüberschiebung *f s.* Reliefüberschiebung
Erosionsunterbrechung *f s.* Erosionslücke
Erosionsvertaubung *f* **im Flöz** symon fault
Erosionswasserbett *n* erosion stream bed
Erosionswelle *f/* **rückschreitende** wave of retrogressive erosion
Erosionszyklus *m* cycle of erosion, geographical cycle, evolutive stages of erosion
erosiv erosive
erratisch erratic, travelled
erregen to induce
Erregung *f* **des Magnetfelds** field excitation
Ersatz *m* replacement
erschlafft relaxed

Erschlaffung *f* relaxation
erschließen to recover, to develop, to open up
Erschließung *f* recovery, development
Erschließungsarbeit *f* prospecting work
erschöpfen to exhaust, to deplete, to work out
~/sich to pinch out
Erschöpfung *f* exhaustion, depletion, working-out
~ einer Erdölbohrung exhaustion of an oil well
~ eines Feldes exhaustion of a mine
~ von Lagerstätten working-out of deposits
Erschöpfungskurve *f/* **exponentielle** exponential decline curve
~/hyperbolische hyperbolic decline curve
Erschöpfungsspeicher *m* depletion-type reservoir
erschreckend frightening, slight damage *(6th stage of the scale of seismic intensity)*
erschürfen to uncover, to discover (reach) by digging
~/eine Lagerstätte to discover a deposit
Erschürfen *n* uncovering
erschüttern to vibrate; to shake
Erschütterung *f* vibration; shaking; quake; tremor
Erschütterungsgebiet *n* region of [seismic] disturbance
Erschütterungsschicht *f* quake sheet
ersetzen to replace; to substitute
Ersetzung *f* replacement; substitution
~/isomorphe isomorphous replacement
ersoffen submerged, drowned *(mining)*
Erstabbildung *f* **einer Spezies** figure type
erstarren 1. to consolidate, to solidify; 2. to congeal, to freeze
Erstarren *n* 1. consolidation, solidification; 2. congealing, gelation, freezing
~/oberflächliches dermolithic solidification
Erstarrungsalter *n* consolidation (solidification) age
Erstarrungsgestein *n* eruptive (magmatic, pyrogenetic, igneous) rock
Erstarrungskruste *f* congealed crust
Erstarrungsphase *f* phase of consolidation
Erstarrungspunkt *m* solidification (congealing, freezing) point
Erstarrungsspalte *f* cooling crack
Erstarrungstemperatur *f* congealing temperature
Erstausscheidungen *fpl* earliest separation products, minerals of early generation, earliest minerals to crystallize (separate out)
Erstbesiedler *mpl* pioneer organisms (species) *(ecology)*
Erstgewinnung *f* primary exploitation
Erstreckung *f* **der Lagerstätte/mutmaßliche** probable extent of the deposit
Ertrag *m* yield, output
~ einer Sonde well yield

ertrunken submerged, drowned
erumpieren to erupt *(volcano)*; to blow out *(well)*
~/stoßweise to flow by heads
Eruptiersonde *f* natural flowing well
Eruption *f* eruption *(of a volcano)*; blow-out *(of a well)*
~/flächenhafte areal eruption
~/intermittierende intermittent eruption
~/subaquatische subaquatic eruption
Eruptionsherd *m* focus of eruption
Eruptionskanal *m s.* Eruptionsschlot
Eruptionskegel *m* eruption cone
Eruptionskrater *m* eruption crater
Eruptionskreuz *n* cross (x-mas) tree, Christmas tree *(drilling technics)*
Eruptionsphase *f* phase of eruptivity
Eruptionsprodukte *npl* ejectamenta
Eruptionssäule *f* eruption column
Eruptionsschlot *m* eruption channel (vent), volcanic vent (tunnel, duct, chimney, throat)
Eruptionsschlund *m* explosion pipe
Eruptionssonde *f* flowing well
Eruptionsspalte *f* eruption fissure, volcanic (fissure) vent, volcanic fissure trough
Eruptionsstopfbüchse *f* blow-out preventer
Eruptionswolke *f* eruption (volcanic, glowing, hot) cloud, volcanic blast
Eruptionszyklus *m* eruption cycle
eruptiv eruptive, subnate
Eruptiva *npl* eruptives
Eruptivbrekzie *f* eruptive breccia
Eruptivfazies *f* eruptive facies
Eruptivgang *m* eruptive (igneous, intrusive) vein; eruptive (igneous) dike
Eruptivgestein *n* eruptive (igneous, volcanic) rock
Eruptivkörper *m* eruptive body
Eruptivkuppe *f* eruptive knob
Eruptivmasse *f* igneous mass
Eruptivpfropfen *m* igneous plug
Eruptivschlot *m s.* Eruptionsschlot
Eruptivstock *m* eruptive stock (boss)
erwachsen adult
Erweichbarkeit *f* mollifiability *(of rocks)*
erweitern/ein Bohrloch to enlarge a borehole
Erweitern *n* **des Bohrlochs** widening (enlarging) of the hole
Erweiterung *f***/flügelartige** alar expansion *(palaeontology)*
~/seeartige lake expansion *(of a river)*
Erweiterungsbohrer *m* enlarging (broaching) bit
Erweiterungsbohrung *f* development drilling; development well, appraisal well
~ auf bekanntem Horizont extension test; extension (step-out) well, outpost
~ auf höherem Horizont shallower pool test
~ auf tieferem Horizont deeper pool test
Erweiterungsmeißel *m* reaming bit
Erweiterungsschuß *m* side shot
Erweiterungssonde *f* outstep [well]

Erweiterungswerkzeug *n* reamer
Erythrin *m* erythrite, red cobalt, cobalt ochre, $Co_3[AsO_4]_2 \cdot 8H_2O$
Erythrosiderit *m* erythrosiderite, $K_2Fe^{\cdot\cdot\cdot}Cl_5H_2O]$
Erythrozinkit *m* erythrozincite, (Zn, Mn)S
Erz *n* ore
~/abbauwürdiges workable (pay, payable, profitable) ore
~/abgeschertes drag ore
~/anstehendes solid (rock) ore, ore in sight (place)
~/armes lean (low-grade, base) ore, raff
~/aszendentes *s.* ~/primäres
~/aufbereitetes dressed ore
~/aufgeschlossenes developed ore
~ aus einheimischen Lagerstätten domestic ore
~/bauwürdiges *s.* ~/abbauwürdiges
~/bedingt bauwürdiges marginal ore
~/durch Zerkleinerung aufschließbares free milling ore
~/eingesprengtes disseminated (powder) ore, sprinkling
~/erschürftes prospective ore
~/fein eingesprengtes chatty ore
~/geringwertiges *s.* ~/armes
~/gewaschenes jigged ore
~/grobgesiebtes hurdled ore
~/handgeklaubtes hand-sorted ore
~/herausgesprengtes blasted ore
~/hochwertiges rich (high-grade) ore
~/kalkiges limy ore
~/karbonatisches carbonate ore
~/lateritisches lateritic ore
~/lettiges argillaceous ore
~/mit Gangart verhaftetes stuff
~ mit niedrigen Metallgehalten milling ore
~/mögliches possible ore
~/mulmiges dust ore
~/nachgewiesenes proven (proved) ore
~/orthotektisches orthotectic ore
~/primäres primary (hypergene) ore, protore
~/pulverförmiges fines
~/reichhaltiges *s.* ~/hochwertiges
~/reines clean ore
~/schwer aufschließbares rebellious ore
~/sekundäres supergene ore
~/selbstgehendes self-fluxing ore
~/sicher nachgewiesenes assured ore
~/sichtbares visible ore
~/strahliges striated ore
~/strengflüssiges refractory (stubborn) ore
~/stückiges lumpy ore
~/toniges argillaceous ore
~/unverändertes protore
~/vermutetes inferred ore
~/verwachsenes intergrown ore
~/vollständig ausgeblocktes positive ore
~/vorgerichtetes developed (blocked-out) ore
~/vorhandenes *s.* ~/nachgewiesenes
~/wahrscheinlich vorhandenes probable ore
~/zweitklassiges boose

Erzabbau

Erzabbau *m* ore mining (breaking), extraction of ore
Erzabscheidung *f* ore separation (precipitation)
Erzader *f* ore vein; streak, rib
Erzanalyse *f* ore assaying
Erzanreicherung *f* ore enrichment (concentration)
Erzaufbereitung *f* preparation (cleansing) of ore, ore dressing (separation); ore benefication
Erzaufbereitungsanlage *f* ore dressing plant
Erzausbringen *n* ore yield
Erzausscheidung *f*/**gangartige** vein
~/**lagenartige** flatwork
~/**weit aushaltende dünne** tape
Erzbank *f* bank of ore
~/**sedimentäre** flat of ore
Erzbehandlung *f* ore handling
Erzbergbau *m* 1. ore (metal) mining; 2. ore mining industry
Erzbergwerk *n* ore (metalliferous) mine
Erzbewertung *f* ore valuation
erzbildend ore-forming
Erzbildung *f* ore formation; mineralization
Erzblock *m*/**erratischer** ore boulder
Erzbrecher *m* ore crusher
Erzbringer *m* belly of ore
Erzbruchbau *m* ore caving
Erzbutze *f* chamber of ore
Erzdruse *f* loch
Erzeinschluß *m* sprinkling
Erzentstehung *f* ore genesis
erzeugen to generate
Erzeugung *f* generation
Erzfall *m* ore shoot, chimney of ore; squat; bonanza; burk
~/**reicher** gulf of ore, shoot of variation
~/**vertikaler** chimney of ore
Erzfalle *f* ore trap
Erzfeld *n* ore field (allotment)
Erzfläche *f* area of ore body
Erzflöz *n* ore bed
Erzförderung *f* output of ore; ore winning
Erzformation *f s.* Erzbildung
erzfrei barren, sterile
erzführend ore-bearing, metalliferous, mineralized
Erzfundort *m* source of ore
Erzgang *m* ore (metalliferous) lode; ore (metalliferous, ledge) vein
~ **in der Oxydationszone** gossany lode
~/**linsenförmiger** lenticular ore body
Erzgattung *f* class of ore
Erzgebiet *n* mineralized area
Erzgemenge *n* brood
Erzgenese *f* ore genesis
Erzgestein *n* ore rock
Erzgrube *f* metalliferous mine
Erzgüte *f* ore quality
Erzhalde *f* ore dump, heap of dead ore
erzhaltig ore-bearing, orey; mineralized
Erzhandstück *n* peasy

Erzhaufen *m* parcel
Erzhütte *f* smelting house
Erzkammer *f* ore chamber
Erzkontrolle *f*/**strukturelle** structural ore control
Erzkonzentrat *n* ore concentrate
erzkonzentrierend ore-concentrating
Erzkörper *m* ore body
~/**abbauwürdiger** payable ore body
~/**reicher** bonanza ore body
Erzlager *n* ore bed (ledge), sill of ore
~/**flaches** blanket deposit
~/**geringmächtiges, großflächiges** flat mass
Erzlagerstätte *f* ore deposit, source of ore
Erzlagerstättenkunde *f* ore geology
Erzlaugung *f* ore leaching
Erzlineal *n s.* Erzschmitze
Erzlösung *f* ore solution
Erzmagma *n* ore magma
Erzmikroskop *n* ore (metallographic) microscope
Erzmikroskopie *f* minera[lo]graphy
Erzmineral *n* ore (metalliferous, metallogenic) mineral
Erzminerale *npl*/**eingeschlossene** locked ore minerals
Erzmulm *m* rubble ore
Erznest *n* nest (chamber) of ore, ore bunch (pocket, shoot)
~/**reiches** treasure box
Erzniere *f* ore nodule (group)
Erzpartikel *fpl*/**kleine** knits
Erzpfeiler *m* pillar (sill) of ore
Erzpocher *m* bucker
Erzprobe *f* ore sample, specimen of ore, assay
Erzprobenahme *f* ore testing (sampling)
Erzprovinz *f* metallogenetic province
Erzputzen *m s.* Erznest
Erzqualität *f* ore grade
Erzquetsche *f* crushing plant, ore crusher
Erzreserve *f*/**geschätzte** estimated ore reserve
Erzrevier *n* ore district
Erzrolle *f* ore chute
Erzscheiden *n* ore sorting
Erzscheider *m* ore separator; bucker
Erzscheidung *f* sorting of ores
Erzschiefer *m* ore-bearing shale
Erzschlamm *m* ore sludge (slime)
Erzschlämmen *n* ore washing
Erzschlauch *m* ore pipe (chimney, shoot)
Erzschlich *m* washed ore slime, concentrate of ore, small (fine-grained) ore
Erzschlot *m* mineral pipe
Erzschmitze *f* ribbon of ore, pod
Erzschnur *f* string ore; column of ore, stringer [lode], streak
~/**reiche** pay streak
Erzschuß *m* shoot of ore
Erzschwebe *f* horizontal ore pillar
Erzsorte *f* class of ore
Erzspur *f* trace of ore

Erzstock m solid ore deposit, ore body, stockwork
Erzstreichen n ore run
Erzstücke npl/**lose** float ore *(on the surface of the earth)*
Erzstufe f glebe, cobble
Erztagebau m open-cast ore mine
Erztasche f s. Erznest
Erztrübe f ore slime
Erztrum n stringer [lead], string, slicking, midfeather
~/**derbes** ore sheet
~/**schmales** rute, vena
Erzverdünnung f dilution of ore *(by deads)*
Erzverhüttung f ore smelting
Erzverluste mpl ore losses
Erzvermahlung f grinding of ore
Erzverunreinigung f ore dilution
Erzvorkommen n ore occurrence (s.a. Erzlagerstätte)
~/**[ab]bauwürdiges** workable ore field
~/**reiches** pride [ore field]
Erzvorrat m ore stock (reserve)
~/**ausgeblockter** blocked-out ore
~/**ausgewiesener** measured ore
Erzwäsche f ore washery
Erzwaschen n ore washing
Erzwäscher m 1. buddler; 2. picking drum *(engine)*
Erzwäscherei f ore-washing plant
Erzwaschmaschine f vanning machine
Erzwaschprobe f assay of washed (buddled) ore
Erzzerkleinerung f ore crushing
Erzzone f ore zone
Esker m esker, osar, esc[h]ar, asar
Eskerablagerung f **mit Moränenkern** beta layers
eskerartig eskerine
Eskolait m escolaite, CrO_3
Esperit m esperite, calcium-larsenite, $PbCa_3Zn_4[SiO_4]_4$
Esse f chimney
Essexit m essexite *(rock of the alkali gabbro clan)*
Essigsäure f acetic acid
Eßkohle f forge coal
Etage f level
Etagen- und Firstenbruchbau m combined shrinkage and caving method
Etalon n test pill
Etappe f/**orogene** orogenic stage
etappenweise by stages
Ethmolith m ethmolith *(intrusive body)*
Ethologie f ethology
Etikette f **für Kerndokumentation** core description
Etroeungt n Etroeungt[ian], Strunian s. str. *(uppermost Devonian)*
Ettringit m ettringite, $Ca_6Al_2[(OH)_4|SO_4]_3 \cdot 24H_2O$
Euchroit m euchroite, $Cu_2[OH|AsO_4] \cdot 3H_2O$

Eudialyt m eudialyte, $(Na, Ca, Fe)_6 Zr[(OH, Cl)|(Si_3O_9)_2]$
Eudidymit m eudidymite, $NaBe[OH|Si_3O_7]$
eugeosynklinal eugeosynclinal
Eugeosynklinale f eugeosyncline
eugranitisch eugranitic
Eukairit m eucairite, $Cu_2Se \cdot Ag_2Se$
Euklas m euclase, $AlBe[OH|SO_4]$
eukristallin eucrystalline, thoroughly crystalline
Eukrit m eucrite *(meteorite)*
Eukryptit m eucryptite, $LiAl[SiO_4]$
Eulytin m eulytine, eulytite, bismuth blende, $Bi_4[SiO_4]_3$
eupelagisch eupelagic
Europium n europium, Eu
euryhalin euryhaline
eustatisch eustatic
Eutektikum n eutectic
eutektisch eutectic
eutektoid eutectoid
Eutonikum n eutonic
eutroph eutrophic
Eutrophierung f eutrophication
Euxenit m euxenite, chlopinite, $(Y,Er,Ce,U,Pb,Ca)(Na,Ta,Ti)_2(O,OH)_6$
euxinisch euxinic, pontic
Evansit m evansite, $Al_3[(OH)_6|PO_4] \cdot 6H_2O$
Evaporit m evaporite
Evaporitgefüge/mit primärem evapocrystic
~/**mit schwach lamelliertem** evapolensive
Evaporitkorn n/**primäres** evapocryst
Evapotranspiration f evapotranspiration, consumptive [water] use
Evenkit m evenkite, $C_{24}H_{50}$
evolut evolute
Evorsion f digging-up, turning-up, raking-up
Exhalation f exhalation, volcanic emanation
Exhalationslagerstätte f exhalation (emanation) deposit
exhumieren to exhume
Exinit m exinite *(coal maceral; maceral group)*
Existenzbedingung f condition of existence *(palaeobiology)*
exogen exogene, exogenous, exogenetic, exogenic
Exogeosynklinale f exogeosyncline, deltageosyncline
exokinetisch exokinetic
Exokontakt m exocontact
exomorph exomorphic
Exomorphismus m exo[meta]morphism
Exosphäre f exosphere, outer atmosphere
exosphärisch exospheric
exotherm[isch] exothermal, exothermic, exoergic
exotisch exotic
Expansion f **des Weltalls** expansion of the universe
Expansionsspeicher m constant pore volume reservoir
Expansionstheorie f expansion theory

Expansionswelle

Expansionswelle f blast wave
Experimentalgeologie f experimental geology
Exploration f exploration, reconnaissance, scouting
Explorationsbohren n exploration drilling
Explorationsbohrloch n exploratory borehole
Explorationsbohrung f exploration well
Explorationsrecht n exploration right
Explorationstätigkeit f exploration activity
Explosion f explosion
Explosionsbeben n explosive earthquake, explosion tremor
Explosionsbrekzie f explosion breccia
Explosionsglutwolke f avalanche of hot gas, blast of incandescent gas, volcanic blast, glowing cloud
~/senkrechte vertically initiated domal nuée ardente
Explosionsherd m explosion focus
Explosionskaldera f caldera of subsidence
Explosionskrater m explosion crater
explosiv explosive
Explosivausbruch m explosive eruption
Expositionsalter n exposure age (of a meteorite)
Exsudanit m exsudanite (coal maceral)
Extensionsüberschiebung f stretch thrust
extern external
Externgefüge n se-fabric
Externiden pl externides
Externrotation f external rotation
Extinktion f extinction (of radiation)
extragalaktisch extragalactic
Extraklast m extraclast (fragments of carbonaceous rocks, descending from outside of the area of sedimentation)
Extraktionsmethode f extraction method
Extraktionswasser n extraction water (for the subsurface dilution of sulphur)
extramagmatisch extramagmatic
extraorogen extraorogenetic
Extrapolation f extrapolation
Extrapolationsmöglichkeit f/**geotektonische** geotectonic possibility of extrapolation
extratellurisch extratelluric
extraterrestrisch extraterrestrial
Extremitätenknochen m limb bone
Extrusion f extrusion
~/magmatische magmatic extrusion
Extrusionsphase f extrusive phase
extrusiv extrusive
Extrusivgestein n extrusive rock
Extrusivkörper m extrusive body
extrusiv-magmatisch extrusive-magmatic
Exudat n exudation
Exuvie f mo[u]lt (palaeontology)
Exzentrizitätswinkel m angle of eccentricity
Exzeptionalismus m exceptionalism
Ezcurrit m ezcurrite, $Na_2[B_5O_6(OH)_5] \cdot H_2O$

F

Fabianit m fabianite, $Ca[B_3O_5(OH)]$
Facette f facet
Facettenaugen npl facetted eyes (arthropodans)
Facettengeschiebe n facetted pebble, windfacetted pebble[s]
facettieren to facet
facettiert facetted, soled
Fächer m fan
~ aus Küstensand wash-over fan
Fächerantiklinale f fan-shaped anticline
Fächerbohrung f multiple (cluster) drilling
Fächerfalte f fan fold
Fächerfilter n fan filter; velocity filter; pie slice filter
fächerförmig fan-shaped, fanlike, fanwise
Fächermarke f s. Fließmarke/fächerförmige
Fächerschießen n fan (arc) shooting, fanning
Fächerstellung f **der Schieferung** cleavage fan
Fächerung f fanning
Fackelgas n flare gas
Fackelkohle f cannel (jet,candle) coal, cannelite
fadenförmig filamentary, filamentous, filiform
Fadenkreuz n crossed threads (hairs)
Fadenlapilli pl pele's hair
Fadenmikrometer n filar micrometer
Fadenströmung f one-dimensional flow
Faheyit m faheyite, $(Mn,Mg,Na)Fe_2Be_2[PO_4]_4 \cdot 6H_2O$
Fahlband n fahlband
Fahlerde f leached soil
Fahlerz n fahlore, tetrahedrite, black (gray) copper ore, Cu_3SbS_{3-4}
Fahrfeld n travelling track (way)
Fährte f trackway (ichnology)
~/fossile ichn[ol]ite
Fährtenkunde f ichnology
Fahrwasser n navigable channel
Fahrwassertiefe f depth of the navigable channel
Fairfieldit m fairfieldite, $Ca_2(Mn,Fe)[PO_4]_2 \cdot 2H_2O$
Faktor m factor (complex of causes)
~/gemeinsamer common factor
~/spezifischer specific factor
Faktoranalyse f factor analysis
Faktorladung f factor loading (weight of a variable on a factor)
Faktorwertkarte f factor value map, map of factor values
Falkenauge n hawk's eye (variety of crocidolite)
Fallabstand m distance of fall
Fallazimut m azimuth (direction) of dip
Fallbeschleunigung f gravity acceleration
Falle f trap
~/antiklinale anticlinal trap
~/fazielle depositional oil trap
~/hydrodynamische hydrodynamic trap

Faltengitter

~ im abgesunkenen Flügel einer Verwerfung hanging trap
~/kombinierte combination trap
~/lithologische lithologic trap
~/stratigrafische stratigraphic trap
~/strukturelle structural trap
~/tektonische reservoir (fault) trap
fallen to fall
Fallen n fall, dip (s. a. Einfallen 1.)
~/periklinales quaquaversal dip
~ und Streichen n dip and strike
fallend on-dip
~/rechtsinnig hading with the dip
~/widersinnig hading against the dip
Fallfilter n descending filter
Fallgewicht n weight drop
Fallhöhe f height of fall
~ des Meißels percussion bit stroke
Fallinie f line of dip (slope)
Fallot n wire-weight gauge (for groundwater level measurement)
Fallrichtung f direction of dip
~/entgegengesetzt der up-dip
~/in der downdip
Fallschutt m gravity scree
Fällung f precipitation
Fallwert m s. Fallwinkel
Fallwind m descending (katabatic) wind
Fallwinkel m dip [angle], angle of incidence
~ der Verwerfung hade of the fault
~ von Schichten angle of bedding
Fallzeichen n dip-strike symbol
Falschfarbenaufnahme f false colour photo (picture, image)
Falschfarbenfilm m false colour film
Falschfarbenfotografie f false colour photography
Falschfarbensynthesebild n false colour composite
Falte f fold
~/allochthone allochthonous (displaced) fold
~/anliegende attached fold
~/antiklinale anticlinal fold
~/asymmetrische asymmetrical (unsymmetrical) fold
~/aufrechte upright (erect, symmetrical) fold
~/ausklingende lessening fold
~/breite wide (broad) fold
~/disharmonische disharmonic fold
~/disjunktive disjunctive fold
~/diskordante discordant fold
~/einfache simple (single) fold
~/flache open fold
~/flachschenklige broad fold
~/fließende smooth fold
~/gemischte mixed fold
~/geneigte inclined (gentle) fold
~/geradlinige rectilinear fold
~/geschlossene closed fold
~/kammartige crest-like fold
~/kielartige keel-like fold
~/konzentrische concentric (distance-true, parallel) fold

~/liegende lying fold
~ mit gefälteten Schenkeln composite fold
~ mit Gleitung auf s flexure-slip fold
~ mit horizontaler Achse non-plunging fold
~ mit horizontaler Sattellinie level fold
~ mit Längenunterschieden der Schenkel inequant fold
~ mit steilen Schenkeln steep limbed fold
~ mit verdicktem Scheitel und ausgedünnter Mulde reverse flowage fold
~ mit verdickten Flanken und ausgedünntem Scheitel reverse similar fold
~/offene open fold
~ parallel zum Schichtstreichen longitudinal fold
~/postume posthumous fold
~/ptygmatische ptygmatic fold
~/quergefaltete complex fold
~/schiefe inclined fold
~/schwach entwickelte feebly developed fold
~/spitze sharp fold
~/stehende s. ~/aufrechte
~/steile steep fold
~/streichende strike (longitudinal) fold
~/stumpfe blunt fold
~/symmetrische symmetrical (normal) fold
~/synsedimentäre intraformationelle slump fold
~/überkippte overturned (inverted, recumbent, reversed) fold, overfold
~/überschobene overthrust fold
~/verdeckte buried fold
~/wiedergefaltete [re]folded fold
fälteln to plicate; to crumple
Fältelung f plication; crumpling; puckering; minute folding
~/enge intimate crumpling
~/synsedimentäre intraformational contortion (folds), intrastratal crumpling
Fältelungsrutschung f convolute bedding
falten to fold; to plicate
Falten fpl/gestaffelte echelon folds
~/rheomorphe rheomorphic folds
~/verschuppte crisscross folds
Faltenabmessung f dimension of fold
Faltenachse f fold axis
Faltenbau m fold[ed] structure
Faltenbildung f formation of folds, folding
Faltenbogen m arc of folding, fold arc
Faltenbreite f width of fold
Faltenbündel n fold bundle
Faltendecke f fold nappe (thrust, carpet)
Faltendurchkreuzung f cross folding
Faltenelement n element of fold
Faltenfirst m crest of fold
Faltenflügel m limb (flank) of fold
Faltengebiet n fold area
Faltengebirge n fold[ed] mountains, mountains formed by folding
~/geradliniges linear-folded mountain range
~/junges recently folded mountain range
Faltengitter n grid pattern

Faltengürtel

Faltengürtel *m*/**alpidischer** Mediterranean belt, Alpides
Faltenhöhe *f* height of fold
Faltenjura *m* folded Jura Mountains
Faltenkern *m* core of fold
Faltenkomplex *m* fold complex
Faltenlänge *f* length of fold
Faltenlinie *f* fold line
Faltenmächtigkeit *f* depth of folding
Faltenmullionstruktur *f* fold mullion
Faltenneigung *f* pitch of fold
Faltenrumpf *m* truncated fold
Faltenscheitel *m* crest of fold
Faltenschenkel *m* flank (limb) of fold
~/**überkippter** inverted limb of fold
Faltenschollengebirge *n* faulted fold mountains
Faltenspiegel *m* enveloping contour (surface)
Faltenstirn *f* front of a thrust
~/**abtauchende** plunging crown
Faltenstruktur *f* fold structure
~/**periklinale** quaquaversal fold structure
~/**steilachsige** fold structure with steep axes
~/**unregelmäßige** am[o]eboid fold *(in disturbed areas)*
Faltensystem *n* fold system
Faltenüberkippung *f* overfolding
Faltenüberschiebung *f* thrust folding, overthrust fault
Faltenvergenz *f* regard, face
Faltenverwerfung *f* overlap (reversed fold, flexure) fault, faulted overfold, folded (lap) fault
Faltenwechsel *m* reversed fold fault
Faltenwinkel *m* angle of fold
Faltung *f* 1. folding, flexing *(bending of stratified rocks);* 2. convolution *(of a seismical wave);* 3. roll *(in a seam)*
~/**alpidische** Alpidic orogeny
~/**andine** Andean orogeny
~/**archäische** Archaean orogeny
~/**assyntische** Assyntian orogeny
~/**ausklingende** dying-out folding
~/**cadomische** Cadomian orogeny
~ **der Erdrinde** terrestrial corrugations
~/**diapire** diapir [folding]
~/**disharmonische** disharmonic (inharmonious) folding
~/**frankonische** Franconian folding
~/**herzynische** Hercynian orogeny
~ **in Störungszonen** fault folding
~ **in Verschuppung** imbricated folding
~/**kaledonische** Caledonian orogeny
~/**karelische** Karelian orogeny
~/**kaskadische** Cascadian orogeny
~/**kimmerische** Cimmerian folding
~/**kongruente** congruent folding
~/**konzentrische** concentric folding
~/**orkadische** Orcadian folding
~/**postume** posthumous (superposed) folding
~/**svekofennidische (svekofennische)** Svecofennian folding
~/**variskische (varistische, variszische)** Variscan orogeny
~/**wiederholte** refolding
~/**zweiseitig abtauchende** doubly plunging folding *(s. a.* Fächerfalte)
Faltungsachse *f* axis of folding, axial line
Faltungsalter *n* age of folding
Faltungsausmaß *n* size of folding
Faltungsbeben *n* earthquake due to folding
Faltungsbecken *n* basin fold
Faltungsepoche *f* epoch of folding
Faltungsphase *f* folding phase, phase of folding
~/**akroorogene** acroorogene phase of folding
~/**altkimmerische** Old-Cimmerian phase of folding
~/**asturische** Asturic phase of folding
~/**attische** Attic phase of folding
~/**austrische** Austrian phase of folding
~/**baikalische** Baikalian orogeny
~/**belomorische** Belomorian orogeny
~/**böhmische** Bohemian phase of folding
~/**bretonische** Bretonic phase of folding
~/**dalslandidische** Dalslandian orogeny
~/**eisengebirgische** Zelesnohorian phase of folding
~/**erische** Erian phase of folding
~/**erzgebirgische** Erzgebirge phase of folding
~/**gotidische** Gothian orogeny
~/**jungkaledonische** Late Caledonian phase of folding
~/**jungkimmerische** Late Cimmerian phase of folding
~/**karelidisch-svekofinnische** Karelian-Svecofennian orogeny
~/**laramische** Laramide orogeny
~/**pasadenische** Pasadenic phase of folding
~/**pfälzische** Palatine phase of folding
~/**pyrenäische** Pyrenean phase of folding
~/**rhodanische** Rhodanic phase of folding
~/**saalische** Saalic phase of folding
~/**saamidische** Saamian orogeny
~/**salairische** Salair phase of folding
~/**sardische** Sardinian phase of folding
~/**savische** Savic phase of folding
~/**steirische** Styrian phase of folding
~/**subherzyn[isch]e** Subhercynian phase of folding, Andean phase of folding
~/**sudetische** Sudetic phase of folding
~/**svekofinnische** Svecofennian orogeny
~/**takonische** Taconic phase of folding
~/**wallachische** Valachian phase of folding
Faltungsstreichen *n* trend of folding; direction of plication
Faltungstal *n* valley due to folding
Faltungstiefe *f* depth of folding
Faltungstyp *m*/**saxonischer** Saxonian type of fold structure
Faltungsüberschiebung *f* break thrust
Faltungszone *f* zone of folding, folded zone, fold belt; bow area
Famenne *n*, **Famennian** *n*, **Famennien** *n* Famennian [Stage] *(of Upper Devonian)*
Familie *f* family

Fangarbeit f recovery, fishing job
Fangbuhne f weir, breakwater
Fangdamm m cofferdam
~/oberer upstream cofferdam
~/unterer downstream cofferdam
Fangdorn m fishing tap
~/lösbarer releasing spear
Fanggebiet n catchment area
Fangglocke f fishing socket (bell), die collar
~/lösbare releasing overshot
Fanghaken m overshot grab, grapnel, bit hook
Fanglomerat n fanglomerate, bockram (Lower New Red)
Fangmuffe f overshot, die collar
Fangschere f fishing jars
Fangspinne f junk basket tube
Fangwerkzeug n fishing tool
Fangzahn m fang
Farallonit m farallonite, $2MgO \cdot W_2O_5 \cdot SiO_2 \cdot nH_2O$
Farbabspielung f coloured display
Farbabweichung f chromatic deviation
Farbanalyse f colour analysis
Farbdichte f colorimetric density
Farbeigenschaft f chromatic property
Farbenskala f colour scale
Farbenvergleich m colour comparison
Farbenwechsel m allochroism
farbenwechselnd allochromatic
Farberde f coloured clay
Farbfehler m chromatic aberration
Farbgleiche f s. Isochromate
Farbintensität f colour intensity
farblos colourless; achromatic
Farblosigkeit f achromatism
Farbspektrum n chromatic spectrum
Färbung f coloration
Farbverstärkung f colour enhancement
Farbversuch m colour dilution method (tracer)
Farbwertbestimmung f colour measurement
Farbzahl f colour index
Farlovien n Farlovian (Upper Devonian, Old Red facies)
Farn m fern
Farnpflanzen fpl fern plants, pteridophytes
Farnwedel m fern frond
Farringtonit m farringtonite, $[Mg,Fe]_3[PO_4]_2$
Faschine f fascine
Faschinendamm m fascine barrier wall
Faser f filament
Faseraggregat n fibrous aggregate
Faseraragonit m flower of iron, flos ferri (variety of aragonite)
Faserasbest m fibrous asbestos
Fasereis n fibrous ice, ice feathers
Fasergips m fibrous gypsum (English talc)
faserig fibrous, stringy
Faserkalk m fibrous limestone, satin spar (stone)
Faserkiesel m s. Sillimanit
Faserkohle f s. Fusain

Faserquarz m fibrous quartz
Faserserpentin m chrysotile (a fibrous silky serpentine)
Faserstruktur f bacillary structure
Fasertalk m fibrous talc
Fasertorf m fibrous (surface) peat
Faserzement m fibrous cement
Faserzeolith m fibrous zeolite
Fassait m fassaite, $Ca(Mg,Fe,Al)[(Si,Al)_2O_6]$
Fassan[ium] n Fassanian [Substage] (of Middle Triassic, Tethys)
Fassungsvermögen n specific capacity (of a well)
Fassungszone f captation zone (for ground water)
Fastebene f peneplain, old plain, base-levelled plain
~/zerschnittene dissected peneplain
Faujasit m faujasite, $Na_2Ca[Al_2Si_4O_{12}]_2 \cdot 16H_2O$
faul putrid
Faulbecken n septic tank
faulen to rot, to putrefy
Faulen n putrefaction
Faulgas n sewage (sludge) gas, gas of putrefaction
Fäulnis f putrefaction, septicity
Fäulnisbakterien fpl bacteria of decay, putrefactive bacteria
fäulnisliebend sapropel[it]ic
Faulschlamm m sapropel, putrid (vegetable) slime, putrid mud, digested sludge
~/gallertartiger slimy sapropel, saprocoll
Faulschlammbildung f saprofication
Faulschlammgestein n sapropel rock, sapropelite
Faulschlammkohle f sapropel coal (s. a. Sapropelkohle)
Faulschlammsediment n foul-bottomed sediment
Fauna f fauna
~/endemische endemic (indigenous) fauna
~/fremdartige exotic fauna
~/laurasische Laurasian fauna (palaeobiogeography of Permo-Carboniferous)
~/marine marine fauna
Faunenfolge f faunal succession
Faunengesellschaft f faunal association
Faunengrenze f faunal boundary
Faunenhorizont m faunal horizon
Faunenprovinz f faunal province
Faunenreich n Faunal Realm
~/boreales Boreal Realm (Mesozoic, North Asia, North America, North Europe)
~/notales Notal Realm (Triassic of New Zealand)
~/tethyales Tethyan Realm
Faunenschnitt m faunal break
Faunensubprovinz f Faunal Subprovince (palaeobiogeography)
Faunenvergesellschaftungsgrenzen fpl faunal community boundaries
Faunenzone f faunizone

faunistisch

faunistisch faunal, faunistic
Fauserit *m* fauserite, $Mn[SO_4] \cdot 7H_2O$
Faustit *m* faustite, $ZnAl_6[(OH)_2|PO_4]_4 \cdot 4H_2O$
Faustregel *f* rule of thumb
Fayalit *m* fayalite, $Fe_2[SiO_4]$
faziell facial
Fazies *f* facies
~/**alpine** Alpine facies
~/**ästuarine** estuarine facies
~/**bayrische** Bavarian facies
~/**euxinische** Euxinic (Black Sea) facies
~/**fluviatile** fluviatile facies
~/**geochemische** geochemical (elemental) facies
~/**germanische** German facies
~/**granulometrische** granulometric (parabolic) facies
~/**heteromerische** heteromeric facies
~/**heteropische** heteropic facies
~/**homotaxe** homotaxe facies
~/**isomerische** isomeric facies
~/**isopische** isopic facies
~/**isotopische** isotopic facies
~/**kalkige** calcareous facies
~/**kontinentale** *s.* ~/**terrestrische**
~/**lakustrine** lacustrine facies
~/**limnische** limnetic facies
~/**magmatische** magmafacies
~/**marine** marine facies
~/**metamorphe** metamorphic facies
~/**ökologische** ecologic[al] facies
~/**pelagische** pelagic facies
~/**rheinische** Rhenish facies
~/**salinarische** saliniferous facies
~/**sandige** arenaceous facies
~/**sedimentäre** origofacies
~/**terrestrische** terrestrial facies
~/**tethyale** Tethyan facies
~/**tonige** argillaceous facies
Faziesänderung *f* facies change
~/**laterale** lateral gradation of facies
~/**lithologische** lithological facies change
~/**vertikale** vertical gradation of facies
Faziesausbildung *f* facial character
Faziesbereich *m* range of facies
~ **mit ruhigen Sedimentationsbedingungen** quiescent-area facies
Faziesdarstellung *f* facies representation
Faziesdecke *f* facies nappe
Faziesdeutung *f* facies interpretation
Faziesdifferenzierung *f* facies differentiation
Faziesfossil *n* facies fossil
Faziesgegensatz *m* facies contrast
Faziesgleichheit *f* isomesia
Faziesindikator *m* facies indicator
Facieskarte *f* facies map
Facieskartierung *f* facies mapping
Facieskontrast *m* facies contrast
Facieskunde *f* facieology
~ **der Sedimente** ecostratigraphy
Faziesserie *f* facies series
~ **vom Abukuma-Typ/metamorphe** Abukuma-type metamorphism

~ **vom Barrow-Typ/metamorphe** Barrovain-type metamorphism
Faziestektonik *f* tectonic selection
Faziesübergang *m* facies transition, change in facies
Faziesunterschied *m* facies difference
Faziesverhältnisse *npl* facies conditions
Faziesverzahnung *f* interdigitations of facies; intergrowth along the facies
Facieswanderung *f* migration of facies
Facieswechsel *m* facies change
federartig featherlike, feathery; plumose
Federerz *n* feather ore (*s. a.* Antimonit; Jamesonit; Plagionit)
federförmig featherlike, feathery; plumose
Federgips *m* striate gypsum, fibrous English talc
Federgravimeter *n* spring gravimeter
Federkielstalaktit *m* straw stalactite
Federsalz *n* feather salt
Fehlbohrung *f* faulty drilling; dry well (hole)
Fehlerkurve *f*/**Gaußsche** Gaussian [error] curve
fehlgeordnet disordered
fehlklassifizieren to misclassify
Fehlordnung *f* disorder, imperfection
Fehn *n* *s.* Fenn
Feinboden *m* fine soil
Feindetritus *m* fine detritus
Feindetritus-Mudde *f* fine-detrital organic mud
Feineinstellung *f* fine adjustment
Feinerde *f* fine ground
Feinerz *n* fine ore, fines, smalls
Feingefüge *n* microstructure
Feingehalt *m* betterness
feingemahlen fine-ground
feingeschichtet finely laminated (layered, stratified, bedded), thin-bedded
feingeschlämmt levigated
Feingliederung *f* refined classification
feinglimmerig fine-micaceous
Feingold *n* fine (greasy) gold
feingranoblastisch decussate
Feinheit *f* fineness; grist *(of grain)*
Feinkies *m* fine gravel *(2–6 mm)*
feinklastisch finely clastic
Feinkohle *f* fine coal, fines, smalls, duff
Feinkorn *n* fine grain
Feinkornbereich *m* fine-size range
feinkörnig finely granular, fine-granular, fine-grained, close-grained
feinkristallin fine-crystalline
Feinlehm *m* light silt
Feinmessung *f* precision measurement
Feinnivellement *n* precise (precision) levelling
Feinortung *f* accurate scanning
feinporig finely porous
Feinsand *m* fine sand *(0,125–0,25 mm)*
~/**schluffiger** loamy fine sand
~/**weißer** silver sand
Feinsandboden *m*/**lehmiger** loamy fine soil

feinsandig fine-sandy
Feinsandschicht f fine-sand layer
Feinsandstein m/**eingekieselter** ganister
~/schluffiger silty fine sandstone
Feinschicht f s. Lamine
Feinschichtung f lamination
feinschiefrig finely foliated
feinschleifen to lap
Feinschleifen n [fine] lapping, fine grinding
Feinskulptur f fine sculpture
Feinstkorn n finest grain
feinstkörnig finest-textured
Feinstratigrafie f refined stratigraphy
feinstratigrafisch microstratigraphical, detailed stratigraphical
feinverteilt intimately disseminated, finely divided
Feinzerkleinerung f secondary comminution
feinzerrieben comminuted
Feld n field; area; ground
~ einer regionalisierten Variablen/geometrisches geometric[al] field of a regionalized variable
~/elektromagnetisches electromagnetic field
~/erdmagnetisches geomagnetic (terrestrial-magnetic, earth's magnetic) field
~/geochemisches geochemical field *(random field of geochemical variables)*
~/gestörtes contorted area
~/hydrothermales hydrothermal field
~/magnetisches magnetic field
~/nicht aufgeschlossenes unexploited field *(oil or gas)*
~/unverritztes unworked area
Feldarbeiten fpl field work *(surveying)*
~/geologische geologic[al] field work, field geological work
Feldaufbaumethode f transient electromagnetic method
Feldbahnwagen m pipe carriage
Feldbeobachtung f field observation
Feldbetrieb/im under field conditions
Feldbreite f s. Feldesbreite
Feldbuch n field record (data notebook)
Felddokumentation f field documentation
Feldenergie f/**magnetische** magnetic field energy
Feldergrenze f boundary system
Felderregung f field excitation
Feldesbreite f width of cut, track width, breast
Feldesgrenze f boundary line
Feldesteil m panel
Feldesteile mpl/**grubenrandliche** parts of the field situated at the border of a mine
Feldfortsetzung f continuation *(of a potential field)*
~ nach oben upward continuation
~ nach unten downward continuation
Feldgeologe m field geologist
Feldgeologie f field geology
feldgeologisch field-geological

feldgeophysikalisch field-geophysical
Feldgleichung f field equation
Feldgrenze f border of a claim
Feldkapazität f field capacity
Feldlabor n field laboratory
Feldlinie f field line
~/magnetische magnetic field line
Feldmagnetband n field tape
Feldmesser m surveyor
Feldmessung f field measurement
Feldmethodik f field technique
Feldort n end of a gallery
Feldortsstoß m toe of stope
Feldresultate npl field data
Feldspat m fel[d]spar
~/glasiger ice spar *(s. a. Sanidin)*
~/kataklasierter (zerscherter) sliced fel[d]spar
feldspatartig fel[d]spathic
feldspatführend fel[d]spathic
Feldspatgneis m fel[d]spathic gneiss
Feldspatgrauwacke f fel[d]spathic (high-rank) graywacke, arkosic wacke
feldspathaltig fel[d]spathic
Feldspatisierung f fel[d]spathization
Feldspatoide mpl fel[d]spathoids, foids
Feldspatsandstein m fel[d]spathic sand-stone
Feldspatvertreter mpl fel[d]spathoids, foids
Feldstärke f field strength (intensity)
~/erdmagnetische geomagnetic field intensity
~/magnetische magnetic field strength (intensity), magnetizing force, field density
Feldstärkemessung f field-intensity measurement
Feldstärkendiagramm n, **Feldstärkenprofil** n field pattern
Feldstativ n field tripod
Feldstecher m binocular [prism-telescope]
Feldstein m cobble [stone], great rubble stone
Feldtrupp m field party
Feldumkehrung f field reversal
Felduntersuchung f field investigation
Feldversuch m field test
Feldwaage f field balance
~/magnetische magnetic field balance
~/Schmidtsche Schmidt field balance
Fels m 1. [solid] rock *(s. a. Gestein)*; 2. fels *(massive metamorphic rocks lacking schistosity)*
~/fauler soft rock
~/gesunder sound rock
~/gewachsener native [bed]rock, [solid] bedrock, ledge [rock]
~/isolierter hervorstehender scar, cicatrix
Felsabsturz m rock precipice
Felsaufreißen n **mittels Reißhakenkraft** ripping
Felsaushub m **für das Planum** rock cutting in formation
Felsbank f ledge
Felsbeckensee m rock-basin lake
Felsbewehrung f rock reinforcement
Felsblock m block of rock, boulder

Felsblock

~/losgelöster crag
Felsboden *m* rock floor, lithosol
Felsböschung *f* rock slope
Felsbruch *m* rock failure
Felsbrücke *f* natural bridge
Felsbuckel *m*/**glazialer** glacial boss
Felsburg *f* tor
Felsebene *f*/**aride** pediment
Felsen *m* rock; ca[i]rn
~/äolisch bearbeiteter ventifact
Felsen *mpl*/**unterseeische** sunken rocks
Felsenbetthöhle *f* rock cave
Felsenkette *f* ledge *(along shore)*
Felsenklippe *f* reef
Felsenmeer *n* stone (block, boulder) field, chaos of rocks
Felsenriff *n* rocky reef (awash), skerry
Felsenspitze *f* crag
Felsentasche *f* water pocket
Felsentor *n* rock (natural) arch
Felsfußfläche *f* pediment
Felsgrat *m* high rocky ridge
Felsgrund *m* rocky bottom
Felsgründung *f* foundation in rock
Felshang *m* rock slope
Felshohlraum *m* rock cavity
felsig rocky, clifty, clifted, cliffy, skerry, ragged, cragged
Felsinjektion *f* rock sealing
Felsinsel *f* rocky island
felsisch felsic
Felsit *m* felsite, felstone, petrosilex
felsitartig felsitoid
Felsitfels *m* felsite rock
felsitisch felsitic
Felsitsphärolit *m* felsosphaerite
Felskap *n* rocky cape
Felskegel *m* rock cone
Felskessel *m* rock tank (basin)
Felskliff *n*/**steilwandiges** mural escarpment
Felsklippe *f* chimney rock, *(Am)* bluff
~ im Fluß cripple
Felsklippengebirge *n* cragged mountains
Felsklotz *m* node of rock, nubbin
Felskriechen *n* rock creeping
Felsküste *f* rocky coast
Felslawine *f* rock avalanche
Felsleiste *f* rock ledge
Felsmechanik *f* rock mechanics
Felsnadel *f* monolith; spire; obelisk; spine
Felsnische *f* niche
Felsöbanyit *m* felsöbanyite, $Al_4[(OH)_{10}|SO_4] \cdot 5H_2O$
Felsophyr *m* felsophyre *(igneous texture)*
felsophyrisch felsophyric
felsosphäritisch spherophyric
Felspanzerbildung *f* mortar bed, hardpan
Felspfeiler *m* rock pillar
Felspflanzen *fpl* rupicolous (saxicolous) plants
Felsplatte *f* shelf of a rock
Felsquarzit *m* rock quartzite
Felsriegel *m* rock bar (threshold, sill)

~/glazialer glacial boss
Felsrücken *m* rocky ridge
Felsrutschgebiet *n* rock slide area
Felsrutschung *f* rock slide
Felsschicht *f*/**horizontale (söhlige)** rock blanket
Felsschlucht *f* mountain gorge, cleugh, cleuch
Felsschüssel *f* rock basin (tank)
Felsschutt *m* rock debris; slide rock; scree
Felsschuttboden *m* rocky debris soil
Felsschwelle *f s.* Felsriegel
Felssicherung *f* rock protection
Felssohle *f* rock floor
Felsspalt *m* rock interstice
Felssprengung *f* rock blasting
Felsstrand *m* rock beach
Felssturz *m* rock fall (slide)
Felstasche *f* water pocket
Felsterrasse *f* rock terrace
Felstrümmer *pl* rock waste
Felsufer *n* rocky shore
Felsuntergrund *m* rock bed, main bottom
Felsvernagelung *f* rock bolting
Felsvorsprung *m* rock spur, buttress
Felswand *f* rock wall (face), cliff
Felswüste *f* rock (rocky, stone, stony) desert, stony waste; hammada *(Sahara)*
Felswüstenplateau *n* rocky desert plateau
Felszacken *m* jag
Felszinne *f* pinnacle
femisch femic
Femur *m* femur, thigh bone
Fenaksit *m* fenaksite, $KNa(Fe,Mn)[Si_4O_{10} \cdot {}^1/_2H_2O$
Fenit *m* fenite
Fenn *n* fen, mire, marshy ground
Fennosarmatia *f* Fennosarmatia
Fennoskandia *f* Fennoscandia
Fenster *n* window, inlier, denuded cutting
~/geologisches geological window
~/stratigrafisches inlier
~/tektonisches tectonic window, fenster, structural inlier
Fenstergefüge *n* fenestral fabric *(in carbonate rocks)*
Fensterzählrohr *n* end-window counter
Ferberit *m* ferberite, $Fe[WO_4]$
Ferghanit *m* ferg[h]anite, $LiH[UO_2)_4|(OH)_4|(VO_4)_2] \cdot 2H_2O$
Fergusit *m* fergusite *(rock of the alkali gabbro clan)*
Fergusonit *m* fergusonite, bragite, tyrite, $Y(Nb,Ta)O_4$
Fermorit *m* fermorite, $(Ca, Sr)_4[Ca(OH, F)][(P, As)O_4]_3$
Fernandinit *m* fernandinite, $CaV_2^{-}[VO_4H_2]_{10} \cdot 4H_2O$
Fernbeben *n* distant earthquake, earthquake with remote epicentre, teleseism
~/weites very distant earthquake
Fernbeobachtung *f* remote sensing

Ferndecke f allochthonous nappe
Ferner m s. Firnfeld
Fernerkundung f remote sensing
~ **zur Nachtzeit** night-time remote sensing
~ **zur Tageszeit** day-time remote sensing
Fernerkundungsaufnahme f remote sensing image (picture)
Fernerkundungsaufnahmegerät n remote sensor
Fernerkundungsdaten pl remote sensing data
Ferngasleitung f gas main
fernmessen to telemeter
Fernmessen n telemetering
Fernmeßgerät n telemeter, remote meter, long-distance recorder, remote measurement device
Fernmeßtechnik f telemetry
Fernmessung f telemetering; telemetry
Fernschub m remote thrust
Fernseite f farside (of the moon)
Fernthermometer n telethermometer
Fernüberschiebung f far-travelled mass; powerful thrust
Fernwirkung f action at a distance
Ferrierit m ferrierite, $(Na,K)_2Mg[OH|Al_3Si_{15}O_{36}] \cdot 9H_2O$
Ferrikarbonat n ferricarbonate
ferrimagnetisch ferrimagnetic
Ferrimagnetismus m ferrimagnetism
Ferrimolybdit m ferrimolybdite, $Fe_2[MoO_4]_3 \cdot 7H_2O$
Ferrinatrit m ferrinatrite, $Na_3Fe[SO_4]_3 \cdot 3H_2O$
Ferrisalz n ferric salt
Ferrisicklerit m ferrisicklerite, $Li(Fe,Mn)[PO_4]$
Ferrisymplesit m ferrisymplesite, $Fe_3[(OH)_3 | (AsO_4)_2] \cdot 5H_2O$
Ferritungstit m ferritungstite, $Ca_2Fe_4[WO_4]_7 \cdot 9H_2O$
Ferrohydroxid n ferrous hydroxide
Ferrokarbonat n ferrous carbonate
Ferromagnesit m mesitite, mesitine [spar], ferroan magnesite
ferromagnetisch ferromagnetic
Ferromagnetismus m ferromagnetism
Ferromangan n ferromanganese
Ferrosalz n ferrous salt
Ferrosilit m ferrosilite (s. a. Pyroxen)
Ferrospinell m hercynite, $FaAl_2O_4$
Fersmanit m fersmanite, $Na_4Ca_4Ti_4[(O,OH,F)_3|SiO_4]_3$
Fersmit m fersmite, $(Ca,Ce,Na)(Nb,Ti,Fe,Al)_2(O,OH,F)_6$
fertigstellen/eine Bohrung to complete a well
Fertigstellung f **als verrohrte Bohrung** cased hole completion
~ **einer Erdölbohrung zur Förderung** completion [work] of an oil well
Fervanit m fervanite, $Fe[VO_4] \cdot H_2O$
fest solid; strong; sturdy; firm
Feste f pillar
Festeis n fast ice
Festfahren n **des Bohrstrangs** tight pull of the drill pipe
Festgestein n solid (hard) rock
Festigkeit f strength; compactness; sturdiness; firmness
festigkeitsanisotrop anisotropic in strength
Festigkeitsberechnung f stress calculation
Festigkeitsgrad m degree of strength
Festigkeitsgrenze f s. Bruchfestigkeit
Festigkeitskoeffizient m coefficient of resistance (of a rock)
Festigkeitskriterien npl strength criteria
Festigkeitsnachweis m stress analysis
Festigkeitsverhalten n strength behaviour
Festigung f **des Untergrunds** soil stabilization
Festkörper mpl/**kristalline** crystalline solids
Festkörperphysik f physics of solids, solid state physics
Festland n earth; continent, mainland; emerged land, onshore
~/**altes** oldland
~/**auf dem** onshore (seen from sea)
Festlandablagerung f continental deposition
Festlandinsel f continental island
Festlandsockel m continental basement
Festpunkt m fixed (observation) point, ground point of control; bench mark
~/**trigonometrischer** altitude point, triangulation station
Festpunktnetz n observation grid
Feststoff m solid
Feststofflagerstätte f solid substance deposit
Feststoffvolumen n solid substance volume
Festungsachat m fortification agate
Festwerden n setting
~ **des Rohrs** sticking (freezing) of the pipe
Fettglanz m greasy (soapy) lustre
fettig greasy, soapy, unctuous
Fettkohle f (Am) medium volatile bituminous coal (28—22 % volatile matter, vitrite basis); low volatile bituminous coal (with less than 22 % volatile matter); fat coal
feucht humid; soggy; muggy
feuchtgemäßigt humid-temperate
Feuchtigkeit f humidity; moisture; dampness
~/**absolute** absolute humidity
~/**relative** relative humidity
Feuchtigkeitsäquivalent n moisture equivalent
Feuchtigkeitsdefizit n moisture deficiency
Feuchtigkeitsgehalt m moisture percentage
feuchtigkeitsisolierend damp-proof
Feuchtigkeitsisolierung f damp-proofing
Feuchtigkeitskorrosion f aqueous corrosion
feuchtigkeitsundurchlässig moisture-proof
Feuchtigkeitszone f **des Bodens** belt of soil water, soil water bed
Feuchtklimaperiode f epoch of humid climate
feuchtwarm muggy
Feuerblende f pyrostilpnite, fire blende, Ag_3SbS_3
feuerfangend inflammable
Feuerfontäne f, **Feuergarben** fpl fire fountain
Feuerkugel f fireball, bolide
Feueropal m fire (sun) opal (variety of opal)

Feuerprobe

Feuerprobe f fire assay
Feuersee m fire lake
Feuerstein m flint, firestone, chert; ignescent stone
~ **in Kreide** chalk flint
feuersteinartig flinty, cherty
Feuersteinband n flint layer (sheet), band of flint nodules, nodular sheet of flint
Feuersteingerölle npl flint boulders
feuersteinhaltig flinty, cherty
Feuersteinknollen m flint pebble
~/**feigenförmiger** sycite
Feuersteinlinie f flint limit
Feuerstrahlbohren n heat drilling
fibroblastisch fibroblastic
Fibroferrit m fibroferrite, $Fe[OH|SO_4] \cdot 5H_2O$
Fichtelit m fichtelite, $C_{19}H_{34}$
Fichten-Eiben-Hasel-Zeit f spruce-yew-hazel period
Fiederchen n pinnule
fiederförmig pennate
Fiedergang m/**kleiner** feeder
Fiederkluft f feather joint
Fiedermarke f chevron mark
Fiederschichtung f chevron (herringbone) cross-bedding
Fiederspalte f feather joint, [open] gash fracture
Fiederspalten fpl tension gashes en échelon
Fiederstörung f auxiliary fault
Fiederstreifen m stria
Fiedlerit m fiedlerite, $Pb_3(OH)_2Cl_4$
Figuren fpl/**Widman[n]stättensche** Widmanstaettian figures
Figurenstein m figured stone (s. a. Agalmatolith)
Fillowit m fillowite, $Na_2(Mn,Fe,Ca,H_2)_5[PO_4]_4$
Filmfeuchtigkeit f pellicular moisture
Filmwasser n film water
Filter n filter, screen
~/**dispersives** dispersive filter
~/**inverses** inverse filter
Filterboden m foundation of filter (in a well)
Filterbrunnen m filter (spring, screen) well
Filtereinbau m running of the filter
Filterfläche f filter area
Filtergeschwindigkeit f speed of filtration; effective (apparent, true) velocity (of ground-water flow); Darcy velocity (in rocks)
Filterkies m filter gravel
Filterkruste f filter cake
Filterkuchen m mud cake
Filterpressung f filter pressing
Filterprozeß m filtering process
Filterrohr n well filter, strainer
Filterrohrziehvorrichtung f liner puller
Filtersand m filter sand
Filterschicht f filter layer
Filterung f filtering
Filterverlust m filter loss
Filterwiderstand m filter resistance
Filtrationsdifferentiation f filtration differentiation

Filtrationskoeffizient m s. Durchlässigkeitsbeiwert
Filtratwassereindringen n filtrate invasion
filzig felted, felty
Filzpolierscheibe f felt bob
Fimmenit m fimmenite (kind of turf)
final final
Finanzierungsquelle f source of financing (for geological investigations)
Findling m erratic block; boulder, bowlder; drift boulder, perched block (boulder); glacial boulder
Findlingskarte f erratic map
Findlingsquarzit m boulder of quartzite
Fingerbildung f fingering
fingerförmig digitate
Fingerlakes[ien] n Fingerlakesian [Stage] (lower Frasnian, North America)
Fingersee m/**glazialer** glacial scour lake
Finnemanit m finnemanite, $Pb_5[Cl|(AsO_3)_3]$
Finsternis f/**partielle** partial eclipse
~/**totale** total eclipse
Fireclay-Mineral n fire-clay mineral, b/3 disordered kaolinite
Firmament n firmament, celestial sphere, vault of heaven, vaulted sky
Firn m firn, névé
Firnbrücke f snow cornice, snowdrift site
Firneis n firn (glacier) ice
Firneisbildung f firnification, nivation
Firnfeld n snowfield, firn field, névé field (slope)
Firngebiet n névé region
Firngletscher m névé (snow) glacier
Firnlinie f firn (névé) line, firn limit
Firnmulde f névé basin
Firnpfeiler m serac
Firnschnee m firn (glacier) snow, granular ice
Firnspalte f névé crevasse
First m crest, top
Firste f back, hanging wall, roof
~ **eines Bogens** crown
~ **eines Stollens** back of a gallery
~/**zubruchgehende** loose roof
Firstenausbau m roof support
Firstenausgasung f roof emission
Firstenbau m overhand (overhead) stoping
~ **mit Versatz** cut-and-fill stoping
~/**versatzloser** open [overhand] stoping
Firstenbohrloch n back borehole
Firstenbruch m top failure, roof foundering
Firstendruck m roof (top) pressure, superincumbent pressure of the ground
Firstendurchbiegung f roof deflection
Firstenerz n roof ore
Firstengewölbe n roof (pressure) arch
Firstenläufer m crown runner
Firstennachreißen n roof ripping
Firstensegment n top section (of 3-piece roadway arch)
Firstensprengung f heading blast
Firstenstoßbau m longwall (shrinkage) stoping

Firstenstrecke f top heading
Firstlinie f crest line
Fischabdruck m ichthyolite
fischähnlich fishlike, piscine
Fische mpl/**kieferlose** jawless fishes
Fischerit m s. Wavellit
Fischrest m ichthyolite, fish remainder
Fischschwanzmeißel m fishtail bit
Fixismus m fixism
Fixpunkt m fixed point, ground point of control; bench mark
Fixstern m fixed star
Fizelyit m fizelyite, $7PbS \cdot 1^1/_2 Ag_2 S \cdot 5 Sb_2 S_3$
Fjord m firth; fjord, fiord, fiard, inlet
Fjordinsel f fjord island
Fjordküste f fjord[ed] coast
flach 1. flat, plane; 2. shallow
Flachbohren n shallow [well] drilling
Flachbohrung f shallow well (hole)
Flachbrunnen m surface well
Fläche f plain, area; surface, face; superficies
~/**bebaute** cultivated area
~/**ebene** plane face, plane
~/**erzführende** ore-bearing surface
~/**gekrümmte** warped surface
~ **gleicher Wellengeschwindigkeit** isovelocity surface (seismics)
~/**isostatische** isostatic surface
~/**listrische** listric surface
~/**morphologische** morphological plain
~/**polierte** polished surface
~/**vertorfte** peaty flat
Flächen fpl/**gleichwertige** similar faces (of crystals)
Flächenaufschluß m areal exposure
Flächenausdehnung f areal extent
Flächenausgleich m surface fitting
Flächenbasalt m shield (multiple vent) basalt
Flächenbelegung f areal (surface) density
Flächenberechnung f computation of area
Flächendichte f areal (surface) density
Flächendruck m contact pressure
Flächenergiebigkeit f areal productiveness (during compacting outpressed water)
Flächenerguß m lava flood
Flächenerosion f sheet erosion
Flächeneruption f areal eruption
Flächengefüge n structure of planes
Flächengewicht n areal (surface) density
flächenhaft two-dimensional
Flächenindizes mpl indices (of crystals)
Flächenleistung f areal capacity (during compacting outpressed water, in area and time)
Flächenmesser m planimeter, area measuring equipment
Flächenmessung f planimetering, area measurement
Flächennivellement n levelling of surface
Flächennormale f normal to a surface
Flächenpaar n pair of faces
Flächenpol m pole of the face
Flächenschrift f variable area recording

Flächenschüsse mpl multiple shot-holes
Flächenseismik f areal seismics, 3D-seismics
Flächenspülung f superficial flushing
Flächenströmung f extending flow
Flächensystem n/**orthogonales** orthogonal system of surfaces
Flächentrend m two-dimensional trend, trend with two coordinates
Flächenwinkel m face (interfacial) angle (of crystals)
flächenzentriert face-centered
~/**kubisch** cubic face-centered
Flachgründung f shallow foundation
Flachküste f flat (low, low-lying) coast, flat shore
Flachland n plain, flat, flat land (country, ground)
~/**durchkratertes** cratered plain
Flachlandmoor n lowland swamp
Flachlandsee m lowland lake
Flachlandstrom m river of the plains
flachliegend flat-lying
Flachmeißel m chisel auger
Flachmoor n low (shallow) moor, flat (low-level, low-lying) bog, low-lying moorland
Flachmoortorf m lower-moor peat
flachschalig flat-valved
Flachsee f shallow (epicontinental) sea, epicontinental (offshore) waters, littoral area (district)
Flachseeablagerung f shoal-water deposit, shallow-sea deposit, continental marine deposit
Flachseefauna f neritic fauna, epifauna
Flachseefazies f neritic (shallow-water) facies
Flachseekalk m shallow-water limestone
Flachseeriff n bank reef
Flachseezone f neritic (action) zone
flachsohlig flat-bottomed, flat-floored
Flachufer n low bank
Flachwasser n shallow water
Flachwasser ... s.a. Flachsee ...
Flachwasservermessung f shallow-water surveys
Flachzapfen m depressed flute cast
Fladenlava f ropy (corded-folded, dermolithic, pahoehoe) lava
Flagstaffit m flagstaffite, $C_{10}H_{18}(OH)_2 \cdot H_2O$
Flajolotit m flajolotite (s.a. Tripuhyit)
Flammbohren n s. Flammenbohren
Flamme f/**reduzierende** carbonizing flame
Flammenbohren n flame-jet drilling, jet (fusion) piercing
Flammenfärbung f flame coloration
Flammenfotometer n flame photometer
Flammenfotometrie f flame photometry
Flammenmergel m flammenmergel
Flammenspektrometrie f flame spectrometry
Flammenspektrum n flame spectrum
Flammenstrahlbohrer m churn drill equipped for jet piercing
Flammenstruktur f flame structure (sedimentary structure)

Flammkohle

Flammkohle *f* 1. *(Am)* high volatile bituminous coal *(stage A/B)*; 2. flame coal *(technical)*
Flammpunkt *m* flash point
Flammstrahlbohren *n s.* Flammenbohren
Flandrien *n* Flandrian *(Holocene of North Sea district)*
Flanke *f* flank, versant
Flankenerguß *m,* **Flankeneruption** *f* flank outflow, flank (lateral) eruption
Flankenschicht *f* flank bed
Flankensonde *f* flank well
Flaschenzugsystem *n* hoisting tackle
Flasergabbro *m* flaser gabbro, gabbroid schist
Flasergneis *m* flaser gneiss
flaserig schlierenlike; phacoidal
Flaserkalk *m* phacoidal limestone
Flaserschichtung *f,* **Flasertextur** *f* flaser bedding (structure), streaked structure
Flechten *fpl* lichens
Flechtströmung *f* turbulent flow
Fleckenriff *n* patch reef
Fleckenstruktur *f*/**sparitische** grumous texture *(of carbonate rock)*
Fleckentextur *f* stictolithic structure
fleckig spotty, spotted, mottled, stained *(s.a.* gefleckt)
Fleckschiefer *m* mottled schist (shale, slate), spotted schist (shale, slate), fleckschiefer
Fledermausguano *m* bat guano, chiropterite
Fleischerit *m* fleischerite, $Pb_3Ge[(OH)_4|(SO_4)_2] \cdot 4H_2O$
fleischfarben sacroline
Fleischnadeln *fpl s.* Mikroskleren
Flexur *f* flexure, downwarp, step fold
Flexurblatt *n* horizontal flexure
Flexurebene *f* flexure plane
Flexurgebirge *n* monoclinal mountains
Flexurgraben *m* synclinal flexure
Flexur-Zonentextur *f* diktyonitic structure *(of migmatites)*
fliegend volant
Fliehkraftklassierer *m* centrifugal classifier
fliesenartig flaggy
Fließballungen *fpl* **in Lavaströmen** accretionary lava balls
Fließbewegung *f* flowage
~/**subaerische** liquid subaerial flow
Fließblattfoliation *f*/**magmatische** orthofoliate
Fließdruck *m* flow pressure
~ **im Steigrohr** flowing tubing pressure
Fließdruckgradient *m* flowing pressure gradient
Fließebene *f* planar (platy) flow structure *(in igneous rocks)*
fließen to flow
~/**in Mäandern** to meander
~/**pulsierend** to surge, to fluctuate, to head, to slug
Fließen *n* flow
~/**laminares** sheet flow
~/**plastisch-elastisches** plasto-elastic flow
~/**plastisches** plastic flow
~/**tektonisches** tectonic flow (transport)
~/**turbulentes** turbulent flow
~ **unverfestigter Sedimente** sedifluction
~/**viskoelastisches** visco-elastic flow
~/**viskoses** viscous (creeping) flow
~ **von gespanntem Grundwasser** confined flow
fließend/entgegen dem Schichtfallen obsequent
~/**träge** sluggish
Fließerde *f* mud
Fließerdezunge *f* mud tongue
Fließfähigkeit *f* fluidity, mobility of fluid
~ **der Zementschlämme** fluidity of the cement grout
~ **des Krustenmaterials** rheidity
Fließfalte *f* flow[age] fold, irregular fold
Fließfältelung *f s.* Wulstschichtung
Fließfaltung *f* flow (incompetent) folding
Fließfestigkeit *f* yield strength
Fließgefälle *n* flow gradient
Fließgefüge *n* flow (fluxion) structure
Fließgeschwindigkeit *f* rapidity (velocity, rate) of flow, velocity of current
Fließgeschwindigkeitslog *n* fluid-velocity log
Fließgrenze *f* flow (liquid, ductility, yield) limit, yield point (stress) *(s.a.* Streckgrenze)
~/**hohe** high liquid limit
~/**niedrige** low liquid limit
Fließgrenzgerät *n* apparatus for plasticity test
Fließkapazität *f (Am)* permeability-thickness product
Fließkraft *f*/**viskose** viscous flow force
Fließkunde *f* rheology
Fließlinie *f* flow line *(in plutonic rocks)*
Fließliniengewölbe *n* flow-line arch *(in plutonic rocks)*
Fließmarke *f* flow[age] cast, flow mark, flute cast, gouge channel
~/**fächerförmige** frondescent cast, cabbage leaf marking
~/**gescharte große** shooting flow cast
~/**schuppenförmige** squamiform load cast
Fließprobe *f* flow test
Fließpunkt *m* flow point
Fließrate *f*/**normierte** dimensionless flow rate
Fließregime *n* flow regime *(fluviatile transport)*
~/**oberes** upper flow regime
~/**unteres** lower flow regime
Fließrichtung *f* direction of flow[age]
~ **des Eises** direction of ice flow
Fließrille *f* scour mark, flute cast
Fließrinne *f* flute
Fließrippel *f* current ripple [mark]
Fließrutschung *f* earth flow
Fließsand *m* float (shifting) sand, quicksand
Fließschicht *f* mollisol, active (annually thawed) layer
Fließtextur *f* flow (fluxion) structure
Fließtheorie *f* flow theory, theory of flow
Fließton *m* quick clay
Fließversatz *m* flow (controlled-gravity) stowing

Fließvorgang *m* flow phenomenon
Fließwiderstand *m* resistance to flow
Fließwirksamkeit *f* flow efficiency
Fließwulst *m* load (flute) cast
~/belasteter load-casted current marking
~/gefurchter rill cast
~/terrassierter terraced flute cast
Fließwulststruktur *f* ball-and-pillow structure
Fließzone *f* zone of flow
flimmern to scintillate
Flimmern *n* scintillation; twinkling *(of stars)*
Flinkit *m* flinkite, $Mn_3[(OH)_4|AsO_4]$
Flint *m* flint *(s.a. Feuerstein)*
Flinteinlagerung *f* bur
Flintknollen *m* flint pebble (nodule)
Flinz *m* flinz
Flinzgraphit *m* flake (flaky) graphite
Flittergold *n* flour (float) gold
Flocke *f* flake
Flockenerz *n* mimet[es]ite, $Pb_5[Cl|(AsO_4)_3]$
Flockengraphit *m* flake (flaky) graphite
flockig flocculent; flaked
Flockung *f* flocculation
Flokit *m* flokite, $(Ca, K_2, Na_2)[AlSi O_{12}]_2 \cdot 6 H_2O$
Flora *f* flora
Florenbestände *mpl* floral species
Florencit *m* florencite, $CeAl_3[(OH)_6|(PO_4)_2]$
Florenelemente *npl* floristic elements
Florengrenze *f* floral boundary
Florenkarte *f* floral chart
Florensprung *m* floral interruption
Florenverwandtschaft *f* floral relationship
Florenzone *f* floral zone
floristisch floristic, floral
Flosse *f* fin; flipper
Flossenstachel *m* fin spine
Flossenstrahlen *mpl* fin rays
Flotation *f* floatation
~/einfache (kollektive) all-floatation
Flotationsanlage *f* floatation plant
Flotationsaufbereitung *f* floatation concentration
flotationsfähig floatable
Flotationsmittel *n* floatation agent
Flotationszelle *f* floatation cell
flotierbar floatable
Flotierbarkeit *f* floatability
Flöz *n* seam
~/ausgasendes fiery seam
~/bedingt [ab]bauwürdiges marginal seam
~/erdölführendes oil measure
~/erschöpftes worked-out seam
~/flach einfallendes gently dipping seam
~/flaches flat seam
~/geneigtes inclined (pitching) seam
~/geringmächtiges thin seam
~/hangendes overlying seam
~ im Liegenden underlying seam
~/in zwei Lager aufgespaltenes simple split seam
~/liegendes underlying seam
~/mächtiges heavy layer

~/Methan führendes fiery seam
~/schwebendes dilated seam
~/seigeres heavily pitching seam
~/söhliges horizontal (level) seam
~/stehendes vertical (edge) seam
~/steil einfallendes rearer seam
~/steiles steep seam
~/tiefgelagertes deep-lying seam
~ von 45° Neigung half-edge seam
~/zusammengesetztes composite seam
Flözanalyse *f* seam analysis
~/mikroskopische microscopical seam analysis, microscopic analysis of the seam section
Flözanschnitt *m* seam cut
Flözarchiv *n* seam memoirs
Flözaufnahme *f*/**makropetrografische** macroscopic seam section
Flözausbauchung *f* seam swell
Flözausgehendes *n* layer exit
Flözauswaschung *f*/**mit Ton gefüllte** clay hog
Flözbildung *f* seam formation
Flöze *npl*/**beieinander gelegene** contiguous seams
~/vereinigte associated sheets
Flözeinfallen *n* seam pitch, dip of the seam
Flözerstreckung *f* course of seam
Flözhorizont *m* seam horizon
Flözidentifizierung *f* seam identification
Flözlage *f* position of the seam
Flözleeres *n* dividing slate
Flözmächtigkeit *f* seam thickness
~/[ab]bauwürdige useful seam thickness
~/gebaute effective seam thickness
Flözpaket *n* seam complex
Flözprofil *n* seam section, *(Am)* coal-bed profile
Flözreichtum *m* abundance of seams
Flözscharung *f* seam swell
Flözschlag *m* coal burst
Flözstrecke *f s.* Abbaustrecke
Flözunterton *m* pan
Flözverdickung *f*/**lokale** swell[y]
Flözverdrückung *f* pinch
Flözvertaubung *f* rock (dirt) fault
flözweise in strata
Flözwelle *f* seam wave
Flözwellenseismik *f* in-seam seismics
fluchten to be in alignment
flüchtig volatile
Flüchtigkeit *f* volatility; fugacity
Fluchtpunkt *m* vanishing point
Fluchtspur *f* escape structure *(ichnology)*
Fluchtstrecke *f* escape way
Fluellit *m* fluellite, $AlF_3 \cdot H_2O$
Flug *m* **im intergalaktischen Raum** intergalactic travel
~/interstellarer interstellar flight
Flugasche *f* fly ash
Flugbahn *f* flight path, trajectory; orbit *(of a satellite)*
Flügel *m* 1. side, limb, leg *(geological)*; 2. ala *(of brachiopodans)*

Flügel

~/**abgesunkener** downdropped (downthrown) side
~/**gehobener** upthrown (upcast, lifted) side, uplifted wall, upleap
~/**gesunkener** thrown side
~/**steiler** steep limb
~/**tiefer** underside
Flügeladerung f wing venation
flügelähnlich pteroid
Flügelbohrer m wing auger
flügelförmig alar
Flügelmeißel m drag bit
Flügelneigung f inclination of limbs
Flügelschnecke f pteropod, sea butterfly
Flughöhe f flight altitude
Flugmagnetometer n airborne (aerial) magnetometer
Flugsand m flying (drift, wind-borne, wind-blown, aeolian) sand, quicksand
Flugstaub m/**schwefelhaltiger** sulphureous flue-dust
Flugweg m s. Flugbahn
Fluid n/**fließunfähiges** immobile fluid
fluidal fluidal
Fluidalblattbänderung f fluxion banding
fluidalstreifig linophyric
Fluidaltextur f s. Fließtextur
Fluidität f s. Fließfähigkeit
Fluidsättigung f fluid saturation *(for crude oil or natural gas)*
Fluktuomutationen fpl fluctuo-mutations
Fluoborit m fluoborite, $Mg_3[(F, OH)_3|BO_3]$
Fluocerit m fluocerite *(variety of tysonite)*
Fluor n fluorine, F
Fluoreszenz f fluorescence
Fluoreszenzanalyse f fluorescence analysis
Fluoreszenzaufnahme f fluorography
Fluoreszenzlampe f fluorescent lamp
Fluoreszenzmesser m fluorimeter
Fluoreszenzmessung f **am Bohrklein** fluorlogging
Fluoreszenzmikroskopie f fluorescence microscopy
Fluoreszenzschirm m fluorescent screen
fluoreszieren to fluoresce
fluoreszierend fluorescent
Fluorinit m fluorinite *(coal maceral)*
Fluorit m fluorite, fluor[spar], CaF_2
Fluorit-Zinkblende-Erz n/**gebändertes** coon-tail ore
Fluormineral n fluorine mineral
Fluoroskop n fluoroscope
Fluoroskopie f fluoroscopy
Fluorsilikat n fluorsilicate
Fluortest m fluorine test
Fluorwasserstoffsäure f fluorohydric acid, hydrofluoric acid, HF
Fluraufnahme f land survey[ing]
Flurform f lie of the land
Flurkarte f cadastral map
Flurneugestaltung f land reorganization, redistribution of land

Fluß m river; stream
~/**abgezapfter** beheaded river
~/**anaklinaler** anaclinal river
~/**antezedenter** antecedent stream
~/**auf einer Antiklinalflanke (Synklinalflanke) abfließender konsequenter** lateral consequent stream
~/**ausgeglichener** graded river
~/**ausgetrockneter** lost river
~/**durch Anzapfung entstandener** pirate stream
~/**durchgehender** continuous stream
~/**durchhaltender** perennial river
~/**epigenetischer** superimposed river
~/**geschwollener** swollen (bank-full) river
~/**grundwasserspendender** influent stream
~/**inkonsequenter** inconsequent stream
~/**kanalisierter** canal river
~/**kleiner** creek, rivulet
~/**komplexer** compound stream
~/**kurzzeitig fließender** ephemeral stream
~ **mit Schwinde** disappearing stream
~ **mit Tiefenerosion** degrading (down-cutting) stream
~/**obsequenter** obsequent stream
~/**pendelnder** swinging river
~/**periodisch wiederkehrender** ressurected stream
~/**periodischer** intermittent stream
~/**schiffbarer** navigable river
~/**schlammiger** heavily silted river
~/**schwindender** disappearing stream
~/**syngenetischer** syngenetic river
~/**überlasteter** overloaded stream
~/**ursprünglicher** antecedent stream
~/**verjüngter** rejuvenated (revived) river
~/**verlegter** diverted river
~/**verschlammter** silted river
~/**vielverzweigter** braided river
~/**wasseraufnehmender** effluent (gaining) stream
~/**wiederkehrender** resurrected stream
~/**zusammengesetzter** composite stream
Flußablagerung f river (river-laid, fluvial, aggradational) deposit
~/**glaziale** glacial outwash
Flußablagerungsboden m fluviogenic soil
Flußableitung f river (stream) diversion
Flußablenkung f river (stream) deflection
Flußabschnitt m river section
Flußabschnürung f raft
Flußabstand m stream spacing
flußabwärts downstream
Flußachse f stream centre line
Flußanzapfung f river capture (beheading, piracy), stream capture (beheading, piracy)
Flußarm m river arm, branch of a river; distributary *(of a delta)*
~/**alter** oxbow lake
Flußaue f [river] flood plain, river (beaver, alluvial) meadow
Flußaufschotterung f dam gradation

Flußspat

Flußaufstauung f/**natürliche** raft lake
flußaufwärts upstream
Flußausbauchung f river widening
Flußausbildung f evolution of river bed
Flußbagger m **mit Schleppsaugrohr** backdigger [dredge]
Flußbauten mpl river structural works
Flußbecken n river basin
Flußbett n river bed (channel), stream bed (channel)
~/altes old course
~/begrabenes palaeochannel
~/epigenetisches ancient geological gorge
~/fossiles buried river
~/stabiles stable channel
~/verlassenes abandoned river bed
~/verzweigtes, pendelndes anastomosing stream
Flußbetterhöhung f river bed elevation (gradation)
Flußbettverlagerung f channel migration
Flußbiegung f river bend (elbow)
Flußbildung f fluvial formation
Flüßchen n river[l]et, rivulet, streamlet
Flußdamm m river wall
Flußdeich m river levee
Flußdelta n river delta; alluvial fan
Flußdichte f drainage density (texture)
~/magnetische magnetic flux density
Flußdurchbruch m river gorge
Flußeinschnitt m stream cut
Flußeis n river (stream) ice
Flußenthauptung f s. Flußanzapfung
Flußerosion f fluvial (river, stream) erosion
~/peneplainisierende fluvial geomorphic cycle
Flußgebiet n river basin, catchment area
Flußgefälle n river gradient, slope of river
Flußgefüge n s. Fließtextur
Flußgeröll n fluvial (river) pebble
~/weit transportiertes lag gravel
Flußgeschiebe n river drift, bottom (tractional) load
Flußgeschwindigkeit f stream velocity
Flußgewässer n **unter dem Eis** tunnel valley, tunneldale
Flußhydraulik f fluvial hydraulics
flüssig fluid, liquid
Flüssiggas n liquid petroleum gas, LPG
Flüssiggasspeicher m liquefied petroleum gas storage
Flüssigkeit f fluid, liquid
~ mit gelöstem Gas liquid containing gas in solution
~/homogene homogeneous fluid
~/nichtbenetzende non-wetting fluid
Flüssigkeitsbahn f path of the liquid
Flüssigkeitsdruck m fluid pressure
Flüssigkeitsdruckmeßdose f hydraulic capsule (load cell)
Flüssigkeitseinschluß m liquid inclusion (vesicle), sealed liquid, fluid cavity
Flüssigkeitsmigration f fluid redistribution
Flüssigkeitsoberfläche f fluid surface
Flüssigkeitssäule f fluid (liquid) column
Flüssigkeitsspiegel m fluid (liquid) level
Flüssigkeitsspiegelmesser m liquid level indicator
Flüssigkeitsszintillator m liquid scintillation spectrometer
Flüssigmethanspeicher m liquefied natural gas storage
Flußinsel f river island (islet)
Flußkappung f s. Flußanzapfung
Flußkies m fluvial (river, stream) gravel
Flußknie n river bend (elbow)
Flußkorrasion f river corrasion
Flußkrümmung f river curve (bend)
Flußkunde f fluviology, potamology
Flußlauf m river course
~/alter abandoned channel
Flußlehm m fluviatile loam
Flußmäander m river meander
Flußmarsch f flood land
Flußmittel n flux, (Am) fluxard
Flußmorast m river swamp
Flußmorphologie f river bed morphology
Flußmündung f river mouth, stream outlet (debouchure), embouchure, estuary
Flußnetz n river system; system of rivers and streams; flow net; drainage pattern
~/ertrunkenes dismembered river system
~/gitterförmiges trellis drainage pattern
~/glaziales glacial drainage pattern
~/verzweigtes dendritic[al] drainage pattern
Flußniederung f river flat (valley), flood plain
Flußpegel m fluviometer
Flußpegelnetz n stream gauging network
Flußplankton n river plankton
Flußquelle f river source
Flußregime n stream-flow regime
Flußregulierung f [artificial] river regulation, watercourse regulation, river realignment, river training [works]
Flußrichtung f fluvial direction
Flußrinne f river (stream) channel
Flußsand m river (warp) sand
Flußsandbank f hirst, channel bar
Flußsäure f fluorohydric acid, hydrofluoric acid, HF
Flußschleife f river curve (bend); meander
Flußschlick m clay-containing river silt
Flußschlinge f river loop, meander
Flußschnelle f rapid
Flußschotter m river gravel
Flußschutt m/**angespülter** river wash
Flußschwinde f swallow (sink, leach) hole
Flußsediment n fluviatile detritus, river-borne (stream-borne, stream-laid) sediment
Flußseife f river (stream) placer
Flußsohle f river floor
~/bewegliche shifting bed
Flußspaltung f branching of a river
Flußspat m fluorite, fluor[spar], CaF_2

Flußspat

~/**violetter** false amethyst
Flußspeisung f river alimentation
Flußstrecke f river course
~/**gerade** reach
~/**obere** upper course of river
Flußsystem n s. Flußnetz
Flußtal n river (alluvial) valley
~/**breites** strath
~/**ertrunkenes** drowned river (stream) valley, drowned (flooded) stream
Flußterrasse f fluvial (river, alluvial, flood-plain) terrace, river (alluvial) bench
Flußterrassenseife f bench placer
Flußtransport m stream transportation
Flußtrübe f sediments carried in suspension
Flußüberschwemmung f river inundation
Flußufer n [river] bank; riverside
~/**flaches** gentle river bank
Flußumkehr f river (stream) inversion
flußverfrachtet river-borne, stream-transported
Flußverjüngung f stream rejuvenation
Flußverlagerung f migration of river, river changing
~ **an der Innenseite von Mäandern** chute cut-off
Flußverlegung f river shifting (diversion), shift of river course
~ **durch Abdämmung** river diversion by ponding
Flußverschmutzung f, **Flußverunreinigung** f river pollution
Flußwassermenge f discharge of river
Flußwasserstand m river stage
Flußwehr n river weir
Flußwirbel m fluxion swirl
flußzerschnitten stream-worn
Flut f flood[-tide]; high tide
Flutbasalt m trap[rock] (s.a. Plateaubasalt)
Flutbrandung f bore, eagre
Flutdelta n flow delta
fluten/eine Grube to flovel a mine
Fluten n water flooding
~ **mit oberflächenaktiven Stoffen** detergent flooding
Flutgrenze f tide mark, land wash, head of the tide
Fluthöhe f tidal range, range (height, lift) of tide
Flutkatastrophe f catastrophic[al] flood
~/**erdumwälzende** cataclysm
Flutkräfte fpl tidal forces
Flutlinie f high-water line
Flutmesser m tide gauge; tide register
Flutstand m high-tide level
Flutstrom m flood current
Fluttank m floatation tank
Fluttrichter m flood channel
Flutung f flushing
Flutwassermenge f volume of flood
Flutwechsel m turn of the tides
Flutwelle f tidal (rising tide) wave; tsunami

~/**seismisch bedingte** seismic sea wave
Flutzeit f flood tide (s.a. Flut)
fluvia[ti]l fluvial
fluvioglazial fluvioglacial, aqueoglacial
fluviolakustrin fluviolacustrine
fluviomarin fluviomarine
Fluxoturbidit m fluxoturbidite
Flysch m flysch, orogenic sediment
flyschähnlich flysch-like
Flyschbrekzie f flysch breccia
Flyschfazies f flysch facies
Flyschzone f flysch zone
Föhn m foehn; chinook
Foide npl foids, fel[d]spathoids
fokussieren to focus
Folge f sequence, succession; suite, column; spit-out (seismics)
Folgefluß m consequent river
~ **in älterem Mäandertal/junger** entrenched meander valley
Folgeformen fpl sequential forms (morphology)
Folgeprodukt n successive product
Foramen n foramen, perforation, opening
Foraminiferen fpl foraminifer[ran]s
~ **der Tiefsee** benthonic foraminifers
~/**sandschalige** arenaceous foraminifers
Foraminiferenablagerung f foraminiferal deposit
Foraminiferenkalk m foraminiferal limestone
Foraminiferenkreide f foraminiferal chalk
Foraminiferenmergel m foraminiferal marl
Foraminiferensand m foraminiferal sand
Foraminiferenschlamm m foraminiferal ooze
Forbesit m forbesite, $(Ni, Co)H[AsO_4] \cdot 3H_2O$
Förde f fjord, fiard, fiord; inlet; narrows; firth
Fördenküste f fjord type of coast line
Förderabfall m production decline
Förderabfallkurve f [production] decline curve
Förderabfallmethode f [production] decline curve method
Förderabgabe f royalty
Förderanlage f hoist
Förderausfall m production downtime
Förderband n band conveyor
Förderbeginn m commencement of production
Förderbohrung f producing (development) well, producer
Förderbrücke f conveying bridge
Förderbrunnen m discharging well
Förderdruck m flowing pressure
Fördererz n crude (current) ore, run-of-mine ore
Förderfähigkeit f productive capacity
Fördergut n 1. mining product; 2. material to be conveyed
Förderhöhe f pressure (discharge) head; head of water
Förderhorizont m production (pay) zone
Förderkapazität f productive capacity
Förderkohle f run-of-mine coal

Förderkonzession *f* production licence
Förderkorb *m* cage
Förderkosten *pl* lifting cost
Förderleistung *f* output; tonnage *(of a mine)*; inflow performance *(of water)*; discharge capacity *(of a pump)*
Förderleistungsvermögen *n*/**tägliches** daily [delivery] capacity
Fördermenge *f* output *(of a mine)*; rate of delivery, [volumetric] delivery, capacity *(of a pump)*
~ **der Spülpumpe** slush (mud) pump delivery
~ **einer Sonde** rate of flow
~/**zulässige** allowables *(oil and gas)*
fördern to produce; to mine; to extract; to raise
Förderrate *f* capacity of well; well production; production rate
~ **einer Bohrung** production rate of a well
~/**eruptive** flush production rate
~/**freie** *(Am)* open-flow potential
~/**spezifische** specific capacity of well; unitary yield
Förderraum *m* discharge chamber
Förderschacht *m* drawing shaft
Förderschlot *m* conduit [of volcano], channel of ascent *(of a volcano)*
Förderseil *n* hoisting cable
Fördersohle *f* track level, haulage horizon
Fördersonde *f* producing well
Förderstillstand *m* off-time
Förderstrecke *f* drawing road
Förderstrom *m* delivery (flow, discharge) rate
Fördertechnik *f* production engineering
Förderteufe *f* depth of pit
Fördertour *f* tubing string
Förderturm *m* shaft tower, production derrick
Förderung *f* 1. production; output; throughput; extraction; offtake; 2. withdrawal *(non eruptive)*; 3. discharge *(of a pump)*
~ **aus zwei Horizonten/gleichzeitige** dual well completion
~/**kumulative** cumulative production
~/**küstennahe** offshore production
~/**mögliche** potential production *(estimate of ultimate production)*
~/**natürliche eruptive** natural flow
Förderunterbrechung *f* production shut-down
Förderverfahren *n*/**künstliches** artificial lift method *(oil)*
Fördervermögen *n* productive capacity
Förderversuch *m* productivity test *(of oil and gas holes)*
Förderwinde *f* rambler rig
Förderzins *m* royalty
Förderzuteilung *f* **innerhalb von Erdöllagerstätten** allocation of oil production within oil pools
Forellenstein *m* troutstone, troctolite *(variety of gabbro)*
Form *f*/**abweichende** aberrant (divergent) type

~/**allotropische** allotropic form
~/**alpine** alpine form
~/**endemische** endemic (indigenous) form
~/**kolloidale** colloidal form
~/**kongruente** congruous form
~/**menschenähnliche** hominoid
~/**rezente** contemporary form
~/**tektonische** tectonic form
~/**unreife** immature form
~/**zackige** serrated form
~/**zwerghafte** dwarfish species
Formähnlichkeit *f* homomorphism
Formänderung *f* deformation
Formänderungsarbeit *f* work of deformation
Formänderungsvermögen *n* deformation capacity
Formart *f* form species
Formation *f* formation *(lithostratigraphic unit, in the former German literature synonym of system)*
~/**gasführende** gas zone
~ **geringen Drucks** lower-pressure formation
~/**liegende** subformation
Formationsanalyse *f* analysis of formation
Formationsbehandlung *f* formation treating
Formationsdruck *m* formation pressure
Formationsfaktor *m* formation resistivity factor
Formationsfaktorformel *f*/**Archiesche** Archie formation-factor equation
Formationsfolge *f* geologic[al] column, succession (suite, column, sequence) of formations, formational record
Formationsfraccen *n* formation fracturing
Formationsglied *n* member *(lithostratigraphic unit)*
Formationsgrenze *f* formation boundary, contact between two formations
Formationskarte *f* formation map
Formationsname *m* formation name
Formationstabelle *f* table of strata
Formationstest *m* formation test
Formationstesten *n* formation testing
Formationstester *m*, **Formationstestgerät** *n* formation tester
Formationsvolumenfaktor *m* formation volume factor
Formationswasser *n* formation water
Formationswiderstandsfaktor *m* formation [resistivity] factor
Formel *f* formula
~/**Faustsche** Faust's equation
Formenergie *f* force of crystallization
Formenschatz *m* forms
Formfaktor *m* shape factor *(of a reservoir)*
Formgattungen *fpl* form genera
Formkohle *f* crumble coal
Formkoks *m* formed coke
formlos amorphous
Formsand *m* moulding sand
Formveränderung *f* deformation
Fornacit *m* fornacite, $Pb_2Cu[OH|CrO_4|AsO_4]$

Forsterit

Forsterit *m* forsterite, boltonite, $Mg_2[SiO_4]$
Förster-Sonde *f* fluxgate magnetometer
Fortpflanzung *f* propagation
~ **seismischer Wellen** seismic wave propagation
Fortpflanzungsgeschwindigkeit *f* velocity (speed) of propagation
~ **der Wellen** velocity of wave propagation
Fortpflanzungskonstante *f* propagation constant
Fortpflanzungsorgane *npl s.* Reproduktionsorgane
Fortpflanzungsrichtung *f* direction of propagation
Fortpflanzungszeit *f* propagation time
forträumen to clear away
Fortschreiten *n* sweeping *(of meanders)*
Fortschritt *m* **je Schicht** advance per shift
Fortschrittsgeschwindigkeit *f* velocity of underground flow
Fortschrittswinkel *m* advance angle
fortschwemmen to wash away, to sweep away; to truncate
Fortschwemmung *f* truncation
Fortsetzung *f* continuation
fortsprengen to blast off
Foshagit *m* foshagite, $Ca_4[(OH)_2|Si_3O_9]$
fossil fossilized; petrified
Fossil *n* fossil
~/**abgeriebenes (abgerolltes)** rolled (partly rounded) fossil
~/**angeätztes** corroded fossil
~/**angebohrtes** fossil with borings
~ **auf primärer Lagerstätte** indigenous fossil, indigene
~ **auf sekundärer Lagerstätte** drifted (derived) fossil
~/**durchlaufendes** persistent fossil
~/**eingebettetes** encased fossil
~/**eingespültes** drifted (derived) fossil
~/**endemisches** indigenous fossil, indigene
~/**pyritisiertes** pyritized fossil
~/**silifiziertes** silicified fossil
~/**tierisches** zoölite, zoölith
~/**umlagertes** drifted (derived, reworked) fossil
~/**verquetschtes** distorted fossil
~/**verschlepptes** *s.* ~/umgelagertes
~/**zweifelhaftes** problematic fossil
Fossilabdruck *m* fossil mould
fossilarm poor in fossils
Fossilarmut *f* paucity of fossils
Fossilart *f* fossil type
Fossilbeleg *m* fossil record
Fossilbestand *m* stock of fossils
Fossilbildung *f* fossilization
Fossildiagenese *f* fossil diagenesis
Fossileinbettung *f* burial of fossils
Fossilfestkalk *m* biolithite
Fossilfolge *f* fossil sequence; fossil record
Fossilfragmente *npl* fossil debris
fossilfrei devoid of fossils, non-fossiliferous, unfossiliferous
fossilführend fossiliferous, fossil-bearing, relic-bearing
Fossilführung *f* fossil sequence; fossil[iferous] record; content of fossils
Fossilfundort *m*, **Fossilfundstätte** *f*, **Fossilfundstelle** *f* fossil locality, fossil-bearing deposit
Fossilgemeinschaft *f*/**wellenschlagsortierte** psephonecrocoenosis
Fossilgesellschaft *f* fossil assemblage
fossilhaltig *s.* fossilführend
Fossilinhalt *m* fossil[iferous] content
Fossilisation *f* fossilization
Fossilisationskunde *f*, **Fossilisationslehre** *f* taphonomy
fossilisieren to fossilify; to fossilate; to petrify; to permineralize; to lithify
fossilisiert/nicht unfossilized
Fossilkunde *f* fossilogy
Fossilmaterial *n* fossil material
fossilreich rich (abundant) in fossils
Fossilrest *m* fossil remain
Fossilsammler *m* bone digger
Fossilspuren *fpl* fossil markings
Fossilvorkommen *n* fossil occurrence
Fossula *f* fossula *(of corals)*
Fotobasis *f* photobase
Fotoflug *m* photographic flight
Fotogeologie *f* photogeology
fotogeologisch photogeologic
Fotografie *f* **aus der Luft** aerophotography
Fotogrammetrie *f* air surveying, photogrammetry
Fotolineationen *fpl* photolineations *(linear features, mostly of geological-geomorphological origin, recognizable in remote sensing images)*
Fotolumineszenz *f* photoluminescence
Fotometrie *f* photometry
Fotomosaik *n* mosaic
Fotosphäre *f* photosphere
Foucherit *m* foucherite, $Ca(Fe, Al)_4[(OH)_8|(PO_4)_2] \cdot 7H_2O$
Fourier-Trend *m* Fourier (harmonic) trend, trend with trigonometric functions
Fourmarierit *m* fourmarierite, $8[UO_2|(OH)_2 \cdot 2Pb(OH)_2 \cdot 4H_2O$
Fowlerit *m* fowlerite *(variety of rhodonite)*
Foyait *m* foyaite *(feldspathoidal syenite)*
Fracortung *f* frac location
Fracstützmaterial *n* proppant
Fracverfahren *n* fracturing
~ **mit Säurebehandlung** acid fracturing
~/**selektives** selective fracturing
Fraipontit *m* fraipontite, $Zn_8Al_4[(OH)_8|(SiO_4)_5] \cdot 7H_2O$
Fraktion *f*/**monomineralische** monomineral fraction
fraktioniert fractional
Fraktionierung *f* fractionation
~/**gravitative** gravity fractionation *(of a magma)*
Fraktionsanalyse *f* fractional analysis

Francevillit m francevillite,
   (Ba,Pb)[(UO$_2$)$_2$|V$_2$O$_8$] · 5H$_2$O
Franckeit m franckeite, lepidolamprite,
   5PbS · 3SnS$_2$ · Sb$_2$S$_3$
Franconien n Franconian [Stage] (of Croixian)
Franklinit m franklinite, ZnFe$_2$O$_4$
Frasch-Verfahren n Frasch process
Fräsen n milling (within the hole)
Fräser m milling tool
Frasne n s. Adorf
Fräsvortriebmaschine f channelling machine
Frauenglas n sparry (specular) gypsum
Freboldit m freboldite, γ-CoSe
frei free
Freibergit m freibergite (Ag-bearing tetrahedrite)
Freieslebenit m freieslebenite,
   4PbS · 2Ag$_2$S · 2Sb$_2$S$_3$
Freigleitung f free gliding
Freigold n free gold
~/sichtbares specimen gold
Freigoldklumpen m gold nugget
Freiheitsgrad n degree of freedom
freilegen to uncover, to lay bare, to reveal; to expose; to exhume
Freilegung f uncovering, revelation; exposure, exposing; exhumation
freiliegend exposed
Freiluftanomalie f free-air anomaly
Freiluftkorrektion f free-air correction
Freiluftreduktion f free-air reduction
freisetzen to release
Freisetzung f release
Freitauchgerät n aqualung
Freiwerden n escape
~ von Gas gas delivery
Fremdasche f foreign ash
Fremdatom n foreign atom
Fremdberge pl imported dirt
Fremdbestäubung f s. Allogamie
fremdfarbig allochromatic
Fremdgesteinseinschlüsse mpl accidentals
Fremdimpulsmethode f artificial impulse method
Fremdion n foreign ion
Fremdkörper m foreign body
Fremdlingsfluß m allogenous river
Fremdmaterial n foreign material
Fremdversatz m imported stowing
Fremdzufluß m imported water (runoff from other areas)
Fremontit m fremontite, (Na,Li)[(OH,F)|PO$_4$]
Frenzelit m s. Guanajuatit
frequenzabhängig frequency-dependent
Frequenzbereich m frequency range; frequency domain
Frequenzcharakteristik f frequency response
Frequenzverzerrung f harmonic distortion
Fresnoit m fresnoite, Ba$_2$ Ti[Si$_2$O$_8$]
Freßrohr n burrow
Freßspur f feeding structure (ichnology)
Freudenbergit m freudenbergite,
   NaFe(Ti,Nb)$_3$O$_7$(O,OH)$_2$

Friedelit m friedelite, (Mn,Fe)$_8$[(OH,Cl)$_{10}$|Si$_6$O$_{15}$]
Friedhof m grave yard
Frieseit m frieseite, Ag$_2$Fe$_5$S$_8$
Friktionsstreifen mpl striation, scratches
frisch fresh
Frischerz n raw ore
Frischwasser n fresh water
fritten to bake, to frit, to vitrify
Frittung f baking, fritting, vitrif[ic]action
Fritzscheit m fritzscheite (variety of autunite)
Prohbergit m frohbergite, FeTe$_2$
Frolovit m frolovite, Ca[B$_2$O(OH)$_6$] · H$_2$O
Frondelit m frondelite, ·
   (Mn,Fe$^{..}$)Fe$_4^{...}$[(OH)$_5$|(PO$_4$)$_3$]
Frontbö f cold front squall
Frontmoräne f frontal moraine
Froodit m froodite, α-PdBi$_2$
Frost m frost; frostiness
Frostabblätterung f frost scaling
Frostaufgang m thaw
Frostauftreibung f s. Frosthebung
Frostbeginn m initiation of freezing
frostbeständig frost-resisting, frost-proof
Frostbeständigkeit f frost resistance
Frostbeule f frost heave (boil)
Frostboden m frozen earth (ground, soil)
Frostbodenkunde f cryopedology
Frostbodenwirkungen fpl congeliturbation
Frosteindringung f frost penetration
Frosteinfall m incidence of frost
Frosteinwirkung f frost action
frostempfindlich frost-susceptible
Frostfiguren fpl frost patterns
frostfrei frost-free
Frostgefahr f danger of freezing
Frostgefügeboden m patterned ground
Frostgraupeln fpl small hail
Frostgrenze f freezing line; frost line
Frosthebung f frost heaving (lifting, heave, boil), earth hummock, thufur
Frostmusterboden m patterned ground
Frostpunkt m freeze point
Frostriß m s. Frostspalte
Frostschäden mpl frost damages
Frostschub m frost thrust (shove)
Frostschuttstück n congelifract
Frostschutzlösung f antifreeze solution
Frostschutzmaßnahme f frost precaution
Frostschutzmittel n antifreeze
Frostschwelle f initiation of freezing
Frostsicherheit f s. Frostunveränderlichkeit
Frostspalte f frost crack, fissure caused by frost
Frostsprengung f congelifraction, frost splitting (weathering, blasting, wedging)
Froststauchung f cryoturbation, kryoturbation
Frosttiefe f frost penetration
Frostunbeständigkeit f frost instability
frostunempfindlich s. frostbeständig
Frostunveränderlichkeit f frost inalterability
Frostveränderlichkeit f frost alterability
Frostverwitterung f s. Frostsprengung

Frostverwitterungsschutt

Frostverwitterungsschutt *m* congelifracts
Frostwirkung *f* frost effect
~ ohne Massenbewegung frost stirring
Frostwürgeboden *m* congeliturbate
Frostzerstörung *f* frost work
Fruchtbarkeit *f* fertility
Fruchtschiefer *m* fruchtschiefer *(s.a.* Fleckschiefer)
Fruchtzapfen *m s.* Fruktifikation
Frühdiagenese *f* early diagenesis
frühdiagenetisch early diagenetic[al]
Frühgeschichte *f* **der Erde** earth's early history
Frühjahrshochflut *f* spring flood
Frühkristallisation *f* early crystallization
Frühlings-Äquinoktium *n,* **Frühlings-Tagundnachtgleiche** *f* spring (vernal) equinox
frühreif early mature
Frühreife *f* early maturity
Fruktifikation *f* fructification, fruiting cone
Fuchsit *m* fuchsite *(s.a.* Muskovit)
Fucoidensandstein *m* fucoidal sandstone
Fuge *f* joint; juncture
~/durch Scherung geöffnete emphasized cleavage
Fugenöffnung *f* joint opening
Fühler *m* transducer; sensitive element *(of an apparatus)*
Führungsmeißel *m* pilot bit
Führungsrahmen *m/***fester** permanent guide structure
Führungsrohr *n,* **Führungstrichter** *m* fishing tap with guide shoe
Fukus *m* bladder wrack
Fulgurit *m* fulgurite, lightning (sand) tube
Fülldruck *m* inflation pressure
Fülleisen *n* plessite *(meteorite)*
füllen/sich to fIll up
Fullererde *f* fuller's earth, malthacite
Füllmineral *n* fillers
Füllmittel *n* fillers
Füllort *n* pit bottom, shaft landing
Füllstoff *m* filling material, filler
Füllung *f* [in]filling *(of a vein)*
~/hydrothermale hydrothermal filling
Füllungsgrad *m* degree of filling
Fülöppit *m* fülöppite, $3PbS \cdot 4Sb_2S_3$
Fumarole *f* fumarole, smoke hole
~/flammende flaming orifice
~/saure acid fumarole
Fumarolenablagerung *f* fumarolic deposit
Fumarolenabsatz *m/***vulkanischer** deposit from volcanic fumaroles
Fumarolenfeld *n* fumarole field
Fumarolengase *npl* fumarolic gases
Fumarolengebiet *n* area of volcanic fumaroles
Fumarolenhügel *m* fumarole mound
Fumarolenstadium *n* fumarole (fumarolic) stage
Fumarolentätigkeit *f* fumarolic action (activity)
Fund *m* discovery, strike
Fundament *n* basement

~/kristallines crystalline floor (fundament)
Fundamentalpunkt *m* basal point
Fundamentoberfläche *f* basement surface
Fundamentplatte *f* base slab
Fundaussichten *fpl* chances of discovery
Fundbewertung *f* evaluation of a discovery
Fundbohrung *f* discovery well
Fundclaim *m* discovery claim *(of a mineral deposit)*
Fundierungsbodenaushebung *f* basement excavation
fündig rich; yielding ore; yielding oil
~ werden to come in[to] production
Fündigkeit *f* discovery
Fundmöglichkeiten *fpl* chances of discovery
Fundort *m* locality, finding (collecting) place, source (point) of discovery
fünfflächig pentahedr[ic]al
Fünfflächner *m* pentahedron
Fünfling *m* fiveling *(crystals)*
fünfseitig five-sided, pentahedr[ic]al
Fünf-Sonden-Anordnung *f (Am)* five-spot network
Fungosclerotinit *m* fungosclerotinite *(submaceral)*
Funkenspektrum *n* spark spectrum
Funkhöhenmesser *m* radio altimeter
Furche *f* furrow, groove; stria; sulcus
furchenblättrig furrow-leaved *(palaeobotany)*
Furchenmarke *f* furrow flute cast
furchig furrowed
Furt *f* ford, shallow, shoal
~/ohne fordless
Fusain *m* fusain *(coal lithotype)*
Fusinisierung *f* fusinitization *(of coal)*
Fusinit *m* fusinite *(coal maceral)*
Fusinitisierung *f* fusinitization *(of coal)*
Fusit *m* fusite *(coal microlithotype)*
Fuß *m* **einer Bruchwand** toe of a bank
Fußabdruck *m* footprint, footmark, foot impression
Fußbefestigung *f/***luftseitige** abutment toe wall
Fußhöhlen *fpl* stack caves
Fußplatte *f* sole plate, foot plate
Fußpunkt *m* base
Fußspur *f s.* Fußabdruck
Fußteil *m* stilt *(of an arch)*
Fusulinenkalk *m* Fusulina limestone
Futtermauer *f* revetment wall
Futterrohr *n* casing
Futterrohrabsetzteufe *f* casing seat
Futterrohrbruch *m* casing break-off
Futterrohreinbeulung *f* casing collapse
Futterrohrroller *m* casing roller
Futterrohrschuh *m* bottom of casing string
Futterrohrstrang *m* casing string

G

Gabbro *m* gabbro

117
gangähnlich

gabbroartig gabbro[it]ic
Gabbrodiorit m gabbro diorite
gabbrohaltig gabbroid[al]
gabbroid gabbro[it]ic
Gabbroschale f gabbro layers
gabelförmig s. dichotom
gabeln/sich to fork; to bifurcate; to intersect (lodes)
Gabelung f forking; bifurcation; intersection (of lodes); divarication
Gadolinit m gadolinite, $Y_2FeBe_2[O|SiO_4]_2$
Gagarinit m gagarinite, $NaCaYF_6$
Gagat m gagate, jet
Gahnit m gahnite, zinc spinel, $ZnAl_2O_4$
Gal n gal (unit of gravity)
galaktisch galactic
Galaktit m galactite (s.a. Natrolith)
Galaxis f galaxy
Galaxit m galaxite, $MnAl_2O_4$
Galeit m galeite, $Na_3[(F,Cl)|SO_4]$
Galenit m galena, blue lead, led glance, PbS
Galenobismutit m galenobismuthite, $PbS \cdot Bi_2S_3$
Galerie f gallery
Galle f nodule, lump
gallertartig jellous, jellylike, gelatinous, slimy
Gallerte f jelly
gallertig s. gallertartig
Gallit m gallite, $CuGaS_2$
Galmei m galmei (partly smithsonite, partly hemimorphite)
galvanometrisch galvanometric
Gamagarit m gamagarite, $Ba_2(Fe,Mn)[VO_4]_2 \cdot 1/2H_2O$
Gamma n gamma (formerly unit of magnetic force)
Gammabohrlochmeßkurven fpl gamma well survey curves
Gamma-gamma-Log n density log
Gammakernen n, **Gammalog** n, **Gammamessung** f gamma[-ray] logging
Gammaspektrometrie f gamma-ray spectrometry
Gammaspektroskopie f gamma-ray spectroscopy
Gammaspektrum n gamma-ray spectrum
Gammastrahler m gamma radiator (emitter)
Gammastrahlung f gamma radiation (emission)
Gammastrahlungsmessung f gamma-ray measurement
Gammazerfall m gamma decay
Gang m 1. vein; lode, alley, lead (a deposit of ore); 2. dike (of igneous rocks); 3. tear (daily changing of the zero of an instrument); 4. course; 5. workability (of coal)
~/abbauwürdiger live lode
~/abgebauter exhausted vein
~/absetziger benchy vein
~/armer coarse lode
~ aus netzförmigen Trümern reticulated vein
~ aus verschiedenen Mineralen compound vein

~/aushaltender continuous vein
~/bauwürdiger live lode
~/boudinierter wavy vein
~/differenzierter differentiated dike
~/drusiger vuggy lode
~/durch Klüfte zerteilter quarry lode
~/durch Querspalten stufig versetzter linked vein
~/durchfallender conjugate vein
~/durchsetzender cross course
~/echter fissure vein
~/edler pay lead
~/epithermaler epithermal vein
~/erzhöffiger likely lode
~/flacher flat vein (lode)
~/flachfallender lode of medium dip
~/geneigter underlay lode
~/gesprenkelter spotty vein
~/horizontaler lode plot
~/hydrothermaler hydrothermal vein
~/hypothermaler hypothermal vein
~/kataklasierter, zerscherter pebble dike
~/kavernöser cavernous (vuggy) lode
~/klastischer clastic dike
~/kleiner veinlet, venule
~/linsenförmiger lentiform (lenticular) vein
~/mächtiger strong vein
~/mesothermaler mesothermal vein
~ mit Krustenstruktur crustified vein
~ mit Lagenstruktur banded (combed) vein
~/mit Nachfall gefüllter gull
~ mit unregelmäßiger versprengter Mineralisation vein of spotty character
~ mit Vererzungsindikationen likely lode
~ mit zeitverschiedenen Füllungen composite dike
~/nach der Teufe auskeilender gash vein
~/nicht abbauwürdiger unkindly lode
~ ohne Ausstrich blind lead
~/pneumatolytischer pneumatolytic dike
~/schmaler narrow vein, whin gaw, scum
~/schwebender plot lode
~/sedimentärer clastic (Neptunian) dike
~/söhliger flat lode
~/steiler steep (rake) vein
~/tauber dead (poor, barren) lode, worthless vein
~/teleskopischer telescoped vein
~/tonnlägiger lode of steep dip
~/unbauwürdiger unkindly lode
~/verdeckter blind lode (vein)
~/verdrückter und überlappend neu einsetzender spliced vein
~/verheilter crustified vein
~/vielfacher multiple vein
~/wiedereröffneter reopened vein
~/zerschlagener branch vein
~/zersetzter rotten lode
~/zusammengesetzter multiple (composite, accretion) vein
Gangachse f axis of lode
gangähnlich veinlike, dikelike

Gangamopteris

Gangamopteris f Gangamopteris
Gangamopterisflora f Gangamopteris flora
Gangapophyse f skew, spray
Gangart f vein (lode) stuff, gangue [material, mineral, rock], rocky (ledge) matter, matrix ore
~/erzhaltige boose
gangartig veined
Gangbergbau m lode mining
Gangbildung f veining
Gangbrekzie f vein breccia
Gangbrekzienstruktur f agmatic structure
Gänge mpl/**sich kreuzende** interlacing veins
Gangeinschnürung f bout
Gangerweiterung f enlargement of the vein
Gangerz n vein (lode) ore
Gangerzanreicherng f/**[ab]bauwürdige** make
Gangerzkörper m/**kleiner** squat
Gangformation f formation of lodes
gangförmig in vein, lianous
Gangfüllung f vein (lode) filling, [vein] infilling
~/zellige, chloritreiche peachy lode
Ganggefolgschaft f vein accompaniment; dike rocks, dikites; satellite (in plutonites)
Ganggefüge n vein structure
Ganggestein n vein (lode, dike) rock, vein (lode) stone, gangue [material, mineral, rock]
~/aplitisches aplitic dike rock
~/aschistes aschistic (undifferentiated) dike rock
~/diaschistes (gespaltenes) differentiated dike rock
~/glimmerreiches basisches mica trap
~/hypoabyssisches hypabyssal rock
~/leukokrates leucocratic dike rock
~/melanokrates melanocratic dike rock
~/taubes castaways
~/ungespaltenes s. ~/aschistes
Ganggruppe f group of lodes, set of dikes
Gangintrusion f dike intrusion
Gangkontakt m dike contact
Gangkontrolle f/**gesteuerte automatische** ganged automatic gain control
Gangkörper m vein matter
Gangkreuz n intersection of lodes, junction of veins, interlacing veins (dikes)
Ganglagerstätte f vein (lode) deposit
Ganglette f gouge clay, douk[e]
Ganglinie f **des Wasserstands** water level isoline (contour line)
Gangmächtigkeit f/**wahre** width
Gangmasse f, **Gangmaterial** n, **Gangmittel** n s. Gangart
Gangnetz n network of veins
Gangpartie f/**harte** huttrill
Gangquarz m vein quartz
~/zelliger floatstone
Gangrichtung f strike of a vein
Gangscharung f jumble
Gangschwarm m cluster of veins, dike swarm (complex), composite (linked) veins
Gangspalte f vein fissure, abra

Gangstrecke f head
Gangstreichen n line (trend) of lode, course of vein, bearing
Gangsystem n 1. vein (dike) system; 2. burrow system (ichnology)
Gangteil m/**[ab]bauwürdiger** paystreaks
Gangtrum n branch (lead) of a lode, veinlet
Gangtrumzone f compound vein
Gangunterschied m path difference; phase difference; relative retardation; maximum retardation (refraction)
~/optischer relative retardation of optical path
Gangverästelung f forking of vein
Gangverdrückung f, **Gangverengung** f pinch, twitch, twith
Gangverfüllung f burrow cast (ichnology)
Gangverzweigung f network of lodes
Gangwand f vein (lode) wall
Gangwandung f burrow lining (ichnology)
Gangzertrümerung f splitting of a lode into branches
Gangzinn n lode tin
Gangzone f zone of a vein
Gangzug m range of veins, sheeted (shear) zone, group of lodes, linked veins
Ganister m ga[n]nister (quartzitic raw material)
Ganoidschuppe f ganoid (enamel) scale
Ganomalith m ganomalite, $Pb_6Ca_4[(OH)_2|(Si_2O_7)_3]$
Ganomatit m ganomatite (Fe-arsenate with Ag and Co)
Ganophyllit m ganophyllite, $(Na,K,Ca)(Mn,Al,Mg)_3[(OH)_2(OH,H_2O)_2|(Si,Al)Si_3O_{10}]$
Gänsekötigerz n s. Ganomatit
ganzblättrig lamprophyll (palaeobotany)
Ganzkarst m deep karst
garbenförmig sheaflike
Garbenschiefer m fascicular schist, garbenschiefer
Gargas[ien] n Gargasian [Stage] (of upper Aptian, Tethys)
Garrelsit m garrelsite, $(Ba,Ca)_2[(BOOH)_3|SiO_4]$
Garronit m garronite, $NaCa_{2.5}[Al_3Si_5O_{16}] \cdot 13^1/_2H_2O$
Gas n gas
~/adsorbiertes adsorbed gas
~/armes lean gas
~/bei Zirkulationsstillstand angesammeltes trip gas
~/brennbares combustible gas
~/brennendes flaming gas
~/eingepreßtes injected gas
~/eingeschlossenes occluded gas
~/entbenziniertes processed (stripped) gas
~/entzündliches combustible gas
~/freies free gas
~/freigemachtes liberated gas
~/freigewordenes released gas
~/gelöstes dissolved gas, gas in solution
~/ideales perfect (ideal) gas
~/kondensatreiches distillate gas
~/magmatisches magmatic gas

~/**nichtideales** imperfect (non-ideal) gas
~/**nichtreagierendes** inactive gas
~/**ölbildendes** olefiant gas
~/**phreatisches** phreatic gas
~/**reales** imperfect (non-ideal) gas
~/**reiches** rich gas
~/**schwefelwasserstoffhaltiges** foul (scour) gas
~/**seltenes** rare gas
~/**teerhaltiges** tarry gas
~/**unbrennbares** incombustible gas
~/**verflüssigtes** liquefied gas
~/**wassergelöstes** gas dissolved in water
Gasabgabe f **aus Untergrundbevorratung** dispatching of gas from underground storage
Gasabscheider m degasser, gas separator
Gasabscheidung f gas discharge
~ **aus der Spülung** mud degassing
Gasanalyse f **der Spülung** mud logging
Gasanalysegerät n gas analyzer
Gasanzeichen n gas show
Gasanzeigegerät n, **Gasanzeiger** m gas indicator (detector)
gasarm gas-poor
gasartig gaseous
Gasaufbereitung f gas processing
Gasauftrieb m gas buoyancy
Gasausbeute f gas yield
Gasausbruch m gas eruption (blow-out), blast (outburst) of gas
~/**gewaltsamer vulkanischer** eructation
~/**plötzlicher** outburst of gas, sudden escape of gas; instantaneous excavation *(in coal mines)*
~/**vulkanischer** volcanic blow piping
Gasausscheidung f gas precipitation; gas discharge
Gasausströmung f s. Gasaustritt
Gasaustritt m gas seep (spurt, escape)
~/**brennender** flaming orifice
Gasbläschen n 1. small bubble of gas; 2. gas pore *(in minerals)*
Gasblase f gas (gaseous) bubble
Gasbläser m gasser (s.a. Gasfördersonde)
Gasbohren n gas drilling
Gasbohrloch n, **Gasbohrung** f gas well, gasser
Gasconade n Gasconadian [Stage] *(Lower Ordovician, North America)*
Gasdetektor m gas detector
Gasdruck m gas pressure
gasdynamisch gas-dynamic
Gase npl/**durch Assimilation freigesetzte** resurgent gases
~/**juvenile** juvenile gases
Gaseinbruch m **in die Bohrung** gas invasion of the well
Gaseinlagerung f gas storage
Gaseinpreßbohrung f gas-input well
Gaseinpressen n gas repressuring
Gaseinpressung f gas injection
Gaseinpressungsmethode f method of injecting gas

Gaseinschluß m gas inclusion (occlusion)
Gasemanation f gas emanation
Gasentlösungspunkt m bubble point
Gas-Erdöl-Verhältnis n oil-gas-ratio
Gaserzeugung f gasification
Gasexpansionstrieb m gas expansion drive, depletion (solution gas) drive
Gasexplosion f gaseous explosion; explosion of the combustible gases
Gasfeld n gas field
Gasflammkohle f *(Am)* high volatile bituminous coal *(stage A)*; gas-flame coal
Gas-Flüssigkeits-Chromatografie f gas-liquid chromatography
Gasfördersonde f gas-producing well, gasser, feeder
gasförmig gasiform, gaseous
gasführend gassy, gas-bearing
Gasgehalt m gas content
~ **der Kohlenschicht** coal-seam gas content
Gasgehaltsbestimmung f gas determination
Gasgesetz n[/**ideales**], **Gasgleichung** f ideal gas law
gashaltig gaseous, gassy; gas-bearing
gashöffig prospective for gas, gas-prone, prolific
Gashöffigkeit f possible gas prospect
Gashorizont m gas horizon (layer)
Gashülle f gaseous atmosphere; gas skin
gasig gaseous
Gaskappe f gas cap
Gaskappentrieb m gas cap drive
Gaskegelbildung f gas coning
Gaskernen n gas logging
Gaskernprobe[nent]nahmegerät n gastight core barrel
Gaskissen n gas cushion
Gaskohle f *(Am)* high volatile bituminous A coal; medium volatile bituminous coal *(with less than 31% volatile matter)*; gas coal
Gaskondensatlager n deposit of gas condensate
Gaskondensatträger m gas-condensate reservoir
Gaskonstante f/**allgemeine** universal gas constant
Gaskopf m gas cap
Gaskreislauf m cycling of gas *(for oil lift)*
Gaskreislaufverfahren n recycling *(for oil lift)*
Gaslagerstätte f reservoir of gas, gas field
Gasleitung f gas pipe (line)
Gasliftförderung f gas lift
~/**intermittierende** intermittent gas lift
Gasliftverfahren n s. Gasliftförderung
Gaslöslichkeit f gas solubility
Gasmantel m gas jacket
Gas-Öl-Förderverhältnis n producing gas-oil ratio
Gas-Öl-Grenzfläche f gas-oil interface
Gas-Öl-Kontakt m gas-oil contact
Gas-Öl-Kontaktfläche f gas-oil interface (level)
Gas-Öl-Lösungsverhältnis n solution gas-oil ratio

Gas-Öl-Sättigung

Gas-Öl-Sättigung f gas-oil saturation
Gas-Öl-Verhältnis n gas-oil ratio
Gaspolster n gas cushion (lock)
Gasprobe f gas sample
Gasprobenahmegerät n, **Gasprobenehmer** m gas sampler
Gasprospektion f gas prospection, atmogeochemical prospecting
Gasprüfer m gas tester
Gasquelle f 1. gas well; 2. air gun *(seismics)*
Gasregime n gas regime
gasreich gas-rich, gas-charged
Gasreinigung f purification of gas
Gasreste mpl remaining gases
Gassammelleitung f gas collecting main
Gassand m gas[-carrying] sand
Gassättigung f gas saturation
Gasschiefer m gas slate
Gasse f lane *(radionavigation)*
Gassonde f gas well
Gasspeicher m gas reservoir
~/nuklear angeregter nuclearly stimulated gas reservoir
Gasspeicherpotential n gas-storage capacity
Gasspeicherung f gas storage
~ im Wasserträger aquifer storage of gas
~ in einem Salzwerk salt-mine storage of gas
~/unterirdische subterranean storage of gas
Gasspur f trace of gas
Gasspürgerät n gas analyzer (detector)
Gasstrahl m gas blast
Gasstrom m gas jet
Gasströmung f migration of gas
Gastaldit m gastaldite *(variety of glaucophane)*
Gastasche f gas pocket
Gasteer m gas tar
Gastelement n guest element
Gastmineral n guest mineral, metasome
Gastralraum m gastric pouch *(palaeontology)*
Gastransport m gas transfer
Gastreibverfahren n s. Gastrieb
Gastrichter m bubble impression
Gastrieb m gas (pressure) drive
~/natürlicher internal gas drive
Gastriebverfahren n gas drive recovery
Gastropoden mpl gastropod[an]s
Gasverflüssigung f liquefaction of gas
Gasvermessung f gasometry
Gasvolumenmessung f metering of gas
Gasvorkommen n gas pool; *(Am)* pay horizon
Gaswanderung f migration *(of gas)*
Gas-Wasser-Kontakt m gas-water contact
Gas-Wasser-Kontaktfläche f gas-water interface (level)
Gaswolke f gas cloud
Gaszulauf m gas influx
Gattung f genus
Gattungsmerkmal n generic feature
Gattungsname m generic name (appellation)
Gaudefroyite m gaudefroyite, $3CaMn^{...}[O|BO_3] \cdot Ca(CO_3)$
Gault n Gault *(uppermost Lower Gretaceous, middle and upper Albian)*

Gault-Ton[mergel] m Gault Clay *(Albian of England)*
Gauß-Kurve f Gaussian [error] curve
Gauß-Verteilung f Gaussian distribution
Gauteit m gauteite *(plagioclase bostonite)*
Gaylussit m gaylussite, $Na_2Ca[CO_3]_2 \cdot 2H_2O$
geadert veiny, interveined; marbled
geantiklinal ge[o]anticlinal
Geantiklinale f ge[o]anticline, ge[o]anticlinal fold
Gearksutit m gearksutite, $Ca[Al(F,OH)_5] \cdot H_2O$
gebändert banded, ribboned, straticulate
gebankt stratified, bedded
Gebäudeschaden m/allgemeiner general damage to buildings *(9th stage of the scale of seismic intensity)*
Gebäudezerstörungen fpl/allgemeine general destruction of buildings *(10th stage of the scale of seismic intensity)*
Geber m transducer
gebeugt bent
Gebiet n area, region, district, zone, territory
~/abflußloses closed drainage
~/abgelegenes und unzugängliches remote and inaccessible area
~/abgetastetes coverage
~/absinkendes sinking area
~/aklinales aclinal area
~/antarktisches Antarctic zone (region)
~/arides aride region
~/arktisches Arctic zone (region)
~/aseismisches aseismic[al] district
~/aufschlußloses area without exposures
~/bekanntes proven territory
~ des Epizentrums epicentral area
~/dräniertes drained area
~/druckleeres inert area
~/erdbebenfreies aseismic[al] district
~/erschöpftes depleted area
~/höffiges prospect, prolific area, favourable locality
~/in den Ozean direkt entwässerndes exorheic region
~/mineralhöffiges glebe, range
~/mit Eis bedecktes glaciated area
~ mit horizontaler Schichtenlagerung aclinic area
~/noch nicht durch Bohrungen untersuchtes area untested by drilling
~/ölführendes proved oil land
~/ölhöffiges prospective oil land
~/seismisches seismical region
~/tektonisch beeinflußtes tectonized region
~/unaufgeschlossenes unexplored (virgin) area
~/untersuchtes proven territory
~/unvergletschertes driftless area
~/vereistes glaciated area
Gebietsniederschlag m regional precipitation; regional rainfall
Gebietsressourcen fpl regional resources
Gebietssenkung f areal subsidence

Gebietsverdunstung f regional evaporation
Gebirge n 1. mountains *(orographical)*; 2. formation, strata *(geological)*; 3. ground, rock masses, measures *(mining, engineering geology)*
~/**anstehendes** solid (native) bedrock, ledge [rock]
~/**bröckliges** friable rock
~/**drückendes** heaving (sticky) formation; heaving rock
~/**festes** stand-up formation; shooting (shutting) ground; solid (stable) rock; shelf
~/**flözführendes** seamy rock
~/**gebräches** broken (teary) ground; unconsolidated rock (strata), friable rock
~/**gestörtes** troubled ground
~/**gewachsenes** bottom rock
~/**gutes** s. ~/standfestes
~/**hartes** hard ground
~/**hereingeschossenes** broken ground
~/**im Schutt ertrunkenes** waste-covered mountains
~/**knallendes** s. Gebirgsschlag
~/**lockeres** loose ground, unconsolidated deposit
~/**loses** s. ~/gebräches
~/**mildes** soft country (ground)
~ **mit tiefer Wurzelzone** thick-shelled mountain
~/**nachfallendes (nachfälliges)** caving (cavey) formation; caving ground (country)
~/**nicht standfestes** unstable ground
~/**nicht standfestes, sich ablösendes** sloughing formation
~/**plastisches (quellendes)** plastic strata, swelling rock (ground)
~/**schlagendes** explosive rock
~/**schwimmendes** light ground; shifting rock; running country (ground); running measures
~/**standfestes** compact[ed] rock, feasible ground
~/**taubes** barren measures
~/**tektonisches** tectonic mountains
~/**überhängendes** rock shelter
~/**unsymmetrisch gefaltetes** asymmetrically folded mountain range
~/**unverritztes** virgin rock
~/**verritztes** rock affected by working
~/**vorgelagertes** mountain spur, limb
~/**vulkanisches** volcanic mountains
~/**wasserführendes** water-bearing strata; watery rock
~/**wassergesättigtes** waterlogged ground
~/**zerklüftetes** broken ground
~/**zu Bruch gehendes** caving rock
gebirgig mountainous; mountainy
Gebirgsanker m roof bolt
Gebirgsart f species of stone
gebirgsartig montiform
Gebirgsausläufer m mountain spur, limb
Gebirgsbach m mountain creek
Gebirgsbewegung f rock (strata, roof, ground) movement
gebirgsbildend mountain-building, mountain-forming
Gebirgsbildung f orogenesis, orogeny; mountain building (development, folding)
~/**alpidische** Alpidic orogenesis
~/**alpinotype** Alpine orogenesis
~/**assyntische** Assyntian orogenesis
~/**baikalische** Baikalian orogenesis
~/**dharwarische** Dharwar orogenesis
~/**germanotype** germanotype orogenesis
~/**gotidische** Gothian orogenesis
~/**kaledonische** Caledonian orogenesis
~/**karelisch-svecofennidische** Karelian-Svecofennian orogenesis
~/**katarchaische** Katarchaean orogenesis
~/**labradorische** Labrador[e]an orogenesis
~/**laurentische** Laurentian orogenesis
~/**saamadische** Saamian orogenesis
~/**saxonische** Saxonian orogenesis
~/**variszische** Varisc[i]an orogenesis
Gebirgsdichte f density of ground
Gebirgsdruck m orogenic (rock, overburden, compaction) pressure
~/**normaler** normal rock pressure
Gebirgsdruckfestigkeit f compressive mass strength
Gebirgsdruckkontrolle f roof control
Gebirgsdruckmessung f measurement of rock pressure
Gebirgsdurchlässigkeit f permeability of ground
Gebirgsfaltung f mountain folding, orographic plication, mountain-building crumpling
Gebirgsfestigkeit f rock strength; strength of the rock mass; strata cohesion
Gebirgsfluß m mountain river; mountain stream; mountain torrent
Gebirgsfuß m base of the mountains
Gebirgsfußfläche f pediment
Gebirgsgelände n mountainous (hilly) ground
Gebirgsgletscher m mountain glacier
Gebirgsglied n terrane
Gebirgsgrat m mountain ridge
Gebirgshang m mountain side
Gebirgskamm m mountain crest (ridge)
~ **mit Gipfelflur/tief eingeschnittener** sawback
Gebirgskette f mountain chain (range)
Gebirgskörper m rock mass *(mining)*
Gebirgskunde f orology
Gebirgslandschaft f mountain topography; mountain side
Gebirgsmechanik f rock mechanics
Gebirgsmoorboden m mountain peaty soil
Gebirgsnormalspannung f normal tension of ground
Gebirgspaß m [mountain] pass, gate, col
Gebirgsrelief n mountain relief
Gebirgsrücken m mountain crest (ridge)
Gebirgssattel m anticlinal ridge, upbending fold, upfold

Gebirgsschichtung 122

Gebirgsschichtung f rock stratification
Gebirgsschlag m fall of country, pressure burst; popping rock
~/leichter bumb
~/schwerer rock burst
Gebirgsschlagablösen n popping
gebirgsschlaggefährdet subject to rock bursts
Gebirgsschlucht f defile
Gebirgsschub m rock (orogenic) thrust
Gebirgsschutt m mountain waste
Gebirgssee m mountain lake
Gebirgsspalte f rock fissure
~/kleine pin crack
Gebirgsstock m massif
Gebirgsstörung f dislocation; disturbance
Gebirgsstück n/**stehengelassenes** scarcement
Gebirgsverankerung f rock bolting; strata bolting
Gebirgsverband m structure of rock mass
Gebirgsverformung f rock deformation
Gebirgsvergletscherung f mountain glaciation
~/gleichzeitige sympathetic mountain glaciation
Gebirgsverhalten n rock behaviour
Gebirgsverlagerung f strata displacement
Gebirgsvorland n piedmont, foreland, frontland
Gebirgswüste f mountainous desert
Gebirgszug m mountain chain (range)
Gebirgszüge mpl/**mittelozeanische** rift mountains
Gebirgszugfestigkeit f tensile strength of rock mass
Gebläsekies m, **Gebläsesand** m abrasive
gebleicht etiolated
gebogen bent; flexed; arcuate
gebräch friable, fractured
Gebrauchswasser n industrial (process, service) water
gebrochen fractured
gebuchtet embayed
gebunden bound-down
~/an das Ganggestein locked to gangue
gebüschelt fasciculate
Gedächtniseffekt m memory effect
Gedanit m gedanite *(a fossil resin similar to amber)*
gediegen native, free *(metals)*
Gedinne n, **Gedinnien** n, **Gedinnium** n Gedinnian [Stage] *(of Devonian)*
gedrängt crowded, packed
gedreht twisted
Gedrit m gedrite *(variety of anthophyllite)*
gedrungen compact, squat
Gefährdungsgrad m endangering degree
Gefälle n incline, slope, [falling] gradient, acclivity, declivity, descent; head
~/gleichsinniges graded slope
~/natürliches natural fall
~/nutzbares useful head
~/rückläufiges reversed gradient
Gefällebruch m break in (of) slope
Gefällestufe f gradient section

Gefälleunterschied m difference of head
Gefällskurve f gradient curve
gefältelt plicated, crumpled, convoluted, goffered
gefaltet folded, flexed
~/eng closely folded
~/isoklinal isoclinally folded
~/schwach slightly (gently, weakly, mildly) folded
~/stark strongly (intensely, highly, tightly, closely) folded
Gefäßpflanzen fpl vascular plants
gefiedert pinnate, fishbone
gefleckt spotty, spotted, mottled, speckled, blotched, stained
~/etwas fair-stained
~/kaum good-stained
~/stark heavy-stained
Gefließmarke f flow[age] cast, flow mark, gouge channel *(s.a. Fließmarke)*
geflutet water-invaded
Gefrierbohrloch n freezing hole
gefrieren to freeze, to congeal
Gefrieren n freeze, freezing, congelation
Gefrierpunkt m freezing point
Gefrierpunktmesser m cryoscope
Gefrier- und Auftauzyklus m freezing and thawing cycle
Gefrierverfahren n freezing method
Gefrierzone f freezing zone
gefritted baked
Gefüge n fabric *(in petrofabrics and especially for metamorphic rock structures, s.a. Struktur, Textur)*; texture, structure
~/agmatisches agmatic fabric
~/amygdaloidisches amygdaloidal fabric
~/biogenes biogenic structure *(ichnology)*
~/blasiges cystose (vesicular, vesiculous) fabric
~/blastisches blastic fabric
~/blastophyrisches blastophyric fabric
~/blättriges lamellar (laminated) structure
~/bröckeliges shredded structure
~/diablastisches diablastic fabric
~/dichtes dense texture *(rock)*; close-grained structure
~/doleritisches s. **~/ophitisches**
~/eugranitisches eugranitic fabric
~/fadenförmiges filiform texture
~/faseriges fibrous (nematoblastic, bacillary, rodlike) fabric
~/feinkörniges close-grained structure
~/feinkristallines fine-crystalline fabric
~/felsitisches felsitic fabric
~/fibroblastisches fibroblastic fabric
~/freisichtiges macrostructure
~/geopetales geopetal fabric
~/geschichtetes bedded structure
~/geschlossenes closed fabric
~/gewundenes convoluted fabric
~/glasiges hyaline fabric
~/glomeroblastisches glomeroblastic structure

Gefügesymmetrie

~/**granitisches** granitic fabric
~/**granoblastisches** granoblastic fabric
~/**granophyrisches** granophyric (granopatic) texture
~/**granulitisches** granulitic texture
~/**haselnußförmiges** nutty fabric, nuciform structure
~/**heteroblastisches** heteroblastic fabric
~/**holokristallines** holocrystalline structure
~/**homöoblastisches** homoeoblastic fabric
~/**hornartiges** puddled fabric
~/**hyalines** hyaline structure
~/**hyaloophitisch-intersertales** hyaloophitic-intersertal fabric
~/**hyalopilitisches** hyalopilitic fabric
~/**hypidiomorphes** subhedral (hypidiomorphic) structure
~/**intergranulares** intergranular (intragranular) fabric
~/**kataklastisches** cataclastic (crush) structure
~/**kavernöses** cavernous structure
~/**kelyphitisches** ocellar fabric
~/**klastisches** fragmental fabric
~/**kompaktes** compact fabric
~/**körniges** grained (granular) fabric
~/**kristallines** crystalline texture
~/**kristalloblastisches** crystalloblastic fabric
~/**kryptokristallines** cryptocrystalline structure
~/**lepidoblastisches** lepidoblastic fabric
~/**linear gestrecktes** linear fabric
~/**makrokristallines** macrocrystalline structure
~/**makroskopisches** macrostructure
~/**massiges** massive fabric
~/**merismitisches** merismitic structure
~/**miarolithisches** miarolit[h]ic fabric
~/**mikrofelsitisches** microfelsitic fabric
~/**mikrogranitisches** microgranitic fabric
~/**mikrokristallines** microcrystalline structure
~/**mosaikartiges** mosaic fabric
~/**mylonitisches** mylonitic fabric
~/**nematoblastisches** nematoblastic fabric
~/**oolithisches** oolitic fabric
~/**ophitisches** ophitic (diabasic, doleritic) fabric
~/**orthophyrisches** orthophyric fabric
~/**pelitisches** argillaceous (pelitic) fabric
~/**phanerisches** phaneric fabric
~/**phanerokristallines** s. ~/makrokristallines
~/**pilotaxitisches** pilotaxitic fabric
~/**planares** planar structure
~/**poikilitisches** poikilitic (poecilitic) fabric
~/**poikiloblastisches** poikiloblastic fabric (structure)
~/**poröses** porous fabric
~/**porphyrisches** porphyric fabric
~/**porphyroblastisches** porphyroblastic fabric
~/**protoklastisches** protoclastic structure
~/**psammitisches** arenaceous (psammitic) fabric
~/**psephitisches** rudaceous (psephitic) fabric
~/**radiales** radiated fabric, stellated structure
~/**radialstrahliges** divergent fabric

~/**richtungsloses** unoriented (non-direction, crisscross) fabric
~/**röhrenförmiges** tubular structure
~/**schichtiges** stratified structure
~/**schieferiges** schistose (foliated) fabric, plane schistosity
~/**schuppiges** tegular (flaky) fabric
~/**sedimentär-diagenetisches** preconsolidation deformation
~/**sehr feines** impalpable fabric
~/**serialkörniges** seriate fabric
~/**skalares** scalar fabric (structure)
~/**spastolithisches** spastolitic fabric
~/**sperriges** wide-spreading fabric
~/**sperrig-insertales** wide-spreading insertal fabric
~/**sperrig-intergranulares** wide-spreading intergranular fabric
~/**sphäroidales** spheroidal structure
~/**sphärolitisches** spherulitic texture, spherulitic (spherule) fabric
~/**stengliges** linear (acicular, columnar) fabric
~/**symplektisches** symplectic fabric
~/**synsedimentäres** penecontemporaneous structure
~/**tektonisches** diastrophic (tectonic) fabric
~/**übernommenes** inherited fabric
~/**vektorielles** vectorial fabric (structure)
~/**verdecktes** buried fabric
~/**verworrenfasriges** reticulate fibrous structure
~/**verzahntes** sutural fabric
~/**vitrophyrisches** s. ~/hyalines
~/**zelliges** cavernous structure
~/**zonales** zonal structure
Gefügeanalyse f petrofabric analysis
~/**röntgenografische** X-ray texture analysis
Gefügeänderung f structural change
Gefügeaufbau m structural composition
Gefügebestandteil m structural constituent
~/**kohlenbildender** maceral
Gefügecharakteristik f textural characteristics
Gefügediagramm n orientation (fabric) diagram
~/**nicht ausgezähltes** point diagram
Gefügeebene f senkrecht zur b-Achse ac-plane
Gefügeeinregelung f fabric regulation
Gefügeelement n fabric element
Gefügekamera f texture goniometer
Gefügekompaß m/**geologischer** geologic[al] stratum compass
Gefügekunde f science of structure
~ **der Gesteine** petrotectonics, structural petrology, petrofabrics, petrofabric studies
gefügelos structureless
gefügemäßig textural
Gefügeregelung f structural orientation
gefügestatistisch fabric-statistical
Gefügestockwerke npl tiers of different structural character *(tectonics)*
Gefügesymmetrie f symmetry of fabric

Gefügeuntersuchung 124

Gefügeuntersuchung *f* fabric research
gefurcht striated; ripple-marked *(sedimentary structure)*
Gegenbalancier *m* counterbalance
Gegendruck *m* counter (back) pressure
Gegendrucktest *m (Am)* back pressure test *(in gas wells)*
Gegeneinfallen *n* counter inclination
Gegenhang *m* reversal of slope
Gegenkraft *f* opposing force
Gegenmonsun *m* antimonsoon
Gegenort *n* counter headway (gangway)
Gegenrippel *f* antidune
Gegenschußverfahren *n* reversed refraction method, reverse control method
Gegenseptum *n* counter (cardinal) septum
gegensinnig reverse
Gegensonne *f* parhelion
Gegenspülen *n* reverse circulation *(of borehole)*
Gegenstandsmarken *fpl* tool marks *(sedimentary structure)*
Gegenstrom *m* countercurrent [flow]
Gegenstromlaugung *f* countercurrent leaching
Gegenströmung *f* countercurrent [flow]
Gegenwind *m* reverse wind
Gegenzeit *f* mutual (reverse-controlled, total) time
Gegenzeitaufstellung *f* interlocking *(of geophones)*
geglättet smooth
gegliedert dissected; indented *(coast)*
~/stark deeply indented
Gehalt *m* content; capacity; amount
~ an Bergen content of shale *(coal dressing)*
~ an Kalziumkarbonat calcium carbonate content
~/mittlerer average content
~/prozentualer percentage content
Gehänge *n* flank; precipice
Gehängebrekzie *f* talus breccia
Gehängegletscher *m* cliff (cornice) glacier
Gehängekriechen *n* slope creep
Gehängelehm *m* slope wash
Gehängemoor *n* hanging bog
Gehängeschutt *m* rubble slope, slide rock, scree (talus) material, colluvial deposits, hillside waste
~/abgespülter slope-wash alluvium
Gehäuse *n* shell; case; test; conch *(of gastropods and cephalopods)*
Gehäusedicke *f* tumidity *(of fossils)*
gehen/zu Bruch to cave [in], to break down, to collapse, to choke
Gehlenit *m* gehlenite, $Ca_2Al[(Si, Al)_2O_7]$
gehoben upfaulted; emerged
~ werden to undergo (suffer) uplift
gehöckert noded *(fossil shell)*
Gehörknöchelchen *n*/**mittleres** incus
Gehörstein *m* ear stone, otolith
Geiger-Müller-Fensterzählrohr *n*, **Geiger-Müller-Glockenzählrohr** *n* end-window-G-M tube

Geiger-[Müller-]Zählrohr *n* Geiger[-Müller] counter, G-M counter, Geiger[-Müller] counter] tube
Geikielith *m* geikielite, $MgTiO_3$
Geiser *m* geyser
Geiserausbruch *m* geyser eruption
Geiserbecken *n* geyser basin
Geiseröffnung *f* geyser vent
Geiserschlot *m* geyser pipe
Geisertätigkeit *f* geyser action
Geisterfauna *f* infiltrated (introduced) fossils
Geistergefüge *n* ghost *(in crystals and fossils)*
Geisterkrater *m* ghost crater *("ghost"-rings, old craters which have been flooded by younger mare material)*
Geisterreflexion *f* ghost [reflection]
gekammert chambered, camerate
gekielt keeled, carinated
gekippt *(Am)* tipped
geklüftet jointed
~/dicht claggy *(coal)*
gekörnelt granulose, granulous
gekörnt grained, grainy, granulated
gekräuselt ripply
Gekriech *n* [hillside] creep, rock creeping, creepwash
gekritzt striated, scratched, scarred *(by ice)*
Gekrösefaltung *f* enterolithic folding *(in vermicular gypsum)*
Gekrösegips *m* tripestone, vermicular gypsum
Gekröselava *f* ropy lava
Gekröseschichtung *f* contorted (distorted) bedding
Gekrösestruktur *f* convoluted structure
Gekrösetextur *f* enterolithic structure
gekrümmt contorted; warped
Gel *n* gel, jelly
~/wäßriges aqueous gel
~/zerreißbares brittle gel
geladen/negativ negatively charged
~/positiv positively charged
gelagert/darüber superincumbent
~/schicht[en]weise lying stratified
~/zwischen Trappdecken intertrappean
Gelände *n* ground, terrain
~/bebautes built-up area
~/durchkratertes cratered terrain
~/verlassenes abandoned lands
~/zerklüftetes jagged terrain
Geländeabschnitt *m* terrain sector; territorial section
Geländearbeit *f* field work *(surveying)*
Geländeaufnahme *f* topographic survey, survey of a country; mapping
~/fotografische terrain photosurvey
Geländeausschnitt *m* ground sector
Geländeauswertung *f* terrain analysis
Geländebegehung *f* field checking
Geländeerkundung *f* terrain reconnaissance
Geländefahrzeug *n* cross-country vehicle; marsh buggy
Geländeform *f* land form; configuration (conformation) of ground

Geländegestalt f configuration of ground (s.a. Geländeform)
Geländeform)
Geländehöhe f ground level
Geländekarte f topographic chart, (Am) topographic map
Geländekontrolle f field checking
Geländekorrektur f terrain (cartographic) correction
Geländemulde f depression of ground
Geländenadir m ground nadir
Geländeoberfläche f terrain surface; ground level
Geländeschnitt m ground cut
Geländeschwierigkeitsgrad m passibility category
Geländestudien npl reconnaissance studies
Geländestufe f terrace
Geländevermessung f s. Geländeaufnahme
Geländeversuch m in-situ test
gelappt lobulate
gelartig jellous
Gelatinierung f gela[tina]tion
gelatinös gelatinous
Gelbbleierz n yellow lead ore, molybdate of lead, wulfenite, $PbMoO_4$
Gelbeisenerz n xanthosiderite, $Fe_2O_3 \cdot 2H_2O$
Gelberde f latosol
Gelberz n s. Krennerit
Gelbildner m gelling agent
Gelbildung f s. Gelatinierung
Gelblatosol m s. Gelberde
Gelbwerden n yellowing
Gelenk n joint (palaeontology)
Gelenkbogen m articulated [roadway] arch
~/nachgiebiger articulated yielding [roadway] arch
Gelenkflächen fpl articular facets (echinoderms)
Gelenkkappe f link bar; hinged (articulated) bar
Gelenkkopf m condyle
Gelenkquarzit m, **Gelenksandstein** n itacolumite, flexible sandstone
Gelenkverbindung f articulation, knuckle joint
Gelifluxion f gelifluxion
Gelinit m gelinite (maceral of brown coals and lignites)
Gelmagnesit m gelatinous magnesite
Gelmineral n gel mineral
Gelocollinit m gelocollinite (submaceral)
Gelstärke f gel strength
gemasert veined; marbled, streaked
gemäßigt temperate
gemäßigt-arid temperate-arid
gemäßigt-humid temperate-humid
Gemeinschaft f s. Vergesellschaftung
Gemenge n aggregate
Gemengteil m constituent; constituent mineral (of rocks)
~/gesteinsbildender rock-forming mineral
~/kohlenbildender maceral
~/melanokrater melanocratic constituent

~/unwesentlicher unessential (medium) constituent
~/wesentlicher essential constituent
Gemme f gem
Gemmenschneiden n lapidary
Genauigkeit f accuracy
~/geometrische geometrical correction
Genauigkeitsgrad m degree of accuracy
geneigt inclined, sloped, sloping, declivous, declivitous, slanting; tilted; pitching
~/allseitig quaquaversal
~/in einer Richtung monoclinal
Generalfallen n general inclination of strata, average dip
Generationsabfolge f sequence of generations
Generotypus m s. Genotypus
Genese f genesis
Genetik f genetics
genetisch genetic[al]
Genotypus m genotype (rules of nomenclature)
Genthelvin m genthelvine, $Zn_8[S_2|(BeSiO_4)_6]$
Genthit m genthite (Ni-antigorite)
Gentnerit m gentnerite, $Cu_8Fe_3Cr_{11}S_{18}$
Genus n genus
Geoastronomie f geoastronomy
Geobarometer n geobarometer
Geobarometrie f geobarometry
Geobiologie f geobiology
geobiologisch geobiologic[al]
geobiotisch geobiotic
Geobotanik f geobotany, phytogeography
Geobotaniker m geobotanist, phytogeographer
geobotanisch geobotanic[al], phytogeographic[al]
Geocerain m, **Geocerit** m geocer[a]in, geocerite, $C_{27}H_{53}O_2$
Geochemie f geochemistry, chemical geology
~ der Gase atmogeochemistry
~ der Gesteine lithogeochemistry
~ der Salze geochemistry of salt, salt geochemistry
~ der Umwelt environmental geochemistry
~ der Verwitterung geochemistry of weathering
~ des Wassers hydrogeochemistry
~/historische historical geochemistry
~/marine marine geochemistry
~/organische organic geochemistry
Geochemiker m geochemist
geochemisch geochemical
Geochore f geochore
Geochronologie f geochron[olog]y, geologic[al] chronology
geochronologisch geochronological
Geodäsie f geodesy, geodetics
Geodät m geodet[ician], geodesist
geodätisch geodetic, geodesic
Geode f geode, potato stone, vug
~/selektiv gelöste rattle stone
geodenreich geodiferous

Geodepression

Geodepression f geodepression
Geodynamik f geodynamics
~/äußere external geodynamics
~/innere internal geodynamics
geodynamisch geodynamic
Geoelektrik f geoelectrics
geoelektrisch geoelectric[al]
Geoelektrizität f terrestrial electricity
Geofotogrammetrie f ground photogrammetry
Geofraktur f geofracture, crust fracture
geogen geogenic
Geogenese f geogenesis, geogeny
geogenetisch geogen[et]ic
Geoglyphe f geoglyphic
Geognosie f geognosy
geognostisch geognostic[al]
Geogonie f geogony
Geografie f geography
~/allgemeine systematic geography
~/physikalische physical geography
geohistorisch geohistorical
Geohydrochemie f geohydrochemistry
Geohydrologie f geohydrology
geohydrologisch geohydrological
Geoid n geoid
geoisothermal isogeothermal
Geoisothermalfläche f isogeothermal surface
Geoisotherme f geoisotherm, isogeotherm
Geoklinaltal n geoclinal valley
Geokorona f geocorona
Geokratie f geocracy
geokratisch geocratic
Geokronit m geocronite, $5PbS \cdot AsSbS_3$
Geologe m geologist, geologian
~/beratender consulting geologist
Geologenhacke f geologist's pick
Geologenhammer m geologist's hammer
Geologenkompaß m geologist's compass
Geologie f geology
~/allgemeine general geology
~/angewandte applied (economical) geology
~/astronomische astronomic[al] geology
~ der Ozeane geology of oceans
~/dynamische dynamic[al] geology
~/extraterrestrische extraterrestrial geology
~/historische historical (geochronic, stratigraphic) geology, stratigraphy
~/kartierende areal geology
~/marine marine geology
~/mathematische mathematical geology (analysis of geologic problems)
~/ökonomische economic[al] geology
~/physiografische physiographic geology
~/praktische s. ~/angewandte
~/tektonische structural geology
Geologieingenieur m geological engineer
geologisch geologic[al]
Geomagnetik f geomagnetics
Geomagnetismus m geomagnetism, terrestrial magnetism
Geomathematik f geomathematics, mathematical geology

Geomechanik f geomechanics
geomikrobiologisch geomicrobiologic[al]
geomorphisch geomorphic
Geomorphogenie f geomorph[ogen]y
Geomorphologe m geomorphologist, geomorph[ogen]ist
Geomorphologie f geomorphology, geomorphic (morphological) geology, orography, physiography
~ des Meeresgrundes ocean-floor topography
geomorphologisch geomorphologic, geomorphogenic
Geomyricit m geomyricite, geomyricin, $C_{32}H_{62}O_2$
Geonomie f geonomy
geonomisch geonomic
Geopetalgefüge n top-bottom determination
Geophon n geophone, geotector
Geophone npl/**multiple** multiple geophones
Geophongruppenabstand m group interval
Geophonleitung f jug line
Geophonträger m juggie, jug hustler
Geophysik f geophysics
~/allgemeine general geophysics
~/angewandte applied geophysics
geophysikalisch geophysical
Geophysiker m geophysicist
Geopotential n geopotential
Georgiadesit m georgiadesite, $Pb_3[Cl_3|AsO_4]$
Georgien n s. Waucobien
Geosphäre f geosphere
Geostatik f geostatics
Geostatistik f geostatistics *(in the strict sense the mathematical theory of regionalized variable according to Matheron)*
Geosutur f geosuture
Geosynklinale f geosyncline, geotectocline
~/innerhalb eines Kontinentalgebiets ausgebildete intrageosyncline
~/intrakontinentale intracontinental (bilateral) geosyncline
~/intrakratonale intracratonal geosyncline
~ zwischen Kontinentalrand und Borderland closed marginal geosyncline
Geosynklinalentwicklung f geosynclinal development
Geosynklinalgebiet n geosynclinal area
Geosynklinalsystem n geosynclinal system
Geosynklinaltrog m geosynclinal trough
Geosynklinalzyklus m geosynclinal cycle
Geotechnik f geotechnics
geotechnisch geotechnic[al]
Geotektonik f geotectonics, geotectonic geology
Geotektoniker m geotectonician
geotektonisch geotectonic
Geotherme f geotherm
Geothermie f geothermy
geothermisch geothermal, geothermic
Geothermometer n geothermometer
geothermometrisch geothermometric
Geotop n geotope

Geotumor *m* geotumor
Geoundation *f s.* Undation
Geowissenschaften *fpl* geosciences
Geowissenschaftler *m* geoscientist
geozentrisch geocentric
Geradbohren *n* straight hole drilling
geradlinig rectilinear
Gerasimovskit *m* gerasimovskite, (Nb, Ti, Mn, Ca)O$_2$ · 1$^1/_2$H$_2$O
Gerät *n*/**aerogeodätisches** instrument for areal survey
~/**jungsteinzeitliches** neolith
~ **zur Bestimmung der Wasserabgabe der Spülung** filter press
Geräusch *n*/**ohrenbetäubendes** roaring noise of a blow-out *(of an oil eruption)*
Geräusche *npl*/**dumpfe** dull rumbling *(volcanism)*
~/**unterirdische** subterranean rumbling *(volcanism)*
Gerdau-Interstadial *n* Gerdau period
Gerechtsame *f* **vor der Küste** offshore lease
Gerhardtit *m* gerhardtite, Cu$_2$[(OH)$_3$|NO$_3$]
gerichtet directional
~/**hangabwärts** in downward direction
~/**nach unten** downfacing
gerieft *s.* gerillt
geriffelt striated
gerillt grooved, furrowed
geringdurchlässig low-permeable
geringhaltig low-grade
geringmächtig thin
Geringwasserleiter *m* aquiclude; aquitarde; semipermeable bed
geringwertig low-grade
Gerinne *n* riverlet, streamlet
~/**offenes** open channel; open gutter
gerinnen to coagulate
Gerinnsel *n* coagulum; clot
gerippelt rippled, ripple-marked, ribbed
gerissen cracked
Germanit *m* germanite, Cu$_3$(Fe, Ge)S$_4$
Germanium *n* germanium, Ge
Germaniumerz *n* germanium ore
germanotyp germanotype
Geröll *n* pebble [stone], rubble [stone], debris, detritus, scree, wash, *(Am)* slide *(s.a.* Geschiebe*)*
~/**eingedrücktes** impressed (indented, pitted) pebble
~/**fluviatiles** fluviatile pebble
~/**goldhaltiges** auriferous alluvium, rimrock
~/**in Schlammströmen transportiertes** kneaded gravel
~/**marines** marine pebble
~/**mit marinen Pflanzen behaftetes** anchor[age] stone
~/**tektonisches** crush conglomerate
Geröllablagerung *f* debris accumulation
Geröllboden *m* bouldery ground
Geröllbrekzie *f* rubble breccia
Gerölldolomit *m* dolorudite

Geröllfächer *m* alluvial fan (apron)
geröllführend pebbly
Geröllgemeinschaft *f* association of boulders
Geröllgestein *n*/**erratisches** boulder (bowlder) rock
Geröllgneis *m* pebble (conglomerate) gneiss
Geröllgröße *f* size of boulders
Geröllhalde *f* scree, slope of boulders
Geröllkalkstein *m* calcirudite, lime rubblerock
Geröllkegel *m* debris (dirt) cone
Geröllkies *m* cobble gravel *(64–256 mm)*
Geröllpanzer *m* pebble armour *(of desert soil)*
Geröllpyrit *m* buckshot pyrite
Geröllsand *m* detrital sand
Geröllschicht *f* caller
~/**erratische** boulder bed
Geröllsedimente *npl* detrital sediments
Geröllwüste *f* gravel desert; serir
Gersdorffit *m* gersdorffite, NiAsS
Gerstleyit *m* gerstleyite, (Na, Li)$_4$As$_2$Sb$_8$S$_{17}$ · 6H$_2$O
Geruch *m*/**brenzliger** empyreuma, empyreumatic odour
~/**erdiger** earthy odour (smell)
gerundet subrounded
gerunzelt corrugated, crenulated, rumpled, crumpled
Gerüst *n* 1. framework; 2. matrix
~/**organisches** organic lattice *(biogenetic framework in reefs)*
Gerüstbildung *f s.* Diktyogenese
Gerüstdruck *m* grain pressure
Gerüstkompressibilität *f* grain (framework) compressibility
Gerüstporosität *f* framework porosity; true porosity
~/**primäre** growth-framework porosity
~/**sekundäre** secondary framework porosity
Gerüstsilikat *n s.* Tektosilikat
Gerüststruktur *f* **von Tonmineralen** scaffold-type structure
Gerüstwerk *n* framework
gesamtarktisch holarctic
Gesamtausbeute *f* total output (recovery)
~/**erwartete** expectation of ultimate recovery
Gesamtertrag *m s.* Gesamtausbeute
Gesamtförderung *f* total production
Gesamtgestein *n* total (whole) rock
Gesamtgesteinsprobe *f* total rock sample
Gesamthöhe *f* **der Energielinie** energy head
Gesamtkerngewinn *m* overall core recovery
Gesamtlaufzeit *f* total time
Gesamtmächtigkeit *f* overall (total, aggregate) thickness
Gesamtporosität *f* total (actual) porosity
Gesamtproduktion *f* ultimate (gross, cumulative) production
Gesamtstrahlung *f* total radiation
Gesamtvarianz *f* total variance
Gesamtverdunstung *f* evapotranspiration
Gesamtvorrat *m* total reserve
Gesamtwassergehalt *m* moisture content

gesättigt

gesättigt saturated
geschart/dicht closely spaced
geschichtet bedded, layered, in layers, sheeted; lamellar; eutaxic *(ore deposits)*
~/**blätterartig** bladed
~/**dickbankig** massively bedded
~/**gleichmäßig** uniformly bedded, even-bedded
~/**gut** well bedded
~/**in Lagen übereinander** bedded, layered
~/**kaum** poorly stratified
~/**lamellenförmig** shaly bedded *(2–10 mm thickness of laminae)*
~/**nicht** unbedded
~/**schlecht** poorly bedded
~/**schräg** obliquely bedded
~/**undeutlich** rudely bedded
~/**unregelmäßig** warped
Geschiebe *n* pebble [stone], rubble [stone], debris, detritus, drift; boulder, bowlder; *(Am)* slide *(s.a.* Geröll); bed load *(in a river or a glacier)*
~/**diluviales** glacial drift
~/**erratisches** erratic boulder, errant block
~/**gekritztes** striated pebble (rock pavement), scratched boulder
~/**geschliffenes** polished boulder
~/**geschrammtes** *s.* ~/gekritztes
geschiebebedeckt drift-covered, drift-mantled
Geschiebebelastung *f* contact load *(of a river)*
Geschiebeblöcke *mpl* till stones
Geschiebefänger *m* bed-load sampler
Geschiebefracht *f* sediment discharge, discharge of solids, bed-load transport, traction load *(of a river)*
geschiebeführend loaded with detritus
Geschiebeführung *f* bed-load discharge (transport), transport of detritus *(of a river)*
Geschiebegrenze *f* drift border
Geschiebeklumpen *m* till ball
Geschiebelast *f s.* Geschiebefracht
Geschiebelehm *m* [boulder, glacial, clay] till, drift (boulder) clay
~/**angewitterter** mesotil
~/**verwitterter** gumbotil, humic gley soil
~/**voreiszeitlicher** preboulder-clay
Geschiebelehmdecke *f* till cover (sheet)
Geschiebemenge *f s.* Geschiebefracht
Geschiebemergel *m* boulder clay, [glacial] till, drift clay
~/**eluvialer** silttil
~/**in Gletscherspalten aufgequetschter** till wall
geschiebemergelartig tilloid
Geschiebemergelschicht *f* till layer
Geschiebesand *m* glacial sands
Geschiebeschichten *fpl* drift beds
Geschiebetrieb *m* dislodging (picking-up) of sediment
Geschiebewall *m* shingle rampart, boulder wall
geschiefert 1. cleaved, foliated; 2. slaty

128

geschlängelt serpentine, festooned
Geschlecht *n* genus
Geschlechtsdimorphismus *m* sexual dimorphism
geschlechtslos *s.* agam
geschleppt dragged
~/**aufwärts** dragged upward
geschmacklos flavourless
geschmeidig malleable
Geschmeidigkeit *f* malleability, ductile tenacity
geschmolzen wasted away
~/**durch Schockmetamorphose** shock-melted
Geschoßkerner *m* sample-taking bullet apparatus
geschrammt striated
Geschwindigkeit *f* **des Leithorizonts** marker velocity
~ **unterhalb der Langsamschicht** subweathering velocity
Geschwindigkeitsabnahme *f* decrease in velocity
Geschwindigkeitsbestimmung *f* velocity survey *(seismics)*
Geschwindigkeitsfilter *n* fan filter; velocity filter; pie slice filter
Geschwindigkeitsisobare *f* isotime curve
Geschwindigkeitskurve *f* hodograph
Geschwindigkeitslog *n* velocity (acoustic) log
Geschwindigkeitsmesser *m* velocity meter *(for water flow)*
Geschwindigkeitsmessung *f* velocity measurement
Geschwindigkeitspotential *n* **einer Grundwasserströmung** velocity potential of a groundwater flow
Geschwindigkeitsprofil *n* velocity profile
Geschwindigkeits-Tiefen-Diagramm *n* velocity-depth diagram
Geschwindigkeitsverteilung *f* velocity distribution
Gesenk *n* winze, staple
gesenkt depressed, downthrown, downfaulted, dropped
Gesetz *n*/**Darcysches** Darcy's law
~ **des radioaktiven Zerfalls** law of radioactive decay
~/**Hookesches** Hooke's law
~/**Stokessches** Stokes' equation
Gesichtsnaht *f* facial suture *(trilobites)*
Gesims *n* cornice
gespalten cracked; flerry
gespannt confined, entrapped
gesprenkelt spotty, spotted, mottled, speckled, blotched, stained, freckled, sprinkled
~/**mit Pyrit** peppered with pyrite
Gestade *n* beach, shore, coast, waterside
Gestalt *f* contour
Gestaltänderung *f* metamorphosis *(organic)*
Gestaltung *f* **des Meeresbodens** bottom configuration of the sea, topography of the sea bottom

Gestein

Gestängeabfangkeil *m* slip
Gestängeabstellvorrichtung *f* racking system
Gestängebohren *n* boring by means of rods
Gestängebruch *m* twist-off, drill pipe failure
Gestängebühne *f* racking platform, pipe-stabbing board
Gestängefangkrebs *m* overshot with slips
Gestängemagazin *n* drill pipe racker
Gestängerampe *f* ramp
Gestängeschlagbohren *n* Canadian drilling
Gestängeschraubvorrichtung *f* power tongs, drill pipe spinner, iron roughneck
Gestängestrang *m* drilling (drill pipe) string
Gestängetest *m* drill stem test
Gestängeverbinder *m* tool joint, drill connector
Gestängezug *m* drill pipe stand
~ aus drei Bohrstangen thribble
Gestängezugverbinder *m* tool joint, drill connector
Gestein *n* rock
~/abreibendes abrasive rock
~/abyssisches abysmal (intrusion) rock
~/alkalisches alkaline rock
~/allochthones allochthonous (exogenetic) rock
~/altvulkanisches palaeotypal (old-volcanic) rock
~/anemoklastisches anemoclastic rock
~/anemopyroklastisches anemopyroclastic rock
~/angefahrenes (angetroffenes) encountered rock
~/anhydritreiches anhydrock, anhydristone
~/anstehendes solid (native, exposed, living) rock, bedrock, rock in situ
~/äolisches aeolian (anemoclastic, wind-formed) rock, anemoclastic
~/aschistes aschistic rock
~/atlantisches Atlantic rock
~/atmogenes atmogenic rock
~/atmoklastisches atmoclastic rock
~/atmopyroklastisches atmopyroclastic rock
~ aus fossilen Wurmausscheidungen vermicular rock
~ aus Pflanzenresten phytophoric rock
~ aus resedimentiertem Material resedimented rock
~ aus Turmalin und Quarz tourmalite, tourmaline rock
~/autoklastisches autoclastic rock
~/basisches basic (subsilicic) rock, basite
~/bergfeuchtes fresh rock
~/biogenes biogenic rock (*s.a.* ~/organogenes)
~/bioklastisches bioclastic rock
~/bröckeliges friable rock
~/bröckeliges schieferiges shab
~/brüchiges shattered rock
~/cenotypes *s.* ~/jungvulkanisches
~ chemischen Ursprungs chemically formed rock
~ der Granitgruppe granitic rock

~/detritisches detrital rock
~/diaschistes diaschistic rock
~/dichtes compact rock
~/dynamometamorphes dynamometamorphic rock
~/effusives extrusive rock
~/eingebettetes involved rock
~/eisenhaltiges hartes kal
~/endogenes endogenetic rock
~/entglastes devitrified rock
~/entwässertes dehydrated rock
~/erdölhaltiges oil rock
~/eruptives eruptive (extrusive) rock
~/erzführendes ore-bearing rock, stoping ground
~/exogenes exogenous (exogenetic) rock
~/faules soft rock, brush
~/festes stone head, solid rock; shelf
~/fluvioklastisches fluvioclastic (potamoclastic) rock
~/frisches unaltered rock
~/gasführendes gas rock
~/gefrittetes fritted (baking) rock
~/gelöstes loosened (blasted) rock
~/geschichtetes bedded rock
~/geschiefertes foliated rock
~/gesundes sound (unaltered) rock
~/gewachsenes main bottom
~/gipsreiches gypsstone
~/goldfreies buckstone
~/goldhaltiges auriferous rock
~/grobklastisches macroclastic rock
~/halitreiches saltstone
~/hartes hard rock, rip
~/hereingewonnenes mine rock
~/hochporöses sucked stone
~/holokristallines holocrystalline rock
~/hybrides hybrid rock
~/hydroklastisches hydroclastic rock
~ in natürlicher Lagerung/aufgeschlossenes day stone
~/intermediäres mediosilicic (intermediate) rock
~/jungvulkanisches kainotype (cenotypal, young volcanic, fresh volcanic) rock
~/kalkhaltiges calcareous rock
~/karbonatisches carbonatic rock
~/kataklastisches cataclastic rock, cataclasite
~/klastisches clastic (fragmental) rock
~/klüftiges seamy rock
~/kohlenhaltiges carbonaceous rock, carbonolite
~/komagmatisches comagmatic rock
~/kompaktes compact rock
~/konsolidiertes cemented (consolidated) rock
~/körniges grained rock
~/kristallines crystalline rock
~/leicht verwitterbares weak rock
~/lockeres loose rock, scall
~/magmatisches magmatic rock
~/magmatogenetisches magmatogenic rock

Gestein

~/massiges bulky (massive) rock
~/metamorphes metamorphic (metamorphosed) rock
~/metasedimentäres metasedimentary rock
~ mit Schockwellenmetamorphose shock-altered rock
~ mit Wabenstruktur honeycombed rock
~ mit Wasseraustritten /poröses weeping rock
~/nachbrechendes afterburst
~/NaCl-reiches saltstone
~/neovulkanisches neovolcanic rock
~/organogenes organ[ogen]ic rock, organogenous (biogenic) rock
~/ortsfremdes exotic rock
~/paläovulkanisches s. ~/altvulkanisches
~/phytogenes phytogenic rock
~/plutonisches plutonic rock, plutonite
~/poröses porous rock
~/potamoklastisches s. ~/fluvioklastisches
~/primäres primary rock
~/psephitisches rudaceous rock
~/pyrogenes pyrogenetic rock
~/pyroklastisches pyroclastic rock
~/regionalmetamorphes regional metamorphic rock
~/rissiges fissured rock
~/sandiges arenaceous rock
~/saures acidic rock
~/schieferiges schistic (shale) rock
~/sedimentogenes sedimentogenic rock
~/sekundäres secondary (deuterogene) rock
~/sprödes brittle rock
~/submarines pyroklastisches hyaloclastite
~/taubes waste (dead, barren) rock, deads, dead heaps, gangue [material, mineral, rock], dirt
~/ton[halt]iges argillaceous (clay) rock, linsey, clunch
~/trockenes heißes hot dry rock, HDR
~/überdecktes buried rock
~/übersättigtes oversaturated rock
~/ultrabasisches ultrabasic rock
~/umgebendes enclosing (environmental) rock
~/umgekehrt magnetisiertes reversed rock
~/undurchlässiges impermeable rock
~/ungestörtes undisturbed bed
~ unter dem Abraum/festes fast stone head
~/untersättigtes undersaturated (insaturated) rock
~/unverwittertes primary rock
~/verfestigtes cemented (consolidated) rock
~/verwandtes related rock
~/verwittertes decomposed (decayed) rock
~/vulkanisches volcanic (igneous, eruptive, extrusive) rock
~/vulkanoklastisches athrogenic rock
~/wabenförmiges sucked stone
~/weiches soft rock
~/weiches chloritisiertes peach stone
~/witterungsempfindliches weak rock

~/zersetztes rotten rock
~/zoogenes zoogenic (zoogenous) rock
~/zu Bruch gegangenes broken-down rock
~/zum Nachfall neigendes *(Am)* drawrock
Gesteine *npl*/anorthositische anorthositic rocks *(moon's highlands)*
~/gleichaltrige synchronogenic rocks
Gesteinsabfall *m* rock waste
Gesteinsabfolge *f*/zeitlich eingegrenzte chronolith, chronolithologic unit
Gesteinsablösung *f* pot[hole], cauldron bottom
Gesteinsabschlag *m* spall *(by weathering)*
Gesteinsanalyse *f* analysis of rocks
Gesteinsanker *m* roof bolt
Gesteinsart *f* nature of rock
gesteinsartig lithoid[al]
Gesteinsaufbereitungsmaschinen *fpl* aggregate production (producing) equipment
Gesteinsaufschluß *m* rock outcrop (exposure)
Gesteinsaufschmelzung *f* rock melting
~ durch radiogen erzeugte Wärme radioactive refusion
Gesteinsausbiß *m* s. Gesteinsaufschluß
Gesteinsauspressung *f* rock sealing, cementation of rock fissures
Gesteinsbestandteil *m* rock component (constituent)
Gesteinsbestimmung *f* rock identification
Gesteinsbezeichnung *f* designation of rock
gesteinsbildend rock-forming, rock-making, lithogenetic, lithogenous
Gesteinsbildung *f* formation of rocks, lithogenesis, lithogenese
Gesteinsbitumen *n* rock bitumen
Gesteinsblock *m* block, boulder, raft, gobbet
Gesteinsboden *m* lithosol, lithogenic (skeletal) soil
Gesteinsbohrer *m* rock drill
Gesteinsbohrung *f* rock drilling
Gesteinsbrekzie *f* brecciated rock
Gesteinsbruch *m* rock failure
Gesteinsbruchstück *n* rock fragment
Gesteinsbrücke *f* strata bridge
Gesteinscharakter *m* lithic (lithologic, petrologic, petrographic) character
Gesteinschemie *f* petrochemistry, lithochemistry
Gesteinsdatierung *f*/radiometrische rock dating
Gesteinsdeformation *f* rock deformation
Gesteinsdichte *f* rock density
Gesteinsdredsche *f* rock dredge
Gesteinsdruck *m* rock pressure
Gesteinsdünnschliff *m* thin rock section
Gesteinsdurchlässigkeit *f* rock permeability
Gesteinseigenschaften *fpl* properties of rocks
Gesteinseinbruch *m* in einer Höhle choke
Gesteinseinheit *f* lithologic unit
Gesteinselastizität *f* rock elasticity
Gesteinsfamilie *f* rock clan
~/komagmatische comagmatic family of rocks

Gewächshauseffekt

Gesteinsfazies f lithologic facies
Gesteinsfeuchte f natural dampness; interstitial water
Gesteinsfließen n flow of rocks, rock flowage
~/laminares single[-group] slip
~/tektonisches tectonic transport
Gesteinsfließfähigkeit f rock plasticity (fluidity)
Gesteinsfolge f rock sequence
Gesteinsformation f rock formation
Gesteinsfragment n rock fragment, talus, scabbling
Gesteinsgang m vein, lode; dike
Gesteinsgenese f lithogeny
Gesteinsglas n volcanic glass
Gesteinsgürtel m belt of rock
Gesteinshalde f attle heap
Gesteinshärte f rock hardness
Gesteinshülle f rock shell
Gesteinskomponente f rock component
Gesteinskörper m body of rock
~/kleiner, linsiger lenticule
~ mit Fließgefüge rheid
Gesteinskruste f rocky crust
Gesteinskunde f petrography, petrology, lithology, science of rocks, lithologic geology
gesteinskundlich petrographic[al], petrologic[al]
Gesteinslinse f lentil
Gesteinsmagma n rock magma
Gesteinsmagnetismus m rock magnetism
Gesteinsmantel m surrounding rock
Gesteinsmasse f rock mass
~/schmelzflüssige molten rock
Gesteinsmaterial n rock material
Gesteinsmehl n rock flour
Gesteinsmeißel m rock bit
Gesteinsmikroskop n petrographic (polarizing) microscope
Gesteinsmikroskopie f petrographic[al] microscopy
Gesteinsmittel n dirt band
Gesteinsplastizität f rock plasticity
Gesteinsplatte f slab of rock, rock beam
Gesteinsplattenkorrektur f stone slab correction
Gesteinsporosität f rock porosity
Gesteinsprobe f rock sample
~/vorgebrochene pre-cracked (pre-fractured) rock specimen
Gesteinsprobe[nent]nahmegerät n rock sample taker
Gesteinsprovinz f petrographic[al] province
~/komagmatische comagmatic province
Gesteinssäge f rock [cutting] saw
Gesteinsschicht f rock bed (stratum); attal; girdle
Gesteinsschichtung f rock stratification
Gesteinsschlacke f scoria
Gesteinsschmitze f pod
Gesteinsschuppe f scale
Gesteinsschutt m rock debris, detritus, detrital (colluvial) deposit, scree

Gesteinsserie f rock series
Gesteinssippe f rock clan
Gesteinssphäre f lithic sphere
Gesteinssplitt m chip[ping]s
Gesteinssplitter mpl chips of rock
Gesteinssprengung f rock blasting
Gesteinssprödigkeit f rock brittleness
Gesteinsstandfestigkeit f rock stability
Gesteinsstaub m stone dust
Gesteinsstaubsperre f stone duster (dust barrier)
Gesteinsstaubverfahren n rock dusting
Gesteinsstrecke f rock (stone) drift
~/abfallende dipping stone drift
~/ansteigende rising stone drift
Gesteinsstück n stone
gesteinstechnisch rock-technical
Gesteinstemperatur f rock (formation) temperature
Gesteinstrümmer pl rock debris
Gesteinstyp[us] m lithic type
Gesteinsüberzug m rock incrustation
Gesteinsumwandlung f rock alteration
~/spätmagmatische deuteric alteration
Gesteinsuntersuchung f rock investigation
Gesteinsverformung f rock deformation
~ mit Minerallängung in b restricted movement
Gesteinsverwandtschaft f consanguinity of rocks
Gesteinsverwitterung f rock weathering (decay)
Gesteinswiderstandsfähigkeit f rock strength
Gesteinswolle f rock wool
Gesteinszerfall m rock breaking (rotting)
~ durch Frost rock breaking by freezing
Gesteinszerkleinerung f clastation, fragmentation of rock
~ durch fluviatilen Transport der Brandung lithofraction
Gesteinszerklüftung f rock fissuring
Gesteinszerschrammung f rock sco[u]ring
Gesteinszerstörung f rock destruction, crushing of rock
~/biogene chelation
~/mechanische mechanical rock destruction
Gesteinszertrümmerung f fragmentation of rock, rock shattering
Gesteinszusammensetzung f petrographic[al] composition
Gestirn n celestial body
Gestirnhöhe f astronomic[al] altitude
gestirnt starry, starred
gestört disturbed, thrown, faulted
~/tektonisch tectonically disturbed
gestreift banded, striped, striated, streaked
gestumpft smooth[ed]
gesund firm
getönt/leicht off-colour *(jewels)*
Geversit m geversite, $PtSb_2$
Gewächshauseffekt m greenhouse effect *(of the atmosphere)*

Gewässer

Gewässer n/**stehendes** standing (stagnant, ponded) water
~/**träge fließendes** sluggish stream
~/**zum Anstau vorgesehenes** (Am) draw
Gewässerkunde f land hydrology (s.a. Hydrologie)
Gewässerniederschlag m channel precipitation (falls directly into rivers or lakes)
Gewässerschutz m water conservation
Gewebe n/**mineralisiertes** mineralized tissue
~/**trübes** cloudy texture (of jewels)
Gewicht n weight
~/**spezifisches** specific weight
Gewichtsanalyse f gravimetric analysis
Gewichtskontrollmesser m weight indicator
Gewichtsschlag m weight drop
Gewichtssperre f, **Gewichtsstaumauer** f gravity dam
Gewichtsverhältnis n ratio by weight
Gewinde n spire (of fossils)
gewinnbar recoverable, exploitable, extractive, excavatable
gewinnen to recover, to exploit, to extract, to mine
~/**einen Kern** to carry out coring
~/**Erz** to raise ore
Gewinnung f recovery, exploitation, extraction; mining, extraction
~/**gemeinschaftliche** unit exploitation
~ **im Tagebau** open-pit mining, mining by the open-cast method
~ **im Tiefbau** mining by deep mine, mining by level workings
~ **mittels Bagger** strip mining
~ **von Kohle** coal getting
Gewinnungsarbeit f mining working
Gewinnungsart f exploitation method
Gewinnungsberechtigung f exploitation permit
Gewinnungsbohrung f exploitation drilling
Gewinnungsfestigkeit f solidity [of rock] for exploitation (e.g. of ore, minerals, coal)
Gewinnungsingenieur m exploitation engineer
Gewinnungskoeffizient m recovery factor
Gewinnungskosten pl cost of winning
Gewinnungsmethode f mining practice (method), exploitation practice, recovery method
Gewinnungsrecht n mineral right
Gewinnungsschicht f winning (coal) shift
Gewinnungsstelle f borrow source
Gewinnungsstoß m face
Gewitter n thunderstorm
~/**magnetisches** magnetic impetuous rush
~/**vulkanisches** volcanic thunderstorm
Gewitterbö f thunder squall
Gewitterhoch n thunderstorm high
gewitterig thundery, thunderous
Gewitterregen m thunder shower
Gewitterwand f thunderhead
Gewitterwolke f thunder cloud; thunderhead

Gewölbe n arch, arched roof (top), quaquaversal structure
Gewölbeachse f anticlinal (saddle) axis
Gewölbegewichtssperre f arch-gravity dam
Gewölbekern m arch core (of pressure arch)
Gewölbelinie crest line (tectonics)
Gewölbemauer f arched dam
Gewölbescheitel m crest (tectonics)
Gewölbescheitelbruch m anticlinal fault
Gewölbescheiteloberfläche f crestal plane
Gewölbeschenkel m arch limb
Gewölbetheorie f arch (dome) theory
Gewölbewirkung f arching effect
gewölbt dome-shaped, domed
~/**stark** strongly arched
gewunden 1. contorted; coiled; 2. sinuous, sinuate, flexuous
Geyserit m geyserite, fioryte (variety of opal)
Geysir m s. Geiser
gezackt ragged, creviced, serrate
gezähnt denticulate
Gezeiten pl tides
~/**erdmagnetische** geomagnetic tides
Gezeitenablagerung f tidal mud deposit
Gezeitenberg m tidal bulge
Gezeitendelta n tidal delta
Gezeitenfluß m tidewater stream
Gezeitenflußmündung f estuary
Gezeitengefüge n ebb-and-flow structure (sedimentary)
Gezeitengravimeter n tidal gravimeter
Gezeitenhub m range of tide
Gezeitenkolk m tidal scourway
Gezeitenkorrektion f tidal correction
Gezeitenkraftwerk n tidal power station
Gezeitenlagune f tidal lagoon
gezeitenlos tideless
Gezeitenmarsch f tidal marsh
Gezeitenpegel m tide gauge (register)
Gezeitenpriel m tidal inlet; tidal outlet
Gezeitenregistrierung f tidal recording
Gezeitenreibung f tidal friction
Gezeitenrinne f/**schmale** chuck
Gezeitensaum m tidal zone
Gezeitenschichtung f tidal bedding
Gezeitenschwankung f tidal fluctuation
Gezeitenstrand m tide beach
Gezeitenstrom m tidal current (stream), tide current
~ **mit großem Tidenhub** e[a]gre
~/**schmaler** chuck
Gezeitenströmung f tidal (tide) current, race
Gezeitenverfrühung f acceleration of the tides, priming
Gezeitenverzögerung f lag[ging] of the tides
Gezeitenwelle f s. Flutwelle
Gezeitenwirbel m rip tide
Gezeugstrecke f level (main) gangway
GGA s. Geophongruppenabstand
Gibbsit m gibbsite, hydrargillite, γ-Al(OH)$_3$
Gieseckit m gieseckite (s.a. Pinit)
Gießbach m torrent, torrential [mountain] stream

gießbachartig torrential
Gießbachbett *n* goulee, gully, barranca
Giessenit *m* giessenite, $8PbS \cdot 3Bi_2S_3$
giftig toxic; irrespirable *(e.g. gas)*
Gigantismus *m* gigantism
Gigantolith *m* gigantolite *(s.a.* Pinit)
Gilbert-Delta *n* Gilbert-type delta
Gillespit *m* gillespite, $BaFe[Si_4O_{10}]$
Gilpinit *m* gilpinite *(s.a.* Johannit)
Gilsonit *m* gilsonite *(asphaltite)*
Ginkgogewächse *npl* Ginkgoales
Ginorit *m* ginorite,
  $Ca_2[B_4O_5(OH)_4][B_5O_6(OH)_4]_2 \cdot 2H_2O$
Gipfel *m* summit, peak
Gipfel *mpl/***gleichhohe** accordant summits
Gipfelausbruch *m* summit eruption
Gipfelberg *m* peaked mountain
Gipfelerguß *m* summit effusion
Gipfelflur *f* summit area (region, surface), peak plain, even-crested ridges (summit area, skyline)
Gipfelflurtreppe *f* storeyed peak plain
Gipfelhöhe *f* summit altitude
Gipfelhöhenkonstanz *f* summit concordance
Gipfelkuppe *f/***submarine** seapeak
Gipfelplateau *n* summit plateau
Gipfelpunkt *m* summit
gipfelständig terminal
Gips *m* plaster stone, gypsum, selenite, $Ca[SO_4] \cdot 2H_2O$
~/blättriger sparry gypsum
~/erdiger earthy gypsum
~/gebrannter plaster of Paris
~ in Rosettenform oulopholite
~/massiger rock gypsum
~/wasserfreier anhydrite, karstenite, $CaSO_4$
Gipsanhydrithut *m* caprock *(of a salt dome)*
gipsartig gypseous
Gipsaufblühungen *fpl* gypsum bulges
Gipsausblühung efflorescence of gypsum
Gipserde *f* gypseous soil
gipsführend gypsiferous, gypseous, gypsum-bearing
Gipsgestein *n* gypsolith, gypsolyte
~/erdiges friable gypsum
~/feinporiges gypsite
~/massiges compact gypsum
Gipsgur *f* gypseous soil
gipshaltig *s.* gipsführend
Gipshut *m* caprock *(of a salt dome)*
Gipskarst *m* gypsum karst
Gipskarsthöhle *f* gypsum cave
Gipskruste *f* gypseous crust
Gipskrustenboden *m* gypsum crust soil
Gipslager *n* gypsum deposit
Gipsmergel *m* gypseous marl
Gipsplättchen *n* gypsum test plate
Gipsstock *m* gypsum body
Girlande *f* festoon *(of islands)*
Girlandenschichtung *f* loop bedding
Gischt *m* sea foam, spray, whitecap, spindrift
Gismondin *m* gismondine, gismondite,
  $(Ca, Na) [Al_2Si_2O_8] \cdot 4H_2O$

Gitter *n* 1. lattice, grating; 2. pattern *(of diagrams)*
~/flächenzentriertes face-centered lattice, plane-centered lattice
~/heterodesmisches heterodesmic lattice
~/hochsymmetrisches highly symmetrical lattice
~/homodesmisches homodesmic lattice
~/raumzentriertes space-centered lattice
gitterähnlich latticelike
Gitteranordnung *f* lattice arrangement (system), packing of particles
gitterartig latticed, latticelike
Gitterdimension *f* lattice dimension
Gitterebene *f* lattice (atomic) plane
Gitterenergie *f* lattice energy; configurational energy
Gitterfehlstelle *f s.* Gitterstörung
gitterförmig latticed
Gittergeometrie *f* lattice geometry
Gitterkonstante *f* lattice (grating) constant
Gitterlamellierung *f* lattice of twinning lamellae
Gitternetz *n* map grid
Gitternetzkarte *f* gridded map
Gitterorientierung *f* lattice orientation
Gitterorientierungsmechanismus *m* lattice-orienting mechanism
Gitterprofil *n* fence diagram
Gitterskelett *n* lattice-work skeleton
Gitterspektrum *n* diffraction spectrum
Gitterstörung *f* lattice imperfection (dislocation, distorsion)
Gitterstörungsbereich *m* displacement spikes
Gitterstruktur *f* reticular (grating) structure
Gittertyp *m* type of lattice
Gitterverband *m* lattice combination
Gitterwerk *n* lattice work
Gitterzelle *f* lattice cell
Givet *n* Givetian [Stage] *(of Devonian)*
Glabella *f* glabella *(trilobites)*
Gladit *m* gladite, $2PbS \cdot Cu_2S \cdot 5Bi_2S_3$
Glanz *m* lustre, sheen; glance, brilliancy
~/diamantartiger adamantine lustre
~/glasartiger subvitreous lustre
~/metallartiger submetallic lustre (sheen)
~/perlmutt[er]artiger pearly lustre (sheen)
~/poikilitischer poikilitic lustre
Glanzbraunkohle *f* subbituminous coal *(stage A/B)*; bright brown coal
Glanzeisenerz *n* [gray] haematite, iron glance, specularite, specular iron [ore]
glänzend lustrous, shiny, shining
~/glasartig subvitreous-shining
Glanzfleckigkeit *f* lustre-mottling
Glanzkobalt *m s.* Kobaltglanz
Glanzkohle *f* vitrain *(coal lithotype); (Am)* bright coal *(partly)*
~/detritische anthraxylous[-attrital] coal
glanzlos lustreless, lacklustre, dull
Glanzschiefer *m* lustrous schist
Glanzsilber *n s.* Argentit

Glanzstreifenkohle

Glanzstreifenkohle f clarain; bright-banded coal
Glanzwinkel m glancing angle
Glas n glass
~/diaplektisches diaplectic glass
~/durch Impaktmetamorphose gebildetes impact glass
~/mineralisches natural glass
~/thetomorphes thetomorphic glass
glasartig vitreous, glassy; hyaline
Glasasche f essential ash
Glasbasalt m hyalo basalt
Glasbasis f glassy base
Glaseinschluß m glass inclusion, interstitial glass
Glaserit m glaserite, aphthitalite, $K_3Na[So_4]_2$
Glasfäden mpl pele's hair
glasführend glassy
Glasglanz m vitreous (glassy) lustre
Glashärte f chilling
Glashauswirkung f greenhouse effect *(of the atmosphere)*
glasig glassy, glasseous, hyaline
Glaskopf m**/brauner** fibrous brown iron ore (s.a. Limonit)
~/roter fibrous red iron ore, wood haematite, kidney ore, Fe_2O_3
~/schwarzer fibrous manganese oxide, pyrolarite, MnO_2
Glaskügelchen npl **im Lunargestein** lunar glassy spherules
Glasmeteorit m tectite, tektite
Glasopal m s. Hyalit
Glaspech n stone pitch
Glasphase f glassy phase
Glasporphyr m glass porphyry
Glassand m glass sand
Glasschlacke f glassy scoria
Glasschwamm m glass sponge
Glasstruktur f glassy texture
Glastuff m vitric tuff
Glätte f smoothness
Glatteis n [ice] glaze, freezing rain
glätten/Bruchsteinflächen to scabble
glattflächig self-faced
glattrandig smooth-edged
glattschalig smooth-shelled
Glättung f grid smoothing *(of a map)*
Glauberit m glauberite, $CaNa_2[SO_4]_2$
Glaubersalz n glauber salt, mirabilite, $Na_2SO_4 \cdot 10H_2O$
Glaukochroit m glaucochroite, $CaMn[SiO_4]$
Glaukodot m glaucodot[e], (Co, Fe)AsS
Glaukokerinit m glaucocerinite, $(Zn, Cu)_{10}Al_4[(OH)_{30}|SO_4] \cdot 2H_2O$
Glaukonit m glauconite, $(K, Ca, Na)_{<1}(Al, Fe^{...}, Fe^{...} Mg)_2[(OH)_2|Al_{0,35}Si_{3,65}O_{10}]$
Glaukonitfazies f glauconitic facies
glaukonitisieren to glauconitize
Glaukonitisierung f glauconitization
Glaukonitkalk m glauconitic limestone
Glaukonitmergel m green sand marl

Glaukonitsand m glauconite (glauconitic, green) sand
Glaukonitsandstein m glauconitic sandstone
Glaukonitton m glauconitic clay
Glaukophan m glaucophane, $Na_2Mg_3Al_2[(OH, F)|Si_4O_{11}]_2$
Glaukophaneklogit m glaucophane eclogite
Glaukophanlawsonitfazies f glaucophane-lawsonite facies
Glaukophanschiefer m blueschist, glaucophane schist
Glaukophanschieferfazies f blueschist facies
glazial glacial, glacic
Glazial n s. Eiszeit
Glazialboden m glacial soil
Glazialdelta n glacial delta
glazialdynamisch glacial-dynamic[al]
Glazialerosion f s. Gletschererosion
glazialgeformt crystic
Glazialgeologie f glacial geology, glaciology
Glazialgeschiebe n glacial pebbles (drift), glaciated boulders
Glazialgeschiebedecke f mantle of glacial drift
Glazialkies m glacial gravel
glaziallakustrisch glaciolacustrine
Glaziallandschaft f**/kuppige** sag-and-swell topography
Glazialmoräne f glacial moraine
Glazialperiode f glacial period
Glazialsandtasche f sandbag
Glazialschotter m glacial[-borne] debris
Glazialschrammen fpl drift scratches
Glazialschutt m glacial detritus
Glazialschuttküste f glacial-deposition coast
Glazialtal n glaciated valley
Glazialtektonik f glacial tectonics
Glazialtheorie f glacialism
Glazialtransport m glacial transport
Glazialzeit f period of glaciation, glacial period (epoch)
glaziär ice-shaped, crystic
glazieluvial glacioeluvial
glazifluviatil s. glaziofluviatil
glazigen glacigenous, glaciogenic, cryogenic
glaziofluvial glaciofluvial
glaziofluviatil glaciofluviatile
Glaziologe m glacialist, glaciologist
Glaziologie f glaciology, glacial geology, cryology
glaziomarin glaciomarine
gleichaltrig contemporaneous; synchronal, synchronous; coeval
Gleichaltrigkeit f contemporaneity; synchroneity
gleichartig homogeneous
gleichfällig of equal terminal velocity, of equal falling speed
Gleichfälligkeit f equal falling
Gleichfälligkeitsapparat m gravitational settler
gleichförmig uniform; accordant; conformable
Gleichförmigkeit f uniformism; conformability
Gleichförmigkeitskoeffizient m coefficient of uniformity *(grain size)*

Gleichgewicht n equilibrium
~/**chemisches** chemical equilibrium
~/**elektrostatisches** electrostatic equilibrium
~/**gestörtes** disequilibrium
~/**instabiles** instable equilibrium
~/**isostatisches** isostatic equilibrium
~/**isothermes** isothermal equilibrium
~/**kapillares** capillary equilibrium
~/**metamorphes** metamorphic equilibrium (maturity)
~/**metastabiles** metastable equilibrium
~/**stabiles** stable equilibrium
~/**thermisches** thermal equilibrium
Gleichgewichtsdruck m equilibrium pressure
Gleichgewichtskonstante f equilibrium constant (for gas-oil mixture)
Gleichgewichtsprofil n profile of equilibrium
Gleichgewichtssättigung f equilibrium saturation
Gleichgewichtsverdampfung f equilibrium liberation (gas-oil ratio)
Gleichgewichtsverschiebung f displacement of equilibrium
Gleichgewichtszustand m state of equilibrium
Gleichheit f **des Drucks** isobarism
~/**areale** areal identity
gleichklappig equivalve[d]
gleichkörnig even-grained, equigranular
Gleichlauf m parallel shot (seismics)
gleichlaufend colinear
Gleichphasigkeit f line-up (seismics)
Gleichrichtung f homoeotropy (of crystals)
gleichschalig equivalve[d]
gleichsinnig equidirectional; concordant
Gleichung f/**chemische** chemical equation
gleichwertig isovalent
gleichzeitig contemporaneous, simultaneous
Gleichzeitigkeit f contemporaneity, simultaneity
Gleichzeitigkeitsgesetz n/**orogenes** orogenetic rule of simultaneity
Gleitbahn f sliding path
Gleitbänder npl glide (slip) bands
Gleitbettbildung f imbricated folding
Gleitbewegung f gliding movement
Gleitblöcke mpl slump balls
Gleitbrett n launching plank; shear slice (tectonics)
Gleitbruch m sliding (shear) fracture
Gleitdecke f slide (downsliding) nappe
~/**gravitative** gravity slide nappe
Gleitebene f 1. slide (slip) plane; 2. T-plane (crystal)
~/**dichtest gepackte** close-packed slip plane
Gleiteffekt m slippage phenomenon
Gleiteigenschaft f antifriction property
gleiten to slide, to glide
Gleiten n s. Gleitung
Gleitfalte f slip (sliding) fold
Gleitfältelung f corrugation, convolute bedding
Gleitfaltung f slip folding (bedding), slump (convolute) bedding

Gleitfläche f sliding (slip, slipping) plane, slip [sur]face, slickenside
Gleitflächenbruch m lateral slide
Gleitflächenmethode f method of slices
Gleitflächenstapelung f/**subaquatische** glide bedding
Gleithang m 1. slip-off slope; 2. inner bank
Gleitkörper m sliding body (mass)
Gleitkörperabmessung f dimension of the sliding body
Gleitkreis m friction circle
Gleitkreisuntersuchung f circular arc analysis
Gleitlager n journal bearing
Gleitlinie f slip line
Gleitlinienstreifung f slip bands
Gleitmarke f 1. slide mark (cast); 2. olistoglyph (of sandstone on clay)
Gleitmodul m modulus of shear
Gleitpacken m slip block
Gleitpaket n sliding mass
Gleitreibung f dynamic[al] friction, skidding friction
Gleitschicht f flow sheet, (Am) sheet of drift, slickensiding
Gleitschlick m sling muds
Gleitsinus m sweep
Gleitspur f trail, foil
Gleitstauchung f s. Gleitfaltung
Gleitstreifung f slip striae
Gleitströmung f slippage phenomenon
Gleitstruktur f slip structure
~/**synsedimentäre** roof-and-wall-structure
Gleittheorie f slip theory
Gleitung f sliding, slip[page]; slide (s.a. Rutschung)
~/**affine einscharige** homogeneous rotational strain
~ **der Schichten längs der Schichtflächen** bedding plane slip
~/**gravitative** gravitational gliding
~/**laminare** laminar gliding
~/**tiefliegende** base failure
Gleitungsbruch m rupture by sliding
Gleitwulst m leaving scar (sedimentary structure)
Glessit m glessite (a resin)
Gletscher m glacier
~/**aktiver** live glacier
~ **aus mehreren Zuströmen** compound valley glacier
~/**fossiler** dead glacier
~ **in Bewegung** active glacier
~ **ins Meer kalbender** tidewater (tidal) glacier
~/**kalbender** calving (discharging) glacier
~/**neuformierter** recemented glacier (after spalling)
~/**nicht gefrorenen Untergrund überfahrender** warm glacier (ice)
~/**stagnierender** dead glacier
~/**überfahrender** overriding glacier
~/**vorrückender** advancing (proceeding, progressing) glacier

Gletscher

~ **zwischen zwei Gebirgszügen/konfluenter** intermont[ane] glacier
Gletscherabbruch m/**seeseitiger** glacier face
Gletscherabfluß m glacier runoff
Gletscherabhobelung f glacial planing
Gletscherablagerung f glacial (drift) deposit; glacier accumulation
~/**alluviale** alluvial apron
Gletscherablation f glacial ablation
Gletscherabtrag m glacial sco[u]ring, glacial ploughing
Gletscherausbruch m glacier outburst
Gletscherbach m glacial river (stream), glacier[-fed] torrent; englacial stream *(within the glacier)*
Gletscherberg m glacier berg
Gletscherbett n glacier bed
Gletscherbewegung f glacial movement
Gletscherbildung f glacial formation
Gletscherbruch m glacier flood, icefall
~ **und Gletschersturz** m glacier burst *(e.g. by volcanic actions)*
Gletschercañon m glacial canyon
Gletschereis n glacial (glacier) ice
~/**aktives** live ice
Gletschereiseinzelkorn n glacier grain
Gletschererosion f glacial erosion (sco[u]ring, sculpturing), glacier screen
~/**abschürfende** glacial abrasion
~/**splitternde** plucking
Gletscherfall m icefall, ice cascade (cataract)
Gletscherfließen n glacier (glacial) flow
Gletscherfluß m s. Gletscherbach
Gletscherforscher m s. Glaziologe
Gletscherfurche f glacial groove
Gletschergeschwindigkeit f rate of glacial movement
Gletschergrotte f ice cavern
Gletscherhaushalt m regimen of a glacier
Gletscherhöhle f ice cavern
Gletscherkanal m ablation funnel
Gletscherkies m glacial gravel
Gletscherkorrasion f glacial corrasion (planing)
Gletscherkritze f s. Gletscherschramme
Gletscherkunde f s. Glaziologie
Gletscherlandschaft f glacier landscape, glacial topography
Gletscherlawine f ice avalanche
Gletscherlehre f s. Glaziologie
Gletschermassenbildung f mass budget of glacier
Gletschermilch f glacial meal, rock milk (flour)
Gletschermoräne f glacial moraine
Gletschermühle f glacial mill (chimney), glacier mill, [glacial] pothole, moulin [pothole]
Gletschermühlenkames mpl moulin kames
Gletscherrandsee m marginal lake
Gletscherrandspalte f bergschrund
Gletscherrückgang m, **Gletscherrücktritt** m glacier recession (shrinkage, retreat)
Gletscherschlamm m glacial mud

Gletscherschliff m glacial polish[ing]; ice mark (striation), glacial scratch (groove, fluting)
Gletscherschram m s. Gletscherabtrag
Gletscherschramme f glacial stria (groove)
Gletscherschurf m glacial ploughing
Gletscherschutt m glacial (glacier) drift, glacial[-borne] debris, morainic debris (material)
Gletscherschuttboden m glacial soil
Gletscherschwankung f glacier oscillation (fluctuation)
Gletscherschwund m **durch Ablation** downcasting
Gletschersee m glacial (glacier) lake, lakelet
Gletschersohle f glacier sole (pavement, foot)
Gletscherspalte f glacial crevasse; glacier crater
Gletscherstausee m ice-barrier lake
Gletscherstirn f glacier front (terminus)
Gletscherströmung f glacier current
Gletschersturz m s. Gletscherfall
Gletschertal n glacier (glacial) valley; glacial-carved valley; glacier-filled valley
Gletschertätigkeit f glacier action
Gletschertheorie f glacial theory
Gletschertisch m glacier table, ice pedestal (pillar, pyramid), ablation cone
Gletschertopf m s. Gletschermühle
Gletschertor n glacier outlet, glacier (ice) cave
Gletschertrichter m s. Gletschermühle
Gletschertrog m glacial trough
Gletschertrübe f s. Gletschermilch
Gletschertyp m glacial type, type of glacier
Gletschervorstoß m glacial advance
~/**plötzlicher** glacier flood
Gletscherwirkung f glacial effect
Gletscherzerkarung f glacial grooving
Gletscherzunge f glacier tongue (snout)
Gletscherzungensee m glacier-lobe lake
Gley m gley, glei
Gleybildung f gleyization, gleying process
Gliederfüßler mpl arthropod[an]s
Gliederung f/**geochemische** geochemical structure (division) *(of the earth)*
~/**großtektonische** major tectonic division
~/**stratigrafische** stratigraphic division
~/**tektonische** tectonic division
~/**vertikale** vertical ordering
Gliederungseinheit f/**stratigrafische** time-rock unit, time-stratigraphic unit *(e.g. system, period, stage)*
Glimmer m mica
~/**dunkler** dark mica
~/**heller** light mica
~ **in transparenten Tafeln** isinglass [stone]
glimmerartig micaceous
Glimmerblättchen n mica flake (scale, spangle)
Glimmergneis m mica gneiss
glimmerhaltig, glimmerig micaceous
Glimmerplättchen n mica flake

Glimmerporphyr *m* micaceous porphyry, micaphyre
Glimmerquarz *m* venturine quartz
Glimmersand *m* micaceous sand
Glimmersandstein *m* micaceous sandstone
Glimmerschiefer *m* mica slate, mica[ceous] schist
Glimmerschieferhülle *f* mica schist envelope
Glimmertextur *f* micaceous structure
Glimmerton *m* micaceous clay
Globalstrahlung *f* global (total, incoming) radiation *(of sky and sun)*
Globaltektonik *f* [new] global tectonics
Globigerinenschlamm *m* globigerina ooze
Globosphärit *m* globosphaerite
Globulit *m* globulite (*s.a.* Mikrolith 1.)
Glockenkurve *f* bell-shaped curve
Glockenzählrohr *n* end-window counter
Glomeroblast *m* glomeroblast
glomeroklastisch glomeroclastic
glomeroporphyrisch glomero[por]phyric
glomeroporphyritisch glomeroporphyritic
Glossopterisflora *f* Glossopteris flora
Glucin *m* glucine, $BaBe_4[(OH)_2|PO_4]_2 \cdot 1/2 H_2O$
Glückshaken *m* overshout, grab, grapnel
Glühen *n* incandescence
glühend incandescent
Glühverlust *m* ignition loss
Glut *f* blaze
Glutbrekzienablagerung *f* glowing avalanche deposit
glutflüssig igneous, fused
Glutlawine *f* glowing avalanche
Glutschein *m* blaze
Gluttuff *m* incandescent tuff (pumice), ignimbrite
Gluttuffstrom *m* incandescent tuff (pumice, ash) flow, hot tuff flow
Glutwolke *f* glowing cloud
~/absteigende descendent glowing cloud
~/überquellende upwelling glowing cloud
~/zurückfallende back-falling glowing cloud
Glyptogenese *f* glyptogenesis
Gmelinit *m* gmelinite, $(Na_2, Ca)[Al_2Si_4O_{12}] \cdot 6 H_2O$
GM-Zählrohr *n* Geiger[-Müller counter] tube
Gneis *m* gneiss
~/gebänderter ribbon gneiss
~/metatektischer veined gneiss
~/pseudotachylitischer trap-shotten gneiss
gneisartig gneissoid, gneissic, gneissose
Gneischarakter *m* gneissosity
Gneisdom *m*/**ummantelter** mantled gneiss dome
Gneisglimmerschiefer *m* gneiss-mica schist
Gneisgranit *m* gneiss[oid] granite, bastard granite
Gneismassiv *n* gneiss massif
Gneisplattung *f* gneissosity
Gneistextur *f* gneissoid structure
Goethit *m* goethite, needle ironstone, α-FeOOH

Gold *n* gold, Au
~/alluviales alluvial gold
~/dendritisches moss gold
~/fein verteiltes flour gold
~/gediegenes native (virgin) gold
~/kleinkörniges shotty gold
~/klumpiges nuggety gold
~/silberhaltiges dore, electrum
Goldader *f* gold vein
goldähnlich chrysomorph
Golderde *f*/**ergiebige** pay dirt
Golderzgang *m* lode gold deposit
Goldfieldit *m* goldfieldite *(Te-tetrahedrite)*
goldführend gold-bearing, auriferous
Goldgang *m* auriferous vein
Goldgewinnung *f* gold extraction
~ auf Decken blanketing
Goldglanz/mit inaurate
Goldgräber *m* digger, tributor, fossicker
Goldgrube *f*/**ergiebige** bonanza
goldhaltig gold-bearing, auriferous
Goldichit *m* goldichite, $KFe[SO_4]_2 \cdot 4 H_2O$
Goldklumpen *m* gold nugget, scad
Goldkonzentrat *n*/**durch Windsichtung gewonnenes** winnowed gold
Goldlagerstätte *f* gold deposit
Goldmanit *m* goldmanite, $Ca_3V_2[SiO_4]_3$
Goldprobe *f* gold assay
Goldpulver *n* dust gold
Goldquarz *m* gold (auriferous) quartz
Goldquarzgang *m* gold quartz vein
Goldquarzgrube *f* gold quartz mine
goldreich highly auriferous
Goldsand *m* auriferous sand
Goldscheidung *f* gold parting
Goldseife *f* gold placer (washings); auriferous alluvium (alluvial)
Goldstaub *m* gold dust
Goldsucher *m* gold finder (washer)
Goldwaschen *n* gold washing (buddling)
~ im Waschtrog panning
Goldwäscher *m* gold washer; chimmer
Goldwäscherei *f s.* Goldwaschen
Goldwaschherd *m* gold buddle
Golf *m* gulf
Golfstrom *m* Gulf Stream
Gondwana-Fauna *f* Gondwana[land] fauna *(Permo-Triassic of South continents)*
Gondwana-Flora *f* Gondwana flora
Gondwana-Kohle *f* Gondwana coal
Gondwanaland *n* Gondwana[land]
Gondwanaland-Fauna *f s.* Gondwana-Fauna
Gondwana-Schichten *fpl* Gondwana layers
Goniatitenkalk *m* goniatite limestone
Goniometer *n* goniometer
Gonnardit *m* gonnardite, $(Ca, Na)_3[(Al, Si)_5O_{10}] \cdot 6 H_2O$
Gonophore *f* gonophore, reproductive sac *(palaeontology)*
Gordonit *m* gordonite, $MgAl_2[OH|PO_4]_2 \cdot 8 H_2O$
Görgeyit *m* görgeyite, $K_2Ca_5[SO_4]_6 \cdot 1 1/2 H_2O$

Gorstium

Gorstium n Gorstian *(upper stage of Ludlow series)*
Gosauschichten fpl Gosau layers *(Upper Cretaceous)*
Goshenit m goshenite *(variety of beryl)*
Goslarit m goslarite, white vitriol (copperas), $Zn[SO_4] \cdot 7H_2O$
Gotland[ium] n Gotlandian [System, Period] *(mostly not used synonym of Silurian)*
Götzenit m götzenite, $(Ca, Na)_3(Ti, Ce)_{<1}[F_2|Si_2O_7]$
Gowerit m gowerite, $Ca[B_3O_4(OH)_2]_2 \cdot 3H_2O$
Goyazit m goyazite, $SrAl_3H[(OH)_6|(PO_4)_2]$
graben to dig
Graben m trench; furrow; gre[a]ve; ditch; channel; trench fault, fault trough *(s.a. Grabenbruch)*
~/kleiner grindlet
~/tektonisch zentraler rift valley
~/tektonischer graben
~/untermeerischer submarine trench
~/V-förmiger V-ditch
~/vulkanotektonischer volcano-tectonic trough
Graben n digging
Grabenabdichtung f lining of channel
Grabenbewässerung f furrow irrigation
Grabenböschung f bank of ditch
Grabenbruch m trough fault, fault-block depression, depressed rift, [fault] graben
Grabenerosion f gully erosion, gullying
Grabenflutung f channel encroachment
Grabengebiet n rift (ramp) zone
Grabengeosynklinale f taphrogeosyncline
Grabenramme f backfill [trench] rammer
Grabensee m fault-trough lake, rift-valley lake
Grabensenke f s. Grabenbruch
Grabensohle f bottom of trench
Grabenstampfer m backfill [trench] rammer
Grabenströmungsgleichung f channel regime equation
Grabensystem n/**Ostafrikanisches** East African rift system
Grabenzone f graben zone
Grabgang m burrow
Grabgemeinschaft f thanatocoenosis
Grabstichel m chipper
Grad m degree; grade; rank
~ der Bodenerosion erosiveness, erodibility of soil
~ der Gefährdung degree of endangering
~ der Setzung degree of consolidation
~ der Umsetzung degree of turn-over
~ des Trendpolynoms degree of trend, order of trend [polynomial]
Gradation f gradation
Gradient m gradient
~/adiabatischer adiabatic gradient
~/geothermischer geothermal gradient
~/hydraulischer hydraulic gradient
~/paläogeothermischer palaeogeothermic gradient

Gradientenprofil n gradient profile
Gradientmesser m gradiometer
Gradientmessung f lateral log *(well logging)*
gradieren to concentrate brine
Gradiersaline f drying (thorn) house
gradiert graded
Gradierwerk n gradation works, brine concentrating house; cooling stack
Gradintervall n degree interval
Gradiometer n gradiometer
Gradnetz n graticule, grid [of parallels and meridians]
Graebeit m graebeite, $C_{18}H_{14}O_8$
Graftonit m graftonite, $(Ca, Fe, Mn)_3[PO_4]_2$
Grahamit m grahamite *(asphaltite)*
Grammatit m grammatite *(s.a. Tremolit)*
Grammatom n gram-atom
Granat m garnet
~/böhmischer Bohemian garnet (ruby)
~/gelber topazolite
~/rotierter pinwheel (spiral) garnet
Granatamphibolit m garnet amphibolite
Granatbildung f garnetization *(in the rock)*
Granatfels m garnet rock, garnetyte
granatführend garnetiferous
Granatglimmerschiefer m garnet mica schist
Granatgneis m garnet gneiss
granathaltig garnetiferous
Granatisierung f garnetization
Granatpegmatit m garnetiferous pegmatite
Granatsand m garnetiferous sand
Granatschiefer m garnetiferous schist
Grandidierit m grandidierite, $(Mg, Fe)Al_3[O|BO_4|SiO_4]$
Grandit m grandite *(variety of garnet)*
Granit m granite
~/anorogener anorogenic granite
~ des Grundgebirges basal granite
~/glimmerarmer, feinkörniger granitelle
~/postorogener postorogenic granite
~/primorogener primary orogenic granite
~/schwarzer black granite *(trade name of diorite and gabbro)*
~/serorogener late orogenic granite
~/synorogener synorogenic granite
~/umkristallisierter recomposed granite
~/zu Grus verwitterter granite crumbled to grit
Granitäderchen n granitic stringer
granitähnlich granitoid[al], granitiform
Granitaplit m granite-aplite
granitartig granitic, granitlike
Granitblock m granite boulder
Granitbuckel m granite boss
granitförmig granitiform
Granitgneis m granite-gneiss
Granitgreisen m granite-greisen
Granitisation f granitization, granitification
granitisch granitic, granitlike
granitisieren to granitize
Granitit m granitite, biotite granite
Granitkomplex m granitic complex

Granitmagma n granitic magma
Granitmassiv n granitic massif
Granitoidgestein n granitoid rock
Granitoidintrusion f granitoid intrusion
Granitoidmassiv n granitoid massif
Granitpegmatit m granite-pegmatite
Granitphyllonit m granite-phyllonite
Granitporphyr m granite-porphyry
Granitrücken m granite ridge
Granitschale f granite layers
Granitsteinbruch m granite quarry
Granitstock m granitic body
Granittektonik f granite tectonics
Granittrum m (n) granitic offshoot
granoblastisch granoblastic
Granodiorit m granodiorite
Granofels m granofels
Granophyr m granophyre (igneous texture type)
granophyrisch granophyric, granopatic
Granosphärit m granosphaerite
Grantsit m grantsite, $(Na, Ca)_2V_6O_{16} \cdot 4H_2O$
granuliert acinose; granulated, grained, grainy
Granulierung f granulation
Granulit m granulite, white stone, weisstein (high-rank metamorphite)
Granulitbildung f granulitization
Granulitfazies f granulite facies
Granulitgneis m granulite gneiss
granulitisch granulitic, decussate
Granulitisierung f granulitization
Granulometrie f granulometry
Grapestone m grapestone
Graphit m graphite, graphitic (mineral) carbon, plumbago, plumbagine
~/flockiger flaky graphite
~ für Ziegel crucible graphite
~/stückiger Ceylon lumps
graphitartig plumbaginous
Graphitbildung f graphitization
Graphitelektrode f graphite electrode
Graphitgestein n graphitic rock
Graphitglimmerschiefer m graphite mica schist
Graphitgneis m graphite (graphitic) gneiss
graphithaltig graphitiferous
graphitisch graphitoid[al]
Graphitisierung f graphitization
Graphitphyllit m graphitic phyllite
Graphitschüppchen n graphite scale
Graphophyr m graphophyre (igneous texture type)
graphophyrisch graphophyric
Graptolithenschiefer m graptolite[-bearing] shale
Gras n grass
Grasboden m sod
Grasbüschel n tussock
Grasebene f grassy plain; prairie
Grashügel m grassy mound
Grasland n grassland; prairie
~/baumloses veld[t] (in South Africa)
Graslandboden m grassland soil
Grasnarbe f grass cover, mat of grass
Grasnarbenstreifen m buffer strip
Grasscholle f turf
Grassteppe f grass[y] steppe; prairie; pampas (Argentina)
Grat m 1. ridge, [sharp-topped] crest; 2. carina (of fossils)
~/schmaler scharfer razor back
Grätenmuster n chevron pattern
Gratonit m gratonite, $9PbS \cdot 2As_2S_3$
Grauerde f s[i]erozemic soil, podsol
Graukalk m gray lime
Graulehm m gray plastosol
Graumanganerz n partly pyrolusite, partly manganite
graupeln to sleet; to hail
Graupeln fpl soft hail
Graupelschauer m graupel shower
Graupenerz n granular ore, ore in grains
Grauplastosol m s. Graulehm
Grausandstein m gray bands
Grauspießglanz m s. Antimonit
Grauwacke f graywacke
~/konglomeratische conglomeratic graywacke
~/körnige grainy graywacke
~/schiefrige splintery (schistous) graywacke
Grauwackensandstein m graywacke (trap) sandstone
Grauwackenschiefer m graywacke slate
Gravimeter n gravimeter, gravity meter
Gravimetervermessung f gravity meter surveying
Gravimetrie f gravimetry
Gravitation f gravitation, gravity, gravitational force
Gravitationsaufbereitung f gravity concentration
Gravitationsbeschleunigung f gravity acceleration
Gravitationsdifferentiation f gravitational differentiation
Gravitationsdrehwaage f gravity balance
Gravitationsenergie f gravitational energy
Gravitationsfeld n gravity field, [earth] gravitational field
Gravitationsfließkraft f gravitational force
Gravitationsgesetz n law of gravitation
Gravitationsgleitmasse f olistostrome
Gravitationsgleitstruktur f flap
Gravitationsgleitung f gravitational sliding (slip)
Gravitationskonstante f gravitation[al] constant
Gravitationskraft f gravity (gravitational) force
Gravitationsparameter m gravitational parameter
Gravitationspotential n gravity (gravitational) potential
Gravitationsseigerung f gravity segregation

Gravitationsströmung

Gravitationsströmung f gravitational flow
Gravitationstektonik f gravitational tectonics
Gravitationsvariometer n gravity variometer
Gravitationswelle f gravitational wave
Greenalith m greenalite, $(Fe^{..}, Fe^{...})_{<6}[(OH)_8|Si_4O_{10}]$
Greenockit m greenockite, cadmium ochre (blende), β-CdS
Greenwich-Meridian m Greenwich meridian
Greenwich-Ortszeit f Greenwich apparent time
~/mittlere Greenwich civil (mean) time
Greenwich-Sternzeit f Greenwich sidereal time
Greenwichzeit f/mittlere universal time
Greifer m grapple, grab
Greiferprobe f grab sample
Greigit m greigite, Fe_3S_4
Greisen m greisen, hyalomite
Greisenalter n old age (geomorphologically)
Greisenbildung f greisening, greisenization
Greisenformen fpl/**topografische** senile topography
Greisenstadium n stage of old age
Grenville n Grenvillian, Grenville (Upper Precambrian in North America, Grenville district)
Grenville-Tektogenese f Grenville folding (Upper-Precambrian in North America)
Grenzbedingung f boundary condition
~/geologische geologic[al] fence
Grenzblatt n folding tear fault
Grenzbohrloch n determining borehole
Grenzdichte f critical density
Grenzdruck m limiting pressure
Grenze f boundary line
~ des Eises glacial boundary
~/geologische geologic[al] barrier
Grenzen fpl/**korrespondierende** compromise boundaries
Grenzfläche f interface; boundary surface (plane, layer), limit plane; bounding surface (of crystals)
~/geneigte dipping interface
~/rauhe aplanetic surface (seismics)
~/seismische elastic discontinuity
~/stratigrafische stratigraphic[al] boundary plane
~/tektonische tectonic contact
~/untere base surface (of a layer)
Grenzflächenkräfte fpl interfacial (film) forces (e.g. of water)
Grenzflächenpotential n interface potential
Grenzflächenreibung f boundary-layer friction
Grenzflächenspannung f interfacial tension
Grenzflächenwelle f interfacial (boundary) wave
Grenzfrequenz f cut-off frequency
Grenzgefälle n critical gradient (slope)
Grenzgehalt m cut-off grade (condition for deposits)
Grenzgeschwindigkeit f critical velocity; permissible velocity; threshold velocity (e.g. for erosion by wind)
Grenzgleichgewicht n limit equilibrium
Grenzkonzentration f critical concentration; threshold concentration (e.g. for mineralization of water)
Grenzkurve f boundary system
Grenzlast f ultimate load; limit load
Grenzlinie f limit line
Grenzmarkierung f hoarstone
Grenzrelief n boundary relief (ichnology)
Grenzschicht f interface, boundary layer
~ eines Speichers confining stratum
~/laminare laminar boundary layer
~/turbulente turbulent boundary layer
Grenzschichtablösung f separation of the boundary layer
Grenzschichterscheinungen fpl barrier layer phenomena
Grenzsieblinie f limiting grading curve
Grenzspannung f limiting (failure) stress
Grenzspannungskreis m circle of stress limit
Grenzwert m limit of concentration (hydrochemics)
Grenzwinkel m limit (critical) angle, angle of draw
~/dynamischer travelling limit angle, dynamic angle of draw
Grenzziehung f **zwischen Zyklen** delimitation between cycles
Grey Beds fpl Grey Beds (Karnian Series in North America)
Grieß m grit
grießförmig calculiform
grießig gritty
Griffelschiefer m grapholite, grapholith, pencil slate
Griffelschieferung f linear schistosity (cleavage)
Griffelstruktur f prismatic jointing
Griffithit m griffithite (variety of saponite)
Griphit m griphite, $(Mn, Na, Ca)_3(Al, Mn)_2[PO_3|(OH, F)]_3$
Griquait m griquaite (magmatic nodules in ultrabasic rock types)
Griquaitschale f griquaite layers
Grit m grit
Grobabtastung f coarse scanning
grobbankig thickly stratified
Grobboden m coarse soil
Grobbrecher m coarse breaker (crusher), stone breaker
grobbrekziös coarsely brecciated
Grobdetritus m coarse detritus
Grobdetritus-Mudde f coarse detrital organic mud
Grobeinstellung f coarse adjustment
Groberz n coarse ore
grobfaserig coarse-fibred
Grobgefüge n macrostructure
grobgeschichtet coarsely bedded, coarse-bedded

Grobkalkschicht f coarse-limestone bed
Grobkies m coarse gravel; pebble; cobble
grobklastisch coarsely clastic
Grobkonglomerat n coarse[-pebbled] conglomerate
grobkörnig coarsely granular, coarse-grained, large-grained; coarse-textured; macrocrystalline
Grobkörnigkeit f coarseness
Grobkreide f coarse chalk
grobkristallinisch coarse-crystalline, granular-crystalline
Grobortung f coarse radiolocation
Grobporen fpl quickly draining pores
grobporig coarse-pored, coarsely porous
grobporphyrisch magnophyric *(diameter > 5 mm)*
Grobrechen m coarse screen
Grobsalz n dairy salt
Grobsand m coarse sand, grit
~/lehmiger loamy coarse sand
Grobsandstein m coarse sandstone
Grobschlamm m coarse slurry
Grobschluff m coarse silt
Grobschotter m coarse crushed stone
Grobsiebung f coarse screening
Grobspalten n blocking, sledging
Grobsplitt m coarse stone chip[ping]s
Grob- und Mittelkies m/**sandiger** sandy coarse and medium gravel
Grobzerkleinerung f coarse crushing (reduction)
Grobzerkleinerungsmaschine f rock (stone) crusher
Grospydit m grospydite *(grossularite-pyrope-disthene rock)*
Großabbau m large workings
Großbeben n [very] catastropic earthquake
Großbohrloch n large[-size] borehole, large-diameter hole
Großbrekzie f/**[platten]tektonische** mélange
Größe f/**natürliche** natural size
Größenordnung f order of magnitude
Größenwachstum n growth of size
Großfalte f large-scale fold, broad warp
Großintrusion f major intrusion
Großkar n compound cirque
Großkluft f major (main, master) joint
Großköpfigkeit f macrocephaly *(of fossils)*
Großkreis m great circle *(of orientation diagram)*
Großkristall m megacryst
Großkristallbildung f **durch Rekristallisation** integration
Großlochbohren n large-hole drilling, big-hole drilling
~/schlagendes hammer-down of the hole
Großlochbohrmaschine f drilling rig
Großlochbohrmeißel m large-diameter bit
großlückig open-grained
Großrippel f sand wave, megaripple, metaripple

Großspeicher m large reservoir
großstückig lumpy, large-sized
Großtektonik f macrotectonics
Grossular m grossularite, $Ca_3Al_2[SiO_4]_3$
Großversuch m large-scale test, full-scale experiment
Grotte f sea cavern
~/torartige cave arch
Groutit m groutite, α-MnOOH
Grovesit m grovesite, $(Mn, Mg, Al)_6[(OH)_8|(Si, Al)_4O_{10}]$
Grube f pit; mine; quarry *(of stones)*
~/ersoffene flooded (drowned) mine
~/fündige discovery shaft
~ mit Stollenförderung drift mine *(without shaft)*
~/schlagwetterfreie non-gassy mine
~/stillgelegte mine shut-down, gotten
~/stilliegende lie
~/unrentable barren mine
Grubenaufnahme f underground survey[ing], latch[ing]
Grubenausbau m pit arch
Grubenbau m mine (underground) working, mine digging
~/abgeworfener goaf
~/enger narrow working
~/unterirdischer closed work
Grubenbemusterung f mine sampling
Grubenbrand m mine fire
Grubeneingang m pit head
Grubeneinsturz m falling-in of mine
Grubenentwässerung f mine dewatering
~/kombinierte combined mine drainage
~/untertägige underground mine drainage
Grubenerz n ore rough from the mine, run-of-mine ore
Grubenfeld n mine field, mining field (district), allotment, set of mine
Grubenfeldriß m mining area plan, claim map
Grubengas n pit (marsh) gas, methane, CH_4
~ mit CO black damp
Grubengasanzeiger m methane detector
Grubengebäude n **mit natürlicher Wasserhaltung** level-free workings
Grubengebiet n minery
Grubengeologe m mining geologist
Grubengeologie f mine (mining) geology
Grubenhydrogeologie f hydrogeology of mines
Grubenkapazität f mine capacity
Grubenklein n smalls
Grubenkompaß m mining compass, miner's dial
Grubenplan m plan of mine
Grubenräume mpl mine openings
Grubenriß m map of mine
Grubenschlamm m sleck
Grubensohle f mine floor
Grubenstaub m mine dust
Grubenstollen m mine adit
Grubenteile mpl/**abgebaute** mined-out stopes of a mine

Grubenversatz

Grubenversatz *m* packing
Grubenvorfeldentwässerung *f* preliminary dewatering of underground mine
Grubenwasser *n* mine (pit) water, swallet
Grubenwässer *npl*/**hochaggressive** highly aggressive mine waters
~/**saure** acid mine drainage
Grubenwasserschutz *m* protection against mine waters
Grubenwetter *pl* mine atmosphere
Grünbleierz *n* green lead ore, pyromorphite, $Pb_5[Cl|(PO_4)_3]$
Grund *m* 1. ground, earth, soil; 2. bottom
~/**sumpfiger** cripple
Grundablagerung *f* bed load *(e.g. in a river)*
Grundablagerungen *fpl*/**geschichtete** bottomset beds
~ **vor dem Delta** prodelta
Grundablaß *m* bottom (scour) outlet, bottom (lower) discharge tunnel, bottom-emptying gallery
Grundanalyse *f* base analysis
Grundanker *m* ground anchor
Grundaufnahme *f s.* Geländeaufnahme
Grundbau *m* foundation engineering (practice)
Grundbelastung *f* basic load
Grundblock *m* basement block
Grundbruch *m* ground failure, subsidence, breach
~/**hydraulischer** seepage (piping) failure, spring
~/**statischer** base failure
Grundbruchuntersuchung *f* soil-failure investigation
Grundebene *f* basal plane
Grundeis *n* ground (bottom, anchor) ice
Grundfalte *f* basic (basement) fold
Grundfeuchtigkeit *f* soil moisture
~/**sich abwärts bewegende** mobile water
Grundfläche *f* basal face
Grundgebirge *n* foundation rock, basement [rocks, complex], substratum of old rock
~/**kristallines** crystalline basement
~/**präkambrisches** Precambrian basement
Grundgebirgsdecke *f* basement nappe
Grundgesamtheit *f* population *(statistics)*
Grundgesetz *n*/**kristallchemisches** basic crystallochemical law
Grundhorizont *m* bottom level
Gründigkeit *f* soil depth
Grundkabel *n* bay cable *(sea seismics)*
Grundkonglomerat *n* base[ment] conglomerate
Grundkörper *m s.* Kluftkörper
Grundlawine *f* ground avalanche, avalanche of earth
Grundlinie *f* base line
Grundluft *f* ground air
~/**gespannte** confined ground air
Grundluftzone *f* zone of aeration
Grundmasse *f* ground mass; matrix; base

~ **eines Porphyrs** base (paste) of a porphyry
Grundmoräne *f* ground (bottom, base, basal) moraine, [basal] till
grundmoränenbedeckt till-covered
Grundmoränendecke *f* cover of till
Grundmoränengeschiebe *n* lodgement till
Grundmoränenlandschaft *f* drift (till-plains) topography
Grundmoränentümpel *m* swale
Grundplatte *f* base slab
Grundpolarisierbarkeit *f* basic polarizability
Grundprobensammler *m* bottom grab
Grundregime *n*/**paläohydrogeologisches** palaeohydrogeological basic regime
Grundriß *m* ground plan, layout
~/**im** in plan, in outline
Grundschicht *f* bottom slice, base course
Grundschotter *m* deep gravel
Grundstrecke *f* bottom road, main (mother) gate
Grundströmung *f* bottom current
Gründung *f* foundation
~ **auf Steinschüttung** riprap foundation
Gründungsfels *m* rock foundation
Gründungskörper *m* foundation body
Gründungstiefe *f* depth of foundation
Grundwasser *n* ground (underground, subsoil, subterranean, level) water, underwater
~/**artesisches** artesian ground water *(overflowing)*
~/**durch magmatische Wärme verdampftes** resurgent vapours
~/**freies** *s.* ~/ungespanntes
~/**gebundenes** *s.* ~/gespanntes
~/**gespanntes** confined (attached) ground water, artesian water
~ **im Permafrost** intrapermafrost water
~/**künstliches** artificial ground water
~ **mit freier Oberfläche** free (unconfined) ground water, phreatic water
~/**oberflächennahes** perched ground water
~/**salinares untermeerisches** submarine salty ground water
~/**schwebendes** suspended subsurface water; perched ground water
~/**süßes untermeerisches** submarine fresh ground water
~ **über dem Permafrost** suprapermafrost water
~/**ungespanntes** free (unconfined) ground water, phreatic [ground] water, non-artesian water
~ **unter dem Permafrost** subpermafrost water
~/**zusitzendes** ground water entering sewers
Grundwasserabdichtung *f* subsoil water packing
Grundwasserabfluß *m* ground-water discharge (runoff)
~/**unechter** interflow
Grundwasserabsenkung *f* ground-water lowering, lowering of the ground-water surface, lowering of subsoil water, subsidence (recession) of ground-water level

Grundwasserabsenkungsanlage *f* ground-water lowering installation
~ **mit Filterbrunnen** well system (point installation), dewatering installation (system)
Grundwasserabsenkungskurve *f* recession curve of ground water
Grundwasserabsinken *n* s. Grundwasserabsenkung
Grundwasserader *f* ground-water artery
Grundwasseraltersdatierung *f* ground-water dating
Grundwasseranreicherung *f*/**induzierte** induced recharge of ground water
~/**künstliche** artificial recharge of ground water
Grundwasseranstieg *m* ground-water increase
Grundwasseraufbrauch *m* ground-water depletion
Grundwasseraußerbilanzvorrat *m* ground-water resource out of balance
Grundwasseraustritt *m* ground-water discharge
~/**flächenhafter** seepage spring
Grundwasserbecken *n* ground-water basin (reservoir)
Grundwasserbedarf *m* ground-water use
Grundwasserbelastung *f* ground-water load
Grundwasserbeobachtung *f* ground-water observation
Grundwasserbeobachtungsnetz *n* groundwater observation network
Grundwasserbeobachtungsrohr *n* gauge well, ground-water check borehole, ground-water observation well
Grundwasserberg *m* ground-water mound
Grundwasserbestandsaufnahme *f* ground-water inventory
Grundwasserbewegung *f* ground-water movement
Grundwasserbewirtschaftung *f* ground-water management
Grundwasserbilanz *f* ground-water balance
Grundwasserbilanzvorrat *m* ground-water balance resource
Grundwasserdargebot *n* ground-water recharge
Grundwasserdeckschicht *f* confining bed, ceiling of an aquiferous layer
Grundwasserdetailerkundung *f* detailed ground-water prospection (exploration)
Grundwassereinzugsgebiet *n* ground-water basin
Grundwasserentnahme *f* tapping of ground water
Grundwassererfassung *f* catchment of ground waters
Grundwasserergiebigkeit *f* yield of an aquiferous layer
Grundwassererhöhung *f* ground-water increase
Grundwassererkundung *f* ground-water prospection (exploration)

Grundwassererschließung *f* capture of underground water
Grundwasserfassung *f* ground-water captation
Grundwasserfläche *f* phreatic surface
Grundwasserfließrichtung *f* direction of ground-water flow
Grundwasserfördermenge *f* ground-water output
Grundwassergewinnung *f* winning of ground water
Grundwassergleiche *f* ground-water [surface] contour, subsoil water-level contour, isopiestic line
Grundwassergleichenkarte *f* contour map of the water table
Grundwasserhaushalt *m* subterranean water system, ground-water resources
Grundwasserhaushaltsgleichung *f* equation for ground-water resources
Grundwasserherkunft *f* ground-water origin
Grundwasserhöhengleiche *f* s. Grundwassergleiche
Grundwasserhöhenlinie *f* water table isohypse
Grundwasserhorizont *m* ground-water horizon
~/**hängender** perched ground water
Grundwasserhydraulik *f* ground-water hydraulics
Grundwasserisohypse *f* ground-water isohypse; ground-water isoline
Grundwasserkunde *f* subsurface hydrology
Grundwasserkuppeln *fpl* ground-water ridges
Grundwasserlagerstätte *f* ground-water deposit
Grundwasserlagerstättenvorrat *m* static ground-water resource; ground-water deposit resource
Grundwasserleiter *m* water-bearing bed (formation, horizon), aquifer [layer] permeable bed
~/**geringpermeabler** aquiclude; aquitarde; semipermeable (leaky) aquifer
~/**küstennaher** coastal (nearshore) aquifer
~ **mit artesischem (gespanntem) Grundwasser** artesian aquifer
Grundwasserleitermächtigkeit *f* aquifer thickness
Grundwasserliefervermögen *n* groundwater deliverability
Grundwassermächtigkeit *f* ground-water thickness; ground-water sheet
Grundwassermeßstelle *f* ground-water measuring point
Grundwassernährgebiet *n* ground-water catchment (drainage) area
Grundwasserneubildung *f* recharge of ground water
Grundwasseroberfläche *f* water table, surface of subsoil water
Grundwasserpflanze *f* phreatophyte

Grundwasserraubbau

Grundwasserraubbau *m* overdraft of ground water
Grundwasserregime *n* ground-water regime
Grundwasserreservoir *n* ground-water reservoir
Grundwasserressourcen *fpl* ground-water resources
Grundwasserschicht *f* ground-water sheet
~/phreatische phreatic surface
Grundwasserschutz *m* ground-water protection
Grundwasserschutzgebiet *n* ground-water protection area
Grundwassersenkung *f s.* Grundwasserabsenkung
Grundwassersohle *f* bottom of an aquifer layer, ground-water bottom, confining stratum (layer)
Grundwassersohlschicht *f* [lower] confining bed, underlying stratum of the ground water
Grundwasserspeicher *m* ground-water reservoir
~/artesischer artesian aquifer
~/leckender leaky aquifer
Grundwasserspeicherung *f* ground-water storage
Grundwasserspende *f* ground-water recharge, module of ground-water flow
~/künstliche artificial recharge
Grundwasserspiegel *m* ground-water level (table), subsoil water level (table), phreatic nappe (surface), water table
~/angespannter *s.* **~/gespannter**
~/artesisch gespannter false water table
~/artesischer piezometric [ground-water] surface
~/gesenkter lowered ground-water level
~/gespannter piezometric [ground-water] surface, perched water table
~/ungesenkter natural ground-water level
Grundwasserspiegelabfall *m* phreatic decline
Grundwasserspiegelanstieg *m* phreatic rise
Grundwasserspiegelgefälle *n* water-table gradient
Grundwasserspiegelschwankung *f* ground-water table fluctuation, phreatic fluctuation
Grundwasserstand *m* ground-water level
Grundwasserstau *m* ground-water swell
Grundwasserstauer *m* aquiclude; aquifuge; impermeable bed
~/begrenzt durchlässiger aquitard
Grundwasserstockwerk *n* ground-water storey, multiaquifer formation
Grundwasserstrom *m* flow of ground water, subterranean current
Grundwasserstromsickerung *f* underground seepage, underseepage
Grundwasserströmung *f* ground-water flow
~/instationäre (nichtstationäre) unsteady flow of ground water, non-steady ground-water flow
~/stationäre steady flow of ground water
Grundwasserströmungsfeld *n* field of ground-water flow, current field of ground water
Grundwassersuche *f* ground-water prospection (exploration)
Grundwassertal *n* ground-water trench
Grundwasserteufenkarte *f* depth-to-water map
Grundwasserträger *m s.* Grundwasserleiter
Grundwasserverunreinigung *f* ground-water pollution (contamination)
Grundwasservorerkundung *f* ground-water preliminary exploration
Grundwasservorkommen *n* ground-water occurrence
Grundwasservorräte *mpl* ground-water resources
Grundwasservorratsprognose *f* ground-water resources (reserve) prognosis
Grundwinkel *m* base angle
Grünerde *f* green earth, terra verte, celadonite *(Fe-, Mg-, K-silicate)*
Grunerit *m*, **Grünerit** *m* grünerite, grunerite, $(Fe,Mg)_7[OH|Si_4O_{11}]_2$
Grünlandmoor *n* lowland (flat) bog, fen
Grünlingit *m* grünlingite, Bi_4Te_2S
Grünsand *m* green (glauconite) sand
~/Oberer Upper Greensand *(middle and upper Albian, England)*
~/Unterer Lower Greensand *(Aptian and lower Albian, England)*
Grünsandstein *m* green sandstone
Grünschiefer *m* greenschist
Grünschieferfazies *f* green schist facies
Grünschlick *m* green mud
grünspanfarbig aeruginous
Grünstein *m* greenstone, metabasalt
Grünsteintuff *m* greenstone tuff
Gruppe *f* group *(lithostratigraphic unit)*
~/funktionelle functional group
~/terminologische terminological group
Gruppennummer *f* group number
Gruppensilikat *n s.* Sorosilikat
gruppieren to group *(seismic shots)*
Grus *m* detritus, grit, grus[h], gruss
Grusboden *m* gritty soil
Guadalcazarit *m* guadalcazarite, $(Hg,Zn)(S,Se)$
Guadalupien *n* Guadalupian *(Permian, North America)*
Guanajuatit *m* guanajuatite, $Bi_2(Se,S)_3$
Guano *m* guano, ornithocorpus
Guarinit *m* guarinite, $Ca_2NaZr[(F,O)_2|Si_2O_7]$
Gudmundit *m* gudmundite, $FeSbS$
Guejarit *m* guejarite *(s.a.* Wolfsbergit*)*
Guerinit *m* guerinite, $Ca_5H_2[AsO_4]_4 \cdot 9H_2O$
Gugiait *m* gugiaite, $Ca_2Be[Si_2O_7]$
Guildit *m* guildite, $Cu_3Fe_4[(OH)_4|(SO_4)_7] \cdot 15H_2O$
Guilleminit *m* guilleminite, $Ba[(UO_2)_3|(OH)_4|(SeO_3)_2] \cdot 3H_2O$
Gulf-Hauptgruppe *f* Gulf [Supergroup] *(Upper Cretaceous, North America, Gulf district)*

Gummit m gummite, eliasite *(alteration of uraninite)*
Gunningit m gunningite, $Zn[SO_4] \cdot H_2O$
Günz-Eiszeit f, **Günz-Kaltzeit** f Günz [Drift] *(Pleistocene of Alps)*
Günz-Mindel-Interglazial n, **Günz-Mindel-Warmzeit** f Günz-Mindel [Interval] *(Pleistocene of Alps)*
Gürtel m belt
~**/metallogenetischer** metallogenic belt
~**/orogenetischer** orogenic belt
~**/planetarischer metallogenetischer** metallogenic planetary belt
Gürteldiagramm n girdle diagram
Gußregen m downpour
Gut n**/ungesiebtes gebrochenes** crusher-run [stone]
Gutsevichit m gutsevichite, $(Al,Fe)_3[(OH)_3|((P,V)O_4)_2] \cdot 8H_2O$
Guyanaschild m Guiana shield
Guyot m guyot, table mount, oceanic bank
Gymnospermen npl gymnosperms, naked-seed plants
Gypsit m gypsite
Gypsum-Spring-Formation f Gypsum Spring Formation, Carmel Formation *(Dogger of North America)*
Gyrolith m gyrolite, centrallasite, $Ca_2[Si_4O_{10}] \cdot 4H_2O$
Gyttja f gyttja
Gzhell-Stufe f Gzhellian [Stage] *(uppermost stage of Upper Carboniferous, East Europe)*

H

Haar n**/Peles** pele's hair
haarfein capillary
Haarkies m millerite, capillary (hair) pyrite, β-NiS
Haarkristall m whisker
Haarkristalle mpl **aus Eis/aufgewachsene** air hoar
Haarperthit m hair perthite
Haarriß m hair[line] crack, microfissure
Haarsilber n wire silver
Habitus m habit[us]
~**/säuliger** columnar habitus
~**/stengeliger** acicular habitus
Hackmanit m hackmanite *(variety of sodalite)*
Hackprobe f picking sample
Haemafibrit m h[a]emafibrite, $Mn_3[(OH)_3|AsO_4] \cdot H_2O$
Haematit m h[a]ematite, red iron ore, Fe_2O_3
~**/nierenförmiger** kidney ore
~**/roter** Indian red
~**/schwammiger** iron froth
Haematiterz n h[a]ematite ore
haematithaltig h[a]ematitic *(aggregal)*; h[a]emataceous *(integral)*
haematitisieren to h[a]ematitize
Haematitisierung f h[a]ematitization

Haematitroheisen n h[a]ematite pig iron
Haematogelit m h[a]ematogelite
Haematolith m h[a]ematolite, $(Mn,Mg,Fe)_5[(OH)_7|AsO_4]$
Haematophanit m h[a]ematophanite, $4PbO \cdot Pb(Cl,OH)_2 \cdot 2Fe_2O_3$
Haematostibiit m h[a]ematostibiite, $8(Mn,Fe)O \cdot Sb_2O_5$
Hafendamm m sea wall
Haff n lagoon, bay, gulf, frith
Haffküste f lagoon-type of coast
Haffwasser n backwater
Hafnium n hafnium, celtium, Hf
Haftfähigkeit f adhesiveness, adhesive power
Haftfestigkeit f adhesive strength, cohesional resistance
Haftfestigkeitsmesser m adhesion meter
Haftöl n non-recoverable oil
Haftreibung f static friction
Haftrippeln fpl adhesion ripples, antiripplets
Haftspannung f adhesion (bond) stress
Haftung f adhesion, bond
~**/scheinbare** coverage
Haftvermögen n adhesiveness, bonding strength; retention force
Haftwasser n irreducible (adhesive, retained, attached) water
Haftwassersättigung f irreducible water saturation
Hagel m hail
Hageleindrücke mpl hail imprints
Hagelkorn n hailstone
hageln to hail, to sleet
Hagelschauer m hailstorm, hailsquall
Hagelschlag m, **Hagelsturm** m, **Hagelwetter** n hailstorm
Hagelwolken fpl hail clouds
Hagendorfit m hagendorfite, $(Na,Ca)_2(Fe,Mn)_3[PO_4]_3$
Häggit m haeggite, $V_2O_2(OH)_3$
Haidingerit m haidingerite, $CaH[AsO_4] \cdot H_2O$
Haifischzahn m shark tooth
Hainit m hainite *(a mineral of the aenigmatite group)*
Haiweeit m haiweeite, $Ca[UO_2)_2](Si_2O_5)_3 \cdot 4H_2O$
Haken m 1. hook; 2. offshore spit *(of a tongue of land)*
~**/V-förmiger** cuspate bar *(of a tongue of land)*
Hakenhöchstlast f **der Bohranlage** hoisting capacity of drilling rig
Hakenlast f hook load
Hakenschlagen n s. Hakenwerfen
Hakenschlinge f looped bar *(of a river)*
Hakenwerfen n outcrop bending; tipping downslope *(of the outcrops)*; sagging *(of the beds)*
hakig hackly
Halbboudinkörper mpl responds
halbdurchlässig semipermeable, semipervious
halbdurchscheinend subtransparent
halbdurchsichtig subtranslucent

Halbedelstein

Halbedelstein *m* semiprecious stone
Halbfenster *n* half window *(tectonics)*
Halbfertigprodukt *n*/**mineralisches** semiprocessed mineral
halbflächig hemihedral
Halbflächner *m* hemihedron
halbgerundet subrounded
Halbhöhle *f* rock shelter
Halbhorst *m* half-horst, semi-fault block
Halbinsel *f* peninsula
~/**angegliederte** attached peninsula, tombolo
~/**spitz zulaufende** bill
Halbkarst *m* shallow karst
halbklastisch hemiclastic
Halbklippe *f* half-klippe *(tectonics)*
halbkristallinisch half-crystalline, semicrystalline, hemicrystalline, subcrystalline
Halbkugel *f* hemisphere
~/**nördliche** northern hemisphere
~/**obere** upper hemisphere
~/**südliche** southern hemisphere
~/**untere** lower hemisphere
halbkugelförmig hemispherical
Halbleitervorrichtung *f*/**ladungsgekoppelte** charge-coupled device
Halbleiterzähler *m* semiconductor counter
Halbmikromethode *f* semi-micromethod
Halbmond *m* half moon, crescent
halbmondähnlich crescentoid
halbmondartig crescentiform
halbmondförmig crescent-shaped, lunar
halbmuschelig semiconchoidal
Halbopal *m* semiopal, hemiopal
halbpolar semipolar
Halbraum *m* half-space
halbsalzig subsaline
Halbsavanne *f* semisavanna
Halbschatten *m* penumbra, incomplete shadow
halbsteil semisteep
halbtäglich semidiurnal
Halbtaucher *m* semisubmersible barge *(drilling barge)*
~/**an Ketten verankerter** catenary-moored semisubmersible
halbversteinert semipetrified
halbvulkanisch metavolcanic
Halbwertsbreite *f* thickness of layer which absorbes half of γ-radiation
Halbwert[s]zeit *f* half-life [period]; half time
~/**biologische** biologic[al] half-life
Halbwüste *f* semidesert
Halbwüstenboden *m*/**brauner** brown steppe soil
Halde *f* stock[pile], waste (attle) heap, spoil bank (dump); [cinder] tip
Haldenbestände *mpl* dump stocks
Haldendüne *f* blow-out dune
Haldenerz *n* dump (waste heap) ore, ore from tailings
Haldenfläche *f* spoil area
Haldenlagerung *f* [stock]piling

Haldenmaterial *n* stockpiled materials, pile-driving materials
Haldenrutsch *m* dump slip
Haldenschüttung *f* [stock]piling
Haldenseilbahn *f* dumping cableway
Haldenton *m* stockpile clay
Halistase *f* halistase
Halit *m* halite, water opal, NaCl
halitisch halitic
Halitit *m* halitite
Hall *m* ringing *(seismics)*
Halle *f* hall
Hälleflint *m* hälleflinta *(porphyroidic rock)*
Hallerit *m* hallerite *(Li-paragonite)*
Hallien *n* Hallian [Stage] *(marine stage, Pleistocene of North America)*
Hallig *f* hallig, marsh island
Halloysit *m* halloysite, $Al_4[(OH)_8|Si_4O_{10}] \cdot (H_2O)_4$
halmyrogen halmyrogenetic
Halmyrolyse *f* halmyro[ly]sis, submarine weathering
Halo *m* halo
halogen halogenic
Halogen *n* halogen
Halogenderivat *n* halide, haloid salt
Halogenese *f* halogenesis
Halogenid *n*, **Haloidsalz** *n* halide, haloid salt
Haloidstadium *n* haloid stage
Halokinese *f* halokinesis
halokinetisch halokinetic
Halokline *f* halocline
halophil halophilic, salt-loving
Halophyten *mpl* halophytes, salt-loving plants
Haloplankton *n s.* Meeresplankton
halotektonisch halotectonic
Halotrichit *m* halotrichite, $FeAl_2[SO_4]_4 \cdot 22 H_2O$
Halswirbel *m s.* Cervicalwirbel
Halurgit *m* halurgite, $Mg_2[B_4O_5(OH)_4]_2 \cdot H_2O$
Häma... *s.* Haema...
Hambergit *m* hambergite, $Be_2(OH)BO_3$
Hamilton-Gruppe *f* Hamilton Group *(Devonian of North America)*
Hammada *f* hammada *(rock desert)*
Hammarit *m* hammarite, $2 PbS \cdot Cu_2S \cdot 2 Bi_2S_3$
Hammer *m*/**geologischer** prospecting pick
~/**hydraulischer** hydraulic hammer *(seismic source)*
Hammerschlag *m* hammer blow
Hammerschlagbohren *n* pneumatic hammer drilling
Hammerschlagseismik *f* hammer-blow (reflection) seismics
Hancockit *m* hancockite, $(Ca,Pb,Sr,Mn)_2(Al,Fe,Mn)_3[O(OH|SiO_4)Si_2O_7]$
Handbohren *n* hand drilling
Handbohrer *m* hand auger
Handbohrung *f* hand-drilled well
Handbrunnen *m* dug well
Handdrehbohrung *f* auger boring
Handklauben *n*, **Handlesen** *n* picking by hand
Handmeißel *m* [hand] chisel
Handprüfsieb *n* hand testing screen

Handschappenbohrung f hand-drilled auger hole
Handscheidung f hand sorting (dressing), cobbing
Handstück n [hand] specimen; geologic[al] specimen
~/orientiertes oriented specimen
Handvollversatz m solid (hand) packing
Handwurzel f wrist, carpus
Handwurzelknochen m carpalia, carpal bone
Hang m slope; acclivity; declivity; flank of hill
~/abfallender declivity, downslope
~/ansteigender acclivity, upslope
~ mit Bodenfließmarken terracette slope
~/sonnenseitiger adret slope
~/terrassierter ledgy slope
hangabwärts downslope
hangaufwärts upslope
Hangböschung f hillside slope
Hängegletscher m hanging glacier, glacieret
Hangeinschnitt m cut slope
Hängekompaß m hanging compass, circumferentor [compass]
Hängemündung f dicordant junction *(of a river)*
hängen an to adhere to
hängend/abwärts pendulous
Hangendabtragung f/**erosive** back erosion
Hangendamputation f back truncation
Hangendbruch m collapsed roof
Hangenden/im stratigraphically above
~ von/im situated above
Hangendes n roof hanging [wall], hanging (overlying) layer, top (upper) wall, back, capping bed; lidstone *(in iron-ore deposits);* horse beans *(of salt deposits)*
~/domartig gewölbtes domed roof
~/gesundes hard roof
~ und Liegendes n cheek
~/unmittelbares immediate roof
~/unsicheres insecure (slippery) roof
~/zu Bruch gegangenes caved roof, shet
Hangendflöz n overlying seam
Hangendgeber m roof strain indicator
Hangendgestein n roof (superincumbent) rock
Hangendgrundwasserleiter m upper aquifer
Hangendkluft f roof fissure
Hangendkohle f top coal
Hangendpflege f strata control
Hangendquelle f perched spring
Hangendrichtung f bent of the roof
Hangendriß m main roof break
Hangendschicht f hanging (overlying, upper) bed
Hangendscholle f upper (uplifted) block
Hangendschwebe f roof pillar
Hangendsperre f top seal *(of oil or gas wells)*
Hangendverhalten n roof behaviour
Hangendwasser n upper (top) water *(in oil and gas wells)*
Hängetal n hanging valley
Hängezeug n miner's compass

Hangfläche f scarp
Hangfußablagerung f hillwash
Hanggefälle n dip of slope
Hangkrater m subterminal crater
Hangkriechen n hill creep
Hangmulde f depression on a slope
Hangnebel m upslope fog
Hangneigung f slope
Hangquelle f slope spring
Hangrutsch m earth slide, landslip
Hangschuttablagerungen fpl talus deposits
Hangschuttquelle f talus spring
Hangseife f hillside placer, hill diggings
Hangsickerung f hillside seepage
Hangtektonik f slope tectonics
Hangwasser n s. Hangendwasser
Hanksit m hanksite, $KNa_{22}[Cl|(CO_3)_2|(SO_4)_9]$
Hannayit m hannayite, $(NH_4)_2Mg_3H_4[PO_4]_4 \cdot 8H_2O$
Haradait m haradaite, $SrV[Si_2O_7] \cdot H_2O$
Hardystonit m hardystonite, $Ca_2ZnSi_2O_7$
Harkerit m harkerite, $Ca_{12}Mg_5Al[Cl(OH)_2|(BO_3)_5(CO_3)_6(SiO_4)_4] \cdot H_2O$
Harmotom m harmotome, $Ba[Al_2Si_6O_{16}] \cdot 6H_2O$
Harnisch m slickenside; polished surface
Harnischriefung f a-lineation
Harnischrillung f fault (slip) striation
Harpolith m harpolith *(magmatic intrusion type)*
Harsch m crusted snow; ice crust
Harschkruste f **aus gefrorenem Regen** rain crust
Harstigit m harstigite, $MnCa_6Be_4[O|OH|Si_3O_{10}]_2$
Hartboden m solution bottom *(crustified sedimentary soil)*
Hartbraunkohle f subbituminous coal; hard brown coal; *(partly)* lignite
~/detritische attrital lignite
~/vitrinitische xyloid lignite (brown coal)
Härte f hardness; sturdiness
~ des Wassers hardness of water
Härtebestimmung f determination of hardness
Härtegrad m degree of hardness
Härtemesser m sclerometer
Härteminderer m rock hardness reducer
härten to indurate
Härter m hardening agent
Härteskala f hardness scale
~/Mohssche Mohs's hardness scale
Härtewert m, **Härtezahl** f hardness number
Hartgestein n hard rock (stone)
Hartgrund m hard ground; solution bottom *(crustified sedimentary soil)*
Hartit m hartite, hartine, josen[ite], $C_{20}H_{34}$
Hartkalkhorizont m lime pan *(soil)*
Hartlaubgewächse npl sclerophyll plants
Härtling m monadnock, relict mountain
Hartmanganerz n 1. braunite, $Mn_7[O_8|SiO_4]$; 2. psilomelane, $(Ba,H_2O)_2Mn_5O_{10}$
Hartmetall n hard-facing metal
Hartmetallbesatz m hard facing; carbide cutters

Hartmetallbohren 148

Hartmetallbohren *n* drilling with hardfaced core bits
Hartmetallkrone *f* core bit with tungsten carbide inserts
Hartmetallschneiden *fpl* carbide cutters
Hartsalz *n* hard salt, sylvinite
~/anhydritisches anhydritic hard salt
Hartschrot *m* [hard] chilled [steel] shot
Harttit *m* harttite, $(Sr,Ca)Al_3[(OH)_6|(SO_4,PO_4)_2]$
Hartton *m* clunch
Hartzerkleinerungsmaschinen *fpl* crushing and grinding machinery (equipment)
Harz *m* Hartz Mountains
Harz *n* resin
~/fossiles fossil resin, mineral resin; amber, succinite; refikite *(in brown coal)*
harzartig resinlike
Harzbildung *f* resinification *(of the oil)*
Harzburgit *m* harzburgite *(rock of the ultramafic clan)*
harzig resin[ace]ous
Harzkörper *mpl* resin rodlets (casts, fibrils, needles); resinite *(coal maceral)*
Harzstäbchen *npl* rodlets *(petrography of coal)*
Harzteer *m* resinous tar
Hastingsit *m* hastingsite, $NaCa_2 Fe_4(Al, Fe)[(OH, F)_2|Al_2Si_6O_{22}]$
Hastit *m* hastite, $CoSe_2$
Hatchettit *m* hatchettine, hatchettite *(a mineral wax)*
Hatchettolith *m* hatchettolite *(variety of pyrochlore)*
Hatchit *m* hatchite *(Th-Pb-sulfoarsenite)*
Hauchecornit *m* hauchecornite, $(Ni,Co)_9(Bi,Sb)_2S_8$
Hauerit *m* hauerite, MnS_2
Haufen *m/* **sternförmiger** stellate cluster
Häufigkeit *f* abundance
~/kosmische cosmic[al] abundance
~/natürliche natural abundance
Häufigkeitsanomalien *fpl* abundance anomalies
Häufigkeitsgrenze *f* abundance limit
Häufigkeitsverhältnis *n* abundance ratio
Haufwerk *n* heap of debris, rubbish; mined rock; rock pile; raw ore; heap of coal; broken material
Haufwerksprobe *f* bulk sample
Hauptabbruch *m/* **Mitteldeutscher** central German main fault
Hauptabteilung *f* phylum
Hauptachse *f* principal axis
Hauptachsentransformation *f* principal component transformation
Hauptantiklinale *f* principal anticline
Hauptbeben *n* principal earthquake (shock)
Hauptbebengürtel *m* major seismic belt
Hauptbestandteil *m* main constituent
~/klastischer major clastic component
Hauptbrechungsindex *m* chief index of refraction

Hauptbruchzone *f* master zone of fracturing
Hauptdehnung *f* principal strain
Hauptdruck *m s.* Periodendruck
Hauptebene *f* principal plane
Haupteinheiten *fpl/* **großtektonische** major tectonic main units
Hauptelement *n* major (main) element
Hauptfalte *f* main (major) fold
Hauptfaltung *f* main folding
Hauptfaltungsperiode *f* major period of folding
Hauptfazies *f* main facies
Hauptflöz *n* bulk bed
Hauptfluß *m* master (trunk) stream
Hauptförderschacht *m* main hoisting shaft
Hauptförderstrecke *f* main haulage road
Hauptgang *m* main (master, mother) lode, master vein
Hauptgemengteil *m* major constituent
Hauptgesteinstyp *m* main type of rock
Hauptgletscher *m* main glacier
Hauptgruppe *f* supergroup *(lithostratigraphic unit)*
Haupthangendes *n* main roof
Haupthorizont *m* main horizon
Hauptkluft *f* main (major, master) joint
Hauptkluftschar *f* set of joints, *(Am)* system of joints
Hauptkomponente *f* main constituent
Hauptkomponentenanalyse *f* principal component analysis
Hauptkomponentenmethode *f* method of principal components
Hauptkrater *m* main crater
Hauptkristallisation *f* main crystallization
Hauptlastfall *m* principal load case
Hauptleitung *f* main
Hauptletten *m* main clay
Hauptmasse *f* matrix
Hauptmeridian *m* central meridian
Hauptmerkmal *n* salient feature
Hauptmeßort *m* main measuring point
Hauptmetallader *f* champion lode
Hauptmineral *n* dominant (essential) mineral
Hauptmulde *f* major trough
Hauptnormalspannung *f* principal normal stress
Hauptphase *f* main phase
Hauptplanet *m* principal planet
Hauptsammelkanal *m* main trunk sewer
Hauptschnitt *m* principal section (plane)
~/zweiter sagittal plane
Hauptseptum *n* major septum
Hauptspalte *f* principal joint
Hauptspannung *f* principal stress
Hauptspannungsachse *f* principal stress axis
Hauptspannungsdifferenz *f* principal stress difference
Hauptspannungslinie *f* stress trajectory
Hauptspannungsrichtungen *fpl* axes of the principal stresses
Hauptspannungstrajektorien *fpl* trajectories of the principal stresses

Hauptstation f master station
Hauptstrecke f main drive (gate)
Hauptstreichen n main (general) trend
Hauptstrom m main river
Haupttätigkeit f main activity
Hauptvereisung f major glaciation
Hauptverschiebung f master displacement
Hauptverwerfung f main (major, master, dominant) fault
Hauptwasserscheide f main (major) divide
Hauptwülste mpl elongate irregular marks
Hauptzone f principal section *(of a mineral)*
Hausmannit m hausmannite, $MnO \cdot Mn_2O_3$
Haustein m quarrystone
Hautabdruck m skin impression
Häutchen n film
Häutchenwasser n pellicular (film) water
Hauterive n, **Hauterivien** n Hauterivian [Stage] *(Lower Cretaceous)*
Hautknöchelchen n dermal ossicle
Hautnadel f dermal spicule
Hautskelett n s. Dermalskelett
Hautspicula npl dermal spicules
Häutung f mo[u]lting
Häutungsrest m mo[u]lt
Hauyn m hauyne, haüynite, $(Na,Ca)_{8-4}[(SO_4)_{2-1}|(AlSiO_4)_6]$
Hauyntephrit m hauyntephrite *(alkali basalt)*
Hawaiit m hawaiite *(trachyandesite)*
Hawaiitätigkeit f Hawaiian activity *(of volcanoes)*
Hawaiitypus m Hawaiian type
Hawleyit m hawleyite, α-CdS
Headdenit m s. Arrojadit
Heazlewoodit m heazlewoodite, Ni_3S_2
Hebeeinrichtung f hoist[ing] equipment, jack
heben to lift, to raise; to [up]heave *(bottom)*
~/sich to rise
Hebewerk n s. Hebeeinrichtung
Hebridenschild m Hebridean shield
Hebung f elevation; raising, rise, lifting; uplift; upheaval *(of the bottom)*; heaving *(by frost)*
~ der Sohle, ~ des Liegenden floor lift (heave, creep)
~/glazialisostatische glacioisostatic rise
~/ruckartige pulsational uplift
~/säkulare secular rise
Hebungsgebiet n area of uplift
Hebungsinsel f upheaved island
Hebungsküste f raised coast (beach), elevated (positive) shore line, shore line of emergence (elevation)
Hebungslinie f line of emergence
Hebungsphase f upheaval phase
Hebungstendenz f tendency of rising
Hectorit m hectorite, $(Mg,Li)_3[(OH,F)_2|Si_4O_{10}]^{0,33-}Na_{0,33}(H_2O)_4$
Hedenbergit m hedenbergite, $CaFe[Si_2O_6]$
Hedleyit m hedleyite, $Bi_{14}Te_6$
Hedyphan m hedyphane *(variety of mimetite)*
Heftband n s. Annulus
Heide f heath, moor

Heideboden m heath soil, barren ground
Heideland n heath
Heidemoor n heath bog
Heidesand m heath sand
Heidornit m heidornite, $Ca_3Na_2[Cl|(SO_4)_2|B_5O_8(OH)_2]$
Heilquelle f medicinal spring
Heilwasser n medicinal (remedial) water
Heinrichit m heinrichite, $Ba[UO_2|AsO_4]_2 \cdot 10-12H_2O$
Heißwasserbecken n hot pool
Heißwasserfluten n hot water flooding
Heißwassergewinnung f **aus Festgestein** *(Am)* hot dry rock method
Heizmaterial n combustible
Heizöl n heating oil, combustion fuel
Heizwert m heating (calorific) value
Heizwertversuch m calorimetric[al] test
Heleoplankton m s. Seenplankton
Heliodor m heliodor *(variety of beryl)*
Heliograf m heliograph
Heliografie f heliography
heliografisch heliographic
Heliophyllit m heliophyllite, $Pb_3AsO_{<4}Cl_{<2}$
Heliothermometer n heliothermometer
Heliotrop m heliotrope *(variety of chalcedony)*
heliozentrisch heliocentric
Helium n helium, He
Heliumalter n helium age
Heliumfusion f helium fusion
helizitisch helicitic
hell/sehr resplendent
Hellandit m hellandite, $(Ca,Y,Er,Mn)_{<3}(Al,Fe)[(OH)_2|Si_2O_7]$
Hellbezugswert m albedo
Hellfeld n bright field
Hellfeldabbildung f bright-field image
Hellfeldbeleuchtung f bright-field illumination
Hellfeldbeobachtung f bright-field observation
Helligkeit f brightness; brilliance
~ der Sterne brightness of stars
Helligkeitsschwankung f brightness fluctuation
Helligkeitswert m brightness value
Hellyerit m hellyerite, $NiCO_3 \cdot 6H_2O$
Helmholtz-Spule f Helmholtz coil
Helophyten mpl helophytes, swamp plants
Helsinkit m helsinkite
Helvet n, **Helvétien** n Helvetian [Stage] *(of Miocene)*
Helvetikum n Helveticum
Helvetium n s. Helvet
Helvin m helvite, helvin[e], $(Mn,Fe,Zn)_8[S_2|(BeSiO_4)_6]$
Hemberg[ium] n, **Hemberg-Stufe** f Hembergian [Stage] *(Upper Devonian, Europe)*
Hemieder n hemihedron
Hemiedrie f hemihedrism, hemihedry
hemiedrisch hemihedral, hemisymmetric
hemimorph hemimorph[ic], hemimorphous
Hemimorphie f hemimorphism, hemimorphy
Hemimorphit m hemimorphite, calamine, $Zn_4[(OH)_2|SiO_7] \cdot H_2O$

Hemingfordien 150

Hemingfordien n, **Hemingfordium** n Hemingfordian [Stage] *(mammalian stage, lower Miocene, North America)*
Hemiphyllien n Hemiphyllian [Stage] *(mammalian stage, upper Miocene to basal Pliocene in North America)*
Hemisphäre f hemisphere
hemitrop hemitropic
hemmen to clog
Hendersonit m hendersonite, $Ca_2V_9O_{24} \cdot 8H_2O$
Hepatit m hepatite *(a bituminous baryte)*
Heptaeder n heptahedron
heptaedrisch heptahedral
Heptagon n heptagon
heptagonal heptagonal
Heptan n heptane, C_7H_{16}
herabrinnen, herabtröpfeln to trickle down[ward]
Herabwandern n sweeping *(of meanders)*
herausarbeiten to carve out *(by erosion)*
Herausdrücken n protrusion
herausfließen to outflow, to issue
Herausfließen n outflow
herausheben to uplift
Heraushebung f uplift
herauskommen to issue
herauslösen to leach
herausnehmen/einen Kern aus dem Kernrohr to remove a core from the barrel
herauspräparieren to clear out
herausschleudern to eject
herausschwemmen to flush out
heraussickern to ooze out
heraussprengen to blast out
heraussprudeln to gush forth
herausströmen to issue
Herbizid n herbicide
Herbsthochflut f fall flood
Herbststürme mpl equinoctial storms
Herbst-Tagundnachtgleiche f autumn[al] equinox
Hercynit m hercynite, $FeAl_2O_4$
Herd m/**subkrustaler** subcrustal focus
Herdarbeit f tabling *(mineral dressing)*
Herdentfernung f distance from the focus
Herderit m herderite, $CaBe[(F,OH)|PO_4]$
Herdlösung f fault plain solution
Herdtiefe f focal depth, depth of [seismic] focus
Herdverschiebungslösung f fault plain solution
Herdzeit f time of origin
Hereinbrechen n **des Hangenden** roof fall *(by longwall working)*; caving-in *(by caving)*
hereingewinnen to get, to mine, to win; to break *(ore)*
hereinschieben/sich to flow into *(rock)*
Herkunft/subkrustaler hypogene
hermatyp hermatypic, reef-building
Herrengrundit m s. Devillin
Herschelit m herschelite *(variety of chabasite)*
heruntergleiten to slide down, to slip down[-ward]

herunterspülen to wash down
herunterströmen to pour down
heruntertropfen to drip from
hervorbringen to generate
Hervorbringung f generation
hervorquellen to bubble forth
hervorströmen to gush [from]
hervortreten/im Gelände to be topographically prominent
Herzenbergit m herzenbergite, SnS
herzyn s. herzynisch
Herzyniden pl hercynids
herzynisch Hercynian *(e.g. direction of strike)*
Hesperornis m Hesperornis
Hessit m hessite, telluric silver, Ag_2Te
Hessonit m [h]essonite, cinnamon stone, cinnamite *(variety of garnet)*
Hetaerolith m hetaerolite, $ZnMn_2O_4$
heteroaxial heteroaxial
heteroblastisch heteroblastic
heterocerk heterocercal, unequally lobed *(type of caudal fin)*
heterodesmisch heterodesmic
heterodont heterodont
heterogen heterogenous
~ **in der Zusammensetzung** polygenous, various
Heterogenit m heterogenite, stainerite, CoOOH
Heterogenität f heterogeneity
heterometrisch heterometric
heteromorph heteromorphous, heteromorphic
Heteromorphismus m heteromorphism, heteromorphosis
Heteromorphit m heteromorphite, $11PbS \cdot 6Sb_2S_3$
heteropisch heteropic
Heterosit m heterosite, $(Fe,Mn)[PO_4]$
heterotherm heterothermal, heterothermic
heterotopisch heterotopic
heterotroph heterotrophic
heterotropisch heterotropical
Hettang[ien] n, **Hettangium** n Hettangian [Stage] *(basal stage of Lias)*
Heubachit m heubachite *(variety of heterogenite)*
Heulandit m heulandite, $Ca[Al_2Si_7O_{18}] \cdot 6H_2O$
Hewettit m hewettite, $CaV_6O_{16} \cdot 9H_2O$
Hexaeder n hexahedron
hexaedrisch hexahedral, hexahedric
Hexaedrit m hexahedrite *(meteorite)*
hexagonal hexagonal
Hexahydrit m hexahydrite, $Mg[SO_4] \cdot 6H_2O$
Hexan n hexane, C_6H_{14}
H-Horizont m H horizon
Hiatalgefüge n hiatal fabric
Hiatus m hiatus, stratigraphic break, lost record; lacuna
~/**struktureller** structural hiatus
Hibbenit m hibbenite, $Zn_7[OH|(PO_4)_2]_2 \cdot 6H_2O$
Hibonit m hibonite, $CaO \cdot 6Al_2O_3$
Hibschit m hibschite, plazolite, $Ca_3Al_2[(Si,H_4)O_4]_3$

Hidalgoit m hidalgoite, $PbAl_3[(OH)_6|SO_4AsO_4]$
Hiddenit m hiddenite *(a green spodumene)*
Hieratit m hieratite, $K_2[SiF_6]$
Hieroglyphe f hieroglyph
Higginsit m higginsite, $CaCu[OH|AsO_4]$
Hilfsbohrloch n slab hole
Hilfsbohrung f service well
Hilfsebene f auxiliary plane
Hilfsleitung f patch *(seismics)*
Hilfsschacht m by-pit
Hilfsstempel m catch prop
Hilgardit m hilgardite, $Ca_2[Cl|B_5O_8(OH)_2]$
Hillebrandit m hillebrandite, $Ca_2[SiO_4] \cdot H_2O$
Himbeerspat m rhodochrosite, dialogite, manganese spar, $MnCO_3$
Himmelsabtastungsgerät n sky screen equipment
Himmelsachse f celestial axis
Himmelsäquator m celestial equator, equator of the heavens, equinoctial
Himmelsbeobachtung f uranoscopy
Himmelsbeschreibung f uranography
Himmelsgewölbe n celestial vault, firmament
Himmelsglobus m celestial globe
Himmelshorizont m celestial horizon
Himmelskörper m celestial (heavenly, stellar) body
Himmelskugel f [celestial] sphere
Himmelskunde f uranology
Himmelsmechanik f celestial mechanics, gravitational astronomy
Himmelsmeridian m celestial meridian
Himmelsmessung f uranometry
Himmelspol m celestial pole, pole of the heavens
Himmelsrichtung f compass point
Himmelsrichtungen fpl/**vier** cardinal points
Himmelsstrahlung f sky radiation
Himmelsstrahlungsmesser m pyranometer
Hinabgleiten n sliding down
Hindernismarken fpl obstacle marks
hineinströmen to pour in; to rush in
Hineinströmen n inpouring; inrush
hinschlängeln/sich to crawl
Hinsdalit m hinsdalite, $PbAl_3[(OH)_6|SO_4PO_4]$
Hinterdüne f back dune
Hinterextremitäten fpl hindlimbs
Hintergrund m background
Hintergrundeffekt m background effect *(tracer)*
Hinterland n back land, hinterland
Hintermauerung f backing
hinterpacken to backfill *(behind arches)*
Hinterrand m posterior margin *(of a fossil shell)*
Hinterriffbereich m zone at the rear of reefs
hinüberragen to overlap
Hin- und Herschwanken n yawing *(of the magnetic needle)*
hipidiomorph hipidiomorph
Hipparion n hipparion
Hippuritenkalk m Hippurite Limestone *(Upper Cretaceous, Tethys)*

Histogramm n histogram
Hitzdrahtanalysator m hot wire analyzer
Hitzegrad m degree of hotness
Hitzewelle f wave of heat
Hjelmit m hjelmite, hielmite *(aggregate of tapiolite and pyrochlore)*
Hoch n high, anticyclone
Hochalpental n high mountain valley
hochalpin high-alpine
hochangereichert high-grade
Hochbohrung f rising borehole
Hochdruck m high (heavy) pressure
Hochdruckausrüstung f high-pressure equipment
Hochdruckbohrung f high-pressure well
Hochdruckbrücke f high-pressure ridge
Hochdruckgebiet n high-pressure area, anticyclone
Hochdruckgürtel m high-pressure belt
Hochdruckmetamorphose f high-pressure metamorphism
Hochdruckwasserkraftwerk n high-head water power plant
Hochdruckzone f high-pressure zone
Hochebene f high (upland) plain, [high] plateau, [elevated] tableland
Hochfläche f flat upland area
Hochflut f high flood
Hochflutbett n high-water bed
Hochflutebene f flood plain
Hochflutsee m overflow lake
Hochflutwelle f flood wave
Hochfrequenzseismik f high-resolution seismics
Hochgebirge n high mountains
Hochgebirgsgletscher m alpine glacier
Hochgebirgssteppe f high mountain steppe
Hochgebirgstal n alpine valley
Hochgeschwindigkeitseinschlag m hypervelocity impact
Hochgewitter n high thunderstorm
Hochglanz m shining lustre
Hochglazial n high glacial
hochkippen to tip up *(tectonically)*
Hochkraton n high craton, hedreocraton
Hochlage f/**epirogene** epeirocracy
Hochland n highland, upland
~/flaches mesa
~/welliges rolling upland
Hochlandgesteine npl highland rocks *(moon)*
Hochleistungspumpe f high-speed pump
hochliegend high-lying
hochmineralisiert highly mineralized
Hochmoor n high (emerged, domed, hill, upland) bog, high moor[land]
Hochmoortorf m high-moor peat
Hochofenkoks m blast-furnace coke
Hochpaßfilter n high-pass filter, low-cut filter
Hochpuffen n boiling-up *(in the floor)*
Hochquarz m high[-temperature] quartz
hochquellen to gush up
Hochschnitt m high cut

Hochscholle 152

Hochscholle f upper (upthrown, uplifted) block, fault ridge, uplifted (upthrown) fault block
Hochsee f high (open) sea, deep water
Hochseeablagerung f oceanic (pelagic, thalassic) deposit
Hochspannungsstörung f high line distortion
Höchstabfluß m maximum flow
Höchstkonzentration f/**zulässige** maximum permissible concentration *(tracer)*
Höchstwassermenge f maximum discharge
Höchstwertigkeit f maximum valence
Hochsumpf m high marsh
Hochtemperaturalbit m analbite
Hochtemperaturminerale npl high-temperature minerals, high-grade minerals
Hochtemperaturphase f high-temperature phase
Hochtemperaturverkokung f high-temperature carbonization
Hochterrasse f high-lying terrace
Hoch-/Tieftemperatur-Umwandlung f high-low inversion *(e.g. of quartz)*
Hochwald m 1. mountain forest; 2. timber forest
hochwarmzeitlich high-interglacial
Hochwasser n high (flood) water; [high] flood
~ **mit Gesteinsmassen** debacle
~/**mittleres jährliches** mean annual flood
~/**plötzlich einsetzendes** freshet
Hochwasserabfluß m flood flow
~/**maximaler** maximum flood discharge
Hochwasserablagerung f flood[-plain] deposit, overbank deposit
Hochwasseranstieg m flood elevation
Hochwasserauffangsperre f flood [control] dam
Hochwasserbarren m chute bar
Hochwasserbecken n flood pool
Hochwasserberechnungen fpl flood estimates
Hochwasserbett n high-water bed (channel)
~ **eines Flusses** major stream bed
Hochwasserdamm m levee
Hochwasserdeich m flood bank
Hochwasserentlastung f flood discharge
Hochwasserganglinie f flood hydrograph
Hochwasserhäufigkeit f flood frequency
Hochwasserkatastrophe f flood disaster (calamity)
Hochwassermarke f high-water mark
Hochwassermeldedienst m flood-warning service
Hochwassermenge f flood discharge
Hochwasserregulierung f flood regulation; flood control; flood routing
Hochwasserrückhaltebecken n high-water basin, retaining (retention, stopping, retardation) basin
Hochwasserschaden m flood damage
Hochwasserschutt m flood debris
Hochwasserschutz m flood protection; flood control
Hochwasserschutzbauten mpl flood protection works

Hochwasserschutzdamm m flood[-control] levee
Hochwasserschutzdeich m flood bank
Hochwasserschutztalsperre f flood[-control] dam
Hochwasserschwall m flood wave; freshet
Hochwasserspeicherung f flood storage
Hochwasserstand m high-water stand (level)
~/**kritischer** flood stage
~/**mittlerer** mean high water level
Hochwasserstandsmesser m high-mark gauge
Hochwasserstollen m spillway tunnel
Hochwasserstrand m storm beach
Hochwasserüberlauf m overfall, overflow *(of a dam)*
Hochwasservorhersage f flood forecast (prediction)
Hochwasserwelle f flood discharge
hochwertig high-value, high-quality; high-class; high-grade
Höcker m 1. hummock, knob; 2. node *(of fossils)*
höckerig hummocky
Hodgkinsonit m hodgkinsonite, $MnZn_2[(OH)_2|SiO_4]$
Hodograph m, **Hodographenkurve** f hodograph
Hoelit m hoelite, $C_{14}H_8O_2$
Hof m halo, corona; aureole
~/**geochemischer** geochemical halo
~/**pleochroitischer (radioaktiver)** pleochroic halo, radiohalo
~ **um die Sonne** solar halo
Hoffnungsgebiet n s. Gebiet/höffiges
Högbomit m hoegbomite, $Na(Al, Fe, Ti)_{24-x}O_{36-x}$
Höhe f 1. height; altitude; 2. peak, summit, top; height, elevation, hill; 3. elevation
~/**absolute** absolute altitude
~/**barometrische** barometric height
~ **der Schneedecke** depth of snow cover
~ **des Ufers über dem Wasserspiegel** height of flood bank above water line
~ **einer Antiklinale** closure
~ **einer Flexur** height of a flexure
~/**hydrostatische** hydrostatic head, head of water
~/**lichte** head room *(e.g. under a bridge)*
~/**morphologische** land-surface altitude
~ **über Normalnull** altitude above [mean] sea level, sea-level elevation
Höhenaufnahme f/**barometrische** barometric levelling
Höhenbeobachtung f upper air observation
Höhenberechnung f/**barometrische** barometric height computation
Höhenbestimmung f/**barometrische** barometric levelling
Höhenforschung f **mit Meßsonden** air sounding
Höhengestaltung f relief features
Höhengleichheit f isometry
Höhengleichmäßigkeit f accordance of summit levels

Höhenklima *n* alpine climate
Höhenkorrektur *f* elevation correction
Höhenkreis *m* circle of altitude
Höhenlage *f* height, altitude
~/relative relative altitude
Höhenlinie *f* isophyse, contour line, topographic contour [line], surface contour line, isohypsometric line
Höhenlinienabstand *m* contour interval
Höhenliniendiagramm *n* contour diagram
Höhenlinienkarte *f* contoured map
Höhenmarke *f* bench mark
Höhenmesser *m* altimeter, altimetric device *(instrument)*
~/elektrodynamischer absolute altimeter
Höhenmessung *f* altimetry, hypsometry
~/barometrische barometric hypsometry (levelling)
Höhenparallaxe *f* parallax in altitude
Höhenplan *m* contoured plan
Höhenrakete *f* sounding (high-altitude) rocket
Höhenrücken *m* ridge
Höhenschicht *f* height (altitude) zone *(stratosphere)*
Höhenschichtenkarte *f* hypsometric map
Höhenschichtlinie *f s.* Höhenlinie
Höhensicherheit *f* altitude stability
Höhenstrahlenschauer *m* cosmic[al-ray] track
Höhenstrahlung *f* cosmic[al-ray] radiation
Höhenstrahlungsintensität *f* cosmic[al-ray] intensity
Höhenunterschied *m* difference in elevation (level)
Höhenvermessung *f s.* Höhenmessung
Höhenweg *m* mountain trail
Höhenwind *m* wind at high altitudes
Höhenzug *m* ridge
~/flacher subdued ridge
Hohlabdruck *m* hollow impress *(of fossils)*
Hohlabguß *m* hollow cast *(of fossils)*
Hohlbohrer *m* box auger
Höhle *f* cave; cavern; hollow
~/kleine niche *(e.g. behind a waterfall)*
~/mehrsohlige galleried cave
~/primäre primary cave
~/sekundäre secondary cave
Höhlenablagerung *f* cave[rn] deposit
~/karbonatische spelaeothem
Höhlenbär *m* cave bear
Höhlenbewohner *m* cave dweller
Höhlenbildung *f* cave formation
Höhlendach *n* cave roof
Höhlenfluß *m* subterranean river
Höhlenforscher *m* spelaeologist
Höhlenforschung *f* exploration of caves
Höhlenfüllung *f* cavity filling
Höhlengebiet *n* cavern region
Höhlengerinne *n* underground streamlet
Höhlenkalkstein *m* cave (spelaeal) limestone
Höhlenkunde *f* spelaeology
Höhlenlehm *m* cave clay
Höhlenmensch *m* cave man

Höhlenperle *f* cave pearl, clusterite, grape formation
Höhlenröhre *f* lead
Höhlensediment *n* cave[rn] deposit
Höhlensee *m* underground lake
Höhlenspalte *f* cavernous fissure
Höhlentier *n* cave-dwelling animal
Hohlform *f* hollow mould
Hohlformporosität *f* intraparticle porosity
Hohlkehle *f* cavetto
Hohlkehlenbildung *f* notching
Hohlladungsperforation *f* jet perforating, bazooka-type system of perforation
Hohlraum *m* cavity; void; open space; subground excavation *(artificial)*
~/becherförmiger calicle
~/bergmännischer mine cavity
~/durch Abbau entstandener gob
~/gaserfüllter gas-filled cavity
~ im Gestein druse
~ im Sediment/kavernöser bird's eye
~/miarolitischer miarolitic cavity
~/subkapillarer subcapillary interstice
~/wassergefüllter cavity filled with water
Hohlraumanteil *m*/**grundwassererfüllbarer** specific yield of pore space
Hohlräume *mpl*/**Webersche** Weber's (bed separation) cavities
Hohlraumgefüge *n* open-space structure
Hohlraumspeicher *m*/**durch Kernexplosion entstandener** nuclear cavity storage
Hohlraumvermessung *f* cavern surveys
Hohlraumvolumen *n* cavity volume
Hohlschliff *m* hollow (concave) grinding
Hohlsog *m* cavitation
Hohltiere *npl* Coelenterata
Höhlung *f* cavity
~/viszerale visceral cavity
Hohlweg *m* narrows, defile
Hohmannit *m* hohmannite, $Fe[OH|SO_4] \cdot 3^{1}/_{2}H_2O$
Holdenit *m* holdenite, $(Mn, Ca)_4(Zn, Mg, Fe)_2[(OH)_5O_2|AsO_4]$
Hollandit *m* hollandite, $Ba_{<2}Mn_8O_{16}$
Hollingworthit *m* hollingworthite, $(Rh, Pd)AsS$
Holm *m* spar
Holmium *n* holmium, Ho
Holmquistit *m* holmquistite, $Li_2Mg_3Al_2[OH|Si_4O_{11}]_2$
holoaxial holoaxial
Holoblast *m* holoblast
Holoeder *n* holohedron
Holoedrie *f* holohedrism, holohedry
holoedrisch holohedral, holosymmetric
Holografie *f* holography
holohyalin holohyaline
Holokopie *f* holocopy
holokristallin holocrystalline; felty
hololeukokrat hololeucocratic
holomelanokrat holomelanocratic
holomorph holomorphic
Holoplankton *n* permanent plankton

Holostratotyp

Holostratotyp *m* holostratotype
Holotypus *m* holotype
holozän Holocene
Holozän *n* Holocene [Series]
Holstein *n* Holsteinian [Stage] *(of Pliocene)*
Holstein-Interglazial *n*, **Holstein-Warmzeit** *f* Holstein [Interval] *(Pleistocene, Northwest Europe)*
Holz *n*/**fossiles** fossil wood
~/silifiziertes (verkieseltes) opalized (silicified) wood, woodstone, dendrolite
~/verkohltes carbonized (coalified, charred) wood
~/versteinertes petrified wood
Holzachat *m* wood agate
Holzasbest *m* mountain wood
Holzausbau *m* wooden supports
Holzeinlagen *fpl* wooden inserts, layers of wooden blocks *(mining)*
holzig woody, ligneous
Holzkappe *f* wooden bar
Holzkohle *f* charcoal
Holzkohlenschicht *f* charcoal layer
Holzopal *m* wood opal, xylopal
Holzpflock *m* wooden peg
Holzstempel *m* wooden prop
Holztorf *m* wood peat
Holzzinn[erz] *n* wood tin, tin wood, fibrous cassiterite
Homeotyp *m* homeotype
Homerium *n* Homerian *(basal stage of Wenlock series)*
Homilit *m* homilite, $Ca_2FeB_2[O|SiO_4]_2$
homocerk homocercal *(type of caudal fin)*
homoedrisch homohedral
homogen homogeneous
Homogenisierung *f* homogenization
Homogenität *f* homogeneity
Homogenitätstest *m* homogeneity test
~/multipler statistischer multiple statistical homogeneity test
~/multivariabler multivariable homogeneity test
homolog homologous
homometrisch homometric
homöoblastisch homoeoblastic
Homoseiste *f* homoseismal curve (line)
homotaktisch homotactic
homotax homotaxial, homotaxeous
homotherm homothermal, homothermic
homothetisch homothetic
Honigblende *f* rosin (resin) jack *(yellow variety of zinc blende)*
Honigstein *m* honeystone *(s.a. Mellit)*
Hopeit *m* hopeite, $Zn_3[PO_4]_2 \cdot 4H_2O$
Hörbarkeitsgebiet *n* area of audibility
Hörbläschen *npl s.* Statocysten
Horizont *m* horizon
~/durchhaltender reflektierender persistent reflecting horizon
~/erdölführender oil horizon
~/erschöpfter depleted layer
~/gasführender gas horizon
~/geoidaler geoidal horizon
~/produktiver productive horizon
~/produzierender producing horizon
~/reflektierender coverage, reflecting horizon *(seismics)*
~/reflexionsseismischer reflection seismic horizon
~/schluckender thieving horizon
~/seismischer seismic horizin
~/sichtbarer visible horizon
~/Spülung aufnehmender thieving horizon
horizontal horizontal; flat; aclinic
Horizontalbewegung *f* horizontal movement
Horizontalbohrung *f* horizontal hole
Horizontaldepression *f* depression angle
Horizontalfilterbrunnen *m* horizontal filter well
Horizontalflexur *f* horizontal flexure
Horizontalkomponente *f* **des Erdmagnetfelds** earth's horizontal field
~/magnetische horizontal intensity
Horizontalmagnetometer *n* horizontal magnetometer
Horizontalpendel *n* horizontal pendulum
Horizontalrippeln *fpl* level-surface ripples
Horizontalschub *m* horizontal thrust
Horizontalseismograf *m* horizontal seismograph
Horizontalseismometer *n* horizontal motion seismometer
Horizontalstylolithen *mpl* transverse (unusual) stylolites
Horizontalverschiebung *f* shift fault, horizontal (lateral) shift
~/große rift
~/transversale transverse (transcurrent, tear) fault, offset, flaw
Horizonte *mpl* **im Flözgebirge/marine** marine bands
horizontieren to level
Horn *n* 1. horn; spine *(animal)*; 2. horn, spine *(a sharp peak)*; 3. horn *(material)*
Hornblei *n* horn lead *(s.a. Phosgenit)*
Hornblende *f* hornblende, amphibole
Hornblendediorit *m* hornblende diorite
Hornblendefels *m* hornblendite
Hornblendegneis *m* hornblende gneiss
Hornblendegranit *m* hornblende granite
Hornblendepikrit *m* hornblende picrite
Hornblendeschiefer *m* hornblende schist, hornschist, hornslate
Hornblendit *m* hornblendite *(rock of the ultramafic clan)*
Hornerz *n* horn silver
Hornfels *m* hornfels
hornig horny, corneous
Hornito *m* hornito, blowing cone, driblet cone (spire)
Hornquecksilber *n* horn mercury *(s.a. Kalomel)*
Hornschale *f* corneous shell

hornschalig horny-shelled
Hornschwämme *mpl* horny sponges
Hornsilber *n* horn (corneous) silver, chlorargyrite, AgCl
Hornstein *m* hornstone, chert *(variety of opal)*
~/chalzedonreicher novaculitic chert
~/gelber rabben
hornsteinartig cherty
Hornsteinbrekzie *f* chert breccia
hornsteinhaltig corniferous
Hornsteinknollen *fpl/***angewitterte** patinated chert
Hornsteinschotter *m* chert gravel
Horobetsuit *m* horobetsuite, $(Sb, Bi)_2S_3$
Horsfordit *m* horsfordite, Cu_6Sb
Horst *m* horst, fault (heaved) block, fault scarp, uplift
Horstgebirge *n* horst (rift-block) mountain
Horstscholle *f s.* Horst
Hortonolith *m* hortonolite, $(Fe, Mg, Mn)_2SiO_4$
Howardit *m* howardite *(a meteorite)*
Howieit *m* howieite, $NaMn_3Fe_7(Fe, Al)_2(OH)_{11}Si_{12}O_{32}$
Howlith *m* howlite, $Ca_2[(BOOH)_5|SiO_4]$
Hoxnien *n* Hoxnian *(Pleistocene of British Islands, corresponding to Mindel-Riss Interval of Alps district)*
Hsianghualith *m* hsianghualite, $Ca_2[(Li, Be, Si)_6O_{12}] \cdot CaF_2$
Hsihutsunit *m* hsihutsunite *(variety of rhodonite)*
Huanghoit *m* huanghoite, $BaCe[F|(CO_3)_2]$
Huantajayit *m* huantajayite, $20NaCl \cdot AgCl$
Hubbein *n* leg
Hubinsel *f* jackup
Hübnerit *m* huebnerite, $MnWO_4$
hufeisenförmig crescentic
Hufeisenwulst *m* horse-shoe flute cast, current crescent
Hügel *m* hill[ock], mound
~/hoher felsiger tor
~/kleiner knoll
~/mit dünner Geschiebedecke bedeckter veneered hill
~ mit zentraler Depression/wurtähnlicher prairie mound
Hügelgegend *f* hummocky region
hügelig hilly, hummocky
Hügelit *m* hügelite, $Pb_2[(UO_2)_3|(OH)_4|(AsO_4)_2] \cdot 3H_2O$
Hügelkette *f* range of hills
Hügelland *n* hill[y] country
~/flachwelliges rolling country
Hügellandschaft *f* hilly landscape
Hügelmoor *n* palsa bog
Hühnerkobelit *m* hühnerkobelite, $(Ca, Na)_2(Fe, Mn)_3[PO_4]_3$
Hülle *f* envelope
Hüllentausch *m* cover substitution *(tectonical)*
Hüllgestein *n* encasing rock
Hüllkurve *f* [/**Mohrsche**] intrinsic curve (line), rupture curve, Mohr's envelope

Hüllzement *m* rim cement
Humangeologie *f* geology of Man
Humboldtin *m* humboldtine, humboldtite, $Fe[C_2O_4] \cdot 2H_2O$
humid humid
humifizieren to humify
Humifizierung *f* humi[di]fication, mouldering
~/saure acid humi[di]fication
Huminit *m* huminite *(maceral group of brown coals and lignites)*
Huminsäure *f* humic (ulmic) acid
Huminstoff *m* humate, ulmous substance
Humit *m* humite, humolith, $Mg_7[(OH, F)_2|(SiO_4)_3]$
humitisch humic
Hummerit *m* hummerite, $K_2Mg_2[V_{10}O_{28}] \cdot 16H_2O$
Humocollinit *m* humocollinite *(maceral subgroup of brown coals and lignites)*
Humodetrinit *m* humodetrinite *(maceral subgroup of brown coals and lignites)*
Humolith *m* humolith
humos humic, humous
humo-siallitisch humo-siallitic
Humotelinit *m* humotelinite *(maceral subgroup of brown coals and lignites)*
Humus *m* humus, soil-ulmin, vegetable mould
~/sandiger sandy muck
Humusbildung *f* formation of humus *(s.a.* Humifizierung)
Humusboden *m* humus (humous, humic, organic, black top) soil, mould *(s.a.* Humuserde)
Humuserde *f* humus (vegetable, ulmous) earth *(s.a.* Humusboden)
Humusgel *n* humic gel
Humusgestein *n* humus-rich rock
Humushorizont *m* humus horizon
Humuskarbonatboden *m* chalkhumus soil, humus carbonate soil, humic carbonated soil
Humuskohle *f* humic coal (coal type)
Humussäure *f s.* Huminsäure
Humusstoff *m* humic matter (substance)
Humusstoffschicht *f* humic layer, leaf mould
Humus-Ton-Komplex *m* clay-humus complex
Humustorf *m* humocoll
Hundsstern *m* Canicula
Hünenstein *m* menhir
Hungchaiot *m* hungchaoite, $Mg[B_4O_5(OH)_4] \cdot 7H_2O$
Huntilith *m* huntilite, (Ag, As)
Huntit *m* huntite, $CaMg_3[CO_3]_4$
Hüpfmarke *f* skip cast (mark)
Huréaulith *m* hureaulite, wenzelite, $(Mn, Fe)_5H_2[PO_4]_4 \cdot 4H_2O$
Hurlbutit *m* hurlbutite, $CaBe_2[PO_4]_2$
Huron[ien] *n*, **Huronium** *n* Huronian *(Middle Precambrian in North America)*
Hut *m* cap
~/anhydritischer anhydritic cap
~/Eiserner iron (oxidized) cap, ore capping, [capping of] gossan

hutbildend

hutbildend gossaniferous
Hutbildung f downward enrichment
Hutchinsonit m hutchinsonite, (Pb, Tl)S · Ag$_2$S · 5As$_2$S$_3$
Hutgebirge n s. Deckgebirge
Hutgestein n capping rock, caprock; katatectic layer
Hutlimonit m limonite gossan
~/zelliger iron gossan
Hüttenwerk n smeltery, smelting plant
Huttonit m huttonite, Th[SiO$_4$]
hyalin hyaline
Hyalit m hyalite, SiO$_2$ · nH$_2$O
Hyalobasalt m hyalobasalt
Hyaloklastit m hyaloclastite *(submarine pyroclastic rock)*
Hyalomylonit m hyalomylonite, pseudotachylite
Hyalophan m hyalophane, (K, Ba)[Al(Al, Si)Si$_2$O$_8$]
hyalopilitisch hyalopilitic
Hyaloporphyr m hyalophyre
Hyalosiderit m hyalosiderite *(highly ferruginous olivine)*
Hyalotekit m hyalotekite, (Pb, Ca, Ba)$_4$B[Si$_6$O$_{17}$(F, OH)]
Hyazinth m hyacinth, jacinth *(variety of zircon)*
hybrid hybrid
Hybridisierung f hybridization, contamination of magma
hydatogen hydatogenic, hydatogenous
Hydatomorphose f hydatomorphism
Hydrargillit m hydrargillite, γ-Al(OH)$_3$
Hydrat n hydrate
Hydratation f hydration
Hydratationswasser n hydration water, water of constitution (crystallization)
Hydratationszustand m state of hydration
Hydratisierung f hydration
Hydratwasser n s. Hydratationswasser
Hydraulik f hydraulics
Hydrid n hydride
hydrieren to hydrogenize
Hydrierung f hydrogenation
hydrisch anhydrous
Hydrit m hydrite *(Japanese Tertiary clarite; coal microlithotype)*
Hydrobiotit m hydrobiotite, (K, H$_2$O)(Mg, Fe, Mn)$_3$[(OH, H$_2$O)$_2$|AlSi$_3$O$_{10}$]
Hydrobohrer m hydrodrill
Hydroboracit m hydroboracite, CaMgB$_6$O$_{11}$ · 6H$_2$O
Hydrocalumit m hydrocalumite, 2Ca(OH)$_2$ · Al(OH)$_3$ · 3H$_2$O
Hydro-Cassiterit m hydrocassiterite, (Sn, Fe)(O, OH)$_2$
Hydrocerussit m hydrocerussite, Pb$_3$[OH|CO$_3$]$_2$
hydrochemisch hydrochemical
Hydrocyanit m hydrocyanite, CuSO$_4$
Hydrodynamik f hydrodynamics

Hydrofraccen n hydrofracturing, formation fracturing *(drilling engineering)*
hydrogenetisch hydrogenetic
Hydrogenie f hydrogenesis
Hydrogeochemie f hydrogeochemistry
hydrogeochemisch hydrogeochemical
Hydrogeologe m hydrogeologist
Hydrogeologie f hydrogeology
hydrogeologisch hydrogeological
Hydrografie f hydrography
Hydrogrossular n s. Hibschit
Hydrohalit m hydrohalite, NaCl · 2H$_2$O
Hydro-Hetaerolith m hydrohetaerolite, Zn(Mn, H$_3$)$_2$O$_4$
Hydroisohypsenplan m piezometric map, ground-water contour map
Hydrokanit m hydrocanite, CuSO$_4$
Hydroklast m hydroclast
hydroklastisch hydroclastic
Hydroleitfähigkeit f hydraulic diffusivity
Hydrolith m hydrolith *(carbonate rock with hydroclasts)*
Hydrologe m hydrologist
Hydrologie f hydrology
~/angewandte (praktische) applied hydrology
hydrologisch hydrologic[al]
Hydrolyse f hydrolysis
hydrolytisch hydrolytic
Hydromagnesit m hydromagnesite, Mg$_5$[OH|(CO$_3$)$_2$]$_2$ · 4H$_2$O
Hydromechanik f hydromechanics, fluid mechanics, mechanics of liquids
Hydromelanothallit m hydromelanothallite, Cu(Cl, OH)$_2$ · 1/2H$_2$O
Hydrometamorphismus m hydrometamorphism
Hydrometeor m hydrometeor
Hydrometeorologie f hydrometeorology
hydrometeorologisch hydrometeorological
Hydrometrie f hydrometry
Hydromonitor m mud gun
Hydromonitorbohren n jet drilling
hydromorph hydromorphic, hydromorphous
Hydromuskovit m hydromuscovite, (K, H$_2$O)Al$_2$[(H$_2$O, OH)$_2$|AlSi$_3$O$_{10}$]
Hydronephelit m hydronephelite, HNa$_2$Al$_3$Si$_3$O$_{12}$ · 3H$_2$O
Hydroparagonit m hydroparagonite, (Na, H$_2$O)Al$_2$[(H$_2$O, OH)$_2$|AlSi$_3$O$_{10}$]
Hydrophan m hydrophane *(variety of opal)*
hydrophil hydrophilic
Hydrophilie f hydrophily
Hydrophilit m hydrophilite, chlorocalcite, CaCl$_2$
Hydrophlogopit m hydrophlogopite, (K, H$_2$O)Mg$_3$[(OH, H$_2$O)$_2$|AlSi$_3$O$_{10}$]
hydrophob hydrophobic, water-repellent, non-absorbent
Hydrophobie f hydrophobicity
Hydrophon n hydrophone, pressure detector
Hydrophyten mpl hydrophytes, aquatic plants
hydrophytisch hydrophytic

Hydrosol *n* hydrosol
Hydrosolfatare *f* hydrosolfatara
Hydrosphäre *f* hydrosphere
~/unterirdische subsurface (subterranean) water
Hydrostatik *f* hydrostatics
hydrostatisch hydrostatic
Hydrotalkit *m* hydrotalcite, $Mg_6Al_2[(OH)_{16}|CO_3] \cdot 4H_2O$
Hydrotechnik *f* hydraulic (water) engineering
hydrothermal hydrothermal
Hydrothermalfeld *n*/**submarines** submarine hydrothermal field
Hydrotherme *f* hydrothermal spring
Hydrothorith *m* hydrothorite, $ThSiO_4 \cdot 4H_2O$
Hydrotroilit *m* hydrotroilite, $FeS \cdot nH_2O$
Hydrotungstit *m* hydrotungstite, $WO_2(OH)_2 \cdot H_2O$
Hydrowissenschaft *f* hydroscience
Hydroxid *n* hydroxide
Hydroxidfällung *f* hydroxide precipitation
Hydrozinkit *m* hydrozincite, $Zn_5[(OH)_3|CO_3]_2$
Hydrozoen *npl* hydrozoans
Hygrograf *m* hygrograph
Hygrometer *n* hygrometer
hygroskopisch hygroscopic, water-absorbing
Hygroskopizität *f* hygroscopicity
hypabyssisch hypabyssal
hypereutektisch hypereutectic
hypersalin hypersaline
Hypersalinar *n* hypersalinity
Hypersthen *m* hypersthene, $(Fe, Mg)_2[Si_2O_6]$
Hypersthendiorit *m* hypersthene diorite
Hypersthengranit *m* charnockite
Hypersthenit *m* hypersthenite *(rock of the ultramafic clan)*
Hyphe *f* hypha
hypidiomorph hypidiomorphic, subhedral
hypidiomorph-körnig hypidiomorphic-granular
hypoabyssisch hypabyssal
hypobarisch hypobaric
hypobatholitisch hypobatholithic
hypogen hypogene, hypogenic
hypogenetisch hypogenetic
Hypoglyphe *f* hypoglyph *(hieroglyph at the subface of stratum)*
hypokristallin hemicrystalline, hypocrystalline, merocrystalline
Hypolimnion *n* hypolimnion
Hypomagma *n* hypomagma
Hyporheon *n* hyporheon
Hyposalinar *n* hyposalinity
hypothermal hypothermal
Hypotyp *m* hypotype
Hypozentrum *n* hypocentre, focus
Hypsografie *f* hypsography
hypsografisch hypsographic
Hypsoisotherme *f* hypsoisotherm
hypsometrisch hypsometric
Hysterese *f* hysteresis

I

Ianthinit *m* ianthinite, $[UO_2|(OH)_2]$
Ichnofossil *n* ichnofossil
Ichnologie *f* ichnology
Ichthyodorulith *m* ichthyodorulite *(fin spine remainder)*
Idait *m* idaite, Cu_5FeS_6
Iddingsit *m* iddingsite *(pseudomorph after olivine)*
Idealaufbau *m* **von Kristallen** crystal perfection
Idealkristall *m* ideal (perfect) crystal
Idealschnitt *m* ideal section
Idealsieblinie *f* ideal grading curve
Identifikation *f (Am)* history matching *(of a reservoir mechanical simulation model)*
Identifikationsprozeß *m (Am)* automatic history match *(of a reservoir mechanical model test)*
Idioblast *m* idioblast
idioblastisch idioblastic
idiochromatisch idiochromatic
Idiogeosynklinale *f* idiogeosyncline, marginal deep (trough), foredeep
idiomorph idiomorphic, idiomorphous
idiophan idiophanous
Idokras *m s.* Vesuvian
Idrialin *m* idrialine, $C_{22}H_{14}$
Ignimbrit *m* ignimbrite, welded tuff (pumice), pyroclastic (tuff, ash) flow
Ijolit *m* ijolite *(rock of the alkali gabbro clan)*
Ikait *m* ikaite, $CaCO_3 \cdot 6H_2O$
Ikosaeder *n* icosahedron
Ikositetraeder *n* icositetrahedron
Ikunolith *m* ikunolithe, $Bi_4(S, Se)_3$
Ilesit *m* ilesite, $Mn[SO_4] \cdot 4H_2O$
Illinois-Eiszeit *f* Illinoisian Ice Age
Illit *m* illite *(s. a.* Hydromuskovit*)*
~/ausgelaugter degraded (stripped) illite
illuvial illuvial
Illuvialboden *m* illuvial soil
Illuvialhorizont *m* illuvial horizon, B-horizon
~ aus Ton und Humus agric horizon
~ mit hohem Tonanteil argillaceous horizon
Illyr[ium] *n* Illyrian [Substage] *(Middle Triassic, Tethys)*
Ilmenit *m* ilmenite, $FeTiO_3$
Ilmenorutil *m* ilmenorutile *(variety of rutile)*
Ilvait *m* ilvaite, $CaFe_3[OH|O|Si_2O_7]$
imbibiert infiltrated
Imbibition *f* imbibition
~/kapillare capillary imbibition
Imgreit *m* imgreite, NiTe
Immersion *f* immersion
Immersionsobjektiv *n* immersion objective
Immigration *f* immigration
Impaktit *m* impactite *(a glassy object produced by fusion of rock)*
Impaktmetamorphose *f* shock (impact) metamorphism
Impedanz *f* impedance
~/akustische acoustical impedance

Implikationsgefüge

Implikationsgefüge *n* implication texture
~/grafisches graphic[al] texture
Implikationsstruktur *f s.* Implikationsgefüge
Implosion *f* implosion
Imprägnation *f* impregnation
Imprägnationserz *n* impregnation (disseminated) ore
Imprägnationserzkörper *m* impregnation ore body
Imprägnationsgang *m* impregnation vein
Imprägnationslagerstätte *f* impregnation (disseminated, interstitial) deposit
imprägnieren to impregnate
~/mit Erdöl to petrolize
~/mit Kupfer to copperize
Imprägnierung *f* impregnation
Impsonit *m* impsonite *(asphaltic pyrobitumen)*
Impuls *m* pulse; spike *(seismic signal)*
Impulsantwort *f* impulse response; transient response
Impulskompression *f* pulse compressing
Impulsmodulation *f* pulse-width modulation
Impulstest *m* pulse test
in situ in situ, indigenous
Inderborit *m* inderborite, $MgCa[B_3O_3(OH)_5]_2 \cdot 6H_2O$
Inderit *m* inderite, $Mg[B_3O_3(OH)_5] \cdot 5H_2O$
Indexmessung *f* measurement of the index
Indexmineral *n* index (critical, diagnostic) mineral
Indialith *m* indialite, $Mg_2Al_3[AlSi_5O_{18}]$
Indianait *m s.* Halloysit
Indigolith *m* indicolite, indigolite *(blue variety of tourmaline)*
Indikator *m*/**geochemischer** geochemical indicator
Indikatorhorizont *m* indicator horizon
Indikatormineral *n* indicator (symptomatic) mineral
Indikatrix *f* indicatrix, index ellipsoid
~/optische optic indicatrix
Indit *m* indite, $FeIn_2S_4$
Indium *n* indium, In
Indizes *mpl*/**Millersche** Miller crystal indices
Indochinit *m* indochinite *(a tectite)*
Induktion *f* induction
Induktionslog *n* induction log[ging], electromagnetic log[ging]
Induktionsmessung *f s.* Induktionslog
Induktionspotential *n* induced polarization
Induktionsverfahren *n* **mit horizontalem Primärkreis** horizontal-loop method
~ mit vertikalem Primärkreis vertical-loop method
induktiv inductive
Induktivität *f* inductance
Industrie *f*/**bergbautreibende** mining industry
Industriediamant *m* industrial grade diamond, bo[a]rt, boort
induzieren to induce
ineinandergreifen to interlock
inelastisch inelastic

inert inert
Inertgas *n* inert gas
Inertinit *m* inertinite *(coal maceral, maceral group)*
Inertodetrinit *m* inertodetrinite *(coal maceral)*
Inertodetrit *m* inertodetrite *(coal microlithotype)*
Inertsubstanz *f* inert substance
Inesit *m* inesite, $Ca_2Mn_7[Si_5O_{14}OH]_2 \cdot 5H_2O$
Infauna *f* infauna
Infiltration *f* infiltration, influent seepage; invasion
Infiltrationsdynamik *f* infiltration dynamics
Infiltrationsetappe *f* infiltration stage
Infiltrationsgebiet *n* infiltration area
Infiltrationsgruppe *f* group of infiltration
Infiltrationsrate *f* infiltration rate
~/aktuelle infiltration rate at a given moment
~/potentielle potential infiltration rate
~/ungesättigte unsaturated infiltration rate
Infiltrationsspende *f* infiltration recharge
Infiltrationsvorgang *m* process of infiltration
Infiltrationszone *f* infiltration (invaded) zone *(logging)*
infiltrieren to infiltrate
Informationskernen *n* spot coring
Infrabasalplatte *f* infrabasal plate
infrakrustal infracrustal
infrarot infrared
Infrarot *n*/**thermisches** thermal infrared
Infrarotabsorption *f* infrared absorption
Infrarotaufnahmen *fpl* infrared imagery
Infrarotdurchlässigkeit *f* infrared transmittancy
Infraroterkundung *f* infrared remote sensing
Infrarotluftfernerkundung *f* infrared aerial remote sensing
Infrarotmikroskop *n* infrared microscope
Infrarot-Satellitenfernerkundung *f* infrared satellite remote sensing
Infrarotspektrometer *n* infrared spectrometer
Infrarotspektrometrie *f* infrared spectrometry
Infrarotspektroskopie *f* infrared spectroscopy
Infrarotstrahlung *f* infrared radiation
Infrarotthermometer *n* infrared thermometer
Infrastruktur *f* infrastructure
Infusorienerde *f* infusorial earth, fossil flour (meal), tellurine, molera, diatomite, kieselgu[h]r
Ingenieurgeologe *m* geologic engineer
Ingenieurgeologie *f* engineering geology
ingenieurgeologisch engineering-geological
Ingenieurgeophysik *f* engineering geophysics
inglazial englacial
Ingression *f* ingression
Ingressionsmeer *n* ingression sea
inhomogen inhomogeneous
Inhomogenität *f* inhomogeneity
initial initial
Initialausbruch *m* initial eruption
Initialdurchbruch *m* initial break (rupture)
Initialsprengstoff *m* booster

Injektion f injection
~/wiederholte staccato injection
Injektionsbeben n injection earthquake
Injektionsfaltung f ejective folding
Injektionsflüssigkeit f injection fluid
Injektionsgebiet n injection section *(tracer)*
Injektionsgneis m injection gneiss
Injektionsgut n injection liquid
Injektionsloch n grout hole
Injektionsmetamorphose f metamorphism by injection
Injektionsmittel n injection liquid
Injektionspunkt m injection patch *(tracer)*
Injektionsrisse mpl injection structures *(in sediments)*
Injektionsschleier m grout curtain
Injektionszeitpunkt m injection time *(tracer)*
Injektionszone f injection area
Injektivfalten fpl diapiric folds
Injektivfaltung f injection folding, diapir [folding]
injizieren to inject, to grout under pressure
injiziert/mit Granit injected with granite
Inklination f inclination
~/magnetische magnetic inclination
Inklinationsnadel f dipping needle
Inklinationsrichtung f direction of dip
Inklinationswinkel m angle of inclination (incline)
Inklinometer n inclinometer
Inklinometermessung f inclinometer measurement
Inklinometerrohr n inclinometer tube
Inklinometrie f hole deviation logging
inkohlen to coalify, to carbonize
Inkohlung f coalification, carbonification
~/biochemische biochemical coalification
Inkohlungsgas n dry natural gas
Inkohlungsgrad m degree of coalification, rank
Inkohlungsgradient m rank gradient
Inkohlungsknick m coalification break
Inkohlungsmodellversuch m coalification model test
Inkohlungsprofil n coalification section
Inkohlungsprozeß m coalification process
Inkohlungssprung m coalification jump
Inkohlungsstadium n coalification stage
Inkohlungsverhältnisse npl coalification conditions
inkompetent incompetent
inkongruent incongruous
Inkrustation f s. Inkrustierung
inkrustieren to incrust[ate], to encrust
Inkrustierung f incrustation, encrustation, clogging
Inlandeis n inland ice; ice sheet (cap)
Inlandserz n domestic ore
Inlandvereisung f continental glaciation
Innelit m innelite, $Ba_2(Na, K, Mn, Ti)_2Ti[(O, OH, F)_2|(S, Si)O_4|SiO_7]$
Innenabguß m internal (interior) cast

Innenbeanspruchung f inner stress
Innenböschung f back slope *(of a moraine)*
innenbürtig endogen
Innendruck m internal pressure
Innendüne f interior dune
Innendurchmesser m calibre
~ des gesteinszerstörenden Werkzeugs inside diameter of drilling tool
Innenfaltenteil m inner part of a fold
Innenküstenlinie f inner shore line
Innenlamelle f inner lamelle
Innenleiste f list *(of a fossil shell)*
Innenmassiv n internal massif
Innenmolasse f interior molasse
Innenmoräne f internal (englacial) moraine
Innenrand m inner margin
Innenreflex m interior reflection
Innenreflexion f internal reflection
Innenschneidegerät n internal cutting tool
Innenschneidmaß n inside diameter of drilling tool
Innensenke f interior depression (trough)
Innenskelett n internal skeleton, endoskeleton
Innenstruktur f internal structure *(of the earth)*
Innenwindungen fpl interior spires
innenzentriert inside-centred
innermolekular intramolecular
innerplanetar innerplanetary
Inoceramenschichten fpl Inoceramus beds
Inoceramus m Inoceramus
Inosilikat n inosilicate, chain silicate
Insectivoren mpl s. Insektenfresser
Insektenbernstein m insect-bearing amber
insektenfressend insectivorous
Insektenfresser mpl insect eaters
Insel f island
~/festlandnahe near-shore island
~/kleine islet; eyot *(in a river or lake)*
~/landfest gewordene land-tied island
~/ozeanische oceanic island
~/schwimmende floating island
~/unbewohnte sea holm
inselartig insular
Inselbank f key
Inselberg m inselberg, outlier, island mountain, monadnock
~/kleiner castle koppie
Inselberglandschaft f inselberg landscape
Inselbogen m island arc
Inselfläche f insulosity
inselförmig insular
Inselgirlande f island festoon
Inselgruppe f s. Archipel
Inselkette f island chain
Inselnehrung f connecting bar, tombolo
Inselreihe f island festoon
Inselschelf m insular shelf
Inselsilikat n s. Nesosilikat
Inselvulkan m island (insular) volcano
Insequenz f insequence
In-situ-Gewinnung f in situ recovery

In-situ-Laugung

In-situ-Laugung f heap (in situ) leaching, leaching in place
In-situ-Verbrennung f in situ combustion, fire flooding
In-situ-Verbrennungsprozeß m underground combustion
Insolation f insolation, incoming solar radiation
Insolationssprengung f, **Insolationsverwitterung** f destruction by insolation
instabil unstable, labile, non-equilibrium
Instabilitätsbedingung f condition of instability (ground-water flow)
Instabilitätsgleichung f non-equilibrium equation (ground-water flow)
Instandhaltung f **der Grubenbaue** support of workings
Instrument n/**seismisches** seismic instrument
Instrumentenfehler m instrumental error
Instrumentierung f instrumentation
insular insular
Integralgefüge/mit integral
Intensität f/**seismische** seismic (sound) intensity
Interambulakralfläche f interambulacral area (palaeontology)
Interferenz f **der von der Ionosphäre reflektierten Wellen** sky-wave interference
Interferenzbild n interference figure (pattern)
Interferenzerscheinung f interference phenomenon
Interferenzfarbe f interference colour
Interferenzrippeln fpl interference ripples (wave ripple marks)
~/hexagonale hexagonal interference ripples
~/rechteckige rectangular interference ripples
Interferenzstreifen m interference fringe
Interferenztest m interference test
interferieren to interfere
interformational interformational
intergalaktisch intergalactic
Intergelisol n intergelisol
interglazial interglacial
Interglazial n interglacial episode (interval), interval of deglaciation
Interglazialschichten fpl interglacial beds
Interglazialton m interglacial clay
Interglazialzeit f interglacial age
Interglazialzeitraum m interglaciation
intergranular intergranular
Intergranular n intergranular, intragranular
Intergranularfilm m intergranular film, interstitial fluid
Intergranulargefüge n intergranular texture
Interkontinentalmeer n intercontinental sea
interkristallin intercrystalline, intergranular
intermediär intermediate
intermittieren to intermit
intermittierend intermittent, interrupted
intermolekular intermolecular
intermontan intermountain, intermont[ane]

Intermontanbecken n intermountain basin
Intermontansenke f intermountain depression
Interngefüge n si-fabric
Interniden pl internides
Internrotation f internal rotation
Interpolationseffekt m grid effect
Interpolationsfehler m map convolution; grid residual
Interpretation f/**geochemische** geochemical interpretation
Interpretator m interpreter
Interpretierbarkeit f interpretability
interseptal interseptal
Interseptalraum m interseptum
Intersertalgefüge n intersertal texture
interstadial interstade, interstadial
Interstadial n interstadial epoch
Interstadialkomplex m interstadial complex
interstellar interstellar
Intervall n/**geochronologisches** geochronologic interval (time span between two geological events)
~/stratigrafisches stratigraphic interval (body of strata between two lithostratigraphic markers)
Intervallgeschwindigkeit f interval velocity
intervulkanisch intervolcanic
intraglazial intraglacial, englacial
intragranular intragranular
Intraklast m intraclast
intrakontinental intracontinental
intrakrustal intracrustal
intramagmatisch intramagmatic
Intramontansenke f intramont depression
Intramontantrog m intramontane trough
intraorogen intraorogenetic
intraozeanisch intraoceanic
intrasalinar intrasaliniferous
intratellurisch intratelluric, intratellural
intrudieren to intrude
Intrusion f intrusion
~ des Magmas in den Erstarrungsraum irruption
~/diskordante discordant intrusion (injection)
~/konkordante concordant intrusion (injection)
~/magmatische magmatic intrusion
~/plutonische plutonic intrusion
~/postkinematische s. ~/serorogene
~/primorogene primary orogenic intrusion, synkinematic intrusion
~/serorogene serorogenic (subsequent) intrusion
~/spätkinematische s. ~/serorogene
~/synkinematische s. ~/primorogene
Intrusionen fpl/**mehrfache** multiple intrusions
Intrusionsbeben npl intrusion tremors
Intrusionsform f intrusion form
Intrusionsmasse f intrusive [mass], intruded mass (body), invading (invaded) igneous mass
Intrusionsphase f intrusive phase

Intrusionstektonik f intrusion displacement
Intrusionstemperatur f temperature of intrusion
intrusiv intrusive, intercalary
Intrusiva npl/**altpaläozoische** earlier Palaeozoic intrusives
Intrusivbrekzie f intrusive breccia
Intrusivgang m intrusive dike
Intrusivgestein n intrusive [rock], intrusion (intruded, penetrative) rock
~/basisches basic intrusive
Intrusivkomplex m intrusive complex
Intrusivkörper m intrusive (intruded, injected, igneous) body
~/irregulärer chonolith
~/keilförmiger sphenolith
Intrusivlager n intrusive sheet
Intrusivmasse f injected mass (s.a. Intrusionsmasse)
Intrusivstock m intrusive stock (boss)
Inundation f inundation
Inundationsbett n alluvial (alluvian) plain
Inundationsfläche f flood plain (ground), alluvial (river) flat
Inundationsgebiet n submerged area
Inundationsgrenze f limit of submersion
Invasionszone f s. Infiltrationszone
invers inverted, reverse
Inversion f inversion
~ des Reliefs inversion of relief
~/hydrochemische hydrochemical inversion
Inversionsachse f inversion rotation axis
Inversionsschicht f inversion layer
Inversionstemperatur f inversion temperature
Inversionszentrum n s. Symmetriezentrum
Invertebraten mpl invertebrates
involut involute
Inyoit m inyoite, $Ca[B_3O_6(OH)_5] \cdot 4H_2O$
Inzisiv m incisor, cutting tooth
Iolith m s. Cordierit
Ionenabstand m distance between ions, interionic distance
Ionen-Äquivalentgewicht n ionic equivalent weight
Ionenart f ionic species
Ionenaustausch m ion exchange
Ionenaustauscher m ion exchanger
Ionenaustauschphänomene npl ion exchange phenomena
Ionenbestand m ion stock
Ionenbindung f ionic bond (compound), ion-dipole bond, ionic link[age]
Ionendiffusion f ionic diffusion
Ionengitter n ion[ic] lattice
Ionenkristall m ionic crystal
Ionenladungszahl f ionic charge number
Ionenleitfähigkeit f ionic conductivity
Ionenpartialdruck m ionic partial pressure
Ionenpotential n ionic potential
Ionenradius m ionic radius
Ionensäule f ion column
Ionenscheider m isotron
Ionensonde f ion detector
Ionenstrahl m ion beam, ionic ray
Ionenstrahlenanalyse f/**massenspektrometrische** ion beam scanning
Ionenstrom m ion flow
Ionenvolumen n ionic volume
Ionenwanderung f migration of ions
Ionenwertigkeit f ionic valence
Ionenwichte f specific gravity of ions
Ionisationspotential n ionization potential
Ionisationsstufe f degree of ionization
ionisch ionic
Ionisierung f ionization
Ionisierungsenergie f ionizing (ionization) energy
ionogen ionogenic
Ionosphäre f ionosphere
Ionosphärenforschung f exploration of the ionosphere
Ionosphärenschicht f ionospheric layer
Ionosphärenstrom m electrojet
Ionosphärenwelle f ionospheric wave
Iowan-Eiszeit f Iowan Ice Age
IP s. Polarisation/induzierte
Ipswichien n Ipswichian (Pleistocene, British Islands, corresponding to Riss-Würm Interval of Alps)
Iranit m iranite, $Pb[CrO_4] \cdot H_2O$
irdisch earthly; sublunar[y]
Iridium n iridium, Ir
Iridosmium n iridosmine, osmiridium
Iriginit m iriginite, $H_2[UO_2|(MoO_4)_2] \cdot 2H_2O$
irisieren to iridize; to iridesce; to aventurize; to schillerize
Irisieren n iridescence; aventurism
irisierend iridescent
irregulär irregular; exocyclic; heterotactous
Isanomale f is[o]anomaly
Isanomalenkarte f isanomalic contour map
Isenit m isenite (variety of trachyandesite)
Ishikawait m ishikawaite (samarskite containing 22% UO_2)
Ishkyldit m ishkyldite (variety of antigorite)
Islandit m icelandite (Fe-rich andesite)
Islandspat m Iceland spar, doubly reflecting spar, optical calcite
isobar isobaric
Isobare f isobar
Isobarenkarte f isobaric chart
Isobase f isobase
Isobathe f isobath, subsurface contour
Isobathenkarte f bathymetric chart, subsurface contour map
Isocardienton m Isocardia clay
isochem isochemical
Isochore f isochor[e]
Isochorenkarte f convergence map
Isochromate f isochromatic [line]
isochromatisch isochromatic
isochron isochronous
Isochronaltest m isochronal test
Isochrone f isochrone, isotime curve

Isochronenplan

Isochronenplan *m* isochrone map
Isodyname *f* isodynamic line; isogam *(geomagnetics)*
isofaziell isofacial
Isofazieskarte *f* isofacies map
Isogamme *f* isogal
Isogammenkarte *f* isogal map
isogen isogenic, isogenous
Isogenese *f* isogeny
isogenetisch isogenetic
isogeothermal isogeothermal, isogeothermic, ge[o]isothermal
Isogeotherme *f* isogeotherm, isogeothermal line, ge[o]isotherm
Isogone *f* isogonic line
Isograd *m* isograd
Isograde *f* isograd
Isohaline *f* isohaline
Isohelie *f* isohelic line
Isohyete *f* isohyet, isohyetal (isopluvial) line, line of equal rainfall
Isohypse *f* isohypse, isohypsometric line, topographic contour [line], surface contour [line]
~ **des Grundwasserspiegels** water table isohypse
Isohypsenkarte *f* contour chart
Isokarbe *f* isocarb line
Isokit *m* isokite, $CaMg[F|PO_4]$
Isoklas *m* isoclasite, $Ca_2[OH|PO_4] \cdot 2H_2O$
isoklinal isoclinal
Isoklinalfalte *f* isoclinic (isoclinal, closed, tight) fold
Isoklinalfaltenbündel *n*, **Isoklinalfaltensystem** *n* isoclinal fold system
Isoklinalfaltung *f* isoclinal folding
Isoklinalkamm *m* isoclinal ridge
Isoklinalschieferung *f* isoclinal foliation
Isoklinaltal *n* isoclinal valley
Isokline *f* isoclinic (isodip) line
Isolator *m* insulator
Isolinie *f* isogram, isoline, contour line
Isolinienkarte *f* isoline map
Isolithe *f* isolith
Isolithenkarte *f* isolith map
Isomagnetik *f* isomagnetics
isomagnetisch isomagnetic
isomorph isomorphous, isomorphic
Isomorphie *f*, **Isomorphismus** *m* isomorphism
Isoorthoklas *m* isoortho[cla]se
Isopache *f* isopach, isopachous line, isopachyte
Isopage *f* isopag
Isopekte *f* isopectic
Isophane *f* isophene, isophane
isopisch isopic
Isoplethe *f* isopleth
isopolymorph isopolymorphic
Isopolymorphismus *m* isopolymorphism
Isopore *f* isopore
Isorade *f* isorad
Isoseiste *f* isoseismal, isoseismal curve (line)
Isostasie *f* isostasy, isostacy

Isostate *f* isostatic line
isostatisch isostatic
isostrukturell isostructural
Isothere *f* isothere
isotherm isothermal
Isotherme *f* isotherm
Isothermenfläche *f* isothermal surface
Isothermenkarte *f* isothermal chart
Isotop *n* isotope
~/**aktivierendes** activating isotope
~/**künstliches radioaktives** man-made radioisotope, artificially produced radioisotope
~/**radioaktives** radioisotope
~/**radiogenes** radiogenic isotope
~/**stabiles** stable isotope
Isotopenaktivierungsquerschnitt *m* isotopic activation cross section
Isotopenanalysator *m* isotope analyzer
Isotopenanalyse *f* isotopic analysis
Isotopenanreicherung *f* isotopic enrichment
Isotopenaustausch *m* isotopic exchange
Isotopenchemie *f* isotopic chemistry
Isotopenfraktionierung *f s*. Isotopentrennung
Isotopengeochemie *f* isotope geochemistry
Isotopengeologie *f* isotope geology
Isotopengewicht *n* isotopic (atomic) mass
Isotopengleichgewicht *n* isotopic equilibrium
Isotopenhäufigkeit *f* isotopic (isotope) abundance
Isotopenhäufigkeitsverhältnis *n* abundance ratio
Isotopenhydrogeologie *f* isotope hydrogeology
Isotopenstandard *m* **für** $^{12}C/^{13}C$ PDB *(CO_2 from Belemnitella americana, Cretaceous, PD formation)*
~ **für Deuterium** standard mean ocean water, SMOW
Isotopenthermometrie *f* isotopic thermometry
Isotopentracer *m* isotope tracer
Isotopentrennung *f* isotope separation (fractionation)
Isotopenverdünnungsanalyse *f* isotope dilution analysis
~/**massenspektrometrische** mass spectrometric isotope dilution analysis
Isotopenverdünnungsmethode *f* isotope dilution method
Isotopenverhältnis *n* isotope (abundance) ratio
~/**natürliches** natural abundance ratio (variation)
Isotopenverteilung *f* **des Kohlenstoffs** isotopic distribution of carbon
Isotopenwerte *mpl* isotope data
Isotopenzusammensetzung *f* isotopic composition (constitution)
Isotopie *f* isotopy
Isotopie-Effekt *m* isotope effect
Isotopieverschiebung *f* isotope shift
Isotron *n* isotron
isotrop isotropic
~/**optisch** optically isotropic

Isotropie *f* isotropy
Isotropisierung *f* isotropization
~ **von Mineralen durch radioaktive Strahlung** metamictization
isotyp isotypic[al]
Isotypie *f* isotypism
Issit *m* issite *(melanocratic dike rock)*
Isthmus *m* isthmus, narrowing
Istisuit *m* istisuite, (Ca, NaH) (Si, AlH)O$_3$
Itabirit *m* itabirite
Itakolumit *m* itacolumite, flexible sandstone
Italit *m* italite *(rock of the alkali-gabbro clan)*
iterativ iterative
Itoit *m* itoite, Pb$_3$[GeO$_2$(OH)$_2$(SO$_4$)$_2$]
Itolith *m* ear stone
Itternit *m* itternite *(zeolitizated nosean)*
Ivanoit *m* ivanoite *(H$_2$O-bearing chloroborate)*
Ixolith *m* ixolyte *(a resin)*

J

Jacupirangit *m* jacupirangite *(nepheline-bearing pyroxenite)*
Jade *f* jade *(cryptocrystalline actinolite)*
Jadeit *m* jadeite, NaAl[Si$_2$O$_6$]
Jadeitit *m* jadeitite *(a fossil resin)*
Jagoit *m* jagoite, Pb$_8$Fe$_2$[(Cl, O)|Si$_3$O$_9$]$_3$
jäh precipitous
Jahr *n* **der aktiven Sonne/Internationales** International Year of the Active Sun *(1968–1970)*
~ **der ruhigen Sonne/Internationales** International Year of the Quiet Sun
~/**hydrologisches** hydrologic (water) year
~/**Internationales Geophysikalisches** International Geophysical Year *(1957–1958)*
~/**nasses** wet year
~/**regnerisches** rainy year
~/**siderisches** sidereal year
~/**trockenes** dry year
Jahresaberration *f* annual aberration
Jahresabflußmenge *f* annual discharge
Jahresablagerung *f* annual deposit
Jahresdurchschnitt *m* annual mean
Jahresförderung *f* annual production (output)
Jahresgang *m* annual variation
Jahreshochwasser *n* annual flood
Jahresmenge *f* annual volume
Jahresmitteltemperaturen *fpl* average annual temperatures
Jahresmittelwert *m* average annual value
Jahresmonsum *m* annual monsoon, etesian winds
Jahresniederschlag *m*/**mittlerer** mean annual precipitation
Jahresproduktion *f s.* Jahresförderung
Jahresregenmenge *f* annual (yearly) rainfall, annual precipitation
Jahresring *m* annual ring
Jahresschichtung *f* annual stratification; varvity
Jahresspeicherung *f* annual storage

Jahreswasserstand *m*/**mittlerer** mean annual water level
Jahreszeit *f* season
jahreszeitlich seasonal
Jaipurit *m* jaipurite, γ-CoS
Jakobsit *m* jacobsite, MnFe$_2$O$_4$
Jakut[ium] *n* Jakutian [Stage] *(Lower Triassic, Tethys)*
Jalpait *m* jalpaite, Cu$_2$S · 3Ag$_2$S
Jamesonit *m* jamesonite, feather ore, plumosite, pilite, 4PbS · FeS · 3Sb$_2$S$_3$
Jamin-Effekt *m* Jamin effect
Janit *m* janite, (Na, K, Ca)(Fe, Al, Mg)[Si$_2$O$_6$] · 2H$_2$O
Japanit *m* japanite *(s. a.* Pennin)
Jarlit *m* jarlite, NaSr$_2$[AlF$_6$] · [AlF$_5$H$_2$O]
Jarosit *m* jarosite, raimondite, cyprusite, KFe$_3$[(OH)$_6$|(SO$_4$)$_2$]
Jaspilit *m* jaspilite, jasper bar
Jaspis *m* jasper[ite] *(variety of chalcedony)*
~ **mit Chalzedonäderchen** agate jasper
jaspisartig jaspideous, jaspidean, jaspoid
Jaspisbildung *f* jasperization
jaspisführend jaspidean, jaspoid
Jasp[is]opal *m* jasper opal, opal jasper, jaspopal
Jatul[ien] *n*, **Jatulium** *n* Jatulian *(Middle Precambrian in Finland)*
Jaulingit *m* jaulingite *(a fossil resin)*
Javanit *m* javanite *(tectite)*
Jefferisit *m* jeffer[i]site *(s. a.* Vermiculit)
Jeffersonien *n* Jeffersonian [Stage] *(Lower Ordovician in North America)*
Jeffersonit *m* jeffersonite *(variety of schefferite)*
Jelinit *m* jelinite *(a fossil resin)*
Jelletit *m* jelletite *(variety of andradite)*
Jeremejewit *m* jeremejevite, AlBO$_3$
Jersey-Vereisung *f* Jerseyan Ice Age
Jet *m (n)* jet, gagate
Jetperforation *f* jet perforating
Jetpumpe *f* jet pump
Jett *m (n)* jet, gagate
Jetztzeit *f* recent epoch, present-time
Jetztzeitform *f* contemporary (present-time) form
Ježekit *m* ježekite *(s. a.* Morinit)
Jimboit *m* jimboite, Mn$_3$[BO$_3$]$_2$
Joaquinit *m* joaquinite, NaBa(Ti, Fe)$_3$[Si$_4$O$_{15}$]
Job-Steuersprache *f* job-control language, JCL *(seismic data processing)*
Joch *n* ridge, col
Jod *n* iodine, J
Jodargyrit *m* iodyrite, β-AgJ
Jodat *n* iodate
Jodbromchlorsilber *n* iodobromite, Ag(Cl, Br, J)
jodhaltig iodic; ioduretted
Jodit *m* iodyrite, β-AgJ
Jodobromit *m* iodobromite, Ag(Cl, Br, J)
Jodsilber *n s.* Jodit
Johachidolith *m* johachidolite, Ca$_3$Na$_2$Al$_4$H$_4$[F, OH]|BO$_3$]$_6$

Johannit

Johannit *m* johannite, $Cu[UO_2|SO_4]_2 \cdot 6H_2O$
Johannsenit *m* johannsenite, $CaMn[Si_2O_6]$
Johnstrupit *m* johnstrupite, $(Ca, Na)_3(Ti, Ce)[F|(SiO_4)_2]$
Jordanit *m* jordanite, $5PbS \cdot As_2S_3$
Jordisit *m* jordisite *(colloidal MoS_2)*
Josefit *m* josefite *(ultramafic dike rock)*
Joseit *m* joseite, Bi_4Te_2S
Josephinit *m* josephinite, $FeNi_3$
Jotnien *n*, Jotnium *n* Jotnian *(Late Precambrian in Finland)*
Joule-Thompson-Effekt *m* Joule-Thompson effect
Jugale *n* jugal, cheek bone
Jugendform *f* phyloneanic form
Jugendstadium *n* young (immature) stage; youth[ful] stage
Jul *n* Julian [Substage] *(Upper Triassic, Tethys)*
Julienit *m* julienite, $Na_2Co[SCN]_4 \cdot 8H_2O$
jungfräulich virgin, maiden, unworked
Jungmoränengebiet *n* young moraine area
Jungpaläozoikum *n* Upper Palaeozoic *(Carboniferous to Permian)*
Jungsteinzeit *f* Neolithic [Age]
jungsteinzeitlich Neolithic
Jungtertiär *n s.* Neogen
jungvulkanisch cenotypal
Jura *m* Jurassic [System] *(chronostratigraphically)*; Jurassic [Period] *(geochronologically)*; Jurassic [Age] *(common sense)*
~/Brauner (Mittlerer) Brown (Middle) Jurassic, Dogger [Series, Epoch]
~/Oberer Upper Jurassic [Series, Epoch], Malm [Series, Epoch]
~/Schwarzer (Unterer) Lower (Black) Jurassic, Lias [Series, Epoch]
~/Weißer *s.* ~/Oberer
Juraaufschluß *m* Jurassic exposure
Jurakalk *m* Jurassic Limestone
Jurameer *n* Jurassic sea
Juraperiode *f* Jurassic [Period]
jurassisch Jurassic
Jurasystem *n* Jurassic [System]
Jurazeit *f* Jurassic [Age]
Jurupait *m* jurupaite, $Ca_6[(OH)_2|Si_6O_{17}]$
Jusit *m* jusite, $(Ca, KH, NaH)(Si, AlH)O_3 \cdot H_2O$
justieren to adjust
Justierung *f* adjustment
Justit *m* justite *(s. a. Koenenit)*
juvenil juvenile
Juxtaposition *f* juxtaposition
Juxtapositionszwilling *m* contact twin

K

Kabelbagger *m* cable excavator
Kabelbaum *m* [seismic] cable
Kabeleinsatz *m* cable break (wave)
Kabelkran *m* cable crane (derrick), cableway, blondin
Kabelschrapper *m* cable excavator
Kabelsonde *f* wire-line log
Kabelwagen *m* reel truck
Kabelwelle *f* cable break (wave)
Kadaver *m* carcass
Kadmium *n* cadmium, Cd
Kadmiumerz *n* cadmium ore
kadmiumhaltig cadmiferous
Kadmiumoxid *n* cadmium oxide, CdO
Kadmiumspat *m* otavite, $CdCO_3$
Kaennelkohle *f s.* Kännelkohle
Kaersutit *m* kaersutite *(basaltic amphibole, rich in TiO_2)*
Käfigschießen *n* cage shooting
Kai *m* quai, wharf; embankment
Kainit *n* kainit[e], $KMg[Cl|SO_4] \cdot 2^3/_4H_2O$
Kainitit *m* kainitite
Kainosit *m* kainosite, cenosite, $Ca_2Y_2[CO_3|Si_4O_{12}] \cdot H_2O$
Kakirit *m* kakirite *(cataclastic rock)*
Kakoxen *m* cacoxenite, $Fe_4[OH|PO_4]_3 \cdot 12H_2O$
Kaktolith *m* cactolith *(a ramified form of intrusion)*
Kalamin *m s.* Hemimorphit
Kalbeis *n* calf
kalben to calve *(glacier)*
Kalbung *f* calving *(of a glacier)*
Kaldera *f* caldera
Kaledoniden *fpl* Caledonids
Kaledonikum *n* Caledonian
kaledonisch Caledonian
Kali *n* potassium, K
Kalialaun *m* potash alaun, $KAl(SO_4)_2 \cdot 12H_2O$
Kali-Argon-Alter *n* K-A-age
Kaliastrakanit *m* kaliastrakanite *(s. a. Leonit)*
Kaliberlog *n* caliper (calibre) log, section gauge log
Kalibermeßgerät *n* caliper
Kalibermessung *f s.* Kaliberlog
Kaliberschneide *f* gauge edge
Kaliberzapfen *m* bore gauge
Kaliblödit *m* kaliblödite, kalibloedite *(s. a. Leonit)*
Kaliborit *m* kaliborite, $KMg_2[B_5O_6(OH)_4|B_3O_3(OH)_5] \cdot 2H_2O$
Kalicinit *m* kalicinite, $KHCO_3$
Kalidüngesalz *n* potash manure, *(Am)* potash fertilizer
Kalifeldspat *m* kalifel[d]spar, potash fel[d]spar
Kaliflöz *n* potash seam
Kalifornit *m* californite, Californian jade
Kaliglimmer *m* potash mica
Kaligrube *f* potash mine
kalihaltig potassic
Kalilager *n* potash deposit
Kalilauge *f* potash lye
Kalimagnesiasalz *n* potash-magnesia salt
Kalinit *m* kalinite, $KAl[SO_4]_2 \cdot 11H_2O$
Kaliophilit *m* kaliophilite, phacelite, $K[AlSiO_4]$
Kalirevier *n* potash district
Kalirohsalz *n* crude potassium (potash) salt, deliquescent salt

Kalisalpeter m nitre, saltpetre, KNO_3
Kalisalz n potassium (potash) salt
Kalisalzlager n deposit (bed) of potash salts
Kalisalzvorratsblock m block of potash-salt, deliquescent salt reserves
Kalistrontit m kalistrontite, $SrK_2[SO_4]_2$
Kalitonerde f aluminate of potash
Kalium n potassium, K
Kaliumkarbonat n potash, K_2CO_3
Kaliumoxid n potash, K_2O
Kalk m lime[stone]
~/**allodaptischer** allodaptic limestone
~/**bituminöser** bituminous limestone
~/**doppelkohlensaurer** calcium bicarbonate
~/**gebrannter** burnt lime
~/**gelöschter** slaked lime
~ **in situ/organogener** accretionary limestone
~/**kohlensaurer** carbonate of lime
~/**ungelöschter** live (quick) lime
kalkablagernd lime-depositing, lime-precipitating; lime-secreting
Kalkablagerung f calcareous deposit
kalkabscheidend lime-secreting
Kalkalgen fpl calcareous (lime-precipitating, lime-secreting) algae
Kalkalgenfazies f algae-mat facies
Kalkalgenriff n algal reef
Kalkalkaligestein n calc-alkali rock
Kalkalkaligesteine npl calc-alkalic series, alkali-calcic series
Kalkalkaligranit m calc-alkali granite
Kalkalkalireihe f calc-alkali (subalkalic, pacific, calcic) series (suite, province)
Kalkarenit m calcarenite, lime sandrock
kalkarm carbonate-poor
Kalkarmut f scarity of lime
kalkartig limey
Kalkasphalt m asphaltic (asphalt-impregnated) limestone
Kalkbakterien fpl lime-depositing bacteria
Kalkbildung f calcification
Kalkboden m ped[o]cal
Kalkbruch m limestone quarry
Kalkdetritus m calcareous detritus
Kalkeisengranat m calcium-iron garnet, andradite, $Ca_3Fe_2(SiO_4)_3$
Kalkeisenstein m calcareous ironstone
Kalkerde f calcareous earth
Kalkfeldspat m lime fel[d]spar, anorthite, $Ca[Al_2Si_2O_8]$
kalkfrei lime-free, non-calcareous
kalkführend calcarinate
Kalkgehalt m lime content, calcium carbonate content
Kalkgehaltsbestimmung f calcimetry
Kalkgerüst n limy (calcareous) skeleton
Kalkgestein n limestone rock
Kalkgesteine npl calcic series
Kalkglimmer m brittle (pearl) mica, margarite, $CaAl_2(OH)_2[Si_2Al_2O_{10}]$
Kalkglimmerschiefer m calcareous (calc-mica) schist

Kalkgrube f lime pit
kalkhaltig lim[e]y, calcareous, calcic, calc[ar]iferous
Kalkhärte f calcium hardness
Kalkhöhle f dene hole
kalkig lim[e]y, calcareous, calciferous
Kalkkarst m carbonate karst
Kalkkies m calcareous gravel
Kalkknollenschiefer m nodulous limestone
Kalkkompensationstiefe f calcite compensation depth
Kalkkonkretion f calcareous concretion
Kalkkruste f calcicrust, calcareous crust; calcrete, caliche, ped[o]cal (on arid soils)
kalkliebend chalk-loving
Kalkmarmor m lime (calcic) marble
Kalkmergel m lime marl, calcareous marl (clay)
Kalkmudde f calcareous mud
Kalknagelfluh f calcareous nagelfluh
Kalknatronfeldspat m soda-lime fel[d]spar (s. a. Plagioklas)
Kalkofen m lime kiln
Kalkoolith m oolitic limestone, limy oolite
Kalkpelit m calcilutite
Kalkphyllit m calcareous phyllite
Kalkquelle f calcareous spring
kalkreich lime-rich
Kalkrotlehm m limestone red loam, siallitic terra rossa
Kalksalpeter m nitrocalcite, $Ca[NO_3]_2 \cdot 4H_2O$
Kalksand m lime (calcareous) sand
Kalksandstein m calcarenite, calcareous (calciferous, lime) sandstone, sandy (arenaceous) limestone, lime sandrock
Kalkschaler mpl calcareous tests
kalkschalig calcareous-shelled
Kalkschicht f limestone layer, limy (calcareous) bed
~ **im Moor** bog lime
Kalkschiefer m limestone shale
Kalkschieferbruch m calcareous-shale quarry
Kalkschlamm m calcareous mud
Kalkschwämme mpl calcisponges, calcispongians, calcareous sponges
Kalkschwarzerde f humus carbonate soil, rendzina
Kalksilikat n lime silicate, calc-silicate
Kalksilikatfels m, **Kalksilikatgestein** n lime silicate rock, calc-silicate rock, erlane
Kalksilikatgneis m calc-silicate gneiss
Kalksilikathornfels m calc-silicate hornfels
Kalksiltstein m calcisiltite
Kalksinter m calcareous sinter (tufa), calc-sinter, calc-tufa, fresh-water limestone
Kalkskelett n skeleton of lime
Kalkspat m calcareous spar, calc-spar, calcite, $CaCO_3$
~/**optischer** optical calcite, Iceland spar, doubly reflecting spar
Kalkspatpolarisationsprisma n double-image prism

Kalkspülung

Kalkspülung *f* lime mud
Kalkstein *m* limestone, lime rock, calcitite, calcilyte, calcilith
~/**argillitischer** cement rock
~/**asphaltimprägnierter** asphalt[ic] rock
~ **aus Korallendetritus** calcarneyte
~/**biogener** biogenic (organic) limestone
~/**brüchiger** malm
~/**detritischer** detrital (petroclastic) limestone
~/**dichter** compact limestone
~/**dolomitischer** dolostone, dolomitite, dolomitic (magnesian) limestone
~/**drusiger** vugular (vuggy) limestone
~/**erbsenförmiger** pisiform limestone
~/**fleckiger dolomitischer** cotton rock
~/**fossilführender** fossiliferous limestone
~/**grobkörniger** coarse limestone
~/**grobkristalliner** sparry limestone
~/**hochprozentiger** high-lime rock
~/**konkretionärer** ballstone
~/**korallenführender** coralliferous limestone
~/**körniger** granular limestone
~/**kristalliner** crystalline limestone
~/**lithografischer** lithographic limestone
~/**löcheriger** *s.* ~/**drusiger**
~/**massiger** massive limestone
~/**organogener mit autochthonen Strukturen** bioframe limestone
~ **ohne Skelettelemente** non-skeletal limestone
~/**oolithischer** oolitic (pisiform) limestone
~/**organogener** bioaccumulated limestone
~/**pelitischer** *s.* Kalzilutit
~/**pillenführender (pillenreicher)** pelletal micritic limestone
~/**pisolitischer** pisosparite, pisiform (pisolitic) limestone
~/**poröser** *s.* Kalksinter
~/**psammitischer** calcarenite, lime sandrock
~/**resedimentierter** calcarneyte
~/**sandiger** arenaceous limestone
~/**schwach pillenführender** micritic limestone
~/**sedimentärer** ortholimestone
~/**spröder brüchiger** ganil
~/**toniger** argillaceous limestone
~/**verkarsteter** karstified limestone
~/**zelliger** vesicular limestone
Kalksteinboden *m* limestone soil
Kalksteinbraunlehm *m s.* Terra fusca
Kalksteinbruch *m* limestone quarry
Kalksteingebirge *n* limestone mountains
Kalksteingeröll *n* limestone pebbles
Kalksteingrube *f* lime[stone] pit
Kalksteinindividuen *npl*/**klastische** limeclasts
Kalkstein-Karst-Morphologie *f* rugged limestone rocky land
Kalksteinkies *m* limestone gravel
Kalksteinkugel *f s.* Kalzitsphärit
Kalksteinlage *f* limestone bed
Kalksteinlinse *f* limestone lens
Kalksteinplatte *f* limestone slab
Kalksteinrotlehm *m s.* Terra rossa

Kalktonboden *m* malm
Kalktonschiefer *m* calcareous slate
Kalktonstein *m* lime mud rock
Kalktuff *m* tufaceous limestone (*s. a.* Kalksinter)
~/**klastischer** clastic (detrital) lime tufa
kalkumhüllt limestone-encased
kalk- und tonhaltig calcareo-argillaceous
Kalkuranglimmer *m s.* Autunit
Kalkvolborthit *m s.* Tangeit
Kallait *m* turquois, $CuAl_6[(OH)_2|PO_4]_4 \cdot 4H_2O$
Kallilith *m* kallilite, $Ni(Sb, Bi)S$
Kalmen *fpl*, **Kalmengürtel** *m* doldrums
Kalomel *m* calomel, mercurial horn ore, $HgCl$
Kalsilit *m* kalsilite, $K[AlSiO_4]$
Kältepol *m* cold pole
Kältewelle *f* cold wave
Kaltfront *f* arctic (cold) front
Kaltluft *f*/**arktische** arctic (polar) air
Kaltlufteinbruch *m* cold wave
Kaltluftfront *f* cold front
Kaltverfestigung *f* strain hardening
Kaltzeit *f s.* Eiszeit
Kalzilutit *m* calcilutite
Kalzimikrit *m* calcimicrite
kalzinieren to calcine
Kalzinierung *f* calcination
kalzinierungsfähig calcinable
Kalzirudit *m* calcirudite, lime rubblerock
Kalzisiltit *m* calcisiltite
Kalzisphären *fpl* calcispheres
Kalzit *m* calcite, calcareous spar, calc-spar, $CaCO_3$
~/**bituminöser** horn tiff
~/**geaderter** onychite
~ **mit Sandinklusionen** sand calcite, sand crystal
Kalziterbse *f* cave pearl
Kalzitgestein *n* calcitite
Kalzitisierung *f* calcitization
Kalzitkompensationstiefe *f* calcite compensation depth, CCD
Kalzitskalenoeder *npl* hog-tooth spar
Kalzitsphärit *m* calcite sphaerite
kalzitverkittet calcicrete (*pebbles*)
Kalzium *n* calcium, Ca
Kalziumalter *n* calcium age
Kalziumchlorid *n* calcium chloride
Kalziumkarbonat *n* calcium carbonate
Kalziumoxid *n* lime, CaO
Kalziumsulfat *n* calcium sulphate, anhydrite, gypsum
Kamarezit *m* kamarezite, $Cu_3[(OH)_4|SO_4] \cdot 6H_2O$
Kamazit *m* kamacite (*Ni-poor iron in meteorites*)
kambrisch Cambrian
Kambrium *n* Cambrian [System] (*chronostratigraphically*); Cambrian [Period] (*geochronologically*); Cambrian [Age] (*common sense*)
Kambriumperiode *f* Cambrian [Period]
Kambriumsystem *n* Cambrian [System]

Kambriumzeit f Cambrian [Age]
Kambrosilur n Cambro-Silurian
Kam m kame *(short moraine crosswise to the flowing direction of the ice)*
Kameslandschaft f kame topography
Kamesterrasse f lateral stream terrace
Kamin m chimney
kaminartig chimneylike
Kamm m ridge, crest, chain of mountains; clay vein, horseback *(of the seam)*
kammartig ridgy, ridgelike
Kammeis n needle ice, mush frost
Kammer f 1. hall; 2. chamber *(of fossil shells)*
Kammerbau m roomwork, room working
Kammerblockbild n isometric stratigraphic diagram
Kammergang m chambered vein
Kammerpfeilerbau m room and pillar method
Kammerschießarbeit f, **Kammerschießen** n chamber blasting
Kammersprengverfahren n *(Am)* coyote tunneling method
Kammgraben m/**medianer** rift valley *(inside the middle-oceanic ridges)*
Kammkies m cockscomb pyrite (s. a. Markasit)
Kammstruktur f comb texture
Kammwasserscheide f dividing crest
Kampf m **ums Dasein** struggle for live
Kämpfer m abutment
Kämpferdruck m abutment pressure, pressure on [a]butment
~/hinterer (rückwärtiger) rear (back) abutment pressure
~/vorderer (voreilender) front abutment pressure
Kämpferdruckzone f abutment zone
Kämpferlinie f springing line
Kämpferpunkt m springing
Kampylit m campylite *(s. a. Phosphor-Mimetesit)*
Kanadabalsam m Canada balsam *(turpentine)*
Kanadit m canadite *(nepheline syenite)*
Kanal m 1. channel *(natural waterway)*; 2. canal *(artificial waterway)*; 3. duct *(passage)*
~ im Einschnitt canal in a cut
~/kleiner thoroughfare *(crosses a cape or a shore barrier)*
Kanalbau m canal construction
Kanaldamm m canal bank (embankment)
Kanalhaltung f canal reach
Kanalisationsgraben m ditch for canalization
Kanalisationstechnik f sewage engineering, sewerage and sewage disposal
Kanalisierung f canalization
Kanalstufe f canal pond
Kanalwellen fpl channel waves; leaking modes
Kaneit m kaneite, MnAs
kännelartig canneloid
Kännel-Boghead-Kohle f cannel-boghead coal *(sapropelic coal)*

Kapillarröhrchenhohlraum

kanneliert channelled, fluted, canaliculate[d]
Kannelierung f channelling, fluting, furrowing, grooving
Kännelkohle f cannel coal, gayet *(sapropelic coal)*
Kännelschiefer m cannel shale *(sapropelic shale)*
Känophytikum n Cainophyticum, Cenophytic
Känozoikum n Caenozoic [Era], Kainozoic [Era]
känozoisch Caenozoic, Kainozoic
Kansan n Kansan *(Pleistocene in North America, corresponding to Menapian to Cromerian in Europe)*
Kansasit m kansasite *(a fossil resin)*
Kante f edge
~/scharfe keen edge
kantenbestoßen smoothed *(pebbles)*
kantendurchscheinend translucent at [the] edges, with translucent edges, transparent on edges
Kanteneffekt m edge effect
Kantengeröll n [wind] faceted pebble[s]
kantengerundet rounded at [the] edges, subangular
Kantenpressung f edge pressure
Kantenriß m edge crack
Kantenspannung f edge pressure
Kantenwinkel m edge angle
kantig angular
Kantigkeit f angularity
Kaolin m kaolin, porcelain clay (earth)
kaolinhaltig kaolinic
kaolinisiert kaolinized
Kaolinisierung f kaolinization
Kaolinit m kaolinite, $Al_4[(OH)_8|Si_4O_{10}]$
kaolinitisch kaolinic
Kaolin-Kohlen-Tonstein m kaoline-coal flint clay
Kaolinlagerstätte f kaolin deposit
Kaolinsandstein m kaolin[iferous] sandstone
Kap n cape; headland
Kapdiamant m cape diamond
kapillar capillary
Kapillarabsorption f capillary absorption
Kapillaranstieg m capillary elevation (rise)
Kapillaranziehung f, **Kapillarattraktion** f capillary attraction
Kapillardruck m capillary pressure
Kapillardruckkurve f capillary pressure curve
Kapillardurchfluß m capillary percolation
Kapillardurchlässigkeit f capillary conductivity
Kapillare f capillary
Kapillarimeter n capillarimeter
Kapillarität f capillarity
Kapillaritätszahl f capillary constant
Kapillarkanal m capillary channel
Kapillarkondensation f capillary condensation
Kapillarkraft f capillary force
Kapillarpotential n capillary potential
Kapillarröhrchen n capillary tube
Kapillarröhrchenhohlraum m capillary bore

Kapillarröhrchenwandung

Kapillarröhrchenwandung f capillary wall
Kapillarsaugkraft f capillary attraction
Kapillarsaum m capillary fringe, boundary zone of capillarity
Kapillarsaumwasser n fringe water
Kapillarspannung f capillary tension
Kapillarwasser n capillary water (moisture)
Kapillarzahl f capillary number
Kapillarzone f zone of capillarity
Kapillarzwischenraum m capillary interstice
Kappe f cap; roof bar (lining)
~/gewölbte cambered girder
kappen to capture, to behead (a river)
Kappen n capture, beheading (of a river)
Kappenkette f row of bars
Kappenquarz m cap[ped] quartz
Kappenreihe f row of bars
Kappschuh m jointing shoe
Kappung f s. Kappen
Kaprubin m cape ruby
Kapselton m sagger (saggar, seggar) clay
Kar n cirque, kar, [glacier] circus, amphitheatre, kettle
~/ausgekerbtes scalloped cirque
Karachait m carachaite, $MgO \cdot SiO_2 \cdot H_2O$
Karat n carat
~/metrisches metric (international) carat (= 200 mg)
Karbildung f cirquation, cirque cutting (erosion)
Karboden m cirque floor
Karbon n Carboniferous [System] (chronostratigraphically); Carboniferous [Period] geochronologically); Carboniferous [Age] (common sense)
Karbonado m carbonado, carbon diamond
Karbonat n carbonate
Karbonatablagerung f/**äolische** parna
Karbonatapatit m carbonate apatite, $Ca_5[F|PO_4,(O_3OH)_3]$
Karbonatbestimmung f calcimetry
Karbonatboden m calcareous soil
Karbonat-CO$_2$ n firmly bound CO_2
Karbonatdetritus m flour
Karbonatgestein n carbonate rock
~/kryptokristallines silifiziertes jasperoid
~/pelitfreies grainstone
Karbonathärte f carbonate hardness (of water)
karbonatisieren to carbonat[iz]e
Karbonatisierung f carbonat[izat]ion; calcification
Karbonatit m carbonatite (rock of the ultramafic clan)
Karbonatkohlenstoff m carbonate carbon
Karbonatkonkretion f algal biscuit (ball) (produced by algae or similar organisms)
Karbonatmetasomatose f carbonat[izat]ion
Karbonatmineral n carbon spar
Karbonatplattform f carbonate platform
Karbonatsand m carbonate sand, calcarneyte
Karbonatspat m carbon spar
Karbonflora f Carboniferous flora

Karbonisierung f carbonat[izat]ion
Karbonperiode f Carboniferous [Period]
Karbonsystem n Carboniferous [System]
Karbonzeit f Carboniferous [Age]
Karborund[um] n carborundum
Kardanring m gimbal
Kardinalseptum n cardinal septum (of corals)
Karelianit m carelianite, V_2O_3
Karerosion f cirquation, cirque cutting (erosion)
Kargebirge n fretted upland
Kargletscher m cirque glacier
Karinthin m carinthine (brown-green pleochroitic eclogite-amphibole)
Karkessel m kettle depression
Karminit m carminite, $PbFe_2[OH|AsO_4]_2$
Karmulde f kettle depression
Karn n Carnian [Stage], Karnian [Stage] (of Triassic)
Karnallit m carnallite, $KMgCl_3 \cdot 6H_2O$
karnallitisch carnallitic
Karnallitit m carnallitite
Karneol m carnelian, carneol[e], cornelian (subvariety of chalcedony)
~/bräunlicher sard (s. a. Quarz)
Karnotit m carnotite, $K_2[(UO_2)_2|(VO_4)_2] \cdot 3H_2O$
Karo n diamond (geophone or shot-point arrangement)
karoartig chequered
Karpathit m carpathite, $C_{32}H_{17}O$
Karpholith m carpholite, $MnAl_2[(OH)_4|Si_2O_6]$
Karphosiderit m carphosiderite, $H_2OFe_3[(OH)_5H_2O|(SO_4)_2]$
Karpinskiit m karpinskiite, $(Na, K, Zn, Mg)_2 [(OH, H_2O)_{1-2}|(Al, Be)_2Si_4O_{12}]$
karpologisch carpological
Karreeboden m polygonal ground (markings, soil)
Karren npl karren, schratten, clints, lapies
Karrenbrunnen m lapie-well
Karrenfeld n karrenfeld
Karrenkarst m lapies
Karrenzone f clint zone
Karru-Formation f Karoo Beds
Karru-Hauptgruppe f Karoo Supergroup (Permo-Carboniferous in South Africa)
Karschwelle f cirque threshold
Karsee m cirque (rock basin) lake, [mountain, alpine] tarn
Karsohle f cirque floor
Karst m karst [region]
~/nackter naked karst
~/subkutaner subcutaneous karst
~/tiefer deep karst
karstartig karstic
Karstberg m/**residualer** hum, butte temoine
Karstbildung f karstification, karst formation (forming)
Karstbrekzie f collapse (founder) breccia
Karstbrunnen m jama
Karstdoline f swallow hole
Karsterscheinungen fpl karst phenomena

Karstfluß m karst stream
~/subterraner estavel
~/wasserabgebender lost river
Karstforschung f karst research
Karstgebiet n karst [region]
Karstgrundwasserleiter m karst aquifer
Karsthochfläche f karst plateau, planina
Karsthöhle f karst hollow (hole, cavity)
Karstinselberg m hum, butte temoine
Karstlandschaft f karst landscape
~/reife cockpit topography
Karstmorphologie f karst morphology
Karstquelle f karst (tubular) spring
Karstrelief n karst topography
Karstrestberg m hum, butte temoine
Karstschlot m sink (leach) hole, lime[stone] sink, ponor, jama
Karstschlotte f karst cave
Karstsee m karst lake
Karsttrichter m karst funnel, doline
Karstufe f headwall
Karstwanne f s. Karsttrichter
Karstwasser n Karst (cavern) water
Karte f map; chart
~/abgedeckte subsurface (deep horizon) map
~/barometrische pressure chart
~ der Ableitungen derivative map *(seismics)*
~ der Glazialablagerungen drift map
~ der Oberflächenformationen/geologische areal map
~ der regionalen Schwere regional gravity map
~ der zweiten Ableitung second-derivative map *(seismics)*
~ des Untergrunds/geologische geologic[al] subsurface map
~/flächentreue equal area chart
~/geologische geologic[al] map
~ gleicher Mächtigkeiten isochore map
~/kleinmaßstäbliche small-scale map
~/lithologische lithologic map
~/metallogenetische metallogenetic map
~/meteorologische meteorologic[al] chart
~/paläogeografische pal[a]eogeographic[al] map
~/paläolithologische pal[a]eolithologic map
~/tektonische structure map
Kartenabriß m base map
Kartenaufnahme f **aus der Luft** aerophotogrammetry
Kartenausschnitt m map section
Kartenblatt n map sheet
~/geologisches geologic[al] map sheet
Kartengenauigkeit f accuracy of map; degree of accuracy of a map
Kartenkunde f cartography
Kartenlesen n map reading, interpretation of maps
Kartenmaßstab m map scale, scale of chart; representative fraction *(distance ratio of two points on the map and in the terrain)*
Kartennetz n map grid

Kartenprojektion f map projection
Kartenskizze f topographic drawing, sketch map
Kartenunterlage f **für geologische Arbeiten/topografische** base map of geological work
Kartenzeichen n map symbol
Kartenzeichner m cartographer
Karterrasse f cirque platform
Kartierbarkeit f mappability
kartieren to map; to chart
Kartieren n s. Kartierung
Kartiergerät n mapping instrument
Kartierung f mapping; charting; profiling *(geoelectrics)*
~ der radiometrischen Intensität radiometric intensity mapping
~ des Überflutungsgebiets mittels Satellitenfernerkundung satellite flood mapping
~ des Untergrunds/geologische geologic[al] subsurface mapping
~/geodätische geodesic mapping
~/geologische geologic[al] mapping
~/großmaßstäbliche large-scale mapping
~/regionale regional mapping
~ vom Flugzeug aus aerial (airplane) mapping
Kartierungsbohrung f drilling for mapping purposes
Kartograf m cartographer
Kartografie f cartography; map printing
kartografisch cartographic[al]
Kartreppe f cirque (glacial) stairway, cirque steps
Karyinit m caryinite, (Na, Ca)$_2$(Mn, Mg, Ca, Pb)$_3$[AsO$_4$]$_3$
Karyopilit m caryopilite, Mn$_6$[(OH)$_8$|Si$_4$O$_{10}$]
Kasan-Eiszeit f Kasan Ice Age
Kascholong m cacholong *(variety of opal)*
Kaskade f cascade, waterfall
Kaskadenfalte f zigzag fold
Kaskadia f Cascadia, Cascadis
Kasolit m kasolite, Pb$_2$[UO$_2$|SiO$_4$]$_2$ · 2H$_2$O
Kasparit m kasparite *(variety of pickeringite)*
Kaspigebiet n Caspian area
Kaspisenke f Caspian depression
Kassiterit m cassiterite, tin spar (ore, stone), SnO$_2$
Kastenfalte f box fold
Kastengreifer m box sampler
Kastenprofil n box section *(for roof bars)*
Kastental n U-shaped valley
Katagenese f catagenesis *(anchimetamorphism)*
Katagestein n kata rock
Kataklase f cataclasis, cataclastic processes
Kataklasit m cataclasite
kataklastisch cataclastic
Kataklinaltal n cataclinal valley
Kataklysmentheorie f cataclysmal (catastrophic) theory, catastrophism, catastrophist concept *(of Cuvier)*
Kataklysmus m cataclysm, convulsion
katamorph katamorphic

Katamorphismus

Katamorphismus m katamorphism
katamorphosieren to katamorphose
Katanorm f catanorm
Katapleit m catapleiite, $Na_2Zr[Si_3O_9] \cdot 2H_2O$
kataseismisch kataseismic
Katasteramt n cadastral office
Katasteraufnahme f cadastral survey
Katasterblatt n survey map
Katastrophe f catastrophe *(11th stage of the scale of seismic intensity)*
Katastrophenbereitschaft f disaster preparedness
Katastrophenhilfe f disaster relief
Katastrophenhochwasser n disastrous flood, *(Am)* superflood, flood of record
Katastrophenlehre f, **Katastrophentheorie** f s. Kataklysmentheorie
Katastrophenverhütung f disaster prevention
Katastrophenwarnung f disaster warning
katathermal katathermal
Katavothre f katavothron
katazonal katazonal
Katazone f katazone, catazone
Kategorie f **der Gesteinshärte** rock hardness category
~ **der Kompliziertheit des geologischen Baus bei Untersuchungsarbeiten** category of geological structure complication
Kation n cation
Kationenaustausch m cation exchange
Kationenaustauschkapazität f cation exchange capacity
Katodenstrahloszillograf m cathode ray oscillograph (tube), CRT
Katophorit m katophorite, $Na_2CaFe_4(Fe, Al)[OH, F)_2|AlSi_7O_{22}]$
Katoptrit m catoptrite, $Mn_{14}Sb_2(Al, Fe)_4[O_{21}|(SO_4)_2]$
Katt n Chattian [Stage] *(of Oligocene)*
Katungit m katungite *(pyroxene-free melilite lava)*
Katzenauge n cat's eye *(partly quartz, partly chrysoberyl)*
Katzenglimmer m cat gold *(weathered biotite)*
Katzengold n fool's gold, golden mica
Katzensteine mpl cat heads
Kauleiste f grinding ridge
Kaulquappennester npl tadpole nests *(interference ripples)*
Kauri n kauri *(a fossil resin)*
kaustisch caustic
Kaustobiolith m caustobiolite, kaustobiolite
Kautschuk m caoutchouc
Kauwulst m basalpib *(cephalopodans jaw element)*
Kaverne f cavern
Kavernenbohrung f cavern well
Kavernendach n cavern roof
Kavernendimensionierung f cavern design
Kavernenkontur f cavern shape
Kavernenkonvergenz f cavern convergence
Kavernenspeicher m cavern storage

~/**bergmännisch hergestellter** mined cavern storage
Kavernenstoß m cavern wall
Kavernensumpf m cavern sump
Kavernenüberwachung f cavity surveillance
Kavernenvermessung f cavern logging
kavernös cavernous
Kavernosität f vugular porosity
Kavitation f cavitation
Kayenta-Formation f Kayenta Formation *(Lower Lias in North America)*
Kazan n Kazanian [Stage] *(of Permian)*
K-Bau m K-support *(mining)*
Kegel m cone
~/**kleiner** conelet
Kegelbildung f coning *(reservoir mechanics)*
Kegelbrecher m cone crusher
Kegeldruckversuch m cone penetration test
kegelförmig, kegelig conic[al], cone-shaped, conoid; coniform
Kegelkarst m cockpit karst
Kegelkarstgebiet n cockpit karst area
Kegelprojektion f conic projection
Kegelrollmeißel m cone bit
Kegelspalten fpl cone sheets *(volcano-tectonic)*
Kegelteilung f [sample] coning
Kegelwinkel m angle of taper
Kegelwulst m flute cast
Kehoeit m kehoeite, $(Zn, Ca)[Al_2P_2(H_3)_2O_{12}] \cdot 4H_2O$
Kehrwert m reciprocal value
Keil m wedge; tongue
keilförmig wedge-shaped, wedgelike, cuneiform
Keilhauit m keilhauite, $(Ca, Y, Ce)(Ti, Al, Fe)[O|SiO_4]$
Keilscholle f fault wedge, wedge block
Keilschollengebirge n fault-wedge mountain
Keiltopf m spider
Keim m nucleus, germ
Keimbildung f nucleation, germination
Keimbildungsgeschwindigkeit f nucleation rate, rate of germination
Kelch m calyx, crown *(of crinoids)*
Kelchdecke f tegmen *(of crinoids)*
~/**ventrale** ventrale tegmen
Keldyshit m keldyshite, $Na_2Zr[Si_2O_7]$
Kelly n kelly, grief stem
Kelyphit m kelyphite *(intergrowth of fibrous amphibole and feldspar)*
kelyphitisch kelyphitic
Kelyphitrinde f kelyphitic rim
Kempit m kempite, $Mn_2(OH)_3Cl$
Kennedyit m kennedyite, $Fe_2MgTi_3O_{10}$
Kennkurve f characteristic curve
Kennlinie f **eines Stempels** s. Last-Weg-Kurve
Kennmarke f gap *(seismogram)*
Kennreihe f characteristic series
Kennuntergruppe f characteristic subgroup
Kentallenit m kentallenite *(alkali gabbro)*
Kentrolith m kentrolite, $Pb_2Mn_2[O_2|Si_2O_7]$

Kenyait *m* kenyaite, $NaSi_{11}O_{20,5}$
Kerabitumen *n s.* Kerogen
Keralith *m* keralite *(quartz-biotite-hornfels)*
Kerargyrit *m* cerargyrite, AgCl
Keratophyr *m* keratophyre *(effusive of the syenite clan)*
Kerbe *f* cut; sco[u]ring
kerben to carve
Kerbtal *n* V-shaped valley
Kerbwirkung *f* notch effect
Kerbzähigkeit *f* impact resistance (strength)
kerbzähnig groove-toothed *(palaeobotany)*
Kermesit *m* kermesite, red antimony, antimony blende, Sb_2S_2O
Kern *m* 1. core *(e.g. drilling)*; 2. nucleus *(of an atom)*
~/abgequetschter detached core *(of a fold)*
~/ausschwitzender bleeding core
~/eingespülter wasserdichter core pool *(earthfill dam)*
~/gewonnener recovered core
~/langlebiger instabiler long-living instable nucleus
~/nichtdeformierter detached core *(of a fold)*
~/ölausschwitzender bleeding core
~/raumorientierter oriented core
~/zermahlener ground-up core
Kernabsorptionsmagnetometer *n* optically pumped magnetometer
Kernapparat *m* core barrel
Kernaufbau *m* nuclear structure
Kernausstoßvorrichtung *f* core extractor (pusher)
Kernbildung *f* nucleation
Kernbohrausrüstung *f* core drill rig
Kernbohren *n* core drilling (boring), core drill boring, auger mining *(with comminution of the coal core)*
Kernbohrer *m* core drill
Kernbohrkrone *f* core bit
~/mit Diamanten besetzte diamond core head
Kernbohrloch *n* core hole
~ mit kleinem Durchmesser slim hole
Kernbohrmaschine *f* core drill machine
Kernbohrung *f s.* 1. Kernbohren; 2. Kernbohrloch
Kernbrecher *m* core catcher
Kernbrennstoff *m* nuclear fuel
Kerndamm *m* core-type dam (embankment)
Kerndurchmesser *m* core diameter
kernen to core
Kernen *n* coring
~ aus der Bohrlochwand lateral (side-wall) coring
~/elektrisches electrical coring (logging)
~/fortlaufendes continuous coring
~ mit Diamantkrone diamond coring
~/seitliches lateral (side-wall) coring
Kernentnahme *f* core extraction, coring *(s. a.* Kernen*)*
Kernexplosionsbruchbau *m* nuclear caving
Kernfänger *m* core catcher (breaker)

~/durch Pumpendruck betätigter core catcher operated by pump pressure
Kernfangring *m* core catcher
Kernfangvorrichtung *f* core-retaining device
Kernfolge *f* suite of cores
Kernforscher *m* atomic scientist
Kerngewinn *m,* **Kerngewinnung** *f* core extraction (recovery)
Kernhalter *m* core holder
Kernheber *m* core lifter
Kernit *m* kernite, rasorite, $Na_2[B_4O_6(OH)_2] \cdot 3H_2O$
Kernkiste *f* core storage box
Kernklemmer *m* core wedging
Kernkronenrille *f* im anstehenden Gestein kerf, annular groove cut by a coring bit
Kernladung *f* nuclear charge
Kernladungszahl *f* atomic number
Kernlochbohren *n,* **Kernlochbohrung** *f* core hole drilling
Kernmasse *f* nuclear mass
Kernmeißel *m* core bit
Kernorientierung *f* core orientation
Kernpräzessionsmagnetometer *n* nuclear (proton) precession magnetometer
Kernprobe *f* core sample
Kernprobenahme *f* coring
Kernprobenehmer *m* core grabber *(person)*
Kernprofil *n* core profil
Kernprozeß *m* nuclear process
Kernreaktion *f* nuclear reaction
Kernresonanzmagnetometer *n* nuclear (proton) resonance magnetometer
Kernrohr *n* core barrel (tube)
~/ausbaubares retrievable core barrel
~/äußeres outer core barrel
~/inneres inner core barrel, core-receiving barrel, core-retaining tube
Kernrohrkopf *m* core barrel head
Kernsatz *m* suite of cores
Kernschatten *m* umbra
Kernschießgerät *n* bullet-type side wall corer
~ für Meeresbodenproben piggot corer
Kernspaltung *f* nuclear (atomic) fission
Kernspaltvorrichtung *f* core splitter
Kernsprung *m* radial (heat) crack
Kernspülen *n* core flushing
Kernstoßbohren *n* punching
Kernstoßbohrer *m* core barrel
Kernstrahlung *f* nuclear radiation
Kernstrecke *f* cored interval
Kernsynthese *f* nuclear synthesis
Kernuntersuchung *f* core examination
Kernverlust *m* core loss, loss of [drill] core
Kernwaffeneffekt *m* bomb effect
Kernzerfall *m* nuclear disintegration (decay)
kernziehen to core
Kernzone *f* supplementary pressure zone
Kerogen *n* kerogen
Kersantit *m* kersantite *(lamprophyre)*
Kerstenit *m* kerstenite, $Pb[SeO_4]$
kerzenartig candlelike

Kessel

Kessel *m* ca[u]ldron *(generally);* [fault] pit, sink, basin, bowl *(geologically);* dome, pothole *(mining)*
Kesselbruch *m* cauldron (circular) subsidence, fault basin (pit) *(tectonically)*
~/unterirdischer subterranean cauldron subsidence
~/vulkanischer volcanic cauldron subsidence
kesselförmig cauldron-shaped, basin-shaped
Kesselkohle *f* boiler coal
Kesselsee *m* kettle lake, cuvette, pingo remnant
Kesselstein *m* rock basin *(form of erosion)*
Kesseltal *n* basin-shaped valley (gorge), closed basin
Kette *f* 1. chain; 2. range *(topographically);* 3. string *(of geophons)*
Kettengebirge *n* mountain chain; mountain range, cordillera
Kettenkoralle *f* chain coral
Kettensilikat *n* chain silicate, inosilicate
Kettenzange *f* chain tongs
Kettnerit *m* kettnerite, CaBi[OF|CO$_3$]
keulenförmig clavate
Keuper *m* Keuper [Stage] *(of Triassic)*
Keupermergel *m* red marls
Keupersandstein *m* Keuper Sandstone
Kewatin-Coutchiching *n* Kewatin-Choutchiching *(Lower Precambrian in North America)*
Keweenaw *n* Keweenawan *(Later Precambrian in North America)*
Khondalit *m* khondalite *(rock in granulitic facies)*
Kiefer-Birken-Zeit *f* pine-birch period
Kieferfüße *mpl* foot jaws, maxillipedes
Kieferknochen *m* mandible, jaw
Kiel *m* keel, carina *(of fossils)*
Kiemen *fpl* branchiae, gills
kiemenförmig branchiform
Kiemenspalte *f* gill cleft (slit)
Kiemenstrahlen *mpl* gill rakers
Kies *m* 1. gravel, gravelstone; pebble; grit; grail; 2. used with respect to a group of sulfidic ores
~/feiner sandy gravel, granule roundstone
~/grober rubble
~/ungesiebter all-in gravel
Kiesabbrand *m* purple ore
Kiesablagerung *f* gravel deposit
~/nicht zementierte granular gravel
kiesähnlich pyritic
kiesartig gravelly; gritty
Kiesaufbereitungsanlage *f* gravel plant
Kiesbank *f* gravel bank (bar)
kiesbedeckt gravel-capped, gravel-sheeted
Kiesboden *m* gravelly soil, cailloutis
Kiesbohrung *f* gravel boring
Kiesdecke *f* gravel covering (sheet, spread)
Kiesel *m* pebble
Kieselalge *f* diatom
kieselartig flinty
Kieselerde *f* siliceous earth

Kieselgallerte *f* *s.* Kieselgel
Kieselgalmei *m* silicate of zinc
Kieselgel *n* silica gel (jelly)
Kieselgeröll *n* shingle
Kieselgerüst *n* framework of silica
Kieselgestein *n* siliceous (silicified) rock
~/kompaktes körniges granular (crystalline) chert
~/kryptokristallines phthanite
Kieselgesteinsknollen *fpl* W-chert *(from weathering)*
Kieselgur *f* kieselgu[h]r *(s. a.* Diatomeenerde)
Kieselgurstein *m* fossil meal brick
Kieselhölzer *npl* silicified woods
kieselig gravelly, cherty, flinty, siliceous
kieselig-klastisch siliceous-clastic
Kieselkalk *m* cornstone
Kieselkalkstein *m* chert[y] limestone, malmstone, hearthstone
Kieselknauer *m* chert nodule
Kieselkonglomerat *n* silcrete
Kieselkonkretion *f* siliceous concretion
Kieselkruste *f* silcrust
Kieselmanganerz *n* *s.* Rhodonit
Kieselmehl *n* siliceous flour
Kieseloolith *m* siliceous oolite
Kieselsandstein *m* ragstone
~/dunkler dark rag
Kieselsäure *f* silicic acid
~/amorphe amorphous silica
~/freie free silica
Kieselsäuregel *n* silica gel
Kieselsäuregestein *n* silica rock
Kieselschaler-Foraminiferen *fpl* arenaceous foraminifers
kieselschalig siliceous-shelled, flinty-shelled
Kieselschiefer *m* [radiolarian] chert, siliceous schist (shale), flinty slate
~/schwarzer touchstone *(s. a.* Lydit)
Kieselschwamm *m* siliceous (glass) sponge
Kieselsinter *m* siliceous sinter; pearl sinter
Kieselskelett *n* siliceous (silica, flinty) skeleton
Kieselstein *m* gravelstone
Kieselstrand *m* shingle beach
Kieselwismut *m* *s.* Eulytin
Kieselzinkerz *n* hemimorphite, Zn$_4$[(OH)$_2$|Si$_2$O$_7$] · H$_2$O
Kieserit *m* kieserite, Mg[SO$_4$] · H$_2$O
Kiesfächer *m/***grober** fanglomerate
Kiesfilter *n* gravel packing *(in wells)*
Kiesgrube *f* gravel pit
kieshaltig 1. gravelly *(with respect to the dimension of grains);* 2. pyritic, pyritaceous *(with respect to a group of sulfidic ores)*
Kieshülle *f* gravel envelope *(in filter wells)*
kiesig gravelly, pebbly *(coarse-grained);* gritty, arenose *(fine-grained)*
Kieskälber *npl* pyritic concretions *(roofing slate)*
Kieslagerstätte *f* gravel deposit
Kiesmantel *m*, **Kiespackung** *f* gravel packing
Kiessand *m* gravel sand, grit

Kiesschicht f gravel layer, pebble bed
Kiesschotter m ballast, boulder gravel
Kiesschutt m gravel wash, gravel[ly] detritus
Kiesschüttung f gravel accretion; gravel pack (envelope) *(in wells)*
Kiesstrand m gravel beach
Kieswälle mpl gravel trains *(in a bed of a river)*
Kieswüste f gravel desert, serir
Kieszuschlag[stoff] m gravel aggregate
Kilchoanit m kilchoanite, $Ca_3[Si_2O_7]$
Kimberlit m kimberlite *(mica peridotite)*
~/verwitterter yellow (blue) ground
Kimmeridge n Kimmeridgian [Stage] *(of Malm)*
Kimmeridge-Ton m Kimmeridge Clay *(Kimmeridgian including lower and middle Tithonian in England)*
Kimmeridgium n s. Kimmeridge
Kimzeyit m kimzeyite, $Ca_3Zr_2[Al_2SiO_{12}]$
Kinematik f kinematics
kinematisch kinematic
Kinetogenese f kinetogenesis
kinetogenetisch kinetogenetic
Kinetometamorphose f kinetometamorphosis
Kingit m kingite, $Al_3[(OH)_3|(PO_4)_2] \cdot 9H_2O$
Kinzigit m kinzigite *(metasomatic gneiss)*
Kippbewegung f tipping movement
Kippe f [overburden] dump, tipper
Kippen n dumping
Kippenboden m dumping floor
Kippscholle f tilted block
Kippung f tilt, roll *(in direction of flight, i.e. along-track)*; swing, pitch *(perpendicular to direction of flight, i.e. across-track)*
Kippwinkel m dip angle *(electromagnetics)*
Kirchheimerit m kirchheimerite, $Co[UO_2|AsO_4]_2 \cdot n\ H_2O$
Kirkfield[ien] n Kirkfieldian [Stage] *(of Champlainian Series, North America)*
Kirrolith m cirrolite, kirrolite, $Ca_3Al_2[OH|PO_4]_3$
Kirschsteinit m kirschsteinite, $CaFe[SiO_4]$
Kissenlava f pillow (cushion) lava
Kissenstruktur f pillow structure
Kitkait m kitkaite, NiTeSe
Kivit m kivite *(variety of leucite basanite)*
Kladnoit m kladnoite, $C_6H_4(CO)_2NH$
klaffend gaping
Klamm f gorge, ravine
Klammbildung f gorge cutting
Klammerorgane npl claspers, tendrils
Klang m sound
Klappe f valve *(palaeontology)*
Klapperstein m rattle stone, aetite, eaglestone
Klappmast m collapsing (jack knife, folding) mast
Klaprothit m klaprothite, klaprotholite *(aggregate of wittichenite and emplectite)*
Kläranlage f clarification plant, detritus pit
Klärbecken n, **Klärbehälter** m settling tank (basin, pond), clearing basin, clarification bed
Klärbrunnen m settling well

klären/sich to clear up
Klären n clearing
Klärmittel n clarifier
klarspülen/das Bohrloch to clean the hole
Klärsumpf m s. Klärbecken
Klarwasserspülung f circulation with clear water
Klasse f class
Klasseneinteilung f classification
Klassieranlage f classifying (screening, sizing) plant
klassieren to classify; to grade, to size; to screen
Klassierer m classifier
Klassiersieb n classifying screen
Klassiertrog m classifying trough
Klassiertrommel f picking drum
Klassierung f classification, sorting; grading, sizing
~ nach der Korngröße sizing
Klassifikation f classification, assorting
~/geochemische geochemical classification
~/stratigrafische stratigraphic classification
klassifizieren to classify, to class, to assort, to range
Klassifizierung f/**überwachte** supervised classification
~/unüberwachte unsupervised classification
Klassifizierungseigenschaft f index property
Klast m clast
klastisch clastic, fragmental
klastogen clastogene
klastokristallin clasto-crystalline
klastomorph clastomorphic
Klaubearbeit f hand picking, selection
Klaubeband n picking belt
Klaubeberge pl picked deads, pickings
klauben to select, to sort [out by hand], to pick; to cull *(ore)*
Klauben n selection, sorting, picking
Klaubetisch m sorting (picking) table
Klebeanker m resin-bedded roof bolt
Klebegrenze f sticky limit
Klebeschnee m damp snow
klebrig sticky
Klebrigkeit f stickiness
~ der Tonkruste adhesion of the filter cake
Klebsand m loam sand, sand for facing
Klebschiefer m adhesive slate
Klei m s. Schlick
Kleinbeben n microseism
kleindimensional choppy *(cross-bedding)*
kleindrusig miarolitic
Kleinfalte f minor (small) fold
~/inkongruente incongruous minor fold
Kleinfältelung f crenulation, crinkles; microfolds *(in the microscopical view)*
Kleinfaltung f minute (small-scale) folding
Kleinintrusion f minor intrusion
Kleinit m kleinite, $[Hg_2N](Cl,SO_4) \cdot xH_2O$
Kleinkies m grouan
kleinklastisch microclastic

Kleinkluft

Kleinkluft f minor joint
kleinkörnig small-grained
Kleinkreis m small circle
Kleinkreisregelung f small-circle orientation
Kleinplanet m minor planet
Kleinrippel-Schrägschichtungs-Flaserung f ripple cross lamination
kleinstückig small-sized, light-sized
Kleintektonik f microtectonics, small-scale structures
Klemmlast f setting load
Klemmscholle f fault wedge
Klettenerz n bur ore
Klettermoor n climbing bog
Kliachit m kliachite, $AlOOH + H_2O$
Kliff n cliff
~/**gehobenes** elevated shore cliff
~/**kleines** nip
~/**untertauchendes** plunging cliff
kliffartig cliffed
kliffbildend cliff-making, cliff-forming
Kliffbildung f cliff formation (cutting)
Kliffdüne f cliff dune
Kliffeinschnitt m sea chasm *(by wave erosion)*
Kliffhang m chine
Kliffkehle f cliff notch
Kliffkreide f cliff chalk
Kliffküste f cliffed coast
Kliffnische f/**kleine** goe
Kliffrutschung f cliff landslide
Kliffüberhang m cliff overhang
Kliffunterhöhlung f sapping *(in weaker layers)*
Klima n climate
~/**äquatoriales** equatorial climate
~/**arktisches** arctic climate
~/**gemäßigtes** temperate climate
~/**gleichartiges** isonomic climate
~/**maritimes** s. ~/**ozeanisches**
~/**nivales** nival climate
~/**ozeanisches** marine (oceanic) climate
~/**polares** polar climate
~/**regionales** regional climate, macroclimate
~/**subarktisches** subarctic climate
~/**tropisches** tropical climate
Klimaänderung f climatic change, climate variation
Klimabedingungen fpl climatic conditions
Klimaentwicklung f development of climate
Klimagebiet n climatic region
Klimagürtel m climatic belt
Klimakarte f climatic chart
Klimakunde f climatology
Klimaperiode f climatic cycle
Klimascheide f climatic (climate) divide
Klimaschwankung f climatal fluctuation, climatic oscillation
klimatisch climatic, climatal
Klimatologie f climatology
klimatophytisch climatophytic
Klimaverbesserung f amelioration of climate
Klimaverschlechterung f climatic deterioration
Klimawechsel m climatal change

Klimax f climax, vigor, culmination, maximum *(palaeontology)*
Klimazone f climatal (climate) zone
Klingstein m sound-stone, clink stone, phonolite
Klinkenberg-Effekt m Klinkenberg effect
Klinoachse f clinoaxis
Klinochlor m clinochlore, $(Mg,Al)_6[(OH)_8|AlSi_3O_{10}]$
Klinodiskordanz f clin[o]unconformity
Klinodoma n clinodome
Klinoedrit m clinoedrite, $Ca_2Zn_2[(OH)_2|Si_2O_7] \cdot H_2O$
Klinoenstatit m clinoenstatite, $Mg_2[Si_2O_6]$
Klinoferrosilit m clinoferrosilite, $Fe_2[Si_2O_6]$
Klinograf m clinograph
Klinohumit m clinohumite, $Mg_9[(OH,F)_2(SiO_4)_4]$
Klinohypersthen m clinohypersthene, $(Mg, Fe)_2 [Si_2O_6]$
Klinoklas m clinoclasite, $Cu_3[(OH)_3AsO_4]$
Klinometer n inclinometer
klinometrisch clinometric
Klinopinakoid n clinopinacoid
Klinopyroxene mpl clinopyroxenes
Klinostrengit m clinostrengite, phosphosiderite, $Fe[PO_4] \cdot 2H_2O$
Klinoungemacht m clinoungemachite, $K_3Na_9Fe[OHI(SO_4)_2]_3 \cdot 9H_2O$
Klinovariscit m clinovariscite, metavariscite, $Al[PO_4] \cdot 2H_2O$
Klinozoisit m clinozoisite, $Ca_2Al_3[O|OH|SiO_4|Si_2O_7]$
Klippe f 1. rock, cliff; crag; 2. klippe, [nappe] outlier
~/**autochthone** autochthonous klippe
~/**geologische** underneath ridge
~/**parautochthone** parautochthonous klippe
Klippen fpl/**sedimentäre** sedimentary blocks
Klockmannit m klockmannite, CuSe
Kluft f cleft, joint, diaclase; feeder *(water- or ore-bearing)*
~/**einfallende** cutter
~/**endokinetische** endokinematic joint
~/**erzführende** feeder [of ore]
~/**exokinetische** exokinematic joint
~/**geschlossene** tightset
~/**kleine** parting
~/**offene** vug[g]
~/**schaufelförmige** toe-nail
~/**schichtungsparallele** strata joint
~/**sekundäre** minor joint
~/**söhlige** bottom joint
~/**verborgene** blind joint
~/**verschlossene** sealed joint
~/**wasserführende** water slip, feeder [of water]
Kluftabstand m joint spacing
Kluftanalyse f fracture analysis
Kluftbesen m cross-joint fan
Kluftbündel n s. Kluftschar
Kluftdichte f closeness of fissures, degree of joining

Kluftdurchlässigkeit f fissure permeability
Klüfte fpl/**streichende** backs, back joints
Kluftebene f joint plane
klüften to joint
Kluftfalle f fracture trap
Kluftfläche f joint plane
Kluftfugenhöhle f fissure cave
Kluftfüllung f filling of a joint
Kluftgrundwasserleiter m joint aquifer
klüftig jointed, jointy, fractured, fissured; crevassed (of ice)
klüftig-kavernös jointable-cavernous
Klüftigkeit f jointing
~/**schichtparallele** reed
Klüftigkeitskoeffizient m jointing coefficient
Kluftinjektion f rock sealing
Kluftkörper m rock fragment, joint-bordered rock body
~/**ausbrechender** cheestone
Kluftkörperverband m joint body complex, rock block system, rock bonding
Kluftletten m gouge, leader stone, flucan
Kluftmaxima npl joint maxima
Kluftmessungen fpl measurements of joints
Kluftmineral n fissure mineral
~/**alpines** alpine mineral
Kluftmuster n joint pattern
Kluftnetz n s. Kluftsystem
Kluftquelle f fracture (fissure) spring
kluftreich chasmy
Kluftrichtung f direction of fissures
Kluftrose f joint diagram
Kluftrosendarstellung f rose diagram
Kluftschar f joint set (family)
Kluftschwarm m zone of jointing, zone with clusters of joints
Kluftspalte f joint crack
Kluftstatistik f s. Kluftrose
Kluftstellung f joint orientation
Kluftsystem n joint system (network), fracture system (network, pattern)
Klufttektonik f joint tectonics
Klufttrum n joint vein
Klüftung f jointing, cleaving, cleavage
~/**griffelige** linear cleavage
~/**konzentrische** ball jointing
~/**kugelschalige** cup-and-ball jointing (effusive rocks)
~/**latente** potential fissuration
~/**oberflächenparallele** lift jointing (in plutonic rocks)
Klüftungszone f zone of jointing
Kluftvolumen n volume of joint
Kluftwasser n joint (fissure, crevice, crack) water
Kluftwasserdruck m joint-water pressure
Kluftwinkel m angle of jointing
Kluftzone f zone of joint
Klumpen m lump, clot; nugget (of native metal)
Klumpenton m ball clay
klumpig lumpy, nodular, cloddy

Klunst f clough
Knäpperschießen n boulder popping, bulldozing
Knappschuß m pop shot
Knauer m hard (slate) rock
Knebelit m knebelite, $(Mn,Fe)_2[SiO_4]$
knetbar plastic
Knetgestein n s. Mylonit
Knetstruktur f mashed texture (of sediments)
Knickbänder npl kink bands
Knickbeanspruchung f buckling load
Knickerscheinung f buckling
Knickfalten fpl drag folds
Knickfaltung f drag folding; buckled folding
Knickfestigkeit f buckling strength
Knicklast f buckling load
Knickpunkt m 1. deflection point (influenced from outside); 2. nickpoint (inclining stage); 3. yield load (of props)
Knickpunktentfernung f crossover (intersection) distance
Knickspannung f buckling stress
Knickung f 1. buckling; 2. kink
Knickversuch m buckling test
Knickwinkel m deflection angle
Knickzonen fpl kink bands
Knie n elbow
Kniefalte f knee fold, flexure
knirschen s. knistern
Knirschen n s. Knistern
Knistergeräusch n rock noise
knistern to crackle, to gnash; to creak (coal)
Knistern n crackling, gnashing
knitterfest crushproof
Knittermarken fpl crinkle marks, creep wrinkles
knittern s. knistern
Knoblaucherz n s. Skorodit
Knoblauchgeruch/mit alliaceous (mineral)
Knochen m bone
~/**kleiner** ossicle
~/**zahntragender** tooth-bearing bone, dentary
Knochen mpl/**pneumatische** pneumatic (air) bones (birds)
Knochenauswuchs m bony prominence
Knochenbau m bone structure
Knochenbrekzie f osseous breccia, bone (fish) bed
Knochenfische mpl bony (osseous) fishes
~/**quastenflossige** lobe-finned bony fishes
~/**strahlenflossige** ray-finned bony fishes
knochenführend ossiferous
Knochenpanzer m bony armature
Knochenplatte f sclerotic (bony) plate
Knochenplattenring m sclerotic plate ring
Knochenskelett n bony skeleton
Knochenstachel m bony spine
Knochenverwachsung f coossification
Knochenwulst m bony ridge
Knochenzapfen m bony core
knochig ossiferous
Knolle f nodule, noddle, nug

Knollenkalk

Knollenkalk *m* nodular limestone
Knollenstein *m s.* Tertiärquarzit
Knollenstruktur *f* nodular structure
Knopit *m* knopite *(variety of perovskite)*
Knorpelfisch *m* cartilaginous (gristly) fish
Knorpelskelett *n* cartilaginous skeleton, chondroskeleton
Knorringit *m* knorringite, $Mg_3Cr_2[SiO_4]_3$
Knospung *f* gemmation *(palaeontology)*
Knoten *m* node
knotenartig nodular, knotty
Knotenebene *f* nodal plane
knotenförmig nodular, knotty
Knotenpunkt *m* nodal point
Knotenschiefer *m* knotenschiefer, maculose rock
Knotenstruktur *f* knotty texture
knotig nodular, knotty; nodose
Knotte *f* nodule
Knottendolomit *m* knotty dolomite
Knotteneisenerz *n* nodular iron ore
Knottensandstein *m* knotten sandstone
Knottenschiefer *m* knotted schist
Koagulation *f* coagulation
Koagulationsmittel *n*, **Koagulator** *m* coagulant
koagulieren to coagulate
Kobalt *n* 1. cobalt, Co; 2. Cobalt *(middle Huronian in North America)*
Kobaltarsenkies *m* danaite *(variety of arsenopyrite)*
Kobaltblüte *f* cobalt bloom (ochre), red cobalt, erythrite, $Co_3[AsO_4]_2 \cdot 8H_2O$
Kobalterz *n* cobalt ore
Kobaltglanz *m* cobalt glance, cobaltine, cobaltite, CoAsS
kobalthaltig cobaltiferous
Kobaltin *m s.* Kobaltglanz
Kobaltkies *m* linnaeite, cobalt pyrites, Co_3S_4
Kobaltmanganerz *n* black earthy cobalt ore, asbolan[e]
Kobaltokalzit *m s.* Kobaltspat
Kobaltomenit *m* cobaltomenite, $Co[SeO_3] \cdot 2H_2O$
Kobaltspat *m* spherocobaltite, cobaltocalcite, $CoCO_3$
Kobellit *m* kobellite, $6PbS \cdot 2Bi_2S_3 \cdot Sb_2S_3$
Koblenz *n* Coblantzian, Coblentzian *(former synonym for Emsian, uppermost Lower Devonian)*
Kochpunkt *m* bubble point
Kochsalz *n* sodium chloride, native salt, NaCl
Koechlinit *m* koechlinite, Bi_2MoO_6
Koeffizient *m* **der Diskriminanzfunktion** discriminance coefficient, coefficient of discriminance function
Koenenit *m* koenenite *(Al-Mg-oxichloride)*
Koerzitivkraft *f* coercive force, coercivity
Koevolution *f* coevolution
Kofferfalte *f* koffer (box) fold
Kog *m s.* Koog
Kohalait *m* kohalaite *(olivine-bearing trachyandesite)*

Kohärenz *f* coherence
Kohäsion *f* cohesion, cohesiveness, cohesive attraction
Kohäsionsboden *m*/**gebrächer** ravelling ground
Kohäsionsfaktor *m* cohesional coefficient
kohäsionslos cohesionless
kohäsiv cohesive
Kohle *f* coal
~/**allochthone** allochthonous (drift, float) coal
~/**anstehende** unworked coal
~/**anthrazitähnliche** anthracitic (flint, flew) coal
~/**aschereiche** ash (dirty, crow) coal, *(Am)* high-ash coal
~/**aufbereitete** cleaned coal
~/**ausgeglühte** cinder coal
~/**autochthone** autochthonous (indigenous) coal
~/**backende** caking coal
~/**bergehaltige** bone coal *(carbonaceous shale)*
~/**bituminöse** bituminous coal
~/**frische** green coal
~/**gasarme** non-gaseous coal
~/**gasreiche** hydrogenous coal
~/**geringinkohlte** low-rank coal
~/**geringwertige** low-grade coal
~/**glimmende** ember
~/**granulierte** granulated coal
~/**graphitisierte** graphitized coal
~/**hochinkohlte** high-rank coal
~/**hochwertige** high-grade coal
~/**holzartig aussehende** board coal *(s.a. Holzkohle)*
~ **in Ausstrichnähe** day coal
~ **in Ausstrichnähe/oxydierte** crop coal
~ **in thermischen Kontakthöfen** humped coal
~/**kurzflammige** furnace (short-flaming) coal
~/**langflammige** long-flaming coal
~/**liegende** ground coal
~/**limnische** limnetic coal
~/**lithologisch homogene** clod coal
~/**magere** *s.* Magerkohle
~/**minderwertige** inferior (humped) coal
~/**minderwertige pyritische** grizzle
~ **mit hohem Gehalt an flüchtigen Bestandteilen** high-volatile coal
~ **mit niedrigem Aschegehalt** *(Am)* low-ash coal
~ **mit niedrigem Schwefelgehalt** *(Am)* low-sulfur coal
~ **mittleren Ranges** medium-rank coal
~/**nicht schlackenbildende** non-clinkering coal
~/**nicht verkokbare** non-coking coal
~/**paralische** paralic coal
~/**sapropelitische** sapropelitic coal
~/**schiefrig-tonige** shaly coal
~/**schlackenbildende** clinkering coal
~/**schwefelreiche** *(Am)* high-sulfur coal
~/**sinternde** sintering coal

~/steil stehende edge coal, rearer
~/thermometamorph veränderte thermally metamorphosed coal
~/trockene mushy coal
~/ungesiebte grubenfeuchte run-of-mine coal
~/unreine bone coal, (Am) boney coal
~/unverritzte sound (unmined) coal
~/verwachsene combined pieces of coal and shale
~/weiche apple (mushy) coal
~/zu Tage anstehende outbreak coal
kohlefrei non-carbonaceous
kohleführend coal-bearing, carboniferous
kohlehöffig s. kohleführend
Kohlehydrierung f coal hydrogenation
Kohlenabbau m coal breaking
Kohlenanalyse f coal analysis
Kohlenart f 1. type of coal (lithotype of coal); 2. rank of coal (degree of coalification)
kohlenartig carbonaceous, coaly
Kohlenasche f/schlackige clinker
Kohlenaufbereitbarkeit f coal washability
Kohlenaufbereitung f coal preparation (dressing), cleaning of coal
Kohlenausstrich m/verwitterter [coal] blossom, smut
Kohlenbank f/obere bench coal (of a seam)
~/untere floor coal (of a seam)
Kohlenbecken n coal basin
~/intramontanes (limnisches) limnetic coal basin
~/paralisches paralic coal basin
Kohlenbergbaugebiet n coal-mining region
Kohlenbildung f coal formation
Kohlenbildungszeit f time of coal formation
Kohlendioxid n carbon dioxide, CO_2
Kohleneisenstein m carbonaceous ironstone, carbonaceous iron ore, black band
Kohlenfazies f coal facies
Kohlenfeld n coal field
~/unverritztes whole coal
Kohlenflöz n coal seam
~/absetziges wandering coal
~/geringmächtiges coal shed
~ mit mächtigen Zwischenmitteln split coal
~ mit Schieferzwischenlage ribbed coal seam
~/pyritreiches pyritiferous coal bed
~/söhliges flat coals
~/stark pyrithaltiges brassy seam
~/unverritztes ungot coal seam
Kohlenflözausstrich m/verwitterter [coal] blossom, smut
Kohlenflözbeschaffenheit f quality of coal seam
Kohlenförderung f coal output
Kohlengas n coal gas
Kohlengebiet n s. Kohlenrevier
Kohlengebirge n coal-bearing rock (formation), carbonaceous rock, coal measures
Kohlengeröll n coal pebble
Kohlengestein n carbonaceous rock, carbonolite

Kohlengewinnung f coal getting
Kohlengewinnungsschicht f coal shift
Kohlengröße f size of coal
Kohlengrube f colliery
Kohlengrus m slack coal
Kohlengürtel m/europäischer European coal-belt
kohlenhaltig coal-bearing, carboniferous, coaly
Kohlenhäutchen npl coal prints
Kohleninsel f coal pillar
Kohlenkalk m carboniferous (carbonaceous) limestone
Kohlenkalkstein m 1. s. Anthrakonit; 2. mountain limestone (in the Lower Carboniferous of England)
Kohlenklein n gum, breeze, rubbles, coombe coal
Kohlenlagerstätte f coal deposit
Kohlenletten m black bed
Kohlenlithotyp m coal lithotype
Kohlenmaceral m coal maceral
Kohlenmikrolithotyp m coal microlithotype
Kohlenmonoxid n carbon monoxide, CO
Kohlenpetrografie f coal petrography
kohlenpetrologisch coal-petrological
Kohlenpfeiler m coal pillar
Kohlenpreßstein m coal-dust brick
Kohlenrestpfeiler m coal pillar
Kohlenrevier n coal region, coal [mining] district, coal basin
Kohlensack m swell
Kohlensandstein m carboniferous (coal-bearing) sandstone, coal grit; rock bind
~/weißer, schiefriger white paste
Kohlensäuerling m acidulous spring
Kohlensäure f carbonic acid
Kohlensäureausbruch m outburst of carbon dioxide
Kohlensäurefumarole f carbonic acid fumarole
Kohlensäuregeiser m carbonate geyser
kohlensäurehaltig carbonic
Kohlensäurequelle f carbonate spring, mofette
Kohlensäuresaturation f carbonation
Kohlensäurespringquelle f carbonate geyser
Kohlenschacht m pit
Kohlenschicht f coal bed (layer), stratum of coal
~/dünne girdle
~/oberste top coal (of a seam)
Kohlenschiefer m black stone
Kohlenschlamm m coal mud (sludge)
Kohlenschlechte f cleat
~/gut ausgebildete face cleat
Kohlensorte f size of coal (sieve)
Kohlenstaub m carbon dust, dust coal
Kohlenstoff m carbon, C
~/gebundener fixed carbon
~/graphitischer graphitic carbon
~/organischer organic carbon

kohlenstoffarm

kohlenstoffarm carbon-lean
kohlenstofffrei carbon-free
Kohlenstoffgehalt m carbon content
kohlenstoffhaltig carbonic, carbonaceous, carboniferous
Kohlenstoffisotop n carbon isotope
kohlenstoffreich carbon-rich
Kohlenstoffverbindung f carbon compound
Kohlenstoffverhältnis n carbon ratio
Kohlentagebau m open-cast coal mine; open-pit coal mining
Kohlenteer m coal tar
Kohlenvorkommen n coal deposit
Kohlenvorräte mpl coal reserves
Kohlenwasserstoff m hydrocarbon
~/aromatischer aromatic hydrocarbon
~/flüssiger fluid (liquid) hydrocarbon
~/hochmolekularer high-molecular-weight hydrocarbon
~/leichter light hydrocarbon
~/mineralisierter mineral resin
~/natürlicher native hydrocarbon
~/schwerer heavy hydrocarbon
Kohlenwasserstoffe mpl/aus Erdgas kondensierte drip gasoline
~ mit dicht benachbarten Siedepunkten close-boiling hydrocarbons
Kohlenwasserstoffentstehung f hydrocarbogenesis
kohlenwasserstoffhaltig hydrocarbonaceous
Kohlenwasserstofflagerstätte f hydrocarbon deposit
Kohlenwasserstoffverbindung f hydrocarbon compound
Kohlenzeche f colliery
Kohlenzwischenlage f shed coal
Kohleschmitz m, Kohlestreifen m coal streak (band)
Kohlevergasung f coal gasification
kohlig carbonous, carbonaceous, carboniferous; coaly
Kokardenbildung f cockade formation
Kokardenerz n cockade (ring, crust) ore
Kokardenstruktur f cockade texture
Kokerei f coking plant
Kokkolith m coccolite (variety of diopside)
Koks m coke, coak
Koksbildung f coke formation
Koksbildungsvermögen n coking capacity
Koksfestigkeit f strength of coke
Kokskohle f coking coal
Kokskohlenstadium n coking-coal stage
Kokszellwand f cell wall of coke
Koktait m koktaite, $(NH_4)_2Ca[SO_4]_2 \cdot H_2O$
Kolbeckit m kolbeckite, $Sc[PO_4] \cdot 2H_2O$
Kolben n swabbing
Kolbenblasenströmung f plug flow
Kolbenlot n piston corer
Kolk m flute; erosional cavity, deep (in a river)
Kolkausguß m s. Kolkmarke
Kolkbildung f cratering

Kolkmarke f flute cast, scour mark
~/diagonale diagonal scour mark
~/transversale transverse scour mark
Kolkriefen fpl scour lineation
Kolkschutz m erosion control, protection against scour
Kollision f collision (plate tectonics)
Kolloid n colloid
kolloidal colloidal
Kolloidalstruktur f colloform texture
Kolloidalzustand m colloidal state
kolloidarm poor in colloids
Kolloidmineral n colloid mineral
Kolloidsubstanz f colloidal material
Kollophan m collophan (CO_3-containing apatite)
kolluvial colluvial
Kolluvialboden m colluvial (transported) soil
Kolluvium n colluvium
Kolmatage f s. Kolmation
Kolmatierung f filling-up, silting-up, aggradation, accretion through alluvium
Kolmation f colmatage, colmation, filling-up, silting-up, accretion through alluvium, aggradation
Kolonne f column
~/verlorene liner
Kolophonium n colophony
Kolorimetrie f colorimetry
kolorimetrisch colorimetric
Kolovratit m kolovratite (vanadate of nickel)
Kolskit m kolskite, $Mg_5[(OH)_8|Si_4O_{10}]$
Kolumbit m columbite, $(Fe,Mn)(Nb,Ta)_2O_6$
Koma f coma
komagmatisch comagmatic
Komarit m s. Connarit
Komatiit m komatiite
Kombination f von Darstellungsarten superimposed mode
Kombinationsfalle f combination trap (hydrocarbons)
Komet m comet
kometenartig cometary
Kometenbahn f cometary orbit
Kometenkern m cometary nucleus
Kometenkopf m head of a comet
Kometenschweif m comet trace
Kometografie f cometography
Kommunalgeologie f urban geology
Kommunalität f communality
kommunizierend intercommunicating
Kompaktheit f compactness
Kompaktion f compaction
Kompaktionsfaktor m packing factor
Kompaktionswasser n water of compaction
Kompaß m compass
~/bergmännischer miner's compass
~/gedämpfter aperiodic[al] compass
Kompaßabweichung f compass declination
Kompaßnadel f [magnetic] compass needle
Kompaßpeilung f compass bearing
Kompaßrichtung f compass direction

konsolidieren

Kompaßrose f compass card
Kompaßzug m compass traverse
Kompensation f/**isostatische** isostatic compensation
Kompensationsfläche f level of compensation *(isostasy)*
Kompensationsmassen fpl compensation masses
Kompensator m compensator
kompetent competent
Kompetentüberschiebung f strut thrust
Komplement n complement *(to unity)*
Komplementarität f complementarity
Komplettierung f **einer Bohrung** well completion
~ **mit offenem Speicher** open-hole completion
Komplex m/**lithologischer** lithologic complex *(lithostratigraphical unit)*
~/**tektonischer** tectonic complex
Komplexaugen npl compound eyes *(arthropods)*
Komplexauswertung f s. Komplexinterpretation
Komplexebene f complex plane
Komplexerkundung f integrated survey
Komplexerz n complex ore
Komplexinterpretation f complex (integrated) interpretation
Komplexkurve f complex curve
Komplexlinie f complex line
Komplexpunkt m complex point
Komplexraum m complex space
Komplexstabilität f complex stability
Komplikation f **im Bohrloch** borehole troubles
Kompressibilität f compressibility
Kompression f compression
Kompressionsmodul m bulk modulus
Kompressionswelle f compression (P) wave
komprimierbar compressible
Komprimierbarkeit f compressibility
komprimieren to compress
Konarit m s. Connarit
Konchylien fpl conchylia
Konchylienbestand m content of conchylia
Kondensatfeld n distillate field
Kondensatförderung f condensate production
Kondensation f condensation
~/**retrograde** retrograde condensation
~/**stratigrafische** stratigraphic condensation
Kondensationskeim m, **Kondensationskern** m condensation centre, nucleus of condensation
Kondensationslager n condensed sequence
Kondensationswasser n condensation water
Kondensatlagerstätte f condensate field
kondensieren/sich to condense
Kondensstreifen m condensation trail
Kondenswasser n condensation water
Konditionen fpl conditions *(of ground-water protection)*
Konfluenzstufe f confluence step
Konformität f **in Mächtigkeit und Lagerung** planoconformity *(of beds)*

Kongeliturbation f congeliturbation
Konglomerat n conglomerate
~ **eines Regressionszyklus** conglomerate of emergency
~/**eingelagertes** intraformational conglomerate
~/**goldführendes** auriferous conglomerate
~/**intraformationales** intraformational conglomerate
~/**kantengestelltes** edgewise structure
~ **mit Schuppentextur** edgewise conglomerate
~/**unsortiertes** immature conglomerate
Konglomerateinlagerung f/**interformationelle (schichtfremde)** interformational conglomerate
Konglomeratfazies f conglomeratic facies
Konglomeratgestein n conglomerate rock
konglomeratisch conglomeratic
Kongruenz f congruency
Kongruenzschmelzpunkt m congruent melting point
Kongsbergit m kongsbergite, mercury argental, α-(Ag,Hg)
Konichalcit m konichalcite, higginsite, CaCu[OH|AsO₄]
Koniferen fpl conifers
Königsberger-Koeffizient m Koenigsberger ratio *(geomagnetics)*
Königswasser n aqua regia
Koninckit m koninckite, FePO₄ · 3H₂O
konisch conic[al]; conoid; coniform
~/**invers** obconic[al]
Konjugationslinie f joint
Konjunktivbruch m compression (thrust) fault
konkav-konvex concavo-convex
konkordant concordant, accordant; conformable
Konkordanz f concordance; conformation, conform[abil]ity
Konkretion f concretion, concrement, lump
~/**fossilführende** bullion
~/**gerundete** nablock
~/**hohle zylindrische** incretion
~/**kleine** extoolite
~/**längliche** lunker
~/**linsenförmige** septata concretion
~/**wurzelförmige** rhyzoconcretion
konkretionär concretionary
Konkretionskruste f mortar bed, hardpan
Könl[ein]it m koenleinite *(carbocyclic hydrocarbon compound)*
Konode f conode, tie line
konoidisch conoidal
Konoskop n conoscope
konoskopisch conoscopic
konsequent consequent
Konservierung f **einer Bohrung** temporary abondon of a well
Konsistenzgrenzen fpl/**Atterbergsche** Atterberg (consistency) limits
Konsistenzprüfer m consistency gauge
konsolidieren/sich to consolidate

Konsolidierung

Konsolidierung f consolidation
Konstante f/**optische** optical constant
Konstellation f constellation
Konstitutionswasser n constitution water
Konstriktionstheorie f constriction theory
Kontakt m/**intermittierender** intermittency contact
~/**mechanischer** abnormal contact
~/**stylolithischer** stylolitic contact
~/**tektonischer** tectonic contact
Kontaktaureole f thermal aureole
Kontaktbildung f contact formation
Kontaktfläche f junction surface
Kontaktgang m contact lode (vein)
Kontaktgestein n contact [altered] rock, contact-metamorphosed rock
Kontakthof m contact [metamorphic] area, exomorphic (anamorphic) area, [metamorphic] aureole, alteration (exomorphic) halo, contact belt
Kontaktlagerstätte f contact deposit
Kontaktlog n contact log
~/**elektrisches** electric tape gauge *(for ground-water level measuring)*
kontaktmetamorph contact-metamorphic
Kontaktmetamorphose f contact (thermal) metamorphism, thermometamorphism, exometamorphism
~ **um magnetische Intrusionskörper** injection metamorphism
kontaktmetasomatisch contact-metasomatic
Kontaktmineral n contact mineral
Kontaktpneumatolyse f contact pneumatolysis
Kontaktrand m contact border
Kontaktring m contact fringe
Kontaktskarn m/**allochthoner** tactite
Kontaktspannung f contact stress
Kontaktwinkel m contact angle
Kontaktwirkung f contact action
~/**endogene** endogenous metamorphism
Kontaktzone f contact zone (area)
Kontaktzwillinge mpl juxtaposition twins
Kontaminant m pollutant *(ground-water pollution)*
Kontamination f pollution, contamination *(of ground water)*
Kontaminationsschutz m pollution control
~ **vor Salzwasser** salinity control
Kontinent m continent, mainland
kontinental continental
Kontinentalabfall m continental slope
Kontinentalanstieg m continental rise
Kontinentalbewegung f continent-making movement
Kontinentalbildung f continent making, epeirogeny
Kontinentalblock m continental plateau (platform, mass)
Kontinentalböschung f continental slope
Kontinentaldrift f s. Kontinentalverschiebung
Kontinentaldüne f inland dune
Kontinentaleffekt m continental effect

180

Kontinentalfazies f continental (terrestrial) facies
Kontinentalfuß m continental base
Kontinentalgletscher m continental glacier
Kontinentalhang m continental slope
Kontinentalkern m continental nucleus, nuclear area
Kontinentalklima n continental (mid-continent) climate
Kontinentalluft f continental air
Kontinentalplattform f s. Kontinentalsockel
Kontinentalrand m shelf edge
Kontinentalsaum m continental margin
Kontinentalschelf m continental shelf
~/**stabiler** stable continental shelf
Kontinentalschelfbildung f continental shelf formation
Kontinentalsockel m, **Kontinentaltafel** f continental terrace
Kontinentalverschiebung f continental drift, land shifting, creep of continents
Kontinentalverschiebungstheorie f continental drift theory, theory of floating continents
Kontinuitätsfläche f surface of conformity
Kontinuitätsgleichung f continuity equation
~ **für stationäre Strömung** continuity equation of steady flow
Kontinuummechanik f continuum mechanics
Kontraktion f contraction
Kontraktionsspalte f joint (fissure) of retreat
Kontraktionstheorie f contraction (shrinkage) theory
Kontrastverstärkung f contrast enhancement (stretching)
Kontrollanalyse f check analysis
Kontrollbohrloch n check borehole
Kontrollbohrung f control boring
Kontrolle f/**äußere** external control
~/**innere** internal control
~ **von Hochdrucksonden** high-pressure well control
Kontrollimpuls m head check pulse *(data processing)*
Kontrollmessung f control measurement, check run
Kontrollmosaik n controlled mosaic
Kontrollprobenahme f check sampling
Kontrollpunkt m control point
Kontrollschuß m check shot
Kontrollstation f control (master) station
Kontur f contour
~/**bewegliche** moving boundary *(reservoir mechanics)*
Konturierungsbohrung f field development well
Konturite mpl contourites
Konturkarte f structure contour map
Konturstrom m contour current
Konus m cone
Konvektion f convection; convective process *(ground-water flow)*
Konvektionsgleichung f convection equation

Konvektionsströmung f convective flow (current, creep)
Konvektionsströmungen fpl **in der subkrustalen Zone** subcrustal convection currents
Konvektionssystem n/**hydrothermales** hydrothermal convection system
Konvektionszelle f convective cell
konvergent convergent
Konvergenz f convergence
~/adaptive adaptive convergence, convergent evolution
~ im Streichen von Gebirgszügen syntaxis
Konvergenzerscheinung f phenomenon of convergence
Konvergenzgeber m s. Konvergenzmesser
Konvergenzlinie f convergence contour, line of equal interval, isochore *(line of equal perpendicular distance between two geological horizons)*
Konvergenzlinse f convergent lens
Konvergenzmesser m convergence indicator, closure meter
Konvergenzschreiber m convergence recorder
Konvexfläche f convexity
Konvexität f convexity
konvex-konkav convexo-concave
Konvolution f convolution *(of a seismic wave)*
Konzentrat n concentrate
Konzentration f concentration; enrichment
~ der Diamanten in der Krone diamond content in core bit
~/molare molar concentration
Konzentrationsangabe f statement of concentration
Konzentrationsfront f concentration front
Konzentrationsgrad m factor of concentration
Konzentrationsvorgang m concentration process
Konzession f grant
~ zur Aufsuchung von Erdöllagerstätten oil grant
~ zur Erforschung und Ausbeutung concession for exploration and exploitation
Konzessionsinhaber m concessionaire
Koog m koog, polder, diked land (marsh), reclaimed marsh land
Koordinatenpapier n coordinate (quadrille) paper
Koordinationsgruppe f coordination group
Koordinationspolyeder npl coordination polyhedra
Koordinationszahl f coordination number
Kopal m/**fossiler** fossil copal
Kopfdruck m casing-head pressure, well head pressure
Kopffüßer m s. Cephalopode
Kopfgebirge n vertical beds
Kopfholz n lid, wooden crusher block
Kopfraum m head clearance
Kopfschild m s. Cephalon
Kopfstrecke f top road, tail gate

Kopfwelle f head (refraction) wave *(seismics)*
Koppit m koppite, $(Ca,Ce)_2(Nb,Fe)_2O_6(O,OH,F)$
koprogen coprogenous
Koprolith m coprolite, petrified excrement
Koprolithenpellet n faecal pellet, casting
koprolithisch coprolitic
Koralle f coral
~/fossile corallite
~/koloniebildende colonia coral
~/riffbildende reef-building coral
~/solitäre four-part coral
Korallenachat m coral agate
Korallenbank f coral shoal
Korallenbauten mpl coral frameworks
korallenförmig coralloid[al]
Korallen-Hydrozoen-Rasen mpl coral hydrozoan biostromes
Koralleninsel f coral island
Korallenkalk m coral lime
Korallen-Kalkalgen-Fazies f coralgal facies
Korallenkalkstein m coral limestone
Korallenkolonie f coral colony
Korallenriff n coral reef
Korallenriffkalk m coral limestone
Korallenriffküste f coral-reef coast
Korallenrifflagune f coral-reef lagoon
Korallensand m coral sand
Korallenschlick m coral mud
Kordierit m cordierite, $Mg_2Al_3[AlSi_5O_{18}]$
Kordieritgneis m cordierite gneiss
Kordillere f cordillera
Kordillerenfaltung f Cordilleran orogeny (revolution)
Kordillerengeosynklinale f Cordilleran geosyncline
Kordilleren-Subprovinz f Cordilleran Subprovince *(palaeobiogeography of Devonian)*
Kordylit m cordylite, kordylite, $Ba(Ce, La, Nd)_2[F_2 | (CO_3)_3]$
Korkasbest m cork fossil *(s.a. Aktinolit)*
Korkenzieherfalte f corkscrew (torsion, contorted) fold
Korkenzieherzapfen m corkscrew flute cast
Korkstein m rock cork *(s.a. Chrysotil)*
Korn n grain; granule
~/mattiertes frosted grain
~/ovoides ovoid grain
~/rundgescheuertes nugget
~/verwachsenes included grain
Kornabbau m grain diminution, degenerative recrystallization
Kornabstufung f granulometric gradation (grading)
~/diskontinuierliche discontinuous granulometry (gradation, grading)
Kornaggregatien f **aus Oolithen** lump
Kornaufbau m granulometric composition
Kornbegrenzung f s. Korngrenze
Kornbindung f grain bond
Körnchen n granule, small grain
Korndichte f grain density
Korndurchmesser m diameter of grain, particle diameter

Körnelgneis

Körnelgneis *m* pearl gneiss
Kornelit *m* kornelite, $Fe_2[SO_4]_3 \cdot 7\frac{1}{2}H_2O$
Körner *npl* **mit Anlagerungsgefüge** aggregation grains
~ **mit konzentrischem Anlagerungsgefüge** coated grains
~/**oolitoide** oolitoid grains
Körnerpräparat *n* grains
Kornerupin *m* kornerupine, $Mg_4Al_6[(O, OH)_2 | BO_4 | (SiO_4)_4]$
Kornform *f* grain (particle) shape
Kornfraktion *f* grain-size category
Korngefüge *n* grain structure, microfabric
~ **des Gletschereises** glacier grain
Korngefügeanalyse *f* analysis of grain structure, microfabric analysis
Korngefügediagramm *n* petrofabric diagram
Korngefügeregelung *f* grain orientation
Korngerüst *n* granular skeleton
Korngrenze *f* grain boundary
Korngrenzendiffusion *f* grain boundary diffusion
Korngrenzenenergie *f* energy of grain boundary
Korngrenzenriß *m* grain boundary crack
Korngröße *f* grain (granular, particle) size, granularity
~/**feinste** fines
~ **von 1–10 cm/in** centimeter-sized
~ **von 100–1000 μm/in** centimicron-sized
~/**wirksame** effective grain size
Korngrößenanalyse *f* granulometric (grain-size) analysis
Korngrößenanteil *m* grain-size content
Korngrößenaufbau *m* granulometry
Korngrößenbereich *m* grain-size range
Korngrößenbestimmung *f s.* Korngrößenanalyse
Korngrößeneinteilung *f* grain[-size] classification
Korngrößenindex *m* grain-size range index
Korngrößenkennzahl *f* average grain diameter
Korngrößenklasse *f* grain-size grade
Korngrößenmeßgerät *n* granulometric gauge
Korngrößenmessung *f* granulometry
Korngrößentrennung *f* screening
Korngrößenverteilung *f* grain (particle) size distribution, grading
Korngrößenverteilungskurve *f* granulometric curve
Korngrößenzusammensetzung *f* granulometric composition
körnig grained, grainy, granular, granulose, granulous, grenu
~/**gleichmäßig** even-grained, equigranular
~/**ungleichmäßig** uneven-grained, inequigranular
Körnigkeit *f* granularity, grain size
~ **der Diamanten in der Krone** diamond size
Kornklasse *f* grain-size range (category)
Kornklasseneinteilung *f* grain grade scale
Kornklassenfraktion *f* grain-size distribution (category) fraction

Kornrauhigkeit *f* roughness of grain surface
Kornregelung *f* grain orientation
Kornspanne *f* grain-size range
Kornumwälzung *f* revolution of the grain
Körnung *f s.* Korngröße
Körnungsart *f* kind of graining (granulation)
Körnungsaufbau *m* grain-size distribution
Körnungsbereich *m* grain-size range
Körnungskennlinie *f* grain-size distribution curve, granulation curve
Körnungsschwankung *f* granular variation
Kornvergröberung *f* increase in grain size
Kornverteilung *f* grain-size distribution, grading
Kornverteilungskurve *f* granulometric curve
Kornverzahnung *f* interlocking grain
~/**suturierte** sutured contacts
Kornwachstum *n* grain growth
Kornzementierung *f* **durch Porenlösungen** granular cementation
Kornzerbruch *m* breakage of grains
Kornzertrümmerung *f* demolition of grains
Kornzusammensetzung *f* granulometric composition
Kornzusammensetzungsfaktor *m* grading factor
Korona *f* corona
~/**Frauenhofersche** Frauenhofer corona
Körper *m*/**Binghamscher** Bingham body
~/**homogener isotoper** homogeneous isotopic body
~/**leitender** conductive body
~/**Prandtlscher** Prandtl body
~/**rheologischer** rheological body
~/**rotationssymmetrischer** body representing rotation symmetry
Körperspicula *npl* body spicules
körperzentriert body-centred
korradieren to corrade
Korrasion *f* corrasion, wind carving
Korrasionskraft *f* corrasive power
Korrasionstätigkeit *f* corrasional work
Korrektur *f* **auf das Bezugsniveau** elevation correction
~/**dynamische** dynamic correction
~ **eines abweichenden Bohrlochs** correction of the hole deviation
~ **geometrischer Verzerrungen** geometrical correction
~/**radiometrische** radiometric correction
~/**statische** static correction
Korrelation *f* correlation
~/**feinstratigrafische** refined stratigraphical correlation
~/**geologische** geologic[al] correlation
~/**lithostratigrafische** lithostratigraphic correlation
~ **von Bohrprofilen** correlation of well logs
Korrelationsaufstellung *f* expanding spread (seismics)
Korrelationsdiagramm *n* correlation diagram
Korrelationslänge *f* correlation distance (length,

radius), range of influence of a sample (value), range of variogram *(minimum distance between uncorrelated random or regionalized variables)*
Korrelationsradius *m* range of semivariogram
Korrelationsschießen *n* correlation shooting *(seismics)*
korrelieren/Schichten to correlate, to put beds in relation with each other
Korrodierbarkeit *f* corrodibility
korrodieren to corrode, to eat away
Korrodieren *n* corroding
korrodierend corrosive
Korrosion *f* corrosion
~ **bei geringem Schwefelanteil des Erdöls** sweet corrosion
~/**chemische** chemical corrosion
~ **durch Schwefelgehalt des Erdöls** sour corrosion
~/**interkristalline** intergranular corrosion
Korrosionsbasis *f* base level of karst erosion
Korrosionsfläche *f* corrosion surface
Korrosionsgeschwindigkeit *f* rate of corrosion
Korrosionsnarbe *f* corrosion pit
Korrosionsschutzmittel *n* corrosion combatant
Korrosionswirkung *f* corrosiveness
Korschinskit *m* korschinskite, $Ca_2[B_4O_6(OH)_4]$
Korund *m* corundum, Al_2O_3
~/**blauer** *s.* Saphir
~/**gemeiner** common corundum
~/**körniger** emery
~/**roter** *s.* Rubin
~/**weißer** *s.* Leukosaphir
korundhaltig corundum-bearing
Korundophilit *m* corundophilite, $(Mg, Fe, Al)_6[(OH)_8 | AlSi_3O_{10}]$
Korundvarietät *f*/**gelbe** oriental topaz
~/**grüne** oriental emerald
koseismisch coseismal
kosmisch cosmic[al], interstellar
Kosmochemie *f* cosmochemistry
kosmochemisch cosmochemic[al]
kosmogen cosmogenic
Kosmogeologie *f* cosmic[al] geology
Kosmogonie *f* cosmogeny, cosmogony
kosmogonisch cosmogonic[al]
Kosmografie *f* cosmography
Kosmonautik *f* cosmonautics, astronautics; interstellar aviation
Kosmophysik *f* cosmophysics
kostbar precious
Kösterit *m* koesterite, Cu_2ZnSnS_4
Kotballen *m*/**fossiler** *s.* Koprolith
kotektisch cotectic
Kotoit *m* kotoite, $Mg_3[BO_3]_2$
Kotschubeit *m* kotschubeite, $(Mg, Al)_{<3}[(OH)_2 | (Cr, Al)Si_3O_{10}] \cdot Mg_3(OH)_6$
Köttigit *m* koettigite, köttigite, $Zn_3[AsO_4]_2 \cdot 8H_2O$
Kotulskit *m* kotulskite, $Pd(Te, Bi)_{1-2}$
Kotypus *m* syntype
Koutekit *m* koutekite, Cu_2As

kovalent covalent
kovalentgebunden covalent-bonded
Kovariogramm *n* covariogram, co-variogram *(geostatistical analog of the covariance function of a homogeneous isotropic random field)*
Kovellin *m* covellite, indigo copper, CuS
Kraft *f* **der Faltung/zusammendrückende** compressive force of folding
~/**wasserbindende** water-holding (water-containing) capacity, retentive power *(of a soil)*
Kraftdrehkopf *m* power swivel
Kräfte *fpl*/**abtragende** denuding agents
~/**außenbürtige** exogenous (exogenetic) agents
~/**externe** external agents (forces)
~/**tellurische** endogenous agents (forces)
Kräftefeld *n* field of force[s]
kräftig sturdy
Kraftlinie *f* line of force
Kraftlinienbündel *n* bundle of lines of force
Kraftlinienfeld *n* field of force
Krakatautätigkeit *f* Plinian activity
Kramenzelkalk *m* kramenzelkalk
Kranbarke *f* crane barge
Krantzit *m* krantzite *(a resin)*
Kranz *m* circlet
Krater *m* crater
~/**aufgesetzter** monticule
~/**endogener** endogenic crater *(predominantly by collapse)*
~/**kesselförmiger** cauldron crater
~/**kleiner** craterlet
~/**meteoritischer** meteoritic crater
~ **mit zentralen Bocchen** nested crater
~/**tätiger** active crater
~/**übergreifender** host crater *(overlapping, overlapped)*
Kraterabtragungsfolge *f* crater denudation chronology
Krateranalyse *f* crater analysis
Krateranordnung *f* crater alignment
Kraterbecken *n* crater basin
Kraterbildung *f* cratering, formation of craters
Kraterboden *m* crater bottom (floor)
Kraterböschung *f* crater slope
Kraterdurchmesser *m* crater diameter
Kratereinsturz *m* crater collapse
Kratereruption *f* crater eruption
Kraterfeld *n* crater field
kraterförmig crater-shaped, crateriform
Kraterfumarole *f* crater fumarole
Kratergipfel *m* crater summit
Kratergrube *f* craterlet *(on the moon)*
Kraterinsel *f* crater island
Kraterkette *f* crater chain
Kraterkreisförmigkeit *f* crater circularity
Krateröffnung *f* crater vent
Kraterrand *m* crater edge (rim, lip)
Kraterreihe *f* row of craters
Kraterschlot *m* channel of ascent
Kraterschlund *m* throat of a volcano

Kratersee

Kratersee m crater lake
Kratertrichter m explosion funnel
Kraterungsdichte f cratering density *(on planets and satellites)*
Kraterungsgeschwindigkeit f cratering velocity *(on planets and satellites)*
Kraterverteilung f crater distribution
Kratervertiefung f crater dimple
Kratervulkan m cratered volcano
Kraterwall m crater wall (ring)
Kraterzerstörung f crater obliteration *(predominantly at high crater densities)*
Kratochwilit m kratochwilite, $C_{13}H_{10}$
Kratogen n s. Kraton
Kraton n craton, cratogen[ic areal], continental nucleus
Kratonbildung f cratonization
Kratongebiet n cratonal area
kratonisch cratonal, cratonic
Kratzer m scratcher
Kratzer mpl abrasion marks
Kratzgeräusche npl crackling
Kräuselmarke f rill mark
Kräuselung f wrinkle, crenulation; ripple *(of water)*
Kräuselwellen fpl ripples
Krausit m krausite, $KFe[SO_4] \cdot H_2O$
Krauskopfit m krauskopfite, $Ba_4[Si_4O_{10}] \cdot 6H_2O$
krautig herbaceous
Krautsteppe f herb (feather grass) steppe
KREEP KREEP *(lunar rocks enriched in potassium, rare-earth elements, and phosphorus)*
Kreide f 1. chalk; 2. Cretaceous [System] *(chronostratigraphically)*; Cretaceous [Period] *(geochronologically)*; Cretaceous [Age] *(common sense)*
~/**klüftige** scaly chalk
~/**lemnische rote** Lemnian ruddle
~/**mergelige** marly chalk
~/**Obere** Upper Cretaceous
~/**sandige** sandy chalk
~/**Untere** Lower Cretaceous
~/**weiße** white chalk
Kreideablagerung f cretaceous (chalk) deposit
Kreideboden m chalky soil
Kreidefelsen m chalk cliff
Kreideflysch m Cretaceous flysch
kreidehaltig chalky, cretaceous
Kreidekalk m/**weißer** white chalk
Kreidekalkstein m chalky limestone
Kreidemergel m calcareous clay, chalk marl
Kreideperiode f Cretaceous [Period]
Kreidesystem n Cretaceous [System]
Kreidezeit f Cretaceous [Age]
kreidig chalky
Kreis m/**Mohrscher** Mohr's circle
Kreisbahn f [circular] orbit
Kreisbewegung f circulation
Kreisbruch m ring fracture
Kreisel m gyroscope, gyro compass
Kreiselbrecher m gyratory breaker

Kreiselkompaß m gyroscope, gyro compass
Kreisfrequenz f angular frequency
Kreislauf m circulation; cycle
~/**exogener** exogenous cycle
~/**geochemischer** geochemical cycle
Kreisprozeß m cyclic process
Kremersit m kremersite, $KCl_2 \cdot NH_4Cl \cdot FeCl_2 \cdot H_2O$
Krennerit m krennerite, $(Au, Ag)Te_2$
kretaz[e]isch Cretaceous
Kreuz n/**Bertrandsches** Bertrand cross
~ **des Südens** Southern cross
Kreuzaufstellung f cross [spread]
Kreuzausgleich m cross equalization
Kreuzbein n sacrum
kreuzen/sich to intersect
kreuzend/sich interfering
Kreuzfadenmikrometer n cross bar micrometer
Kreuzgang m cross vein
kreuzgeschichtet cross-stratified, false-bedded, current-bedded
Kreuzgürtel m cross girdle
Kreuzkluft f cross flookan (flucan)
Kreuzkorrelationsfunktion f cross-correlation function
Kreuzlinien fpl traces
Kreuzmeißel m cross auger (bit)
Kreuzrille f cross groove
Kreuzriß m cross section
Kreuzschichtung f cross-bedding, cross stratification (lamination), false (crisscross) bedding
~/**äolische** aeolian cross-bedding
Kreuzschichtungstyp m/**girlandenartiger** festoon
Kreuzschieferung f crisscross schistosity
Kreuzschießen n dip shooting
Kreuzschlitten m cross (compound) slide
Kreuzsee f choppy sea
Kreuzstück n cross tee
Kreuztisch m cross table, mechanical stage
~/**aufsetzbarer** attachable mechanical stage
Kreuzübertragung f cross talk
Kreuzung f intersection *(of lodes)*
Kreuzvergleich m cross equalization
Kreuzzwilling m crossed (gridiron) twin
Kriechdehnung f creep strain
kriechen to creep
Kriechen n creep
~/**plastisches** creep buckling
Kriechfestigkeit f resistance to creep, creep strength
Kriechgrenze f creep limit; limiting [creep] stress
Kriechschutt m creeping waste
Kriechspur f crawling trace *(ichnology)*
Kriechvorgang m process of creeping
Kriechweg m amount of creep
Kriging n kriging *(principle of moving average established by Krige estimating the expectation value of a regionalized variable in a*

Kristallisationsdifferentiat

point, region or geometric field under consideration of correlations)
~/stetiges continuous kriging, kriging with a continuous weighting function
Kriging-Koeffizient *m* kriging coefficient
Kriging-Varianz *f* kriging variance, variance of [estimation by] kriging
Kristall *m* crystal
~/allothigener xenocryst, c[h]adacryst
~/allotriomorpher anhedron, allotriomorphic crystal
~/angeschmolzener brotocryst, eocryst, corroded crystal
~/angrenzender contiguous crystal
~/anisotroper anisotropic crystal
~/dichroitischer dichroic crystal
~/einachsiger uniaxial crystal
~/endomorpher endomorphic crystal
~/fehlgeordneter disordered crystal
~/freigewachsener free crystal
~/gestreckter elongate crystal
~/hemiedrischer hemihedral crystal
~/idiochromatischer idiochromatic crystal
~/idiomorpher euhedron, euhedral crystal
~/isomorpher isomorphous crystal
~/kleiner microlite
~/korrodierter brotocryst, eocryst, corroded crystal
~/linksdrehender left-handed crystal
~/lumineszierender luminescent crystal
~/mimetischer mimetic crystal
~/nadelförmiger acicular crystal, bacillite
~/optisch negativer negative crystal
~/optisch positiver positive crystal
~/piezoelektrischer piezoelectric crystal
~/realer imperfect crystal
~/rechtsdrehender right-handed crystal
~/resorbierter reabsorbed crystal
~/sargdeckelförmiger hopper-shaped crystal
~/teilweise resorbierter *s.* **~/korrodierter**
~/unvollkommener imperfect crystal
~/xenomorpher xenomorphic crystal, anhedron
~/zweiachsiger biaxial crystal
~/zweifarbiger merochrome
~/zweiseitig zugespitzter doubly terminated crystal
Kristallabdrücke *mpl* crystal imprints *(in sediments)*
Kristallabscheidung *f* separation of crystals
Kristallabseigerung *f* crystal settling (sedimentation)
~/gravitative gravitational crystal settling
Kristallachse *f* crystal[lographic] axis
Kristallachsenabschnitt *m* parameter of a crystal axis
Kristallachsenmesser *m* conoscope
Kristallachsenrichtung *f* crystallographic axis orientation
Kristallaggregat *n* crystal aggregate
kristallähnlich crystalloid
Kristallarten *fpl*/**isotype** isotypical crystal types

kristallartig crystalliform
Kristallaufbaufehler *m* crystal lattice imperfection
Kristallaufstellung *f* crystallographic setting
Kristallbaustein *m* structural unit of a crystal
Kristallbezeichnung *f* crystallographic notation
Kristallbildung *f* crystallizing, crystal formation
Kristallbrechung *f* crystal diffraction
Kristallbrei *m* crystal mush
Kristallchemie *f* crystal chemistry
kristallchemisch crystallochemical
Kriställchen *n* minute crystal
Kristalldiamagnetismus *m* crystal diamagnetism
Kristalldruse *f* cluster crystal, cluster of crystals, druse lines with crystals
Kristalle *mpl* **gleicher Größe** equidimensional crystals
~/gesetzmäßig verwachsene symmetrically related crystals
~/reine pure goods
~/verzahnte interlocking crystals, crystals felted together
Kristallebene *f* crystal face
kristallelektrisch piezoelectric
Kristallembryo *m* incipient crystal, crystallite
Kristallfehler *m* crystal (lattice) imperfection
Kristallfläche *f* crystal face, facet
Kristallflotation *f* crystal (gas) floatation
Kristallform *f* crystal[line] form
kristallförmig crystalliform
Kristallgebilde *n* grain colony
kristallgeometrisch crystallogeometric
Kristallgerippe *n*/**inneres** internal crystal framework
Kristallgitter *n* crystal (molecular) lattice
Kristallgitterabstand *m* crystal lattice spacing
Kristallgitterhohlraum *m* empty position of a crystal lattice
Kristallgrenze *f* crystal outline; grain boundary
Kristallgrenzlinie *f s.* **Kristallgrenze**
Kristallgruppe *f* crystal group
Kristallhabitus *m* crystal habit
kristallhaltig crystalliferous
Kristallhaufen *m* glomerocryst
kristallin crystalline
~/undeutlich obscurely crystalline
Kristallin *n* crystalline
Kristallinikum *n* crystalline floor
kristallinisch crystalline
kristallin-körnig crystalline-granular
Kristallinscholle *f* crystalline block
Kristallinzone *f* crystalline zone
Kristallisation *f* crystallization
~/fraktionierte fractional crystallization
~ in mehrfacher Form pleomorphism
~/posttektonische posttectonic crystallization
~/primäre primary crystallization
Kristallisationsbahn *f* crystalline path
Kristallisationsdifferentiat *n* crystallization differentiate

Kristallisationsdifferentiation 186

Kristallisationsdifferentiation f/**gravitative** gravitational crystallization differentiation
~/**komplexe gravitative** complex gravitational crystallization differentiation
Kristallisationsdruck m crystallizing pressure
kristallisationsfähig crystallizable
Kristallisationsfolge f sequence (order) of crystallization
Kristallisationsform f form of crystallization
Kristallisationsgrad m crystallinity
Kristallisationskern m nucleus of crystallization
Kristallisationskraft f crystallizing force
Kristallisationsprozeß m crystallizing process
Kristallisationsregelung f crystallizing orientation
Kristallisationsreihe f s. Kristallisationsfolge
Kristallisationsschieferung f foliation due to crystallization, crystallization (true, flow) cleavage
Kristallisationsstadium n state of crystallization
Kristallisationsvermögen n crystalline force
Kristallisationsvorgang m s. Kristallisationsprozeß
Kristallisationswasser n water of crystallization (constitution, hydration)
Kristallisationszentrum n centre of crystallization
Kristallisationszustand m state of crystallization
Kristallisator m crystallizer
kristallisierbar crystallizable
kristallisieren to crystallize; to vegetate
kristallisiert/nicht uncrystallized
~/**schlecht** dyscrystalline
Kristallisierversuch m crystallizing experiment
Kristallit n crystallite
~/**nadelförmiger** belonite
Kristallkante f crystal edge
Kristallkeim m crystal nucleus, nucleus of crystal[lization]
Kristallkeimbildung f crystal seeding
Kristallkeller m crystal cave
Kristallkern m crystal core
Kristallklasse f crystal (symmetry) class, space group
~/**symmetrielose** pedial class
Kristallkorn n/**sekundäres** neocryst
Kristallkörperchen n/**rundes** spherulite, sphaerolite
Kristallkunde f crystallography
Kristallmorphologie f crystal morphology
Kristallnadel f needle
Kristallnegativ n negative crystal
Kristallnetzebene f plane lattice
Kristalloblast m [crystallo]blast
Kristalloblastese f [crystallo]blastesis
kristalloblastisch [crystallo]blastic
Kristallograf m crystallographer
Kristallografie f crystallography
kristallografisch crystallographic

kristalloid crystalloid
Kristallometrie f crystallometry
Kristalloptik f crystal optics
Kristallorientierung f crystal orientation
Kristallphysik f crystal physics, physical crystallography (mineralogy)
Kristallprojektion f crystal projection
Kristallpseudomorphosen fpl crystal casts
Kristallregenerierung f crystal recovery (regeneration)
Kristallsandstein m crystallized sandstone, gritstone
Kristallschnee m fine snowy crystals
Kristallschnitt m crystal section
Kristallseitenkante f lateral edge of a crystal
Kristallskelett n crystal skeleton
Kristallspektrometer n Bragg spectrometer
Kristallstrukturlehre f theory of the crystalline texture
Kristallstrukturuntersuchung f crystal analysis
Kristallsymmetrie f crystal symmetry, symmetry of crystals
~/**äußere** external symmetry of crystals
Kristallsystem n crystal[lographic] system
Kristalltuff m crystal tuff
Kristallüberzug m drusy coating
Kristallumgrenzung f crystal boundary
Kristallumineszenz f crystalloluminescence
Kristallverheilung f crystal recovery
Kristallverwachsung f crystalline overgrowth
Kristallwachstum n crystal (crystallite, grain) growth, crystal growing
~ **durch plötzliche Abschreckung** quench crystal growth
Kristallwasser n s. Kristallisationswasser
kristallwasserhaltig hydrous
Kristallwinkel m crystal angle
Kristallwinkelmessung f crystal[line] goniometry
Kristallzusammenballung f/**unregelmäßige** glomerocryst
Kristallzustand m crystalline state
Kritze f striation
kritzen to striate
Kröhnkit m kröhnkite, kroehnkite, $Na_2Cu[SO_4]_2 \cdot 2H_2O$
Krokoit m crocoite, $PbCrO_4$
Krokydolith m crocidolite, blue-cape asbestos (fibrous riebeckite)
Krone f 1. crown, coping (of a dam); 2. core bit (drilling)
~/**selbstschärfende** self-sharpening core bit
Kronenblock m crown block
Kronenbohrer m annular auger
Kronstedtit m cronstedtite, $Fe_4Fe_2(OH)_8 | Fe_2Si_2O_{10}]$
Krückelführer m driller
Krümel m crumb, clot
krümelig friable, cloddy; acinose
Krümeltextur f clod (crumb, aggregate, bean-shaped) structure

Krümelzerbröckelung f size degradation
Krumentiefe f depth of top soil
krummlinig curvilinear
Krümmung f bend; curvature; sinuosity
Krümmungsform f **von Schichten** shape of strata curvature
Krümmungsradius m curvature radius
~ **der Bohrlochachse** radius of deviation
Krümmungssinn m curvature direction
Krümmungswinkel m angle of curvature
Krümmungszentrum n centre of bend (of plots)
Kruste f crust; incrustation
~/**basaltische** basaltic crust
~/**dünne** illinition (mineral)
~/**eisenschüssige** ferricrust
~/**granitische** granitic crust
~/**kontinentale** continental crust
~/**ozeanische** oceanic crust
~/**starre** rigid crust
~/**wandständige** wallbound crust
Krustenabbiegung f/**plötzliche** downbuckle
Krustenabkühlung f crustal cooling
Krustenabschnitt m/**in Absenkung begriffener** negative segment
~/**in Hebung begriffener** positive segment
Krustenalgen fpl incrusting algae
krustenartig crustaceous
Krustenbau m crustal structure
Krustenbereich m crust range (zone)
~/**tieferer** deeper range of the crust
Krustenbewegung f crustal movement
~/**ausgleichende** crustal readjustment
~/**rezente** recent crustal movement
Krustenbildung f crustification; overcrusting, scale; encrustation (well); clogging
Krustenboden m incrusted soil
Krustendeformation f diastrophe
Krusteneinengung f crustal shortening
Krustengleitung f **auf dem Erdmantel** phorogenesis
Krustenhebung f crustal upheaval
Krusteninstabilität f tectonism
Krustenmächtigkeit f crustal thickness
Krustenriff n coral shoal, patch reef
Krustenruhe f crustal rest (quiescence)
Krustensegment n crustal segment
Krustenspannung f crustal stress
Krustenstörung f crustal disturbance
Krustentiere npl crustaceans, crustaceous animals
Krustenunruhe f crustal unrest
Krustenverbiegung f warping
Krustenverformung f crustal deformation
Krustenverkippung f/**seismische** earth tilting
Krustenverkürzung f crustal shortening
Krustenversteifung f **durch Ausfaltung** cratonization
kryogen cryogenic
Kryogenik f cryogenics
Kryolith m cryolite, Greenland spar, Na_3AlF_6
Kryolithionit m cryolithionite, $Na_3Li_3[Al, F_6]_2$

Kryometer n cryometer
Kryopedologie f cryopedology
Kryoplankton n cryoplankton
Kryoskop n cryoscope
kryoskopisch cryoscopic
Kryosphäre f cryosphere
kryoturbat cryoturbate
Kryoturbation f cryoturbation
Kryoturbationshorizont m strangling horizon
Kryptogamen fpl cryptogams; cryptogamic (cryptogamous) plants
kryptogranitisch cryptogranitic
Kryptohalit m cryptohalite, $(NH_4)_2SiF_6$
kryptoklastisch cryptoclastic
kryptokristallin cryptocrystalline, microfelsitic, microaphanitic
kryptomagmatisch cryptomagmatic
kryptomer cryptomerous
Krypton n krypton, Kr
Kryptopedometer n cryptopedometer
Kryptopherit m cryptopherite (extremly fine interlamination of albite and orthoclase)
Kryptophytikum n Cryptophytic
Kryptoschichtung f cryptic layering
Kryptostruktur f cryptic texture
kryptovulkanisch cryptovolcanic
Kryptovulkanismus m cryptovolcanism
Kryptozoikum n Cryptozoic [Eon]
Kryshanovskit m kryshanovskite, $MnFe_2[OH | PO_4]_2 \cdot H_2O$
Kubanit m cubanite, chalmersite, $CuFe_2S_3$
Kubatur f cubage, cubature
Kubergand n Kubergandian [Stage] (basal stage of Middle Permian)
Kubikmeter n cubic metre
kubisch cubic[al]
kubisch-flächenzentriert face-centered cubic
kubisch-raumzentriert body-centered cubic
kubizieren/die Masse to calculate the volume of a solid
Kubooktaeder n cub[o-]octahedron
Kubus m hexahedron
Kuckersit m kukersite (Ordovician algal rock from Estonia)
Kugel f ball, globe, orbicule, sphere
kugelähnlich spheroidal
Kugelbasalt m ellipsoidal basalt
Kugelblitz m globe (ball) lightning
Kügelchen n globule, globulite; small globe; spherule; pellet
~/**kosmisches** cosmic spherule
Kügelchen npl/**schwarze magnetische** black magnetic spherules (extraterrestrial)
Kugeldiorit m ball (globular, orbicular) diorite
Kugeldruckhärteprüfer m ball-indentation testing apparatus
Kugeldruckhärteprüfung f ball-indentation test
Kugelerz n sphere ore
kugelförmig globular, globe-shaped; spherical; ball-shaped
Kugelgelenkklappe f ball-joint roof bar
Kugelgelenkstempel m ball-joint prop

Kugelgranit

Kugelgranit *m* globular (orbicular, spheroidal) granite
Kugelgraphit *m* nodular graphite
kugelig globular, globe-shaped; orbicular; spherical; nodular; mammillary *(mineral aggregates)*
Kugeljaspis *m* ball jasper, Egyptian pebble
Kugelkörperchen *n* globulite, spherulite
Kugelmühle *f* ball mill
Kugelpackung *f* sphere packing *(crystallography)*
~/dichteste close-packed structure
Kugelperforation *f* gun (bullet) perforation
Kugelschlagbohren *n* pellet impact drilling
Kugeltextur *f* orbicular (nodular) structure
Kühlbodenhypothese *f* Wundt's thermic-gravitative contraction theory of earth with regard to the differentiated terrestrial heat between ocean soils and land
kulissenartig interlocking
Kulissenfalte *f* overlapping (echelon) fold
kulissenförmig en echelon
Kulissenverwerfung *f* kulissen fault
Kullenberg-Probenehmer *m* Kullenberg corer *(for deep-sea sediments)*
Kullerudit *m* kullerudite, $NiSe_2$
Kulm *n* Culm [facies] *(Lower Carboniferous in Thuringia)*
Kulmination *f* culmination
Kulminationspunkt *m* culminating point
kulminierend culminant
kultivierbar arable
Kultosol *m* anthropogenetic-changed soil
Kulturboden *m* cultivated (agricultural, arable) soil
Kulturland *n* cultivated land
Kultursteppe *f* cultivated steppe land
Kulturterrasse *f* field terrace
Kümmerfauna *f* poorly developed fauna
Kümmerfluß *m* misfit river, underfit stream
Kungur *n* Kungurian [Stage] *(of Permian in the Permian district)*
Kunzit *m* kunzite *(variety of spodumene)*
Kupfer *n* copper, Cu
~/arsenhaltiges arsenical copper
~/gediegenes native copper, barrel copper, mass copper
~ im Moränenschutt drift copper
Kupferantimonglanz *m* chalcostibite, $Cu_2S \cdot Sb_2S_3$
kupferartig coppery, cupreous
Kupferbergwerk *n* copper mine
Kupferbleiglanz *m* alisonite, $3Cu_2S \cdot PbS$
Kupfererz *n* copper ore
~/in Porphyr eingesprengtes disseminated porphyry copper ore
Kupferfahlerz *n* black copper ore
Kupfergehalt *m* copper content
Kupferglanz *m* chalcocite, chalcosine, copper glance, Cu_2S
Kupfergrün *n s.* Chrysokoll
kupferhaltig copper-bearing, cupriferous, cupreous

Kupferindigo *m* indigo copper, blue copper, covellite, CuS
Kupferkies *m* chalcopyrite, copper pyrite, cupriferous (yellow) pyrite, yellow [copper] ore, $CuFeS_2$
Kupferkonzentrationslagerstätte *f/aride* red-bed deposit
Kupferlagerstätte *f* copper deposit
Kupferlasur *m* azurite, blue copper ore, $Cu_3[OH \mid CO_3]_2$
Kupferlebererz *n* liver-coloured copper ore
Kupfermanganerz *n* lampadite *(variety of wad)*
Kupfermelanterit *m* pisanite, $(Fe, Cu)[SO_4] \cdot 7H_2O$
Kupfernickel *m s.* Niccolit
Kupfersandstein *m* copper-bearing sandstone
Kupferschiefer *m* copper shale (slate, schist), kupferschiefer
Kupferspat *m s.* Malachit
Kupferstein *m* copper matte
Kupfersulfat *n s.* Kupfervitriol
Kupferuranglimmer *m* copper uranite, torbernite, $Cu[UO_2 \mid PO_4]_2 \cdot 10(12-8)H_2O$
Kupferverhüttung *f* copper smelting
Kupfervitriol *m* chalcanthite, blue copperas (vitriol), $CuSO_4 \cdot 5H_2O$
Kupferwismutglanz *m* emplectite, $Cu_2S \cdot Bi_2S_3$
Kupferzeit *f* Copper Age
Kupletskit *m* kupletskite, $(K_2, Na_2, Ca)(Mn, Fe)_4(Ti, Zr)[OH \mid Si_2O_7]_2$
Kuppe *f* dome; top, head; knoll *(of ocean floor)*
Kuppel *f* cupola; quaquaversal structure *(tectonical)*
Kuppeldach *n* **des Batholithen** cupola of the batholith, plutonic cupola
Kuppelfalte *f* dome-shaped fold
Kuppelflanke *f* domal flank
kuppelförmig domal
Kuppelgebirge *n* dome-shaped mountains
Kuppelkarst *m* cupola karst
Kuppelstaumauer *f* dome dam
Kuppenberg *m* knob
Kuppenriff *n* patch reef, pinnacle
Kuprit *m* cuprite, ruby copper [ore], red copper oxide, Cu_2O
Kurgantait *m* kurgantaite, $(Sr, Ca)_2[B_4O_8] \cdot H_2O$
Kurnakovit *m* kurnakovite, $Mg[B_3O_3(OH)_5] \cdot 5H_2O$
Kurtosis *f* kurtosis
Kurumsakit *m* kurumsakite, $(Zn, Ni, Cu)Al_8[(VO_4)_2 \mid (SiO_4)_5] \cdot 27H_2O$
Kurve *f/bathygrafische* bathymetric curve
~/spitze peaked curve
Kurvendiagramm *n* graph
Kurvenschar *f* master curves, target
Kurventrend *m* one-dimensional trend, trend with one coordinate
Kurzanker *mpl* bolts
kurzköpfig brachycephalic *(palaeontology)*
Kurzköpfigkeit *f* brachycephaly, brachycephalism

kurzsäulig short-columnar
Kurzwegmultiple f short-path multiple
Kurzzeitgebiet n time lead area
Küste f coast, shore, sea side
~/an der inshore
~/aufgetauchte emerged shore line, shore line of emergency
~/befestigte man-made shore line
~/buchtenreiche much indented coast
~/[ein]gebuchtete embayed coast
~/gegliederte indented coast
~/gelappte lobate coast
~/geradlinige straight coast line
~/tiefeingebuchtete deeply embayed coast
~/untergetauchte submerged (negative) shore line, shore line of submergence
~/vorspringende projecting coast
~/zerlappte lobate coast
~/zerrissene ragged coast
Küstenabdachung f coast[al] slope
Küstenablagerung f coastal (shore, beach) deposit, shore-laid sediment
Küstenaufnahme f coast survey
Küstendüne f coast[al] dune, littoral dune
Küstenebene f coastal plain
~/zonar gegliederte belted coastal plain
Küsteneis n shore ice
Küstenfauna f epifauna
Küstenfazies f coastal (littoral) facies
küstenfern offshore
Küstengebiet n coastal area (region, territory)
Küstengebirge n coastal mountain, coast[al] range
Küstengestaltung f configuration of coast
Küstengewässer npl coastal (offshore) waters
Küstengliederung f indentation of the coast
Küstenhebung f coastal uplift, elevation of coast
Küsteninsel f cay *(consisting of sand or corals)*
Küstenkliff n shore (sea) cliff
Küstenlagune f coastal lagoon
Küstenlinie f coast[al] line, shore line
~/ehemalige ancient coast line
~/langgestreckte gerade rectilinear shore line
küstennah near-shore, inshore
Küstennebel m sea fog
Küstenniederung f low-lying coast region, low-lying coastal land, coastal lowland
Küstenplattform f littoral (shore) platform
Küstenprofil n shore profile
Küstenriff n shore (onshore, fringing) reef
Küstenrifflagerstätte f strand-line pool *(of oil)*
Küstenschlick m hemipelagic muds
Küstenschutt m coastal debris
Küstenschutz m coast[al] protection; shore protection; coastal engineering
Küstenschutzbauten mpl coast [protection] works
Küstenschutzgebiet n coast-defence zone
Küstenschutzmaßnahmen fpl measures of coast protection

Küstensediment n shore sediment
Küstensee m coastal lake
Küstensenkung f submergence (subsidence) of coast
Küstensicherung f s. Küstenschutz
Küstenspitzen fpl beach cusps
Küstenstrich m seaboard
Küstenstrom m littoral (longshore) current, coastal stream
Küstenströmung f littoral drift, shore drift
Küstensumpf m marine marsh, coastal swamp, dismal
Küstenterrasse f coastal (shore, beach, face) terrace, wave-cut platform, marine bench
Küstenüberschwemmung f coastal flooding
Küstenveränderung f coastal change
Küstenvermessung f coast[al] geodetic survey
Küstenversetzung f shifting of shores, coastal drifting, longshore drift[ing]
Küstenwall m s. Strandwall
Küstenwüste f coastal desert
Küstenzerstörung f coast[al] destruction
Küstenzone f littoral zone
Kutikularanalyse f cuticular analysis
Kutikulen fpl cuticules
Kutinit m s. Cutinit
Kutnahorit m kutnahorite, $CaMn[CO_3]_2$
Kuverwasser n seepage through dikes
K-Wert m transmission constant
Kyanit m kyanite, cyanite, disthene, Al_2SiO_5
Kylindrit m cylindrite, $6PbS \cdot 6SnS_2 \cdot Sb_2S_3$

L

labil labile, unstable
Labit m labite, $Mg_3H_6[Si_8O_{22}] \cdot 2H_2O$
Labormagnetscheider m laboratory magnetic separator
Laboruntersuchung f laboratory investigation
Labradit m labradite *(phaneric labradorite)*
Labrador m labrador
labradorisieren to aventurize, to iridesce, to schillerize
Labradorisieren n labradorescence, aventurism, iridescence
Labradorit m labradorite
Labradoritdazit m labradorite dacite
Labradoritit m labradoritite *(anorthosite)*
Labuntsovit m labuntsovite, $(K, Ba, Na, Ca, Mn) (Ti, Nb) (Si, Al)_2(O, OH)_7 \cdot H_2O$
Lacertilier mpl lacertilians
Lack m s. Wüstenlack
Lackfolie f lacquer disk
Lackfolienaufnahme f lacquer original
Lacroixit m lacroixite, $Na_4Ca_2Al_3[(OH, F)_8 | (PO_4)_3]$
Lacus m lacus *(sea on Mars or moon)*
Ladedruckhöhe f critical altitude
Ladestange f loading pole
Ladin n Ladinian [Stage] *(of Triassic)*
Ladung f charge

Ladung

~/vorbesetzte sleeper charge
Ladungsdichte f charge density
Ladungszahl f charge number
Lage f 1. layer, bed, stratum, bank; seam; sheet; 2. position
~/fossilführende fossiliferous layer
~/horizontale horizontality
~ im Kohlenflöz/erdige dirt bed
Lagekarte f layout chart
Lagen fpl/**abwechselnde** interlaminate layers
Lagengneis m layered gneiss
Lageninjektion f ribbon injection
Lagenkugel f locus sphere
Lagenkugeldiagramm n sphere diagram
~/ausgezähltes contoured stereogram
Lagentextur f layered (banded, laminated, ribbon) structure; stromatic texture *(in migmatites)*
Lageplan m site plan, *(Am)* location plane; layout
Lager n bed; layer; ledge; assise; pool *(of oil, natural gas)*
~ für radioaktive Abfälle nuclear wastes deposit
~ mit Gasexpansionstrieb depletion (solution gas) drive pool
~ mit Gaskappentrieb free gas cap drive pool
~ mit Randwassertrieb water drive pool
~ mit Schwerkrafttrieb gravity drainage pool
Lagergang m bed[ded] vein, fissure vein, sill, intrusive sheet
~/basischer whinsill
~/horizontaler blanket vein
~/interformationeller interformational sill
~/zusammengesetzter composite sill
Lagergestein n bedrock, rockhead
Lagerhaltung f stockpiling
Lagerkluft f flat-lying joint, L-joint
Lagerstätte f deposit
~/abbauwürdige payable deposit
~/adernförmige network deposit
~/alluviale alluvial deposit
~/als Porenraumfüllungen ausgebildete interstitial deposit
~/antiklinale anticlinal reservoir
~/apomagmatische apomagmatic deposit
~/ausgebeutete depleted field
~/autochthone in situ deposit
~/bauwürdige payable deposit
~/durch submarinen Erdrutsch entstandene submarine landslide deposit
~/eluviale eluvial deposit
~/epigenetische epigenetic (subsequent) deposit
~/epithermale epithermal deposit
~/erkundete proved deposit
~/erschöpfte exhausted deposit; depleted field
~/flachliegende blanket deposit
~/gangartige gangue deposit
~/geringmächtige, flache narrow-reef mine

~/gestörte dislocated deposit, faulted reservoir
~/hydrothermale hydrothermal deposit
~/hypotaxische hypotaxic deposit
~ in einer Scherzone shear-zone deposit
~ in situ in situ deposit
~/intramagmatische intramagmatic deposit
~/intrusive intrusive deposit
~/katathermale katathermal deposit
~/kontaktmetamorphe contact-metamorphic deposit
~/kontaktmetasomatische contact-metasomatic deposit
~/kontaktpneumatolytische contact-pneumatolytic deposit
~/linsenförmige lenticular deposit
~/liquidmagmatische liquid magmatic deposit
~/marine marine deposit
~/massige solid ore deposit
~/mesothermale mesothermal deposit
~/metasomatische metasomatic (replacement) deposit
~ mit angereicherten Schwerölen und Asphalten inspissated oil deposit
~ mit Liegendwassertrieb bottom water drive field
~ mit mehreren Trägern multilayer field
~/nutzbare workable (minable) deposit
~/nutzbare mineralische useful mineral deposit
~/oberflächennahe superficial deposit
~/perimagmatische perimagmatic deposit
~/plattenförmige tabular deposit
~/schichtige stratified deposit
~/sedimentäre sedimentary deposit
~/sedimentär-exhalative sedimentary exhalative deposit
~/submarin-exhalativ-sedimentäre submarine exhalative sedimentary deposit
~/subvulkanische subvolcanic deposit
~/telemagmatische telemagmatic deposit
~/tiefliegende deep-seated deposit
~ unter dem Meeresgrund deep-water reservoir
~/verdeckte blind deposit
~/verworfene faulted deposit
~ von nutzbaren Mineralen mineral deposit
~/wasserfreie dry field
~/wasserführende water-bearing deposit
Lagerstättenabschreibung f depreciation of deposit
Lagerstättenarchiv n deposit archive
Lagerstättenart f form of deposit
Lagerstättenbedingungen fpl in situ conditions
Lagerstättenbemusterung f deposit sampling
Lagerstättenbewertung f deposit (mine) evaluation
Lagerstättenbildung f formation of deposits; reservoir sedimentation *(aquifer)*
Lagerstättendruck m formation (reservoir) pressure

~/mit natürlichem oleostatic
~/mittlerer average reservoir pressure
Lagerstätteneinschätzung f [/technisch-ökonomische] evaluation of deposits
Lagerstättenenergie f formation (reservoir) energy
Lagerstättenerkundung f exploration of deposits
Lagerstättenfeld n/unverritztes virgin field
Lagerstättenforschung f/gravimetrische gravitational method of prospecting
Lagerstättengenese f genesis of deposits
Lagerstättengeochemie f exploration geochemistry, geochemistry of mineral deposits
Lagerstättengeophysik f exploration geophysics
Lagerstättengeschichte f (Am) field case history
Lagerstätteninhalt m well effluent
Lagerstättenkartierung f mapping of deposits
Lagerstättenkonditionen fpl conditions (requirements) for deposits
Lagerstättenkunde f geology (science) of mineral deposits, economic[al] geology
Lagerstättenmächtigkeit f thickness of deposit
Lagerstättenmodellierung f simulation of reservoir
Lagerstättennutzung f exploitation of deposits
Lagerstättenparameter m deposit parameter
Lagerstättenperspektive f deposit perspective
Lagerstättenpflege f conservation of mineral resources
Lagerstättenplanungsmodell n model for planning deposits
Lagerstättenprofil n deposit profile
Lagerstättenprognose f prognosis of deposits
Lagerstättenschätzung f valuation of deposits
Lagerstättensuche f search for deposits
Lagerstättenumriß m deposit outline
Lagerstättenuntersuchung f field evaluation
Lagerstättenveränderlichkeit f variability of deposits
Lagerstättenvolumen n/gesamtes bulk reservoir volume
Lagerstättenvorräte mpl deposit resources; reservoir storage (of groundwater)
Lagerstättenwasser n formation (oil-field) water
Lagerstein m bearing stone
Lagerung f attitude; bedding, stratification
~/diskordante s. ~/ungleichförmige
~/gestörte dislocation, disturbed stratification
~/gleichförmige concordance, conformability of strata, conformable (plan-parallel) structure
~/inverse inversion, inverted (reserved) order
~/konkordante s. ~/gleichförmige
~/linsenförmige lensing
~/normale origin order, original position
~/rechtsinnige s. ~/gleichförmige
~/schichtenförmige foliation
~/söhlige horizontal bedding (stratification)
~/transgredierende transgressive superposition (overlap)

~/übergreifende on-lap
~/umgekehrte s. ~/inverse
~/ungestörte undisturbed stratification
~/ungleichförmige discordance, non-conformity, disconformity, disconformable contact
~/zurückbleibende off-lap
~ zwischen den Randsenken zweier Salzstöcke/ antiklinale residual anticlines
Lagerungsbedingungen fpl 1. stratigraphic conditions; 2. reservoir conditions (oil field)
Lagerungsdichte f compactness
Lagerungsform f bedding form; nature of deposition
Lagerungsstörung f dislocation, disturbance [of beds], displacement
Lagerungsteufe f depth of occurrence
Lagerungsverhältnisse npl bedding conditions, mode of occurrence, attitude
lagunär lagoonal, lagoon-derived
Lagune f lagoon, lagune
~ hinter dem Riff back-reef lagoon
~/in Verlandung begriffene lagoon in process of being filled
Lagunenablagerung f lagoonal deposit[ion]
Lagunenküste f lagoon-type of coast
Lagunenriff n atoll [reef], reef ring
Lahar m lahar
Lahngang m debris avalanche
Laitakarit m laitakarite, Bi_4Se_2S
Lakkolith m laccolite, laccolith
lakustrin, lakustrisch lacustrine, limnetic
lakustroglazial glaciolacustrine
Lamarckismus m Lamarck[ian]ism
Lambertit m s. Uranophan
lamellar lamellar
Lamellargefüge n lamination
Lamelle f lamella
Lamellenstempel m lamellar prop
Lamellibranchiaten npl lamellibranchs, pelecypods
laminar laminar
Laminargefüge n lamellar (laminated, platy) structure
Laminarie f laminaria
Laminarströmung f laminar flow
Lamination f lamination
Lamine f lamina
Laminit m laminite (sedimentology)
Lampadit m lampadite (variety of wad)
Lamprophyllit m lamprophyllite, molengraaffite, $Na_3Sr_2Ti_3[(O, OH, F)_2|Si_2O_7]_2$
Lamprophyr m lamprophyre (dark dike rock)
~/metamorpher lamproschist
Lanarkit m lanarkite, $Pb_2[O|SO_4]$
Lance-Formation f Lance Formation (upper parts of Campanian to Maastrichtian, North America)
Land n land; ground, soil; earth
~/an ashore
~/angeschwemmtes alluvium, alluvion
~/bestelltes tilth
~/verwehtes blow land

Landbedeckung

Landbedeckung f land cover
Landbrücke f land bridge
landen/auf dem Mond to moon
Landenge f isthmus, neck of land
Landénien n Landénian [Stage] *(of Palaeocene, Paris Basin)*
Landenippel m landing nipple
Landesaufnahme f geodetic survey, survey of a country, topographic reconnaissance
Landesit m landesite, $(Mn, Fe)_{<3}[PO_4]_2 \cdot 3H_2O$
Landesplanung f regional planing
Landgewinnung f land reclamation
Landhebung f elevation of land
Landkarte f map
~ **im Maßstab 1:62 500** fifteen minute[s] map
~ **im Maßstab 1:250 000** degree map
Landmarke f landmark
landnah near-shore
Landnutzungspotential n land potential
Landpfeiler m abutment
Landpflanze f land (terrestrial) plant
Landraubtiere npl land carnivores
Landregen m steady (general) rain
Landsbergit m landsbergite γ-(Ag, Hg)
Landschaft f/**durch Abtragung geschaffene** destructional landforms
Landschaften fpl/**mehrzyklische** multicycle landscapes
Landschaftsplanung f landscape planning
Landschaftsschutz m protection of the environment
landschaftsverändernd landscape changes *(12th stage of the scale of seismic intensity)*
Landschutt m land waste, terrigenous detritus
Landseismik f onshore seismics
landseitig onshore
Landspitze f cape, headland, promontory, tongue
~/**krumme** hook
Landstufe f escarpment
landumschlossen land-locked
Landvermessung f cadastral survey
Landwind m offshore wind (breeze), landwind
Landwirtschaftsgeologie f agricultural geology, agrogeology
Landzunge f tongue, headland, promontory, spine, neck of land
Langbanit m langbanite $(Mn\cdot Mn_6\cdots[O_8|SiO_4]$
Langbeinit m langbeinite, $K_2Mg_2(SO_4)_3$
Länge f/**geografische** [terrestrial] longitude
~/**Petersche** Peter's length *(seismics)*
~ **und Breite** geographic[al] coordinates
Längenfehler m linear error
Längengrad m longitude degree
Längenkreis m [geographical] meridian, circle of longitude
Längenmaßstab m linear scale factor
längentreu equidistant
Längenunterschied m difference of longitude
Längenverstellbarkeit f extensibility *(of prop)*
Langhien n Langhian [Stage] *(of Miocene)*
Langit m langite, $Cu_4[(OH)_6|SO_4] \cdot H_2O$

langköpfig dolichocephalic *(palaeontology)*
Langlebigkeit f longevity
länglich elongate
Langlochbohren n long-hole drilling
Langsamschicht f weathering *(seismics)*
~/**doppelte** double-layer weathering
Langsamschichtkorrektur f weathering correction *(seismics)*
Langsamschichtschluß m short (pop) shot *(seismics)*
Langsamschichtunterkante f base of weathering *(seismics)*
Längsdruck m longitudinal pressure
Längsdüne f longitudinal dune
Längsfaserasbest m slip fibre asbestos
Längsholm m spar
Längskluft f longitudinal joint, S-joint
Längsküste f/**ertrunkene** drowned longitudinal coast
Längsmoräne f longitudinal moraine
Längsplattung f longitudinal slab joints
Längsprofil n longitudinal profile
Längsrippung f intrastratified ribs
Längsschnitt m longitudinal section
Längsspalte f longitudinal crevasse, strike joint
Längsstreifen m longitudinal stria
Längstal n longitudinal [strike] valley
Längsüberdeckung f forward lap
Längsverformung f longitudinal deformation
Längsverwerfung f longitudinal (strike) fault
Längung f lengthening, elongation, stretching
~ **in b** lengthening in b
Langwegmultiple f long-path multiple *(seismics)*
Langzeitverhalten n long-term behaviour
Lansfordit m lansfordite, $MgCO_3 \cdot 5H_2O$
Lanthanidengruppe f lanthanide group
Lanthanidenkontraktion f lanthanide contraction
Lanthanit m lanthanite, $(La, Dy, Ce)_2[CO_3]_3 \cdot 8H_2O$
Lanthinit m lanthinite, $2UO_2 \cdot 7H_2O$
Lapilli pl lapilli
lapilliartig lapilliform
Lapillituff m lapilli tuff
Lapislazuli m lazurite, lazuli, lapis-lazuli, $(Na, Ca)_8[(SO_4, S, Cl)_2|(AlSiO_4)_6]$
Laplace-Transformation f Laplace transform
Lappen m lobe
läppen to lap
Läppen n lapping
lappig lobate
Läppmittel n lapping abrasive
Läppscheibe f lapping wheel
laramisch laramic
Larderellit m larderellite, $NH_4[B_5O_6(OH)_4]$
Larnit m larnite, β-$Ca_2[SiO_4]$
Larsenit m larsenite, $PbZn[SiO_4]$
Larvikit m larvikite *(rock of the syenite clan)*
Laserhöhenmesser m airborne laser profiler
Lasermessung f **für geophysikalische Zwecke** laser geophysical measurement

Lasermikrospektralanalyse *f* laser microspectrographic analysis
Last *f* load
~/aufgebrachte imposed (superimposed, additional) load, surcharge, loading
~/kritische critical load
~/zulässige design load
Lastangriff *m* application of load
Lastannahme *f* assumed load, assumption of load
Lastaufbringung *f* application of load
Lastaufnahme *f* load-bearing capacity
Lastboden *m* foundation soil
Lastdehnungskurve *f* load-deflection curve, stress-strain curve
Lastsenkungskurve *f* load-settlement curve
Lastsenkungsschreiber *m* load-yield recorder
Lastspiel *n* cycle of stress
Laststufe *f* load range
Lastübertragung *f* transference of load *(Potts)*
Lastwechsel *m* cycle of stress, stress reversal
Last-Weg-Kurve *f* load-yield curve, resistance-yield curve
Lasurit *m*, **Lasurstein** *m* lazurite, lasurite, lapis-lazuli, lazuli, $(Na, Ca)_8[(SO_4, S, Cl)_2|(AlSiO_4)_6]$
Latdorf[ien] *n*, **Latdorfium** *n*, **Latdorf-Stufe** *f* Latdorfian [Stage] *(of Oligocene)*
latent latent
Lateralgraben *m* lateral ditch
Laterallobus *m* lateral lobe
Laterallogaufnahme *f* lateral curve
Lateralmigration *f* lateral migration
Lateralsegregation *f* lateral segregation
Lateralsekretion *f* lateral secretion
Laterit *m* laterite
~/allochthoner low-level laterite
Lateritbildung *f* laterization
Lateritboden *m* laterite (ferallitic) soil
lateritisch lateritic
Lateritkieshorizont *m* lateritic gravel horizon
Lateritpanzer *m* lateritic crust
Laterolog *n* laterolog, focussed-current logging
Latit *m* latite *(trachyandesite)*
Latiumit *m* latiumite, $Ca_6(K, Na)_2Al_4[(O, CO_3, SO_4)|(SiO_4)_6]$
Latosol *m* latosol
Latrappit *m* latrappite, $(Ca, Na, SE)(Nb, Ti, Fe)O_3$
Lattenpegel *m* staff gauge
Laubanit *m* laubanite *(variety of natrolite)*
Laubbaldachin *m* plant canopy
Laubbäume *mpl* leaf-bearing trees
Laubmannit *m* laubmannite, $(Fe, Mn)_3Fe_6[(OH)_3|PO_4]_4$
Laubwald *m* deciduous forest (wood)
Laue-Diagramm *n* Laue diffraction pattern, Laue [X-ray] pattern
Laueit *m* laueite, $MnFe_2[OH|PO_4]_2 \cdot 8H_2O$
Läufer *m* runner
Laufrichtung *f*/**umgekehrte** inverted stream
Laufverkürzung *f* **eines Flusses infolge Mäanderdurchschneidung** neck cut-off

Laufweg *m*/**kleinster** brachistochrone
Laufzeit *f* travel (propagation, transit) time
~ der Reflexion am Schußpunkt reflection arrival time at zero offset
~/einfache one-way time
~/reduzierte reduced travel time
~/vertikale vertical time
Laufzeitdifferenz *f* **am Geophon** geophone delay time
~ am Schußpunkt shot delay time
Laufzeitfehler *m* phase delay error
Laufzeitkette *f* delay line
Laufzeitkurve *f* travel time curve, time-distance curve, time-travel curve
~ einer Reflexion reflection curve
~/reduzierte reduced-scale travel time curve
~/refraktionsseismische refraction time-distance curve
~/rückläufige reverse travel time curve
~/zusammengesetzte continous time-distance curve, composite travel time curve
Laufzeitmessung *f* transit-time measurement
Laufzeitprofil *n* cross section
Laufzeitverzerrung *f* envelope delay frequency distortion
Laufzeit-Weg-Diagramm *n* time-distance graph
Lauge *f* lye
~/aggressive leaching liquor
laugen to lye; to buck
laugenartig lixivial
Laugenit *m* laugenite *(oligoclase diorite)*
Laugenrückfluß *m* **durch den Porenraum zum Meer** seepage refluxion
Laugenrückstau *m* backflow of the lye *(in a saliniferous region)*
Laugenzufluß *m* inflow of lye, brine affluent (feeder)
Laugung *f* leaching
~/alkalische carbonate leaching
~/bakterielle bacterial leaching
~/karbonatische carbonate leaching
~ mit Lösungsmittel solvent leaching
~/natürliche natural percolation
~/saure acid leaching
Laugungsmittel *n* lixiviant, leaching agent
Laumontit *m* laumontite, leonhardite, lomonite, $Ca[AlSi_2O_6]_2 \cdot 4H_2O$
Laurdalit *m* laurdalite *(nepheline syenite)*
Laurentium *n* Laurentium *(Precambrian in North America)*
Laurionit *m* laurionite, $PbOHCl$
Laurit *m* laurite, RuS_2
Laurvigit *m*, **Laurvikit** *m* laurvigite, laurvikite *(alkaline syenite)*
Lausenit *m* lausenite, $Fe[SO_4]_3 \cdot 6H_2O$
Lautarit *m* lautarite, $Ca(JO_3)_2$
Lautit *m* lautite, $CuAsS$
Lava *f* lava
~/aus lavatic
~/ausfließende effluent (outpouring, issuing) lava

Lava

~/eindringende intruding (invading) lava
~/erstarrte solidified (consolidated) lava
~/geschrammte grooved lava
~/schlackige scorified lava
~/tauförmig ausgezogene ropelike lava
~/zähflüssige viscous lava
lavaartig lav[at]ic
Lavaasche f accessory ash
Lavaausbruch m lava eruption
Lavaausfluß m effusion (outflow) of lava
~/subterminaler subterminal outflow of lava
~/terminaler superfluent lava flow, summit overflow of lava
Lavaauswurf m projection (protrusion) of lava
Lavaball m s. Lavabombe
Lavabaum m lava tree [mould, cast]
Lavablasen fpl lava blisters
Lavabombe f lava bomb, pseudobomb, floatation bomb
Lavadecke f lava sheet
Lavadom m lava dome (tumefaction, cupola)
Lavadorn m lava (volcanic) spine, monolith, obelisk
Lavaeinlagerung f rib of lava
Lavaerguß m/unterirdischer interfluent lava flow
Lavafeld n lava plain (plateau, field)
Lavaflatschen m lump (blob) of slag
Lavaflut f lava flood
Lavafontäne f lava fountain
Lavagestein n lava stone
Lavahöhle f lava cave[rn]
Lavaklumpen m lump (clot) of lava
Lavakruste f lava crust
~/erhärtete rigid lava crust
Lavakugel f lava ball
Lavamantel m coating of lava
Lavamurgang m hot lahar
Lavaorgel f lava colonnade
Lavapfropfen m lava plug
Lavarippe f levee (of lava)
Lavaschornstein m blowing cone, driblet cone (spire), spiracle, hornito
Lavaschrammen fpl lava scratches
Lavasee m lava lake, fire pit
Lavastalagmit m lava spine
Lavastrom m lava stream (river, flow), volcanic flow
Lavastücke npl fragments of lava
Lavaträne f lava tear, tear-shaped bomb
Lavatunnel m lava tunnel
Lavendulan m lavendulane, $(Ca, Na)_2Cu_5[(Cl|AsO_4)_4] \cdot 4-5H_2O$
Låvenit m låvenite, la[a]venite, $(Na, Ca, Mn)_3Zr[(F, OH, O)_2|Si_2O_7]$
Lavierung f hachuring; hill shading (in topographic maps)
Lawine f avalanche, snowslide, snowslip
~ aus verschiedenen Schneesorten combination avalanche
Lawinenbahn f avalanche (snowslide) track
Lawinendach n, Lawinengalerie f avalanche roof

Lawinengasse f s. Lawinenbahn
Lawinengraben m avalanche trench (chute)
Lawinenmoräne f avalanche moraine
Lawinenschutt m avalanche debris
Lawinenschutzmauer f avalanche baffle works
Lawinenwind m avalanche wind (blast)
Lawrencit m lawrencite, $FeCl_2$
Lawrowit m lawrowite (variety of diopside)
Lawsonit m lawsonite, $CaAl_2[(OH)_2|SiO_7] \cdot H_2O$
Lazarevicit m lazarevicite, Cu_3AsS_4
Lazulith m lazulite, blue (azure) spar, $(Mg, Fe^{...})Al_2[OH|PO_4]_2$
Leadhillit m leadhillite, $Pb_4[(OH)_2|SO_4|(CO_3)_2]$
Leben n im marinen Milieu halobios
~/tierisches animal life
lebend/in Nähe des Tiefseebodens engybenthic
~/in O_2-armem Milieu microaerophil
~/noch heute extant
Lebendform f live form
Lebendstellung f life position (biostratinomy)
Lebensdauer f lifetime
~ einer Sonde well life
~/geologische geological (stratigraphic) range (of a fossil)
Lebensform f life form
Lebensgemeinschaft f bioc[o]enosis, biocenose, biologic[al] association (community), symbiosis, life community
Lebenslauf m/geochemischer geochemical course of life
Lebensraum m life district (realm)
Lebensspur f trace of life; animal trail
Lebenszeit f lifetime, life duration
Leberkies m liver pyrite, hepatitic marcasite
Leberopal m s. Menilit
Leberstein m hepatite
Lebertorf m black glossy fuel peat
Lebewelt f einer Region biota
Lebewesen n living being
Lebewesen npl/koloniebildende colonial organisms
Lechatelierit m lechatelierite, SiO_2
Lecontit m lecontite, $(Na, NH_4, K)_2SO_4 \cdot 2H_2O$
Lectostratotyp m lectostratotype
Lectotypus m lectotype
Léd[ien] n, Lédium n Lédian [Stage] (of Eocene in the Belgian basin)
Leeblatt n foreset bed
Leeblattschichtung f/zusammengesetzte compound foreset bedding
Leehang m lee[ward] slope, downstream slope
Leeküste f lee shore
leer empty, hollow
leerpumpen to pump off
leerschöpfen/eine Bohrung to bail out a well
Leerstelle f vacancy (within a crystal lattice)
Leeschicht f foreset bed
Leeseite f lee[ward] side, downwind side
Leeufer n lee shore
Legende f legend

Lesestein

Lehiit m lehiite,
  $Na_2Ca_5Al_8[(OH)_{12}|(PO_4)_8] \cdot 6H_2O$
Lehm m loam
~/**fetter** heavy loam
~/**harter** clunch (clod) clay
~/**klebriger** lute
~/**leichter** silt loam to silt
~/**lockerer** mellow loam
~/**mergeliger** marl loam
~ **mit Trocknungsrissen** mud-cracked loam
~/**sandiger** paddy field soil
~/**sandig-toniger** sandy clay loam
~/**schiefriger** bind, bina
~/**schluffiger** silt loam
~/**schluffig-toniger** silty clay loam
~/**toniger** medium silt
Lehmbildung f loam formation
Lehmboden m loamy soil (ground)
~/**sandiger** argillaceous sand ground
Lehmerde f fat clay
Lehmgrube f loam pit
lehmhaltig clayey
lehmig loamy; muddy
Lehmwüste f loamy desert
Lehne f ramp
Leibeshöhle f coelenteron
Leiche f carcass
Leichenfeld n churchyard
leicht/sehr very slight *(2nd stage of the scale of seismic intensity)*
Leichtbenzin n casing-head gasoline
leichtflüchtig easily volatilized
leichtflüssig free-flowing
Leichtmineral n light[-weight] mineral
leichtschmelzbar easily fusible
Leidleit m leidleite *(vitreous variety of dacite)*
Leifit m leifite, $Na_2(F, OH, H_2O)_{1-2}[(Al, Si)Si_5O_{12}]$
Leightonit m leightonite,
  $K_2Ca_2 2Cu[SO_4]_4 \cdot 2H_2O$
leimig sticky
Leiste f ridge *(palaeontology)*
leistenförmig lath-shaped, lathlike
Leistungsabfallkurve f drawdown curve
Leistungsfähigkeit f deliverability *(of a gas well)*
Leistungsplan m/**technischer** technical and economical plan of geological exploration
Leistungsspektrum n power spectrum
Leitbank f key layer
Leiter m/**elektrischer** conductor of electricity
Leitergang m ladder lode (vein)
Leitfähigkeit f conductivity, conducting power, conductance
~/**asymmetrische** unilateral conductance
~/**hydraulischer** hydraulic conductivity
~/**kapillare** capillary conductivity
~/**magnetische** permeance
~/**spezifische** specific conductivity *(of a water-bearing bed)*
~/**spezifische elektrische** specific electrical conductance

~/**ungesättigte** unsaturated conductivity
Leitfähigkeitsgrenze f conductivity horizon
Leitfähigkeitsmessung f conductivity logging, conductimetry
Leitflöz n leading (marker, guide) seam
Leitform f key (type) form
Leitformation f key formation
Leitfossil n leading (key, type, index, dominant, guide) fossil
Leitgang m/**erzfreier** indicator vein
Leitgeschiebe n indicator stone
Leitgestein n key rock
Leitgesteinsbank f key layer
~/**dolomitische** S-dolostone
~/**kieselige** S-chert
Leithorizont m marker, marker (key) bed, stratigraphic[al] level, lithostratigraphic[al] horizon
~/**lithologischer** lithologic key bed
Leitmineral n index (guide, typomorphic) mineral
Leitmineralanalyse f index mineral analysis
Leitpflanze f indicator plant
Leitprobe f standard sample
Leitrohr n surface casing, guide column
Leitrohrtour f conductor (surface) string, conductor pipe
~ **für die Verbindung Bohrinsel-Meeresboden** riser
Leitschicht f s. Leithorizont
Leitstern m lodestar, load star
Leitung f 1. s. Leithorizont; 2. conduction
Leitungsgraben m ditch for conduits
Leitungsrohr n line pipe
Leitungsvermögen n s. Leitfähigkeit
Leitungswasser n tap water
Leitverbindungen fpl/**biologische** biological markers
Lemniskate f lemniscate
Lendenwirbel m lumbar vertebra
Lengenbachit m lengenbachite, $7PbS \cdot 2As_2S_3$
lentikular lenticular *(s.a. linsenförmig)*
Lentikulargang m wavy (beaded) vein
Lentikulartextur f lenticular texture
~/**mit senkundärer** neolensic
Leonard[ium] n Leonardian [Stage] *(of Lower Permian)*
Leonit m leonite, $MgSO_4 \cdot K_2SO_4 \cdot 4H_2O$
Leopardit m leopardite *(variety of quartz porphyry)*
lepidoblastisch lepidoblastic
Lepidokrokit m lepidocrocite, needle ironstone, goethite, α-FeOOH
Lepidolith m lepidolite, lithionite, lithiamica, $KLi_2Al[F, OH)_2|Si_4O_{10}]$
Lepidomelan m lepidomelane *(iron-rich biotite)*
Leptinit m leptynite *(metamorphic rock)*
Leptit m leptite
Lermontovit m lermontovite, (U, Ca, Ce...)$_3[PO_4]_4 \cdot 6H_2O$
Leseberge pl picked deads, pickings
Lesestein m fragment of bedrock, float [mineral, ore], boulder

13*

Lesetisch

Lesetisch *m* sorting (picking) table
Lestiwarit *m* lestivarite *(syenite aplite)*
Letovicit *m* letovicite, $(NH_4)_3H[SO_4]_2$
Lette *f* lean (plastic) clay, loam, clay, argil
~/**bunte** varicoloured clay
~/**eisenschüssige** ferriferous clay
~/**harte** clod clay
~/**ockerhaltige** gossaniferous clay
~/**weiche** flucan, pug
Letten *m s.* Lette
Lettenbesatz *m* clay stemming
Lettenbesteg *m* gouge [clay], clay gouge (course, wall, parting), selvage, flucan, pug
lettenhaltig clayey
Lettenkluft *f s.* Lettenbesteg
Lettensalband *n* flookan course *(s.a.* Lettenbesteg)
lettig clayey, clayish, lettenlike, loamy
leuchtend luminous
Leuchtkraft *f* luminosity
Leuchtöl *n* illuminating oil, kerosene
Leuchtschirm *m* fluorescent screen
Leucit *m s.* Leuzit
Leukochalcit *m s.* Olivenit
Leukogranit *m* leucogranite
leukokrat leucocratic
Leukophan *m* leucophanite, $(Ca, NaH)_2Be[Si_2O_6(OH, F)]$
Leukophoenicit *m* leucophoenicite, $Mn_5(MnOH)_2(SiO_4)_3$
Leukophosphit *m* leucophosphite, $K(Fe, Al)_2[OH|(PO_4)_2] \cdot 2H_2O$
Leukophyr *m* leucophyre *(variety of diabase)*
Leukosaphir *m* leucosapphire, white sapphire
Leukosom *n* leucosome
Leukosphenit *m* leucosphenite, $Ba(Na, Ca)_4Ti_3[BO_3|Si_8O_{24}]$
Leukoxen *m* leucoxene *(aggregate of Ti-minerals)*
Leuzit *m* leucite, white garnet, $K[AlSi_2O_6]$
leuzitähnlich leucitic
Leuzitbasanit *m* leucite basanite *(rock of the alkali gabbro clan)*
leuzitführend leucitic
Leuzitgestein *n* leucitic rock *(rock of the alkali gabbro clan)*
Leuzitit *m* leucitite, $K[AlSi_2O_6]$
Leuzitophyr *m* leucitophyre *(rock of the alkali gabbro clan)*
Leuzittephrit *m* leucite tephrite *(rock of the alkali gabbro clan)*
Leuzittrachyt *m* leucite trachyte, amphegenyte *(rock of the alkali gabbro clan)*
Leuzituff *m* pozzuolana
Leverett-Funktion *f* Leverett function
Levyn *m* levynite, $Ca[Al_2Si_4O_{12} \cdot 6H_2O$
Lewisit *m* lewisite, $(Ca, NaH)Sb_2O_6(O, OH, F)$
Lewistonit *m* lewistonite *(variety of apatite)*
Lherzolit *m* lherzolite *(variety of peridotite)*
Liard *n* Liardian *(Ladinian, North America)*
Lias *m s.* Jura/Schwarzer
Liaskalk *m* Lias Limestone

Liasscholle *f* Liassic block
liassisch Liassic
Libelle *f* bubble, level *(geodesy)*
Libethenit *m* libethenite, $Cu_2(OH)PO_4$
Libration *f* lunar libration
Licht *n*/**auffallendes** reflected (impinging) light
~/**durchfallendes** transmitted light, transparency
~/**durchfallendes, polarisiertes** transmitted polarized light
~/**polarisiertes** polarized light
~/**reflektiertes** reflected light
~/**unpolarisiertes** unpolarized (ordinary, plane) light
~/**zirkular polarisiertes** circularly polarized light
~/**zurückgestreutes** backscattered light
Lichtbeugung *f* diffraction of light
lichtbrechend refractive, refracting, refringent
Lichtbrechung *f* refraction of light, optical refraction
lichtdurchlässig diaphanous; translucent
Lichtdurchlässigkeit *f* diaphaneity; translucence, translucency
Lichtgeschwindigkeit *f* light velocity (speed)
Lichthof *m* halo
Lichthofbildung *f* halo formation
Lichtjahr *n* light year
Lichtkreis *m* **der Sonne** photosphere
Lichtlinie *f* light line
~/**Beckesche** Becke line
Lichtlot *n* electric light gauge, ammeter, light plumb line *(for ground-water level measurement)*
Lichtmikroskop *n* light[-optical] microscope, optical microscope
Lichtnebel *m* nebulous fog, luminous haze, haze of light
Lichtspiel *n* **der Augensteine** chatoyancy
Lichtstrahl *m* light ray
~/**einfallender** luminous incident ray
Lichtstreuung *f* light scatter
lichtundurchlässig opaque [to light]
Lichtundurchlässigkeit *f* opaqueness [to light]
Lido *n* offshore bar, offshore (barrier) beach, beach sand barrier
Liebigit *m* liebigite, $Ca_2[UO_2|(CO_3)_3] \cdot 10H_2O$
Liegemarke *f* repose imprint *(of an animal)*
liegen/zutage to outcrop
liegend/darüber superjacent
~/**darunter** subjacent
~/**nahe der Küste** sublittoral
Liegenddurchbruch *m* floor breaking
Liegenden von / im underlain by, situated below
~ **zum Hangenden/vom** from bottom to top
Liegendes *n* subjacent bed, underlying bed (stratum), lying (bottom) wall, bottom rock, seat, underwall, footwall, ledger wall, floor *(e.g. of a seam)*
~ **eines Flözes** seat rock (stone)

~ **eines Ganges** heading side (wall)
~/**nichtstandhaftes** false floor
Liegendfläche f einer sedimentären Schicht sole
Liegendflöz n underseam
Liegendgestein n basement rock
Liegendgrundwasserleiter m lower aquifer
Liegendgruppe f floor group
Liegendkohle f ground coal
Liegendschicht f s. Liegendes
Liegendscholle f lower block, underside
~/**überschobene** overridden mass
Liegendsperre f seat seal
Liegendton m sods
Liegendverhalten n floor behaviour
Liegendwasser n bottom (lower) water
Ligament n ligament *(palaeontology)*
~/**äußeres** external ligament
~/**inneres** internal ligament
Ligamentfalte f ligamental inflection *(molluscans)*
Lignit m brown coal; xyloid brown coal; *(Am)* lignite
lignitartig ligneous
lignitisch lignitic
lignitisieren to lignitize
Lignitisierung f lignitization, lignification
Lignitkohle f s. Lignit
Likasit m likasite, $Cu_6[(OH)_7|(NO_3)_2|PO_4]$
Lillianit m lillianite, $3PbS \cdot Bi_2S_3$
Limanküste f liman coast
Limburgit m limburgite *(rock of the ultramafic clan)*
Limnimeter n limnimeter, limnometer, water level gauge
limnisch limn[et]ic, limnal
limno-aphotisch limno-aphotic
limno-biotisch limno-biotic
limnogen limnogenic
Limnologe m limnologist
Limnologie f limnology
limnologisch limnologic[al]
Limnoplankton n limnoplankton
limno-terrestrisch limno-geotic
Limonit n limonite, xanthosiderite, $FeOOH \cdot nH_2O$
~/**autochthoner** indigenous limonite
limonitisch limonitic
limonitisieren to limonitize
Limonitisierung f limonitization
Limurit m limurite *(metasomatite with axinite)*
Linarit m linarite, $PbCu[(OH)_2|SO_4]$
Lindackerit m lindackerite, $(Cu, H_2)_3[AsO_4]_2 \cdot 4H_2O$
Lindgrenit m lindgrenite, $Cu_3[OH|MoO_4]_2$
Lindströmit m lindstromite, lindströmite, $2PbS \cdot Cu_2S \cdot 3Bi_2S_3$
Lineament n lineament, geosuture
Lineamenttektonik f lineageny
linear linear
Linear n linear
Linearbeiwert m linear coefficient
Lineareruption f linear eruption

Linearprojektion f linear projection
Linearschieferung f linear cleavage
Linearstreckung f s. Lineation
Lineation f lineation, linear parallelism, stretching
~ **auf der Schichtunterseite** substratal lineation
Liner m liner
~ **mit Lochöffnungen** screen liner
~ **mit Schlitzöffnungen** slotted liner
~/**präperforierter** preperforated liner
Linerhänger m liner hanger
Linguoidrippeln fpl linguoid ripple marks
Linie f line, curve
~/**Beckesche** Becke line
~/**deklinationslose** isogonic zero line
~ **des gleichzeitigen Schalleintritts des ersten Donners** isobront
~/**eutektische** eutectic curve
~/**geschlossene** closure *(seismics)*
~ **gleichen artesischen Drucks** isopiestic line
~ **gleichen Bedeckungsgrads des Himmels** isoneph
~ **gleichen C-Gehalts** isocarb line *(in coal seams)*
~ **gleichen Eintritts einer Vegetationsphase** isophene, isophane
~ **gleichen Feuchtigkeitsgehalts** isohume
~ **gleichen Heizwerts** isocal line *(in coal seams)*
~ **gleichen Inkohlungsgrads** isorank line
~ **gleichen Luftdrucks** isobar
~ **gleichen optischen Reflexionsvermögens** isoreflectance line *(coal petrology)*
~ **gleichen reduzierten Luftdrucks** isobar
~ **gleichen Reflexionsvermögens** isoreflectance line *(coal petrology)*
~ **gleichen Salzgehalts** isohaline
~ **gleicher Eisbedeckungsdauer** isopage
~ **gleicher Erdbebenstärke** isoseismal [line]
~ **gleicher Erdbebenzeit** coseismal (coseismic) line
~ **gleicher Erdbodentemperatur** geoisotherm, isogeotherm
~ **gleicher erdmagnetischer Größe** isomagnetic
~ **gleicher erster Eisbildung** isopectic
~ **gleicher Flutzeiten** cotidal line
~ **gleicher Gehalte an flüchtigen Bestandteilen** isovol [line]
~ **gleicher Geschwindigkeit** line of equal rate of flow
~ **gleicher Gesteinsmächtigkeit** isolith, line of aggregate thickness
~ **gleicher Insolation** isohele, isohelic line
~ **gleicher Intensität des erdmagnetischen Feldes** isodynamic line, isogam
~ **gleicher Konzentration** isocon
~ **gleicher Luftdichte** isopycnic, isopycnal
~ **gleicher Lufttemperatur zum gleichen Zeitpunkt** isotherm
~ **gleicher Mächtigkeit** isopach, isopachous line, isopachyte

Linie

~ gleicher magnetischer **Deklination** isogonic line
~ gleicher magnetischer **Inklination** isoclinic line
~ gleicher **Meerestemperatur** isothermobath, isobathytherm, isobathythermal line
~ gleicher **Meerestiefen** bathymetric line
~ gleicher **Mitteltemperatur des kältesten Wintermonats** isocrynal line
~ gleicher **mittlerer Sommertemperatur** isothere
~ gleicher **mittlerer Sonnenscheindauer** isohel
~ gleicher **mittlerer Wintertemperatur** isocheim
~ gleicher **Niederschlagsmenge** isohyet[al]
~ gleicher **Polarlichthäufigkeit** isoaurore, isochasm
~ gleicher **Schichtmächtigkeit** isopach
~ gleicher **Schwere** isogal
~ gleicher **Schwerkraftwerte** isogam
~ gleicher **Strahlungsstärke** isophot[e]
~ gleicher **Strömungsgeschwindigkeit** isotach
~ gleicher **tektonischer Hebung** isobase
~ gleicher **Verdunstung** isoatmic line
~ gleicher **Vereisungsdauer** isopag
~ gleicher **Wassertiefe** isobath
~ **maximaler Geschwindigkeit** line of fastest flow *(flow glaciers)*
~ **maximaler Sedimentation während eines geologischen Zeitabschnitts** depoaxis
~ **mit konstanten Werten** isogram *(of temperature, pressure or rainfall)*
~/**tektonische** tectonic line
Linien *fpl*/**Fraunhofersche** Fraunhofer lines
~/**Hartmannsche (Lüderssche)** Lüders' lines
Linienabtaster *m* **im Bereich des nahen Infrarot** near-infrared scanner
~ **im thermischen Infrarotbereich** thermal-infrared scanner
~/**optisch-mechanischer** optical-mechanical scanner
Linienblitz *m* streak lightning
Linienbö *f* line squall
Linienfluten *n* line flooding
Linienschrift *f* dual polarity display *(seismics)*
Linienschriftspur *f* wiggle trace *(seismics)*
Linienspektrum *n* line spectrum
Linienverschiebung *f* line displacement
linksdrehend levorotatory, levogyrate
Linksdrehsinn *m* sense of left-hand screw motion
Linksdrehung *f* levorotation
Linksquarz *m* levogyrate (left-hand) quartz
Linksspülen *n* reverse circulation *(of drill hole)*
Linneit *m* linnaeite, Co_3S_4
Linse *f* lens *(optics);* lentil *(of rock)*
~/**Bertrandsche** Bertrand lens
~/**kleine** lenticle
~/**langgestreckte** elongated lens
linsenähnlich lenticulated

linsenförmig lenticular, lentiform, lenslike, lens-shaped
Linsengang *m* lenticular (beaded, wavy) vein
Linsengefüge *n* phacoidal structure, beaded texture
Linsenschichtung *f* lenticular bedding
Linsenwolke *f* lenticular cloud
linsig phacoidal
Liparit *m* liparite
Liparitglas *n*/**wasserarmes** lithiodyre
Liparittuff *m* liparite tuff
Liptinit *m* liptinite *(maceral group of brown coals and lignites)*
Liptit *m* liptite *(coal microlithotype)*
Liptobiolithe *mpl* liptobioliths *(coal lithotypes unusually liptinite-rich)*
Liptodetrinit *m* liptodetrinite *(coal maceral)*
Liquation *f* liquation
Liquidierung *f* **einer Bohrung** plugging and abandonment of a well
Lirokonit *m* liroconite, $Cu_2Al[(OH)_4|AsO_4] \cdot 4H_2O$
Liskeardit *m* liskeardite, $Al_2[(OH)_3|AsO_4] \cdot 2^1/_2H_2O$
Listvenit *m* listwanite *(metasomatite)*
Litchfieldit *m* litchfieldite *(nepheline syenite)*
Lithargit *m* lithargite, α-PbO
Lithidionit *m* lithidionite, $(K, Na)_2Cu[Si_3O_7]_2$
Lithifikation *f* lithification, lithifaction
Lithionglimmer *m* lithia mica, lepidolite, lithionite, $KLi_2Al[(F, OH)_2|Si_4O_{10}]$
Lithiophilit *m* lithiophilite, triphyline, $Li(Mn, Fe)PO_4$
Lithiophosphatit *m* lithiophosphatite, $Li_3[PO_4]$
lithisch lithic
Lithium *n* lithium, Li
Lithocalcarenit *m* lithocalcarenite *(sedimentite)*
Lithocalcilutit *m* lithocalcilutite *(sedimentite)*
Lithocalcirudit *m* lithocalcirudite *(sedimentite)*
Lithocalcisiltit *m* lithocalcisiltite *(sedimentite)*
Lithodolarenit *m* lithodolarenite *(sedimentite)*
Lithodololutit *m* lithodololutite *(sedimentite)*
Lithodolorudit *m* lithodolorudite *(sedimentite)*
Lithodolosiltit *m* lithodolosiltite *(sedimentite)*
Lithofazies *f* lithofacies
Lithofazieskarte *f* lithofacies map; lithologic percentage map
lithogen lithogenous, lithogenetic, rockforming
Lithogenese *f* lithogenese, lithogenesis
lithogenetisch *s.* lithogen
Lithogeochemie *f* lithogeochemistry
lithogeochemisch lithogeochemical
Lithografieschiefer *m* lithographic [lime]stone
Lithokalkarenit *m* lithocalcarenite *(sedimentite)*
Lithokalzilutit *m* lithocalcilutite *(sedimentite)*
Lithokalzirudit *m* lithocalcirudite *(sedimentite)*
Lithokalzisiltit *m* lithocalcisiltite *(sedimentite)*
Lithoklase *f* lithoclase
lithoklastisch lithoclastic

Lithologie f lithology
lithologisch lithologic[al], lithic
lithologisch-ökologisch lithological-ecological
lithologisch-paläogeografisch lithological-palaeogeographical
lithophil lithophile, lithophilic, lithophilous
Lithophysen fpl stone bubbles (in magmatic rocks)
Lithosiderit m lithosiderite, stony iron meteorite
Lithosphäre f lithosphere, oxysphere
Lithosphärenplatte f lithospheric plate (slab), slab of lithosphere
~/abtauchende descending slab of lithosphere
lithostatisch lithostatic
Lithostratigrafie f lithostratigraphy
lithostratigrafisch lithostratigraphic[al]
Lithothamnium n lithothamnion
Lithotop n lithotope
Lithotyp m lithotype, rock type; banded ingredient (constituent), zone type
litoral littoral
Litoral n littoral zone
Litoralströmung f shore drift
Li[t]torinatransgression f Lit[t]orina transgression
Li[t]torinazeit f Li[t]torina Time[s] (Holocene)
Liveingit m liveingite, 4PbS · 3As$_2$S$_3$
Livingstonit m livingstonite, HgSb$_4$S$_8$
Lizardit m lizardite (serpentine mineral)
L-Kluft f primary flat joint, L-joint
Llandeilo n Llandeilian [Stage] (of Ordovician)
Llandoverium n, **Llandovery** n Llandovery, Llandoverian [Series, Epoch] (Lower Silurian)
Llanvirn[ium] n Llanvirnian [Stage] (Lower Ordovician)
Loben mpl denticulate (crenated, crenelated, crenulated) lobes (ammonites)
Lobenlinie f lobe (suture, sutural) line, lobed (septal) suture
~/ammonitische ammonitic suture
~/ceratitische ceratitic suture
~/goniatitische goniatitic suture
Lobus m lobe
Loch n/**vorgebohrtes** drilled hole
löcherig pitted
Lochkov[ium] n, **Lochkov-Stufe** f Lochkovian [Stage] (of basal Devonian including the uppermost Silurian)
Lochkrater m pit crater
Lochleibungsdruck m bearing stress
Lochverwitterung f pitted weathering
locker comminuted
Lockerboden m friable soil, hover ground, mantle rock; regolith; sathrolith
Lockergestein n loose (unconsolidated) rock
~/anorganisches inorganic soil
~/organisches organic loose rock
Lockermassen fpl loose masses
Lockermassenausbruch m detritus eruption

Lockermaterial n loose material
Lockerprodukt n loose product
~/pyroklastisches volcanic ejecta
Lockerschnee m loose snow
Lockersediment n loose sediment
Lockersedimente npl/**waschfähige goldführende** wash dirt, washing stuff
Lockerung f loosening
~ des Bodens soil loosening
~ des Gesteinszusammenhalts rock disintegration
Lockport-Dolomit m Lockport Dolomite (basal part of the Lockport Group, North America)
Lockport-Gruppe f Lockport Group (upper Wenlockian to Ludlowian in North America)
Lodranit m lodranite (siderolite)
Loferit m loferite (a carbonate rock)
Löffelbagger m dipper (shovel) dredger, digger
löffeln to bail (drilling engineering)
Löffelprobe f spoon sample
Log n log
Logauswertung f log interpretation
lokal local
Lokalanomalie f local anomaly
Lokalisieren n pinpointing (with great precision)
Lokalmoräne f local moraine
Lokation f location
Löllingit m löllingite, FeAs$_2$
Lomonossowit m lomonossovite, Na$_2$MnTi$_3$[O|Si$_2$O$_7$]$_2$ · 2Na$_3$PO$_4$
longitudinal longitudinal
Longitudinaldüne f sief
Longitudinalwelle f longitudinal (dilatational, compressional, pressure) wave, P-wave
Longobard[ium] n Longobard [Substage] (Middle Triassic, Tethys)
Loparit m loparite, (Na, Ce, Ca)TiO$_3$
Lopezit m lopezite, K$_2$[Cr$_2$O$_7$]
Lopolith m lopolith (funnel intrusion)
Lorandit m lorandite, TlAsS$_2$
Lorenzenit m lorenzenite (variety of ramsayite)
Lorettoit m lorettoite, PbCl$_2$ · 6PbO
lose discrete (gobbet)
lösen/ein Flöz to drain a seam
Lösen n bedding plane (mining)
Löser m plane of separation
Loseyit m loseyite, (Mn, Zn)$_7$[(OH)$_5$ | CO$_3$]$_2$
losgelöst/vom Frost frost-broken, frost-detached
löslich soluble
~/schwer difficultly soluble
Löslichkeit f solubility
Löslichkeitsgrad m degree of solubility
Löslichkeitsprodukt n solubility product
Löslichkeitsverminderung f decrease in solubility
Löslichkeitszunahme f increase in solubility
loslösen to detach
~/sich to break loose
Loslösung f **von Gesteinsteilchen** detachment of rock particles

losreißen

losreißen to pluck out
Löß *m* loess, bluff formation
~ aus Wüstenstaub warm loess
~/glazialen Auswaschungen entstammender cold loess
~/umgelagerter reassorted (reworked) loess
lößähnlich loessoid, loesslike, loessial
lößartig loesslike
Lößboden *m* loess soil
~/fossiler fossil loess soil
Lößdecke *f* loessial cover
Lößgürtel *m* belt of loess
Lößkeil *m* loessial wedge
Lößkindl *n* loess doll (nodule), puppet of loess
Lößlehm *m* loess loam (clay)
~/podsolierter podzolized loess loam
Lößmergel *m* marl loess
Lößpuppe *f s.* Lößkindl
Lößschnecke *f* loess snail
Lößstaub *m* loess dust
Lößsteilufer *n* loess bluff
Lößvorkommen *n* loess deposit
Lösung *f* solution
~/absteigende descending solution
~/äquimolekulare equimolecular solution
~/aufsteigende ascending (rising) solution
~/erzbildende ore-forming solution
~/ideale ideal solution *(hydrochemistry)*
~/Thouletsche Thoulet solution
~/wäßrige aqueous solution
Lösungsbrekzie *f* solution breccia
Lösungseigenschaft *f* solvent property
Lösungsfacetten *fpl* solution facets
Lösungshohlraum *m* solution cavity (opening), vugular pore space
Lösungskraft *f* solvent power
Lösungsmittel *n* solvent
Lösungsmobilisierung *f* solution mobilization
Lösungsnäpfe *mpl* solution hollows
Lösungsporosität *f* solution porosity
Lösungsrippeln *fpl* solution ripples, instratified ribs
Lösungsrückstand *m* solution residue
Lösungsrückstände *mpl* katatectic layer
Lösungsspalte *f* solution fissure
Lösungstätigkeit *f* solvent action
Lösungsumsatz *m* solution transfer
Lot *n* plumb line
Lotablenkung *f,* **Lotabweichung** *f* deflection of the vertical (plumb line)
Lotapparat *m* sounder
loten to sound
Lotgerät *n* sounding device
Lotharingien *n s.* Sinemur
lotrecht vertical, perpendicular, normal, straight down
Lotrit *m* lotrite, $Ca_2(Mg, Fe, Mn, Al)(Al, Fe, Ti)_2[(OH, H_2O)_2|SiO_4|Si_2O_7]$
Lötrohr *n* blowpipe
Lötrohrprobe *f* blowpipe proof (test, assay, analysis)
Lötrohrprobierkunst *f* blowpipe assaying

Lotung *f* sounding
Lotungsanlage *f* sounding device
Lotungslinie *f* sounding line
Lotzeit *f* vertical (two-way travel) time, reflection time [at zero offset]
Louderbackit *m* louderbackite, $Fe(Fe, Al)_2[SO_4]_4 \cdot 14H_2O$
Loughlinit *m* loughlinite, $Na_2Mg_3[(OH)_2|Si_6O_{15}] \cdot 2H_2O + 4H_2O$
Love-Welle *f* Love wave
Löweit *m* loeweite, $Na_{12}Mg_7[SO_4]_{13} \cdot 15H_2O$
Löwigit *m s.* Alunit
Lowozerit *m* lovozerite, $(Na, K)_2(Mn, Ca)ZrSi_6O_{16} \cdot 3H_2O$
Loxoklas *m* loxoclase *(variety of orthoclase)*
Lücke *f* 1. hiatus, cessation, gap; 2. blank *(in the map)*
~ in der Schichtenfolge, ~/stratigrafische stratigraphic gap (hiatus), lost record, cessation of deposition
Lückenwolken *fpl* hiatus clouds
Lud *n* Ludian [Stage] *(of Eocene)*
Ludfordium *n* Ludfordian *(basal stage of Ludlow series)*
Ludien *n,* **Ludium** *n s.* Lud
Ludlamit *m* ludlamite, $Fe_3[PO_4]_2 \cdot H_2O$
Ludlow[ium] *n* Ludlovian [Series, Epoch] *(Upper Silurian)*
Ludwigit *m* ludwigite, $(Mg, Fe)_2Fe[O_2|BO_3]$
Lueshit *m* lueshite, $NaNbO_3$
Luft *f/*staubhaltige dusty (dust-laden) air
~/verunreinigte contaminated air
Luftabschluß *m* exclusion of air
Luftantiklinale *f* aerial anticline
Luftätzung *f* etching by air
Luftaufnahme *f* aerial photograph (survey, view), air photo[graph]
Luftaufnahmeverfahren *npl* aerial methods
Luftbild *n s.* Luftaufnahme
Luftbildauswertung *f* restitution from air photographs
Luftbildgeologie *f* aerology
Luftbildkamera *f* aerial (airborne) camera
Luftbildkarte *f* aerial mosaic, photomap
Luftbildmeßkamera *f* aerial-mapping camera
Luftbildplan *m/*entzerrter rectified photoplane
Luftbildtechnik *f* air photography
Luftbildvermessung *f* air surveying, photographic aerial survey
luftdicht air-tight, air-sealed
Luftdruck *m* air (atmospheric, barometric) pressure
Luftdruckmessung *f* barometry
Luftdruckwelle *f* air wave
Lufteinströmung *f* air ingress
Luftfalte *f* aerial fold
Luftfarbfilm *m* aerial colour film
Luftfeuchte *f.*atmospheric moisture
Luftfeuchtemesser *m* psychrometer
Luftfeuchtigkeit *f* air humidity (moisture)
Luftflimmern *n* terrestrial scintillation
Luftfotografie *f* aerial photography

Luftfotogrammetrie f aerial photogrammetry
Luftgewebe n s. Aerenchym
Luftgewölbe n aerial arch
Lufthaltewert m specific yield
Lufthebebohren n air drilling
Lufthebetest m air lift test
Lufthebeverfahren n air lift
Lufthülle f atmosphere *(of earth)*
Luftkammer f s. Pneumatophor
Luftkartierung f aerial (airplane) mapping
Luftklassierer m air classifier (separator)
Luftleuchten n airglow
Luftlinie f bee-line
Luftlinienentfernung f crow-fly distance
Luftloch n air bump
Luftmantel m layer of air
Luftmasse f air mass
Luftpore f air void
Luftporenanteil m air space ratio
Luftprobenahme f atmosphere sampling
Luftpulser m air gun *(seismics)*
Luftraum m air space
Luftriß m mud crack *(sedimentary fabric)*
Luftsattel m saddle, aerial arch (fold)
Luftsauerstoff m atmospheric oxygen
Luftsäule f air column
Luftschaumschwimmverfahren n air-froth floatation, air-bubble floatation
Luftschicht f air layer (stratum)
Luftschußtechnik f air shooting *(seismics)*
Luftseite f downstream (air-side) face *(of a dam)*
Luftsichtung f air elutriation
Luftspalt m air gap
Luftspülung f air flushing, blowing
Luftstrom m, **Luftströmung** f air current (flow)
Luftstrudel m air eddy
Lufttemperatur f air temperature
Lufttriangulation f aerotriangulation
lufttrocken air-dry
Luftvermessung f air (aerial) surveying
Luftverschmutzung f air pollution
Luftvolumen n air volume
Luftwirbel m air eddy, wind burble
Luftwirbelung f air whirling
Luftwurzel f aerial root
Luftziegel m adobe clay
Luftzirkulation f circulation of the atmosphere
Luftzusammensetzung f atmospheric[al] composition
Luftzutritt m access of air
Lugarit m lugarite *(variety of techenite)*
Luisien n Luisian [Stage] *(marine stage of middle Miocene of North America)*
Lujavrit m lujavrite *(nepheline syenite)*
Lumachelle f lumachelle
~/verfestigte coquinite
Lumachellenkalkstein m coquinoid (biostromal) limestone
Lumbalwirbel m lumbar vertebra
Lumineszenz f luminescence
Lumineszenzanalyse f luminescence analysis

Lumineszenzemission f luminescent emission
Lumineszenzlöschung f luminescence quenching
lumineszieren to luminesce
lumineszierend luminescent
lunar lunar
Lunar... s. Mond...
Lüneburgit m lüneburgite, $Mg_3[(PO_4)_2|B_2O(OH)_4] \cdot 6H_2O$
Lungenfisch m lung fish
Lungenschnecke f air-breathing gastropod
Lunit m *synthetically produced regolith (moon mineral)*
Lupe f magnifier, magnifying glass, hand lens
~/stark vergrößernde high magnifier
Lurche mpl amphibians
Lusakit m lusakite *(variety of staurolite)*
Lusitanien n Lusitanian *(facies of upper Oxford, Swiss Jura)*
Lussatit m lussatite *(chalcedony)*
Lusungit m lusungite, $(Sr,Pb)Fe_3H[(OH)_6|(PO_4)_2]$
Lutalit m lutalite *(variety of leucite nephelinite)*
Lutet n, **Lutétien** n, **Lutetium** n Lutetian [Stage] *(of Eocene)*
lutro s. lufttrocken
Luv f s. Luvseite
Luvblattschichtung f backset bedding (beds)
Luvgraben m current crescent
Luvhang m upstream slope
Luvseite f weather (upwind, windward) side
Luvwirbel m windward eddy
Luxullianit m luxullianite *(tourmaline-granite)*
Luzonit m luzonite, Cu_3AsS_4
Lydit m lydite, touchstone, radiolarian [chert]
Lymnaeazeit f Lymnaea Time *(Holocene)*
Lyndochit m lyndochite *(s.a. Euxenit)*
Lysimeter n lysimeter
Lysimetertechnik f lysimeter technique

M

Mäander m meander
~/abgeschnittener cut-off meander
~/eingeschnittener (eingesenkter) incised (entrenched) meander
~/freier free meander
~ mit Ausgleich zwischen Abtrag und Anlandung forced-cut meander
~/verlassener abandoned meander (loop), false river
Mäanderabschneidung f meander cut-off
Mäanderbildung f meandering
Mäanderdurchbruch m meander cut-off
Mäanderfluß m meandering (snaking) stream
mäanderförmig meandriform
Mäandergürtel m meander belt
Mäanderhals m meander neck
mäandern to meander, to wind about
Mäanderschlinge f meander loop
Mäanderstrom m s. Mäanderfluß
Mäandertal n meandering valley

Mäanderunterschneidung

Mäanderunterschneidung f crescentic wall niche
Mäanderzunge f meander lobe
Maar n maar
Maarsee m maar lake
Maastricht[ien] n, **Maastrichtium** n Maastrichtian *(uppermost stage of Upper Cretaceous)*
Macdonaldit m macdonaldite, $BaCa_4[Si_{15}O_{35}] \cdot 11H_2O$
Maceral n maceral *(coal)*, *(Am)* component, constituent
Maceralbeschreibung f description of the macerals
Maceralgruppe f maceral group
Maceralsubgruppe f maceral subgroup
Macgovernit m macgovernite, $Mn_9Zn_2Mg_4[O|(OH)_{14}|(AsO_4)_2|(SiO_4)_2]$
mächtig thick
Mächtigkeit f thickness, depth
~/**[ab]bauwürdige** minable thickness
~ **der Schicht** thickness of layer (stratum)
~ **des Hangenden** roof thickness
~/**durchschnittliche** average thickness
~/**effektive** net pay thickness
~/**erbohrte** drilled thickness
~/**geringe** slight thickness
~/**horizontale** horizontal thickness
~/**mittlere** average thickness
~/**reduzierte** reduced thickness
~/**scheinbare** apparent thickness
~/**sichtbare** visible thickness
~/**wahre** actual (true) thickness
~/**vertikale** vertical thickness
Mächtigkeitsänderung f variation of thickness
Mächtigkeitsanomalie f thickness anomaly
Mächtigkeitsdifferenz f thickness difference
Mächtigkeitsdifferenzierung f thickness differentiation
Mächtigkeitskarte f isopach map
~ **der Schichten einer stratigrafischen Einheit** isobed map
Mächtigkeitslinie f isopach, line of equal thickness, isopachous line, isopachyte
Mächtigkeitsverlust m loss of thickness
Mächtigkeitsverringerung f convergence *(s.a. Konvergenz)*
Mächtigkeitszunahme f thickening *(of a layer)*; inspissation *(of sediment)*
Mackayit m mackayite, $Fe[TeO_3]_3 \cdot xH_2O$
Mackensit m mackensite *(mineral of the chlorite group)*
Mackintoshit m mackintoshite, $(Th,U)[Si_2O_4,(OH)_4]$
Macrinit m macrinite *(coal maceral)*
Macroit m macroite *(coal microlithotype)*
Madeirit m madeirite *(porphyraceous alkaline picrite)*
Madreporarier npl madreporarians
Madupit m madupite *(ultrapotassic rock)*
Maenit m maenite *(Ca-bearing bostonite)*
mafisch mafic
Mafite mpl mafites

Mafitmineral n dark[-coloured] mineral
Mafurit m mafurite *(olivine leucitite)*
Magadiit m magadiite, $NaSi_7O_{18}(OH)_3 \cdot 3H_2O$
Magallanit m magallanite *(asphaltlike substance)*
Magenstein m gastrolith, gizzard (stomach) stone
mager lean
Magererz n lean ore
Magergas n lean gas
Magerkalk m lean lime
Magerkohle f lean coal; *(Am)* semianthracite
Magerton m lean clay
Maghaemit m maghemite, γ-Fe_2O_3
Magma n magma, flow of rock
~/**anatektisches** anatectic magma
~/**basisches** basic magma
~/**hybrides** hybride magma
~/**juveniles** primitive magma
~/**lunares** lunar magma
~/**nicht differenziertes** primitive magma
~/**palingenes** palingenetic magma
~/**partiell kristallisiertes** crystal mush
~/**primäres** primary magma
~/**schmelzflüssiges** molten magma
~/**sekundäres** secondary magma
~/**sialisches** sialic magma
~/**simatisches** simatic magma
~/**syntektisches** syntectic magma
~/**ursprüngliches** primitive magma
Magmagestein n magmatic rock *(s.a. Magmatit)*
Magmaherd m, **Magmakammer** f magma hearth (focus, chamber), volcanic chamber
Magmanest n pocket of magma
Magmasippe f s. Magmensippe
Magmaspaltung f differentiation of magma
magmatisch magmatic, igneous, ignigenous
Magmatismus m magmatism
~/**initialer** initial phase of magmatism
Magmatit m magmatic rock
~/**fluidalstreifiger** linophyre
magmatogen magmatogene, magmatogenic
Magmawülste mpl wrinkle ridges *(on the moon)*
Magmenderivat n derivative magma
Magmendurchbruch m magmatic extrusion
Magmenerstarrung f consolidation of magma
Magmenherd m s. Magmaherd
Magmenkörper m magmatic body
Magmensippe f magmatic family (series, suite, tribe)
~/**atlantische** Atlantic [alkali-calcic] series (suite)
~/**mediterrane** Mediterranean [alkalic] series (suite)
~/**pazifische** Pacific [calc-alkalic] series (suite)
Magmenspiegel m magmatic level
Magmentektonik f magma tectonics
Magnesia f magnesia, MgO
Magnesiaglimmer m s. Phlogopit
magnesiahaltig magnesian

Magnesiakalk m magnesian limestone
Magnesiasalpeter m nitromagnesite, $Mg(NO_3)_2 \cdot 2H_2O$
Magnesiastäbchen n splinter of magnesia
Magnesiochromit m magn[esi]ochromite, $MgCrO_4$
Magnesio-Copiapit m magnesiocopiapite, $MgFe_4(SO_4)_6(OH)_2 \cdot 20H_2O$
Magnesioferrit m magn[esi]oferrite, $MgFeO_4$
Magnesiokatophorit m magnesiokatophorite, $Na_2CaMg_4(Fe, Al)[(OH, F)_2|AlSi_7O_{22}]$
Magnesioludwigit m magnesioludwigite *(variety of ludwigite)*
Magnesioniobit m magnesioniobite, $(Mg,Fe,Mn)(Nb,Ta,Ti)_2O_6$
Magnesioriebeckit m magnesioriebeckite, $Na_2Mg_3Fe_2[(OH, F)|Si_4O_{11}]_2$
Magnesiosussexit m magnesiosussexite *(variety of sussexite)*
Magnesiotriplit m magnesiotriplite *(variety of triplite)*
Magnesit m magnesite, $MgCO_3$
Magnesium n magnesium, Mg
Magnesium-Chlorophoenicit m magnesium-chlorophoenicite, $(Zn, Mn)_5[(OH)_7|AsO_4]$
magnesiumhaltig magnesian
Magnesiumoxid n magnesia, MgO
Magnet m[/natürlicher] magnet
Magnetachse f magnetic axis
Magnetanomalie f magnetic anomaly
Magneteisenerz n, **Magneteisensand** m, **Magneteisenstein** m s. Magnetit
Magnetfänger m fishing magnet
Magnetfeld n magnetic field
~ **der Erde** earth's magnetic field
~/**inhomogenes** inhomogeneous magnetic field
~/**pulsierendes** pulsating magnetic field
~/**sich periodisch umkehrendes** periodically reversing magnetic field
~/**stellares** stellar magnetic field
Magnetfeldwaage f magnetic field balance
Magnetik f magnetics
magnetisch magnetic
~/**schwach** feebly magnetic
~/**stark** strongly magnetic
magnetisieren to magnetize
Magnetisierung f magnetization
~/**bleibende** remanent magnetization, remanence
~/**hysteresefreie** anhysteretic magnetization
~/**remanente** residual magnetization
~/**reverse (umgekehrte)** reverse[d] magnetization
~/**umkehrbare** reversible magnetization
~/**von kleinen Teilchen hervorgerufene** detrital remanent magnetization
Magnetisierungsintensität f intrinsic induction
Magnetisierungsrichtung f direction of magnetization
Magnetismus m magnetism
~/**thermoremanenter** thermoremanent magnetism

Magnetit m magnetite, magnetic (black) iron ore, natural magnet, load stone, lodestone, Fe_3O_4
~/**vulkanischer** iozite
Magnetitskarn m magnetite skarn
Magnetkies m pyrrhotine, pyrrhotite, magnetic pyrites, FeS
Magnetkopf m head
Magnetnadel f magnetic [compass] needle
Magnetometer n magnetometer
~/**astatisches** astatic magnetometer
Magnetoplumbit m magnetoplumbite, $PbO \cdot 6Fe_2O_3$
Magnetopyrit m s. Magnetkies
Magnetosphäre f magnetosphere
Magnetostriktion f magnetostriction
Magnetostriktionsbohren n magnetostrictive drilling
Magnetotellurik f magnetotellurics, magnetotelluric method
Magnetscheider m magnetic [ore] separator
Magnetscheidung f magnetic [ore] separation
Magnitude f magnitude
Magnoferrit m magn[esi]oferrite, $MgFeO_4$
Magnolit m magnolite, $Hg_2[TeO_4]$
Magnophorit m magnophorite *(variety of richterite)*
Magnussonit m magnussonite, $(Mn, Mg, Cu)_5[(OH, Cl)|(AsO_3)_3]$
Mahlen n milling
Mahlkörper m grinding body
Mahlung f grinding
Mäkinemit m mäkinemite, NiSe
Makkalube f mud volcano
Makonit m maconite *(vermiculite)*
makrochemisch macrochemical
Makrochemismus m macrochemism
Makrodoma n macrodome *(crystallography)*
Makrogefüge n macrostructure
Makrointegration f macrointegration
Makrointegriervorrichtung f macrointegrating device
makroklastisch macroclastic
Makroklima n macroclimate, regional climate
Makrokosmos m macrocosm
makrokristallin macrocrystalline
Makrorhythmen mpl macrorhyths *(distance of 35–40 millions of years)*
Makroseismik f macroseismics
makroskopisch macroscopic[al]
Makrospore f macrospore
Malachit m malachite, green carbonate of copper, green copper ore, green mineral, $Cu_2[(OH)_2|CO_3]$
malakofaunistisch malacofaunistic
Malakolith m malacolite *(variety of diopside)*
Malakon m malacon *(variety of zircon)*
Malayait m malayaite, $CaSn[O|SiO_4]$
Malchit m malchite *(lamprophyric dike rock)*
Maldonit m maldonite, Au_2Bi
Malignit m malignite *(nepheline syenite)*
Malinowskit m malinowskite *(variety of tetrahedrite)*

Malladrit 204

Malladrit m malladrite, Na_2SiF_6
Mallardit m mallardite, $MnSO_4 \cdot 7H_2O$
Malm m s. Jura/Weißer
Maltesit m s. Chiastolith
Malthait m maltha, pittasphalt, sea wax
Mammalia pl, **Mammalier** pl mammal[ian]s
Mammut n mammoth
~/wollhaariges hairy mammoth
Mammutgehalt m extreme contents (capacity)
Mammutpumpe f mammoth pump
Mammutstoßzahn m mammoth tusk
Manandonit m manandonite, $LiAl_2[(OH)_2|AlBSi_2O_{10}]Al_2(OH)_6$
Manasseit m manasseite, $Mg_6Al_2[(OH)_{16}|CO_3] \cdot 4H_2O$
Mandel f amygdule, amygdale, geode
mandelartig amygdaline
Mandeleinschluß m amygdular inclusion
mandelförmig amygdaloidal, almond-shaped
Mandelfüllung f amygdaloidal infilling
Mandelgestein n, **Mandelstein** m amygdaloid, amygdaloidal rock, amandola
mandelsteinartig amygdaloidal
Mandeltextur f amygdaloidal texture
Mandibel f mandible, jaw
Mandibularfurche f mandibular groove
Mandschurit m mandshurite (nepheline basanite)
Mangan n manganese, Mn
Mangan-Alluaudit m manganalluaudite, $Na(Mn, Fe)[PO_4]$
Mangananreicherung f enrichment of manganese
Mangan-Berzeliit m manganberzeliite, $(Ca, Na)_3(Mn, Mg)_2[AsO_4]_3$
Manganblende f alabandine, alabandite, MnS
Mangandendrit m dendritic[al] manganese
Manganeisen n manganous iron
Manganeisenerz n manganiferous iron ore
Manganepidot m s. Piemontit
Manganerz n manganese ore
Mangangranat m s. Spessartin
manganhaltig manganous, manganiferous, manganese-bearing
Mangan-Hörnesit m manganhoernesite, $(Mn, Mg)_3[AsO_4]_2 \cdot 8H_2O$
Manganit m manganite, grey manganese, γ-MnOOH
Manganknolle f manganese nodule, manganese-rich pellet
~ des Ozeanbodens ocean-floor manganese nodule
Manganknollenlagerstätte f nodular manganese deposit
Manganolangbeinit m manganolangbeinite, $K_2Mn_2(SO_4)_3$
Manganomelan m manganomelane, MnO_2 (amorphous)
Manganoniobit m manganoniobite, $(Mn,Fe)Nb_2O_6$
Manganophyllit m manganophyllite (a manganiferous biotite)

Manganosit m manganosite, MnO
Manganostibiit m manganostibiite, $8(Mn, Fe)O \cdot Sb_2O_5$
Manganotantalit m manganotantalite, $(Mn, Fe)Ta_2O_6$
Manganschaum m bog manganese
Manganschiefer m manganese slate
Manganschwärze f s. Wad
Manganspat m manganese (rose) spar, rhodochrosite, dialogite, $MnCO_3$
Manganspinell m galaxite, $MnAl_2O_4$
Mangerit m mangerite
Mangrovenboden m mangrove soil
Mangrovensumpf m mangrove marsh
Mangroventorf m mangrove peat
Manjak m manjak (asphalt)
Mann m/**Alter** goaf, abandoned workings, old excavation
Mansfieldit m mansfieldite, $Al[AsO_4] \cdot 2H_2O$
Mantel m mantle; surrounding rock (of a roadway)
Mantelbucht f pallial sinus (palaeontology)
Manteldruck m surface pressure; peripheral (lateral) pressure
Manteldruckfestigkeit f strength under peripheral pressure
Mantelfläche f outer surface (of a cylinder)
Mantelkurve f envelope curve
Mantellinie f pallial (mantle) line (molluscans)
~/integripalliate entire pallial line
Mantelrohr n outer core barrel
Mantelsinus m pallial sinus (palaeontology)
Mäot n Maot (part of the Pontian in USSR)
Marahunit m marahunite (boghead formation in the brown coal stage)
Marcellus-Schiefer mpl Marcellus Shales (middle Devonian of North America)
Mare n mare (moon or Mars)
Maregesteine npl mare rocks (moon)
Marestadium n mare stage (of the moon)
Margarit m margarite, pearl (brittle) mica, $CaAl_2(OH)_2[Si_2Al_2O_{10}]$
Margarosanit m margarosanite, $Pb(Ca, Mn)_2[Si_3O_9]$
marginal marginal
Marialith m marialite, $Na_8[Cl_2, SO_4, CO_3]|(AlSi_3O_8)_6]$
Marienglas n gypseous spar, sparry (specular) gypsum, selenite
marin marine
Mariposit m mariposite (variety of phengite)
Mariupolit m mariupolite (albite nepheline syenite)
Markasit m marcasite, cellular (white iron, radiated) pyrite, FeS_2
~/massiger liver pyrite
Marke f mark; surface (bedding plane) marking; gap (of a seismogram)
Markierer mpl/**biologische** biological markers
Markierung f marking; tracing; labelling (of water)
~/dendritische dendritic[al] marking

~ mit radioaktiven Isotopen *s.* ~/radioaktive
~/radioaktive radioactive labelling [process], radioactive tracing
~/vorübergehende stake *(seismics)*
Markscheide *f* boundary [line], border [of a claim]
Markscheidegerät *n* mining survey instrument
Markscheidekunde *f,* **Markscheidekunst** *f* [mine] surveying, mining goedesy
markscheiden to survey underground, to adjoin, to dial
Markscheiden *n* underground surveying
Markscheider *m* surveyor [of mines], underground surveyor, bounder
Markscheidearbeiten *fpl* mine surveying
Markscheiderei *f* mine surveying
Markscheidergehilfe *m* deputy surveyor
Markscheiderriß *m* plot of a mine
Markscheidesicherheitspfeiler *m* boundary pillar
Markscheidewesen *n s.* Markscheidekunde
Markscheidezug *m* dialling
Markstrahlen *mpl* medullary rays *(wood)*
Marmor *m* marble
~/bunter fancy marble
~/dichter polierfähiger compact polishable limestone
~/kalksilikatischer calc-silicate marble, calciphyre
~/schwarzer jet
marmorartig marbled, marmoraceous, marmoreal, marblelike
Marmorbruch *m* marble quarry
Marmorfolge *f* marble series
Marmorgips *m* alum-soaked Keene's cement
marmoriert marbled, mottled, veined
Marmorierung *f* marbling, mottling
marmorisieren to marmorize
Marmorisierung *f* marmarosis, marmorosis, marmorization
Marmorkalk *m* marble lime
Marmorplatte *f* marble slab
Marmorsteinbruch *m* marble quarry
Marokit *m* marokite, $CaMn_2O_4$
Maronage *f* surface crazing, *(Am)* map cracking
Marosit *m* marosite *(variety of shonkinite)*
Marrit *m* marrite, $PbAgAsS_3$
Marsch *f* marsh, estuarine (low-lying) flat, low meadow, shore moorland
~/eingedeichte diked marsh (land)
Marschboden *m* marshy soil
Marschenton *m* marine clay
Marschheide *f* lande
Marschinsel *f* marsh island
Marschland *n* bog land, fen[land]
~/eingedeichtes polder
Marshit *m* marshite, CuJ
Marskanäle *mpl* Martian canals, canals of Mars
Marsmonde *mpl* Martian moons
Marsupialier *pl* marsupials, marsupial mammals

Martinit *m* martinite *(variety of whitlockite)*
Martit *m* martite *(pseudomorphous hematite after magnetite)*
Martitisierung *f* martitization
Mascagnit *m* mascagnite, $(NH_4)_2[SO_4]$
Maschentextur *f* mesh (netted) texture, reticulated structure; beam texture *(in serpentine)*
Maschinenhaus *n* engine and pump housing
Maschinenmonat *m* rig-month
Maschinenschicht *f* rig-shift
Maschinenstunde *f* rig-hour
Maskelynit *m* maskelynite *(a bywtonite melted to glass)*
Masrit *m* masrite *(Mn-Co-bearing pickeringite)*
Maß *n* 1. measure; 2. gauge
Maßanalyse *f* measure (volumetric) analysis, analysis by measure
Masse *f* mass, block, massif *(s.a.* Massiv*)*
~/kritische critical mass
~/stationäre stationary (steady) mass
~/träge inertial mass
~/überschobene overthrust mass
~/wurzellose aberrant mass *(tectonics)*
Massebilanz *f* material balance
Masseeinheit *f* mass unit
Massekonzentration *f* concentration of mass, mass concentration
Masseleisen *n* pig-iron
Massenanziehung *f/***allgemeine** universal gravitation
Massenausgleich *m/***isostatischer** isostatic mass compensation
Massenbewegung *f* mass movement
Massendefekt *m* mass defect, crustal unloading *(gravimetry)*
Massendefizit *n* mass deficiency *(gravimetry)*
Massenelement *n* mass element
Massengestein *n* compact[ed] rock, unstratified rock
Massenkalk *m* compact[ed] limestone, massive limestone
Massenkonzentration *f* mascon *(on the moon)*
Massenkorrektur *f* mass correction *(gravimetry)*
Massenprobe *f* bulk sample
Massenselbstbewegung *f s.* Massenbewegung
Massenspektrograf *m* mass spectrograph
Massenspektrogramm *n* mass spectrogram
Massenspektrometer *n* mass spectrometer
Massenspektrometrie *f* mass spectrometry
massenspektrometrisch mass spectrometric
Massenspektroskopie *f* mass spectroscopy
Massenstörung *f* derangement of masses
Massenströmung *f* mass flow
Massentransport *m* mass transport
Massenüberschiebung *f* mass thrust
Massenüberschuß *m* mass excess (surplus), crustal accumulations *(isostasy)*
Massenverschiebung *f* mass shift[ing]
Massenwert *m* mass value

Massenwertskala

Massenwertskala f mass value scale
Massenzahl f mass number
Massicot[it] m massicot[ite], plumbic ochre, PbO
massig massive
Massigkeit f massiveness
massiv massive
Massiv n massif
~/altes oldland
~/Armorikanisches Armorican massif
~/autochthones autochthonous massif
~/Böhmisches Bohemian massif
~/Brabanter Brabant massif
~/Lausitzer Lusatian massif
~/Rheinisches Rhenish massif
Massivbetonmauer f massive concrete dam
Massive npl/starre rigid (resistant) masses
Massivität f compactness
Maßstab m scale
~/verkleinerter reduced scale
~/verzerrter non-uniform scale division
Maßsystem n system of measurement
Material n/alluviales fill
~/angeschwemmtes drifted (washed-up) material
~/anstehendes in-place material, in-situ material
~/ausgeschleudertes vulkanisches clinker
~/diskontinuierlich abgestuftes gap-graded material
~/feuerfestes refractory
~/loses incoherent material
~/pulvriges fines (of ore)
~/spannungsoptisches photoelastic material
~/suspendiertes material in suspension
~/unkonsolidiertes pyroklastisches volcanic debris (rubble)
Materialbilanz f regimen
Materialbilanzmethode f material balance method
Materialwanderung f s. Stoffwanderung
Materie f matter
~/anorganische inorganic matter
~/fossile organische fossil organic matter
~/intergalaktische intergalactic matter
~/interstellare interstellar matter
~/kosmische cosmic matter
~/lebende living matter
~/leuchtende luminous matter
~/organische organic matter
Matildit m matildite (s.a. Schapbachit)
Matlockit m matlockite, PbFCl
Matratzenlava f pillow (cushion) lava
Matrix f ground mass
Matsch m sludge
matschig sludgy
matt 1. dull; lacklustre; 2. irrespirable (mine damp)
Mattbraunkohle f lignite; subbituminous coal (stage C); dull brown coal
Matteuccit m matteuccite, $NaH[SO_4] \cdot H_2O$
Mattglanz m dull lustre
Mattkohle f durain; dull coal
Mattschliff m frosting
Mattstreifenkohle f clarain; dull banded coal
Maturität f maturity
Maucherit m maucherite, Ni_3As_2
Mauerdamm m masonry dam
Maufit m maufite, $(Mg, Fe, Ni)Al_3[(OH)_8|AlSi_3O_{10}]$
Maulwurfdränage f mole drainage
Maulwurfpflug m mole plow
Mauzeliit m mauseliite, romeite, $(Ca, NaH)Sb_2O_6(O, OH, F)$
Maximalwert m des Variogramms sill of variogram, sill variance (value) (of a variogram)
Maximalwertigkeit f maximum valence
Maximum n des Eisvorstoßes glacial maximum
Mayenit m mayenite, $12CaO \cdot 7Al_2O_3$
Mazapilit m mazapilite (arseniosiderite)
Mazedonit m macedonite (olivine-bearing trachyte)
Mazeral n s. Maceral
Mazerierung f maceration
McAllisterit m mcallisterite, $Mg[B_6O_9(OH)_2] \cdot 6^1/_4 H_2O$
Mckelveyit m mckelveyite, $(Na, Ba, Ca, Y, SE, U)_9[CO_3]_9 \cdot 5H_2O$
mechanisch mechanical
Median m median grain size
Medianlobus m median lobe
Medina n, Medinien n Medinian, Oswegan (lower Llandovery in North America)
Medium n/dispergierendes dispersive medium
~/elastisches elastic medium
~/mehrschichtiges multilayered medium
~/transportierend-sedimentäres transporting-sedimentary medium
~/unelastisches anelastic medium
Meer n 1. sea, ocean; 2. mare (of the moon)
~ mit Gezeiten tidal sea
~/transgredierendes transgressing (encroaching) sea
Meerbusen m gulf, bay
~/ins Land eingreifender reach
Meereis n sea (field) ice
Meerenge n strait, narrows, sea gate
Meeresablagerung f marine deposit
Meeresarm m arm of the sea, [sea] inlet
Meeresbecken n sea basin
Meeresbergbau m marine mining
Meeresboden m sea (ocean) bottom, ocean floor
~ ohne unverfestigte Sedimentdecke hard bottom
Meeresbohranlage f offshore oil rig
Meeresbohrung f subsea drilling
Meeresbrandung f surf
Meeresbucht f gulf, bay
Meeresdeich m sea dike
Meereseinbruch m invasion of the sea, marine invasion

~ in Grabenbruchzonen fault embayment
Meeresforschung f oceanology; oceanography; marine research
Meeresgebiet n sea area
Meeresgeologie f marine geology
meeresgeologisch marine-geological
Meeresgrund m sea bottom, ocean floor
Meereshöhe f absolute altitude
Meereskunde f oceanography
meereskundlich oceanologic[al]; oceanographic[al]; mareographic
Meeresküste f sea coast (shore, beach), seaboard, seaside
Meeresküstenseife f sea-beach placer
Meereslagerstätte f marine deposit
Meeresleuchten n sea fire, phosphorescence of the sea
Meeresorganismen mpl/**bodenbewohnende** epibionta
Meeresplankton n marine plankton
Meeresregression f regression (retreat) of the sea, oceanic retreat
Meeressaline f salt pan
Meeressalz n/**grobkörniges** bay salt
Meeressalzgarten m/**künstlich angelegter** artificial marginal salt pan
Meeresschaum m sea foam
Meeressediment n marine sediment
Meeresspiegel m sea level, oceanic level
~ **bei maximaler ep[e]irogener Hochlage** ep[e]irocratic sea level
~/**mittlerer** mean sea level
~/**über dem** above sea level
Meeresspiegelkontur f contour of zero elevation
Meeresspiegelschwankung f sea level fluctuation
~/**eustatische** eustatic change of the sea level
Meeresstrand m [sea, ocean, marine] beach
Meeresstraße f/**intermarine** intermarine street
Meeresströmung f ocean (sea, marine) current; drift
Meerestechnik f offshore technology
Meerestemperatur f ocean temperature
Meeresterrasse f marine terrace
Meerestiefe f ocean depth
Meerestransgression f sea transgression
Meeresufer n sea shore
Meeresuferlinie f shore line
Meeresumwelt f marine environment
Meeresvorstoß m marine invasion
Meermühle f sea mill
Meerschaum m meerschaum, sepiolite (s.a. Sepiolith)
Meerwasser n ocean (sea) water
Meerwasserentsalzung f sea-water desalination
Meerwassersalinität f salinity of sea water
Megablast m megablast, phenoblast
Megagäa f Megagaea
Megalosaurier m megalosaur
Megantiklinale f meganticline

Megantiklinorium n meganticlinorium
megaskopisch megascopic[al], macroscopic[al]
Megaspore f macrospore
Megasynklinale f megasyncline, area of tectonic depression
Megasynklinorium n megasynclinorium
Mehlsand m mealy (flour, impalpable, very fine) sand
Mehlsandstein m very fine sandstone
mehrachsig multiaxial
Mehrausbruch m overbreak
Mehrbrunnenanlage f installation consisting of several wells
Mehrelektrodensonde f multielectrode sonde
Mehrentölung f improved oil recovery
Mehrfachfließratentest m multiple-rate test
Mehrfachreflexion f multiple reflection
Mehrfach-Ring-Bassin n multiring basin
Mehrfachschußlöcher npl multiple shot-holes
Mehrfachstufenzementation f multistage cementing
Mehrfachüberdeckung f common-depth-point shooting, multiple coverage (seismics)
Mehrfachüberdeckungsverfahren n common-depth-point technique (seismics)
mehrfarbig polychromatic, polychroic
Mehrfarbigkeit f polychromatism
mehrjährig perennial
Mehrkanalaufnahmen fpl s. Multispektralaufnahmen
Mehrkanalfilterung f multichannel filtering
Mehrkanalkamera f multiband camera
~/**einlinsige** single-lens multiband camera
Mehrkristall m polycrystal
mehrlagig multilayer[ed]; laminated
Mehrlochbohrung f multihole drilling
Mehrphasenströmung f multiphase (multiple-phase) flow
Mehrreihenschießen n more row shooting
Mehrsatellitenstart m tandem launch
mehrschichtig multilayer[ed]; laminated
Mehrschichttonmineralwasser n excessive water interlayer
Mehrsohlenbohren n multihole drilling
Mehrstrangsonde f multiple completion well
Mehrstufendatensammlung f multistage sampling (data sampling at various levels of altitude or detail, respectively)
Mehrstufenrakete f multistage rocket
mehrstufig multistage
Mehrzweckspeicher m multiple-purpose reservoir (aquifer)
Meilerstellung f inverted fan (of schistosity); periclinal structure (of basaltic columns)
Meißel m bit; auger drill
~/**abgenutzter** dull bit
Meißelbelastung f bit pressure
Meißeldirektantrieb m down-hole motor
Meißeldrehzahl f bit speed
Meißeldurchmesser m bit size
Meißeldüse f bit nozzle

Meißellebensdauer

Meißellebensdauer f bit life
Meißelprobe f bit sample
Meißelschablone f bit gauge
Meißelspiel n bit clearance
Meißelstandzeit f bit life
Meißelvorschub m feed of the bit
Mejonit m meionite, $Ca_8[(Cl_2, SO_4, CO_3)_2 | (Al_2Si_2O_8)_6]$
Melange f mélange, olisthostrom[a]
Melanit m melanite *(variety of andradite)*
Melanocerit m melanocerite, Na_4Ca_{16} (Y, La)$_3$(Zr, Ce)$_6$[F$_{12}$|(BO$_3$)$_3$|(SiO$_4$)$_{12}$]
melanokrat melanocratic
Melanophlogit m melanophlogite *(modification of SiO_2)*
Melanosom n melanosome
Melanotekit m melanotekite, $Pb_2Fe_2[O_2|Si_2O_7]$
Melanothallit m melanothallite, $Cu(Cl, OH)_2$
Melanovanadit m melanovanadite, $Ca_2V_{10}O_{25} \cdot 7H_2O$
Melanterit m melanterite, copperas, green vitriol, $FeSO_4 \cdot 7H_2O$
Melaphyr m melaphyre *(basalt)*
Melaphyrmandelstein m amygdaloidal melaphyre
Melaphyrtuff m melaphyre tuff
Melilith m melilite, (Ca, Na)$_2$(Al, Mg) [(Si, Al)$_2$O$_7$]
Melilithbasalt m melilite basalt
Melilithit m melilitite *(rock of the ultramafic clan)*
Melinophan m melinophane, (Ca, Na)$_2$(Be, Al) [Si$_2$O$_6$F]
Melioration f amelioration
meliorieren to meliorate
Melksonde f marginal well, stripper [well]
Mellit m mellite, $Al_2[C_{12}O_{12}] \cdot 18H_2O$
Melonit m melonite, $NiTe_2$
Melteigit m melteigite *(alkaline rock)*
Menap-Eiszeit f, **Menap-Kaltzeit** f Menap [Drift] *(Pleistocene of Northwest Europe)*
Mendelejewit m mendelyeevite *(variety of koppite)*
Mendipit m mendipite, $PbCl_2 \cdot 2PbO$
Mendozit m mendozite, $NaAl(SO_4)_2 \cdot 12H_2O$
Meneghinit m meneghinite, $4PbS \cdot Sb_2S_3$
Menge f quantity; amount
~/wirtschaftlich nutzbare commercial quantity
Menilit m menilite *(variety of opal)*
Mennige f minium, Pb_3O_4
Mensch m **und Umwelt** f man and environment
menschenähnlich manlike, anthropoid
Mercallit m mercallite, $KH[SO_4]$
Mergel m marl
~/bituminöser anthraconite, anthracolite
~/dolomitischer dolomitic marl
~/harter ga[u]lt
~/lehmiger loamy marl
mergelartig marly
Mergelbank f marly bed
Mergelboden m marly soil, marl earth

Mergelfazies f marly facies
Mergelgrube f marlpit
mergelig marlaceous, marly
Mergelkalk m marlaceous lime
Mergelsandstein m marly sandstone
Mergelschicht f marly bed
Mergelschiefer m marl[y] slate, marlslate, marly shale, margode
~/bituminöser bituminous marl
Mergelstein m marlstone, marlite
Mergelton m marl (gault) clay, argillaceous marl
Mergelung f marling
Meridian m meridian
~/erdmagnetischer geomagnetic meridian
~/geografischer geographic[al] meridian
~/magnetischer magnetic meridian
~ von Greenwich meridian of Greenwich
~/wahrer true meridian
Meridiandurchgang m meridian passage (transit)
Meridianhöhe f meridian altitude
meridional meridional
merklich/kaum scarcely noticeable, very slight *(2nd stage of the scale of seismic intensity)*
Merkmal n/**geologisches** geologic[al] feature
~/lithologisches lithologic character
~/tektonisches structural feature
Merkmale npl/**analytische** analytic (structural) characteristics *(taxonomy)*
~/linienhaft ausgebildete linear features
Merkmalsanalyse f signature analysis
Merkmalserkennung f feature recognition
Merkmalsgewinnung f feature extraction
Merkmalsverschiebung f character displacement
Merkurhornerz n horn quicksilver
Meroedrie f merohedrism
meroedrisch merohedral, merohedric
merokristallin hemicrystalline, hypocrystalline
Meroxen m meroxene *(biotite poor in iron)*
Merrihueit m merrihueite, (K, Na)$_2$(Fe, Mg)$_5$Si$_{12}$O$_{30}$ *(meteoric mineral)*
Merwinit m merwinite, $Ca_3Mg(SiO_4)_2$
Mesenterien npl mesenteries *(corals)*
Mesitinspat m mesitite, breunnerite
Mesocoquina f mesocoquina
Mesoeuropa n Meso-Europe
Mesogeosynklinale f mesogeosyncline
mesohalin mesohaline
Mesolith m mesolite, $Na_2Ca_2[Al_2Si_3O_{10}]_3 \cdot 8H_2O$
Mesomerie f mesomerism
Mesoperthit m mesoperthite *(between perthite and antiperthite)*
Mesophytikum n Mesophytic
Mesorhythmen mpl mesorhythms
Mesosiderit m mesosiderite *(meteorite)*
Mesostasis f mesostasis, base
mesothermal mesothermal
Mesozoikum n Mesozoic [Era]
mesozoisch Mesozoic
mesozonal mesozonal

Mesozone f mesozone
Meßanker m measurement bolt
Meßanordnung f measuring arrangement; field layout *(geophysics)*
Meßbake f surveying rod
Meßband n measuring tape
Meßbasis f [measuring] platform
Meßbereich m range of measurement
Meßdose f dynamometer; pressure capsule
Meßdübel m measuring plug
Meßebene f measuring plane
Meßelektrode f measuring electrode
Messelit m messelite, Ca$_2$(Fe, Mn) [PO$_4$]$_2$ · 2H$_2$O
messen to measure; to gauge; to log
Meßergebnis n measuring result
Meßergebnisse npl **am Kern** core data
Meßfahrzeug n recording truck
Meßflügel m hydrometric current meter
Meßfühler m measurement transducer, sensitive element
Meßgenauigkeit f accuracy of measurement
Meßgerät n measuring instrument (device); gauge; meter
Meßgeräteausrüstung f instrumentation
Messinium n Messinian [Stage] *(Miocene)*
Meßkopf m measuring head; probe
Meßlänge f live section *(of a streamer)*
Meßlatte f rod, staff
Meßlinie f measuring (observation) line
Meßlot n sounding weight *(for ground-water level measurement)*
Meßlupe f scale magnifying glass
Meßmarke f measurement point
Meßmöglichkeit f possibility of measurement
Meßpatrone f bore gauge
Meßpflock m measuring plug
Meßplatz m measuring position
Meßprofil n measuring profile
Meßpunkt m measuring point, station, exposure site
Meßpunktabstand m stationary interval, interval of stations
Meßsatellit m satellite carrying instruments
Meßschiff n recording boat
Meßsonde f probe
Meßstelle f s. Meßpunkt
Meßtechnik f mensuration technique
Meßtisch m surveyor's table
~/topografischer topographic drawing board
Meßtischaufnahme f plane table survey[ing]
Meßtischblatt n plane table map (sheet), survey sheet
Meßtrupp m survey[ing] party
~/seismischer seismic party (crew), seismic surveying unit
Meßuhr f dial indicator
Messung f measurement, mensuration; gauging; logging
~/abbaudynamische measurement of strata behaviour
~ bei offenem Bohrloch open flow test

~ der magnetischen Permeabilität magnetic permeability logging
~ des Bohrlochquerschnitts calibre log
~/gaschromatografische gas chromatographic measurement
~/gravimetrische gravimetric measurement
~/hammerschlagseismische hammer-blow-seismic measurement
~ induzierter Potentiale induced potential logging
~/markscheiderische survey measurement
~/massenspektrometrische mass-spectrometric measurement
~ mit Meßband taping
~/stationäre deadbeat measurement
~/vibratorseismische vibrator-seismic measurement
~ während des Bohrvorgangs [/geophysikalische] measuring while drilling
Meßverfahren n measuring (logging) technique
Meßwagen m logging truck
Meßwehr n measuring weir
Meßwertfehler m datum error
Meßwertschreiber m data recorder
Meßwertwandler m transmitter
Meta-Ankoleit m metaankoleite, K$_2$[UO$_2$|PO$_4$]$_2$ · 6H$_2$O
Metaarkose f metaarkose
Meta-Autunit m metaautunite, Na$_2$[UO$_2$|PO$_4$]$_2$ · 8H$_2$O
Metabasalt m metabasalt
Metabasit m metabasite
Meta-Bassetit m metabassetite, Fe[UO$_2$|PO$_4$]$_2$ · 8H$_2$O
Metabentonit m potassium bentonite
Metablastese f metablastesis
Metablastit m metablastite
Metabolismus m metabolism
Metacinnabarit m metacinnabarite, HgS
Meta-Heinrichit m metaheinrichite, Ba[UO$_2$|AsO$_4$]$_2$ · 8H$_2$O
Metahewettit m metahewettite, CaV$_6$O$_{16}$ · 3H$_2$O
Metahohmannit m metahohmannite, Fe[OH|SO$_4$] · 1$^1/_2$H$_2$O
Meta-Kahlerit m metakahlerite, Fe[UO$_2$|AsO$_4$]$_2$ · 8H$_2$O
Metakieselsäure f metasilicic acid
Meta-Kirchheimerit m metakirchheimerite, Co[UO$_2$|AsO$_4$]$_2$ · 8H$_2$O
metakristallinisch metacrystalline
Metall n metal
~ der Platingruppe platinoid
~/edles noble metal
~/gediegenes native metal
~/unedles ignoble (base) metal
Metallablagerung f metalliferous deposit[ion]
Metallagerstätte f metallic deposit
metallähnlich metalline
metallartig metalloid; metalliform
Metallatom n metal atom

metallen

metallen metalline
Metallerzlagerstätte f metalliferous ore deposit
Metallfaktor m metal factor *(geoelectrics)*
metallfrei barren
metallführend metal-bearing, metalliferous
Metallgehalt m metal[lic] content, amount of metal; ore grade
~/durchschnittlicher tenor, average ore grade
Metallglanz m metallic[-splendent] lustre
metallglänzend metallic-shining, metallic-splendent
metallhaltig metalliferous
metallisch metallic
Metallisierung f metallization
Metallkern m metal core
Metallogenese f metallogenesis
metallogenetisch metallogenetic[al], metallogenic
Metallogenie f metallogeny
Metallometrie f metallometry
metallometrisch metallometric
Metallprovinz f metallogenic province
Metallstück n prill *(small piece of native metal)*
metamorph metamorphic, metamorphous
~/nicht unmetamorphosed
Metamorphiden pl metamorphides
Metamorphit m metamorphic rock
metamorphogen metamorphogenic
Metamorphose f metamorphism, metamorphosis
~/allocheme allochemical metamorphism
~/ansteigende s. **~/progressive**
~/beginnende incipient metamorphism
~ durch Dislokation cataclastic metamorphism
~ durch Druck metamorphism by pressure
~ durch Kontakt mit Intrusionsmassen contact metamorphism
~ durch Versenkung [regional] burial metamorphism, load metamorphism
~/hydrothermale hydrothermal metamorphism
~/ischeme isochemical metamorphism
~/katazonale s. **~/starke**
~/kaustische caustic metamorphism
~/kinetische kinetic metamorphism
~/lokale local metamorphism
~/mechanische s. **~/kinetische**
~/mittlere medium-rank metamorphism, medium-grade metamorphism
~/pneumatolytische pneumatolytic (additive) metamorphism
~/progressive progressive (prograde) metamorphism
~/regionale regional [dynamothermal] metamorphism
~/regressive (retrograde, rückläufige) retrogressive (retrograde) metamorphism
~/schwache low-rank metamorphism, low-grade metamorphism
~/starke high-rank metamorphism, high-grade metamorphism
~/statische static metamorphism
Metamorphosegrad m degree of metamorphism, metamorphic grade (rank)
Metamorphosegürtel mpl/**paarige** paired metamorphic belts
metamorphosieren to metamorphose
Meta-Novačekit m metanovačecite, $Mg[UO_2|AsO_4]_2 \cdot 4H_2O$
Metaquarzit m metaquartzite
Metarossit m metarossite, $Ca[V_2O_6] \cdot 2H_2O$
Metaschoderit m metaschoderite, $Al[(P,V)O_4] \cdot 3H_2O$
Metasom n metasome *(of migmatites)*
metasomatisch metasomatic
Metasomatit m metasomatite
Metasomatosestockwerk n metasomatic stockwork
Metastibnit m metastibnite, Sb_2S_3
Metatekt n metatect, neosome
Metatexis f metatexis
Metatexit m metatexite *(a migmatite)*
Metathenardit m metathenardite, $\delta\text{-}Na_2SO_4$
Metatorbernit m metatorbernite, $Cu[UO_2|PO_4]_2 \cdot 8H_2O$
Metatyp[us] m metatype
Meta-Uramphit m metauramphite, $(NH_4)_2[UO_2|PO_4]_2 \cdot 6H_2O$
Meta-Uranocircit m metauranocircite, $Ba[UO_2|PO_4]_2 \cdot 8H_2O$
Meta-Uranospinit m metauranospinite, $Ca[UO_2|AsO_4]_2 \cdot 8H_2O$
Metavariscit m metavariscite, $AlPO_4 \cdot 2H_2O$
Metavoltin m metavoltine, $\alpha\text{-}K_5Fe_3[OH|(SO_4)_3]_2 \cdot 8H_2O$
Meta-Zeunerit m metazeunerite, $Cu[UO_2|AsO_4]_2 \cdot 8H_2O$
Metazoen npl metazoans
Meteor m meteor
~/pfeifender whistling meteor
Meteorbahn f meteor orbit (path)
Meteoreisen n meteoric iron
Meteoreisenstein m aerosiderite
Meteorfall m meteoric fall (shower)
meteorisch meteoric
Meteorit m meteorite, aerolite, uranolite
~/achondritischer howardite, chassignite, amphoterite
~ mit Titanaugit/achondritischer angrite
Meteoriteneinschlag m meteoric impact
Meteoriten-Einsturz-Theorie f impact theory
Meteoritenfall m meteorite (meteoritic) fall, fall [of meteorites]
Meteoritenfund m meteorite (meteoritic) find, find [of meteorites]
Meteoritengruppe f meteoritic group
Meteoritenkrater m meteor[itic] crater, meteorite crater
Meteoritenkunde f meteoritics
Meteoritenmineral n meteoric mineral
Meteoritensubstanz f meteoritic matter
meteoritisch meteoritic
Meteoritphase f meteoritic phase

Meteormasse f meteoritic mass
Meteorologe m meteorologist
Meteorologie f meteorology
~/physikalische physical meteorology
~/synoptische synoptic meteorology
meteorologisch meteorologic[al]
Meteorschwarm m meteor swarm (shower), shoal of meteors
Meteorschweif m meteor train
Meteorsplitter m meteoroid
Meteorspur f meteor wake
Meteorstein m meteorite, meteoric (falling, air) stone, siderite, aerolite
~/eisenhaltiger siderolite
Meteorstrom m meteor stream
Methan n methane, formene, CH_4
Methanabsaugung f methane (firedamp) drainage
Methanoldosierung f methanol inhibition
Methode f/**auf dem Zufall beruhende** hit or miss method
~/biometrische biometric[al] method
~/deduktive deductive method
~/induktive inductive method
~/lithostratigrafische lithostratigraphic[al] method
~/mikrofazielle method of microfacies
~/orthoskopische orthoscopic method
~/polarisationsoptische polarization-optical method
~/volumetrisch-genetische volumetric-genetic method
Methodik f **geologischer Untersuchungsarbeiten** geological prospecting technique
Meyerhofferit m meyerhofferite, $Ca[B_5O_3(OH)_5] \cdot H_2O$
Miargyrit m miargyrite, $AgSbS_2$
miarolithisch miarolitic
Miaskit m miaskite *(nepheline syenite)*
Michenerit m michenerite, $PdBi_2$
Micrinit m micrinite *(coal maceral)*
Miersit m miersite, α-AgJ
Miesmuschel f mussel
Migma n migma
Migmatisierung f migmatization
Migmatit m migmatite
Migration f migration, travel
~/geochemische geochemical migration
~/innere internal migration
~/laterale (schichtparallele) lateral (parallel) migration
migrationsfähig mobile *(components)*
Migrationsfähigkeit f migration capability
Migrationsfaktor m migration factor
~/äußerer external migration factor
~/geochemischer geochemical migration factor
~/innerer internal migration factor
Migrationsfalle f migration accretion
Migrationsgebiet n gathering area *(of hydrocarbons)*
Migrationsgefüge n migration fabric

Migrationsstapelung f migration stack *(seismics)*
Migrationsweg m avenue of migration *(of oil)*
migrieren to migrate, to travel
Miharait m miharaite *(quartz-bearing hypersthene basalt)*
Mijakit m mijakite *(variety of andesite)*
Mikrinit m s. Micrinit
Mikrit m micrite *(carbonate<0,005 mm)*
~/oolithischer oomicrite
~ mit Ooiden > 1 mm/oolithischer oomicrudite
Mikroanalyse f microanalysis
mikroaphanatisch felsiphyric, aphanophyric *(porphyrites)*
Mikrobe f microbe
Mikrobentätigkeit f microbian action
Mikrobild n microdrawing, micrograph
Mikrobiologie f microbiology
mikrobiologisch microbiological
Mikrobion n microbe
Mikrobrekzie f microbreccia
mikrochemisch microchemical
Mikrochemismus m microchemism
Mikrocoquine f microcoquina
Mikroelement n minor element
mikrofaunistisch microfaunistic
mikrofelsitisch microfelsitic, microaphanitic
mikrofloristisch microfloristic
Mikrofossil n microfossil
mikrofotometrisch microphotometric
Mikrogranit m microgranite
mikrogranitisch microgranitic
mikrogranophyrisch microgranophyric
Mikrogravimeter n microgravimeter
Mikrohärte f microhardness
Mikrohärteprüfung f microhardness test
mikroklastisch microclastic
Mikroklima n microclimate
Mikroklimatologie f microclimatology
Mikroklin m microcline, $KAlSi_3O_8$
~/grüner amazonite
Mikroklinisierung f microclinization
Mikrokosmos m microcosm
mikrokristallin microcrystalline
Mikrokristallografie f microcrystallography
Mikrolith m 1. microlite *(small crystal);* 2. microlite, $(Ca,Na)_2(Ta,Nb)_2O_6(O,OH,F)$
mikrolithisch microlitic
Mikrolithotyp m microlithotype *(coal)*
Mikrolog n microlog, contact log
Mikrologmessung f resistivity micrologging
Mikromagnetik f micromagnetics
Mikromaßanalyse f micromeasure analysis
mikromeritisch micromeritic
Mikrometeorit m micrometeorite
Mikromethode f micromethod
Mikropaläontologie f micropal[a]eontology
mikropaläontologisch micropal[a]eontologic[al]
mikropegmatitisch micropegmatic
Mikropellets npl pseudo-oolite, false oolites

Mikroperthit

Mikroperthit *m* microperthite
mikropetrografisch micropetrographical
Mikrophänokristall *m* microphenocryst
Mikroporosität *f* microporosity
mikroporphyrisch microporphyric
~/körnig magnifyric *(0,2–0,4 mm)*
Mikroreste *mpl* microremains
Mikroriß *m* microcrack
Mikroschichtung *f* fissible bedding *(<2 mm)*
Mikroseismik *f* microseismics
mikroseismisch microseismic
Mikroseismograf *m* microseismograph
Mikroseismometer *n* microseismometer
Mikroskleren *fpl* microscleres, flesh spicules *(poriferans)*
Mikroskop *n* microscope
~/heizbares hot-stage microscope
Mikroskopie *f* microscopy
mikroskopisch microscopic[al]
Mikroskoptisch *m* microscope stage
Mikrosonde *f s.* Elektronenmikrosonde
Mikrosparit *m* microsparite *(sedimentite)*
mikrosphärulithisch microspherulitic
Mikrospore *f* mi[cr]ospore
Mikrostruktur *f* microstructure
Mikrotektonik *f* microtectonics
Mikrotomschnitt *m* microtome slide
Mikrowelle *f* microwave
Mikrowellen *fpl* crenulation
Mikrowellenantenne *f* microwave antenna
Mikrowellenempfänger *m* microwave receiver
Mikrowellenradiometrie *f* microwave radiometry
Mikrowellenstreuung *f* microwave scattering
Milarit *m* milarite, $KCa_2AlBe_2[Si_{12}O_{30}] \cdot 1/2H_2O$
milchig milky
Milchopal *m* milky opal
Milchquarz *m* milky (greasy) quartz
Milchstein *m* galactite
Milchstraße *f* galaxy, milky way
Milchstraßennebel *m* galactic nebula
Milchstraßensystem *n* galactic (milky way) system
Milchzahn *m* milk (deciduous) tooth
Milieu *n* environment
~/durchlüftetes küstennahes oxygenated inshore environment
~/geologisches geologic[al] environment
~ in der Gezeitenzone/benthonisches littoral, littorine
~/küstennahes inshore environment
~/limnisches limnic environment
~/mooriges paludal environment
~/oxydierendes oxidizing environment
~/reduzierendes reducing environment
~/sedimentfeindliches non-depositional environment
Milieuindex *m* environmental index
Milieuindikator *m* environmental criterion
Militärgeologie *f* military geology

Millerit *m* millerite, capillary (hair) pyrite, NiS
milliäquivalent milliequivalent
Millisit *m* millisite, $(Na,Ca)Al_3[(OH,O)_4|(PO_4)_2] \cdot 2H_2O$
Mimetesit *m* mimet[es]ite, mimetene, campylite, $Pb_5[Cl|(AsO_4)_3]$
mimetisch mim[et]ic
Minasragrit *m* minasragrite, $V_2[(OH)_2|(SO_4)_3] \cdot 15H_2O$
Mindel-Eiszeit *f*, **Mindel-Kaltzeit** *f* Mindel [Drift] *(Pleistocene of Alps district)*
Mindel-Riß-Interglazial *n*, **Mindel-Riß-Warmzeit** *f* Mindel-Riß [Interval] *(Pleistocene of Alps district)*
minderwertig low-grade
Mindestabfluß *m* minimum flow
Mindestabflußmenge *f* minimum discharge
Mindestfördermenge *f* minimum output, minimum (amortization) tonnage
Mineral *n* mineral
~/akzessorisches accessory mineral
~/alkalisches leach mineral
~/amorphes gel mineral
~/authigenes authigenic mineral
~/basisches mafic mineral, melane
~/charakteristisches diagnostic (symptomatic) mineral
~/detritisches detrital mineral
~/diagnostisches diagnostic (symptomatic) mineral
~/diamagnetisches diamagnetic mineral
~/eingesprengtes interspersed mineral
~/erdiges earthy mineral
~/farbiges idiochromatic mineral
~/fazieskritisches critical (diagnostic, index) mineral
~/felsisches felsic mineral
~/festes hard mineral
~/flüssiges liquid mineral
~/gefärbtes allochromatic mineral
~/gepreßtes mineral under strain
~/gesteinsbildendes rock-forming mineral
~/harzartiges resinous mineral
~/hydroxylhaltiges hydatogenic mineral
~/idiochromatisches idiochromatic mineral
~/isotropisiertes metamict mineral
~/nutzbares economic (industrial, useful) mineral
~/paramagnetisches paramagnetic mineral
~/persistentes persistent mineral
~/pleochroitisches pleochroic mineral
~/pneumatolytisches pneumatolytic mineral
~/primäres origin mineral
~/pyrogenes pyrogenetic mineral
~/spatiges tiff
~/synantetisches synantetic mineral
~/wachsartiges waxy mineral
Mineralabfolge *f s.* Mineralfolge
Mineralabscheidung *f* mineral separation
Mineralaggregat *n* mineral aggregate
Mineralanalyse *f* mineral analysis
Mineralanhäufung *f* mineral aggregate

Mineralanordnung *f*/**linearparallele (lineationsbildende)** mineral streaming
Mineralassoziation *f* mineral association
Mineralausstattung *f* **eines Gebiets** mineral endowment
Mineralbestandteil *m* mineral constituent (ingredient)
~/kennzeichnender essential mineral
Mineralbestimmung *f* identification of minerals
mineralbildend mineralizing, mineral-forming
Mineralbildner *m* mineralizer, mineralizing agent
Mineralbildung *f* mineral formation
Mineralboden *m* mineral soil
Mineralchemie *f* chemical mineralogy
Mineralchemismus *m* mineral chemism
Mineraldiagnostik *f* mineral diagnostics
Mineraldichte *f* mineral density
Mineraldünger *m* inorganic fertilizer
Minerale *npl*/**beibrechende** ancillary minerals (coal mines)
~ des maritimen Raums/ökonomisch interessierende submarine minerals
~/durchwachsene intergrown minerals
~/koexistierende coexisting minerals
~/verwachsene intergrown minerals
Mineraleinschluß *m* mineral inclusion
Mineralfazies *f* mineral facies
Mineralfaziesprinzip *n* principle of mineral facies
Mineralfolge *f* mineral sequence
Mineralformel *f* minèral formula
Mineralformen *fpl*/**gestrickte** skeletal mineral forms
Mineralfraktion *f* mineral fraction
Mineralgang *m* mineral[ized] vein
~/eine Verwerfungsspalte ausfüllender fault vein
Mineralgefüge *n* mineral fabric
Mineralgehalt *m* mineral content
Mineralgemisch *n*/**hohlraumarmes** dense[-graded] aggregate, close[-graded] aggregate, dense (close) mineral aggregate, DGA
Mineralgewinnung *f* **aus Küstensanden** beach sand mining
Mineralgitterwasser *n* lattice-bound water
Mineralglanz *m* **mit guter Oberflächenreflexion** glistening *(e.g. of talcum)*
~ mit unvollständiger Oberflächenreflexion glimmering *(e.g. of chalcedony)*
Mineralgleichgewichte *npl* mineral equilibria
Mineralgruppe *f* mineral group
Mineralidentifizierung *f* mineral recognition
Mineraliensammlung *f* mineral[ogic] collection
Mineralisation *f* mineralization
Mineralisationsperiode *f* mineralization period
Mineralisator *m* mineralizer, mineralizing agent
mineralisch mineral

mineralisieren to mineralize
Mineralisierung *f* mineralization
Mineralkautschuk *m* mineral rubber
Mineralkomponente *f* mineral component
Mineralkonkretionen *fpl* **auf dem Meeresgrund** deep-sea nodules
Mineralkonzentrat *n* mineral concentrate
Mineralkunde *f s.* Mineralogie
Mineralmasse *f*/**hohlraumarme** *s.* Mineralgemisch/hohlraumarmes
Mineraloge *m* mineralogist
Mineralogie *f* mineralogy, oryctognosy
~/allgemeine (beschreibende) descriptive mineralogy
~/spezielle determinative mineralogy
mineralogisch mineralogic[al], oryctognostic
Mineralöl *n* mineral oil
~/reines straight mineral oil
Mineralölerzeugnisse *npl* petrochemicals
Mineralölwirtschaft *f* mineral oil industry
Mineralparagenese *f* mineral paragenesis
Mineralphasen *fpl*/**miteinander im Gleichgewicht stehende** coexisting (compatible) phases
Mineralprobe *f* mineral sample
Mineralquelle *f* mineral spring (well), spring of mineral water
Mineralreich *n* mineral kingdom
Mineralreichtum *m* mineral wealth
Mineralressourcen *fpl* mineral resources
~ in Handelsform mineral commodities
~/maritime subsea mineral resources
Mineralschuppe *f* mineral scale
Mineralseife *f* mineral placer
~/tief liegende deep lead
Mineralstreckung *f* mineral streaking (streaming)
~ durch plastisches Fließen/lineare flow stretching
Mineralstruktur *f* mineral structure
Mineralsubstanz *f* mineral matter *(e.g. in coal)*
~/eingebettete paste
Mineralteer *m* mineral tar, maltha, pittasphalt, sea wax
Mineraltrum *n*/**sehr dünnes** thread
Mineraltrümchen *n* leader
Mineralvergesellschaftung *f* mineral association
Mineralverteilung *f*/**zonale** mineral zoning
Mineralverwachsung *f* mineral intergrowth (*s. a.* Verwachsung)
~/parallele parallel growth
~/symplektitische dactylotype intergrowth
Mineralvorräte *mpl*/**nachgewiesene** discovered reserves
Mineralwachs *n* mineral (fossil) wax, paraffin
Mineralwasser *n* mineral water
Mineralwasserfront *f* mineral water interface
Mineralzoning *n* mineral zoning
Mineralzusammensetzung *f* mineral composition
minerogen minerogenic (*s. a.* anorganogen)

minerogenetisch

minerogenetisch minerogenetic
minerogenetisch-kristallografisch minerogenetic-crystallographic
Minerogenie f minerogeny
Minette f minette *(lamprophyre)*
Minetteerz n minette ore
Minguzzit m minguzzite, $K_3Fe[C_2O_4]_3 \cdot 3H_2O$
Minimalgehalt m**/industrieller** industrial minimum percentage (quality)
Minium n minium, Pb_3O_4
Minnesotait m minnesotaite, $(Fe^{..}, Mg, H_2)_3[(OH)_2I(Si, Al, Fe^{...})_4O_{10}]$
Mintrop-Welle f Mintrop (refraction, conical) wave *(seismics)*
Minyulit m minyulite, $KAl_2[OH,F)I(PO_4)_2] \cdot 4H_2O$
miogeosynklinal miogeosynclinal
Miogeosynklinale f miogeosyncline
miohalin miohaline
miozän Miocene
Miozän n Miocene [Series, Epoch] *(Tertiary)*
Mirabilit m mirabilite, $Na_2SO_4 \cdot 10H_2O$
mischbar miscible
~/nicht inmiscible, non-miscible
Mischbarkeit f miscibility
~/lückenlose uniform miscibility
~/vollständige complete miscibility
Mischbindung f mixed bond
Mischgestein n hybrid rock
Mischkorrosion f mixing corrosion
Mischkristall m mix[ed] crystal; solid solution
Mischkristallbildung f mixed-crystal formation
~/lückenlose continuous crystalline solution
Mischkristallreihe f series of mixed crystals
Mischphasenfluten n miscible flooding
Mischphasenströmung f mixing flow
Mischphasentrieb m, **Mischphasenverdrängung** f miscible drive (phase displacement) *(oil lift)*
Mischprobe f s. Sammelprobe
Mischungslücke f [im]miscibility gap
Mischverhältnis n mixing ratio *(of different water mineralization)*
Mischwald m mixed forest
Misenit m misenite, $K_8H_6[SO_4]_7$
Miserit m miserite, $KCa_5[Si_5O_{14}OH] \cdot H_2O$
Mispickel m s. Arsenkies
Mißbildung f malformation, aberration
Mississippian n Mississippian [Series] *(Lower Carboniferous and basal Namurian in North America)*
Missourit m missourite *(variety of leucite basalt)*
Mißweisung f compass error
~/magnetische magnetic declination, variation (aberration) of the magnetic needle, grid variation
Mistral m mistral
Mitfördern n **von Sand** sand heaving
mitnehmen to carry *(e.g. a dirt pack)*
Mitnehmerstange f kelly, grief stem
Mitnehmerstangeneinsatz m kelly bushing

Mitrafalten fpl mitre folds
Mitridatit m mitridatite *(alteration product of vivianite)*
Mitscherlichit m mitscherlichite, $K_2[CuCl_4(H_2O)_2]$
mitschleppen to drag [along]
Mittag m**/mittlerer** mean noon
Mittel n 1. medium; 2. stone band
~/gleitendes moving average *(statistics)*
~/reiches ore shoot
~/taubes vein stone, sterile mass
Mitteldamm m intermediate pack
Mitteldevon n Middle Devonian [Series, Epoch]
Mittelfurche f median sulcus
Mittelfußknochen m cannon bone
Mittelgebirge n hill country, hills; average (secondary, subdued) mountain
Mittelgebirgsformen fpl subdued mountain forms
Mittelgebirgsrelief n medium relief
Mittelhandknochen m cannon bone
Mittelkambrium n Middle Cambrian [Series, Epoch]
Mittelkarbon n Middle Carboniferous [Series, Epoch]
Mittelkies m medium gravel *(6–20 mm)*
mittelkörnig medium-grained
Mittellauf m middle course *(of a river)*
Mittellinie f**/erste** acute bisectrix
Mittelmeer n Mediterranean
Mittelmeerklima n Mediterranean climate
Mittelmeerregion f Mediterranean region
Mittelmoräne f medial (median, interlobate) moraine
Mittelperm n Middle Permian [Series, Epoch]
Mittelpräkambrium n Middle Precambrian [Series, Epoch]
Mittelsand m medium[-grained] sand *(0,25–0,5 mm)*
Mittelschenkel m middle (common) limb
~/ausgequetschter (reduzierter, verdünnter) drawn-out middle limb, stretched-out middle limb, squeezed-out middle limb, reduced limb
Mittelschenkelbruch m anticlinal fault
Mittelschenkelreste mpl overthrust slice
Mittelschluff m middle silt *(0,02–0,0063 mm)*
Mittelsteinzeit f Mesolithic [time]
mittelsteinzeitlich Mesolithic
Mittelung f averaging
Mittelwasser n mean tide (water), half tide
Mittelwasserführung f**/jährliche** mean annual discharge
Mittelwert m**/quadratischer** root mean square, rms
Mittelwertbildung f averaging
Mitternachtssonne f midnight sun
Mixit m mixite, $(Bi,Fe,Zn H, CaH)Cu_{12}[(OH)_{12}I(AsO_4)_6] \cdot 6H_2O$
Mixtinit m mixtinite *(coal maceral)*
Mizzonit m mizzonite *(a mineral of the scapolite*

group intermediate between meionite and marialite)
Mobilisation *f* mobilization
Mobilismus *m* mobilism
Mobilitätsfaktor *m* mobility factor
Mobilitätsreihe *f* mobility series
Mobilitätsverhältnis *n* mobility ratio
Modal[wert] *m* mode *(grain size)*
Moddergrund *m* muddy ground
Modderit *m* modderite, CoAs
Modell *n* model; template
~ **für den Laufweg einer Refraktion** model of refraction travel path
Modellalter *n* model age
Modellierung *f* **der Grundwasserdynamik** simulation analysis of ground-water flow
~/**strahlengeometrische** ray tracing *(seismics)*
Modellkurven *fpl* master curves
Modellmaßstab *m* model scale
Modellrechnung *f* modelling *(geophysics)*
Modellseismik *f* model seismics
Modellversuch *m* model (scaled-down) test
Moder *m* mould[ering]; rottenness, decay
Modifikation *f* **der Schalenöffnung** apertural modification
~/**polymorphe** polymorphic modification, polymorph
Modul *m*/**dynamischer** dynamic[al] modulus
Modulationsübertragungsfunktion *f* modular transfer function, MTF *(e.g. of a remote sensor)*
Modus *m* mode
Mofette *f* mof[f]ette
~/**nasse** carbonic acid fumarole
Mogoten *pl* mogotes *(tropical form of karst)*
Mohnien *n* Mohnian [Stage] *(marine stage, Miocene of North America)*
Moho-Diskontinuität *f s.* Mohorovičić-Diskontinuität
Mohorovičić-Bohrung *f* Mohole project
Mohorovičić-Diskontinuität *f* Mohorovičić discontinuity, M boundary
Mohrenkopf *m s.* Turmalin
Mohrit *m* mohrite, $(NH_4)_2Fe[SO_4]_2 \cdot 6H_2O$
Moiréglanz *m* moiré
Moissanit *m* moissanite, SiC *(meteoritic mineral)*
Mol *n* mole
Molasse *f* molasse
Molassebecken *n* molasse basin
~/**intramontanes** molasse intra-deep
Molassefazies *f* molasse facies
Moldanubikum *n* Moldanubicum
Moldavit *m* moldavite *(tectite)*
Mole *f* mole, pier, jetty
Molekül *n* molecule
~/**Tschermaks** Ca-Tschermak's molecule, $CaAl_2SiO_6$
molekular molecular
Molekulardiffusion *f* molecular diffusion
Molekularquotient *m,* **Molekularverhältnis** *n* molecular ratio

Molekülbindung *f* molecular bond
Molekülgitter *n* molecule lattice
Molekülparameter *m* molecular parameter
Molekülspektroskopie *f* molecular spectroscopy
Molengraaffit *m s.* Lamprophyllit
Mollisol *m* mollisol, active (annually thawed) layer
Mollusken *fpl* mollusc[an]s
Molluskenfauna *f* molluscan fauna
Molluskoiden *fpl* molluscoids
Moluranit *m* moluranite, $H_6[(UO_2)_3I(MoO_4)_5] \cdot 9H_2O$
Molwärme *f* molar heat
Molybdän *n* molybdenum, Mo
Molybdänglanz *m* molybdenite, MoS_2
molybdänhaltig molybdeniferous
Molybdänit *m* molybdenite, MoS_2
Molybdänocker *m,* **Molybdit** *m* molybdite, molybdenic ochre, MoO_3
Molybdomenit *m* molybdomenite, $Pb[SeO_3]$
Molybdophyllit *m* molybdophyllite, $Pb_2Mg_2[(OH)_2ISi_2O_7]$
Molysit *m* molysite, $FeCl_3$
Moment *n*/**erdmagnetisches** geomagnetic moment
~/**erstes** first moment *(granulometric analysis)*
Momentangeschwindigkeit *f* instantaneous velocity
Momente *npl* moment measures *(granulometric analysis)*
Momnouthit *m* momnouthite *(variety of urtite)*
Monadnock *m* monadnock, unaka, relict mountain, isolated hard rock hill
Monalbit *m* monalbite *(monocline high-temperature phase of albite)*
Monat *m*/**siderischer** sidereal month
Monatsisotherme *f* monthly isotherm
Monatsmittel *n* monthly mean
Monatsniederschlag *m* monthly precipitation
~/**mittlerer** mean monthly precipitation
Monazit *m* monacite, monazite, cryptolite, $C[PO_4]$
Monazitsand *m* monazite sand
Moncheit *m* moncheite, $(Pt,Pd)(Te,Bi)_2$
Monchiquit *m* monchiquite *(lamprophyric dike rock)*
Mond *m* moon
Mondablösungstheorie *f* moon's separation theory
Mondalter *n* moon's age
Mondaufgang *m* moonrise
Mondbahn *f* moon's orbit (path), lunar path
Mondbasalt *m* moon (lunar) basalt
Mondbeschreibung *f* selenography
Mondbewegung *f* lunar libration
Mondboden *m* lunar regolith (dust)
Mondentfernung *f* lunar distance
Mondes/diesseits des cislunar
~/**jenseits des** translunar
Mondferne *f* apocynthion
Mondfinsternis *f* eclipse of the moon, lunar eclipse, moon's black-out

Mondfinsternis

~/partielle partial eclipse of the moon
~/totale total lunar eclipse
mondförmig lunate
Mondforscher *m* lunarian
Mondforschung *f* lunar research
Mondfurche *f* [lunar] rill
Mondgebirge *n* lunar mountain[s]
Mondgeologie *f* lunar geology
Mondgestein *n* lunar rock
Mondgraben *m s.* Mondfurche
Mondhaldeit *m* mondhaldeite *(monzonitic dike rock)*
Mondhof *m* lunar aurora
Mondjahr *n* lunar year
Mondkrater *m* lunar crater (circus)
Mondkruste *f* moon's crust
Mondkunde *f* selenology
mondkundlich selenographic
Mondlandschaft *f* lunar landscape (topography)
Mondmassenkonzentration *f* lunar mass concentration
Mondmaterial *n*/**pulvriges** lunar fines ($< 1\ cm$)
Mondmeere *npl* lunar maria
mondmittelpunktbezogen selenocentric
Mondnähe *f* pericynthion
Mondnarbe *f*/**irdische** lunar scar [of earth]
Mondoberfläche *f* lunar (moon's) surface
Mondoberflächenmaterial *n*/**zu Brekzie geschweißtes (kompaktiertes)** lunar microbreccia
Mondoberflächenmerkmal *n* lunar surface feature
Mondphase *f* lunar phase
Mondphasenwechsel *m* quartering
Mondrakete *f* moon rocket
Mondring *m* lunar halo
Mondrückseite *f* back of the moon
Mondsatellit *m* moon's satellite
Mondschatten *m* moon's (lunar) shadow
Mondscheibe *f* lunar disk
Mondschwerefeld *n* lunar gravitational field
Mondsonde *f* lunar probe
Mondspalte *f* lunar cleft
Mondstein *m* moonstone *(variety of feldspar)*
Mondstrahlen *mpl* lunar streaks
Mondtag *m* lunar day
Mondtektonik *f* selenotectonics
Mondumlauf *m* lunar circuit, lunation
Mondumlaufbahn *f s.* Mondbahn
Monduntergang *m* moonset
Mondvermessungskunde *f* selenodesy
Mondviertel *n* quarter of the moon
Mondvorderseite *f* front of the moon
Mondvulkanismus *m* lunar volcanism
Monetit *m* monetite, $CaH[PO_4]$
monochromatisch monochromatic
monogenetisch monogenetic
Monogeosynklinale *f* monogeosyncline, simple geosyncline
monoklin monoclinic, monoclinal, homoclinal, uniclinal

Monoklinale *f* monocline, homocline
Monoklinalfalte *f* monoclinal (step) fold
Monoklinalkamm *m* monoclinal mountain
Monoklinaltal *n* monoclinal (homoclinal) valley
Monokotyledonen *fpl* monocotyls, monocots
Monolith *m* monolith
monolithisch monolithic
monometallisch monometallic
monometrisch monometric[al]
monomikt monomict
monomineralisch monomineralic, monogene
Monongahela *n* Monongahela *(upper Pennsylvanian in North America)*
monophyletisch monophyletical
monotrop monotropic
Monotypie *f* monotypy *(rules of nomenclature)*
Monrepit *m* monrepite *(Fe-rich biotite)*
Mons *m* mons *(mountain on Mars or moon)*
Monsun *m* monsoon
Monsunklima *n* monsoon climate
Monsunwind *m* monsoon wind
Mont *n* Montian [Stage] *(of Palaeocene)*
Montage *f* **und Demontage** *f* rig-up and rig-down operations
Montagebrigade *f* rigging-up crew
Montangeologe *m* mining geologist
Montangeologie *f* mining (economic) geology
montangeologisch mining-geological
Montangeophysik *f* mining geophysics
montanhydrogeologisch mining-hydrogeological
Montanindustrie *f* mining industry
Montanit *m* montanite, $[(BiO)_2|TeO_4] \cdot 2H_2O$
Montanwachs *n* mineral (montan) wax, ozocerite
Montbrayit *m* montbrayite, Au_2Te_3
Monte-Carlo-Probenahme *f* Monte Carlo sampling *(sampling with random numbers from theoretical distributions)*
Montebrasit *m* montebrasite, $LiAl[OH|PO_4]$
Monteponit *m* cadmium oxide, CdO
Montgomeryit *m* montgomeryite, $Ca_4Al_5[(OH)_5|(PO_4)_6] \cdot 11H_2O$
Monticellit *m* monticellite, $CaMgSiO_4$
Montien *n*, **Montium** *n s.* Mont
Montmorillonit *m* montmorillonite, $(Na,Mg,Al)_2[(OH)_8|Si_4O_{10}] \cdot nH_2O$
Montmorillonitgruppe *f* montmorillonite (smectite) group
Montrealit *m* montrealite *(variety of olivine essexite)*
Montroseit *m* montroseite, $(V,Fe)OOH$
Montroydit *m* montroydite, HgO
Monzonit *m* monzonite *(rock between syenite and diorite)*
monzonitisch monzonitic
Moor *n* moor, fen, bog, swamp, mire, marsh; hill peat
~/unter Wasser wachsendes immersed bog

moorbildend peat-forming
Moorbildung f mire (peat) formation
Moorboden m fenny (boggy, marshy, peaty) soil, swampy land, quagmire
Moorbruch m (n) bog burst
Moordecke f peat cover
Mooreit m mooreite, $(Mg,Zn,Mn)_8[(OH)_{14}|SO_4] \cdot 4H_2O$
Moorentwässerung f marsh drainage
Moorerde f bog earth
Moorerz n morass ore
Moorgebiet n moor country, bog land
Moorgley m moor clay
Moorgrund m morass
Moorhouseit m moorhouseite, $(Co,Ni,Mn)[SO_4] \cdot 6H_2O$
moorig moory, fenny, peaty, swamped, paludal
Moorkunde f peat land science, investigation of bogs and marshes
Moorland n moorland, fenland, swampland
Moorlandschaft f moorland
Moormarsch f swampy marsh
Moormergel m marsh marl
Moorpodsol m turf podzol
Moorsee m bog pool
Moorsenke f slew
Moorsprengung f bog (peat) blasting
Moortorf m bog (mouldy, limnetic) peat, drag turf
~/tonüberdeckter dary
Moorwasser n boggy water
Moos n/**schwach angetorftes** moss slightly converted into peat
Moosachat m moss agate, mocha pebble (stone) (s. a. Chalzedon)
moosähnlich mosslike
Moosbedeckung f mossiness
Moosdecke f moss cover
moosförmig mossy
moosig mossy
Mooskunde f bryology
Moosmoor n moos fen (bog)
Moostorf m moss peat
Moraesit m moraesite, $Be_2[OH|PO_4] \cdot 4H_2O$
Moräne f moraine
~/angehäufte dumped moraine
~ einer Eisstillstandslage retreatal moraine
~/sollbedeckte kettle moraine
~/tektonische mélange
Moränenablagerung f morainic (moraine) deposit
Moränenbecken n morainic basin
moränenbedeckt moraine-covered
Moränenbogen m morainic arc, morainal lobe (loop), moraine lobe (loop)
Moränenbrekzie f scree breccia
Moränendecke f morainic cover
Moränengebiet n moraine district
Moränengirlanden fpl festooned moraines
Moränengürtel m moraine belt

Moränengürtels/innerhalb des intramorainic
Moränenhügel m morainic mound (hill, hummock)
Moränenkessel m moraine kettle
Moränenlandschaft f morainic (moraine) topography
~/kuppige knobby (pitted morainal, knob-and-kettle, kame-and-kettle) topography
Moränenlappen m, **Moränenlobus** m s. Moränenbogen
~/kleiner doughnut
Moränenmaterial n/**im Eis transportiertes** englacial (upper) till
Moränenschotter m morainic (morainal) gravel
Moränenschutt m moraine debris, till, iceland drift
Moränensee m morainic lake
Moränenstausee m moraine-dammed lake
Moränenwall m moraine rampart, morainic coteau
Moränenzug m morainic (moraine) tracts, morainic (moraine) dams
Moränenzuwachs m plastering-on (glacier)
Morast m morass, marsh, bog, mire
Morasterz n morass ore
morastig morassic, marshy, boggy
Moravikum n Moravicum
Mordenit m mordenite, ptilotite, $(Ca,K_2,Na_2)[AlSi_5O_{12}]_2 \cdot 6H_2O$
Morenosit m morenosite, nickel vitriol, $NiSO_4 \cdot 7H_2O$
Morganien n Morganian (Westphalian D in England)
Morganit m morganite (variety of beryl)
Morgendämmerung f dawn
Morgenstern m morning star
Morinit m morinite, $Ca_2NaAl_2[(F,OH)_5|(PO_4)_2] \cdot 2H_2O$
Morion m morion (variety of quartz)
Mornes pl mornes (tropical form of karst)
Morphogenese f morphogenesis, morphogeny
morphogenetisch morphogen[et]ic
Morphografie f morphography
morphografisch morphographic
Morphologie f morphology
~/der Erdoberfläche geomorphology
~/genetische genetic[al] morphology
morphologisch morphologic[al]
Morphometrie f morphometry
morphometrisch morphometric[al]
Morphoskopie f s. Morphometrie
Morphotropie f morphotropism, morphotropy
morphotropisch morphotropic
Morrison-Formation f Morrison Formation (Malm in North America)
Morrow n Morrowan [Stage] (of Pennsylvanian)
morsch rotten
Mörtelstruktur f mortar texture
Mosaikgefüge n mosaic texture

Mosaikzerlegung

Mosaikzerlegung f disintegration into mosaics
Mosandrit m mosandrite, rinkolite, $(Ca, Na, Y)_3(Ti, Zr, Ce)[(F, OH, O)_2 | Si_2O_7]$
Mosesit m mosesite, $[Hg_2N]Cl \cdot H_2O$
Moskau-Stufe f Moskovian [Stage] *(of Middle Carboniferous, East Europe)*
Mößbauer-Effekt m Moessbauer effect
Mottramit m mottramite, $Pb(Cu, Zn)[OH | VO_4]$
Mountainit m mountainite, $KNa_2Ca_2[HSi_9O_{20}] \cdot 5H_2O$
Mourit m mourite, $[(UO_2)_2 | (MoO_4)_5] \cdot 5H_2O$
Moveout n move-out
Mozambikit m mozambikite, $(Th, SE, U)(O, OH)_2$
Mud[d] m s. Schlick
Mudde f mud
Muffe f coupling
Mugearit m mugearite *(trachybasalt)*
Mühlsandstein m grindstone grit, burrstone, *(Am)* millstone
Muirit m muirite, $Ba_5CaTi[O_4 | Si_4O_{12}] \cdot 3H_2O$
Mulchen n mulching
Mulde f hollow, tray, downfold, syncline, synclinal fold, low ground[s]
~/falsche pseudosyncline
~/tektonische trough, structural syncline
Muldenachse f synclinal axis, axis of the trough
muldenartig trough-shaped, synclinal
Muldenbiegung f synclinal turn, trough curve
Muldenbildung f downfolding, synclinal formation
Muldeneinsenkung f synclinal depression
Muldenflügel m synclinal limb, flank of a basin
muldenförmig basinlike, alveolate
Muldengebiet n trough area
Muldenkern m trough core, core of syncline
Muldenlinie f bottom line
Muldenquelle f synclinal spring
Muldenscharnier n synclinal turn
Muldenschenkel m s. Muldenflügel
Muldenschichtung f trough cross stratification, festoon cross lamination
Muldenschluß m nose of synclinal fold, hairpin synclinal fold
Muldensee m synclinal lake
Muldenstellung f der Schieferung cleavage trough
Muldental n trough[-shaped] valley
Muldentiefstes n trough (bottom line) of a syncline
Mull m mild humus, mull
Müll m waste; garbage
Mullboden m mull soil
Mülldeponie f waste repository (storage site)
Mullion n mullion
Mullionstruktur f mullion (rodding) structure
~/irreguläre irregular mullion structure
Mullit m mullite, $Al_8O_3(OH, F) Si_3AlO_{16}$
mulmig pasty

Multiple f/einfache simple multiple
Multiplexer m multiplexer
Multishotgerät n multiple shot photoclinometer
Multispektralaufnahmen fpl multispectral (multiband, multichannel) images
Multispektralkamera f multispectral camera
Multispektralprojektor m additive colour viewer
Mumie f mummy
mumifizieren to mummify
Münder-Mergel m Münder Marl *(uppermost Malm, Lower Saxony basin)*
Mundfeld n s. Peristom
Mundloch n orifice, opening hole, adit opening
Mündung f 1. mouth, embouchure, debouchure *(of a river)*; estuary *(of a tidal river)*; 2. aperture *(palaeontology)*; 3. head *(of a well)*
~/gleichsohlige accordant junction
~/septale septal aperture
~/ungleichsohlige discordant junction
~/verschleppte delayed river junction
Mündungsbarren m mouth bar
Mündungsbecken n/**verschlammtes** silted estuary
Mündungsfortsätze mpl auricles, ears, lappets *(cephalopodans)*
Mündungsrand m s. Peristom
Mundwerkzeuge npl mouth parts *(arthropods)*
Murambit m murambite *(variety of leucite basanite)*
mürbe friable
Mürbheit f friability
Murbruch m s. Mure
Murdochit m murdochite, $PbCu_6O_8$
Mure f mud flow (avalanche, rock flow, stream, torrent), torrential wash, [cold] lahar
Murgang m s. Mure
Murit m murite *(olivine-bearing nepheline phonolite)*
Murkegel m torrential fan, talus
Murmanit m murmanite, $Na_2MnTi_3[SiO_4]_4 \cdot 8H_2O$
Murtobel m ravine, gully, *(Am)* gulch
Muschel f mussel; shell, pelecypod
Muschelbank f mussel bed, shell bank
Muschelbrekzie f shell breccia, lumachelle
muschelförmig conchiform
muschelig conchoidal, shelly, shell-like
~ bis splitterig semiconchoidal
Muschelkalk m 1. shell[y] limestone, coquina; 2. Muschelkalk [Series] *(Triassic)*
Muschelkunde f conchology
Muschelmarmor m shell marble
Muschelmergel m shell marl
Muschelsand m shell[y] sand
Muschelsandstein m shell[y] sandstone, beach rock
Muskeg m muskeg
Muskelfleck m, **Muskelnarbe** f muscle scar
Muskovit m muscovite, mirror stone, $KAl_2[(OH, F)_2 | AlSi_3O_{10}]$

Muskovit-Chlorit-Schiefer *m* muscovite phyllade
Muskovitgneis *m* muscovite gneiss
Muskovitgranit *m* muscovite granite
Muskovitquarzit *m* muscovite quartzite
Muskovitschiefer *m* muscovite schist
Muster *n* 1. sample; 2. pattern *(e.g. of a diagram)*
Musterabgrenzung *f* pattern delimitation (delineation)
Musteranalyse *f* pattern analysis
Musterbeutel *m* sample bag
Mustererkennung *f* pattern recognition
muten to claim
Muter *m* claimholder
Muting *n* muting
Mutteratom *n* parent atom
Mutterboden *m* native (parent, undisturbed, surface) soil, topsoil
Mutterelement *n* parent element
Muttergestein *n* bedrock *(e.g. of soils)*; native (mother, parent, country, source) rock
Mutterisotop *n* parent isotope
Mutterkristall *m* mother crystal
Mutterlauge *f* mother lye (liquor, liquid), leach brine
Muttermagma *n* parent[al] magma
Mutterpause *f* transparent positive original
Muttersubstanz *f* parent substance
Mutung *f* claim, concession
~/blinde demand for concession without previous discovery
Mutungskarte *f* claim map, concession plan
Mylonit *n* mylonite
mylonitisch mylonitic
mylonitisieren to myloni[ti]ze
Mylonitisierung *f* myloni[ti]zation
Mylonityzone *f* fractured (shatter) zone
Myrmekit *m* myrmekite

N

Nabel *m* umbilicus
Nachauftragnehmerschaft *f* staring *(geological prospecting)*
Nachbarfeld *n* adjoining concession (property)
Nachbargestein *n* adjoining (adjacent) rock
Nachbarkristall *m* contiguous crystal
Nachbarschaft *f* adjacency
Nachbarschichten *fpl* adjacent beds
Nachbarsonde *f* offset[ting] well
Nachbearbeitung *f* postprocessing
Nachbeben *n* aftervibrations, aftershock, trailer
nachbohren to underream, to bore again, to rebore
Nachbohren *n* underreaming, boring again, reboring
Nachbohrer *m* broaching bit
nachbrechen to crumble away

Nacheil[ungs]winkel *m* angle of lag
Nacheiszeit *f* postglacial time
nacheiszeitlich postglacial
Nacherkundung *f* postexploration
Nachfall *m* caving, cave[-in], false roof; clod, detritus; drawslate *(only slate in the roof of coal)*; sloughing *(within the borehole)*
nachfallen to cave in
Nachfaltung *f* posthumous folding
Nachfolgeintrusion *f* afterintrusion
Nachfolgetal *n* subsequent (strike) valley
nachgeben to yield *(e.g. telescoping of friction props)*
nachgiebig yielding
nachgiebig-gelenkig yielding and articulated
Nachgiebigkeit *f* capacity to yield
Nachinkohlung *f* recoalification
Nachintrusion *f* afterintrusion
Nachlaßvorrichtung *f* drilling control
Nachläufer *m* end portion, trailer *(seismics)*
nachnehmen to dint *(the floor)*
nachorogen postorogenic
Nachphase *f*/**hydrothermale** hydrothermal subsequent stage
Nachproduktion *f* afterflow
nachräumen to underream
Nachräumen *n* underreaming
Nachräumer *m* reamer
nachreißen to rip
Nachreißen *n* ripping
~ der Sohle floor dinting
Nachreißstelle *f* ripping lip, canch
Nachrichtensatellit *m* communications satellite
Nachriß *m* **im Liegenden** bottom canch
Nachsacken *n* settling
nachschießen to trim *(an adit)*
nachschleifen to regrind
Nachschliff *m* regrind
Nachsenkung *f* delayed subsidence
Nachsinken *n* downsagging
nachtleuchtend noctilucent
nachträglich subsequent
Nachtwolke *f*/**leuchtende** luminous cloud
Nachweis *m* 1. proof; 2. detection, indication
~ von gasförmigem Kohlenwasserstoff in Bohrkernen hydrocarbon gas detection in cores
nachweisbar traceable
Nachweisempfindlichkeit *f* detecting sensitivity
nachweisen 1. to prove; 2. to detect, to indicate
Nachweisgerät *n* detection instrument, detector
~ für Gammastrahlen gamma detector
Nachweisglied *n* detecting element
Nachweisgrenze *f* detection limit
Nachwirkung *f*/**elastische** elastic aftereffect, creep recovery
~/magnetische magnetic aftereffect
nackt bare
Nacktsamer *mpl* *s.* Gymnospermen

Nadel

Nadel f needle
Nadelbäume mpl conifers
Nadeleisenerz n needle ironstone, goethite, α-FeOOH
Nadelerz n s. Aikinit
nadelförmig acicular, aciculate
Nadelharnisch m slickolites
nadelig acicular, needlelike
Nadelkohle f leaf (needle) coal
Nadelsonde f needle probe
Nadelstein m needlestone
Nadelzinn m s. Zinnstein
Nadirabstand m nadir distance
Nadirpunkt m nadir point
Nadirwinkel m nadir angle
Nadorit m nadorite, $PbSbO_2Cl$
Naegit m naegite (variety of zircon)
Nagatelith m nagatelite (variety of allanite)
Nagelfluh f nagelfluh, pudding stone, gompholite
~/bunte partly coloured pudding stone
Nagelkalk m styolitic (cone-in-cone) limestone
Nagelkalkstruktur f cone-in-cone structure
Nagelkopfschramme f nail head scratch
Nagelung f piling (of a rock)
Nagyagit m nagyagite, tellurium glance, black telluride, $AuTe_2 \cdot Pb(S, Te)$
Nahansicht f close-up view
Nahbeben n near earthquake (shock), neighbouring earthquake
Nahcolith m nahcolite, $NaHCO_3$
naheliegend close-set
Näherung f approximation
Näherungsformel f approximation formula
Nährboden m vegetable soil
Nährelement n nutritive element
Nährgebiet n alimentation (nourishment) area, feeding (gathering) ground, intake place; collecting (catchment) basin
Nährhumus m fertile mould
nährstoffarm oligotrophic
Nährstoffgehalt m nutrient content
nährstoffreich eutrophic
Naht f 1. juncture; 2. suture (of fossils)
Nahtzone f konvergierender Platten trench
Nakhlit m nakhlite (achondritic, diopside-, and olivine-bearing meteorite)
Nakrit m nacrite, stone marrow, $Al_4[(OH)_8 \mid Si_4O_{10}]$
Name m/**gültiger** valid name (rules of nomenclature)
~/ungültiger invalid name (rules of nomenclature)
Namur[ien] n, **Namurium** n, **Namur-Stufe** f Namurian [Stage] (basal stage of Upper Carboniferous in West and Central Europe)
Nannofossil n nannofossil
Nannoplankton n nannoplankton
Nantokit m nantokite, CuCl
Napalith m napalite (hydrocarbon compound)
Naphthenöl n naphthenic oil
Narbe f [root] scar, cicatrix
Narbenverwitterung f pitted weathering
Narbenzone f s. Narbe
narbig scarred (by ice)
Narizien n Narizian [Stage] (marine stage, middle Eocene of North America)
Narsarsukit m narsarsukite, $Na_2Ti[O \mid Si_4O_{10}]$
Nashorn n/**wollhaariges** woolly rhinoceros
Nasinit m nasinite, $Na_2[B_5O_6(OH)_5] \cdot H_2O$
Nasonit m nasonite, $Pb_6Ca_4[Cl_2 \mid (Si_2O_7)_3]$
Naßanalyse f analysis by wet way
Naßaufbereitung f wet cleaning (dressing)
Naßbagger m dredge[r]
naßbaggern to dredge
Naßbaggerung f dredging
Nässe f wetness; moisture
Naßfestigkeit f green strength
Naßgas n wet natural gas, combination gas
Naßklassieren n hydraulic classification
Naßkugelmühle f ball mill for wet grinding
Naßmahlen n wet grinding; wet crushing
Naßmoor n soggy moor
Naßöl n wet oil
Naßreiniger m wet washer
Naßreinigung f wet washing
Naßschliff m wet grinding
Naßsiebung f wet screening
Naßsortierung f wet cleaning
Naßzerkleinerung f wet crushing
Nasturan n s. Uranpechblende
Natrit m natron, $Na_2CO_3 \cdot 10H_2O$
Natrium n sodium, Na
Natriumchlorid n sodium chloride, NaCl
Natriumglimmer m paragonite, $NaAl_2[(OH, F)_2 \mid AlSi_3O_{10}]$
Natroalunit m natroalunite, $NaAl_3[(OH)_6 \mid (SO_4)_2]$
Natrochalcit m natrochalcite, $NaCu_2[OH \mid (SO_4)_2] \cdot H_2O$
Natrojarosit m natrojarosite, cyprusite, $NaFe[(OH)_6 \mid (SO_4)_2]$
Natrolith m natrolite, $Na_2[Al_2Si_3O_{10}] \cdot 2H_2O$
Natromontebrasit m natromontebrasite, $(Na, Li)[(OH, F) \mid PO_4]$
Natron n s. Natrit
Natronalaun m sodium alaun, mendozite, $NaAl(SO_4)_2 \cdot 12H_2O$
Natronfeldspat m sodium feldspar, albite, $NaAlSi_3O_8$
Natronhornblende f glaucophane schist
Natronkalk m soda lime
Natronlauge f caustic soda solution
Natronsalpeter m soda nitre, nitratine, nitratite, caliche, $NaNO_3$
Natronsee m soda (alkali) lake
Natronvormacht f preponderance of soda rocks (in igneous rocks)
Natrophilit m natrophilite, $Na(Mn, Fe)[PO_4]$
Natur f/**belebte** animate nature
Naturasphalt m natural (rock) asphalt
Naturbimsstein m pumice
Naturbitumen n native asphalt, asphaltic bitumen

Naturbrücke f natural bridge
Naturdenkmal n nature sanctuary
Naturgas n natural gas
~/**an Öldämpfen reiches** gas rich in oil vapours
~/**gasolinfreies** dry natural gas
Naturgasolin n natural (casing-head) gasoline
Naturgraphit m plumbago, plumbagine
Naturkatastrophe f natural disaster
Naturkoks m natural (geological) coke; burnt (cinder) coal
Naturphosphat n phosphorite
Natursalzsole f natural brine
Naturschacht m jama
Naturschätze mpl natural resources
Naturschutz m nature preservation (conservation)
Naturschutzgebiet n nature reserve
Naturstein m natural stone, quarrystone
Natursteinplatte f quarry tile
Naturwerkstein m natural freestone
Naujakasit m naujakasite, $Na_4FeAl_4H_4Si_8O_{27}$ (Na, K)$_6FeAl_4[O_3$ I $Si_4O_{10}]_2 \cdot H_2O$
Naumannit m naumannite, Ag_2Se
Navajo-Formation f Navajo Formation *(Lias and lower part of Dogger in North America)*
Navajoit m navajoite, $V_2O_5 \cdot 3H_2O$
Navarro-Gruppe f Navarro Group *(upper Campanian and Maastrichtian, North America)*
Navier-Stokes-Gleichung f Navier-Stokes equation
neanisch neanic
Nebel m mist; fog
~/**dichter** [thick] fog
~/**feuchter** wet fog
~/**galaktischer** galactic nebula
~/**leichter** haze
~/**planetarischer** planetary nebula
Nebelbank f fog bank
Nebelbildung f formation of fog
Nebeleis n mist ice
Nebelfleck m nebula, nephelium
Nebelhülle f nebulosity
nebelig misty; foggy; hazy
Nebeligkeit f mistiness; fogginess; haziness
Nebelschicht f cloudy layer
Nebelschleier m misty veil; nebula
Nebelschwaden m, **Nebelstreifen** m fog band
Nebelströmung f mist flow
Nebeltröpfchen n fog (cloud) droplet
Nebenarm m arm of a river
Nebenarme mpl/**verzweigte** branching distributaries *(of a delta)*
Nebenbereich m side lobes
Nebenbestandteil m secondary (incidental) constituent
nebenblattlos exstipulate *(palaeobotany)*
nebenblattständig side-leaved *(palaeobotany)*
Nebencañon m tributary (side) canyon
Nebeneinanderlagerung f juxtaposition
nebeneinanderstellen to juxtapose
Nebeneinanderstellung f juxtaposition

Nebenerscheinungen fpl/**vulkanische** paravolcanic phenomena
Nebenfluß m [con]tributary, affluent, influent, confluent, feeder
~/**linker** left-bank tributary
~/**rechter** right-bank tributary
Nebenflußsystem n system of tributaries
Nebengang m secondary vein
Nebengemengteil m accessory (medium) constituent
Nebengestein n wall (adjoining, inclosing, neighbouring, surrounding, dead) rock, rock wall, associated strata
~/**mildes** teary ground
Nebengesteinsbruchstück n fragment of country rock
Nebengesteinseinschluß m inclusion of country rock
Nebengesteinsumwandlung f wall rock alteration
Nebengesteinswände fpl vein skirts *(of a lode)*
Nebengletscher m distributary glacier
Nebengrundwasserspiegel m apparent water table
Nebengruppe f subgroup
Nebenkarte f inset
Nebenkegel m secondary (subsidiary, subordinate) cone
Nebenkluft f subjoint, auxiliary joint
Nebenkrater m secondary crater
Nebenmeer n border (marginal, minor) sea
Nebenmineral n accessory (associated, accompanying, subordinate) mineral
Nebenmond m paraselena, paraselene
Nebenmulde f minor trough
Nebenprodukt n by-product
Nebenschlechte f butt cleat
Nebenschlot m subordinate vent
Nebenschlucht f tributary ravine
Nebenschuß m side shot
Nebensepten npl minor septa
Nebensonne f parhelion
Nebenspalte f subsidiary (auxiliary) fissure
Nebenstation f slave station
Nebenstörung f auxiliary fault
Nebental n side (branch) valley
Nebentief n secondary depression
Nebentrum n ancillary vein
~/**einen Hauptgang schneidendes** counterlode, countervein
Nebenverwerfung f associated (auxiliary, minor, subsidiary, branch) fault
Nebenvulkan m subordinate volcano
Nebenwasserscheide f secondary divide
Nebraska-Vereisung f Nebrascan [Ice Age] *(Pleistocene of North America corresponding to Eburonian in Europe)*
Nebularhypothese f nebular hypothesis
Nebulit m nebulite *(migmatite)*
Neck m neck, stump
negativ/optisch optically negative

Negative

Negative *npl* **von Dolomitkristallen** dolocasts, dolomoulds
~ von Ooiden oomoulds
Nehden *n*, **Nehden-Stufe** *f* Nehdenian [Stage] *(of Upper Devonian, Europe)*
nehmen/Probe to take sample
Nehrung *f* beach ridge, [sand] bar, bay[mouth] bar, sand reef
~/angelehnte headland bar
neigen/sich to dip
Neighborit *m* neighborite, $NaMgF_3$
Neigung *f* 1. incline, inclination, dip, hade *(of a fault plane);* slope, [falling] gradient, acclivity; 2. tilt, roll *(in direction of flight, i.e. alongtrack);* swing, pitch *(perpendicular to direction of flight, i.e. across-track)*
~ der Erdachse tilt of the earth's axis
~/magnetische magnetic bias
Neigungsauflösung *f* dip resolution *(seismics)*
Neigungsebene *f* inclined plane
Neigungsgleiche *f s.* Isokline
Neigungsgröße *f* amount of dip
Neigungsmesser *m* [in]clinometer; gradiometer; tiltmeter; deviation recorder, directional recording instrument *(for boreholes)*
Neigungsmessung *f* directional deviation logging, directional surveying *(in boreholes)*
~/geophysikalische geophysical slope measurement
Neigungsschießen *n* dip shooting
Neigungswinkel *m* angle of incline (inclination, pitch, deviation)
~ des Bohrlochs borehole inclination angle
Nekoit *m* necoite, $Ca_{1,5}[Si_3O_6(OH)_3] \cdot 2^1/_2 H_2O$
Nekonit *m* nekonite *(apatite-ilmenite rock)*
Nekrosalinar *n* necrosalinity
Nekton *n* nekton
nektonisch nektonic
nematoblastisch nematoblastic, fibroblastic
NE-Metall *n s.* Nichteisenmetall
Nenndruck *m* rated pressure
Nenndurchmesser *m* nominal diameter
Nennlast *f* nominal load-bearing capacity
Neodigenit *m* neodigenite, Cu_9S_5
Neoeuropa *n* Neo-Europe
Neogäa *f* Neogaea
neogen Neogenic
Neogen *n* Neogene *(Miocene and Pliocene)*
Neokom *n* Neocomian *(lower part of Lower Cretaceous)*
Neolithikum *n* Neolithic [Age, Times]
Neomorphismus *m* neomorphism
Neosom *n* neosome
Neostratotyp *m* neostratotype
Neotantalit *m s.* Mikrolith
Neotektonik *f* neotectonics
Neotypus *m* neotype
neovulkanisch neovolcanic
Neovulkanismus *m* neovolcanism
Neozoikum *n* Neozoic [Era]
neozoisch Neozoic
Nephelin *m* nepheline, nephelite, elaeolite, $KNa_3[AlSiO_4]_4$

Nephelinbasalt *m* nepheline basalt
Nephelindiorit *m* nepheline diorite
Nephelindolerit *m* nepheline dolerite
Nephelingestein *n* nephelitic rock
Nephelinisierung *f* nephelinization
Nephelinit *m* nephelinite *(rock of the alkali gabbro clan)*
Nephelinphonolith *m* nepheline phonolite
Nephelinsyenit *m* nepheline syenite, elaeolite syenite
Nephrit *m* nephrite; jade; y[o]ustone
Nepouit *m* nepouite *(variety of antigorite)*
Neptunismus *m* Neptunism, Neptunian theory
Neptunit *m* neptunite, carlosite, $Na_2FeTi[Si_4O_{12}]$
neritisch neritic
Nesosilikat *n* nesosilicate
Nesquehonit *m* nesquehonite, $MgCO_3 \cdot 3H_2O$
Nest *n* node, kidney *(of ore)*
Nestbohren *n* cluster drilling, grouping of wells
nesterweise by groups
Nettoförderung *f* net production
Nettomächtigkeit *f* net pay
Nettostrahlung *f* net radiation
Netz *n* net[work]; canvas *(of a survey)*
~/hydrologisches hydrologic network
~/synoptisches synoptic network
~/Wulffsches Wulff's net
netzartig reticulated, reticular
Netzbildung *f* netting
Netzdichte *f* reticular density
Netzebene *f* lattice (atomic) plane
Netzebenenabstand *m* interplanar [crystal] spacing, space-lattice distance, interface
netzförmig netlike, reticulated, reticular
Netzgefüge *n* cancellated structure
Netzleiste *f* mud crack *(sedimentary fabric)*
Netzleisten *fpl***/gefältelte** crumpled mud-crack casts
Netzmikrometer *n* cross-line micrometer
Netzmittel *n* wetting agent
Netzstruktur *f* reticulated (cellular) structure
Netztextur *f* welted texture
Netzwerk *n* net[work]
Netzwerkgefüge *n* network fabric
Netzwerktechnik *f* network planning
neuaktivieren to reactivate
Neuaktivierung *f* reactivation
neubeleben to rejuvenate, to reactivate
Neubelebung *f* rejuvenation, reactivation
Neubruch *m* new rupture
Neueis *n* sludge ice
neugebildet neogenic *(petrographically)*
Neukristallisation *f* recrystallization
neukristallisieren to recrystallize
Neuland *n* virgin soil
Neulandgewinnung *f* reclamation of land
Neumond *m* new moon
neuordnen to rearrange
Neuordnung *f* rearrangement
~ von Kristallen rearrangement of crystals

Neuozean *m* new ocean
Neuschnee *m* fresh[ly fallen] snow
~/nasser clog snow
Neuseeland-Subprovinz *f* New Zealand Sub-province *(palaeobiogeography, Devonian)*
Neusprossung *f* new growth
Neutralebene *f* neutral plane
neutralisieren to neutralize
Neutronenabsorption *f* absorption (capture) of neutrons
Neutronenaktivierungsanalyse *f* neutron activation analysis
Neutronenbestrahlung *f* irradiation by neutrons
Neutroneneinfang-Gamma-Spektrometrie *f* neutron capture gamma-ray spectrometry
Neutronenfluß *m* neutron flux
Neutronen-Gamma-Spektrometrie *f* neutron-gamma-ray spectrometry
Neutronenlog *n*, **Neutronenmessung** *f* neutron logging
Neutronenquelle *f* atom smasher *(for logging)*
Neutronenstrahlung *f* neutron radiation
Neutronenüberschuß *m* neutron excess
Neutronenzahl *f* number of neutrons
Neutron-Neutron-Log *n* neutron-neutron logging
Neu- und Brachland *n* virgin and idle lands
Neuzeit *f* Recent Epoch
Newberyit *m* newberyite, $HMgPO_4 \cdot 3H_2O$
N'hangellit *m* n'hangellite *(kind of bitumen)*
Niagara *n*, **Niagarien** *n* Niagaran [Series] *(upper Llandoverian to lower Budnanian in North America)*
Niccolit *m* niccolite, copper nickel, NiAs
nichtausgelaugt non-leached
nichtaushaltend discontinuous
nichtbindig cohesionless, uncohesive, incoherent, friable
Nicht-Darcy-Strömung *f* non-Darcy flow
nichtdissoziiert non-dissociated
nichtdrusig non-drusy
Nichteisenmetall *n* non-ferrous metal
Nichterze *npl* non-metallics
Nichterzmineral *n* non-metallic mineral
nichtflüchtig non-volatile
nichtglazial non-glacial
Nichtgleichgewicht *n* disequilibrium
nichtkristallin non-crystalline
nichtleuchtend non-luminous
Nichtlinearität *f* non-linearity
nichtmagmatisch non-magmatic, amagmatic
nichtmagnetisch non-magnetic
Nichtmetall *n* non-metal
nichtmetallführend non-metalliferous
nichtmetallisch non-metallic
nichtmischbar insoluble
Nichtmischbarkeit *f* immiscibility
nichtstationär non-steady
nichtstrahlend non-radiating, non-radiative
nichtvergasbar non-gasifiable
nichtwäßrig non-aqueous

Nickel *n* nickel, Ni
Nickel-Antigorit *m* s. Garnierit
Nickelarsenkies *m* s. Gersdorffit
Nickelblüte *f* nickel bloom (green, ochre), annabergite, $Ni_3[AsO_4]_2 \cdot 8H_2O$
Nickeleisen *n* nickel-iron, nickeliferous iron, α-(Fe, Ni)
Nickel-Eisen-Kern *m* nickel-iron core
Nickelerz *n* nickel ore
~/lateritisches lateritic nickel ore
nickelführend nickeliferous, nickel-bearing
nickelhaltig nickelous, nickeliferous
Nickelin *m* copper nickel, niccolite, NiAs
Nickelsmaragd *m* emerald nickel, zaratite, $Ni_3[(OH)_4 | CO_3] \cdot 4H_2O$
Nicol *n* nicol [prism]
Nicols *npl*/**gekreuzte** crossed nicols
niederbrechen to cave [in]
Niederbrechen *n* **des Hangenden** roof foundering *(magma hearth)*
niederbringen to carry down, to lower, to sink, to put down *(a well)*
Niederbringen *n* sinking, well drilling, drilling of a well
~ von Aufschlußbohrungen wild-cat drilling
niedergehen to descend
Niedermoorboden *m* humus fen soil
Niedermoortorf *m* low-moor peat
Niederschlag *m* 1. rainfall; 2. precipitation; precipitate; sediment; fallout
~/effektiver effective precipitation
~/feiner flowers
~/künstlicher artificial precipitation
~/radioaktiver fallout
~/reicher abundant rainfall
niederschlagen to precipitate
Niederschlagen *n* **von Feuchtigkeit** condensation of moisture
Niederschlags-Abfluß-Beziehung *f* rainfall runoff relation
Niederschlagsänderung *f* modification of precipitation
Niederschlagsatlas *m* rainfall frequency atlas
Niederschlagserosion *f* rainfall erosion
Niederschlagsfolge *f* cycles in precipitation
Niederschlagsgebiet *n* area of precipitation; gathering ground, catchment area
Niederschlagshäufigkeit *f* precipitation frequency
Niederschlagshöhe *f* rainfall coefficient, depth of rain[fall], altitude of precipitation
~/mittlere average precipitation (rainfall figure)
~/tägliche daily amount of rainfall
Niederschlagshöhenkurve *f* rainfall curve, isohyet[al line]
Niederschlagskoeffizient *m* rainfall coefficient
Niederschlagsmenge *f* amount of precipitation; net rainfall *(to the surface)*; gross rainfall *(above the vegetation)*; throughfall *(to the surface without vegetation)*; stemflow *(to the surface along trees)*

Niederschlagsmenge

~/jährliche annual (yearly) rainfall, annual precipitation
Niederschlagsmesser *m* precipitation gauge; rain gauge
Niederschlagsprognose *f* forecasting of precipitation; forecasting of rainfall
Niederschlagsregistrierung *f* rainfall record
niederschlagsreich rainy
Niederschlagsschwankung *f* variation of precipitation
Niederschlagsstärke *f* average rainfall intensity *(mm/min)*
Niederschlagsüberschuß *m* precipitation excess
Niederschlags-Verdunstungs-Verhältnis *n* precipitation-evaporation ratio
Niederschlagswasser *n* rainwater; atmospheric water; meteoric water
Niederterrasse *f* lower terrace
Niederung *f* lowland, low ground[s], flat [land]
~/überschwemmungsgefährdete flood-menaced land
Niederungsgebiet *n* [/ **sumpfiges**] backswamp area *(of a river)*
Niederungsmoor *n* low moor, flat (lowland, low-lying, black) bog, humus fen
Niederungsmoorboden *m* low moor soil
Niederungstorf *m* fen peat
Niedrigwasser *n* low water (tide)
Niedrigwasserabfluß *m* low[-water] flow, low-level discharge
Niedrigwasserabflußprognose *f* low-flow forecast
Niedrigwasserbett *n* minor bed *(of a river)*
Niedrigwasserlinie *f* low-water line; tide mark
Niedrigwassermenge *f* low-water discharge
Niedrigwasserprognose *f* low-flow forecast
Niedrigwasserstand *m* low-water level (stage)
~/mittlerer mean low-water level
Niefrostboden *m* subgelisol, never frozen soil
Niere *f* node, nodule, bunch [of ore]
Nierenerz *n* nodular (kidney) ore
nierenförmig reniform; kidney-shaped
nierig reniform
nieseln to drizzle
Nieseln *n* drizzle
Nife *n*, **Nife-Kern** *m* nife
Nifontovit *m* nifontovite, $CaB_2O_4 \cdot 2,3H_2O$
Niggliit *m* niggliite, Pt(Su, Te)
Niggli-Wert *m* Niggli value
Nigrin *m* nigrine *(variety of rutile)*
Niob *n* niobium, columbium, Nb
Niobit *m* niobite, columbite, (Fe, Mn) $(Nb, Ta)_2O_6$
Niobium *n s.* Niob
Nioboloparit *m* nioboloparite, (Na, Ce, Ca) $(Ti, Nb)O_3$
Niocalit *m* niocalite, $Ca_3(Nb, Ca, Mg)[(O, F)_2 \mid Si_2O_7]$
Nippebbe *f* neap low tide[s]
Nippflut *f* neap tide[s]
Nipphochwasser *n* high water of ordinary neap tide
Nippniedrigwasser *n* low water of ordinary neap tide
Nipptide *f* neap tide[s]
Nische *f* niche; cave; recess
~/ökologische ecologic[al] niche
Nischenhöhle *f* shelter cave
Niton *n* niton, Rn
Nitrat *n* nitrate
Nitrierung *f* nitrification
Nitrifikation *f* nitrification
Nitrobaryt *m* nitrobarite, $Ba(NO_3)_2$
Nitrocalcit *m* nitrocalcite, $Ca[NO_3]_2 \cdot 4H_2O$
Nitrokalit *m* nitre, petre, KNO_3
Nitromagnesit *m* nitromagnesite, $Mg(NO_3)_2 \cdot 2H_2O$
Nitronatrit *m* nitratine, nitratite, soda nitre, $NaNO_3$
nival nival
nival-äolisch niveo-aeolian
Niveau *n* level
~/hydrostatisches hydrostatic level
~/piezometrisches piezometric level
Niveauänderung *f* change (shift) of level
Niveaudifferenz *f s.* Niveauunterschied
Niveaufläche *f* **des Geopotentials** geopotential surface
~ gleichen Zeitalters isochronous surface
Niveaulinie *f* contour line
Niveauschwankung *f* level fluctuation
Niveauschwankungen *fpl* **des Meeres/glazialeustatische** glacioeustatic fluctuations of the sea level
Niveauunterschied *m* difference of level, head
Nivellement *n* levelling
nivellieren to level
Nivellierinstrument *n* stadia
~ mit Fernrohr telescope level
Nivellierlatte *f* levelling rod
Nivellierung *f* levelling
Nivellierzeichen *n* bench mark
Nobleit *m* nobleite, $Ca[B_6O_9(OH)_2] \cdot 3H_2O$
Nocerin *m* nocerite, $Mg_3[Fe_3 \mid BO_3]$
Nodus *m* node
Nomenklatur *f*/**binäre** binomial nomenclature
~/stratigrafische stratigraphic[al] nomenclature
Nontronit *m* nontronite, morencite *(mineral of the montmorillonite group)*
Nor *n* Norian [Stage] *(of Triassic)*
Norbergit *m* norbergite, $Mg_3[(OH, F)_2 \mid SiO_4]$
Nord/geografisch geographical (true) north
~/magnetisch magnetic north
Norden *m*/**geografischer** geographical (true) north
Nordenskiöldin *m* nordenskioldine, $CaSn(BO_3)_2$
Nordhemisphäre *f* Northern hemisphere
nördlich North[ern] *(area)*; northerly *(wind)*; boreal, septentrional
Nordlicht *n* northern lights
Nordpol *m* north pole

Nordpolarexpedition f arctic expedition
Nordrichtung f/**magnetische** magnetic compass north
Nordwind m north wind, norther
Norit m norite (variety of gabbro)
Normalbeschleunigung f normal acceleration
Normalbett n mean water bed (channel)
Normale f normal
Normalfeld n reference (normal) field
~/**magnetisches** normal magnetic field
Normalgranit m biotite granite
Normalkorrektur f latitude correction
Normallast f normal load
Normalnull n [mean] sea level, zero of level
Normal-Ozeanwasser-Standard m standard mean ocean water, SMOW (deuterium)
Normalprofil n/**geologisches** columnar section
Normalschichtung f true bedding
Normalschwere f normal [value of] gravity
Normalspannung f normal stress (traction)
~/**wirkliche** normal effective stress
Normalspannungszustand m normal stress state
Normalsphäroid n normal sphäroid
Normalspülen n direct circulation (of borehole)
Normalverformung f pure strain
Normalverteilung f normal (Gaussian) distribution
Normalverteilungskurve f s. Glockenkurve
Normalzeit f standard time
Normativmineral n normative (standard) mineral
Normdruck m standard condition pressure
Normenvorschrift f standard specification
Northupit m northupite, $Na_3Mg[Cl \mid (CO_3)_2]$
Nosean m nosean, noselite, $Na_8[SO_4 \mid (AlSiO_4)_6]$
Noumeait m s. Garnierit
Nováčekit m nováčecite, $Mg[UO_2 \mid AsO_4]_2 \cdot 10H_2O$
Novaculit m novaculite (variety of hornstone)
Novakit m novacite, Cu_4As_3
Nsutit m nsutite, $Mn_2(O, OH)_2$
Nugget n nugget
nuggetähnlich nuggety
Nuggeteffekt m nugget effect
Nuggetsuche f nuggeting
Nuggetvarianz f nugget variance, variance of the nugget effect
Nukleon n nucleon
Nuklid n nuclide
~/**radioaktives** radionuclide
Nulleffekt m background count
Nullisogone f isogonic zero line
Nullmeridian m zero (reference, Greenwich) meridian
Nullpegel m zero gauge
Nullpunktenergie f zero of energy
Nummulitenkalk m nummulitic limestone
Nummulitensandstein m nummulitic sandstone

Nunatak m nunatak (ice-free hill in polar regions)
Nutzanwendung f/**geologische** geologic[al] application
Nutzbarmachung f utilization
~ **von Salzböden** reclamation of salterns
Nutzdruck m effective pressure
Nutzeffekt m coefficient of performance
Nutzlast f payload
Nutzporosität f effective (practical) porosity
Nutz-Stör-Verhältnis n signal-to-noise ratio, SNR
Nutzung f beneficial use
~ **mineralischer Rohstoffe/komplexe** complex utilization of mineral raw materials
Nutzwasser n process (service, industrial) water
Nyerereit m nyerereite, $Na_2Ca[CO_3]_2$

O

Oase f oasis
Oberbank f top layer (of a seam)
Oberbau m superstructure
Oberbecken n upper reservoir
Oberboden m upper floor
Oberbohrmeister m toolpusher
Oberdevon n Upper Devonian [Series, Epoch]
Oberfläche f surface; superficies
~/**apikalische** apical plane
~ **des Muldentiefsten** trough plane
~/**freie** open condition of surface; free surface (of ground water)
~/**hügelige** hummocky surface
~/**löcherige** scalloped surface
~/**mit Grübchen bedeckte** dimpled surface
~/**mit Schmelzrinde bedeckte** crusted surface (of meteorites)
~/**narbige** pitted surface
~/**schaumige** scoriaceous surface
~/**spezifische** specific surface (of a rock particle)
~/**windgefurchte** wind-grooved surface, wind-channelled surface
Oberflächenabdruck m replica
Oberflächenabfluß m surface (direct) runoff, overland flow
Oberflächenablagerung f surface (surficial) deposit
Oberflächenabrasion f surface abrasion
Oberflächenabspülung f surface wash of rain
Oberflächenabtragung f surface removing
Oberflächenanschnitt m eines Batholithen acrobatholithic stage
Oberflächenanzeichen npl **von Erdöllagerstätten** surface oil shows
Oberflächenareal n surface area
Oberflächenbau m surface structure
Oberflächenbeobachtung f examination of surface
Oberflächenberäumung f **durch fließendes Wasser** fluviraption

Oberflächenbeschaffenheit 226

Oberflächenbeschaffenheit f surface conditions
Oberflächenbestrahlung f surface irradiation
Oberflächenbewässerung f surface irrigation
Oberflächendecke f superficial covering
Oberflächeneinebnung f durch Frostwirkung cryoplanation
Oberflächenenergie f surface energy *(of a rock particle)*
Oberflächenentwässerung f surface drainage
Oberflächenerguß m superficial outflow
Oberflächenerkundung f surface prospecting
~/elektrische electrical surface prospecting
Oberflächenfalten fpl superficial folds
Oberflächenfaltung f superficial folding
Oberflächenfestigkeit f surface stability
Oberflächenform f surface (land) form
Oberflächengeber m surface strain indicator
Oberflächengefälle n surface slope
Oberflächengeologie f surface (areal) geology, cenology
Oberflächengestalt[ung] f [surface] configuration, topography
Oberflächengestein n surface (surficial, supercrust) rock
Oberflächengewässer n surface waters
Oberflächengrenzschicht f surface boundary layer
Oberflächenhaftwasser n/zusammenhängendes funicular regime
Oberflächenhärte f surface hardness
Oberflächenhorizont m surface horizon
Oberflächenkartierung f surface mapping
Oberflächenkonservierung f surface conservation
Oberflächenmagma n surface magma
Oberflächenmoräne f surface (superglacial) moraine
oberflächennah close to the surface; superficial; inframundane
Oberflächenprospektion f s. Oberflächenerkundung
Oberflächenrauhigkeit f surface roughness
Oberflächenreibung f surface friction
Oberflächenschicht f surface layer (bed)
~/dünne surface film
Oberflächenschießen n air shooting *(seismics)*
Oberflächenschliff m surface grinding
Oberflächenschutt m surface debris
~ des Gletschers glacier rubbish
Oberflächensenkung f surface depression
Oberflächenspannung f surface tension
Oberflächenströmung f epicurrent *(of the ocean)*; surface stream
Oberflächenstruktur f surface structure
Oberflächentemperatur f surface temperature
Oberflächentrendanalyse f trend-surface analysis
Oberflächenverdichtung f superficial compaction
Oberflächenverdunstung f surface evaporation

Oberflächenvulkanismus m external volcanism
Oberflächenwasser n surface (superficial, land) water; suspended subsurface water
Oberflächenwasserbindung f surface retention
Oberflächenwelle f surface (ground) wave; ground roll *(seismics)*
~/Rayleighsche Rayleigh wave *(seismics)*
~/seismische circumferential wave
oberflächlich superficial
Oberhang m high slope
oberirdisch above ground
Oberjura m s. Jura/Oberer
Oberkambrium n Upper Cambrian [Series, Epoch]
Oberkante f top [side]
~/multiple multiple top
~/rekonstruierte reconstructed (projected, estimated) top
~/scheinbare apparent top
~/wahre true top
Oberkantensonde f reciprocal sonde
Oberkarbon n 1. Upper Carboniferous [Series, Epoch], Silesian [Series, Epoch] *(in West and Middle Europe corresponding to Namurian A to Stephanian)*; 2. s. Stefan
Oberkohle f bench coal *(of a seam)*
Oberkreide f Upper Cretaceous [Series, Epoch]
Oberland n upland areas
Oberlauf m upper course, headwaters *(of a river)*
Obermoräne f surface (superglacial) moraine
Operm Upper Permian [Series, Epoch]
Oberschenkelknochen m s. Femur
Oberstrom m superficial current (s.a. Oberflächenströmung)
Oberwasser n headwater, suspended subsurface water
oberwasserseitig upstream
Oberwasserspiegel m upstream water line
Objektführer m attachable mechanical stage *(stereomicroscope)*
Objektiv n objective
Objektivträger m object-glass carrier, base board
Objektmarkierer m object marker
Objektmikrometer n stage micrometer
Objekttisch m revolving stage
Objektträger m object carrier (support, slide)
Objektträgerplättchen n object-support slide (lamina), specimen-support grid
Obruchevit m obruchevite, $(Y, Na, Ca)_2(Nb, Ti, Ta)_2O_6(O, OH, F)$
obsequent obsequent
Observatorium n observatory
~/magnetisches magnetic observatory
Obsidian m obsidian, volcanic glass
~/echter Iceland agate
~/edler marecanite
Occipitalfurche f occipital lobe *(trilobites)*

Ochoan *n* Ochoan *(uppermost Permian in North America)*
Ochrolith *m s.* Nadorit
Ocker *m* ochre, yellow earth
~/brauner (gelber) spruce ochre
~/roter rud[d]
ockerartig ochr[e]ous
Ockererde *f/gelbe* sil
~/rote red bole
ockerfarben ochr[e]y
ockergelb ochre-yellow
Ockergestein *n* ochr[e]ous rock
ockerhaltig, ockerig ochr[e]ous
Ockerschiefer *m* ochre schist
Ockerschlamm *m* ochr[e]ous mud
öde barren
Odinit *m* odinite *(basaltic dike rock)*
Ödland *n* waste (barren) land; heathland; badlands
Öffnermuskeln *mpl s.* Deduktores
Öffnung *f* 1. opening; orifice; 2. vent, throat *(of a volcano)*
~/klaffende gaping hole
Offretit *m* offretite, $(Ca, Na, K)_2[Al_3Si_9O_{24}] \cdot 9H_2O$
Offshore-Versorgung *f* offshore supply
Ogive *f* ogive, dirt band *(glacier)*
Öhningium *n* Öhningian [Stage] *(continental stage, Pliocene)*
Öhrchen *npl s.* Mündungsfortsätze
Okait *m* okaite *(feldspathoidal ultramafite)*
Okenit *m* okenite, $Ca_{1.5}[Si_3O_6(OH)_3] \cdot 1^{1}/_{2} H_2O$
okkludieren to occlude
Okklusion *f* occlusion
Okklusionswasser *n* occlusion water
Ökologie *f* ecology
ökologisch ecologic[al]
Ökospezies *f* ecospecies
Ökosystem *n* ecosystem
Ökotyp *m* ecotype
Oktaeder *n* octahedron
Oktaederfläche *f* octahedral face
Oktaederschicht *f* octahedral sheet (layer)
oktaedrisch octahedral
Oktaedrit *m* octahedrite *(meteorite)*
Oktave *f* octave
Okular *n* ocular, eye piece
Okularmikrometer *n* ocular (eye-piece) micrometer
Okularnetz *n* graticule
Öl *n* oil *(s.a.* Erdöl*)*
~/gasleeres inert oil
~/gasreiches live oil
~/gewinnbares recoverable (drainable) oil
~/paraffinöses paraffinic[-base] oil
~/reines clean (pure) oil
~/schwefelhaltiges sulphureous oil
~/totes dead oil
~/wasserfreies dry oil *(s.a.* ~/reines*)*
~/zurückgebliebenes by-passed oil
Ölanzeichen *n* oil show
Ölaustritt *m* [oil] seepage

Ölbohrung *f/freifließende* flowing oil well
Old Red *n* Old Red
~/Mittleres Orcadian
~/Oberes Farlovian *(Upper Devonian, Old Red facies)*
Oldhamit *m* oldhamite, CaS
Öldichte *f* oil density, *(Am)* oil gravity
Old-Red-Kontinent *m* Old-Red-Continent
öldurchtränkt oil-impregnated
Ölemulsion *f* crude-oil emulsion
Olenek *n* Olenekian [Stage] *(Lower Triassic, Tethys)*
Olenellus *m* Olenellus
Olenellus-Reich *n* Olenellid Realm *(palaeobiogeography, Lower Cambrian)*
Olenellus-Stufe *f* Olenellus Stage *(Lower Cambrian of the Acado-Baltic Province)*
Olenus *m* Olenus
Olenus-Stufe *f* Olenus Stage
Ölfalle *f s.* Falle
Ölfeld *n* oil field
~/erschöpftes exploited oil field
~/marines marine oil field
Ölfeldverhältnisse *npl* field conditions
Ölfilm *m* film (pellicle) of oil
~/haftender adhesive film of oil
Ölfleck *m* stain of oil
ölfrei barren of oil
Ölgeschrei *n* oil excitement
ölgetränkt oil-impregnated
Ölgewinnung *f* oil recovery
~/sekundäre secondary oil recovery
~ vom Rande eines Salzstocks flank production
Ölhäutchen *n s.* Ölfilm
Oligoelement *n* trace element
oligohalin oligohaline
Oligoklas *m* oligoclase, aventurine feldspar *(a mineral of the plagioclase series)*
oligotroph oligotrophic
Oligozän *n* Oligocene [Series, Epoch] *(Tertiary)*
Ölimmersion *f* oil immersion
ölimprägniert oil-impregnated
Olistolith *m* olistolith, sedimentary klippe
Olistostrom *n* olistostrome
Oliveirait *m* oliveiraite, $3ZrO_2 \cdot 2TiO_2 \cdot 2H_2O$ *(amorphous)*
Olivenit *m* olivenite, olive ore, $Cu_2(OH)AsO_4$
Olivin *m* olivine, peridot[e], $(Mg, Fe)_2[SiO_4]$
Olivinbasalt *m* olivine basalt
Olivindiabas *m* olivine diabase
Olivingabbro *m* olivine gabbro
Olivingestein *n* olivine rock
Olivinit *m* olivinite *(peridotite in high-grade metamorphosed rocks)*
Olivinknolle *f* olivine nodule
Olivinnephelinit *m* olivine nephelinite
Ölkalk *m* oil-bearing limestone
Öllager *n* **unter Gaskappe** oil leg
Ollenit *m* ollenite *(hornblende schist)*
Ölmergel *m* kerosine shale

Ölmigration

Ölmigration f travel of the oil
ölnaß oil-wet
Ölsandstein m oil sandstone
Ölschiefer m oil (petroliferous, bituminous) shale, pyroschist
~/dickplattiger plain shale
Ölschieferindustrie f shale oil industry
Ölschieferwerk n shale oil factory
Ölsickerung f oil seepage
Ölspringer m gusher oil well
~/nicht kontrollierbarer wild well
Ölspur f trace of oil
Ölsumpf m seepage
~/feuchter wet sump
Ölträger m petroliferous bed
Ölwanne f oil spotting around the drilling string
Ölwasser n petroleum water
Öl-Wasser-Grenze f oil-water surface
Ombrometer n pluviometer
Omphacit m omphacite, (Ca, Na) (Mg, Fe, Al) $[Si_2O_6]$
Onesquethawan n Onesquethawan (upper Siegenian to Couvinian in North America)
Onkilonit m onkilonite (olivine nephelinite)
Onkolith m oncolite
Onofrit m onofrite, Hg(S, Se)
Onondaga n, **Onondaga-Gruppe** f Onondaga Group (Couvinian in North America)
Ontarien n Ontarian (lower Old Precambrian in North America)
Ontogenese f ontogenesis, individual development
ontogenetisch ontogenetic[al]
Ontogenie f ontogeny
Onyx m onyx (subvariety of chalcedony)
Ooid n ooid
Oolith m oolite
Oolithhohlformporosität f oomouldic porosity
Oolithhorizont m oolitic horizon
oolithisch oolitic, ovoid
Oolithkalk m oolitic lime
Oopellet n oopellet
opak opaque
Opakilluminator m vertical illuminator
Opaksubstanz f **/körnige** granular opaque matter
Opal m opal, SiO_2 + aq, amorphous
~/gemeiner common opal
opalartig opaline
Opaleszenz f opalescence
opalisieren to opalesce
Opalisieren n opalescence, opaline iridescence
opalisierend opalescent
Opazit m opacite, ferrite
Opdalit m opdalite (variety of hypersthene diorite)
Opferkessel m rock basin, water eye, weather pit, sacrificial table (erosional form)
Ophikalzit m ophicalcite, serpentine marble
Ophiolith m ophiolite

Ophiolithserie f ophiolite suite
Ophit m ophite (igneous texture type)
ophitisch ophitic, granitotrychytic
~/teilweise subophitic
Ophthalmit m ophthalmite
Optimalfilter n optimum filter
Optimierung f optimization
optisch optic[al]
oral oral
Orangit m thorite, $ThSiO_4$
Orbikulit m orbiculite (s.a. Kugelgranit)
Orbitalbewegung f orbital motion
Orbitalstation f orbital station
Orcadien n Orcadian
Orcelit m orcelite, $Ni_{<5}As_2$
Ordauchit m ordauchite (olivine-bearing hauyn tephrite)
Ordnung f order
Ordnungsgrad m degree of order
Ordnungszahl f atomic number
Ordoñezit m ordoñezite, $ZnSb_2O_6$
ordovizisch Ordovician
Ordovizium n Ordovician [System] (chronostratigraphically); Ordovician [Period] (geochronologically); Ordovician [Age] (common sense)
~/Mittleres Middle Ordovician [Series, Epoch] (Llandeilo, Caradoc without the zone of Pleurograptus linearis)
~/Oberes Upper Ordovician (uppermost Caradocian and Ashgillian)
~/Unteres Lower Ordovician [Series, Epoch]
Ordoviziumperiode f Ordovician [Period]
Ordoviziumsystem n Ordovician [System]
Ordoviziumzeit f Ordovician [Age]
Oregonit m oregonite, Ni_2FeAs_2
Orellan n Orellan (mammalian stage, upper Oligocene of North America)
Orenburg[ium] n Orenburgian [Stage] (uppermost stage of Upper Carboniferous, East Europe)
Orendit m orendite (ultrapotassic mafic rock)
Organ n**/trichterförmiges** infundibulum
organisch organic
Organismen mpl**/bodenbewohnende** bottom-dwelling organisms
~/eutrophe eutropic organisms (ecology)
~/gerüstbildende frame-building organisms
~/gesteinsbildende lithogenous organisms
~/im Sediment wühlende sediment-infesting organisms
~/sessile sedentary (sessile) organisms
Organismenreste mpl remains of organism
organogen organogen[et]ic, organogenous
Organotonkomplexe mpl organoclays
Orgel f**/geologische** sand pipe (gall)
orientieren to orient[ate]
~/eine Karte to set up a map
orientiert oriented
~/nicht bevorzugt randomly oriented
~/nicht non-oriented
Orientierung f orientation; bearing (of a seismometer)

~/**bevorzugte** non-random orientation
~ **der Diamanten in der Krone** diamond orientation in core bit
~/**regellose (ungeregelte)** random orientation; isotropic fabric
Orientierungskontrolle f attitude control
Orientierungsvorrichtung f device for deflecting tool orientation
Orientit m orientite, $Ca_4Mn_4[SiO_4] \cdot 4H_2O$
Oriskanien n, **Oriskany** n Oriskanian [Stage] (of Lower Devonian in North America)
Orkan m hurricane
Ornamentierung f ornamentation (on fossil shells)
Ornoit m ornoite (hornblende diorite)
orogen orogen[et]ic
Orogen n orogen
~ **aus mehreren parallelen Geosynklinaltrögen** composite mobile belt
~/**herzynisches** Hercynian (Variscan) orogen
~/**kaledonisches** Caledonian orogen
~/**variszisches** Variscan (Hercynian) orogen, Variscides
~/**zweiseitiges** bilateral orogen
Orogenese f orogenesis, orogeny
~/**algomane** Algomane orogeny
~/**alpine** Alpine orogeny
~/**kaledonische** Caledonian orogeny
~/**laramische** Laramide (Laramidian) orogeny
~/**neva[di]dische** Nevadian orogeny
~/**variszische** Variscan orogeny
Orogengebiet n orogenetic area
Orogengürtel m orogenic belt
Orogenhypothese f orogen hypothesis
orogentektonisch orogen-tectonic
Orogentheorie f hypothesis of orogeny
Orografie f orography
orografisch orographic[al]
Orohydrografie f orohydrography
Orokinese f s. Orogenese; Tektogenese
Orologie f orology
Örterbau m entry working
Orterde f orterde, pan soil
Orthit m s. Allanit
Orthoachse f orthoaxis
Orthocheme npl orthochems
orthochronologisch orthochronological
Orthodolomit m orthodolomite
Orthofoto n orthophoto (satellite or aerial photo with orthographic mapping accuracy, i.e. corrected with respect to perspective and inclination distortions)
Orthogenese f orthogenesis, orthogenetic (directed) evolution
Orthogeosynklinale f orthogeosyncline
Orthogestein n orthorock
Orthogneis m orthogneiss, igneous gneiss
Orthokieselsäure f orthosilicic acid
Orthoklas m orthoclase, $KAlSi_3O_8$
~/**optisch positiver** isoorthoclase, isorthose
Orthoklasporphyr m s. Orthophyr
orthoklastisch orthoclastic

Orthometamorphit m s. Orthogestein
Orthomikrit m orthomicrite (sedimentite)
Orthophyr m ortophyre (rock of the syenite clan)
orthorhombisch orthorhombic, trimetric
Orthostratigrafie f orthostratigraphy
Orthotropie f orthotropy
örtlich local
Ortsbeben n local earthquake (shock)
Ortsbestimmung f positioning; position finding (navigation)
Ortsboden m autochthonal (primary) soil
Ortsbrust f drift (heading) face
ortsfremd allochthonous, strange
Ortsgeschwindigkeit f instantaneous (local) velocity
Ortsmeridian m local meridian
Ortsstoß m [working] face, end of a gallery
~ **mit angeschnittenem Hangenden** highwall
Ortstein m ortstein, hardpan, iron pan, moorband [pan], swamp ore
Ortsteinhorizont m layer of iron pan
Ortszeit f local time
~/**mittlere** local mean time
~/**scheinbare (wahre)** local apparent time
Oryktogeologie f oryctogeology
Oryktognosie f oryctognosy
Os m esker, osar
Osannit m osa[n]nite (variety of riebeckite)
Osar m s. Os
Osbornit m osbornite, TiN (meteoric mineral)
Oser m s. Os
Osmiridium n s. Iridosmium
Ossipit m ossipite (olivine gabbro)
Osteichthyes mpl s. Knochenfische
Osterwaldphase f Osterwald phase
Ostracum n-ostracum, porcellaneous layer (molluscans)
Ostsee f Baltic Sea
Oszillation f oscillation
Oszillationsrippeln fpl oscillation (oscillatory) ripples, oscillation ripple marks
Oszillationstheorie f oscillation theory
Oszillator m oscillator
oszillieren to oscillate
oszillierend oscillatory
Oszillogramm n oscillogram
Otavit m otavite, $CdCO_3$
Ottajanit m ottajanite (leucite tephrite)
Ottemannit m ottemannite, Sn_2S_3
Ottrelith m ottrelite, $Mn_2AlAl_3[(OH)_4 | O_2 | (SiO_4)_2]$
Ottrelithschiefer m ottrelite slate
Ouachitit m ouachitite (variety of monchiquite)
Ovarieneindrücke mpl ovarian impressions, genital markings (brachiopods)
Overit m overite, $Ca_3Al_8[(OH)_3|(PO_4)_4]_2 \cdot 15H_2O$
ovoid ovoid
Owyheeit m owyheeite, $5PbS \cdot Ag_2S \cdot 3Sb_2S_3$
Oxammit m oxammite, $(NH_4)_2[C_2O_4] \cdot H_2O$
Oxford[ien] n, **Oxfordium** n Oxfordian [Stage] (basal stage of Malm)

Oxid 230

Oxid n oxide
oxidhaltig oxidic
Oxidüberzug m oxide coating
Oxydation f oxidation, oxidization
Oxydationsflamme f oxidizing flame
Oxydationshut m/**unechter** false gossan
~ **von Zinnerzgängen** brown face of tin lodes
Oxydationsstufe f degree of oxidation, oxidation state (stage)
Oxydationszahl f oxidation number
Oxydationszone f oxidation (oxidizing) zone
Oxydierung f s. oxidation
Ozean m ocean
~/**Atlantischer** Atlantic ocean
~/**offener** open (main) ocean
Ozeanbecken n ocean[ic] basin
Ozeanbeckengrund m ocean-basin floor
Ozeanbodenmetamorphose f ocean-floor metamorphism
Ozeanien n Oceania
ozeanisch oceanic
Ozeanit m oceanite *(picrite basalt)*
Ozeanität f oceanity
Ozeankruste f oceanic crust
Ozeanograf m oceanographer
Ozeanografie f oceanography, thalassography, thalassology
ozeanografisch oceanographic[al], mareographic
Ozeanologie f oceanology
ozeanologisch oceanologic[al]
Ozeanrand m border of ocean
Ozeanschwelle f ocean swell
Ozeantief n ocean deep
Ozellartextur f ocellar structure
Ozokerit m ozocerite (fossil, mineral, ader) wax
Ozon n ozone
Ozonschicht f ozone layer

P

Paare npl/**homometrische** homometric pairs
Pabstit m pabstite, $BaSn[Si_3O_9]$
Pachnolith m pachnolite, $NaCa[AlF_6] \cdot H_2O$
Packeis n pack (rafted) ice
Packer m packer *(drilling)*
~/**durchbohrbarer** drillable packer
~ **für Mehrzonenförderung** multiple-zone packer
Packertest m packer test *(during well drilling)*
Packung f/**kubisch dichteste** cubic close packing
Packungsart f packing of particles
Packungsdichte f packing (reticular) density
Padangboden m padang soil
Pädogenese f paedogenesis
Pagodit m s. Agalmatolith
Pahoehoe-Lava f pahoehoe [lava]
Painit m painite, $5Al_2O_3 \cdot Ca_2[(Si, BH)O_4]$
Paisanit m paisanite *(dike rock containing riebeckite)*

Paket n group *(e.g. of strata)*
Palaeoniscus m Pal[a]eoniscum, Pal[a]eoniscus
Palagonit m palagonite *(variety of basaltic glass)*
Palagonitbildung f palagonitization
Palagonittuff m palagonite tuff
Palait m s. Huréaulith
Paläobiochemie f pal[a]eobiochemistry
paläobiochemisch pal[a]eobiochemical
Paläobiogeografie f pal[a]eobiogeography
Paläobiologie f pal[a]eobiology
Paläobotanik f pal[a]eobotany, pal[a]eophytology, phytopal[a]eontology, fossil botany
Paläobotaniker m pal[a]eobotanist
paläobotanisch pal[a]eobotanical
Paläobreite f pal[a]eomeridian
Paläoendemismus m pal[a]eoendemism
paläofloristisch pal[a]eofloristic
Paläogen n Pal[a]eogene
Paläogeograf m pal[a]eogeographer
Paläogeografie f pal[a]eogeography
paläogeografisch pal[a]eogeographic[al]
Paläogeologie f pal[a]eogeology
paläogeologisch pal[a]eogeologic
Paläogeophysik f pal[a]eogeophysics
Paläoglaziologie f pal[a]eoglaciology
Paläohistologie f pal[a]eohistology
Paläohöhe f pal[a]eolatitude
Paläohydrochemie f pal[a]eohydrochemistry
Paläohydrodynamik f pal[a]eohydrodynamics
Paläohydrogeochemie f pal[a]eohydrogeochemistry
Paläohydrogeologie f pal[a]eohydrogeology
paläohydrogeologisch pal[a]eohydrogeological
Paläohydrologie f pal[a]eohydrology
paläoklimatisch pal[a]eoclimatic
Paläoklimatologie f pal[a]eoclimatology
Paläolimnologie f pal[a]eolimnology
Paläolithikum n Pal[a]eolithic, Old Stone Age
paläolithisch Pal[a]eolithic
paläolithologisch pal[a]eolithologic
Paläolithschicht f pal[a]eolithic layer
paläomagnetisch pal[a]eomagnetic
Paläomagnetismus m pal[a]eomagnetism
Paläomeridian m pal[a]eomeridian
Paläontologe m pal[a]eontologist, fossilist
Paläontologie f pal[a]eontology, fossilism, fossilogy, biologic[al] geology
~/**analytische** analytical pal[a]eontology
~/**geografische** geographic[al] pal[a]eontology
~/**stratigrafische** stratigraphical pal[a]eontology
paläontologisch pal[a]eontologic[al]
Paläoökologie f pal[a]eoecology
paläoökologisch pal[a]eoecologic[al]
Paläoozeanografie f pal[a]eooceanography
Paläophytologie f s. Paläobotanik
Paläophytikum n Pal[a]eophytic
Paläopikrit m pal[a]eopicrite *(basaltic rock)*
Paläorelief n pal[a]eorelief
Paläosom n pal[a]eosome

Paläostrukturen *fpl* pal[a]eostructures
Paläotektonik *f* pal[a]eotectonics
Paläotemperaturen *fpl* pal[a]eotemperatures
Paläotemperaturmessungen *fpl* pal[a]eotemperature measurements
paläothermometrisch pal[a]eothermometric
Paläotopografie *f* pal[a]eotopography
paläotopografisch pal[a]eotopographic
paläotyp, paläovulkanisch pal[a]eovolcanic, pal[a]eotypal
Paläovulkanismus *m* pal[a]eovolcanism
paläozän Pal[a]eocene
Paläozän *n* Pal[a]eocene [Series, Epoch] *(Tertiary)*
Paläozoikum *n* Pal[a]eozoic [Era]
paläozoisch Pal[a]eozoic
Paläozoografie *f* pal[a]eozoography
paläozoografisch pal[a]eozoographic
Paläozoologe *m* pal[a]eozoologist
Paläozoologie *f* pal[a]eozoology
paläozoologisch pal[a]eozoological
Paleozän *n* s. Paläozän
Palermoit *m* palermoite, $SrAl_2[OH \mid PO_4]_2$
Palimpsest *m(n)* palimpsest
Palimpsest-Gefüge *n* palimpsest structure
Palimpsest-Sedimente *npl* palimpsest sediments
palingen palingen
Palingenese *f* palingenesis, palingeny
Palisadenfaltung *f* Palisadian disturbance
Palladinit *m* palladinite *(earthy PdO)*
Palladium *n* palladium, Pd
Pallasit *m* pallasite, pallas iron *(olivine-bearing iron meteorite)*
Pallialeindrücke *mpl* pallial markings *(brachiopodans)*
Pallit *m* pallite, $Ca(Al, Fe)_3[(OH_3)O \mid (PO_4)_2] \cdot 2H_2O$
Palmerit *m* palmerite, $K_3Al_5H_6[PO_4]_8 \cdot 18H_2O$
Palmierit *m* palmierite, $PbK_2[SO_4]_2$
Palsa *f* palsa, earth hummock, pingo, thufur
Palsa-Moor *n* palsa bog
Paludinenbank *f*, **Paludinenschicht** *f* Paludina bed
Palus *m* palus *(swamp, marsh, fen, bog on moon or Mars)*
Palygorskit *m* palygorskite, fuller's earth, $(Mg, Al)_2[OH \mid Si_4O_{10}] \cdot 2H_2O + 2H_2O$
Palynologie *f* s. Pollenanalyse
panallotriomorph panallotriomorphic
panautomorph panautomorphic
Pandait *m* pandaite, $Ba(Nb, Ti, Ta)_2O_6(H_2O)$
Pandermit *m* pandermite, $Ca_2[B_5O_8(OH)_7]$
Paneeldiagramm *n* fence diagram
Panethit *m* panethite, $(Na, Ca)_2(Mg, Fe)_2(PO_4)_2$ *(meteoric mineral)*
panidiomorph panidiomorphic
panidiomorph-körnig panidiomorphic-granular
Pannon[ien] *n*, **Pannonium** *n* Pannonian [Stage] *(of Tertiary)*
Pantellerit *m* pantellerite *(alkaline rhyolite)*
Panzerfische *mpl* placoderms

Papagoit *m* papagoite, $CaCuAlH_2[OH \mid (SiO_4)_2]$
Papierchromatografie *f* paper chromatography
papierförmig papyraceous
Papierkaolin *m* paper clay
Papierkohle *f* paper coal *(cutinite-rich sapropelitic coal beds)*; leaf coal; dysodile
Papierschiefer *m* paper shale (schist)
Papyrusmoor *n* sudd, sedd
Paraaluminit *m* para-aluminite, $Al_4[(OH)_{10} \mid SO_4] \cdot 6H_2O$
parabraun para-brown
Parabraunerde *f* para-brown earth
Parabutlerit *m* parabutlerite, $Fe[OH \mid SO_4] \cdot 2H_2O$
Parachronologie *f* parachronology
Paradamin *m* paradamine, $Zn_2[OH \mid AsO_4]$
Paraffin *n* paraffin
Paraffinablagerung *f* paraffin deposition
Paraffine *npl*/**geradkettige** straight-chain paraffins
Paragen *n* paragene
Paragenbegriff *m* paragene concept
Paragenese *f* paragenesis, association, assemblage
paragenetisch paragenetic, associate
parageosynklinal parageosynclinal
Parageosynklinale *f* parageosyncline, minor (marginal, intracratonal) geosyncline
Paragestein *n* para-rock
Paragneis *m* paragneiss, sedimentary gneiss
Paragonit *m* paragonite, $NaAl_2[(OH, F)_2 \mid AlSi_3O_{10}]$
Paragonitschiefer *m* paragonite schist
Parahopeit *m* parahopeite, $Zn_3[PO_4]_2 \cdot 4H_2O$
Paraklase *f* paraclase *(s.a. Spalt)*
parakristallin paracrystalline
Paralaurionit *m* paralaurionite, PbOHCl
paralisch paralic
parallaktisch parallactic
Parallaxe *f* parallax
~/heliozentrische heliocentric parallax
Parallaxenwinkel *m* parallactic angle
Parallelanordnung *f* parallel arrangement (alignment), parallelism
Paralleldiskordanz *f* parallel unconformity
Parallelentwicklung *f* parallel development
Parallelfalte *f* parallel (concentric, competent, similar, distance-true) fold
Parallelfaltung *f* parallel (concentric) folding
parallelfaserig parallel fibrous
Paraaluminit *m* para-aluminite, $Al_4[(OH)_{10} \mid SO_4] \cdot 6H_2O$
parallelisieren to parallelize
Parallelkreis *m* parallel of latitude
Parallelorientierung *f* parallel orientation *(mineral structure)*
parallelperspektivisch in parallel perspective
Parallelprobe *f* comparison test
Parallelrippelmarken *fpl* parallel ripple marks
Parallelschichten *fpl* conformable strata
Parallelschichtung *f*/**horizontale** primary stratification

Parallelschieferung

Parallelschieferung f bedding cleavage
Parallelschuß m parallel shot *(seismics)*
Parallelstellung f parallel orientation
Parallelstriemung f/**feine** parting lineation
Parallelstrukturierung f bedway
Paralleltextur f parallel texture
Parallelverschiebung f parallel displacement *(crystallography)*; translatory shift
Parallelverwachsung f parallel growth
Parallelverwerfung f translational (translatory) fault
paramagnetisch paramagnetic
Paramagnetismus m paramagnetism
Parametamorphit m s. Paragestein
Parameter m parameter, intercept *(of crystals)*
Parameteranpassung f *(Am)* history matching *(reservoir mechanics)*
Parameterbohrung f stratigraphic well
parameterfrei non-parametric
paramorph paramorphous, paramorphic
Paramorphose f paramorphosis, paramorphism
Paranaphthalin n paranaphthalene, $C_{14}H_{10}$
Para-Rammelsbergit m pararammelsbergite, $NiAs_2$
Pararendzina f pararendzina
Pararippel f para-ripple
Paraschiefer m paraschist
parasitär parasitic
Parasitärkrater m parasitic crater (cone)
parasitisch parasitic
Parastratigrafie f parastratigraphy
parastratigrafisch parastratigraphic
Parastratotyp m parastratotype
paratektonisch paratectonic
Paratellurit m paratellurite, TeO_2
Paratenorit m paratenorite, CuO
Paratypus m paratype, allotype
parautochthon parautochthonous
Paravauxit m paravauxite, $FeAl_2[OH \mid PO_4]_2 \cdot 8H_2O$
Pardonet[ium] n Pardonetian *(Norian and Rhaetian in North America)*
Pargasit m pargasite, $NaCa_2Mg_4(Al, Fe^{\cdot\cdot})[(OH, F)_2 \mid Al_2Si_6O_{22}]$
Parhelium n parhelium
Parisit m parisite, $[(Ce, LA, Di)F]_2CaCO_3$
Parkettverzwillingung f parquet-twinning
Paroxysmus m paroxysm
Parsettensit m parsettensite, $(K, H_2O)(Mn, Fe, Mg, Al)_3[(OH)_2 \mid Si_4O_{10}] \cdot nH_2O$
Parsonsit m parsonsite, $Pb_2[UO_2 \mid (PO_4)_2] \cdot 2H_2O$
Partialdruck m partial pressure
partiell partial
Partikelporosität f intraparticle porosity
Partridgeit m patridgeite, Mn_2O_3
Partschin m s. Spessartin
Pascoit m pascoite, $Ca_3[V_{10}O_{28}] \cdot 16H_2O$
Paß m pass
Passat m trade [wind], geostrophic wind
Passatgürtel m trade wind belt

Passatströmung f equatorial current
Passatwind m s. Passat
Passatwindströmung f trade wind current
Paßgenauigkeit f registration accuracy
Paßkreuze npl fiducial marks
Passung f fitting *(breccia)*
Pastonien n Pastonian *(Pleistocene, British Islands)*
patelliform patelliform, disk-shaped, basin-shaped
Paternoit m paternoite, $KMg_2[B_5O_6(OH)_4 \mid B_3O_3(OH)_5] \cdot 2H_2O$
Patrinit m s. Aikinit
Patronit m patronite, VS_4
Paxit m paxite, Cu_2As_3
Peak m peak point *(tracer test)*
Pearceit m pearceite, $8(Ag, Cu)_2S \cdot As_2S_3$
pechartig pitchlike, pitchy
Pechblende f pitchblende, black blende, nasturan, uraninite, UO_2
Pecheisenerz n s. Stilpnosiderit
Pechglanz m pitch glance, pitchy lustre
Pechkohle f s. Glanzkohle
Pechstein m pitchstone
Pechtorf m pitch (black fuel) peat
Pechuran n uraninite, retinic uranium
~/rotes gummite
Pectoralflosse f pectoral fin
Pediment n pediment
Pedimentrumpffläche f pediment peneplain, *(Am)* pan-fan
Pedogeochemie f pedogeochemistry
pedogeochemisch pedogeochemical
Pedologe m pedologist, agrogeologist
Pedologie f pedology
pedologisch pedological
Pedosphäre f pedosphere, pedological sphere
Peganit m s. Variscit
Pegel m level, [water] gauge, water post
Pegelablesung f gauge reading
Pegelbrunnen m gauge well
Pegeldruck m gauge pressure *(water level in a gauge)*
Pegelhöhe f gauge height, level of the water gauge
Pegellatte f staff gauge
Pegelmesser m level indicator
Pegelmeßstelle f flood measuring point
Pegelmessung f level measurement, gauging
Pegelnullpunkt m gauge datum
Pegelstation f gauge (limnimetrical) station
Pegelwasserstand m gauge pressure
Pegelzeiger m level indicator, hypsometer
pegmatisieren to pegmatize
Pegmatisierung f pegmatization
Pegmatit m pegmatite
pegmatitähnlich pegmatoid
Pegmatitgang m pegmatitic vein, pegmatite dike
pegmatitisch pegmatitic
pegmatoid pegmatoid
Pegmatophyr m pegmatophyre

peilen to bear; to sound
Peilstange f sounding rod
Peilung f bearing, direction finding; sounding
~/magnetische magnetic bearing
Pektolith m pectolite, $Ca_2Na[Si_3O_8OH]$
Pelagial n pelagic region
pelagisch pelagian, pelagic
Pelagosit m pelagosite *(carbonate deposit with high contents of $MgCO_3$, $SrCO_3$, $CaSO_4$, SiO_2 and H_2O)*
Peleeit m peleeite *(variety of dacite)*
Peléetätigkeit f Pelean activity *(of volcanoes)*
Peleträne f tear-shaped bomb
Pelit m pelite, mudstone, lutite
pelitisch pelitic
pelitomorph pelitomorphic
Pelitschiefer m pelitic slate
Pellet n pellet
pelletartig pelletoid
pelletführend pelletal, pelleted
pelletisieren to pelletize, to nodulize
Pelletisierung f pelletization, nodulizing
pelletoid pelletoid
Pellikularwasser n pellicular (film) water
Pelmatozoen fpl Pelmatozoa
Pelosol m pelosol
Pelson[ium] n Pelsonian [Substage] *(Middle Triassic, Tethys)*
Pelvis f pelvis *(palaeontology)*
Pendel n**/aperiodisch gedämpftes** aperiodic[al] pendulum
~/astatisiertes astatic pendulum
~/gedämpftes damped pendulum
~/physikalisches physical pendulum
Pendeleffekt m pendulum effect *(drilling engineering)*
Pendellänge f**/äquivalente** length of equivalent pendulum
Peneplain f peneplain, old plain
~/fossile fossil erosion surface
peneseismisch peneseismic
Penetrationszwillinge mpl penetration twins
Penetrometer n consistency gauge
Penfieldit m penfieldite, Pb_2OHCl_3
Penitentes mpl s. Büßerschnee
Pennantit m pennantite, $(Mn, Al, Fe)_3 [(OH)_2 | (Al, Si)Si_3O_{10}]Mn_3(OH)_6$
Pennin m pennine, penninite *(a chloritic mineral)*
penninisch Penninic
Pennsylvanien n Pennsylvanian *(Upper Carboniferous without basal Namurian in North America)*
Penroseit m penroseite, $(Ni, Cu, Co)Se_2$
Pentaeder n pentahedron
pentaedrisch pentahedr[ic]al
Pentagondodekaeder n pentagonal dodecahedron, pyritohedron
Pentagonikositraeder n pentagonal icositetrahedron
Pentahydrit m pentahydrite, $Mg[SO_4] \cdot 5H_2O$
Pentahydroborit m pentahydroborite, $CaB_2O_4 \cdot 5H_2O$

Pentan n pentane, C_5H_{12}
Pentlandit m pentlandite, iron nickel pyrite, nicopyrite, folgerite, $(Fe, Ni)_9S_8$
Penutien n Penutian [Stage] *(marine stage, lower Eocene in North America)*
Percentile mpl percentiles *(grain size parameter)*
Percylith m percylite, $PbCl_2 \cdot CuO \cdot H_2O$
perennierend perennial
~/nicht non-perennial
perfemisch perfemic
Perforation f perforation
Perforierung f perforating
~ einer Bohrung well perforating
Pergelisol n pergelisol
Periastron n, **Periastrum** n periastron
Peribaltikum n Peribalticum
Peridot m peridot[e] *(s.a. Olivin)*
Peridotit m peridotite *(rock of the ultramafic clan)*
Peridotitschale f peridotite shell
Perigäum n perigee
periglazial periglacial, cryergic
Periglazialerscheinungen fpl periglacial phenomena
Periglazialgebiet n periglacial region
Perihel[ium] n perihelion
Periklas m periclase, MgO
Periklin m pericline *(variety of feldspar)*
periklinal periclinal, quaquaversal
Periklinale f pericline
~/flache parma
perimagmatisch perimagmatic
Periode f period *(1. a division of geological time longer than epoch and included in an era; 2. seismics)*
~/geokratische geocratic period
Periodenabsenkung f periodic settling
Periodendruck m periodic weight
periodisch periodic[al]
Periodizität f periodicity
Periphract n s. Annulus
Periprokt n periproct
Periselenion n pericynthian
Perisphinctes m Perisphinctes
Perissodaktylen mpl perissodactyls
Peristerit m peristerite *(low-temperature plagioclase)*
Peristom n peristome, mouth (apertural) border *(palaeontology)*
Perit m perite, $PbBiO_2Cl$
Peritektikum n peritectic
Peritidalkomplex m peritidal complex
perkristallin percrystalline
perlartig pearly
Perle f 1. pearl; 2. bead *(blowpipe)*
perlenförmig moniliform
Perlenverfahren n bead system
Perlerz n pearl ore
Perlglanz m pearly lustre (sheen)
Perlglimmer m brittle (pearl) mica, margarite, $CaAl_2(OH)_2[Si_2Al_2O_{10}]$

Perlgneis

Perlgneis m pearl gneiss
Perlit m perlite, pearl stone
~/streifiger lamellar perlite
Perlitgefüge n perlitic structure
perlitisch perlitic
Perlmutt n mother-of-pearl, nacre
perlmuttartig nacreous, pearly
Perlmuttglanz m pearly lustre (sheen), nacreous lustre
Perlmuttschicht f nacreous layer
Perlmuttwolke f nacreous cloud
perlschnurartig in the form of strings of pearls
Perlsinter m pearl sinter
Perlspat m pearl spar *(variety of dolomite)*
Perm n Permian [System] *(chronostratigraphically)*; Permian [Period] *(geochronologically)*; Permian [Age] *(common sense)*
Permafrost m permafrost
Permafrostboden m permafrost soil, pergelisol
~/eisfreier dry permafrost (pergelisol)
Permafrostbodenbildung f pergelation
Permafrostsee m cryogenic lake
permanent permanent; perennial
Permanenz f **der Ozeane** permanence of the ocean basins
permeabel permeable
Permeabilität f permeability
~/absolute absolute permeability
~/anisotrope anisotropic permeability
~/effektive effective permeability
~/gerichtete directional permeability
~/magnetische magnetic permeability
~/relative relative permeability
Permeabilitätsfalle f permeability trap
Permeabilitätskoeffizient m permeability coefficient
Permeabilitätsprofil n permeability profile log
Permokarbon n Permo-Carboniferous, Carbo-Permian, Anthracolithic
Permosiles n s. Permokarbon
permosilesisch Permosilesian
Permotrias f Permo-Triassic
Permperiode f Permian [Period]
Permsystem n Permian [System]
Permzeit f Permian [Age]
Perowskit m perovskite, $CaTiO_3$
Perryit m perryite, Ni_3Si *(meteoritic mineral)*
Perthit m perthite
perthitisch perthitic
Petalit m petalite, $Li[AlSi_4O_{10}]$
Petrefakt n petrifact[ion], fossil
Petrefaktenkunde f petrifactology
Petrochemie f petrochemistry, lithochemistry
Petrofazies f petrofacies
Petrogenese f petrogenesis, petrogeny
petrogenetisch petrogenetic
Petrograf m petrographer
Petrografie f petrography
petrografisch petrographic[al]
petrografisch-lithologisch petrographical-lithological

Petrolchemie f petrol chemistry
Petrologe m petrologist
Petrologie f petrology
petrologisch petrologic[al]
Petrolpech n petroleum pitch
Petrophysik f petrophysics
petrophysikalisch petrophysical
Petrotektonik f petrotectonics, structural petrology
Petzit m petzite, $(Ag, Au)_2Te$
Pfadfinderelement n indicator element
Pfahl m pile
Pfahlbauten mpl pile dwellings
Pfahlgründungen fpl pile foundations
Pfannenbildung f water eye, weather pit, sacrificial table
Pfeife f pipe
pfeifenartig pipelike
Pfeifenstein m/**indianischer**, **Pfeifenton** m pipestone, catlinite
Pfeiler m pillar
Pfeilerbau m pillar exploitation, open stope with pillar, bord-and-pillar work (system), bord-and-wall work
Pfeilerbruchbau m room and pillar caving
Pfeilerstärke f pillar thickness
Pferdeschwanzstruktur f horsetail structure
Pflanze f plant
~/amphibische amphiphyte
~/farnähnliche fernlike plant
~/feuchtigkeitsliebende hygrophytic plant
~/fossile fossil plant, plant fossil, eophyte
~/kalkfliehende calcifuge
~/kalkliebende calcicole
~/krautige herbaceous plant
~/salzempfindliche salt-sensitive plant
~/torfbildende peat formation plant
~/versteinerte lithifled (petrified) plant
Pflanzenabdruck m plant impression, vegetation print
Pflanzenablagerung f plant[-bearing] deposit, vegetable deposit
Pflanzenassoziation f plant assemblage (association, community)
Pflanzenballen mpl sea balls *(marine sediments)*
Pflanzendecke f plant (vegetable, vegetation, vegetative) cover[ing], plant canopy; vegetable blanket
Pflanzenerde f vegetable mould
Pflanzenfossil n/**kohlebildendes** coal [measures] plant
pflanzenfressend plant-eating, vegetable-eating, herbivorous
Pflanzenfresser m plant eater (feeder), herb eater (feeder), herbivore, vegetarian
Pflanzengeograf m phytogeographer, geobotanist
Pflanzengeografie f botanic geography, phytogeography, geobotany
pflanzengeografisch phytogeographic[al], geobotanic[al]

Pflanzengesellschaft *f s.* Pflanzenassoziation
Pflanzenhäcksel *m* fragmental plant remains
Pflanzenknäuel *m*/**lakustrischer** lake ball
Pflanzenmaterial *n*/**mazeriertes** macerated plant material
~/verrottetes sudd, sedd
Pflanzenökologie *f* phytoecology
Pflanzenpaläontologie *f* phytopal[a]eontology
Pflanzenregion *f* floral region
Pflanzenreich *n* plant kingdom
Pflanzenreste *mpl* plant remains
~/fossile plant fossils, vegetable debris (remains)
~/strukturzeigende structure-indicating plant remains
Pflanzensubstanz *f*/**vergelte** fundamental jelly (substance)
Pflanzenwelt *f* flora
Pflanzenwuchs *m* vegetable carpet
pflanzlich vegetable; floral
Pflasterstruktur *f* mosaic texture
Pflege *f* **des Hangenden** roof control
Pflockgefüge *n* peg structure *(e.g. of melilite)*
Pforte *f* gate [way]
Pfropfen *m* plug
Phacoid *n* phacoid
Phacoidgefüge *n* phacoidal structure
Phakolith *m* 1. phacolith *(form of migmatic intrusion)*; 2. phacolite *(variety of chabasite)*
phanerogen phanerogenic
phanerokristallin phanerocrystalline, visibly crystalline, phaneric
phaneromer phaneromerous
Phanerozoikum *n* Phanerozoic [Eon]
phanerozoisch Phanerozoic
Phänoklast *m* phenoclast
phänoklastisch phenoclastic
Phänokrist *m* phenocryst
phänokristisch phenocrystic
Phänologie *f* phenology
phänomenologisch phenomenological
Phänoplast *m* phenoplast
Phänotyp[us] *m* phenotype
Phantomhorizont *m* phantom [horizon] *(seismics)*
Pharmakolith *m* pharmacolite, $CaH[AsO_4] \cdot 2H_2O$
Pharmakosiderit *m* pharmacosiderite, $KFe_4[(OH)_4 \mid (AsO_4)_3] \cdot 6H_2O$
Phase *f* phase *(tectonical and physicochemical)*
~/böhmische Bohemian phase of folding
~/fluide fluid phase
~/gotidische Gothian phase
~/Ilseder Ilsede phase
~/instabile unstable phase
~/karelisch-svekofennidische Karelian-Svecofennian phase
~/laramische Laramide phase
~/liquidmagmatische liquid magmatic phase
~/pasadenische Pasadenic phase
~/pegmatitische pegmatitic phase

~/pfälzische Palatine phase
~/pneumatolytische pneumatolytic phase
~/pyrenäische Pyrenean phase
~/regressive regressive phase
~/rhodanische Rhodanic phase
~/saalische Saalic phase
~/saamidische Saamidic phase
~/sardische Sardic phase
~/stabile stable phase
~/steirische Styrian phase
~/subherzynische Subherzynian phase
~/sudetische Sudetic phase
~/synorogene magmatische synorogenic phase
~/takonische Taconic phase
~/transgressive transgressive phase
~/vorbereitende preparatory phase
~/vulkanische volcanic phase
~/walachische Wallachian phase
~/Wernigeröder Wernigerode phase
Phasen *fpl*/**koexistierende** coexisting (compatible) phases
Phasenanalyse *f* phase analysis
~/röntgengeografische x-ray phase analysis
Phasenausbreitungsgeschwindigkeit *f* phase propagation velocity
Phasencharakteristik *f* phase response
Phasendiagramm *n* phase diagram
Phasendifferenz *f* phase difference
Phasendispersion *f* dispersion of phases
Phasengang *m* phase response
Phasengeschwindigkeit *f* phase velocity
Phasengleichgewicht *n* phase equilibrium
Phaseninversion *f* phase inversion
Phasenkontrastverfahren *n* phase contrast microscopy
Phasennacheilung *f* phase lag
Phasenregel *f* phase rule
~/Gibbssche Gibbs's phase rule
~/Goldschmidtsche (mineralogische) mineralogic[al] phase rule
Phasenresonanz *f* phase resonance
Phasensprung *m* [jump of a] leg
Phasentrennungsrate *f* segregation rate
Phasenübergang *m* phase transition (transfer)
Phasenumkehrung *f* phase inversion
Phasenumverteilung *f* phase redistribution
Phasenumwandlung *f* phase change
Phasenveränderung *f* phasing
Phasenverhalten *n* phase response
Phasenverschiebung *f* phase shift[ing]
Phasenverteilung *f* phase distribution
Phasenverzerrung *f* phase distortion
Phasenvoreilung *f* phase lead
Phasenzustandsverhalten *n* phase behaviour
Phenakit *m* phenacite, Be_2SiO_4
Phengit *m* phengite, $K(Fe, Mg)Al[(OH)_2 \mid (Al, Si)Si_3O_{10}]$
Phenoblast *m s.* Porphyroblast
Philadelphit *m* philadelphite *(decomposition product of biotite)*
Philippinit *m* philippinite *(tektite)*

Phillipsit

Phillipsit *m* phillipsite, $KCa[Al_3Si_5O_{16}] \cdot 6H_2O$
Phlebit *m* phlebite *(migmatite)*
Phlobaphinit *m* phlobaphinite *(maceral of brown coals and lignites)*
Phlogopit *m* phlogopite, rhombic mica, $KMg_3[(F,OH)_2 \mid AlSi_3O_{10}]$
Pholadiden *fpl* pholadids
Phönikochroit *m* phoenicochroite, $Pb_3[O \mid (CrO_4)_2]$
Phonolith *m* phonolite, clinkstone, sound-stone *(effusive of alkali syenite)*
Phonolithtuff *m* phonolite tuff
Phorogenese *f* phorogenesis
Phosgenit *m* phosgenite, $Pb_2[Cl_2 \mid CO_3]$
Phosphat *n* phosphate
Phosphatablagerung *f*/**erdige** earthy phosphates
~/feste petrous phosphates
Phosphatgestein *n* phosphatic rock
Phosphatgrube *f* phosphate mine
phosphatisch phosphatic
phosphatisiert phosphatized
Phosphatkreide *f* phosphatic chalk
Phosphatlagerstätte *f* phosphatic deposit
Phosphatverwitterungslagerstätte *f* phosphatic deposit due to weathering, residual phosphatic deposit
Phosphoferrit *m* phosphoferrite, $(Fe,Mn)_3[PO_4]_2 \cdot 3H_2O$
Phosphophyllit *m* phosphophyllite, $Zn_2Fe[PO_4]_2 \cdot 4H_2O$
phosphorartig phosphatic
Phosphoreszenz *f* phosphorescence
phosphoreszieren to phosphoresce
phosphorhaltig phosphoric
Phosphorit *m* phosphorite, rock phosphate
~/knolliger pebble phosphates
Phosphoritbänder *npl*/**harte** hard rock
phosphoritisch phosphoritic
Phosphoritknolle *f* phosphorite nodule
Phosphosiderit *m* phosphosiderite, $Fe[PO_4] \cdot 2H_2O$
Phosphuranylit *m* phosphuranylite, $Ca[(UO_2)_4 \mid (OH)_4 \mid (PO_4)_2] \cdot 8H_2O$
Photon *n* photon
Phragmokon *n* phragmocone, phragmacone
phreatisch phreatic
pH-Wert *m* pH value; pH index *(of water)*
pH-Wert-Messer *m* pH meter
Phyllit *m* phyllite
Phyllitisierung *f* phyllitization
Phyllonit *m* phyllonite
Phylloretin *n* phylloretine, $C_{18}H_{18}$
Phyllosilikat *n* phyllosilicate
Phylogenese *f* phylogenesis, phylogeny
Phylogenetik *f* phylogenetics
phylogenetisch phylogenetic
Phylogenie *f s.* Phylogenese
physikalisch-chemisch physico-chemical
Physiografie *f* physiography
phytogen[etisch] phytogenetic, phytogenic
Phytogeograf *m* phytogeographer, geobotanist

Phytogeografie *f* phytogeography, geobotany
phytogeografisch phytogeographic[al], geobotanic[al]
Phytolith *m* phytolite, phytolith
phytomorph phytomorphic
Phytoplankton *n* phytoplankton
Piacenta *n*, **Piacenza** *n*, **Piacenzium** *n* Piacenzian [Stage] *(of Pliocene)*
Pickeringit *m* pickeringite, $MgAl_2[SO_4]_4 \cdot 22H_2O$
Pickprobe *f* chip sample
Piedmontebene *f* piedmont plain
~/alluviale piedmont alluvial plain, mountain apron
Piedmontfläche *f* piedmont [slope, flat]
Piedmontgletscher *m* piedmont glacier
Piedmontterrassen *fpl* piedmont terraces
Piedmonttreppe *f* piedmont stairway (steps, benchlands)
Piemontit *m* piemontite, $Ca_2(Mn,Fe)Al_2[O \mid OH \mid SiO_4 \mid Si_2O_7]$
Pierre-Schiefer *m* Pierre Shale *(Santonian to Maastrichtian, North America)*
piezoelektrisch piezoelectric
Piezoelektrizität *f* piezoelectricity
Piezoklase *f* piezoclase
Piezokristall *m* piezoelectric crystal
Piezokristalleinheit *f* piezoelectric crystal unit
Piezokristallisation *f* piezocrystallization
Piezokristallplatte *f* piezoelectric crystal plate
piezomagnetisch piezomagnetic
Piezometer *n* piezometer
piezometrisch piezometric
Pigeonit *m* pigeonite *(variety of pyroxene)*
Pigotit *m* pigotite, $Al_4[O_6 \mid C_6H_5O_4] \cdot 13^{1}/_{2} H_2O$
Pikosekunde *f* picosecond
Pikotit *m* chrome spinel
Pikrit *m* picrite *(olivine diabase)*
Pikromerit *m* picromerite, $K_2Mg[SO_4]_2 \cdot 6H_2O$
Pikropharmakolith *m* picropharmacolite, $(Ca,Mg)_3[AsO_4]_2 \cdot 6H_2O$
Pilbarit *m* pilbarite, $Pb,Th[UO_2 \mid (SiO_4)_2] \cdot 4H_2O$
Pillenkalkstein *m* pelletal limestone
~/matrixführender micritic-pelletal limestone
Pillowlava *f* pillow (cushion, ellipsoidal) lava
Pilotbohrung *f* pilot hole
Pilotmeißel *m* pilot (lead) bit
Pilzaktivität *f* fungal activity *(destruction)*
pilzartig mushroom-shaped
Pilzfaden *m* hypha
Pilzfalte *f* mushroom fold
Pilzfels[en] *m* mushroom (pedestal) rock
Pilzsporen *fpl* fungal spores
Pilzwolke *f* mushroom cloud
Pinakiolith *m* pinakiolite, $(Mg,Mn)_2Mn[O_2 \mid BO_3]$
Pinakoid *n* pinacoid
Pinge *f* surface depression, sink, fault pit, glory hole, local depression
Pingenbergbau *m* open diggings, glory-hole mining
~ mit untertägiger Förderung milling

Pingo *m* pingo, frost mound
Pinienwolke *f* pine-tree[-shaped] cloud *(volcanism)*
Pinit *m* pinite *(mineral aggregate pseudomorph after cordierite)*
Pinnoit *m* pinnoite, $Mg[B_2O(OH)_6]$
Pinnulae *fpl* pi[n]nules
Pinolith *m* pinolite *(aggregate of coarse crystalline magnesite with lime shale)*
Pintadoit *m* pintadoite, $CaH[VO_4] \cdot 4H_2O$
Pionierarten *fpl* pioneer species
Pionierbohrung *f* wildcat [well]
Pionierpflanze *f* pioneer plant
Pipeline *f* pipeline
Pirssonit *m* pirssonite, $Na_2Ca[CO_3]_2 \cdot 2H_2O$
Pisanit *m* pisanite, $(Fe,Cu)[SO_4] \cdot 7H_2O$
Pisekit *m* pisekite *(U-, Ce-, ect. niobate and titanate)*
Pisolithe *mpl* pisolites
~/vulkanische volcanic pisolites, mud pellets, fossil raindrops, accretionary lapilli
Pisolithgestein *n* pisolites, peastone
pisolithhaltig, pisolithisch pisolitic; pea-grit *(sandstone)*
Pisolithkalk *m* pisolitic limestone
Pisolithtuff *m* pisolitic tuff
Pissasphalt *m* pissasphalt
Pistazit *m s.* Epidot
Pitotrohr *n* Pitot (gauge) tube
Pitticit *m* pitticite, $Fe_{20}[(OH)_{24}|(AsO_4,PO_4,SO_4)_{13}] \cdot 9H_2O$
Pivotabilität *f* pivotability, rollability *(of clastic grains)*
Placodermen *npl* placoderms
Placodus *m* Placodus
Plagiogranit *m* plagiogranite
Plagioklas *m* plagioclase *(isomorphous mixed crystals between $NaAlSi_3O_8$ and $CaAl_2Si_2O_8$)*
~/anorthitreicher calciclase
Plagionit *m* plagionite, $5PbS \cdot 4Sb_2S_3$
Plakoidschuppe *f* placoid scale
plakoidschuppig placoid
Plan *m* der geologischen Erkundungsarbeiten technical and economical plan of geological exploration
~ nach Luftbildaufnahme air-survey plan
Plancheit *m* plancheite, $Cu_8[(OH)_2|Si_4O_{11}]_2 \cdot H_2O$
Pläner *m* pläner sandstone *(marly sedimentite)*
Planet *m* planet
~/äußerer outer (superior) planet
planetarisch planetary
Planeten *mpl*/**transneptunische** extra-Neptunian planets
Planetenbahn *f* planet orbit
Planetensystem *n* planetary system
Planetesimalhypothese *f* planetesimal hypothesis
Planetoid *m* planetoid, asteroid
Planetologie *f* planetology
Planimeter *n* planimeter
Planimetrierung *f* planimetering

planktogen planktogenic
Plankton *n* plankton, floating organisms
Planktonforaminiferen *fpl* planktonic foraminifers
planktonisch planktonic
Planktonorganismus *m* plankter
Planoferrit *m* planoferrite, $Fe_2[(OH)_4|SO_4] \cdot 13H_2O$
Planparallelgefüge *n* plan-parallel structure
Planum *n* levelled ground
~/aufgeschüttetes artificial subgrade
Planumauskofferung *f* subgrade excavation
Planung *f* der Bodennutzung land-use planning
~ der Schußbohrungen preplot
Plasma *m* plasma *(s.a.* Chalzedon*)*
plastifizierend plasticizing
Plastiklast *m* plasticlast
plastisch plastic
Plastizität *f* plasticity
~/ökologische ecological plasticity
Plastizitätsbedingung *f* criterion of yielding
Plastizitätsbeiwert *m* plasticity index
Plastizitätsgrenze *f* plastic limit
~/untere liquid limit
Plastizitätszahl *f* plasticity index
Plastosol *m* plastosol
Plastosphäre *f* plastosphere
Plateau *n* plateau
~ an den Flanken der Riftgebirge high fractured plateau
Plateaubasalt *m* plateau (flood) basalt
Plateaubewegung *f* plateau movement
Plateaufläche *f* plateau surface
Plateaugletscher *m* plateau glacier
Platin *n* platinum, Pt
~/gediegenes native platinum
platinartig, platinführend platinous, platinic
platinhaltig platiniferous, platinous
Plättchen *n* lamina, flake
plättchenförmig lamellose
Platte *f* plate; slab
~/dünne fehlerfreie film *(quality of mica)*
~/fehlerfreie block *(quality of mica)*
~/Moesische Moesian plate
~ unter 0,10 mm Dicke splitting *(quality of mica)*
λ/4-Platte *f* quarter-wave [length] plate
plattenartig slab-shaped, slablike, sheetlike
Plattenbelastungsversuch *m* plate [load] bearing test
Plattenbiegungssteifigkeit *f* flexural rigidity of a plate
Plattendiagramm *n* plate diagram *(of echinoderm skeleton)*
Plattendolomit *m* sheet dolomite
Plattendruckversuch *m* plate [load] bearing test
plattenförmig platy; slabby
Plattenglimmer *m* book mica
Plattengrenze *f* plate juncture (margin, boundary)

Plattengrenzen 238

Plattengrenzen *fpl*/**divergierende** accreting plate margins
~/konvergierende (krustenaufzehrende) consuming plate margins
~/krustenproduzierende accreting plate margins
Plattenkalk *m* platy limestone
~/Solnhofener Solnhofen Platy Limestones *(Malm in South Germany)*
Plattenschiefer *m* plate shale
Plattentektonik *f* plate tectonics
Plattentextur *f* slab structure
Plattentheorie *f* theory of fixed beams
Plattform *f* platform
~ einer Schichtstufe cuesta back slope
~/horizontal stabilisierte gimbal *(drilling engineering)*
~/Osteuropäische Eastern-European platform
~/Russische Russian platform
~/stabilisierte stabilized platform
Plattformelement *n* platform element *(conodonts)*
plattig plate-shaped, platy; laminate[d]; slabby
Plattnerit *m* plattnerite, PbO_2
plattstengelig bladed
Plättung *f* flattening
Plättungsebene *f* plane of flattening
Platyclymenia-Stufe *f s.* Hemberg-Stufe
Platynit *m* platynite, $Pb_4Bi_7Se_7S_4$
Platzaustauschhypothese *f s.* Aufstemmungstheorie
platzen to crack
Platznahme *f* emplacement *(of rock or magma)*
Platzregen *m* torrent[ial] rain, rainstorm, heavy shower, storm precipitation
Playa *f* playa *(southern California)*
Plazolith *m s.* Hibschit
pleistozän Pleistocene
Pleistozän *n* Pleistocene, Drift Period, Ice Age
Pleochroismus *m* pleochroism; dichroism; trichroism
pleochroitisch pleochroic; dichroic; trichroic
Pleomorphie *f* pleomorphism
Pleonast *m* pleonaste *(black spinel)*
plesiomorph plesiomorphic
Plesiomorphie *f* plesiomorphy
Plessit *m* plessite *(in meteorites)*
Pliensbach[ien] *n*, **Pliensbachium** *n* Pliensbachian [Stage] *(of Jurassic)*
~/oberes *s.* Domer
~/unteres *s.* Carix
pliohalin pliohaline
Plio-Pleistozän *n* Plio-Pleistocene
Pliozän *n* Pliocene [Series, Epoch] *(Tertiary)*
Plombierit *m* plombierite, $Ca_5H_2[Si_3O_9]_2 \cdot 6H_2O$
Plotter *m* plotter
Plumbocalcit *m* plumbocalcite *(mixed crystal of calcite and cerussite)*
Plumboferrit *m* plumboferrite, $PbO \cdot 2Fe_2O_3$
Plumbojarosit *m* plumbojarosite, vegasite, $PbFe_6[(OH)_6|(SO_4)_2]_2$

Plumboniobit *m* plumboniobite (Y, Yb, $Gd)_2(Fe,Pb,Ca,U)[Nb_2O_7]_2$
Plutogenese *f* plutogenesis
Pluton *m* pluton
~/anorogener atectonic pluton
plutonisch plutonic, plutonian
Plutonismus *m* plutonism, vulcanian theory
~/synorogener synorogeneous plutonism
Plutonist *m* plutonist
Plutonit *m* plutonite, plutonic (intrusion, deep-seated igneous) rock
pluvial pluvial
Pluvialperiode *f*, **Pluvialzeit** *f* pluvial period (phase)
Pluviograf *m* pluviograph
Pluviometer *n* pluviometer
pneumatogen pneumatogenic, pneumatogene[tic]
Pneumatolyse *f* pneumatolysis, pneumatolytic process
~/endogene endogenous pneumatolysis
pneumatolytisch pneumatolytic
Pneumatophor *n* pneumatophore, air chamber *(palaeontology)*
pochen to crush
Pocherz *n* poor (milling) ore
Pochwerk *n* stamp mill
Podsol *m* podzol [soil], podsol [soil]
~/tropischer tropical podzol
~/verborgener latent podzol
Podsolboden *m s.* Podsol
podsolieren to podzolize
Podsolierung *f* podzolization
podsolisch podzolic
podsolisieren to podzolize
Podsolisierung *f* podzolization
Poechit *m* poechite *(Mn-rich Fe-, Si-gel)*
poikilitisch poikilitic
poikiloblastisch poikiloblastic
Pointcounter *m* point counter
Pol *m* pole
~/antiloger antilogous pole
~/ekliptischer ecliptic pole
~/erdmagnetischer geomagnetic pole, [terrestrial] magnetic pole
~/geografischer geographic[al] pole
~/magnetischer magnetic pole
~/paläomagnetischer pal[a]eomagnetic pole
Polabstand *m* polar distance
Polachse *f* magnetic axis
polar polar, arctic
~/nicht non-polar
Polarachse *f s.* Polachse
Polardiagramm *n* polar plot
Polareiskappe *f* polar ice cap
Polargletscher *m* Arctic glacier
Polarisation *f* polarization
~/dielektrische dielectric polarization
~/induzierte induced polarization
~/lineare plane polarization
~/magnetische magnetic polarization
Polarisationsebene *f* polarization plane

Polarisationseigenschaft f polarization property
Polarisationsenergie f polarization energy
Polarisationsfilter n polarization filter
Polarisationsmesser m polarimeter
Polarisationsmikroskop n polarizing (polarization, petrological) microscope
Polarisationspotentialfeld n polarizing potential field
Polarisationsvermögen n polarizing ability
Polarisationswinkel m polarizing (Brewster) angle
Polarisator m polarizer
polarisierbar polarizable
Polarisierbarkeit f polarizability
polarisieren to polarize
polarisiert/eben (linear) plane-polarized
Polarität f polarity
Polarkappe f polar cap
Polarklima n polar climate
Polarkreis m polar circle
~/nördlicher Arctic Circle
~/südlicher Antarctic Circle
Polarlicht n polar light (aurora), auroral light (display)
Polarlichtzone f auroral zone (belt)
Polarluft f polar air
Polarografie f polarography
polarografisch polarographical
Polarstern m polestar, lodestar, loadstar
Polarwirbel m polar eddy
Polbahn f polhody
Polder m polder, diked land (marsh)
Poldistanz f polar distance
Poleck n summit *(crystallography)*
Polfigur f polar point
Polflucht f drift away from the poles
Polfluchtkraft f pole-fleeing force
Polhöhe f altitude of the pole
Polhöhenschwankung f variation of altitude of the pole
Polianit n polianite, $\beta\text{-MnO}_2$
polieren to polish
Polierfähigkeit f amenability to receive polish
Polierkratzer m polishing scratch
Poliermittel n polishing powder
Polierschatten mpl polishing shadows
Polierscheibe f polishing wheel
~/feste solid bob
Polierschiefer m polishing (adhesive) slate, tripoli
poliert/schlecht insufficiently polished
Polierung f polishing
Polje n polje
Pollen m pollen
Pollenanalyse f pollen analysis (statistics)
Pollenform f pollen form
Pollenit m pollenite *(nepheline phonolite)*
Pollenkorn n pollen grain
Pollenprofil n pollen profile
Pollensäckchen n anther
Pollentorf m torch peat

Pollucit m pollucite, caesium silicate, $(Cs, Na)[AlSi_2O_6] \cdot H_2O$
Polradius m polar radius
Polreduktion f reduction to the pole *(geomagnetics)*
Polstärke f/**magnetische** magnetic intensity
Polster n cushion
Polstergas n cushion gas
Polverlagerung f s. Polwanderung
Polverschiebung f/**absolute** shift in the earth's axis
Polwanderung f polar wandering (drift)
polwärts poleward[s]
Polyargyrit m polyargyrite, $Ag_{24}Sb_2S_{15}$
polyaszendent polyascendent
Polybasit m polybasite, $8(Ag,Cu)_2S \cdot Sb_2S_3$
Polydymit m polydymite, Ni_3S_4
Polyeder n polyhedron
polyedrisch polyhedral, polyhedric
polygen polygenous
polygenetisch polygenetic
Polygeosynklinale f polygeosyncline
Polygonalstrukturen fpl stone rings
Polygonboden m polygonal ground (soil), stone polygon soil
Polygonisation f polygonization
Polygonzug m/**geknickter** chain traverse
Polyhalit m polyhalite, $K_2Ca_2Mg[SO_4]_4 \cdot 2H_2O$
Polyklase f polyclase
Polykras m polycrase, $(Y, Ce, Ca, U, Th)(Ti, Nb, Ta)_2(O, OH)_6$
Polymerisation f polymerization
polymerisieren to polymerize
Polymetallerzgang m compound vein
polymetamorph polymetamorphic
Polymetamorphose f polymetamorphism
Polymignit m polymignite, $(Ce,La,Y,Th,Mn,Ca)[(Ti,Zr,Nb,Ta)_2O_6]$
polymikt polymict
polymorph polymorphic, polymorphous
Polymorphie f polymorphy, polymorphism
Polymorphismus m polymorphism, polymorphy
Polynomtrend m polynomial trend
polynuklear polynuclear
Polzenit m polzenite *(melilite basalt)*
Ponor m ponor, katavothron, sink (leach) hole, swallow [hole], lime[stone] sink
Pont[ien] n, **Pontium** n Pontian [Stage] *(of Miocene)*
Ponzit m ponzite *(variety of trachyte)*
Populationsdynamik f population dynamics
Pore f pore
~/syngenetische fenestra
~/wasserhaltige water-holding pore
Porenanteil m/**auffüllbarer** effective porosity (pore volume)
~/entwässerbarer specific porosity, specified yield of pore space
Porendruck m pore pressure
Porendruckabnahme f pore pressure dissipation

Poreneintrittsradius 240

Poreneintrittsradius *m* pore entry radius
Porenflüssigkeit *f* pore liquid
Porenflüssigkeitsdruck *m* formation (pore liquid) pressure
Porenform *f* pore form
Porenfüllung *f* pore (interstitial) filling
Porengas *n* interstitial gas
Porengefüge *n*/**syngenetisches** fenestral fabric
Porengehalt *m* porosity
Porengeschwindigkeit *f* velocity of flow in pores, velocity through the pores
Porengröße *f* pore size
Porengrößenverteilung *f* pore size distribution
Porengrundwasserleiter *m* pore aquifer
Poreninhalt *m* pore content
Porenkanal *m* pore canal
Porenkontinuität *f* pore continuity
Porenlosigkeit *f* non-porosity, imporosity
Porenluft *f* pore air
Porenquerschnitt *m* pore cross section
Porenraum *m* void, pore space (volume), interspace
~/**effektiver** *s.* ~/**wirksamer**
~/**freier** void space (volume)
~/**nutzbarer** specified yield of pore space
~/**relativer** void ratio
~/**wirksamer** effective pore volume, reservoir voidage
Porenräume *mpl*/**untereinander verbundene** intercommunicating pore spaces
Porenraumverteilung *f* porosity distribution
Porenrestwasser *n* residual pore water
Porensaugsaum *m* capillary fringe
Porensaugwasser *n* capillary water (moisture)
~/**ruhendes** suspended water
Porensinter *m* porous sinter
Porenvolumen *n s.* Porenraum
Porenwasser *n* pore (void, interstitial) water
~/**fest gebundenes** monolayer water, last (single) water layer
~/**haftendes** interstitial water; combined pore water
~/**labil gebundenes** polylayer water
Porenwasserabgabe *f* pore water drainage (expulsion, loss)
Porenwasserdruck *m* pore water pressure, neutral stress
~/**zurückbleibender** residual pore water pressure
Porenwasserdruckabnahme *f* pore water dissipation
Porenwasserdruckhöhe *f* pore water pressure head
Porenweg *m* avenue of migration
Porenwinkelwasser *n* pore angle water
Porenwinkelwasserregime *n* pendular regime
Porenziffer *f* void ratio
porig mushy; pored, porous (*s.a.* porös)
~/**syngenetisch** fenestral *(sediments)*
Porigkeit *f s.* Porosität
porös porous, pory, spongy, spongiform, pervious

~ **durch Ooidauslösung** oocastic
~/**nicht** imporous
Porosität *f* porosity, porousness, voidage, perviousness, perviousity
~/**effektive** effective porosity
~/**freie** unfilled porosity
~ **im frühdiagenetischen Stadium** eogenetic porosity
~ **in situ** in-situ porosity
~ **infolge mechanischer Auflockerung** fracture porosity
~/**intergranulare** intergranular porosity
~/**kavernöse** vugular porosity
~/**nutzbare** specific porosity (yield of pore space)
~/**primäre** depositional porosity
~/**scheinbare** air space ratio
~/**sekundäre** induced porosity
~/**syngenetische** fenestral porosity
~ **vor der Zementbildung** minus-cement porosity
~/**wahre** actual porosity
Porositätsänderung *f* change of porosity
Porositätsfalle *f* porosity trap
Porositätsgrad *m* degree of porosity
Porositätslog *n* porosity log
Porpezit *n* porpezite, palladium gold
Porphyr *m* porphyry *(effusive rock of the granite clan)*
~/**quarzfreier** quartz-free porphyry
Porphyrgang *m* porphyry dike
porphyrhaltig porphyraceous
porphyrisch porphyric
~/**lagenartig** planoporphyric
~/**nicht** aphyric
Porphyrit *m* porphyrite *(effusive rock of diorite)*
porphyritisch porphyritic
Porphyrittuff *m* porphyrite tuff
Porphyrkupfererz *n* porphyry copper ore
Porphyroblast *m* porphyroblast, megablast, metacryst
porphyroblastisch porphyroblastic
Porphyroid *n* porphyroid
Portland *n* Portlandian [Stage] *(upper Malm in South England)*
Portlandit *m* portlandite, Ca(OH)$_2$
Portlandium *n s.* Portland
porzellanartig porcelain-like
Porzellanerde *f* kaolin, porcelain earth (clay), China clay
Porzellanit *m* porcellanite *(decomposed scapolithe)*
Porzellanjaspis *m* porcelain jasper
Porzellanschicht *f s.* Ostracum
Porzellanspat *m s.* Porzellanit
Porzellanton *m s.* Porzellanerde
Posidonienschiefer *m* Posidonia shale
Positionierung *f*/**dynamische** dynamic positioning *(of drilling barks)*
Positionierungssystem *n* position-reference system

Positionswechsel *m* positional change
positiv/optisch optically positive
Postdiagenese *f* postlithification
postdiagenetisch postdiagenetic
postdiluvial postdiluvial
postgeosynklinal postgeosynclinal
postglazial postglacial, superglacial
Postglazial *n* postglacial period
postgranitisch postgranitic
postkristallin postcrystalline
postmagmatisch postmagmatic
postmagmatisch-metasomatisch postmagmatic-metasomatic
postorogen postorogenic, epikinematic
postpleistozän Recent
postsedimentär postsedimentary
posttektonisch posttectonic, apotectonic
postum posthumous
postvariszisch post-Variscan
postvulkanisch postvolcanic
potamogen potamogenic
Potamologie *f* potamology
Potamoplankton *n s.* Flußplankton
Potarit *m* potarite, PdHg
Potential *n* potential
~/elektrokinetisches electrokinetic potential
~/gewinnbares geothermisches recoverable geothermal potential
~/hochenthalpes geothermisches high enthalpy geothermal potential
~/induziertes induced potential
~/niedrigenthalpes geothermisches low enthalpy geothermal potential
~/thermodynamisches thermodynamic potential
Potentialfeld *n*/**geoelektrisches** geoelectric potential field
Potentialfeldtransformation *f* potential-field transformation
Potentialgefälle *n*, **Potentialgradient** *m* potential gradient
Potentialsprung *m* change in potential
Potentialströmung *f* potential flow
Potentialwert *m* potential value
Potentiometrie *f* potentiometry
Potomac-Gruppe *f* Potomac Group *(Lower Cretaceous, North America, Atlantic shore)*
Potsdam *n s.* Croixien
Powellit *m* powellite, $Ca[MoO_4]$
Pozzuolan *n* pozzuolana
pozzuolanartig pozzuolanic
Pozzuolanerde *f* pozzuolana
pozzuolanhaltig pozzuolanic
Präadaptation *f* preadaptation
präbasaltisch prebasaltic
Präboreal *n* Preboreal [Time] *(Holocene)*
präexistent preexistent
präexistieren to preexist
Prag[ium] *n* Pragian [Stage] *(of Lower Devonian)*
präglazial preglacial
Prag-Stufe *f s.* Prag[ium]

prähistorisch prehistoric
präkambrisch Precambrian
Präkambrium *n* Precambrian [Eon], Cryptozoic [Eon]
Prallhang *m* outer (cut) bank, undercut slope
präorogen preorogenic
präpaläozoisch pre-Pal[a]eozoic
Präparat *n* preparation
Präparationstechnik *f* preparation technique
Präparieren *n* **einer Lagerstätte** mineral salting *(simulation of deposits)*
Präparierlupe *f* preparing lens
präpermisch pre-Permian
Prä-planorbis-Schichten *fpl* Pre-planorbe Beds *(basal Lias)*
Prärie *f* prairie
Prärieboden *m* prairie soil
~/brauner brunizem (brunigra) soil
Prasem *m* prase *(subvariety of quartz)*
Prasinit *m* prasinite, ophidite
prätektonisch pretectonic
prätertiär pre-Tertiary
Prätertiäroberfläche *f* pre-Tertiary surface
prätremadocisch pre-Tremadocian
prävariszisch pre-Variscan
Präzession *f* precession
Präzipitatgestein *n* chemically deposited sedimentary rock
Präzisionsisotopenanalyse *f* precision isotopic analysis
Predazzit *m* predazzite *(marble with brucite)*
Prehnit *m* prehnite, $Ca_2Al_2[(OH)_2|Si_3O_{10}]$
Preßkohle *f s.* Preßstein
Preßluftbohrer *m* compressed-air drill
Preßluftbohrhammer *m* compressed-air hammer drill
Preßlufthammer *m* jackhammer
Preßluftspeicher *m* compressed-air storage
Preßschnee *m* drifted snow
Preßstein *m* briquette, coal-dust brick
Pressung *f* compression
Pressungsform *f* compression form
Pressungsgebiet *n* compressing zone
Pressungsmaximum *n*/**kritisches** critical compression maximum
Pressungsmetamorphose *f* pressure metamorphism
Preventer *m* [blow-out] preventer
Preventergarnitur *f* blow-out-preventer assembly
Priabon[ien], Priabonium *n* Priabonian [Stage] *(of Eocene)*
Priceit *m* priceite, $Ca_5[B_4O_5(OH)_5]_3 \cdot H_2O$
Priderit *m* priderite, $(K,Ba)[(Ti,Fe)_8O_{16}]$
Priel *m* marsh creek, wash-out, gully, slough
Prielfüllung *f* channel cast
Primäräste *mpl* primary order of branches
Primärboden *m* primary (autochthonal, sedentary) soil
Primärbrekzie *f* edgewise structure
Primärförderung *f* primary recovery *(crude oil)*

Primärgefüge

Primärgefüge *n* primary (apposition) fabric
Primärkristallisation *f* primary crystallization
Primärlöß *m* true loess
primärmagmatisch protogenic
Primärmigration *f* primary migration
Primäröl *n* mother oil
Primärradioisotop *n* primordial radioisotope
Primärreflexion *f* primary reflection *(seismics)*
Primärriß *m* primary crack
Primärrohstoff *m* primary raw material
Primärrücken *m* primary back
primorogen *s.* synorogen
Prinzip *n*/**Beckesches** Becke's principle
~ **der gleichen Gegenzeit** reciprocity principle *(seismics)*
~/**Rieckesches** Riecke's principle
Prisma *n* prism
~/**dihexagonales** dihexagonal prism
~/**ditetragonales** ditetragonal prism
~/**Nicolsches** nicol [prism]
prismaähnlich prismoidal
prismatisch prismatic[al]
Prismenfläche *f* prism face
prismenförmig prismatic[al]
Prjevalskit *m* prjevalskite, $Pb[UO_2|PO_4]_2 \cdot 4H_2O$
Probe *f* 1. sample, specimen; 2. trial, assay *(s.a.* Prüfung)
~ **aus der Bohrlochwand** side wall sample
~/**gestörte** disturbed sample
~ **kleiner Dimensionen** small-size sample
~/**lufttrockene** air dry sample
~/**orientierte** oriented specimen
~/**repräsentative** representative sample
~/**reproduzierbare** reproducible sample
~/**unausgesuchte** unpicked sample
~/**unkontaminierte** uncontaminated sample
~/**verunreinigte** contaminated sample
~ **vom Boden eines Bohrlochs** bottomhole sample
~/**zuverlässige** reliable sample
Probeabsenkung *f* pumping test, trial pumping *(hydrology)*
Probebohrung *f* trial boring (drilling), exploration (experimental) drilling; test hole
Probebrunnen *m* sampling well
Probeflasche *f* sample bottle
Probegerät *n* tester
Probegut *n* sampled material
Probekörper *m* test specimen
~/**zylindrischer** control cylinder
Probemenge *f* [test] sample quantity
Probenahme *f* sampling, taking of samples
~ **aus dem Bohrloch** borehole testing
~/**differenzierte** stratified sampling
~/**geschichtete** stratified sampling *(sampling strategy in complex areas by subdividing them in more homogeneous parts)*
~ **mit systematischem Fehler** biased sampling, sampling with a systematic error
~/**neue** resampling
~ **ohne systematischen Fehler** unbiased sampling, sampling without a systematic error

242

~/**repräsentative** representative sampling
~/**systematische** systematic sampling
~/**ununterbrochene** continuous sampling
~/**unverfälschte** *s.* ~ ohne systematischen Fehler
~/**verfälschte** *s.* ~ mit systematischem Fehler
~ **von Bohrklein** sampling of cuttings
~ **von Staub** dust sampling
~ **während des Niederbringens** operational sampling
~/**zufällige** random sampling
Probenahmeabstand *m* sampling distance
Probenahmefehler *m* sampling error
Probenahmegebiet *n* sample section
Probenahmegerät *n* sampling device (tool)
Probenahmerepräsentanz *f* sampling reliability
Probenahmeschema *n* scheme of sampling
Probenanzahl *f* number of samples
Probenbeutel *m* sample bag
Probenehmer *m* 1. sampler, sample grabber; 2. sampler, sample device
~ **im Bohrloch** bottom-hole sampler
Probenentnahme *f s.* Probenahme
Probenhomogenität *f* homogeneity of sample
Probenkasten *m* sample box
Probenreduktion *f* sample reducing (splitting)
Probensammlung *f* collection of samples
Probenstelle *f* sampling point
Probenteiler *m* sample divider
Probenteilung *f* sample splitting (dividing)
Probenuntersuchung *f* assaying
Probenviertelung *f* sample quartering, quartering of sample
Probenvorbereitung *f* preparation of samples
Probepumpversuch *m* preliminary pumping test
Probertit *m* probertite, $NaCa[B_5O_6(OH)_6] \cdot 2H_2O$
Probestück *n* test specimen
Probewürfel *m* cube test specimen
Probezylinder *m* control cylinder
Probierkunde *f* fire assay
Probierstein *m* touchstone
Problematikum *n* problematical fossil
Prochlorit *m* prochlorite *(Fe-, Mg-chlorite)*
Proctor-Dichte *f* Proctor compactness
Proctor-Kurve *f* Proctor [compaction] curve
Prodelta *n* prodelta
Produkte *npl*/**biogene** biogenic products
~/**pyroklastische** pyroclastics, pyroclasts
Produktion *f* production
~ **je Kopf der Belegschaft** output per man employed
~/**stabilisierte** settled production
~/**wirtschaftlich lohnende** commercial production
~/**zu erwartende** expected output
~/**zulässige** allowable production
Produktionsabfall *m* output decline (fall)
Produktionsbohrung *f* production hole drilling
Produktionseinschränkung *f* restriction of production, proration

Produktionskreuz n Christmas tree (drilling technics)
Produktionskurve f production (output) curve
Produktionspacker m production packer
Produktionsrate f/**gleichmäßige** settled production rate
Produktionsrohrtour f production casing string
Produktionsrückgang m s. Produktionsabfall
Produktionssonde f producing well
Produktionsversuch m production (productivity) test
Produktivitätsindex m productivity index
produzieren to produce
Profil n profile, [cross] section (of a body); shape, section (form)
~/**feinstratigrafisches** refined stratigraphical profile
~/**generelles** generalized section
~/**geologisches** geologic column (section, profile)
~/**lithologisches** lithological profile
~/**schematisches** generalized section
Profilabfolge f succession of profile
Profilaufnahme f profiling
~/**refraktionsseismische** refraction seismic profiling
Profilbau m sectional structure (e.g. of sedimentary rocks)
Profildurchlässigkeit f transmissibility, transmissivity
Profilgitter n graticule
Profilierung f/**elektrische** electrical profiling
~/**kontinuierliche** continuous profiling
Profilmaßstab m abacus
Profilmessung f profile measurement
Profilschießen n profile shooting, profiling (seismics)
Profilschnitt m cross section; plot
Profilserie f serial section
Profilskizze f sketch profile
Prognoseabschnitt m prognostic sector
Prognosekarte f prognostic map
Prognoseproblem n problem of prognosis
Prognosetest m predictivity test
programmieren to program
Programmregelung f preset (programmed) gain control
Projekt n **zur Erforschung des oberen Erdmantels** Upper Mantle Project
Projektdokumentation f design estimates
Projektion f/**abstandstreue** equidistant projection
~/**flächentreue** equiareal (equal area, equivalent) projection
~/**gnomonische** gnomonic projection
~/**stereografische** stereographic projection
~/**winkeltreue** conformal projection
Projektionspunkt m projection point
Projektnachtrag m addendum to a project
Prologismus m prologism (palaeontology)
Proportionalitätsfaktor m proportionality factor

Proportionalitätsgrenze f limit of proportionality
Proportionalitätszählrohr n proportional counter tube
Propylit m propylite (deuteric alteration of andesite)
propylitisch propylitic
Propylitisierung f propylitization
Prosopit m prosopite, $Ca[Al(F,OH)_4]_2$
prospektieren to prospect
~/**mit UV-Lampe** to lamp
Prospektieren n prospecting (s.a. Schürfen)
~/**bohrlochgeochemisches** geochemical borehole prospection
~ **durch Widerstandsmessungen** resistivity prospecting
~/**elektrisches** electrical prospecting
~/**geochemisches** geochemical prospecting
~/**geoelektrisches** electrical prospecting
~/**geophysikalisches** exploration geophysics
~ **im Meer/elektrisches** offshore electrical prospection
~/**radiometrisches** radiometric prospecting
Prospektion f prospection (s.a. Prospektieren)
Prospektionsbohrung f prospect well
Prospektionsmethode f prospecting method
~/**mit Quecksilberdispersionshof arbeitende** mercury-halo method
Prospektor m prospector
Proterobas m proterobase (variety of diabase)
Proterophytikum n Proterophytic
Proterozoikum n Proterozoic [Era]
proterozoisch Proterozoic
Protoconch m protoconch, initial (apical) chamber (molluscs)
Protodolomit m protodolomite (unstable dolomite)
protogen protogene, protogenous
Protogin m protogine, protogene (variety of gneiss)
Protoklase f protoclase
Protokristallisation f protocrystallization
Protolyse f protolysis
Protoplanet m protoplanet
Protoplatte f protoplate
Prototafel f protoplatform
Prototyp m prototype, archetype, arquetype, antetype
Protozoen npl protozoans, eozoans
protozoisch protozoic
Protrusion f protrusion
Protuberanz f protuberance, prominence
Proustit m proustite, Ag_3AsS_3
Provinz f/**Akado-baltische** Acado-Baltic Province (palaeobiogeography, Lower Cambrian)
~/**biochemische** biochemic[al] province
~/**geologische** geologic[al] province
~/**magmatische** magmatic province
~/**Malvino-kaffrische** Austral (Malvinokaffric) Province (palaeobiogeography, Devonian)
~/**metallogenetische** metallogenetic (minerogenetic) province

Provinz

~/pazifische Pacific Province *(palaeobiogeography, Lower Cambrian)*
~/petrografische petrographic[al] province
~/zoogeografische zoogeographic[al] province, biofacies realm
Prozentgehalt *m* an Gesamtporenraum percentage of [total] pore space
Prozeß *m*/Detritus erzeugender detrition
~/exogenetischer exogenetic process
~/lagerstättenbildender process forming deposits
~/thermisch-katalytischer thermal-catalytic process
~/tiefgreifender tektonischer diastrophic process
Prozeßabfolge *f* sequence of processes
Prozeßgliederung *f* geologischer Untersuchungsarbeiten nach Stadien performance of geological prospecting by stage
Prüfdruck *m* test pressure
Prüfgelände *n* test site
Prüfgerät *n* tester
Prüfkörper *m* [test] specimen; sample piece
Prüfsieb *n* testing screen
Prüfsiebung *f* grading test
Prüfstand *m* test rig
Prüfung *f* durch Augenschein visual inspection
~/mikroskopische microscopic[al] examination
Psammit *m* psammite, arenite
psammitisch psammitic, arenaceous
Psephit *m* psephite, rudite
psephitisch psephitic, rudaceous
Pseudoantiklinale *f* pseudoanticline
Pseudobergschaden *m* apparent mining damage
Pseudoboleit *m* pseudoboleite, $5PbCl_2 \cdot 4Cu(OH)_2 \cdot 2^1/_2 H_2O$
Pseudobrekzie *f* pseudobreccia
Pseudobrookit *m* pseudobrookite, Fe_2TiO_5
Pseudocotunnit *m* pseudocotunnite, K_2PbCl_4
Pseudodruck *m* pseudopressure
Pseudofossil *n* pseudofossil
pseudogeschichtet pseudobedded
pseudoglazial pseudoglacial
Pseudogley *m* similigley
pseudohexagonal pseudohexagonal
Pseudokonglomerat *n* pseudoconglomerate, crush conglomerate
pseudokonkordant pseudoconformable
Pseudokonkordanz *f* pseudoconformity
pseudokristallin pseudocrystalline
Pseudolaueit *m* pseudolaueite, $MnFe_2[OH|PO_4]_2 \cdot 8H_2O$
Pseudomalachit *m* pseudomalachite, $Cu_5[(OH)_2|PO_4]_2$
Pseudomikrit *m* pseudomicrite *(sedimentite)*
Pseudomoräne *f* pseudomoraine, scoria moraine

pseudomorph pseudomorph[ic]
~ nach Dolomit dolomorphic
Pseudomorphie *f*, Pseudomorphose *f* pseudomorphism
Pseudomulde *f* pseudotrough
Pseudo-Ooid *n s.* Pseudo-Oolith
Pseudo-Oolith *m* pseudo-oolite, false oolite
Pseudopegmatit *m* pseudopegmatite
Pseudoplankton *n* pseudoplankton
Pseudoschichtung *f* pseudobedding, pseudostratification
Pseudoschrägschichtung *f* pseudo-cross stratification
Pseudosymmetrie *f* pseudosymmetry, mimetry
Pseudotachylit *m* pseudotachylite, flinty crush rock
pseudovulkanisch pseudovolcanic
Pseudowollastonit *m* pseudowollastonite, $Ca_3[Si_3O_9]$
PSF *s.* Punktspreizfunktion
Psilomelan *m* psilomelane, black hematite, manganese hydrate, $(Ba,H_2O)_2Mn_5O_{10}$
Psilophyt *m* psilophyte
Psychrometer *n* psychrometer
Pteranodon *n* Pteranodon
Pterocerien *n* Pterocerian *(Kimmeridgian in Northwest Germany)*
Pteropodenschlamm *m* pteropod ooze
Ptilolith *m s.* Mordenit
ptygmatisch ptygmatic
Pucherit *m* pucherite, $BiVO_4$
Puddinggranit *m* pudding granite
Puddingstein *m* [plum-]pudding stone
Puercan/Dragon *n* Puercan-Dragonian [Stage] *(mammalian stage, lower Palaeocene in North America)*
Puffer *m* buffer *(chemical)*
Pulaskit *m* pulaskite *(alkaline syenite)*
Pulsationstheorie *f* pulsation theory
pultartig, pultförmig desk-like, shed-roof-like
Pultschole *f* desk-like fault block
Pulveranalysenverfahren *n* method of powder analysis
pulverartig powdery, pulverulent
Pulverdiagramm *n* powder pattern
pulverförmig, pulverig pulverulent, powdery
pulverisieren to pulverize; to triturate
Pulverisierung *f* pulverization; trituration
Pulvermethode *f* powder method of analysis
Pulverprobe *f* powder sample
Pulverschnee *m* powder[y] snow
Pumpanlage *f* pumping installation (unit, outfit)
Pumpellyit *m* pumpellyite, $Ca_2(Mg,Fe,Mn,Al)(Al,Fe,Ti)_2[(OH,H_2O)_2|SiO_4|Si_2O_7]$
Pumpen *n*/kombiniertes back crank pumping
Pumpenbock *m* pumping jack
Pumpensonde *f s.* Pumpsonde
Pumpenstation *f s.* Pumpstation
Pumpfähigkeit *f* pumpability
Pumprohr *n* pumping string

Pumpsonde f pumping (beam) well, pumper
Pumpspeicherkraftwerk n pumped-storage hydropower plant
Pumpspeicherung f pumped storage
Pumpstation f pumping station (plant)
Pumpversuch m pumping test
Punkt m**/kritischer** critical point
~/trigonometrischer trigonometrical point
Punktbelastung f point loading
Punktdiagramm n point (scatter) diagram
Punkteruption f explosion-pipe eruption
Punktfestigkeit f spot strength
Punktinjektionsmethode f constant-rate injection method
Punktkarte f dot chart
Punkt-Kriging n point kriging
Punktpaar n pair of convergence points
Punktprobe f points (spot) sample
Punktprobenehmer m point-integrating sampler (of water in wells)
Punktquelle f dimple spring
Punktspreizfunktion f point spread function, PSF
Punktvermarkung f marking of points
Punktwanderung f displacement of observation points
Purbeck n Purbeckian [Stage] *(uppermost Malm including basal Lower Cretaceous in South England)*
Purpurit m purpurite, $(Mn,Fe)[PO_4]$
Pußta f puszta
Putzen n pocket of ore
Putzsand m abrasive
Puzzolan n s. Pozzuolan
P-Welle f longitudinal wave
Pygidium n pygidium, tailshield, caudal shield (arthropods)
Pyknit m pycnite *(variety of topaz)*
Pyknometer n pycnometer
pyramidal pyramidal
Pyramide f pyramid
pyramidenförmig pyramidal
Pyranometer n pyranometer
Pyrargyrit m pyrargyrite, [dark] red silver ore, Ag_3SbS_3
Pyrgeometer n pyrgeometer
Pyrheliometer n pyrheliometer
Pyrheliometrie f pyrheliometry
Pyrigarnit m pyrigarnite
Pyriklasit m pyriclasite
Pyrit m [iron] pyrite, sulphur ore, FeS_2
~/goldhaltiger auriferous pyrite
~/konkretionärer brass balls
~/massiger liver pyrite
pyritartig pyritaceous
Pyritband n **in der Kohle** steel band
Pyriteinlagerung f coal brass
Pyriterz n pyritic ore
pyrithaltig pyritiferous, pyritous
pyritisch pyritic
pyritisieren to pyritize
Pyritisierung f pyritization

Pyritknolle f pyrite nodule
Pyritkonkretion f pyrite (pyritic) concretion
Pyritoeder n pyritohedron
Pyritschiefer m pyritiferous shale
Pyritzwischenlage f scud
Pyroaurit m pyroaurite, $Mn_6Fe_2[(OH)_{16}|CO_3] \cdot 4H_2O$
Pyrobelonit m pyrobelonite, $PbMn[OH|VO_4]$
Pyrobitumen n pyrobitumen
Pyrochlor m pyrochlore, pyrrhite, chalcolamprite, $(Ca, Na)_2(Nb, Ta)_2O_6(O, OH, F)$
Pyrochroit m pyrochroite, $Mn(OH)_2$
pyroelektrisch pyroelectric
Pyroelektrizität f pyroelectricity
Pyrofusinit m pyrofusinite *(submaceral)*
pyrogen pyrogenic
pyroklastisch pyroclastic
pyrokristallin pyrocrystalline
Pyrolit m pyrolite
Pyrolusit m pyrolusite, black manganese, MnO_2
Pyrolyse f pyrolysis
Pyromagma n pyromagma
pyrometamorph pyrometamorphic
Pyrometamorphose f pyrometamorphism
pyrometasomatisch pyrometasomatic
Pyrometasomatose f pyrometasomatism
pyromorph pyromorphous
Pyromorphit m pyromorphite, $Pb_5[Cl|(PO_4)_3]$
Pyrop m pyrope, $Mg_3Al_2[SiO_4]_3$
Pyrophanit m pyrophanite, $MnTiO_3$
Pyrophyllit m pyrophyllite, $Al_2[(OH)_2|Si_4O_{10}]$
Pyropissit m pyropissite *(wax-rich brown coal)*
Pyrosmalith m pyrosmalite, $(Mn, Fe)_8[(OH, Cl)_{10}|Si_6O_{15}]$
Pyrostilpnit m pyrostilpnite, fire blende, Ag_3SbS_3
Pyroxen m pyroxene *(Ca-, Mg-, Fe-silicate mineral)*
~/orthorhombischer orthopyroxene
Pyroxengneis m pyroxene gneiss
Pyroxengruppe f pyroxene group
Pyroxenit m pyroxenite *(rock of the ultramafic clan)*
Pyroxenquarzporphyr m pyroxene quartz porphyry
Pyroxferroit m pyroxferroite, $[Fe, Ca, Mg, Mn]SiO_3$ *(mineral of the moon)*
Pyroxmanganit m pyroxmanganite *(mineral of the moon)*
Pyroxmangit m pyroxmangite, sobralite, $(Fe, Mn)_7[Si_7O_{21}]$
Pyrrhotin m pyrrhotine, pyrrhotite, magnetic pyrites, FeS

Q

Q-Kluft f Q-joint
Quader m square (cut, dimension) stone, ashlar
Quadermauerwerk n ashlar stonework, ashlar stone walling

Quadersandstein

Quadersandstein m block sandstone, mitchell
Quaderstein m s. Quader
Qualität f/hohe bonanza quality *(of mining products)*
Qualmwasser n seepage water
Quartär n Quaternary [System] *(chronostratigraphically);* Quaternary [Period] *(geochronologically);* Quaternary [Age] *(common sense)*
Quartärperiode f Quaternary [Period]
Quartärsystem n Quaternary [System]
Quartärzeit f Quaternary [Age]
Quarz m quartz, SiO_2
~/blauer sapphire quartz
~/brasilianischer Brazilian (optical) pebble
~/drusiger mineral blossom
~/gelber Scotch topaz
~/gemeiner common quartz
~/goldfreier buck quartz
~/laminierter laminated quartz
~/linksdrehender levogyrate (left-handed) quartz
~ mit eingewachsenen Goethitnadeln hedgehog stone
~/mit Erz verwachsener live quartz
~ mit Rutilnadeln sagenitic quartz
~/optisch inaktiver racemic quartz
~/optischer optical (Brazilian) pebble
~/piezoelektrischer piezoelectric quartz
~/rechtsdrehender dextrogyrate (right-handed) quartz
~/sandiger arenaceous quartz
~/tauber dead quartz
Quarzader f s. Quarzgang
Quarzäderchen n quartz veinlet, stringer of quartz
quarzähnlich, quarzartig quartzose, quartzous, quartzy
Quarzdiabas m quartz diabase
Quarzdiorit m quartz diorite, tonalite
Quarzdolerit m quartz dolerite
Quarzeinschluß m interstitial quartz
Quarzfels m s. Quarzit
Quarzfluoritachromatlinse f achromatic quartz fluorite salt lens
Quarzflußspatachromatlinse f achromatic quartz rock salt lens
quarzfrei quartz-free
Quarzgang m quartz dike (vein)
~/goldführender quartz reef
Quarzgeneration f generation of quartz
Quarzgestein n quartz rock
Quarzglimmerfels m quartz mica rock
Quarzglimmerschiefer m quartz mica schist
quarzhaltig quartz-bearing, quartziferous, quartzose, quartzous, quartzy
quarzig s. quarzhaltig
Quarzin m quartzine *(s.a. Chalzedon)*
Quarzit[fels] m quartzite, quartz rock, granular quartz
Quarzitgestein n quartzitic rock
quarzitisch quartzitic
Quarzitstein m ganister brick *(refractory industry)*

Quarzkeil m quartz wedge
Quarzkeratophyr m quartz keratophyre
Quarzkies m quartzous gravel
Quarzknauern fpl quartz lenses
Quarzkornfarbe f colour of the quartz grains
Quarzlagergang m blanket
Quarzphyllit m quartz phyllite
Quarzplättchen n quartz plate
Quarzporphyr m quartz porphyry
Quarzporphyrit m quartz porphyrite
quarzreich quartz-rich, quartzose
Quarzsand m quartz[ose] sand, arenaceous quartz
Quarzschieferton m arenaceous shale
Quarzspektrograf m quartz spectrograph
Quarzsyenit m quartz syenite
Quarztapeten fpl laminated quartz
Quarztrümer npl/**horizontal gelagerte** floating spurs
Quarzuhr f quartz[-crystal] clock
Quarz-Uraninit-Kalzit-Gang m quartz-uraninite-calcite vein
Quastenflosser mpl s. Crossopterygier
Quastenmarke f brush cast
Quecksilber n mercury, quicksilver, Hg
~/gediegenes native mercury
Quecksilberbergwerk n quicksilver mine
Quecksilberbranderz n idrialite
Quecksilbererz n quicksilver ore
Quecksilberfahlerz n s. Schwazit
Quecksilbergrube f quicksilver mine
quecksilberhaltig mercurial; mercuric; mercurous
Quecksilberhochdruckporosimeter n mercury high-pressure porosimeter
Quecksilberhornerz n horn quicksilver, mercurial horn ore, calomel, $HgCl$
Quecksilberinjektionsmessung f mercury injection measurement
Quecksilberinjektionsmessungsmethode f mercury injection method
Quecksilberlebererz n hepatic cinnabar (mercurial ore)
Quecksilberprovinz f mercury province
quellbar swellable
Quellbrunnen m spring well
Quelle f source, spring; well
~/artesische artesian spring
~/hypogene hypogene spring
~/intermittierende intermittent (periodic, pulsating) spring; ebbing and flowing spring
~/juvenile juvenile (deep) spring
~/kalte cold spring
~/kleine springlet
~/kochende boiling spring
~/periodische non-uniform spring
~/permanente perennial spring
~/springende gushing spring
~/submarine submarine (submerged) spring
~/tektonische contact spring
~/unterseeische s. ~/submarine
~/vadose vadose spring

~/warme warm spring
quellen 1. to spring, to flow, to gush; 2. to swell [up]; 3. to heave, to raise, to creep
Quellen n 1. floor heave, creeping; 2. raising, upheaval, floor lift; 3. gelling *(by frost)*
Quelleneis n c[h]rystocrene
Quellenergiebigkeit f strength of a source; productiveness of a source (spring)
quellenfrei solenoidal
Quellenlinie f line of springs
Quellergiebigkeit f discharge of spring
Quellfähigkeit f rock swelling; expansive force *(of soil and clay)*
Quellfaltung f *a kind of flow folding caused by water intake of the rock*
Quellfassung f capture (tapping) of spring
Quellfluß m river source, headwater stream
Quellgebiet n head[water] of a river; headwater region; field of source
Quellgebietsanzapfung f capturing of headwaters
Quellhorizont m, **Quellinie** f line of springs
Quellkuppe f intrusive (lava) dome, intumescence of lava, tumulus
Quellmoor n spring fen
Quellmulde f 1. valley head; 2. reception basin *(of a river)*
Quellrohr n geyser pipe
Quellschüttung f delivery of a source (spring)
Quellteich m headpool
Quelltrichter mpl spring pits
Quellung f s. Quellen
Quellungsfältelung f enterolithic structure
Quellungsvermögen n swelling property
Quellwasser n spring water
Quenselit m quenselite, $PbO \cdot MnOOH$
Quenstedtit m quenstedtite, $Fe_2(SO_4)_3 \cdot 10H_2O$
Queraufstellung f cross spread; broadside shooting
Querbruch m cross fracture
Querbruchbau m top slicing
Querdehnungsziffer f transverse expansion, Poisson's ratio
Querdüne f transverse dune
Querfalte f cross (oblique) fold
Querfaltung f cross (transverse) folding
~/kontemporäre simultaneous cross folding
~/verschiedenzeitliche subsequent cross folding
Querfluß m right-angled stream
Quergang m cross vein (lode, course)
Querglimmer m transverse mica
Querkluft f dip joint, Q-joint
Querkraft f lateral load
Querkraftbeiwert m side-force coefficient
quermagnetisiert cross-magnetized, cross-magnetic
Quermagnetisierung f cross magnetization
Quermoment n lateral moment
Querneigung f cross dip
Querplattung f longitudinal slab joints
Querprofil n cross profile, transverse section

~ eines Tals transverse valley profile
~/geologisches geologic[al] cross section
Quersattel m transverse anticline
Querschieferung f s. Transversalschieferung
Querschlag m cross cut, cross-cut level, transverse heading
querschlägig cross-cutting
Querschnitt m cross (transverse, lateral) section
~/geologischer geologic[al] cross section
Querschnittsprobenahme f averaging [of samples]
Querschnittsverminderung f closure, reduction of cross section
Querschwelle f transverse ridge
Querschwingung f contour vibration
Querspalte f transverse crevasse *(of a glacier)*; cross crack
Querstörung f s. Querverwerfung
Querstörungszone f transverse fault zone
Querstrecke f cross heading, transverse gallery
Querströmung f cross current
Quertal n cross valley
Querverformung f lateral deformation
Querverkürzung f lateral contraction
Querverstrebung f cross bracing
Querverwerfung f cross (transverse, dip) fault
Quetenit m s. Botryogen
Quetschfalte f compressed (constricted, squeezed) fold
Quetschholz n crusher block, lid
Quetschschieferung f induced cleavage
Quicksand m quicksand, running sand
Quickton m quick clay
Quisqueit m quisqueite *(lignite with a higher content of V and S)*

R

Rabbittite m rabbittite, $Ca_3Mg_3[(UO_2)I(OH)_2I(CO_3)_3]_2 \cdot 18H_2O$
Racemisierung f racemization
Rachel f s. Erosionsrinne
Radar n radar
~ mit synthetischer Apertur synthetic aperture radar, SAR
Radarecho n radar echo (return)
Radarhöhenmesser m radar altimeter
Radarmeteorologie f radar meteorology
Radarrichtstrahl m radar beam
Radarstreuquerschnitt m radar scattering cross-section, RCS
Radarsystem n radar system
Radarverkürzung f radar foreshortening *(of the slant range of sensorward points in hilly and mountaneous terrain)*
Rädelerz n wheel ore (s. a. Bournonit)
radial radial
radialblättrig lamellar-stellate
radialfaserig radially fibrous, radial-columnar, radiating-columnar

radialförmig 248

radialförmig actiniform
Radialfurche f radial furrow
Radialgänge mpl radiating dikes
Radialkartiergerät n radial line plotter
radialstengelig s. radialfaserig
Radialströmung f radial flow
Radialverwerfungen fpl radial faults
radiär radial
Radienquotient m radii quotient
radioaktiv [radio]active
Radioaktivität f [radio]activity
~ **der Luft** airborne radioactivity
~/**induzierte** induced radioactivity
~/**künstliche** artificial radioactivity
~/**natürliche** natural[-occuring] radioactivity
Radioaktivitätslog n radioactivity (nuclear) log
Radioaktivitätsmessung f measuring of the radioactivity (s.a. Radiometrie)
Radioastronomie f radio astronomy
Radioautografie f radioautograph
Radioballon m/**automatischer** automatic radioballoon
Radioblei n radiolead
Radio-Echo-Beobachtung f radio echo observation
radiogen radiogenic
Radiogeochronometrie f radiogeochronometry
Radiogramm n radiograph
Radioindikator m radioactive tracer
Radioisotop n radioisotope
Radiokarbon n radiocarbon, ^{14}C
Radiokarbondatierung f radiocarbon dating
Radiokarbonmethode f radiocarbon [dating] method
Radiokarbonzyklus m radiocarbon cycle
Radiolarienfaulschlammkalk m radiolarian mudstone
Radiolarienschlamm m radiolarian ooze
Radiolarit m radiolarite, radiolarian chert (earth)
Radiologie f radiology
radiologisch radiologic
Radiolumineszenz f radioluminescence
Radiometeor m radio meteor
Radiometeorologie f radiometeorology
Radiometer n radiometer
~ **zur Messung der wahren Objektstrahlung** truth radiometer
Radiometrie f radiometry, radioactivity logging
radiometrisch radiometric
Radionuklid n/**kosmisches** cosmogenic radionuclide
Radioteleskop n radio telescope
Radiothorium n radiothorium, ^{228}Th
Radiowellen fpl/**galaktische** galactic radio waves
Radium n radium, Ra
Radiumalter n radium age
Radiumemanation f radium emanation, radon, Rn

Radiumquelle f radioactive spring
Radiumzerfall m disintegration of radium
Radon n radon, radium emanation, Rn
Radula f radula
Radulazähnchen npl radula teeth
Raffinieren n refining
Raglanit m raglanite (diorite containing nepheline and corundum)
Raguinit m raguinite, $TlFeS_2$
Rahmen m/**geologischer** rock framework
Rahmenausbau m frame support
Rahmenfaltung f s. Diktyogenese
Rahmenmarken fpl fiducial marks
Raimondit m raimondite, $KFe_3[(OH)_6|(SO_4)_2]$
Rakete f/**mehrstufige** multistage rocket
~/**meteorologische** meteorologic[al] rocket
Raketensonde f sounding rocket
Ralstonit m ralstonite, $Al_2(F, OH)_6 \cdot H_2O$
Raman-Spektroskopie f Raman spectroscopy
Ramdohrit m ramdohrite, $Pb_6Ag_4Sb_{10}S_{23}$
Rammbär m ram
Rammbrunnen m driven well
Rammelsbergit m rammelsbergite, niccolite, NiAs
Rammsonde f driving rod, percussion probe
Rammsondierung f driving test, drop-penetration testing, percussion penetration method
Ramsayit m ramsayite, $Na_2Ti_2[O_3|Si_2O_6]$
Ramsdellit m ramsdellite, γ-MnO_2
Ranciéit m ranciéite, $(Ca, Mn)Mn_4O_9 \cdot 3H_2O$
Rand m edge; rim; margin
~/**aktiver** s. ~/mobiler
~ **eines Öllagers** edge of a pool
~/**mit gekerbtem** emarginate
~/**mobiler** mobile rim (of a geosyncline)
Randbecken n **am Fuße des Kontinentalabhangs** marginal basin
Randbedingung f boundary condition
Randbohrung f marginal well
Randbruch m marginal fault
Randeis n marginal ice
Randfalte f marginal fold
Randfazies f marginal (border) facies
~/**dichte** chilled contact (edge)
Randfläche f lateral face (of crystals)
Randgebiet n marginal region, borderland
~/**glaziales** periglacial region
Randgebirge n border mountains, bordering mountain chain, foothill
Randlage f marginal position
Randlamelle f/**innere** duplicature (palaeontology)
Randmeer n border (marginal, adjacent) sea
Randmoräne f border (marginal, peripheral) moraine
Randmulde f rim syncline (e.g. of a salt plug)
Randplateau n marginal plateau
Randpotentialfläche f marginal potential area (of an artesian basin)
Randschicht f surface layer
Randscholle f marginal crustal block
Randschwelle f marginal well

Randsee *m*/**alpiner** piedmont lake
~/glazialer ice-marginal lake
Randsenke *f* rim syncline, idiogeosyncline, marginal deep (trough); peripheral sink *(salt stock)*
Randsonde *f* edge well
Randspalte *f* marginal crevasse *(of a glacier)*
Randstaffel *f* marginal step
Randstörung *f* peripheral fault, marginal dislocation
Randstromfläche *f* marginal stream area
Randstufe *f*/**steile** marginal escarpment *(in the continental slope)*
Randsumpf *m* lagg
Randüberschiebung *f* marginal overthrust
Randverwerfung *f* border (boundary) fault
Randwasser *n* edge (syncline) water
~ mit großem Auftrieb high-head edge water
Randwasserlinie *f* edge-water line (limit)
Randwasserspiegel *m* oil-water contact, edge water surface
Randwassertrieb *m* [edge-]water drive
Randwulst *m* marginal well
Randzone *f* marginal (boundary) zone
Randzonensättigung *f* boundary saturation
Rang *m* rank, degree of coalification
Ranquilit *m* ranquilite, $Ca[(UO_2)_2|(Si_2O_5)_3] \cdot 12H_2O$
Ransomit *m* ransomite, $CuFe_2\text{-}[SO_4]_4 \cdot 7H_2O$
Rapakivi *m* rapakivi *(variety of granite)*
Rasen *m* turf, grass, sward, green
Rasenboden *m* soddy (sevardy) soil
~/schwarzer black turf soil
Rasenböschung *f* sodded (turfed) slope
Rasendecke *f* sod *(s.a. Rasenböschung)*
Raseneisenerz *n* meadow (marsh, swamp) ore, bog (lake, natural) iron ore
Raseneisenstein *m*, **Rasenerz** *n s.* Raseneisenerz
Rasenhängebank *f* surface (pit-bank) level, shaft mouth
Rasenhügel *m* earth hummock
Rasennarbe *f* mat of turf
Rasenpodsolboden *m* sod podzol
Rasensohle *f* surface level, grass roots
Rasenstufen *fpl* terracettes
Rasentorf *m* light surface peat
Rasorit *m s.* Kernit
Raspit *m* raspite, $\alpha\text{-}PbWO_4$
Raster *m*, **Rasterbild** *n* scanner
Rasterelektronenmikroskop *n* scanning electron microscope
Rastrites *m* rastrites
Rät *n s.* Rhät
Rathit *m* rathite, $Pb_7As_9S_{20}$
Ratsche *f* circle jack
Raubbau *m* destructive exploitation, overcutting
rauben to draw off, to withdraw
Raubfisch *m* predatory fish
Räucherer *m*/**schwarzer** "black smoker" *(chimney in the sea bottom)*
~/weißer "white smoker" *(submarine gas and smoke exhalation)*
Rauchfahne *f* wreath of smoke plume
Rauchgas *n* chimney gas
Rauchquarz *m* smoky quartz (topaz), smokestone
~/dunkler morion
Rauchsäule *f* smoke (steam) column
Rauchtopas *m s.* Rauchquarz
Rauchwacke *f. s.* Rauhwacke
Rauchwolke *f* smoke cloud
rauh rough; rugged
Rauheit *f* roughness; ruggedness
Rauhfrost *m s.* Rauhreif
Rauhigkeit *f* asperity *(of a joint)*
Rauhigkeitsfeld *n* roughness pattern
Rauhigkeitskoeffizient *m* coefficient of roughness
Rauhigkeitsverteilung *f* roughness pattern
Rauhreif *m* hoarfrost, [hard] rime
rauhsandig gritty
Rauhwacke *f* rauhwacke, smoke wacke, cellular dolomite
Raum *m* space
~/eurasiatischer Eurasian area
~/gefalteter consolidated area
~/geologischer geologic[al] space *(a defined set of geographic and geodetic coordinates of geological objects)*
~/intergalaktischer intergalactic space
~/interplanetarischer interplanetary space
~/interstellarer interstellar space
~/konsolidierter consolidated area
~ maximaler Sedimentation depocenter
~/säkular sich senkender zone of permanent downwarp[ing]
~/substanzfreier substance-free space *(in salt rocks)*
~/versteifter consolidated area
räumen to deplete
Räumer *m* reamer
Raumflugkörper *m* spacecraft
~ mit automatischem Filmrücktransport zur Erde film-return spacecraft
Raumgeologie *f* space geology
Raumgewicht *n* unit weight
~ unter Auftrieb buoyant unit weight
Raumgitter *n* space [group] lattice, three-dimensional lattice
Raumgruppe *f* lattice (space, point) group
Raumkoordinaten *fpl* three-dimensional coordinates
Raumlage *f* **einer Schicht/primäre** facing
räumlich three-dimensional
Raummodell *n* spatial model
Raumschaffung *f* **durch Intrusion** emplacement
Raumsonde *f* space probe
Raumstrahlung *f* cosmic[al] radiation, space radiation
Raumtrend *m* three-dimensional trend
Räumung *f* land clearing

Räumungsarbeit

Räumungsarbeit f stripping, [land] clearing
Raumwelle f body wave
Raumwinkel m solid angle
raumzeitlich space-time
raumzentriert body-centered, space-centered
~/kubisch cubic body-centered *(crystals)*
~/tetragonal tetragonal body-centered
Raurac[ien] n, **Rauracium** n Rauracian [Substage] *(of Lusitanian)*
Rauschen n [random] noise, background
~/weißes white noise
Rauschgelb n yellow arsenic (ratebane), orpiment, As_2S_3
Rauschleistung f/äquivalente noise-equivalent power
Rauschrot n red arsenic, realgar, ruby sulphur, ruby arsenic, As_4S_4
Rautenböden mpl rhumbs
Rautenflach n rhombohedron
Rautenfläche f facet
rautenförmig rhombic[al], rhomboidal
Rauvit m rauvite, $Ca[(UO_2)_2|V_{10}O_{28}] \cdot 16H_2O$
Rayleigh-Welle f Rayleigh wave
Rayonnierung f regional division
reagieren to react
Reaktion f reaction
~/chemische chemical reaction
~/endotherme endothermic reaction
reaktionsfreudig reactive
Reaktionsgrad m reaction rate
Reaktionspaar n reaction pair
Reaktionsprinzip n/**Bowensches** Bowen's reaction series
Reaktionsrand m reaction border
Reaktionsreihe f reaction series
~/Bowensche Bowen's reaction series, Bowen's petrogenetic grid
Reaktionssaum m reaction rim
reaktionsträge inert, weakly reactive
Reaktionsvermögen n responsivity *(e.g. of a sensor)*
Reaktionswärme f heat of reaction
Reaktionszone f reaction zone
Reaktionszonung f reaction zoning
Reaktivität f **der Kohle** reactivity of coal
Realgar m realgar, red arsenic, As_4S_4
Realgasfaktor m gas deviation factor
Realgasverhalten n supercompressibility
Realkristall m real (imperfect) crystal
Rechteckfunktion f step function
rechtsdrehend dextrorotatory, dextrogyrate
Rechtsdrehsinn m sense of right-hand screw motion
rechtsgewunden dextral *(molluscan tests)*
Rechtsquarz m dextrogyrate (right-hand) quartz
Rechtsspülen n direct circulation *(of borehole)*
Reddingit m reddingite, $(Mn, Fe)_3[PO_4]_2 \cdot 3H_2O$
Redingtonit m redingtonite, $(Fe, Mg, Ni)(CrAl)_2[SO_4]_4 \cdot 22H_2O$

Redledgeit m redledgeite, $(Mg, Ca, OH, H_2O)[(Ti, Cr, Si)_8O_{16}]$
Redlichia-Reich n Redlichiid Realm *(palaeobiogeography, Lower Cambrian)*
Redondit m redondite *(Fe-bearing variscite)*
Redoxnormalpotential n redox normal potential
Redoxpotential n redox (oxidation-reduction) potential
Redoxreaktion f redox reaction
Reduktion f/**adaptive** adaptive reduction *(palaeontology)*
~/topografische topographic correction *(gravimetry)*
Reduktionsflamme f reducing (carbonizing) flame
Reduktionsmittel n reducing agent
Reduktionsvorgang m reduction process
Reduktionszone f reducing zone
Redundanz f redundancy
reduzieren to reduce
Reduzierung f reduction
Reedmergnerit m reedmergnerite, $NaBSi_3O_8$
Referenzellipsoid n reference ellipsoid
Refizit m reficite, $C_{20}H_{32}O_2$
Reflektanz f reflectance
Reflektor m mirror; reflecting horizon
Reflektorlänge f subsurface coverage *(seismics)*
Reflex m s. Reflexion
Reflexion f reflection
~ an einer Störung fault plain reflection
~/diffuse diffuse reflection
~/einfache simple reflection
~/seismische seismic reflection
~/spiegelnde specular reflection
Reflexionen fpl/**multiple** multiple (repeated) reflections
Reflexionsebene f plane of reflection
Reflexionselement n segment
Reflexionsgesetz n law of reflection
Reflexionshorizont m reflection horizon
Reflexionskoeffizient m reflection coefficient
Reflexionsmessung f reflection measurement, reflectometry
Reflexionspleochroismus m reflection pleochroism, bireflectance
Reflexionspunkt m depth point
~/gemeinsamer common reflection point, CRP
Reflexionsschießen n reflection shooting *(seismics)*
Reflexionsseismik f seismic reflection method (technique)
Reflexionsstandard m reflection standard
Reflexionsverfahren n photoelastic reflection method
Reflexionsvermögen n reflectivity, reflectance, reflecting power
~/relatives spektrales spectral reflectance
~ von Blättern leaf reflectance
Reflexionswinkel m angle of reflection

Reformieren *n*, **Reforming** *n* reforming
Refraktion *f* refraction; refraction (conical) wave
~/flache shallow refraction
~/reflektierte reflected refraction
~/seismische seismic refraction
Refraktionsaufstellungen *fpl*/**radiale** radial refraction
Refraktionsberichtigung *f* refraction correction
Refraktionshorizont *m* refraction marker, refractor
Refraktionsprofil *n* refraction profile
Refraktionsschießen *n* refraction shooting
Refraktionsseismik *f* refraction seismics
Refugien *n* Refugian [Stage] *(marine stage, upper Eocene in North America)*
Regel *f*/**Fersmansche** Fersman's rule
~/Goldschmidtsche Goldschmidt's rule
~/Hiltsche Hilt's law
~/Nernstsche Nernst's rule
~/Oddo-Harkinssche Oddo-Harkins' rule
Regelation *f* regelation
Regeln *fpl* **für die Zoologische Nomenklatur/Internationale** International Rules of Zoological Nomenclature
Regelung *f* **nach dem Kornbau** lattice orientation
~ nach der Korngestalt dimensional orientation
Regelungsbild *n* pattern *(of diagrams)*
Regelungsdiagramm *n* orientation diagram
Regelungsmechanismus *n* orienting mechanism
Regen *m* rain
Regenabflußmenge *f* runoff from rainfall
Regenabtragung *f* pluvial denudation
regenarm lacking (deficient) in rain
Regenauffangbehälter *m* rain trap
Regenbande *f* rainband
Regenbö *f* rainsquall
Regenbogen *m* rainbow
Regenbogenachat *m* irisated agate
Regenbogenfarben *fpl* rainbow colours
regenbogenfarbig rainbow-coloured
Regendichte *f* rainfall intensity
Regeneration *f* regeneration; regrowth *(of crystals)*
regeneriert resurrected
Regenerosion *f* pluvial erosion
Regenfall *m* rainfall
Regenfront *f* rain front
Regenfurche *f* rain (wet-weather) rill
Regengleiche *f* isohyet[al line], isopluvial line, line of equal rainfall
Regenguß *m* rainsquall, rainpour, [torrential] downpour
Regenhochwasser *n* flood resulting from rain
Regenhöhe *f* depth of the rain
Regenjahr *n* rainy year
Regenkarte *f* isohyetal map
Regenlahar *m* rain lahar

Regenlinie *f* rainband
regenlos rainless
Regenmenge *f* rainfall
Regenmesser *m* rain gauge, pluviometer, ombrometer, udometer
~/registrierender *s.* Regenschreiber
Regenmeßstelle *f* rain-gauge station
Regenmessung *f* rain measurement, pluviometry, udometry
Regenperiode *f s.* Regenzeit
regenreich rainy, abundant with rain
Regenriefe *f*, **Regenrille** *f* rain (wet-weather) rill
Regenschatten *m* rain shadow
Regenschauer *m* rain shower
Regenschichtflut *f* overland flow, rainsheet
Regenschlag *m* rain beat
Regenschreiber *m* rainfall recorder, pluviograph, ombrograph, hyetograph
Regenstein *m* ooid, ovulite, ammite
Regensturm *m* rainstorm
Regentag *m* rainy (wet) day
Regentropfen *m* raindrop
Regentropfen *mpl*/**fossile** fossil raindrops, accretionary lapilli
Regentropfeneindrücke *mpl*, **Regentropfenmarken** *fpl* rain prints
Regenwasser *n* rainwater, storm water
Regenwetter *n* rainy weather
Regenwolke *f* rain cloud
Regenzeit *f* pluvial phase (period), rainy period (season)
Regenzone *f* rain belt
Regime *n* regime
~/hydraulisches hydraulic regime
Region *f* region, area, zone; region *(palaeobiogeography)*
~/abyssische abyssal region
~/aphotische aphotic region
~/aseismische aseismic[al] region, non-seismic region
~/dysphotische dysphotic region
~/peneseismische peneseismic region
regional regional
Regionalaufnahme *f* regional survey
Regionaldiskordanz *f* regional unconformity
Regionalgeologie *f* regional (areal) geology
regionalgeologisch regional-geological
regionalmetamorph regional-metamorphic
Regionalmetamorphose *f* regional metamorphism
Regionalprofil *n* regional profile
Regionalprognose *f* regional prognosis
Regionalvermessung *f* reconnaissance *(seismics)*
Registrierer *m* operator
Registriergerät *n* recorder, recording device (instrument)
~ für Bohrlochmessungen logging recorder
Registriergeschwindigkeit *f* speed of registration
Registrierpapier *n* registration paper

Registrierstreifen 252

Registrierstreifen *m* registration sheet
Registriertrommel *f* recording drum
Registrierung *f* registration, registering, record[ing]
~ **aus der Bewegung** smearing
~/**elektromagnetische** electromagnetic registration
~ **in Linienschrift/seismische** seismic record in wiggle-trace form
Registriervorrichtung *f* registering arrangement
Registrierzeit *f* record time
Registrierzylinder *m* recording cylinder
regnerisch pluvious, pluvial
Regolith *m* regolith; loipon *(by chemical weathering)*
Regression *f* regression, reliction
~/**fortschreitende** progressive off-lapping
Regressionsanalyse *f* regression analysis
Regressionslinie *f* regression line *(water)*
regressiv regressive
regulär regular
Reibung *f* friction
~/**innere** internal friction
Reibungsbeiwert *m* friction coefficient
~ **der Bewegung** dynamic[al] friction coefficient
~ **der Ruhe** static friction coefficient
Reibungsbrekzie *f* friction (fault, fresh, crush, tectonic) breccia
Reibungsdrehmoment *n* frictional torque
Reibungserwärmung *f* friction heating
Reibungsfläche *f* friction surface
Reibungsgeschwindigkeit *f* friction velocity
Reibungskoeffizient *m s.* Reibungsbeiwert
Reibungskopf *m* friction cap
Reibungskraft *f* frictional force; shear drag *(of fluids)*
Reibungsschluß *m* friction grip
Reibungsstempel *m* friction prop
Reibungsteppich *m* friction carpet
Reibungsverankerung *f* anchoring by friction
Reibungswiderstand *m* frictional resistance
Reibungswinkel *m* friction angle, angle of [internal] friction
Reibungsziffer *f s.* Reibungsbeiwert
Reicherz *n* rich (high-grade) ore
reichhaltig rich, high-grade
Reichweite *f* reach
~/**mittlere** mean range *(ground-water depression)*
Reichweitenbegrenzung *f* zero drawdown boundary
Reifbildung *f* ice frost
Reife *f* maturity
~/**strukturelle** textural maturity
Reifestadium *n* stage of maturity
Reihe *f*/**diskontinuierliche** discontinuous series
~/**isomorphe** isomorphous series
~/**kristalloblastische** crystalloblastic series
~/**ökologische** ecological series
~/**phänomenologische** phenomenological series
~/**phylogenetische** phylogenetic series, lineage, line of descent
Reihenfolge *f* **der Lagerung** succession of beds
~/**paragenetische** paragenetic sequence
Reihenpegel *m* chain gauge
Reihenstempel *mpl* breaker props
Reihenüberschiebung *f* base vubbing
rein pure, neat
Reindichte *f* solids density
Reinerit *m* reinerite, $Zn_3[AsO_3]_2$
Reingut *n* concentrate
Reinhaltung *f* antipollution
Reinheitsgrad *m* degree of purity
Reinheitsprüfung *f* purity test
reinigen to clean; to purify; to clear; to clarify
~/**vom tauben Gestein** to clear the rock
Reinigen *n* **des Bohrlochs** cleaning of the borehole
Reinigungssystem *n* solid control system
Reinit *m* reinite *(pseudomorph after ferberite)*
Reinjektion *f* reinjection
Reinkohle *f* clean coal
Reißblei *n* plumbago, plumbagine
Reißen *n* **des Hangenden** roof break
Reißfuge *f*, **Reißkluft** *f* ac-point, tension point
Rejuvenation *f* rejuvenation
rekonstruieren to reconstruct
Rekonstruktion *f* reconstruction
Rekristallisation *f* recrystallization, rejuvenation of crystals
Rekristallisationsgefüge *n* percrystalline structure
rekristallisieren to recrystallize
rekristallisiert neocrystic *(in the fabric of evaporites)*
Rekultivierung *f* recultivation
Rekurrenz *f* recurrence
Rekurrenzfläche *f* recurrence horizon
Relaisfalten *fpl* overlapping folds
Relaxation *f* relaxation
Relaxationszeit *f* relaxation time
Relief *n* relief
~/**alpines** alpine relief
~/**geringes** subdued relief
~/**topografisches** topographic[al] relief
Reliefdiskordanz *f* relief unconformity
Reliefeinebnung *f* deplanation, equiplanation
Reliefeinfluß *m* **auf oberirdischen Abfluß** roughness factor for overland flow
Reliefenergie *f* relief intensity (ratio); measure of relief; amount of local relief; fall *(of a river)*
Reliefinversion *f* relief inversion
Reliefkarte *f* relief (embossed) map
Reliefüberschiebung *f* erosion (surface) thrust
Reliefumkehr[ung] *f* relief inversion; inverted relief
Relikt *n* relict *(biological)*; relic *(remainder)*; palimpsest
~/**gepanzertes** armoured relict

~/instabiles unstable relict
~/stabiles stable relict
Reliktboden m relict soil
Reliktendemismus m palaeoendemism
Reliktfauna f relict fauna
Reliktflora f relict flora
Reliktgefüge n relict fabric
Reliktlösung f/salinare saliniferous residual water
Reliktstruktur f relic structure
Relikttextur f relic texture
Reliktwässer npl residual waters
Relizien n Relizian [Stage] (marine stage, lower Miocene in North America)
remanent remanent, residual
Remanenz f remanence, remanent (residual) magnetization
Remission f diffuse reflection
Renardit m renardite, Pb[(UO$_2$)$_4$|(OH)$_4$|(PO$_4$)$_2$] · 8H$_2$O
Rendzina f rendzina, humus carbonate (calcareous) soil
Reniérit m reniérite, Cu$_3$(Fe, Ge)S$_4$
Rentabilität f geologischer Untersuchungsarbeiten profitability of geological prospecting
Reomorphose f reomorphism
Repetitionsschichtung f repetitive bedding, alternate structure, cyclic sedimentation
Repetitionsverwerfung f repetitive fault
Repetitionszwilling m repetition twin
Repettien n Repettian [Stage] (Pliocene)
Reproduktionsorgane npl reproductive (generative) organs
Reptil n reptile
Resedimentationsgefüge n secondary (indirect) stratification
Reserveblock m reserve block
Reservelagerstätte f reserve deposit
Reserveschätzung f reserve estimate
Reservoir n/geschlossenes bounded reservoir
~/klüftig-poröses fractured-matrix reservoir, fissured-porous reservoir
~/unendliches infinite reservoir
Reservoirabgrenzungstest m reservoir limit test
Reservoirgitternetz n reservoir grid
Reservoirheterogenitäten fpl reservoir heterogeneities
Reservoirmechanik f reservoir mechanics, [petroleum] reservoir engineering
Residualanreicherung f residual enrichment
Residualerzlagerstätte f residual ore deposit
Residualgebirge n residual mountain
Residuallagerstätte f residual deposit
Residualsediment n/grobes lag concentrate
Residuum n residual
Resilifizierung f resilication
Resinit m resinite (coal maceral); (partly) resinous substance; resin rodlets
Resistivimetrie f mud resistivity logging
Resistivität f der Tonspülung mud resistivity

Resonanz f resonance; singing
Resonanzkraft f resonance force
Resonanzmessung f/kernmagnetische nuclear magnetic resonance logging
resorbieren to reabsorb
Resorption f resorption
Ressourcen fpl/bekannte, gegenwärtig wirtschaftlich nicht bauwürdige identified subeconomic resources
~ des Tiefseebodens deepsea bed resources
~/mutmaßliche probable resources
~/nachgewiesene identified resources
~/nicht nachgewiesene unproven resources
Ressourcenerkundung f resources survey
Rest m residual, remnant, remainder
Restabtragungsfläche f residual erosion surface
Restauration f reconstruction
restaurieren to restore; to reconstruct
Restberg m residual mountain (hill), [erosional] outlier, [residual] butte, monadnock
Restentgasung f/magmatische magmatic residual degassing
Restfeld n grid residual, residual disturbance, map convolution
Resthügel m residual hill
Restintrusion f afterintrusion
Restion n ionic radical
Restit m restite
Restkrater m submorphic crater (rest of an collapsed crater)
Restlagerstätte f residual deposit
Restlösung f residual solution; aliquot solution (after subrosion)
~/kalziumreiche calciferous residual solution
~/kieselsäurereiche siliceous residual solution
~/magmatische residual [magmatic] liquor
Restmagma n residual (rest) magma
Restmagnetisierung f residual magnetization
Restmagnetismus m residual magnetism
Restmoveout n rest move-out
Restöl n/nicht gewinnbares residual oil
Restpfeiler m coal (ore) pillar
Restregelung f residual orientation (tectonite fabric)
Restsättigung f residual saturation (crude oil)
Restscherfestigkeit f residual shear strength
Restschmelze f residual melt
Restschwere f residual gravity
Restsediment n residual sediment
Restsee m residual (relic) lake
Restspannung f residual stress
~/tangentiale residual hoop stress
Reststörung f residual disturbance
Reststrahlung f residual radiation
Reststreuung f residual scattering
Restwasser n residual water
Restwasseranteil m residual water content
Restzeit f residual [time]
resurgent resurgent
Retardationszeit f retardation time
Retention f retention (for water)

Retgersit 254

Retgersit m retgersite, α-Ni[SO$_4$] · 6H$_2$O
retikuliert reticulated
Retinasphalt m retinasphalt[um]
Retinit m retinite *(a fossil resin)*
Retortengraphit m retort graphite
Retro[meta]morphose f retrogressive metamorphism
Retzian m retzian *(Y-, Mn-, Ca-arsenate)*
Rewdanskit m rewdanscite *(variety of antigorite)*
Reyerit m reyerite, truscottite, Ca$_2$[Si$_4$O$_{10}$]H$_2$O
Rézbányit m rézbányite, 3PbS · Cu$_2$S · 5Bi$_2$S$_3$
rezent recent, modern
Rhabdit m rhabdite, (Ni, Fe)$_3$P *(mineral in meteorites)*
Rhabdophan m rhabdophan[it]e, Ce[PO$_4$] · $^1/_2$H$_2$O
Rhagit m s. Atelestit
Rhät n Rhaetian [Stage], Rhaetic [Stage] *(uppermost stage of Triassic)*
Rhätizit m rhaeticite *(variety of disthene)*
Rhätsandstein m Rhaetic sandstone
Rhegmagenese f rhegmagenesis
Rheintalgraben m Rhine graben
Rhenoherzynikum n Rheno-Hercynian zone
rhenotyp rhenotype
Rheologie f rheology
rheologisch rheological
Rheomorphose f rheomorphism
Rhipidolith m s. Prochlorit
Rhodesit m rhodesite, KNaCa$_2$[H$_2$Si$_8$O$_{20}$] · 5H$_2$O
Rhodit m rhodite, rhodium gold *(natural alloy of gold and rhodium)*
Rhodium n rhodium, Rh
Rhodizit m rhodizite, KNaLi$_4$Al$_4$[Be$_3$B$_{10}$O$_{27}$]
Rhodochrosit m rhodochrosite, dialogite, manganese spar, MnCO$_3$
Rhodolith m rhodolite
Rhodonit m rhodonite, CaMn$_4$[Si$_5$O$_{15}$]
Rhombendodekaeder n rhombododecahedron, rhombic[al] dodecahedron, granatohedron
rhombenförmig rhombic[al]
Rhombenporphyr m rhomb porphyry *(effusive rock from laurvikite)*
rhombisch rhombic[al]
Rhomboeder n rhombohedron
rhomboedrisch rhombohedral
Rhomboid n rhomboid
rhomboidisch rhomboidal
Rhomboklas m rhomboclase, FeH[SO$_4$]$_2$ · 4H$_2$O
Rhombus m rhomb
Rhuddenium n Rhuddenian [Stage] *(basal stage of Llandovery series)*
Rhyakolit m s. Sanidin
Rhyodazit m rhyodacite
Rhyolith m rhyolite
rhyolithisch rhyolitic
Rhyolithlava f rhyolitic lava
rhyotaxitisch rhyotaxitic
rhythmisch rhythmic

Rhythmit m rhythmite, laminite *(sedimentite)*
Ria[s]küste f ria coast (shore line)
Richellit m richellite, Ca$_3$Fe$_{10}$[(OH, F)$_3$I(PO$_4$)$_2$]$_4$ · nH$_2$O
Richetit m richetite *(uranium mineral)*
Richmond[ien] n Richmondian [Stage] *(of Cincinnatian in North America)*
Richmondit m richmondite, Al[PO$_4$] · 4H$_2$O
Richtbohren n directional drilling
~ **mit einer Ablenkturbine** jet deflection drilling
Richtbohrung f inclined bore
Richtbohrwerkzeuge npl deflecting tools
Richtcharakteristik f directivity graph
Richterit m richterite, Na$_2$Ca (Mg, Fe$^{..}$, Mn, Fe$^{...}$, Al)$_5$[(OH, F)ISi$_4$O$_{11}$]$_2$
Richtgelenk n knuckle joint
Richtlinien fpl/**stratigrafische** stratigraphic guide lines
Richtschnitt m determination profile
Richtstrecke f driftway, main road, *(Am)* lateral road
Richtung f direction; course
~ **der Kristallachse** crystallographic axis orientation
~ **der tektonischen Durchbewegung** tectonic flow (transport), a-direction
~ **des Streichens** bearing of the trend
~/**eggische** Eggish direction *(NNW–SSE)*
~/**erzgebirgische** direction of the Erzgebirge *(NE–SW)*
~/**herzynische** Hercynian direction *(NW–SE)*
~ **quer zur Fallinie** side-basse
~/**rheinische** Rhenish direction *(NNE-SSW)*
~ **senkrecht zur Hauptspaltbarkeit** bord ways course
Richtungsabweichung f deviation in azimuth
Richtungsbohren n directional drilling
Richtungsbohrung f directional well
Richtungsfilter n velocity filter *(seismics)*
richtungslos 1. directionless; 2. non-oriented
Richtungsmessung f direction measurement
Richtungsrose f rose diagram
Richtungswechsel m change in direction
Richtungswinkel m heading *(sea seismics)*
Rickardit m rickardite, Cu$_3$Te$_3$
Riebeckit m riebeckite, Na$_2$Fe$_3^{..}$Fe$_2^{...}$[(OH, F) I Si$_4$O$_{11}$]$_2$
Ried n fen[land], peat bog
Riedmoor n black bog
Riedtorf m marsh peat
Riefe f flute, groove, stria
Riefenbildung f s. Riefung
Riefenmarke f striation cast (mark)
Riefung f striation, fluting, channelling
~/**geradlinige** parting lineation
Riese m/**Roter** red giant *(star)*
Rieselanlage f irrigation plant
Rieselfeld n irrigation field (district)
Rieselmarke f rill mark
Rieselmuster n rill pattern

Rippelmarken

Rieselregen m gentle rain
Rieselwasser n irrigation (sewage) water
Rieselwerk n cooling stack
Riesenfaultier n Megatherium
Riesenhirsch m giant deer
Riesenklüfte fpl gigantic joints
Riesenkristall m giant crystal
Riesenmeteorit m giant bolide
Riesenrippeln fpl giant ripples
Riesenstern m giant star
Riesenwuchs m giant growth
Riff n reef, shelf
~/**aufgetauchtes** emerged reef
~/**erhöhtes** uplifted reef
~/**ringförmiges** annular reef
riffartig reeflike
Riffazies f reef facies
riffbildend reef-building, hermatypic
~/**nicht** ahermatypic
Riffbild[n]er m reef builder (former)
Riffbildung f reef building (formation)
Riffelteiler m riffle splitter (bank)
Rifffläche f reef flat
Riffflankenschichtung f reef-flank bedding
Riffgestein n hermatolith
~/**organogenes** hermatobiolith
riffig reefy
Riffkalkstein m reef limestone
~/**massiger** klintite
Riffkern m reef core
Riffkoralle f reef coral
Rifflagunenfazies f lagoon facies near reef
Riffmauer f reef wall
Riffmilch f reef milk (opaque calcareous mud)
Riffplatte f reef flat
Riffrand m reef edge
Riffspeicher m reef-type reservoir
Rifftuff m reef tufa
Rift n rift
Riftgebirge npl rift mountains
Riftzone f rift zone
Righeit f rigidity
Rille f rill; groove; furrow
Rillenerosion f rill erosion
Rillenmarke f groove cast
~/**gefiederte** ruffled groove cast
~/**kleine** microgroove cast
Rillenspülung f rill erosion, rill-wash[ing erosion]
Rillensteine mpl rill stones
Rillung f a-lineation, stries, striations (tectonical)
Rima f rima (rill, groove, furrow on moon or Mars)
Rindenkörner npl coated grains
Ring m annulus
~/**pleochroitischer** [pleochroic] halo
Ringe mpl/**Liesegangsche** diffusion banding
~/**planetare** planetary rings
Ringelerz n ring (sphere, cockade) ore
ringförmig annular
Ringgang m ring dike, ring-fracture intrusion

Ringgebirge n walled plain (of the moon)
Ringintrusion f ring-fracture intrusion, ring dike
Ringkörper m annular body
Ringlagune f lagoon moat
Ringmarke f ring mark
Ringraum m annular space, annulus (of a bore)
~ **zwischen Bohrloch und Rohrstrang** clearance between casing and hole
~ **zwischen zwei Rohrsträngen** clearance between casing, annular space
Ringraumdruck m casing pressure
Ringraumfließdruck m flowing casing pressure
Ringraumkopfdruck m casing-head pressure
Ringraumruhedruck m static casing pressure
Ringraumzementierung f casing cementing job
Ringriff n reef ring, atoll [reef]
Ringschicht f annular layer
Ringschluß m loop
Ringspalte f concentric[al] rift
Ringstruktur f ring structure
Ringwall m ring wall; rampart
Ringwanne f rim syncline (around salt plugs)
Ringwoodit m ringwoodite (cubic olivine)
Rinkit m rinkite, (Na, Ca, Ce)$_3$(Ti, Ce)[(F, OH, O)$_2$ I Si$_2$O$_7$]
Rinkolith m rinkolite (Sr-bearing rinkite)
Rinne f channel, groove, flute, furrow, runway
~/**glaziale** dorr
~/**submarine** submarine channel
Rinneit m rinneite, K$_3$Na[FeCl$_6$]
Rinnenausfüllung f, **Rinnenausguß** m groove cast
Rinnenerosion f rill-wash[ing erosion], shoestring gully erosion
rinnenförmig furrowed
Rinnenfüllung f channel cast
Rinnenkarren npl gully clints
Rinnenmarke f channel cast
Rinnenmuster n channel pattern
~ **eines geradlinig verlaufenden Flusses** straight channel pattern
~ **eines mäandrierenden Flusses** meandering channel pattern
~ **eines vielverzweigten Flusses** braided channel pattern
Rinnenprofil n [U-]channel section
Rinnensande mpl/**deltaische** barfinger sands
Rinnensediment n channel sand (fill)
Rinnensee m groove lake
~/**glazialer** fosse lake
Rinnental n gutter valley
Rinnsal n runnel, riverlet, streamlet
Rippe f rib, ridge
~/**frei endende** floating rib
Rippel f ripple
Rippelfaserung f ripple cross lamination
Rippelmarken fpl ripple (rill) marks, ripples

Rippelmarken

~/**flachkämmige** flat-topped ripple marks
~/**gekrümmte** curved ripple marks
~/**isolierte** incomplete (isolated) ripples
~/**kletternde** climbing ripples
~/**longitudinale** longitudinal ripple marks
~/**mit Anlagerungs-Schrägschichtungsblättern/ flache** accretion ripple marks
~/**normale** normal ripple marks
~/**periklinale** pericline ripple marks
~/**rautenförmige** rhomboid ripple marks
~/**regressive** regressive ripples
~/**rhombenförmige** rhomboid ripple marks
~/**schlammbedeckte** mud-buried ripple marks
~/**sichelförmige** cuspate ripple marks
~/**symmetrische** symmetrical ripple marks
~/**unsymmetrische** asymmetric[al] ripple marks
~/**zungenförmige** linguloid ripple marks
~/**zusammengesetzte** compound ripple marks
Rippelmarkenbildung f rippling, ripple marking
Rippeln fpl s. Rippelmarken
Rippelschichtung f ripple bedding (drift), ripple cross lamination, lee-side concentration, rolling strata
Rippeltal n ripple trough
Rippelungen fpl s. Rippelmarken
Rippen fpl wrinkle ridges (on the moon)
Rippenversatz m strip (partial) packing
Rippströmung f rip current
Risörit m risörite (variety of fergusonite)
Riß m tear; cleft, rupture, fracture, fissure (tectonically); crevasse (in a glacier)
~ **im Gestein** cranny
~/**innerkristalliner** intracrystalline crack
~/**interkristalliner** intercrystalline (grain boundary) crack
~/**mikroskopischer** microfissure
~/**senkrechter** shake
Riß n s. Riß-Eiszeit
rißartig chinkshaped
Rißausbreitung f crack propagation
Rißbildung f cracking, fissuration
~/**feine** s. Maronage
~/**hydraulische** [hydra]frac, hydraulic fracturing
~/**karoartige** checking
~/**mehrstufige hydraulische** multifrac
~ **mittels Druckschwankungen/hydraulische** vibrofrac
~/**netzartige** alligatoring, alligator cracking
Rißbreite f fracture width
Risse mpl/**senkrecht zum Einfallen gerichtete** shuttles
Rißeindringen n penetration of fracture
Riß-Eiszeit f Riss [Drift] (Pleistocene of Alps district)
Rißhöhe f fracture height
rissig fissured, chinky, crannied, cracky, cracked, slippy; crevassed
~ **werden** to crack
Riß-Kaltzeit f s. Riß-Eiszeit

Rißlänge f fracture length
Riß-Mindel-Interglazial n Riss-Mindel [Interval] (Pleistocene of Alps district)
Rißorientierung f fracture direction
Rißporosität f crack porosity
Rißweite f fracture width
Ritze f scratch; interstice; chink
ritzen to scratch
Ritzhärte f scratch (abrasive) hardness; resistance to scratching
Ritzhärteprobe f surface scratching test
Ritzhärteprüfer m scratch hardness tester
Ritzhärteprüfung f abrasive hardness test
Ritzhärtezahl f scratch hardness number
Ritzverfahren n scratch test
Robinsonit m robinsonite, $7PbS \cdot 6 Sb_2S_3$
Rockbridgeit m rockbridgeite, $(Fe\ddot{}Mn)Fe_4\ddot{}[(OH)_5 | (PO_4)_3]$
Rockland[ien] n, **Rocklandium** n Rocklandian [Stage] (Champlaining, North America)
Rockwellhärte f Rockwell hardness
Rodingit m rodingite (garnet pyroxene rock)
Roeblingit m roeblingite, $PbCa_3H_6[SO_4|(SiO_4)_3]$
Rogeis n frazil [ice]
Rogenpyrit m framboidal pyrite
Rogenstein m roestone, oolite
roh crude
Rohanalyse f rough analysis
Rohbauxit m crude bauxite
Rohblock m rough quarry block
Rohboden m virgin soil
Rohbraunkohle f raw brown coal, rough (raw) lignite
Rohdiamant m rough diamond, dob
~ **mit zahlreichen Einschlüssen** rejection stone
Roheisen n pig iron
Roherdöl n s. Rohöl
Roherz n crude (raw, mine, run-of-mine) ore, crudes
Roherzhalde f bouse team
Rohfördergut n run of mine
Rohgips m gypsum rock
Rohglimmer m natural (block) mica
Rohgold n gold bullion
Rohhumus m duff, mor
Rohkaolin m crude (raw) kaolin, China clay
Rohkohle f crude (raw, green, run-of-mine) coal
Rohkristall m crystal blank
Rohkupfer n copper matte
Rohmaterial n raw material
Rohöl n crude (raw, base, rock) oil, crude petroleum (naphtha), crude
Rohölasche f crude petroleum ash
Rohölbasis f crude oil base
Rohphosphat n rock phosphate
Rohr n tube, pipe
Rohrbrunnen m borehole well
Röhre f tube
röhrenartig tubular, tubulous, tubelike

röhrenförmig tubiform
Röhrentour f s. Rohrfahrt
Röhrenwand f tube wall
Röhrenwürmer mpl tubicolar worms
Rohrfahrt f casing
~/erste [surface] string
Rohrfangkrebs m casing spear
Rohrkaliber n drift diameter gauge, drift mandrel
Rohrkopf m casing head
Rohrkopfbenzin n casing-head gasoline
Rohrleitung f pipeline
~/untermeerische submarine pipeline
Rohrmuffe f casing collar
Rohrperforation f casing perforation
Rohrreduzierflansch m adapter casing flange
Rohrschneider m pipe (tube) cutter, casing cutter (knife)
Rohrschraubvorrichtung f power tongs
Rohrschuh m casing shoe
~ mit Rückschlagventil float shoe
Rohrstempel m tubular prop
Rohrstrang m string of casing
Rohrtiefe f casing depth
Rohrtorf m reed (telmatic) peat
Rohrtour f casing string, tour
~/präperforierte liner, preperforated section
~/technische intermediate casing string
~/verlorene liner
Rohrüberlauf m pipe spillway (for water volume measurement)
Rohrwagen m pipe carriage
Rohrzange f casing tongs, pipe wrench
Rohsalz n crude salt
~/erdiges caliche
Rohstapelung f brute stack (seismics)
Rohstoff m raw material
~/angearbeiteter mineralischer semiprocessed mineral
~/keramischer ceramic raw material
~/mineralischer mineral raw material
~/verarbeiteter mineralischer processed (manufactured) mineral
Rohstofferkundung f exploration of raw materials
Rohstoffgewinnung f aus geologischen Untersuchungsarbeiten side recovery
~ im Übertagebau quarrying
~/maritime undersea (ocean) mining
Rohteer m crude tar
Rohton m raw clay
Rohzink n spelter
Rollbereitschaft f pivotability, rollability (of clastic grains)
Rollen n rumbling (volcanology)
~/dumpfes dull rumbling
Rollenkernbohrer m, **Rollen[kern]krone** f rock core bit, cutter head
Rollenlager n crown block
Rollenmeißel m roller (rock) bit
Rollenmeißelbohren n rock bit drilling
Roller m ground roll (seismics)

Rollfalten fpl **in Decken** nappe involutions
Rollgrenze f plastic limit
rollig non-plastic (soil)
Rollkiesel m roundstone
Rollmarke f roll mark
Rollsteine mpl cobbles, rubble stones
Rollstruktur f/**synsedimentäre** pseudonodule, sand roll
Rollwinkel m angle of roll
Roméit m romeite, $(Ca, NaH)Sb_2O_6(O,OH,F)$
Römerit m roemerite, $Fe\ddot{F}e_2[SO_4]_4 \cdot 14H_2O$
Röntgenanalyse f X-ray analysis
Röntgenbeugungsanalyse f X-ray diffraction analysis
Röntgenbeugungsdiagramm n X-ray diffraction pattern
Röntgendiffraktometrie f X-ray diffractometry
Röntgenfluoreszenzanalyse f fluorescent X-ray analysis
Röntgenfluoreszenzspektralanalyse f fluorescent X-ray spectrographic analysis
Röntgenfluoreszenzspektrometrie f X-ray fluorescence spectrometry
Röntgenfluoreszenzspektroskopie f X-ray fluorescence spectroscopy
Röntgenit m roentgenite, $Ca_2Ce_3[Fe_3|(CO_3)_5]$
röntgenkristallin roentgencrystalline
Röntgenmetallografie f radiometallography
Röntgenografie f radiography
Röntgenstrahlenbild n X-ray target
Röntgenstruktur f X-ray crystal structure
Röntgenuntersuchung f X-ray investigation
Röntgenzählrohrgoniometer n X-ray counting-tube goniometer
Rooseveltit m rooseveltite, $\alpha\text{-}Bi[AsO_4]$
Roquésit m roquésite, $CuInS_2$
Rosasit m rosasite, $(Zn,Cu)_2[(OH)_2|CO_3]$
Rösche f gullet
Roscherit m roscherite, $(Ca,Mn,Fe)\ B[OH|PO_4] \cdot {}^2/_3H_2O$
Roscoelith m roscoelite, $KV_2[(OH)_2|AlSi_3O_{10}]$
Roselith m roselite, $\alpha\text{-}Ca_2Co[AsO_4]_2 \cdot 2H_2O$
Rosenbuschit m rosenbuschite, $(Ca,Na)_6Zr(Ti,Mn,Nb)\ [(F,O)_2|Si_2O_7]_2$
Rosenquarz m rose (rosy) quartz (variety of quartz)
Rosenspat m s. Manganspat
Rosickyit m rosickyite (γ-sulphur)
Rosieresit m rosieresite (Pb-, Cu-bearing evansite)
Rossit m rossite, $Ca[V_2O_6] \cdot 4H_2O$
rostbraun rusty-brown
Rösterz n calcined ore
röstfähig calcigenous
rostfarben rust-coloured
rostfleckig rusty
rostig rusty
Rostrum n gaine (palaeontology)
Roststreifen m rusty band
Röt n Roethian [Stage] (of Lower Triassic)
Rotalgen fpl red algae
Rotarybohren n rotary drilling, drilling with rotary table

Rotarybohrgerät

Rotarybohrgerät *n* rotary drilling rig
Rotarysprenglochverfahren *n* rotary blast hole drilling
Rotationsachse *f* rotational axis, axis of rotation
Rotationsellipsoid *n* ellipsoid of rotation, revolution (oblate) ellipsoid
Rotationsenergie *f* angular kinetic energy
Rotationsgeschwindigkeit *f* speed (rate) of rotation
Rotationspol *m* pole of rotation
Rotationssphäroid *n* revolution spheroid
rotationssymmetrisch axially symmetrical
Rotationszwilling *m* rotation twin
Rotbleierz *n* red lead ore, crocoite, $PbCrO_4$
Roteisenerz *n* haematite, red iron ore, bloodstone, Fe_2O_3
Roteisenocker *m* red iron ochre
Rötel *m* 1. ruddle, reddle; 2. *s.* Roteisenerz
Rötelerde *f* adamic earth
Roterde *f* red earth (soil), laterite soil, latosol
~/mediterrane Mediterranean red soil
Rotfärbung *f* rubefaction
Rotfazies *f* red bed facies
rotglänzend rutilant
Rotgültigerz *n* red silver ore
~/dunkles dark red silver ore, pyrargyrite, Ag_3SbS_3
~/lichtes light red (ruby) silver ore, proustite, Ag_3AsS_3
rotieren to rotate
Rotkupfererz *n* ruby (red) copper ore, cuprite, Cu_2O
Rotlatosol *m s.* Roterde
Rotlehm *m* red loam
Rotliegenderuptiva *npl* igneous rocks of the Lower Permian
Rotliegendes *n* Rotliegendes, New Red (facies of Upper Carboniferous to Middle Permian Age)
Rotnickelkies *m* copper nickel, niccolite, NiAs
Rotplastosol *m s.* Rotlehm
Rotsandsteinfazies *f* red bed facies
Rotsandsteinfolge *f/devonische* Old Red
~/permische Lower New Red
Rotschichten *fpl* red beds
Rotsedimente *npl* red sediments
Rotspießglanz *m* antimony blende, red antimony, kermesite, Sb_2S_2O
Rotspülung *f* red mud
rotstrahlend rutilant
Rotverwitterung *f* red weathering
Rotzinkerz *n* red zinc ore, zincite, spartalite, ZnO
Roweit *m* roweite, $CaMn[B_2O_5] \cdot H_2O$
Rowlandit *m* rowlandite, $(Y, Fe, Ce)_3[(F, OH)|(SiO_4)_2]$
Rozenit *m* rozenite, $Fe[SO_4] \cdot 4H_2O$
R-Tektonit *m* R-tectonite
Rubellit *m* rubellite (variety of tourmaline)
Rubidium *n* rubidium, Rb
Rubidiumdampfmagnetometer *n* rubidium vapour magnetometer
Rubin *m* ruby (red variety of corundum)
~/brasilianischer Brazilian ruby
~/industrieller corubin
Rubinblende *f* ruby blende, α-ZnS
Rubinglimmer *m* needle ironstone, goethite, α-FeOOH
Rubrit *m* rubrite, $MgFe_2[SO_4]_4 \cdot 18H_2O$
Rückblick *m* backsight (geometry)
Rückdruck *m* back pressure (well)
Rücken *m* crest
~/dammartiger embankment
~/magmatischer magmatic crest
~/Mittelatlantischer Mid Atlantic ridge
~/ozeanischer ocean ridge
~/überdeckter buried hill
~/untermeerischer submerged ridge; submarine ridge
~/unveränderter primary back (of a nappe)
~/vulkanischer volcanic ridge
Rückenansicht *f* dorsal view
Rückenflosse *f* back (dorsal) fin
Rückengebirge *n* subdued mountains
Rückenklappe *f* dorsal valve
Rückenmoräne *f* ablation moraine
Rückentrage *f* back-pack
Rückfaltung *f* backfolding, backward folding
Rückfluß *m* reflux, return flow (of irrigation water into the river)
Rückformung *f/elastische* elastic rebound
Rückführungsleitung *f* repressure line
Rückgang *m* recession, retreat (of a glacier)
rückgreifend retrogressive
Rückhaltebecken *n* retention (retaining, retardation, high-water) basin
Rückhaltevermögen *n* retention (of water); seal capacity (of traps)
~ der Grasnarbe retardancy of grassed waterways
Rückhaltevolumen *n* retention storage, detention storage
Rückkopplung *f* feedback
Rückland *n* back land, hinterland
Rückprallmarke *f* bounce cast
Rückschlagventil *n* float valve
Rückschmelzen *n* remelting
rückschreitend regressive
Rücksenke *f* backdeep [basin]
Rückspielung *f* playback (seismics)
Rückspielzentrale *f* playback centre
Rückspülung *f* indirect flushing
Rückstand *m/silikatischer* siliceous residue
~/unlöslicher insoluble residue
Rückstandsboden *m/toniger* residual clay soil
Rückstandsgestein *n* in situ saprolite
Rückstandston *m* residual clay
Rückstau *m* backflow, backwash, afflux
Rückstauwasser *n* backwater
Rückstreuung *f* backscattering
Rückstrom *m* backwash
Rückstromrippelmarken *fpl* backwash ripple marks
Rücktiefe *f* backdeep

Rücküberschiebung f backthrusting
Rückverdampfung f revaporization *(condensate)*
Rückverwitterung f cliff sapping
Rückzug m recession, retreat
Rückzugsmoräne f recessional (retreatal) moraine
Rückzugsstadium n recessional stage
Rückzugsstaffel f recessional step
Rudiment n vestige
rudimentär rudimentary, vestigal
Ruhe f tranquillity, quiescence *(e.g. of a volcano)*
Ruhedruck m earth pressure at rest
~ **im Steigrohr** static tubing pressure
Ruhedruckziffer f ratio between horizontal and vertical pressure in undisturbed ground
Ruheform f dead form
Ruheklifff n abandoned cliff
Ruhemasse f rest mass
ruhend stationary *(e.g. mountains);* quiescent *(e.g. volcano)*
Ruheperiode f repose period
Ruhereibung f static friction
Ruhespur f resting trace *(ichnology)*
Ruhewasserspiegel m standing (static) level
Ruhewinkel m angle of repose (rest)
ruhig quiet
Rumoren n, **Rumpeln** n rumbling *(volcanism)*
Rumpf m thorax *(of trilobites)*
Rumpfebene f s. Rumpffläche
Rumpffläche f peneplain, old plain
~/**abgedeckte** exhumed (stripped) peneplain
~/**alte** pal[a]eoplain
~/**gehobene** uplifted peneplain
Rumpfgebirge n truncated (bevelled), upland, uplifted peneplain
Rumpfscholle f bevelled fault block, truncated upland
Rundberg m s. Rundhöcker
rundblättrig teretifolious *(palaeobotany)*
Rundbrecher m gyratory breaker
Rundfalte f circular fold
Rundhöcker m roche moutonnée, sheepback, hump, mamillated rock
Rundholz n spar
Rundkarren npl rounded clints
Rundnischenquelle f tubular spring
Rundung f roundness
Runse f ravine, rill
Runzelbildung f dünner Schichten warping of beds
Runzelmarken fpl creep wrinkles, wrinkle marks; Kinneya ripples
Runzeln fpl rumples, puckerings
Runzelschicht f wrinkle layer *(cephalopods)*
Runzelschichtung f crinkled bedding
Runzelschieferung f fracture (strain-slip, fault-slip, false, crenulation) cleavage
Runzelung f plication, minute folding, crumpling; corrugation, fluting
~/**starke** intimate crumpling

~/**synsedimentäre** intraformational corrugation
Rupel n, **Rupélien** n, **Rupelium** n Rupelian [Stage] *(of Oligocene)*
Rupes f rupes *(furrow, groove on the moon)*
Ruptur f rupture
Rusakovit m rusakovite, $Fe_5[(OH)_9|((V,P)O_4)_2] \cdot 3H_2O$
Ruschel f scale
Ruschelerz n drag ore
Ruschelzone f fractured (crushing) zone, zone of jointing
Ruscinium n Ruscinian [Stage] *(continental stage of Pliocene)*
Russellit m russellite, $(Bi_2,W)O_3$
Russia f s. Fennosarmatia
rußig smoky
Rustumit m rustumite, $Ca_4[(OH)_2|Si_2O_7]$
Ruthenium m ruthenium, Ru
Rutherfordin m rutherfordine, $[UO_2|CO_3]$
Rutil m rutile, TiO_2
Rutsch m slide; creeping
~/**progressiver** progressive slide
Rutschbahn f slide slope
Rutschbelag m leather coat (bed)
Rutschebene f plane of sliding
Rutschfalte f slump overfold
Rutschfältelung f s. Wulstschichtung
Rutschfaltung f slip (convolute, slump) bedding
Rutschfläche f glide (gliding, slipping) plane, slip face; slickenside
Rutschfließung f flow slide
Rutschgebiet n slip area
Rutschharnisch m slickenside
Rutschkörper mpl slump balls
Rutschmarke f slump mark
Rutschmassen fpl slide masses
Rutschrille f stria
Rutschrinne f slide furrow
Rutschschere f drilling jars
Rutschschramme f stria, scratch, furrow
Rutschschuppe f scale
Rutschspiegel m slickenside
Rutschstreifen m s. Rutschschramme
Rutschung f earth slip (fall), landslide, shear slide, rapid flowage *(s. a. Gleitung)*
~ **einer Böschung** slide of a bank
~/**subaquatische** subaquatic slide
~/**submarine** submarine (sea) slide
Rutschungsballen m ball-and-pillow structure, flow roll
~/**verknäuelter** crumpled ball
Rutschungsschicht f slump sheet
Rutschungsstruktur f collapse structure
Rutschungsterrasse f landslip terrace
Rutschungstyp m type of slide
Rutschvorgang m sliding phenomenon
Rutschwülste mpl slump balls
Rüttelsieb n shaker
Rütteltisch m bumping table

Ryazan *n*, **Ryazan-Stufe** *f* Ryazanian [Stage] *(basal stage of Lower Cretaceous in the Boreal Realm)*

S

Saal *m* hall
Saale-Eiszeit *f*, **Saale-Kaltzeit** *f* Saale Ice Age *(Pleistocene)*
Sabugalit *m* sabugalite, $(AlH)_{0.5}[UO_2|PO_4]_2 \cdot 10H_2O$
Sackhöhle *f* bottle
Sackung *f* settling; creep
Sackungsstruktur *f* sag structure
Sacrum *n* sacrum
Safflorit *m* safflorite, $CoAs_2$
sägeartig serrate
Sägeblattanordnung *f* saw-tooth system
Sagenit *m* sagenite *(variety of rutile)*
Sägeschmant *m* sawing residue
Sagvandite *mpl* sagvandites *(magnesite and enstatite rocks)*
Sahamalith *m* sahamalith, $(Ce,La,Nd)_2 (Mg,Fe)[CO_3]_4$
Saharabecken *n* Saharan basin
Sahlinit *m* sahlinite, $Pb_{14}[Cl_4|O_9|(AsO_4)_2]$
saiger *s.* seiger
Sakmara *n*, **Sakmarien** *n*, **Sakmarium** *n* Sakmarian [Stage] *(of Lower Permian)*
säkular secular
Säkularvariation *f* secular variation
Sal *n s.* Sial
Salairfaltungsphase *f* Salair [Bohemian] phase of folding
Salammoniak *m s.* Salmiak
Salar *n* alkali flat
Salband *n* selvage, flucan [course], clay gouge (course, parting, wall), vein wall, caple, cab
~/fest aufgewachsenes frozen wall
Saléeit *m* saléeite, $Mg[UO_2|PO_4]_2 \cdot 10H_2O$
Salesit *m* salesite, $Cu[OH | JO_3]$
salin saline
salinar saliniferous
Salinartektonik *f* salt tectonics
Saline *f* saline, salina, saltworks
Salinenwasser *n* saline water
Salinität *f* salinity
~/von variabler poikilohaline
Salinitätsgrad *m* degree of salinity
salisch salic
Salit *m* sa[h]lite *(pyroxene)*
Salmiak *m*[/**natürlicher**] salmiac, α-NH_4Cl
Salmiakfumarole *f*/**alkalische** alkalic (alkaline) ammoniacal fumarole
Salmoit *m* salmoite *(zinc phosphate)*
Salmonsit *m* salmonsite, $(Mn,Fe)_5H_2[PO_4,(OH)_4]_4 \cdot 4H_2O$
Salpeter *m* saltpetre, nitre
Salpeterausblühung *f* wall saltpetre
Salpeterbildung *f* nitrification
Salpetersäure *f* nitric acid, HNO_3
salpetrig nitrous
Salse *f* salse *(s.a.* Schlammsprudel)
Salz *n* salt
~/gelöstes dissolved salt
~/kohlensaures carbonate
~/leicht lösliches deliquescent salt
Salzablagerung *f* salt deposit
~ in der Wüste salar
Salzabwanderungsbecken *n* salt withdrawal basin
salzähnlich haloid
salzartig salinous, saline
Salzauftrieb *m s.* Salzdiapirismus
Salzausblühung *f* salt efflorescence
~ auf Alkaliböden white alkali
salzausscheidend salitral
Salzausscheidung *f* salt secretion, saline precipitate
Salzausstrich *m s.* Salzausblühung
Salzauswaschung *f* salt dilution
Salzbergwerk *n* salt mine
salzbildend salt-forming, saligenous, halogenous
Salzbildner *m* salt former, halogen
Salzbildung *f* salt forming, salification, halification
Salzboden *m* saline (halomorphic) soil
Salzbodenkruste *f* duricrust
Salzbodenvegetation *f* halophytic vegetation
Salzdiapir *m* salt diapir
Salzdiapirismus *m* salt diapirism
Salzdom *m* salt (saline) dome, acromorph
~/konkordant durchbrechender non-piercement salt dome
~/schmaler gestreckter salt ridge
~/tiefliegender deep-seated salt dome, deeply buried salt dome
Salzebenen *fpl* salinas *(South America)*
salzförmig saliniform
salzfrei non-saline
salzführend salt-bearing, sali[ni]ferous
Salzgarten *m* salt garden, saltern, salt pan
Salzgebirge *n* salt (saliferous, saline) rock
Salzgehalt *m* salt content, saltiness, [degree of] salinity; mineralization
~ der Spülung mud salinity
~/mangelnder deficiency in salt
Salzgehaltsmessung *f* halometry
Salzgenese *f* salt genesis
Salzgeochemie *f* salt geochemistry, geochemistry of salt
Salzgeschmack *m* saline taste
Salzgestein *n* salt (saliferous, saline) rock
Salzgletscher *m* salt glacier
Salzgrube *f* salt (brine) pit, saltworks
salzhaltig salty; salt-containing, salt-bearing; sali[ni]ferous, salinous
Salzhaltigkeit *f s.* Salinität
Salzhang *m* salt table
Salzhaushalt *m* salt balance
Salzhorst *m* salt plug (stock), acromorph
Salzhut *m* caprock

salzig salty, briny, saline
Salzinkrustation f salt incrustation
Salzintrusion f salt intrusion
Salzkarst m salt karst
Salzkavernenspeicher m salt caverns
Salzkissen n salt pillow
Salzkissenstadium n salt pillow stage
Salzkohle f salt coal
Salzkörper m body of salt
Salzkraut n saltbush
Salzkruste f salt (saline) crust
Salzkuppel f s. Salzdom
Salzlager n salt bed
Salzlagerstätte f salt deposit
~/**marine** halogenic deposit
Salzlake f brine solution
Salzlauge f [salt] brine
~/**frische** eluent
Salzlaugenspülung f brine mud
Salzlecke f salt lick
salzliebend salt-loving
Salzlöslichkeit f salt solubility
Salzlösung f brine [solution]
Salzmauer f salt diapir *(of elongated form)*
Salzmoor n salt-water marsh
Salzpaar n/**reziprokes** reciprocal salt pair
Salzpfanne f salt pan
Salzpflanzen fpl s. Halophyten
Salzquelle f salt (saline) spring
Salzrücken m salt ridge
Salzsattel m salt anticline
Salzsäure f hydrochloric (muriatic) acid, HCl
Salzschicht f salt bed
~/**harte** salt pan
Salzsee m salt (saline) lake
Salzsole f salt brine
Salzspiegel m salt wash (leaching) surface
Salzsprengung f salt wedging, wedgework of salts
Salzsteppe f salt steppe
Salzstock m salt stock (plug), acromorph
Salzstruktur f salt structure
Salzsumpf m salt marsh
Salztektonik f salt tectonics
salztektonisch halokinetic
Salzton m saliferous clay
~/**grauer** grey salt pelite
~/**roter** red salt pelite
Salztonbecken n takyr, takir
Salztonboden m saline clay soil
Salztonebene f alkali flat, salt plain
Salztonkruste f clay-and-salt crust
Salzüberhang m salt overhang (cornice)
Salzungsversuch m salt-dilution method *(tracer test)*
Salzvegetation f saline vegetation
Salzverstopfung f **einer Bohrung** salt plugging of well
Salzvorkommen n salt deposit
Salzwanne f salt pan
Salzwasser n salt[y] water, sea (saline) water
Salzwasserbeseitigung f salt-water disposal

Salzwassereinbruch m salt-water intrusion
Salzwasserintrusion f salt-water intrusion
Salzwasserlagune f salt-water lagoon
Salzwassermarsch f salt marsh
Salzwasserquelle f salt-water source
Salzwassersumpf m salt-water bog
Salzwasser-Süßwasser-Grenze f salt-water and fresh-water boundary
Salzwasserzutritt m ingress of salt water
Salzwerk n s. Saline
Salzwiese f salt meadow
Salzwüste f salt desert
Samarskit m samarskite, $(Y,Er,Fe,Mn,Ca,U,Th,Zr)(Nb,Ta)_2(O,OH)_6$
Samen m seed
Sammelbecken n catchment (water storage, drainage) basin
Sammelflotation f all-floatation
Sammelgebiet n 1. catchment (drainage) area, drain[age] district; 2. sampling area *(area selected for data sampling often by random procedures)*
Sammelgraben m catch water drain
Sammelkanal m collecting channel
Sammelkristallisation f accretive crystallization
~/**von Crinoidenstielgliedern ausgehende** syntaxial enlargement
Sammelleitung f gathering system *(in the oil or gas field)*
Sammellinse f condensing lens
Sammelloch n s. Sammelbecken
Sammelmulde f reception basin
sammeln/Fossilien to fossilize
Sammelprobe f composite sample
Sammelprofil n composite section
Sammeltypen mpl composite types *(of fossils)*
Sammlung f collection
~/**geowissenschaftliche** geoscientific collection
~/**systematisch geordnete** systematically arranged collection
Sampleit m sampleite, $CaNaCu_5[Cl|(PO_4)_4] \cdot 5H_2O$
Samplerlog n strip chart
Samsonit m samsonite, $2Ag_2S \cdot MnS \cdot Sb_2S_3$
Samtblende f needle ironstone *(aggregate of α-FeOOH and γ-FeOOH)*
Sanbornit m sanbornite, $Ba_2[Si_4O_{10}]$
Sand m sand
~/**bei Überflutung abgelagerter** sud
~/**bindiger** heavy sand
~/**diagonalgeschichteter** cross-bedded sand
~/**dränierter** depleted sand
~/**durchtränkter** impregnated sand
~/**entölter** depleted sand
~/**erdölabsorbierender** thief sand
~/**erdölgesättigter** oil-saturated sand
~/**fossilführender mariner** crag
~/**gasführender** gas-carrying sand
~/**grubenfeuchter** freshly quarried sand
~/**gut durchlässiger** open sand

Sand

~/**humoser** humous sand
~/**im Wasser abgerundeter** water-worn sand
~/**kalkhaltiger** calcareous sand
~/**kreuzgeschichteter** cross-bedded sand
~/**lockerer vulkanischer** menaccanite
~ **mit hellen und dunklen Komponenten** salt and pepper sand
~/**nicht ölführender** barren sand
~/**pyroklastischer** ashy grit
~/**saugender** thief sand
~/**scharfkörniger** sharp sand
~/**schlammiger** miry sand
~/**schwer durchlässiger** tight (close) sand
~/**standfester** calist
~/**steriler** barren sand
~/**tönender** singing sand
~/**toniger** argillaceous (clay, shaly) sand
~/**trockener (unergiebiger, unproduktiver)** dry (barren) sand
~/**verfestigter** consolidated sand
~/**windgefurchter** wind-rippled sand
~/**windtransportierter** millet-seed sand
sandartig sandy; sandlike
Sandaufbruch m boiling of sand
Sandauftrieb m inrush of sand
Sandausscheuerung f sand erosion
Sandausschliff m sand cutting
Sandbank f sand bank, shoals, shallows; sand bar
~/**längliche** sand bar (reef)
~/**spitz zulaufende** sand spit
~ **zwischen Insel und Festland** tombolo
Sandboden m sandy soil (ground); regosol
Sandbohrung f sand boring
Sanddeckkultur f cultivation of peat by covering with sand
Sanddüne f sand dune
Sander m [glacial] outwash, [alluvial, ice, morainic] apron, fluvioglacial deposit, overwash plain (apron)
Sanderebene f apron plain, [glacial] outwash plain
~ **mit Toteislöchern** pitted outwash plain
Sanderfläche f s. Sanderebene
Sanderit m sanderite, Mg[SO$_4$] · 2H$_2$O
Sandfahne f spindrift
Sandfänger m bailer (deep boring)
Sandfeld n sand plain
Sandfrac-Verfahren n sandfracing
sandführend sandy, sabulous
Sandgegend f sandy country
Sandgehalt m sand content
sandgeschlämmt blinded with sand
Sandgestein n arenaceous rock
Sandgrube f sand pit (quarry)
sandhaltig sabulous
~/**stark** arenaceous
Sandhaltigkeit f grittiness
Sandheide f sand heath, barren
sandig sandy, arenose; arenaceous; gravelly
sandig-oolithisch sandy-oolitic
Sandinsel f sandkey, sand cay

Sandkegel m sand volcano (sedimentary fabric)
Sand-Kies-Wüste f sandy-pebble desert
Sandkörper m/**linsenförmiger** lenticular sand
Sandlehm m loamy sand
Sandlinse f/**erdölhaltige** oil lens
~ **im Flöz** swell
~/**schmale, langgestreckte** shoestring sand
~/**zufällig auftretende** stray sand
Sandlöß m sandy loess
Sand-Luft-Gemisch n air-sand mixture
Sandmergel m sandy marl, clay grit
Sandmeßglas n sand content set
Sandmischkultur f cultivation of peat by mixing with sand
Sandmodell n sand-packed model
Sand-Öl-Fracverfahren n sand oil fracturing
Sandr m s. Sander
Sandriefung f sand lineation
Sandriff n offshore sand bar
Sandrippeln fpl sand (wind) ripples
Sandrohr n bailer (deep boring)
Sandröhre f sand pipe (gall)
Sandrücken m sand bar
~ **im Flachwasser/submariner** bore
~/**subaquatischer** subaqueous bar
Sandschaler mpl arenaceous tests
Sandschicht f sand stratum (layer)
Sandschichten fpl **mit Kalklagen** calcareous grits
Sandschiefer m sandy (arenaceous) shale, slaty grit
Sandschliff m aeolian corrasion; sand cutting (scratch)
Sandschmitze f sand streak
Sand-Siltstein m sandy siltstone
Sandstein m sandstone, sandrock, psammite, arenite
~/**allseitig gleich spaltender** freestone
~/**bimodaler** bimodal sandstone
~/**bitumenhaltiger** asphaltic sandstone
~/**dunkelgrauer quarziger** ragstone
~/**eisenhaltiger** brownstone, iron sandstone
~/**feinkörniger** packsand
~/**feldspathaltiger** feldspathic sandstone
~/**flözleerer** farewell rock
~/**gasführender** gas sand
~/**gekneteter** kneaded sandstone
~/**geschichteter** lea stone
~/**gestreifter** tiger sandstone
~/**grobkörniger** coarse-grained sandstone, sandstone grit, gritstone
~/**harter, glatter** galliard
~/**kalkreicher** calcareous sandstone
~/**konglomeratischer** conglomeratic sandstone
~/**laminierter** lea stone
~ **mit kalkigem Bindemittel** lime-cemented sandstone, calcareous-cemented sandstone
~ **mit 80–90 % Quarz** sublabile sandstone
~/**plattiger** flags
~/**roter** sleck, redstone (trade name)

~/**sehr feiner** hone
~/**silifizierter** grays
~/**toniger** argillaceous sandstone
~/**weicher** holystone *(cleaning material)*
~/**weicher brüchiger** rotch[e]
sandsteinartig arenilitic
Sandsteinblock *m*/**erratischer** sarsen stone
Sandsteinbruch *m* sandstone quarry
Sandsteingang *m* sandstone vein (dike)
Sandsteinlage *f* sandstone bed
Sandsteinplatte *f* flagstone
Sandsteinrolle *f* snowball structure *(sedimentary fabric)*
Sandsteinwulst *m* flute (load) cast
Sandsteinzwischenlage *f* sandstone band (intercalation)
Sandstoß *m* face of sand
Sandstrand *m* sand[y] beach
Sandstreifen *m* dene
Sandsturm *m* sandstorm, dust storm
Sandton *m* sandy (mild) clay
Sandtragfähigkeit *f* sand carrying capacity
Sandtreiben *n* sand drift
Sanduhrbau *m* hour-glass structure *(of crystals)*
Sand-Ton-Linie *f* sand line *(well logging)*
Sand- und Kiesablagerung *f*/**inselförmige** archipelagic apron
Sandur *m* s. Sander
Sandvorkommen *n* sand deposit
Sandvulkan *m* sand volcano
Sandwalze *f* shoestring sand
Sandwanderung *f* migration of sand
Sandwatt *n* sand flat
Sandwehen *n* sand drift
Sandwelle *f* sand wave *(in river beds)*
~/**flache** antidune
~/**progressive** progressive sand wave
~/**regressive** regressive sand wave
Sandwüste *f* sand desert, waste of sand
sanft smooth
Sangamon-Interglazial *n*, **Sangamon-Warmzeit** *f* Sangamon [Interglacial Age] *(Pleistocene of North America corresponding to Eemian in Northwest Europe)*
Sanidin *m* sanidine, $K[AlSi_3O_8]$
Sanidinit *m* sanidinite
Sanidinitfazies *f* sanidinite facies
Sannois[ien] *n*, **Sannoisium** *n* Sannoisian [Stage] *(of Oligocene)*
Santon[ien] *n*, **Santonium** *n* Santonian [Stage] *(of Upper Cretaceous)*
Santorinerde *f* santorin
Saphir *m* sapphire
~/**weißer** leucosapphire
Saphirin *m* sapphirine, $Mg_2Al_4[O_6|SiO_4]$
Saphirquarz *m* sapphire, blue quartz
Saponit *m* saponite, piotine, soapstone, steatite, $Mg_3[(OH)_2Al_{0.33}Si_{3.67}O_{10}]_{0.33}(H_2O)_4$
Saprokoll *n* saprocol
Sapropel *n (m)* sapropel, putrid (vegetable) slime, putrid mud, digested sludge *(s. a.* Faulschlamm*)*

Sapropelit *m* sapropelite, sapropel rock
~/**sandiger** sapropsammite
~/**verfestigter** metasapropel
sapropelitisch sapropel[it]ic
Sapropelkohle *f* sapropelic coal *(coal type)*
saprophytisch saprophytic
Saratogan *n* Saratogan [Stage] *(of Cambrian)*
Sardachat *m* sardachate
Sardonyx *n* [chalcedony] sardonyx *(variety of chalcedony)*
Sargassotang *m* Sargassum
Sargdeckel *m* cauldron bottom, pothole
Sarkinit *m* sarkinite, $Mn_2[OH|AsO_4]$
Sarkolith *m* sarcolite, $(Ca,Na)_8[O_2|(Al(Al,Si)Si_2O_8)_6]$
Sarkopsid *m* sarcopside, $(Fe,Mn,Ca)_3[PO_4]_2$
Sarkosepten *npl* mesenteries *(corals)*
Sarmat[ien] *n*, **Sarmatium** *n* Sarmatian [Stage] *(of Miocene)*
Sartorit *m* sartorite, $PbAs_2S_4$
Sassolin *m* sassolite, $B(OH)_3$
Satellit *m* satellite
~/**geostationärer** geostationary satellite *(artificial earth satellite orbiting the earth in its equatorial plane in the direction and with the period of earth rotation)*
~/**geosynchroner** geosynchronous satellite *(artificial earth satellite with an orbital period that equals the period of earth rotation)*
~/**künstlicher** artificial satellite
~/**meteorologischer** meteorologic[al] satellite
~/**polumkreisender** polar-orbiting satellite
~/**sonnensynchroner** sun-synchronous satellite *(artificial earth satellite with near-polar orbit passing points on the ground always at the same local time)*
~/**stationärer** fixed satellite
~/**synodischer** synodic satellite
Satellitenaufnahmen *fpl* satellite imagery
Satellitenfotografie *f*/**geologische** geologic[al] orbital photography
Satellitenkamera *f* satellite-borne camera
Satellitenkörper *m* satellite body
Satellitensystem *n* satellite system
Satellitenüberwachung *f* satellite monitoring
Sattel *m* saddle, anticline, arch, upfold *(s. a.* Antiklinale*)*
~/**falscher** pseudoanticline
~/**tektonischer und topografischer** geanticline
~/**überkippter** overturned (recumbent) anticline
Sattelachse *f* anticlinal (saddle) axis
Sattelbiegung *f* ridge uplift
Sattelbildung *f* anticlinal formation
Sattelboden *m* upfold
Sattelfalte *f* uparching fold, [arched] upfold
Sattelfaltung *f* anticlinal folding
Sattelflügel *m* flank (slope) of a saddle, side of an anticline
sattelförmig saddle-form, selliform
Sattelgang *m* saddle vein (reef)
Sattelgebiet *n* anticlinal area

Sattelhöchstes

Sattelhöchstes *n* crown of anticline
Sattelkern *m* anticlinal (arch) core
Sattellinie *f* anticlinal [crest] line, ridge line
Sattelreef *n* saddle reef (vein)
Sattelscharnier *n* saddle (arch) bend
Sattelscheitel *m* saddle back
Sattelschenkel *m* anticlinal limb
Sattelspalte *f* anticlinal fissure
Sattelstellung *f* **der Schiebung** cleavage arch
Satteltal *n* saddle (anticlinal) valley
Sattelvererzung *f s.* Sattelgang
Sattelwendung *f point at which the contour line of an anticline changes direction*
sättigen to saturate
Sättigung *f* saturation
~/unvollkommene subsaturation
Sättigungsdampfdruck *m* saturation vapour pressure
Sättigungsdichte *f* saturation density
Sättigungsdruck *m* saturation (bubble point) pressure
sättigungsfähig saturable
Sättigungsgebiet *n* saturation region
Sättigungsgrad *m* saturation value (degree)
Sättigungskernmagnetometer *n* fluxgate magnetometer
Sättigungskurve *f* saturation curve
Sättigungsspiegel *m* level of saturation
Sättigungswert *m* water inhibition value
Sättigungszone *f* saturation (phreation) zone
Sättigungszustand *m* saturation state
Saucesien *n* Saucesian [Stage] *(marine stage, lower Miocene in North America)*
sauer acid
Sauerbrunnen *m s.* Kohlensäuerling
Sauergas *n* acid (sour) gas
Säuerling *m*, **Sauerquelle** *f s.* Kohlensäuerling
Sauerstoff *m* oxygen, O
sauerstofffrei anaerobic
Sauerstoffisotop *n* oxygen isotope
Sauerstoffisotopenverteilung *f* oxygen isotope distribution
sauerstoffreich oxygen-rich
sauerstoffverarmt dysaerobic
Säuerung *f* acidizing *(of a well)*
Saugamonien *n* Saugamonian [Stage] *(of Pleistocene)*
Saugamon-Interglazial *n* Saugamon Interglacial Age
Saugbagger *m* suction (hydraulic) dredger
Saugbohrverfahren *n* suction counter flush drilling
Saugbrunnen *m* sinkhole
Säugetier *n* mammal
~/marines sea mammal
Saughöhe *f* suction head (lift) *(pump)*; capillary rise, absorptive height
Saugkorb *m* suction pipe check valve and screen
Saugleitung *f* suction line
Saugsaumwasser *n* fringe water
Saugschiefer *m* absorbent shale, adhesive slate

Saugspannung *f* water tension
Saugvermögen *n* suction
Saugwirkung *f* suction
~/osmotische osmotic suction
Säule *f* column
Säulenabsonderung *f* columnar segregation
Säulenaggregat *n* columnar aggregate
säulenartig columnar, prismatic
Säulenbasalt *m* columnar (palisade) basalt
Säulenbildung *f* **im oberen Teil einer Lavadecke** entablature
~ im unteren Teil einer Lavadecke colonnade
säulenförmig column-shaped, pillarlike; basaltiform
Säulenprobe *f* pillar sample *(coal seam)*
Säulenprofil *n* pillar section *(coal)*
Säulentextur *f* columnar structure
säulig columnar
Saum *m* 1. margin, border, fringe *(relating to space)*; 2. selvage *(of fossils)*
~ der Polkappe polar fringe
Saumriff *n* fringing reef
Saumsenke *f*, **Saumtiefe** *f* marginal deep (trough), foredeep, idiogeosyncline
Säure *f/freie* free acid
~/organische organic acid
säurearm acid-poor
Säurebehandlung *f* **von Ölbohrungen** acidation (acidizing, acid treatment) of oil wells
säurebildend acid-forming
Säurebildner *m* acidifier
Säureflasche *f* acid bottle
Säurefracung *f* acid fracturing
Säuregehalt *m* acidity
Säuregrad *m* acidity *(pH value)*
säurehaltig acidic, acidiferous
säurelöslich soluble in acids
Säuremesser *m* acidimeter
Säurereinigung *f* **von Brunnen** acid treatment of wells
Säureschlamm *m* acid sludge
Säurewanne *f* acid spotting around the drilling string
Saurier *mpl* saurians
Saussurit *m* saussurite *(pseudomorph after plagioclase)*
Saussuritgabbro *m* saussurite-gabbro, allalinite
saussuritisieren to saussuritize
Saussuritisierung *f* saussuritization
Savanne *f* savanna, *(Am)* savannah
Savannenlichtwald *m* savanna forest
Sawkill[ien] *n* Sawkillian [Stage] *(of Ulsterian in North America)*
Saxon[ien] *n* Saxonian [Stage] *(of Permian in Central and West Europe)*
Saxonit *m* saxonite *(variety of peridotite)*
Saxonium *n s.* Saxon
Sborgit *m* sborgite, $Na[B_5O_6(OH)_4] \cdot 3H_2O$
Scacchit *m* scacchite, $MnCl_2$
Scarbroit *m* scarbroite, $Al(OH)_3$
Scawtit *m* scawtite, $Ca_6[Si_3O_9]_2 \cdot CaCO_3 \cdot 2H_2O$

Schachbrettalbit *m* chequered albite
Schachbrettboden *m* tundra polygons
Schachbrettmuster *n* chequer-board pattern
Schachbrettstruktur *f* chess-board texture
Schacht *m* shaft, gruff
~/**abgeteufter** sunk shaft
~/**auflässiger** disused shaft
~ **im Liegenden eines Ganges/tonnlägiger** underlay shaft
~/**tonnlägiger** hading shaft
Schachtabteufen *n* shafting
Schachtausbau *m* shaft lining (support)
Schachtausgang *m* shaft head
Schachtbohren *n* shaft drilling (boring)
Schachtbrunnen *m* dug well
Schachtmundloch *n* shaft mouth
Schachtscheibe *f* shaft cross section
Schachtsicherheitspfeiler *m* shaft [safety] pillar
Schachtsohle *f* shaft bottom
Schachtsumpf *m* sump
Schachtwand *f* pit wall
Schädel *m* skull, cranium
Schädeldach *n* cranial roof
Schädelfragment *n* cranial fragment
Schädelkalotte *f* brain pan
Schäden *mpl* **an Gebäuden** damage to buildings *(7th stage of the scale of seismic intensity)*
Schadenszone *f* zone of damage
Schädigungsgrad *m* damage factor
Schädigungsradius *m* radius of well damage
Schädigungsverhältnis *n* damage ratio
Schadstoff *m* aggressive substance; pollutant
Schadwasser *n* aggressive water
Schafarzikit *m* schafarzicite, $FeSb_2O_4$
Schäfchenhimmel *m* mackerel sky
Schäfchenwolken *fpl* fleecy clouds
Schairerit *m* schairerite, $Na_3[(F,Cl)|SO_4]$
Schale *f* 1. shell; test, conch *(e.g. of gastropods)*; 2. disk *(mechanically)*
~/**agglutinierte** agglutinated test, granular shell
~/**äußere** outer shell
~/**äußerste** outermost shell
~/**gedrungene** distally compressed valve
~/**gleichklappige** equivalve (equilateral) shell
~/**längliche** elongate valve
Schalenblatt *n* lamella
~/**äußeres** outer lamella
~/**inneres** inner lamella
Schalenblende *f s.* Wurtzit
Schalenerhaltung *f* preservation of shells
Schalenfragment *n* shell fragment
Schalenkalk *m* pisiform limestone
Schalenöffnung *f* aperture of the shell
Schalenstein *m* rock basin, weather pit, water eye
Schalentrümmerkalkstein *m* coquina
Schalenverdopplung *f* duplicature *(palaeontology)*
schalig shelly, valvate; scaly
Schall *m* sound

Schallaufzeit *f* sound travel time
Schallbohren *n* sonic drilling
Schallempfänger *m* air wave receiver, blastophone
schallen to sound
Schallerit *m* schallerite, $(Mn,Fe)_8[(OH)_{10}|(Si,As)_6O_{15}]$
Schallerscheinungen *fpl*/**vulkanische** volcanic sounds
Schallfeld *n* area of audibility
Schallgeschwindigkeit *f* sonic speed (velocity), speed (velocity) of sound
schallhart non-absorbing
Schallhärte *f* acoustic resistance, acoustical (elastic) impedance
Schallhöhenmesser *m* sonic altimeter
Schallkernen *n* sonic log[ging]
Schallot *n* **nach Behm** Behm depth indicator
Schallwelle *f* sound (acoustic, air) wave
Schallwiderstand *m* acoustic resistance
Schalstein *m* schalstein, greenstone
Schaltjahr *n* leap-year
Schalwolke *f* scarf cloud
Schamotte *f*, **Schamotteton** *m* fireclay, refractory clay
Schapbachit *m* schapbachite, α-$AgBiS_2$
Schappe *f* mud (shell) auger
Schappenbohren *n* auger boring
Schappenbohrer *m* shell auger, wimble scoop
Schappenbohrung *f* auger boring
Schäre *f* reef, rocky island, skerry
Scharen *fpl s.* Scharung
Schärenküste *f* schären-type of coast line, skerry coast
Scharfeinstellung *f* sharp focussing
scharfkantig sharp[-edged]; angular
Scharkreuz *n* intersection of lodes
Scharnier *n* bend; hinge *(tectonics)*
Scharnierfalte *f* hinge (angular) fold
Scharte *f* notch *(mountains)*
Scharung *f* crossing, junction, point of intersection *(of lodes)*
~ **der Gangtrümer** linked (composite) veins
Schatten *m* umbra; shadow
~/**seismischer** seismic shadow zone
Schattenkegel *m* shadow cone
schätzen to estimate *(mathematical statistics)*
~/**durch Kriging** krige/to
Schätzung *f* estimation *(mathematical statistics)*
Schaubild *n* **der Oberflächenbeschaffenheit** contourogram
~/**räumliches** three-dimensional diagram
Schaufelfläche *f* **[/listrische]** listric surface
Schaufelprobenahme *f* shovel sampling
Schaufelradbagger *m* bucket wheel[-type] excavator
Schauhöhle *f* developed (commercial) cave
Schaum *m* foam
schäumen to effervesce
Schäumen *n* effervescence
Schäumer *m* frother, frothing (foaming) agent

Schaumflotation

Schaumflotation f foam (froth) floatation
schaumig foamy
Schaumkalk m aphrite
schaumkalkartig oo[li]castic
Schaumkrone f/**weiße** whitecap
Schaumlava f foam[y] lava, pumiceous lava, froth flow
Schaummarke f foam mark
Schaumschwimmaufbereitung f froth floatation
Schaumton m foamclay
Schaumzelle f frother cell
scheckig variegated
Scheelbleierz n stolzite, lead tungstate, β-$PbWO_4$
Scheelit m scheelite, $CaWO_4$
Scheererit m scheererite (earth wax)
Schefferit m schefferite (pyroxene-mixed crystal)
Scheibenbruchbau m top slicing
scheibenförmig discoid[al]
Scheibenmeißel m disk bit
Scheibenschwingmühle f disk vibratory (swing sledge) mill
Scheideanalyse f arbitration analysis
Scheideanlage f sorting plant, screening device
Scheideapparat m sorting unit
Scheidebank f bucking plate
Scheideerz n picked (screened, bucking, bucked) ore
Scheidegold n parting gold
Scheidehaus n sorting house
scheiden to sort, to buck (s. a. klauben)
~/**Erze** to cop ores
Scheiden n sorting, bucking (s. a. Klauben)
~/**elektrostatisches** electrostatic separation
Scheidesilber n parting silver
Scheidetrichter m separating funnel
Scheideverfahren n parting process
Scheidewand f partition wall
Scheidewände fpl septa (e.g. of corals)
Scheidung f s. Scheiden
scheinbar apparent
Scheindiskordanz f false discordance
Scheinfazieskomplex m wrong facies complex
Scheingeschwindigkeit f apparent velocity
Scheinlotrichtung f direction of the apparent perpendicular
Scheinplankton n s. Pseudoplankton
Scheinreflexion f fake reflection
Scheinrippeln fpl pseudoripples
Scheinserie f pseudoseries
Scheinwiderstand m apparent resistivity; impedance
Scheitel m crest, ridge, crown, apex; top (e.g. of a salt plug)
Scheiteldruck m top pressure
Scheitelfläche f crestal plane
Scheitelgebiet n crestal area
Scheitelgräben mpl **der ozeanischen Rücken** mid ocean ridges

Scheitelgrabenbildung f keystone faulting
Scheitelkegel m apex cone
Scheitellagerstätte f **über dem Deckgebirge** supercap sand
Scheitellinie f crest line
Scheitelpfeiler m crown pillar
Scheitelsonde f crestal well
Scheitelstörung f crest fault
Scheitelung f, **Scheitelzone** f median crest of a bilateral orogen
Schelf m shelf
~/**äußerer** outer shelf
~/**erhöhter** uplifted shelf
~/**innerer** inner shelf
~/**labiler** labile shelf
~/**mobiler** mobile (unstable) shelf
~/**stabiler** stable shelf
~ **unterhalb der tiefsten Brandungseinwirkung** offshore
Schelfabbruch m shelf break
Schelfablagerung f shelf deposit
Schelfaufschüttungen fpl topsets
Schelfbildung f shelf formation
Schelfbucht f shelf embayment
Schelfeis n shelf (barrier) ice
Schelferkundung f/**geophysikalische** offshore surveys
Schelfküste f shelf coast
Schelfmeer n shelf (epicontinental, epeiric) sea, offshore waters
Schelfrand m shelf margin
Schelfrinnen fpl shelf channels
Schelfsandkörper m offshore sandbody
Schelfsediment n marginal deposit
Schelfvorschüttungen fpl foresets
Schenkel m limb; wing (of an anticline)
~/**aufrechter (hangender)** normal (upper, roof) limb
~/**liegender** lower (floor, reversed) limb, underlimb
~/**steiler** forelimb (of an asymmetric fold)
~/**überkippter** overturned limb
Schenkelbruch m anticlinal fault
Schenkelüberschiebung f break thrust
schenklig limbed
Scherapparat m **nach Casagrande** Casagrande shear test apparatus, box shear apparatus
Scherbakovit m scherbakovite, $(K,Na,Ba)_3(Ti,Nb)_2[Si_2O_7]_2$
Scherbeanspruchung f s. Scherspannung
Scherbelastung f shear load
Scherbenkobalt m shard cobalt, native arsenic, As
Scherbenlava f slab pahoehoe
Scherbruch m shear rupture, sliding fracture
Scherbüchse f Casagrande shear test apparatus, box shear apparatus
Scherdehnung f shear strain
Scherebene f shear[ing] plane
Scherenfenster n scissors window (tectonics)
Scherfalte f shear fold
Scherfaltung f shear folding

Schicht

Scherfestigkeit f shear strength; shear resistance *(of a rock complex)*
~/kritische critical shear strength
~/maximale peak shear strength
Scherflächenpaar n pair of shear planes
Scherfuge f s. Scherkluft
Scherkastengerät n s. Scherbüchse
Scherkluft f shear joint
Scherklüfte fpl/**gefiederte** pinnate shear joints
Scherkörper m s. Kluftkörper
Scherling m dislodged slice; exotic block
Schermodul m shear modulus
Scherspalte f shear fissure
~/geöffnete emphasized cleavage
Scherspannung f shearing stress
Schertelit m schertelite, $(NH_4)_2MgH_2[PO_4]_2 \cdot 4H_2O$
Scherung f shear[ing]
~/einfache (reine) simple (pure) shear
Scherungsüberschiebung f scissions (shear, shearing-off) thrust
Scherungsverschiebung f/**laterale** detrusion
Scherversuch m shear[ing] test
~/direkter direct shear[ing] test
Scherwelle f shear wave, S wave
Scherwinkel m angle of shear
Scherzone f shear zone
Scherzugversuch m tensile shear test
Schicht f lay[er], bed, stratum, blanket; sheet *(thin)*
~/abbauwürdige workable bed
~/aklinale (anliegende) aclinal bed
~/aufgerichtete upturned (ridged-up, ended-up) bed, straightened-up layer
~/aufliegende superposed bed
~/ausstreichende outcropping bed, exposed stratum
~/bauwürdige workable bed
~/dünne sheet; lamina
~/durchbohrte penetrated bed
~/durchgehende persistent stratum
~/durchhaltende continuous bed
~/durchlässige permeable bed (layer), pervious bed (stratum)
~/durchlaufende persistent stratum
~/einfallende dipping bed
~/eingelagerte interstratified bed
~/eingeschobene intercalated bed
~/einschließende enclosing bed
~/einseitig aufgerichtete monocline
~/einseitig geneigte homoclinal bed
~/erdölführende petroliferous bed, oil-bearing stratum, oil producer
~/erdölspeichernde oil storer
~/faltbare foldable layer
~/feste rough sheet
~/flach einfallende flat-dipping bed, low-dipping stratum, gently inclined stratum, feeble-dipping stratum
~/flachliegende flat-lying stratum
~/fossilführende fossil-bearing bed
~/gasabgebende plank

~/gebogene bent stratum
~/gefaltete folded bed
~/gekippte tilted stratum
~/gekräuselte contorted bed
~/geneigte inclined bed
~/gestauchte contorted (convoluted) bed
~/gestörte dislocated bed
~/gut aufgeschlossene well exhibited bed
~/hangende capping bed
~ hohen Widerstands high-resistivity stratum
~/horizontalgelagerte level-bedded stratum, horizontal stratum, horizontally laid (bedded) stratum
~/inkompetente incompetent bed
~/isotrope isotropic stratum
~/karbonatische carbonatic bed
~/kohleführende coal measure
~/kompetente competent bed
~/liegende subjacent bed
~/minderwertige buzzard
~ mit Drucklösungserscheinungen presolved bed
~ mit geringer Geschwindigkeit low velocity layer *(seismics)*
~ mit hoher Geschwindigkeit high-speed layer *(seismics)*
~/nicht durchspießte unpenetrated bed
~/nicht verhärtete non-indurated pan
~/obere superstratum, cledge
~/oberste top layer, uppermost bed
~/ölführende oil measure
~/schallharte high-speed layer
~/schallharte dünne stringer
~/seiger stehende vertical bed
~/stark gestörte highly disturbed layer
~/stark wasserführende heavily watered stratum
~/steil einfallende steep-dipping bed, high-dipping stratum, steep-dipping stratum, steeply (highly) inclined stratum, high-angle dipping stratum, strong-dipping stratum
~/steil gelagerte steep seam
~/steil stehende s. ~/aufgerichtete
~/tiefere substratum
~/transgredierende transgressive (overlapping) stratum
~/überlagernde superimposed bed stratum, high-angle dipping stratum, stratum, cover, capping, superficial layer
~/überschossene hidden layer *(seismics)*
~/unberührte virgin bed
~/undurchlässige impermeable bed (layer), impervious bed (layer)
~/ungestörte undisturbed bed
~/unnachgiebige s. ~/kompetente
~/untere bottom layer
~/unterlagernde subjacent stratum, underlayer, sublayer
~/unterste lowermost bed; bench floor
~/unverritzte virgin bed
~/verbogene warped (flexed, crumpled) stratum

Schicht

~/**verfestigte** concretionary horizon
~/**verformte** deformed layer
~/**versetzte** displaced stratum
~/**Versteinerungen führende** fossil-bearing bed
~/**verwitternde** weathering layer
~/**verworfene** disrupted bed, faulted stratum
~/**V-förmig abtauchende** nose-in stratum
~/**wasserdurchlässige** permeable stratum
~/**wasserführende** water-bearing layer (bed, formation, horizon), carrier of water, water-bearing stratum
~/**wasserstauende** s. ~/**undurchlässige**
~/**zerbrechliche harte** brittle pan, fragipan
Schichtaufrichtung f tilting of strata
Schichtbeprobung f bed sampling
Schichtbericht m drilling report
Schichtbesetzung f shift
Schichtblatt n stratification lamina, flaggy
Schichtdeformation f durch differentielle Kompaktion draping
Schichtdicke f thickness of layer
Schichtdruckänderung f change of the formation pressure
Schichtebene f surface of bedding (stratification, lamination), plane of bedding (stratification, lamination)
~/**verworfene** faulted bedding plane
schichten to stratify, to arrange in layers, to straticulate
Schichten fpl strata (s. a. Schicht)
~/**äquivalente** equivalent (contemporary, homotaxial) beds
~/**gleichaltrige** contemporaneous beds
~/**präsalinare** presaliferous beds
~/**steil stehende** beds dipping at high angles
~ **von Deltaablagerungen/obere** topset beds
~/**Waderner** Wadern Beds (Permian in West Europe)
~/**wechsellagernde** alternating beds
Schichtenablösen n bed separation
Schichtenaufbau m s. **Schichtenfolge**
Schichtenaufbiegung f upwarp[ing]
Schichtenaufblätterung f bed separation
Schichtenaufrichtung f upridging of the beds
Schichtenausfall m omission of beds
Schichtenausstrich m/**V-förmiger** nose-out
Schichtenbau m/**mantelförmiger** periclinal bedding
~/**trichterförmiger** centroclinal bedding
Schichtenblock m block of strata
Schichtenbruch m bedding fault
Schichtendepression f/**trogförmige** troll[e]y
Schichtendruck m formation pressure
Schichtenfaltung f folding of strata
Schichtenfolge f stratigraphic sequence (succession), succession of beds, sequence of bedding, strata series
~/**erdölführende** oil-bearing series
~/**isoklinal gefaltete** isocline
~/**lückenhafte** incomplete (abbreviated) record

~/**lückenlose** uninterrupted sequence of strata
~/**umgekehrte** reversed stratigraphical sequence
~/**unterlagernde** underlying series of beds
schichtenförmig stratiform
Schichtenfuge f s. **Schichtfuge**
Schichtenglied n member (of strata)
Schichtengruppe f, Schichtenkomplex m s. **Schichtenfolge**
Schichtenkonkordanz f conformability of strata
Schichtenkopf m s. **Schichtkopf**
Schichtenlage f s. **Schichtfuge**
Schichtenlücke f s. **Schichtlücke**
Schichtenmächtigkeit f thickness of beds
Schichtenmuldentiefstes n bottom-lines of beds
Schichtenneigung f s. **Schichtneigung**
Schichtenpaket n series of strata
Schichtenprofil n strata profile, stratigraphic section
Schichtenreihe f s. **Schichtenfolge**
Schichtenschnitt m strata section
Schichtenserie f s. **Schichtenfolge**
Schichtenstörung f s. **Schichtstörung**
Schichtenstreichen n strike line of beds, direction of strata
Schichtenströmung f sheet (parallel) flow
Schichtenüberkippung f overturning of strata
Schichtenunterbrechung f, Schichtenunterdrückung f break in the succession, elimination (omission) of beds, disappearance of outcrop
Schichtenverdopplung f duplication (repetition) of beds
Schichtenverschiebung f strata displacement
Schichtenwechsel m s. **Schichtwechsel**
schichtenweise s. **schichtweise**
Schichtenwiederholung f duplication (repetition) of beds
Schichtfallen n bedding dip, dip (decline) of stratum
~/**synsedimentäres** original (initial, primary) dip
Schichtfallwinkel m bedding angle
Schichtfläche f bedding (cleat, stratification, deposition) plane, cleat
~/**gegen den Stoß einfallende** face slip
Schichtflächenerscheinung f, Schichtflächenmarke f sole mark
Schichtflexur f monocline
Schichtfließen n bedding flow
Schichtflut f sheetwash [flow], sheet flood
Schichtflutebene f adobe flat
Schichtfluterosion f sheet erosion
Schichtflutkreuzschichtung f torrential cross-bedding
Schichtfolge f s. **Schichtenfolge**
Schichtfuge f bedding plane (joint), joint of bedded rocks, stratification line, cleaving grain
~ **im Liegenden** bottom break
~/**wasserstauende** permissive bedding plane

Schichtfugenhöhle f bedding cave
Schichtführer m drilling foreman driller
Schichtgefüge n/**biogenes** biostratification structure *(ichnology)*
Schichtgestein n bedded (stratified) rock
Schichtgitterstruktur f layer-lattice structure
Schichtgleitfalte f bedding slip fold
Schichtgrenze f boundary of the bed
Schichtgruppe f s. Schichtenfolge
schichtig imbedded, floored
Schichtkante f s. Schichtkopf
Schichtkomplex m s. Schichtenfolge
Schichtkopf m basset, [outcropping] edge of a stratum, seam exit
~/**aufgerichteter** upturned edge of the strata
Schichtkörper m bedded body
Schichtlagerstätte f/**sedimentäre** stratiform (strata-bound) deposit
Schichtlagerung f/**regressive** regressive overlap, off-lap
~/**transgressive** side lap, overlap
Schichtlänge f stratum length
Schichtleistung f output per shift
Schichtlinie f s. Isohypse
Schichtlücke f stratigraphic gap (hiatus, break), lost interval, lack of sedimentation
~/**lokale** want
Schichtmächtigkeit f layer (stratum) thickness
schichtmäßig by layers
Schichtneigung f slope of stratum
Schichtneigungsmesser m dipmeter
Schichtneigungsmessung f dipmeter survey, dip logging *(in a borehole)*
Schichtoberfläche f bed surface, superface of stratum
Schichtoberkante f/**aus Bohrlochmessungen abgeleitete** projected downward top
Schichtpaket n s. Schichtenfolge
schichtparallel concordant
Schichtquelle f strata (outcrop, contact, gravity) spring
Schichtreihe f s. Schichtenfolge
Schichtrichtung f direction of strata
Schichtrippe f hogback
Schichtrippelung f slate ribbons
Schichtsattel m anticlinal flexure
Schichtschnitt m strata section
Schichtserie f s. Schichtenfolge
Schichtsilikate npl sheet silicates, phyllosilicates
Schichtspalte f bedding fissure (joint)
~/**offene** riving seam
Schichtspaltung f delamination
Schichtstörung f disturbance, dislocation, leap
~/**synsedimentäre** contemporaneous disturbance of bedding
Schichtstreichen n strike (trend) of beds, direction of strata, bearing
Schichtstufe f benchland; cuesta
Schichtstufenlandschaft f cuesta landscape (topography), alcove lands

Schichtstunde f shift-hour
Schichttafelland n structural plateau
Schichttag m shift-day
Schichtterrasse f structural terrace; benchland
Schichttiefe f layer depth
Schichtung f bedding, stratification, layering, sheeting, arrangement in layers
~/**äolische** aeolian bedding
~/**deutliche** distinct bedding
~/**diskordante** discordant (irregular) bedding
~/**ebene** even bedding
~/**fleckige** mottled bedding (structure)
~/**geneigte** inclined bedding
~/**gradierte** graded bedding, density stratification, didactic structure
~/**knollige** nodular bedding
~/**konkordante** concordant bedding
~/**linsige** lenticular bedding
~/**mächtige** heavy stratification
~ **nach dem Salzgehalt** salinity stratification
~/**natürliche** natural bedding
~/**nicht erkennbare [magmatische]** cryptic layering
~ **parallel zur liegenden Erosionsbasis** compound stratification
~/**primäre horizontale** origin stratification
~/**rhythmische** rhythmic bedding (layering)
~/**sichtbare** actual bedding
~/**sortierte** sorted bedding
~/**undeutliche** obscure bedding
~/**waagerechte** horizontal bedding
~/**wellige** wavy bedding
~/**zusammengefaltete** prolapsed bedding
Schichtungsbänderung f slate ribbons
Schichtungsdiskordanz f discordance of bedding, discontinuity of deposition
Schichtungsebene f s. Schichtebene
Schichtungsfazies f phyllofacies
Schichtungsfläche f s. Schichtfläche
schichtungslos unstratified
Schichtungslosigkeit f absence of bedding
Schichtungslücke f s. Schichtlücke
Schichtungsmullion n bedding mullion
Schichtungsoberfläche f s. Schichtebene
Schichtungstyp m bedding type
Schichtungswinkel m bedding angle
Schichtunterfläche f subface of stratum
Schichtvulkan m stratovolcano
Schichtwasser n stratum (formation, layer, held) water
Schichtwechsel m alternation of beds
~/**kleiner rhythmischer** intracyclothem
~/**rhythmischer** cyclothem
schichtweise in layers, layer in layer
Schichtwolke f stratus
schichtwolkenförmig stratiform
Schiebekappe f slide bar
schieben über/sich to ride over, to override
Schieber m gate
Schiebewinkel m angle of sideslip
schief skew, oblique, inclined, slopy

Schiefe

Schiefe f **der Ekliptik** obliquity of the ecliptic
~ **von Kornverteilungskurven** skewness of grain-size distribution curves
Schiefer m slate; schist *(metamorphous)*; bind, shale[stone] *(argillaceous)*
~/**bituminöser** naphtholithe
~/**durch Kompaktion verfestigter** compaction shale
~/**feinkörniger** honestone
~/**gasführender** gas[-carrying] schist
~/**gut laminierter** bibliolite, bookstone
~/**hangender** rag
~/**kohlig-kieseliger** coal-containing siliceous slate
~/**kristalliner** crystalline schist
~/**metamorpher** metamorphosed schist
~ **mit belteroporem Mineralwachstum in der s-Fläche** fascicular schist
~ **mit Bindemittelverkittung** cemented shale
~ **mit Schubklüftungsrunzelung** creased (puckered) slate
~/**phosphatischer** phosphatic shale
~/**sandiger** rock bind
~/**schwach metamorpher** metashale
~/**schwarzer** cannel
~ **sedimentären Ursprungs/kristalliner** sedimentary schist
~/**von Kohle durchsetzter** coaly rashing
Schiefer mpl/**Dörntener** Dörnten Shales *(upper Toarcian in Northwest Europe)*
schieferähnlich s. schieferartig
schieferartig slaty, shaly, schistous, schistic
Schieferbank f slate bed
Schieferbruch m slate quarry
Schiefereinlage f slate break
Schiefereinschaltung f slaty intercalation
Schiefergebirge n slate mountains
~/**Thüringer** Thuringian Slate Mountains
Schiefergneis m foliated gneiss
Schiefergrube f slate pit
schieferig slaty, shaly foliated, flaky, schistous, schistic
~/**dünnlamelliert** thin-lamellar shaly
Schieferigkeit f 1. fissility; 2. s. Schieferungsfläche
Schieferkalk m shaly limestone
Schieferlage f/**sulfidimprägnierte** fahlband
Schieferletten m clay shale
Schiefermehl n slate flour (powder)
Schiefermergel m slaty marl
Schiefermittel n shale band, parting shale
Schieferöl n shale oil
~/**rohes** crude shale oil
Schieferölgewinnung f shale distillation
Schiefersandstein m shaly sandstone
Schieferteer m shale tar
Schiefertextur f slaty structure
Schieferton m shaly (slate, laminated) clay, (argillaceous) shale, mud rock, rock (stone) bind *(aleuritic)*
~/**dünnblättriger** leaf (laminated) shale
~/**dünnschiefriger** clives, clift

~/**erhärteter** pitcher brasses
~/**haftender** sticky shale
~/**harter** plate shale
~/**kalkiger** calcareous shale
~/**klebender** sticky shale
~/**kohlehaltiger** shaly clay with coal
~/**kohliger** black stone
~ **mit Toneisensteinknollen** pimpley
~/**pyritischer** pyritic shale
~/**quellender** heaving (sloughing) shale
~/**sandiger** sandy shale, metal stone
~/**schmieriger** sticky shale
Schiefertoneinlage f shale break
~/**sehr dünne** shale parting
Schiefertonschmitze f shale crescent
Schiefertonzwischenlage f shale break
Schieferung f foliation [cleavage], foliated (schistose) structure; schistosity *(in micaschists and gneiss)*; cleavage *(in non-metamorphic argillaceous rocks)*
~/**ebene** plane schistosity
~/**falsche** pseudoschistosity, close foliation, oblique lamination
~/**fiedrig angeordnete** pinnate cleavage
~/**parallele** bedding cleavage
~/**transversale** slaty (fracture, flow) cleavage, transverse lamination
Schieferungsebene f cleavage (foliation) plane, plane of schistosity
Schieferungsfächer m cleavage fan
schieferungsfähig cleavable
Schieferungsfähigkeit f cleavability
Schieferungsfläche f foliation (cleavage) plane
Schieferungsfuge f foliation (cleavage) joint
Schieferungsmulde f cleavage trough
Schieferungsmullionstruktur f cleavage mullion
Schieferungssattel m cleavage arch
Schieferzwischenmittel n layer of shale
Schiefgürtelregelungsbild n oblique girdle pattern
Schieflage f inclined position, tilt; subsidence slope *(of soil)*
schiefrig s. schieferig
schiefrigschuppig foliated, foliaceous, fissile
Schiefstellung f tilt, deviation [from plumb]
Schießen n shooting, blasting
Schießloch n shot-hole
Schießpunkte mpl shot points
Schiff n **zum Verlegen von Rohrleitungen** pipe-laying ship
Schiffsprahm m/**versenkbarer** submersible barge
Schild m shield
~/**Äthiopischer** Ethiopian shield
~/**Australischer** Australian shield
~/**Baltischer** Baltic shield, Fennoscandia
~/**Finnisch-Skandinavischer** s. ~/Baltischer
~/**Indischer** Indian shield
~/**Kanadischer** Canadian shield
~/**kristalliner** crystalline shield
~/**präkambrischer** Precambrian shield

~/Skandinavischer Scandinavian shield
~/Ukrainischer Ukrainian shield
Schildbasalt m shield (multiple vent) basalt
schildförmig shield-shaped
Schildkröte f turtle
Schildkrötenstruktur f turtle-structure anticline (salt tectonics)
Schildvulkan m shield volcano, [exogenous] lava dome
Schilf n reed; cane
Schilfrand m reedy margin
Schilfrohr n reed
Schilfröhricht n reed swamp
Schilftorf m reed peat
Schill m shells; lumachelle (fossil)
Schillbank f shell bank
Schillerglanz m varying (changeable) lustre
schillern to schillerize, to iridize, to iridesce, to aventurize
Schillern n aventurism, schillerization, iridescence, allochroism
schillernd iridescent, chatoyant, allochroic
Schillkalk m coquina
Schimmer m lustre
Schirmerit m schirmerite, $PbS \cdot 2Ag_2S \cdot 2Bi_2S_3$
Schirokko m sirocco
Schizolith m schizolite (Mn-bearing variety of pectolite)
Schlachtfeld n churchyard
Schlacke f slag, cinder, scoria
~/vulkanische volcanic cinder (scoria)
schlackenähnlich slaggy, slaglike, scoriaceous, scoriform
schlackenartig scoriaceous
Schlackenbasalt m scoriaceous basalt
Schlackenbildung f scorification
Schlackenbombe f slag bomb
Schlackenbruch m slag shingle
Schlackendecke f covering of scoriae
Schlackenfontäne f lava fountain
Schlackenkegel m slag (cinder, scoria) cone
Schlackenkruste f crust of scoriae
Schlackenkuchen m cow-dung bomb
Schlackenlapilli mpl scoriaceous lapilli
Schlackenlava f aa lava, aphrolite, aphrolith
Schlackenlavafeld n aa field
Schlackensand m scoriaceous sand
Schlackenschicht f bed of scoriae
Schlackenschornstein m blowing (driblet) cone
Schlackentuff m lithic tuff
Schlackenwall m spatter rampart
Schlackenwolle f mineral (slag, cinder) wool
Schlackenwurftätigkeit f cinder eruption activity, Strombolian activity
schlackig slaggy, cindery, scoriated
Schlagbär m ram
Schlagbiegefestigkeit f notch impact strength
Schlagbohren n hammer (percussion) drilling
~/hydraulisches hydraulic hammer drilling
~/pneumatisches pneumatic hammer drilling
Schlagbohrer m percussion drill, spudder

Schlamminjektion

Schlagbohrgerät n percussion drilling rig
Schlagbohrwerk n hammer drill
Schlageinrichtung f thumper (seismics)
Schlägel m und Eisen n hammer and wedge
Schlagfestigkeit f resistance to impact
Schlagfigur f chatter mark
Schlaghärte f impact hardness
Schlagkreis m target
Schlagmarken fpl percussion marks, crescentic impact scars
Schlagmeißel m percussion bit
Schlagschere f jar
Schlagschotter m broken stone (rock)
Schlagsonde f percussion probe, driving rod
Schlagwetter pl firedamps
Schlagwetteransammlung f body of gas
Schlagwetteranzeiger m methane indicator
Schlagwetterexplosion f explosion of firedamp
schlagwetterfest, schlagwettergeschützt firedamp-proof
schlagwettersicher non-fiery, flameproof
Schlagzahl f number of strokes
Schlamm m mud, mire; slurry; silt, ooze; sludge
~/feiner pulp
~/gritfreier gritless mud
~/organogener copropel
~/vulkanischer mud lava
~/weicher slush
Schlammablagerung f mud (silting) deposit, sullage
Schlämmanalyse f elutriation (settling) analysis, hydrometer analysis (test)
~ im aufsteigenden Wasserstrom elutriation by rising currents
Schlämmapparat m elutriator (granulometric analysis)
Schlämmarbeit f clearing
schlammartig muddy, sludgy, uliginous
Schlammaufbruch m mud lump
Schlammausbruch m mud eruption
schlammbedeckt silt-covered
Schlammboden m muddy soil (ground), silt soil
Schlammeinpressung f mud jacking
Schlammeis n slush
schlämmen 1. to elutriate; 2. to wash [down] (ore); to screen (gold)
Schlämmen n 1. elutriation; 2. washing (of ore); screening (of gold)
Schlammfang m sediment sump (of a well)
Schlammfeld n mud field
schlammführend mud-bearing
Schlämmgraben m box buddle
Schlammgrube f mud (slush) pit
Schlammhügel m mud mound
schlammig muddy, miry, sludgy; silty, slimy, oozy; swamped, uliginous
Schlammigkeit f muddiness, miriness, sliminess, ooziness
Schlamminjektion f mud jacking

Schlamminsel

Schlamminsel f mud island
Schlammkegel m puff cone
Schlämmklassierer m desliming classifier
Schlammkohle f smudge coal
Schlämmkorn n/grobes coarse silt
Schlammkrater m mud pot
Schlämmkreide f prepared (precipitated) chalk
Schlammlast f load of silt (of a river)
Schlammlava f aqueous lava
Schlammlawine f mud avalanche
Schlammleitung f mud line suspension equipment
Schlammniederung f mud flat
Schlämmprobe f outwash sample
Schlämmprodukt n outwash product
Schlammregen m mud rain
Schlammriß m mud crack
Schlammrißbildung f mud cracking
Schlammrohr n sludge barrel
Schlammrutschung f sludging
Schlammschicht f mud (warp) bed
~/harte silt pan
Schlammschüttelsieb n shale shaker
Schlammschwelle f mud sill
Schlämmseil n sand line
Schlammsprudel m mud spring (geyser, volcano), salse, macaluba
~/heißer paint pot
Schlammstrom m mud flow, torrent of mud; [cold] lahar
Schlammstruktur f/diapirartige mud lump
Schlammsumpf m slime pit
Schlammteich m tailings pond
Schlämmtrommel f sand reel
Schlammtrübe f sludge water
Schlammtuff m lahar deposit
Schlämmung f s. Schlämmen
Schlammvulkan m mud vulcano, monroe (s.a. Schlammsprudel)
Schlammwasser n slurry
schlängeln/sich to meander
Schlangengips m tripestone
Schlangenstern m brittle star
Schlankheitsgrad m slenderness ratio
Schlauchalgen fpl siphoneous algae
Schlauchbohren n flexodrilling
Schlauchwaage f hose levelling instrument
Schlechte f cleat, cleavage; parting, slip
~/abfallende back slip
~/gegen den Stoß einfallende face slip
~ senkrecht zur Hauptschlechtenrichtung end cleat
~/vertikale slippy back
Schlechtenrichtung f cleat direction
Schlechtwetterstrecke f bad weather line
Schlechtwetterwolken fpl fractonimbus clouds
Schleierwolke f veil (scarf) cloud
Schleifdiamant m abrasive diamond
Schleife f loop, bend (of a river)
Schleifen n mit Sand sand bobbing
Schleifenschlußfehler m loop error

Schleiffläche f polished surface
Schleifgranat m abrasive garnet
Schleifhärte f resistance to polish
Schleifkratzer m grinding scratch
Schleiflinie f bobbing mark
Schleifmarke f slide (drag) mark, groove cast
Schleifmittel n abrasive, abrader; grinding powder
~/sanft wirkendes soft abrasive
Schleifnarbe f s. Schleiflinie
Schleifpolieren polish-grinding
Schleifpulver n polishing powder
Schleifriefen fpl drag striae
Schleifrille f drag groove
~/gefiederte chevron mark
Schleifsand m cutting sand
Schleifschmant m grinding residue
Schleifspur f trail, foil
Schleifstein m grindstone
Schleif- und Poliertechnik f abrasive engineering practice
Schleifwirkung f abrasive action
schleimig slimy
Schlenke f hollow
Schleppblatt n drag sheet
Schleppdecke f drag nappe
Schleppfalte f drag fold
~/inkongruente incongruous drag fold
~/kongruente congruous drag fold
Schleppfalt[enbild]ung f drag folding
Schleppkeil m drag wedge
Schleppkraft f tractive force, carrying power (of the water)
Schlepplast f traction load (of a river)
Schleppsynklinale f dragged syncline
Schleppung f drag, distortion, bending
~ nach oben upward drag
~ nach unten downward drag
~/umgekehrte reverse drag
Schleppverwerfung f drag fault
Schleuse f gate, lock, sluice
Schleusenkammer f lock [chamber]
Schleusentor n lock gate
Schlich m concentrate
Schlichanalyse f s. Schwermineralanalyse
Schlick m silt, ooze, tidal mud deposits; sludge
~/kalkiger calcareous ooze
~/sandiger sandy mud
~/schluffiger silty mud
~/toniger argillaceous mud, clay-containing silt
Schlickablagerung f mud deposit
Schlickebene f mud (silt) plain, mud flat
Schlickgerölle npl mud pebbles, plasticlasts
~/eingerollte clay galls
schlickig muddy, slimy, oozy
Schlicksand m silty sand
Schlickstrand m mud beach
Schlickton m/rezenter gumbo clay
Schlickwatt n mud flat
Schlier m clay marl

Schliere f schliere, streak
Schlierentextur f schlieric (streaked) structure
schlierig schlieric, streaked, streaky
Schließdauer f closure (shut-in) time *(of a well)*
Schließdruck m closing pressure
Schließdruckkurve f build-up curve
Schließen n 1. shutting-in *(of a well)*; 2. closing *(plate tectonics)*
Schließmuskel m adductor muscle
Schließmuskeleindruck m/**hinterer** posterior muscular impression
Schließmuskelgrube f pit
Schließmuskelnarbe f adductor muscle scar
Schliffbild n micrograph
Schlifffläche f surface slide
Schliffkratzer m scratch on the section
Schlingenbau m vortex structure, folding about vertical axis
Schlitzband n slit band, selenizone, anal fasciola *(gastropods)*
schlitzen to carve
Schlitzfenster n slit window *(tectonics)*
Schlitzgefäß n slotted sampling vessel
Schlitzkeilanker m slot-and-wedge [roof] bolt
Schlitzprobe f channel (slit) sample
Schlitzrohr n screen pipe *(in wells)*
Schloß n 1. hinge *(palaeontology);* 2. yoke *(of a friction prop)*
~/adontes (zahnloses) adont hinge *(ostracods)*
Schloße f sleet, hailstone
Schloßfurche f hinge groove *(palaeontology)*
Schloßgrube f socket *(palaeontology)*
Schloßleiste f hinge bar *(palaeontology)*
Schloßplatte f hinge plate *(palaeontology)*
Schloßrand m hinge (posterior) margin, cardinal area *(palaeontology)*
Schloßzahn m tooth *(palaeontology)*
Schlot m 1. pipe, vent, funnel, tube, feeder; 2. neck, stump *(palaeontology)*
~/flacher flattish pipe
Schlotfüllung f pipe filling
Schlotgang m spine neck
Schlothohlraum m/**vulkanischer** pan
Schlotponor m pit ponor
Schlotte f pipe, sink
Schlotverlagerung f shifting of the volcanic vent
Schlucht f ravine, gorge, cleft, narrow, chasm
~/enge tiefe gully, goulee
~/kleine clough
Schluchtenbildung f gorge cutting
Schluchtmeander m meander channel
Schluckbrunnen m recharging image well, invaded well
~ für Salzwasser salt-water disposal well
Schluckloch n ponor, swallow [hole], swallet, katavothron
~ am Meeresgrund founder
Schluckvermögen n disposal power of a well
Schluff m schluff, silt, loam watery clay
~/steifer tough silt

Schluffauswaschung f silt sluicing
Schluffboden m silty soil
schluffhaltig silt-bearing
schluffig silty
Schluffkorn n silt fraction
Schlufflehm m silty loam
~/toniger clay silty loam
Schluffmergel m/**verfestigter** siltstone, siltite
Schluffstein m silt rock, siltstone, siltite, mudstone
Schluffton m silty clay
Schlumberger-Anordnung f Schlumberger electrode array
Schlumberger-Logs npl Schlumberger logs, Slumberjag
schlummernd quiescent
Schlund m throat, abyss
Schlundloch n s. Schluckloch
Schlüpfrigkeit f lubricity
Schlüsseldoline f uvala
Schmalfalte f narrow-crested anticline
Schmantbüchse f bailer
Schmarotzerkrater m s. Adventivkrater
Schmelzanlage f smelter
schmelzbar fusible
Schmelzbarkeit f fusibility
Schmelzbasalt m fused (cast) basalt
Schmelzbasaltwolle f s. Schlackenwolle
Schmelzbohren n fusion piercing
Schmelze f/**lunare** lunar melt
schmelzen 1. to thaw, to melt, to be wasted away; 2. to fuse *(rocks);* 3. to smelt *(metals)*
Schmelzen n 1. fusion *(of rocks);* 2. smelting *(of metals)*
~/selektives selective melting
~ und Wiedergefrieren n thaw and freeze, regelation
Schmelzer m smelter
Schmelzerz n smelting ore
Schmelzfluß m melt, flow of rock *(magma)*
schmelzflüssig molten, liquid
Schmelzgesteinsbombe f/**poröse** impact bomb
Schmelzhütte f smeltery
Schmelznäpfe mpl melt cups *(within the glacier)*
Schmelzpunkt m melting (fusing) point
~/inkongruenter incongruent melting point
~/kongruenter congruent melting point
Schmelzpunktniedrigung f lowering (depression) of melting point
Schmelzpunktverhalten n melting point behaviour
Schmelzrinde f baked crust *(of meteorites)*
Schmelzschupper mpl scaly ganoids, ganoid fishes
schmelzschuppig enamel-scaled
Schmelztektonite mpl fusion tectonites
Schmelztemperatur f melting (fusion) temperature
Schmelztuff m welded tuff (pumice), tuff (ash, pyroclastic) flow, aso lava, ignimbrite

Schmelzung 274

Schmelzung f melting; fusion
~/innere englacial melting *(of a glacier)*
Schmelzwärme f heat of fusion
Schmelzwasser n melt water; snow water; glacial water
Schmelzwasserabfluß m snowmelt runoff
Schmelzwasserablagerungen fpl aqueoglacial (melt-water) deposits
Schmelzwasserbach m superglacial (melt-water) stream
Schmelzwasserebene f glacial outwash plain, outwash [gravel] plain, sand[u]r
Schmelzwasserfluß m/**gletscherfrontparalleler** interlobular stream
Schmelzwasserformen fpl/**glaziale** scabland forms (features)
Schmelzwasserkies m melt-water gravel
Schmelzwasserrinne f glacial spillway (stream channel), melt-water gully
Schmelzwassersedimente npl overwash
Schmelzwassersee m glacier (glacial) lake
Schmelzwasserspur f strake *(on the glacial surface)*
Schmelzwasserstrom m torrent of melt water
Schmelzwassertal n valley formed by melt water, glacial spillway
Schmerkluft f clay-filled fissure
Schmiermittel n lubricant
Schmierschicht f lubricating layer
Schmirgel m emery [rock]
Schmirgelhärte f abrasive hardness
Schmirgelsand m abrasive sand
Schmitze f streak, thin seam, buzzard
Schmöllnitzit m s. Szomolnokit
Schmuckstein m decorative stone
Schmutzband n, **Schmutzstreifen** m dirt-band [ogive]
Schmutzwasser n dirty (foul) water *(s.a. Abwasser)*
Schnabel m beak; umbo *(of bivalved fossils)*
Schnecke f snail
Schneckenbohren n auger drilling
Schneckenbohrer m auger bit, worm auger
~/zylindrischer spiral auger
Schneckenförderer m screw conveyor
Schneckenschale f conchylium
Schnee m snow
~/durchtränkter slush
~/ewiger eternal (perpetual, perennial) snow
~/frischgefallener deposited snow
~/körniger nasser corn (spring, granular) snow
~/nasser waterlogged snow
~/vereister névé *(of a glacier)*
~/windgepackter drifted snow
Schneeanhäufung f snow wreath
Schneeballstruktur f snowball structure
schneebedeckt snowclad, snow-covered
Schneebergit m s. Roméit
Schneebrettlawine f snow-slab avalanche, wind-slab avalanche
Schneebrücke f snowbridge

Schneedecke f snow cover, blanket of snow
Schneedurchlässigkeit f air permeability of snow
Schnee-Erosion f nivation
Schneefahne f spindrift
Schneefall m snowfall
Schneefeld n snowfield
Schneeflocke f snowflake
schneefrei snow-free, snowless
Schneegebiet n snow region
Schneegekriech n snow creep
Schneegestöber n snow flurry (squall)
Schneegipfel m snow-capped peak
Schneegrenze f snow limit (line); permanent snow line
~/nördliche northern limit of snow fall
~/südliche southern limit of snow fall
Schneehöhe f depth of snow cover
Schneelawine f snow avalanche
Schneemenge f snowfall
Schneemesser m snow gauge
Schneemuldenboden m nival snow basin soil
schneereich snowy
Schneeschauer m snow shower
Schneeschicht f snow layer
Schneeschmelze f snowmelt, snowbreak
Schneesturm m snowstorm, snow blast
Schneesturz m snowslip, snowslide
Schneetreiben n drifting of snow
Schneeverwehung f snowdrift, drifted snow
Schneewächte f snow cornice (plume), overhanging snow, snowdrift site
Schneewehe f snowdrift, snowbank
Schneewolke f snow cloud
schneidbar sectil
Schneide f cutting edge blade
schneiden/sich to intersect *(lodes)*
Schneidezahn m cutting tooth, incisor
Schneidfläche f cutting surface
Schneidmaß n outside diameter of drilling tool
Schnellanalyse f/**spektrofotometrische** rapid spectrophotometric analysis
Schnellmethode f/**spektrochemische** rapid spectrochemical method
Schnitt m 1. intersection; 2. section; 3. cut, incision
~/biostratigrafischer biostratigraphic[al] break
~/schematischer schematic section
~ von Schieferung und Schichtung cleavage-bedding intersection
Schnittfläche f surface of section
Schnitthöhe f cutting height *(of a dredger)*
Schnittlage f cutting position
Schnittlinien fpl traces, cutting lines
Schnittmodell n cut-away model
Schnittpunkt m intersection point; cut point
Schnittwinkel m angle of intersection
Schnur f loading *(of ore)*
Schnurlot n plumb line
Schockwelle f shock (impact) wave
Schoderit m schoderite, $Al[(P,V)O_4] \cdot 4H_2O$

Schoepit m schoepite, 8 [UO$_2$ I (OH)$_2$] · 8H$_2$O
Scholle f block, fault[ed] block, clod; massif *(of earth's crust)*; raft *(in magmatites)*
~/abgesunkene downfaulted (depressed, sunken, downthrown, downwarped, subsided, lowered) block
~/aufgeschobene thrusted block
~/eingeklemmte horse[back], rider
~/gehobene upper (upthrown, uplifted) block
~/gekippte tilted fault block
~/geschleppte dragged overthrust block
~/gesenkte s. ~/abgesunkene
~/hangende upthrow side
~/mitgeschleppte dragged overthrust block
Schollenabkippung f tipping of blocks
Schollenbau m block structure *(tectonics)*
Schollenbruch m block fault
Scholleneinkippung f s. Schollenkippung
Scholleneis n floe ice, ice floe
Schollenfaltung f block folding
Schollenfazies f block facies
schollenförmig blocklike
Schollengebirge n fault-block mountains, plateau, basin range
Schollenkante f fault ridge
Schollenkippung f tilting of blocks
Schollenland n basin range
Schollenlava f block lava
Schollenrotation f block rotation
Schollenrutschung f cambering
Schollensystem n block system
Schollentextur f raft structure *(of migmatites)*
Schollenüberschiebung f overthrusting, overthrust faulting, block overthrust
Schollenunterschiebung f underthrusting, underthrust fault[ing]
Schollenverschiebung f block faulting
schollig cloddy
Scholzit m scholzite, CaZn$_2$[PO$_4$]$_2$ · 2H$_2$O
Schongebiet n reserve zone
Schönit m schoenite, picromerite, K$_2$Mg[SO$_4$]$_2$ · 6H$_2$O
Schöpfbüchse f bailer
Schöpfsonde f bailing well
Schöpfversuch m bailing
Schörl m schorl, schorlite, black tourmaline, NaFe$_3$Al$_6$[(OH) I (BO$_3$)$_3$ I Si$_6$O$_{18}$]
schörlartig schorlaceous
Schorlomit m schorlomite *(variety of melanite)*
schornsteinartig chimneylike
Schorre f shore (wave-cut) platform, marine-cut terrace
Schott m shott, chott *(dune area in the Sahara)*
Schotter m boulder flint, gravel, crushed rock (stone); macadam, road stone
~/quarzreicher gravel rich in quartz
Schotter mpl/**fluvioglaziale** valley train
Schotterablagerung f gravel deposit
Schotterakkumulation f accumulation of gravels
Schotterbank f bank of gravel

schotterbedeckt gravel-capped, gravel-sheeted
Schotterboden m waste gravel soil
Schotterbrecher m stone breaker, coarse crusher
Schotterdecke f alluvial cover, gravel covering (sheet)
Schotterfächer m gravel fan
Schotterkegel m alluvial cone
Schottermasse f heap of gravel
Schotterschicht f gravel layer
Schotterstraße f macadam road
Schotterterrasse f alluvial (gravel, aggradational) terrace
Schotterung f gravelling; ballasting
Schotterwerk n rock (stone-crushing) plant
schraffieren to hatch
Schraffierung f hatching
schräg oblique, sloping, slant, skew, inclined
Schrägaufnahme f oblique photograph
Schrägbelastung f oblique load
Schrägbohrloch n angle borehole
Schrägbohrung f 1. inclined (slant) drilling; 2. slant hole
Schrägbohrungslöcher npl raking holes
schräggeschichtet cross-bedded, cross-stratified, false-bedded
schräggestellt tilted, tipped
Schrägheitswinkel m angle of obliquity
Schräglichtbeleuchtung f obliquity of illumination
Schrägschacht m inclined shaft
schrägschichtig s. schräggeschichtet
Schrägschichtung f cross-bedding, cross stratification (lamination), oblique bedding (lamination), false bedding
~/bogige concave [inclined] bedding, tangential cross-bedding, festoon cross lamination
~/ebenflächig begrenzte tabular (planar) cross stratification
~/einfache simple cross stratification
~/gerade gestreckte tabular (planar) cross-bedding
~/großdimensionale large-scale cross-bedding
~/keilförmige wedge-shaped cross-bedding
~/kleindimensionale microcross lamination
~/konvexe convex inclined bedding
~/linsige lenticular cross-bedding
~/schaufelförmige (synklinale) s. ~/bogige
~/tafelige tabular (planar) cross-bedding
~/trogförmige s. ~/bogige
~/überkippte overturned cross-bedding
~/verformte deformed cross-bedding
~/winkelige angular cross-bedding
~/zusammengesetzte furious cross lamination
Schrägschichtungsbögen mpl rib-and-furrow
Schrägschichtungseinheit f set
Schrägstellung f tilting; inclination
Schrägstollen m inclined shaft
Schrägungswinkel m angle of skew
Schrägzuschnitt m/**basaler** oblique truncation *(of base)*

Schram

Schram *m s.* Schrämen
schrämen to carve
Schrämen *n* carving, cross cutting; bannocking
Schrämklein *n* cuttings
Schrämmaschine *f* cross cutter, channelling machine
Schramme *f* scratch, stria[tion]
schrammen to scratch
Schrammen *fpl* abrasion marks *(e.g. on a film)*
Schrämvortriebmaschine *f* channelling machine
Schrapper *m* scraper
Schrapperversatz *m* stowing with scraper buckets
Schratten *fpl* karren, schratten, clints, grikes, rain channels
Schrattenbildung *f* karren (schratten) formation
Schrattenfeld *n* karrenfeld, schrattenfeld, rugged limestone rock
Schrattenkalk *m* schrattenkalk
Schraubenachse *f* screw axis
Schraubenbewegung *f* screw (helical) motion
Schraubeneis *n* pack ice
Schraubentute *f* overshot
Schraubstempel *m* screw jack prop
Schraubung *f* spiral axis
Schraubungsachse *f* axis of the screw motion
Schraubungssinn *m* direction of screwing
Schreiber *m* recorder
Schreibersit *m* schreibersite, rhabdite, $(Fe,Ni,Co)_3P$
Schreiberz *n s.* Sylvanit
Schreibkreide *f* chalk
~/Mittlere Middle Chalk *(Turonian, England)*
~/Obere Upper Chalk *(Cenomanian to Maastrichtian, British Islands)*
~/Untere Lower Chalk *(British Islands)*
Schreibpegel *m* limnograph, limnigraph; water-level recorder
Schreibregenmesser *m* self-recording rain gauge
Schrifterz *n s.* Sylvanit
Schriftgranit *m* graphic (Hebraic) granite, runite
Schriftstruktur *f* graphical (eutectic) texture
Schröckingerite *m* schroeckingerite, $NaCa_3[UO_2 \mid F \mid SO_4 \mid (CO_3)_3] \cdot 10H_2O$
schroff cragged, craggy, precipitous
Schroffheit *f* craggedness, cragginess
Schrot *n* drilling shot
Schrotbohren *n* shot drilling
Schrotbohrer *m* adamantine drill
Schrotkrone *f* [chilled-]shot bit, core bit for shot drilling
Schrotmeißel *m* blacksmith's chisel
schrumpfen to shrink; to contract
Schrumpfpore *f* shrinkage pore
Schrumpfspalte *f* fissure of retreat
Schrumpfung *f* shrinkage; contraction

Schrumpfungsfaktor *m* shrinkage factor *(crude oil)*
Schrumpfungskluft *f* contraction joint
Schrumpfungsriß *m* shrinkage (desiccation, mud, contraction) crack, joint (fissure) of retreat
Schrumpfungstheorie *f* contraction (shrinkage) theory
Schrund *m* crevice
Schub *m* thrust, push, shoving; shear
~/seitlicher lateral pressure
~/tangentialer tangential thrust
Schubbelastung *f* thrust loading
Schubdecke *f* [over]thrust sheet, overthrust nappe (plate)
Schubfestigkeit *f s.* Scherfestigkeit
Schubfläche *f* thrust (slip) plane
~/basale basal thrust plane
Schubhöhe *f* vertical throw (displacement)
~/flache thrust slip
~/scheinbare stratigrafische perpendicular throw
Schubklüftung *f* crenulation (close-joint, fracture, false, fault-slip) cleavage, strain[-slip] cleavage
Schubkraft *f* thrusting force
Schublänge *f*/**horizontale (söhlige)** horizontal displacement, strike slip, shove
~/wahre total displacement, net slip
Schubmasse *f* overthrust (overriding, displaced) mass
Schubmodul *m* shear[ing] modulus, modulus of rigidity
Schubpakete *npl*/**abgescherte** thrust slices (wedges)
Schubrichtung *f* direction of thrust[ing]
Schubspannung *f* shear stress
Schubweite *f* distance (width) of thrust
Schuchardtit *m* schuchardtite *(variety of antigorite)*
Schuetteit *m* schuetteite, $Hg_3[O_2 \mid SO_4]$
Schulp *m* pen *(cephalopods)*
Schultenit *m* schultenite, $HPbAsO_4$
Schulter *f* shoulder
Schulzenit *m* schulzenite *(variety of heterogenite)*
Schummerung *f* shading
Schungit *m* s[c]hungite, graphitite
Schuppe *f* flake, scale, shingle, wedge *(tectonical)*
schuppenartig imbricated
Schuppenbau *m s.* Schuppengefüge
Schuppenfaltung *f* imbricated folding
schuppenförmig squamiform
Schuppengefüge *n* imbricate (scaly) structure
Schuppenglimmer *m* flake mica
Schuppengraphit *m* flake (flaky) graphite
Schuppenstruktur *f* flaky texture
schuppig scaly, flaky, imbricated
Schuppung *f* imbrication, imbricate structure
Schurf *m* exploratory excavation
Schürfarbeit *f* prospecting [work], prospect, costeaning

Schürfbohranlage f prospecting rig
Schürfbohrloch n cast (slim) hole
Schürfbohrung f test well, prospection drilling
~/geologische post (structure) hole, structural test hole
schürfen to prospect, to search, to explore
Schürfen n prospecting, search[ing], exploration (s.a. Prospektieren)
~/geochemisches geochemical prospecting
~/geophysikalisches geophysical prospecting
~/gravimetrisches gravitational prospecting
~/magnetisches magnetic survey
Schürfer m prospector, searcher
Schürffreiheit f freedom prospect
Schürfgebiet n prospecting area
Schürfgraben m prospecting trench
Schürfgrube f test (trial) pit
Schürfling m dislodged slice
Schürflizenz f exploration permit
Schürfloch n s. Schürfgrube
Schürfmarke f gouge mark
Schürfmethode f prospecting method
Schürfschacht m prospecting shaft, prospect hole, prospecting (test) pit
Schürfschein m exploration permit
Schürfstelle f prospect
Schürfstrecke f prospecting drift
Schürftätigkeit f exploration
Schürfung f search[ing], prospection, exploration
Schürfverfahren n/**geophysikalisches** geophysical [method of] prospecting
Schürfzeit f digging (dig-and-turn) time
Schurre f chute
Schuß m shot
Schußanregung f shot incitement (of waves)
Schußbohrloch n shot hole
Schußbohrung f/**seismische** seismic shot drilling
Schüsse mpl/**versetzte** broadside
Schüssel f basin, bowl; centroclinal fold
Schüsseldoline f polye, polje
schüsselförmig 1. basin-shaped, bowl-shaped; 2. s. patelliform
Schüsselklassierer m bowl classifier
Schußgebirge n shooting ground
Schußkanal m channel of ascent, conduit [of volcano]
Schußloch n shot hole
Schußmoment m shot break
Schußperforierung f gun perforation
Schußpunkt m shot point
Schußpunktabstand m distance between shot points; offset, gap (to the first geophone group)
Schußtiefe f shot depth
Schutt m rubble, wast[age], [float, scree] debris, talus
~/glazialer drift
Schuttablagerung f detrital (debris) accumulation, detritus

Schuttbildung f detrital formation
Schuttboden m detrital (waste gravel, talus) soil
Schuttböschung f detrital (waste) slope
Schuttbrekzie f scree (talus) breccia
Schuttdecke f cover (mantle, blanket) of debris, regolith, sathrolith
~/alluviale coverhead
~/fluvioglaziale glaciofluviatile mantle
~/glaziale drift sheet, overburden of glacial drift
~/kriechende sheet of creeping waste
Schuttebene f detrital (waste) plain, plain of debris
Schüttelherd m shaking (oscillating) table (dressing)
Schüttelprobe f shaking test
Schüttelsieb n vibrating screen, shale shaker; mud screen
Schütteltisch m shaking (shaker) table
Schüttergebiet n region of [seismic] disturbance
Schütterlinie f seismic line
schüttern to quake
Schütterzone f seismic zone
Schuttfächer m talus (boulder) fan, [morainic] apron, moraine plain, overwash plain (apron)
~/alluvialer alluvial fan
~ durch Auswaschung outwash fan
Schuttfazies f detrital facies
Schuttfracht f solid discharge
Schuttgesteine npl detrital rocks, land waste
~/terrestrische terrestrial detritus
Schuttgletscher m rock glacier
Schutthalde f rubble (detrital, talus) slope, spoil bank (dump), rock fan
~/submarine submarine detrital slope
Schutthang m s. Schutthalde
Schuttkegel m talus (alluvial) cone, detrital (alluvial outfall) fan, heap of debris
Schuttkriechen n talus (hillside, downhill) creep
Schuttlast f solid load, load of waste (debris) (of a river)
Schuttlawine f debris avalanche
Schuttlawinenbrekzie f avalanche breccia
Schuttmantel m mantle of rock waste
~/dünner alluvial veneer
Schuttmasse f/**durch Frostwirkung entstandene** congelifractate
Schuttmaterial n detrital (waste) material, waste matter
Schuttquelle f detrital spring
Schuttrutschung f debris slide
Schuttschicht f detrital layer
Schüttsprengverfahren n muck-blasting operation
Schuttstrom m flow of debris, earth glacier
~/glühender glowing avalanche
Schüttung f accretion, embankment, flow (of sparing)

Schüttungskoeffizient

Schüttungskoeffizient *m* discharging coefficient
Schüttungsmenge *f* discharge
Schüttungswinkel *m* angle of repose (rest)
Schüttungszahl *f* coefficient of bulk increase
Schüttungszentrum *n* talus centre
Schüttvolumen *n* bulk volume
Schüttwinkel *m* angle of discharge
Schuttwulst *m* corrugation
Schutz *m* **gegen Unterspülungen** protection against underwashing, cut-off walls, cut-offs
Schutzband *n*/**spitzbogiges** glacier (forbes) band
Schutzdach *n* canopy
Schutzdamm *m* levee
Schutzdecke *f* protecting cover
Schützenwehr *n* sluice weir
Schutzflöz *n* protective seam
Schutzgasatmosphäre *f* protective atmosphere
Schutzgebiet *n* protection (offset) area, reserve zone
Schutzgebiete *npl*/**geologische** geologic[al] preservation areas
Schutzkolloid *n* protective colloid
Schutzrinde *f* pellicle
Schutzschicht *f* protective layer; confining bed
~ gegen Unterspülungen overwash plain (apron)
Schutzsonde *f* offset[ting] well
Schutzzone *f* 1. protective zone; 2. zone of sanitary protection
schwach weak, partially observed only *(3rd stage of the scale of seismic intensity)*
Schwächezone *f* zone of weakness
Schwachgas *n* lean gas
schwachgradig low-grade
schwachmuschelig semiconchoidal
schwachsandig slightly sandy
Schwadbreite *f* swath width *(width of the strip on the ground from which remote sensing pictures are taken by an overflying satellite or aircraft)*
schwalbenschwanzförmig dovetailed, culvertailed
Schwalbenschwanzzwilling *m* butterfly (fish-tail) twin
schwammartig spongiform
Schwammerz *n* sponge ore
schwammig spongious, spongy
Schwammnadel *f* sponge needle (spicule)
Schwammnadelschlamm *m* [sponge] spicule ooze
Schwanenhals *m* gooseneck
Schwankung *f* **des Wasserspiegels** water table fluctuation
Schwankungen *fpl*/**jährliche** annual variations
~/tägliche diurnal variations
~/tägliche magnetische diurnal magnetic changes
Schwanzflosse *f* caudal fin

Schwanzschild *m s.* Pygidium
Schwanzsegment *n s.* Telson
Schwanzskelett *n* tail skeleton
Schwanzstachel *m* caudal spine
Schwanzwirbel *m* caudal vertebra
Schwarm *m* swarm
Schwarmbeben *npl* swarm earthquakes, earthquake series
Schwartenbildung *f* shingle-block structure
Schwartzembergit *m* schwartzembergite, $Pb_5[Cl_3O_3 \mid JO_3]$
Schwarzdecke *f* 1. black top pavement *(road building)*; 2. black earth (soil), chernozem *(pedology)*
~/tropische black adobe
schwarzglänzend black lustrous
Schwarzgültigerz *n s.* Stephanit
Schwarzkohle *f* pit coal
Schwarzkupfererz *n s.* Tenorit
Schwarzmanganerz *n* partly psilomelane, partly hausmannite
Schwarzmeerfazies *f* Euxinic (Black Sea) facies
Schwarzöl *n* hot oil
Schwarzpulver *n* **in Pulverform** blasting powder
~ in Tablettenform blasting pellet
Schwarzschiefer *m* black shale
Schwarzschieferfazies *f* black-shale facies
Schwarzspießglanz *m s.* Bournonit
Schwarzstreif *m* black band
Schwärzungsklassifizierung *f* density (level) slicing
Schwazit *m* schwazite *(mercurial tetrahedrite)*
Schweb *n* slime
Schwebeblase *f s.* Pneumatophor
Schwebefracht *f,* **Schwebelast** *f* suspension load *(of a river)*
schweben to float, to be suspended
schwebend 1. suspended; 2. up-dip, overhand, to the rise *(exploitation)*
Schwebstoffbelastung *f* silt charge
Schwebstoffe *mpl* suspensoids, suspended matter (solids); suspended (sediment) load
Schwebstofffracht *f* sediment runoff
Schwebstoffschöpfer *m* silt (suspended load) sampler
Schwebstoffführung *f* suspended load discharge
Schwefel *m* sulphur, *(Am)* sulfur, S
~/gediegener native sulphur
schwefelartig sulphur[e]ous
Schwefelbakterien *fpl* sulphur bacteria
Schwefeldämpfe *mpl* sulphur fumes
Schwefeldiapir *m* sulphur dome
Schwefelerz *n* sulphur ore
schwefelgelb sulphur-coloured
Schwefelgeruch *m s.* Schwefelwasserstoffgeruch
Schwefelgrube *f* sulphur mine (pit)
schwefelhaltig sulphur[e]ous
Schwefelkies *m* [sulphur] pyrite, FeS_2
Schwefelkieskonkretion *f* pyrite concretion

Schwefellagerstätte f sulphur deposit
Schwefelquelle f sulphur[e]ous (sulphur) spring, solfataric vent
schwefelsauer sulphuric
Schwefelsäure f sulphuric acid, H_2SO_4
Schwefelschlammstrom m sulphur mud flow
Schwefelung f sulphurization
Schwefelwasser n sulphur[ic] water
Schwefelwasserstoff m hydrogen sulphide, sulphuretted hydrogen, H_2S
Schwefelwasserstoffgeruch m sulphur smell; fire stink
~/mit fetid
Schwefelwasserstoffumarole f sulphuretted-hydrogen fumarole
schweflig sulphur[e]ous
Schweif m tail, train, beard *(of a comet)*
Schweißschlackenkegel m spatter cone
Schwelbraunkohle f brown coal for [low-temperature] carbonization; bituminous (retort) brown coal
Schwelkohle f low-temperature carbonization coal
Schwelkoks m low-temperature coke
Schwellast f pulsating stress
Schwelldruck m swelling pressure
Schwelle f swell, sill
~/mittelatlantische Mid-Atlantic rise, Mid-Atlantic ridge
~/mitteldeutsche Central-German ridge
~/mittelozeanische mid-oceanic rise, mid-oceanic ridge
~/untermeerische submarine sill
~/vindelizische Vindelician rise
Schwellen fpl **und Rinnen** fpl runnels and ridges, submarine bars
schwellend tumid; heaving
Schwellenfazies f sill facies
Schwellengehalt m/**geologischer** cut-off grade
Schwellung f tumidity; bulkage, bulking
Schwellvermögen n expansibility
Schwellwert m coefficient of elastic recovery
Schwelung f low-temperature carbonization
Schwemmbagger m flushing dredge[r]
Schwemmboden m alluvial soil
Schwemmdelta n fan delta
schwemmen to sweep, to rinse, to float, to wash
Schwemmgebilde n alluvial formation
Schwemmkegel m alluvial cone
Schwemmland n alluvium, alluvion, alluvial accumulation (soil), bottom land
Schwemmlandboden m alluvial floor
Schwemmlandebene f alluvial plain (slope)
Schwemmlandküste f alluvial shore, alluvial plain shore line
Schwemmlaterit m low-level laterite
Schwemmlöß m aqueous (reworked, reassorted) loess
Schwemmsand m alluvial (blanket) sand
Schwemmstein m alluvial stone

Schwenkkeil m swinging wedge
Schwere f/**verminderte** subgravity
Schwereanomalie f gravitational (gravity) anomaly; mascon *(on the moon)*
Schwereanziehung f gravitational (gravity) attraction
Schwerebeschleunigung f gravity acceleration, acceleration due to gravity, acceleration of gravity
Schwereeffekt m **des Salzhuts** cap[rock] effect
Schwerefeld n gravitational (gravity) field
Schwerefeldmessung f gravity field measurement
Schwereformel f gravity formula
Schweregradient m gravity gradient
~/horizontaler horizontal gradient of gravity
~/vertikaler vertical gradient of gravity
Schwerehoch n maximum of gravity
Schwerekarte f isogal map
schwerelos weightless
Schwerelosigkeit f weightlessness
Schwerelösung f gravity solution, heavy liquid
Schwerelotkern m gravity core
Schweremasse f gravitational mass
Schweremesser m gravity meter, gravitometer
Schweremessung f gravity (gravimetric) measurement, gravity determination; barymetry
Schwerepotential n gravitational (gravity) potential
Schwereprofil n/**regionales** regional gravity profile
Schwereschichtung f segregation
Schwereschwankung f gravity change
Schweresystem n/**Potsdamer** Potsdam system of gravity
Schweretief n minimum of gravity
Schwereuntersuchung f gravity exploration
Schwereverteilung f gravity distribution
Schwerewellen fpl gravity waves
Schwerewert m[/**Potsdamer**] Potsdam gravity value
~/reduzierter reduced gravity value
Schwerewirkung f gravitational (gravimetric) effect
Schwerezunahme f gravity increment
schwerflüchtig difficultly volatile
Schwerflüssigkeit f s. Schwerelösung
Schwerflüssigkeitsaufbereitung f dense-medium washing
Schwergewichtsmauer f gravity dam
Schwerkraft f force of gravity, gravitational force, gravity, gravitation
Schwerkraftdrainage f gravity drive (drainage)
Schwerkraftentölung f gravity drainage of oil
Schwerkraftentwässerung f gravity drainage
Schwerkraftgefälle n, **Schwerkraftgradient** m gravity gradient
Schwerkraftkomponente f component of gravity

Schwerkraftmessung 280

Schwerkraftmessung f measurement of gravity
Schwerkraftquelle f gravity spring
Schwerkraftströmung f gravity flow
Schwerkrafttrennung f gravity segregation
Schwerkraftverfahren n gravitational method
Schwerkraftverteilung f gravity distribution
Schwermetall n heavy metal
Schwermineral n heavy mineral
Schwermineralanalyse f heavy-mineral analysis
Schwermineralauflösung f während der Diagenese intrastratal solution of heavy minerals
Schwermineralgehalt m im Küstensand beach concentrate of heavy minerals
Schwermineralllagerstätte f/küstennahe coastal placer deposit of heavy minerals
Schwermineralvergesellschaftung f heavy-mineral assemblage
Schweröl n heavy (low-gravity) oil
~/rohes heavy (low-gravity) crude oil
Schwerpunkt m gravity centre
Schwerpunktskoordinate f centre of mass coordinate
Schwerspat m heavy spar (earth), baryte, BaSO$_4$
Schwerspülung f heavy mud
Schwerstange f drill[ing] collar, sinker bar
~/nicht magnetische non-magnetic drill collar
Schwerstangenstabilisator m drill collar stabilizer
Schwestergruppe f sister group
Schwimmanalyse f s. Schlämmanalyse
Schwimmaufbereitung f floatation [concentration], froth floatation
Schwimmbagger m [floating] dredge[r]
schwimmen to float
Schwimmerpegel m float level gauge
schwimmfähig floatable
Schwimmfähigkeit f floatability
Schwimmgold n floating gold
Schwimmkran m floating crane
Schwimmsand m float (shifting, running, wet) sand, quicksand
Schwimmschuh m float shoe
Schwimm- und Sinkaufbereitung f sink and float separation
Schwindriß m s. Schwundriß
schwingen to vibrate, to oscillate
schwingend vibratory, oscillatory; ringy (seismics)
Schwinger m oscillator
Schwingerde f floating earth
Schwingkristall m oscillating crystal
Schwingkristallmethode f oscillating-crystal method
Schwingmoor n swing moor, trembling (quaking) bog, quagmire
Schwingsaitendehnungsmesser m vibrating-wire strain gauge
Schwingtisch m shaking (shaker) table
Schwingung f vibration, oscillation

~/gedämpfte damped vibration (oscillation)
schwingungsartig ringy (seismics)
Schwingungsbauch m vibration antinode (loop)
Schwingungsbewegung f movement of oscillation, oscillatory movement
Schwingungsdauer f period of oscillation, periodic time
Schwingungsempfänger m oscillating receiver
Schwingungsfrequenz f frequency of oscillation
Schwingungsmarke f vibration mark
Schwingungsrichtung f vibration direction
Schwingungsschreiber m vibrograph
Schwingungssender m oscillating transmitter
Schwingungsweite f amplitude
Schwingwiese f s. Schwingmoor
Schwitzwasser n condensation water
Schwundgebiet n wastage (dissipating) area (of a glacier)
Schwundriß m mud (desiccation) crack, reduction (contraction) fissure
Sclerotinit m sclerotinite (coal maceral)
Scolecodonten mpl scolecodonts
Scorzalith m scorzalite, (Fe, Mg)Al$_2$[OH | PO$_4$]$_2$
Seamanit m seamanite, Mn$_3$[PO$_4$ | BO$_3$] · 3H$_2$O
Searlesit m searlesite, NaB(SiO$_3$)$_2$ · H$_2$O
Sechseck n hexagon
Sechserkoordination f octahedral coordination
sechsflächig hexahedral, hexahedric
sechswertig hexavalent, sexivalent
Sechswertigkeit f hexavalence, sexivalence
sechszählig hexagonal, sixfold
sedentär sedentary
Sedentärboden m sedentary soil
Sedifluktion f sedifluction
~/endostratische intraformational corrugation (contortion folds), convolute bedding
Sediment n sediment
~/anemogenes anemogenic sediment
~/äolisches wind-deposited sediment, windborne sediment
~ aus eckigen Körpern sharpstone (< 2 mm)
~ aus Kalkalgen und Sapropel sapropel calc
~ aus Sapropel und Ton sapropel clay
~/ausgesondertes winnowed sediment
~/chemisches evaporite
~/diagenetisch verfestigtes consolidated sediment
~/entlastetes lightened sediment (by erosion)
~/euxinisches euxinic sediment
~/flyschoides flyschoid sediment
~/goldhaltig glazigenes reef wash
~ in Meteorkratern/verglastes impact slag
~/klassiertes graded sediment
~/klastisches clastic sediment, clasolite
~/lamellenförmig strukturiertes laminite
~/limnisches limnic sediment
~/lösungsverfestigtes exosolutional sediment
~/marines marine sediment

Sedimentrolle

~ mit schwachem Schiefergefüge/toniges immature shale
~ ohne makroskopische Schalenreste/marines aqueous desert
~/orogenes orogenic sediment
~/pelitisches pelitic sediment
~/plattig spaltendes flagstone
~/sich verdichtendes compacting sediment
~/suspendiertes suspensate
~/terrigenes terrigenous (terrigene) sediment
Sedimentanhäufung f/laterale depositional strike deposit
Sedimentanschwemmung f berm
sedimentär sedimentary
Sedimentärbrekzie f sedimentary breccia
Sedimentation f sedimentation (s.a. Ablagerung)
~/äolische aeolian sedimentation
~/aquatische aquatic sedimentation
~/extensive fluviatile Huangho sedimentation
~/fluviatile fluvial (fluviatile) sedimentation
~/fluvioglaziale fluvioglacial sedimentation
~/glaziale glacial sedimentation
~/gleichmäßige continuous sedimentation
~/interne internal sedimentation
~/kondensierte condensed deposition
~/limnische limnic sedimentation
~/marine marine sedimentation
~/reduzierte diastem (interruption of sedimentation)
~/rhythmische rhythmic sedimentation
~/vorherrschende dominant sedimentation
~/zyklische cyclic sedimentation
Sedimentationsablauf m sedimentary process
Sedimentationsanalyse f size analysis by sedimentation
Sedimentationsbecken n sedimentary (sedimentation) basin
Sedimentationsdynamik f ground-water flow in sedimentation basins
Sedimentationseinheit f sedimentation unit
Sedimentationsetappe f sedimentation stage
Sedimentationsfolge f sequence of strata (s.a. Schichtenfolge)
Sedimentationsgebiet n area of sedimentation, depositional (sedimentary) environment
Sedimentationsgefüge n depositional fabric
Sedimentationsgeschwindigkeit f rate of sedimentation (deposition)
Sedimentationslücke f hiatus
~/kleine diastem
Sedimentationsmodell n s. Ablagerungsmodell
Sedimentationsprobe f sedimentation test
Sedimentationsraum m s. Sedimentationsgebiet
Sedimentationsterrasse f depositional terrace
Sedimentationsumkehr f reverse by-passing of sedimentation
Sedimentationsunterbrechung f diastem
Sedimentationswasser n sedimentary water
Sedimentationswechsel m sedimentary change

Sedimentationszentrum n depocenter
Sedimentationszyklus m cycle of sedimentation, sedimentary cycle
sedimentaufnehmend geophagous (organisms)
Sedimentaustrag m an der Gletscherstirn overwash drift
Sedimentbank f an der Innenseite einer Mäanderschleife point-bar deposit
~ im Fluß channel-mouth bar
Sedimentbasis f interstitial matrix (between coarse grains)
Sedimentbecken n sedimentary basin
~/großes ungefaltetes geobasin
Sedimentbildung f s. Sedimentation
Sedimentblatt n in gradierten Sedimenten/strukturloses symmict structure
Sedimentboudinage f sedimentary boudinage structure (by sedifluction)
Sedimentdecke f sedimentary cover, blanket of sediment
Sedimentdiagenese f diagenesis of sediments
Sedimentdichte f bulk (natural) density
Sedimenteinheit f/durch ihre Fossilführung abgegrenzte isobiolith
~/durch ihre Lithologie abgegrenzte isogeolith
Sedimentfahne f sand shadow
sedimentführend sediment-bearing
Sedimentgefüge n/biogenes biogenic sedimentary structure (ichnology)
Sedimentgestein n sedimentary (stratified, bedded) rock, sedimentite
~/äolisches aeolianite
~/aquatisches aqueous rock
~/chemisches chemically deposited sedimentary rock
~/fluvioglaziales fluvioglacial sediment
~/glazigenes ice-borne sediment
~/küstenfern gebildetes thalassic rock
~/partiell metamorphes metasedimentary rock
sedimentieren to sedimentate
Sedimentierung f s. Sedimentation
Sedimentit n s. Sedimentgestein
Sedimentkern m sedimentary core
Sedimentkompaktion f [gravity] compaction of sediment
Sedimentkomplex m sedimentary complex
Sedimentlast f load (burden) of sediments
Sedimentmarke f hieroglyph in sediments
Sedimentologie f sedimentology
sedimentologisch sedimentological
Sedimentorium n s. Sedimentationsgebiet
Sedimentpartikel f sediment particle
Sedimentpetrografie f sedimentary petrography
sedimentpetrografisch sedimentary-petrographical
Sedimentrohr n sludge barrel
Sedimentrolle f flow roll, spiral (slump) ball, ball-and-pillow structure

Sedimentschlamm

Sedimentschlamm *m* detritus ooze
Sedimentstruktur *f* sedimentary fabric
Sedimenttransport *m* sediment transport
Sedimentverfestigung *f* [gravity] compaction; lithification *(generally for diagenesis, crystallization, fossilization)*
Sedimentwalze *f s.* Sedimentrolle
Sedimentzuwachs *m* aggradation [of sediments]
See *m* lake
~/abflußloser lake without outflow, imprisoned lake
~/eintrocknender evanescent lake
~/glazialer glacial lake
~ in einem toten Flußarm mortlake
~/kleiner lakelet
~/kleiner, natürlich gebildeter pondlet
~ mit Abfluß drainage (open) lake
~/periodischer seasonal (temporary, intermittent) lake
~/verlandeter extinct (filled) lake
~/zuflußloser dead lake
See *f* sea
~/hohe (offene) high (open, main) sea
~/überbrechende overfall
Seeablagerung *f* lake deposit (bed); sea drift
Seeasphalt *m* lake asphalt
Seebeben *n* submarine earthquake
~/vulkanisches submarine volcanic earthquake
Seebecken *n* lake basin
Seebildung *f* **innerhalb eines Wasserlaufs/natürliche** ponding
Seeboden *m* lake floor
Seebrise *f* onshore breeze
Seebuhne *f* beach groin, shore jetty
Seedeich *m* sea dike
Seedelta *n* lake delta
See-Erz *n* lake [iron] ore
Seegangsrippeln *fpl* oscillation ripples, wave ripple marks
Seegeophysik *f* marine geophysics
Seegras *n* sea grass, seaweed
Seegravimeter *n* shipboard gravity meter
Seegurke *f* sea cucumber
Seehöhe *f*/**mittlere** mean sea level
Seeigel *m* sea urchin
~/fossiler echinite
Seeigelstachel *mpl* echinoid spines
Seekarte *f* nautical (marine, naval) chart; hydrographic[al] map
Seeklima *n* marine (maritime, ocean) climate
Seekreide *f* lake marl, calcareous mud, bog lime
Seeküste *f* sea coast, seaboard
Seelandschaft *f* lake side, lake-land country
Seelilie *f* sea lily, [lily] crinoid
Seelilienkrone *f* crinoid head
Seelöwenguano *m* sea-lion guano
Seemarsch *f* marine (salt) marsh
Seemessungen *fpl* sea surveys
Seen *mpl*/**dystrophe** dystrophic lakes

Seenebel *m* sea fog
Seengebiet *n* lake district
Seenkette *f* chain (string) of lakes
Seenkunde *f* limnology
Seenplankton *n* lake plankton
Seenverlandung *f* lake filling
Seepegelmesser *m* limnimeter
Seepocken *fpl* balanids
Seesand *m* sea (beach) sand
Seeschlick *m* lake silt
Seesediment *n* lacustrine deposit
~/fossiles lake bed
Seeseismik *f* offshore seismics; marine seismic surveying
Seespiegel *m* lake surface (level)
~ im Maximum einer Transgression thalassocratic sea level
Seespiegelabsenkung *f* fluctuation of level in lake
Seestern *m* starfish, sea star
Seeströmung *f* lake current
Seetang *m* seaweed, fucus
~/angeschwemmter cast-up seaweed
Seeterrasse *f* lake terrace
Seeton *m* lacustrine clay
Seetorf *m* dy peat
Seeufer *n* lake shore, foreshore
Seewarte *f* marine (naval) observatory
seewärts forereef
Seewetterdienst *m* sea weather service
Seewind *m* onshore wind, ocean breeze
Seggenmoor *n* sedge moor
Seggentorf *m* sedge (carex) peat
Segmentalfurchen *fpl* facial grooves
Segregationsgang *m* segregated (exudation) vein
Seiche *f* seiche
seicht shallow, shoaly
Seichtwasser *n* shallow water
Seichtwassersee *m* shallow lake
Seichtwerden *n* shallowing
Seidenglanz *m* silk, silky lustre
Seidozerit *m* seidozerite, $Na_4MnTi(Zr, Ti)[O|(F, OH)|Si_2O_7]_2$
Seife *f* placer [deposit], alluvial deposit
~/äolische eolian placer, dry digging
~ auf Alluvialterrasse high-level placer
~/eluviale eluvial ore deposit
~/fluviatile alluvial ore deposit
~/fossile fossil placer
~/verdeckte buried placer
Seifen[ab]bau *m* placer mining, alluvial working
Seifenclaim *n*/**kleines** patch
Seifenerz *n* alluvial (diluvial, wash) ore
Seifenerzgewinnung *f* streaming
Seifengold *n* placer (alluvial, driftal, river) gold
Seifenlagerstätte *f* placer [deposit]
Seifenmaterial *n* alluvial diggings
Seifenmineral *n* placer mineral
Seifenstein *m s.* Saponit

Seifenwerk n alluvial washing [plant]
Seifenzinn n alluvial (stream) tin
seifig unctuous (rock)
seiger vertical, perpendicular, upright
Seigergang m rake vein
Seigerriß m vertical section
Seigersprung m vertical fault
Seigerteufe f vertical (perpendicular) depth
Seigerung f segregation
Seigerungserscheinungen fpl liquation phenomena
Seigerungsprodukt n segregate, cumulate
Seigerungsschichtung f graded bedding, didactic structure
Seigerungsstreifen m segregated band
Seilbohranlage f cable rig
Seilbohren n cable [tool] drilling
Seilfangspeer m wire line grab
Seilfangspirale wire line spiral fishing tool
Seilkernbohren n cable tool coring
Seilkernen n wire line coring
Seilkernrohr n cable core bit, retrievable (wire line) core barrel
Seilmesser m wire line
Seilschlagbohren n churn (Pennsylvanian) drilling
Seilschlagbohrgerät n churn drill
Seilstrang m line
Seiltrommel f reel
Seismik f [prospection] seismics; seismology
seismisch seism[ograph]ic, seism[ic]al
Seismizität f seismicity
seismogeologisch seismogeological
Seismograf m seismograph
Seismografenabstand m seismograph spacing
Seismografenaufstellung f seismograph spread
Seismogramm n seismogram, seismographic record
~/synthetisches synthetic seismogram
Seismologe m seismologist
Seismologie f seismology
seismologisch seismological
Seismometer n seismometer
~/elektromagnetisches electromagnetic seismometer
Seismometer npl/**gebündelte** bunched (grouped) seismometers
Seismometerabstand m seismometer spacing
Seismometeraufstellung f seismometer spread
Seismometerprofil n seismometer (seismic) profile
Seismoskop n seismoscope
Seismotektonik f seismotectonics
seismotektonisch seismotectonic
Seite f/**gehobene** heaved (uplifted) side (e.g. of a flexure)
Seiten/mit ungleichen inequilateral
Seitenabrutsch m sideslip
Seitenansicht f lateral view
Seitenausbruch m flank eruption
Seitenböschung f side slope

Selbstentzündung

Seitendruck m lateral pressure
Seitenerosion f lateral erosion
Seitenfläche f lateral face (of crystals)
Seitenfluß m lateral stream
Seitengang m branch gallery, by-lane
Seitengletscher m tributary glacier
Seitenkegel m lateral cone
Seitenkern m side wall core
Seitenkraftkomponente f lateral-force component
Seitenmoräne f lateral (border, marginal) moraine
seitennervig side-veined (palaeobotany)
Seitenrichtradar n side-looking radar
Seitenschub m lateral thrust (push, shoving)
Seitenseptum n alar septum (of corals)
Seitental n lateral (branch) valley
Seitentrum n branch of a vein, dropper
Seitenverschiebung f lateral shift (faulting), transverse thrust; shift (lateral shearing, strike) fault
~ durch Dehnung transform faulting (in the central region of the ocean ridge)
Seitenverschiebungssystem n transcurrent fault system
Seitenverstellung f offset
Seitenverwitterung f weathering back (of the slopes)
Sekretion f secretion
~/biologische biologic[al] secretion
Sektor m segment
sekundär secondary; neogenic (petrography)
Sekundäräste mpl second order of branches
Sekundärelektronenvervielfacher m secondary electron multiplier, photomultiplier [tube]
Sekundärentölung f secondary oil recovery
Sekundärfeld n/**elektromagnetisches** secondary electromagnetic field
Sekundärförderung f secondary recovery
Sekundärgefüge n secondary fabric
Sekundärgestein n secondary rock
Sekundärgewinnungsverfahren n **von Erdöl** petroleum secondary recovery, secondary recovery [method]
Sekundärpodsolboden m secondary podzolized soil
sekundärporphyrisch neoporphyric, neoporphyrocrystic
Sekundärquarzit m secondary (metasomatic) quartzite
Sekundärreflexion f ghost
Sekundärschichtung f secondary (indirect) stratification
Sekundärschieferung f refoliation
Sekundärstrahlung f secondary radiation
~/kosmische secondary cosmic radiation
Sekundärstruktur f secondary structure
Seladonit m seladonite, celadonite (Fe-, Mg-, K-silicate)
Selbstanzapfung f autocapture, self-capture
Selbstbestäubung f s. Autogamie
Selbstentzündung f spontaneous ignition

Selbsthemmung

Selbsthemmung f self-locking *(of props)*
Selbstionisation f autoionization
selbstregistrierend self-recording, self-registering
Selbstreinigung f self-purification
selbsttragend self-sustaining
Selbstumkehrung f self-reversal
Selbstversorgung f self-supply *(by water)*
Selektion f/**tektonische** selection by tectonic processes
selektiv selective
Selektivbestimmung f selective determination
Selektivfalte f selective fold
Selen n selenium, Se
Selenblei n s. Clausthalit
selenhaltig seleniferous
Selenit m selenite *(gypsum)*
Selenodäsie f selenodesy
Selenogeologie f selenogeology
Selenografie f selenography
selenografisch selenographic
Selenolith m selenolite, SeO_2
Selenologie f selenology
Selenotektonik f selenotectonics
selenozentrisch selenocentric
Selenwismutglanz m s. Guanajuatit
Seligmannit m seligmannite, $2PbS \cdot Cu_2S \cdot As_2S_3$
Sellait m sellaite, MgF_2
semiarid semiarid
Semifusinit m semifusinite *(coal maceral)*
Semifusit m semifusite *(coal microlithotype)*
semihumid semihumid
semiklastisch semiclastic
semikristallin hemicrystalline, merocrystalline
Semipodsol m semipodzol
semiterrestrisch semiterrestrial
Semivariogramm n semivariogram
Semivitrinit m semivitrinite *(coal maceral)*
Semseyit m semseyite, $9PbS \cdot 4Sb_2S_3$
Semurium n s. Sinemur
Senait m senaite, $(Fe^{..}, Fe^{...}, Mn, Pb)_2(Ti, Fe^{...})_5O_{12}$
Senarmontit m senarmontite, Sb_2O_3
Sender m transmitter
Senecan n Senecan [Series] *(Adorfian including the upper part of Givetian, North America)*
Sengierit m sengierite, $Cu_2[(OH)_2|(UO_2)_2|V_2O_8] \cdot 6H_2O$
Senkbrunnen m sunk well, cesspool
Senke f depression, depressed area, fault trough
~/**Aralo-Kaspische** Aralo-Caspian depression
~/**geochemische** geochemical negative anomaly
~/**intramontane** intramontane trough
~/**norddeutsch-polnische** North German-Polish depression
~/**vulkanotektonische** volcano-tectonic depression
senken/sich to subside
Senken n **des Hangenden** swag

Senkkasten m caisson
Senkkastengründung f foundation by caissons
senkrecht vertical, perpendicular, straight down
~ **zur Kluftfläche** on plane
Senkrechtaufnahme f vertical aerial photograph
Senkstoffablagerung f silt of precipitates
Senkung f 1. lowering; subsidence; decline; fall; 2. depression; hollow; declivity
~ **der Tagesoberfläche** crop fall
~/**isostatische** isostatic[al] settling
~/**säkulare** secular sinking
~/**tektonische** tectonic subsidence
Senkungsgebiet n depression area
Senkungsgeschwindigkeit f subsidence velocity, rate of subsidence
Senkungskurve f subsidence (recession) curve
Senkungsküste f depressed coast (shore line), coast (shore line) of submergence
Senkungsperiode f period of subsidence
Senkungssee m depression lake
Senkungstrichter m cone of depression
Senkungstrog m subsidence trough
Senkungsvorgang m process of subsidence
Senkungswanne f subsidence trough
Senkungswelle f subsidence wave
Senkungswinkel m depression angle
Senkungs-Zeit-Kurve f time-subsidence curve
Senkungszentrum n centre of subsidence
Senkungszone f zone (area) of subsidence
Senkwasser n gravitation water
Senon[ien] n [sensu D'Orbigny] Senonian *(Coniacian to Maastrichtian)*
Sensibilitätsanalyse f sensibility analysis, sensi[ti]vity analysis *(by the estimation of a project)*
Sensor m/**aktiver** active [remote] sensor
~/**passiver** passive [remote] sensor
Sensoreichung f sensor calibration
Sepiolith m sepiolite, $Mg_4[(OH)_2|Si_6O_{15}] \cdot 2H_2O + 4H_2O$
Septalgrube f fossula *(of corals)*
Septarie f septarium, septarian nodule
Septarienstruktur f septarian texture
Septen/mit septa-bearing
Sequanien n Sequanian *(facies development of upper Oxfordian in the Swiss Jura)*
Sequentialverfahren n sequential method
Sequenz f/**positive** fining upward sequence
Sérandit m serandite, $(Mn,Ca)_2Na[Si_3O_8OH]$
Serendibit m serendibite, $(Ca,Mg)_5(AlO)_5[BO_3|(SiO_4)_3]$
Serie f 1. series, division *(biostratigraphic unit)*; 2. suite, succession
~ **flacher Überschiebungen** shingle-block structure series
~/**stratigrafische** stratigraphic[al] column
Serienanalyse f serial analysis
Serienprobe f series sample
Serir m serir

Serizit *m* sericite *(dense muscovite)*
serizitisieren to sericitize
Serizitisierung *f* sericitization
Serizitphyllit *m* sericite phyllite
Serizitquarzit *m* sericite quartzite
Serizitschiefer *m* sericite slate
serokristallin hypocrystalline
serorogen serorogenic
Serpentin *m* serpentine, $Mg_6[(OH)_8|Si_4O_{10}]$
~/edler precious serpentine
~/gemeiner common serpentine
Serpentinasbest *m* serpentine asbestos
serpentinisieren to serpentinize
Serpentinisierung *f* serpentinization
Serpentinit *m* serpentinite, serpentine rock
Serpentinschiefer *m* serpentine schist
Serpierit *m* serpierite, $Ca(Cu,Zn)_4[(OH)_3|SO_4]_2 \cdot 3H_2O$
Serpophit *m* serpophite *(variety of serpentinite)*
Serpuchov-Stufe *f* Serpuchovian [Stage] *(uppermost Lower Carboniferous in East Europe)*
Serpuliden *fpl* serpulids
Serravil[ium] *n* Serravilian [Stage] *(of Miocene)*
Sesquioxid *n* sesquioxide
sessil sessile
Seston *n* seston
Setzarbeit *f s.* Setzen 2.
Setzdehnungsmesser *m* hand displacement meter
Setzdruck *m/erster* first weight
setzen to erect, to set *(props)*
~/Futterrohre to set casing
~/sich to subside
~/unter Wasser to flood, to down *(e.g. a mine)*
Setzen *n* 1. settling, consolidation; 2. jigging *(dressing)*
~ des Gebirges roof settlement
Setzkasten *m* jig, concentrator
Setzlast *f* settling load
Setzmaschine *f s.* Setzkasten
Setzriß *m* first (main roof) break
Setzung *f* settlement
~/fortschreitende progressive settlement
~ in Bergwerksgebieten mining subsidence
~/initiale first weight
~/ungleichmäßige differential settlement
Setzungsanalyse *f* settlement (settling) analysis
Setzungsklassierung *f* classification by settlement
~ durch Luft air classification
Setzungsmessung *f* settlement measurement
Setzungsunterschied *m* differential settlement
Setzungsvorgang *m* 1. process of settlement; 2. jigging action *(dressing)*
Setzwäsche *f* tub washing *(of ores)*
SEV *s.* Sekundärelektronenvervielfacher
Sevat[ium] *n* Sevatian [Substage] *(Upper Triassic, Tethys)*

Sexualdimorphismus *m* sexual dimorphism
s-Fläche *f/nicht verstellte* s-plane
Shackanit *m* shackanite *(analcite trachyte)*
Shandit *m* shandite, β-$Ni_3Pb_2S_2$
Sharpit *m* sharpite, $[UO_2|CO_3] \cdot H_2O$
Shastait *m* shastaite *(dacite)*
Shastalit *m* shastalite *(andesite glass)*
Shattuckit *m* shattuckite *(mineral of the dioptase group)*
Shermanien *n s.* Trenton
Sherwoodit *m* sherwoodite, $Ca_3[V_8O_{22}] \cdot 15H_2O$
Shoestring-Falle *f* shoestring trap
Shonkinit *m* shonkinite *(nepheline syenite)*
Shore-Härte *f* Shore hardness
Shortit *m* shortite, $Na_2Ca_2[CO_3]_3$
Shoshonit *m* shoshonite *(alkaline basalt)*
Sial *n* sial
sialisch sialic
siallitisch siallitic
Sibirskit *m* sibirskite, $Ca_2[B_2O_5] \cdot H_2O$
Sichel *f des Mondes* crescent of the moon
Sichelbruch *m s.* Sichelwanne
Sicheldüne *f* crescentic (crescent-shaped) dune, barchan
sichelförmig crescentic, sickle-shaped, falciform
Sichelwanne *f* gouge, friction crack *(glacial erosion)*
Sicherheitsbereich *m* safety zone
Sicherheitseinrichtungen *fpl* **am Bohrlochmund** well control equipment
Sicherheitsfaktor *m* safety factor
Sicherheitsgrenze *f* safety margin
Sicherheitsgurt *m* safety belt
Sicherheitskoeffizient *m* safety factor
Sicherheitslampe *f* safety lamp
Sicherheitsmaßnahmen *fpl* safety precautions
Sicherheitspfeiler *m* safety pillar
Sicherheitsseil *n* safety line
Sicherheitsventil *n* safety valve
Sicherheitsverbinder *m* safety joint
Sicherheitszone *f* safety zone
Sicherschüssel *f*, **Sichertrog** *m* [miner's] batea; bowl classifier
Sicherungsarbeiten *fpl* stabilizing workings
Sichsetzen *n s.* Setzung
Sichtbarkeitsgebiet *n* area of visibility
Sichtgerät *n* monitor
Sichtweite *f* range of visibility
Sickerbach *m* seepage runnel
Sickerdrainage *f* weep (blind) drain
Sickerfeld *n* infiltration field
Sickerfläche *f* seepage [sur]face, phreatic surface
Sickergeschwindigkeit *f* seepage rate, percolation velocity
Sickergraben *m* swamp ditch
Sickerkanal *m* percolation channel, canal with filter bed
Sickerlinie *f* seepage path, phreatic line
sickern to seep, to percolate, to leak

Sickerquelle

Sickerquelle f filtration spring
Sickerrate f percolation rate
Sickerschacht m recharge pit
Sickerstelle f swallow hole
Sickerstrecke f 1. infiltration gallery; 2. seepage face (distance), surface ground-water level distance; recharge distance *(in wells)*
Sickerströmung f seepage flow; [underground] seepage
Sickerung f percolation [creep], bleeding
Sickerverlust m leakage
Sickerwasser n drain[age] water, percolation (infiltration) water; gravitation water
~/austretendes seepage water
Sickerwasserdruck m seepage pressure *(per unit length)*; seepage force *(per unit volume)*
Sickerweg m infiltration routing, path of percolation
Sicklerit m sicklerite, $Li_{<1}(Mn, Fe)[PO_4]$
Sicula f sicula
Siderazot m siderazot[e], silvestrite *(telluric Fe_5N_2)*
Siderit m siderite, sparry (spathic) iron ore, $FeCO_3$
~/massiger siderite rock, iron carbonate
sideritisch sideritic
Siderolith m sider[aer]olite *(stony iron)*
Sideromelan m sideromelane *(vitreous basalt)*
Sideronatrit m sideronatrite, $Na_2Fe[OHI(SO_4)_2] \cdot 3H_2O$
siderophil siderophil[ic]
Siderophyr m siderophyre *(meteorite)*
Siderosphäre f siderosphere
Siderotil m siderotil, $Fe[SO_4] \cdot 5H_2O$
Siebanalyse f sieve (screen, grading) analysis
Siebdurchgang m screen underflow, duff
Siebdurchgangsdiagramm n cumulative direct plot of screen test
Siebdurchgangskurve f cumulative size distribution curve of the underflow
Siebdurchlauf m s. Siebdurchgang
sieben to sieve, to screen
siebenatomig heptatomic
Siebeneck n heptagon
siebenflächig heptahedral
Sieben-Sonden-Anordnung f *(Am)* seven-spot network
siebenwertig heptavalent, septivalent
Siebenwertigkeit f heptavalence, septivalence
Siebfeines n [screen] undersize, siftings, duff
Siebgrobes n [screen] oversize, coarse of screen
Siebgut n material to be graded
Siebkennlinie f gradation limit
Siebklassierung f screening, screen classifying (grading)
Siebkurve f [aggregate] grading curve, grain-size distribution curve, particle-size distribution curve
~/einfache direct plot of screen test
Sieblinie f s. Siebkurve

Siebrückstand m sieve residue
Siebrückstandsdiagramm n cumulative direct plot of screen test
Siebstruktur f sieve (diablastic) texture
Siebtextur f poikiloblastic structure
Siebvorrichtung f screening device
Sieden n/**retrogrades** retrograde boiling
Siedepunkt m boiling point
Siedlungsort m biotope
Siegelerde f bole
Siegen n, **Siegénien** n Siegenian [Stage] *(of Devonian)*
Siegenit m siegenite, $(Co, Ni)_3S_4$
Siegenium n s. Siegen
Sienaerde f Siena [earth]
Siggeis n frazil [ice]
Sigillarien npl Sigillaria
Sigloit m sigloite, $FeAl_2[O|PO_4]_2 \cdot 8H_2O$
sigmoidal sigmoidal, S-shaped
Sigmoidalfalte f sigmoidal fold
Sigmoidalklüftung f longitudinal slab joints
Sigmoide f sigmoidal fold
Signaleinrichtung f alarm
Signalkorrektur f signal correction
Signal-Rausch-Verhältnis n signal-to-noise ratio, SNR
Signaltrennung f demultiplexing
Signalverbesserung f signal enhancement
Signatur f conventional sign; signature
Silber n silver, Ag
~/dendritisches moss silver
~/gediegenes native silver
~/goldhaltiges dore silver
silberähnlich argentine
Silberamalgam m mercury argental, α-(Ag,H)
Silberantimonglanz m s. Miargyrit
silberartig argentine
Silbererz n silver ore
Silbererzlagerstätte f silver deposit
silberführend argentiferous
Silberglanz m argentite, acanthite, Ag_2S
Silberglätte f silver litharge
Silberhalogen n halide of silver
silberhaltig argentic; argentiferous
Silberhornerz n s. Chlorargyrit
Silberkupferglanz m s. Stromeyerit
silbern argentic
silberreich highly argentiferous
silbrig argent
Siles n Siles[ian] [Series, Epoch] *(s. a. Oberkarbon 1.)*
Silex n silex
Silexknolle f chert nodule
Silicomagnesiofluorit m silicomagnesiofluorite, $Ca_4Mg_3H_2F_{10}Si_2O_7$
Silifikation f, **Silifizierung** f silicatization, silicating; silicification
Silikaklastika n siliciclastics
Silikastein m silica brick
Silikat n silicate
Silikat-Eisen-Meteorit m siderolite, syssiderite
Silikatgestein n silicate rock

Silikatkruste *f* silicate crust
Silikatphase *f* silicate phase
Silikoflagellaten *mpl* silicoflagellates
Silizifikat *n* silicified material
Silizium *n* silicon, Si
Siliziumdioxid *n* silica, SiO_2
Siliziumkarbid *n* carbide of silicon, carborundum
Sill *m* sill
Sillénit *m* sillénite, $\gamma\text{-}Bi_2O_3$
Sillimanit *m* sillimanite, Al_2SiO_5
Sillimanitgneis *m* sillimanite gneiss
Silt *m* silt *(0,05–0,005 mm)*
Silt-Sommerlage *f* summer silt *(of varves)*
Siltstein *m* siltstone, siltite
~/kalkhaltiger calcareous siltstone
Silur *n* Silurian [System] *(chronostratigraphically;* Silurian [Period] *(geochronologically);* Silurian [Age] *(common sense)*
Silurperiode *f* Silurian [Period]
Silursystem *n* Silurian [System]
Silurzeit *f* Silurian [Age]
Silvestrit *m* silvestrite, siderazot[e] *(telluric Fe_5N_2)*
Sima *n* sima
simatisch simatic
Simonellit *m* simonellite, $C_{15}H_{20}$
Simplotit *m* simplotite, $CaV_4O_9 \cdot 5H_2O$
Simpsonit *m* simpsonite, $Al_4Ta_3(O_{13}OH)$
Simsentorf *m* bulrush peat
Simulationsmethode *f* method of images *(ground-water flow)*
Simulationsmodell *n (Am)* model of simulation *(reservoir mechanics)*
Simultanbearbeitung *f* time sharing
Simultanbohren *n* simultaneous drilling
Sincosit *m* sincosite, $Ca[V(OH)_2|PO_4]_2 \cdot 3H_2O$
Sinemur[ien] *n*, **Sinemurium** *n* Sinemurian [Stage], Lotharingian [Stage] *(of Lower Jurassic)*
Singing *n* singing
Single-shot-Gerät *n* single-shot-photoclinometer
Sinhalit *m* sinhalite, $MgAlBO_4$
Sinium *n* Sinian *(Late Precambrian in China)*
Sinkanalyse *f s.* Schlämmanalyse
Sinken n des Hochwassers flood decline
~ des Wasserstands level decrease
Sinkgeschwindigkeit *f* sinking (settling) velocity
Sinkstoffe *mpl* water-borne sediments *(s.a.* Schweb, Flußtrübe)
Sinkstoffgehalt *m* stream-borne materials discharge
Sinkströmung *f* down structure flow
Sinoit *m* sinoite, Si_2N_2O *(meteoric mineral)*
Sinter *m* sinter
Sinterablagerung *f* sinter deposit
Sinterbecken *n* rimstone pool
Sinterbildung *f* sinter formation
Sinterblähton *m* sintered expanded clay
Sinterdamm *m* rimstone bar

Sinterkalk *m* calc-sinter
Sinterkiesel *m* fioryte
Sinterkruste *f* sinter incrustation
sintern to sinter; to vitrify
Sinterterrasse *f* sinter terrace
Sinterung *f* sintering; vitrification
Sintervorhang *m* curtain
Sintflut *f* Deluge of Noah
Sinus *m* sinus *(bay on Mars or moon)*
Sinusfalte *f* sinusoidal fold
Sipho *m* siphuncle
Siphonalausscheidungen *fpl* siphonal deposits *(cephalopodans)*
Siphonaldüte *f* septal neck *(cephalopodans)*
Siphonquelle *f* siphon spring
Sippe *f* suite, tribe, kindred
~/atlantische Atlantic suite
~/mediterrane Mediterranean suite
~/pazifische Pacific suite
Sirius *m* canicula
Sitaparit *m* sitaparite, $(Mn, Fe)_2O_3$
Situationsplan *m* site plan, *(Am)* location plan
Situationsskizze *f* layout plan, site sketch, *(Am)* location sketch
sitzen/auf den Schlechten to work with the cleats lying back
~/unter den Schlechten to work with the cleats lying forward
Sjerosjom *m* serozemic soil
Sjögrenit *m* sjögrenite, $Mg_6Fe_2[(OH)_{16}|CO_3] \cdot 4H_2O$
Skala *f/***geochronologische** geochronological scale
skalar scalar
Skalenoeder *n* scalenohedron
Skandik *m* Scandic [Ocean]
Skandium *n* scandium, Sc
Skapolith *m* scapolite, dipyre *(mixed crystal of meionite and marialite)*
Skapolithisierung *f* scapolitization, dipyrization
Skarn *m* skarn, scarn, calc-silicate marble, calc-silicate hornfels, calciphyre
Skarnerzlagerstätte *f* skarn deposit
Skarnisierung *f* skarnization
Skarnpyroxen *m* skarn pyroxene
Skelett *n* skeleton
~/artikuliertes articulated skeleton
~/aus dem Verband gelöstes disarticulated skeleton
~ im Zusammenhang articulated skeleton
Skelettboden *m* skeletal (skeleton) soil
Skelettelemente *npl* skeletal elements
Skelettfasern *fpl* skeletal strands
skelettförmig skeletal
Skelettfragmente *npl* skeletal debris
Skelettkristall *m* skeleton crystal
Skelettreste *mpl* skeletal remains
~/abgeworfene exuviae
Skelettstruktur *f* skeleton structure
Skemmatit *m* skemmatite *(aggregate of psilomelane and polianite)*

Skiagit

Skiagit *m* skiagite *(garnet end member)*
Skiddaw-Schiefer *m* Skiddavian Slate *(group, Tremadocian to Llanvirnian)*
Skineffekt *m* skin effect
Skleroblasten *mpl* scleroblasts *(bone, spiculae producing cells)*
Skleroklas *m s.* Sartorit
Sklerometer *n* sclerometer
Sklerosphäre *f* sclerosphere
Sklerotisation *f* sclerotization
Sklodowskit *m* sklodowskite, chinkolobwite, $MgH_2[UO_2|SiO_4]_2 \cdot 5H_2O$
S-Kluft *f* S-joint, longitudinal joint
Skolezit *m* scolecite, $Ca[Al_2Si_3O_{10}] \cdot 3H_2O$
Skorodit *m* scorodite, $Fe^{\cdots}[AsO_4] \cdot 2H_2O$
Skulptur *f* 1. surface (bedding plane) marking *(depositional fabric)*; 2. sculpture, ornamentation *(palaeontology)*
~/gitterartige reticulation
skulpturieren to sculpture, to carve *(by erosion)*
Skutterudit *m* skutterudite, $CoAs_3$
Skyth *n* Skythian [Stage] *(of Triassic)*
Slavikit *m* slavikite, $Fe[OH|SO_4] \cdot 8H_2O$
Slingram-Verfahren *n* horizontal electromagnetic method
Smaltin *m* smaltite, smaltine, gray cobalt, $CoAs_2$
Smaragd *m* smaragd, emerald *(green variety of beryl)*
smaragdfarben smaragdine, emeraldine
smaragdgrün emerald green
Smaragdit *m* smaragdite *(actinolite-like amphibole)*
Smaragdspat *m* amazonite, microcline, green feldspar
Smektit *m s.* Montmorillonit
Smithit *m* smithite, $Ag_2S \cdot As_2S_3$
Smithsonit *m* smithsonite, zinc spar, $ZnCO_3$
Sobralit *m s.* Pyroxmangit
Sockel *m* basement
Soda *f* soda, natron, $NaCO_3 \cdot 10H_2O$
Sodaboden *m* soda soil
Sodalith *m* sodalite, $Na_8[Cl_2(AlSiO_4)_6]$
Soddyit *m* soddyite, $(UO_2)_{15}[(OH)_{20}|Si_6O_{17}] \cdot 8H_2O$
Soffione *f* soffione
Sog *m* 1. wake; undertow; 2. suction
Sohlbanktyp *m* **eines klastischen Zyklus** fining upward sequence
Sohlblatt *n* toe set
Sohldruck *m* base pressure
Sohle *f* bottom, floor *(of an adit)*; base surface *(of a layer)*; underlier, horizon *(of a working)*
~/undurchlässige impervious sole
Sohlenauftrieb *m* floor swelling
Sohlenaufwölbung *f* floor pressure arch
Sohlenausgasung *f* floor emission
Sohlenbreite *f* bottom width
Sohlendruck *m* bottom-hole pressure
~/statischer shut-in formation pressure

Sohlendruckmeßgerät *n* bottom-hole pressure gauge
Sohlenfließdruck *m* bottom-hole flow[ing] pressure, flowing formation pressure
Sohlengewölbe *n* floor pressure arch
Sohlenhebung *f* floor heave (lift)
Sohlenhöhe *f* height of level
Sohlenquellung *f* floor swelling
Sohlenschließdruck *m* shut-in bottom-hole pressure
Sohlenstrecke *f* level gangway
Sohlenströmung *f* bottom current
Sohlental *n* flood-plain valley
Sohlentemperatur *f* bottom-hole temperature
Sohlenwasserdruck *m* uplift (foundation water) pressure
Sohlenwassertrieb *m* bottom water drive
Sohlfläche *f* base, subface [of stratum]
söhlig bottomed, aclinal, aclinic, horizontal
~/nicht unlevelled
Söhligbohrung *f* horizontal hole
Sohlmarke *f* sole mark
Sohlpressung *f* base pressure
Sohlquellen *n s.* Sohlenhebung
Sohlrisse *mpl* floor breaks
Sohlstrecke *f*, **Sohlvortrieb** *m* bottom heading, level drift
Söhngeit *m* soehngeite, $Ga(OH)_3$
Sol *n* sol *(mineral in solution)*
~/ausgeflocktes flocculated sol
solar solar
Solarkonstante *f* solar constant
Solarmaterie *f* solar matter
solar-terrestrisch solar-terrestrial
Solbad *n* salt-water bath
Solbrunnen *m* salt well
Sole *f* [salt] brine
~/fossile fossilized brine
Solebohrung *f* brine well
solehaltig briny
Solerohr *n* brine pipe *(in salt caverns)*
Soleverdampfer *m* brine evaporator
Solfatare *f* solfatara
~/saure acid solfatara
~/ständige permanent solfatara
~/temporäre temporary solfatara
Solfatarenfeld *n* solfatara field
Solfatarenhügel *m* solfatara mound
Solfatarentätigkeit *f* solfataric action (activity)
Solifluktion *f* solifluction, soil flow, slow creeping of wet soil
Solifluktionsmasse *f* solifluction mass
Solifluktionstasche *f* solifluction pocket
Solifluktionsterrasse *f* solifluction terrace
Solitär *m* solitaire
Soll *n* kettle hole; morainic lake
Solod *m/grauer* gray solodic soil
Solodierung *f* solodization
Solone[t]z *m* black alkali soil *(with more than 1–3 % salt)*
~/schwarzer kara
solone[t]zartig solonetzlike, solonetzic

Solontschak *m s.* **Solone[t]z**
Solquelle *f* saline (salt, brine) spring
~/in Ausbeutung stehende brine pit
Solstitialpunkt *m* solstitial point
Solstitium *n* solstice
Solvan *n* Solvan [Stage] *(of Cambrian)*
Sommait *m* sommaite *(leucite-monzonite)*
Sommakrater *m* somma crater
Sommavulkan *m* somma volcano
Sommawall *m* somma ring
Sommerhochwasser *n* summer flood
Sommermonsun *m* summer monsoon
Sommerschichtung *f* summer stratification
Sommersolstitium *n,* **Sommersonnenwende** *f* summer solstice, midsummer
Sommerwasserstand *m* summer water level
Sonde *f* 1. bore, hole; 2. probe, sonde, well; 3. potential electrode *(geoelectrics)*
~/erschöpfte dead well
~/freie open hole
~/gedrosselt fließende well flowing under back pressure control
~/gekolbte swabbing well
~/geschlossene closed-in well
~/selbsttätig ausfließende natural flowing well
~/torpedierte shot hole
~/unverrohrte open hole
~/verwässerte well gone to water
~/vorübergehend geschlossene temporarily shut-in well
~/wild eruptierende wild (blowing) well
~ zur elektrischen Bohrlochmessung electrical [logging] sonde
Sondenbrand *m* well fire
Sondengas *n* casing-head gas
Sondenprobe *f* spoon sample
Sondenrammung *f* driver probing
Sondentechnik *f* probe technique
Sondenzahl *f/***optimale** optimum number of boreholes
Sonderung *f/***gravitative** gravitative sorting
Sondierstollen *m* exploration tunnel, trial heading
Sondierung *f/***elektrische** electrical sounding
~/geoelektrische geoelectric[al] sounding
Sondierungsbohrung *f* probing of a bore
Sondierungskurven *fpl* sounding graphs
Soniclog *n* sonic log[ging]
Sonne *f* sun
~/fleckenarme quiet sun
~/gestörte disturbed sun
~/ruhige quiet sun
Sonnenatmosphäre *f* solar atmosphere
Sonnenaufgang *m* sunrise
Sonnenbahn *f* orbit (path) of the sun, ecliptic
Sonnenbestrahlung *f* sun irradiation, irradiation by solar rays
Sonnenbewegung *f* sun's motion
Sonneneinstrahlung *f* insolation, solar irradiation
Sonnenenergie *f* solar energy (power)

Sonnenerhebungswinkel *m* sun elevation angle
Sonneneruption *f* solar eruption (flare)
Sonnenferne *f* aphelion
Sonnenfernrohr *n* helioscope
Sonnenfinsternis *f* solar eclipse, sun's blackout
~/partielle partial solar eclipse
~/totale total solar eclipse
Sonnenfleck *m* sunspot
Sonnenfleckenaktivität *f* sunspot activity
Sonnenfleckengruppe *f* sunspot group
Sonnenfleckenhäufigkeit *f* frequency of sunspots
Sonnenfleckenperiode *f* sunspot period
Sonnenfleckenrand *m* penumbra
Sonnenfleckenzahl *f/***relative** relative sunspot number
Sonnenfleckenzyklus *m* sunspot cycle
sonnengehärtet sun-baked
Sonnengezeiten *pl* solar tides
Sonnenhof *m* solar corona
Sonnenhöhe *f* sun's altitude
Sonneninneres *n* sun's interior
Sonnenjahr *n* solar year
Sonnenkorona *f* solar (sun's) corona
Sonnenlicht *n* sunlight
sonnenlos sunless
Sonnenmagnetismus *m* solar (sun's) magnetism
Sonnenmesser *m* heliometer
Sonnennähe *f* perihelion
Sonnenoberfläche *f* solar surface
Sonnenprotuberanz *f* solar prominence
Sonnenradius *m* solar radius
Sonnenscheibe *f* solar (sun's) disk
Sonnenschein *m* sunlight
Sonnenscheinautograf *m* heliograph
Sonnenseite *f* sunny side
Sonnenspektrum *n* solar spectrum
Sonnenspiegelung *f* superior mirage
Sonnenstrahl *m* sunray
Sonnenstrahlung *f* solar radiation
Sonnenstrahlungsmesser *m* solarimeter, pyrheliometer
Sonnenstrahlungsmessung *f* pyrheliometry
Sonnensystem *n* solar system
Sonnentag *m* solar day
~/mittlerer mean solar day
~/wahrer apparent solar day
Sonnentätigkeitsperiode *f* solar activity period
Sonnentemperaturmesser *m* heliothermometer
Sonnenuntergang *m* sunset
Sonnenwende *f* solstice
Sonnenwendepunkt *m* solstitial point
Sonnenwind *m* solar wind
Sonnenzeit *f* solar time
~/mittlere mean solar time
~/wahre apparent solar time
Sonolith *m* sonolite, $Mn_9[(OH, F)_2 | SiO_4]_4$
Sonomait *m* sonomaite, $Mg_3Al_2[SO_4]_6 \cdot 33H_2O$

Sonoprobe 290

Sonoprobe f sonoprobe
Sorosilikat n sorosilicate
Sorotiit m sorotiite *(siderolite)*
Sorption f sorption
Sorptionswasser n pellicular water
sortiert [as]sorted; graded
~/gut poorly graded *(prevailing one grain size)*
~/schlecht 1. ill sorted; 2. well graded *(all grain sizes present)*
Sortiertisch m sorting table
Sortiertrommel f sizing trommel
Sortierung f [as]sorting, grading
~/rohe ragging
Sortierungsgrad m sorting index
Sortierungskoeffizient m sorting coefficient
Souxit m s. Hydro-Cassiterit
Souzalith m souzalite, $(Mg, Fe^{\cdot\cdot})_3 (Al, Fe^{\cdot\cdot\cdot})_4[(OH)_3|(PO_4)_2]_2 \cdot 2H_2O$
Spallation f spallation
Spalt m gap; fissure *(of the soil)*; crevice, scissure; split, cleft, break, fracture, paraclase *(of a rock)*; crevasse *(of a glacier)*
~/enger confined space
~/gefüllter infilled fissure
~/klaffender gaping fissure
~/kleiner cranny
~/offener open joint
~/schwebender bathroclase, bottom joint
~/verdeckter blind joint
~/wasserführender water vein
Spaltausfüllung f fissure occupation
spaltbar fissile; cleavable *(crystals)*
~/nur in einer Richtung axotomous
~/parallel zur Basis acrotomous
~/uncharakteristisch heterotomous
Spaltbarkeit f fissility; splitting; cleavability, cleavage *(of crystals)*
~/deutliche distinct (easy) cleavage
~/kubische cubic cleavage
~/mit deutlicher eutomous
~/mit unvollkommener dystomic
~/oktaedrische octahedral cleavage
~ parallel zur Seitenfläche lateral cleavage
~/pseudokubische pseudocubic cleavage
~/rhomboedrische rhombohedral cleavage
~/schlechte poor cleavage
~/undeutliche (unvollkommene) indistinct (imperfect) cleavage
~/vollkommene perfect cleavage
Spaltbildung f fissuring
Spaltbruch m fracture cleavage
Spalte f s. Spalt
Spaltebene f cleavage face
~/schräge clinoclase
spalten to fissure, to split; to cleave *(crystals)*; to septate *(septaria)*
~ nach to cleave (split) along
~/sich to chap
Spaltenanordnungen fpl fracture patterns
Spaltenausbiß m fissure outcrop
Spaltenausbruch m fissure (labial) eruption

Spaltenbildung f fissuring; formation of clefts; crevassing *(glaciers)*
~ mit Verwerfung fissuring with dislocation
spaltend/rechtwinklig orthoclastic
~/schiefwinklig oblique-angled dividing
Spaltenerguß m fissure effusion
Spalteneruption f fissure (labial) eruption
Spaltenfrost m ice wedging; congelifraction
Spaltenfrostverwitterung f frost weathering, frost shattering
Spaltenfrostwirkungen fpl nivation
Spaltenfüllung f fissure (joint) filling
Spaltenfumarole f fissure fumarole
Spaltengang m fissure vein
Spaltenhöhle f fissure cave
Spaltenlagerstätte f crevice deposit
Spaltenöl n crevice oil
Spaltenquelle f fracture (fissure) spring, rock fracture (fissure) spring
Spaltensystem n system of cracks
Spaltenwasser n fissure (joint, crevice, crack) water
Spalter m demulsifying chemical
Spaltfestigkeit f cleavage strength
Spaltfläche f cleavage [sur]face, cleavage plane, cleat face
~/zur Verwerfung gleichlaufende slip (shear) cleavage
Spaltform f cleavage form
Spaltglimmer m laminated mica
spaltig creviced; crevassed *(glaciers)*
Spaltkorrosion f crevice corrosion
Spaltlänge f gap length
Spaltmaterial n fissile (fissionable fuel) material
Spaltplatte f book *(quality of mica)*
Spaltprodukt n fission product
~ des Muttermagmas diaschistic rock
~/radioaktives radioactive fission product
Spaltrhomboeder n cleavage rhombohedron
Spaltrichtung f direction of fissures
Spaltriß m cleavage crack (fissure, line)
Spaltspur f [fossil] track
Spaltspurenmethode f fission-track method *(bei der radioaktiven Altersbestimmung)*
Spaltstoff m fissile fuel
Spaltung f 1. fissuring; cleavage *(of crystals)*; splitting; [nuclear] fission; 2. reforming *(of natural gas)*
~/unvollkommene parting *(of crystals)*
Spaltungsebene f cleavage plane
~/glatte self-faced cleavage plane
Spaltungsrhomboeder n cleavage rhombohedron
Spaltweite f gap width
Spaltwinkel m cleavage angle
Spangolith m spangolite, $Cu_6Al[(OH)_{12}|Cl|SO_4] \cdot 3H_2O$
Spannanker m anchorage fixture
Spannkopf m chuck
Spannkraft f **des Bodens** tensile strength of soil

Spannung f stress; tension
~/innere internal stress
~/latente latent (residual) stress
~/spezifische unit stress
~/zulässige allowable stress
Spannungsabfall m stress drop
Spannungsabweichung f deviator stress
Spannungsanhäufung f bulb pressure, stress concentration
Spannungsanreicherung f concentration (accumulation) of stress
Spannungsauslösung f stress release
Spannungs-Dehnungs-Beziehung f stress-strain relation
Spannungs-Dehnungs-Diagramm n stress-strain diagram, tensile test diagram
Spannungsdeviator m stress deviator
Spannungsfeld n stress field
Spannungsfreisetzung f stress release*
Spannungsgefälle n stress gradient
Spannungsgleiche f s. Isostate
Spannungsgrad m degree of tension
Spannungskomponente f stress component
Spannungskreis m/**Mohrscher** Mohr's stress circle
Spannungsoptik f photoelasticity
spannungsoptisch photoelastic
Spannungsrelaxation f stress relaxation
Spannungsriß m tension crack
Spannungstensor m stress tensor
Spannungstrajektorien fpl stress trajectories
Spannungsüberlagerung f superposition of stresses
Spannungsverteilung f stress distribution (pattern)
Spannungszonung f tension zoning
Spannungszustand m stress condition, state of stress
~/dreiachsiger triaxial stress
~/ebener plane state of stress
~/räumlicher general state of stress
~/zweiachsiger biaxial stress
Spannweite f span (of pressure arch); apices distance (of folds)
Spannweitenbelastung f span loading
Sparagmit m sparagmite
Sparit m sparite, sparry calcite
~ mit Ooiden >1 mm/**oolithischer** oosparrudite
~/oolithischer oosparite
Sparnac[ien] n, **Sparnacium** n Sparnacian [Stage] (of Palaeocene)
Sparren m spar
Sparsamkeitsregel f parsimony rule
Sparwerkstoff m critical material
Spastoide npl spastolites (deformed ovoids)
Spat m spar
spatartig spathic, spathose, sparry
Spätdiagenese f late diagenesis
spätdiagenetisch late diagenetic
Spateisenstein m sparry iron, siderite, $FeCO_3$
~/kohlehaltiger black band

spatförmig s. spatartig
spätglazial late glacial
spathaltig spathic, spathose, sparry
spatig spathiform, spathic, spathose, sparry
Spatiopyrit m s. Safflorit
spätjurassisch Late Jurassic
spätmagmatisch deuteric
spätorogen late orogenic
Spätpaläozoikum n Neopal[a]eozoic [Period]
Spätpräkambrium n Neocryptozoic [Era]
Spätreife f advanced maturity
spättektonisch epitectonic
spätvariszisch Late Varisc[i]an
Speckstein m soapstone, lard stone, lardite, steatite, $Mg_3[(OH)_2|Si_4O_{10}]$
~/chinesischer Chinese soapstone
specksteinartig steatitic
Specktorf m black fuel peat
Specularit m specularite, specular (rhombohedral) iron ore, haematite, Fe_2O_3
Speerkies m spear pyrite (variety of marcasite)
Speicher m reservoir bed
~ für mehrere Jahre carry-over storage
~/klüftig-poröser jointable-porous reservoir
~/ölnasser oil-wet reservoir
~/zerklüfteter fractured reservoir
Speicherabdeckung f reservoir seal
Speicherbecken n storage basin
Speichereigenschaften fpl storage properties
~ in situ in situ reservoir properties
Speichereigenschaftserkennung f reservoir parameter identification
Speichereinschätzung f formation evaluation
Speichererkundung f exploration of the reservoir
Speicherflüssigkeit f reservoir fluid
Speichergasverlust m loss in gas storage
Speichergestein n reservoir (carrier, container, source) rock, pay sand
~/chemisches chemical reservoir rock
~/klastisches clastic reservoir rock
Speichergesteinsschicht f carrier bed
Speicherhöhe f/**nutzbare** closure
Speicherhorizont m reservoir horizon
Speicherinhalt m (Am) inventory
Speicherkapazität f storage capacity
Speicherkoeffizient m storage coefficient (aquifer)
Speichermächtigkeit f sand thickness
Speichermethode f storage method (radioactive dating)
Speichermodell n reservoir simulator (model)
Speichermodellierung f simulation of reservoir
Speicherschädigung f damage at well bore (in the near of a borehole)
Speicherschicht f reservoir stratum
Speicherumstellung f conversion of storage
Speicherundichtheit f leakage of storage
Speicherung f storage
Speicherverbreitung f reservoir hold-out

Speichervermögen 292

Speichervermögen n storage capacity
Speichervolumen n reservoir storage; reservoir capacity
Speichervolumen-Ergänzungsmengen-Verhältnis n capacity-inflow ratio of reservoirs
Speicherwegsamkeit f routing through reservoirs
Speicherzyklus m storage cycle
speisen to feed
Speisewasser n feed water
Speisewasseraufbereitung f feed water make-up
Speiskobalt m smaltite, smaltine, gray cobalt, $CoAs_2$
~/gestrickter netted (reticulated) smaltite, $CoAs_3$
Speisung f **durch Gletscherschmelzwasser** alimentation by glaciers
~ durch Schneeschmelzwasser alimentation by snowmelt
Speisungsfaktor m alimentation factor (ground water)
Spektralanalyse f spectrum (spectrographic, spectroscopical) analysis, spectrology
spektralanalytisch spectroanalytic
Spektralband n spectral band
Spektralband-Quotientenbildung f band rationing
Spektralfotometer n spectrophotometer
Spektralfotometrie f/grobe abridged spectrophotometry
Spektralkohleerzeugnis n spectral carbon product
Spektrallinie f spectral line
Spektrallinienverbreiterung f broadening of line
Spektralmerkmal n s. Spektralsignatur
Spektralmessung f spectral measurement
Spektralsignatur f spectral signature (e.g. of remote sensing object)
Spektrenauswertung f evaluation of spectra
Spektrograf m spectrograph
Spektrohelioskop n spectrohelioscope
Spektrometer n spectrometer
~/Braggsches Bragg spectrometer
Spektroskop n spectroscope
Spektroskopie f spectroscopy
spektroskopisch spectroscopic[al]
Spektrum n spectrum
~/elektromagnetisches electromagnetic spectrum
Speläologie f spelaeology
Spencerit m spencerite, $Zn_2[OH|PO_4] \cdot 1^1/_2H_2O$
Spergenit m spergenite (carbonate rock with fragments of fossils)
Sperre f seal
Sperrfilter n notch filter
Sperrfrequenz f cut-off [frequency]
sperrig bulky
Sperrmauer f barrage dam
Sperrylith m sperrylite, $PtAs_2$

Spessartin m spessartine, spessartite, partschinite, $Mn_3Al_2[SiO_4]_3$
Spezialfalten fpl special folds
Spezialisierung f/geochemische geochemical specialization
Spezialkarte f/geologische detailed geological map
Spezialkartierung f special mapping
Spezies f species
Sphaerit m sphaerite (s.a. Variscit)
Sphaerokobaltit m sphaerocobaltite, cobaltocalcite, $CoCO_3$
Sphaerosiderit m spherosiderite, argillaceous ironstone, clay ironstone, iron clay; clay band (in concretionary layers)
Sphagnum n sphagnum, bog moss
Sphagnumtorf m moor peat
Sphalerit m sphalerite, zinc blende, false galena, α-ZnS
Sphäre f sphere
~/geochemische geochemical sphere
sphärisch spherical
Sphärit m s. Sphärolith
Sphäroid n spheroid
sphäroidisch spheroidal; orbicular
Sphärokristall m sph[a]erocrystal
Sphärolith m spherulite, sph[a]erolite
sphärolithisch spherulitic, sph[a]erolitic, spherophyric, globuliferous
Sphen m sphene, $CaTi[O|SiO_4]$
Sphenolith m sphenolith
Spiculit m spicular chert (s.a. Spongolit)
~/poröser spiculite, spicularite
Spiegel m polished surface, fault striations, slickensiding (tectonical)
Spiegelabsenkung f water level decrease
spiegelbildlich homologous
Spiegelbohrung f image well
Spiegelebene f mirror plane, reflection plane (of a crystal)
Spiegeleisscholle f glare ice
Spiegelerhebung f banked-up water level
Spiegelgefälle n fall of level, loss of head (of water)
Spiegelkompaß m mirror compass, Brunton [compass]
Spiegelpunkt m mirror point
Spiegelschwankung f variation (fluctuation) of level
Spiegelung f reflection
Spiegelungsfläche f reflection plane (of crystals)
Spielart f variety
Spielraum m zwischen Bohrlochwand und Gestänge hole clearance
Spiere f spar
Spilit m spilite (albite basalt)
spilitisch spilitic
Spill n cathead
Spillseil n spinning rope
Spilosit m spilosite (contact metamorphic rock)

Spilsby-Sandstein *m* sandstone *(sandstone of Upper Jurassic and Lower Cretaceous age in eastern England)*
Spindel *f* spindle-shaped bomb
Spindelachse *f* mesotergum *(of fossil tests)*
Spindelbohrgerät *n* spindle-type drilling rig
spindelförmig spindle-shaped, fusiform, fusoid
Spinell *m* spinel, $MgAl_2O_4$
~/blauer blue spinel
~/grüner pleonaste, ceylonite
~/rosa (roter) Brazilian ruby
Spinifex-Gefüge *n* spinifex structure
Spiralbohrer *m* screw (pointed twist) auger
Spirale *f*/**schneckenartige** helicoid spiral
Spiralgefüge *n* spiral structure
Spiralnebel *m* spiral nebula
Spiroffit *m* spiroffite, $(Mn, Zn)_2Te_3O_8$
spitz acute; acicular
Spitzbohrer *m* pointed auger
Spitze *f* apex
~ der Schale apex of the shell
Spitzenabfluß *m* peak runoff, maximum discharge
Spitzenapparat *m* multitube elutriator *(elutriation analysis)*
Spitzenproduktion *f* peak production
Spitzfänger *m* taper tap
Spitzhacke *f* double-pointed drifting pick
Spitzkasten *m* box classifier
Spitzkuppe *f* butte
Splitt *m* grit
Splitter *m* chip
splitterig splintery
Splittermarke *f* chatter mark
Splitterprobe *f* chip sample
Spodumen *m* spodumene, triphane, $LiAl(Si_2O_6)$
Spongien *fpl* spongians
Spongienriff *n* sponge reef
Spongolit *m* spongolite, spongoline
Sporangium *n* sporangia, spore vessel (case)
Spore *f* spore
Sporenbildung *f* sporulation
Sporenkapsel *f s.* Sporangium
Sporenkunde *f* palynology
Sporenpflanzen *fpl* cryptogams
Sporinit *m* sporinite *(coal maceral)*
Sporit *m* sporite *(coal microlithotype)*
Sporoclarit *m* sporoclarite *(coal microlithotype)*
Sporodurit *m* sporodurite *(coal microlithotype)*
Sporogelit *m s.* Alumogel
Spratzlava *f* aa lava, aphrolite, aphrolith
Spratzlavafeld *n* aa field
Spreizanker *m* expanding anchor
Spreizbewegung *f* spreading
~ des Meeresbodens sea-floor spreading
Spreize *f* sprag
Spreizhülsenanker *m* expansion shell bolt
Spreizkeil *m s.* Spreize

Spreizstempel *m s.* Spreize
Sprengarbeit *f* shot-firing, blasting operation
Sprengbohren *n* drilling with explosives
Sprengbohrloch *n* shot hole, blasthole
Sprengbohrlochgerät *n* blasthole drill
sprengen to shoot, to blast
Sprengen *n* shooting, blasting
Sprengfestigkeit *f* bursting strength
Sprengkegel *m* cone of blast
Sprengloch *n* shot hole, blasthole
Sprenglochbohren *n* blasthole drilling
Sprengmoment *m* break
Sprengöl *n* blasting oil
Sprengpulver *n* powder
Sprengriß *m* expansion (burst) crack
Sprengschnur *f* detonation cord, primacord
Sprengstoff *m* powder
Sprengtrichter *m* explosion crater
Sprengung *f* shooting, blasting
~ im Bohrloch shooting of (in) wells
~ im Steinbruch quarry blasting
~/nukleare nuclear blasting
~/seismische shot
Sprengwirkung *f* wedge effect, wedgework *(e.g. by frost)*
Springbrunnen *m* flowing (gushing) well
Springdecke *f* rising nappe
springen to crack
Springenlassen *n*/**stoßweises** stop-cocking *(of an oil well)*
Springer *m* gusher, blowing well, blow-out
Springflut *f* [high water of] spring tide
Springmarken *fpl* saltation marks
Springniedrigwasser *n* low water of spring tide
Springquelle *f* pulsating spring
~/intermittierende geyser
~/kontinuierliche spouting spring
Springsonde *f s.* Springquelle
Springtide *f* spring tide
Springwasser *n* flowing artesian water
Springwelle *f* tsunami
Spritzbeton *m s.* Torkretbeton
Spritzer *m s.* Springer
Spritzlava *f* aa lava, aphrolite, aphrolith
Spritzlavafeld *n* aa field
Spritzwasser *n* spray
Sprödbruch *m* brittle fracture (displacement)
sprödbruchempfindlich brittle
Sprödbruchempfindlichkeit *f* brittleness
sprödbruchunempfindlich tough
Sprödbruchunempfindlichkeit *f* toughness
spröde brittle
Sprödglaserz *n s.* Stephanit
Sprödigkeit *f* brittleness
Sprödigkeitsbruch *m* brittle fracture
Sprudel *m* spouting spring
Sprudelbohrung *f s.* Springquelle
Sprudelquelle *f* bubbling spring
Sprudelstein *m* pisolite, pisolith
Sprühregen *m* drizzle
Sprung *m* 1. [normal] fault, displacement, up-

Sprung 294

slide jump, leap, throw (*s.a.* Verwerfung); 2. crack, fissure, cleft (*s.a.* Riß, Spalt)
~/**gewöhnlicher** hade-slip fault
~ **im alternden Gel** syneresis crack
~ **ins Hangende** upcast slip
~ **ins Liegende** dowthrown fault
Sprungbildung *f* faulting, faultage
Sprungfunktion *f* step function
Sprunghöhe *f* fault throw, displacement of fault
~/**flache** dip separation (slip)
~/**flache allgemeine** total throw (displacement)
~/**scheinbare seigere** apparent throw (slip)
~/**scheinbare stratigrafische** apparent stratigraphic separation, [apparent] perpendicular throw
~/**seigere** perpendicular (vertical, fault) throw, vertical (normal) displacement
~ **senkrecht zur Schichtung** perpendicular separation
~/**stratigrafische** stratigraphic separation (throw)
~/**streichende** strike slip
~/**totale** net slip
~/**vertikale** *s.* ~/seigere
Sprungkreuzung *f* intersecting faults
Sprungschicht *f* layer of discontinuity, interface
Sprungschwall *m* freshet
sprungweise by leaps and bounds
Sprungweite *f* fault heave, horizontal throw, shift of the fault
~/**flache** perpendicular displacement (slip), lateral separation
~/**horizontale** heave
~ **in der Schichtebene/scheinbare** apparent stratigraphic[al] gap, apparent gap in bedding plane
~/**scheinbare horizontale (söhlige)** apparent heave
~/**söhlige** heave
~/**streichende** horizontal separation along fault line strike, total heave
Sprungwinkel *m* angle of slip, pitch
Spülbagger *m* flushing dredge[r]
Spülbogen *m s.* Spülmarke
Spülbohren *n* wash boring, flush (circulation) drilling
Spülbohrgerät *n* wash-boring rig
Spülbohrung *f* wash boring; jetted well
Spüldamm *m* hydraulic fill embankment
Spülen *n* **des Bohrlochs** scavenging of the hole
Spulenabstand *m* intercoil spacing
Spülflüssigkeit *f* wash (flush) fluid, watery mud (*s.a.* Spülung 2.)
Spülgas *n* flush gas
Spülkippe *f* hydraulic fill
Spülkopf *m* circulating head, swivel
~/**angetriebener** power swivel
Spülkopfkrümmer *m* gooseneck

Spülmarke *f* wavemark, swash mark *(sedimentary fabric)*
Spülprobe *f* catch sample
Spülproben *fpl* sludge (ditch) samples; drill cuttings (chips)
Spülprobenlog *n* sample log
Spülpumpe *f* slush (flushing mud) pump
Spülpumpendruck *m* slush (flushing, mud) pump pressure
Spülsaum *m* trash (drift) line
Spülschappe *f* flushing auger
Spülschlamm *m* drilling fluid (mud), mud flush
Spülschlauch *m* flexible hose
Spültrübe *f* flush[ing] fluid
Spülung *f* 1. flushing, washing; circulation; 2. mud, drilling fluid (*s.a.* Spülflüssigkeit)
~/**belüftete** aerated mud
~/**beschwerte** weighted mud
~/**direkte** straight circulation [of the mud]
~/**indirekte** reversed circulation [of the mud]
~ **mit Inhibitoren** inhibited mud
~ **mit oberflächenaktiven Zusätzen** surfactant mud
~/**natürliche** natural mud
~/**ölbasische** oil-base mud
~/**wiederaufbereitete** regenerated mud
Spülungsanalysenlog *n* mud log
Spülungsaufbereitungsanlage *f* mud plant
Spülungsdruck *m* mud (circulating, gas) pressure
Spülungsflüssigkeit *f s.* Spülung 2.
Spülungsgaslog *n* mud-gas log
Spülungsingenieur *m* mud engineer
Spülungskanal *m* mud circulating opening (channel)
Spülungskasten *m* mud saver bucket
Spülungsmengenmesser *m* flowmeter
Spülungsmessung *f* mud test
Spülungsprobe *f* mud sample
Spülungssäule *f* mud column
Spülungssystem *n* mud system
Spülungstemperatur *f* mud temperature
Spülungsüberwachung *f* mud control
Spülungsumlauf *m* circulation of the mud
~/**direkter** straight circulation [of the mud]
~/**umgekehrter** reversed circulation [of the mud]
Spülungsverlust *m s.* Spülverlust
Spülungsvolumenstrom *m* pump delivery
Spülungswaage *f* mud balance
Spülungswiderstandsmessung *f* mud resistivity logging
Spülungszusatz *m* mud additive
Spülverlust *m* mud loss, loss of circulation (returns), lost circulation, absorption rate
Spülverlustzone *f* loss-circulation zone
Spülversatz *m* hydraulic stowing
Spülwasser *n* drilling water
Spundwand *f*/**verankerte** anchored sheet [pile] wall
Spur *f* 1. track, trail, trace *(of animal)*; 2. trace;

vestige *(residual)*; 3. train, track; show *(e.g. of oil)*
Spuranalyse *f* trace analysis *(seismics)*
Spurenanalyse *f* detection of trace elements
Spurenelement *n* trace[r] element, microelement, minor element
Spurenfossil *n* trace fossil
Spurengehalt *m* trace amount *(in ground water)*
Spurengruppe *f* gather *(seismics)*
Spurennachweis *m* detection of trace elements
Spurrit *m* spurrite, $Ca_5[CO_3|(SiO_4)_2]$
Spuruntersuchung *f* trace analysis *(seismics)*
Spurwahlschalter *m* roll-along switch *(in CDP-seismics)*
S$_1$-Schieferung *f* slaty (flow) cleavage, axial plane foliation
S$_2$-Schieferung *f* fracture (fault-slip, strainslip, crenulation, false, strain) cleavage
Sserir *m* serir
Stabalge *f* diatom
stabil stable
Stabilisierung *f* **des Strömungszustands** stabilization of flow conditions
~ **des Untergrunds** soil stabilization
Stabilisierungsgrad *m* grade of a stabilization *(of a ground-water depression)*
Stabilität *f* stability
~/**thermodynamische** thermodynamic stability
Stabilitätsabfolge *f*/**Goldichs** Goldich's stability sequence
Stabilitätsfeld *n* stability field
Stabilitätsfläche *f* acceptance area
Stabilitätsgrenze *f* **einer Böschungsneigung** critical slope
Stabilkomplex *n* stable complex
Stachelhäuter *mpl* echinoderms
Stadium *n* 1. stage; 2. stade *(glacial)*
~/**aktives** active stage *(of a volcano)*
~/**frühdiagnetisches** eogenetic stage
~/**hydrothermales** hydrothermal stage
~/**kohlensaures** carbonic stage
~/**magmatisches** magmatic stage
~ **mit geringmächtiger Sedimentbedeckung** shallow-burial stage
~ **mit mächtiger Sedimentbedeckung** deep-burial stage
~ **ohne Sedimentbedeckung** preburial stage
~/**orogenes** orogenic stage
~/**orthomagmatisches** orthomagmatic (orthotectic) stage
~/**pneumatolytisches** pneumatolytic stage
~/**sulfidisches** sulphidic stage
~/**vorletztes** penultimate stage
Staffel *f* step
Staffelbruch *m* step (echelon) fault
~/**gleichsinniger** progressive step fault
~ **mit fortläufigen und rückläufigen Staffeln** faults with balance of throw
Staffelfalte *f* chevron (zig-zag, accordion, concertina) fold

staffelförmig echeloned
Staffelgirlanden *fpl* echelon festoons
Staffelverwerfungen *fpl*/**antithetische** step faults hading against the dip
~/**synthetische** step faults hading with the dip
stagnieren to stagnate
stagnierend stagnant, stagnating
Stagnogley *m* soil with permanent stagnant water
Stahlquelle *f* ferruginous (chalybeate) spring
Stainierit *m* stainierite, CoOOH
Stalagmeter *n* stalagmeter
Stalagmit *m* stalagmite
stalagmitartig, stalagmitisch stalagmitic[al]
Stalaktit *m* stalactite
~ **mit versetzter Wachstumsachse** anemolite, helictite, heligmite
stalaktitisch stalactic[al], stalactital, stalactitic[al], stalactiform
Stamm *m* 1. stem; 2. phylum *(division of the animal kingdom)*
Stammagma *n* parent[al] magma
Stammbaum *m* genealogic succession (tree), phylogenic tree
Stammdecke *f* primary nappe, trunk (major, master) sheet
Stammesgeschichte *f* phylogeny, phylogenesis
stammesgeschichtlich phylogenetic
Stammrest *m*/**kohliger** coal pipe
Stamp *n s.* Stampien
Stampfbeton *m* tamped concrete
Stampfen *n* ramming, beating
Stampien *n*, **Stampium** *n* Stampian [Stage] *(of Oligocene)*
Stand *m*/**ufervoller** bank-full stage
Standardgestein *n* standard rock
Standardmeßverfahren *n*/**elektrisches** standard electric logging
Standardmineral *n* standard (normative) mineral
Standardoberfläche *f* standard surface
Standardprobe *f* standard sample, paradigm
~/**geochemische** geochemical standard sample
Standardprofil *n* standard section
Standardskala *f*/**internationale stratigrafische** international stratigraphic standard scale
Standardzelle *f* standard cell *(according to Eskola)*
Standdauer *f* 1. standing time *(e.g. of props); age (e.g. of shafts)*; 2. time after circulation stops
standfest stable; sturdy; consistent *(mountains)*
Standfestigkeit *f* stability; sturdiness
~ **von Böschungen** slope stability
ständig perennial
Standlinie *f* lane *(navigation)*
Standort *m* habitat; location, site
Standpfeiler *m* [permanent] chock
Standrohr *n* standpipe, surface string (casing), gauge tube, outer (conductor) casing

Standrohrsetzen

Standrohrsetzen *n* setting of conductor
Standrohrspiegelhöhe *f* **des Grundwassers** ground-water level in a gauge
Standsicherheit *f* stability
Standsicherheitsuntersuchung *f* stability analysis
Standwasser *n* stagnant water
Standzeit *f* s. Standdauer
Stangenbohrer *m* auger
Stangenschwefel *m* stick sulphur
Stannin *m* stannite, tin pyrite, Cu_2FeSnS_4
Stannopalladinit *m* stannopalladinite, Pd_3Sn_2
Stapelgeschwindigkeit *f* stacking velocity
Stapelgrad *m* stack multiplicity *(seismics)*
Stapelmoräne *f* deposited moraine
Stapelung *f* storing, stack[ing] *(seismics)*
~ **für einen gemeinsamen Tiefenpunkt** common depth point stack[ing], horizontal mixing
~/**gewichtete** diversity stack[ing]
~/**vertikale** vertical (uphole) stack[ing]
Stärke *f* **der Doppelbrechung** degree of double refraction
Starkniederschlag *m* excessive precipitation
starr rigid
Starrheit *f* rigidity
Staßfurtit *m* stassfurtite, α-$Mg_3[Cl|B_7O_{13}]$
Staszizit *m* staszicite, 5(Ca, Cu, Zn)O · As_2O_5 · $2H_2O$
Station *f* station
~ **für Schweremessungen** gravity station
~/**meteorologische** meteorologic[al] station, weather station
~/**trigonometrische** trigonometrical station
stationär stationary *(mountains)*
Stationsabstand *m* station[ary] interval
Stativ *n*/**standfestes** crowfoot
Statocysten *fpl* staticysts, lithocysts *(palaeontology)*
Statolithen *mpl* statoliths, lithites *(palaeontology)*
Statuenmarmor *m* statuary marble
Stau *m* storage, impoundage, swell of water; raised water level; water-surface ascent
Stauanlage *f* weir
Staub *m*/**atmosphärischer** dust
~/**kosmischer** cosmic[al] dust, interstellar dust
~/**meteorischer** meteor dust
~/**meteoritischer** meteoritic dust
~/**vulkanischer** volcanic dust
Staubablagerung *f* dust deposit
staubartig powdery, pulverulent
staubbeladen dusty
Staubboden *m* pulverulent (silty) soil
staubdicht dust-proof
Staubecken *n* water storage basin, impounding reservoir (basin), artificial lake
Staubfahne *f* spindrift
Staubfall *m* dust fall
staubfrei dustfree, dustless
staubgeschützt dust-proof
Staubgold *n* flour (float) gold
staubhaltig dusty, dust-laden

Staubhaut *f* dust skin
staubig dusty
Staubkalk *m* air-slaked lime
Staubkohle *f* dust coal
Staubkruste *f* dusty crust
Staublawine *f* dust (powdery, dry, drift) avalanche
~/**vulkanische** ash avalanche
Staubodenwasser *n* internal stagnant water
Staubregen *m* dust shower
Staubsand *m* sand dust, impalpable sand
~/**feinster** rock flour
Staubsäule *f* whirling pillar of dust
Staubschicht *f* dust layer
~ **des Mondes** lunar regolith
Staubsturm *m* dust storm, *(Am)* duster
Staubtuff *m* dust tuff
Staubwirbel *m* dust whirl (swirl)
Staubwolke *f* dust cloud
stauchen to compress
Stauchfältelung *f* convolute bedding
Stauchfaltung *f* crumpling folding
Stauchmoräne *f* push (upset) moraine
Stauchung *f* compression, swell
Stauchwall *m* ice-pushed ridge *(of a moraine)*
Staudamm *m* barrage [dam], retaining dam (weir)
~/**überflutbarer** submergible dam
Staudruck *m* stagnation pressure
stauen to dam up, to impound
Staufläche *f* backwater surface
Staugebiet *n* backwater area (zone)
Staugley *m* similigley
Staugrenze *f* limit of backwater
Staugrundwasser *n* ponded ground water
Stauhöhe *f* height of damming; top water level; water rise head, water surface elevation
Stauinhalt *m* capacity of reservoir
~ **einer Talsperre** volume of the reservoir of a barrage
Staukuppe *f* intrusive (endogenous) dome
Staukurve *f* backwater curve, banking[-up] curve
Staulänge *f* backwater length
Staulinie *f* s. Staukurve
Staumauer *f* barrage dam (wall), retaining wall
Staumauerwiderlager *n* dam abutment
Staumoräne *f* s. Stauchmoräne
Staunässe *f* damming wetness, perched ground water
Staunässebereich *m* stagnation (saturation) layer
Staunässeboden *m* similigley
Stauquelle *f* barrier (contact) spring
Stauraum *m* storage capacity
Staurolith *m* staurolite, $AlFe_2O_3(OH) \cdot 4Al_2[O|SiO_4]$
Staurolith-Isograd *m* staurolite-in isograd
Stauschleuse *f* retaining sluice
Stausee *m* artificial (storage, impounded, dammed) lake, storage reservoir
~/**glazialer** proglacial lake

Staustufenkraftwerk n barrage power station
Stauung f damming, ponding
Stauungsbogen m arc of folding
Stauwall m s. Stauchwall
Stauwasser n dam (dammed-up, impounded, ponded) water, backwater
Stauwasserdruck m impounded water pressure
Stauwehr n barrage, retaining dam (weir)
Stauwerk n barrage, penstock
Steatit m steatite, lard stone, lardite, soapstone, $Mg_3[(OH)_2|Si_4O_{10}]$
stechen/Torf to dig turf
Stechmarke f prod cast
Stechpegel m hook (needle) gauge
Stechzylinder m metal cylinder for determination of bulk density
Steenstrupin m steenstrupine, $Na_2Ce(Mn, Ta, Fe,\cdots)H_2[(Si, P)O_4]_3$
Stefan[ien] n, **Stefanium** n Stephanian [Stage] (of Upper Carboniferous in West and Central Europe)
Steg m web
stehen/seiger to be ended up
Steifezahl f stiffness coefficient, resistance modulus (of the soil)
Steifheit f rigidity
Steifheitsmodul m stiffness coefficient
Steifigkeit f stiffness
Steifigkeitskoeffizient m, **Steifigkeitszahl** f coefficient of rigidity
steifplastisch stiff-plastic
Steigen n des **Hochwassers** flood rise
Steigerit m steigerite, $Al[VO_4] \cdot 3H_2O$
Steigerrohrstrang m s. Steigleitung
Steiggeschwindigkeit f rising velocity
Steighöhe f head; artesian [pressure] head
~ **des Wassers** hydrostatic head
~/**kapillare** capillary head (height, rise)
Steigleitung f rising main, flow string, production flow well; stand pipe
Steigmarke f air heave structure
Steigrohr n tubing
~/**engkalibriges** macaroni tubing
Steigung f gradient, incline, inclination, slope, rise; taper (of a wedge)
Steigungswinkel m angle of lead
steil steep; aslope, scarped; abrupt, precipitous
Steilabbruch m s. Steilabfall
Steilabfall m precipice, [steep] escarpment
~ **einer Stufe** cuesta scarp
Steilabhang m steep slope
~/**unterseeischer** marine bench; seascarp
Steilaufnahme f low oblique photograph (aerogeology)
steilbegrenzt steep-sided
Steilböschung f s. Steilabhang
Steildüne f steep (shelving) dune
Steilhang m steep face, escarpment
Steilheit f steepness, precipitousness
Steilküste f steep (precipitous, shelving) coast

Steilrand m scarp, cliff
Steilsattel m steep saddle
Steilufer n steep (high) bank, river bluff
Steilwand f precipitous wall (cliff), cliff wall, scarp face
steilwandig steep-walled, steep-sided, steep-sloped
Steilwinkelreflexion f steep angle reflection
Stein m stone
~/**großer abgerundeter** cobblestone
Steinalaun m stone alum
Steinarbeit f carving
steinartig stony; petrous
Steinausklaubung f picking-out of slate
Steinbänder npl stone strings
Steinbank f stone bed
Steinblock m large stone
~/**erratischer** erratic boulder, errant block
Steinboden m stony soil; lithosol
~/**netzartiger** netlike stone soil
Steinböschung f riprapped slope
Steinbrechen n quarrying
Steinbrecher m stone breaker (crusher), rock crusher
Steinbruch m [stone] quarry, stone (barrow) pit
~ **mit horizontaler Klüftung** sheet quarry
Steinbruchabbau m quarrying [operation]
~/**terrassenförmiger** multiple-bench quarrying
Steinbruchbetrieb m quarrying
Steinbruchlager n quarry bed
Steinbruchsohle f quarry floor
Steinchen n lapillus
Steindamm m/**gerüttelter** vibrated rockfill dam
Steindräne f stone drain
Steine mpl/**eckige** angular cobbles
~/**kleine** ratchel[l]
~/**sich gegenseitig eindrückende** mutually indenting pebbles
Steineis n fossil ice
steinern stony
Steine- und Erdenindustrie f pit and quarry industry
Steinfall m rock fall (inrush); roof fall (in a mine)
Steinfülldamm m rock-fill dam
Steingeröll n shingle, scree
Steingeschiebe n boulder shingle
Steingirlande f stone garland
Steingitter n stone grating
Steingletscher m rock glacier
Steingrubenabfall m quarry rubbish
Steingutton m white ware clay, ball clay
Steinhauer m quarrier
Steinhaufen m karn, ca[i]rn
Steinhügel m bourock
steinig stony; rocky; petrous; lithoid[al]; pebbly
Steinkern m stony cast, rock kernel, internal cast (mould)
~ **einer Sigillarie** bell mould (mouth)

Steinkohle 298

Steinkohle f bituminous coal; hard coal; black coal
~/hochflüchtige high-volatile bituminous coal
~/niedrigflüchtige low-volatile bituminous coal
Steinkohlenbergwerk n colliery, coal mine
Steinkohlendestillation f carbonization of bituminous coal
Steinkohlenflöz n bituminous coal seam
Steinkohlenformation f coal formation
Steinkohlengebirge n carboniferous rock (strata)
~/flözführendes hard-coal-bearing strata
Steinkohlenhorizont m coal horizon
Steinkohlenlager n coal deposit
Steinkohlenmoor n coal moor
Steinkohlenteeröl n mineral tar oil
Steinkohlenwald m coal-forming forest
Steinlage f bench
Steinlawine f stone (rock, debris) avalanche
Steinmark n lithomarge, stone marrow
Steinmehl n rock meal
Steinmeteorit m stone (stony) meteorite, aerolite, asiderite
~/chondritischer chondrite
Steinnetzboden m polygonal ground (markings, soil)
Steinöl n mineral (rock, stone, fossil) oil
Steinpech n stone pitch
Steinpflaster n bowlder (desert) pavement
~/fossiles plaster conglomerate
Steinringboden m patterned ground
Steinringe mpl stone rings
Steinsalz n mineral (rock, native, fossil) salt, halite, NaCl
steinsalzhaltig halitic
Steinsalzhorizont m rock-salt horizon
Steinsäule f menhir
Steinschlag m rock fall (burst), debris fall, falling stones, broken stone; bats (ballast stone broken by hand)
Steinschliff m stone grinding
Steinschotter m ballast
Steinschutt m rock waste, detritus rubbish
Steinschüttung f rock fill
Steinsohle f gravel[ly] layer
Steinsplitter mpl stone chips
Steinstreifen mpl stone stripes (frost soil)
Steinstreifenboden m soil with stone stripes
Steinstrom m stone river
Steintrümmer pl rock waste
Steinwolle f rock wool
Steinwüste f stone desert, stony desert (waste), rock[y] desert; hammada (Sahara)
Steinzeit f Stone Age
~/jüngere Neolithic [Age, Times]
Steinzeugton m pipeclay, stoneware clay
S-Tektonit m S-tectonite
stellar stellar
Stellarit m stellarite, stellar (oil) coal
Stellerit m stellerite (s.a. Stibnit)
Stellung f/**taxonomische** taxonomic position

Stelznerit m s. Antlerit
Stempel m prop
Stempelabstand m prop spacing
Stempeldichte f prop density
Stempeldruckfestigkeit f stamp-load bearing strength (of rock)
Stempeldruckversuch m stamp-load bearing experiment
Stempeleinschubpresse f s. Stempelprüfpresse
Stempelprüfpresse f testing press for props
Stengel m stalk, footstalk, stem; column
~/flacher blade (of crystals)
stengelförmig cauliform (s.a. stengelig)
Stengelgneis m pencil gneiss
stengelig stalked, caulescent, cauliferous; spiky; acicular; [long-]columnar
Stengelkristalle mpl fringe crystals
Stengelung f pencil structure
stenohalin stenohaline
Stenonit m stenonite, $Sr_2Al[F_5|CO_3]$
Stepanowit m stepanovite, $NaMgFe[C_2O_4]_3 \cdot 8-9H_2O$
Stepback n stepback (correction for measuring on sea)
Stephanit m stephanite, black silver, brittle silver ore, $5Ag_2S \cdot Sb_2S_3$
Steppe f steppe, grass-covered plain; pampa (Argentina); scrub (Australia); veld[t] (South Africa); llano (Orinoco)
Steppenbildung f steppization
Steppenboden m steppe soil
~/schwarzer steppe black earth
Steppenfauna f steppe fauna
Steppengürtel m/**eurasiatischer** Eurasian steppe region
Steppenhochebene f barren plateau
Steppenvegetation f steppe vegetation
Steppenzone f steppe zone
Stercorit m stercorite, $(NH_4)NaH[PO_4] \cdot 4H_2O$
Stereobasis f stereobase
Stereobetrachtung f stereoscopic viewing
Stereobildauswertung f stereoscopic interpretation of imagery
stereografisch stereographic
Stereomodell n stereoscopic model
Stereopaar n stereoscopic pair
Stern m star
~ erster Größe first magnitude star
~/Roter red star
sternartig starlike; starry; asteroid; astral
Sternbeobachtung f astroscopy, astronomic[al] observation
Sternbergit m sternbergite, flexible silver ore, $AgFe_2S_3$
Sternbild n stellar constellation
Sternbildfigur f zodiacal figure
sternchenartig stellular
Sternenasche f star (stellar) ash
sternenhell starry
Sternenhelle f starriness
Sternenlicht n starlight

sternenlos starless
sternförmig star-shaped; stellar; stellate[d]; asteroid
Sternforschung f astral exploration
Sternhaufen m [star] cluster
sternhell starlit
Sternjahr n sidereal year
Sternkarte f star map
sternklar starlit
Sternkompaß m astrocompass
Sternkunde f astronomy
Sternmaterie f stellar matter
Sternmesser m astrometer
Sternnähe f periastron
Sternquarz m star (asteriated) quartz, crosscourse spar
Sternsaphir m star sapphire
Sternschießen n radial refraction, arc shooting
Sternschnuppe f shooting (falling) star, meteor
Sternschnuppenschwarm m meteor shower
Sternschüsse mpl multiple shot holes
Sternspektrum n stellar spectrum
Sternströme mpl star streaming
Sternstunde f sidereal hour
Sternsystem n sidereal system
Sterntafel f star map
Sterntag m sidereal (star) day
Sternum n sternum, breast bone
Sternwarte f observatory, astronomic[al] station
Sternwolke f star cloud
Sternzeit f sidereal (stellar) time
~/mittlere mean sidereal time
Sterrettit m sterrettite, Sc[PO$_4$] · 2H$_2$O
Stetefeldtit m stetefeldtite, Ag$_{1-2}$Sb$_{2-1}$(O, OH, H$_2$O)$_7$
Stewartit m stewartite, MnFe$_2^{...}$[OH|PO$_4$]$_2$ · 8H$_2$O
Stibarsen m stibarsenic, AsSb
Stibiconit m stibiconite, antimony ochre, SbSb$_2$O$_6$OH
Stibio-Domeykit m stibiodomeykite, 3Cu$_3$(As, Sb)
Stibioluzonit m stibioluzonite, Cu$_3$SbS$_4$
Stibiopalladinit m stibiopalladinite, Pd$_3$Sb
Stibiotantalit m stibiotantalite, Sb(Ta, Nb)O$_4$
Stiblith m s. Stibiconit
Stibnit m stibnite, gray antimony, Sb$_2$S$_3$
Stichprobe f random (spot, chance) sample
~/wahllose grab sample
Stichprobenahme f work sampling, spot checking
Stichprobenerhebung f sampling
Stichprofil n single-ended spread (seismics)
Stichtit m stichtite, Mg$_6$Cr$_2$[(OH)$_{16}$|CO$_3$] · 4H$_2$O
Stichtorf m dug peat
Stickstoff m nitrogen, N
stickstoffarm nitrogen-poor
Stickstoffbakterien fpl nitrifying bacteria
stickstoffhaltig azotic

Stielforamen n pedicle foramen (of brachiopods)
Stielgang m neck, stump
Stielglieder npl stem ossicles
Stielklappe f ventral (pedicle) valve (of brachiopods)
Stigmarien fpl stigmarian roots
Stilbit m stilbite, [epi]desmine, Ca[Al$_2$Si$_7$O$_{18}$] · 7H$_2$O
stillegen to abandon
~/eine Grube to abandon a mine
~/vorläufig to suspend (shut down) temporarily
Stilleit m stilleite, ZnSe
Stillstandsperiode f der Vereisung interstadial epoch
Stillstandszeit f shut-down time (boring technique)
Stillwasser n stillwater, dead water
Stillwasserbereich m quiet reach, environment of quiet marine water
Stillwasserfazies f quiescent-area facies
Stillwellit m stillwellite, (Ce, La)$_3$[B$_3$O$_6$|Si$_3$O$_9$]
Stilpnomelan m stilpnomelane, (K, H$_2$O) (Fe, Fe$^{...}$, Mg, Al)$_{<3}$ [(OH)$_2$|Si$_4$O$_{10}$]X$_n$(H$_2$O)$_2$
Stilpnosiderit m stilpnosiderite (amorphous brown ironstone)
Stimulationsmethode f stimulation method (of a well)
Stimulierung f einer Sonde stimulation of a well
Stinkkalk m stinkstone, fetid limestone, swinestone
Stinkschiefer m stinking schist, fetid shale
Stinkspat m antozonite
Stinkstein m stinkstone, swinestone, anthraconite
Stirn f front, face, end
~ der Deckfalte frontal overthrust
Stirnabsatz m foreset bed (cross stratification)
Stirneinrollung f, Stirnfalte f frontal lobe
Stirnhang m cuesta scarp
Stirnmoräne f frontal (terminal, end) moraine
Stirnplatte f frontal sheet
Stirnrand m anterior end
Stirnschuppe f frontal wedge
Stishovit m stishovite, SiO$_2$ tetragonal
Stochastik f stochastics
Stöchiometrie f stoichiometry
stöchiometrisch stoichiometric
Stock m sill, stock (magmatic)
Stockpunkt m pour point (of oil)
Stockwerk n floor
~/tektonisches tectonic store[y]; tectonic level (Wegmann and others)
~/zeitlich begrenztes metallogenetisches chronologically limited metallogenetic stockwork
Stockwerklagerstätte f stockwork deposit
Stockwerktektonik f tectonic level (Ampferer and others)
Stoff m/betonangreifender concrete-attacking substance

Stoff

~/**diamagnetischer** diamagnetic substance
~/**mineralischer** mineral matter
~/**oberflächenaktiver** surfactant, surface-active agent, tenside
~/**organischer** organic matter
~/**poröser** porous medium
~/**suspendierter** suspensoid
Stoffabfuhr f evacuation of material
Stoffaustausch m zwischen Nebengestein und Magma cross assimilation
Stoffbilanz f balance of composition
Stoffe mpl/**im Flußwasser gelöste** river-dissolved load
Stoffkonzentration f **durch Migration** migration accretion
stofflich-gefügemäßig material-textural
Stoffwanderung f migration (migrating, travel, wandering) of substance
Stoffwechsel m s. Metabolismus
Stokesit m stokesite, $Ca_2Sn_2[Si_6O_{18}] \cdot 4H_2O$
Stollen m adit, gallery; day level
~/**schiffbarer** boat level
Stollenbergbau m mining by galleries, adit mining
Stollendeformationen fpl deformations of galleries
Stolleneingang m s. Stollenmundloch
Stollenfirste f gallery roof (head, back)
Stollenfräse f mole
Stollenloch n adit opening
Stollenmund m gallery mouth
Stollenmundloch n adit (pit) entrance, tunnel face, level entry
Stollenrichtung f direction of heading
Stollenrösche f day level
Stollensohle f adit level
Stollen- und Tunnelbau m heading and tunnel construction
Stollenvortrieb m heading, drift of a gallery
Stolzit m stolzite, $PbWO_4$
Stopfbauten mpl stuffed burrows (ichnology)
Stopfbuchsenbildung f **im Bohrloch** balling
Stopfgefüge n stuffed structure (ichnology)
Störanomalien fpl/**magnetische** magnetic anomalies
stören to disturb
Störgeräusch n background noise
Störimpuls m pulse disturbance
Störkörper m disturbing (perturbing) body; causative body
Störkörper mpl/**magnetische** magnetic artefacts
Störpegel m noise level
~ **des weißen Rauschens** white noise level
Störung f disturbance, fault; perturbation
~/**an einer älteren Störung abgelenkte jüngere** trailed fault
~/**durch Faltung induzierte** fold fault
~/**elektrische** hum
~ **entlang einer Schichtfläche** bedding fault
~ **im hangenden Schenkel einer asymetrischen Falte** lag

300

~/**ionosphärische** ionospheric disturbance
~/**kleine** thurm
~/**kurzperiodische** short-period perturbation
~/**langperiodische** long-period perturbation
~/**magnetische** magnetic disturbance (storm)
~/**periphere** circumferential fault
~/**säkulare** secular perturbation
~/**streichende** strike fault
~/**tektonische** disturbance, fault trouble
~/**über Tage ausstreichende** disturbance trace on surface
~/**widersinnig einfallende** reverse (reversal) fault
~/**wiederbelebte** renewed (revived) fault
~/**zufällige** random noise
Störungen fpl/**äquidistante** equidistant faults
~/**divergierende** splays (at the end of a break line)
~/**periodische** periodic perturbations (inequalities)
Störungsfläche f dislocation plane
~/**gefaltete** folded fault
Störungsfunktion f disturbing (perturbing) function
Störungsgleichung f perturbation equation
Störungsglied n perturbing term
Störungsgraben m rift trough
Störungspaar n/**gegensinnig fallendes** trough fault
Störungssystem n fault bundle
Störungszone f fault (fractured) zone
Stoß m 1. shock; 2. face, bank, wall (mining)
~ **parallel zu den Schlechten** face on board
~/**überhängender** overhanging side
~/**unterirdischer** underground shock
~/**verschrämter** carved face
stoßartig discontinuous
Stoßbau m shortwall working
Stoßbohren n percussion (hammer) drilling
Stoßbohrer m percussion drill (jumper)
Stoßdämpfer m pulsation damper
Stoßdruck m 1. shock pressure; 2. side pressure
Stoßeindruck m impact (prod) cast
stoßen/auf Gold to strike gold
~/**auf Öl** to strike oil
Stoßherd m percussion frame
Stoßkernrohr n biscuit cutter
Stoßkraft f push
Stoßkuppe f plug dome
~/**nadelförmige** blocked spine
Stoßmarke f impact (prod) cast
Stoßseite f scour side
Stoßsieb n impact screen
Stoßstärke f shock magnitude
Stoßtisch m bumping table
Stoßverschiebungen fpl impact displacements
stoßweise intermittent
Stoßwelle f shock (impact) wave
Stoßwiderstand m resistance to impact
Stoßwind m gust
Stoßzahn m tusk

~/gerader straight tusk
Stottit m stottite, FeGe(OH)$_6$
Strahl m/außerordentlicher extraordinary ray
~/ordentlicher ordinary ray
strahlenbrechend refractive
Strahlenbrechung f refraction
Strahlenbündel n, Strahlenbüschel n luminous pencil, pencil of rays
strahlend lustrous
Strahlendosis f radiation dose
Strahlenflosser mpl ray-finned bony fishes
strahlenförmig radiating
Strahlengang m path of rays
Strahlengeometrie f ray geometry
Strahlenglimmer m striated mica
Strahlenkupfer n s. Klinoclas
Strahlenschema n source-receiver product (seismics)
Strahlensystem n im Mondkrater bright ray system (in the lunar crater)
Strahlenverlauf m ray path
Strahlenverseuchung f radioactive contamination
Strahlenweg m ray path
~ mit minimaler Laufzeit least (minimum) time path
Strahler m emitter
Strahlerz n s. Klinoklas
strahlig radiated, radiating; radiated-crystalline
Strahlkies m radiated pyrite (s. a. Markasit)
Strahlpumpe f jet pump
Strahlstein m actino[li]te, Ca$_2$(Mg, Fe)$_5$(OH, F)|Si$_4$O$_{11}$]$_2$
Strahlstrom m jet stream
Strahlung f radiation
~/atmosphärische atmospheric radiation
~/effektive terrestrische effective terrestrial radiation
~ eines grauen Körpers gray body radiation
~ eines schwarzen Körpers black body radiation
~/elektromagnetische electromagnetic radiation
~/extraterrestrische extraterrestrial radiation
~/ionisierende ionizing radiation
~/kosmische cosmic[al] radiation
~/nächtliche nocturnal radiation
~/schwache low-level radiation
~/solare kosmische solar cosmic radiation
Strahlungsdichte f radiance, radiancy
Strahlungsdruck m radiation pressure
Strahlungseigenschaft f radiation property
Strahlungsenergie f radiation (radiant) energy
Strahlungsgürtel m radiation belt (zone) (of the earth)
~/äußerer outer radiation region
~/innerer inner radiation region
~/Van Allenscher Van Allen belt
Strahlungshaushalt m radiation budget
Strahlungshelligkeit f radiance, radiancy
Strahlungshof m/radioaktiver radioactive halo

Strahlungsintensität f intensity of radiation
Strahlungsintensitätsmesser m radiometer
Strahlungskorrektur f radiometric[al] correction
Strahlungskurve f radiation curve
Strahlungsmesser m actinometer
Strahlungsmessung f actinometry
Strahlungsnebel m radiation fog
Strahlungsstärke f intensity of radiation
Strahlungstemperatur f radiation temperature
Strahlungsvermögen n intrinsic radiance
Strahlungszeit f time of radiation (radioisotope)
Strahlungszunahme f enhanced radiation
Strain m strain
Strainseismograf m strainmeter
Strand m beach, shore, strand
~/abfallender shelving beach
Strandablagerung f beach (shore, littoral) deposit
Strandbildung f beach building
Strandbuhne f beach groin, shore jetty
Stranddamm m beach ridge
Stranddüne f beach (shore, strand) dune
Strandebene f beach (strand) plain
Strandentwicklung f coastal evolution
Stranderneuerung f beach restoration
Stranderosion f beach (littoral) erosion
Strandgerölle npl beach pebbles
Strandhafer m beach grass
Strandhaff n marginal lagoon
Strandhörner npl beach cusps
Strandkies m beach (shore) gravel
Strandlinie f shore (strand) line, sea limit (coast)
~/gehobene raised shore line
~/vorrückende prograding shore line
Strandmauer f sea wall
Strandpriel m low
Strandriff n onshore reef
Strandrille f rill mark
Strandrippel f ripple mark
Strandsand m beach sand
~/lose verkitteter beach rock
Strandschotter m beach (shore) gravel
Strandsee m shore (coastal) pool, coastal lake
Strandseife f beach placer
Strandstufe f in der Brecherzone shore, face
Strandterrasse f beach (shore, marine) terrace, beach berm, elevated beach (shore, terrace)
Strandverdriftung f shore drift
Strandverschiebung f shift in the shore line
~/negative negative shift in the shore line
~/positive positive shift in the shore line
Strandversetzung f drifting of beach
Strandwall m beach ridge, barrier beach, beach sand barrier
~/angelehnter fixed coastal barrier
~/fossiler shoestring sand
~/freier (vorgelagerter) offshore bar (beach)
Strandwallinsel f barrier island

Strandzone

Strandzone f beach zone
Strang m string
Strangkomplex m ridge-pool complex *(bog)*
Strangmoor n string (patterned) bog
Stranskiit m stranskiite, $CuZn_2[AsO_4]_2$
Straße f strait
Straßenbauschotter m macadam, road stone, crushed stone (rock), paving gravel
Straßeneinschnitt m trench along roads
Straßenschotter m s. Straßenbauschotter
Straßenunterbau m road bed
Stratamerie f, **Stratamessung** f dip logging
Stratameter n dipmeter
Strataskop n stratascope
Strate f stratum *(consisting of many laminas)*
Stratigraf m stratigrapher, stratigraphic geologist
Stratigrafie f stratigraphy, stratigraphic geology
stratigrafisch stratigraphic[al]
Stratocumulus m stratocumulus cloud
Stratosphäre f stratosphere
Stratosphärenballon m skyhook balloon
Stratosphärenstrahlung f stratosphere radiation
Stratotyp m stratotype, type section
~ einer stratigrafischen Grenze boundary stratotype
Stratovulkan m stratovolcano, composite cone
~/schildförmiger pseudo-shield volcano
Stratus m stratus
Stratuswolke f stratus cloud
Strauchwüste f shrub desert
Streb m longwall [face]
~/einfallender dip face
~/gestundeter standing (stationary) face
~/zweiflügeliger double-unit face
Strebausgang m face end
Strebbau m longwall working system
~/streichender strike face
Strebbreite f face width
Strebbruch m roof fall
Strebbruchbau m longwall caving
Strebdurchgang m passage of a face *(under an observation line)*
Streblänge f face length
Strebpfeiler m supporting pillar
Strebquerschnitt m working thickness *(of a seam)*
Strebraum m face excavation
Strebstoß m/**anstehender** breast side of work
Strecke f 1. drift, gallery, heading, roadway; 2. reach
~/einfallende dipping heading, incline
~/gekernte cored interval
~/vorgesetzte advance heading
Streckenauffahren n drifting
Streckenausbau m roadway supports
Streckenbemusterung f road sampling
Streckenfirste f drift (gallery) roof
Streckenförderung f haulage
Streckennetz n roadway system
Streckenort n road head
Streckensohle f gallery level
Streckenstoß m roadway wall (side)
Streckenvortrieb m drifting of a gallery, tunnel (roadway) driving
Streckenvortriebsmaschine f tunnelling machine
Streckfläche f plane of stretching *(in an intrusive body)*
Streckflächen fpl flat-lying gravity faults *(in plutonic contacts)*
Streckgrenze f yield point
~/obere upper yield point
~/untere lower yield point
Streckung f 1. stretching, linear stretching *(parallel arrangement of minerals)*; 2. elongation *(of fossils)*
Streckungshöfe mpl stretching haloes, pressure fringes
streichen to strike, to trend
~ von to run from
Streichen n strike; trend; course
~/durchschnittliches average trend
~/eggisches Eggish trend *(NNW-SSE)*
~ einer Verwerfung fault strike
~/erythräisches Erythrean trend *(NS)*
~/erzgebirgisches Ergebirge trend *(NE-SW)*
~/herzynisches Hercynian trend *(NW-SE)*
~/im along the strike
~/periklinales periclinal trend
~/quer zum across the strike
~/rheinisches Rhenish trend *(NNE-SSW)*
~ und Fallen n attitude
~/variszisches Varisc[i]an trend
streichend along (on) the strike, longitudinal
Streichlinie f strike line; boundary *(of a bank)*
Streichlinienkarte f [structure] contour map
Streichrichtung f strike direction (line), striking, line of bearing; trend *(s.a. Streichen)*
Streich- und Fallmessungen fpl strike and dip readings
Streichwert m, **Streichwinkel** m angle of strike
Streifen m stripe; streak; lamella
Streifenart f rock type
Streifenbild n/**spannungsoptisches** photoelastic fringe pattern
Streifenboden m striped ground, striated ground (soil)
Streifenerz n banded ore
streifenförmig lamellar
Streifenkohle f banded coal; clarain *(very finely stratified coal layers)*
~/vitritreiche s. Glanzstreifenkohle
streifig striped; streaky, streaked; banded; interstratified
Streifigkeit f streakiness
strengflüssig calcitrant *(ore)*
Strengit m strengite, $Fe[PO_4] \cdot 2H_2O$
Streß m stress
Streßmineral n stress mineral

Streubereich *m* [range of] scatter
Streukoeffizient *m* scattering coefficient
Streustrahlung *f* diffuse radiation
Streustrahlungsmesser *m* nephelometer
Streustrahlungsmessung *f* nephelometry
Streustrom *m* parasitic (stray) current
Streuung *f* scattering
~ **des Lichts** light scatter
Streuungsbeiwert *m* spreading coefficient
Streuungskegel *m* fan talus
Streuungsmesser *m*, **Streuwellenmesser** *m* scatterometer
Strich *m* streak *(of a mineral)*
Strichfarbe *f* streak colour *(of a mineral)*
Strichkreuzokular *n* cross-line eyepiece
Strichplatte *f* streak plate
Strichprobe *f* streak test
Strichregen *m* local rains, scattered showers
Strichzeichnung *f* line drawing
Stricklava *f* corded[-folded] lava, ropy lava, pahoehoe [lava]
Striemung *f* lineation, linear parallelism
Strigovit *m* strigovite *(mineral of the chlorite group)*
Stringocephalenkalk *m* Stringocephalus Limestone *(Givetian)*
Stripperbohrung *f* stripper [well]
Strom *m* 1. stream; river *(s.a.* Fluß); 2. current, flow *(s.a.* Strömung)
~/**intermittierender** intermittent stream
~/**tellurischer** earth (ground) current
~/**vagabundierender** vagabondary current
stromabwärts downstream, downcurrent
Stromatolith *m* stromatolite, gymnosolen, algal biscuit
Stromatolithenfazies *f* stromatolitic (algal-mat) facies
stromatolithisch stromatolitic
Stromatoporenkalk *m* Stromatopora limestone
stromaufwärts upcurrent, upstream, upgrade
Strombank *f* sand wave
Strombett *n* stream bed (channel)
Strombettdurchlaßfähigkeit *f* conveyance of a channel
Strombettrelief *n* roughness of channel bed
Strombolitätigkeit *f* Strombolian activity
Ströme *mpl*/**pyroklastische** pyroclastic flows
Stromebene *f* plane of a plane flow
strömen to stream
Strömen *n* streaming
Stromenge *f* narrows
Stromeyerit *m* stromeyerite, $Cu_2S \cdot Ag_2S$
Stromfläche *f* stream surface
Stromfunktion *f* stream function
Stromgebiet *n* drainage area; river basin
Stromgefälle *n* stream gradient
Stromlauf *m* course of river
Stromlinie *f* line of flow, stream line
Strommündung *f* river mouth
Stromrinne *f* navigable channel
Stromröhre *f* streamtube, tube of flow
Stromschnelle *f* rapid, riffle

Stromstreifung *f* parting lineation
Stromstrich *m* stream line, thread of maximum velocity, thread of the current
Stromsystem *n* stream system
Stromteilung *f* bifurcation of a river
Strömung *f* current; flow
~/**aufsteigende** rising current
~/**ebene** plane (two-dimensional) flow
~/**eindimensionale** one-dimensional flow
~/**fossile** pal[a]eocurrent *(sedimentation)*
~/**geschichtete** stratified flow
~/**gleichförmige** uniform flow
~ **in offenen Gerinnen** flow in open channels, open-channel flow
~/**instationäre** transient (unsteady-state) flow
~/**kugelsymmetrische** spherical flow
~/**laminare** laminar (stream-line) flow
~/**lineare** linear (one-dimensional) flow
~/**ozeanische** ocean current
~/**periodische** periodic current
~/**quasistationäre** quasi-steady flow
~/**radiale** radial flow
~/**räumliche** three-dimensional flow
~/**regulierte** regulated flow
~/**reißende** flashy flow
~/**rücklaufende** backwash
~/**stationäre** steady-state flow
~/**turbulente** turbulent (sinuous) flow
~/**unbeeinflußte (ungestörte)** virgin flow
~/**unperiodische** non-periodic current
~/**verzögerte** retarded flow
Strömungsenergie *f* stream power
Strömungsfeld *n* field of flow, flow pattern
Strömungsfunktion *f* stream function
Strömungsganglinie *f* stream hydrograph
strömungsgeregelt current-oriented
Strömungsgeschwindigkeit *f* current (stream) velocity
Strömungsgleichung *f* flow equation
Strömungsgradient *m* current gradient
Strömungshindernis *n* flow barrier
Strömungskamm *m* current crescent
Strömungsmarke *f s.* Fließwulst
Strömungsmesser *m* current meter, flowmeter
~/**sensitiver** sensitive current-measuring device
Strömungsphase *f*/**späte instationäre** late transient period
Strömungspotential *n* streaming potential
Strömungsprofil *n* flow profile
Strömungsrate *f*/**vertikale** transmission rate
Strömungsrichtung *f* direction of flow (current)
Strömungsriefe *f* sand streak
Strömungsriefung *f* current (parting) lineation, linear parallelism
Strömungsrinne *f* scour mark, channel
Strömungsrippel *f* current ripple [mark]
~/**zungenförmige** linguoid [current] ripple
Strömungsrippelschichtung *f* current-ripple bedding (lamination)

Strömungsrippelschichtung 304

~/verfältelte convolute current-ripple lamination
Strömungsrippelschrägschichtung f current-ripple cross lamination
Strömungsschreiber m recording stream gauge
Strömungsstreifung f s. Strömungsriefung
Strömungsvorgang m process of flow
Strömungswiderstand m flow resistance, resistance to fluid flow
Strömungswulst m s. Fließwulst
Strömungszustand m pattern of flow; type of flow; state of flow
~/quasistationärer semisteady state
Stromwasser n current water
Strontianit m strontianite, carbonate of strontium, $SrCO_3$
Strontium n strontium, Sr
Strontiumkarbonat n s. Strontianit
Strosse f stope; bottom; bench, bank
Strossenbau m stoping, underhand stoping; benching, benching work[ing]
Strossenbohrung f bench drilling
Strudel m whirlpool, eddy, vortex
Strudelkessel m whirlpool, plunge pool, pothole, rock mill
Strudelloch n s. Strudelkessel
strudellos non-eddying
Strudeltopf m s. Strudelkessel
Strudler m filter feeder *(pelaeontology)*
Struktur f 1. structure *(general and structural-geological);* fabric; 2. texture *(for rocks equivalent to the German „Struktur", but not uniform in application)*
~/antiklinale anticlinal structure
~/astige dendritic[al] structure
~/atomare atomic structure
~/außerhalb der off-structure
~/baumförmige dendritic[al] structure
~/breitsattelförmige s. ~/antiklinale
~/daktylitische dactylitic structure
~/dendritische dendritic[al] texture, arborescent structure
~ des Untergrunds subsurface structure
~/diktyonitische diktyonitic structure
~/embryonale embryonic structure
~/erdölführende petroliferous (oil-bearing) structure
~/gekrümmte contorted structure
~/kubisch raumzentrierte body-centred cubic structure
~/nebulitische nebulitic structure
~/ophthalmitische ophthalmitic structure
~/perlitische perlitic structure
~/phlebitische phlebitic structure
~/plattenförmige blanket structure
~/ptygmatische ptygmatic structure
~/speicherhöffige structure prospective for reservoirs
~/stromataktische stromatactis *(complex open space structure in micrite limestone)*
~/stromatische stromatic structure

~/stylolithische stylolitic structure
~/zuckerkörnige saccharoidal texture
~/zylindrische cylindrical structure
strukturaufwärts upstructure
Strukturboden m polygonal ground (soil), patterned ground
Strukturbohrung f structure drilling; structure [drilling] well
~/geologische structural [test] hole
Strukturdiskordanz f structural discordance (disconformity)
Struktureigenschaft f structural character
Struktureinheit f structural unit
~/überschobene downward facing structure
~/von Scherzonen begrenzte stabile tessera
Strukturelement n structural element
strukturell structural
Strukturen fpl/**an- und abschwellende** pinch and swell structures
~ in Meteoriten/fossile organized elements
Strukturform f structural form
Strukturforschung f structural research work
strukturgeologisch structural-geological
strukturgeometrisch structural-geometric
Strukturgruppe f structure group
Strukturkarte f structural map
~ der Oberfläche surface-structure map
Strukturkomplex m structural complex
Strukturlehre f/**allgemeine geologische** structural geology
Strukturlinie f/**halokinetische** halokinetic structure contour
strukturlos structureless; amorphous; anhistous
Strukturmerkmal n structural characteristic
Strukturoberfläche f structural surface
Strukturprofil n structure section
Strukturscheitel m structural crest, crest of structure
Strukturschema n structural scheme
Strukturstockwerk n structural stage (layer)
strukturtektonisch structural-tectonic
Strukturtensor m structural tensor
Strukturtheorie f structural theory
Strukturtiefstpunkt m spill point *(aquifer storage)*
Strukturvorsprung m nose
Strunien s. str. n. n s. Etroeungt
Strunzit m strunzite, $MnFe'''[OH|PO_4]_2 \cdot 6H_2O$
Struvit m struvite, $NH_4Mg[PO_4] \cdot 6H_2O$
Stubben m stub
Stubbenhorizont m stump horizon *(coal)*
~/interglazialer interglacial forest bed, black drift
Stückerz n lump (coarse) ore, ore in pieces
stückig lumpy
Stückigkeit f lumpiness
Stückkalk m lump lime *(burnt)*
Stückkohle f lump coal
Stufe f 1. stage *(biostratigraphic unit);* 2. step; 3. range
~/Baschkirische s. Baschkir

~/Dänische s. Dan
~/hangende upper[most] stage
~/Ludische s. Lud
~/Tatarische s. Tatar
stufenartig scalariform; echeloned
Stufendüne f cliff dune
Stufenfolge f succession of stages
stufenförmig stepped
Stufenland n/treppenförmiges scarped tableland
Stufenlandschaft f terraced landscape
Stufenlehne f cuesta back slope
Stufenmeißel m pilot (ear) bit
Stufenmündung f discordant junction (of a river)
Stufensee m[/glazialer] glint lake
Stufenstirn f cuesta scarp
Stufenterrasse f bench terrace
Stufenversetzung f edge dislocation
Stufenzementation f stage cementing
Stufenziehen n rate growth (of crystals)
Stufferz n s. Stückerz
stumpfwinklig amblygon[i]al
stunden to abandon
Stundenkreis m circle of compass
Stundenwinkel m hour angle
Sturm m strong gale (number 9 of Beaufort scale)
~/erdmagnetischer geomagnetic storm
~/magnetischer magnetic storm (disturbance)
~/orkanartiger storm (number 11 of Beaufort scale)
~/starker full (whole) gale (number 10 of Beaufort scale)
Sturmflut f storm tide (surge), high tide, sea flood
Sturmflutablagerung f s. Tempestit
Sturmflutschichtung f storm-surge lamination
Sturmstärke f gale force
Sturmwarnung f gale warning
Sturmwelle f storm wave, billow
Sturmwirbel m storm vortex
Sturmwolke f/niedrigziehende storm scud
Sturmzentrum n storm centre
Sturzbach m torrent, torrential (ravine) stream
stürzen/auf Halde to throw over the dump, to discard
Sturzflut f flash flood
Sturzhöhe f height of fall
Sturzregen m storm rainfall, torrential downpour
Sturzsee f heavy sea, breaker, surge
Sturzseite f slip face
Sturzversatz m drop stowing
Sturzwelle f breaker, roller
Stützdruck m support pressure
Stützgerüst n 1. supporting skeleton (anatomical); 2. supporting frame (e.g. in mines)
Stützit m stützite, Ag_5Te_3
Stützkraft f supporting force
Stützmauer f bearing wall
Stützpfeiler m supporting pillar

Stützweite f span
Styliolinenkalk m Styliolina Limestone (Devonian)
Stylolith m stylolite
Stylolithenharnisch m slickolites
stylolithisch stylolitic
Stylotyp m s. Tetraedrit
Suanit m suanite, $Mg_2[B_2O_5]$
subaerisch subaerial
subalpin subalpine
subangular subangular
subantarktisch subantarctic
subaquatisch subaquatic; subaqueous
subarktisch subarctic
Subatlantikum n Subatlanticum (higher part of Flandrian)
Subboreal n Subboreal (higher part of Flandrian)
Subduktion f subduction (after Rittmann, a kind of undercurrent)
Subduktionszone f subduction (Benioff) zone
subeffusiv subeffusive
Suberinit m suberinite (maceral of brown coals and lignites)
Suberosion f concealed erosion
Subfazies f subfacies
subfossil subfossil
subglazial subglacial, infraglacial
Subgrauwacke f subgraywacke, lithic (lowrank) graywacke
subkapillar subcapillary
subkrustal subcrustal
sublakustrin sublacustrine
Sublimation f sublimation
Sublimationswärme f heat of sublimation
sublitoral sublittoral, infralittoral
Sublitoral n sublittoral, subtidal
~/äußeres circalittoral
sublunarisch sublunar[y]
submarin submarine
submarin-pyroklastisch hyaloclastic
Submergenzdecke f onlap
submers submersed (parts of plants)
Submersion f submersion
submikroskopisch submicroscopic[al]
subozeanisch suboceanic
Subprovinz f subprovince
~/Rheinisch-böhmische Rhenish-Bohemian Subprovince (palaeobiogeography, Lower and Middle Devonian)
Subrosion f subrosion
subrosiv subrosive
subsalinar subsaliniferous
Subsalinar n subsaliniferous bed
subsequent subsequent
Subsolifluktion f subsolifluction
Subsolifluktionsbrekzie f glide breccia
Subsolution f subsolution
Subspezies f subspecies
Substanz f substance, material, matter
~/an Sedimentpartikel adsorbierte organische pelogloea

Substanz 306

~/anisotrope non-isotopic material
~/fluoreszierende fluorescent substance
~/fossile brennbare pyricaustate, thermite
~/kohlige coal organic matter
~/organische organic matter
Substituierbarkeit f substitutability
substituieren to substitute, to replace
Substitution f substitution, replacement
~/isomorphe isomorphous substitution (replacement)
Substrat n substratum
subterran subterranean
Subtraktionsstapelung f plus-minus stacking (seismics)
Subtropen pl subtropics
subtropisch subtropic[al], semitropical
Subvulkan m subvolcano
subvulkanisch subvolcanic
Subzone f subzone
Succinit m s. Sukzinit
Sucharbeiten fpl prospection
~ auf Erdöl und Erdgas prospecting for oil and gas
~ auf Lagerstätten prospecting for deposits
Suchbohrung f 1. exploratory drilling (boring); 2. exploratory borehole, prospecting well
~ untertage/kleine gopher hole
Suche f/geobotanische geobotanical prospecting
~/geochemische geochemical prospecting
Suchstrategie f strategy of prospection
südlich south[ern]; austral
Südlicht n southern lights, aurora australis
Südmulde f southern syncline
Südpol m south pole
Südpolarland n Antarctic Continent
Suess-Effekt m Suess effect
Suevit m suevite
Sukzession f succession
sukzinisch succinic
Sukzinit n succinite, amber
Sulfation n sulphate ion
Sulfatreduktion f sulphate reduction
Sulfid n/massives massive sulphide
Sulfitablauge f sulphite liquor
Sulfoborit m sulphoborite, $Mg_3[SO_4|(BO_2OH)_2] \cdot 4H_2O$
Sulfohalit m sulphohalite, $Na_6[F|Cl|(SO_4)_2]$
sulfophil sulphophil[e]
Sulvanit m sulvanite, Cu_3VS_4
Sulzeis n bottom ice, frazil [ice]
Summationskurvenauftragung f cumulative logarithmic plot
Summationsverfahren n summation method
Summenkurve f cumulative curve
Summenlinie f cumulative line
Sumpf m swamp, marsh, fen, bog; [quag]mire; morass
~/mariner paralic swamp
Sumpfablagerung f paludal (palustrine) deposit
Sumpfbildung f paludification

Sumpfboden m swampy soil, marshy ground, quagmire
~/schwarzer silty bog
Sumpfbutter f bog butter, butyr[ell]ite
Sumpfebene f mud flat
Sumpfeisenstein m s. Sumpferz
sümpfen to bail, to drain
~/eine Grube to clear a mine from water
Sümpfen n bailing, drainage
Sumpferz n bog [iron] ore, swamp (marsh, morass) ore
Sumpffläche f quagmire
Sumpfgas n marsh (peat) gas
Sumpfgebiet n swampy (marshy) area
~ mit Salzquellen lick
sumpfig swampy, marshy, fenny, boggy, morassic, paludal
Sumpfküste f marshy coast
Sumpfland n bog land
Sumpfloch n quagmire
Sumpfmoos n sphagnum [moss]
Sumpfniederung f swampy flat, marshy depression (flat)
Sumpfpflanzen fpl swamp plants, helophytes
Sumpfstrecke f drainway
Sumpfvegetation f swamp vegetation
Sumpfwaldboden m swamp forest soil
Sumpfwasser n water from marshy soils
Sumpfwiese f swamp meadow
Sund m straights, sound
Sundance-Formation f Sundance Formation (upper Dogger and lower Malm, North America)
superkapillar supercapillary
superkrustal supercrustal
Supernova f supernova
Superpositionsprinzip n superposition principle
Superpositionsverfahren n method of superposition
Superprovinz f/metallogenetische metallogenetic superprovince
supraaquatisch supra-aquatic
suprakrustal supracrustal
Supraleitungsmagnetometer n superconducting magnetometer, superconducting quantum interference device, SQUID
Suprastruktur f suprastructure
Sursassit m sursassite, $Mn_2H_3Al_2[O|OH|SiO_4|Si_2O_7]$
Suspension f suspension
Suspensionsstrom m suspension current, turbidity current (flow)
Sussexit m sussexite, $Mn_2[B_2O_5] \cdot H_2O$
Süß-Salzwasser-Grenzfläche f interface, fresh-water interface
Süßwasser n fresh water
Süßwasserablagerung f lacustrine (fresh-water) deposit
Süßwasserbenthos n limnaean benthos
Süßwasserbereich m fresh-water zone
Süßwasserbildung f fresh-water formation

System

Süßwasserfazies *f* fresh-water facies
Süßwasserfossil *n* fresh-water fossil
Süßwasserkalk *m* lacustrine (fresh-water) limestone
Süßwassermarsch *f* fresh-water marsh
Süßwassermolasse *f* fresh-water molasse
Süßwassermoor *n* fresh-water marsh (bog)
Süßwasserplankton *n* limnoplankton
Süßwasserquarzit *m* limnoquartzite
~/kavernöser buhrstone
Süßwassersee *m* fresh-water lake
Süßwassersumpf *m* fresh-water marsh (bog)
Suszeptibilität *f* susceptibility
~/elektrische electrical susceptibility
~/magnetische magnetic susceptibility
~/spezifische specific (mass) susceptibility
Suszeptibilitätsnomogramm *n* susceptibility nomogram
Sutur *f* suture [line]
~/gewellte waved suture [line]
~/gezackte angled suture [line]
~/wellige waved suture [line]
Svabit *m* svabite, $Ca_5[Fl(AsO_4)_3]$
Svanbergit *m* svanbergite, $SrAl_3[(OH)_6|SO_4PO_4]$
Swabben *n* swabbing
Swabbkolben *m* swab
Swartzit *m* swartzite, $CaMg[UO_2|(CO_3)_3] \cdot 12H_2O$
Swedenborgit *m* swedenborgite, $NaSbBe_4O_7$
Sweep *m* sweep *(signal form in vibroseis method)*
Syenit *m* syenite
syenitisch syenitic
Syenodiorit *m* syenodiorite
Sylvanit *m* sylvanite, white tellurium, graphic[al] gold, (Au, Ag) Te_4
Sylvin *m* sylvin[e], sylvite, leopoldite, KCl
Sylvinit *m* sylvinite
Symbiose *f* symbiosis
Symmetrie *f*/**bilaterale** bilateral symmetry
~/meridionale meridional symmetry
Symmetrieachse *f* axis of symmetry
~/dreizählige axis of threefold symmetry
~/optische optic axis of symmetry, axis of optic symmetry
~/vierzählige axis of fourfold (tetragonal) symmetry
~/zweizählige axis of twofold (binary) symmetry
Symmetrieebene *f* plane of symmetry
Symmetrieelement *n* symmetry element
symmetriegleich of the same symmetry
Symmetriegrad *m* degree of symmetry
Symmetrieklasse *f* symmetry class
Symmetrieoperation *f* symmetry operation
Symmetriezentrum *n* centre of symmetry
Symmicton *n* symmicton
~/verfestigtes symmictite
Symplesit *m* symplesite, $Fe_3[AsO_4]_2 \cdot 8H_2O$
Synadelphit *m* synadelphite, $Mn_4[(OH)_5|AsO_4]$
Synärese *f* synaeresis

Synäreseriß *m* syneresis crack
Synchisit *m* synchisite, $CaCe[Fl(CO_3)_2]$
synchron synchronous, synchronal
Synchronsatellit *m* synchronous satellite
Syneklise *f* syneclise
Syngenese *f* syngenesis
syngenetisch syngenetic, idiogenous, contemporaneous
Syngenit *m* syngenite, $K_2Ca[SO_4]_2 \cdot H_2O$
synkinematisch synkinematic
synklastisch synclastic
synklinal synclinal
Synklinalachse *f* synclinal axis
Synklinale *f* syncline, synclinal curve
~/isoklinal gefaltete carinate syncline
Synklinalfalte *f* synclinal fold, downfold
Synklinaltal *n* synclinal valley
Synklinalumbiegung *f* keystone of a synclinal fold
Synklinalwasser *n* syncline water
Synklinalzone *f* synclinal zone
Synklinorium *n* synclinorium, synclinore
Synökologie *f* synecology
Synonym *n*/**jüngeres** junior synonym *(rules of nomenclature)*
synoptisch synoptic
synorogen synorogene[ous], synorogenic
Synorogenese *f* synorogeny
synplutonisch synplutonic
synsedimentär synsedimentary, penecontemporaneous, intraformational
synsedimentär-tektonisch synsedimentary-tectonic
Synsedimentation *f* synsedimentation
syntektonisch syntectonic, principal tectonic
Syntexis *f* syntexis
Synthese *f* synthesis
synthetisch synthetic
Syntypus *m* syntype
Syrosjom *m* syrosjom
Sysserskit *m* sysserskite, osmite (Os,Ir,...)
System *n* system *(biostratigraphic unit)*
~ einer Bohranlage/hydraulisches drilling-rig hydraulic control system
~ einer Bohranlage/pneumatisches drilling-rig pneumatic control system
~/geologisches geological system
~/gesättigtes saturated system
~/granitisches granitic system
~/heterogenes heterogeneous system
~/hexagonales hexagonal system
~/homogenes homogeneous system
~/hydrothermales hydrothermal system
~/kubisches cubic (regular, isometric) system
~/monoklines monoclinic (oblique) system
~/offenes open system
~/orthorhombisches orthorhombic system
~ paralleler Gänge dike set
~/passives passive system *(seismics)*
~/quadratisches quadratic system
~/reguläres *s.* **~/kubisches**
~/rhombisches prismatic[al] system

System 308

~/**rhomboedrisches** rhombohedral system
~/**statisch bestimmtes** statically determined system
~/**statisch unbestimmtes** statically undetermined system
~/**tetragonales** tetragonal (quadratic) system
~/**trigonales** trigonal system
~/**triklines** triclinic system
~ **von Grundwasserleitern** multiaquifer formation
Systemkunde f systematics, taxonomy
Szaibelyit m szaibelyite, $Mg_2[B_2O_5] \cdot H_2O$
Szepterwachstum n scepterlike growth
Szik-Boden m szik soil
~/**toniger** clay szik soil
Szintillation f scintillation
Szintillationszähler m photomultiplier counter, scintillation counter (detector)
Szintillator m scintillator
szintillieren to scintillate
Szintillometer n scintillometer, scintillation tube
~ **für Flugvermessung** airborne scintillation counter
Szmikit m szmikite, $Mn[SO_4] \cdot H_2O$
Szomolnokit m szomolnokite, schmöllnitzite, $Fe[SO_4] \cdot H_2O$

T

Taaffeit m taaffeite, Al_4MgBeO_8
Tabelle f/**stratigrafische** geologic[al] column
Tabetisol m tabetisol, talik
Tabetisolbildung f tabetification
Tachometer n tachometer, revolution counter
Tachyhydrit m tachyhydrite, $CaCl_2 \cdot 2MgCl_2 \cdot 12H_2O$
Tachylit m tachylite, tachylyte
Taeniolith m taeniolite, $KLiMg_2[F_2|Si_4O_{10}]$
Tafel f platform (macrotectonic structural form)
~/**Osteuropäische** Eastern European platform
~/**Russische** Russian platform
~/**Sibirische** Siberian platform
~/**Westeuropäische** Western European platform
tafelartig tablelike
Tafelberg m table mountain
~/**aus einer Ebene aufragender** mesa
Tafelbruchbildung f block faulting
Tafeldeckgebirge n platform cover
Tafeldeckgebirgssedimente npl cover sediments of a platform
Tafeleisberg m tabular iceberg
tafelförmig tabular
Tafelgebirge n table mountains
tafelig tabular
Tafelland n tableland, plateau
Tafelrestberg m mesa
Tafelschiefer m grapholite
Tafelschollengebirge n plateau block mountains

Tafelsenke f platform basin
Tafelstruktur f table structure
Tafoniverwitterung f tafoni-type of weathering
Tag m/**astronomischer** astronomic[al] day
Tage/über above ground, overground, bank head
~/**unter** underground, below ground
Tagebau m open mine (cut, pit, cast); surface (strip, open-cut) mining, opencasting, opencast working
~/**abgeworfener** abandoned strip mine
~/**neuaufgeschlossener** recently opened cast working
~/**strossenförmiger** benching working
Tagebauaufschluß m opencast development
Tagebaubetrieb m surface mining (winning, workings)
Tagebauentwässerung f drainage of opencast mines
Tagebaufeld n open-pit field, stripping site
Tagebaugrenze f open-pit boundary
~/**obere** open-pit top outline
~/**untere** open-pit bottom outline
Tagebaukohle f strip (opencast) coal
Tagebauneuaufschluß m new exposure
Tagebausohle f open-pit bottom
Tagebaustoß m open-pit bank
Tagesänderung f diurnal variation
~ **der Erdströme** telluric diurnal variation
~/**magnetische** magnetic diurnal variation
Tagesanlage f surface plant
Tagesaufschluß m surface exposure
Tagesausbeute f daily exploitation (excavation, winning)
Tagesbericht m daily report
Tagesbruch m cave to the surface (mining damage)
Tagesförderung f, **Tagesleistung** f daily output, output per day
Tagesmittel n daily mean
Tagesoberfläche f day (ground) surface, surface of the ground
Tagesstrecke f day level
Tagesvariation f daily variation
Tageswasser n surface (outcrop) water
Taghanic[um] n Taghanican [Stage] (basal stage of Senecan in North America)
Tagilit m tagilite, $Cu_2[OH|PO_4] \cdot H_2O$
Tagundnachtgleiche f equinox
Tahitit m tahitite (alkali-basaltic rock)
Taifun m typhoon
Taifunbahn f typhoon track
Taiga f taiga
Tailing n tailing
takonisch Taconic
Takonit m taconite (banded ironstone ore)
Taktit m tactite
Takyr m takyr, salt desert
Takyr-Boden m takyr soil
Tal n valley
~/**abgeriegeltes** blocked-up valley

~/**abgesperrtes** obstructed valley
~ **am Rande einer Blockkippung** fault-angle valley
~/**antezedentes** antecedent valley
~/**aufgepfropftes** engrafted valley
~/**aufgesetztes** super[im]posed valley
~/**auflandiges** filled valley
~/**autogenes** autogenous valley
~/**blindes** blind valley
~/**breitsohliges** wide-bottomed valley, broad-floored valley
~/**durch Geschiebe abgeriegeltes** valley encumbered (blocked up) by drift
~/**entgletschertes** deglaciated valley
~/**epigenetisches** super[im]posed valley
~/**ertrunkenes** drowned valley
~ **in Richtung des Schichtfallens** cataclinal valley
~/**insequentes** insequent valley
~/**jungreifes** early mature valley
~/**konsequentes** consequent valley
~/**mehrzyklisches** polycyclic valley
~/**reifes** mature valley
~/**resequentes** resequent valley
~/**spätreifes** late mature valley
~/**steilwandiges** sinking creek
~/**submarines** submarine valley (canyon)
~/**subsequentes** subsequent (strike) valley
~/**tektonisches** tectonic (structural) valley
~/**tiefeingeschnittenes** sharply incised valley
~/**trockenes** uadi
~/**überreifes** old-age valley
~/**überstautes** drowned valley
~/**ursprüngliches** consequent valley
~/**verlängertes** extended valley
~/**vermurtes** debris-filled valley
~/**V-förmiges** V-shaped valley
~/**vollreifes** full-mature valley
~ **zwischen zwei Überschiebungseinheiten** ramp valley
Talaue f valley plain (flat), flood (river) plain, alluvial flat
Talaufschüttung f valley fill
Talausgang m valley mouth
Talbecken n/**glaziales** glacial basin
Talbeginn m valley head
Talbett n valley channel
Talbildung f valley formation
Talboden m valley bottom (floor)
Taleinschnitt m valley cut (section)
Talerweiterung f valley broadening (widening)
Talfüllungen fpl alluvial fills
Talgabelung f bifurcation of the valley
Talgefälle n channel slope
Talgehänge n overhanging valley side
Talgletscher m valley glacier
~/**in ein Nebental überlaufender** diffluence glacier
Talhang m valley side (slope)
Talk m talc[um], $Mg_3[(OH)_2|Si_4O_{10}]$
~/**massiger** talcite
Talkar n valley car

talkartig talcous, talcose, talcoid
Talkessel m deep circular valley (gorge)
Talkesselboden m basin soil
Talkgestein n/**unreines** pot stone
talkhaltig talcous, talcose
talkig talcky, talcous, talcose
Talkschiefer m talcous schist (slate), talc schist (slate)
Talkum n s. Talk
Tallandschaft f valley landscape
Tallehm m valley loam
Tallehne f ramp
Talmäander m valley meander
Talmessit m talmessite, $Ca_2Mg[AsO_4]_2 \cdot 2H_2O$
Talmoor n valley bog (mire)
Talmulde f hollow, dale, swale, combe
Talquelle f valley spring
Talsand m valley sand
Talschlucht f defile, glen, dingle
Talschluß m valley head
Talschotter m valley gravel
Talschutt m valley fill
Talsohle f valley bottom (floor)
Talsperre f dam, barrage
~ **mit festem Überfall** permanent overfall weir
~ **mit Vielfachkuppeln** multiple dome dam
Talsperrenbaustelle f dam site, (Am) dam location
Talsperrenbecken n storage (impounding) reservoir, impounding basin
Talsperrenmauer f concrete dam
Talsystem n/**verzweigtes** dendritic[al] valley system
Talterrasse f valley terrace
Talvereng[er]ung f constriction of a valley
Talverlegung f migration of a valley
Talwand f valley wall
talwärts downhill
Talwasserscheide f valley-floor divide
Talwind m valley breeze, upslope wind
Talzuschub m closing-up of a valley, valley thrust, creeping towards the valley
Tamarugit m tamarugite, $NaAl[SO_4]_2 \cdot 6H_2O$
Tamiskaming n Tamiskaming [System] (Precambrian in North America)
Tamponieren n packing
Tandemrakete f tandem rocket
Tang m seaweed, kelp
tangähnlich fucoidal
Tangeit m tangeite, calciovolborthite, $CaCu[OH|VO_4]$
Tangentialebene f tangential plane
Tangentialspannung f tangential stress
tannenbäumchenartig arborescent
Tannenbaumkristall m pine crystal
Tannen-Hainbuchen-Zeit f fir-hornbeam period
Tansanit m tanzanite (blue-coloured zoisite)
Tantal n tantalum, Ta
Tantalerz n tantalum ore
Tantalit m tantalite, (Fe, Mn) (Ta, Nb)$_2O_6$
Tanteuxenit m s. Delorenzit

Tapalpit

Tapalpit *m* tapalpite, $3Ag_2(S, Te) \cdot Bi_2(S,Te)_3$
taphrogen taphrogenic
Taphrogenese *f* taphrogenesis, taphrogeny
Tapiolit *m* tapiolite, ixiolite, $(Fe, Mn)(Ta, Nb)_2O_6$
Taramellit *m* taramellite, $Ba_2(Fe, Ti, Fe)_2[(OH)_2|Si_4O_{12}]$
Taranakit *m* taranakite, palmerite, $K_3Al_5H_6[PO_4]_8 \cdot 18H_2O$
Tarapacait *m* tarapacaite, K_2CrO_4
Tarbuttit *m* tarbuttite, $Zn_2[OH|PO_4]$
Tarnowitzit *m* tarnowitzite *(Pb-aragonite)*
Tarnung *f* **eines Spurenelements** camouflage of a trace element
Tasche *f* pocket
Taschenboden *m* involution layer
Tasmanit *m* tasmanite *(oil-algal formation, oil shale)*
Tastatur *f* keyboard
Tastdilatometer *n* feeling dilatometer
Tatar[ium] *n* Tatarian [Stage] *(of Upper Permian)*
Tätigkeit *f* activity
~/ausklingende vulkanische declining volcanic activity
~/bergbauliche mining activity
~ des Eises ice action
~/effusive effusive activity
~/explosive explosive activity
~/hypoabyssische hypabyssal activity
~/unregelmäßige spasmodic activity
~/vulkanische volcanic activity
Tau *m* dew
taub dead, barren
Taubenblutrubin *m* pigeon-blood ruby
Taubfeld *n* barren track
Taubildung *f* dew formation
Taubkohle *f* blind coal
Taubodenrutschung *f* über Frostboden gelifluxion, gelifluction
Tauchboot *n/unbemanntes* unmanned submersible (diving boat)
Tauchdecke *f* plunging nappe, underthrust sheet
Taucherglocke *f* diving bell
Tauchfalte *f* plunging fold (anticline), returned fold
Tauchhammer *m* hammer drill
Tauchsonde *f* immersion probe
Tauchsystem *n* diving system
Tauchwelle *f* dipping (diving) wave; refraction wave
tauen to thaw
Taufließtextur *f* ropy flow structure
Tau-Frost-Wechsel *m* freezing and thawing cycle
Tau-Gefrier-Prozeß *m/mehrfacher* multigelation
Tauprozeß *m* depergelation *(in permafrost);* mollition *(in mollisol)*
Taupunkt *m* dew point
Taupunktdruck *m* dew-point pressure

Tauriscit *m* tauriscite, $Fe[SO_4] \cdot 7H_2O$
Tautemperatur *f* defrosting temperature
Tautirit *m* tautirite *(nepheline monzonite)*
tautozonal tautozonal, cozonal
Tauwasser *n* dripping water
Tauwetter *n* thaw [weather]
Tavistockit *m* tavistockite, $Ca_3Al_2[OH|PO_4]_3$
Tavorit *m* tavorite, $LiFe[OH|PO_4]$
Tawmawit *m* tawmawite *(Cr-epidote)*
Taxon *n/nominelles* nominal taxon *(rules of nomenclature)*
Taxonomie *f* taxonomy
~/biologische biological (genetical) taxonomy
taxonomisch taxonomic[al]
Taylorit *m* taylorite, $(K,NH_4)_2[SO_4]$
T-Bau *m* T-support
T-D-Kurve *f* T-D curve, time-depth curve
Teallit *m* teallite, $PbSnS_2$
Technogeochemie *f* technogeochemistry
Technosphäre *f* technosphere
Tectorium *n* tectorium, deposition layer *(foraminiferans)*
Teepleit *m* teepleite, $Na_2[Cl|B(OH)_4]$
Teer *m* tar
teerartig tarry
Teerasphalt *m* tar asphalt
teerfrei tarless
teerig tarry
Tegel *m s.* Tonmergel
Tegelen-Warmzeit *f* Tegelen stadial
Teich *m* pool, pond
teigartig, teigig pasty
Teil *m/[ab]bauwürdiger* pay shoot
~ der Erdkruste/oberflächennaher supercrust of earth
~ einer Felswand/vorspringender ledge of a rock
~ einer Subzone zonule *(fossil-recorded)*
~/hangender upper leaf *(of a seam)*
~/oberster top part
~/wasserführender terraqueous zone *(of the lithosphere)*
Teilabbau *m* partial extraction
Teilabschnitt *m* partial section
teilbar divisible; fissile
Teilbarkeit *f* divisibility; fissility
~/beste rift *(in plutonites)*
Teilbereich *m* leg
Teilbeweglichkeit *f* part movability, componental mobility
Teilbodenentwässerung *f* dewatering through the partially perforated base
Teilchen *n* particle
~/suspendiertes suspended solid
Teildecke *f* branch (subsidiary) sheet, subordinate nappe
Teildruck *m* partial pressure
teilen to reduce *(samples)*
Teilfluß *m* fraction of flow
Teilgebiet *n* subarea
~/morphologisch exponiertes partial area exposed morphologically

Teilkonvergenz f incomplete convergence
Teilkreis m graduated circle
~ am Kompaß circle of compass
Teilmagma n partial (fractional) magma
teilorientiert partially oriented
Teilprobe f subsample
Teilprobenahme f subsampling *(a special case of cluster sampling)*
Teilschmelzenbildung f fractional (partial) melting
Teilsenkung f partial subsidence
Teilsohle f sublevel
Teilsohlen[bruch]bau m sublevel [space] stoping
Teilsohlenstrecke f sublevel
Teilstrecke f leg
Teilung f reduction *(of samples)*
Teilungsebene f parting plane
Teilungsfläche f plane of division, joint
Teilversatz m partial stowing
Teilversetzung f partial dislocation
Teilwegmultiple f interformational (peg-leg) multiple *(seismics)*
Teilzone f local range zone
Teilzyklus m partial cycle
Teineit m teineite, $Cu[TeO_3] \cdot 2H_2O$
Tektit m tektite
~/tasmanischer Darwin glass, queenstownite
Tektitenglas n **von Macedon** Macedon glass
Tektitenstreufeld n strewn field of tektites
Tektofazies f tectofacies
Tektogen n tectogene
Tektogenese f tectogenesis
~/algomane Algoman folding *(Late Precambrian in North America)*
~/laurentische Laurentian folding *(Lower Precambrian in North America)*
tektogenetisch tectogenetic
tektomagmatisch tectomagmatic
Tektonik f tectonics, [archi]tectonic geology
~/regionale regional tectonics
tektonisch tectonic, structural
tektonisch-lithologisch tectonic-lithological
Tektonisierung f tectonization
Tektonit m tectonite
Tektonitgefüge n tectonite fabric
Tektonogramm n tectonogram
tektonometamorph tectonometamorphic
Tektonophysik f tectonophysics
Tektonosphäre f tectonosphere
Tektosilikat n tectosilicate
Tektotop n tectotope
telemagmatisch telemagmatic
Teleosteer npl teleosts
Teleseismologie f teleseismology
Teleskoping n telescoping
telethermal telethermal
Telinit m telinite *(coal maceral)*
Tellerbohrer m earth auger
Tellereis n pancake ice
Tellur n tellurium, Te
Tellurblei n altaite, PbTe

Tellurerz n tellurium ore
tellurführend telluriferous
Tellurgold n calaverite, $(Au, Ag)Te_2$
tellurhaltig telluriferous
tellurig tellurous
Tellurik f tellurics
tellurisch telluric, tellurian
Tellurit m, **Tellurocker** m tellurite, TeO_2
Telocollinit m telocollinite *(submaceral)*
Telson n telson, caudal spine, tail segment *(crustaceans)*
Telychium n Telychian *(uppermost stage of Llandovery)*
Temperatur f temperature
~ auf Bohrlochsohle bottom-hole temperature
~ der Wasseroberfläche water surface temperature
~/kritische critical temperature
Temperaturabnahme f decrease in temperature
Temperaturanstieg m temperature rise
Temperaturaufbau m temperature build-up
Temperaturbereich m temperature range
Temperaturbestimmung f geothermometry *(in geological processes)*
Temperaturerhöhung f increase (elevation) of temperature
Temperaturfixpunkt m fixed point of temperature
Temperaturgradient m temperature gradient
Temperaturgradientenlog n temperature gradient log
Temperaturinversion f temperature inversion
Temperaturleitfähigkeit f thermal diffusivity
Temperaturmeßsonde f thermometer probe
Temperaturmessung f temperature survey (logging)
Temperaturschwankung f fluctuation of temperature, temperature variation
~/tägliche diurnal temperature variation
Temperaturskale f temperature scale
Temperatursturz m precipitous drop in temperature
Temperaturunterschied m difference in temperature
Temperaturverwitterung f destruction by insolation
Temperaturwechsel m change of temperature
Tempestit m tempestite
Tengerit m tengerite (H_2O-bearing Y carbonate)
Tennantit m tennantite, $3Cu_2S \cdot As_2S_3$
Tenorit m tenorite, melaconite, CuO
Tensid n tenside
Tensiometer n tensiometer
Tentakel mpl tentacles
Tentakulitenschicht f Tentaculites bed
Tentakulitenschiefer m Tentaculites schist
Tenuidurit m tenuidurite *(coal microlithotype)*
Tephra f tephra, volcanic ejecta
Tephrit m tephrite
Tephroit m tephroite, Mn_2SiO_4

Teppichfaltung

Teppichfaltung f carpet folding
Terebratelbank f Terebratula bed
Terebratuliden fpl terebratulids
Tergit n, **Tergum** n tergum, dorsum (arthropods)
Terlinguait m terlinguaite, $2HgO \cdot Hg_2Cl_2$
Terminologie f/**stratigrafische** stratigraphic[al] terminology
Terra f **fusca** terra fusca
~ **rossa** terra rossa
Terrainaufnahme f ground survey
Terrainbeschaffenheit f topographic features
Terrakotta f terracotta, burnt clay
terran terranean
Terrasse f terrace
~/**alluviale** aggradation[al] terrace
Terrassen fpl/**niveaugleiche** matched terraces
~/**parallele** parallel roads
Terrassenbildung f terracing, development of terraces
Terrassenböschung f terrace slope (front)
terrassenförmig terraciform, terraced, bench-like
Terrassensand m terrace sand
Terrassenschotter m terrace (bench) gravel
Terrassentreppe f terrace flight
Terrassierung f terracing, benching
terrestrisch terrestrial; land-derived
terrigen terrigenous, terrigene
Territorium n territory
tertiär Tertiary
Tertiär n Tertiary [System] (chronostratigraphically); Tertiary [Period] (geochronologically); Tertiary [Age] (common sense)
Tertiärperiode f Tertiary [Period]
Tertiärquarzit m Tertiary quartzite
Tertiärsystem n Tertiary [System]
Tertiärzeit f Tertiary [Age]
Tertschit m tertschite, $Ca_2[B_5O_6(OH)_7] \cdot 6\,^1/_2 H_2O$
Teschemacherit m teschemacherite, NH_4HCO_3
Teschenit m teschenite (alkali rock)
tesseral tesseral
Test m test (method applied to prove statistical hypotheses)
Testgebiet n test site
Testmessung f pilot run, test line
Testort m test site
Tetartoeder n tetartohedron
tetartoedrisch tetartohedral, tetartosymmetric
Tetradymit m tetradymite, Bi_2Te_3S
Tetraeder n tetrahedron
Tetraedertheorie f tetrahedral theory of the earth
tetraedrisch tetrahedral
Tetraedrit m tetrahedrite, silver fahlerz, gray copper ore, $3Cu_2S \cdot Sb_2S_3$
tetragonal tetragonal, dimetric
Tetragonalboden m tetragonal soil, tundra polygons
Tetrakishexaeder n tetrakishexahedron

Tetrakorallen fpl tetracorals
Teufe f depth
~ **einer Bohrung** well depth
~/**ewige** unlimited depth
Teufenabschnitt m/**produzierender** producing interval
Teufenanzeiger m depth indicator
Teufenkapazität f depth capacity
Teufenlage f position of depth
Teufenmeßgerät n depthometer, depth finder, fathometer
Teufenunterschied m/**primärer** zoning of primary mineralization
~/**sekundärer** secondary downward change, secondary variation in depth
Textinit m textinite (maceral of brown coals and lignites)
Textur f 1. texture, structure (for rocks equivalent to the German „Textur", but not uniform in application, s.a. Gefüge, Struktur); 2. texture (palaeontology)
~/**bioturbate** bioturbate texture (ichnology)
~/**schlackige** slaggy (scoriaceous) texture
~/**schwammige** spongy texture
~/**sphäroidische** orbicular (nodular) texture
~/**surreitische** surreitic texture
~/**syngenetische** syngenetic texture
~/**variolitische** variolitic texture
Texturboden m structure ground
Texturdiagramm n texture diagram
texturell textural
Texturgoniometer n texture goniometer
texturlos anhistous
Texturmerkmal n textural character
thalassogen thalassogenic
thalassokratisch thalassocratic
Thalattogenese f thalattogenesis
Thalattokratie f thalattocracy
Thalenit m thalenite, $Y_2[Si_2O_7]$
Thallium n thallium, Tl
Thanatocoenose f, **Thanatokönose** f, **Thanatozönose** f thanatocoenosis
Thanet n, **Thanétien** n, **Thanetium** n Thanetian [Stage] (of Palaeocene)
Thaumasit m thaumasite, $Ca_3H_2[CO_3|SO_4|SiO_4] \cdot 13H_2O$
Theken fpl thecae (of graptolites)
Thenardit m thenardite, verde salt, $\alpha\text{-}Na_2[SO_4]$
Theodolit m theodolite
Theodolitfernrohr n alidade
Theorie f **der Kontinentalverschiebungen** theory of continental drift
~ **der Vorzerklüftung** theory of induced cleavage
~ **des Diskontinuums** discontinuum theory
~/**Huttonsche** Huttonian theory
Theralith m theralite (rock of the alkali gabbro clan)
Thermalfeld n thermal field
Thermalquelle f thermal (hot) spring
Thermalquellenablagerung f thermal spring deposit

Thermalwasser n thermal water
Thermalwasseraustritt m thermal water outlet
Therme f thermal (hot) spring
Thermenlinie f thermal fault fissure
thermisch thermal
Thermoanalyse f thermal analysis
Thermochemie f thermochemistry
thermochemisch thermochemical
Thermodynamik f **der Erde** terrestrial thermodynamics
thermodynamisch thermodynamic
thermoelektrisch thermoelectric
Thermoelektrizität f thermoelectricity
Thermogravimetrie f thermogravimetry
Thermokarst m thermokarst
Thermokarstniederung f thaw depression
Thermolumineszenz f thermoluminescence
Thermomagnetismus m thermomagnetism
Thermometamorphose f thermometamorphism, thermal metamorphism
Thermometer n **für Tiefbohrungen** bottom-hole thermometer
~/geologisches geologic[al] thermometer
thermometrisch thermometric
Thermonatrit n thermonatrite, $Na_2CO_3 \cdot H_2O$
thermophil thermophilic
Thermoremanenz f **magnetischer Minerale** detritional remanent magnetization
thixotrop thixotropic
Thixotropie f thixotropy
Thixotropieeffekt m thixotropic hardening
Tholeiit m tholeiite *(basaltic rock)*
Thomsenolith m thomsenolite, $NaCa[AlF_6] \cdot H_2O$
Thomsonit m thomsonite, mesole, $NaCa_2[Al_2(Al,Si)Si_2O_{10}]_2 \cdot 6H_2O$
Thomsonitgeröll n/**grünes** bagotite
Thor n thorium, Th
Thorakalfüße mpl thoracic legs *(arthropods)*
Thorax m thorax *(of trilobites)*
Thoraxring m thoracic ring *(of trilobites)*
Thoraxsegment n thoracic somite *(of trilobites)*
Thoreaulith m thoreaulite, $Sn[(Ta, Nb)_2O_7]$
Thorerde f thoria
Thorianit n thorianite, ThO_2
Thorit m thorite, $ThSiO_4$
Thorium n thorium, Th
Thoriumerz n thorium ore
thoriumhaltig thoriated
Thorogummit m thorogummite, mackintoshite, $(Th, U)[SiO_4, (OH)_4]$
Thorotungstit m thorotungstite, $2W_2O_3 \cdot H_2O + (ThO_2, Ce_2O_3, ZrO_2) + H_2O$
Thortveitit m thortveitite, $Sc_2[Si_2O_7]$
Thoruranin m *s.* Bröggerit
Thufur m *s.* Palsa
Thulit m thulite *(Mn-zoisite and Mn-epidote)*
Thuring[ien] n Thuringian [Stage] *(of Permian)*
Thuringit m thuringite, $(Mg, Fe)_3(Fe, Al)_3[(OH)_8|AlSi_3O_{10}]$
Thurnien n Thurnian *(part of preglacial complex in England, lowermost Pleistocene)*

Tide f tide
Tidefluß m tidal river
Tideneffekt m tidal effect
Tidenhub m tidal range
Tief n low, deep
~/ozeanisches oceanic deep
Tiefanker mpl tie rods
Tiefbau m underground mining, [level] deep mining, deep [mine] working
Tiefbohranlage f deep-well drilling plant (rig)
Tiefbohrausrüstung f deep-well drilling equipment
Tiefbohren n deep boring (drilling)
Tiefbohrer m depth drill
Tiefbohrgeräte npl deep-well drilling equipment
Tiefbohrloch n deep hole (well)
Tiefbohrlochschießen n deep-hole blasting
Tiefbohrpumpe f subsurface pump
Tiefbohrung f deep boring (drilling)
Tiefbohrzement m cement for packing, oil-well cement
Tiefbrunnen m deep well
Tiefdruckgebiet n low-pressure area
Tiefdruckrinne f trough
Tiefe f depth; abysm
~ bis zum Grundgebirge depth to the basement rocks
~ des Weltmeers/mittlere mean sea depth
~/erwartete expected depth
~/geringe slight (shallow) depth
~/lichtlose aphotic region
~/mittlere intermediate depth
~ von Gebirgsleitschichten depth of formation markers
~/voraussichtliche expected depth
Tiefebene f lowland plain
Tiefenbereich m depth range
Tiefenbruch m depth fracture
Tiefenerkundung f deep exploration
Tiefenerosion f deep (downward, vertical) erosion
Tiefengestein n plutonite, plutonic (deep-seated, abyssal, intrusion) rock
Tiefengesteine npl/**gleichaltrige** plutonic equivalents
Tiefenintrusionen fpl abyssal activity
Tiefenkarstvorkommen n deep karst occurrence
Tiefenkarte f bathymetric (bathygraphic) chart
Tiefenkartierung f depth mapping
tiefenkorrelierbar pickable, willing to pick
~/nicht unwilling to pick
Tiefenkorrelierung f subsurface stratigraphic correlation
Tiefenkurve f bathymetric curve
Tiefenlinie f isobath, subsurface contour (line), bottom contour line
Tiefenlinienkarte f subsurface contour map
Tiefenmagma n hypomagma
Tiefenprobe f depth sample
Tiefenprobenahme f depth-integrating sampling

Tiefenprobenehmer 314

Tiefenprobenehmer *m* depth-integrating sampler
Tiefenprofil *n* depth profile (section)
Tiefenpunkt *m* depth point
~/gemeinsamer common depth point
Tiefenregion *f* abyssal zone
Tiefenschicht *f* subsurface bed
Tiefenschnitt *m* depth section
Tiefenschurf *m* scour *(within a river bed)*
Tiefensondiergerät *n* deep-sounding apparatus
Tiefensondierung *f* deep sounding
~/elektromagnetische electromagnetic deep sounding
~/erdmagnetische geomagnetic deep sounding
~/seismische deep seismic sounding, DSS
Tiefenstrom *m* deep current, bathycurrent, underflow
Tiefenstruktur *f* subsurface structure
Tiefenstufe *f*/**geothermische** geothermal step (degree of depth)
Tiefentektonik *f* deep tectonics
Tiefenunterschiede *mpl*/**primäre** primary downward changes
Tiefenverwitterung *f* downward weathering
Tiefenvorgang *m* deep-seated process
Tiefenvulkan *m* deep-seated volcano
Tiefenwasser *n* deep (subterranean, juvenile) water
Tiefenwasserströmung *f* deep-water current
Tiefenwinkel *m* depression angle
Tiefenzirkulation *f* subsurface circulation *(of vadose waters)*
Tiefenzone *f* deep (depth) zone
Tiefenzunahme *f* increase in depth
Tieffaltungszone *f* hinge belt *(between geosyncline and continental foreland)*
Tiefgründung *f* deep foundation
Tiefherdbeben *n* deep-focus earthquake, deep-seated tremors
Tiefkraton *n* low craton, thalassocraton
tiefkrustal deep-crustal
Tiefland *n* lowland, bottom land
tiefliegend deep-seated, deeply buried, low-lying
tieforogen cataorogenic
Tiefpaßfilter *n* low-pass filter, high-cut filter
Tiefpumpe *f*/**gestängelose** hydraulic subsurface pump
~ mit Gestänge sucker-rod-type pump
Tiefpumpenförderung *f* pumping with sucker rods
Tiefquarz *m* low (alpha) quartz
Tiefschnitt *m* deep cut
Tiefscholle *f* sunken (downthrown) block, downthrown (downdropped) fault block, fault trough, trench fault
Tiefsee *f* deep sea (ocean), abyssal sea (depths), oceanic abyss
Tiefseeablagerung *f* abyssal (deep-sea, pelagic) deposit, deposit of the abyssal depths

Tiefseeberg *m* sea mount[ain]
Tiefseebergbau *m* deep-sea mining
Tiefseeboden *m* deep-sea bottom, abyssal floor
Tiefseebohrung *f* deep-sea drilling
Tiefseedredge *f* deep-sea dredge
Tiefsee-Ebene *f* abyssal plain
Tiefsee-Erhebung *f* seaknoll; sea mount
Tiefseefächer *m* deep-sea fan
Tiefseefauna *f* hypobenthos
Tiefseefazies *f* deep-sea facies, deep-water marine facies
Tiefseeforschung *f* deep-sea exploration
Tiefseegraben *m* [deep] trench, [oceanic] deep
Tiefseehügel *m* abyssal hill
Tiefseekuppe *f* sea mount[ain]
Tiefseelot *n* bathometer, bathymeter
Tiefseelotung *f* bathymetry, oceanographic (deep-sea) sounding
Tiefseemanganknolle *f* pelagite
Tiefseemessung *f* bathymetry
Tiefseerinne *f* deep-sea furrow (channel), abyssal gap
Tiefseeschlamm *m* deep-sea ooze (mud), pelagic ooze
Tiefseeschleppnetz *n* deep-sea dredge
Tiefseeschwellen *fpl* abyssal rises
Tiefseesediment *n* deep-sea sediment, abyssal deposit
Tiefseeton *m*/**brauner (roter)** deep-sea brown (red) clay
Tiefseezone *f* pelagic zone
Tiefsttemperatur *f* cryogenic temperature
Tieftemperaturverkokung *f* low-temperature carbonization
Tiemannit *m* tiemannite, HgSe
Tierfraß *m* grazing
Tiergeografie *f* zoogeography
Tierkreis *m* zodiac
Tierkreislicht *n* zodiacal light
Tierreich *n* animal kingdom, fauna
Tierreste *mpl*/**fossile** animal debris (remains), faunal remains
Tierspur *f* animal trail
Tierversteinerung *f* zoolite
Tiffanien *n* Tiffanian [Stage] *(of Palaeocene)*
Tigerauge *n* tiger's-eye *(subvariety of quartz)*
Tigersandstein *m* tiger (mottled) sandstone
Tikhonenkovit *m* tikhonenkovite, $(Sr, Ca)[AlF_4OH \cdot H_2O]$
Tilasit *m* tilasite, $CaMg[F|AsO_4]$
Tilleyit *m* tilleyite, $Ca_5[(CO_3)_2|Si_2O_7]$
Tillit *m* tillite
Timiskaming *n* Timiskaming *(upper Lower Precambrian in North America)*
Tinguait *m* tinguaite *(alkali syenite)*
Tinkal *m* tincal, native borax
Tinkalconit *m* tincalconite, $Na_2[B_4O_5(OH)_4] \cdot 3H_2O$
Tinkalsee *m* alkaline lake
Tinticit *m* tinticite, $Fe_3[(OH)_3|(PO_4)_2] \cdot 3H_2O$

Tinzenit *m* tinzenite *(variety of axinite)*
Tioughnioga *n* Tioughniogan [Stage] *(of Givetian in North America)*
Tirolit *m* tyrolite, $Ca_2Cu_9[(OH)_{10}|(AsO_4)_4] \cdot 10H_2O$
Tischfels *m* pedestal (mushroom) rock
Titan *n* titanium, Ti
Titan-Augit *m* titanaugite *(3–5% TiO_2)*
Titaneisenerz *n* titanic iron ore, ilmenite, menaccanite, $FeTiO_3$
Titanerz *n* titanium ore, octahedrite
titanführend, titanhaltig titaniferous, titanous
Titanit *m* titanite, sphene, $CaTi[O|SiO_4]$
Titanomagnetit *m* titanomagnetite *(magnetite-ulvite solid solution)*
Titanomorphit *m* titanomorphite
Titanoxid *n*/**schwarzes** ilmenorutile
Tithon[ien] *n*, **Tithonium** *n* Tithonian [Stage] *(upper stage of Malm, Tethys)*
Tjäle *m*/**perenner** *s.* Dauerfrostboden
Toad[ien] *n* Toadian *(Scythian to lower Ladinian, North America)*
Toarc[ien] *n*, **Toarcium** *n* Toarcian [Stage] *(uppermost stage of Lias)*
Tobel *m* ravine, defile, gully
Tobermorit *m* tobermorite, $Ca_5H_2[Si_3O_9]_2 \cdot 4H_2O$
Tochteratom *n* daughter atom
Tochterelement *n* daughter element
Tochterisotop *n* daughter isotope
Tochtermagma *n* derivative magma
Tochterprodukt *n* daughter product
Tochtersubstanz *f* daughter substance
Tochtersubstanzabtrennung *f* separation of daughter substance
Todesgemeinschaft *f* thanatocoenosis, death assemblage
Tommot *n* Tommotian [Stage] *(Lower Cambrian, Siberia)*
Ton *m* 1. clay; argil, potter's earth (clay); 2. sound *(acoustics)*
~/alaunhaltiger astringent clay
~/aufgeblähter *s.* **~/geschwellter**
~/bildsamer ball clay
~/bituminöser bituminous clay
~/brandrissiger drawn clay
~/dünngeschichteter banded (leaf, varved) clay
~/eisenhaltiger sinople
~/eisenhaltiger schieferiger paint rock
~/erhärteter clay-stone; mudstone
~/fetter fat (rich, heavy, soapy) clay
~/feuerfester refractory (fire) clay
~/gebänderter bedded clay
~/gebrannter burnt (baked) clay
~/geschwellter expanded (expansive) clay
~/gewöhnlicher low-grade clay
~/glimmerführender micaceous shale
~/hochplastischer long clay
~/hochwertiger high-grade clay
~/kalkhaltiger calcareous clay
~/klebriger sticky clay; gutta-percha clay

Tongestein

~/knetbarer plastic (soft) clay
~/magerer meagre (sandy, green) clay
~/mergeliger marly clay
~ mit geringer Plastizität lean clay
~ mit Kalkkonkretionen clay with race
~/mulmiger crumbly clay
~/ockerhaltiger ochreous clay
~/ockeriger ochrey clay
~/plastischer plastic (soft) clay
~/schlickiger clay-containing silt
~/schluffiger silty clay
~/schmutzfarbiger drab clay
~/schwerer *s.* **~/fetter**
~/steifer geklüfteter stiff fissured clay
~/strukturempfindlicher sensitive clay
~/tropischer schwerer black cotton soil
~ unter dem Flöz sods
~/verfestigter consolidated clay
~ von muscheligem Bruch/harter flint clay
~/weicher muckle
~/weißbrennender white-burning clay
~/zermürbter shattered clay
~/zerruschelter slickensided clay
Tonalit *m* tonalite *(quartz-dioritic rock)*
Tonanteil *m* clay fraction
tonartig clayey, claylike, argill[ace]ous, argillic
Tonaufbereitung *f* clay preparation
tonbedeckt lutose
Tonbildung *f* argillization
Tonbindemittel *n* clay bond
Tonboden *m* clay ground, clayey soil
~/kompakter tile earth
Tonbrandgestein *n* procelainite
Tonbrei *m* watery clay
Tondinasstein *m* clay dinas brick
Toneinlagerung *f* sloam
Toneisenstein *m* clay (argillaceous) ironstone, iron clay, spherosiderite
~/koprolithischer beetle stone
Toneisensteinband *n* pennystone
~/dünnes chitter
Toneisensteingalle *f* ironstone concretion, siderite nodule
Toneisensteinkonkretionen *fpl* argillaceous iron ore concretions
tönen to sound
Tonerde *f* alumina, argillaceous earth
Tonerdeeinschluß *m* alumina inclusion
Tonerdegehalt *m* alumina content
tonerdehaltig aluminiferous
Tonerdemineral *n* aluminium mineral
tonerdereich [high-]aluminous
Tonerdesilikat *n* aluminium silicate
Tonerdeverbindung *f* compound of alumina
Tonerdezement *m* alumina (aluminous, calcium aluminate) cement
Tongalle *f* clay gall (lenticule)
Tongehalt *m* clay content
Tongerölle *npl*/**gespickte** pudding (armoured mud) balls
Tongestein *n* clay (argillaceous, pelitic) rock
~/angewittertes claycrete

Tongestein

~/bituminöses jet rock
Tongewinnung f getting of clay
Tongrien n Tongrian [Stage] (of Tertiary)
Tongrube f clay pit (quarry)
Tongyttja f clay gyttja
tonhaltig clayey, argill[ace]ous, argillic, argilliferous
tonig clayish, clayey, argillaceous
tonig-kalkig argillo-calcareous
tonig-schluffig clayey-silty
Toninjektion f clay grouting
Tonkalk m argillaceous limestone, argillocalcite
Tonkonkretion f in Sandstein stonegall
Tonlage f clay bed
Tonlager n clay bed
Tonlagerstätte f clay deposit
Tonlehm m clay loam
Tonlinse f clay lens
Tonmergel m clay (clayey, argillaceous) marl, loam
Tonmineral n clay mineral
Tonmischer m mud mixer
Tonne f ton
Tonnengewölbe n barrel vault
Tonnest n clay pocket
Tonnlage f hade, dip
tonnlägig hading, inclined
Tonrolle f clay gall
Tonsandstein m argillaceous sandstone
Tonscherbenbrekzie f desiccation breccia
Tonschicht f clay bank (bed)
~/verdichtete clay pan, claypan
Tonschiefer m clay schist (slate), argillaceous slate (shale, schist); grapholith
~ mit Toneisenstein sideritic shale
~/schluffiger silty slate
~/schwachsandiger slightly sandy shale
Tonschlempe f clay slurry
Tonschlick m clayey mud
Tonspülung f clay base mud
Tonstein m mudstone, clay stone
~/mergeliger marly mudstone
~ mit Gips gypsiferous mudstone
~/sandiger sandy mudstone
Tontrübe f clay detritus held in suspension
Tonüberzug m clay film
ton- und sandhaltig argillo-arenaceous
Ton-Winterlage f winter clay (of varves)
Tonzwischenlage f clay parting, scud
Topas m topaz, $Al_2[F_2|SiO_4]$
Topasbildung f topazization
Topasfels m topaz rock, topazfels
Topasit m topazite
Topazolith m topazolite (variety of andradite)
Töpfererde f, Töpferton m potter's clay (earth), ball clay
Topfstein m soapstone, steatite, $Mg_3[(OH)_2|Si_4O_{10}]$
Topografie f topography
~ des Meeresgrundes submarine topography
topografisch topographic[al]

Topotypus m topotype
Torbanit m torbanite (boghead coal)
Torbernit m torbernite, copper uranite, chalcolite, $Cu[UO_2|PO_4]_2 \cdot 10(12-8)H_2O$
Torf m peat, turf
~/allochthoner allochthonous peat
~ aus Süßwasseralgen conferva peat
~/blättriger laminated moor
~/dichter stone turf
~/dunkelbrauner fetter lard peat
~/erdiger crumble peat
~/getrockneter vag
~ in Glazialablagerungen drift peat
~/leicht entzündlicher tallow peat
~ mit stückigen Pflanzenresten chaff peat
~/oberhalb des Wasserspiegels gebildeter terrestrial peat
~/schlammiger dredged peat
~/umgelagerter peat breccia (slime)
~/unreifer unripe peat
~/unreiner muck
~/vergelter amorphous peat
~/von Gestrüpp bedeckter brushwood peat
torfartig peaty, turfy
torfbildend peat-forming, turf-forming
Torfbildung f peat (turf) formation
Torfboden m peat (turfy, boggy) soil
Torfbrekzie f peat breccia
Torfdiagenese f peat diagenesis (peatification)
Torfdolomit m coal ball (apple), clayat, seam nodule
Torfeinschluß m peat pocket, concealed bed of peat
Torferde f/schwarze muck
Torfgas n peat gas
Torfgel n dopplerite
Torfgewinnung f peat digging (extraction)
Torfgräber m peat digger
Torfgrube f peat (turf) pit
torfhaltig, torfig peaty, turfy
Torflage f peaty layer
Torflager n peat bed (deposit), peatery
Torfland n moorland
Torfmoor n swamp, peat-bog, peaty moor (bog)
Torfmoorbildung f swamp formation
Torfmoos n high (peat, bog) moss, sphagnum
Torfmudde f limn[et]ic peat, liver peat
Torfmull m peat dust (moss litter)
Torfnest n peat pocket, concealed bed of peat
Torfniederung f peaty flat
torfreich peaty, turfy
Torfschicht f peat (turf) bed
Torfschlamm m meermolm
Torfstecher m peat digger
Torfstich m moss fallow
Torfstück n peat sod
Torfteer m peat tar
Torfvergasung f peat gasification
Torfverkohlung f turf carbonization, peat charring

Torkretbeton *m* gunite, air-placed concrete, gunned (gun-applied) concrete, jetcrete, shotcrete
torkretieren to gunite
Tornado *m* tornado, *(Am)* twister
Tornadowirbel *m* tornado vortex
Tornadowolke *f* tornado cloud
Törnebohmit *m* törnebohmite, (Ce, La, Al)$_3$[OH|(SiO$_4$)$_3$]
torpedieren to shoot
Torpedieren *n* torpedoing, shooting *(of wells)*
~ einer Erdölbohrung oil-well shooting
Torrejonien *n* Torrejonian [Stage] *(mammalian stage, Palaeocene in North America)*
Torreyit *m* torreyite, (Mg, Zn, Mn)$_7$[(OH)$_{12}$|SO$_4$] · 4H$_2$O
Torridon-Sandstein *m* Torridonian sandstone
Torsion *f* torsion
Torsionsbruch *m* twist-off
Torsionsmodul *m* torsion modulus
Torsionsseismograf *m* torsion seismograph
Torsionsseismometer *n* torsion seismometer
Torsionsspannung *f* torsional stress
Torsionswinkel *m* angle of twist
Tortenstück *n* pie slice *(seismics)*
Torton[ien] *n*, **Tortonium** *n* Tortonian [Stage] *(of Miocene)*
Tortuosität *f* tortuosity
~ der Porenkanäle pore tortuosity
Tosbecken *n* stilling basin (pool, well)
Totalflotation *f* all-floatation
Totalintensität *f* total intensity
Totalisator *m* totalizator
Totalreflexion *f* total reflection
totdrücken to kill *(a well)*
Totdrücken *n* killing *(of a well)*
Toteis *n* dead ice
Toteisloch *n* dead ice kettle
Toteispinge *f* kettle hole
Toteisrand *m* dead ice margin
Toteisschmelzsee *m* pingo remnant
Toteissee *m* kettle
Totform *f* dead form
Totlast *f* dead load
Totöllagerstätte *f* tar-sand deposit, heavy (dead) oil deposit
Totölsandstein *m* tar sand
Totpore *f* dead-end pore
Totporosität *f* isolated porosity
totpumpen to kill *(a well)*
Totpumpen *n* killing *(of a well)*
Totpunktflüssigkeit *f* kick mud
Totraum *m* dead space
totsöhlig absolutely horizontal
Totwasser *n* dead waters
Totwinkel *m* dead angle
Totzeit *f* dead time *(in radiometric devices)*
Totzeitkorrektur *f* dead time correction
Tournai *n* Tournaisian [Stage] *(of Carboniferous)*
T-Profil *n* T-section *(microsection parallel to the bedding or to the sample surface)*

Trabant *m* satellite
~/begleitender attendant satellite
Tracer *m* tracer
Trachee *f* trachea
Trachyandesit *m* trachyandesite
Trachybasalt *m* trachybasalt
Trachydolerit *m* trachydolerite
Trachyt *m* trachyte
trachytartig trachytoid[al]
trachytisch trachytic
Trachyttuff *m* trachyte tuff
Tragdecke *f* base
träge inert
Träger *m* 1. beam *(e.g. in mines)*; 2. reservoir bed, container bed *(layer bearing e.g. oil or water)*
~/geschlossener closed reservoir
~/produktiver producing rock
Trägerdecke *f* carrier nappe
Trägerfolie *f* support film
Trägergestein *n* reservoir (carrier) rock
Trägergesteinsschicht *f* carrier bed
tragfähig bearing
Tragfähigkeit *f* [load-]bearing capacity
~ des Bodens soil bearing capacity
Tragfähigkeitsfaktor *m* bearing capacity factor
Tragfähigkeitsindex *m* bearing index
Tragfähigkeitsminderung *f* reduction of load-bearing capacity
Tragfähigkeitsversuch *m* bearing test
Trägheit *f*/**thermische** thermal inertia
Trägheitsachse *f* axis of inertia
Trägheitshalbmesser *m* radius of inertia
Trägheitsmoment *n* moment of inertia
Trägheitspol *m* pole of inertia
Tragring *m* ring support
Tragschicht *f* base
Tragvermögen *n* bearing capacity
Tränenbombe *f* tear-shaped bomb
tränken to soak
~/mit Erdöl to naphthalize
Transformation *f* transformation *(of a potential field)*
~/geotektonische geotectonic transformation
~/substratbedingte transformation conditioned by the substratum
transgredieren to transgress; to overlap
Transgression *f* transgression, encroachment; overlap
~/fortschreitende progressive overlap
Transgressionsdiskordanz *f* unconformability of transgression
Transgressionsfalle *f* truncation trap
Transgressionskonglomerat *n* basal conglomerate
Transgressionsmeer *n* transgression sea
Transgressionszyklus *m* cycle of submergence
transgressiv transgressive
Transkaspi-Gebiet *n* Transcaspia
Translation *f* translation; parallel displacement *(of crystals)*

Translationsebene

Translationsebene *f* slip (translation) plane
Translationsgitter *n* translation lattice (grating)
Translationsgleitung *f* translation gliding
Translationsgruppe *f* translation group
Translationslinie *f* slip band
Translationsstreifung *f* translation banding (gliding striae), slip bands
Translationstheorie *f* translation theory
translatorisch translatory
translunar translunar
Transmissibilität *f* transmissibility
Transmissionskurve *f* transmittance curve
Transmitter *m* transmitter
transparent transparent, diaphanous
Transparenz *f* transparency, diaphaneity
Transpiration *f*/**pflanzliche** vegetable discharge
Transport *m* transport[ation]
~ **durch Flußströmung**, ~/**fluviatiler** fluviatile (potamic) transport
~/**sprungweiser** saltation
~/**tektonischer** tectonic transport (flow)
Transportanalyse *f* transport analysis *(e.g. of sediments)*
Transportfähigkeit *f* transporting (carrying) capacity
Transportkräfte *fpl* transportational agents
Transportweite *f* distance of transport
Transural-Gebiet *n* Transural region
Transuran *n* transuranium (transuranic) element
Transvaporisation *f* transvaporization
transversal transverse
Transversalbeben *n* transverse earthquake
transversalgeschichtet false-bedded
Transversalkluft *f* transverse joint
Transversalrippeln *fpl* transverse ripple marks
Transversalschichtung *f* false (oblique, diagonal) bedding, false (oblique, diagonal) lamination
Transversalschieferigkeit *f* slatiness
Transversalschieferung *f* slaty (fracture, flow) cleavage, transverse lamination
Transversalverschiebung *f* wrench (strike-slip) fault
Transversalwelle *f* transverse (transversal, shear) wave, S wave
Trapezoeder *n* trapezohedron
trapezoedrisch trapezohedral
Trapezoid *n* trapezoid
trapezoidförmig trapezoidal
Trapp *m* trap[rock] *(s.a. Plateaubasalt)*
trappartig trappoid
Trappdecken *fpl* trap flows
Trappfels *m* trappean rock
Traskit *m* trascite, $Ba_5FeTi[(OH)_4|Si_6O_{18}]$
Traß *m* [Rhenish] trass
Trasse *f* alignement
Trassierung *f* route selection
traubenartig grapelike
traubenförmig botryoid[al]
Traubentextur *f* botryoid[al] texture
traubig botryoid[al]

Trauf *f* cuesta scarp
Traverse *f* traverse
Travertin *m* travertine, calc tufa, calcareous tufa (sinter)
Travertinprofil *n* travertine profile
Travertinvorkommen *n* travertine occurrence
Trechmannit *m* trechmannite, $Ag_2S \cdot As_2S_3$
Treibanker *m* drift anchor
Treibeis *n* drift (floating, flow, floe, pancake) ice
~/**arktisches** Arctic pack
Treibeisgrenze *f* limit of drift ice
treiben/einen Stollen to run a drift
~/**Raubbau** to rob
Treibholz *n* drift wood, floating timber
Treibmaterial *n* rafted material
Treibsand *m* drift (running, shifting) sand
Treibsandablagerung *f* blown-sand deposit
Treibsandgrund *m* shifting beach
Tremadoc *n* Tremadocian [Stage], Salmian [Stage] *(of Ordovician)*
Tremolit *m* tremolite, $Ca_2Mg_5[(OH, F)|Si_4O_{11}]_2$
Trempealeauen *n* Trempealeaunian [Stage] *(at the Cambrian/Ordovician boundary in North America)*
Trend *m* trend [function]
~/**gewöhnlicher** ordinary trend
~/**lokaler** local trend
~ **mit orthogonalen Polynomen** trend with orthogonal polynomials
~/**regionaler** regional trend
Trendanalyse *f* trend analysis
Trendansatz *m* set-up of trend functions
Trendfläche *f* **hohen Grades** high-order trend surface, trend surface of high-degree polynomial
~ **niedrigen Grades** low-order trend surface, trend surface of low-degree polynomial
Trendflächenabbildung *f* trend-surface mapping
Trendflächenanalyse *f* trend-surface analysis, analysis of trend surface
Trendflächenkarte *f* trend-surface map, map of trend surface
Trendfunktion *f* trend [function]
Trendhyperfläche *f* trend hypersurface
Trendkoeffizient *m* trend coefficient, coefficient of trend function
Trendkurve *f* trend curve, one-dimensional trend function
Trendrest *m* trend residual, residual-value function of trend *(difference between observation and trend function)*
Trennbruch *m* parting rupture, cleavage fracture, rupture by separation, stretching fault
trennen to separate; to septate *(septaria)*
Trennfläche *f* parting (dividing) surface, parting (separation) plane, interface, joint, plane of division
Trennfunktion *f s.* Diskriminanzfunktion
Trennlinie *f* tie line, conode
Trennschnitt *m* cut point

Trennung f separation
Trennungsfläche f s. Trennfläche
Trennungsgrad m **von Klassierapparaten** classifier efficiency
Trennungspunkt m cut-off point
Trenton[ien] n Trentonian, Shermanian [Stage] (of Champlainian in North America)
Treppe f step (in rock layers)
treppenartig scalariform
treppenförmig echeloned
Treppenverwerfung f step fault
treten/zutage to basset, to come up to the grass
Trevorit m trevorite, $NiFe_2O_4$
Triangulation f triangulation
~/terrestrische ground triangulation
Triangulationsnetz n triangulation net
Trias f Triassic [System] (chronostratigraphically); Triassic [Period] (geochronologically); Triassic [Age] (common sense)
~/alpine Alpine Triassic
~/germanische Germanic Triassic
~/Mittlere Middle Triassic [Series, Epoch] (Anisian and Ladinian)
~/Obere Upper Triassic [Series, Epoch] (Karnian, Norian, Rhaetian)
~/pelagische s. ~/germanische
~/Untere Lower Triassic [Period]
Triasperiode f Triassic [Period]
Triasplatte f Triassic plate
triassisch Triassic
Triassystem n Triassic [System]
Triaszeit f Triassic [Age]
Triaxialbelastung f triaxial load
Triaxialgerät n triaxial compression cell
~ mit fest angeordneter Gummihülle fixed sleeve cell
Trichalcit m trichalcite, $Cu_3[AsO_4]_2 \cdot 5H_2O(?)$
Trichit m fibrous (hair-like) crystal
Trichroismus m trichroism
trichroitisch trichroic
Trichter m 1. funnel; 2. infundibulum (organ)
Trichterauslaufzeit f mud viscosity
Trichterbildung f **des Randwassers** coning-in of edge water
Trichterdoline f solution sink
trichterförmig funnel-shaped; crateriform; bottle-necked
Trichterinhalt m depression storage (of depression cone)
Trichtermeer n funnel sea
Trichtermündung f tidal estuary, flaring mouth
Trichter- und Kegelstruktur f pit-and-mound structure
Trichterwasservolumina npl funnel-water volumes
Tridymit m tridymite, SiO_2
Triebsand m s. Treibsand
Triebwasserleitungen fpl intake conduits
Trieder n trihedron
triedrisch trihedral

Trift f drift
triften to drift
trigonal trigonal
Trigonit m trigonite, $Pb_3MnH[AsO_3]_3$
triklin triclinic, anorthic
Triklinität f triclinicity
Trimacerit m trimacerite (coal microlithotype)
Trimerit m trimerite, $CaMn_2[BeSiO_4]_2$
trimorph trimorph[ic], trimorphous
Trimorphismus m trimorphism
Trinidadasphalt m Trinidad pitch
Trinkbrunnen m drinking fountain
Trinkerit m trinkerite (a resin)
Trinkwasser n drinking (potable) water
Trinkwasserstandard m drinking water standard
Trinkwasserversorgung f drinking water supply
Trinkwasserwerk n domestic water supply [plant]
Tripel m, **Tripelerde** f tripoli [earth, powder]
Tripelpunkt m triple point
Triphan m s. Spodumen
Triphylin m triphylite, $Li(Fe\ddot{},Mn\dot{})[PO_4]$
Triplet n triplet (method with three readings)
Triplit m triplite, $(Mn,Fe\ddot{})_2[F|PO_4]$
Triploidit m triploidite, $(Mn,Fe\ddot{})_2[OH|PO_4]$
Tripoli m tripoli
Trippkeit m trippkeite, $CuAs_2O_4$
Tripton n tripton
Tripuhyit m tripuhyite, $FeSb_2O_6$
Trisoktaeder n trisoctahedron
Tristetraeder n tristetrahedron
Tritium n tritium, T
~ kosmischer Herkunft cosmic-ray produced tritium
Tritomit m tritomite (Th-, Ce-, Y-,Ca-borosilicate)
Trittsiegel n track (ichnology)
Trochiten mpl trochites, columnals
Trochitenkalk m crinoidal limestone
Trochitenschalentrümmerkalkstein m encrinitic coquina
trocken arid
Trockenanalyse f analysis by dry way
Trockenaufbereitung f dry concentration (treatment)
Trockenbagger m dredger excavator
trockenbohren to drill dry
Trockenbohren n dry drilling (boring)
Trockenfestigkeit f dry strength
Trockengas n dry [natural] gas
Trockengebiet n arid region (area)
Trockengründung f foundation in the dry
Trockenheit f aridity, aridness, drought
trockenheitsliebend xerophilous
Trockenlawine f dry (dust) avalanche
trockenlegen to drain; to dewater, to unwater
Trockenlegung f drainage, draining; dewatering, unwatering
Trockenmasse f dry residue
Trockenraumgewicht n dry unit weight, dry bulk density

Trockenresistenz 320

Trockenresistenz *f* drought resistance
Trockenrinne *f* coomb[e]
Trockenriß *m* drying (desiccation, mud) crack, desiccation fissure (joint); air shrinkage *(clay)*
~/falscher false mud crack
Trockenrißbildung *f* mud cracking
Trockenrißnetzwerk *n* desiccation polygons
Trockenrohdichte *f* bulk density
Trockenrückstand *m* dry residue
Trockenschlucht *f* dry defile (gap, narrow, rift)
Trockenschrank *m* drying cabinet
Trockenschwarzerde *f* dry chernozem
Trockenschwindung *f* drying shrinkage
Trockensee *m* dry lake
Trockensiebung *f* dry screening
Trockensortierung *f* dry cleaning
Trockental *n* dry (dead) valley, wadi
Trockenwald *m* xerophytic forest
Trockenwetterabfluß *m* arid (fair-weather) runoff, dry-weather flow
Trockenzeit *f* dry (rainless) season, drought duration
trocknen 1. to dry; to drain; 2. to desiccate; to dehumidify
Trocknung *f* 1. drying; drainage; 2. desiccation; dehumidification
Trog *m* trough, tray, basin
~ auf der konvexen Seite eines Inselbogens hinterdeep
~/intramontaner intramontane trough
~ zwischen innerem und äußerem Inselbogen interdeep
Trogachse *f* trough axis
Trogeintiefung *f* deepening of trough
Trögerit *m* trögerite, $(H_3O)_2[UO_2|AsO_4]_2 \cdot 6H_2O$
trogförmig trough-shaped
Trogtal *n* trough (U-shaped) valley, glacial trough
Trogtalit *m* trogtalite, $CoSe_2$
Troilit *m* troilite, FeS
Troilitphase *f* troilite phase *(of meteorites)*
Troktolith *m* troctolite *(variety of gabbro)*
Trolleit *m* trolleite, $Al_4[OH|PO_4]_3$
Trombe *f* waterspout
Trommel *f* reel *(winding)*
Trommelsieb *n* rotational sieve
Trommelwelle *f* drum shaft
trompetenförmig trumpet-shaped
Trona *f* trona, $Na_3H[CO_3]_2 \cdot 2H_2O$
Trondhjemit *m* trondhjemite *(granitic plutonite)*
Troostit *m* troostite *(variety of willemite)*
Tropen *pl* tropics
~/feuchte wet tropics
Tropenklima *n* tropical climate
Tropenmoor *n* tropical swamp
Tropenwald *m* tropical forest
Tropfarbeit *f* rain-drop impact
Tröpfchen *n* spherule; globule
tröpfeln to drop, to drip

tropfen to drop, to drip
Tropfen *m* drop
Tropfenbildung *f* **im Bohrloch** balling
tropfenförmig drop-shaped
Tropfenmesser *m* stalagmeter
Tropfenquarz *m* drop quartz
Tropfloch *n* driphole
Tropfstein *m* dropstone, dripstone, spelaeothem; stalactite; stalagmite
tropfsteinartig stalactiform
Tropfsteinhöhle *f* stalactite cavern
Tropfwasser *n* dripping (trickling) water
Tropwasseraustritt *m* kettle bottom
tropfwassergeschützt drip-proof
tropisch tropic[al]
Troposphäre *f* troposphere
trübe muddy; milky, opaque, cloudy, turbid *(crystals)*
Trübe *f* slurry, pulp, slush; suspended matter
~/absetzbare settling slurry
Trübestrom *m* slurry slump, suspension (density) current, turbidity current (flow)
Trübheit *f* cloudiness, turbidity *(of crystals)*
Trübung *f*/**atmosphärische** atmospheric[al] turbidity
Trudellit *m* trudellite, $Al_{10}[(OH)_4|Cl|SO_4]_3 \cdot 30H_2O$
Trum *n* stringer, compartment, vein[let]
Trümerzone *f* stringer zone (lead)
Trümmer *pl* debris, fragments
Trümmerablagerung *f* debris (detrital, fragmental, clastic) accumulation
Trümmerachat *m* broken (fracture, ruin, brecciated) agate
trümmerartig frustulent
Trümmerbrekzie *f* rubble breccia
Trümmererzlagerstätte *f* residual ore deposit
Trümmerfeld *n* debris plain
Trümmergestein *n* fragmental (detrital, clastic) rock, breccia, conglomerate
~/glaziales glacial clastic
Trümmergesteinsmaterial *n* fragmental (disintegrated) material
Trümmergesteinszone *f* fractured zone
Trümmerkalk *m* detrital limestone
Trümmerlagerstätte *f* clastic (detrital) deposit
Trümmermasse *f* detritus, land waste
Trümmermaterial *n* detrital material
Trümmersedimente *npl* clastic sedimentary rocks
~/lose disjunctive rocks
Trümmerstruktur *f* breccialike structure
Trümmerzone *f* shatter zone (belt)
Truscottit *m* truscottite, $Ca_2[Si_4O_{10}] \cdot H_2O$
Tscheffkinit *m* tscheffkinite, $(Ce,La)_2Ti_2[O_4|Si_2O_7]$
Tschermakit *m* tschermakite, $Ca_2Mg_3(Al,Fe)_2[(OH,F)_2|Al_2Si_6O_{22}]$
Tschermigit *m* tschermigite, $NH_4Al[SO_4]_2 \cdot 12H_2O$
Tschernosem *m* [t]chernozem, [steppe] black earth

Tschkalowit m tschkalowite, $Na_2[BeSi_2O_6]$
Tsumebit m tsumebite,
  $Pb_2Cu[(OH)_3|PO_4] \cdot 3H_2O$
Tsunami m tsunami, seismic wave
Tübbingausbau m tubbing supports
Tuff m tuff *(volcanic);* tufa *(sedimentary)*
~/lithischer lithic tuff
~/verfestigter tuffstone
tuffablagernd tufa-depositing
Tuffablagerung f tufa deposit
tuffartig tuffaceous *(volcanic);* tufaceous *(sedimentary)*
Tufferde f tufaceous earth
Tuffgestein n tufa rock
~/vulkanisches volcanic tuff
Tuffisit m tuffisite *(hybrid rock consisting of tuff and fragments of country rock)*
Tuffit m tuffite
tuffitisch igneoaqueous
Tuffkalk m tufaceous limestone
Tuffkegel m/**vulkanischer** tuff cone
Tufflava f tuffolava
~/irreguläre ataxite
Tuffschiefer m tufaceous shale
Tuffstein m 1. tuffaceous rock; 2. tuffaceous sandstone; 3. trass
tuffführend tuffaceous *(volcanic);* tufaceous *(sedimentary)*
Tuffvulkan m tuff cone
Tugtupit m tugtupite, $Na_8[Cl_2|(BeAlSi_4O_{12})_2]$
Tujamunit m s. Tyuyamunit
Tümpel m [muddy, stagnant] pool, puddle
Tundra f tundra
Tundraboden m tundra soil, muskeg
Tundramoor n muskeg
Tundramoorboden m swampy tundra soil
Tunellit m tunellite, $Sr[B_6O_9(OH)_2] \cdot 3H_2O$
Tungstein m s. Scheelit
Tungstenit m tungstenite, WS_2
Tungstit m tungstite, $WO_2(OH)_2$
Tunnelbau m tunnelling
Tunneltal n gutter valley
Turanit m turanite, $5CuO \cdot V_2O_5 \cdot 2H_2O$
Turbidit m turbidite, resedimented rock
~ mit synsedimentärer Gleitstruktur fluxoturbidite
Turbiditzonen fpl/**ausgedünnte** nepheloid layers
Turbinenbohren n turbodrilling
Turbinenmeißel m turbobit
Turbozyklon m centrifuge
turbulent turbulent
Turbulenz f turbulence
Turbulenzströmung f turbulent flow
Türkis m turquois[e], calaite,
  $CuAl_6[(OH)_2|PO_4]_4 \cdot 4H_2O$
~/fossiler bone turquoise
Turm m **aus Gitterwerk** latticed tower
Turmalin m tourmaline *(complex borosilicate)*
~/blauer indigolite, indicolite
~/gemeiner s. **~/schwarzer**
~/roter raspberry spar

~/schwarzer schorl, jet stone,
  $NaFe_3 \cdot Al_6[(OH)_{1+3}|(BO_3)_3|Si_6O_{18}]$
turmalinartig tourmalinic
Turmalinfels m schorl rock
turmalinführend tourmaline-bearing
Turmalingranit m tourmaline granite
turmalinhaltig tourmalinic
turmalinisieren to tourmalinize
Turmalinisierung f tourmalinization
Turmalin-Quarz-Knolle f tourmaline-quartz nodule
Turmalinschiefer m tourmaline schist; schorl schist
Turmalinsonne f tourmaline sun
turmförmig turritiform
Turmkarst m tower (needle) karst
Turmkronenbühne f crown platform
Turolium n Turolian [Stage] *(continental stage of Pliocene)*
Turon[ien] n, **Turonium** n Turonian [Stage] *(of Upper Cretaceous)*
Türstock m timber set
Türstockausbau m frame timbering
Tütenkalk m s. Tutenmergel
Tutenmergel m styolithic (cone-in-cone) limestone
Tutenmergelstruktur f cone-in-cone structure
Tuval n Tuvalian [Substage] *(Upper Triassic, Tethys)*
Tychit m tychite, $Na_6Mg_2[SO_4|(CO_3)_4]$
typomorph typomorphic
Typus m/**lagunärer** lagoonal type
~/persistenter persistent type
Typusart f type specimen
Typusgebiet n type area
Typuslokalität f type (reference) locality
Tyrrellit m tyrrellite, $(Cu,Co,Ni)_3Se_4$
Tysonit m tysonite, $(Ce,La)F_3$
Tyuyamunit m tyuyamunite, calcium carnotite,
  $Ca[(UO_2)_2|V_2O_8] \cdot 5-8^1/_2 H_2O$

U

überarbeiten to review
Überarbeitung f review
Überbau m superstructure
überbaut influenced by overlying workings
überbeanspruchen to overload
Überbeanspruchung f overstress
Überbleibsel npl remnants
~/organische relics, reliquiae
überbohren to wash over
Überbolid m giant bolide
überdecken to lap
Überdeckung f 1. lap[ping]; 2. smearing *(seismics)*
Überdeckungsgrad m coverage
Überdrehungsbruch m twist-off
Überdruck m excess pressure
~/hydrostatischer excess hydrostatic pressure
~/tektonischer tectonic overpressure

Übereinanderfolge 322

Übereinanderfolge f order of superposition
~ **mehrerer Paragenesen** telescoping
übereinandergelagert superimposed
übereinandergreifen to lap
Übereinandergreifen n lap[ping]
übereinanderlegen to superpose
übereinanderliegen/dachziegelartig (schuppenartig) to imbricate
Übereinanderliegen n/**dachziegelartiges (schuppenartiges)** imbrication
übereinanderliegend superposed
Übererkundung f excess exploration
übereutektisch hypereutectic
Überfall m 1. weir, escape, waste-way; overfall (measuring weir); 2. spillway (of a glacier)
~/**vollkommener** perfect weir
Überfallbreite f width of overfall
Überfalldamm m overflow dam
Überfallhöhe f height of overfall
Überfallkante f overfall crest (crown), crest (crown) of overfall
Überfallquelle f overflow (depression, pocket) spring
Überfallwehr n overfall (overflow) weir
überfalten to overfold
Überfaltung f overfolding, overturning, inversion
Überfaltungsdecke f fold nappe (carpet, thrust), overthrust fold
Überfaltungsgebirge n overfolded rocks, overthrust mountains
überfluten to overflow; to flood; to inundate; to submerge
Überflutung f overflow; [over]flooding; inundation
~/**kurzzeitige** marining
Überflutungsebene f flood plain (ground), river flat
überformt/durch Belastung load-casted
Übergang m 1. transition, passage; 2. gradation
Übergangsbindung f transitional bond
Übergangsfazies f transition (passage) facies
Übergangsmoor n transition bog
Übergangsmoorboden m carr
Übergangsregime n transition regime (between lower and upper flow regime)
Übergangsschicht f transition (passage) bed
Übergangswiderstand m **der Elektrodenstäbe** electrode (stake) resistance (geoelectrics)
Übergangszeit f transit time
Übergangszone f 1. transition zone (belt), gradational zone; 2. transitional zone (palaeontology)
~/**kapillare** capillary transition zone
~/**schwach durchlichtete** disphotic zone (between 80 and 600 m ocean depth)
übergehen in to pass (grade) into
~ **in/nach dem Liegenden** to grade downward into
~ **in/seitwärts** to grade laterally into
Übergemengteil m accessory mineral, minor constituent

Übergleitung f overslide
übergreifen to overlap, to [on]lap
Übergreifen n overlap[ping], [on]lap
~/**allmähliches** regular progressive overlap
übergreifend overlapping
Übergußschichtung f reef-slope bedding
Überhang m overhang
überhängend overhanging, coving
überhauen to raise
Überhauen n rise drift
überhitzt superheated
überhöht exaggerated (scale)
~/**zweimal** vertical scale twice horizontal, vertical scale exaggerated twice
Überhöhung f exaggeration (scale); exaggeration of heigths
~/**vertikale** vertical exaggeration
Überhöhungsverhältnis n ratio of exaggeration
Überindividuum n superindividual
Überjahresspeicherbecken n conservation reservoir
Überjahresspeicherung f conservation storage
überkippt overturned, overthrown, overtilted, inverse, reversed, recumbent; underthrust (more than 180°)
Überkippung f overturning, overthrust, overfault, inversion, recumbency
überkragen to project, to protrude
überkritisch overcritical, supercritical, above critical
überkrusten to encrust, to overcrust; to incrust
Überkrustung f encrustation, overcrusting; incrustation
überladen overloaded
überlagern to overlap, to overlie, to superpose
überlagernd overlapping, overlaying, superimposed, superincumbent
~/**sich** superimposed
überlagert overlaid, overlain
Überlagerung f overlapping, superposition; overlay; mantle
Überlagerungsdruck m geopressure, normal rock pressure; rock weight pressure; overburden [rock] pressure, pressure of overlying strata, cover load
Überlagerungsprinzip n principle of superimposition
Überlagerungsweite f/**tektonische** minimum breadth
überlappen to [over]lap
überlappend overlapping
Überlappung f overlap[ping], [side] lap, overlap fault
Überlappungspunkt m tie point
Überlast f surcharge
überlasten to overload
überlastet overloaded; overburdened
Überlastung f overload; overburden

Überlauf m 1. overflow; 2. escape, waste-way, spill-over *(of a dam);* 3. spillway *(of a glacier);* 4. tailings, rejects
Überlaufdamm m overflow dam
Überlaufdeich m overfall
Überlaufgletscher m spill-over glacier
Überlaufpunkt m escape (spill) point *(of traps)*
Überlaufquelle f overflow (depression, pocket) spring
Überlaufstollen m spillway tunnel
Überlaufwehr n overflow (effluent) weir
Übermurung f *covering of the river banks with slime, mud or stones*
überprägt superimposed
Überprägung f superimposition, overprint, superprint
überragen to overlook
überreif postmature, fully mature
Überrest m relic
~/organischer organic remain
übersättigen to oversaturate, to supersaturate
Übersättigung f oversaturation, supersaturation
Überschallströmung f supersonic flow
überschichten to stratify
überschieben to overthrust
Überschiebung f overthrusting, upthrow, upthrust, overfolding, overlapping; overfault, overthrust (upthrust, reversed, overlap) fault
~/gefaltete fold[ed] thrust
~/progressive progressive thrust
γ-Überschiebung f gamma structure
Überschiebungsbau m overthrust tectonics
Überschiebungsbewegung f thrusting movement
Überschiebungsblock m overthrust (overriding) block
Überschiebungsdecke f shear-thrust sheet
Überschiebungsfalte f faulted overfold, reversed fold fault
Überschiebungsfläche f [over]thrust plane, slide
Überschiebungsklippe f small thrust outlier
Überschiebungsmasse f [over]thrust mass, displaced mass
Überschiebungsrest m nappe outlier
Überschiebungsschieferung f thrust cleavage
Überschiebungsscholle f overthrust (overriding) block
Überschiebungszone f overthrust zone
überschoben thrust-over, thrust-faulted
Überschuß-Niederschlagsschreiber m excess rain hyetograph
überschütten to overwhelm
überschwemmen to inundate, to flood, to deluge
überschwemmt submerged
Überschwemmung f inundation, flood[ing], deluge, submersion
überschwemmungsbedroht floodable
Überschwemmungsbett n high-water bed
Überschwemmungsfläche f, **Überschwem-**mungsgebiet n inundated (flooded, submerged) area, flood plain (land)
Überschwemmungsniveau n overflow level
Übersicht f survey
Übersichtsaufnahme f reconnaissance survey
Übersichtsbetrachtung f synoptic view
Übersichtsbild n general view
Übersichtskarte f general map
~/geologische generalized geological map
Übersichtsvermessung f reconnaissance survey
Übersichtswetterkunde f synoptic meteorology
Übersprechen n cross talk *(in measuring circuits)*
Übersprung m overfault
überspülen to wash over
Überspülung f overwash
überstaut drowned
übersteil oversteepened
Übersteilung f oversteepening
Übersteuerung f overload
Übertageanlage f surface equipment (installation), decking plant
Übertiefung f overdeepening
Übertiefungsmulde f overdeepened basin
Übertrager m transducer
Übertragszeit f transit time
Übertragungsfaktor m propagation constant
Übertragungsfunktion f/**optische** optical transfer function
Überwasserspiegelzone f zone of aeration
überwintern to winter, to hibernate
überwinternd perennial
Überwinterung f hibernation
überzogen coated; encrusted; incrusted
Überzug m coating; encrustation; incrustation
Überzugsverfahren n coat system
übrigbleibend residual
Ufer n shore, sea coast; bank, embankment *(of a river)*
~/abfallendes shelving shore
~/anlandendes accreting bank
~/ans ashore
~/ansteigendes shelving shore
~/äußeres outer bank
~/exponiertes weather shore
~/inneres inner bank
~/konvexes convex bank
~/verlandetes accreting bank
~/windseitiges windward bank
Uferabbruch m erosion of a bank
uferanliegend riparian
Uferausbesserung f bank reinstatement *(of a river)*
Uferbank f bar, terrace
~/angeschwemmte depositional terrace
Uferbefestigung f bank stabilization
Uferböschung f slope of bank *(of a river)*
Uferclaim n bank claim
Uferdamm m flood bank; natural levee
Ufereinfassung f embankment

Ufereis 324

Ufereis *n* marginal ice
Uferentwicklung *f* shore development
Ufererosion *f* bank erosion *(of a river)*
Uferfiltrat *n* bank filtrate
Uferfiltration *f* bank filtration
Ufergelände *n* riparian lands *(of a river)*
Uferland *n* foreshore
Uferlinie *f* coast (strand) line; bank line *(of a river)*
~/veränderliche changeable coast line
~/vermutete supposed coast line
Ufersandbank *f* point bar
Uferschutz *m* bank protection *(of a river)*
Uferströmung *f* coastal stream
Ufervorsprung *m* outward bend of bank *(of a river)*
Uferwall *m* beach [sand] barrier
~/natürlicher natural levee
Uferwalldurchbruch *m* crevasse splay
Uhligit *m* uhligite, $Ca(Zr, Ti)_2O_5$ with Al_2TiO_5
Uinta[h]it *m* uinta[h]ite *(asphaltite)*
Uintan[ien] *n* Uintan [Stage] *(mammalian stage, Eocene in North America)*
Ukrainit *m* ukrainite *(variety of monzonite)*
Ulatisien *n* Ulatisian [Stage] *(marine stage, Eocene in North America)*
Ulexit *m* ulexite, boronatrocalcite, $NaCa[B_5O_6(OH)_6] \cdot 5H_2O$
Ullmannit *m* ullmannite, NiSbS
Ulminit *m* ulminite *(maceral of brown coals and lignites)*
ultrabasisch ultrabasic
Ultrabasit *m* ultrabasite *(s. a. Diaphorit)*
ultramafisch ultramafic
ultrametamorph ultrametamorphic
Ultrametamorphose *f* ultrametamorphism
Ultramylonit *m* ultramylonite, flinty crush rock
ultramylonitisch ultramylonitic
Ultrarotspektrometrie *f s.* Infrarotspektrometrie
Ultraschall *m* ultrasound, ultrasonics, supersonics
Ultraschallbohren *n* ultrasonic drilling
Ultraschallecholot *n* active sonar
Ultraschallimpulsgerät *n* ultrasonic impulse transmitter
Ultraschallimpulsverfahren *n* pulsed ultrasonic technique
Ultraschallmessung *f* measurement of ultrasonic
Ultraschallortungsanlage *f* active sonar
Ultraschallot *n* supersonic sounder
Ultraschallströmungsmesser *m* ultrasonic flowmeter
Ultraschallwelle *f* ultrasonic wave
Ultraschallwirkung *f* action of ultrasounds
Ultraviolettaufnahmen *fpl* ultraviolet imagery
Ultraviolettlampe *f* ultraviolet lamp, UV-lamp
Ulvit *m* ulvite, Fe_2TiO_4
Umangit *m* umangite, Cu_3Se_2
Umarbeitung *f/tektonische* tectonization

Umbau *m* rig-up and rig-down operations *(drilling engineering)*
Umbiegung *f* einer Antiklinale keystone of an anticlinal fold
Umbiegungskante *f* bend *(palaeontology)*
Umbiegungspunkt *m* einer gefalteten Schicht nose
Umbildung *f/* deszendente supergene alteration
~/lösungsmetamorphe solution-metamorphic reshaping
Umbildungsvorgang *m* process of alteration
Umbra *f* umber *(manganiferous clay)*
Umbruch *m* regeneration
~/Laurentischer Laurentian revolution *(Precambrian)*
Umfangsgeschwindigkeit *f* circumferential speed
~ des gesteinszerstörenden Werkzeugs peripheral speed of the drilling tool
Umformung *f/bruchlose* deformation without shearing
Umgang *m* whorl *(of fossil shells, s. a.* Windung 3.*)*
~/letzter body whorl
~/spiraliger whorl of spire
Umgebungsisotop *n* environmental isotope
umgehen to side-track *(a bore)*
umgekehrt reverse
umgelagert reassorted
umgestalten to rework
Umgestaltung *f* reworking
Umgestaltungskräfte *fpl* agents of alteration
umgliedern to regroup
Umgliedern *n* regrouping
Umgrenzungslinie *f* clearance line
umgruppieren to rearrange
Umgruppierung *f* rearrangement
umhüllen to encrust
Umhüllungskurve *f/Mohrsche* intrinsic (rupture) curve
Umkehrpunkt *m* stagnation point *(ground-water flow)*
Umkehrspülbohren *n s.* Bohren mit Umkehrspülung
Umkehrung *f* der Polarität reversal of polarity
~ des Erdmagnetfeldes reversal of the earth's magnetic field
~ von Schichten upturning of beds
umkreisen to orbit
Umkristallisation *f* recrystallization, crystalling transformation
~ unter starker Erwärmung durch Temperung annealing recrystallization
umkristallisieren to recrystallize
umkrustet encrusted
Umkrustung *f* encrusting
umlagern to rearrange; to redeposit; to redistribute
Umlagerung *f* rearrangement; redeposition; redistribution; regrouping; rebedding
~/innermolekulare intramolecular rearrangement

Umlagerungsschichtung f secondary (indirect) stratification
Umlagerungssedimente npl redeposited sediments
Umlagerungsvorgang m process of redeposition
Umlauf m circulation
Umlaufbahn f orbit
~/geostationäre geostationary orbit *(satellite orbit in the earth's equatorial plane with a nominal altitude of 35787 km and an orbital period of 23 hours and 56 minutes)*
~/polare polar orbit
Umlaufberg m meander core, cut-off meander spur
Umlaufbewegung f orbital motion
umlaufend centroclinal *(strike)*
Umlaufgeschwindigkeit f rotating speed
Umlaufperiode f orbital period
Umlaufzeit f orbital period
~ der Gestirne sidereal period
Umleitungskanal m diversion channel, by-channel, by-wash
Umleitungsstollen m diversion (by-pass) tunnel
Umlenkbohrung f deviated borehole, doglegged hole
Ummineralisierung f remineralization
Umohoit m umohoite, [UO$_2$|MoO$_4$] · 4H$_2$O
Umordnung f rearrangement
~/atomare atomic rearrangement
Umorientierung f reorientation
Umpolung f/**geomagnetische** geomagnetic reversal
Umptekit m umptekite *(alkali syenite)*
Umriß m contour, outline
~/lateraler lateral outline
Umrißform f contour form
Umrißkarte f outline map
Umrißverfahren n **mit Ermittlung der Erdmassen aus dem Lageplan** contour method of grade design and earthwork calculation
Umscherung f transposition
Umschließungsdruck m confining pressure
umschmelzen to remelt
Umschmelzung f remelting
Umsetzen n changing *(e.g. of the bit)*
Umsetzwinkel m **des Meißels** turning angle of the percussion bit
Umtauschkapazität f cation exchange capacity
Umverteilung f/**kapillare** capillary redistribution
Umwälzung f/**tektonische** diastrophism
Umwandelbarkeit f/**enantiotrope** enantiotropic transformation
umwandeln to change, to convert; to alter
~/in Anthrazit to anthracitize
~/in Dolomit to dolomitize
~/in Glimmer to micatize
~/in Granit to granitize
~/in Jaspis to jasperize
~/in Pegmatit to pegmatize
~/in Pyrit to pyritize
Umwandlung f change, conversion; alteration
~/deuterische deuteric alteration, synantexis
~/diagenetische diagenetic change
~/hydrothermale hydrothermal alteration
~ in Anthrazit anthracitization
~ in Glimmer micatization
~ in Pegmatit pegmatization
~ in Pyrit pyritization
~ in Tonminerale argillaceous alteration
~/metamorphe metamorphic change
~/pneumatolytische pneumatolytic alteration
~/polymorphe polymorphous inversion
~/randliche peripheral change
~ von Anhydrit zu Gips gypsification
Umwandlungslösung f solution of replacement
Umwandlungsprodukt n alteration product
Umwandlungspunkt m change point
Umwandlungssaum m resorption rim *(of minerals)*
Umwandlungszone f zone of alteration, anamorphic zone
Umwelt f environment
Umweltfaktor m environmental factor
Umweltfazies f ecologic[al] facies
Umweltgeochemie f environmental geochemistry
Umweltgeologie f environmental geology; urban geology
Umweltisotop n environmental isotope
Umweltschutz m environment[al] protection
Umweltüberwachung f environmental monitoring
Umweltveränderung f environmental change
Umweltverschmutzung f environmental pollution
unbauwürdig inexploitable, unworkable, unprofitable
unbeansprucht fresh
Unbeweglichkeit f immobility
unbewölkt unclouded
unbrennbar unburnable
Undation f undation
Undationstheorie f undation theory
undehnbar non-ductile
undicht leaky
Undichtheit f **der Gestängeverbindungen** leaks in the casing joints
Undulation f undulation
undulatorisch undulatory
undurchdringlich impermeable, impenetrable
Undurchdringlichkeit f impermeability, impenetrability
undurchlässig impervious, impermeable; moisture-proof; opaque *(optical)*
Undurchlässigkeit f impermeability, imperviousness; opacity *(optical)*
undurchsichtig opaque
Undurchsichtigkeit f opacity, opaqueness
uneben uneven; rough; rugged, cragged, craggy

Unebenheit

Unebenheit f roughness; ruggedness; craggedness, cragginess
~ des Reliefs roughness of relief
unerschlossen undeveloped
unerschöpflich inexhaustible
~/nicht exhaustible
unfruchtbar sterile; infertile *(soil);* barren
ungangbar impassable
ungefrierbar incongealable
ungegliedert massive
Ungemachit m ungemachite, $K_3Na_9Fe[OH|(SO_4)_2]_3 \cdot 9H_2O$
ungemischt straight *(seismics)*
ungesättigt unsaturated
ungeschichtet unstratified, non-bedded, unbedded; ataxic *(ore deposits)*
ungeschmolzen unfused
ungespalten undifferentiated; aschistic
ungestört undisturbed; unfaulted; unmoved; undeformed
~/tektonisch tectonically undisturbed
ungleichartig heterogeneous
Ungleichartigkeit f heterogeneity
ungleichförmig 1. non-uniform; 2. unconformable, disconformable
Ungleichförmigkeit f 1. non-uniformity; 2. unconformity, disconformity
Ungleichgewicht n non-equilibrium
ungleichklappig inequivalved
ungleichkörnig varisize-grained, inequigranular
ungleichschalig inequivalve
ungleichseitig inequilateral
ungleichzeitig heterochronous
Ungula f ungula, hoof
unhaltig barren
univariant univariant *(having one degree of freedom)*
Universaldrehtisch m universal stage
~/dreiachsiger universal three-axis stage
Universum n universe
unklassiert unassorted
unlöslich insoluble
Unlöslichkeit f insolubility
unmagnetisch non-magnetic
unmerklich instrumental *(1st stage of scale of seismic intensity)*
unpolarisiert non-polarized
unregelmäßig irregular
Unregelmäßigkeit f irregularity
unrein impure
unschmelzbar infusible
unsortiert unsorted, unsized
unspaltbar uncleavable
unstabil unstable; astatic
unstetig discontinuous
Unstetigkeitsfläche f discontinuity surface, surface of instability
unstreckbar non-ductile
unsymmetrisch asymmetric[al]
Unterart f subspecies, subvariety
Unterbank f bottom layer (bench) *(of a seam)*

Unterbau m substructure; basement; undermass
Unterbecken n lower reservoir
Unterboden m bottom soil, subsoil
~/steiniger ratchel
unterbrechen to interrupt; to break; to intermit
Unterbrechung f interruption; break; discontinuity; lacuna; intermittency
~/stratigrafische stratigraphic[al] break, gap in the geologic record, range of lost strata
~/tektonische tectonic termination
Unterbringung f von Bergen dirt disposal
unterbrochen interrupted; discontinuous
Unterdevon n Lower Devonian [Series, Epoch]
Unterdruck m subpressure
Unterdrückung f omission; suppression
Unterfamilie f subfamily
Unterfläche f undersurface
Unterflurdrainage f lithic drainage
Unterform f subvariety
Untergattung f subgenus
untergehen to set
untergetaucht s. submers
Untergliederung f subdivision
~/fazielle subdivision of the facies
~/paläontologische palaeontologic subdivision
~/stratigrafische stratigraphic subdivision
untergraben to sap
Untergrund m 1. subsoil, underground, undersoil, earth (soil) subgrade; 2. background
~ des Bauwerks seat of settlement
~/geologischer geologic[al] set-up
~/kristalliner crystalline floor
~/magmatischer igneous floor
~/subsalinarer subsaliniferous bottom
~/tieferer deeper basement
~/unregelmäßiger erratic subsoil
Untergrundbewässerung f subirrigation, subterranean irrigation
Untergrundentwässerung f underdrainage, subsoil (subsurface) drainage
Untergrundfließen n subsolifluction
Untergrundforschung f soil exploration, soil (subsurface) investigation, site exploration
Untergrundgasspeicher m underground gas store (reservoir)
Untergrundgasspeicherung f underground gas storage
Untergrundkarte f/**strukturelle** structural subsurface map
Untergrundlockerung f subsoiling
Untergrundspeicher m underground storage chamber, underlying reservoir
Untergrundspeicherung f underground (subterranean) storage
Untergrundstauwerk n underground dam
Untergrundstrahlung f background radiation
Untergrundwasser n deep subsoil water
Unterhaltungskosten pl cost of maintenance
unterhöhlen to undercut; to undermine

unterirdisch underground; subterranean, subterraneous; subsurface; hypogeal, hypogeic, hypogeous *(part of plants)*
Unterkambrium *n* Lower Cambrian [Series, Epoch]
Unterkante *f* **der Langsamschicht** base of weathering
~/stratigrafische stratigraphic bottom edge
Unterkantenmessung *f* lateral log *(well logging)*
Unterkarbon *n* 1. Lower Carboniferous, Dinantian *(in West and Central Europe, Gattendorfia to Goniatites Stages)*; 2. Lower Carboniferous *(in East Europe, Gattendorfia Stage to Namurian A)*
unterkarbonisch Lower Carboniferous
Unterkiefer *m* lower jaw
Unterkonstruktion *f* substructure
Unterkorn *n* undersize
Unterkreide *f* Lower (Early) Cretaceous [Series, Epoch]
unterkritisch subcritical
unterkühlt supercooled
Unterkühlung *f* supercooling
Unterlage *f* basement; substratum
unterlagern to underlie
unterlagert underlain
Unterlagerung *f* subdeposit
Unterlauf *m* lower course *(of a river)*
untermeerisch subsea, submarine
Unterordnung *f* suborder
Unterperm *n* Lower Permian [Series, Epoch]
unterpermisch Lower Permian
untersättigt undersaturated, subsaturated
Untersättigung *f* undersaturation, subsaturation
Unterscheidbarkeit *f* discriminability
Unterscheidung *f* discrimination
Unterscheidungskriterium *n* discriminator
Unterscheidungsvermögen *n* discriminability
Unterschicht *f* underlayer, substratum, lower bed
Unterschiebung *f* underthrust
Unterschiebungsinsel *f* outlier
Unterschießen *n* **eines Salzstocks** saltdome undershooting
unterschneiden to undercut, to underream
Unterschneider *m* underreamer
Unterschneidung *f* undercutting, underreaming
Unterschneidungshang *m* undercut slope; concave bank
Unterschottern *n* ballasting
unterschrämen to undercut
Unterschwere *f* subgravity
unterseeisch submarine, subsea
Unterseeschlamm *m* gyttja
Unterseite *f* **eines Ganges** ledger
Unterseitenwulst *m* load cast
unterspülen to underwash, to undercut
Unterspülung *f* underwashing, undercutting
Unterstamm *m* subphylum

Unterstrom *m* downstream
Unterströmung *f* underflow, undercurrent
Unterströmungshypothese *f*, **Unterströmungstheorie** *f* hypothesis of convection currents
Unterstufe *f* substage
Unterstützungsausbau *m* standing supports *(e.g. conventional supports, as opposed to roof)*
Unterstützungspunkt *m* centre of support
untersuchen to examine; to investigate; to explore; to study; to analyze
~/geologisch *(Am)* to geologize
Untersuchung *f* examination; investigation; exploration; study; analyzation
~/faziell-ökologische investigation of the facies and ecology
~/gefügekundliche investigation of fabrics
~/geophysikalische geophysical investigation
~/geröllstatistische statistical boulder analysis
~/isotopengeochemische isotope geochemical study
~/lagerstättentektonische tectonic investigation of deposits
~/makroskopische macroscopic[al] examination
~/mikroskopische microscopic[al] study
~/tiefenseismische deep seismic sounding
Untersuchungsarbeiten *fpl* research (exploration) work
~/geologische geological prospecting
Untersuchungsbohren *n* exploration drilling; prospecting bore, core drill; exploration well, structure hole
Untersuchungsgrad *m* stage of investigation
Untersuchungskosten *pl* exploration expenses
Untersuchungsobjekt *n*/**geologisches** object of geological prospecting
Untersuchungsstadium *n*/**geologisches** stage of geological prospecting
Untersuchungsstrecke *f* trial heading
Untertageabbau *m* deep mining (working)
Untertagearbeit *f* underground workings
Untertageaufbereitung *f* underground milling
Untertagebau *m* underground mining
Untertagebetrieb *m* underground operations
Untertagebohren *n* underground drilling
Untertagegrube *f* mine
Untertagespeicherungsmöglichkeiten *fpl* bottom storage facilities
Untertageverdampfung *f* underground vaporization
Untertagevergasung *f* underground gasification
untertauchen to submerge, to immerse
Untertauchen *n* submersion, submergence, immersion
~/teilweises partial submergence
Untertauchküste *f* shore line of submergence
Unterteilung *f* subdivision
Untervorschiebung *f* lag fault
unterwaschen *s.* unterspülen

Unterwaschung

Unterwaschung f s. Unterspülung
Unterwasserablagerung f subaqueous deposit
Unterwasserausbruch m subaquatic eruption
Unterwasserausrüstung f subsea equipment
Unterwasserbaggern n dredging
Unterwasserbank f/**küstenparallele** offshore beach
Unterwasserboden m subaqueous soil
Unterwasserbohren n offshore drilling
Unterwasserbohrung f subsea drilling venture
Unterwasserdamm m submerged dam
Unterwasserentlastung f submerging of outlet
Unterwassereruptionskreuz n subsea christmas tree
Unterwasserkanal m off-take, tailrace
Unterwasserkomplettierung f subsea completion
Unterwasserplattform f submarine platform
Unterwasserproduktionssystem n subsea production system
Unterwasserquelle f drowned (subaqueous) spring
Unterwasserriff n submerged reef, offshore bar
~ eines Eisbergs ram
Unterwassersandbank f/**küstenparallele** offshore bar
unterwasserseitig downstream
Unterwasserspiegel m downstream water line
Unterwasserstollen m tailrace tunnel
Unterwasservulkan m subaquatic volcano
Unterzone f infrazone
untief shallow, shoaly
Untiefe f shallow[ness], shoal[iness], flat; sandbank
~ der Lagune lagoon shoal
unverändert unaltered
unverfestigt unconsolidated, uncompacted
unverformt undeformed
unvergletschert non-glaciated
unverritzt unworked, virgin, maiden
unverrohrt unlined
unverwittert unweathered, unaltered, undecayed
unverzerrt undistorted
unzersetzbar undecomposable
unzersetzt undecomposed
unzufällig antichance
Uphole-Geophon n uphole geophone (seis)
Uphole-Schießen n uphole shooting
Uraconit m uraconite (partly zippeite, partly uranopilite)
Uralborit m uralborite, $CaB_2O_4 \cdot 2H_2O$
Ural-Faltenorogen n Ural orogene
Ural-Faltensystem n Ural fold system
Uraliden pl uralids
Uralit m uralite (an amphibole resulting from alteration of pyroxene)
Uralitdiabas m uralitic diabase
uralitisieren to uralitize
Uralitisierung f uralitization
Uralitschiefer m uralite schist

328

Uralolith m uralolite, $CaBe_3[OH|PO_4]_2 \cdot 4H_2O$
Ural-Randsenke f Uralian marginal deep
Ural-Subprovinz f Uralian Subprovince (palaeobiogeography, Lower Devonian)
Uramphite uramphite, $(NH_4)_2[UO_2|PO_4]_2 \cdot xH_2O$
uranartig uranous
Uranblüte f zippeite, $[6UO_2|3(OH)_2|3SO_4] \cdot 12H_2O$
urandatiert uranium-dated
Urandioxid n brown oxide, UO_2
Uranerz n uranium ore
uranfänglich primordial
Urangehalt m uranium content
uranhaltig uranous, uraniferous, uranium-bearing
Uraninfiltrationslagerstätte f uranium infiltration deposit
Uraninit m uraninite, pitchblende, UO_2
Uranium n uranium, U
~/an organische Substanz gebundenes urano-organic ore
Uranmikrolith m djalmaite (a mixed mineral closely related to betafite)
Uranmineral n uranium mineral
Uranocircit m uranocircite, $Ba[UO_2|PO_4]_2 \cdot 10H_2O$
Uranocker m s. Uranopilit
Uranografie f uranography
Uranometrie f uranometry
Uranophan m uranophane, uranotil[e], $CaH_2[UO_2|SiO_4]_2 \cdot 5H_2O$
Uranopilit m uranopilite, $[6UO_2|5(OH)_2|SO_4] \cdot 12H_2O$
Uranospathit m uranospathite (a hydrous uranyl phosphate)
Uranosphärit m uranosphaerite, $[UO_2|(OH)_2|BiOOH]$
Uranospinit m uranospinite, $Ca[UO_2|AsO_4]_2 \cdot 10H_2O$
Uranothallit m s. Liebigit
Uranothorit m uranothorite, $(ThU)[SiO_4]$
Uranpechblende f, **Uranpecherz** n uraninite, UO_2
Uranspaltung f uranium fission
Uranvitriol n gilpinite (s.a. Johannit)
Uranzerfall m uranium decay
Uratmosphäre f primitive (primordial, initial) atmosphere
urban urban
Urbarmachung f **von Land** cultivating of lands
Ureilit m ureilite (meteorite)
Urelbe f original Elbe
Urformen fpl initial forms (morphology)
Urgebirge n primary mountains
Urgesteinsmassiv n terrane
Urheimat f ancestral (aboriginal) home
Urhydrosphäre f primordial hydrosphere
Urkarte f original map
Urkontinent m early (primary) continent, early (primary) mainland
Urkraton n early (primary) craton

Urlandschaft f primeval landscape
Urleben n primordial life
Urmeer n primeval (primordial) ocean
Urmensch m prehistoric (aboriginal, primitive) man
Urozean m s. Urmeer
Urplanet m protoplanet
Ursilit m ursilite, $(Ca,Mg)_2[(UO_2)_2|Si_5O_{14}] \cdot 9-10H_2O$
Ursonne f protosun
Ursprung m origin, source
~/anorganischer inorganic origin
~/organischer biological origin
ursprünglich primordial
Ursprungsart f mode of origin
Ursprungsbäche mpl headwaters
Ursprungsfestigkeit f original strength
Ursprungsgebiet n source area
Ursprungsgestein n origin rock
Ursprungsstelle f starting place
Urstromtal n Pleistocene watercourse, ice-marginal valley, glacial spillway (stream channel)
Ursubstanz f/**organische** primitive organic substance
Urtit m urtite (nepheline-rich alkali gabbro)
Urtyp m proterotype
Urwald m primeval (virgin) forest
~/tropischer tropical primeval forest
Urwaldsumpf m primeval swamp
Urwelt f primeval world
Urzeit f s. Archaikum
urzeitlich primeval, archaic
Usbekit m uzbekite, $3CuO \cdot V_2O_5 \cdot 3H_2O$
Ussingit m ussingite, $Na[OH | AlSi_3O_8]$
Ustarasit m ustarasite, $PbS \cdot 3Bi_2S_3$
Utahit m s. Jarosit
U-Tal n U-shaped valley, glacial gorge
Uvala f uvala
Uvanit m uvanite, $[(UO_2)_2 | V_6O_{17}] \cdot 15H_2O$
Uvit m uvite, $CaMg_3(Al_5Mg)[(OH)_{1+3} | (BO_3)_3 | Si_6O_{18}]$
Uwarowit m uvarovite, uwarowite, $Ca_3Cr_2(SiO_4)_3$
Uzbekit m s. Usbekit

V

vados vadose
Vaesit m vaesite, NiS_2
vagil vagile
Vaginatenkalk m Vaginatum limestone (Lower Ordovician)
Vakuumspektrograf m vacuum spectrograph
Valangin[ien] n, **Valanginium** n Valanginian [Stage] (Lower Cretaceous)
Valent n s. Llandoverium
Valentinit m valentinite, Sb_2O_3
Valentium n s. Llandoverium
Valleriit m valleriite, $CaFeS_2$
Vallesium n Vallesien [Stage] (continental stage of Pliocene)

Vallis f vallis (valley on Mars or moon)
Vanadin n vanadium, V
vanadinartig vanadous
Vanadinbleierz n s. Vanadinit
Vanadinerz n vanadium ore
vanadinhaltig vanadous, vanadiferous
Vanadinit m vanadinite, $Pb_5[Cl | (VO_4)_3]$
Vanadium n s. Vanadin
Vanalit m vanalite, $NaAl_8V_{10}O_{38} \cdot 30H_2O$
Vandenbrandeit m vandenbrand[e]ite, $[UO_2 | (OH)_2] \cdot Cu(OH)_2$
Vandendriesscheit m vandendriesscheite, $8[UO_2 | (OH)_2] \cdot Pb(OH)_2 \cdot 4H_2O$
Vanoxit m vanoxite, $2V_2O_4 \cdot V_2O_5 \cdot 8H_2O$
Vanthoffit m vanthoffite, $Na_6Mg[SO_4]_4$
Vanuralit m vanuralite, $Al[OH | (UO_2)_2 | VO_8] \cdot 8H_2O$
Variable f/**regionalisierte** regionalized variable
Varianz f **des zufälligen Effekts** dispersion variance
~ einer Zufallsvariablen variance (measure of variability of a random variable)
Varianzanalyse f variance [component] analysis, analysis of variances
Varianzanalysemodell n **mit festen Effekten** fixed effects model of variance analysis, model I of variance analysis, model of variance analysis with fixed effects
~ mit gemischten Effekten mixed effects model of variance analysis, model of variance analysis with mixed (fixed and random) effects
~ mit zufälligen Effekten random effects model of variance analysis, model II of variance analysis, model of variance analysis with random effects
Varianzkomponente f variance component
Variation f variation
~/erdmagnetische variation of terrestrial magnetism
~/jahreszeitliche seasonal variation
~/zeitliche time variation
Variationsbreite f range of variation
Variationsmerkmal n varietal character
Variationsreihe f variation range
Varietät f variety
Variogramm n variogram
Variolit m variolite, pearl diabase
Variscit m variscite, sphaerite, amatrice, $Al[POH_4] \cdot 2H_2O$
variskisch s. variszisch
Varistikum n/**mitteleuropäisches** Central European Variscan belt
varistisch s. variszisch
variszisch Variscan, Hercynian
Varlamoffit m s. Hydro-Cassiterit
Varmouth n Varmouth[ian] (Pleistocene in North America)
Varulith m varulite, $(Na, Ca)_2(Fe, Mn)_3[PO_4]_3$
Vaterit m vaterite ($CaCO_3$ hexagonal)
Vaugnerit m vaugnerite (variety of granodiorite)

Vauquelinit

Vauquelinit *m* vauquelinite, $PbCu[OH \mid CrO_4 \mid PO_4]$
Vauxit *m* vauxite, $Fe\cdot Al_2[OH\mid PO_4]_2 \cdot 7H_2O$
Väyrynenit *m* vaeyrynenite, $MnBe[(OH,F) \mid PO_4]$
Veatchit *m* veatchite, $Sr[B_3O_4(OH)_2]_2$
Vegasit *m s.* Plumbojarosit
Vegetation *f* vegetation
Vegetationsdecke *f* vegetation cover[ing], vegetable layer (blanket, cover), mantle of vegetation
Vegetationseinheit *f* unit of vegetation
Vegetationsgeschichte *f* history of vegetation
~/interglaziale history of interglacial vegetation
Vegetationsgürtel *m* belt of vegetation
Vegetationskarte *f* ecologic[al] map
vegetationslos barren of vegetation
Vektordiagramm *n* tadpole plot *(in geophysical borehole measurements)*
vektoriell vectorial
Velum *n* frill
Vendium *n s.* Wendium
Venit *m* venite *(a migmatite)*
Ventilbohrer *m*, **Ventilschappe** *f* valve auger
Ventralansicht *f* ventral view
Ventralkanal *m* ventral furrow
Ventralklappe *f* ventral (pedicle) valve
Ventraltasche *f* pouch
Venturien *n* Venturian [Stage] *(marine stage, upper Pliocene to lower Pleistocene in North America)*
Venushaar *n* Venus' hair stone
Veränderlichkeit *f* alterability
verändert/sekundär deuteromorphic *(crystals)*
Veränderung *f* variation
~ in der Werteauswahl resample
~/paläoklimatische palaeoclimatic change
Verankerung *f* anchorage
~des Hangenden strata bolting
~/unterirdische buried anchorage
Verankerungspunkt *m* point of anchorage
Verankerungssystem *n* mooring system
verarbeitbar workable
Verarbeitbarkeit *f* workability
verarbeiten to treat
Verarbeitung *f* treatment
verarmen to impoverish
Verarmung *f* impoverishment
Veraschung *f* incineration
verästeln to ramify
Verästelung *f* ramification
Verband *m* bond
~/orientierter oriented intergrowth
Verbandsfestigkeit *f* bond[ing] strength
Verbesserung *f* amendment
Verbiegung *f* buckling, bending; flexure
verbinden to agglutinate
Verbinder *m* joint, coupling
Verbindung *f*[**/chemische**] compound
~/hydraulische hydraulic connection
~/metallorganische organometallic compound
~/optisch aktive optically active compound
~ von Futterrohren/gasdichte integral joint
Verbindungsgewicht *n* combining weight
Verbindungsleitung *f* bus
verblasen to stow pneumatically
verbogen bent; warped
Verbolzung *f* strutting
verborgen concealed
verbreiten to disseminate
Verbreiterung *f* **der Ozeanräume** sea-floor spreading, spreading of the ocean floor
Verbreitung *f*/**stratigrafische (vertikale)** stratigraphic (geologic) range
Verbreitungswege *mpl* dispersion routes
Verbrennungsprodukt *n* product of combustion
Verbruch *m* collapse
verbunden/untereinander interconnected; intercommunicating
verdämmen to tamp, to plug
Verdämmen *n* tamping, plugging
verdampfen to vaporize, to evaporate, to volatilize
Verdampfung *f* vaporization, evaporation, volatilization
Verdampfungswärme *f* [latent] heat of evaporation
verdeckt concealed
Verdichtbarkeit *f* condensability; compactibility
verdichten to condense; to compact; to pack; to reconstitute
Verdichtung *f* condensation; compaction; packing; compression; consolidation
~ der Sedimente mit zunehmender Belastung compaction of sediments with increasing load
Verdichtungsapparat *m* consolidation apparatus
Verdichtungsbeiwert *m* coefficient of compressibility *(of soils)*
Verdichtungseffekt *m* packing effect
Verdichtungsfähigkeit *f s.* Verdichtbarkeit
Verdichtungsfaktor *m* packing factor *(of loose particles)*
Verdichtungsgerät *n* compact apparatus
Verdichtungsgrad *m* degree of compaction; degree of consolidation
Verdichtungshorizont *m* hardened horizon, [hard]pan
Verdichtungskoeffizient *m* coefficient of compaction *(diagenesis)*
Verdichtungsmaschinen *fpl* compaction (compression) equipment
Verdichtungssetzung *f* consolidation settlement
Verdichtungsversuch *m* compaction test
~ nach Proctor Proctor compaction test
Verdichtungswalze *f* compaction roller, compactor
Verdichtungswellen *fpl* condensational waves *(seismics)*

Verdichtungsziffer *f s.* Verdichtungskoeffizient
Verdickung *f* thickening *(of a layer)*
Verdopplung *f* duplication
verdorren to dry up
verdrängen to displace, to replace; to substitute
Verdrängendes *n* metasome
Verdrängung *f* metasomatism, displacement, replacement; substitution
~ **des Öls durch Wasser** water-oil displacement
~/**frontale** immiscible displacement
~/**hydrothermale** hydrothermal alteration
~/**pneumatolytische** pneumatolytic alteration
~/**selektive** selective replacement
Verdrängungsarbeit *f* work of displacement
Verdrängungsdruck *m* displacement pressure
Verdrängungserzlagerstätte *f* replacement ore deposit
Verdrängungsfront *f* displacement front
Verdrängungsgang *m* replacement vein
Verdrängungskörper *m* replacement body
Verdrängungslagerstätte *f* replacement (metasomatic) deposit
~/**pneumatolytische** pneumatolytic replacement deposit
Verdrängungspunkt *m* centre of displacement
Verdrängungsreste *mpl* replacement remnants
Verdrängungszentrum *n* centre of displacement
Verdrängungszonung *f* replacement zoning
verdreht contorted, twisted
Verdrehung *f* torsion, twist[ing]
Verdrehungsbruch *m* torsion failure
Verdrehungswinkel *m* angle of torsion
Verdriftung *f* shore (beach) drifting
verdrücken to contract, to squeeze out
~/**sich** to pinch out, to die away, to peter out, to wedge out, to feather
verdrückt pinched[-out], nipped
Verdrückung *f* contraction, pinching[-out], nip[-out], thinning, petering
Verdunkelung *f* obscuration
verdünnen 1. to dilute; to rarefy; 2. *s.* verdrücken
verdünnt dilute
Verdünnung *f* 1. dilution; rarefaction; 2. *s.* Verdrückung
Verdünnungsmethode *f* radioactive tracer dilution method
Verdünnungsmittel *n* diluent
verdunsten to evaporate, to vaporize, to volatilize
Verdunstung *f* evaporation, vaporization, volatilization, evapotranspiration
~/**latente** latent evaporation
~/**potentielle** potential evapotranspiration
~/**selektive** selective evaporation
Verdunstungsfläche *f* evaporation area
Verdunstungsgleichung *f* evapotranspiration equation

Verfestigung

Verdunstungshöhe *f* amount of evaporation, height of [natural] evaporation
Verdunstungsmesser *m* evaporimeter
Verdunstungsrate *f* rate of evaporation
Verdunstungsunterdrückung *f* evaporation suppression
Verdunstungsverlust *m* evaporation loss, loss by evaporation
Verdunstungsvermögen *n* evaporating capacity, evaporativity
verebnen to planate
Verebnung *f* [pene]planation
Verebnungsfläche *f* erosion surface
veredeln to enrich
~/**sich** to become enriched
Vereinbarkeit *f* compatibility *(of data)*
vereinigen/sich to coalesce
Vereinigung *f* coalescence
vereisen to ice, to glaciate
vereist icy; glaciated
~/**nicht** unglaciated
Vereisung *f* icing, glaci[eriz]ation, ice frost; ice accretion
Vereisungszustand *m* icing condition
Verengung *f* reduction in diameter
~ **des Bohrlochs** borehole diameter decreasing
vererzbar mineralizable
vererzen to mineralize, to metallize
Vererzung *f* mineralization, metallization
~/**hydrothermale** hydrothermal mineralization
~/**verborgene** hidden mineralization
Vererzungsknoten *m* ore knot
Verfahren *n* **der Probe[nent]nahme** sample collecting techniques
~ **der Wasserzuflußmessung/fotoelektrisches** photoelectric logging *(in boreholes)*
~ **des verbesserten Stapelns von Mehrspurfiltern** optimum horizontal wide band stack *(seismics)*
~/**elektromagnetisches** electromagnetic method
~/**geoelektrodynamisches** geoelectric-dynamic method
~/**geotechnisches** geotechnic[al] process
~/**gravimetrisches** gravimetric method
~/**naßmechanisches** wet process
~/**radiografisches** radiographic method
Verfall *m* decay
verfallen to decay
verfälschen/eine Probe to salt a sample
Verfärbung *f*/**radioaktive** radioactive discoloration
verfaulen to putrefy, to rot
Verfaulen *n* putrefaction
verfeldspaten to feldspathize
Verfeldspatung *f* feldspathization
verfestigen to cement [together]; to consolidate by injection
~/**diagenetisch** to lithify
~/**sich** to consolidate; to solidify
Verfestigung *f* consolidation; solidifaction; bonding *(of the rock)*

Verfestigung   332

~/**chemische** chemical grouting
~/**diagenetische** induration, lithifaction
~ **durch Impaktmetamorphose** shock lithifaction
~ **mit Zement** cement stabilization
~ **von Sedimenten** consolidation of sediments
~ **zu Konglomerat** conglomeration
Verfestigungsbeiwert m coefficient of consolidation
Verfestigungsfaktor m compaction factor
Verfestigungsgrad m degree of consolidation
verfinstern/sich to be eclipsed, to occult
Verfinsterung f eclipse, occultation
Verfirnung f firnification
verflachen to slope down, to flatten
~/**sich** to flatten, to become shallow
Verflachen n flattening[-out]
verflechten to intertongue
Verflechtung f intertonguing
~/**fingerförmige** interdigitation
verflochten/miteinander interlacing
~ **sein/fingerartig** to interdigitate
Verflochtenheit f interlacing
verflüchtigen/sich to volatilize
Verflüchtigung f volatilization
verflüssigen to liquefy
Verflüssigung f liquefaction
~ **durch Meteoritenaufschlag** impact fluidization
~ **untertage** underground liquefaction
verfolgen/eine Schicht to trace a bed (on the surface)
Verfolgung f **eines Gangs im Streichen** chasing
verformbar deformable
~/**bruchlos unter Druck** malleable
Verformbarkeit f deformability
~ **unter Druck/bruchlose** malleability
verformen to deform; to distort (crystals)
verformt deformed; distorted (crystals)
Verformung f deformation; distortion (of crystals)
~/**affine** affine transformation
~/**atektonische** non-diastrophic deformation
~/**bleibende** permanent (residual) deformation
~/**diagenetische** diagenetic compaction
~/**elastische** elastic deformation
~/**elastoplastische** elastic-plastic deformation
~/**plastische** plastic deformation
~/**tektonische** diastrophic deformation
Verformungsarbeit f deformation energy
Verformungsbruch m deformation fracture
Verformungsgeschwindigkeit f rate of deformation
Verformungskreis m deformation circle
Verformungsstruktur f deformation structure
Verformungszustand m/**räumlicher** three-dimensional state of deformation
Verformungszwilling m deformation twin
Verfrachtung f transport
~/**küstenparallele** longshore transport
Verfügbarkeit f **von Rohstoffen** availability of raw material

Verfüllboden m backfilling
verfüllen to fill in; to refill; to backfill; to plug
Verfüllen n refilling; backfilling; plugging[-back]
~/**aktive** active fill (ichnology)
~ **des Bohrlochs** plugging and abandonment of a well
Vergangenheit f/**geologische** geologic[al] past
vergasbar gasifiable
vergasen to gasify
Vergasung f gasification
~ **in der Lagerstätte** underground gasification
vergelen to gel
Vergelung f 1. gelification (peat, coal); 2. gelation
~/**biochemische** biochemical gelification (peat, soft brown coal)
~/**geochemische** geochemical gelification (vitrinitization)
Vergenz f vergency, overturn
Vergenzfächer m vergency fan
vergesellschaften to associate, to assemble
Vergesellschaftung f association, assemblage, paragenesis
Vergesellschaftungsgrenzen fpl community boundaries [of organisms]
verglasen to vitrify
Vergleichbarkeit f compatibility (of data)
Vergleichsprobe f check (reference) sample
Vergleichsprüfung f comparison test
Vergleichsschießen n turkey shoot (seismics)
vergletschern to glaciate, to glacierize
vergletschert glacierized, (Am) glacier-covered
~/**nicht** unglaciated
Vergletscherung f glaciation, glacierization
~/**alpine** alpine mountain glaciation
Vergletscherungsgebiet n area of glaciation
Vergletscherungsgrenze f glacial boundary
vergleyt gleyed
Vergleyung f gleying process, gleyization
Verglimmerung f micatization
vergneisen to alter to gneiss
Vergneisung f alteration to gneiss, gneissification
Vergrabungsstelle f grave yard (for radioactive waste)
vergreisenen to greisenize
Vergreisenung f greisening, greisenization
Vergreisenungsmetasomatose f greisening metasomatism
vergrößern to magnify
Vergrößerung f magnification
~ **des Einfallens** steepening of dip
~/**lineare** linear magnification
~/**stärkere** stronger magnification
Vergrößerungsglas n magnifier, magnifying glass
vergrust crumbly
Vergrusung f granular disintegration
Verhalten n **eines Gesteins nach dem Bruch** post-failure behaviour
~/**gebirgsdynamisches** rock-burst behaviour

~/optisches optical behaviour
~/unelastisches inelasticity
Verhaltensforschung f ethology
Verhältnis n ratio
~ Abraum zu Kohle overburden-to-coal ratio
~ des gemessenen Evaporationsbetrags zur potentiell möglichen Evaporation relative evaporation
~ Signal zu Störungen signal-to-noise ratio
~ von Fehl- zu Fundbohrungen dry-hole-to-producer ratio
Verhältniszahl f ratio
verharscht crusted, hardened
Verharschung f hardening
verhärten/sich to indurate
Verhärtung f induration; concretion
Verhieb m face advance, extraction, working
Verhiebrichtung f direction of advance (working)
Verhiebsbreite f increment of face advance
Verhiebsfläche f area worked (exposed)
verholzen to lignify
Verholzung f lignification
verhüttbar smeltable
verhütten to smelt
Verhüttung f smelting
verhüttungsfähig smeltable
verjüngen to rejuvenate, to revive, to reinvigorate (a river)
Verjüngung f rejuvenation, rejuvenescence, revival, reinvigoration (of a river); foreshortening (on maps)
Verjüngungsmethode f increment method (sampling)
verkalken to calcify
Verkalkung f calcification
verkanten to tilt
verkarsten to karstify
Verkarstung f karstification
Verkehrsbelastbarkeit f/ingenieurgeologische trafficabilty
Verkehrtspülung f reversed circulation [of the mud]
Verkeilung f invection
Verkieseln n silicating, treatment with silicate
verkieselt silicious, cherty
~/mit Jaspis jasperated
Verkieselung f silification, silicatization, chertification
Verkippung f dumping
verkitten to cement [together]
verkittend cementitious
Verkittung f cementation (of rock); secondary cementation (of sediment)
verklausen to jam
Verklausen n, Verklausung f jam
verkleben to plaster off
verkleinern/im Maßstab to reduce in scale
Verklemmen n des Meißels bit wedging
Verknäuelung f crumpled ball
Verknetung f mashing, kneading; involution (cryoturbate form)

Vermessungsingenieur

Verknöcherung f ossification
Verknorpelung f chondrification
Verknüpfungsgesetz n scaling law (seismology)
verkohlen to carbonize
Verkohlung f carbonization
verkoken to coke, to carbonize
Verkokung f coking, carbonization
Verkokungseigenschaften fpl coking properties
verkrusten to encrust
verkrustet crustified
Verkrustung f crustification, encrustation
verkümmert rudimentary, dwarfed; aborted
Verkümmerung f dwarfing
verkürzt abbreviated (e.g. development)
Verkürzung f shortening; foreshortening (on maps)
verlagern to displace; to transfer (pressure)
Verlagerung f displacement
verlanden to silt up
Verlandung f 1. process of alluviation, filling-up [process], silting-up; 2. alluvial deposit, alluvium
Verlandungsmoor n ancient lake mire
Verlandungsprozeß m s. Verlandung
Verlängerung f elongation; prolongation; extension; tailing (e.g. of seismical waves)
Verlauf m in Richtung des Schichtenstreichens level course
~ einer Tiefenstörung/schaufelförmiger listric surface
verlegen to transfer, to shift, to move
~/einen Fluß to divert a river
~/Ölleitung unterflur to bury a line
Verlegung f der Küstenlinie/seewärtige advance of a beach
~ eines Flußbetts clearing of a river bed
~/seitliche swinging (meander)
~ von Erdölleitungen pipelining
Verlehmung f loamification, weathering to loam
verletten to waxwall
Verletten n claying (e.g. of a borehole)
verlieren/Spülung to loose circulation
vermarken to demarcate, to set out observation points
vermessen to survey
~/eine Grube to survey a mine
~/geophysikalisch to survey geophysically
Vermessung f survey[ing]; mensuration
~/geodätische geodetic survey
~/geomagnetische geomagnetic survey
~/geophysikalische geophysical survey
~/untertägige surveying of underground
~ vom Flugzeug aus/magnetische aerial magnetometry
Vermessungsarbeiten fpl im Bergbau mine surveying
Vermessungsflugzeug n survey plane
Vermessungsingenieur m geodetic engineer

Vermessungsinstrument 334

Vermessungsinstrument *n* surveying instrument
Vermessungskunde *f* surveying
Vermessungsmethode *f*/**luftgeophysikalische** airborne exploration method
Vermessungsplan *m* survey plan
Vermessungsschiff *n* survey[ing] vessel
Vermessungstechnik *f* mensuration technique
Vermessungstrupp *m* survey[ing] party
Vermiculit *m* vermiculite, $(Mg, Fe)_3[(Si, Al)_4O_{10}][OH_2] \cdot 4H_2O$
Verminderung *f* **seismischer Energie** attenuation of seismic energy
Vermischungsgrad *m* entropy *(of different sedimentary types)*
Vermischungskoeffizient *m* dispersion coefficient
Vermischungsstrecke *f* mixing distance *(of water)*
vermodern to moulder, to decay
Vermoderung *f* mouldering
Vermoderungsprozeß *m* process of rotting
vermoort converted into peat
Vermoorung *f* peat formation
Vermörtelung *f* cement stabilization
Vermullung *f* mouldering
Vermurung *f* overwash of debris *(covering of the river banks with slime, mud or stones)*
Vernadit *m* vernadite, $H_2MnO_3 + H_2O$
Vernadskyit *m* vernadskite *(a mineral consisting of a hydrous basic sulphate of copper)*
Verödung *f* desolation
Verplanckit *m* verplanckite, $Ba_6Mn_3[(OH)_6 |Si_6O_{18}]$
verpressen to inject; to grout under pressure
Verpreßloch *n* grout hole
verquarzt quartzose
Verquetschung *f* nip-out
verrichten/Aufschlußarbeiten to carry on explorations
verrieseln to seep in
verrohren to case
Verrohren *n* casing
Verrohrung *f* 1. casing, tubing; 2. casing pipe *(material)*
~ **mit eingelassener Verschraubung** inserted joint-casing
~/**volle** full string of casing
~/**vorläufige** temporary casing
Verrohrungsabmaße *npl* casing size
Verrohrungsdruck *m* casing pressure
Verrohrungsprogramm *n* casing program
Verrohrungsteufe *f* casing depth (point)
Versalzung *f* salting, salification, salinization *(of soil)*
versanden to sand up
Versanden *n* sanding-up, sand silting, *(Am)* sand filling
Versatz *m* fill rock, stowage, stowing, packing, backfilling; tamp[ing]
~/**mechanischer** power stowing
~ **mit taubem Gestein** waste fill

~/**verfestigter** consolidated fill
Versatzarbeit *f* gobbing
Versatzbau *m* 1. cutting and filling, extraction with stowing; 2. backfill *(ichnology)*
Versatzberge *pl* stowing material, rubbish
Versatzböschung *f* slope of the stowed material
Versatzdichte *f* degree of filling
Versatzdruck *m* 1. pressure acting upon the stowed goaf; 2. pressure exerted by the stowing material
Versatzdruckdose *f* pack-pressure dynamometer
Versatzfeld *n* stowed goaf
Versatzgut *n* filling (stowing) material
Versatzkante *f* pack line, edge of the stowed zone
Versatzrippe *f* pack
Versatzschicht *f* stowing shift, attle
Versatzschild *m* flushing shield
Versauerung *f* acidification *(of soil)*
verschieben to thrust, to shift, to slide; to displace *(e.g. within crystals)*
Verschiebung *f* thrusting, shifting, sliding; thrust, shift, fault, break; displacement *(e.g. within crystals)*
~ **der Wasserscheiden** shifting (migration) of divides
~ **des Bezugspunkts** lag
~ **im Streichen** strike shift
~/**räumliche** space lag
~/**transversale** heave fault
Verschiebungsbruch *m* sliding (shear) fracture, sliding rupture, rupture by shearing
Verschiebungsdichte *f* density of dislocation *(crystallography)*
Verschiebungsfläche *f* fault surface
Verschiebungsgeber *m* displacement indicator
Verschiebungskurve *f* displacement curve
Verschiebungsrichtung *f* direction of slip in the fault plane
verschiedenartig heterovalent
verschiedenkörnig varigrained
verschlacken to scorify
verschlackt scorious
Verschlackung *f* scorification
verschlammen to choke
verschlämmen to clog
verschlammt silted-up
Verschlammung *f* [mud] silting, *(Am)* mud filling
~ **des Bohrlochs** cutting settling, deposition of cuttings
Verschlammungsprozeß *m* process of silting-up
Verschleiß *m* wear
Verschleißfestigkeit *f* resistance to wear
Verschleißwiderstand *m* abrasion resistance
Verschlickung *f* filling-up
verschließen to block
Verschließen *n* **des Ringraums zwischen den**

Rohren packing of the space between casings
Verschlingen n, **Verschlucken** n engulfment, downsucking
Verschluckung f subduction *(tectonics)*
Verschluckungszone f subduction zone
~ **konvergierender Platten** trench
Verschluffung f conversion into silt
verschlungen/eng interlacing
Verschlüsselung f encoding
verschmelzen s. verwachsen
Verschmelzung f s. Verwachsung
verschmieren/mit Ton to clay
Verschmutzung f pollution
Verschmutzungsgefahr f danger of contamination
Verschmutzungsquelle f source of contamination (pollution)
Verschmutzungssubstanz f pollutant
Verschotterung f **des Flußlaufs** choking of the river course
verschrämen to carve
verschütten to bury
verschweißt/mit dem Nebengestein frozen to the walls
verschwelen to carbonize at a low temperature
Verschwelung f [low-temperature] carbonization
verschwinden to disappear; to taper out
Verschwinden n extinction *(e.g. of a lake)*; disappearance *(e.g. of species)*
versehen/mit Gletschertöpfen potholed
~/**mit Kanälen** canaliculate[d]
~/**mit Knötchen** noded
~/**mit Loben** lobulate
verseifen to saponify
Verseifung f saponification
Versenkungsbohrung f, **Versenkungsbrunnen** m disposal well
Versenkungsmetamorphose f burial (load) metamorphism
~/**regionale** regional burial metamorphism
Versenkungstiefe f depth of burial
versetzen 1. s. verfüllen; 2. to dislocate *(within crystals)*; 3. to add, to mix; 4. to stow *(mechanically)*; to pack *(by hand)*
Versetzen n 1. s. Verfüllen; 2. dislocation *(within crystals)*; 3. adding, addition
~ **mit CO₂** carbonation
Versetzung f dislocation *(within crystals)*
~/**partielle** partial dislocation
~ **von Bildpunkten** relief displacement
Versetzungsgrenze f, **Versetzungslinie** f dislocation line
Verseuchung f/**radioaktive** radioactive contamination
versickern to seep, to soak in[to], to infiltrate, to percolate, to ooze away, to zigger
Versickerung f seepage, soaking-in, infiltration, percolation, intake, recharge
~ **im Boden** infiltration in the subsoil

Versickerungsbrunnen m absorbing (recharge, diffusion, inverted) well
Versickerungsbrunnenkette f recharge line
Versickerungsfläche f intake area
Versickerungsverlust m loss by percolation
versiegen to dry up, to run dry *(well)*
Versiegen n drying up *(of wells)*; exhaustion, depletion *(of oil wells)*
Versinkung f influation *(of water)*
versintern to incrustate
Versinterung f scale deposit
Verskarnung f skarnization
Versorgungsbrunnen m supply well
Verspannung f aggregate interlock[ing] *(of mineral mass)*
versteinern to fossilize, to petrify, to lithify, to permineralize
versteinert fossil, petrified, petrous
Versteinerung f 1. fossilization, petrifaction, petrification, lithifaction; 2. fossil, petrifact
~/**eozoische** eozoon
Versteinerungskunde f petrifactology
Versteinerungsvorgang m s. Versteinerung 1.
Verstellwinkel m setting angle
verstopfen to stop, to clog
~/**Poren** to clog up pores
~/**sich** to choke
Verstopfen n s. Verfüllen
verstopft/mit Schlamm laired
Verstopfungsmaterial n fibrous material, propping agent
verstreuen to scatter
Versuch m test, trial; experiment
Versuchsbank f test bench
Versuchsbohrloch n test hole, trial borehole
Versuchsbohrung f 1. test (trial) boring, exploration drilling; 2. s. Versuchsbohrloch
Versuchsbrunnen m test well
Versuchsgebiet n test site
Versuchsprofil n test line
Versuchsschacht m prospecting shaft, test pit
Versuchsstrecke f exploring drift, test gallery
versumpfen to become swampy
Versumpfung f swamp formation, swamping, paludification
versunken submerged
vertauben/sich to impoverish
Vertaubung f impoverishment, getting barren
vertauschbar interchangeable
Vertebraten mpl Vertebrata
verteilen to distribute
~/**willkürlich** to randomize
verteilt/äußerst fein highly dispersed
~/**statistisch** statistically distributed
~/**unregelmäßig** randomly distributed
Verteilung f distribution; spread *(e.g. of the geophones)*
~ **auf Zonen** zonation
~ **der Körnungen** grain-size distribution
~/**Gaußsche** Gaussian distribution
~/**lognormale** log-normal distribution
~/**willkürliche** randomization

Verteilungsbahn

Verteilungsbahn *f*/**geochemische** geochemical distribution path
Verteilungsbild *n* **von Leitgeschieben** indicator fan
Verteilungsgesetzmäßigkeit *f* law of distribution
Verteilungskoeffizient *m* distribution coefficient (ratio)
vertiefen to deepen
Vertiefung *f* deepening; hollow; depression; swelly
~/geschlossene closed depression
~/schüsselförmige bowlike (bowl-shaped) hollow
vertikal vertical, perpendicular
Vertikalabweichungswinkel *m* angle of deviation from the vertical
Vertikalfilterbrunnen *m* vertical filter well
Vertikalintensität *f* vertical intensity
Vertikalmagnetometer *n* vertical magnetometer
Vertikalmigration *f* vertical migration
Vertikalpendel *n* vertical pendulum
Vertikalprofilierung *f*/**seismische** vertical seismic profiling
Vertikalseismograf *m* vertical [component, motion] seismograph
Vertikalvariationskarte *f* vertical variability map
Vertikalverwerfung *f* vertical fault
Vertonung *f* weathering to clay, argillation, argillaceous alteration; shale-out, shalification
vertorft peaty, peatified, converted into peat
Vertorfung *f* peatification, peat formation; ulmification
Verträglichkeit *f* compatibility *(of data)*
Vertretbarkeit *f* substitutability; diadochy
vertrocknen to dry up
verunreinigt impure
Verunreinigung *f* impurity, pollution, contamination
verwachsen to intergrow, to aggregate
verwachsen/fein disseminated, intimately associated
Verwachsenes *n* interstratified material
Verwachsung *f* intergrowth, aggregation, intercrescence; combination *(of twinned crystals)*
~/orientierte oriented intergrowth
~/parallele parallel intergrowth *(of minerals)*
~/schriftgranitische graphic[al] intergrowth, graphic[al] texture
Verwachsungsbedingungen *fpl* intergrowth conditions
Verwachsungsfläche *f* composition plane (face)
~ eines Zwillingskristalls composition surface of a twin crystal
Verwachsungszone *f* zone of concrescence
verwandeln to change; to alter; to metamorphose
~/in ein Salz to salify

336

~/in Gas to gasify
Verwandlung *f* change; alteration; metamorphosis
Verwaschungszone *f* blurred zone
verwässern to water out *(oil deposits)*
Verwässerung *f* water incursion (intrusion, invasion); ingress of water
~ einer erdölführenden Schicht inundation of a petroliferous bed
verwechseln/Schichten to jump to beds
Verweildauer *f* retention period
Verweilzeit *f* residence time
verwerfen to fault [down, off], to disturb; to displace
~/ins Hangende to cast over (up)
~/ins Liegende to cast down
Verwerfer *m* riser
Verwerfung *f* faulting, [normal] fault, dip-slip fault, throw, shift[ing], dislocation [of strata], displacement, upslide
~/abfallende hading-against-the-dip fault
~/aktive active fault
~/antiklinale anticlinal fault
~/antithetische *s.* **~/gegensinnige**
~/diagonale oblique[-slip] fault
~ durch Heben eines Flügels overthrust fault
~/ebene plane fault
~/eigentliche dipper, downcast
~/flachwinklige low-angle fault
~/gegensinnige overfault, reverse (reversal) fault, hading-against-the-dip fault
~/geneigte inclined fault
~/geschlossene close fault
~/gestaffelte echelon fault
~/glatte plane fault
~/gleichsinnige conformable (dip) fault
~/homothetische *s.* **~/rechtsinnig fallende**
~/inaktive dead fault
~ ins Hangende upcast [fault], upthrow fault, jump-up
~ ins Liegende downcast [fault], downthrown (downthrust) fault, jump-down
~/inverse upthrow (thrust, overlap) fault
~/klaffende gap (open) fault
~/kleine slip, thurm, hitch, stib
~/kreisförmige ring fault
~/krummlinige curvilinear fault
~/normale slip (drop, centripetal) fault
~/offene *s.* **~/klaffende**
~ ohne Bruch fault without rupture
~/rechtsdrehende dextral fault
~/rechtsinnig fallende synthetic (hading-with-the-dip) fault
~/schichtenparallele bedding fault, slide
~/schräge oblique fault
~/sekundäre secondary (minor) fault
~/spießeckige semilongitudinal (semitransverse) fault
~/steiler als 45° fallende high-angle fault
~/streichende longitudinal fault
~/synthetische *s.* **~/rechtsinnig fallende**
~/tiefgreifende profound fault

Verwitterungsschutt

~/verästelte branching fault
~/widersinnig fallende, ~/widersinnige s. ~/gegensinnige
~/wiederaufgelebte renewed (revived) fault
~/zusammengesetzte compound (complex) fault
Verwerfungen fpl/kleine microfaulting
~/konjugierte conjugate faults
Verwerfungsabsturz m fault scarp
Verwerfungsausstrich m fault outcrop
Verwerfungsbildung f faultage
Verwerfungsbreite f heave
Verwerfungsbrekzie f fault breccia
Verwerfungsbüschel n compound fault
Verwerfungsebene f fault plane
Verwerfungsfalle f fault trap
Verwerfungsfläche f fault (slip) plane, slip[ping] surface
Verwerfungsfront f fault face
Verwerfungsgang m slip vein
Verwerfungsgebiet n area of faulting
Verwerfungsgraben m trough fault
Verwerfungsgruppe f set of faults
Verwerfungshöhe f perpendicular throw
Verwerfungshöhle f fault cave
Verwerfungskliff n fault cliff (scarp)
Verwerfungskluft f fault crevice
Verwerfungskontakt m fault contact
Verwerfungskörper m faulted body
Verwerfungsküste f fault coast (shore line)
Verwerfungsletten m fault gouge
Verwerfungslinie f fault line (trace, outcrop)
~/vorherrschende dominant fault line
Verwerfungsnetz n network of faults
Verwerfungsquelle f fault[-dam] spring
Verwerfungsrichtung f fault strike
Verwerfungsschar f fault set (bundle)
Verwerfungssenke f depression of downfaulting
Verwerfungsspalte f fault fissure (cleft, rift)
Verwerfungsstreichen n fault trend
Verwerfungsstufe f fault scarp (bench), cliff of displacement
Verwerfungssystem n fault system
~/verzweigtes distributive faulting
Verwerfungstal n fault[-line] valley
Verwerfungstektonik f faulting tectonics
Verwerfungston m fault gouge
Verwerfungswand f fault wall (scarp)
Verwerfungswinkel m angle of hade
Verwerfungszone f fault zone (space)
verwertbar/wirtschaftlich commercially valuable
Verwesung f putrefaction
Verwitterbarkeit f alterability
verwittern to weather; to decay
~/chemisch to decompose; to effloresce
~/mechanisch to disintegrate, to disaggregate
verwitternd/rostbraun rusty-weathering
verwittert weathered; detrital; rotten
~/chemisch decomposed
~/stark deeply weathered (disintegrated); finely broken up

Verwitterung f weathering; decay; surface disintegration
~/chemische chemical weathering; decomposition; efflorescence
~/frische immature weathering
~/humose humic decomposition
~/kug[e]lige concentric (spheroidal) weathering
~/lateritische laterite weathering
~/mechanische mechanical (physical) weathering; disintegration; disaggregation
~/schalige onion weathering
~/selektive selective weathering
~/stufenweise degradation
~/submarine submarine weathering, halmyro[ly]sis
~ von innen heraus cavernous weathering
~ zu Karbonaten carbonation
Verwitterungsbasis f base of weathering
verwitterungsbegünstigend conductive to weathering
Verwitterungsboden m residual earth (soil), regolith, sathrolith
~/unreifer immature residual soil
Verwitterungsdolomit m W-dolostone
verwitterungsfähig disintegrable
Verwitterungsfaktor m factor of weathering
Verwitterungsfazies f eksedofacies
verwitterungsfest resistant to weathering
Verwitterungsform f/kammförmige coomb rock
Verwitterungsgrad m degree of weathering
Verwitterungskorrektur f low-velocity correction (of seismic measurements)
Verwitterungskräfte fpl weathering (subaerial) agents
Verwitterungskrume f mantle rock
Verwitterungskruste f weathering crust
Verwitterungslagerstätte f deposit formed by weathering
Verwitterungslehm m eluvial (residual) loam
Verwitterungslösung f solution resulting from rock decomposition
Verwitterungsmantel m regolith
Verwitterungsmaterial n weathered material
Verwitterungsprodukt n weathering (disintegration, decomposition, residual) product
Verwitterungsprozeß m weathering (decomposition, disintegration, rotting) process, process of decay
Verwitterungsrestblock m/autochthoner residual boulder
Verwitterungsrinde f weathering crust (rind)
~/helle patina
Verwitterungsrückstand m weathering (decomposed) residuum, residuum of weathered rocks
Verwitterungsschicht f weathering layer, weathered layer (bed)
Verwitterungsschießen n microspread, walkaway; noise profile
Verwitterungsschutt m mantle rock, residual

Verwitterungsschutt 338

detritus, eluvium, subaerial (atmospheric) waste
~/alluvialer alluvial mantle rock
~/glazialer glacial mantle rock
~/kolluvialer colluvial mantle rock
Verwitterungsterrasse f denudation (structural) terrace
Verwitterungston m residual clay
Verwitterungsvorgang m weathering process
Verwitterungszone f zone (belt) of weathering, weathered zone
~/eisenhaltige ferreto zone *(moraine)*
Verwitterungszustand m state of weathering
verwoben/miteinander interlacing
verworfen faulted, thrown, disturbed, dislocated
~/ins Hangende thrown-up
~/ins Liegende thrown-down, down-faulted
~/nicht unfaulted
~/stark badly faulted
Verwurf m s. Verwerfung
Verwüstung f desolation
verzahnen/sich to interwedge; to intertongue; to interfinger
verzahnt/miteinander intercrystallized
~/wechselseitig interlocking
Verzahnung f [aggregate] interlocking
~ von Schichten interlocking of strata
~/wechselseitige interlocking, interfingering, interdigitation
verzerrt distorted *(e.g. crystals);* clipped *(e.g. waveform)*
~/homogen homogeneously strained
Verzerrung f distortion *(e.g. of crystals);* flattening *(of fossils)*
~/geometrische geometric[al] distortion
Verzerrungsenergie f energy of distortion
verzerrungsfrei distortionless
Verzerrungszustand m/räumlicher general state of strain
Verzögerung f retardation; lag; [time] delay
~ der Erdrotation retardation of earth's rotation
Verzögerungszeit f delay (intercept) time
Verzögerungszünder m delay cap
Verzug m lagging
Verzugsbrett n cover board *(timber)*
Verzugsplatte f cover board *(concrete)*
verzweigen/sich to branch [off]; to ramify; to split off
verzweigt ramose
Verzweigung f branching; ramification
~/gabelförmige s. Dichotomie
~/netzartige anastomosis *(of a river)*
Verzweigungsstruktur f lineage structure *(of crystals)*
Verzweigungsverhältnis n branching ratio *(nuclear decay)*
verzwillingt twinned
Verzwillingung f twinning
Vesuvian m vesuvianite, $Ca_{10}(Mg,Fe)_2Al_4[(OH)_4 | (SiO_4)_5 | (Si_2O_7)_2]$

Vesuvit m vesuvite *(variety of tephrite)*
Vesuvtypus m Vesuvian type
Veszelyit m veszelyite, $(Cu,Zn)_3[(OH)_3PO_4] \cdot H_2O$
Vibration f vibration
Vibrationsbohren n vibratory drilling
Vibrationsrotarybohren n vibratory rotary drilling
Vibrationsschlagbohren n vibratory percussion drilling
Vibrator m vibrator *(seismic source)*
vibrieren to vibrate
Vibrograf m vibrograph
Vibroseis n vibroseis
Vielfachübertragung f multiplexing
vielfarbig polychromatic
Vielfarbigkeit f polychromatism
Vielfaziesdecke f nappe with several facies
vielfingrig polydactyl
vielflächig polyhedral, polyhedric
Vielflächner m polyhedron
vielgestaltig polymorphous, polymorphic, pleomorphous
Vielkanter m polyfacetted pebble
Vielling m compound (repeated, multiple) twin
Viellingslamellierung f banded (lamellar) twinning
Viellingsverzwillingung f multiple twinning
vielseitig polyhedral, polyhedric; manysided
Vielstoffsystem n multicomponent (polynary) system
Viererkoordination f tetrahedral coordination
Vierflächner m tetrahedron
vierfüßig tetrapod
Vierpunktmethode f four-point method
Vierrollenmeißel m trigger bit
vierseitig four-sided
Vierstoffsystem n quaternary system
Viertelflächner m tetartohedron
vierteln to reduce by quartering
Viertelung f quartering, inquartation
Viertelwellen[längen]plättchen n quarter-wave plate
vierundzwanzigflächig icositetrahedral
Vierundzwanzigflächner m icositetrahedron
vierwertig quadrivalent
Vierwertigkeit f quadrivalence
vielzählig fourfold *(symmetry axis)*
Villafranchien n, Villafranchium n Villafranchian *(Pliocene and lower Pleistocene in Italy)*
Villamaninit m villamaninite, $(Cu,Ni,Co,Fe)(S,Se)_2$
Villiaumit m villiaumite, NaF
Vindobon[ien] n, Vindobonium n Vindobonian [Stage] *(of Miocene)*
Violarit m violarite, $FeNi_2S_4$
Virenzzeit f s. Klimax
Virgation f virgation
Virgatitenschichten fpl Virgatites beds
Virgil n Virgilian [Stage] *(uppermost stage of Pennsylvanian in North America)*

Viridin *m* viridine *(variety of andalusite)*
Visé *n* Visean [Stage] *(of Lower Carboniferous)*
Visiergraupe *f* beak of tin
viskoplastisch viscoplastic
viskos viscous
Viskosimeter *n* viscosimeter, marsh funnel
Viskosität *f* viscosity
~ **der Spülung/bedingte** mud viscosity
~/**dynamische** dynamic viscosity
~/**kinematische** kinematic viscosity
Viskositätskraft *f* viscous flow force
Viszeralhöhle *f* visceral cavity
Viszeralskelett *n* visceral skeleton
Viterbit *m* viterbite *(variety of leucite phonolite)*
Vitrain *m* vitrain *(coal lithotype)*
Vitrinertit *m* vitrinertite *(coal microlithotype)*
Vitrinertoliptit *m* vitrinertoliptite *(coal microlithotype)*
Vitrinit *m* vitrinite *(coal maceral, maceral group);* (Am partly) anthraxylon *(vitrinite< 14 μm)*
~ **in Sapropeliten** saprovitrinite
Vitriolbleierz *n* lead vitriol, anglesite, $PbSO_4$
Vitriolschiefer *m* alum schist (shale, slate)
Vitrit *m* vitrite *(coal microlithotype)*
Vitrodetrinit *m* vitrodetrinite *(coal maceral)*
vitroklastisch vitroclastic
vitrophyrisch vitrophyric
Vivianit *m* vivianite, blue ochre (iron earth), native Prussian blue, $Fe_3[PO_4]_2 \cdot 8H_2O$
Vladimirit *m* vladimirite, $Ca_3[AsO_4]_2 \cdot 4H_2O$
Vlasovit *m* vlasovite, $Na_2Zr[O|Si_4O_{10}]$
Vogelguano *m* bird guano
Vogelperspektive *f* bird's eye view
Vogesit *m* vogesite *(lamprophyre)*
Voglit *m* voglite, $Ca_2Cu[UO_2|(CO_3)_4] \cdot 6H_2O$
Volborthit *m* volborthite, $Cu_3[VO_4]_2 \cdot 3H_2O$
Volkovit *m* volkovite, $(Sr,Ca)_2[B_4O_5(OH)_4][B_5O_6(OH)_4]_2 \cdot 2H_2O$
Vollanalyse *f* bulk analysis
Vollausbruch *m* full-face method
Vollbodenentwässerung *f* draining through the whole area of the bottom
Vollbohren *n* full-hole drilling
Volldruckhöhe *f* critical altitude
Volleinwirkungsfläche *f* critical area of extraction
Vollergiebigkeit *f* **einer Sonde** open flow of well
Vollfläche *f* critical area of extraction
vollflächig holohedral
Vollflächigkeit *f* holohedry, holohedrism
Vollflächner *m* holohedron
vollglasig holohyaline
vollidiomorph panidiomorphic
vollkristallin[isch] holocrystalline, eucrystalline, fully crystalline
Vollmond *m* full moon
Vollreife *f* full maturity
Vollrelief *n* full relief *(ichnology)*

Vollsenkung *f* subsidence
Volltroggleitung *f* full-trough gliding
Vollversatz *m* solid stowing
Vollwegmultiple *f* long-patch multiple, two-way multiple
Voltait *m* voltaite, $K_2Fe_5^{..}Fe_4^{...}[SO_4]_{12} \cdot 18H_2O$
Voltziensandstein *m* Voltzia Sandstone
Voltzin *m* voltzite, $Zn(S,As)$
Volumenänderung *f* change of volume
Volumendehnung *f* volume strain
Volumendiagramm *n* volume diagram
Volumengewicht *n* volume weight
Volumenkonzentration *f* volume concentration
Volumenprozent *n* percentage by volume
Volumenschwund *m* **beim Brennprozeß** fire shrinkage
Volumenstrom *m* **der Spülpumpe** slush (mud) pump delivery
Volumenverminderung *f* **beim Erstarren** contraction of volume on solidification
Volumenzähler *m* volumetric flowmeter
Vonsenit *m* vonsenite, $(Fe,Mg)_2Fe[O_2|BO_3]$
Vorabsenkung *f* initial convergence
Voralpen *pl* Prealps
Voranreicherung *f* preconcentration
Vorbeanspruchung *f* **des Gebirges** ground conditions
Vorbeben *n* preliminar tremor (shock, tremblings), foreshock, forerunner
Vorbehandlung *f* pretreatment
Vorbeibohren *n* side tracking
Vorbelastung *f* preloading
vorbereiten/eine Bohrung zur Förderung to complete a well
Vorberg *m* outlier
vorbohren to predrill, to rathole
Vorbohrer *m* spudder
Vorbohrloch *n* predrilled (pilot) hole, exploratory drill hole; advance borehole, rathole
Vorbohrung *f* 1. primary (preliminary) drilling, predrilling, preboring; 2. *s.* Vorbohrloch
~ **zur Entwässerung des Gesteins** weep hole, weeper
Vordamm *m* advanced dam (dike)
Vorderansicht *f* anterior view
Vorderende *n* anterior end
Vordergliedmaßen *pl* forelimbs
Vorderrand *m* anterior margin
vordringen to encroach *(water)*
Vordringen *n* encroachment *(of water)*
~ **von Randwasser** edge-water encroachment
Vordüne *f* foredune, littoral dune
Voreiszeit *f* preglacial period
voreiszeitlich preglacial
Vorentwässerung *f* preliminary drainage
Vorerkundung *f* preliminary exploration, previous prospecting, reconnaissance survey
Vorerkundungsflug *m* reconaissance flight
Vorfahren *mpl* ancestors *(palaeobiology)*
Vorfeld *n* zone in front of the face
Vorfeldentwässerung *f* drainage of forefields

Vorfeldkonvergenz

Vorfeldkonvergenz f convergence in the coal ahead of the face
Vorflut f outfall
Vorfluter m receiver, receiving stream, watercourse
Vorgang m/**endogener** endogenous event
~/**exogener** exogenous event
~/**geologischer** geological event
~/**zerstörender** destructive (wasting) process
Vorgänge mpl/**gebirgsbildende** diastrophism
~/**salztektonische** salt-tectonic processes
~/**tiefvulkanische** deep-seated volcanicity
Vorgebirge n promontory, headland, foreland, foothill, mountain spar, submountain region
vorgebohrt previously bored
vorgeologisch pregeological
Vorgeschichte f prehistory
Vorhang m drapery (e.g. in a stalactite cave)
vorherrschen to predominate
Vorhersage f/**hydrologische** hydrologic[al] forecast
~/**kurzfristige** short-range forecast
~/**langfristige** long-range forecast
Vorhersagefilter n prediction filter
vorkesseln to pot
Vorklassierung f preclassification
vorkommen to occur (deposits)
Vorkommen n occurrence, deposit
~/**[ab]bauwürdiges** workable deposit
~/**gangförmiges** occurrence in veins
~/**lagerförmiges** occurrence in beds
~/**nesterförmiges** occurrence in pockets
~/**stockförmiges** occurrence in floors
vorkommend/als Nugget nuggety
~/**natürlich** natural-occuring, native
~/**zerstreut** sporadic[al]
Vorland n piedmont [slope], foreland (s.a. Vorgebirge); foreshore (s.a. Vorstrand)
Vorlandebene f piedmont plain
Vorlandgletscher m piedmont glacier
Vorlast f initial load
Vorläufer m 1. precursor (palaeontology); 2. forerunner, foreshock (seismics)
~/**erster** primary wave
~/**zweiter** secondary (equivolumnar) wave, S-wave
Vormagnetisierung f magnetic biasing
vororogen preorogenic
Vorphase f preliminary stage
Vorrat m reserve, stock
~/**bauwürdiger** commercial reserve
~/**geologischer** geologic[al] reserve
~/**gewinnbarer** recoverable reserve
~/**industrieller** expected tonnage
~/**mineralischer** mineral reserve
~/**möglicher** possible (discounted) reserve
~/**nachgewiesener** positive (proved) reserve
~/**prognostischer** prognostic reserve
~/**sicherer** known (actual) reserve
~/**sichtbarer** visible reserve
~/**teilweise ausgewiesener** partimesurate body (of ore)

340

~/**vermuteter** inferred reserve
Vorräte mpl/**ausgerichtete** developed reserves
~/**erkundete** measured reserves
~ **Gruppe Delta 1/prognostische** hypothetical resources
~ **Gruppe Delta 2/prognostische** speculative resources
~/**nachgewiesene** developed resources
Vorratsabschätzung f mineral assessment
Vorratsabschreibung f depreciation of ore reserves
Vorratsangaben fpl reserve data
Vorratsbegrenzung f delimitation of reserves
Vorratsberechnung f calculation of resources, reserve calculation
Vorratsbilanz f balance of mineral reserves
Vorratsblock m reserve block
~/**unverritzter** virgin reserve block
Vorratseinschätzung f/**volumetrische** volumetric reserve estimation
Vorratsergänzungskurve f storage-draught curve
Vorratsgruppe f group of reserves
Vorratshalde f stockpile
Vorratsklasse f class of resources
Vorratsklasseneinstufung f classification of reserve class
Vorratsklassifikation f classification of reserves
Vorratsmengenberechnung f calculation of reserves
Vorratsschätzung f estimation of reserves
Vorratsvorlauf m **mineralischer Rohstoffe** providing of mineral resources
Vorrichtung f development work (e.g. in coal)
Vorriff n forereef
Vorriffbereich m zone in the front of reefs
Vorrücken n advance, accretion
~ **des Gletschers** glacial advance
Vorschiebung f accretion, advance, overslide
Vorschleifen n rough (initial coarse) grinding
Vorschliff m preliminary grinding
Vorschub m feed-off (of the drill rods)
Vorschüttsande mpl frontal apron (of a glacier)
Vorschüttsedimente npl foreset beds (of a delta)
Vorschüttungsblatt n foreset bed (cross-bedding)
Vorsenke f foredeep
Vorsetzschichten fpl foresets
Vorspannung f prestressing, prestraining
~/**statische** static prestrain
vorspringen to project, to protrude
vorspringend projecting, protruding
Vorsprung m salient, offset
Vorstoß m advance (of a glacier)
~/**erneuter** readvance
Vorstrand m foreshore, barrier beach
Vortiefe f foredeep

~/subvariszische sub-Varisc[i]an foredeep
Vortrieb *m* advance
Vortriebsstrecke *f* heading
vorvariszisch pre-Varisc[i]an
Vorvermessung *f* preliminary survey
vorwiegend ultradominant
Vorzeichen *npl* premonitory events
Vorzeichnungen *fpl*/epirogen-fazielle epirogenetic and facies patterns
Vorzeit *f* past ages
Vorzeitform *f* form of past ages, past (prerecent) form
Vorzerkleinerung *f* coarse crushing (reduction), preliminary comminution
Vorzerklüftung *f* induced cleavage
Vorzugsorientierung *f* preferred orientation
Vraconne *n* Vraconnian [Stage] *(upper Albian, Tethys)*
Vrbait *m* vrbaite, $Tl_4Hg_3Sb_2As_8S_{20}$
Vredenburgit *m* vredenburgite, $(Mn,Fe)_3O_4$
V-Tal *n* V-shaped valley
Vulcanit *m* vulcanite, CuTe
Vulkan *m* volcano
~/abgetragener dissected volcano
~/aufgesetzter supravolcano, accumulation volcano
~/ausbrechender discharge volcano
~/dampfender fuming volcano
~/erloschener extinguished (extinct, dead) volcano
~/ineinandergesetzter nested volcano
~/junger young volcano
~/kleiner volcanello
~ mit Ringwall somma volcano
~ mit zentralen Kegeln nested volcano
~/ruhender quiescent (dormant) volcano
~/submariner submarine volcano
~/tätiger active (burning) volcano
~/untätiger inactive volcano
~/unterseeischer submarine volcano
Vulkanausbruch *m* volcanic eruption (outbreak, outburst)
Vulkanauswürfling *m* accidental block
Vulkanbauten *mpl* volcanic edifices
Vulkanbogen *m* arc of volcanoes, volcanic arc
Vulkanböschung *f* flank of volcano
Vulkanembryo *m* volcanic embryo, embryonic (abortive) volcano
Vulkanexhalationen *fpl* volcanic exhalations
Vulkanforscher *m* volcanologist
Vulkangebiet *n* volcanic area
Vulkangebirgsküste *f* volcanic coast
Vulkanglas *n* volcanic glass
Vulkanglasscherbe *f* shard
Vulkangruppe *f* volcanic cluster
Vulkangürtel *m* volcanic belt
~/zirkumpazifischer circumpacific volcanic belt
Vulkanhang *m* volcanic slope
Vulkanherd *m* volcanic focus
Vulkaninsel *f* volcanic island

vulkanisch volcanic, plutonic; extrusive; igneous, ignigenous
Vulkanismus *m* volcanism; volcanicity
~/initialer initial volcanism
~/subsequenter late-orogenic phase
Vulkanit *m* volcanic (extrusive) rock
Vulkanizität *f* volcanicity
Vulkankegel *m* volcanic cone (butte)
~/parasitärer epigone
Vulkankette *f* chain of volcanoes
Vulkankunde *f* volcanology
Vulkankuppe *f* volcanic dome (head, knob)
vulkanoaquatisch igneoaqueous
vulkanoklastisch athrogenic
Vulkanologe *m* volcan[olog]ist
Vulkanologie *f* volcanology
Vulkanotektonik *f* volcano-tectonics
vulkanotektonisch volcano-tectonic
Vulkanpfropfen *m* volcanic (igneous) plug
Vulkanreihe *f* linear volcanoes
Vulkanruine *f* volcanic wreck (skeleton)
Vulkanschlot *m* volcanic channel (chimney, duct, throat, funnel, vent)
Vulkanschlotbrekzie *f* vent breccia
Vulkanspalte *f* volcanic fissure
Vulpinit *m* vulpinite *(variety of anhydrite)*
Vysotskit *m* vysotskite, (Pd, Ni)S

W

Waage *f*/hydrostatische hydrostatic balance
~/magnetische magnetic balance
waagerecht horizontal
Waal *n*, Waal-Warmzeit *f* Waal[ian] *(lower Pleistocene in Northwest Europe)*
Wabenboden *m* stone polygon soil
wabenförmig honeycombed, alveolar
Wabenstruktur *f* honeycomb structure
Wabenverwitterung *f* honeycomb weathering
Wabenverwitterungsstruktur *f* fretwork
Wachsabdruck *m* impression in wax
Wachsen *n* von Kristallen accretion of crystals
wachsend/nach außen hin exogenous
~/nach innen hin endogenous
Wachsglanz *m* waxy lustre
Wachstum *n*/akkretionäres accretionary growth
~/gestricktes crocketed growth
~ in unregelmäßigen Knollen glomeration
~/kristalloblastisches crystalloblastic growth
~/radialstrahliges radial growth
~/wandständiges wallbound growth
Wachstumsachse *f* axis of growth
Wachstumsanlagerung *f* accretion
Wachstumserwärmung *f* accretional heating (heating by increasing planetary bodies)
wachstumsfördernd growth-promoting
Wachstumsgefüge *n* growth fabric
wachstumshemmend inhibiting growth
Wachstumskurve *f* growth curve

Wachstumsperiode

Wachstumsperiode f growing season
Wachstumsring m growth ring
Wachstumsspirale f growth spiral
Wachstumsstruktur f/**zonale** zonal structure
Wachstumstreppe f growth step
Wachstumszonung f growth zoning
Wachstumszwilling m growth twin
Wächte f cornice
Wacke f wacke
Wackelstein m perched block (boulder), rock[ing] stone, balanced rock
Wad m wad, black ochre, earthy manganese
Wadeit m wadeite, $K_2Zr[Si_3O_9]$
Wadi n wadi, *(Am)* dry river bed
Wagnerit m wagnerite, $Mg[F(PO_4)]$
Wahrscheinlichkeitsnetz n, **Wahrscheinlichkeitspapier** n probability paper
Wairakit m wairakite, $Ca[AlSi_2O_6]_2 \cdot 2H_2O$
Wairauit m wairauite, CoFe
Walchowit m walchowite, $(C_{15}H_{26}O)_4$
Wald m/**versteinerter** petrified (silicified) forest
~/versunkener submerged forest
Waldboden m forest (wooded) soil
~/brauner brown forest (podzolic) soil
~/saurer brauner acid brown forest soil
~/schwarzer black forest earth
Wälderton m s. Wealdenton
Waldgelände n woodland
Waldgrenze f limit of forest growth
Waldhochmoor n high moor forest, timbered upland moor
Waldhorizont m/**interglazialer** woodyard
Waldinseln fpl forest islands
Waldland n forest land, woodland
Waldmoor n forest swamp (bog)
Waldmoorboden m woody peat
Waldregion f forested area
Waldreichtum m abundance of forests
Waldschutzstreifen m forest shelterbelt
Waldsteppe f wooded (forested, timbered) steppe
Waldsteppentschernosem m wood steppe chernozem
Waldsteppenzone f prairie-timber zone
Waldung f woodland
Walkerde f, **Walkton** m fuller's earth, malthacite
Wall m dam, dike
Wallberg m s. Os
Wallebene f walled plain *(of the moon)*
Wallmoräne f morainic ridge, dumped moraine
Wallriff n barrier (encircling) reef
Walpurgin m walpurgite, $[(BiO)_4|UO_2|(AsO_4)_2] \cdot 3H_2O$
Walstromit m walstromite, $BaCa_2[Si_3O_9]$
Walzenmühle f roller mill
Walzfalten fpl nappe involutions
Wand f wall
~ des Porensystems flow-channel wall
~/überhängende overhang

342

~/übersteilte oversteepened wall
Wanderdüne f wandering (travelling, shifting, marching, mobile, migratory) dune, quicksand
Wandergeschiebe n shore drift
Wandermoräne f moving moraine, moraine in transit
wandern to migrate, to move *(points)*
Wanderpunkt m moving point *(reservoir mechanics)*
Wandersand m drift[ed] sand
Wanderschutt m creeping waste (rubble), migratory detritus
Wanderschuttdecke f sheet of creeping waste
Wanderstation f slave station *(geoelectrics)*
Wanderung f migration
~ der Kontinente creep (drift) of continents
~/kapillare capillary migration
Wanderwege mpl dispersion routes
Wanderwelle f travelling wave
Wandung f wall
Wangen fpl cheeks *(of the trilobite headshield)*
Wangenstacheln mpl genal spines *(of the trilobite headshield)*
Wanne f [closed] basin, furrow
wannenförmig troughlike, trough-shaped
Wannenlandschaft f closed-basin topography
Wardit m wardite, $NaAl_3[(OH)_4|(PO_4)_2] \cdot 2H_2O$
Warft f dwelling mond; embankment
Wärme f heat
~/latente latent heat
~/radiogene radiogenic (radioactive) heat
~/sensible sensible heat
~/spezifische specific heat
Wärmeabgabe f heat emission
Wärmeäquator m thermal (heat) equator
Wärmeausdehnung f **des Wassers** thermal expansion of water
Wärmeausstrahlung f s. Wärmestrahlung
Wärmeaustausch m heat exchange (transfer)
Wärmebilanz f heat balance
Wärmediffusionsvermögen n thermal diffusivity
Wärmedom m heat dome
Wärmeentwicklung f evolution (development) of heat
Wärmefeld n thermal field
Wärmefluß m heat flux (flow)
Wärmeflußmessung f heat flow measurement
Wärmegewitter n heat thunderstorm
Wärmegradient m heat gradient
Wärmehaushalt m heat budget
Wärmeinhalt m heat content
Wärmekapazität f heat (thermal) capacity
~ des Wassers thermal capacity of water
Wämekartiergerät n thermal mapper
Wärmeleiter m heat conductor
Wärmeleitfähigkeit f thermal (heat) conductivity
Wärmeleitzahl f thermal conductibility factor
Wärmemenge f amount of heat

343 Wasser

Wärmepotential *n* thermal potential
Wärmepumpe *f* heat pump
Wärmequelle *f* source (origin) of heat
Wärmeschichtung *f* thermal stratification
Wärmeschwankung *f* heat variation
wärmespeichernd heat-storing
Wärmestrahlung *f* radiation of heat, heat radiance, thermal radiation
Wärmestrom *m* heat flow
Wärmestromdichte *f* heat flow density
Wärmestromeinheit *f* heat flow unit
Wärmeströmung *f* heat convection
Wärmetönung *f* heat effect
Wärmeträgheit *f* thermal inertia
Wärmeübergangszahl *f* heat transfer number
Wärmeübertragung *f* heat transfer
wärmeundurchlässig adiathermal, adiathermanous, adiathermic
Wärmeunterschied *m* difference in temperature
Wärmeverlust *m* heat loss
Wärmewirkung *f* thermal effect
Wärmezufuhr *f* heat supply
Warmfront *f* warm front
Warmlufteinbruch *m* heat wave
Warmluftfront *f* warm-air front
Warmzeit *f* interglacial episode (interval), interval of deglaciation
warmzeitlich interglacial
Warve *f* varve
~ **mit gradiertem Kornaufbau** diatectic varve
~ **ohne gradierten Kornaufbau** symmict varve
Warvenschichtung *f* varvity
Warventon *m* [bedded] varved clay
~/**metamorpher** varved slate
Warwickit *m* warwickite, $(Mg,Fe)_3 Ti[O|BO_3]_2$
Warwit *m* slaty varved rock *(of elder glacial periods)*
warzenförmig verrucose
Warzenmeißel *m* tungsten carbide button (insert) bit, knobby bit
warzig nodular
Wasatch[ien] *n* Wasatchian [Stage] *(mammalian stage, uppermost Palaeocene and lower Eocene in North America)*
waschbar washable
Waschberge *pl* washed dirt
Wäsche *f* dressing floor
waschen to clean, to flush
~/**Erz** to stream
Waschen *n* cleaning, flushing
~ **mit Sichertrog** panning
Wascherz *n* wash (diluvial) ore
Wascherzablagerung *f*/**erdige** wash[ing] stuff
Waschgold *n* placer gold
Waschrinne *f* box buddle
Waschschüssel *f* batea
Waschtrog *m* tray, gold pan
Waschtrommel *f* trommel
Wasser *n* water
~/**abfließendes** tail water
~/**aktiviertes** activated water

~/**artesisches** artesian water
~/**aszendentes** ascending (hypogene) water
~/**atmosphärisches** atmospheric water
~/**aufgestautes** imponded water
~ **aus dem Oberlauf des Stroms** upgrade-stream water
~ **aus Schichten zwischen zwei produzierenden Horizonten** intermediate water
~/**ausgepreßtes** water of compaction
~/**ausgetriebenes** rejuvenated (rehabilitation) water
~/**bewegtes** agitated water
~/**chemisch gebundenes** chemically combined water
~/**darüberliegendes** superjacent water
~ **der Aerationszone** perched water
~/**deszendentes** descending water
~/**durch magmatische Wärme aus hydratisierten Gesteinen ausgetriebenes** resurgent water
~/**emulgiertes** emulsified water
~/**enthärtetes** softened water
~/**fallendes** subsiding water; falling tide
~/**filtriertes** filtered water
~/**fossiles** fossil (native) water
~/**freies** free water *(in crude oil, as opposed to emulsified water)*
~/**geschichtetes** stratified water *(by temperature or grade of salinity)*
~/**hartes** hard water
~/**hygroskopisches** hygroscopic water
~ **in abgeschlossenen Poren** water in unconnected pores
~/**in der Aerationszone schwebendes** suspended subsurface water
~/**juveniles** juvenile (primitive, magmatic) water
~/**karbonattrübes** *s.* Bergmilch
~/**kohlensaures** acidulated (acidulous) water
~/**kohlensaures moussierendes** aerated water
~/**konnates** connate water
~/**magmatisches** plutonic water
~/**metamorphes** metamorphic water
~/**niedersinkendes** supergene water
~/**penduläres** pendular water
~/**quirlendes** swirling water
~/**ruhiges** calm water
~/**sauerstoffhaltiges** oxygenated water
~/**stagnierendes** stagnant (dead) water
~/**stehendes** stagnant backwater
~/**steigendes** flood water; rising tide
~/**stilles** backwater
~/**strömendes** current waters
~/**tellurisches** telluric water
~/**terrestrisches** terrestrial water
~/**tritiiertes** tritiated water
~/**trübes** muddled water
~/**überflurgespanntes** flowing artesian water
~/**uferfiltriertes** bank-filtered water
~/**umlaufendes** circulating water
~/**unter** subaqueous

Wasser 344

~/**unterirdisches** subsurface (subterranean) water
~/**vadoses** vadose (suspended subsurface) water
~/**versalzenes** salinized (saliferous) water
~/**vollentsalztes** fully desalted water
~/**vulkanisches** volcanic water
~/**weiches** soft water
~/**wiedereingepreßtes** recirculated water
~/**wirbelndes** swirling water
~/**zeitweilig auftretendes** temporary water
~/**zirkulierendes** circulating water
Wasserabfluß m water run-off
Wasserabgabe f water yield; filter loss; doling-out of water *(of soil)*
~ **der Spülung** water loss of mud
Wasserabgabefähigkeit f **des Gesteins** rock bleeding
~/**spezifische** relative rock bleeding
Wasserabgabevermögen n water separation capability
Wasserableitung f water drainage, drawing-off of the water
Wasserabsenkungsbereich m area of dewatering
Wasserabsperrung f water shut-off
Wasserabstoßen n sweating
Wasseransammlung f body of water
Wasserarmut f shortage of water
Wasseraufbereitung f water treatment (conditioning)
Wasseraufnahme f water intake
Wasseraufnahmekapazität f water-absorbing capacity
Wasseraufnahmevermögen n moisture-holding capacity; water inhibition value
Wasseraufspeicherung f **des Flußbetts** channel storage
Wasserausnutzung f water utilization
Wasseraustausch m water exchange
Wasseraustritt m water outlet
Wasserbau m water (hydraulic) engineering, hydraulic works, waterworks
Wasserbauingenieur m hydraulic engineer
Wasserbautechnik f hydrotechnics
Wasserbauten mpl hydraulic structures
Wasserbecken n water basin
Wasserbedarf m water need (demand, requirement)
Wasserbekämpfung f water control *(mining)*
Wasserberieselung f water spraying, irrigation by water
Wasserbeschaffenheit f water quality (constitution, conditioning)
Wasserbewegung f water movement
Wasserbilanz f water balance
Wasserblock m water block
Wasserbrunnen m water well
Wasserdampf m water (aqueous) vapour
Wasserdampffumarole f/**reine** cold fumarole
wasserdicht watertight, waterproof, impermeable; aquifuge

Wasserdichtigkeit f watertightness, impermeability to water
Wasserdruck m water pressure
Wasserdruckversuch m squeeze injection
Wasserdurchbruch m water outbreak, rush of water
wasserdurchlässig permeable (pervious) to water
Wasserdurchlässigkeit f water permeability
~ **durch Fugen und Spalten** secondary permeability
Wasserdurchlässigkeitsprüfung f water permeability test
wasserdurchtränkt water-impregnated, water-charged, water-logged
Wassereinbruch m water inflow, inrush of water, swallet
Wassereinlaß m water inlet
Wassereinpreßbohrung f water-input well
Wassereinpressen n water injection
Wassereintritt m water inlet
Wasserenthärtung f softening of water
Wasserenthärtungsanlage f water softening plant
Wasserentnahmekanal m intake channel
Wassererosion f wash
Wasserfall m waterfall; cataract; cascade
Wasserfassung f gathering of water, water catchment; captation
Wasserfassungsdamm m water procuring dike
Wasserfeindlichkeit f hydrophobicity
Wasserfläche f/**gekräuselte** choppy (ruffled) water surface
Wasserfluten n water flooding
Wasserförderanteil m water cut
Wasserfrac-Verfahren n river fracturing
wasserfrei anhydrous, anhydric
Wasserfreundlichkeit f hydrophily
wasserführend water-bearing, water-carrying, aquiferous; enhydrous *(minerals)*
Wasserführung f rate of stream-flow, flow, run-off, delivery
Wasserfüllung f water fill
Wassergehalt m water content; moisture equivalent (percentage)
wassergesättigt water-saturated, water-logged
Wassergesetz n water law
Wasser-Gestein-Wechselwirkung f water-rock interaction
Wassergewinnung f water winning (catchment), producing of water; water development (exploitation)
Wasserglanz m moiré *(of minerals)*
Wassergraben m water ditch
wasserhaltend water-retaining
Wasserhaltevermögen n retention force
Wasserhaltewert m specific retention
wasserhaltig water-base, water-carrying; aqueous
Wasserhaltung f water drainage; mine pumping; dewatering *(of a foundation pit)*

~/geschlossene closed drainage
~/offene catch water drain
Wasserhaltungsniveau n drainage level
Wasserhaltungsstollen m s. Wasserstollen
Wasserhaltungsstrecke f mine drainage gallery
Wasserhärte f water hardness
~/permanente permanent hardness
Wasserhaushalt m water balance; water conservation (budget); [water] regime *(of a river)*
Wasserhaushaltsgleichung f regime (water balance) equation
Wasserhaushaltsprognose f water-supply forecast
Wasserhebung f water pumpage; water hoisting
wasserhell water-clear *(precious stone)*
Wasserhöffigkeit f water yield
Wasserhorizont m/**artesischer** artesian [pressure] head
~/liegender inferior water horizon
Wasserhose f waterspout
Wasserhülle f water film
Wasserkapazität f water capacity *(of soil)*
~ **des Bodens/gesamte** total soil moisture capacity
~/natürliche field capacity
~/nutzbare available water
Wasserkegelbildung f [water] coning
Wasserkissen n water cushion
Wasserkläranlage f water-clearing plant, water-purifying plant
Wasserknappheit f water scarcity (shortage)
Wasserkörper m body of water
Wasserkorrosion f aqueous corrosion
Wasserkraft f water power, hydropower; white coal
Wasserkraftanlage f hydroplant
Wasserkraftnutzung f utilization of water power, hydroelectric exploitation
Wasserkreislauf m water cycle (circulation), hydrologic[al] cycle
Wasserlauf m watercourse
~ **im Kohlenflöz/fossiler** horseback
~/intermittierender (jahreszeitlicher) ephemeral stream
~/kleiner rivulet
~/künstlicher artificial water conduit
~/natürlicher natural water conduit
~/unterirdischer subterranean stream, subsurface flow
~/versumpfter slough
Wasserloch n 1. water hole; 2. slush pit *(drilling mud)*
wasserlöslich soluble in water
Wasserlösung f drainage
~ **durch Stollen** adit drainage
Wasserlösungsstollen m water (deep) adit, drainage gallery, offtake (delivery) drift
Wassermangel m water scarcity (shortage), dearth of water
Wassermenge f water volume (discharge)

Wassermengenmessung f discharge measurement; stream gauging *(of river water)*
Wassermengenprognose f runoff forecast
Wassermengenschwankung f discharge fluctuation
Wasseroberfläche f water surface
Wasserpflanzen fpl aquatic plants, hydrophytes
Wasserpfütze f puddle
Wasserplatz m water place
Wasserprobe f water sample
Wasserprobe[nent]nahmegerät n water sample taker
Wasserqualität f water quality
Wasserrecht n water right
Wasserregime n water regime
wasserreich abundant in water
Wasserreinigung f water purification
Wasserreserven fpl/**gewinnbare** exploitable reserves of water
Wasserreservoir n water store (reservoir)
Wasserressourcen fpl water resources
Wasserrinne f wash-out, gut
~/fossile dumb fault
Wasserriß m gully
Wasserrißbildung f gullying
Wasserrösche f [subterranean, submountain] water ditch, drainage ditch, ditch drain, water tunnel
Wasserrückhaltevermögen n water-retaining capacity, water retentiveness (retentivity), specific retention
Wassersaphir m water sapphire, iolite *(variety of cordierite)*
Wassersättigung f water saturation, waterlogging
Wassersäule f water column
Wassersäulenhöhe f water head
Wasserscheide f watershed, water divide (parting), *(Am)* [watershed] divide
~/oberirdische topographic divide
~/unterirdische subterranean water parting
~/wandernde shifting divide
Wasserschichtung f water layering
Wasserschloß n surge tank
Wasserschutz m water pollution control
Wasserschwierigkeiten fpl water trouble
Wasserseige f s. Wasserrösche
Wasserseite f waterside (upstream) face
Wassersortierung f washing *(of sediments)*
Wasserspeicherung f water storage
~ **an der Oberfläche** pocket storage
Wasserspeicherungsvermögen n water storage capacity
Wasserspende f discharge
~/maximale peak discharge
Wassersperre f water shut-off
Wasserspiegel m water level (table, surface)
~/unbeeinflußter original water table
~/wirklicher actual water table
Wasserspiegelabsenkung f decline of water table

Wasserspiegelmeßgerät 346

Wasserspiegelmeßgerät *n* liquid level indicator; water-stage recorder
Wasserspiegelmessung *f* water-stage measurement; checking of the water table
Wasserspiegelschwankung *f* **durch Winddrift** wind denivellation
Wassersprühregen *m* water spray
Wassersprung *m* hydraulic jump
Wasserstand *m* water (sea) level
~/höchster maximum water level
~/mittlerer mean water level
~/oberer headwater
Wasserstandsanzeiger *m* water-level gauge (indicator); river gauge
~/selbstregistrierender water-level recorder
Wasserstandsganglinie *f* stage hydrograph
Wasserstandslinie *f* water line
Wasserstandsmarke *f* water [level] mark
Wasserstandsmesser *m*, **Wasserstandsmeßgerät** *n* liquid level indicator, piezometer
Wasserstandsmessung *f* water-stage measurement; checking of the water table
Wasserstandspegel *m*/**elektrischer** electrical variable-resistance level gauge
Wasserstandsvorhersage *f* water-stage forecast
Wasserstandverhältnisse *npl* water-stage regime
Wasserstau *m* piling-up of water
Wasserstauer *m* impermeable bed
Wasserstoff *m* hydrogen, H
wasserstoffarm hydrogen-poor
wasserstofffrei hydrogen-free
wasserstoffhaltig hydrogenous
Wasserstoffperoxid *n* hydrogen peroxide, H_2O_2
wasserstoffreich hydrogen-rich
Wasserstollen *m* water (drainage) adit, water tunnel
Wasserstrahl *m* water jet
Wasserstrahlbohren *n* jet drilling
Wasserstrahlmischer *m* mud gun
Wasserstraße *f* [navigable] waterway
Wasserströmung *f* water current
Wasserströmungsrippeln *fpl* water-current ripples
Wasserstrudel *m* whirlpool
Wassertiefe *f* depth of water
Wassertiefen *fpl*/**lotbare** soundings
Wassertrieb *m* water drive
~/aktiver active water drive
~/partieller partial water drive
Wassertröpfchen *n* water droplet (particle)
Wassertropfen *m* water drop (particle)
Wassertrübe *f* fine detritus held in suspension
Wasserüberlauf *m* water overflow
Wasserüberleitungsstollen *m* water conduct gallery
Wasserüberschwemmung *f* water flooding
wasserundurchlässig waterproof, watertight, impervious
Wasserundurchlässigkeit *f* watertightness, imperviousness

wasserunlöslich insoluble in water
Wasserunlöslichkeit *f* insolubility in water
Wasserverbrauch *m* water consumption
wasserverfrachtet water-borne, water-drifted
Wasserverschmutzung *f* water pollution
Wasserversorgung *f* water supply (delivery)
~/städtische municipal water supply
Wasserversorgungsleitung *f* water supply line
Wasserverunreinigung *f* water pollution, contamination of water
Wasservolumen *n* water volume
Wasservorrat *m* water reserve, stock of water
Wasservorratsplanung *f* water resources planning
Wasservorratsprojekt *n* water resources project
Wasserwaage *f*/**fossile** fossil spirit level
Wasserwanderung *f* water migration
~/weiträumige large area migration of water
Wasserwanne *f* water spotting around the drilling string
Wasserwegsamkeit *f* water routing; hydraulic routing
Wasserwiderstand *m* water resistance
~/scheinbarer apparent water resistivity
Wasserwirbel *m* water whirlpool, eddy
Wasserwirkung *f* water action
Wasserwirtschaft *f* water economy, water resources management (policy); water supply service
Wasserzone *f*/**durchlichtete** [eu]photic (diaphanous) zone
Wasserzubringer *m* water feeder
Wasserzufluß *m* 1. water inflow (influx), intrusion (inrush) of water; water feeder; 2. rate of inflow
~ in eine Grube/normaler (regelmäßiger) come water
~/starker rush of water
Wasserzulauf *m* water influx
wäßrig aqueous
Watergun *f* watergun *(marine seismic energy source)*
Watt *n* tidal (low-tide) flat, watt
Wattboden *m* tidal marsh, sea mud
Wattengebiet *n* tidal[-flat] area, intertidal region
Wattenküste *f* coast with tidal flats
Wattenmeer *n* shallows, tideland
Wattensand *m* sand of tidal flat
Wattenschlick *m* tidal silts, mud tidal deposits
Wattrinne *f* tidal channel
Wattsand *m s.* Wattensand
Waucobien *n* Waucobian [Series], Georgian [Series] *(Lower Cambrian in North America)*
Wavelet *n* wavelet
Wavellit *m* wavellite, lasionite, $Al_3[(OH)_3|(PO_4)_2] \cdot 5H_2O$
Waylandit *m* waylandite, $(Bi, Ca)Al_3[(OH)_6|(PO_4)_2]$
Wealden *n* Wealden *(brakish to limnic development of Lower Cretaceous)*

Wealdensandstein m Wealden Sandstone
Wealdenton m Wealden Clay
Wealdien n, **Wealdium** n s. Wealden
Weberit m weberite, $Na_2Mg[AlF_7]$
Websterit m s. Aluminit
Wechsel m im Einfallen reversal of dip
Wechselbreite f/**scheinbare söhlige** apparent horizontal overlap
Wechselfeld n/**magnetisches** periodic magnetic field
Wechselfeldentmagnetisierung f alternating field demagnetization
wechsellagernd interbedded
~/**feinschichtig** interlaminated
Wechsellagerung f interbedding, interstratification, alternated stratification, alternate bedding
~/**flasrige** lenticular alternation
Wechsellagerungsminerale npl alternate bedding minerals
Wechsellagerungsstruktur f mixed-layer structure (of clay minerals)
Wechselschichtung f interlayered bedding
~/**feine** thinly interlayered bedding, rhythmites
~/**grobe** coarsely interlayered bedding
Wechselschlund m estavelle
Wechselwelle f converted (transformed) wave
Wechselwellen fpl alternating waves
Wechselwirkung f interaction
Wechselwirkungsenergie f interaction energy
Weddelit m weddelite, $Ca[C_2O_4] \cdot 2H_2O$
Wedel m frond
~/**fruktifizierender** fructiferous frond
Weeksit m weeksite, $K_2[(UO_2)_2|(Si_2O_5)_3] \cdot 4H_2O$
Wegdifferenz f relative retardation
Wegeinschnitt m cut of path
weggespült truncated
Wegscheiderit m wegscheiderite, $Na_2CO_3 \cdot 3NaHCO_3$
wegsprengen to blow off
Wegspülung f subsurface erosion
Weg-Zeit-Diagramm n s. Zeit-Weg-Diagramm
Wehr n weir, dam
~/**festes gemauertes** solid masonry weir
Wehranlage f weir plant
Wehrgeologie f military geology
Wehrhöhe f height of weir
Wehrkörper m body of weir
Wehrlit m wehrlite, BiTe
Wehrmauer f body of weir
Weibullit m weibullite, $PbS \cdot Bi_2Se_3$
weich soft (rock); late-bearing (prop)
Weichbraunkohle f soft brown coal; attrital brown coal; brown coal; (partly) lignite
~/**xylitische** xyloid brown coal, lignite
Weichmacher m softener
Weichmanganerz n pyrolusite, $\beta\text{-}MnO_2$
Weichsel-Kaltzeit f Weichsel Glacial Period
Weichsepten npl mesenteries (corals)
Weichtiere npl soft-bodied invertebrates
Weidespur f grazing trace (ichnology)

Weiher m pond
Weilit m weilite, $CaH[AsO_4]$
Weinschenkit m weinschenkite (variety of hornblende)
Weiselbergit m weiselbergite (vitreous augite porphyrite)
Weißbleierz n s. Zerussit
weißglühend incandescent
Weißgolderz n graphic[al] tellurium (gold) (s.a. Sylvanit)
Weissit m weissite, Cu_2Te
Weißkupfer n arsenical copper, domeykite, Cu_3As
Weißkupfererz n cubanite, chalmersite, $CuFe_2S_3$
Weißliegendes n weißliegendes, white underlying (of the German copper slate)
Weißmoos n sphagnum moss
Weißnickelkies m s. Chloanthit
Weißspießglanz m, **Weißspießglanzerz** n s. Valentinit
Weißstein m white stone, weisstein
Weite f width, span (of pressure arch)
Weitung f excavation
Weitungen fpl **im Alten Mann** gaps in the unconsolidated goaf
Weitungsbau m cavity working
Weitwinkelreflexion f overcritical (wide angle) reflection
Weitwinkelstapelung f wide-aperture CDP
Welkepunkt m[/**permanenter**] wilting point
Welle f wave; surge; breaker
~/**ankommende** oncoming wave
~/**einfallende** incident wave
~/**elastische** seismic (elastic) wave
~/**elektromagnetische** electromagnetic wave
~/**fortschreitende** progressive (travelling) wave
~/**gebrochene** refracted wave
~/**gedämpfte** damped wave
~/**geführte** guided wave (seismic prospection, seismics)
~/**gesteuerte** sustained wave
~/**hydrodynamische** hydrodynamic wave
~/**kleine** wavelet, ripplet
~/**konische** refraction (conical) wave
~/**linear polarisierte** linearly polarized wave
~/**planpolarisierte** plane-polarized wave
~/**primäre** primary wave
~/**reflektierte** reflected (indirect, sky) wave
~/**rückgekoppelte** sustained wave
~/**rücklaufende** reflected wave
~/**schrägauftreffende** incident wave
~/**seismische** seismic wave
~/**sekundäre** secondary wave
~/**sich überschlagende** combing wave, comber
~/**transformierte** transformed wave
~/**wandernde** travelling (progressing) wave
~/**Webersche** Weber's wave
~/**zurückgeworfene** s. ~/**reflektierte**
~/**zurückziehende** backwash
Wellenanprall m wave impact

wellenartig

wellenartig wavy, wavelike
Wellenausbreitung *f* wave propagation
Wellenband *n* leggy
Wellenbasis *f* wave base
Wellenbereich *m* wave range
Wellenberg *m* wave crest
wellenbespült wave-washed
Wellenbewegung *f* wave (undulatory) motion
Wellenbrecher *m* water breaker
Wellendolomit *m* wellendolomite
Wellendruck *m* wave pressure
Wellenerosion *f* wave erosion
wellenförmig undulatory
Wellenfortpflanzung *f* wave propagation
Wellenfront *f* wave front
Wellenfrontdiagramm *n* wave front chart
Wellenfurchen *fpl* ripple (rill, current) marks, ripples
~/asymmetrische asymmetrical ripples (ripple marks)
~/symmetrische symmetrical ripples (ripple marks)
Wellengeschwindigkeit *f* wave velocity
Wellengeschwindigkeitsfläche *f* elastic discontinuity
Wellengleichung *f* wave equation
Wellenhöhe *f* wave height
Wellenkalk *m* wellenkalk
Wellenkamm *m* wave crest
Wellenlänge *f* wave length
Wellenlängenbereich *m* wavelength range
Wellenlinie *f* trash line
Wellenmaximum *n* peak *(seismics)*
Wellenrippeln *fpl s.* Wellenfurchen
Wellenschlag *m* wave action; wave attack, beating (pounding, dash) of the waves
Wellenstreifen *mpl* intrastratified ribs
Wellenströmung *f* wave flow
Wellental *n* wave trough
Wellentätigkeit *f* wave action
Wellenweg *m* wave path
Wellenzahlfilter *n* wave number filter
wellenzerfressen wave-worn
Wellenzug *m* wave train
wellig wavy, ripply, undulating; sinuate
Welligkeit *f* waviness, undulation
Wellsit *m* wellsite *(variety of harmotome)*
Wellung *f* corrugation, scalloping *(sedimentary structure)*
Weltachse *f* celestial axis
Weltall *n* [cosmic, sidereal] universe, macrocosm
Weltbeben *n* world quake, megaseism
Weltkarte *f/*geologische geological map of the world
~/tektonische tectonic map of the world
Weltklimaprogramm *n* world climate program
Weltmeer *n* ocean
Weltraum *m* cosmic (extraterrestrial, interstellar, outer) space
~/erdferner deep space
Weltraumforschung *f* space exploration, astrionics

348

Weltraumlaboratorium *n* space laboratory
Weltraumschiff *n* interstellar craft
Weltraumschiffahrt *f* interstellar aviation
Weltraumsonde *f* space probe
Weltsystem *n* cosmic system
weltweit hologeodic
Weltzeit *f* universal time, Greenwich mean time, GMT
Wemmel[ien] *n,* **Wemmélium** *n* Wemmélian *(Tertiary)*
Wendekreis *m* tropic
~ des Krebses tropic of Cancer
~ des Steinbocks tropic of Capricorn
Wendekreisen/zwischen den subsolar
Wendepunkt *m* apsis
Wendium *n* Wendian, Vendian *(uppermost part of the Cryptozoic aeonothem)*
Wenkit *m* wenkite,
(Ba, K)$_{4,5}$(Ca, Na)$_{4,5}$[(OH)$_4$|(SO$_4$)$_2$|Al$_9$Si$_{12}$O$_{48}$]
Wenlock[ien] *n,* **Wenlockium** *n* Wenlockian [Series, Epoch]
Wenzelit *m* wenzelite,
(Mn, Fe)$_5$H$_2$[PO$_4$]$_4 \cdot$ 4H$_2$O
Werder *m* island in a river
Werkanlage *f* plant
Werkblei *n* raw lead
Werksgeologe *m* company geologist
Werkstein *m* building (dimension, cut) stone, quarrystone, ashlar
Werksteinmauerwerk *n* ashlar stonework
Werkzinn *n* raw tin
Wernerit *m* wernerite *(variety of scapolite)*
Wert *m* **der zweiten Ableitung** second-derivative value
Wertigkeit *f* valency, valence
Wertstoffmineral *n* valuable mineral
Westfal[ien] *n,* **Westfalium** *n* Westphalian [Stage] *(Upper Carboniferous in Central and West Europe)*
Westgrenit *m* westgrenite,
(Bi, Ca)(Ta, Nb)$_2$O$_6$OH
Wetter *n* weather
~/böiges squally weather
Wetter *pl/*CO$_2$-führende damps
~/explosive explosive atmosphere
~/faule foul (vitiated) air
~/matte dead (bad) air
~/schlagende firedamps
~/schlechte dead air
~/stinkende stink damps
Wetteränderung *f* weather modification
Wetterbeobachtung *f* aeroscopy
Wetterbericht *m* weather report
wetterbeständig weather-resistant
Wetterdienst *m* weather (meteorological) service
Wetterdienststelle *f* weather station
Wetterfunk *m* meteorologic[al] broadcasts
Wetterkarte *f* weather (meteorological) chart, weather map
Wetterkunde *f* meteorology
Wetterlage *f* weather (meteorological) conditions

Wetterleuchten n summer (heat) lightning
Wetterrakete f meteorological rocket
Wettersatellit m weather (meteorological) satellite
Wetterschacht m ventilation (air) shaft
Wetterscheide f weather limit, weather parting
Wetterseite f weather (windward) side
Wettersohle f air level
Wetterstation f weather station
Wetterstrecke f air way
Wetterstrom m air flow (current)
~/einziehender downcast
Wettervorhersage f weather forecast[ing]
Wetterwarte f weather station (observatory)
Wetterwolke f storm cloud
Wetzschiefer m whet slate, coticule, novaculite, honestone
Wetzstein m 1. rubstone *(type of rock)*; 2. whetstone, grindstone
Wheelerien n Wheelerian [Stage] *(marine stage, Lower Pleistocene in North America)*
Wheelerit m wheelerite *(a fossil resin)*
Wherryit m wherryite *(variety of caledonite)*
Whewellit m whewellite, $Ca[C_2O_4] \cdot H_2O$
Whisker m whisker
Whitesmoker m white smoker *(chimney in the sea bottom)*
Whitlockit m whitlockite, $\beta\text{-}Ca_3[PO_4]_2$
Whitneyan n Whitneyan [Stage] *(mammalian stage, Oligocene in North America)*
Whitneyit m whitneyite, (Cu, As)
Wichtemesser m density meter
Wickelfalte f convolutional (spiral, roll-up) ball, flow roll
Wickelstruktur f convolute bedding, ball-and-pillow structure
Wicklung f **von Faltendecken** involution of overthrust folds
Widerlager n abutment
widersinnig reverse; discordant; disconformable; antithetic[al]; anticlinal
Widerstand m**/akustischer** acoustic resistance
~ der Spülung/elektrischer mud resistivity
~ des Formationswassers/elektrischer water resistivity
~/elektrischer electrical resistance
~ im Invasionsbereich des Spülungsfiltrats/elektrischer invaded zone resistivity
~/magnetischer magnetic resistance
~/scheinbarer spezifischer apparent resistivity
~/spezifischer resistivity
~/wahrer elektrischer true resistivity *(e.g. of a formation)*
~Widerstand-Elektroden-Abstandskurve f resistivity-spacing curve
Widerstandsbeiwert m drag coefficient
Widerstandsbohrlochmessung f **mit verschiedenen Meßlängen** multiple spacings electric logging
Widerstandsdiagramm n**/elektrisches** electric log

widerstandsfähig resistant; stable
Widerstandsfähigkeit f resistivity; stability
Widerstandsgradient m resistivity gradient
Widerstandskurve f resistivity curve
Widerstandslog n resistivity log
Widerstandsmeßgerät n resistivimeter
Widerstandsmessung f resistivity survey
~/elektrische electrical logging
~/elektromagnetische electromagnetic logging
~/inverse inverse lateral logging
~ mit verschiedenen Meßlängen multiple spacings electronic logging
Widerstandsmoment n moment of resistance
Widerstandsnetzwerk n resistance network
Widerstandsverfahren n resistivity method
~/geoelektrisches geoelectric[al] resistivity method
Widerstandsziffern fpl resistance quotient *(of rock block systems)*
widerstehen to resist
Wiederablagerung f redeposition
Wiederabtragung f reerosion
Wiederanstieg m uplift, reuplift *(of ground-water level)*
Wiederaufleben n rejuvenation
wiederaufschmelzen to remelt
Wiederaufschmelzung f remelting
Wiederauftauchen n reemergence
Wiederausfällung f reprecipitation; redeposition *(by water)*
Wiederaustritt m resurgence *(of a river)*
Wiederbeginn m **der vulkanischen Tätigkeit** recrudescence of volcanic action
wiederbelebt revived
Wiedereinbruch m **des Meeres** reinvasion of the sea
Wiedereintritt m reentry
wiederfreilegen to reexpose
Wiederfreilegung f reexposure
Wiedergabevermögen n degree of fidelity *(tracer test)*
Wiedergabezentrale f playback centre
wiedergefrieren to refreeze, to recongeal
Wiedergefrieren n refreezing, recongealing
Wiederherstellung f **der wahren Amplitude** true-amplitude recovery
~ einer Aufnahme image restitution
Wiederholungsüberdeckung f repetitive coverage *(of the same scene on the ground by means of remote sensing pictures)*
Wiederholungsverzwilligung f repeated (polysynthetic, multiple) twinning
Wiederholungszwillinge mpl multiple twins
Wiederkehrwelle f W-wave
wiederverfestigen f to resolidify
Wiederverfestigung f resolidification
wiederverkitten to recement
Wiederverkittung f recementation
Wiederzusammenfrieren n regelation
Wiederzuwerfen n backfilling
Wiese f meadow

Wiesenboden

Wiesenboden *m* meadow soil, lacovishte
~/saurer schwarzer black acid prairie soil
Wiesenerz *n* meadow ore, bog [iron] ore
Wiesenkalk *m* meadow chalk, bog lime
Wiesenmoor *n* meadow (black) bog, fenland
Wiesenmoorboden *m* meadow bog soil
Wiesentorf *m* meadow peat
Wiese-Pfeil *m* tipper *(geomagnetics)*
Wightmanit *m* wightmanite, $Mg_9[(OH)_6|BO_3] \cdot 2H_2O$
Wildbach *m* [mountain] torrent, mountain (torrential, violent) stream
Wildbachablagerung *f* torrent deposit
Wildbachbett *n* ravine
Wildbachschlucht *f* gully, ravine
Wildbachverbauung *f* torrent regulation (control work)
Wildflysch *m* pebbly mudstones
Wildwasser *n* mountain torrent, rapid
Wilkeit *m* wilkeite, $Ca_5[(F, O)|(PO_4, SiO_4, SO_4)_3]$
Willemit *m* willemite, hebetine, $Zn_2[SiO_4]$
Wind *m* wind
~/ablandiger offshore wind (breeze), land-wind, land-breeze
~/auflandiger onshore wind (breeze), sea breeze
~/frischer fresh wind
~/geostrophischer geostrophic wind
~/mäßiger moderate breeze
~/stürmischer fresh gale
~/vorherrschender prevailing (dominant) wind
Windabdrift *f* wind drift
Windablagerung *f* aeolian (wind-laid) deposit
Windablation *f* deflation
Windabsatzboden *m* aeolian (wind-borne) soil
Windaktivität *f* aeolian activity
Windaufschüttung *f* aeolian accumulation
Windauskolkung *f* wind scour
windbewegt wind-borne, wind-drifted, wind-blown
Windbö *f* squall (scud) of wind
Winddenudation *f* deflation
Winddruck *m* wind pressure
Windduine *f* aeolian dune
Winde *f* hoist
winderodiert wind-worn
Winderosion *f* wind (aeolian, blowing) erosion, aeolation, deflation
Windfahne *f* wind vane
windgeglättet wind-polished
windgeschliffen wind-carved
Windgeschwindigkeit *f* wind velocity (speed)
Windgeschwindigkeitsschreiber *m* air-speed recorder
Windgeschwindigkeitszähler *m* air-speed computer
Windhose *f* whirlwind
Windkanter *m* wind-shaped pebble, aeolian-carved pebble, windkanter, ventifact, glyptolith
Windkessel *m* deflation basin
Windkorrasion *f* wind (aeolian) corrasion

Windmesser *m* wind gauge, anemometer
Windmeßvorrichtung *f* wind-measuring device
Windmulde *f* blow-out
Windreihenkämme *mpl* windrow ridges
Windrichtung *f* wind direction
Windrichtungswinkel *m* angle of wind direction
Windrippelmarken *fpl* wind-ripple marks, aeolian ripple marks
Windrippeln *fpl* wind[-current] ripples, aeolian current ripples, air-current ripples
Windrose *f* wind rose, compass card
Windschattensand *m* wind-shadow drift
Windschliff *m* 1. wind erosion (abrasion, carving, corrasion); 2. wind-polished rock
Windschlifffläche *f* deflation surface
Windschutzstreifen *m* wind (protective) forest belt, shelterbelt
Windschwelle *f/***geostrophische** geostrophic wind level
Windsediment *n* wind-borne sediment
Windseite *f* windward side
Windsichter *m* air separator (classifier)
Windsichtung *f* wind assortment, winnowing *(of sediments)*
Windstärke *f* wind force (strength)
Windstau *m* raising of the water level by the effect of wind
Windstille *f* calm
Windstoß *m* gust of wind, flurry
Windtransport *m* wind (aeolian) transport
Windufer *n* weather shore
Windung *f* 1. winding; 2. meander, loop, sinuosity *(of a river)*; 3. whorl, volution *(of molluscans, s.a. Umgang)*
~/evolute evolute whorl
~/involute involute whorl
Windungen/mit offenen loose-coiled, loose-coiling
Windungsachse *f* axis of the screw motion
Windungsbreite *f* whorl thickness *(of molluscan test)*
Windungsquerschnitt *m* cross section of volutions
windverfrachtet wind-carried, wind-transported, wind-laid
Windverfrachtung *f* wind transport
Windwirbel *m* eddy
windzerfressen wind-eroded
Winebergit *m* winebergite, $Al_4[(OH)_{10}|SO_4] \cdot 7H_2O$
Winkel *m* angle
~/ausspringender salient angle
~/Braggscher Bragg (glancing) angle
~ der inneren Reibung angle of internal friction
~ der wahren inneren Reibung angle of true internal friction
~/eingeschlossener included angle
~/einspringender reentrant angle
~/flacher plane angle

~/optischer visual angle
Winkelauflösungsvermögen *n* angular resolution
Winkeldiskordanz *f* angular unconformity, clin[o]unconformity, unconformability of dip
Winkelgeschwindigkeit *f* angular velocity
winkelig angular
Winkelmesser *m* angulometer
Winkelträger *m* angle beam
Winkelverformung *f* angular deformation
Winkelverlagerung *f*, Winkelverschiebung *f* angular displacement
Winterhochwasser *n* winter flood
Wintermonsun *m* winter monsoon
Winterschneehöhe *f* hibernal snow level
Wintersolstitium *n*, Wintersonnenwende *f* winter solstice
Wirbel *m* 1. whirlpool, eddy, vortex; 2. vertebra; beak, umbo *(of bivalves)*
~/am subumbonal
Wirbel *mpl*/klaffende separated beaks
~/sich berührende contiguous beaks
Wirbelbälle *mpl* whirl-balls
Wirbelbewegung *f* vortex (eddy) motion, eddying
Wirbelbildung *f* vortex (eddy) formation
Wirbelerosion *f* evorsion
wirbelfrei non-eddying
Wirbelgebiet *n* vorticity zone
Wirbeligkeit *f* vorticity
Wirbelkolk *m* pothole
wirbellos invertebrate
Wirbelmarken *fpl* eddy markings
Wirbelsäule *f* spinal (vertebral) column
Wirbelstörung *f* whirl disturbance
Wirbelströmung *f* turbulent flow
Wirbelsturm *m* cyclone, tornado
~/tropischer tropical cyclone
Wirbeltier *n* vertebrate
Wirbeltierfauna *f* vertebrate fauna
Wirbeltierstamm *m* vertebrate phylum
Wirbeltierstufe *f* mammalian stage
Wirbelung *f* eddying
Wirbelwind *m* whirlwind
Wirbelzone *f* vorticity zone
wirkend/von außen *s.* exogen
~/von innen *s.* endogen
Wirksamkeit *f*/areale areal efficiency *(by flushing)*
Wirkung *f*/abscheuernde abrasive (grinding) action
~/abschleifende corrading action
~/abtragende gradational effect
~/erodierende erosive effect
~/fällende precipitating action
~/polarisierende polarizing effect
~/scheuernde scouring *(e.g. of a glacier)*
Wirkungsgrad *m*/spektraler spectral efficiency
Wirkungsquerschnitt *m* effective cross section

Wirkungsrichtung *f* effective direction
Wirkungstiefe *f* penetration depth
Wirkungszone *f* area of influence
wirr choppy *(cross lamination)*
Wirtschaftlichkeit *f* profitability
Wirtschaftlichkeitsgrenze *f* einer Bohrung economic[al] limit of exhaustion of a well
Wirtschaftlichkeitsuntersuchung *f* feasibility study
Wirtschaftsgeologie *f* economical (industrial) geology
Wirtsgestein *n* host rock
Wirtsmineral *n* host mineral
Wisaksonit *m* wisaksonite *(variety of uranothorite)*
Wisconsin-Eiszeit *f* Wisconsin [Ice Age] *(corresponding to Würm II Glacial)*
Wiserit *m* wiserite, $Mn_4[(OH, Cl)_4|B_2O_5]$
Wismut *n* bismuth, Bi
~/gediegenes native bismuth
Wismutblende *f s.* Eulytin
Wismutglanz *m* bismuthinite, bismuth glance, Bi_2S_3
Wismutkupfererz *n* emplectite, $Cu_2S \cdot Bi_2S_3$
Wismutocker *m* bismuth ochre, bismite, α-Bi_2O_3
Wissenschaften *fpl*/geognostische geognosy
Witherit *m* witherite, barium carbonate, $BaCO_3$
Witterung *f* weather; atmospheric condition
Witterungsbeschreibung *f* meteorography
Witterungseinflüsse *mpl* atmospheric actions, climatic effects
Witterungsverhältnisse *npl* weather conditions
Witterungsverlauf *m* course of weather
Wittichenit *m* wittichenite, $3Cu_2S \cdot Bi_2S_3$
Wittit *m* wittite, $5PbS \cdot 3Bi_2(S, Se)_3$
Wocklum *n* Wocklum [Stage] *(uppermost stage of Upper Devonian)*
Wodginit *m* wodginite, $(Ta, Nb, Sn, Mn, Fe)_2O_4$
Woge *f* wave *(s.a.* Welle); billow, breaker, roller
Wogenprall *m s.* Wellenschlag
Wöhlerit *m* wöhlerite, $Ca_2NaZr[(F, OH, O)_2|Si_2O_7]$
Wohnbau *m* dwelling structure *(ichnology)*
Wohngang *m* dwelling burrow *(ichnology)*
Wohngebiet *n* residential area
Wohnkammer *f* living (body) chamber *(palaeontology)*
Wohnröhre *f* dwelling tube *(ichnology)*
wölben to arch
Wölbung *f* arching; buckling
Wolchonskoit *m* wolchonskoite *(a mineral belonging to the montmorillonites)*
Wolfachit *m* wolfachite, Ni(As, Sb)S
Wolfcamp[ien] *n*, Wolfcampium *n* Wolfcampian [Stage] *(of Permian)*
Wolfram *n* tungsten, wolfram, W
Wolframerz *n* tungsten ore

wolframhaltig

wolframhaltig tungsteniferous
Wolframit m wolframite, (Fe, Mn) WO_4
Wolframocker m tungstite, tungstic ochre, $WO_2(OH)_2$
Wolfsbergit m chalcostibite, $Cu_2S \cdot Sb_2S_3$
Wolga n, **Wolga-Stufe** f Volganian [Stage] *(uppermost Malm in the Boreal Realm)*
Wolke f cloud
~/nachtleuchtende noctilucent cloud
wolkenartig nepheloid
Wolkenbank f cloud bank
Wolkenbeobachtung f nephelognosy
Wolkenbildung f cloud formation
Wolkenbruch m cloud burst, torrent[ial] rain, deluge of rain
Wolkendecke f cloud cover
Wolkenfetzen m cloud shred
Wolkenflug m cloud flight
Wolkenform f cloud form
Wolkengrenze f cloud top
~/untere cloud base
Wolkenhimmel m overcast sky
Wolkenhöhe f cloud ceiling (height)
Wolkenhöhenmesser m cloud ceilometer (altimeter)
Wolkenkappe f cloud cap
Wolkenkarte f cloud map
Wolkenkunde f nephology
Wolkenkuppe f cloud dome
Wolkenloch n cloud gap
wolkenlos cloudless
Wolkenmessung f cloud measurement
Wolkenschicht f cloud layer
Wolkenspiegel m cloud reflector
Wolkenstraße f cloud street
Wolkenstreifen m cloud banner
Wolkental n cloud trough
Wolkenturm m towering cloud
Wolkenvorhang m cloud curtain
Wolkenwand f cloud bank
Wolkenwelle f cloud wave
Wolkenzerstreuung f dispersion of clouds
Wolkenzone f troposphere
Wolkenzug m cloud train
wolkig 1. cloudy, clouded, nepheloid; 2. milky *(crystals)*
Wollastonit m wollastonite, table (tabular) spar, $Ca_3[Si_3O_9]$
Wollsack m woolsack
Wollsackabsonderung f sacklike structure *(of granites)*
Wollsackverwitterung f spheroidal weathering
Wölsendorfit m wölsendorfite, $2[UO_2|(OH)_2] \cdot PbO$
Wolstonien n Wolstonian *(Pleistocene of British Islands corresponding to Riss Drift of Alps district)*
Woodhouseit m woodhouseite, $CaAl_3[(OH)_6|SO_4PO_4]$
Word n Wordian [Stage] *(of Middle Permian)*
worfeln to winnow

Wühlgefüge n bioturbation *(ichnology)*
Wühlmarke f foralite
Wulfenit m wulfenite, yellow lead ore, $PbMoO_4$
Wulst m [geanticlinal] welt
Wulstbank f s. Wulstschichtung
Wülste mpl/**magmatische** wrinkle ridges
Wulstfaltung f s. Wulstschichtung
wulstig torose
Wulstschichtung f, **Wulststruktur** f, **Wulsttextur** f, **Wulstung** f convolute bedding, ball-and-pillow structure
Wünschelrute f dowsing (divining) rod
Wünschelrutengänger m waterfinder, water diviner, dowser
Wünschelrutengehen n dowsing, [water] divining, witching
Würfel m cube, hexahedron
Würfeldruckfestigkeit f crushing strength of a cube
Würfelerz n pharmacosiderite, $KFe_4|(OH)_4|(AsO_4)_3 \cdot 6-7H_2O$
Würfelfestigkeit f cube strength
würfelig blocky
Würfelprobe f cube test
Wurfschlacke f lava rag
Würgehorizont m strangling horizon
wurmartig vermicular, worm-shaped *(mineral)*
Wurmausscheidungen fpl worm castings (excrements)
Würm-Eiszeit f Würm [Drift] *(Pleistocene, Alps district)*
Würm-Interstadial n Würmian [Interstadial] *(Pleistocene, Alps district)*
Würm-Kaltzeit f s. Würm-Eiszeit
Wurtzilit m wurtzilite *(asphaltite)*
Wurtzit m wurtzite, ZnS
Wurzel f 1. root; 2. radix *(crinoids)*
~ der Überschiebungsdecke nappe root
Wurzelboden m underclay, rootled (stigmarian) bed, root clay *(in the floor of a seam)*; cauldron bottom *(in the roof of a seam)*
Wurzelhaar n root hair
Wurzelregion f root region
Wurzelstock m root stock
Wurzelstruktur f root cast
Wurzeltorf m fibrous (surface) peat
Wurzelzone f root zone
Wüste f desert
~/kiesbedeckte gravelly desert
~/tote harsh desert
~/winterkalte cold desert
Wüstenbildung f desertification
Wüstenboden m desert soil (floor)
Wüstendüne f desert dune
Wüstengebiet n desert area (region)
Wüstengürtel m desert belt
Wüstenklima n desert climate
Wüstenlack m desert varnish (lacquer), patina
Wüstenlandschaft f desert topography
Wüstenpflaster n desert pavement (mosaic)
Wüstenpolitur f desert polish

Wüstenrinde f s. Wüstenlack
Wüstensand m desert sand
Wüstensee m desert lake
Wüstensteppe f semidesert
Wüstental n/**ebenes** bolson
Wüstentheorie f desert theory
Wüstenwind m desert wind
Wüstenzone f desert zone
Wyomingit m wyomingite *(leucitic phonolite)*

X

Xanthiosit m xanthiosite, $Ni_3[AsO_4]_2$
Xanthit m xanthite *(yellow variety of vesuvianite)*
Xanthochroit m xanthochroite, CdS
Xanthokon m xanthoconite, Ag_3AsS_3
Xanthophyllit m xanthophyllite, $Ca(Mg, Al)_{3-2}[(OH)_2|Al_2Si_2O_{10}]$
Xanthosiderit m s. Limonit
Xenoblast m xenoblast
xenoblastisch xenoblastic
Xenocryst m xenocryst, c[h]adacryst
Xenolith m xenolith, exogenous enclosure, foreign (accidental) inclusion
xenomorph xenomorphic, anhedral
Xenotim m xenotime, YPO_4
xerophil xerophilous
Xonotlit m xonotlite, $Ca_6[(OH)_2|Si_6O_{17}]$
Xylit m xylite

Y

Yardan m yardang, yarding
Yarmouth-Interglazial n, **Yarmouth-Warmzeit** f Yarmouth [Interglacial]
Yavapaiit m yavapaiite, $KFe[SO_4]_2$
Yeatmanit m yeatmanite, $Mn_9Zn_2Mg_4[O|(OH)_{14}|(AsO_4)_2|(SiO_4)_2]$
Ynez[ien] n, **Ynezium** n Ynezian [Stage] *(marine stage, Palaeocene in North America)*
Yoderit m yoderite, $(Al, Mg, Fe)_2[(O, OH)|SiO_4]$
Yoldiameer n Yoldia Sea
Yosemit m yosemite *(rock of the granite group)*
Yoshimurait m yoshimuraite, $(Ba, Sr)_2(Mn, Fe, Mg)_2(Ti, Fe)[(OH, Cl)_2|(S, P, Si)O_4|Si_2O_7]$
Yo-Yo-Verfahren n yo-yo technique *(marine geophysics)*
Ypern n, **Yprésien** n, **Ypresium** n Ypresian [Stage] *(of Eocene)*
Ytterbit m s. Gadolinit
Yttererde f yttria
ytterhaltig yttric, yttriferous
Ytterspat m s. Xenotim
Yttrialith m yttrialite *(Y-Th-silicate)*
Yttrium n yttrium, Y
Yttrocerit m s. Cerfluorit
Yttrofluorit m yttrofluorite, $(Ca_3, Y_2)F_6$
Yttrokras[it] m yttrocrasite, YTi_2O_5OH

Yttrotantalit m yttrotantalite, yttrocolumbite, $(Y, U, Ca)(Ta, Fe)_2(O, OH)_6$
Yugawaralith m yugawaralite, $Ca[Al_2Si_5O_{14}] \cdot 3H_2O$
Yukonit m yukonite, $(Ca_3, Fe_2^{..})(AsO_4)_2 \cdot 2Fe(OH)_3 \cdot 5H_2O$

Z

Zackenfirn m penitent snow, nieve penitente, pinnacles
Zackengrat m comblike ridge
zäh tough; tenacious; viscous
zähflüssig viscous
Zähflüssigkeit f viscosity
~/dynamische absolute viscosity
Zähigkeit f toughness; tenacity; viscosity
~/kinematische kinematic ductility
zähigkeitsfrei non-viscous
Zähigkeitskoeffizient m coefficient of dynamic viscosity, coefficient of internal friction
Zähigkeitskraft f viscous force
Zahl f **der Freiheitsgrade** number of degrees of freedom
~/Poissonsche Poisson's ratio
~/Reynoldssche Reynolds number
Zählrate f counting rate *(radioisotope)*
Zählrohr n counter (counting) tube
Zählrohr-Texturgoniometer n X-ray texture goniometer
zahnähnlich dentaloid
Zahnarztbohrer m dentist borer
Zähnchenmarke f crenulation
Zähne mpl/**pflasterartige** pavement-like teeth
~/plattige platy teeth
~/scharnierartige hinge teeth
~/scharfe sharp teeth
~/spitze pointed teeth
~/stumpfe pointless teeth
Zahnformel f dental formula, dentition
Zahngrube f socket
Zahnkrone f saw-toothed core bit
Zahnpaar n pair of teeth
Zahnplatten fpl teeth plates
Zahnschmelz m tooth enamel, dentine
Zahnstützen fpl teeth supports
Zahntürkis m odontolite, bone (fossil) turquoise *(a mineral consisting of fossil bone or tooth)*
Zanclium/Tabianium n Zanclian/Tabianian [Stage] *(basale stage of Pliocene)*
Zapfenwulst m conical flute cast
Zaratit m zaratite, $Ni_3[(OH)_4|CO_3] \cdot 4H_2O$
Zäsium n caesium, *(Am)* cesium, Cs
Zäsiumdampfmagnetometer n caesium vapour magnetometer
Zavariskit m zavariskite, BiOF
Zebedassit m zebedassite *(variety of saponite)*
Zeche f [coal] mine; colliery; pit
Zechstein m Zechstein Subdivision
Zechsteintransgression f Zechstein transgression

Zederbaumlakkolith

Zederbaumlakkolith *m* cedar-tree laccolith
zehnflächig decahedral
Zehnflächner *m* decahedron
Zehrgebiet *n* depletion area
~ **eines Gletschers** zone of glacier ablation, region of melting
Zeichengerät *n* plotter
Zeichenprisma *n* camera lucida
zeichnen/maßstabgetreu to draw to scale
Zeichnung *f*/**wolkige** clouding *(of marble)*
Zeigermeßgerät *n* dial gauge
Zeigerokular *n* pointer eyepiece
Zeigerpflanze *f* indicator (accumulative) plant
Zeilenstruktur *f* slip bands
Zeit *f*/**absolute** absolute (abstract) time
~/**astronomische** astronomic[al] time
~ **für das Niederbringen einer Bohrung/volle** time of a drilling cycle
~/**produktive** productive time
~/**siderische** sidereal time
~/**unproduktive** unproductive time
Zeitabschnitt *m*/**geologischer** geologic[al] era
Zeitalter *n* 1. age; 2. era *(geologic time table)*
~/**abiotisches** abiotic era
~/**geologisches** geologic[al] age
~/**vorgeschichtliches** prehistoric period
Zeitanschluß *m* time tie
Zeitäquivalenz *f* synchroneity, isochroneity
Zeitbereich *m* time domain
Zeitbestimmung *f*/**absolute** absolute chronology
~/**relative** relative chronology
Zeitdauer *f* **bis zum Anfangseinsatz** arrival time
~ **einer biostratigrafischen Zone** intrazonal time
~ **eines stratigrafischen Hiatus** interzonal time
Zeitdilatation *f* time dilatation
Zeiteinheit *f*/**geologische** geochronologic[al] unit, chronostratigraphic unit
Zeitfaktor *m* time factor
Zeitfeld *n* delay time plot
Zeitfenster *n* time window
Zeitintervall *n* interval of time
Zeitkonstante *f* *s.* Zerfallskonstante
Zeitmarke *f* time mark, timer line, adjacent timing line
Zeitmarkierung *f* time registration
Zeitmessung *f* measurement of time
~/**geologische** geochronometry, geologic[al] time measurement
Zeit-Mittel-Gleichung *f* time-average relationship
Zeiträume *mpl*/**geologische** geologic[al] ages
Zeitrechnung *f*/**absolute** absolute chronology
~/**astronomische** astronomic[al] time reckoning
~/**biostratigrafische** biostratigraphic chronology
~/**geologische** geologic[al] chronology
Zeitreihen *fpl* stationary time series
Zeitschnitt *m* time section

Zeit-Senkungs-Kurve *f* time-subsidence curve
Zeit-Setzungs-Kurve *f* consolidation-time curve
Zeitskala *f*/**erdgeschichtliche** geologic time scale
~/**geochronologische** geochronological scale
~/**paläomagnetische** palaeomagnetic time scale
Zeitspanne *f* span
~/**geologische** geological span
Zeittafel *f*/**geochronologische** geochronological time table
~/**geologische** table of geologic[al] chronology, chart of geologic[al] time
Zeitverminderung *f* time lead *(in fan shooting)*
Zeit-Versatz-Kurve *f* time-pressure curve for stowed goaf
Zeitverzögerung *f* time delay, lag
Zeit-Weg-Diagramm *n*, **Zeit-Weg-Kurve** *f* path-time diagram, displacement-time diagram
Zeitzone *f* time zone, *(Am)* time belt
Zellenboden *m* cellular soil
Zellendolomit *m* cellular dolomite
Zellenrauhwacke *f* boxwork rauhwacke
zellig cellular; cavernous; vesicular; honeycombed
Zellulose *f*/**mineralische** sapperite
Zementation *f* cementation, cementing[-together]
~/**absatzweise** stage cementing
~/**sekundäre** secondary cementation
Zementationsfaktor *m* cementation factor
Zementationszone *f* cementation zone, zone of reduction, belt of cementation, supergene sulphide zone
Zementaufnahme *f* **bei Injektion** grout[ing] acceptance
Zementbrücke *f* cement bridge
Zementieranlage *f* cementing unit
Zementierdruck *m* injection pressure
Zementierkopf *m* plug container
Zementierpacker *m* cement retainer
Zementierpumpe *f* cementing pump
Zementierstopfen *m* cementing plug
zementiert/mit Gips gypsinate
~/**mit Limonit** ferruginate
~/**mit SiO$_2$** silicinate
Zementierung *f* *s.* Zementation
Zementinjektion *f* cement grouting
Zementkalkstein *m* hydraulic limestone
Zementkopf *m* cement top
Zementlog *n* cement log
Zementmantel *m* cement sheath
Zementmilch *f* cement grout (slurry)
Zementquarzit *m* *s.* Tertiärquarzit
Zementschlämme *f* cement grout (slurry)
Zementtone *mpl* cement clays
Zementvermörtelung *f* cement grouting
Zemorrien *n* Zemorrian [Stage] *(marine stage, Oligocene to lowermost Miocene in North America)*
Zenit *m* zenith

~/astronomischer astronomic[al] zenith
Zenitwinkel *m* zenith angle
~ des Bohrlochs zenith angle of the hole
Zentralaufstellung *f* split[-dip] spread *(seismics)*
Zentralausbruch *m* central (summit) eruption
Zentralberg *m* central peak *(of the moon)*
Zentraleruption *f* central (summit) eruption
Zentralkörper *m* centrosphere
Zentrallasit *m* centrallasite, $Ca_2[Si_4O_{10}] \cdot 4H_2O$
Zentralmassiv *n* central massif
Zentrierhaken *m* fishing hook
zentriert centred
zentrifugal centrifugal
Zentrifugalbeschleunigung *f* centrifugal acceleration
Zentrifugalkraft *f* centrifugal force
Zentrifuge *f* centrifuge
Zentriklinale *f* centricline
zentripetal centripetal
Zentripetalbeschleunigung *f* centripetal acceleration
Zentripetalkraft *f* centripetal force
zentroklinal periclinal
Zeolith *m* zeolite
Zeolithbildung *f* zeolitization
Zeolithfazies *f* zeolite facies
zeolithisch zeolitic
Zeolithisierung *f* zeolitization
Zeophyllith *m* zeophyllite, $Ca_4[F_2|(OH)_2|Si_3O_8] \cdot 2H_2O$
Zer *n* cerium, Ce
Zerargyrit *m* chlorargyrite, AgCl
zerbohren to drill up
zerbrechen to break
zerbrechlich fragile
Zerbrechlichkeit *f* fragility
zerbrochen/durch Gasausbruch gasoclastic
zerbröckeln to crumble [away, down]
Zerbröckelung *f* crumbling
Zerfall *m* decay, disintegration; decomposition, breakdown; disaggregation
~/körniger granular disintegration
~/radioaktiver radioactive decay (disintegration)
~/spontaner spontaneous decay (disintegration)
zerfallen to decay, to disintegrate; to decompose; to disaggregate; to fall into crumbs
Zerfallsart *f* type of decay
Zerfallsenergie *f* decay energy
Zerfallsgeschwindigkeit *f* rate of decay, disintegration rate
Zerfallsgesetz *n*[/radioaktives] [radioactive] decay law
Zerfallskette *f s.* Zerfallsreihe
Zerfallskonstante *f* decay constant
Zerfallsmethode *f* decay method *(of radioactive dating)*
Zerfallsmodul *m* modulus of decay
Zerfallsphase *f* crumbling phase
Zerfallsprodukt *n* decay (disintegration) product *(geological)*; fission product, daughter element
~/aktives active product
Zerfallsrate *f* decay rate
Zerfallsreihe *f* decay (disintegration) series, disintegration chain
~ mit n-Gliedern/radioaktive n-membered chain
~/radioaktive radioactive series (family)
Zerfallsschema *n* disintegration scheme
Zerfallswärme *f* heat of radioactivity
Zerfallszeit *f* decay time
Zerfluorit *m s.* Cerfluorit
zerfressen eroded; fretted
zerfurchen to furrow
Zerinit *m* cerinite *(wax from Eocene brown-coal plants)*
Zerit *m* cerite, $(Ca,Fe)Ce_3H[(OH)_2|SiO_4|Si_2O_7]$
zerkart kettled, channelled
Zerkarung *f* cirquation, cirque erosion (cutting); nivation
~/schwache upland grooving
~/starke upland fretting
zerkleinern to crush, to break; to comminute
Zerkleinerung *f* crushing, breaking; comminution
~ des Gesteins rock fragmentation (comminution)
~ von großen Gesteinsblöcken boulder breaking
zerklüften to fracture
zerklüftet fractured, jointed, fissured [by joints]; crevassed *(ice)*
~/schwach distantly jointed
~/stark highly jointed
Zerklüftung *f* fissuring, fissuration, fracturing, jointing, breaking, crevasse
Zerklüftungszone *f* fissured zone
zerknistern to decrepitate
Zerknistern *n* decrepitation
Zerknitterungslamellen *fpl* crumpled lamellae
zerlegt/durch Brüche fractured
zermalmen to crush
zermürben to mellow
zermürbt fragmented, mouldered
Zermürbung *f* mellowing
zernagt corroded
zerquetschen to crush
zerracheln to gully
Zerrachelung *f* gullying, gully (badland-type) of erosion
zerreiben to triturate; to grind
zerreiblich friable
Zerreibung *f* trituration
zerreißen to disrupt
Zerreißen *n* disruption
Zerreißungsspalte *f* fissure of disruption (discission)
zerrieben detrital
zerrissen ragged
Zerrkluft *f* tension joint
Zerrung *f* stretching; extension; tear

Zerrungsbruch

Zerrungsbruch *m* stretching fault
Zerrungsgebiet *n* tearing zone
Zerrungsspalte *f* rupture fissure
Zerrungstextur *f* pull-apart structure
Zerrüttungszone *f* fractured (shatter) zone
~/mineralisierte stringer zone
Zerscherung *f* shearing *(e.g. of microremains)*
Zerschluchtung *f* ravining, gullying
zerschneiden to dissect
zerschnitten/jung youthfully dissected
zersetzbar/in Wärme thermolabile
zersetzen/sich to decay, to decompose
zersetzt rotten
Zersetzung *f* decay, disintegration, decomposition
~/hydrothermale hydrothermal decomposition
Zersetzungsgrad *m* rate of decomposition
Zersetzungsprodukt *n* product of decomposition (weathering)
Zersetzungsprozeß *m* decay process
Zersetzungsreaktion *f* decomposition reaction
Zersetzungsschlick *m* decay ooze
zerspalten to fissure, to cleave
Zerspaltung *f* fissuring, cleavage
zersplittern/sich to shatter
zerstörend destructive
Zerstörung *f* decay, destruction
Zerstörungen *fpl* **an Gebäuden** destruction of buildings *(8th stage of the scale of seismic intensity)*
Zerstörungsarbeit *f* destructional work
Zerstörungsbeben *n* strong motion earthquake
Zerstörungsform *f* destructed form
Zerstörungsprodukt *n* destruction product
zerstreuen to diffuse
zertalen to dissect
zertalt/stark maturely dissected
zerteilt flerry *(rock)*
Zertrümmerung *f* crushing; fragmentation; fracturing
Zertrümmerungskräfte *fpl* agents of clastation
Zertrümmerungszone *f* crushed (fissured) zone
Zerussit *m* cerussite, white (earthy) lead ore, lead spar, $PbCO_3$
Zetapotential *n* zeta potential
Zeugenberg *m* outlier, erosional outlier (remnant), island mount, relict mountain, monadnock
Zeugogeosynklinale *f* zeugogeosyncline
Zeunerit *m* zeunerite, $Cu[UO_2|AsO_4]_2 \cdot 10(16-10)H_2O$
Zickzackfalte *f* zigzag fold
Zickzackmuster *n* zigzag pattern
Ziegelerz *n* tile ore
Ziegelstapelgefüge *n* pile-of-brick texture
Ziegelsteinmauerung *f* brick walling
Ziegelton *m* brick clay (earth), potter's clay
Ziegenrücken *m* hogback
Ziehbrunnen *m* draw well

ziehen/einen Kern to extract a core
~/Gräben to ditch
~/Rohre to pull
~/Schürfgräben to costean, to costeen
Zielbohren *n* directional drilling
Zielbohrung *f* directional hole
Zielobjekt *n* target
Zielpunkt *m* target
zigarrenförmig cigar-shaped
Zinckenit *m* zin[c]kenite, $PbS \cdot Sb_2S_3$
Zincobotryogen *m* zincobotryogene, $(Zn,Mg,Mn,Fe)Fe[OH\,|\,(SO_4)_2] \cdot 6,6H_2O$
Zincocopiapit *m* zincocopiapite, $(Zn,Fe,Mn)Fe_4[OH\,|\,(SO_4)_3]_2 \cdot 18H_2O$
Zink *n* Zinc, Zn
Zinkaluminit *m* zincaluminite, $Zn_3Al_3[(OH)_{13}|SO_4] \cdot 2H_2O$
zinkartig zin[c]ky, zincous
Zinkblende *f* sphalerite, zinc (garnet) blende, false galena, black (steel) jack, α-ZnS
~/hell gefärbte resin tiff
~/rote ruby zinc
Zinkblüte *f* hydrozincite, zinc bloom, $Zn_5[(OH)_3|CO_3]_2$
Zinkdibraunit *m* zincdibraunite, $ZnMn_2O_3 \cdot 2H_2O$
Zinkeisenerz *n* franklinite, $ZnFe_2O_4$
Zinkerz *n*/**verwachsenes** zinc chat
zinkführend, zinkhaltig zinciferous, zinkiferous, zinc-bearing, zinc-containing
Zinkit *m* zincite, spartalite, red oxide of zinc, ZnO
Zinklavendulan *m* zinclavendulane, $(Ca,Na)_2(Zn,Cu)_5[Cl|(AsO_4)] \cdot 4-5H_2O$
Zinkosit *m* zinkosite, $Zn[SO_4]$
Zinkrockbridgeit *m* zincrockbridgeite, $ZnFe_4[(OH)_5|(PO_4)_3]$
Zinkspat *m* smithsonite, zinc spar, $ZnCO_3$
Zinkspinell *m* gahnite, zinc spinel, $ZnAl_2O_4$
Zinn *n* tin, stannum, Sn
zinnartig tinny
Zinnausbringen *n* tin yield
Zinnbergbau *m* tin mining, tinning
Zinnbergwerk *n* tin mine, stannary
Zinne *f* pinnacle
Zinnerz *n* tin ore (stone), cassiterite, SnO_2
~ mit Gangart squat
~/rohes tin stuff
~/unregelmäßig verteiltes tin floor
Zinnerzgang *m* tin (scovan) lode
Zinnerzgrube *f* tin ore mine
zinnführend tin-bearing, stanniferous
Zinngang *m s.* Zinnerzgang
Zinngraupen *fpl* tin gravels
Zinngrube *f* stannary
zinnhaltig tinny, stannic, stannous, tin-bearing, stanniferous
Zinnkies *m* tin pyrite, stannite, Cu_2FeSnS_4
Zinnlagerstätte *f* tin deposit
Zinnober *m* cinnabar, HgS
Zinnschlich *m* fine (small, dressed) tin
Zinnseife *f* tin placer, stream tin

Zinnstein *m* tin ore (stone), cassiterite, SnO_2
~/fein eingesprengter floran
Zinnstufe *f* lump of tin ore
Zinnwaldit *m* zinnwaldite, $KLiFeAl[(F,OH)_2|AlSi_3O_{10}]$
Zinnwäsche *f* tin buddle
Zinn-Wolfram-Gang *m* cassiterite wolframite vein
Zinnzwitter *m* tin stuff
Zipolin *m* cipolin
Zippeit *m* zippeite, $[6UO_2|3(OH)_2|3SO_4] \cdot 12H_2O$
Zirkelit *m* zirkelite, $(Ca,Ce,Y,Fe)(Ti,Zr,Th)_3O_7$
Zirklerit *m* zirklerite, $9FeCl_2 \cdot 4AlOOH$
Zirkon *m* zircon, $Zr[SiO_4]$
Zirkon[ium] *n* zirconium, Zr
Zirkulation *f* circulation
Zirkulationsdauer *f* circulation time
zirkulieren to circulate
zirkumboreal circumboreal
Zirkumferentor *m* circumferentor [compass]
zirkumpolar circumpolar
Zirrostratus *m* stratocirrus cloud
zirrusartig cirriform
Zirruswolke *f* cirrus cloud
Zitrin *m* citrine, false topaz, topaz quartz *(a semiprecious yellow stone)*
Zittern *n* vibration
Zlichov *n*, **Zlichov-Stufe** *f* Zlichovian [Stage] *(of Lower Devonian)*
Zodiakallicht *n* zodiac[al] light
Zodiakus *m* zodiac
Zoisit *m* zoisite, $Ca_2Al_3[O|OH|SiO_4|Si_2O_7]$
Zölestin *m* celestine, celestite, $SrSO_4$
Zonalität *f* zonality, zoning
~/hydrochemische hydrochemical zoning
zonar zonary
Zonarkristall *m* zoned crystal
Zonarstruktur *f* zoning
Zone *f* zone, area, region, belt; zone *(smallest biostratigraphic unit)*
~/abyssale abyssal zone
~/abyssopelagische abyssopelagic zone
~/bathypelagische bathypelagic zone
~ der maximalen Entwicklung zone of maximum development *(of species)*
~ des Sickerwassers vadose zone
~/diaphoritische diaphoritic zone
~/durch ihren Radioaktivitätsgrad charakterisierte stratigrafische radiozone
~/euphotische euphotic zone
~/geflutete flushed zone
~/gemäßigte temperate zone
~ gleichmäßiger Absenkung zone of regular subsidence
~/hadale hadal zone
~/heiße torrid zone
~/infiltrierte infiltrated zone
~/labile mobile belt
~/lichtlose aphotic zone
~/lithologisch definierte stratigrafische lithozone, lithizone

~/litorale littoral zone *(down to 200 m)*
~/metallogenetische metallogenetic zone
~/metamorphe metamorphic belt
~/moldanubische Moldanubian zone
~/neritische neritic zone
~/nördliche gemäßigte north temperate zone
~/nördliche kalte north frigid zone, Arctic region
~ oberhalb des Grundwasserspiegels gathering zone
~/penninische Penninic zone
~/rhenoherzynische Rheno-Hercynian zone
~/saxothuringische Saxo-Thuringian zone
~/schiefrige reef
~/subtropische subtropic[al] region
~/südliche gemäßigte south temperate zone
~/südliche kalte south frigid zone, Antarctic region
~/taube barren spots
~/Trompetersche Trompeter's zone
~/tropische tropical zone
~/westphalische Westphalian zone
Zonenachse *f* zone axis
Zonenanordnung *f* zonation
Zonenbau *m* zoning *(of crystals)*
Zonenfolge *f* zone succession
zonenförmig zonal, zonated
Zonenfossil *n* zone fossil
Zonengrenze *f* zonal boundary
Zonenkreis *m* zone circle
Zonenschmelzverfahren *n* zone melting
zonenverteilt zoned
Zonenzeit *f* zone time
Zoning *n* zoning
~/inverses (umgekehrtes) reversed zoning
zoogen zoogenous, zoogenic
Zoogeografie *f* zoogeography
zoogeografisch zoogeographic[al]
Zoolith *m* zoolite
Zooplankton *n* zooplankton
Zubringer[fluß] *m* contributary, tributary, feeder
Zubruchbauen *n* caving
zubruchgehen to stope in
Zubußzeche *f* non-paying mine
zuckerkörnig saccharoidal, sugary, sucrosic
zufällig incidental
Zufallsprobe *f* grab sample
Zufallsprobenahme *f* random sampling
Zufluß *m* 1. influx, inflow; direct intake *(to the ground water)*; 2. inflowing stream, affluent, contributary, tributary, feeder
~/dauernder continuous inflow
~/höchster greatest head flow
Zuflußkanal *m* feeding channel
Zuflußmenge *f* rate of flow
Zuflußmesser *m* head meter
zufrieren to freeze over
Zufuhrkanal *m* feeding channel, channelway, feeder
Zug *m* tensile force, pull
Zugang *m* adit

Zugänglichkeit 358

Zugänglichkeit *f* accessibility
zugbeansprucht subjected to tension
Zugbruch *m* tension failure
Zugehen *n* **des Bohrlochs** borehole diameter decreasing
Zugfestigkeit *f* tensile strength
Zugkluft *f* tension joint
Zugklüfte *fpl***/gefiederte** pinnate tension joints
Zugspannung *f* tensile stress
Zugversuch *m* tensile test
Zulauf *m s.* Zufluß 1.
Zumischung *f* 1. admixture, addition, 2. *s.* Zusatzstoff
Zündmaschine *f* blaster, shooting device
zunehmen/an Mächtigkeit to thicken [up]
Zungenbecken *n* tonguelike basin
Zungenbeckensee *m* finger lake, glacial piedmont lake
Zungenbildung *f* fingering
zungenförmig linguiform, linguloid
Zunyit *m* zunyite, $Al_{12}[AlO_4|(OH,F)_{18}Cl|Si_5O_{16}]$
zurücktreten to retreat *(glacier)*
Zurücktreten *n* retreat *(of a glacier)*
zurückweichen to retreat
Zurückweichen *n* retreat
~ der Küste retreat of the coast
Zurückwitterung *f* back weathering
Zurundung *f* roundness
Zurundungsgrad *m* degree of roundness
zusammenbacken, zusammenballen[/sich] to agglomerate
Zusammenballung *f* agglomeration, aggregation, concrement
Zusammenbruch *m* caving-in, falling-in, foundering
~ der Bohrlochwand[ung] caving of the walls of a drill hole
zusammendrückbar compressible
Zusammendrückbarkeit *f* compressibility
~ von Gasen compressibility of gases
zusammendrücken to compress
Zusammendrückung *f* compression
zusammenfallen to cave in
zusammenfließen to coalesce
Zusammenfluß *m* confluence, junction
zusammenfrieren to congeal
zusammengebacken welded
zusammengekittet cemented together *(e.g. rocks)*
zusammengeschwemmt colluvial
zusammengesetzt composite
zusammenkleben to clog
zusammenrollen/sich to coil up *(trilobites)*
Zusammenrücken *n* closing *(plate tectonics)*
Zusammenschub *m* [lateral] compression *(orogeny)*
Zusammensetzen *n* **von Bodengemischen** blending of soils
Zusammensetzung *f* compound, composition
~/chemische chemical composition
~/durchschnittliche granulometrische average grading

~/geochemische geochemical composition
~/granulometrische grain-size composition
Zusammenstellung *f* **von Registrierungen** record section
Zusammenstoß *m* 1. collision *(plate tectonics)*; 2. junction *(of plates)*
zusammenstürzen to cave in
zusammenwachsen 1. to coalesce; 2. to become coossified
Zusammenwachsen *n* coalescence
zusammenziehen/sich to contract
Zusatzdruck *m* additional pressure
Zusatzstoff *m* admixture, addition, additive
Zuschlag *m* flux
Zuschlagerz *n* fluxing ore
Zuschlagkalkstein *m* flux limestone, limestone for flux
Zuschlagstoff *m* aggregate, additament
~/feiner fine aggregate
~/grober coarse aggregate
~/ungesiebter all-in aggregate
Zuschüttung *f* **eines Tals** aggradation of a valley
Zussmanit *m* zussmanite, $KFe_{11}(Mg,Mn)_2[OH|Si_{5,5}Al_{0,5})O_{14}(OH)_4]$
Zustand *m* state
~/ausgeglichener poised state *(of a river without erosion or sedimentation)*
~/bergfeuchter fresh condition
~/geschmolzener state of fusion
~/kristalliner crystalline state
~/metastabiler metastable state
Zustandsdiagramm *n* equilibrium (constitution, phase) diagram, diagram of state
Zustandsfeld *n* equilibrium region
Zustandsgleichung *f* **der idealen Gase** ideal gas law
~ der Wasserströmung equilibrium equation of water flow
Zustandsgrenzen *fpl***/Atterbergsche** Atterberg (consistency) limits
Zustrom *m*, **Zuströmung** *f* influx, inflow, afflux
Zutageliegen *n* outburst
Zutageliegendes *n* [out]crop, outbreak
Zutageziehen *n* **[verlorener Geräte]** recovery
Zutritt *m* adit
Zuverlässigkeit *f* **der Probenahme** reliability of sampling, sampling reliability
Zuwachs *m* accretion
Zuwachsen *n* filling by plant growth
Zuwachslinie *f* growth line
Zwanzigeck *n* eiconagon
zwanzigflächig icosahedral
Zwanzigflächner *m* icosahedron
zweiachsig biaxial
~/optisch optically biaxial
zweiatomig diatomic, biatomic
Zweideutigkeit *f* **magnetischer Aufnahmen** ambiguity of magnetic surveys
Zweiflach *n* dihedron
zweiflächig dihedral

Zweiflächner *m* dihedron
Zweig *m* branch *(of a travel-time curve)*
Zweigbohren *n* multihole drilling
Zweigcañon *m* tributary canyon
Zweiglimmergranit *m* two-mica granite
Zwei-Glocken-Tauchsystem *n* two-bell diving system
Zweiphasenströmung *f* biphase (two-phase) flow
Zweischaler *m* bivalve [mollusk]
zweispitzig bicuspid
Zwei-Stationen-Vergleichsmethode *f* remote reference method
Zweistoffsystem *n* binary system
Zweistrangfördersonde *f* two-string well
Zweitgewinnung *f* secondary exploitation
zweiwertig divalent, bivalent
Zweiwertigkeit *f* divalence, bivalence
zweiwinklig digonal
zweizählig binary, twofold *(symmetry axis)*
Zwergentwicklung *f* dwarfed development
Zwergfauna *f* dwarfed fauna
Zwergform *f* dwarfed form
Zwergpodsol *m*/**nördlicher** northern dwarf podzol
Zwergstern *m* dwarf star
Zwergstrauchsteppe *f* steppe covered with low bushes
Zwergwuchs *m* nanism, dwarfism *(palaeontology)*
Zwickelporosität *f* interparticle porosity
Zwiebelstruktur *f* concentric[al] jointing
Zwielicht *n* twilight
Zwieselit *m* zwieselite, $(Fe,Mn)_2[F|PO_4]$
Zwilling *m* twin *(crystal)*
Zwillingsachse *f* twin-axis
Zwillingsarten *fpl* sibling species
Zwillingsbildung *f* twinning, twin formation
~/polysynthetische polysynthetic twinning
Zwillingsbohrung *f* twin hole
Zwillingsdoline *f* twin doline
Zwillingsebene *f*, **Zwillingsfläche** *f* twinning plane, twin-plane
Zwillingsfördersonde *f* dual-zone well
Zwillingsgesetz *n* twinning law
Zwillingsgleitung *f* twin gliding
Zwillingsgrenze *f* twin boundary
Zwillingskrater *m* twin crater
Zwillingskristall *m* twin (compound, geminate) crystal, macle, hemitrope *(s.a. Zwilling)*
Zwillingslamellen *fpl* twinning lamellae
Zwillingslamellierung *f* lamellar twinning [structure]
Zwillingsnaht *f* suture of the twin plane
Zwillingsrakete *f* tandem rocket
Zwillingsstellung *f* twinning position
Zwillingsstern *m* twin star
Zwillingsstreifung *f* twin striation
zwischenblättrig intrafoliaceous *(palaeobotany)*
Zwischenbohrloch *n* intermediate borehole

Zwischeneiszeit *f* interglacial episode (interval), interval of deglaciation
zwischeneiszeitlich interglacial
Zwischenelement *n* intermediate element
Zwischenfelderkundung *f* hole-to-hole measurement
Zwischenfläche *f* interface
Zwischenform *f* intermediate (intergrading, linking) form *(palaeontology)*
Zwischengebirge *n* intermediate massif, intermountain, intermont[ane] area, median mass
zwischengelagert interstratified
zwischengeschichtet interbedded, interstratified
Zwischengitteratom *n* interstitial [atom]
Zwischengittermechanismus *m* interstitial mechanism
Zwischengitterplatz *m* interstice
Zwischengitterwanderung *f* interstitial migration
Zwischenglied *n* connecting link *(palaeontology)*
Zwischenherd *m* intermediate focus
Zwischenklemmasse *f* interstitial material, mesostasis
Zwischenkornspannung *f* intergranular stress
zwischenkristallin intercrystalline
Zwischenlage *f* interlayer, intercalary (interstratified) bed, parting, intercalation
~/dünne break
~/gasführende gas streak
~/taube dirt bed
~/undurchlässige impervious break
zwischenlagern to intercalate
~/schichtenweise to interlay
Zwischenlagerung *f* interbedding, interstratification, intercalation
~/linsenförmige interlensing
Zwischenmasse *f* matrix
Zwischenmassiv *n* intermediate massif, median mass
Zwischenmaterial *n* interstitial material
Zwischenmeßpunkt *m* interpolation (fill-in) station
Zwischenmittel *n* interbed, intercalated bed, intercalation, cleave, intermediate medium; parting, dirt band *(in coal)*; fillings *(in joints)*; intermediate rock *(between two seams)*
~/erdiges drift band *(in coal)*
~ im Flöz want
~ im unteren Teil eines mächtigen Flözes underply
Zwischenniveau *n* interface level
zwischenozeanisch interoceanic
Zwischenprodukte *npl* middlings, middling particles
Zwischenpumpstation *f* booster station
Zwischenraum *m* interspace, interstice
~/durchgehender continuous interstice
~/nichtdurchgehender discontinuous interstice

Zwischenriffbecken

Zwischenriffbecken *n* interreef (off-reef, intershoal) basin
Zwischenrohrtour *f* intermediate casing string
zwischenschalten to intercalate, to interstratify, to interpose
Zwischenschaltung *f s.* Zwischenlagerung
Zwischenschicht *f* interbed, interlayer, intermediate layer
zwischenschichten to interstratify
Zwischenschichtung *f* interstratification
Zwischenschichtwasser *n* middle (interlayer) water
Zwischensohle *f* sublevel
Zwischensonde *f* intermediate (infilling) well
Zwischenstreifen *m* zwischen **Haft- und Grundwasser** intermediate belt
Zwischenstrom *m* intermediate current
Zwischenstromland *n* interstream area, interfluve
Zwischensubstanz *f* cement
~/verkittende cementing material
Zwischenverwerfungen *fpl/***wechselsinnige** faults with balance of throw
Zwischenwand *f* partition wall

Zwischenzustand *m/***bindungsmäßiger** intermediate state of bonding
Zwölfeck *n* dodecagon
Zwölfflächner *m* dodecahedron
Zyklentheorie *f* cycle theory
zykloidschuppig cycloid
Zyklon *m* cyclone
Zyklone *f* cyclone
Zyklopenmauerwerk *n* cyclopic wall
Zyklosilikat *n* cyclosilicate
Zyklothem *n* cyclothem
Zyklus *m/***elfjähriger** 11-year cycle *(of sunspot activity)*
~/geochemischer geochemical cycle
~/geotektonischer geotectonical cycle
~/litoraler shore-line cycle
~/magmatischer magmatic cycle
~/mariner shore-line cycle
~/orogener orogenic cycle
~/tektonischer tectonic cycle
~/thermischer thermic cycle
~/unterbrochener interrupted cycle
~/warmzeitlicher interglacial cycle
Zylinderprojektion *f* cylindrical projection

Jutta Vesper
Diplom-Dolmetscherin AIIC
Haffstrasse 12
5300 Bonn 3

TECHNIK-WÖRTERBUCH
Geowissenschaften
Englisch-Deutsch

TECHNIK-WÖRTERBUCH

Geowissenschaften

Englisch-Deutsch

Herausgegeben von
Prof. Dr. rer. nat. Adolf Watznauer

Mit etwa 40 000 Wortstellen

3., bearbeitete Auflage

VEB VERLAG TECHNIK BERLIN

AUTOREN
Prof. Dr. *Werner Arnold;* Prof. Dr. *Horst Bachmann;* Dr. *Walter Bachmann;* Prof. Dr. *Hans-Jürgen Behr;* Ing. *Gerhard Bochmann;* Dr. *Peter Bormann;* Prof. Dr. *Klaus Dörter;* Prof. Dr. sc. *Klaus Fröhlich;* Dr. *G. Haas;* Dr. *Roland Hähne;* Prof. Dr. *Christian Hänsel;* Dr. *Christian Knothe;* Dr. sc. techn. *Hans-Jürgen Kretzschmar;* Dr. *Eberhard Künstner;* Dr. sc. *Manfred Kurze;* Dr. *Gerhard Mathé;* Prof. Dr. *Rudolf Meinhold;* Doz. Dr. *Christian Oelsner;* Dipl.-Ing. *Yadlapalli Venkateswara Rao;* Dr. sc. *Winfried Rasemann;* Geol.-Ing. *Wolfgang Reichel;* Prof. Dr. *Hans-Jürgen Rösler;* Dr. *Jörg Schneider;* Dr. *Karl-Armin Tröger;* Dr. *Richard Wäsch*

GUTACHTER
Prof. Dr. *Eberhard Kautzsch,* Dr. *Hans Prescher,* Dr. *Helmut Schmidt*

Eingetragene (registrierte) Warenzeichen sowie Gebrauchsmuster und Patente sind in diesem Wörterbuch nicht ausdrücklich gekennzeichnet. Daraus kann nicht geschlossen werden, daß die betreffenden Bezeichnungen frei sind oder frei verwendet werden können.

Geowissenschaften : engl.-dt. ; mit etwa 40 000 Wortstellen / hrsg. von Adolf Watznauer. – 3., bearb.
Auflage – Berlin : Verl. Technik, 1987. – 388 S.
NE: Watznauer, Adolf [Hrsg.]

ISBN 3-341-00323-1

3., bearbeitete Auflage
© VEB Verlag Technik, Berlin, 1987
Lizenz 201 · 370/104/87
Printed in the German Democratic Republic
Gesamtherstellung: Grafischer Großbetrieb Völkerfreundschaft Dresden
Lektor: Dipl. phil. *Gisela Rütz*
Schutzumschlag: *Kurt Beckert*
LSV 1407 · VT 4/4350-3
Bestellnummer: 553 779 2
03200

Vorwort zur dritten Auflage

Die günstige Aufnahme des Wörterbuchs für den Sektor Geowissenschaften in den angesprochenen Fachdisziplinen haben Verlag und Herausgeber bewogen, eine 3., bearbeitete Auflage vorzulegen.
Die Zahl der Wörter wurde um etwa 2000 auf 40000 erhöht. Die Erweiterung betrifft vor allem jene Wissenschaftsbereiche, deren Einfluß auf die Geowissenschaften nicht mehr übergangen werden kann. An einer Reihe von Wortstellen wurden darüber hinaus Korrekturen oder Präzisierungen vorgenommen.
Die Begriffe für die Erweiterungen und Ergänzungen wurden wie bisher unmittelbar dem Schrifttum entnommen. Dem in einzelnen Fällen von der üblichen Form abweichenden Wortgebrauch durch bedeutende Autoren wurde dabei in manchen Fällen Rechnung getragen. Dies entspricht dem Charakter des Buches als dem eines „Wörter"-Buches. Eine Tendenz zur Entwicklung eines Thesaurus bzw. Begriffslexikons wurde damit nicht angestrebt. Ein solches Vorhaben ist für das Gesamtgebiet der Geowissenschaften undurchführbar.
Der Herausgeber dankt allen Fachkollegen, deren unmittelbare Mitarbeit bzw. mittelbare Hinweise zur Fertigstellung dieser Auflage wesentlich beigetragen haben. Dem Verlag gebührt vollste Anerkennung und Dank für die vertrauensvolle Zusammenarbeit.
Sachdienliche Hinweise für die weitere Verbesserung des Buches sollten wie bisher an den VEB Verlag Technik, Oranienburger Str. 13/4, Berlin, DDR – 1020 gegeben werden.

Adolf Watznauer

Vorwort zur zweiten Auflage

In der vorliegenden zweiten Auflage ist der Wortschatz der ersten Auflage im wesentlichen erhalten geblieben. Die Entwicklung einzelner Untergebiete sowie die sich gegenwärtig vollziehende starke Verzahnung der Geowissenschaften mit anderen wissenschaftlichen und technischen Fachdisziplinen erforderten eine Überarbeitung und Erweiterung des erfaßten Wortschatzes. Es wurden etwa 3800 neue Stichwörter aufgenommen. Gleichzeitig wurden bei der Überarbeitung der vorhandenen Begriffe veraltete Termini herausgenommen, wobei jedoch in jenen Fällen, wo der alte Begriff noch gebräuchlich ist bzw. zum Verständnis der älteren Literatur als notwendig erscheint, dieser beibehalten wurde.
In einigen Spezialfächern sind die nomenklatorischen Diskussionen noch im Fluß. Dies betrifft vor allem die kohlenpetrografischen Begriffe. Hier wurde – insbesondere bei den Maceralen und Mikrolithotypen der Kohlen – auf das „Internationale Lexikon für Kohlenpetrologie" zurückgegriffen. Dabei wurden überwiegend die im System Stopes-Heerlen definierten Begriffe berücksichtigt. Die Schreibweise der stratigrafischen Einheiten im englischsprachigen Text bezieht sich auf die Vorschläge im „International Stratigraphic Guide (a Guide to Stratigraphic Classification, Terminology and Procedure)".
Der zweiten Auflage wurden zwei Tabellen beigefügt. Die stratigrafische Tabelle erleichtert dem Benutzer des Buches die Einordnung eines diesbezüglichen Terminus in das geologische Zeitschema. Die seismische Intensitätsskala, die Bezeichnungen der Umgangssprache verwendet, vermeidet die Hereinnahme solcher Begriffe in den Textteil bzw. deren umständliche begriffliche Definition als seismische Parameter. Von der Beigabe einer mineralogischen Tabelle wurde abgesehen, da das Mineral zweifellos im Stichwortverzeichnis unter seinem Namen gesucht wird, dagegen wurde die Schreibung des Mineralchemismus einheitlich gestaltet.
Die Ergänzungen und Veränderungen wären ohne die tätige Mithilfe zahlreicher Fachkollegen nicht möglich gewesen. Ihnen allen sei herzlichst für ihre mühevolle Arbeit gedankt, den Herren Dr. Kurze, Dr. Mathé und Dr. Schneider auch für ihre Hilfe beim Korrekturlesen.
Dank gebührt auch dem VEB Verlag Technik für sein verständnisvolles Eingehen auf die Wünsche des Herausgebers und der Bearbeiter.

Adolf Watznauer

Vorwort zur ersten Auflage

Der Verlag legt mit diesem Band ein englisch-deutsches Fachwörterbuch für den Bereich der Geowissenschaften vor, das mit etwa 35 000 englischen Termini und den dazugehörigen deutschen Äquivalenten zu den umfangreichsten Terminologiesammlungen dieses Fachgebietes gehört.
Ein Fachwörterbuch soll den Übersetzer und Dokumentalisten bei der Übersetzung bzw. Auswertung fremdsprachiger Fachliteratur unterstützen und dem Wissenschaftler helfen, die Ergebnisse seiner Forschungen auf Tagungen und Kongressen in Form und Inhalt adäquat darzustellen.
Um diese Ziele zu erreichen, wurden ein Fachmann für Geowissenschaften und ein Fachphilologe für die Erarbeitung des Wortschatzes gewonnen. So konnten eine sachgemäße und umfassende Wortauswahl und sprachliche Genauigkeit in gleicher Weise berücksichtigt werden. Beiden Mitarbeitern sei an dieser Stelle für ihre Mühe herzlichst gedankt.
In den Fällen, in denen englische Fachbegriffe nicht durch einen exakten und üblichen deutschen Terminus wiedergegeben werden konnten oder die Möglichkeit einer Doppeldeutigkeit im deutschen Ausdruck bestand, wurden Umschreibungen und kurze Erklärungen gegeben. Die Auswahl jener Fälle ist zweifellos subjektiv, und die Gefahr, den Begriffsbestimmungen zu großen Raum zu geben, ist groß. Durch einen streng angelegten Maßstab hoffen die Autoren und der Herausgeber, dieser Tendenz entgegengewirkt zu haben.
Der Wortschatz wurde zum größten Teil der Fachliteratur entnommen. Starke Betonung erfuhr die praktische Seite der Geowissenschaften. Hier gingen die Autoren oft weit in den Bereich der technischen Praxis hinein. Nachbarwissenschaften, wie physikalische Chemie, Geochemie, Geophysik, Paläontologie, Gebirgsmechanik u. a. wurden nur in dem Umfange berücksichtigt, wie es zum Verständnis der geowissenschaftlichen Kerngebiete erforderlich ist. Stärker betont wurden Mineralogie, Petrografie und Lagerstättenlehre. Die Mineralformeln sind hauptsächlich dem Standardwerk von H. Strunz entnommen worden. Die Gesteinsnamen lehnen sich an die bewährten Lehrbücher von H. Rosenbusch an. Beim Wortschatz der Lagerstättenlehre wurde die Auswahl so getroffen, daß praktische Gesichtspunkte im Vordergrund stehen. Außer der wissenschaftlichen Terminologie sind auch Handelsnamen von Rohstoffen, Vulgärbezeichnungen von Mineralen und Gesteinen, Slangausdrücke u. ä. berücksichtigt. Der Entwicklungstendenz der Geologie entsprechend fanden auch auf die Geologie bezogene astronomische und astrophysikalische Termini und solche der Raumfahrt sowie der Wortschatz der sich stürmisch entwickelnden Lithologie und marinen Geologie Aufnahme in das Wörterbuch. Hierbei wurde allerdings nur der schon gefestigte Sprachgebrauch erfaßt. Es besteht die Absicht, diese beiden Sparten bei einer der späteren Auflagen stark auszubauen. Als zweckmäßig erwies es sich, die in den Geowissenschaften gebräuchlichen Abkürzungen zu erfassen. Hier ist eine Vollständigkeit weder angestrebt noch zu erreichen.
Nachdem im Akademie-Verlag das „Wörterbuch der Geowissenschaften" von H. J. Teschke in der russisch-deutschen und deutsch-russischen Sprachrichtung erschienen ist, fehlte ein ähnlicher Titel für die englisch-deutsche und deutsch-englische Sprachrichtung, und das um so mehr, als das Englische als Publikations- und Kongreßsprache in den Geowissenschaften eine große Rolle spielt. Zu dem vorliegenden englisch-deutschen Band wird voraussichtlich 1973 der deutsch-englische Band erscheinen.
Hinweise, die zur Verbesserung weiterer Auflagen beitragen können, sind an den Verlag zu richten.

Adolf Watznauer

Benutzungshinweise

1. Alphabetische Ordnung

Die Stichwörter sind alphabetisch geordnet. Zusammengesetzte Begriffe stehen unter dem ersten Wort und sind dort zu einem „Nest" zusammengefaßt. Für das Stichwort, bzw. Nestwort, ist innerhalb des Nestes eine Tilde gesetzt.
Haben Verb, Adjektiv und Substantiv die gleiche Form, so stehen sie in der Regel auch in dieser Reihenfolge. Mit dem Verb gebildete Begriffe bilden ein eigenes Nest, mit Adjektiv oder Substantiv gebildete Begriffe stehen zusammen unter dem Substantiv. Wenn ein Wort klein und groß geschrieben werden kann, steht zuerst das kleingeschriebene, dann das großgeschriebene (wobei sich jeweils das Nest anschließt).
Zusammengesetzte Begriffe, die mit angelsächsischem Genitiv gebildet werden, bilden ein eigenes Nest, wobei das 's als zum Wort gehörig alphabetisch mitgezählt wird.

earth	lower/to	wave
~ anchor	~ the water table	~-built terrace
~ load	lower aquifer	~-cut
~ wax	~ bed	~ ripple marks
earth...	~ block	~-washed
earthly	~ water	~-worn
earthmoving	~ yield point	waved suture
earthquake	Lower Cambrian	wavelike
earth's	~ Carboniferous	wavellite
~ attraction	~ Chalk	waves of condensation
~ surface	~ Triassic	waviness

Anmerkung

Eine große Anzahl von Begriffen kann im Englischen zusammen- oder auseinandergeschrieben werden. Der Gebrauch des Kopplungsbindestrichs bei Auseinanderschreibung schwankt ebenfalls. Der Benutzer sollte, wenn er einen Begriff vermißt, daher bei der anderen Schreibungsmöglichkeit nachsehen, da Verweise nicht in allen Fällen eingefügt wurden.

2. Bedeutung der Zeichen und Abkürzungen

/   gibt die Umstellung in der Wortfolge an:
       abandon/to = to abandon
       mineralized/well = well mineralized

( )   Die in ( ) stehenden Wörter können für das unmittelbar vorhergehende Wort eingesetzt werden:
       mocha pebble (stone) = mocha pebble *oder* mocha stone
       verschlepptes (eingespültes, umgelagertes) Fossil = verschlepptes Fossil *oder* eingespültes Fossil *oder* umgelagertes Fossil

[ ]   In [ ] stehende Wörter oder Wortteile können entfallen, ohne daß sich der Bedeutungsinhalt ändert:
       [im Flußbett] ablagern = ablagern *oder* im Flußbett ablagern
       [ab]bauwürdig = bauwürdig *oder* abbauwürdig
       Agnotozoic [Period] = Agnotozoic *oder* Agnotozoic Period
       geologic[al] = geologic *oder* geological

( )	kursive Klammern enthalten Erklärungen
=	verbindet Abkürzung und Klartext
s.	siehe/see verweist auf einen anderen Begriff mit gleicher Bedeutung. Wird auf einen Begriff im gleichen Nest verwiesen, so wird das erste Wort, wie im Nest üblich, abgekürzt.
s.a.	siehe auch/see also gibt einen Hinweis auf weitere Übersetzungsmöglichkeiten oder bei zusammengesetzten Begriffen darauf, daß die gesuchte Kombination unter dem Begriff, auf den verwiesen wird, nachzuschlagen ist.
Am	Amerikanismus/Americanism
sl	Slang/slang

Anmerkung

Ausgenommen sind die in den mineralogischen Formeln auftretenden ( ) und [ ] Klammern.

3. Allgemeine Hinweise

In der Regel wurde bei unterschiedlicher englischer und amerikanischer Schreibung die englische Version gewählt. Wenn allerdings Fachbegriffe aus der amerikanischen Literatur stammen, wurde auch die dort verwendete Schreibung übernommen, ohne daß die Begriffe durch *(Am)* gekennzeichnet wurden.

Kursiv gesetzt sind erklärende Hinweise (sie stehen in Klammern) und Umschreibungen des Bedeutungsinhalts von englischen Stichwörtern, für die keine einfache Entsprechung gefunden wurde.

Bedeutungsunterschiede werden wie folgt angegeben:

,	trennt inhaltsgleiche Begriffe
;	trennt Bedeutungsvarianten
1.;2.	trennt Homonyme oder stark voneinander abweichende Bedeutungsvarianten

A

a axis a-Achse *f (mineralogische und tektonische Koordinate)*
a-direction a-Richtung *f*, Richtung *f* des tektonischen Transports
A-horizon A-Horizont *m*, Auslaugungshorizont *m*, oberer Bodenhorizont *m*
Ao-horizon Humusteil des A-Horizonts im Bodenprofil
Aoo-horizon höchster Teil des A-Horizonts im Bodenprofil mit unzersetztem Pflanzenmaterial
a-lineation a-Lineation *f*, Rillung *f*, Harnischriefung *f*
aa field Spratzlavafeld *n*, Schlackenlavafeld *f*, Spritzlavafeld *n*
aa-lava Spratzlava *f*, Schlackenlava *f*, Spritzlava *f*
Aalenian [Stage] Aalen[ium] *n (Stufe des unteren Doggers)*
aasar s. esker
Aasby diabase Aasbydiabas *m (Olivindiorit)*
ab-plane ab-Ebene *f (Gefügeebene, in der die tektonische a- und b-Achse liegen)*
abacus Profilmaßstab *m*
abandon/to auflassen; einstellen; stillegen
~ **a mine** eine Grube auflassen (aufgeben, stillegen)
~ **a well** eine Bohrung aufgeben (einstellen)
~ **at a depth of** in einer Teufe von ... einstellen
abandoned channel Altwasser *n*, toter Arm *m*, alter Flußlauf *m*
~ **cliff** Ruhekliff *n*
~ **gas mill** verlassene Gasfundstelle *f*
~ **lands** verlassenes Gelände *n*
~ **loop (meander)** verlassener Mäander *m*
~ **river bed** verlassenes Flußbett *n*
~ **river course** Altarm *m*
~ **stream channel** s. ~ channel
~ **strip mine** abgeworfener Tagebau *m*
~ **support** verlorener Ausbau *m*
~ **well** verlassene (eingestellte) Bohrung *f*
~ **workings** Alter Mann *m*, verlassene (aufgegebene) Baue *mpl*
abbreviated verkürzt *(z.B. Entwicklung)*
~ **record** lückenhafte Schichtenfolge *f*
aberrant mass wurzellose Masse *f (Tektonik)*
~ **type** abweichende Form *f*
aberration Aberration *f*, Abweichung *f*
~ **of the magnetic needle** Abweichung *f* der Magnetnadel, magnetische Mißweisung *f*
abioglyph Abioglyphe *f (Hieroglyphe anorganischen Ursprungs)*
ablation Ablation *f*, Abhebung *f*
~ **area** Ablationsgebiet *n*, Ablationsfläche *f (eines Gletschers)*
~ **cone** Gletschertisch *m (Ablationsform)*
~ **form** Ablationsform *f*
~ **funnel** Gletscherkanal *m*
~ **moraine** Rückenmoräne *f*

ablykite Ablykit *m (halloysitähnliches Tonmineral)*
abnormal abnormal; abnorm, anormal
~ **contact** mechanischer Kontakt *m (bei einer Verwerfung)*
abnormality Abnormalität *f*, Abnormität *f*
aboral aboral
aboriginal home Urheimat *f*
~ **man** Urmensch *m*
aborted verkümmert
abortive unvollkommen entwickelt
~ **volcano** Vulkanembryo *m*
above critical überkritisch
~ **ground** oberirdisch, über Tage
~ **sea level** über dem Meeresspiegel
abra Gangspalte *f*, Kluft *f*
abradant Schleifmittel *n*
abrade/to abschleifen, abtragen, abradieren, abscheuern
abraded by ice eisgeschrammt
abrader Schleifmittel *n*
abrasion Abschleifung *f*, Abtragung *f*, Abrasion *f*, Abscheuern *n*
~ **coast (embayment)** Abtragungsküste *f*
~ **of briquette** Brikettabrieb *m*
~ **pH** Abrasions-pH-Wert *m*
~ **plain** Abrasionsebene *f*, Brandungsebene *f*
~ **platform** Abrasionsplattform *f*
~ **resistance** Verschleißwiderstand *m*
~ **strength** Abriebfestigkeit *f*
abrasive Schleifmittel *n*; Gebläsesand *m*, Putzsand *m*, Blassand *m*, Gebläsekies *m*
~ **action** abscheuernde Wirkung *f*, Schleifwirkung *f*
~ **diamond** Schleifdiamant *m*
~ **engineering practice** Schleif- und Poliertechnik *f*
~ **garnet** Schleifgranat *m*
~ **hardness** Ritzhärte *f*, Schmirgelhärte *f*
~ **hardness test** Ritzhärteprüfung *f*
~ **rock** abreibendes Gestein *n*
~ **sand** Schmirgelsand *m*
abrasiveness Abrasivität *f*
abraum [salts] Abraumsalze *npl*, KMg-Salze *npl*
abridged spectrophotometry grobe Spektralfotometrie *f*
abrupt steil, abschüssig
absarokite Absarokit *m (basisches Ergußgestein)*
absence of bedding Schichtungslosigkeit *f*
absolute age absolutes Alter *n*
~ **altimeter** elektrodynamischer Höhenmesser *m*
~ **altitude** absolute Höhe *f*, Meereshöhe *f*
~ **chronology** absolute Zeitrechnung (Zeitbestimmung, Zeitmessung) *f*
~ **humidity** absolute Feuchtigkeit *f*
~ **permeability** absolute Permeabilität *f*
~ **pressure** absoluter Druck *m*
~ **rest precipitation tank** Absetzbecken *n* für aussetzenden Betrieb, Absetzbecken *n* mit ruhendem Abwasser

absolute

~ time absolute Zeit f *(durch radiogene Altersbestimmung festgelegt)*
~ viscosity dynamische Viskosität (Zähflüssigkeit) f
absolutely horizontal totsöhlig
absorb/to absorbieren
absorbability Absorbierbarkeit f, Aufsaugbarkeit f
absorbed water Absorptionswasser n
absorbency Absorptionsfähigkeit f, Absorptionsvermögen n, Aufnahmefähigkeit f
absorbent Absorptionsmittel n
~ shale Saugschiefer m
absorber Absorptionsturm m *(für Erdöl)*
absorbing power Absorptionsfähigkeit f
~ well Versickerungsbrunnen m
absorptance Absorptionsvermögen n, Absorptionsfähigkeit f
absorption Absorption f
~ basin Tosbecken n
~ of neutrons Neutronenabsorption f
~ plant Absorptionsanlage f *(für Erdöl)*
~ rate Spülungsverlust m
~ spectrum Absorptionsspektrum n
absorptive capacity for water Wasseraufnahmevermögen n, Wasseraufsaugefähigkeit f
~ height Ansaughöhe f
absorptivity Absorptionsfähigkeit f, Absorptionsvermögen n, Aufnahmefähigkeit f
abstract time s. absolute time
abstraction Entziehung f, Anzapfung f *(z.B. Bohrung)*
Abukuma type Abukuma-Typ m *(Metamorphose)*
~-type metamorphism metamorphe Faziesserie f vom Abukuma-Typ *(temperaturbetonte Regionalmetamorphose)*
abundance Abundanz f, Häufigkeit f
~ anomalies Häufigkeitsanomalien fpl
~ of forests Waldreichtum m
~ of seams Flözreichtum m
~ ratio Häufigkeitsverhältnis n, Isotopen[häufigkeits]verhältnis n; Clarke-Wert m
abundant in fossils fossilreich
~ in water wasserreich
~ rainfall reiche Niederschläge mpl
~ vitrain gebänderte Kohle f *(mit 30 bis 60% Vitrit)*
~ with rain regenreich
abut/to stumpf aneinanderfügen
~ against abstoßen, absetzen *(eine Schicht)*
abutment Landpfeiler m, Widerlager n
~ pressure Kämpferdruck m
~ toe wall luftseitige Fußbefestigung f *(eines Damms)*
~ zone Kämpferdruckzone f
abysm Abgrund m, Tiefe f
abysmal s. abyssal
abyss Abgrund m, Schlund m
abyssal abyssisch, abyssal, bathyal, abgründig
~ activity Tiefenintrusionen fpl
~ area abyssische Region f

10

~ deposit Tiefseeablagerung f, Tiefseesediment n, bathyale Ablagerung f
~ depths Tiefsee f
~ floor Tiefseeboden m
~ gaps Tiefseerinnen fpl
~ hills Tiefseehügel mpl
~ magma Tiefenmagma n
~ plain Tiefsee-Ebene f
~ region abyssische Region f, Abyssalregion f (s.a. ~ zone)
~ rise Tiefseeschwelle f
~ rock Tiefengestein n
~ sea Tiefsee f
~ zone abyssale Zone f, Tiefenregion f, Abyssal n (s.a. ~ region)
Abyssinian pump Abessinierpumpe f
~ well Abessinierbrunnen m
abyssolith Batholith m
abyssopelagic district abysso-pelagische Zone f
ac-girdle ac-Gürtel m
ac-joint ac-Kluft f, Reißfuge f
ac-plane ac-Ebene f, Gefügeebene f senkrecht zur b-Achse
Acadian [Stage] s. Albertan
Acado-Baltic Province Akado-Baltische Provinz f *(Paläobiogeografie, Unterkambrium)*
acanthite Akanthit m, Argentit m, Silberglanz m, Ag_2S
acaustobiolith Akaustobiolith m *(nicht brennbares organisches Sedimentgestein)*
accelerating agent Abbindebeschleuniger m
acceleration due to gravity Erdbeschleunigung f, Fallbeschleunigung f, Schwerebeschleunigung f
~ of the tides Gezeitenverfrühung f
accelerator Abbindebeschleuniger m
~ mass spectrometry Beschleunigermassenspektrometrie f
accelerometer Beschleunigungsmesser m
acceptance angle Einfangwinkel m
~ area Stabilitätsfläche f
access gallery Zugangsstollen m
~ of air Luftzutritt m
accessibility Zugänglichkeit f
accessories 1. Zubehör n *(z.B. einer Bohrung)*; 2. Nebenanlagen fpl *(über Tage)*; 3. s. accessory mineral
accessory akzessorisch
accessory s. ~ mineral
~ ash resurgente Asche f, Lavaasche f
~ constituent Nebengemengteil m
~ ejecta resurgent-authigene Auswürflinge mpl
~ element Spurenelement n
~ mineral akzessorisches Mineral n, Nebenmineral n, Begleitmineral n, Übergemengteil m
accidental block Vulkanauswürfling m *(aus dem nicht vulkanischen Untergrund)*
~ discharges Auswürflinge mpl
~ ejecta allothigene Auswürflinge mpl

~ **inclusion** s. xenolith
~ **products** Auswürflinge mpl
accidentals Fremdgesteinseinschlüsse mpl in Vulkaniten (Autolithe und Xenolithe)
acclivity ansteigender Hang m, Böschung f, Böschungsanstieg m, Gefälle n, Neigung f
acclivous abschüssig
accompanying bed Begleitflöz n
~ **mineral** Nebenmineral n, Begleitmineral n
accordant gleichförmig, konkordant
~ **junction** gleichsohlige Mündung f
~ **summit level** Gipfelflur f
~ **summits** gleichhohe Gipfel mpl, Gipfelflur f
~ **unconformity** unterbrochene gleichförmige Auflagerung f
accordion fold s. chevron fold, zigzag fold
accretic s. clastic
accreting bank anlandendes Ufer n; verlandetes Ufer
~ **plate margins** divergierende (krustenproduzierende) Plattengrenzen fpl
accretion 1. Aufschüttung f, Schüttung f, Anhäufung f; 2. Anlandung f, Ablagerung f, Anschwemmung f, Wachstumsanlagerung f; Aufspülung f durch Sedimentanlagerung; 3. Vorschieben n, Vorrücken n
~ **along a bank** Anlandung f an einem Ufer
~ **coast** Anschwemmungsküste f
~ **of crystals** Wachsen n von Kristallen
~ **ripples** flache Rippeln fpl mit Anlagerungs- Schrägschichtungsblättern
~ **theory** Einfanghypothese f
~ **through alluvium** Auflandung f, Kolmation f, Anschwemmung f, Aufschwemmung f, Kolmatierung f
~ **vein** zusammengesetzter Gang m
accretional heating Wachstumserwärmung f (Erwärmung durch das Wachsen planetarer Körper)
accretionary angelagert (durch Überwachsen von Körnern oder Korngerüsten)
~ **lapilli** vulkanische Pisolithe mpl, fossile Regentropfen mpl
~ **lava balls** Fließballungen fpl in Lavaströmen
~ **limestone** organogener Kalk m in situ
accumulate/to sich anhäufen, anwachsen, sich vermehren
accumulation Anhäufung f, Ansammlung f, Anreicherung f
~ **of debris** Schuttablagerung f
~ **of petroleum** Erdölanreicherung f
~ **of stress** Spannungsanreicherung f
~ **of talus** Schutthalde f
~ **zone** Anreicherungszone f (von mineralisiertem Wasser)
accumulative plant Zeigerpflanze f
accuracy Genauigkeit f (einer Analyse)
~ **of map** Kartengenauigkeit f
~ **of measurement** Meßgenauigkeit f
~ **of observation** Genauigkeit f der Beobachtung
accurate scanning Feinortung f

acentrous acentrisch, ohne Wirbelzentrum
acervation Anhäufung f
acetate peel Azetatfilm m; Azetatfolie f
acetic acid Essigsäure f
achondrite Achondrit m
achroite Achroit m (Varietät von Turmalin)
achromatic achromatisch, farblos
~ **quartz fluorite lens** Quarzfluoritachromatlinse f
~ **quartz rock salt lens** Quarzflußspatachromatlinse f
achromatism Achromatismus m, Farblosigkeit f
acicular nadelförmig, nadelig, stengelig, spitz
~ **bismuth** s. aikinite
~ **crystal** nadelförmiger Kristall m
~ **fracture** nadelförmiger Bruch m
~ **habitus** stengeliger Habitus m
aciculate s. acicular
aciculite s. akikinite
acid bottle Säureflasche f (für Neigungsmessungen in Bohrlöchern)
~ **brown forest soil** saurer brauner Waldboden m
~ **clay** saure Bleicherde f
~ **fracturing** Fracverfahren n mit Säurebehandlung, Säurefracung f (Bohrtechnik)
~ **fumarole** saure Fumarole f
~ **gas** Sauergas n
~ **humification** saure Humifizierung f
~ **leaching** saure Laugung f
~ **mine drainage** saure Grubenwässer npl
~-**poor** säurearm
~ **sludge** Säureschlamm m
~ **soil** saurer Boden m
~ **solfatara** saure Solfatare f
~ **spotting around the drilling string** Säurewanne f
~ **treatment of wells** Säurereinigung f von Brunnen
acidic sauer, säurehaltig
~ **rock** saures Gestein n
acidification Versauerung f (des Bodens)
acidifier Säurebildner m
acidity Säuregrad m, Säuregehalt m
~ **of peat** Säuregrad (pH-Wert) m des Torfs
acidizing Säuerung f, Säurebehandlung f (von Erdölbohrungen)
acidulous spring Sauerbrunnen m, Kohlensäuerling m (Mineralquelle)
~ **water** kohlensäurehaltiges Wasser n
acinose krümelig, granuliert (Textur)
acknowledgement of receipt Empfangsanzeige f (z. B. von seismischen Wellen)
aclinal s. aclinic
aclinic söhlig, horizontal, ohne Einfallen
~ **area** Gebiet n mit horizontaler Schichtenlagerung
~ **line** s. magnetic equator
acme-zone biostratigrafische Einheit, gekennzeichnet durch die maximale Häufigkeit einer Art, Gattung bzw. eines anderen Taxons

acmite

acmite Akmit *m*, NaFe[Si$_2$O$_6$]
~-trachýte Ägirintrachyt *m*
acoelous acöl
ACOH = Advisory Committee for Operational Hydrology
acoustic[al] impedance akustische Impedanz *f*, Schallhärte *f*
~ log Geschwindigkeitslog *n*, Akustiklog *n* (Bohrlochmessung)
~ [velocity] logging akustische Bohrlochmessung *f*
~ wave Schallwelle *f*
acre-foot Wassermenge, die auf 1 acre 1 Fuß hoch steht
~-yield gewinnbare Menge eines Bodenschatzes pro acre Fläche
acritical unkritisch
acrobatholithic stage Oberflächenanschnitt *m* eines Batholiten
acromorph Salzdom *m*, Salzhorst *m*, Salzstock *m*, Diapir *m*
acrotomous parallel zur Basis spaltbar
acrozone *s*. range zone
actiniform radialförmig
actinolite Aktinolith *m*, Strahlstein *m*, Ca$_2$(Mg, Fe)$_5$ [(OH, F)Si$_4$O$_{11}$]$_2$
~ schist Aktinolithschiefer *m*
actinometer Aktinometer *n*, Strahlungsmesser *m*
actinometry Aktinometrie *f*, Strahlungsmessung *f*
action at a distance Fernwirkung *f*
~ of ultrasounds Ultraschallwirkung *f*
~ zone *s*. neritic zone
activate/to beleben, aktivieren
activated water aktiviertes Wasser *n*
activating isotope aktivierendes Isotop *n*
activation Aktivierung *f*
~ analysis Aktivierungsanalyse *f*
~ logging Aktivierungslog *n*, Aktivierungsmessung *f*
~ of deposits Aktivierung *f* des Erkundungsaufwands von Lagerstätten
activator Anreger *m*
active aktiv; radioaktiv
~ crater tätiger Krater *m*
~ earth Bleicherde *f*, Bleichton *m*
~ earth pressure aktiver Erddruck *m*
~ fault aktive Verwerfung *f*
~ fill aktive Verfüllung *f (Ichnologie)*
~ glacier Gletscher *m* in Bewegung
~ lateral earth pressure aktiver Erddruck *m*
~ layer Auftauschicht *f (im Permafrost)*
~ occurrence lebende Lagerstätte *f (von Kohlenwasserstoffen)*
~ oil seeps tätige Erdölaustrittsstellen *fpl*
~ product [radio]aktives Zerfallsprodukt *n*
~ sensor aktiver Sensor *m (registriert das Antwortsignal des Untersuchungsobjekts auf die vom Sensor selbst ausgesandte Strahlung)*
~ soil eutropher Boden *m*
~ sonar Ultraschallecholot *n*, Ultrasonarortungssystem *n*

~ state aktives Stadium *n (eines Vulkans)*
~ volcano tätiger Vulkan *m*
~ water drive aktiver Wasserbetrieb *m*
activity Aktivität *f*, Wirksamkeit *f*, Radioaktivität *f*
~ index Aktivitätsindex *m (von Wasserinhaltsstoffen)*
actual age tatsächliches Alter *n*
~ bedding sichtbare Schichtung *f*
~ drilling time reine Bohrzeit *f*
~ level Augenblickspegel *m*
~ porosity Gesamtporosität *f*
~ reserves sichere Vorräte *mpl*
~ thickness wahre Mächtigkeit *f*
~ water table wirklicher Wasserspiegel *m*
actualism Aktualismus *m*
acute spitz
~ bisectrix erste (spitze) Mittellinie *f*
adamantine diamantartig
~ drill Diamantbohrer *m*, Schrotbohrer *m*
~ lustre diamantartiger Glanz *m*, Diamantglanz *m*
adamellite Adamellit *m (Quarzmonzonit)*
adamic earth Röterde *f*
adamine, adamite Adamin *m*, Zn$_2$[OH|AsSO$_4$]
adapter casing flange Rohrreduzierflansch *m*
adaption Anpassung *f (Paläobiologie)*
adaptive convergence adaptive Konvergenz *f*
~ divergence adaptive Divergenz *f*
~ radiation *s*. ~ divergence
~ reduction adaptive Reduktion *f*
adarce *(sl)* Kalkablagerungen von Mineralquellen
addendum to a project Projektnachtrag *m*
additament Zuschlag[stoff] *m*, Beimengung *f*
addition 1. Beimischung *f*, Zumischung *f*; 2. Zusatzstoff *m*
additional load Auflast *f*
additive Zusatzstoff *m*, Beimischung *f*, Zumischung *f*
~ colour process Methode der Erzeugung praktisch aller Farben durch Addition des Lichts der additiven Primärfarben Blau, Grün und Rot in verschiedenen Anteilen
~ colour viewer Multispektralprojektor *m (Gerät zur Betrachtung additiver Farbmischbilder)*
~ metamorphism *s*. pneumatolytic metamorphism
~ soil stabilization Bodenvermörtelung *f* mit Stabilisatorbeigabe
additives Reagenzien *npl*
adductor Adduktor *m*
~ impression Adduktoreindruck *m*
~ muscle Schließmuskel *m*
~ muscle scar Schließmuskelnarbe *f*
adelite Adelit *m*, CaMg[OH|AsO$_4$]
adelomorphic adelomorph
ader wax Erdwachs *n*, Bergwachs *n*, Ozokerit *m*
adhere to/to hängen an
adhesion Adhäsion *f*, Haftfähigkeit *f*, Haftvermögen *n*
~ meter Haftfestigkeitsmesser *m*

~ **of the filter cake** Klebrigkeit *f* der Tonkruste
~ **ripples** Haftrippeln *fpl*
~ **tension** Haftspannung *f*
adhesive film of oil haftender Ölfilm *m*
~ **ground** klebriger Boden *m*
~ **slate** 1. Klebschiefer *m*, Saugschiefer *m*, Polierschiefer *m*; 2. Tripel *m* (dünn geschichtete Kieselgur)
~ **strength** Haftfestigkeit *f* (eines Ankers)
~ **water** Haftwasser *n*
adhesiveness Adhäsionsvermögen *n*
adiabatic adiabatisch
~ **gradient** adiabatischer Gradient *m*
adiagnostic adiagnostisch
adiathermal, adiathermanous, adiathermic, adiathermous wärmeundurchlässig
adinole Adinol *m* (hauptsächlich aus Quarz und Albit bestehendes Gestein)
adipocerite, adipocire *s*. hatchettite
adit 1. Zugang *m*, Zutritt *m*; 2. Stollen *m*, Zugangsstollen *m*
~ **drainage** Wasserlösung *f* durch Stollen
~ **entrance** Stolleneingang *m*, Stollenmundloch *n*
~ **level** Stollensohle *f*
~ **mining** Stollenbergbau *m*
~ **opening** Mundloch *n*, Stollenloch *n*
adjacent angrenzend, anliegend, benachbart
~ **beds** Nachbarschichten *fpl*
~ **rock** Nebengestein *n*, Nachbargestein *n*
~ **sea** Randmeer *n*
~ **structure** benachbartes Bauwerk *n*
~ **timing lines** Zeitmarken *fpl* (Seismik)
adjoin/to 1. [an]grenzen; 2. markscheiden
adjoining concession (property) Nachbarfeld *n*
~ **rock** Nebengestein *n*, Nachbargestein *n*
~ **well** Nachbarschacht *m*
adjusted photobase angepaßte Bildbasis *f*
adjusting Justieren *n*, Einstellen *n*
adjustment Justierung *f*, Einstellung *f*, Einregulierung *f*
admission *s*. admittance
admittance Abfangen *n* (Kristallchemie)
admix/to beimischen
admixture Beimischung *f*, Zumischung *f*, Zusatzstoff *m*
adobe [clay] (Am) 1. kalkhaltiger sandiger Schluff *m*, sandigschluffiger Ton *m*, Alluvialton *m*; 2. Trockenstein *m*, Luftziegel *m*
~ **flat** Schichtflutebene *f*
adont adont (Ostracoden)
~ **hinge** adontes (zahnloses) Schloß *n* (Ostracoden)
Adorfian [Stage] Adorf[ium] *n*, Frasne *n* (Stufe des Oberdevons in Europa)
adret slope sonnenseitiger Hang *m*
adsorb/to adsorbieren
adsorbed gas adsorbiertes Gas *n*
~ **[soil] water** Adsorptionswasser *n*, äußeres Haftwasser *n*
adsorbing capacity Adsorptionsvermögen *n*

adsorption Adsorption *f*
~ **capacity** Adsorptionsvermögen *n*
~ **isotherm** Adsorptionsisotherme *f*
~ **potential** Adsorptionspotential *n*
~ **water** Adsorptionswasser *n*
adsorptive adsorptiv
adular Adular *m* (*s. a.* orthoclase)
adult adult, ausgewachsen, erwachsen, geschlechtsreif
advance a theory/to eine Theorie aufstellen
advance Vortrieb *m*
~ **angle** Fortschrittswinkel *m*
~ **borehole** Vorbohrloch *n*
~ **heading** Richtstollen *m*
~ **of a beach** seewärtige Verlegung *f* der Küstenlinie
~ **of a glacier** Vorwärtsschreiten *n* eines Gletschers, Gletschervorstoß *m*
~ **of the ice** Eisvorstoß *m*
~ **of the sea** Einbrechen *n* des Meeres
~ **per shift** Vortrieb *m* je Schicht
advanced dam (dike) Vordamm *m*
~ **maturity** Spätreife *f*
advancing glacier vorrückender Gletscher *m*
advection Advektion *f*
advent of the sea Einbrechen *n* des Meeres
adventive cone Adventivkegel *m*
~ **lobes** Adventivloben *mpl*
~ **saddles** Adventivsättel *mpl*
~ **vent** Adventivschlot *m*
AE *s*. aeon
Aegean [Substage] Aegean *n* (Unterstufe, Mittlere Trias, Tethys)
aegirine, aegirite *s*. acmite
aenigmatite Aenigmatit *m*, $Na_4Fe_{10}Ti_2[O_4|(Si_2O_6)_6]$
aeolation Winderosion *f*
aeolian äolisch
~ **accumulation** Windaufschüttung *f*
~ **activity** Windaktivität *f*
~ **bedding** äolische Schichtung *f*
~ **-carved pebble** Windkanter *m*
~ **corrasion** Windkorrasion *f*, Sandschliff *m*
~ **current ripples** Windrippeln *fpl*
~ **deposit** Windablagerung *f*
~ **dune** Windüne *f*
~ **erosion** Winderosion *f*
~ **ripple marks** Windrippeln *fpl*
~ **rocks** äolische Gesteine *npl* (hauptsächlich aus windtransportierten Gesteinen bestehend)
~ **sand** Flugsand *m*, Dünensand *m*
~ **soil** Windabsatzboden *m*, windtransportierter Boden *m*
~ **transport** Windtransport *m*
aeolianite äolische Sedimentablagerung *f*; verfestigter Dünensand *m*
aeolic deposit äolische Ablagerung *f*
aeolotropic *s*. anisotropic
aeolotropy *s*. anisotropy
aeon 1. Äon *f* (größte geochronologische Einheit); 2. Äonothem *n* (größte biostratigrafische Einheit)

aeonothem 14

aeonothem Äonothem *n (größte biostratigrafische Einheit)*
aerate/to belüften, bewettern; durchlüften *(z. B. Wasser)*
aerated mud belüftete Spülung *f*
~ soil zone lufterfüllte Bodenzone *f*
~ spring Sauerbrunnen *m*, Säuerling *m*
~ water kohlensaures, moussierendes Wasser *n*
aeration Belüftung *f*, Bewetterung *f*, Durchlüftung *f (z. B. von Wasser)*
~ of soil Bodendurchlüftung *f*
~ of water Durchlüftung *f* des Wassers
~ tissue *s.* aerenchyma
~ zone Aerationszone *f (des Bodens)*
aerenchyma Aerenchym *n*, Luftgewebe *n (bei Pflanzen)*
aerial äolisch
~ arch Luftsattel *m*
~ camera Luftbildkamera *f*
~ colour film Luftfarbfilm *m*
~ current Luftstrom *m*
~ fold Luftsattel *m*
~ magnetometry Aeromagnetik *f (magnetische Vermessung vom Flugzeug aus)*
~ mapping Luftkartierung *f*, Kartierung *f* vom Flugzeug aus
~ mapping camera Luftbildmeßkamera *f*
~ methods Luftaufnahmeverfahren *npl*
~ mosaic Luftbildkarte *f*
~ photogrammetry Luftfotogrammetrie *f*
~ photograph Luftaufnahme *f*, Luftbild *n*
~ photography Luftfotografie *f*
~ pterosaur Flugsaurier *m*
~ root Luftwurzel *f*
~ survey Luft[bild]aufnahme *f*
~ surveying Luftvermessung *f*
~ view Luftaufnahme *f*, Luftbild *n*
aerobic bacteria aerobische Bakterien *fpl*
aerocartograph Aerokartograf *m*
aerodynamics Aerodynamik *f*
aerogeology Aerogeologie *f*, Luftbildgeologie *f*
aerogeophysics Aerogeophysik *f*
aerogravimeter Aerogravimeter *n*
aerolimnology Aerolimnologie *f*
aerolite Aerolith *m*, Meteorit *m*
aerolitic Meteor...
aerologic aerologisch
aerology Aerologie *f*
aeromagnetics Aeromagnetik *f (magnetische Vermessung vom Flugzeug aus)*
aeronautic[al] aeronautisch
~ astronomy aeronautische Astronomie *f*
aeronautics Aeronautik *f*
Aeronian [Stage] Aeronium *n (Stufe des Llandovery)*
aerophotogrammetric survey luftfotogrammetrische Aufnahme *f*
aerophotogrammetry Aerofotogrammetrie *f*, Kartenaufnahme *f* aus der Luft
aerophotographic reconnaissance luftfotografische Erkundung *f*

aerophototopography Aerofototopografie *f*, Fototopografie *f* aus der Luft
aeroscopy Wetterbeobachtung *f*
aerosiderite Meteoreisenstein *m*, Eisenmeteorit *m*
aerosiderolite Aerosiderolit *m (Eisen-Stein-Meteorit)*
aerosite *s.* pyrargyrite
aerosol Aerosol *n*
aerothermodynamics Aerothermodynamik *f*
aerotriangulation Lufttriangulation *f*
aeruginous grünspanfarbig
aeschynite Äschynit *m*,
(Ce, Th, Ca) [(Ti, Nb, Ta)$_2$O$_6$]
aestival Sommer...
aetite Klapperstein *m*, hohle Eisenhydroxidkonkretion *f*, Eisenniere *f*
affine deformation affine Deformation *f*
~ transformation affine Verformung *f*
affinity Affinität *f*
affluent Zufluß *m*, Nebenfluß *m*
afflux 1. Zustrom *m*; 2. Rückstau *m*
afforestation, afforesting Aufforstung *f*
AFMAG method AFMAG Verfahren *n (magnetisches Audiofrequenzverfahren)*
afterburst nachbrechendes Gestein *n (nach einem Gebirgsschlag)*
aftereffect Nachwirkung *f*
afterflow Nachproduktion *f*
afterintrusion Nachfolgeintrusion *f*, Restintrusion *f*
aftershock, aftervibrations Nachbeben *n*
Aftonian [Interglacial Age] Afton-Interglazial *n (entspricht dem Günz/Mindel-Interglazial)*
afwillite Afwillit *m*, Ca$_3$[SiO$_3$OH]$_2$·2H$_2$O
agalite Varietät von Talk
agalmatolite Agalmatolith *m*, Bildstein *m (dichte Varietät von Porphyllit)*
agamous agam *(geschlechtslos)*
agaric mineral Bergmilch *f*, karbonattrübes Wasser *n*
agate Achat *m (s.a.* chalcedony)
~ jasper Achatjaspis *m*, Jaspis *m* mit Chalzedonäderchen
~ mill Achatschleiferei *f*
agatiferous achathaltig
agatiform, agatine achatartig, achatähnlich
agatized wood verkieseltes Holz *n*
agatoid, agaty achatähnlich
AGC *s.* automatic gain control
AGC distorsion AGC-Verzerrung *f*
AGC time constant AGC-Zeitkonstante *f*
age 1. Alter *n*, Zeitalter *n*; 2. Standzeit *f (z.B. eines Bohrers)*
~ assignment Altersbestimmung *f*
~ characteristic Alterskriterium *n*
~ determination Altersbestimmung *f*
~ hardening Alterung *f*
~ of folding Faltungsalter *n*
~ of the universe Alter *n* des Weltalls
~ trend Alterstrend *m*
Age of Bronze Bronzezeit *f*

air

~ **of Ferns** s. Carboniferous
~ **of Fishes** s. Devonian
ageing s. aging
agency Einwirkung f
agent Agens n
agents Agenzien npl
~ **of alteration** Umgestaltungskräfte fpl
~ **of clastation** Zertrümmerungskräfte fpl
~ **of denudation** Abtragungskräfte fpl
~ **of transport[ation]** Transportkräfte fpl, Transportmittel npl
~ **of weathering** Verwitterungskräfte fpl
agglomerate/to agglomerieren, zusammenballen, zusammenbacken; sich zusammenballen, sich anhäufen
agglomerate Agglomerat n
agglomerated structure Agglomeratstruktur f
agglomeratic lava Agglomeratlava f
agglomeration Zusammenballung f, Anhäufung f
agglutinate/to agglutinieren, verbinden
agglutinated test agglutinierte Schale f
aggradate/to [im Flußbett] ablagern
aggradation Aggradation f, Auflandung f, Kolmation f, Anschwemmung f, Kolmatierung f, Aufschüttung f, Ablagerung f, Versandung f, Aufschotterung f, Sedimentzuwachs m
~ **deposit** Flußablagerung f
~ **of a valley** Zuschüttung f eines Tals
~ **plain** Anschwemmungsebene f
~ **terrace** Aufschüttungsterrasse f, alluviale Terrasse f, Schotterterrasse f
aggregal mit Aggregalgefüge (für Sedimente mit diskretem Einzelkornverband)
aggregate/to sich ansammeln
aggregate Aggregat n, Gemenge n; Zuschlagstoff m
~ **crushing value** Druckfestigkeit f (Straßenbaugestein)
~ **grading curve** Siebkurve f, Sieblinie f
~ **impact value** Schlagfestigkeit f (Straßenbaugestein)
~ **interlock[ing]** Verspannung f, Verzahnung f (Mineralmasse)
~ **of minerals** Mineralanhäufung f, Mineralaggregat n
~ **of polarization** Aggregatpolarisation f
~ **of producing (production) equipment** Gesteinsaufbereitungsmaschinen fpl
~ **retention** Gesteinsbildung f (auf bituminösen Verschleißdecken)
~ **structure** Krümelstruktur f (des Bodens)
~ **thickness** Gesamtmächtigkeit f
aggregated ore (sulfide) Sulfiderz n (mit mehr als 20% Sulfiden)
aggregation Zusammenballung f, Aggregation f, Verwachsung f (von Mineralen)
~ **grains** Körner npl mit Anlagerungsgefüge (z.B. Oolithe, Pellets)
aggressive substance Schadstoff m
~ **water** Schadwasser n
aging Alterung f

~ **of well** Brunnenalterung f
agitated water bewegtes Wasser n
agmatic structure agmatische Textur f, Gangbrekzientextur f (bei Migmatit)
agmatite Agmatit m (Migmatit)
agonic line Agone f
agpaite Agpait m (Gruppenname für in Grönland auftretende Feldspatgesteine)
agric horizon Illuvialhorizont m aus Ton und Humus (infolge Bebauung)
agricolite Agricolit m, $Bi_4[SiO_4]_3$
agricultural geology Landwirtschaftsgeologie f
~ **hydrology** Agrarhydrologie f
~ **limestone** Düngekalk m
~ **meteorology** Agrarmeteorologie f
~ **region** Agrargebiet n
~ **soil** Kulturboden m
~ **topsoil** Ackerkrume f
agriculture Ackerbau m, Bodennutzung f
agrogeochemistry Agrogeochemie f (Geochemie der Landwirtschaft)
agrogeologist Bodengeologe m, Pedologe m
agrogeology s. agricultural geology
agron Anreicherungshorizont m (des Bodens)
aguilarite Aguilarit m, $Ag_2(S, Se)$
ahermatypic ahermatyp, nicht riffbildend
aikinite Aikinit m, $2PbS \cdot Cu_2S \cdot Bi_2S_3$
aimless drainage unvollkommenes Entwässerungssystem n (z.B. im Karst)
air base Aufnahmebasis f (Luftbild)
~ **bones** s. pneumatic bones
~-**breathing gastropod** Lungenschnecke f
~-**bubble floatation** Luftschaumschwimmverfahren n
~ **bump** Luftloch n
~-**burst pattern** Lufttreffbild n, Sprengwolkenbild n
~ **chambers** Luftkammern fpl (bei Cephalopoden)
~ **classification** Setzungsklassierung f durch Luft
~ **classifier** Windsichter m, Luftklassierer m
~ **column** Luftsäule f
~ **current** Luftstrom m, Wetterstrom m; Luftströmung f
~-**current ripples** Windrippeln fpl
~ **drill** Druckluftbohrer m
~ **drilling** Bohren n mit Luftspülung, Luftheberbohren n
~ **dry** lufttrocken, lutro
~ **dry sample** lufttrockene Probe f
~ **eddy** Luftstrudel m, Luftwirbel m
~ **elutriation** Luftsichtung f
~ **flow** Wetterstrom m
~-**flush drill** Luftspülung f
~ **froth floatation** Luftschaumschwimmverfahren n
~ **gap** Luftspalt m
~ **gun** 1. Gasquelle f (hochkomprimierte Gasblase im Wasser für seismische Messungen); 2. Luftpulser m (Ingenieurgeophysik)
~ **heave structure** Steigmarke f, Entgasungskanal m, Entgasungsspur f (im Sediment)

air 16

- ~ **hoar** aufgewachsene Haarkristalle *mpl* aus Eis
- ~ **humidity** Luftfeuchtigkeit *f*
- ~ **ingress** Lufteinströmung *f*
- ~ **layer** Luftschicht *f*
- ~ **level** Wettersohle *f*
- ~ **lift** 1. Lufthebeverfahren *n*, Druckförderung *f* von Flüssigkeiten *(mit Hilfe von Luft)*; 2. Windsichtung *f*
- ~ **lift test** Lufthebetest *m*
- ~ **mass** Luftmasse *f*
- ~ **moisture** Luftfeuchtigkeit *f*
- ~ **permeability of snow** Schneedurchlässigkeit *f*
- ~ **photo[graph]** Luftaufnahme *f*, Luftbild *n*
- ~ **photographic[al] survey** Luftbildaufnahme *f*
- ~ **photography** Luftbildtechnik *f*
- ~-**placed concrete** Spritzbeton *m*, Torkretbeton *m*
- ~ **pollution** Luftverschmutzung *f*
- ~ **pressure** Luftdruck *m*
- ~ **return** Ausziehstrom *m*
- ~ **saddle** Luftsattel *m*
- ~-**sand mixture** Sand-Luft-Gemisch *n*
- ~-**sealed** luftdicht
- ~ **separator** Windsichter *m*, Luftklassierer *m*
- ~ **shaft** Wetterschacht *m*
- ~ **shooting** Oberflächenschießen *n*, Luftschußtechnik *f (Seismik)*
- ~ **shrinkage** Trockenriß *m (in Ton)*
- ~-**side face** Luftseite *f (z.B. einer Talsperre)*
- ~-**slaked lime** Staubkalk *m*
- ~-**soil interface** Luft-Boden-Grenzschicht *f (Übergangsschicht zwischen Luft und Boden)*
- ~ **sounding** Höhenforschung *f* mit Meßsonden
- ~ **space** Luftraum *m*
- ~ **space ratio** scheinbare Porosität *f*, Luftporenanteil *m*
- ~-**speed computer** Windgeschwindigkeitszähler *m*
- ~-**speed recorder** Windgeschwindigkeitsschreiber *m*
- ~ **stone** Meteorstein *m*
- ~ **stratum** Luftschicht *f*
- ~ **survey** Luftbildaufnahme *f*
- ~-**survey plan** Plan *m* nach Luftbildaufnahme
- ~ **surveying** Luft[bild]vermessung *f*, Fotogrammetrie *f*
- ~ **temperature** Lufttemperatur *f*
- ~-**tight** luftdicht
- ~ **view** Luftbild *n*
- ~ **void** Luftpore *f*
- ~ **wave** Luftdruckwelle *f*, Schallwelle *f*
- ~ **wave receiver** Schallempfänger *m (registriert die Ankunftszeit der Explosionswellen)*
- ~ **way** Wetterstrecke *f*
- ~ **whirling** Luftwirbelung *f*
- **airborne camera** Luftbildkamera *f*
- ~ **exploration method** luftgeophysikalische Vermessungsmethode *f*
- ~ **geophysics** luftgeophysikalische Vermessung (Erkundung) *f*

- ~ **magnetics** Aeromagnetik *f*
- ~ **magnetometer** Flugmagnetometer *n*
- ~ **platform** luftgetragene Meßbasis *f (in einem Flugzeug, Hubschrauber bzw. Ballon montierte Beobachtungsplattform)*
- ~ **radioactivity** Radioaktivität *f* der Luft
- ~ **sand** Flugsand *m*
- ~ **scanner** Flugzeugscanner *m (in einem Flugzeug montiertes Linienabtastgerät)*
- ~ **scintillation counter** Szintillometer *n* für Flugvermessung
- **airglow** Luftleuchten *n*
- **airgun** Luftpulser *m (Entspannung komprimierter Luft)*
- **airplane mapping** Luftkartierung *f*, Kartierung (Kartenaufnahme) *f* vom Flugzeug aus
- **ajoite** Ajoit *m*, $Cu_2Al[OH|Si_3O_9]\cdot 2H_2O$
- **akaganeite** Akaganeit *m*, ß-FeOOH
- **akaustobiolite** Akaustobiolith *m*
- **akenobeite** Akenobeit *m (dioritisches Ganggestein)*
- **akerite** Akerit *m (quarzführender Augitsyenit)*
- **akermanite** Akermanit *m*, $Ca_2Mg[Si_2O_7]$
- **akmolith** Akmolith *m (zungenförmige Intrusionsform)*
- **akrochordite** Akrochordit *m*, $(Mn, Mg)_5[(OH)_2|AsO_4]_2 \cdot 5H_2O$
- **aksaite** Aksait *m*, $Mg[B_3O_4(OH)_2]_2 \cdot 3H_2O$
- **Aktian deposits** Ablagerungen *fpl* am Kontinentalabhang
- **ala** Flügel *m (bei Brachiopoden)*
- **alabandine, alabandite** Alabandin *m*, Manganblende *f*, MnS
- **alabaster** Alabaster *m (s.a. gypsum)*
- **alabastrite** Alabastergips *m*
- **alaite** Alait *m*, $V_2O_5 \cdot H_2O$
- **alamosite** Alamosit *m*, $PbSiO_3$
- **alar expansion** flügelartige Erweiterung *f*
- ~ **septum** Seitenseptum *n (bei Korallen)*
- **alarm** Signaleinrichtung *f*
- **alaskaite** Alaskait *m*, $Ag_2S \cdot 3Bi_2S_3$
- **Alaskan band** *s.* dirt-band
- **alaskite** Alaskit *m (leukokratischer Granit)*
- **Alaunian [Substage]** Alaun *n (Unterstufe, Obere Trias, Tethys)*
- **albanite** Albanit *m (Leuzitit)*
- **albedo** Albedo *f*, Hellbezugswert *m*
- **Albert coal** *s.* albertite
- **Albertan [Stage]** Albertan *n*, Acadian *n (Serie, Mittelkambrium in Nordamerika)*
- **albertite** Albertit *m (asphaltisches Pyrobitumen)*
- **Albian [Stage]** Alb *n (Stufe der Unterkreide)*
- **albite** Albit *m*, $NaAlSi_3O_8$
- ~ **schist** Albitschiefer *m*
- ~ **twin** Albitzwilling *m*
- **albitic** albitisch
- ~ **schist** Albitschiefer *m*
- **albitite** Albitit *m (Na-Syenit oder Albitporphyr)*
- **albitization** Albitisierung *f*
- **albitophyre** Albitophyr *m (Albiteinsprenglinge enthaltendes porphyrisches Gestein)*

allochemical

alboranite Alboranit *m (Hypersthenandesit)*
albuminoid eiweißhaltig
albuminoid Eiweißstoff *m*
alcove schichtparallele Erosionsnische *f (eines Flusses)*
~ **lands** Schichtstufenlandschaft *f*
alee basin *durch Trübeströme gebildete Beckenstruktur*
aleotropic material Anisotropiematerial *n*
aleurite Aleurit *m*; Schluff *m*; Silt *m (feinkörniges klastisches Sediment)*
aleurolite Aleurolith *m*; Schluffstein *m*; Siltstein *m (feinkörniges verfestigtes klastisches Gestein)*
alexandrite Alexandrit *m (Varietät von Chrysoberyll)*
algae Algen *fpl*
~ **threads** Algenfäden *mpl*
algal ball (biscuit) Stromatolith *m*, Karbonatkonkretion *f (verursacht durch Algen oder ähnliche Organismen)*
~ **coal** Bogheadkohle *f*
~ **dust** Algenstaub *m (Karbonatstaub von 1–5 µm aus Algenrückständen)*
~ **growth structure** Algenwachstumsstruktur *f*
~-**mat facies** *s.* stromatolitic facies
~ **reef** Algenriff *n*, Kalkalgenriff *n*
~ **remains** Algenreste *mpl*; Alginit *m (Kohlenmaceral)*
~ **secretion** Algenabscheidung *f*
~ **structure** Algenstruktur *f*
alginate Alginat *n*
alginite Alginit *m (Kohlenmaceral)*
algite Algit *m (Kohlenmikrolithotyp)*
algodonite Algodonit *m*, Cu_6As
Algoman folding algomane Tektogenese *f (Altpräkambrium in Nordamerika)*
Algonkian Algonkium *n (höheres Archaikum und Proterozoikum in Nordamerika)*
~ **coal** algonkische Kohle *f*
algous accumulation Algenanhäufung *f*
algovite Algovit *m (Gruppenname für Augit-Plagioklas-Gesteine)*
aliasing effect Aliasing-Effekt *m*
alidade Theodolitfernrohr *n*
align/to ausrichten; einfluchten; einregeln
~ **the sights on** anvisieren
aligned orientiert
alignment Ausrichten *n*, Ausrichtung *f*; Einfluchtung *f*; Absteckungslinie *f*; Einregelung *f*
alimentation area Nährgebiet *n*
~ **by glaciers** Speisung *f* durch Gletscherschmelzwasser
~ **by snowmelt** Speisung *f* durch Schneeschmelzwasser
~ **factor** Speisungsfaktor *m (Grundwasser)*
alinement *s.* alignment
aliquot solution Restlösung *f (nach Ablaugung)*
alisonite Alisonit *m*, Kupferbleiglanz *m*, $3Cu_2S \cdot PbS$
alizarine complex Alizarinkomplex *m*

alkalescent schwach alkalisch
alkali-calcic series Alkalikalkgesteine *npl*, Kalkkaligesteine *npl*, pazifische Sippe *f*
~ **compound** Alkaliverbindung *f*
~ **flat** Salar *n*, Salztonebene *f*
~ **granite** Alkaligranit *m*
~ **lake** Natronsee *m*
~ **metal** Alkalimetall *n*
~ **rock** Alkaligestein *n*
~ **silicate** Alkalisilikat *n*
~ **soil** Alkaliboden *m*
~ **syenite** Alkalisyenit *m*
alkalic ammoniacal fumarole alkalische Salmiakfumarole *f*
~ **series** Alkaligesteine *npl*, atlantische Sippe *f*
alkaline alkalisch
~ **ammoniacal fumarole** alkalische Salmiakfumarole *f*
~-**earth** erdalkalisch
~ **earth** Erdalkali *n*
~-**earth deposit** Lagerstätte *f* alkalischer Erden
~-**earth metal** Erdalkalimetall *n*
~ **group** Alkalimetallgruppe *f*
~ **lake** Tinkalsee *m*
~ **podzol** Alkaliboden *m*
~ **soil** alkalischer Boden *m*, Alkaliboden *m*
alkalinity Alkali[ni]tät *f*, Alkaleszenz *f*
alkalinous alkalisch (*s.a.* alkaline)
alkalization Alkalisierung *f*
alkalize/to alkalisieren
all-floatation einfache (kollektive) Flotation *f*, Sammelflotation *f*, Totalflotation *f*
~-**in aggregate** ungesiebter Zuschlagstoff *m (Straßenbau)*
~-**in gravel** ungesiebter Kies *m*
~-**weather remote sensing** Allwetterfernerkundung *f*
allactite Allaktit *m*, $Mn_7[(OH)_4|AsO_4]_2$
allalinite Allalinit *m*, Saussuritgabbro *m (Gabbro mit zersetztem Mineralbestand)*
allanite Allanit *m*, Orthit *m*, $(La, Ce)_2FeAl_2[O|OH|SiO_4|Si_2O_7]$
allargentum Allargentum *n*, ε-(Ag, Sb)
alleghanyite Alleghanyit *m*, $Mn_5[(OH)_2|(SiO_4)_2]$
allemontite Allemontit *m*, Antimonarsen *n*, $SbAs_3$
alley Gang *m*, Erzgang *m*
~ **stone** *s.* websterite
alliaceous mit Knoblauchgeruch *(z.B. arsenhaltige Minerale)*
alligator cracking, alligatoring netzartige Rißbildung *f*
Alling scale Alling-Skala *f (für Korngrößenklassifizierung)*
allite Allit *m (Gesteinsname für Bauxite und Laterite)*
allitic allitisch
allocation of oil production within oil pools Förderzuteilung *f* innerhalb von Erdöllagerstätten *(Maßnahme zur Einschränkung der Förderung)*
allochemical metamorphism allocheme Metamorphose *f*

allochems

allochems Allocheme *npl (Sammelbegriff für alle „organisierten Karbonataggregate", die transportiert wurden oder transportfähig sind)*
allochroic allochroitisch, schillernd
allochroism Farbwechsel *m*, Schillern *n*
allochroite Allochroit *m*, brauner Eisengranat *m (s.a. andradite)*
allochromatic allochromatisch, farbenwechselnd, andersfarbig *(als es der Substanz zukommt)*
~ **mineral** gefärbtes Mineral *n*
allochthon[al], allochthonic allochthon *(s.a. allochthonous)*
allochthonous allochthon, ortsfremd, bodenfremd
~ **deposit** allochthone Ablagerung *f*
~ **fold** allochthone Falte *f*
~ **geochemical anomaly** allochthone geochemische Anomalie *f*
~ **nappe** Ferndecke *f*
~ **rock** allochthones Gestein *n*
allocthonous s. allochthonous
allodapic limestones allodapische Kalke *mpl*
allodelphite s. synadelphite
allogamy Allogamie *f*, Fremdbestäubung *f*
allogene, allogenic allothigen
allogenous allogen
~ **river** Fremdlingsfluß *m*
allomicrite Allomikrit *m (allochtoner Orthomikrit)*
allomorph[ic] allomorph
allomorphism Allomorphismus *m*
allomorphous allomorph
allopalladium Allopalladium *n*, gediegenes Palladium *n (hexagonale Modifikation)*
allopatric *in verschiedenen geografischen Gebieten vorkommend*
allophane Allophan *m*, $Al_2SiO_5 \cdot nH_2O$
allothigene, allothigenic, allothigenous, allothogenic allothigen
~ **discharges,** ~ **ejecta[menta]** Auswürflinge *mpl*
allotment Grubenfeld *n*
~ **of ore** Erzfeld *n*
allotriomorphic allotriomorph
~**-granular** allotriomorph-körnig
allotropic allotrop
~ **form** allotrope Form *f*
allotropism, allotropy Allotropie *f*
allotype s. paratype
allowable maximum of hole deviation zulässige Bohrlochabweichung *f*
~ **production** zulässige Produktion *f*
~ **stress** zulässige Spannung *f*
allowables zulässige Fördermenge *f (z.B. von Erdöl, Erdgas)*
alluvial alluvial, angespült, angeschwemmt
~ **accumulation** Schwemmland *n*
~ **apron** alluviale Gletscherablagerung *f*, Alluvialfächer *m*, Geröllfächer *m*, Sander *m*
~ **bench** Alluvialterrasse *f*, Flußterrasse *f*
~ **coast** Anschwemmungsküste *f*

~ **cone** Aufschüttungskegel *m*, Schotterkegel *m*, Schuttkegel *m*, Schwemmkegel *m*
~ **cover** Schotterdecke *f*
~ **deposit** 1. Verlandung *f*, Anschütte *f*, Anlandung *f*, Alluvium *n*, Auflandung *f*; 2. alluviale Lagerstätte *f*, Seife *f*
~ **diggings** Seifenmaterial *n*
~ **epoch** Alluvium *n*
~ **fan** Alluvialfächer *m*, alluvialer Schuttfächer *m*, Geröllfächer *m*, Schuttkegel *m*; Flußdelta *n*; Anschwemmland *n*
~ **fan accumulations** Alluvialfächerschutt *m*
~ **fills** Alluvionen *fpl*, Talfüllungen *fpl*
~ **flat** Talaue *f*, Inundationsfläche *f*
~ **floor** Alluvialboden *m*, Schwemmlandboden *m (eines Tals)*
~ **formation** Schwemmgebilde *n*
~ **gold** Seifengold *n*, alluviales Gold *n*
~ **gravel** Alluvialkies *m*
~ **mantle rock** alluvialer Verwitterungsschutt *m*
~ **meadow** Flußaue *f*
~ **meadow soil** Auenboden *m*
~ **ore** Seifenerz *n*
~ **ore deposit** alluviale Erzlagerstätte *f*, fluviatile Seife *f*
~ **period** Alluvium *n*
~ **piedmont plain** alluviale Piedmontebene *f*
~ **plain** Alluvialebene *f*, Inundationsbett *n*, Schwemmlandebene *f*
~**-plain shore line** Schwemmlandküste *f*
~ **sand** Schwemmsand *m*
~ **sheet** Alluvialdecke *f*
~ **shore** Schwemmlandküste *f*
~ **slime** Alluvialschlamm *m*
~ **slope** Schwemmlandebene *f*
~ **soil** Alluvialboden *m*, angeschwemmter Boden *m*, Schwemmland *n*, Schwemmboden *m*, Aueboden *m*
~ **stone** Schwemmstein *m*
~ **swamping soil** Alluvialmoorboden *m*
~ **terrace** Aufschüttungsterrasse *f*, Schotterterrasse *f*, Flußterrasse *f*
~ **time[s]** Alluvium *n*
~ **tin** Seifenzinn *n* in Flußseifen
~ **veneer** dünner Schuttmantel *m*
~ **washing [plant]** Seifenwerk *n*
~ **working** Seifenbau *m*
alluvian angeschwemmt
~ **plain** Alluvialebene *f*, Inundationsbett *n*, Schwemmlandebene *f*
alluviated angeschwemmt
alluviation Ablagerung *f*, Anschwemmung *f*, Anlandung *f*
alluvion Alluvium *n*; angeschwemmtes Land *n*, Schwemmland *n*; Versandung *f*
alluvious alluvial, angeschwemmt
alluvium Alluvium *n*; angeschwemmtes Land *n*, Schwemmsand *m*, Schwemmland *n*; Auflandung *f*, Verlandung *f*, Anschütte *f*, Anlandung *f*
~**-covered** alluviumbedeckt

alunitize

~ period Alluvialepoche *f*
alm *(sl)* Seekreide *f*
almandine, almandite Almandin *m*, Eisentongranat *m*, $Fe_3Al_2[SiO_4]_3$
almeraite Almerait *m*, $KCl \cdot NaCl \cdot MgCl_2 \cdot H_2O$
almond-shaped mandelförmig
almost atoll Atoll *n* mit vulkanischer Laguneninsel
alnoite Alnöit *m (Melilithbasalt)*
alongshore current Küstenstrom *m*
alpha counter tube Alphazählrohr *n*
~ decay Alphazerfall *m*, Alphaumwandlung *f*
~ emitter Alphastrahler *m*
~ meter Alphazähler *m*
~ particle Alphateilchen *n*
~ quartz Tiefquarz *m*, α-Quarz *m*
~ radiation Alphastrahlung *f*
~ radioactivity Alphaaktivität *f*
~-ray emitter Alphastrahler *m*
Alpide folding alpidische Faltung *f*
Alpides Alpiden *pl*, alpidischer Faltengürtel *m*
alpine alpin
~ climate Höhenklima *n*
~ form alpine Form *f*
~ glacier Hochgebirgsgletscher *m*
~ metamorphism alpine Metamorphose *f*
~ mineral alpines Kluftmineral *n*
~ mountain glaciation alpine Vergletscherung *f*
~ orogenesis alpinotype Gebirgsbildung *f*
~ relief alpines Relief *n*
~ tarn Karsee *m*
~ valley Hochgebirgstal *n*
Alpine facies alpine Fazies *f*
~ foot-hills Alpenvorland *n*
~ glow Alpenglühen *n*
~ orogeny alpine Orogenese *f*
~ piedmont Alpenvorland *n*
~ Triassic alpine Trias *f*
~ tunnel Alpentunnel *m*
alpinotype alpinotyp *(tektonischer Baustil)*
Alps Alpen *pl*
alsbachite Alsbachit *m (Aplit)*
alstonite Alstonit *m (Bariumaragonit)*
altaite Altait *m*, Tellurblei *n*, PbTe
alter/to abändern, verwandeln; metamorphosieren
alterability Veränderlichkeit *f*; Verwitterbarkeit *f*
alteration Abänderung *f*, Verwandlung *f*; Metamorphose *f*
~ fringe Kontakthof *m*
~ from contact Kontaktmetamorphose *f*
~ halo Kontakthof *m*
~ product Umwandlungsprodukt *n*
~ to gneiss Vergneisung *f*
altered to gneiss vergneist
alternate structure Repetitionsschichtung *f*, Wechsellagerung *f*
alternated stratification *s.* alternate structure
alternating beds wechsellagernde Schichten *fpl*

field demagnetization Wechselfeldentmagnetisierung *f*
~ of stress Lastwechsel *m*
alternation of beds Wechsellagerung *f (von Schichten)*, Schichtenwechsel *m*
altimeter Höhenmesser *m*
altimetric device (instrument) Höhenmesser *m*
altimetry Höhen[ver]messung *f*
altitude Höhe *f*
~ above [mean] sea level Höhe *f* über NN
~ of a place Höhenlage *f* eines Orts
~ of precipitation Niederschlagshöhe *f*
~ of the pole Polhöhe *f*
~ point trigonometrischer Festpunkt *m*
~ stability Höhensicherheit *f*
~ zone Höhenschicht *f (Stratosphäre)*
alto-stratus hohe Schichtwolke *f*
alum Alaun *m*
~ coal ton- und pyritreiche Braunkohle *f*
~ earth Alaunerde *f*
~ ore Alaunerz *n*
~ schist (shale, slate) Alaunschiefer *m*, Vitriolschiefer *m*
~-soaked Keene's cement Marmorgips *m*, Alabastergips *m*
~ stone *s.* alunite
~ works Alaunsiederei *f*
alumian Alumian *m*, Natroalunit *m*, $NaAl_3[(OH)_6|(SO_4)_2]$
alumina Tonerde *f*
~ cement Tonerdezement *m*
~ content Tonerdegehalt *m*
~ hydrate Bauxit *m*
~ inclusion Tonerdeeinschluß *m*
aluminate Aluminat *n*
~ of potash Kalitonerde *f*
aluminiferous aluminiumhaltig; tonerdehaltig
aluminite Aluminit *m*, $Al_2[(OH)_4|SO_4] \cdot 7H_2O$
aluminium Aluminium *n*, Al
~-bearing aluminiumhaltig
~ iron Aluminiumeisen *n*
~ mineral Tonerdemineral *n*
~ ore Aluminiumerz *n*
~ silicate Tonerdesilikat *n*
aluminosilicate Alumosilikat *n*
aluminous alaunartig, alaunhaltig; tonderreich
~ cement Tonerdezement *m*
~ silicate Alumosilikat *n*
aluminum *(Am) s.* aluminium
alumogel *s.* kliachite
alumohydrocalcite Alumohydrokalzit *m*, Alumohydrocalcit *m*, $CaAl_2[(OH)_4|(CO_3)_2] \cdot 3H_2O$
alumy alaunerdehaltig
alumyte *s.* bauxite
alunite Alunit *m*, Alaunstein *m*, Alaunerz *n*, $KAl_3[(OH)_6|(SO_4)_2]$
alunitic alunitisch
alunitization Alunitisierung *f*, Alunitisation *f*, Alunitbildung *f*
alunitize/to alunitisieren

alunogen

alunogen Alunogen m, $Al_2[SO_4]_3 \cdot 18H_2O$
alveolar wabenförmig
~ weathering Alveolarverwitterung f *(supralitorale Verkarstung)*
alveolate muldenförmig
Alveolina limestone Alveolinenkalk m
amalgam Amalgam m, (Ag, Hg)
amandola Mandelstein m
amarantite Amarantit m, $Fe[OH|SO_4] \cdot 3H_2O$
amatrice s. variscite
Amazon Amazonas m
~ stone s. amazonite
Amazonian shield Amazonasschild m
amazonite grüner Mikroklin m, Amazonenstein m, Smaragdspat m *(s.a. microcline)*
ambatoarinite Ambatoarinit m, $Sr(Ce, La, Nd)[O|(CO_3)_3]$
amber gelbrot
amber Bernstein m; Sukzinit m, Succinit m
~ forest Bernsteinwald m
~ inclusion Bernsteineinschluß m
ambiguity Zweideutigkeit f, Mehrdeutigkeit f, Vieldeutigkeit f, *(z.B. von geomagnetischen, gravimetrischen oder Radarmessungen)*
amblygonal, amblygonial stumpfwinklig
amblygonite Amblygonit m, $LiAl[(F,OH)|PO_4]$
ambonite Ambonit m *(Kordierit-Andesit)*
ambrite fossiles Harz n
ambulacral area Ambulakralfeld n
Amburcen-type dam Amburcen-Staumauer f
ameboid fold unregelmäßige Faltenstruktur f *(in schwachdeformierten Gebieten)*
amelioration Melioration f, Bodenverbesserung f
~ of [the] climate Klimaverbesserung f
amenability to receive polish Polierfähigkeit f
amendment 1. Verbesserung f; 2. Melioration f
amesite Amesit m, $(Mg, Fe)_4Al_2[(OH)_8|Al_2Si_2O_{10}]$
amethyst Amethyst m *(s.a. quartz)*
amethystine amethystartig, amethystfarben
~ quartz Blauquarz m
amherstite Amherstit m *(Syenodiorit)*
amianthus Amianth m *(Varietät von Asbest)*
amiantine s. amianthus
aminoffite Aminoffit m, $Ca_3(BeOH)_2Si_3O_{10}$
Ammanian [Stage] Ammanien n *(Westfal A + B in England)*
ammeter Lichtlot n *(Grundwasserspiegelmessung)*
ammite s. ooid
ammonia Ammoniak n
ammonification Ammonifikation f
ammonioborite Ammonioborit m, $NH_4[B_5O_6(OH)_4] \cdot 2/3H_2O$
ammoniojarosite Ammoniojarosit m, $(NH_4)_2Fe_6(OH)_{12}(SO_4)_4$
ammonite Ammonit m
ammonitic suture ammonitische Lobenlinie f
ammonoid zones Ammonitenzonen fpl
ammonoids Ammoniten mpl
amorphous amorph, formlos, strukturlos

~ admixtures amorphe Beimengungen fpl
~ silica amorphe Kieselsäure f
amortization tonnage Mindestfördermenge f
amount Betrag m, Menge f, Gehalt m
~ of creep Kriechweg m
~ of evaporation Verdunstungshöhe f
~ of local relief Reliefenergie f
~ of metal Metallgehalt m
~ of precipitation Niederschlagsmenge f
~ of runoff Abflußhöhe f
ampangabeite s. samarskite
ampelite Ampelit m *(schwarzer, bituminöser, pyritreicher Schiefer)*
amphegenyte Leuzitophyr m, Leuzittrachit m
amphibian amphibisch
amphibian Amphibie f
amphibious amphibisch
amphibole Amphibol m, Hornblende f
~ schist Amphibolschiefer m
amphibolic amphibolisch
amphibolite Amphibolit m, Amphibolfels m
~ facies Amphibolitfazies f
amphibolization Amphibolisierung f
amphiphytes Amphiphyten mpl, amphibische Pflanzen fpl
amphitheatre Kar n
amphoteric amphoter
amphoterite achondritischer Meteorit m
amplitude Amplitude f, Schwingungsweite f
~-frequency distortion Amplituden-Frequenz-Verzerrung f
~ modulation Amplitudenmodulation f
~ response Amplitudencharakteristik f
~ spectrum Amplitudenspektrum n
amputation of a nappe Amputation f einer Decke
AMS s. accelerator mass spectrometry
Amstelian Amstelien n, Amstelium n *(Präglazialfolge Niederrhein, Grenzbereich Tertiär/Pleistozän)*
amygdale Mandel[füllung] f *(bei Vulkaniten)*
amygdaline mandelartig
amygdaloid s. amygdaloidal
amygdaloid Mandelstein m
amygdaloidal amygdaloidisch, mandelsteinartig; Mandel ...; mandelförmig
~ basalt Basaltmandelstein m
~ diabase Diabasmandelstein m
~ infilling Mandelfüllung f
~ melaphyre Melaphyrmandelstein m
~ rock Mandelgestein n, Mandelstein m
~ structure amygdaloidische Struktur f, Mandelstruktur f
~ texture amygdaloidische Textur f, Mandeltextur f
amygdalophyre Amygdalophyr m
amygdular inclusion Mandeleinschluß m
amygdule Mandel f, kleine Mandelfüllung f
anabatic aufsteigend *(Luftstrom)*
anabohitsite Anabohitsit m *(Olivinpyroxenit)*
anaclinal river anaklinaler Fluß m *(Fluß mit Strömungsrichtung entgegen dem Schichtfallen)*

angle

~ **valley** Anaklinaltal *n*
anadiagenese Anadiagenese *f*, Diagenesehauptstadium *n (mit Übergang zur Metamorphose)*
anadiagenetic anadiagenetisch *(z.B. sekundäre Dolomitisierung)*
anaerobic[al] anaerob
~ **bacteria** anaerobe Bakterien *fpl*
anaerobiosis Anaerobiose *f*
anagenesis Anagenese *f*, progressive Entwicklung *f*
anal anal
~ **fasciola** *s.* slit band
~ **tube** Analtubus *m*, Afterröhre *f*
~ **X** Analplatte X *f*, Anale X *n (Echinodermata)*
analbite Analbit *m*, Hochtemperaturalbit *m*
analcidite, analcime *s.* analcite
analcimite Analzimit *m (Nephelinsyenit)*
analcite Analzim *m*, $NaAlSi_2O_6 \cdot H_2O$
analogue model study Analogmodelluntersuchung *f*
analysis Analyse *f*
~ **by dry way** Trockenanalyse *f*
~ **by measure** volumetrische Analyse *f*
~ **of rocks** Gesteinsanalyse *f*
~ **sample** Analysenprobe *f*
analytic characteristics analytische Merkmale *npl (Taxonomie)*
analyzer Analysator *m*
analyzing Nicol Analysator-Nikol *n*
anamesite Anamesit *m*
anamorphic area (fringe) Kontakthof *m*
~ **zone** Umwandlungszone *f*
anamorphism Anamorphose *f*
ananthous blütenlos
anapaite Anapait *m*, $Ca_2Fe[PO_4]_2 \cdot 4H_2O$
anastomosing deltoid branch verzweigtes Delta *n*
~ **stream** verzweigtes, pendelndes Flußbett *n*
anastomosis 1. netzartige Verzweigung *f (eines Flusses)*; 2. Anastomose *f*, Querverbindung *f (von Nervaturen)*
anatase Anatas *m*, TiO_2
anatectic magma anatektisches Magma *n*
anatexis Anatexis *f*
anatexite Anatexit *m*
anauxite Anauxit *m*, $(Al, H_3)_4[(OH)_8|Si_4O_{10}]$
ancestor Ausgangsform *f*, Ahnenform *f*
ancestors Vorfahren *mpl*
ancestral elephant Urelefant *m*
~ **home** Urheimat *f*
anchimetamorphism Anchimetamorphose *f*
anchor bolt Ankerbolzen *m (Ausbau)*
~ **ice** Bodeneis *n*, Grundeis *n*
~ **line** Ankerseil *n*
~ **log** Ankerbalken *m*
~ **stone** *s.* anchorage stone
~ **wall** durchlaufende Ankerwand *f*
anchorage Verankerung *f*
~ **fixture** Spannanker *m*
~ **point** Ankerpunkt *m*
~ **stone** mit marinen Pflanzen verhaftetes Geröll *n*

anchored craft verankertes Bohrschiff *n*
~ **dune** [ingenieurbiologisch] befestigte Düne *f*
~ **sheet [pile] wall** verankerte Spundwand *f*
anchoring by friction Reibungsverankerung *f*
anchorite Anchorit *m (Varietät von Diorit)*
ancient alt, ehemalig; fossil
~ **coast line** ehemalige Küstenlinie *f*
~ **geological gorge** epigenetisches Flußbett *n*
~ **lake mire** Verlandungsmoor *n*
~ **soil bed** fossiler Boden *m*
ancillary minerals at coal mines beibrechende Minerale *npl* in Kohlenbergwerken
ancylite Ankylit *m*, $Sr_3(Ce, La, Dy)_4[(OH)_4|(CO_3)_7] \cdot 3H_2O$
Ancylus lake Ancylussee *m*
~ **time** Ancyluszeit *f*
andalusite Andalusit *m*, Al_2SiO_5
~ **biotite schist** Andalusit-Biotit-Schiefer *m*
~ **mica rock** Andalusit-Glimmerfels *m*
Andean folding andine Faltung *f*
~ **phases of folding** subherzyn[isch]e Faltungsphasen *fpl*
andesine Andesin *m (Mischkristall aus $NaAlSi_3O_8$ und $CaAl_2Si_2O_8$)*
andesinite Andesinit *m (andesinreiches Ergußgestein)*
andesite Andesit *m*
~ **line** Andesitlinie *f*
andesitic andesitisch
andorite Andorit *m*, $Pb_4Ag_4Sb_{12}S_{24}$
andradite Andradit *m*, Kalkeisengranat *m*, $Ca_3Fe_2(SiO_4)_3$
anelastic medium unelastisches Medium *n*
anemoarenyte Flugsand *m*, Dünensand *m*
anemoclastic anemoklastisch, aeroklastisch *(zerfallen und gerundet durch Windeinwirkung)*
~ **rocks** äolische Gesteine *npl*
anemoclastics äolische Gesteine *npl*
anemogenic anemogen, äolisch
anemolite Anemolith *m*, Stalaktit *m* mit versetzter Wachstumsachse
anemometer Anemometer *n*, Windmesser *m*
anemosilicarenite, anemosilicarenyte äolischer Arenit *m*
aneroid barometer Aneroidbarometer *n*
angaralite Angaralith *m*, $(Mg, Ca)_2(Al, Fe)_{10}[O_9|(SiO_4)_6]$
angiospermatous (angiospermous) plants, angiosperms Angiospermen *npl*
angle Winkel *m*
~ **beam** Winkelträger *m*
~ **of bedding** Fallwinkel *m* von Schichten
~ **of break** Bruchwinkel *m*
~ **of contact** Berührungswinkel *m*
~ **of curvature** Krümmungswinkel *m*
~ **of deflection** Abweichungswinkel *m*, Ausschlagwinkel *m (eines Zeigers)*
~ **of deviation** Neigungswinkel *m*
~ **of deviation from the vertical** Abweichungswinkel *m* von der Lotrechten, Vertikalabweichungswinkel *m*

angle

- ~ of diffraction Beugungswinkel m
- ~ of dip[ping] Einfallswinkel m, Fallwinkel m
- ~ of discharge Schüttwinkel m
- ~ of draw Grenzwinkel m
- ~ of eccentricity Exzentrizitätswinkel m
- ~ of elevation Böschungswinkel m
- ~ of emergence Emergenzwinkel m, Austrittswinkel m
- ~ of extinction Auslöschungswinkel m
- ~ of friction Reibungswinkel m
- ~ of hade Verwurfswinkel m, Deklinationswinkel m
- ~ of incidence Einfallswinkel m, Fallwinkel m
- ~ of inclination (incline) Inklinationswinkel m, Neigungswinkel m
- ~ of internal friction Reibungswinkel m, Winkel m der inneren Reibung
- ~ of intersection Schnittwinkel m
- ~ of lag Nacheilungswinkel m
- ~ of lead Steigungswinkel m
- ~ of obliquity Schrägheitswinkel m
- ~ of pitch Neigungswinkel m
- ~ of polarization Polarisationswinkel m
- ~ of reflection Ausfallswinkel m, Reflexionswinkel m
- ~ of refraction Brechungswinkel m
- ~ of repose (rest) Ruhewinkel m, natürlicher Böschungswinkel m, Schüttungswinkel m
- ~ of roll Rollwinkel m
- ~ of rotation Drehwinkel m
- ~ of setting the whipstock Ablenkwinkel m, Einstellwinkel m des Ablenkelements
- ~ of shear Scherwinkel m
- ~ of sideslip Schiebewinkel m
- ~ of skew Schrägungswinkel m
- ~ of slip Sprungwinkel m
- ~ of slope Böschungswinkel m
- ~ of strike Streichwinkel m
- ~ of taper Kegelwinkel m
- ~ of torsion Verdrehungswinkel m
- ~ of true internal friction Winkel m der wahren inneren Reibung
- ~ of twist Torsionswinkel n
- ~ of unconformity Diskordanzwinkel m
- ~ of wind direction Windrichtungswinkel m

angled suture line gezackte Sutur f
anglesite Anglesit m, Vitriolbleierz n, $PbSO_4$
Anglian Anglien n (Pleistozän der britischen Inseln, entspricht dem Mindel-Glazial der Alpen)
angling [drill] hole Bohrloch n mit schiefer Richtung
angrite Angrit m (Meteorit)
anguclast 1. eckiges Bruchstück n; 2. s. breccia
angular Angulare n (Paläontologie)
angular eckig, winkelig, kantig, scharfkantig
- ~ blocky structure eckig-kantige Blockstruktur f
- ~ clast eckiges Bruchstück n
- ~ cobble eckiger Stein m
- ~ cross-bedding winkelige Schrägschichtung f

- ~ deformation Winkelverformung f
- ~ displacement Winkelverschiebung f
- ~ fold Scharnierfalte f (Falte mit winkelig gestaltetem Scheitel, z.B. Zickzackfalte)
- ~ fragment eckiges Bruchstück n
- ~ frequency Kreisfrequenz f
- ~ kinetic energy Rotationsenergie f
- ~ momentum Drehmoment n, Drehimpuls m
- ~ resolution Winkelauflösungsvermögen n (z.B. eines Fernerkundungssensors)
- ~ unconformity Winkeldiskordanz f
- ~ velocity Winkelgeschwindigkeit f

angularity Eckigkeit f, Kantigkeit f
angulometer Winkelmesser m
anhedral allotriomorph, xenomorph
anhedron allotriomorpher (xenomorpher) Kristall m
anhistous texturlos; strukturlos
anhydric anhydrisch, wasserfrei
anhydriceous anhydrithaltig
anhydristone s. anhydrock
anhydrite Anhydrit m, $CaSO_4$
- ~ band Anhydritschnur f

anhydritic anhydrithaltig
- ~ concretion Anhydritknolle f

anhydrock anhydritreiches Gestein n
anhydrokainite Anhydrokainit m, $KMg[Cl|SO_4]$
anhydrous anhydrisch, wasserfrei
- ~ gypsum s. anhydrite

anhysteretic magnetization hysteresefreie Magnetisierung f
animal debris [fossile] Tierreste mpl
- ~ kindom Tierreich n
- ~ life tierisches Leben n
- ~ remains [fossile] Tierreste mpl
- ~ trail Lebensspur f, Tierspur f

animate nature belebte Natur f
Animikian [Period] Animikie n (Oberhuron in Nordamerika)
animikite Animikit m, (Ag, Sb)
anion exchange Anionenaustausch m
anionic potential Anionenpotential n
Anisian [Stage], Anisic [Stage] anisische Stufe f, Anis n (alpine Trias)
anisometric anisometrisch, nichtisometrisch
anisotropic anisotrop
- ~ crystal anisotroper Kristall m
- ~ in strength festigkeitsanisotrop
- ~ permeability anisotrope Permeabilität f

anisotropism Anisotropie f
- ~ of the subsurface Anisotropie f des Untergrunds

anisotropous s. anisotropic
anisotropy Anisotropie f
ankaramite Ankaramit m (basaltisches Ergußgestein)
ankaratrite Ankaratrit m (Olivinnephelinit)
ankerite Ankerit m, Braunspat m, $CaFe[CO_3]_2$
annabergite Annabergit m, Nickelblüte f, $Ni_3[AsO_4]_2 \cdot 8H_2O$
annealing Tempern n, Temperung f
- ~ recrystallization Umkristallisation f (unter starker Erwärmung durch Temperung)

annite Annit *m*, KFe$_3$[(OH)$_2$|AlSi$_3$O$_{10}$]
annivite Annivit *m (Bi-haltiger Tetraedrit)*
annotated image mit Erläuterungen versehene Fernerkundungsaufnahme *f (z.B. über Ort, Datum, Höhe, Sonnenwinkel, Spektralkanal)*
annotation of an outcrop Erläuterung *f* eines Aufschlusses
annual aberration Jahresaberration *f*
~ deposit Jahresablagerung *f*
~ discharge Jahresabflußmenge *f*
~ flood Jahreshochwasser *n*
~ mean Jahresdurchschnitt *m*
~ monsoon Jahresmonsun *m*
~ output Jahresförderung *f*
~ precipitation jährliche Niederschlagsmenge *f*
~ production Jahresförderung *f*
~ rainfall jährliche Niederschlagsmenge *f*
~ ring Jahresring *m (Kalisalz; Bäume)*
~ runoff jährlicher Abfluß *m*
~ storage Jahresspeicherung *f*
~ stratification Jahresschichtung *f*
~ variation Jahresgang *m*
~ variations jährliche Schwankungen *fpl*
~ volume Jahresmenge *f*
annually layered glacial lake clay Bänderton *m*
~ thawed layer *s.* mollisol
annular ringförmig
~ auger Kronenbohrer *m*
~ body Ringkörper *m*
~ groove cut by a coring bit Kernkronenrille *f* im anstehenden Gestein
~ layer Ringschicht *f*
~ reef ringförmiges Riff *n*
~ space Ringraum *m (einer Bohrung)*
annulus 1. Annulus *m*, Periphract *n*, Haftband *n (Cephalopoda)*; 2. Ring *m*; Ringraum *m (einer Bohrung)*
anomalous anomal
anomaly Anomalie *f*, Abweichung *f*, Unregelmäßigkeit *f*
anomite Anomit *m (Varietät von Biotit)*
anorogenetic *s.* anorogenic
anorogenic anorogen
~ granite anorogener Granit *m*
anorthic triklin
anorthite Anorthit *m*, Kalkfeldspat *m*, Ca[Al$_2$Si$_2$O$_8$]
~-basalt Anorthitbasalt *m*
anorthitic anorthitisch
anorthoclase Anorthoklas *m*, (Na, K)AlSi$_3$O$_8$
anorthoclasite Anorthoklasit *m (anorthoklasreiches Tiefgestein)*
anorthose *s.* anorthoclase
anorthosite Anorthosit *m*
anorthositic rocks anorthositische Gesteine *npl (Mondhochländer)*
ant mound *(sl)* Schlammvulkan *m*, Schlammkegel *m*, Salse *f (durch Kohlenwasserstoffgase hervorgebrachter Schlammsprudel an der Golfküste von Texas und Louisiana)*

ANT-rocks ANT-Gesteine *npl (anorthositische, noritische, troktolitische Gesteine)*
ANT-series Mondgesteine *npl* der Serie Anorthosit, Norit, Troktolith
antarctic antarktisch
Antarctic Antarktis *f*
~ Circle südlicher Polarkreis *m*
~ Continent Südpolarland *n*
~ ice sheet antarktischer Eisschild *m*
~ mountains Gebirge *npl* der Antarktis
~ Ocean Südliches Eismeer *n*
~ region südliche kalte Zone *f*
Antarctica Antarktika *f*, Antarktis *f*
antecedent soil moisture epigenetische Bodenfeuchte *f*
~ stream antezedenter Fluß *m*
~ valley antezedentes Tal (Durchbruchstal) *n*
antenna footprint vom Antennenrichtstrahl bestrahlte Fläche
anterior end Stirnrand *m*, Vorderende *n*
~ margin Vorderrand *m*
~ view Vorderansicht *f*
antetype *s.* prototype
anthodite Gips oder Aragonit in Nadel- oder Haarkristallen an Höhlenwänden
anthoinite Anthoinit *m*, Al[OH|WO$_4$]·H$_2$O
anthonyite Anthonyit *m*, Cu(OH, Cl)$_2$·3H$_2$O
anthophyllite Anthophyllit *m*, (Mg, Fe)$_7$[OH|Si$_4$O$_{11}$]$_2$
anthraciferous anthrazithaltig
anthracite Anthrazit *m*
anthracitic anthrazitisch, anthrazitartig
~ shale Anthrazitschiefer *m*
anthracitization Anthrazitisierung *f (Umwandlung in Anthrazit, s.a. coalification)*
anthracitize/to in Anthrazit umwandeln
anthracitous *s.* anthracitic
anthracolite *s.* anthraconite
Anthracolithic Permokarbon *n*
anthraconite Anthrakonit *m*, bituminöser Mergel *m*, Kohlenspat *m*, Stinkstein *m*
anthragenesis *s.* coalification
anthraxylon 1. *(Am)* Vitrinit *m (in Lagen mit über 14 Mikron Breite)*; 2. Vitrit *m*
anthraxylous[-attrital] coal detritische Glanzkohle *f*
anthropic[al], anthropogenic anthropogen
~ soil type anthropogener Bodentyp *m*
anthropogeny Anthropogenie *f*
anthropoid anthropoid, menschenähnlich
anthropologic[al] anthropologisch
anthropology Anthropologie *f*
anthroposphere Anthroposphäre *f*
Antian Antien *n (tieferes Pleistozän der Britischen Inseln)*
anticentre Antizentrum *n*
antichance unzufällig
anticlastic antiklastisch
anticlinal antiklinal, widersinnig *(von Gängen und Schichten)*
~ axis Antiklinalachse *f*, Sattelachse *f*, Gewölbeachse *f*

anticlinal 24

~ **core** Antiklinalkern m, Sattelkern m
~ **crest** Antiklinalsattel m
~ **crest line** Antiklinallinie f, Sattellinie f
~ **fault** antiklinale Verwerfung f, Schenkelbruch m, Gewölbescheitelbruch m, Mittelschenkelbruch m
~ **fissure** Sattelspalte f
~ **flank** Antiklinalflanke f
~ **flexure** Schichtsattel m
~ **fold** antiklinale Falte f
~ **folding** Sattelfaltung f
~ **formation** Sattelbildung f
~ **limb** Antiklinalschenkel m, Sattelschenkel m
~ **line** Antiklinallinie f, Sattellinie f
~ **mountain** Antiklinalkamm m
~ **reservoir** Antiklinalspeicher m, antiklinale Lagerstätte f
~ **ridge** Antiklinalkamm m, Antiklinalrücken m, Antiklinalsattel m, Gebirgssattel m, Scheitel m einer Antiklinale
~ **spring** Antiklinalquelle f
~ **structure** antiklinale (breitsattelförmige) Struktur f
~ **trap** Antiklinalfalle f
~ **uplift** Aufsattelung f
~ **valley** Antiklinaltal n, Satteltal n; aufgebrochene Antiklinale f
anticline Antiklinale f, Sattel m
~ **cut off by a fault plane** durch eine Verwerfungsfläche abgeschnittene Antiklinale f
anticlinorium Antiklinorium n, Faltenbündel n (s.a. geanticline)
anticyclone Antizyklone f, Hoch[druckgebiet] n
antidistortion device Entzerrer m, Entzerrereinrichtung f
antidune Gegenrippel f, flache Sandwelle f
antiepicentre Anti-Epizentrum n
antiferromagnetism Antiferromagnetismus m
antiflushing measures Bruchsicherung f
antifoaming agent Entschäumer m
antifouling paint bewuchsverhindernder Anstrich m
antifreeze Frostschutzmittel n
~ **solution** Frostschutzlösung f
antifriction property Gleiteigenschaft f
antigorite Antigorit m, $Mg_6[(OH)_8|Si_4O_{10}]$
Antillis Antillia f
antilogous pole antiloger Pol m
antimonial, antimonic antimonhaltig
antimoniferous arsenic s. allemontite
antimonious antimonhaltig
antimonite Antimonit m, Antimonglanz m, Sb_2S_3
antimonous s. antimonious
antimonsilver s. dyscrasite
antimonsoon Gegenmonsun m
antimony Antimon n, Sb
~ **blende** s. kermesite
~ **bloom** Antimonblüte f (s.a. valentinite)
~ **glance** s. antimonite
~ **ochre** s. stibiconite

~ **ore** Antimonerz n
antiperthite Antiperthit m
antipollution Reinhaltung f (der Umwelt)
Antiquus time Antiquuszeit f
antiripplets Haftrippeln fpl
antistress mineral Antistreßmineral n
antithetic[al] antithetisch, widersinnig
~ **fault** antithetische (widersinnige) Verwerfung f
antitropal ventilation gegenläufige Bewetterung f
antlerite Antlerit m, $Cu_3[(OH)_4|SO_4]$
antozonite Antozonit m, Stinkspat m (radioaktiv verfärbter Flußspat)
apachite Apachit m (Nephelinphonolith)
apatite Apatit m, $Ca_5[F|(PO_4)_3]$
aperiodic[al] aperiodisch
~ **compass** gedämpfter Kompaß m
~ **damping** aperiodische Dämpfung f
~ **pendulum** aperiodisch gedämpftes Pendel n
apertural margin s. peristome
~ **modification** Modifikation f der Schalenöffnung
aperture Mündung f, Apertur f (Paläontologie)
~ **of the shell** Schalenöffnung f
apex Apex m, Scheitel m, Spitze f
~ **cone** Scheitelkegel m
~ **of a vein** Ausbiß m eines Ganges
~ **of an anticline** Antiklinalkamm m, Scheitel m einer Antiklinale
~ **of the shell** Spitze f der Schale
aphanese s. clinoclasite
aphanic s. aphanitic
aphanite Aphanit m
aphanitic aphanitisch
aphanophyric s. felsiphyric
aphelion Aphel[ium] n, Sonnenferne f
~ **distance** Aphelabstand m
aphotic region (zone) lichtlose Tiefe (Zone) f (des Ozeans)
aphrite Schaumkalk m
aphrolite, aphrolith s. aa lava
aphrosiderite Aphrosiderit m (Varietät von Chlorit)
aphthitalite Aphthitalit m, Glaserit m, $K_3Na[SO_4]_2$
aphyllous blattlos
aphyric nicht porphyrisch
API = American Petroleum Institute
API gamma-ray unit API-Gammastrahlungseinheit f
API gravity Öldichte f nach API
API neutron unit API-Neutronenstrahlungseinheit f
apical apical, am Apex gelegen
~ **chamber** s. initial chamber
apices distance Spannweite f (von Falten)
apjohnite Apjohnit m, $MnAl_2[SO_4]_4 \cdot 22H_2O$
aplanetic surface rauhe Grenzfläche f (Seismik)
aplite Aplit m
~ **dike** Aplitgang m

aplitic aplitisch
~ dike rock aplitisches Ganggestein *n*
aplogranite Aplogranit *m (Granit mit wenig Biotit)*
aplome Aplom *m (Al-Andradit)*
aplowite Aplowit *m*, (Co, Mn, Ni)[SO$_4$]·4H$_2$O
apobsidian Apobsidian *m (entglaster Obsidian)*
apochromatic apochromatisch
apocynthion Mondferne *f*
apogee Apogäum *n*, Erdferne *f*
apogrit *s.* graywacke
apomagmatic apomagmatisch
~ deposit apomagmatische Lagerstätte *f*
apomorphic apomorph, abgeleitet
apomorphy Apomorphie *f*
apophyllite Apophyllit *m*, KCa$_4$[F|(Si$_4$O$_{10}$)$_2$]·8H$_2$O
apophyse, apophysis Apophyse *f (Abzweigung vom Hauptgang)*
aporhyolite Aporhyolith *m (entglaster Rhyolith)*
aposandstone *s.* quartzite
apotectonic *s.* posttectonic
Appalachia Appalachia *f*
Appalachian oldland Appalachia *f*
~ Province Appalachen-Provinz *f (Paläobiogeografie, Devon)*
Appalachis Appalachia *f*
apparatus for plasticity test Fließgrenzengerät *n*
~ for rectification Entzerrungsgerät *n*
apparent scheinbar
~ age scheinbares Alter *n*
~ density Porigkeit *f*, Porosität *f*
~ dip scheinbares Einfallen *n*
~ gap in bedding plane scheinbare Sprungweite *f* in der Schichtebene
~ heave (horizontal overlap) scheinbare söhlige (horizontale) Sprungweite *f*
~ mining damage Pseudobergschaden *m*
~ resistivity scheinbarer spezifischer Widerstand *m (bedingt durch Meßanordnung)*
~ slip flache Sprunghöhe *f*
~ solar day wahrer Sonnentag *m*
~ solar time wahre Sonnenzeit *f*
~ stratigraphic[al] gap scheinbare Sprungweite *f* in der Schichtebene
~ stratigraphic[al] separation scheinbare stratigrafische Sprunghöhe (Schubhöhe) *f*
~ thickness scheinbare Mächtigkeit *f (Bohrlochmächtigkeit, Ausstrichbreite)*
~ throw scheinbare seigere Sprunghöhe *f*
~ top scheinbare Oberkante *f*
~ velocity Scheingeschwindigkeit *f*
~ velocity of ground-water flow Filtergeschwindigkeit *f* des Grundwassers
~ water resistivity scheinbarer Wasserwiderstand *m*
~ water table Nebengrundwasserspiegel *m*
appear/to auftreten
appearance of fracture Bruch[flächen]aussehen *n*

appinite Appinit *m (hornblendereiche Syenite, Monzonite, Diorite)*
applanation Einebnung *f (eines Reliefs)*
apple coal weiche Kohle *f*
application of load Lastaufbringung *f*, Lastangriff *m*
applied geology angewandte (praktische) Geologie *f*
~ geophysics angewandte (praktische) Geophysik *f*
~ hydrology angewandte (praktische) Hydrologie *f*
apposition Anlagerung *f*
~ fabric Primärgefüge *n*
appraisal well Erweiterungsbohrung *f*
appraise/to schätzen, taxieren
approximate scale mittlerer Bildmaßstab *m*
approximation Näherung *f*
apron Sander *m*, Schuttfächer *m*; Schuttschicht *f* gegen Unterspülung
~ plain Sanderebene *f*
apse, apsis Apside *f*, Wendepunkt *m*
Aptian [Stage] Apt *n (Stufe der Unterkreide)*
Aptychus Marl Aptychenmergel *m (pelagische Entwicklung in Malm und Unterkreide, Alpen)*
aqua regia Königswasser *n*
aquafact durch Wellenschlag geglättetes Küstengeröll *n*
aquafer *s.* aquifer
aqualung Aqualunge *f*; Freitauchgerät *n*
aquamarine blaugrün
aquamarine Aquamarin *m (s.a. beryl)*
aquapulse Aquapulse *n (eine seeseismische Energiequelle)*
aquathermal pressuring Überdruck durch thermische Ausdehnung des Poreninhalts
aquatic aquatisch
~ carnivora Wasserraubtiere *npl*
aqueduct Aquädukt *m*
aqueoglacial fluvioglazial
~ deposits Schmelzwasserablagerungen *fpl*
aqueous wäßrig, wasserhaltig; durch Wasser gebildet
~ corrosion Wasserkorrosion *f*, Feuchtigkeitskorrosion *f*
~ current ripple marks *s.* water current ripples
~ desert marines Sediment *n* ohne makroskopische Schalenreste
~ gel wäßriges Gel *n*
~ lava Schlammlava *f*
~ loess Schwemmlöß *m*
~ oscillation ripple marks *s.* wave ripple marks
~ rock Sedimentgestein *n*
~ solution wäßrige Lösung *f*
~ vapour Wasserdampf *m*
aquiclude wasserdicht
aquiclude geringpermeabler Grundwasserleiter *m*, Geringwasserleiter *m*
aquifer [layer] Wasserleiter *m*, Grundwasserträ-

aquifer 26

ger *m*, Grundwasserleiter *m*, wasserführende Schicht *f*
~ **packing** Abdichten *n* eines Grundwasserleiters
~ **storage** Aquiferspeicherung *f*, Gasspeicherung *f* im Wasserträger
~ **thickness** Grundwasserleitermächtigkeit *f*
aquiferous wasserdurchlässig, wasserführend, Wasser enthaltend
aquifuge wasserdicht
aquifuse Grundwasserstauer *m*
Aquitanian [Stage] Aquitan[ium] *n*, Aquitanien *n* *(Stufe des Miozäns)*
aquitarde *s.* aquiclude
arable ackerfähig, kultivierbar
~ **earth** Ackerkrume *f*
~ **land** Ackerland *n*
~ **meadow** Ackerwiese *f*
~ **soil** Ackerboden *m*, Kulturboden *m*, kulturfähiger (urbarer) Boden *m*
araeoxene Araeoxen *m (Varietät von Deskloizit)*
aragonite Aragonit *m*, $CaCO_3$
aramayoite Aramayoit *m*, $Ag(Sb, Bi)S_2$
arandisite Arandisit *m (Gemenge von Hydrocassiterit und Quarz)*
arapahite Arapahit *m (magnetitreicher Basalt)*
arborescent dendritisch, tannenbäumchenartig, baumförmig
~ **agate** Baumachat *m*
~ **crystal** Dendrit *m*
~ **fern** Baumfarn *m*
~ **structure** dendritische Struktur *f*
arborization baumförmige Bildung *f*, Verästelung *f*
arc excitation Bogenanregung *f (Spektralanalyse)*
~ **of folding** Stauungsbogen *m*, Faltenbogen *m*
~ **of volcanoes** Vulkanbogen *m*
~ **shooting** Sternschießen *n*, Fächerschießen *n (Refraktionsschießen)*
~-**trench systems** Systeme von Inselbögen und Tiefseegräben
arch/to [auf]wölben
arch Gewölbe *n*, Sattel *m*
~ **bend** Sattelscharnier *n*
~ **core** Sattelkern *m*
~ **dam** Bogenstaumauer *f*
~-**gravity dam** Bogengewichtsmauer *f*, Bogengewichtssperre *f*, Gewölbegewichtssperre *f*
~ **limb** Gewölbeschenkel *m (Falte)*
~ **theory** Gewölbetheorie *f*
Archaean archäisch, archäozoisch
Archaean [Era] Archaikum *n*, Archäozoikum *n*, Urzeit *f*
~ **folding** archäische Faltung *f*
Archaeozoic archäozoisch, archäisch
Archaeozoic [Era] 1. Archäozoikum *n*, Kryptozoikum *n*, Unterpräkambrium *n*; 2. Archaikum *n*, Archäozoikum *n*, Urzeit *f*
archaic archäisch, urzeitlich

arche... *s.a.* archae...
arched dam Bogensperrmauer *f*, Bogen[stau]mauer *f*, Gewölbemauer *f*
~ **roof (top)** Gewölbe *n*
~-**up** aufgewölbt
~ **upfold** Sattelfalte *f*
archetype *s.* prototype
Archie formation-factor equation Archiesche Formationsfaktorformel *f*
Archie's law Archie-Gleichung *f*
arching bogig
arching Auffaltung *f*, Beulung *f*, Aufwölbung *f*, Wölbung *f*
~ **effect** Bogenwirkung *f*, Gewölbewirkung *f (Erddruckverteilung)*
archipelagic apron inselförmige Sand- und Kiesablagerung *f*
archipelago Archipel *m*, Inselgruppe *f*
architectonic geology Tektonik *f*
arcilla Ton *m*, Kaolin *m (Mexiko)*
arcose Arkose *f (s.a.* arkose*)*
arcosic Arkose... *(s.a.* arkosic*)*
arctic arktisch, polar
~ **air** arktische Kaltluft *f*
~ **expedition** Nordpolarexpedition *f*
~ **front** Kaltfront *f*
Arctic Circle nördlicher Polarkreis *m*
~ **glacier** Polargletscher *m*
~ **mountains** Gebirge *npl* der Arktis
~ **Ocean** Nördliches Eismeer *n*
~ **pack** arktisches Treibeis *n*
~ **region** Arktis *f*; arktisches Gebiet *n*
~ **zone** arktisches Gebiet *n*
arcuate gebogen, bogenförmig
ardennite Ardennit *m (Al-, Mn-, V-Silikat)*
area Fläche *f*, Gebiet *n*, Zone *f*; Feld *n (im Abbau)*
~ **affected by dammed water** Staugebiet *n*
~ **in advance** Vorland *n*
~ **measurement** Flächenmessung *f*
~ **measuring equipment** Flächenmeßgerät *n*
~ **occupied by settlements** Besiedlungsgebiet *n*
~ **of audibility** Schallfeld *n*, Hörbarkeitsgebiet *n*
~ **of dewatering** Wasserabsenkungsbereich *m*
~ **of discontinuity** Unstetigkeitsfläche *f*
~ **of dissipation** *s.* ablation area
~ **of extraction** Einwirkungsfläche *f (Bergschaden)*
~ **of fracture** Bruchgebiet *n*
~ **of glaciation** Vergletscherungsgebiet *n*
~ **of high pressure** Hochdruckgebiet *n*
~ **of influence** Wirkungszone *f*
~ **of low pressure** Tiefdruckgebiet *n*
~ **of ore body** Erzfläche *f*
~ **of precipitation** Niederschlagsgebiet *n*
~ **of protection** Schutzgebiet *n*
~ **of sedimentation** Sedimentationsgebiet *n*
~ **of settlement** Einwirkungsfläche *f (Bergschaden)*
~ **of subsidence** Senkungszone *f*

~ **of tectonic culmination** Auffaltungsfeld *n*, Megaantiklinale *f*
~ **of tectonic depression** Einfaltungsfeld *n*, Megasynklinale *f*
~ **of truncation** Abtragungsgebiet *n*
~ **of uplift** Hebungsgebiet *n*
~ **of visibility** Sichtbarkeitsgebiet *n*
~ **sampling frame** Flächenrahmen *m* für Datensammlung
~ **without exposures** aufschlußloses Gebiet *n*
~ **without exposures and untested by drilling** aufschlußloses, noch nicht durch Bohrungen untersuchtes Gebiet *n*
areal capacity Flächenleistung *f* (je Fläche und Zeit bei Kompaktion ausgepreßte Wassermenge)
~ **degradation** flächenhafte Abtragung *f*
~ **density** Flächendichte *f*, Flächengewicht *n*, Flächenbelegung *f*
~ **efficiency** areale Wirksamkeit *f* (bei Flutung)
~ **eruption** Arealeruption *f*, Flächeneruption *f*, flächenhafte Eruption *f*
~ **exposure** Flächenaufschluß *m*
~ **extent** Flächenausdehnung *f*
~ **features** flächenhafte Merkmale *npl* (Eigenschaften *fpl*)
~ **geology** Regionalgeologie *f*, Oberflächengeologie *f*
~ **map** geologische Karte *f* der Oberflächenformationen
~ **productiveness** Flächenergiebigkeit *f* (bei Kompaktion ausgepreßte Wassermenge)
~ **seismics** Flächenseismik *f*, 3D-Seismik *f*
~ **subsidence** Gebietssenkung *f*
arenaceous sandig; stark sandhaltig; psammitisch
~ **facies** sandige Fazies *f*
~ **foraminifera** sandschalige Foraminiferen *fpl*, Kieselschaler-Foraminiferen *fpl*
~ **limestone** Kalksandstein *m*, sandiger Kalkstein *m*
~ **quartz** Quarzsand *m*, sandiger Quarz *m*
~ **rock** Sandgestein *n*, sandiges Gestein *n*
~ **shale** Sandschiefer *m*, Quarzschieferton *m*
~ **tests** Sandschaler *mpl*
~ **texture** psammitische Struktur *f*
Arenigian [Stage] Arenig *n* (Stufe des Unterordoviziums)
arenilitic sandsteinartig
arenite *s.* psammite
arenose kiesig, grießig, grittig, sandig
arenyte *s.* psammite
areola of [contact] metamorphism Kontakthof *m*
arête Grat *m*
arfvedsonite Arfvedsonit *m*, $Na_3Fe_4Al[(OH)_2|Si_8O_{22}]$
argent silbern, silbrig
argentic silberhaltig, Silber...
argentiferous silberführend, silberhaltig
argentine silberartig, silberähnlich
argentite Argentit *m*, Silberglanz *m*, Akanthit *m*, Ag_2S

argentojarosite Argentojarosit *m*, $AgFe_3[(OH)_6|(SO_4)_2]$
argentopyrite Argentopyrit *m*, $AgFe_2S_3$
argil Ton *m*, Letten *m*
argilla Ton *m* (natürliches Aluminiumsilikat)
argillaceous tonig; tonhaltig, tonartig
~ **alteration** Vertonung *f*, Umwandlung *f* in Tonminerale
~ **bauxite** tonhaltiger Bauxit *m* (Tongehalt bis 50%)
~ **cementing material** toniges Bindemittel *n*
~ **earth** Tonerde *f*
~ **facies** tonige Fazies *f*
~ **horizon** Illuvialhorizont *m* mit hohem Tonanteil
~ **iron ore concretions** Toneisensteinkonkretionen *fpl*
~ **iron-stone** Toneisenstein *m*, Sphärosiderit *m*
~ **limestone** Tonkalk *m*, toniger Kalkstein *m*
~ **marl** Tonmergel *m*, Mergelton *m*
~ **material** toniges Bindemittel *n*
~ **mud** toniger Schlick *m*
~ **ore** toniges (lettiges) Erz *n*
~ **rock** Tongestein *n*, tonhaltiges (toniges) Gestein *n*
~ **sand** toniger Sand *m*
~ **sand ground** sandiger Lehmboden *m*
~ **sandstone** Tonsandstein *m*, toniger Sandstein *m*
~ **schist** Tonschiefer *m*
~ **shale** Schieferton *m*
~ **slate** Argillit *m*
~ **texture** pelitische Struktur *f*
argillation Vertonung *f* (durch Verwitterung)
argillic *s.* argillaceous
argilliferous tonhaltig
argillite Argillit *m* (vorgefestigter Ton)
argillitic argillitisch
argillization Tonbildung *f*
argillo-arenaceous ton- und sandhaltig
argillous tonhaltig; tonartig
argon Argon *n*, Ar
~ **age** Argonalter *n*
Argovian [Substage] Argov[ium] *n* (Unterstufe des Lusitans)
argyrite *s.* argentite
argyrodite Argyrodit *m*, $4Ag_2S \cdot GeS_2$
argyrose *s.* argentite
argyrthrose *s.* pyrargyrite
arid arid, dürr, trocken
~ **area (region)** Trockengebiet *n*
~ **runoff** Trockenwetterabfluß *m*
aridity, aridness Aridität *f*, Dürre *f*, Unfruchtbarkeit *f*, Trockenheit *f*
ariegite Ariégit *m* (Pyroxenit)
Arikareean [Stage] Arikareean *n* (Wirbeltierstufe des oberen Oligozäns und unteren Miozäns in Nordamerika)
arite Arit *m*, Ni(As, Sb)
arizonite 1. Arizonit *m*, $Fe_2O_3 \cdot 3TiO_2$; 2. Arizonit *m* (orthoklasreiches Ganggestein)

arkite 28

arkite Arkit *m (alkalisches Ergußgestein)*
arkose Arkose *f*
~ **quartzite** Arkosequarzit *m*
arkosic arkosig
~ **bentonite** Bentonit *m* mit kristallinem Detritus
~ **grit** Arkosesandstein *m*
~ **wacke** Feldspatgrauwacke *f (mehr Feldspatals Gesteinsbruchstücke)*
arkosite *s.* arkose quartzite
arm of a delta Deltaarm *m*
~ **of a river** Nebenarm *m*
~ **of the sea** Meeresarm *m*
~ **support** Armgerüst *n (der Brachiopoden)*
armalcolite Armalkolith *m*, $(Fe_{0,5} \cdot Mg_{0,5})Ti_2O_5$ *(Mondmineral)*
armangite Armangit *m*, $Mn_3[AsO_3]_2$
Armorica Armorika *f*
Armorican massif armorikanisches Massiv *n*
armoured mud balls gespickte Tongerölle *npl*
~ **relict** gepanzertes Relikt *n*
aromatic hydrocarbon aromatischer Kohlenwasserstoff *m*
aromatics Aromaten *mpl (Kohlenwasserstoffe)*
arquetype *s.* prototype
arrangement Anordnung *f*, Aufbau *m*; Lagerung *f*
~ **in layers** Schichtung *f*
~ **in rows** Aufreihung *f*
array 1. Anordnung *f (von Geophonen oder Schüssen);* 2. Array *n (Netz seismischer Stationen)*
arresting nitrogen gebundener Stickstoff *m*
arrival time Einsatzzeit *f*, Zeitdauer *f* bis zum Anfangseinsatz *(Seismik);* Laufzeit *f (einer Reflexion)*
~ **time of seismic waves** Ankunftszeit *f* seismischer Wellen
arrojadite Arrojadit *m*, Headdenit *m (Fe-, Mn-Phosphat)*
arroyo Arroyo *n (Relikttal)*
arsenic Arsen *n*, As
~ **ore** Arsenerz *n*
arsenical arsenhaltig, arsenführend
~ **copper** *s.* domeykite
~ **nickel** *s.* niccolite
~ **pyrite** *s.* arsenopyrite
arseniferous arsenführend
arseniopleite Arseniopleit *m (Varietät von Karyinit)*
arseniosiderite Arseniosiderit *m*, $Ca_3Fe_4[OH|AsO_4]_4 \cdot 4H_2O$
arsenious arsenhaltig
arsenite *s.* arsenolite
arsenobismite Arsenobismit *m*, $Bi_4[OH|AsO_4]_3 \cdot H_2O$
arsenoclasite Arsenoklasit *m*, $Mn_5[(OH)_2|AsO_4]_2$
arsenoferrite Arsenoferrit *m*, $FeAs_2$
arsenolamprite Arsenolamprit *m (Arsenmodifikation)*
arsenolite Arsenolith *m*, Arsenit *m*, Arsenblüte *f*, As_2O_3

arsenopalladinite Arsenopalladinit *m*, Pd_3As
arsenopyrite Arsenkies *m*, Arsenopyrit *m;* Mispickel *m*, FeAsS
arsenpolybasite Arsenpolybasit *m*, $8(Ag, Cu)_2S \cdot As_2S_3$
arsensulvanite Arsensulvanit *m*, $Cu_3(As,V)S_4$
arsenuranylite Arsenuranylit *m*, $Ca[(UO_2)_4|(OH)_4|(AsO_4)_2] \cdot 6H_2O$
artefact Artefakt *n*
arterite Arterit *m (ein Migmatit)*
artesian artesisch
~ **aquifer** Grundwasserleiter *m* mit artesischem Wasser, Grundwasserleiter *m* mit gespanntem Grundwasser, artesischer Grundwasserspeicher *m*
~ **basin** artesisches Becken *n*
~ **discharge** Ergiebigkeit *f* eines artesischen Brunnens
~ **ground water** artesisches Grundwasser *n (überflurgespannt)*
~ **[pressure] head** artesischer Wasserhorizont *m*, artesische Druckhöhe *f*, Steighöhe *f (artesischer Brunnen)*
~ **spring** artesischer Brunnen *m*, artesische Quelle *f*
~ **uplift pressure** artesischer Auftrieb *m*
~ **water** artesisches Wasser *n*, gespanntes (unter Spannung stehendes) Grundwasser *n*
~ **well** 1. Brunnen *m* mit gespanntem Grundwasserspiegel; 2. frei ausfließende Bohrung *f;* artesischer Brunnen *m*
article of antiquity Ausgrabungsfund *m*
articular facets Gelenkflächen *fpl*
Articulata Articulaten *pl*
articulated skeleton Skelett *n* im Zusammenhang
articulation Gelenkverbindung *f*
articulite Gelenkquarzit *m*
artifact Artefakt *n*
artificial cementation Bodenstabilisierung *f*, Baugrundverbesserung *f*, Baugrundverfestigung *f*
~ **consolidation** künstliche Bodenverdichtung *f*
~ **earth satellite** künstlicher Erdsatellit *m*
~ **earthquake** künstliches Erdbeben *n*
~ **gemstone** synthetischer Edelstein *m*
~ **ground water** künstliches Grundwasser *n*
~ **impulse method** Fremdimpulsmethode *f*
~ **lake** Sammelbecken *n*, Staubecken *n*, Stausee *m*
~ **lift method** künstliches Förderverfahren *n (Erdöl)*
~ **magnetic anomalies** magnetische Störanomalien *fpl (z.B. durch Hochspannungsleitungen)*
~ **marginal salt pan** künstlich angelegter Meeressalzgarten *m*
~ **method of cementation by the injection of chemicals** chemische Baugrundverbesserung *f*
~ **precipitation** künstlicher Niederschlag *m*
~ **radioactivity** künstliche Radioaktivität *f*
~ **recharge of ground water** künstliche Grundwasseranreicherung *f*

associated

~ **river regulation** Flußregulierung f
~ **roof** künstliches Dach n
~ **satellite** künstlicher Satellit m
~ **subgrade** aufgeschüttetes Planum (Erdplanum) n
~ **water conduit** künstlicher Wasserlauf m
artificially excited earth waves künstlich erregte Bodenerschütterungswellen fpl
~ **produced radioisotope** künstliches radioaktives Isotop n
artinite Artinit m, $Mg_2[(OH)_2|CO_3]\cdot 3H_2O$
Artinskian [Stage] Artinsk n (basale Stufe des Unterperms)
arzrunite Arzrunit m, $Pb_2Cu_4[O_2|Cl_6|SO_4]\cdot 4H_2O$
asar s. esker
asbestic, asbestine 1. asbestführend; 2. unbrennbar
asbestoid asbestartig
asbestos Asbest m
~ **slate** Asbestschiefer m
asbestous s. asbestic
asbolan[e] Asbolan m (s.a. asbolite)
asbolite Erdkobalt m, Kobaltmanganerz n (Kobaltoxid)
ascend/to aufsteigen
ascending aufsteigend (Luftstrom, Wasser)
~ **solution** aufsteigende Lösung f
~ **water** aszendendes Wasser n
ascension theory Aszensionstheorie f
ascent of water Aufsteigen n des Wassers
~ **path** Aufstiegsbahn f
aschaffite Aschaffit m (Lamprophyr)
ascharite Ascharit m, $Mg_2[B_2O_5]\cdot H_2O$
aschistic aschist[isch], ungespalten
~ **dike rock** aschistes (ungespaltenes) Ganggestein n
aseismic[al] aseismisch, erdbebenfrei, erdbebensicher
~ **district** erdbebenfreies Gebiet n
~ **region** aseismische Region f
ash Asche f
~ **cloud** Aschewolke f
~ **cone** Aschekegel m
~ **constituent** Aschebildner m
~ **content** Aschegehalt m
~ **fall** Aschefall m
~ **flows** Aschenströme mpl
~-**free** aschefrei (Kohlenanalyse)
~ **rain (shower)** Ascheregen m
~ **slate** Aschetonschiefer m
ashcroftine Ashcroftin m, $KNa(Ca, Mg, Mn)[Al_4Si_5O_{18}]\cdot 8H_2O$
ashes vulkanische Ascheschicht f
Ashgillian [Stage] Ashgill n, Ashgillstufe f (Stufe des Oberordoviziums)
ashlar Werkstein m, Quader[stein] m
~ **stone walling**, ~ **stonework** Werksteinmauerwerk n, Quadermauerwerk n
ashless aschefrei
ashore an Land, ans Ufer
ashy component Aschebildner m
~ **grit** pyroklastischer Sand m

~ **shale** Ascheschieferton m
asiderite Steinmeteorit m
aslope abschüssig, steil
aso lava s. ignimbrite
asowskite Asowskit m, $Fe_3[(OH)_6|PO_4]$
asparagus stone Varietät von Apatit
asperity Rauhigkeit f (einer Kluft)
asphalt Asphalt m, Erdpech n
~-**base crude petroleum** asphaltbasisches Rohöl n
~-**base oil** Asphaltöl n
~-**base petroleum** asphaltbasisches Erdöl n
~ **deposit** Asphaltlager n, Asphaltvorkommen n
~ **from petroleum oil** Erdölasphalt m
~-**impregnated limestone** Asphaltkalkstein m, Kalkasphalt m
~ **membrane** (Am) Bitumendichtungshaut f
~ **rock** Asphaltgestein n, Bergasphalt m, asphaltimprägnierter Kalkstein m
~ **seepage** Asphaltausbiß m
~ **stone** s. ~ rock
asphaltene Asphalten n
asphaltic aus Asphalt, asphaltisch; asphalthaltig, erdpechhaltig
~ **bitumen** Erdölbitumen n, Naturbitumen n
~ **bitumen membrane** Bitumendichtungshaut f
~ **coal** s. albertite
~ **concrete** Asphaltbeton m
~ **limestone** Asphaltkalkstein m, Kalkasphalt m
~ **pyrobituminous shale** Ölschiefer m
~ **rock** Asphaltgestein n, Bergasphalt m, asphaltimprägnierter Kalkstein m
~ **sand** Asphaltsand m
~ **sandstone** bitumenhaltiger Sandstein m
asphaltite Asphaltit m (z.B. Gilsonit, Grahamit)
asphaltlike asphaltähnlich
asphaltum s. asphalt
assay Probe f, Erzprobe f, Lötrohrprobe f
~ **of buddled (washed) ore** Erzwaschprobe f
assaying Probenuntersuchung f (Rohstoff)
Asselian [Stage] Assel[ium] n (höchste Stufe des Oberkarbons)
assemblage 1. Vergesellschaftung f, Gemeinschaft f (Paläobiologie); 2. Paragenese f (von Mineralen)
~ **zone** biostratigrafische Einheit, gekennzeichnet durch die vertikale Verbreitung einer bestimmten Gesamtfauna oder -flora innerhalb einer Gesteinsabfolge
assembly Anordnung f, Aufbau m
assignment Bestimmung f, Angabe f
assimilation Assimilation f
assise zwei oder mehr aufeinander folgende fossilhaltige Zonen
associate/to 1. vergesellschaften (Paläobiologie); 2. paragenetisch vorkommen (Minerale)
associated fault Nebenverwerfung f, Begleitverwerfung f
~ **mineral** Begleitmineral n, Nebenmineral n
~ **natural gas** freies Erdölbegleitgas n
~ **rocks** Begleitgesteine npl

associated

~ **sheets** vereinigte Flöze *npl*
~ **strata** Nebengestein *n*
association 1. Vergesellschaftung *f*, Gemeinschaft *f (Paläobiologie)*; 2. Paragenese *f (von Mineralen)*
assort/to 1. einteilen, klassifizieren; 2. sortieren; 3. aufarbeiten *(durch Wasser)*
assorting 1. Einteilung *f*, Klassifikation *f*; 2. Sortierung *f*; 3. Aufarbeitung *f (durch Wasser)*
assumption of load Belastungsannahme *f*, Lastannahme *f*
assured ore sicher vorhandenes Erz *n*
Assynt folding assyntische Faltung *f*
astatic astatisch, unstabil
~ **magnetometer** astatisches Magnetometer *n*
~ **pendulum** astasiertes Pendel *n*
asteriated quartz Sternquarz *m*
asteriation, asterism Asterismus *m*
asteroid sternartig, sternförmig
~ **belt** Asteroidengürtel *m*
asteroid Asteroid *m*, Planetoid *m*
asthenolith Asthenolit *m*
asthenosphere Asthenosphäre *f*
Astian [Stage] Ast *n*, Asti-Stufe *f (Stufe des Pliozäns)*
astillen Salband *n*
astite Astit *m (Varietät von Hornfels)*
astrak[h]anite Astrakanit *m*, Blödit *m*, $Na_2Mg(SO_4)_2 \cdot 4H_2O$
astral sternartig, Stern...
~ **exploration** Sternforschung *f*
astringent mit zusammenziehendem Geschmack *(bei bestimmten Mineralen)*
~ **clay** alaunhaltiger Ton *m*
astrionics Weltraumforschung *f*
astrobiology Astrobiologie *f*
astrobleme Astroblem *n*, Meteoritenkrater *m*
astrobotany Astrobotanik *f*
astrochemistry Astrochemie *f*
astrocompass Sternkompaß *m*
astrodynamics Astrodynamik *f*
astrogeologist Astrogeologe *m*
astrogeology Astrogeologie *f*
astrolite Astrolith *m*, $(Na, K)_2Fe(Al, Fe)_2(SiO_3)_5 \cdot H_2O$
astrological astrologisch
astrometry Astrometrie *f*
astronautics Astronautik *f*
astronavigation Astronavigation *f*
astronomer Astronom *m*
astronomic[al] astronomisch
~ **altitude** Gestirnhöhe *f*
~ **day** astronomischer Tag *m*
~ **geology** astronomische Geologie *f*
~ **latitude** astronomische Breite *f*
~ **navigation** Astronavigation *f*
~ **observation** Sternbeobachtung *f*
~ **observatory (station)** Sternwarte *f*
~ **time reckoning** astronomische Zeitberechnung *f*
~ **zenith** astronomischer Zenit *m*
astronomy Astronomie *f*, Sternkunde *f*

astrophyllite Astrophyllit *m*, $(K_2, Na_2, Ca)(Fe, Mn)_4(Ti, Zr)[OH|Si_2O_7]_2$
astrophysical astrophysikalisch
astrophysicist Astrophysiker *m*
astrophysics Astrophysik *f*
astroscopy Sternbeobachtung *f*
astrospectroscopy Astrospektroskopie *f*
asymmetric[al] unsymmetrisch
~ **anticline** unsymmetrische Antiklinale *f*
~ **fold** asymmetrische Falte *f*
~ **ripple marks** unsymmetrische Rippelmarken *fpl*
asymmetrically folded mountain range unsymmetrisch gefaltetes Gebirge *n*
asymmetry Asymmetrie *f*
asynchronous deposits ungleichaltrige Ablagerungen *fpl*
atacamite Atakamit *m*, $Cu_2(OH)_3Cl$
atatschite Atatschit *m (glasreicher Orthophyr)*
atavism Atavismus *m (Paläontologie)*
ataxic ungeschichtet *(bei Erzlagerstätten)*
ataxite 1. Ataxit *m (Eisenmeteorit)*; 2. irreguläre Tufflava *f*
Atdabanian [Stage] Atdaban[ium] *n (Stufe, höheres Unterkambrium Sibiriens)*
atectonic atektonisch
~ **pluton** anorogener Pluton *m*
atelestite Atelestit *m*, $Bi_2[O|OH|AsO_4]$
athrogenic vulkanoklastisch
~ **rock** vulkanoklastisches Gestein *n*
Atlantic atlantisch
~ **Ocean** Atlantischer Ozean *m*
~ **rock** atlantisches Gestein *n*
~ **suite** atlantische Sippe *f*
Atlantica Atlantika *f*
Atlanticum Atlantikum *n (Holozän)*
atmochemistry Chemie *f* der Atmosphäre
atmoclastic atmoklastisch
~ **rock** atmoklastisches Gestein *n*
atmogeochemical prospecting Gasprospektion *f*
atmogeochemistry Atmogeochemie *f*
atmologic[al] meteorologisch
atmophil[ic] atmophil
~ **element** atmophiles Element *n*
atmopyroclastic atmopyroklastisch
atmosphere Atmosphäre *f*
atmospheric[al] atmosphärisch
~ **absorption** atmosphärische Absorption *f*
~ **action** Witterungseinfluß *m*
~ **composition** Luftzusammensetzung *f*
~ **condition** Witterung *f*
~ **constituents** atmosphärische Bestandteile *mpl*
~ **entry** Eintauchen *n* in die Atmosphäre
~ **exposure** Witterungseinfluß *m*
~ **moisture** Luftfeuchte *f*
~ **oxygen** Luftsauerstoff *m*
~ **pressure** Luftdruck *m*
~ **radiation** atmosphärische Strahlung *f*
~ **turbidity** atmosphärische Trübung *f*
~ **waste** Verwitterungsschutt *m*

auriferous

~ **water** atmosphärisches Wasser n, Niederschlagswasser n
Atokan [Stage] Atokan n (Stufe des Pennsylvaniens)
atoll [reef] Atoll n, Lagunenriff n, Ringriff n (aus Korallen)
atom Atom n
~ **smasher** Neutronenquelle f (für Bohrlochmessungen)
atomic absorption spectrometry Atomabsorptionsspektrometrie f
~ **arrangement** atomarer Aufbau m
~ **blast** Atomexplosion f
~ **chart** Atomgewichtstabelle f
~ **concentration** Atomkonzentration f
~ **decay (disintegration)** Atomzerfall m
~ **energy** Atomenergie f
~ **fission** Kernspaltung f
~ **forces** Atomkräfte fpl
~ **group** Atomgruppe f
~ **heat** Atomwärme f
~ **irradiation** radioaktive Bestrahlung f
~ **kernel** Atomkern m
~ **mass** Atommasse f, Isotopengewicht n
~ **mass number** Atommassenzahl f
~ **nucleus** Atomkern m
~ **number** Atomzahl f, Kernladungszahl f, Ordnungszahl f
~ **physicist** Atomphysiker m
~ **physics** Atomphysik f
~ **plane** Gitterebene f, Netzebene f
~ **radiation** Atomstrahlung f
~ **rearrangement** atomare Umordnung f
~ **scientist** Atomforscher m, Atomwissenschaftler m, Kernforscher m
~ **space lattice** Atomgitter n
~ **spectrum** Atomspektrum n
~ **structure** atomare Struktur f, Atom[auf]bau m, atomarer Aufbau m
~ **symbol** Atomsymbol n
~ **theory** Atomtheorie f, Atomlehre f
~ **transformation** Atomumwandlung f
~ **volume** Atomvolumen n
~ **weight** Atomgewicht n
atopite Atopit m (Varietät von Romeit)
attachable mechanical stage aufsetzbarer Kreuztisch m, Objektführer m (Stereomikroskop)
attached fold anliegende (verwachsene) Falte f
~ **ground water** gebundenes Grundwasser n
~ **island** Angliederungsinsel f
~ **water** Haftwasser n, Adhäsionswasser n
attal Bergeschicht f, Gesteinsschicht f
~ **stuff** Alter Mann m, taubes Gestein n
attendant satellite begleitender Trabant m
attenuation Dämpfung f
~ **of seismic energy** Verminderung f seismischer Energie
attenuator Dämpfungseinrichtung f
Atterberg limits Atterbergsche Konsistenzgrenzen (Zustandsgrenzen) fpl
attitude Lagerung f, Schichtenlagerung f, Strei-

chen n und Fallen n (als Gesamtheit der Lagerungsform)
~ **control** Orientierungskontrolle f (Kontrolle der räumlichen Orientierung eines Fernerkundungsaufnahmesystems bezüglich eines äußeren Bezugssystems)
attle Versatzschicht f, Bergeschicht f, Berge pl, taubes Gestein n
~ **heap** Halde f, Bergehalde f, Gesteinshalde f
attraction Anziehung f
~ **of gravitation** Schwereanziehung f
attractional force Anziehungskraft f
attrinite Attrinit m (Braunkohlenmaceral)
attrital brown coal erdige Braunkohle f
~ **lignite** (Am) detritische Hartbraunkohle f
attrition Abrasion f, Abschleifung f, Abrieb m
~ **clay** Lettenbesteg m
~ **of the wind** Windschliff m
~ **rate** Abrasionsrate f
attritus Attritus m (Am, Maceralgemisch der Vitrinit-, Exinit- und Inertinit-Gruppe; meist in feinstreifiger Wechsellagerung)
aubrite Aubrit m (achondritischer enstatitführender Meteorit)
auerlite Auerlith m, Th[(Si, P)O$_4$]
auganite Auganit m (Augitandesit)
augelite Augelith m, Al$_2$[(OH)$_3$|PO$_4$]
augen gneiss Augengneis m
auger Erdbohrer m, Gesteinsbohrer m, Schappe f, Schappenbohrer m; Stangenbohrer m
~ **bit** Schneckenbohrer m
~ **boring** Schappenbohren n, Schappenbohrung f, Handdrehbohrung f
~ **drill** Meißel m (zur Durchteufung harter felsiger Schichtglieder)
~ **drilling** Schneckenbohren n
~ **mining** Bohrlochbergbau m (Gewinnungsverfahren von Kohle mittels großkalibriger Schlangenbohrer)
augite Augit m, (Ca, Mg, Fe, Ti, Al)$_2$[(Si, Al)$_2$O$_6$]
~ **amphibolite** Augitamphibolit m
~ **andesite** Augitandesit m
~ **gneiss** Augitgneis m
~ **schist** Augitschiefer m
augitic augithaltig
~ **basalt** Augitbasalt m
augitite Augitit m (augitreiches Ergußgestein)
augitophyre Augitporphyr m (Augitbasalt)
aulacogene Aulakogen n (tektonische Strukturform)
auralite Auralith m (zersetzter Cordierit)
aureole Aureole f, Kontakthof m, Hof m
aurichalcite Aurichalcit m, (Zn, Cu)$_5$[(OH)$_3$|CO$_3$]$_2$
auricles Auricula npl, Aurikel npl (Mündungsfortsätze an Cephalopodenschalen, Schloßlamellen bei Muscheln, Coronafortsätze bei Seeigeln)
auriferous goldführend, goldhaltig
~ **alluvial (alluvium)** Goldseife f, goldhaltiges Geröll n

auriferous 32

~ **conglomerate** goldführendes Konglomerat n
~ **deposit** goldhaltige Ablagerung f
~ **gravels** goldführende Alluvionen fpl
~ **pyrite** goldhaltiger Pyrit m
~ **quartz** Goldquarz m
~ **rock** goldhaltiges Gestein n
~ **sand** Goldsand m
~ **vein** Goldgang m
aurora australis Südlicht n
~ **borealis (polaris)** Polarlicht n, Nordlicht n
auroral belt Polarlichtzone f
~ **display (light)** Polarlicht n
~ **zone** Polarlichtzone f
aurostibite Aurostibit m, $AuSb_2$
Austin Chalk Austin n (Coniac und Santon in Nordamerika, Golf-Gebiet)
austinite Austinit m, $CaZn[OH|AsO_4]$
austral südlich
Austral Province Malvino-Kaffrische Provinz f (Paläobiogeografie, Devon)
Australian shield australischer Schild m
australite Australit m (ein Tektit)
Austrian method österreichische Bauweise f
autecology Autökologie f
authigene[tic], authigenic authigen
~ **constituent** authigener Bestandteil m
~ **ejecta** juvenil-authigene Auswürflinge mpl
~ **minerals** authigene Minerale npl
authigenous s. authigene
autocapture Selbstanzapfung f
autochthonous autochthon, bodenständig
~ **anomaly** autochthone Anomalie f
~ **deposit** autochthone Ablagerung f
~ **klippe** autochthone Klippe (Deckenklippe) f
~ **massif** autochthones Massiv n
~ **nappe** autochthone Decke f
~ **soil** Ortsboden m, Primärboden m
autoclastic autoklastisch
~ **breccia** autoklastische Brekzie f (infolge diagenetischer Schrumpfung)
autogamy Autogamie f, Selbstbestäubung f (bei Pflanzen)
autogenetic s. autogenous
autogenous autogen
~ **valley** autogenes Tal n
autogeosyncline Autogeosynklinale f
autohydration Autohydratation f
autolith Autolith m (endogener Einschluß)
automatic gain control automatische Amplitudenregelung f, ARA
~ **history match** (Am) Identifikationsprozeß m (einer reservoirmechanischen Modellsimulation)
autometamorphic autometamorph
autometamorphism Autometamorphose f
autometasomatism Autometasomatose f
automicrite Automikrit m (autochthoner Orthomikrit)
automolite Automolit m (Varietät von Gahnit)
automorphic automorph
automorphous automorph
autopneumatolysis Autopneumatolyse f
autoradiograph Autoradiografie f

autotheca Autothek f (bei Graptolithen)
autrophic autroph
autumn[al] equinox Herbst-Tagundnachtgleiche f
Autunian Autun[ien] n (oberstes Karbon, französisches Zentralplateau)
autunite Autunit m, Kalkuranglimmer m, $Ca[UO_2|PO_4]_2 \cdot 10(12-10)H_2O$
Auversian [Stage] Auvers n (Stufe des Eozäns)
auxiliary fault Begleitverwerfung f, Nebenverwerfung f, Nebenstörung f, Fiederstörung f
~ **fissure** Nebenspalte f
~ **fracture** Begleitbruch m
~ **gauge** Begleitpegel m (eines Brunnens)
~ **joint** Nebenkluft f, Begleitkluft f
~ **lobe** Auxiliarlobus m
~ **plane** Hilfsebene f
availability of raw material Verfügbarkeit f von Rohstoffen
available porosity Nutzporosität f
~ **water** [für den Bewuchs] nutzbare Wasserkapazität f
avalanche Lawine f; Schneelawine f
~ **baffle works** Lawinenschutzmauer f
~ **blast** Lawinenwind m
~ **breccia** Schuttlawinenbrekzie f
~ **chute** Lawinengraben m
~ **debris** Lawinenschutt m
~ **moraine** Lawinenmoräne f
~ **of earth** Grundlawine f
~ **of ice** Eislawine f
~ **of stone** Steinlawine f
~ **ripples** steile Rippeln mit Übergußsedimentation
~ **roof** Lawinengalerie f, Lawinendach n
~ **track** Lawinenbahn f
~ **trench** Lawinengraben m
~ **wind** Lawinenwind m
aventurine Aventurin m (s.a. quartz)
~ **feldspar** Aventurinfeldspat m, Oligoklas m
~ **glass** Aventuringlas n
~ **quartz** Aventurinquarz m
aventurism Aventurisieren n, Irisieren n, Labradorisieren n, Schillern n
aventurize/to aventurisieren, irisieren, labradorisieren, schillern
avenue of migration Migrationsweg m, Porenweg m (Fließkanal des Öls im Speicher)
average up/to auf Durchschnitt[sgehalt] bringen
average abundance Durchschnittshäufigkeit f
~ **annual value** Jahresmittelwert m
~ **content** Durchschnittsgehalt m, mittlerer Gehalt m
~ **dip** Generalfallen n
~ **grading** durchschnittliche granulometrische Zusammensetzung f
~ **grain diameter** Korngrößenkennzahl f
~ **hade** allgemeines Einfallen n
~ **mountain** Mittelgebirge n
~ **ore grade** durchschnittlicher Metallgehalt m des Erzes
~ **photobase** mittlere Bildbasis f

~ **precipitation (rainfall figure)** mittlere Niederschlagshöhe (Niederschlagsmenge) *f*
~ **rainfall intensity** Niederschlagsstärke *f (mm/ min)*
~ **reservoir pressure** mittlerer Lagerstättendruck (Speicherdruck) *m*
~ **species number** mittlere Artenzahl *f*
~ **thickness** durchschnittliche Mächtigkeit *f*
~ **trend** durchschnittliches Streichen *n*
averaging Querschnittprobenahme *f*, Mittelung *f*, Mittelwertbildung *f*
avezacite Avezakit *m (augit- und hornblendereiches Ganggestein)*
avicennite Avicennit *m*, Tl_2O_3
aviolite Aviolith *m (Varietät von Hornfels)*
avogadrite Avogadrit *m*, $(K, Cs)BF_4$
Avonian *s.* Carboniferous Limestone
avulsion Durchstich *m*
awakening aufweckend *(5. Stufe der Erdbebenstärkeskala)*
awaruite Awaruit *m*, (Ni_3, Fe)
axes of the principal stresses Hauptspannungsrichtungen *fpl*
axial angle Achsenwinkel *m*
~ **compression** mittiger Druck *m*
~ **direction** Axialrichtung *f*
~ **line** Faltungsachse *f*
~ **load** *s.* ~ pressure
~ **loading** mittige Belastung *f*
~ **plane** Achsenebene *f*
~ **plane foliation** S_1-Schieferung *f*, Achsenflächenschieferung *f*, Transversalschieferung *f*
~ **pressure** 1. axiale Belastung *f*; 2. axialer Bohrdruck *m*
~ **ratio** Achsenverhältnis *n*
~ **revolution** Achsendrehung *f (der Erde)*
~ **stress** Axialspannung *f*
axially symmetrical rotationssymmetrisch, achsensymmetrisch
axinite Axinit *m*, $Ca_2(Fe, Mn)AlAl[BO_3OH|Si_4O_{12}]$
axiolitic axiolitisch *(von Oolithgefügen mit radialnadligem Wachstum senkrecht zur Zentralachse)*
axis culmination Achsenkulmination *f*
~ **elevation and depression** Achsenkulmination *f* und Achsendepression *f*
~ **of anticline** Sattelachse *f*
~ **of binary symmetry** zweizählige Symmetrieachse *f*
~ **of crystal** Kristallachse *f*
~ **of elevation** Elevationsachse *f*
~ **of fourfold symmetry** vierzählige Symmetrieachse *f*
~ **of growth** Wachstumsachse *f*
~ **of inertia** Trägheitsachse *f*
~ **of lode** Gangachse *f*
~ **of optic symmetry** optische Symmetrieachse *f*
~ **of rotation** Rotationsachse *f*
~ **of symmetry** Symmetrieachse *f*
~ **of tetragonal symmetry** vierzählige Symmetrieachse *f*

~ **of the arch** Sattelachse *f*
~ **of the earth** Erdachse *f*
~ **of the screw motion** Schraubungsachse *f*, Windungsachse *f*
~ **of the trough** Trogachse *f*
~ **of threefold symmetry** dreizählige Symmetrieachse *f*
~ **of twofold symmetry** zweizählige Symmetrieachse *f*
axissymmetric[al] achsensymmetrisch
axotomous nur in einer Richtung spaltbar
azimuth Azimut *m (n)*
~ **angle** Azimutwinkel *m*
~ **frequency diagram** Häufigkeitsdiagramm *n* der Azimute
~ **of the hole** Azimut *m* des Bohrlochs
azimuthal azimutal
~ **equal area projection** flächentreue Azimutalprojektion *f*
Azoic azoisch
~ **Age (Era)** Azoikum *n*
azonal soil Boden *m* ohne Horizontbildung
azotic stickstoffhaltig
azure spar *s.* lazulite
azurite Azurit *m*, Kupferlasur *f*, $Cu_3[OH|CO_3]_2$

B

b axis b-Achse *f (mineralogische und tektonische Koordinate)*
b/3 disordered kaolinite *s.* fire-clay mineral
B-horizon B-Horizont *m*, Anreicherungshorizont *m*, Illuvialhorizont *m*
B-tectonite B-Tektonit *m*
babel quartz Babelquarz *m (gestaltliche Varietät von Quarz)*
babingtonite Babingtonit *m*, $Ca_2Fe_2[Si_5O_{14}OH]$
Babylonia quartz *s.* babel quartz
bacalite Varietät von Bernstein
bacillary structure faserige Struktur *f*, Faserstruktur *f*
bacillite nadelförmiger Kristall *m*
back 1. Hangendes *n*, Firste *f (s.a.* face 2.); 2. Hauptschlechte *f*
~ **abutment pressure** hinterer (rückwärtiger) Kämpferdruck *m*
~ **borehole** Firstenbohrloch *n*
~ **crank pumping** kombiniertes Pumpen *n (von Erdöl)*
~ **-deep basin** *s.* backdeep
~ **dune** Hinterdüne *f*
~ **erosion** erosive Hangendabtragung *f (einer Decke)*
~ **fin** *s.* dorsal fin
~ **folding** *s.* backfolding
~ **furrow** *s.* esker
~ **joints** *s.* backs
~ **land** Rückland *n (Tektonik)*
~ **leads** Hochwasserspülsaum *m* aus dunklen Sanden
~ **of the gallery** Firste *f* eines Stollens

back 34

~ **of the hole** Bohrlochtiefstes *n*
~-**pack** Rückentrage *f*
~ **pressure** 1. Gegendruck *m*; 2. Rückdruck *m* (Sonde)
~ **pressure test** *(Am)* Gegendrucktest *m* (in Gasbohrungen)
~-**reef** 1. landwärts (leeseitig) vom Riff gelegener Lagunenbereich; 2. „Rückriff", der Brandungsseite abgewandter Bereich eines Riffkomplexes, der noch stark vom Riffkörper beeinflußt wird
~-**reef lagoon** Lagune *f* hinter dem Riff
~ **slips** abfallende Schlechten *fpl*
~ **slope** 1. Innenböschung *f*; 2. Hinterhang *m*
~ **swamp** Auesumpf *m*
~-**swamp area** [sumpfiges] Niederungsgebiet *n* (eines Flusses)
~-**thrusting** Rücküberschiebung *f (Tektonik)*
~ **truncation** Hangendamputation *f (Tektonik)*
~ **weathering** Zurückwitterung *f*
backarc area Gebiet (Becken) zwischen Inselbogen und Kontinent
backbarrier complex Bezeichnung zur Kennzeichnung aller Ablagerungsmilieus und Sedimente, die zwischen einer Uferwall-Insel und dem Festland bzw. einer großen Insel anzutreffen sind
backbreak Ausbruch *m (Steinbruch)*
backcleat Ablösen *n (Ablösungsfuge im Gestein)*
backdeep Rücksenke *f*, Rücktiefe *f*
backdigger [dredge] Flußbagger *m* mit Schleppsaugrohr
backfill/to 1. versetzen, Versatz einbringen; 2. verfüllen, einfüllen (z.B. Graben)
backfill 1. Versatz *m*; 2. Versatzbau *m (Ichnologie)*
~ **[trench] rammer** Grabenramme *f*, Grabenstampfer *m*
backfilling 1. Verfüllboden *m*; 2. Versatzeinbringen *n*; 3. Wiederzuwerfen *n*
backflow Rückstau *m*
backfolding Rückfaltung *f*, Einfaltung *f*
background 1. Untergrund *m*, Hintergrund *m*; 2. Nulleffekt *m*, Störpegel *m*, Rauschen *n*
~ **count** Nulleffekt *m*
~ **effect** Hintergrundeffekt *m (Tracer)*
~ **noise** Störgeräusch *n*
backing Hintermauerung *f*
backs streichende Klüfte *fpl (parallel zum Schichtstreichen)*
backscattered light zurückgestreutes Licht *n*
backscattering Rückstreuung *f*
backset bedding (beds) Luvblattschichtung *f*
backshore 1. Ufer *n*, Vorland *n*; 2. oberer Teil des Strandes, der nur gelegentlich überflutet wird
backsight Rückblick *m (bei Vermessungsarbeiten)*
backslides Gravitationsgleitung in eine strukturelle Depression
bäckströmite Bäckströmit *m*, Mn(OH)$_2$

backward erosion rückschreitende Erosion *f*
~ **folding** *s.* backfolding
backwash 1. Rückstau *m*; 2. zurückziehende Welle *f*, rücklaufende Strömung *f*, Rückstrom *m*
~ **ripple marks** Rückstromrippelmarken *fpl*
backwater Rückstauwasser *n*, Stauwasser *n*, stilles Wasser *n*, Haffwasser *n*; Aufstau *m*, Anstauung *f*
~ **area** Staugebiet *n*
~ **curve** Staukurve *f*
~ **length** Staulänge *f*
~ **surface** Staufläche *f*
~ **zone** Staugebiet *n*
bacon stone *s.* steatite
bacteria of decay Fäulnisbakterien *fpl*
bacterial action (activity) Bakterientätigkeit *f*
~ **leaching** bakterielle Laugung *f*
Baculites limestone Baculitenkalk *m*
bad lands *s.* badlands
~ **weather line** Schlechtwetterstrecke *f*
baddeleyite Baddeleyit *m*, ZrO$_2$
badland-type of erosion Zerrachelung *f*
badlands Ödland *n (pflanzenwuchsloses, von engen Schluchten und scharfen Kämmen durchzogenes Gelände)*
badly faulted stark verworfen
baeckstroemite *s.* bäckströmite
bafertisite Bafertisit *m*, BaFe$_2$Ti[O$_2$|Si$_2$O$_7$]
bafflestone boundstone, bei dem die Organismen als Sedimentfänger wirkten
bagotite grüne Lintonitgerölle *npl*
bagshot sands Serie im unteren Tertiär von Hampshire
bahama grain *s.* pellet
bahamite Bahamit *m (körniges Karbonatgestein analog den rezenten Sedimenten im Inneren der Bahama Banks)*
bahiaiite Bahiait *m (Varietät von Hypersthenit)*
baikalite Baikalit *m (1. Varietät von Ozokerit; 2. Varietät von Salit)*
baikerinite Baikerinit *m (teerartiger Kohlenwasserstoff, reich an Baikerit)*
baikerite Baikerit *m (an Ozokerit reiches, festes Kohlenwasserstoffgemenge)*
bail/to löffeln (das vom Meißel losgeschlagene Gestein aus dem Bohrloch entfernen)
~ **out a well** eine Bohrung leerschöpfen
bailer 1. Schöpfbüchse *f (Erdöl)*; 2. Schmantbüchse *f*, Sandfänger *m*, Sandrohr *n (Tiefbohrung)*
bailing 1. Ausschöpfen *n*, Sümpfen *n*, Wasserziehen *n*; 2. Schöpfversuch *m*
~ **well** Schöpfsonde *f*
Bajocian [Stage] Bajocien *n*, Bajocium *n (Stufe des Mittleren Juras)*
baked gefrittet
~ **crust** Schmelzrinde *f (bei Meteoriten)*
~ **shale** Erdbrandgestein *n*, gebrannter Ton *m*
bakerite Bakerit *m (Varietät von Datolith)*
baking Frittung *f*

~ **coal** s. caking coal
~ **rock** gefrittetes Gestein n
bal (sl) Grube f
balance of composition Stoffbilanz f
~ **of mineral reserves** Vorratsbilanz f von Mineralen
balanced rock Wackelstein m
Balas[s ruby] Ballasrubin m (Spinell)
bald-headed anticline gekappte und überlagerte Antiklinale f
balk 1. Auskeilen n; 2. mit Schutt gefüllte Auswaschungszonen in Kohlenflözen
balkhashite Balkaschit m (brennbares, rezentes Algengestein im Torfstadium)
balkstone (sl) unreiner, schichtiger Kalkstein m
ball-and-pillow structure Sedimentrolle f, Wikkelfalte f, Wulstbank f, Rutschungsballen m, Rutschungskörper m, Fließwulst m, Ballenstruktur f
~ **clay** Töpferton m, Backsteinton m, Steingutton m, bildsamer Ton m, Klumpenton m, Ballclay m (Fireclay mit nur geringen Beimengungen)
~ **diorite** Kugeldiorit m
~-**indentation testing apparatus** Kugeldruckhärteprüfer m
~ **ironstone** konkretionäres Eisenkarbonat n
~ **jasper** Kugeljaspis m
~ **jointing** konzentrische Klüftung f
~ **mill** Kugelmühle f
~ **mill for wet grinding** Naßkugelmühle f
~-**pressure test** Kugeldruckhärteprüfung f
~ **structure [parting]** kugelige Absonderung f
balland (sl) mulmiges Bleierz n
ballas Bort m (Industriediamant)
ballast 1. Kiesschotter m, Steinschotter m, Gleisschotter m, Bahnschotter m; 2. Ballast m
~ **element** Ballastelement n
~ **pit** Kiesgrube f
ballasting Schotterung f, Unterschottern n
balling Stopfbuchsenbildung f im Bohrloch (Tonmännern)
balloon satellite Ballonsatellit m
~ **sonde** Ballonsonde f
ballstone konkretionärer Kalkstein m
bally (sl) Gebirge n
balmstone (sl) hangendes Gestein n
balneology Balneologie f
Baltic Sea Ostsee f
~ **shield** Baltischer Schild m
banakite Banakit m, BaNa$_2$[Al$_2$Si$_2$O$_8$]$_2$
banatite Banatit m (orthoklasreicher Quarzdiorit)
band Zwischenlage f, Bergemittel n
~ **conveyor** Bandförderer m, Förderband n
~ **of flint nodules** Feuersteinband n
~ **rationing** Spektralband-Quotientenbildung f (Bildung des Quotienten aus verschiedenen Spektralbändern)
~-**reject filter** Bandsperrfilter n

bandaite Bandait m (Labradoritdazit)
banded gebändert, gestreift, streifig
~ **agate** Bandachat m
~ **arrangement** lagenförmige Anordnung f
~ **clay** Bänderton m, dünngeschichteter Ton m
~ **coal** Streifenkohle f
~ **constituent** (Am) Lithotyp m (Kohlentyp der Steinkohle)
~ **gneiss** Bändergneis m
~ **ingredient** s. ~ constituent
~ **ironstone** Eisenjaspilit m
~ **jasper** Bandjaspis m
~ **ore** Streifenerz n, Bändererz n
~ **slate** Bänderschiefer m
~ **structure** Lagentextur f
~ **twinning** Viellingslamellierung f
~ **vein** Gang m mit Lagentextur
banding Bänderung f
bandpass Bandpaß m
~ **filter** Bandpaßfilter n; Banddurchlaßfilter n (Fernerkundung)
bandstone verkieseltes Schichtblatt n
bandwidth Bandbreite f (z.B. eines Seismografen)
bandy clay Bänderton m
bandylite Bandylith m, Cu[Cl|B(OH)$_4$]
bank in/to eindeichen
~ **out** auf Halde bringen
bank 1. Flußufer n; 2. Sandbank f; 3. Erdböschung f; 4. Bruchwand f, 5. Stoß m (im Abbau); Strosse f (im Steinbruch); 6. Bank f, Lage f, Wall m; 7. in-situ Karbonatablagerung aus Skelettresten
~ **and bottom infiltration** Uferfiltration f
~ **claim** Uferclaim f
~ **erosion** Infererosion f (eines Flusses)
~-**filtered water** uferfiltriertes Wasser n
~ **filtration** Uferfiltration f
~-**full river** geschwollener Fluß m
~-**full stage** Ausuferungshöhe f, Ausuferungswasserstand m, ufervoller Stand m
~ **head** über Tage
~ **line** Uferlinie f (eines Flusses)
~ **of ditch** Grabenböschung f
~ **of gravel** Schotterbank f
~ **of sand** Sandbank f
~ **of the river** Flußufer n
~ **protection** Uferschutz m
~ **reef** Flachseeriff n
~ **reinstatement** Uferausbesserung f (eines Flusses)
~ **shooting** Banksprengarbeit f (Steinbruch)
~ **stabilization** Uferbefestigung f
~ **storage** Uferfiltration f
banked structure plattenförmige Struktur f
~-**up water level** Spiegelerhebung f
banket goldführendes Konglomerat n (Transvaal)
banking structure Bankung f
~-**up curve** Staulinie f, Staukurve f
bannocking Schrämen n (von Kohle)

3*

baotite

baotite Baotit m, $Ba_4(Ti,Nb)_8[Cl|O_{16}|Si_4O_{12}]$
bardown/to abräumen, beräumen *(den Stoß mit der Brechstange)*
bar 1. Barre f, Unterwasserriff n, Uferbank f; Nehrung f, Landspitze f; 2. Bohrstange f, Bohrsonde f, Gestänge n
~-enclosed durch eine Nehrung abgeschlossen
~ gravels Bankschotter m
~ of sand Sandbank f
~ sands marine Barrensande mpl
~ trap Barrenfalle f
baraboo begrabener und teilweise exhumierter Restberg
barachois *s.* lagoon
bararite Bararit m, $(NH_4)_2[SiF_6]$
barbierite Barbierit m, $NaAlSi_3O_8$
barbosalite Barbosalith m, $Fe_2[OH|PO_4]_2$
barchan Barchan m, Sicheldüne f
bare/to freilegen
bare entblößt, nackt
~ ground nackter Boden m
~ ice schneefreies Eis n
~ soil unbebauter Boden m
barefoot completion Vorbereitung einer Bohrung zur Förderung aus unverrohrtem Speicher
barefooted well Bohrung f ohne Filterrohre, Bohrung f mit unverrohrtem Ölträger
barfinger sands deltaische Rinnensande mpl
bargh *(sl)* Bergwerk n, Grube f
baring Abräumen n des Deckgebirges
barite *s.* baryte
barium Barium n, Ba
~-bearing bariumhaltig
~ carbonate *s.* witherite
~ sulphate *s.* baryte
barkevikite Barkevikit m *(Varietät von Amphibol)*
barnesite Barnesit m, $Na_2V_6O_{16} \cdot 3H_2O$
barnyard *(sl)* interglazialer Bodenhorizont m
barolite Gestein mit Baryt und Zölestin
barometer Barometer n
barometric column Barometersäule f
~ height barometrische Höhe f
~ height computation barometrische Höhenberechnung f
~ hypsometry barometrische Höhenmessung f
~ levelling barometrische Höhenbestimmung (Höhenaufnahme, Höhenmessung) f
~ pressure Luftdruck m, barometrischer Druck m
barometry Luftdruckmessung f
barracks shale Ölschiefer m *(Schottland)*
barrage Stauwerk n, Staudamm m, Talsperre f, Stauwehr n
~ dam Staudamm m, Sperrmauer f, Staumauer f
~ power station Staustufenkraftwerk n
~ wall Staumauer f
barranca Gießbachrinne f
barrandite Barrandit m, $(Al,Fe)PO_4 \cdot 2H_2O$

barred basin durch Barre vom offenen Ozean getrenntes Teilbecken
barrel Barrel n, Faß n *(Erdölraummaß = 0,15898 m³)*
~ copper gediegenes Kupfer n *(z.B. in Form von Blechen)*
~ vault Tonnengewölbe n
barrels of oil per hour Faß Öl je Stunde
Barremian [Stage] Barrême n *(Stufe der Unterkreide)*
barren 1. unhaltig, metallfrei, erzfrei, taub; 2. öde, unfruchtbar; 3. unvollkommen entwickelt
barren 1. Auslaugungszone f; 2. Sandheide f
~ ground 1. taubes Gestein n; 2. Heideboden m
~ land Ödland n
~ lode tauber Gang m
~ measure taubes Gebirge n
~ mine unrentable Grube f
~ of fossils fossilfrei
~ of oil ölfrei, nicht ölführend
~ of timber baumlos
~ of vegetation vegetationslos
~ plateau Steppenhochebene f
~ rock taubes Gestein n, Abraum m
~ sand steriler (trockener, nicht ölführender, unproduktiver) Sand m
~ solution Abstoßlösung f, Ablauge f
~ spots taube Zone f
~ track Taubfeld n
~ well unergiebige Bohrung f
barrier Strandwall m, Uferwall m, Lido m
~ basin Bassin n mit natürlicher Dammschüttung
~ beach Vorstrand m; Strandwall m, Uferwall m, Lido m *(s.a. offshore bar)*
~ complex alle Ablagerungsmilieus und Sedimente, die mit Uferwallinseln im Zusammenhang stehen
~ ice *s.* shelf ice
~ island Strandwallinsel f
~ lake Abdämmungssee m
~ layer phenomena Grenzschichterscheinungen fpl
~ of pressure Druckbarriere f
~ reef Wallriff n, Barriereriff n
~ ridge Barre f
~ spring Stauquelle f
barroisite Barroisit m *(Na-Amphibol)*
Barrovian-type metamorphism metamorphe Faziesserie f vom Barrow-Typ *(druckbetonte Regionalmetamorphose)*
barrow Halde f
~ pit Steinbruch m
barsanovite Barsanovit m, $(Na, Ca, Sr, SE)_9(Fe,Mn)_2(Zr,Nb)_2[Cl|Si_{12}O_{36}]$
barsowite Barsowit m *(s.a. anorthite)*
Barstovian [Stage] Barstovien n *(Wirbeltierstufe des Miozäns in Nordamerika)*
barthite Barthit m *(Varietät von Austinit)*
Bartonian [Stage] Barton[ium] n *(Stufe des Eozäns)*

barylite Barylith m, $Be_2Ba[Si_2O_7]$
barymetry Schweremessung f *(der Luft)*
barysilite Barysilit m, $Pb_3[Si_2O_7]$
baryte Baryt m, Schwerspat m, $BaSO_4$
barytes *s.* baryte
barytic barytartig
barytocalcite Barytokalzit m, $BaCa[CO_3]_2$
basal basal
~ **breccia** Basalbrekzie f
~ **cleavage** Basisspaltbarkeit f
~ **conglomerate** Basalkonglomerat n, Grundkonglomerat n
~ **face** Basalfläche f, Grundfläche f, Basisfläche f
~ **fauna** Basalfauna f
~ **flora** Basalflora f
~ **granite** Granit m des Grundgebirges
~ **moraine** Grundmoräne f
~ **plane** Grundebene f, Basisebene f
~ **point** Bezugspunkt m
~ **quartzite** Basalquarzit m
~ **runoff** Basisabfluß m
~ **thrust plane** basale Schubfläche f
~ **till** Grundmoräne f
basalpib Basalwulst m *(der Säugerzähne);* Kauwulst m *(am Cephalopodenkiefer); s.a.* cingulum
basals Basaltäfelchen *npl (Paläontologie)*
basalt Basalt m *(basisches Ergußgestein)*
~-**kainite** *s.* anhydrokainite
~-**type VHA** basaltisches Mondgestein mit hohem Aluminiumgehalt **(V**ery **H**igh **A**luminium)
basaltic basaltisch, Basalt...
~ **clay** Basaltton m
~ **column** Basaltsäule f
~ **crust** basaltische Kruste f
~ **cupola** Basaltkuppe f
~ **debris** Basaltschutt m
~ **dike** Basaltgang m
~ **iron ore** Basalteisenerz n
~ **jointing** säulenförmige Absonderung f
~ **knob** Basaltkuppe f
~ **lava** Basaltlava f
~ **magma** Basaltmagma n
~ **ridge** Basaltrücken m
~ **scoria** Basaltschlacke f
~ **scree** Basaltschutt m
~ **sheet** Basaltdecke f
~ **structure** säulenförmige Absonderung f *(bei Migmatiten)*
~ **tuff** Basalttuff m
~ **wacke** Basaltwacke f
basaltiform säulenförmig
basaltine *s.* basaltic
basaltite Basaltit m *(olivinfreier Basalt)*
basanite 1. Basanit m *(basisches Ergußgestein);* 2. Lydit m *(s.a.* touchstone*)*
Baschkirian [Stage] Baschkir n, Baschkirische Stufe f *(Stufe des Mittelkarbons, Osteuropa)*
basculating fault *s.* wrench fault
base 1. Basis f, Sohlfäche f; Bett n; Fußpunkt m;

2. Tragschicht f, Tragdecke f; 3. Endfläche f *(Kristallografie);* 4. Mesostasis f, Grundmasse f; 5. Base f
~ **adjustment** Basiseinstellung f
~ **analysis** Grundanalyse f
~ **angle** Grundwinkel m, Bezugswinkel m
~ **board** Objektivträger m *(Mikroskopie)*
~ **conglomerate** Basalkonglomerat n, Grundkonglomerat n
~ **content** Basengehalt m
~ **course** Grundschicht f
~ **exchange** Basenaustausch m
~ **exchange capacity** Basenaustauschkapazität f
~ **failure** statischer Grundbruch m, tiefliegende Gleitung f, Bruch m am Fuße einer Rutschung
~ **flow** Basisabfluß m
~-**flow separation** Abflußseparation f *(Trennung A_u/A_o)*
~-**height ratio** Basis-Höhen-Verhältnis n *(Verhältnis zwischen der Luftbasis und der Flughöhe eines stereoskopischen Aufnahmepaars)*
~ **level** 1. Ausgangshorizont m; 2. Denudationsniveau n, Erosionsbasis f
~ **level of erosion** Erosionsbasis f
~ **level of karst erosion** Korrosionsbasis f
~ **level of river** Mittellauf m eines Flusses
~-**levelled plain** gleichmäßige Ebene f, Fastebene f
~ **levelling** Bildung f der Fastebenen
~ **line** Basis f, Grundlinie f
~ **map** Kartenabriß m
~ **map for drilling work** Bohrkarte f
~ **map for geological work** topografische Kartenunterlage f für geologische Arbeiten
~ **metal** unedles Metall n
~ **moraine** Grundmoräne f
~ **of a rock** Grundmasse f eines Gesteins
~ **of weathering** Basis (Unterkante) f der Langsamschicht *(Seismik)*
~ **oil** Rohöl n
~ **ore** armes (geringwertiges) Erz n
~ **pressure** Sohldruck m, Sohlpressung f
~ **runoff** Basisabfluß m
~ **saturation** Basensättigung f
~ **slab** Fundamentplatte f, Grundplatte f
~ **station** Basisstation f
~ **surface** Sohle f, untere Grenzfläche f *(einer Schicht)*
~ **surge deposits** reliefabhängige Tuffablagerungen, deren Material lawinenartig in Bodennähe transportiert wurde
~ **truncation** Basalamputation f
~ **vubbing** Basalüberschürfung f, Reihenüberschiebung f *(Deckenbau)*
basement 1. Fundament n, Unterlage f, Sockel m, Untergrund m, Unterbau m; 2. Grundgebirge n
~ **complex** Grundgebirge n
~ **conglomerate** Basalkonglomerat n, Grundkonglomerat n

basement

~ **excavating** Aufgrabung f für Fundamente
~ **fold** Grundfalte f
~ **nappe** Grundgebirgsdecke f
~ **rocks** 1. Grundgebirge n; 2. Liegendgestein n
~ **uplift** Anstieg m des Grundgebirges
basic 1. Grund ..., Basis ...; 2. basisch
~ **clot** Anhäufung großer Kristalle basischer Minerale in Magmatiten
~ **fold** Grundfalte f
~ **intrusive** basisches Intrusivgestein n
~ **load** Grundbelastung f
~ **magma** basisches Magma n
~ **material** Ausgangsmaterial n
~ **measurement** Grundmaß n; Ausgangsmaß n
~ **mesh size** Bezugskorngröße f
~ **rock** basisches Gestein n
~ **sediment** Öltanksediment n
~ **specific gravity** Bezugskornwichte f
basicity basische Beschaffenheit f, Basizität f
basification Basifizierung f, SiO_2-Abwanderung f [in Gesteinen], Entkieselung f
basifier Basenbildner m
basifixed mit einer Basis befestigt
basin Bassin n, Kessel m, Mulde f, Wanne f, Trog m (Strukturform); Becken n
~ **desert** Beckenwüste f
~ **facies** Beckenfazies f
~ **for the settling of slimes** Klärbecken n, Klärteich m (Aufbereitung)
~ **of deposition** Ablagerungsraum m
~ **range** Schollengebirge n, Schollenland n
~ **-shaped** beckenförmig, kesselförmig, schüsselförmig
~ **-shaped gorge (valley)** Kesseltal n
~ **soil** Talkesselboden m
~ **topography** Beckenlandschaft f
basinal lake Dauersee m
basining Beckenbildung f, Einmuldung f
basinlike muldenförmig
basis Basis f
~ **of classification** Einteilungsgrundlage f
basite Basit m, basisches Gestein n
bass (sl) 1. dichter Ton m; 2. schieferige Kohle f, Brandschiefer m
bassanite Bassanit m, $Ca[SO_4] \cdot 1/2 H_2O$
basset/to ausstreichen, ausbeißen, ausgehen, zutage treten (Lagerstätte)
basset Schichtkopf m, Schichtkante f; Ausgehendes n, Ausstrich m, Ausbiß m
~ **edge** Ausgehendes n, Ausstrich m, Ausbiß m
~ **edge of a stratum** Schichtkopf m, Schichtkante f
basseting Ausstreichendes n
bassetite Bassetit m, $Fe[UO_2|PO_4]_2 \cdot 10-12H_2O$
bastard (sl) Zwischenlage f, Einlage[rung] f, Einschaltung f; hartes Gestein n
~ **granite** Gneisgranit m
~ **quartz** (sl) tauber Gangquarz m
~ **shale** (sl) bituminöser Schiefer m
~ **whin** (sl) harte Gesteinsbank f

38

bastite Bastit m (angewitterter Enstatit)
bastnaesite Bastnäsit m, $Ce[F|CO_3]$
bat (sl) Kohlenschiefer m
~ **guano** Fledermausguano m
batea Sichertrog m, Waschschüssel f
bath stone englischer Muschelkalkstein aus dem Jura
batholite, batholith Batholith m (ausgedehnter Tiefengesteinskörper)
batholithic batholithisch
batholyth Batholith m
batholytic batholithisch
bathometer Bathometer n, Tiefseelot n
Bathonian [Stage] Bathonien n (Stufe des Mittleren Juras)
bathosphere Bathosphäre f
bathroclase Bathroklase f, schwebende Spalte f
bathyal bathyal
~ **deposit** bathyale Ablagerung f (in 200 bis 800 m Meerestiefe)
~ **facies** Bathyalfazies f
bathycurrent Tiefenstrom m (des Ozeans)
bathygraphic bathygrafisch
~ **chart** Tiefenkarte f (des Ozeans)
bathylite, bathylith s. batholite
bathymeter s. bathometer
bathymetric bathymetrisch
~ **chart** Tiefenkarte f, Isobathenkarte f
~ **curve** bathygrafische Kurve f, Tiefenkurve f
~ **lines** Linien fpl gleicher Meerestiefen
bathymetry Tiefseelotung f, Tiefseemessung f
bathypelagic zone bathypelagische Zone f (Tiefenzone des offenen Meeres im Bereich des Kontinentalabhangs)
bathyrheal underflow subkrustale Ausgleichsströmung f
bathyseism Beben n mit tiefliegendem Epizentrum
bathythermograph Bathythermograf m
bating Abteufen n
bats 1. Abfallstücke npl; 2. Steinschlag m (handgeschlagener Schotter)
batt (sl) Schieferton m, harter Ton m
batter Böschungsneigung f (eines Dammes)
battery of wells Brunnengalerie f
batukite Batukit m (Varietät von Leuzitbasalt)
baulk s. balk
baumhauerite Baumhauerit m, $Pb_5As_9S_{18}$
bäumlerite Bäumlerit m, $KCaCl_3$
bauxite Bauxit m (Al-reiches Verwitterungsprodukt)
~ **deposit** Bauxitlagerstätte f
bauxitization Bauxitisierung f
Bavarian facies Bayrische Fazies f
bavenite Bavenit m, $Ca_4Al_2Be_2[(OH)_2|Si_9O_{26}]$
Baveno law Bavenoer Zwillingsgesetz n
Baventian Baventien n (Pleistozän, Britische Inseln)
bavin (sl) unreiner Kalkstein m
bay 1. Meeresbucht f, Meerbusen m, Bai f; 2. Bogenstaumauer f; 3. Baistörung f

bedabble

~ **bar** Nehrung *f*
~ **cable** Grundkabel *n (Seeseismik)*
~ **head** *s.* bayhead
~**-mouth bar** Nehrung *f*
~ **salt** grobkörniges Meeressalz *n*
bayate *(sl)* brauner Jaspis *m*
bayerite Bayerit *m*, α-Al(OH)
bayhead Buchtinneres *n*, Buchtende *n*
bayldonite Bayldonit *m*, $PbCu_3[OH|AsO_4]_2$
bayou Ausflußgraben *m*; *(Am)* Altwasser *n (s.a.* oxbow lake)
bazooka-type system of perforation Hohlladungsperforation *f (Perforation nach dem System der Panzerfaust)*
BCD [code] BCD-Kode *m*
beach Meeresstrand *m*, Gestade *n (s.a.* shore); Bucht *f*, Golf *m*
~ **berm** *s.* ~ terrace
~ **building** Strandbildung *f*
~ **concentrate** Schwermineralgehalt *m* im Küstensand
~ **cúsps** Strandhörner *npl*, Brandungskiesrücken *mpl*, Küstenspitzen *fpl*
~ **deposit** Strandablagerung *f*, Küstenablagerung *f*
~ **drift[ing]** Stranddrift *f*, Strandvertriftung *f*, Küstenversetzung *f*, Strandversetzung *f*
~ **dune** Stranddüne *f*
~ **erosion** Stranderosion *f*
~ **grass** Strandhafer *m*
~ **gravel** Strandschotter *m*, Strandkies *m*
~ **groin** Seebuhne *f*, Strandbuhne *f*
~ **pebble** Strandgeröll *n*
~ **placer** Strandseife *f*
~ **plain** Strandebene *f*
~ **restoration** Stranderneuerung *f*
~ **ridge** Stranddamm *m*, Strandwall *m*; Nehrung *f*
~ **rock** lose verkitteter Strandsand *m*; Muschelsandstein *m*
~ **sand** Strandsand *m*, Seesand *m*
~ **sand barrier** Strandwall *m*, Uferwall *m*, Lido *m*
~ **sand mining** Mineralgewinnung *f* aus Küstensanden
~ **terrace** Strandterrasse *f*, Küstenterrasse *f*
bead Perle *f (am Lötrohr)*
~ **system** Perlenverfahren *n*
beaded texture Linsenstruktur *f*
~ **vein** Linsengang *m*, Lentikulargang *m*
beadlet Flitter *m (z.B. von Zinn)*
beak 1. Wirbel *m*, Schnabel *m (bei Fossilschalen)*; 2. Kap *n*
~ **of tin** Visiergraupe *f (Zinnsteinzwillingsform)*
beam texture Maschenstruktur *f (bei Serpentin)*
~ **well** Pumpsonde *f*, im Pumpbetrieb fördernde Bohrung *f*
bean ore Bohnerz *n*
~**-shaped structure** Krümeltextur *f*
bear/to peilen
beard Schweif *m (eines Kometen)*

bearing 1. Schichtstreichen *n*, Gangstreichen *n*; 2. Kompaßpeilung *f*; 3. Orientierung *f (z.B. eines Seismometers)*
~ **capacity** Tragfähigkeit *f*, Tragvermögen *n*
~ **capacity factor** Tragfähigkeitsfaktor *m*
~ **index** Tragfähigkeitsindex *m*
~ **of the trend** Richtung *f* des Streichens
~ **point** Angriffspunkt *m*
~ **pressure** Auflagerdruck *m*
~ **stone** Lagerstein *m*
~ **stress** Lochleibungsdruck *m*
~ **surface** Auflagefläche *f*
~ **test** Belastungsversuch *m*, Belastungsprüfung *f*, Tragfähigkeitsversuch *m*
~ **thrust** Drucklagerschub *m*
~ **value** Tragfähigkeit *f*
~ **wall** Stützmauer *f*
bears *(sl)* Toneisensteinkonkretionen *fpl*
bearsite Bearsit *m*, $Be_2[OH|AsO_4] \cdot 4H_2O$
beat Ausgehendes *n*, Ausbiß *m*, Ausstrich *m*
beating Abrammen *n*, Stampfen *n*
~ **of the waves** Wogenprall *m*, Wellenschlag *m*
~ **rain** Platzregen *m*
beauxite *s.* bauxite
beaver meadow Flußaue *f*
beaverite Beaverit *m*, $Pb(Cu, Fe)_3[(OH)_6|(SO_4)_2]$
Becke line Beckesche Linie (Lichtlinie) *f*
Becke's principle Beckesches Prinzip *n*
beckelite Beckelith *m*, $(Ca, Ce, La, Nd)_5$
become coossified/to zusammenwachsen *(Knochen)*
~ **enriched** sich veredeln *(Erz)*
~ **exposed** ausapern
~ **extinct** 1. aussterben; 2. erlöschen *(Vulkan)*
~ **flocculated** ausgeflockt werden
~ **hardened** erhärten
~ **swampy** versumpfen
becquerelite Becquerelit *m*, $6[UO_2(OH)_2] \cdot Ca(OH)_2 \cdot 4H_2O$
bed 1. Bank *f*, Lage *f*, Horizont *m (kleinste lithostratigrafische Einheit)*; 2. Flußbett *n*
~ **joint** Bankungskluft *f*
~ **load** Bodenlast *f*, Grundablagerung *f*
~**-load discharge** Geschiebeführung *f*
~**-load sampler** Geschiebefänger *m*
~**-load transport** Geschiebeführung *f*, Geschiebefracht *f*
~ **of passage** Übergangsschicht *f*
~ **of potash salts** Kalisalzlager *n*
~ **of river** Flußbett *n*
~ **of scoriae** Schlackenschicht *f*
~ **plane** Schichtfläche *f*, Schichtfuge *f*
~ **sampling** Schichtbeprobung *f*
~ **separation** Schichtenablösen *n*, Schichtenaufblätterung *f*
~ **set** von angrenzenden sedimentären Einheiten deutlich abgegrenzte Schichtengruppe
~ **succession** Schichtenfolge *f*
~ **surface** Schichtenoberfläche *f*
~ **vein** Lagergang *m*
bedabble/to berieseln, bewässern

bedded

bedded [in Lagen übereinander] geschichtet, gebankt, bankig
~ **clay** Bänderton *m*, gebänderter Ton *m*
~ **deposit** *s.* blanket deposit
~ **jointing** bankförmige Absonderung *f*
~ **rock** Sedimentgestein *n*, Schichtgestein *n*, geschichtetes Gestein *n*
~ **structure** geschichtetes Gefüge *n*
~ **varved clay** Warventon *m (Bänderton)*
~ **vein** Lagergang *m*
~/**well** gut geschichtet
bedding Schichtung *f*, Lagerung *f*
~ **angle** Schichtfallwinkel *m*
~ **cave** Schichtfugenhöhle *f*
~ **cleavage** Parallelschieferung *f*
~ **fault** Störung *f* entlang einer Schichtfläche
~ **fissure** Schichtspalte *f*
~ **flow** Schichtfließen *n*, Biegefließen *n*
~ **joint** Schichtfuge *f*, Bankungsspalte *f*
~ **mullion** Schichtungsmullion *n*
~ **plane** Schichtfläche *f*, Ablagerungsfläche *f*, Schichtfuge *f*
~ **plane fault** *s.* ~ fault
~ **plane markings** Marken *fpl*, Skulpturen *fpl*
~ **plane slip** Gleitung *f* der Schichten längs der Schichtflächen
~ **slip fold** Schichtgleitfalte *f*
~ **slippage** Abrutschung *f*
~ **surface** Schichtungsoberfläche *f*, Schichtebene *f*
bedenite Bedenit *m*, $Ca_2(Mg, Fe, Al)_5[OH|(Si, Al)_4O_{11}]_2$
Bedoulian [Stage] Bedoulien *n (Stufe, Unterapt, Tethys)*
bedrock Anstehendes *n*, anstehendes Gestein *n*, gewachsener Fels *m*, Muttergestein *n*, Lagergestein *n*
beds dipping at high angles steil stehende Schichten *fpl*
~ **of passage** Übergangsschichten *fpl*
bedway Parallelstrukturierung *f (im Granit)*
bee-line Luftlinie *f*
beef *(Am)* schichtparallele Kalzitfäden und -schmitzen in Sedimenten
beegerite Beegerit *m*, $6PbS \cdot Bi_2S_3$
beekite Beekit *m (kryptokristalline Varietät von Quarz)*
beerbachite Beerbachit *m (Varietät von Aplit)*
Beestonian Beestonien *n (Pleistozän, britische Inseln)*
beetle stone koprolithischer Toneisenstein *m*
begin to bear on/to sich auflegen *(Hangendes)*
behaviour to etching Ätzverhalten *n*
behead/to anzapfen, enthaupten, kappen *(z.B. einen Fluß)*
beheaded river angezapfter Fluß *m*
beheading Anzapfung *f*, Enthauptung *f*, Kappung *f (des Oberlaufs eines Flusses)*
behierite Behierit *m*, $(Ta, Nb)[BO_4]$
Behm depth indicator Behmlot *n*, Echolot *n*
beidellite Beidellit *m*, $Al_2[(OH)_2|Si_4O_{10}] \cdot 4H_2O$

bekinkinite Bekinkinit *m (alkalisches Ergußgestein)*
belch/to ausstoßen *(Vulkan)*
belch Ausstoß *m (eines Vulkans)*
belching well stoßweise eruptierende Bohrung *f*
belemnite Belemnit *m*, Donnerkeil *m*
~ **marl** Belemnitenmergel *m*
bell-metal ore *s.* stannite
~-**mould**, ~-**mouth** Steinkern *m* einer Sigillarie, Sigillarienausguß *m*
~ **sand** Flugsand *m*
~-**shaped curve** Glockenkurve *f*, Normalverteilungskurve *f (bei Korngrößenverteilungen)*
belland *(sl)* mulmiges Bleierz *n*
Bellerophon limestone Bellerophonkalk *m*
bellingerite Bellingerit *m*, $Cu_3[JO_3]_6 \cdot 2H_2O$
bellite Bellit *m*, $(Pb, Ag)_5[Cl|(CrO_4, AsO_4, SiO_4)_3]$
belly *(sl)* Ausbauchung *f*, Kohlensack *m (Kohlenbergbau)*
~ **of ore** Erzbringer *m*
bellying Ausbauchung *f*
belonite Belonit *m (nadelförmiger Mikrolith)*
belovite Belovit *m*, $Sr_5[OH|(PO_4)_3]$
belt Band *n*, Gürtel *m*, Zone *f*, Gebiet *n*
~ **of cementation** Zementationszone *f*
~ **of deposition** Ablagerungsgürtel *m*
~ **of loess** Lößgürtel *m*
~ **of rock** Gesteinsgürtel *m*
~ **of soil water** Feuchtigkeitszone *f* des Bodens
~ **of vegetation** Vegetationsgürtel *m*
~ **of weathering** Verwitterungszone *f*
belted coastal plain zonar gegliederte Küstenebene *f*
belteroporic belteropor
Beltian Belt *n (Präkambrium in Nordamerika)*
belugite Belugit *m (Gestein zwischen Diorit und Gabbro)*
bementite Bementit *m*, $Mn_8[(OH)_{10}|Si_6O_{15}]$
bench Strosse *f*, Bank *f*, Steinlage *f*, Schicht *f*; Berme *f*, Absatz *m*, Bankett *n*
~ **coal** Oberkohle *f*, obere Kohlenbank *f (Flöz)*
~ **floor** untere Kohlenbank *f (Flöz)*
~ **gravel** Terrassenschotter *m*, Terrassenkies *m*
~ **mark** Festpunkt *m*, Fixpunkt *m*, Höhenmarke *f*, Nivellierzeichen *n*
~ **placer** Flußterrassenseife *f*
~ **surface** Berme *f*, Absatz *m*, Bankett *n*
~ **terraces** Stufenterrassen *fpl*
benching 1. Abtreppen *n*, Terrassieren *n*; 2. Strossenbau *m*; 3. Sicherheitsbankett *n*
~ **work[ing]** strossenweiser (stufenweiser) Abbau *m (Steinbruch)*
benchland Piedmonttreppe *f*, Schichtstufe *f*, Schichtterrasse *f*
benchlike terrassenförmig
benchmark *s.* bench mark
benchy vein absetziger Gang *m*
bend 1. Krümmung *f*, Biegung *f*; 2. Scharnier *(von Falten)*; 3. Schleife *f (eines Flusses)*; 4. Umbiegungskante *f (Paläontologie)*

bending Schleppung f, Verbiegung f, Durchbiegung f
~ **axis** Biegeachse f
~ **coefficient** Biegezahl f
~ **fold** Beule f *(vertikaltektonische Struktur)*
~ **moment** Biegemoment n
~ **resistance** Biegesteifigkeit f
~ **shooting** stufenweises Abschießen n *(Steinbruch)*
~ **strength** Biegefestigkeit f
~ **stress** Biegespannung f
~ **test** Biegeversuch m
~ **waves** Biegewellen fpl
beneficial use Nutzung f
~ **use of water** Wassernutzung f
beneficiate/to aufbereiten
beneficiation Aufbereitung f, Anreicherung f *(von Erzen)*
Benioff zone Benioff-Zone f, Subduktionszone f
benitoite Benitoit m, $BaTiSi_3O_9$
benstonite Benstonit m, $Ba_6Ca_7[CO_3]_{13}$
bent gebogen, gebeugt
benthal, benthic s. benthonic
bentho-pelagic benthopelagisch
benthonic benthonisch
~ **fauna** Bodenfauna f
~ **foraminifers** Foraminiferen fpl der Tiefsee
benthos Benthos n *(als Lebensraum) und als Lebewelt im benthonischen Milieu*
bentonite Bentonit m
bentonitic bentonitisch
beraunite Beraunit m, $Fe_3[(OH)_3|(PO_4)_2]\cdot 2^1/_2H_2O$
beresite Beresit m *(Varietät von Aplit)*
beresitization Beresitisierung f
berg Eisberg m
~ **crystal** Bergkristall m
~ **till** s. subaqueous till
bergalite Bergalit m *(alkalisches Ganggestein)*
bergenite Bergenit m, $Ba[(UO_2)_4|(PO_4)_2]\cdot 8H_2O$
bergschrund Bergschrund m, Gletscherrandspalte f
bergy bit Eisbergstück n
beringite Beringit m *(Alkalitrachyt)*
berlinite Berlinit m, $Al[PO_4]$
berm oberer Strand m, Böschungsabsatz m, Berme f, Sedimentanschwemmung f *(dem Strand vorgelagert)*
bermanite Bermanit m, $(Mn, Mg)_5(Mn, Fe)_8[(OH)_5|(PO_4)_4]_2\cdot 15H_2O$
berme s. berm
bermudite Bermudit m *(monchiquitisches Ergußgestein)*
berondrite Berondrit m *(Varietät von Theralith)*
Berriasian [Stage] Berrias[ium] n, Berrias-Stufe f *(basale Stufe der Unterkreide, Thetys)*
berthierite Berthierit m, $FeS \cdot Sb_2S_3$
Bertrand cross Bertrandsches Kreuz n
~ **lens** Bertrandsche Linse f
bertrandite Bertrandit m, $Be_4[(OH)_2|Si_2O_7]$
beryl Beryll m, $Al_2Be_3[Si_6O_{18}]$

beryllia Beryllerde f
beryllium Beryllium n, Be
beryllonite Beryllonit m, $NaBePO_4$
berzelianite Berzelianit m, Cu_2S_2
berzeliite Berzeliit m, $(Ca, Na)_3(Mg, Mn)_2[AsO_4]_3$
beschtanite Beschtanit m *(Quarzkeratophyr)*
BESS = Bottom Environmental Sensing System
beta activity Betaaktivität f
~ **decay** Betazerfall m
~ **emitter** Betastrahler m
~ **layer** Eskerablagerung f mit Moränenkern
~ **particle** Betateilchen n
~ **quartz** Betaquarz m
~ **radiator** Betastrahler m
~-**radioactive** betaradioaktiv
~ **radioactivity** Betaaktivität f
~-**ray emission** Betastrahlung f
~ **uranium** Betauran n
betafite Betafit m, $(Ca, U)_2(Nb, Ti, Ta)_2O_6(O, OH, F)$
betechtinite Betechtinit m, $Pb_2(Cu, Fe)_{21}S_{15}$
betpakdalite Betpakdalit m, $CaFe_2H_8[(MoO_4)_5|(AsO_4)_2]\cdot 10H_2O$
betterment of land Melioration f
betterness Feingehalt m *(von Gold und Silber über dem Standard)*
betwixt-mountains Zentraliden pl *(s.a. median mass)*
beudantite Beudantit m, $PbFe_3[(OH)_6|SO_4AsO_4]$
bevel [off]/to abschrägen
bevel Abschrägung f
bevelled abgeschrägt
~ **fault block** Rumpfscholle f
~ **upland** Rumpfgebirge n
bevelling Abschrägung f
beyerite Beyerit m, $CaBi_2[O|CO_3]_2$
Beyrichia limestone Beyrichienkalk m
BHP s. bottom-hole pressure
BHT s. bottom-hole temperature
bianchite Bianchit m, $(Zn, Fe)[SO_4]\cdot 6H_2O$
biased sampling Probenahme f mit systematischem Fehler, verfälschte Probenahme f
biaxial zweiachsig
~ **crystal** zweiachsiger Kristall m
~ **ellipsoid** Rotationsellipsoid n
~ **stress** zweiachsiger Spannungszustand m
bibbley-rock (sl) Konglomerat n
bibliolite gut laminierter Schiefer m
bicarbonate hardness Bikarbonathärte f
bicuspid zweispitzig
bieberite Bieberit m, $Co[SO_4]\cdot 7H_2O$
bifurcate/to sich gabeln, abzweigen
bifurcation Bifurkation f, Gabelung; Stromteilung f
~ **of the valley** Talgabelung f
big hole drilling Großlochbohren n
bigging Pfeiler m *(aus Bergen)*
bight Bai f, Bucht f
bikitaite Bikitait m, $Li[AlSi_2O_6]\cdot H_2O$

bilateral 42

bilateral geosyncline s. intracontinental geosyncline
~ **orogen** zweiseitiges Orogen n
~ **symmetry** bilaterale Symmetrie f
bilibinite Bilibinit m (metamikter Coffinit)
bilinite Bilinit m, $Fe_3[SO_4]_4 \cdot 22H_2O$
bill spitz zulaufende Halbinsel f
billietite Billietit m, $6[UO_2|(OH)_2] \cdot Ba(OH)_2 \cdot 4H_2O$
billitonite Billitonit m (indischer Tektit)
billow Sturmwelle f, Woge f
bimodal sandstones bimodale Sandsteine mpl (Sandsteine mit zweigipfliger Korngrößenverteilung)
bina s. bind
binary binär, zweizählig (Symmetrieachse)
~ **star** Doppelstern m
~ **system** 1. s. ~ star; 2. Zweistoffsystem n
binches Pyritkristalle in Goldkonglomeraten
binching Liegendes n
bind (sl) schiefriger Lehm (Letten) m, bituminöser Tonschiefer m
binder Bindemittel n
~ **shale** (sl) Schieferpacken m (Kohlenbergbau)
~ **soil** Bindeerde f
bindheimite Bindheimit m, $Pb_{1-2}Sb_{2-1}(O, OH, H_2O)_{6-7}$
binding agent Bindemittel n
~ **force** Bindekraft f
~ **material (medium)** Bindemittel n
bindstone boundstone, bei dem die Organismen als Sedimentbinder wirkten
bing/to aufhalden
bing Bergehalde f
~ **ore** hochwertiges Bleierz n
Bingham body Binghamscher Körper m
binocular Feldstecher m
~ **microscope** Binokular n
~ **prism telescope** Feldstecher m
binomial nomenclature binäre Nomenklatur f
bioaccumulated limestone organogener Kalkstein m (vorwiegend aus unzerbrochenen und nicht sortierten Schalen seßhafter Organismen)
biocalcarenite Biokalkarenit m (psammitischer Kalkstein aus vorwiegend organischem Material)
biocalcirudite Biokalzirudit m (psephitischer Kalkstein aus vorwiegend organischem Material)
biochemical biochemisch
~ **coalification** biochemische Inkohlung (Karbonifikation) f
~ **gelification** biochemische Vergelung f
biochore Biochor n, Großlebensraum m, Lebensbezirk m
biochronological biochronologisch
bioclastic bioklastisch
~ **rock** bioklastisches Gestein n
bioclasts Bioklasten mpl (Bruchstücke von Organismenhartteilen)
bioclimatology Bioklimatologie f
biocoenosis Biozönose f, Lebensgemeinschaft f

bioconstructed limestone deposit organogene Kalksteinablagerung f aus koloniebildenden Organismen
biodeformational structure Biodeformation f, Wühlgefüge n (Ichnologie)
bioerosion structure Bioerosion f (Ichnologie)
biofacial biofaziell
biofacies Biofazies f
~ **realm** s. zoogeographic province
bioframe limestone organogener Kalkstein m mit autochthonen Strukturen
biogenic biogen, organischen Ursprungs
~ **composition** Biogengehalt m
~ **limestone** biogener Kalkstein m
~ **product** biogenes Produkt n
~ **rock** biogenes Gestein n, Biolith m
~ **sedimentary structure** biogenes Sedimentgefüge n (Ichnologie)
~ **structure** biogenes Gefüge n (Ichnologie)
biogens Biogene npl (alle Organismenhartteile)
biogeochemical prospection biogeochemische Erkundung f
~ **province** biogeochemische Provinz f
biogeochemistry Biogeochemie f
biogeographer Biogeograf m
biogeographic[al] biogeografisch
biogeography Biogeografie f
bioglyph Bioglyphe f (Marke, Spur organischen Ursprungs)
bioherm Bioherm n (hügel- oder linsenförmiger organogener Gesteinskörper)
biohermal bed Biohermbank f
~ **reef** Biohermriff n
biohieroglyph Biohieroglyphe f
biolite Biolith m (organogenes Gestein); Fossilfestkalk m
biolith s. biolite
biologic[al] association (community) Biozönose f, Lebensgemeinschaft f
~ **half life** biologische Halbwertzeit f
~ **origin** organischer Ursprung m
~ **secretion** biologische Sekretion f
~ **taxonomy** biologische Taxonomie f
biomass Biomasse f
biometeorology Biometeorologie f
biometric[al] method biometrische Methode f
biomicrite Biomikrit m
bionomic[al] bionomisch
biophil[e] biophil
~ **biosparite** Biosparit m
biosphere Biosphäre f
biostratification structure biogenes Schichtgefüge n (Ichnologie)
biostratigraphic[al] biostratigrafisch
~ **break** biostratigrafischer Schnitt m
~ **unit** biostratigrafische Einheit f
biostratigraphy Biostratigrafie f
biostratonomy Biostratonomie f
biostromal limestone s. coquinoid limestone
biostrome Biostrom n (bankförmiger geschichteter In-situ-Fossilkalk)

biota Bios *n*, Lebewelt *f* einer Region
biotic biotisch
biotite Biotit *m (Mg-Fe-Glimmer)*
~ **flake** Biotitschüppchen *n*
~ **gneiss** Biotitgneis *m*
~ **granite** Granitit *m*
~ **schist** Biotitschiefer *m*
biotitization Biotitisierung *f*
biotope Biotop *m (n)*, Siedlungsort *m*
bioturbate texture bioturbate Textur *f*, Wühlgefüge *n (Ichnologie)*
bioturbation 1. Bioturbation *f*, biogene Schichtdestruktion *f*; 2. Wühlgefüge *n (Ichnologie)*
biphase flow Zweiphasenströmung *f*
biprism Biprisma *n*
bipyramid Bipyramide *f*
bird Flugkörper *m*, Sonde *f (am Flugzeug befestigtes geophysikalisches Meßgerät)*
~ **guano** Vogelguano *m*
bird's eye 1. Vogelauge *n (spätiges Karbonatauge im Sediment)*; 2. kavernöser Hohlraum im Sediment *(s.a.* fenestra)
~ **porosity** *s.* fenestral porosity
~ **view** Vogelschau *f*, Vogelperspektive *f*
birdseye *s.* bird's eye
bireflectance Reflexionspleochroismus *m*
bireflection Bireflexion *f*
birefringence Doppelbrechung *f*
birefringent doppelbrechend
biringuccite Biringuccit *m*, $Na_2[B_5O_7(OH)_3] \cdot 1/2 H_2O$
birkremite Birkremit *m (Quarzsyenitvarietät)*
birth line Bildungslinie *f*, „Geburtslinie" *f (an den Inkohlungsgrad gebundener Begriff bei der Erdölbildung)*
~ **stone** Monatsstein *m*, Glücksstein *m (im Volksaberglauben)*
bischofite Bischofit *m*, $MgCl_2 \cdot 6H_2O$
biscuit cutter Stoßkernrohr *n*
bisectrix Bisektrix *f*
bishop's stone *volkstümlich für Amethyst*
bismite Bismit *m*, Wismutocker *m*, $\alpha\text{-}Bi_2O_3$
bismoclite Bismoclit *m*, BiOCl
bismuth Wismut *n*, Bi
~ **blende** *s.* eulytite
~ **glance** *s.* bismuthinite
~ **ochre** *s.* bismite
~ **spar** *s.* bismutite
bismuthinite Bismuthinit *m*, Wismutglanz *m*, Bi_2S_3
bismuthite *s.* bismutite
bismutite Bismutit *m*, $Bi_2[O_2|CO_3]$
bismutoferrite Bismutoferrit *m*, $BiFe_2[OH|(SiO_4)_2]$
bismutoplagionite Bismutoplagionit *m*, $5PbS \cdot 4Bi_2S_3$
bismutosphaerite *s.* bismutite
bismutotantalite Bismutotantalit *m*, $Bi(Ta, Nb)O_4$
bit Meißel *m*, Bohrmeißel *m*, Bohrer *m*, Bohrkopf *m*, Bohrkrone *f*
~ **clearance** Meißelspiel *n*

~ **hook** Fanghaken *m*, Glückshaken *m*
~ **life** Meißelstandzeit *f*, Meißellebensdauer *f*
~ **nozzle** Meißeldüse *f*
~ **of ground** Bodenprobestück *n*
bite/to beizen, ätzen, anfressen
bitheca Bithek *f (bei Graptolithen)*
Bithynian [Substage] Bithyn[ium] *n (Unterstufe, Mittlere Trias, Tethys)*
bitter lake Bittersee *m*
~ **salt** Bittersalz *n*
~ **spar** *s.* dolomite
bittern Mutterlauge *f*
bitumen Bitumen *n*, Bergteer *m*
bituminiferous asphalthaltig, bitumenhaltig
bituminite Bituminit *m (Kohlenmaceral der Liptinit-Gruppe)*
bituminization Bituminierung *f*
~ **range** Bituminierungsbereich *m*
bituminological method Bitumenmethode *f*
bituminous bituminös, bitumenhaltig
~ **brown coal** Schwelbraunkohle *f*
~ **clay** bituminöser Ton *m*
~ **coal** 1. Steinkohle *f*; 2. bituminöse Kohle *f*
~ **coal seam** Steinkohlenflöz *n*
~ **earth** Bitumen *n*
~ **limestone** bituminöser Kalk *m*, Stinkkalk *m*
~ **marl** bituminöser Mergelschiefer *m*
~ **mastic** Bitumenkitt *m*
~ **oil shale** Ölschiefer *m*
~ **rock** Asphaltgestein *n*, Bergasphalt *m*
~ **sandstone** Asphaltsandstein *m*
~ **shale** 1. bituminöser (bitumenhaltiger) Schiefer *m*; 2. kohlenhaltiger Schiefer *m*
bityite Bityit *m*, $CaLiAl_2[(OH)_2|AlBeSi_2O_{10}]$
bivalence Zweiwertigkeit *f*
bivalent zweiwertig
bivalve [mollusk] Zweischaler *m*
bivalved, bivalvular doppelschalig
bixbyite Bixbyit *m*, $(Fe, Mn)_2O_3$
black acid prairie soil saurer schwarzer Wiesenboden *m*
~ **adobe** tropische Schwarzerde *f*
~ **alkali soil** Solone[t]z *m*, Solontschak *m*, schwarzer Alkaliboden *m (Salzboden mit mehr als 1–3% Salzgehalt)*
~ **antimony** *s.* antimonite
~ **band** Blackband *n*, Kohleneisenstein *m*, kohlehaltiger Spateisenstein *m*, Schwarzstreif *m*
~ **bat** *(sl) s.* ~ batt
~ **batt** Brandschiefer *m*
~ **bed** Kohlenletten *m*
~ **blende** *s.* uraninite
~ **blizzard** *(Am)* Staubsturm *m*
~ **body radiation** Strahlung *f* eines schwarzen Körpers
~ **bog** Nieder[ungs]moor *n*, Riedmoor *n*, Wiesenmoor *n*
~ **coal** Steinkohle *f*
~ **copper ore** *s.* tenorite
~ **cotton soil** tropischer schwerer Ton *m*
~ **damp** Grubengas *n* mit CO
~ **diamond** schwarzer Diamant *m*, Bohrdiamant *m*

black

- ~ **drift** s. forest bed
- ~ **durain** sporenreicher Durit m (Steinkohlenmikrolithotyp)
- ~ **earth** Schwarzerde f, Tschernosem m
- ~ **earthy cobalt ore** schwarzer Erdkobalt m, Kobaltmanganerz n
- ~ **forest earth** schwarzer Waldhumusboden m
- ~ **fuel peat** Specktorf m, Pechtorf m
- ~ **glossy fuel peat** Lebertorf m
- ~ **granite** schwarzer Granit m (Handelsbezeichnung für Diorit und Gabbro)
- ~ **haematite** s. psilomelane
- ~ **iron ore** s. magnetite
- ~ **jack** s. sphalerite
- ~ **lead** s. graphite
- ~ **lead ore** schwarze Abart des Zerussit
- ~ **lead spar** s. cerussite
- ~ **lustrous** schwarzglänzend
- ~ **magnetic spherules** schwarze magnetische Kügelchen npl (5–580 μm groß, extraterrestrischer oder terrestrischer Herkunft)
- ~ **manganese** s. pyrolusite
- ~ **meadow soil** dunkler Aueboden m
- ~ **mettle** (sl) schwarzer Schiefer m
- ~ **mica** s. biotite
- ~ **ochre** s. wad
- ~ **oil** Sammelbegriff für dunkle Öle mit relativ viel Asphalt
- ~ **regur** Bodenart in Indien
- ~ **sand** 1. Schliech m, Schlich m; 2. durch dunkle Schwerminerale angereicherte Seifen
- ~ **shale** Schwarzschiefer m
- ~ **-shale facies** Schwarzschieferfazies f
- ~ **silver** s. stephanite
- ~ **smoker** „Blacksmoker" m, „Schwarzer Räucherer" m (Kamin im Meeresboden)
- ~ **soil** Schwarzerde f
- ~ **stone** Kohlenschiefer m, kohliger Schieferton m (sehr karbonatreicher Schiefer)
- ~ **telluride** s. nagyagite
- ~ **top pavement** (Am) Schwarzerde f
- ~ **top soil** Humusboden m
- ~ **tourmaline** Eisenturmalin m, Schörl m
- ~ **turf soil** schwarzer Rasenboden m
- **Black Jura** Schwarzer Jura m, Lias m (f)
- ~ **Sea facies** Schwarzmeerfazies f, euxinische Fazies f
- **blackband** s. black band
- **blackbox** Blackbox f
- **Blackriveran [Stage]** Blackriver[ien] n (Stufe des Champlainiens in Nordamerika)
- **blackroller** (Am) Staubsturm m
- **blacks** (sl) milder schwarzer Schiefer m
- **blacksmiths' chisel** Schrotmeißel m
- **bladder wrack** Blasentang m, Fukus m
- **blade** flacher Stengel m (von Kristallen)
- **bladed** blätterartig geschichtet, plattig, blattstenglig
- **blae** (sl) s. blairmorite
- **blaes** 1. kluftfreier harter Sandstein m; 2. s. bind

- **blairmorite** Blairmorit m (alkalisches Ergußgestein)
- **blaize** (sl) harter Sandstein m
- **Blancan [Stage]** Blancan n (Wirbeltierstufe des Pliozäns in Nordamerika)
- **blanch** (sl) Bleierz n
- **blank** Lücke f (z.B. auf der Karte)
- **blanket** 1. Schicht f, Flöz n, Decke f; 2. Quarzlagergang m; 3. Dichtungsschürze f
- ~ **basalt** Deckenbasalt m
- ~ **deposit** flaches Erzlager n (sedimentäre Lagerstätte geringer Mächtigkeit, aber großer Ausdehnung)
- ~ **of debris** Schuttdecke f
- ~ **of sediment** Sedimentdecke f
- ~ **of snow** Schneedecke f
- ~ **sand** Decksand m, Schwemmsand m
- ~ **vein** horizontaler Lagergang m
- **blanketing** Goldgewinnung f auf Decken
- **blast/to** sprengen
- ~ **off** wegsprengen
- ~ **out** heraussprengen
- **blast** Blast m (metamorph gebildetes Kristallindividuum)
- ~ **furnace coke** Hochofenkoks m
- ~ **of gas** Gasausbruch m
- ~ **wave** Druckwelle f, Expansionswelle f
- **blasted ore** herausgesprengtes Erz n
- ~ **rock** gelöstes Gestein n
- **blaster** Zündmaschine f
- **blastesis** Blastese f, Kristalloblastese f
- **blasthole** Sprengbohrloch n, Bohrloch n
- ~ **drill** Sprengbohrlochgerät n
- ~ **drilling** Sprenglochbohren n
- **blastic** [kristallo]blastisch umkristallisiert
- ~ **fabric** blastisches Gefüge n, Blastitgefüge n
- **blasting** Schießen n, Sprengen n
- ~ **oil** Sprengöl n
- ~ **operations** Sprengarbeiten fpl
- ~ **pellet** Schwarzpulver n in Tablettenform
- ~ **powder** Schwarzpulver n in Pulverform
- ~ **technician** Sprengmeister m
- **blastogranitic** blastogranitisch
- **Blastoidea** Blastoideen fpl
- **blastomycetous** s. blastomylonitic
- **blastomylonite** Blastomylonit m
- **blastomylonitic** blastomylonitisch
- **blastopelitic** blastopelitisch
- **blastophone** Schallempfänger m (Seismik)
- **blastophyric** blastophyrisch
- **blastophytic** blastophytisch
- **blastoporphyric** blastoporphyrisch
- **blastopsammitic** blastopsammitisch
- **blastopsephitic** blastopsephitisch
- **blaze** Glut f, Glutschein m
- **bleach/to** bleichen
- **bleached layer** Bleichschicht f
- ~ **zone** Bleichungszone f
- **bleaching** Bleichung f, Entfärbung f, Ausbleichung f
- ~ **clay (earth)** Bleicherde f
- ~ **podzolization** Ausbleichung f, Podsolisierung f

bleb s. bubble
bleed [off] pressure/to Druck ablassen
bleeder well Entlastungsbrunnen m, Abzapfbrunnen m in artesisch gespanntem Grundwasser
bleeding 1. Sickerung f, Durchsickerung f; 2. Anzapfen n
~ **core** [öl]ausschwitzender Kern m
bleischweif Bleischweif m
blende s. sphalerite
blending of soils Zusammensetzen n von Bodengemischen
blind chimney verdeckter Gang m
~ **creek** zeitweiliger Bach m
~ **deposit** verdeckte Lagerstätte f
~ **drain** Sickerdrän m
~ **drilling** Bohren n ohne geologische Vorarbeiten
~-**end bore** Blindloch n
~ **hole** Blindbohrung f
~ **joint** verborgene Kluft f, verdeckte Spalte f
~ **lead** Gang m ohne Ausstrich
~ **lode** verdeckter Gang m
~ **valley** blindes Tal n
~ **vein** s. ~ lode
blinde s. sphalerite
blinded with sand sandverschlämmt
blister cone Entgasungskegel m (auf Lavadekken)
blistered schwammig
blizzard (Am) Schneesturm m
bloating Blähen n
~ **clay** Blähton m
~ **property** Blähvermögen n
blob of slag Lavaflatschen m
block/to verschließen
block 1. Block m, Massiv n, Scholle f; 2. fehlerfreie Platte f (Handelsglimmersorte)
~ **caving** Blockbruchbau m
~ **coal** (sl) Würfelkohle f
~ **diagram** Blockdiagramm n
~ **disintegration** Blockzerfall m
~ **embankment** Blockwall m
~ **fault** Schollenbruch m
~-**faulted area** Bruchschollengebiet n
~ **faulting** Blockverwerfung f, Bruchschollenbildung f, Schollenverschiebung f
~ **field** Blockmeer n, Felsenmeer n
~ **folding** Schollenfaltung f
~ **ice** Blockeis n, Eis n in Blöcken
~-**in-course walling** Quadermauerwerk n
~ **lava** Blocklava f, Schollenlava f
~ **levee** Blockwall m
~ **mica** Rohglimmer m
~ **mountains** Bruchschollengebirge n
~ **of ice** Eisscholle f
~ **of rock** Felsblock m
~ **of strata** Schichtenblock m
~ **overthrust** Schollenüberschiebung f
~ **packing** Blockpackung f
~ **rampart** Blockwall m
~ **reef** Blockriff n

~ **sandstone** Quadersandstein m
~ **stream** Blockstrom m
~ **structure** Schollenbau m
blocked-out ore vorgerichtetes Erz n, ausgeblockter Erzvorrat m
~ **spine** nadelförmige Stoßkuppe f
~-**up valley** abgeriegeltes Tal n
blocking Grobspalten n (Steine mit Keilen)
~-**up** Auflandung f, Auffüllung f, Verlandung f
blocklike schollenförmig
blocky würfelig, Block...
blödite, bloedite Blödit m (s.a. astrakanite)
blomstrandine Blomstrandin m, (Y, Ce, Th, Ca, Na, U) [(Ti, Nb, Ta)$_2$O$_6$]
blondin Kabelkran m
blood rain Blutregen m
bloodstone Blutstein m, Blutachat m, Roteisenstein m (s.a. haematite)
bloom 1. Erdölfluoreszenz f; 2. Blüte f (z.B. Kobaltblüte); 3. Ausblühung f (von Mineralen in ariden Gebieten)
blossom 1. Ausbiß m (von Kohle oder Erz); 2. s. bloom 2.
~ **of coal** s. coal smut
blotched gesprenkelt, gefleckt
blow down/to anschießen (das Hangende)
~ **down pressure** Druck ablassen
~ **off** wegsprengen
~ **out** ausbrechen, wild erumpieren
blow hole Durchschlagsloch n, Blasloch n
~ **land** verwehtes Land n
~-**out** 1. Ausbruch m, Eruption f (einer Bohrung); 2. Deflationskessel m, Windmühle f
~-**out dune** Haldendüne f
~-**out dust storm** Staubsturm m
~-**out preventer** Eruptionsstopfbüchse f, Preventer m, Bohrlochabsperrarmatur f
~-**out prevention** Ausbruchsverhütung f
~-**out valve** Absperrventil n
~-**out well** Springer m, Springquelle f, Springsonde f (Erdöl)
~ **well** artesischer Brunnen m
blowing Luftspülung f
~ **cone** Lavaschornstein m, Schlackenschornstein m, Hornito m
~ **dune** Wanderdüne f
~ **erosion** Winderosion f
~-**out** Auswurf m, Ausschleudern n
~-**out preventer assembly** Preventergarnitur f, Bohrlochabsperrvorrichtung f
~ **well** 1. artesischer Brunnen m; 2. wild erumpierende Sonde f; Springer m, Springquelle f, Springsonde f (Erdöl)
blown-out hole Bohrlochpfeife f
~-**out shot** Ausbläser m
~ **sand** Flugsand m
~-**sand deposit** Treibsandablagerung f
blowpipe Lötrohr n
~ **analysis (assay)** Lötrohranalyse f, Lötrohrprobe f
~ **assaying** Lötrohrprobierkunst f
~ **proof (test)** s. ~ analysis

blue

blue asbestos Blauasbest *m*
~ **bands** Blaublätter *npl (im Gletscher)*
~-**cape asbestos** *s.* crocidolite
~ **clay** Blauton *m*
~ **copper** *s.* covellite
~ **copper ore** *s.* azurite
~ **copperas** *s.* chalcanthite
~ **earth** *s.* ~ ground
~-**green algae** Blaualgen *fpl*
~ **ground** Blauerde *f (Diamantenpipes)*
~ **ice** Altgletschereis *n*
~ **iron earth** *s.* vivianite
~ **john** *(sl)* blauer Flußspat *m (s.a.* fluorite)
~ **lead** *s.* galena
~ **mud** Blauschlick *m*
~ **ochre** *s.* vivianite
~ **quartz** Saphirquarz *m*
~-**remaining covellite** blaubleibender Covellin *m*
~ **spar** *s.* lazulite
~ **vitriol** *s.* chalcanthite
~ **whin** *(sl)* Basalt *m*
blueschist Glaukophanschiefer *m,* Glaukophanit *m,* glaukophanitischer Grünschiefer *m*
~ **facies** Glaukophanschieferfazies, *f,* Grünschieferfazies *f,* Hochdruckgrünschieferfazies *f*
bluestone *s.* chalcanthite
bluff *(Am)* Felsufer *n,* Steilufer *n,* Felsenklippe *f*
~ **formation** Löß *m*
blunt fold stumpfe Falte *f*
blurr pan verzerrte Panoramaaufnahme *f*
blurred zone Verwaschungszone *f*
board Abbaustrecke *f*
~-**and-pillar work** *s.* bord and pillar work
~ **coal** *(sl)* holzartig aussehende Kohle *f*
boar's back *(sl) s.* hogback
boart Bort *m,* Industriediamant *m*
boat channel Rinne zwischen Saumriff und Küste
~ **level** schiffbarer Stollen *m*
bobbing Bearbeiten *n* einer Scheibe *(Schleifen, Polieren von Kristallen)*
~ **mark** Schleiflinie *f,* Schleifnarbe *f*
bobierrite Bobierrit *m,* $Mg_3[PO_4]_2 \cdot 8H_2O$
bocca Bocca *f,* Ausbruchsöffnung *f*
bodden Bodden *m*
~ **type of coast line** Boddenküste *f*
body-centred cubic structure kubisch-raumzentrierte Struktur *f*
~ **chamber** Wohnkammer *f (Paläontologie)*
~ **of coal** brennbarer Bestandteil der Kohle
~ **of gas** Schlagwetteransammlung *f*
~ **of rock** Gesteinskörper *m*
~ **of salt** Salzkörper *m*
~ **of surface waters** Oberflächengewässer *n*
~ **of water** Wasserkörper *m,* Wasseransammlung *f*
~ **of weir** Wehrkörper *m,* Wehrmauer *f*
~ **presenting rotation symmetry** rotationssymmetrischer Körper *m*
~ **spicules** Körperspicula *npl (Paläontologie)*
~ **stress** Eigenspannung *f*

~ **wave** Raumwelle *f*
~ **whorl** letzter Umgang *m (bei spiraligen Fossilgehäusen)*
boeggildite Böggildit *m,* $Na_2Sr_2Al_2[F_9PO_4]$
boehmite Böhmit *m,* γ-AlOOH
bog Sumpf *m;* Moor *n*
~ **blasting** Moorsprengung *f*
~ **burst** Moorbruch *m*
~ **butter** Sumpfbutter *f*
~ **earth** Moorerde *f*
~ **iron ore** Rasen[eisen]erz *n,* Raseneisenstein *m,* Sumpferz *n,* Sumpfeisenstein *m,* Wiesenerz *n*
~ **land** Moorgebiet *n,* Marschland *n,* Sumpfland *n*
~ **lime** Kalkschicht *f* im Moor, Seekreide *f,* Wiesenkalk *m*
~ **manganese** Manganschaum *m (s.a.* wad)
~ **moor** Torfmoor *n*
~ **moss** Torfmoos *n,* Sphagnum *n*
~ **ore** *s.* iron ore
~ **peat** Moortorf *m*
~ **pool** Moorsee *m,* Blänke *f*
~ **soil** Moorboden *m*
bogginess sumpfige Beschaffenheit *f*
boggy sumpfig, morastig
~ **soil** Moorboden *m,* Torfboden *m*
~ **water** Moorwasser *n*
boghead coal Bogheadkohle *f (Sapropelkohle)*
~ **seam** Boghead[kohlen]flöz *n*
~ **shale** Bogheadschiefer *m*
boghedite *s.* torbanite
Bohemian garnet böhmischer Granat *m*
~ **massif** Böhmisches Massiv *n*
~ **phase of folding** Böhmische Phase *f (Oberkambrium, Prager Mulde)*
~ **ruby** *s.* ~ garnet
boiling down Abdampfen *n*
~ **of sand** Sandaufbruch *m (Grundbruch bei kritischem Gefälle)*
~ **point** Siedepunkt *m*
~ **spring** kochende Quelle *f*
~ **up** Hochpuffen *n (Sohle)*
bojite Bojit *m (Hornblendegabbro)*
boke *(sl)* kleines Erztrum *n*
bolar bolusartig
bold cliff Steilwand *f*
~ **coast** Steilküste *f*
~ **precipice (scarps)** Steilabfall *m*
~ **shore** Steilküste *f*
boldyrevite Boldyrevit *m,* $CaNaMg[AlF_5,(F,H_2O)]_3$
bole Bol[us] *m,* Boluserde *f,* Siegelerde *f*
boleite Boleit *m,* $5PbCl_2 \cdot 4Cu(OH)_2 \cdot AgCl \cdot 1\tfrac{1}{2}H_2O$
Bolerian [Stage] *s.* Blackriveran
bolide Bolid *m,* Feuerkugel *f*
bolivarite Bolivarit *m,* $Al_2((OH)_3|PO_4) \cdot 5H_2O$
bolly *(sl) s.* bally
bolson ebenes Wüstental *n*
boltonite *s.* forsterite
bolts Kurzanker *mpl*
boltwoodite Boltwoodit *m,* $K_2H_2[UO_2|SiO_4] \cdot 4H_2O$

bomb Lavabombe f, [vulkanische] Bombe f
~ **effect** Kernwaffeneffekt m
~ **pit** Einschlagtrichter m *(vulkanischer Bomben)*
bombiccite s. hartite
bomblike hole Bombenloch n *(Meteorit)*
bonanza ergiebige Goldgrube f, Erzfall m
~ **ore body** reicher Erzkörper m
~ **quality** hohe Qualität f *(von Bergbauprodukten)*
bonattite Bonattit m, $Cu[SO_4] \cdot 3H_2O$
bonchevite Bonchevit m, $PbS \cdot 2Bi_2S_3$
bond 1. Bindemittel n; 2. Bindung f, Aneinanderlagerung f; Verband m; Haftung f
~ **clay** Bindeton m *(hochplastisch)*
~ **stress** Haftspannung f
~ **type** Bindungsart f
bonding Verfestigung f *(des Gebirges)*
~ **strength** Verbandsfestigkeit f, Haftvermögen n
bone 1. Knochen m; 2. *(Am)* Brandschiefer m
~ **bed** Knochenbrekzie f
~ **coal** *(Am)* bergehaltige (unreine) Kohle f
~ **digger** Fossilsammler m
~ **structure** Knochenbau m
~ **turquoise** fossiler Türkis m
boney Schieferton m *(im Kohlengebirge)*
~ **coal** *(Am)* bergehaltige (unreine) Kohle f
boning Nivellement n; Visieren n
~-**in** Einvisieren n
boninite Boninit m *(glasreicher Andesit)*
bonney Erznest n
bonny s. bonney
bony armature Knochenpanzer m
~ **coal** s. bone coal
~ **core** Knochenzapfen m
~ **fish** Knochenfisch m
~ **plate** Knochenplatte f
~ **prominence** Knochenauswuchs m
~ **ridge** Knochenwulst m
~ **skeleton** Knochenskelett n
~ **spine** Knochenstachel m
bonze *(sl)* nicht aufbereitetes Bleierz n, Bleiroherz n
book feinste Spaltplatte f *(Handelsglimmersorte)*
~ **clay** Bänderton m, dünngeschichteter Ton m
~ **mica** Plattenglimmer m
bookstone s. bibliolite
boomer Boomer m *(1. Energiequelle; 2. scharfer niederfrequenter Reflexionseinsatz)*
booming Ausschlämmethode f *(für Seifen)*
boort s. bort
boose erzhaltige Gangart f; zweitklassiges Erz n
booster Initialsprengstoff m
~ **station** Zwischenpumpstation f
boothite Boothit m, $Cu[SO_4] \cdot 7H_2O$
BOPD = barrel oil per day
BOPH = barrel oil per hour
boracite Borazit m, $\beta\text{-}Mg_3[Cl|B_7O_{13}]$

borax Borax m, $Na_2[B_4O_5(OH)_4] \cdot 8H_2O$
~ **lake** Boraxsee m
bord s. ~ way
~-**and-pillar work** Pfeilerbau m
~-**and-stall working** Kammer- und Pfeilerbau m, Örterbau m
~-**and-wall work** Pfeilerbau m
~ **way** Vorrichtungsstrecke f, Grundstrecke f
~ **ways course** Richtung f senkrecht zur Hauptspaltbarkeit
border Markscheide f, Feld[es]grenze f
~ **facies** Randfazies f
~ **moraine** Randmoräne f, Endmoräne f
~ **mountains** Randgebirge n
~ **of a claim** Markscheide f, Feld[es]grenze f
~ **sea** Randmeer n, Nebenmeer n
bordering mountain chains Randgebirge npl
borderland Randgebiet n
bore/to bohren *(s.a.* drill/to)
~ **again** nachbohren
~ **sound** tiefbohren, abbohren
bore 1. Bohrloch n, Sprengloch n, Sonde f; 2. Stollen m, Tunnel m; 3. Springflut f, Flutbrandung f; 4. submariner Sandrücken m im Flachwasser
~ **detritus** Nachfall m im Bohrloch
~ **dust** Bohrmehl n, Bohrsand m
~ **gauge** Kaliberzapfen m; Meßpatrone f
~ **surface** Bohrfläche f, Bohrwandung f
~ **well** Bohrbrunnen m
boreal nördlich
Boreal Boreal n *(Teil des Flandriens, Holozän)*
~ **Realm** boreales Faunenreich n *(Mesozoikum in Nordasien, Nordamerika, Nordeuropa)*
bored pile Bohrpfahl m
~ **well** Bohrbrunnen m
borehole Bohrung f, Bohrloch n
~ **axial strain transmitter** Bohrlochlängsgeber m
~ **camera** Bohrlochkamera f
~ **deformation meter** Bohrlochverformungsgeber m
~ **depth** Bohrlochtiefe f
~ **detritus** Nachfall m im Bohrloch
~ **diameter decreasing** Verengung f des Bohrlochs, Zugehen n
~ **diametral strain** Bohrlochkaliberdeformation f
~ **direction** Bohrlochrichtung f
~ **fluid** Bohrflüssigkeit f
~ **gravimeter** Bohrlochgravimeter n
~ **inclination angle** Neigungswinkel m des Bohrlochs
~ **logging** Bohrlochuntersuchung f
~ **measurement** Bohrlochmessung f
~ **pump** Bohrlochpumpe f
~ **sample** Bohrlochprobe f
~ **sealing** Bohrlochverfüllung f
~ **shooting** Torpedieren n
~ **spacing** Bohrlochdistanz f
~ **survey[ing]** Bohrlochmessung f
~ **testing** Probeentnahme f aus dem Bohrloch

borehole 48

- ~ to prove strata Versuchsbohrloch *n*
- ~ troubles Komplikation *f* im Bohrloch
- ~ wall Bohrlochwand *f*
- ~ well Rohrbrunnen *m*

borickyite Borickyit *m*, $CaFe_4[(OH)_8]$
boring Bohrung *f* (*s.a.* drilling)
- ~ again Nachbohren *n*
- ~ capacity Bohrleistung *f*
- ~ depth Bohrtiefe *f*
- ~ for soil investigation Bodenuntersuchungsbohrung *f*
- ~ head Bohrkopf *m*
- ~ kernel Bohrkern *m*
- ~ log durch bohrende Organismen verursachte Porosität
- ~ mud Bohrschmand *m*, Bohrtrübe *f*
- ~ porosity *s.* ~ log
- ~ record sheet, ~ report Bohrprotokoll *n*
- ~ rod Bohrgestänge *n*
- ~ sludge Bohrschmand *m*, Bohrtrübe *f*
- ~ spindle Bohrspindel *f*
- ~ tackle Bohrgerät *n*
- ~ test Bohrversuch *m*
- ~ tool Bohrmeißel *m*, Bohrwerkzeug *n*
- ~ tower Bohrturm *m*
- ~ trestle Bohrbock *m*, Bohrturm *m*, Bohrgerüst *n*
- ~ tube Erdbohrer *m*
- ~ unit Bohreinheit *f*

borings Bohrmehl *n*, Bohrsand *m*, Bohrklein *n*
bornhardtite Bornhardtit *m*, Co_3Se_4
bornite Bornit *m*, Buntkupferkies *m*, Cu_5FeS_4
Born's exponent of repulsion Bornscher Abstoßungsexponent *m*
boron Bor *n*, B
boronatrocalcite *s.* ulexite
borrow excavation material Entnahmematerial *n*
- ~ pit Entnahmegrube *f*
- ~ soil Entnahmeboden *m*
- ~ source Entnahmestelle *f*, Gewinnungsstelle *f*

borse (*sl*) Gesteinsstrum *n*
bort schwarzer Diamant *m*, Industriediamant *m*
bortz *s.* bort
bosjemanite Bosjemanit *m* (*Mn-Pickeringit*)
boss 1. Lakkolith *m*; 2. Buckel *m*
bostonite Bostonit *m* (*Alkalisyenitaplit*)
botallackite Botallackit *m*, $Cu_2(OH)_3Cl$
botanic geography Pflanzengeografie *f*
botryogen Botryogen *m*, $MgFe[OH|(SO_4)_2]\cdot 7H_2O$
botryoidal traubig, traubenförmig
- ~ blende Schalenblende *f* (*s.a.* sphalerite)
- ~ structure Traubentextur *f*

bottle Sackhöhle *f*
~-necked trichterförmig
bottom Füllort *n*, Sohle *f*, Strosse *f*, Liegendes *n*
- ~ agitation Aufwirbeln *n* des Bodens
- ~ assembly for side-tracking operations Ablenkungsbohrgarnitur *f*

- ~ bench of a seam Unterbank *f* eines Flözes
- ~ break Schichtfuge *f* im Liegenden
- ~ canch Nachriß *m* im Liegenden
- ~ catcher Bodengreifer *m*
- ~ configuration of the sea Gestaltung *f* des Meeresbodens
- ~ contour line Tiefenlinie *f*
- ~ current Grundströmung *f*, Bodenstrom *m*, Sohlenströmung *f*
- ~ discharge tunnel Grundablaß *m*
- ~ drift Bodendrift *f*
- ~-dwelling organism bodenbewohnender Organismus *m*
- ~-emptying gallery Grundablaß *m*
- ~ frictional layer Bodenreibungsschicht *f*
- ~ grab Grundprobensammler *m*
- ~ heading Sohlvortrieb *m*
- ~ hole Bohrlochsohle *f*
- ~-hole equipment Bohrlochausrüstung *f*
- ~-hole flow[ing] pressure Sohlenfließdruck *m*
- ~-hole flowmeter Durchflußmeßgerät *n* an der Bohrlochsohle
- ~-hole inclinometer Bohrlochneigungsmesser *m*
- ~-hole pressure Druck *m* an der Bohrlochsohle, Sohl[en]druck *m* (*Erdöl*)
- ~-hole pressure gauge Sohl[en]druckmeßgerät *n*
- ~-hole sample Probe *f* vom Boden eines Bohrlochs, Bodenprobe *f*
- ~-hole sample taker, ~-hole sampler Bohrlochsohlenprobenehmer *m*, Bodenprobenehmer *m*, Probenehmer *m* im Bohrloch
- ~-hole spacing Sohlenabstand *m* der Bohrungen
- ~-hole temperature Bohrlochsohlentemperatur *f*
- ~-hole thermometer Thermometer *n* für Tiefbohrungen
- ~ ice Grundeis *n*, Sulzeis *n*
- ~ joint schwebende Spalte *f*
- ~ land Schwemmland *n*, Tiefland *n*, Aue *f*
- ~ layer untere Schicht *f*; Unterbank *f* (*eines Flözes*)
- ~ lift Grundhorizont *m*
- ~ line Muldenlinie *f*, Muldentiefstes *n*
- ~-living life Benthos *n*
- ~ load Bodenlast *f*, Flußgeschiebe *n*
- ~ measure liegende Bank *f*
- ~ moraine Grundmoräne *f*
- ~ of an aquifer layer Grundwassersohle *f*
- ~ of casing string Futterrohrschuh *m*
- ~ of the bed Sohle *f* des Flözes
- ~ of the borehole Bohrlochsohle *f*
- ~ of the crater Kraterboden *m*
- ~ of the hole Bohrlochsohle *f*
- ~ of the nappe Deckenbasis *f*, Deckensohle *f* (*tektonisch*)
- ~ of the well bore Bohrlochsohle *f*
- ~ of trench Grabensohle *f*
- ~ outlet Grundablaß *m*
- ~ peat Flachmoortorf *m*
- ~ plug Bodenpfropfen *m* (*Bohrung*)

box

~ **rock** Liegendes *n*, gewachsenes Gebirge *n*
~ **slice** Grundschicht *f*
~ **soil** Unterboden *m*
~ **stone** *s.* fire clay 2.
~ **storage facilities** Untertagespeicherungsmöglichkeiten *fpl*
~ **to top/from** vom Liegenden zum Hangenden
~ **wall** Liegendes *n*
~ **water** Liegendwasser *n*, Sohlenwasser *n*, Bodenwasser *n*
~ **water drive** Sohlenwassertrieb *m*
~ **water drive field** Lagerstätte *f* mit Liegendwassertrieb
~ **width** Sohlenbreite *f*
bottomed söhlig
~ **well** eingestellte Bohrung *f*
bottomset Basisschicht *f*, Bodensediment *n*
~ **bed** Bodenablagerung *f*
~ **beds** geschichtete Grundablagerungen *fpl*
boudinage Boudinage *f*
boudiner/to boudinieren
Bouguer anomaly Bouguersche Anomalie *f*, Bouguer-Anomalie *f*
~ **correction** Bouguer-Reduktion *f*
boulangerite Boulangerit *m*, 5PbS·2Sb$_2$S$_3$
boulder 1. Geschiebe *n*, Geröll *n*; Findling *m*, Felsblock *m*; 2. Erzklumpen *m*
~ **bed** [erratische] Geröllschicht *f*, Blockpackung *f*
~ **breaking** Zerkleinern *n* von großen Gesteinsblöcken
~ **clay** Geschiebelehm *m*, Geschiebemergel *m*, Blocklehm *m*
~ **fan** Schuttfächer *m*
~ **field** Felsenmeer *n*, Blockmeer *n*
~ **flint** Schotter *m*
~ **gravel** unverfestigte Blockablagerung *f*; Kiesschotter *m*
~ **masses** Blockpackung *f*
~ **moraine** Blockmoräne *f*
~ **of quartzite** Findlingsquarzit *m*, Süßwasserquarzit *m*
~ **pavement** Blockschicht *f*, Steinpflaster *n*
~ **period** Eiszeit *f*
~ **popping** Knäpperschießen *n (Steinbruch)*
~ **rock** erratisches Geröllgestein *n*
~ **shingle** Steingeschiebe *n*
~ **stream (train)** Blockstrom *m*
~ **till** Geschiebelehm *m (petrografisch)*
~ **wall** Blockmoränenwall *m*
boulderet *s.* cobble
bouldery blockreich
~ **deposit** Blockpackung *f*
~ **ground** Geröllboden *m*
Bouma sequence Bouma-Sequenz *f (ideale vertikale Abfolge in einem Turbidityzyklus)*
bounce cast Aufprallmarke *f*, Aufstoßmarke *f*, Rückprallmarke *f*
bound-down gebunden
boundary 1. Markscheide *f*, Feld[es]grenze *f*; 2. Streichlinie *f (von Flußufern)*

~ **condition** Grenzbedingung *f*, Randbedingung *f*
~ **effect** Endeffekt *m (Reservoirtechnik)*
~ **fault** Randverwerfung *f*
~ **layer** Grenzfläche *f*, Grenzschicht *f*
~-**layer friction** Grenzflächenreibung *f*
~ **line** Markscheide *f*, Feld[es]grenze *f*
~ **pillar** Bergefeste *f*
~ **plane** Grenzfläche *f*
~ **problem** Randwertaufgabe *f*
~ **relief** Grenzrelief *n (Ichnologie)*
~ **saturation** Grenzsättigung *f*
~ **stratotype** Stratotyp *m* einer stratigrafischen Grenze
~ **surface** Grenzfläche *f*
~ **system** Grenzkurve *f*, Feldesgrenze *f*
~ **wave** Grenzflächenwelle *f*
~ **zone** Randzone *f*
~ **zone of capillarity** Kapillarsaum *m*
bounded reservoir geschlossenes Reservoir *n*
bounder Markscheider *m*
bounding plane (surface) Grenzfläche *f (von Kristallen)*
boundstone Karbonatgestein aus primär organogen verbundenen Komponenten
bourne Trockentälchen *n*
bournonite Bournonit *m*, Schwarzspießglanz *m*, Bleifahlerz *m*, 2 PbS·Cu$_2$S·Sb$_2$S$_3$
bourock Steinhügel *m*
bouse *(sl)* 1. verwachsenes Erz *n*; 2. hereingewonnenes Gangbleierz *n*
~ **team** Roherzhalde *f*
boussingaultite Boussingaultit *m*, (NH$_4$)$_2$Mg[SO$_4$]$_2$·6H$_2$O
bout Gangeinschnürung *f*
bouze *s.* bouse
Bovey coal Boveykohle *f (eine Art Braunkohle)*
bow up/to aufwölben
bow area Faltungszone *f*
~-**shaped dune** Bogendüne *f*
bowenite *(sl)* Serpentin *m*
Bowen's petrogenetic grid *s.* ~ reaction series
~ **reaction series** Bowensche Reaktionsreihen *fpl (Kristallisationsreihen für verschiedene Magmentypen)*
bowing-up Aufwölbung *f*
bowl Erdvertiefung *f*, Kessel *m*
~ **classifier** Schüsselklassierer *m*, Sichertrog *m*
~-**shaped** schüsselförmig
~-**shaped hollow** schüsselförmige Vertiefung *f*
bowlder *s.* boulder
bowldery *s.* bouldery
bowlike hollow schüsselförmige Vertiefung *f*
bowr *s.* bort
bowralite Bowralith *m (Alkalipegmatit)*
bowse *s.* bouse
box auger Hohlbohrer *m*
~ **buddle** Schlämmgraben *m*, Waschrinne *f*
~ **classifier** Spitzkasten *m*

box 50

~ fold Kofferfalte f, Kastenfalte f
~ sampler Kastengreifer m; Bodengreifer m
~ shear apparatus Scherapparat m nach Casagrande, Scherkastengerät n, Scherbüchse f
boxwork rauhwacke Zellenrauhwacke f
BPD = barrel per day
BPWPD = barrel per well per day
Brabant mass Brabanter Massiv n
braccianite Braccianit m (Varietät von Leuzittephrit)
brachial supports s. brachidium
~ valve Dorsalklappe f, Brachialklappe f (der Brachiopoden)
brachidium Brachidium n, Armgerüst n (der Brachiopoden)
brachiopod Brachiopode m
brachistochrone 1. kleinster Laufweg m; 2. Tabelle mit Laufzeiten einer Reflexion abhängig von der Tiefe
brachyanticline Brachyantiklinale f
brachyaxis Brachyachse f
brachycephalic kurzköpfig
brachycephalism, brachycephaly Kurzköpfigkeit f
brachydome Brachydoma n
brachyhaline brachyhalin
brachypinacoid Brachypinakoid n
brachysyncline Brachysynklinale f
brackebuschite Brackebuschit m, $Pb_2(Mn,Fe)[VO_4]_2 \cdot H_2O$
brackish brackisch; brackig
~ water Brackwasser n
~ water limestone Brackwasserkalk m
~ water swamp Brackwassermoor n
Bradfordian [Stage] Bradford[ien] n (Stufe, höheres Famenne in Nordamerika)
bradyseism Bradyseismus m (Hebungen und Senkungen des Landes infolge vulkanischer Aktivität)
brae Hügel m
Bragg angle Braggscher Winkel m
~ spectrometer Braggsches Spektrometer n, Kristallspektrometer n
braggite s. fergusonite
Brahmanian [Stage] Brahman[ium] n (Stufe, Untere Trias, Tethys)
braided channel pattern Rinnenmuster n eines vielverzweigten Flusses
~ river vielverzweigter Fluß m
brain pan Schädelkalotte f
brammallite Brammallit m, $(Na,H_2O)Al_2[(H_2O,OH)_2|AlSi O_{10}]$
brances (sl) Pyriteinschlüsse mpl (in Kohle)
branch [off]/to sich verzweigen
branch 1. Zweig m (der Laufzeitkurve); 2. Flügelort n
~ fault Nebenverwerfung f (s.a. auxiliary fault)
~ of a delta Deltaarm m
~ of a lode Gangtrum n
~ of a river Flußarm m
~ of a vein Seitentrum n
~ sheet Teildecke f

~ valley Seitental n, Nebental n
~ vein zerschlagener Gang m
branchiae Kiemen fpl
branchiform kiemenähnlich, kiemenförmig
branching Verzweigung f
~ dendrites Dendritenverästelung f
~ distributaries verzweigte Nebenarme mpl (eines Deltas)
~ fault verästelte Verwerfung f
~ of a river Flußspaltung f
brandbergite Brandbergit m (Varietät von Aplit)
brandtite Brandtit m, $CaMn[AsO_4]_2 \cdot 2H_2O$
brannerite Brannerit m, $(U, Ca, Th, Y)[(Ti,Fe)_2O_6]$
brash (sl) Trümmergestein n
brasilianite Brasilianit m, $NaAl_3[(OH)_2|PO_4]_2$
brass balls konkretionärer Pyrit m
brasses Pyriteinlagerungen fpl (in Kohle)
brassil (sl) 1. Pyrit m; 2. schwefelkieshaltige Kohle f
brassy seam stark pyrithaltiges Kohlenflöz n
brat dünnes Kohlenflöz n (mit Pyrit oder Karbonaten verunreinigtes Kohlenflözchen)
braunerde Braunerde f
braunite Braunit m, Hartmanganerz n, $Mn_7[O_8|SiO_4]$
Bravais lattice Bravais-Gitter n, Translationsgitter n
bravaisite Bravaisit m (ein Hydromuskovit)
bravoite Bravoit m, $(Fe, Ni)S_2$
Brazilian emerald grüne Varietät von Turmalin
~ pebble brasilianischer (optischer) Quarz m
~ ruby brasilianischer Rubin m, rosa Spinell m
~ sapphire blaue Varietät von Turmalin
~ twin Brasilianer Zwilling m
brazilly coal pyritführende Kohle f
brazzil s. brassil
brea Naturasphalt m
breach Grundbruch m, Durchbruch m
~ in a dike Deichbruch m
breadth of outcrop Ausstrichbreite f
break/to [zer]brechen; hereingewinnen; sich zertrümern (Gänge)
~ down zu Bruch gehen
~ loose sich loslösen
~ out ausbrechen (Vulkan)
~ up aufhacken, aufbrechen
break 1. Verschiebung f; Spalte f; Bruch m; 2. Schichtungslücke f; 3. dünne Einlagerung (Einlage, Zwischenlage, Einschaltung) f; 4. Einsatz m, Unterbrechung f; 5. Abriß m, Sprengmoment m
~ in slope Gefällebruch m
~ in the succession Schichtenunterbrechung f
~ line Bruchlinie f
~ of slope Gefällebruch m
~ phenomena Brucherscheinungen fpl
~-through Durchbruch m
~-thrust Faltungsüberschiebung f (Tektonik)

breakability Brechbarkeit f
breakage Bruch m
breakages Abbruchstufen fpl
breakdown 1. Durchschlag m, Durchbruch m; 2. Zerfall m, Abbau m
breaker 1. Woge f, Welle f, Sturzwelle f, Brandung f; 2. Steinbrecher m; Grobbrecher m, Schotterbrecher m
breaking 1. Zerklüftung f, Auflockerung f; 2. Brechen n, Vorzerkleinern n
~ **deformation** Bruchdeformation f
~-**down** Einsturz m
~ **edge** Bruchkante f
~ **flow** Bruchfließen n
~-**forth** Ausbruch m, Vulkanausbruch m
~ **limit** Bruchgrenze f
~ **limit circle** Bruchspannungskreis m
~ **line** Bruchlinie f
~ **load** Bruchlast f, Bruchbelastung f
~ **of a dike** Deichbruch m
~ **of ground** Einschnittherstellung f
~ **of ore** Abbau m von Erz
~ **plane** Bruchfläche f
~ **plant** Brechanlage f
~ **strength** Bruchfestigkeit f
~ **stress** Bruchspannung f
~-**through** Durchbruch m
~-**up** 1. Auflockerung f (des Gebirges); 2. Aufschluß m
~-**up of the ice** Eisbruch m, Aufgehen n der Eisdecke
~ **waves** Brandung f
breakthrough Durchbruch m
breakwater Fangbuhne f, Wellenbrecher m
breast Feld[es]breite f
~ **bone** s. sternum
~ **side of work** anstehender Strebstoß m
breccia Brekzie f, Trümmergestein n
~ **porosity** Brekzienporosität f
~ **tuff** Brekzientuff m
breccialike structure Trümmerstruktur f
brecciated brekzienartig, brekziös
~ **agate** Trümmerachat m
~ **rock** Gesteinsbrekzie f
~ **structure** Brekzientextur f
~ **vein** Brekziengang m
brecciation Brekzienbildung f
brecciform[ous] brekzienartig
Breconian [Stage] Brecon[ium] n (höheres Unterdevon, Old Red-Fazies)
bredigite Bredigit m, γ-Ca$_2$[SiO$_4$]
breeze Brise f
breithauptite Breithauptit m, NiSb
breunnerite Breunnerit m, Mesitinspat m (Ferromagnesit)
Brewster angle Polarisationswinkel m
~ **effect of double refraction** Brewsterscher Doppelbrechungseffekt m
brewsterite Brewsterit m, (Sr, Ba, Ca)[Al$_2$Si$_6$O$_{16}$]·5H$_2$O
brianite Brianit m, Na$_2$MgCa(PO$_4$)$_2$ (Meteoritenmineral)
brick clay (earth) Ziegelton m

Bridgerian [Stage] Bridgerian n (Wirbeltierstufe des mittleren Eozäns in Nordamerika)
bright banded coal Glanzstreifenkohle f, Clarain m
~ **brown coal** Glanzbraunkohle f
~ **coal** 1. Glanzkohle f, Vitrain m (Lithotyp der Humuskohlen-Steinkohle); 2. Vitrit m; Clarit m
~ **field** Hellfeld n
~-**field image** Hellfeldabbildung f
~-**field observation** Hellfeldbeobachtung f
~ **fireball** heller Bolid m (Meteor)
~-**line spectrum** Emissionsspektrum n
~ **ray system** Strahlensystem n im Mondkrater
~ **spot** Bright Spot m (starke, lagerstättenkundlich interessante Überhöhung seismischer Amplituden)
brightness fluctuation Helligkeitsschwankung f
~ **of stars** Helligkeit f der Sterne
~ **temperature** Strahlungstemperatur f
~ **value** Helligkeitswert m
brights Glanzkohle f
brilliance Helligkeit f, Brillanz f
brilliancy Glanz m
brilliant Brillant m
~ **cut[ting]** Brillantschliff m
brimstone (sl) Bergschwefel m
brine Sole f, Salzlauge f, Salzwasser n, Salzlösung f
~ **affluent** Laugenzufluß m
~ **concentrating house** Gradierwerk n
~ **evaporator** Soleverdampfer m
~ **feeder** Laugenzufluß m
~ **handling** Einsatz m von Solen (beim Bohren)
~ **leachate** Ablaugungssole f
~ **mud** Salzlaugenspülung f
~ **pipe** Solerohr n (in Salzkavernen)
~ **pit** 1. Salzgrube f; 2. in Ausbeutung stehende Solquelle f
~ **solution** Salzlake f, Salzlösung f
~ **spring** Solquelle f
~ **well** Solebohrung f
Brinell hardness [number] Brinellhärte f
~ **hardness test** Brinellprüfung f
bring in a well/to eine Bohrung in Produktion bringen
~ **into production** zur Produktion bringen
~ **up the drillings** das Bohrklein austragen
briny salzig, solehaltig
briquette/to brikettieren
briquette Brikett n, Preßstein m, Preßkohle f
briquetting Brikettierung f
~ **of mineral grains** Einbettung f von Mineralkörnern (für Anschliffe)
~ **plant** Brikettieranlage f
~ **press** Brikettpresse f
~ **process** Brikettierverfahren n
britholite Britholith m, (Na, Ce, Ca)$_5$[F|(SiO$_4$,PO$_4$)$_3$]
brittle spröde, brüchig, sprödbruchempfindlich
~ **displacement (fracture)** Sprödbruch m

brittle 52

~ **gel** zerreibbares Gel *n*
~ **mica** *s.* margarite
~ **pan** zerbrechliche harte Schicht *f*
~ **silver ore** *s.* stephanite
~ **star** Schlangenstern *m*
brittleness Sprödigkeit *f,* Brüchigkeit *f*
broaching bit Erweiterungsbohrer *m,* Nachbohrer *m*
broad-crested anticline Breitsattel *m,* breite Antiklinale *f*
~-**floored valley** breitsohliges Tal *n*
~ **fold** flachschenklige Falte *f*
~ **irrigation** Oberflächenbewässerung *f*
~-**leaved tree** Laubbaum *m*
~ **warp** Großfalte *f*
broadening of line Spektrallinienverbreiterung *f*
~ **of valley** Talerweiterung *f*
broadside versetzte Schüsse *mpl (Seismik)*
~ **offset** Heraussetzung *f,* seitlicher Abstand *m (eines seismischen Schusses)*
~ **shooting** Queraufstellung *f*
broadstone bind großplattig brechender Schieferton *m*
brochantite Brochantit *m,* $Cu_4[(OH)]_6SO_4$
brockite Brockit *m* $CaTh[PO_4]_2 \cdot H_2O$
brodel structure Brodeltextur *f*
bröggerite Bröggerit *m,* Thoruranin *m (Varietät von Uranit)*
broil *s.* gossan
broken agate Trümmerachat *m*
~-**down bank** Abbruch *m*
~-**down rock** zu Bruch gegangenes Gestein *n*
~ **fold** Bruchfalte *f*
~ **ground** 1. hereingeschossenes Gestein *n;* 2. zerklüftetes Gebirge *n;* gebräches Gestein *n;* 3. unproduktive Schichten *fpl*
~ **material** Haufwerk *n*
~ **rock (stone)** Schlagschotter *m,* Steinschlag *m*
bromargyrite *s.* bromyrite
bromellite Bromellit *m,* BeO
bromine Brom *n,* Br
bromlite Bromlit *m,* $BaCa(CO_3)_2$
bromyrite Bromit *m,* Bromsilber *n,* Bromargyrit *m,* AgBr
brontolith Belemnit *m,* Donnerkeil *m*
Bronze Age Bronzezeit *f*
bronzite Bronzit *m,* $(Mg, Fe)_2[Si_2O_6]$
bronzitite Bronzitit *m (bronzitreiches Tiefengestein)*
brood Erzgemenge *n*
~ **pouch** Brutkammer *f,* Brutraum *m,* Bruttasche *f (Paläontologie)*
brook Bach *m*
~ **bed** Bachbett *n*
brookite Brookit *m,* TiO_2
brooklet kleiner Bach *m*
brotocrystal korrodierter (angeschmolzener, teilweise resorbierter) Kristall *m*
brown coal Braunkohle *f;* Weichbraunkohle *f*
~-**coal briquette** Braunkohlenbrikett *n*

~-**coal facies** Braunkohlenfazies *f*
~ **coal for low temperature retort process** Schwelkohle *f*
~-**coal formation** Braunkohlenbildung *f*
~-**coal grit** Braunkohlensandstein *m*
~-**coal high-temperature coke** Braunkohlenhochtemperaturkoks *m*
~-**coal low-temperature coke** Braunkohlenschwelkoks *m*
~-**coal opencast mining** Braunkohlentagebau *m*
~-**coal stage** Braunkohlenstadium *n (Inkohlungs- oder Karbonifikationsstadium)*
~ **face** Oxydationshut *m* von Zinnerzgängen
~ **forest soil** brauner Waldboden *m*
~ **haematite [iron ore]** Brauneisenerz *n,* Brauneisenstein *m,* Braunerz *n (s.a. limonite)*
~ **lead ore** Braunbleierz *n (s.a. pyromorphite)*
~ **lime** *(sl)* Magerkalk *m*
~ **matter** *(Am)* zersetzte Zellwandsubstanz und Zellfüllungen, die in Kohledünnschliffen braun und halbdurchsichtig sind
~ **ochre** Braunocker *m*
~ **oxide** Urandioxid *n*
~ **podsolic soil** brauner Waldboden *m*
~ **spar** Braunspat *m (Fe-arme Abart von Ankerit)*
~ **steppe soil** brauner Halbwüstenboden *m*
~ **turf** Brauntorf *m*
Brown Jura [Epoch, Series] Brauner Jura *m,* Dogger *m*
brownmillerite Brownmillerit *m,* $2CaO \cdot AlFeO_3$
brownstone eisenhaltiger Sandstein *m*
Bruce Bruce *n (unteres Huron in Nordamerika)*
brucite Brucit *m,* $Mg(OH)_2$
brugnatellite Brugnatellit *m,* $Mg_6Fe[(OH)_{13}|CO_3] \cdot 4H_2O$
brunigra (brunizem) soil brauner Prärieboden *m*
brunsvigite Brunsvigit *m,* $(Fe, Al, Mg)_3[(OH)_2|AlSi_3O_{10}](Fe,Mg)_3(OH)_6$
Brunton [compass] Brunton-Kompaß *m,* Spiegelkompaß *m*
brush faules Gestein *n*
~ **cast** Quastenmarke *f*
~ **discharge** Elmsfeuer *n*
~ **ore** stalaktitisches Brauneisenerz *n*
brushite Brushit *m,* $HCa[PO_4] \cdot 2H_2O$
brushwood peat von Gestrüpp bedeckter Torf *m*
brute stack Rohstapelung *f (Seismik)*
Bruxellian [Stage] Bruxellien *n (Stufe des Eozäns, Belgisches Becken)*
bryalgal limestone Kalkstein aus gerüstbildenden Bryozoen und Algen
bryle *s.* gossan
bubble/to aufsprudeln, aufbrodeln
~ **forth** hervorquellen, hervorsprudeln
bubble 1. Blase *f,* Libelle *f,* Bläschen *n;* 2. Blubber *m (schwingende Gasblase durch Explosion im Wasser)*

~ **hole** Blähpore f
~ **impression** Gastrichter m
~ **of gas** Gasblase f
~ **point** Kochpunkt m, Blasenpunkt m, Entgasungsbeginn m, Gasentlösungspunkt m
~ **point of crude** Entgasungsbeginn m von Erdöl in der Lagerstätte
bubbling spring Sprudelquelle f
bubbly blasig
buchite Buchit m (Hyalomylonit)
buchonite Buchonit m (Varietät von Tephrit)
buck/to laugen, scheiden
buck quartz goldfreier Quarz m
bucker Erzscheider m
bucket wheel[-type] excavator Schaufelradbagger m
bucking Scheidung f (der Erze)
~ **ore** Scheideerz n
~ **plate** Scheidebank f
buckle/to aufwölben
~ **up** aufbuckeln
buckled folding Knickfalte f
Buckley-Leverett theory Buckley-Leverett-Theorie f
buckling Ausbeulung f, Ausknickung f, Knickerscheinung f, Verbiegen n; Wölbung f, Aufwölbung f
~ **load** Knickbeanspruchung f
~ **strength** Knickfestigkeit f
~ **stress** Knickspannung f
~ **test** Knickversuch m
buckshot Eisenmangankonkretion im Boden
~ **pyrite** Geröllpyrit m
buckstone goldfreies Gestein n
buddler Erzwäscher m
buddling Schlämmung f (der Erze)
~ **hole** Drusenhöhle f
Budnanian [Epoch, Series] Budnany n, Budnanium n (Oberes Silur)
buffer Puffer m (chemisch)
~ **stock** Ausgleichslager n zur Stabilisierung von Rohstoffmärkten
~ **strip** Grasnarbenstreifen m
buffering of soil Bodenpufferung f
bugs (sl) Foraminiferen fpl
buhr 1. s. buhrstone; 2. (sl) Kalkstein m
buhrstone kavernöser Süßwasserquarzit m
build up pressure/to Druck aufbauen (ansammeln)
build-up analysis Druckaufbaumessung f
~-**up curve** Schließdruckkurve f
building ground Baugrund m
~-**ground map** Baugrundkarte f
~ **industry** Bauindustrie f, Bauwirtschaft f
~ **lime** Baukalk m
~ **material** Baumaterial n, Baustoff m
~ **pit** Baugrube f
~ **preservation** Bautenschutz m
~ **stone** Baustein m, Werkstein m
~-**up** Aufbau m
bulb of pressure Druckzwiebel f
~ **pressure** Spannungsanhäufung f, Druckanhäufung f (Baugrund)

bulge Achsensattel m
~ **of the earth** Erdkrümmung f
bulging Aufbeulung f, Aufquellen n (der Talsohle)
~ **of the slope** Ausbauchung f der Böschung
Bulitian [Stage] Bulitien n (Wirbeltierstufe, oberes Paläozän in Nordamerika)
bulk analysis Bauschanalyse f, Vollanalyse f (chemisch)
~ **bed** Hauptflöz n
~ **density** 1. Trockenrohdichte f; 2. Sedimentdichte f (Mineralsubstanz plus Poren)
~ **modulus** Kompressionsmodul m (das Stress-Strain-Verhältnis bei einfachem hydrostatischem Druck)
~ **reservoir volume** gesamtes Lagerstättenvolumen n
~ **sample** Massenprobe f, Haufwerksprobe f
~ **volume** Schüttvolumen n
bulkage Schwellung f, Quellen n
bulkhead Damm m, Wehr n
bulking Schwellung f, Quellen n, Auflockerung f
bulldozing Knäpperschießen n (mit aufgelegter Ladung)
bullet perforating Kugelperforation f
~-**type side wall corer** Kernschießgerät n
bullion 1. fossilführende Konkretion f; 2. Barren m (Gold oder Silber)
bull's eyes Pyritkonkretionen im Dachschiefer
bulrush peat Simsentorf m
bultfonteinite Bultfonteinit, $Ca_2[F|SiO_3OH]\cdot H_2O$
bump Bergschlag m, schlagendes Gebirge n
bumping table Stoßtisch m, Rütteltisch m, Schüttelherd m
bunch [of ore] Erzputzen m, Erznest n, Butzen, Niere f
bunched seismometers gebündelte Seismometer npl, Mehrfachgeophone npl
bunchy unregelmäßig
bundle of lines of force Kraftlinienbündel n
bungum Londoner Name für jungen alluvialen Schluff
bunny Erznest n
bunsenite Bunsenit m, NiO
bunter [sandstone] Buntsandstein m
buoyancy Auftrieb m, Tragfähigkeit f
buoyant effect (force) Auftrieb m
~ **unit weight** Raumgewicht n unter Auftrieb
bur 1. s. burrstone 2.; 2. Flinteinlagerung f
~ **ore** Klettenerz n
burbankite Burbankit m, $Na_2(Ca, Sr, Ba, Ce, La)_4[CO_3]_5$
burden Deckgebirge n
~ **of sediments** Sedimentlast f
~ **over** Abraumgebirge n
Burdigalian [Stage] Burdigal[ien] n, Burdigalium n (Stufe des Miozäns)
burial metamorphism Versenkungsmetamorphose f
~ **of fossils** Fossileinbettung f
buried eingebettet

buried

- **~ anchorage** unterirdische Verankerung *f*
- **~ electrode** versenkte Elektrode *f*
- **~ fold** verdeckte Falte *f*
- **~ hill** überdeckter Rücken *m*
- **~ outcrop** verdeckter Ausstrich *m*, maskiertes Ausgehendes *n*
- **~ placer** verdeckte Seife *f*
- **~ river** fossiles Flußbett *n*
- **~ rock** überdecktes Gestein *n*
- **~ soil** fossiler Boden *m*
- **~ structure** verdeckte Struktur *f*

burk Erzfall *m*
burkeite Burkeit *m*, $Na_6[CO_3|(SO_4)_2]$
burn off/to abfackeln
burn line Kontakt *m* zwischen verkokter und unverkokter Kohle *(unter der Erdoberfläche)*
burning mountain Vulkan *m*
- **~ volcano** tätiger Vulkan *m*

burnt clay gebrannter Ton *m*, Terrakotta *f*
- **~ coal** Naturkoks *m*
- **~ lime** gebrannter Kalk *m*

burr 1. Erzfall *m*; 2. *(sl)* hartes Gestein *n*
burrow/to schürfen
burrow Bau *m*, Baute *f*; 2. Grabgang *m*, Bohrgang *m*; Wohnrohr *n*, Freßrohr *n*; 3. taubes Gestein *n*; 4. Halde *f*
- **~ cast** Gangverfüllung *f (Ichnologie)*
- **~ lining** Gangwandung *f (Ichnologie)*
- **~ system** Gangsystem *n (Ichnologie)*

burrowing animal wühlendes Bodentier *n*
burrstone 1. Mühlsandstein *m*; 2. *(sl)* Feuerstein *m*, Flint *m*
burst/to bersten
burst-crack Sprengriß *m*
- **~ out** Vulkanausbruch *m*

bursting-out Vulkanausbruch *m*
- **~ pressure** Berstdruck *m*
- **~ strength** Sprengfestigkeit *f*

bury/to begraben, verschütten
- **~ a line** Ölleitung unterflur verlegen

bus Verbindungsleitung *f*, Datenbus *m*
bush mould gewachsener Boden *m*
bushland Buschland *n*
bustamite Bustamit *m*, $(Mn, Ca)_3[Si_3O_9]$
bustite Bustit *m (Meteorit)*
butlerite Butlerit *m*, $Fe[OH|SO_4]\cdot 2H_2O$
bütschliite Bütschliit *m*, $K_6Ca_2[CO_3]_5\cdot 6H_2O$
butt cleat Nebenschlechte *f*
- **~ entry** Abbaustrecke *f* parallel zu den Schlechten

butte Restberg *m*, Zeugenberg *m*, Einzelberg *m*, Spitzkuppe *f*
- **~ temoine** *s.* hum

butterfly twin Schwalbenschwanzzwilling *m*
buttgenbachite Buttgenbachit *m*, $Cu_{19}[Cl_4|(OH)_{32}|(NO_3)_2 + 2H_2]$
buttock Abbaustoß *m*
buttress Felsvorsprung *m*
butyrellite, butyrite Sumpfbutter *f*
buzzard minderwertige Schicht (Schmitze) *f*
b.y. = billion years
by-channel Umleitungskanal *m*
~-coke Zechenkoks *m*

~-lane Seitengang *m*
~-pass tunnel Umleit[ungs]stollen *m (einer Talsperre)*
~-passed oil zurückgebliebenes Öl *n*
~-pit Hilfsschacht *m*
~-product Nebenprodukt *n*, Abfallprodukt *n*
~-wash Umleitungskanal *m*
~-work Nebengestein *n*

byerite bituminöse Kohlenart
bysmalith Bysmalith *m*
byssal notch Byssusfurche *f*
byssolite Byssolith *m (Aktinolithasbest, s.a. actinolite)*
byssus Byssus *m (Haftfasern bei Muscheln)*
bytownite Bytownit *m (anorthitreicher Plagioklas)*

C

c axis c-Achse *f (mineralogische und tektonische Koordinate)*
C[14] [14]C *(instabiles C-Isotop)*
C[14] age determination (measurement) Altersbestimmung *f* mit [14]C
C-horizon C-Horizont *m (Boden)*
Ca femic Ca-femisch *(Ca-, Fe-, Meg-haltig)*
Ca-Tschermak's molecule Tschermaks Molekül *n*, $CaAl_2SiO_6$ *(hypothetisches Ca-Endglied)*
cab Salband *n*
cabbage-head structures kopfartig aufgewölbte Laminen *fpl (von Stromatolithen)*
- **~ leaf marking** Fächermarke *f*, fächerförmige Fließmarke *f*

cable break Kabelwelle *f*, Kabeleinsatz *m*
- **~ core bit** Seilkernrohr *n*
- **~ crane (derrick)** Kabelkran *m*
- **~ drilling** Seilbohren *n*
- **~ drum** Kabeltrommel *f*
- **~ excavator** Kabelschrapper *m*, Kabelbagger *m*
- **~ rig** Seilbohranlage *f*
- **~ tool coring** Seilkernbohren *n*
- **~ tool drilling** Seilbohren *n*

cableway Kabelkran *m*
cabrerite Cabrerit *m (Varietät von Annabergit)*
cacholong Kascholong *m (Varietät von Opal)*
cacoxenite Kakoxen *m*, $Fe_4[OH|PO_4]_3\cdot 12H_2O$
cactolith Kaktolith *m (verzweigte Intrusionsform)*
cadacryst *s.* xenocryst
cadaite *s.* turquois
cadastral map Flurkarte *f*
- **~ office** Katasteramt *n*
- **~ survey** Katasteraufnahme *f*, Landvermessung *f*

cadmia *s.* 1. calamine; 2. cadmium oxide
cadmiferous kadmiumhaltig
cadmium Kadmium *n*, Cadmium *n*, Cd
- **~ blende (ochre)** *s.* greenockite
- **~ ore** Kadmiumerz *n*
- **~ oxide** Kadmiumoxid *n*, Monteponit *m*, CdO

calcimetry

cadmoselite Cadmoselit m, β-CdSe
Cadomian folding cadomische Faltung f
cadwaladerite Cadwaladerit m, $Al(OH)_2Cl\cdot 4H_2O$
Caenozoic [Era] s. Cenozoic
caesium Zäsium n, Caesium n, Cs
~ silicate s. pollucite
~ vapour magnetometer Zäsiumdampfmagnetometer n
cafetite Cafetit m, $(Ca, Mg)[(Ti, Fe)_6O_{12}]\cdot 4H_2O$
CAG = Caribbean-Atlantic Geotraverse
cage Förderkorb m
~ shooting Käfigschießen n (Seismik)
cahnite Cahnit m, $Ca_2[AsO_4|B(OH)_4]$
cailloutis Kiesboden m
cainophyticum Känophyticum n
Cainozoic s. Cenozoic
cairn Felsen m, Steinhaufen m
cairngorm Rauchtopas m, gelber Quarz m (s.a. Scotch topaz)
caisson Senkkasten m
cake/to einen Filterkuchen an der Bohrlochwand bilden
cake Filterkruste f, verfestigter Bohrschlamm m
caking capacity Backfähigkeit f (der Kohle)
~ coal backfähige (backende) Kohle f; Kokskohle f
~ properties Backvermögen n, Backeigenschaften fpl (Kohle)
cal s. wolframite
calaite s. turquois
calamine Calamin m (ein Zinkerz)
calamite Calamit m
calamitean peat Calamitentorf m
~ reed Calamitenröhricht n
calaverite Calaverit m, Tellurgold n, $(Au, Ag)Te_2$
calc-alkali granite Kalkalkaligranit m
~-alkali rock Kalkalkaligestein n
~-alkalic series Kalkalkaligesteine npl, Alkalikalkgesteine npl, pazifische Sippe f
~-mica schist Kalkglimmerschiefer m
~-silicate Kalksilikat n
~-silicate gneiss Kalksilikatgneis m
~-silicate hornfels Kalksilikathornfels m, Skarn m
~-silicate marble kalksilikatischer Marmor m, Skarn m
~-silicate rock Kalksilikatgestein n
~-sinter Sinter[kalk] m, Kalksinter m
~-spar s. calcite
~-tufa Kalktuff m, Kalksinter m, Travertin m
calcarenite Kalkarenit m, Calcarenit m, psammitischer Kalkstein m, Kalksandstein m
calcareo-argillaceous kalk- und tonhaltig
calcareous kalkhaltig, kalkig
~ algae Kalkalgen fpl
~ bed Kalkschicht f
~ cement Bindemittel n aus Kalk
~-cemented sandstone Sandstein m mit kalkigem Bindemittel

~ cementing material Bindemittel n aus Kalk
~ clay kalkhaltiger Ton m, Kreidemergel m, Kalkmergel m
~ concretion Kalkkonkretion f
~ crust Kalkkruste f
~ deposit Kalkablagerung f
~ earth Kalkerde f
~ facies kalkige Fazies f
~ gravel Kalkkies m
~ grits Sandschichten fpl mit Kalkalgen
~ iron-stone Kalkeisenstein m
~ marl Kalkmergel m
~ mud Seekreide f, Kalkschlamm m; Kalkmudde f (bei Torfbildung in Mooren)
~ ooze kalkiger Schlick m
~ phyllite Kalkphyllit m
~ rock kalkhaltiges Gestein n
~ sand Kalksand m, kalkhaltiger Sand m
~ sandstone kalkreicher Sandstein m, Kalksandstein m
~ schist Kalkglimmerschiefer m
~ shale kalkiger Schieferton m
~-shale quarry Kalkschieferbruch m
~-shelled kalkschalig
~ siltstone kalkhaltiger Siltstein m
~ sinter Kalksinter m, Kalktuff m, Travertin m
~ skeleton Kalkgerüst n
~ slate Kalktonschiefer m
~ soil Karbonatboden m
~ spar s. calcite
~ sponge Kalkschwamm m
~ spring Kalkquelle f
~ test Kalkschaler m
calcarinate kalkführend
calcarneyte 1. Karbonatsand m; 2. resedimentierter Kalkstein m, Kalkstein m aus Korallendetritus
calcedony s. chalcedony
calciborite Kalziborit m, Calciborit m, CaB_2O_4
calcic kalkhaltig
~ marble Kalkmarmor m
~ series Kalkgesteine npl
calciclase anorthitreicher Plagioklas m
calcicole kalkliebende Pflanze f
calcicrete kalzitverkittet (Gerölle)
calcicrust Kalkkruste f
calciferous kalkig, kalkhaltig; Ca-Karbonat führend
~ residual solution kalziumreiche Restlösung f
~ sandstone Kalksandstein m
calcification 1. Karbonatisierung f, Kalkbildung f; 2. Verkalkung f (des Bodens)
calcifuge kalkfliehende Pflanze f
calcify/to verkalken
calcigenous röstfähig, Röstoxide bildend (Erze)
calcilith Kalkstein m
calcilutite Kalzilutit m, Calcilutit m, pelitischer Kalkstein m, Kalkpelit m
calcilyte Kalkstein m
calcimetry Kalkgehaltsbestimmung f, Karbonatbestimmung f

calcimicrite 56

calcimicrite Kalzimikrit *m*
calcinable kalzinierungsfähig
calcination Kalzinierung *f*, Kalzination *f*, Kalzinieren *n*
calcine/to kalzinieren
calcined dolomite gebrannter Dolomit *m*
~ **ore** Rösterz *n*
calcioferrite Calcioferrit *m*, (Ca, Mg)$_3$Fe, Al)$_3$[(OH)$_3$|(PO$_4$)$_4$]·8H$_2$O
calciovolborthite Kalkvolborthit *m*, CaCu[OH|VO$_4$]
calciphyre *s.* calc-silicate marble
calcirudite Kalzirudit *m*, Calcirudit *m*, Geröllkalkstein *m*
calcisiltite Kalzisiltit *m*, Calcisiltit *m*, Kalksiltstein *m*
calcispheres Kalzisphären *fpl (kalkige Mikroproblematika)*
calcite Kalzit *m*, Calcit *m*, Kalkspat *m*, Doppelspat *m*, CaCO$_3$
~ **compensation depth** Kalzitkompensationstiefe *f*, Kalkkompensationstiefe *f*
calcitite Kalzitgestein *n*, Kalkstein *m*
calcitization Kalzitisierung *f (Umwandlung von Aragonit in Kalzit)*
calcitrant strengflüssig *(Erz)*
calcium Kalzium *n*, Calcium *n*, Ca
~ **age** Kalziumalter *n*
~ **aluminate cement** Tonerdezement *m*
~ **bicarbonate** doppelkohlensaurer Kalk *m*
~ **borate** Boraxkalk *m*
~ **carbonate** Kalziumkarbonat *n*
~ **carbonate content** Kalkgehalt *m*, Gehalt *m* an Kalziumkarbonat
~ **carnotite** *s.* tyuyamunite
~ **chloride** Kalziumchlorid *n*, Chlorkalzium *n*
~ **hardness** Kalkhärte *f*
~--**iron garnet** Kalkeisengranat *m*
~ **larsenite** Esperit *m*, PbCa$_3$Zn$_4$[SiO$_4$]$_4$
~ **phosphate** *s.* apatite
~ **sulphate** *s.* anhydrite; gypsum
calclacite Calclacit *m*, Ca[Cl|(C$_2$H$_3$O$_2$)$_2$]·5H$_2$O
calclithite Calclithit *m (Karbonatgestein mit mehr als 50% umgelagertem Karbonatanteil)*
calcrete *s.* caliche 5.
calcspar *s.* calcite
calcspathization Entwicklung *f* spätigen Kalzits
calculate the volume of a solid/to die Masse kubizieren
calculated reserves berechnete Vorräte *mpl (noch nicht bestätigt durch die staatliche Vorratskommission)*
calculiform grießförmig
calculous grießig
calcurmolite Calcurmolit *m*, Ca[(UO$_2$)$_3$(OH)$_2$|(MoO$_4$)$_5$]·9H$_2$O
caldera Kaldera *f*, Caldera *f*, vulkanischer Einbruchskessel *m*
~ **island** Kaldera-Insel *f*
~ **of subsidence** Explosionskaldera *f (eines Vulkans)*
calderite Calderit *m*, Mn$_3$Fe$_2$[SiO$_4$]$_3$

caldron *s.* cauldron
Caledonian Kaledonikum *n*
~ **folds** kaledonische Faltung *f*
~ **orogen** kaledonisches Orogen *n*
caledonids Kaledoniden *pl*
caledonite Caledonit *m*, Pb$_5$Cu$_2$[(OH)$_6$|CO$_3$|(SO$_4$)$_3$]
calf Kalbeis *n*
calibrate/to eichen
calibration Eichung *f (z.B. eines Analysenverfahrens)*
~ **curve** Eichkurve *f (z.B. eines Gebers)*
calibre Innendurchmesser *m*
~ **log** Kalibermessung *f*, Messung *f* des Bohrlochquerschnitts
caliche 1. Chilesalpeter *m*, Natronsalpeter *m*; 2. erdiges Rohsalz *n*; 3. zersetzter Kalkstein mit Schluff- und Tonanteilen; 4. Kalkkruste auf Böden durch Evaporation; 5. Karbonatzement in verkitteten Sanden, Kiesen und Geröllen
calicinal zum Kelch gehörend
calicle becherförmiger Hohlraum *m*
calico marble triassisches Kalksteinkonglomerat *n (Maryland)*
calicular becherförmig
Californian jade *s.* californite
californite Kalifornit *m*, dichter Vesuvian *m*, massiges Vesuviangestein *n (s.a. vesuvianite)*
caliper Kalibermeßgerät *n*
~ **log** Kaliberlog *n*
~ **logging** Kalibermessung *f*
calipering device Kalibrierungsgerät *n*
calist standfester Sand *m*
calitreras Calichelagerstätte *f (Nitrat)*
calkinsite Calkinsit *m*, (Ce, La)$_2$[CO$_3$]$_3$·4H$_2$O
callaghanite Callaghanit *m*, Cu$_2$Mg$_2$[(OH)$_6$|CO$_3$]·2H$_2$O
callainite Callainit *m*, Al[PO$_4$]·2½H$_2$O
callen eisenschüssig, reich an Fe-Oxiden
caller Geröllschicht *f*, loses Deckgebirge *n*
calley stone *(sl)* harter Sandstein *m (im Kohlenbergbau)*
Callovian [Stage] Callovien *n (Stufe des Mittleren Juras)*
callow 1. Aue *f*; 2. Abraumgestein *n.*
Callow method Callow-Methode *f (zur grafischen Darstellung von Siebanalysen)*
callys *(sl)* Nebengestein der Sn-Gänge in Cornwall
calm 1. Windstille *f*; 2. *(sl)* heller kohliger Schiefer *m*
~ **water** ruhiges Wasser *n*, Stillwasser *n*
calomel Kalomel *m*, Quecksilberhornerz *n*, HgCl
calorific value Heizwert *m*
calorimetric[al] test Heizwertbestimmung *f*
calp *(sl)* dunkler (grauer) Kalkstein *m*
calumetite Calumetit *m*, Cu(OH, Cl)$_2$·2H$_2$O
calvarium Calvarium *n (Schädel ohne Unterkiefer)*
calve/to kalben *(Gletscher)*

calving Kalbung f *(eines Gletschers)*
calx Rostrückstände von Erzen
calycular becherförmig
calyx Kelch m *(von Crinoiden)*
cambering Schollenrutschung f
Cambrian kambrisch
Cambrian Kambrium[system] n *(chronostratigrafisch)*; Kambrium n, Kambriumperiode f *(geochronologisch)*; Kambrium n, Kambriumzeit f *(allgemein)*
~ **Age** Kambrium n, Kambriumzeit f
~ **Period** Kambrium n, Kambriumperiode f
~ **System** Kambrium n, Kambriumsystem n
Cambro-Silurian Kambrosilur n
camel back *(sl)* Ausbucklungen fpl des Firstgesteins
camera lucida Zeichenprisma n
camerae Luftkammern fpl *(bei Cephalopoden)*
camerate gekammert
camouflage of a trace element Tarnung f eines Spurenelements
campanian [Stage] Campan[ium] n *(Stufe der Oberkreide)*
campanite Campanit m *(Nephelinsyenit)*
camper *(sl)* angewitterte Kohle f
campo Grassteppe f *(in Brasilien)*
camptonite Camptonit m *(Lamprophyr)*
camptospessartite Camptospessartit m *(Lamprophyr)*
campylite Kampylit m, Phosphormimetesit m
camsellite Camsellit m, Ascharit m, $Mg_2[B_2O_5] \cdot H_2O$
camstone *(sl)* 1. kompakter weißer Kalkstein; 2. blauweißer Ton
Canada balsam (turpentine) Kanadabalsam m
Canadian Canadien n *(Tremadoc und Arenig in Nordamerika)*
~ **drilling** Gestängeschlagbohren n
~ **Series** s. Canadian
~ **shield** Kanadischer Schild m
canadite Canadit m, Kanadit m *(Nephelinsyenit)*
canal Kanal m
~ **bank** Kanaldamm m
~ **construction** Kanalbau m
~ **embankment** Kanaldamm m
~ **in a cut** Kanal m im Einschnitt
~ **pond** Kanalstufe f
~ **reach** Kanalhaltung f
~ **river** kanalisierter Fluß m
~ **with filter bed** Sickerkanal m
canaliculate[d] kanneliert; mit Kanälen versehen
canalization Kanalisierung f
canals of Mars Marskanäle mpl
canary stone gelbe Varietät von Karneol
canasite Canasit m, $(Na, K)_5Ca_4[(OH, F)_3|Si_{10}O_{25}]$
cancelled structure Netzgefüge n
cancrinite Cancrinit m, $(Na_2, Ca)_4[CO_3|(H_2O)_{0-3}|AlSiO_4)_6]$
cand *(sl)* Flußspat m *(als Gangfüllung)*
candle coal s. cannel coal

~ **-like** kerzenartig
canfieldite Canfieldit m, $4Ag_2S \cdot (Sn, Ge)S_2$
canga *(sl)* eisenhaltige Brekzie f
Canicula Hundsstern m, Sirius m
cank [stone] *(sl)* 1. s. burr 2.; 2. s. whinrock
cann s. cand
cannel schwarzer Schiefer m
~ **-boghead coal** Kännel-Boghead-Kohle f *(Sapropelkohle)*
~ **coal** Kännelkohle f *(Sapropelkohle)*
~ **shale** Kännelschiefer m *(sapropelischer Schiefer)*
cannelite s. cannel coal
canneloid kännelartig
cannizzarite Cannizzarit m, $Pb_3Bi_5S_{11}$
cannon bone Mittelhandknochen m, Mittelfußknochen m
canny s. cand
cañon s. canyon
cant 1. einseitiges Abrutschen n; 2. Neigung f
canted leg jackup Hubinsel f
cantilever Auskragung f
~ **mast** Klappmast m *(Erdölgeologie)*
cantonite s. covellite
canvas Netz n *(einer Vermessung)*
canyon Cañon m, Klamm f
~ **cutting (formation)** Cañonbildung f
~ **-shaped** cañonartig
canyoning Cañonbildung f
caoutchouc Kautschuk m (n)
cap/to 1. unter Kontrolle bringen, fassen; 2. überlagern
cap 1. Hut m, Kappe f, Decke f; 2. Zünder m
~ **effect** s. caprock effect
~ **of rock** Deckgebirge n
~ **quartz** Kappenquarz m
~ **rock** s. caprock
capable of being opened aufschließbar
capacity Ausbringung f, Gehalt m, Fördermenge f
~ **-inflow ratio of reservoirs** Speichervolumen-Ergänzungsmengen-Verhältnis n
~ **of deformation** Formänderungsvermögen n
~ **of reservoir** Stauinhalt m
~ **of root penetration** Durchdringungsfähigkeit f der Wurzeln
~ **of storage** Speicherkapazität f
~ **of well** Brunnenergiebigkeit f, Förderrate f *(Hydrogeologie)*; Ergiebigkeit f der Bohrung, Förderrate *(Erdölgeologie)*
~ **to yield** Nachgiebigkeit f
cape Kap n, Landspitze f
~ **diamond** Kapdiamant m, gelber Diamant m
~ **ruby** Kaprubin m *(roter Granat im Kimberlit)*
capel s. caple
capillarimeter Kapillarimeter n
capillarity Kapillarität f
capillary kapillar, haarfein
capillary Kapillare f
~ **apparatus** Kapillarimeter n
~ **attraction** Kapillarattraktion f, Kapillaranziehung f, Kapillarsaugkraft f

capillary 58

- ~ **bore** Kapillarröhrchenhohlraum *m*
- ~ **channel** Kapillarkanal *m*
- ~ **condensation** Kapillarkondensation *f*
- ~ **conductivity** kapillare Leitfähigkeit *f*, Kapillardurchlässigkeit *f*
- ~ **constant** Kapillaritätszahl *f*
- ~ **depression** kapillare Absenkung *f*
- ~ **elevation** kapillare Steighöhe *f*, Kapillaranstieg *m*
- ~ **equilibrium** kapillares Gleichgewicht *n*
- ~ **force** Kapillarkraft *f*
- ~ **fringe** Porensaugsaum *m*, Kapillarsaum *m*
- ~ **head (height)** s. ~ elevation
- ~ **imbibition** kapillare Imbibition *f*
- ~ **interstice** Kapillarzwischenraum *m*
- ~ **migration** kapillare Wanderung *f*
- ~ **moisture** Kapillarwasser *n*, Porensaugwasser *n*
- ~ **number** Kapillarzahl *f*
- ~ **potential** Kapillarpotential *n*
- ~ **pressure** Kapillardruck *m*
- ~ **pyrite** s. millerite
- ~ **rise** s. ~ elevation
- ~ **tension** Kapillarspannung *f*
- ~ **transition zone** kapillare Übergangszone *f*
- ~ **tube** Kapillarröhrchen *n*
- ~ **wall** Kapillarröhrchenwandung *f*
- ~ **water** Kapillarwasser *n*, Porensaugwasser *n*
- ~ **yield** kapillare Aufstiegsmenge *f*

Capitanian [Stage] Capitan[ium] *n (hangende Stufe des Mittelperms)*
caple Salband *n*
capped quartz Kappenquarz *m*
cappelenite Cappelenit *m*, $(Ba, Ca, Ce, Na)_3(Y, Ce, La)_6[(BO_3)_6|Si_3O_9]$
capping Deckschichten *fpl*, überlagernde Schichten *fpl*
- ~ **bed** Hangendes *n*, hangende Schicht *f*
- ~ **mass** Deckgebirge *n*
- ~ **of gossan** Eiserner Hut *m*, Eisenhut *m*
- ~ **rock** Deckgestein *n*, Hutgestein *n*

caprocianite s. laumontite
caprock 1. Deckgebirge *n*, Deckschicht *f*; 2. Gipsanhydrithut *m*, Salzhut *m*, Hutgestein *n (eines Salzstocks)*
- ~ **effect** Schwereeffekt *m* des Salzhuts

captation Wasserfassung *f*
- ~ **zone** Fassungszone *f (für Grundwasser)*

capture a river/to eine Fluß anzapfen
capture 1. Enthauptung *f*, Anzapfung *f*, Kappen *n (eines Flusses)*; 2. Abfangen *n (Kristallchemie)*; 3. Einfang *m (Atomphysik)*
- ~ **cross section** Einfangquerschnitt *m*
- ~ **hypothesis** Einfanghypothese *f*
- ~ **of neutrons** Neutronenabsorption *f*
- ~ **of spring** Quellfassung *f*
- ~ **of underground water** Grundwassererschließung *f*

capturing of headwaters Quellgebietsanzapfung *f*
carachaite Karachait *m*, $MgO \cdot SiO_2 \cdot H_2O$
caracolite Caracolit *m* $PbNa_2[OH|Cl|SO_4]$

Caradocian [Stage] Caradoc[ium] *n (Stufe, Mittelordivizium bis basales Oberordovizium)*
carapace Carapax *m*, Panzer *m*
carat Karat *n (1 metrisches Karat = 200 mg; 1 englisches Karat = 205,3 mg)*
carbankerite Carbankerit *m (Verwachsung von Kohlenmikrolithotypen mit 20–60 Vol.-% Karbonatspäten)*
carbargilite Carbargilit *m (Vermengung von Kohlenmikrolithotypen mit 20–60 Vol.-% Tonmineralen)*
carbide cutters Hartmetallbesatz *m*, Hartmetallschneiden *fpl (Bohrkronen)*
- ~ **of silicon** Siliziumkarbid *n*

Carbo-Permian s. Permo-Carboniferous
carboborite Carborit *m*, $Ca_2Mg[Co_3|B_2O_5] \cdot 10H_2O$
carbocernaite Carbocernait *m*, $(Ca, Na, La, Ce)[CO_3]$
carbominerite Carbominerit *m (Vergesellschaftung von Kohlenmikrolithotypen mit verschiedenen Mineralen)*
carbon 1. Kohlenstoff *m*, C; 2. s. carbonado
- ~ **black** Erdgasruß *m*
- ~ **compound** Kohlenstoffverbindung *f*
- ~ **content** Kohlenstoffgehalt *m*
- ~ **diamond** s. carbonado
- ~ **dioxide** Kohlendioxid *n*, CO_2
- ~ **dust** Kohlenstaub *m*
- ~-**free** kohlenstofffrei
- ~-**lean** kohlenstoffarm
- ~ **monoxide** Kohlenmonoxid *n*, CO
- ~ **oil** Handelsname für Kerosen
- ~ **ratio** 1. Kohlenstoffisotopenverhältnis *n*,C-Isotopenverhältnis *n* $(^{12}C/^{13}C)$; 2. Brennstoffverhältnis *n* (Verhältnis von festem Kohlenstoff zu flüchtigen Bestandteilen einer Kohle)
- ~ **ratio theory** Carbon-ratio-Theorie *f*, Kohlenstoffverhältnistheorie *f*
- ~-**rich** kohlenstoffreich
- ~ **spar** Karbonatspat *m*, Karbonatmineral *n*
- ~ **spot** schwarzer Fleck in einem Diamanten

carbona unregelmäßige Sn-Imprägnationen neben einem Gang
carbonaceous kohlenartig; kohlenstoffhaltig; kohlig
- ~ **chondrite** kohlenstoffhaltiger Chondrit *m*
- ~ **iron ore**, ~ **iron-stone** Kohleneisenstein *m*
- ~ **limestone** Kohlenkalk *m*
- ~ **rock** kohlenhaltiges Gestein *n*
- ~ **rocks** Kohlengebirge *n*
- ~ **shale** Brandschiefer *m*

carbonado Karbonado *m*, schwarzer Diamant *m*, Bohrdiamant *m*
carbonate/to karbonatisieren
carbonate Karbonat *n*, kohlensaures Salz *n*
- ~ **apatite** Karbonatapatit *m*, $Ca_5[F|(PO_4,(O_3OH)_3]$
- ~ **carbon** Karbonatkohlenstoff *m*
- ~ **geyser** Kohlensäuregeiser *m*, Kohlensäurespringquelle *f*
- ~ **hardness** Karbonathärte *f (Wasser)*
- ~ **karst** Kalkkarst *m*

~ **leaching** karbonatische (alkalische) Laugung f
~ **of barium** s. witherite
~ **of iron** s. siderite 1.
~ **of lead** s. cerussite
~ **of lime** kohlensaurer Kalk m
~ **of strontium** s. strontianite
~ **ore** karbonatisches Erz n
~ **platform** Karbonatplattform f
~ **rock** Karbonatgestein n (mehr als 50% Karbonat)
~ **sand** Karbonatsand m
~ **spring** Säuerling m, Sauerquelle f, Sauerbrunnen m, Kohlensäurequelle f
carbonated spring s. carbonate spring
carbonateous rock s. carbonate rock
carbonation 1. Kohlensäuresaturation f; 2. Karbonisierung f, Versetzen n mit CO_2; 3. Verwitterung f zu Karbonaten
carbonatite Karbonatit m
carbonatization Karbonatisierung f
carbonatize/to karbonatisieren
carbonic kohlenstoffhaltig; kohlensäurehaltig
~ **acid** Kohlensäure f
~ **acid fumarole** Kohlensäurefumarole f, nasse Mofette f
~ **acid gas** Kohlendioxid[gas] n, Kohlenstoffdioxid f
Carbonic s. Carboniferous
carboniferous 1. kohlenstoffhaltig, kohlig; 2. kohleführend
~ **rock** Steinkohlengebirge n
~ **sandstone** Kohlensandstein m
~ **slate** Kohlenschiefer m
~ **strata** Steinkohlengebirge npl
Carboniferous das Karbon betreffend, Karbon...
Carboniferous Karbon[system] n (chronostratigrafisch); Karbon n, Karbonperiode f (geochronologisch); Karbon n, Karbonzeit f (allgemein)
~ **Age** Karbon n, Karbonzeit f
~ **flora** Karbonflora f
~ **Limestone** Unterkarbon n (Süd- und Mittelengland)
~ **Period** Karbon n, Karbonperiode f
~ **System** Karbon n, Karbonsystem n
carbonification s. coalification
carbonitization Karbonatmetasomatose f
carbonization Verkokung f, Verschwelung f
~ **of bituminous coal** Steinkohlendestillation f
~ **of brown coal** Braunkohlenverschwelung f
carbonize/to verkohlen, verschwelen, verkoken
~ **under vacuum at a low temperature** verschwelen, abschwelen
carbonized verkohlt, verschwelt, verkokt
~ **lignite** Braunkohlenkoks m, Schwelkoks m
~ **wood** verkohltes Holz n
carbonizing flame reduzierende Flamme f, Reduktionsflamme f
carbonolite s. carbonaceous rock

carbonous kohlig
carbopolyminerite Carbopolyminerit m (Verwachsung von Kohlenmikrolithotypen mit 20–60 Vol.-% Mineralsubstanz)
carbopyrite Carbopyrit m (Verwachsung von Kohlenmikrolithotypen mit 5–20 Vol.-% sulfidischen Erzen)
carborne exploration Erkundung f vom Fahrzeug aus
carborund[um] Karborund[um] n, Siliziumkarbid n
carbosilicite Carbosilicit m (Verwachsung von Kohlenmikrolithotypen mit 20–60 Vol.-% Quarz)
carcass Kadaver m, Leiche f
cardinal angle Dorsalwinkel m
~ **area** Schloßrand m (Brachiopoden)
~ **points** vier Himmelsrichtungen fpl
~ **septum** Kardinalseptum n, Gegenseptum n (Korallen)
carelianite Karelianit m, V_2O_3
carex peat Seggentorf m
Caribbean arc Karibischer Bogen m
~ **Sea** Karibisches Meer n
carina Kiel m, Grat m (von Fossilien)
carinate anticline isoklinal gefaltete Antiklinale f
~ **fold** s. isoclinal fold
~ **syncline** isoklinal gefaltete Synklinale f
carinated gekielt
carinthine Karinthin m (braungrün pleochroitische Eklogithornblende)
Carixian [Stage] Carix n, unteres Pliensbach n (Stufe des Unteren Juras)
carlosite Carlosit m, Neptunit m (s.a. neptunite)
Carlsbad twin Karlsbader Zwilling m
Carmel formation Carmel-Formation f, Gypsum-Spring-Formation f (Dogger, Nordamerika)
carminite Carminit m, $PbFe_2[OH|AsO_4]_2$
carn Steinhaufen m, Felsen m
carnack (sl) Hornstein m
carnallite Karnallit m, Carnallit m, $KMgCl_3 \cdot 6H_2O$
carnallitite Karnallitit m, Carnallitit m
carnegieite Carnegieit m, $NaAlSiO_4$ (aus Nephelin bei Erhitzen)
carnelian, carneol[e] Karneol m (s.a. chalcedony)
Carnian [Stage] Karn n (alpine Trias)
carnotite Karnotit m, Carnotit m, $K_2[(UO_2)_2|(VO_4)_2] \cdot 3H_2O$
carobbiite Carobbiit m, KF
carpal bone Carpalium n, Handwurzelknochen m
carpathite Karpathit m, $C_{32}H_{17}O$
carpet folding Teppichfaltung f
carpholite Karpholith m, $MnAl_2[(OH)_2|Si_2O_6]$
carphosiderite Karphosiderit m, $H_2OFe_3[(OH)_5H_2O|(SO_4)_2]$
carpolite Fruchtversteinerung f, fossile Frucht f

carpus

carpus Carpus m, Handwurzel f, Handgelenk n
carr Übergangsmoorboden m
carrack s. caple
Carrara [marble] Carraramarmor m
carried soil verschwemmter Boden m
carrier Träger m
~ **bed** Trägergesteinsschicht f, Speichergesteinsschicht f
~ **nappe** Trägerdecke f (Tektonik)
~ **of water** wasserführende Schicht f
~ **rock** Trägergestein n, Speichergestein n
carrion eater (feeder) Aasfresser m
carrollite Carrollit m, $CuCo_2S_4$
carry down/to abteufen, niederbringen
~ **on explorations** Aufschlußarbeiten verrichten (betreiben)
~ **out coring** einen Kern bohren, kernen
carry [on] explorations Aufschlußarbeiten fpl, Abbau m
~-**over storage** Speicher m für mehrere Jahre
carrying capacity Transportfähigkeit f
~ **power** Schleppkraft f
carse flache Alluvion in Ästuarmündung
carstone eisenschüssiger Sandstein m
cartilaginous fish Knorpelfisch m
~ **skeleton** Knorpelskelett n
cartographer Kartenzeichner m, Kartograf m
cartographic[al] kartografisch
~ **correction** Geländekorrektur f (bei geophysikalischen Messungen)
~ **rectification** kartografische Entzerrung f (z.B. einer Fernerkundungsaufnahme)
~ **reference system** kartografisches Bezugssystem n
~ **survey** kartografische Erkundung (Vermessung) f
cartography Kartografie f, Kartenkunde f
carve/to kerben, schlitzen, [ver]schrämen
~ **out** skulpturieren, herausarbeiten (durch Erosion)
carved face verschrämter Stoß m
carving Steinarbeit f, Bildhauerarbeit f, Schram m
caryinite Karyinit m, $(Na, Ca)_2(Mn,Mg,Ca,Pb)_3[AsO_4]_3$
caryopilite Karyopilit m, $Mn_6[(OH)_8|Si_4O_{10}]$
Casagrande shear test apparatus Scherapparat m nach Casagrande, Scherkastengerät n, Scherbüchse f
casalties (sl) Zinnschlämme mpl
cascade Wasserfall m, Kaskade f
Cascadian disturbance (orogeny) kaskadische Faltung f
cascadite Cascadit m (Varietät von Lamprophyr)
case/to verrohren, ausrohren, auskleiden
case Gehäuse n
cased [bore]hole verrohrtes Bohrloch n
~ **hole completion** Fertigstellung f als verrohrte Bohrung
~-**in bore** verrohrte Bohrung f

cash (sl) milder Schieferton m (in Kohleflözen)
cashy blaes (sl) milder kohliger Tonschiefer m
casing 1. Verrohrung f, Röhrentour f, Rohrfahrt f, Rohrstrang m, Futterrohr n; 2. Verrohren n, Verrohrung f (Arbeitsprozeß); 3. Salband n
~ **break-off** Bohrstrangbruch m, Futterrohrbruch m
~ **cementing job** Ringraumzementierung f, Ringraumzementation f
~ **collapse** Einbeulen (Eindrücken) n der Verrohrung, Futterrohreinbeulung f
~ **collar** Rohrmuffe f
~ **depth** Verrohrungsteufe f
~ **head** Rohrkopf m
~-**head gas** Bohrlochkopfgas n, Sondengas n, feuchtes Erdgas n
~-**head gasoline** Naturgasbenzin n, Rohrkopfbenzin n, aus dem Naturgas zurückgewonnenes Leichtbenzin n
~-**head pressure** Kopfdruck m, Druck m am Bohrlochkopf, Ringraumkopfdruck m
~ **perforation** Rohrperforation f
~ **pipe** Verrohrung f (Material)
~ **point** Verrohrungsteufe f
~ **pressure** Verrohrungsdruck m, Ringraumdruck m
~ **program** Bohrlochkonstruktion f, Verrohrungsprogramm n
~ **roller** Futterrohrroller m
~ **seat** Futterrohrabsetzteufe f
~ **shoe** Rohrschuh m
~ **size** Verrohrungsabmaße npl
~ **spear** Rohrfangkrebs m
~ **string** Futterrohrstrang m, Futterrohrtour f
~ **tongs** Rohrzange f
Cassadagan [Stage] Cassadaga n (Stufe des Famenne in Nordamerika)
Casselian [Stage] s. Chattian
Cassian Beds Cassianer Schichten fpl
Cassinian [Stage] Cassinien n (hangende Stufe des Unterordoviziums in Nordamerika)
cassidyite Cassidyit m, $Ca_2(Ni,Mg)(PO_4)_2 \cdot 2H_2O$ (Meteoritenmineral)
cassiterite Kassiterit m, Zinnstein m, SnO_2
~ **wolframite vein** Zinn-Wolfram-Gang m
cast down/to ins Liegende verwerfen
~ **over** ins Hangende verwerfen
cast Ausguß m, Abguß m
~ **basalt** Schmelzbasalt m
~ **hole** Schürfbohrloch n
~ **in relief** erhabener Abguß m
~-**up seaweed** angeschwemmter Seetang m
castaways (sl) taube Gangfüllung f
castillite Castillit m (Gemenge von Zn-, Cu-, Ag-Erzen)
casting s. coprolite
castle koppie kleiner Inselberg m
castorite s. petalite
cat feuerfester Ton m (in Kohleschichten)
~ **claw** (sl) Markasitlage in Kohle
~ **dirt** (sl) 1. Kohle mit Pyrit; 2. harter, feuerfester Ton

~ face Pyritkonkretionen in der Kohle
~ gold (sl) Katzenglimmer m, Katzengold n (angewitterter Biotit)
~ heads Katzensteine mpl (Gestein mit eisenhaltigen Knoten)
cataclasis Kataklase f
cataclasite Kataklasit m; kataklastisches Gestein n
cataclastic kataklastisch
~ metamorphism Dislokationsmetamorphose f
~ processes Kataklase f
~ structure kataklastisches Gefüge n
cataclinal valley Kataklinaltal n, Tal n in Richtung des Schichtfallens
cataclysm Kataklysmus m, erdumwälzende Flutkatastrophe f
cataclysmal theory Kataklysmentheorie f
catagenesis Katagenese f (Anchimetamorphose)
catalinite Achatmandel f (als Flußgeröll)
catamorphism Katamorphismus m
catanorm Katanorm f
cataorogenic tieforogen
catapleiite Katapleit m, $Na_2Zr[Si_3O_9] \cdot 2H_2O$
cataract Wasserfall m
catarinite Ni-reicher Eisenmeteorit
catastrophe Katastrophe f (11. Stufe der Erdbebenstärkeskala)
catastrophic[al] flood Flutkatastrophe f
~ theory Katastrophentheorie f
catastrophism Katastrophentheorie f
catastrophist concept Katastrophentheorie f
catazone Katazone f
catch basin Sammelloch n
~ drain s. ~ water drain
~ earth s. cat
~ sample Spülprobe f
~ water drain Sammelgraben m, Drainagegraben m; offene Wasserhaltung f
catchment area Einzugsgebiet n, Sammelgebiet n; Fanggebiet n, Auffangfläche f; Niederschlagsgebiet n; Entwässerungsgebiet n, Abflußgebiet n; Ernährungsgebiet n; Flußbecken n
~ area of an aquifer Einzugsgebiet n eines Grundwasserleiters
~ basin Nährgebiet n (eines Gletschers); Abflußgebiet n, Sammelbecken n
~ drainage area, ~ ground Einzugsgebiet n
~ of ground waters Grundwassererfassung f
~ surface Auffangfläche f
category of geological structure complication Kategorie f der Kompliziertheit des geologischen Baus bei Untersuchungsarbeiten
catenary-moored semisubmersible an Ketten verankerter Halbtaucher m
cathead Spill n
cathode ray tube Katodenstrahloszillograf m
cation exchange capacity Kationenaustauschkapazität f, Umtauschkapazität f
catlinite s. pipestone
catoctin s. monadnock

catoptrite Katoptrit m, $Mn_{14}Sb_2(Al, Fe)_4[O_{21}|(SO_4)_2]$
cat's brain Sandstein m mit Kalzitdurchtrümerung
~ eye (quartz) Katzenauge n (Quarz mit Asbest)
cattierite Cattierit m, CoS_2
cauce Flußbett n
caudal fin Schwanzflosse f
~ shield s. pygidium
~ spine s. telson
~ vertebra Schwanzwirbel m
cauk 1. Kalk m (in Schottland); 2. (sl) Baryt m
cauldron Kessel m
~ bottom 1. Sargdeckel m; 2. fossiler Wurzelboden m (im Hangenden eines Flözes)
~-shaped kesselförmig
~ subsidence Einbruchsbecken n
cauliflower structure Blumenkohlstruktur f (stromatolithische Limonitkruste)
caulm (sl) s. calm
causative body Störkörper m
caustic kaustisch
caustic Brennpunkt m
~ metamorphism kaustische Metamorphose f, Kontaktmetamorphose f
~ soda solution Natronlauge f
caustobiolite Kaustobiolith m
cave/to zu Bruch gehen, einstürzen, niederbrechen
~ in zusammenstürzen; zusammenfallen (Bohrloch, Grubenräume); nachfallen (Bohrloch); zu Bruch gehen, einsinken, niederbrechen
cave 1. Höhle f; 2. Einsturz m, Bruch m; Nachfall m (Bohrloch)
~ arches torartige Grotten fpl
~ bear Höhlenbär m
~ clay Höhlenlehm m
~ deposit Höhlenablagerung f, Höhlensediment n
~ dweller Höhlenbewohner m
~-dwelling animal Höhlentier n
~-in Einsturz m, Bruch m, Nachfall m (Bohrloch)
~ limestone Höhlenkalkstein m
~ man Höhlenmensch m
~ onyx (Am) Sinter[kalk] m, Kalksinter m
~ pearl Kalziterbse f, Höhlenperle f
~ roof Höhlendach m
~ to the surface Tagesbruch m (Bergschaden)
caved goaf Bruchfeld n
~ roof zu Bruch gegangenes Hangendes n
cavern Kaverne f
~ convergence Kavernenkonvergenz f
~ deposit Höhlenablagerung f, Höhlensediment n
~ design Kavernendimensionierung f
~ leaching process Aussolen n von Kavernen
~ logging Kavernenvermessung f (Bohrlochgeophysik)
~ region Höhlengebiet n
~ roof Kavernendach n

cavern 62

~ **shape** Kavernenkontur f
~ **storage** Kavernenspeicher m
~ **sump** Kavernensumpf m
~ **surveillance** Kavernenüberwachung f
~ **survey** s. ~ logging
~ **wall** Kavernenstoß m
~ **well** Kavernenbohrung f
cavernous blasig, zellig, kavernös
~ **dolomite** kavernöser Dolomit m
~ **fissure** Höhlenspalte f
~ **lode** s. ~ vein
~ **sand** Blasensand m
~ **structure** kavernöses (zelliges) Gefüge n
~ **vein** kavernöser (offener) Gang m *(Oxydationszone)*
~ **weathering** Verwitterung f von innen heraus, Auswitterung f
cavetto Hohlkehle f
cavey formation nachfallendes Gebirge n
caving Nachfall m
~ **country (formation, ground)** nachfallendes (nachfälliges) Gebirge n
~-**in** Zusammenbruch m; Hereinbrechen n des Hangenden *(Bruchbau)*
~ **line** Bruchlinie f
~ **of the walls of a drill hole** Zusammenbruch m der Bohrlochwand[ung]
~ **rocks** zu Bruch gehendes Gebirge n
~ **zone** Bruchzone f
cavitation Kavitation f
cavities Bruchfeld n
cavity Hohlraum m; Auskesselung f, Bohrlochauskesselung f
~ **filling** Höhlenfüllung f
~ **volume** Hohlraumvolumen n
~ **working** Weitungsbau m
cawk [stone] *(sl)* 1. Kalk m; 2. unreiner Baryt m
cay Küsteninsel f *(aus Sand oder Korallen)*
Cayugan [Series] Cayugan n *(Obersilur in Nordamerika)*
Cazenovian [Stage] Cazenovien n *(Stufe des Eriens in Nordamerika, Devon)*
CCD s. 1. calcite compensation depth; 2. charge-coupled device
CCOP/SOPAC = Committee for Co-ordination of Joint Prospecting for Mineral Resources in Offshore Areas/East Asia
CCT s. computer compatible tape
CDP s. common depth point
CDPS s. common depth point stack
cebollite Cebollit m, $Ca_5Al_2[(OH)_4(SiO_4)_3]$
cedar-tree laccolith Zederbaumlakkolith m
cedarite Cedarit m *(bernsteinähnliches Harz)*
ceiling cavity Klufthöhlenreihe f
~ **of an aquiferous layer** Grundwasserdeckschicht f
celadonite Seladonit m, Grünerde f *(Fe-, Mg-, K-Silikat)*
celestial Himmels...
~ **axis** Himmelsachse f, Weltachse f
~ **body** Gestirn n, Himmelskörper m

~ **equator** Himmelsäquator m
~ **globe** Himmelsglobus m
~ **horizon** Himmelshorizont m
~ **mechanics** Himmelsmechanik f
~ **meridian** Himmelsmeridian m
~ **navigation** Astronavigation f
~ **observation** Himmelsbeobachtung f
~ **pole** Himmelspol m
~ **space** Weltraum m
~ **sphere** Himmelskugel f, Firmament n
~ **vault** Himmelsgewölbe n
celestine s. celestite
celestite Cölestin m, $SrSO_4$
cell wall of coke Kokszellwand f
cellar Bohrturmkeller m
cellular zellig
~ **dolomite** Rauhwacke f, Zellendolomit m
~ **lava** Blasenlava f
~ **pyrite** s. marcasite
~ **soil** Zellenboden m
~ **structure** Netz[werk]struktur f
celsian Celsian m, $Ba[Al_2Si_2O_8]$
celtium s. hafnium
celyphitic s. kelyphitic
cement [together]/to verfestigen, verkitten
cement Bindemittel n, Zwischensubstanz f
~ **bridge** Zementbrücke f
~ **clay** Zementton m *(für Portlandzement)*
~ **for packing** Tiefbohrzement m
~ **grout** Zementschlämme f, Zementmilch f
~ **grouting** Zementinjektion f
~ **log** Zementlog n *(Bohrlochmessung)*
~ **retainer** Zementationspacker m
~ **rock** argillitischer Kalkstein m *(für hydraulischen Zement)*
~ **sheath** Zementmantel m *(Bohrtechnik)*
~ **slurry** Zementschlämme f, Zementmilch f
~ **stabilization** Verfestigung f mit Zement, Vermörtelung f
~ **stone** s. ~ rock
~ **top** Zementkopf m
cementation 1. Zementation f, Zementierung f; 2. Verkittung f *(von Gestein);* 3. Baugrundverfestigung f
~ **by enlargement** Zementierung f durch Kornvergröberung *(Rekristallisation)*
~ **factor** Zementationsfaktor m
~ **of rock fissures** Gesteinsauspressung f
~ **zone** Zementationszone f
cementative accumulation zementative Ansammlung f
cemented verkittet
~ **rock** verfestigtes Gestein n
~ **shale** Schiefer m mit Bindemittelverkittung
~ **together** zusammengekittet *(Gestein)*
cementing Zementation f *(Bohrtechnik);* Zementieren n, Zementtränkung f *(Bauwesen, Bohrtechnik)*
~ **material** Bindemittel n, [verkittende] Zwischensubstanz f
~ **on glass slide** Aufkitten n *(auf Objektglas)*
~ **plug** Zementierstopfen m

~ **property** Bindefähigkeit f, Backvermögen n
~ **pump** Zementierpumpe f
~**-together** Zementierung f
~ **unit** Zementieranlage f
cementitious verkittend *(für Material mit Stabilisierungseigenschaften, z.B. Kalk, Tuff)*
cenology s. surface geology
Cenomanian [Stage] Cenoman n *(Stufe der Oberkreide)*
~ **transgression** Cenomane Transgression f
Cenophytic Känophytikum n
cenosite Kainosit m, $Ca_2Y_2[CO_3|Si_4O_{12}]\cdot H_2O$
cenotypal jungvulkanisch
~ **rock** jungvulkanisches Gestein n
Cenozoic [Era] Känozoikum n
cenozone s. assemblage zone
centimeter-sized in Korngröße von 1–10 cm
centimicron-sized in Korngröße von 100 bis 1000 μm
central core [of the earth] Erdkern m
~ **eruption** Zentraleruption f
~ **loading** mittige Belastung f
~ **massif** Zentralmassiv n
~ **meridian** Hauptmeridian m
~ **peak** Zentralberg m *(des Mondes)*
Central European Variscan belt mitteleuropäisches Varistikum n
centrallasite Zentrallasit m, Gyrolith m, $Ca_2[Si_4O_{10}]\cdot 4H_2O$
centre of accumulation Nährgebiet n *(eines Gletschers)*
~ **of crystallization** Kristallisationszentrum n
~ **of displacement** Verdrängungszentrum n, Verdrängungspunkt m
~ **of eruption** Ausbruchszentrum n
~ **of mass coordinate** Schwerpunktskoordinate f
~ **of origin** Entstehungszentrum n
~ **of pressure** 1. Druckmittelpunkt m; 2. Druckzentrum n *(im Grundwasserleiter)*
~ **of support** Unterstützungspunkt m
~ **of symmetry** Symmetriezentrum n
~ **of the earth** Erdmittelpunkt m
centrifugal zentrifugal
~ **air separator** Windsichter m
~ **classifier** Fliehkraft[naß]klassierer m
~ **fault** Aufschiebung f
~ **force** Zentrifugalkraft f
centrifuge Zentrifuge f, Turbozyklon m *(Spülungstechnik)*
centripetal zentripetal
~ **acceleration** Zentripetalbeschleunigung f
~ **fault** normale Verwerfung f
~ **force** Zentripetalkraft f
centroclinal umlaufend *(Streichen)*
~ **bedding** trichterförmiger Schichtenbau m
~ **dip** periklinales Einfallen n
~ **fold** Schüssel f *(Struktur)*
centrocline s. pericline 2.
centrosphere Erdkern m
cenuglomerate zementierte Brekzie f
cephalopod Kopffüßer m, Cephalopode m

~ **facies** Cephalopodenfazies f
ceramic raw material keramischer Rohstoff m
cerargyrite Kerargyrit m, Chlorsilber n, Silberhornerz n, Chlorargyrit m, AgCl
ceratite Ceratit m
~ **limestone** Ceratitenkalk m
~ **marl** Ceratitenmergel m
ceratitic ceratitisch
~ **suture** ceratitische Lobenlinie f
ceratophyre s. keratophyre
cerepidote s. allanite
cerfluorite Cerfluorit m, $(Ca, Ce)F_2$
cerianite Cerianit m, $(Ce, Th)O_2$
cerinite Zerenit m *(pflanzliche Wachsbildung in Braunkohlen)*
cerite Zerit m, Cerit m, $(Ca, Fe)Ce_3H[(OH)_2|SiO_4|Si_2O_7]$
cerium Zer n, Cer n, Ce
cerussite Zerussit m, Cerussit m, Weißbleierz n, $PbCO_3$
cervantite Cervantit m, Sb_2O_4
cervical vertebra Halswirbel m, Cervicalwirbel m
cesium *(Am)* Zäsium n, Caesium n, Cs *(s.a. caesium)*
cessation of deposition Lücke f in der Schichtenfolge
cesspool Senkbrunnen m
ceylanite s. ceylonite
Ceylon lumps stückiger Graphit m
~ **plumbago** Ceylongraphit m
ceylonite Ceylonit m, Pleonast m *(schwarzer Spinell)*
CFGPD = cubic feet gas per day
CGMW = Commission for the Geological Map of the World *(IUGS)*
chabasite, chabazite Chabasit m, $Ca,Na_2[Al_2Si_4O_{12}]\cdot 6H_2O$
chad Schotter m
chadacryst s. xenocryst
Chadronian [Stage] Chadron[ien] n *(Wirbeltierstufe des Oligozäns in Nordamerika)*
chafe away/to abscheuern
chaff peat Torf m mit stückigen Pflanzenresten
chafing Abscheuerung f
chain 1. Kette f, Zerfallsreihe f; 2. Längeneinheit von 66 Fuß; 3. direkte Entfernungsmessung *(mit Stahlband)*
~ **coral** Kettenkoralle f
~ **gauge** Reihenpegel m
~ **of islands** Inselkette f
~ **of lakes** Seenkette f
~ **of mountains** Kettengebirge n
~ **of vulcanoes** Vulkankette f
~ **silicate** Kettensilikat n, Inosilikat n
~ **tongs** Kettenzange f
~ **traverse** geknickter Polygonzug m *(Vermessungskunde)*
chaining arrows Stäbe mit Markierungsfähnchen für Prospektionsarbeiten
chalazoidites s. accretionary lapilli
chalcanthite Chalkanthit m, $Cu[SO_4]\cdot 5H_2O$

chalcedonic

chalcedonic chalzedonisch
~ **chert** glasiger, muschelig brechender Hornstein bzw. Kieselschiefer
chalcedony Chalzedon m, SiO_2 (kryptokristallin)
chalchnite s. turquois
chalcoalumite Chalkoalumit m, $CuAl_4[(OH)_{12}|SO_4]\cdot 3H_2O$
chalcocite Chalkosin m, Kupferglanz m, Cu_2S
chalcocyanite Hydrocyanit m, Chalcocyanit m, $Cu[SO_4]$
chalcolamprite Chalkolamprit m, Pyrochlor m, $(Ca,Na)_2(Nb, Ta)_2O_6(O, OH, P)$
chalcolite s. torbernite
chalcomenite Chalkomenit m, $Cu[SeO_3]\cdot 2H_2O$
chalconatronite Chalkonatronit m, $Na_2Cu[CO_3]_2\cdot 3H_2O$
chalcophanite Chalkophanit m, $ZnMn_3O_7\cdot 3H_2O$
chalcophil[e] s. chalcophilic
chalcophilic chalkophil
~ **element** chalkophiles Element n
chalcophyllite Chalkophyllit m, $(Cu,Al)_3[(OH)_4|(AsO_4,SO_4)]\cdot 6H_2O$
chalcopyrite Chalkopyrit m, Kupferkies m, $CuFeS_2$
chalcosiderite Chalkosiderit m, $CuFe_6[(OH)_2|PO_4]_4\cdot 4H_2O$
chalcosine s. chalcocite
chalcostibite Chalkostibit m, Kupferantimonglanz m, Wolfsbergit m, $Cu_2S\cdot Sb_2S_3$
chalcotrichite Chalkotrichit m (nadliger Cuprit)
chalk Schreibkreide f
~ **cliff** Kreidefelsen m
~ **deposit** Kreideablagerung f
~ **flint** Feuerstein m in Kreide
~-**loving** kalkliebend
~ **marl** Kreidemergel m
~ **period** Kreidezeit f
chalkhumus soil Humuskarbonatboden m
chalky kreidehaltig, kreidig
~ **limestone** Kreidekalkstein m
~ **soil** Kreideboden m
chalmersite s. cubanite
chalybeate eisenähnlich; eisenhaltig
~ **spring** Stahlquelle f, Eisensäuerling m, Eisenquelle f
chalybite s. siderite 1.
chalypite Chalypit m, Fe_2C (in Meteoriten)
chamber 1. Abbaukammer f; 2. Kammer f (von Fossilgehäusen)
~ **blasting** Kammersprengen n, Kammersprengarbeit f
~ **of ore** Erzbutze f, Erznest m
chambered gekammert
~ **vein** Kammergang m
chambersite Chambersit m, $Mn_3[Cl|B_7O_{13}]$
chamfer/to abschrägen, böschen
chamfer schräger Anschnitt m
chamfering Abschrägen n, Abkanten n
chamo[i]site Chamosit m, $(Fe, Mg)_6[O|(OH)_8|AlSi_3O_{10}]$

champion lode Hauptgang m
Champlainian [Series] Champlainien n (Llanvirn, Llandeilo und Teile des Caradocs in Nordamerika)
chance sample Stichprobe f, Einzelprobe f
chances of discovery Fundaussichten fpl, Fundmöglichkeiten fpl
change detection Feststellung f von Veränderungen
~ **in direction** Richtungswechsel m
~ **in facies** Faziesübergang m
~ **in potential** Potentialsprung m
~ **of climate** Klimawechsel m
~ **of colours** Labradorisieren n
~ **of facies** Fazieswechsel m
~ **of level** Niveauänderung f
~ **of shift** Schichtwechsel m (lithologisch)
~ **of temperature** Temperaturwechsel m
~ **of volume** Volumenänderung f
~ **point** Umwandlungspunkt m
changeable coast line veränderliche Uferlinie f
~ **lustre** Schillerglanz m
changing of colours Labradorisieren n
~ **of the bit** Umsetzen n des Bohrgeräts
channel 1. Rinne f; Auswaschungsrinne f, Erosionsrinne f, Strömungsrinne f; 2. Graben m
~ **bar** Flußsandbank f
~ **cast** Rinnenfüllung f, Rinnenmarke f, Prielfüllung f
~ **encroachment** Grabenflutung f
~ **fill** Rinnensediment n
~-**floor lag** grobe Ablagerung auf dem Boden von Strömungs- oder Flußrinnen
~ **migration** Flußbettverlagerung f
~-**mouth bar** Sedimentbank f im Fluß (durch Strömungsverringerung)
~ **net** Entwässerungsnetz n (eines Einzugsgebiets)
~ **of a river** Flußbett n
~ **of ascent** Förderschlot m, Schußkanal m
~ **of drainage** Abflußrinne f
~ **of marginal glacial streamwash** Schmelzwasserrinne f
~ **pattern** Rinnenmuster n, Flußbettmuster n
~ **precipitation** Gewässerniederschlag m (Niederschlag, der in Flüsse oder Seen fällt)
~ **regime equation** Grabenströmungsgleichung f
~ **roughness** Bettrauhigkeit f (des Wassers)
~ **sample** Schlitzprobe f
~ **sand** Rinnensediment n, Rinnensand m
~ **slope** Talgefälle f
~ **storage** Wasseraufspeicherung f des Flußbetts
~ **wave** Kanalwelle f (elastische Welle mit geringer Ausbreitungsgeschwindigkeit)
channelled zerkart, kanneliert
~ **by ice** eisgeschrammt
channelling Kannelierung f, Riefenbildung f, Auskehlung f

~ **machine** Schrämm[vortriebs]maschine f, Fräsvortriebsmaschine f
channelway Zufuhrkanal m
chaos of rocks Felsenmeer n
chap/to sich spalten
chap Spalte f
chapmanite Chapmanit m, SbFe$_2$[OH|(SiO$_4$)$_2$]
character displacement Merkmalsverschiebung f
characteristic curve Ausbaukennlinie f
~ **fossil** Leitfossil n
~ **pulse method** Eigenimpulsverfahren n
~ **series** Kennreihe f
~ **subgroup** Kennuntergruppe f
charcoal 1. Holzkohle f; 2. Brandfusit m (in Torfmooren oder Kohlenflözen)
~ **heap** Holzkohlenmeiler m
~ **layer** Holzkohlenschicht f
charge Ladung f (auch chemisch)
~**-coupled device** ladungsgekoppelte Halbleitervorrichtung f (Linearanordnung ladungsgekoppelter Festkörperdetektoren, als Fernerkundungssensor genutzt)
~ **density** Ladungsdichte f
charged with water wasserdurchtränkt
Charmouthian [Stage] Charmoutien n (Stufe des Unteren Juras)
charnockite Charnockit m
charred wood verkohltes Holz n
chart/to kartieren, auf eine Karte eintragen
chart Karte f, grafische Darstellung f
~ **of geologic time** geologische Zeittafel f
charting Kartieren n
chasing Verfolgung f eines Gangs im Streichen
chasm Abgrund m, Kluft f, Schlucht f
chasmy kluftreich
chassignite Chassignit m (Meteorit)
chat verwachsen, fein eingesprengt
chat klastischer Chalzedon als Bestandteil der Gangart
chathamite Chathamit m, (Fe, Co, Ni)As$_3$
chatoyancy Lichtspiel n der Augensteine (z.B. Tigerauge, Falkenauge)
chatoyant changierend, schillernd
chatter mark Splittermarke f, Schlagfigur f
Chattian [Stage] Chatt[ium] n, Katt n (Stufe des Oligozäns)
chatty ore fein eingesprengtes Erz n
Chazyan [Stage] Chazy n, Chazy-Kalk m (Stufe des Champlainiens in Nordamerika)
check analysis Kontrollanalyse f
~ **borehole** Kontrollbohrloch n
~ **irrigation** geregelte Bewässerung f
~ **run** Kontrollmessung f
~ **sample** Vergleichsprobe f, Parallelprobe f
~ **shot** Kontrollschuß m (bei der Bohrlochmessung)
checker ... s. chequer ...
checkered s. chequered
checking karoartige Rißbildung f
~ **of borehole depth** Bohrlochlängenkontrolle f

~ **of the water table** Wasserstandsmessung f, Wasserspiegelmessung f
cheek off/to beräumen
cheek 1. Wange f (bei Fossilien); 2. Hangendes n und Liegendes n, Nebengestein n, Salbänder npl
~ **bone** Backenknochen m, Jugale n
~ **tooth** Backenzahn m
cheeks Wangen fpl (des Trilobitenkopfschilds)
cheestone ausbrechender Kluftkörper m
chelation biogene Gesteinszerstörung f
chemical chemisch
~ **analysis** chemische Analyse f
~ **attack** chemischer Angriff m
~ **autotrophic bacterial activity** bakterielle chemoautotrophe Aktivität f
~ **bond** chemische Bindung f
~ **composition** chemische Zusammensetzung f
~ **corrosion** chemische Korrosion f
~**-deposited sedimentary rock** chemisches Sedimentgestein n, Ausscheidungssedimentgestein n, Präzipitatgestein n
~ **element** chemisches Element n
~ **equation** chemische Gleichung f
~ **equilibrium** chemisches Gleichgewicht n
~ **geology** Geochemie f
~ **grouting** chemische Verfestigung f
~ **mineralogy** Mineralchemie f
~ **properties** chemische Eigenschaften fpl
~ **reaction** chemische Reaktion f
~ **reservoir rock** chemisches Speichergestein n
~ **soil solidification** chemische Bodenverfestigung f
~ **substitution** chemischer Austausch m
~ **weathering** chemische Verwitterung f
~ **well service** chemische Bohrlochbehandlung f
chemically bound water Konstitutionswasser n
~ **formed rock** Gestein n chemischen Ursprungs
chemism Chemismus m
chenevixite Chenevixit m, Cu$_2$Fe$_2$[(OH)$_2$|AsO$_4$]$_2$·H$_2$O
chequer-board pattern Schachbrettmuster n
~ **coal** in parallelepipedische Stücke zerfallender Anthrazit
chequered karoartig
~ **albite** Schachbrettalbit m
cheralite Cheralith m, (Ca, Ce, La, Th)[PO$_4$]
chernier Strandwall m
chernozem Schwarzerde f, Tschernos[j]em m (n), Tschernosjom m (n)
cherry coal Sinterkohle f
chert Kieselschiefer m, Hornstein m, Feuerstein m
~ **bit** Cobra-Meißel m (Bohrkrone)
~ **breccia** Hornsteinbrekzie f
~ **gravel** Hornsteinschotter m
~ **limestone** Kieselkalkstein m
~ **nodule** Silexknolle f, Kieselknauer m
chertification Verkieselung f

cherty

cherty kieselig, verkieselt, hornsteinartig
~ **limestone** Kieselkalkstein *m*
chervetite Chervetit *m*, $Pb_2V_2O_7$
chess-board texture Schachbrettstruktur *f*
chessy copper, chessylite *s.* azurite
Chesterian [Stage] Chester *n (Stufe des Mississippiens)*
chestnut-brown soil kastanienfarbiger Boden *m*
chevron cross-bedding Fiederschichtung *f*, Kreuzschichtung *f*
~ **fold** Staffelfalte *f (s.a.* zigzag fold)
~ **mark** Fiedermarke *f*, gefiederte Schleifrille *f*
~ **pattern** Grätenmuster *n*
chi-square test Chi-Quadrat-Test *m (Wahrscheinlichkeitstest einer Verteilungsanalyse)*
chiastolite Chiastolith *m (s.a.* andalusite)
chibinite Chibinit *m*
chief index of refraction Hauptbrechungsindex *m*
Chihsian [Stage] Chihsia *n (hangende Stufe des Unterperms)*
childrenite Childrenit *m*, $(Fe,Mn)Al[(OH)_2|PO_4]\cdot H_2O$
Chile nitre (salpetre) Chilesalpeter *m*, $NaNO_3$
chilenite Chilenit *m*, (Ag,Bi)
chill/to abkühlen, abschrecken
chillagite Chillagit *m*, $Pb[(Mo, W)O_4]$
chilled contact (edge) dichte Randfazies *f (Kontaktmetamorphose)*
~ **shot** Hartschrot *n*
~-**shot bit** Schrotkrone *f*
~ **surface** Abkühlungsfläche *f*
chilling 1. Abkühlung *f*; 2. Glashärte *f*
chim Goldsand *m*
chimmer Goldwäscher *m*, Aufbereiter *m (mit Mulden)*
chimming Erzaufbereitung *f (mit Mulden)*
chimney 1. Vulkanschlot *m*, Kamin *m*, Esse *f*, 2. Gletschermühle *f*; 3. vertikaler Erzfall *m*
~ **gas** Rauchgas *n*
~ **of ore** Erzfall *m*
~ **rock** Erdpyramide *f*, Erdpfeiler *m*
~ **rocks** Felsklippen *fpl*
chimneylike kaminartig, schornsteinartig
China clay Porzellanerde *f*, Rohkaolin *m*
~ **stone** kaolinisierter Granit *m*, pneumatolytischer Kaolin *m (von Cornwall)*
chine Kliffhang *m*
~ **of mountains** Bergrücken *m*, Kamm *m*
Chinese figure stone Agalmatolith *m*
~ **soapstone** chinesischer Speckstein *m (s.a.* talc)
chink Ritze *f (im Gestein)*
chinkolobwite Chinkolobwit *m*, Sklodowskit *m*, $MgH_2[UO_2|SiO_4]_2\cdot 5H_2O$
chinley coal Stückkohle *f*
chinook Föhn *m*
chiolite Chiolith *m*, $Na_5[Al_3F_{14}]$
chip Splitter *m*
~ **sample** Splitterprobe *f*, Pickprobe *f*
~ **yard** Waldboden *m*

chipper Grabstichel *m*
chippings 1. Grobkies *m*, Gesteinssplitt *m*; 2. Bohrklein *n*
chips Gesteinssplitt *m*
~ **of rock** Gesteinssplitter *mpl*
chiropterite Fledermausguano *m*
chirotype Chirotyp *m (noch nicht publizierte Spezies)*
chirt[t] *s.* chert
chisel Handmeißel *m*, Beitel *m*
~ **auger** Flachmeißel *m*
chitinous chitinös
~ **integument** Chitinhülle *f*
chitter *(sl)* 1. hangendes Begleitflöz *n*; 2. [dünnes] Toneisensteinband *n*
chiviatite Chiviatit *m*, $Pb_2Bi_6S_{11}$
chladnite achondritischer Meteorit mit viel Enstatit
chloanthite Chloanthit *m*, Weißnickelkies *m*, $NiAs_3$
chlopinite Chlopinit *m (Varietät von Euxinit)*
chlorapatite Chlorapatit *m*, $Ca_5[Cl|(PO_4)_3]$
chlorargyrite Hornsilber *n*, Kerargyrit *m*, AgCl
chlorastrolite *s.* pumpellyite
chloride of sodium Kochsalz *n*
chlorine Chlor *n*, Cl
chlorite Chlorit *m*
~ **albite schist** Chloritalbitschiefer *m*
~ **group** Chloritgruppe *f (Gruppe von glimmerigen Fe-, Mg-, Al-Silikatmineralen mit H_2O-Gruppen)*
~ **muscovite schist** Chloritmuskovitschiefer *m*
~ **phyllite** Chloritphyllit *m*
~ **schist (slate)** Chloritschiefer *m*
chloritic chloritisch
~ **gneiss** Chloritgneis *m*
~ **marl** Chloritmergel *m*
~ **rock** Chloritgestein *n*
~ **schist** Chloritschiefer *m*
chloritization Chloritbildung *f*, Chloritisierung *f*
chloritize/to chloritisieren
chloritoid Chloritoid *m*, $Fe_2AlAl_3[(OH)_4|O_2|(SiO_4)_2]$
~ **mica schist** Chloritglimmerschiefer *m*
chlornatrokalite Chlornatrokalit *m*, 6KCl + 1NaCl
chlorocalcite *s.* hydrophilite
chloromagnesite Chloromagnesit *m*, $MgCl_2$
chloromanganokalite Chloromanganokalit *m*, $K_4[MnCl_6]$
chloromelanite Varietät von Jadeit
chloropal Chloropal *m (Gemenge von Nontronit mit Opal)*
chlorophoenicite Chlorophönizit *m*, $(Zn, Mn)_5[(OH)_7|AsO_4]$
chlorophyllinite Chlorophyllinit *m (Braunkohlenmaceral)*
chlorophyllite Chlorophyllit *m (pinitartiges Zersetzungsprodukt von Kordierit)*
chlorospinel Chlorospinell *m (Varietät von grünem Spinell)*

chlorotile Chlorotil m, $(Cu, Fe)_2Cu_{12}[(OH, H_2O)_{12}|(AsO_4)_6] \cdot 6H_2O$
chloroxiphite Chloroxiphit m, $Pb_3O_2Cl_2 \cdot CuCl_2$
choana Choana f, innere Nasenöffnung f
choke/to 1. verstopfen, verschlammen; 2. drosseln
choke Gesteinseinbruch m in einer Höhle
choking of the river course Verschotterung f des Flußlaufs
chondre s. chondrule
chondrification Verknorpelung f
chondrite Chondrit m, chondritischer Steinmeteorit m
chondritic chondritisch
chondrodite Chondrodit m, $Mg_5[(OH, F)_2|(SiO_4)_2]$
chondroskeleton Knorpelskelett n
chondrostibian Chondrostibian m (komplexes Sb-Oxid)
chondrule Chondrum n (kugeliges Mineralaggregat in Meteoriten und Mondgestein)
chonolith irregulärer Intrusionskörper m
chop Verwerfung f
choppy wirr, kleindimensional (Schrägschichtung)
~ sea Kreuzsee f
~ water surface gekräuselte Wasserfläche f
chorismite Chorismit m (Migmatit)
chott Schott m (Dünengebiet in der Sahara)
Christmas tree Produktionskreuz n, Eruptionskreuz n, Christbaum m (Bohrtechnik)
chromatic aberration Farbfehler m
~ deviation Farbabweichung f
~ property Farbeigenschaft f
~ spectrum Farbspektrum n
chromatite Chromatit m, $Ca[CrO_4]$
chromatography Chromatografie f
chrome Chrom n, Cr
~ garnet s. uvarovite
~ iron ore Chromeisenstein m, Chromit m (s.a. chromite)
~ ore Chromerz n
~ spinel Chromit m, Pikotit m, Chromeisenstein m (s.a. chromite)
chromic chromhaltig
chromiferous chromhaltig
chromite Chromit m, Chromeisenstein m, $FeCr_2O_4$
chromitite Chromit m (als massiges Erz)
chromium s. chrome
chromosol stark farbiger Boden m
chromosphere Chromosphäre f
chron Chron n (kleinste Einheit der chronologischen Skala)
chronogenesis Entwicklungsgeschichte f
chronolith zeitlich eingegrenzte Gesteinsabfolge f
chronology Chronologie f
chronometer Chronometer n
chronospecies Chronospezies f
chronostratigraphic[al] unit chronostratigrafische Einheit f (z.B. Äonothem, Ärathem, System, Serie, Stufe, Chronozone)

chronostratigraphy Chronostratigrafie f (künstliches Gliederungsschema der Erdgeschichte)
chrysoberyl Chrysoberyll m, Al_2BeO_4
chrysocolla Chrysokoll m, $Cu_4H_4[(OH)_8|Si_4O_{10}]$
chrysolite Chrysolith m (Olivin von Edelsteinqualität)
chrysomorph goldähnlich
chrysopal 1. s. chrysoberyl; 2. opalisierender Chrysolith m
chrysoprase Chrysopras m (s.a. chalcedony)
chrysotile Chrysotil m, kanadischer Asbest m
chrystocrene s. crystocrene
chuchrovite Chuchrovit m, $(Ca, Y, Ce)_3[(AlF_6)_2|SO_4] \cdot 10H_2O$
chuck 1. schmale Gezeitenrinne f; 2. schmaler Gezeitenstrom m; 3. Spannkopf m (einer Bohranlage)
chuco Calichelager n (Chile)
chudobaite Chudobait m, $(Na, K)(Mg, Zn)_2H[AsO_4]_2 \cdot 4H_2O$
chumbe (sl) s. sphalerite
chunck mineral Bleierzhaufwerk n
chunckie stones Fremdgesteinsgerölle in Kohleschichten
churchite Churchit m, $(Ce,Ca)(PO_4) \cdot 2H_2O$
churchyard Leichenfeld n, Schlachtfeld n
churn drill Seilschlagbohrgerät n
~ drill equipped for jet piercing Flammenstrahlbohrer m
~ drilling Seilschlagbohren n
churning Umrührung f
chute 1. Schurre f; 2. s. shoot of ore
~ bar Hochwasserbarren m (fluviatilen Ursprungs)
~ cut-off Flußverlagerung f an der Innenseite von Mäandern
Cl s. contour interval
cigar-shaped zigarrenförmig
ciminite Ciminit m (olivinführender Trachydolerit)
Cimmerian disturbance (folding, orogeny) kimmerische Faltung f
cimolite Cimolit m (Gemenge von Ton und Alunit)
Cincinnatian [Series] Cincinnatien n (oberes Caradoc und Ashgill in Nordamerika)
cinder Schlacke f
~ coal 1. Naturkoks m; 2. ausgeglühte Kohle f
~ cone Schlackenkegel m, Aschenkegel m
~ tip Halde f
~ wool s. mineral wool
cindery schlackig
cinerite Aschesediment n (vulkanisch)
cingulum Cingulum n, Basalwulst m, Äquatorleiste f (bei Sporomorphen; s.a. basalpib)
cinnabar Cinnabarit m, Zinnober m, HgS
cinnamite s. cinnamon stone
cinnamon-coloured soil zimtfarbener Boden m
~ stone Hessonit m (Granat)
cinnamonic soil zimtfarbener Boden m

cipolin 68

cipolin Zipolin *m (Kalkstein mit Glimmer)*
CIPW *Normsystem nach Cross, Iddings, Pirsson, Washington*
circalittoral äußeres Sublitoral *n*
circle jack Ratsche *f*
~ **of altitude** Höhenkreis *m*
~ **of compass** Teilkreis *m* am Kompaß, Stundenkreis *m*
~ **of latitude** Breitenkreis *m*
~ **of longitude** Längenkreis *m*
~ **of stress limit** Grenzspannungskreis *m*
circlet Kranz *m*
circular 1. kreisförmig, [kreis]rund; rundlich; 2. zirkulierend, umlaufend
~ **arc analysis** Gleitkreisuntersuchung *f*
~ **coal** Augenkohle *f*
~ **fold** Rundfalte *f*
~ **orbit** Kreisbahn *f*
~ **reef** Atoll *n*
~ **slip** Grundbruch *m*, Böschungsbruch *m*
~ **spirit level** Dosenlibelle *f*
~ **subsidence** Kesselbruch *m*
circularly polarized light zirkular polarisierendes Licht *n*
circulate/to zirkulieren
circulating head Spülkopf *m*
~ **pressure** Spülungsdruck *m*
~ **water** zirkulierendes (umlaufendes) Wasser *n*
circulation Zirkulation *f*, Kreisbewegung *f*, Kreislauf *m*, Umlauf *m*
~ **drilling** Spülbohren *n*
~ **of the atmosphere** Luftzirkulation *f*
~ **of the mud** Spülungsumlauf *m*
~ **time** Zirkulationsdauer *f (Bohrlochspülung)*
~ **with clear water** Klarwasserspülung *f*
~ **with mud** Dickspülung *f (Verfahren)*
circumboreal zirkumboreal
circumcontinental terrace *s.* continental shelf
circumference of the earth Erdumfang *m*
circumferential fault periphere Störung *f*
~ **speed** Umfangsgeschwindigkeit *f*
~ **wave** seismische Oberflächenwelle *f*
circumferentor [compass] Hängekompaß *m*; Zirkumferentor *m (Markscheidekunde)*
circumpacific volcanic belt zirkumpazifischer Vulkangürtel *m*
circumpolar zirkumpolar
circumsolar 1. die Sonne umgebend; 2. sich um die Sonne drehend
circus Kar *n (s.a.* cirque)
cirquation Karbildung *f*, Karerosion *f*, Zerkarung *f*
cirque Kar *n*
~ **cutting (erosion)** Karbildung *f*, Karerosion *f*, Zerkarung *f*
~ **floor** Karboden *m*
~ **glacier** Kargletscher *m*
~ **lake** Karsee *m*
~ **platform** Karterrasse *f*
~ **stairway (steps)** Kartreppe *f*
~ **threshold** Karschwelle *f*

cirriform zirrusartig
cirrolite Kirrolith *m*, $Ca_3Al_2[OH|PO_4]_3$
cirrus cloud Zirruswolke *f*
cislunar diesseits des Mondes
citrine Zitrin *m (s.a.* quartz)
cladgy, claggy dicht geklüftet *(Kohle)*
claim/to muten, Mutung einlegen
claim Bergwerksanspruch *m*, Mutung *f*
~ **map** Mutungskarte *f*, Grubenfeldriß *m*
claimholder Muter *m*
clammy zähe
clan Sippe *f*, Familie *f (Gestein)*
clarain Clarain *m*, Halbglanzkohle *f (Lithotyp der Humuskohlen; Steinkohle)*
Clarendonian [Stage] Clarendonien *n (Wirbeltierstufe des mittleren Miozäns in Nordamerika)*
clarification bed Klärbecken *n*
~ **plant** Kläranlage *f*
~ **tank** Klärbrunnen *m*
clarifier 1. Klärmittel *n*; 2. Klärbehälter *m*
clarify/to abklären, reinigen
clarite Clarit *m (Kohlenmikrolithotyp)*
Clarke value Clarke[wert] *m*
clarkeite Clarkeit *m*, $Na_2U_2O_7$
Clarkforkian [Stage] Clarkforkien *n (Wirbeltierstufe des Paläozons in Nordamerika)*
clarodurite Clarodurit *m (Kohlenmikrolithotyp)*
clarovitrinite Clarovitrinit *m (Kohlenmaceral)*
clasmoschist *s.* graywacke
clasolite klastisches Sediment *n*
claspers Klammerorgane *npl*
class/to klassifizieren
class Klasse *f*
~ **of ore** Erzgattung *f*, Erzsorte *f*
~ **of symmetry** Symmetrieklasse *f*
~ **100 room** Raum *m* mit weniger als 100 Partikel (> 5 μm) im Kubikmeter Luft
classical earth pressure theory orthodoxe Erddrucktheorie *f*
classification 1. Eingliederung *f*, Klasseneinteilung *f*, Klassenordnung *f*, Klassifikation *f*; 2. Setzungsklassierung *f*
~ **of reserves** Vorratsklassifikation *f*
~ **of rocks** Einteilung *f* der Gesteine
classifier Klassierer *m*
~ **efficiency** Trennungsgrad *m* von Klassierern
classify/to 1. klassifizieren, einteilen; 2. klassieren
classifying Klassierung *f*, Setzungsklassierung *f*
~ **screen** Klassiersieb *n*
~ **trough** Klassiertrog *m*
clast Klast *m*, Bruchstück *n*
clastation Gesteinszerkleinerung *f*
clastic klastisch
clastic Trümmergestein *n*
~ **accumulation** Trümmerablagerung *f*
~ **deposit** Trümmerlagerstätte *f*
~ **dike** sedimentärer Gang *m*
~ **discharges**, ~ **ejecta[menta]** Auswürflinge *mpl*

~ **iron-ore deposit** Eisentrümmerlagerstätte f
~ **lime tuff** klastischer Kalktuff m
~ **marl** Brockenmergel m
~ **products** Auswürflinge mpl
~ **ratio** Verhältnis klastisch zu nichtklastisch auf Lithofazieskarten
~ **reservoir rock** klastisches Speichergestein n
~ **rock** klastisches Gestein n, Trümmergestein n
~ **sediment** klastisches Sediment n
~ **sedimentary rocks** Trümmersedimente npl
clasto-crystalline klastokristallin
clastomorphic klastomorph
claudetite Claudetit m, As_2O_3
clausthalite Clausthalit m, Selenblei n, PbSe
clavate keulenförmig
clay/to mit Ton verschmieren
clay Ton m, Letten m
~-**and-salt crust** Salztonkruste f
~ **band** s. ~ ironstone
~ **bank** Tonschicht f
~ **base mud** Tonspülung f
~ **bed** Tonschicht f, Tonlage f; Tonlager n
~ **bond** Tonbindemittel n
~-**bond silica brick** tongebundener Dinasstein m
~-**containing river silt** toniger Flußschlick m
~-**containing silt** toniger Schlick m, schlickiger Ton m
~ **content** Tongehalt m
~ **course** s. ~ parting
~ **detritus held in suspension** Tontrübe f
~ **dinas brick** Tondinasstein m
~-**filled fissure** Lettenkluft f
~ **film** Tonüberzug m
~ **fraction** Tonanteil m
~ **gall** Tongalle f, Tonrolle f, eingerolltes Schlickgeröll n
~ **gouge** s. ~ parting
~ **grit** Sandmergel m
~ **ground** Tonboden m
~ **grouting** Toninjektion f
~ **gyttja** Tongyttja f
~ **hog** mit Ton gefüllte Flözauswaschung f
~-**humus complex** Humus-Ton-Komplex m
~ **ironstone** Toneisenstein m, Sphärosiderit m
~ **lens** Tonlinse f
~ **lenticule** Tongalle f
~ **loam** Tonlehm m
~ **marl** Tonmergel m, Schlier m
~ **mineral** Tonmineral n
~ **pan** verdichtete Tonschicht f
~ **parting** Tonzwischenlage f, Lettenbesteg m, Salband n
~ **pit** Tongrube f
~ **plug** Tonmuck m (in Mäanderschleifen)
~ **pocket** Tonnest n
~ **preparation** Tonaufbereitung f
~ **quarry** Tongrube f
~ **rock** toniges Gestein n, Tongestein n
~ **sand** tonhaltiger Sand m
~ **schist** Tonschiefer m

~ **shale** Schieferton m, Schieferletten m
~ **silty loam** toniger Schlufflehm m
~ **slate** Tonschiefer m
~ **slurry** Tonschlempe f
~ **soil** Lehmboden m
~ **stemming** Lettenbesatz m
~ **stone** erhärteter Ton m, Tonstein m
~ **szik soil** schwarzer Alkaliboden m, toniger Szik-Boden m
~ **till** Geschiebelehm m
~ **vein** Kamm (Tonrücken) m im Flöz
~ **wall** s. ~ parting
~ **with race** Ton m mit Kalkkonkretionen
clayat Torfdolomit m (mineralisierte, meist karbonatspatige Knolle im Kohlenflöz)
claycrete angewittertes Tongestein n (unter der Oberfläche)
clayey lehmhaltig, tonartig; lettenhaltig, lettig
~ **marl** Tonmergel m
~ **mud** Tonschlick m
~ **shale** Tonschiefer m
~ **soil** Tonboden m
~ **till** Geschiebelehm m
claying of a borehole Verletten n eines Bohrlochs
clayish tonig, lettig
claylike tonartig
claypan verdichtete Tonschicht f
clean/to 1. reinigen, abschlämmen, waschen (Aufbereitung); 2. beräumen (im Steinbruch)
~ **the hole** das Bohrloch klarspülen
clean[-cut] fracture glatter Bruch m
~ **ore** reines Erz n
~ **oil** reines (wasserfreies) Öl n
cleaned coal aufbereitete Kohle f, Reinkohle f
cleaning of coal Kohlenaufbereitung f
~ **of the borehole** Reinigen n des Bohrlochs
~ **plant** Aufbereitungsanlage f (für Kohle)
cleanse/to aufbereiten (Erze)
cleansing Aufbereitung f (von Erzen)
cleap s. cleat
clear/to aufwältigen (eine Strecke)
~ **a mine from water** eine Grube sümpfen
~ **away** forträumen
~ **off surface soil** Mutterboden entfernen
~ **out of** herauspräparieren
~ **the rock** vom tauben Gestein reinigen
~ **up** sich klären (Aufbereitung)
~ **up a mine** aufwältigen (eine Strecke)
clear and slightly stained völlig durchsichtig (Glimmerqualität)
~ **distance** lichte Weite f
clearance between casing and hole Ringraum m (zwischen Bohrloch und Rohrstrang)
~ **line** Umgrenzungslinie f
clearing 1. Klären n, Schlämmarbeit f (Aufbereitung); 2. Beräumungsarbeiten fpl (im Steinbruch)
~ **basin** Klärsumpf m, Klärbecken n
~ **of a river bed** Verlegung f eines Flußbetts
~-**out** Aufwältigung f (einer Strecke)
cleat Absonderungsfläche f, Ablösungsfläche f, Schichtfläche f

cleat

~ **direction** Schlechtenrichtung f
~ **plane** Absonderungsfläche f, Ablösungsfläche f, Schichtfläche f
cleavability Spaltbarkeit f (nach ebenen Flächen); Spaltfähigkeit f
cleavable spaltbar (nach ebenen Flächen)
cleavage Spaltbarkeit f (nach ebenen Flächen); Schieferung f (im engeren Sinne: Schieferung in nicht metamorphen Tongesteinen)
~ **angle** Spaltwinkel m
~ **arch** Sattelstellung f der Schieferung, Schieferungssattel m
~-**bedding intersection** Schnitt m von Schieferung und Schichtung
~ **brittleness** interkristalline Brüchigkeit f
~ **crack** Spaltriß m
~ **face** Spaltebene f, Spaltfläche f
~ **fan** Fächerstellung f der Schieferung, Schieferungsfächer m
~ **fissure** Spaltriß m
~ **form** Spaltform f
~ **fracture** Trennbruch m
~ **joint** Schieferungsfuge f
~ **line** Spaltriß m
~ **mullion** Schieferungsmullionstruktur f
~ **plane** Spaltebene f, Spaltfläche f, Schieferungsebene f, Schieferungsfläche f
~ **rhombohedron** Spalt[ungs]rhomboeder n
~ **strength** Spaltfestigkeit f
~ **surface** Spaltfläche f
~ **trough** Muldenstellung f der Schieferung, Schieferungsmulde f
cleavages Schlechten fpl
cleave/to aufspalten, [zer]spalten
~ **along** spalten nach
cleave Bergemittel n, Zwischenmittel n
cleaved geschiefert
cleavelandite Cleavelandit m (blättriger Albit)
cleaving 1. Klüftung f; 2. Ausspalten n (Pflasterstein)
~ **grain** Schichtfuge f
cledge obere Schicht f
cleek coal Rohkohle f
cleet s. cleat
cleft Riß m, Sprung m, Spalte f, Kluft f, Erdspalt m
clench/to abdichten
Clerici's solution Clerici-Lösung f
cleuch, cleugh Felsschlucht f, Wand f einer Schlucht (Schottland)
cleve steiler Berghang m
cleveite s. uraninite
clevelandite s. cleavelandite
cliff/to unterschneiden
cliff Kliff n, Steilrand m; Felswand f
~ **bank** Bergufer n (eines Flusses)
~ **chalk** Kliffkreide f
~ **cutting** Kliffbildung f
~ **dune** Kliffdüne f, Stufendüne f
~ **formation** Kliffbildung f
~-**forming** kliffbildend
~ **glacier** Hängegletscher m

~ **landslide** Kliffrutschung f
~-**marking** kliffbildend
~ **notch** Kliffkehle f
~ **of displacement** Verwerfungsstufe f
~ **overhang** Kliffüberhang m
~ **sapping** Rückverwitterung f
~ **wall** Steilwand f
cliffed kliffartig
~ **coast** Kliffküste f
cliffy felsig
clift 1. dünnschiefriger Schieferton m; 2. s. cliff
clifted felsig
cliftonite Cliftonit m (C in Meteoriten)
clifty felsig
climatal Klima... (s.a. climatic)
~ **change** Klimawechsel m
~ **fluctuation** Klimaschwankung f
~ **zone** Klimazone f
climate Klima n
~ **divide** Klimascheide f
~ **variation** Klimaänderung f
~ **zone** Klimazone f
climatic klimatisch (s.a. climatal)
~ **belt** Klimagürtel m
~ **change** Klimaänderung f
~ **chart** Klimakarte f
~ **conditions** Klimabedingungen fpl
~ **cycle** Klimaperiode f
~ **deterioration** Klimaverschlechterung f
~ **divide** Klimascheide f
~ **effects** Witterungseinflüsse mpl
~ **oscillation** Klimaschwankung f
~ **region** Klimagebiet n
~ **zone** Klimagürtel m
climatology Klimatologie f, Klimakunde f
climatophytic klimatophytisch
climax Klimax f, Virenzzeit f, Blütezeit f
climbing bog Klettermoor n
~ **ripples** kletternde Rippeln fpl
clime s. climate
cling kleiner Kalksteinausstrich m
clinker 1. schlackige Kohlenasche f; 2. ausgeschleudertes vulkanisches Material n
~ **field** Blocklavafeld n
clinkstone Klingstein m, Phonolith m
clinoaxis Klinoachse f
clinochlore Klinochlor m, $(Mg, Al)_6[(OH)_8|AlSi_3O_{10}]$
clinoclase 1. s. clinoclasite; 2. schräge Spaltebene f
clinoclasite Klinoklas m, Strahlerz n, Strahlenkupfer n, $Cu_3[(OH)_3|AsO_4]$
clinodome Klinodoma n
clinoedrite Klinoedrit m, $Ca_2Zn_2[(OH)_2|Si_2O_7] \cdot H_2O$
clinoenstatite Klinoenstatit m, $Mg_2[Si_2O_6]$
clinoferrosilite Klinoferrosilit m, $Fe_2[Si_2O_6]$
clinoforms Sammelbezeichnung für verschiedene marine Abhänge
clinograph Klinograf m, Neigungsschreiber m
clinohedrite s. clinoedrite

clinohumite Klinohumit m, $Mg_9[(OH,F)_2|(SiO_4)_4]$
clinohypersthene Klinohypersthen m, $(Mg, Fe)_2[Si_2O_6]$
clinometer Neigungsmesser m, Neigungsmeßgerät n
clinopinacoid Klinopinakoid n
clinostrengite Klinostrengit m, $Fe[PO_4]\cdot 2H_2O$
clinotherms Sammelbezeichnung für alle Sedimente, die an subaquatischen Hängen abgelagert wurden
clinounconformity Winkeldiskordanz f
clinoungemachite Klinoungemachit m, $K_3Na_8Fe[OH|(SO_4)_2]_3\cdot 9H_2O$
clinovariscite Klinovariscit m, $Al[PO_4]\cdot 2H_2O$
clinozoisite Klinozoisit m, $Ca_2Al_3[O|OH|SiO_4|Si_2O_7]$
clint zone Karrenzone f
Clinton Group Clinton-Gruppe f *(Wenlock in Nordamerika)*
~ **ore** Clinton-Erz n
clintonite Clintonit m, $Ca(Mg, Al)_{2-3}[(OH)_2|Al_2Si_2O_{10}]$
clints Karren pl, Schratten pl
clinunconformity s. clinounconformity
clipped verzerrt *(in der Wellenform)*
clives dünnschiefriger Schieferton m
clod Erdklumpen m, Scholle f; harter Lehm m
~ **clay** harter Letten (Lehm) m
~ **coal** lithologisch homogene Kohle f
~ **structure** Krümelstruktur f
clodded klumpig
cloddy schollig, klumpig, krümelig
clog/to hemmen, verstopfen, zusammenkleben, verschlämmen
~ **up pores** Poren verstopfen
clog snow nasser Neuschnee m
clogged [up] verstopft
clogging Inkrustierung f, Krustenbildung f *(Verstopfung der Brunnen)*
cloggy klumpig, klebrig
close a well in/to Förderbohrung absperren
close boiling hydrocarbons Kohlenwasserstoffe mpl mit dicht benachbarten Siedepunkten
~ **boring** dichtes Abbohren n *(eines Feldes)*
~-**coiled** engaufgerollt
~ **fault** geschlossene Verwerfung f
~ **foliation** falsche Schieferung f
~-**graded mineral aggregate** hohlraumarme Mineralmasse f
~-**grained** feinkörnig, dicht
~-**grained structure** dichtes (feinkörniges) Gefüge n
~-**in operation** Absperren n *(z.B. einer Fördersonde)*
~-**joint cleavage** s. fracture cleavage
~-**packed slip plane** dichtest gepackte Gleitebene f
~-**packed structure** dichteste Kugelpackung f
~ **sand** schwer durchlässiger Sand m
~-**set** naheliegend
~ **to the surface** oberflächennah[e]
~-**up view** Nahansicht f
closed anticline geschlossene Antiklinale f

~ **basin** Wanne f, geschlossenes Becken n, Kesseltal n
~-**basin topography** Wannenlandschaft f
~ **depression** geschlossene Vertiefung f
~ **drainage** abflußloses Gebiet n, geschlossene Wasserhaltung f
~ **fold** steile Falte f
~-**in bottom hole pressure** Bohrlochsohldruck m bei geschlossenem Schieber
~-**in pressure** hydrostatischer Druck m
~-**in well** geschlossene Sonde f
~ **marginal geosyncline** Geosynklinale f zwischen Kontinentalrand und Borderland
~ **reservoir** geschlossener Träger m, geschlossenes Trägergestein n
~ **structure** geschlossene Struktur f
closely coiled eng aufgerollt
~ **folded** stark (eng) gefaltet
~ **spaced** dicht geschart
closeness of fissures Kluftdichte f
closing Schließen n, Zusammenrücken n *(in der Plattentektonik)*
~ **error** Abschlußfehler m *(Vermessungskunde)*
~ **of an arm of the sea** Abschließung f eines Meeresarms
~ **pressure** Schließdruck m
~ **rate** Annäherungsgeschwindigkeit f
~-**up of the valley** Talzuschub m
closure 1. geschlossene Linie f *(Seismik);* 2. Querschnittsverminderung f, Zusammendrückung f; 3. Höhe f einer Antiklinale; 4. nutzbare Speicherhöhe f *(vom Überlaufpunkt bis Scheitelpunkt)*
~ **meter** Konvergenzmesser m
~ **of an anticline** vom tiefsten umlaufenden Streichen eingeschlossener Raum einer Antiklinale
~ **time of a well** Schließdauer f einer Bohrung
clot 1. Gerinnsel n; 2. Klumpen m, Krümel m; 3. Aggregation femischer Minerale in Magmatiten
~ **of lava** Lavaklumpen m
clotted klumpig
~ **texture** s. grumous texture
clotty klumpig
cloud Wolke f
~ **altimeter** Wolkenhöhenmesser m
~ **bank** Wolkenwand f, Wolkenbank f
~ **banner** Wolkenstreifen m
~ **base** untere Wolkengrenze f
~ **burst** Wolkenbruch m
~ **cap** Wolkenkappe f
~ **ceiling** Wolkenhöhe f
~ **ceilometer** Wolkenhöhenmesser m
~ **cover** Wolkendecke f
~ **curtain** Wolkenvorhang m
~ **dome** Wolkenkuppe f
~ **droplet** Nebeltropfen m
~ **flight** Wolkenflug m
~ **form** Wolkenform f
~ **formation** Wolkenbildung f; Bewölkung f
~ **gap** Wolkenloch n

cloud 72

- ~ **height** Wolkenhöhe f
- ~ **layer** Wolkenschicht f
- ~ **map** Bewölkungskarte f, Wolkenkarte f
- ~ **measurement** Wolkenmessung f
- ~ **motion** Wolkenzug m
- ~ **of haze** Dunstwolke f
- ~ **of vapour** Dampfwolke f
- ~ **reflector** Wolkenspiegel m
- ~ **shred** Wolkenfetzen m
- ~ **street** Wolkenstraße f
- ~ **train** Wolkenzug m
- ~ **trough** Wolkental n
- ~ **wave** Wolkenwelle f

cloudburst s. cloud burst
clouded 1. bewölkt, bedeckt, wolkig; 2. trübe *(bei Kristallen)*
cloudiness 1. Bewölkung f; 2. Trübheit f *(von Kristallen)*
clouding wolkige Zeichnung f *(von Marmor)*
cloudless wolkenlos
cloudy 1. bewölkt, bedeckt, wolkig; 2. trübe *(Edelsteine)*
- ~ **diamond** trüber Diamant m
- ~ **layer** Nebelschicht f
- ~ **texture** Trübung f *(bei Edelsteinen)*

clough kleine Schlucht f, Klunst f
clucking schaufelförmige, schalige Bruchfläche im Gestein
clunch 1. Hartton m *(eisenhaltig)*; 2. tonhaltiges Gestein n
- ~ **clay** harter Lehm m

clunchy tonhaltig
cluster 1. Haufen m, Schwarm m; Sternhaufen m; 2. durch Clusteranalyse erhaltene Klasse f von ähnlichen Objekten
- ~ **analysis** Clusteranalyse f *(mathematische Behandlung von Klassifizierungsproblemen)*
- ~ **crystal** Drusenkristall m
- ~ **drilling** Fächerbohrung f, Nestbohrung f
- ~ **of crystal** Kristalldruse f
- ~ **of veins** Gangschwarm m
- ~ **sampling** Aggregatprobenahme f *(Konzentration der Probenahme auf wenige, jeweils benachbarte Bereiche)*

clustered traubig
clusterite Höhlenperlen fpl; kleine glatte Kalzitkonkretionen fpl
clusters of exsolution Entmischungsspindeln fpl
Clymenia Limestone Clymenienkalk m *(höheres Oberdevon)*
CMG = International Union of Geophysical Sciences Commission for Marine Geology
coagulate/to koagulieren, gerinnen, ausflokken
- ~ **into lumps** ausflocken

coagulation Koagulation f, Ausflockung f
coagulum Gerinnsel m
Coahuila Supergroup Coahuila-Hauptgruppe f *(Valangin-Barrême, Nordamerika, Golf-Gebiet)*
coak s. coke
coal Kohle f

- ~ **apple (ball)** Torfdolomit m *(mineralisierte, meist karbonspatige Knolle im Kohlenflöz)*
- ~ **analysis** Kohlenanalyse f
- ~ **band** Kohlestreifen m, Kohleschmitz m
- ~ **basin** Kohlenbecken n
- ~-**bearing** kohleführend, kohlenhaltig; kohlehöffig; flözführend
- ~-**bearing formaton (rock)** kohleführender (kohlenhaltiger, flözführender) Schichtenkomplex m; flözführendes Gebirge n, Kohlengebirge n
- ~-**bearing sandstone** Kohlensandstein m
- ~ **bed** Kohlenschicht f; Kohlenlage f
- ~-**bed profile** *(Am)* Flözprofil n
- ~ **blossom** verwitterter Kohlenausstrich m
- ~ **brass** Pyriteinlagerung f *(in der Kohle)*
- ~ **breaking** Kohlenabbau m
- ~ **burst** Flözschlag m
- ~ **clay** s. fire clay
- ~ **deposit** Kohlenvorkommen n, Steinkohlenlager n
- ~ **district** Kohlengebiet n, Kohlenrevier n
- ~ **dressing** Kohlenaufbereitung f
- ~ **duns** Schieferlagen fpl im Kohlenflöz
- ~-**dust brick** Brikett n, Preßstein m, Kohlenpreßstein m
- ~ **facies** Kohlenfazies f
- ~ **field** Kohlenlagerstätte f; Kohlenrevier, Kohlengebiet n; Kohlenfeld n
- ~ **formation** 1. Kohlenbildung f; 2. Kohlenformation f *(stratigrafisch)*
- ~-**forming forest** Steinkohlenwald m
- ~-**forming plants** kohlenbildende Pflanzen fpl
- ~ **gas** Kohlengas n
- ~ **gasification** Kohlevergasung f
- ~ **getting** Kohlengewinnung f
- ~ **grit** Kohlensandstein m
- ~ **hydrogenation** Kohlehydrierung f
- ~ **layer** Kohlenschicht f; Kohlenlage f
- ~ **measures** 1. Kohlengebirge n, Kohlenschichten fpl, Kohlenlager n; 2. kohleführende Schichten des Karbons
- ~ **measures plant** s. ~ plant
- ~ **metals** kohleführende Schichten fpl *(Schottland)*
- ~-**mining region** Kohlenbergbaugebiet n
- ~ **mud** Kohlenschlamm m
- ~ **organic matter** kohlige Substanz f
- ~ **output** Kohlenförderung f
- ~ **pebble** Kohlengeröll n
- ~ **pillar** Kohlen[rest]pfeiler m
- ~ **pipe** kohliger Stammrest m *(ins Hangende des Flözes reichend)*
- ~ **plant** kohlebildendes Pflanzenfossil n
- ~ **preparation** Kohlenaufbereitung f
- ~ **prints** Kohlenhäutchen npl *(im Schiefer)*
- ~ **properties** Kohleneigenschaften fpl
- ~ **rake** *(sl)* Kohlenflöz n
- ~ **rash** tonig verunreinigte Kohle f
- ~ **region** Kohlengebiet n, Kohlenrevier n
- ~ **reserves** Kohlenvorräte mpl
- ~ **seam** Kohlenflöz n
- ~-**seam formation** Flözbildung f

~-seam gas content Gasgehalt m des Kohlenflözes
~ seat s. underclay
~ shale Kohlenschiefer m, Brandschiefer m
~ shed nichtbauwürdiges (geringmächtiges) Kohlenflöz n
~ shift Kohlengewinnungsschicht f
~ slate Kohlenschiefer m, Brandschiefer m
~ sludge Kohlenschlamm m
~ smits erdige Kohle f
~ smut Ausbiß m eines Kohlenflözes
~ strata Kohlenschichten fpl
~ streak Kohlenschmitz m
~ tar Kohlenteer m
~ vein Kohlenflöz n, Kohlenschicht f
~ washability Kohlenaufbereitbarkeit f (im Naßverfahren)
coalesce/to zusammenfließen, sich vereinigen; verschmelzen
coalescence Vereinigung f; Verschmelzung f; Zusammenwachsen n
coalescing Zusammenwachsen n
coalheugh Kohlenfundstelle f (Schottland)
coalification Inkohlung f
~ break Inkohlungsknick m
~ conditions Inkohlungsverhältnisse npl
~ jump Inkohlungssprung m
~ pattern Inkohlungsverhältnisse npl
~ process Inkohlungsprozeß m
~ section Inkohlungsprofil
~ stage Inkohlungsstadium n
coalified wood verkohltes Holz n
coaly kohlenartig; kohlig; kohlehaltig
~ facies Kohlenfazies f
~ rashings von Kohle durchsetzter Schiefer m
coarse adjustment Grobeinstellung f
~ aggregate grober Zuschlagstoff m
~-bedded grobgeschichtet
~ breaker s. ~ crusher
~ chalk Grobkreide f
~ conglomerate Grobkonglomerat n
~-crushed stone Grobschotter m
~ crusher Grobbrecher m, Schotterbrecher m
~ crushing Grobzerkleinerung f, Vorzerkleinerung f
~-crystalline grobkristallinisch
~ detrital organic mud Grobdetritus-Mudde f (bei Torfbildung in Mooren)
~-fibred grobfaserig
~-grained grobkörnig
~-grained sandstone grobkörniger Sandstein m
~ gravel Grobkies m (20–60mm Durchmesser)
~ limestone grobkörniger Kalkstein m
~ lode armer Gang m
~ ore Groberz n, Stückerz n
~-pebbled conglomerate Grobkonglomerat n
~-pored grobporig
~ radiolocation Grobortung f
~ reduction s. ~ crushing
~ sand Grobsand m (0,6–2mm Durchmesser)
~ sandstone Grobsandstein m

~ scanning Grobabtastung f
~ screen Grobrechen m (Abwasserwesen)
~ screening Grobsieben n, Grobsiebung f
~ silt grobes Schlämmkorn n
~ slurry Grobschlamm m
~ stone chip[ping]s Grobsplitt m
~-textured grobkörnig
coarsely bedded grobgeschichtet
~ brecciated grobbrekziös
~ clastic grobklastisch
~ crystalline grobkristallin
~ granular grobkörnig
~ interlayered bedding grobe Wechselschichtung f
~ porous grobporig
coarseness Grobkörnigkeit f
coast Küste f, Gestade n
~ defence zone Küstenschutzgebiet n
~ destruction Küstenzerstörung f
~ dune Küstendüne f
~ geodetic survey Küstenvermessung f
~ line Küstenlinie f
~ line with tidal flats Wattenküste f
~ of emergence Hebungsküste f
~ of submergence Senkungsküste f
~ protection Küstenschutz m
~ protection works Küstenschutzbauten mpl
~ range Küstengebirge n
~ slope Küstenabdachung f
~ survey Küstenaufnahme f
~ with tidal flats Wattenküste f
~ works Küstenschutzbauten mpl
coastal Küsten...
~ aquifer küstennaher Grundwasserleiter m
~ area Küstengebiet n
~ deposit Küstenablagerung f
~ desert Küstenwüste f
~ destruction Küstenzerstörung f
~ drifting Küstenversetzung f
~ dune Küstendüne f
~ engineering Küstenschutz m
~ facies Küstenfazies f
~ flooding Küstenüberschwemmung f
~ geodetic survey Küstenvermessung f
~ lake Strandsee m
~ line Küstenlinie f
~ lowland Küstenniederung f
~ mountain Küstengebirge n
~ placer deposit küstennahe Schwermineralagerstätte f
~ plain Küstenebene f
~ pool Strandsee m
~ protection Küstenschutz m
~ range Küstengebirge n
~ region Küstengebiet n
~ sebkha Küstensebkha f
~ slope Küstenabdachung f
~ stream Küstenströmung f, Uferströmung f
~ swamp Küstensumpf m
~ terrace Küstenterrasse f
~ territory Küstengebiet n
~ uplift Küstenhebung f
~ waters Küstengewässer npl

coasting

coasting Küstenlinie f
coat system Überzugsverfahren n
coated grains Rindenkörner npl (Körner mit konzentrischem Anlagerungsgefüge, z.B. Oolithe, Pisolithe)
coating Überzug m
~ **of ash** Aschendecke f
~ **of lava** Lavamantel m
coba lockeres Sediment unter den Nitratlagerstätten von Chile
cobalt Kobalt n, Co
~ **bloom** Kobaltblüte f (s.a. erythrite)
~ **glance** Kobaltglanz m (s.a. cobaltite)
~ **ochre** s. erythrite
~ **ore** Kobalterz n
~ **pyrites** s. linnaeite
Cobalt Kobalt n, Cobalt n (mittleres Huron in Nordamerika)
cobaltiferous kobalthaltig
cobaltine s. cobaltite
cobaltite Kobaltin m, Glanzkobalt m, Kobaltglanz m, CoAsS
cobaltocalcite Kobaltokalzit m, Sphärokobaltit m, $CoCO_3$
cobaltomenite Kobaltomenit m, Cobaltomenit m, $Co[SeO_3] \cdot 2H_2O$
cobbing Handscheidung f
cobble Feldstein m, Rollstein m
~ **gravel** Geröllkies m (64–256 mm Durchmesser)
cobbles 1. Stufferz n, Erzstufen fpl; 2. Grobkies m
cobblestone großer abgerundeter Stein m
cobbly soil steiniger Boden m
Coblenzian [Stage], Coblentzian [Stage] Ems n, Koblenz n (früher gebräuchliche Bezeichnung, höchste Stufe des Unterdevons)
coccinite Coccinit m, HgJ_2
coccolite Kokkolith m (Varietät von Diopsid)
coccospheres Coccosphären fpl
cocinerite Cocinerit m, Cu_4AgS
cockade formation Kokardenbildung f
~ **ore** Kokardenerz n, Ringelerz n
~ **texture** Kokardenstruktur f
cockle Schörl m, schwarzer Turmalin m
cockpit 1. Tagesbruch m, Erdfall m (Karstform aus Trichterdolinen mit zwischengelagerten Spitzkegeln); 2. steilflankiger Kegelberg m
~ **country** Dolinenkarst m
~ **karst area** Kegelkarstgebiet n
~ **landscape** Dolinenkarst m
~ **topography** reife Karstlandschaft f
cockschute silifizierte Einlagerung in den Kohlenlagern von Wales
cockscomb pyrite Kammkies m (s.a. marcasite)
codazzite Codazzit m (Gemenge von Ankerit und Parisit)
coefficient of bulk increase Schüttungszahl f
~ **of compaction** Verdichtungskoeffizient m
~ **of consolidation** Verfestigungsbeiwert m
~ **of discharge** Abflußkoeffizient m; Entlastungskoeffizient m

~ **of dissociation** Dissoziationsgrad m
~ **of dynamic viscosity** Zähigkeitskoeffizient m
~ **of earth pressure** Erddruckkoeffizient m
~ **of elastic recovery** Schwellwert m
~ **of expansion** Ausdehnungskoeffizient m
~ **of friction** Reibungskoeffizient m, Reibungsbeiwert m
~ **of hydraulic conductivity** Durchlässigkeitsbeiwert m
~ **of internal friction** Zähigkeitskoeffizient m
~ **of intrinsic permeability** Durchlässigkeit f für Wasser
~ **of performance** Nutzeffekt m
~ **of permeability** Durchlässigkeitsbeiwert m
~ **of rainfall** Niederschlaghöhe f, Niederschlagkoeffizient m
~ **of resistance** Festigkeitskoeffizient m (eines Gesteins)
~ **of rigidity** Steifigkeitskoeffizient m, Steifigkeitszahl f
~ **of roughness** Rauhigkeitskoeffizient m
~ **of runoff** Abflußkoeffizient m, Abflußbeiwert m
~ **of soil reaction** Bettungsziffer f
~ **of uniformity** Gleichförmigkeitskoeffizient m
coelenteron Leibeshöhle f
coelestine s. celestite
coenosteum Coenosteum n, Coenenchym n (Skelettmaterial bei Korallen und Bryozoen)
coercive force Koerzitivkraft f
coercivity Koerzitivkraft f
coeruleolactite Coeruleolaktit m, $CaAl_6[(OH)_2|PO_4]_4 \cdot 4H_2O$
coesite Coesit m, SiO_2 (monoklin)
coeval gleichaltrig
coevolution Koevolution f
coexisting minerals koexistierende (im stabilen Gleichgewicht befindliche) Minerale npl
coffer/to abdichten (z.B. einen untertägigen Wasserzufluß im Gebirge)
cofferdam Fangdamm m
coffin strossenförmiger Tagebau m
coffinite Coffinit m, $U[SiO_4]$
cog Gesteinsgang m
cognate inclusion (xenolith) s. autolith
cohenite Cohenit m, Cementit m, Fe_3C
coherence Kohärenz f
coherent optical processing kohärente optische Bearbeitung (Bildbearbeitung) f (z.B. von Radaraufnahmen)
cohesion Kohäsion f, Bindigkeit f
cohesional coefficient Kohäsionsfaktor m
~ **resistance** Haftfestigkeit f
cohesionless kohäsionslos, nichtbindig
~ **soil** nichtbindiger Boden m
cohesive kohäsiv, bindig (Boden)
~ **attraction** Kohäsion f
~ **water** Adhäsionswasser n
cohesiveness Kohäsion f, Bindigkeit f
Cohoctonian [Stage] Cohocton[ien] n (Stufe des oberen Frasne in Nordamerika)
coil up/to sich zusammenrollen (Trilobiten)
coiled gewunden, aufgerollt

coke/to verkoken
coke Koks *m*
~ **formation** Koksbildung *f*
~ **strength** Koksfestigkeit *f*
cokeite Naturkoks *m*
coking Verkoken *n*, Verkokung *f*
~ **capacity** Koksbildungsvermögen *n*
~ **coal** Kokskohle *f*
~ **plant** Kokerei *f*
~ **properties** Verkokungseigenschaften *fpl*, Verkokungsverhalten *n*, Koksbildungsvermögen *n*
col Gebirgspaß *m*
~-**fed glacier** Subtyp eines „drift glacier"
cold desert winterkalte Wüste *f*
~ **front** Kaltluftfront *f*
~ **front squall** Frontbö *f*
~ **fumarole** reine Wasserdampffumarole *f*
~ **lahar** Mure *f*, Murbruch *m*, Schlammstrom *m*
~ **loess** glazialen Auswaschungen entstammender Löß *m*
~ **pole** Kältepol *m*
~ **spring** kalte Quelle *f*
~ **wave** Kältewelle *f*, Kaltlufteinbruch *m*
~ **work** Kaltverformung *f*
colemanite Colemanit *m*, Ca[B$_3$O$_4$(OH)$_3$]·H$_2$O
colina *s.* colline
colinear gleichlaufend
collapse/to einstürzen, zu Bruch gehen
collapse Einsturz *m*, Verbrauch *m*
~ **breccia** Einsturzbrekzie *f*, Karstbrekzie *f*
~ **caldera** Einbruchkaldera *f*, Einsturzkaldera *f*
~ **dolina** Einsturzdoline *f*
~ **of [the] casing** Eindrücken (Einbeulen) *n* der Verrohrung, Futterrohreinbeulung *f*
~ **sink** Einsturzdoline *f*
~ **structure** Rutschungsstruktur *f*
~ **valley** Einsturztal *n*
collapsed eingesunken
~ **roof** Hangendbruch *m*
collapsing mast Klappmast *m*
collar Bohrlochmund *m*
collecting basin Nährgebiet *n* (*z.B. eines Gletschers*)
~ **channel** Sammelkanal *m*
~ **locality (place)** Fundort *m*
collection Sammlung *f*
~ **of minerals** Mineraliensammlung *f*
~ **of samples** Probensammlung *f*
colliery Kohlengrube *f*, Kohlenzeche *f*, Steinkohlenbergwerk *n*, Zeche *f*
colline kleine Erhebung *f*, Hügel *m*
collinite Collinit *m* (*Kohlenmaceral der Vitringruppe*)
collinsite Collinsit *m*, Ca$_2$(Mg, Fe)[PO$_4$]$_2$·2H$_2$O
collision Kollision *f*, Zusammenstoß *m* (*Plattentektonik*)
colloform texture Kolloidalstruktur *f*
colloid[al] kolloidal
~ **form** kolloidale Form *f*
~ **material** Kolloidsubstanz *f*
~ **minerals** Kolloidminerale *npl*

~ **properties of coal** kolloidale Eigenschaften *fpl* von Kohlen
~ **state** Kolloidalzustand *m*
collophane Kollophan *m* (*CO$_3$-haltiger Apatit*)
colluvial kolluvial, zusammengeschwemmt
~ **accumulations** Schwemmland *n*
~ **deposits** Gesteinsschutt *m*, Gehängeschutt *m*
~ **mantle rock** kolluvialer Verwitterungsschutt *m*
~ **soil** Kolluvialboden *m*, Absatzboden *m*, Anschwemmungsboden *m*
colluvium Kolluvium *n*, Zusammenschwemmung *f*
colmatage, colmation Kolmatage *f*, Kolmation *f*, Aufschwemmung *f* von Erde, Auflandung *f*
colonial coral koloniebildende Koralle *f*
~ **organism** koloniebildendes Lebewesen *n*
colonization Besiedlung *f*
colonnade Säulenbildung *f* (*z.B. im liegenden Teil eines Lavastroms*)
colophony Kolophonium *n*
Colorado [Stage], Coloradoan [Stage] mittlere Oberkreide in Nordamerika
coloradoite Coloradoit *m*, HgTe
coloration Färbung *f*
colorimetric density Farbdichte *f*
colorimetry Kolorimetrie *f*
colour aerial film Luftfarbfilm *m*
~ **analysis** Farbanalyse *f*
~ **comparison** Farbenvergleich *m*
~ **dilution method** Farbversuch *m* (*Tracer*)
~ **enhancement** Farbverstärkung *f*
~ **filter** Farbfilter *n*
~ **index** Farbzahl *f*
~ **measurement** Farbwertbestimmung *f*
~ **scale** Farbenskala *f*
coloured clay Farberde *f*
~ **display** Farbabspielung *f*
colourless farblos
columbite Columbit *m*, Niobit *m*, (Fe, Mn) (Nb, Ta)$_2$O$_6$
columbium Niob[ium] *n*, Nb
column 1. Säule *f*, Kolonne *f*; 2. Schichtenfolge *f*
~ **of fluid** Flüssigkeitssäule *f*
~ **of formations** Formationsfolge *f*, Schichtenfolge *f*
~ **of liquid** Flüssigkeitssäule *f*
~ **of mud** Spülungssäule *f*
~ **of ore** Erzschnur *f*
~ **of steam (vapour)** Dampfsäule *f*
~ **of water** Wassersäule *f*
~-**shaped** säulenförmig
columnar stengelig, säulig
~ **aggregate** Säulenaggregat *n*
~ **basalt** Säulenbasalt *m*
~ **coal** Säulenkohle *f* (*an thermischen Kontakten*)
~ **habitus** säuliger Habitus *m*
~ **jointing** säulenförmige Absonderung *f*
~ **section** geologisches Normalprofil *n*
~ **structure** Säulentextur *f*

colusite

colusite Colusit *m*, $Cu_3(Fe, As, Sn)S_4$
comagmatic komagmatisch
~ **family of rocks** komagmatische Gesteinsfamilie *f (dem gleichen Muttermagma entstammend)*
~ **province** komagmatische Gesteinsprovinz *f*
~ **rock** komagmatisches Gestein *n*
Comanche Supergroup Comanche-Hauptgruppe *f (Apt und Alb in Nordamerika)*
comb texture Kammstruktur *f*
combe Talmulde *f*; Senkung *f*
combed vein *s.* banded vein
combeite Combeit *m*, $Na_4Ca_3[Si_6O_{16}(OH,F)_2]$
comber sich überschlagende Welle *f (Brandung)*
combination Verwachsung *f (von Zwillingskristallen)*
~ **avalanche** Lawine *f* aus verschiedenen Schneesorten
~ **gas** feuchtes Erdgas *n*, Naßgas *n*
~ **system of drilling** kombiniertes Bohren *n*
~ **trap** Kombinationsfalle *f (für Kohlenwasserstoffe)*
combined mine drainage kombinierte Grubenentwässerung *f*
~ **pieces of coal and shale** verwachsene Kohle *f*
~ **pore water** haftendes Porenwasser *n*
~ **rotation and reflection** Drehspiegelung *f*
~ **shrinkage and caving method** Etagen- und Firstenbruchbau *m*
~ **stress** zusammengesetzte Beanspruchung *f*
~ **water** chemisch gebundenes Wasser *n*
combing wave sich überschlagende Welle *f (Brandung)*
combining weight Verbindungsgewicht *n*
comblike crest Grat *m*
~ **ridge** Zackengrat *m*
combustibility Brennbarkeit *f*
combustible brennbar, entzündlich
combustible Brennstoff *m*, Heizmaterial *n*
~ **gas** brennbares (entzündliches) Gas *n*
~ **shale** brennbarer Schiefer *m*; Brennschiefer *m*
combustion fuel Heizöl *n*
~ **metamorphism** Erdbrandmetamorphose *f*
~ **rock** Erdbrandgestein *n*
come into production/to fündig werden *(Erdölsonden)*
~ **out of solution** entlösen; frei werden
~ **out to the day** zu Tage ausstreichen
~ **up to daylight** zu Tage ausstreichen
~ **up to the grass** ausblühen, ausgehen, ausbeißen, zutage treten *(Lagerstätten)*
come water normaler (regelmäßiger) Wasserzufluß *m (in eine Grube)*
comendite Comendit *m (Alkalirhyolith)*
comet Komet *m*
~ **trace** Kometenschweif *m*
cometary kometenartig, Kometen...
~ **nucleus** Kometenkern *m*
~ **orbit** Kometenbahn *f*
cometography Kometografie *f*

Comleyan [Stage] Unterkambrium *in Nordamerika*
commencement of drilling Bohrbeginn *m*
~ **of production** Förderbeginn *m*
commercial cave Schauhöhle *f*
~ **producer** wirtschaftlich fördernde Bohrung *f*
~ **production** wirtschaftlich lohnende Produktion *f*
~ **quantity** wirtschaftlich nutzbare Menge *f*
~ **reserves** bauwürdige Vorräte *mpl*
commercially valuable wirtschaftlich verwertbar
comminuted feinzerrieben, locker
comminution Zerkleinerung *f*
~ **of the rock** Zerkleinerung *f* des Gesteins
common depth point gemeinsamer Tiefenpunkt *m (Seismik)*
~ **depth point shooting** Schießen *n* in Bezug auf den gleichen Reflexionspunkt, Mehrfachüberdeckung *f (Seismik)*
~ **depth point stack[ing]** Stapelung *f* für einen gemeinsamen Tiefenpunkt *(Seismik)*
~ **factor** gemeinsamer (allgemeiner) Faktor *m*
~ **limb** Mittelschenkel *m*
~ **mica** *s.* muscovite
~ **opal** gemeiner Opal *m*
~ **quartz** gemeiner Quarz *m*
~ **range gathering** Aufstellung der zu stapelnden Spuren nach gleichen Entfernungsbereichen *(Seismik)*
~ **reflection point** gemeinsamer Reflexionspunkt *m*
~ **salt** *s.* halite
communality Kommunalität *f (Grad der Verbundenheit eines Merkmals mit den durch die Faktoranalyse extrahierten Faktoren)*
communications satellite Nachrichtensatellit *m*
community boundaries Grenzen *fpl* der Vergesellschaftungen *(von Organismen)*
compact dicht
~ **apparatus** Verdichtungsgerät *n (Bodenprüfung)*
~ **gypsum** massiges Gipsgestein *n*
~ **limestone** Massenkalk *m*, dichter Kalkstein *m*
~ **polishable limestone** dichter polierfähiger Marmor *m*
~ **rock** kompaktes (dichtes) Gestein *n*
~ **rocks** Massengestein *n*, standfestes Gebirge *n*
~ **soil** fester Boden *m*
compacted limestone Massenkalk *m*, dichter Kalkstein *m*
~ **rocks** Massengestein *n*, standfestes Gebirge *n*
compactibility Verdichtbarkeit *f*, Verdichtungsfähigkeit *f*
compacting pressure Differenz zwischen hydrostatischem und Überlagerungsdruck
~ **sediment** sich verdichtendes Sediment *n*
compaction 1. Verdichtung *f*; 2. Kompaktion *f*, Sedimentverfestigung *f*

~ **equipment** Verdichtungsmaschinen *fpl*
~ **factor** Verfestigungsfaktor *m*
~ **of sediments with increasing load** Verdichtung *f* der Sedimente mit zunehmender Belastung
~ **pressure** Gebirgsdruck *m*
~ **roller** Verdichtungswalze *f*, Bodenverfestigungswalze *f*
~ **shale** durch Kompaktion verfestigter Schiefer *m*
compactness Kompaktheit *f*, Dichtigkeit *f*, Festigkeit *f*, Massivität *f*, Lagerungsdichte *f*
compactor Verdichtungswalze *f*, Bodenverfestigungswalze *f*
companion Begleiter *m* *(von Erzen)*
~ **fault** Nebenverwerfung *f*
company geologist Werksgeologe *m*
comparison test Vergleichsprobe *f*, Parallelprobe *f*
compartment Trum *m (n)*
compass Kompaß *m*
~ **bearing** Kompaßpeilung *f*
~ **card** Kompaßrose *f*, Windrose *f*
~ **declination** Kompaßabweichung *f*
~ **direction** Kompaßrichtung *f*
~ **error** Mißweisung *f*
~ **needle** Kompaßnadel *f*
~ **point** Himmelsrichtung *f*
~ **traverse** Kompaßzug *m*
compatibility Verträglichkeit *f*, Vereinbarkeit *f*, Vergleichbarkeit *f (z.B. von Daten)*
compatible verträglich, vereinbar, passend
~ **data** verträgliche Daten *pl*
~ **element** kompatibles Element *n (einem bestimmten chemischen System zugehörig)*
~ **phases** koexistierende Phasen *fpl*, miteinander im Gleichgewicht stehende Mineralphasen *fpl*
compensation Ausgleichszahlung *f (bei geologischen Untersuchungsarbeiten)*
~ **level** Ausgleichsfläche *f*
~ **masses** Kompensationsmassen *fpl*
compensator Kompensator *m*
competence, competency Grenzgröße eines Sedimentkorns bekannter Dichte, bei der durch Strömung Transport eintritt
competent kompetent
~ **bed** kompetente Schicht *f*
~ **fold** Parallelfalte *f*, konzentrische Falte *f*
~ **stratum** unnachgiebige Schicht *f*
compile a subsurface map of the key bed/to eine Tiefenlinienkarte der Leitschicht herstellen
complement Komplement *n (Ergänzung eines Werts zur Skaleneinheit)*
complementarity Komplementarität *f*, Ergänzbarkeit *f (z.B. von Fernerkundungsdaten)*
complementary remote sensing systems sich ergänzende Fernerkundungssysteme *npl*
complete a well/to eine Bohrung fertigstellen (zur Förderung vorbereiten)
complete melting [vollständige] Aufschmelzung *f*

~ **miscibility** vollständige Mischbarkeit *f*
~ **well** vollkommener Brunnen *m*
completion 1. Komplettierung *f (einer Sonde);* 2. Inproduktionssetzung *f*
~ **[work] of an oil well** Fertigstellung *f* einer Erdölbohrung zur Förderung
complex curve Komplexkurve *f*
~ **fault** zusammengesetzte Verwerfung *f*
~ **fold** quergefaltete Falte *f*
~ **gravitational crystallization differentiation** komplexe gravitative Kristallisationsdifferentiation *f*
~ **interpretation** Komplexinterpretation *f*, Komplexauswertung *f (z.B. von geophysikalischen Daten)*
~ **line** Komplexlinie *f*
~ **ore** Komplexerz *n*
~ **plane** Komplexebene *f*
~ **point** Komplexpunkt *m*
~ **space** Komplexraum *m*
~ **targets** komplex zusammengesetzte Objekte *npl (Fernerkundung)*
~ **utilization of mineral raw materials** komplexe Nutzung *f* mineralischer Rohstoffe
component Bestandteil *m*
~ **mineral** Bestandmineral *n*
~ **of gravity** Schwerkraftkomponente *f*
~ **of movement** Bewegungskomponente *f*
componental mobility Teilbeweglichkeit *f*
composite zusammengesetzt
~ **anticline** zusammengesetzte Antiklinale *f*
~ **boundary** Verwachsungsebene verschieden orientierter Kristalle, die keiner Kristallfläche entspricht
~ **cone** Stratovulkan *m*
~ **dike** zusammengesetzter Gang *m*, Gang *m* mit zeitverschiedenen Füllungen
~ **fan structure** Antiklinorium *n*
~ **fold** Falte *f* mit gefältelten Schenkeln
~ **gneiss** s. injection gneiss
~ **grain** Verwachsung mehrerer Körner mit Anlagerungsgefügen
~ **mobile belt** Orogen *n* aus mehreren parallelen Geosynklinaltrögen
~ **sample** Sammelprobe *f*, Mischprobe *f*
~ **seam** zusammengesetztes Flöz *n (durch Auskeilen von Zwischenmitteln)*
~ **section** Sammelprofil *n*
~ **sill** zusammengesetzter Lagergang *m*
~ **stream** zusammengesetzter Fluß *m*
~ **travel time curve** zusammengesetzte (gegengeschossene) Laufzeitkurve *f*
~ **unconformity of erosion** mehrfache Erosionsdiskordanz *f*
~ **veins** Scharung *f* der Gangtrümer, Gangschwarm *m*
composition Zusammensetzung *f*
~ **face** *s.* ~ plane
~ **of the ground** Bodenbeschaffenheit *f*
~ **plane (surface)** Verwachsungsfläche *f (von Kristallen)*
compound zusammengesetzt

compound

compound 1. Zusammensetzung *f*; 2. [chemische] Verbindung *f*
- **~ arch** Antiklinorium *n*
- **~ cirque** Großkar *n*
- **~ crystal** Zwillingskristall *m*
- **~ eyes** Komplexaugen *npl (Arthropoda)*
- **~ fault** zusammengesetzte Verwerfung *f*, Verwerfungsbüschel *n*
- **~ foreset bedding** zusammengesetzte Leeblattschichtung *f*
- **~ of alumina** Tonerdeverbindung *f*
- **~ pellet** *Pellet mit mikritischem oder sparitischem Zement*
- **~ ripple marks** zusammengesetzte Rippelmarken *fpl*
- **~ slide** Kreuzschlitten *m*
- **~ stratification** Schichtung *f* parallel zur liegenden Erosionsbasis
- **~ stream** komplexer Fluß *m*
- **~ twins** Viellinge *mpl*
- **~ valley glacier** Gletscher *m* aus mehreren Zuströmen
- **~ vein** 1. Gangtrumzone *f*; 2. Gang *m* aus verschiedenen Mineralen, Polymetallerzgang *m*

compreignacite Compreignacit *m*, $6[UO_2|(OH)_2]\cdot 2K(OH)\cdot 4H_2O$
compress/to zusammendrücken, zusammenpressen, komprimieren
compressed-air drill Preßluftbohrer *m*
~-air hammer drill Preßluftbohrhammer *m*
~-air storage Preßluftspeicher *m*
~ fold Quetschfalte *f*
compressibility Kompressibilität *f*; Zusammendrückbarkeit *f*, Komprimierbarkeit *f*
- **~ of gases** Zusammendrückbarkeit *f* von Gasen

compressible zusammendrückbar, komprimierbar
compressing zone Pressungsgebiet *n*
compression Zusammendrückung *f*, Pressung *f*, Kompression *f*, Verdichtung *f*, Stauchung *f*, Zusammenschub *m*
- **~ equipment** Verdichtungsmaschinen *fpl*
- **~ fault** Konjunktivbruch *m*
- **~ joint** Druckspalte *f*
- **~ of ground (soil)** Bodendruckpressung *f*
- **~ test** Druckversuch *m*
- **~-test specimen** Druckprobe *f*, Druckprobekörper *m*
- **~ wave** Kompressionswelle *f*, Druckwelle *f*
- **~ zone** Druckzone *f*

compressional deformation Druckmetamorphose *f*
- **~ folding** Druckfaltung *f*
- **~ joint** Druckspalte *f*
- **~ wave** *s.* longitudinal wave

compressive force zusammendrückende Kraft *f* (z. B. einer Faltung)
- **~ mass strength** Gebirgsdruckfestigkeit *f*
- **~ strain** Druckbeanspruchung *f*
- **~ strength** Druckfestigkeit *f*
- **~ strength test** Druckprüfung *f*

- **~ stress** Druckspannung *f*
- **~ twin formation** Druckzwillingsbildung *f*
- **~ yield strength** Kriechgrenze *f*

compromise boundaries korrespondierende Grenzen (Korngrenzen) *fpl*, verzahnte Grenzen (Korngrenzen) *fpl*
computation of area Flächenberechnung *f*
computer compatible tape rechnerkompatibles Band *n*
computing Auswertung *f*
conarite *s.* connarite
conca Oberflächensenkung *f (durch Magmenausfluß)*
concave bank Unterschneidungshang *m*
- **~ cross-bedding, ~ inclined bedding** bogige Schrägschichtung *f*
- **~ grinding** Hohlschliff *m*

concealed verdeckt, verborgen *(vom Ausgehenden einer Lagerstätte)*
- **~ bed of peat** Torffeinschluß *m*, Torfnest *n*
- **~ erosion** Suberosion *f*, verdeckte Erosion *f*
- **~ outcrop** verstecktes Ausgehendes *n*

concentrate/to anreichern, aufbereiten
- **~ brine** gradieren

concentrate Konzentrat *n*, Anreicherungsprodukt *n*, Reingut *n*; Schlich *m*
- **~ of ore** Erzschlich *m*

concentrating ore Anreicherungserz *n*
- **~ plant** Aufbereitungsanlage *f*, Anreicherungsanlage *f*

concentration Anreicherung *f*, Aufbereitung *f*
- **~ front** Konzentrationsfront *f*
- **~ of mass** Massekonzentration *f*
- **~ of stress** Spannungsanreicherung *f*
- **~ of volume** Volumenkonzentration *f*
- **~ plant** Aufbereitungsanlage *f*, Anreicherungsanlage *f*
- **~ process** Konzentrationsvorgang *m*
- **~ table** Aufbereitungsherd *m*

concentrator Setzkasten *m*
concentric[al] fold konzentrische Falte *f*, Parallelfalte *f*
- **~ fractures** konzentrisches Bruchbild *n*
- **~ jointing** konzentrischschalige (zwiebelschalige) Absonderung *f*, Zwiebelstruktur *f*
- **~ rift** Ringspalte *f*
- **~ weathering** kugelige Verwitterungsformen *fpl*

concertina fold Staffelfalte *f (s.a. zigzag fold)*
concession Konzession *f*, Erlaubnis *f*, Mutung *f*
- **~ for exploration and exploitation** Konzession *f* zur Erforschung und Ausbeutung
- **~ plan** Mutungskarte *f*

concession[n]aire Konzessionsinhaber *m*
conch Schale *f*, Gehäuse *n (bei Gastropoden und Cephalopoden)*
conchiform muschelförmig
conchoidal muschelig
- **~ fracture** muscheliger Bruch *m*

conchology Muschelkunde *f*
conchylium Schneckenschale *f*
concomitant begleitend, gleichzeitig

confluence

concordance Konkordanz f
concordant konkordant, gleichsinnig schichtparallel
~ **bedding** konkordante Schichtung f
~ **injection** konkordante Intrusion f
concrement Konkretion f, Zusammenballung f
concrete aggregate Betonzuschlagstoffe mpl
~-**attacking substance** betonangreifender Stoff m
~ **dam** Staumauer f, Talsperrenmauer f
concretion Konkretion f, Verhärtung f
~ **of anhydrite** Anhydritknolle f
concretionary konkretionär
~ **granite** Kugelgranit m
~ **horizon** verfestigte Schicht f
condensability Verdichtbarkeit f
condensate field Kondensatlagerstätte f
~ **production** Kondensatförderung f
condensation Kondensation f
~ **centre** Kondensationskern m
~ **moisture** Niederschlagen n von Feuchtigkeit
~ **trail** Kondensstreifen m
~ **water** Schwitzwasser n, Kondenswasser n; Kondensationswasser n
condensational waves Verdichtungswellen fpl
condense/to sich kondensieren
condensed deposit kondensierte Sedimentation f (langsame, aber nicht unterbrochene Sedimentation)
~ **sequence** Kondensationslager n (geringmächtiger Gesteinskörper, in dem verschieden alte Faunen nicht trennbar nebeneinander liegen)
condensing lens Sammellinse f
condition for deposits Lagerstättenkondition f
~ **of existence** Existenzbedingung f (Paläobiologie)
~ **of flow** Durchflußbedingung f
~ **of instability** Instabilitätsbedingung f (Grundwasserströmung)
~ **of soil** Bodenbeschaffenheit f
~ **of stress** Spannungszustand m
conditions Konditionen fpl (z.B. der Grundwassererkundung)
conductance Leitfähigkeit f
conductimetry Leitfähigkeitsmessung f
~ **nducting power** Leitfähigkeit f, Leitungsvermögen n
conduction Leitung f; Leitfähigkeit f
conductive body leitender Körper m
conductivity Leitfähigkeit f, Leitungsvermögen n
~ **horizon** Leitfähigkeitsgrenze f
~ **logging** Leitfähigkeitsmessung f
conductor casing Standrohr n
~ **of electricity** elektrischer Leiter m
~ **of heat** Wärmeleiter m
~ **pipe** Leitrohrtour f, erste Rohrfahrt f, Standrohr n
~ **shaft** Vorbohrloch n
~ **string** s. ~ pipe

conduit Wasserseige f; Wasserrösche f
~ **of vulcano** Vulkanschlot m, Förderschlot m, Schußkanal m
condyle Gelenkkopf m (Paläontologie)
cone 1. Bergkegel m, Konus m; Vulkankegel m; 2. Zapfen m, Fruchtzapfen m
~ **bit** Kegelrollenmeißel m
~ **crusher** Kegelbrecher m
~ **cup** Innenform der Tutenstrukturen
~ **delta** Alluvion an der Mündung von Gebirgsströmen
~-**in-cone coal** Tutenkohle f
~-**in-cone limestone** Tutenmergel m, Nagelkalk m, Tütenmergel m, Dütenmergel m
~-**in-cone structure** Tutenmergelstruktur f, Nagelkalkstruktur f
~-**in-crater structure** Doppelvulkan m
~ **of blast** Sprengkegel m
~ **of debris** Schuttkegel m
~ **of dejection** Alluvialkegel m
~ **of depression** Absenkungstrichter m, Senkungstrichter m, Entnahmetrichter m
~ **of detritus** Alluvialkegel m
~ **of influence** s. ~ of depression
~ **of light** Beleuchtungskegel m
~ **of pressure relief,** ~ **of pumping depression** s. ~ of depression
~ **of talus** Schuttkegel m
~ **of waterable depression** s. ~ of depression
~ **penetration test** Kegeldruckversuch m
~-**shaped** kegelig, kegelförmig
~ **sheets** Kegelspalten fpl (Vulkanotektonik)
conelike kegelförmig
Conewangoan [Stage] Conewangoan n (Stufe des Oberdevons in Nordamerika)
Conferva peat Torf m aus Süßwasseralgen
configuration Oberflächengestaltung f; Struktur f
~ **of coast** Küstengestaltung f
~ **of ground** Geländegestaltung f, Geländeform f
~ **of soil** Bodengestaltung f
configurational energy Gitterenergie f
confined gespannt (bei Grundwasser)
~ **aquifer** gespannter Grundwasserspeicher m
~ **flow** Fließen n von gespanntem Grundwasser
~ **ground air** gespannte Grundluft m
~ **ground water** gespanntes (artesisches) Grundwasser n
~ **space** enge Spalte f
confining bed (layer) Grundwasserdeckschicht f, Grundwassersohlschicht f, Dichtungsschicht f; Schutzschicht f (bezogen auf Umweltschutz)
~ **pressure** allseitiger (hydrostatischer) Druck m, Umschließungsdruck m
~ **stratum** undurchlässige Schicht f, Grenzschicht f eines Speichers, Grundwassersohle f

confirmed reserves bestätigte Vorräte mpl (durch die staatliche Vorratskommission)
confluence Zusammenfluß m

confluence

~ plain durch Zusammenfluß zweier Ströme gebildete Ebene
~ step Konfluenzstufe f
confluent Nebenfluß m
conformability Konkordanz f
~ of strata Schichtenkonkordanz f, gleichförmige Lagerung f
conformable konkordant, gleichförmig
~ fault gleichsinnige Verwerfung f
~ strata Parallelschichten fpl
~ structure gleichförmige Lagerung f
conformal projection winkeltreue Projektion f
conformation Konkordanz f
~ of the ground Geländegestalt f, Geländeform f
conformity s. conformability
congeal/to 1. einfrieren, gefrieren, zusammenfrieren; 2. erstarren, erhärten
congealed crust Erstarrungskruste f
congealing 1. Zusammenfrieren n; 2. Erstarren n, Erhärten n
~ point Erstarrungspunkt m
~ temperature Erstarrungstemperatur f
congela s. coba
congelation 1. Gefrieren n, Vereisen n; 2. Erstarren n, Erhärten n
congelifluction Bodenfließen n im Permafrostgebiet
congelifract Frostverwitterungsschuttstück n
congelifraction Frostsprengung f, Frostverwitterung f, Spaltenfrost m
congelifracts Frostverwitterungsschutt m
congeliturbate Frostwürgeboden m
congeliturbation Kongeliturbation f, Frostbodenwirkungen fpl
congenial für Gesteine, die erzführende Gänge enthalten
~ climate passendes Klima n
congenital angeboren
conglomerate Konglomerat n, Trümmergestein n
~ of emergence Konglomerat n eines Regressionszyklus
~ of submergence Konglomerat n eines Transgressionszyklus
~ rock Konglomeratgestein n
conglomeratic konglomeratisch
~ facies Konglomeratfazies f
~ sandstone konglomeratischer Sandstein m
conglomeration Verfestigung f zu Konglomerat (z.B. von Geröll)
conglomeritic s. conglomeratic
congregated sands Sandbänke fpl
congruency Kongruenz f
congruent melting point Kongruenzschmelzpunkt m
congruous drag folds geometrisch zur Hauptfalte kongruente Schleppfalten fpl
~ form kongruente Form f
Coniacian [Stage] Coniac n (Stufe der Oberkreide)
conic kegelförmig, konisch (s.a. conical)

80

~ projection Kegelprojektion f
conical kegelförmig, konisch
~ flute cast Zapfenwulst m
~ mound konischer Erdhügel m (Auswurfshügel über Mündungen von Grabgängen von Organismen)
~ wall niche Ausbruchsnische f bei Hangunterschneidung
~ wave s. refraction wave
Coniferales Koniferengewächse npl
coniferous tree Konifere f
conifers Koniferen fpl, Nadelbäume mpl
coniform kegelförmig, konisch
coning Kegelbildung f (reservoirmechanisch)
~-in of edge water Trichterbildung f des Randwassers
~ of water Wasserkegelbildung f
conjugate centre übertragener Bildmittelpunkt m
~ faults konjugierte Verwerfungen fpl
~ joint sets konjugierte Kluftscharen fpl
~ vein durchfallender Gang m
connarite Connarit m, Konarit m, Komarit m (Varietät von Antigorit)
connate water konnates Wasser n (syngenetisch eingefangenes, marines Wasser); Adhäsionswasser n, fossiles Wasser
connecting bar Inselnehrung f
~ link Zwischenglied n (Paläontologie)
connellite Connellit m, $Cu_{19}[Cl_4(OH)_{32}|SO_4+4H_2O]$
conode Konode f
conoid[al] konoidisch
conoscope Konoskop n, Kristallachsenmesser m
conoscopic konoskopisch
Conrad discontinuity Conrad-Diskontinuität f, Conrad-Fläche f
consanguineous s. comagmatic
consanguinity of rocks Gesteinsverwandtschaft f
consequent konsequent (von der geologischen Struktur oder Oberflächenform bestimmt)
~ divide konsequente Wasserscheide f
~ river Folgefluß m
~ valley konsequentes Tal n
consertal für Gesteinsgefüge ohne Zwischenklemmasse
conservation 1. Erhaltung f; 2. Naturschutz m; Naturschutzgebiet n
~ of mineral resources Lagerstättenpflege f
~ of soil Bodenerhaltung f
~ principle Erhaltungssatz m
~ reservoir Überjahresspeicherbecken n
~ storage Überjahresspeicherung f
consistency gauge Penetrometer n, Konsistenzprüfer m, Drucksonde f
~ limits Konsistenzgrenzen fpl nach Atterberg, Atterbergsche Konsistenzgrenzen fpl
consistent standfest (Gebirge)
consolidate/to sich konsolidieren, sich verfestigen, fest werden, erstarren
~ by injection verfestigen

consolidated konsolidiert, verfestigt, erstarrt
~ **area** konsolidierter (versteifter, gefalteter) Raum *m*
~ **clay** verfestigter Ton *m*
~ **fill** verfestigter Versatz *m*
~ **ground** verfestigter Boden *m*
~ **lava** erstarrte Lava *f*
~ **rock** verfestigtes (konsolidiertes) Gestein *n*
~ **sand** verfestiger Sand *m*
~ **sediment** diagenetisch verfestigtes Sediment *n*
consolidation Konsolidierung *f*, Verfestigung *f*, Erstarrung *f*
~ **age** Erstarrungsalter *n*
~ **apparatus** Verdichtungsapparat *m*
~ **of ground** Bodenverdichtung *f*
~ **of magma** Magmenerstarrung *f*
~ **of sediments** Verfestigung *f* von Sedimenten
~ **of the subsoil** Bodenpressung *f*
~ **settlement** Verdichtungssetzung *f*
~ **time curve** Zeit-Setzungs-Kurve *f*
conspecific zur gleichen Spezies gehörend
constant head permeability test Durchlässigkeitsversuch *m* mit gleichbleibender Wasserhöhe
~ **head permeameter** Durchlässigkeitsmeßgerät *n* mit gleichbleibender Wasserhöhe
~ **pore volume reservoir** Expansionsspeicher *m*, geschlossenes Reservoir *n*
~-**rate injection method** Punktinjektionsmethode *f (einmalige Tracerzugabe)*
constellation Konstellation *f*, Sternbild *n*
constituent 1. Bestandteil *m*, Gemengteil *m*; 2. *(Am)* Maceral *n (Kohle)*
~ **mineral** Gemengteil *m (des Gesteinsgefüges)*
~ **of high volatility** leichtflüchtiger Bestandteil *m*
constitution Aufbau *m*, Bau *m*, Beschaffenheit *f*, Struktur *f*
~ **diagram** Zustandsdiagramm *n*
~ **water** Konstitutionswasser *n*, Kristallwasser *n*
constricted fold Quetschfalte *f*
constriction Einschnürung *f*
~ **of the channel** Bettvereng[er]ung *f (eines Flusses)*
~ **of the valley** Talvereng[er]ung *f*
construction industry Bauindustrie *f*, Bauwirtschaft *f*
~ **lime** Baukalk *m*
~ **material** Baustoff *m*
~ **of levees** Abdeichung *f*
~ **of roads** Straßenbau *m*
constructional coast Aufbauküste *f*
~ **form** Aufbauform *f*
consulting geologist beratender Geologe *m*
consuming plate margins konvergierende (krustenaufzehrende) Plattengrenzen *fpl*
consumptive use Aufbrauch *m (von Wasservorrat)*

contact action Kontaktwirkung *f*
~-**altered rock** Kontaktgestein *n*
~ **angle** Kontaktwinkel *m*
~ **area** Kontaktzone *f*
~ **belt** Kontakthof *m*
~ **between two formations** Formationsgrenze *f*
~ **deposit** Kontaktlagerstätte *f*
~-**erosion valley** Erosionsrinne *f (entlang dem Kontakt zweier Gesteinseinheiten)*
~ **formation** Kontaktbildung *f*
~ **goniometer** Anlegegoniometer *n*
~ **load** Geschiebebelastung *f (eines Flusses)*
~ **lode** Kontaktgang *m*
~ **log** Kontaktlog *n*, Mikrolog *n (Geophysik)*
~ **metamorphic** kontaktmetamorph
~-**metamorphic area** Kontakthof *m*
~-**metamorphic deposit** kontaktmetamorphe Lagerstätte *m*
~-**metamorphic rock** Kontaktgestein *n*
~ **metamorphism** Kontaktmetamorphose *f*
~-**metamorphosed rock** Kontaktgestein *n*
~-**metasomatic deposit** kontaktmetasomatische Lagerstätte *f*
~ **mineral** Kontaktmineral *n*
~ **pneumatolysis** Kontaktpneumatolyse *f*
~-**pneumatolytic deposit** kontaktpneumatolytische Lagerstätte *f*
~ **pressure** Flächendruck *m*
~ **rock** Kontaktgestein *n*
~ **spring** Schichtquelle *f*, Stauquelle *f*; tektonische Quelle *f*
~ **twin** Berührungszwilling *m*, Juxtapositionszwilling *m*
~ **vein** Kontaktgang *m*
~ **zone** Kontaktzone *f*
container rock Speichergestein *n*, Träger *m (von Erdöl oder Wasser)*
contaminant Schadstoff *m*, Schmutzstoff *m*
contaminated rocks Magmatite mit aufgenommenem Nebengesteinsmaterial
~ **sample** verunreinigte Probe *f*
contamination Vermischung *f*, Verunreinigung *f (von Mineralen)*; Kontamination *f*, Verschmutzung *f (von Grundwasser)*
~ **of magma** Hybridisierung *f (chemische Veränderung durch Aufnahme von Fremdmaterial)*
~ **of water** Wasserverunreinigung *f*
contemporaneity Gleichzeitigkeit *f*, Gleichaltrigkeit *f*
contemporaneous syngenetisch, gleichzeitig, gleichaltrig
~ **beds** gleichaltrige Schichten *fpl*
~ **deposition** gleichzeitig entstandene Ablagerung *f*
~ **disturbance of bedding** synsedimentäre Schichtstörung *f*
contemporary beds äquivalente Schichten *fpl*
~ **form** rezente Form *f*, Jetztzeitform *f*
content of fossils Fossilführung *f*
contiguous beaks sich berührende Wirbel *mpl*

contiguous

- ~ **crystal** angrenzender Kristall *m*, Nachbarkristall *m*
- ~ **rock** Nebengestein *n*
- ~ **seams** beieinander gelegene Flöze *npl*
- **continent** Festland *n*
- ~-**making** Kontinentalbildung *f*
- ~-**making movement** Kontinentalbewegung *f*
- **continental** kontinental, binnenländisch
- ~ **air** Kontinentalluft *f*
- ~ **apron** Böschung *f* am Fuße des Kontinentalabhangs
- ~ **block** Kontinentalblock *m*
- ~ **bridge** Brückenkontinent *m*
- ~ **climate** Kontinentalklima *n*, Binnenklima *n*
- ~ **crust** kontinentale Kruste *f*
- ~ **deposition** Festlandsablagerung *f*
- ~ **development** kontinentale Entwicklung *f*
- ~ **drift** Kontinentaldrift *f*, Kontinentalverschiebung *f*
- ~ **effect** Kontinentaleffekt *m*
- ~ **facies** Kontinentalfazies *f*
- ~ **formation** kontinentale Bildung *f*
- ~ **glaciation** Inlandvereisung *f*
- ~ **glacier** Kontinentalgletscher *m*
- ~ **ice sheet** Binneneisdecke *f*
- ~ **island** Festlandsinsel *f*
- ~ **margin** Kontinentalsaum *m*
- ~ **marine deposit** Flachseeablagerung *f*
- ~ **mass** Kontinentalblock *m*
- ~ **nucleus** Kontinentalkern *m*; Krato[ge]n *n*
- ~ **origin** Entstehung *f* der Kontinente
- ~ **plateau (platform)** Kontinentalblock *m*
- ~ **rise** Kontinentalanstieg *m*
- ~ **shelf** Kontinentalschelf *m (n)*
- ~ **shelf formations** Kontinentalschelfbildungen *fpl*
- ~ **slope** Kontinentalabfall *m*, Kontinentalböschung *f*, Kontinentalhang *m*
- ~ **terrace** Kontinentalsockel *m (Kontinentalschelf und Kontinentalhang)*
- **continuation** Fortsetzung *f (z.B. eines Potentialfeldes nach oben)*
- **continuity equation** Kontinuitätsgleichung *f*
- ~ **equation of steady flow** Kontinuitätsgleichung *f* für stationäre Strömung
- ~ **of a bed (stratum)** Durchhalten *n* einer Schicht *(von Bohrung zu Bohrung)*
- **continuous areal** kontinuierliches Areal *n (Ökologie)*
- ~ **bed** durchhaltende Schicht *f*
- ~ **coring** fortlaufendes Kernen *n*
- ~ **crystalline solution** lückenlose Mischkristallbildung *f*
- ~ **inflow** dauernder Zufluß *m*
- ~ **interstice** durchgehender Zwischenraum *m*
- ~ **kriging** stetiges Kriging *n*, Kriging *n* mit einer stetigen Gewichtsfunktion
- ~ **profiling** kontinuierliches Profilieren *n*
- ~ **running** kontinuierlicher Betrieb *m*
- ~ **sampling** ununterbrochene Probe[ent]nahme *f*
- ~ **sedimentation** gleichmäßige Sedimentation *f*

- ~ **stream** durchgehender Fluß *m*
- ~ **stress** Dauerbeanspruchung *f*
- ~ **time-distance curve** zusammengesetzte Laufzeitkurve *f*
- ~ **vein** aushaltender Gang *m*
- ~ **velocity log** Akustiklog *n*
- ~ **wave** ungedämpfte Welle *f*
- **continuum mechanics** Kontinuumsmechanik *f*
- **contorted** gekrümmt, gewunden, verdreht
- ~ **area** gestörtes Feld *n*
- ~ **bedding** Gekröseschichtung *f*
- ~ **beds** gekräuselte Schichten *fpl*
- ~ **fold** Korkenzieherfalte *f*
- ~ **strata** gekräuselte Schichten *fpl*
- **contortion** Fältelung *f*, Verdrehung *f*
- **contour** 1. Umriß *m*, Gestalt *f*, Kontur *f*; 2. Isolinie *f*; Isohypse *f*
- ~ **chart** Isohypsenkarte *f*
- ~ **current** Konturstrom *m*
- ~ **diagram** Höhenliniendiagramm *n*
- ~ **form** Umrißform *f*
- ~ **interval** Höhenlinienabstand *m*
- ~ **line** Höhenschichtlinie *f*, Isohypse *f*, Äquipotentiallinie *f*, Niveaulinie *f*
- ~ **map** Streichlinienkarte *f*
- ~ **map of the water table** Grundwassergleichenkarte *f*
- ~ **of zero elevation** Meeresspiegelkontur *f*
- ~ **vibration** Querschwingung *f (von Kristallen)*
- **contoured map** Höhenlinienkarte *f*
- ~ **plan** Höhenplan *m*
- ~ **stereogram** ausgezähltes Lagenkugeldiagramm *n*
- **contourites** Konturite *mpl (Ablagerungen von Konturströmen)*
- **contourogram** Schaubild *n* der Oberflächenbeschaffenheit
- **contours of subsurface structures** Tiefenlinien *fpl* der Strukturen im Untergrund
- **contract/to** auskeilen, verdrücken, schrumpfen, sich zusammenziehen
- **contract work** Auftragsarbeit *f (in der geologischen Erkundung)*
- **contracting industry** Bauindustrie *f*, Bauwirtschaft *f*
- **contraction** Schrumpfung *f*, Verdrückung *f*; Kontraktion *f (der Erde)*
- ~ **crack (fissure)** Schrumpfungsriß *m*, Schwindriß *m*
- ~ **joint** Schrumpfungskluft *f*
- ~ **of a lode** Verdrückung *f* eines Ganges
- ~ **of volume on solidification** Volumenverminderung *f* beim Erstarren
- ~ **theory** Kontraktionstheorie *f*
- ~ **vein** durch Austrocknung oder Abkühlung gebildeter Gang
- **contrast enhancement (stretching)** Kontrastverstärkung *f*, Kontrasterhöhung *f*
- **contributary** *s.* tributary
- **control cylinder** Probezylinder *m*, zylindrischer Probekörper *m*
- ~ **of leakage** Dichtheitskontrolle *f*

~ **of torrent works** Wildbachverbauung f
~ **points** Kontrollpunkte mpl (genau vermessene markante Geländepunkte)
~ **station** Kontrollstation f, Basisstation f
controlled directional drilling Richtbohrung f
~ **mosaic** Kontrollmosaik n, Kontrollnetz n (zusammengesetzte Luftaufnahme eines Kontrollgebiets)
convection Konvektion f
~ **current** Konvektionsströmung f (Unterströmung im oberen Erdmantel)
~ **equation** Konvektionsgleichung f
convectional rain Aufgleitregen m, Strichregen m
convective cell Konvektionszelle f (Unterströmungstheorie)
~ **creep** Konvektionsströmung f (Tektonik)
~ **current (flow)** Konvektionsströmung f
~ **process** Konvektion f (Grundwasserströmung)
conventional age konventionelles Alter n
~ **signs** Signatur f (auf Karten)
convergence Konvergenz f
~ **contour** Konvergenzlinie f (Linie gleichen senkrechten Abstands zwischen zwei gegebenen geologischen Horizonten)
~ **in the coal ahead of the face** Vorfeldkonvergenz f
~ **indicator** Konvergenzgeber m, Konvergenzmesser m
~ **map** Isochorenkarte f
convergency s. convergence
convergent konvergent
~ **evolution** s. adaptive convergence
~ **lens** Konvergenzlinse f
conversion of storage Speicherumstellung f
converted into peat vertorft, vermoort
~ **wave** Wechselwelle f
convex bank konvexes Ufer n
~ **inclined bedding** konvexe Schrägschichtung f
convexity 1. Konvexität f; 2. Konvexfläche f
conveyance of a channel Strombettdurchlaßfähigkeit f
conveyed by ice eisverfrachtet
conveying bridge Förderbrücke f
~ **bridge for open cuts** Abraumförderbrücke f
conveyor sieve Bandsieb n
convolute bedding endostratische Sedifluktion f (synsedimentäre Faltung); subaquatische Rutschung f, Wulstbank f, Wulstschichtung f, Wulstung f, Wulsttextur f; Wickelfalte f, Wicklungsstruktur f; Gleitfältelung f, Gleitfaltung f, Gleitstauchung f, Stauchfältelung f, Rutschfaltung f, Fältelungsrutschung f
~ **current-ripple lamination** verfältelte Strömungsrippelschichtung f
convoluted gefältelt
~ **structure** gewundene Struktur f, Gekrösestruktur f
convolution 1. Fältelung f; 2. Konvolution f, Faltung f (einer seismischen Welle)

convolutional ball Wickelfalte f
convulsion s. cataclysm
cookeite Cookeit m, $LiAl_4[(OH)_8|AlSi_3O_{10}]$
cooking time Dauer der Temperaturbeanspruchung bei der Diagenese
cool/to abkühlen; abschrecken
cool spring Akratopege f
cooling Abkühlung f; Abschreckung f
~ **constant** Abkühlungskonstante f
~ **crack** Abkühlungsspalte f, Erstarrungsspalte f
~-**down** Akühlung f, Erkaltung f
~ **fissure** s. ~ crack
~ **rate** Abkühlungsgeschwindigkeit f
~ **stack** Gradierwerk n, Rieselwerk n
~ **surface** Abkühlungsfläche f
coom Kohlenstaub m
coomb[e] Trockenrinne f (am Hang)
~ **rock** 1. kammförmige Verwitterungsform; 2. Verwitterungsschutt m
coon-tail ore gebändertes Fluorit-Zinkblende-Erz n
cooperite Cooperit m, PtS
coor (sl) Schicht f
coordinate paper Koordinatenpapier n
coorongite Coorongit m (brennbares, rezentes Algengestein im Torfstadium)
coose s. coarse lode
coossification Knochenverwachsung f
cop ores/to Erze scheiden
copi verwitterter Gips m
copiapite Copiapit m, $(Fe, Mg)Fe_4[OH|SO_4)_3]_2 \cdot 20H_2O$
coping Krone f (eines Damms)
copious mine Ausbeutezeche f
copper Kupfer n, Cu
~-**bearing** kupferführend
~-**bearing sandstone** Kupfersandstein m
~-**bearing shale** Kupferschiefer m
~ **content** Kupfergehalt m
~ **deposit** Kupferlagerstätte f
~ **glance** s. chalcocite
~ **matte** Kupferstein m, Rohkupfer n
~ **mine** Kupferbergwerk n
~ **nickel** s. niccolite
~ **ore** Kupfererz n
~ **pyrites** s. chalcopyrite
~ **schist (shale, slate)** Kupferschiefer m
~ **smelting** Kupferverhüttung f
~ **sulphate** s. chalcanthite
~ **uranite** s. tobernite
~ **vitriol** s. chalcanthite
Copper Age Kupferzeit f
copperas s. melanterite
copperization Imprägnierung f mit Kupfer
coppery kupferartig
coprolite Koprolith m, fossiler Kotballen m
copropel organogener Schlamm m
coquimbite Coquimbit m, $Fe_2[SO_4]_3 \cdot 9H_2O$
coquina Muschelkalk m, Schalentrümmerkalkstein m, Schillkalk m
~ **encrinite** Schalentrümmer-Trochitenkalkstein m

coquinite

coquinite Coquinit *m*, verfestigte Lumachelle *f*
coquinoid limestone Lumachellenkalkstein *m*, autochthoner Coquinit *m*
coral Koralle *f*
~ **agate** Korallenachat *m*
~ **colony** Korallenkolonie *f*
~-**hydrozoan biostromes** Korallen-Hydrozoen-Rasen *mpl*
~ **island** Koralleninsel *f*
~ **limestone** Korallenkalkstein *m*, Korallenriffkalk *m*
~ **mud** Korallenschlick *m*
~ **reef** Korallenriff *n*
~-**reef coast** Korallenriffküste *f*
~ **sand** Korallensand *m*
~ **shoal** Krustenriff *n*
coralgal facies Korallen-Kalkalgen-Fazies *f*
~ **limestone** Kalkstein aus einem Gerüst verwachsener Korallen und Algen
coralliferous limestone korallenführender (korallenreicher) Kalkstein *m*
corallite fossile Koralle *f*
coralloid[al] korallenförmig
corbond Druse *f*, Erznest *n*
Cordaitales Cordaitengewächse *npl*
Cordaite Cordait *m*
Cordatus beds Cordatenschichten *fpl*
corded[-folded] lava Stricklava *f*, Fladenlava *f*
Cordevolian [Substage] Cordevol[ium] *n* (Unterstufe, Obere Trias, Tethys)
cordierite Kordierit *m*, Cordierit *m*, $Mg_2Al_3[AlSi_5O_{18}]$
~ **gneiss** Kordieritgneis *m*
cordillera Kordillere *f*, Kettengebirge *n*
Cordilleran geosyncline Kordillerengeosynklinale *f*
~ **orogeny (revolution)** Kordillerenfaltung *f*
~ **Subprovince** Kordilleren-Subprovinz *f (Paläobiogeografie, Devon)*
cordylite Kordylit *m*, $Ba(Ce, La, Nd)_2[F_2|(CO_3)_2]$
core/to kernen, kernziehen, einen Kern bohren
core Kern *m*
~ **analysis** Bohrkernuntersuchung *f*
~ **barrel** Kernstoßbohrer *m*, Kernapparat *m*; Kernrohr *n*
~ **barrel head** Kernrohrkopf *m*
~ **barrel tube** Kernrohr *n*
~ **bit** Bohrkrone *f*, Kernbohrkrone *f*; Kernmeißel *m*
~ **bit for shot drilling** Schrotkrone *f*
~ **bit with tungsten carbide inserts** Hartmetallkrone *f*
~ **boring** Kernbohren *n*, Kernbohrung *f*
~ **breaker (catcher)** Kernfangeinrichtung *f*, Kernfänger *m*
~ **catcher operated by pump pressure** durch Pumpendruck betätigter Kernfänger *m*
~ **data** Meßergebnisse *npl* am Kern
~ **description** Etikette *f* für Kerndokumentation
~ **diameter** Kerndurchmesser *m*
~ **dip** Einfallen *n* an Bohrkernen
~ **drill** Kernbohrer *m*; Kernbohrgarnitur *f*
~ **drill boring** Kernbohren *n*, Kernbohrung *f*
~ **drill machine** Kernbohrmaschine *f*
~ **drill rig** Kernbohrausrüstung *f*
~ **drilling** Kernbohren *n*, Kernbohrung *f*; Untersuchungsbohrung *f (für geologische Aufschlüsse)*
~ **examination** Kernuntersuchung *f*
~ **extraction** Kernentnahme *f*, Kerngewinnung *f*
~ **extractor** Kernausstoßvorrichtung *f*
~ **flushing** Kernspülen *n*
~ **grabber** Kernprobenehmer *m (Person)*
~ **holder** Kernhalter *m*
~ **hole** Kernbohrloch *n*
~ **hole drilling** Kernlochbohren *n*, Kernlochbohrung *f*
~ **lifter** Kernheber *m*
~ **losses** Kernverluste *mpl*
~ **of anticline** Antiklinalkern *m*, Sattelkern *m*
~ **of earth** Erdkern *m*
~ **of syncline** Muldenkern *m*
~ **orientation** Kernorientierung *f*
~ **pool** eingespülter wasserdichter Kern *m (Erddamm)*
~ **pusher** Kernausstoßvorrichtung *f*
~-**receiving barrel** inneres Kernrohr *n*
~ **recovery** Kerngewinn *m*
~-**retaining device** Kernfangvorrichtung *f*
~-**retaining tube** inneres Kernrohr *n*
~ **sample** Kernprobe *f*
~ **shack** *(sl)* Kernbude *f*
~ **splitter** Kernspaltvorrichtung *f*
~ **storage box** Kernkiste *f*
~-**type dam (embankment)** Kerndamm *m (einer Talsperre)*
~ **wall** Dammkernmauer *f (einer Talsperre)*
~ **wedging** Kernklemmer *m*
cored interval gekernte Strecke *f*, Kernstrecke *f*
coring Kernprobenahme *f*
Coriolis force Coriolis-Kraft *f*
cork fossil Korkasbest *m (s.a. actinolite)*
corkite Corkit *m*, $PbFe_3[(OH)_6|SO_4PO_4]$
corkscrew fold Korkenzieherfalte *f*
~ **flute cast** Korkenzieherzapfen *m (Strömungswulst)*
corn snow körniger, nasser Schnee *m*
cornbrash *(sl)* rauher Kalksandstein *m*
corneite *s.* hornfels
cornelian Karneol *m (s.a. chalcedony)*
corneous hornig
~ **shell** Hornschale *f*
~ **silver** Hornsilber *n*, Silberhornerz *n (s.a. cerargyrite)*
cornetite Cornetit *m*, $Cu_3[(OH)_3|PO_4]$
cornice Gesims *n*, Wächte *f*
~ **glacier** Gehängegletscher *m*
corniferous hornsteinhaltig
Cornish clay kalkhaltiger Kaolin von Cornwall
~ **diamond** Quarzkristall aus Cornwall
~ **stone** kalkhaltiger Kaolin von Cornwall

cornubite Cornubit m, $Cu_5[(OH)_2|AsO_4]_2$
cornwallite Cornwallit m, $Cu_5[(OH)_2|AsO_4]_2$
corona Korona f
coronadite Coronadit m, $Pb_2Mn_8O_{16}$
coronoid Coronoid n, Kronenbein n
corpocollinite Corpocollinit m (Kohlensubmaceral)
corpohuminite Corpohuminit m (Braunkohlenmaceral)
corrade/to abschleifen, korradieren
corrading action abschleifende Wirkung f
corrasion Korrasion f, Sandschliff m, Windschliff m
corrasional work Korrasionstätigkeit f
corrasive power Korrasionskraft f
correction of the hole deviation Korrektur f eines abweichenden Bohrlochs
correlate beds/to Schichten korrelieren
correlation Korrelation f
~ diagram Korrelationsdiagramm n
~ of well logs Korrelation f von Bohrprofilen
~ shooting Korrelationsschießen n (Seismik)
corrie Kar n (Schottland)
~ glacier Kargletscher m
corrode/to ätzen, korrodieren
~ superficially anätzen
corroded korrodiert, zernagt
~ crystal teilweise resorbierter Kristall m
~ fossil angeätztes Fossil n
~-off abgeätzt
corrodibility Korrodierbarkeit f
corroding Korrodieren n
corrosion Korrosion f
~ embayment Abrasionsbucht f
~ pit Korrosionsnarbe f
~ surface Korrosionsfläche f
corrosional phenomenon Ätzungserscheinung f
corrosive korrodierend, ätzend
corrosiveness Korrosionswirkung f
corrugated gerunzelt
corrugation 1. Wellung f; 2. Schuttwulst m
corry Kar n (Schottland)
cortlandite Cortlandit m (Varietät von Peridotit)
corubin industrieller Rubin m
corundophilite Korundophilit m, $(Mg,Fe,Al)_6[(OH)_8|AlSi_3O_{10}]$
corundum Korund m, Al_2O_3
corvusite Corvusit m, $V_{14}O_{34} \cdot nH_2O$
cosalite Cosalit m, $2PbS \cdot Bi_2S_3$
cosedimentation gleichzeitige Ablagerung f
cosmic[al] kosmisch
~ abundance kosmische Häufigkeit f
~ dust kosmischer Staub m
~ energy kosmische Energie f
~ geology Kosmogeologie f
~ matter kosmische Materie f
~ origin kosmische Entstehung f
~ radiation Höhenstrahlung f, kosmische Strahlung f, Raumstrahlung f
~-ray intensity Höhenstrahlungsintensität f

~-ray produced tritium Tritium n kosmischer Herkunft
~-ray track Höhenstrahlenschauer m
~ space Weltraum m
~ spherule kosmisches Kügelchen n
~ system Weltsystem n
~ universe Weltall n
cosmochemic[al] kosmochemisch
cosmochemistry Kosmochemie f
cosmogenic kosmogen
cosmogonic[al] kosmogonisch
cosmogony Kosmogonie f
cosmography Kosmografie f
cosmophysics Kosmophysik f
cost of cleaning Aufbereitungskosten pl
~ of coal getting Gewinnungskosten pl für Kohle
~ of drilling Bohrkosten pl
~ of exploitation Abbaukosten pl
~ of maintenance Unterhaltungskosten pl
~ of rock blasting Gesteinssprengungskosten pl
~ of upkeep Unterhaltungskosten pl
~ of winning Gewinnungskosten pl
~ per meter of hole Bohrmeterkosten pl
~ price Gestehungskosten pl
costean/to Schürfgräben ziehen
costeaning Schürfarbeit f
~ ditch Schürfgraben m
costeen/to s. to costean
costeening s. costeaning
coteau Moränenwall m, Moränenplateau n
cotectic kotektisch
coticule Wetzschiefer m
cotidal lines Linien fpl gleicher Flutzeiten
cotton ball s. ulexite
~ rock 1. fleckig zersetztes Kieselsediment n; 2. fleckiger dolomitischer Kalkstein m
cotunnite Cotunnit m, $PbCl_2$
cotype Cotyp m, Syntyp m (Paläontologie)
coulee (Am) Schlucht f, Klamm f
Coulomb's condition Coulombsche Bedingung f
coulometry Coulometrie f (elektrochemisches Analysenverfahren)
coulsonite Coulsonit m, FeV_2O_4
counter Gang m quer zum Streichen
~ inclination Gegeneinfallen n
~ pressure Gegendruck m
~ rock Nebengestein n
~ septum Gegenseptum n
~ tube Zählrohr n
counterbalance Gegenbalancier m (Fördertechnik)
countercurrent [flow] Gegenstrom m, Gegenströmung f
~ leaching Gegenstromlaugung f
counterflush drilling Bohren n nach dem Gegenstromprinzip, Bohren n mit Umkehrspülung
counterlode, countervein einen Hauptgang schneidendes Nebentrum n

counting

counting rate Zählrate f *(Radioisotop)*
~ **tube** Zählrohr n
country mass (rock) Muttergestein n; Nebengestein n
course Streichen n; Gang m
~ **flookan** Salband n, Lettenbesteg m
~ **of orbit** Bahnverlauf m
~ **of ore** Erzgang m
~ **of outcrop** Ausgehendes n
~ **of river** Stromlauf m, Flußlauf m
~ **of weather** Witterungsverlauf m
Couvinian [Stage] Couvin n, Eifel n, Eifel-Stufe f *(Stufe des Mitteldevons)*
covariogram Kovariogramm n *(geostatisches Analogon der Kovarianzfunktion eines homogenen isotropen zufälligen Feldes)*
cove 1. Bucht f, kleine Bai f; 2. Brandungsnische f
coved edge Böschungskante f
covellite Kovellin m, Covellin m, Kupferindig[o] m, CuS
cover Decke f *(s.a. covering)*; Deckgebirge n, Deckschichten fpl, überlagernde Schichten fpl; Überdeckung f
~ **load** Überlagerungsdruck m
~ **of debris** Schuttdecke f
~ **of glacial till** eiszeitliche Ablagerungen fpl
~ **of till** Grundmoränendecke f, Geschiebelehmdecke f
~ **sand** Decksand m
~ **substitution** Hüllentausch m *(Tektonik)*
coverage 1. abgetastetes Gebiet n; 2. Überdeckungsgrad m; 3. scheinbare Haftung f *(Bitumen am Gestein)*
~ **diagram** Umriß m des abgetasteten Gebiets
covered with ruts gekritzt *(durch Eis)*
coverhead alluviale Schuttdecke f
covering Decke f
~ **of moss** Moosdecke f
~ **of scoriae** Schlackendecke f *(Lava)*
~ **of the river banks with slime, mud or stones** Vermurung f, Übermurung f
~ **of vegetation** Vegetationsdecke f
~ **rocks** Deckgebirge n
~ **strata** Deckschichten fpl
coving überhängend
cow-dung bomb Schlackenkuchen m
~-**stone** *(sl)* Grünsandsteinblock m
coyote hole s. gopher hole
~ **tunnelling method** *(Am)* Kammersprengverfahren n
cozonal tautozonal
crack/to springen, bersten, platzen, rissig werden
crack Sprung m, Riß m, Spalt m; Bruchfuge f
~ **porosity** Rißporosität f
~ **propagation** Rißausbreitung f
~ **water** Kluftwasser n
cracked gerissen, gespalten, rissig
cracking Rißbildung f
crackle/to knirschen, knistern, knittern
crackling Knirschen n, Knistern n, Kratzgeräusche npl *(im Gestein)*

cracky rissig, brüchig
Craelius drilling Craelius-Bohren n
crag 1. fossilführender mariner Sand m; 2. Felsenspitze f, Klippe f; 3. losgelöster Felsblock m
cragged felsig, schroff, uneben
~ **mountains** Felsklippengebirge n
craggedness, cragginess Schroffheit f, felsige Beschaffenheit f, Unebenheit f
craggy s. cragged
crandallite Crandallit m, $CaAl_3H[(OH)_6](PO_4)_2$
crane barge Kranbarke f
cranial roof Schädeldach n, Schädeldecke f
cranium Cranium n, Schädel m
cranny kleine Spalte f, Riß m im Gestein
crassidurite Crassidurit m *(Kohlenmikrolithotyp)*
crater Krater m, Sprengtrichter m
~ **alignment** Krateranordnung f [in Reihe]
~ **analysis** Krateranalyse f
~ **basin** Kraterbecken n
~ **chain** Kraterkette f
~ **circularity** Kraterkreisförmigkeit f
~ **collapse** Kratereinsturz m
~ **denudation chronology** Kraterabtragungsfolge f
~ **diameter** Kraterdurchmesser m
~ **dimple** Kratervertiefung f
~ **distribution** Kraterverteilung f
~ **edge** Kraterrand m
~ **eruption** Katereruption f
~ **floor** Kraterboden m
~ **fumarole** Kraterfumarole f
~ **island** KraterInsel f
~ **lake** Kratersee m
~ **obliteration** Kraterzerstörung f *(typisch bei hohen Kraterdichten)*
~ **of eruption** Ausbruchskrater m
~ **rim** Kraterrand m
~ **ring** Kraterwall m
~-**shaped** kraterförmig
~ **slope** Kraterböschung f
~ **summit** Kratergipfel m
~ **vent** Krateröffnung f
~ **wall** Kraterwall m
cratered plain durchkraterte Ebene f, durchkratertes Flachland n
~ **terrain** durchkratertes Gelände n
crateriform kraterförmig, trichterförmig
cratering Auskolken n, Auskolkung f, Kolkbildung f
~ **density** Kraterungsdichte f *(auf Planeten und Satelliten)*
~ **velocity** Kraterungsgeschwindigkeit f *(auf Planeten und Satelliten)*
craterlet 1. Erdbebentrichter m; 2. Kratergrube f *(auf dem Mond)*
craton Krato[ge]n n
cratonal, cratonic kratonisch
cratonization Kratonbildung f, Krustenversteifung f durch Ausfaltung
craw coal s. crow coal
crawl/to sich hinschlängeln

crawling trace Kriechspur f
CRCM = Commission on Recent Crustal Movements
creak/to knistern *(Kohle)*
creased slate Schiefer m mit Schubklüftungsrunzelung
crednerite Crednerit m, $CuMnO_2$
creedite Creedit m, $Ca_3[(Al(F, OH, H_2O)_6)_2]SO_4]$
creek 1. Bach m; 2. kleine schmale Bucht f
~ **bed** Bachbett n
creep/to kriechen
creep 1. Gekriech n, Kriechen n; 2. Schuttkriechen n; 3. Sackung f *(Felssackung)*; 4. Aufquellen n des Liegenden, Sohlendruck m
~ **buckling** plastisches Kriechen n
~ **limit** Kriechgrenze f
~ **of continents** Wanderung f der Kontinente, Kontinentalverschiebung f
~ **of ground (soil)** Bodenkriechen n
~ **recovery** elastische Nachwirkung f
~ **strain** Kriechdehnung f
~ **strength** Kriechfestigkeit f
~ **wrinkles** Knittermarken fpl, Runzelmarken fpl
creeping 1. Rutsch m, Bodenkriechen n; 2. Quellen n der Sohlschichten
~ **flow** s. viscous flow
~ **rubble** Wanderschutt m
~ **towards the valley** Talzuschub m
~ **waste** Schuttkriechen n; Kriechschutt m
creepwash Gekriech n
crenated lobes gezähnte Loben mpl *(Ammoniten)*
crenulated gerunzelt
~ **lobes** gezähnte Loben mpl *(Ammoniten)*
crenulation 1. Kleinfältelung f, Mikrowellung f; 2. Zähnchenmarke f
~ **cleavage** S_2-Schieferung f, Schubklüftung f, Runzelschieferung f
crepitate/to knistern, knacken
crepitation Zerknistern n
crescent Halbmond m
~ **of the moon** Sichel f des Mondes
~**-shaped** halbmondförmig
~**-shaped dune** s. crescentic dune
crescentic sichelförmig, hufeisenförmig
~ **dune** Barchan m, Bogendüne f, Sicheldüne f
~ **fracture** bogiger Bruch m
~ **grooves** Druckmarken fpl *(Tektonik)*
~ **impact scars** Schlagmarken fpl *(Sedimentologie)*
~ **lake** halbmondförmiges Altwasser n
~ **moraine** Bogenmoräne f
~ **wall niche** Mäanderunterschneidung f
crescentiform halbmondartig
crescentoid halbmondähnlich
crest 1. Scheitel m, Rücken m, First m, Kamm m, Grat m; 2. Schwingungsbauch m
~ **fault** Scheitelstörung f
~ **line** Scheitellinie f, Sattellinie f, Firstlinie f
~ **of anticline** Antiklinalkamm m, Scheitel m einer Antiklinale
~ **of dam** Dammkrone f
~ **of dune** Dünenkamm m
~ **of fold** Faltenfirst m, Scheitel m einer Falte
~ **of mountain** Gebirgskamm m
~ **of overfall** Überfallkante f
~ **of structure** Strukturscheitel m
~ **of wave** Wellenberg m, Wellenkamm m
crestal area Scheitelgebiet n
~ **plane** Scheitelfläche f
~ **well** Scheitelsonde f
crestmoreite Crestmoreit m *(Gemenge von Tobermorit und Wilkeit)*
cretaceous kreidehaltig, Kreide...
~ **deposit** Kreideablagerung f
Cretaceous Kreide f, Kreidesystem n *(chronostratigrafisch)*; Kreide[periode] f *(geochronologisch)*; Kreide[zeit] f *(allgemein)*
~ **Age** Kreide[zeit] f
~ **flysch** Kreideflysch m
~ **formation** Kreideformation f
~ **Period** Kreide[periode] f
~ **System** Kreide f, Kreidesystem n
crevasse Riß m; Gletscherspalte f
~ **splay** Uferwalldurchbruch m
crevassed spaltig, rissig, zerklüftet, klüftig *(bei Eis)*
crevassing Spaltenbildung f
crevice Spalt m *(Erdspalt)*
~ **corrosion** Spaltkorrosion f
~ **oil** Spaltenöl n *(in Gesteinsspalten vorkommendes Erdöl)*
~ **water** Kluftwasser n
creviced zackig, spaltig
crichtonite Crichtonit m, $Fe_2(Ti, Fe)_5O_{12}$
crinkle marks Knittermarken fpl
crinkled bedding Runzelschichtung f
crinkles Kleinfältelung f
crinoid column Crinoidenstengel m
~ **fauna** Crinoidenfauna f
~ **garden** Crinoidenrasen m
~ **head** Seelilienkrone f
~ **plate** Seelilienplatte f
~ **stalk** Crinoidenstengel m
~ **stem fragments** Crinoidenstielglieder npl
crinoidal limestone Crinoidenkalk m, Trochitenkalk m
~ **sand** Crinoidensand m
cripple 1. sumpfiger Grund m; 2. Felsklippe f im Fluß
criquina Crinoidenlumachelle f
criquinite verfestigte Crinoidenlumachelle f
crisscross bedding Kreuzschichtung f
~ **folds** verschuppte Falten fpl
~ **schistosity** Kreuzschieferung f
~ **texture** richtungslose Struktur f
cristobalite Cristobalit m, SiO_2
criterion of failure Bruchkriterium n
~ **of yielding** Plastizitätsbedingung f
critical altitude Volldruckhöhe f, Ladedruckhöhe f
~ **angle** Grenzwinkel m
~ **area of extraction** Vollfläche f *(Bergschaden)*

critical 88

- ~ **compression maximum** kritisches Pressungsmaximum n
- ~ **concentration** Grenzkonzentration f
- ~ **damping** kritische Dämpfung f, periodischer Grenzfall m *(Seismik)*
- ~ **density** Grenzdichte f
- ~ **gradient** Grenzgefälle n
- ~ **head** kritische Druckhöhe f
- ~ **load** kritische Belastung (Last) f
- ~ **mass** kritische Masse f
- ~ **material** Sparwerkstoff m
- ~ **mineral** [fazies]kritisches Mineral n, Indexmineral n
- ~ **point** kritischer Punkt m; Wendepunkt m
- ~ **pressure** kritischer Druck m
- ~ **shear stress** kritische Schubfestigkeit f
- ~ **slope** Stabilitätsgrenze f einer Böschungsneigung; Grenzgefälle n
- ~ **temperature** kritische Temperatur f
- ~ **velocity** Grenzgeschwindigkeit f
- **crocheted growth** gestricktes Wachstum n
- **crocidolite** Krokydolith m *(fasriger Riebeckit)*
- **crocoite** Krokoit m, Rotbleierz n, $Pb[CrO_4]$
- **Croixian [Series]** Croixien n, Potsdam n *(Serie des Oberkambriums in Nordamerika)*
- **Cromerian Complex** Cromer-Komplex m *(Pleistozän der britischen Inseln, entspricht dem Günz-Mindel-Interglazial der Alpen)*
- **cronstedtite** Kronstedtit m, $Fe_4Fe_2[(OH)_8|Fe_2Si_2O_{10}]$
- **crooked hole** abgewichene (gekrümmte) Bohrung f
- **crookesite** Crookesit m, $(Cu, Tl, Ag)_2Se$
- **crop out/to** ausstreichen, ausbeißen
- **crop** 1. s. outcrop, 2. Scheideerz n
- ~ **coal** minderwertige Kohle f, oxydierte Kohle f in Ausbißnähe
- ~ **fall** Senkung f der Tagesoberfläche
- **cropland** Ackerland n
- **cropping** s. outcropping
- **cross a lode/to** einen Gang durchörtern
- **cross** Kreuzaufstellung f, Queraufstellung f *(Seismik)*
- ~ **auger** Kreuzmeißel m
- ~ **assimilation** Stoffaustausch m zwischen Nebengestein und Magma
- ~ **bar micrometer** Kreuzfadenmikrometer n
- ~ **bearing** Anschnitt m
- ~-**bedded** schräggeschichtet, kreuzgeschichtet, diagonalgeschichtet
- ~-**bedding** Schrägschichtung f, Kreuzschichtung f, Diagonalschichtung f, Winkelschichtung f
- ~ **bit** Kreuzmeißel m
- ~-**bracing** Querverstrebung f
- ~-**correlation function** Kreuzkorrelationsfunktion f *(Seismik)*
- ~-**country gas line** Ferngasleitung f
- ~-**country pipeline** Überlandrohrleitung f
- ~-**country vehicle** Geländefahrzeug n
- ~ **course** durchsetzender Gang m, Quergang m
- ~ **course spar** Sternquarz m
- ~ **current** Querströmung f
- ~ **cut** Querschlag m, Ortsquerschlag m
- ~-**cut** durchbrochen *(z.B. von Granit)*
- ~-**cut level** Querschlag m
- ~ **cutter** Schrämmaschine f
- ~ **cutting** Schrämen n
- ~-**dip** Querneigung f
- ~ **equalization** Kreuzvergleich m, Kreuzausgleich m *(Seismik)*
- ~ **fault** Querverwerfung f, Querstörung f
- ~ **fertilization** s. allogamy
- ~ **fiber asbestos** Asbest m mit Fasern senkrecht zum Salband *(Rohqualität)*
- ~ **flookan (flucan)** Kreuzkluft f *(mit Letten ausgefüllt)*
- ~ **fold** Querfalte f
- ~ **folding** Querfaltung f, Faltendurchkreuzung f
- ~ **fracture** Querbruch m
- ~ **girdle** Kreuzgürtel m
- ~ **groove** Kreuzrille f
- ~-**joint fan** Kluftbesen m
- ~ **lamination** Schrägschichtung f, Kreuzschichtung f, Diagonalschichtung f
- ~ **level bubble** Dosenlibelle f
- ~-**line eyepiece** Strichkreuzokular n
- ~-**line micrometer** Netzmikrometer n
- ~ **lode** Quergang m
- ~-**magnetic** quermagnetisiert
- ~ **magnetization** Quermagnetisierung f
- ~-**magnetized** quermagnetisiert
- ~ **profile** Querprofil n
- ~ **section** 1. Querschnitt m, Profil n, Profilschnitt m; Kreuzriß m; 2. Laufzeitprofil n *(Seismik)*
- ~ **section of flow** Durchflußquerschnitt m
- ~ **section of passage** Durchgangsquerschnitt m
- ~ **section of volutions** Windungsquerschnitt m *(z.B. bei Ammoniten)*
- ~ **slide** Kreuzschlitten m
- ~ **spread** Kreuzaufstellung f, Queraufstellung f
- ~ **spur** einen Gang schneidendes Quartztrümchen n
- ~ **stone** s. andalusite
- ~ **stratification** Schrägschichtung f, Kreuzschichtung f, Diagonalschichtung f
- ~-**stratified** schräggeschichtet, kreuzgeschichtet, diagonalgeschichtet
- ~ **talk** Übersprechen n *(in Meßleitungen)*
- ~ **tee** Eruptionskreuz n, Kreuzstück n *(Bohrtechnik)*
- ~ **valley** Quertal n
- ~ **vein** Quergang m
- **crossed nicols** gekreuzte Nicols npl
- ~ **threads** Fadenkreuz n
- ~ **twinning** Kreuzzwillingsbildung f
- **crossing** Scharung f *(zweier Gänge)*
- **crossite** Crossit m *(Na-Amphibol)*
- **Crossopterygia** Crossopterygier mpl, Quastenflosser mpl
- **crossover distance** Knickpunktentfernung f
- **crosstable** Kreuztisch m

crouan *(sl)* Granit *m (Cornwall)*
crow coal aschereiche Kohle *f*
~-fly distance Luftlinienentfernung *f*
crowfoot standfestes Stativ *n*
crown 1. Bohrkrone *f*; 2. Krone *f (eines Damms)*, 3. Kelch *m (bei Crinoiden)*
~ **block** Kronenblock *m*, Rollenlager *n*
~ **of anticline** Sattelhöchstes *n*
~ **of overfall** Überfallkante *f*
~ **pillar** Scheitelpfeiler *m*
~ **platform** Turmkronenbühne *f*
CRP *s.* common reflection point
CRT *s.* cathode ray tube
crucible graphite Graphit *m* für Ziegel
cruciform twin Durchkreuzungszwilling *m*
crucite *s.* andalusite
crude roh *(im natürlichen Zustand)*
crude Rohöl *n*
~ **asphalt** Asphaltgestein *n*, Asphaltstein *m*
~ **bauxite** Rohbauxit *m*
~ **kaolin** Rohkaolin *m*
~ **naphtha (oil)** Erdöl *n*, Roh[erd]öl *n*
~ **oil base** Rohölbasis *f*
~ **ore** Fördererz *n*, Roherz *n*
~ **petroleum** Erdöl *n*, Roh[erd]öl *n*
~ **potassium salt** Kalirohsalz *n*
~ **shale oil** rohes Schieferöl *n*
~ **tar** Rohteer *m*
crudes Roherz *n*
crumb structure Krümelstruktur *f (des Bodens)*
crumble/to zerbröckeln, zerfallen
~ **away** zerbröckeln, nachbrechen
~ **down** zerbröckeln
crumble coal Formkohle *f*
~ **peat** erdiger Torf *m*
crumbling Zerbröckelung *f*
~ **phase** Zerfallsphase *f*
crumbly bröckelnd, bröcklig; vergrust
~ **clay** mulmiger Ton *m*
~ **soil** gekrümelter Boden *m*
crump Steinschlag *m*
crumpled gerunzelt, gefältelt
~ **ball** verknäulter Rutschungsballen *m*, Verknäulung *f*
~ **lamellae** Zerknitterungslamellen *fpl*
~ **mud-crack casts** gefältelte Netzleisten *fpl*
~ **stratum** verbogene Schicht *f*
crumpling Fältelung *f*
~ **folding** Stauchfaltung *f*
crush/to 1. zerquetschen, zermalmen; 2. pochen *(Erz)*
crush breccia Reibungsbrekzie *f*
~ **conglomerate** tektonisches Geröll *n*, Pseudokonglomerat *n*
~ **resistance** Knitterfestigkeit *f*
~ **rock** Kataklasit *m*, Trümmergestein *n*
~ **structure** kataklastisches Gefüge *n*
crushed zerklüftet
~ **material** Brechgut *n*
~ **rock (stone)** Straßen[bau]schotter *m*, Schotter *m*

~ **zone** Zertrümmerungszone *f*
crusher Brecher *m*, Grobzerkleinerungsmaschine *f*
~ **block** Quetschholz *n*
~**-run [stone]** ungesiebtes gebrochenes Gut *n*
crushing Zerkleinern *n*, Zerkleinerung *f*
~ **and grinding equipment (machinery)** Hartgesteinszerkleinerungsmaschinen *fpl*, Maschinen *fpl* für die Zerkleinerung im Hartgestein
~ **of rock** Gesteinszerstörung *f*
~ **plant** Brechanlage *f*; Erzquetsche *f*
~ **strength** Druckfestigkeit *f (von Gesteinen)*
~ **strength of a cube** Würfeldruckfestigkeit *f*
~ **zone** Ruschelzone *f*, Bruchzone *f*
crushproof knitterfest
crust fracture Geofraktur *f*
~ **of earth** Erdrinde *f*, Erdkruste *f*
~ **of scoriae** Schlackenkruste *f*
~ **ore** Kokardenerz *n*
crustaceous krustenartig, Krustentier...
crustal Krusten...
~ **accumulation** Massenüberschuß *m (isostatisch)*
~ **cooling** Krustenabkühlung *f*
~ **deformation** Krustenverformung *f*
~ **disturbance** Krustenstörung *f*, Tiefenbruchzone *f* bedeutender Größe
~ **movement** Krustenbewegung *f*
~ **quiescence** Krustenruhe *f*
~ **readjust**ment ausgleichende Krustenbewegung *f*
~ **rest** Krustenruhe *f*
~ **shortening** Krusteneinengung *f*, Krustenverkürzung *f*
~ **stress** Krustenspannung *f*
~ **thickness** Krustenmächtigkeit *f*
~ **unloading** Massendefekt *m (isostatisch)*
~ **unrest** Krustenunruhe *f*
~ **upheaval** Krustenhebung *f*
crusted-over überkrustet
~ **surface** mit Schmelzrinde bedeckte Oberfläche *f (bei Meteoriten)*
crustification Krustenbildung *f*
crustified vein verheilter Gang *m*, Gang *m* mit Krustenstruktur
cryergic periglazial *(im allgemeinen Sinne)*
cryogenic kryogen; glazigen
~ **lake** Permafrostsee *m*
~ **temperature** Tiefsttemperatur *f*
cryogenics Kryogenik *f*
cryolite Kryolith *m*, $Na_3[AlF_6]$
cryolithionite Kryolithionit *m*, $Na_3Li_3[Al,F_6]_2$
cryology Glaziologie *f*
cryometer Kryometer *n*
cryomorphic soil Frostboden *m*
cryopedology Kryopedologie *f*, Frostbodenkunde *f*
cryopedometer Kryopedometer *n*, Bodenfrostmesser *m*
cryoplanation Oberflächeneinebnung *f* durch Frostwirkung

cryoscope

cryoscope Kryoskop *n*, Gefrierpunktmesser *m*
cryosphere Kryosphäre *f*
cryoturbation Kryoturbation *f*, Froststauchung *f*
cryptic verborgen, nicht sichtbar
~ **layering** Kryptoschichtung *f*, nicht erkennbare [magmatische] Schichtung *f*
~ **texture** Kryptostruktur *f (mit bloßem Auge nicht sichtbare Struktur)*
cryptoclastic kryptoklastisch
cryptocrystalline kryptokristallin
cryptohalite Kryptohalit *m*, $(NH_4)_2[SiF_6]$
cryptolite *s.* monazite
cryptomagmatic ore deposit kryptomagmatische Erzlagerstätte *f*
cryptomerous kryptomer
cryptoperthite Kryptoperthit *m*
Cryptophytic Kryptophytikum *n*
cryptovolcanic kryptovulkanisch
~ **earthquake** magmatisches Beben *n*
Cryptozoic [Eon] Kryptozoikum *n*, Archäozoikum *n*, Präkambrium *n*
crystal Kristall *m*
~ **aggregate** Kristallaggregat *n*
~ **analysis** Kristallstrukturuntersuchung *f*
~ **angle** Kristallwinkel *m*
~ **axis** Kristallachse *f*
~ **blank** Rohkristall *m*
~ **boundary** Kristallgrenze *f*, Kristallgrenzlinie *f*
~ **casts** Kristallpseudomorphosen *fpl*
~ **cave** Kristallkeller *m*
~ **chemistry** Kristallchemie *f*
~ **class** Kristallklasse *f*
~ **core** Kristallkern *m*
~ **diamagnetism** Kristalldiamagnetismus *m*
~ **diffraction** Kristallbrechung *f*
~ **edge** Kristallkante *f*
~ **face** Kristallfläche *f*, Kristallebene *f*
~ **floatation** Kristallflotation *f (im Magma)*
~ **form** Kristallform *f*
~ **formation** Kristallbildung *f*
~ **goniometry** Kristallwinkelmessung *f*
~ **group** Kristallgruppe *f*
~ **growing (growth)** Kristallwachstum *n*
~ **habit** Kristallhabitus *m*
~ **imperfection** Kristallfehler *m*
~ **imprints** Kristallabdrücke *mpl (in Sedimenten)*
~ **lattice** Kristallgitter *n*, Raumgitter *n*
~ **lattice imperfection** Kristallbaufehler *m*
~ **lattice spacing** Kristallgitterabstand *m*
~ **morphology** Kristallmorphologie *f*
~ **mush** Kristallbrei *m*, partiell kristallisiertes Magma *n*
~ **orientation** Kristallorientierung *f*
~ **outline** Kristallgrenzlinie *f*, Kristallgrenze *f*
~ **perfection** Idealaufbau *m* von Kristallen
~ **physics** Kristallphysik *f*
~ **recovery** Kristallregenerierung *f*, Kristallverheilung *f*
~ **section** Kristallschnitt *m*
~ **sedimentation** Kristallabseigerung *f*
~ **seeding** Kristallkeimbildung *f*
~ **settling** Kristallabseigerung *f*
~ **skeleton** Kristallskelett *n*
~ **symmetry** Kristallsymmetrie *f*
~ **system** Kristallsystem *n*
~ **tuff** Kristalltuff *m*
crystalliferous kristallhaltig
crystalliform kristallartig; kristallförmig
crystalline kristallin[isch]
~ **basement** kristallines Grundgebirge *n*
~ **chert** *s.* granular chert
~ **floor** Kristallinikum *n*, kristallines Fundament *n*, kristalliner Untergrund *m*
~ **force** Kristallisationsvermögen *n*
~ **form** Kristallform *f*
~ **goniometry** Kristallwinkelmessung *f*
~-**granular** kristallin-körnig
~ **limestone** kristalliner Kalkstein *m*
~ **overgrowth** Kristallverwachsung *f*
~ **path** Kristallisationsbahn *f*
~ **rock** kristallines Gestein *n*
~ **schist** kristalliner Schiefer *m*
~ **state** Kristallzustand *m*, kristalliner Zustand *m*
~ **texture** kristallines Gefüge *n*
crystalling transformation Umkristallisation *f*
crystallinity Kristallisationsgrad *m*
crystallite Kristallit *m*, Kristallembryo *m*
~ **growth** Kristallwachstum *n*
crystallizable kristallisierbar, kristallisationsfähig
crystallization Kristallisation *f*
~ **differentiate** Kristallisationsdifferentiat *n*
crystallize/to kristallisieren
~ **out** auskristallisieren
crystallized sandstone Kristallsandstein *m*
crystallizer Kristallisator *m*
crystallizing Kristallbildung *f*
~ **force** Kristallisationskraft *f*
~ **process** Kristallisationsprozeß *m*
crystalloblast Kristalloblast *m*
crystalloblastic kristalloblastisch
~ **growth** kristalloblastisches Wachstum *n*
~ **series** kristalloblastische Reihe *f*
~ **texture** kristalloblastische Struktur *f*
crystallochemical kristallchemisch
crystallographer Kristallograf *m*
crystallographic kristallografisch
~ **axis** Kristallachse *f*, kristallografische Achse *f*
~ **axis orientation** Kristallachsenrichtung *f*, Richtung *f* der Kristallachse
~ **notation** Kristallbezeichnung *f*
~ **setting** kristallografische Aufstellung *f*, Kristallaufstellung *f*
~ **system** Kristallsystem *n*
crystallography Kristallografie *f*
crystalloid kristallähnlich, kristalloid
crystalloluminescence Kristallumineszenz *f*
crystallometry Kristallometrie *f*
crystals felted together verzahnte Kristalle *mpl*
crystic eisgeformt, glazialgeformt

crystocrene Quelleneis n
csiklovaite Csiklovait m, $Bi_2Te(S, Se)_2$
ctenoid cast Ctenoidmarke f, kammförmige Aufstoßmarke f
~ **scale** Ctenoidschuppe f, Kammschuppe f *(bei Fischen)*
cubage Kubatur f *(Massenberechnung)*
cubanite Kubanit m, Chalmersit m, Weißkupfererz n, $CuFe_2S_3$
cubature s. cubage
cube Würfel m
~ **strength** Würfeldruckfestigkeit f
~ **test** Würfelprobe f
~ **test specimen** Probewürfel m
cubic[al] kubisch
~ **body-centered** kubisch-raumzentriert
~ **cleavage** kubische Spaltbarkeit f
~ **close packing** kubisch dichteste Packung (Kugelpackung) f
~ **face-centered** kubisch-flächenzentriert
~ **metre** Kubikmeter n
~ **spar** s. boracite
~ **system** kubisches (reguläres) System n
~ **yardage** Kubatur f
cuesta Schichtstufe f, Abtragungsstufe f, Cuesta f
~ **back slope** Schichtfläche f, Stufenlehne f, Plattform f einer Schichtstufe
~ **inface** Schichtköpfe mpl
~ **landscape** Schichtstufenlandschaft f
~ **scarp** Stirnhang m, Stufenstirn f, Steilabfall m einer Stufe, Trauf f
~ **topography** Schichtstufenlandschaft f
cull/to klauben *(Erz)*
Culm Kulm m (n) *(Dinant in Mitteleuropa)*
culminant kulminierend
culminating point Kulminationspunkt m
culmination Kulmination f
cultivated area bebaute Fläche f
~ **land** Kulturland n
~ **soil** Kulturboden m
~ **steppe land** Kultursteppe f
cultivating of lands Urbarmachung f von Land
cultivation of peat by covering with sand Sanddeckkultur f
~ **of peat by mixing with sand** Sandmischkultur f
culvert Entwässerungsstollen m, Entwässerungsgraben m
culvertailed schwalbenschwanzförmig
cumeng[e]ite Cumengeit m, $5PbCl_2 \cdot 5Cu(OH)_2 \cdot 1/2 H_2O$
cummingtonite Cummingtonit m, $(Mg,Fe)_7[OH|Si_4O_{11}]_2$
cumulate 1. Akkumulation f *(von Mineralen)*; 2. Bodensatz m *(eines Magmas)*; 3. Seigerungsprodukt n; 4. Knolle f, Schliere f
cumulative curve Summenkurve f
~ **direct plot of screen test** Siebrückstandsdiagramm n, Siebdurchlaufdiagramm n
~ **line** Summenlinie f
~ **logarithmic plot** Summationskurvenauftragung f in logarithmischem Maßstab

~ **production** Gesamtproduktion f; kumulative Förderung f
~ **size distribution curve of the underflow** Siebdurchgangskurve f
cumuliform cumulusartig
cumulose deposit Ablagerung f organischer Materialien
cuneiform keilförmig
cup-and-ball jointing kugelschalige Klüftung f *(in den Säulen von Effusivgesteinen)*
~-shaped becherförmig
cupola Kuppe f
~ **karst** Kuppelkarst m
~ **of the batholith** Kuppeldach n des Batholithen
cupreous kupferhaltig; kupferartig
cupriferous kupferhaltig
~ **pyrite** s. chalcopyrite
~ **slate** Kupferschiefer m
cuprite Kuprit m, Cuprit m, Rotkupfererz n, Cu_2O
cuprobismuthite Cuprobismuthit m, $Cu_2S \cdot Bi_2S_3$
cuprocopiapite Cuprocopiapit m, $CuFe_4(SO_4)_6(OH)_2 \cdot 20H_2O$
cuprorivaite Cuprorivait m, $CaCu[Si_4O_{10}]$
cuprosklodowskite Cuprosklodowskit m, $CuH_2[UO_2|SiO_4]_2 \cdot 5H_2O$
cuprotungstite Cuprotungstit m, $Cu_2[(OH)_2|WO_2]$
cuprouranite s. torbernite
cuprum s. copper
curdle into lumps/to ausflocken
Curie point Curie-Punkt m
curite Curit m, $3PbO \cdot 8UO_3 \cdot 4H_2O$
curly bedding s. glide bedding
current Strom m; Strömung f
~-bedded s. cross-bedded
~-bedding s. cross-bedding
~ **crescent** Auskolkung f, Kolkmarke f, Luvgraben m, Strömungskamm m, Hufeisenwulst m
~ **electrode** Stromelektrode f, Erdungspunkt m
~ **field of ground water** Grundwasserströmungsfeld n
~ **gradient** Strömungsgradient m
~ **lineation** Strömungsriefung f
~ **marks** Wellenfurchen fpl
~ **meter** Strömungsmesser m
~ **of the sea** Meeresströmung f
~ **ore** Fördererz n, Roherz n
~-oriented strömungsgeregelt
~ **ripple** Fließrippel f, Strömungsrippel f
~-ripple bedding Strömungsrippelschichtung f
~-ripple cross lamination Strömungsrippelschrägschichtung f
~ **ripple mark** Fließrippel f, Strömungsrippel f
~ **velocity** Strömungsgeschwindigkeit f
~ **water** strömendes Wasser n; Stromwasser n, Bachwasser n
curtisite Curtisit m, $C_{24}H_{18}$ *(bernsteinähnliches Harz)*

curvature

curvature Krümmung f
~ **direction** Krümmungssinn m
~ **of earth** Erdkrümmung f
~ **of field** Bildfeldwölbung f
~ **of hole** Bohrlochkrümmung f
~ **radius** Krümmungsradius m
curve apex Bogenscheitel m
~ **of equal rainfall** Isohyete f, Niederschlagshöhenkurve f, Regengleiche f
~ **of lowering** Absenkungskurve f (des Grundwasserspiegels)
curved ripple marks gekrümmte Rippelmarken fpl
~ **well** abgewichene (gekrümmte) Bohrung f
curvilinear fault krummlinige Verwerfung f
Cuselian Cuseler Schichten fpl
cuselite Cuselit m (Augitporphyr)
cushion Polster n (von Kohlenwasserstofflagerstätten)
~ **gas** Polstergas n, Kissengas n (Untergrundgasspeicher)
~ **lava** s. pillow lava
cuspate bar V-förmiger Haken m (einer Nehrung)
~ **ripple marks** sichelförmige Rippelmarken fpl
cut a core/to kernen, einen Kern bohren
~ **a lode** einen Gang anfahren
~ **across** durchschneiden; durchörtern, durchfahren
~ **across the ground** Gebirge durchörtern
~ **off** abschneiden
~ **slots in the casing** feine Schlitze in der Verrohrung anbringen
cut Kerbe f
~ **and fill** Einschnitt m und Damm m
~-**and-fill stoping** Firstenbau m mit Versatz
~-**away model** Schnittmodell n
~ **bank** Prallufer n
~ **of path** Wegeinschnitt m
~-**off** 1. Durchbruch m (eines Mäanders); 2. Sperrfrequenz f, Grenzfrequenz f (Seismik)
~-**off coefficient** Einstellwert m
~-**off grade** Grenzgehalt m, geologischer Schwellengehalt m (Lagerstättenkondition)
~-**off meander** abgeschnittener Mäander m
~-**off meander spur** Umlaufberg m
~-**off point** Trennungspunkt m
~-**off trench** Abdichtungsgraben m
~-**off walls** Schutzbauten mpl gegen Unterläufigkeit
~-**offs** s. ~-off walls
~ **oil** teilweise emulgiertes Erdöl n (in Gegenwart von Gas oder Luft)
~ **point** Trennschnitt m; Schnittpunkt m einer Bohrung mit einer Störung
~ **slope** Hangeinschnitt m
~ **stone** Werkstein m, Quader[stein] m
~-**through** Durchhieb m
cuticoclarite Cuticoclarit m (Kohlenmikrolithotyp)
cuticule Kutikula f

cutinite Cutinit m (Kohlenmaceral der Exinit/Liptinitgruppe)
cutoff s. cut-off
cutter Querkluft f
~ **head** Rollenkrone f
cutting 1. Abbau m (z.B. eines Flözes); 2. Einschnitt m (z.B. im Gelände)
~ **and filling** Versatzbau m
~ **edge blade** Schneide f
~ **height** Schnitthöhe f (eines Baggers)
~ **inserts** Stifte aus Hartmetall, die in Bohrungen oder Schlitze eingesetzt werden
~ **of peat** Abtorfen m
~ **position** Schnittlage f
~ **sand** Schleifsand m
~ **settling** Verschlammung f des Bohrlochs
~ **surface** Schneidfläche f; Schnittfläche f
~ **tooth** s. incisor
cuttings Schrämklein n; Bohrklein n, Bohrschmant m
~ **analysis** Bohrkleinanalyse f
cuvette Kesselsee m (Glazialform)
CVL s. continuous velocity log
cwm Kar n (Wales)
cyanite Cyanit m, Kyanit m, Al_2SiO_5
cyanochroite Cyanochroit m, $K_2Cu[SO_4]_2 \cdot 6H_2O$
Cyanophyta Blaualgen fpl
cyanotrichite Cyanotrichit m, $Cu_4Al_2[(OH)_{12}|SO_4] \cdot 2H_2O$
cycle of development Entwicklungszyklus m
~ **of erosion** Erosionszyklus m
~ **of sedimentation** Sedimentationszyklus m
~ **of stress** Lastwechsel m; Lastspiel n
~ **of submergence** Transgressionszyklus m
cycles in precipitation Niederschlagsfolge f
cyclic character zyklische Ausbildung f
~ **sedimentation** Repetitionsschichtung f, zyklische Sedimentation f
cycling of gas Gaskreislauf m (durch eine Lagerstätte)
cycloid zykloidschuppig
cyclone 1. Zyklone f; 2. Zyklon m
cyclopic wall Zyklopenmauerwerk n
cyclothem Zyklothem n, rhythmischer Schichtwechsel m
cyclowollastonite Cyclowollastonit m, $Ca_3[Si_3O_9]$
cylindrical projection Zylinderprojektion f
~ **structure** zylindrische Struktur f
cylindrite Kylindrit m, $6PbS \cdot 6SnS_2 \cdot Sb_2S_3$
cymophane s. chrysoberyl
cymrite Cymrit m, $Ba[OH|AlSi_3O_8]$
Cypridina Shale Cypridinenschiefer m
cyprine Cyprin m (blauer Vesuvian)
cyprusite Cyprusite m, Jarosit m, Natrojarosit m (s.a. jarosite)
cyrilovite Cyrilovit m, $NaFe_3[(OH)_4(PO_4)_2] \cdot 2H_2O$
cystoidean limestone Cystoideenkalk m
cystoideans Cystoideen fpl

D

D-horizon D-Horizont *m (Boden)*
3-D-seismics flächenhafte seismische Aufnahme *f*, 3-D-Seismik *f*
dachiardite D'Achiardit *m*, (K, Na, $Ca_{0,5})_5[Al_5Si_{19}O_{48}] \cdot 12H_2O$
Dacian [Stage] Dacien *n (Stufe des Pliozäns)*
dacite Dazit *m*
~ **porphyry** Dazitporphyr *m*
dacitic dazitisch
dactylotype intergrowth symplektitische Mineralverwachsung *f*
daf *s.* dry, ash-free
dahllite Dahllit *m (Oxi-Karbonat-Apatit)*
dailies Tagesberichte *mpl*
daily Tagesausbeute *f*
~ **amount of rainfall** tägliche Niederschlagshöhe *f*
~ **[delivery] capacity** tägliches Förderleistungsvermögen *n*
~ **mean** Tagesmittel *n*
~ **output** Tagesleistung *f*, Tagesförderung *f*
~ **variation** Tagesvariation *f*
dairy salt Grobsalz *n*
dale Talmulde *f*
dalyite Dalyit *m*, $K_2Zr[Si_6O_{15}]$
dam in/to eindeichen
~ **up** [auf]stauen, anstauen; eindeichen
dam Damm *m*, Staudamm *m*, Staumauer *f*, Talsperre *f*, Wehr *n*
~ **abutment** Staumauerwiderlager *n*
~ **break** Dammbruch *m*
~ **embankment** Dammkörper *m*
~ **failure** Dammbruch *m*
~ **gradation** Flußaufschotterung *f*
~ **lake** Stausee *m*
~ **location** Talsperrenbaustelle *f*, Standort *m* der Talsperre
~ **shale** schottischer Ölschiefer *m*
~ **site** *s.* ~ location
~ **water** Stauwasser *n*
damage at well bore Speicherschädigung *f* in Bohrlochnähe
~ **due to mining operations, ~ due to subsidence** Bergschaden *m*
~ **factor** Schädigungsgrad *m*
~ **ratio** Schädigungsverhältnis *n*
~ **to buildings** Schäden *mpl* an Gebäuden *(7. Stufe der Erdbebenstärkeskala)*
dammed lake Stausee *m*
~-**up water** Stauwasser *n*
damming[-off] Abdämmung *f*, Absperrung *f*; Eindämmen *n*
~-**up** Stauung *f*
~ **wetness** Staunässe *f*
damourite Damourit *m (feinschuppiger Muskovit)*
damp-proof feuchtigkeitsisolierend
~-**proof membrane** Dichtungshaut *f*
~-**proofing** Feuchtigkeitsisolierung *f*, Abdichtung *f (Bauwerk gegen Bodenfeuchte)*
~ **snow** Klebeschnee *m*
damped oscillation gedämpfte Schwingung *f*
~ **pendulum** gedämpftes Pendel *n*
~ **vibration** gedämpfte Schwingung *f*
~ **wave** gedämpfte Welle *f*
damping Dämpfung *f*
~ **apparatus** *s.* ~ device
~ **arrangement** Dämpfungsvorrichtung *f*, Dämpfungseinrichtung *f (z.B. eines Seismometers)*
~ **basin** Tosbecken *n*
~ **device** Dämpfungsvorrichtung *f (z.B. eines Seismometers)*
dampness Feuchtigkeit *f*
damps CO_2-führende Wetter *pl*
danaite Danait *m*, Kobaltarsenkies *m (Varietät von Arsenopyrit)*
danalite Danalith *m*, $Fe_8[S_2|(BeSiO_4)_6]$
danburite Danburit *m*, Kalziumborosilikat *n*, $Ca[B_2Si_2O_8]$
dandered coal *(sl)* unreine selbstentzündliche Kohle *(Schottland)*
danger of freezing Frostgefahr *f*
Danian [Stage] Danien *n*, Dan[ium] *n*, dänische Stufe *f (basale Stufe des Tertiärs)*
danks *(sl)* Schwarzschiefer mit Kohleflitter *(Newcastle)*
dannemorite Dannemorit *m (Mn-haltiger Cummingtonit)*
Dano-Montian Dano-Mont *n (tiefstes Tertiär)*
dansite D'Ansit *m*, $Na_{21}Mg[Cl_3|(SO_4)_{10}]$
dant *(sl)* minderwertige fusitreiche Kohle *(Newcastle)*
daphnite Daphnit *m*, $(Fe, Al)_6[(OH)_8|AlSi_3O_{10}]$
darapskite Darapskit *m*, $Na_3[SO_4|NO_3] \cdot H_2O$
Darcy Darcy *(Maß für die Permeabilität von Gesteinen)*
~ **flow** Darcy-Strömung *f*
~ **velocity** Darcy-Geschwindigkeit *f*, Filtergeschwindigkeit *f*, Durchgangsgeschwindigkeit *f*
Darcy's law Darcysches Gesetz *n* $(v=k \cdot i)$
darg Tagesproduktion *f (Schottland)*
dark field Dunkelfeld *n (Mikroskopie)*
~ **field illumination** Dunkelfeldbeleuchtung *f*
~ **field image** Dunkelfeldabbildung *f*
~ **field observation** Dunkelfeldbeobachtung *f*
~ **field stop** Dunkelfeldblende *f*
~ **ground** *s.* ~ field
~-**line spectrum** Absorptionsspektrum *n*
~ **nebula** Dunkelnebel *m*
~ **position** Dunkelstellung *f*
~ **radiation** Dunkelstrahlung *f*
~ **red silver ore** *s.* pyrargyrite
Darwin glass tasmanischer Tektit *m*
dary tonüberdeckter Moortorf *m*
Dasberg Limestone Dasberger Kalk *m (Oberdevon)*
Dasbergian [Stage] Dasberg *n (Stufe des Oberdevons in Europa)*
dash geringe Beimengung *f*
~ **of the waves** Wellenschlag *m*, Wogenprall *m*

data

data acquisition Datengewinnung f, Datenerfassung f
- ~ **characteristics** Datenmerkmale npl, Datencharakteristika npl
- ~ **compression** Datenverdichtung f (Fernerkundung, Seismik)
- ~ **direct reception** Datendirektempfang m (Fernerkundung)
- ~ **handling** Datenverwaltung f (z.B. in Fernerkundungszentren)
- ~ **pre-processing** Datenvorverarbeitung f (Fernerkundung, Seismik)
- ~ **processing** Datenverarbeitung f
- ~ **rate** Daten[fluß]rate f
- ~ **recorder** Meßwertschreiber m
- ~ **retrieval** Datenwiederauffindung f
- ~ **storage** Datenspeicherung f
- ~ **transmission** Datenübertragung f (z.B. von geophysikalischen Meßstationen oder Fernerkundungssatelliten)

date line Datumsgrenze f
datolite Datolith m, $CaB[OH|SiO_4]$
datum error Meßwertfehler m
- ~ **horizon (level)** Bezugshorizont m, Leithorizont m
- ~ **plane** Bezugsniveau n

daubreeite Daubréeit m (Bi-Oxichlorid)
daubreelite Daubréelith m, $FeCr_2S_4$
daubreite s. daubreeite
daugh (sl) Tonlager n
daughter element Tochterelement n, radioaktives Zerfallsprodukt n
dauk (sl) Sandtonboden m
Dauphiné twin Dauphinézwilling m
davidite Davidit m, $(Fe, U, Ce, La)_2(Ti, Fe, Cr, V)_5O_{12}$
daviesite Daviesit m (s.a. mendipite)
davisonite Davisonit m (s.a. apatite)
davyne Davyn m, $(Na, K)_6Ca_2[(SO_4)_2|(AlSiO_4)_6]$
dawk s. dauk
dawn Morgendämmerung f
- ~ **organisms** s. eobionts

dawsonite Dawsonit m, $NaAl[(OH)_2|CO_3]$
day coal Kohle f in Ausstrichnähe
- ~ **level** Stollen m, Stollenrösche f, Tagesstrecke f
- ~ **output** Tagesförderung f
- ~ **stone** Ausgehendes n, aufgeschlossenes Gestein n in natürlicher Lagerung
- ~ **surface** Tagesoberfläche f
- ~-**time remote sensing** Fernerkundung f zur Tageszeit

daze (sl) Glimmer m
deacidification Entsäuerung f
dead air matte Wetter pl
- ~ **angle** Totwinkel m
- ~ **arm (channel)** toter Arm m
- ~ **coal** nicht verkokbare Kohle f
- ~-**end pore** Totpore f, unverbundene Pore n
- ~ **fault** inaktive Verwerfung f
- ~ **form** Totform f, Ruheform f
- ~ **glacier** stagnierender (fossiler) Gletscher m
- ~ **heaps** taubes Gestein n
- ~ **ice** Toteis n, fossiles Eis n
- ~ **ice kettles** Toteislöcher npl
- ~ **lake** zuflußloser See m
- ~ **level** tischglatte Ebene f
- ~ **line** 1. Grenzbedingung f, Grenztermin m; 2. Totlinie f (an Inkohlungsstadium gebundener erdölgeologischer Begriff für Grenzlinie, außerhalb derer mit Kohlenwasserstofflagerstätten nicht mehr gerechnet werden kann)
- ~ **litter** tote Bodendecke f
- ~ **load** Eigenmasse f
- ~ **lode** tauber Gang m
- ~ **man** s. guy anchor
- ~ **oil** totes (entgastes) Öl n
- ~ **quartz** tauber Quarz m
- ~ **rock** taubes Gestein n, Nebengestein n
- ~ **space** Totraum m
- ~ **time** Totzeit f (radiometrischer Meßgeräte)
- ~ **time correction** Totzeitkorrektur f
- ~ **valley** Trockental n
- ~ **volcano** erloschener Vulkan m
- ~ **water** stagnierendes Wasser n, Stillwasser n, Totwasser n (eines Flusses)
- ~ **weight** Eigenmasse f
- ~ **well** erschöpfte Bohrung (Sonde) f
- ~ **work** Ausrichtung f und Vorrichtung f (einer Grube, Aufschlußarbeit)

deadbeat measurement stationäre Messung f
deads Abfall m, Berge pl, taubes Gestein n
deaf ore Gangart f mit fein eingesprengtem Erz
dealkalization Entbasung f, Entalkalisierung f
dean s. dene 1.
deaquation Trocknung f, Wasserentziehung f
dearth of water Wassermangel m
death assemblage Todesgemeinschaft f
debacle 1. Eisaufbruch m (in Flüssen); 2. Hochwasserflut f mit Gesteinsmassen
debouchement, debouchure Mündung f (eines Flusses)
debris 1. Schutt m, Geröll n, Geschiebe n, Trümmer pl, Erosionsprodukte npl; 2. Bohrgut n, Bohrschmant m, Bohrmehl n
- ~ **accumulation** Schuttablagerung f, Geröllablagerung f, Trümmerablagerung f
- ~ **avalanche** Lahngang m, Steinlawine f, Schuttlawine f
- ~ **cone** Geröllkegel m
- ~ **fall** Steinschlag m
- ~-**filled valley** vermurtes Tal n
- ~ **flow** Schlammstrom m (aus einer Mischung von feinen und gröberen Partikeln)
- ~ **plain** Trümmerfeld n
- ~ **slide** Bergsturz m, Schuttrutschung f

Debye-Scherrer ring Debye-Scherrer-Ring m
Debyeogram Debye-Scherrer-Aufnahme f
decahedral dekaedrisch, zehnflächig
decahedron Dekaeder n, Zehnflächer m
decalcification Entkalkung f
decalcify/to entkalken
decantation basin Ablagerungsbecken n, Absetzbecken n

~ **test** Sedimentationsprobe f, Dekantationstest m
decanter Dekantiergefäß n
decapitate/to enthaupten, köpfen
decapod crustaceans, decapodans Dekapoden mpl
decay/to verwittern, verfallen, sich zersetzen
decay Verwitterung f, Zerstörung f, Zerfall m, Verfall m, Zersetzung f; Abbau m *(radioaktiver Schadstoffe)*
~ **constant** Zerfallskonstante f, Zeitkonstante f
~ **energy** Zerfallsenergie f
~ **family** [radioaktive] Zerfallsreihe f
~ **law** Zerfallsgesetz n
~ **method** Zerfallsmethode f *(radioaktive Altersbestimmung)*
~ **of rocks** Gesteinsverwitterung f
~ **ooze** Zersetzungsschlick m
~ **process** Zersetzungsprozeß m
~ **product** Zerfallsprodukt n
~ **rate** Zerfallsrate f
~ **series** [radioaktive] Zerfallsreihe f
~ **time** Zerfallszeit f, Abklingzeit f
decayed rock verwittertes Gestein n
dechenite Dechenit m, PbV_2O_6
deciduous forest Laubwald m
~ **tooth** Milchzahn m
~ **tree** Laubbaum m
declination Deklination f *(der Magnetnadel)*
~ **tides** Deklinationstiden pl
decline to grant a concession/to eine Mutung abweisen
decline Neigung f, Senkung f; Abhang m *(s.a. slope)*
~ **curve** Förderabfallkurve f
~ **curve method** Fördermengenabfallmethode f *(Vorratsberechnung)*
~ **of pressure** Druckabfall m
declining volcanic activity ausklingende vulkanische Tätigkeit f
declivate abschüssig
declivitous geneigt, abschüssig, steil
declivity Abschüssigkeit f, Gefälle n; Abhang m
~ **of the mountain** Berghang m
declivous geneigt, abschüssig, steil
decoding Entziffern n, Entschlüsseln n, Dechiffrieren n
decollation, decollement Abgleitung f, Abscherung f *(von Sedimenten)*
~ **structure** Abscherungsstruktur f
decolourize/to entfärben
decompose/to [chemisch] verwittern, sich zersetzen, zerfallen
decomposed verwittert
~ **outcrop** verwitterter Ausstrich m
~ **residuum** Verwitterungsrückstand m
~ **rock** verwittertes Gestein n
decomposition Verwitterung f, Zersetzung f, Zerfall m; Abbau m *(chemischer und biologischer Schadstoffe)*
~ **process** Verwitterungsprozeß m

~ **product** Verwitterungsprodukt n
~ **reaction** Zersetzungsreaktion f
deconsolidation Entfestigung f
deconvolution Dekonvolution f *(Wiederherstellung des ursprünglichen Signals)*
decorative stone Schmuckstein m
decrease in solubility Löslichkeitsverminderung f
~ **in temperature** Temperaturabnahme f
~ **in velocity** Geschwindigkeitsabnahme f
decrepitate/to dekrepitieren, zerknistern
decrepitation Dekrepitieren n, Zerknistern n
decussate feingranoblastisch, granulitisch
decussation Durchkreuzung f *(von Kristallen)*
dedolomitization Entdolomitisierung f
dedolomitize/to entdolomitisieren
deductor muscles Deduktores mpl, Divarikatores mpl, Öffnermuskeln mpl *(bei Brachiopoden)*
deed of surrender of geological prospecting works Abschlußdokument n über durchgeführte geologische Untersuchungsarbeiten
deep 1. Kolk m *(im Fluß);* 2. Tiefseegraben m, Ozeantief n
~ **adit** Wasserlösungsstollen m
~ **boring** Tiefbohren n, Tiefbohrung f *(tiefer als 3000 m)*
~ **boring tool** Bohrgerät n für Tiefbohrungen
~-**burial stage** Stadium n mit mächtiger Sedimentbedeckung
~ **circular gorge (valley)** Talkessel m
~ **current** Tiefenstrom m
~ **digging** Erdfall m
~-**dipping** steil einfallend
~ **drilling** s. ~ boring
~ **erosion** Tiefenerosion f
~-**focus earthquake** Tiefherdbeben n
~ **foundation** Tiefgründung f
~ **gravel** Grundschotter m
~ **hole** Tiefbohrloch n, Tiefbohrung f
~ **karst** tiefer Karst m, Ganzkarst m
~ **lead** tiefliegende Mineralseife f
~ **level mining** s. ~ mining
~ **level workings** Tiefbauarbeiten fpl
~-**lying seam** tiefgelagertes Flöz n
~ **mine workings** s. ~ mining
~ **mining** unterirdischer Abbau m, Tiefbau m
~ **ocean** s. ~ sea
~ **sea** Tiefsee f
~-**sea bed resources** Ressourcen fpl des Tiefseebodens
~-**sea bottom** Tiefseeboden m
~-**sea brown clay** brauner Tiefseeton m
~-**sea channels** Tiefseerinnen fpl
~-**sea deposit** bathyale Ablagerung f, Tiefseeablagerung f
~-**sea depth** mittlere Tiefe f der Meere
~-**sea dredge** Tiefseeschleppnetz n
~-**sea drilling** Tiefseebohrung f
~-**sea exploration** Tiefseeforschung f
~-**sea facies** Tiefseefazies f
~-**sea fan** Tiefseefächer m *(Sedimentfächer, der*

deep

an der Öffnung eines submarinen Cañons gegen das Ozeanbecken ansetzt und sich auf dem Tiefseeboden ausbreitet)
~-sea furrow Tiefseerinne f
~-sea mining Tiefseebergbau m
~-sea mud (ooze) Tiefseeschlamm m
~-sea red clay roter Tiefseeton m
~-sea sediment Tiefseesediment n
~-sea sounding Tiefseelotung f
~-sea terrace Tiefseeterrasse f
~-seated tiefliegend, in der Tiefe entstanden
~-seated igneous rock Tiefengestein n, Plutonit m
~-seated magma Tiefenmagma n
~-seated process Tiefenvorgang m
~-seated rock Tiefengestein n, Plutonit m
~-seated salt dome tiefliegender Salzdom m
~-seated tremors Tiefherdbeben npl
~-seated volcanicity tiefvulkanische Vorgänge mpl
~-seated volcano Tiefenvulkan m
~ seismic sounding seismische Tiefensondierung f
~ sounding Tiefensondierung f
~-sounding apparatus Tiefensondiergerät n
~ space erdferner Weltraum m
~ spring juvenile Quelle f
~ subsoil water Untergrundwasser n
~ trench Tiefseegraben m
~ water 1. Tiefsee f, Hochsee f; 2. Tiefenwasser n
~-water current Tiefenwasserströmung f
~-water marine facies Tiefseefazies f
~-water reservoir Lagerstätte f unter dem Meeresgrund
~ well Tiefbrunnen m
~-well drilling equipment Tiefbohrgeräte npl, Tiefbohrausrüstung f
~-well drilling plant (rig) Tiefbohranlage f
~ working s. ~ mining
~ zone Tiefseezone f
deepen/to 1. abteufen; 2. vertiefen
deepening 1. Abteufen n; 2. Eintiefung f, Vertiefung f
~ of a well Abteufen n des Bohrlochs
deeper pool test Erkundungsbohrung f auf tieferen Horizont (Speicher)
deeply buried tiefliegend
~ buried salt dome tiefliegender Salzdom m
~ disintegrated s. ~ weathered
~ embayed tief eingebuchtet (Küste)
~ incised tief eingeschnitten (Tal)
~ indented stark gegliedert (Küste)
~ rotten s. ~ weathered
~ weathered tiefgründig (stark) verwittert
deerite Deerit m, $MnFe_{12}^{\cdot\cdot}Fe_7^{\cdot\cdot\cdot}(OH)_{11}Si_3O_{44}$
defence of dunes Dünenschutzwerk n
deferred tributary junction s. Yazoo river
deficiency in salt mangelnder Salzgehalt m
~ of mass Massendefizit n (bei Schweremessungen)
deficient in rain regenarm

defile Schlucht f, Talschlucht f, Gebirgsschlucht f, Engpaß m, Hohlweg m, Tobel m
deflation Abwehung f, Deflation f, äolische Ablation f, Windablation f, Winderosion f, Winddenudation f
~ basin Deflationsbecken n, Windkessel m
~ hole Deflationskessel m
~ peneplain Deflationsebene f
~ residue Deflationsrückstand m
~ surface Windschlifffläche f
~ valley Deflationstal n
deflect/to ablenken
~ a river einen Fluß ablenken
deflected hole abgelenkte Bohrung f
deflecting tools Richtbohrwerkzeuge npl
deflection Ablenkung f; Abbiegung f; Durchbiegung f
~ angle Knickwinkel m; Ablenkungswinkel m
~ of the plumb line Lotablenkung f
~ of the vertical Lotabweichung f
~ point Knickpunkt m
deflocculate/to ausflocken
deflocculation Ausflockung f
deforest/to abholzen
deforestation Abholzung f, Entwaldung f
deform/to verformen, deformieren
deformability Verformbarkeit f
deformation 1. Verformung f, Form[ver]änderung f, Deformation f; 2. Dislokation f, Störung f
~ bands Deformationsbänder npl
~ circle Verformungskreis m
~ energy Verformungsarbeit f
~ fabric Deformationsgefüge n
~ fracture Verformungsbruch m
~ of river bed Flußverlegung f
~ plane Deformationsebene f, ac-Ebene f
~ structure Verformungsstruktur f
~ twin Deformationszwilling m, Verformungszwilling m
~ without shearing bruchlose Umformung f
deformed verformt
~ cross-bedding verformte Schrägschichtung f
~ layer verformte Schicht (Bank) f
defrosting Auftauen n
~ temperature Tautemperatur f
degas/to entgasen, degasieren
degasification Entgasung f, Degasierung f
degasifier Entgaser m
degasify/to entgasen, degasieren
degasifying Entgasung f, Degasierung f
degasser Gasabscheider m
degassing Entgasung f, Degasierung f
~ phenomenon Entgasungsprozeß m
~ tremors Entgasungsbeben npl
degaussing Entmagnetisierung f
degeneracy Degenerierung f, Entartung f
degenerate/to degenerieren, entarten
degenerate degeneriert
degeneration Degeneration f, Entartung f
~ of atoms Atomzerfall m

degenerative recrystallization s. grain diminution
deglaciated entgletschert
deglaciation Entgletscherung f
degradation Abtragung f, stufenweise Verwitterung f, Degradierung f
degrade/to 1. abtragen, degradieren; 2. erniedrigen *(Topografie)*
degraded abgebösht
~ **illite** ausgelaugter Illit m
~ **soil** ausgelaugter Boden m
degrading stream Fluß m mit Tiefenerosion
degradinite Degradinit m *(Kohlenmaceral, in japanischen tertiären Kohlen)*
degradofusinite Degradofusinit m *(Kohlensubmaceral)*
degree map Landkarte f im Maßstab 1:250 000
~ **of accuracy** Genauigkeitsgrad m
~ **of accuracy of a map** Kartengenauigkeit f
~ **of cloudiness** Bewölkungsgrad m
~ **of coalification** Inkohlungsgrad m
~ **of compaction** Verdichtungsgrad m
~ **of consolidation** Grad m der Setzung, Verdichtung f, Verfestigungsgrad m
~ **of deformation** Deformationsgrad m
~ **of double refraction** Stärke f der Doppelbrechung
~ **of endangering** Grad m der Gefährdung
~ **of fidelity** Wiedergabevermögen n *(Tracermessung)*
~ **of filling** Versatzdichte f
~ **of freedom** Freiheitsgrad m
~ **of hardness** Härtegrad m
~ **of hotness** Hitzegrad m
~ **of joining** Kluftdichte f
~ **of latitude** Breitengrad m
~ **of longitude** Längengrad m
~ **of metamorphism** Metamorphosegrad m
~ **of oxidation** Oxydationsstufe f
~ **of porosity** Porositätsgrad m
~ **of proof** Bewertungsgrad m
~ **of purity** Reinheitsgrad m
~ **of roundness** Rundungsgrad m
~ **of salinity (saltness)** Salzgehalt m
~ **of saturation** Sättigungsgrad m
~ **of separation** Durchtrennungsgrad m *(von Klüften)*
~ **of slope** Böschungsgrad m
~ **of strength** Festigkeitsgrad m
~ **of symmetry** Symmetriegrad m
~ **of tension** Spannungsgrad m
~ **of trend** Grad m des Trendpolynoms
~ **of turnover** Grad m der Umsetzung
~ **of weathering** Verwitterungsgrad m
dehrnite Dehrnit m *(Varietät von Apatit)*
dehumidify/to Feuchtigkeit entziehen, [aus]trocknen
dehydrate/to entwässern, dehydrieren
dehydrated rock entwässertes Gestein n
dehydration Entwässerung f, Dehydratation f
dejection rocks lose vulkanische Auswurfsmassen fpl

delafossite Delafossit m, $CuFeO_2$
delamination Schichtspaltung f
delatynite Delatynit m *(fossiles Harz)*
delay cap Verzögerungszünder m
~ **distorsion** Laufzeitverzerrung f, Phasenverzerrung f
~ **equalizer** Laufzeitentzerrer m, Phasenentzerrer m
~ **line** Laufzeitglied n, Verzögerungsleitung f, Verzögerungslinie f, Zeitlinie f, Laufzeitkette f *(Seismik)*
~ **time** Verzögerung[szeit] f *(Seismik)*
~ **time characteristic** Laufzeitcharakteristik f
~ **time plot** Zeitfeld n
~ **time variation** Laufzeitverlauf m
delayed river junction verschleppte Mündung f
~ **subsidence** Nachsenkung f
delessite Delessit m *(Varietät von Chlorit)*
delf *(sl)* Kohle- oder Eisensteinlager
delhayelite Delhayelith m, $(Na, K)_{10}Ca_5[(Cl_2, F_2SO_4)_3|O_4|Al_6Si_{32}O_{76}] \cdot 18H_2O$
delime/to entkalken
deliming Entkalken n
delimitation Abgrenzung f
deliquescent salt leicht lösliches Salz n
deliverability Leistungsfähigkeit f *(z. B. einer Gasbohrung)*
delivery Abflußmenge f, Wasserführung f
~ **drift** Wasserlösungsstollen m
~ **loss** Austrittsverlust m *(von Wasser)*; Abgabeverlust m *(eines genutzten Grundwasserleiters)*
~ **of a source (spring)** Quellschüttung f
~ **of a well** Brunnenergiebigkeit f
~ **rate** Förderstrom m
dell Doline f
dellenite Dellenit m *(Quarzlatit)*
Delmontian [Stage] Delmont[ien] n *(marine Stufe, oberes Miozän bis Pliozän in Nordamerika)*
delorenzite Delorenzit m *(Tanteuxinit)*
delrioite Delrioit m, $SrCaH_2[VO_4]_2 \cdot 2H_2O$
delta Delta n
~ **bay** Deltabucht f
~ **bedding** Deltaschichtung f, Deltaaufschüttung f
~ **built into the sea** vorgeschobenes Delta n
~ **fill** Deltaaufschüttung f
~ **flats** Deltaniederung f
~ **formation** Deltabildung f
~ **-front sheet sand** Deltafrontflächensand m
~ **growth** Deltawachstum n
~ **lake** Deltasee m
~ **margin** Deltarand m
~ **-margin island sand** Deltafrontinselsand m
~ **plain** Deltaebene f
~ **shape** Deltaform f
deltafication Deltabildung f
deltageosyncline s. exogeosyncline
deltaic embankment Deltadamm m
~ **fan** Deltaablagerungskegel m

deltaic

- ~ **gravel deposit** Deltakiesablagerung f
- ~ **sediment** Deltasediment n
- ~ **stratification** Deltaschichtung f
- **deltaite** Deltait m, Crandallit m, CaAl$_3$H[(OH)$_6$|(PO$_4$)$_2$]
- **deltohedron** Deltoeder n
- **deltoid dodecahedron** Deltoiddodekaeder n
- ~ **icositetrahedron** Deltoidikositetraeder n
- **deltoids** Deltoidplatten fpl (Paläontologie)
- **deluge/to** überschwemmen
- **deluge** Überschwemmung f
- ~ **of rain** Wolkenbruch m
- **Deluge of Noah** Sintflut f
- **delvauxite** Delvauxit m, Fe[(OH)$_3$|PO$_4$]·5$^1/_2$H$_2$O
- **demagnetization** Entmagnetisierung f
- **demagnetize/to** entmagnetisieren
- **demand for concession without previous discovery** blinde Mutung f
- **demant** s. diamond 1.
- **demantoid** Demantoid m (grüne Granatvarietät; s.a. andradite)
- **demarcate/to** vermarken
- **demicron-sized** in Korngröße von 10–100 μm
- **Demingian [Stage]** Demingien n (Stufe des Unterordoviziums in Nordamerika)
- **demoiselle** Erdpyramide f
- **demonstrated reserves** Summe aus berechneten und angezeigten Vorräten
- **demonstration pumping test** Demonstrationspumpversuch m
- **demorphism** Verwitterungsprozeß m
- **demulsifier** Demulgator m
- **demulsify/to** demulgieren
- **demulsifying chemical** Entemulgierungsmittel n, Demulgator m, Spalter m (Bohrtechnik)
- **demultiplexing** Signaltrennung f (beim Multiplexverfahren)
- **dendrachate** Baumachat m
- **dendriform** baumähnlich
- **dendrite** Dendrit m
- **dendritic[al]** dendritisch
- ~ **agate** Baumachat m
- ~ **drainage pattern** verzweigtes Flußnetz n
- ~ **manganese** Mangandendriten mpl
- ~ **markings** dendritische Markierungen fpl
- ~ **texture** dendritische (baumförmige, astige) Struktur f
- ~ **valley system** verzweigtes Talsystem n
- **dendrochronology** Dendrochronologie f, Baumringmessung f
- **dendrogram** Dendrogramm n
- **dendrograph** Dendrograph m (grafische Darstellung der Ähnlichkeiten innerhalb und zwischen hierarchisch geordneten Clustern)
- **dendrolite** Dendrolith m, versteinerter Baumstamm m, verkieseltes Holz n
- **dene** 1. Tal n; 2. Sandstreifen m, kleine Düne f
- ~ **hole** Kalkhöhle f
- **denitrification** Denitrifikation f
- **denitrifying** Denitrifizieren n
- ~ **bacteria** denitrifizierende Bakterien fpl

denningite Denningit m, (Mn, Ca, Zn)Te$_2$O$_5$
dennisonite s. davisonite
dense[-graded] aggregate hohlraumarmes Mineralgemisch n
~ **-medium washing** Schwerflüssigkeitssortierung f
~ **mineral aggregate** hohlraumarmes Mineralgemisch n
~ **texture** dichtes Gefüge n (Gestein)
densinite Densinit m (Braunkohlenmaceral)
densitometer Densitometer n, Dichtemesser m
densitometric[al] analysis densitometrische Analyse f
density Dichte f
- ~ **contrast** Dichteunterschied m
- ~ **current** s. turbidity current
- ~ **difference** Dichteunterschied m
- ~ **log** Dichtelog n, Gamma-gamma-Log n
- ~ **logging** Dichtemessung f
- ~ **meter** Wichtemesser m
- ~ **of dislocation** Verschiebungsdichte f (Kristallgitter)
- ~ **of exploration (exposure)** Aufschlußdichte f (eines Erkundungsgebietes)
- ~ **of ground** Gebirgsdichte f
- ~ **profile** Dichteprofil n
- ~ **slicing** Äquidensitendarstellung f (stufenförmige Klassifizierung der Schwärzungsniveaus)
- ~ **stratification** gradierte Schichtung f
dental formula Zahnformel f
~ **sockets** Zahngruben fpl
dentaloid zahnähnlich
dentary Dentale n, zahntragender Knochen m
dentation Bezahnung f
denticles Dentikel mpl, Zähnchen npl
denticulate gezähnt
~ **lobes** gezähnte Loben mpl
dentine s. tooth enamel
dentist borer Zahnarztbohrer m
dentition Zahnformel f
denudation Abtragung f, Denudation f
- ~ **level** Abtragungsebene f, Abtragungsniveau n, Denudationsniveau n
- ~ **limit** Denudationsgrenze f
- ~ **plain** Denudationsebene f
- ~ **remnant** Denudationsrelikt n
- ~ **ridge** Erosionsrücken m
- ~ **surface** Denudationsfläche f
- ~ **terrace** Denudationsterrasse f, Verwitterungsterrasse f
- ~ **valley** Erosionstal n
denude/to abtragen, denudieren, bloßlegen
denuded cutting Fenster n (Deckenfenster)
deoxidation sphere Bleichungshof m (in Rotsedimenten)
departure Abweichung f (z.B. von der Basislinie)
depauperate fauna s. dwarfed fauna
depergelation Tauprozeß m im Permafrost
deplanation Reliefeinebnung f

deplete/to 1. erschöpfen; 2. entleeren, räumen
depleted erschöpft
~ **area** erschöpftes Gebiet n
~ **field** erschöpfte (ausgebeutete) Lagerstätte f
~ **layer** erschöpfter Horizont m
~ **sand** dränierter (entölter) Sand m
~ **soil** verarmter Boden m
~ **well** 1. erschöpfte Bohrung f; 2. versiegter Brunnen m
depletion Erschöpfung f (von Lagerstätten durch fortschreitenden Abbau)
~ **area** Zehrgebiet n
~ **drive** Gasexpansionstrieb m
~ **drive pool** Gasexpansionstrieblager n
~ **layer** Auslaugungsschicht f
~ **of oil wells** Erschöpfung f (Versiegen n) von Erdölbohrungen
~-**type reservoir** Erschöpfungsspeicher m
depoaxis Linie f maximaler Sedimentation während eines geologischen Zeitabschnitts
depocenter Sedimentationszentrum n, Raum m maximaler Sedimentation
depolarize/to depolarisieren
depoldering Entpolderung f
deposit/to ablagern
deposit Lagerstätte f
~ **evaluation** Lagerstättenbewertung f
~ **formed by exhalations** Exhalationslagerstätte f
~ **formed by weathering** Verwitterungslagerstätte f
~ **from volcanic fumaroles** vulkanischer Fumarolenabsatz m
~ **of natural gas** Erdgasvorkommen n
~ **of ore** Erzlager n
~ **of petroleum** Erdöllagerstätte f
~ **of potash salts** Kalisalzlager n
~ **of the abyssal depths of the deep sea** Tiefseeablagerung f
~ **precipitated in sea water** Ausscheidungslagerstätte f im Meer
~ **produced by weathering** Verwitterungslagerstätte f
deposited moraine Stapelmoräne f
~ **snow** frischgefallener Schnee m, Neuschnee m
depositing medium Ablagerungsmedium n
deposition Ablagerung f, Absatz m
~ **area** Ablagerungsgebiet n
~ **bluff** Anwachsufer n
~ **layer** s. tectorium
~ **of cuttings** Verschlammung f des Bohrlochs
~ **place** Ablagerungsstelle f
~ **plane** Schichtfläche f, Ablagerungsfläche f
depositional basin Ablagerungsbecken n
~ **environment** 1. Ablagerungsmilieu n; 2. Sedimentationsraum m, Sedimentationsgebiet n
~ **fabric** Anlagerungsgefüge n, Sedimentationsgefüge f
~ **factors** Ablagerungsbedingungen fpl
~ **magnetization** remanente Magnetisierung, festgelegt durch sedimentäre Korneinregelung
~ **model** Ablagerungsmodell n, Sedimentationsmodell n
~ **oil trap** fazielle Falle f
~ **pattern** Ablagerungsmuster n
~ **porosity** primäre Porosität f
~ **rate** Ablagerungsgeschwindigkeit f
~ **strike deposit** laterale Sedimentanhäufung f
~ **terrace** angeschwemmte Uferbank f, Sedimentationsterrasse f
~ **trap** lithologische Falle f
depositories Ablagerungsplätze mpl
depotassication Kaliumentzug m aus Tonmineralen
depreciation of deposit Lagerstättenabschreibung f
~ **of ore reserves** Abschreibung f von Erzvorräten
depressed gesenkt
~ **area** Depression f, Niederung f, Senke f
~ **block** abgesenkte Scholle f
~ **coast** Senkungsküste f
~ **flute cast** Flachzapfen m (Strömungswulst)
~ **rift** Grabenbruch m
~ **shore line** Senkungsküste f
depression Vertiefung f, Senkung f, Senke f, Einsenkung f, Niederung f; Depression f, Mulde f
~ **angle** 1. Senkungswinkel m; 2. Tiefwinkel m, Horizontaldepression f, Depressionswinkel m
~ **area of nappe** Deckenmulde f
~ **funnel** Absenkungstrichter m
~ **lake** Senkungssee m
~ **of downfaulting** Bruchsenke f, Verwerfungssenke f
~ **of ground** Bodensenke f, Bodensenkung f; Geländemulde f
~ **of melting point** Schmelzpunkterniedrigung f
~ **on a slope** Hangmulde f
~ **spring** Überfallquelle f, Überlaufquelle f
~ **storage** Trichterinhalt m (Absenkungstrichter)
depressuring of reservoirs Auflast f von Staubecken
depth Tiefe f, Teufe f
~ **capacity** Teufenkapazität f
~ **drill** Tiefbohrer m
~ **finder** Teufenmeßgerät n
~ **gauge** Tiefenmesser m
~ **hoar** durch Sublimation im Schneekörper wachsender Eiskristall
~ **indicator** Teufen[an]zeiger m
~-**integrating sampler** Tiefprobenehmer m (Grundwasser)
~-**integrating sampling** Tiefprobenahme f (Grundwasser)
~ **measuring device** Tiefenmesser m
~ **of bore** Bohrtiefe f
~ **of burial** Einbettungstiefe f, Versenkungstiefe f

depth 100

~ of drilling Bohrtiefe f
~ of focus Herdtiefe f
~ of formation markers Tiefe f von Gebirgsleitschichten
~ of foundation Gründungstiefe f
~ of frost penetration Frosttiefe f
~ of mining Abbauteufe f
~ of mud invasion Eindringtiefe f der Spülung
~ of occurrence Lagerungsteufe f
~ of penetration Eindringtiefe f
~ of pit Schachttiefe f
~ of rain[fall] Regenhöhe f, Niederschlagshöhe f
~ of runoff Abflußhöhe f
~ of seismic focus Herdtiefe f
~ of snow cover Höhe f der Schneedecke, Schneehöhe f
~ of soil Bodentiefe f
~ of stratum Mächtigkeit f
~ of the navigable channel Fahrwassertiefe f
~ of top soil Krumentiefe f
~ of water Wassertiefe f
~ point Tiefenpunkt m, Reflexionspunkt m
~ probe Tiefenprobe f
~ profile Tiefenprofil n
~ range Tiefenbereich m
~ section Tiefenschnitt m, Tiefenprofil n
~ sounder Echolot n
~ sounding Tiefensondierung f (durch Echolot)
~ to the basement rocks Tiefe f bis zum Grundgebirge
~-to-water map Grundwasserteufenkarte f
~ zone Tiefenzone f
depthometer Teufenmeßgerät n
deputy surveyor Markscheidergehilfe m
derangement of masses Massenstörung f
Derby spar (sl) s. fluorite
derbylite Derbylith m, Fe$_3$Ti$_3$SbO$_{11}$OH
Derbyshire spar (sl) s. fluorite
dereliction s. accretion
dereption subaquatische Erosion durch Strömung
derivative Ableitung f (eines Potentialfeldes)
~ magma Tochtermagma n, Differentiat n, Magmenderivat n
~ map Karte f der Ableitungen (eines Potentialfeldes)
derived fossil Fossil n auf sekundärer Lagerstätte, verschlepptes Fossil n
dermal ossicle Hautknöchelchen n
~ skeleton Dermalskelett n, Exoskelett n, Hautskelett n
~ spicule Dermale n, Dermalspiculum n, Hautnadel f (bei Schwämmen)
dermolithic lava Fladenlava f
~ solidification oberflächliche Erstarrung f
deroofing Durchschmelzung f des Daches (Magmatismus)
derrick Bohrturm m
~ floor Arbeitsbühne f (Bohrturm)
~ foundation Bohrturmsockel m, Bohrturmfundament n

~ platform Bohrbühne f
~ substructure Bohrturmunterbau m
desalination Entsalzung f
desalinification Entsalzung f (bei Diagenese)
desalinify/to entsalzen
desalinization Entsalzung f
~ of soil Bodenentsalzung f
desalting Entsalzung f
~ of water Entsalzung f des Wassers
desander, desanding device Entsander m (Bohrtechnik)
descend/to 1. sich abwärts bewegen, niedergehen; 2. abstammen (Paläontologie)
~ into a mine einfahren, eine Grube befahren
descendance Abstammung f (Paläontologie)
descendant deszendent (Paläontologie)
descending absteigend, deszendent
~ filter Fallfilter n
~ slab of lithosphere abtauchende Lithosphärenplatte f
~ solution absteigende Lösung f
~ water deszendentes Wasser n
~ wind Fallwind m
descent 1. Abstammung f; 2. Gefälle n, Neigung f
~ of water Einsickern n des Wassers
descloizite Descloizit m, Descloizit m, Pb(Zn,Cu)[OH|VO$_4$]
descriptive mineralogy beschreibende (allgemeine) Mineralogie f
desert Wüste f
~ area Wüstengebiet n
~ belt Wüstengürtel m
~ climate Wüstenklima n
~ floor Wüstenboden m
~ lacquer s. ~ varnish
~ lake Wüstensee m, Endsee m
~ mosaic s. ~ pavement
~ of sand Sandwüste f
~ of stones Steinwüste f
~ pavement Wüstenpflaster n, Steinpflaster n, Deflationsrückstand m
~ polish Wüstenpolitur f
~ region Wüstengebiet n
~ sand Wüstensand m
~ soil Wüstenboden m
~ topography Wüstenlandschaft f
~ varnish Wüstenlack m, Wüstenrinde f
~ wind Wüstenwind m
~ zone Wüstenzone f
desertification Wüstenbildung f
desiccate/to austrocknen, eintrocknen
desiccated ausgetrocknet
desiccation Austrocknen n, Austrocknung f
~ breccia Tonscherbenbrekzie f
~ crack Schrumpfungsriß m, Schwundriß m, Trockenriß m (Sedimentgefüge)
~-cracked von Trockenrissen durchzogen
~ fissure Trockenriß m, Austrocknungsspalte f
~ form Austrocknungsform f
~ fracture (joint) Trockenriß m
~ polygons Trockenrißnetzwerk n

desiccative [aus]trocknend
design estimates Projektdokumentation f
~ **flood** Flut, gegen die Schutzmaßnahmen getroffen werden
~ **load** Lastannahme f; zulässige Last f
designation of rock Gesteinsbezeichnung f
desilicate/to entkieseln, desilifizieren
desilication Entkieselung f, Desilifizierung f
desilt/to entschlammen
desilting Entschlammung f
desliming classifier Schlämmklassierer m
desmine s. stilbite
desmocollinite Desmocollinit m (Kohlensubmaceral)
Desmoinesian [Stage] Desmoines n (Stufe des Pennsylvaniens in Nordamerika)
desmosite Desmosit m (Kontaktgestein)
desolation Verödung f, Verwüstung f
desorption Desorption f
desquamation Abschuppen n, Abschuppung f
destinezite Destinezit m, $Fe_4[(OH)_4|(PO_4,SO_4)_3]\cdot 13H_2O$
destrengthening Entfestigung f
destruction Destruktion f, Zerstörung f
~ **by insolation** Insolationsverwitterung f, Temperaturverwitterung f, Insolationssprengung f
~ **of buildings** Zerstörungen fpl an Gebäuden (8. Stufe der Erdbebenstärkeskala)
~ **product** Zerstörungsprodukt n
destructional form Destruktionsform f, Zerstörungsform f
~ **landforms** durch Abtragung geschaffene Landschaft f
~ **work** Zerstörungsarbeit f
destructive zerstörend
~ **exploitation** Raubbau m
~ **process** zerstörender Vorgang m
desulphurate/to entschwefeln
desulphur[iz]ation Entschwefelung f
~ **unit** Entschwefelungsanlage f
desulphurize/to entschwefeln
detach/to ablösen, abtrennen, loslösen; abscheren
detached coffin in the roof Sargdeckel m
~ **core** nichtdeformierter Kern m (einer Isoklinalfalte)
detachment Ablösung f, Abtrennung f, Loslösung f; Abscherung f; Absonderung f
~ **of rock particles** Loslösung f von Gesteinsteilchen
~ **of the current** Abreißen n der Strömung
detailed geological map geologische Spezialkarte f
~ **ground-water exploration (prospection)** Grundwasserdetailerkundung f
~-**stratigraphical** feinstratigrafisch
detect/to entdecken, nachweisen, auffinden
detecting element Nachweisglied n
~ **sensitivity** Nachweisempfindlichkeit f
detection Entdeckung f, Nachweis m, Auffindung f

~ **limit** Nachweisgrenze f
~ **of trace elements** Spurenanalyse f, Spurennachweis m
detector Nachweisgerät n; Aufnehmer m, Geophon n (Seismik); Empfänger m (Radiometrie)
~ **element** fotoelektrisches Halbleiterelement n
~ **spread** Seismometerprofil n
detention basin Rückhaltebecken n
~ **storage** Rückhaltevolumen n
detergent flooding Fluten n mit oberflächenaktiven Stoffen
deterioration of climate Klimaverschlechterung f
determination fossil Leitfossil n
~ **of age** Altersbestimmung f
~ **of character of ore** Erzbewertung f
~ **of epicentre** Bestimmung f des Epizentrums
~ **of gravity** Schweremessung f
~ **of hardness** Härtebestimmung f
~ **of orbit** Bahnbestimmung f
~ **of trace elements** Bestimmung f von Spurenelementen
determinative mineralogy spezielle Mineralogie f
~ **test** Bestimmungsprobe f
determining borehole Grenzbohrloch n, Abgrenzungsbohrloch n
detonation Detonation f
~ **cord** Sprengschnur f
detrital 1. verwittert, zerrieben, detritisch; 2. Geröll..., Schutt...
~ **accumulation** Schuttablagerung f, Trümmerablagerung f
~ **deposit** detritische Ablagerung f, Gesteinsschutt m, Trümmerlagerstätte f
~ **facies** Schuttfazies f
~ **fan** Schuttkegel m
~ **formation** Schuttbildung f
~ **lime tufa** klastischer Kalktuff m
~ **limestone** detritischer Kalkstein m (aus Detritus älterer Kalksteine)
~ **material** Schuttmaterial n, Trümmermaterial n
~ **mineral** detritisches Mineral n
~ **plain** Schuttebene f
~ **ratio** Verhältnis von klastisch zu nichtklastisch in einem Profil
~ **remanent magnetization** von kleinen Teilchen hervorgerufene Magnetisierung f
~ **rock** detritisches Gestein n, Trümmergestein n
~ **sand** Geröllsand m
~ **sediments** Geröllsedimente npl
~ **slope** Schutthang m, Schuttböschung f, Schutthalde f
~ **soil** Schuttboden m
~ **spring** Schuttquelle f
detrited s. detrital 2.
detrition Detritus erzeugender Prozeß m
detritovore Detritus fressendes Tier n

detritus 102

detritus Detritus *m*, Geröll *n*, Grus *m*, Gesteinsschutt *m*, Schuttablagerung *f*, Schutt *m*, Geschiebe *n*, Trümmermasse *f*
~ **eruption** Lockermassenausbruch *m*
~ **rubbish** Steinschutt *m*
detrusion Scherungsverschiebung *f*
deuteric deuterisch, autometamorph, spätmagmatisch
~ **alteration** deuterische Umwandlung *f*, spätmagmatische Gesteinsumwandlung *f*
deuterium Deuterium *n*
deuterogene rock sekundäres Gestein *n*
deuterogenic aus anderen Gesteinen gebildet
deuterogenotypic zum gleichen Genotyp gehörend
deuterogenous *s.* deuterogenic
deuteromorphic deuteromorph, sekundär verändert *(Kristalle)*
deuterosomatic regeneriert, umgewandelt *(Gesteine)*
develop/to erschließen, aufschließen, ausrichten; entwickeln *(ein Ölfeld)*
developable abwickelbar
developed cave Schauhöhle *f*
~ **ore** vorgerichtetes (aufgeschlossenes) Erz *n*
~ **reserves** ausgerichtete (nachgewiesene) Vorräte *mpl*
development Erschließung *f*, Aufschluß *m*, Ausrichtung *f*; Entwicklung *f (eines Ölfelds)*
~ **curve** Bodensenkungskurve *f*
~ **drilling** Erweiterungsbohrung *f*
~ **of heat** Wärmeentwicklung *f*
~ **of pressure** Druckverlauf *m*
~ **of terraces** Terrassenbildung *f*
~ **well** Förderbohrung *f*, Erweiterungsbohrung *f*
~ **work** Aus- und Vorrichtungsarbeiten *fpl*
developmental history Entwicklungsgeschichte *f*
~ **series** Entwicklungsreihe *f*
~ **stage** Entwicklungsstadium *n*
Devensian Devensien *n (Pleistozän, Britische Inseln, entspricht etwa der Würmeiszeit der Alpen)*
deviated borehole Umlenkbohrung *f*; abgewichene Bohrung *f*
~ **well** *s.* ~ borehole
deviation Ablenkung *f*, Abweichung *f*
~ **from plumb** Schiefstellung *f (Schacht)*
~ **in azimuth** Richtungsabweichung *f*
~ **of the hole** Bohrlochkrümmung *f*
~ **of well** Abweichung *f* der Bohrung
~ **recorder** Abweichungsanzeiger *m*
deviator Deviator *m (Abweichung des dreiachsigen Spannungszustands vom hydrostatischen)*
device for deflecting tool orientation Orientierungsvorrichtung *f (Bohrtechnik)*
devilline Devillin *m*, $CaCu_4[(OH)_3|SO_4]_2 \cdot 3H_2O$
devil's dice *(sl)* Limonit pseudomorph nach Pyrit
devitrification Entglasung *f*

devitrified rock entglastes Gestein *n*
devitrify/to entglasen
devoid of fossils fossilfrei
~ **of trees** baumlos
devolatilization Entgasung *f (bei Inkohlung)*
Devonian Devon[system] *n (chronostratigrafisch);* Devon *n*, Devonperiode *f (geochronologisch);* Devon *n*, Devonzeit *f (allgemein)*
~ **Age** Devon *n*, Devonzeit *f*
~ **Period** Devon *n*, Devonperiode *f*
~ **System** Devon[system] *n*
Devono-Carboniferous devono-karbonisch
dew Tau *m*
~ **formation** Taubildung *f*
~ **point** Taupunkt *m*
~-**point pressure** Taupunktdruck *m*
dewater/to entwässern, trockenlegen
dewatering Entwässerung *f*, Trockenlegung *f*; Wasserhaltung *f (einer Baugrube)*
~ **installation** Grundwasserabsenkungsanlage *f* mit Filterbrunnen
~ **method** Entwässerungsverfahren *n*
~ **roadway system** Entwässerungsstreckennetz *n*
~ **system** *s.* ~ installation
~ **through the partially perforated base** Teilbodenentwässerung *f*
deweylite Deweylit *m (Serpentinmineral)*
dewindtite Dewindtit *m*, $Pb[(UO_2)_4|(OH)_4|(PO_4)_2]\cdot 8H_2O$
dextral rechtsgewunden *(bei Molluskenschalen)*
~ **fault** rechtsdrehende Verwerfung *f*
dextrogyrate quartz Rechtsquarz *m*
dextrorotatory rechtsdrehend
DGA *s.* dense-graded aggregate
diabantite Diabantit *m (Chloritmineral)*
diabase Diabas *m*
~ **porphyry** Diabasporphyr *m*
~ **tuff** Diabastuff *m*
diabasic diabasisch
~ **lava** Diabaslava *f*
~ **texture** Diabasstruktur *f*, ophitisches Gefüge *n*
Diablan orogeny Diablan-Orogenese *f (Orogenese im Grenzbereich Tithon/Berrias, Nordamerika)*
diablastic diablastisch
~ **texture** diablastische Struktur *f*, Siebstruktur *f*
diaboleite Diaboleit *m*, $Pb_2[Cu(OH)_4Cl_2]$
diabrochite Diabrochit *m (Migmatit)*
diachronic *s.* diachronous
diachronism Diachronismus *m (verschieden zeitliche Position einer Transgressionsfläche)*
diachronous im geologischen Alter differierend
diaclase Diaklase *f*, Bruchstelle *f*, normaler Bruch *m*, Kluft *f (ohne Verschiebungsbetrag)*
diaclasis *s.* diaclase
diaclinal valley Diaklinaltal *n (Tal, das eine Falte schneidet)*

diacritical diakritisch
diadochite Diadochit *m*, $Fe_4[(OH)_4(PO_4, SO_4)_3] \cdot 13H_2O$
diadochy Diadochie *f*, Vertretbarkeit *f*
diagenesis Diagenese *f*
~ **of sediments** Sedimentdiagenese *f*
diagenetic diagenetisch
~ **change** diagenetische Umwandlung *f*
diagenism *s.* diagenesis
diagnosis 1. Differentialprozeß *m*; 2. Beschreibung *f (der Spezies oder Art)*
diagnostic mineral [fazies]kritisches Mineral *n*, Indexmineral *n*
diagonal bedding Diagonalschichtung *f*, Transversalschichtung *f*
~ **joint** Diagonalkluft *f*
~ **lamination** Transversalschichtung *f*
~ **position** Diagonalstellung *f*
~ **scour marks** diagonale Kolkmarken *fpl*
~ **slip fault** schräge Auf- *oder* Abschiebung *f*
diagram of state Zustandsdiagramm *n*
diagrammatic section Querschnittaufriß *m*
dial/to mit dem Kompaß aufnehmen; markscheiden *(mit der Bussole)*
dial Bussole *f*
~ **gauge** Zeigermeßgerät *n*
~ **indicator** Meßuhr *f*
diallage Diallag *m (monokliner Pyroxen)*
dialling Markscheidezug *m*
dialogite *s.* rhodochrosite
dialysis Dialyse *f*
diamagnetic diamagnetisch
~ **mineral** diamagnetisches Mineral *n*
~ **substance** diamagnetischer Stoff *m*
diamagnetism Diamagnetismus *m*
diamantiferous *s.* diamondiferous
diamantine diamantartig; diamantführend
diameter Durchmesser *m*
~ **of drill hole** Bohrlochdurchmesser *m*
~ **of the grains** Korndurchmesser *m*
diamictite Diamiktit *m*
diamond 1. Diamant *m*, β-C; 2. Karo *n (Geophon oder Schußpunktanordnung)*
~ **content in core bit** Konzentration *f* der Diamanten in der Krone
~ **core barrel** Diamantkernbohrapparat *m*
~ **core bit** Diamantkernkrone *f*
~ **core drilling** Diamantkernbohren *n*
~ **core head** mit Diamanten besetzte Kernbohrkrone *f*
~ **coring** Kernen *n* mit Diamantkrone
~ **crown** Diamantkrone *f*
~ **drill** Diamantbohrer *m*
~ **drilling** Bohren *n* mit Diamantkronen
~ **drilling bit** Diamantbohrmeißel *m*
~ **dust** Diamantstaub *m*
~ **-impregnated** mit Diamantstaub durchsetzt
~ **lustre** Diamantglanz *m*
~ **of the purest water** Diamant *m* von reinstem Wasser
~ **orientation in core bit** Orientierung *f* der Diamanten in der Krone

~ **size** Körnigkeit *f* der Diamanten in der Krone
~ **spar** *s.* corundum
~ **tin** großer Zinnsteinkristall *m*
~ **-type cutter head** Diamantbohrkrone *f*
diamondiferous diamantenführend, diamanthaltig
diamorphism Diamorphismus *m*
diamorphous diamorph
diaphaneity Lichtdurchlässigkeit *f*; Transparenz *f (Qualitätsbegriff bei Mineralen)*
diaphanous lichtdurchlässig *(Porzellan)*; durchscheinend *(Kristalle)*; transparent *(Minerale)*
diaphorite Diaphorit *m*, $4PbS \cdot 3Ag_2S \cdot 3Sb_2S_3$
diaphragm Dichtungsschirm *m*, Dichtungsgürtel *m*
diaphthoresis Diaphthorese *f*
diaphthorite Diaphthorit *m*
diaphthoritic diaphthoritisch
~ **zone** diaphthoritische Zone *f*
diaphthoritization Diaphthoritisierung *f*
diapir Diapir *m (s.a. piercement fold)*
~ **folding** diapire Faltung *f*, Durchspießungsfaltung *f*, Injektivfaltung *f*
diapiric folds Injektivfalten *fpl*, Diapirfalten *fpl*
diapirism Diapirismus *m*
diaplectic glass diaplektisches Glas *n (amorphe Phase, erzeugt durch Schockmetamorphose ohne Schmelzung)*
diaschistic diaschist
~ **rock** diaschistes Gestein *n*, Spaltprodukt *n* eines Muttermagmas
diaspore Diaspor *m*, α-AlOOH
diastatic diastatisch *(für Krustendeformationen erzeugende Kräfte)*
diastem Diastem *n*, Sedimentationsunterbrechung *f*, kleine Sedimentationslücke *f*, Omissionsfläche *f*
diastrophe Krustendeformation *f*
diastrophic diastrophisch
~ **cycle** krustengestaltender Deformationszyklus *m*
~ **deformation** tektonische Verformung *f*
~ **process** tiefgreifender tektonischer Prozeß *m*
~ **structure** tektonische Struktur *f*
diastrophism Diastrophismus *m*, krustengestaltende Deformationsprozesse *mpl*, tektonische Umwälzung *f*, diastrophische Bewegungen *fpl*, gebirgsbildende Vorgänge *mpl*
diatectic diatektisch
~ **varve** Warve *f* mit gradiertem Kornaufbau
diatexis Diatexis *f*
diathermal, diathermanous, diathermic, diathermous wärmedurchlässig
diatom Diatomee *f*, Kieselalge *f*
~ **case (frustule)** Diatomeenschale *f*
~ **ooze** Diatomeenschlamm *m*, Diatomeenschlick *m*
~ **shell** Diatomeenschale *f*
diatomaceous Diatomeen...
~ **chert** *s.* diatomite 1.

diatomaceous 104

~ **clay** Diatomeenton m
~ **earth** Diatomeenerde f, Kieselgur f, Infusorienerde f
~ **ooze** Diatomeenschlamm m, Diatomeenschlick m
diatomic zweiatomig
diatomite 1. Infusorienerde f, Kieselgur f, Diatomit m; 2. Kieselgurpulver n *(als Rohstoff)*
diatonous schief auslöschend *(Kristalle)*
diatreme Diatrema n, Durchschlagsrohr n, Förderkanal m *(vulkanisch)*
dice coal *(sl)* würflig brechende Kohle f
dichotomous dichotom, gabelförmig
~ **branching** Dichotomie f, gabelförmige Verzweigung f
dichroic dichroitisch, pleochroitisch
~ **crystal** dichroitischer Kristall m
~ **mineral** pleochroitisches Mineral n
dichroism Dichroismus m, Pleochroismus m
dichroite s. cordierite
dickinsonite Dickinsonit m, $Na_2(Mn, Fe)_5[PO_4]_4$
dickite Dickit m, $Al_4[(OH)_8|Si_4O_{10}]$
dictyogenesis Diktyogenese f, Rahmenfaltung f
dictyogenetic diktyogenetisch
didactic structure s. graded bedding
didecahedral didekaedrisch
didodecahedron Dyakisdodekaeder n
didymograptus shale Didymograptenschiefer m
didymolite Didymolith m, $(Ca, Mg, Fe)Al_2[Si_3O_{10}]$
die away (out)/to sich verdrücken, auskeilen
dle collar Fangglocke f *(Bohrtechnik)*
dielectric[al] dielektrisch
~ **constant** Dielektrizitätskonstante f
~ **logging** Dielektrizitätsmessung f
~ **polarization** dielektrische Polarisation f
~ **properties** Dielektrizitätseigenschaften fpl *(z.B. von Gesteinen)*
dienerite Dienerit m, Ni_3As
dietrichite Ditrichit m, $ZnAl_2[SO_4]_4 \cdot 22H_2O$
dietzeite Dietzeit m, $Ca_2[CrO_4 \cdot (JO_3)_2]$
difference in density Dichteunterschied m
~ **in elevation (level)** Höhenunterschied m
~ **in temperature** Wärmeunterschied m, Temperaturunterschied m
~ **of head** Gefälleunterschied m
~ **of latitude** Breitenunterschied m
~ **of level** Niveauunterschied m
~ **of longitude** Längenunterschied m
~ **of path** Gangunterschied m
differential compaction unterschiedliche Setzung f
~ **erosion** ungleichmäßige (selektive) Erosion f
~ **liberation** Differentialverdampfung f *(Gas/Öl-Verhältnis)*
~ **movement** Differentialbewegung f
~ **pressure** Differenzdruck m
~ **sediment (settlement)** ungleichmäßige Setzung f, Setzungsunterschied m
~ **thermal analysis** Differentialthermoanalyse f

differentiate Differentiat n
differentiated dike differenzierter Gang m
differentiation Differentiation f, Entmischung f
~ **by gas transfer** Differentiation f durch Gastransport
~ **due to gravity** gravitative Differentiation f
~ **due to gravity sinking of crystals** gravitative Kristallisationsdifferentiation f
~ **of species** Differenzierung f der Arten
~ **process** Differentiationsvorgang m
~ **product** Differentiationsprodukt n
difficultly soluble schwer löslich
~ **volatile** schwerflüchtig
diffision Diffision f, Gesteinsabtrag m durch Wolkenbrüche
diffluence Diffluenz f, Auseinanderlaufen n, Auffächern f
~ **glacier** in ein Nebental überlaufender Talgletscher m
diffraction Diffraktion f, Beugung f, Strahlenbrechung f
~ **grating** Beugungsgitter n
~ **image** Beugungsbild n
~ **of light** Lichtbrechung f
~ **pattern** Beugungsfigur f, Beugungsbild n, Beugungsaufnahme f
~ **spectrum** Beugungsspektrum n, Gitterspektrum n
diffuse/to 1. diffundieren; 2. zerstreuen
diffuse diffus
~ **radiation** Streustrahlung f
~ **reflection** diffuse Reflexion f, Remission f
~ **sky radiation** diffuse Himmelsstrahlung f
diffusibility Diffusionsvermögen n
diffusion Diffusion f
~ **banding** Liesegangsche Ringe mpl
~ **equation** Diffusionsgleichung f
~ **process** Diffusionsvorgang m
~ **rate** Diffusionsgeschwindigkeit f
~ **well** Versickerungsbrunnen m
diffusivity Diffusionsvermögen n
~ **coefficient** Diffusionskoeffizient m
dig/to schürfen; graben; baggern
~ **turf** Torf stechen
~ **up** ausgraben
dig-and-turn time Schürfzeit f
digenite Digenit m, Cu_9S_5
digested sludge Faulschlamm m *(Abwasserwesen)*
digger 1. Bagger m, Löffelbagger m; 2. Goldgräber m; Erzgräber m
digging 1. Schürfen n; 2. Graben n; Baggern n
~ **height** Abtraghöhe f
~ **pit** Schürfschacht m
~ **time** Schürfzeit f
digital digital
digitate fingerförmig
digitation Digitation f, Auffingerung f von Faltendeckenstirnen
digitize/to digitalisieren
digonal zweiwinklig

dihedral zweiflächig
dihedron Zweiflach n, Zweiflächner m
dihexagonal dihexagonal
~ **prism** dihexagonales Prisma n
dihydrite Dihydrit m, Pseudomalachit m, $Cu_5[(OH)_2|PO_4]_2$
dike [in]/to eindeichen
dike 1. Deich m; 2. Gesteinsgang m, Eruptivgang m
~ **burst** Deichbruch m
~ **complex** Gangschwarm m
~ **intrusion** Gangintrusion f
~ **land** Deichland n
~ **rock** Ganggestein n
~ **rocks** Ganggefolgschaft f
~ **set** System n paralleler Gänge
~ **swarm** Gangschwarm m
~ **system** Gangsystem n
diked eingedeicht *(Küste)*
~ **land (marsh)** eingedeichte Marsch f, Ko[o]g m, Polder m
dikelet Apophyse f eines Ganges
dikelike gangähnlich
diking Eindeichung f
dikites Ganggefolgschaft f
diktyonite Diktyonit m *(Migmatit)*
diktyonitic structure diktyonitische Textur f, Flexur-Zonentextur f *(bei Migmatit)*
dilatancy Dilatanz f
dilatation Dilatation f, Ausdehnung f
~ **veins** durch Kristallisationsdruck geöffnete, linsige Gangtrümer im Schiefergestein
dilatational wave s. longitudinal wave
dilated seam schwebendes Flöz n
dilation s. dilatation
dilatometer Dehnungsmesser m, Dilatometer n
dilsh *(sl)* Schicht f geringwertiger Kohle
dilute verdünnt
dilution Verdünnung f, Auswaschung f
~ **of ore** Erzverdünnung f *(durch taubes Gestein)*
diluvial Diluvial..., Eiszeit...
~ **ore** Seifenerz n, Wascherz n
dimension Dimension f *(z.B. von Sonne, Planeten)*
~ **stone** Werkstein m, Quader[stein] m
dimensional orientation Regelung f nach der Korngestalt
dimensionless flow rate normierte Fließrate f
~ **pressure drop** normierte Druckänderung f
dimetric 1. tetragonal; 2. hexagonal
dimorphic dimorph
dimorphine s. dimorphite
dimorphism 1. Dimorphismus m *(Paläontologie)*; 2. Dimorphie f *(Mineralogie)*
dimorphite Dimorphin m, As_4S_3
dimorphous s. dimorphic
dimple spring Punktquelle f
dimpled surface mit Grübchen bedeckte Oberfläche f
Dinantian s. Lower Carboniferous 1.

dingle Talschlucht f, enges Tal n
dinite Dinit m *(kristalline Kohlenwasserstoffverbindung in Braunkohle)*
dinoflagellates Dinoflagellaten mpl
dinosaur[ian] Dinosaurier m
~ **egg shell** Dinosauriereierschale f
~ **fauna** Dinosaurierfauna f
~ **track** Dinosaurierfährte f
dint/to durchsenken
dioctahedral dioktaedrisch
dioctahedron Dioktaeder n
diogenite Diogenit m *(achondritischer hypersthenführender Meteorit)*
diopside Diopsid m, $CaMg[Si_2O_6]$
dioptase Dioptas m, $Cu_6[Si_6O_{18}]\cdot 6H_2O$
diorite Diorit m, Aphanit m
~ **magma** Dioritmagma n
dioritic dioritartig
~ **dike** Dioritgang m
~ **rock** Dioritgestein n
dip/to einfallen; sich neigen
~ **at high angles** steil einfallen
~ **at low angles** flach einfallen
~ **gently** flach einfallen
~ **steeply** steil einfallen
dip Fallen n, Einfallen n; Neigung f, Tonnlage f
~ **and strike** Fallen n und Streichen n
~ **angle** 1. Fallwinkel m, Einfallwinkel m; 2. Kippwinkel m *(elektromagnetisches Verfahren)*
~ **at high angles** steiles Einfallen n
~ **at low angles** flaches Einfallen n
~ **face** einfallender Streb m
~ **fault** Querverwerfung f, gleichsinnige Verwerfung f *(Störung quer zur Schichtung oder Schieferung)*
~ **heading** Abhauen n, Gesenk n
~ **joint** Querkluft f *(Kluft quer zur Schichtung oder Schieferung)*
~ **logging** Stratamessung f, Stratametrie f, Schichtneigungsmessung f *(im Bohrloch)*
~ **needle** Inklinationsnadel f
~ **of slope** Hanggefälle n
~ **resolution** Neigungsauflösung f *(Seismik)*
~ **separation** flache Sprunghöhe f
~ **shift** s. ~ slip
~ **shooting** Neigungsschießen n, Kreuzschießen n
~ **slip** flache Sprunghöhe f
~ **-slip fault** Abschiebung f, normale Verwerfung f *(Störung mit vertikaler Verschiebung)*
~ **strike symbol** Fallzeichen n
diphycercal diphycerk *(ein Typ der symmetrischen Schwanzflosse)*
diplopore dolomite Diploporendolomit m
diplopores Diploporen fpl
dipmeter Schichtneigungsmesser m, Stratameter n
~ **survey** s. dip logging
dipole sonde Dipolmeßsonde f
dipper eigentliche Verwerfung f *(Absenkung)*
~ **dredger** Löffelbagger m

dipping

dipping einfallend
dipping Eintauchen *n*
~ **bed** einfallende Schicht *f*
~ **heading** einfallende Strecke *f*
~ **interface** geneigte Grenzfläche *f*
~ **needle** Inklinationsnadel *f*
~ **towards** einfallend gegen
~ **wave** Tauchwelle *f*
dipyre Dipyr *m*, Skapolith *m* (*s.a.* mizzonite)
dipyrite *s.* dipyre
dipyrization Skapolithisierung *f*
direct alluvial stream *s.* meandering stream
~ **circulation** Rechtsspülen *n*, Normalspülen *n* (des Bohrlochs)
~ **-finding method** Direktnachweisverfahren *n*
~ **intake** Zufluß *m* (zum Grundwasser)
~ **-light electron microscope** Auflichtelektronenmikroskop *n*
~ **plot of screen test** einfache Siebkurve *f*
~ **recording** Direktaufzeichnung *f* (auf Magnetband)
~ **runoff** direkter Abfluß *m*, Oberflächenabfluß *m*
~ **shear test** direkter Scherversuch *m*
directed evolution Orthogenese *f*
~ **stress** gerichtete Beanspruchung *f*
direction finding Peilung *f*
~ **indicator** Neigungsmesser *m* (für Bohrungen)
~ **of advance** Verhiebrichtung *f*
~ **of dip** Inklinationsrichtung *f*, Fallrichtung *f*, Einfallrichtung *f*
~ **of fissures** Kluftrichtung *f*, Spaltrichtung *f*
~ **of flowage** Fließrichtung *f*
~ **of ground-water flow** Grundwasserfließrichtung *f*
~ **of heading** Streckenrichtung *f*
~ **of holes** Bohrlochrichtung *f*
~ **of ice flow** Fließrichtung *f* des Eises
~ **of magnetization** Magnetisierungsrichtung *f*
~ **of mining** Abbaurichtung *f*
~ **of motion (movement)** Bewegungsrichtung *f*
~ **of plication** Streichrichtung *f* der Faltung
~ **of propagation** Fortpflanzungsrichtung *f*
~ **of screwing** Schraubungssinn *m*
~ **of slip in the fault plane** Verschiebungsrichtung *f*
~ **of strata** Schichtstreichen *n*
~ **of strike** Streichrichtung *f*
~ **of the apparent perpendicular** Scheinlotrichtung *f*
~ **of thrust[ing]** Schubrichtung *f*
~ **of trend** Streichrichtung *f*
~ **of vibration** Schwingungsrichtung *f*
~ **of winds** Windrichtung *f*
~ **of working** Verhiebrichtung *f*
directional gerichtet, in Bewegungsrichtung
~ **deviation logging** Neigungsmessung *f*
~ **drilling** gerichtetes Bohren *n*, Richtbohren *n*
~ **force** Richtungskraft *f*
~ **hole** Zielbohrung *f*
~ **load cast** gerichtete Belastungsmarke *f*

~ **log** Abweichungsmessung *f*
~ **permeability** gerichtete Permeabilität *f*
~ **pressure** einseitiger Druck *m*
~ **recording instrument** Neigungsmeßgerät *n* (für Bohrungen)
~ **surveying** Neigungsmessung *f* (bei Bohrungen)
~ **well** Richt[ungs]bohrung *f*
~ **well drilling** *s.* ~ drilling
directionless richtungslos, allseitig
~ **pressure** allseitiger Druck *m*
directivity graph Richtcharakteristik *f*
dirt Boden *m*, Lockergestein *n*; taubes Gestein *n*, Berge *pl*
~ **band [ogive]** Zwischenmittel *n*, Bergemittel *n*, Gesteinsmittel *n*, Schmutzstreifen *m* (in der Kohle); Schmutzband *n*, Ogive *f* (im Gletscher)
~ **bed** 1. fossiler Bodenhorizont *m* mit Pflanzenresten; 2. erdige Lage *f* im Kohlenflöz; 3. *s.* ~ band
~ **cone** *s.* debris cone
~ **fault** Flözvertaubung *f*
~ **heap** Bergehalde *f*
dirty bergehaltig
~ **coal** aschereiche Kohle *f*
~ **sand** toniger Sandstein *m*
~ **water** Schmutzwasser *n*
disaggregate/to zerfallen, mechanisch verwittern
disaggregation Zerfall *m*, mechanische Verwitterung *f*
disappearance of outcrop Schichtenunterdrückung *f*
~ **of species** Aussterben (Verschwinden) *n* von Arten
~ **stream** verschwindender Fluß *m*, Flußschwinde *f*
disarticulated skeleton aus seinem Verband gelöstes Skelett *n*
disaster preparedness vorbeugende Katastrophenbereitschaft *f* (z.B. in erdbebengefährdeten Siedlungsgebieten)
~ **prevention** Katastrophenverhütung *f*
~ **relief** Katastrophenhilfe *f*
~ **warning** Katastrophenwarnung *f*
disastrous earthquake verwüstendes Beben *n*
~ **flood** Katastrophenhochwasser *n*
discard/to auf Halde stürzen, abräumen
discard Berge *pl*, Abgänge *mpl*
discharge/to ablassen; auswerfen
discharge Abfluß *m*, Ablauf *m*, Ausfluß *m*; Abflußmenge *f*; Wasserspende *f*, Wasserergiebigkeit *f*, Schüttungsmenge *f*; Auswurf *m*
~ **area** Entlastungsgebiet *n* (Wasser)
~ **chamber** Förderraum *m*
~ **curve** Abflußkurve *f*
~ **fluctuation** Wassermengenschwankung *f*
~ **-frequency curve** Abflußganglinie *f*
~ **head** Förderhöhe *f*
~ **hydrograph** Abflußmengenkurve *f*

~ **measurement** Wassermengenmessung f
~ **of a well** Brunnenergiebigkeit f
~ **of solids** Geschiebefracht f, Geschiebemenge f
~ **of spring** Quellergiebigkeit f
~ **outlet (tunnel)** Entlastungsstollen m
~ **volcano** ausbrechender Vulkan m
discharging coefficient Schüttungskoeffizient m
~ **well** Förderbrunnen m
discoid[al] scheibenförmig
disconformable ungleichförmig, widersinnig, diskordant
~ **contact** ungleichförmige Lagerung f
disconformity ungleichförmige Lagerung f, Diskordanz f
discontinuity Unterbrechung f, Diskontinuität f; Unstetigkeitsfläche f
~ **of deposition** Schichtungsdiskordanz f
~ **surface** Unstetigkeitsfläche f
discontinuous unterbrochen, diskontinuierlich, unstetig; nichtaushaltend; stoßartig
~ **area** disjunktes Areal n (Ökologie)
~ **grading (granulometry)** diskontinuierliche Kornabstufung f
~ **interstice** nichtdurchgehender Zwischenraum m
~ **series** diskontinuierliche Reihe f
discontinuously graded aggregate Ausfallkörnung f
discontinuum theory Theorie f des Diskontinuums, Diskontinuumlehre f
discordance Diskordanz f, ungleichförmige Lagerung f
~ **of bedding** Schichtungsdiskordanz f
discordant diskordant, widersinnig
~ **bedding** diskordante Schichtung f
~ **fold** s. disharmonic fold
~ **injection (intrusion)** diskordante Intrusion f
~ **junction** Stufenmündung f, Hängemündung f, ungleichsohlige Mündung f (eines Flusses)
discounted reserves s. possible reserves
discover/to entdecken
~ **a deposit** eine Lagerstätte entdecken (erschürfen)
~ **a mine** ein Bergwerk fündig machen
~ **by digging** erschürfen
discovered reserves nachgewiesene Mineralvorräte mpl
discoverer Schürfer m, Erzsucher m
discovery Entdeckung f, Fund m; Fündigkeit f
~ **claim** erster Fundclaim m (einer Lagerstätte)
~ **shaft** fündige Grube f
~ **well** erste Fundbohrung f
discrete lose (Gesteinsblock)
~ **element** gesondertes Element n
discriminability Unterscheidbarkeit f, Unterscheidungsvermögen n (z.B. zwischen Fernerkundungsobjekten, seismischen Ereignissen)
discriminance analysis Diskriminanzanalyse f
~ **coefficient** Koeffizient m der Diskriminanzfunktion (Gewicht eines Diskriminanzmerkmals bei der Diskriminanzfunktion)
~ **function** Diskriminanzfunktion f, Trennfunktion f
discrimination Unterscheidung f
discriminator Unterscheidungskriterium n (z.B. zwischen natürlichen und künstlichen seismischen Ereignissen)
disequilibrium Nichtgleichgewicht n; gestörtes [radiometrisches] Gleichgewicht n
~ **assemblage** nicht im thermodynamischen Gleichgewicht stehende Mineralassoziation
disharmonic fold disharmonische Falte f
~ **folding** disharmonische Faltung f
~ **relations** Abweichungen fpl vom Schichtungsparallelismus
dished ballig, konvex
disintegrable verwitterungsfähig
disintegrate/to zerfallen, mechanisch verwittern
disintegrated material Trümmergesteinsmaterial n
disintegrating process Verwitterungsprozeß m
disintegration Zerfall m, mechanische Verwitterung f, Zerstörung f, Zersetzung f
~ **chain** Zerfallsreihe f, Zerfallskette f
~ **of atom** Atomzerfall m
~ **of radium** Radiumzerfall m
~ **of the nucleus** Kernzerfall m
~ **process** Verwitterungsprozeß m
~ **product** Zerfallsprodukt n, Verwitterungsprodukt n
~ **rate** Zerfallsgeschwindigkeit f
~ **series** Zerfallsreihe f
disintegrative process Verwitterungsprozeß m
disinter/to ausgraben
disinterment Ausgrabung f
disjunction Disjunktion f
disjunctive folds disjunktive Falten fpl
~ **rocks** lose Trümmersedimente npl
disk Schale f (mechanisch)
~ **bit** Scheibenmeißel m
~ **-shaped** s. patelliform
~ **swing sledge mill, ~ vibratory mill** Scheibenschwingmühle f
dislocate/to dislozieren
dislocated verworfen
~ **bed** gestörte Schicht f
~ **deposit** gestörte Lagerstätte f
dislocation 1. Dislokation f, Verwerfung f, Lagerungsstörung f, Gebirgsstörung f, Schichtenstörung f, gestörte Lagerung f; 2. Versetzung f (Kristall)
~ **breccia** Dislokationsbrekzie f
~ **earthquake** Dislokationsbeben n, tektonisches Beben n
~ **in crystals** Versetzung f in Kristallen
~ **line** Versetzungsgrenze f, Versetzungslinie f
~ **metamorphism** Dislokationsmetamorphose f, Dynamometamorphose f
~ **mountains** Dislokationsgebirge n

dislocation

- **~ of strata** Verwerfung *f*
- **~ plane** Dislokationsfläche *f*, Störungsfläche *f*
- **~ valley** Dislokationstal *n*

dislodged slice Schürfling *m*, Abscherkörper *m*, Scherling *m*

dislodging of sediment Geschiebetrieb *m*

dismal Küstensumpf *m*

dismantling Demontage *f*, Abbrechen *n (einer Bohrung)*

dismembered river system ertrunkenes Flußnetz *n*

disomatic *für Kristalle, die als Einschluß in anderen vorkommen*

disorder Fehlordnung *f*

disordered fehlgeordnet
- **~ crystal** fehlgeordneter Kristall *m (s.a. imperfect crystal)*

dispatching of gas from underground storage Gasabgabe *f* aus Untergrundbevorratung

dispersal pattern Elementverteilung *f* im geochemischen Kreislauf

disperse/to dispergieren

dispersed elements Elemente *npl* mit geringem Anreicherungsfaktor, Spurenelemente *npl*
- **~ organic matter** disperse organische Substanz *f*

dispersion Dispersion *f*
- **~ coefficient** Vermischungskoeffizient *m*
- **~ halo** Dispersionshof *m (geochemische Prospektion)*
- **~ of clouds** Wolkenzerstreuung *f*
- **~ of phases** Phasendispersion *f*
- **~ train** *s.* ~ halo
- **~ variance** Varianz *f* des zufälligen Effektes *(z.B. einer bestimmten Probenahmestrategie)*

dispersive filter dispersives Filter *n (Filter mit Phasenverschiebung)*
- **~ medium** dispergierendes Medium *n*
- **~ model** Dispersionsmodell *n (Isotopenhydrogeologie)*

disphotic zone schwach durchlichtete Übergangszone *f (zwischen 80 und etwa 600 m Meerestiefe)*

displace/to verlagern, verschieben, verwerfen, dislozieren

displaced fold allochthone Falte *f*
- **~ mass** Überschiebungsmasse *f*, Schubmasse *f*
- **~ strata** versetzte Schichten *fpl*

displacement 1. Lagerungsstörung *f*, Verschiebung *f*, Verwerfung *f*, Verlagerung *f*, Sprung *m*, Verdrängung *f*, Dislokation *f*; 2. Verschiebung *f*, Punktwanderung *f (Geomechanik)*; 3. Gitterstörung *f*
- **~ curve** Verschiebungskurve *f*
- **~ front** Verdrängungsfront *f*
- **~ of equilibrium** Gleichgewichtsverschiebung *f*
- **~ of fault** Sprunghöhe *f (einer Verwerfung)*
- **~ of oil** Erdölverdrängung *f*
- **~ of stress** Spannungsumlagerung *f*
- **~ plane** ab-Gefügeebene *f*

- **~ pressure** Verdrängungsdruck *m*
- **~ reaction** Austauschreaktion *f*
- **~ rupture** Verschiebungsbruch *m*
- **~ spikes** Gitterstörungsbereich *m*
- **~-time diagram** Zeit-Weg-Diagramm *n*, Zeit-Weg-Kurve *f*

displacing 1. Verdrängen *n*; 2. Versetzen *n*, Verschieben *n (in Kristallen)*

displacive shearing stress scherende Durchbewegung *f (bei Metamorphose)*

disposal of brine Entfernung *f* des Salzwassers
- **~ power of a well** Schluckvermögen *n*
- **~ site** Deponie *f*
- **~ well** Versenkungsbohrung *f*, Versenkungsbrunnen *m (für Schadwässer)*

disrupt/to zerreißen

disrupted bed verworfene Schicht *f*
- **~ fold** Bruchfalte *f*

disruption Zerreißen *n*, Spaltung *f*

dissect/to zertalen, zerschneiden

dissected zerschnitten, gegliedert
- **~ by faults** von Verwerfungen durchsetzt
- **~ peneplain** zerschnittene Fastebene *f*

disseminate/to ausstreuen, verbreiten; einsprengen

disseminated eingesprengt, fein verwachsen
- **~ deposit** Imprägnationslagerstätte *f*
- **~ ore** eingesprengtes Erz *n*, Imprägnationserz *n*
- **~ porphyry copper ore** in Porphyr eingesprengtes Kupfererz *n*

dissemination Einsprengung *f*, Dissemination *f*; disperse Auskristallisation *f*

dissipating area Schwundgebiet *n*

dissipator *s.* ablation area

dissociate/to dissoziieren

dissociation Dissoziation *f*
- **~ constant** Dissoziationskonstante *f*

dissolution Auflösung *f*; Aufschmelzung *f*

dissolve/to sich auflösen; aufschmelzen

dissolved gas gelöstes Gas *n*
- **~-gas drive** Entlösungstrieb *m*, Gasexpansionstrieb *m (Erdölförderung)*
- **~ natural gas** im Öl gelöstes Erdgas *n*
- **~ salt** gelöstes Salz *n*

dissolving of rocks 1. Aufschmelzen *n* von Gestein; 2. Auslaugen *n* von Gestein

dissymmetric[al] asymmetrisch; enantiomorph

dissymmetry Asymmetrie *f*; Enantiomorphismus *m*

distal distal
- **~ end** Distalende *n*

distance from the earth Erdferne *f*, Entfernung *f* von der Erde
- **~ from the focus** Herdentfernung *f*
- **~ measurement** Entfernungsmessung *f*
- **~ of epicentre** Epizentralentfernung *f*
- **~ of fall** Fallabstand *m*
- **~ of thrust** flache Schubhöhe *f*, Schubweite *f*
- **~ of transport** Transportweite *f*, Transportentfernung *f*
- **~-true fold** *s.* parallel fold

108

distant earthquake Fernbeben n
distantly jointed undeutlich zerklüftet
distensional fault Disjunktivbruch m
disthene Disthen m, Kyanit m, Cyanit m, Al_2SiO_5
distichous zweireihig angeordnet
distillate field Kondensatfeld n
~ **gas** kondensatreiches Gas n
distillation Chitinzersetzung f bei Fossilisation
distinct bedding deutliche Schichtung f
~ **cleavage** deutliche Spaltbarkeit f
distorted verformt; verzerrt *(Kristalle)*
~ **bedding** Gekröseschichtung f
~ **fossil** verquetschtes Fossil n
distortion 1. Verformung f; Verzerrung f *(von Kristallen)*; 2. Schleppung f *(von Schichten)*
~ **correction** Entzerrung f *(z.B. von Fernerkundungsaufnahmen)*
distortional wave Distorsionswelle f
distortionless verzerrungsfrei
distributary Flußarm m, Deltaarm m
~ **glacier** Nebengletscher m
distribution coefficient (number, ratio) Verteilungskoeffizient m
distributive faulting verzweigtes Verwerfungssystem n
district Bezirk m
disturb/to stören
disturbance Störung f, Dislokation f, Gebirgsstörung f, Schichtenstörung f, Lagerungsstörung f, Bruch m
~ **of beds** Lagerungsstörung f
~ **trace on surface** über Tage ausstreichende Störung f
disturbed gestört, verworfen
~ **sample** gestörte Probe f
~ **stratification** gestörte Lagerung f
~ **sun** gestörte Sonne f
disturbing function Störungsfunktion f
disuse/to auflassen
disused shaft auflässiger Schacht m
ditch Graben m *(mit abgeböschten Wänden)*; Entwässerungsgraben m
~ **cuttings** Bohrgut n, Bohrschmant m, Bohrmehl n
~ **drain** Wasserseige f, Wasserrösche f
~ **for canalization** Kanalisationsgraben m
~ **for conduits** Leitungsgraben m
~ **sample** Spülprobe f
ditetragonal ditetragonal
dithizone method Dithizonmethode f
ditrigonal ditrigonal
ditroite Ditroit m *(feldspatoider Syenit)*
dittmarite Dittmarit m, $(NH_4)Mg_3H_2[PO_4]_3 \cdot 8H_2O$
Dittonian [Stage] Ditton[ium] n, Unteres Old Red n *(tieferes Unterdevon, Old-Red-Fazies)*
diurnal aberration tägliche Aberration f
~ **magnetic changes** tägliche magnetische Schwankungen fpl
~ **temperature variation** täglicher Temperaturgang m, tägliche Temperaturschwankung f
~ **variation** Tagesänderung f, tägliche Schwankung f

divalence Zweiwertigkeit f
divalent zweiwertig
divarication Gabelung f
divaricator Öffnungsmuskel m *(bei Brachiopoden)*
diverge/to divergieren
divergence, divergency Divergenz f
divergent structure radialstrahlige Struktur f
~ **type** abweichende Form f
diversion Ablenkung f *(eines Flusses)*
~ **channel (cut)** Umleitungskanal m
~ **tunnel** Umleit[ungs]stollen m *(Talsperre)*
diversity Diversität f, Mannigfaltigkeit f
~ **stacking** gewichtete Stapelung f
divert/to ablenken
~ **a river** einen Fluß verlegen
diverted river verlegter Fluß m
diverter Raubfluß m, Ablenker m
divide *(Am)* Wasserscheide f
dividing range *(Am)* Wasserscheide f
~ **slate** Bergemittel n; Flözleeres n *(Braunkohlentagebau)*
~ **surface** Trennfläche f
diviner Wünschelrutengänger m
diving bell Taucherglocke f
~ **system** Tauchsystem n
~ **wave** Tauchwelle f
divining Wassersuche f mit der Wünschelrute
~ **rod** Wünschelrute f
divisibility Teilbarkeit f
divisible teilbar
division s. series
divisional plane Absonderungsfläche f, Trennungsfläche f
dixenite Dixenit m, $Mn_5As_2[O_6|SiO_4] \cdot H_2O$
djalindite Djalindit m, $In(OH)_3$
djalmaite Djalmait m, Uranmikrolith m *(Varietät von Mikrolith)*
djerfisherite Djerfisherit m, $K_3CuFe_{12}S_{14}$ *(Meteoritenmineral)*
Djulfian [Stage] Dzhulfa n *(Stufe des Oberperms)*
doab *(sl)* Sandton m
doak *(sl)* Ganglette f
dob Rohdiamant m, ungeschliffener Diamant m
doctrine of catastrophism Katastrophenlehre f
~ **of descent** Deszendenztheorie f, Abstammungslehre f
~ **of uniformitarianism** Aktualitätstheorie f
dodecahedral dodekaedrisch, zwölfflächig
~ **slip** Dodekaedergleitung f
dodecahedron Dodekaeder n, Zwölfflächner m
dog leg Richtungsänderung f *(der Aufstiegbahn, der Profiltrasse)*
~ **leg severity** Bohrlochkrümmung f
~**-legged hole** Umlenkbohrung f
dogger band *(sl)* rauhe Toneiseneinlage f
Dogger [Epoch, Series] Dogger m, Brauner Jura m *(Serie des Juras)*
doghouse *(sl)* Bohrmeisterbude f

dogtooth

dogtooth spar *(sl)* besondere Kalzitkristallform
dohyalin für ein Gefüge glasreicher Magmatite
dol *(sl)* Tal *n*
dolarenaceous von dolarenitischer Struktur
dolarenite arenitischer Dolomit *m*
doldrums Kalmen *fpl*, Kalmengürtel *m*
dolerite Dolerit *m* *(Gabbrogestein)*
doleritic texture doleritische Struktur *f*, ophitisches Gefüge *n*
dolerophanite Dolerophanit *m*, $Cu_2[O|SO_4]$
dolichocephalic langköpfig *(Paläontologie)*
doline Doline *f*, Karstwanne *f*, Kasttrichter *m*
~ **lake** Dolinensee *m*
dolinen *s.* doline
doling-out of water Wasserabgabe *f (Boden)*
dolocasts *s.* dolomoulds
dolomicrite Dolomikrit *m (dolomitisierter mikritischer Kalkstein)*
dolomite 1. Dolomit *m*, $CaMg[Co_3]_2$; 2. Dolomit *m (dolomitreiches Karbonatgestein)*
~ **rocks** Dolomitgestein *n*
dolomitic dolomitisch, dolomithaltig
~ **limestone** dolomitischer Kalkstein *m*
~ **marl** dolomitischer Mergel *m*, Dolomitmergelstein *m*
~ **mottling** Dolomitfleckigkeit *f (durch unvollständige Dolomitisierung)*
~ **sandstone** Dolomitsandstein *m*
dolomitite *s.* dolostone
dolomitization Dolomitbildung *f*, Dolomitisation *f*, Dolomitisierung *f*
dolomitize/to dolomitisieren, in Dolomit umwandeln
dolomization *s.* dolomitization
dolomorphic pseudomorph nach Dolomit
dolomoulds Abdrücke von Dolomitkristallen oder Pseudomorphosen nach Dolomit
doloresite Doloresit *m*, $V_3O_4(OH)_4$
dolorudite Dolorudit *m*, Gerölldolomit *m*
dolosiltite Dolosiltit *m*, Dolomitsiltstein *m*
dolostone Dolomitgestein *n*
domain of definition Definitionsbereich *m*
~ **of dependence** Abhängigkeitszone *f*
domal domartig
~ **flank** Kuppelflanke *f*
~ **uplift** Aufwölbung *f*
dome up/to aufwölben
dome Dom *m*, Kuppe *f*, Staukuppe *f*, periklinale Aufwölbung *f*
~-**shaped** domartig, gewölbt
~-**shaped fold** Kuppelfalte *f*
~-**shaped mountains** Kuppelgebirge *n*
~ **theory** Gewölbetheorie *f*
domed domartig, gewölbt *(s.a.* domeshaped*)*
~ **bog** Hochmoor *n*, Torfmoor *n*
~ **roof** domartig gewölbtes Hangendes *n*
domelike domartig
Domerian [Stage] Domer[ium] *n*, Domero *n (Stufe des Unteren Juras)*
domestic ore Erz *n* aus einheimischen Lagerstätten, Inlandserz *n*

110

~ **water supply [plant]** Trinkwasserwerk *n*
~ **wells** *(Am)* in den USA gelegene Sonden
domeykite Domeykit *m*, Weißkupfer *n*, Cu_3As
dominant fault Hauptverwerfung *f*, Hauptverwerfer *m*
~ **fault line** vorherrschende Verwerfungslinie *f*
~ **fossil** Leitfossil *n*
~ **mineral** Hauptmineral *n*
~ **sedimentation** vorherrschende Sedimentation *f*
~ **species** dominierende Art *f*
~ **wind** vorherrschender Wind *m*
doming Dombildung *f*, Aufwölbung *f*
donbassite Donbassit *m*, (Na, Ca, Mg)$Al_4[(OH)_8|AlSi_3O_{10}]$
Donez coalfield Donezbecken *n*
~ **phase of folding** Donezphase *f*
donga Rinne *f*, Schlucht *f (Südafrika)*
donk *s.* doak
donnick, don[n]ock *s.* dornick 1.
doodle bug *(Am)* unwissenschaftliches Lagerstättensuchgerät
dopatic in Gefügeform von Porphyriten
dopplerite Dopplerit *m (Humusgele in Torfen)*
~-**sapropel** Huminsäuresapropel *m*
Dorashamian [Stage] Dorasham *n (hangende Stufe des Oberperms)*
Dordonian [Stage] *s.* Maastrichtian
dore silberhaltiges Gold *n*
~ **silver** goldhaltiges Silber *n*
dormant volcano untätiger (ruhender) Vulkan *m*
dornick *(sl)* 1. kleiner Block *m*; 2. Eisenerzklumpen *m*
dornock *s.* dornick 1.
Dörnten Shales Dörntener Schiefer *mpl (oberes Toarc in Nordwesteuropa)*
dorr glaziale Rinne *f*
dorsal corner Dorsalecke *f*
~ **cup** Dorsalkapsel *f*
~ **fin** Dorsalflosse *f*, Rückenflosse *f*
~ **margin** Dorsalrand *m*
~ **valve** Dorsalklappe *f*, Rückenklappe *f (von Brachiopoden)*
~ **view** Rückenansicht *f*
dorsoventral axis dorsoventrale Achse *f*
dorsum *s.* tergum
dorversal limb Deckenrücken *m*
dot chart Punktkarte *f*
dote *(sl)* Fäulnis *f*, Moder *m*
dott[-hole] kleine Gangöffnung *f*, Drusenspalte *f*
double-arch[ed] dam Doppelbogenmauer *f*
~ **crater** Doppel[wall]krater *m*
~ **gate preventer** Doppelsicherheitsschieber *m (Bohrtechnik)*
~-**image prism** Kalkspatpolarisationsprisma *n*
~-**layer weathering** doppelte Langsamschicht *f (Seismik)*
~-**pointed drifting pick** Spitzhacke *f*
~ **quartz wedge** Doppelquarzkeil *m*

~-**refracting** doppelbrechend
~ **refraction** Doppelbrechung *f*
~ **salt** Doppelsalz *n*
~ **stars** Doppelsterne *mpl*
~ **tombolo** Doppelnehrung *f*
~ **tube core barrel** Doppelkernrohr *n*
~ **window** Doppelfenster *n (Tektonik)*
doublet Doublette *f (auch Bohrungspaar)*
doubly plunging fold zweiseitig abtauchende Falte *f*
~ **reflecting spar** Doppelspat *m*, Islandspat *m* *(s.a.* calcite)
~ **refracting** doppelbrechend
~ **terminated crystal** zweiseitig zugespitzter Kristall *m*
doughnut kleiner Moränenlobus *m*
douglasite Douglasit *m*, $K_2[FeCl_4(H_2O)_2]$
douk[e] Gangletten *m*
doverite Doverit *m*, $CaY[F|(CO_3)_2]$
dovetailed schwalbenschwanzförmig
dowk *s.* douk[e]
down *s.* dune
down-... *s.a.* down...
~-**structure deflection of the hole** Bohrlochabweichung *f* mit dem Schichtenfallen
~-**structure flow** Sinkströmung *f*
~-**the-hole drilling** Bohren *n* mit Vorort-Antriebsmaschine
downbuckle plötzliche Krustenabbiegung *f*
downcast *s.* downfaulted
~ **breeze** Bergwind *m*
~ **fault** Verwerfung *f* ins Liegende
downcasting Gletscherschwund *m* durch Ablation
downcoast *(Am)* südwärts streichende Küste *f*
downcurrent stromabwärts
downcutting Tiefenerosion *f*
~ **stream** Fluß *m* mit Tiefenerosion
downdip 1. mit dem Fallen, in der Richtung des Einfallens; 2. bergab
downdip Fallrichtung *f*
downdropped fault block abgesunkene Scholle *f*, Tiefscholle *f*
~ **side** abgesunkener Flügel *m (an einer Störung)*
downedging Absinken *n*
downfacing nach unten gerichtet
downfaulted nach unten verworfen, ins Liegende verworfen, gesenkt
~ **block** abgesenkte Scholle *f*
downflexed abgebogen
downfold Synklinalfalte *f*, Mulde *f*
downfolding Muldenbildung *f*
downgrade bergab
downhill bergab, talwärts
~ **creep** Schuttkriechen *n*
downhole camera Bohrlochkamera *f*
~ **drilling assembly** niedergebrachte Bohrgarnitur *f*
~ **motor** Bohrlochsohlenmotor *m*, Meißeldirektantrieb *m*

downleap *s.* downthrow
downpour 1. Tropfwasser *n*; 2. Regenguß *m*, Platzregen *m*, Gußregen *m*
~ **of rain** Platzregen *m*
downsagging Nachsinken *n*
downsinking Absinken *n*
downslide level Abgleitfläche *f*
~ **motion** Abgleiten *n*
downsliding nappe Gleitdecke *f*
downslope hangabwärts, bergab
~ **wind** Bergwind *m*
downstream unterwasserseitig, stromabwärts, flußabwärts
~ **cofferdam** unterer Fangdamm *m*
~ **face** Luftseite *f (eines Damms)*
~ **slope** Leehang *m*
~ **water line** Unterwasserspiegel *m*
downstroke Abwärtsbewegung *f*
downsucking Verschluckung *f*
downthrow abgesunkene Scholle *f*
downthrown gesenkt
~ **block** abgesunkene (gesenkte) Scholle *f*, Tiefscholle *f*
~ **fault** Verwerfung *f* ins Liegende, Abschiebung *f*, Absenkung *f*
~ **fault block** *s.* ~ block
~ **side** abgesunkener Flügel *m (einer Verwerfung)*
downthrust Senkung *f*
Downtonian [Stage] Downtonstufe *f (Stufe des Silurs)*
downward block faulting Bruchsenkung *f*
~ **bowing** Abwölbung *f*, Abbiegung *f*
~ **continuation** Feldfortsetzung *f* nach unten
~ **direction/in** hangabwärts gerichtet
~ **drag** Schleppung *f* nach unten
~ **enrichment** Hutbildung *f (Erzanreicherungsprozeß in der Verwitterungszone)*
~ **erosion** Tiefenerosion *f*
~ **facing structure** überschobene Struktureinheit *f*
~ **flexure** Abbiegung *f*
~ **pressure** Abwärtsdruck *m*
~ **progress/in the** während des Niederbringens
~ **sucking zone** Verschluckungszone *f (Geotektonik)*
~ **weathering** Tiefenverwitterung *f*
downwarp Flexur *f*, Absenkung *f*, Abbiegung *f*
downwarped eingesunken
~ **block** abgesunkene Scholle *f*, Tiefscholle *f*
downwarping *s.* downwarp
downwash Abspülung *f*
~ **velocity** Abströmgeschwindigkeit *f*
downwind side Leeseite *f*
dowser Wünschelrutengänger *m*
dowsing Wünschelrutengehen *n*
~ **rod** Wünschelrute *f*
doxenic *für spezielle poikilitische Gefüge*
drab clay schmutzfarbiger Ton *m*
drag along/to mitschleppen

drag

drag Schleppung f (von Schichten bei Verwerfungen)
~ **bit** Drehmeißel m; Blattmeißel m; Flügelmeißel m
~ **coefficient** Widerstandsbeiwert m
~ **fault** Schleppverwerfung f
~ **fold** Schleppfalte f
~ **folding** Schleppfaltenbildung f, Schleppfaltung f
~ **groove** Schleifrille f
~ **mark** Driftmarke f, Driftspur f, Schleifmarke f
~ **nappe** Schleppdecke f
~ **ore** abgeschertes Erz n, Ruschelerz n
dragged [mit]geschleppt
~ **overthrust block** [mit]geschleppte Scholle f
~ **syncline** Schleppsynklinale f
~ **upward** aufwärts geschleppt (Schichten)
dragging Aufkrempen n (Tektonik)
Dragonian [Stage] Dragonien n (Stufe des Paläzäons in Nordamerika)
dragon's skin Lepidodendronabdruck m
drain/to 1. entwässern, dränieren, dränen; sümpfen; trockenlegen; 2. entölen, entgasen (bei Kohlenwasserstofflagerstätten)
~ **a seam** ein Flöz lösen
~ **off** abfließen; ablassen
drain Entwässerungsgraben m
~ **channel** Abflußkanal m
~ **district** Einzugsgebiet n, Entwässerungsgebiet n, Sammelgebiet n
~ **water** Sickerwasser n
drainable oil gewinnbares Öl n
drainage 1. Entwässerung f, Dränung f, Dränage f; Trockenlegung f; Sümpfung f, Wasserlösung f, Wasserhaltung f; 2. Entölen n, Entgasen n (bei Kohlenwasserstofflagerstätten)
~ **adit** Wasser[haltungs]stollen m
~ **area** Einzugsgebiet n, Niederschlagsgebiet n, Entwässerungsgebiet n, Sammelgebiet n, Abflußgebiet n, Stromgebiet n
~ **at the toe** Böschungsfußentwässerung f
~ **basin** Abflußbecken n
~ **blanket** Entwässerungsteppich m
~ **by closed canals** unterirdische Entwässerung f
~ **channel (course)** Abflußrinne f
~ **density** Flußdichte f
~ **district** s. ~ area
~ **ditch** Drängraben m, Entwässerungsgraben m, Abzugsgraben m
~ **divide** Entwässerungsscheide f
~ **funnel** Entwässerungstrichter m
~ **furrow** Abflußrinne f
~ **gallery** Wasserlösungsstollen m
~ **lake** See m mit Abfluß
~ **large** Abflußgröße f
~ **level** Wasserhaltungsniveau n
~ **network** Entwässerungsnetz n
~ **path** Entwässerungsweg m
~ **pattern** Entwässerungsnetz n
~ **ratio** Abflußkoeffizient m

~-**recovery factor** Entölungsgrad m (bei Kohlenwasserstofflagerstätten)
~ **relief** Entwässerungsrelief n
~ **shaft** Entwässerungsschacht m
~ **slope** Entwässerungshang m
~ **system** Entwässerungsnetz n
~ **texture** Flußdichte f
~ **trench** s. ~ ditch
~ **water** Sickerwasser n
drained area dräniertes Gebiet n
draining Entwässerung f, Trockenlegung f; Wasserhaltung f (s.a. drainage 1.)
~ **through the whole area of the bottom** Vollbodenentwässerung f
drainway Abflußrinne f; Sumpfstrecke f
drape folds Draperiefalten fpl
drapery Vorhang m (z.B. Tropfsteinvorhang)
draping Schichtdeformation f durch differentielle Kompaktion
dravite Dravit m (Varietät von Turmalin)
draw off/to rauben (Ausbau)
draw (Am) 1. Trockenschlucht f; 2. natürlicher Drainagegraben m; 3. zum Anstau vorgesehenes Gewässer n
~ **well** Ziehbrunnen m
drawdown Absenkung f des Grundwasserspiegels
~ **component** Absenkung[shöhe] f
~ **curve** Leistungsabfallkurve f
drawing-off of water Wasserableitung f
~ **road** Förderstrecke f
~ **shaft** Förderschacht m
drawn clay brandrissiger Ton m
~-**out middle limb** ausgequetschter Mittelschenkel m
drawrock (Am) zum Nachfall neigendes Gestein n
drawslate Nachfall m (brüchiger Schiefer im Hangenden der Kohle)
drawworks Hebeeinrichtung f
dredge/to [aus]baggern, naßbaggern
dredge 1. Naßbagger m, Schwimmbagger m; 2. Dredge f
dredged peat schlammiger Torf m
dredger Naßbagger m, Schwimmbagger m
~ **excavator** Trockenbagger m
dredging 1. Baggerungen n, Naßbaggerung f, Unterwasserbaggern n; 2. Baggergut n
dreikanter Dreikanter m
Dreissensia Beds Dreissensienbänke fpl
drench/to durchtränken
Dresbachian [Stage] Dresbachien n (basale Stufe des Croixiens)
dress/to bereißen (Firste, Stoß)
dressed ore aufbereitetes Erz n
~ **rock** Rundhöcker m
~ **tin** Zinnschlich m
dressing Aufbereitung f
~ **expenses** Aufbereitungskosten pl
~ **floor** Wäsche f, Aufbereitung f
~ **of ore** Erzaufbereitung f
~ **plant** Aufbereitungsanlage f

driblet cone (spire) Lavaschornstein *m*, Schlakkenschornstein *m*, Hornito *m*
dries durch Anwitterung sichtbar werdende Feinschichtung *f*
drift/to driften
drift 1. glazialer Schutt *m*, Grundmoräne *f*; Geschiebe *n*; 2. Meeresströmung *f*; 3. Abdrift *f*, Drift *f*; 4. Schneewehe *f*; 5. Eisdecke *f*; 6. Strecke *f*
~ **anchor** Treibanker *m*
~ **angle** Ablenkungswinkel *m*, Abweichungswinkel *m (Bohrloch)*
~ **avalanche** Staublawine *f*
~ **away from the poles** Polflucht *f*
~ **band** erdiges Zwischenmittel *n (in der Kohle)*
~-**barrier lake** Moränenstausee *m*
~ **beds** Geschiebeschichten *fpl*
~ **border** Geschiebegrenze *f*
~ **boulder** Findling *m*, erratischer Block *m*, Driftblock *m*
~ **clay** *s.* boulder clay
~ **coal** allochthone Kohle *f*
~ **copper** Kupfer *n* im Moränenschutt
~-**covered** geschiebebedeckt
~ **current** Driftströmung *f*
~-**dam lake** Moränenstausee *m*
~ **deposit** Gletscherablagerung *f*
~ **diameter gauge** Rohrkaliber *n*
~ **face** Ortsbrust *f*, Ortsstoß *m*
~ **glacier** bewegter Eiskörper *m (unterhalb der klimatischen Schneegrenze ausgebildet)*
~ **hill** Düne *f*
~ **ice** Treibeis *n*
~ **indicator** Abweichungsmeßgerät *n*, Neigungsmesser *m (Bohrtechnik)*
~ **line** Spülsaum *m*
~ **mandrel** Rohrkaliber *n*
~-**mantled** geschiebebedeckt
~ **map** Karte *f* der Glazialablagerungen
~ **mine** Grube *f* mit Stollenförderung *(ohne Schacht)*
~ **mobility** Driftgeschwindigkeit *f*
~-**obstructed valley** durch Geschiebe abgeriegeltes Tal *n*
~ **of a gallery** Streckenvortrieb *m*
~ **of ice** Eisdrift *f*
~ **of the continents** Kontinentaldrift *f (A. Wegener)*
~ **peat** Torflager *n* in Glazialablagerungen
~ **recorder** Abweichungsmeßgerät *n*
~ **sand** Flugsand *m*, Triebsand *m*, Triebsand *m*, Wandersand *m*
~ **scratch** Glazialschramme *f*
~ **sheet** glaziale Schuttdecke *f*
~ **survey** Neigungsmessung *f*
~ **topography** Grundmoränenlandschaft *f*
~ **wood** Treibholz *n*
Drift Epoch (Period) Pleistozän *n*, Diluvium *n*, Eiszeit *f*
driftal gold Seifengold *n*
drifted fossil Fossil *n* auf sekundärer Lagerstätte,
verschlepptes (eingespültes, umgelagertes) Fossil *n*
~ **material** angeschwemmtes Material *n*
~ **sand** Flugsand *m*, Triebsand *m*, Triebsand *m*, Wandersand *m*
~ **snow** windgepackter Schnee *m*, Preßschnee *m*
drifting 1. Abdrift *f*; 2. Auffahren *n*, Streckenauffahren *n*
~ **ice** Treibeis *n*
~ **of beach** Strandversetzung *f*
~ **of ice** Eistreiben *n*
~ **of snow** Schneetreiben *n*
~ **of soil** Bodenverlagerung *f*
~ **sand** *s.* drift sand
driftless area [während der Eiszeit] unvergletschertes Gebiet *n*
driftway Richtstrecke *f*, söhlige Strecke *f*
driftwood *s.* drift wood
drill/to bohren *(s.a.* bore/to)
~ **dry** trockenbohren
~ **in den Ölträger anfahren**
~ **into** anbohren
~ **through** durchbohren
~ **up** zerbohren
drill barge Bohrinsel *f*
~ **bit** Bohrkrone *f*, Bohrmeißel *m*
~ **chips** *s.* ~ cuttings
~ **collar** Schwerstange *f*
~-**collar stabilizer** Schwerstangenstabilisator *m*
~ **connector** Gestängeverbinder *m*
~ **core** Bohrkern *m*
~ **crew** *s.* drilling crew
~ **cuttings** Spülproben *fpl*, Bohrklein *n*
~ **dust** Bohrmehl *n*
~-**hole depth** Bohrlochtiefe *f*
~-**hole direction** Bohrlochrichtung *f*
~-**hole surveying** Bohrlochmessung *f*
~ **log** Bohrprofil *n*, Bohrlochvermessung *f*
~ **pipe** Bohrgestänge *n (insgesamt)*
~ **pipe failure** Gestängebruch *m*
~ **pipe racker** Gestängemagazin *n*
~ **pipe spinner** Gestängeverschraubvorrichtung *f*
~ **pipe stand** Gestängezug *m*
~ **pipe string** Bohrgestängestrang *m*, Gestängestrang *m*
~ **rig** Bohranlage *f*
~ **rod** Bohrgestänge *n*
~ **shaft** *s.* ~ string
~ **stem test** Gestängetest *m*
~ **string** Gestängestrang *m*, Bohrgarnitur *f*, Bohrzeug *n*
~ **string break-off** Bohrstrangbruch *m*, Futterrohrbruch *m*
~ **tower** Bohrturm *m*
~ **tube** Bohrrohr *n*
~ **unit** Bohranlage *f*
drillability Bohrbarkeit *f*
drillable packer durchbohrbarer Packer *m (Bohrtechnik)*
drilled footage Bohrleistung *f* in englischen Fuß

drilled

~ **hole** 1. Bohrloch n, Bohrung f; 2. vorgebohrtes Loch n
~ **thickness** erbohrte Mächtigkeit f
~ **well** Bohrbrunnen m
driller Bohrarbeiter m; Bohrmeister m, Krückelführer m
driller's log Bohrprotokoll n, Bohrmeisterlog n
drilling Bohren n, Bohrverfahren n, Bohrung f, Bohrarbeiten fpl (s.a. boring)
~ **activity** Bohrtätigkeit f
~ **barge** Bohrinsel f
~ **breaks** Änderungen fpl des Bohrfortschritts
~ **bridge** Bohrbrücke f
~ **by means of a rope** Seilbohren n
~ **by percussion** Schlagbohren n, schlagendes Bohren n
~ **by rotation** Drehbohren n, drehendes Bohren n
~ **cable** Bohrseil n
~ **capacity** Bohrleistung f
~ **collar** Schwerstange f
~ **control** Nachlaßvorrichtung f
~ **crew** Bohrmannschaft f, Bohrbelegschaft f, Bohrbrigade f
~ **depth** Bohrtiefe f
~ **diamond** Bohrdiamant m
~ **diary** Bohrjournal n
~ **efficiency** Bohrproduktivität f
~ **engineer** Bohringenieur m
~ **engineering** Bohrtechnik f
~ **equipment** Bohrausrüstung f
~ **fluid** Dickspülung f, Spülschlamm m, Bohrschlamm m, Bohrspülung f, Spülung[sflüssigkelt] f
~ **foreman driller** Schichtführer m
~ **grip** Bohrgreifer m
~ **implement** Bohrgerät n
~~**in** Anbohrung f einer Schicht, Anfahren n des Ölträgers
~ **island** Bohrinsel f
~ **jars** Rutschschere f
~ **jig** Bohrvorrichtung f
~ **journal** Bohrjournal n
~ **lance** Bohrlanze f
~ **mast** Bohrmast m
~ **meterage** Bohrmeterleistung f
~ **method** Bohrverfahren n
~ **mud** Dickspülung f, Spülschlamm m, Bohrschlamm m, Bohrspülung f
~ **mud additives** Bohrspülungszusatzmittel npl
~ **of a well** 1. Niederbringen (Abteufen) n einer Bohrung; 2. Bohrprozeß m
~ **operations** Bohrarbeiten fpl
~ **outfit** Bohrausrüstung f
~ **pipe string** Bohrgestängestrang m, Gestängestrang m
~ **platform** Bohrbühne f, Bohrinsel f
~ **program** Bohrprogramm n
~ **progress** Bohrfortschritt m
~ **rate** Bohrfortschritt m, Bohrgeschwindigkeit f
~ **report** Schichtbericht m

~ **rig** Bohranlage f
~ **rig hydraulic control system** hydraulisches System n eines Bohrgeräts, hydraulisches System n einer Bohrung
~ **rig performance** Bohranlagenleistung f
~ **rig pneumatic control system** pneumatisches System n eines Bohrgeräts, pneumatisches System n einer Bohranlage
~ **shaft** s. ~ string
~ **ship** Bohrschiff n
~ **shot** Bohrschrot m, Schrot m
~ **site** Bohransatzpunkt m
~ **speed** Bohrgeschwindigkeit f
~ **string** Gestängestrang m, Bohrgarnitur f, Bohrzeug n
~ **string break-off** Bohrstrangbruch m, Futterrohrbruch m
~ **technique** Bohrregime n
~ **time** Bohrzeit f, Bohrdauer f
~~**time break** Bohrfortschrittswechsel m
~~**time log** Bohrfortschrittslog n
~ **tool** Bohrwerkzeug n
~ **tower** Bohrturm m
~ **unit** Bohraggregat n
~ **vessel** Bohrschiff n
~ **water** Spülwasser n (Tiefbohren)
~ **with explosives** Bohren n mit Sprengstoffen, Sprengbohren n
~ **with hard-faced core bits** Hartmetallbohren n
~ **with reversed circulation** Bohren n mit Umkehrspülung
~ **with rotary table** Rotarybohren n
~ **without a drill pipe** Bohren n ohne Gestänge
~ **work** Bohrarbeit f
drillings Bohrmehl n, Bohrklein n
drillometer Drillometer n (Bohrdruckanzeiger)
drillstock Bohrvorrichtung f
drinking fountain Trinkbrunnen m
~ **water** Trinkwasser n
~ **water standard** Trinkwasserstandard m
~ **water supply** Trinkwasserversorgung f
drip from/to heruntertropfen
drip gasoline aus Erdgas kondensierte Kohlenwasserstoffe mpl
~~**proof** tropfwassergeschützt
driphole Tropfloch n, Aufschlagloch n von Tropfwasser
dripping tröpfelnd
dripping Tröpfeln n
~ **water** Tropfwasser n; Kondenswasser n; Tauwasser n
dripstone Tropfstein m
drive/to auffahren (Grubenbaue)
drive bushing Drehtischeinsatz m (Bohrtechnik)
driven well Bohrbrunnen m, Rammbrunnen m
driver pricking (probing) Sondenrammung f
driving rod Rammsonde f, Schlagsonde f
~ **test** Rammsondierung f
drizzle/to nieseln

drizzle Sprühregen *m*, Nieseln *n*
drop/to 1. absinken; 2. tropfen, tröpfeln; sickern
~ **off** aussterben
drop Tropfen *m*
~ **fault** normale Verwerfung *f*
~ **in bottom-hole pressure** Druckabfall *m* an der Bohrlochsohle
~ **in pressure** Druckabfall *m*
~-**penetration sounding apparatus** Rammsonde *f*, Schlagsonde *f*
~-**penetration testing** Rammsondierung *f*
~ **quartz** Tropfenquarz *m*
~ **stowing** Sturzversatz *m*
dropped gesenkt
~ **block** abgesunkene Scholle *f*
dropper Nebengang *m*, Seitentrum *n*
dropstone Dropstein *m* (triftend verfrachtetes Gesteinsfragment)
dross dilution of ore Gangart *f*
drossy coal (sl) schwefelkiesführende Kohle *f*
drought Trockenheit *f*, Dürre *f*, Trockenzeit *f*
~ **duration** Trockenzeit *f*
~ **resistance** Trockenresistenz *f*
drown/to unter Wasser setzen (z.B. eine Grube)
drowned ertrunken; ersoffen (Schacht); überstaut
~ **longitudinal coast** ertrunkene Längsküste *f*
~ **mine** ersoffene Grube *f*
~ **river** ertrunkener Fluß *m*
~ **river valley** ertrunkenes Flußtal *n*
~ **spring** Unterwasserquelle *f*
~ **stream** ertrunkenes Flußtal *n*
~ **valley** ertrunkenes Tal *n*
~ **well** verwässerte Bohrung *f*
drowning Einsattelung *f*
drum shaft Trommelwelle *f*
drumlins Drumlins *mpl* (wallartige Anhäufungen von Moränenmaterial)
drums s. drumlins
druse Druse *f*
~ **lined with crystals** Kristalldruse *f*
drused drusig
drusy drusenartig, drusig, Drusen...
~ **cavity** Drusenraum *m*
~ **coating** Kristallüberzug *m* (um Kalkarenit-Körner)
dry up/to vertrocknen, verdorren; eintrocknen, austrocknen; versiegen (Brunnen)
dry (sl) maskierte Kluft *f* (in der Firste)
~ ,**ash-free** wasser- und aschefrei (Kohlenanalyse)
~ **avalanche** Trockenlawine *f*, Aschenlawine *f*, Staublawine *f*
~-**bone ore** s. smithsonite
~ **bulk density** Trockenraumgewicht *n*
~ **chernozem** Trockenschwarzerde *f*
~ **cleaning** Trockensortierung *f*
~ **concentration** Trockenaufbereitung *f*
~ **delta** s. alluvial fan
~ **diggings** äolische Seifen *fpl*

~ **drilling** Trockenbohren *n*
~ **field** trockene Lagerstätte *f*
~ **firn** trockener Altschnee *m*
~ **gas** trockenes Erdgas *n*, Kohlengas *n*, Trockengas *n*
~ **hole** ergebnislose Bohrung *f*, Fehlbohrung *f*
~ **hole-to-producer ratio** Verhältnis *n* von Fehl- zu Fundbohrungen
~ **lake** Trockensee *m*
~ **natural gas** trockenes Erdgas *n*, Trockengas *n*, gasolinfreies Naturgas *n*, Inkohlungsgas *n*
~ **oil** wasserfreies Öl *n*
~ **pergelisol (permafrost)** eisfreier Permafrostboden *m*
~ **residue** Trockenmasse *f*
~ **river bed** (Am) Wadi *n*
~ **sand** trockener (unergiebiger) Sand *m* (bei Öllagerstätten)
~ **screening** Trockensiebung *f* (von Erzen)
~ **sea-floor well head** trockener Bohrlochabschluß *m* auf dem Meeresboden
~ **season** Trockenzeit *f*
~ **strength** Trockenfestigkeit *f*
~ **treatment** Trockenaufbereitung *f*
~ **unit weight** Trockenraumgewicht *n*
~ **valley** Trockental *n*
~-**weather flow** Trockenwetterabfluß *m*
~ **well** ergebnislose Bohrung *f*, Fehlbohrung *f*
~ **year** trockenes Jahr *n*
drying Trocknung *f*
~ **cabinet** Trockenschrank *m*
~ **crack** Trockenriß *m*
~ **house** Gradiersaline *f*
~ **shrinkage** Trockenschwindung *f*
~-**up** Austrocknung *f*, Eindunstung *f*; Versiegen *n* (Brunnen)
DSS s. deep seismic sounding
DSSP Deep Submergence Systems Program
dual polarity display Linienschrift *f* (Seismik)
~ **well completion,** ~ **zone well** Zwillingsfördersonde *f* (gleichzeitige Förderung aus zwei Horizonten)
Duchesnian [Stage] Duchesnien *n* (Wirbeltierstufe des oberen Eozäns in Nordamerika)
duct Kanal *m*, Durchgang *m*
ductile dehnbar, duktil
~ **tenacity** Geschmeidigkeit *f*
ductilimeter Dehnbarkeitsmesser *m*, Duktilometer *n*
ductility Dehnbarkeit *f*, Duktilität *f*
~ **limit** Fließgrenze *f*
dudley rock fossilführender Kalkstein *m*
duff 1. Rohhumus *m*; 2. Siebdurchgang *m*, Siebfeines *n*
dufrenite Dufrenit *m*, $Fe_3 \cdot Fe_6 \cdots [(OH)_3|PO_4]_4$
dufrenoysite Dufrenoysit *m*, $2PbS \cdot As_2S_3$
duftite Duftit *m*, $PbCu[OH|AsO_4]$
dug peat Stichtorf *m*
~ **well** Handbrunnen *m*, Schachtbrunnen *m*
dull glanzlos, matt
~ **banded coal** Mattstreifenkohle *f*, Clarain *m*

dull

~ **bit** abgenutzter Meißel *m*
~ **brown coal** Mattbraunkohle *f*
~ **coal** Mattkohle *f*, Durain *m*
~ **lustre** Mattglanz *m*
~ **rumbling** dumpfe Geräusche *npl*, dumpfes Rollen *n (Vulkanismus)*
dumb fault fossile Wasserrinne *f*
dumontite Dumontit *m*, $Pb[(UO_2)_3|(OH)_4|(PO_4)_2] \cdot 3H_2O$
dumortierite Dumortierit *m*, $(Al, Fe)_7[O_3|BO_3|(SiO_4)_3]$
dump Kippe *f*, Halde *f*, Bergehalde *f*, Schutthalde *f*, Abraumkippe *f*
~ **of overburden** Abraumkippe *f*
~ **ore** Haldenerz *n*
~ **slip** Haldenrutsch *m*
~ **stocks** Haldenbestände *mpl*
dumped abgesetzt
~ **moraine** angehäufte Moräne *f*, Wallmoräne *f*
dumping Kippen *n*
~ **cableway** Haldenseilbahn *f*
~ **ground** Absturzhalde *f*
dumreicherite Dumreicherit *m*, $Mg_4Al_2[SO_4]_7 \cdot 36H_2O$
dundasite Dundasit *m (H$_2$O-haltiges PbAl-Karbonat)*
dune Düne *f*
~ **belt** Dünengürtel *m*
~ **chain** Dünenzug *m*, Dünenkette *f*, Dünenreihe *f*
~ **cliff** Dünenkliff *n*
~ **coast** Dünenküste *f*
~-**covered** dünenbedeckt
~ **field** Dünenfeld *n*
~ **lake** Dünensee *f*
~ **on the march** Wanderdüne *f*
~ **range** Dünenzug *m*, Dünenkette *f*, Dünenreihe *f*
~ **ridge** Dünenrücken *m*
~ **sand** Dünensand *m*
~ **system** Dünensystem *n*
~ **valley** Dünental *n*
Dunham classification Dunham-Klassifikation *f (Klassifikation von Karbonatgesteinen nach Gefügetypen aufgestellt von Dunham 1962)*
dunite Dunit *m*, Peridotit *m*
Dunlap orogeny Dunlap-Orogenese *f (Orogenese im Pliensbach, Nordamerika)*
dunn dickschiefriger Schieferton *m*
~ **bass** *(sl)* Schieferton *m* in Kohlenschichten
dunnet shale Ölschiefer *m (Schottland)*
duns *(sl) s.* dunn
dunstone *(sl)* Amygdaloidbasalt *m*
duplication Verdopplung *f*
~ **of beds** Schichtenverdopplung *f*, Schichtenwiederholung *f (an einer Verwerfung)*
duplicature Duplikatur *f*, Schalenverdopplung *f*; innere Randlamelle *f (der Ostracodenschale)*
Dupuit-Forchheimer assumption Dupuit-Forchheimer-Näherung *f*

Dupuit's well equation Dupuit-Brunnengleichung *f*
durable crumbling soil klumpiger Boden *m*
durain Durain *m*, Mattkohle *f (Lithotyp der Steinkohle)*
durangite Durangit *m*, $NaAl[F|AsO_4]$
durbachite Durbachit *m*
durdenite *s.* emmonsite
duricrust harte Bodenkruste *f (Bodenzementation durch Karbonate, Salze, Kieselsäure u.a.)*
durite Durit *m (Kohlenmikrolithotyp)*
duroclarite Duroclarit *m (Kohlenmikrolithotyp)*
dussertite Dussertit *m*, $BaFeH[(OH)_6|(AsO_4)_2]$
dust [atmosphärischer] Staub *m*
~ **avalanche** Staublawine *f*, Trockenlawine *f*, Aschenlawine *f*
~ **cloud** Staubwolke *f*
~ **coal** Kohlenstaub *m*; Staubkohle *f*
~ **deposit** Staubablagerung *f*
~ **devil** Staubsturm *m*
~ **fall** Staubfall *m*
~ **gold** Goldpulver *n*
~-**laden** staubhaltig
~-**laden air** staubhaltige Luft *f*
~-**layer** Staubschicht *f*
~ **ore** mulmiges Erz *n*
~-**proof** staubdicht, staubgeschützt
~ **sampling** Probenahme *f* von Staub
~ **skin** Staubhaut *f*
~ **storm** Staubsturm *m*, Sandsturm *m*
~ **swirl** Staubwirbel *m*
~ **tuff** Staubtuff *m*
~ **whirl** Staubwirbel *m*
duster *(Am)* 1. Staubsturm *m*; 2. *(sl)* Fehlbohrung *f*
dustfree, dustless staubfrei
dusty staubhaltig, staubbeladen
~ **air** staubhaltige Luft *f*
~ **crust** Staubkruste *f*
duxite Duxit *m (schwarzglänzendes, sekundär durch Thermometamorphose entstandenes Braunkohlenharz, Tschechoslowakei)*
dwang Brechstange *f*, Brecheisen *n*
dwarf star Zwergstern *m*
dwarfed development Zwergentwicklung *f*
~ **fauna** Zwergfauna *f*
~ **form** Zwergform *f*
dwarfing Verkümmerung *f*
dwarfish species zwerghafte Form *f*
dwarfism Zwergwuchs *m*
dwelling burrow Wohngang *m (Ichnologie)*
~ **mond** Wurt *f*, Warft *f*
~ **structure** Wohnbau *m (Ichnologie)*
~ **tube** Wohnröhre *f (Ichnologie)*
dwindle/to auskeilen
dwindling-away Auskeilung *f*
dy Dy *m*
~ **ore** Erzfall *m*
~ **peat** Seetorf *m*
Dyas *s.* Permian
dying-out Ausschwänzen *n* eines Ganges
dyke *s.* dike

earthquake

dyked s. diked
dyktyonite s. diktyonite
dynamic[al] angle of draw dynamischer Grenzwinkel m
~ **breccia** tektonische Brekzie f
~ **correction** dynamische Korrektur f
~ **friction** Gleitreibung f
~ **friction coefficient** Reibungsbeiwert m der Bewegung
~ **geology** dynamische Geologie f
~ **load** dynamische Belastung f
~ **metamorphism** Dynamometamorphose f, Dislokationsmetamorphose f
~ **modulus** dynamischer Modul m
~ **positioning** dynamische Positionierung f (von Bohrschiffen und Halbtauchern)
~ **pressure** dynamischer Druck m
~ **viscosity** dynamische Viskosität f
dynamics Dynamik f
dynamiting Dynamitsprengung f
dynamometamorphic dynamometamorph
~ **rock** dynamometamorphes Gestein n
dynamometamorphism Dynamometamorphose f
dynamometer Dynamometer n
~ **prop** Dynamometerstempel m
dysaerobic dysaerobisch, sauerstoffverarmt
dysanalyte Dysanalyt m, (Ca, Na, Ce)(Ti, Nb, Fe)O$_3$
dyscrasite Dyskrasit m, Antimonsilber n, Ag$_3$Sb
dysodile Papierkohle f
dysprosium Dysprosium n, Dy
dystomic mit unvollkommener Spaltbarkeit
dystrophic lakes dystrophe Seen mpl
~ **peat** Moosmoor n

E

eager s. eagre
Eagle Ford Shale Eagle Ford-Schiefer m (Cenoman und Turon in Nordamerika)
eagle stone s. eaglestone
eaglestone Eisenniere f, Adlerstein m
eagre Gezeitenstrom m mit großem Tidenhub; Flutbrandung f, Springflut f
ear bit Stufenmeißel m
~ **stone** Gehörstein m, Itolith m (Paläontologie)
eardleyite Eardleyit m, Ni$_6$Al$_2$[(OH)$_{16}$|CO$_3$]·4H$_2$O
earlandite Earlandit m, Ca$_3$[C$_6$H$_5$O$_7$]$_2$·4H$_2$O
earlier Palaeozoic intrusives altpaläozoische Intrusiva npl
earliest minerals to crystallize Erstausscheidungen fpl (von Mineralen im kristallisierenden Magma)
~ **separation products** Erstausscheidungen fpl
early diagenetic[al] frühdiagenetisch
~ **magmatic ore deposit** frühmagmatische Erzlagerstätte f
~ **mature** frühreif
~ **mature valley** jungreifes Tal n

~ **maturity** Frühreife f
Early Cretaceous Unterkreide f
~ **Jurassic** Unterer Jura m
~ **Precambrian** Frühpräkambrium n
ears s. auricles
earth 1. Erde f, Erdball m; 2. Erde f, Erdboden m; 3. Land n, Festland n; 4. [seltene] Erde f
~ **anchor** Erdanker m
~ **auger** Tellerbohrer m
~ **brown coal** erdige Braunkohle f
~ **coal** erdige Kohle f
~ **column** Erdpyramide f, Erdpfeiler m
~ **compaction** künstliche Bodenverdichtung f
~ **consolidation** natürliche Bodenverdichtung f, Eigenverfestigung f, Eigensetzung f
~ **dam** Erddamm m
~ **densification** künstliche Bodenverdichtung f
~ **din** (sl) Erdbeben n
~ **fall** s. landslide
~ **fill dam** Erd[schüttungsstau]damm m
~ **flax** s. amianthus
~ **flow** Bodenfließen n, Erdfließen n, Fließrutschung f, Erdschlipf m
~ **-formed sediment** Ablagerung f terrestrischer Herkunft
~ **glacier** Schuttstrom m
~ **hummocks** 1. Bülten fpl, Palsen fpl, Rasenhügel mpl; 2. Frosthebung f
~ **load** (Am) Erddruck m
~ **materials laboratory** Erdbaulabor[atorium] n
~ **-moon system** Erde-Mond-System n
~ **movement** Erdbewegung f, Bodenbewegung f
~ **pillar** Erdpyramide f, Erdpfeiler m
~ **pitch** Bergpech n
~ **pressure** Bodendruck m, Erddruck m
~ **pressure at rest** Ruhedruck m
~ **pyramid** Erdpyramide f, Erdpfeiler m
~ **runs** kleinlobiges Bodenfließen n (unter der Rasensohle)
~ **shock** Erdstoß m
~ **slide** Hangrutsch m (s.a. landslip)
~ **slip** kleiner Erdrutsch m, Rutschung f, Bergrutsch m
~ **solidification** Bodenverfestigung f
~ **subgrade** Erdplanum n, Untergrund m
~ **subsidence** Erdfall m
~ **terrain camera** Präzisionskamera f für Erdterrainbeobachtungen
~ **tide** Erdgezeitenbewegung f
~ **tilting** seismische Krustenverkippung f
~ **tremor** schwaches Erdbeben n
~ **vibration** Bodenerschütterung f
~ **waterproofing** Bodenabdichtung f
~ **wave** 1. Bodenerschütterungswelle f; 2. Bodenwelle f, wellenförmige Bodenerhebung f
~ **wax** Erdwachs n, Bergwachs n (s.a. ozocerite)
earthly irdisch
earthmoving Erdbewegung f, Erdbewegungsarbeiten fpl (künstlich)
earthquake Erdbeben n
~ **area** Erdbebengebiet n

earthquake

~ **damage** Erdbebenzerstörung f
~ **due to collapse** Einsturzbeben n
~ **due to folding** Faltungsbeben n
~ **engineering** erdbebensichere Bauweise f
~ **focus** Erdbebenherd m
~ **forecast** Erdbebenvorhersage f
~ **hazard** s. ~ risk
~ **intensity** Erdbebenstärke f
~ **observatory** Erdbebenstation f
~ **of distant origin** Fernbeben n
~ **precursor** Erdbebenvorläufer m, Vorbeben n
~ **prediction** Erdbebenvorhersage f
~-**proof** erdbebensicher
~-**proof constructions** erdbebensichere Bauten mpl
~ **record** Erdbebenaufzeichnung f
~ **region** Erdbebengebiet n
~ **research** Erdbebenforschung f
~-**resistant** erdbebensicher
~ **rift** Erdbebenspalte f
~ **risk** Erdbebengefahr f, Erdbebengefährdung f
~ **series** Erdbebenschwarm m, Schwarmbeben npl
~ **shock** Erd[beben]stoß m
~ **wave** Erdbebenwelle f
~ **with remote epicentre** Fernbeben n
earth's attraction Erdanziehung f
~ **axis** Erdachse f
~ **bodily tides** Erdgezeiten pl
~ **centre** Erdmittelpunkt m
~ **circumference** Erdumfang m
~ **core** Erdkern m
~ **crust** Erdkruste f, Erdrinde f
~ **current** [natürlicher] Erdstrom m, tellurischer Strom m
~ **curvature** Erdkrümmung f
~ **ellipsoid** Erdellipsoid n
~ **equator** Erdäquator m
~ **field** Erdfeld n
~ **flattening** Erdabplattung f
~ **genesis** Erdentstehung f
~ **globe** Erdkugel f
~ **gravitational field** Erdschwerefeld n, Gravitationsfeld n
~ **interior** Erdinneres n
~ **magnetic field** erdmagnetisches Feld n, Magnetfeld n der Erde, magnetisches Feld n der Erde, magnetisches Erdfeld n
~ **magnetic pole** magnetischer Erdpol m
~ **magnetism** Erdmagnetismus m
~ **motion** Erdbewegung f (des Erdballs)
~ **nucleus** Erdkern m
~ **oblateness** Erdabplattung f
~ **orbit** Erd[umlauf]bahn f
~ **origin** Erdentstehung f
~ **path** Erdbahn f
~ **pole** Erdpol m
~ **radiation belt** Strahlungsgürtel m der Erde
~ **rotation** Erd[um]drehung f
~ **satellite** Erdtrabant m, Erdsatellit m

118

~ **shadow** Erdschatten m
~ **shell** Erdkruste f, Erdhülle f, Erdrinde f
~ **shine** Erdschein m
~ **sphere** Erdkugel f
~ **surface** Erdoberfläche f
earthwork Erdbau m
~ **dam** Erd[schüttungsstau]damm m
earthworks Erdarbeiten fpl, Erdbau m
earthy erdig
~ **brown haematite** Brauneisenmulm m
~ **cobalt** schwarzer Erdkobalt m (s.a. asbolite)
~ **dilution of ore** Gangart f, Ganggestein n
~ **dolomite** Dolomitasche f
~ **gypsum** erdiger Gips m
~ **iron ore** Eisenmulm m, Eisenmohr m
~ **lead ore** s. cerussite
~ **limonite**, ~ **magnetic iron ore** s. ~ iron ore
~ **manganese** s. wad
~ **minerals** erdige Minerale npl
~ **odour** erdiger Geruch m, Erdgeruch m
~ **psilomelane** Manganschwärze f
~ **smell** erdiger Geruch m, Erdgeruch m
~ **turf** Erdtorf m
~ **vivianite** Eisenblauerde f (s.a. vivianite)
easily catching fire leicht entzündbar
~ **fusible** leichtschmelzbar
~ **set on fire** leicht entzündbar
~ **volatilized** leichtflüchtig
~ **volatilized constituent** leichtflüchtiger Bestandteil m
East African rift system Ostafrikanisches Grabensystem n
~ **African rift valley** Ostafrikanischer Graben m
easy cleavage deutliche Spaltbarkeit f
eat away/to korrodieren
ebb Ebbe f
~ **and flow** Ebbe f und Flut f
~-**and-flow structure** Gezeitengefüge n (Sedimentgefüge)
~ **channel** Ebbetrichter m
~ **current** Ebbeströmung f, Ebbestrom m, Ebbestromrichtung f
~ **delta** Ebbedelta n
~ **tide** Ebbestrom m, Ebbe f
ebbing Ebbe f
~ **and flowing spring** intermittierende Quelle f
ebelmenite s. psilomelane
ebullition Aufsprudeln n, Aufkochen n
Eburonian [Drift] Eburon-Eiszeit f, Eburon-Kaltzeit f (Pleistozän in Nordwesteuropa)
eccentering arm Anpreßarm m (Bohrlochmessung)
ecdemite Ekdemit m, $Pb_3AsO_4Cl_2$
echelle s. natrolite
echelon arrangement staffelförmige Anordnung f
~/**en** kulissenförmig
~ **fault** Staffelbruch m, gestaffelte Verwerfung f
~ **festoons** Staffelgirlanden fpl

~ **folds** Kulissenfalten *fpl*, gestaffelte Falten *fpl*
echeloned staffelförmig, stufenartig, treppenförmig
echinite fossiler Seeigel *m*
echinoid spines Seeigelstacheln *mpl*
echinoidal limestone Echinodermenkalk *m*
echinoids Echinoiden *fpl*
echinosphaerites limestone Echinosphaeritenkalk *m*
echinus Seeigel *m*
echo depth sounding Echolotung *f (Tiefenbestimmung)*
~ **prospecting** Echoschürfung *f*
~ **pulse receiver** Echoimpulsempfänger *m*
~ **sounder** Echolot *n*
~ **sounding** Echolotung *f*
~ **sounding apparatus (device)** Echolot *n*
echogram Echogramm *n*
eclipse Finsternis *f*, Verfinsterung *f*
~ **of the moon** Mondfinsternis *f*
~ **of the sun** Sonnenfinsternis *f*
ecliptic ekliptisch
ecliptic Ekliptik *f*, Sonnenbahn *f*, Erdbahn *f*
~ **coordinates** Ekliptikkoordinaten *fpl*
~ **pole** ekliptischer Pol *m*
ecliptical *s.* ecliptic
eclogite Eklogit *m*
~ **facies** Eklogitfazies *f*
~ **shell** Eklogitschale *f*
ecologic[al] ökologisch
~ **facies** ökologische Fazies *f*, Umweltfazies *f*
~ **map** Vegetationskarte *f*
~ **niche** ökologische Nische *f*
~ **plasticity** ökologische Plastizität *f*
~ **series** ökologische Reihe *f*
ecology Ökologie *f*
economic[al] geological substantiation geologisch-ökonomische Begründung *f*
~ **geology** ökonomische Geologie *f*, Wirtschaftsgeologie *f*; angewandte (praktische) Geologie *f*; Montangeologie *f*, Lagerstättenlehre *f* [der nutzbaren Minerale und Gesteine]
~ **limit of exhaustion of a well** Wirtschaftlichkeitsgrenze *f* einer Bohrung
~ **mineral** nutzbares Mineral *n*, Hauptmineral *n*
~ **production** wirtschaftliche Ausbeute *f*
~ **valuation** ökonomische Bewertung *f*
ecophenotype Ökophenotyp *m*
ecospecies Ökospezies *f*
ecostratigraphic unit fazielle Einheit *f*
ecostratigraphy Fazieskunde *f* der Sedimente
ecosystem Ökosystem *n*
ecotype Ökotyp *m*
ectodynamic (ectodynamomorphic) soil Boden, *f*, dessen Eigenschaften durch äußere Einflüsse bestimmt wird
ectropite Ektropit *m*, Rhodonit *m*, $Mn_2Si_8O_{28} \cdot 7H_2O$
eddy out/to auskolken
eddy 1. Wasserwirbel *m*, Strudel *m*; 2. Windwirbel *m*, Luftwirbel *m*

~ **markings** Wirbelmarken *fpl*
eddying Wirbelung *f*, Wirbelbewegung *f*
edenian [Stage] Eden *n (Stufe des Cincinnatiens in Nordamerika)*
edenite Edenit *m*, $Na\ Ca_2Mg_5[(OH?F)_2|AlSi_7O_{22}]$
edge away/to auskeilen
edge Kante *f*, Rand *m*
~ **angle** Kantenwinkel *m*
~ **coal** steil stehende Kohle *f*
~ **crack** Kantenriß *m*
~ **dislocation** Stufenversetzung *f*
~ **effect** kanteneffekt *m*
~ **of a crystal** Kristallkante *f*
~ **of a pool** Rand *m* eines Erdöllagers
~ **of the stowed zone** Versatzkante *f*
~ **pressure** Kantenpressung *f*
~ **seam** stehendes Flöz *n*
~ **water** Randwasser *n*
~-**water drive** Randwassertrieb *m*
~-**water encroachment** Vordringen *n* von Randwasser
~-**water limit** Randwassergrenze *f*
~ **water line** Randwasserlinie *f*
~ **well** Randsonde *f*
edgewise conglomerate Konglomerat *n* mit Schuppentextur
~ **structure** 1. kantengestelltes Konglomerat *n*; 2. Primärbrekzie *f*
Ediacara fauna Ediacara-Fauna *f*, Metazoen-Fauna *f (des höchsten Präkambrium, Wendium)*
edingtonite Edingtonit *m*, $Ba[Al_2Si_3O_{10}] \cdot 3H_2O$
Eem [Interval], Eemian Eem-Warmzeit *f*, Eem-Interglazial *n (Pleistozän in Nordwesteuropa)*
effective cross section Wirkungsquerschnitt *m*
~ **direction** Wirkungsrichtung *f*
~ **grain size** wirksame Korngröße *f*
~ **overburden pressure** effektiver Belastungsdruck *m*
~ **permeability** effektive Permeabilität *f*
~ **pore volume** wirksamer Porenraum *m*; auffüllbarer Porenanteil *m*
~ **porosity** effektive Porosität *f*, Nutzporosität *f*; auffüllbarer Porenanteil *m*
~ **precipitation** effektiver Niederschlag *m*
~ **pressure** Nutzdruck *m*
~ **radiometric resolution element** effektives radiometrisches Auflösungselement *n*
~ **resolution element** effektives Auflösungselement *n*
~ **terrestrial radiation** effektive terrestrische Strahlung *f*
~ **thickness of seam** gebaute Flözmächtigkeit *f*
~ **velocity** Filtergeschwindigkeit *f (Grundwasser)*
effervesce/to schäumen, Aufwallen, aufbrausen
effervescence Schäumen *n*, Aufwallen *n*, Aufbrausen *n*
effloresce/to ausblühen, verwittern, effloreszieren

efflorescence

efflorescence Ausblühung f, Auswitterung f, Effloreszenz f
~ **of gypsum** Gipsausblühung f
~ **of salt** Salzausblühung f
efflorescing clayey iron ore Eisenschwärze f, Eisenmulm m
effluent Abfluß m, Ausfluß m
~ **channel** Abflußgraben m
~ **disposal** Abwasserbeseitigung f
~ **lava** ausfließende Lava f
~ **stream** wasseraufnehmender Fluß m
~ **waste water** Abwasser n
~ **weir** Überlaufwehr n
efflux Ausflußmenge f, Abflußmenge f
effort 1. Aufwand m; 2. Anzahl f *(der Schüsse einer Gruppe, der Geophone bei Bündelung der zu stapelnden Spuren)*
effosion Effosion f, Ausgrabung f *(aus der Erde, z.B. von Fossilien)*
effusion 1. Effusion f; 2. Lavaausfluß m, Erguß m
effusive activity effusive Tätigkeit f
~ **body** Effusivkörper m
~ **rock** Ergußgestein n, Effusivgestein n
egeran Egeran m *(Vesuvian in strahligen Aggregaten)*
egg stone s. ooid
eglestonite Eglestonit m, Hg_6Cl_4O
egre s. eagre
Egyptian pebble Kugeljaspis m
eiconagon Zwanzigeck n
Eifelian [Stage] s. Couvinian
eight-fold achtzählig
~**-sided** achtseitig
eject/to [her]ausschleudern, auswerfen, ausstoßen
ejecta Auswurf m, Auswürflinge mpl
~ **blanket** oberflächenbedeckendes Auswurfmaterial n *(durch Meteoriteneinschläge herausgeschleudertes Material)*
ejectamenta, ejected material Auswurf m, Auswürflinge mpl
ejection Ejektion f, Ausschleudern n, Auswerfen n, Auswurf m, Ausstoßung f
~ **pressure** Abspritzdruck m
ejective folding Injektionsfaltung f *(ausgelöst durch magmatisches Strömen)*
ekdemite s. ecdemite
eksedofacies Verwitterungsfazies f
ekzema s. salt dome
elaeolite s. nepheline
elasmosaur Elasmosaurier m
elastic elastisch
~ **aftereffect (afterworking)** elastische Nachwirkung f
~ **bitumen** s. elaterite
~ **deformation** elastische Deformation f
~ **discontinuity** seismische Grenzfläche f
~ **impedance** Schallhärte f
~ **limit** Elastizitätsgrenze f
~ **line** elastische Linie f

~ **mineral pitch** s. elaterite
~**-plastic deformation** elastoplastische Verformung f
~ **rebound** elastische Rückformung f
~ **wave** 1. elastische Welle f *(Geophysik)*; 2. seismische Welle f
elasticity Elastizität f
~ **modulus** Dehnungsmodul m
elaterite Elaterit m, elastisches Erdpech n *(asphaltisches Pyrobitumen)*
elbaite Elbait m *(Varietät von Turmalin)*
elbow Knie n
~ **of capture** Ablenkungsknie n, Anzapfungsknie n
~ **of stream capture** s. ~ of capture
elbrussite Elbrussit m *(Mineral der Montmorillonitreihe)*
electric ... s.a. electrical ...
~ **calamine** s. calamine
~ **conductance** elektrischer Leitwert m
~ **conductivity** elektrische Leitfähigkeit f, elektrisches Leitvermögen n
~ **drill** Elektrobohrgerät n
~ **survey** elektrische Bohrlochmessung f
electrical ... s.a. electric ...
~ **coring** elektrisches kernen n
~ **discharge** elektrische Entladung f
~ **disintegration drilling** Bohren n mittels elektrischer Gesteinszertrümmerung
~ **drainage** Entwässerung f durch Elektroosmose
~ **light gauge** Lichtlot n *(Grundwasserspiegelmessung)*
~ **log** elektrisches Widerstandsdiagramm (Bohrprofil) n
~ **logging** elektrisches Kernen n, elektrische Bohrlochmessung (Formationsmessung, Widerstandsmessung) f
~ **logging sonde** Sonde f zur elektrischen Bohrlochmessung
~ **profiling** elektrische Profilierung f
~ **prospecting** elektrisches Prospektieren n, geoelektrische Prospektion f
~ **resistance (resistivity)** elektrischer Widerstand m
~ **sonde** Sonde f für elektrische Widerstandsmessung
~ **sounding** elektrische Sondierung f
~ **surface prospecting** elektrische Oberflächenerkundung f
~ **susceptibility** elektrische Suszeptibilität f
~ **tape gauge** elektrisches Kontaktlot n *(für Grundwasserspiegelmessung)*
~ **variable-resistance level gauge** elektrischer Wasserstandspegel m
~ **well logging** s. ~ logging
electrified ash cloud elektrisch geladene Aschewolke f
electrode resistance Übergangswiderstand m der Elektrodenstäbe *(Geoelektrik)*
electrodrill Elektrobohrer m
electrodrilling Elektrobohren n

electrohydraulic drilling elektrohydraulisches Bohren *n*
electrojet Ionosphärenstrom *m*
electrokinetic potential elektrokinetisches Potential *n*
electromagnetic elektromagnetisch
~ **depth sounding** elektromagnetische Tiefensondierung *f*
~ **field** elektromagnetisches Feld *n*
~ **logging** Induktionslog *n*, elektrische Widerstandsmessung *f*
~ **method** elektromagnetisches Verfahren *n*
~ **prospecting** elektromagnetische Erkundung *f*
~ **radiation** elektromagnetische Strahlung *f*
~ **registration** elektromagnetische Registrierung *f (z.B. von Erdbeben)*
~ **seismometer** elektromagnetisches Seismometer *n*
~ **spectrum** elektromagnetisches Spektrum *n*
~ **wave** elektromagnetische Welle *f*
electrometeor Elektrometeor *m*
electromicroprobe Elektronenmikrosonde *f*
~ **analysis** Elektronenstrahlmikroanalyse *f*
electron beam magnetometer Elektronenstrahlmagnetometer *n*
~ **micrograph** elektronenmikroskopische Aufnahme *f*
~ **microprobe** Elektronenmikrosonde *f*
~ **probe** Elektronensonde *f*
~ **spin resonance spectra** Elektronenspin-Resonanzspektren *npl*
electronegativity Elektronegativität *f*
electronic sky screen equipment elektronisches Himmelsabtastungsgerät *n*
electroosmosis Elektroosmose *f*
electroosmotic solidification elektroosmotische Baugrundverbesserung *f*
electrostatic separation elektrostatische Scheidung *f*
electrum Elektrum *n*, silberhaltiges Gold *n*
element distribution Elementverteilung *f*
~ **geochemistry** Elementgeochemie *f*
~ **of an orbit** Bahnelement *n*
~ **of symmetry** Symmetrieelement *n*
~ **ratio** Elementverhältnis *n*
elemental facies geochemische Fazies *f*
elementary cell Elementarzelle *f*
~ **crystal cell** Elementarkristallzelle *f*
eleolite *s.* nepheline
eleonorite *s.* beraunite
elevate/to emporheben
elevated beach gehobene Strandterrasse *f*
~ **cliff** gehobenes Kliff *n*
~ **shore face terrace** Strandterrasse *f*
~ **shore line** Hebungsküste *f*
~ **tableland** Hochebene *f*
~ **wave-cut terrace** gehobene Abrasionsterrasse *f*
elevation Aufsteigen *n*; Hebung *f*, Heraushebung *f*; Erhebung *f*, Erhöhung *f*, Höhe *f*; Elevation *f*

~ **correction** Höhenkorrektur *f*, Korrektur *f* auf das Bezugsniveau
~ **head** Druckhöhe *f*
~ **of coast** Küstenhebung *f*
~ **of land** Landhebung *f*
~ **of temperature** Temperaturerhöhung *f*
ELF = extra low frequency
eliasite *s.* gummite
ellestadite Ellestadit *m*, $Ca_5[OH|(SiO_4,SO_4)_3]$
ellipsoid of rotation Rotationsellipsoid *n*
ellipsoidal ellipsoidisch
~ **basalt** Kugelbasalt *m*
~ **lava** Pillowlava *f*
elliptic[al] elliptisch
ellsworthite Ellsworthit *m (Uran-Pyrochlor)*
Elmo's fire Elmsfeuer *n*
elongate länglich
~ **crystal** gestreckter Kristall *m*
~ **irregular marks** Hauptwülste *mpl*
~ **valve** längliche Schale *f*
elongation Längung *f*, Streckung *f*, Dehnung *f*
~ **curve** Dehnungsverlauf *m*
elpasolite Elpasolith *m*, $K_2Na[AlF_6]$
elpidite Elpidit *m*, $Na_2Zr[Si_6O_{15}]\cdot 3H_2O$
Elsterian Elster-Eiszeit *f*, Elster-Kaltzeit *f (Pleistozän in Nordwesteuropa)*
eluent frische Salzlauge *f*, Sole *f*
elution Auslaugung *f*
elutriate/to abschlämmen, [aus]schlämmen; feine Korngrößen nach der Sedimentationsgeschwindigkeit bestimmen
elutriation Schlämmung *f*, Abschlämmung *f*, Ausschlämmung *f*, Aufschlämmen *n*, Entschlämmen *n*
~ **analysis** Schlämmanalyse *f*
~ **by rising currents** Schlämmanalyse *f* im aufsteigenden Wasserstrom
elutriator Schlämmapparat *m (zur Korngrößenbestimmung unterhalb der Siebgrenze)*
eluvial eluvial
~ **deposit** eluviale Lagerstätte *f*
~ **horizon** Eluvialhorizont *m*, A-Horizont *m*
~ **loam** Verwitterungslehm *m*
~ **ore deposit** eluviale Erzlagerstätte (Seife) *f*
~ **soil** Ausschwemmungsboden *m*
eluviated horizon *s.* eluvial horizon
eluviation Auslaugung *f*, Auswaschung *f (des Bodens)*
eluvium Eluvium *n*, Eluvialboden *m*, Verwitterungsschutt *m*
elvan *(sl)* 1. pneumatolytischer Gang *m*; 2. Quarzporphyr *m*
~ **course** *(sl)* Tiefengesteinsgang *m (Schottland)*
EM *s.* electromagnetic method
emanate/to ausströmen
emanation Emanation *f*, Ausströmen *n*, Ausstrahlung *f*; Entgasung *f*
~ **deposit** Exhalationslagerstätte *f*
~ **of natural gas** Erdgasaustritt *m*
emarginate mit gekerbtem Rand
embacle Eisgang *m*

embank 122

embank/to eindämmen, eindeichen
embankment 1. Eindeichung f, Anschüttung f, Schüttung f; kleiner Erddamm m; Kai m; Ufer n, Ufereinfassung f; 2. dammartiger Rücken m (Glazialform)
embayed gebuchtet
~ **coast** [ein]gebuchtete Küste f, zerlappte Küste f, Buchtenküste f
embayment Einbuchtung f
embed/to [ein]betten
embedded eingebettet, eingelagert
embedding Einbettung f
~ **material** Einbettungsmedium n (Dünnschliff)
embedment Einlagerung f
ember glimmende Kohle f
embolite Embolit m, Bromchlorargyrit m, Bromchlorsilber n, Ag(Br, Cl)
emboss/to bossieren
embossed map Reliefkarte f (Landkarte)
embosser Bossierer m (Natursteinindustrie)
embossing hammer Bossierhammer m
embouchure Mündung f, Einmündung f, Flußmündung f
embrasure Leibung f
embrechite Embrechit m (Mischgestein)
embryonic folds Embryonalfalten fpl
~ **soil** primärer Boden m
~ **structures** embryonale Strukturen fpl
~ **type** Embryonaltyp m
~ **volcano** Vulkanembryo m
emerald Smaragd m, grüne Beryllvarietät f (s.a. beryl)
~ **copper** s. dioptase
~ **green** smaragdgrün
~ **nickel** s. zaratite
emeraldine smaragdfarben
emerge/to auftauchen
emerged gehoben, aufgetaucht
~ **bog** Hochmoor n
~ **land** Festland n
~ **reef** aufgetauchtes Riff n
emergence Emportauchen n (von Land)
~ **angle** Emergenzwinkel m (Seismik)
~ **of coast** Auftauchen n der Küste
~ **of the axes** Achsenaustritt m
~ **point** Austrittsstelle f
emersed emers, aufgetaucht
emersion Emersion f, Auftauchen n
~ **plane** Emersionsfläche f
emery Schmirgel m, körniger Korund m
~ **bob** Schleifscheibe f mit Schmirgelbelag
~ **rock** Schmirgel m (Gestein aus Korund und Fe-Mineralen, Handelsbezeichnung)
eminence Bodenerhebung f, Anhöhe f; Aufragung f
emission 1. Emission f, Eigenstrahlung f (eines Körpers); 2. Ausschleudern n, Auswurf m
~ **of gas** Entgasung f
~ **of rays** Aussendung f von Strahlen
~ **spectrum** Emissionsspektrum n
~ **spectrum analysis** Emissionsspektralanalyse f

emissive emittierend, ausstrahlend, aussendend
emissivity Emissionsvermögen n, Strahlungsvermögen n, Ausstrahlungsvermögen n
emit/to 1. emittieren, ausstrahlen, aussenden; 2. auswerfen, [her]ausschleudern
emitter Strahler m
emmonsite Emmonsit m, $Fe_2[TeO_3]_3 \cdot 2H_2O$
emphasized cleavage geöffnete Scherspalte f, durch Scherung geöffnete Fuge f
emplacement Platznahme f, Raumgewinnung f (eines Gesteins oder Magmas)
emplectite Emplektit m, Kupferwismutglanz m, Wismutkupfererz n, $Cu_2S \cdot Bi_2S_3$
employing of explosives Torpedieren n (Bohrtechnik)
empressite Empressit m, AgTe
empty leer, taub
~ **position of a crystal lattice** Kristallgitterhohlraum m
empyreuma, empyreumatic odour brenzliger Geruch m
Emscherian Emscher n (Coniac bis mittleres Santon in Nordwestdeutschland)
Emsian [Stage] s. Coblenzian
emulsibility Emulgierbarkeit f
emulsification Emulgierung f, Emulsionsbildung f
emulsified water emulgiertes Wasser n, Emulsionswasser n
emulsifier Emulsionsbildner m
emulsifracturing Emulsifrac n (Bohrtechnik)
emulsify/to emulgieren
emulsion Emulsion f
~ **breaker** Demulgator m (Bohrtechnik)
~ **mud** Emulsionsspülung f
emulsive emulgierend, emulsionsbildend
emulsoid Emulsionskolloid n
enallogenous enclave s. xenolith
enamel Zahnschmelz m
~ **scale** Ganoidschuppe f (bei Fischen)
~ **-scaled** schmelzschuppig
enantiomorphic enantiomorph
~ **allotropy** enantiomorphe Allotropie f
enantiomorphous enantiomorph
enantiotropic enantiotropisch
enantiotropy Enantiotropie f
enargite Enargit m, Cu_3AsS_4
encallowing Abtragen n des Abraums
encasing rock s. enclosing rock
encatchment area Einzugsgebiet n
encircling reef Dammriff n, Wallriff n
enclave Einschluß m in Magmatiten
enclose/to einschließen
enclosed sea Binnenmeer n
enclosing beds einschließende Schichten fpl
~ **rock** umgebendes Gestein n, Nebengestein n
enclosure Einschluß m
encoding Verschlüsselung f
encounter/to anfahren (in die Grube)
encountered rock angefahrenes (angetroffenes) Gestein n

encrinal limestone s. encrinite limestone
encrinite Enkrinit m (Kalkstein mit über 50% Crinoidenresten)
~ limestone Crinoidenkalk m
~ with shell debris s. encrinitic limestone
encrinitic coquina schalentrümmerführender Trochitenkalkstein m, Trochitenschalentrümmerkalkstein m
encroach/to eindringen, vordringen (Wässer in Speicherhorizonte)
encroaching sea transgredierendes Meer n
encroachment 1. Eindringen n, Vordringen n (von Wässern in Speicherhorizonte); 2. Transgression f, Überflutung f (Ozean)
~ by sand Versandung f
~ of the sea Einbrechen n des Meeres
encrust/to inkrustieren, überkrusten, beschlagen, umhüllen
encrustation 1. Inkrustation f, Inkrustierung f, Überkrustung f, Verkrustung f; 2. Kruste f, Belag m, Überzug m, Ansatz m; Krustenbildung f (im Brunnen)
encrusted überkrustet, überzogen
~ soil Krustenboden m
encrusting Umkrustung f
~ algae inkrustierende Algen fpl, Krustenalgen fpl
end off/to auskeilen
end-centered basis-flächenzentriert
~ cleat Schlechte f senkrecht zur Hauptschlechtenrichtung
~ effect Endeffekt m (bei Kerndurchströmung)
~ face Endfläche f (z.B. eines Kristalls)
~ joint s. ~ cleat
~ moraine Endmoräne f, Stirnmoräne f
~ of a gallery Feldort n, Ortsstoß m
~-on spread einseitige Aufstellung f (z.B. von Geophonen)
~ plane Abschlußfläche f; Endfläche f
~ portion Nachläufer m, Endphase f
~ thrust Axialschub m
~-window counter Fensterzählrohr n, Glockenzählrohr n
~-window G-M tube Geiger-Müller-Fensterzählrohr n, Geiger-Müller-Glockenzählrohr n
endangering degree Gefährdungsgrad m
ended-up/to be seiger stehen
~-up bed aufgerichtete (steil stehende) Schicht f
endellionite Bournonit m, Spießglanzbleierz n (s.a. bournonite)
endellite s. halloysite
endemic endemisch
~ fauna endemische Fauna f
~ form endemische Form f
~ species bodenständige Art f
enderbite Enderbit m (Gestein in Granulitfazies)
endoblastesis Endoblastese f
endocast Ausfüllung f eines geschlossenen Hohlraums
endodynamics endogene Dynamik f

endodynamomorphic soil endodynamomorpher Boden m
endoergic endotherm
endogenetic 1. endogen (Gestein); 2. s. endogenous
~ rock endogenes Gestein n
endogenic endogen
~ crater endogener Krater m (Entstehung meist durch Zusammenbruch)
endogenous endogen, innenbürtig
~ agents tellurische Kräfte fpl
~ dome Staukuppe f
~ enclosure endogener Einschluß m
~ event endogener Vorgang m
~ forces tellurische Kräfte fpl
~ metamorphism endogene Kontaktwirkung f
~ pneumatolysis endogene Pneumatolyse f
endokinetic endokinetisch
endolithic endolithisch
~ breccia autoklastische Brekzie f
endomorph endomorpher Kristall m
endomorphic endomorph
endomorphism Endomorphose f
endorheic basin abflußloses Binnenbecken n
~ drainage area abflußloses Einzugsgebiet n
endoskeleton Innenskelett n
endothermic endotherm, wärmeabsorbierend, Wärme aufnehmend
~ reaction endotherme Reaktion f
energy budget Energiehaushalt m
~ coefficient Energiekoeffizient m
~ dissipation Dissipation f der Energie
~ grade line Energielinie f
~ head Gesamthöhe f der Energielinie
~ loss Energieverlust m
~ of activation Aktivierungsenergie f
~ of distortion Verzerrungsenergie f
~ of grain boundary Korngrenzenenergie f
~ source Energiequelle f
engine and pump housing Maschinenhaus n
engineering geology Ingenieurgeologie f
~ geophysics Ingenieurgeophysik f
englacial in[tra]glazial
~ melting innere Schmelzung f (eines Gletschers)
~ moraine Innenmoräne f
~ stream Gletscherbach m (im Gletscher)
~ till im Eis transportiertes Moränenmaterial n
englishite Englishit m, $K_2Ca_4Al_6[(OH)_{10}(PO_4)_8] \cdot 9H_2O$
engrafted river aufgepfropfter Fluß m
~ valley aufgepfropftes Tal n
engulfment Verschlingen n, Verschlucken n
engybenthic in Nähe des Tiefseebodens lebend
enhanced oil recovery gesteigerte Erdölgewinnung f
enhydrite Enhydrit m (Mineral mit großen Lösungseinschlüssen)
enhydros Enhydros m (Chalzedonknolle mit Flüssigkeitseinschlüssen)

enhydrous

enhydrous hydrisch, wasserführend *(Minerale)*
enlarge a borehole/to ein Bohrloch erweitern
enlargement of the dike (vein) Gangerweiterung *f*
enlarging bit Erweiterungsbohrer *m*
~ of the hole Erweitern *n* des Bohrlochs
enrich/to anreichern *(Aufbereitung)*; veredeln *(Erzgang)*
enrichment Anreicherung *f*, Konzentration *f*
~ factor Anreicherungsfaktor *m*
~ zone Anreicherungszone *f*
enroll/to sich einrollen
enstatite Enstatit *m*, $Mg_2[Si_2O_6]$
entablature Säulenbildung *f (im oberen Teil eines Lavastroms)*
enter/to anfahren, einfahren
enterolithic folding Gekrösefaltung *f (im Schlangengips)*
~ structure Quellungsfältelung *f*
entire pallial line integripalliate Mantellinie *f (der Molluskenschale)*
entomolite, entomolith fossiles Insekt *n*
entoolitic 1. amygdaloidisch; 2. für Oolithstrukturen, die durch Ausfüllung von Blasenräumen entstanden
entrain/to eindringen, einwandern *(z.B. Wasser)*
entrainment Eindringen *n*, Einwanderung *f (z.B. von Wasser)*
entrance Einfahrt *f*
~ gallery Zugangstrecke *f*
~ loss Eintrittsverlust *m (von Grundwasser in den Brunnen)*
~ surface Einfallsfläche *f*
entrapment Einfang *m (von Flüssigkeiten und Gasen)*
~ burrow Begräbnisbau *m*, Begräbnisstätte *f (von Fossilien)*
entrapped gespannt *(Grundwasser)*
entrenched meander eingesenkter Mäander *m*
~ meander valley junger Folgefluß *m* in älterem Mäandertal
entropy 1. Entropie *f*; 2. Vermischungsgrad *m (verschiedener Sedimenttypen)*
~ function facies map Fazieskarte, die die Übergangstypen von drei Fazies ausweist
~-ratio lithofacies map Fazieskarte, die die reinen Endglieder eines Faziesdiagramms ausweist
entry corridor Entrittskorridor *m*
~ working Örterbau *m*
envelope 1. Hülle *f*; 2. Kontakthof *m*
~ curve Mantelkurve *f*, Hüllkurve *f*
~ delay frequency distortion Laufzeitverzerrung *f*
enveloping contour (surface) Faltenspiegel *m*
environment Milieu *n*, Umwelt *f*, Bildungsmilieu *n*
~ isotope Umweltisotop *n*, Umgebungsisotop *n*
~ of quiet marine water Stillwasserbereich *m*
~ protection Umweltschutz *m*
environmental Umgebungs...
~ change Umweltveränderung *f*
~ criterion Milieuindikator *m*
~ geochemistry Umweltgeochemie *f*
~ geology Umweltgeologie *f*
~ influence Einfluß *m* der Umgebung
~ isotope Umweltisotop *n*, Umgebungsisotop *n*
~ monitoring Umweltüberwachung *f*
~ pollution Umweltverschmutzung *f*
~ protection Umweltschutz *m*
eobionts Eobionten *npl (älteste Organismen)*
Eocambrian [Period] Eokambrium *n*
Eocarboniferous *s.* Mississippian
Eocene eozän
Eocene [Epoch, Series] Eozän *n (Serie des Tertiärs)*
Eocryptozoic Frühpräkambrium *n*
eocrystal *s.* brotocrystal
eogenetic porosity Porosität *f* im frühdiagenetischen Stadium
~ stage frühdiagenetisches Stadium *n*
eolation *s.* aeolation
eolian *s.* aeolian
eolianite *s.* aeolianite
eolith Eolith *m (primitiver Artefakt)*
eon *s.* aeon
eonothem *s.* aeonothem
Eopalaeozoic Altpaläozoikum *n*
eosite Eosit *m (V-haltiger Wulfenit)*
eosphorite Eosphorit *m*, $(Mn, Fe)Al[(OH)_2|PO_4]\cdot H_2O$
Eötvös torsion balance Eötvössche Drehwaage *f*
~ unit Eötvös *n*, Eötvös-Einheit *f (inkohärente Einheit des Gradienten der Beschleunigung in der Geodäsie)*
Eozoic eozoisch
Eozoic [Era, Time] Eozoikum *n*, Präkambrium *n*
epeiric für flache Golfseen auf epirogen gehobenen Kontinentaltafeln
~ sea Epikontinentalmeer *n*, Schelfmeer *n*
epeirocracy epirogene Hochlage *f (eines Gebiets)*
epeirocratic sea level Meeresspiegel *m* bei maximaler epirogener Hochlage
epeirogenesis *s.* epeirogeny
epeirogenetic *s.* epeirogenic
epeirogenic epirogen[etisch]
~ movement epirogene Bewegung *f*
epeirogeny Epirogenese *f*, Kontinentalbildung *f*
epeirophoresis Epirophorese *f*, Kontinentalverschiebung *f*
epeirophoris Großfaltungsprozeß *m*
ephemeral activity einmalige Ausbruchstätigkeit *f (eines Vulkans)*
~ stream intermittierender (jahreszeitlicher) Wasserlauf *m*, kurzzeitig fließender Fluß *m*
ephemerid Ephemeride *f*

ephesite Ephesit m, (Na, Ca)Al$_2$[(OH)$_2$|Al(Al, Si)Si$_2$O$_{10}$]
epibiont benthonisch
epibiota Benthos n, bodenbewohnende Meeresorganismen mpl
epibole biostratigrafische Einheit, gekennzeichnet durch die maximale Häufigkeit einer Art, Gattung bzw. eines anderen Taxons
epicentral area Gebiet n des Epizentrums, Epizentralgegend f
~ **distance** Epizentralentfernung f
epicentre Epizentrum n
epiclastic epiklastisch
epicontinental basin epikontinentales Becken n
~ **development** epikontinentale Entwicklung f
~ **sea (waters)** Epikontinentalmeer n, Schelfmeer n, Flachsee f
epicurrent Oberflächenströmung f (Ozean)
epidermic folding s. Jura-type folding
epidesmine s. stilbite
epidiagenese Diagenesespätstadium n (mit Übergang zur Verwitterung)
epididymite Epididymit m, NaBe[OH|Si$_3$O$_7$]
epidiorite Epidiorit m (Orthoamphibolit)
epidosite Epidosit m (Kalksilikatgestein)
epidote Epidot m, Ca$_2$(Fe, Al)Al$_2$[O|OH|SiO$_4$|Si$_2$O$_7$]
epidotization Epidotisierung f
epidotize/to epidotisieren
epieugeosyncline Epieugeosynklinale f
epifauna Epifauna f (auf dem Meeresboden lebende Fauna)
epigenesis Epigenese f
epigenetic epigenetisch
~ **deposit** epigenetische Lagerstätte f
epigone parasitärer Vulkankegel m
epiianthinite Epiianthinit m, [UO$_2$|(OH)$_2$]·H$_2$O
epikinematic s. postorogenic
epimagmatic epimagmatisch, deuterisch
epineritic epineritisch
epiphysis Epiphyse f
epiphytic epiphytisch
epiro... s. epeiro...
epirock Epigestein n
episcopic illumination Auflichtbeleuchtung f
epistilbite Epistilbit m, Ca[Al$_2$Si$_6$O$_{16}$]·5H$_2$O
epistolite Epistolit m, (Na, Ca)(Nb, Ti, Mg, Fe, Mn)[OH|SiO$_4$]
epitaxy Epitaxie f
epitectonic spättektonisch
epithermal epithermal
~ **deposit** epithermale Lagerstätte f
epizoa Epizoen npl
epizone Epizone f
epizootical Abdrücke von Tierresten enthaltend
epoch Epoche f (geochronologische Einheit)
~ **of folding** Faltungsepoche f
~ **of humid climate** Feuchtklimaperiode f
epoptic figures Absorptionsfiguren fpl (im Kristallschnitt senkrecht zur optischen Achse)

epoxy-embedded in Epoxi[d]harz eingebettet
epsom salt s. epsomite
epsomite Epsomit, Bittersalz n, Mg[SO4]·7H$_2$O
equal area chart flächentreue Karte f
~ **area projection** flächentreue Projektion f
~ **falling** Gleichfälligkeit f
~ **falling speed/of, ~ terminal velocity/of** gleichfällig (Aufbereitung)
equalizing reservoir Ausgleichbecken n
equant s. equigranular
equation of motion Bewegungsgleichung f
equator Äquator m
~ **of the heavens** Himmelsäquator m
equatorial äquatorial, Äquator...
~ **axis** parallaktische Achse f
~ **circumference** Äquatorumfang m
~ **climate** äquatoriales Klima n
~ **current** Äquatorialstrom m, Passatströmung f
~ **drift** Äquatorströmung f
~ **forest** Äquatorialwald m
~ **plane** Äquatorebene f
~ **radius** Äquatorradius m
equiareal projection flächentreue Projektion f
equidimensional crystals Kristalle mpl gleicher Größe
equidistance Äquidistanz f
equidistant äquidistant, abstandsgleich, abstandstreu, längentreu
~ **projection** abstandstreue Projektion f
equigranular gleichkörnig, gleichmäßig körnig
equilateral shell gleichklappige Schale f
equilibrium Gleichgewicht n
~ **constant** Gleichgewichtskonstante f (für Gas-Öl-Gemisch)
~ **diagram** Zustandsdiagramm n
~ **equation of water flow** Zustandsgleichung f der Wasserströmung
~ **liberation** Gleichgewichtsverdampfung f (Gas-Öl-Verhältnis)
~ **pressure** Gleichgewichtsdruck m
~ **region** Zustandsfeld n
~ **saturation** Gleichgewichtssättigung f
equimolecular solution äquimolekulare Lösung f
equinoctial äquinoktial, Äquinoktial...
equinoctial Äquinoktiallinie f; Himmelsäquator m
~ **gales (storms)** Äquinoktialstürme mpl, Herbststürme mpl
equinoctials s. equinoctial gales
equinox Äquinoktium n, Tagundnachtgleiche f
equiplanation Reliefeinebnung f (ohne Massendefizit)
equipotential äquipotential
~ **line** Äquipotentiallinie f
~ **surface** Äquipotentialfläche f
equivalence Äquivalenz f
~ **beds** äquivalente Schichten fpl
~ **projection** flächentreue Projektion f
~ **weight** Äquivalentgewicht n

equivalent 126

equivalent photographic resolution äquivalentes fotografisches Auslösungsvermögen n
equivalve[d] gleichschalig, gleichklappig
~ **shell** gleichklappige Schale f
equivolumnar wave s. shearing wave
era Ära f *(geochronologische Einheit)*
eradiation Ausstrahlung f, Strahlung f
erathem Ärathem n *(Einheit der biostratigrafischen Skala)*
erbium Erbium n, ER
ERE s. effective resolution element
erect fold aufrechte (stehende) Falte f
erg Sandwüste f
Erian [Series] Eri n *(Serie des Devons in Nordamerika, entspricht etwa dem Mitteldevon Europas)*
~ **phase of folding** erische Faltungsphase f
ericaite Ericait m, $(Fe, Mg, Mn)_3[Cl|B_7O_{13}]$
erikite Erikit m *(Monazit pseudomorph nach Eudialit)*
erinite Erinit m *(s.a. cornwallite)*
eriochalcite Eriochalcit m, $Cu Cl_2 \cdot 2H_2O$
erionite Erionit m *(s.a. offretite)*
erlane Erlan m *(Kalksilikatfels)*
erode/to erodieren, abspülen, abtragen, auswaschen
erodibility Erosionsempfindlichkeit f
~ **of soil** Grad m der Bodenerosion
erodible erosionsempfindlich, erodierbar
erosion Erosion f, Ausnagung f, Abtragung f
~ **base level** Erosionsbasis f
~ **control** Kolkschutz m
~ **drilling** Erosionsbohren n
~ **groove** Erosionsrille f
~ **gully** Erosionsgraben m
~ **interval** Erosionslücke f, Erosionsintervall n, Erosionsunterbrechung f
~ **level** Abtragungsniveau n, Erosionsbasis f
~ **of a bank** Uferabbruch m
~ **plain (plane)** Erosionsebene f
~ **stream bed** Erosionswasserbett n
~ **surface** Erosionsfläche f, Abtragungsfläche f, Verebnungsfläche f
~ **thrust** Reliefüberschiebung f
~ **trench** Erosionsgraben m
~ **unconformity** Erosionsdiskordanz f
~ **valley** Erosionstal n
erosional action (activity) Erosionstätigkeit f
~ **break** s. ~ disconformity; ~ interval
~ **cavity** Kolk m
~ **channel** Erosionsrinne f
~ **disconformity** Erosionsdiskordanz f
~ **fenster** Erosionsfenster n
~ **form** Abtragungsform f
~ **gap** s. ~ interval
~ **outlier** Restberg m, Zeugenberg m; Erosionsrest m
~ **rate** Erosionsgeschwindigkeit f
~ **remnant** s. ~ outlier
~ **terrace** Erosionsterrasse f, ausgewaschene Uferbank f
~ **window** Erosionsfenster n

~ **work** Erosionstätigkeit f
erosive erosiv, erodierend, Erosions...
~ **action (activity)** Erosionstätigkeit f
~ **effect** erodierende Wirkung f
~ **work** Erosionstätigkeit f
erosiveness 1. Erosionsfähigkeit f; 2. Grad m der Bodenerosion
errant block s. erratic block
erratic erratisch
~ **block** erratischer Block m, Findling m
~ **boulder (bowlder)** s. ~ block
~ **map** Findlingskarte f
~ **soil** Alluvialboden m
~ **subsoil** unregelmäßiger Untergrund m
erratics erratische Blöcke mpl, Findlinge mpl
ERRE s. effective radiometric resolution element
error of closure Abschlußfehler m *(einer Vermessung)*
erubescite s. bornite
eructate/to ausschleudern
eructation gewaltsamer vulkanischer Gasausbruch m, Ausschleudern n, Auswurf m
erupt/to erumpieren, ausbrechen *(von Vulkanen)*
erupted blocks Auswürflinge mpl
eruption Eruption f, [vulkanischer] Ausbruch m
~ **channel** Eruptionsschlot m, Eruptivschlot m, Eruptionskanal m
~ **cloud** Eruptionswolke f
~ **column** Eruptionssäule f
~ **cone** Eruptionskegel m
~ **crater** Eruptionskrater m
~ **cycle** Eruptionszyklus m
~ **fissure** Eruptionsspalte f
~ **of lava** Lavaausbruch m
eruptive eruptiv
~ **body** Eruptivkörper m
~ **breccia** Eruptivbrekzie f
~ **dike** Eruptivgang m
~ **facies** Eruptivfazies f
~ **knob** Eruptivkuppe f
~ **rocks** Eruptivgestein n, Erstarrungsgestein n, vulkanisches Gestein n
~ **vein** Eruptivgang m
~ **vent** s. eruption channel
eruptives Eruptiva npl
Erythr[a]ean trend erythräische Streichrichtung f
erythrite Erythrin m, Kobaltblüte f, $Co_3[AsO_4]_2 \cdot 8H_2O$
erythrosiderite Erythrosiderit m, $K_2[FeCl_5H_2O]$
erythrozinkite Erythrozinkit m, $(Zn, Mn)S$
Erzgebirgian orogeny Erzgebirgische Orogenphase f
escape/to entweichen
escape 1. Entweichen n, Freiwerden n; 2. Überfall m, Überlauf m *(einer Talsperre)*
~ **of natural gas** Erdgasaustritt m
~ **of the volatile constituents** Entweichen n der flüchtigen Bestandteile

~ **point** Überlaufpunkt m
~ **structure** Fluchtspur f *(Ichnologie)*
~ **velocity** Entweichgeschwindigkeit f
~ **way** Fluchtstrecke f
escar s. esker
escarpment Steilhang m, Steilabfall m, Steilabbruch m, steile Böschung f; Landstufe f
eschar s. esker
eschwegeite s. euxenite
eschynite s. aeschynite
escolaite Eskolait m, CrO_3
escutcheon Area f, Schildchen n *(bei Muscheln)*
eskar s. esker
esker Esker m, Os m, Ås m *(glazialer Kiesrükken)*
eskerine eskerartig
esperite Esperit m, $PbCa_3Zn_4[SiO_4]_4$
essential ash Glasasche f
~ **constituent** wesentlicher Gemengteil m
~ **ejecta** juvenil-authigene Auswürflinge mpl
~ **mineral** Hauptmineral n, kennzeichnender Mineralbestandteil m *(eines Gesteins)*
essexite Essexit m
essonite Hessonit m *(Fe-Grossular, s.a. garnet)*
estavel subterraner Karstfluß m
estavelle Wechselschlund m
estimated reserves geschätzte Vorräte mpl *(noch nicht berechnet und durch die staatliche Vorratskommission bestätigt)*
~ **top** rekonstruierte Oberkante f *(einer Schicht)*
estimation Schätzung f *(mathematische Statistik)*
~ **of reserves** Vorratsschätzung f
estuarine ästuarin
~ **facies** ästuarine Fazies f
~ **flat** Marsch f
~ **type** Ästuartypus m
~ **water** Brackwasser n
estuary 1. Ästuar[ium] n, Flußmündung f, Trichtermündung f, Gezeitenflußmündung f; 2. Meeresarm m, Meeresbucht f
~ **coast** Ästuarküste f
etch/to [an]ätzen
etch figure Ätzfigur f
etching Ätzung f, Anätzung f
~ **by air** Luftätzung f
~ **figure** Ätzskulptur f, Ätzgrübchen n
~ **pit** Ätzgrübchen n
~ **structure** Ätzstruktur f
eternal frost Permafrost m, Dauerfrost m
~ **snow** ewiger Schnee m
etesian winds Jahresmonsun m
ethane Äthan n, C_2H_6
Ethiopian shield Äthiopischer Schild m
ethmolith Ethmolith m
ethology Ethologie f, Verhaltensforschung f
etiolated gebleicht
Etroeungt [Stage], Etroeungtian [Stage] Etroeungt n *(Stufe des höchsten Oberdevons, Ardennen)*

ettringite Ettringit m, $Ca_6Al_2[(OH)_4|SO_4]_3 \cdot 24H_2O$
eucairite Eukairit m, $Cu_2Se \cdot Ag_2Se$
euchroite Euchroit m, $Cu_2[OH|AsO_4] \cdot 3H_2O$
euclase Euklas m, $AlBe[OH|SO_4]$
eucrite Eukrit m *(1. Varietät von Gabbro; 2. Meteorit aus Anorthit und Augit)*
eucryptite Eukryptit m, $LiAl[SiO_4]$
eucrystalline eukristallin, vollkristallin
eudialyte Eudialyt m, $(Na,Ca,Fe)_6Zr[(OH,Cl)|(Si_3O_9)_2]$
eudidymite Eudidymit m, $NaBe[OH|Si_3O_7]$
eugeosyncline Eugeosynklinale f
eugranitic eugranitisch
~ **texture** eugranitische Struktur f
euhedral crystal, euhedron idiomorpher Kristall m
eulytine s. eulytite
eulytite Eulytin m, Kieselwismut m, Wismutblende f, $Bi_4[SiO_4]_3$
eupelagic eupelagisch
~ **deposit** eupelagische Ablagerung f
euphotic zone euphotische Zone f, durchlichtete Wasserzone f
Eurasian steppe region eurasiatischer Steppengürtel m
euritic s. microgranitic
europium Europium n, Eu
euryhaline euryhalin
eustatic eustatisch
~ **change of the sea level** eustatische Meeresspiegelschwankung f
~ **movements** eustatische Bewegungen fpl
eusynchite s. descloizite
eutaxic geschichtet *(bei Erzlagern)*
eutectic eutektisch
eutectic Eutektikum n
~ **curve** eutektische Linie f
~ **ratio** Eutektikumsverhältnis n
~ **texture** Schriftstruktur f
eutectiferous Eutektikum enthaltend
eutectoid eutektoid
eutomous mit deutlicher Spaltbarkeit
eutonic Eutonikum n
eutrophic eutroph, nährstoffreich
~ **organisms** eutrophe Organismen mpl *(Ökologie)*
eutrophication Eutrophierung f
euxenite Euxenit m, $(Y,Er,Ce,U,Pb,Ca)(Na,Ta,Ti)_2(O,OH)_6$
euxinic euxinisch
~ **facies** Schwarzmeerfazies f, euxinische Fazies f, Schwarzschieferfazies f
~ **sediment** euxinisches Sediment n
evacuation of material Stoffabfuhr f
evaluation [technisch-ökonomische] Lagerstätteneinschätzung f
~ **of discovery** Fundbewertung f
evanescent lake eintrocknender See m
evansite Evansit m, $Al_3[(OH)_6|PO_4] \cdot 6H_2O$
evapocryst primäres Evaporitkorn n
evapocrystic mit primärem Evaporitgefüge
evapolensive mit schwach lamelliertem Evaporitgefüge

evaporate 128

evaporate/to verdampfen, verdunsten
evaporating capacity Verdunstungsvermögen n
evaporation Verdampfung f, Verdunstung f, Eindampfen n
~ **area** Verdunstungsfläche f
~ **from soil** Bodenausdünstung f
~ **loss** Verdunstungsverlust m
~ **opportunity** s. relative evaporation
~ **pressure** Dampfdruck m
~ **suppression** Verdunstungsunterdrückung f
evaporativity Verdunstungsvermögen n, Verdunstungshöhe f
evaporimeter Verdunstungsmesser m
evaporite Evaporit m (chemisches Sediment)
~-**solution breccia** Auslaugungsbrekzie f (Karsterscheinung)
evapotranspiration Evapotranspiration f, produktive Verdunstung f, Gesamtverdunstung f (einschließlich Pflanzentranspiration)
~ **equation** Verdunstungsgleichung f
even-bedded gleichmäßig geschichtet
~ **bedding** ebene Schichtung f
~-**crested ridges** Gipfelflur f
~-**crested skyline (summit area, upland)** Gipfelflurebene f
~ **fracture** ebener Bruch m
~-**grained** gleichkörnig, gleichmäßig körnig
evenkite Evenkit m, $C_{24}H_{50}$
evenly bedded gleichmäßig geschichtet
~ **laminated** ebengeschichtet
~ **surfaced** ebenflächig
evenness Ebenflächigkeit f, Ebenheit f
event Einsatz m (Seismik)
ever-frost Permafrost m, Dauerfrost m
~ **frozen layer** Dauerfrostschicht f
~ **frozen soil** Permafrostboden m, Dauerfrostboden m
everglade (Am) sumpfige Steppe f, Küstensumpf m
evidence of erosion Erosionsanzeichen n
eviscerated aufgerissen
evolute whorls evolute Windungen fpl (bei Ammoniten)
evolving course Entwicklungsgang m
evolution of heat Wärmeentwicklung f
~ **of river bed** Flußausbildung f
~ **of species** Entwicklung f der Arten
evolutional ... s. evolutionary ...
evolutionary course Entwicklungsgang m
~ **doctrine** Entwicklungslehre f
~ **history** Entwicklungsgeschichte f
~ **line** Entwicklungslinie f
~ **process** Entwicklungsvorgang m
~ **progress** Entwicklungsfortschritt m
~ **record** Entwicklungsgeschichte f
~ **series** Entwicklungsreihe f
~ **spurt** Entwicklungssprung m
~ **stage** Erdölstadium n
~ **trend** Entwicklungsrichtung f
evolutionism Entwicklungslehre f
evolutive stages of erosion s. geographical cycle

evorsion Wirbelerosion f, Ausstrudelung f, Auskolkung f
exaggerated überhöht (Maßstab)
exaggeration of heights Überhöhung f (im Profil)
~ **of the vertical scale** Überhöhung f (Maßstab)
exalbuminous eiweißlos
examination of soil Bodenuntersuchung f
~ **of subsoil** Baugrunduntersuchung f
~ **of surface** Oberflächenbeobachtung f
exarate/to auskolken
exaration Auskolken n
excavatability Gewinnbarkeit f (durch Ausbruch)
excavate/to 1. [aus]baggern, ausschachten, aushöhlen; 2. ausgraben, ausstrudeln, auskolken
excavated cross-section lichter Ausbruchsquerschnitt m
excavation 1. Ausbruch m, Ausschachtung f, Aushöhlung f; Aushub m; Ausgrabung f; 2. Weitung f; 3. Ausstrudelung f, Auskolkung f
excavator Bagger m
excess hydrostatic pressure hydrostatischer Überdruck m
~ **of mass** Massenüberschuß m (Gravimetrie)
~ **pressure** Überdruck m
~ **rain hyetograph** Überschuß-Niederschlagsganglinie f
excessive precipitation Starkniederschlag m
~ **water interlayer** Mehrschichttonmineralwasser n
exchange capacity Austauschkapazität f; Austauschvermögen n
~ **reaction** Austauschreaktion f
exclusion of air Luftabschluß m
excretory Ausscheidungs...
executive program Ausführungsprojekt n
exfoliate/to abblättern
exfoliation Abblätterung f, schalenförmige Abschuppung f, Desquamation f, Abschieferung f
exhalation Exhalation f, Aushauchung f; Ausdünstung f
~ **deposit** Exhalationslagerstätte f
exhale/to aushauchen; ausdünsten; ausströmen
exhaust/to völlig abbauen; erschöpfen; versiegen
exhausted soil erschöpfter Boden m
~ **vein** abgebauter Gang m
~ **well** 1. erschöpfte Bohrung f; 2. versiegter Brunnen m
exhaustible begrenzt, nicht unerschöpflich
exhaustion of a mine Erschöpfung f eines Feldes
~ **of an oil well** Erschöpfung f (Versiegen n) einer Erdölbohrung
exhibited beds/well gut aufgeschlossene Schichten fpl
exhumation Ausgrabung f, Freilegung f

exhume/to exhumieren, ausgraben, freilegen
exhumed peneplain abgedeckte Rumpfebene *f*
exinite Exinit *m (Kohlenmaceral; Maceralgruppe)*
exit Austrittsstelle *f*
~ **gradient** Austrittsgefälle *n*
exocast Außenabdruck *m* eines Fossils
exocontact Exokontakt *m*
exocyclic irregulär
exodynamics exogene Dynamik *f*
exoergic exotherm
exogene, exogenetic, exogenic s. exogenous
exogenous exogen, von außen wirkend, außenbürtig
~ **agents** außenbürtige Kräfte *fpl*
~ **cycle** exogener Kreislauf *m*
~ **dome** s. volcanic dome
~ **effects** Auswirkungen *fpl* im Intrusionsdach
~ **enclosure** s. xenolith
~ **inclusion** exogener Einschluß *m*
~ **lava dome** s. shield volcano
~ **process** exogenetischer Prozeß *m*
~ **rock** exogenes Gestein *n*
exogeosyncline Exogeosynklinale *f*
exokinetic exokinetisch
exometamorphism Kontaktmetamorphose *f*
exomorphic exomorph
~ **area (halo)** Kontakthof *m*
exomorphism s. exometamorphism
exorheic region in den Ozean entwässerndes Gebiet *n*
exoskeleton Außenskelett *n*
exosmose Ausschwitzung *f*
exosphere Exosphäre *f*
exospheric exosphärisch
exothermal, exothermic exotherm[isch]
exotic exotisch
~ **block** exotischer Block *m*, Scherling *m (bei Überschiebungen)*
~ **fauna** fremdartige Fauna *f*
~ **rock** ortsfremdes Gestein *n*
expand/to sich ausdehnen
expanded entspannt
~ **clay** Blähton *m*, aufgeblähter (geschwellter) Ton *m*
expanding anchor Spreizanker *m*
~ **spread** Korrelationsaufstellung *f (Seismik)*
expansibility Schwellvermögen *n*
expansion coefficient Ausdehnungskoeffizient *m*
~ **crack** Sprengriß *m*
~ **measuring strip** Dehnungsmeßstreifen *m*
~ **of the gas cap** Ausdehnung *f* der Gaskappe
~ **of the universe** Expansion *f* des Weltalls
expansive clay s. expanded clay
~ **force** Quellfähigkeit *f (von Böden, Tonen)*
expectation of ultimate recovery erwartete Gesamtausbeute *f*
expected depth voraussichtliche (erwartete) Tiefe *f*
~ **output** zu erwartende Produktion *f*

~ **tonnage** industrieller (abbauwürdiger) Vorrat *m*
expel/to ausschleudern
expenses of exploration Untersuchungskosten *pl*, Aufschlußkosten *pl*
experimental drilling Probebohrung *f*
~ **geology** Experimentalgeologie *f*
~ **verification** experimenteller Beweis *m*
exploit/to abbauen, ausbeuten, gewinnen
exploitable abbauwürdig, gewinnbar
~ **reserves of water** gewinnbare Wasserreserven (Wasserressourcen) *fpl*
exploitation Abbau *m*, Ausbeutung *f*, Gewinnung *f*
~ **drilling** Gewinnungsbohrung *f*
~ **engineer** Gewinnungsingenieur *m*
~ **factor** Ausnutzungsfaktor *m*
~ **method** Abbaumethode *f*, Gewinnungsart *f*
~ **permit** Gewinnungsberechtigung *f*
exploited oil field erschöpftes Ölfeld *n*
exploration Exploration *f*, Erkundung *f*, Aufsuchen *n*, Schürfen *n*
~ **activity** Explorationstätigkeit *f*
~ **boring** s. ~ drilling
~ **drilling** 1. Explorationsbohren *n*, Untersuchungsbohren *n*, Aufschlußbohren *n*; 2. Versuchsbohrung *f*, Probebohrung *f*
~ **expenses** Untersuchungskosten *pl*, Aufschlußkosten *pl*
~ **geochemistry** Lagerstättengeochemie *f*
~ **geophysics** Erkundungsgeophysik *f*
~ **licence** Aufschlußkonzession *f*
~ **of caves** Höhlenforschung *f*
~ **of space** Weltraumforschung *f*
~ **of the ionosphere** Ionosphärenforschung *f*
~ **permit** Schürfschein *m*, Schürflizenz *f*
~ **right** Explorationsrecht *n*
~ **tunnel** Sondierstollen *m*
~ **well** Aufschlußbohrung *f*, Explorationsbohrung *f*, Untersuchungsbohrung *f*, Erkundungsbohrung *f*
~ **work** Aufschlußarbeiten *fpl*, Untersuchungsarbeiten *fpl*
explorative drilling s. exploration drilling 1.
exploratory borehole Explorationsbohrloch *n*
~ **boring** s. exploration drilling 1.
~ **drift** Untersuchungsstrecke *f*, Erkundungsstrecke *f*
~ **drill hole** Vorbohrloch *n*
~ **drilling** s. exploration drilling 1.
~ **excavation** Schurf *m*
~ **hole** Aufschlußbohrung *f*
~ **rocket** meteorologische Rakete *f*
~ **well** s. exploration well
~ **work** Aufschlußarbeiten *fpl*, Untersuchungsarbeiten *fpl*
explore/to erkunden, aufsuchen, untersuchen, schürfen, erforschen
exploring Erforschung *f*, Erkundung *f*
~ **drift** Versuchsstrecke *f*, Untersuchungsstollen *m*
~ **mining** bergmännische Erkundungsarbeiten *fpl*

explosion

explosion Explosion f, Ausbruch m
~ **breccia** Explosionsbrekzie f
~ **crater** Explosionskrater m
~ **focus** Explosionsherd m
~ **of fire damp** Schlagwetterexplosion f
~ **of the combustible gases** Gasexplosion f, Schlagwetterexplosion f
~ **pipe** Eruptionsschlund m
~-**pipe eruption** Punkteruption f
~ **pit** Maar n
~ **tremors** Explosionsbeben npl
explosive Sprengstoff m
explosive explosiv
~ **activity** explosive Tätigkeit f
~ **atmosphere** explosive Wetter pl
~ **earthquake** Explosivbeben n
~ **eruption** Explosivausbruch m
~ **index** pyroklastischer Anteil an der Gesamtförderung eines Vulkans
~ **rock** schlagendes Gebirge n
exponential decline curve exponentielle Erschöpfungskurve f (Lagerstättenabbau)
expose/to bloßlegen, freilegen, aufschließen
exposed freiliegend, freigelegt, bloßgelegt, aufgeschlossen
~ **anticline** bloßgelegte Antiklinale f
~ **area** Verhiebsfläche f
~ **rock** anstehendes Gestein n
~ **strata** ausstreichende Schichten fpl
exposing Freilegung f
exposure Freilegung f, Aufschluß m, Bloßlegung f
~ **site** Meßstelle f
~ **time** 1. Belichtungszeit f; 2. Einwirkungszeit f (Strahlung)
expulsion Ausschleudern n, Auswurf m
exsiccation Austrocknung f, Vertrocknung f
exsolution Entmischung f
~ **lamellae** Entmischungslamellen fpl
~ **minerals** Entmischungsminerale npl
exsolutional sediment lösungsverfestigtes Sediment n
exstipulate nebenblattlos
exsudanite Exsudanit m (Kohlenmaceral der Liptinitgruppe; sekundäre Bildung bei der Diagenese)
extant noch heute lebend
extended exposures flächenhafte Aufschlüsse mpl
~ **valley** verlängertes Tal n
extending flow Flächenströmung f
extensibility Dehnbarkeit f
extension Zerrung f
~ **joint** Dehnungskluft f
~ **strain fracture** Entspannungskluft f
~ **test** Erweiterungsbohrung f
~ **well** Erweiterungsbohrung f (auf bekanntem Horizont)
extensometer Dehnungsmesser m
extensometric method Dehnungsmeßverfahren n
exterior cast Außenabguß m (eines Fossils)
~ **dune** Außendüne f

~ **mould** Außenabguß m (eines Fossils)
external extern, exogen
~ **agencies** externe Kräfte fpl
~ **cast** Außenabguß m (eines Fossils)
~ **dynamic processes** s. exodynamics
~ **geodynamics** äußere Geodynamik f
~ **ligament** äußeres Ligament n
~ **migration factor** äußerer Migrationsfaktor m
~ **mould** Außenabguß m (eines Fossils)
~ **pressure** Außendruck m
~ **rotation** Externrotation f
~ **skeleton** Außenskelett n
~ **symmetry of crystals** äußere Kristallsymmetrie f
~ **volcanism** Oberflächenvulkanismus m
externides Externiden pl (orogene Strukturform)
extinct ausgestorben, erloschen
~ **lake** verlandeter See m
~ **species** ausgestobene Art f
~ **volcano** erloschener Vulkan m
extinction 1. Auslöschung f (optisch); 2. Extinktion f, Schwächung f (der Strahlung); 3. Aussterben n, Erlöschen n, Artentod m; 4. Verschwinden n (z.B. eines Sees)
~ **angle** Auslöschungsschiefe f
~ **direction** Auslöschungsrichtung f
~ **position** Auslöschungslage f
extinguished volcano erloschener Vulkan m
extoölite kleine Konkretion f
extra low frequency exploration Erkundung f mittels extrem niederfrequenter [elektromagnetischer] Wellen
~-**Neptunian planets** transneptunische Planeten mpl
extraclast Extraklast m (Karbonatgesteinsfragment von außerhalb des Sedimentationsraums)
extract/to 1. fördern; abbauen, gewinnen; 2. auskohlen
~ **a core** einen Kern ziehen
extraction Verhieb m, Abbau m, Gewinnung f, Förderung f
~ **method** Extraktionsmethode f
~ **of oil** Erdölgewinnung f
~ **of ore** Erzabbau m
~ **water** Extraktionswasser n (zur Untertageverflüssigung von Schwefel)
~ **with stowing** Versatzbau m
extractive gewinnbar
~ **industry** Aufbereitungsindustrie f
extragalactic extragalaktisch
extramagmatic extramagmatisch
extramorainic außerhalb der Endmoräne gelegen
extramundane außerirdisch
extraneous ash syngenetische Aschebestandteile mpl (von Kohle)
extraordinary ray außerordentlicher Strahl m
extrapolation Extrapolation f
extratelluric extratellurisch
extraterrestrial extraterrestrisch, extratellurisch, außerirdisch, außerhalb der Erde

~ **geology** extraterrestrische Geologie *f*
~ **radiation** extraterrestrische Strahlung *f*
~ **source** extraterrestrische Quelle *f*
~ **space** Weltraum *m*
extravasate/to ausströmen
extravasating lava ausfließende Lava *f*
extravasation of lava Ausfließen *n* von Lava, Lavaausbruch *m*
extreme pressure Höchstdruck *m*
extrude/to ausstoßen
extrusion Extrusion *f*, Erguß *m*, Auswurf *m*
extrusive extrusiv, vulkanisch
~ **body** Extrusivkörper *m*
~ **magmatic** extrusiv-magmatisch
~ **phase** Extrusionsphase *f*
~ **rock** Extrusivgestein *n*, Ergußgestein *n*, vulkanisches Gestein *n*, Vulkanit *m*
exudation Ausschwitzung *f*, Ausgasung *f*, Exudat *n*
~ **of oil** Ausschwitzung *f* von Erdöl
~ **vein** *s.* segregated vein
eye-ball interpretation visuelle Auswertung *f*
~ **clean** augenrein *(bei Edelsteinen)*
~ **coal** Augenkohle *f*
~ **node** Augenknoten *m*
~ **piece** Okular *n*
~-**piece micrometer** Okularmikrometer *n*
~ **tubercle** Augenhöcker *m*
eyed structure Augengefüge *n*
eyot kleine Insel *f (im Fluß oder See)*
ezcurrite Ezcurrit *m*, $Na_2[B_5O_6(OH)_5] \cdot H_2O$

F

fabianite Fabianit *m*, $Ca[B_3O_5(OH)]$
fabric Gefüge *n (im gefügekundlichen Sinne)*
~ **element** Gefügeelement *n*
face 1. Fläche *f (z.B. eines Kristalls);* 2. Abbaustoß *m*, Gewinnungsstoß *m*, Ortsbrust *f*, Ortsstoß *m*, Stoß *m (s.a.* back 1.); 3. Faltenvergenz *f (Tektonik)*
~ **advance** Verhieb *m*; Abbaufortschritt *m*, Vortriebsfortschritt *m*
~ **angle** Flächenwinkel *m (z.B. eines Vielflächners)*
~-**centered** flächenzentriert *(Kristall)*
~-**centered cubic** kubisch-flächenzentriert
~-**centered lattice** flächenzentriertes Gitter *n*
~ **cleat** gut ausgebildete Kohlenschlechte *f*
~ **end** Strebausgang *m (Abbau)*
~**entry** Abbaustrecke *f* senkrecht zu den Schlechten
~ **excavation** STrebraum *m*
~ **length** Streblänge *f*
~ **of crystal** Kristallfläche *f*
~ **of lode** Salband *n (eines Erzganges)*
~ **of sand** Sandstoß *m*
~ **of well** Bohrlochsohle *f*
~ **on board** Arbeitsstoß *m* parallel zu den Schlechten
~ **on end** Arbeitsstoß *m* senkrecht zu den Schlechten

~ **slips** gegen den Stoß einfallende Schichtflächen (Schlechten) *fpl*
~ **support** Strebausbau *m*
~ **terrace** Küstenterrasse *f*
~ **working space** Abbauraum *m*
facet/to facettieren
facet Facette *f*, Kristallfläche *f*, Rautenfläche *f*
facetted eyes Facettenaugen *npl*, Komplexaugen *npl (der Arthropoden)*
~ **pebble** Kantengeröll *n*, Facettengeschiebe *n*
facial faziell
~ **grooves** Segmentalfurchen *fpl*
~ **suture** Gesichtsnaht *f (Trilobiten)*
facieology Fazieskunde *f*
facies Fazies *f*
~ **change** Fazieswechsel *m*, Faziesänderung *f*
~ **fossil** Faziesfossil *n*
~ **map** Fazieskarte *f*
~ **nappe** Faziesdecke *f*
~ **of coal** Kohlenfazies *f*
facing 1. Bestimmung *f* der ursprünglichen Schichtenoberkante; primäre Raumlage *f* einer Schicht
~ **of strata** Bestimmung *f* der primären Schichtorientierung
facsimile crystallization Abbildungskristallisation *f*
factor Faktor *m*, Merkmalskomplex *m*, Ursachenkomplex *m*
~ **analysis** Faktor[en]analyse *f*
~ **loading** Faktorladung *f (Gewicht eines Merkmals bei einem Faktor)*
~ **of concentration** Konzentrationsgrad *m*
~ **of outflow variation** Abflußschwankungskoeffizient *m*
~ **of safety** Sicherheitsgrad *m*, Sicherheitskoeffizient *m*
~ **of weathering** Verwitterungsfaktor *m*
~ **value map** Faktorwertkarte *f*
fade Abschwächung *f*, Amplitudenunterdrückung *f*
faecal pellet Fäkalpellet *n*, Kotpellet *n*
faheyite Faheyit *m*, (Mn, Mg, Na)$Fe_2Be_2[PO_4]_4 \cdot 6H_2O$
fahlband Fahlband *n*, sulfidimprägnierte Schieferlage *f*
fahlore Fahlerz *n (s.a.* tetrahedrite, tennantite)
fahlunite Falunit *m (zersetzter Kordierit)*
faik[e]s *(sl) s.* fake
failing of dike (embankment) Deichbruch *m*
~ **well** versiegender Brunnen *m*
failure Bruch *m (Tektonik)*
~ **by spreading** Böschungsrutschung *f*
~ **of surface controls** Versagen *n* der Bohrlochabsperrvorrichtung
~ **stress** Bruchspannung *f*
~ **surface** Bruchfläche *f*
fair-stained etwas gefleckt *(Glimmerqualität)*
~-**weather runoff** Trockenwetterabfluß *m*
fairfieldite Fairfieldit *m*, $Ca_2(Mn, Fe)[PO_4]_2 \cdot 2H_2O$
fairy stone *(sl)* 1. *exotisch geformte Konkretion;* 2. fossiler Seeigel *m*

fake

fake *(sl)* Sandschiefer *m*
~ **diamond** unechter Diamant *m*
~ **reflection** Scheinreflexion *f*
falciform sichelförmig
fall/to [ein]fallen
~ **in** einstürzen
~ **into crumbs** zerbröckeln
fall 1. Fallen *n*, Einfallen *n*; 2. Reliefenergie *f (eines Flusses)*; 3. Bruch *m*, Niederwasser *n*; 4. Wasserfall *m*
~ **flood** Herbsthochflut *f*
~ **in output** Produktionsabfall *m*, Produktionsrückgang *m*
~ **of country** Gebirgsschlag *m*
~ **of ground** 1. Einsinken *n* des Bodens; 2. Gebirgsschlag *m*
~ **of level** Spiegelgefälle *n (Wasser)*
~ **of meteorites** Meteoritenfall *m (der frisch niedergegangen ist, im Gegensatz zu „find")*
~ **of rock** Bergrutsch *m*, Bergsturz *m*, Steinschlag *m*
~ **of roof** Hereinbrechen *n* des Hangenden
falling Ebbe *f*
~ **gradient** Gefälle *n*, Neigung *f*
~-**head permeameter** Durchlässigkeitsmeßapparatur *f* mit fallender Druckhöhe
~-**in** Einsturz *m*; Zusammenbruch *m*
~-**in of mine** Grubeneinsturz *m*
~ **of dike** Deichbruch *m*
~ **star** Sternschnuppe *f*
~ **stone** Meteorstein *m*
~ **stones** Steinschlag *m*
~ **tide** fallendes Wasser *n*
fallout radioaktiver Niederschlag (Ausfall) *m*
fallow land Brachland *n*
false amethyst violetter Flußspat *m (Schmuckstein)*
~ **anticline** sedimentäre Abbildungsantikline *f*
~-**bedded** kreuzgeschichtet, diagonalgeschichtet, schräggeschichtet, Transversalgeschichtet
~ **bedding** Kreuzschichtung *f*, Diagonalschichtung *f*, Schrägschichtung *f*, Transversalschichtung *f*
~ **cleavage** S_2-Schieferung *f*; Runzelschieferung *f (nach A. Born)*; Schubklüftung *f (nach H. Scholtz)*
~ **colour composite** Falschfarbensynthesebild *n*
~ **colour film** Falschfarbenfilm *m*
~ **colour image** Falschfarbenbild *n*, Falschfarbenaufnahme *f*
~ **colour photography** Falschfarbenfotografie *f*
~ **floor** nicht standhaftes Liegendes *n*
~ **galena** *s.* sphalerite
~ **gossan** unechter Oxydationshut *m*
~ **lamination** Transversalschichtung *f*
~ **mud crack** falscher Trockenriß *m*
~ **oolites** Pseudo-Oolithe *mpl*, Pseudo-Ooide *npl*, Mikropellets *npl*
~ **river** verlassener Mäander *m*
~ **roof** Nachfall *m*

~ **topaz** *s.* quartz
~ **water table** artesisch gespannter Grundwasserspiegel *m*
Famennian [Stage] Famenne *n (Stufe des Oberdevons)*
family Familie *f*
famp verwitterter Kalkstein *m*
fan 1. Fächer *m*, Fächerstellung *f (der Schieferung)*; 2. Schuttkegel *m*
~ **delta** Schwemmdelta *n*
~ **filter** Fächerfilter *n*; Geschwindigkeitsfilter *n*
~ **fold** Fächerfalte *f*
~ **mesa** Erosionsrest *m* eines Schuttfächers
~ **of alluvium** Alluvialfächer *m*
~-**shaped** fächerförmig
~ **shooting** Fächerschießen *n*
~ **talus** Schuttfächer *m*, Streuungskegel *m*, Schuttkegel *m*
~-**topped pediments** mit Schuttkegeln bedeckte Pedimentflächen *f*
fancy marble bunter Marmor *m*
~ **stones** farbige Diamanten *mpl*
fang Fangzahn *m*
fanglomerate Fanglomerat *n*, grober Kiesfächer *m*
fanlike fächerförmig
fanning 1. Fächerung *f*; 2. Fächerschießen *n*
fanwise fächerförmig
far-travelled mass Fernüberschiebung *f*
farallonite Farallonit *m*, $2MgO \cdot W_2O_5 \cdot SiO_2 \cdot nH_2O$
farewell rock 1. flözleerer Sandstein *m*; 2. Zeugenberg *m*
Farlovian Farlovien *n*, Oberes Old Red *n (Oberdevon, Old-Red-Fazies)*
farmout Konzessionsübertragung oder -verkauf (Grundeigentümerbergbau)
faro Atoll *n* zweiter Ordnung, Atollon *n*
farringtonite Farringtonit *m*, $[Mg, Fe]_3[PO_4]_2$
farside Fernseite *f (Mond)*
fascicular schist Garbenschiefer *m*, Schiefer *m* mit belteroporem Mineralwachstum in der S-Fläche
fasciculate gebüschelt
fascine Faschine *f*
~ **barrier wall** Faschinendamm *m*
fassaite Fassait *m*, $Ca(Mg, Fe,Al)[(Si,Al)_2O_6]$
Fassanian [Substage] Fassan[ium] *n (Unterstufe, Mittlere Trias, Tethys)*
fast *s.* ~ stone head
~ **dip** steiles Einfallen *n*
~ **ice** Festeis *n*
~ **stone head** festes Gestein *n (unter dem Abraum)*
fat clay fetter (stark plastischer) Ton *m*, Lehmerde *f*
~ **coal** Fettkohle *f*
~ **soil** fetter Boden *m*
fathometer Teufenmeßgerät *n*, Echolot *n*
fatigue break Ermüdungsbruch *m*, Dauerbruch *m*
~ **crack** Ermüdungsriß *m*

faults

~ **failure (fracture)** Ermüdungsbruch *m*, Dau... bruch *m*
~ **strength** Dauerfestigkeit *f*
~ **test** Dauerfestigkeitsversuch *m*
faujasite Faujasit *m*, $Na_2Ca[Al_2Si_4O_{12}]_2 \cdot 16H_2O$
fault [down, off]/to verwerfen
fault Verwerfung *f*, Verschiebung *f*, Sprung *m*
~-**angle valley** Tal *n* am Rande einer Blockkippung
~ **basin** tektonisches Becken *n*, Bruchbecken *n*, Bruchsenke *f*, Kesselbruch *m*
~ **belt** Bruchzone *f*
~ **bench** Verwerfungsstufe *f*
~ **block** Bruchscholle *f*, Scholle *f*, Horst *m*
~-**block depression** Grabenbruch *m*
~-**block mountains** Bruch[schollen]gebirge *n*, Schollengebirge *n*
~-**bounded** von Verwerfung begrenzt
~ **breccia** Reibungsbrekzie *f*, Verwerfungsbrekzie *f*
~ **bundle** Störungssystem *n*, Verwerfungsschar *f*, Bruchbündel *n*
~ **cave** Verwerfungshöhle *f*
~ **cleft** Verwerfungsspalte *f*
~ **cliff** Verwerfungskliff *n*, Bruchstufe *f*
~ **coast** Verwerfungsküste *f*
~ **crevice** Verwerfungskluft *f*
~-**dam spring** Verwerfungsquelle *f*
~ **dip** Einfallen *n* der Verwerfung
~ **dipping against the beds** widersinnig fallende Verwerfung *f*
~ **embayment** Meereseinbruch *m* in Grabenbruchzonen
~ **face** Verwerfungsfront *f*
~ **fissure** Verwerfungsspalte *f*
~ **fold** Bruchfalte *f*
~-**fold structure** Bruchfaltenbau *m*
~ **folding** Faltung *f* in Störungszonen
~ **gouge** Verwerfungston *m*
~ **graben** Grabenbruch *m*
~ **hading against the dip** widersinnig fallende Verwerfung *f*
~ **line** Verwerfungslinie *f*, Bruchlinie *f*
~-**line scarp** Bruchlinienwand *f*, Bruchlinienstufe *f*
~-**line valley** Verwerfungstal *n*
~ **mosaic** Bruchfeld *n (tektonisch)*
~ **mountains** Bruchgebirge *n*
~ **movement** Bewegung *f* entlang der Verwerfungsfläche
~ **outcrop** Verwerfungsausstrich *m*, Verwerfungslinie *f*
~ **outlier** Deckscholle *f*
~ **pit** Kessel[bruch] *m*, Pinge *f*
~ **plain reflection** Reflexion *f* an einer Störung
~ **plain solution** Herd[verschiebungs]lösung *f*
~ **plane** Verwerfungsebene *f*, Verwerfungsfläche *f*
~ **polish** Rutschfläche *f*
~ **ridge** Schollenkante *f*, Hochscholle *f*
~ **rift** Verwerfungsspalte *f*
~ **scarp** Verwerfungsabsturz *m*, Verwerfungskliff

n, Verwerfungswand *f*, Verwerfungs[steil]stufe *f*, Bruchwand *f*, Bruchstufe *f*, Horst *m (Staffelbruch)*
~-**scarp coast** Bruchlinienküste *f*
~-**scarp topography** Bruchstufenlandschaft *f*
~ **set** Verwerfungsschar *f*
~ **shore line** Verwerfungsküste *f*
~-**slip cleavage** S_2-Schieferung *f*; Runzelschieferung *f (nach A. Born)*; Schubklüftung *f (nach H. Scholtz)*
~ **space** Verwurfszone *f*, Verwerfungszone *f*
~ **spring** Verwerfungsquelle *f*
~ **striae** Harnischrillen *fpl*, Bewegungsstreifen *mpl (auf einer Störungsfläche)*
~ **striation** Harnisch *m*
~ **strike** Streichen *n* einer Verwerfung, Verwerfungsrichtung *f*
~ **surface** Verwerfungsfläche *f*, Verschiebungsfläche *f*
~ **system** Verwerfungssystem *n*
~ **terrace** Bruchterrasse *f*
~ **throw [seigere]** Sprunghöhe *f*
~ **trace** Verwerfungslinie *f*, Bruchlinie *f*
~ **trap** Verwerfungsfalle *f*, Ölfalle *f* an einer Verwerfung
~ **trend** Verwerfungsstreichen *n*
~ **trough** Graben *m*, Bruch *m*, Senke *f*; Tiefscholle *f*
~-**trough lake** Grabensee *m*
~ **valley** Dislokationstal *n*, Bruchtal *n*, Verwerfungstal *n*
~ **vein** eine Verwerfungsspalte ausfüllender Mineralgang *m*
~ **wall** Verwerfungswand *f*
~ **wedge** Keilscholle *f*
~-**wedge mountain** Keilschollengebirge *n*
~ **zone** Verwerfungszone *f*, Bruchzone *f*, Störungszone *f*
faultage Sprungbildung *f*
faulted verworfen, gestört *(Flöz, Gebirge)*
~ **anticline** Faltenverwerfung *f*, Bruchsattel *m*, Bruchfalte *f*
~ **area** Bruchgebiet *n*
~ **bedding plane** verworfene (verschobene) Schichtebene *f*
~ **block** *s*. fault block
~ **body** Verwerfungskörper *m*
~ **deposit** verworfene Lagerstätte *f*
~-**down block** abgesunkene Scholle *f*
~ **fold mountains** Faltenschollengebirge *n*
~ **mountains** Bruchgebirge *n*
~-**out** ausgequetscht *(an einer Störung)*
~ **overfold** Faltenüberschiebung *f*, Faltenverwerfung *f*; Bruchfalte *f*, Überschiebungsfalte *f*
~ **reservoir** gestörte Lagerstätte *f*
~ **strata** verworfene Schichten *fpl*
~ **zone** Störungszone *f*, Verwerfungszone *f*
faulting Verwerfung *f*, Verwurf *m*, Bruchbildung *f*, Sprungbildung *f*
~ **in reverse** widersinnige Verwerfung *f*
~ **tectonics** Verwerfungstektonik *f*
faults with balance of throw wechselsinnige

faulty 134

Zwischenverwerfungen *fpl*, Staffelbruch *m* mit fortläufigen und rückläufigen Staffeln
faulty drilling Fehlbohrung *f*
~ **interpretation** fehlerhafte Auswertung *f*
fauna Fauna *f*, Tierreich *n*
faunal faunistisch, Faunen...
~ **association** Faunengesellschaft *f*
~ **boundary** Faunengrenze *f*
~ **break** Faunenschnitt *m*
~ **community boundaries** Grenzen *fpl* von Faunenvergesellschaftungen
~ **horizon** Faunenhorizont *m*
~ **province** Faunenprovinz *f*
~ **realm** Faunenreich *n*
~ **remains** fossile Tierreste *mpl*
~ **subprovince** Faunensubprovinz *f*
~ **succession** Faunenfolge *f*
faunistic *s.* faunal
faunizone Faunenzone *f*
fauserite Fauserit *m*, $Mn[SO_4] \cdot 7H_2O$
faustite Faustit *m*, $ZnAl_6[(OH)_2|PO_4]_4 \cdot 4H_2O$
Faust's equation Faustsche Formel *f*
favas transportierte Mineralgerölle *npl (Brasilien)*
favourable locality höffiges Gebiet *n*
fayalite Fayalit *m*, $Fe_2[SiO_4]$
feasibility study Durchführbarkeitsstudie *f*, Projektstudie *f (z.B. für den Aufschluß einer Lagerstätte)*
feasible ground standfestes (gutes) Gebirge *n*
feather/to sich verdrücken, auffiedern, fingerförmig endigen
~ **out** fingerförmig endigen, auffiedern
feather alum *s.* halotrichite
~ **grass steppe** Krautsteppe *f*
~ **joint** Fiederspalte *f*, Fiederkluft *f*
~ **ore** Federerz *n*, Jamesonit *m (s.a. jamesonite)*
~ **salt** Federsalz *n*
feathering gestaffelte Aufstellung *f (z.B. von Geophonen)*
featherlike, feathery federartig, federförmig
feature extraction Herausarbeitung *f* charakteristischer Merkmale, Merkmalsgewinnung *f (z.B. aus Fernerkundungsaufnahmen)*
~ **recognition** Merkmalserkennung *f*
fecal pellet *s.* faecal pellet
feeble-dipping strata flach einfallende Schichten *fpl*
feebly developed fold schwach entwickelte Falte *f*
~ **magnetic** schwach magnetisch
feed/to speisen
feed ditch Bewässerungsrinne *f*
~ **of the bit** Meißelvorschub *m*
~ **-off** Vorschub *m (des Bohrgestänges)*
~ **stock** Einsatzmaterial *n*, Ausgangsstoff *m*
~ **water** Speisewasser *n*
~ **water make-up** Speisewasseraufbereitung *f*
feedback Rückkopplung *f*
feeder 1. Kluft *f (wasser- oder erzführend)*; kleiner Fiedergang *m*; 2. Nebenfluß *m*; Zufluß *m*; Zubringer *m*, Zufuhrkanal *m*; 3. Gasbläser *m*; Schlot *m*
~ **beach** Anlandungsstrand *m*
~ **of ore** erzführende Kluft *f*
~ **of water** Wasserzubringer *m (z.B. Gebirgsspalten)*
feeding channel Zufuhrkanal *m*
~ **ground** Einzugsgebiet *n*, Nährgebiet *n*
~ **structure** Freßspur *f (Ichnologie)*
~ **vent** Vulkanschlot *m*
feeling Untersuchung *f (des Hangenden)*
~ **dilatometer** Tastdilatometer *n*
feigh Berge *pl*
feldspar Feldspat *m (s.a. orthoclase; plagioclase)*
feldspathic feldspatführend, feldspathaltig, feldspatartig
~ **gneiss** Feldspatgneis *m*
~ **graywacke** Feldspatgrauwacke *f*
~ **sandstone** feldspathaltiger Sandstein *m*, Feldspatsandstein *m*, Arkosesandstein *m*
feldspathization Feldspatisierung *f*
feldspathize/to verfeldspaten
feldspathoids Feldspatvertreter *mpl (z.B. Leuzit, Nephelin)*
fell 1. Hügel *m*; 2. Moorland *n (in Nordengland)*; 3. Bleierz *n*
felsic felsisch
~ **mineral** felsisches Mineral *n*
felsiphyric mikroaphanitisch *(bei Porphyriten)*
felsite Felsit *m*
felsitic felsitisch
~ **texture** felsitische Struktur *f*
felsitoid felsitartig
felsöbányite Felsöbányit *m*, $Al_4[(OH)_{10}|SO_4] \cdot 5H_2O$
felsophyre felsophyr *m*
felsophyric felsophyrisch
felsosphaerite Felsitsphärolit *m*
felspar *s.* feldspar
felspathic *s.* feldspathic
felstone Felsit *m*
felsyte *s.* felsite
felt bob Filzpolierscheibe *f*
felted *s.* felty
felty filzig, dicht, holokristallin *(Grundmasse)*
femic femisch
femur Femur *n*, Oberschenkelknochen *m*
fen Fehn *n*, Fenn *n*, Venn *n*, Bruch *m (n)*, Ried *n*, Moor *n*, Flachmoor *n*, Niederungsmoor *n*, Grünlandmoor *n*, Marschland *n*
~ **peat** Niederungstorf *m*
fenaksite Fenaksit *m*, $KNa(Fe, Mn)[Si_4O_{10}] \cdot 1/2 H_2O$
fence diagram Paneeldiagramm *n*, Gitterprofil *n*
fenestra syngenetische Pore *f (bei Sedimenten)*
fenestral syngenetisch porig *(bei Sedimenten)*
~ **fabric** syngenetisches Porengefüge *n*, Hohlraumgefüge *n*, Fenstergefüge *n (in Karbonatgesteinen)*

~ porosity syngenetische Porosität *f*
fenite Fenit *m*
fenland Ried *n*, Wiesenmoor *n*, Marschland *n*
Fennoscandia Finnisch-Skandinavischer Schild *m*, Baltischer Schild *m*
fenny sumpfig, moorig
~ soil Moorboden *m*
fenster tektonisches Fenster *n*
ferallitic soil Lateritboden *m*
ferberite Ferberit *m*, Fe[WO$_4$]
ferg[h]anite Ferghanit *m*, LiH[(UO$_2$)$_4$|(OH)$_4$|(VO$_4$)$_2$]·2H$_2$O
fergusite Fergusit *m*
fergusonite Fergusonit *m*, YNbO$_4$
fermorite Fermorit *m*, (Ca, Sr)$_4$[Ca(OH, F)|[(P, As)O$_4$]$_3$
fern Farn *m*
~ frond Farnwedel *m*
~ impression Farnabdruck *m*
~ plant Farnpflanze *f*
fernandinite Fernandinit *m*, CaV$_{12}$O$_{30}$·14H$_2$O
fernlike plant farnähnliche Pflanze *f*
Ferrel's law *s.* Coriolis force
ferreous eisenhaltig, eisenschüssig
ferreto zone 1. Fe-Hydroxid-Ausfällungszone *f (in Entwässerungsgebieten)*; 2. Fe-haltige Verwitterungszone *f (auf Moränenmaterial)*
ferric eisenhaltig *(dreiwertiges Eisen enthaltend)*
~ hydroxide Eisenhydroxid *n*, Eisen(III)-hydroxid *n*, Eisenoxidhydrat *n*
~ salt Eisen(III)-salz *n*, Ferrisalz *n*
ferricarbonate Ferrikarbonat *n*, Eisen(III)-karbonat *n*
ferricrete mit Fe-Oxiden zementierte Bodenzone *f*
ferricrust eisenschüssige Kruste *f*
ferrierite Ferrierit *m*, (Na, K)$_2$Mg[OH|Al$_3$Si$_{15}$O$_{36}$]·9H$_2$O
ferriferous 1. eisenhaltig, eisenschüssig *(s.a. ferruginous)*; 2. für Fe-Minerale mit Integralgefüge
~ clay eisenschüssiger Letten *m*
~ quartz Eisenkiesel *m*
ferrific 1. eisenhaltig; 2. für Fe-Minerale mit Aggregalgefüge
ferrimagnetic ferrimagnetisch
ferrimagnetism Ferrimagnetismus *m*
ferrimolybdite Ferrimolybdit *m*, Molybdänocker *m*, Fe$_2$[MoO$_4$]$_3$·7H$_2$O
ferrinatrite Ferrinatrit *m*, Na$_3$Fe[SO$_4$]$_3$·3H$_2$O
ferrisicklerite Ferrisicklerit *m*, Li(Fe, Mn)[PO$_4$]
ferrisymplesite Ferrisymplesit *m*, Fe$_3$[(OH)$_3$|(AsO$_4$)$_2$]·5H$_2$O
ferrite *s.* opacite
ferritozone eisenhaltige Ausfällungszone *f*
ferritungstite Ferritungstit *m*, Ca$_2$Fe$_4$[WO$_4$]$_7$·9H$_2$O
ferroan dolomite *bis zu 50% durch Fe-Karbonat verdrängter Dolomit*
ferrolite Eisengestein *n*
ferromagnesian silicate Eisenmagnesiumsilikat *n*

ferromagnetic ferromagnetisch
ferromagnetism Ferromagnetismus *m*
ferromanganese Ferromangan *n*, Eisenmangan *n*
ferrosilite Ferrosilit *m (s.a. clinoferrosilite)*
ferrosoferric oxide *s.* magnetite
ferrous eisenhaltig *(zweiwertiges Eisen enthaltend)*
~ carbonate Ferrokarbonat *n*, Eisen(II)-karbonat *n*
~ hydroxide Ferrohydroxid *n*, Eisen(II)-hydroxid *n*, Eisendihydroxid *n*
~ oxide Eisen(II)-oxid *n*, Eisen[mon]oxid *n*
~ salt Ferrosalz *n*, Eisen(II)-salz *n*
~ sulphate Eisensulfat *n*, Eisen(II)-sulfat *n*
ferruginate mit Limonit zementiert
ferrugineous *s.* ferruginous
ferruginization Eisensteinbildung *f (im Boden)*
ferruginous eisenhaltig, eisenschüssig
~ cementing material eisenschüssiges Bindemittel *n*
~ chert 1. Eisenjaspilit *m*; 2. Eisenkiesel *m*
~ conglomerate Eisenkonglomerat *n*
~ deposit abbauwürdige Eisenlagerstätte *f*
~ limestone Eisenkalkstein *m*
~ outcrop Eiserner Hut *m (einer Lagerstätte)*
~ quartz Eisenkiesel *m*
~ sandstone Eisensandstein *m*
~ schist Eisenglimmerschiefer *m*
~ spring Eisenquelle *f*, Stahlquelle *f*
~ top-layer Eiserner Hut *m*
ferrum Eisen *n*, Fe
fersman[n]ite Fersmanit *m*, Na$_4$Ca$_4$Ti$_4$[(O, OH, F)$_3$|SiO$_4$]$_3$
Fersman's rule Fersmansche Regel *f*
fersmite Fersmit *m*, (Ca, Ce, Na) (Nb, Ti, Fe, Al)$_2$ (O, OH, F)$_6$
fertile fruchtbar
fertility Fruchtbarkeit *f*
~ of well Brunnenergiebigkeit *f*
fertilization Düngung *f*
fertilizing salt *(Am)* Düngesalz *n*
fervanite Fervanit *m*, Fe[VO$_4$]·H$_2$O
festoon 1. girlandenartiger Kreuzschichtungstyp *m*; 2. Girlande *f (Inseln)*
~ cross-bedding synklinale (trogförmige) Schrägschichtung *f*
~ cross lamination bogige Schrägschichtung *f*, Muldenschichtung *f*
festooned geschlängelt
~ moraines Moränengirlanden *fpl*
fetid mit Schwefelwasserstoffgeruch
~ limestone Stinkkalk *m*
~ shale Stinkschiefer *m*
fiard fjordähnliche Bucht *f*, Förde *f (Jütland)*
~-type of coast line Fördenküste *f*
fibroblastic fibroblastisch
~ texture fibroblastische Struktur *f*
fibroferrite Fibroferrit *m*, Fe[OH|SO$_4$]·5H$_2$O
fibrolite *s.* sillimanite
fibrous faserig
~ aggregate Faseraggregat *n*

fibrous 136

~ **asbestos** Faserasbest m
~ **brown iron ore** brauner Glaskopf m (s.a. limonite)
~ **cassiterite** Holzzinn[erz] n (s.a. cassiterite)
~ **cement** Faserzement m
~ **coal** (sl) Faserkohle f (fossile Holzkohle mit deutlicher Pflanzenstruktur; s.a. fusain)
~ **crystal** Trichit m (haarförmiger Mikrolith)
~ **English talc** Fasergips m, Federgips m
~ **fracture** fasriger Bruch m, fasrige Bruchfläche f
~ **gypsum** Fasergips m
~ **ice** Fasereis n
~ **limestone** Faserkalk m
~ **manganese oxide** schwarzer Glaskopf m, MnO_2
~ **material** Verstopfungsmaterial n (Bohrtechnik)
~ **peat** Fasertorf m, Wurzeltorf m
~ **quartz** Faserquarz m
~ **red iron ore** roter Glaskopf m, Fe_2O_3
~ **sphalerite** Schalenblende f (s.a. sphalerite)
~ **structure** fasrige Textur f
~ **talc** Fasertalk m
~ **zeolite** Faserzeolith m
fichtelite Fichtelit m, $C_{19}H_{34}$
fiducial marks Rahmenmarken fpl
fiedlerite Fiedlerit m, $Pb_3(OH)_2Cl_4$
field 1. Kohlenfeld n; Erdölfeld n; 2. Kraftlinienfeld n
~ **capacity** Feldkapazität f, natürliche Wasserkapazität f
~ **case history** (Am) Lagerstättengeschichte f
~ **checking** Geländebegehung f, Geländekontrolle f (Vergleich der Fernerkundungsdaten mit den tatsächlichen Gegebenheiten am Erdboden)
~ **conditions** Ölfeldverhältnisse npl
~ **data** Feldresultate npl
~ **data notebook** Feldbuch n
~ **development well** Konturierungsbohrung f (Aufschlußbohrung in einem Erdöl- oder Erdgasfeld)
~ **documentation** Felddokumentation f
~ **equation** Feldgleichung f
~ **evaluation** Lagerstättenuntersuchung f
~ **excitation** Felderregung f, Erregung f des Magnetfelds
~ **exploitation** Ausbeutung f eines Felds
~ **gas processing** Feldgasaufbereitung f
~ **geological works** geologische Feldarbeiten fpl
~ **geologist** Feldgeologe m
~ **geology** Feldgeologie f
~ **ice** s. sea ice
~ **intensity** [magnetische] Feldstärke f
~ **-intensity measurement** Feldstärkemessung f
~ **laboratory** Feldlabor n
~ **layout** Meßanordnung f; Aufnahmegeometrie f
~ **line** Feldlinie f
~ **-moisture deficiency** Bodenfeuchtedefizit n

~ **observation** Feldbeobachtung f
~ **of flow** Strömungsfeld n
~ **of force** Kräftefeld n
~ **of gravity** Schwerefeld n
~ **of ground-water flow** Grundwasserströmungsfeld n
~ **of source** Quellgebiet n
~ **of view** Blickfeld n
~ **party** Feldtrupp m
~ **pattern** Feldstärkendiagramm n, Feldstärkenprofil n
~ **record** Feldbuch n
~ **reversal** Feldumkehrung f (Erdmagnetfeld)
~ **strength** [magnetische] Feldstärke f
~ **tape** Feldmagnetband n
~ **terrace** Anbauterrasse f, Kulturterrasse f
~ **test** Feldversuch m
~ **tripod** Feldstativ n
~ **work** Feldarbeit f, Geländearbeit f (Vermessung)
fiery seam ausgasendes (Methan führendes) Flöz n
fifteen minute map Landkarte f im Maßstab 1:62 500
figure type Erstabbildung f einer Spezies
figured stone Figurenstein m, Agalmatolith m (dichte Varietät von Pyrophyllit)
filamentary fadenartig
filamentous fadenförmig
filar micrometer Fadenmikrometer n
filiation of species Abzweigung f von Arten
filiform texture fadenförmiges Gefüge n
fill in/to 1. verfüllen, einfüllen; 2. versetzen
~ **up** versenden, sich füllen
fill alluviales Material n
~ **-in station** Zwischenmeßpunkt m, Ergänzungspunkt m
~ **rock** Versatz m
~ **terrace** Aufschotterungsterrasse f
filled lake verlandeter See m
~ **valley** auflandiges Tal n
filler Füllstoff m (Bohrtechnik)
fillers Füllmittel n, Füllmineral n
filling 1. Bergeversatz m; 2. Einstau m (einer Talsperre); 3. Besteg m (Geomechanik)
~ **by plant growth** Zuwachsen n, Verlandung f
~ **-in** Ausfüllung f
~ **material** Füllstoff m (Bohrtechnik)
~ **of a joint** Kluftfüllung f
~ **-up** Ausfüllung f; Auflandung f, Anschwemmung f, Aufschwemmung f, Verschlickung f, Versandung f, Kolmation f, Kolmatierung f
~ **-up process** Verlandungsprozeß m
~ **-up with alluvium** Anschwemmung f
fillings Bestege mpl, Zwischenmittel npl (auf Klüften)
fillowite Fillowit m, $Na_2(Mn, Fe, Ca, H_2)_5[PO_4]_4$
fillstrath terrace erodierte Aufschotterungsterrasse f
filltop terrace vollständig erhaltene Aufschotterungsterrasse f

film 1. Belag *m*, Häutchen *n*; 2. dünne fehlerfreie Platte *f (Handelsglimmersorte)*
~ **forces** Grenzflächenkräfte *fpl (z.B. von Erdöl, Wasser)*
~ **of oil** Ölfilm *m*, Ölhäutchen *n*
~-**return spacecraft** Raumflugkörper *m* mit automatischem Filmrücktransport zur Erde
~ **water** Häutchenwasser *n*, Haftwasser *n*, Filmwasser *n*
filter area Filterfläche *f*
~ **cake** Filterkruste *f*
~ **feeder** Strudler *m (Paläontologie)*
~ **gravel** Filterkies *m*
~ **layer** Filterschicht *f*
~ **loss** Filterverlust *m (bei Preßwasser)*; Wasserabgabe *f (der Spülung)*
~ **press** Gerät zur Bestimmung der Wasserabgabe der Spülung
~ **pressing** Filterpressung *f*, Auspressungsdifferentiation *f*, Filtrationsdifferentiation *f*
~ **resistance** Filterwiderstand *m (für Wassereintritt)*
~ **sand** Filtersand *m*
~ **well** Filterbrunnen *m*
filtered water filtriertes Wasser *n*
filtering Filterung *f*
filtrate invasion Filtratwassereindringen *n*
filtration differentiation *s.* filter pressing
~ **pressing** Abpressungsfiltration *f*
~ **spring** Sickerquelle *f*
fimmenite Fimmenit *m (Sporentorf)*
fin Flosse *f*
~ **rays** Flossenstrahlen *mpl*
~ **spine** Flossenstachel *m*
final brine Endlauge *f*
~ **depth** Endteufe *f*
~ **diameter of drilling** End[bohr]durchmesser *m*
~ **form** Endform *f*
~ **pressure** Enddruck *m*
~ **shut-in pressure** Endschließdruck *m*
~ **subsidence** Endabsenkung *f*
find of meteorites Meteoritenfund *m (im Gegensatz zu „fall" mit unbekannter Verweildauer auf der Erdoberfläche)*
finding of a meteorite Meteoritenfund *m*
~ **place** Fundort *m*
fine adjustment Feineinstellung *f*
~ **aggregate** feiner Zuschlagstoff *m*
~-**bedded** feingeschichtet
~-**crystalline** feinkristallin
~ **detrital organic mud** Feindetritus-Mudde *f (bei Torfbildung in Mooren)*
~ **detritus held in suspension** Wassertrübe *f*
~ **gold** Feingold *n*
~-**grained** feinkörnig
~-**grained ore** Erzschlich *m*
~-**granular** feinkörnig
~ **gravel** Feinkies *m (2–6 mm Durchmesser)*
~ **grinding** Feinschleifen *n*
~-**ground** feingemahlen
~ **lapping** Feinschleifen *n*

~-**layered** feingeschichtet
~-**micaceous** feinglimmerig
~ **ore** Feinerz *n*
~ **sand** Feinsand *m (0,125–0,25 mm Durchmesser)*
~-**sandy** feinsandig
~-**size range** Feinkornbereich *m*
~ **snowy crystals** Kristallschnee *m*
~-**stratified** feingeschichtet
~ **tin** Zinnschlich *m*
finely bedded feingeschichtet
~ **broken up** stark verwittert
~ **clastic** feinklastisch
~ **divided** feinverteilt
~ **foliated** feinschiefrig
~ **granular** feinkörnig
~ **laminated (layered)** feingeschichtet
~ **porous** feinporig
~ **stratified** feingeschichtet
fineness of grain Feinheit *f* des Korns
fines 1. feinste Korngröße *f*; Feinstkorn *n*; 2. pulvriges Material *n*; pulverförmiges Erz *n*, Feinerz *n*
finest grain Feinstkorn *n*
~-**textured** feinstkörnig
finger/to Finger (Zungen) bilden
~ **out** fingerförmig endigen, auffiedern
finger lake Zungenbeckensee *m*
~ **stone** Donnerkeil *m*
fingering Fingerbildung *f*, Zungenbildung *f*
Fingerlakesian [Stage] Fingerlakes[ien] *n (Stufe, unteres Frasne in Nordamerika)*
fining upward sequence nach oben feiner werdende Abfolge *f*, Sohlbanktyp *m* eines klastischen Zyklus, „positive Sequenz" *f*
finite-element method Finite-Elemente-Methode *f*
finnemanite Finnemanit *m*, $Pb_5[Cl|(AsO_3)_3]$
fiord Fjord *(Norwegen)*
~ **coast** Fjordküste *f*
~ **island** Fjordinsel *f*
fiorded coast (shore line) *s.* fiord coast
~ **stream** ertrunkenes Flußtal *n*
fioryte Sinterkiesel *m*, Geiserit *m*
fir crystal Dendrit *m*
fire assay Probierkunde *f*, Feuerprobe *f*
~ **blende** *s.* pyrostilpnite
~ **clay** 1. Schamotteton *m*, feuerfester Ton *m*; 2. Liegendton *m*, Unterton *m (von Kohlenflözen)*
~-**clay mineral** Fireclay-Mineral *n (Kaolinit mit schlechtem Ordnungsgrad und Beimengungen)*
~ **drilling** Bohren *n* mit der Sauerstofflanze
~ **flooding** In-situ-Verbrennung *f*, Ölförderung *f* durch unterirdische Verbrennung
~ **fountain** Feuerfontäne *f*, Feuergarben *fpl*
~ **lake** Feuersee *m*
~ **opal** Feueropal *m*
~ **pit** Lavasee *m*
~ **shrinkage** Brennschwindung *f*, Volumenschwund *m* beim Brennprozeß

fire 138

~ **stink** Schwefelwasserstoffgeruch m *(in Kohlengruben)*
~ **styth** s. ~ stink
fireball Bolid m, Feuerkugel f
firedamp schlagende Wetter pl, Schlagwetter pl
~-**proof** schlagwetterfest, schlagwettergeschützt
firestone 1. s. fire clay 2.; 2. Flint m
firm fest; gesund *(Gebirge)*
firmament Firmament n, Himmelsgewölbe n
firmly bound CO$_2$ Karbonat-CO$_2$ n
firmness Festigkeit f
firn Firn[schnee] m
~ **field** Firnfeld n
~ **ice** Firneis n
~ **limit (line)** Firnlinie f
~ **snow** Firnschnee m
firnification Firneisbildung f, Verfirnung f
first arrival erster Einsatz m, Anfangseinsatz m *(Seismogramm)*
~ **break** 1. Setzriß m *(Geomechanik)*; 2. s. ~ arrival
~ **impetus** s. ~ arrival
~ **magnitude star** Stern m erster Größe
~ **meridian** Nullmeridian m
~ **minerals to separate out** Erstausscheidungen fpl
~ **moment** erstes Moment n *(nach der Momentmethode ermitteltes Maß für die mittlere Korngröße)*
~ **weight** erster Setzdruck m, initiale Setzung f
firth Meeresarm m, Förde f, Fjord m *(England)*
fischerite s. wavellite
fish Fangobjekt n, „Fisch" m *(Bohrung)*
~ **tail** Fischschwanzmeißel m
~-**tail twin** Schwalbenschwanzzwilling m
~ **vertebrae** Fischwirbel mpl
fishbone gefiedert *(Qualitätsbegriff bei Glimmer)*
fishing Fangarbeiten fpl
~ **bell** Fangglocke f
~ **hook** Zentrierhaken m
~ **jars** Fangschere f
~ **job** Fangarbeiten fpl
~ **magnet** Magnetfänger m
~ **socket** Fangglocke f
~ **tap** Fangdorn m
~ **tap with guide shoe** Führungsrohr n, Führungstrichter m
~ **tool** Fangwerkzeug n
fishlike fischähnlich
fishtail bit Fischschwanzmeißel m
fissile 1. teilbar, spaltbar; 2. schiefrigschuppig, blättrig
~ **bedding** Mikroschichtung f *(<2 mm)*
~ **element** spaltbares Element n
~ **fuel** Spaltstoff m, Kernbrennstoff m
~ **material** Spaltmaterial n
fissility 1. Teilbarkeit f, Spaltbarkeit f; 2. Schiefrigkeit f *(von Gesteinen)*

fission product Zerfallsprodukt n
~-**track method** Spaltspurenmethode f, Fission-track-Methode f *(der radioaktiven Altersbestimmung)*
fissionable material Spaltmaterial n
fissuration Rißbildung f, Zerklüftung f
fissure/to spalten
fissure Spalte f, Kluft f
~ **caused by frost** Frostspalte f, Eiskeil m
~ **cave** Kluftfugenhöhle f, Spaltenhöhle f
~ **effusion** Spaltenerguß m
~ **eruption** Spaltenausbruch m, Spalteneruption f
~ **filling** Spaltenfüllung f
~ **fumarole** Spaltenfumarole f
~ **mineral** Kluftmineral n
~ **occupation** Spaltenausfüllung f
~ **of discission (disruption)** Zerreißungsspalte f
~ **of eruption** Eruptionsspalte f, Ausbruchsspalte f
~ **of retreat** Kontraktionsspalte f, Schrumpfungsriß m
~ **outcrop** Spaltenausbiß m
~ **permeability** Kluftdurchlässigkeit f
~ **spring** Spaltenquelle f, Kluftquelle f
~ **vein** Spaltengang m, echter Gang m, Lagergang m, Gangspalte f
~ **vent** Eruptionsspalte f, Ausbruchsspalte f
~ **water** Spaltenwasser n, Kluftwasser n
fissured rissig, klüftig, zerklüftet, mit Spalten durchsetzt
~ **by joints** durchklüftet, zerklüftet
~-**porous reservoir** klüftig-poröses Reservoir n
~ **rock** rissiges Gestein n
~ **zone** Zerklüftungszone f, Zertrümmerungszone f
fissuring Rißbildung f, Spaltbildung f, Zerspaltung f, Zerklüftung f, Spaltung f
~ **of rock** Gesteinszerklüftung f
fit Anpassung f
fitness Anpassungsfähigkeit f, Adaptivwert m
fitting Passung f *(korrespondierende Trümmergrenzen bei Brekzien)*
five-rayed symmetry fünfstrahlige Symmetrie f
~-**sided** fünfseitig
~-**spot network** *(Am)* Fünf-Sonden-Anordnung f
fiveling Fünfling m *(Kristallverzwillingung)*
fixed carbon gebundener Kohlenstoff m
~ **coastal barrier** angelehnter Strandwall m
~ **derrick** ortsfester Bohrturm m
~ **dune** befestigte (ruhende) Düne f
~ **effects model of variance analysis** Varianzanalysemodell n mit festen Effekten
~ **ground water** Haftwasser n
~ **platform** feststehende Bohrplattform f
~ **point** Festpunkt m, Fixpunkt m
~ **satellite** stationärer Satellit m
~ **sleeve cell** Triaxialgerät n mit fest angeordneter Gummihülle

~ star Fixstern m
fizelyite Fizelyit m, $7PbS \cdot 1,5Ag_2S \cdot 5Sb_2S_3$
fjord s. fiord
flaggy plattig, fliesenartig
flaggy Schichtblatt n (zwischen 10–100 mm Mächtigkeit)
flags plattiger Sandstein m
flagstaffite Flagstaffit m, $C_{10}H_{18}(OH)_2 \cdot H_2O$
flagstone 1. plattig spaltendes Sediment n; 2. Sandsteinplatte f, Schieferplatte f (für Straßenbau, Fußbodenbelag)
flajolotite Flajolotit m (s.a. tripuhyite)
flake off/to abblättern
flake Blättchen n, Schuppe f, Flocke f, Plättchen n
~ graphite Flockengraphit m, Schuppengraphit m, Flinzgraphit m
~ mica Schuppenglimmer m
~ of mica Glimmerblättchen n
flaked flockig, schuppig
flakes schalenförmige Ablösung f
flaking[-off] Abblättern n, Abplatzen n
flaky schiefrig, schuppig, blättrig
~ graphlte s. flake graphite
flame coal Flammkohle f
~ coloration Flammenfärbung f
~-jet drilling Flammenbohren n
~ photometer Flammenfotometer n
~ photometry Flammenfotometrie f
~ spectrometry Flammenspektrometrie f
~ spectrophotometric determination flammenspektrofotometrische Bestimmung f
~ spectrum Flammenspektrum n
~ structure Flammenstruktur f (Sedimentgefüge)
flameproof schlagwettersicher
flaming orifice flammende Fumarole f, brennender Gasaustritt m
flammable leicht brennbar
flammenmergel Flammenmergel m
Flandrian Flandrien n (Holozän, Nordseegebiet)
flange Außenleiste f
flank Flanke f, Gehänge n (s.a. limb)
~ bed Flankenschicht f
~ eruption Flankeneruption f, Flankenerguß m, Seitenausbruch m
~ of a basin Muldenflügel m
~ of anticline Antiklinalflügel m
~ of fold Faltenschenkel m
~ of hill Hang m, Abhang m
~ of saddle Sattelflügel m
~ outflow s. ~ eruption
~ production Ölgewinnung f am Rande eines Salzstocks
~ well Flankensonde f
flanking sand Flankenlagerstätte f an einem Salzstock
flap Gravitationsgleitstruktur f
flare gas/to Gas abfackeln
flare gas Fackelgas n
flaring mouth Trichtermündung f (eines Flusses)

flaser bedding Flaserschichtung f
~ gabbro Flasergabbro m
~ gneiss Flasergneis m
~ structure Flasertextur f, Flaserschichtung f
flash flood Sturzflut f; Wolkenbruch m
~ point Flammpunkt m
flashy flow reißende Strömung f
flat horizontal, söhlig; flach (Lagerung)
flat 1. Ebene f; Flachland n; 2. Sandbank f, Untiefe f; 3. Watt n
~ bog Flachmoor n, Niederungsmoor n, Gründlandmoor n
~-bottomed flachsohlig
~ coals söhliges Kohlenflöz n
~ country Flachland n
~-dipping bed flach einfallende Schicht f
~-floored flachsohlig
~ ground Flachland n
~ hade flaches Einfallen n
~ land Flachland n, Niederung f
~ lode söhliger Gang m (bis 15° Einfallen)
~ low-lying coast Flachküste f
~-lying flachliegend
~-lying gravity fault Streckfläche f (in Plutonkontakten)
~-lying joints Lagerklüfte fpl
~-lying strata flachliegende Schichten fpl
~ mass geringmächtiges, großflächiges Erzlager n
~ of ore sedimentäre Erzbank f
~ seam flaches Flöz n
~ sheet s. ~ mass
~ shore Flachküste f
~-topped ripple marks flachkämmige Rippelmarken fpl
~ upland area flache Hochfläche f
~-valved flachschalig
~ work s. flatwork
flatness Abplattung f
flatten/to sich verflachen; abplatten
~ out ausplätten (tektonischer Vorgang)
flattening 1. Plättung f, Einebnung f, Planierung f, Abplattung f, Abböschen n, Abflachen n; 2. Verzerrung f (von Fossilien)
~ at the poles Erdabplattung f
~ index Abplattungsindex m
~ of the earth Abplattung f der Erde
~-out Verflachen n
flattish abgeplattet
~ pipe flacher Schlot m
flatwork lagenartige Erzausscheidung f
flavourless geschmacklos
flaw 1. transversale Horizontalverschiebung f; Blattverschiebung f (Tektonik); 2. Bö f; 3. federartiger Einschluß m (in Edelsteinen)
~ fault Blattverschiebung f; Seitenverschiebung f
flawless gem fehlerloser Edelstein m
flaxseed coal (sl) feinkörniger Anthrazit m
~ ore Clinton-Erz n
fleckschiefer Fleckschiefer m
fleecy clouds Schäfchenwolken fpl

fleischerite

fleischerite Fleischerit m, $Pb_3Ge[(OH)_4(SO_4)_2] \cdot 4H_2O$
flemish down/to aufschießen
flerry gespalten, zerteilt *(Gestein)*
flesh spicules s. microscleres
fletz *(sl)* Flöz n
flew coal *(sl)* anthrazitähnliche Kohle f
flexed gebogen, gefaltet
~ **stratum** verbogene Schicht f
flexibility Biegsamkeit f
flexible biegsam
~ **hose** Spülschlauch m
~ **sandstone** Gelenkquarzit m, Gelenksandstein m, Itakolumit m
~ **silver ore** s. sternbergite
flexing Biegung f, Faltung f, Beugung f
flexodrilling Schlauchbohren n
Flexotir Flexotir-Verfahren n *(seeseismisches Sprengverfahren)*
flexuous gewunden, zickzackgebogen
flexural gliding Biegegleitung f
~ **rigidity** Biegesteifigkeit f
~ **rigidity of a plate** Plattenbiegungssteifigkeit f
flexure Flexur f, Abbiegung f, Biegung f; Verbiegung f; Falte f, Kniefalte f
~ **fault** Faltenverwerfung f
~ **fold** Biegefalte f
~ **folding** Biegefaltung f
~ **plane** Flexurebene f
~-**slip fold** Falte f mit Gleitung auf s, Biegegleitfalte f
flight altitude Flughöhe f
~ **path** Flugbahn f, Flugweg m
~ **pattern** Flugroute f für Messungen vom Flugzeug aus
flinders diamond Topasvarietät
flinkite Flinkit m, $Mn_3[(OH)_4AsO_4]$
flint Feuerstein m, Flint m
~ **brick** Silikastein m *(aus Flint hergestellt)*
~ **clay** harter Ton m von muscheligem Bruch
~ **coal** *(sl)* anthrazitähnliche Kohle
~ **layer** Feuersteinband n
~ **nodule** s. ~ pebble
~ **pebble** Feuersteinknollen m, Flintknollen m
~ **sheet** Feuersteinband n
flinty feuersteinartig, feuersteinhaltig; kieselartig, kieselig, Flint...
~ **crush rock** Ultramylonit m, Pseudotachylit m
~ **fracture** muscheliger Bruch m
~-**shelled** kieselschalig
~ **skeleton** Kieselskelett n
~ **slate** Kieselschiefer m
flipper Flosse f
float/to schwimmen, schweben
~ **off** abschwemmen
float 1. Lesestein m; 2. s. pneumatophore
~ **coal** allochthone Kohle f
~ **debris** Schutt m, Erosionsprodukte npl
~ **gold** s. flour gold
~ **level gauge** Schwimmerpegel m

~ **mineral (ore)** Lesestein m, lose Erzstücke npl *(an der Erdoberfläche)*
~ **sand** Fließsand m, Schwimmsand m
~ **shoe** Schwimmschuh m, Rohrschuh m mit Rückschlagventil
~ **valve** Rückschlagventil n
floatability Schwimmfähigkeit f, Flotierbarkeit f
floatable schwimmfähig, flotationsfähig, flotierbar
floatation Flotation f, Schwimmaufbereitung f
~ **agent** Flotationsmittel n
~ **bombs** Lavabälle mpl
~ **cell** Flotationszelle f
~ **concentration** Flotationsaufbereitung f, Schwimmaufbereitung f
~ **plant** Flotationsanlage f
~ **tank** Fluttank m
floater s. float 1.
floating crane Schwimmkran m
~ **derrick** schwimmender Bohrturm m, Bohrinsel f
~ **dredge[r]** Schwimmbagger m
~ **drilling vessel** Bohrschiff n
~ **earth** Schwingerde f
~ **fault block** wurzellose Deckscholle f
~ **gold** Schwimmgold n
~ **ice** Treibeis n
~ **island** schwimmende Insel f
~ **organism** Plankton n
~ **peat** allochthoner Torf m
~ **ribs** frei endende Rippen fpl, Costae fluctuantes fpl
~ **spurs** schwebende Quarztrümer npl
~ **timber** Treibholz n
floatstone 1. schlammgestütztes Karbonatgestein mit mehr als 10% Komponenten > 2 mm; 2. poröser Opal m; 3. zelliger Gangquarz m
flocs kleine Seifenzinnaggregate npl
flocculate/to ausflocken
flocculated sol ausgeflocktes Sol n
flocculating agent Koagulator m, Koagulationsmittel n
flocculation Ausflockung f, Flockung f
flocculent flockig
floe schwimmendes Eisfeld n, Treibeis n
~ **ice** Scholleneis n, Treibeis n
~ **till** s. subaqueous till
floeberg aufgetürmte Eisschollen fpl *(an der Küste)*
floetz s. fletz
flokite s. mordenite
floocan s. flucan
flood/to überschwemmen, [über]fluten
~ **a mine** eine Grube unter Wasser setzen
flood Hochwasser n, Flut f, Überschwemmung f
~ **bank** Hochwasserdeich m, Uferdamm m, Hochwasserschutzdamm m
~ **basalt** Plateaubasalt m
~ **calamity** Hochwasserkatastrophe f
~ **channel** Fluttrichter m

~ **control** Hochwasserregulierung f, Hochwasserschutz m
~-**control dam** s. ~ dam
~-**control levee** Hochwasserschutzdeich m
~ **control storage** Hochwasserspeicherung f
~ **current** Flutstrom m
~ **dam** Hochwasserschutztalsperre f, Hochwasserauffangsperre f
~ **damage** Hochwasserschaden m
~ **debris** Hochwasserschutt m
~ **decline** Sinken n des Hochwassers
~ **deposit** Hochwasserablagerung f
~ **disaster** Hochwasserkatastrophe f
~ **discharge** Hochwassermenge f; Flutwelle f, Hochwasserwelle f; Hochwasserentlastung f
~ **district** Überschwemmungsgebiet n
~ **elevation** Hochwasseranstieg m
~ **estimates** Hochwasserberechnungen fpl
~ **flow** Hochwasserabfluß m
~ **forecast** Hochwasservorhersage f
~ **frequency** Hochwasserhäufigkeit f
~ **ground** Überflutungsebene f, Inundationsfläche f, Talaue f
~ **hydrograph** Hochwasserganglinie f
~ **land** Überschwemmungsgebiet n, Flußmarsch f, Aue f
~ **levee** Hochwasserschutzdeich m
~ **measuring point** Pegelmeßstelle f; Hochwassermeßpunkt m
~ **measuring post** Pegel m
~-**menaced land** überschwemmungsgefährdete Niederung f
~ **of record** (Am) Katastrophenhochwasser n
~ **plain** Überschwemmungsfläche f, Inundationsfläche f, Überflutungsebene f, Talaue f; Flußaue f, Flußniederung f; Hochflutbett n, Hochflutebene f
~-**plain deposit** Hochwasserablagerung f
~-**plain soil** Aueboden m
~-**plain terrace** Flußterrasse f
~-**plain valley** Sohlental n
~ **pool** Hochwasserbecken n
~ **prediction** Hochwasservorhersage f
~ **protection** Hochwasserschutz m
~ **protection works** Hochwasserschutzbauten mpl
~ **regulation** Hochwasserregulierung f
~ **resulting from rain** Regenhochwasser n
~ **retention basin** Rückhaltebecken n, Hochwasserrückhaltebecken n
~ **rise** Steigen n des Hochwassers
~ **routing** Hochwasserregulierung f, Hochwasserableitung f
~ **stage** kritischer Hochwasserstand m
~ **tide** Flut[zeit] f
~-**warning service** Hochwassermeldedienst m
~ **water** Hochwasser n, steigendes Wasser n
~ **wave** Hochflutwelle f, Hochwasserschwall m

floodable überschwemmungsbedroht
flooded area Überschwemmungsgebiet n
~ **mine** ersoffene Grube f
~ **stream** s. drowned stream
flooding Überflutung f, Überschwemmung f
~ **soil** Schwemmlandboden m
flookan s. flucan
floor 1. Sohle f, Liegendes n; 2. Stockwerk n (einer Lagerstätte); 3. Meeresboden m
- **arch** Sohlengewölbe n
~ **bolting** Ankern n der Sohlen
~ **breaking** Liegenddurchbruch m
~ **breaks** Abbaurisse mpl im Liegenden, Sohlrisse mpl
~ **emission** Sohlenausgasung f
~ **heading** Sohlenstrecke f
~ **heave (lift)** Sohlenquellung f, Sohlenauftrieb m, Sohlenhebung f
~ **limb** liegender Schenkel m (Falte)
~ **of crater** Kraterboden m
~ **of sea** Meeresboden m
~ **pressure arch** Sohlenaufwölbung f
~ **ripping** Nachreißen n der Sohle
~ **swelling** s. ~ heave
floored schichtig
flora Flora f, Pflanzenwelt f
floral floristisch, Floren...
~ **boundary** Florengrenze f
~ **chart** Florenkarte f
~ **region** Pflanzenregion f
~ **relationship** Florenverwandtschaft f
~ **zone** Florenzone f
floran fein eingesprengter Zinnstein m
florencite Florencit m, $CeAl_3[(OH)_6|(PO_4)_2]$
floristic floristisch
~ **elements** Florenelemente npl
florule endemische Florengemeinschaft f
flos ferri Eisenblüte f, Faseraragonit m (s.a. aragonite)
flotation s. floatation
flour Karbonatdetritus m (gebildet in der Brandungszone)
~ **gold** Flittergold n, fein verteiltes Gold n, Staubgold n
~ **sand** Mehlsand m
flovel a mine/to eine Grube fluten
flow/to fließen
~ **by heads** stoßweise [frei] ausfließen, stoßweise erumpieren
~ **off** abfließen
~ **out** ausfließen
flow Flut f, Strömung f, Strom m; Abflußmenge f, Wasserführung f
~ **and ebb** Ebbe f und Flut f
~ **barrier** Strömungshindernis n
~ **bean** Düse f, Drossel f
~ **by rupture** Bruchfließen n
~ **capacity** Durchflußfähigkeit f
~ **cast** Fließmarke f, Gefließmarke f
~-**channel walls** Wände fpl des Porensystems
~ **cleavage** S_1-Schieferung f, Transversalschieferung f, Kristallisationsschieferung f
~ **deficit** Abflußdefizit n
~ **delta** Flutdelta n
~ **detector** Farbindikator zur Verfolgung unterirdischer Wasser

flow

~ **efficiency** Fließwirksamkeit f
~ **equation** Strömungsgleichung f
~ **failure** Bruchfließen n
~ **fold** Fließfalte f
~ **folding** Fließfaltung f
~ **gauge** Abflußmesser m, Pegel m
~ **gauging** Abflußmengenmessung f
~ **ice** Treibeis n
~ **in open channels** Strömung f in offenen Gerinnen
~ **indicator** s. ~ detector
~ **limit** Fließgrenze f (nach Atterberg)
~ **line** Fließlinie f (in Plutoniten)
~-**line arch** Fließliniengewölbe n (in Plutoniten)
~-**line connector** Anschluß m der Förderleitung
~ **mark** Fließmarke f, Gefließmarke f
~ **measurement** Durchflußmessung f
~ **net** Flußnetz n
~ **of basalt** Basaltfluß m
~ **of ground water** Grundwasserstrom m
~ **of rock** Schmelzfluß m, Magma n
~ **of seepage** Sickerströmung f
~ **of spring** Schüttung f (einer Quelle)
~ **pattern** Strömungsfeld n
~ **phenomenon** Fließvorgang m
~ **point** Fließpunkt m (z.B. von Asphalt)
~ **pressure** Fließdruck m
~ **profile** Durchflußprofil n
~ **record** Abflußmengenmessung f
~ **regime** 1. Abflußgeschehen n (Summe aller Abflußerscheinungen); 2. Fließregime n (fluviatiler Transport)
~ **resistance** Durchflußwiderstand m, Strömungswiderstand m
~ **roll** Rutschungsballen m, Rutschungskörper m, Sedimentrolle f, Sedimentwalze f, Wickelfalte f
~ **section** Durchflußquerschnitt m
~ **sheet** Gleitschicht f
~ **slide** Rutschfließung f
~ **stowing** Fließversatz m
~ **stretching** lineare Mineralstreckung f durch plastisches Fließen
~ **string** Steigleitung f, Steigrohrstrang m
~ **structure** Fließtextur f, Fließgefüge n, Fluidaltextur f
~ **test** Fließprobe f
~ **velocity** Durchflußgeschwindigkeit f
flowage Fließbewegung f (fester Körper unter Druck)
~ **cast** Fließmarke f, Gefließmarke f
~ **differentiation** Bewegungsdifferentiation f
~ **fold** Fließfalte f (Falte mit Materialfluß vom Sattel zur Mulde)
flower of iron s. flos ferri
flowers durch Sublimierung erzeugter feiner Niederschlag m
flowing artesian water überflurgespanntes Wasser n, Springwasser n
~ **bottom hole pressure** Sohlenfließdruck m
~ **casing pressure** Ringraumfließdruck m
~ **formation pressure** Sohlenfließdruck m
~ **lava** ausfließende Lava f
~ **oil well** freifließende Ölbohrung f
~ **pressure** Förderdruck m
~ **pressure gradient** Fließdruckgradient m
~ **tubing pressure** Fließdruck m im Steigrohr
~ **well** artesischer Brunnen m, Eruptionssonde f, Springbrunnen m
flowmeter 1. Strömungsmesser m, Durchflußmeßgerät n, Durchflußmesser m; 2. Spülungsmengenmesser m (Bohrtechnik)
flucan [course] Salband n, Lettenbesteg m, Kluftlette f, weicher Letten m
fluccan s. flucan
fluctuate/to pulsierend fließen
fluctuation of level in lake Seespiegelabsenkung f
fluctuations of glaciers Gletscherschwankungen fpl
~ **of level** Niveauschwankungen fpl, Spiegelschwankungen fpl
~ **of temperature** Temperaturschwankungen fpl
fluctuo-mutation Fluktuomutation f
fluellite Fluellit m, $AlF_3 \cdot H_2O$
fluid flüssig
fluid Flüssigkeit f
~ **cavity** Flüssigkeitseinschluß m
~ **hydrocarbon** flüssiger Kohlenwasserstoff m
~ **inclusion** Flüssigkeitseinschluß m
~ **level** Flüssigkeitsspiegel m
~ **loss additives** Chemikalien fpl zur Reduktion der Filtrationsverluste
~ **mechanics** Hydromechanik f
~ **metering** Durchflußmessung f
~ **phase** fluide Phase f, Gasphase f
~ **pressure** Flüssigkeitsdruck m
~ **recovery** Erdölgewinnung f; Erdgasgewinnung f
~ **redistribution** Flüssigkeitsmigration f
~ **saturation** Fluidsättigung f (für Öl oder Gas)
~ **surface** Flüssigkeitsoberfläche f
~-**velocity log** Fließgeschwindigkeitslog n
fluidal fluidal
fluidity Fluidität f, Fließfähigkeit f
~ **of coking coals** Fluidität f von Kokskohlen
~ **of the cement grout** Fließfähigkeit f der Zementschlämme
flukan s. flucan
flume 1. (Am) Wildbachschlucht f; 2. Überfallrinne f, Rinne f
fluoborite Fluoborit m, $Mg_3[(F, OH)_3|BO_3]$
fluocerite Fluocerit m (Varietät von Tysonit)
fluor [spar] s. fluorite
fluoresce/to fluoreszieren
fluorescence Fluoreszenz f
~ **analysis** Fluoreszenzanalyse f
~ **microscopy** Fluoreszenzmikroskopie f
~ **of petroleum** Erdölfluoreszenz f (schillernde Färbung von Erdöl und dessen Produkten)
fluorescent fluoreszierend, fluoreszent

~ **screen** Fluoreszenzschirm *m*, Leuchtschirm *m*
~ **substance** fluoreszierende Substanz *f*
~ **X-ray analysis** Röntgenfluoreszenzanalyse *f*
fluorimeter Fluoreszenzmesser *m*
fluorine Fluor *n*, F
~ **mineral** Fluormineral *n*
fluorinite Fluorinit *m (Kohlenmaceral der Liptinitgruppe)*
fluorite Fluorit *m*, Flußspat *m*, CaF₂
fluorlogging Fluoreszenzmessung *f* am Bohrklein
fluorography Fluoreszenzaufnahme *f*
fluorohydric acid Fluorwasserstoffsäure *f*, Flußsäure *f*, HF
fluorophore Fluoreszenz verursachend
fluoroscope Fluoroskop *n*
fluoroscopy Fluoroskopie *f*
fluorspar s. fluorite
fluosilicate Fluorsilikat *n*
flurry leichte Brise *f*; Windstoß *m*, Bö *f*
~ **of rain** *(Am)* Regenschauer *m*, Regenguß *m*
~ **of snow** Schneegestöber *n*
flush out/to austragen, herausschwemmen
flush drilling Spülbohren *n*
~ **eliberation** plötzliche Entlösung *f (von Gas aus Erdöl)*
~ **fluid** Spülflüssigkeit *f*, Spültrübe *f*
~ **gas** Spülgas *n*
~ **production rate** eruptive Förderrate *f*
flushed zone geflutete Zone *f*
flushing Flutung *f*, Spülung *f*, Waschen *n*
~ **auger** Spülschappe *f*
~ **dredge[r]** Schwimmbagger *m*, Spülbagger *m*
~ **fluid** s. flush fluid
~ **pump** Spülpumpe *f*
~ **shield** Bruchabschirmung *f*, Versatzschild *m*
flute Rinne *f*, Riefe *f*; Erosionsfurche *f*, Erosionsrinne *f*; Fließrinne *f*; Auskolkung *f*, Kolk *m*
~ **cast** Fließmarke *f*, Fließwulst *m*, Fließrille *f*; Strömungsmarke *f*, Strömungswulst *m*; Kegelwulst *m*, Kolkausguß *m*, Kolkmarke *f*, Sandsteinwulst *m*
fluted kanneliert
fluting Kannelierung *f*
fluvial Fluß... (*s.a.* fluviatile)
~ **deposit** Flußablagerung *f*
~ **erosion** Flußerosion *f*
~ **formation** Flußbildung *f*
~ **geomorphic cycle** peneplainisierende Flußerosion *f*
~ **gravel** Flußkies *m*
~ **hydraulics** Flußhydraulik *f*
~ **lacustrine** fluviolakustrisch
~ **pebble** Flußgeröll *n*
~ **terrace** Flußterrasse *f*
fluviatile fluviatil; Fluß... (*s.a.* fluvial)
~ **dam** natürliche Dammbildung *f* durch Nebenflußeinspülung
~ **detritus** Flußsediment *n*
~ **erosion** fluviatile Erosion *f*

~ **facies** fluviatile Fazies *f*
~ **loam** Flußlehm *m*
fluviation Wirkungen *fpl* des fließenden Oberflächenwassers
fluvioclastics fluvioklastische Gesteine *npl*
fluviogenic soil Flußablagerungsboden *m*
fluvioglacial fluvioglazial
~ **deposit (drift)** fluvioglaziale Ablagerung *f*, Sander *m*
fluviolacustrine fluviolakustrin
fluviology Flußkunde *f*
fluviomarine fluviomarin, brackig
fluviometer Flußmesser *m*, Flußschreiber *m*
fluviraption Oberflächenberäumung *f* durch fließendes Wasser
flux Flußmittel *n*, Zuschlag *m*
~ **and reflux** Ebbe *f* und Flut *f*
~-**gate magnetometer** Sättigungskernmagnetometer *n*, Fördersonde *f*
~ **limestone** Zuschlagkalkstein *m*
fluxing ore Zuschlagerz *n*
fluxion banding Fluidalblattbänderung *f*
~ **structure** s. flow structure
~ **swirl** Flußwirbel *m*
fluxoturbidite Fluxoturbidit *m (meist grobkörnige sandige Ablagerungen in Flyschbecken, deren Charakteristika zwischen denen von Turbiditen und gravitativen Gleitmassen liegen)*
fly ash Flugasche *f*
flyer Bündelungskabelbaum *m*
flying sand Flugsand *m*
flysch Flysch *m*
~ **breccia** Flyschbrekzie *f*
~ **facies** Flyschfazies *f*
~ **zone** Flyschzone *f*
flyschoid sediment flyschoides Sediment *n*
foam Schaum *m*
~ **clay** s. foamclay
~ **floatation** Schaumflotation *f*
~ **lava** Schaumlava *f*
~ **mark** Schaummarke *f*
foamclay Schaumton *m*, Blähton *m*
foaming agent Schäumer *m*
foamy schaumig
focal depth Herdtiefe *f*
~ **length** Brennweite *f*
~ **point of subsidence** Absenkungsschwerpunkt *m*
focus/to fokussieren
focus 1. Hypozentrum *n*, Erdbebenherd *m*; 2. Brennpunkt *m (seismischer Strahlen bei gekrümmtem Reflektor)*
~ **of eruption** Eruptionsherd *m*, Ausbruchsherd *m*
focussed-current logging Laterolog *n (Meßverfahren mit gebündeltem Stromsystem)*
foehn Föhn *m*
fog dichter Nebel *m*
~ **band** Nebelschwaden *m*, Nebelstreifen *m*
~ **bank** Nebelbank *f*
~ **droplet** Nebeltröpfchen *n*

foggy

foggy neblig
foids Foide *npl*, Feldspatvertreter *mpl*
foil *s.* trail
~-stone Edelsteinimitation *f*
fold/to falten
fold Falte *f*
~ **arc** Faltenbogen *m*
~ **axis** Faltenachse *f*
~ **belt** Faltungszone *f*
~ **bundle** Faltenbündel *n*
~ **carpet** Überfaltungsdecke *f*, Faltendecke *f*
~ **fault** Bruchfalte *f*, durch Faltung induzierte Störung *f*
~ **line** Faltenlinie *f*
~ **mountain** Faltengebirge *n*
~ **mullion** Faltenmullionstruktur *f*
~ **nappe** Überfaltungsdecke *f*, Faltendecke *f*
~ **structure** Faltenbau *m*, Faltenstruktur *f*
~ **structure with steep axes** steilachsige Faltenstruktur *f*
~ **system** Faltensystem *n*
~ **thrust** Überfaltungsdecke *f*, Faltendecke *f*
foldable layers faltbare Schichten *fpl*
folded gefaltet
~ **beds** gefaltete Schichten *fpl*
~ **fault** gefaltete Störungsfläche *f*
~ **folds** gefaltete Falten *fpl*
~ **Jura Mountains** Faltenjura *m*
~ **mountain** Faltengebirge *n*
~ **structure** *s.* fold structure
~ **thrust** *s.* fold thrust
folding Faltung *f*
~ **about vertical axis** Schlingenbau *m*
~ **mast** Klappmast *m*
~ **phase** Faltungsphase *f*
~ **tear fault** Grenzblatt *n* (Blattverschiebung)
~ **tectonics** Faltungstektonik *f*
~ **within a frame** Rahmenfaltung *f*
folgerite *s.* pentlandite
foliaceous blättrig, Blatt..., Blätter..., schiefrigschuppig
~ **structure** Blättertextur *f*
~ **tree** Laubbaum *m*
foliated blättrig, schiefrig, geschiefert, schiefrigschuppig
~ **clay** Blätterton *m*
~ **coal** *(sl)* schiefrige blättrige Kohle *f*; schiefrige Kohle *f*
~ **galena** Bleischweif *m* *(s.a. galena)*
~ **gneiss** Schiefergneis *m*
~ **rock** geschiefertes Gestein *n*
~ **structure** schiefrige Textur *f*, Schieferung *f*; Blättertextur *f*
foliation Bänderung *f*, Blätterung *f*, Schieferung *f*, schichtenförmige Lagerung *f*, Blättrigkeit *f*; s-Flächen *fpl* (in metamorphen Gesteinen nach Turner-Weiss)
~ **cleavage** Schieferung *f*
~ **due to crystallization** Kristallisationsschieferung *f*
~ **joint** Schieferungsfuge *f*
~ **plane** Schieferungsebene *f*, Schieferungsfläche *f*

~ **structure** schiefrige Textur *f*
fondo *s.* basin
fondoform Oberfläche eines gravitativ gebildeten (umgelagerten) Sedimentkörpers
fool's gold Katzengold *n*
foot impression *s.* footprint
~ **jaws** Kieferfüße *mpl*, Maxillipeden *mpl*
~ **of glacier** Gletschersohle *f*
footage 1. Bohrstrecke *f*, Bohrmeterleistung *f*; 2. Längengedinge *n*, Metergedinge *n*
foothill Vorgebirge *n*, Randgebirge *n*
footmark *s.* footprint
footprint Laufspur *f*, Fußabdruck *m*, Fußspur *f*
footwall Liegendes *n*, Sohle *f*
~ **swelling** Anschwellen *n* des Liegenden
foralite Bohrmarke *f*, Wühlmarke *f* (Sedimentgefüge)
foramen Foramen *n*, Perforation *f*, Öffnung *f*
foraminiferal deposit Foraminiferenablagerung *f*
~ **limestone** Foraminiferenkalk *m*
~ **marl** Foraminiferenmergel *m*
~ **ooze** Foraminiferenschlamm *m*
~ **sand** Foraminiferensand *m*
~ **shell** Foraminiferenschälchen *n*
foraminifers, forams Foraminiferen *fpl*
forbes band *s.* ogive
forbesite Forbesit *m*, (Ni, Co)H[AsO$_4$]·3H$_2$O
force of crystallization Kristallisationskraft *f*, Formenergie *f*
~ **of gravity** Schwerkraft *f*, Gravitation *f*, Erdbeschleunigung *f*
~ **of wind** Windstärke *f*
forced-cut meander Mäander *m* mit Ausgleich zwischen Abtrag und Anlandung
ford Furt *f*
fordable durchwatbar
fordless ohne Furt
forecasting of precipitation (rainfall) Niederschlagsprognose *f*
foredeep Vortiefe *f*, Vorsenke *f*, Saumsenke *f*
foredune Vordüne *f*
foreign ash Fremdasche *f*
~ **atom** Fremdatom *n*
~ **body** Fremdkörper *m*
~ **inclusion** Xenolith *m*
~ **ion** Fremdion *n*
~ **material** Fremdmaterial *n*
foreland Vorland *n*, Gebirgsvorland *n*, Vorgebirge *n*
forelimb steiler Schenkel *m* (einer asymmetrischen Falte)
forelimbs Vordergliedmaßen *fpl*
forereef seewärts (luvseitig = „vor dem Riff gelegen")
forereef Vorriff *n* (der Brandungsseite zugewandter Bereich eines Riffkomplexes, der noch stark vom Riffkörper beeinflußt wird)
forerunner Vorläufer *m*, Vorbeben *n*
foreset bed Leeblatt *n*, Leeschicht *f*, Vorschüttungsblatt *n*, Stirnabsatz *m* (bei Schrägschichtung)

~ **beds** Vorschüttungssedimente *npl (eines Deltas)*
foresets 1. Vorsetzschichten *fpl*; 2. Schelfvorschüttungen *fpl*
foreshock Vorbeben *n*
foreshore Uferland *n*; Strand *m*, Seeufer *n*; Vorland *n*, Vorstrand *m*; Watt *n*
foreshortening Verjüngung *f*, Verkürzung *f (bei Karten)*
forest bed interglazialer Stubbenhorizont *m*
~ **bog** Waldmoor *n*
~-**clad swamp** Waldmoor *n*
~ **islands** Waldinseln *fpl*
~ **land** Waldland *n*
~ **moor** Waldmoor *n*; Bruchwaldmoor *n*
~ **shelter-belt** Waldschutzstreifen *m*
~ **soil** Waldboden *m*
~ **swamp** *s.* ~ moor
forestation Aufforstung *f*
forested bewaldet
~ **area** Waldregion *f*
~ **steppe** Waldsteppe *f*
forge coal Eßkohle *f*
fork/to sich gabeln
forked branching *s.* dichotomous branching
forking Bifurkation *f*, Gabelung *f*
form into crystals/to auskristallisieren, Kristalle bilden
form genera Formgattungen *fpl*
~ **of crystallization** Kristallisationsform *f*
~ **of deposit** Lagerstättenart *f*
~ **of past ages** Vorzeitform *f*
~ **of structure** Strukturform *f*
~ **species** Formart *f*
formation 1. Formation *f (lithostratigrafische Einheit, im älteren deutschen Schrifttum auch als biostratigrafische Einheit verwendet)*; 2. Gebirge *n (im Sinne von Gebirgsart)*
~ **boundary** Formationsgrenze *f*
~ **energy** Lagerstättenenergie *f*
~ **evaluation** Speichereinschätzung *f*
~ **factor** Formations[widerstands]faktor *m*
~ **fracturing** Hydrofraccen *n*, Formationsfraccen *n*
~ **map** Formationskarte *f*
~ **name** Formationsname *m*
~ **of clefts** Spaltenbildung *f*
~ **of cliffs** Kliffbildung *f*
~ **of clouds** Wolkenbildung *f*
~ **of coal** Kohlenbildung *f*
~ **of cracks** Rißbildung *f*
~ **of craters** Kraterbildung *f*
~ **of crystal layers** Schichtkristallbildung *f*
~ **of eddies** Wirbelbildung *f*
~ **of fissures** Rißbildung *f*
~ **of fog** Nebelbildung *f*
~ **of humus** Humusbildung *f*
~ **of lodes** Gangformation *f*
~ **of rocks** Gesteinsbildung *f*
~ **pressure** 1. Formationsdruck *m*, Lagerstättendruck *m*; Schichtendruck *m*; 2. Porenflüssigkeitsdruck *m*; Schichtdruck *m (Hydrogeologie)*

~ **process** Bildungsvorgang *m*
~ **resistivity factor** Formations[widerstands]faktor *m*
~ **temperature** Gesteinstemperatur *f*
~ **test** Formationstest *m*
~ **test tool,** ~ **tester** Formationstester *m*, Formationstestgerät *n*
~ **testing** Formationstesten *n*
~ **treating** Formationsbehandlung *f*
~ **volume factor** Formationsvolumenfaktor *m*
~ **water** Schichtwasser *n*; Formationswasser *n*
formed coke Formkoks *m*
forms Formenschatz *m*
formula Formel *f*
fornacite Fornacit *m*, $Pb_2Cu[OH|CrO_4|AsO_4]$
forsterite Forsterit *m*, $Mg_2[SiO_4]$
fortification agate Festungsachat *m*
forward lap Längsüberdeckung *f*
foshagite Foshagit *m*, $Ca_4[(OH)_2|Si_3O_9]$
fosse lake glazialer Binnensee *m*
fossicker Goldgräber *m*
fossil alt, fossil; versteinert
fossil Fossil *n*, Versteinerung *f*, Petrefakt *n*
~ **assemblage** Fossilgesellschaft *f*
~-**bearing** fossilhaltig, fossilführend
~-**bearing bed** Versteinerungen führende Schicht *f*
~-**bearing deposit** *s.* ~ locality
~ **botany** Paläobotanik *f*
~ **charcoal** Fusit *m (Kohlenmikrolithotyp)*
~-**collecting locality** *s.* ~ locality
~ **content** Fossilinhalt *m*
~ **copal** fossiler Kopal *m*
~ **debris** Fossilfragmente *npl*
~ **droppings** fossiler Darmkot *m*
~ **dust** *s.* ~ meal
~ **earthquake** fossiles Beben *n*
~ **erosion surface** *s.* ~ peneplain
~ **flour** *s.* ~ meal
~ **fuel** fossiler Brennstoff *m*
~ **ice** Steineis *n*, fossiles Eis *n*, Bodeneis *n*
~ **ivory** fossiles Elfenbein *n*
~ **locality** Fossilfundstätte *f*, Fossilfundstelle *f*, Fossilfundort *m*
~ **meal** Infusorienerde *f*, Kieselgur *f*
~ **meal brick** Kieselgurstein *m*
~ **mould** Fossilabdruck *m*
~ **occurence** 1. Fossilvorkommen *n*; 2. Totöllagerstätte *f*, energielose Lagerstätte *f*
~ **oil** Erdöl *n*, Steinöl *n*, Petroleum *n*
~ **organic matter** fossile organische Materie *f*
~ **peneplain** fossile Peneplain *f*
~ **placer** fossile Seife *f*
~ **plant** fossile Pflanze *f*
~ **raindrops** *s.* accretionary lapili
~ **record** Fossilfolge *f*, Fossilführung *f*
~ **rejectamenta** fossiler Darmkot *m*
~ **remain** Fossilrest *m*
~ **resin** fossiles Harz *n*; Erdharz *n*, Bergharz *n*
~ **salt** Steinsalz *n*
~ **sequence** Fossilfolge *f*, Fossilführung *f*
~ **spirit level** fossile Wasserwaage *f*

fossil

- ~ **track** Spaltspur *f*
- ~ **tripoli** *s*. ~ meal
- ~ **type** Fossilart *f*
- ~ **volcano** erloschener Vulkan *m*
- ~ **water** fossiles Wasser *n*
- ~ **wax** Mineralwachs *n*, Bergwachs *n*, Ozokerit *m*, Erdwachs *n*
- ~ **with borings** von Organismen angebohrtes Fossil *n*

fossilate/to fossilieren, versteinern
fossiliferous fossilführend, fossilhaltig, Versteinerungen enthaltend
- ~ **content** Fossilinhalt *m*
- ~ **layer** fossilführende Lage *f*
- ~ **record** *s*. fossil record

fossilify/to fossilisieren, versteinern
fossilism Paläontologie *f*, Fossilkunde *f*
fossilist Paläontologe *m*, Fossilienkundiger *m*
fossilization Fossilisation *f*, Fossilienbildung *f*, Versteinerung *f*, Versteinerungsvorgang *m*
fossilize/to 1. fossilisieren, versteinern; 2. Fossilien sammeln
fossilized fossil
- ~ **brine** fossile Sole *f*
- ~ **excrements** fossiler Darmkot *m*

fossilogy Paläontologie *f*, Fossilkunde *f*
fossula Fossula *f*, Septalgrube *f* (von Korallen)
foucherite Foucherit *m*, Ca(Fe,Al)$_4$[(OH)$_8$|(PO$_4$)$_2$]·7H$_2$O
foul air faule Wetter *pl*
- ~ **-bottomed sediment** Faulschlammsediment *n*
- ~ **gas** schwefelwasserstoffhaltiges Gas *n*
- ~ **water** Schmutzwasser *n*, Abwasser *n*

foumarierite Foumarierit *m*, 8[UO$_2$|(OH)$_2$]·2Pb(OH)$_2$·4H$_2$O
foundation Fundierung *f*, Gründung *f*, Fundament *n*, Unterlage *f*, Sockel *m*, Baugrund *m*
- ~ **by caissons** Senkkastengründung *f*
- ~ **exploration** *s*. ~ testing
- ~ **in rock** Felsgründung *f*
- ~ **in the dry** Trockengründung *f*
- ~ **of filter** Filterboden *m* (im Brunnen)
- ~ **rock** Grundgebirge *n*
- ~ **soil** Untergrund *m*, Baugrund *m*, Lastboden *m*
- ~ **test boring** Baugrunduntersuchungsbohrung *f*
- ~ **testing** Bodenuntersuchung *f*, Untergrundforschung *f*, Baugrunduntersuchung *f*
- ~ **water pressure** Sohlenwasserdruck *m*

founder Schluckloch *n* am Meeresgrund
- ~ **breccia** Karstbrekzie *f*

foundered block abgesunkene Scholle *f*
foundering Zusammenbruch *m*, Einsturz *m*, Absinken *n*
four-part coral solitäre Koralle *f*
~-point method Vierpunktmethode *f*
~-sided vierseitig
fourble aus vier Stangen bestehender Gestängezug *m*
fourfold vierzählig *(Symmetrieachse)*
Fourier trend *s*. harmonic trend

fourling twinning Durchkreuzungsverzwillingung *f (Vierlingsbildung bei Feldspat)*
fowlerite Fowlerit *m (Varietät von Rhodonit)*
foyaite Foyait *m*
frac *s*. fracturing 2.
- ~ **location** Frac-Ortung *f*

fraction of flow Teilfluß *m*
fractional fraktioniert
- ~ **crystallization** fraktionierte Kristallisation *f*
- ~ **distillation** fraktionierte Destillation *f*
- ~ **magma** Teilmagma *n*
- ~ **melting** Teilschmelzenbildung *f*; partielle Aufschmelzung *f*

fractionation Fraktionierung *f*
fractonimbus clouds Schlechtwetterwolken *fpl*
fracture/to zerklüften
fracture Bruch *m*, Spalte *f*, Kluft *f*, Riß *m*
- ~ **across the grains** intrakristalliner Bruch *m*
- ~ **agate** Trümmerachat *m*
- ~ **analysis** Kluftanalyse *f*, Bruchanalyse *f (statistische Auswertung der Häufigkeit, Dichte und Orientierung von Brüchen und Klüften)*
- ~ **angle** Bruchwinkel *m*
- ~ **cleavage** S$_2$-Schieferung *f*; Runzelschieferung *f (nach A. Born)*; Schubklüftung *f (nach H. Scholtz)*; Bruchschieferung *f*, Transversalschieferung *f*; Spaltbruch *m*
- ~ **direction** Rißorientierung *f*
- ~ **frequency** Bruchflächenhäufigkeit *f*
- ~ **height** Rißhöhe *f*
- ~ **length** Rißlänge *f*
- ~ **line** Bruchlinie *f*
- ~ **origin** Bruchentstehung *f*
- ~ **pattern** Bruchbild *n*
- ~ **patterns** Bruchmuster *npl*, Kluftnetze *npl*, Spaltenanordnungen *fpl*
- ~ **plane** Bruchfläche *f*
- ~ **porosity** Porosität *f* infolge mechanischer Auflockerung
- ~ **spring** Spaltenquelle *f*, Kluftquelle *f*
- ~ **strength** Bruchfestigkeit *f*
- ~ **stress** Bruchspannung *f*
- ~ **trap** Kluftfalle *f*
- ~ **width** Rißweite *f*, Rißbreite *f*
- ~ **zone** *s*. fractured zone

fractured gebrochen, klüftig, zerklüftet, durch Brüche zerlegt; gebräch
- ~ **area** Bruchgebiet *n*
- ~ **matrix reservoir** klüftig-poröses Reservoir *n*
- ~ **region** Bruchgebiet *n*
- ~ **reservoir** zerklüfteter Speicher *m*
- ~ **zone** 1. Zerrüttungsstreifen *m*, Ruschelzone *f*, Störungszone *f*, Trümmergesteinszone *f*, Mylonitzone *f*; 2. Bruchfeld *n*

fracturing 1. Zerstückelung *f*, Zertrümmerung *f*, Zerklüftung *f*, Bruchbildung *f*; 2. Rißbildung *f*, Frac-Behandlung *f (Bohrtechnik)*; 3. Aufreißen *n*
- ~ **fluid** Brechflüssigkeit *f (Bohrtechnik)*

fragile bröcklig, brüchig, zerbrechlich
fragility Zerbrechlichkeit *f*

fragipan zerbrechliche harte Schicht f
fragment Bruchstück n
~ **of bedrock** Lesestein m
~ **of country rock** Nebengesteinsbruchstück n
~ **of lava** Lavastück n
~ **of rock** Gesteinsbruchstück n
fragmental bruchstückartig, klastisch
~ **accumulation** Trümmerablagerung f
~ **discharges (ejectamenta)** Auswürflinge mpl
~ **material** Trümmergesteinsmaterial n
~ **plant remains** Pflanzenhäcksel m (n)
~ **products** Auswürflinge mpl
~ **rocks** Trümmergesteine npl, klastische Gesteine npl
~ **texture** klastische Struktur f
fragmentary s. fragmental
fragmentation Zertrümmerung f
~ **of rock** Gesteinszerkleinerung f, Gesteinszertrümmerung f
fragmented zermürbt
fragments Trümmer pl
fraipontite Fraipontit m, $Zn_8Al_4[(OH)_8|(SiO_4)_5] \cdot 7H_2O$
framboidal pyrite Pyritsphäroid n aus Pyritoedern, Rogenpyrit m
frame-building organisms gerüstbildende Organismen mpl
~ **work** s. framework
framestone boundstone, bei dem die Organismen als Gerüstbildner wirkten
framework Gerüst[werk] n
~ **compressibility** Gerüstkompressibilität f
~ **of silica** Kieselgerüst n
~ **silicate** Gerüstsilikat n
francevillite Francevillit m, $(Ba, Pb)[(UO_2)_2|(V_2O_8)] \cdot 5H_2O$
franckeite Franckeit m, $5PbS \cdot 3SnS_2 \cdot Sb_2S_3$
Franconian Franconien n (Stufe des Croixiens)
~ **disturbance** Frankonische Faltung f
~ **Stage** s. Franconian
frangibility Brüchigkeit f, Sprödigkeit f
frangible brüchig, spröde
franklinite Franklinit m, Zinkeisenerz m, $ZnFe_2O_4$
Frasch process Frasch-Verfahren n (Schwefelabbau mit Heißwasser)
Frasnian [Stage] Frasne n, Frasnien n, Frasnium n (Stufe des Oberdevons)
Fraunhofer corona Fraunhofersche Korona f
~ **lines** Fraunhofersche Linien fpl
fray out/to auskeilen
frazil [ice] Rogeis n, Sulzeis n, Eisbrei m, Grundeis n, Siggeis n
freboldite Freboldit m, γ-CoSe
freckled gesprenkelt
free 1. frei; 2. gediegen
~ **acid** freie Säure f (z.B. im rohen Erdöl)
~-**air anomaly** Freiluftanomalie f
~-**air correction** Freiluftkorrektion f
~-**air reduction** Freiluftreduktion f
~-**burning coal** Magerkohle f, Sandkohle f
~ **crystal** freigewachsener Kristall m

~-**flowing** dünnflüssig, leichtflüssig
~ **from hydrogen** wasserstofffrei
~ **gas** freies Gas n
~ **gas cap drive** Gaskappentrieb m
~ **gas cap drive pool** Gaskappentrieblager n
~ **gliding** Freigleitung f
~ **gold** Freigold n
~ **ground water** Grundwasser n mit freier Oberfläche; ungespanntes Grundwasser n
~ **milling ore** durch Zerkleinerung aufschließbares Erz n
~-**moving benthos** vagiles Benthos n
~ **of ice** eisfrei
~ **silica** freie Kieselsäure f
~-**standing portable mast** freistehender, ortsbeweglicher Mast m
~ **surface** freie Oberfläche f (des Grundwassers)
~ **water** freies Wasser n (im rohen Erdöl, im Unterschied zum Emulsionswasser)
freedom prospect Schürffreiheit f
freestone allseitig gleich spaltender Sandstein m, Bausandstein m, Quaderstein m
freeze/to gefrieren, erstarren
~ **off** abfrieren
~ **over** zufrieren
~ **up** zufrieren
freeze Gefrieren n, Erstarren n
freezing 1. Erstarrung f, Gefrieren n; Gefrierverfahren n; 2. Festwerden n (von Rohren im Bohrloch)
~ **and thawing cycle** Gefrier- und Auftauzyklus m, Tau-Frost-Wechsel m
~ **hole** Gefrierbohrloch n
~ **line** Frostgrenze f
~ **of the pipe** Festwerden n des Rohrs
~ **point** Frostpunkt m, Gefrierpunkt m; Eispunkt m
~ **rain** Glatteis n
~ **shaft sinking** Abteufen n von Gefrierschächten
~ **zone** Gefrierzone f
freibergite Freibergit m (Ag-haltiger Tetraedrit)
freieslebenite Freieslebenit m, $4PbS \cdot 2Ag_2S \cdot 2Sb_2S_3$
fremontite s. natramblygonite
French chalk Speckstein m (s.a. talc)
frequency domain Frequenzbereich m
~ **of oscillation** Schwingungsfrequenz f
~ **of sunspots** Sonnenfleckenhäufigkeit f
~ **response** Frequenzcharakteristik f
fresh frisch, unbeansprucht
~ **breccia** Reibungsbrekzie f
~ **breeze** frische Brise f
~ **cleavage** frischer Bruch m
~ **condition** bergfeuchter Zustand m
~ **fracture plane** frisch angeschlagene Bruchfläche f
~ **gale** stürmischer Wind m
~ **rock** bergfeuchtes Gestein n
~ **snow** Neuschnee m

fresh

~ **volcanic rocks** jungvulkanische Gesteine *npl*
~ **water** Süßwasser *n*, Frischwasser *n*
~-**water bog** Süßwassermoor *n*
~-**water deposit** Süßwasserablagerung *f*
~-**water facies** Süßwasserfazies *f*
~-**water formations** Süßwasserbildungen *fpl*
~-**water fossil** Süßwasserfossil *n*
~-**water interface** Süß-Salzwasser-Grenzfläche *f*
~-**water lake** Süßwassersee *m*
~-**water limestone** Süßwasserkalk *m*, Kalksinter *m*
~-**water marsh** Süßwassersumpf *m*, Süßwassermoor *n*, Süßwassermarsch *f*
~-**water molasse** Süßwassermolasse *f*
~ **wind** frischer Wind *m*
freshen/to ausgesüßt werden; aussüßen, entsalzen
freshened aufgefrischt
freshening Aussüßung *f*, Entsalzung *f*
freshet Sprungschwall *m*; plötzlich einsetzendes Hochwasser *n*
freshly fallen snow Neuschnee *m*
~ **quarried sand** grubenfeuchter Sand *m*
Fresnel's ellipsoid Fresnelsches Ellipsoid *n*
fresnoite Fresnoit *m*, $Ba_2Ti[Si_2O_8]$
fretted zerfressen
~ **upland** Kargebirge *n*
fretwork Wabenverwitterungsstruktur *f*
freudenbergite Freudenbergit *m*, $NaFe(Ti, Nb)_3O_7(O, OH)_2$
friability Brüchigkeit *f*, Mürbheit *f*
friable bröcklig, zerbröckelnd, krümelig, zerreiblich, mürbe, gebräch, nichtbindig, kohäsionslos
~ **aggregate** *s.* pellet
~ **gypsum** erdiges Gipsgestein *n*
~ **iron ore** mulmiges Eisenerz *n*
~ **rock** bröckliges (gebräches, loses) Gebirge *n*
~ **soil** Lockerboden *m*
friction Reibung *f*
~ **breccia** Reibungsbrekzie *f*
~ **carpet** Reibungsteppich *m*
~ **circle** Gleitkreis *m*
~ **coefficient** Reibungsbeiwert *m*
~ **grip** Reibungsschluß *m*, Haftreibung *f*
~ **heating** Reibungserwärmung *f*
~ **surface** Reibungsfläche *f*
~ **velocity** Reibungsgeschwindigkeit *f*
frictional force Reibungskraft *f*
~ **resistance** Reibungswiderstand *m*
~ **torque** Reibungsdrehmoment *n*
friedelite Friedelit *m*, $(Mn, Fe)_8[(OH, Cl)_{10}|Si_6O_{15}]$
frieseite Frieseit *m*, $Ag_2Fe_5S_8$
frightening erschreckend *(6. Stufe der Erdbebenstärkeskala)*
frigid wave Kältewelle *f*
frill Velum *n*
fringe crystals Stengelkristalle *mpl*
~-**finned ganoids** Crossopterygier *mpl*, Krossopterygier *mpl*

148

~ **pattern** spannungsoptisches Bild *n*
~ **water** Kapillarsaumwasser *n*, Saugsaumwasser *n*
fringing reef Saumriff *n*, Küstenriff *n*
frit/to fritten
frith *s.* estuary
fritted rock gefrittetes Gestein *n*
fritting Fritten *n*, Frittung *f*
fritzscheite Fritzscheit *m* (Mn-, VO_4-haltige Varietät von Autunit)
frohbergite Frohbergit *m*, $FeTe_2$
frolovite Frolovit *m*, $Ca[B_2O(OH)_6]\cdot H_2O$
frond Wedel *m*
frondelite Frondelit *m*, $(Mn, Fe^{\cdot\cdot})Fe_4^{\cdot\cdot\cdot}[(OH)_5|(PO_4)_3]$
frondescent cast Fächermarke *f*, fächerförmige Fließmarke *f*
front abutement pressure vorderer (voreilender) Kämpferdruck *m*
~ **of a thrust** Faltenstirn *f*
~ **range** Vorgebirge *n*
frontal apron Vorschüttsande *mpl (glazial)*
~ **lobe** Stirneinrollung *f*, Stirnfalte *f*
~ **moraine** Stirnmoräne *f*, Frontmoräne *f*
~ **overthrust** Stirn *f* der Deckfalte *(Überschiebung)*
~ **sheet** Stirnplatte *f*
~ **wedge** Stirnschuppe *f*
frontland *s.* foreland
froodite Froodit *m*, α-$PdBi_2$
frost Frost *m*
~ **action** Frosteinwirkung *f*
~ **blasting** Frostsprengung *f*
~ **boil** Frosthebung *f*, Frostbeule *f*
~-**broken** vom Frost losgelöst
~ **crack** Frostspalte *f*, Frostriß *m*
~ **damages** Frostschäden *mpl*
~-**detached** von Frost losgelöst
~ **effect** Frostwirkung *f*
~-**free** frostfrei
~ **heave** Frosthebung *f*, Frostbeule *f*, Frostauftreibung *f*
~ **heaved mound** *s.* ~ mound
~ **heaving (lifting)** Frosthebung *f*, Frostbeule *f*, Auffrieren *n*, Aufwulstung *f* des Lockerbodens durch Eis
~ **line** Frostgrenze *f (im Boden)*
~ **mound** Pingohydrolakkolith *m*, Aufeishügel *m*
~ **patterns** Frostfiguren *fpl*
~ **penetration** Frosteindringung *f*, Frosttiefe *f*
~ **precaution** Frostschutzmaßnahme *f*
~-**proof** frostbeständig, frostunempfindlich
~ **rending** Frostsprengung *f*
~ **resistance** Frostbeständigkeit *f*
~-**resisting** frostbeständig, frostunempfindlich
~ **scaling** Frostabblätterung *f*
~ **shattering** Frostverwitterung *f*, Frostsprengung *f*
~ **shove** Frostschub *m*
~ **splitting** Frostsprengung *f*
~ **stirring** Frostwirkung *f* ohne Massenbewegung

~-susceptible frostempfindlich
~ thrust Frostschub *m*
~ weathering Frostverwitterung *f*, Frostsprengung *f*; Spaltenfrost *m*; Spaltenfrostverwitterung *f*
~ wedging Frostsprengung *f*
~ work Frostzerstörung *f*
frosted mattgeschliffen, mattiert *(Sandkörner)*
~ grain mattiertes Korn *n*
frostiness Frost *m*, Eiskälte *f*
frosting Mattschliff *m (Sandkörner)*
frostwork *s.* frost work
froth floatation Schaumschwimmverfahren *n*, Schwimmaufbereitung *f*
~ flow 1. turbulente Blasenströmung *f*; 2. Schaumlava *f*
frother cell Schaumzelle *f*
frothing agent Schäumer *m (Flotation)*
frozen earth (ground, soil) Frostboden *m*
~ to the walls mit dem Nebengestein verschweißt *(Gangmasse)*
~ wall fest aufgewachsenes Salband *n*
fruchtschiefer Fruchtschiefer *m*
fructiferous frond fruktifizierender Wedel *m*
fruiting cone Fruchtzapfen *m*, Fruktifikation *f*
frustule of a diatom Diatomeenschale *f*
frustulent klastisch
FT *s.* field tape
fuchsite Chromglimmer *m*, Fuchsit *m (s.a.* muscovite)
fucoidal tangähnlich
~ sandstone Fukoidensandstein *m*
fuel Brennstoff *m*; Spaltstoff *m*, Kernbrennstoff *m*
~ gas Brenngas *n*
~ material Spaltmaterial *n*
fugacity Flüchtigkeit *f*
fulgurite Blitzröhre *f*, Blitzsinter *m*, Fulgurit *m*
fulja Depression zwischen zwei Barchanen
full *s.* beach ridge
~ dip stärkstes (wahres) Einfallen *n*
~-face method Vollausbruch *m*
~ gale starker Sturm *m*
~-gauge hole Bohrlochnenndurchmesser *m*
~ hole drilling Vollbohren *n*, kernloses Bohren *n*
~ mature valley vollreifes Tal *n*
~ maturity Vollreife *f*
~ moon Vollmond *m*
~ of fissures zerklüftet
~ relief Vollrelief *n (Ichnologie)*
~-scale experiment (test) Großversuch *m*
~-seam extraction Abbau *m* des Flözes in voller Mächtigkeit
~ string of casing volle Verrohrung *f*
~-trough gliding Volltroggleitung *f*
fuller's earth Fullererde *f*, Palygorskit *m*, Walkerde *f*, Smektit *m*, Walkton *m*, fetter Ton *m*, weißer Bolus *m*
fully crystalline vollkristallin
~ desalted water vollentsalztes Wasser *n*
~ mature überreif

fülöppite Fülöppit *m*, $3PbS \cdot 4Sb_2S_3$
fumarole Fumarole *f*
~ field Fumarolenfeld *n*
~ mound Fumarolenhügel *m*
~ stage Fumarolenstadium *n*
fumarolic action (activity) Fumarolentätigkeit *f*
~ gases Fumarolengase *npl*
~ stage Fumarolenstadium *n*
functional group funktionelle Gruppe *f*
fundamental complex Grundgebirge *n*
~ jelly (substance) vergelte Pflanzensubstanz *f* (biochemische Inkohlung)
fungal activity Pilzaktivität *f (Zerstörung durch Pilze)*
~ spores Pilzsporen *fpl*
fungosclerotinite Fungosclerotinit *m (Kohlensubmaceral)*
funicular regime zusammenhängendes Oberflächenhaftwasser *n*
funnel Eruptionskanal *m*, Eruptionsschlot *m*, Vulkanschlot *m*, Schlot *m*, Trichter *m*
~ intrusion Lopolith *m*
~ sea Trichtermeer *n*
~-shaped trichterförmig
funnellike trichterförmig
furious cross lamination zusammengesetzte Schrägschichtung *f*
furrow/to zerfurchen
furrow Furche *f*, Graben *m*, Rinne *f*, Rille *f*, Abflußrinne *f*, Wanne *f*, Einsenkung *f*
~ flute cast Furchenmarke *f*
~ irrigation Grabenbewässerung *f*
~-leaved furchenblättrig
furrowed furchig, zerfurcht, rinnenförmig, gerillt
furrowing Ausfurchung *f*, Kannelierung *f*
furrows Rutschstreifen *mpl*, Rutschschrammen *fpl*
fusain 1. Fusain *m*, Faserkohle *f (Lithotyp der Humussteinkohle);* 2. *(Am)* Mikrolithotyp *m*, Fusit *m*
fuse/to schmelzen *(Gestein)*
fused glutflüssig
~ basalt Schmelzbasalt *m*
fusibility Schmelzbarkeit *f*
fusible schmelzbar
fusiform spindelförmig
fusing point Schmelzpunkt *m*
~ temperature Schmelztemperatur *f*
fusinite Fusinit *m (Kohlenmaceral)*
fusinitization Fusini[ti]sierung *f*
fusion 1. Schmelzen *n*, Schmelzung *f*; 2. Fusion *f*
~ piercing Schmelzbohren *n*, Flammbohren *n*
~ tectonites Schmelztektonite *mpl*
~ temperature Schmelztemperatur *f*
fusite Fusit *m (Kohlenmikrolithotyp)*
fusoid spindelförmig
Fusulina limestone Fusulinenkalk *m*

gabbro 150

G

gabbro Gabbro m
~ diorite Gabbrodiorit m
gabbroic gabbroid, gabbroartig
gabbroid[al] gabbrohaltig
~ schist Flasergabbro m
gabbroitic s. gabbroic
gadolinite Gadolinit m, $Y_2FeBe_2[O|SiO_4]_2$
gagarinite Gagarinit m, $NaCaYF_6$
gagate Gagat m, Jet m (n) (Sapropelit, bituminiertes fossiles Holz)
gage (Am) s. gauge
gahnite Gahnit m, Zinkspinell m, $ZnAl_2O_4$
gain control Amplitudenregelung f
gaining stream s. effluent stream
gaist s. ghost
gait road Hauptförderstrecke f
gaize feinkörniger Glaukonitsandstein m
gal Gal n (inkohärente Einheit der Beschleunigung in der Geophysik)
galactic galaktisch, Milchstraßen...
~ nebula galaktischer Nebel m, Milchstraßennebel m
~ radio waves galaktische Radiowellen fpl
~ system Milchstraßensystem n
galactite Milchstein m (s.a. natrolite)
galaxite Galaxit m, Manganspinell m, $MnAl_2O_4$
galaxy Galaxis f, Milchstraße f
gale Sturm m (Windstärke 9 der Beaufortskala)
~ force Sturmwindstärke f
~-warning Sturmwarnung f
galeate mit helmartiger Bedeckung
galeite Galeit m, Na_3 [(F, Cl)|SO_4]
galena Galenit m, Bleiglanz m, PbS
galenical bleihaltig
galeniferous bleiglanzhaltig, bleiglanzführend
galenite s. galena
galenobismuthite Galenobismutit m, $PbS \cdot Bi_2S_3$
galera s. hogback
galleried cave mehrsohlige Höhle f
gallery Strecke f, Stollen m
~ back s. ~ roof
~ driven through the rock Gesteinsstrecke f
~ level Streckensohle f, Stollensohle f
~ mouth Stollenmund m
~ roof Stollenfirste f, Streckenfirste f
galliard harter, glatter Sandstein m (für Schotter)
gallite Gallit m, $CuGaS_2$
galmei Galmei m (teils Zinkspat, teils Hemimorphit)
galt harter Mergel m
galvanometric galvanometrisch
gamagarite Gamagarit m, $Ba_2(Fe, Mn)[VO_4] \cdot 1/2 H_2O$
gamma Gamma n (alte Einheit der magnetischen Feldstärke, 1 y ≙ 1 nT)
~ decay Gammazerfall m
~ emitter Gammastrahler m
~-gamma log Gamma-gamma-Log n (radiometrische Dichtemessung im Bohrloch)

~ logging Gammalog n, Gammamessung f, Gammakernen n
~ radiation Gammastrahlung f
~ radiator Gammastrahler m
~-ray logging s. ~ logging
~-ray spectroscopy Gammaspektroskopie f
~-ray spectrum Gammaspektrum n
~ structure y-Überschiebung f (Überschiebung mit flach, dann steil fallender Fläche)
gang of wells Brunnengalerie f
ganged automatic gain control gesteuerte automatische Gangkontrolle f (Seismik)
gangstock gangartige Ausstülpung f (von Intrusivkörpern)
gangue s. ~ material
~ deposit gangartige Lagerstätte f
~ material (mineral, rock) Gangart f, Ganggestein n, taubes Gestein n, Gangmasse f
ganil spröder brüchiger Kalkstein m
ganister Ganister m, eingekieselter Feinsandstein (quarzitischer Rohstoff für Silikatsteine)
~ brick Quarzitstein m (Feuerfestindustrie)
gank (sl) 1. zerklüftete Oxydationszone f; 2. Erzanzeiger m
gannister s. ganister
ganoid fish Schmelzschupper m, Ganoide m
~ scale Ganoidschuppe f (bei Fischen)
ganomalite Ganomalith m, $Pb_6Ca_4[(OH)_2|(Si_2O_7)_3]$
ganomatite Ganomatit m, Gänsekötigerz n (Fe-Arsenat mit Ag- und Co-Gehalt)
ganophyllite Ganophyllit m, (Na, K, Ca) (Mn, Al, Mg)$_3$[(OH)$_2$(OH, H$_2$O)$_2$(Si, Al) Si$_3$O$_{10}$]
gap 1. Spalte f, Kluft f; 2. Lücke f (stratigrafisch); 3. Kennmarke f, Marke f, Markierung f (Seismogramm)
~ fault klaffende Verwerfung f
~ graded material diskontinuierlich abgestuftes Material n
~ grading diskontinuierliche Abstufung f (der Körnung)
~ in geologic record Schichtenlücke f, stratigrafische Unterbrechung f
~ in range of miscibility Mischungslücke f
~ in the unconsolidated goaf Weitung f im Alten Mann
~ length Spaltlänge f
~ of miscibility Mischungslücke f
~ width Spaltweite f
gaping klaffend
gaping Spalt m
~ fault klaffende (offene) Verwerfung f
~ fissure klaffende Spalte f
~ hole klaffende Öffnung f
garbage Müll m
garbenschiefer Garbenschiefer m
Gargasian [Stage] Gargas n (Stufe, oberes Apt, Tethys)
garnet Granat m (Mineralgruppe, $3RO \cdot R_2O_3 \cdot 3SiO_2$; R=Ca, Mg, Fe, Mn, Al, Cr, Ti)
~ amphibolite Granatamphibolit m

~ blende s. sphalerite
~ gneiss Granatgneis m
~ mica schist Granatglimmerschiefer m
~ rock Granatfels m
garnetiferous granathaltig, granatführend
~ pegmatite Granatpegmatit m
~ sand Granatsand m
~ schist Granatschiefer m
garnetization Granatbildung f (im Gestein)
garnetyte Granatfels m
garnierite Garnierit m, Nickelantigorit m (Varietät von Antigorit)
garrelsite Garrelsit m, (Ba, Ca)$_2$[(BOOH)$_3$|SiO$_4$]
garronite Garronit m, NaCa$_{2,5}$[Al$_3$Si$_5$O$_{16}$]$_2$·13^1/$_2$H$_2$O
gas Gas n
~ analyzer Gasanalysegerät n, Gasspürgerät n
~ barren infolge vulkanischer Exhalationen unfruchtbares Gebiet
~-bearing gashaltig, gasführend
~ blast Gasstrahl m
~ blow-out Gasausbruch m
~ bubble Gasblase f
~ buoyancy Gasauftrieb m
~ cap Gaskappe f, Gaskopf m, Gashut m
~ cap drive Gaskappentrieb m
~ cap of a structure Gaskappe f einer Struktur
~-carrying sand Gassand m, gasführender Sand m
~-carrying schist gasführender Schiefer m
~-charged gasreich
~ chromatographic measurement gaschromatografische Messung f
~ chromatography Gaschromatografie f
~ cloud Gaswolke f
~ coal Gaskohle f
~-collecting main Gassammelleitung f
~-condensate field Kondensatlagerstätte f
~-condensate reservoir Gaskondensatträger m
~ coning Gaskegelbildung f
~ content Gasgehalt m
~ cushion Gaspolster n (Gasspeicher)
~ delivery Freiwerden n von Gas
~ detector Gasspürgerät n, Gasanzeigegerät n, Gasdetektor m
~ determination Gasgehaltsbestimmung f
~ deviation factor Realgasfaktor m
~ discharge Gasausscheidung f, Gasabscheidung f
~ discovery Erdgasfund m
~ drilling Gasbohren n, Bohren n mit Gasspülung, Drehbohren n mit Luftspülung
~ drive Gastrieb m, Gastreibverfahren n (Erdöl)
~ emission Entgasung f, Ausgasung f
~ envelope Dampfhülle f
~ eruption Gasausbruch m
~ escape (extraction) Entgasung f
~ expansion drive Gasexpansionstrieb m
~ field Gaslagerstätte f, Erdgasfeld n
~-filled cavity gaserfüllter Hohlraum m

~-flame coal Gasflammkohle f
~ floatation s. crystal floatation
~ horizon Gashorizont m
~ in solution gelöstes Gas n
~ inclusion Gaseinschluß m
~ indicator Gasanzeiger m (s.a. ~ detector)
~ influx Gaszulauf m
~-input well Gaseinpreßbohrung f
~ invasion Gaseinbruch m (in Bohrungen)
~ layer Gashorizont m
~ lift Gasliftverfahren n, Gasliftförderung f
~ line Gasleitung f
~-liquid chromatography Gas-Flüssig[keits]-Chromatografie f
~ lock Gaspolster n
~ logging Gaskernen n, Gaskarrotage f
~ main Ferngasleitung f
~ mound Schlammvulkan m, Salse f (Golfküste von Texas und Louisiana)
~ occlusion Gaseinschluß m
~ of putrefaction Faulgas n
~-oil contact Gas-Öl-Kontakt m
~-oil interface (level) Gas-Öl-Kontaktfläche f, Gas-Öl-Grenzfläche f
~-oil ratio Gas-Öl-Verhältnis n
~-oil saturation Gas-Öl-Sättigung f
~-oil surface s. ~-oil interface
~ pipe Gasleitung f
~ pit s. ~ spurt
~ pocket Gastasche f
~ pool Erdgasakkumulation f, Erdgaslagerstätte f
~-poor gasarm
~ pore Gasbläschen n (im Mineralkorn)
~ precipitation Gasausscheidung f
~ pressure Gasdruck m
~ processing Gasaufbereitung f
~ processing equipment Erdgasverarbeitungsanlage f
~-producing well Gasfördersonde f
~ prospecting Gasprospektion f
~ province Erdgasprovinz f
~ repressuring Gaseinpressen n zur Druckerhaltung
~ reserve Gashöffigkeit f
~-rich gasreich
~ rich in oil vapours an Öldämpfen reiches Naturgas n
~ rock gasführendes Gestein n
~ sampler Gasprobenehmer m, Gasprobenahmegerät n
~ sand Gassand m, gasführender Sandstein m
~ schist gasführender Schiefer m
~ seep Gasaustritt m, Gasausströmung f
~ seepage Erdgasausbiß m
~ separating barge Barke f zur Gasabscheidung und -aufbereitung
~ separator Gasabscheider m
~ show Gasanzeichen n
~ skin Gashülle f
~ solubility Gaslöslichkeit f
~ spurt Gasblubberstelle f, Gasaustritt m

gas

~ **storage** Gaseinlagerung f, Gasspeicherung f
~ **streak** gasführende Zwischenlage f
~ **tester** Gasprüfer m
~-**tight core barrel** Gaskernprobe[nent]nahmegerät n
~ **transfer** Gastransport m
~-**water contact** Gas-Wasser-Kontakt m
~-**water interface (level, surface)** Gas-Wasser-Kontaktfläche f
~ **well** Gasbohrung f, Gasbohrloch n; Gassonde f, Gasquelle f
~ **yield** Gasausbeute f
~ **zone** gasführende Formation f
Gasconadian [Stage] Gasconade n (Stufe des Unterordoviziums, Nordamerika)
gaseous gasförmig, gasig, gasartig, gashaltig
~ **bubble** Gasblase f
~ **explosion** Gasexplosion f
gash s. ~ vein
~ **fractures** Fiederspalten fpl (diagonale Dehnungsfugen an Störungen)
~ **vein** kleine mineralisierte Dehnungsfuge f; mineralisierte ac-Fuge f in inkompetenten Lagen; nach der Teufe auskeilender Gang m
gasifiable vergasbar
gasification Gaserzeugung f, Vergasung f
gasiform gasförmig
gasify/to in Gas verwandeln, vergasen
gasoclastic durch Gasausbruch zerbrochen (Sedimente im Schlammvulkan)
gasoline (Am) Benzin n
gasometry Gasvermessung f
gasser Gasfördersonde f, Gasbläser m, Gasbohrung f
gassi schmale Dünenpassage f
gassy gasführend, gashaltig
gastaldite Gastaldit m (s.a. glaucophane)
gastric pouche Gastralraum m, Magen m
gastrolith s. stomach stone
gate 1. Gebirgspaß m, Pforte f; 2. Schieber m; 3. Fenster n, Zeitabschnitt m
gateway Pforte f
gather Spurengruppe f (Seismik)
gathering area Migrationsgebiet n (von Kohlenwasserstoffen)
~ **ground** Niederschlagsgebiet n, Einzugsgebiet n; Nährgebiet n
~ **of water** Wasserfassung f
~ **system** Sammelleitung f (im Öl- oder Gasfeld)
~ **zone** Zone f oberhalb des Grundwasserspiegels
gaudefroyite Gaudefroyit m, 3 CaMn···[O|BO$_3$]·Ca(CO$_3$)
gauge 1. Maß n, Eichmaß n; 2. Meßgerät n; 3. Pegel m
~ **datum** Pegelnullpunkt m
~ **edge** Kaliberschneide f
~ **height** Pegelhöhe f
~ **pressure** Pegeldruck m (Wasserspiegelhöhe im Beobachtungsrohr)
~ **reading** Pegelablesung f

152

~ **station** Pegelstation f
~ **tube** Pitotrohr n, Standrohr n; Grundwasserbeobachtungsrohr n
~ **well** Pegelbrunnen m, Beobachtungsbrunnen m, Grundwasserbeobachtungsrohr n
gauged oil rohes Erdöl n (nach dem Ablassen des mitgeförderten Wassers)
gauging Pegelmessung f
~ **by measuring** Überfallabflußmessung f
~ **station** Abflußmeßstelle f
Gault Gault n (höchste Unterkreide, mittleres und oberes Alb)
~ **Clay** Gault-Ton[mergel] m (in England)
Gaussian curve Gauß-Kurve f, Gaußsche Fehlerkurve f
~ **distribution** Gauß-Verteilung f, Gaußsche Verteilung f, Normalverteilung f
~ **error curve** s. ~ curve
gauteite Gauteit m (Alkaligestein)
gauton Wasserseige f; Wasserrösche f
gayet Kännelkohle f (Sapropelkohle)
gaylussite Gaylussit m, Na$_2$Ca[CO$_3$]$_2$·5H$_2$O
geanticlinal fold Geoantiklinale f
geanticlinal welt s. welt
geanticline Geoantiklinale f (tektonischer und topografischer Sattel)
gearksutite Gearksutit m, Ca[Al(F, OH)$_5$H$_2$O]
gedanite Gedanit m (bernsteinähnliches Harz)
Gedinnian [Stage] Gedinne n (Stufe des Unterdevons)
gedrite Gedrit m, (Mg, Fe)$_6$ (Al, Fe) [OH|(Si, Al)$_4$O$_{11}$]$_2$
geest 1. Gesteinszerfallsprodukte npl in situ; 2. Aufschotterungsgebiet n; 3. alluviale Ablagerung f
gehlenite Gehlenit m, Ca$_2$Al[(Si, Al)$_2$O$_7$]
Geiger[-Müller] counter, ~[-Müller counter] tube Geiger-Zähler m, Geiger-Müller-Zählrohr n, GM-Zählrohr n
geikielite Geikielith m, MgTiO$_3$
geisotherm s. isogeotherm
geisothermal s. isogeothermal
gel Gel n
~ **mineral** Gelmineral n, amorphes Mineral n
~ **strength** Gelstärke f
gelatination 1. Gelbildung f, Gelatinierung f; 2. Vergelung f (im Moor)
gelatinization s. gelatination
gelatinous gallertartig, gelatinös
~ **magnesite** Gelmagnesit m
gelation 1. Gelatinierung f; 2. Erstarrung f
gelification s. gelatination 2.
gelifluction s. gelifluxion
gelifluxion Gelifluxion f, Taubodenrutschung f über Frostboden
gelinite Gelinit m (Braunkohlenmaceral)
gelling Quellung f
~ **agent** Gelbildner m
gelocollinite Gelocollinit m (Kohlensubmaceral)
gem Gemme f, Edelstein m
~ **cutter** Edelsteinschneider m

geochemical

~ **magnifier** Edelsteinlupe f
~ **mineral** Edelmineral n
~ **placer** Edelsteinseife f
geminate crystal Doppelkristall m, Zwillingskristall m
gemination Doppelbildung f (von Kristallen)
gemmary Edelsteinkunde f
gemmation Knospung f (Paläontologie)
gem[m]ology Edelsteinkunde f
gemstone Edelstein m
genal spines Wangenstacheln mpl (des Trilobitenkopfschilds)
genealogic[al] succession (tree) Stammbaum m
general collapse Einsturz m (des Grubengebäudes)
~ **damage to buildings** allgemeiner Gebäudeschaden m (9. Stufe der Erdbebenstärkeskala)
~ **destruction of buildings** allgemeine Gebäudezerstörungen fpl (10. Stufe der Erdbebenstärkeskala)
~ **geology** allgemeine Geologie f
~ **geophysics** allgemeine Geophysik f
~ **inclination of strata** Generalfallen n
~ **map** Übersichtskarte f
~ **state of strain** räumlicher Verzerrungszustand m
~ **state of stress** räumlicher Spannungszustand m
~ **trend** Hauptstreichen n
~ **view** Übersichtsbild n
generalized geological map geologische Übersichtskarte f
~ **section** schematisches (generelles) Profil n
generate/to erzeugen, hervorbringen
generation Erzeugung f, Hervorbringung f; Entstehung f
generative organs s. reproductive organs
generic appellation Gattungsname m
~ **feature** Gattungsmerkmal n
~ **name** Gattungsname m
generotype s. genotype
genesis Genese f, Entstehung f, Bildung f
~ **of the earth** Erdentstehung f
genetic[al] genetisch
~ **line** Entwicklungslinie f
~ **morphology** genetische Morphologie f
~ **taxonomy** biologische Taxonomie f
genetics Genetik f
genital markings s. ovarian impressions
genotype Gen[er]otypus m, Typusart f (Nomenklaturregeln)
genthelvine Genthelvin m, $Zn_8[S_2|(BeSiO_4)_6]$
genthite Genthit m (Nickelantigorit)
gentle breeze schwache Brise f
~ **dip** flaches Einfallen n
~**-dipping strata** flach einfallende Schichten fpl
~ **grade** schwaches Einfallen n
~ **rain** Rieselregen m
~ **river bank** flaches Flußufer n

~**-sloped talus** sanft geneigte Böschung f
gently dipping seam flach einfallendes Flöz f
~ **folded** schwach gefaltet
~ **inclined strata** flach einfallende Schichten fpl
gentnerite Gentnerit m, $Cu_8Fe_3Cr_{11}S_{18}$ (Meteoritenmineral)
genus Geschlecht n, Gattung f, Genus n
geo kleine Bucht in steiler Kliffküste (Island)
geoanticline s. geanticline
geoastronomy Geoastronomie f
geobarometer Geobarometer n
geobarometry Geobarometrie f, Druckbestimmung f (bei geologischen Prozessen)
geobasin großes ungefaltetes Sedimentbecken n
geobiologic[al] geobiologisch
geobiologist Geobiologe m
geobiology Geobiologie f
geobiotic geobiotisch
geobotanic[al] geobotanisch, phytogeografisch, pflanzengeografisch
~ **prospecting** geobotanische Erkundung (Suchmethode) f
geobotanist Geobotaniker m, Phytogeograf m, Pflanzengeograf m
geobotany Geobotanik f, Phytogeografie f, Pflanzengeografie f
geocentre Erdmittelpunkt m
geocentric geozentrisch
geocerase s. geocerite
geocerite Geozerit m, $C_{27}H_{53}O_2$ (eine Erdwachsart in Braunkohle)
geochemical geochemisch
~ **anomaly** geochemische Anomalie f
~ **aureole** geochemischer Hof m
~ **balance** geochemische Bilanz f
~ **barrier** geochemische Barriere f
~ **borehole prospection** bohrlochgeochemische Prospektion f
~ **calculation** geochemische Berechnung f
~ **character** geochemischer Charakter m
~ **classification** geochemische Klassifikation f
~ **composition** geochemische Zusammensetzung f
~ **cycle** geochemischer Zyklus (Kreislauf) m
~ **element** geochemisches Indikatorelement n
~ **exploration** geochemische Erkundung f
~ **facies** geochemische Fazies f
~ **field** geochemisches Feld n (zufälliges Feld geochemischer Merkmale)
~ **gelification** geochemische Vergelung f
~ **halo** geochemischer Hof m
~ **indicator** geochemischer Indikator m
~ **interpretation** geochemische Interpretation f
~ **migration** geochemische Migration f
~ **negative anomaly** geochemische Senke f
~ **prospecting** geochemisches Prospektieren n
~ **specialization** geochemische Spezialisierung f
~ **standard sample** geochemische Standardprobe f

geochemical

~ **structure** geochemische Gliederung *f (der Erde)*
~ **well logging** geochemische Bohrlochmessung *f*
geochemist Geochemiker *m*
geochemistry Geochemie *f*
~ **of salt** Geochemie *f* der Salze, Salzgeochemie *f*
~ **of weathering** Geochemie *f* der Verwitterung
geochore Geochore *f*
geochronologic[al] geology historische Geologie *f*
~ **interval** geochronologisches Intervall *n*
~ **scale** geochronologische Zeitskala *f*
~ **unit** geochronologische Einheit *f*
geochronology Geochronologie *f*
geochronometry Geochronometrie *f (geologische Zeitmessung in Jahren bezogen auf die Dauer des irdischen Jahres)*
geochrony *s.* geochronology
geoclinal valley Geoklinaltal *n (einer Krustendepression folgendes Tal)*
geocorona Geokorona *f*
geocratic period geokratische Periode *f*
geocronite Geokronit *m*, 5PbS·AsSbS₃
geode Geode *f*, Mandel *f*
geodepression Geodepression *f*
geodesic *s.* geodetic
geodesist Geodät *m*
geodesy Geodäsie *f*, Erdvermessung *f*
geodete Geodät *m*
geodetic geodätisch
~ **engineer** Vermessungsingenieur *m*
~ **mapping** geodätische Abbildung *f*
~ **survey** geodätische Vermessung *f*, Landesaufnahme *f*
~ **surveying** Geodäsie *f*, Erdvermessung *f*
geodetics Geodäsie *f*
geodiferous geodenreich
geodynamic geodynamisch
geodynamics Geodynamik *f*
geoelectric[al] geoelektrisch
~ **resistivity method** geoelektrische Widerstandsmethode *f*
~ **sounding** geoelektrische Sondierung *f*
geoelectrics Geoelektrik *f*
geofracture Geofraktur *f*
geogenesis Geogenese *f*
geogen[et]ic geogenetisch
geogeny Geogenese *f*
geoglyphic Geoglyphe *f (Fossilspur)*
geognostic[al] geognostisch
geognosy geognostische Wissenschaften *fpl*, Geognosie *f*
geogony Geogonie *f*, Erdbildungslehre *f*
geographic[al] coordinates Länge *f* und Breite *f*
~ **cycle** Erosionszyklus *m*
~ **meridian** geografischer Meridian *m*, Längenkreis *m*
~ **north** geografischer Norden *m*
~ **palaeontology** geografische Paläontologie *f*

~ **pole** geografischer Pol *m*
geography Geografie *f*, Erdkunde *f*
geohydrochemistry Geohydrochemie *f*
geohydrological geohydrologisch
geohydrology Geohydrologie *f (Hydrologie des Grundwassers)*
geoid Geoid *n*
geoidal horizon geoidaler Horizont *m*
geoisotherm Geoisotherme *f*
geoisothermal surface Geoisothermalfläche *f*
geologian Geologe *m*
geologic[al] geologisch, erdgeschichtlich
~ **age** geologisches Alter *n*
~ **age determination** geologische Altersbestimmung *f*
~ **ages** geologische Zeitalter *npl (Zeiträume mpl)*
~ **application** geologische Nutzanwendung *f*
~ **atlas** geologischer Atlas *m*
~ **barrier** geologische Grenze *f*
~ **chronology** Geochronologie *f*, geologische Zeitrechnung *f*
~ **clock** geologische Zeittafel *f*
~ **coke** Naturkoks *m*
~ **column** geologisches Profil *n*, Schichtfolge *f*, Formationsfolge *f*, stratigrafische Tabelle (Serie) *f*
~ **conditions** Lagerungsverhältnisse *npl*
~ **correlation** geologische Korrelation *f*
~ **cross section** geologischer Querschnitt *m*, geologisches Querprofil *n*
~ **environment** geologisches Milieu *n*
~ **era** geologischer Zeitabschnitt *m*
~ **events** geologische Vorgänge *mpl*
~ **exploratory drill hole** geologische Aufschlußbohrung *f*
~ **feature** geologisches Merkmal *n*
~ **fence** geologische Grenzbedingungen *fpl*
~ **field work** geologische Feldarbeit *f*
~ **ground survey** geologische Aufnahme *f* eines Gebiets
~ **hammer** Geologenhammer *m*
~ **history** Erdgeschichte *f*
~ **map** geologische Karte *f*
~ **map sheet** geologisches Kartenblatt *n*
~ **mapping** geologisches Kartieren *n*
~ **orbital photography** geologische Satellitenfotografie *f*
~ **past** geologische Vergangenheit *f*
~ **preservation area** geologisches Schutzgebiet *n*
~ **prospecting** geologische Untersuchungsarbeiten *fpl*
~ **prospecting efficiency** Effektivität *f* geologischer Untersuchungsarbeiten
~ **prospecting technique** Methodik *f* geologischer Untersuchungsarbeiten
~ **province** geologische Provinz *f*
~ **range** *s.* stratigraphic range
~ **reconnaissance map** geologische Übersichtskarte *f*
~ **reconnaissance work** geologische Erkundungsarbeiten *fpl*

~ **record** 1. geologische Dokumentation f; 2. s.
~ **column**
~ **reserves** geologische Vorräte mpl
~ **section (sequence of strata)** s. ~ column
~ **set-up** geologischer Untergrund m
~ **space** geologischer Raum m (definierte Menge der geografischen und geodätischen Koordinaten geologischer Objekte)
~ **span** geologische Zeitspanne f
~ **specimen** Handstück n
~ **stratum compass** geologischer Gefügekompaß m
~ **structure** geologischer Bau m
~ **subsurface map** geologische Karte f des Untergrunds
~ **subsurface mapping** geologisches Kartieren n des Untergrunds (nach Bohrergebnissen)
~ **succession** s. ~ column
~ **surveying** geologische Aufnahme f
~ **target** geologische Aufgabenstellung f
~ **thermometer** geologisches Thermometer n
~ **time measurement** geologische Zeitmessung f
~ **window** tektonisches Fenster n
geologist Geologe m
geologist's compass Geologenkompaß m
~ **hammer** Geologenhammer m
~ **pick** Geologenhacke f
geologize/to geologisch untersuchen
geograph Bohrfortschrittsschreiber m
geology Geologie f
~ **of oceans** Geologie f der Ozeane
~ **of man** Humangeologie f
~ **of mineral deposits** Lagerstättenlehre f
geolith s. rock-stratigraphic unit
geomagnetic geomagnetisch, erdmagnetisch
~ **activity** erdmagnetische Aktivität f
~ **anomaly** erdmagnetische Anomalie f
~ **axis** erdmagnetische Achse f
~ **deep sounding** erdmagnetische Tiefensondierung f
~ **equator** erdmagnetischer Äquator m
~ **field** erdmagnetisches Feld n
~ **field intensity** erdmagnetische Feldstärke f
~ **meridian** erdmagnetischer Meridian m
~ **moment** erdmagnetisches Moment n
~ **pole** erdmagnetischer Pol m
~ **reversal** geomagnetische Umpolung f
~ **storm** erdmagnetischer Sturm m
~ **tides** erdmagnetische Gezeiten pl
geomagnetism Geomagnetismus m, Erdmagnetismus m
geomalic auf den Einfluß der Gravitation bezogen
geomathematics Geomathematik f, mathematische Geologie f
geomechanics Geomechanik f
geometric[al] accuracy geometrische Genauigkeit f (von Karten und Fernerkundungsaufnahmen)
~ **base of a regionalized variable** geometrische Basis f einer regionalisierten Variablen

~ **correction** Korrektur f geometrischer Verzerrungen
~ **distortion** geometrische Verzerrung f
~ **field of a regionalized variable** geometrisches Feld n einer regionalisierten Variablen
geometrics quantitativ statistische Methoden in den Geowissenschaften
geomicrobiologic[al] geomikrobiologisch
geomorphic geology Geomorphologie f
geomorphist Geomorphologe m
geomorphogenic geomorphologisch
geomorphogenist Geomorphologe m
geomorphogeny Geomorphogenie f
geomorphologic geomorphologisch
geomorphologist Geomorphologe m
geomorphology Geomorphologie f
geomorphy Geomorphogenie f
geomyricin s. geomyricite
geomyricite Geomyricit m, $C_{32}H_{62}O_2$ (Erdwachs in Braunkohle)
geonomic geonomisch
geonomy Geonomie f
geopetal fabric geopetales Gefüge n, Anlagerungsgefüge n
geophagous sedimentaufnehmend (Organismen)
geophone Geophon n
~ **delay time** Laufzeitdifferenz f am Geophon
geophysical geophysikalisch
~ **exploration** geophysikalische Erforschung f
~ **field study** geophysikalische Baugrunduntersuchung f
~ **investigation** geophysikalische Untersuchung f
~ **method of prospecting** geophysikalisches Schürfverfahren n
~ **surveying** geophysikalische Vermessung f
~ **well logging** geophysikalische Bohrlochmessung f
geophysicist Geophysiker m
geophysics Geophysik f
geopolar den Erdpol betreffend
geopotential Geopotential n
~ **surface** Niveaufläche f des Geopotentials
geopressure Überlagerungsdruck m
georgiadesite Georgiadesit m, $Pb_3[Cl_3AsO_4]$
Georgian [Series] s. Waucobian
geoscientist Geowissenschaftler m
geoscopy Erdbeobachtung f
geosphere Geosphäre f, Erdsphäre f
geostatics Geostatik f
geostationary orbit geostationäre Umlaufbahn f
~ **satellite** geostationärer Satellit m
geostatistics Geostatistik f (i.e. Sinne auch mathematische Theorie der regionalisierten Variablen nach Matheron)
geostrophic wind geostrophischer Wind m, Passatwind m
~ **wind level** geostrophische Windschwelle f
geosuture Geosutur f, Lineament n
geosynchronous satellite geosynchroner Satellit

geosynclinal

m (Erdsatellit, dessen Umlaufperiode gleich der Periode der Erdrotation ist)
geosynclinal cycle Geosynklinalzyklus *m*
~ system Geosynklinalsystem *n*
~ trough Geosynklinaltrog *m*
geosyncline Geosynklinale *f*
geotechnic[al] geotechnisch
~ process geotechnisches Verfahren *n*
geotechnics Geotechnik *f*
geotectocline *s.* geosyncline
geotectology Geotektonik *f*
geotectonic geotektonisch
~ geology Geotektonik *f*
geotectonics Geotektonik *f*
geotector *s.* geophone
geotherm Geotherme *f*
geothermal geothermisch
~ degree of depth *s.* ~ gradient
~ energy geothermische Energie *f*
~ energy recovery geothermische Energiegewinnung *f*
~ gradient geothermischer Gradient *m*
~ logging geothermische Bohrlochmessung *f*
~ prospecting geothermische Erkundung *f*
~ steam geothermaler Dampf *m*
~ step geothermische Tiefenstufe *f*
geothermic geothermisch *(s.a. geothermal)*
geothermometer Geothermometer *n*
geothermometric geothermometrisch
geothermometry Geothermometrie *f*, Temperaturbestimmung *f (bei geologischen Prozessen)*
geothermy Geothermie *f*
geotope Geotop *n*
geotumor Geotumor *m*
gerasimovskite Gerasimovskit *m*, (Nb, Ti, Mn, Ca)O$_2 \cdot 1^1/_2$H$_2$O
gerhardtite Gerhardtit *m*, Cu$_2$[(OH)$_3$|NO$_3$]
German facies Germanische Fazies *f*
Germanic basin Germanisches Becken *n*
~ Triassic Germanische Trias *f*
germanite Germanit *m*, Cu$_3$(Fe, Ge)S$_4$
germanium ore Germaniumerz *n*
germanotype orogenesis germanotype Gebirgsbildung *f*
germination Keimbildung *f (z.B. bei Kristallen in Metallgefügen)*
gersdorffite Gersdorffit *m*, Nickelarsenkies *m*, Nickelglanz *m*, NiAsS
gerstleyite Gerstleyit *m*, (Na, Li)$_4$As$_2$Sb$_8$S$_{17} \cdot$6H$_2$O
getter Hauer *m*, Häuer *m*
getting barren Vertaubung *f (von Erzen)*
~-down of coal Auskohlen *n*
~ of clay Tongewinnung *f*
geversite Geversit *m*, PtSb$_2$
geyser Geiser *m*, Geysir *m*, intermittierende Springquelle *f*
~ action Geisertätigkeit *f*
~ basin Geiserbecken *n*
~ eruption Geiserausbruch *m*
~ jet Dampf- und Wasserstrahl *m* eines Geisers

~ pipe Quellrohr *n*, Geiserschlot *m*
~ vent Geiseröffnung *f*
geyserite Geiserit *m (Opalvarietät)*
gha[u]t Gebirgspaß *m (Indien)*
ghost 1. Relikt *n*, Gefügerelikt *n*, schemenhaft erkennbares älteres Inventar *n*; 2. Geisterreflexion *f*, Sekundärreflexion *f (Seismik)*
~ coal Geisterkohle *f (Kohle mit hellem Glühlicht)*
~ crater Geisterkrater *m ("Geister"-Ringe, durch jüngeres Maremateriel überflutete alte Krater)*
~ structure Geistergefüge *n*, Reliktgefüge *n*
giant bolide Riesenmeteorit *m*, Überbolid *m*
~ crystal Riesenkristall *m*
~ granite *s.* pegmatite
~ growth Riesenwuchs *m*
~ kettle Erosionstopf *m*, Gletschermühle *f*
~ ripples Riesenrippeln *fpl (Rippeln mit über 30 m Länge)*
~ stairway *s.* glacial stairway
~ star Riesenstern *m*
gibber Dreikanter *m (Australien)*
gibbous ausgebaucht, angeschwollen
gibbsite Gibbsit *m*, γ-Al(OH)$_3$
Gibbs's phase rule Gibbssche Phasenregel *f*
gieseckite Gieseckit *m (zu dichter Muskovitsubstanz veränderter Nephelin)*
giessenite Giessenit *m*, 8PbS·3Bi$_2$S$_3$
gigantic joint Riesenkluft *f*
gigantism Gigantismus *m*, Riesenwuchs *m*
gigantolite Gigantolit *m (s.a. pinite)*
Gilbert-type delta Delta *n* vom Gilbert-Typ, Gilbert-Delta *n (Delta mit sandigen, beckenwärts einfallenden Vorsetzschichten)*
gill 1. Kieme *f (Atmungsorgan)*; 2. schmales Tal *n*, Schlucht *f*
~ cleft Kiemenspalte *f*
~ rakers Kiemenstrahlen *mpl*
~ slit Kiemenspalte *f*
gillespite Gillespit *m*, BaFe[Si$_4$O$_{10}$]
gilpinite *s.* johannite
gilsonite Gilsonit *m (Asphaltit)*
gimbal 1. Kardanring *m*; 2. horizontal stabilisierte Plattform *f*
~ mounting kardanische Aufhängung *f*
ginorite Ginorit *m*, Ca$_2$[B$_4$O$_5$(OH)$_4$][B$_5$O$_6$(OH)$_4$]$_2 \cdot$2H$_2$O
girasol *s.* opal
girdle Gesteinsschicht *f*, dünne Kohlenschicht *f*
~ diagram Gürteldiagramm *n (Gefügeregelung)*
~ maximum Gürtelbesetzung *f (in einem Gefügediagramm)*
gismondine, gismondite Gismondin *m*, (Ca, Na)[Al$_2$Si$_2$O$_8$]·4H$_2$O
Givetian [Stage] Givet *n (Stufe des Mitteldevons)*
gizzard stone *s.* stomach stone
glabella Glabella *f (Zentralteil eines Trilobitenkopfes)*

glacially

glabellar zur Glabella gehörig
glacial glazial, eiszeitlich
~ **abrasion** glaziale Abrasion f, [abschleifende] Gletschererosion f
~ **action** Gletschertätigkeit f
~ **advance** Vorrücken n des Gletschers, Gletschervorstoß m
~ **age** Eiszeitalter n
~ **basin** glaziales Talbecken n
~-**borne** eisverfrachtet
~-**borne debris** Gletscherschutt m, Glazialschotter m
~ **boss** glazialer Felsriegel (Felsbuckel) m
~ **boulder** Findling m
~ **boundary** Grenze f des Eises
~-**carved valley** Gletschertal n, Trogtal n
~ **catchment basin** Firnfeld n
~ **chimney** Gletschermühle f, Gletschertopf m, Gletschertrichter m
~ **clastics** glaziale Trümmergesteine npl
~ **clay** glazialer Bänderton m
~ **corrasion** Gletscherkorrasion f
~ **crevasse** Gletscherspalte f
~ **crowding** Eisdruck m
~ **crust** Eiskruste f
~ **debris** Gletscherschutt m, Glazialschotter m
~ **delta** Glazialdelta n
~ **deposit** Gletscherablagerung f, glaziale Ablagerung f
~-**deposition coast** Glazialschuttküste f
~ **detritus** s. ~ drift
~ **drainage pattern** glaziales Flußsystem n
~ **drift** 1. Glazialgeschiebe n, diluviales Geschiebe n, Gletscherschutt m; 2. Eisdrift f
~ **effect** Gletscherwirkung f
~ **epoch** Glazialzeit f, Eiszeit f
~ **erosion** Gletschererosion f, Glazialerosion f, glaziale Abtragung f
~ **flow** s. glacier flow
~ **flutings** s. ~ grooves
~ **formation** Gletscherbildung f
~ **geologist** Glaziologe m
~ **geology** s. glaciology
~ **gorge** glaziales Trogtal n, U-Tal n
~ **gravel** Gletscherkies m, Glazialkies m
~ **grooves** Gletscherschliffe mpl, Gletscherfurchen fpl, Gletscherschrammen fpl
~ **grooving** Gletscherzerkarung f
~ **ice** Gletschereis n
~ **isostasy** Eisisostasie f
~ **lake** Gletschersee m, glazialer See m, Eisstausee m, Moränenstausee m, Schmelzwassersee m
~ **limit** Eisgrenze f
~ **lobe** Gletscherzunge f, Eiszunge f
~ **mantle rock** glazialer Verwitterungsschutt m
~ **marking** Eisabscheuerung f
~ **maximum** Maximum n des Eisvorstoßes
~ **meal (milk)** Gletschermilch f, Gletschertrübe f
~ **mill** Gletschermühle f, Gletschertopf m, Gletschertrichter m

~ **moraine** Glazialmoräne f
~ **movement** Gletscherbewegung f
~ **mud** Gletscherschlamm m
~ **outwash** glaziale Flußablagerung f, Sander m, Sandur m
~ **outwash plain** Sanderebene f, Schmelzwasserebene f
~ **pebbles** Glazialgeschiebe npl
~ **period** Glazialperiode f, Glazialzeit f, Eiszeit f
~ **piedmont lake** Zungenbeckensee m
~ **planing** Gletscherabhoblung f
~ **ploughing** Gletscherabtrag m
~ **polish[ing]** Gletscherschliff m
~ **pothole** Gletschermühle f, Gletschertopf m, Gletschertrichter m
~ **push** Eisdruck m
~ **retreat** Gletscherrückgang m
~ **river** Gletscherfluß m, Gletscherbach m
~ **sand plain** s. ~ delta
~ **sands** Geschiebesand m
~ **scoring** Gletschererosion f, Gletscherabtrag m
~ **scour** Gletscherabtrag m, Gletscherschramm m
~ **scour lake** glazialer Fingersee m
~ **scouring** Eisabscheuerung f, Auskolken n durch Eis
~ **scratches** s. ~ grooves
~ **sculpturing** Gletschererosion f
~ **shove** Eisdruck m
~ **shrinkage** Eisschrumpfung f
~ **soil** Gletscherschuttboden m, Glazialboden m, Moränenschuttboden m
~ **spillway** Urstromtal n, [glaziale] Schmelzwasserrinne f, Schmelzwassertal n
~ **stage** Eiszeit f
~ **stairway** Kartreppe f
~ **stream** Gletscherfluß m, Gletscherbach m
~ **stream channel** Schmelzwasserrinne f, Urstromtal n
~ **stria** Gletscherschramme f, Gletscherkritze f
~ **table** Gletschertisch m
~ **thrust** Eisdruck m
~ **till** Geschiebemergel m, Geschiebelehm m
~ **time[s]** Eiszeit f
~ **topography** Gletscherlandschaft f
~ **transport** Glazialtransport m
~ **trough** glaziales Ausräumungsbecken (Eintiefungsbecken) n, Trogtal n; Gletschertrog m
~ **trough coast** ertrunkene glaziale Erosionsküste f
~ **valley** Gletschertal n
~ **varve** glazialer Bänderton m
~ **waters** Schmelzwässer npl
~ **wear** Eisabscheuerung f
Glacial Epoch s. Pleistocene
glacialism Glazialtheorie f
glacialist Glaziologe m, Gletscherforscher m
glacialized glazialer Einwirkung unterworfen
glacially eroded vom Eise ausgeräumt
~ **impounded lake** Eisstausee m

glacially

~ **striated** eisgeschrammt
~ **transported** eisverfrachtet
glaciate/to vereisen, vergletschern
glaciated area vereistes (mit Eis bedecktes) Gebiet *n*
~ **boulders** Glazialgeschiebe *npl*
~ **valley** Glazialtal *n*
glaciation Vereisung *f*, Vergletscherung *f*
glacic *s.* glacial
glacier Gletscher *m*
~ **accumulation** Gletscherablagerung *f*
~ **action** Gletschertätigkeit *f*
~ **band** *s.* ogive
~ **bed** Gletscherbett *n*
~ **berg** Gletscherberg *m (Eisberg)*
~ **bulb** Gletscherkopf *m (Gletschererweiterung bei Austritt aus einem engen Tal)*
~ **burst** Gletscherausbruch *m (verbunden mit Wasserausbruch)*
~ **cap** *s.* ice cap
~ **cave** Gletschertor *n*
~ **circus** Kar *n*
~ **cliff** Eiskliff *n*
~ **corn** Blaueisstück *n (aus einem Gletscher stammend)*
~-**covered** *(Am)* vergletschert
~ **crater** Gletscherspalte *f*
~ **current** Gletscherströmung *f*
~ **drift** Gletscherschutt *m*
~ **erosion** Gletschererosion *f*
~ **face** seeseitiger Gletscherabbruch *m*
~-**fed torrent** Gletscherbach *m*
~-**filled valley** Gletschertal *n (mit glazialem Schutt gefüllt)*
~ **flood** plötzlicher Gletschervorstoß *m*, Gletscherbruch *m*
~ **flow** Gletscherfließen *n*, Eisbewegung *f* im Gletscher
~ **front** Gletscherstirn *f*
~ **grain** 1. Korngefüge *n* des Gletschereises; 2. Gletschereiseinzelkorn *n*
~ **ice** Gletschereis *n*; Firneis *n*
~ **lake** Gletschersee *m*, Moränenstausee *m*, Schmelzwassersee *m*
~ **landscape** Gletscherlandschaft *f*
~ **lobe** Eislobus *m*, Gletscherzunge *f*
~-**lobe lake** Gletscherzungensee *m*
~ **meal (milk)** *s.* glacial meal
~ **mill** Gletschermühle *f*, Gletschertopf *m*, Gletschertrichter *m*
~ **oscillation** Gletscherschwankung *f*
~ **outburst** Gletscherausbruch *m*
~ **outlet** Gletschertor *n*
~ **pavement** Gletschersohle *f (abgeschliffener Felsuntergrund unter einem Gletscher)*
~ **recession** Gletscherrückgang *m*
~ **reservoir** Akkumulationszone *f* eines Gletschers
~ **rubbish** Oberflächenschutt *m* eines Gletschers
~ **run** plötzlicher Wasserausbruch *m* aus einem Gletscher

~ **runoff** Gletscherabfluß *m*
~ **shrinkage** Gletscherrückgang *m*
~ **snout** Gletscherzunge *f*
~ **snow** Firnschnee *m*
~ **sole** Gletschersohle *f*
~ **table** Gletschertisch *m*
~ **terminus** Gletscherstirn *f*
~ **tongue** Gletscherzunge *f*
~ **torrent** Gletscherbach *m*
~ **valley** Gletschertal *n*
~ **well** *s.* ~ mill
glacieret Hängegletscher *m*
glacierization *s.* glaciation
glacierized vergletschert
glacigenous glazigen
glacioeluvial glazieluvial
glacioeustatic fluctuations of the sea level glazial-eustatische Niveauschwankungen *fpl* des Meeres
glaciofluvial, glaciofluviatile fluvioglazial, von eiszeitlichen Schmelzwässern gebildet
~ **mantle** fluvioglaziale Schuttdecke *f*
glacioisostatic rise glazialisostatische Hebung *f*
glaciolacustrine glaziallakustrisch, in Schmelzwasserseen abgelagert
glaciologist Gletscherforscher *m*
glaciology Glaziologie *f*, Glazialgeologie *f*, Gletscherlehre *f*
glaciomarine glaziomarin
~ **till** *s.* subaqueous till
glacionatant till *s.* subaqueous till
glacis flache Abdachung *f*
glacon Eisscholle *f*
gladite Gladit *m*, $2PbS \cdot Cu_2 \cdot 5Bi_2S_3$
glance Glanz *m (in Verbindung mit Mineralnamen, besonders Sulfiden, z.B. Bleiglanz)*
~ **cobalt** *s.* cobaltite
~ **copper** *s.* chalcocite
~ **pitch** reiner Asphalt *m*
glancing angle Glanzwinkel *m*, Braggscher Winkel *m*
glandular drüsenartig
glaposition Abgrenzung *f* von Gletscherverbreitungsräumen
glare ice Spiegeleisscholle *f*
glarosion glaziogene Erosions- und Transporttätigkeit *f*
glaserite Glaserit *m (s.a.* aphthitalite)
glass Glas *n*, Gesteinsglas *n*
~ **inclusion** Glaseinschluß *m*
~ **porphyry** Glasporphyr *m*
~ **rock** kryptokristalliner Kalkstein aus dem Trenton
~ **sand** Glassand *m*
~ **seam** *mit Kalzit oder Quarz verheilte Kluft*
~ **sponge** Glasschwamm *m*, Kieselschwamm *m*
~ **stiff** *(sl) s.* calcite
~ **wool** *s.* mineral wool
glasseous *s.* glassy
glassy glasig, amorph, glasartig; glasführend

~ **base** Glasbasis f
~ **lustre** Glasglanz m
~ **scoria** Glasschlacke f
~ **texture** Glasstruktur f
glauber salt Glaubersalz n (s.a. mirabilite)
glauberite Glauberit m, $CaNa_2[SO_4]_2$
glaucocerinite Glaukokerinit m, $(Zn, Cu)_{10}Al_4[(OH)_{30}|SO_4] \cdot 2H_2O$
glaucochroite Glaukochroit m, $CaMn[SiO_4]$
glaucodot[e] Glaukodot m, (CO, Fe)AsS
glauconite Glaukonit m, $(K, Ca, Na)_{<1}(Al, Fe^{\cdot\cdot\cdot}, Fe^{\cdot\cdot}, Mg)_2[(OH)_2|Al_{0,35}Si_{3,65}O_{10}]$
~ **sand** Glaukonitsand m, Grünsand m
glauconitic clay Glaukonitton m
~ **facies** Glaukonitfazies f
~ **limestone** Glaukonitkalk m
~ **sand** Glaukonitsand m, Grünsand m
~ **sandstone** Glaukonitsandstein m
glauconitization Glaukonitisierung f
glauconitize/to glaukonitisieren
glaucophane Glaukophan m, $Na_2Mg_3Al_2[(OH, F)|Si_4O_{11}]_2$
~ **eclogite** Glaukophaneklogit m
~-**lawsonite facies** Glaukophanlawsonitfazies f, Blauschieferfazies f
~ **schist** Glaukophanschiefer m
glaze Glatteis n
glazy glasig
glebe 1. mineralhöffiges Gebiet n; 2. Erzstufe f
glei s. gley
gleitbrett fold s. shear fold
gleization s. gleying process
glen Talschlucht f, Bergschlucht f, Schlucht f
glessite Glessit m (fossiles Harz)
gley Gley m
gleyed vergleyt
gleying process, gleyization Vergleyung f, Gleybildung f
glide/to gleiten
glide bands Gleitbänder npl
~ **bedding** subaquatische Gleitflächenstapelung f
~ **breccia** Subsolifluktionsbrekzie f
~ **plane** Gleitebene f, Rutschfläche f
gliding Gleiten n, Gleitung f
~ **movement** Gleitbewegung f
~ **plane** s. glide plane
glimmering Mineralglanz m mit unvollständiger Oberflächenreflexion (z.B. bei Chalzedon)
glint Böschung f (durch Austritt verschieden harter Schichten verursachte Stufe)
~ **lake** [glazialer] Stufensee m
~ **line** s. cuesta
glist (sl) 1. Glimmer m; 2. schwarzer Turmalin m; 3. Schimmer m, Funkeln n
glistening Mineralglanz m mit guter Oberflächenreflexion (z.B. bei Talk)
glo (sl) Kohle f
global atmospheric research program globales Atmosphärenforschungsprogramm n
~ **radiation** Globalstrahlung f (von Himmel und Sonne)

~ **tectonics** Globaltektonik f, Geotektonik f
globbing Bergeversatz m; Abraum m
globe Erdglobus m, Erdkugel f
~ **lightning** Kugelblitz m
~-**shaped** kugel[förm]ig
globigerina ooze Globigerinenschlamm m
globigerine facies Globigerinenfazies f
globosphaerite Globosphärit m
globular kugel[förm]ig
~ **bomb** kugelige Bombe f
~ **diorite** Kugeldiorit m
~ **granite** Kugelgranit m
globule Tröpfchen n, Kügelchen n
globuliferous Globulite enthaltend, sphärolithisch
globulite Globulit m, Kügelchen n, Kugelkörperchen n
glomerate/to in dichten Haufen zusammenwachsen
glomerate s. agglomerate; conglomerate
glomeration Wachstum n in unregelmäßigen Knollen
glomeroblast Glomeroblast m
glomeroblastic structure glomeroblastisches Gefüge n
glomeroclastic glomeroklastisch
glomerocryst Kristallhaufen m, unregelmäßige Kristallzusammenballung f
glomero[por]phyric glomeroporphyrisch
glomeroporphyritic glomeroporphyritisch
glory hole Pinge f, Abbautrichter m
~-**hole mining** Pingenbergbau m, Trichterbergbau m
gloss s. polish
~ **coal** Pechkohle f, Hartbraunkohle f
glossopteris flora Glossopterisflora f
gloup 1. Blasloch n (im Brandungskliff); 2. Entgasungslöcher npl (auf einem Lavastrom)
glowing avalanche Glutlawine f, glühender Schuttstrom m
~ **avalanche deposit** Glutbrekzienablagerung f
~ **cloud** Eruptionswolke f, Glutwolke f
glucine Glucin m, $BaBe_4[(OH)_2|PO_4]_2 \cdot 1/2 H_2O$
gluing rock (sl) hangender eisenschüssiger Ton m (der mit der Kohle gewonnen wird)
glutinous dickflüssig
glyptogenesis Glyptogenese f, Entstehung f der Landformen
glyptolith Dreikanter m, Windkanter m
G-M counter s. Geiger-Müller counter
gmelinite Gmelinit m, $(Na_2, Ca)[Al_2Si_4O_{12}] \cdot 6H_2O$
GMT s. Greenwich mean time
gnamma mit Wasser gefüllte Verwitterungshohlräume längs Gesteinsklüften (Australien)
gnash/to knistern, knirschen
gnashing Knistern n, Knirschen n
gneiss Gneis m
~ **massif** Gneismassiv n
~-**mica schist** Gneisglimmerschiefer m
gneissic gneisartig (s.a. gneissoid)
gneissification Vergneisung f

gneissoid

gneissoid gneisartig
~ granite Gneisgranit m
~ structure Gneistextur f
gneissose gneisartig (s.a. gneissoid)
gneissosity Gneisplattung f, Gneischarakter m
gnomonic projection gnomonische Projektion f
go dry/to versiegen
goaf Alter Mann m, abgeworfener Grubenbau m
gob 1. durch Abbau entstandener Hohlraum m; 2. taubes Gestein n
gobbet Gesteinsblock m
gobbing 1. Versatzarbeit f; 2. Bergeversatz m
goe kleine Kliffnische f
goethite Goethit m, Nadeleisenerz n, Lepidokrokit m, Rubinglimmer m, Samtblende f, α-FeOOH
goffered gefältelt
goffering Fältelung f
gog Sumpf m
going s. trafficability
gold Gold n, Au
~ assay Goldprobe f
~ aventurine s. aventurine; quartz
~-bearing goldführend, goldhaltig
~ beryl s. chrysoberyl
~ buddle Goldwaschherd m
~ buddling Goldwäscherei f
~ bullion Rohgold n
~ deposit Goldlagerstätte f
~ dust Goldstaub m
~ extraction Goldgewinnung f
~ finder Goldsucher m
~ flux s. aventurine; quartz
~ nugget Nugget n, Freigoldklumpen m
~ pan Sicherschüssel f, Waschtrog m
~ parting Goldscheidung f
~ placer Goldseife f
~ quartz vein Goldquarzgang m
~ screening Schlämmen n von Gold
~ washer Goldwäscher m, Goldsucher m
~ washing Goldwäscherei f
~ washings Goldseife f
golden mica (sl) Katzengold n, angewitterter Glimmer m
goldfieldite Goldfieldit m (Te-Tetraedrit)
goldichite Goldichit m, KFe⁻[SO₄]₂·4H₂O
Goldich's stability sequence Goldichs Stabilitätsabfolge f (Abfolge der wichtigsten gesteinsbildenden Minerale nach der Stabilität gegen chemische Verwitterung)
goldmanite Goldmanit m, Ca₃V₂⁻[SiO₄]₃
Goldschmidt's rule Goldschmidtsche Regel f
goldstone s. aventurine; quartz
gole 1. Schleuse f; 2. Graben m; 3. Tal n
golt s. galt
gompholite Nagelfluh f
Gondwana coal Gondwana-Kohle f
~ fauna Gondwana[land]-Fauna f (Permokarbon und Trias der Südkontinente)
~ layers Gondwana-Schichten fpl

160

Gondwanaland fauna s. Gondwana fauna
goniatite Goniatit m
~ limestone Goniatitenkalk m
goniatitic suture goniatitische Lobenlinie f
goniometer Goniometer n
gonnardite Gonnardit m, (Ca, Na)₃[(Al, Si)₅O₁₀]₂·6H₂O
gonophore Gonophor m
good-stained kaum gefleckt (Glimmerqualität)
~ tilth Bodengare f
gooseneck Schwanenhals m, Spülkopfkrümmer m
gopher/to planlos abbauen
gopher hole horizontales Bohrloch n; kleine Suchbohrung f unter Tage
gophering unsystematisch durchgeführte Schürfarbeiten fpl
GOR s. gas-oil ratio
gordonite Gordonit m, MgAl₂[OH|PO₄]₂·8H₂O
gore of schist Bergemittel n
gorge Schlucht f, enge Felsschlucht f, Engpaß m, Klamm f
~ cutting (making) Schluchtenbildung f, Klammbildung f
görgeyite Görgeyit m, K₂Ca₅[SO₄]₆·1¹/₂H₂O
Gorstian [Stage] Gorstium n (obere Stufe des Ludlow)
goshenite Goshenit m (farblose Varietät von Beryll)
goslarite Goslarit m, Zn[SO₄]·7H₂O
gossan Eiserner Hut m, Oxydationszone f
gossaniferous hutbildend; Hutmaterial führend, Produkte der Oxydationszone enthaltend, okkerhaltige Letten führend
~ clay ockerhaltiger Letten m
gossany lode Erzgang m in der Oxydationszone
Gothian folding gotidische Faltung f
Gotlandian [Period, System] Gotland[ium] n (nicht mehr gebräuchliche Bezeichnung für das Silursystem)
gotten abgebaut
gotten stillgelegte Grube f
götzenite Götzenit m, (Ca, Na)₃(Ti, Ce)<₁[F₂|Si₂O₇]
gouge [out]/to auskolken
gouge 1. Lettenbesteg m, Verwerfungsletten m, Salband n; Kluftletten m; 2. unsystematischer Abbau m
~ channel Fließmarke f, Gefließmarke f
~ clay Lettenbesteg m, Ganglette f
~ mark Schürfmarke f
gouging-out Auskolken n
goulee enge tiefe Schlucht f, Gießbachbett n
gowan zersetzter Granit m
gowerite Gowerit m, Ca[B₃O₄(OH)₂]₂·3H₂O
goyazite Goyazit m, SrAl₃H[(OH)₆|(PO₄)₂]
goz großer Sandrücken m (Sudan)
gozzan s. gossan
grab Fanghaken m, Glückshaken m, Greifer m
~ sample 1. wahllose Stichprobe f, Zufallsprobe f; 2. Greiferprobe f (vom Meeresgrund)

graben Grabenbruch m, Grabensenke f, [tektonischer] Graben m
gradation 1. Abstufung f, Übergang m, Gradation f; 2. Abtragung f
~ **limit** Siebkennlinie f
~ **works** Gradierwerk n
gradational effect abtragende Wirkung f
~ **surface** Abtragungsebene f
~ **zone** Übertragungszone f
grade downward into/to nach dem Liegenden übergehen in
~ **into** übergehen in
~ **laterally into** seitwärts übergehen in
grade 1. Gefälle n, Neigung f, Einfallen n; 2. Neigungswinkel m (z.B. einer Straße); 3. Grad m, Größe f, Güte f (als relative Qualitätsbezeichnung)
~ **of ore** Metallgehalt m
~ **of stabilization** Stabilisierungsgrad m (einer Grundwasserabsenkung)
~ **scale** Kornklasseneinteilung f
graded 1. gradiert; klassiert; 2. abgetragen
~ **bedding** gradierte Schichtung f, Seigerungsschichtung f, Abstufungsschichtung f
~ **revolving stage** graduierter Drehtisch m
~ **river** ausgeglichener Fluß m
~ **sediments** klassierte Sedimente npl
~ **shore line** Ausgleichsküste[nlinie] f
~ **slope** gleichsinniges Gefälle n
~ **unconformity** Diskordanz f ohne scharfe Grenzfläche
~/**well** schlecht sortiert, gut abgestuft (alle Korngrößenklassen vertreten)
gradient Gradient m, Neigung f, Gefälle n
~ **curve** Absenkungskurve f, Gefällskurve f
~ **of gravity** Schweregradient m
~ **profile** Gradientenprofil n
~ **section** Gefällestufe f
grading Korn[größen]verteilung f
~ **analysis** Siebanalyse f
~ **curve** Siebkurve f, Sieblinie f
~ **factor** Kornzusammensetzungsfaktor m
~ **test** Prüfsiebung f
gradiometer Gradientmesser m, Gradiometer m
graduated circle Teilkreis m
graebeite Graebeit m, $C_{18}H_{14}O_8$
graftonite Graftonit m, $(Ca, Fe^{..}, Mn)_3[PO_4]_2$
grahamite Grahamit m (Asphaltit)
grail Kies m; Sand m; Feinkorn n
grain 1. Korn n; 2. Teilbarkeitsrichtung in Plutoriten senkrecht zu hardway
~ **boundary** Kornbegrenzung f, Korngrenze f, Kristallgrenze f
~ **boundary crack** Korngrenzenriß m, interkristalliner Riß m
~ **boundary diffusion** Korngrenzendiffusion f
~ **classification** Korngrößeneinteilung f
~ **colony** Kristallgebilde n
~ **compressibility** Gerüstkompressibilität f
~ **density** Korndichte f
~ **diameter** Korndurchmesser m

~ **diminution** Kornabbau m
~ **flow** Trägheitsstrom, bei dem die Partikel durch Kornwechselwirkung in Suspension gehalten werden
~ **growth** Kornwachstum n; Kristallwachstum n
~ **interaction** Kornwechselwirkung f
~ **plane** Ebene f der Teilbarkeit senkrecht zur Schieferung (von Metamorphiten)
~ **pressure** Gerüstdruck m (Parameter für Porenkompressibilität)
~ **shape** Kornform f
~ **size** Korngröße f; Körnigkeit f
~ **size content** Korngrößenanteil m
~ **size distribution** Korn[größen]verteilung f
~ **size distribution curve** Siebkurve f, Sieblinie f
~ **structure** Korngefüge n
grained körnig, gekörnt
~ **rock** körniges Gestein n
~ **texture** körnige Struktur f
grainstone Karbonatgestein aus sich gegenseitig abstützenden Partikeln
grainy körnig, gekörnt
grammatite Grammatit m (Ca-Mg-Amphibol, s.a. tremolite)
granatohedron Rhombendodekaeder n
grandidierite Grandidierit m, (Mg, Fe)Al$_3$[O|BO$_4$|SiO$_4$]
grandite Grandit m (Varietät von Granat)
graniform kornartig; aus Körnern zusammengesetzt
graniphyric s. granophyric
granite Granit m
~ **aplite** Granitaplit m
~ **boss** Granitbuckel m
~ **boulder** Granitblock m
~ **boulder slope** Granitgeröllhalde f
~ **crumbled to grit** zu Grus verwitterter Granit m
~-**gneiss** Granitgneis m
~-**greisen** Granitgreisen m
~-**pegmatite** Granitpegmatit m
~-**phyllonite** Granitphyllonit m
~-**porphyry** Granitporphyr m
~ **ridge** Granitrücken m
~ **tectonics** Granittektonik f
granitelle glimmerarmer, feinkörniger Granit m
granitic granitartig, granitisch, Granit...
~ **body** Granitstock m
~ **boulder** Granitblock m
~ **complex** Granitkomplex m
~ **crust** granitische Kruste f
~ **magma** Granitmagma n
~ **massif** Granitmassiv m
~ **off-shoot** Granittrum n
~ **rock** Gestein n der Granitgruppe
~ **stringer** Granitäderchen n
~ **system** granitisches System n, System n Quarz-Kalifeldspat-Albit-Anorthit-Wasser
~ **texture** granitische Struktur f

granitification

granitification *s.* granitization
granitiform granitförmig, granitähnlich
granitite Granitit *m*, Biotitgranit *m*
granitization Granitisation *f*, Granitisierung *f*
granitize/to in Granit umwandeln, granitisieren
granitlike *s.* granitic
granitoid[al] granitoid, granitähnlich
granitotrychytic *s.* ophitic
granoblastic granoblastisch
~ **texture** granoblastische Struktur *f*
granodiorite Granodiorit *m*
granofels Granofels *m*
granopatic *s.* granophyric
granophyre Granophyr *m*
granophyric granophyrisch
~ **texture** granophyrisches Gefüge *n*
granosphaerite Granosphärit *m*
grant Konzession *f*
grantsite Grantsit *m*, $(Na, Ca)_2V_6O_{16} \cdot 4H_2O$
granular körnig
~ **cementation** Kornzementierung *f* durch Porenlösungen
~ **chert** kompaktes körniges Kieselgestein *n*
~**-crystalline** grobkristallin, kristallinisch, körnig
~**-crystalline fracture** grobkörnige Bruchfläche *f*
~ **disintegration** körniger Zerfall *m*, Vergrusung *f*
~ **gravel** nicht zementierte Kieselablagerung *f*
~ **ice** *s.* firn
~ **limestone** körniger Kalkstein *m*
~ **opaque matter** körnige Opaksubstanz *f*, Feinmikrinit *m* (*Kohlenpetrografie*)
~ **ore** Graupenerz *n*
~ **quartz** *s.* quartzite
~ **shell** agglutinierte Schale *f*
~ **size** Korngröße *f*
~ **skeleton** Korngerüst *n*
~ **snow** *s.* spring snow
~ **texture** körnige Struktur *f* (*Korngröße über 2 mm Durchmesser in Sedimenten*)
~ **variation** Körnungsschwankung *f*
granularity Körnigkeit *f*, körnige Beschaffenheit *f*, Korngröße *f*
granulated gekörnt
granulation Körnung *f*
~ **curve** Körnungskurve *f*
granule Körnchen *n*
~ **roundstone** feiner Kies *m*
granulite Granulit *m*
~ **facies** Granulitfazies *f*
~ **gneiss** Granulitgneis *m*
granulitic granulitisch
~ **texture** granulitisches Gefüge *n*
granulitization Granulitbildung *f*, Granulitisierung *f*
granulometric analysis Korngrößenanalyse *f*, Korngrößenbestimmung *f*
~ **composition** Kornaufbau *m*, Kornzusammensetzung *f*

~ **curve** Korn[größen]verteilungskurve *f*
~ **facies** granulometrische Fazies *f*
~ **gauge** Korngrößenmeßgerät *n*
~ **gradation** Kornabstufung *f*
granulometry Granulometrie *f*, Korngrößenmessung *f*
granulose, granulous körnig; Körnchen tragend (*bei Fossilien*)
granulyte *s.* granulite
grape-shaped traubig
grapelike traubenartig
grapestone Grapestone *m* (*Karbonatgestein aus Lumps*)
grapevine drainage *s.* trellised drainage
graph Kurvendiagramm *n*
graphic[al] gold *s.* ~ tellurium
~ **granite** Schriftgranit *m*
~ **intergrowths** schriftgranitische Verwachsungen *fpl*
~ **measures** grafisch bestimmte Körnungskennwerte *mpl*
~ **representation** grafische Darstellung *f*
~ **tellurium** Schreiberz *n*, Sylvanit *m*, Weißgolderz *n*
~ **texture** grafisches Implikationsgefüge *n*, schriftgranitische Verwachsung *f*, Schriftstruktur *f*
graphite Graphit *m*, α-C
~ **gneiss** Graphitgneis *m*
~ **mica schist** Graphitglimmerschiefer *m*
~ **scale** Graphitschüppchen *n*
graphitic carbon graphitischer Kohlenstoff *m*, Graphit *m*
~ **gneiss** Graphitgneis *m*
~ **phyllite** Graphitphyllit *m*
~ **rock** Graphitgestein *n*
graphitiferous graphithaltig
graphitite *s.* shungite
graphitization Graphitbildung *f*, Graphitisierung *f*
graphitized coal graphitisierte Kohle *f*
graphitoid[al] graphitisch
grapholite, grapholith Tafelschiefer *m*, Griffelschiefer *m*, Tonschiefer *m* (*für Schreibgriffel*)
graphophyre Graphophyr *m*
graphophyric graphophyrisch
grapnel Fanghaken *m*, Glückshaken *m*
grapple Greifer *m*
graptolite Graptolith *m*
~**[-bearing] shale** Graptolithenschiefer *m*
graptolith *s.* graptolite
graptolitic facies Graptolithenfazies *f*
grass Gras *n*
~ **cover** Grasnarbe *f*
~**-covered plain** Steppe *f*
~ **roots** Rasensohle *f* (*Tagesoberfläche im bergmännischen Sinne*)
~ **steppe** Grassteppe *f*
~ **temperature** Erdbodentemperatur *f*
grassland Grasland *n*
~ **soil** Graslandboden *m*

gravity

grassy mound Grashügel *m*
~ **plain** Grasebene *f*
~ **savannah** Grassteppe *f (Afrika)*
~ **steppe** Grassteppe *f*
graticule 1. Okularnetz *n*; 2. Gradnetz *n*, Profilgitter *n*
grating constant Gitterkonstante *f*
~ **structure** Gitterstruktur *f*
gratonite Gratonit *m*, $9PbS \cdot 2As_2S_3$
graupel shower Graupelschauer *m*
grave wax s. hatchettite
gravel Kies *m*, Schotter *m*
~ **accretion** s. ~ envelope
~ **aggregate** Kieszuschlag[stoff] *m*
~ **bank (bar)** Kiesbank *f*
~ **beach** Kiesstrand *m*
~**-capped** kiesbedeckt, schotterbedeckt
~ **covering** Kiesdecke *f*, Schotterdecke *f*
~ **deposit** Kiesablagerung *f*, Schotterablagerung *f*
~ **desert** Kieswüste *f*, Geröllwüste *f*, Serir *m*
~ **detritus** Kiesschutt *m*
~ **envelope** Kiesschüttung *f*, Kieshülle *f (im Filterbrunnen)*
~ **fan** Schotterfächer *m*
~ **layer** 1. Kiesschicht *f*, Schotterschicht *f*; 2. Steinsohle *f* von Flußkiesen
~ **pack[ing]** s. ~ envelope
~ **pit** Kiesgrube *f*
~ **plant** Kiesaufbereitungsanlage *f*
~ **sand** Kiessand *m*
~ **sheet** Kiesdecke *f*, Schotterdecke *f*
~**-sheeted** kiesbedeckt, schotterbedeckt
~ **spread** Kiesdecke *f*, Schotterdecke *f*
~ **terrace** Schotterterrasse *f*
~ **trains** Kieswälle *mpl (im Flußbett)*
~ **wash** Kiesschutt *m*
gravelling Schotterung *f*
gravelly kiesartig, kieselig, kieshaltig, kiesig, grießig, sandig *(von Korngrößen)*
~ **detritus** Kiesschutt *m*
~ **layer** s. gravel layer
~ **soil** Kiesboden *m*
gravelstone 1. Kieselstein *m*; 2. Kies *m (als Korngröße)*
graveyard Friedhof *m*, Vergrabungsstelle *f (für radioaktiven Abfall)*
gravimeter Gravimeter *n*
gravimetric analysis Gewichtsanalyse *f*
~ **measurement** gravimetrische Messung *f*, Schweremessung *f*
~ **method** gravimetrisches Verfahren *n*
gravimetry Gravimetrie *f*
gravitation Gravitation *f*, Schwerkraft *f*
~ **constant** Gravitationskonstante *f*
~ **water** Sickerwasser *n*, Senkwasser *n*
gravitational Gravitations..., Schwere...
~ **anomaly** Schwereanomalie *f*
~ **astronomy** Himmelsmechanik *f*
~ **attraction** Schwereanziehung *f*
~ **constant** Gravitationskonstante *f*
~ **crystal settling** gravitative Kristallseigerung *f*

~ **differentiation** Gravitationsdifferentiation *f*
~ **effect** Schwerewirkung *f*
~ **field** s. gravity field
~ **flow** Gravitationsströmung *f*
~ **force** Gravitation *f*, Schwerkraft *f*; Gravitationsfließkraft *f*
~ **mass** Schweremasse *f*
~ **method** Schwerkraftverfahren *n*
~ **method of prospecting** gravimetrische Lagerstättenforschung *f*
~ **parameter** Gravitationsparameter *m*
~ **potential** Gravitationspotential *n*, Schwerepotential *n*
~ **prospecting** gravimetrisches Schürfen *n*
~ **pull** Schwereanziehung *f*
~ **settler** Gleichfälligkeitsapparat *m*
~ **sliding (slip)** Gravitationsgleitung *f*, Abgleitung *f* infolge Schwerkraftwirkung
~ **tectonics** Gravitationstektonik *f*
~ **wave** Gravitationswelle *f*
gravitative s. gravitational
gravitometer Schweremesser *m*
gravity 1. Gravitation *f*, Schwerkraft *f*; Schwerebeschleunigung *f*, Fallbeschleunigung *f*; 2. *(Am)* spezifisches Gewicht *n* von Erdöl
~ **acceleration** Schwerebeschleunigung *f*, Fallbeschleunigung *f*
~ **anomaly** Schwereanomalie *f*
~ **attraction** Schwereanziehung *f*
~ **balance** Drehwaage *f*
~ **centre** Schwerpunkt *m*
~ **change** Schwereschwankung *f*
~ **compaction** Sedimentkompaktion *f (durch Auflast)*
~ **concentration** Gravitationsaufbereitung *f*
~ **core** Schwerelotkern *m*
~ **dam** Schwergewichtsmauer *f*, Gewichtssperre *f*
~ **depletion** s. ~ drainage
~ **determination** Schweremessung *f*
~ **distribution** Schwerkraftverteilung *f*
~ **drainage** Schwerkraftentwässerung *f*, Schwerkraftdrainage *f*
~ **drainage of oil** Schwerkraftentölung *f*
~ **effect** Schwerewirkung *f*
~ **exploration** Schwereuntersuchung *f*
~ **fault** Abschiebung *f*
~ **field** Gravitationsfeld *n*, Schwerefeld *n*
~ **field measurement** Schwerefeldmessung *f*
~ **flow** Schwerkraftströmung *f*
~ **force** Gravitationskraft *f*
~ **fractionation** gravitative Fraktionierung (Differentiation) *f (eines Magmas)*
~ **gradient** Schweregradient *m*, Schwerkraftgradient *m*, Schwerkraftgefälle *n*
~ **measurement** Schweremessung *f*
~ **meter** Gravimeter *n*
~ **meter surveying** Gravimetervermessung *f*
~ **potential** Gravitationspotential *n*, Schwerepotential *n*
~ **pull** Schwereanziehung *f*
~ **scree** Fallschutt *m*

gravity

~ **segregation** Gravitationsseigerung f, Schwerkrafttrennung f
~ **sinking** gravitatives Absinken n
~ **slide nappes** gravitative Gleitdecken fpl
~ **solution** Schwerelösung f (für Schwermineralanalyse)
~ **spring** Schwerkraftquelle f
~ **station** Station f für Schweremessungen
~ **variometer** Gravitationsvariometer n
~ **waves** Schwerewellen fpl
gray antimony s. stibnite
~ **bands** Grausandstein m; feingeschichteter Sandstein m
~ **body radiation** Strahlung f eines grauen Körpers
~ **cobalt** s. smaltite
~ **copper [ore]** s. tetrahedrite
~ **durain** sporenarmer Durit m (Steinkohlenmikrolithotyp)
~ **haematite** s. haematite
~ **lime** Graukalk m
~ **manganese [ore]** s. manganite
~ **post** (sl) grauer Sandstein m
~ **salt pelite** grauer Salzton m (Zechstein)
~ **soil** Bleicherde f
~ **solodic soil** grauer Solod m
~ **warp soil** grauer Alluvialboden m
grayheads zylindrische Klüfte fpl (Australien)
grays silifizierter Sandstein m
graywacke Grauwacke f
~ **sandstone** Grauwackensandstein m
~ **slate** Grauwackenschiefer m
grayweather blockförmiger Rückstand m erodierter Tertiärschichten
grazing Tierfraß m
~ **trace** Weidespur f (Ichnologie)
greasy fettig
~ **gold** Feingold n
~ **lustre** Fettglanz m
~ **quartz** Milchquarz m
great circle Großkreis m (im Gefügediagramm)
~ **fireball** großer Bolid m (Meteor)
~ **rubble stone** Feldstein m
greatest head flow höchster Zufluß m (zur Talsperre)
green Rasen m
green grubenfeucht
~ **carbonate of copper** s. malachite
~ **clay** magerer Ton m
~ **copper ore** s. malachite
~ **copperas** s. melanterite
~ **earth** 1. s. glauconite; 2. s. chlorite
~ **feldspar** Smaragdspat m, Amazonit m
~ **iron ore** s. dufrenite
~ **john** (sl) grüner Flußspat m
~ **lead ore** Grünbleierz n
~ **marble** Serpentin m (Handelsbezeichnung)
~ **mineral** s. malachite
~ **mud** Grünschlick m
~ **ore** Roherz n
~ **sand** Glaukonitsand m, Grünsand m
~ **sand marl** Glaukonitmergel m

~ **sandstone** Grünsandstein m
~ **stone** Grünstein m; Schalstein m (Diabastuff)
~ **strength** Naßfestigkeit f
~ **vitriol** Melanterit m, Eisenvitriol n (s.a. melanterite)
greenalite Greenalith m, $(Fe^{..},Fe^{...})_{<6}[(OH)_8|Si_4O_{10}]$
greenhouse effect Gewächshauseffekt m (der Atmosphäre)
Greenland spar Eisstein m, Kryolith m (s.a. cryolite)
greenockite Greenockit m, Kadmiumsulfid n, β-CdS
greenschist Grünschiefer m
greenstone Grünstein m, Schalstein m (Diabastuff)
~ **belt** Ophiolithgürtel m
~ **tuff** Grünsteintuff m
Greenwich civil time mittlere Greenwich-Ortszeit f
~ **mean time** Greenwich-Zeit f, Weltzeit f
~ **meridian** Greenwich-Meridian m, Nullmeridian m
~ **sidereal time** Greenwich-Sternzeit f
greigite Greigit n, Fe_3S_4
greisen Greisen m
greisening, greisenization Greisenbildung f, Vergreisenung f
greisenize/to vergreisenen
grenate s. garnet
grenatite s. staurolite
grenu granitisch, körnig
Grenville s. Grenvillian
~ **folding** Grenville-Tektogenese f (Oberpräkambrium in Nordamerika)
Grenvillian Grenville n (Oberpräkambrium in Nordamerika, Grenville-Provinz)
grewt als Leithorizont bei Prospektionsarbeiten verwendeter farbiger Boden
grey ...s. gray ...
Grey Beds Grey Beds fpl (Karn in Nordamerika)
grid Gradnetz n
~ **effect** Interpolationseffekt m
~ **of parallels and meridians** Gradnetz n
~ **pattern** Faltengitter n
~ **residual** 1. Restfeld n; 2. Interpolationsfehler m
~ **smoothing** Glätten n (einer Karte)
~ **variation** magnetische Mißweisung f
gridded map Gitternetzkarte f
gridiron drainage Dränage f in Rechteckform
~ **twinning** s. crossed twinning
grief stem Mitnehmerstange f, Kelly n
griff steile Bergschlucht f
griffithite Griffithit m (Varietät von Saponit)
Griffith's failure theory Griffithsche Bruchtheorie f
~ **theory** Griffithsche Theorie f
grikes Schratten pl, Karren pl
grind [down]/to abschleifen (durch Gletscher)

grinding 1. Abschleifen *n (durch Gletscher)*; 2. Mahlung *f*, Vermahlung *f*, Zerreiben *n (Aufbereitung)*
~ **action** abscheuernde Wirkung *f*
~ **body** Mahlkörper *m (Aufbereitung)*
~ **of ore** Erzvermahlung *f*
~ **powder** Schleifmittel *n*
~ **residue** Schleifschmant *m*
~ **ridge** Kauleiste *f*
~ **scratch** Schleifkratzer *m*
grindlet kleiner Graben *m*
grindstone Schleifstein *m*, Wetzstein *m*
~ **grit** Mühlsandstein *m*
griphite Griphit *m*, (Mn, Na, Ca)₃(Al, Mn)₂[PO₃(OH, F)]₃
griquaite Griquait *m*
grist Feinheit *f (des Korns)*
grit Grit *m*, Kies *m*, Kiessand *m*, Grobsand *m*, grobkörniger Sandstein *m*, Grus *m*; Grieß *m*, Splitt *m*, Flußsand *m*
gritless mud gritfreier Schlamm *m*
gritstone grobkörniger Sandstein *m*, Kristallsandstein *m*
grittiness kiesige Beschaffenheit *f*, Sandhaltigkeit *f*
gritty grittig, kiesig, kiesartig, [rauh-]sandig, grießig
~ **soil** Grusboden *m*
grizzle minderwertige pyritische Kohle *f*
groin *(Am) s.* groyne
groining *(Am) s.* groyning
gronan lode mit zersetztem Granit gefüllte Kluft *f*
groove [out]/to auskolken
groove Riefelung *f*, Kannelierung *f*, Riefe *f*, Furche *f*, Rinne *f*, Rille *f*
~ **cast** 1. Schleifmarke *f*, Rillenmarke *f*, Driftmarke *f*, Driftspur *f*; 2. Rinnenausfüllung *f*, Rinnenausguß *m*
~ **lake** Rinnensee *m*
~-**toothed** kerbzähnig
grooved gerillt, gerieft, furchig, rinnenförmig; schwach zerkart
~ **lava** geschrammte Lava *f*
grospydite Grospydit *m (Grossular-Pyrop-Disthen-Gestein)*
gross oil rohes Erdöl *n (nach dem Ablassen des mitgeförderten Wassers)*
~ **production** Gesamtproduktion *f*, Bruttoproduktion *f*
~ **rainfall** Niederschlagsmenge *f (oberhalb der Vegetation)*
grouan Grus *m*, Kleinkies *m*
ground 1. Erdboden *m*, Erde *f*; 2. Grund *m*, Boden *m*, Feld *n*; Gelände *n*; 3. Grund *m*, Basis *f*, Nullpunkt *m* Nullpotential *n*
~/**above** oberirdisch, über Tage
~ **air** Bodenluft *f*
~ **anchor** Grundanker *m*
~ **avalanche** Grundlawine *f*
~/**below** unter Tage
~ **coal** Liegendkohle *f*, liegende Kohle *f*
~ **conditions** Gebirgsverhältnisse *npl*, Vorbeanspruchung *f des Gebirges*
~ **consolidation** natürliche Baugrundverdichtung *f*
~ **current** *s.* earth's current
~ **data** Bodendaten *pl (Daten über die Beschaffenheit der Objekte am Erdboden zur Verifizierung von Fernerkundungsdaten)*
~ **density** Bodendichte *f*
~ **draining** Ableitung *f* von unterirdischem Wasser
~ **failure** Grundbruch *m*
~ **fog** Bodennebel *m*
~ **frost** Bodenfrost *m*
~ **gas** Bodenluft *f*, Bodengas *n*
~ **heat** Erdwärme *f*
~ **heat flow** Bodenwärmefluß *m*, Wärmefluß *m*
~ **humidity** Bodenfeuchtigkeit *f*
~ **ice** Grundeis *n*
~-**ice mound** *s.* pingo
~ **level** Geländeoberfläche *f*
~-**living forms (organisms)** Benthos *n*
~ **mass** Grundmasse *f*, Matrix *f*
~ **moraine** Grundmoräne *f*
~ **movement** Gebirgsbewegung *f*
~ **nadir** Geländenadir *m*
~ **noise** seismischer Störpegel *m*
~ **photogrammetry** Erdbildmessung *f*, Geofotogrammetrie *f*
~ **plan** Grundriß *m*
~ **point of control** Festpunkt *m*, Fixpunkt *m*
~ **pressure** Bodendruck *m*
~ **range** horizontaler Abstand des Bodenobjekts von der Bodenspur des Flugzeugs bzw. Satelliten
~ **receiving station** bodengebundene Empfangsstation *f (z.B. für Daten der Satellitenfernerkundung)*
~ **roll** Oberflächenwelle *f*, Roller *m (Seismik)*
~ **section** Geländeschnitt *m*
~ **sector** Geländeausschnitt *m*
~ **submergence (subsidence)** Bodensenkung *f*
~ **surface** Tagesoberfläche *f*
~ **survey** Geländeaufnahme *f*, Terrainaufnahme *f*, Grundaufnahme *f*
~ **temperature** Bodentemperatur *f*
~ **track** Bodenspur *f (z.B. des Flugzeugs oder Satelliten)*
~ **triangulation** terrestrische Triangulation *f*
~ **truth** Daten bzw. Informationen über die tatsächlichen Gegebenheiten am Boden zur Eichung bzw. Verifizierung von Fernerkundungsdaten
~ **unrest** Bodenerschütterung *f*, Bodenunruhe *f*
~-**up core** zermahlener Kern *m*
~ **vegetation** Bodenvegetation *f*
~ **verification** Bestätigung *f* durch Bodendaten, Bodenbeleg *m (Fernerkundung)*
~ **vibration** Bodenerschütterung *f*
~ **water** Grundwasser *n*

ground

~-water artery Grundwasserader *f*
~-water balance Grundwasserbilanz *f*
~-water balance resource Grundwasserbilanzvorrat *m*
~-water basin Grundwasserbecken *n*, Grundwassereinzugsgebiet *n*
~-water bottom Grundwassersohle *f*
~-water captation Grundwasserfassung *f*
~-water catchment area Grundwassernährgebiet *n*
~-water check borehole Grundwasserbeobachtungsrohr *n*
~-water contour Grundwassergleiche *f*
~-water contour map Hydroisohypsenplan *m*
~-water dating Grundwasseraltersdatierung *f*
~-water deliverability Grundwasserliefervermögen *n*
~-water depletion Grundwasseraufbrauch *m*
~-water deposit Grundwasserlagerstätte *f*
~-water deposit resource Grundwasserlagerstättenvorrat *m*
~-water discharge Grundwasserabfluß *m*
~-water drainage area Grundwassernährgebiet *n*
~ water entering sewers zusitzendes Grundwasser *n*
~-water exploration Grundwassererkundung *f*; Grundwassergewinnung *f*
~-water flow Grundwasserströmung *f*
~-water flow in sedimentation basins Sedimentationsdynamik *f*
~-water hydrology Grundwasserkunde *f*
~-water inventory Grundwasserbestandsaufnahme *f*
~-water isohypse Grundwasserisohypse *f*
~-water level Grundwasserspiegel *m*; Grundwasserstand *m*
~-water level in a gauge Standrohrspiegelhöhe *f* des Grundwassers
~-water lowering Grundwasser[ab]senkung *f*
~-water lowering installation Grundwasser[ab]senkungsanlage *f*
~-water management Grundwasserbewirtschaftung *f*
~-water measuring point Grundwassermeßstelle *f*
~-water mound Grundwasserberg *m*
~-water movement Grundwasserbewegung *f*
~-water observation Grundwasserbeobachtung *f*
~-water observation gauge Grundwasserbeobachtungsrohr *n*
~-water observation network Grundwasserbeobachtungsnetz *n*
~-water observation well Grundwasserbeobachtungsrohr *n*
~-water occurrence Grundwasservorkommen *n*
~-water origin Grundwasserherkunft *f*
~-water pollution Grundwasserverunreinigung *f*
~-water preliminary exploration Grundwasservorerkundung *f*

~-water prospecting Grundwassererkundung *f*; Grundwassersuche *f*
~-water protection Grundwasserschutz *m*
~-water protection area Grundwasserschutzgebiet *n*
~-water recharge Grundwasserneubildung *f*; Grundwasserdargebot *n*
~-water regime Grundwasserregime *n*
~-water resource out of balance Grundwasseraußerbilanzvorrat *m*
~-water resources Grundwasserressourcen *fpl*, Grundwasservorräte *mpl*
~-water resources prognosis Grundwasservorratsprognose *f*
~-water ridges Grundwasserkuppeln *fpl*
~-water runoff Grundwasserabfluß *m*
~-water sheet Grundwassermächtigkeit *f*
~-water storage Grundwasserspeicherung *f*
~-water storeys Grundwasserstockwerke *npl*
~-water surface contour Grundwassergleiche *f*
~-water swell Grundwasserstau *m*
~-water table Grundwasserspiegel *m*
~-water table fluctuation Grundwasserspiegelschwankung *f*
~-water thickness Grundwassermächtigkeit *f*
~-water trench Grundwassertal *n*
~-water use Grundwasserbedarf *m*
~ wave Bodenwelle *f*, Oberflächenwelle *f*
grounding Erdung *f*
grounds *s.* ground coal
group Gruppe *f (lithostratigrafische Einheit)*
~ interval Geophongruppenabstand *m*
~ of beddings (beds) Schichtengruppe *f*, Schichtenkomplex *m*
~ of lodes Gangzug *m*, Ganggruppe *f*
~ of strata *s.* ~ of beddings
grouping 1. Gruppieren *n (von Schüssen)*; 2. Bündeln *n (von Geophonen)*
~ of wells Nestbohren *n*
groups/by nesterweise
grout under pressure/to injizieren, einpressen, verpressen
grout Zementmilch *f*
~ acceptance Zementaufnahme *f* bei Injektion
~ curtain Dichtungsschürze *f*, Dichtungsgürtel *m*, Injektionsschleier *m*
~ hole Injektionsloch *n*, Einpreßloch *n*, Verpreßloch *n*
grouted cut-off Abdichtungsschleier *m*
grouting acceptance *s.* grout acceptance
groutite Groutit *m*, α-MnOOH
grovesite Grovesit *m*, (Mn, Mg, Al)$_6$[(OH)$_8$(Si, Al)$_4$O$_{10}$]
growan zersetzter Granit *m*
growing season Wachstumsperiode *f*
growler in Wasser treibendes Eisstück *n*
grown in situ autochthon
growth curve Wachstumskurve *f*
~ fabric Wachstumsgefüge *n*
~-framework porosity primäre Gerüstporosität *f*

~ **line** Anwachslinie f, Zuwachslinie f
~ **of water** im Gebirge angesammelte Wassermassen fpl
~-**promoting** wachstumsfördernd
~ **rings** Wachstumsringe mpl
~ **spiral** Wachstumsspirale f
~ **step** Wachstumstreppe f
~ **zoning** Wachstumszonung f
groyne/to Buhnen bauen
groyne Buhne f
~ **head** Buhnenkopf m
groyning Buhnenbau m
grubben (sl) s. gubbin
gruel Kohle f
gruff Grube f, Schacht m
grumous texture sparitische Fleckenstruktur f (in Karbonatgesteinen)
grunerite Grunerit m, (Fe, Mg)$_7$[OH|Si$_4$O$_{11}$]$_2$
grünlingite s. joseite
grus, grush, gruss Grus m
grykes Schratten pl, Karren pl
guadalcazarite Guadalcazarit m, (Hg, Zn) (S, Se)
Guadalupian Guadalupien n (Perm in Nordamerika)
gual (sl) Kohle f (Irland)
guanajuatite Guanajuatit m, Selenwismutglanz m, Frenzelit m, Bi$_2$(Se, S)$_3$
guano Guano m
guard electrode Abschirmelektrode f
guarinite Guarinit m, Ca$_2$NaZr[(F, O)$_2$|Si$_2$O$_7$]
gubbin (sl) Toneisenstein m
gudmundite Gudmundit m, FeSbS
guejarite Guejarit m (s.a. chalcostibite)
guerinite Guerinit m, Ca$_5$H$_2$[AsO$_4$]$_4$·9H$_2$O
guest element Gastelement n
gugiaite Gugiait m, Ca$_2$Be[Si$_2$O$_7$]
guhr Kieselgur f
Guiana shield Guyanaschild m
Guianis-Amazonis Brasilianische Masse f
guide bed Leitschicht f
~ **column** Leitrohr n (Bohrtechnik)
~ **fossil** Leitfossil n
~ **mineral** Leitmineral n
~ **seam** Leitflöz n
guided wave geführte Welle f (Seismologie)
guildite Guildit m, Cu$_3$Fe$_4$[(OH)$_4$|(SO$_4$)$_7$·15H$_2$O
guilleminite Guilleminit m, Ba[(UO$_2$)$_3$|(OH)$_4$(SeO$_3$)$_2$]·3H$_2$O
gulch (Am) tiefe Schlucht f, Talriß m; Murtobel m, Tobel m, Wildbachschlucht f
~ **gold** Seifengold n
gulf 1. Meeresbucht f, Meer[es]busen m, Golf m; 2. Gangerzanreicherung f
~ **of ore** reicher Erzfall m
Gulf Stream Golfstrom m
~ **Supergroup** Gulf-Hauptgruppe f (Oberkreide in Nordamerika, Golf-Gebiet)
gull 1. Einsturzstruktur f; 2. mit Nachfall gefüllter Gang m
gullet Kluft f, Schlucht f, Rösche f
gully/to zerracheln

gully Gießbachbett n, Erosionsrinne f, Rachel f, Wasserriß m; Brandungsschlucht f; Priel m; Murtobel m, Tobel m, Wildbachschlucht f
~ **clints** Rinnenkarren pl
~ **erosion** rinnenartige Erosion f, Grabenerosion f, Zerrachelung f
~ **glacier** Kargletscher m
gullying rinnenartige Erosion f, Grabenerosion f, Zerrachelung f, Zerschluchtung f, Auswaschung f, Wasserrißbildung f
gulph of ore s. gulf of ore
gum Kohlenklein n
gumbo haftender Schieferton m, zäher, klebriger Ton m
~ **clay** rezenter Schlickerton m
gumbotil verwitterter Geschiebelehm m
gummite Gummit m, Gummierz n, rotes Pechuran n (Verwitterungsprodukt von Uraninit und anderen Uranmineralen)
gun-applied concrete Spritzbeton m, Torkretbeton m
~ **perforation** Schußperforieren n, Kugelperforation f
gunite/to torkretieren
gunite Spritzbeton m, Torkretbeton m
gunned concrete Spritzbeton m, Torkretbeton m
gunningite Gunningit m, Zn[SO$_4$]·H$_2$O
Günz [Drift] Günz-Eiszeit f, Günz-Kaltzeit f (Pleistozän, Alpen)
~-**Mindel [Interval]** Günz-Mindel-Warmzeit f, Günz-Mindel-Interglazial n (Pleistozän, Alpen)
gurmy Grubensohle f
gurt Wasserseige f; Wasserrösche f
gush/to selbsttätig laufen, eruptiv ausfließen, hervorströmen, heftig ausströmen
~ **forth** heraussprudeln
~ **up** hochquellen
gusher s. ~ well
~ **of natural gas** Erdgasquelle f
~ **oil well** Ölspringer m
~ **well** Springer m, Springquelle f, Springsonde f, Sprudelbohrung f
gushing spring springende Quelle f
~ **well** s. gusher well
gust Bö f, Stoßwind m
~ **meter** Böenmesser m
~ **of wind** Windstoß m
~ **recorder** Böenschreiber m
gustiness Böigkeit f
gusty böig
gut/to Reicherzpartien abbauen
gut schmale Verbindungsrinne f, Wasserrinne f
gutsevichite Gutsevichit m, (Al, Fe)$_3$[(OH)$_3$|(P, V)O$_4$)$_2$]·8H$_2$O
gutta-percha clay klebriger Ton m
gutter Rinne f
~ **valley** Tunneltal n, Rinnental n (Glazialform)
guy anchor Erdanker m
~ **lines** Abspannseile npl

guyot

guyot Guyot m *(abgestumpfter Tiefseeberg)*
gwag abgeworfener Grubenbau m *(Cornwall)*
gwythyen Mineralgang m *(Wales)*
gymnosolen s. stromatolite
gymnosperms Gymnospermen npl, Nacktsamer mpl
gypseous gipsartig; gipshaltig, gipsführend
~ **crust** Gipskruste f
~ **marl** Gipsmergel m
~ **soil** Gipserde f, Gipsgur f
~ **spar** Marienglas n
gypsiferous gipshaltig, gipsführend
~ **dolomite** gipsführender Dolomit m
~ **mudstone** Tonstein m mit Gips
gypsification Umwandlung f von Anhydrit zu Gips
gypsinate mit Gips zementiert
gypsite Gypsit m, feinporiges Gipsgestein n
gypsitic 1. gipshaltig; 2. s. aggregal
gypsolith, gypsolyte Gipsgestein n
gypsstone gipsreiches Gestein n
gypsum Gips m, $Ca[SO_4] \cdot 2H_2O$
~-**bearing** gipshaltig, gipsführend *(s.a. gypsiferous)*
~ **body** Gipsstock m
~ **bulges** Gipsaufblühungen fpl
~ **cave** Gipskarsthöhle f
~ **crust soil** Gipskrustenboden m
~ **deposit** Gipslager n
~ **karst** Gipskarst m
~ **rock** Rohgips m
~ **test plate** Gipsplättchen n
Gypsum Spring Formation Gypsum Spring-Formation f, Carmel-Formation f *(Dogger in Nordamerika)*
gyratory breaker Kreiselbrecher m, Rundbrecher m
gyrolite Gyrolith m, $Ca_2[Si_4O_{10}] \cdot 4H_2O$
gyroscope Kreisel[kompaß] m
gyrosine compass Erdinduktionskompaß m
gyttja Gyttja f
Gzhelian [Stage] Gzhell-Stufe f *(hangende Stufe des Oberkarbons in Osteuropa)*

H

H horizon H-Horizont m *(Boden, Humusschicht)*
habit Habitus m
habitat Standort m
habitus Habitus m
hachure Bergschraffierung f *(auf Landkarten)*
hachuring Lavierung f *(einer Landkarte)*
hacking 1. mildes Gebirge n *(Tunnelbau);* 2. Hackboden m *(Erdbau)*
hackly fracture splittriger Bruch m
hackmanite Hackmanit m *(Varietät von Sodalith)*
hadal zone hadale Zone f *(Bodenzone im Bereich der Tiefseegräben)*
hade/to einfallen

hade Einfallen n; Tonnlage f
~ **of the fault** Fallwinkel m der Verwerfung
~-**slip fault** gewöhnlicher Sprung m
hading tonnlägig
~ **against the dip** widersinnig fallend
~-**against-the-dip fault** widersinnig fallende Verwerfung f
~ **shaft** tonnlägiger Schacht m
~ **with the dip** rechtsinnig fallend
~-**with-the-dip fault** rechtsinnig fallende Verwerfung f
haeggite Häggit m, $V_2O_2(OH)_3$
haemachate Blutachat m
haemafibrite Haemafibrit m, $Mn_3[(OH)_3|AsO_4] \cdot H_2O$
haemataceous 1. haematithaltig; 2. s. integral
haematite Haematit m, Eisenglanz m, Specularit m, Roteisenstein m, Fe_2O_3
~ **ore** Haematiterz n
~ **pig iron** Haematitroheisen n
~ **rose** Eisenrose f
haematitic 1. haematithaltig; 2. s. aggregal
haematitization Haematitisierung f
haematize/to haematitisieren
haematitogelite s. haematogelite
haematogelite Haematogelit m *(kolloidales Eisenferrioxid im Bauxit)*
haematolite Haematolith m, $(Mn, Mg, Fe)_5[(OH)_7|AsO_4]$
haematophanite Haematophanit m, $4PbO \cdot Pb(Cl,OH)_2 \cdot 2Fe_2O_3$
haematostibiite Haematostibiit m, $8(Mn, Fe)O \cdot Sb_2O_5$
hafnium Hafnium n, Hf
hag 1. Durchstich m, Graben m *(Schottland);* 2. Moorloch n
hagendorfite Hagendorfit m, $(Na, Ca)_2(Fe, Mn)_3[PO_4]_3$
haiarn Eisen n *(Wales)*
haidingerite Haidingerit m, $CaH[AsO_4] \cdot H_2O$
hail Hagel m
~ **clouds** Hagelwolken fpl
~ **imprints** Hageleindrücke mpl
~ **shower** Hagelschauer m
hailsquall Hagelschauer m
hailstone Hagelkorn n, Schloße f
hailstorm Hagelschauer m, Hagelsturm m, Hagelschlag m, Hagelwetter n
hainite Hainit m *(nadliges Na-, Ca-, Ti-, Zr-Silikat)*
hair crack Haarriß m
~ **perthite** Haarperthit m
~ **pyrite** s. millerite
~ **salt** nadelförmiger Epsomit m
hairlike crystal Trichit m
hairline crack Haarriß m
hairpin synclinal fold Muldenschluß m
hairy mammoth wollhaariges Mammut n
haiweeite Haiweeit m, $Ca[(UO_2)_2|(Si_2O_5)_3] \cdot 4H_2O$
half bog soil anmooriger Boden m
~-**crystalline** halbkristallinisch
~-**edge seam** Flöz n von 45° Neigung

hardening

~-klippe Halbklippe f *(Tektonik)*
~-life [period] Halbwert[s]zeit f
~ moon Halbmond m
~ space Halbraum m
~ tide Mittelwasser n
~ time Halbwert[s]zeit f
~ window Halbfenster n *(Tektonik)*
halide Halogenid n, Haloidsalz n, Halogenderivat n
~ of silver Silberhalogen n
halidification Salzbildung f
halistas tiefe Löcher npl im Meeresboden
halistase Halistase f
halite Halit m, Steinsalz n, NaCl
halitic halitisch, steinsalzhaltig
halitite Halitit m
hall Halle f, Saal m, Kammer f
hälleflinta Hälleflint m *(Porphyroidgestein)*
hallerite Hallerit m *(Li-Paragonit)*
Hallian [Stage] Hallien n *(marine Stufe, Pleistozän in Nordamerika)*
hallig Hallig f
hallite Hallit m *(Vermiculit)*
halloysite Halloysit m, $Al_4[(OH)_8|Si_4O_{10}](H_2O)_4$
halmyro[ly]sis Halmyrolyse f, submarine Verwitterung f
halo Halo m, Lichthof m
~ formation Lichthofbildung f
halobios Leben n im marinen Milieu
halocline Halokline f *(Zone in einem geschichteten Wasserkörper, in der sich die Dichte infolge einer Veränderung des Salzgehalts rasch ändert)*
halogen Halogen n, Salzbildner m
halogenous halogen, salzbildend
~ deposit marine Salzlagerstätte f
haloid salzähnlich
~ salt Haloidsalz n
halokinetic halokinetisch, salztektonisch
halometry Salzgehaltsmessung f
halomorphic soil Salzboden m
halophilic halophil
halophytes Halophyten mpl, Salzpflanzen fpl
halophytic vegetation Salzbodenvegetation f
halotrichite Halotrichit m, $FeAl_2[SO_4]_4 \cdot 22H_2O$
halurgite Halurgit m, $Mg_2[B_4O_5(OH)_4]_2 \cdot H_2O$
halvan, halving Pocherz n; stark verunreinigtes Erz n *(Cornwall)*
hambergite Hambergit m, $Be_2[OH|Bo_3]$
Hamilton Group Hamilton-Gruppe f *(Devon in Nordamerika)*
hamlet Weiler m
hammada Hammada f, Steinwüste f, Felswüste f *(Sahara)*
hammarite Hammarit m, $2PbS \cdot Cu_2S \cdot 2Bi_2S_3$
hammer and wedge Schlegel m und Eisen n
~ blow Hammerschlag m, Schlag m mit dem Hammer
~-down of the hole schlagendes Großlochbohren n *(bei dem das Schlagwerk unmittelbar dem Bohrkopf folgt)*
~ drill Bohrhammer m, Tauchhammer m

~ drilling Stoßbohren n
~ reflection seismics Hammerschlagseismik f
hammock s. hummock
~ structure zwei Flächensysteme, die sich unter spitzem Winkel schneiden
hanaways Pocherz n, Pochgänge mpl
hancockite Hancockit m, $(Ca, Pb, Sr, Mn)_2(Al, Fe, Mn)_3[O|OH|SiO_4|Si_2O_7]$
hand auger Handbohrer m *(für Bodenproben)*
~ chisel Handmeißel m, Beitel m
~ displacement meter Setzdehnungsmesser m
~ dressing Handscheidung f
~-drilled well Handbohrung f
~ drilling Handbohren n
~ lens Lupe f
~ picking Klaubearbeit f
~-sorted ore handgeklaubtes Erz n
~ sorting Handscheidung f
~ specimen Handstück n
~ testing screen Handprüfsieb n
hanging Hangendes n
~ beds Hangendschichten fpl
~ bog Gehängemoor n
~ compass Hängekompaß m
~ glacier Hängegletscher m
~ layer Hangendes n
~ trap Ölfalle f im abgesunkenen Flügel einer Verwerfung
~ valley Hängetal n
~ wall Hangendes n
~ water Haftwasser n
hanksite Hanksit m, $KNa_{22}[Cl|(CO_3)_2|(SO_4)_9]$
hannayite Hannayit m, $(NH_4)_2Mg_3H_4[PO_4]_4 \cdot 8H_2O$
haradaite Haradait m, $SrV[Si_2O_7] \cdot H_2O$
hard bottom Meeresboden m ohne unverfestigte Sedimentdecke
~ brown coal Hartbraunkohle f
~ chilled steel shot Hartschrot n (m) *(Bohrtechnik)*
~ coal Steinkohle f
~-coal-bearing strata flözführendes Steinkohlengebirge n
~ facing Hartmetallbesatz m *(Bohrkronen)*
~-facing metal Hartmetall n
~ ground 1. Hartgrund m; 2. hartes Gebirge n
~ mineral festes Mineral n *(im Gegensatz zu flüssigem Mineral)*
~ rime Rauhfrost m
~ rock 1. Festgestein n, Hartgestein n; 2. harte Phosphoritbänder npl
~ roof gesundes Hangendes n
~ seat s. seat rock
~ spar s. 1. corundum; 2. andalusite
~ stone Hartgestein n
~ stony ground fester steiniger Boden m
~ water hartes Wasser n
harden/to erhärten
hardened 1. erhärtet; 2. verharscht
~ horizon Verdichtungshorizont m *(Boden)*
hardening 1. Erhärtung f; 2. Verharschung f
~ agent Härter m
~ process Erhärtungsprozeß m

hardness

hardness Härte f
~ number Härtewert m, Härtezahl f
~ of water Härte f des Wassers
~ scale Härteskala f
hardpan 1. harte, verkittete Akkumulate npl (von Sanden und Kiesen); 2. Verdichtungshorizont m (Boden); 3. Ortstein m; 4. Konkretionskruste f; Felspanzerbildung f
hardway Teilbarkeitsrichtung in Plutoniten senkrecht zu grain und rift
hardystonite Hardystonit m, $Ca_2Zn[Si_2O_7]$
harkerite Harkerit m, $Ca_{12}Mg_5Al[Cl(OH)_2|(BO_3)_5(CO_3)_6(SiO_4)_4] \cdot H_2O$
harmful substance Schadstoff m
harmonic distortion Frequenzverzerrung f
~ oscillation harmonische Schwingung f
~ system of working harmonischer Abbau m
~ trend harmonischer Trend m, Fourier-Trend m, Trend m in trigonometrischen Funktionen
harmotome Harmotom m, $Ba[Al_2Si_6O_{16}] \cdot 6H_2O$
harpolith Harpolith m (magmatischer Intrusionstyp)
harsh desert tote Wüste f
harstigite Harstigit m, $(Ca, Mn, Mg)_8Al_2[(OH)_4|(Si_2O_7)_3]$
hartine s. hartite
hartite Hartit m, $C_{20}H_{34}$
hartsalz Hartsalz f
harttite Harttit m, $(Sr, Ca)Al_3[(OH)_6|(SO_4, PO_4)_2]$
harzburgite Harzburgit m (ultrabasisches Gestein)
hassock structure s. glide bedding
hastingsite Hastingsit m, $NaCa_2Fe_4(Al, Fe)[(OH, F)_2|Al_2Si_6O_{22}]$
hastite Hastit m, $CoSe_2$
hatch/to schraffieren
hatchettine s. hatchettite
hatchettite Hatchettin m (Erdwachs)
hatchettolite Hatchettolith m, U-Pyrochlor m
hatching Schraffierung f
hatchite Hatchit m (Th-Pb-Sulfoarsenit)
hauchecornite Hauchecornit m, $(Ni, Co)_9(Bi, Sb)_2S_8$
hauerite Hauerit m, MnS_2
haulage Streckenförderung f
~ horizon Fördersohle f
~ road Abbauförderstrecke f
hausmannite Hausmannit m, Schwarzmanganerz n, $MnMn_2O_4$
Hauterivian [Stage] Hauterive n, Hauterivien n (Stufe der Unterkreide)
haüyne s. haüynite
haüynite Hauyn m, $(Na, Ca)_{8-4}[(SO_4)_{2-1}|(AlSiO_4)_6]$
Hawaiian activity Hawaiitätigkeit f (von Vulkanen)
~ type Hawaiitypus m
~-type bomb s. pancake-shaped bomb
hawaiite Haiwaiit m (Alkali-Olivinbasalt)
hawk's eye Falkenauge n (blaue Varietät von Krokydolit)
hawleyite Hawleyit m, α-CdS

haystack s. cockpit
hazardous waste Schadstoff m
haze [trockener] Dunst m
~ of light Lichtnebel m
haziness Nebligkeit f
hazle (sl) fester schiefriger Sandstein m
hazy neblig, dunstig
HDR s. hot dry rock
HDT s. high density tape
head/to pulsierend fließen
head 1. Gangstrecke f; Abbaustrecke f; 2. Hangschutt m; 3. Gefälle n; Niveaudifferenz f, Druckhöhe f, Energiehöhe f, Steighöhe f; 4. Flußhaupt n; 5. Magnetkopf m; 6. s. headland
~ check pulse Kontrollimpuls m (auf Magnetband)
~ clearance Kopfraum m
~ erosion fortschreitende Erosion f
~ meter Zuflußmesser m
~ of a comet Kometenkopf m
~ of a dike (groyne) Buhnenkopf m
~ of a landslide Abrißstelle f (einer Rutschung)
~ of a river Quellgebiet n
~ of an adit Stollenfirste f
~ of pressure Druckhöhe f
~ of the tide Flutgrenze f
~ of water hydrostatische Höhe f, Druckhöhe f, Förderhöhe f, Auftriebshöhe f, Steighöhe f (von Wasser)
~ room lichte Höhe f (z.B. unter einer Brücke)
~ slope obere Böschung f
~ wave Kopfwelle f (Seismik)
heading 1. Stollenvortrieb m; Vortriebsstrecke f; 2. Anzahl f geschlossener Klüfte; 3. Richtungswinkel m (eines Schiffes, Seeseismik)
~ and tunnel construction Stollen- und Tunnelbau m
~ blast Firstensprengung f
~ error Kursfehler m (Navigation)
~ face Ortsbrust f, Ortsstoß m
~ side (wall) Liegendes n [eines Ganges]
headland Vorgebirge n; Landspitze f; Bergvorsprung m
~ bar angelehnte Nehrung f
headpool Quellteich m
headshield Kopfschild m, Cephalon n (bei Trilobiten)
headwall Karstufe f
headwater oberer Wasserstand m
~ of a river, ~ region Quellgebiet n
~ stream Quellfluß m
headwaters Ursprungsbäche mpl, Oberlauf m (eines Flusses)
heap Meiler m, Bergehalde f
~ leaching Haufenlaugung f
~ of dead ore Erzhalde f
~ of debris Haufwerk n; Schuttkegel m
~ of gravel Schottermasse f
hearthstone Kieselkalkstein m
heat Wärme f

~ **balance** Wärmebilanz f
~ **budget** Wärmehaushalt m
~ **capacity** Wärmekapazität f
~ **conductivity** Wärmeleitfähigkeit f
~ **conductor** Wärmeleiter m
~ **content** Wärmeinhalt m
~ **convection** Wärmeströmung f
~ **crack** Kernsprung m
~ **dome** Wärmedom m
~ **drilling** Feuerstrahlbohren n
~ **effect** Wärmetönung f
~ **equator** Wärmeäquator m
~ **exchange** Wärmeaustausch m
~ **flow** 1. Wärmestrom m, Wärmefluß m; 2. Wärmeströmung f
~ **flow density** Wärmestromdichte f
~ **flow unit** Wärmestromeinheit f
~ **flux** Wärmefluß m
~ **gradient** Wärmegradient m
~ **lightning** Wetterleuchten n
~ **loss** Wärmeverlust m
~ **of ablation** Ablationswärme f
~ **of radioactivity** radioaktive Zerfallswärme f
~ **of reaction** Reaktionswärme f
~ **of the earth** Erdwärme f
~ **pump** Wärmepumpe f
~ **radiance** Wärmestrahlung f
~-**storing** wärmespeichernd
~ **supply** Wärmehaushalt m
~ **thunderstorm** Wärmegewitter n
~ **transfer** Wärmeübergang m
~ **transfer number** Wärmeübergangszahl f
~ **wave** Warmlufteinbruch m
heath Heide f, Heideland n
~ **bog** Heidemoor n
~ **sand** Heidesand m
~ **soil** Heideboden m
heathland Ödland n
heating oil Heizöl n
~ **value** Heizwert m
heave/to quellen, heben (Sohle)
heave horizontale Sprungweite (Sprungbreite) f, söhlige Sprungbreite f, Verwerfungsbreite f
~ **fault** transversale Verschiebung f
heaved gehoben, verworfen
~ **block** Horst m, Horstscholle f
~ **side** gehobene Seite f
heavenly body Himmelskörper m
heavily pitching seam seigeres Flöz n
~ **silted river** schlammiger Fluß m
~ **watered strata** stark wasserführende Schichten fpl
heaving schiebend, quellend, schwellend
heaving Quellung f; Hebung f (durch Frost)
~ **bottom** schwellender Boden m
~ **country (formation, ground)** quellendes (drückendes) Gebirge n
~ **of the floor** Sohlquellen n
~ **rock** quellendes (drückendes) Gebirge n
~ **sands** Flugsand m
~ **shale** quellender Schieferton m
~ **soil** frostgefährdeter Boden m

heavy-bedded dickbankig
~-**carburetted hydrogen** Äthylen n, C_2H_4
~ **clay** fetter Ton m
~ **crude oil** schweres, rohes Erdöl n, rohes Schweröl n
~-**duty derrick** Bohrturm m für höchste Beanspruchung
~ **earth** Baryt m, Schwerspat m (s.a. baryte)
~ **hydrocarbons** schwere Kohlenwasserstoffe mpl
~ **layer** mächtiges Flöz n
~ **liquid** Schwerflüssigkeit f
~ **liquids** Schwerelösungen fpl (für Schwermineralanalyse)
~ **loam** fetter Lehm m
~ **metal** Schwermetall n
~ **mineral** Schwermineral n
~-**mineral analysis** Schwermineralanalyse f
~-**mineral assemblage** Schwermineralvergesellschaftung f
~ **mud** Schwerspülung f
~ **oil** Schweröl n
~ **pressure** Hochdruck m, hoher Druck m
~ **roof fall** Strebbruch m
~ **sand** bindiger Sand m
~ **sea** Seegang m, hohe See f
~ **shower** Platzregen m
~ **spar** s. baryte
~-**stained** stark fleckig (Glimmerqualität)
~ **stratification** mächtige Schichtung f
~ **tiff** s. baryte
heazlewoodite Heazlewoodit m, Ni_3S_2
hebetine s. willemite
Hebraic granite s. graphic granite
Hebridean shield Hebridenschild m
hebronite s. amblygonite
hectorite Hektorit m (Mineral der Saponitreihe)
hedenbergite Hedenbergit m, $CaFe[Si_2O_6]$
hedgehog stone Quarz m mit eingewachsenen Goethitnadeln
hedleyite Hedleyit m, $Bi_{14}Te_6$
hedreocraton Hochkraton n
hedyphane Hedyphan m, Kalziumbarium-Mimetesit m (Varietät von Mimetesit)
heel Bohrlochöffnung f
~ **of water** Druckhöhe f
heft (Am) spezifisches Gewicht n
heidornite Heidornit m, $Ca_3Na_2[Cl(SO_4)_2|B_5O_8(OH)_2]$
height 1. Höhe f, Anhöhe f; 2. Höhenlage f
~ **of damming** Stauhöhe f
~ **of derrick** Bohrgerüsthöhe f
~ **of fall** Fallhöhe f; Sturzhöhe f
~ **of flood bank above water line** Höhe f des Ufers über dem Wasserspiegel
~ **of land** s. watershed
~ **of level** Sohlenhöhe f
~ **of natural evaporation** Verdunstungshöhe f
~ **of overfall** Überfallhöhe f
~ **of the tide** Fluthöhe f
~ **of water** Druckhöhe f des Wassers
~ **of weir** Wehrhöhe f

height

~ **zone** Höhenschicht f *(Stratosphäre)*
heightening Aufwölbung f
heinrichite Heinrichit m, Ba[UO$_2$|AsO$_4$]$_2$·10–12H$_2$O
held water Schichtwasser n
Helderbergian [Stage] Helderbergien n, Helderberger Kalk m *(Stufe des Ulsteriens, Unterdevon in Nordamerika)*
heliacal Sonnen...
helical motion s. screw motion
helicitic helizitisch
helicoid spiral schneckenartige Spirale f
helictite, heligmite s. anemolite
heliocentric heliozentrisch
~ **parallax** heliozentrische Parallaxe f
heliodor Heliodor m *(Varietät von Beryll)*
heliograph Heliograf m
heliographic heliografisch
heliography Heliografie f
heliometer Sonnenmesser m
heliophyllite Heliophyllit m, Pb$_3$AsO$_{<4}$Cl$_{<2}$
helioscope Sonnenfernrohr n
heliothermometer Heliothermometer n, Sonnentemperaturmesser m
heliotrope Heliotrop m *(grüne, rotgefleckte Varietät von Chalzedon)*
helium Helium n, He
~ **age** Heliumalter n
~ **fusion** Heliumfusion f
hellandite Hellandit m, (Ca, Y, Er, Mn)$_{<3}$(Al,Fe)[(OH)$_2$|Si$_2$O$_7$]
hellyerite Hellyrit m, NiCO$_3$·6H$_2$O
Helmholtz coil Helmholtz-Spule f
helophytes Helophyten mpl, Sumpfpflanzen fpl
helsinkite Helsinkit m
Helvetian [Stage] Helvet n *(Stufe des Miozäns)*
Helvetic nappes Helvetische Decken fpl, Decken fpl helvetischen Typs
Helveticum Helvetikum n
helvin[e] s. helvite
helvite Helvin m, (Mn, Fe, Zn)$_8$[S$_2$|(BeSiO$_4$)$_6$]
hema... s. haema...
Hembergian [Stage] Hemberg[ium] n *(Stufe des Oberdevons in Europa)*
hemicrystalline hypokristallin, merokristallin, semikristallin
hemihedral hemiedrisch
~ **crystal** hemiedrischer Kristall m
hemihedrism Hemiedrie f
hemihedron Hemieder n, Halbflächner m
hemimorph[ic] hemimorph
hemimorphite Hemimorphit m, Zn$_4$[(OH)$_2$|Si$_2$O$_7$]·H$_2$O
hemimorphous hemimorph
Hemingfordian [Stage] Hemingfordien n, Hemingfordium n *(Wirbeltierstufe des unteren Miozäns in Nordamerika)*
hemiopal Halbopal m
hemipelagic-abyssal der Tiefsee angehörend mit terrestrischem Detritus *(für Sedimente)*

172

~ **deposit** hemipelagische Ablagerung f
~ **muds** Küstenschlick m
Hemiphyllian [Stage] Hemiphyllien n *(Wirbeltierstufe, oberes Miozän bis unterstes Pliozän in Nordamerika)*
hemisphere Erdhalbkugel f, Halbkugel f, Hemisphäre f
hemispherical halbkugelförmig
hemisymmetric s. hemihedral
hemitrope Zwilling[skristall] m
hemitropic hemitrop
hepatic cinnabar Quecksilberlebererz n *(s.a. cinnabar)*
~ **iron ore** Eisenlebererz n *(s.a. marcasite)*
~ **marcasite** Leberkies m *(s.a. marcasite)*
~ **mercurial ore** s. cinnabar
hepatite Hepatit m, Leberstein m *(s.a. baryte)*
heptagon Heptagon n, Siebeneck n
heptagonal heptagonal
heptahedral heptaedrisch, siebenflächig
heptahedron Heptaeder n
heptane Heptan n, C$_7$H$_{16}$
heptatomic siebenatomig
heptavalence Siebenwertigkeit f
heptavalent siebenwertig
herb eater (feeder) Pflanzenfresser m
~ **steppe** Krautsteppe f
herbaceous krautartig
~ **plants** krautige Pflanzen fpl
herbicide Herbizid n
herbivore Pflanzenfresser m
herbivorous pflanzenfressend
Hercynian 1. herzynisch, variskisch *(s.a. Variscan)*; 2. herzyn *(Streichrichtung)*
~ **disturbance (folding)** herzynische Faltung f
~ **orogen** herzynisches (variskisches) Orogen n
~ **orogeny** herzynische Faltung f
~ **trend** herzynische Streichrichtung f
hercynite Herzynit m, Ferrospinell m, FeAl$_2$O$_4$
herderite Herderit m, CaBe[(F, OH)|PO$_4$]
hermatobiolith organogenes Riffgestein n
hermatolith Riffgestein n
hermatypic hermatyp, riffbildend
herringbone cross-bedding Fiederschichtung f
herschelite Herschelit m *(Varietät von Chabasit)*
herzenbergite Herzenbergit m, SnS
hessite Hessit m, Ag$_2$Te
hessonite Hessonit m *(Varietät von Granat)*
hetaerolite Hetaerolith m, ZnMn$_2$O$_4$
heteroaxial heteroaxial
heteroblastic heteroblastisch
heterocercal heterocerk *(unsymmetrische Schwanzflosse)*
heterochronous ungleichzeitig
heterodont heterodont
heterogeneity Heterogenität f, Ungleichartigkeit f
heterogenetic von verschiedenem Ursprung
heterogenite Heterogenit m, CoOOH

heterogenous heterogen, ungleichartig
~ **system** heterogenes System n
heteromesic[al] heteromesisch, in verschiedenen Medien gebildet
~ **deposit** heteromesische Ablagerung f
heterometric heterometrisch
heteromorphic heteromorph
heteromorphism Heteromorphismus m
heteromorphite Heteromorphit m, Federerz n, 11 PbS·6Sb$_2$S$_3$
heteromorphous heterometrisch
heteromorphic heteromorph
heteropic[al] heteropisch
~ **facies** heteropische Fazies f (gleichzeitige, aber verschiedenartige Fazies)
heterosite Heterosit m, (Fe, Mn)[PO$_4$]
heterotactous irregulär
heterotaxial deposits ungleichaltrige Ablagerungen fpl
heterothermal, heterothermic heterotherm
heterotomous mit uncharakteristischer Spaltbarkeit
heterotopic heterotopisch, an verschiedenen Plätzen gebildet
~ **deposit** heterotopische Ablagerung f
heterotrophic heterotroph
heterotropical heterotropisch
heterovalent verschiedenwertig
Hettangian [Stage] Hettang[ien] n, Hettangium n (basale Stufe des Lias)
heubachite Heubachit m (Varietät von Heterogenit)
heudersonite Heudersonit m, Ca$_2$V$_9$O$_{24}$·8H$_2$O
heugh Mineralgewinnungsstelle f, Grube f, Schacht m (Schottland)
heulandite Heulandit m, Ca[Al$_2$Si$_7$O$_{18}$]·6H$_2$O
hew trenches/to ausschrämen
hewettite Hewettit m, CaV$_6$O$_{16}$·9H$_2$O
hexad sechszählige Achse f
hexagon Sechseck n
hexagonal hexagonal, sechszählig
~ **interference ripples** hexagonale Interferenzrippeln fpl
~ **system** hexagonales System n
hexagonally centred hexagonal zentriert (Kristallgitter)
hexahedral, hexahedric hexaedrisch, sechsflächig
hexahedrite Hexaedrit m (Meteorit)
hexahedron Hexaeder n, Kubus m, Würfel m
hexahydrite Hexahydrit m, Mg[SO$_4$]·6H$_2$O
hexakisoctahedron Hexakisoktaeder n
hexakistetrahedron Hexakistetraeder n
hexane Hexan n, C$_6$H$_{14}$
hexavalence Sechswertigkeit f
hexavalent sechswertig
HFU s. heat flow unit
hiatal fabric Hiatalgefüge n
hiatus Hiatus m, Lücke f, Schichtlücke f
~ **clouds** Lückenwolken fpl
hibbenite Hibbenit m, Zn$_7$[OH|(PO$_4$)$_2$]$_2$·6H$_2$O
hibernal snow level Winterschneehöhe f

hibernate/to überwintern
hibernation Überwinterung f
hibonite Hibonit m, CaO·6Al$_2$O$_3$
hibschite Hibschit m, Hydrogrossular m, Ca$_3$Al$_2$[(SiH$_4$)O$_4$]$_3$
hidalgoite Hidalgoit m, PbAl$_3$[(OH)$_6$|SO$_4$AsO$_4$]
hidden layer überschossene Schicht f (Seismik)
hiddenite Hiddenit m (grüner Spodumen)
hielmite Hjelmit m (Gemenge von Tapiolit und Pyrochlor)
hieratite Hieratit m, K$_2$[SiF$_6$]
hieroglyph Hieroglyphe f, Sedimentmarke f
higginsite Higginsit m, Konichalcit m, CaCu[OH|AsO$_4$]
high-alpine hochalpin
~-**altitude photography** Aufnahmen fpl aus großer Flughöhe
~-**altitude rocket** Höhenrakete f
~-**alumina basalt** Al-Basalt m (Basalt mit > 17% Al$_2$O$_3$)
~-**aluminous** tonerdereich
~-**angle dipping strata** steil einfallende Schichten fpl
~-**angle fault** steiler als 45° fallende Verwerfung f
~-**ash** aschereich
~-**ash coal** (Am) aschereiche Kohle f (> 15% Asche)
~ **bank** Steilufer n
~ **bending strength/of** biegefest
~ **bog** Hochmoor n
~ **bog peat** Hochmoortorf m
~-**class** hochwertig
~ **craton** Hochkraton m
~-**cut filter** Tiefpaßfilter n
~ **density tape** Band n hoher Belegungsdichte
~-**drift angle well** Bohrung f mit starker Vertikalabweichung
~ **enthalpy geothermal potential** hochenthalpes geothermisches Potential n
~ **flood** Hochflut f, Hochwasser n
~ **fractured plateau** Plateau n an den Flanken der Riffgebirge
~-**grade** hochhaltig
~-**grade chippings** Edelsplitt m
~-**grade clay** Edelton m, hochwertiger Ton m
~-**grade metamorphism** starke (katazonale) Metamorphose f
~-**grade mineral** Hochtemperaturmineral n
~-**grade ore** hochwertiges (reichhaltiges) Erz n, Reicherz n
~-**head edge water** Randwasser n mit großem Auftrieb
~-**head water power plant** Hochdruckwasserkraftwerk n
~-**level placer** Seife f auf Alluvialterrasse
~-**lime rock** hochprozentiger Kalkstein m
~ **line distortion** Störung f durch Hochspannung
~-**liquid limit** hohe Fließgrenze f eines bindigen Materials (> 50)

high

~-low inversion Hoch-/Tieftemperatur-Umwandlung f (bei Quarz)
~-lying hochliegend
~-lying terrace Hochterrasse f
~ magnifier stark vergrößernde Lupe f
~-mark gauge Hochwasserstandsmesser m
~ marsh Hochsumpf m
~-molecular-weight hydrocarbons hochmolekulare Kohlenwasserstoffe mpl
~ moor Hochmoor n
~-moor forest Waldhochmoor n
~-moor peat Hochmoortorf m
~ moorland Hochmoor n
~ moss Hochmoor n, Torfmoor n
~ mountain steppe Hochgebirgssteppe f
~ mountain valley Hochalpental n
~ mountains Hochgebirge n
~ oblique photograph Schrägaufnahme f (Luftbildgeologie)
~-order trend surface Trendfläche (Polynomtrendfläche) f hohen Grades
~ ore s. ~-grade ore
~-pass filter Hochpaßfilter n
~-permeable stark durchlässig
~ plain (plateau) Hochebene f
~ pressure Hochdruck m, hoher Druck m
~-pressure area Hochdruckgebiet n
~-pressure belt Hochdruckgürtel m
~-pressure equipment Hochdruckausrüstung f
~-pressure metamorphism Hochdruckmetamorphose f
~-pressure ridge Hochdruckbrücke f
~-pressure well Hochdruckbohrung f
~-pressure well control Kontrolle f von Hochdrucksonden
~-pressure zone Hochdruckzone f
~-quality hochwertig
~ quartz Hochquarz m
~-rank coal hoch inkohlte Kohle f; Anthrazit m
~-rank graywacke Feldspatgrauwacke f
~-rank metamorphism starke Metamorphose f
~-resistivity stratum Schicht f hohen Widerstands
~-resolution seismics Hochfrequenzseismik f
~ rocky ridge Felsgrat m
~ sea hohe (offene) See f
~-silica stones (Am) Reinstquarzite mpl
~ slope Oberhang m
~-speed bed (layer) schallharte Schicht f (Schicht mit hoher Geschwindigkeit für seismische Wellen)
~-speed pump Hochleistungspumpe f
~-speed stratum s. ~-speed bed
~-sulfur coal (Am) schwefelreiche Kohle f (>3% Schwefel)
~-temperature carbonization Hochtemperaturverkokung f
~-temperature mineral Hochtemperaturmineral n
~-temperature phase Hochtemperaturphase f
~ thunderstorm Hochgewitter n

~ tide Flut f, Sturmflut f
~-tide level Flutstand m
~ value/of hochwertig
~-volatile bituminous coal (Am) hochflüchtige (gering inkohlte) Steinkohle f (auf wasseraschefreie Basis bezogen; flüchtige Bestandteile >31%)
~-volatile coal Kohle f mit hohem Gehalt an flüchtigen Bestandteilen
~ water Hochwasser n
~-water basin Rückhaltebecken n, Hochwasserrückhaltebecken n
~-water bed Hochflutbett n, Überschwemmungsbett n; Hochwasserbett n
~-water channel Hochwasserbett n
~-water line Flutlinie f
~-water mark Hochwassermarke f, Flutmarke f
~-water neap Nipphochwasser n
~ water of ordinary neap tide Nipphochwasser n
~ water of spring tide Springflut f
~-water regulation Hochwasserregulierung f
highland Hochland n
~ rocks Hochlandgesteine npl (Mond)
highly argentiferous silberreich
~ auriferous goldreich
~ dispersed äußerst fein verteilt
~ disturbed strata stark gestörte Schichten fpl
~ fluid dünnflüssig
~ folded stark gefaltet
~ inclined strata steil einfallende Schichten fpl
- jointed stark zerklüftet
highwall Abbaustoß m, Ortsstoß m mit angeschnittenem Hangenden
hilgardite Hilgardit m, $Ca_2[Cl|B_5O_8(OH)_2]$
hill Hügel m, Berg m
~ country Mittelgebirge n; Hügelland n
~ creep Hangkriechen n
~ diggings Hangseife f
~ hachure Bergschraffe f
~ moor Hochmoor n
~ peat Moor n in kalten Berggebieten
~ shading Lavierung f
~ top Bergspitze f
hillebrandite Hillebrandit m, $Ca_2[SiO_4]\cdot H_2O$
hillock Hügel m, Buckel m; Bult m
~ bog Bültenmoor n
hills Mittelgebirge n
hillside Berghang m, Berglehne f, Abhang m
~ creep Schuttkriechen n, Gekriech n
~ placer Hangseife f
~ seepage Hangsickerung f
~ slope Hangböschung f
~ waste Gehängeschutt m
hillwash Hangfußablagerung f
hilly hügelig, bergig
~ country Hügelland n
~ ground Gebirgsgelände n
Hilt's law Hiltsche Regel f
hindlimbs Hinterextremitäten fpl

holotype

hinge 1. Schloß n *(Paläontologie)*; 2. Scharnier n *(Tektonik)*
~ **bar** Schloßleiste f
~ **belt** Tieffaltungszone f *(zwischen Geosynklinale und kontinentalem Vorland)*
~ **fold** Scharnierfalte f
~ **groove** Schloßfurche f
~ **line** 1. Zone, die den vorlandwärtigen Teil der Randsenke vom orogenwärtigen Teil trennt; 2. Schloßrand m *(Paläontologie)*
~ **margin** Schloßrand m
~ **plate** Schloßplatte f
~ **teeth** Schloßzähne mpl, Scharnierzähne mpl
hinging coal stark einfallendes Kohlenflöz n *(Schottland)*
hinsdalite Hinsdalit m, $PbAl_3[(OH)_6|SO_4PO_4]$
hinter surf beds Schelfablagerungen fpl
hinterdeep Trog m auf der konvexen Seite eines Inselbogens
hinterland Rückland n
hippurite limestone Hippuritenkalk m
hirst Flußsandbank f
histogram Histogramm n
~ **equalization** Egalisierung der Häufigkeitsverteilung von Schwärzungs- bzw. Farbdichteniveaus
historic[al] character historischer Charakter m *(geochemischer Gesetze)*
~ **geochemistry** historische Geochemie f
~ **geology** historische Geologie f
history match model *(Am)* Anpassungsmodell n *(reservoirmechanisch)*
~ **matching** *(Am)* Parameteranpassung f, Identifikation f *(eines reservoirmechanischen Simulationsmodells)*
~ **of earth** Erdgeschichte f
~ **of vegetation** Vegetationsgeschichte f
hit or miss method auf dem Zufall beruhende Methode f
hitch kleine Verwerfung f
hjelmite s. hielmite
hoarfrost Rauhfrost m, Rauhreif m
hoarstone Landmarke f, Grenzmarkierung f
hodgkinsonite Hodgkinsonit m, $MnZn_2[(OH)_2|SiO_4]$
hodograph Hodograph m, Hodographenkurve f, Geschwindigkeitskurve f
hoegbomite Högbomit m, $Na_x(Al,Fe,Ti)_{24-x}O_{36-x}$
hoelite Hoelit m, $C_{14}H_8O_2$
hog-tooth spar Kalzitskalenoeder npl
hogback 1. Grat m, Ziegenrücken m; 2. Schichtrippe f; 3. Isoklinalkamm f
hogbacked bottom gewellter Boden m
hohmannite Hohmannit m, $Fe[OH|SO_4]·3^1/_2H_2O$
hoist/to ausbauen *(Gestänge)*
hoist 1. Förderanlage f; 2. Winde f, Hebewerk n
hoisting cable Förderseil n
~ **capacity of drilling rig** Hakenhöchstlast f der Bohranlage
~ **drum** Bohrseiltrommel f

~ **tackle** Flaschenzugsystem n
holarctic gesamtarktisch
hold/to abfangen *(eine Schicht)*
holdenite Holdenit m, $(Mn, Ca)_4(Zn, Mg, Fe)_2[(OH)_5O_2|AsO_4]$
hole Sonde f, Bohrloch n
~ **blow** Ausbläser m
~ **bottom** Bohrlochtiefstes n
~ **calibre** Bohrlochkaliber n
~ **clearance** Spielraum m zwischen Bohrlochwandung und Gestänge
~ **deviation** Bohrlochabweichung f
~ **deviation logging** Abweichungsmessung f, Inklinometrie f
~ **of impact** Einschlaggrube f *(z.B. eines Meteoriten)*
~ **plug** Bohrlochpfropfen m, Bohrlochverschluß m
~ **sloughing** Ablösen n *(der Bohrlochwandung)*
~ **straightening** Ausrichten n der Bohrung
~**-to-hole measurement** Zwischenfelderkundung f
~ **wall** Bohrlochwand f
~ **with deviation in a plane** in einer Ebene gekrümmtes Bohrloch n
~ **with deviation not in a plane** räumlich gekrümmtes Bohrloch n
hollandite Hollandit m, $Ba_{<2}Mn_8O_{16}$
hollingworthite Hollingworthit m, (Rh, Pd)AsS
hollow out/to aushöhlen
hollow leer, taub
hollow Höhle f, Mulde f, Senkung f, Talmulde f
~ **cast** Hohlabguß m *(von Fossilien)*
~ **grinding** Hohlschliff m
~ **impress** Hohlabdruck m *(von Fossilien)*
~ **lode** Drusengang m
~ **mould** Hohlform f
~ **spar** s. andalusite
holmium Holmium n, Ho
holmquistite Holmquistit m, $Li_2Mg_3Al_2[OH|Si_4O_{11}]_2$
holoaxial holoaxial
holoblast Holoblast m
Holocene holozän
Holocene Holozän n
~ **series** Holozän n
holocrystalline holokristallin, vollkristallin
~ **rock** holokristallines Gestein n
holohedral holoedrisch, vollflächig
holohedrism Holoedrie f, Vollflächigkeit f
holohedron Holoeder n, Vollflächner m
holohedry Holoedrie f, Vollflächigkeit f
holohyaline holohyalin, vollglasig
hololeucocratic hololeukokrat
holomelanocratic holomelanokrat
holomorphic holomorph
holosiderite Eisenmeteorit m *(ohne Silikatkomponenten)*
holostratotype Holostratotyp m
holosymmetric s. holohedral
holotype Holotypus m

Holstein 176

Holstein [Interval] Holstein-Warmzeit f, Holstein-Interglazial n *(Pleistozän in Nordwesteuropa)*
holystone weicher Sandstein m *(als Reinigungsmaterial)*
homeoblastic homöoblastisch
homeogene enclaves endogene Einschlüsse mpl
homeomorphic, homeomorphous homöomorph
homeotropy Gleichrichtung f
homeotype Homeotyp m
Homerian [Stage] Homerium n *(basale Stufe des Wenlock)*
homilite Homilit m, $Ca_2FeB_2[O|SiO_4]_2$
hominoids menschenähnliche Formen fpl
homocercal homocerk *(ein Typ der symmetrischen Schwanzflosse)*
homoclinal bed einseitig geneigte Schicht f
~ **valley** Monoklinaltal n
homocline Monoklinale f
homogeneity Homogenität f
~ **of sample** Probenhomogenität f
~ **test** Homogenitätstest m
homogeneous homogen, gleichartig
~ **deformation** affine Deformation f
~ **fluid** homogene Flüssigkeit f
~ **isotropic body** homogener isotroper Körper m
~ **rotational strain** affine einscharige Gleitung f
~ **system** homogenes System n
homogeneously strained homogen verzerrt
homohedral homoedrisch
homologous homolog; spiegelbildlich
homometric homometrisch
~ **pairs** homometrische Paare npl
homomorphism Formähnlichkeit f
homoseismal curve (line) Homoseiste f
homotactic homotaktisch, mit gleichem Gefüge *(s.a. homotaxial)*
homotaxeous *s.* homotaxial
homotaxial homotax, äquivalent
~ **beds** äquivalente Schichten fpl
~ **deposit** homotaxe (äquivalente) Ablagerung f
~ **facies** homotaxe Fazies f
homotaxic *s.* homotaxial
homotaxis gleichartige Anordnung f
homothermal, homothermic homotherm
homotropal ventilation gleichlaufende Bewetterung f
hone Abziehstein m, sehr feiner Sandstein m *(für Schleifzwecke)*
honestone feinkörniger Schiefer m, Wetzschiefer m
honeycomb corrosion narbenartige Anfressung f
~ **structure** Wabenstruktur f
~ **weathering** Wabenverwitterung f
honeycombed wabenförmig, zellig
~ **rock** Gestein n mit Wabenstruktur

honeystone Honigstein m *(s.a. mellite)*
hoo cannel unreine Kännelkohle f
hoodoo *s.* earth pyramid
hook Haken m, krumme Landspitze f
~ **gauge** Stechpegel m
~ **load** Hakenlast f
Hooke's law Hookesches Gesetz n
hopeite Hopeit m, $Zn_3[PO_4]_2 \cdot 4H_2O$
hopper-shaped crystal sargdeckelförmiger Kristall m
horde of meteors Meteorschwarm m
horizon 1. Horizont m; 2. Abbausohle f
horizontal horizontal, waagerecht; söhlig
~ **bedding** waagerechte Schichtung f, söhlige Lagerung f
~ **displacement** horizontale Schublänge f
~ **electromagnetic method** Slingram-Verfahren n
~ **extent** horizontale Ausdehnung f
~ **fault** Blattverschiebung f
~ **filter well** Horizontalfilterbrunnen m
~ **flexure** Horizontalflexur f, Flexurblatt n
~ **gradient of gravity** horizontaler Schweregradient m
~ **hole** Horizontalbohrung f, Söhligbohrung f
~ **intensity** magnetische Horizontalkomponente f
~ **-loop method** Induktionsverfahren n mit horizontalem Primärkreis
~ **magnetometer** Horizontalmagnetometer n
~ **mixing** Stapelung f für einen gemeinsamen Tiefenpunkt *(Seismik)*
~ **motion seismograph** Horizontalseismograf m
~ **movement** Horizontalbewegung f
~ **ore pillar** Erzschwebe f
~ **pendulum** Horizontalpendel n
~ **seam** söhliges Flöz n
~ **seismograph** Horizontalseismograf m
~ **seismometer** Horizontalseismometer n
~ **separation along the fault line strike** streichende Sprungweite f
~ **stacking** *s.* ~ mixing
~ **strata** horizontalgelagerte Schichten fpl
~ **stratification** waagerechte Schichtung f, söhlige Lagerung f
~ **throw** Sprungweite f *(Verwerfung)*
~ **thrust** Horizontalschub m
horizontality horizontale Lage f
horizontally bedded (laid) strata horizontalgelagerte Schichten fpl
horn Horn n
~ **lead** Hornblei n, Bleichlorid n *(s.a. phosgenite)*
~ **mercury** Merkurhornerz n, Quecksilberhornerz n *(s.a. calomel)*
~ **silver** Hornerz n, Hornsilber n *(s.a. cerargyrite)*
~ **tiff** bituminöser Kalzit m
hornblende Hornblende f, Amphibol m
~ **granite** Hornblendegranit m
~ **schist** Hornblendeschiefer m

hornblendic schist Hornblendeschiefer *m*
hornblendite Hornblendit *m*, Hornblendefels *m*
hornfels Hornfels *m*
hornito Hornito *m*, Ofen *m*, vulkanischer Lavakegel *m (Südamerika)*
hornschist, hornslate Hornblendeschiefer *m*
hornstone Hornstein *m*
horny minderwertige Gaskohle *f (Schottland)*
horny hornig
~-shelled hornschalig
~ sponges Hornschwämme *mpl*
horobetsuite Horobetsuit *m*, (Sb, Bi)$_2$S$_3$
horse Pferdeschwanz *m (ausgeschwänzter Gang)*
~ beans laugenhaltiges Hangendes *n (von Salzlagerstätten)*
~ flesh ore *s.* bornite
~-shoe flute cast Hufeisenwulst *m (f)*
horseback 1. *s.* horse; 2. fossiler Wasserlauf *m* im Kohlenflöz; 3. Kamm *m (im Flöz)*
horses teeth *(sl)* Feldspatmegablasten im Granit
horseshoe lake *s.* oxbow
horsetail structure Pferdeschwanzstruktur *f*
horsfordite Horsfordit *m*, Cu$_6$Sb
horst Horst *m*, Horstscholle *f*
~ mountain Horstgebirge *n*
hortonolite Hortonolith *m*, (Fe, Mg, Mn)$_2$[SiO$_4$]
hose levelling instrument Schlauchwaage *f*
host crater übergreifender Krater *m (auf einen anderen)*
~ mineral Wirtsmineral *n*
~ rock Nebengestein *n*; Muttergestein *n*
hot ash avalanche vulkanische Staublawine *f*
~ cloud absteigende Eruptionswolke *f*
~ dry rock trockenes heißes Gestein *n (zur Gewinnung geothermischer Energie)*
~ dry rock method *(Am)* Heißwassergewinnung *f* aus Festgestein
~ lahar Lavamurgang *m*
~ mud flow heißer Schlammstrom *m*
~ oil Schwarzöl *n*
~ pool Heißwasserbecken *n*
~ spot Hot spot *m (sehr starke, geologisch interessante geothermische Anomalie)*
~ spring Thermalquelle *f*, Therme *f*
~-spring deposit Ablagerung *f* von heißen Quellen
~-stage microscope heizbares Mikroskop *n*
~ tuff flow Gluttuffstrom *m*
~ water flooding Heißwasserfluten *n*
~ wire analyzer Hitzdrahtanalysator *m*
houppes *s.* epoptic figures
hour angle Stundenwinkel *m*
~ glass structure Sanduhrbau *m (in Kristallen)*
hover ground Lockerboden *m*, Gare *f*
howardite Howardit *m (achondritischer hypersthen- und plagioklasführender Meteorit)*
howieite Howieit *m*, NaMn$_3$Fe$_7$(Fe, Al)$_2$(OH)$_{11}$Si$_{12}$O$_{32}$
howlite Howlith *m*, Ca$_2$[(BOOH)$_5$|SiO$_4$]

Hoxnian Hoxnien *n (Pleistozän der britischen Inseln, entspricht etwa dem Mindel-Riss-Interglazial der Alpen)*
hsianghualite Hsianghualith *m*, Ca$_2$[(Li, Be, Si)$_6$O$_{12}$]·CaF$_2$
hsihutsunite Hsihutsunit *m (Varietät von Rhodonit)*
Huangho sedimentation extensive fluviatile Sedimentation *f*
huanghoite Huanghoit *m*, BaCe[F|(CO$_3$)$_2$]
huantajayite Huantajayit *m*, 20NaCl·AgCl
Huber's fracture condition Hubersche Bruchbedingung *f*
huebnerite Hübnerit *m*, Wolframit *m*, MnWO$_4$
huel *(sl)* Bergwerk *n*, Grube *f*, Zeche *f*
hügelite Hügelit *m*, Pb$_2$[(UO$_2$)$_3$(OH)$_4$|(AsO$_4$)$_2$]·3H$_2$O
hühnerkobelite Hühnerkobelit *m*, (Ca, Na)$_2$(Fe, Mn)$_3$[PO$_4$]$_3$
Hull ring Debye-Scherrer-Ring *m*
hum 1. Karstrestberg *m*, Karstinselberg *m*, residualer Karstberg *m*; 2. Brummen *n*, elektrische Störung *f*
humates Huminstoffe *mpl*
humboldtine Humboldtin *m*, Fe[C$_2$O$_4$]·2H$_2$O
humboldtite 1. *s.* datolite; 2. *s.* humboldtine
humic humos, humitisch
~ acid Huminsäure *f*, Humussäure *f*
~ cannel coal *s.* pseudocannel coal
~ carbonated soil Humuskarbonatboden *m*
~ coal Humuskohle *f*
~ decomposition humose Verwitterung *f*
~ deposit humitische Ablagerung *f*
~ detritus humoser Detritus *m*
~ gel Humusgel *n*
~ gley soil *s.* gumbotil
~ layer Humusschicht *f*
~ matter Humussubstanz *f*, Humus[stoff] *m*
~ soil Humusboden *m*
~ substance Humusstoff *m*
humid humid, feucht
~-temperate feuchtgemäßigt
humidity Feuchtigkeit *f*
~ of air Luftfeuchtigkeit *f*
humification Humifizierung *f*, Humusbildung *f*
humify/to humifizieren
huminite Huminit *m (Maceralgruppe der Braunkohle)*
humite 1. Humit *m*, Mg$_7$[(OH, F)$_2$|(SiO$_4$)$_3$]; 2. humose (humitische) Kohle *f*
hummerite Hummerit *m*, K$_2$Mg$_2$[V$_{10}$O$_{28}$]·16H$_2$O
hummock 1. Bodenschwelle *f*, Bult *m*, Buckel *m*; 2. Eishügel *m*
hummocky höckerig
~ region Hügelgegend *f*
~ surface hügelige Oberfläche *f*
~ topography kuppige Moränenlandschaft *f*
humo-siallitic humo-siallitisch
humocoll Humustorf *m*
humocollinite Humocollinit *m (Maceralsubgruppe der Braunkohle)*
humodetrinite Humodetrinit *m (Maceralsubgruppe der Braunkohle)*

humolith Humolith m *(Gruppe der Kaustobiolithe, Torf, Braunkohle und Steinkohle umfassend)*
humonigrite schwarze bituminöse Substanz im Sediment
humotelinite Humotelinit m *(Maceralsubgruppe der Braunkohle)*
humous humos *(s.a. humic)*
~ **sand** humoser Sand m
~ **soil** Humusboden m
hump up/to aufbuckeln
hump Rundhöcker m
humped coal 1. Kohle f in thermischen Kontaktöfen; 2. minderwertige (erdige) Kohle f
humus Humus m
~ **calcareous (carbonate) soil** Rendzina f, Kalkschwarzerde f, Humuskarbonatboden m
~ **earth** Humuserde f
~ **fen soil** Niedermoorboden m
~ **horizon** Humushorizont m
~-**rich rock** Humusgestein n
~ **soil** Humusboden m, Humuserde f
hundred percent section kontinuierliche seismische Profilierung f, Einfachüberdeckung f
hungchaoite Hungchaoit m, $Mg[B_4O_5(OH)_4] \cdot 7H_2O$
hungry soil magerer Boden m
huntilite Huntilith m, (Ag, As)
huntite Huntit m, $CaMg_3[CO_3]_4$
hurdled ore grobgesiebtes Erz n
hureaulite Huréaulith m, $(Mn, Fe)_5H_2[PO_4]_4 \cdot 4H_2O$
hurlbutite Hurlbutit m, $CaBe_2[PO_4]_2$
Huronian Huron[ien] n, Huronium n *(Mittelpräkambrium in Nordamerika)*
hurricane Hurrikan m, Orkan m
~ **tidal wave** Sturmflut f
hushing Gangsuche f durch Bodenabschwemmung
hutchinsonite Hutchinsonit m, $(Pb, Tl)S \cdot Ag_2S \cdot 5As_2S_3$
huttonite Huttonit m, $Th[SiO_4]$
huttrill harte Gangpartie f
hyacinth Hyazinth m *(Varietät von Zirkon)*
hyaline glasig, glasartig
~ **texture** glasige Struktur f
hyalinocrystalline s. hyalocrystalline
hyalite Hyalit m, Glasopal n, $SiO_2 \cdot nH_2O$
hyalobasalt Hyalobasalt m, Glasbasalt m
hyaloclastic submarin-pyroklastisch
hyaloclastite Hyaloklastit m, submarines pyroklastisches Gestein n
hyalocrystalline hyalokristallin
hyalomite Greisen m *(vergreister Granit)*
hyalophane Hyalophan m, $(K, Ba)[Al, Si)Si_2O_8]$
hyalopilitic hyalopilitisch
~ **texture** hyalopilitische Struktur f
hyalosiderite Hyalosiderit m *(Fe-reicher Olivin)*
hyalotekite Hyalotekit m, $(Pb, Ca, Ba)_4B[Si_6O_{17}(F, OH)]$

hybrid hybrid
~ **rock** hybrides Gestein n, Mischgestein n
hybridism Hybridismus m, Mischbildung f
hybridization Hybridisierung f
hydatogenic hydatogen
~ **mineral** hydroxylhaltiges Mineral n *(Mineral mit OH-Gruppen)*
hydatogenous s. hydatogenic
hydatomorphism Hydatomorphose f
hydrargillite s. gibbsite
hydrate Hydrat n
hydration Hydratisierung f, Hydratation f
hydraulic barrier hydraulische Barriere f
~ **capsule** Flüssigkeitsdruckmeßdose f
~ **classification** Naßklassierung f, Hydroklassierung f, Stromklassierung f
~ **conductivity** hydraulische Leitfähigkeit f
~ **connection** hydraulische Verbindung f
~ **construction** Wasserbau m
~ **diffusivity** Hydroleitfähigkeit f
~ **dredger** Saugbagger m
~ **drilling** hydraulisches Bohren n
~ **engineer** Wasserbauingenieur m
~ **engineering** Wasserbau m, Hydrotechnik f
~ **fill** Spülkippe f, Aufspülung f
~ **fill dam** gespülter Erddamm m
~ **fill embankment** Spüldamm m
~ **fracturing** hydraulische Rißbildung f
~ **gradient** Druckgefälle n, hydraulischer Gradient m
~ **hammer** hydraulischer Hammer m *(seismische Energiequelle)*
~ **hammer drilling** hydraulisches Schlagbohren n
~ **head** Druckhöhe f
~ **jump** Wassersprung m
~ **lifting cylinder** hydraulische, unter Tage befindliche Pumpe f
~ **limestone** Zementkalkstein m
~ **load cell** Flüssigkeitsdruckmeßdose f
~ **mining** Abbau m mit Druckwasser
~ **routing** Wasserwegsamkeit f
~ **stowing** Spülversatz m
~ **structures** Wasserbauten mpl
~ **subsurface pump** gestängelose Tiefpumpe f
~ **works** Wasserbau m
hydraulicking hydraulischer Abbau m
hydraulics Hydraulik f
hydride Hydrid n
hydrite Hydrit m *(Kohlenmikrolithotyp; claritähnlich)*
hydrobiotite Hydrobiotit m, $(K, H_2O) (Mg, Fe, Mn)_3[(OH, H_2O)_2|AlSi_3O_{10}]$
hydroboracite Hydroboracit m, $MgCa[B_3O_4(OH)_3]_2 \cdot 3 H_2O$
hydrocalumite Hydrocalumit m, $2Ca(OH)_2 \cdot Al[OH]_3 \cdot 3 H_2O$
hydrocarbogenesis Kohlenwasserstoffentstehung f
hydrocarbon Kohlenwasserstoff m
~ **compound** Kohlenwasserstoffverbindung f
~ **deposit** Kohlenwasserstofflagerstätte f

~ **gas detection in cores** Nachweis m von gasförmigem Kohlenwasserstoff in Bohrkernen
hydrocarbonaceous kohlenwasserstoffhaltig
hydrocassiterite Hydrocassiterit m, Souxit m, Varlamoffit m, (Sn, Fe) (O, OH)$_2$
hydrocerussite Hydrocerussit m, Pb$_3$[OH|CO$_3$]$_2$
hydrochemical hydrochemisch
~ **anomaly** hydrochemische Anomalie f
~ **inversion** hydrochemische Inversion f
~ **zoning** hydrochemische Zonalität f
hydrochemistry Chemie f der Hydrosphäre
hydrochloric acid Salzsäure f, HCl
hydroclast Hydroklast m (litho- oder bioklastischer Karbonatdetritus, in aquatischem Milieu gebildet)
hydroclastic hydroklastisch
~ **eruption** Eruption, bei der eine Schmelze mit Wasser in Berührung kommt
~ **rock** hydroklastisches Gestein n
hydrocyanite s. chalcocyanite
hydrodrill Hydrobohrer m
hydrodynamic oil trap hydrodynamische Ölfalle f
~ **trap** hydrodynamische Falle f
~ **wave** hydrodynamische Welle f
hydrodynamics Hydrodynamik f
hydroelectric exploitation Wasserkraftnutzung f
hydrofluoric acid Fluorwasserstoffsäure f, Flußsäure f, HF
hydrofracturing Hydrofracverfahren n (Bohrtechnik)
hydrogen Wasserstoff m, H
~ **peroxide** Wasserstoffperoxid n
~-**poor** wasserstoffarm
~-**rich** wasserstoffreich
~ **sulphide** Schwefelwasserstoff m, H$_2$S
hydrogenation Hydrierung f
hydrogenesis Hydrogenie f
hydrogenize/to hydrieren
hydrogenous wasserstoffhaltig
~ **coal** gasreiche Kohle f
hydrogeochemical prospecting hydrogeochemische Erkundung (Prospektion) f
hydrogeochemistry Hydrogeochemie f, Geochemie f des Wassers
hydrogeology Hydrogeologie f
hydrograph [curve of discharges] Abflußmengenkurve f
hydrographic[al] area Abflußgebiet n
~ **map** Seekarte f
hydrography Hydrografie f, Gewässerkunde f
hydrohalite Hydrohalit m, NaCl·2H$_2$O
hydrohetaerolite Hydrohetaerolith m, Zn(Mn, H$_3$)$_2$O$_4$
hydrolaccolith Eislakkolith m, Pingo m
hydrolith Hydrolith m (Karbonatgestein mit Hydroklasten)
hydrologic[al] hydrologisch
~ **budget** Wasserhaushalt m
~ **cycle** Wasserkreislauf m
~ **dating** hydrologische Datierung f

~ **forecast** hydrologische Vorhersage f
~ **network** hydrologisches Netz n
~ **triangle** hydrologisches Dreieck n
~ **year** hydrologisches Jahr n
hydrologist Hydrologe m
hydrology Hydrologie f
hydrolysis Hydrolyse f
hydrolytic hydrolytisch
hydromagnesite Hydromagnesit m, Mg$_5$[OH|(CO$_3$)$_2$]$_2$·4 H$_2$O
hydromechanics Hydromechanik f
hydromelanothallite Hydromelanothallit m, Cu(Cl, OH)$_2$·$^1/_2$H$_2$O
hydrometamorphism Hydrometamorphose f
hydrometeor Hydrometeor m
hydrometeorological hydrometeorologisch
hydrometeorology Hydrometeorologie f
hydrometer analysis (test) Aräometeranalyse f, Schlämmanalyse f
hydrometric current meter Meßflügel m (für Wasserströmung)
hydrometry Hydrometrie f
hydromorphic, hydromorphous hydromorph
hydromuscovite Hydromuskovit m, (K, H$_2$O)Al$_2$[(H$_2$O, OH)$_2$|AlSi$_3$O$_{10}$]
hydronephelite Hydronephelit m, HNa$_2$Al$_3$Si$_3$O$_{12}$·3 H$_2$O
hydroparagonite Hydroparagonit m, (Na, H$_2$O)Al$_2$[(H$_2$O, OH)$_2$|AlSi$_3$O$_{10}$]
hydrophane Hydrophan m (s.a. opal)
hydrophilic hydrophil, wasseranziehend
hydrophilite Hydrophilit m, CaCl$_2$
hydrophily Hydrophilie f, Wasserfreundlichkeit f
hydrophlogopite Hydrophlogopit m, (K, H$_2$O) Mg$_3$[(OH, H$_2$O)$_2$|AlSi$_3$O$_{10}$]
hydrophobic hydrophob
hydrophobicity Hydrophobie f, Wasserfeindlichkeit f
hydrophone Hydrophon n (Seeseismik)
hydrophytic hydrophytisch
hydroplant Wasserkraftanlage f
hydropower Wasserkraft f
hydropressure hydrostatischer Druck m
hydroscience Hydrowissenschaft f
hydrosol Hydrosol n
hydrosphere Hydrosphäre f
hydrostatic hydrostatisch
~ **balance** hydrostatische Waage f
~ **head** hydrostatische Höhe f, Auftriebshöhe f, Steighöhe f
~ **level** hydrostatisches Niveau n
~ **pressure** hydrostatischer Druck m
~ **pressure distribution** hydrostatische Druckverteilung f (im Grundwasserleiter)
hydrostatics Hydrostatik f
hydrotalcite Hydrotalkit m, Mg$_6$Al$_2$[(OH)$_{16}$|CO$_3$]·4H$_2$O
hydrotechnics Wasserbautechnik f
hydrothermal hydrothermal
~ **alteration** hydrothermale Umwandlung f

hydrothermal

~ **convection system** hydrothermales Konvektionssystem n
~ **decomposition** hydrothermale Zersetzung f
~ **deposit** hydrothermale Lagerstätte f
~ **field** Hydrothermalfeld n
~ **filling** hydrothermale Füllung f
~ **metamorphism** hydrothermale Metamorphose f
~ **spring** Hydrotherme f
~ **stage** hydrothermales Stadium n
~ **system** Hydrothermalsystem n
~ **vein** hydrothermaler Gang m
hydrothorite Hydrothorith m, $ThSiO_4 \cdot 4 H_2O$
hydrotroilite Hydrotroilit m, $FeS \cdot nH_2O$
hydrotungstite Hydrotungstit m, $WO_2(OH)_2 \cdot H_2O$
hydrous kristallwasserhaltig
hydroxide Hydroxid n
hydrozincite Zinkblüte f, Hydrozinkit m, $Zn_5[(OH)_3|CO_3]_2$
hyetograph Regenschreiber m
hygrograph Hygrograf m
hygrometer Hygrometer n
hygrophytes Hygrophyten mpl, Wasserpflanzen fpl
hygroscopic hygroskopisch
~ **water** hygroskopisches Wasser n
hygroscopicity Hygroskopizität f
hypabyssal hyp[o]abyssisch
~ **activity** hypoabyssische Tätigkeit f
~ **rock** hypoabyssisches Ganggestein n
hyperbolic decline curve hyperbolische Erschöpfungskurve f (Lagerstättenabbau)
hypereutectic hypereutektisch, übereutektisch
hypergene ore primäres Erz n
hypersaline hypersalin
hypersalinity Hypersalinar n
hypersthene Hypersthen m, $(Fe, Mg)_2[Si_2O_6]$
hypersthenite Hypersthenit m
hypervelocity impact Hochgeschwindigkeitseinschlag m
hypha Hyphe f, Pilzfaden m
hypidiomorphic hypidiomorph
~ **granular** hypidiomorph-körnig
~ **structure** hypidiomorphes Gefüge n
Hypnum moss bog Braunmoor n
hypobaric hypobarisch, Unterdruck...
hypobatholithic hypobatholitisch
hypobenthos Tiefseebodenfauna f
hypocentre Hypozentrum n, Erdbebenherd m
hypocrystalline s. hemicrystalline
hypogaean, hypogeal, hypogean, hypogeic unterirdisch
hypogene hypogen, subkrustaler Herkunft
~ **spring** hypogene Quelle f
~ **water** aszendierendes Wasser n
hypogenetic hypogenetisch
hypogeous unterirdisch
hypolimnion Hypolimnion n
hyposalinity Hyposalinar n
hypotaxic deposit hypotaxische Lagerstätte f
hypothermal hypothermal

~ **vein** hypothermaler Gang m
hypothesis of convection currents Unterströmungshypothese f
hypothetical resources prognostische Vorräte mpl Gruppe Delta 1
hypotype Hypotyp m
hypsographic hypsografisch
hypsography Hypsografie f
hypsoisotherm Hypsoisotherme f
hypsometer Hypsometer n
hypsometric map Höhenschichtenkarte f
hypsometry Höhenmessung f
hysteresis Hysterese f, Hysteresis f, Nachwirkung f

I

IACC = International Association of Geochemistry and Cosmochemistry
IAEA = International Atomic Energy Agency
IAEG = International Association of Engineering Geology
IAH = International Association of Hydrogeologists
IAHR = International Association for Hydraulic Research
IAHS = International Association of Hydrological Sciences
ianthinite Ianthinit m, $[UO_2(OH)_2]$
IAS = International Association of Sedimentology
IASH = International Association of Scientific Hydrology
IASPEI = International Association of Seismology and Physics of the Earth's Interior
IASY s. International Year of the Active Sun
IATME = International Association of Terrestrial Magnetism and Electricity
IAV = International Association of Volcanology
ICCP = International Committee for Coal Petrology
ice Eis n
~ **accretion** Vereisung f
~ **accumulation** Eisanhäufung f
~ **action** Tätigkeit f des Eises
~ **advance** Eisvorstoß m
~ **agency** s. action
~ **apron** Sander m
~ **avalanche** Eislawine f, Gletscherlawine f
~ **bank** Packeis n
~ **barrier** Eisbarriere f
~-**barrier lake** Gletscherstausee m
~ **blink** s. ~ cliff
~ **boom** Eisaufbruch m, Eisgang m
~ **border** Eisrand m
~-**borne** eisverfrachtet
~-**borne sediment** glaziges Sedimentgestein n; fluvioglaziales Sedimentgestein n
~-**bound** vom Eis eingeschlossen
~ **cake** Eisscholle f

~ **cap** s. ~ sheet
~-**carried** eisverfrachtet
~ **cascade (cataract)** Eiskaskade f, Gletscherfall m
~ **cave** Eiskeller m, Eishöhle f, Gletschertor n
~ **cavern** Gletschergrotte f, Gletscherhöhle f
~ **cliff** Eiskliff n
~ **cloud** Eiswolke f
~ **cone** Eiskegel m
~ **core** Eiskern m
~ **cover** Eisdecke f (eines Sees)
~ **crowding** Eisdruck m
~-**crumpled** eisgefältelt, eisgestaucht
~ **crust** Eiskruste f, Harsch m
~ **crystal** Eisnadel f, Eiskristall m
~ **crystal marks** Eiskristallmarken fpl (Spuren, Abdrücke, Pseudomorphosen)
~ **dam** Eisbarr[ier]e f, Eisdamm m, Eisstau m
~-**dammed lake** Eisstausee m
~ **divide** Eisscheide f
~ **drift** Eisgang m, Treibeis n, Eisdrift f
~ **edge** Eisrand m
~ **feathers** Fasereis n
~ **fern** Eisblumen fpl
~ **field** Eisfeld n
~-**floated** eisverfrachtet
~ **floats** Treibeis n
~ **floe** Eisscholle f, Scholleneis n
~ **floes** Treibeis n
~ **flowers** Eisblumen fpl
~ **fog** Eisnebel m
~-**free** eisfrei
~ **front** Eisfront f
~ **frost** Vereisung f; Reifbildung f
~ **glaze** Glatteis n
~ **gorge** s. ~ dam
~ **jam** Eisstoß m, Eisstauung f
~-**laid drift** s. till
~ **layer** Eisschicht f
~ **lens** Eislinse f
~ **line** Eislinie f
~ **load** Eislast f
~ **lobe** s. glacier lobe
~ **margin** Eisrand m
~-**marginal channel** s. ~-marginal valley
~-**marginal lake** glazialer Randsee m
~-**marginal valley** Urstromtal n, Eisrandtal n
~ **mark** Gletscherschliff m
~ **marking** Eisabscheuerung f
~ **motion** Eisgang m
~ **needle** Eisnadel f
~ **pedestal** Gletschertisch m
~ **period** Eiszeit f
~ **pillar** Gletschertisch m
~ **plateau** Eisplateau n
~-**ponded lake** Eisstausee m
~ **push** s. ~ thrust
~-**pushed ridge** Stau[ch]wall m (einer Moräne)
~ **pyramid** s. ablation cone
~ **quake** Eiskrachen f
~-**rafted** eisverfrachtet
~ **rafts** Treibeis n

~ **rain** Eisregen m
~ **rampart** Eiswall m
~ **recession** Eisrückzug m
~ **remnant** Eisrest m
~ **retreat** Eisrückzug m
~ **ridge** Eisrücken m
~ **river** s. glacier
~-**scoured** vom Eise ausgekolkt
~ **scouring** Eisabscheuerung f
~-**scratched** eisgeschrammt
~ **seismics** seismische Eisdickenmessung f
~-**shaped** eisgeformt
~ **sheathing** Eisüberzug m
~ **shed** Eisscheide f
~ **sheet** Eisschicht f, Eisdecke f, Inlandeis n
~ **shove** s. ~ thrust
~-**smoothed** eisgeglättet
~ **spar** glasiger Feldspat m, Eisspat m (s.a. sanidine)
~ **spicule** Eisnadel f
~ **stream** Eisstrom m
~ **striation** Gletscherschliff m
~ **strip** Eisband n
~ **thrust** Eisdruck m, Eisschub m, Eispressung f
~-**transported** eisverfrachtet
~ **vein** Eiskeil m
~ **veneer** Eisfläche f
~ **waste** Eiswüste f
~ **wear** Eisabscheuerung f
~ **wedge** Eiskeil m
~ **wedging** Spaltenfrost m
~-**worn** eisgeschrammt
Ice Age Glazial n, Eiszeit f, Eiszeitalter n, Pleistozän n
iceberg Eisberg m
icefall Gletscherbruch m, Eisbruch m; Gletscherfall m; Eissturz m
Iceland agate echter Obsidian m
~ **spar** isländischer Doppelspat m, optischer Kalkspat m (s.a. calcite)
icelandite Islandit m (Fe-reicher Andesit)
ichnite fossile Fährte f
ichnofossil Ichnofossil n
ichnolite fossile Fährte f
ichnology Ichnologie f, Fährtenkunde f
ichthyodorulite Ichthyodorulith m (Flossenstachelrest)
ichthyolite Fischrest m
ichthyosaur Ichthyosaurus m
icicle Eiszapfen m
ICID = International Commission on Irrigation and Drainage
icing Vereisung f
~ **condition** Vereisungszustand m
icosahedral zwanzigflächig
icosahedron Ikosaeder n, Zwanzigflächner m
icositetrahedral vierundzwanzigflächig
icositetrahedron Ikositetraeder m, Deltoidikositetraeder n, Vierundzwanzigflächner m
I.C.S.G. = International Commission of Snow and Glaciers

icy

icy eisartig, eisig, vereist
idaite Idait m, Cu_5FeS_6
iddingsite Iddingsit m (komplexes Zersetzungsprodukt von Olivin)
ideal crystal Idealkristall m
~ **gas** ideales Gas n
~ **gas law** [ideales] Gasgesetz n, Gasgleichung f, Zustandsgleichung f der idealen Gase
~ **grading curve** Idealsieblinie f
~ **section** Idealschnitt m
~ **solution** ideale Lösung f (Hydrochemie)
identification method [**of reservoir properties**] Erkennungsverfahren n [für Speichereigenschaften]
~ **of minerals** Mineralbestimmung f
~ **of soils** Bodenkennzeichnung f
identified resources nachgewiesene Ressourcen fpl (Lage, Quantität und Qualität durch geologische Untersuchungsarbeiten bekannt)
~ **subeconomic resources** bekannte, gegenwärtig wirtschaftlich nicht bauwürdige Ressourcen fpl
idioblast Idioblast m
idioblastic idioblastisch
idiochromatic idiochromatisch
~ **crystal** idiochromatischer Kristall m
~ **mineral** idiochromatisches Mineral n
idiogen syngenetisch
idiogeosyncline Idiogeosynklinale f, Saumtiefe f, Randsenke f
idiomorphic, idiomorphous idiomorph, automorph, isometrisch
idiophanous idiophan
idocrase Idokras m (s.a. vesuvianite)
idrialine Idrialin m, $C_{22}H_{14}$
idrialite Quecksilberbranderz n (Kohlenwasserstoffe mit Zinnober)
IGC = International Geological Congress
IGCP = International Geological Correlation Programme
igneoaqueous vulkanoäquatisch, tuffitisch (vulkanische Aschen)
igneous glutflüssig, vulkanisch, magmatisch
~ **body** Intrusivkörper m
~ **dike** Eruptivgang m
~ **floor** magmatischer (kristalliner) Untergrund m
~ **gneiss** Orthogneis m
~ **mass** Eruptivmasse f
~ **plug** Eruptivpfropfen m, Vulkanpfropfen m
~ **rock** Erstarrungsgestein n, vulkanisches Gestein n, Eruptivgestein n
~ **vein** Eruptivgang m
ignescent stone Feuerstein m
ignigenous s. igneous
ignimbrite Ignimbrit m, Gluttuff m, Schmelztuff m
ignition loss Glühverlust m
ignoble metal unedles Metall n
IGP = International Geodynamics Project
iguanodonts Iguanodonten mpl
IGY = International Geophysical Year

IHD = International Hydrological Decade
ijolite Ijolith m (Alkaligestein)
ikaite Ikait m, $CaCO_3 \cdot 6H_2O$
ikunolite Ikunolith m, $Bi_4(S, Se)_3$
ilesite Ilesit m, $Mn[SO_4] \cdot 4H_2O$
illinition dünne Kruste f (auf einem Mineral)
Illinoisian [**Ice Age**] Illinois-Eiszeit f (entspricht der Riß-Eiszeit)
illiquation Schmelzung einer Substanz in einer anderen
illite Illit m (Hydroglimmer mit K-Einbau)
illuminating oil Leuchtöl n
illuvial horizon Illuvialhorizont m, B-Horizont m
~ **soil** Illuvialboden m, Anreicherungsboden m
illuviation Einspülung f
Illyrian [**Substage**] Illyr[ium] n (Unterstufe, Mittlere Trias, Tethys)
ilmenite Ilmenit m, Titaneisen n, $FeTiO_3$
ilmenorutile Ilmenorutil m, schwarzes Titanoxid n (Varietät von Rutil mit Fe-Titanat, -Niobat, -Tantalat)
ilvaite Ilvait m, $CaFe_3[OH|O|Si_2O_7]$
image Abbild n
~ **analysis** Bildauswertung f
~ **correlation** Bildkorrelation f
~ **display** 1. Bildwiedergabe f; 2. Bildwiedergabegerät n
~ **distortion** Bildverzerrung f
~ **interpretation** Bildauswertung f
~ **of interference** Interferenzbild n
~ **point** Spiegelpunkt m
~ **processing** Bildbearbeitung f
~ **registration** paßgerechte Überlappung bzw. Überlagerung z.B. von Luftbildern der mehrkanaligen Fernerkundungsaufnahmen
~ **restoration** Wiederherstellung f einer Aufnahme (z.B. aus einer digitalen Magnetband- oder analogen Hologrammaufzeichnung)
~ **scale** Abbildungsmaßstab m
~ **well** Spiegelbohrung f
imagery Bildmaterial n, Aufnahmen fpl
imaging radar Bildradar n
~ **system** Bildaufnahmegerät n, bilderzeugendes System n
imbedded eingebettet, schichtig
imbibe/to durchtränken
imbibition Imbibition f, Aufsaugung f, Einsaugung f, Durchtränkung f
imbricate structure Dachziegellagerung f (von Geröllen); Schuppengefüge n, Schuppenbau m, Schuppung f
imbricated schuppenartig
~ **folding** Schuppenfaltung f, Faltung f mit Verschuppung, Gleitbettbildung f
imbricating dachziegelartig (schuppenartig) übereinanderliegend
imbrication s. imbricate structure
imgreite Imgreit m, NiTe
immature in unreifen Formen
~ **conglomerate** unsortiertes Konglomerat n
~ **form** unreife Form f

impregnation

~ **residual soil** unreifer Verwitterungsboden *m*
~ **shale** toniges Sediment *n* mit schwachem Schiefergefüge
~ **stage** Jugendstadium *n*
~ **weathering** frische Verwitterung *f*
immediate roof unmittelbares Hangendes *n*; Dachschichten *fpl*
immersed bog unter Wasser wachsendes Moor *n*
immersion Immersion *f*, Eintauchung *f*, Untertauchen *n*
~ **objective** Immersionsobjektiv *n*
~ **probe** Tauchsonde *f*
immigrate/to einwandern
immigration Einwanderung *f*
immiscibility Nichtmischbarkeit *f*
immiscible entmischt; nicht mischbar
~ **displacement** frontale Verdrängung *f*
immobile fluid fließunfähiges Fluid *n*
immobility Unbeweglichkeit *f*
impact Anprall *m*; Schlagenergie *f*
~ **bomb** poröse Schmelzgesteinsbombe *f (an Meteorkratern)*
~ **cast** Stoßmarke *f*, Stoßeindruck *m*; Einschlagmarke *f (Sedimentgefüge)*
~ **coefficient** Aufschlagsbeiwert *m*
~ **displacements** Stoßverschiebungen *fpl*
~ **fluidization** Verflüssigung *f* durch Meteoritenaufschlag
~ **glass** durch Impaktmetamorphose gebildetes tektitartiges Glas *n*
~ **hardness** Schlaghärte *f*
~ **hypothesis** Aufsturzhypothese *f (Mond)*
~ **mark** Aufschlagspur *f (eines Meteoriten)*
~ **melting** Einschlagschmelzen *n (durch Meteorite)*
~ **metamorphism** s. shock metamorphism
~ **resistance** Kerbzähigkeit *f*
~ **screen** Stoßsieb *n*
~ **slag** verglastes Sediment *n* in Meteorkratern
~ **strength** s. ~ resistance
~ **theory** Meteoriten-Einsturz-Theorie *f (Mond)*
~ **velocity** Einschlaggeschwindigkeit *f*
~ **wave** s. shock wave
impactite Impaktit *m (Schmelzgestein durch Impaktmetamorphose)*
impalpable sand Staubsand *m*, Mehlsand *m*
~ **structure** sehr feine Struktur *f*
impassable ungangbar
impedance Impedanz *f*, Scheinwiderstand *m*
~ **matching** [optimale] Ankopplung *f*
impenetrability Undurchdringlichkeit *f*
imperfect cleavage unvollkommene (undeutliche) Spaltbarkeit *f*
~ **crystal** unvollkommener (realer) Kristall *m*, Realkristall *m*
imperfection Fehlordnung *f (im Kristall)*
~ **of crystal** Kristallfehler *m*
impermeability Undurchlässigkeit *f*, Undurchdringlichkeit *f*
~ **of the soil** Bodenundurchlässigkeit *f*
~ **to water** Wasserundurchlässigkeit *f*

impermeable undurchlässig, undurchdringlich
~ **bed** undurchlässige Schicht *f*; Grundwasserstauer *m*
~ **rock** Wasserstauer *m*, undurchlässiges Gestein *n*
~ **stratum** undurchlässige Bodenschicht *f*
impervious undurchlässig; wasserundurchlässig, wasserdicht
~ **bed** undurchlässige (wasserstauende) Schicht *f*
~ **blanket** Dichtungsvorlage *f*, Dichtungsteppich *m*
~ **break** undurchlässige Zwischenlage *f*
~ **core** Dichtungskern *m (einer Talsperre)*
~ **diaphragm** Dammkernmauer *f (einer Talsperre)*
~ **layer** undurchlässige Schicht *f*
~ **sole** undurchlässige Sohle *f*
imperviousness Undurchlässigkeit *f*; Wasserundurchlässigkeit *f*
~ **of the soil** Bodenundurchlässigkeit *f*
impetus Anstoß *m*, Antrieb *m*
impinge/to aufschlagen *(Meteoriten)*
impingement optisch diskordante Verdrängung von Kalzit durch Dolomit
impinging light auffallendes Licht *n (Mikroskopie)*
implication texture Implikationsgefüge *n*
implosion Implosion *f*
imponded water aufgestautes Wasser *n*
imporosity Mangel *m* an Porosität, Porenmangel *m*
imporous nicht porös
imported dirt Fremdberge *pl*
~ **water** Fremdzufluß *m (von A_o von außerhalb des Betrachtungsraums)*
imposed load aufgebrachte Last *f*, Auflast *f*
impossible of fossilization fossil nicht erhaltungsfähig
impound/to [auf]stauen, anstauen
impound water Stauwasser *n*
impoundage Stau *m*, Aufstau *m*, Anstauung *f*
impounded lake Stausee *m*
~ **reservoir** Staubecken *n*, Talsperrenbecken *n*
~ **water pressure** Stauwasserdruck *m*
impounding basin Staubecken *n*, Talsperrenbecken *n*
~ **dam** Staudamm *m*
~ **reservoir** Staubecken *n*, Talsperrenbecken *n*
impoverish/to verarmen, sich vertauben
impoverished soil magerer Boden *m*
impoverishment Verarmung *f*, Vertaubung *f*
impregnate/to imprägnieren, durchtränken
impregnated sand durchtränkter Sand *m*
~ **with iron** eisenhaltig, eisenschüssig
~ **with oil** ölgetränkt, ölimprägniert, öldurchtränkt
impregnation Durchtränkung *f*, Imprägnation *f*, Imprägnierung *f*
~ **deposit** Imprägnationslagerstätte *f*
~ **ore** Imprägnationserz *n*
~ **vein** Imprägnationsgang *m*

impressed

impressed pebbles eingedrückte Gerölle *npl*
impression Abdruck *m (eines Fossils)*
~ **in wax** Wachsabdruck *m*
~ **of plants** Pflanzenabdruck *m*
~ **of the foot** Fußabdruck *m*
imprint Eindruck *m*, Abdruck *m*
~ **of a leaf** Blattabdruck *m*
imprisoned lake abflußloser See *m*
improved oil recovery Mehrentölung *f*
improvement of a river channel Flußregulierung *f*
~ **of land (soil)** Bodenmelioration *f*, Bodenverbesserung *f*
impsonite Impsonit *m (asphaltisches Pyrobitumen)*
impulse response Impulsantwort *f*
impulsive beginning deutlicher (scharfer) Einsatz *m (Seismik)*
impure unrein, verunreinigt
~ **coal** *(Am)* unreine (aschereiche) Kohle *f*
~ **iron alum** Bergbutter *f (s.a. halotrichite)*
impurity Beimengung *f*, Verunreinigung *f*
in-line offset Offset *n*; Anlauf *m (Abstand des Schußpunkts zur ersten Geophongruppe)*
~**-place material** anstehendes Material *n*
~**-seam seismics** Flözwellenseismik *f*
~ **situ** am Ort, an Ort und Stelle, in situ
~**-situ combustion** In-situ-Verbrennung *f (einer Lagerstätte)*
~**-situ conditions** Lagerstättenbedingungen *fpl*
~**-situ deposit** Lagerstätte *f* in situ, autochthone Lagerstätte *f*
~**-situ leaching** In-situ-Laugung *f*
~**-situ material** anstehendes Material *n*
~**-situ porosity** Porosität *f* in situ
~**-situ recovery** In-situ-Gewinnung *f*
~**-situ reservoir properties** Speichereigenschaften *fpl* in situ
~**-situ soil** anstehender Boden *m*
~**-situ test** Geländeversuch *m*
inactive gas nichtreagierendes Gas *n*
~ **volcano** untätiger Vulkan *m*
inaurate mit Goldglanz
inbiota Infauna *f*, Substratbewohner *mpl*
inbreak crater Einbruchskrater *m*, Einsturzkrater *m*, Caldera *f*
incandescence Glühen *n*
incandescent [weiß]glühend
~ **ash flow** Gluttuffstrom *m*
~ **detritus** glühender Auswürfling *m*
~ **pumice (tuff) flow** Gluttuffstrom *m*
incarbonization Inkohlung *f (s.a. coalification)*
incidence Einfallen *n (von Licht)*
~ **of frost** Auftreten *n* von Frost
incident einfallend
~ **angle** Einfallswinkel *m*
~ **wave** einfallende (schrägauftreffende) Welle *f*
incidental zufällig
~ **constituent** zufälliger Bestandteil *m*, Nebenbestandteil *m*
incipient crystal Kristallembryo *m*
~ **folding** Embryonalfaltung *f*
~ **form** Embryonalform *f (bei Kristallen)*
~ **metamorphism** beginnende Metamorphose *f (Übergangsbereich zwischen Diagenese und Metamorphose)*
~ **stage** Anfangsstadium *n*
incise/to einschneiden
incised meander eingeschnittener (eingesenkter) Mäander *m*
incision Einschneiden *n*
incisor Inzisiv *m*, Schneidezahn *m*
inclination 1. Schrägstellung *f*, Neigung *f*, Abböschung *f*; 2. *s.* continental slope; 3. Inklination *f (der Magnetnadel)*
~ **angle** Neigungswinkel *m*
~ **dip** Einfallrichtung *f*
incline 1. Gefälle *n*, Neigung *f*, Einfallen *n*; 2. einfallende Strecke *f*
inclined geneigt, tonnlägig
~ **bed** geneigte Schicht *f*
~ **bedding** geneigte Schichtung *f*, Diagonalschichtung *f*
~ **borehole** Schrägbohrung *f*, Schrägbohrloch *n*
~ **drilling** Schrägbohren *n*
~ **extinction** schiefe Auslöschung *f*
~ **fault** geneigte Verwerfung *f*
~ **fold** schiefe (geneigte) Falte *f (mit nicht vertikaler Achsenebene)*
~ **plane** Neigungsebene *f*
~ **seam** geneigtes Flöz *n*
~ **shaft** Schrägschacht *m*
inclinometer Neigungsmesser *m*, Inklinometer *n*, Klinometer *n*
~ **log** Diagramm *n* einer Neigungsmessung
inclosing rock Nebengestein *n*
included angle eingeschlossener Winkel *m*
~ **grain** verwachsenes Korn *n*
inclusion Einlagerung *f*, Einschluß *m*
incoalation Inkohlung *f*
incoherent nichtbindig *(Boden)*
~ **material** loses Material *n*
incombustible constituent unbrennbarer Bestandteil *m*
incoming radiation Globalstrahlung *f (von Himmel und Sonne)*
~ **solar radiation** Sonneneinstrahlung *f*, Insolation *f*
incompatible element inkompatibles Element *n (nicht einbaufähig in die wesentlichsten gesteinsbildenden Minerale)*
incompetent bed inkompetente Schicht *f*
~ **folding** *s.* flow folding
incomplete convergence Teilkonvergenz *f*
~ **record** lückenhafte Schichtenfolge *f*
~ **ripples** isolierte Rippeln *fpl*, Einzelrücken *mpl*
~ **shadow** Halbschatten *m*
~ **well** unvollkommener Brunnen *m*
incompressibility modulus Elastizitätsmodul *m*
incongealable ungefrierbar
incongruent melting point inkongruenter Schmelzpunkt *m*

incongruous inkongruent
- ~ **drag fold** inkongruente Schleppfalte f *(nicht parallel zur Großfalte)*
- ~ **minor fold** inkongruente Kleinfalte f *(nicht parallel zur Großfalte)*

inconsequent stream inkonsequenter Fluß m *(unabhängig von der geologischen Struktur)*
inconstant fold Faltenschwarm mit Streuung der Achsen in Streichen und Fallen
increase in depth Tiefenzunahme f
- ~ **in solubility** Löslichkeitszunahme f
- ~ **in temperature** Temperaturerhöhung f
- ~ **of pressure** Druckerhöhung f
- ~ **of soil fertility** Erhöhung f der Bodenfruchtbarkeit
- ~ **of temperature** Temperaturerhöhung f

increment method Verjüngungsmethode f *(Probenahme)*
incretion hohle zylindrische Konkretion f
incrop verdeckter fossiler Ausstrich m
incrust[ate]/to s. to encrust
incrustation s. encrustation
incrusted s. encrusted
incrusting s. encrusting
incursion Einströmen n *(von Wasser)*
- ~ **of the sea** Einbrechen n des Meeres

incus Amboß m, mittleres Gehörknöchelchen n
indentation Einbuchtung f
- ~ **of the coast** Küstengliederung f

indented coast gegliederte Küste f
- ~ **pebbles** eingedrückte Gerölle npl

inderborite Inderborit m, $MgCa[B_3O_3(OH)_5]_2 \cdot 6H_2O$
inderite Inderit m, $Mg[B_3O_3(OH)_5] \cdot 5H_2O$
index bed Leitschicht f
- ~ **ellipsoid** Indikatrix f
- ~ **fossil** Leitfossil n
- ~ **mineral** Leitmineral n
- ~ **of friction** Reibungskoeffizient m
- ~ **of mining intensity** Abbaugeschwindigkeitswert m
- ~ **of refraction** Brechungsindex m
- ~ **property** Klassifizierungseigenschaft f
- ~ **well** Einpreßbohrung f

indialite Indialith m, $Mg_2Al_3[AlSi_5O_{18}]$
Indian pipestone Varietät von Argillit
- ~ **red** Eisenglanz m, roter Haematit m
- ~ **road** s. esker
- ~ **shield** Indischer Schild m

indianaite Indianait m *(weißer Porzellanton, s.a. halloysite)*
indianite s. anorthite
indicated reserves angezeigte Vorräte mpl *(nach Quantität und Qualität teilweise aus Proben berechnet, teilweise aufgrund geologischer Schlüsse abgeleitet)*
indication of age Alterszeichen n
- ~ **of oil** Erdölanzeichen n

indicator element Pfadfinderelement n
- ~ **fan** Verteilungsbild n von Leitgeschieben
- ~ **horizon** Indikatorhorizont m

- ~ **mineral** Indikatormineral n
- ~ **plant** Leitpflanze f *(Geobotanik)*
- ~ **stone** Leitgeschiebe n
- ~ **vein** erzfreier Leitgang m

indices Flächenindizes mpl *(bei Kristallen)*
indicolite Indigolith m, blauer Turmalin m *(s.a. tourmaline)*
indigene endemisches Fossil n
indigenous bodenständig, eigenbürtig, in situ
- ~ **coal** autochthone Kohle f
- ~ **fauna** endemische Fauna f
- ~ **form** endemische Form f
- ~ **fossil** Fossil n auf primärer Lagerstätte
- ~ **limonite** autochthoner Limonit m *(Eiserner Hut)*

indigo copper Covellin m, Kupferindigo m *(s.a. covellite)*
indigolite s. indicolite
indirect flushing Rückspülung f
- ~ **stratification** s. secondary stratification
- ~ **wave** reflektierte Welle f

indistinct cleavage undeutliche Spaltbarkeit f
indite Indit m, $FeIn_2S_4$
indium Indium n, In
individual crystal Einzelkristall m
- ~ **development** Ontogenese f

indochinite Indochinit m *(zur Gruppe der Tektite gehörig)*
induce/to induzieren, erregen
induced cleavage Druckschieferung f
- ~ **polarization** induzierte Polarisation f
- ~ **porosity** sekundäre Porosität f
- ~ **potential** induziertes Potential n, Induktionspotential n
- ~ **potential logging** Messung f induzierter Potentiale
- ~ **radioactivity** induzierte Radioaktivität f
- ~ **recharge of ground water** Grundwasseranreicherung f

inductance Induktivität f
induction Induktion f
- ~ **logging** Induktionslog n, Induktionsmessung f

inductive induktiv
- ~ **method** induktive Methode f

indurate/to härten, sich verhärten, hart werden
indurated talc Talkschiefer m
induration Erhärtung f, Verhärtung f, diagenetische Verfestigung f
- ~ **process** Erhärtungsprozeß m

industrial geology Wirtschaftsgeologie f
- ~ **grade diamond** Industriediamant m
- ~ **mineral** nutzbares Mineral n
- ~ **water** Brauchwasser n, Nutzwasser n, Gebrauchswasser n

industry of building materials Baustoffindustrie f
inelasticity unelastisches Verhalten n
inequant fold Falte f mit beträchtlichen Längenunterschieden der Schenkel
inequigranular ungleichmäßig körnig, ungleichkörnig

inequilateral

inequilateral mit ungleichen Seiten
inequivalved ungleichklappig
inert inert, [reaktions]träge
~ area druckleeres Gebiet *n*
~ gas Inertgas *n*
~ material Ballastmaterial *n*
~ oil gasleeres Öl *n*
inertia Beharrungsvermögen *n*
inertial mass träge Masse *f*
inertinite Inertinit *m (Kohlenmaceral, Maceralgruppe)*
inertite Inertit *m (Kohlenmikrolithotyp, Mikrolithotypengruppe)*
inertodetrite Inertodetrit *m (Kohlenmikrolithotyp)*
inesite Inesit *m*, $Ca_2Mn_7[Si_5O_{14}OH]_2 \cdot 5H_2O$
inexhaustible unerschöpflich
inexploitable abbauunwürdig, unbauwürdig
inface Kliffteil einer Cuesta
infauna Infauna *f (im Bodensediment lebende Fauna)*
inferior coal minderwertige Kohle *f*
~ stones minderwertige Diamanten *mpl*
inferred ore vermutetes Erz *n*
~ reserves geschlußfolgerte Vorräte *mpl (in nicht erkundeten Teilen bekannter Lagerstätten. Quantität und Qualität geologisch geschlußfolgert)*
infertile unfruchtbar
infill/to auffüllen
infilled fissure gefüllte Spalte *f*
infilling Füllung *f*, Gangfüllung *f*
~ well Zwischensonde *f*
infiltrability Eindringkapazität *f*
infiltrate/to infiltrieren, einsickern, versickern, durchsickern
infiltrated imbibiert
~ fossils Geisterfauna *f*
~ zone infiltrierte Zone *f*
infiltration Infiltration *f*, Einsickern *n*, Einsickerung *f*, Versickern *n*, Versickerung *f*
~ area Infiltrationsgebiet *n (Wasser)*
~ area of well Brunneneinsickerungsbereich *m*
~ capacity Einsickerungskapazität *f*
~ dynamics Infiltrationsdynamik *f*
~ field Sickerfeld *n*
~ gallery Sickerstrecke *f*
~ in the subsoil Versickerung *f* im Boden
~ rate Infiltrationsrate *f*, Einsickerungsfaktor *m*
~ rate at a given moment aktuelle Infiltrationsrate *f*
~ recharge Infiltrationsspende *f*
~ routing Sickerweg *m*
~ stage Infiltrationsetappe *f*
~ water Sickerwasser *n*
infinite electrode Dreielektrodenanordnung *f*
~ reservoir unendliches Reservoir *n*
infinitesimal strain infinitesimale Deformation *f*
inflammability Entzündbarkeit *f*
inflammable feuerfangend, entzündbar

186

inflated aufgebläht
inflation pressure Fülldruck *m*
inflow Zustrom *m*, Zufluß *m*, Einfließen *n*, Einfluß *m*
~ performance Förderleistung *f (Wasser)*
inflowing stream Zufluß *m*
influation Versinkung *f (Wasser)*
influence zone of a well Brunnenwirkungsbereich *m*
influent 1. Nebenfluß *m*; 2. s. ~ stream
~ seepage Infiltration *f*, Versickerung *f*
~ stream Grundwasser spendender Fluß *m*
influx Zuströmung *f*, Zufluß *m*, Zulauf *m*, Einfließen *n*, Einfluß *m*
infrabasal plate Infrabasalplatte *f (Paläontologie)*
infracrustal infrakrustal
infraglacial subglazial
infralittoral sublitoral
inframundane oberflächennah, unter der Erdoberfläche
infrared infrarot
~ absorption Infrarotabsorption *f*
~ aerial remote sensing Infrarot-Luftfernerkundung *f (Luftfernerkundung im infraroten Bereich des Spektrums)*
~ analysis Infrarotspektroskopie *f*
~ imagery Infrarotaufnahmen *fpl*
~ microscope Infrarotmikroskop *n*
~ radiation Infrarotstrahlung *f*
~ remote sensing Infraroterkundung *f (Fernerkundung unter Nutzung des infraroten Spektralbereichs)*
~ rock discrimination Unterscheidung *f* von Gesteinen nach ihrer unterschiedlichen Wärmeausstrahlung im Infrarotbereich
~ satellite remote sensing Infrarot-Satellitenfernerkundung *f (Satellitenfernerkundung im infraroten Bereich des Spektrums)*
~ spectrometer Infrarotspektrometer *n*
~ thermometer Infrarotthermometer *n*
~ transmittancy Infrarotdurchlässigkeit *f*
infrastructure Infrastruktur *f*, migmatischer Unterbau *m*
infundibulum Trichter *m*, trichterförmiges Organ *n*
infusible unschmelzbar
infusorial earth Diatomeenerde *f*, Infusorienerde *f*, Kieselgur *f*
ingrained eingesprengt
ingress of salt water Salzwasserzutritt *m*
~ of the sea Einbrechen *n* des Meeres
~ of water Verwässerung *f*
ingression Ingression *f*, Einbruch *m (des Meeres)*
~ sea Ingressionsmeer *n*
inharmonious folding disharmonische Faltung *f*
inherent ash Eigenasche *f (Kohle)*
~ moisture Bergfeuchte *f*
~ stability Eigenstabilität *f*
inherited structure übernommene Struktur *f*

inhibited mud Spülung *f* mit Inhibitoren
inhibiting growth wachstumshemmend
inhomogeneity Inhomogenität *f*
inhomogenous magnetic field inhomogenes Magnetfeld *n*
initial activity Anfangsaktivität *f (eines Tracers)*
~ **atmosphere** Uratmosphäre *f*
~ **chamber** Bursa *f* primordialis, Protoconch *m*, Anfangskammer *f (der Gastropoden- und Cephalopodenschale)*
~ **coarse grinding** Vorschleifen *n*
~ **concentration** Anfangskonzentration *f (Tracer)*
~ **diameter of drilling** Anfangs[bohr]durchmesser *m*
~ **dip** synsedimentäres Schichtfallen *n*
~ **forms** Urformen *fpl (Morphologie)*
~ **gas in place** geologischer Erdgasvorrat *m*
~ **impulse** erster Einsatz *m*, Anfangseinsatz *m (Seismik)*
~ **loading** Anfangsbelastung *f*, Vorlast *f*
~ **melt** Ausgangsschmelze *f*
~ **meridian** Nullmeridian *m*
~ **oil in place** geologischer Erdölvorrat *m*
~ **phase** initialer Magmatismus *m*
~ **pressure** Anfangsdruck *m*
~ **production** Anfangsproduktion *f*
~ **shell** Embryonalkammer *f*
~ **solution** Ausgangslösung *f (der Sedimentationswassergenese)*
~ **stage** Anfangsstadium *n*
~ **stress** Anfangsspannung *f*; Eigenspannung *f*
~ **suppression** Anfangsdämpfung *f*
~ **volcanism** initialer Vulkanismus *m*
initiation of freezing Frostschwelle *f*, Frostbeginn *m*
inject/to injizieren, einpressen, verpressen, einspritzen
injected body Intrusivkörper *m*
~ **gas** eingepreßtes Gas *n (für Flutung oder Speicherung)*
~ **mass** Intrusivmasse *f*
~ **with granite** durchbrochen von Granit, mit Granit injiziert
injection Injektion *f*, Einpressung *f*, Einspritzung *f*; Wasserdruckversuch *m*
~ **area** Injektionszone *f*
~ **earthquake** Injektionsbeben *n*
~ **fluid** Einpreßflüssigkeit *f*, Injektionsflüssigkeit *f*
~ **folding** Injektivfaltung *f*
~ **gneiss** Injektionsgneis *m (Migmatitgneis)*
~ **hole** Einpreßbohrloch *n*
~ **liquid** Injektionsmittel *n*, Injektionsgut *n*
~ **metamorphism** Kontaktmetamorphose *f* um magmatische Intrusionskörper
~ **patch** Injektionspunkt *m (Tracer)*
~ **pressure** Einpreßdruck *m*, Zementierdruck *m*
~ **section** Injektionsgebiet *n (Tracer)*
~ **structures** Injektionsrisse *mpl (in Sedimenten)*

~ **time** Injektionszeitpunkt *m (Tracer)*
~ **well** Einpreßbohrung *f*, Einpreßsonde *f*
injectivity Einpreßindex *m*
~ **profile** Einpreßprofil *n*
ink stone s. melanterite
inland dune Binnendüne *f*, Kontinentaldüne *f*
~ **earthquake** kontinentales Beben *n*, Beben *n* mit kontinentalem Herd
~ **ice** Inlandeis *n*, Binneneis *n*
~ **lake** Binnensee *m*
~ **-moving dune** Binnenwanderdüne *f*
~ **sea** Binnenmeer *n*
~ **sebkha** Inlandsebkha *f*
~ **waters** Binnengewässer *n*
inlet Bucht *f*, Meeresarm *m*, Meeresenge *f*, Förde *f (Jütland)*, Fjord *m*
~ **well** Einpreßbohrung *f*
inlier 1. stratigrafisches Fenster *n (Tektonik)*; 2. Einlieger *m (älterer geologischer Komplex umgeben von jüngeren Ablagerungen)*
innate angeboren
innelite Innelit *m*, $Ba_2(Na, K, Mn, Ti)_2Ti[(O, OH, F)_2|(S, Si)O_4|SiO_7]$
inner bank Gleithang *m*, inneres Ufer *n*
~ **core barrel** inneres Kernrohr *n*
~ **lamella** Innenlamelle *f*, inneres Schalenblatt *n*
~ **margin** Innenrand *m*
~ **radiation region (zone)** innerer Strahlungsgürtel *m (der Erde)*
~ **shelf** innerer Schelf *m*
~ **shore line** Innenküstenlinie *f*
~ **stress** Innenbeanspruchung *f*
innings Anschwemmland *n*, Deichland *n (durch Abdeichung gegen das Meer gewonnenes Land)*
Inoceramus beds Inoceramenschichten *fpl*
inorganic anorganisch
~ **fertilizer** Mineraldünger *m*
~ **origin** anorganischer Ursprung *m*
~ **soil** anorganisches Lockergestein *n*
inosilicate Inosilikat *n*, Kettensilikat *n*
inpouring Einströmen *n*, Hineinströmen *n (von Wasser)*
input gas Einpreßgas *n*
~ **pressure** Einpreßdruck *m*
~ **well** Einpreßbohrung *f*, Einlaßsonde *f*
inquartation Viertelung *f (bei Probenahme)*
inroad of the sea Einbrechen *n* des Meeres
inrush Einbruch *m*, Einströmen *n (von Wasser)*
~ **of sand** Sandauftrieb *m*
~ **of water** Wassereinbruch *m*, Wasserzufluß *m*
insaturated rock untersättigtes Gestein *n*
insect-bearing amber Insektenbernstein *m*
~ **eaters** Insektenfresser *mpl*
Insectivora Insektenfresser *mpl*
insectivorous insektenfressend
insecure roof unsicheres Hangendes *n*
inselberg Inselberg *m*
~ **landscape** Inselberglandschaft *f*
insequent valley insequentes Tal *n*

insert

insert a string of casing/to eine Futterrohrtour einbauen
insert Einlagerung f, Zwischenschicht f
~ **bit** Hartmetallschneide f *(als Einsatzschneide)*
inserted joint-casing Verrohrung f mit eingelassener Verschraubung
insertion Einbringen n *(in die Bohrung)*
inset 1. Nebenkarte f; 2. s. phenocryst
inshore an der Küste, küstennah, Küsten...
~ **environment** küstennahes Milieu n
inside diameter of drilling tool Innenschneidmaß n (Innendurchmesser m) des gesteinszerstörenden Werkzeugs
~ **pool drilling** Abbohren einer ihrer Begrenzung nach bereits bekannten Erdöllagerstätte
insolation Insolation f, Sonneneinstrahlung f
insolubility Unlöslichkeit f
~ **in water** Wasserunlöslichkeit f
insoluble unlöslich, nichtmischbar
~ **in water** wasserunlöslich
~ **residue** unlöslicher Rückstand m
inspection gallery Beobachtungsstrecke f
inspissate/to eindicken
inspissated deposit zerstörte (eingetrocknete) Erdöllagerstätte f
~ **oil deposit** Lagerstätte f mit angereicherten Schwerölen und Asphalten
inspissation 1. Eindickung f; Austrocknung f *(von Erdöl)*; 2. Mächtigkeitszunahme f *(von Sediment)*
instable equilibrium instabiles Gleichgewicht n
installation for mineral water abstraction Mineralwasserfassung f
instant 1. *Anfangs- oder Endzeit einer Sedimentation*; 2. *geologische Zeitdauer einer biostratigrafischen Zone*
instantaneous excavation plötzlicher Gasausbruch m *(im Kohlenbergbau)*
~ **velocity** Momentangeschwindigkeit f, Ortsgeschwindigkeit f
instratified s. interstratified
instreaming Einströmen n *(von Wasser)*
instrument for areal survey aerogeodätisches Gerät n
~ **for tracing hydrocarbons** Gerät n zum Aufspüren von Kohlenwasserstoffen
instrumental error Instrumentenfehler m
instrumentation Instrumentierung f, Meßgerätausrüstung f
insufficiently polished schlecht poliert
insular inselartig, inselförmig, insular, Insel...
~ **shelf** Inselschelf m
~ **volcano** Inselvulkan m
insulator Isolator m
insulosity Inselfläche f *(innerhalb der Küstenlinie eines Sees)*
intake Versickerung f
~ **area** Versickerungsfläche f
~ **channel** Wasserentnahmekanal m
~ **conduit** Druckrohrleitung f, Triebwasserleitung f

~ **place** Nährgebiet n
~ **pressure** Einlaßdruck m
~ **shaft** einziehender Schacht m, Einziehschacht m
~ **valve** Einlaßventil n
~ **well** Einpreßbohrung f, Einpreßsonde f
integral mit Integralgefüge *(für Sediment ohne diskreten Einzelkornverband)*
~ **joint** gasdichte Verbindung von Futterrohren
integrated interpretation Komplexinterpretation f
~ **program for mineral commodities** integriertes Rohstoffprogramm der UNTAD für mineralische Rohstoffe (Bauxit, Kupfer, Eisenerz, Mangan, Phosphat, Zinn)
~ **survey** Komplexerkundung f
integration Großkristallbildung f *(durch Rekristallisation)*
intemperateness Atmosphärilien pl
intensely folded stark gefaltet
intensity of magnetic field magnetische Feldstärke f
~ **of radiation** Strahlungsintensität f
~ **of relief** Reliefenergie f
intentional deviation of the hole Ablenkung f des Bohrlochs
interact/to austauschen
interaction Wechselwirkung f
~ **energy** Wechselwirkungsenergie f *(zwischen Teilchen)*
interambulacral area Interambulakralfläche f *(Paläontologie)*
interbed Zwischenmittel n, Zwischenschicht f
interbedded eingelagert, eingebettet, zwischengeschichtet, eingeschaltet, wechsellagernd
interbedding Einlagerung f, Einbettung f, Zwischenlagerung f, Zwischenschaltung f, Wechsellagerung f
intercalary eingelagert, eingeschaltet, intrusiv
~ **bed** Zwischenlage f, Einlage[rung] f, Einschaltung f
intercalate/to einbetten, einlagern, zwischenlegen, zwischenschalten
intercalated bed eingeschobene Schicht f, Zwischenmittel n
intercalation Einlage[rung] f, Einschaltung f, Zwischenlage f, Zwischenlagerung f, Zwischenmittel n, Zwischenschaltung f
intercept a blowing well/to eine ausbrechende Sonde durch Richtbohrung abfangen
intercept Abschnitt m, Achsenabschnitt m, Parameter m *(bei Kristallen)*
~ **time** Intercept-time f *(Ordinatenabschnitt auf der Laufzeitkurve)*
interchangeable vertauschbar, austauschbar
intercoil spacing Spulenabstand m
intercolline zwischen vulkanischen Erhebungen gelegen
intercommunicating kommunizierend, untereinander verbunden
~ **pore spaces** untereinander verbundene Porenräume mpl

interconnected untereinander verbunden
intercontinental sea Interkontinentalmeer n, Binnenmeer n
intercrescence Verwachsung f
intercrystalline interkristallin
~ **brittleness** interkristalline Brüchigkeit f
~ **crack** interkristalliner Riß m
intercrystallized miteinander verzahnt (Kristalle)
intercutaneous nappe interkutane Decke f (Tektonik)
interdeep Trog m zwischen innerem und äußerem Inselbogen
interdigitate/to fingerartig verflochten sein (von Flachwasserablagerungen)
interdigitation wechselseitige Verzahnung f
~ **of facies** Fazieszahnung f
interdistributary bays Buchten zwischen den Loben der Mündungsarme eines Deltas
interdune passage Dünental n
interface 1. Grenzfläche f, Grenzschicht f, Trennungsfläche f, Zwischenfläche f; Süß-Salzwasser-Grenzfläche f; 2. Sprungschicht f; 3. Netzebenenabstand m; 4. Interface n, Anpassungselement n
~ **level** Zwischenniveau n
~ **potential** Grenzflächenpotential n
interfacial angle Flächenwinkel m (von Kristallen)
~ **forces** Grenzflächenkräfte fpl (z.B. von Erdöl, Wasser)
~ **tension** Grenzflächenspannung f
~ **waves** Grenzflächenwellen fpl
interfere/to interferieren
interference colour Interferenzfarbe f
~ **effect** Druckbeeinflussung f (reservoirmechanisch)
~ **figure** Interferenzbild n
~ **fringe** Interferenzstreifen m
~ **of wells** 1. gegenseitige Beeinflussung f von Sonden; 2. Brunneninterferenz f
~ **pattern** Interferenzbild n
~ **phenomenon** Interferenzerscheinung f
~ **ripples**, ~ **wave ripple marks** Interferenzrippeln fpl
~ **test** Interferenztest m
interfering sich kreuzend
interfinger/to sich verzahnen
interfingering wechselseitige Verzahnung f
interflow hypodermischer Abfluß m (fließt dem Vorfluter aus der ungesättigten Bodenzone direkt zu, ohne den Grundwasserspiegel erreicht zu haben)
interfluent lava flow unterirdischer Lavaerguß m
interfluve Zwischenstromland n, Wasserscheide f
interfolding Einfaltung f
interformational interformationell, zwischen den Schichtlagen auftretend
~ **conglomerate** interformationelle (schichtfremde) Konglomerateinlagerung f

~ **multiple** Teilwegmultiple f
~ **sill** interformationeller Lagergang m
intergalactic intergalaktisch
~ **matter** intergalaktische Materie f
~ **space** intergalaktischer Raum m
~ **travel** Flug m im intergalaktischen Raum
intergelisol Intergelisol n (schwankende Bodenfrostzone zwischen Mollisol und Pergelisol)
interglacial zwischeneiszeitlich, interglazial
interglacial [age] s. ~ episode
~ **clay** Interglazialton m
~ **deposit** interglaziale Ablagerung f
~ **episode (interval)** Interglazial n, Zwischeneiszeit f, Warmzeit f
interglaciation Interglazialzeitraum m
intergrading form Zwischenform f (Paläontologie)
intergranular intergranular
~ **corrosion** interkristalline (von Korngrößen ausgehende) Korrosion f
~ **film** Intergranularfilm m
~ **porosity** intergranulare (primäre) Porosität f
~ **stress** Zwischenkornspannung f
~ **texture** Intergranulargefüge n
intergrow/to verwachsen
intergrown minerals durchwachsene (verwachsene) Minerale npl
~ **ore** verwachsenes Erz n
intergrowth Durchwachsung f, Verwachsung f (von Mineralen)
~ **along the facies** Fazieszahnung f
interior basin intrakontinentales Becken n
~ **cast** Innenabguß m (von Fossilien)
~ **delta** Binnendelta n
~ **depression** Innensenke f
~ **drainage** Binnenentwässerung f
~ **dune** Innendüne f
~ **of the earth** Erdinneres n
~ **reflections** Innenreflexe mpl
~ **spires** Innenwindungen fpl
~ **strain** innere Spannung f
~ **trough** Innensenke f
~ **water** Binnengewässer n
interjacent eingebettet, eingeschaltet, dazwischenliegend
interjointal zwischen den Kluftflächen gelegen
interlacing miteinander verflochten (verwoben), eng verschlungen
interlacing Verwachsung f, Verflochtenheit f
~ **dikes (veins)** sich kreuzende Gänge mpl, Gangkreuz n
interlaminate/to durchsetzen, einlagern
interlaminated feinschichtig wechsellagernd
interlay/to [schichtenweise] zwischenlagern, einlagern
interlayer Zwischenschicht f, Zwischenlage f
~ **water** Zwischenschichtwasser n (im Tonmineral)
interlayered bedding Wechselschichtung f
interleaved flözförmig eingelagert
interlensing linsenförmige Zwischenlagerung f

interlobate

interlobate zwischen benachbarten Gletscherloben gelegen
~ **moraine** Mittelmoräne f
interlobular stream gletscherfrontparalleler Schmelzwasserfluß m
interlock/to ineinandergreifen
interlocked texture Durchwachsungsstruktur f
interlocking wechselseitig verzahnt, ineinandergreifend, kulissenartig
interlocking 1. [wechselseitige] Verzahnung f (von Schichten); 2. Gegenzeitaufstellung f (von Geophonen)
~ **crystals** verzahnte Kristalle mpl
~ **grain** Kornverzahnung f
~ **of strata** Verzahnung f von Schichten
intermarine strait intermarine Meeresstraße f
intermediary s. intermediate
intermediate intermediär
~-**base oil** Erdöl n mit Paraffin- und Asphaltbasis, gemischt-basisches Erdöl n
~ **belt** Zwischenstreifen m zwischen Haft- und Grundwasser
~ **borehole** Zwischenbohrloch n
~ **casing string** Zwischenrohrtour f, technische Rohrtour f
~ **current** Zwischenstrom m
~ **depth** mittlere Tiefe f
~ **focus earthquake** Beben n mit Epizentrum zwischen 65 und 300 km
~ **form** Zwischenform f (Paläontologie)
~ **forms** Mittelgebirgsformen fpl
~ **igneous rock** intermediäres Gestein n (Erstarrungsgestein mit 55 bis 66% Kieselsäure)
~ **layer** Zwischenschicht f
~ **massif** Zwischenmassiv n, Zwischengebirge n
~ **medium** Zwischenmittel n
~ **principal stress** mittlere Hauptspannung f
~ **rock** 1. Zwischenmittel n (zwischen zwei Flözen); 2. hybrides Gestein n; intermediäres Gestein n
~ **water** Wasser n aus Schichten zwischen zwei produzierenden Horizonten
~ **well** Zwischensonde f
intermine von Grubenbauen durchsetzt
intermingled durchwachsen, eingesprengt
intermit/to intermittieren, unterbrechen
intermittency zeitweilige Unterbrechung f
~ **contact** intermittierender Kontakt m
intermittent intermittierend, stoßweise, aussetzend, diskontinuierlich
~ **eruptions** intermittierende Eruptionen fpl
~ **gas-lift** intermittierende Gasliftförderung f
~ **lake** periodischer See m
~ **spring** intermittierende (periodische) Quelle f
~ **stream** periodischer Fluß m, intermittierender Strom m
intermolecular intermolekular
intermont[ane] intermontan
~ **area** s. intermountain
~ **basin** intermontanes Becken n

~ **depression** Intermontansenke f
~ **floor** Gebirgsfußebene f
~ **glacier** konfluenter Gletscher m zwischen zwei Gebirgszügen
intermountain Intermontan...
intermountain Zwischengebirge n (orogene Strukturform)
~ **basin** intermontanes Becken n
~ **depression** Intermontansenke f
internal Innen...; endogen
~ **cast** Steinkern m, Innenabguß m (Ausguß des Innenhohlraums eines Fossils)
~ **constitution** innerer Aufbau m
~ **cutting tool** Innenschneidegerät n
~ **deformation** innere Deformation f
~ **drainage** Binnenentwässerung f
~ **dynamic processes** s. endodynamics
~ **erosion** von Porenräumen ausgehende Erosion f
~ **flush tool joint** Gestängeverbinder m mit freiem Durchflußquerschnitt
~ **friction** innere Reibung f
~ **gas drive** natürlicher Gastrieb m (einer Lagerstätte)
~ **geodynamics** innere Geodynamik f
~ **migration factor** innerer Migrationsfaktor m (Geochemie)
~ **moraine** Innenmoräne f
~ **mould** s. ~ cast
~ **pressure** Innendruck m
~ **reflection** Innenreflexion f
~ **resistance** Eigenwiderstand m
~ **rotation** Internrotation f
~ **sedimentation** interne Sedimentation f (in Hohlräumen von Sedimentgesteinen)
~ **skeleton** Innenskelett n
~ **stagnant water** Staubodenwasser n
~ **stress** Eigenspannung f
~ **structure** Innenstruktur f
~ **water** Tiefenwasser n
international date line Datumsgrenze f
~ **stratigraphic standard scale** internationale stratigrafische Standardskala f
International Geophysical Year Internationales Geophysikalisches Jahr (1957–1958)
~ **Hydrological Decade** Internationale Hydrologische Dekade (1965–1974)
~ **Rules of Zoological Nomenclature** Internationale Regeln für die Zoologische Nomenklatur
~ **Year of the Active Sun** Internationales Jahr der aktiven Sonne (1968–1970)
~ **Year of the Quiet Sun** Internationales Jahr der ruhigen Sonne
internides Interniden pl (orogene Strukturform)
interoceanic zwischenozeanisch
interparticle porosity Zwickelporosität f
interpenetrate/to sich gegenseitig durchdringen, durchwachsen
interpenetration gegenseitige Durchdringung f

~ twin Durchdringungszwilling *m*
interplanar [crystal] spacing Netzebenenabstand *m*, Abstand *m* der Kristallebenen
interplanetary space interplanetarer Raum *m*
interpose/to zwischenschalten
interposed eingebettet, eingeschaltet
interpretability Interpretierbarkeit *f*, Auswertbarkeit *f (z.B.* von Luftbildern)
interpretation equipment Auswertegerät *n*; Auswertegeräte *npl*
~ of maps Kartenlesen *n*
~ technique Auswertetechnik *f*
interpreter Interpretator *m*, Auswerter *m (für geophysikalische Aufnahmen)*
interradials Interradialia *npl*
interreef basin Zwischenriffbecken *n*
interrupted unterbrochen, absätzig, intermittierend
~ cycle unterbrochener Zyklus *m*
intersect/to sich schneiden; durchsetzen, sich kreuzen, sich gabeln *(Gänge)*
~ the ground das Gebirge durchörtern
intersecting faults Sprungkreuzung *f*
Intersection Durchsetzung *f*, Durchörterung *f*, Kreuzung *f (von Gängen)*
~ distance Knickpunktentfernung *f*
~ of lodes Gangkreuz *n*, Scharkreuz *n*
~ point Schnittpunkt *m*
intersertal texture Intersertalgefüge *n*
intershoal basin Zwischenriffbecken *n*
interspace Zwischenraum *m*; Porenraum *m*
intersperse/to einsprengen, einsprenkeln
interspersed mineral eingesprengtes Mineral *n*
interstade, interstadial interstadial
~ epoch Interstadial *n*, Stillstandsperiode *f* der Vereisung
interstellar interstellar, kosmisch
~ dust kosmischer Staub *m*
~ matter interstellare Materie *f*
~ space Weltraum *m*, interstellarer Raum *m*
interstice 1. Ritze *f*, Zwischenraum *m*; Pore *f*; 2. Zwischengitterplatz *m*
interstitial [atom] Zwischengitteratom *n*
~ deposit Imprägnationslagerstätte *f*, als Porenraumfüllungen ausgebildete Lagerstätte *f*
~ filling Porenfüllung *f*
~ fluid *s.* intergranular film
~ gas Porengas *n*
~ glass Glaseinschluß *m*
~ material Zwischenklemmasse *f*, Zwischenmaterial *n*, Mestasis *f (Gesteinsgefüge)*
~ matrix Sedimentbasis *f (zwischen dem Grobkorn)*
~ mechanism Zwischengittermechanismus *m*
~ migration Zwischengitterwanderung *f*
~ quartz Quarzeinschluß *m*
~ water Porenwasser *n*, Kluftwasser *n*, Haftwasser *n*, haftendes Porenwasser *n*; Bergfeuchtigkeit *f*
interstratification Zwischenlagerung *f*, Zwischenschichtung *f*, Zwischenschaltung *f*, Einlagerung *f*, Wechsellagerung *f*

interstratified zwischengelagert, zwischengeschichtet, eingelagert, streifig; durchzogen
~ bed eingelagerte Schicht *f*, Zwischenlage *f*
~ material Verwachsenes *n (Material)*
interstratify/to zwischenschichten, zwischenschalten, einschalten, einlagern, einsprengen, durchziehen, durchsetzen
interstream area Zwischenstromland *n*
intertidal flat (region) Watt *n*
intertongue/to sich verzahnen
intertrappean zwischen Trappdecken gelagert
interval of deglaciation Zwischeneiszeit *f*, Interglazial *n*
~ of stations Meßpunktabstand *m*, Stationsabstand *m*
~ of time Zeitintervall *n*
~ velocity Intervallgeschwindigkeit *f*
interveined geadert
intervolcanic intervulkanisch
interwedge/to sich verzahnen
interzonal soil unreifer Boden *m (ohne Horizontbildung)*
~ time Zeitdauer *f* eines stratigrafischen Hiatus
intimate crumpling Fältelung *f*, starke Runzelung *f*
intimately associated fein verwachsen
~ disseminated feinverteilt
intra-arc basin Becken *n* innerhalb eines Inselbogens
intraclast Intraklast *m*
intracontinental intrakontinental
~ geosyncline intrakontinentale Geosynklinale *f*
~ trough intramontane Senke *f*, intramontaner Trog *m*, intramontanes Becken *n*
intracratonal geosyncline Parageosynklinale *f*, intrakratonale Geosynklinale *f*
intracratonic auf einem Kraton gelegen
intracrustal intrakrustal
intracrystalline fracture intrakristalliner Bruch *m*
intracyclothem kleiner rhythmischer Schichtenwechsel *m (innerhalb eines größeren Verbands)*
intrafoliaceous zwischenblättrig *(Paläobotanik)*
intraformational synsedimentär, innerhalb einer Schichtlage auftretend
~ conglomerate intraformationales Konglomerat *n*
~ contortion *s.* ~ corrugation
~ corrugation endostratische Sedifluktion *f*, synsedimentäre Faltung *f*, schichtlagengebundene Gleitfältelung *f*
~ folds *s.* ~ corrugation
intrageosyncline innerhalb eines Kontinentalgebiets ausgebildete Geosynklinale *f*
intraglacial intraglazial, eingebettet im zentralen Teil eines Gletschers
intragranular intragranular
intramagmatic intramagmatisch
~ deposit intramagmatische Lagerstätte *f*

intramolecular

intramolecular innermolekular
~ rearrangement innermolekulare Umlagerung f
intramont depression Intramontsenke f
intramontane trough Intramontantrog m
intramontanous basin intramontanes Becken n
intramorainic innerhalb des Moränengürtels
intraoceanic intraozeanisch
intraparticle porosity Hohlformporosität f, Partikelporosität f
intrapermafrost water Grundwasser n im Permafrost
intrastratal flow structure endostratische Sedifluktion f, synsedimentäre Faltung f
~ solution Schwermineralauflösung f während der Diagenese
intrastratified ribs Längsrippung f, Lösungsrippeln fpl, Wellenstreifen mpl
intratellural, intratelluric intratellurisch
intrazonal time Zeitdauer f einer biostratigrafischen Zone
intrinsic curve Mohrsche Umhüllungskurve f, Hüllkurve f
~ induction Magnetisierungsintensität f
~ line s. ~ curve
~ magnetic moment magnetisches Eigenmoment n
~ permeability absolute Permeabilität f
~ radiance Strahlungsvermögen n
introduced fossils s. infiltrated fossils
introscope [optische] Bohrlochsonde f
intrude/to intrudieren, eindringen
Intruded body Intrusivkörper m, Intrusionsmasse f
~ by granite durchbrochen von Granit
~ mass Intrusionsmasse f
~ rock Intrusivgestein n
intrusion Intrusion f
~ displacement Intrusionstektonik f
~ of water Wasserzufluß m
~ rock Tiefengestein n, abyssisches Gestein m, Plutonit m, Intrusivgestein n
~ tremors Intrusionsbeben npl
intrusive intrusiv
intrusive Intrusionsmasse f, Intrusivgestein n
~ body Intrusivkörper m
~ boss Intrusivstock m
~ breccia Intrusivbrekzie f
~ deposit intrusive Lagerstätte f
~ dike Intrusivgang m
~ dome Quellkuppe f, Staukuppe f
~ mass Intrusionsmasse f
~ phase Intrusionsphase f
~ rock Intrusivgestein n (s.a. intrusion rock)
~ sheet Intrusivlager n, Lagergang m
~ stock Intrusivstock m
~ vein Eruptivgang m
intumescence 1. Aufpressung f; 2. Aufblähung f (in der Hitze)
~ of lava Lavadom m, Quellkuppe f
inundate/to überfluten, überschwemmen

inundated area Überschwemmungsgebiet n
inundation Überflutung f, Überschwemmung f, Hochwasser n
~ of a petroliferous bed Verwässerung f einer erdölführenden Schicht
invaded by granite durchbrochen von Granit
~ igneous mass Intrusionsmasse f
~ well Schluckbrunnen m
~ zone Infiltrationszone f, Invasionszone f
~ zone resistivity elektrischer Widerstand m im Invasionsbereich des Spülungsfiltrats
invaders eindringende Art f (Ökologie)
invading igneous mass Intrusionsmasse f
invalid name ungültiger Name m (Nomenklaturregeln)
invasion Infiltration f; Einbruch m
~ of the sea Einbrechen n des Meeres, Meereseinbruch m
invection Verkeilung f (Tektonik)
inventory (Am) Speicherinhalt m
inverse überkippt
~ filter inverses Filter n
~ lateral logging inverse Widerstandsmessung f
inversion Überfaltung f, Überkippung f, inverse Lagerung f
~ layer Inversionsschicht f
~ nappe verkehrte Decke f (Tektonik)
~ of relief Inversion f des Reliefs, Reliefumkehr[ung] f
~ temperature Inversionstemperatur f
invertebrate wirbellos
invertebrates Invertebraten npl
inverted invers, überkippt
~ capacity of well Brunnenaufnahmevermögen n
~ fan Meilerstellung f (der Schieferung)
~ fault widersinnige Verwerfung f
~ fold überkippte Falte f
~ limb überkippter Faltenschenkel m
~ order inverse Lagerung f
~ plunge Abtauchen n einer Falte mit inverser Schichtung
~ relief Reliefumkehr f
~ stratigraphic sequence inverse Lagerung f
~ stream umgekehrte Laufrichtung f (eines Flusses)
~ well Versickerungsbrunnen m
investigation of bogs and marshes Moorkunde f
~ of foundation Baugrundforschung f
~ of foundation conditions Baugrunduntersuchung f
~ of rock Gesteinsuntersuchung f
~ of soil Bodenuntersuchung f
involute whorl involute Windung f
involution 1. Wickelung f von Faltendecken; 2. s. cryoturbation
~ layer Taschenboden m, Auftauboden m
involutions Brodelstrukturen fpl, Verknetungen fpl (kryoturbate Formen)
involved rock eingebettetes Gestein n

inward dipping nach innen einfallend
inwash *aus dem Vorland stammende alluviale Ablagerung am Gletscherrand*
inyoite Inyoit m, $Ca[B_3O_8(OH)_5]\cdot 4H_2O$
iodargyrite *s.* iodyrite
iodate Jodat n
iodic jodhaltig
iodine Jod n, J
iodite *s.* iodyrite
iodobromite Jodobromit m, Jodbromchlorsilber n, Ag(Cl, Br, J)
ioduretted jodhaltig
iodyrite Jodit m, Jodsilber n, Jodargyrit m, β-AgJ
iolite Iolith m, Wassersaphir m *(Varietät von Cordierit)*
ion-beam scanning massenspektrometrische Ionenstrahlungsanalyse f
~ **column** Ionensäule f
~ **detector** Ionensonde f
~-**dipole bond** Ionenbindung f, heteropolare Bindung f
~ **exchange** Ionenaustausch m
~ **exchange phenomena** Ionenaustauschphänomene npl
~ **exchanger** Ionenaustauscher m
~ **flow** Ionenstrom m
~ **lattice** Ionengitter n
ionic ionisch
~ **bond** Ionenbindung f, heteropolare Bindung f
~ **cleavage** Ionenspaltung f
~ **compound** Ionenverbindung f, heteropolare Verbindung f
~ **conductivity** Ionenleitfähigkeit f
~ **crystal** Ionenkristall m
~ **diffusion** Ionendiffusion f
~ **lattice** Ionengitter n
~ **link[age]** Ionenbindung f, heteropolare Bindung f
~ **potential** Ionenpotential n
~ **radius** Ionenradius m
~ **ray** Ionenstrahl m
~ **species** Ionenart f
ionization Ionisierung f
~ **potential** Ionisationspotential n
ionizing radiation ionisierende Strahlung f
ionogenic ionogen
ionosphere Ionosphäre f
ionospheric disturbance ionosphärische Störung f
~ **layer** Ionosphärenschicht f
~ **wave** Ionosphärenwelle f
IOR *s.* improved oil recovery
Iowan [Ice Age] Iowan-Eiszeit f *(entspricht dem Würm I-Glazial)*
iozites vulkanischer Magnetit m, schwarze magnetische Kügelchen npl in der Lava
IP *s.* induced polarization
Ipswichian Ipswichien n *(Pleistozän, Britische Inseln, entspricht etwa dem Riß-Würm-Interglazial der Alpen)*

IPU = International Paleontological Union
IQSY *s.* International Year of the Quiet Sun
IR *s.* infrared
iranite Iranit m, $Pb[CrO_4]\cdot H_2O$
irestone *(sl)* harter Schieferton m; Hornstein m
iridesce/to irisieren, schillern, labradorisieren
iridescence Irisieren n, Schillern n, Labradorisieren n
iridescent irisierend, [in den Regenbogenfarben] schillernd
iridium Iridium n, Ir
iridize/to irisieren, [in den Regenbogenfarben] schillern
iridizing Changieren n
iridosmine Iridosmium n *(isomorphe Mischung von Os und Ir)*
iriginite Iriginit m, $H_2[UO_2(MoO_4)_2]\cdot 2H_2O$
iris in Regenbogenfarben schillernder Bergkristall m
irisated agate Regenbogenachat m
Irish coal *(sl)* Gesteinsberge pl *(Kohlenbergbau)*
~ **touchstone** *(sl)* Basalt m
iron [gediegenes] Eisen n, Fe
~ **algae** Eisenalgen fpl
~ **alum** Eisenalaun m *(s.a. halotrichite)*
~ **and manganese concretion** Eisenmangankonkretion f
~ **bacteria** Eisenbakterien fpl
~-**bearing** eisenhaltig
~ **black** fein verteiltes Antimon n
~ **cap** Eiserner Hut m
~ **carbonate** *s.* siderite rock
~-**clad** eisenummantelt
~ **clay** Toneisenstein m, Sphärosiderit m
~ **concretion** Eisenkonkretion f
~ **crust** Eisenkruste f
~ **deposit due to weathering** Eisenverwitterungslagerstätte f
~-**depositing bacteria** Eisenbakterien fpl
~ **dolomite** *s.* ankerite
~ **dross** Eisensinter m
~ **formation** Eisenformation f *(nur für präkambrische Fe-Ablagerungen üblich)*
~ **froth** schwammiger Haematit m *(s.a. haematite)*
~ **glance** Glanzeisenerz n, Eisenglanz m *(s.a. specular iron, haematite)*
~ **gossan** zelliger Hutlimonit m
~ **hat** Eiserner Hut m
~-**humus ortstein (pan)** Eisenhumusortstein m
~ **hydroxide coating** Eisenhydroxidüberzug m
~ **lode** Eisenerzgang m
~-**magnesium rich** eisen-magnesiumreich
~ **manganese ore** Eisenmanganerz n
~ **meteorite** Eisenmeteorit m
~ **mica** Eisenglimmer m *(s.a. haematite)*
~ **nickel core** Eisennickelkern m *(der Erde)*
~ **nickel pyrite** Eisennickelkies m, Pentlandit m *(s.a. pentlandite)*
~ **ochre** Berggelb n, Eisenocker m *(s.a. limonite)*

iron

~ oolite Eisenoolith *m*
~ ore Eisenerz *n*
~-ore deposit Eisenerzlager *n*
~-oxide coat Eisenoxidhaut *f*
~ pan Eisenortstein *m*
~ pyrite Eisenkies *m*, Pyrit *m* (*s.a.* pyrite)
~ sandstone Eisensandstein *m*, eisenschüssiger Sandstein *m*
~-shot Eisenoolithe führend
~ silicate ore Eisensilikaterz *n*
~-stained eisenfleckig
Iron Age Eisenzeit *f*
ironlike eisenartig
ironstone 1. Eisenstein *m (üblich für postpräkambrische Fe-Ablagerungen)*; 2. *s.* clay ironstone
~ blow *s.* gossan
~ concretion Toneisensteingalle *f*
irony eisenhaltig
irradiation by solar rays Sonnenbestrahlung *f*
irreducible water saturation Haftwassersättigung *f*
irregular unregelmäßig
~ bedding diskordante Schichtung *f*
~ fold *s.* flow fold
~ mullion nicht näher klassifizierbare Mullionsstruktur *f*
irreparable well damage nicht zu beseitigende Bohrlochverstopfung *f*
irrespirable nicht atembar, matt; giftig *(Grubengase)*
irrigate/to bewässern, berieseln
irrigation Bewässerung *f*, Berieselung *f*
~ agriculture Bewässerungswirtschaft *f*
~ by water Wasserberieselung *f*
~ channel Bewässerungsrinne *f*, Bewässerungsgraben *m*
~ district Rieselfeld *n*
~ engineering Bewässerungstechnik *f*
~ field Rieselfeld *n*
~ net Bewässerungsnetz *n*, Berieselungsnetz *n*
~ plant Bewässerungsanlage *f*, Rieselanlage *f*
~ system Bewässerungssystem *n*
~ tower Berieselungsturm *m*
~ water Rieselwasser *n*; Beregnungswasser *n*
~ works Bewässerungsanlage *f*
irrotational wave *s.* longitudinal wave
irruption Intrusion *f* des Magmas in den Erstarrungsraum
irruptive rock *s.* intrusive rock
Irvingtonian [Stage] Stufe des unteren Pleistozäns
IRWA = International Water Resources Association
IRZN *s.* International Rules of Zoological Nomenclature
isanomal[ic] *s.* isoanomal
isanomaly *s.* isoanomaly
isenite Isenit *m (Varietät von Trachyandesit)*
ishikawaite Ishikawait *m* (U-Niobat)
ishkyldite Ishkyldit *m (Varietät von Antigorit)*
isinglass [stone] Glimmer *m* in transparenten Tafeln

island Insel *f*, Eiland *n*
~ arc Inselbogen *m*
~ chain Inselkette *f*
~ festoon Inselgirlande *f*, Inselreihe *f*
~ formed by aggradation Aufschüttungsinsel *f*
~ in a river Werder *m*
~ mount Zeugenberg *m*
~ mountain Inselberg *m*
~ volcano Inselvulkan *m*
Isle of Wight diamond *(sl)* transparente Varietät von Quarz
islet kleine Insel *f*
isoanomal Isanomale *f*, Linie *f* gleicher Störwerte
~ contour map Isanomalenkarte *f*
isoanomaly Isanomalie *f*
isobar Isobare *f*
isobaric isobar, bei konstantem Druck
~ chart Isobarenkarte *f*
isobarism Gleichheit *f* des Drucks
isobase Isobase *f*
isobath Isobathe *f*, Linie *f* gleicher Wassertiefe, Tiefenlinie *f*
isobatherm, isobathythermal line Linie *f* gleicher Meerestemperatur
isobed map Mächtigkeitskarte *f* der Schichten einer stratigrafischen Einheit
isobiolith durch ihre Fossilführung abgegrenzte Sedimenteinheit *f*
isocal line Linie *f* gleichen Heizwerts (in Kohlenflözen)
isocarb line Linie *f* gleichen Kohlenstoffverhältnisses (Carbon-ratio-Theorie)
Isocardia clay Isocardienton *m*
isochione Linie *f* gleicher Schneegrenze
isochore Konvergenzlinie *f* (Linie gleichen senkrechten Abstands zwischen zwei gegebenen geologischen Horizonten)
~ map Karte *f* gleicher (erbohrter, nicht wahrer) Mächtigkeiten
isochromatic isochromatisch
isochronal test Isochronaltest *m*
isochrone Isochrone *f* (in der Geochronologie)
~ map Isochronenplan *m*
isochroneity Zeitäquivalenz *f*
isochronous isochron
~ surface Niveaufläche *f* gleichen Zeitalters (in einer sedimentären Einheit)
isoclasite Isoklas *m*, $Ca_2[OH|PO_4] \cdot 2H_2O$
isoclinal isoklinal
~ fold Isoklinalfalte *f*
~ fold system Isoklinalfaltenbündel *n*
~ folding Isoklinalfaltung *f*
~ ridge Isoklinalkamm *m*
~ valley Isoklinaltal *n*
isoclinally folded isoklinal gefaltet
isocline 1. isoklinal gefaltete Schichtserie *f*; 2. *s.* isoclinic line
isoclinic fold Isoklinalfalte *f*
~ line Isokline *f*, Linie *f* gleicher magnetischer Inklination

isocon Linie *f* gleicher Konzentration
isocrynal line Linie *f* gleicher Mitteltemperatur des kältesten Wintermonats
isodip line *s.* isoclinic line
isodynamic separator Magnetscheider *m*
isofacial isofaziell
isofacies map Isofazieskarte *f*
isogal Isogamme *f*, Linie *f* gleicher Schwere
~ **map** Isogammenkarte *f*, Schwerekarte *f*
isogam Isodyname *f*, Linie *f* gleicher magnetischer Intensität
isogenetic isogenetisch
isogeny Isogenese *f*
isogeolith lithofazielle Einheit *f (Sedimenteinheit, die durch ihre Lithologie abgegrenzt wird)*
isogeotherm Geoisotherme *f*, Linie *f* gleicher Erdtemperatur
isogeothermal geoisothermal
~ **line** *s.* isogeotherm
isogonic line Isogone *f*, Linie *f* gleicher magnetischer Deklination
~ **zero line** Nullisogone *f*, deklinationslose Linie *f*
isograd Isograd *m (Fläche gleichen Metamorphosegrads)*; 2. Isograde *f*, Linie *f* gleicher Temperatur
isohaline Isohaline *f*, Linie *f* gleichen Salzgehalts
isohele, isohelic line Linie *f* gleicher Insolation
isohume Linie *f* gleichen Feuchtigkeitsgehalts *(in Kohlenflözen)*
isohyet *s.* isohyetal line
isohyetal line Isohyete *f*, Niederschlagshöhenkurve *f*, Regengleiche *f*
~ **map** Regenkarte *f*
isohypse, isohypsometric line Isohypse *f*, Höhenlinie *f*
isokite Isokit *m*, CaMg[F|PO$_4$]
isolated hard-rock hill Monadnock *m*
~ **porosity** Totporosität *f*
~ **ripples** *s.* incomplete ripples
isolith Isolithe *f*, Linie *f* gleicher Gesteinsmächtigkeit
~ **map** Isolithenkarte *f (Lithofazieskarte mit Darstellung der reinen Mächtigkeit eines lithologischen Typs)*
isomagnetic isomagnetisch
isomatic line Linie *f* gleicher Verdunstung
isomesia Faziesgleichheit *f (gleiche Umgebung bzw. Fazies)*
isometric stratigraphic diagram Kammerblockbild *n*
~ **system** reguläres (kubisches) System *n*
isometry Höhengleichheit *f*
isomorphic isomorph *(s.a. isomorphous)*
isomorphism Isomorphie *f*
isomorphous isomorph
~ **crystal** isomorpher Kristall *m*
~ **replacement** *s.* ~ substitution
~ **series** isomorphe Reihe *f*
~ **substitution** isomorphe Substitution *f*

isonomic climate gleichartiges Klima *n*
isoorthoclase Isoorthoklas *m*, optisch positiver Orthoklas *m*
isopach Isopache *f*, Linie *f* gleicher Mächtigkeit, Mächtigkeitslinie *f*
~ **map** Mächtigkeitskarte *f*
isopachous von gleicher Mächtigkeit
~ **line** *s.* isopach
isopachyte *s.* isopach
isopage Linie *f* gleicher Eisbedeckungsdauer
isopectic Isopekte *f (Isochrone des Gefrierens)*
isopic isopisch
~ **facies** isopische Fazies *f (gleichzeitige und gleichartige Fazies)*
isopiestic level isostatische Ausgleichsfläche *f*
~ **line** Grundwassergleiche *f*, Linie *f* gleichen artesischen Drucks
isopleth Isoplethe *f*, Abstandsgleiche *f*
isopluvial line *s.* isohyetal line
isopolymorphic isopolymorph
isopolymorphism Isopolymorphismus *m*
isopore Isopore *f*, Linie *f* gleicher zeitlicher Änderung
isorad Isorade *f*, Linie *f* gleicher Radioaktivität
isorank line Linie *f* gleichen Inkohlungsgrads *(in Kohlenflözen oder kohlehaltigen Sedimenten)*
isoreflectance line of coaly materials Linie *f* gleichen [optischen] Reflexionsvermögens von kohligem Material *(in Sedimenten)*
isorthose *s.* isoorthoclase
isoseism Isoseiste *f*, Linie *f* gleicher Erdbebenstärke
isoseismal isoseismisch
~ **curve (line)** Isoseiste *f*, Linie *f* gleicher Erdbebenstärke
isoseismic isoseismisch *(s.a. isoseismal)*
isostasy Isostasie *f*
isostatic isostatisch
~ **adjustment** isostatischer Ausgleich *m*
~ **anomaly** isostatische Anomalie *f*
~ **balance** isostatisches Gleichgewicht *n*
~ **compensation** isostatische Kompensation *f*
~ **compensation current** isostatische Ausgleichsströmung *f*
~ **equilibrium** isostatisches Gleichgewicht *n*
~ **mass compensation** isostatischer Massenausgleich *m*
~ **settling** isostatische Senkung *f*
~ **surface** isostatische Fläche *f*
isotherm Isotherme *f*, Temperaturgleiche *f*
isothermal isotherm[isch]
~ **chart** Isothermenkarte *f*
~ **equilibrium** isothermes Gleichgewicht *n*
~ **surface** Isothermenfläche *f*
isothermobath Linie *f* gleicher Meerestemperatur
isotime curve Geschwindigkeitsisobase *f*, Isochrone *f (alle Punkte gleicher Laufzeit für seismische Wellen verbindende Kurve)*
isotope Isotop *n*

isotope

~ **abundance** Isotopenhäufigkeit f
~ **analyzer** Isotopenanalysator m
~ **calibration curve** Eichkurve f für Isotope
~ **dilution** Isotopenverdünnung f
~ **dilution analysis** Isotopenverdünnungsanalyse f
~ **fractionation** s. ~ separation
~ **geochemistry** Isotopengeochemie f
~ **hydrogeology** Isotopenhydrogeologie f
~ **ratio** Isotopenverhältnis n
~ **separation** Isotopentrennung f, Isotopenfraktionierung f
~ **shift** Isotopieverschiebung f
~ **tracer** Isotopentracer m
isotopic abundance Isotopenhäufigkeit f
~ **activation cross section** Isotopenaktivierungsquerschnitt m
~ **age determination** radiometrische (radioaktive, absolute) Altersbestimmung f
~ **composition (constitution)** Isotopenzusammensetzung f
~ **dating** s. ~ age determination
~ **enrichment** Isotopenanreicherung f
~ **equilibrium** Isotopengleichgewicht n
~ **exchange** Isotopenaustausch m
~ **facies** isotopische Fazies f
~ **fractionation** Isotopentrennung f, Isotopenfraktionierung f
~ **mass** Isotopengewicht n, Atommasse f
~ **thermometry** Isotopenthermometrie f
isotron Isotron n, Ionenscheider m
isotropic isotrop
~ **fabric** s. random orientation
~ **stratum** isotrope Schicht f
isotropization Isotropisierung f
isotropy Isotropie f
isotypism Isotypie f
isovalent gleichwertig
isovelocity surface Fläche f gleicher Wellengeschwindigkeit (Seismik)
isovol [line] Linie f gleicher Gehalte an flüchtigen Bestandteilen (in Kohlenflözen)
issite Issit m (melanokrates Ganggestein)
issue/to herausfließen, herausströmen, herauskommen
issuing lava ausfließende Lava f
isthmus Isthmus m, Landenge f
istisuite Istisuit m, (Ca, NaH)(Si, AlH)O₃
itabirite Itabirit m, Eisenglimmerschiefer m
itabiritic iron ore itabiritisches Eisenerz n
itabyryte s. itabirite
itacolumite Gelenkquarzit m, Gelenksandstein m, Itakolumit m
italite Italit m (leuzitreiches alkalisches Effusivgestein)
iterative iterativ
itoite Itoit m, $Pb_3[GeO_2(OH)_2(SO_4)_2]$
itternite Itternit m (zeolithisierter Nosean)
IUGG = International Union of Geodesy and Geophysics
IUGS = International Union of Geological Sciences

ivanoite Ivanoit m (H_2O-haltiges Chloroborat)
IWSA = International Water Supply Association
ixiolite s. tapiolite
ixolyte Ixolith m (fossiles Harz)

J

jacinth s. hyacinth
jack 1. Hebevorrichtung f; 2. s. sphalerite
~ **knife mast** Klappmast m (Bohrturm)
~ **up** Hubinsel f
jacket unter Wasser befindliche Stahlrohrkonstruktion von Bohrinseln
jackhammer Preßlufthammer m
jackup Hubinsel f
jacobsite Jakobsit m, $MnFe_2O_4$
jacupirangite Jacupirangit m (nephelinführender Pyroxenit)
jade Jade f, Nephrit m (kryptokristalliner Aktinolith)
jadeite Jadeit m, $NaAl[Si_2O_6]$
jadeitite Jadeitit m
jag Felszacken m
jagged terrain zerklüftetes Gelände n
jagoite Jagoit m, $Pb_8Fe_2[(Cl, O)|Si_3O_9]_3$
jaipurite Jaipurit m, γ-CoS
Jakutian [Stage] Jakut[ium] n (Stufe, Untere Trias, Tethys)
jalpaite Jalpait m, $Cu_2S \cdot 3Ag_2S$
jam/to verklausen
jam Verklausung f
jama Karstschlot m, Karstbrunnen m, Naturschacht m
jamb (sl) 1. Steinschicht f; großer Block m; 2. störendes Begleittrum n
jamesonite Jamesonit m, $4PbS \cdot FeS \cdot 3Sb_2S_3$
Jamin effect Jamin-Effekt m
janite Janit m, (Na, K, Ca)(Fe, Al, Mg)[Si_2O_6]·$2H_2O$
Japanese twin Japaner Zwilling m
japanite Japanit m (s.a. penninite)
jargon 1. farbloser oder rauchiger Ceylonzirkon; 2. minderwertiger gelber Diamant
jarlite Jarlit m, $NaSr_2[AlF_6] \cdot [AlF_5H_2O]$
jarosite Jarosit m, $KFe_3[(OH)_6|(SO_4)_2]$
jars Schlagschere f
jasper Jaspis m (s.a. chalcedony)
~ **bar** Jaspilit m (Australien)
~ **opal** Jaspopal m
jasperated mit Jaspis vermengt
jasperite s. jasper
jasperization Jaspisbildung f
jasperize/to in Jaspis umwandeln
jasperoid kryptokristallines silifiziertes Karbonatgestein n
jaspidean jaspisartig; jaspisführend
jaspideous jaspisartig
jaspilite Jaspilit m
jaspoid s. jaspidean
jaspopal Jaspopal m

jaspure marmoriert (gefärbt) wie Jaspis
Jatulian Jatul[ien] *n*, Jatulium *n (Mittelpräkambrium in Finnland)*
jaulingite Jaulingit *m (fossiles Harz)*
javanite Javanit *m (zur Gruppe der Tektite gehörig)*
jaw *s.* mandible
~ breaker Backenbrecher *m*
jawless fishes kieferlose Fische *mpl*, Agnathen *mpl*
jay *(sl)* Dachkohle *f*, Kohle *f* im Hangenden
JCL *s.* job-control language
jefferisite Jefferisit *m (s.a.* vermiculite)
jeffersite *s.* jefferisite
Jeffersonian [Stage] Jeffersonien *n (Stufe des Unterordoviziums in Nordamerika)*
jeffersonite Jeffersonit *m (Varietät von Schefferit)*
jelinite Jelinit *m (fossiles Harz)*
jelletite Jelletit *m (lichtgrüner Andradit)*
jellous gelartig, gallertartig
jelly Gallerte *f*
jellylike gallertartig
jeremejevite Jeremejewit *m*, $AlBO_3$
Jerseyan Jersey-Vereisung *f*
jeso zerkarstete Gipsschicht *f*
jet 1. Gagat *m*, Jett *m*; 2. schwarzer Marmor *m*; 3. Düse *f*
~ bit Düsenmeißel *m*
~ coal *s.* cannel coal
~ deflection drilling Richtbohren *n* mit einer Ablenkturbine
~ drilling Wasserstrahlbohren *n*, Hydromonitorbohren *n*
~ of ash Aschenwurf *m*
~ of steam Dampfstrahl *m*
~ perforating Jetperforation *f*, Hohlladungsperforation *f*
~ piercing Flamm[strahl]bohren *n*
~ pump Strahlpumpe *f*, Jetpumpe *f*
~ rock bituminöses Tongestein *n*
~ screen Schüttelsieb *n*
~ stone schwarzer Turmalin *m*
~ stream Strahlstrom *m (Atmosphäre)*
jetcrete Spritzbeton *m*, Torkretbeton *m*
jetonized wood *s.* vitrain
jetted particle drilling Erosionsbohren *n*
~ well Spülbohrung *f*
jetty Buhne *f*, Mole *f*
jewel Edelstein *m*
jewstone *(sl)* 1. *s.* marcasite; 2. Basalt oder Kalkstein
jeyekite *s.* morinite
jhama Naturkoks *m*
jig Setzmaschine *f*, Setzkasten *m*
jigged ore gewaschenes Erz *n*
jigging Setzen *n*, Setzarbeit *f*
~ action Setzvorgang *m*
jimboite Jimboit *m*, $Mn_3[BO_3]_2$
joaquinite Joaquinit *m*, $NaBa(Ti, Fe)_3[Si_4O_{15}]$
job-control language Job-Steuersprache *f (seismische Datenverarbeitung)*

~ site Baustelle *f*
johachidolite Johachidolith *m*, $Ca_3Na_2Al_4H_4[(F, OH)|BO_3]_6$
johannite Johannit *m*, $Cu[UO_2|OH|SO_4]_2 \cdot 6H_2O$
johannsenite Johannsenit *m*, $CaMn[Si_2O_6]$
johnstrupite Johnstrupit *m (s.a.* mosandrite)
JOIDES = Joint Oceanographic Institutes Deep Earth Sampling
JOIDES program Tiefseebohrprogramm *n* von Schiffen *(bis in layer 2)*
joint/to klüften
joint 1. Kluft *f*; Teilungsfläche *f*, Fuge *f*, Absonderungsfläche *f*, Trennungsfläche *f*, Bruch *m* ohne Verwerfung ; 2. Konjugationslinie *f (im Phasendiagramm)*; 3. Verbinder *m*; 4. Bohrstange *f*; 5. Gelenk *n (Paläontologie)*
~ aquifer Kluftgrundwasserleiter *m*
~ body complex Kluftkörperverband *m*
~-bordered rock body Kluftkörper *m*
~ crack Kluftspalte *f*
~ diagram Kluftrose *f*
~ due to cooling Abkühlungskluft *f*
~ exploitation agreement Ausbeutungsgemeinschaft *f*
~ family Kluftschar *f*
~ network Kluftnetz *n*, Kluftsystem *n*
~ of bedded rocks Schichtfuge *f*
~ of bedding Schichtfuge *f*
~ of retreat Schrumpfungsriß *m*, Kontraktionsspalte *f*
~ opening Fugenöffnung *f*
~ orientation Kluftstellung *f*
~ pattern Kluftmuster *n*
~ plane Kluftfläche *f*
~ set Kluftschar *f*
~ spacing Kluftabstand *m*
~ system Kluftsystem *n*, Kluftnetz *n*
~ vein mineralisierte Kluft *f*, Klufttrum *n*
~ venture gemeinsames Unternehmen *n (zur Finanzierung und Durchführung von Erkundungs- und Gewinnungsarbeiten von mineralischen Rohstoffen)*
~ water Kluftwasser *n*, Spaltenwasser *n*
~-water pressure Kluftwasserdruck *m*
jointable klüftig
jointed klüftig, zerklüftet, geklüftet, von Klüften durchzogen
jointing 1. Klüftung *f*, Zerklüftung *f*, Klüftigkeit *f*; 2. Ablösefähigkeit *f (von Gesteinen)*
jointy klüftig, zerklüftet, voller Schlechten
jordanite Jordanit *m*, $5PbS \cdot As_2S_3$
jordisite Jordisit *m (kolloidales MoS_2)*
josefite Josefit *m (feinkörniges ultrabasisches Ganggestein)*
joseite Joseit *m*, Bi_4Te_2S
josen[ite] *s.* hartite
josephinite Josephinit *m*, $FeNi_3$
Jotnian Jotnien *n*, Jotnium *n (Jungpräkambrium in Finnland)*
Joule Thompson effect Joule-Thompson-Effekt *m (für Gase)*
jug *s.* geophone

jug

~ **hustler** Geophonträger *m*, Meßgehilfe *m*
~ **line** Geophonleitung *f*
juggie Geophonträger *m*, Meßgehilfe *m*
Julian [Substage] Jul *n* (Unterstufe, Obere Trias, Tethys)
julienite Julienit *m*, $Na_2Co[SCN]_4 \cdot 8H_2O$
jumble Gangscharung *f*
jumbo Bohrwagen *m*
jump to beds/to Schichten verwechseln
jump Sprung *m* (kleine Verwerfung)
~-**down** *s.* downthrown fault
~ **of a leg** Fehler *m* bei der Korrelation, Phasensprung *m* (Seismik)
~-**up** *s.* upthrow fault
junction 1. Zusammenfluß *m* (von Flüssen); 2. Zusammenstoß *m* (von Lithosphärenplatten)
~ **of lodes (veins)** Gangkreuz *n*, Scharung *f* von Gängen
~ **surface** Kontaktfläche *f* (einer Störung)
juncture Naht *f*, Grenzlinie *f*, Fuge *f* (von tektonischen Einheiten)
~ **plane** Kontaktfläche *f*
jungle Dschungel *m* (*f*, *n*)
junior synonym jüngeres Synonym *n* (Nomenklaturregeln)
junk basket Brockenfänger *m* (Bohrtechnik)
~ **basket tube** Fangspinne *f*
Jura Jura *m*
~-**type folding** Faltung *f* vom Helvetischen Typ (eigenständige Faltung oberhalb des Grundgebirges)
Jurassic jurassisch, Jura...
Jurassic Jura *m*, Jurasystem *n* (chronostratigrafisch); Jura *m*, Juraperiode *f* (geochronologisch); Jura *m*, Jurazeit *f* (allgemein)
~ **Age** Jura *m*, Jurazeit *f*
~ **coal** Jurakohle *f*
~ **fold** *s.* Jura-type folding
~ **Limestone** Jurakalk *m*
~ **Period** Jura *m*, Juraperiode *f*
~ **System** Jura *m*, Jurasystem *n*
jurupaite Jurupait *m*, $Ca_6[(OH)_2|Si_6O_{17}]$ (*s.a.* xonothite)
jusite Jusit *m*, $(Ca, KH, NaH)(Si, A|H)O_3 \cdot H_2O$
justite Justit *m* (*s.a.* koenenite)
jut out/to überkragen
juvenile juvenil
~ **ejecta** juvenil-authigene Auswürflinge *mpl*
~ **water** juveniles Wasser *n*
juxtapose/to nebeneinanderstellen
juxtaposition Juxtaposition *f*, Anlagerung *f*; Nebeneinanderlagerung *f*, Nebeneinanderstellung *f*, Überlagerung *f*
~ **twins** Juxtapositionszwillinge *mpl*, Berührungszwillinge *mpl*, Kontaktzwillinge *mpl*

K

K-A-age Kali-Argon-Alter *n*
kaersutite Kaersutit *m* (Ti-Amphibol)
kainit[e] Kainit *m*, $KMg[Cl|SO_4] \cdot 2^3/_4H_2O$

kainitite Kainitit *m*
kainosite Kainosit *m*, $Ca_2Y_2[CO_3|Si_4O_{12}] \cdot H_2O$
kainotype rock jungvulkanisches Gestein *n*
Kainozoic känozoisch, neozoisch
Kainozoic [Era] Känozoikum *n*
kakirite Kakirit *m* (grobkataklastisches Gestein)
kakortokite *s.* agpaite
kal eisenhaltiges hartes Gestein *n*
kaliastrak[h]anite Kaliastrakanit *m* (*s.a.* leonite)
kaliblödite, kalibloedite Kaliblödit *m* (*s.a.* leonite)
kaliborite Kaliborit *m*, $KMg_2[B_5O_6(OH)_4][B_3O_3(OH)_5] \cdot 2H_2O$
kalicinite Kalicinit *m*, $KHCO_3$
kalinite Kalinit *m*, $KAl[SO_4]_2 \cdot 11H_2O$
kaliophilite Kaliophilit *m*, $K[AlSiO_4]$
kalistrontite Kalistrontit *m*, $SrK_2[SO_4]_2$
kalkowskite Kalkowskyn *m* (Teilpseudomorphose von Rutil und Haematit nach Ilmenit)
kallaite Türkis *m* (*s.a.* turquois)
kallar Salzausblühung *f*
kallen *s.* callen
kallilite Kallilith *m*, $Ni(Sb, Bi)S$
kalsilite Kalsilit *m*, $K[AlSiO_4]$
kamacite Kamazit *m* (Ni-armes Balkeneisen in Meteoriten)
kamarezite Kamarezit *m*, $Cu_3[(OH)_4|SO_4] \cdot 6H_2O$
kame Kam *m* (kurzer Geschieberücken senkrecht zur Fließrichtung des Eises)
~-**and-kettle topography** kuppige Moränenlandschaft *f*
~ **topography** Kameslandschaft *f*
kampylite *s.* campylite
Kanawhan [Stage] Kanawhan *n* (Stufe des Pennsylvaniens, Appalachen)
kand, kann (*sl*) *s.* cand
kaneite Kaneit *m*, $MnAs$
kansan Kansan *n* (Pleistozän in Nordamerika, entspricht etwa dem Menap bis Chromer Europas)
kansasite Kansasit *m* (fossiles Harz)
kaolin[e] Kaolin *m*, Porzellanerde *f*
~ **coal flint clay** Kaolin-Kohlen-Tonstein *m*
~ **deposit** Kaolinlagerstätte *f*
~ **sandstone** Kaolinsandstein *m*
kaolinic kaolinhaltig, kaolinitisch
kaoliniferous sandstone Kaolinsandstein *m*
kaolinite Kaolinit *m*, $Al_4[(OH)_8|Si_4O_{10}]$
kaolinization Kaolinisierung *f*
kaolinized kaolinisiert
kapel, kaple *s.* caple
kar *s.* cirque
kara schwarzer Solone[t]z *m*
Karelian folding karelische Faltung *f*
karn Steinhaufen *m*, fester Felsen *m*
Karnian [Stage] Karn *n* (Stufe der alpinen Trias)
karoo land unfruchtbarer Boden *m*
Karoo Supergroup Karru-Hauptgruppe *f* (Permokarbon in Südafrika)
karpinskiite Karpinskiit *m*, $(Na, K, Zn, Mg)_2[(OH, H_2O)_{1-2}|(Al, Be)_2 Si_4O_{12}]$

karren Karren *pl*, Schratten *pl*
~ **formation** Schrattenbildung *f*
karrenfeld Karrenfeld *n*, Schrattenfeld *n*
karst Karst *m*, Karstbildung *f*
~ **aquifer** Karstgrundwasserleiter *m*
~ **depression** Karstwanne *f*, Karsttrichter *m*
~ **formation** Karstbildung *f*
~ **funnel** Karsttrichter *m*
~ **lake** Karstsee *m*
~ **landscape** Karstlandschaft *f*
~ **phenomena** Karsterscheinungen *fpl*
~ **plateau** Karsthochfläche *f*
~ **region** Karst *m*, Karstgebiet *n*
~ **spring** Karstquelle *f*
~ **stream** Karstfluß *m*
~ **topography** Karstrelief *n*
karsten *s.* karren
karstenite *s.* anhydrite
karstic karstartig
karstification Verkarstung *f*, Karstbildung *f*
karstified limestone verkarsteter Kalkstein *m*
karstify/to verkarsten
Kasan Ice Age Kasan-Eiszeit *f*, Kasan-Kaltzeit *f* *(entspricht der Mindel-Eiszeit)*
kasolite Kasolit *m*, $Pb_2[UO_2|SiO_4]_2 \cdot 2H_2O$
kasparite Kasparit *m* *(Co-haltiger Pickeringit)*
kata-rock Katagestein *n*, metamorphes Gestein *n* der Katazone
katabatic absteigend *(Luftstrom)*
~ **wind** Fallwind *m*
katagenesis Katagenese *f*, regressive Entwicklung *f*
katamorphic katamorph
katamorphism Katamorphose *f*
katamorphose/to katamorphosieren
kataseismic kataseismisch
katatectic layer Hutgestein *n*, Lösungsrückstände *mpl*
katavothron Katavothre *f*, Ponor *m*, Schluckloch *n*
katazone Katazone *f*
katophorite Katophorit *m*, $Na_2CaFe_4(Fe,Al)[(OH,F)_2|AlSi_7O_{22}]$
katungite Katungit *m* *(pyroxenfreier Melilithit)*
kauri Kauri *n* *(Harzart)*
kaustobiolite Kaustobiolith *m*
kawk *(sl)* Flußspat *m* *(in Cornwall)*
kay *s.* key
Kayenta Formation Kayenta-Formation *f* *(unterer Lias, Nordamerika)*
Kazanian [Stage] Kazan *n* *(Stufe des Perms)*
kebble opaker Kalkspat *m*
keel Kiel *m* *(an Fossilschalen)*
keeled gekielt
keen edge scharfe Kante *f*
Keewatin [Period] Keewatin *n* *(System des Präkambriums von Nordamerika)*
kehoeite Kehoeit *m*, $(Zn, Ca)[Al_2P_2(H_3)_2O_{12}] \cdot 4H_2O$
keilhauite Keilhauit *m*, $(Ca, Y, Ce)(Ti, Al, Fe)[O|SiO_4]$
keldyshite Keldyshit *m*, $Na_2Zr[Si_2O_7]$
kelly Kelly *n*, Mitnehmerstange *f* *(Bohrtechnik)*

~ **bushing** Mitnehmerstangeneinsatz *m*
kelp Tang *m*
kelve *(sl)* Flußspat *m* *(in Cornwall)*
kelyphite Kelyphit *m* *(Verwachsung von Faseramphibol und Feldspat)*
kelyphitic kelyphitisch
~ **rim** Kelyphitrinde *f*
kempite Kempit *m*, $Mn_2(OH)_3Cl$
kennedyite Kennedyit *m*, $Fe_2MgTi_3O_{10}$
kentallenite Kentallenit *m* *(Alkaligabbro)*
kentrolite Kentrolith *m*, $Pb_2Mn_2[O_2|Si_2O_7]$
kenyaite Kenyait *m*, $NaSi_{11}O_{20.5}$
keralite Keralith *m* *(Quarz-Biotit-Hornfels)*
keratophyre Keratophyr *m*
kerf Kernkronenrille *f* im anstehenden Gestein
kermesite Kermesit *m*, Antimonblende *f*, Rotspießglanz *m*, Sb_2S_2O
kern but Bruchstufe *f*
~-**stone** grobkörniger Sandstein *m*
kernite Kernit *m*, Rasorit *m*, $Na_2[B_4O_6(OH)_2] \cdot 3H_2O$
kerogen Kerogen *n*, Schieferöl *n*
kerogenic shale *s.* bituminous shale
kerosene Leuchtöl *n*, Leuchtpetroleum *n*
~ **coal** Ölschiefer *m*
~ **shale** *s.* bituminous shale
kersanite Kersanit *m* *(basisches Ganggestein)*
kerstenite Kerstenit *m*, $Pb[SeO_4]$
kettle Kar *n*; Toteissee *m*
~ **bottom** Tropfwasseraustritt *m* *(am Gestein)*
~ **depression** Karkessel *m*, Karmulde *f*
~ **drift** *s.* ~ moraine
~ **hole** Soll *n*, Toteispinge *f*
~ **lake** Kesselsee *m* *(Glazialform)*
~ **moraine** sollbedeckte Moräne *f*
kettleback *s.* horse
kettled zerkart; ausgehöhlt
kettnerite Kettnerit *m*, $CaBi[OF|CO_3]$
Keuper Keuper *m*
~ **Sandstone** Keupersandstein *m*
kevel *(sl)* 1. Gangfüllung *f*; 2. Fördermenge *f* pro Zeiteinheit *(Nordengland)*
~ **horizon** Leitschicht *f*
kevil *s.* kevel
Kewatin-Coutchiching Kewatin-Coutchiching *n* *(Altpräkambrium in Nordamerika)*
Keweenawan Keweenaw *n* *(Oberpräkambrium in Nordamerika)*
key Inselbank *f*
~ **bed** *s.* marker 1.
~ **form** Leitform *f*
~ **formation** Leitformation *f*
~ **fossil** Leitfossil *n*
~ **horizon** Leithorizont *m*, Bezugshorizont *m*
~ **rock** Leitgestein *n*
~ **well** Einpreßbohrung *f*
keyboard Tastatur *f*, Bedienpult *n*
keystone faulting Scheitelgrabenbildung *f*
khondalite Khondalit *m* *(Gestein in Granulitfazies)*
kick a well/to Ausbruch unter Kontrolle bringen

kick

~ **off** ablenken
kick Einsatz *m (Seismik)*
~ **mud** Totpunktflüssigkeit *f*
~-**off toll** Ablenkwerkzeug *n*
~-**out** Abweichen *n* einer Bohrung
kicking plötzlicher Zufluß *m* im Bohrloch
kidney Nest *n (Erz)*
~ **ore** Nierenerz *n*, nierenförmiger Haematit *m*, roter Glaskopf *m*
~-**shaped** nierenförmig
kieselgu[h]r Kieselgur *f*, Diatomeenerde *f*, Infusorienerde *f*
kieserite Kieserit *m*, $Mg[SO_4] \cdot H_2O$
kilchoanite Kilchoanit *m*, $Ca_3[Si_2O_7]$
Kilkenny coal *s.* anthracite
kill a well/to totpumpen, totdrücken *(eine Bohrung)*
killas *(sl)* Tonschiefer *m (in Cornwall)*
killing of a well Totpumpen *n* einer Sonde
killow Blauerde *f*, Schwarzerde *f*
kimberlite Kimberlit *m*
Kimmeridge Clay Kimmeridge-Ton *m (Kimmeridge, unteres und mittleres Tithon in England)*
Kimmeridgian [Stage] Kimmeridge *n (Stufe des Oberen Juras)*
kimzeyite Kimzeyit *m*, $Ca_3Zr_2[Al_2SiO_{12}]$
kind weich, leicht zu bearbeiten *(Erz)*
kind Art *f*, Gattung *f*
~ **ground** Nebengestein mit topomineralischer Wirkung auf Erzgänge
~ **of deposition** Ablagerungsart *f*
~ **of energy** Energieart *f*
Kinderhookian [Stage] Kinderhookien *n (Stufe des Mississippiens)*
kinematic kinematisch
~ **ductility** kinematische Zähigkeit *f*
~ **viscosity** kinematische Viskosität *f*
kinematics Kinematik *f*
kinetic friction Bewegungsreibung *f*
~ **metamorphism** mechanische Metamorphose *f*
~ **resistance** Bewegungswiderstand *m*
kingite Kingit *m*, $Al_3[(OH)_3(PO_4)_2] \cdot 9H_2O$
kink Biegung *f*, Knickung *f*
~ **bands** Knickbänder *npl*, Knickzonen *fpl*
~ **fold** *s.* chevron fold; zigzag fold
Kinneya ripples Runzelmarken *fpl*
kinoully loses, mildes Nebengestein *n*
kinzigite Kinzigit *m (metasomatischer Gneis)*
kirchheimerite Kirchheimerit *m*, $Co[UO_2|AsO_4]_2 \cdot nH_2O$
Kirkfieldian [Stage] Kirkfieldien *n (Stufe des Champlainings in Nordamerika)*
kirrolite Kirrolith *m*, $Ca_3Al_2[OH|PO_4]_3$
kirschsteinite Kirschsteinit *m*, $CaFe[SiO_4]$
kitkaite Kitkait *m*, NiTeSe
kivite Kivit *m (Varietät von Leuzitbasanit)*
kladnoite Kladnoit *m*, $C_6H_4|(CO)_2NH$
klaprothite, klaprotholite Klaprothit *m (Gemenge von Wittichenit und Emplektit)*
kleinite Kleinit *m*, $[Hg_2N](Cl, SO_4) \cdot xH_2O$

kliachite Kliachit *m*, Alumogel *m*, $AlOOH + H_2O$
Klinkenberg effect Klinkenberg-Effekt *m (für Gase)*
klint karbonatischer Erosionshärtling *m*
klintite massiger Riffkalkstein *m*
klippe Klippe *f*, tektonische Deckscholle *f*
klockmannite Klockmannit *m*, CuSe
kloof tiefe Schlucht *f*
knead into/to einkneten
kneaded gravel in Schlammströmen transportiertes Geröll *n*
~ **sandstone** gekneteter Sandstein *m*
~ **texture** Brodelstruktur *f (kryoturbate Form)*
kneading Verknetung *f*
knebelite Knebelit *m*, $(Mn, Fe)_2[SiO_4]$
knee fold Kniefalte *f*
knits kleine Erzpartikel *fpl*
knob Höcker *m*, Kuppenberg *m*
~-**and-basin topography**, ~-**and-kettle topography** kuppige Moränenlandschaft *f*
~-**and-trail** geschwänzte Buckelstruktur *f*
knobby bit Warzenmeißel *m*
~ **topography** kuppige Moränenlandschaft *f*
knoblike buckelförmig
knock off/to abbauen
knoll 1. kleiner Hügel *m*, Erdhügel *m*, Kuppe *f*; 2. rundliche Erhebung *f (des Meeresbodens)*
~-**reef** *s.* reef-knoll
knopite Knopit *m (Varietät von Perowskit)*
knorringite Knorringit *m*, $Mg_3Cr_2[SiO_4]_3$
knotenschiefer Knotenschiefer *m*
knotted schist Knotenschiefer *m*
knotten sandstone Knottensandstein *m*
knotty dolomite Knottendolomit *m*
~ **texture** Knotenstruktur *f*
known reserves sichere Vorräte *mpl*
knuckle joint Richtgelenk *n*, Gelenkverbindung *f*
kobellite Kobellit *m*, $6PbS \cdot 2Bi_2S_3 \cdot Sb_2S_3$
koechlinite Koechlinit *m*, Bi_2MoO_6
koenenite Koenenit *m (Al-Mg-Oxidchlorid)*
Koenigsberger ratio Königsberger Koeffizient *m (Geomagnetik)*
koenleinite Könl[ein]it *m (karbozyklische Kohlenwasserstoffverbindung)*
koesterite Kösterit *m*, Cu_2ZnSnS_4
koettigite Köttigit *m*, $Zn_3[AsO_4]_2 \cdot 8H_2O$
koffer fold Kofferfalte *f*
kohalaite Kohalait *m (olivinführender Trachyandesit)*
koktaite Koktait *m*, $(NH_4)_2Ca[SO_4]_2 \cdot H_2O$
kolbeckite *s.* sterrettite
kolovratite Kolovratit *m (Ni-Vanadat)*
kolskite Kolskit *m*, $Mg_5[(OH)_8|Si_4O_{10}]$
komatiite Komatiit *m*
kongsbergite Kongsbergit *m*, α-(Ag, Hg)
konichalcite Konichalcit *m*, $CaCu[OH|AsO_4]$
koninckite Koninckit *m*, $Fe[PO_4] \cdot 3H_2O$
koog Koog *m*
koppite Koppit *m*, $(Ca, Ce)_2(Nb, Fe)_2O_6(O, OH, F)$

kordylite Kordylit m, $Ba(Ce, La, Nd)_2[F_2(CO_3)_3]$
kornelite Kornelit m, $Fe_2[SO_4]_3 \cdot 7^1/_2H_2O$
kornerupine Kornerupin m, $Mg_4Al_6[(O, OH)_2|BO_4|(SiO_4)_4]$
korschinskite Kirschinskit m, $Ca_2[B_4O_6(OH)_4]$
kotoite Kotoit m, $Mg_3[BO_3]_2$
kotschubeite Kotschubeit m, $(Mg, Al)_{<3}[(OH)_2|(Cr,Al)Si_3O_{10}] \cdot Mg_3OH]_6$
köttigite s. koettigite
kotulskite Kotulskit m, $Pd(Te, Bi)_{1-2}$
koutekite Koutekit m, Cu_2As
kramenzelkalk Kramenzelkalk m
krantzite Krantzit m (fossiles Harz)
kratochwilite Kratochwilit m, $C_{13}H_{10}$
kratogen[ic], kraton s. craton
kraurite s. dufrenite
krausite Krausit m, $KFe[SO_4]_2 \cdot H_2O$
krauskopfite Krauskopfit m, $Ba_2[Si_4O_{10}] \cdot 6H_2O$
KREEP stark radioaktives gabbroides Mondgestein, angereichert mit **K**alium, seltenen (raren) **E**rdelementen und **P**hosphor)
kremersite Kremersit m, $KCl_2 \cdot NH_4Cl \cdot FeCl_2 \cdot H_2O$
krennerite Krennerit m, $(Au, Ag)Te_2$
krige/to schätzen durch Kriging
kriging Kriging n (nach Krige benanntes Schätzprinzip für den Erwartungswert einer regionalisierten Variablen)
~ coefficient Kriging-Koeffizient m
~ variance Kriging-Varianz f
kroehnkite, kröhnkite Kröhnkit m, $Na_2Cu[SO_4]_2 \cdot 2H_2O$
kryo... s. cryo
krypto... s. crypto...
krypton Krypton n
kryshanovskite Kryshanovskit m, $MnFe_2OH|PO_4]_2 \cdot H_2O$
Kubergandian [Stage] Kubergand n (basale Stufe des Mittelperms)
kukersite Kuckersit m (ordovizisches brennbares Algengestein; Ölschiefer)
kulaite Kulait m (Hornblende-Nephelin-Tephrit)
kulissen fault Kulissenverwerfung f
Kullenberg corer Kullenberg-Probenehmer m (für Tiefseesedimente)
kullerudite Kullerudit m, $NiSe_2$
Kungurian [Stage] Kungur n (Stufe des Perms im westlichen Uralvorland)
kunzite Kunzit m (rosarote Varietät von Spodumen)
kupferschiefer Kupferschiefer m
kupletskite Kupletskit m, $(K_2, Na_2, Ca)(Mn, Fe)_4(Ti, Zr)[OH|Si_2O_7]_2$
kurgantaite Kurgantait m, $(Sr, Ca)_2[B_4O_8] \cdot H_2O$
kurnakovite Kurnakovit m, $Mg[B_3O_3(OH)_5] \cdot 5H_2O$
kurtosis Kurtosis f (statistischer Parameter zur Kennzeichnung eines Korngemisches)
kurumsakite Kurumsakit m, $(Zn, Ni, Cu)Al_8[(VO_4)_2|(SiO_4)_5] \cdot 27H_2O$
kutnahorite Kutnahorit m, $CaMn[CO_3]_2$
kyanite s. cyanite

L

L-joint Lagerkluft f, L-Kluft f (Granittektonik)
laavenite s. lavenite
labelling Markierung f (von Wasser)
labial eruption Spalteneruption f
labile labil, instabil
~ sandstone s. subgraywacke
labite Labit m, $Mg_3H_6[Si_8O_{22}] \cdot 2H_2O$
laboratory investigation Laboruntersuchung f
labradite Labradit m (phanerokristallines Labradoritgestein)
labradorescence Labradorisieren n, Farbwechsel m im Labradorit
labradorite Labradorit m (Mischkristall aus $NaAlSi_3O_8$ und $CaAl_2Si_2O_8$)
labradoritite Labradoritit m (Anorthosit)
labuntsovite Labuntsovit m, $(K, Na, Ba)(Ti, Nb)[(Si, Al)_2(O, OH)_7]_3 \cdot H_2O$
laccolite, laccolith Lakkolith m
lack 1. Mangel m; 2. s. leck
~ of sedimentation Schichtlücke f
lacking in rain regenarm
lacklustre glanzlos, matt
lacovishte Wiesenboden m
lacquer disk Lackfolie f
~ original Lackfolienaufnahme f
lacroixite Lacroixit m, $Na_4Ca_2Al_3[(OH,F)_8|(PO_4)_3]$
lacuna Hiatus m, Diskordanz f, Unterbrechung f
lacus Lacus m (See auf Mars oder Mond)
lacustral, lacustrian s. lacustrine
lacustrine lakustrisch
~ clay Seeton m
~ deposit Süßwasserablagerung f, Seesediment n
~ facies lakustrine Fazies f
~ limestone Süßwasserkalk m
ladder lode (vein) Leitergang m
Ladinian [Stage] Ladin n (Stufe der alpinen Trias)
ladu s. glowing avalanche
lag 1. Zeitverzögerung f; 2. Verschiebung f (des Bezugspunkts); 3. Störung f im hangenden Schenkel einer asymmetrischen Falte
~ concentrate grobes Residualsediment n
~ deposit grobe fluviatile Ablagerung f
~ fault verzögerte Abscherung f; Untervorschiebung f (Tektonik)
~ gravel weit transportiertes Flußgeröll n
~ of the tides Gezeitenverzögerung f
lagg Randsumpf m
lagging [of tides] Gezeitenverzögerung f
lagoon Lagune f, Haff n
~ deposit Lagunenablagerung f
~-derived lagunär
~ facies near reef Riffschattenfazies f
~ in process of being filled in Verlandung begriffene Lagune f
~ island Atoll n
~ moat Ringlagune f
~ shoal Untiefe f der Lagune

lagoon 202

~-type of coast Lagunenküste f, Haffküste f
lagoonal lagunär
~ deposit Lagunenablagerung f
~ type lagunärer Typus m
lagune s. lagoon
lahar Lahar m *(pyroklastischer Schlammstrom)*
~ deposit Schlammtuff m
laid bare bloßgelegt
laired mit Schlamm verstopft
laitakarite Laitakarit m, Bi_4Se_2S
lake See m, Binnensee m
~ asphalt Seeasphalt m
~ ball lakustrischer Pflanzenknäuel m
~ basin Seebecken n
~ bed Seeablagerung f, fossiles Seesediment n
~ current Seeströmung f
~ delta Seedelta n
~ deposit Seeablagerung f
~ district Seengebiet n
~ drainage Einzugsgebiet n eines Sees
~ due to landslide Bergsturzsee m
~ expansion seeartige Erweiterung f *(eines Flusses)*
~ extinction Verschwinden n eines Sees
~ filling Seenverlandung f
~ floor Seeboden m
~ iron ore Raseneisenerz n, See-Erz n
~-land country Seelandschaft f
~ level Seespiegel m
~ marl Seekreide f
~ ore s. ~ iron ore
~ shore Seeufer n
~ side Seelandschaft f
~ silt Seeschlick m
~ surface Seespiegel m
~ swamp Niederungsmoor n
~ terrace Seeterrasse f
~ with subterranean outlet Karstsee m
~ without outflow (outlet) abflußloser See m, Endsee m
Lake Constance Bodensee m
lakelet kleiner See m; Eissee m, Gletschersee m
Lamarcki[ani]sm Lamarckismus m
lamb and slack *(sl)* minderwertige Kohle f
lambertite s. uranophane
lambskin minderwertige Varietät von Anthrazit in Wales
lamella 1. Schalenblatt n; 2. Lamelle f, Blättchen n, Streifen m; 3. Balken m *(Meteorit)*
lamellar lamellar, geschichtet, blättrig, blättchenförmig, streifenförmig
~ fracture blättriger Bruch m
~ pearlite streifiger Perlit m
~-stellate radialblättrig
~ structure Lamellargefüge n, blättriges Gefüge n
~ twinning [structure] Viellingslamellierung f, Zwillingslamellierung f
lamellated s. lamellar
Lamellibranchia[ta] Lamellibranchiaten npl

lamelliferous blätterartig
lamelliform blättchenartig
lamellose plättchenförmig, blättchenförmig
lamellosity Blattschichtung f, Lamellenschichtung f
lamina Plättchen n, dünne Schicht f, Lamine f, Feinschicht f, Lamelle f
laminable in dünne Plättchen deformierbar
laminar boundary layer laminare Grenzschicht f
~ flow laminare Strömung f
laminaria Laminarie f, Riementang m
laminate[d] plattig, blättrig, feingeschichtet, mehrlagig
~ brown coal Blätterkohle f
~ clay Bänderton m
~ mica Spaltglimmer m
~ moor blättriger Torf m
~ quartz laminierter Quarz m, Quarztapeten fpl
~ shale Blätterschiefer m, dünnblättriger Schieferton m
~ structure Laminargefüge n, blättriges Gefüge n, Lagentextur f
lamination Lamellargefüge n, Lamination f, Bänderung f, Feinschichtung f
~ plane Schichtebene f
laminite Laminit m, Rhythmit m, lamellenförmig strukturiertes Sediment n
lamp/to mit UV-Lampe prospektieren
lamp shell s. brachiopod
lampadite Lampadit m, Kupfermanganerz n *(Cuhaltiges Wad)*
lamprophyllite Lamprophyllit m, $Na_3Sr_2Ti_3[(O, OH, F)_2|Si_2O_7]_2$
lamprophyllous lamprophyll, ganzblättrig
lamprophyre Lamprophyr m *(dunkles Ganggestein)*
lamproschist metamorpher Lamprophyr m
lanarkite Lanarkit m, $Pb_2[O|SO_4]$
Lance Formation Lance-Formation f *(Maastricht bis höchstes Campan in Nordamerika)*
lancelet Lanzettfisch m, Amphioxus m
land casing/to Verrohrung absetzen
land amelioration Bodenmelioration f
~ asphalt mit Nebengestein verunreinigter Asphalt m
~ breeze ablandiger Wind m, Landwind m
~ bridge Landbrücke f
~ carnivora Landraubtiere npl
~ clearing Räumung f, Räumungsarbeiten fpl
~ cover Landbedeckung f, Oberflächenbedeckung f des Landes
~-derived terrestrisch
~ evaluation Bodenbewertung f
~ floe Küsteneisfeld n
~ form Geländeform f, Bodenform f, Oberflächenform f
~ hydrology Gewässerkunde f
~ ice Küsteneis n
~ improvement Bodenmelioration f
~-locked landumschlossen

~-locked sea Binnenmeer *n*
~ operations Bohrarbeiten *fpl* auf dem Festland
~ potential Landnutzungspotential *n*
~ reclamation Bodenmelioration *f*; Landgewinnung *f*
~ reorganization Flurneugestaltung *f*
~ sediments kontinentale Ablagerungen *fpl*
~ shifting Kontinentaldrift *f (A. Wegener)*
~ subsidence Bodensetzung *f*
~-surface altitude morphologische Höhe *f*
~ survey[ing] Fluraufnahme *f*
~-tied island landfest gewordene Insel *f*, Angliederungsinsel *f*
~ treatment Bodenbearbeitung *f*
~ upheaval Bodenhebung *f*
~ use Bodennutzung *f*
~-use capability classes Bodennutzungsklassen *fpl*
~-use planning Planung *f* der Bodennutzung
~ value Bodenwert *m*
~ wash Flutgrenze *f*
~ waste Landschutt *m*, Trümmermasse *f*
~ water Oberflächenwasser *n*
~ wind *s*. ~ breeze
lande Heide *f*, Marschheide *f*
Landénian [Stage] Landénien *n (Stufe des Paläozäns, Pariser Becken)*
landesite Landesit *m*, $(Mn, Fe)<_3[PO_4]_2 \cdot 3H_2O$
landfall Erdfall *m*
landfill Deponie *f*
landing depth Einbautiefe *f*, Absetzteufe *f (der Verrohrung)*
~ nipple Landenippel *m*
landsbergite Landsbergit *m*, γ-(Ag,Hg)
landscape planning Landschaftsplanung *f*
landslide Erdrutsch *m*, Rutschung *f*, Bergsturz *m*
~ lake Bergsturzsee *m*
~ scar Abrißnische *f (z.B. von Bergstürzen)*
landslip Erdrutsch *m*
~ terrace Rutschungsterrasse *f*
landward slope of trench kontinentseitiger Abhang *m* eines Tiefseegrabens
lane 1. Gasse *f (Funknavigation)*; 2. Standlinie *f*
langbanite Långbanit *m*, $Mn^{..}Mn_6^{...}[O_8|SiO_4]$
langbeinite Langbeinit *m*, $K_2Mg_2[SO_4]_3$
Langhian [Stage] Langium *n (Stufe des Miozäns)*
langite Langit *m*, $Cu_4[(OH)_6|SO_4] \cdot H_2O$
Langobardian [Substage] Langobardium *n (Unterstufe, Mittlere Trias, Tethys)*
lansfordite Lansfordit *m*, $MgCO_3 \cdot 5H_2O$
lanthanite Lanthanit *m*, $(La, Dy, Ce)_2[CO_3]_3 \cdot 8H_2O$
lanthinite Lanthinit *m*, $2UO_2 \cdot 7H_2O$
lap/to 1. überlappen, überdecken, übergreifen, überstehen; 2. läppen, feinschleifen
lap Überlappung *f*, Überdeckung *f*
~ fault Überschiebung *f*, Faltenwerfung *f*
~-out map Karte der Verbreitung einer postdiskordanten Formation

lapidary 1. Edelsteinschleifer *m*; 2. Gemmenschneiden *n*
lapidification *s*. petrifaction
lapidify/to *s*. fossilize/to 1.
lapidofacies Diagenesefazies *f*
lapie-well Karrenbrunnen *m*
lapies, lapiez Karren *pl (Karstform)*
lapilli Lapilli *pl*
~ tuff Lapillituff *m*
lapilliform lapilliartig, in Form kleiner Steinchen
lapillus Steinchen *n*
lapis-lazuli *s*. lazurite
Laplace transform Laplace-Transformation *f*
lappets Öhrchen *npl (Mündungsfortsätze an Cephalopodenschalen, s.a. auricles)*
lapping 1. Übereinandergreifen *n*; 2. Läppen *n*, Feinschleifen *n*
~ abrasive Läppmittel *n*
~ wheel Läppscheibe *f*
lapse rate Temperaturgradient *m*
Laramide (Laramidian) orogeny laramische Orogenese *f*
lard peat dunkelbrauner fetter Torf *m*
~ stone Speckstein *m*, Steatit *m (s.a. talc)*
larderellite Larderellit *m*, $NH_4[B_5O_6](OH)_4$
lardite *s*. lard stone
large-diameter bit Großlochbohrmeißel *m*
~-diameter hole Großbohrloch *n*
~ grained grobkörnig
~ hole Großbohrloch *n*
~-hole drilling Großlochbohren *n*
~ reservoir Großspeicher *m*
~-scale cross-bedding großdimensionale Schrägschichtung *f*
~-scale fold Großfalte *f*
~-scale imagery großmaßstäbliche (großformatige) Aufnahmen *fpl*
~-scale mapping großmaßstäbliche Kartierung *f*
~-scale mining Bergbau *m* großen Maßstabs, Bergbau *m* hoher Förderleistung
~-scale test Großversuch *m*
~-size borehole Großbohrloch *n*
~-sized derbstückig, großstückig
~ stone Steinblock *m*
~ workings Großabbau *m*
largely observed größtenteils beobachtet *(4. Stufe der Erdbebenstärkeskala)*
larnite Larnit *m*, β-$Ca_2[SiO_4]$
larsenite Larsenit *m*, $PbZn[SiO_4]$
larvikite Larvikit *m (Syenitgestein)*
laser geophysical measurement Lasermessung *f* für geophysikalische Zwecke
~ microspectrographic analysis Lasermikrospektralanalyse *f*
lasionite *s*. wavellite
last water layer fest gebundenes Porenwasser *n (im Tonmineral)*
lasurite Lasurit *m*, $(Na, Ca)_8[(SO_4, S, Cl)_2|(AlSiO_4)_6]$
latch[ing] Markscheiden *n*, Grubenaufnahme *f*

Latdorfian 204

Latdorfian [Stage] Latdorf-Stufe f *(Oligozän)*
late-glacial spätglazial
~-magmatic ore deposit spätmagmatische Erzlagerstätte f
~-mature valley spätreifes Tal n
~-orogenic spätorogen
~-orogenic phase subsequente Phase f
~ transient period späte instationäre Strömungsphase f
latent latent, verdeckt
~ evaporation latente Verdunstung f
~ heat of evaporation latente Verdampfungswärme f
~ heat of fusion latente Schmelzwärme f
~ ore Erzvorrat, der in Zukunft abbauwürdig werden kann
~ podzol verborgener Podzol m
~ stress latente Spannung f
later arrival späterer Einsatz m *(Seismik)*
~ diagenesis Spätdiagenese f
Later Precambrian Spätpräkambrium n, Jungpräkambrium n, Oberpräkambrium n
lateral cleavage Spaltbarkeit f parallel zur Seitenfläche *(Kristall)*
~ compression Zusammenschub m *(Gebirgsbildung)*
~ cone Seitenkegel m
~ consequent stream auf einer Antiklinal- oder Synklinalflanke abfließender konsequenter Fluß m
~ coring Kernen n (Entnahme f von Gesteinsproben) aus der Bohrlochwandung
~ crater Adventivkrater m
~ curve Laterallogaufnahme f
~ deformation Querverformung f
~ ditch Lateralgraben m
~ edge of a crystal Kristallseitenkante f
~ erosion Seitenerosion f
~ eruption Flankeneruption f, Seitenausbruch m, Flankenerguß m
~ extent seitliche Ausdehnung f
~ face Seitenfläche f *(bei Kristallen)*
~ fault Blattverschiebung f
~-force component Seitenkraftkomponente f
~ gradation of facies laterale Faziesänderung f
~ load Querkraft f
~ lobe Laterallobus m
~ log Gradientmessung f, Unterkantenmessung f
~ migration laterale (schichtparallele) Migration f
~ moment Quermoment n
~ moraine Seitenmoräne f
~ outline lateraler Umriß m
~ pressure Seitendruck m
~ push Seitenschub m
~ secretion Lateralsekretion f
~ section Querschnitt m
~ segregation Lateralsegregation f
~ separation flache Sprungweite f *(einer Verwerfung)*
~ shearing fault (shift) Seitenverschiebung f

~ shoving Seitenschub m
~ slide Gleitflächenbruch m
~ spread Anlandung f
~ stream Seitenfluß m
~ stream terrace Kamesterrasse f
~ thrust Seitenschub m
~ valley Seitental n
~ view Seitenansicht f
laterite Laterit m
~ soil Lateritboden m, Roterde f
~ weathering lateritische Verwitterung f
lateritic lateritisch
~ nickel ore lateritisches Nickelerz n
~ ore lateritisches Erz n
laterization Lateritbildung f
laterolog Laterolog n (spezielles Widerstandsmeßverfahren in Bohrungen mit stark salzhaltiger Spülung)
lath-shaped, lathlike leistenförmig
latite Latit m *(Trachyandesit)*
latitude geografische Breite f
~ circle Breitenkreis f
~ correction Breitenkorrektur f, Normalkorrektur f
~ degree Breitengrad m
latiumite Latiumit m, $Ca_6(K, Na)_2Al_4[(O, CO_3, SO_4)|(SiO_4)_6]$
latosol Roterde f, Gelberde f
latrappite Latrappit m, $(Ca, Na, SE)(Nb, Ti, Fe)O_3$
lattice Kristallgitter n, Gitter n
~ arrangement Gitteranordnung f
~-bound water Mineralgitterwasser n
~ constant Gitterkonstante f
~ defect s. ~ imperfection
~ dislocation (distorsion) Gitterstörung f
~ energy Gitterenergie f
~ group Raumgruppe f
~ imperfection Gitterfehlstelle f, Gitterstörung f, Kristallfehler m
~ of twinning lamellae Gitterlamellierung f
~ orientation Regelung f nach dem Kornbau
~ plane Gitterebene f
~ system Gitteranordnung f
~ work Gitterwerk n
~-work skeleton Gitterskelett n
latticed gitterartig
~ tower Turm m aus Gitterwerk *(Bohrturm)*
latticelike gitterartig, gitterähnlich
laubanite Laubanit m *(Varietät von Natrolith)*
laubmannite Laubmannit m, $(Fe, Mn)_3Fe_6[(OH)_3|PO_4]_4$
Laue diffraction (X-ray) pattern Laue-Diagramm n *(Röntgendiagramm)*
laueite Laueit m, $MnFe_2[OH|PO_4]_2 \cdot 8H_2O$
laugenite Laugenit m *(Oligoklasdiorit)*
laumontite Laumontit m, $Ca[AlSi_2O_6]_2 \cdot 4H_2O$
Laurasian fauna laurasische Fauna f *(Permokarbon, Trias)*
laurdalite Laurdalit m *(Nephelinsyenit)*
Laurentian folding laurentische Tektogenese f *(Altpräkambrium, Nordamerika)*

~ **revolution** Laurentischer Umbruch m (Präkambrium)
laurionite Laurionit m, PbOHCl
laurite Laurit m, RuS$_2$
laurvigite, laurvikite Laurvigit m, Laurvikit m (Alkalisyenit)
lausenite Lausenit m, Fe[SO$_4$]$_3$·6H$_2$O
lautarite Lautarit m, Ca[JO$_3$]2
lautite Lautit m, CuAsS
lava Lava f
~ **blisters** Lavablasen fpl, Entgasungsaufblähungen fpl aus dem Lavastrom
~ **colonnade** Lavaorgel f
~ **cupola** s. ~ dome
~ **dome** Schildvulkan m, Quellkuppe f, Lavadom m
~ **eruption** Lavaausbruch m
~ **field** Lavafeld n, Deckenerguß m
~ **flood** Lavaflut f, Flächenerguß m
~ **flow** Lavastrom m
~ **fountain** Lavafontäne f, Schlackenfontäne f
~ **lake** Lavasee m
~ **plain (plateau)** Lavafeld n, Deckenerguß m
~ **plug** Lavapfropfen m
~ **pumice** Bimssteinlava f
~ **rag** Wurfschlacke f
~ **river** Lavastrom m
~ **scratches** Lavaschrammen fpl
~ **sheet** Lavadecke f
~ **spine** Lavastalagmit m
~ **stone** Lavagestein n, Ergußgestein n
~ **stream** Lavastrom m
~ **tree [cast]** s. ~ tree mould
~ **tree mould** Lavabaum m (Abbildung bzw. Umkrustung eines in Lava aufgenommenen verbrannten Baums)
~ **tumefaction** s. ~ dome
~ **tunnel** Lavatunnel m
laval Lava...
lavatic lavaartig, aus Lava
lavendulane Lavendulan m, (Ca, Na)$_2$Cu$_5$[(Cl|(AsO$_4$)]$_4$·4—5H$_2$O
lavenite Låvenit m, (Na, Ca, Mn)$_3$Zr[(F,OH,O)$_2$|Si$_2$O$_7$]
lavialite metamorpher Basalt m mit Einsprenglingsrelikten
lavic s. lavatic
law of distribution Verteilungsgesetzmäßigkeit f (von chemischen Elementen)
~ **of radioactive decay** Gesetz n des radioaktiven Zerfalls
~ **of refraction** Brechungsgesetz n, Reflexionsgesetz n
lawrencite Lawrencit m, FeCl$_2$
lawrosite Lawrosit m (Varietät von Diopsid)
lawsonite Lawsonit m, CaAl$_2$[(OH)$_2$|Si$_2$O$_7$]·H$_2$O
lay bare/to entblößen, bloßlegen, freilegen
~ **down** ablagern
lay Schicht f, Flöz n
layer Schicht f, Lage f
~ **2** ein Schallhorizont im Ozeanboden unter dem Tiefseesediment

~ **depth** Schichttiefe f
~ **exit** Flözausgehendes n
~ **in layers** schichtweise
~ **-lattice structure** Schichtgitterstruktur f
~ **of air** Luftmantel m
~ **of discontinuity** Sprungschicht f
~ **of flint** Feuersteinband n
~ **of iron pan** Ortsteinhorizont m
~ **of shale** Schieferzwischenmittel n
~ **of shale chips** Borkenlehm m
~ **of weather-worn material** Verwitterungsschicht f
~ **thickness** Schichtmächtigkeit f
~ **water** Schichtwasser n
layered [in Lagen übereinander] geschichtet
~ **structure** Lagentextur f
layering Schichtung f
layers/by schichtmäßig
~/**in** schichtenweise, geschichtet
laying-bare Bloßlegung f
~-**down** Ablagerung f
~-**up basin** Rückhaltebecken n
layland Brache f
layout 1. Lageplan m, Grundriß m; 2. Auslage f (von Kabeln)
~ **chart** Lagekarte f, Tiefenkarte f
~ **plan** Situationsskizze f
lazarevicite Lazarevicit m, Cu$_3$AsS$_4$
lazuli s. lazurite
lazulite Lazulith m, Blauspat m, (Mg, Fe)Al$_2$[OH|PO$_4$]$_2$
lazurite Lasurit m, Lapislazuli m, Lasurstein m, (Na, Ca)$_8$[(SO$_4$, S, Cl)$_2$|(AlSiO$_4$)$_6$]
lea Wiese f
~ **stone** geschichteter (laminierter) Sandstein m
leach/to 1. auslaugen, herauslösen; 2. einsikkern, versickern, durchsickern
leach brine Mutterlauge f
~ **hole** s. sinkhole
~ **mineral** alkalisches Mineral n
leachability Auslaugbarkeit f
leachable auslaugfähig
leachate Auslaugprodukt n
leached soil ausgelaugter (entbaster) Boden m
~ **zone** Auslaugungszone f
leaching Auslaugung f, Auslaugen n, Ausschwitzung f, Laugung f
~ **agent** Laugungsmittel n, Laugemittel n
~ **cavity** durch Laugen entstandener Hohlraum m, Laughöhle f
~ **in place** In-situ-Laugung f
~ **liquor** aggressive Lauge f
~ **residue** Auslaugungsrückstand m
~ **waters** Auslaugungswässer npl
lead 1. Leitung f, Leithorizont m; Gang m (s.a. lode); 2. Höhlenröhre f; 3. Phasenvoreilung f
~ **bit** Pilotmeißel m
~-**in section** Anlauflänge f (Teil des seeseismischen Kabelbaums)
~ **of a lode** Gangtrum n, Ausläufer m

lead

lead Blei n, Pb
~ age Bleialter n (Geochronologie)
~-bearing bleiführend
~ glance Bleiglanz n, Galenit m, PbS
~ mine Bleibergwerk n, Bleigrube f
~ ore Bleierz n
~ tungstate s. stolzite
~ vitriol s. anglesite
leader Mineraltrümchen n, Ader f
~ stone Kluftlette f
leadhillite Leadhillit m, $Pb_4[(OH)_2|SO_4|(CO_3)_2]$
leading 1. Abraum über einer Seife; 2. Schnur f (von Erz)
~ fossil Leitfossil n
~ seam Leitflöz n
leadlike bleiartig
leady bleiartig; bleihaltig
leaf-bearing trees Laubbäume mpl
~ clay Bänderton m, dünngeschichteter Ton m
~ coal Blätterkohle f, Papierkohle f (kutikulenreiche Braunkohle); Nadelkohle f
~ gneiss Blättergneis m
~ impression Blattabdruck m
~ injection Blatt-für-Blatt-Injektion f (parallel den s-Flächen)
~ mould Humusstoffschicht f
~ primordium Blattanlage f
~ reflectance Reflexionsvermögen n (von Blättern)
~ scar Blattnarbe f
~ shale Blätterschiefer m, dünnblättriger Schieferton m
leaflike blättrig
league 1. Längeneinheit, entspricht 15,840 Fuß; 2. Flächenmaß, entspricht 6,919 Quadratmeilen
leak/to sickern
~ downward durchsickern
~-off test Dichtheitstest m
~ proof Dichtheitsprüfung f
leakage 1. Undichtheit f; 2. Lecken n, Leckage f; 3. Versickerung f, Sickerverlust m
~ halo Kohlenwasserstoff-Bodengas-Anomalie über einer Öl-Gas-Lagerstätte
~ of storage Speicherundichtheit f
~ of well Bohrungsundichtheit f
leaking modes Leaking-Moden mpl (Kanalwellen mit Sickerverlust)
leaks in the casing joints Undichtheit f der Gestängeverbindungen
leaky undicht
~ aquifer semipermeabler Grundwasserleiter m
lean arm (Erz, Gas); mager (Kohle, Ton)
lean Armerz n
~ clay Ton m mit geringer Plastizität, Magerton m, Lette f
~ coal Magerkohle f
~ gas Armgas n, armes Gas n, Schwachgas n
~ lime Magerkalk m

~ ore geringwertiges (armes) Erz n, Magererz n
leap Dislokation f, Schichtenstörung f, Sprung m
~ year Schaltjahr n
leaps [and bounds]/by sprungweise
lease Abbaurecht n, Erwerb m von Abbaurechten (im Grundeigentümerbergbau)
least squares fit Anpassung f nach dem Verfahren der kleinsten Quadratsumme
~ time path Strahlenweg m mit minimaler Laufzeit
leat Graben m, Wasserlauf m (in Cornwall)
leath weiches Trum n, weicher Teil m eines Ganges (Derbyshire)
leather bed (coat) Rutschbelag m (einer Störungsfläche); Lettenbesteg m
leatherstone Bergleder n (Varietät von Palygorskit)
leaving scar Gleitwulst m (Sedimentgefüge)
leavings Scheideerze npl
lechatelierite Lechatelierit m, SiO_2, amorph
leck toniger Schiefer m
leckstone körniges Trappgestein n
lecontite Lecontit m, $(NH_4)Na[SO_4]\cdot 2H_2O$
lectostratotype Lektostratotyp m
lectotype Lectotypus m
ledge 1. Felsbank f, Riff n; Felsenkette f (entlang der Küste); 2. gewachsener Fels m, Anstehendes n, anstehendes Gestein n; 3. Erzlager n, Erzgang m; 4. Berme f (Tagebau)
~ matter Gangmittel n, Gangart f
~ of a rock vorspringender Teil m einer Felswand
~ rock gewachsener Fels m, Anstehendes n, anstehendes Gebirge n
~ vein Erzlager n, Erzgang m
ledger Unterseite f eines Ganges
~ wall s. footwall
ledgy slope terrassierter Hang m
Lédian [Stage] Léd[ien] n, Lédium n (Stufe des Eozäns, Belgisches Becken)
lee shore Leeufer n
~ side Leeseite f
~-side concentration Rippelschichtung f
leelite fleischrote Varietät von Orthoklas
leeward dem Winde abgekehrt
~ side Leeseite f
~ slope windabseitiger Abhang m
left-bank tributary linker Nebenfluß m
~-hand quartz Linksquarz m
~-handed crystal linksdrehender Kristall m
~ quartz Linksquarz m
leg 1. Teilstrecke f, Teilbereich m; 2. Phasensprung m; 3. Hubbein n; 4. s. limb
legend Legende f (zur Karte)
leggy Wellenband n
lehiite Lehiit m, $Na_2Ca_5Al_8[(OH)_{12}|(PO_4)_8]\cdot 6H_2O$
leidleite Leidleit m (glasige Varietät von Dazit)
leifite Leifit m, $Na_2[(F,OH,H_2O)_{1-2}|(Al,Si)Si_5O_{12}]$
leightonite Leightonit m, $K_2Ca_2Cu[SO_4]_4\cdot 2H_2O$

Lemnian bole (earth) lemnische Erde f
~ ruddle lemnische rote Kreide f
lemniscate Lemniskate f
lengenbachite Lengenbachit m, 7PbS·2As$_2$S$_3$
length of equivalent pendulum äquivalente Pendellänge f
~ of pipe (tube) Bohrstangenlänge f
lengthening in b Längung f in b
lens out/to linsenförmig auskeilen
lens Linse f
~-shaped linsenförmig
lensing Ausdünnen n einer Schicht, linsenförmige Lagerung f
~-out auskeilend
lenslike linsenförmig
lenticle kleine Linse f
lenticular linsenförmig
~ alternation flasrige Wechsellagerung f
~ bedding Linsenschichtung f, linsige Schichtung f
~ cloud Linsenwolke f
~ cross-bedding linsige Schrägschichtung f
~ field linsenförmige Lagerstätte f
~ intercalation linsenförmige Einlagerung f
~ ore body linsenförmiger Erzgang m
~ sand linsenförmiger Sandkörper m
~ vein Linsengang m
~ vug linsenförmige Druse f
lenticularity linsenförmiges Auftreten n
lenticulated linsenähnlich
lenticule kleiner, linsiger Gesteinskörper m
lentiform linsenförmig
lentil Gesteinslinse f, Linse f
Leonardian [Stage] Leonard n (Stufe des Unterperms)
leonhardite s. laumontite
leonite Leonit m, K$_2$Mg[SO$_4$]$_2$·4H$_2$O
leopardite Leopardit m (Varietät von Quarzporphyr)
leopoldite s. sylvite
lepidoblastic lepidoblastisch
~ structure Blättertextur f
lepidocrocite Lepidokrokit m, γ-FEOOH
lepidolamprite s. franckeite
lepidolite Lepidolith m, Lithiumglimmer m, KLi$_2$Al[(F,OH)$_2$|Si$_4$O$_{10}$]
lepidomelane Lepidomelan m (eisenreicher Biotit)
leptite Leptit m
leptynite Leptinit m (metamorphes Gestein)
lermontovite Lermontovit m, (U, Ca, Ce⋯)$_3$[PO$_4$]$_4$·6H$_2$O
lessening fold ausklingende Falte f
lessingite Lessingit m, (Ca,Ce,La,Nd)$_5$[(O,OH,F)|(SiO$_4$)$_3$]
lestiwarite Lestiwarit m (Syenitaplit)
letdowns abgesunkene Erosionshärtlinge mpl (auf tiefere stratigraphische Horizonte)
letovicite Letovicit m, (NH$_4$)$_3$H[SO$_4$]$_2$
lettenlike lettig
leucite Leuzit m, K[AlSi$_2$O$_6$]
leucitic leuzitführend; leuzitähnlich

leucitite Leuzitit m
leucitohedron s. trapezohedron
leucitophyre Leuzitophyr m
leucocratic leukokrat, hell
leucogranite Leukogranit m
leucophanite Leukophan m, (Ca, NaH)$_2$Be[Si$_2$O$_6$(OH, F)]
leucophoenicite Leukophönicit m, Mn$_7$[(OH)$_2$|(SiO$_4$)$_3$]
leucophosphite Leukophosphit m, K(Fe, Al)$_2$[OH|(PO$_4$)$_2$·2H$_2$O
leucophyre Leukophyr m (Varietät von Diabas)
leucosapphire Leukosaphir m, weißer Saphir m (s.a. corundum)
leucosome Leukosom m
leucosphenite Leukosphenit m, Ba(Na, Ca)$_4$Ti$_3$[BO$_3$|Si$_8$O$_{24}$]
leucoxene Leukoxen m (Gemenge von Titanmineralen)
levee/to eindeichen (einen Fluß)
levee 1. Damm, Schutzdamm m, Hochwasserdamm m; 2. Lavarippe f
level/to nivellieren, horizontieren
level 1. Abbausohle f, Etage f, Höhenlinie f, Niveau n, Pegel m, Bausohle f; 2. Pegel m, Niveau n; 3. Libelle f (Vermessungswesen)
~-bedded strata horizontalgelagerte Schichten fpl
~ country Flachland n
~ course Verlauf m in Richtung des Schichtstreichens
~ decrease Sinken n des Wasserstandes
~ entry Stollenmundloch n
~ fluctuation Niveauschwankung f
~ fold Falte f mit horizontaler Sattellinie
~-free workings 1. Abbau m im Ausbiß einer Lagerstätte; 2. Grubengebäude n mit natürlicher Wasserhaltung
~ gangway Gezeugstrecke f, Sohlstrecke f
~ of abrasion Abrasionsebene f
~ of compensation Ausgleichsfläche f (Isostasie)
~ of organic metamorphism [linearer] Maßstab m für die Inkohlung
~ of reference Bezugsniveau n, Bezugsfläche f
~ of saturation Sättigungsspiegel m
~ of the lake Seespiegel m
~ of the ocean (sea) Meeresspiegel m
~ of the water gauge Pegelhöhe f
~ of underground water Grundwasserspiegel m
~ seam söhliges Flöz n
~ slicing s. density slicing
~-surface ripples Horizontalrippeln fpl
~ water Grundwasser n
levelled ground Planum n
levelling Nivellement n, Nivellierung f
~ of surface Flächennivellement n
~ rod Nivellierlatte f
levelness Ebenheit f (Topografie)
Leverett function Leverett-Funktion f
levigated feingeschlämmt

levigation

levigation Abschlämmen *n*, Dekantieren *n*, Auslaugung *f*
levogyrate crystal Linksquarz *m*
levorotation Linksdrehung *f*
levorotatory linksdrehend
levynite Levyn *m*, Ca[Al$_2$Si$_4$O$_{12}$]·6H$_2$O
lewisite *s.* romeite
Lewistonian [Stage] Stufe des Silurs
lewistonite Lewistonit *m (Varietät von Apatit)*
lherzolite Lherzolit *m (Varität von Peridotit)*
lianous gangförmig
Liardian Liard *n (Ladin, Nordamerika)*
Lias [Epoch] Lias *m*, Schwarzer Jura *m (Serie des Juras)*
~ **Limestone** Liaskalk *m*
~ **Series** Lias *m*, Schwarzer Jura *m (Serie des Juras)*
Liassic liassisch
liberated gas freigemachtes Gas *n*
libethenite Libethenit *m*, Cu$_2$[OH|PO$_4$]
libolite asphaltartige Kohle *f*
lichens Flechten *fpl*
lick Sumpfgebiet *n* mit Salzquellen
lidded eingeschnürt *(auf den Ausstrich eines Erzschlauchs begrenzt)*
lidstone Hangendes *n (in Eisenerzlagerstätten)*
lie 1. stilliegende Grube *f*; 2. Richtung *f*, Lage[rung] *f*
~ **of the land** Flurform *f*
liebigite Liebigit *m*, Ca$_2$[UO$_2$|(CO$_3$)$_3$·10H$_2$O
Liesegang banding Liesegangsche Bänderung *f*
lievrite *s.* ilvaite
life community Lebensgemeinschaft *f*
~ **district** Lebensraum *m*
~ **duration** Lebenszeit *f*
~ **form** Lebensform *f*
~ **of a well** Lebensdauer *f* einer Sonde
~ **position** Lebendstellung *f (Biostratonomie)*
~ **realm** Lebensraum *m*
lifetime Lebenszeit *f*; Lebensdauer *f (z.B. einer Bohrlochdoublette)*
lift/to heben
lift Saughöhe *f*
~ **coefficient** Auftriebsbeiwert *m*, Auftriebskoeffizient *m*
~ **joint** Bankung *f*, oberflächenparallele Klüftung *f (in Plutoniten)*
~ **of tide** Fluthöhe *f*
lifted side gehobener Flügel *m (einer Verwerfung)*
lifting Hebung *f*
~ **cost** Förderkosten *pl*
~ **effect (force)** Auftrieb *m*
~ **into an arch** Aufwölbung *f*
liftings schwebende Örter *npl*
ligamental inflection Ligamentfalte *f (bei Muscheln)*
light ground schwimmendes Gebirge *n*
~ **hole** Einsturzschlot *m (Karst)*
~ **hydrocarbons** leichte Kohlenwasserstoffe *mpl*

~ **layers of brown coal** helle Braunkohlenschichten *fpl (sog. „helle Bänder ", meist bitumenreich)*
~ **line** Lichtlinie *f*
~ **microscope** Lichtmikroskop *n*
~ **mineral** Leichtmineral *n*
~~**optical microscope** Lichtmikroskop *n*
~ **plumb line** Lichtlot *n (Grundwasserspiegelmessung)*
~ **red silver ore**, ~ **ruby silver** *s.* proustite
~ **scatter** Lichtstreuung *f*
~ **silt** Feinlehm *m*
~~**sized** kleinstückig
~ **surface peat** Rasentorf *m*
~ **transmission** Lichtdurchlässigkeit *f*
~~**weight mineral** Leichtmineral *n*
~ **year** Lichtjahr *n*
lighten/to entlasten
lightened sediment entlastetes Sediment *n (durch Erosion)*
lightning Blitz *m*
~ **tube** Fulgurit *m*, Blitzröhre *f*
ligneous lignitartig, holzig
~ **coal** Braunkohle *f*
lignification Verholzung *f (der Zellwände)*
lignify/to verholzen
lignite 1. Braunkohle *f (Weich- bis Mattbraunkohle nach Inkohlungsgrad)*; Lignit *m*; 2. xylitische Braunkohle *f (Kohlenart)*; 3. Xylit *m (biochemisch verändertes, fossiles Holz)*
~~**bearing** braunkohleführend, braunkohlehaltig
~ **coal mine** Braunkohlengrube *f*
~ **coal tar** Braunkohlenteer *m*
~ **deposit** Braunkohlenlager *n*
~ **mine** Braunkohlenbergwerk *n*
~ **mining** Braunkohlenbergbau *m*
lignitic braunkohlehaltig, lignitisch
~ **field** Braunkohlenfeld *n*
lignitiferous braunkohleführend, braunkohlehaltig
lignitization *s.* lignification
lignitize/to lignitisieren
likasite Likasit *m*, Cu$_6$[(OH)$_7$|(NO$_3$)$_2$|PO$_4$]
likely lode erzhöffiger Gang *m*, Gang *m* mit Vererzungsindikationen
lillianite Lillianit *m*, 3PbS·Bi$_2$S$_3$
lily crinoid Seelilie *f*
~ **pond** Quellbecken *n* mit Kalksinterterrassen
liman coast Limanküste *f*
limb 1. Schenkel *m*, Flügel *m*; 2. Gebirgsausläufer *m*
~ **bone** Extremitätenknochen *m*
~ **of fold** Faltenschenkel *m*
~ **of syncline** Muldenflügel *m*
limbed schenklig
limburgite Limburgit *m (glasführender Nephelinbasalt)*
lime 1. Kalziumoxid *n*, CaO; 2. *allgemein auch* Kaliumkarbonat und Kalziumhydroxid
~~**bearing** kalkhaltig
~~**cemented sandstone** Sandstein *m* mit kalkigem Bindemittel

~-containing kalkhaltig
~ content Kalkgehalt m
~ craig anstehender Kalkstein m; Wand f eines Kalksteinbruchs *(Schottland)*
~-depositing kalkablagernd
~-depositing bacteria Kalkbakterien fpl
~ feldspar Kalkfeldspat m
~-free kalkfrei
~ kiln Kalkofen m
~ marble Kalkmarmor m
~ marl Kalkmergel m
~ mud Kalkspülung f *(Bohrtechnik)*
~ mud rock Kalktonstein m
~ nodule Lößkindl n
~ pan Hartkalkhorizont m *(Boden)*
~ pit Kalksteinbruch m, Kalkgrube f
~-precipitating kalkablagernd
~-precipitating algae Kalkalgen fpl
~-rich kalkreich
~ rock Kalkstein m
~ rubblerock s. calcirudite
~ sand Kalksand m
~ sandrock (sandstone) s. calcarenite
~-secreting kalkablagernd, kalkabscheidend
~-secreting algae Kalkalgen fpl
~ silicate Kalksilikat n
~ silicate rock Kalksilikatfels m
~ sink s. sinkhole
~ stone s. limestone
~ uranite s. autunite
limeclasts klastische Kalksteinindividuen npl
limestone Kalkstein m
~ bed Kalksteinlage f
~-encased kalkumhüllt
~ for flux Zuschlagkalkstein m
~ gravel Kalksteinkies m
~ layer Kalkschicht f
~ mountains Kalkgebirge n
~ pebbles Kalksteingeröll n
~ pit Kalksteingrube f
~ quarry Kalk[stein]bruch m
~ red loam Kalkrotlehm m
~ rock Kalkgestein n
~ shale Kalkschiefer m
~ sink s. sinkhole
~ slab Kalksteinplatte f
~ soil Kalksteinboden m
limey kalkartig, kalkhaltig, kalkig
limit angle Grenzwinkel m
~ equilibrium Grenzgleichgewicht n
~ line Grenzlinie f
~ load Grenzlast f
~ of backwater Staugrenze f
~ of concentration Grenzwert m *(Hydrochemie)*
~ of creep Kriechgrenze f
~ of detection Nachweisgrenze f *(eines Elements)*
~ of drift ice Treibeisgrenze f
~ of forest growth Waldgrenze f
~ of pay Bauwürdigkeitsgrenze f
~ of proportionality Proportionalitätsgrenze f

~ of resolution Auflösungsgrenze f
~ of snow Schneegrenze f
~ of submersion Inundationsgrenze f
~ of trees Baumgrenze f
~ plane Grenzfläche f
~ stress Grenzspannung f, Dauerstandfestigkeit f
limiting grading curve Grenzsieblinie f
~ pressure Grenzdruck m
~ stress Grenzspannung f
limnaean benthos Süßwasserbenthos n
limnal s. limnetic
limnetic limnisch, zum Süßwasser gehörend, Süßwasser..., lakustrisch
~ coal limnische Kohle f
~ coal basin limnisches Kohlenbecken n
~ facies limnische Fazies f
~ formation limnische Bildung f
~ peat Moorttorf m, Torfmudde f
limnic s. limnetic
limnigraph Schreibpegel m
limnimeter Seepegelmesser m
limnimetrical station Pegelstation f
limnite s. bog iron ore
limno-aphotic limno-aphotisch
~-biotic limno-biotisch
~-geotic limno-terrestrisch
limnogenic limnogen
limnograph Schreibpegel m
limnologic[al] limnologisch
limnology Limnologie f, Seenkunde f
limnoplankton Limnoplankton n
limnoquartzite Süßwasserquarzit m
limonite Limonit m, Brauneisenerz n, $FeOOH \cdot nH_2O$
~ ore Brauneisenerz n
limonitic limonitisch
limonitization Limonitisierung f
limonitize/to limonitisieren
limous schlammig
limurite Limurit m *(Metasomatit mit mehr als 50% Axinit)*
limy kalkig, kalkhaltig
~ bed Kalkschicht f
~ ore kalkiges Erz n
~ skeleton Kalkgerüst n
linarite Linarit m, $PbCu[(OH)_2|SO_4]$
lindackerite Lindackerit m, $(Cu, H_2)_3[AsO_4]_2 \cdot 4H_2O$
lindgrenite Lindgrenit m, $Cu_3[OH|MoO_4]_2$
lindstromite, lindströmite Lindströmit m, $2PbS \cdot Cu_2S \cdot 3Bi_2S_3$
line 1. Profil n, Profillinie f; 2. Seilstrang m
~ displacement Linienverschiebung f
~ drawing Strichzeichnung f
~ flooding Linienfluten n
~ of aggregate thickness Linie f gleicher Gesteinsmächtigkeit, Isolithe f
~ of ascent Entwicklungslinie f
~ of bearing Ausstrichlinie f
~ of breakage Bruchlinie f
~ of cleavage Spaltriß m, Absonderungsfuge f

line

- ~ **of development** Entwicklungslinie *f*
- ~ **of dip** Fallinie *f*, Einfallrichtung *f*
- ~ **of dislocation (displacement)** Bruchlinie *f*
- ~ **of emergence** Hebungslinie *f*
- ~ **of equal interval** Konvergenzlinie *f*, Isochore *f* *(Linie gleichen senkrechten Abstands zwischen zwei gegebenen geologischen Horizonten)*
- ~ **of equal magnetic dip** Linie *f* gleicher magnetischer Inklination, Isokline *f*
- ~ **of equal rainfall** Regengleiche *f*, Niederschlagshöhenkurve *f*, Isohyete *f*
- ~ **of equal rate of flow** Linie *f* [der Punkte] gleicher Geschwindigkeit *(z.B. bei Gletschern)*
- ~ **of equal thickness** Linie *f* gleicher Mächtigkeit, Mächtigkeitslinie *f*, Isopache *f*
- ~ **of equal value of gravity** Linie *f* gleicher Schwerewerte, Isogamme *f*
- ~ **of evolution** Entwicklungslinie *f*
- ~ **of fastest flow** Linie *f* [der Punkte] maximaler Geschwindigkeit *(z.B. bei Gletschern)*
- ~ **of faulting** Bruchlinie *f*
- ~ **of flow** Stromlinie *f*
- ~ **of force** Kraftlinie *f*
- ~ **of fracture** Bruchlinie *f*
- ~ **of junction** Anheftungslinie *f (bei Fossilschalen)*
- ~ **of lode** Gangstreichen *n*
- ~ **of movement** Bewegungssinn *m*
- ~ **of outcrop** Ausstrichlinie *f*
- ~ **of rent** Bruchlinie *f*
- ~ **of saddle** Sattellinie *f*
- ~ **of saturation** *s.* ground-water level
- ~ **of slope** Fallinie *f*, Einfallrichtung *f*
- ~ **of springs** Quellhorizont *m*, Quellinie *f*
- ~ **of stratification** Schichtfuge *f*
- ~ **of strike** Streichrichtung *f*, Streichlinie *f*
- ~ **of wells** Brunnengalerie *f*
- ~ **pipe** Leitungsrohr *n*
- ~ **spectrum** Linienspektrum *n*
- ~ **squall** Linienbö *f*
- ~**-up** Gleichphasigkeit *f (Seismik)*
- **lineage** Entwicklungsreihe *f*, phylogenetische Reihe *f*
- ~ **structure** Verzweigungsstruktur *f (bei Kristallen)*
- **lineagenic movements** lineamentäre Bewegungen *fpl*
- **lineageny** Lineamenttektonik *f*
- **lineament** Lineament *n*
- **linear cleavage** Griffelung *f*, Griffelschieferung *f*, griffelige Klüftung *f*
- ~ **coefficient** Linearbeiwert *m*
- ~ **earthquake** lineares Beben *n*
- ~ **eruption** Lineareruption *f*
- ~ **features** linear ausgeprägte Merkmale *npl*, Merkmale *npl* mit dominierender Längsstreckung, linienhaft ausgebildete Merkmale *npl*
- ~ **flow** lineare Strömung *f*
- ~**-folded mountain range** geradliniges Faltengebirge *n*
- ~ **magnification** lineare Vergrößerung *f*

210

- ~ **parallelism** *s.* lineation
- ~ **projection** Linearprojektion *f*
- ~ **scale factor** Längenmaßstab *m (Modelltechnik)*
- ~ **schistosity** stengelige Textur *f*, Griffelschieferung *f*
- ~ **stretching** Streckung *f*
- ~ **structure** linear gestreckte Textur *f*, Linear *n*
- ~ **volcanoes** Vulkanreihen *fpl*
- **linearly polarized wave** linear polarisierte Welle *f*
- **lineation** 1. Linearstreckung *f*, Lineation *f*, Striemung *f*; 2. Strömungsriefen *fpl (Sedimentgefüge)*
- **lined borehole** verrohrtes Bohrloch *n*
- **liner** verlorene Kolonne (Rohrtour) *f*, Liner *m*
- ~ **hanger** Linerhänger *m (Aufhängevorrichtung für eine im Bohrloch eingebaute verlorene Rohrtour)*
- ~ **puller** Filterrohrziehvorrichtung *f*
- **linguiform, linguoid** zungenförmig
- ~ **current ripples** zungenförmige Strömungsrippeln *fpl*
- ~ **ripple marks, ~ ripples** Linguoidrippeln *fpl (sichelförmige Rippeln)*
- **lining of channel** Grabenabdichtung *f*
- **linkage** scharfes Abbiegen *n* eines Gebirgsrückens
- **linked vein** durch Querspalten stufig versetzter Gang *m*, Kettengang *m*
- ~ **veins** Scharung *f* der Gangtrümer, Gangschwarm *m*, Gangzug *m*
- **linking form** Zwischenform *f*
- **linn** Wasserfall *m*
- ~ **and wool** *(sl)* streifiger grauer Sandstein *m*
- **linnaeite** Linneit *m*, Kobaltkies *m*, Co_3S_4
- **linnets** oxidiertes Bleierz *n*
- **linophyre** fluidalstreifiger Magmatit *m*
- **linophyric** fluidalstreifig
- **linseed earth** *(sl)* grauer Ziegelton *m*
- **linsey** tonhaltiges Gestein *n*
- **lip of the crater** Kraterrand *m*
- **liparite** Liparit *m (ein Rhyolith)*
- ~ **tuff** Liparittuff *m*
- **liptinite** Liptinit *m (Kohlenmaceral, Maceralgruppe)*
- **liptite** Liptit *m (Kohlenmikrolithotyp)*
- **liptobioliths** Liptobiolithe *mpl (liptinreiche Kohlenlithotypen)*
- **liptodetrinite** Liptodetrinit *m (Kohlenmaceral)*
- **liquation** Liquidentmischung *f*
- ~ **phenomena** Seigerungserscheinungen *fpl*
- **liquefaction** Verflüssigung *f*
- ~ **of gas** Gasverflüssigung *f*
- **liquefied [natural] gas** verflüssigtes Erdgas *n*
- ~ **natural gas storage** Flüssigmethanspeicher *m*
- ~ **petroleum gas storage** Flüssiggasspeicher *m (Propan-Butan-Speicher)*
- **liquefy/to** flüssig machen, verflüssigen

liquid schmelzflüssig
- ~ **capacity** Wasserhaltevermögen n, wasserbindende Kraft f (eines Bodens)
- ~ **column** Flüssigkeitssäule f
- ~ **containing gas in solution** Flüssigkeit f mit gelöstem Gas
- ~ **hydrocarbons** flüssige Kohlenwasserstoffe mpl
- ~ **inclusion** Flüssigkeitseinschluß m
- ~ **level** Flüssigkeitsspiegel m
- ~ **level indicator** 1. Wasserspiegelmesser m; 2. Flüssigkeitsspiegelmesser m, Wasserstandsmeßgerät n
- ~ **limit** Fließgrenze f, unterer Plastizitätszustand m
- ~ **limit device** Gerät n zur Bestimmung der Fließgrenze
- ~ **magmatic deposit** liquidmagmatische Lagerstätte f
- ~ **petroleum gas** [natürliches] Flüssiggas n
- ~ **scintillation spectrometer** Flüssigkeitsszintillator m
- ~ **subaerial flow** subaerische Fließbewegung f
- ~ **vesicle** Flüssigkeitseinschluß m

liroconite Lirokonit m, $Cu_2Al[(OH)_4|AsO_4]\cdot 4H_2O$
liskeardite Liskeardit m, $Al_2[(OH)_3|AsO_4]\cdot 2^1/_2H_2O$
lissen Gesteinsspalt m
list Innenleiste f (bei Fossilschalen)
listric surface lystrische Fläche f, schaufelförmiger Verlauf m einer Tiefenstörung, Schaufelfläche f
listwanite Listvenit m (Metasomatit)
litchfieldite Litchfieldit m (Nephelinsyenit)
lithargite Lithargit m, α-PbO
lithia mica Lithiumglimmer m (s.a. lepidolite)
lithic 1. lithisch; 2. lithologisch
- ~ **arenite** s. ~ sandstone
- ~ **character** Gesteinscharakter m
- ~ **drainage** Unterflurdrainage f
- ~ **graywacke** s. subgraywacke
- ~ **sandstone** Standstein mit mehr Gesteinsfragmenten als Feldspatanteilen
- ~ **sphere** Gesteinssphäre f
- ~ **tuff** lithischer Tuff m, Blocktuff m, Schlackentuff m
- ~ **type** Gesteinstyp[us] m

lithidionite Lithidionit m, $(K, Na)_2Cu[Si_3O_7]_2$
lithification Lithifikation f, Sedimentverfestigung f, Diagenese f (allgemein für Diagenese, Kristallisation, Fossilisation)
lithify/to diagenetisch verfestigen, fossilisieren, versteinern
lithionite s. lepidolite
lithiophilite Lithiophilit m, $Li(Mn, {}^Fe)[PO_4]$
lithiophosphatite Lithiophosphatit m, $Li_3[PO_4]$
lithites s. statoliths
lithizone s. lithostratigraphic zone
lithocalcarenite Lithokalkarenit m, Lithocalcarenit m (lithoklastischer Kalksandstein)
lithocalcilutite Lithokalzilutit m, Lithocalcilutit m (Sedimentit)

lithocalcirudite Lithokalzirudit m, Lithocalcirudit m (Sedimentit)
lithocalcisiltite Lithokalzisiltit m (Sedimentit)
lithochemistry Petrochemie f, Gesteinschemie f
lithoclase Lithoklase f (Kluft- oder Störungsfläche)
lithoclastic lithoklastisch
lithocysts s. statocysts
lithodolarenite Lithodolarenit m (Sedimentit)
lithodololutite Lithodololutit m (Sedimentit)
lithodolorudite Lithodolorudit m (Sedimentit)
lithodolosiltite Lithodolosiltit m (Sedimentit)
lithodomous im Sediment bohrend (für Organismen, z.B. Bohrmuschel)
lithofacies Lithofazies f
- ~ **map** Lithofazieskarte f

lithofraction Gesteinszerkleinerung f durch fluviatilen Transport der Brandung
lithogenese, lithogenesis Lithogenese f, Gesteinsbildung f
lithogenetic gesteinsbildend, lithogen
lithogenic soil Gesteinsboden m
lithogenous gesteinsbildend, lithogen
- ~ **organism** gesteinsbildender Organismus m

lithogeny Lithogenese f, Gesteinsbildung f
lithogeochemistry Lithogeochemie f
lithographic limestone lithografischer Kalkstein m
lithoid[al] steinig; gesteinsartig
lithoidyre wasserarmes Liparitglas n
lithologic[al] lithologisch
- ~ **association** lithologische Assoziation f
- ~ **character** Gesteinscharakter m, lithologisches Merkmal n
- ~ **complex** lithologischer Komplex m (lithostratigrafische Einheit, zusammengesetzt aus verschiedenen Gesteinsklassen oder Typen einer Gesteinsklasse)
- ~ **facies** Gesteinsfazies f
- ~ **geology** Lithologie f, Gesteinskunde f
- ~ **key bed** lithologischer Leithorizont m
- ~ **map** lithologische Karte f
- ~ **percentage map** Lithofazieskarte f (mit Darstellung des Prozentanteils eines Sedimenttyps am Aufbau einer lithologischen Einheit)
- ~ **trap** lithologische Falle f
- ~ **unit** lithologische Einheit f, Gesteinseinheit f

lithology Lithologie f, Gesteinskunde f
lithomarge Steinmark n
lithophagous s. lithodomous
lithophile, lithophilic, lithophilous lithophil
- ~ **element** lithophiles Element n

lithophyl fossile Blätter führend
lithophyl versteinertes Blatt n, Blattabdruck m
lithosol Steinboden m, Felsboden m, Gesteinsboden m
lithosome aufgefingerte (verzahnte) lithostratigrafische Einheit f
lithosphere Lithosphäre f
lithospheric plate (slab) Lithosphärenplatte f
lithostatic[al] pressure lithostatischer (petrostatischer) Druck m

lithostratigraphic 212

lithostratigraphic[al] lithostratigrafisch
~ **correlation** lithostratigrafische Korrelation f
~ **horizon** s. marker 1.
~ **method** lithostratigrafische Methode f
~ **unit** lithostratigrafische Einheit f
~ **zone** allgemeine lithostratigrafische Einheit zur Kennzeichnung bestimmter lithologischer Merkmale
lithostratigraphy Lithostratigrafie f
lithostrome parallelschichtige lithostratigrafische Einheit f
lithotope Lithotop n
lithotype Lithotyp m (Kohlentyp der Steinkohle)
lithozone s. lithostratigraphic zone
littoral Küsten..., Ufer...
littoral 1. s. ~ zone; 2. benthonisches Milieu n in der Gezeitenzone
~ **area** Flachsee f
~ **current** Küstenstrom m
~ **deposit** Strandablagerung f
~ **district** Flachsee f
~ **drift** Küstenströmung f
~ **dune** Küstendüne f, Vordüne f
~ **erosion** Stranderosion f
~ **facies** Küstenfazies f
~ **zone** litorale Zone f, Litoral n, Küstenzone f (bis 200 m Wassertiefe)
Littorina time[s] Littorinazeit f
live form Lebendform f
~ **glacier** aktiver Gletscher m
~ **ice** aktives Gletschereis n
~ **lime** ungelöschter Kalk m, Ätzkalk m
~ **lode** [ab]bauwürdiger Gang m
~ **oil** gasreiches Öl n
~ **quartz** mit Erz verwachsener Quarz m
~ **section** Meßlänge f (Teil des seeseismischen Kabelbaums)
liveingite Liveingit m, $4PbS \cdot 3As_2S_3$
liver-coloured copper ore Kupferlebererz n (Gemenge von erdigem Kuprit)
~ **peat** Torfmudde f
~ **pyrite** Leberkies m, massiger Pyrit (Markasit) m
living being Lebewesen n
~ **chamber** Wohnkammer f (Paläontologie)
~ **matter** lebende Materie f
~ **rock** anstehendes Gestein n
livingstonite Livingstonit m, $HgSb_4S_8$
lixivial laugenartig, alkalisch
lixiviant Laugungsmittel n, Lauge f
lixiviate/to auslaugen
lixiviation Auslaugung f, Auswaschung f
lizardite Lizardit m (Serpentinmineral)
Llandeilian [Stage] Llandeilo n (Stufe des Mittelordoviziums)
Llandoverian [Epoch, Series] Llandovery n (unteres Silur), Valent[ium] n (veraltete Bezeichnung)
llano Steppe f (Orinoko)
Llavirnian [Stage] Llanvirn[ium] n (Stufe des Unterordoviziums)

LME = London Metal Exchange
load Belastung f, Last f
~-**bearing capacity, load-carrying capacity** Tragfähigkeit f, Belastbarkeit f
~ **cast** Sandsteinwulst m, Unterseitenwulst m, Fließwulst m, Belastungsmarke f
~-**cast lineation** Belastungslineation f, Belastungsriefen fpl
~-**casted** durch Belastung überformt
~-**casted current markings** belastete Strömungsmarken fpl
~ **cell** Druckmeßdose f
~ **curve** Belastungskurve f
~-**deflection curve** Last-Dehnungs-Kurve f
~ **fold** Belastungsfalte f
~ **limit** Belastungsgrenze f
~ **metamorphism** Versenkungsmetamorphose f, Belastungsmetamorphose f
~ **mould** Belastungsmarke f, Belastungseindruck m
~ **of debris** Schuttlast f (eines Flusses)
~ **of ice** Eislast f
~ **of sediments** Sedimentlast f
~ **of silt** Schlammlast f (eines Flusses)
~ **of waste** Schuttlast f (eines Flusses)
~ **pocket** Belastungstasche f
~ **pressure** Belastungsdruck m
~ **range** Belastungsbereich m; Laststufe f
~-**settlement curve** Belastungssetzungsdiagramm n, Lastsenkungskurve f
~ **stone** Magneteisenstein m, Magneteisenerz n (s.a. magnetite)
~ **test** Belastungsversuch m
~ **wave** Belastungsfahne f (Sedimentgefüge)
~ **yield recorder** Lastsenkungsschreiber m
loaded with detritus geschiebeführend
loading aufgebrachte Last f, Auflast f
~ **function** Belastungsfunktion f
~ **plate** Belastungsplatte f
~ **pole** Ladestange f
~ **test** Belastungsversuch m
loadstar Leitstern m; Polarstern m
loadstone s. lodestone
loaflike brotlaibartig
~ **jointing** brotlaibartige Absonderung f (durch Klüfte)
loam Lehm m; Letten m, Ton[mergel] m
~ **formation** Lehmbildung f
~ **pit** Lehmgrube f
~ **sand** Klebsand m
~ **watery clay** Schluff m
loamification Verlehmung f
loamy lehmig, lettig
~ **coarse sand** lehmiger Grobsand m
~ **desert** Lehmwüste f
~ **fine sand** schluffiger Feinsand m
~ **fine soil** schluffiger Feinsandboden m
~ **ground** Lehmboden m
~ **marl** lehmiger Mergel m
~ **sand** Sandlehm m
~ **soil** Lehmboden m
lob of gold kleine Reichgoldlagerstätte f

lobate lappig
~ **coast** gelappte Küste *f*
~ **rill mark** *s.* flute cast
~ **type of coast line** gelappte Küste *f*
lobe Lappen *m*, Lobus *m*
~**-finned bony fishes** quastenflossige Knochenfische *mpl*, Crossopterygier *mpl*
~ **line (suture)** Lobenlinie *f*
lobulate gelappt, mit Loben versehen
local lokal, örtlich
~ **anomaly** lokale Anomalie *f*
~ **apparent time** scheinbare Ortszeit *f*
~ **depression** Pinge *f*
~ **earthquake** Ortsbeben *n*
~ **magnetic anomaly** lokale magnetische Anomalie *f*
~ **mean time** mittlere Ortszeit *f*
~ **meridian** Ortsmeridian *m*
~ **metamorphism** lokale Metamorphose *f (z.B. Kontaktmetamorphose)*
~ **range zone** Teilzone *f*
~ **shock** Ortsbeben *n*
~ **time** Ortszeit *f*
~ **trend** lokaler Trend *m*
~ **velocity** Ortsgeschwindigkeit *f*
locality Fundort *m*
locate a well/to eine Bohrung ansetzen
location Standort *m*, Ansatzpunkt *m*
~ **of a well** Bohransatzpunkt *m*
~ **plan** *(Am)* Lageplan *m*, Situationsplan *m*
~ **sketch** Situationsskizze *f*
loch 1. See *m*; schmaler Seearm *m*; 2. Druse *f*, Erzdruse *f*
~ **hole** große Druse *f*
Lochkovian [Stage] Lochkov *n*, Lochkov-Stufe *f (Stufe des basalen Unterdevons einschließlich des höchsten Silurs)*
lock 1. *s.* ~ chamber; 2. *s.* loch
~ **chamber** Schleusenkammer *f*
~ **gate** Schleusentor *n*
~ **of water** Wassermenge *f*
locked ore minerals eingeschlossene Erzminerale *npl*
~ **to gangue** an das Ganggestein gebunden
Lockport Dolomite Lockport-Dolomit *m (unterer Teil der Lockport-Gruppe, Nordamerika)*
~ **Group** Lockport-Gruppe *f (oberes Wenlock und Ludlow Nordamerikas)*
locus of the vent Ausbruchsstelle *f*
~ **sphere** Lagenkugel *f*
lode 1. Erzgang *m*, Gang[zug] *m (s.a.* vein 1.); 2. Deich *m*, Wasserlauf *m*
~ **deposit** Ganglagerstätte *f*
~ **filling** Gangfüllung *f*
~ **gold deposit** Golderzgang *m*
~ **matter** Gangmasse *f*, Gangkörper *m*
~ **of medium dip** flachfallender Gang *m*
~ **of steep dip** tonnläger Gang *m*
~ **ore** Gangerz *n*
~ **plot** horizontaler Gang *m*
~ **rock (stone)** Ganggestein *n*
~ **stuff** Gangmasse *f*, Gangkörper *m*

~ **tin** Gangzinn *n*
~ **wall** Gangwand *f*, Salband *n*
lodestar Leitstern *m*; Polarstern *m*
lodestone *(Am)* Magneteisenstein *m*, Magneteisenerz *n (s.a.* magnetite)
lodestuff Gangart *f*
lodge 1. Sumpf *m*; 2. Wasserreservoir *n*
lodgement Ablagerung *f*
~ **till** Grundmoränengeschiebe *n*
lodranite Lodranit *m (Eisen-Stein-Meteorit)*
loess Löß *m*
~ **bluff** Lößsteilufer *n*
~ **clay** Lößlehm *m*
~ **deposit** Lößvorkommen *n*
~ **doll** Lößpuppe *f*, Lößkindl *n*
~ **loam** Lößlehm *m*
~ **nodule** *s.* ~ doll
~ **snail** Lößschnecke *f*
~ **soil** Lößboden *m*
loessial lößähnlich
~ **cover** Lößdecke *f*
loesslike, loessoid lößähnlich, lößartig
loewelte Löweit *m*, $Na_{12}Mg_7[SO_4]_{13} \cdot 15H_2O$
loferite Loferit *m (durch Fenstergefüge charakterisiertes Karbonatgestein)*
log/to [ver]messen, aufnehmen
log 1. Log *n*, Bohrlochaufnahme *f*; 2. Baumstamm *m*
~ **interpretation** Logauswertung *f*
~ **jam** Barre *f*, Sperre *f*
log[g]an stone Wackelstein *m*
logger Datenauswerter *m*
logging Bohrlochmessung *f*
~ **recorder** Registriergerät *n* für Bohrlochmessungen
~ **stone** *s.* log[g]an stone
~ **technique** Meßverfahren *n*
~ **truck** Meßwagen *m*
~ **unit** Bohrlochmeßapparatur *f*
loipon 1. Regolith *m (durch chemische Verwitterung verändertes Gestein)*; 2. Mondgestein *n*
löllingite Löllingit *m*, Arsenikalkies *m*, Arseneisen *n*, $FeAs_2$
LOM *s.* level of organic metamorphism
loma niedrige langgestreckte Bodenerhebung *f*
lomonite *s.* laumontite
lomonossovite Lomonossowit *m*, $Na_2MnTi_3[O|Si_2O_7]_2 \cdot 2Na_3PO_4$
long clay hochplastischer Ton *m*
~**-columnar** stengelig
~**-distance migration** Lateralmigration *f*
~**-distance recorder** Fernmeßgerät *n*
~**-distance water-level recorder** Wasserstandsfernmelder *m*
~**-duration static test** Dauerstandversuch *m*
~**-hole drilling** Langlochbohren *n*, Tieflochbohren *n*
~**-path multiple** Langwegmultiple *f*, Vollwegmultiple *f (Seismik)*
~**-period perturbations** langperiodische Störungen *fpl*

long 214

~-range forecast langfristige Vorhersage f
~-term behaviour Langzeitverhalten n
~-time pumping test Dauerpumpversuch m
~ ton Langtonne f (1010,05 kg, Einheit der Masse in den USA)
~ wall s. longwall
longevity Langlebigkeit f
longitude geografische Länge f
~ circle Längenkreis m
~ degree Längengrad m
longitudinal longitudinal, Längs...; streichend
~ crevasse Längsspalte f (im Gletscher)
~ deformation Längsverformung f
~ dune Längsdüne f
~ fault streichende Verwerfung f, Längsverwerfung f
~ fold s. strike fold
~ joint Längskluft f, S-Kluft f (Granittektonik)
~ moraine Längsmoräne f
~ pressure Längsdruck m
~ profile Längsprofil n
~ ripple marks longitudinale Rippelmarken fpl
~ section Längsschnitt m
~ slab joints Längsplattung f, Sigmoidalklüftung f
~ stria Längsstreifen m
~ [strike] valley Längstal n
~ wave Longitudinalwelle f, Kompressionswelle f, P-Welle f (Seismik)
longshore current Küstenstrom m
~ drift[ing], ~ transport of material Küstenversetzung f
longwall Streb m
~ caving Strebbruchbau m
~ face Streb m
~ stoping Firstenstoßbau m
~ working system Strebbau m
loop 1. Armgerüst n (bei Brachiopoden); 2. Schleife f (z.B. eines Flusses); 3. Schleife f; Ringschluß m
~ bedding Girlandenschichtung f
~ error Schleifenschlußfehler m
~ lake s. oxbow
looped bar Hakenschlinge f (eines Flusses)
loose circulation/to Spülung verlieren
loose-coiled mit offenen Windungen (Ammoniten)
~ grain soil strukturloser Boden m
~ ground lockeres Gebirge n
~ masses Lockermassen fpl
~ material Lockermaterial n
~ rock Lockergestein n
~ roof zubruchgehende Firste f
~ snow Lockerschnee m
loosened rock gelöstes Gestein n
loosening Auflockerung f (des Bodens); Lockerung f (des Gesteins)
loparite Loparit m, (Na, Ce, Ca)TiO$_3$
lopezite Lopezit m, K$_2$[Cr$_2$O$_7$]
lopolith Lopolith m (Intrusionsform)
lopsided pultförmig
lorandite Lorandit m, TlAsS$_2$

lorenzenite Lorenzenit m (Varietät von Ramsayit)
lorettoite Lorettoit m, PbCl$_2$·6PbO
loseyite Loseyit m, (Mn, Zn)$_7$[(OH)$_5$|CO$_3$]$_2$
loss by evaporation Verdunstungsverlust m
~ by percolation Versickerungsverlust m
~ in cleaning Aufbereitungsverlust m
~ in gas storage Speichergasverlust m
~ of circulation Spül[ungs]verlust m
~ of [drill] core Kernverlust m
~ of energy Energieverlust m
~ of head Spiegelgefälle n (des Wassers)
~ of heat Wärmeverlust m
~ of returns Spül[ungs]verlust m
lossenite Lossenit m (Gemenge von Skorodit und Beudantit)
lost circulation Spül[ungs]verlust m
~-circulation zone Spülverlustzone f
~ interval Schichtenlücke f
~ record Hiatus m, stratigrafische Lücke f
~ river ausgetrockneter Fluß m; wasserabgebender Karstfluß m
Lotharingian [Stage] s. Sinemurian
lotrite Lotrit m, Pumpellyit m, Ca$_2$(Mg, Fe, Mn, Al)(Al, Fe, Ti)$_2$[(OH, H$_2$O)$_2$|SiO$_4$|Si$_2$O$_7$]
louderbackite Louderbackit m, Fe(Fe, Al)$_2$[So$_4$]$_4$·14H$_2$O
lough 1. See m, Lagune f (Irland); 2. unregelmäßiger Hohlraum m (einer Eisenerzgrube in Lancashire)
loughlinite Loughlinit m, Na$_2$Mg$_3$[(OH)$_2$|Si$_6$O$_{15}$]·2H$_2$O+4H$_2$O
loup Verschiebung f, Störung f (Schottland)
lovchorrite s. mosandrite
Love wave Love-Welle f (Seismik)
lovozerite Lowozerit m, (Na, K)$_2$(Mn, Ca)ZrSi$_6$O$_{16}$·3H$_2$O
low 1. Tief n (Meteorologie); 2. Strandpriel m, Auswaschung f; 3. fossile Auswaschung f in Kohlenflözen
~-angle dipping stratum flach einfallende Schicht f
~-angle fault flachwinklige Verwerfung f
~-ash coal (Am) Kohle f mit niedrigem Aschegehalt (<«8%)
~ bank Flachufer n
~ coast Flachküste f
~ craton Tiefkraton n
~-cut filter Hochpaßfilter n
~ dip flaches Einfallen n
~-dipping stratum flach einfallende Schicht f
~ enthalpy geothermal potential niedrigenthalpes geothermisches Potential n
~ flow Niedrigwasserabfluß m
~-flow forecast Niedrigwasserabflußprognose f
~-grade arm, geringhaltig, geringwertig, minderwertig
~-grade clay gewöhnlicher Ton m
~-grade metamorphism schwache Metamorphose f

~-grade ore geringwertiges (armes) Erz *n*, Armerz *n*
~-gravity crude oil rohes Schweröl *n*
~-gravity oil Schweröl *n*
~ ground[s] Niederung *f*, Mulde *f*
~-level bog Flachmoor *n*, Niederungsmoor *n*
~-level discharge Niedrigwasserabfluß *m*
~-level laterite allochthoner Laterit *m*, Schwemmlaterit *m*
~-level radiation schwache Strahlung *f*
~ liquid limit niedrige Fließgrenze *f (eines bindigen Materials, <50)*
~-lying tiefliegend
~-lying bog Flachmoor *n*, Niederungsmoor *n*
~-lying coast Flachküste *f*
~-lying coast region, ~-lying coastal land Küstenniederung *f*
~-lying flat Marsch *f*
~-lying moorland Flachmoor *n*, Niederungsmoor *n*
~ marsh Talmoor *n*
~ meadow *s.* ~-lying flat
~ moor Flachmoor *n*, Niederungsmoor *n*
~-moor peat Flachmoortorf *m*
~-moor soil Niederungsmoorboden *m*
~ oblique photograph Steilaufnahme *f (Aerogeologie)*
~-order trend surface Trendfläche (Polynomtrendfläche) *f* niedrigen Grades
~-pass filter Tiefpaßfilter *n*
~-permeable geringdurchlässig
~-pressure area Tiefdruckgebiet *n*
~-productive soil armer Boden *m*
~ quartz Tiefquarz *m*
~-rank coal gering inkohlte Kohle *f*; Braunkohle *f (überwiegend)*
~-rank graywacke *s.* subgraywacke
~-rank metamorphism schwache Metamorphose *f*
~-sulfur coal *(Am)* Kohle *f* mit niedrigem Schwefelgehalt *(≤ 1%)*
~-temperature carbonization Schwelung *f*, Verschwelung *f*, Tieftemperaturverkokung *f*
~ tide Niedrigwasser *n*, Ebbe *f*
~-tide flat Watt *n*
~-velocity correction Verwitterungskorrektur *f (bei seismischen Messungen)*
~-velocity layer Schicht *f* mit geringerer seismischer Wellengeschwindigkeit
~-volatile bituminous coal *(Am)* niedrigflüchtige (hochinkohlte) Steinkohle *f (auf wasser-aschefreie Basis bezogen: flüchtige Bestandteile: 14 bis 22%, C_{fix}: 78 bis 86%)*
~ volatility/of schwerflüchtig
~ water Niedrigwasser *n*, Ebbe *f*
~-water discharge Niedrigwassermenge *f*
~-water flow Niedrigwasserabfluß *m*
~-water level Niedrigwasserstand *m*
~-water line Niedrigwasserlinie *f*
~ water of ordinary neap tide Nippniedrigwasser *n*
~ water of spring tides Springniedrigwasser *n*

~-water stage Niedrigwasserstand *m*
lower/to 1. niederbringen, einbauen *(Bohrung, Verrohrung)*; 2. erniedrigen *(ein Relief durch Erosion)*; 3. absenken
~ the water table den Grundwasserspiegel absenken
lower aquifer Liegendgrundwasserleiter *m*
~ bed Unterschicht *f*
~ block Tiefscholle *f*, Liegendscholle *f*
~ bottom water Liegendwasser *n (bei Erdöllagerstätten)*
~ confining bed Grundwassersohlschicht *f*
~ course Unterlauf *m (eines Flusses)*
~ discharge tunnel Grundablaß *m*
~ flow regime unteres Fließregime *n (fluviatiler Transport)*
~ hemisphere untere Halbkugel *f (Schmidtsches Netz)*
~ jaw Unterkiefer *m*
~ limb liegender Schenkel *m*
~ limit of the tenor of ore Bauwürdigkeitsgrenze *f*
~ mantle unterer Erdmantel *m*, unterer (tieferer) Mantel *m*
~-pressure formation Formation *f* geringeren Drucks
~ rank lignite Weichbraunkohle *f*
~ reservoir Unterbecken *n*
~ water Liegendwasser *n*
~ yield point untere Streckgrenze *f*
Lower Cambrian [Epoch, Series] Unterkambrium *n*
~ Carboniferous [Epoch, Series] 1. Unterkarbon *n*, Dinant *n (in Westeuropa und Mitteleuropa, Gattendorfia- bis Goniatites-Stufe)*; 2. Unterkarbon *n (in der UdSSR, Gattendorfia-Stufe bis einschließlich Namur A)*
~ Chalk Untere Schreibkreide *f (Cenoman, England)*
~ Cretaceous [Epoch, Series] Unterkreide *f*
~ Devonian [Epoch, Series] Unterdevon *n*
~ Greensand Formation Unterer Grünsand *m (Apt und unteres Alb, England)*
~ Jurassic [Epoch, Series] Unterer (Schwarzer) Jura *m*, Lias *m*
~ Ordovician [Epoch, Series] Unteres Ordovizium *n*, Unterordovizium *n (Tremadoc, Arenig und Llanvirn)*
~ Palaeozoic Altpaläozoikum *n (Kambrium bis Devon)*
~ Permian [Epoch, Series] Unterperm *n*
~ Pliensbachian unteres Pliensbach *n*, Carix *n (Stufe des Unteren Juras)*
~ Precambrian Altpräkambrium *n*
~ Triassic [Epoch, Series] Untere Trias *f (Skyth)*
lowered block abgesunkene Scholle *f*
~ ground-water level gesenkter Grundwasserspiegel *m*
lowering Absinken *n*; Senkung *f*
~ of subsoil water Grundwasserabsenkung *f*
~ of the ground-water surface Grundwasserabsenkung *f*

lowering 216

~ **of the melting point** Schmelzpunkterniedrigung f
~ **of the water table** Absenkung f des Grundwasserspiegels
lowermost bed unterste Schicht f
lowground s. low ground
löwigite s. alunite
lowland Niederung f, Tiefland n, Tiefebene f
~ **bog (moor)** Grünlandmoor n, Niederungsmoor n
~ **plain** Tiefebene f
loxoclase Loxoklas m (Na-reicher Orthoklas)
lubricant Schmiermittel n (auf tektonischen Flächen)
lubricating layer Schmierschicht f
lubricity Schlüpfrigkeit f
Lüders' lines Lüderssche (Hartmannsche) Linien fpl
Ludfordian [Stage] Ludfordium n (basale Stufe des Ludlow)
Ludhanian [Stage] Ludhanien n (Stufe des Pleistozäns)
Ludian [Stage] Lud[ium] n, Ludien n, Ludische Stufe f (Stufe des Eozäns)
ludlamite Ludlamit m, $Fe_3[PO_4]_2 \cdot H_2O$
Ludlovian [Epoch, Series] Ludlow[ium] n (oberes Silur)
ludwigite Ludwigit m, $(Mg, Fe)_2Fe[O_2|BO_3]$
lueshite Lueshit m, $NaNbO_3$
lugarite Lugarit m (Varietät von Techenit)
Luisian [Stage] Luisien n (marine Stufe, mittleres Miozän in Nordamerika)
lujavrite Lujavrit m (Nephelinsyenit)
lum Partie geringerer Härte im Kohlenflöz
lumachelle Lumachelle f; Muschelbrekzie f
lumbar vertebra Lendenwirbel m, Lumbalwirbel m
luminesce/to lumineszieren
luminescence Lumineszenz f
~ **quenching** Lumineszenzlöschung f
luminescent lumineszierend
~ **crystal** lumineszierender Kristall m
~ **emission** Lumineszenzemission f
luminosity Leuchtkraft f
luminous leuchtend
~ **clouds** leuchtende Nachtwolken fpl
~ **haze** Lichtnebel m
~ **incident ray** einfallender Lichtstrahl m
~ **matter** leuchtende Materie f
~ **pencil** Strahlenbündel n
lump Klumpen m, Kornaggregation f (aus Oolithen oder Pellets); Galle f, Konkretion f
~ **coal** Stückkohle f, Grobkohle f
~ **lime** Stückkalk m (gebrannt)
~ **of slag** Lavaflatschen f
~ **of tin ore** Zinnstufe f
~ **ore** Stückerz n
lumpiness Stückigkeit f
lumpy ballig, stückig, derbstückig, grobstückig, klumpig
~ **ore** stückiges Erz n
lunar halbmondförmig, lunar

~ **aurora** Mondhof m
~ **circuit** Mondumlauf m
~ **circus** Mondkrater m
~ **cleft** Mondspalte f (Oberflächenform)
~ **crater** Mondkrater m
~ **day** Mondtag m
~ **disk** Mondscheibe f
~ **dust** s. ~ regolith
~ **eclipse** Mondfinsternis f
~ **fines** pulvriges Mondmaterial n (Bestandteile des Mondbodens < 1cm)
~ **geology** Mondgeologie f
~ **glassy spherules** Glaskügelchen npl im Lunargestein
~ **halo** Mondhalo m, Mondring m
~ **landscape** Mondlandschaft f
~ **libration** Libration f, Mondbewegung f
~ **microbreccia** zu Brekzie kompaktiertes (geschweißtes) Mondoberflächenmaterial n
~ **mountain[s]** Mondgebirge n
~ **orbit** Mond[umlauf]bahn f
~ **path** Mondbahn f
~ **phase** Mondphase f
~ **probe** Mondsonde f
~ **regolith** Mondboden m, Staubschicht f des Mondes
~ **rock** Mondgestein n
~ **shadow** Mondschatten m
~ **topography** Mondlandschaft f
~ **year** Mondjahr n
lunarian Mondforscher m
lunate mondförmig
lunation Mondumlauf m
luncart längliche Konkretion f (Schottland)
lüneburgite Lüneburgit m, $Mg_3[(PO_4)_2|B_2O(OH)_4] \cdot 6H_2O$
lung fish Lungenfisch m
lunker s. luncart
lusakite Lusakit m (Co-haltige Varietät von Staurolith)
Lusitanian Lusitanien n (fazielle Entwicklung, oberes Oxford, Schweizer Jura)
lussatite Lussatit m (s.a. chalcedony)
luster (Am) s. lustre
lustre Glanz m, Schimmer m
~**-motting** Glanzfleckigkeit f (bei Sandsteinen mit sparitischem Zement)
lustreless glanzlos
lustrous glänzend, strahlend
~ **coal** (sl) s. bright coal
~ **schist** Glanzschiefer m
lusungite Lunsungit m, $(Sr, Pb)Fe_3H[(OH)_6|(PO_4)_2]$
lutaceous s. argillaceous
lutalite Lutalit m (Varietät von Leuzitnephelinit)
lute klebriger Lehm m
Lutetian [Stage] Lutet[ium] n (Stufe des Eozäns)
lutetium Lutetium n, Lu
lutite Pelit m
lutose tonbedeckt
luxullianite Luxullianit m (Turmalingranit)

luzonite Luzonit *m*, Cu_3AsS_4
lycopodiaceous bärlappähnlich
~ **tree** Bärlappbaum *m*
Lydian stone, lydite Lydit *m*, Kieselschiefer *m*
lye/to laugen
lye Lauge *f*
lying fold liegende Falte *f*
~ **stratified** schichtweise gelagert
~ **wall** Liegendes *n*
lyndochite Lyndochit *m* (*s.a.* euxenite)

M

M-boundary Moho-Diskontinuität *f*
maar Maar *n*
Maastrichtian [Stage] Maastricht[ien] *n*, Maastrichtium *n* (*höchste Stufe der Oberkreide*)
macadam Straßen[bau]schotter *m*, Schotter *m*
~ **effect** Zementationseffekt *m* (*in Karbonatgesteinen durch Evaporation*)
~ **road** Schotterstraße *f*
macadamize/to beschottern
macaluba Schlammvulkan *m*
macaroni tubing engkalibrige Steigrohre *npl*
macdonaldite Macdonaldit *m*, $BaCa_4[Si_{15}O_{35}] \cdot 11H_2O$
Macedon glass Tektitenglas *n* von Macedon (*Australien*)
macedonite Mazedonit *m* (*olivgrüner Trachyt*)
maceral Maceral *n* (*Gefügebestandteil, Gemengteil der Kohle*)
~ **group** Maceralgruppe *f*
~ **subgroup** Maceralsubgruppe *f*
macerated plant material mazeriertes Pflanzenmaterial *n*
maceration Mazerierung *f*
macgovernite Macgovernit *m*, $Mn_9Zn_2Mg_4[O|(OH)_{14}|(AsO_4)_2|(SiO_4)_2]$
mackayite Mackayit *m*, $Fe[TeO_3]_3 \cdot xH_2O$
mackensite Mackensit *m* (*Mineral der Chlorit-Gruppe*)
mackerel sky Schäfchenhimmel *m*
mackintoshite Mackintoshit *m*, Thorogummit *m*, $(Th, U)[SiO_4, (OH)_4]$
macle 1. Zwillingskristall *m*; 2. dunkler Fleck *m*
maconite Makonit *m* (*Übergangsmineral von Hydrobiotit zu Vermiculit*)
macrinite Macrinite *m* (*Kohlenmaceral*)
macro... *s.a.* mega...
macrocephaly Großköpfigkeit *f* (*bei Fossilien*)
macrochemical makrochemisch
macroclastic makroklastisch
macroclimate Makroklima *n*, regionales Klima *n* (*Ökologie*)
macrocosm Makrokosmos *m*, Weltall *n*
macrocrystalline makrokristallin, grobkörnig
macrodome Makrodoma *n* (*Kristallografie*)
macroite Macroit *m* (*Kohlenmikrolithotyp*)
macropetrographic seam section makropetrografisches Flözprofil *n* (*Kohle*)

macroscopic makroskopisch, megaskopisch
~ **examination** makroskopische Untersuchung *f*
macroseism Makrobeben *n*
macroseismic makroseismisch
macrospore Makrospore *f*, Megaspore *f*
mactrostructure Makrogefüge *n*, makroskopisches (freisichtiges) Gefüge *n*, Grobgefüge *n*
macrotype *s.* microlithotype
maculose rock Knotenschiefer *m*; Fleckschiefer *m*
made ground Auffüllung *f*
madeirite Madeirit *m* (*porphyrischer Alkalipikrit*)
madre 1. Flußbett *n*; 2. Mutterlauge *f*; 3. lockeres Oberflächengestein *n* (*Kolumbien*)
madupite Madupit *m* (*Glimmerleuzitit*)
maenite Maenit *m* (*Ca-reicher Bostonit*)
mafic mafisch
~ **mineral** Dunkelmineral *n*, basisches Mineral *n*
mafites Mafite *mpl* (*Dunkelminerale in magmatischen Gesteinen*)
mafurite Mafurit *m* (*Olivinleuzitit*)
magadiite Magadiit *m*, $NaSi_7O_{18}(OH)_3 \cdot 3H_2O$
magallanite Magallanit *m* (*eine asphaltartige Substanz*)
maggie (*sl*) 1. minderwertige Kohle; 2. minderwertige Eisenkarbonaterze in Schottland
~ **blaes** (*sl*) minderwertige Eisensulfiderze (in Schottland)
maghemite Maghemit *m*, $\gamma\text{-}Fe_2O_3$
magma Magma *n*
~ **chamber** Magmakammer *f*, Magmaherd *m*
~ **focus (hearth)** Magmaherd *m*
~ **reservoir** Magmakammer *f*, Magmaherd *m*
magmatic magmatisch
~ **body** Magmenkörper *m*
~ **cycle** magmatischer Zyklus *m*
~ **differentiation** magmatische Differentiation *f*
~ **digestion** *s.* assimilation
~ **eruption** magmatischer Ausbruch *m*
~ **extrusion** Magmendurchbruch *m*, magmatische Extrusion *f*
~ **intrusion** magmatische Intrusion *f*
~ **province** magmatische Provinz *f*
~ **rock** Magmatit *m*, magmatisches Gestein *n*, Erstarrungsgestein *n*
~ **stage** magmatisches Stadium *n*
~ **stoping** magmatische Aufstemmung *f* (*mechanische Raumschaffung bei magmatischer Intrusion*)
~ **tremor** magmatisches Beben *n*
~ **tribe** Magmasippe *f*
~ **water** *s.* juvenile water
magmatism Magmatismus *m*
magmatogene magmatogen
magmatogenic rock magmatogenes Gestein *n*
magmosphere Zone unterhalb der Mohorovičić-Diskontinuität *f*

magnesia

magnesia Magnesia f, Magnesiumoxid n, MgO
magnesian 1. magnesiumhaltig; 2. magnesiahaltig
~ **limestone** dolomitischer Kalkstein m, Magnesiakalk m, Dolomit[kalk] m
~ **slate** Talkschiefer m
magnesiochromite Magnesiochromit m, $MgCr_2O_4$
magnesiocopiapite Magnesiocopiapit m, $MgFe_4(SO_4)_6(OH)_2 \cdot 20H_2O$
magnesioferrite Magnesioferrit m, Magnoferrit m, $MgFeO_4$
magnesiokatophorite Magnesiokatophorit m, $Na_2CaMg_4(Fe,Al)[(OH,F)_2AlSi_7O_{22}]$
magnesioludwigite Magnesioludwigit m *(Varietät von Ludwigit)*
magnesioniobite Magnesioniobit m, $(Mg, Fe, Mn)(Nb, Ta, Ti)_2O_6$
magnesioriebeckite Magnesioriebeckit m, $Na_2Mg_3Fe_2[(OH, F)|Si_4O_{11}]_2$
magnesiosussexite Magnesiosussexit m *(Mg-haltige Varietät von Sussexit)*
magnesiotriplite Magnesiotriplit m *(Mg-haltiger Triplit)*
magnesite Magnesit m, Bitterspat m, $MgCO_3$
magnesium Magnesium n, Mg
~-**chlorophoenicite** Magnesium-Chlorophoenicit m, $(Zn, Mn)_5[(OH)_7|AsO_4]$
magnet natürlicher Magnet m; Magneteisenstein m
magnetic magnetisch
~ **aftereffect** magnetische Nachwirkung f
~ **anisotropy** magnetische Anisotropie f
~ **anomaly** magnetische Anomalie f
~ **artefacts** [künstliche] magnetische Störkörper mpl
~ **attraction** magnetische Anziehung f
~ **axis** Magnetachse f, Pol[ar]achse f
~ **balance** magnetische Waage f, Feldwaage f
~ **bearing** magnetisches Azimut n, magnetische Peilung f
~ **bias** magnetische Vorspannung f
~ **biasing** Vormagnetisierung f
~ **cobber** Magnetscheider m
~ **compass needle** Kompaßnadel f, Magnetnadel f
~ **compass north** magnetische Nordrichtung f
~ **concentrating** magnetische Aufbereitung f
~ **declination** magnetische Abweichung (Deklination, Mißweisung) f
~ **dip** s. ~ inclination
~ **dipole** magnetischer Dipol m
~ **dipole radiation** magnetische Dipolstrahlung f
~ **disturbance** magnetische Störung f, magnetischer Sturm m
~ **diurnal variation** magnetische Tagesvariation f
~ **dressing** magnetische Aufbereitung f
~ **equator** erdmagnetischer Äquator m
~ **field** magnetisches Feld n, Magnetfeld n
~ **field balance** Magnetfeldwaage f, magnetische Feldwaage f
~ **field energy** magnetische Feldenergie f
~ **field intensity** magnetische Feldstärke f
~ **field line** magnetische Feldlinie f
~ **field strength** magnetische Feldstärke f
~ **flux density** magnetische Flußdichte f
~ **inclination** magnetische Inklination f
~ **intensity** magnetische Feldstärke f
~ **iron ore** s. magnetite
~ **logging** magnetisches Bohrlochmeßverfahren n, magnetische Bohrlochaufnahme f
~ **meridian** magnetischer Meridian m
~ **needle** Magnetnadel f
~ **north** magnetisch Nord
~ **observatory** magnetisches Observatorium n
~ **ore separator** Magnetscheider m
~ **permeability** magnetische Permeabilität f
~ **permeability logging** Messung f der magnetischen Permeabilität
~ **polarization** magnetische Polarisierung f
~ **pole** [erd]magnetischer Pol m
~ **pyrite** s. pyrrhotine
~ **resistance** magnetischer Widerstand m
~ **screening** magnetische Abschirmung f
~ **separation** magnetische Aufbereitung f, Magnetscheidung f
~ **separator** Magnetscheider m
~ **shielding** magnetische Abschirmung f
~ **storm** magnetischer Sturm m, magnetische Störung f
~ **survey** magnetisches Schürfen n, geomagnetische Vermessung f
~ **susceptibility** magnetische Suszeptibilität f
~ **susceptibility logging** Meßverfahren n mit Hilfe der magnetischen Suszeptibilität
~ **variation** s. ~ declination
magnetics Magnetik f
magnetism Magnetismus m
magnetite Magnetit m, Magneteisenstein m, Fe_3O_4
magnetization Magnetisierung f
magnetize/to magnetisieren
magnetizing force magnetische Feldstärke f
magnetometer Magnetometer n
magnetoplumbite Magnetoplumbit m, $PbO \cdot 6Fe_2O_3$
magnetosphere Magnetosphäre f
magnetostriction Magnetostriktion f
magnetostrictive drilling Magnetostriktionsbohren n
magnetotelluric method, magnetotellurics Magnetotellurik f
magnification Vergrößerung f
magnifier Vergrößerungsglas n, Lupe f
magnify/to vergrößern
magnifying glass Vergrößerungsglas n, Lupe f
magniphyric körnig mikrophyrisch *(zwischen 0,2–0,4 mm)*
magnitude Magnitude f *(Maß für die Energie eines Erdbebens)*
magnochromite s. magnesiochromite

magnoferrite s. magnesioferrite
magnolite Magnolit m, $Hg_2[TeO_4]$
magnophorite Magnophorit m *(Varietät von Richterit)*
magnophyric grobporphyrisch *(< 5mm)*
magnussonite Magnussonit m, $(Mn,Mg,Cu)_5[(OH, Cl)(AsO_3)_3]$
maiden jungfräulich, unverritzt
~ **field** unverritztes Abbaufeld n
main activity Haupttätigkeit f
~ **bottom** gewachsenes Gestein n, Felsuntergrund m
~ **constituent** Hauptbestandteil m, Hauptkomponente f
~ **divide** Hauptwasserscheide f
~ **drive** Hauptstrecke f
~ **element** Hauptelement n
~ **fault** Hauptverwerfung f
~ **fold** Hauptfalte f
~ **gangway** Gezeugstrecke f
~ **gate** Grundstrecke f
~ **glacier** Hauptgletscher m
~ **haulage road** Hauptförderstrecke f
~ **hoisting shaft** Hauptförderschacht m
~ **joint** Hauptkluft f, Großkluft f
~ **level road** Richtstrecke f
~ **lode** Hauptgang m
~ **ocean** offener Ozean m
~ **phase** Hauptphase f
~ **river** Hauptstrom m
~ **roof** Haupthangendes n
~ **roof break** Setzriß m, Hangendriß m
~ **sea** hohe (offene) See f
~ **trend** Hauptstreichen n
~ **trunk sewer** Hauptsammelkanal m
mainland Festland n, Kontinent m
maintenance of the strata in undisturbed condition Erhaltung f des ungestörten Schichtenzusammenhangs
major clastic component klastischer Hauptbestandteil m
~ **constituent** Hauptgemengteil m
~ **divide** Hauptwasserscheide f
~ **element** Hauptelement n
~ **fault** Hauptverwerfung f
~ **fold** Hauptfalte f
~ **glaciation** Hauptvereisung f
~ **intrusion** Großintrusion f
~ **joint** Hauptkluft f, Großkluft f
~ **period of folding** Hauptfaltungsperiode f
~ **seismic belt** Hauptbebengürtel m
~ **septum** Hauptseptum n
~ **sheet** Stammdecke f
~ **stream bed** Hochwasserbett n eines Flusses
~ **trough** Hauptmulde f
makatea erhöhter Rand eines Korallenriffs
make hole/to Bohrfortschritt machen
~ **watertight** abdichten
make [ab]bauwürdige Gangerzanreicherung f
~-**up** Ausgehen n *(einer Lagerstätte)*
mäkinenite Mäkinenit m, NiSe
malachite Malachit m, $Cu_2[(OH)_2|CO_3]$

malacolite Malakolith m *(Varietät von Diopsid)*
malacon Malakon m *(isotropisierter Zirkon)*
Malaspina glacier s. piedmont glacier
malayaite Malayait m, $CaSn[O|SiO_4]$
malchite Malchit m *(lamprophyrisches Ganggestein)*
maldonite Maldonit m, Au_2Bi
malformation Mißbildung f; Aberration f
malignite Malignit m *(Nephelinsyenit)*
malinowskite Malinowskit m *(Varietät von Tetraedrit, Cu-armes Silberbleifahlerz)*
malladrite Malladrit m, $Na_2[SiF_6]$
mallardite Mallardit m, $Mn[SO_4] \cdot 7H_2O$
malleability Geschmeidigkeit f, bruchlose Verformbarkeit f
malleable geschmeidig, bruchlos verformbar
malm 1. brüchiger Kalkstein m; 2. Kalktonboden m
Malm [Epoch, Series] Malm m, Weißer Jura m *(Serie des Juras)*
malmstone Kieselkalkstein m
maltesite Maltesit m *(Varietät von Andalusit)*
maltha Bergteer m, Erdteer m, Malthait m, Mineralteer m *(Asphaltmineral)*
malthacite s. fuller's earth
malting coal Anthrazitkohle f *(Wales)*
Malvinokaffric Province Malvino-kaffrische Provinz f *(Devon, Paläobiogeografie)*
mamelon kleine Bodenerhebung f mit rundem Top
mammalian stage Wirbeltierstufe f
mammillary warzig, kugelig *(Mineralaggregate)*
~ **hills** s. drumlins
mammillated rock Rundhöcker m, Rundberg m
mammoth Mammut n
~ **pump** Mammutpumpe f
~ **tusk** Mammutstoßzahn m
man and environment Mensch m und Umwelt f
~-**made radioisotope** künstliches radioaktives Isotop n
~-**made shore line** befestigte Küste f
manandonite Manandonit m, $LiAl_2[(OH)_2|AlBSi_2O_{10}]Al_2(OH)_6$
manasseite Manasseit m, $Mg_6Al_2[(OH)_{16}|CO_3] \cdot 4H_2O$
manatee Seekuh f
mandible Mandibel f, Kiefer[knochen] m
mandibular groove Mandibularfurche f
mandshurite Mandschurit m *(Nephelinbasanit)*
Manebach twins Manebacher Zwillinge mpl
manganalluaudite Mangan-Alluaudit m, $Na(Mn, Fe)[PO_4]$
manganberzeliite Mangan-Berzeliit m, $(Ca, Na)_3(Mn, Mg)_2[AsO_4]_3$
manganese Mangan n, Mn
~-**bearing** manganhaltig
~ **hydrate** s. psilomelane
~ **nodule** Manganknolle f
~ **ore** Manganerz n, Braunstein m

manganese

~-rich pellets Manganknollen *fpl (im marinen Bereich)*
~ slate Manganschiefer *m*
~ spar *s.* rhodochrosite
manganesian manganhaltig
manganhoernesite Mangan-Hörnesit *m*, $(Mn, Mg)_3[AsO_4]_2 \cdot 8H_2O$
manganiferous manganhaltig
~ iron ore Manganeisenerz *n*
manganite Manganit *m*, γ-MnOOH
manganolangbeinite Manganolangbeinit *m*, $K_2Mn_2[SO_4]_3$
manganomelane Manganomelan *m (kolloidal ausgeschiedenes MnO_2)*
manganoniobite Manganoniobit *m*, $(Mn, Fe)Nb_2O_6$
manganophyllite Manganophyllit *m (Mn-reicher Biotit)*
manganosite Manganosit *m*, MnO
manganostibiite Manganostibiit *m*, $8(Mn, Fe)O \cdot Sb_2O_5$
manganotantalite Manganotantalit *m*, $(Mn, Fe)Ta_2O_6$
manganous manganhaltig
~ iron Manganeisen *n*
mangerite Mangerit *m (Monzonit)*
mangrove marsh Mangrovensumpf *m*
~ peat Mangroventorf *m*
~ soil Mangrovenboden *m*
manjak Manjak *m (Asphalt)*
manlike *s.* anthropoid
mansfieldite Mansfieldit *m*, $Al[AsO_4] \cdot 2H_2O$
mantle 1. Überlagerung *f*; Decke *f*; Schwemmland *n*, Alluvion *f*; Aufschüttung *f*; 2. Mantel *m*; Erdmantel *m*
~ line Mantellinie *f (bei Mollusken)*
~ of debris Schuttdecke *f*
~ of glacial drift Glazialgeschiebedecke *f*
~ of rock waste Schuttmantel *m*
~ of vegetation Vegetationsdecke *f*
~ rock 1. Lockerboden *m*, Verwitterungskrume *f*, Deckgebirge *n*, Regolith *m*; 2. Erdmantelgestein *n*
mantled gneiss dome ummantelter Gneisdom *m*
manufacture of thin section Dünnschliffherstellung *f*
manufactured mineral verarbeiteter mineralischer Rohstoff *m*
manuring salt Düngesalz *n*
manyside vielseitig
manystage mehrstufig, Mehrstufen...
map/to kartieren
map Karte *f*, Landkarte *f*
~ convolution Interpolationsfehler *m*, Restfeld *n*
~ cracking *(Am)* Maronage *f*, feine Rißbildung *f*
~ grid Gitternetz *n (einer Karte)*, Kartennetz *n*
~ of mine Grubenriß *m*
~ printing Kartografie *f*
~ projection Kartenprojektion *f*

~ reading Kartenlesen *n*
~ scale Kartenmaßstab *m*
~ section Kartenausschnitt *m*
~ sheet Kartenblatt *n*
~ symbol Kartenzeichen *n*
mappability Kartierbarkeit *f*
mapping Kartierung *f*, Geländeaufnahme *f*
~ instrument Kartiergerät *n*
~ of soil Bodenkartierung *f*
~-out Kartierung *f*
~ radar Bildradar *n*
marahunite Marahunit *m (tertiäres Algengestein, Bogheadbildung im Braunkohlenstadium)*
marble Marmor *m*
~ lime Marmorkalk *m*
~ quarry Marmor[stein]bruch *m*
~ slab Marmorplatte *f*
marbled marmoriert, geädert, gemasert
marblelike marmorartig
marbling Marmorisierung *f*
marcasite Markasit *m*, FeS_2
Marcellus Shales Marcellus-Schiefer *mpl (Mitteldevon in Nordamerika)*
marching dune Wanderdüne *f*
mare Mare *n (Meer auf Mars oder Mond)*
~ rocks Maregesteine *npl (Mond)*
marecanite edler Obsidian *m*, Marekanit *m*
mareographic *s.* oceanographic
margarite Margarit *m*, Perlglimmer *m*, Kalkglimmer *m*, $CaAl_2[(OH)_2|Si_2Al_2O_{10}]$
margarosanite Margarosanit *m*, $Pb(Ca, Mn)_2[Si_3O_9]$
margin Rand *m*, Ufer *n*, Saum *m*
~ of safety Sicherheitsgrenze *f*
marginal am Rand befindlich, Rand...; bedingt [ab]bauwürdig
~ basin Randbecken *n (am Fuße des Kontinentalabhangs)*
~ cord Dorsalstrang *m (bei Foraminiferen)*
~ crevasse Bergschrund *m*, Randspalte *f (eines Gletschers)*
~ deep Saumtiefe *f*, Saumsenke *f*, Randsenke *f*, Idiogeosynklinale *f*
~ deposit 1. Schelfsediment *n*; 2. bedingt [ab]bauwürdige Lagerstätte *f*
~ escarpment steile Randstufe *f (im Kontinentalabhang)*
~ fault Randbruch *m*
~ geosyncline Parageosynklinale *f*
~ ice Ufereis *n*, Randeis *n*
~ lagoon Strandhaff *n*
~ lake Gletscherrandsee *m*
~ moraine Seitenmoräne *f*
~ ores bedingt [ab]bauwürdige Erze *npl*
~ overthrust Randüberschiebung *f*
~ plateau Randplateau *n (auf dem Schelf)*
~ platform submarine Ebene *f (am Kontinentalabhang)*
~ potential area Randpotentialfläche *f (eines artesischen Beckens)*
~ sea Randmeer *n*, Nebenmeer *n*
~ seam bedingt [ab]bauwürdiges Flöz *n*

~ **selvage** Salband *n*
~ **stream area** Randstromfläche *f*
~ **trench** *dem Kontinentalabhang vorgelagerter tiefer Randgraben*
~ **trough** *s.* ~ deep
~ **well** 1. Randschwelle *f*, Randwulst *m*; 2. Melksonde *f*; Randbohrung *f*
~ **zone** Randzone *f*
margode Mergelschiefer *m*
marialite Marialith *m* *(Mischkristall der Skapolithreihe)*
marigram grafische Aufzeichnung *f* des Tidenhubs
marine marin, Meer[es]...
~ **abrasion** Brandungserosion *f*, marine Erosion *f*
~ **arch** Brandungstor *n*
~ **band** mariner Horizont *m* im Flözgebirge
~ **beach** Meeresstrand *m*
~ **bench** Küstenterrasse *f*, Brandungsterrasse *f*
~ **chart** Seekarte *f*
~ **clay** Marschenton *m*
~ **climate** maritimes (ozeanisches) Klima *n*, Seeklima *n*
~ **concrete structure** Betongerüst *n* einer permanent installierten Betonbohr- und -förderinsel
~ **current** Meeresströmung *f*
~ **-cut terrace** Brandungsterrasse *f*, Brandungsplatte *f*, Schorre *f*
~ **deposit** marine Lagerstätte *f*, Meeresablagerung *f* *(Ablagerung am Seeboden)*
~ **drilling** Bohren *n* in der See
~ **environment** marine Umwelt *f*, Meeresumwelt *f*
~ **erosion** marine Erosion *f*, Brandungserosion *f*
~ **fauna** marine Fauna *f*
~ **geochemistry** marine Geochemie *f*
~ **geology** marine Geologie *f*
~ **geosyncline development** marine gesoynklinale Entwicklung *f*
~ **invasion** Meereseinbruch *m*, Meeresvorstoß *m*
~ **marsh** Küstensumpf *m*
~ **mining** Meeresbergbau *m*
~ **observatory** Seewarte *f*
~ **oil field** marines Ölfeld *n*
~ **sediment** marines Sediment *n*, Meeresablagerung *f*
~ **seismic surveying** seeseismische Vermessung *f*
~ **stage** marine Stufe *f*
~ **terrace** Strandterrasse *f*, Meeresterasse *f*
~ **till** *s.* subaqueous till
~ **time** durch marine Fossilien belegte geologische Zeit *f*
marining 1. kurzzeitige Überflutung *f*; 2. Vordringen *n* eines Epikontinentalmeeres
mariposite Mariposit *m* *(Varietät von Phengit)*
maritime climate *s.* marine climate

mariupolite Mariupolit *m* *(Albit-Nephelinsyenit)*
mark Marke *f*
marker 1. Leithorizont *m* *(lithostratigrafische Einheit)*; 2. Markierung *f*; 3. Pegel *m*
~ **bed** *s.* marker 1.
~ **velocity** Geschwindigkeit *f* des Leithorizonts *(Seismik)*
marking of points Punktvermarkung *f*
marl Mergel *m*
~ **ball** *s.* algal biscuit
~ **clay** Mergelton *m*
~ **earth** Mergelboden *m*
~ **loam** mergeliger Lehm *m*
~ **slate** Mergelschiefer *m*
marlaceous mergelig
~ **lime** Mergelkalk *m*
marling Mergelung *f*
marlite *s.* marlstone
marlpit Mergelgrube *f*
marlslate Mergelschiefer *m*
marlstone 1. eisenschüssiger Kalkstein *m* *(des mittleren Lias in England)*; 2. Mergelstein *m*
marly mergelartig, mergelig, Mergel...
~ **bed** Mergelbank *f*, Mergelschicht *f*
~ **chalk** mergelige Kreide *f*
~ **clay** mergeliger Ton *m*
~ **facies** Mergelfazies *f*
~ **mudstone** mergeliger Tonstein *m*
~ **sandstone** Mergelsandstein *m*
~ **shale (slate)** Mergelschiefer *m*
~ **soil** Mergelboden *m*
marmarosis Marmorisierung *f* *(Rekristallisation zu Marmor)*
marmatite Marmatit *m*, Eisenzinkblende *f* *(Fereiches ZnS)*
marmoraceous, marmoreal marmorartig
marmorization *s.* marmarosis
marmorize/to marmorisieren
marmorosis *s.* marmarosis
marokite Marokit *m*, $CaMn_2O_4$
marosite Marosit *m* *(Varietät von Shonkinit)*
marrite Marrit *m*, $PbAgAsS_3$
marsh Marsch *f*, Sumpf *m*, Bruch *m*, Morast *m*
~ **border soil** anmooriger Boden *m*
~ **buggy** Geländefahrzeug *n* *(für Sumpf und Moor)*
~ **creek** Priel *m*
~ **drainage** Moorentwässerung *f*
~ **funnel** *s.* viscosimeter
~ **gas** Grubengas *n*, Sumpfgas *n* *(Methan)*
~ **island** Marschinsel *f*, Hallig *f*
~ **marl** Moormergel *m*
~ **ore** Sumpferz *n*, Raseneisenerz *n*
~ **peat** Riedtorf *m*
Marshall line Andesitlinie *f*
marshes Polder *m*
marshiness sumpfige Beschaffenheit *f*
marshite Marshit *m*, CuJ
marshy sumpfig, morastig
~ **area** Sumpfgebiet *n*

marshy 222

~ **depression (flat)** Sumpfniederung f
~ **ground (soil)** Fehn n, Fenn n, Bruch m, Marschboden m, Moorboden m
martial vitriol s. melanterite
Martian canals Marskanäle mpl
~ **moons** Marsmonde mpl
martinite Martinit m (Varietät von Whitlockit)
martite Martit m (Pseudomorphose von Haematit nach Magnetit)
martitization Martitisierung f
mascagnite Mascagnit m, $(NH_4)_2[SO_4]$
mascon Schwereanomalie f, Massenkonzentration f (auf dem Mond)
mash/to einkneten
mash structure Maschentextur f (bei Mineralen)
mashed texture Knetstruktur f (bei Sedimenten)
mashing 1. Verknetung f, Einknetung f; 2. Korngranulierung f durch Deformation
maskelynite Maskelynit m (durch Schockmetamorphose entstandenes Plagioklasglas)
masonite s. chloritoid
masonry dam Mauerdamm m, Staumauer f
masrite Masrit m (Mn-Co-haltiger Pickeringit)
mass budget of glacier Gletschermassenbilanz f
~ **copper** gediegenes Kupfer n
~ **correction** Massenkorrektur f (Gravimetrie)
~ **defect** Massendefekt m (Gravimetrie)
~ **deficiency** Massendefizit m, Schweretief n (Gravimetrie)
~ **excess** Massenüberschuß m, Schwerehoch n (Gravimetrie)
~ **fiber asbestos** verfilzter Asbest m (Rohqualität)
~ **flow** Schlammstrom m mit plastischem Materialverhalten
~ **movement** Massenbewegung f
~ **shift[ing]** Massenverschiebung f
~ **spectrogram** Massenspektrogramm n
~ **spectrograph** Massenspektrograf m
~ **spectrographic analysis** massenspektrografische Analyse f
~ **spectrometer** Massenspektrometer n
~ **spectrometric** massenspektrometrisch
~ **spectrometric isotope dilution** massenspektrometrische Isotopenverdünnung f
~ **spectrometry** Massenspektrometrie f
~ **spectroscopy** Massenspektroskopie f
~ **surplus** Massenüberschuß m (Gravimetrie)
~ **susceptibility** s. specific susceptibility
~ **thrust** Massenüberschiebung f
~ **wasting** Bodenverlagerung f
massicot[ite] Massicot[it] m, Bleiglätte f, β-PbO
massif 1. Gebirgsmassiv n, Gebirgsstock m; 2. Scholle f (der Erdrinde)
massive massiv, ungeschichtet, ungegliedert, massig
~ **bed** Bank f
~ **bedding** Bankung f (bei Sedimentgesteinen)
~ **concrete dam** Massivbetonmauer f

~ **layer** Bank f
~ **limestone** massiger Kalkstein m, Massenkalk m
~ **rock** massiges Gestein n
~ **structure** massige Textur f
~ **sulphide** massives Sulfid n
massively bedded dickbankig geschichtet
massiveness Massigkeit f
master bushing Haupteinsatz m (im Bohrdrehtisch)
~ **curves** Modellkurven fpl, Kurvenschar f
~ **displacement** Hauptverschiebung f
~ **fault** Hauptverwerfung f
~ **joint** Großkluft f, Hauptkluft f, lang aushaltende Kluft f
~ **lode** Hauptgang m
~ **sheet** Stammdecke f
~ **station** Hauptstation f, Kontrollstation f
~ **stream** Hauptfluß m
~ **vein** Hauptgang m
~ **zone of fracturing** Hauptbruchzone f
mat of grass Grasnarbe f
~ **of turf** Rasennarbe f
matched terraces niveaugleiche Terrassen fpl
material balance Massebilanz f
~ **balance method** Materialbilanzmethode f, Stoffbilanzmethode f
~ **in suspension** suspendiertes Material n
~ **to be conveyed** Fördergut n
~ **to be graded** Siebgut n
mathematical geology mathematische Geologie f
~ **processing** mathematische Behandlung f (geochemischer Daten)
matildite s. schapbachite
matlockite Matlockit m, PbFCl
matrice s. matrix
matrix 1. Grundmasse f, Hauptmasse f, Bindemittel n, Zwischenmasse f; 2. Gerüst n
~ **of lodes** Gangart f, Muttergestein n (von Erzgängen)
~ **ore** Gangart f
matter Materie f
matteuccite Matteuccit m, $NaH[SO_4] \cdot H_2O$
mature shore line Ausgleichsküste f
~ **valley** reifes Tal n
maturely dissected stark zertalt
maturity Maturität f, Reife f (bei Sedimenten bezogen auf Stoffbestand und Gefüge)
maucherite Maucherit m, Ni_3As_2
maufite Maufit m, $(Mg, Fe, Ni)Al_3[(OH)_8|AlSi_3O_{10}]$
mauzeliite s. romeite
maximum discharge Höchstwassermenge f, Spitzenabfluß m
~ **elongation** Bruchdehnung f
~ **flood discharge** maximales Hochwasser n
~ **flow** Höchstabfluß m
~ **level** höchster Wasserstand m
~ **permissible concentration** zulässige Höchstkonzentration f (Tracer)
~ **retardation** Gangunterschied m (Lichtbrechung)

~ **slope of stratum** maximale Schichtenneigung f
mayenite Mayenit m, $12CaO \cdot 7Al_2O_3$
Maysvillian [Stage] Maysville n (Stufe des Cincinnatiens)
mazapilite Mazapilit m (Arseniosiderit pseudomorph nach Skorodit)
mcallisterite McAllisterit m, $Mg[B_6O_9(OH)_2] \cdot 6^1/_2H_2O$
MCFGPD = thousand cubic feet gas per day
mckelveyite Mckelveyit m, $(Na, Ba, Ca, Y, SE, U)_9[CO_3]_9 \cdot 5H_2O$
meadow bog soil Wiesenmoorboden m
~ **chalk** Wiesenkalk m
~ **loam** Auenlehm m
~ **ore** Wiesenerz n, Raseneisenerz n
~ **peat** Wiesentorf m
~ **soil** Auboden m, Wiesenboden m
mealy sand Mehlsand m
mean annual discharge jährliche Mittelwasserführung f
~ **annual flood** mittleres jährliches Hochwasser n
~ **annual precipitation** mittlerer Jahresniederschlag m
~ **annual water level** mittlerer Jahreswasserstand m
~ **anomaly** mittlere Anomalie f
~ **equinox** mittleres Äquinoktium n
~ **high water level** mittlerer Hochwasserstand m
~ **level of the ocean** s. ~ sea level
~ **low water level** mittlerer Niedrigwasserstand m
~ **monthly precipitation** mittlerer Monatsniederschlag m
~ **noon** mittlerer Mittag m
~ **range** mittlere Reichweite f (Grundwasserabsenkung)
~ **sea depth** mittlere Tiefe f des Weltmeeres
~ **sea level** mittlerer Meeresspiegel (Wasserstand) m, mittlere Seehöhe f, Normalnull n, NN
~ **sidereal time** mittlere Sternzeit f
~ **solar day** mittlerer Sonnentag m
~ **solar time** mittlere Sonnenzeit f
~ **tide** Mittelwasser n
~ **value** Durchschnittswert n
~ **water** Mittelwasser n
~ **water bed (channel)** Normalbett n
~ **water level** mittlerer Wasserstand m
meander/to sich schlängeln, in Mäandern fließen
meander Mäander m, Flußschlinge f
~ **belt** Mäandergürtel m
~ **channel** Schluchtmäander m
~ **core** Umlaufberg m (bei Mäandern)
~ **cut-off** Mäanderdurchbruch m
~ **lobe** Mäanderzunge f
~ **loop** Mäanderschlinge f
~ **neck** Mäanderhals m
~ **scrolls lake** Altwassersee m

meandering Mäanderbildung f
~ **channel pattern** Rinnenmuster n eines mäandrierenden Flusses
~ **stream** Mäanderstrom m
~ **valley** Mäandertal n
measure 1. Maß n; Messung f; 2. kohleführende Schicht f; Bank f, Schichtgruppe f, Schichtfolge f
~ **analysis** Maßanalyse f
~ **of gravity** Schweremessung f
~ **of relief** Reliefenergie f
measured level Pegel m
~ **ore** ausgewiesener Erzvorrat m
~ **reserves** erkundete, aufgrund von Analysen und Messungen berechnete Vorräte mpl
measurement bolt Meßanker m
~ **of geologic time** geologische Zeitmessung f
~ **of gravity** Schwerkraftmessung f
~ **of reflectivity** Reflexionsmessung f
~ **of rock pressure** Gebirgsdruckmessung f
~ **of the index** Indexmessung f
~ **of time** Zeitmessung f
~ **of ultrasonics** Ultraschallmessung f
~ **transducer** Meßfühler m
measures Gebirge n (in bergmännischem Sinne)
measuring electrode Meßelektrode f
~ **plane** Meßebene f
~ **plug** Meßdübel m, Meßpflock m
~ **profile** Meßprofil n
~ **tape** Meßband n
~ **weir** Meßwehr n
~ **while drilling** [geophysikalische] Messung f während des Bohrvorgangs
meat-earth Dammerde f
mechanical mechanisch
~ **logging** Bohrfortschrittsmessung f
~ **stage** Kreuztisch m
~ **twins** mechanisch erzeugte Zwillingsstreifung f
~ **weathering** mechanische Verwitterung f
mechanics of liquids Hydromechanik f
medial moraine Mittelmoräne f
median chambers Äquatorialkammern fpl (Foraminifera)
~ **grain size** Median m (aus der Summenkurve abgeleitetes Maß der mittleren Korngröße)
~ **lobe** Medianlobus m (Paläontologie)
~ **mass** Zwischenmassiv n, Zwischengebirge n (orogene Strukturform)
~ **moraine** Mittelmoräne f
~ **sulcus** Mittelfurche f (Paläontologie)
medicinal spring Heilquelle f
Medinan [Series] Medinien n, Medina n (unteres Llandovery in Nordamerika)
Mediterranean Mittelmeer n
~ **belt** alpidischer Faltengürtel m
~ **climate** Mittelmeerklima n, Etesienklima n
~ **red soil** mediterrane Roterde f
~ **suite (tribe)** mediterrane Sippe f (magmatische Gesteine)
medium constituent unwesentlicher Gemengteil m, Nebengemengteil m

medium

~-grained mittelkörnig
~-grained sand s. ~ sand
~ gravel Mittelkies m (6–20 mm)
~-rank coal Kohle f mittleren Rangs; Steinkohle f (überwiegend)
~ relief Mittelgebirgsrelief n
~ sand Mittelsand m (0,25–0,5 mm)
~ silt toniger Lehm m
~ volatile bituminous coal [stage] (Am) [mittelflüchtige] Steinkohle f (Bereich: Gaskohlenbis Fettkohlenstadium)
medullary rays Markstrahlen mpl (Holz)
meermolm Torfschlamm m
meerschaum Meerschaum m (s.a. sepiolite)
mega... s.a. macro...
megacryst Großkristall m, Einsprengling m
megaripples Großrippeln fpl
megascopic[al] megaskopisch, makroskopisch
megaseism Weltbeben n
meionite Mejonit m (Mischkristall der Skapolithreihe)
melaconite Melakonit m, Schwarzkupfererz n, Tenorit m, CuO
melanasphalt s. albertite
melane s. mafic mineral
mélange Melange f, [platten]tektonische Großbrekzie f, tektonische Moräne f
melanite Melanit m (Ti-haltiger Andradit, s.a. garnet)
melanocerite Melanocerit m, $Na_4Ca_{16}(Y, La)_3(Zr, Ce)_6[F_{12}|(BO_3)_3|(SiO_4)_{12}]$
melanocratic melanokrat, dunkel
~ constituent melanokrater Gemengteil m
melanophlogite Melanophlogit m (SiO_2-Modifikation)
melanosome Melanosom n
melanotekite Melanotekit m, $Pb_2Fe_2[O_2|Si_2O_7]$
melanothallite Melanothallit m, $Cu(Cl, OH)_2$
melanovanadite Melanovanadit m, $Ca_2V_{10}O_{25} \cdot 7H_2O$
melanterite Melanterit m, Eisenvitriol m, $Fe[SO_4] \cdot 7H_2O$
melaphyre Melaphyr m
~ tuff Melaphyrtuff m
melilite Melilith m, $(Ca, Na)_2(Al, Mg)[(Si, Al)_2O_7]$
~ basalt Melilithbasalt m
melilitite Melilithit m (Melilithgestein)
melinophane Melinophan m, $(Ca, Na)_2(Be, Al)[Si_2O_6F]$
meliorate/to meliorieren (Boden)
mellite Mellit m, $Al_2[C_{12}O_{12}] \cdot 18H_2O$
mellow/to zermürben
mellow loam lockerer Lehm m
mellowing Zermürbung f
melonite Melonit m, $NiTe_2$
melt/to schmelzen
~ away abschmelzen
melt Schmelzfluß m (Magma)
~ cup Schmelznapf m (im Gletscher)
~ water Schmelzwasser n

~-water gully Schmelzwasserrinne f
~-water stream Schmelzwasserbach m
melteigite Melteigit m (Alkaligestein)
melting Schmelzung f, Abschmelzen n, Aufschmelzen n
~ point Schmelzpunkt m
~ temperature Schmelztemperatur f
member Formationsglied n (lithostratigrafische Einheit)
memory effect Gedächtniseffekt m
~ function of strain Erinnerungsvermögen n (an ältere Deformationen)
menaccanite 1. s. ilmenite; 2. lockerer vulkanischer Sand m
Menap [Drift] Menap-Kaltzeit f (Pleistozän in Nordwesteuropa)
mendelyeevite Mendelejewit m (Varietät von Koppit)
mendipite Mendipit m, Bleioxidchlorid n, $PbCl_2 \cdot 2PbO$
mendozite Mendozit m, Sulfatarit m, Natronalaun m, $NaAl[SO_4]_2 \cdot 12H_2O$
meneghinite Meneghinit m, $4PbS \cdot Sb_2S_3$
menhir Hünenstein m, Steinsäule f
menilite Menilit m, Leberopal m
mensuration Abmessen n, Messung f, Vermessung f
~ technique Vermessungstechnik f, Meßtechnik f
Meotian [Stage] Meotien n (Stufe des Pliozäns)
mephitic air s. black damp
Meramecian [Stage] Stufe des Mississippiens
mercallite Mercallit m, $KH[SO_4]$
mercurial quecksilberhaltig
~ horn ore s. calomel
~ tetrahedrite Quecksilberfahlerz n, Schwazit m (Hg-haltiger Tetraedrit)
mercuric quecksilberhaltig (vorwiegend in Verbindung mit zweiwertigem Hg)
mercurous quecksilbrig (vorwiegend in Verbindung mit einwertigem Hg)
mercury Quecksilber n, Hg
~ argental Silberamalgam m, Kongsbergit m, α-(Ag, H)
~-halo method mit Quecksilberdispersionshof arbeitende Prospektionsmethode f
mere 1. kleiner See m; 2. Auslaugungswanne f; 3. Grenzlinie f, 4. Claimmaß n
merge/to zusammenfließen
~ into übergehen in
merging Scharung f
meridian Meridian m, Längenkreis m
~ altitude Meridianhöhe f
~ of Greenwich Meridian m von Greenwich, Nullmeridian m
~ passage (transit) Meridiandurchgang m
meridional meridional
merismitic fabric merismitisches Gefüge n
merochrome zweifarbiger Kristall m
merocrystalline hypokristallin, semikristallin
merohedral, merohedric meroedrisch

merohedrism Meroedrie f
meroxene Meroxen m *(eisenarmer Biotit)*
merrihueite Merrihueit m, (K, Na)$_2$(Fe, Mg)$_5$Si$_{12}$O$_{30}$ *(Meteoritenmineral)*
merrillite Merrillit m, Ca$_3$(PO$_4$)$_2$ *(Meteoritenmineral)*
merwinite Merwinit m, Ca$_3$Mg[SiO$_4$]$_2$
mesa aus einer Ebene aufragender Tafelberg m, Tafelrestberg m, flaches Hochland n, Tafelland n
mesenteries Mesenterien fpl, Weichsepten npl, Sarkosepten npl
mesh texture Maschenstruktur f
mesitite Mesitinspat m, Ferro-Magnesit m *(Mischkristall der Kalzitreihe)*
mesocoquina Mesocoquina f *(Schelldetritus in Sand- bis Siltfraktion)*
mesogeosyncline Mesogeosynklinale f
mesohaline mesohalin, brackig
mesole s. thomsonite
mesolite Mesolith m, Na$_2$Ca$_2$[Al$_2$Si$_3$O$_{10}$]$_3$·8H$_2$O
Mesolithic mittelsteinzeitlich
Mesolithic [Times] Mittelsteinzeit f
mesoperthite Mesoperthit m *(Mittelglied zwischen Perthit und Antiperthit)*
Mesophytic Mesophytikum n
mesosiderite Mesosiderit m *(Meteorit)*
mesostasis Mesostasis f, Zwischenklemmasse f
mesotergum Mesotergum n *(bei Fossilgehäusen)*
mesothermal mesothermal
~ **vein** mesothermaler Gang m
mesotil halbplastisches Moränenverwitterungsprodukt n
Mesozoic mesozoisch
Mesozoic [Era] Mesozoikum n
mesozone Mesozone f
messelite Messelit m, Ca$_2$(Fe, Mn)[PO$_4$]$_2$·2H$_2$O
Messinian [Stage] Messinium n *(Stufe des Miozäns)*
meta-arcose Metaarkose f, Arkose f von granitartigem Habitus
~-argillite schwach metamorpher Argillit m
metaankoleite Meta-Ankoleit m, K$_2$[UO$_2$|PO$_4$]$_2$·6H$_2$O
metaautunite Meta-Autinit m, Na$_2$[UO$_2$|PO$_4$]$_2$·8H$_2$O
metabasalt Metabasalt m, Grünstein m
metabasite Metabasit m *(metamorphes basisches Gestein)*
metabassetite Meta-Bassetit m, Fe[UO$_2$|PO$_4$]$_2$·8H$_2$O
matabolism Metabolismus m, Stoffwechsel m
metacinnabarite Metacinnabarit m, HgS
metacryst Porphyroblast m
metacrystalline metakristallinisch
metaheinrichite Meta-Heinrichit m, Ba[UO$_2$|AsO$_4$]$_2$·8H$_2$O
metahewettite Metahewettit m, CaV$_6$O$_{16}$·3H$_2$O
metahohmannite Metahohmannit m, Fe[OH|SO$_4$]·1^1/$_2$H$_2$O

metakahlerite Meta-Kahlerit m, Fe[UO$_2$|AsO$_4$]$_2$·8H$_2$O
metakirchheimerite Meta-Kirchheimerit m, Co[UO$_2$|AsO$_4$]$_2$·8H$_2$O
metal Metall n
~-bearing metallführend
~ **conductivity** Elektronenleitfähigkeit f
~ **content** Metallgehalt m
~ **core** Metallkern m *(Erde)*
~ **cylinder for determination of bulk density** Stechzylinder m
~ **factor** Metallfaktor m *(Geoelektrik)*
~ **mining** Erzbergbau m
~ **stone** sandiger Schieferton m
metallic metallisch
~ **content** Metallgehalt m
~ **deposit** Metallagerstätte f
~ **lustre** Metallglanz m
~-shining metallglänzend
~-splendent metallgänzend
~-splendent lustre Metallglanz m
metalliferous metallhaltig, metallführend, erzführend
~ **deposit[ion]** Metallablagerung f
~ **lode** Erzgang m
~ **mine** Erzgrube f, Erzbergwerk n
~ **mineral** Erzmineral n
~ **ore deposit** Metallerzlagerstätte f
~ **vein** Erzgang m
metalliform metallartig
metalline metallen, metallähnlich
metallization Metallisierung f, Vererzung f
metallogenetic[al], metallogenic metallogenetisch
~ **belt** metallogenetischer Gürtel *(sehr große lineare erzführende Fläche)*
~ **epoch** metallogenetische Epoche f
~ **mineral** Erzmineral n
~ **planetary belt** planetarischer metallogenetischer Gürtel m
~ **province** metallogenetische Provinz f *(sehr große nichtlineare erzführende Fläche)*
~ **region** metallogenetischer Bezirk m *(große nichtlineare erzführende Fläche)*
~ **superprovince** metallogenetische Superprovinz f *(planetarische nichtlineare erzführende Fläche)*
~ **zone** metallogenetische Zone f *(große lineare erzführende Fläche)*
metallographic microscope Erzmikroskop n
metalloid metallartig
metallometry Metallometrie f *(geochemische Methode der Metallbestimmung)*
metamict metamikt, durch radioaktive Strahlung isotropisiert
~ **mineral** isotropisiertes Mineral n
metamictization Isotropisierung f von Mineralen durch radioaktive Strahlung
metamorphic metamorph
~ **area (aureole)** Kontakthof m
~ **belt** metamorphe Zone f
~ **change** metamorphe Umwandlung f

metamorphic

- ~ **differentiation** metamorphe Differentiation f
- ~ **equilibrium** metamorphes Gleichgewicht n
- ~ **facies** metamorphe Fazies f
- ~ **grade** Metamorphosegrad m
- ~ **maturity** s. ~ equilibrium
- ~ **rank** s. ~ grade
- ~ **rock** Metamorphit m, metamorphes Gestein n
- ~ **water** metamorphes Wasser n

metamorphism Metamorphose f
- ~ **by injection** Injektionsmetamorphose f

metamorphites Metamorphite mpl
metamorphose/to metamorphosieren
metamorphosed rock metamorphes Gestein n
- ~ **schist** metamorpher Schiefer m

metamorphosis Metamorphose f, Gestaltänderung f (im organischen Bereich)
metamorphous s. metamorphic
metanovačecite Meta-Novačekit m, $Mg[UO_2|AsO_4]_2 \cdot 4H_2O$
metaquartzite Metaquarzit m
metaripples Großrippeln fpl
metarossite Metarossit m, $Ca[V_2O_6] \cdot 2H_2O$
metasapropel verfestigter Sapropelit m
metaschoderite Metaschoderit m, $Al[(P,V)O_4] \cdot 3H_2O$
metasedimentary rock partiell metamorpher Sedimentit m
metashale schwach metamorpher Schiefer m (ohne Rekristallisation und Mineralregelung)
metasilicic acid Metakieselsäure f
metasomatic metasomatisch
- ~ **deposit** metasomatische Lagerstätte f, Verdrängungslagerstätte f

metasomatism Metasomatose f, Verdrängung f
metasomatite Metasomatit m
metasomatosis s. metasomatism
metasome Metasom n, Verdrängendes n (bei Migmatiten)
metastable equilibrium metastabiles Gleichgewicht n
- ~ **state** metastabiler Zustand m

metastibnite Metastibnit m, Sb_2S_3
metathenardite Metathenardit m, $\delta\text{-}Na_2SO_4$
metatorbernite Metatorbernit m, $Cu[UO_2|PO_4]_2 \cdot 8H_2O$
metatype Metatyp[us] m
metauramphite Meta-Uramphit m, $(NH_4)_2[UO_2|PO_4]_2 \cdot 6H_2O$
metauranocircite Meta-Uranocircit m, $Ba[UO_2|PO_4]_2 \cdot 8H_2O$
metauranospinite Meta-Uranospinit m, $Ca[UO_2|AsO_4]_2 \cdot 8H_2O$
metavariscite Metavariscit m, Klinovariscit m, $Al[PO_4] \cdot 2H_2O$
metavoltine Metavoltin m, $\alpha\text{-}K_5Fe_3^{3+}[OH|(SO_4)_3]_2 \cdot 8H_2O$
metazeunerite Meta-Zeunerit m, $Cu[UO_2|AsO_4]_2 \cdot 8H_2O$
meteor Meteor m; Sternschnuppe f
- ~ **crater** Meteoritenkrater m
- ~ **dust** meteorischer Staub m
- ~ **orbit (path)** Meteorbahn f
- ~ **shower** Meteorschwarm m, Sternschnuppenschwarm m
- ~ **stream** Meteorstrom m
- ~ **swarm** s. ~ shower
- ~ **train** Meteorschweif m
- ~ **wake** Meteorspur f

meteoric meteorisch, vados, Meteor...
- ~ **fall** Meteorfall m
- ~ **impact** Meteoriteneinschlag m
- ~ **iron** Eisenmeteorit m, Meteoreisen n
- ~ **shower** Meteorfall m
- ~ **stone** Meteorit m
- ~ **theory** Meteoritenhypothese f (Mond)
- ~ **water** Niederschlagswasser n, vadoses Wasser n

meteorite Meteorit m, Meteorstein m
- ~ **crater** Meteoritenkrater m
- ~ **fall** Meteoritenfall m
- ~ **impact** Aufschlag m eines Meteoriten

meteoritic meteoritisch
- ~ **crater** Meteoritenkrater m
- ~ **dust** meteoritischer Staub m
- ~ **fall** Meteoritenfall m
- ~ **group** Meteoritengruppe f
- ~ **matter** Meteoritensubstanz f
- ~ **seism** meteoritisches Beben n
- ~ **theory** Meteoritenhypothese f (Mond)

meteoritics Meteoritenkunde f
meteorography Witterungsbeschreibung f
meteoroid 1. um die Sonne kreisender Meteor m; 2. Meteorsplitter m
meteorologic[al] meteorologisch, Wetter...
- ~ **broadcast** Wetterfunk m
- ~ **chart** Wetterkarte f, meteorologische Karte f
- ~ **conditions** Wetterlage f
- ~ **limit** Wetterscheide f
- ~ **observatory (office)** meteorologische Station f, Wetterwarte f
- ~ **rocket** meteorologische Rakete f, Wetterrakete f
- ~ **satellite** meteorologischer Satellit m, Wettersatellit m
- ~ **service** Wetterdienst m
- ~ **station** meteorologische Station f, Wetterwarte f

meteorologist Meteorologe m
meteorology Meteorologie f, Wetterkunde f
metering of gas Gasvolumenmessung f
methane Methan[gas] n, Grubengas n, CH_4
- ~ **detector** Grubengasanzeiger m
- ~ **drainage** Entgasung f (Methangewinnung)
- ~ **indicator** Schlagwetteranzeiger m

methanol inhibition Methanoldosierung f
method of images Simulationsmethode f (Grundwasserdynamik)
- ~ **of principal components** Hauptkomponentenmethode f (zur Schätzung der Faktorladungen)
- ~ **of slices** Gleitflächenmethode f

microscopic

metric carat metrisches Karat n *(= 200 Milligramm)*
~ ton metrische Tonne f *(1000 kg, Einheit der Masse in den USA)*
meyerhofferite Meyerhofferit m, $Ca[B_3O_3(OH)_5]\cdot H_2O$
mgal mGal n *(Einheit für die Schwerebeschleunigung, entspricht $10^{-6}cm/sec$)*
miargyrite Miargyrit m, Silberantimonglanz m, $AgSbS_2$
miarolitic miarolithisch, kleindrusig
~ cavity miarolithischer Hohlraum m
~ texture miarolithische Struktur f
miaskite Miaskit m *(Varietät von Nephelinsyenit)*
mica Glimmer m *(Mineral der Glimmergruppe)*
~ flake (scale) Glimmerblättchen n
~ schist (slate) Glimmerschiefer m
~ spangle Glimmerblättchen n
~ trap glimmerreiches basisches Ganggestein n *(allgemein)*
micaceous glimmerig, glimmerhaltig, glimmerartig
~ clay Glimmerton m
~ haematite (iron ore) Eisenglimmer m *(s.a. haematite)*
~ porphyry Glimmerporphyr m
~ sand Glimmersand m
~ sandstone Glimmersandstein m
~ schist Glimmerschiefer m
~ shale glimmerführender Ton m
~ structure Glimmertextur f, Blättertextur f
micaphyre Glimmerporphyr m
micatization Umwandlung f in Glimmer, Verglimmerung f
micatize/to in Glimmer umwandeln
michenerite Michenerit m, $PdBi_2$
micrinite Micrinit m *(Kohlenmaceral)*
micrite Mikrit m *(primärer Typ von feinkörniger Karbonatgrundmasse bzw. feinkörniges Karbonatgestein; Korngrößen nach FOLK< 0,004 mm)*
micritic limestone mikritischer Kalkstein m
~-pelletal limestone matrixreicher Pillenkalkstein m
microaerophil in O_2-armem Milieu lebend
microanalysis Mikroanalyse f
microaphanitic mikrofelsitisch, kryptokristallin
microbial acticity s. microbian action
microbian action Mikrobentätigkeit f, mikrobielle Aktivität f
microbreccia Mikrobrekzie f, kataklastisches Gestein n
microchemical mikrochemisch
microclastic mikroklastisch, kleinklastisch
microclimate Mikroklima n
microclimatology Mikroklimatologie f
microcline Mikroklin m, $K[AlSi_3O_8]$
microclinization Mikroklinisierung f
microcontinent Insel vom Kontinentaltyp, umgeben von ozeanischem Krustenmaterial

microcoquina Mikrocoquina f *(sehr feiner Schelldetritus)*
microcosm[os] Mikrokosmos m
microcross lamination kleindimensionale Schrägschichtung f
microcrystalline mikrokristallin
microdiorite feinkörniger Diorit m
microdrawing Mikrobild n *(zeichnerische Darstellung eines mikroskopischen Bildes)*
microelement Spurenelement n
microfabric Korngefüge n
~ analysis Korngefügeanalyse f
microfacies Mikrofazies f
microfaulting kleine Verwerfungen fpl *(im mikroskopischen Bild)*
microfelsitic mikrofelsitisch, kryptokristallin
~ texture mikrofelsitische Struktur f
microfissure mikroskopischer Riß m, Haarriß m
microfolds Kleinfältelung f *(im mikroskopischen Bild)*
microgeology Mikrogeologie f
microgranite Mikrogranit m
microgranitic mikrogranitisch
~ texture mikrogranitische Struktur f
microgranophyric mikrogranophyrisch
micrograph Mikrobild n, Mikrofoto n; Schliffbild n
microgravimeter Mikrogravimeter n
microgroove casts kleine Rillenmarken fpl
microhardness Mikrohärte f
microlaterolog Mikrolaterolog n
microlite 1. Mikrolith m, $(Ca, Na)_2(Ta, Nb)_2O_6(O, OH, F)$; 2. kleiner Kristall m
microlithotype 1. Mikrolithotyp m; 2. Streifenart f *(Kohle)*
microlitic mikrolithisch
microlog Mikrolog n
micromagnetics Mikromagnetik f
micromeasure analysis Mikromaßanalyse f
micromeritic mikromeritisch, mikrokristallin
micromeritics mikroskopische Untersuchung f kristalliner Strukturen
micrometeorite Mikrometeorit m
micron-sized in Korngröße von 1–10µm
micronutrient Spurenelement n
micropalaeontologic[al] mikropaläontologisch
micropalaeontology Mikropaläontologie f
micropegmatitic mikropegmatitisch
microperthite Mikroperthit m *(Orthoklas mit orientierten Albitspindeln)*
microphyric mikrophyrisch
microporosity Mikroporosität f
microscleres Mikroskleren fpl, Fleischnadeln fpl *(bei Schwämmen)*
microscope Mikroskop n
~ stage Mikroskoptisch m
microscopic[al] mikroskopisch
~ analysis of the seam section mikroskopische Flözanalyse f
~ examination mikroskopische Prüfung f
~ section (slide) Dünnschliff m

microscopic

~ **study** mikroskopische Untersuchung f
microscopy Mikroskopie f
microsection Dünnschliff m
microseism mikroseismische Bodenunruhe f, Kleinbeben n, leichtes Erdbeben n
microseismic mikroseismisch
~ **movement** mikroseismische Bewegung (Bodenunruhe) f
microseismograph Mikroseismograf m
microseismometer Mikroseismometer n
microsparite Mikrosparit m
microspherulitic mikrosphärulithisch
microspore Mikrospore f
microspread Verwitterungsschießen n
microstratigraphical feinstratigrafisch
microstructure Feingefüge n, Mikrostruktur f
microtectonics Kleintektonik f
microtome slide Mikrotomschnitt m
microwave antenna Mikrowellenantenne f
~ **radiometry** Mikrowellenradiometrie f
~ **receiver** Mikrowellenempfänger m
~ **scattering** Mikrowellenstreuung f
mid-continent climate Kontinentalklima n
~-ocean[ic] ridge mittelozeanische Schwelle f
Mid Atlantic ridge Mittelatlantischer Rücken m
middle band flözteilende Bergeschicht f
~ **course** Mittellauf m (eines Flusses)
~ **limb** Mittelschenkel m
~ **man** s. ~ band
~ **water** Zwischenschichtwasser n
Middle Bunter Mittlerer Buntsandstein m (Germanisches Becken, Trias)
~ **Cambrian [Epoch, Series]** Mittelkambrium n
~ **Carboniferous [Epoch, Series]** Mittelkarbon n (UdSSR – Namur B bis einschließlich Westfal)
~ **Chalk** Mittlere Schreibkreide f (Turon in England)
~ **Devonian [Epoch, Series]** Mitteldevon n
~ **Jurassic [Epoch, Series]** Mittlerer (Brauner) Jura m, Dogger m
~ **Ordovician [Epoch, Series]** Mittelordovizium n, Mittleres Ordovizium n (Llandeilo und Caradoc ohne Zone Pleurograptus linearis)
~ **Permian [Epoch, Series]** Mittelperm n
~ **Precambrian** Mittleres Präkambrium n
~ **Triassic [Epoch, Series]** Mittlere Trias f (Anis und Ladin)
middling particles Zwischenprodukte npl
middlings 1. Zwischenprodukte npl; 2. zweite Qualität bei Wascherzen
midfeather Erztrum n, Erzschnur f (zwischen zwei größeren Vorkommen)
midnight sun Mitternachtssonne f
midsummer Sommersonnenwende f
Midwayan [Stage] Stufe des Pliozäns
midwinter Wintersonnenwende f
miersite Miersit m, α-AgJ
migma Migma f
migmatite Migmatit m
migmatization Migmatisierung f

migrate/to migrieren, wandern
migration 1. Migration f (von Elementen); 2. Migration (Lagekorrektur seismischer Elemente)
~ **accretion** Migrationsfalle f, Stoffkonzentration f durch Migration
~ **factor** Migrationsfaktor m
~ **of divides** Verschiebung f der Wasserscheiden
~ **of facies** Fazieswanderung f
~ **of gas** Gaswanderung f
~ **of ions** Ionenwanderung f
~ **of sand** Sandwanderung f
~ **of valleys** Talverlegung f
~ **stack** [direkte] Migrationsstapelung f
migratory detritus Wanderschutt m
~ **dune** Wanderdüne f
miharaite Miharait m (quarzführender Hypersthenbasalt)
mijakite Mijakit m (Varietät von Andesit)
milarite Milarit m, $KCa_2AlBe_2[Si_{12}O_{30}] \cdot 1/2 H_2O$
mild clay Sandton m
mildly folded schwach gefaltet
military geology Wehrgeologie f, Militärgeologie f
milk tooth Milchzahn m
milky milchig, trübe, wolkig
~ **opal** Milchopal m
~ **quartz** Milchquarz m
~ **way** Milchstraße f
~ **way system** Milchstraßensystem n
mill Aufbereitungsanlage f
~ **slurries** Aufbereitungsschlämme mpl
Miller crystal indices Millersche Indizes mpl
millerite Millerit m, Haarkies m, β-NiS
millet-seed sand windtransportierter Sand m
milligal s. mgal
millimeter-sized in Korngröße von 1–10 mm
milling 1. Mahlen n; Aufbereiten n; 2. Fräsen n (bei Havarien im Bohrloch); 3. Pingenabbau mit untertägiger Förderung
~ **ore** Pocherz n, Erz n mit niedrigen Metallgehalten
~ **tool** Fräser m
millisite Millisit m, $(Na, Ca)Al_3[(OH, O)_4|(PO_4)_2] \cdot 2H_2O$
millstone (Am) Mühlsandstein m (zähes, zum Mahlen geeignetes Gestein, meist grobkörniger Sandstein)
~ **grit** Basissandstein m des Oberkarbons in England, Kohlensandstein m
mimetene s. mimetite
mimetesite s. mimetite
mimetic mimetisch
~ **crystal** mimetischer Kristall m
~ **crystallization** Abbildungskristallisation f
mimetite Mimetesit m, Flockenerz n, Grünbleierz n, $Pb_5[Cl|(AsO_4)_3]$
mimetry Pseudosymmetrie f
mimic s. mimetic
minability Bauwürdigkeit f, Abbauwürdigkeit f, Abbaufähigkeit f

minable [ab]bauwürdig, abbaufähig
~ **deposit** nutzbare Lagerstätte *f*
~ **thickness** bauwürdige Mächtigkeit *f*
minasragrite Minasragrit *m*, $V_2[(OH)_2I(SO_4)_3] \cdot 15H_2O$
Mindel [Drift] Mindel-Eiszeit *f (Pleistozän, Alpen)*
~-**Riss [Interval]** Mindel-Riß-Interglazial *n (Pleistozän, Alpen)*
mine/to abbauen, Bergbau betreiben
~ **by banks** abstrossen
mine Untertagegrube *f*
~ **adit** Grubenstollen *m*
~ **atmosphere** Grubenwetter *pl*
~ **claim** Bergbauschutzgebiet *n*
~ **coal** Zechenkohle *f*
~ **dewatering** Grubenentwässerung *f*
~ **digging** Grubenbau *m*
~ **drainage gallery** Wasserhaltungsstrecke *f*
~ **dump** Abraumhalde *f*
~ **field** Grubenfeld *n*
~ **floor** Grubensohle *f*
~ **geology** Grubengeologie *f*
~ **layout** Abbauplan *m*
~ **openings** Grubenräume *mpl*
~ **ore** Roherz *n*
~ **pumping** Wasserhaltung *f*
~ **rock** hereingewonnenes Gestein *n*
~ **sampling** Grubenbemusterung *f*
~ **storage** Bergwerksspeicher *m*
~ **subsidence area** Bergbausenkungsgebiet *n*
~ **survey instrument** Markscheideinstrument *n*
~ **surveying** 1. Markscheidekunde *f*, Markscheiderei *f*; 2. Markscheiderarbeiten *fpl*, Vermessungsarbeiten *fpl* im Bergbau
~ **surveyor** Markscheider *m*
~ **valuation** Lagerstättenbewertung *f*
~ **water** Grubenwasser *n*
~ **working** Grubenbau *m*
~ **workings** bergmännische Auffahrungen *fpl*, Aufschlüsse *mpl*
mined cavern storage bergmännisch hergestellter Kavernenspeicher *m*
~-**out stopes of a mine** abgebaute Grubenteile *mpl*
~ **rock** Haufwerk *n*
mineragraphic microscope Auflichtmikroskop *n*
mineragraphy Erzmikroskopie *f*
mineral mineralisch, Mineral...
mineral Mineral *n*
~ **adipocire** s. hatchettite
~ **aggregate** Mineralanhäufung *f*, Mineralaggregat *n*
~ **amber** wolkiger Bernstein *m*
~ **analysis** Mineralanalyse *f*
~ **assessment** Vorratsabschätzung *f*
~ **association** Mineralvergesellschaftung *f*
~ **blossom** drusiger Quarz *m*
~ **blue** s. azurite
~ **caoutchouc** Mineralkautschuk *m (s.a. elaterite)*

~ **carbon** Graphit *m*
~ **charcoal** 1. Fusain *m*, Faserkohle *f*, 2. Fusit *m*
~-**chemical calculation** mineralchemische Berechnung *f*
~ **chemism** Mineralchemismus *m*
~ **claim** Anspruch auf Mineralerkundung und -gewinnung in einem Gebiet
~ **collection** Mineraliensammlung *f*
~ **commodities** Mineralrohstoffe *mpl* in Handelsform
~ **composition** Mineralzusammensetzung *f*
~ **concentrate** Mineralkonzentrat *n*
~ **constituent** Mineralbestandteil *m*
~ **content** Mineralgehalt *m*
~ **cotton** s. ~ wool
~ **deposit** Lagerstätte *f* von nutzbaren Mineralen
~ **dressing** Aufbereitung *f (von Erzen)*
~ **endowment** Mineralausstattung *f* eines Gebiets
~ **facies** Mineralfazies *f*
~-**forming** mineralbildend
~ **inclusion** Mineraleinschluß *m*
~ **ingredient** Mineralbestandteil *m*
~ **kingdom** Mineralreich *n*
~ **matter** Mineralsubstanz *f (z.B. in der Kohle)*
~ **oil** Mineralöl *n (Erdöl)*
~ **oil extraction** Erdölgewinnung *f*
~ **oil industry** Mineralölwirtschaft *f*
~ **oil processing** Erdölverarbeitung *f*
~ **paragenesis** Mineralparagenese *f*
~ **pipe** Erzschlot *m*
~ **pitch** Erdpech *n*, Bergpech *n*, Asphalt *m*
~ **processing** Mineralaufbereitungs- und -verhüttungsverfahren *n*
~ **raw materials** mineralische Rohstoffe *mpl*
~ **resin** fossiles Harz *n*
~ **resources** Mineralressourcen *fpl*
~ **right** Abbaurecht *n*, Gewinnungsrecht *n*
~ **rubber** Mineralkautschuk *m (s.a. elaterite)*
~ **salt** Steinsalz *n*
~ **salting** Präparieren *n* einer Lagerstätte *(zur Vortäuschung von Vorräten)*
~ **sequence** Mineralfolge *f*
~ **soil** Mineralboden *m*
~ **spring** Mineralquelle *f*
~ **streaking (streaming)** Mineralstreckung *f*, lineationsbildende Mineralanordnung *f*
~ **tar** Bergteer *m*, Erdteer *m*, Mineralteer *m*, Asphaltteer *m*
~ **tar oil** Steinkohlenteeröl *n*
~ **time** geologische Zeit *f* basierend auf Mineralaltern
~ **tin** Bergzinn *n*
~ **under strain** gepreßtes Mineral *n*
~ **water** Mineralwasser *n*
~ **water interface** Mineralwasserfront *f*
~ **wax** Erdwachs *n*, Mineralwachs *n*, Bergwachs *n*, Ozokerit *m*
~ **wealth** Bodenschätze *mpl*
~ **well** Mineralquelle *f*

mineral 230

~ **wool** Schlackenwolle *f*, Schmelzbasaltwolle *f*
~ **zoning** zonale Mineralverteilung *f*, Mineralzoning *n*
mineralizable vererzbar
mineralization 1. Mineralisierung *f*, Mineralisation *f*, 2. Erzbildung *f*, Vererzung *f*
~ **period** Mineralisationsperiode *f*
mineralize/to 1. mineralisieren; 2. vererzen
mineralized 1. mineralisiert; 2. erzführend, erzhaltig
~ **area** Erzgebiet *n*
~ **bacteria** vererzte Bakterien *fpl*
~ **carbon** Salzkohle *f*
~/**well** reich an Mineralen
mineralizer Mineralisator *m*, Mineralbildner *m*
mineralizing mineralbildend
~ **agent** Mineralisator *m*, Mineralbildner *m*
mineralogic[al] mineralogisch
~ **collection** Mineraliensammlung *f*
~ **phase rule** mineralogische (Goldschmidtsche) Phasenregel *f*
mineralogist Mineraloge *m*
mineralography Auflichtmikroskopie *f* von Mineralen
mineralogy Mineralogie *f*
minerals of early generation Erstausscheidungen *fpl (von Mineralen in Gesteinen)*
minerogenic minerogen
~ **province** *s.* metallogenetic province
miner's batea Sichertrog *m*, Sicherschüssel *f*
~ **compass** bergmännischer Kompaß *m*, Hängezeug *n*
~ **works plan** Vorrichtungsplan *m*
minery 1. Abbaudistrikt *m*, Grubengebiet *n*; 2. Steinbruch *m*
minette 1. Minette *f (oolithisches Fe-Erz);* 2. lamprophyrisches Ganggestein *n*
~ **ore** Minetteerz *n*
minge weiche, brüchige Kohle *f*
minguzzite Minguzzit *m*, $K_3Fe[C_2O_4]_3 \cdot 3H_2O$
mingy coal *s.* minge
minimum breadth tektonische Überlagerungsweite *f*
~ **discharge** Mindestabflußmenge *f*
~ **flow** Mindestabfluß *m*
~ **output** Mindestfördermenge *f*
~ **time path** Strahlenweg *m* mit minimaler Laufzeit *(Seismik)*
~ **tonnage** Mindestfördermenge *f*
mining activity bergbauliche Tätigkeit *f*
~ **by deep mine** Gewinnung *f* im Tiefbau
~ **by galleries** Stollenbau *m*
~ **by level workings** Gewinnung *f* im Tiefbau
~ **by the open-cast method** Gewinnung *f* im Tagebau
~ **conditions** Abbaubedingungen *fpl*
~ **damage** Bergschaden *m*
~ **debris** Abgänge *mpl* bei hydraulischem Abbau
~ **district** Grubenfeld *n*
~ **engineer** Bergingenieur *m*
~ **excavation** bergbaulicher Hohlraum *m*
~ **geodesy** Markscheidekunst *f*, Markscheidekunde *f*, Markscheidewesen *n*
~-**geological** montangeologisch
~ **geologist** Montangeologe *m*, Grubengeologe *m*
~ **geology** Montangeologie *f*, Grubengeologie *f*
~ **geophysics** Bergbaugeophysik *f*
~ **horizon** Abbauhorizont *m*
~ **in open pits** Tagebaubetrieb *m*
~ **industry** Montanindustrie *f*
~ **law** Bergrecht *n*, Berggesetz *n*
~ **leases** bergrechtliche Pachtverträge *mpl*
~ **method** Abbauverfahren *n*
~ **operation** Abbauvorgang *m*
~ **ply** dünne Bergeschicht *f*
~ **product** Fördergut *n*
~ **regulations** Bergordnung *f*
~ **science** Bergbauwissenschaften *fpl*
~ **sequence** Abbauablauf *m*
~ **subsidence** Setzungen *fpl* in Bergwerksgebieten
~ **survey instrument** Markscheidegerät *n*
~ **surveyor** Markscheider *m*
~ **with filling** Abbau *m* mit Bergeversatz
~ **working** Gewinnungsarbeit *f*
Mining Academy Bergakademie *f*
miniphyric von porphyrischer Struktur *(<0,008 mm)*
minium Minium *n*, Mennige *f*, Pb_3O_4
minnesotaite Minnesotait *m*, $(Fe, Mg, H_2)_3[(OH)_2|(Si, Al, Fe)|O_{10}]$
minophyric von porphyrischer Struktur *(zwischen 1–0,2 mm)*
minor bed Niedrigwasserbett *n (eines Flusses)*
~ **constituent** Übergemengteil *m*, Beimengung *f*
~ **element** Spurenelement *n*
~ **fault** Nebenverwerfung *f*, sekundäre Verwerfung *f*
~ **fold** Kleinfalte *f*
~ **geosyncline** Parageosynklinale *f*
~ **intrusion** Kleinintrusion *f*
~ **joint** Kleinkluft *f*, sekundäre Kluft *f*
~ **nutrient element** Spurenelement *n*
~ **planet** Kleinplanet *m*
~ **sea** Nebenmeer *n*
~ **septa** Nebensepten *npl (Paläontologie)*
~ **trough** Nebenmulde *f*
Mintrop wave *s.* refraction wave
minus-cement porosity Porosität *f* vor der Zementbildung *(im Sediment)*
minute crystal Kriställchen *n*
~ **folding** Kleinfaltung *f*, Fältelung *f*
minutely grooved spirifer Spirifer *m* mit Chagrin-Skulptur
miny reich an Bergwerken
minyulite Minyulit *m*, $KAl_2[(OH, F)|(PO_4)_2]4H_2O$
Miocene miozän
Miocene [Epoch, Series] Miozän *n (Serie des Tertiärs)*

miogeosyncline Miogeosynklinale f
miohaline miohalin
Miolithic s. Mesolithic
miospore s. microspore
mirabilite Mirabilit m, Glaubersalz n, $Na_2[SO_4]\cdot 10H_2O$
mire 1. Moor n, Fenn n, Bruch m (n); 2. Schlamm m, Sumpf m
~ **formation** Moorbildung f
mirror Reflektor m
~ **compass** Spiegelkompaß m
~ **plane** Spiegelebene f
~ **stone** s. muscovite
miry schlammig, moorig
~ **sand** schlammiger (mooriger) Sand m
miscibility Mischbarkeit f
~ **displacement (drive, flooding)** Mischphasenverdrängung f, Mischphasentrieb m, Mischphasenfluten n (sekundäres Ölgewinnungsverfahren)
~ **gap** Mischungslücke f
~ **phase displacement** s. ~ displacement
misclassify/to fehlklassifizieren
misenite Misenit m, $K_8H_6[SO_4]_7$
miserite Miserit m, $KCa_5[Si_5O_{14}OH]\cdot H_2O$
misfit river Kümmerfluß m
mispickel s. arsenopyrite
Mississippian [Series, System] Mississippien n (wird in Amerika im Gegensatz zu Europa teilweise als System angesprochen. Entspricht dem Unterkarbon und basalen Namur Westeuropas)
Missourian [Stage] Stufe des Pennsylvaniens
missourite Missourit m (Varietät von Leuzitbasalt)
mist Nebel m
~ **flow** Nebelströmung f
~ **ice** Nebeleis n
mistiness Nebligkeit f
mistral Mistral m, Fallwind m (kalter Nordwind des Rhonetals)
misty veil Nebelschleier m
mitchell Quadersandstein m
mitre folds Mitrafalten fpl
mitridatite Mitridatit m (Umwandlungsprodukt von Vivianit)
mitscherlichite Mitscherlichit m, $K_2[CuCl_4(H_2O)_2]$
mix crystal Mischkristall m
mixed avalanche gemischte Aschen- und Schuttlawine f
~ **base oil** Erdöl n mit Paraffin- und Asphaltbasis, gemischtbasisches Erdöl n
~ **crystal** Mischkristall m
~-**crystal formation** Mischkristallbildung f
~ **displacement** Mischphasenverdrängung f
~ **distance** Vermischungsstrecke f (Wasser)
~ **effects model of variance analysis** Varianzanalysemodell m mit gemischten (festen und zufälligen) Effekten
~ **flow** Mischphasenströmung f
~ **fold** disharmonische Falte f

~ **forest** Mischwald m
~-**layer structure** Wechsellagerungsstruktur f (Tonminerale)
~ **oak forest** Eichenmischwald m
~ **water** 1. gemischt juvenil-vadoses Wasser; 2. Wasser mit hohem Chlorid-Sulfat-Gehalt
~ **wettability** gemischte Benetzbarkeit f
mixing displacement Mischphasenverdrängung f
~ **flow** Mischphasenströmung f
~ **ratio** Mischverhältnis n (von Wasser unterschiedlicher Mineralisation)
mixite Mixit m, $(Bi, Fe, ZnH, CaH)Cu_{12}[(OH)_{12}|(AsO_4)_6]\cdot 6H_2O$
mixolimnion im Austausch befindlicher Teil eines Wasserbeckens
mixtinite Mixtinit m (Kohlenmaceral)
mizzonite Mizzonit m (Mischkristall von Mejonit und Marialith)
MLA s. multiple linear array
moat 1. Graben m, 2. Schmelzgraben m (um Nunataker)
mobile barge bewegliche Bohrplattform f
~ **belt** labile Zone f
~ **benthos** vagiles Benthos n
~ **components** migrationsfähige Komponenten fpl, flüchtige Substanzen fpl
~ **dune** Wanderdüne f
~ **oil** fließfähiges Erdöl n
~ **platform** bewegliche Bohrplattform f
~ **rig** bewegliche Bohranlage f
~ **rim** mobiler (aktiver) Rand m (einer Geosynklinale)
~ **shelf** mobiler Schelf m
~ **water** sich abwärts bewegende Grundfeuchtigkeit f
mobility Beweglichkeit f (geochemisch, von Elementen)
~ **factor** Mobilitätsfaktor m
~ **of fluid** Fließfähigkeit f
~ **ratio** Mobilitätsverhältnis n
mobilization Mobilisation f
mocha pebble (stone) Moosachat m (s.a. chalcedony)
mock lead s. sphalerite
~ **moon** Nebenmond m
~ **ore** s. sphalerite
~ **sun** Nebensonne f, Parhelium n
modderite Modderit m, CoAs
mode 1. Modus m, Modalbestand m (Mineralzusammensetzung eines Gesteins); 2. Modal[wert] m (am häufigsten vorkommende Korngröße)
~ **of occurrence** Lagerungsverhältnisse npl
~ **of origin** Enstehungsart f, Ursprungsart f
~ **of preservation** Erhaltungszustand m
MODE = Mid-Ocean Dynamics Experiment
model of refraction travel path Modell n für den Laufweg einer Refraktion
~ **of simulation** (Am) Simulationsmodell n (reservoirmechanisch)
~ **scale** Modellmaßstab m

model 232

~ **seismics** Modellseismik f
~ **test** Modellversuch m
modelling Modelling n, Modellrechnung f (Geophysik)
moderate breeze mäßiger Wind m
modern rezent
modification of precipitation Niederschlagsänderung f
modified drift s. stratified flow
modular transfer function Modulationsübertragungsfunktion f (z. B. eines Fernerkundungssensors)
module of ground-water flow Grundwasserspende f
modulus Absolutwert m (einer komplexen Zahl)
~ **of decay** Zerfallsmodul m
~ **of elasticity in shear** s. ~ of rigidity
~ **of rigidity** Schubmodul m, Gleitmodul m, Gleitmaß n
~ **of rupture** Bruchspannungsmodul m
~ **of shear** s. ~ of rigidity
~ **of subgrade reaction** Bettungsziffer f
Moessbauer effect Mößbauer-Effekt m
mofette Mofette f, Kohlensäurequelle f
mogotes Mogoten pl (tropische Karstform)
Mohnian [Stage] Mohnien n (marine Stufe, Miozän in Nordamerika)
Moho s. Mohorovičič discontinuity
Mohole project Mohorovičič-Bohrung f (zur Erkundung des oberen Erdmantels)
Mohorovičič discontinuity Mohorovičič-Diskontinuität f
mohrite Mohrlt m, $(NH_4)_2Fe[SO_4]_2 \cdot 6H_2O$
Mohr's circle Mohrscher Kreis m
~ **envelope** Mohrsche Hüllkurve f
~ **stress circle** Mohrscher Spannungskreis m
~ **theory** Hypothese f des elastischen Grenzzustands von Mohr
Mohs's hardness scale Mohssche Härteskala f
moil sample Pickprobe f (mit dem Hammer gewonnene Splitterprobe)
moiré Moiréglanz m, Wasserglanz m (von Mineralen)
moissanite Moissanit m, SiC (Meteoritenmineral)
moisten/to befeuchten
moistening Durchfeuchtung f, Anfeuchten n (einer Gesteinsprobe)
~ **power** Benetzungsfähigkeit f
moisture Feuchtigkeit f, Nässe f
~ **content** Gesamtwassergehalt m
~ **deficiency** Feuchtigkeitsdefizit n
~ **density test** Verdichtungsversuch m
~ **equivalent** Feuchtigkeitsäquivalent n
~-**holding capacity** Wasseraufnahmevermögen n; Wasserhaltevermögen n
~-**laden** mit Feuchtigkeit gesättigt
~ **percentage** Feuchtigkeitsgehalt m
~-**proof** feuchtigkeitsundurchlässig
Molasse Molasse f

~ **basin** Molassebecken n
~ **intra-deep** intramontanes Molassebecken n
mold (Am) s. mould
moldauite s. moldavite
moldavite Moldavit m (Glasmeteorit)
mole 1. Buhne f; 2. Stollenfräse f
~ **drainage** Maulwurfdränage f
~ **plow** Maulwurfpflug m
molecular molekular
~ **diffusion** Molekulardiffusion f
~ **lattice** Kristallgitter n
~ **ratio** Molekularverhältnis n
molecule Molekül n
molengraaffite Molengraaffit m, Lamprophyllit m, $Na_3Sr_2Ti_3[(O, OH, F)_2|Si_2O_7]_2$
molera Diatomeenerde f, Infusorienerde f, Kieselgur f
mollifiability Erweichbarkeit f (von Gesteinen)
mollisol Mollisol m, Fließschicht f (Taubodenhorizont im Permafrost)
mollition Tauprozeß m (bei Mollisol)
molt s. moult
molten schmelzflüssig
~ **magma** schmelzflüssiges Magma n
~ **rocks** schmelzflüssige Gesteinsmassen fpl
moluranite Moluranit m, $H_6[(UO_2)_3|(MoO_4)_5] \cdot 9H_2O$
molybdate of lead Gelbbleierz n, Wulfenit m (s.a. wulfenite)
molybdenic ochre s. molybdite
molybdeniferous molybdänhaltig
molybdenite Molybdänit m, Molybdänglanz m, MoS_2
molybdenum Molybdän n, Mo
molybdite Molybdit m, Molybdänocker m, MoO_3
molybdomenite Molybdomenit m, $Pb[SeO_3]$
molybdophyllite Molybdophyllit m, $Pb_2Mg_2[(OH)_2|Si_2O_7]$
molysite Molysit m, $FeCl_3$
moment measures Momente npl (nach der Momentmethode ermittelte Körnungskennwerte)
~ **of inertia** Trägheitsmoment n
momnouthite Momnouthit m (Varietät von Urtit)
monadnock Härtling m, Restberg m, Inselberg m, Monadnock m, Zeugenberg m
monalbite Monalbit m (monokline Hochtemperaturphase von Albit)
monazite Monazit m, $Ce[PO_4]$
~ **sand** Monazitsand m
moncheite Moncheit m, $(Pt, Pd)(Te, Bi)_2$
monchiquite Monchiquit m (lamprophyrisches Ganggestein)
monchiquitic dike Monchiquitgang m
mondhaldeite Mondhaldeit m (monzonitisches Ganggestein)
monetite Monetit m, $CaH[PO_4]$
moniliform perlenförmig, tropfenförmig
monimolimnion permanent stagnierender Teil eines Wasserbeckens

monitor Kontrollgerät *n*, Sichtgerät *n*
monkey board Gestängebühne *f*
~ **hair** Affenhaar *n (fossile Kautschukwolle in Braunkohle)*
monochromatic monochromatisch, einfarbig
monoclinal monoklin, in einer Richtung geneigt
~ **fold** Monoklinalfalte *f*
~ **mountain** Monoklinalkamm *m*
~ **valley** Monoklinaltal *n*
monocline einseitig aufgerichtete Schicht *f*, Flexur *f*, Monoklinale *f*
monoclinic monoklin, in einer Richtung geneigt
~ **system** monoklines System *n*
monocots *s.* monocotyls
monocotyls monokotyle[done] Pflanzen *fpl*, Monokotyle[do]nen *fpl*
monocrystal Einkristall *m*
monogene *s.* monomineralic
monogenetic monogenetisch
monogeosyncline Monogeosynklinale *f*
monolayer water fest gebundenes Porenwasser *n*
monolith Monolith *m*, Lavadorn *m*, Felsnadel *f*
monolithic monolithisch
monometric[al] monometrisch
monomineral fraction monomineralische Fraktion *f*
monomineralic monomineralisch
Monongahela Monongahela *n (oberes Pennsylvanien in Nordamerika)*
monophyletical monophyletisch
monorefringent einfachbrechend *(Lichtbrechung)*
monotropic monotrop
monotypy Monotypie *f (Nomenklaturregeln)*
monovalent einwertig
monrepite Monrepit *m (eisenreicher Biotit)*
monroes besonderer Typ von Schlammvulkanen auf Gezeitenebenen kalter Regionen
mons Mons *m (Berg auf Mars oder Mond)*
monsoon Monsun *m*
~ **climate** Monsunklima *n*
~ **wind** Monsunwind *m*
montanite Montanit *m*, $[(BiO)_2|TeO_4] \cdot 2H_2O$
montbrayite Montbrayit *m*, Au_2Te_3
Monte Carlo sampling Monte-Carlo-Probenahme *f*, Probenahme *f* nach dem Monte-Carlo-Prinzip
montebrasite Montebrasit *m*, $LiAl[OH|PO_4]$
montgomeryite Montgomeryit *m*, $Ca_4Al_5[(OH)_5|(PO_4)_6] \cdot 11H_2O$
monthly isotherm Monatsisotherme *f*
~ **mean** Monatsmittel *n*
~ **precipitation** Monatsniederschlag *m*
Montian [Stage] Mont[ium] *n (Stufe des Paläozäns)*
monticellite Monticellit *m*, $CaMg[SiO_4]$
monticle *s.* monticule

monticulate mit kleinen Hügeln besetzt
monticule kleiner Hügel *m*; Nebenkrater *m*, aufgesetzter Krater *m*
montiform gebirgsartig
montmorillonite Montmorillonit *m*, $(Na, Mg, Al)_2[(OH)_6|Si_4O_{10}] \cdot nH_2O$
~ **group** Montmorillonitgruppe *f*
montrealite Montrealit *m (Varietät von Olivin-Essexit)*
montroseite Montroseit *m*, $(V, Fe)OOH$
montroydite Montroydit *m*, HgO
monzonite Monzonit *m*
moon/to auf dem Mond landen
moon Mond *m*
~ **basalt** Mondbasalt *m*
~-**dog** Nebenmond *m*
~ **probe (rocket)** Mondrakete *f*
moonrise Mondaufgang *m*
moon's age Mondalter *n*
~ **black-out** Mondfinsternis *f*
~ **crust** Mondkruste *f*
~ **orbit (path)** Mondbahn *f*
~ **satellite** Mondsatellit *m*
~ **shadow** Mondschatten *m*
~ **surface** Mondoberfläche *f*
moonset Monduntergang *m*
moonstone Mondstein *m (Abart des Feldspats)*
moor Moor *n*, Torfmoor *n*, Heide *f*
~ **coal** zerreibliche Braunkohle *f (weiche Lignitabart)*
~ **country** Moorgebiet *n*
~ **peat** Moostorf *m*, Sphagnumtorf *m*
moorband [pan] Ortstein *m*
mooreite Mooreit *m*, $(Mg, Zn, Mn)_8[(OH)_{14}|SO_4] \cdot 4H_2O$
moorhouseite Moorhouseit *m*, $(Co, Ni, Mn)[SO_4] \cdot 6H_2O$
mooring system Verankerungssystem *n*
moorland Moorlandschaft *f*, Moor[land] *n*
moorpan *s.* moorband
moorstone Sumpferz *n*, Raseneisenerz *n*
moory moorig
mor Rohhumus *m*
moraesite Moreasit *m*, $Be_2[OH|PO_4] \cdot 4H_2O$
morainal Moränen... *(s.a. morainic)*
~ **lobe (loop)** Moränenbogen, Moränenlappen *m*, Moränenlobus *m*
moraine Moräne *f*, Moränenschutt *m*
~-**covered** moränenbedeckt
~-**dammed lake** Moränenstausee *m*
~ **dams** Moränenzug *m*
~ **deposit** Moränenablagerung *f*
~ **district** Moränengebiet *n*
~ **in transit** Wandermoräne *f*
~ **lobe (loop)** *s.* morainal lobe
~ **plain** *s.* apron
~ **rampart** Moränenwall *m*
~ **topography** Moränenlandschaft *f*
~ **tracts** Moränenzug *m*
morainic Moränen...
~ **arc** Moränenbogen *m*

morainic

- **~ basin** Moränenbecken *n*
- **~-belt topography** Endmoränenlandschaft *f*
- **~ cover** Moränendecke *f*
- **~ dams** Moränenzug *m*
- **~ debris** Gletscherschutt *m*
- **~ deposit** Moränenablagerung *f*
- **~ hill (hummock)** Moränenhügel *m*
- **~ lake** Moränensee *m*, Soll *n*
- **~ lobe (loop)** *s.* morainal lobe
- **~ material** Gletscherschutt *m*
- **~ mound** Moränenhügel *m*
- **~ ridge** Wallmoräne *f*
- **~ topography** Moränenlandschaft *f*
- **~ tracts** Moränenzug *m*

morass Sumpf *m*
- **~ ore** Sumpferz *n*, Moorerz *n*

morassic morastig, sumpfig
mordenite Mordenit *m*, $(Ca, K_2, Na_2)[AlSi_5O_{12}]_2 \cdot 6H_2O$
more Erzvorrat bezogen auf einen Gangteil *(Cornwall)*
- **~ row shooting** Mehrreihenschießen *n*

morencite *s.* nontronite
morenosite Morenosit *m*, $Ni[SO_4] \cdot 7H_2O$
Morganian Morganien *n (Westfal D in England)*
morganite Morganit *m (s.a. beryl)*
morinite Morinit *m*, $Ca_2NaAl_2[(F, OH)_5|(PO_4)_2] \cdot 2H_2O$
morion Morion *m*, dunkler Rauchquarz *m*
mornes Mornes *pl (tropische Karstform)*
morning star Morgenstern *m*
morphogenesis Morphogenese *f*
morphogen[et]ic morphogenetisch
morphogeny Morphogenese *f*
morphographic morphografisch
morphography Morphografie *f*
morphologic[al] morphologisch
- **~ geology** Geomorphologie *f*
- **~ plains** morphologische Flächen *fpl*
- **~ unit** morphologisch charakterisierte lithostratigrafische Einheit *f*

morphology Morphologie *f*
morphometric[al] morphometrisch
- **~ analysis** morphometrische Analyse *f (von Schotter)*

morphometry Morphometrie *f*
morphotropic morphotropisch
- **~ effect** morphotropische Beeinflussung *f*

morphotropism, morphotropy Morphotropie *f*
morriner *s.* esker
Morrison Formation Morrison-Formation *f (Oberer Jura in Nordamerika)*
Morrowan [Stage] Morrow *n (Stufe des Pennsylvaniens)*
mortar bed Konkretionskruste *f*, Felspanzerbildung *f*
- **~ structure** Mörtelgefüge *n*

mortlake See *m* in einem toten Flußarm
mosaic Fotomosaik *n*, Bildplan *m (Luftbildgeologie)*
- **~ texture** Pflasterstruktur *f*

234

mosaizing mosaikartiges Zusammensetzen *n (z.B. benachbarter Luft- und Satellitenaufnahmen zu Bildplänen größerer Gebiete)*
mosandrite Mosandrit *m*, $(Ca, Na, Y)_3(Ti, Zr, Ce)[(F, OH, O)_2|Si_2O_7]$
moscovite *s.* muscovite
mosesite Mosesit *m*, $[Hg_2N]Cl \cdot H_2O$
Moskovian [Stage] Moskau-Stufe *f (höheres Mittelkarbon, Osteuropa)*
moss sumpfiger Boden *m*; Torfmoor *n*
- **~ agate** Moosachat *m (s.a. chalcedony)*
- **~ bog** Moosmoor *n*
- **~ cover** Moosdecke *f*
- **~ fallow** Torfstich *m*
- **~ fen** Moosmoor *n*
- **~ gold** dendritisches Gold *n*
- **~ hag** Moorboden *m*, Torfboden *m*
- **~ peat** Moostorf *m*
- **~ silver** dendritisches Silber *n*

mossiness Moosbedeckung *f*, Moosboden *m*
mosslike moosähnlich
mossy moosförmig, moosig
mother crystal Mutterkristall *m*
- **~ gate** Grundstrecke *f*
- **~ liquid (liquor)** Mutterlauge *f*
- **~ lode** Hauptgang *m*
- **~ lye** Mutterlauge *f*
- **~ of coal** *s.* mineral charcoal 1.
- **~-of-pearl** Perlmutt *n*, Perlmutter *f*
- **~-of-pearl lustre** Perlmutt[er]glanz *m*
- **~ oil** Primäröl *n*
- **~ rock** Muttergestein *n*

mottle irregulärer Sedimentkörper mit abweichendem Gefüge
mottled fleckig, gefleckt, gesprenkelt, marmoriert
- **~ bedding** fleckige Schichtung *f*
- **~ clay** Buntton *m*
- **~ sandstone** Buntsandstein *m*, Tigersandstein *m*
- **~ schist (shale, slate)** Fleckschiefer *m*
- **~ structure** gefleckte Schichtung *f*, Wühlgefüge *n*

mottling Marmorierung *f*
mottramite Mottramit *m*, $Pb(Cu, Zn)[OH|VO_4]$
mould 1. Abdruck *m*, Abformung *f*, 2. Humusboden *m*, Ackererde *f*
mouldered zermürbt
mouldering Humifikation *f*, Humusbildung *f*, Vermoderung *f*, Vermullung *f*
mouldy peat Moortorf *m*
moulin Gletschermühle *f*, Gletschertopf *m*
- **~ kames** Gletschermühlenkames *mpl*
- **~ pothole** Gletschermühle *f*, Gletschertopf *m*

moult Exuvie *f*, Haut *f*, Panzer *m (Häutungsrest von Arthropoden und Reptilien)*
moulting Häutung *f*
mound Anhöhe *f*, Hügel *m*, Erdhaufen *m*, Halde *f*, Erdwall *m*, Erdaufwurf *m*
- **~ of eroded material** Schuttkegel *m*

moundlike beulenförmig
mount Berg *m (in geografischen Namen)*

mountain Berg m
~ **apron** s. piedmont alluvial plain
~ **birth** Gebirgsbildung f
~ **blue** s. azurite
~ **breeze** Bergwind m
~ **building** Gebirgsbildung f
~-**building** gebirgsbildend
~-**building crumpling** Gebirgsfaltung f
~ **butter** s. alunogen
~ **chain** Gebirgskette f, Gebirgszug m, Bergkette f, Kettengebirge n
~ **chain bordering on a plateau** Randgebirge n
~ **coast** Steilküste f
~ **cork** Bergkork m (Erscheinungsform von Asbest)
~ **creek** Gebirgsbach m
~ **creep** Bergsturz m
~ **crest** Gebirgskamm m, Bergkamm m
~ **crystal** Bergkristall m (s.a. quartz)
~ **declivity** Bergabhang m
~ **development** Gebirgsbildung f
~ **face** Bergwand f
~ **flax** Bergflachs m, Amiant m (s.a. actinolite)
~ **flour** Kieselgur f, Infusorienerde f, Diatomeenerde f
~ **folding** Gebirgsfaltung f, Gebirgsbildung f
~ **forest** Bergwald m, Hochwald m
~ **formed by folding** Faltungsgebirge n
~ **formed by plateau-forming movements** Schollengebirge n
~ **formed of disrupted folds** Bruchfaltengebirge n
~ **formed of folds** Faltengebirge n
~ **formed of overthrust (recumbent) folds** Deckfaltengebirge n
~-**forming** gebirgsbildend
~ **glacier** Gebirgsgletscher m
~ **gorge** Felsschlucht f
~ **green** s. malachite
~ **gulch** Bergtobel m
~ **lake** Gebirgssee m
~ **leather** Bergleder n (Erscheinungsform von Asbest)
~ **limestone** Kohlenkalkstein m (im Unterkarbon von England)
~ **meal** s. ~ flour
~ **milk** schwammartige Kalzitausscheidung f
~ **of denudation** Denudationsgebirge n
~ **of erosion** Abtragungsgebirge n
~ **paper** Bergpapier n (Erscheinungsform von Asbest)
~ **pass** Gebirgspaß m
~ **peak** Berggipfel m
~ **peaty soil** Gebirgsmoorboden m
~ **range** s. ~ chain
~ **region** Bergland n
~ **ridge** Bergrücken m, Gebirgsrücken m, Bergkamm m, Gebirgskamm m, Gebirgsgrat m
~ **river** Gebirgsfluß m
~ **side** Berglehne f, Berghang m, Gebirgshang m; Gebirgslandschaft f

~ **slope** Berghang m
~ **soap** Bergseife f (s.a. halloysite)
~ **spar** Vorgebirge n, vorgelagertes Gebirge n
~ **splitting** Bergzerreißung f
~ **spur** Bergsausläufer m, Bergnase f
~ **stream** Bergstrom m, Gebirgsfluß m, Wildbach m
~ **tallow** s. hatchettite
~ **tarn** Karsee m
~ **top** Berggipfel m
~ **topography** Gebirgslandschaft f, Berglandschaft f
~ **torrent** Bergstrom m, Gebirgsfluß m, Wildwasser n, Wildbach m
~ **trail** Höhenweg m
~ **wall** Bergwand f
~ **waste** Gebirgsschutt m
~ **wood** Holzasbest m
~ **wool** Bergwolle f (Asbestart)
mountainite Mountainit m, $KNa_2Ca_2[HSi_8O_{20}] \cdot 5H_2O$
mountainous bergig, gebirgig, Gebirgs...
~ **country** Bergland n
~ **desert** Gebirgswüste f
~ **formation** Gebirgsbildung f
~ **ground** Gebirgsgelände n
~ **region** Bergland n
mountainy gebirgig, hügelig
mounting medium Einbettungsmedium n (für Dünnschliffe)
mourite Mourit m, $[(UO_2)_2(MoO_4)_5] \cdot 5H_2O$
mouth Mündung f (eines Flusses)
~ **bar** Mündungsbarren m (Sandablagerungen der Flußarmmündungen im Bereich der Deltafront-Plattform)
~ **of a river** Flußmündung f
~ **of an adit** Stollenmundloch n
~ **of well** Brunnenmundloch n
~ **parts** Mundwerkzeuge npl (bei Arthropoden)
move-out Moveout n (Zeitdifferenz zwischen den Laufzeiten von Wellen)
movement of oscillation Schwingungsbewegung f
~ **of rotation** Drehbewegung f
~ **of the crust** Krustenbewegung f
~ **of the ground** Bodenbewegung f
moving average gleitendes Mittel n (Statistik)
~ **boundary** bewegliche Kontur f (reservoirmechanisch)
~ **dune** Wanderdüne f
~ **moraine** Wandermoräne f
~ **picture borehole camera** Bohrlochfilmkamera f
~ **point** Wanderpunkt m (reservoirmechanisch)
moya s. mud lava
mozambikite Mozambikit m, (Th, SE, U)(O, OH)$_2$
MSID s. mass spectrometric isotope dilution
MTF s. modular transfer function
much indented coast buchtenreiche Küste f

much 236

~ **weathered** stark verwittert
muck 1. Berge *pl*, Haufwerk *n*; 2. schwarze Torferde *f*, Wiesentorf *m*, anmooriger Boden *m*, unreiner Torf *m*
~-**blasting operation** Schüttsprengverfahren *n*
~ **stack** Bergehalde f
muckle weicher Ton *m (im Hangenden oder Liegenden der Kohle)*
mucks minderwertige erdige Kohle
mucky aus Sumpferde bestehend
mud-off/to abdichten
mud 1. Mudde *f*, Schlamm *m*, Schlick *m*; 2. Spülung[sflüssigkeit] *f*, Dickspülung *f*, Spülschlamm *m*, Tonspülung *f (Bohrung)*
~ **additive** Spülungszusatz *m*
~ **analysis log** Spülungsanalysenlog *n*
~ **auger** Schappe *f*, Schappenbohrer *m*, Bohrschappe *f*
~ **avalanche** *s*. ~ flow
~ **balance** Spülungswaage *f*
~ **balls** *s*. accretionary lapilli
~ **beach** Schlickstrand *m*
~-**bearing** schlammführend
~ **bed** Schlammschicht *f*
~-**buried ripple marks** schlammbedeckte Rippelmarken *fpl*
~ **cake** Filterkuchen *m (an der Bohrlochwandung)*
~-**circulating channel (opening)** Spülungskanal *m*
~ **column** Spülungssäule *f*
~ **control** Spülungsüberwachung *f*
~ **crack** Schwundriß *m*, Schrumpfungsriß *m*, Luftriß *m*, Trockenriß *m*, Schlammriß *m*, Netzleiste *f (Sedimentgefüge)*
~-**cracked** von Schlammrissen durchzogen
~-**cracked loam** Lehm *m* mit Trocknungsrissen
~ **cracking** Schlammrißbildung *f*, Trockenrißbildung *f*
~ **degassing** Gasabscheidung *f* aus der Spülung
~ **density** Dichte *f* der Spülung
~ **deposit** Schlammablagerung *f*, Schlickablagerung *f*
~ **engineer** Spülungsingenieur *m*
~ **eruption** Schlammausbruch *m*
~ **field** Schlammfeld *n*
~ **filling** *(Am)* Verschlammung *f*
~ **filtrate resistivity** elektrischer Widerstand *m* des Spülungsfiltrats
~ **flat** Schlammniederung *f*, Sumpfebene *f*, Schlickwatt *n*, Schlickebene *f*
~ **flow** Mure *f*, Murgang *m*, Murbruch *m*, Schlammstrom *m*
~ **flush** Dickspülung *f*, Spülschlamm *f*
~-**gas log** Spülungsgaslog *n*
~ **geyser** Schlammsprudel *m*
~ **gun** Wasserstrahlmischer *m*, Hydromonitor *m*
~ **hose** Druckleitung *f*
~ **island** Schlamminsel *f*

~ **jacking** Schlamminjektion *f*, Schlammeinpressung *f*
~ **lava** vulkanischer Schlamm *m*
~ **line** Bohrspülungsleitung *f*
~ **line suspension equipment** Schlammleitung *f*
~ **log** Spülungsanalysenlog *n*
~ **logging** Spülungsbefund *m (auf Gas)*, Gasanalyse *f* der Spülung
~ **losses** Spülungsverluste *mpl*
~ **lump** Schlammaufbruch *m*, diapirartige Schlammstruktur *f*
~ **mixer** Tonmischer *m*
~ **mixture** Spülung *f*
~ **mound** Schlammhügel *m*
~ **pebbles** Schlickgerölle *npl*
~ **pellets** *s*. accretionary lapilli
~ **pit** Schlammgrube *f*
~ **plain** Schlickebene *f*
~ **plant** Spülungsaufbereitungsanlage *f*
~ **pot** Schlammkrater *m*
~ **pressure** Spülungsdruck *m*
~ **pump** Spülpumpe *f*
~ **pump delivery** Volumenstrom *m* (Fördermenge *f*) der Spülpumpe
~ **pump pressure** Spülpumpendruck *m*
~ **rain** Schlammregen *m*
~ **resistivity** elektrischer Widerstand *m* der Spülung, Resistivität *f* der Tonspülung
~ **resistivity logging** Spülungswiderstandsmessung *f*, Resistivimetrie *f*
~ **rock** Schieferton *m*
~ **rock flow** *s*. ~ flow
~ **salinity** Salzgehalt *m* der Spülung
~ **sample** Spülungsprobe *f*
~ **saver bucket** Spülungskasten *m*
~ **screen** Schüttelsieb *n*
~ **settling trap pit** Absetzbehälter *m*
~ **sill** Schlammschwelle *f*
~ **silting** Verschlammung *f*
~ **smeller** *(sl)* Erdölgeologe *m*
~ **spring** Schlammsprudel *m*
~ **stream** *s*. ~ flow
~ **system** Spülungssystem *n*
~ **temperature** Spülungstemperatur *f*
~ **test** Spülungsmessung *f*
~ **tidal deposits** Wattenschlick *m*
~ **volcano** Schlammvulkan *m*, Schlammsprudel *m*, Salse *f*, Makkalube *f*
muddiness Schlammigkeit *f*
mudding-off Eindringen *n* von Bohrspülung in die Formation
muddled water trübes Wasser *n*
muddy schlammig, schlammartig, schlickig, trübe, lehmig
~ **ground** Schlammboden *m*, Moddergrund *m*
~ **pool** Tümpel *m*
~ **soil** Schlammboden *m*
mudspate *s*. mud flow
mudstone 1. übergeordneter Begriff für Silt- und Tonsteine; 2. verfestigter Ton *m*, Tonstein *m*; Pelit *m*; 3. schlammgestütztes Karbo-

natgestein mit < 10% Komponenten (Dunham-Klassifikation 1962)
mugearite Mugearit *m (Trachybasalt)*
muggy feucht[warm], schwül
muirite Muirit *m*, $Ba_5CaTi[O_4|Si_4O_{12}]\cdot 3H_2O$
mulatto kretazischer Grünsand *m (Irland)*
mulching Mulchen *n*
mull 1. Vorgebirge *n (Schottland);* 2. an anorganischen Stoffen reicher Waldboden
~ **soil** Mullboden *m*
mullion structure Mullionstruktur *f*
mullite Mullit *m*, $Al_6[O_3|(OH, F)|Si_3AlO_{16}]$
mullock taubes Gestein *n*
multi-... *s.* multi...
multiaquifer formation System *n* von Grundwasserleitern, Grundwasserstockwerk *n*
multiaxial mehrachsig
multiband camera Mehrkanalkamera *f*
~ **images** Mehrkanalaufnahmen *fpl*, Multispektralaufnahmen *fpl*
multibranched drilling Bohren *n* mit mehrfacher Richtungsänderung
multichannel filtering Mehrkanalfilterung *f*
multicomponent system Vielstoffsystem *n*
multicycle landscapes mehrzyklische Landschaften *fpl*
multidate images Aufnahmen der gleichen Szene zu verschiedenen Zeitpunkten
multidirectional drilling Bohren *n* mit mehrfacher Richtungsänderung
multidisciplinary analysis multidisziplinäre Auswertung *f*
multielectrode sonde Mehrelektrodensonde *f*
multifrac mehrstufige hydraulische Rißbildung *f*
multigelation mehrfacher Tau-Gefrier-Prozeß *m*
multihole drilling Mehrlochbohrung *f*, Zweigbohren *n*, Mehrsohlenbohren *n*
multilayer mehrschichtig
~ **field** Lagerstätte *f* mit mehreren Trägern (ölführenden Horizonten)
multilayered mehrschichtig
multipartite map lithologische Mächtigkeitskarte *f (für eine stratigrafische Einheit)*
multiphase flow Mehrphasenströmung *f*
multiple Multiple *f*, Mehrfachreflexion *f*
~ **bench quarrying** terrassenförmiger Steinbruchabbau *m (Strossenbau)*
~ **completion well** Mehrstrangsonde *f*
~ **coverage** Mehrfachüberdeckung *f*, Stapelung *f*
~ **dike** *s.* ~ vein
~ **drilling** Fächerbohrung *f*
~ **fault** wiederholte Bruchbildung *f*
~ **geophones** multiple Geophone *npl*, Geophongruppe *f*
~ **intrusions** mehrfache Intrusionen *fpl*
~ **linear array** Mehrfachanordnung *f* linearer ladungsgekoppelter Festkörperdetektoren *(als Fernerkundungssensor genutzt)*
~-**purpose reservoir** Mehrzweckspeicher *m (Grundwasserleiter)*
~-**rate** Mehrfachfließratentest *m*
~ **reflections** multiple Reflexionen *fpl*
~ **shot holes** Mehrfachschußlöcher *npl*, Sternschüsse *mpl*, Flächenschüsse *mpl*
~ **spacings electric logging** Widerstandsbohrlochmessung *f* mit verschiedenen Meßlängen
~ **top** multiple Oberkante *f* einer Schicht *(durch Überschiebung, Überkippung)*
~ **twinning** Viellingsverzwillingung *f*
~ **twins** Wiederholungszwillinge *mpl*
~ **vein** vielfacher (zusammengesetzter) Gang *m*
~ **vent basalt** Schildbasalt *m*, Flächenbasalt *m (von zahlreichen kleinen Schloten gefördert)*
~-**well derrick** Bohrturm *m* zum gleichzeitigen Bohren von mehreren Bohrungen
~-**well system** Brunnengruppe *f*
~-**zone packer** Packer *m* für Mehrzonenförderung
multiplexer Multiplexer *m*
multiplexing Vielfachübertragung *f*; Multiplexverfahren *n*
multiring basin Mehrfachringbassin *n*
multispectral camera Multispektralkamera *f*
multistage cementing Mehrfachstufenzementation *f*
~ **sampling** Mehrstufendatensammlung *f (in mehreren Höhenniveaus bzw. Arbeitsstufen zunehmenden Detailliertheitsgrades)*
multitemporal sampling *s.* multitime sampling
multithematic presentation multithematische Darstellung *f (z.B. der Auswertungsergebnisse der Fernerkundung)*
multitime sampling Datensammlung *f* zu verschiedenen Zeitpunkten
multitube elutriator Spitzenapparat *m (für die Schlämmanalyse)*
mummify/to mumifizieren
mummy Mumie *f*
mundane ball Erdball *m*
Münder Marl Münder-Mergel *m (oberer Malm, Niedersächsisches Becken)*
mundic *(sl)* Schwefelkies *m (s.a. pyrite)*
mungle shale Ölschiefer *m (Schottland)*
municipal water supply städtische Wasserversorgung *f*
mural escarpment steilwandiges Felskliff *n*
~ **jointing** parallelepipedische (quaderförmige) Absonderung *f*, engständige Bankungsklüftung *f*
murambite Murambit *m (Varietät von Leuzitbasanit)*
murbruk texture Mörtelstruktur *f*
murdochite Murdochit *m*, $PbCu_6O_8$
muriatic acid Chlorwasserstoffsäure *f*, Salzsäure *f*, HCl
murite Murit *m (olivinführender Nephelinphonolith)*
murmanite Murmanit *m*, $Na_2MnTi_3[SiO_4]_4\cdot 8H_2O$

muscle

muscle scar Muskelfleck *m*, Muskelnarbe *f*
muscovite Muskovit *m*, $KAl_2[(OH,F)_2|AlSi_3O_{10}]$
~ **granite** Muskovitgranit *m*
~-**out isograd** Isograd *m* des Muskovitzerfalls, obere [metamorphe] Stabilitätsgrenze *f* von Muskovit
~ **phyllade** Muskovit-Chlorit-Schiefer *m*
~ **quartzite** Muskovitquarzit *m*
~ **schist** Muskovitschiefer *m*
mush frost Kammeis *n*
mushroom cloud Pilzwolke *f*
~ **fold** Pilzfalte *f*
~ **rock** Pilzfels[en] *m*
~-**shaped** pilzartig
mushy porig
~ **coal** weiche (trockene, erdige) Kohle *f*
muskeg 1. mit Moos überwachsene sumpfige Landschaft *f*; 2. Muskeg *m* *(organogener Boden)*; Moor *n*, Tundramoor *n*, nasser Tundraboden *m*
mussel Miesmuschel *f*, Muschel *f*
~ **band** *s.* marine band
~ **bed** Muschelbank *f*
~ **bind** *s.* marine band
mute taub *(Gestein)*
muting Muting *n*; Abschwächen *n (früher Einsätze)*; Auslöschen *n*
mutual time Gegenzeit *f*
mutually cross-cutting sich wechselseitig durchkreuzend
~ **indenting pebbles** sich gegenseitig eindrückende Steine *mpl*
muzgas initiale Karrenform *f (Karst)*
m. y. – million years
mylonite Mylonit *m*
mylonitic mylonitisch
~ **texture** mylonitische Struktur *f*
mylonitization Mylonitisierung *f*
mylonitize/to mylonitisieren
mylonization Mylonitisierung *f*
mylonize/to mylonitisieren
myrmekite Myrmekit *m*
myrmekitic exsolution myrmekitische Entmischung *f*

N

n-membered chain radioaktive Zerfallsreihe *f* mit n-Gliedern
nablock gerundete Konkretion *f*
nacre Perlmutt *n*, Perlmutter *f*
nacreous perlmutt[er]artig
~ **cloud** Perlmutt[er]wolke *f*
~ **layer** Perlmutt[er]schicht *f*
~ **lustre** Perlmutt[er]glanz *m*
nacrite Nakrit *m*, $Al_4[(OH)_8|Si_4O_{10}]$
nadir angle Nadirwinkel *m*
~ **distance** Nadirabstand *m*
~ **point** Nadirpunkt *m*
nadorite Nadorit *m*, $PbSbO_2Cl$
naegite Naegit *m (s.a. zircon)*

naes *s.* ness
nagatelite Nagatelith *m (Varietät von Allanit)*
nagelfluh Nagelfluh *f (tertiäres Konglomerat)*
nagyagite Nagyagit *m*, Blättertellur *m*, $AuTe_2 \cdot Pb(S, Te)$
nahcolite Nahcolith *m*, $NaHCO_3$
nail head scratch Nagelkopfschramme *f (glaziale Schramme)*
naked karst nackter Karst *m*
nakhlite Nakhlit *m (achondritischer diopsid- und olivinführender Meteorit)*
namies Schlechten *fpl (Yorkshire)*
Namurian [Stage] Namur[ien] *n*, Namurium *n (basale Stufe des Oberkarbons in Mittel- und Westeuropa)*
nanism Zwergwuchs *m*
nannofossil Nannofossil *n*
nannoplankton Nannoplankton *n*
nantokite Nantokit *m*, $CuCl$
napalite Napalith *m (Kohlenwasserstoffverbindung)*
napheteine *s.* hatchettite
naphtha 1. schweres Erdöl *n*; 2. benzinartiges Destillationsprodukt von Erdöl
naphthalize/to mit Erdöl tränken
naphthene basic oil naphthenbasisches Erdöl *n*
naphthenic oil Naphthenöl *n*
naphthine *s.* hatchettite
naphtholithe bituminöser Schiefer *m*
naphthology Erdölwissenschaft *f*
naphtine *s.* hatchettite
nappe Decke *f*, Überschiebungsmasse *f*, Überschiebungsdecke *f*, Schubdecke *f*, Ferndecke *f*
~ **inlier** geologisches Fenster *n*, Deckenfenster *n*
~ **involutions** Rollfalten *fpl* in Decken, Walzfalten *fpl*
~ **outlier** Deckscholle *f*, Überschiebungsrest *m*, Klippe *f*
~ **root** Wurzel *f* der Überschiebungsdecke
~ **structure** Deckenbau *m*
~ **system** Deckensystem *n*
~ **tectonics** Deckenfaltung *f*
~ **with several facies** Vielfaziesdecke *f*
Narizian [Stage] Narizien *n (marine Stufe, mittleres Eozän in Nordamerika)*
narrow/to sich verdrücken
narrow Einschnürung *f*, Enge *f*, Schlucht *f*
~-**crested anticline** Schmalsattel *m*, enge Antiklinale *f*
~ **pass** Engpaß *m*
~-**reef mine** geringmächtige, flache Lagerstätte *f*
~ **working** enger Grubenbau *m*
narrowing Isthmus *m*
narrows Förde *f*, Meerenge *f*, Engpaß *m*, Hohlweg *m*, Stromenge *f*
narsarsukite Narsarsukit *m*, $Na_2Ti[O|Si_4O_{10}]$
nasinite Nasinit *m*, $Na_2[B_5O_6(OH)_5] \cdot H_2O$
nasonite Nasonit *m*, $Pb_6Ca_4[Cl_2|(Si_2O_7)_3]$

nasturan s. uraninite
native gediegen, natürlich vorkommend
~ **antimony** gediegenes Antimon n, Sb
~ **arsenic** gediegenes Arsen n, Scherbenkobalt n, As
~ **asphalt** Naturbitumen n, Erdasphalt m
~ **bedrock** s. ~ rock
~ **bismuth** gediegenes Wismut n, Bi
~ **coke** Naturkoks m
~ **copper** Bergkupfer n, gediegenes Kupfer n, Cu
~ **country** Mutterboden m
~ **gold** gediegenes Gold n, Au
~ **hydrocarbons** natürliche Kohlenwasserstoffe mpl
~ **iron** gediegenes Eisen n, Fe
~ **lead** gediegenes Blei n, Pb
~ **mercury** gediegenes Quecksilber n, Hg
~ **metal** gediegenes Metall n
~ **paraffine** Erdwachs n
~ **platinum** gediegenes Platin n, Pt
~ **Prussian blue** s. vivianite
~ **rock** gewachsener Fels m, anstehendes Gestein n, Muttergestein n
~ **salt** Steinsalz n, NaCl
~ **silver** gediegenes Silber n, Ag
~ **soil** Mutterboden m
~-**state core** unberührter Bohrkern m
~ **state/in a** in gediegenem Zustand
~ **sulphur** gediegener Schwefel m, S
~ **water** fossiles Wasser n
natramblygonite Natramblygonit m, (Na,Li)[(OH,F)|PO$_4$]
natroalunite Natroalunit m, NaAl$_3$[(OH)$_6$|(SO$_4$)$_2$]
natrochalcite Natrochalzit m, NaCu$_2$[OH|(SO$_4$)$_2$]·H$_2$O
natrojarsoite Natrojarosit m, NaFe$_3$[(OH)$_6$|(SO$_4$)$_2$]
natrolite Natrolith m, Na$_2$[Al$_2$Si$_3$O$_{10}$]·2H$_2$O
natromontebrasite s. natramblygonite
natron Natrit m, Soda f, Natron n, (Na$_2$CO$_3$·10H$_2$O)
natrophilite Natrophilit m, Na(Mn,Fe)[PO$_4$]
natural abundance variation natürliches Isotopenverhältnis n
~ **angle of slope** natürlicher Böschungswinkel m, Ruhewinkel m
~ **arch** Fels[en]tor n
~ **asphalt** Naturasphalt m, Erdpech n
~ **background radiation** natürliche Untergrundstrahlung f
~ **bed** natürliche Schichtung f
~ **bridge** Naturbrücke f, Felsbrücke f
~ **brine** Natursalzsole f
~ **coke** Naturkoks m
~ **current** Erdstrom m
~ **density** s. bulk density
~ **dike** s. ~ levee
~ **disaster** Naturkatastrophe f
~ **earth current** natürlicher Erdstrom m
~ **fall** natürliches Gefälle n
~ **flow** natürliche eruptive Förderung f

~ **flowing well** selbstlaufende (selbsttätig ausfließende) Sonde f, Eruptiersonde f
~ **frequency** Eigenfrequenz f
~ **gas** Erdgas n, Naturgas n
~ **gas liquefaction plant** Erdgasverflüssigungsanlage f
~ **gas well** Erdgasquelle f
~ **gasoline** Erdgasbenzin n, Naturgasolin n
~ **glass** mineralisches Glas n
~ **ground** gewachsener Boden m
~ **ground-water level** ungesenkter Grundwasserspiegel m
~ **iron ore** Raseneisenerz n
~ **levee** natürlicher Damm m, Uferdamm m, natürlicher Uferwall m
~ **magnet** s. magnetite
~ **mica** Rohglimmer m
~ **mud** natürliche Spülung f
~-**occurring** natürlich vorkommend
~-**occuring radioactivity** natürliche Radioaktivität f
~ **oscillation** Eigenschwingung f (Seismometer)
~ **radioactivity** natürliche Radioaktivität f
~ **resources** Naturschätze mpl, Bodenschätze mpl
~ **selection** natürliche Auslese f
~ **size** natürliche Größe f
~ **soil** gewachsener Boden m
~ **stone** Naturstein m
~ **tar** Bergteer m
~ **vibration** Eigenschwingung f (Seismometer)
~ **water conduit** natürlicher Wasserlauf m
nature of deposition Lagerungsform f
~ **of ground** Bodenbeschaffenheit f
~ **of rock** Gesteinsart f
~ **of soil** Bodenbeschaffenheit f
~ **preservation** Naturschutz m
~ **reserve** Naturschutzgebiet n
~ **sanctuary** Naturdenkmal n
naujacasite Naujakasit m, (Na,K)$_6$FeAl$_4$[O$_3$|Si$_4$O$_{10}$]$_2$·H$_2$O
naumannite Naumannit m, Ag$_2$Se
nautical chart Seekarte f
Navajo Formation Navajo-Formation f (Lias und teilweise Dogger, Nordamerika)
navajoite Navajoit m, V$_2$O$_5$·3H$_2$O
naval chart Seekarte f
~ **observatory** Seewarte f
Navarro Group Navarro-Gruppe f (oberes Campan und Maastricht, Nordamerika)
Navier-Stokes equation Navier-Stokes-Gleichung f
navigable channel Fahrwasser n, Stromrinne f
~ **river** schiffbarer Fluß m
~ **waterway** Wasserstraße f
naze s. ness
neanic neanisch, spätjugendlich (Wachstumsstadium)
neap tide[s] Nippflut f, Nipptide f
near nahe gelegen
~ **earthquake** Nahbeben n

near 240

~-infrared scanner Linienabtaster m im Bereich des nahen Infrarot
~ shock Nahbeben n
~-shore küstennah
~-shore deposit küstennahe Ablagerung f
~-shore island festlandnahe Insel f
~-shore sediment strandnahe Ablagerung f
nearshore s. near-shore
neat rein, unvermischt, unverdünnt
Nebraskan [Ice Age] Nebraska-Vereisung f (Pleistozän in Nordamerika, entspricht etwa dem Eburon in Europa)
nebula Nebelfleck m, Nebelschleier m, planetarischer Nebel m
nebular hypothesis Nebularhypothese f, Nebulartheorie f
nebulite Nebulit m (Migmatit)
nebulitic structure nebulitische Textur f (bei Migmatit)
nebulosity Nebelhülle f
nebulous neblig
~ fog Lichtnebel m
neck 1. Neck m, Stielgang m, Schlotgang m, Bühl m; 2. Meerenge f, Landenge f
~ cut-off Laufverkürzung f eines Flusses infolge Mäanderdurchschneidung
~ of land Landzunge f
~ vertebra Halswirbel m
necoite Nekoit m, $Ca_{1,5}[Si_3O_6(OH)_3]\cdot 2^1/_2H_2O$
necrophagous nekrophag, von abgestorbener Substanz lebend
necrosalinity Nekrosalinar n
needle Nadel f; Kristallnadel f
~ gauge Stechpegel m
~ ice Kammeis n
~ ironstone s. goethite
~ karst Turmkarst m
~ ore s. aikinite
~ probe Nadelsonde f (für Wärmeleitfähigkeitsmessungen)
~ spar s. aragonite
needlelike nadelig
needless well unnötige Bohrung f
needlestone s. natrolite
negative crystal 1. optisch negativer Kristall m; 2. Kristallnegativ n
~ segment in Absenkung begriffener Krustenabschnitt m
~ shore line s. shore line of submergence
Nehdenian [Stage] Nehden n (Stufe des Oberdevons in Europa)
neighborite Neighborit m, $NaMgF_3$
neighbouring earthquake Nahbeben n
~ rock Nebengestein n
nekonite Nekonit m (Apatit-Ilmenit-Gestein)
nekton Nekton n
nektonic nektonisch
nektoplanktonic s. pelagic
nematoblastic nematoblastisch
~ structure faserige Textur f
Neocomian Neokom n (tieferer Teil der Unterkreide)

Neocryptozoic [Era] Spätpräkambrium n
neocryst sekundäres Kristallkorn n (in Evaporiten)
neocrystic rekristallisiert, mit sekundärer, nicht laminierter Textur (in Evaporiten)
neodigenite Neodigenit m, Cu_9S_5
Neogene Neogen n, Jungtertiär n (Miozän und Pliozän)
neogenic neugebildet, sekundär (Petrografie)
neolensic mit sekundärer Lentikulartextur (bei Evaporiten)
neolith jungsteinzeitliches Gerät n
Neolithic jungsteinzeitlich
Neolithic [Age, Times] Neolithikum n, Jungsteinzeit f, jüngere Steinzeit f
neomorphism Neomorphismus m
Neopalaeozoic Jungpaläozoikum n, Spätpaläozoikum n
neoporphyrocrystic sekundärporphyrisch (bei Evaporitgefügen)
neosome Neosom n, Metatekt n
neostratotype Neostratotyp m
neotantalite Neotantalit m (Fe-Tantalit)
neotectonics Neotektonik f
neotype Neotypus m
neovolcanic neovulkanisch
~ rock neovulkanisches Gestein n
Neozoic neozoisch
Neozoic [Era] s. Cenozoic
~ Formation neozoische Formation f
~ Period Neozoikum n
nepheline Nephelin m, $KNa_3[AlSiO_4]_4$
~ basalt Nephelinbasalt m
~ dolerite Nephelindolerit m
~ syenite Eläolithsyenit m, Nephelinsyenit m
nephelinite Nephelinit m
nephelinization Nephelinisierung f
nephelite s. nepheline
nephelitic rock Nephelingestein n
nephelium Nebelfleck m
nephelognosy Wolkenbeobachtung f
nepheloid wolkig, wolkenartig
~ layers ausgedünnte Turbiditzonen fpl (auf dem Tiefseeboden)
nephelometer Streustrahlungsmesser m, Bewölkungsmesser m
nephelometry Streustrahlungsmessung f
nephology Wolkenkunde f
nephometer Bewölkungsmesser m
nephrite Nephrit m, Beilstein m (dichter Aktinolith oder Anthophyllit)
nepouite Nepouit m (Varietät von Antigorit)
neptunian sedimentär, angeschwemmt
~ dike sedimentärer Gang m
Neptunian theory, Neptunism Neptunismus m
neptunite Neptunit m, $Na_2FeTi[Si_4O_{12}]$
neritic neritisch, Flachsee...
~ facies Flachseefazies f
~ fauna Flachseefauna f
~ zone neritische Zone f, Flachseezone f
Nernst's rule Nernstsche Regel f

nesh weich, staubig, pulvrig
nesquehonite Nesquehonit m, $MgCO_3 \cdot 3H_2O$
ness Vorgebirge n, Landspitze f, Kap n
nest of ore Erznest n, Erztasche f
nested crater Krater m mit zentralen Bocchen
~ **sampling** s. cluster sampling
~ **volcano** Vulkan m mit zentralen Kegeln
net s. network
~ **pay thickness** Nettomächtigkeit f, effektive Mächtigkeit f
~ **production** Nettoförderung f
~ **radiation** Nettostrahlung f
~ **rainfall** Niederschlagsmenge f *(erreicht den Erdboden)*
~ **slip** wahre Schublänge f, totale Sprunghöhe f
nether coal untere Kohlenbank (Flözpartie) f *(eines mächtigen Kohlenflözes)*
netlike netzförmig
~ **stone soil** netzartiger Steinboden m
netted smaltite gestrickter Speiskobalt m, $CoAs_3$
~ **structure** Maschentextur f
netting Netzbildung f
network Netz[werk] n
~ **of faults** Verwerfungsnetz n
~ **of lodes** Gangverzweigung f
~ **of veins** Gangnetz n
~ **planning** Netzwerktechnik f
~ **structure** Netzwerkgefüge n
neutral plane Neutralebene f
~ **stress** s. pore-water pressure
~ **surface fold** s. flexure fold
neutralize/to neutralisieren
neutron activation analysis Neutronenaktivierungsanalyse f
~ **logging** Neutronenlog n, Neutronenmessung f
~-**neutron logging** Neutron-Neutron-Log n
Nevadan orogeny neva[di]dische Orogenese f
nevadyte grobkörniger Quarztrachit von Nevada
névé vereister Schnee m *(eines Gletschers)*, Firn m, Firnfeld n
~ **basin** Firnmulde f
~ **crevasse** Firnspalte f
~ **field** Firnfeld n
~ **glacier** Firngletscher m
~ **line** Firnlinie f
~ **penitente** Büßerschnee m
~ **region** Firngebiet n
~ **slope** Firnfeld n
never frozen soil Niefrostboden m
new field wildcat Erkundungsbohrung f auf unbekannte Lagerstätten
~ **global tectonics** neue Globaltektonik f, Geotektonik f, Plattentektonik f, gegenwärtige geotektonische Grundvorstellung f
~ **growth** Neusprossung f
~ **moon** Neumond m
~ **pool wildcat** Erkundungsbohrung f auf neues Lager *(in bekanntem Feld)*

New Red Rotliegendes n *(Fazies, Oberkarbon bis Mittelperm)*
~ **Zealand Subprovince** Neuseeland-Subprovinz f *(Paläobiogeografie, Devon)*
newberyite Newberyit m, $HMg[PO_4] \cdot 3H_2O$
n'hangellite N'hangellit m *(Bitumenart)*
Niagaran [Series] Niagara n, Niagarien n *(oberes Llandovery, Wenlock und unteres Budnanium Nordamerikas)*
nib sehr grobes Überkorn n
niccolite Niccolit m, Rotnickelkies m, Nickelin m, NiAs
niche kleine Höhle f *(hinter einem Wasserfall)*; Felsnische f
nickel Nickel n, Ni
~-**bearing** nickelführend
~ **bloom** s. annabergite
~ **glance** Nickelglanz m *(teils Gersdorffit, teils Ullmannit)*
~ **green** s. annabergite
~ **gymnite** s. genthite
~-**iron core** Nickel-Eisen-Kern m
~ **ochre** s. annabergite
~ **ore** Nickelerz n
~ **skutterudite** s. chloanthite
~ **vitriol** s. morenosite
nickeliferous nickelhaltig, nickelführend
~ **iron** Nickeleisen n
nickelous nickelhaltig
nickpoint Knickpunkt m *(im Gefälle)*
nicol [prism] Nicol[sches Prisma] n
nicopyrite s. pentlandite
nieve penitente Zackenfirn m, Büßerschnee m
nife Nife n *(Erdkern)*
nifontovite Nifontovit m, $CaB_2O_4 \cdot 2,3H_2O$
Niggli value Niggli-Wert m
niggliite Niggliit m, Pt(Su, Te)
night-time remote sensing Fernerkundung f zur Nachtzeit
nigrine Nigrin m (1. *Rutil mit viel Fe*; 2. *Ilmenit mit Rutil*)
nigrite s. asphalt, albertite
niobite Niobit m, $(Fe, Mn)(Nb, Ta)_2O_6$
niobium Niob n, Nb
nioboloparite Nioboloparit m, $(Na, Ce, Ca)(Ti, Nb)O_3$
niocalite Niocalit m, $Ca_3(Nb, Ca, Mg)[(O, F)_2|Si_2O_7]$
nip 1. kleines Kliff n, Absatz m; 2. Verdrückung f, Verquetschung f
~-**out** Verdrückung f, Verquetschung f
nipped verdrückt, eingeschnürt *(Gang)*
niton Niton n, Radon n, Radiumemanation f
nitrate Nitrat n
nitratine, nitratite s. soda nitre
nitre Kalisalpeter m, Nitrokalit m, KNO_3
nitric acid Salpetersäure f, HNO_3
nitrification Nitrierung f, Salpeterbildung f; Nitrifikation f
nitrifying bacteria Stickstoffbakterien fpl
nitrobarite Nitrobaryt m, Barytsalpeter m, $Ba(NO_3)_2$

nitrocalcite

nitrocalcite Nitrokalzit m, Kalksalpeter m, Ca[NO$_3$]$_2$·4H$_2$O
nitrogen Stickstoff m, N
~-poor stickstoffarm
nitromagnesite Nitromagnesit m, Magnesiasalpeter m, Mg(NO$_3$)$_2$·2H$_2$O
nitrous salpetrig
nittings Bleierzstückchen npl
nival nival, Schnee...
~ soil Frostboden m
nivation Firneisbildung f, Karbildung f, Zerkarung f, Schnee-Erosion f, Spaltenfrostwirkungen fpl
nivenite s. uraninite
niveo-aeolian nival-äolisch
NMO s. normal move-out
no pick nicht tiefenkorrelierbar (seismische Horizonte)
noble earths seltene Erden fpl
~ gas Edelgas n
~ metal Edelmetall n
~ opal Edelopal m
nobleite Nobleit m, Ca[B$_6$O$_9$(OH)$_2$]·3H$_2$O
nocerite Nocerin m, Mg$_3$[Fe$_3$|BO$_3$]
noctilucent nachtleuchtend
~ cloud nachtleuchtende Wolke f
nocturnal radiation nächtliche Strahlung f
nodal plane Knotenebene f
~ point Knotenpunkt m
noddle Knolle f, Niere f
node 1. Nest n, Niere f; 2. Höcker m (bei Fossilien); 3. Knoten m, Nodus m
~ of rock Felsklotz m
noded gehöckert, mit Knötchen versehen (Fossilschalen)
nodose Knötchen tragend
nodular warzig, knotenartig, knollig, klumpig, kugelig, knotenförmig
~ bedding knollige Schichtung f
~ galenite Bleiknottenerz n
~ graphite Kugelgraphit m
~ iron ore Knotteneisenerz n
~ limestone Knollenkalk m
~ manganese deposit Manganknollenlagerstätte f
~ ore Nierenerz n
~ sheet of flint Feuersteinband n
~ structure s. orbicular structure
nodule Knotte f, Knolle f, Galle f, Niere f, Druse f
~ of olivine Olivinknolle f
~ of ore Erzniere f
noduliferous Knollen enthaltend
nodulize/to pelletisieren, agglomerieren
nodulizing Pelletisierung f, Agglomerierung f
nodulous limestone Kalkknollenschiefer m
noise Rauschen n, Störpegel m
~-equivalent power äquivalente Rauschleistung f
~ profile Verwitterungsschießen n
nominal diameter Nenndurchmesser m
~ gross capacity Ausnahmelast f

~ load-bearing capacity Nennlast f
~ taxon nominelles Taxon n (Nomenklaturregeln)
non-absorbent hydrophob
~-absorbing schallhart (Seismik)
~-affine deformation nichtaffine Deformation f
~-angular unconformity Erosionsdiskordanz f
~-aqueous nichtwäßrig
~-artesian water ungespanntes Grundwasser n
~-associated natural gas freies Erdgas n
~-baking coal nichtbackende (nichtkokende) Kohle f
~-bedded ungeschichtet
~-caking coal nichtbackende (nichtkokende) Kohle f
~-calcareous kalkfrei
~-carbonaceous kohlefrei
~-clinkering coal schlackenreine Kohle f
~-cognate block s. accidental block
~-coherent soil, ~-cohesive soil nichtbindiger (kohäsionsloser) Boden m
~-coiling nicht aufgerollt
~-conformable diskordant
~-conformity Diskordanz f, Winkeldiskordanz f, ungleichförmige (diskordante) Lagerung f
~-conformity spring Diskordanzquelle f
~-coring diamond bit Diamantvollbohrkrone f
~-crystalline nichtkristallin
~-Darcy effect Abweichungseffekt m vom Darcy-Gesetz
~-Darcy flow Nicht-Darcy-Strömung f
~-depositional environment sedimentfeindliches Milieu n
~-diastrophic deformation atektonische Verformung f
~-dissociated undissoziiert
~-ductile undehnbar, unstreckbar
~-eddying strudellos, wirbelfrei
~-equilibrium instabil
~-equilibrium Ungleichgewicht n
~-equilibrium equation Instabilitätsgleichung f (Grundwasserströmung)
~-erodible erosionsfest
~-evident disconformity maskierte Diskordanz f
~-ferrous metal Buntmetall n, Nichteisenmetall n, NE-Metall n
~-fiery schlagwettersicher
~-fossiliferous fossilfrei
~-fuel minerals nichtenergetische Minerale npl
~-gaseous coal gasarme Kohle f
~-gasifiable nichtvergasbar
~-gassy mine schlagwetterfreie Grube f
~-glaciated unvergletschert
~-ideal gas reales (nicht ideales) Gas n
~-imaging sensor nichtabbildendes Aufnahmesystem n
~-indurated pan nicht verhärtete Schicht (Bodenschicht) f
~-isotropic material anisotrope Substanz f

~-leached nicht ausgelaugt
~-linearity Nichtlinearität f
~-luminous nichtleuchtend
~-magnetic unmagnetisch, nichtmagnetisch, antimagnetisch
~-magnetic drill collar nichtmagnetische Schwerstange f
~-metal Nichtmetall n
~-metallic nichtmetallisch
~-metallic mineral Nichterzmineral n
~-metallics Nichterze npl
~-miscible nicht mischbar
~-oriented nicht orientiert, richtungslos
~-paying mine Zubußzeche f
~-perennial nicht perennierend
~-periodic current unperiodische Strömung f
~-permitted explosive Gesteinssprengstoff m
~-piercement salt dome konkordant durchbrechender Salzdom m
~-plastic rollig (Boden)
~-plunging fold Falte f mit horizontaler Achse
~-polar unpolar
~-polarized unpolarisiert
~-porosity Porenlosigkeit f
~-radiating, ~-radiative nichtstrahlend
~-random orientation bevorzugte Orientierung f
~-recoverable oil Haftöl n
~-saline salzfrei
~-seismic aseismisch, erdbebenfrei
~-seismic region aseismische Region f
~-skeletal limestone Kalkstein m ohne Skelettelemente
~-stationary process instationärer Vorgang m (im Grundwasser)
~-steady nicht stationär
~-uniform ungleichförmig
~-uniform spring periodische Quelle f
~-viscous zähigkeitsfrei, dünnflüssig
~-volatile nichtflüchtig
~-wetting fluid nichtbenetzende Flüssigkeit f
nontronite Nontronit m (Mineral der Montmorillonitreihe)
norbergite Norbergit m, $Mg_3[(OH,F)_2SiO_4]$
nordenskioldine Nordenskiöldin m, $CaSn[BO_3]_2$
nordmarkite s. 1. staurolite; 2. alkali syenite
Norian [Stage] Nor n (Stufe der alpinen Trias)
norite Norit m (Varietät von Gabbro)
normal acceleration Normalbeschleunigung f
~ displacement seigere Sprunghöhe f
~ distribution Normalverteilung f
~ effective stress effektive Normalspannung f
~ fault Verwerfung f, Sprung m
~ fold symmetrische Falte f
~ gravity Normalschwere f (Schwerkraft in Meereshöhe)
~ limb aufrechter (hangender) Schenkel m (einer Falte)
~ load Normallast f
~ magnetic field magnetisches Normalfeld n
~ move-out normales Moveout n

~ position normale Lagerung f
~ ripple marks normale Rippelmarken fpl
~ rock pressure Überlagerungsdruck m, normaler Gebirgsdruck m
~ stress Normalspannung f
~ stress state Normalspannungszustand m
~ tension of ground Gebirgsnormalspannung f
~ to the stratification bankrecht
~ traction s. ~ stress
~ value of gravity Normalschwere f
normative mineral Standardmineral n
north frigid zone nördliche kalte Zone f
~ pole Nordpol m
~ temperate zone nördliche gemäßigte Zone f
norther Nordwind m
northerly nördlich (Wind)
northern dwarf podzol nördlicher Zwergpodsol m
~ lights Nordlicht n
~ limit of snowfall nördliche Schneegrenze f
~ semipodzol nordischer podsoliger Boden m
Northern nördlich (Gebiet)
~ hermisphere Nordhemisphäre f
northupite Northupit m, $Na_3Mg[Cl(CO_3)_2]$
nose 1. offene (abtauchende, halbentwickelte) Antiklinale f; 2. Umbiegungspunkt m einer gefalteten Schicht (auf der Karte); 3. Strukturvorsprung m
~-in stratum V-förmig [unter eine Bergseite] abtauchende Schicht f
~ of synclinal fold Muldenschluß n
~-out V-förmiger Schichtenausstrich m
nosean s. noselite
noselite Nosean m, $Na_8[SO_4(AlSiO_4)_6]$
not noticeable unmerklich (1. Stufe der Erdbebenstärkeskala)
Notal Realm notales Faunenreich n (Trias, Neuseeland)
notch/to auskehlen
notch 1. Einschnitt m, Scharte f (im Hochgebirge); 2. Brandungskehle f
~ effect Kerbwirkung f
~ filter Sperrfilter n, Bandsperre f
~ impact strength Schlagbiegefestigkeit f
notching Hohlkehlenbildung f
noumeite s. garnierite
nourishment area Nährgebiet n
~ of the glacier Ernährung f des Gletschers
novačekite Novačekit m, $Mg[UO_2|AsO_4]_2 \cdot 10H_2O$
novacite Novakit m, Cu_4As_3
novaculite Novaculit m (Hornsteinart)
novaculitic chert chalzedonischer Hornstein m
nsutite Nsutit m, $Mn_2(O, OH)_2$
nubbins Felsklötze mpl
nubble hügelförmiges Inselchen n
nuciform structure haselnußförmiges Gefüge n
nuclear area Kontinentalkern m
~ basin intramontanes Becken n

nuclear 244

~ **blasting** nukleare Sprengung f
~ **caving** Hohlraumbildung f durch Kernexplosion
~ **cavity storage** durch Kernexplosion entstandener Hohlraumspeicher m
~ **decay** Kernzerfall m
~ **disintegration** Kernzerfall m, Atomkernzerfall m
~ **fission** Kernspaltung f
~ **log** Radioaktivitätslog n
~ **magnetic resonance logging** kernmagnetische Resonanzmessung f
~ **precession magnetometer** Kernpräzessionsmagnetometer n
~ **process** Kernprozeß m
~ **radiation** Kernstrahlung f
~ **structure** Kernaufbau m
~ **synthesis** Kernsysnthese f
~ **waste[s] deposit** Lager n für radioaktive Abfälle
nuclearly stimulated gas reservoir durch Kernsprengung stimulierter Gasspeicher m
nucleation Bildung f von Kondensationskernen, Keimbildung f, Kernbildung f
~ **rate** Keimbildungsgeschwindigkeit f
nucleus Kern m, Keim m
~ **of condensation** Kondensationskern m
~ **of crystal** Kristallkeim m
~ **of crystallization** Kristallisationskern m
nug Knolle f; Block m
nugget 1. Klümpchen n, rundgescheuertes Korn n; 2. Nugget n, natürlicher Klumpen m (von gediegenem Metall)
~ **effect** Nuggeteffekt m (beschreibt den Einfluß sprunghafter, nuggetartiger Merkmalsänderungen im geologischen Feld)
~ **variance** Nuggetvarianz f
nuggeting Nuggetsuche f
nuggety nuggetähnlich, als Nugget vorkommend
~ **gold** klumpiges Gold n
number of boreholes Bohrlochanzahl f
~ **of degrees of freedom** Zahl f der Freiheitsgrade
~ **of strokes** Schlagzahl f
numerical aperture numerische Apertur f
nummulitic limestone Nummulitenkalk m
~ **sandstone** Nummulitensandstein m
Nummulitic [Epoch] s. Eocene
nunatak Nunatak m (eisfreier Hügel in Polargebieten)
nutrient content Nährstoffgehalt m
nutritive element Nährelement n
nutty structure haselnußförmige Struktur f
nyerereite Nyerereit m, $Na_2Ca[CO_3]_2$

O

oasis Oase f
obconic[al] invers konisch
obelisk Lavadorn m, Felsnadel f

object carrier Objektträger m
~-**glass carrier** Objektivträger m
~ **marker** Objektmarkierer m
~ **of geological prospecting** geologisches Untersuchungsobjekt n
~ **slide (support)** Objektträger m
~-**support lamina (slide)** Objektträgerplättchen n
objective Objektiv n
oblate abgeplattet
~ **spheroid** Rotationsellipsoid n
oblateness Abplattung f
~ **of the earth** Erdabplattung f
oblique schief
~ **bedding** Schrägschichtung f, Diagonalschichtung f, Transversalschichtung f
~ **fault** diagonale (schräge, spießeckige) Verwerfung f, Diagonalverwerfung f
~ **fold** s. cross fold
~ **girdle pattern** Schiefgürtelregelungsbild n
~ **joint** Diagonalkluft f
~ **lamination** Transversalschichtung f, Schrägschichtung f, falsche Schieferung f
~ **load** Schrägbelastung f
~ **slip fault** Verwerfung f mit diagonaler Verschiebung
~ **system** monoklines System n (Kristallografie)
~ **truncation** basaler Schrägzuschnitt m (einer Deckenbasis)
obliquely bedded schräg geschichtet, schrägschichtig
obliquity of illumination Schräglichtbeleuchtung f
~ **of the ecliptic** Schiefe f der Ekliptik
obruchevite Obruchevit m, $(Y,Na,Ca)_2(Nb, Ti,Ta)_2O_6(O, OH, F)$
obscuration Verdunklung f
obscure bedding undeutliche Schichtung f
obscured exposure verdeckter Aufschluß m
obscurely crystalline undeutlich kristallin[isch]
obsequent obsequent, entgegen dem Schichtfallen fließend
~ **stream** obsequenter Fluß m
observation Beobachtung f
~ **angle** Beobachtungswinkel m
~ **balloon** Beobachtungsballon m
~ **error** Ablesefehler m
~ **grid** Festpunktnetz n
~ **instrument** Beobachtungsinstrument n
~ **line** Meßlinie f
~ **pipe** Beobachtungsrohr n (im Grundwasserleiter)
~ **point** Festpunkt m
~ **station** Beobachtungsstation f
~ **well** 1. Beobachtungsbohrung f; 2. Beobachtungsbrunnen m
observational material Beobachtungsmaterial n
~ **place** Beobachtungsort m
observatory 1. Wetterwarte f; 2. Observatorium n, Sternwarte f

observe with the naked eye/to mit bloßem Auge beobachten
observed altitude Beobachtungshöhe *f*
~ data Beobachtungsdaten *pl*
observer Beobachter *m*
observing station Beobachtungsstation *f*
obsidian Obsidian *m (natürliches Glas)*
obsidianite Australit *m (Tektitenglas)*
obstacle marks Hindernismarken *fpl*
obtuse angle stumpfer Winkel *m*
occipital Occipital..., Nacken ... *(bei Arthropoden)*
~ lobe Occipitalfurche *f (bei Trilobiten)*
occlude/to einschließen, okkludieren
occluded gas eingeschlossenes Gas *n*
occlusion Einschluß *m*, Okklusion *f*
~ water Okklusionswasser *n*
occult/to sich verfinstern
occultation Verfinsterung *f*
occur/to auftreten, vorkommen *(Lagerstätten)*
occurrence Auftreten *n*, Vorkommen *n (von Lagerstätten)*
~ in beds lagerförmiges Vorkommen *n*
~ in floors stockförmiges Vorkommen *n*
~ in pockets nesterförmiges Vorkommen *n*
~ in veins gangförmiges Vorkommen *n*
ocean Ozean *m*, Weltmeer *n*
~ basin Ozeanbecken *n*
~-basin floor Ozeanbeckengrund *m*
~ beach Meeresstrand *m*
~ bed Meeresgrund *m*
~ bottom *s.* **~ floor**
~ breeze Seewind *m*
~ climate Seeklima *n*
~ current Meeresströmung *f*, ozeanische Strömung *f*
~ depth Meerestiefe *f*
~ exploration Meeresforschung *f*
~ floor Meeresgrund *m*, Meeresboden *m*
~-floor manganese nodules Manganknollen *fpl* des Ozeanbodens
~-floor metamorphism Metamorphose *f* der ozeanischen Kruste, Ozeanbodenmetamorphose *f*
~-floor topography Geomorphologie *f* des Meeresgrundes
~ mining maritime Rohstoffgewinnung *f*, unterseeischer Abbau *m*
~ ridge ozeanischer Rücken *m*
~ shore Meeresstrand *m*
~ temperature Meerestemperatur *f*
~ water Meerwasser *n*
Oceania Ozeanien *n*
oceanic ozeanisch, Ozean..., Meeres...
~ abyss Tiefsee *f*
~ bank Guyot *m (abgestumpfter Tiefseeberg)*
~ basin Ozeanbecken *n*
~ climate ozeanisches Klima *n*
~ crust ozeanische Kruste *f*
~ deep Tiefseegraben *m*
~ deposit ozeanische (eupelagische) Ablagerung *f*, Hochseeablagerung *f*

~ island ozeanische Insel *f*
~ level Meeresspiegel *m*
~ retreat Meeresregression *f*
oceanite Ozeanit *m (Olivinbasalt)*
oceanity Ozeanität *f*
oceanographer Ozeanograf *m*
oceanographic[al] ozeanografisch, meereskundlich
~ exploration Meeresforschung *f*
~ sounding Tiefseelotung *f*
oceanography Ozeanografie *f*, Meereskunde *f*, Meeresforschung *f*
oceanologic[al] ozeanologisch, meereskundlich
oceanologist Ozeanologe *m*
oceanology Ozeanologie *f*, Meeresforschung *f*
ocellar structure Ozellartextur *f*, kelyphitische Textur *f*
ocellus sphärolithisches Mineralaggregat *n*, Auge *n*
ocher *s.* ochre
ocherous *s.* ochreous
ochery *s.* ochrey
Ochoan Ochoan *n (höchstes Oberperm in Nordamerika)*
ochre Berggelb *n*, Ocker *m*, Eisenocker *m*
~ schist Ockerschiefer *m*
~-yellow ockergelb
ochreous ockerartig, ockerig, ockerhaltig
~ clay ockerhaltiger Ton *m*
~ deposit eisenhaltige Ablagerung *f*
~ iron ore ockeriger Brauneisenstein *m*, Eisenocker *m*
~ mud Ockerschlamm *m*
~ rock Ockergestein *n*
ochrey ockerfarben
~ brown iron ore Brauneisenerz *n*
~-clay ockeriger Ton *m*
ochrolite Ochrolith *m (s.a. nadorite)*
ochrous *s.* ochreous
ochry *s.* ochrey
octadecagon Achtzehneck *n*, Achtflach *n*
octaedrite 1. *s.* anatase; 2. Oktaedrit *m (Meteorit)*
octagon Achteck *n*
octagonal achteckig
octahedral oktaedrisch, achtflächig, achtseitig
~ cleavage oktaedrische Spaltbarkeit *f*
~ coordination oktaedrische Koordination *f*, Sechserkoordination *f*
~ face Oktaederfläche *f*
~ iron *s.* magnetite
~ layer (sheet) Oktaederschicht *f*
octahedrite *s.* octaedrite
octahedron Oktaeder *n*, Achtflächner *m*
octavalent achtwertig
octave Oktave *f*
ocular Okular *n*
~ micrometer Okularmikrometer *n*
Oddo-Harkins rule Oddo-Harkinssche Regel *f*
odinite Odinit *m (basische Schliere in Granitoiden)*
odontolite Zahntürkis *m*

oersted

oersted Oersted n *(alte Einheit der magnetischen Feldstärke, 1 Oe = 10^5 nT)*
off-colour leicht getönt *(Edelsteine)*
~-end spread einseitige Aufstellung f *(z.B. von Geophonen)*
~-lap zurückbleibende Lagerung f, regressive Schichtlagerung f
~-reef basin s. interreef basin
~-reef facies s. reef talus
~-shoot 1. Ausläufer m, Apophyse f; 2. Ausstülpung f
~-shooting tongue Ausläufer m, Apophyse f
~-spring Abkömmling m
~-structure außerhalb der Struktur
~-time Förderstillstand m
offlap s. off-lap
offretite Offretit m, (Ca, Na, K)$_2$[Al$_3$Si$_9$O$_{24}$]·9H$_2$O
offset verstellt
offset 1. kürzeste horizontale Distanz der Ausbisse einer verworfenen Schicht; 2. Seitenverstellung f; 3. kurzer Querschlag m; 4. kleine Abzweigung f *(eines Gangs oder Gebirgszugs)*; 5. Schußpunktentfernung f
~ **area** Schutzgebiet n
~ **of the bed** Ausläufer m, Apophyse f
~ **well** Schutzsonde f; Nachbarsonde f
offshoot s. off-shoot
offshore 1. ablandig, küstenfern; 2. auf dem Schelf gelegen
offshore Schelf m unterhalb der tiefsten Brandungseinwirkung
~ **activitiy** Bohrtätigkeit f in Küstennähe
~ **bar** küstenparallele Unterwassersandbank f, vorgelagerter (freier) Strandwall m, Lido m, Unterwasserriff n
~ **beach** s. ~ bar
~ **breeze** Landwind m, ablandiger Wind m
~ **clay** Basisschichten fpl *(von Sinkstoffen in Deltas)*
~ **crib** Bohrinsel f
~ **deposit** küstennahe Ablagerung f
~ **drilling** Bohren n vor der Meeresküste, Bohren n in der See, Unterwasserbohren n
~ **drilling barge (platform)** schwimmende Bohranlage f, mobile Bohrinsel f, Bohrplattform f
~ **electrical prospection** elektrische Prospektion f im Meer
~ **lease** Gerechtsame f vor der Küste
~ **location** Bohransatzpunkt m in Küstennähe
~ **oil** Offshore-Erdöl n
~ **oil field** küstennahes Erdölfeld n
~ **oil rig** Bohrinsel f, Meeresbohranlage f
~ **production** küstennahe Förderung f
~ **sand bar** Sandriff n
~ **sandbody** Schelfsandkörper m
~ **seismics** Seeseismik f
~ **slope** meeresseitige Böschung f
~ **spit** Haken m *(Beginn einer Nehrung)*
~ **suction dredge** Saugbagger m für Offshore-Betrieb
~ **supply** Offshore-Versorgung f

~ **surveys** geophysikalische Schelferkundung f
~ **technology** Meerestechnik f
~ **waters** Schelfmeer n, Flachsee f, Küstengewässer n
~ **wind** Landwind m, ablandiger Wind m
offtake 1. Unterwasserkanal m, Abzugskanal m; 2. Förderung f
~ **drift** Wasserlösungsstollen m
ogive Ogive f, spitzbogiges Schmutzband n *(Gletscherbänder mit Geschiebe)*
Öhningian [Stage] Öhningium n *(kontinentale Stufe des Pliozäns)*
oil Erdöl n *(s.a. petroleum)*
~ **accumulation** Erdölakkumulation f
~ **asphalt** Erdölasphalt m
~ **bank** Erdölbank f
~-**base mud** ölbasische Spülung f
~-**basin** Erdölbecken n
~-**bearing** erdölführend, erdölhaltig
~-**bearing bed** Erdölschicht f
~-**bearing capacity** mögliche Erdölführung f
~-**bearing formation** erdölführende Formation f
~-**bearing limestone** Ölkalk m
~-**bearing series** erdölführende Schichtenfolge f
~-**bearing stratum** erdölführende Schicht f
~-**bearing structure** erdölführende Struktur f
~ **belt** Erdölgürtel m
~ **coal** s. stellarite
~ **concession** Erdölkonzession f
~-**containing** erdölführend, erdölhaltig
~ **deposit** Erdöllagerstätte f
~ **derrick** Erdölbohrturm m
~ **district** Erdölgebiet n
~ **drilling vessel** Erdölbohrschiff n
~ **excitement** Ölgeschrei n
~ **extraction** Erdölgewinnung f
~ **exudation** Ausschwitzung f von Erdöl
~ **field** Erdölfeld n, Erdöllagerstätte f
~-**field gathering system** Erdölfeldleitungssystem n
~ **finding** Erdölexploration f
~-**forming** erdölbildend
~ **gas** Erdgas n
~ **gas tar** Erdölgasteer m
~ **gasification** Erdölvergasung f
~ **geologist** Erdölgeologe m
~ **geology** Erdölgeologie f
~ **grant** Konzession f zur Aufsuchung von Erdöllagerstätten
~ **horizon** erdölführender Horizont m
~ **hydrogeology** Erdölhydrogeologie f
~ **immersion** Ölimmersion f
~-**impregnated** ölgetränkt, ölimprägniert, öldurchtränkt
~ **in palce** Erdölvorrat m
~ **indication** Erdölanzeichen n
~ **influx** Erdölzulauf m
~ **leakage** Erdölaustritt m
~ **lease** Erdölgerechtsame f
~ **leg** Öllager n unter Gaskappe

~ **lens** erdölhaltige Sandlinse *f*
~ **maturity** Erdölreife *f*
~ **maturity stage** Erdölreifestadium *n*
~ **measure** erdölführendes Flöz *n*
~ **mine** Erdölbergwerk *n*, Erdölgrube *f*
~ **mining** Erdölbergbau *m*, Erdölschachtbau *m*
~ **occurrence** Erdölvorkommen *n*
~ **pipeline** Erdölfernleitung *f*
~ **plant** Erdölraffinerie *f*
~ **pool** Erdöllagerstätte *f*, Erdölakkumulation *(bezogen auf einen Speicher)*
~ **pool waters** Erdöllagerstättenwasser *npl*
~ **producer** Erdölfördersonde *f*
~ **production** Erdölförderung *f*
~ **production outfit** Erdölgewinnungsanlage *f*
~-**proof** erdöldicht, erdölundurchlässig
~ **property** Erdölgerechtsame *f*, Bergwerkseigentum *n* auf Erdöl
~ **prospecting** Erdölprospektion *f*
~ **recovery** 1. Erdölgewinnung *f*; 2. Entölung *f*
~ **region** Erdölgebiet *n*
~ **reservoir rock** Erdölspeichergestein *n*
~ **rig vessel** Bohrschiff *n*
~ **rights** Erdöl[ausbeutungs]rechte *npl*
~ **rock** erdölhaltiges Gestein *n*
~ **sandstone** Ölsandstein *m*
~-**saturated** erdölgesättigt
~-**saturated sand** erdölgesättigter Sand *m*
~ **saturation** Erdölsättigung *f*
~ **search** Erdölsuche *f*
~ **seep[age]** Erdölaustritt *m*, Erdölaustrittsstelle *f*, Erdölsickerstelle *f*
~ **separation** Erdölabscheidung *f*
~ **shale** Ölschiefer *m*
~ **sheet** Erdöllagerstätte *f*
~ **show** Ölanzeichen *n*
~ **shrinkage** Erdölschrumpfung *f*
~ **sludge** Erdölschlamm *m*
~ **source rock** Erdölmuttergestein *n*
~ **spotting around the drilling string** Ölwanne *f*
~ **spring** Erdölquelle *f*
~ **stain** Erdölfleck *m*
~-**stained** erdölfleckig
~ **storer** erdölspeichernde Schicht *f*
~ **strata** Erdölschichten *fpl*
~ **tar** Erdölteer *m*
~ **trace** Erdölspur *f*
~ **trap** Erdölfalle *f*
~-**water contact** Erdöl-Wasser-Kontakt *m*, Randwasserspiegel *m*
~-**water interface** Erdöl-Wasser-Grenzfläche *f*
~-**water surface** Erdöl-Wasser-Grenze *f*
~-**water zone** Erdöl-Wasser-Zone *f*
~ **well** Erdölquelle *f*, Erdölbohrung *f*, ölführende Bohrung *f*
~-**well blowing** Erdölausbruch *m*
~-**well cement** Tiefbohrzement *m*
~-**well derrick** Bohrturm *m* für Erdölbohrungen
~-**well drill** Erdölbohrgerät *n*
~-**well drilling** Erdölbohrung *f*

~-**well microorganisms** Erdölbakterien *fpl*
~-**well shooting** Torpedieren [einer Erdölbohrung]
~-**well surveying instrument** Erdölsondenmeßgerät *n*
~-**wet reservoir** ölnasser Speicher *m*
~ **withdrawal** Erdölentzug *m*, Erdölentnahme *f*
~ **zone** Erdölzone *f*
oilless erdölfrei
oilsand (Am) 1. Speichergestein *n*; 2. Erdölsand *m*
oily erdölhaltig
okaite Okait *m (basisches Gestein mit Feldspatvertretern)*
okenite Okenit, $Ca_{1,5}[Si_3O_6(OH)_3] \cdot 1^1/_2H_2O$
old age Greisenalter *n (geomorphologisch)*
~-**age valley** überreifes Tal *n*
~-**aged** alt *(geomorphologisch)*
~ **branch** Altarm *m (eines Flusses)*
~ **course** altes Flußbett *n*
~ **excavation** Alter Mann *(abgeworfene Grubenbaue)*
~ **landmass** Altland *n*
~ **plain** *s.* peneplain
~ **snow** Altschnee *m*
~-**volcanic** altvulkanisch
~-**volcanic rock** altvulkanisches Gestein *n*
Old Palaeolithic [Times] Altpaläolithikum *n*
~ **Red** Old Red *n (devonische Molasse-Formation)*
~-**Red Continent** Old-Red-Kontinent *m*
~ **Stone Age** Paläolithikum *n*
~ **Tertiary [Age]** Alttertiär *n*
older moraine Altmoräne *f*
oldhamite Oldhamit *m*, CaS
oldland Altland *n*, Abtragungsgebiet *n*
oleaginous erdölhaltig
olefiant gas ölbildendes Gas *n*, Äthylen *n*, C_2H_4
oleiferous erdölhaltig
Olenekian [Stage] Olenek *n (Stufe, Untere Trias, Tethys)*
Olenellid Realm Olenellus-Reich *n (Paläobiogeografie, Unterkambrium)*
oleogenesis Erdölbildung *f*
oleostatic mit natürlichem Lagerstättendruck *(Erdöl)*
oligiste iron [ore] *s.* haematite
Oligocene [Epoch, Series] Oligozän *n (Serie des Tertiärs)*
oligoclase Oligoklas *m (Mischkristall von $NaAlSi_3O_8$ und $CaAl_2Si_2O_8$)*
oligohaline oligohalin
oligon spar *s.* siderite
oligotrophic oligotroph, nährstoffarm
olistoglyph Gleitmarke *f (von Sandstein auf Ton)*
olistolith Olistolith *m (exotischer Block in Olistostromen)*
olistostrome Olistostrom *n*, Gravitationsgleitmasse *f*
olive ore *s.* olivenite

oliveiraite

oliveiraite Oliveirait m, 3ZrO$_2$·2TiO$_2$·2H$_2$O
olivenite Olivenit m, Cu$_2$[OH|AsO$_4$]
olivine Olivin m, Peridot m, Chrysolith m, (Mg, Fe)$_2$[SiO$_4$]
~ **basalt** Olivinbasalt m
~ **nodule** Olivinknolle f
~ **rock** Dunit m
olivinite Olivinit m (Varietät von Hornblendepikrit)
ollenite Ollenit m (Hornblendeschiefer)
ollite s. soapstone
ombrogenous peat Torf, dessen Charakter vom Niederschlagsbetrag bestimmt wird
ombrograph Regenschreiber m
ombrometer Regenmesser m
omission Unterdrückung f
~ **of beds** Schichtenausfall m, Schichtenunterdrückung f (an einer Verwerfung)
omitted size fraction Auslaßkörnung f
omphacite Omphacit m, (Ca, Na)(Mg, Fe, Al)[Si$_2$O$_6$]
on-dip fallend
oncolite 1. Onkolith m (Gestein aus Onkoiden); 2. Onkoid n (als Einzelkorn)
oncoming of water Vordringen n des Randwassers (im Ölträger)
~ **wave** ankommende (einfallende) Welle f
one-celled animal Einzeller m
~-**dimensional flow** eindimensionale Strömung f
~-**dimensional trend** Kurventrend m
~-**phase system** Einstoffsystem n
~-**sided** einseitig
~-**way time** einfache Laufzeit f
Onesquethawan [Stage] Onesquethawen n (oberes Siegen bis Eifel in Nordamerika)
onion-skin exfoliation zwiebelschalige Abblätterung f
~ **weathering** schalige Verwitterung f
onkilonite Onkilonit m (Olivinnephelinit)
onlap/to übergreifen
onlap Submergenzdecke f, übergreifende Lagerung f
onofrite Onofrit m, Hg(S, Se)
Onondaga Group Onondaga n, Onondaga-Gruppe f (Eifel in Nordamerika)
onset Einsatz m (Seismogramm)
onshore auf dem Festland, landseitig (von der See gesehen)
onshore Festland n
~ **breeze** Seebrise f
~ **reef** Küstenriff n, Strandriff n
~ **seismics** Landseismik f
~ **well** Bohrung f auf dem Festland
~ **wind** Seewind m, auflandiger Wind m
Ontarian Ontarien n (tieferes Altpräkambrium in Nordamerika)
ontogenesis Ontogenese f
ontogenetic[al] ontogenetisch
ontogeny Ontogenese f
onychite 1. geaderter Alabaster; 2. geaderter Kalzit

onyx Onyx m (s.a. chalcedony)
oocastic schaumkalkartig, porös durch Ooidauslösung
ooid eiförmig
ooid Ooid n
oolicastic s. oocastic
oolite 1. Oolith m (Gestein aus Ooiden); 2. s. ooid
oolitic oolithisch
~ **iron ore** oolithisches Eisenerz n
~ **lime** Oolithkalk m
~ **limestone** oolithischer Kalkstein m, Kalkoolith m
~ **texture** oolithische Struktur f
oolitoid grains oolitoide Körner npl (ohne Interngefüge)
oomicrite oolithischer Mikrit m
oomicrudite oolithischer Mikrit m mit Ooiden <1mm
oomouldic porosity Oolithhohlformporosität f
oomoulds Negative npl von Ooiden
oopellet Oopellet n (mit pelletoidem Interngefüge)
oosparite oolithischer Sparit m
oosparrudite oolithischer Sparit n mit Ooiden >1mm
oovoids Poren fpl in unvollständig verdrängten Ooiden
ooze away/to versickern
~ **out** heraussickern, durchsickern
ooze Schlamm m, Schlick m; hauptsächlich aus Skelettresten von Mikroorganismen bestehende pelagische Sedimente
oozing Durchsickerung f, Aussickerung f
~-**out** Ausschwitzung f
oozy schlammig, schlickerig
opacite Opazit m (mikroskopische Opaksubstanz)
opacity Undurchsichtigkeit f
opal Opal m, SiO$_2$ + aq, amorph
~ **jasper** Jaspopal m
opalesce/to opalisieren
opalescence Opaleszenz f, Opalisieren n
opalescent opalisierend
opaline opalartig
~ **iridescence** Opalisieren n
opalized wood silifiziertes Holz n (mit Opal durchsetzt)
opaque opak, [licht]undurchlässig, undurchsichtig, trübe
~ **attritus** Durit m (im weiteren Sinne)
~ **to light** lichtundurchlässig
opaqueness Undurchsichtigkeit f, Lichtundurchlässigkeit f
opdalite Opdalit m (Abart von Hypersthendiorit)
open up/to aufschließen, erschließen
open channel offenes Gerinne n
~-**channel flow** Strömung f in offenen Gerinnen
~ **condition of surface** freie Oberfläche f
~ **diggings** Tagebau m, Pingenbau m

~ fault klaffende Verwerfung f
~-flow delivery Ergiebigkeit f einer Sonde
~ flow of well Vollergiebigkeit f einer Sonde
~-flow potential (Am) freie Förderrate f
~-flow test Messung f bei offenem Bohrloch
~ fold flache Falte f
~ gash fractures Fiederspalten fpl
~-grained großlückig
~ gutter offenes Gerinne n
~ hole unverrohrtes Bohrloch n, unverrohrte (freie) Sonde f
~-hole completion Komplettierung f mit offenem Speicher
~ joint offene Spalte f
~ lake See m mit Ausfluß
~-lake current Ausfluß m aus Seen
~ ocean offener Ozean m, offene See f
~ pit Tagebau m
~-pit bank Tagebaustoß m
~-pit bottom Tagebausohle f
~-pit bottom outline untere Tagebaugrenze f
~-pit boundary Tagebaugrenze f
~-pit coal mining Kohlentagebau m
~-pit field Tagebaufeld n
~-pit mining Gewinnung f m Tagebau
~-pit top outline obere Tagebaugrenze f
~ sand gut durchlässiger Sand m
~ sea offene (hohe) See f
~ space Hohlraum m
~-space structures Hohlraumgefüge npl (in Karbonatgesteinen mit interner Sedimentation)
~ stope versatzloser Firstenbau m
~ stope with pillar Pfeilerbau m, Abbau m in regelmäßigen Abständen
~ system offenes System n
~ working Tagebau m
opencast Tagebau m
~ coal Tagebaukohle f
~ coal mine Kohlentagebau m
~ development Tagebauaufschluß m
~ lignite mine Braunkohlentagebau m
~ mining Gewinnung f im Tagebau
~ ore mine Erztagebau m
~ working Tagebau m
opencasting Tagebau m
opencut s. opencast
openhole s. open hole
opening Aufschluß m; Ausrichtung f
~ hole Mundloch n
~ in mineral beds, ~-up Aufschluß m; Ausrichtung f
~ pressure Anfangsdruck m
operational sampling Probenahme f während des Niederbringens (einer Bohrung)
operator Registrierer m (Seismik)
ophicalcite Ophikalzit m
ophidite Prasinit m
ophiolite Ophiolith m
~ suite Ophiolithserie f
ophite Ophit m
ophitic ophitisch, divergentstrahlig
~ texture ophitische Struktur f, ophitisches Gefüge n

ophthalmite Ophthalmit m
ophthalmitic structure ophthalmitische Textur f, Augentextur f
Oppel zone biostratigrafische Einheit, gekennzeichnet durch die vertikale Verbreitung mehrerer ausgewählter Elemente aus einer Gesamtfauna oder -flora
opposing force Gegenkraft f
oppressive weather Schwüle f
optic optisch (s.a. optical)
~ angle Achsenwinkel m
~ axial angle optischer Achsenwinkel m
~ axis optische Achse f
~ axis of symmetry optische Symmetrieachse f
~ indicatrix optische Indikatrix f
~ plane Achsenebene f
optical optisch (s.a. optic)
~ activity optische Aktivität f (Fähigkeit, die Polarisationsebene zu drehen)
~ behaviour optisches Verhalten n
~ calcite optischer Kalkspat m, Doppelspat m, Islandspat m
~ constant optische Konstante f
~ crystallogy Kristalloptik f
~ double refraction optische Doppelbrechung f
~-mechanical scanner optisch-mechanischer Linienabtaster m
~ microscope Lichtmikroskop n
~ refraction Lichtbrechung f
~ rotation Drehpolarisation f, optische Drehung f
~ rotatory power optisches Drehungsvermögen n
~ thickness optische Dicke f (z.B. der Atmosphäre)
~ transfer function optische Übertragungsfunktion f
optically active compound optisch aktive Verbindung f
~ biaxial optisch zweiachsig
~ isotropic optisch isotrop
~ negative optisch negativ
~ positive optisch positiv
~ pumped magnetometer Kernabsorptionsmagnetometer n
~ uniaxial optisch einachsig
optimization Optimierung f
optimum annular return velocity of mud optimale Aufstiegsgeschwindigkeit f der Spülung
~ filter Optimalfilter n
~ horizontal wide band stack Verfahren n des verbesserten Stapelns von Mehrspurfiltern (Seismik)
orbicular kugelig, sphäroidisch
~ diorite Kugeldiorit m
~ granite Kugelgranit m
~ structure sphäroidische Textur f, Augentextur f, Kugeltextur f
orbicule Kugel f

orbiculite

orbiculite Orbikulit *m*
orbit/to umkreisen, sich auf einer Kreisbahn bewegen
orbit Bahn *f*, Umlaufbahn *f*, Kreisbahn *f*, Planetenbahn *f*
~ **of earth** Erdbahn *f*
~ **of moon** Mondbahn *f*
~ **of planet** Planetenbahn *f*
~ **of sun** Sonnenbahn *f*
orbital Bahn...
~ **moment** Bahnmoment *n*
~ **motion** Orbitalbewegung *f*, Umlaufbewegung *f*
~ **period** Umlaufzeit *f*, Umlaufperiode *f*
~ **plane** Bahnebene *f*
~ **revolution** Bahnumdrehung *f*
~ **velocity** Bahngeschwindigkeit *f*
Orcadian Orcadien *n*, Orcadium *n*, Mittleres Old Red *n* *(Mitteldevon, Old Red-Fazies)*
orcelite Orcelit *m*, $Ni_{<5}As_2$
ordauchite Ordauchit *m* *(olivinführender Haüyntephrit)*
order Ordnung *f*
~ **of age** Altersfolge *f*
~ **of crystallization** Kristallisationsfolge *f*, Kristallisationsreihe *f*
~ **of magnitude** Größenordnung *f*
~ **of superposition** Übereinanderfolge *f*, Schichtenfolge *f*
ordinary light unpolarisiertes Licht *n*
~ **ray** ordentlicher Strahl *m*
~ **trend** gewöhnlicher Trend *m*
ordoñezite Ordoñezit *m*, $ZnSb_2O_6$
Ordovician Ordovizium[system] *n* *(chronostratigrafisch)*; Ordovizium *n*, Ordoviziumperiode *f* *(geochronologisch)*; Ordovizium *n*, Ordoviziumzeit *f* *(allgemein)*
~ **Age** Ordovizium *n*, Ordoviziumzeit *f*
~ **Period** Ordovizium *n*, Ordoviziumperiode *f*
~ **System** Ordovizium[system] *n*
ore Erz *n*
~ **allotment** Erzfeld *n*
~ **assaying** Erzanalyse *f*
~-**bearing** erzhaltig, erzführend
~-**bearing shale** Erzschiefer *m*
~ **bed** Erzlager *n*
~ **benefication** Erzaufbereitung *f*
~ **body** Erzvorkommen *n*, Erzstock *m*, Erzkörper *m*
~ **boulder** erratischer Erzblock *m*
~ **breaking** Erzabbau *m*
~ **bunch** Erznest *n*, Erztasche *f*
~ **capping** Eiserner Hut *m*
~ **caving** Erzbruchbau *m*
~ **chamber** Erzkammer *f*
~ **chimney** Erzschlauch *m*
~ **chute** Erzrolle *f*
~ **concentration** Erzanreicherung *f*
~ **crusher** Erzbrecher *m*
~ **crushing** Erzzerkleinerung *f*
~ **deposit** Erzlagerstätte *f*, Erzvorkommen *n*
~ **dilution** Erzverunreinigung *f*
~ **district** Erzrevier *n*
~ **dressing** Erzaufbereitung *f*
~ **dressing plant** Erzaufbereitungsanlage *f*
~ **dry** Erzfall *m*
~ **enrichment** Erzanreicherung *f*
~ **field** Erzfeld *n*
~ **for crushing** Walzerz *n*
~ **formation** Erzformation *f*; Erzbildung *f*
~-**forming** erzbildend
~-**forming solution** erzbildende Lösung *f*
~ **from tailings** Haldenerz *n*
~ **genesis** Erzentstehung *f*, Erzgenese *f*
~ **geology** Erzlagerstättenkunde *f*
~ **grade** Erzqualität *f*
~ **groups** Erznieren *fpl*
~ **handling** Erzbehandlung *f (Aufbereitung)*
~ **in grains** Graupenerz *n*
~ **in pieces** Stufferz *n*, Stufenerz *n*
~ **in place (sight)** anstehendes Erz *n*
~ **knot** Vererzungsknoten *m*
~ **leaching** Erzlaugung *f*
~ **lode** Erzgang *m*
~ **losses** Erzverluste *mpl*
~ **magma** Erzmagma *n*
~ **mass** Roherz *n*
~ **microscope** Erzmikroskop *n*
~ **mine** Erzbergwerk *n*
~ **mineral** Erzmineral *n*
~ **mining** Erzbergbau *m*, Erzabbau *m*
~ **mining industry** Erzbergbau *m*
~ **nodules** Erznieren *fpl*
~ **occurrence** Erzvorkommen *n*
~ **pipe** Erzschlauch *m*
~ **pocket** Erznest *n*, Erztasche *f*
~ **precipitation** Erzabscheidung *f*
~ **quality** Erzgüte *f*
~ **reserves** Erzvorräte *mpl*
~ **rough from the mine** Grubenerz *n*, Fördererz *n*
~ **separation** Erzaufbereitung *f*; Erzabscheidung *f*
~ **separator** Erzscheider *m*
~ **sheet** derbes Erztrum *n*
~ **shoot** Erzfall *m*, Erzschlauch *m*, Erztasche *f*, reiches Mittel *n*
~ **sludge** Erzschlamm *m*
~ **smelting** Erzverhüttung *f*
~ **solution** Erzlösung *f*
~ **sorting** Erzscheiden *n*
~ **stock** Erzvorrat *m*
~ **testing** Erzprobenahme *f*
~ **trap** Erzfalle *f*
~ **treatment** Erzverhüttung *f*
~ **valuation** Erzbewertung *f*
~ **vein** Erzgang *m*
~ **washing** Erzschlämmen *n*, Erzwaschen *n*
~ **washing plant** Erzwäscherei *f*
~ **winning** Erzförderung *f*
~ **yield** Erzausbringen *n*
~ **zone** Erzzone *f*
oregonite Oregonit *m*, Ni_2FeAs_2
Orellan [Stage] Orellan *n* *(Wirbeltierstufe, oberes Oligozän in Nordamerika)*

Orenburgian [Stage] Orenburg[ium] n *(höchste Stufe des Oberkarbons in Osteuropa)*
orendite Orendit m *(Kalimafit)*
orey erzhaltig, Erz enthaltend
organic organisch
~ **acid** organische Säure f
~ **carbon** organischer Kohlenstoff m
~ **geochemistry** organische Geochemie f
~ **lattice** organisches Gerüst n *(biogenes In-situ-Gerüst bei Riffbildung)*
~ **limestone** s. biogenic limestone
~ **matter** organische Substanz (Materie) f, organische (organogene) Stoffe mpl
~ **remains** organische Überreste mpl
~ **rock** organogenes Gestein n
~ **silt** Mudde f, Mudd m
~ **soil** Humusboden m
organoclay organische Substanz führender Ton m
organogenetic organogen[etisch] *(s.a. organogenic)*
organogenic organogen[etisch]
~ **rock** organogenes Gestein n
~ **sediments** organogene Sedimente npl
organogenous organogen[etisch] *(s.a. organogenic)*
organometallic compounds metallorganische Verbindungen fpl
orient/to orientieren
~ **strongly** einregeln
orient Sonnenaufgang m
oriental emerald grüne Korundvarietät f *(Edelstein)*
~ **topaz** gelbe Korundvarietät f *(Edelstein)*
orientate/to s. orient/to
orientation Ausrichtung f, Einregelung f
~ **diagram** Gefügediagramm n, Regelungsdiagramm n
oriented core [raum]orientierter Kern m
~ **exsolution** orientierte Entmischung f
~ **inclusions** orientierte Einschlüsse mpl
~ **intergrowth** orientierte Verwachsung f, orientierter Verband m
~ **specimen** orientiertes Handstück n, orientierte Probe f
~ **twins** orientierte Zwillinge mpl
orienting mechanism Regelungsmechanismus m
orientite Orientit m, $Ca_4Mn_4[SiO_4] \cdot 4H_2O$
orifice Öffnung f; Mundloch n
origin Entstehen n
~ **mineral** primäres Mineral n
~ **of elements** Elemententstehung f
~ **of heat** Wärmequelle f
~ **order** normale Lagerung f
~ **rock** Ursprungsgestein n
~ **stratification** primäre horizontale Schichtung f
original dip synsedimentäres Schichtfallen n
~ **map** Urkarte f
~ **position** normale Lagerung f
~ **soil** gewachsener Boden m

~ **strength** Ursprungsfestigkeit f, Anfangsfestigkeit f
~ **stresses** Krustenspannungen fpl *(in der Erdkruste)*
~ **water table** unbeeinflußter Wasserspiegel m
origofacies sedimentäre Fazies f
Oriskanian [Stage] Oriskany n, Oriskanien n *(Stufe des Unterdevons in Nordamerika)*
ornamentation Ornamentierung f, Skulptur f *(z.B. des Exoskeletts, von Schalen)*
ornithocopros s. guano
ornoite Ornoit m *(Hornblendediorit)*
orogen Orogen n
orogenesis Orogenese f, Orogenie f, Gebirgsbildung f
orogen[et]ic orogen[etisch]
~ **belt** orogenetischer Gürtel m, Orogengürtel m
~ **cycle** orogener Zyklus m
~ **pressure** Gebirgsdruck m
~ **sediment** orogenes Sediment n, Flysch m
~ **thrust** Gebirgsschub m
orogeny Orogenese f, Orogenie f, Gebirgsbildung f
orographic[al] orografisch
~ **plication** Gebirgsfaltung f
orography Orografie f, Geomorphologie f
orology s. orography
orpiment Auripigment n, Rauschgelb n, As_2S_3
orterde Orterde f
orthite Orthit m *(s.a. allanite)*
orthoaxis Orthoachse f
orthochems Orthocheme npl *(vor allem karbonatische Abscheidungen, die keine oder nur sehr schwache Merkmale eines Transports zeigen)*
orthochronological orthochronologisch
orthoclase Orthoklas m, Kalifeldspat m, $K[AlSi_3O_8]$
orthoclastic orthoklastisch, rechtwinklig spaltend
orthodolomite Orthodolomit m, primärer Dolomit m
orthofoliate mit magmatischer Fließblattfoliation
orthogenesis Orthogenese f
orthogenetic evolution Orthogenese f
orthogeosyncline Orthogeosynklinale f
orthogneiss Orthogneis m
orthogonal system of surfaces orthogonales Flächensystem n
ortholimestone sedimentärer Kalkstein m
orthomagmatic stage orthomagmatisches Stadium n
orthomicrite Orthomikrit m *(nicht rekristallisierter Mikrit)*
orthophotograph Orthofoto n *(bezüglich perspektivischer und Neigungsverzerrungen korrigierte Satelliten- oder Luftbildaufnahme mit kartengemäßer orthografischer Geometrie)*
orthophyre Orthophyr m *(Orthoklasporphyr)*
orthophyric texture orthophyrische Struktur f

orthopyroxene 252

orthopyroxene orthorhombischer Pyroxen *m*
orthorhombic system orthorhombisches System *n*
orthoscopic method orthoskopische Methode *f*
orthosilicic acid Orthokieselsäure *f*
orthostratigraphy Orthostratigrafie *f*
orthotectic ore orthotektisches Erz *n*
~ **stage** *s.* orthomagmatic stage
orthotropy Orthotropie *f*
ortstein Ortstein *m*
ory erzhaltig
oryctognostic mineralogisch
oryctognosy Mineralogie *f*, Mineralkunde *f*, Oryktognosie *f*
Osagian [Stage] Osagien *n (Stufe des Mississippiens)*
osanite *s.* osannite
osannite Osannit *m (Varietät von Riebeckit)*
Osann's triangle Osannsches Dreieck *n*
osar Os *n*, Osar *m*, Aser *m*, Asar *m*, Wallberg *m*
osbornite Osbornit *m*, TiN *(Meteoritenmineral)*
oscillate/to oszillieren, schwingen
oscillating crystal Schwingkristall *m*
~-**crystal method** Schwingkristallmethode *f*
~ **table** Schüttelherd *m (Aufbereitung)*
oscillation Oszillation *f*, Schwingung *f*
~ **period** Schwingungsdauer *f*
~ **ripple marks**, ~ **ripples** Oszillationsrippeln *fpl*, Seegangsrippeln *fpl*, Wellenrippeln *fpl*
~ **theory** Oszillationstheorie *f*
oscillator Schwinger *m*, Oszillator *m*; Schwingungsmesser *m*
oscillatory oszillierend, schwingend
~ **movement** Schwingungsbewegung *f*
~ **ripples** *s.* oscillation ripple marks
~ **twin** polysynthetischer Zwilling *m*
osmiridium *s.* iridosmine
osmotic force osmotischer Druck *m*
~ **suction** osmotische Saugwirkung *f*
osseous breccia Knochenbrekzie *f*
~ **fish** Knochenfisch *m*
ossicle kleiner Knochen *m*
ossiferous knochig; knochenführend
ossification Verknöcherung *f*
ossipite Ossipit *m (Olivingabbroart)*
osteolite erdiger Apatit *m*
Oswegan [Series] *s.* Medinan
otavite Otavit *m*, Kadmiumspat *m*, $CdCO_3$
OTF *s.* optical transfer function
otolith Otolith *m*, Gehörstein *m*
ottajanite Ottajanit *m (Leuzittephrit)*
ottemannite Ottemannit *m*, Sn_2S_3
ottrelite Ottrelith *m*, $Mn_2AlAl_3[(OH)_4|O_2|(SiO_4)_2]$
~ **slate** Ottrelithschiefer *m*
ouachitite Ouachitit *m (Varietät von Monchiquit)*
ouady *s.* wadi
ouges Nebengestein *n* eines Ganges
oulopholite Gips *m* in Rosettenform

outbreak 1. *s.* outcrop; 2. Vulkanausbruch *m*
~ **coal** zu Tage anstehende Kohle *f*
outburst 1. Zutageliegen *n*, Anstehen *n*; 2. Ausbruch *m*
~ **of carbon dioxide** Kohlensäureausbruch *m*
~ **of gas** [plötzlicher] Gasausbruch *m*
outcrop/to zutage liegen, ausstreichen, anstehen, ausbeißen, ausgehen
outcrop Ausbiß *m*, Ausgehendes *n*, Zutageliegendes *n*, Aufschluß *m (einer Lagerstätte)*
~ **bending** Hakenwerfen *n*, Hakenschlagen *m*
~ **curvature** durch Rutschung verbogene Ausstrichlinie *f*
~ **of a vein** Ausbiß *m* eines Ganges
~ **spring** Schichtquelle *f*
~ **water** Tageswasser *n*
outcropping Ausgehendes *n*
~ **beds** ausstreichende Schichten *fpl*
~ **egde of a stratum** Schicht[en]kopf *m*, Schichtkante *f*
outer atmosphere äußere Atmosphäre *f*, Exosphäre *f*
~ **bank** Prallhang *m*
~ **casing** Standrohr *n*
~ **core barrel** äußeres Kernrohr *n*, Mantelrohr *n*
~ **lamella** äußeres Schalenblatt *n*
~ **layer** Außenschicht *f*
~ **planet** äußerer Planet *m*
~ **radiation region** äußerer Strahlungsgürtel *m (der Erde)*
~ **shelf** äußerer Schelf *m*
~ **shell** äußere Schale *f*
~ **shore line** Außenküstenlinie *f*
~ **space** Weltraum *m*
outfall 1. Mündung *f (eines Flusses)*; 2. Vorflut *f*
~ **fan** Schuttkegel *m*
outflow Herausfließen *n*, Ausfluß *m*, Abfluß *m*, Erguß *m*
~ **of lava** Lavaausfluß *m*
outgassing Entgasung *f*
outgrowth of crystals Kristallwachstum *n*
outlet Ableitungskanal *m*, Austrittsstelle *f*, Ausfluß *m*, Abfluß *m*
~ **channel** Abführkanal *m*
~/**without** abflußlos
outlier 1. Restberg *m*, Inselberg *m*, Zeugenberg *m*, Einzelberg *m*, Vorberg *m*; 2. Überschiebungsinsel *f*, Deckscholle *f*, Klippe *f (tektonisch)*
outline/in im Grundriß
~ **map** Umrißkarte *f*
outpost Erweiterungsbohrung *f* auf bekanntem Speicher *(Horizont)*
outpoured ausgeflossen *(Lava)*
outpouring Erguß *m*, Ausfluß *m*
~ **lava** ausfließende Lava *f*
output Ausbringen *n*, Förderung *f*, Gewinnung *f*; Ausbeute *f*, Förderquantum *n*, Ertrag *m*, Fördergut *n*
~ **curve** Produktionskurve *f*

~ **decline** Produktionsabfall *m*
~ **of ore** Erzförderung *f*
~ **of well** Brunnenergiebigkeit *f*
~ **per day** Tagesleistung *f*, Tagesförderung *f*
~ **per man employed** Produktion *f* je Kopf der Belegschaft
~ **per shift** Schichtleistung *f*
~ **per year** Jahresproduktion *f*
outside diameter of drilling tool Schneidmaß *n*, Außendurchmesser *m* des gesteinszerstörenden Werkzeugs
outstep [well] Erweiterungssonde *f*
outward bend of bank Ufervorsprung *m*
~ **dipping** nach außen einfallend
outwash Sander *m (Schmelzwasserablagerung vor dem Gletscher)*
~ **apron** *s.* ~ plain
~ **fan** Schuttfächer *m (durch Auswaschung)*
~ **gravel** Anschwemmschotter *m*
~ **gravel plain** *s.* ~ plain
~ **plain** Schmelzwasserebene *f*, Sanderebene *f*
~ **product** Schlämmprodukt *n*
~ **sample** Schlämmprobe *f*
~ **sand** Auswaschsand *m*
outwelling lava ausfließende Lava *f*
ouvarovite *s.* uvarovite
ovarian impressions Ovarien *mpl*, Ovarieneindrücke *mpl (bei Brachiopoden)*
overall core recovery Gesamtkerngewinn *m*
~ **thickness** Gesamtmächtigkeit *f*
overbank area Ausuferungsgebiet *n*
~ **deposit** *s.* flood-plain deposit
overbreak Mehrausbruch *m*
overburden 1. Deckschichten *fpl*, Abraum *m*, Deckgebirge *n*; 2. Überlastung *f*, Gebirgsdruck *m*
~ **dregder** Abraumbagger *m*
~ **dump** Abraumhalde *f*, Abraumkippe *f*
~ **load** Druck *m* der hangenden Gesteinsschichten
~ **of glacial drift** glaziale Schuttdecke *f*
~ **pressure** Auflast *f*, Überlagerungsdruck *m*, Gebirgsdruck *m*, Druck *m* der Deckschichten
~ **removing** Abräumen *n* des Deckgebirges
~ **rock** Deckgebirge *n*
~ **rock pressure** Überlagerungsdruck *m*
~**-to-coal ratio** Verhältnis *n* Abraum zu Kohle
overburdened überlastet
overcast 1. bedeckt, bewölkt; 2. überkippt
~ **sky** Wolkenhimmel *m*
overcritical überkritisch
~ **reflection** Weitwinkelreflexion *f*
overcrusting Krustenbildung *f*, Überkrustung *f*
overcutting Raubbau *m*
overdeepened basin Übertiefungsmulde *f*
overdraught of ground water Grundwasserraubbau *m*
overfall Hochwasserüberlauf *m (einer Talsperre)*; Überfall *m (eines Meßwehrs)*; Überlaufdeich *m*
~ **crest** Überfallkante *f*

~ **weir** Überfallstauwehr *n*
overfault Überkippung *f*, Überschiebung *f*, Übersprung *m*, antithetische (gegensinnige, widersinnige) Verwerfung *f*
overflooding Überflutung *f*
overflow/to überfluten, überschwemmen, ausufern
overflow 1. Überlauf *m*, Hochwasserüberlauf *m (einer Talsperre)*; 2. Überflutung *f*, Überschwemmung *f*
~ **dam** Überfalldamm *m*, Überlaufdamm *m*
~ **lake** Hochflutsee *m*
~ **land** Überschwemmungsgebiet *n*
~ **level** Überschwemmungsniveau *n*
~ **of dike** Deichsiel *n*
~ **spring** Überlaufquelle *f*
~ **weir** Überlaufwehr *n*, Überfallwehr *n*
overflowing Überschwemmung *f*
~ **spring** Überlaufquelle *f*
overfold/to überfalten
overfold *s.* overturned fold
overfolded rocks mehrfach gefaltete Gesteine *npl*
overfolding Faltenüberkippung *f*, Überfaltung *f*, Überschiebung *f*
overgrowth Aufwuchs *m*
overhand stoping Firstenbau *m*
overhang 1. Salzüberhang *m (Salzdom)*; 2. überhängende Wand *f*, Überhang *m*, Balme *f*
overhanging überhängend
~ **side** überhängender Stoß *m*
~ **snow** Schneewächte *f*
~ **valley side** Talgehänge *n*
overhead irrigation Beregnung *f*
~ **stoping** 1. Übersichbrechen *n*, Aufstemmen *n (z.B. von Intrusionen)*, Dachaufschmelzung *f*; 2. Firstenbau *m*
overite Overit *m*, $Ca_2Al_8[(OH)_3](PO_4)_4]_2 \cdot 15H_2O$
overlaid, overlain überlagert
overland flow oberirdischer Abfluß *m*
overlap/to übergreifen, überlagern, hinüberragen, überlappen, transgredieren
overlap Überlappung *f*, transgressive Schichtlagerung *f*
~ **fault** Überschiebung *f*, Faltenverwerfung *f*, Überlappung *f*, inverse Verwerfung *f*
~ **seal** Diskordanzfalle *f*
overlapping übergreifend, überlappend, überlagernd, transgredierend
overlapping Überlappung *f*, Überlagerung *f*, Überschiebung *f*
~ **folds** Kulissenfalten *fpl*, Relaisfalten *fpl*
~ **stratum** transgredierende Schicht *f*
overlay 1. Deckschutt *m*; 2. Deckblatt *n*, Deckpause *f*
~ **shelf** Abraum *m*
overlaying überlagernd
overlie/to darüberliegen, überlagern
overload/to überlasten, überbeanspruchen
overload 1. Überlastung *f*; 2. Übersteuerung *f*
overloaded überladen
~ **stream** überlasteter Fluß *m (mit transportierten Feststoffen)*

overlook

overlook/to überragen
overlying darüberliegend
~ **beds** Hangendschichten *fpl*
~ **cover** Deckgebirge *n*
~ **layer** Hangendes *n*
~ **rock** Deckgestein *n*, Deckgebirge *n*, Dachgestein *n*
~ **seam** hangendes Flöz *n*, Hangendflöz *n*
~ **strata** Deckschichten *fpl*, überlagernde Schichten *fpl*, Deckgebirge *n*
~ **weight** Auflast *f*
overpressure Überdruck *m*
overprint[ing] Überprägung *f (tektonisch)*
overridden mass Basalscholle *f*, [überschobene] Liegendscholle *f*
override/to sich schieben über, aufgleiten
overriding Überschiebung *f*
~ **block** Überschiebungsblock *m*
~ **glacier** überfahrender Gletscher *m*
~ **mass** Schubmasse *f*
oversaturated übersättigt
~ **rock** übersättigtes Gestein *n*
oversaturation Übersättigung *f*
overshot Fangglocke *f*, Fangmuffe *f*, Schraubentute *f*; Fanghaken *m*, Glückshaken *m*
~ **with slips** Gestängefangkrebs *m*
overslide Vorschiebung *f*, Übergleitung *f (Tektonik)*
oversteepened übersteilt
~ **wall** übersteilte Wand *f*
oversteepening Übersteilung *f*
overstress Überbeanspruchung *f*
overthrow fault *s.* overthrust fault
overthrown überkippt
overthrust/to überschieben
overthrust Überschiebung *f*, Überkippung *f*
~ **block** Überschiebungsscholle *f*, Überschiebungsblock *m*
~ **fault** Verwerfung *f* durch Heben eines Flügels, Überschiebung *f*, Faltenüberschiebung *f*, Überkippung *f*
~ **faulting** Schollenüberschiebungen *fpl*
~ **fold** Faltenüberschiebung *f*, Deckenfalte *f*, Überfaltungsdecke *f*
~ **folding** Deckenfaltung *f*
~ **mass** Überschiebungsmasse *f*, überschobene Masse *f*, Schubmasse *f*
~ **mountains** Überfaltungsgebirge *n*, Deckengebirge *n*
~ **nappe** Abscherungsdecke *f*, Schubdecke *f*, Überschiebungsdecke *f*
~ **plane** Überschiebungsfläche *f*
~ **plate (sheet)** *s.* ~ nappe
~ **slice** Mittelschenkelreste *mpl (bei Decken)*
~ **zone** Überschiebungszone *f*
overthrusting Schollenüberschiebung *f*
overtilted überkippt
overturn/to überkippen
overturn Überkippung *f*, Vergenz *f*
overturned überkippt
~ **anticline** überkippter Sattel *m*
~ **cross-bedding** überkippte Schrägschichtung *f*

254

~ **fold** überkippte (liegende) Falte *f*
~ **limp** überkippter Schenkel *m (einer Falte)*
overturning 1. Schichtenüberkippung *f*, Überkippung *f*; 2. Überfaltung *f (tektonisch)*
overvoltage method Verfahren der induzierten Polarisation *(Geophysik)*
overwash 1. Schmelzwassersedimente *npl (Moränenüberschüttung vor der Gletscherstirn)*; 2. Überspülung *f*
~ **apron** *s.* apron
~ **drift** Sedimentaustrag *m* an der Gletscherstirn
~ **of debris** Vermurung *f*
~ **plain** *s.* apron
overwhelm/to überschütten, begraben
ovoid ovoid, eifömig, oolithisch
~ **grain** ovoides Korn *n*
ovulite *s.* ooid
owyheeite Owyheeit *m*, $5PbS \cdot Ag_2S \cdot 3Sb_2S_3$
oxammite Oxammit *m*, $(NH_4)_2[C_2O_4] \cdot H_2O$
oxbow Altwasser *n*
~ **lake** Altwassersee *m (infolge Mäanderdurchschneidung)*, halbmondförmiges Altwasser *n*, alter Flußarm *m*, toter Arm *m*
Oxfordian [Stage] Oxford[ien] *n*, Oxfordium *n (basale Stufe des Malms)*
oxidation Oxydation *f*, Oxydierung *f*
~-**reduction potential** Redoxpotential *n*
~ **state** Oxydationsstufe *f*
~ **zone** Oxydationszone *f*
oxide Oxid *n*
~ **coating** Oxidüberzug *m*
oxidic oxidhaltig
oxidization *s.* oxidation
oxidized cap (zone) Eiserner Hut *m*
oxidizing environment oxydierendes Milieu *n*
~ **flame** Oxydationsflamme *f*
~ **zone** Oxydationszone *f*
oxyde *s.* oxide
oxygen Sauerstoff *m*, O
~-**rich** sauerstoffreich
oxygenated inshore environment durchlüftetes küstennahes Milieu *n*
~ **water** sauerstoffhaltiges Wasser *n*
oxysphere Lithosphäre *f*
oyster Auster *f*
~ **bed** Austernbank *f*
ozocerite Ozokerit *m*, Erdwachs *n (Gemenge hochmolekularer Kohlenwasserstoffe)*
ozone Ozon *n*
~ **layer** Ozonschicht *f*

P

P-wave P-Welle *f*, Kompressionswelle *f*, Longitudinalwelle *f (Seismik)*
pabstite Pabstit *m*, $BaSn[Si_3O_9]$
pachnolite Pachnolith *m*, $NaCa[AlF_6] \cdot H_2O$
Pacific province pazifische Magmensippe *f*
~ **Province** pazifische Provinz *f (Paläobiogeografie, Unterkambrium)*

palpebral

~ **series (suite)** pazifische Magmensippe *f*
pack/to verdichten
pack ice Packeis *n*
~-**pressure dynamometer** Versatzdruckdose *f*
packer Packer *m*
~ **test** Packertest *m (bei Brunnenbohrungen)*
packing 1. Verdichtung *f*; Tamponieren *n*, Abdichten *n*; 2. Grubenversatz *m*
~ **density** Belegungsdichte *f (Seismik)*
~ **effect** Verdichtungseffekt *m*
~ **factor** Verdichtungsfaktor *m*
~ **material** Dichtungsmaterial *n*
~ **of particles** Packungsart *f*, Gitteranordnung *f*
~ **of the space between casings** Verschließen *n* des Ringraums zwischen den Rohren
packsand feinkörniger Sandstein *m*
packstone Packstone *m (Kalkstein mit selbststützendem Korngerüst und geringem Matrixanteil)*
padang soil Padangboden *m*
paddy field soil sandiger Lehm *m (mit rund 20% Ton und 40% Sand)*
paedogenesis Pädogenese *f*
pagodite Agalmatolith *m*, Pagodit *m*, Bildstein *m*
pahoehoe [lava] Pahoehoe-Lava *f*, Stricklava *f*, Fladenlava *f*
painite Painit *m* , $5Al_2O_3 \cdot Ca_2[(Si,BH)O_4]$
paint pot heißer Schlammsprudel *m*
~ **rock** eisenhaltiger, schieferiger Ton *m (s.a. ochre)*
pair of faces Flächenpaar *n*
~ **of teeth** Zahnpaar *n*
paired metamorphic belts paarige Metamorphosegürtel *mpl*, Hoch- und Niederdruckgürtel *mpl* regionalmetamorpher Gebiete
paisanite Paisanit *m (Ganggestein mit Riebeckkit)*
palaebotany Paläobotanik *f*
Palaeocene paläozän
Palaeocene [Epoch, Series] Paläozän *n (Serie des Tertiärs)*
palaeochannel begrabenes Flußbett *n*
palaeoclimatic change paläoklimatologische Veränderung *f*
palaeoclimatology Paläoklimatologie *f*
palaeocurrent fossile Strömung *f (sedimentbildend)*
palaeoendemism Paläoendemismus *m*, Reliktendemismus *m*
Palaeogene Paläogen *n*, Alttertiär *n*
palaeogeographer Paläogeograf *m*
palaeogeographic[al] paläogeografisch
~ **map** paläogeografische Karte *f*
palaeogeography Paläogeografie *f*
palaeogeothermic gradient paläogeothermischer Gradient *m*
palaeohydrodynamics Paläohydrodynamik *f*
palaeohydrogeochemistry Paläohydrogeochemie *f*
palaeohydrogeological analysis paläohydrogeologische Analyse *f*

~ **basic regime** paläohydrogeologisches Grundregime *n*
palaeohydrogeology Paläohydrogeologie *f*
palaeohydrology Paläohydrologie *f*
palaeolatitude Paläohöhe *f*
Palaeolithic paläolithisch
Palaeolithic Paläolithikum *n*
~ **map** paläolithologische Karte *f*
palaeomagnetic pole paläomagnetischer Pol *m*
palaeomagnetism Paläomagnetismus *m*
palaeomeridian Paläomeridian *m*, Paläobreite *f*
palaeontologic[al] paläontologisch
palaeontologist Paläontologe *m*
palaeontology Paläontologie *f*
Palaeophytic Paläophytikum *n*
palaeophytology Paläobotanik *f*
palaeopicrite Paläopikrit *m*
palaeosol fossiler Bodenhorizont *m*
palaeosome Paläosom *n*
palaeotectonics Paläotektonik *f*
palaeotemperature Paläotemperatur *f*
palaeotypal paläotyp, altvulkanisch
~ **rock** altvulkanisches Gestein *n*
palaeovolcanic paläovulkanisch, altvulkanisch
Palaeozoic paläozoisch
Palaeozoic [Era] Paläozoikum *n*
palaeozoology Paläozoologie *f*
palagonite Palagonit *m*
~ **tuff** Palagonittuff *m*
palagonitization Palagonitbildung *f*
palaite Palait *m (s.a. huréaulith)*
paleo... s. palaeo...
palermoite Palermoit *m*, $SrAl_2[OH|PO_4]_2$
palimpsest Palimpsest *m (n)*, Relikt *n*
~ **sediments** Palimpsest-Sedimente *npl (hydrodynamisch und biologisch aufgearbeitete Reliktsedimente des Kontinentalschelfs)*
~ **structure** Palimpsest-Gefüge *n*
palingenesis Palingenese *f*
palingenetic magma palingenes Magma *n*
palingeny Palingenese *f*
palinspastic map paläogeografische Karte der prädeformativen Bildungsräume lithofazieller Einheiten
palisade basalt Säulenbasalt *m*
palisadian disturbance Palisadenfaltung *f*
palladinite Palladinit *m*, erdiges PdO
palladium Palladium *n*, Pd
~ **gold** s. porpezite
pallas iron, pallasite Pallasit *m (Eisenmeteorit mit Olivin)*
pallial line Mantellinie *f (bei Fossilschalen)*
~ **markings** Pallialeindrücke *mpl (bei Brachiopoden)*
~ **sinus** Mantelsinus *m*, Mantelbucht *f*
pallite Pallit *m*, $Ca(Al, Fe)_3[(OH)_3O|(PO_4)_2 \cdot 2H_2O$
palmerite Palmerit *m*, Taranakit *m*, $K_3Al_5H_6[PO_4]_8 \cdot 18H_2O$
palmierite Palmierit *m*, $PbK_2[SO_4]_2$
palpebral lobe of the eye Augenhügel *m (bei Trilobiten)*

palsa

palsa bog Hügelmoor n, Palsa-Moor n
paludal sumpfig, moorig
~ deposit Sumpfablagerung f
~ environment mooriges Milieu n
paludification Sumpfbildung f, Versumpfung f
palus Palus m (Sumpf auf Mars oder Mond)
palustrine deposit Sumpfablagerung f
palygorskite Palygorskit m,
  $(Mg,Al)_2[OH|Si_4O_{10}] \cdot 2H_2O + 2H_2O$
palynology Palynologie f, Sporenkunde f
pampa Steppe f, Grassteppe f (Argentinien)
pan 1. Trockensee m, Salzwanne f; 2. vulkanischer Schlothohlraum m; 3. Flözunterton m; 4. Verdichtungshorizont m, Ortsteinhorizont m
~-fan (Am) Pedimentrumpffläche f
~ ice s. pancake ice
~ soil Orterde f
panabase s. tetrahedrite
panallotriomorphic panallotriomorph
panautomorphic s. panidiomorphic
pancake ice Eisscholle f, Treibeis n, Tellereis n
~-shaped bomb abgeflachte vulkanische Bombe f
pandaite Pandait m, $Ba(Nb, Ti, Ta)_2O_6(H_2O)$
pandermite Pandermit m, $Ca_2[B_5O_6(OH)_7]$
panel Bauhöhe f
panethite Panethit m, $(Na, Ca)_2(Mg, Fe)_2(PO_4)_2$ (Meteoritenmineral)
panidiomorphic panidiomorph, vollidiomorph
~-granular panidiomorph-körnig
panning Goldwaschen n im Waschtrog, Waschen n mit Sichertrog
Pannonian Pannon[ien] n, Pannonium n (Stufe des Miozäns)
~ basin Pannonisches Becken n, Ungarische Tiefebene f
~ geosyncline Pannonisches Senkungsfeld n
~ Stage s. Pannonian
panplane tafelförmige Erosionsebene f
pantellerite Pantellerit m (Alkalirhyolith)
papagoite Papagoit m, $CaCuAlH_2[OH|(SiO_4)_2]$
paper chromatography Papierchromatografie f
~ clay Papierkaolin m (hochplastischer, weißer Kaolin)
~ coal Papierkohle f, Blätterkohle f
~ schist s. papery shale
papery shale Papierschiefer m; Stinkschiefer m
papyraceous papierförmig
~ lignite s. paper coal
para-aluminite Paraaluminit m,
  $Al_4[(OH)_{10}|SO_4] \cdot 6H_2O$
para-ripples Pararippeln fpl
~-rock Paragestein n
parabutlerite Parabutlerit m, $Fe[OH|SO_4] \cdot 2H_2O$
parachronologic unit parachronologische Einheit f
parachronology Parachronologie f (Biostratigrafie)

paraclase Bruch m (Spaltenbildung f) mit Verwerfung, Paraklase f
paraconformity maskierte Diskordanz f
paracrystalline deformation parakistalline Deformation f
paradamine Paradamin m, $Zn_2[OH|AsO_4]$
paradigm Standardprobe f
paradox of anisotropy Anisotropieparadoxon n (Geoelektrik)
paraffin Paraffin n, Erdwachs n, Mineralwachs n
~-asphalt petroleum Erdöl n mit Paraffin- und Asphaltbasis
~-base oil paraffinöses Erdöl n, Erdöl mit Paraffinbasis
~-base petroleum s. ~-base oil
~ deposition Paraffinablagerung f
paraffinic (paraffinous) oil s. paraffin-base oil
paragenesis Paragenese f, Vergesellschaftung f
~ of elements Elementparagenese f
~ of minerals Mineralparagenese f
paragenetic paragenetisch
~ sequence paragenetische Abfolge f
parageosyncline Parageosynklinale f
paragneiss Paragneis m
paragonite Paragonit m, Natriumglimmer m, $NaAl_2[(OH, F)_2|AlSi_3O_{10}]$
~ schist Paragonitschiefer m
parahopeite Parahopeit m, $Zn_3[PO_4]_2 \cdot 4H_2O$
paralaurionite Paralaurionit m, PbOHCl
paralic paralisch
~ coal paralische Kohle f
~ coal basin paralisches Kohlenbecken n
~ deposit paralische Ablagerung f
~ swamp mariner Sumpf m
parallactic parallaktisch
~ angle Parallaxenwinkel m
~ ellipse parallaktische Ellipse f
parallax Parallaxe f
~ in altitude Höhenparallaxe f
parallel Breitenkreis m, Parallelkreis m
~ acicular aggregate parallelstengliges Aggregat n
~ alignment (arrangement) Parallelanordnung f
~ columnar aggregate parallelstrahliges Aggregat n
~ development Parallelentwicklung f
~ displacement Parallelverschiebung f, Translation f (bei Kristallen)
~ extinction parallele Auslöschung f
~ fibrous parallelfaserig
~ flow Schichtenströmung f
~ fold Parallelfalte f, konzentrische Falte f
~ growth Parallelverwachsung f
~ migration s. lateral migration
~ of declination Deklinationsparallele f
~ of latitude Breitenkreis m, Parallelkreis m
~ orientation Parallelstellung f, Parallelorientierung f (Mineralgefüge)
~ perspective/in parallelperspektivisch

~ **ripple marks** Parallelrippelmarken *fpl*
~ **roads** parallele Terrassen *fpl*
~ **shot** Parallelschuß *m*, Gleichlauf *m (Seismik)*
~ **structure** Paralleltextur *f*
~ **unconformity** Paralleldiskordanz *f*, Erosionsdiskordanz *f*
parallelepipedal structure parallelepipedische Absonderung *f*
parallelism Parallelanordnung *f*
parallelize/to parallelisieren
paramagnetic paramagnetisch
~ **mineral** paramagnetisches Mineral *n*
paramagnetism Paramagnetismus *m*
paramarginal reserves nicht [ab]bauwürdige Ressourcen *fpl (an der Grenze wirtschaftlich bauwürdiger Teile oder nicht verfügbar wegen gesetzlicher oder politischer Umstände)*
parameter Parameter *m*, Kristallachsenabschnitt *m*
paramorphic paramorph
paramorphism, paramorphosis Paramorphose *f*
paramorphous paramorph
paramoudras Feuersteinknollen *fpl (an der englischen Kreideküste)*
paranaphthalene Paranaphthalin *n*, $C_{14}H_{10}$
parapet Terrasse *f*
parapitchblende Nasturan *n*, UO_2
pararammelsbergite Pararammelsbergit *m*, $NiAs_2$
paraschist Paraschiefer *m*
paraselene Nebenmond *m*
parasitic parasitisch, parasitär
~ **cone (crater)** Adventivkrater *m*, Parasitärkrater *m*
~ **currents** Streuströme *mpl*
parastratotype Parastratotyp *m*
paratellurite Paratellurit *m*, TeO_2
paratenorite Paratenorit *m*, CuO
paratype Paratypus *m*
parautochthonous parautochthon
~ **klippe (nappe)** parautochthone Decke *f*, Deckscholle *f*
paravauxite Paravauxit *m*, $FeAl_2[OH|PO_4]_2 \cdot 8H_2O$
paravolcanic phenomena vulkanische Nebenerscheinungen *fpl*
parcel Erzhaufen *m*
Pardonetian Pardonet[ium] *n (Nor und Rhät in Nordamerika)*
parent Mutter...
~ **lodge** Abrißgebiet *n (von Rutschkörpern)*
~ **magma** Muttermagma *n*, Stammagma *n*
~ **rock** Ausgangsgestein *n*, Muttergestein *n*, anstehendes Gestein *n*
~ **soil** Mutterboden *m*
parental magma Muttermagma *n*, Stammagma *n*
pargasite Pargasit *m*, $NaCa_2Mg_4(Al, Fe)[(OH, F)_2|Al_2Si_6O_{22}]$
parhelion Nebensonne *f*, Gegensonne *f*
parianite Asphalt *m (vom Asphaltsee in Trinidad)*

parisite Parisit *m*, $[(Ce, La, Di)F]_2 \cdot CaCO_3$
park 1. Graslandebene *f* im Waldgelände; 2. flache Auslaugungswanne *f*
parma flacher Dom *m*, flache Periklinale *f*
parna äolische Karbonatablagerung *f*
paroptesis Gesteinsbeanspruchung *f* durch trockene Erhitzung, Backung *f*
paroxysm Paroxysmus *m*
parquet-twinning Parkettverzwilligung *f*
parrot coal Sapropelkohle *f (analog Boghead- und Kännelkohle)*
parsettensite Parsettensit *m*, $(K,H_2O)(Mn, Fe, Mg, Al)_3[(OH)_2|Si_4O_{10}] \cdot nH_2O$
parsonsite Parsonsit, $Pb_2[UO_2|(PO_4)_2] \cdot 2H_2O$
part movability Teilbeweglichkeit *f*
partial partiell
~ **cycle** Teilzyklus *m*
~ **diagram** Diagramm *n* eines Kornteilgefüges
~ **dislocation** partielle Versetzung *f*, Teilversetzung *f*
~ **eclipse** partielle Finsternis *f*
~ **eclipse of the moon** partielle Mondfinsternis *f*
~ **eclipse of the sun** partielle Sonnenfinsternis *f*
~ **extraction** Teilabbau *m*
~ **magma** Teilmagma *n*
~ **melting** partielle Aufschmelzung *f*, Teilschmelzenbildung *f*
~ **penetrating well** Bohrung *f* mit unvollständigem Speicheraufschluß
~ **pressure** Partialdruck *m*
~ **solar eclipse** partielle Sonnenfinsternis *f*
~ **submergence** teilweises Untertauchen *n*
~ **subsidence** Teilsenkung *f*
~ **water drive** partieller Wassertrieb *m*
partially observed nur teilweise beobachtet, schwach *(3. Stufe der Erdbebenstärkeskala)*
~ **oriented** teilorientiert
particle Teilchen *n*
~ **diameter** Korndurchmesser *m*
~ **shape** Kornform *f*
~ **size** Korngröße *f*
~-**size analysis** Bestimmung *f* der Korngrößenanteile
~-**size distribution** Korngrößenverteilung *f*
~-**size distribution curve** Sieblinie *f*, Siebkurve *f*
particular colour Eigenfarbe *f*
partimesurate body teilweise ausgewiesener Vorrat *m (eines Erzkörpers)*
parting 1. Absonderung *f*; Absonderungsfläche *f*, kleine Kluft *f*, Schlechte *f*; 2. unvollkommene Spaltung *f (von Kristallen)*; 3. Riß *m*, Trennschicht *f*; 4. taubes Gestein *n*, Bergemittel *n*, Zwischenlage *f*, Zwischenmittel *n*
~ **cast** Dehnungsmarke *f*
~ **gold** Scheidegold *n*
~ **lineation** Strömungsstreifung *f*, Stromstreifung *f*, geradlinige Riefung *f*, feine Parallelstriemung *f*, Strömungsriefen *fpl*
~ **plane** Trennfläche *f*, Grenzfläche *f*, Teilungsebene *f*

parting

- ~ **process** Scheideverfahren *n*
- ~ **rupture** Trennungsbruch *m*
- ~ **shale** Schiefermittel *n*
- ~ **silver** Scheidesilber *n*
- ~ **surface** *s.* ~ plane
- **partition** 1. Scheidewand *f*, Zwischenwand *f*; 2. Bifurkation *f*
- ~ **rock** Nebengestein *n*
- ~ **wall** Zwischenwand *f*
- **partitioning** [of elements] Elementverteilung *f*
- **partiversal dip** umlaufendes Einfallen *n*
- **partly rounded fossil** abgerolltes Fossil *n*
- **partridgeite** Partridgeit *m*, Mn_2O_3
- **partschinite** Spessartin *m*, Partschin *m*, $Mn_3Al_2[SiO_4]_3$
- **party** Trupp *m* (Seismik)
- ~ **manager** Truppleiter *m* (Seismik)
- **pascoite** Pascoit *m*, $Ca_3[V_{10}O_{28}] \cdot 16H_2O$
- **pass into/to** übergehen in
- ~ **into vapour** verdampfen
- **pass** 1. Gebirgspass *m*, Paß *m*; 2. Durchgang *m* (eines Gestirns oder Satelliten zur Ortsbestimmung)
- **passage** Durchfluß *m*
- ~ **bed** Übergangsschicht *f*
- ~ **facies** Übergangsfazies *f*
- ~ **of a screen** Siebdurchgang *m*, Siebdurchlauf *m*
- **passband filter** Bandpaßfilter *n*
- **possibility category** Geländeschwierigkeitsgrad *m*
- **passive earth pressure** passiver Erddruck *m*
- ~ **resistance** Erdwiderstand *m*
- ~ **sensor** passiver Sensor *m* (registriert lediglich die vom Untersuchungsobjekt ausgehende reflektierte oder emittierte Strahlung)
- ~ **system** passives System *n* (Seismik)
- **past ages** Vorzeit *f*
- ~ **form** Vorzeitform *f*
- **paste** Grundmasse *f* (Porphyr); einbettende Mineralsubstanz *f*
- **Pastonian** Pastonien *n* (Pleistozän, Britische Inseln)
- **pasty** teigartig, teigig
- **patch** 1. kleines Seifenclaim *n*; 2. Eisbank *f*
- ~ **of ore** Erznest *n*
- ~ **reef** 1. Fleckenriff *n*, Kuppenriff *n*, Krustenriff *n*; 2. umgeschichtete Karbonatlinsen in faziesfremder Umgebung
- **patched slate** Fleckschiefer *m*
- **patching** vom Ausstrich ansetzender Abbau *m*
- **patchy** unregelmäßig verteilt
- **patelliform** patelliform, schüsselförmig
- **paternoite** Paternoit *m*, Kaliborit *m*, $KMg_2[B_5O_6(OH)_4][B_3O_3(OH)_5] \cdot 2H_2O$
- **paternoster lakes** Seen auf den Stufen einer Kartreppe
- **path** Bahn *f*
- ~ **difference** Gangunterschied *m*
- ~ **of percolation** Sickerweg *m*
- ~ **of rays** Strahlengang *m*
- ~ **of seepage** Sickerlinie *f*
- ~ **of the earth** Erdbahn *f*
- ~ **of the liquid** Flüssigkeitsbahn *f*
- ~ **of the moon** Mondbahn *f*
- ~ **of the sun** Sonnenbahn *f*
- ~ **speed** Bahngeschwindigkeit *f*
- ~ **-time curve** Weg-Zeit-Diagramm *n*
- **patina** 1. Wüstenlack *m*; 2. helle Verwitterungsrinde *f*
- **patinated chert** angewitterte Hornsteinknolle *f*
- **patrinite** *s.* aikinite
- **patronite** Patronit *m*, VS_4
- **pattern** 1. Gitter *n*, Muster *n*; Anordnung *f*; 2. Regelungsbild *n* (von Diagrammen)
- ~ **analysis** Musteranalyse *f* (Fernerkundung)
- ~ **delimitation** Musterabgrenzung *f* (Fernerkundung)
- ~ **of drainage** Entwässerungsnetz *n*
- ~ **of flow** Strömungszustand *m*
- ~ **of well spacing** Bohrlochanordnung *f*
- ~ **recognition** Mustererkennung *f* (Fernerkundung)
- **patterned bog** Strangmoor *n*
- ~ **ground** Strukturboden *m*, Frostgefügeboden *m*, Eismusterboden *m*, Frostmusterboden *m*
- **paucity of fossils** Fossilarmut *f*
- **paulopost** autometamorph
- **pavement** Liegendes *n*
- **paving gravel** Straßenschotter *m*
- ~ **sett** Pflasterstein *m*
- **paxite** Paxit *m*, Cu_2As_3
- **pay/to** produzieren (Sonde)
- **pay dirt** ergiebige Golderde *f*, goldführender Boden *m*
- ~ **horizon** Erdöl (Erdgas) abgebende Schicht *f*
- ~ **ore (rock)** [ab]bauwürdiges Erz *n*
- ~ **sand** Speichergestein *n* (für Erdöl oder Erdgas)
- ~ **shoot** [ab]bauwürdiger Teil *m* (in einer Lagerstätte)
- ~ **zone** Förderhorizont *m*
- **payability** Ergiebigkeit *f*, Abbauwürdigkeit *f*, Bauwürdigkeit *f*
- ~ **ore** [ab]bauwürdiges Erz *n*
- **payable** ergiebig, [ab]bauwürdig
- ~ **deposit** [ab]bauwürdige Lagerstätte *f*
- ~ **ore** [ab]bauwürdiges Erz *n*
- ~ **ore body** [ab]bauwürdiger Erzkörper *m*
- ~ **place** ergiebiger Ausbeutungsplatz *m*
- **paying** [ab]bauwürdig
- ~ **well** produzierende Bohrung *f*
- **payload** Nutzlast *f*
- **paystreaks** 1. Goldanreicherungen in fossilen Strömungsrinnen (Witwatersrand); 2. [ab]bauwürdiger Gangteil *m*, Erzfall *m*
- **PDB** Chicagoer Isotopenstandard für $^{12}C/^{13}C$ (CO_2 aus Belemnitella americana, Kreide, P-D-Formation)
- **pea-grit** pisolithisch (bei Sandstein)
- ~ **ore** Bohnerz *n*
- **peach** hydrothermal zersetztes Nebengestein *n* (Cornwall)
- ~ **stone** weiches chloritisiertes Gestein *n*

peachy lode zellige, chloritreiche Gangfüllung f
peacock copper (ore) s. bornite
peak 1. Bergspitze f, Gipfel m; 2. Wellenmaximum n (Seismik)
~ **discharge** maximale Grundwasserspende f
~ **of wave** Wellenberg m
~ **plain** Gipfelflur f
~ **point** Peak m (Tracerversuch)
~ **production** Spitzenproduktion f
~ **run-off** Spitzenabfluß m
~ **shear strength** maximale Scherfestigkeit f
~ **zone** s. acme-zone
peaked curve spitze Kurve f
~ **mountain** Gipfelberg m
pearceite Pearceit m, Arsenpolybasit m, 8(Ag, Cu)$_2$S·As$_2$S$_3$
pearl Perle f
~ **diabase** Variolith m
~ **gneiss** Perlgneis m, Körnelgneis m, blastischer Gneis m
~ **mica** s. margarite
~ **ore** Perlerz n
~ **sinter** Kieselsinter m, Perlsinter m
~ **spar** Perlspat m (Varietät von Dolomit)
~ **stone** Perlit m
pearlaceous perlmutt[er]artig
pearlite Perlit m
pearly perlmutt[er]artig, perlartig
~ **lustre (sheen)** perlmutt[er]artiger Glanz m, Perlglanz m, Perlmutt[er]glanz m
peastone s. pisolite
peasy 1. Erzhandstück n; 2. bohnkorngroßes Bleierz n
peat bed Torflager n, Torfschicht f
~ **blasting** Moorsprengung f
~ **bog** Torfmoor n, Torflager n, Hochmoor n, Ried n
~ **breccia** umgelagerter Torf m
~ **charcoal** 1. Torffusain m; 2. Torffusit m
~ **charring** Torfverkohlung f
~ **clay** Mudde f, Mudd m
~ **cover** Moordecke f
~ **deposit** Torflager n
~ **diagenesis** Torfdiagenese f
~ **digger** Torfgräber m, Torfstecher m
~ **digging** Torfgewinnung f
~ **dust** Torfmull m
~ **extraction** Torfgewinnung f
~ **formation** Torfbildung f, Moorbildung f, Vertorfung f, Vermoorung f
~-**forming** torfbildend, moorbildend
~ **gas** Torfgas n, Sumpfgas n
~ **gasification** Torfvergasung f
~ **hillock** Aufwölbung f im Torfmoor
~ **land** Moorboden m
~ **land science** Moorkunde f
~ **moor** Torfmoor n
~ **moss** Torfmoos n
~ **moss litter** Torfmull m
~ **pit** Torfgrube f
~ **pocket** Torfeinschluß m, Torfnest n
~ **slime** s. ~ breccia
~ **sod** Torfstück n
~ **soil** Torfboden m
~ **swamp** Torfbruch n, Moor n, Marsch f
~ **tar** Torfteer m
peatery Torflager n
peatification Vertorfung f
peatified vertorft
peaty torfartig, torfhaltig, vertorft, torfig, moorig
~ **bog** Torfmoor n
~ **earth** Moorboden m
~ **fibrous coal** Torffaserkohle f
~ **flat** vertorfte Fläche f, Torfniederung f
~ **lay** Torfschicht f
~ **layer** Torflage f
~ **moor** Torfmoor n
~ **soil** Moorboden m
~ **swamp** Torfmoor n
pebble Kies m; Kiesel m; Geröll n
~ **armour** Geröllpanzer m (auf Wüstenböden)
~ **bed** Kiesschicht f
~ **dike** kataklasierter, zerscherter Gang m
~ **gneiss** Geröllgneis m, Konglomeratgneis m
~ **gravel** Geröll n
~ **jack** (sl) Zinkblende f
~ **phosphates** knolliger Phosphorit m
~ **stone** Geröll n, Geschiebe n
pebbly geröllführend, kiesig, steinig
~ **mudstones** intraformationales Konglomeratslumping n, Wildflysch m
pecos ore Eiserner Hut mit Pb- und Ag-Erzen
pectolite Pektolith m, Ca$_2$Na[Si$_3$O$_8$OH]
pectoral fin Pectoralflosse f, Brustflosse f
pedalfer Al- und Fe-reiche Bodenart f
pedcal s. pedocal
pedestal rock Pilzfels m, Tischfels m
pedial class symmetrielose Kristallklasse f
pedicle foramen Stielforamen n (Brachiopoden)
~ **valve** Ventralklappe f, Bauchklappe f, Stielklappe f (Brachiopoden)
pediment Pediment n, Gebirgsfußfläche f, aride Felsebene f, Felsfußfläche f
~ **pass** verbindende Depression f (zwischen zwei Pedimentflächen)
ped'n-cairn Erznest n (Cornwall)
pedocal Kalkboden m, Kalkkruste f (auf ariden Böden)
pedochemistry Bodenchemie f
pedogenesis Bodenbildung f
pedological pedologisch, bodenkundlich
pedologist Pedologe m, Bodenkundler m
pedology Pedologie f, Bodenkunde f
pedostratigraphic unit pedostratigrafische Einheit f
pedrigal Lavaschicht f (Kalifornien)
peds natürliche Aggregate von Bodenmineralen
pee 1. Gangkreuz n; 2. Bleierzstück n (Derbyshire)
peel off/to abblättern, abbröckeln, abplatzen

peeling

peeling[-off] schalige Absonderung f, Abschuppung f, Abblätterung f
peg Meßdübel m, Meßpflock m
~-leg multiple Teilwegmultiple f (Seismik)
~ structure Pflockgefüge n (z.B. bei Melilith)
peganite s. variscite
pegmatite Pegmatit m
~ dike Pegmatitgang m
pegmatitic pegmatitisch
~ vein Pegmatitgang m
pegmatization Pegmatitisierung f, Umwandlung f in Pegmatit
pegmatize/to pegmatitisieren, in Pegmatit umwandeln
pegmatoid pegmatitähnlich
pelagian s. pelagic
pelagic pelagisch, Tiefsee...
~ deposit pelagische (ozeanische) Ablagerung f, Tiefseeablagerung f, Hochseeablagerung f
~ facies pelagische Fazies f
~ ooze Tiefseeschlamm m
~ zone Tiefseezone f
pelagite Tiefseemanganknolle f
pelagochthonous aus Treibholz (überfluteten Wäldern) entstanden (Kohle)
pelagosite Pelagosit m (Karbonatablagerung mit hohen $MgCO_3$-, $SrCO_3$-, $CaSO_4$-, H_2O- und SiO_2-Gehalten)
pelean activity Pelétätigkeit f (von Vulkanen)
pelecypods Muscheln fpl, Lamellibranchiaten mpl
peleeite Peleeit m (Varietät von Dazit)
pele's hair Fadenlapilli pl, Glasfäden mpl, Peles Haar n
pelite Pelit m (s.a. mudstone, calcilutite)
pelitic pelitisch (s.a. argillaceous)
~ rock Tongestein n
pelitomorphic pelitomorph (pelitisch als Korngröße bei Karbonatgesteinen)
pell-mell structure Gefügebezeichnung für schichtungsfreie Sedimentation
pellet Pellet n, Kügelchen n (unregelmäßiger Rundkörper ohne internes Richtungsgefüge)
~ impact drilling Düsenschrotbohren n, Kugelschlagbohren n
~ of ice Eiskügelchen n
pelletal, pelleted pelletführend
~ limestone Pillenkalkstein m
~-micritic limestone pillenreicher Kalkstein m
pelletize/to pelletisieren (Erz)
pelletoid pelletoid, pelletartig
pellicle Schutzrinde f
~ of oil Ölfilm m, Ölhäutchen n
pellicular moisture Filmfeuchtigkeit f
~ water Pellikularwasser n, Sorptionswasser n, Anlagerungswasser n, Haftwasser n, Häutchenwasser n
pellodite Bänderton m, dünngeschichteter Ton m
pelogloea an Sedimentpartikel adsorbierte organische Substanz f
Pelsonian [Substage] Pelson[ium] n (Unterstufe, Mittlere Trias, Tethys)

pelvis Pelvis f, Becken n
pen Schulp m
pencil gneiss Stengelgneis m
~ of rays Strahlenbüschel n
~ slate Griffelschiefer m
~ structure Stengelung f
pendular regime Porenwinkelwasserregime n
~ water penduläres Wasser n, Haftwasser n
pendulous abwärts hängend
pendulum effect Pendeleffekt m (Bohrtechnik)
penecontemporaneous autometamorph, synsedimentär
~ structure synsedimentäres Gefüge n
peneplain Fastebene f, Peneplain f, Rumpffläche f, Rumpfebene f, Denudationsfläche f
peneplanation Verebnung f
peneplane s. peneplain
peneseismic peneseismisch
~ countries (regions) peneseismische Regionen fpl
penetrate/to 1. durchbohren; 2. durchtrümern
penetrated bed durchbohrte Schicht f
~ by joints durchklüftet
penetrating twin Durchdringungszwilling m
penetration Durchdringung f, Eindringung f
~ advance Bohrfortschritt m
~ by joints Durchklüftung f
~ depth Eindringtiefe f, Wirkungstiefe f
~ effect on build-up analysis Erfassungsgrad m einer Druckaufbaumessung
~ of fracture Rißeindringen n
~ rate Bohrfortschritt m, Bohrleistung f
~ rate recorder Bohrfortschrittsregistriereinrichtung f
~ speed Bohrgeschwindigkeit f
~ twins Durchwachsungszwillinge mpl, Penetrationszwillinge mpl
penetrative durchdringend
~ rock Intrusivgestein n
penetrometer Eindringmeßgerät n
penfieldite Penfieldit m, Pb_2OHCl_3
peninsula Halbinsel f
penitent ice Büßereis n
~ snow Büßerschnee m, Zackenfirn m
pennantite Pennantit m, $(Mn, Al, Fe)_3[(OH)_2|(Al, Si)Si_3O_{10}]Mn_3(OH)_6$
pennate fiederförmig
pennine s. penninite
Pennine nappes Penninische Decken fpl
Penninic penninisch
~ zone penninische Zone f
penninite Pennin m (Chloritmineral)
~ drilling Seilschlagbohren n
Pennsylvanian s. ~ Series
~ drilling Seilschlagbohren n
~ Series (System) Pennsylvanien n (wird in Amerika im Gegensatz zu Europa teilweise als System aufgefaßt. Entspricht etwa dem Oberkarbon Europas)
pennystone Toneisensteinband n
penroseite Penroseit m, $(Ni, Cu, Co)Se_2$

penstock Stauwerk n
pentagonal dodecahedron Pentagondodekaeder n, Dyakishexaeder n
~ **icositetrahedron** Pentagonikositetraeder n
pentahedral pentaedrisch, fünfflächig, fünfseitig
pentahedron Pentaeder n, Fünfflächner m
pentahydrite Pentahydrit m, $Mg[SO_4] \cdot 5H_2O$
pentahydroborite Pentahydroborit m, $CaB_2O_4 \cdot 5H_2O$
pentane Pentan n, C_5H_{12}
pentlandite Pentlandit m, Eisennickelkies m, $(Fe, Ni)_9S_8$
penumbra Sonnenfleckenrand m, Halbschatten m
Penutian [Stage] Penutien n (marine Stufe, unteres Eozän in Nordamerika)
pepino tropische Karstform f
peppered with pyrite mit Pyrit gesprenkelt
peralkaline Alkaliüberschuß..., alkalisch (bezüglich Al_2O_3-Gehalt)
peraluminous Aluminiumüberschuß..., Al-reich (molekularer Anteil Al_2O_3 größer als $CaO + Na_2O + K_2O$)
percentage by volume Volumenprozent n
~ **content** prozentualer Gehalt m
~ **distribution** prozentuale Verteilung f
~ **elongation** Bruchdehnung f
~ **of pore space** Prozentgehalt m an Porenraum
~ **of total pore space** Prozentgehalt m an Gesamtporenraum (an wegsamen und geschlossenen Poren)
~ **subsidence** Absenkungsfaktor m, effektive Senkung f (in Prozent der Vollsenkung)
percentiles Percentile mpl (grafisch bestimmte Körnungskennwerte)
perched block (boulder) erratischer Block m, Findling m, Wackelstein m
~ **ground water** 1. hängender Grundwasserhorizont m, oberflächennahes (schwebendes) Grundwasser n; 2. Staunässe f
~ **spring** Hangendquelle f
~ **water** Wasser n der Aerationszone
~ **water table** [an]gespannter Grundwasserspiegel m
percolate/to [ein]sickern, versickern, durchsickern, eindringen
percolating rate Sickerrate f
~ **water** Sickerwasser n
percolation Einsickern n, Durchsickerung f, Versickerung f, Sickerung f
~ **channel** Sickerkanal m
~ **creep** Sickerung f
~ **rate** Durchflußgeschwindigkeit f
~ **test** Durchlässigkeitsversuch m
~ **velocity** Sickergeschwindigkeit f
~ **water** Sickerwasser n
percrystalline structure Rekristallisationsgefüge n
percussion bit Schlagmeißel m
~ **bit stroke** Fallhöhe f des Meißels

~ **drill** Stoßbohrer m
~ **drilling** schlagendes Bohren n, Schlagbohrverfahren n
~ **drilling rig** Schlagbohrgerät n
~ **frame** Stoßherd m
~ **jumper** Stoßbohrer m
~ **marks** Schlagmarken fpl
~ **penetration method** Rammsondierung f
~ **probe** Rammsonde f, Schlagsonde f
percylite Percylith m, $PbCl_2 \cdot Cu(OH)_2$
perennial permanent, ständig, perennierend, ausdauernd, überwinternd, mehrjährig
~ **ice** fossiles Eis n
~ **irrigation** Dauerbewässerung f
~ **river** durchhaltender Fluß m
~ **snow** ewiger Schnee m
~ **spring** permanente Quelle f, Dauerquelle f
~ **yield** Dauerspende f
perennially frozen ground s. permafrost
perfect cleavage vollkommene Spaltbarkeit f
~ **crystal** Idealkristall m
~ **gas** ideales Gas n
~ **weir** vollkommener Überfall m
perfemic perfemisch
perforating Perforieren n
perforation Perforation f (von Öl- oder Gassonden)
performance of geological prospecting by stage Prozeßgliederung f geologischer Untersuchungsarbeiten in Stadien
pergelation Permafrostbodenbildung f
pergelisol Permafrostboden m, Dauerfrostboden m, Pergelisol n
periastron Periastron n, Periastrum n, Sternnähe f
periclase Periklas m, MgO
periclinal periklinal, zentroklinal, mit umlaufendem Einfallen
~ **bedding** mantelförmiger Schichtenbau m
~ **structure** Meilerstellung f (Basaltsäulen)
pericline 1. Dom m; 2. Periklin m (Feldspatabart)
~ **ripple marks** perikline Rippelmarken fpl
pericynthion Periselenion n, Mondnähe f
peridot[e] s. chrysolite
peridotite Peridotit m
perigee Perigäum n, Erdnähe f
periglacial periglazial
~ **region** Periglazialgebiet n, glaziales Randgebiet n
perihelion Perihelium n, Sonnennähe f
perimagmatic perimagmatisch
~ **deposit** perimagmatische Lagerstätte f
period 1. Schwingungsdauer f (Seismik); 2. Periode f (Stratigrafie, Einheit der chronologischen Skala)
~ **of glaciation** Glazialzeit f, Eiszeit f
~ **of half life** Halbwertzeit f
~ **of oscillation** Schwingungsdauer f
~ **of submergence** Senkungsperiode f
~ **of sun spots** Sonnenfleckenperiode f
periodic[al] change periodische Änderung f

periodic

~ **current** periodische Strömung f
~ **inequalities** periodische Störungen fpl
~ **magnetic field** magnetisches Wechselfeld n
~ **pertubations** periodische Störungen fpl
~ **settling** Periodenabsenkung f
~ **spring** intermittierende Quelle f
~ **time** Schwingungsdauer f
~ **weight** Periodendruck m
periodically reversing magnetic field sich periodisch umkehrendes Magnetfeld n
periodicity Periodizität f, periodisches Auftreten n
peripheral change randliche Umwandlung f
~ **counter** Auszähllineal n (für Gefügediagramme)
~ **faults** Randstörungen fpl (eines tektonischen Beckens)
~ **moraine** Randmoräne f
~ **pressure** Manteldruck m
~ **sink** Randsenke f (Salzstock)
~ **speed of drilling tool** Umfangsgeschwindigkeit f des gesteinszerstörenden Werkzeugs
peristerite Peristerit m (Tieftemperatur-Plagioklas)
peristome Peristom n, Mündungsrand m, Mundfeld n
perite Perit m, $PbBiO_2Cl$
peritectic peritektisch
peritectic Peritektikum n
peritidal complex Peritidalkomplex m (Sammelbezeichnung für alle Ablagerungsmilieus und Ablagerungen, die von Gezeiten beeinflußt sind)
perlite Perlit m
perlitic perlitisch
~ **structure** perlitische Textur f, Perlitgefüge n
permafrost Permafrost m
~ **line** Dauerfrostbodengrenze f (regional)
~ **soil** Permafrostboden m, Dauerfrostboden m
~ **subsoil** Dauerfrostuntergrund m
~ **table** Dauerfrostbodenoberfläche f
permanence of the ocean basins Permanenz f der Ozeane
permanent deformation bleibende Verformung f
~ **guide structure** fester Führungsrahmen m (auf dem Meeresboden am Bohrlochabschluß abgesetzte Einrichtung)
~ **hardness** permanente Wasserhärte f
~ **magnet** Dauermagnet m
~ **overfall weir** Talsperre f mit festem Überfall
~ **plankton** Holoplankton n
~ **snow line** Schneegrenze f
~ **solfatara** ständige Solfatare f
permeability Permeabilität f, Durchlässigkeit f
~ **coefficient** Durchlässigkeitskoeffizient m, Durchlässigkeitsbeiwert m
~ **of ground** Gebirgsdurchlässigkeit f
~ **profile log** Permeabilitätsprofil n
~-**thickness product** (Am) Fließkapazität f
~ **to water** Wasserdurchlässigkeit f

~ **trap** Permeabilitätsfalle f (für Öl oder Gas)
permeable permeabel, durchlässig
~ **bed** Grundwasserleiter m
~ **layer** durchlässige Schicht f
~ **to water** wasserdurchlässig
permeameter Durchlässigkeitsmeßgerät n (Durchströmungsversuch)
permeance magnetische Leitfähigkeit f
permeate/to durchsickern, durchdringen
permeating water Sickerwasser n
permeative boundary Durchlässigkeitsgrenze f
Permian Perm[system] n (chronostratigrafisch); Perm n, Permperiode f (geochronologisch); Perm n, Permzeit f (allgemein)
~ **Age** Perm n, Permzeit f
~ **glaciation** permische Vereisung f
~ **Limestone** Zechsteinkalk m
~ **Period** Perm n, Permperiode f
~ **System** Perm[system] n
permineralize/to versteinern, fossilisieren
permissible load zulässige Belastung f
~ **velocity** Grenzgeschwindigkeit f, zulässige Geschwindigkeit f
permissive bedding plane wasserstauende Schichtfuge f
Permo-Carboniferous Permokarbon n
~-**Triassic** Permotrias f
perovskite Perowskit m, $CaTiO_3$
perpendicular vertikal, seiger
~ **depth** Seigerteufe f
~ **displacement** flache Sprungweite f
~ **separation** Sprunghöhe f senkrecht zur Schichtung
~ **slip** flache Sprungweite f
~ **throw** scheinbare stratigrafische Sprunghöhe (Schubhöhe) f, seigere Sprunghöhe (Verwerfungshöhe) f
~ **to the stratification** bankrecht
perpetual snow ewiger Schnee m
perpetually snow-capped mit ewigem Schnee bedeckt
perryite Perryit m, Ni_3Si (Meteoritenmineral)
persistence Beständigkeit f
~ **of a bed** Durchhalten n einer Schicht (von Bohrung zu Bohrung)
persistent fossil durchlaufendes Fossil n
~ **mineral** Durchläufer m (Mineral)
~ **reflecting horizon** durchhaltender reflektierender Horizont m
~ **stratum** durchgehende (durchlaufende) Schicht f
perspective block Blockdiagramm n
perthite Perthit m (Orthoklas mit orientierten Albitentmischungskörpern)
perthitic perthitisch
perturbation Störung f (z.B. physikalischer Parameter)
~ **equation** Störungsgleichung f
perturbing body Störkörper m
~ **function** Störungsfunktion f
~ **term** Störungsglied n

pervade/to durchtrümern, durchdringen
pervious durchlässig
~ **bed** durchlässige Schicht f
~ **blanket** Entwässerungsschicht f
~ **ground** durchlässiger Boden m
~ **shell** Dränschicht f *(einer Talsperre)*
~ **stratum** durchlässige Schicht f
~ **subsoil** durchlässiger Baugrund m
~ **to water** wasserdurchlässig
perviousness Durchlässigkeit f
petalite Petalit m, Li[AlSi$_4$O$_{10}$]
peter out/to sich verdrücken, auskeilen
petering Verdrückung f, Auskeilen n
Peter's length Petersche Länge f *(Seismik)*
petre s. nitre
petrescence Versteinerungsvorgang m
petrifaction 1. Versteinerung f *(als Vorgang)*; 2. Petrefakt n, Versteinerung f *(als Ergebnis)*
petrifactology Petrefaktenkunde f, Versteinerungskunde f
petrified versteinert, fossil
~ **excrement** Koprolith m
~ **forest** versteinerter Wald m
~ **peat** versteinerter (fossiler) Torf m
~ **wood** versteinertes (fossiles) Holz n
petrify/to versteinern
petrochemical calculation petrochemische Berechnung f
petrochemicals Mineralölerzeugnisse npl; Erdölderivate npl
petrochemistry 1. Petrochemie f, Gesteinschemie f; 2. *(z.T. auch für)* Petrolchemie f, Erdölchemie f
petroclastic limestone s. detrital limestone
petrofabric analysis Gefügeanalyse f
~ **diagram** Korngefügediagramm n
~ **studies** Gefügekunde f
petrofabrics Gefügekunde f
petrogenesis Petrogenese f
petrogenetic petrogenetisch
~ **grid** petrogenetische Darstellung f
petrogeny Petrogenese f
petrographer Petrograf m
petrographic[al] petrografisch, gesteinskundlich
~ **character** Gesteinscharakter m
~ **composition** Gesteinszusammensetzung f
~ **microscopy** Gesteinsmikroskopie f
~ **province** petrografische Provinz f, Gesteinsprovinz f
petrography Petrografie f, Gesteinskunde f
petrol Benzin n
petroleum Petroleum n, Erdöl n *(s.a. oil)*
~-**bearing** petroleumhaltig, erdölhaltig
~ **coke** Petroleumkoks m
~ **deposit** Erdöllager n
~ **exploitation** Erdölgewinnung f, Erdölausbeutung f
~ **field** Erdölfeld n
~ **gas** Petroleumgas n, Erdölgas n
~ **geologist** Erdölgeologe m
~ **geology** Erdölgeologie f

~ **hydrogeology** Erdölhydrogeologie f
~ **pitch** Petrolpech n, Erdölpech n
~ **production engineering (technology)** Erdölfördertechnik f
~ **prospect** Erdölhoffnungsgebiet n
~ **refinery plant** Erdölraffinerieanlage f
~ **reservoir engineer** Erdöllagerstätteningenieur m
~ **reservoir engineering** Reservoirmechanik f
~ **secondary recovery** Sekundärgewinnungsverfahren n von Erdöl
petroliferous erdölhaltig, erdölführend
~ **area** Erdölgebiet n *(im engeren Sinne)*
~ **bed** erdölführende Schicht f, Ölträger m
~ **horizon** Erdölhorizont m
~ **shale** Ölschiefer m
~ **strata** erdölführende Schichten fpl
~ **structure** erdölführende Struktur f
petrolized mit Erdöl imprägniert
petrologic[al] petrologisch, gesteinskundlich
~ **character** Gesteinscharakter m
~ **microscope** Polarisationsmikroskop n
petrologist Petrologe m
petrology Petrologie f, Gesteinskunde f
petrophysics Petrophysik f
petrosilex 1. Felsit m; 2. kompakte Feuersteinmassen, Hornstein in Kalkschichten
petrotectonics Petrotektonik f, Gefügekunde f der Gesteine
petrous steinartig, steinig, versteinert
~ **phosphates** feste Phosphatablagerung f *(im Gegensatz zu erdig)*
petunse, petuntse, petuntze halb zersetzter leicht kaolinisierter Granit m
petzite Petzit m, Ag$_3$AuTe$_2$
PGC = programmed gain control
pH index pH-Wert m
pH meter pH-Wert-Messer m
pH value pH-Wert m
phacelite Kaliophilit m, K[AlSiO$_4$]
phacoidal flaserig, linsig
~ **structure** Phakoidgefüge n, Linsengefüge f
phacolite Phakolith m *(Varietät von Chabasit)*
phacolith Phakolith m *(Intrusionsform)*
phaneric phanerokristallin
~ **texture** phanerokristalline Struktur f *(bei Karbonatgesteinen; Korngrößen über 0,01 mm)*
phanerocrystalline phanerokristallin
Phanerogamia Phanerogamen fpl, Blütenpflanzen fpl
phanerogenic phanerogen
phaneromerous phaneromer
phanerozoic phanerozoisch
Phanerozoic [Eon] Phanerozoikum n *(Äon)*
phantom [horizon] Phantomhorizont m *(Seismik)*
pharmacolite Pharmakolith m, Arsenblüte f, CaH[AsO$_4$]·2H$_2$O
pharmacosiderite Pharmakosiderit m, Würfelerz n, KFe$_4$[(OH)$_4$|(AsO$_4$)$_3$]·6−7H$_2$O
phase behaviour Phasenzustandsverhalten n
~ **change** Phasenumwandlung f

phase

- ~ **contrast microscopy** Phasenkontrastverfahren n *(Mikroskopie)*
- ~ **delay error** Laufzeitfehler m
- ~ **diagram** Phasendiagramm n, Zustandsdiagramm n
- ~ **difference** Phasendifferenz f, Gangunterschied m
- ~ **distortion** Phasenverzerrung f, Phasenverschiebung f *(Seismik)*
- ~ **distribution** Phasenverteilung f
- ~ **equilibrium** Phasengleichgewicht n
- ~ **inversion** Phaseninversion f, Phasenumkehrung f *(Seismik)*
- ~ **of consolidation** Erstarrungsphase f
- ~ **of eruptivity** Eruptionsphase f
- ~ **of folding** Faltungsphase f
- ~ **redistribution** Phasenumverteilung f
- ~ **resonance** Phasenresonanz f
- ~ **response** Phasencharakteristik f, Phasengang m, Phasenverhalten n *(Seismik)*
- ~ **rule** Phasenregel f
- ~ **shift[ing]** Phasenverschiebung f
- ~ **spectrum** Phasencharakteristik f *(Seismik)*
- ~ **transfer** Phasenübergang m
- ~ **transition** Phasenübergang m
- ~ **velocity** Phasengeschwindigkeit f *(Seismik)*

phasing Phasenveränderung f *(Seismik)*
phassachate bleifarbener Achat m
phenacite Phenakit m, $Be_2[SiO_4]$
phengite Phengit m, $K(Fe,Mg)Al[(OH,F)_2|(Al,Si)Si_3O_{10}]$
phenhydrous unter Wasser abgelagert *(Pflanzenmaterial)*
phenoblast Phänoblast m, Megablast m, Porphyroblast m
phenoclast Phänoklast m
phenoclastic phänoklastisch
phenocryst Einsprengling m *(in magmatischen Gesteinen)*
phenocrystic phänokristisch, ungleichmäßig körnig
phenology Phänologie f
phenomena of interference Interferenzerscheinungen fpl
phenomenologic[al] phänomenologisch
phenoplast Phänoplast m
phenotype Phänotyp[us] m
philadelphite Philadelphit m *(Zersetzungsprodukt von Biotit)*
philippinite Philippinit m *(Tektitengruppe)*
phillipsite Phillipsit m, $KCa[Al_3Si_5O_{16}]\cdot 6H_2O$
phlebite Phlebit m
phlebitic structure phlebitische Textur f, Adertextur f *(bei Migmatit)*
phlobaphinite Phlobaphinit m *(Maceraltyp des Humocollinits)*
phlogopite Phlogopit m, Magnesiaglimmer m, $KMg_3[(F, OH)_2|AlSi_3O_{10}]$
phoenicochroite Phönikochroit m, $Pb_3[O|(CrO_4)_2]$
phonolite Phonolith m
- ~ **tuff** Phonolithtuff m

phorogenesis Krustengleitung f auf dem Erdmantel
phosgenite Phosgenit m, $Pb_2[Cl_2|CO_3]$
phosphate Phosphat n
- ~ **mine** Phosphatgrube f
- ~ **of iron** Eisenphosphat n
- ~ **rock** Apatitgestein n

phosphatic phosphatisch, phosphorartig
- ~ **chalk** Phosphatkreide f
- ~ **deposit** Phosphatlagerstätte f
- ~ **deposit due to weathering** Phosphatverwitterungslagerstätte f
- ~ **iron ore** phosphathaltiges Eisenerz n
- ~ **rock** Phosphatgestein n
- ~ **shale** phosphatischer Schiefer m

phosphatized phosphatisiert
phosphoferrite Phosphoferrit m, $(Fe, Mn)_3[PO_4]_2\cdot 3H_2O$
phosphophyllite Phosphophyllit m, $Zn_2Fe[PO_4]_2\cdot 4H_2O$
phosphoresce/to phosphoreszieren
phosphorescence Phosphoreszenz f
- ~ **of the sea** Meeresleuchten n

phosphorescent phosphoreszierend
phosphoric phosphorhaltig
phosphorite Phosphorit m, Naturphosphat n
- ~ **nodule** Phosphoritknolle f

phosphoritic phosphoritisch
phosphosiderite Phosphosiderit m, Klinostrengit m, $Fe[PO_4]\cdot 2H_2O$
phosphuranylite Phosphuranylit m, $Ca[(UO_2)_4|(OH)_4|(PO_4)_2]\cdot 8H_2O$
photic zone durchlichtete Wasserzone f
photobase Bildbasis f, Fotobasis f *(Fotogeologie)*
photoelastic spannungsoptisch
- ~ **fringe patterns** spannungsoptische Streifenbilder npl
- ~ **material** spannungsoptisches Material n
- ~ **reflection method** Reflexionsverfahren n *(Spannungsoptik)*

photoelasticity Spannungsoptik f
photoelectric logging fotoelektrisches Verfahren n der Wasserzuflußmessung *(in Bohrungen)*
photogeology Fotogeologie f
photogrammetric plotting fotogrammetrische Auswertung f
- ~ **rectification** fotogrammetrische Entzerrung f

photogrammetry Fotogrammetrie f, Bildmeßwesen n
photographic aerial survey Luftvermessung f
- ~ **flight** Fotoflug m
- ~ **reconnaissance** Bilderkundung f

photolineations Fotolineationen fpl *(in Fernerkundungsaufnahmen erkennbare Lineationen)*
photoluminescence Fotolumineszenz f
photomap Luftbildkarte f
photometry Fotometrie f
photomicrograph Mikrofoto n, Mikrobild n
photomultiplier s. ~ tube
- ~ **counter** Szintillationszähler m

~ **tube** Sekundärelektronenvervielfacher *m*, SEV
photosphere Fotosphäre *f*, Lichtkreis *m* der Sonne
Phragmites peat Rohrtorf *m*
phreatic phreatisch, unterirdisch
~ **decline** Grundwasserspiegelabfall *m*
~ **eruption** phreatischer Ausbruch *m*
~ **fluctuation** Grundwasserspiegelschwankung *f*
~ **gases** phreatische Gase *npl*
~ **ground water** freies (ungespanntes) Grundwasser *n*
~ **line** Sickerlinie *f*
~ **nappe** Grundwasserspiegel *m*
~ **rise** Grundwasserspiegelanstieg *m*
~ **surface** phreatische Grundwasserschicht *f*, Grundwasserspiegel *m*, Grundwasserfläche *f*, Sickerfläche *f*
~ **water** freies (ungespanntes) Grundwasser *n*
~ **zone** Sättigungszone *f*
phreatomagmatic eruption phreatomagmatischer Ausbruch *m*
phreatophyte Grundwasserpflanze *f*
phtanite *s.* phthanite
phthanite kryptokristallines Kieselgestein *n* (*z.B. Jaspilit*)
phyllite Phyllit *m*
phyllitization Phyllitisierung *f*
phyllofacies Schichtungsfazies *f* (*Faziesunterschiede nach spezifischen Schichtungsmerkmalen*)
phylloid blattförmig
phyllonite Phyllonit *m*
phylloretine Phylloretin *n*, $C_{18}H_{18}$
phyllosilicates Schichtsilikate *npl*, Phyllosilikate *npl*
phylogenesis Phylogenie *f*, Stammesgeschichte *f*
phylogenetic phylogenetisch
phylogenic tree Stammbaum *m*
phylogeny Phylogenie *f*, Stammesgeschichte *f*
phyloneanic form Jugendform *f*
phylum Hauptabteilung *f*, Stamm *m*
physical crystallography Kristallphysik *f*
~ **geography** physikalische Geografie *f*
~ **meteorology** physikalische Meteorologie *f*
~ **mineralogy** Kristallphysik *f*
~ **pendulum** physikalisches Pendel *n*
~ **time measurement** physikalische Altersbestimmung *f*
~ **weathering** physikalische (mechanische) Verwitterung *f*
physico-chemical physikalisch-chemisch
physics of solids Festkörperphysik *f*
physiographic factor affecting run-off morphologische Abflußbedingung *f*
~ **geology** physiografische Geologie *f*
physiography Physio[geo]grafie *f*, Geomorphologie *f*
phyteral erkennbares pflanzliches Fossil in der Kohle

phytoecology Pflanzenökologie *f*
phytogenetic, phytogenic phytogen[etisch], pflanzlichen Ursprungs
~ **rock** phytogenes Gestein *n*
phytogeographic[al] phytogeografisch, pflanzengeografisch, geobotanisch
phytogeography Phytogeografie *f*, Pflanzengeografie *f*, Geobotanik *f*
phytoliths Phytolithe *mpl* (*von pflanzlichen Organismen gebildete marine Kalksteine*)
phytomorphic phytomorph
phytopalaeontology Paläobotanik *f*
phytophoric rock Gestein *n* aus Pflanzenresten
phytoplankton Phytoplankton *n*, Schwebeflora *f*
Piacenzian [Stage] Piacenza *n*, Piacenta *n*, Piacenzium *n* (*Stufe des Pliozäns*)
pick/to aussondern (*Seismik*)
~ **out the ore** ausklauben
~ **up** aufnehmen (*Meßdaten*)
pick Einsatz *m* (*Seismik*); Tiefenbestimmung *f* eines Leithorizonts
~-**up** Detektor *m* (*Geophysik*); Geophon *n*; Hochspannungsleitung *f* (*Seismik*)
picked deads Leseberge *pl*, Klaubeberge *pl*
~ **ore** Scheideerz *n*
pickeringite Pickeringit *m*, $MgAl_2[SO_4]_4 \cdot 22H_2O$
picket Buhnenpfahl *m*
picking Klauben *n*, Auslesen *n* [mit Hand]
~ **belt** Klaubeband *n*
~ **by hand** Handklauben *n*, Handlesen *n*
~ **drum** Erzwäscher *m*, Klassiertrommel *f*
~ **sample** Hackprobe *f*
~ **table** Klaub[e]tisch *m*, Lesetisch *m*
~-**up of sediment** Geschiebetrieb *m*
pickings Leseberge *pl*, Klaubeberge *pl*
picrite Pikrit *m*
picromerite Pikromerit *m*, Schönit *m*, $K_2Mg[SO_4]_2 \cdot 6H_2O$
picropharmacolite Pikropharmakolith *m*, $(Ca, Mg)_3[AsO_4]_2 \cdot 6H_2O$
pie slice „Tortenstück" *n* (*Fächer- oder Geschwindigkeitsfilterung in der Seismik*)
piecemeal stoping *s.* magmatic stoping
piedmont Piedmontfläche *f*, Vorland *n*, Gebirgsvorland *n*
~ **alluvial plain** alluviale Piedmontebene *f*
~ **benchlands (flats)** Piedmontflächen *fpl*, Piedmonttreppe *f*
~ **glacier** Piedmontgletscher *m*, Vorlandgletscher *m*
~ **lake** alpiner Randsee *m*
~ **plain** Piedmontebene *f*, Vorlandebene *f*, Bergfußebene *f*
~ **scarp** *s.* scarplet
~ **slope** Piedmontfläche *f*, Vorland *n*, Bergfußfläche *f*
~ **stairway (steps)** Piedmonttreppe *f*
~ **terraces** Piedmontterrassen *fpl*
piedmontite *s.* piemontite
piemontite Piemontit, Manganepidot *m*, $Ca_2(Mn, Fe)Al_2[O|OH|SiO_4|Si_2O_7]$

pierce 266

pierce/to durchspießen, durchstoßen
pierced rock Felstor n
piercement fold Durchspießungsfalte f, Diapirfalte f
~-type salt dome Durchspießungssalzdom m
piercing folds Durchspießungsfalten fpl
~ klippe Durchspießungsklippe f
Pierre Shale Pierre-Schiefer m (Santon bis Maastricht, Nordamerika)
piezoclase Piezoklase f, Druckspalte f
piezocrystallization Piezokristallisation f, Druckkristallisation f
piezoelectric piezoelektrisch
~ crystal piezoelektrischer Kristall m, Piezokristall m
~ crystal plate Piezokristallplatte f
~ crystal unit Piezokristalleinheit f
~ quartz piezoelektrischer Quarz m
piezoelectricity Piezoelektrizität f
piezomagnetic piezomagnetisch
piezometer Wasserstandsmesser m
piezometric piezometrisch
~ contour Äquipotentiallinie f
~ ground-water surface gespannter (artesischer) Grundwasserspiegel m
~ head piezometrische Druckhöhe f
~ level Druckspiegel m (von Grundwasser)
~ map Hydroisohypsenplan m
~ surface gespannter (artesischer) Grundwasserspiegel m
pig iron Roheisen n, Masseleisen n
~-iron production Roheisenerzeugung f
pigeon-blood ruby Taubenblutrubin m (Edelsteinqualität)
pigeonite Pigeonit m (Pyroxenmineral)
piggot corer Kernschußgerät n für Meeresbodenproben
pigotite Pigotit m, $Al_4[O_6|C_6H_5O_4] \cdot 13^{1}/_{2}H_2O$
pigtail Anschlußkabel n
pilbarite Pilbarit m (Gemenge von Thorogummit und Kasolit)
pile 1. Pfahl m, Rammpfahl m; 2. Haufwerk n
~-driving materials Haldenmaterial n
~ dwellings Pfahlbauten mpl
~ foundations Pfahlgründungen fpl
~-of-brick texture Ziegelstapelgefüge n (bei Anhydrit)
~ of nappe Deckenpaket n
piling 1. Haldenschüttung f, Haldenlagerung f; 2. Nagelung f (eines Felsens)
~-up of water Wasserstau m
pilite s. jamesonite
pillar 1. Pfeiler m; 2. Feste f, Bergfeste f
~ exploitation Pfeilerbau m
~ of coal Kohlenpfeiler m
~ of ore Erzpfeiler m
~ sample Säulenprobe f (Probe aus dem Kohlenflöz als Profilsäule)
~ thickness Pfeilerstärke f
~ work Pfeilerbau m
pillarlike säulenförmig
pillow lava Pillowlava f, Kissenlava f, Matratzenlava f

~ stage s. salt pillow stage
~ structure wollsackförmige Absonderung f, Kissenstruktur f
pillowy lava s. pillow lava
pilot bit Stufenmeißel m, Führungsmeißel m, Pilotmeißel m
~ hole Pilotbohrung f, Basisbohrung f, Vorbohrloch n
~ run Testmessung f
pilotaxitic texture pilotaxitische Struktur f
pimple stone s. pebble stone
pimpley Schieferton m mit Toneisensteinknollen
pin cracks 1. kleine Gebirgsspalten fpl; 2. Dehnungsschlechten fpl (mit Wasser und Gas gefüllte Spalten in der Kohle)
pinacoid Pinakoid n
~ face Endfläche f (Kristall)
pinacoidal plane Endfläche f (Kristall)
pinakiolite Pinakiolith m, $(Mg, Mn^{"})_2Mn^{"'}[O_2|BO_3]$
pinch out/to ausgehen, auskeilen, sich erschöpfen, sich verdrücken
pinch Gangverdrückung f; Flözverdrückung f; Einschnürung f
~ and swell structures an- und abschwellende Strukturen fpl (ähnlich der Boudinage, besonders bei Mineralgängen)
~-out Verdrückung f
~-out trap durch Auskeilen einer porösen Schicht hervorgerufene Erdölfalle f
pinched[-out] verdrückt
pinching Einschnürung f, Einklemmung f, Verdrückung f
~-out Verdrückung f
pindy Brandschiefer m (Cornwall)
pine crystal Dendrit m
~-tree cloud Pinienwolke f (Vulkanismus)
pingo Aufeis n, Palsa f
~ remnant Toteisschmelzsee m, Kesselsee m
pingok s. pingo
pinite Pinit m (glimmerartiges Mineral pseudomorph nach Cordierit)
pinnacle Kuppenriff n, Felszinne f, Zinne f
pinnacles Zackenfirn m
pinnate gefiedert
~ cleavage fiedrig angeordnete Schieferung f (z.B. in bezug auf eine Störung)
~ leaf gefiedertes Blatt n
~ shear joints gefiederte Scherklüfte fpl
~ tension joints gefiederte Zugklüfte fpl
pinnoite Pinnoit m, $Mg[B_2O(OH)_6]$
pinnule Fiederchen n
pinolite Pinolith m (Gemenge aus Magnesit- und Kalkschiefer, z.T. metamorph)
pinpointing Lokalisieren n (mit größter Genauigkeit)
pintadoite Pintadoit m, $CaH[VO_4] \cdot 4H_2O$
pinwheel garnet rotierter Granat m
pioneer organisms Erstbesiedler mpl
~ species Pionierarten fpl
piotine s. saponite

pipe 1. Pfeife f, Schlot m, Vulkanschlot m, vulkanische Durchschlagsröhre f; 2. Schlotte f; 3. Rohr n *(Bohrtechnik)*
~ **amygdules** s. ~ vesicles
~ **carriage** Feldbahnwagen m, Rohrwagen m
~ **coupling** 1. Rohrverbindung f; 2. Gestängeverbinder m *(Tiefbohrtechnik)*
~ **cutter** Rohrschneider m
~ **filling** Schlotfüllung f
~-**laying barge** Barke f zum Verlegen von Rohrleitungen
~-**laying ship** Schiff n zum Verlegen von Rohrleitungen
~ **setback** Gestängezug m, Gestängetisch m
~ **spillway** Rohrüberlauf m *(zur Wassermengenmessung)*
~-**stabbing board** Aushängebühne f, Gestängebühne f *(Tiefbohrung)*
~ **vesicles** Blasenzüge mpl *(in Vulkaniten)*
~ **wrench** Rohrzange f
pipeclay Pfeifenton f, Steinzeugton m
piped oil rohes Erdöl n *(nach dem Ablassen des mitgeförderten Wassers)*
pipelike pfeifenartig
pipeline Pipeline f, Überlandrohrleitung f
pipelining Verlegen n von Überlandrohrleitungen
pipestone Catlinit m, indianischer Pfeifenstein m
piping hydraulischer Grundbruch m *(innere Erosion)*
piracy Anzapfung f, Enthauptung, Kappen n *(eines Flusses im Oberlauf)*
pirate stream durch Anzapfung entstandener Fluß m
pirssonite Pirssonit m, $Na_2Ca[CO_3]_2 \cdot 2H_2O$
pisanite Pisanit m, Kupfermelanterit m, $(Fe,Cu)[SO_4] \cdot 7H_2O$
piscine fischähnlich
piscis Fisch m
pisekite Pisekit m *(U-, Ce-, usw. -Niobat und -Titanat)*
pisiform erbsenförmig
~ **iron ore** Bohnerz n
~ **limestone** erbsenförmiger (oolitischer) Kalkstein m, Schalenkalk m, Erbsenstein m
pisolite Pisolithgestein n
pisolith Pisolith m, Schlammkügelchen n *(aus vulkanischer Asche)*
pisolitic pisolithhaltig, pisolithisch, erbsenförmig
~ **iron ore** s. pisiform iron ore
~ **limestone** s. pisiform limestone
~ **tuff** Pisolithtuff m
pisosparite pisolithischer Kalkstein m
pissasphalt Bergteer m, Pissasphalt m
pisselaeum Varietät von Bitumen
pistacite Epidot m, Pistazit m, $Ca_2(Fe,Al)Al_2[O|OH|SiO_4|Si_2O_7]$
piston corer Kolbenlot m
pit 1. Grube f, Schließmuskelgrube f *(auf der Lateralfläche von Fossilschalen)*; 2. Kohlenschacht m, Grube f, Zeche f; 3. Kessel m, Kolk m; 4. Ausbruch m *(z.B. bei Schliffen)*
~-**and-mound structure** Trichter- und Kegelstruktur f, Sandkegel mpl *(sedimentäre Struktur)*
~ **and quarry industry** Steine- und Erdenindustrie f
~ **arch** Grubenausbau m
~ **bottom** Füllort n
~ **coal** Förderkohle f
~ **crater** Einbruchskrater m, Einsturzkrater m, Einsturzkessel m, Caldera f
~ **entrance** Stollenmundloch n
~ **gas** Grubengas n
~ **heap** Bergehalde f
~ **ponor** Schlotponor m
~ **wall** Schachtwand f
~ **water** Grubenwasser n
pitch 1. Neigung f, Einfall m, Einfallen n, Abtauchen n, Sprungwinkel m *(z.B. von Gesteinsschichten)*; 2. Pech n, Teer m
~ **coke** Pechkoks m
~ **glance** Pechglanz m
~ **of fold axis** Abtauchen n einer Faltenachse
~ **ore** s. uraninite
~ **peat** Pechtorf m
pitchblende s. uraninite
pitcher brasses erhärteter Schieferton m
pitching geneigt
~ **axis** eintauchende Achse f *(Falte)*
~ **seam** geneigtes Flöz n
pitchlike pechartig
pitchstone Pechstein m
pitchy pechartig
~ **lustre** Pechglanz m
pith weiches Trum n *(eines Ganges)*
pitman Brunnengräber m
pittasphalt Malthait m, Mineralteer m
pitted löcherig
~ **morainal topography** kuppige Moränenlandschaft f
~ **outwash plain** Sanderebene f mit Toteislöchern (Söllen)
~ **pebbles** eingedrückte Gerölle npl
~ **surface** narbige Oberfläche f
~ **weathering** Lochverwitterung f, Narbenverwitterung f
pitticite Pitticit m, Arseneisensinter m, $Fe_{20}[(OH)_{24}|(AsO_4, PO_4, SO_4)_{13}] \cdot 9H_2O$
pittinite Pittinit m *(unreiner Gummit)*
pivotability Pivotabilität f, Rollbereitschaft f *(von klastischen Körnern)*
pivotal axis Drehachse f
~ **fault** Drehverwerfung f
place/in autochthon, in situ
placer [deposit] Seife[nlagerstätte] f
~ **gold** Seifengold n, Waschgold n
~ **mineral** Seifenmineral n
~ **mining** Seifenabbau m
placoid plakoidschuppig
~ **scale** Plakoidschuppe f *(bei Fischen)*
plagioclase Plagioklas m *(Feldspat, Mischkristall)*

plagiogranite

mit den Endgliedern Na[AlSi$_3$O$_8$] und Ca [Al$_2$Si$_2$O$_8$])
plagiogranite Plagiogranit *m*
plagionite Plagionit *m*, 5PbS·4Sb$_2$S$_3$
plain Ebene *f*, Flachland *n*
~ **of abrasion** Abrasionsfläche *f*
~ **of debris** Schuttebene *f*
~ **of degradation** Abtragungsebene *f*
~ **of denudation** Abrasionsfläche *f*
~ **of erosion** Abtragungsebene *f*, Erosionsebene *f*
~ **of marine abrasion**, ~ **of [sub]marine denudation** Brandungsterrasse *f*, Brandungsplatte *f*, Schorre *f*, marine Abrasionsfläche *f*
~ **shale** dickplattiger Ölschiefer *m*
~ **tract** Flußniederung *f (im Unterlauf)*
~**-type fold** *s.* bending fold
Plaisancian [Stage] *s.* Piacenzian
plan/in im Grundriß
~ **of mine** Grubenplan *m*
~ **of site** Lageplan *m*
~ **of the concession** Mutungsriß *m*
~**-parallel structure** Planparallelgefüge *n*, gleichförmige Lagerung *f*
planar cross-bedding gerade (gestreckte) Schrägschichtung *f*, Diagonalschichtung *f*
~ **cross stratification** ebenflächig begrenzte Schrägschichtung *f*
~ **flow structure** Fließebene *f (Magmatitgefüge)*
planate/to abhobeln *(Gletschererosion)*; einebnen, verebnen *(Gebirge durch Denudation)*
planation Abhobelung *f (Gletschererosion)*; Einebnung *f*, Verebnung *f (von Gebirgen durch Denudation)*
plancheite Plancheit *m*, Cu$_8$[(OH)$_2$Si$_4$O$_{11}$]$_2$·H$_2$O
plane/to abhobeln; ebnen
~ **down** abhobeln
plane eben, flach
plane Ebene *f*, ebene Fläche *f*
~ **angle** flacher Winkel *m*
~**-centred lattice** flächenzentriertes Gitter *n*
~ **face** ebene Fläche *f*
~ **fault** glatte (ebene) Verwerfung *f*
~ **flow** ebene Strömung *f*
~ **lattice** Kristallnetzebene *f*
~ **light** einfaches (nicht polarisiertes) Licht *n*
~ **of a plane flow** Stromebene *f*
~ **of bedding** Schichtfläche *f*, Schichtebene *f*, Ablagerungsfläche *f*
~ **of break** Bruchfläche *f*, Bruchebene *f*
~ **of cleavage** Spalt[ungs]fläche *f*
~ **of denudation** Erosionsebene *f*
~ **of deposition** *s.* ~ **of bedding**
~ **of division** Teilungsfläche *f*, Absonderungsfläche *f*, Trennungsfläche *f*
~ **of emersion** Emersionsfläche *f*
~ **of erosion** Erosionsebene *f*
~ **of flattening** Plättungsebene *f*
~ **of foliation** Schieferungsebene *f*
~ **of fracture** Bruchfläche *f*, Bruchebene *f*
~ **of incidence** Einfallsebene *f*

268

~ **of isostatic compensation** isostatische Ausgleichsfläche *f*
~ **of lamination** Schichtebene *f*
~ **of motion** Bewegungsebene *f*
~ **of polarization** Polarisationsebene *f*
~ **of reflection** Reflexionsebene *f*
~ **of refraction** Brechungsebene *f*
~ **of rupture** Bruchfläche *f*, Bruchebene *f*
~ **of schistosity** Schieferungsebene *f*
~ **of separation** Trennungsfläche *f*, Löser *m*; Absonderungsfläche *f*
~ **of shear** Scher[ungs]fläche *f*
~ **of sliding** Rutschebene *f*
~ **of stratification** Schichtfläche *f*, Ablagerungsfläche *f*, Schicht[ungs]ebene *f*
~ **of stretching** Streckfläche *f (bei Intrusivkörpern)*
~ **of symmetry** Symmetrieebene *f*, Spiegelebene *f*
~ **of thrust** Schubfläche *f*
~**/on** senkrecht zur Kluftfläche
~ **polarization** lineare Polarisation *f*
~**-polarized** linear (eben) polarisiert
~**-polarized wave** planpolarisierte (linear polarisierte) Welle *f*
~ **schistosity** schieferige Textur *f*, ebene Schieferung *f*
~ **state of stress** ebener Spannungszustand *m*
~ **strain** ebene Deformation *f*
~ **table map (sheet)** Meßtischblatt *n*
~ **table survey** Meßtischaufnahme *f*
~ **table survey sheet** Meßtischblatt *n*
~ **table surveying** Meßtischaufnahme *f*
planed-down eingeebnet
planeness Ebenheit *f*
planet Planet *m*
planetary planetarisch, Planeten...
~ **nebula** planetarischer Nebel *m*
~ **rings** planetare Ringe *mpl*
~ **system** Planetensystem *n*
planetesimal Meteorstein *m*
planetoid Planetoid *m*, Asteroid *m*
planetology Planetologie *f*
planimeter Planimeter *n*, Flächen[inhalts]messer *m*
planimetering Planimetrierung *f*
planina Karsthochfläche *f*
planing-down Abhobelung *f*
plank gasabgebende Schicht *f*
plankter Planktonorganismus *m*
plankton Plankton *n*
planktonic planktonisch
~ **foraminifers** Planktonforaminiferen *fpl*
planned subsidence planmäßige Absenkung *f*
planoconformity Konformität *f* in Mächtigkeit und Lagerung *(von Schichten)*
planoferrite Planoferrit *m*, Fe$_2$[(OH)$_4$|SO$_4$]·13H$_2$O
planophyric lagenartig porphyrisch *(von Gefügen mit Anreicherung der Einsprenglinge in Fließebenen)*
planosol Boden *m* mit verhärtetem Untergrund

plant/to Geophone aufstellen
plant 1. Pflanze *f*; 2. Werkanlage *f*
~ **assemblage** Pflanzengesellschaft *f*, Pflanzenassoziation *f*
~-**bearing deposit** Pflanzenablagerung *f*
~ **bullion** Dolomitknolle *f* im Kohlenflöz
~ **canopy** Pflanzendecke *f*, Blattbaldachin *m*, Laubstockwerk *n* *(Fernerkundung)*
~ **community** *s.* ~ assemblage
~ **cover[ing]** Pflanzendecke *f*
~ **deposit** Pflanzenablagerung *f*
~ **eater** Pflanzenfresser *m*
~-**eating** pflanzenfressend
~ **feeder** Pflanzenfresser *m*
~ **fossils** fossile Pflanzen *fpl* (Pflanzenreste *mpl*)
~ **impression** Pflanzenabdruck *m*
~ **kingdom** Pflanzenreich *n*
~ **remains** Pflanzenreste *mpl*
Plantae Pflanzenreich *n*
planting Bepflanzung *f*
plasma Plasma *m* (*s.a.* chalcedony)
plaster off/to verkleben
plaster conglomerate fossiles Steinpflaster *n (auf einer Erosionsfläche)*
~ **of Paris** gebrannter Gips *m*
~ **stone** Mergel *m*, Gips *m*
plastering-on Moränenzuwachs *m (an der Gletscherbasis)*
plastic plastisch, knetbar; bindig *(Boden)*
~ **clay** plastischer (knetbarer) Ton *m*, Bindeton *m*
~ **deformation** plastische Verformung *f*
~ **fire clay** feuerfester Bindeton *m*
~ **flow** plastisches Fließen *n*
~ **limit** Ausrollgrenze *f*, Rollgrenze *f*, obere Plastizitätsgrenze *f*
~ **strata** plastisches Gebirge *n*
~ **zone** plastische Zone *f (Steinkohlenverkokung)*
plasticity Plastizität *f*, Bildsamkeit *f*
~ **index** Plastizitätszahl *f*
~ **of soil** Bodenzähigkeit *f*
plasticizing plastifizierend
plasticlast Plastiklast *m*, Schlickgeröll *n*
plasto-elastic flow plastisch-elastisches Fließen *n*
plate bearing test Plattenbelastungsversuch *m*, Plattendruckversuch *m*
~ **diagram** Plattendiagramm *n (Lageschema der Echinodermenplatten)*
~ **juncture** Plattengrenze *f*
~ **load bearing test** *s.* ~ bearing test
~ **shale** Plattenschiefer *m*; harter Schieferton *m*
~-**shaped** plattig
~ **tectonics** Plattentektonik *f*
plateau Plateau *n*, Hochebene *f*, Hochfläche *f*, Tafelland *n*, Schollengebirge *f*
~ **basalt** Plateaubasalt *m*, Deckenbasalt *m*
~ **block mountains** Tafelschollengebirge *n*
~-**forming movement** Plateaubewegung *f*

~ **glacier** Plateaugletscher *m*
~ **of ice** Eisplateau *n*
~ **surface** Plateaufläche *f*
platey *s.* platy
platform 1. Plattform *f*, Tafel *f (großtektonische Strukturform)*; 2. Meßbasis *f*, Beobachtungsbasis *f*
~ **basin** Tafelsenke *f*
~ **cover** Tafeldeckgebirge *n*
~ **element** Plattformelement *n (Conodonten)*
~ **on legs** schwimmendes Bohrgerüst *n* mit senkbaren Stützen
platina *s.* platinum
platinic *s.* platinous
platiniferous platinhaltig
platinoids Metalle *npl* der Platingruppe
platinous platinartig, platinführend
platinum Platin *n*, Pt
~ **wire** Platindraht *m*
plattnerite Plattnerit *m*, PbO_2
platy plattenförmig, plattig, bankförmig
~ **flow structure** Fließebene *f (Magmatitgefüge)*
~ **limestone** Plattenkalk *m*
~ **parting** plattenförmige Absonderung *f*
~ **structure** Laminargefüge *n*
platynite Platynit *m*, $Pb_4Bi_2Se_7S_4$
play out/to auskeilen
play Aufschlußgebiet *n*, Schürfgebiet *n*
playa *(Am)* 1. Playa *f*, Salztonebene *f (flaches Evaporationsbecken der Wüste in Südkalifornien)*; 2. sandiger Strand *m*, Sandbank *f (im Fluß)*
~ **lake** Playa *f* mit gelegentlicher Wasserführung
playback Rückspielung *f*, Abspielung *f (Seismik)*
~ **centre** Rückspielzentrale *f*, Wiedergabezentrale *f*
plazolite Plazolith *m*, Hibschit *m*, Hydrogrossular *m*, $Ca_3Al_2[(Si, H_4)O_4]_3$
Pleiocene *s.* Pliocene
Pleistocene Pleistozän *n*, Diluvium *n*
~ **watercourse** Urstromtal *n*
pleochroic pleochroitisch
~ **halo** pleochroitischer Hof *m*
pleochroism Pleochroismus *m*, Mehrfarbigkeit *f*
pleomorphism Pleomorphie *f*, Kristallisation *f* in mehrfacher Form
pleomorphous *s.* polymorphous
pleonaste Pleonast *m*, Ceylonit *m (schwarzer Spinell)*
plesiomorphic plesiomorph, ancestral
plesiomorphy Plesiomorphie *f*
plessite Fülleisen *n*, Plessit *m (in Meteoriten)*
plicate/to biegen, falten
plicated gefältelt
plication Fältelung *f*, Runzelung *f*
Pliensbachian [Stage] Pliensbach[ium] *n (Stufe des Lias)*
Plinian activity Plinianische Auswurfsform *f (Vulkanismus)*

Pliocene

Pliocene [Epoch, Series] Pliozän *n (Serie des Tertiärs)*
pliohaline pliohalin
plombierite Plombierit *m*, $Ca_5H_2[Si_3O_9]_2 \cdot 6H_2O$
plot/to auftragen, aufzeichnen, eintragen *(Meßdaten)*
plot Profilschnitt *m*, Darstellung *f* als Profilschnitt *(Seismik)*
~ **lode** schwebender Gang *m*
~ **of a mine** Markscheiderriß *m*
plotted section Tiefenprofil *n (Seismik)*
plotter Plotter *m*; Zeichengerät *n (an einer Datenverarbeitungsanlage)*
plotting Auftragen *n*, Aufzeichnen *n*, Eintragen *n (von Meßdaten)*
~ **apparatus** Auswertungsgerät *n*
~ **from photographs** Bildauswertung *f*, Bildkartierung *f*
ploughshare pflugscharartige Ablationsform *f*
pluck/to abreißen *(Gletscher)*
~ **out** losreißen
plucking splitternde Gletschererosion *f*; Herausbrechen von Felspartien aus dem Anstehenden durch Gletschereis
plug/to verdämmen, verfüllen
plug Pfropfen *m*, Eruptionspfropfen *m*, Quellkuppe *f*
~ **container** Zementierkopf *m*
~ **flow** Kolbenblasenströmung *f*
plugging Abdichten *n (bestimmter Bohrlochbereiche)*
~ **and abandonment of a well** Verfüllen *n* des Bohrlochs, Liquidierung *f* einer Bohrung
~**-back** Verstopfen *n*, Verfüllen *n (Bohrung)*
plum-pudding stone Puddingstein *m (Konglomeratform)*
plumb/to ausloten
plumb line Lot *n*, Schnurlot *n*
plumbagine *s.* plumbago
plumbaginous graphitartig, Graphit...
plumbago Graphit *m*, Naturgraphit *m*, Reißblei *n*
plumbeous bleifarbig, bleifarben, bleiig
plumbic aus Blei
~ **ochre** *s.* massicot
plumbiferous bleihaltig, bleiführend
plumbocalcite Plumbokalzit *m (Mischkristall von Kalzit und Cerussit)*
plumboferrite Plumboferrit *m*, $PbO \cdot 2Fe_2O_3$
plumbogummite Plumbogummit *m*, $PbAl_3H[(OH)_6|(PO_4)_2$
plumbojarosite Plumbojarosit *m*, $PbFe_6[(OH)_6|(SO_4)_2]_2$
plumboniobite Plumboniobit *m (Y-, U-, Pb-, Fe-Niobat)*
plumbum Blei *n*, Pb
plumose federförmig, federartig
plumosite *s.* jamesonite
plunge Abtauchen *n*
~ **of a fold** Abtauchen *n* einer Falte
~ **of an ore body** Eintauchen *n* eines Erzkörpers

~ **pool** Strudelkessel *m*
plunging anticline Tauchfalte *f*
~ **axis** eintauchende Achse *f*
~ **cliff** untertauchendes Kliff *n*
~ **crown** abtauchende Faltenstirn *f*
~ **fold** Tauchfalte *f*
~ **nappe** Tauchdecke *f*
plus-minus stacking Subtraktionsstapelung *f (Seismik)*
plush copper ore *s.* chalcotrichite
~**-shaped twins** rechtwinklige Durchwachsungszwillinge *mpl*
plutology *(Am)* Teil der Geophysik, der sich mit der festen Erdkruste beschäftigt
pluton Pluton *m (in der Tiefe erstarrter Gesteinskörper)*
plutonian plutonisch *(s.a.* plutonic)
plutonic plutonisch, vulkanisch
~ **cupola** Kuppeldach *n* des Batholithen
~ **equivalents** gleichaltrige Tiefengesteine *npl*
~ **intrusion** plutonische Intrusion *f*
~ **ore deposit** plutonische Erzlagerstätte *f*
~ **rock** plutonisches Gestein *n*, Tiefengestein *n*, Plutonit *m*
~ **water** magmatisches Wasser *n*
plutonism Plutonismus *m*
plutonist Plutonist *m*
plutonite Plutonit *m*, Tiefengestein *n*, plutonisches Gestein *n*
pluvial pluvial, durch Regen entstehend
~ **erosion** Regenerosion *f*
~ **period** Pluvialperiode *f*, Regenperiode *f*
~ **phase** Pluvialzeit *f*, Regenzeit *f*
pluviograph Pluviograf *m*, Regenschreiber *m*
pluviometer Pluviometer *n*, Regenmesser *m*
pluviometry Regenmessung *f*
pluvious regnerisch, Regen...
ply *(sl)* Schieferzwischenmittel *n*
PMT *s.* photomultiplier tube
pneumatic bones pneumatische Knochen *mpl (der Vögel)*
~ **hammer drilling** Hammerschlagbohren *n*, pneumatisches Schlagbohren *n*
~ **level gauge** Druckluftpegel *m*
pneumatically placed concrete Spritzbeton *m*, Torkretbeton *m*
pneumatogene pneumatogen
~ **enclave** pneumatogener Einschluß *m*
pneumatogenetic pneumatogen
~ **inclusion** pneumatogener Einschluß *m*
pneumatogenic pneumatogen
pneumatolysis Pneumatolyse *f*
pneumatolytic pneumatolytisch
~ **alteration** pneumatolytische Umwandlung (Verdrängung) *f*
~ **dike** pneumatolytischer Gang *m*
~ **metamorphism** pneumatolytische Metamorphose *f (Metasomatose)*
~ **mineral** pneumatolitisches Mineral *n*
~ **process** Pneumatolyse *f*
~ **replacement deposit** pneumatolytische Verdrängungslagerstätte *f*
~ **stage** pneumatolytisches Stadium *n*

pneumatophore Pneumatophor *n*, Luftkammer *f*, Schwebeblase *f*; Luftwurzel *f*
pocket Nest *n*, Niere *f*, Tasche *f*, Druse *f*, Einschluß *m*
~ **of magma** Magmanest *n*
~ **of ore** Butze *f*, Butzen *m*, Putzen *m*, Erznest *n*, Erztasche *f*
~ **spring** Überfallquelle *f*, Überlaufquelle *f*
~ **storage** Wasserspeicherung *f* an der Oberfläche
pockety drusig, [nur] vereinzelt Erznester führend
pocosin *(Am)* Waldmoor *n*
pod Erzlineal *n*, Erzschmitze *f*; Gesteinsschmitze *f*
podolite *s.* dahllite
podsol *s.* podzol
podzol [soil] Podsolboden *m*, humider Boden *m*, Bleicherde *f*
podzolic podsolisch
~ **soil** podsoliger Boden *m*, Bleicherde *f*
podzolization Podsol[is]ierung *f*
podzolize/to podsol[is]ieren
podzolized loess loam podsol[is]ierter Lößlehm *m*
poechite Poechit *m* (Mn-reiches Eisensiliziumgel)
poecilitic *s.* poikilitic
poeciloblastic *s.* poikiloblastic
poikilitic 1. poikilitisch; 2. *als Texturbezeichnung für gefleckte Triassandsteine und -kalke*
~ **lustre** poikilitischer Glanz *m*
~ **texture** poikilitische Struktur *f*
poikiloblastic poikiloblastisch
~ **structure** Siebtextur *f*, poikiloblastisches Gefüge *n*
poikilohaline von variabler Salinität
point bar Ufersandbank *f*
~-**bar deposit** Sedimentbank *f* an der Innenseite einer Mäanderschleife
~ **counter** Pointcounter *m* (Integriervorrichtung mit springender Präparatvorstellung)
~ **diagram** Punktdiagramm *n*, nicht ausgezähltes Gefügediagramm *n*
~ **group** Raumgruppe *f*
~-**integrating sampler** Punktprobenehmer *m* (von Wasser in Brunnen)
~ **kriging** Punkt-Kriging *n*
~ **loading** Punktbelastung *f*
~ **of anchorage** Verankerungspunkt *m*
~ **of application** Angriffspunkt *m*
~ **of discovery** Fundpunkt *m*
~ **of emergence** Austrittsstelle *f*
~ **of impact** Aufschlagspunkt *m* (eines Meteors)
~ **of inflection** Knickpunkt *m*
~ **of intersection** Schnittpunkt *m*, Scharung *f*
~ **of issue** Ausflußstelle *f*
~ **of penetration** Durchstoßpunkt *m*
~ **of withdrawal** Entnahmestelle *f*
~ **plotting** punktweise Auftragung *f*, Auswertung *f* Spur für Spur

~ **sample** Punktprobe *f*
~ **spread function** Punktspreizfunktion *f*
pointed auger Spitzbohrer *m*
~ **twist auger** Spiralbohrer *m*
pointer eyepiece Zeigerokular *n*
poised state ausgeglichener Zustand *m* (eines Flusses ohne Erosion und Sedimentation)
Poisson's ratio Poissonsche Zahl *f*, Querdehnungsziffer *f*
poker chips Blätterschiefer *m*, dünnblättriger Schieferton *m*
polar polar, Polar...
~ **air** Polarluft *f*, arktische Kaltluft *f*
~ **aurora** Polarlicht *n*
~ **cap** Polarkappe *f*
~ **circle** Polarkreis *m*
~ **climate** Polarklima *n*, polares Klima *n*
~ **distance** Poldistanz *f*, Polabstand *m*
~ **drift** Polwanderung *f*
~ **eddy** Polarwirbel *m*
~ **flattening** Abplattung *f* an den Polen
~ **fringe** Saum *m* der Polarkappe
~ **ice cap** Polareiskappe *f*
~ **light** Polarlicht *n*
~ **orbit** polare Umlaufbahn *f*
~-**orbiting satellite** polumkreisender Satellit *m*
~ **plot** Polardiagramm *n*
~ **point** Polfigur *f* (Kristallprojektion)
~ **sea** Eismeer *n*
~ **wandering** Polwanderung *f*
polarity Polarität *f*
polarization Polarisation *f*
~ **microscope** Polarisationsmikroskop *n*
~ **plane** Polarisationsebene *f*
polarize/to polarisieren
polarized light polarisiertes Licht *n*
polarizer Polarisator *m*
polarizing angle Polarisationswinkel *m*
~ **microscope** Polarisationsmikroskop *n*
polarography Polarografie *f*
polder Polder *m*, Koog *m*, eingedeichtes Marschland *n*
pole Pol *m*
~-**fleeing force** Polfluchtkraft *f*
~ **of cold** Kältepol *m*
~ **of inertia** Trägheitspol *m*
~ **of magnetic verticality** magnetischer Pol *m*
~ **of rotation** Rotationspol *m*
~ **of the face** Flächenpol *m*
~ **of the heavens** Himmelspol *m*
polestar Polarstern *m*
poleward[s] polwärts
polhody Polbahn *f*
polianite Polianit *m* (idiomorpher Pyrolusit)
polish/to abschleifen, polieren
polish Politur *f*, Glanz *m*
~-**grinding** Schleifpolieren *n*
polished boulders geschliffene Geschiebe *npl*
~ **section** [polierter] Anschliff *m*
~ **surface** polierte Fläche *f*, Harnisch *m*, Spiegel *m*, Schleiffläche *f*
polishing Polierung *f*, Abschleifung *f*

polishing

~ **powder** Poliermittel n, Schleifpulver n
~ **scratch** Polierkratzer m
~ **shadows** Polierschatten mpl
~ **slate** Polierschiefer m
~ **wheel** Polierscheibe f
pollen Pollen m
~ **analysis** Pollenanalyse f
~ **grain** Pollenkorn n
~ **profile** Pollenprofil n
~ **statistics** Pollenanalyse f
pollenite Pollenit m (Nephelinphonolith)
pollucite Pollucit m, (Cs, Na)[AlSi$_2$O$_6$]·H$_2$O
pollutant Schadstoff m, Schmutzstoff m
pollution Verunreinigung f; Verschmutzung f, Kontamination f (von Grundwasser)
~ **abatement** Gewässerschutz m
~ **control** Kontaminationsschutz m
~ **of the air** Luftverunreinigung f
~ **of the environment** Umweltverschmutzung f
polybasite Polybasit m, 8(Ag,Cu)$_2$S·Sb$_2$S$_3$
polychroic s. pleochroic
polychromatic vielfarbig, mehrfarbig
polychromatism Vielfarbigkeit f, Mehrfarbigkeit f
polycrase Polykras m, (Y, Ce, Ca, U, Th)(Ti, Nb, Ta)$_2$(O, OH)$_6$
polycrystal Vielkristall m
polycyclic valley mehrzyklisches Tal n
polydactyl vielfingerig
polydymite Polydymit m, Ni$_3$S$_4$
polye s. uvala
polyfacetted pebble Vielkanter m
polygenetic polygenetisch
polygenous polygen, heterogen in der Zusammensetzung
polygeosyncline Polygeosynklinale f
polygonal ground (markings, soil) Polygonboden m, Karreeboden m, Strukturboden m, Steinnetzwerk n
polygonization Polygonisation f
polyhalite Polyhalit m, K$_2$Ca$_2$Mg[SO$_4$]$_4$·2H$_2$O
polyhedral, polyhedric polyedrisch, vielflächig, vielseitig
~ **parting** polyedrische Absonderung f
polyhedron Polyeder n, Vielflächner m
polylayer water labil gebundenes Porenwasser n
polymerization Polymerisation f
polymerize/to polymerisieren
polymetamorphic polymetamorph
polymetamorphism Polymetamorphose f
polymignite Polymignit m, (Ce, La, Y, Th, Mn, Ca)[(Ti, Zr, Nb, Ta)$_2$O$_6$]
polymorph [polymorphe] Modifikation f
polymorphic polymorph, vielgestaltig
~ **modification** [polymorphe] Modifikation f
~ **transition** polymorphe Umwandlung f, Phasenumwandlung f (mit zunehmender Tiefe)
polymorphism Polymorphie f, Polymorphismus m
polymorphous polymorph, vielgestaltig
~ **inversion** polymorphe Umwandlung f

polymorphy Polymorphie f, Polymorphismus m
polynary system Vielstoffsystem n
polynomial trend Polynomtrend m, Trendpolynom n
polysynthetic twinning Wiederholungszwillingsbildung f, polysynthetische Zwillingsbildung f, Vielling m
polzenite Polzenit m (Melilithbasalt)
pond/to abdämmen
~ **back** aufstauen
pond Teich m, Weiher m
ponded ground water Staugrundwasser n
~ **lake** Stausee m
~ **water** Stauwasser n; stehendes Gewässer n
ponderous spar s. baryte
ponding Stauung f (von Wasser); natürliche Seebildung f innerhalb eines Wasserlaufs
pondlet kleiner, natürlich gebildeter See m
ponor Ponor m, Schluckloch n
Pontian [Stage] Pontien n, Pontium n (Stufe des Miozäns)
pontic s. euxinic
ponzite Ponzit m (Varietät von Trachyt)
pool 1. Tümpel m, Teich m; 2. Lager n (Erdöl, Erdgas); 3. Nest n, Fleck m, Kornaggregat n (von Mineralen im Dünnschliff)
poor cleavage schlechte Spaltbarkeit f
~ **in colloids** kolloidarm
~ **in fossils** fossilarm
~ **lode** tauber Gang m
~ **ore** Pocherz n
poorly bedded schlecht geschichtet
~ **developed fauna** Kümmerfauna f
~ **graded** gut sortiert (eine Korngrößenklasse vorherrschend)
~ **stratified** kaum geschichtet
pop shot Knappschuß m
popping Bergschlag m, Gebirgsschlagablösen n
~ **rock** Steinschlag m, Gebirgsschlag m, knallendes Gebirge n
population 1. Population f (paläontologisch); 2. Grundgesamtheit f (statistisch)
~ **dynamics** Populationsdynamik f
porcelain clay (earth) Porzellanerde f, Kaolin m
~ **jasper** Porzellanjaspis m (natürlich gefritteter Ton)
~-**like** porzellanartig
porcelainite Tonbrandgestein n
porcellaneous layer Porzellanschicht f, Ostracum n (mittlere Schalenschicht der Mollusken)
porcellanite Porzellanit m, Porzellanspat f
pore Pore f
~ **air** Porenluft f
~ **angle water** Porenwinkelwasser n
~ **aquifer** Porengrundwasserleiter m
~ **canals** Porenkanäle mpl
~ **content** Poreninhalt m
~ **continuity** Porenkontinuität f

~ cross section Porenquerschnitt *m*
~ entry radius Poreneintrittsradius *m*
~ filling Porenfüllung *f*
~ form Porenform *f*
~ liquid Porenflüssigkeit *f*
~ liquid pressure Porenflüssigkeitsdruck *m*
~ pressure Poren[wasser]druck *m*
~ pressure dissipation Poren[wasser]druckabnahme *f*
~ size Porengröße *f*
~ size distribution Porengrößenverteilung *f*
~ space Porenraum *m*, Porenvolumen *n*
~ tortuosity Tortuosität *f* der Porenkanäle
~ volume Porenvolumen *n*, Porenraum *m*
~ water Porenwasser *n*
~-water drainage (expulsion) Porenwasserabgabe *f*
~-water head Porenwasserdruckhöhe *f*
~-water loss Porenwasserabgabe *f*
~-water pressure Porenwasserdruck *m*
poriness *s.* porosity
porosity Porosität *f*, Porigkeit *f*, Porengehalt *m*
~ distribution Porenraumverteilung *f*
~ log Porositätslog *n*
~ trap Porositätsfalle *f*
porous porös, durchlässig
~ haematite Eisenrahm *m*
~ medium poröser Stoff *m*
~ pot unpolarisierbare Elektrode *f*
~ rock poröses Gestein *n*
porousness *s.* porosity
porpezite Porpezit *m*, natürliche Gold-Palladium-Legierung *f*
porphyraceaous porphyrhaltig
porphyrite Porphyrit *m*
~ tuff Porphyrittuff *m*
porphyritic porphyrisch
~ texture porphyrische Struktur *f*
porphyroblast Porphyroblast *m*
porphyroblastic porphyroblastisch
~ texture porphyroblastische Struktur *f*
porphyroid Porphyroid *n*
porphyry Porphyr *m*
~ copper ore Porphyrkupfererz *n*
~ dike Porphyrgang *m*
~ ores Imprägnationserze *npl* in porphyrischen Gesteinen
portable drilling rig tragbare Bohranlage *f*
portal Stollenmundloch *n*
Portlandian [Stage] Portland *n (Stufe des oberen Malms, Südengland)*
portlandite Portlandit *m*, $Ca(OH)_2$
position finding Ortsbestimmung *f*
~-reference-system Positionierungssystem *n*
positioning Ortsbestimmung *f*
positive crystal optisch positiver Kristall *m*
~ ore vollständig ausgeblocktes Erz *n*
~ reserves nachgewiesene Vorräte *mpl*
~ segment in Hebung begriffener Krustenabschnitt *m*
~ shore line Hebungsküste *f*

positively charged positiv geladen
possible reserves mögliche Vorräte *mpl*
possuolana *s.* pozzuolana
post failure behaviour Verhalten *n* eines Gesteins nach dem Bruch
postcrystalline deformation postkristalline Deformation *f*
postdepositional movement postsedimentäre Bewegung *f*
posterior margin Schloßrand *m*, Hinterrand *m (Fossilschalen)*
~ muscular impression hinterer Schließmuskeleindruck *m*
postglacial postglazial, nacheiszeitlich
~ time[s] Nacheiszeit *f*
posthole geologische Schürfbohrung (Strukturbohrung) *f*
posthumous postum
~ fold postume Falte *f*
~ folding postume Faltung *f*, Nachfaltung *f*
~ movement postume (nachträgliche) Bewegung *f*
postkinematic *s.* posttectonic
postlithification Postdiagenese *f*
postmature überreif
postorogenic nachorogen, postorogen
~ granite postorogener Granit *m*
postprocessing Nachbearbeitung *f*
posttectonic posttektonisch
postvolcanic postvulkanisch
pot/to vorkesseln
pot 1. [kegelförmige] Gesteinsablösung *f*, Sargdeckel *m*; 2. *(sl)* Detektor *m (Geophysik)*
~ growan *(sl)* zersetzter (verkrusteter) Granit *m*
~ lead *s.* graphite
~ stone unreines Talkgestein *n*
potable water Trinkwasser *n*
potamic transport Transport *m* durch Flußströmung (Meeresströmung)
potamoclastics potamoklastische (fluvioklastische) Gesteine *npl*
potamogenic potamogen
potamology Potamologie *f*, Flußkunde *f*
potarite Potarit *m*, PdHg
potash 1. Kaliumkarbonat *n*, K_2CO_3; 2. Kaliumoxid *n*, K_2O
~ alum Kalialaun *m*, $KAl[SO_4]_2 \cdot 12H_2O$
~ feldspar Kalifeldspat *m*, $KAlSi_3O_8$
~ fertilizer *(Am)* Kalidüngesalz *n*
~ kettles Depressionen *fpl* der Moränenmorphologie
~-magnesia salt Kalimagnesiasalz *n*
~ manure Kalidüngesalz *n*
~ mica Kaliglimmer *m*, Muskowit *m*
~ mine Kaligrube *f*
~ salt Kalisalz *n*
potassic kalihaltig
potassium Kali[um] *n*, K
~ bentonite Metabentonit *m (Ton vom Illittyp)*
~ salt Kalisalz *n*
potato stone Geode *f*

potential

potential Potential n
- ~ **difference** Druckdifferenz f (Wasser)
- ~ **electrode** Sonde f (Geoelektrik)
- ~ **evapotranspiration** potentielle Verdunstung f
- ~ **fissuration** latente Klüftung f
- ~ **flow** Potentialströmung f
- ~ **for ground-water movement** Strömungspotential n
- ~ **gradient** Potentialgradient m, Potentialgefälle n
- ~ **infiltration rate** potentielle Infiltrationsrate f
- ~ **production** mögliche Förderung f (Schätzung der abbauwürdigen Vorräte)
- ~ **rate of evaporation** Verdunstungsvermögen n

potentiometry Potentiometrie f
pothole 1. Strudelloch n, Brandungstopf m, Strudelkessel m; Wirbelkolk m, Auskolkung f; Gletschermühle f, Gletschertopf m; 2. [kegelförmige] Gesteinsablösung f, Sargdeckel m
- ~ **excavation** Ausstrudelung f; Auskolkung f

potholed mit Gletschertöpfen versehen
potlid jurassische Konkretion f
Potomac Group Potomac-Gruppe f (Unterkreide, Nordamerika, Atlantikküste)
pots and kettles Depressionen fpl der Moränenmorphologie
Potsdam system Potsdamer Schweresystem n (Schwerewert m)
Potsdamian s. Croixian
potter's clay (earth) Töpferton m, Backsteinton m, Ziegelton m, Töpfererde f
Pottsvillian [Stage] Stufe des Pennsylvaniens
pouch Ventraltasche f (Paläontologie)
pouched mammal Beuteltier n, Marsupialier m
poudrin feine feste Schneekristalle mpl
Poulter method s. air shooting
pound-day concept (Am) Druck-Zeit-Regime n (Aquifergasspeicher)
pounding of the waves Wellenschlag m, Wogenprall m
pour down/to herunterströmen
- ~ **in** hineinströmen
- ~ **out** ausfließen (z.B. Lava)

pour point Stockpunkt m (bei Öl)
powder Sprengstoff m, Sprengpulver n
- ~ **method of analysis** Pulvermethode f, Debye-Scherrer-Methode f
- ~ **ore** eingesprengtes Erz n
- ~ **pattern** Pulverdiagramm n, Debye-Scherrer-Diagramm n
- ~ **snow** Pulverschnee m

powdered brown coal Braunkohlenstaub m
powdery pulverartig, pulverig, staubartig
- ~ **avalanche** Staublawine f
- ~ **snow** Pulverschnee m

powellite Powellit m, Ca[MoO$_4$]
power of coiling up, ~ of enrollment Einrollungsvermögen n (Paläontologie)

274

- ~ **response function** Antwortfunktion eines Punktobjekts auf ein Radarsignal; s. point spread function
- ~ **slip** Abfangkeil m
- ~ **spectrum** Energiespektrum n, Leistungsspektrum n (Seismik)
- ~ **swivel** angetriebener Spülkopf m, Kraftdrehkopf m (Tiefbohrung)
- ~ **tongs** Gestängeschraubvorrichtung f, Rohrschraubvorrichtung f

powerful rig schwere Bohranlage f
- ~ **thrust** Fernüberschiebung f

pozzuolana Puzzuolanerde f, Bröckeltuff m, Leuzittuff m
pozzuolanic puzzolanartig, puzzolanhaltig
ppb = part per billion
practical porosity Nutzporosität f
practice of dressing and preparation Aufbereitungstechnik f
Pragian [Stage] Prag n, Prag-Stufe f (Stufe des Unterdevons)
prairie Prärie f, Grasebene f, Grasland n, Grassteppe f
- ~ **mound** wurtähnlicher Hügel m mit zentraler Depression
- ~ **soil** Prärieboden m
- ~ **-timber zone** Waldsteppenzone f

Prandtl body Prandtlscher Körper m
prase Prasem m (Varietät von Quarz mit Strahlstein, s.a. chalcedony)
prasinite Prasinit m
Pre-planorbe Beds Prä-planorbis-Schichten fpl (tiefster Lias)
preadaptation Präadaptation f
Prealps Voralpen pl
preboring Vorbohrung f
preboulder clay voreiszeitlicher Lehm m
preburial stage Stadium n ohne Sedimentbedeckung
Precambrian präkambrisch
Precambrian Präkambrium n, Archäozoikum n, Kryptozoikum n
- ~ **basement** präkambrisches Grundgebirge n
- ~ **glaciation** präkambrische Vereisung f
- ~ **shield** präkambrischer Schild m
- ~ **System** Präkambrium n

precession Präzession f
precious kostbar, edel
- ~ **metal** Edelmetall n
- ~ **opal** Edelopal m
- ~ **stone** Edelstein m

precipice Steilabfall m, Absturz m, Steilabbruch m, Abgrund m, Gehänge n
precipitant Ausfällmittel n
precipitate/to niederschlagen, ausfällen
precipitate Niederschlag m, Ausfällung f
precipitated chalk Schlämmkreide f
- ~ **deposit** Ausscheidungslagerstätte f
- ~ **sedimentary rock** Ausscheidungssediment m

precipitating action fällende Wirkung f
precipitation 1. Ausfällung f, Fällung f, Nieder-

schlag *m*, Ausscheidung *f*; 2. [atmosphärischer] Niederschlag *m*
~-evaporation ratio Niederschlags-Verdunstungs-Verhältnis *n*
~ excess Niederschlagsüberschuß *m (fließt direkt oberirdisch ab)*
~ frequency Niederschlagshäufigkeit *f*
~ gauge Niederschlagsmesser *m*
precipitous steil, abschüssig, jäh, schroff
~ cliff Steilwand *f*
~ coast Steilküste *f*
~ drop in temperature Temperatursturz *m*
~ wall Steilwand *f*
precipitousness Steilheit *f*
precise levelling Feinnivellement *n*
precision levelling Feinnivellement *n*
~ measurement Feinmessung *f*
~ of reading Ablesegenauigkeit *f*
preclassification Vorklassierung *f*
preconsolidation deformation sedimentärdiagenetisches Gefüge *n*
precrystalline deformation präkristalline Deformation *f*
precursor 1. Vorläufer *m (Paläontologie)*; 2. *s.* earthquake precursor
predatory fish Raubfisch *m*
predazzite Predazzit *m (Marmor mit Brucit)*
prediction filter Vorhersagefilter *n*
predictivity test Prognosetest *m*
predominate/to vorherrschen
predrill/to vorbohren
predrilled hole Vorbohrung *f*
predrilling Vorbohren *n*
preemphasis Hervorhebung *f* von Frequenzen vor der Bearbeitung *(Seismik)*
preexist/to präexistieren, vorher vorhanden sein
preexisting präexistierend, vorher vorhanden
prefeasibility study vorläufige Durchführbarkeitsstudie (Projektstudie) *f (z.B. für den Aufschluß einer Lagerstätte)*
preferred orientation Vorzugsorientierung *f*, bevorzugte Ausrichtung *f*
preglacial präglazial, vor der Eiszeit
~ period Voreiszeit *f*
prehistoric prähistorisch
~ man Urmensch *m*
~ period vorgeschichtliches Zeitalter *n*
prehistory Vorgeschichte *f*
prehnite Prehnit *m*, $Ca_2Al_2[(OH)_2|Si_3O_{10}]$
preliminary comminution Vorzerkleinerung *f*
~ dewatering of underground mine Grubenvorfeldentwässerung *f*
~ drilling Vorbohren *n*
~ grinding Vorschliff *m*
~ pumping test Probepumpversuch *m*
~ shock *s.* ~ tremor
~ stage Vorphase *f*
~ survey Vorvermessung *f*
~ trembling *s.* ~ tremor
~ tremor Vorbeben *n*, Vorläufer *m*, Vorphase *f (Seismik)*

preloading Vorbelastung *f*
PREMODE = Preliminary Mid-Ocean Dynamics Experiment
premolar vorderer Backenzahn *m*
premonitory events Vorzeichen *npl*
~ shock *s.* preliminary tremor
preorogenic vororogen
prepalaeozoic präpaläozoisch
preparation 1. Aufbereitung *f*; 2. Präparat *n*
~ of ore Erzaufbereitung *f*
~ of samples Probenvorbereitung *f*
~ plant Aufbereitungsanlage *f*
preparatory phase vorbereitende Phase *f*
prepare ores/to Erze aufbereiten
prepared chalk Schlämmkreide *f*
preperforated liner präperforierter Liner *m (Tiefbohrung)*
~ section präperforierte Rohrtour *f (Tiefbohrung)*
preplot Planung *f* der Schußbohrungen *(Seismik)*
preponderance of soda rocks Natronvormacht *f (in Magmatiten)*
prerecent form Vorzeitform *f*
presaliniferous beds präsalinare Schichten *fpl*
present-time form Jetztzeitform *f*
preserval, preservation Erhaltung *f (von Fossilien)*
preserved erhalten *(Fossil)*
preset gain control Programmregelung *f (Seismik)*
presolved bed Schicht *f* mit Drucklösungserscheinungen
~ quartzite porenfreier Druckquarzit *m*
pressure Druck *m*
~ acting in all directions allseitiger Druck *m*
~ acting upon the stowed goaf Versatzdruck *m*
~ balance Druckausgleich *m (bei Erdöl- und Gasförderung)*
~ behaviour Druckentwicklung *f*
~ bomb Druckbombe *f*, Bodendruckmeßgerät *n*
~ build-up Druckaufbau *m (bei Erdöl- und Gasförderung)*
~ build-up curve Druckaufbaukurve *f*
~ bulb Druckzwiebel *f*
~ burst Gebirgsschlag *m*
~ capsule (cell) Druckmeßdose *f*
~ change Druckänderung *f*
~ chart barometrische Karte *f*
~ conditions Druckbedingungen *fpl*
~ curve Druckverlauf *m*
~ decline Druckabfall *m*
~ detector Hydrophon *n (Seismik)*
~ determination by acoustic (ultrasonic) means Drucksondierung *f (akustische Druckbestimmung)*
~ difference Druckdifferenz *f*
~ distribution Druckverteilung *f*
~ drilling Bohren *n* unter Druck
~ drive Gastrieb *m (Erdölförderung)*

pressure

~ **drop** Druckabfall *m*, Druckverlust *m*
~ **drop curve** Druckabfallkurve *f*
~ **drop in circulation system** Druckverlust *m* im Spülungssystem
~ **effect** Druckwirkung *f*
~ **field** Druckfeld *n*
~ **flow** Druckströmung *f*
~ **fringes** Streckungshöfe *mpl*
~ **function** Druckfunktion *f*
~ **gauge** Druckmesser *m*
~ **gradient** Druckgefälle *n*
~ **head** Druckhöhe *f*, Förderhöhe *f*
~ **instrument** Druckmeßgerät *n*
~ **level** Druckniveau *n*
~ **level-off** Druckstabilisierung *f (bei Erdöl- und Gasförderung)*
~ **log** Druckprofil *n*
~ **maintenance** Druckerhaltung *f (bei Erdöl- und Gasförderung)*
~ **measurement** Druckmessung *f*
~ **metamorphism** Pressungsmetamorphose *f*, Druckmetamorphose *f*, Belastungsmetamorphose *f*
~ **observation well** Druckbeobachtungssonde *f*
~ **of mountain mass** Gebirgsdruck *m*
~ **of overlying strata** Überlagerungsdruck *m*
~ **of the overburden** Belastungsdruck *m*
~ **on [a]butment** Kämpferdruck *m*
~ **partings** Drucklagen *fpl (in Kohle)*
~ **peak** Druckspitze *f*
~ **potential** potentielle Druckhöhe *f*, Druckpotential *n*
~ **production history** *(Am)* Abbaugeschichte *f*
~ **release** Druckentlastung *f*
~ **replacement** Druckwiederaufbau *m*
~ **resistance** Druckfestigkeit *f (eines Gesteins)*
~ **restoration** Druckaufbauverfahren *n (bei Erdöl- und Gasförderung)*
~-**solution phenomena** Drucklösungserscheinungen *fpl*
~ **surge** Druckwelle *f*
~ **survey** Drucküberwachung *f*
~ **trace loop** *(Am)* Druckspielcharakteristik *f*
~ **transient** Druckänderung *f*
~ **tunnel** Betriebswasserstollen *m*, Druckwasserstollen *m*
~ **twinning** Druckzwilling *m*
~ **wave** *s.* longitudinal wave
~ **well** Einpreßsonde *f*
prestraining Vorspannung *f (Felsanker)*
prestressing Vorspannung *f*
presuppression Anfangsdämpfung *f (Seismik)*
pretreatment Vorbehandlung *f*
prevailing wind vorherrschender Wind *m*
preventer Preventer *m*, Absperrschieber *m*
previously bored (drilled) vorgebohrt
~ **drilled hole** Vorbohrung *f*
PRF *s.* power response function
Priabonian [Stage] Priabon[ium] *n (Stufe des Eozäns)*
prian *(sl)* weicher weißer Ton *m*

276

priceite Priceit *m*, $Ca_5[B_4O_9(OH)_5]_3 \cdot H_2O$
pride reiches Erzvorkommen *n*
~ **of the country** Reicherzkörper *m* in Oberflächennähe *(Cornwall)*
priderite Priderit *m*, $(K, Ba)[(Ti, Fe)_8O_{16}]$
prill Metallstück *n (kleines Stück gediegenes Metall)*
primacord Sprengschnur *f*
primal jungle Urwaldsumpf *m*
primary back Primärrücken *m (tektonisch)*; unveränderter Rücken *m (einer Decke)*
~ **crack** Primärriß *m*
~ **crystallization** primäre Kristallisation *f*, Primärkristallisation *f*
~ **dip** synsedimentäres Schichtfallen *n*
~ **downward changes** primäre Tiefenunterschiede *mpl*
~ **drilling** Vorbohrung *f*
~ **exploitation** Erstgewinnung *f*
~ **fabric** Primärgefüge *n*
~ **flat joint** *s.* L-joint
~ **geosyncline** Orthogeosynklinale *f*
~ **halo** primärer Dispersionshof *m (bei der Mineralisation festgelegt)*
~ **impact** primärer Einschlag *m (Meteorit)*
~ **industry** Rohstoff verarbeitende Industrie *f*
~ **migration** Primärmigration *f (der Kohlenwasserstoffe vom Muttergestein zum Speicher)*
~ **mountains** Urgebirge *n*
~ **nappe** Stammdecke *f*
~ **order of branches** Primäräste *mpl*
~ **ore** primäres (aszendentes) Erz *n*
~ **raw material** Primärrohstoff *m (Bergbauproduktion)*
~ **recovery** Primärförderung *f*
~ **reflection** Primärreflexion *f (Seismik)*
~ **rock** unverwittertes Gestein *n*
~ **soil** Primärboden *m*, Ortsboden *m*
~ **stratification** horizontale Parallelschichtung *f*
~ **wave** erster Vorläufer *m*, primäre Welle *f (Seismik)*
prime meridian Nullmeridian *m*
primeval urzeitlich
~ **forest** Urwald *m*
~ **landscape** Urlandschaft *f*
~ **ocean** Urmeer *n*
~ **world** Urwelt *f*
priming Gezeitenverfrühung *f*
primitive atmosphere Uratmosphäre *f*
~ **magma** ursprüngliches (juveniles, nicht differenziertes) Magma *n*
~ **man** Urmensch *m*
~ **water** juveniles Wasser *n*
primordial ursprünglich, uranfänglich
~ **atmosphere** Uratmosphäre *f*
~ **hydrosphere** Urhydrosphäre *f*
~ **life** Urleben *n*
~ **ocean** Urmeer *n*
~ **radioisotope** Primärradioisotop *n*
principal axis Hauptachse *f*
~ **component analysis** Hauptkomponentenanalyse *f*

~ **component transformation** Hauptachsentransformation f
~ **joint** Hauptspalte f
~ **load case** Hauptlastfall m
~ **normal stress** Hauptnormalspannung f
~ **plane** Hauptebene f
~ **planet** Hauptplanet m
~ **point** Bildmittelpunkt m
~ **section** Hauptschnitt m, Hauptzone f *(eines Minerals)*
~ **strain** Hauptdehnung f
~ **stress** Hauptspannung f
~ **stress difference** Hauptspannungsdifferenz f
~**-tectonic** s. syntectonic
principle of actualism Aktualitätsprinzip n
~ **of superimposition** Überlagerungsprinzip n
print Abdruck m
priorite s. blomstrandine
prism Prisma n
~ **face** Prismenfläche f
prismatic[al] prismatisch, prismenförmig, säulenartig
~ **colours** Beugungsfarben fpl
~ **jointing** Griffelstruktur f, prismatische Absonderung f
~ **spectrum** Brechungsspektrum n
~ **system** rhombisches System n
prismoidal prismaähnlich
prjevalskite Prjevalskit m, Pb[UO$_2$|PO$_4$]$_2$·4H$_2$O
probability paper Wahrscheinlichkeitspapier n, Wahrscheinlichkeitsnetz n
probable extent of the deposit mutmaßliche Erstreckung f der Lagerstätte
~ **ore** wahrscheinlich vorhandenes Erz n
~ **reserve** vermutliche (mutmaßliche) Reserve f
probe Sonde f, Meßkopf m, Meßsonde f
~ **technique** Sondentechnik f
probertite Probertit m, NaCa[B$_5$O$_6$(OH)$_6$]·2H$_2$O
probing of a bore Sondierungsbohrung f
problematical fossil Problematikum n, zweifelhaftes Fossil n
procedure of evolution Entwicklungsgang m
proceeding glacier vorrückender Gletscher m
process of alluviation Verlandung f
~ **of alteration** Umbildungsvorgang m
~ **of decay** Verwitterungsprozeß m
~ **of filling-up** Verlandungsprozeß m
~ **of flow** Strömungsvorgang m
~ **of rotting** Vermoderungsprozeß m
~ **of silting-up** Verschlammungsprozeß m
~ **of subsidence** Senkungsvorgang m
~ **of weathering** Verwitterungsprozeß m
~ **water** Brauchwasser n, Nutzwasser n, Gebrauchswasser n
processed gas entbenziniertes Gas n
~ **mineral** verarbeiteter mineralischer Rohstoff m
processing Aufbereitung f
prochlorite Prochlorit m, Rhipidolith m *(Fe-, Mg-Chlorit)*
Proctor compaction test Verdichtungsversuch m nach Proctor

procuring of water Wassergewinnung f
prod cast Stechmarke f, Stoßmarke f, Stoßeindruck m
prodelta Grundablagerungen fpl vor dem Delta
~ **slope** Deltaabhang m
produce/to fördern, produzieren
producer Förderbohrung f
producing formation erdölliefernde Formation f
~ **gas-oil ratio** Gas-Öl-Förderverhältnis n
~ **horizon** produzierender Horizont m *(Erdöl, Gas)*
~ **interval** produzierender Teufenabschnitt m *(Erdöl- und Gasförderung)*
~ **oil field** produktives Erdölfeld n
~ **rate** Förderrate f
~ **rock** produktiver Träger m
~ **well** Förderbohrung f, fördernde Bohrung f, Produktionssonde f, Fördersonde f
product of combustion Verbrennungsprodukt n
~ **of decay** Verwitterungsprodukt n
~ **of decomposition** Zersetzungsprodukt n
~ **of destruction** Zerstörungsprodukt n
~ **of volcanic ejection** Auswurfprodukt n
~ **of weathering** Verwitterungsprodukt n
~ **withdrawal** Entnahme f von Erdöl (Gas) *(aus der Lagerstätte)*
production Produktion f, Förderung f
~ **casing string** Produktionsrohrtour f
~ **curve** Produktionskurve f
~ **decline** Förderabfall m
~ **derrick** Förderturm m
~ **downtime** Förderausfall m
~ **engineering** Fördertechnik f *(Erdöl- und Gasförderung)*
~ **flow well** Steigleitung f *(Tiefbohrung)*
~ **graph** Produktionskurve f
~ **hole drilling** Produktionsbohrung f
~ **licence** Förderkonzession f
~ **packer** Produktionspacker m *(Erdöl- und Gasförderung)*
~ **rate of a well** Förderrate f einer Bohrung
~ **shut-down** Förderunterbrechung f
~**-stimulation technique** Verfahren n zur Erhöhung der Ausbeute
~ **test** Produktionsversuch m; Dauerpumpversuch m *(Grundwasser)*
~ **zone** Förderhorizont m
productive capacity Förderkapazität f; Förderfähigkeit f, Fördervermögen n
~ **horizon** produktiver Horizont m
~ **mine** Ausbeutezeche f, Ausbeutegrube f
~ **time** produktive Zeit f
productiveness Ergiebigkeit f
~ **of a source (spring)** Quellenergiebigkeit f
productivity index Produktivitätsindex m
~ **test** Förderversuch m, Produktionstest m *(bei Erdöl- und Gassonden)*
profile Profil n
~ **of a hole** Bohr[loch]profil n

profile

~ **of equilibrium** Gleichgewichtsprofil n, Ausgleichsprofil n
~ **of slope** Böschungsprofil n
~ **shooting** Profilschießen n (Seismik)
profiling 1. Profilschießen n (Seismik); 2. Kartierung f (Elektrik)
profitability of geological prospecting Rentabilität f geologischer Untersuchungsarbeiten
profitable ore [ab]bauwürdiges Erz n
profound fault tiefgreifende Verwerfung f
proglacial channel Urstromtal n
~ **lake** glazialer Stausee m
prognostic reserves prognostische Vorräte mpl
prograde metamorphism ansteigende (progressive) Metamorphose f
prograded coast Anschwemmungsküste f
prograding shore line vorrückende Strandlinie f
program/to programmieren
programmed gain control Programmregelung f
progress of mining Abbaufortschritt m
progressing glacier vorrückender Gletscher m
~ **wave** wandernde Welle f
progressive failure fortschreitender (progressiver) Bruch m
~ **metamorphism** progressive Metamorphose f
~ **off-lapping** fortschreitende Regression f
~ **overlap** fortschreitende Transgression f
~ **sand waves** progressive Sandwellen fpl
~ **settlement** fortschreitende Setzung f
~ **slide** progressiver Rutsch m
~ **step fault** gleichsinniger Staffelbruch m
~ **thrust** progressive Überschiebung f
project/to 1. ausschleudern; 2. überkragen, vorspringen
project site Baustelle f
projected downward top aus Bohrlochmessungen abgeleitete Schichtoberkante (unterhalb der Bohrlochsohle)
~ **top** rekonstruierte Oberkante f eines Horizonts
projecting vorspringend
~ **coast** vorspringende Küste f
projection Ausschleudern n, Auswurf m
~ **of lava** Lavaauswurf m
~ **point** Projektionspunkt m
prolapsed bedding zusammengefaltete Schichtung f
prologism Prologismus m (Paläontologie)
prominence Protuberanz f
promontory Vorgebirge n, Landzunge f, Landspitze f
proof undurchlässig
~ **copy** Belegexemplar n
propagation Ausbreitung f, Fortpflanzung f
~ **conditions** Ausbreitungsbedingungen fpl
~ **constant** Fortpflanzungskonstante f, Übertragungsfaktor m

~ **of seismic waves** Fortpflanzung f seismischer Wellen
~ **time** Fortpflanzungszeit f, Laufzeit f
~ **velocity** Fortpflanzungsgeschwindigkeit f, Ausbreitungsgeschwindigkeit f
proppant Fracstützmaterial n
propping agent Verstopfungsmaterial n
propylite Propylit m (Varietät von Andesit)
propylitic propylitisch
propylitization Propylitisierung f
proration Produktionseinschränkung f (Erdöl- und Gasförderung)
prosopite Prosopit m, Ca[Al(F, OH)$_4$]$_2$
prospect/to prospektieren, schürfen
prospect 1. Erkundungsobjekt n; 2. Schürfstelle f, höffiges Gebiet n, Hoffnungsgebiet n; 3. Schürfarbeit f
~ **hole** s. ~ well
~ **sampling** Bohrprobenahme f
~ **well** Prospektionsbohrung f, Aufschlußbohrung f
prospecting Schürfen n, Schürfarbeit f, Prospektieren n
~ **bore** Suchbohrung f
~ **drift** Schürfstrecke f
~ **for minerals** Erforschung f von Bodenschätzen
~ **method** Schürfmethode f, Prospektionsmethode f
~ **pick** geologischer Hammer m
~ **pit** Schürfschacht m
~ **rig** Schürfbohranlage f
~ **shaft** Versuchsschacht m, Schürfschacht m
~ **trench** Schürfgraben m
~ **well** Suchbohrung f
~ **work** Ausrichtungsarbeit f, Schürfarbeit f, Erschließungsarbeit f
prospection drilling Schürfbohrung f
prospective oil land öIhöffiges Gebiet n
~ **ore** erschürftes (sichtbares) Erz n
prospector Prospektor m, Schürfer m
protecting cover Schutzdecke f
protection against scour Kolkschutz m
~ **against underwashing** Schutz m gegen Unterspülungen
~ **area** Schutzgebiet n, Schutzzone f
~ **of the bank** Uferschutz m
~ **of the environment** Landschaftsschutz m
protective area Schutzgebiet n, Schutzzone f
~ **atmosphere** Schutzgasatmosphäre f
~ **colloid** Schutzkolloid n
~ **cover[ing]** Schutzdecke f
~ **forest belt** Windschutzstreifen m
~ **layer** Schutzschicht f
~ **seam** Schutzflöz n
~ **zone** Schutzzone f
proterobase Proterobas m (basisches Ganggestein)
Proterophytic Proterophytikum n
Proterozoic proterozoisch
Proterozoic [Era] Proterozoikum n
protoclastic structure protoklastisches Gefüge n

protoconch Embryonalkammer f, Protoconch n (Embryonalteil der Gehäuse von Gastropoden und Cephalopoden)
protodolomite Protodolomit m (unstabiler, Ca-reicher Dolomit)
protogene protogen
protogenic primärmagmatisch
protogenous s. protogene
protogine Protogin m (Varietät von Gneis)
protolysis Protolyse f
proton precession magnetometer Kernpräzessionsmagnetometer n
~ resonance magnetometer Kernresonanzmagnetometer n
protoplanet Urplanet m, Protoplanet m
protoplate Protoplatte f
protore unverändertes (primäres) Erz n, Ausgangserz n
protosun Ursonne f
prototype Prototyp m
protozoic protozoisch
protozoon Einzeller m
protract/to kartieren; maßstabgetreu zeichnen
protractor Anlegegoniometer n
protrude/to auswerfen
protruding vorspringend
~ delta vorgeschobenes Delta n
protrusion Protrusion f, Auswurf m, Herausdrücken n
~ of lava Lavaauswurf m
protuberance Protuberanz f
proustite Proustit m, lichtes Rotgültigerz n, Arsensilberblende f, Ag_3AsS_3
proved deposit erkundete Lagerstätte f
proven oil land ölführendes Gebiet n
~ ore nachgewiesenes (vorhandenes) Erz n (Erzreservenberechnung)
~ reserves nachgewiesene Vorräte mpl
~ territory Gebiet n mit nachgewiesener Ölführung; untersuchtes (bekanntes) Gebiet n
providing of mineral resources Vorratsvorlauf m mineralischer Rohstoffe
proving hole Aufschlußbohrung f
provision Vorsorge f
proximate sensing Beobachtung (Messung) f in unmittelbarer Objektnähe
pry apart/to aussprengen
~ off absprengen
psammite Psammit m, Sandstein m (mikroklastisches Gestein)
psammitic psammitisch
psammyte s. psammite
psephicity psephitische Struktur f
psephite Psephit m (makroklastisches Gestein)
psephitic psephitisch
psephonecrocoenosis wellenschlagsortierte Fossilgemeinschaft f
pseudo cannel coal Pseudokännelkohle f (Saprohumolith)
~-cross stratification Pseudoschrägschichtung f
~-oolites Pseudo-Oolithe mpl, Pseudo-Ooide npl, Mikropellets npl

~-shield volcano schildförmiger Stratovulkan m
pseudoanticline falscher Sattel m
pseudobedded pseudogeschichtet
pseudobedding Pseudoschichtung f
pseudoboleite Pseudoboleit m, $5PbCl_2 \cdot 4Cu(OH)_2 \cdot 2^1/_2H_2O$
pseudobombs Lavabälle mpl
pseudobreccia Pseudobrekzie f
pseudobrookite Pseudobrookit m, Fe_2TiO_5
pseudoconformable pseudokonkordant
pseudoconformity Pseudokonkordanz f
pseudoconglomerate Pseudokonglomerat n
pseudocotunnite Pseudocotunnit m, K_2PbCl_4
pseudocrystalline pseudokristallin
pseudocubic cleavage pseudokubische Spaltbarkeit f
pseudodiorite Pseudodiorit m
pseudofossil Pseudofossil n
pseudohexagonal pseudohexagonal
pseudolaueite Pseudolaueit m, $MnFe_2[OH|PO_4]_2 \cdot 8H_2O$
pseudomalachite Pseudomalachit m, $Cu_5[(OH)_2|PO_4]_2$
pseudomicrite Pseudomikrit m (sekundär durch Kornabbau aus organischem Karbonatdetritus entstandener Mikrit)
pseudomoraine Pseudomoräne f
pseudomorph pseudomorph
pseudomorph Pseudomorphose f
pseudomorphic pseudomorph
pseudomorphism Pseudomorphose f
pseudonodule synsedimentäre Rollstruktur f
pseudopressure Pseudodruck m
pseudoripples Scheinrippeln fpl
pseudoschistosity falsche Schieferung f
pseudoseries Scheinserie f (Tektonik)
pseudosymmetry Pseudosymmetrie f
pseudosyncline falsche Mulde f
pseudotachylite Pseudotachylit m
pseudotrough Pseudomulde f
pseudovolcanic pseudovulkanisch
pseudowollastonite Pseudowollastonit m, Cyclowollastonit m, $Ca_3[Si_3O_9]$
PSF s. point spread function
PSFG = Permanent Service on the Fluctuation of Glaciers
psilomelane Psilomelan m, Hartmanganerz n, $(Ba, H_2O)_2Mn_5O_{10}$
psilophyte flora Psilophytenflora f
psychrometer Psychrometer n, Luftfeuchtemesser m
Pteridophyta Farnpflanzen fpl
Pterocerian Pterocerien n (Kimmeridge, Nordwestdeutschland und Oberrheingebiet)
pteroid flügelähnlich
pteropod Pteropode f, Flügelschnecke f
~ ooze Pteropodenschlamm m
ptilolite Ptilolith m, Mordenit m, $(Ca, K_2, Na_2)[AlSi_5O_{12}]_2 \cdot 6H_2O$
ptygmatic ptygmatisch
~ fold ptygmatische Falte f

ptygmatic

~ **structure** ptygmatische Textur f
pucherite Pucherit m, Bi[VO$_4$]
puckered slate s. creased slate
puckering Fältelung f
puckerings Runzeln fpl
pudding balls s. armoured mud balls
~ **granite** Kugelgranit m, Puddinggranit m
~ **stone** Puddingstein m, Nagelfluh f
puddle Wasserpfütze f, Tümpel m
puddled soil verschlämmter Boden m
~ **structure** hornartige Struktur f
Puercan/Dragonian [Stages] Puercan/Dragon n (Wirbeltierstufen, unteres Paläozän in Nordamerika)
puff cone Schlammkegel m
puffing hole s. blow hole
pug s. flucan
pulaskite Pulaskit m (Alkalisyenit)
pull/to entrohren, Rohre ziehen
~ **out** aufholen, ausbauen, ausfahren
pull-apart structure Zerrungsstruktur f
~ **of gravity** Zug m der Schwerkraft, Schwereanziehung f
pulling of the drill[ing] string Ausbau m (Ziehen n) des Bohrgestänges
~ **rate (speed) of drill[ing] string** Ausbaugeschwindigkeit f des Bohrstrangs
pulp feiner Schlamm m, Trübe f
pulsating magnetic field pulsierendes Magnetfeld n
~ **spring** intermittierende Quelle f, Springquelle f
~ **stress** Schwellast f
pulsation dampener Stoßdämpfer m
pulsational uplift ruckartige Hebung f
pulse Impuls m (Seismik)
~ **compressing** Impulskompression f
~ **disturbance** Störimpuls m
~ **test** Impulstest m
~-**width modulation** Impulsbreitenmodulation f (Verfahren zur Registrierung auf Magnetband bei der Seismik)
pulsed ultrasonic technique Ultraschallimpulsverfahren n
pulverized pulverisiert
pulverulent pulverförmig, pulverartig, pulverig, staubartig
~ **brown coal** mulmige Braunkohle f
~ **silica** Kieselgur f, Infusorienerde f, Diatomeenerde f
~ **soil** Staubboden m
pumice Naturbimsstein m, Bims[stein] m
~ **concrete** Bimsbeton m
~ **stone** Bimsstein m
~ **tuff** Bimssteintuff m
pumiceous bimssteinartig, Bimsstein...
~ **bomb** Bimssteinbombe f
~ **lava** Schaumlava f
~ **structure** Bimssteingefüge n
pumicing Bimssteinschliff m
pump off/to leerpumpen
~ **out** auspumpen
pump delivery Spülungsvolumenstrom m

~ **discharge** Förderung f (einer Pumpe)
pumpability Pumpfähigkeit f (Erdöl- und Gasförderung)
pumped storage Pumpspeicherung f
~-**storage hydropower plant** Pumpspeicherkraftwerk n
pumpellyite Pumpellyit m, Ca$_2$(Mg, Fe, Mn, Al)(Al, Fe, Ti)$_2$[(OH, H$_2$O)$_2$|SiO$_4$|Si$_2$O$_7$]
pumper s. pumping well
pumping depression cone Absenkungstrichter m
~ **installation** Pumpanlage f
~ **jack** Pumpenbock m
~ **out** Auspumpen n
~ **outfit** Pumpanlage f
~ **station** Pumpstation f
~ **string** Pumprohr n
~ **test** Pumpversuch m (Erdöl)
~ **unit** Pumpanlage f
~ **well** Pumpsonde f, im Pumpbetrieb fördernde Bohrung f
~ **with sucker rods** Tiefpumpenförderung f
punching Kernstoßbohren n
puppet of loess Lößpuppe f, Lößkindl n
Purbeckian [Stage] Purbeck n (Stufe des obersten Juras einschließlich der tiefsten Unterkreide, Südengland)
pure rein
~ **goods** reine Kristalle mpl (Edelsteine)
~ **oil** reines (wasserfreies) Öl n
~ **shear** reine Scherung (Schiebung) f
~ **strain** Normalverformung f
purification of gas Gasreinigung f
purple copper ore s. bornite
~ **ore** Kiesabbrand m
purpurite Purpurit m, (Mn, Fe)[PO$_4$]
push Stoßkraft f, Schub m
~ **moraine** Stauchmoräne f, Aufpressungsmoräne f
~ **of ice** Eisdruck m
puszta Pußta f
put beds in relation with each other/to Schichten korrelieren
~ **down a well** eine Bohrung niederbringen
putrefaction Verwesung f, Fäulnis f, Verfaulen n, Faulen n
putrefactive bacteria Fäulnisbakterien fpl
putrefy/to faulen
putrid faul
~ **mud (slime)** Sapropel n (m), Faulschlamm m
puzzolana s. pozzuolana
pycnite Pyknit m (grobstengelige Varietät von Topas)
pycnometer Pyknometer n, Dichtemesser m
pygidium Pygidium n, Schwanzschild m (Arthropoden, Trilobiten)
pyramid Pyramide f
~ **pebble** s. dreikanter
pyramidal pyramidenförmig, pyramidal
pyranometer Pyranometer n, Himmelsstrahlungsmesser m
pyrargyrite Pyrargyrit m, dunkles Rotgültigerz n, Antimonsilberblende f, Ag$_3$SbS$_3$

Pyrenean phase of folding pyrenäische Faltungsphase f
pyrgeometer Pyrgeometer n, Erdstrahlungsmesser m
pyrgeometry Pyrgeometrie f, Erdstrahlungsmessung f
pyrheliometer Pyrheliometer n, Sonnenstrahlungsmesser m
pyrheliometry Pyrheliometrie f, Sonnenstrahlungsmessung f
pyricaustate fossile brennbare Substanz f
pyriclasite Pyriklasit m; Pyroxengranulit m *(Pyroxen-Plagioklas-Gestein)*
pyrigarnite Pyrigarnit m *(Pyroxen-Granat-Gestein)*
pyritaceous pyritartig, kieshaltig
pyrite Pyrit m, Schwefelkies m, Eisenkies m, FeS_2
~ **ammonite** s. pyritized ammonite
~ **concretion** Pyritkonkretion f, Schwefelkieskonkretion f
~ **nodule** Pyritknolle f
pyritic[al] pyritisch, kieshaltig; kiesähnlich
~ **concretions** Pyritkonkretionen fpl, Kieskälber npl *(im Dachschiefer)*
~ **ore** Pyriterz n
~ **shale** pyritischer Schieferton m
pyritiferous pyrithaltig
~ **coal seam** pyritreiches Kohlenflöz n
~ **shale** Pyritschiefer m
pyritization Pyritisierung f, Umwandlung f in Pyrit
pyritize/to pyritisieren, in Pyrit umwandeln
pyritized ammonite pyritisierter (verkiester) Ammonit m
pyritohedron Pyritoeder n, Pentagondodekaeder n
pyritous pyrithaltig
pyroaurite Pyroaurit m, $Mg_6Fe_2[(OH)_{16}|CO_3]\cdot 4H_2O$
pyrobelonite Pyrobelonit m, $PbMn[OH|VO_4]$
pyrobitumen Pyrobitumen n
pyrochlore Pyrochlor m, $(Ca, Na)_2(Nb, Ta)_2O_6(O, OH, F)$
pyrochroite Pyrochroit m, $Mn(OH)_2$
pyroclastic pyroklastisch
~ **flow** s. ignimbrite
~ **flows** pyroklastische Ströme mpl
~ **material** Auswürfling m
~ **rock** pyroklastisches Gestein n
pyroclast[ic]s pyroklastische Produkte npl
pyroelectric pyroelektrisch
pyroelectricity Pyroelektrizität f
pyrofusinite Pyrofusinit m *(Kohlensubmaceral)*
pyrogenetic pyrogen
~ **mineral** pyrogenes Mineral n
~ **rock** pyrogenes Gestein n, Erstarrungsgestein n
pyrogenic, pyrogenous s. pyrogenetic
pyrolite Pyrolit m *(hypothetisches Mantelgestein)*
pyrolusite Pyrolusit m, Weichmanganerz n, $\beta\text{-}MnO_2$

pyrolysis Pyrolyse f
pyrometamorphism Pyrometamorphose f
pyrometric effect Heizwert m
pyromorphite Phyromorphit m, Buntbleierz n, $Pb_5[Cl|(PO_4)_3]$
pyromorphous pyromorph
pyrope Pyrop m, $Mg_3Al_2[SiO_4]_3$
pyrophanite Pyrophanit m, $MnTiO_3$
pyrophyllite Pyrophyllit m, $Al_2[(OH)_2|Si_4O_{10}]$
pyropissite Pyropissit m *(Liptobiolith; wachsreiche Schwelbraunkohle)*
pyroschist Ölschiefer m, Brennschiefer m
pyrosmalite Pyrosmalith m, $(Mn, Fe)_8[(OH, Cl)_{10}|Si_6O_{15}]$
pyrostilpnite Pyrostilpnit m, Feuerblende f, Ag_3SbS_3
pyroxene group Pyroxengruppe f *(gesteinsbildende Ca-, Mg-, Fe-Silikatminerale)*
pyroxenite Pyroxenit m *(ultrabasisches Gestein)*
pyroxferroite Pyroxferroit m, $[Fe, Ca, Mg, Mn]SiO_3$
pyroxmanganite Pyroxmanganit m *(triklines pyroxenähnliches Mondmineral)*
pyroxmangite Pyroxmangit m, $(Fe, Mn)_7[Si_7O_{21}]$
pyrrhite s. pyrochlore
pyrrhotine, pyrrhotite Pyrrhotin m, Magnetkies m, FeS

Q

Q-joint Q-Kluft f, Querkluft f *(Granittektonik)*
quadrangle *(Am)* Kartenblatt n *(bei 15° Breite und 15° Länge 1:62500; bei 30° Breite und 30° Länge 1:125000; bei 1° Breite und 1° Länge 1:250000)*
quadratic system quadratisches (tetragonales) System) n
quadrille paper Koordinatenpapier n
quadrivalence Vierwertigkeit f
quadrivalent vierwertig
quadruple platform Aushängebühne f *(Tiefbohrung)*
quagmire Sumpf[boden] m, Moorboden m, Sumpffläche f, Sumpfloch n, Schwingmoor n
quake/to [er]beben, schüttern *(seismisch)*
quake 1. Beben n, Erdbeben n, Erschütterung f; 2. plötzlicher Einbruch m *(von Gestein oder Kohle)*
~-**proof** erdbebensicher
~ **sheet** Erschütterungsschicht f
quaking bog s. quagmire
qualitative analysis qualitative Analyse f
quality of coal seam Kohlenflözbeschaffenheit f
~ **of soil** Bodenbeschaffenheit f
~ **of the lode** Verhalten n des Ganges
quantity available for water Wasserdargebot n

quaquaversal

quaquaversal allseitig geneigt, periklinal
~ **dip** periklinales Fallen n, umlaufendes Einfallen n *(von einem Mittelpunkt nach allen Richtungen)*
~ **dome** kreisförmige Domstruktur f
~ **structure** periklinale Faltenstruktur f, Kuppel f, Gewölbe n
quarpit s. quarry
quarrel Steinbruch m
quarrier Steinbrecher m, Steinhauer m, Steinbrucharbeiter m
quarring Rohstoffgewinnung f im Übertagebau *(s.a. plucking)*
quarry/to im Steinbruch arbeiten, [Steine] brechen
quarry Steinbruch m, Bruch m, Grube f
~ **bed** Steinbruchlager n
~ **blasting** Sprengung f im Steinbruch
~ **block** Bruchstein m
~ **face** Bruchwand f
~ **floor** Steinbruchsohle f, Bruchsohle f
~ **lode** durch Klüfte zerteilter Gang m
~ **rocks** Bruchgestein n
~ **rubbish** Steingrubenabfall m
~ **sap** s. ~ water
~ **tile** Natursteinplatte f
~ **water** Bergfeuchtigkeit f *(im frisch gebrochenen Gestein)*
quarrying Steinbrechen n, Steinbruchbetrieb m
~ **operation** Steinbrucharbeit f
quarryman s. quarrier
quarrystone Bruchstein m, Naturstein m, Werkstein m, Haustein m
quarter Mondviertel n
~-**wave [length] plate** Viertelwellen[längen]plättchen n, λ/4-Platte f
quartering 1. Viertelung f; 2. Mondphasenwechsel m
~ **way** Teilbarkeit[srichtung] f *(von Massengesteinen)*
quartz Quarz m, SiO_2
~-**bearing** quarzhaltig
~ **boil** Ausstrich m eines Quarzganges
~[-**crystal**] **clock** Quarzuhr f
~ **diabase** Quarzdiabas m
~ **dike** Quarzgang m
~ **diorite** Quarzdiorit m
~ **dolerite** Quarzdolerit m
~-**free** quarzfrei
~-**free porphyry** quarzfreier Porphyr m
~ **keratophyre** Quarzkeratophyr m
~ **latite** Quarzlatit m
~ **lenses** Quarzknauern fpl
~ **mica rock** Quarzglimmerfels m
~ **mica schist** Quarzglimmerschiefer m
~ **mine** Goldquarzgrube f
~ **phyllite** Quarzphyllit m
~ **plate** Quarzplättchen n
~ **porphyrite** Quarzporphyrit m
~ **porphyry** Quarzporphyr m
~ **reef** Quarzgang m

~-**rich** quarzreich
~ **rock** Quarzfels m, Quarzit[fels] m
~ **rocks** Quarzgestein n
~ **sand** Quarzsand m
~ **syenite** Quarzsyenit m
~ **vein** Quarzader f
~ **veinlet** Quarzäderchen n
~ **wedge** Quarzkeil m
quartzic quarzhaltig, quarzig
quartziferous quarzhaltig, kieselig; verquarzt, verkieselt
quartzine Quarzin m *(s.a. chalcedony)*
quartzite Quarzit[fels] m, Quarzfels m
quartzitic quarzitisch
~ **rock** Quarzitgestein n
quartzose quarzähnlich, quarzartig, quarzhaltig, quarzreich, verquarzt
~ **sand** Quarzsand m
quartzous, quartzy s. quartzose
quasi-steady flow quasistationäre Strömung f
quaternary system Vierstoffsystem n
Quaternary Quartär[system] n *(chronostratigrafisch)*; Quartär n, Quartärperiode f *(geochronologisch)*; Quartär n, Quartärzeit f *(allgemein)*
~ **Age** Quartär n, Quartärzeit f
~ **Period** Quartär n, Quartärperiode f
~ **System** Quartär[system] n
queenstownite tasmanischer Tektit m
queere s. quere
quench crystal growth Kristallwachstum n durch plötzliche Abschreckung *(z.B. schockgeschmolzenen Glases)*
quenching [plötzliche] Abkühlung f, Abschreckung f; Löschung f
quenselite Quenselit m, PbO·MnOOH
quenstedtite Quenstedtit m, $Fe_2(SO_4)_3 \cdot 10H_2O$
quere Kluft f
quetenite Quetenit m, Botryogen m, $MgFe[OH|(SO_4)_2] \cdot 7H_2O$
quick clay Quickton m, Fließton m
~ **ground** schwimmendes Gebirge n
~ **lime** Ätzkalk m, ungelöschter Kalk m
quickly draining pores Grobporen fpl
quicksand Wanderdüne f, Treibsand m, Flugsand m, Quicksand m, Schwimmsand m, Fließsand m
quicksilver Quecksilber n, Hg *(s.a. mercury)*
~ **mine** Quecksilberbergwerk n, Quecksilbergrube f
~ **ore** Quecksilbererz n
quiescence Ruhe f *(z.B. eines Vulkans)*
quiescent ruhend, schlummernd *(z.B. Vulkan)*
~-**area facies** Stillwasserfazies f, Faziesbereich m mit ruhigen Sedimentationsbedingungen
~ **volcano** Vulkan m im Ruhezustand
quiet ruhig *(z.B. Vulkan)*
~ **reach** Stillwasser n, Stille f
~ **sun** ruhige (fleckenarme) Sonne f
quisqueite Quisqueit m *(vanadinreiche Braunkohle mit S-Gehalt)*
qweear s. quere

R

R-tectonites R-Tektonite *mpl*
rabban Eiserner Hut *m (Cornwall)*
rabben gelber Hornstein *m*
rabbittite Rabbittit *m*,
  $Ca_3Mg_3[(UO_2)(OH)_2(CO_3)_3]_2 \cdot 18H_2O$
race 1. Gezeitenströmung *f*; 2. Pyrit *m* in Wurzelform
racemic quartz optisch inaktiver Quarz *m*
racemization Razemisierung *f (Umwandlung optisch aktiver Substanzen in optisch inaktive)*
rachel, rachen, rachill *s.* ratchel
racking platform Gestängebühne *f*, Aushängebühne *f (Tiefbohrung)*
~ **system** Gestängeabstellvorrichtung *f*
radar Radar *n*
~ **altimeter** Radarhöhenmesser *m*
~ **beam width** Breite *f* des Radar[richt]strahls
~ **echo** Radarecho *n*
~ **foreshortening** Radarverkürzung *f (der Entfernung zu luvseitig gelegenen Punkten in hügelig-bergigem Terrain)*
~ **meteorology** Radarmeteorologie *f*
~ **returns** Radarechos *npl*
~ **scattering cross section** Radarstreuquerschnitt *m*
~ **system** Radarsystem *n*
raddle erdiger Haematit *m (in Kohle, Yorkshire)*
radial radial, radiär
~-**columnar** radialstengelig, radialfaserig
~ **crack** Kernsprung *m*
~ **faults** Radialverwerfungen *fpl*
~ **flow** Radialströmung *f*, radiale Strömung *f*
~ **furrow** Radialfurche *f*
~ **growth** radialstrahliges Wachstum *n*
~ **line plotter** Radialkartiergerät *n (für Luftbildauswertung)*
~ **refraction** radiale Refraktionsaufstellungen *fpl*, Sternschießen *n (Seismik)*
radially arranged strahlig angeordnet
~ **fibrous** radialfaserig, radialstengelig
radiance Strahlungsdichte *f*, spezifische Ausstrahlung *f*, Strahlungshelligkeit *f*
radiancy *s.* radiance
radiant emittance spezifische Ausstrahlung *f*
~ **energy** Strahlungsenergie *f*
~ **intensity** Strahlungsintensität *f*
~ **temperature** Strahlungstemperatur *f*
radiate/to 1. abstrahlen, ausstrahlen; 2. bestrahlen
radiated strahlig, strahlenförmig
~ **crystalline** strahlig
~ **pyrite** *s.* marcasite
~ **structure** radiale Struktur *f*
radiating strahlig, strahlenförmig
~ **columnar** radialstengelig, radialfaserig
~ **dikes** Radialgänge *mpl*
radiation Ausstrahlung *f*, Strahlung *f*
~ **age** Bestrahlungsalter *n*
~ **belt** Strahlungsgürtel *m (der Erde)*
~ **budget** Strahlungshaushalt *m*
~ **damage** Strahlungsschaden *m*, Defekt *m* [im Kristallgitter], radioaktive Spur *f*
~ **energy** Strahlungsenergie *f*
~ **fog** Strahlungsnebel *m*
~ **logging** Aufnahme *f* radioaktiver Profile
~ **of heat** Wärmeausstrahlung *f*
~ **pressure** Strahlungsdruck *m*
~ **temperature** Strahlungstemperatur *f*
~ **zone** Strahlungsgürtel *m (der Erde)*
radio altimeter Funkhöhenmesser *m*
~ **astronomy** Radioastronomie *f*
~ **echo observation** Radioechobeobachtung *f*
~ **meteor** Radiometeor *m*
~ **telescope** Radioteleskop *n*
radioactive radioaktiv
~ **coalification** radioaktive Inkohlung *f*
~ **contamination** radioaktive Verseuchung *f*, Strahlenverseuchung *f*
~ **dating** radioaktive Altersbestimmung *f*
~ **decay** radioaktiver Zerfall *m*
~ **decay law** radioaktives Zerfallsgesetz *n*
~ **discoloration** radioaktive Verfärbung *f*
~ **disintegration** radioaktiver Zerfall *m*
~ **element** radioaktives Element *n*
~ **emission** radioaktive Ausstrahlung *f*
~ **fission product** radioaktives Spaltprodukt *n*
~ **halo** radioaktiver Strahlungshof *m*
~ **heat** radiogene Wärme *f*
~ **labelling [process]** *s.* ~ tracing
~ **refusion** Gesteinsaufschmelzung *f* durch radiogen erzeugte Wärme
~ **series** radioaktive Zerfallsreihe *f*
~ **spring** Radiumquelle *f*
~ **tracer** Radioindikator *m*
~ **tracer dilution method** Verdünnungsmethode *f (Tracerversuch)*
~ **tracing** Markierung *f* mit radioaktiven Isotopen, radioaktive Markierung *f*
~ **waste disposal** Beseitigung *f* radioaktiver Abfälle
~ **wastes** radioaktive Abfälle *mpl*
~ **water** radioaktives Abwasser *n*
radioactivity Radioaktivität *f*
~ **log** Radioaktivitätsmessung *f*, Radioaktivitätslog *n*
~ **logging** Radiometrie *f*
radioautography Radioautografie *f*
radiocarbon Radiokarbon *n*, ^{14}C
~ **cycle** Radiokarbonzyklus *m*
~ **dating** Radiokarbondatierung *f*
~ **method** Radiokarbonmethode *f*
radiogenic radiogen
~ **argon** radiogenes Argon *n*
~ **heat** radiogene Wärme[produktion] *f*
radiograph Radiogramm *n*
radiographic method radiografisches Verfahren *n*
radiography Röntgenografie *f*
radiohalo radioaktiver (pleochroitischer) Hof *m*
radioisotope radioaktives Isotop *n*, Radioisotop *n*

radiolarian

radiolarian chert Radiolarit *m*, Kieselschiefer *m*, Lydit *m*
~ **earth** *s.* radiolarite
~ **mudstone** Radiolarienfaulschlammkalk *m*
~ **ooze** Radiolarienschlamm *m*, Radiolarienschlick *m*
radiolarite Radiolarit *m*
radiolated strahlig *(z.B. Bruch)*
radiolead Radioblei *n*, ^{206}Pb, ^{207}Pb, ^{208}Pb *(Blei als Endprodukt radioaktiver Zerfallsreihen)*
radiolite *s.* natrolite
radioluminescence Radiolumineszenz *f*
radiometeorology Radiometeorologie *f*
radiometer Radiometer *n*, Strahlungsintensitätsmesser *m*
radiometric[al] radiometrisch
~ **age** radiometrisches Alter *n*
~ **correction** Strahlungskorrektur *f*, radiometrische Korrektur *f*, Korrektur *f* gemessener Strahlungswerte
~ **intensity mapping** Kartierung *f* der radiometrischen Intensität
~ **resolution** radiometrisches Auflösungsvermögen *n (eines Fernerkundungssensors)*
radiometry Radiometrie *f*
radionuclide radioaktives Nuklid *n*
radiotelescope Radioteleskop *n*
radiothorium Radiothorium *n*, ^{228}Th
radiozone durch ihren Radioaktivitätsgrad charakterisierte stratigrafische Zone *f*
radium Radium *n*, Ra
~ **age** Radiumalter *n*
~ **emanation** Radiumemanation *f*
radius of deviation Krümmungsradius *m* der Bohrlochachse
~ **of drainage** Dränageradius *m*
~ **of external boundary** Einzugsradius *m*
~ **of influence of depression** Absenkungsreichweite *f (eines Brunnens)*
~ **of investigation** Eindringtiefe *f*
~ **of well damage** Schädigungsradius *m*
radix Wurzel *f (Crinoiden)*
radon Radon *n*, Rn
radula teeth Radulazähnchen *npl (bei Gastropoden und Cephalopoden)*
raff armes Erz *n*
raft 1. Scholle *f*, Gesteinsblock *m*; Einschluß *m (in Magmatiten)*; 2. Flußabschnürung *f (durch Ufereinbruch)*
~ **lake** natürliche Flußaufstauung *f*
~ **structure** Schollentextur *f (bei Migmatit)*
rafted ice Packeis *n*
~ **material** Treibmaterial *n (in Meeresströmungen)*; Treibholz *n*
rafting Transport durch Anheftung an Eis oder anderes Schwimmgut
rag 1. dunkler Kieselsandstein *m*; harter Bildhauerkalkstein *m*; für *Wetzsteine geeignetes hartes Gestein*; 2. hangender Schiefer *m*; 3. Vorbrechen *n* des Erzes *(zur Sortierung)*
ragged zackig, felsig, zerrissen
~ **coast** zerrissene Küste *f*

~ **stone** schiefriger Bruchstein *m*
ragging Vorsortieren *n*, rohes Sortieren *n (von Erzen)*
raglanite Raglanit *m (korundhaltiger Nephelindiorit)*
ragstone 1. Kalksandstein *m*, Kieselsandstein *m*; dunkelgrauer quarziger Sandstein *m*; 2. Bruchstein *m* für Kleinpflasterherstellung
raguinite Raguinit *m*, TlFeS$_2$
raimondite Raimondit *m*, Jarosit *m (s.a.* jarosite)
rain Regen *m*
~ **beat** Regenschlag *m*
~ **belt** Regenzone *f*
~ **channels** Schratten *fpl*
~ **cloud** Regenwolke *f*
~ **crust** Harschkruste *f* aus gefrorenem Regen
~ **front** Regenfront *f*
~ **gauge** Niederschlagsmesser *m*, Regenmesser *m*
~ **-gauge station** Regenmeßstelle *f*
~ **lahar** Regenschlammstrom *m*
~ **measurement** Regenmessung *f*
~ **prints** Regentropfenmarken *fpl*, Regentropfeneindrücke *mpl*
~ **rill** Regenfurche *f*, Regenrinne *f*
~ **shadow** Regenschatten *m*
~ **shower** Regenschauer *m*
~ **trap** Regenauffangbehälter *m*
rainband Regenlinie *f*, Regenbande *f*
rainbow Regenbogen *m*
~ **chalcedony** irisierende Chalzedonlagen *fpl*
~ **-coloured** regenbogenfarbig
~ **colours** Regenbogenfarben *fpl*
raindrop Regentropfen *m*
~ **impact** Tropfarbeit *f (des Regens)*
~ **impressions** *s.* rain prints
rainfall Regenfall *m*, Regenmenge *f*, Niederschlag *m*, Niederschlagsmenge *f*
~ **coefficient** Niederschlagshöhe *f*, Niederschlagskoeffizient *m*
~ **curve** Niederschlagshöhenkurve *f*
~ **erosion** Niederschlagserosion *f*
~ **frequency atlas** Niederschlagsatlas *m*
~ **intensity** Regendichte *f*
~ **record** Niederschlagsregistrierung *f*
~ **recorder** registrierender Regenmesser *m*, Regenschreiber *m*
~ **-runoff relation** Niederschlags-Abfluß-Beziehung *f*
rainless regenlos
~ **season** Trockenzeit *f*
rainpour Regenguß *m*
rainsheet Regenschichtflut *f*
rainsquall Regenbö *f*, Regenguß *m*
rainstorm Platzregen *m*, Regensturm *m*
rainwash 1. Abschwemmung *f* durch Regen; 2. durch Regen abgeschwemmtes Erdreich *n*
rainwater Regenwasser *n*, Niederschlagswasser *n*
rainy niederschlagsreich, regenreich
~ **day** Regentag *m*

~ **period (season)** Regenzeit f
~ **weather** Regenwetter n
~ **year** regnerisches Jahr n, Regenjahr n
raise/to fördern, [zutage] heben; aufhauen, überhauen
~ **ore** Erz gewinnen
raise 1. Aufhauen n, Überhauen n; 2. ins Hangende getriebener Schacht m
~ **boring** Aufwärtsbohrung f
raised beach Hebungsküste f
~ **bog** Hochmoor n, Torfmoor n
~ **coast** Hebungsküste f
~ **reef** über die Wasserfläche ragendes Riff n
~ **shore line** gehobene Strandlinie f
~ **water level** Stau m, Aufstau m, Anstauung f
raising 1. Hebung f; 2. Quellen n (des Gebirges); 3. Aufwirbelung f (von Staub, Schnee)
~ **of the water level by the effect of wind** Windstau m (einer Wasserfläche)
rake 1. Einfallen n; 2. Querspalte f
~ **vein** steiler Gang m, Seigergang m
raking holes Schrägbohrungen fpl
ralstonite Ralstonit m, $Al_2(F, OH)_6 \cdot H_2O$
ram 1. Unterwasserriff n eines Eisbergs; 2. Rammbär m, Schlagbär m
~ **preventer** Backenpreventer m
Raman spectroscopy Raman-Spektroskopie f
ramble im Alten Mann zu Bruch gegangenes Hangendes n
rambler rig fahrbares Bohrgerät n; Förderwinde f
ramdohrite Ramdohrit m, $Pb_6Ag_4Sb_{10}S_{23}$
ramification Stamm m, Verzweigung f (Phylogenie)
ramifying verästelt
rammelly für Wechsellagerung argillitischer und sandiger Sedimente
rammelsbergite Rammelsbergit m, Weißnickelkies m, $NiAs_2$
ramming Abrammen n, Stampfen n
ramose verzweigt
ramp 1. Lehne f, Tallehne f, Abdachung f; 2. Überschiebung f, Aufschiebung f; 3. geneigte Schneefläche f (Land- und Seeeis verbindend); 4. Gestängerampe f (Tiefbohrung)
~ **trough** s. ~ **valley**
~ **valley** Tal n zwischen zwei Überschiebungseinheiten
~ **zone** s. **rift zone**
rampart Ringwall m (vulkanisch)
ramsayite Ramsayit m, $Na_2Ti_2[O_3Si_2O_6]$
ramsdellite Ramsdellit m, $\gamma\text{-}MnO_2$
rance schmaler Kohlenpfeiler m (Schottland)
Rancholabrean [Stage] Stufe des Pleistozäns
ranciéiteRanciéit m, $(Ca, Mn^{..})Mn_4^{....}O_9 \cdot 3H_2O$
randanite Infusorienerde f, Kieselgur f, Diatomeenerde f
randing Schürfen n
random zufällig, unregelmäßig
random Richtung eines steilen Ganges
~ **drilling** Bohren n auf gut Glück
~ **effects model of variance analysis** Varianzanalysemodell n mit zufälligen Effekten

~ **noise** Rauschen m, zufällige Störungen fpl
~ **orientation** regellose (ungeregelte) Orientierung f
~ **pattern** regellose (ungeregelte) Anordnung f
~ **sample** Stichprobe f, Einzelprobe f
~ **sampling** Zufallsprobenahme f
randomization willkürliche Verteilung f
randomize/to willkürlich verteilen
randomly distributed statistisch verteilt
~ **oriented** nicht bevorzugt orientiert
range/to einordnen, einreihen, klassifizieren
range 1. Bereich m, Stufe f; 2. Kette f (topografisch); 3. Abstand m (zwischen Schußpunkt und Geophongruppe); 4. mineralhöffiges Gebiet n; 5. Linie f mit drei Beobachtungspunkten; 6. (Am) Reihe f (gibt an, in der wievielten Reihe östlich oder westlich von einem Basismeridian eine „Township" gelegen ist. Beispiel: Section 29, Township 24 North, Range 12 East)
~ **ambiguity** Entfernungsunbestimmtheit f (z.B. bei Seitensichtradar in hügelig-bergigem Gelände)
~ **distortion** Entfernungsverzerrung f, Abstandsverzerrung f
~ **finder** Entfernungsmesser m (Seismik)
~ **of a fossil** vertikale Verbreitung f eines Fossils
~ **of depression** Absenkungsbereich m (eines Brunnens)
~ **of hills** Hügelkette f
~ **of lost strata** stratigrafische Unterbrechung f
~ **of mountains** Gebirgszug m, Gebirgskette f
~ **of semivariogram** Korrelationsradius m, Korrelationslänge f, Einflußbereich m einer Probe (Mindestabstand zweier unkorrelierter regionalisierter Variabler bzw. Zufallsvariabler)
~ **of species** Artreichweite f
~ **of tide** Gezeitenhub m, Fluthöhe f
~ **of variation** Variationsbreite f
~ **of veins** Gangzug m
~ **zone** biostratigrafische Einheit, gekennzeichnet durch die vertikale Verbreitung eines ausgewählten Elements der Flora oder Fauna innerhalb einer Gesteinsabfolge
rank Inkohlungsgrad m, Rang m
~ **determination** Rangbestimmung f (Bestimmung des Inkohlungsgrads)
~ **gradient** Inkohlungsgradient m
ranks of coal Kohlenarten fpl
ranquilite Ranquilit m, $Ca[(UO_2)_2(Si_2O_5)_3] \cdot 12H_2O$
ransomite Ransomit m, $CuFe_2(SO_4)_4 \cdot 7H_2O$
rapakivi Rapakivi m, Rapakiwi m (Varietät von Granit)
raphite s. **ulexite**
rapid Stromschnelle f, Flußschnelle f, Wildwasser n
~ **flowage** s. **landslide**
~ **spectrophotometric analysis** spektrofotometrische Schnellanalyse f
rapidity of diffusion Diffusionsgeschwindigkeit f

rapidity

~ **of flow** Fließgeschwindigkeit f
rare earth seltene Erde f
~-**earth elements** seltene Erden fpl
~ **gas** Edelgas n, seltenes Gas n
rarefaction Verdünnung f, Dilatation f
rash unreine Kohle f (aus dem Hangenden oder Liegenden eines Flözes)
rasorite s. kernite
raspberry spar 1. roter Turmalin m; 2. s. rhodochrosite
raspite Raspit m, α-$PbWO_4$
ratch reich mit Steinen durchsetzter toniger Unterboden m
ratchel[l] steiniger Unterboden m; kleine Steine mpl
rate growth Stufenziehen n (bei Kristallen)
~ **of advance** Abbaufortschritt m
~ **of corrosion** Korrosionsgeschwindigkeit f
~ **of decay** Zerfallsgeschwindigkeit f
~ **of decomposition** Zersetzungsgrad m
~ **of deposition** Sedimentationsgeschwindigkeit f
~ **of discharge** Abflußmenge f
~ **of drilling** Bohrgeschwindigkeit f
~ **of erosion** Erosionsgeschwindigkeit f
~ **of evaporation** Verdunstungsrate f
~ **of flow** 1. Fließgeschwindigkeit f; Durchflußmenge f, Zuflußmenge f; 2. Fördermenge f einer Sonde; 3. Durchflußintensität f
~-**of-flow meter** Durchflußmesser m
~ **of glacial movement** Gletschergeschwindigkeit f
~ **of inflow** Wasserzufluß m
~ **of nucleation** Keimbildungsrate f
~ **of penetration** Bohrfortschritt m
~ **of production** Förderrate f
~ **of rotation** Rotationsgeschwindigkeit f
~ **of stream flow** Wasserführung f
~ **of subsidence** Senkungsgeschwindigkeit f
rated pressure Nenndruck m
rathite Rathit m, $Pb_7As_9S_{20}$
rathole/to vorbohren
rathole Vorbohrloch n; Abstelloch n für das Kelly
ratio Verhältnis n; Verhältniszahl f, Beiwert m
~ **between horizontal and vertical pressure in undisturbed ground** Ruhedruckziffer f
~ **by weight** Gewichtsverhältnis n
~ **of enrichment** Anreicherungsverhältnis n
~ **of exaggeration** Überhöhungsverhältnis n
~ **of void volume to total volume of body** Porenvolumen n
~-**type lithofacies map** das Verhältnis zweier Komponenten darstellende Lithofazieskarte (z.B. klastisch zu sandig)
rattle jack Kohlenschiefer m, Brandschiefer m
~ **stone** Klapperstein m, selektiv gelöste Geode f
rattler 1. Kännelkohle f; minderwertige Gaskohle f; 2. Sandschiefer m
rauhwacke Rau[c]hwacke f
Rauracian [Substage] Raurac[ium] n (Unterstufe des Lusitans)

rauvite Rauvit m, $Ca[(UO_2)_2|V_{10}O_{28}\cdot 16H_2O$
ravelling ground gebrächer Kohäsionsboden m
ravine Runse f, Tobel m, Murtobel m, Wildbachbett n, Wildbachschlucht f, Klamm f
~ **stream** Sturzbach m, Wildbach m
ravinement Sedimentationsunterbrechung in Deltaablagerungen durch marine Transgressionen
ravining Zerschluchtung f
raw brown coal Rohbraunkohle f
~ **clay** Rohton m
~ **kaolin** Rohkaolin m
~ **lead** Werkblei n
~ **lignite** Rohbraunkohle f
~ **material** Rohstoff m, Rohmaterial n
~ **oil** Rohöl n
~ **ore** Haufwerk n, Roherz n
~ **tin** Werkzinn n
ray-finned bony fishes Strahlenflosser mpl, strahlenflossige Knochenfische mpl, Actinopterygier mpl
~ **geometry** Strahlengeometrie f
~ **of light** Lichtstrahl m
~ **path** Strahlenweg m, Strahlenverlauf m
~ **tracing** strahlengeometrische Modellierung f (Seismik)
Rayleigh wave Rayleigh Welle f (Seismik)
razor back schmaler scharfer Grat m
~ **stone** Wetzschiefer m
RCS s. scattering cross section
reabsorb/to resorbieren
reabsorbed crystal resorbierter Kristall m
reabsorption Resorption f
reach by digging/to erschürfen
reach 1. Weite f, Strecke f; Reichweite f; 2. gerade Flußstrecke f; 3. ins Land eingreifender Meeresbusen m; 4. Landzunge f, Vorgebirge n
react/to reagieren
reaction Reaktion f
~ **border** Reaktionsrand m
~ **pair** Reaktionspaar n
~ **pressure** Gegendruck m
~ **rate** Reaktionsgrad m
~ **rim** Reaktionsrinde f, Reaktionssaum m
~ **series** Reaktionsreihe f
~ **zone** Reaktionszone f
~ **zoning** Reaktionszonung f
reactive reaktionsfreudig
reactivity of coal Reaktivität f der Kohle
reading Ablesung f; Ablesewert m
~ **accuracy** Ablesegenauigkeit f
~ **position** Aufstellung f (eines Kristalls)
readvance erneuter Vorstoß m
real crystal Realkristall m
~ **time** Echtzeit f
realgar Realgar m, Rauschrot n, As_4S_4
reamer Erweiterungswerkzeug n, Nachräumer m
reaming bit Erweiterungsmeißel m
reappear/to wieder einsetzen, wieder aufleben, wieder aufreißen, sich wieder auftun

rearer s. 1. ~ seam; 2. edge coal
~ seam steil einfallendes Flöz n
rearrange/to neuordnen, umgruppieren, umlagern
rearrangement Neuordnung f, Umgruppierung f, Umlagerung f
~ of crystals Neuordnung f von Kristallen
reassorted loess Schwemmlöß m, umgelagerter Löß m
rebedding Umlagerung f (von Sedimenten)
rebellious ore schwer aufschließbares Erz n
rebore/to nachbohren
reboring Nachbohrung f
recede/to zurückweichen
receiver 1. Empfänger m; 2. Vorfluter m
~ calibration Empfängereichung f
receiving canal Aufnahmekanal m, Einlaufkanal m
~ stream Vorfluter m
recement/to wiederverkitten
recementation Wiederverkittung f
recemented glacier neuformierter Gletscher m (nach einem Abbruch)
recent rezent
~ crustal movement rezente Krustenbewegung f
~ formations rezente Bildungen fpl, heutige Ablagerungen fpl
Recent postpleistozän
~ Epoch Jetztzeit f, Neuzeit f
recently folded ranges rezente Faltengebirge npl
~ opened cast working neuaufgeschlossener Tagebau m
reception basin Sammelmulde f, Quellmulde f (eines Flusses)
receptor s. geophone
recess Nische f
recession Rückzug m
~ curve Senkungskurve f
~ curve of ground water Grundwasserabsenkungskurve f
~ hydrograph s. ~ curve
~ of the ground-water level Grundwasserabsenkung f
~ of the ice Eisrückzug m
recessional moraine Rückzugsmoräne f
~ stage Rückzugsstadium n
recharge/to durch Versickerung anreichern (Grundwasser)
recharge Versickerung f
~ area Einzugsgebiet n, Ernährungsgebiet n (Wasser)
~ distance Sickerstrecke f (in Brunnen)
~ line Versickerungsbrunnenkette f
~ of ground water Grundwasserdargebot n
~ pit Sickerschacht m
~ well Versickerungsbrunnen m
recharging image well Schluckbrunnen m
recipient Vorfluter m
reciprocal salt pair reziprokes Salzpaar n
~ sonde Oberkantensonde f, [inverse] Gradientsonde f

reciprocity principle Prinzip n der gleichen Gegenzeit (Seismik)
recirculated water wiedereingepreßtes Wasser n
reclaim/to entwässern, trockenlegen
~ land from the sea dem Meer Land abgewinnen
reclaimed marsh land Koog m
reclamation Entwässerung f, Trockenlegung f
~ of land Landgewinnung f, Neulandgewinnung f
~ of salterns Nutzbarmachung f von Salzböden
recoalification Nachinkohlung f
recomposed granite umkristallisierter Granit m
recongeal/to wiedergefrieren
reconnaissance 1. Exploration f, Erkundung f; 2. topografische Aufnahme f; geologische Übersichtskartierung f; 3. Regionalvermessung f (Seismik)
~ flight Aufklärungsflug m, Vorerkundungsflug m
~ map geologische Übersichtskarte f
~ satellite Aufklärungssatellit m
~ studies Geländestudien fpl
~ survey 1. Übersichtsvermessung f, Übersichtsaufnahme f; 2. Vorerkundung f, aufklärende Erkundung f
reconnoitre/to Aufschlußarbeiten betreiben
reconnoitring Exploration f
reconstitute/to verdichten
reconstruct/to rekonstruieren; restaurieren
reconstructed top rekonstruierte Oberkante f (eines Horizonts)
reconstruction Rekonstruktion f; Restauration f
record 1. Aufzeichnung f, Registrierung f; 2. [geologischer] Beleg m
~ of the rocks penetrated Aufzeichnung f der durchfahrenen Schichten
~ section Zusammenstellung f von Registrierungen
~ time Registrierzeit f, Laufzeit f
recorder Registriergerät n, Schreiber m
recording Aufzeichnung f, Registrierung f
~ apparatus Registriergerät n
~ boat Meßschiff n (Seeseismik)
~ cylinder Registrierzylinder m
~ device Registriergerät n
~ drum Registriertrommel f
~ meter Registriergerät n
~ stream gauge Strömungsschreiber m
~ truck Meßfahrzeug n
recover/to gewinnen, erschließen
recoverable abbaufähig, [ab]bauwürdig
~ geothermal potential gewinnbares geothermisches Potential n
~ oil gewinnbares Öl n
~ reserve gewinnbarer Vorrat m
recovered core gewonnener Kern m
~ diamonds rückgewonnene Diamanten npl

recovery

recovery 1. Gewinnung f; Erschließung f; 2. gewinnbarer Anteil m einer Lagerstätte; 3. Zutageziehen n verlorener Geräte, Fangarbeit f (bei Bohrungen)
- ~ **factor** Gewinnungsfaktor m, Ausbeutefaktor m
- ~ **method** Gewinnungsmethode f
- ~ **of core** Kerngewinn m
- ~ **of oil** Erdölausbeute f

recreation Erholung f (von Kristallen)
recrudescence of volcanic action Wiederbeginn m der vulkanischen Tätigkeit
recrystallization Umkristallisierung f, Umkristallisation f, Rekristallisation f, Neukristallisation f
recrystallize/to umkristallisieren, rekristallisieren, neukristallisieren
rectangular interference ripples rechteckige Interferenzrippeln fpl
rectified entzerrt
- ~ **photoplane** entzerrter Luftbildplan m

rectifier Entzerrungsgerät n
rectifying Entzerrung f
- ~ **apparatus** Entzerrungsgerät n, Gleichrichter m

rectilinear geradlinig
- ~ **fold** geradlinige Falte f
- ~ **shore line** langgestreckte gerade Küstenlinie f

recultivation Rekultivierung f
recumbence, recumbency Überkippung f
recumbent überkippt
- ~ **anticline** überkippte (liegende) Antiklinale f
- ~ **fold** überkippte (liegende) Falte f, Deckenfalte f

recurrence Rekurrenz f
- ~ **horizon** Rekurrenzfläche f

recurrent faulting wiederbelebter Bruch m
recycling Gaskreislaufverfahren n (Ölförderung)
red algae Rotalgen fpl
- ~ **antimony** s. kermesite
- ~ **arsenic** s. realgar
- ~ **-bed deposit** aride Cu-Konzentrationslagerstätte f
- ~ **-bed facies** Rotfazies f, Rotsandsteinfazies f
- ~ **beds** Rotschichten fpl, Ablagerungen fpl arider Schuttwannen
- ~ **bole** rote Ockererde f
- ~ **clay** roter Tiefseeton m
- ~ **cobalt** s. erythrite
- ~ **copper ore (oxide)** s. cuprite
- ~ **crumbly shale** roter Bröckelschiefer m
- ~ **earth** Roterde f
- ~ **giant** Roter Riese m (Stern)
- ~ **iron froth** Varietät von Haematit
- ~ **iron ochre** Roteisenocker m
- ~ **iron ore** Roteisenstein m, Haematit m (s .a. haematite)
- ~ **lead ore** s. crocoite
- ~ **loam** Rotlehm m
- ~ **manganese** s. 1. rhodochrosite; 2. rhodonite
- ~ **measures** Schichten des Perms oder der Trias
- ~ **mud** Rotspülung f (Bohrung)
- ~ **ochre** roter Eisenocker m
- ~ **orpiment** s. realgar
- ~ **oxide of zinc** s. zincite
- ~ **salt pelite** roter Salzton m (Zechstein)
- ~ **sediments** Rotsedimente npl
- ~ **silver ore** s. 1. pyrargyrite; 2. proustite
- ~ **soil** Roterde f
- ~ **star** Roter Stern m
- ~ **tide** Dinoflagellaten- und Diatomeenblüte f, Meeresblühen n
- ~ **zinc ore** s. zincite

Red Sea Rotes Meer n
- ~ **Marls** Keupermergel m

reddening zur Gesteinsrötung führender metasomatischer Prozeß m
reddingite Reddingit m, $(Mn, Fe)_3[PO_4]_2 \cdot 3H_2O$
reddle s. ruddle
redeposit/to umlagern, wieder ablagern, wieder absetzen (durch Wasser)
redeposition Umlagerung f, Wiederablagerung f, Wiederausfällung f (durch Wasser)
redingtonite Redingtonit m, $(Fe, Mg, Ni)(Cr, Al)_2[SO_4]_4 \cdot 22H_2O$
redistribute/to umlagern (durch Wind)
redistribution Umlagerung f (von chemischen Elementen)
- ~ **of land** Flurneugestaltung f
- ~ **of stresses** Spannungsumlagerung f

redledgeite Redledgeit m, $(Mg, Ca, OH, H_2O)[(Ti, Cr, Si)_8O_{16}]$
Redlichiid Realm Redlichia-Reich n (Paläobiogeografie, Unterkambrium)
redondite Redondit m (Fe-haltiger Variscit)
redox potential Redoxpotential n
redrilling Nachbohren n
redruthite s. chalcocite
redstone roter Sandstein m (Handelsbezeichnung)
reduce/to reduzieren; teilen (Proben)
- ~ **by quartering** vierteln
- ~ **in scale** im Maßstab verkleinern

reduced angle of draw reduzierter Grenzwinkel m
- ~ **gravity values** reduzierte Schwerewerte mpl
- ~ **limb** ausgequetschter, reduzierter Mittelschenkel m
- ~ **scale** 1. verkleinerter Maßstab m; 2. reduzierte Laufzeitkurve f
- ~ **thickness** reduzierte Mächtigkeit f
- ~ **travel time** reduzierte Laufzeit f (Seismik)

reducing agent Reduktionsmittel n
- ~ **environment** reduzierendes Milieu n
- ~ **flame** Reduktionsflamme f
- ~ **zone** Reduktionszone f, Zementationszone f (Erz)

reduction Reduzierung f; Teilung f (von Proben)
- ~ **fissure** Schwundriß m
- ~ **of cross section** Querschnittsverminderung f, Einschnürung f

~ of load Entlastung f
~ sphere Bleichungshof m (im Sediment)
~ to the pole Polreduktion f (Magnetik)
redundance Redundanz f, Weitläufigkeit f
reduzate in reduzierendem Milieu gebildetes Sediment n
reed 1. Schilf[rohr] n; 2. schichtparallele Klüftigkeit f; Querkluft f, Schlechte f
~ peat Rohrtorf m
~ swamp Schilfröhricht n
reedmergnerite Reedmergnerit m, $NaBSi_3O_8$
reedy coal s. banded coal
~ margin Schilfrand m (eines Sees)
reef 1. Riff n; Felsenklippe f, Schäre f; 2. goldführender Quarzgang m; 3. Reef n (bauwürdig vererzte Konglomeratlagen); 4. schiefrige Zone f
~ builder Riffbild[n]er m
~-building riffbildend
~-building coral riffbildende Koralle f
~ conglomerate s. ~ talus
~ coral Riffkoralle f
~ core Riffkern m
~ drive Deckgebirgseinschnitt m (über Goldseifen)
~ edge Riffrand m
~ facies Riffazies f
~-flank bedding Riffflankenschichtung f
~ flank deposit s. ~ talus
~ flat Rifffläche f, Riffplatte f
~ formation Riffbildung f
~ former Riffbild[n]er m
~-forming riffbildend
~-knoll Bioherm n, Kuppenriff n, Fleckenriff n
~ limestone Riffkalkstein m
~ milk Riffmilch f (Kalkschlamm)
~ of algal growth Algenriff n
~ ring s. atoll
~ shoal Seeklippe f
~-slope bedding Übergußschichtung f (Riff)
~ talus Riffschuttschichten fpl am seeseitigen Riffrand
~ tufa Rifftuff m (Ablagerung nadliger Kalzitkriställchen im biogenen Riffgerüst)
~-type reservoir Riffspeicher m
~ wall Riffmauer f
~ wash goldhaltige glazigene Sedimente npl
reefal zum Riff gehörig
reefing Abbau m von Goldquarzgängen
reeflike riffartig
reefy riffig
reel Trommel f, Seiltrommel f
~ truck Kabelwagen m (Seismik)
reemergence Wiederauftauchen n (von Land)
reentrant Einbuchtung f
~ angle einspringender Winkel m
reentry 1. Wiedereintritt m, Eintauchen n; 2. Wiedereinführung f (des Gestänges in das Bohrloch auf dem Meeresboden)
~ stress Eintauchbeanspruchung f
reerosion Wiederabtragung f, wiederholte Erosion f

reestablish/to entzerren (Luftbildaufnahme)
reexpose/to wiederfreilegen
reexposure Wiederfreilegung f
reference datum Bezugsniveau n
~ field Bezugsfeld n; Normalfeld n
~ horizon Leithorizont m
~ locality Typuslokalität f, locus typicus m
~ meridian Nullmeridian m
~ point Bezugspunkt m
~ sample Vergleichsprobe f
reficite Refizit m, $C_{20}H_{32}O_2$
refikite fossiles Harz n (in Braunkohle)
refill/to verfüllen, einfüllen
refilling Verfüllung f, Einfüllung f
refining Raffinieren n, Raffination f
reflectance Reflektanz f, Reflexionsvermögen n
reflected light reflektiertes Licht n, Auflicht n
~ refraction reflektierte Refraktion f (Seismik)
~ wave reflektierte (zurückgeworfene, rücklaufende) Welle f
reflecting horizon Reflektor m, Reflexionshorizont m
~ power Reflexionsvermögen n
reflection Reflexion f, Spiegelung f; reflektiertes Licht n, Auflicht n
~ arrival time at zero offset 1. Laufzeit f der Reflexion am Schußpunkt; 2. Lotzeit f
~ coefficient Reflexionskoeffizient m
~ curve Laufzeitkurve f einer Reflexion
~ factor Reflexionsvermögen n
~ measurements Reflexionsmessungen fpl
~ of seismic wave Reflektierung f der seismischen Welle
~ plane Spiegelungsfläche f (von Kristallen)
~ pleochroism Reflexionspleochroismus m
~ seismic technique Reflexionsseismik f
~ shooting Reflexionsschießen n (Seismik)
~ sounding Echolotung f
~ time Lotzeit f
reflectivity Reflexionsvermögen n
~ measurement on coking coals [optische] Reflexionsmessung f an Kokskohlen
~ of vitrinite Reflexionsvermögen n des Vitrinits (optische Größe zur Kennzeichnung des Inkohlungsgrads)
reflectogram Reflektogramm n (grafische Darstellung der optisch bestimmten Reflexionswerte von Kohlenvitriniten)
reflectometry Reflexionsmessung f
reflexed fold s. overturned fold
reflux Rückfluß m, Ebbe f
refolded fold wiedergefaltete Falte f
refolding wiederholte Faltung f
refoliation Sekundärschieferung f, zweite Schieferung f
reforest/to aufforsten
reforestation Aufforstung f
reforming of natural gas Reforming n, Spaltung f von Erdgas
refract/to brechen
refracted wave gebrochene Welle f

refraction

refraction Brechung f, Refraktion f
~ **correction** Refraktionsberichtigung f
~ **index** Brechungsindex m
~ **marker** Refraktionshorizont m *(Seismik)*
~ **of light** Lichtbrechung f
~ **profile** Refraktionsprofil n
~ **seismic profiling** refraktionsseismische Profilaufnahme f
~ **seismics** Refraktionsseismik f
~ **shooting** Refraktionsschießen n
~ **time-distance graph** refraktionsseismische Laufzeitkurve f
~ **wave** Refraktionswelle f, Tauchwelle f
refractive [strahlen]brechend
~ **index** Brechungsindex m, Brechungsexponent m
refractivity Brechungsvermögen n, Brechungskraft f; Lichtbrechung f
refractor s. refraction marker
refractories feuerfeste Materialien npl
refractory clay feuerfester Ton m, Schamotteton m
~ **ore** strengflüssiges (schwer aufschließbares) Erz n *(muß vor der Aufbereitung geröstet werden)*
refrangibility Brechungsvermögen n, Brechungskraft f
refreezing Wiedergefrieren n
refrigerate/to [ab]kühlen, zum Gefrieren bringen
refringence, refringency Brechungsvermögen n, Brechungskraft f; Lichtbrechung f
refringent licht[strahlen]brechend
Refugian [Stage] Refugien n *(marine Stufe, oberes Eozän in Nordamerika)*
refuse Berge pl
~ **dump** Bergehalde f
~ **extractor** Bergeaustrag m
~ **heap** Bergehalde f
~ **rocks** Berge pl, taubes Gestein n
~ **tip** Bergehalde f
refusion Anatexis f
reg mit kleinen Geröllen gespickte Wüstenoberfläche f
regard Faltenvergenz f *(Tektonik)*
regelation Regelation f, Schmelzen n und Wiedergefrieren n, Wiederzusammenfrieren n
regenerated anhydrite durch Gipsdehydratation entstandener Anhydrit m
~ **mud** wiederaufbereitete Spülung f
regeneration Regeneration f
~ **of well** Brunnenregenerierung f
regime equation Wasserhaushaltsgleichung f
regimen 1. Wasserhaushalt m *(eines Flusses)*; 2. Materialbilanz f
~ **of a glacier** Gletscherhaushalt m
region Region f, Gebiet n, Bereich m, Zone f; Region f *(Paläobiogeografie)*
~ **of denudation** Abtragungsgebiet n
~ **of disturbance** Erschütterungsgebiet n, Schüttergebiet n
~ **of melting** Abschmelzgebiet n

~ **of saturation** Sättigungsgebiet n
~ **of seismic disturbance** s. ~ of disturbance
regional regional
~ **earthquake** Flächenbeben n
~ **evaporation** Gebietsverdunstung f
~-**geological conditions** regionalgeologische Verhältnisse npl
~ **geology** Regionalgeologie f
~ **gravity map** Karte f der regionalen Schwere
~ **mapping** regionale Kartierung f
~ **metamorphic rocks** regionalmetamorphe Gesteine npl
~ **metamorphism** Regionalmetamorphose f
~ **planning** Landesplanung f
~ **precipitation (rainfall)** Gebietsniederschlag m
~ **tectonics** regionale Tektonik f
~ **trend** regionaler Trend m
~ **unconformity** Regionaldiskordanz f
regionalized variable regionalisierte Variable f *(von Matheron geprägter Begriff für eine ortsabhängige, auf einem Raumelement definierte Zufallsvariable)*
registering Registrierung f
~ **apparatus** Registriergerät n
~ **arrangement** Registriervorrichtung f
registration Registrierung f
~ **accuracy** Paßgenauigkeit f *(von Fernerkundungsaufnahmen)*
~ **paper** Registrierpapier n
~ **sheet** Registrierstreifen m
regolith Regolith m, Lockerboden m, Verwitterungsboden m, Schuttdecke f, Verwitterungsmantel m
regosol Sandboden m
regradation Bildung eines neuen Gleichgewichtsniveaus zwischen Abtragung und Sedimentation nach einer Deformation
regression Regression f
~ **line** Regressionslinie f *(Wasser)*
~ **of the sea** Meeresregression f
regressive regressiv
~ **overlap** s. off-lap
~ **ripples** regressive Rippeln fpl
~ **sand wave** regressive Sandwelle f
regrind/to nachschleifen
regrind Nachschliff m
regroup/to umgliedern, umlagern
regrouping Umgliedern n, Umlagerung f
regular regulär
~ **progressive overlap** allmähliches Übergreifen n [mariner Schichten]
~ **subsidence** gleichmäßige Absenkung f
~ **system** reguläres (kubisches) System n
regulated flow regulierte Strömung f, Abfluß m nach der Regulierung
regulation of a river Flußregulierung f
~ **of torrents** Wildbachverbauung f
rehabilitation water ausgetriebenes (ausgepreßtes) Wasser n
reid ridges parallele Bänder npl *(im Eis)*
reinerite Reinerit m, $Zn_3[AsO_3]_2$

reinite Reinit m *(Ferberit pseudomorph nach Scheelit)*
reinjection Reinjektion f, Wiedereinpressen n
reinvasion of the sea Wiederhereinbrechen n der See, Wiedereinbruch m des Meeres
reinvigorate/to sich verjüngen *(Fluß)*
reinvigoration Verjüngung f *(eines Flusses)*
rejection stone Rohdiamant m mit zahlreichen Einschlüssen
rejects Überlauf m; Berge pl
rejuvenate/to sich verjüngen *(Fluß)*
~ **a producer** eine Fördersonde wieder beleben
rejuvenated neubelebt; verjüngt
~ **river** verjüngter Fluß m
~ **water** verjüngtes (ausgetriebenes) Wasser n
rejuvenation Rejuvenation f; Verjüngung f; Neuaktivierung f; Wiederaufleben n
~ **of crystals** Rekristallisation f
rejuvenescence Verjüngung f *(eines Flusses)*
related rocks verwandte Gesteine npl
relative altitude relative Höhenlage f
~ **chronology** relative Zeitbestimmung f
~ **evaporation** Verhältnis n des gemessenen Evaporationsbetrages zur potentiell möglichen Evaporation
~ **mobility** relative Beweglichkeit f
~ **permeability** relative Permeabilität (Durchlässigkeit) f
~ **retardation** Wegdifferenz f, Gangunterschied m *(von Strahlen)*
~ **retardation of optical path** optischer Gangunterschied m
~ **rock bleeding** spezifische Wasserabgabefähigkeit f
~ **sunspot number** relative Sonnenfleckenzahl f
relaxation Relaxation f, Entlastung f, Erschlaffung f, Entspannung f
~ **joint** Entspannungskluft f
~ **method** Entlastungsmethode f
~ **of internal stresses** Auslösung f innerer Spannungen
~ **time** Relaxationszeit f
relaxed entlastet, erschlafft, entspannt
release pressure/to Druck ablassen
~ **stresses** Spannungen auslösen
release Freisetzung f, Auslösung f, Entlastung f, Entweichen n, Freiwerden n
~ **joint** Entlastungskluft f
~ **of internal stresses** Auslösung f innerer Spannungen
~ **of pressure** Druckentlastung f
released gas freigewordenes Gas n
releasing overshot lösbare Fangglocke f *(Tiefbohrung)*
~ **spear** lösbarer Fangdorn m *(Tiefbohrung)*
reliable sample zuverlässige Probe f
relic Überrest m, Relikt n
~**-bearing** fossilführend
~ **lake** Restsee m
~ **structure** Reliktgefüge n

relict Relikt n *(meist biologisch)*
~ **fauna** Reliktfauna f
~ **flora** Reliktflora f
~ **mountain** s. monadnock
reliction Regression f
relief 1. Relief n; 2. Entlastung f
~ **displacement** radialer Versatz m von Bildpunkten
~ **features** Höhengestaltung f
~ **from pressure** Druckentlastung f
~ **intensity** Reliefenergie f
~ **inversion** Reliefinversion f, Reliefumkehr f
~ **map** Reliefkarte f
~ **mould** erhabener Abguß m
~ **of load** Entlastung f
~ **of stress** Spannungsauslösung f
~ **ratio** Reliefenergie f
~ **unconformity** Reliefdiskordanz f
~ **well** Entlastungsbrunnen m
relieve/to entspannen
reliquiae organische Überbleibsel npl
Relizian [Stage] Relizien n *(marine Stufe, unteres Miozän in Nordamerika)*
remainder Rest m
remaining gases Gasreste mpl
remains of organism Organismenreste mpl
remanence s. remanent magnetization
remanent magnetization bleibende Magnetisierung f
remanié umgelagertes Fossil n
~ **glacier** s. recemented glacier
remedial water Heilwasser n
remelt/to umschmelzen, wiederaufschmelzen
remelting Umschmelzung f, Wiederaufschmelzung f
remineralization Ummineralisation f, Ummineralisierung f
remission Remission f, Rückstrahlung f *(meist nur eines Teils der zuvor empfangenen Strahlung)*
remnant Rest m, Überbleibsel n
~ **of denudation** Denudationsrelikt n
remote and inaccessible area abgelegenes und unzugängliches Gebiet n
~ **from the coast** küstenfern
~ **measurement device** Fernmeßgerät n
~ **reference method** zwei-Stationen-Vergleichsmethode f
~ **sensing** Fernerkundung f, Fernbeobachtung f
~ **sensor** Fernerkundungsaufnahmegerät n
removal Entfernung f, Beseitigung f, Abtransport m; Abtragung f
~ **of debris (overburden)** Abraumbeseitigung f
removable well damage auflösbare Bohrlochverstopfung f
remove/to entfernen, beseitigen, abtransportieren, abtragen
~ **a core from the barrel** einen Kern aus dem Kernrohr herausnehmen
renardite Renardit m, $Pb[(UO_2)_4|(PO_4)_2] \cdot 8H_2O$
rendzina Rendzina f, Kalkschwarzerde f

renewed

renewed fault wiederaufgelebte Verwerfung f, wiederbelebte Störung f
~ faulting wiederholte Bruchbildung f
reniérite Reniérit m, $Cu_3(Fe, Ge)S_4$
reniform nierenförmig, nierig
rent Bruch m, Kluft f, Spalte f, Riß m
reomorphism Reomorphismus m
reopened vein wiedereröffneter Gang m
reorientation Umorientierung f
repeated reflections multiple Reflexionen fpl (Seismik)
~ twinning Wiederholungsverzwillingung f
~ twins Viellinge mpl
repel/to abstoßen
repetition of beds Schichtenverdopplung f, Schichtenwiederholung f (an einer Verwerfung)
repetitive bedding Repetitionsschichtung f
~ coverage Wiederholungsüberdeckung f (des gleichen Gebietes durch Fernerkundungsaufnahmen)
~ fault Repetitionsverwerfung f
~ stress Schwellast f
Repettian [Stage] Repettien n (Stufe des Pliozäns)
replace/to ersetzen, auswechseln, verdrängen, substituieren (Metasomatose)
replacement Ersatz m, Auswechslung f, Verdrängung f, Metasomatose f, Substitution f
~ body Verdrängungskörper m (Metasomatose)
~ deposit Verdrängungslagerstätte f, metasomatische Lagerstätte f
~ ore deposit Verdrängungserzlagerstätte f
~ reaction Austauschreaktion f
~ remnants Verdrängungsreste mpl
~ vein Verdrängungsgang m
~ zoning Verdrängungszonung f
replacing of the fauna Erneuerung f der Fauna
replenish/to anreichern (Grundwasser)
replenishment Anreicherung f (von Grundwasser)
replica Oberflächenabdruck m
repose imprint Liegemarke f (eines Tieres)
~ period Ruheperiode f (eines Vulkans)
reprecipitation Wiederausfällung f
representative fraction Kartenmaßstab m (Distanzverhältnis zweier Punkte auf der Karte und im Gelände)
~ sample repräsentative Probe f
~ species vikariierende Art f
repressure line Rückführungsleitung f, Einpreßleitung f (Erdöl- oder Erdgasgewinnung)
repressuring Gastriebverfahren n, Gaseinpressung f (zur Erhaltung des Lagerstättendrucks)
reproducible sample reproduzierbare Probe f
reproductive organs Reproduktionsorgane npl, Fortpflanzungsorgane npl
~ sac s. gonophore
reptile Reptil n

requirement for deposits Lagerstättenkondition f
resaca ein schmales Meandertal ausfüllender See
resample Veränderung f in der Werteauswahl (Seismik)
resampling neue Probenahme f
resedimented rock 1. Gestein n aus resedimentiertem Material; 2. Turbidit m
resequent fault-line scarp Verwerfungsstufe, bei der der gehobene Flügel auch topografisch höher liegt
~ valley resequentes Tal n
reserve calculation Vorratsberechnung f
~ estimate Reserveschätzung f
~ zone Schongebiet n, Schutzgebiet n (Grundwasser)
reserves Vorräte mpl (einer Lagerstätte)
reservoir 1. Stausee m; 2. Erdölspeicher m; Erdgasspeicher m
~ bed Speicher m, Träger m (im Sinne von Öl-träger, Wasserträger)
~ capacity Speicherkapazität f, Speichervolumen n
~ conditions Lagerungsbedingungen fpl (des Speichers)
~ energy Lagerstättenenergie f
~ engineering Reservoirmechanik f
~ fluid Speicherflüssigkeit f
~ grid Reservoirgitternetz n
~ heterogeneities Reservoirheterogenitäten fpl
~ hold-out Speicherverbreitung f
~ limit test Reservoirabgrenzungstest m
~ mechanics Reservoirmechanik f
~ model Speichermodell m
~ parameter identification Speichereigenschaftserkennung f
~ performance Abbauverlauf m (für Erdöl und Erdgas)
~ pressure Lagerstättendruck m, Speicherdruck m
~ rock Speichergestein n, Trägergestein n
~ seal Speicherabdeckung f
~ sedimentation Lagerstättenbildung f (Grundwasserleiter)
~ simulator Speichermodell n
~ storage Speichervolumen n; Lagerstättenvorrat m (bei Grundwasser)
~ stratum Speicherschicht f
~ trap tektonische Falle f (in einem Speicher)
~ voidage effektives Porenvolumen n (des Speichers)
residence time Verweilzeit f (radioaktiver Produkte)
residential area Wohngebiet n
residual übrigbleibend, remanent, eluvial, Rest...
residual Rest m, Restfeld n, Residuum n; Restzeit f; Residual n
~ anticlines antiklinale Lagerung f zwischen den Randsenken zweier Salzstöcke

~ **bond** Van-der-Waalssche Bindung *f*
~ **boulder** autochthoner Verwitterungsrestblock *m*
~ **butte** Restberg *m*
~ **clay** Verwitterungston *m*, Rückstandston *m*
~ **clay soil** toniger Rückstandsboden *m*
~ **deformation** bleibende Verformung *f*
~ **deposit** Residuallagerstätte *f*
~ **detritus** Verwitterungsschutt *m*
~ **disturbance** Reststörung *f*, Restfeld *n*
~ **domes** *s*. ~ anticlines
~ **earth** *s*. ~ soil
~ **enrichment** Residualanreicherung *f*
~ **erosion surface** Restabtragungsfläche *f*
~ **glacier** Restgletscher *m*
~ **gravity** Restschwere *f (nach Abzug der Korrekturen in der Gravimetrie)*
~ **hill** Restberg *m*, Resthügel *m*
~ **hoop stress** tangentiale Restspannung *f*
~ **lake** Restsee *m*
~ **liquor** magmatische Restlösung *f*
~ **loam** Verwitterungslehm *m*
~ **magma** Restmagma *n*
~ **magnetism** Restmagnetismus *m*
~ **magnetization** remanente Magnetisierung *f*, Restmagnetisierung *f*
~ **melt** Restschmelze *f*
~ **mountain** Restberg *m*
~ **oil** nicht gewinnbares Restöl *n (einer Lagerstätte)*
~ **ore deposit** Residualerzlagerstätte *f*, Trümmererzlagerstätte *f*
~ **orientation** Restregelung *f (Tektonitgefüge)*
~ **phosphatic deposit** Phosphatverwitterungslagerstätte *f*
~ **pore pressure** zurückbleibender Porenwasserdruck *m*
~ **pore water** Porenrestwasser *n*
~ **product** Verwitterungsprodukt *n*
~ **radiation** Reststrahlung *f*
~ **saturation** Restsättigung *f (an Erdöl)*
~ **sediment** Restsediment *n*
~ **shear strength** Restscherfestigkeit *f*
~ **soil** Verwitterungsboden *m*, Eluvialboden *m*, Rückstandsboden *m*, Ortsboden *m*
~ **solution** Restlösung *f*
~ **stress** Restspannung *f*, latente Spannung *f*
~ **water** 1. Restwasser *n*, Haftwasser *n*; 2. Abwasser *n*
~ **water content** Restwasseranteil *m*
residualize/to das Restfeld bestimmen
residuary eluvial
residue Rückstand *m*, Überrest *m*
~ **of weathered rocks** Verwitterungsrückstand *m*
~ **on evaporation** Abdampfrückstand *m*
residuum 1. Residuat *n*; 2. Rückstand *m*, Residuum *n (Erdöl)*; 3. *s*. residue
resilication Resilifizierung *f*
resin Harz *n*
~-bedded roof bold Klebeanker *m*
~ **[canal] casts**, ~ **fibrils** *s*. ~ rodlets 1.

~ **jack** Honigblende *f (gelbe Varietät von Zinkblende)*
~ **needles** *s*. ~ rodlets 1.
~ **rodlets** 1. Harzkörper *mpl*; 2. Resinit *m*
~ **rods** *s*. ~ rodlets 1.
~ **tiff** hell gefärbte Zinkblende *f (s.a.* sphalerite)
resinaceous *s*. resinous
resinification Harzbildung *f*
resinite Resinit *m (Kohlenmaceral)*
resinlike harzartig
resinous harzig
~ **bands** lagenförmige Harzanreicherungen *fpl* im Kohlenflöz
~ **bodies (components, constituents)** *s*. ~ rodlets 1.
~ **mineral** harzartiges Mineral *n*
~ **tar** Harzteer *m*
resist/to widerstehen, aushalten; aufnehmen *(Kraft)*; abfangen *(Druck)*
resistance modulus Steifeziffer *f (des Bodens)*
~ **network** Widerstandsnetzwerk *n*
~ **quotient of rock block system** Widerstandsziffern *fpl* des Kluftkörperverbandes
~ **to creep** Kriechfestigkeit *f*
~ **to crushing** Druckfestigkeit *f (von Gesteinen)*
~ **to flow** Fließwiderstand *m*
~ **to fluid flow** Strömungswiderstand *m (als Vorgang)*
~ **to impact** Schlagfestigkeit *f*, Stoßwiderstand *m*
~ **to polish** Schleifhärte *f*
~ **to scratching** Ritzhärte *f*
~ **to wear** Verschleißfestigkeit *f*
~ **to yield** Einsinkwiderstand *m*, Einschubwiderstand *m*
resistant widerstandsfähig
~ **masses** starre Massive *npl*
~ **to bending** biegesteif
~ **to weathering** verwitterungsfest
resistivimeter Widerstandsmeßgerät *n*
resistivity elektrischer Eigenwiderstand *m (z.B. eines Horizonts)*; spezifischer [elektrischer] Widerstand *m*
~ **curve** Widerstandskurve *f*
~ **departure curves** Kurven *fpl* bei der elektrischen Bohrlochmessung
~ **gradient** Widerstandsgradient *m*
~ **log** Widerstandslog *n*
~ **method** Widerstandsverfahren *n*
~ **micrologging** Mikrolog *n (Widerstandsverfahren)*
~ **of wetting** Benetzungswiderstand *m*
~ **prospecting** Prospektieren *n* durch Widerstandsmessungen
~ **survey** Widerstandsmessung *f*
resolidification Wiederverfestigung *f*
resolidify/to wiederverfestigen
resolution Auflösung *f*
resolving power Auflösungsvermögen *n (eines Mikroskops)*

resorption

resorption Auflösung f, Resorption f
~ **rim** Umwandlungssaum m *(bei Mineralen im Schliff)*
resources Ressourcen fpl, Vorräte mpl *(eines Lagerstättenbezirks)*
~ **survey** Ressourcenerkundung f
resplendent mit Brillantglanz scheinend; sehr hell
responds Halbboudinkörper mpl
responsitivity Reaktionsvermögen n *(z.B. eines Sensors)*
rest magma Restmagma n, magmatische Restlösung f
~ **move-out** Restmoveout n *(nach Abzug des normalen Moveout)*
~ **of the melt** Restschmelze f
resting trace Ruhespur f *(Ichnologie)*
restite Restit m, Rückstandsgestein n
restitution from air photographs Luftbildauswertung f
restocking Aufforstung f
restore/to restaurieren
restricted basin durch Flachwasserzonen begrenztes marines Becken n
~ **movement** Gesteinsverformung f mit Minerallängung in b
restriction of production Produktionseinschränkung f
resue/to freilegen *(einen Gang vom Nebengestein)*
resurgence Wiederaustritt m *(eines versiegten Flusses)*
resurgent resurgent
~ **gases** durch Assimilation freigesetzte Gase npl
~ **vapours** durch magmatische Wärme verdampftes Grundwasser n
~ **water** durch magmatische Wärme aus hydratisierten Gesteinen ausgetriebenes Wasser n
resurrected regeneriert
~ **stream** [periodisch] wiederkehrender Fluß m
retained water Haftwasser n
retainer 1. undurchlässiges Gestein n; 2. Zementierpacker m
retaining basin Rückhaltebecken n, Hochwasserrückhaltebecken n
~ **dam** Staudamm m, Stauwehr n
~ **sluice** Stauschleuse f
~ **wall** Staumauer f, Böschungsmauer f
~ **weir** Stauwehr n, Staudamm m
retardancy of grassed waterways Rückhaltevermögen n der Grasnarbe
retardation Verzögerung f
~ **basin** Rückhaltebecken n, Hochwasserrückhaltebecken n
~ **of earth' rotation** Verzögerung f der Erdrotation
~ **time** Retardationszeit f
retarded flow verzögerte Strömung f
retarder Abbindeverzögerer m *(Bohrlochzementierung)*
retention Retention f, Rückhaltevermögen n

~ **basin** Rückhaltebecken n, Hochwasserrückhaltebecken n
~ **force** Haftvermögen n, Wasserhaltevermögen n
~ **period** Verweildauer f
~ **storage** Rückhaltevolumen n
~ **water** Haftwasser n
retentive power Wasserhaltevermögen n, wasserbindende Kraft f *(eines Bodens)*
retgersite Retgersit m, α-Ni[SO$_4$]·6H$_2$O
reticular netzförmig, netzartig, Netz...
~ **density** Netzdichte f, Packungsdichte f
~ **structure** Gitterstruktur f
reticulate netzförmig, retikuliert
~ **fibrous structure** verworrenfasriges Gefüge n
reticulated netzförmig, retikuliert
~ **smaltite** gestrickter Speiskobalt m, CoAs$_3$
~ **structure** Maschentextur f, Netztextur f
~ **vein** Gang m aus netzförmigen Trümern
reticulation gitterartige Skulptur f *(bei Fossilien)*
reticulite basaltischer Bimsstein m
retinasphalt[um] Retinasphalt n *(fossiles Harz)*
retinic uranium Pechuran n *(s.a. uraninite)*
retinite Retinit m *(Sammelname für bernsteinartige Harze)*
retort brown coal Schwelbraunkohle f
~ **graphite** Retortengraphit m
retreat/to zurückweichen, zurücktreten *(Gletscher)*
retreat Zurückverlegung f, Zurückweichen n, Rückgang m, Rückzug m *(eines Gletschers)*
~ **of the coast** Zurückweichen n der Küste
~ **of the ice** Eisrückzug m
~ **of the sea** Meeresrückgang m
retreatal moraine Rückzugsmoräne f *(der letzten Vereisung)*; Moräne f einer Eisstillstandslage
retrievable ausbaubar *(z.B. Gestänge)*
~ **core barrel** ausbaubares Kernrohr n, Seilkernrohr n
retrieve/to wiedergewinnen *(Ausbau, Verrohrungen)*
retrograde boiling retrogrades Sieden n
~ **condensation** retrograde Kondensation f
~ **metamorphism** s. retrogressive metamorphism
retrogressive rückgreifend, rückschreitend
~ **erosion** rückschreitende Erosion f
~ **metamorphism** regressive (retrograde, rückläufige) Metamorphose f, Retrometamorphose f, Diaphthorese f
return air Abwetter pl
~~**beam vidicon** modifizierte Vidicon-Fernsehkamera für Fernsehaufnahmen höchster Auflösung; wird in der Satellitenfernerkundung eingesetzt
~ **flow** Rückfluß m *(von überschüssigem Beregnungswasser in den Vorfluter)*
returned fold Tauchfalte f
returns Bohrgut n, Bohrschmant m, Bohrmehl n

~ of a mine Ausbeute f
retzian Retzian m (Y-, Mn-, Ca-Arsenat)
reuplift Wiederanstieg m (des Grundwasserspiegels)
revaporization Rückverdampfung f (Kondensat)
reveal/to freilegen, bloßlegen, aufdecken, abdecken
revelation Freilegung f, Bloßlegung f, Aufdeckung f, Abdeckung f
reverberation multiple Reflexion f einer seismischen Welle zwischen zwei Schichten
reversal dip entgegengesetztes Einfallen n
~ fault s. reverse fault
~ of dip Wechsel m im Einfallen
~ of polarity Umkehrung f der Polarität
~ of slope Gegenhang m
~ of the earth's magnetic field Umkehrung f des Erdmagnetfeldes
reverse umgekehrt, gegensinnig, widersinnig, invers
~ branch rückläufiger Ast m (einer Laufzeitkurve)
~ by-passing Sedimentationsumkehr f (wenn Grobkorn weiter als Feinkorn transportiert wird)
~ circulation Linksspülen n, Gegenspülen n (des Bohrlochs)
~ circulation drilling Bohren n mit Umkehrspülung
~ control Gegenschießen n (Seismik)
~ drag umgekehrte Schleppung f
~ fault gegensinnige (antithetische) Verwerfung f, widersinnig einfallende Störung f
~ flowage fold Falte f mit verdicktem Scheitel und ausgedünnter Mulde
~ magnetization reverse Magnetisierung f
~ position umgekehrte (inverse) Lagerung f
~ rotary drilling Bohren n mit Umkehrspülung
~ similar fold Falte f mit verdickten Flanken und ausgedünntem Scheitel
~ travel time curve rückläufige Laufzeitkurve f
~ wind Gegenwind m
reversed überkippt
~ circulation [of the mud] umgekehrter Spülungsumlauf m, indirekte Spülung f, Verkehrtspülung f
~ dip entgegengesetztes Einfallen n
~ fault widersinnige (antithetische) Verwerfung f
~ fold fault Faltenverwerfung f, Faltenwechsel m, Überschiebungsfalte f
~ gradient rückläufiges Gefälle n
~ limb liegender (verkehrter) Schenkel m (einer Falte)
~ magnetization umgekehrte Magnetisierung f
~ order inverse Lagerung f
~ refraction method Gegenschußverfahren n
~ rocks umgekehrt magnetisierte Gesteine npl
~ stratigraphical sequence umgekehrte Schichtenfolge f
reversible magnetization umkehrbare Magnetisierung f

revetment Futtermauer f, Uferschutzschicht f
~ of the banks Uferschutz m
review Überarbeitung f (Neuinterpretation von Messungen)
revival Verjüngung f (eines Flusses)
revive/to [sich] verjüngen (Fluß)
revived wiederbelebt
~ fault wiederaufgelebte Verwerfung f, wiederbelebte Störung f
~ faulting wiederbelebter Bruch m
~ river verjüngter Fluß m
revolution 1. Zeitabschnitt m mit kräftiger Krustendeformation; 2. jährliche Umdrehung f (Erde)
~ counter Drehzahlmesser m, Tachometer n
~ ellipsoid Rotationsellipsoid n
~ of earth Erdumlauf m
~ spheroid Rotationssphäroid n
revolving stage Drehtisch m, Objekttisch m (Mikroskopie)
rewdanscite Rewdanskit m (Varietät von Antigorit)
rework/to aufarbeiten; umgestalten
reworked fossils umgelagerte Fossilien npl (Fossilien auf sekundärer Lagerstätte)
~ loess Schwemmlöß m, umgelagerter Löß m
reworking Aufarbeitung f; Umgestaltung f
reyerite Reyerit m, $Ca_2[Si_4O_{10}] \cdot H_2O$
Reynolds number Reynoldssche Zahl f
rézbányite Rézbányit m, $3PbS \cdot Cu_2S \cdot 5Bi_2S_3$
rhabdite Rhabdit m, $(Ni, Fe)_3P$ (Meteoritenmineral)
rhabdophanite Rhabdophan m, $Ce[PO_4] \cdot \frac{1}{2}H_2O$
Rhaetian [Stage] Rät n (Stufe der Trias)
Rhaetic [Stage] s. Rhaetian
rhaeticite Rhätizit m (gelbliche Varietät von Disthen)
rhagite Rhagit m (s.a. atelestite)
rhegmagenesis Rhegmagenese f
rheid Gesteinskörper m mit Fließgefüge
rheidity Fließfähigkeit f des Krustenmaterials
Rhenish-Bohemian Subprovince Rheinisch-böhmische Subprovinz f (Paläobiogeografie, Unter- und Mitteldevon)
~ massif Rheinisches Massiv n
~ trass Traß m (fein gemahlener vulkanischer Tuffstein)
~ trend rheinische Streichrichtung f
Rheno-Hercynian zone Rhenoherzynische Zone f, Rhenoherzynikum n
rheological rheologisch
~ properties rheologische Eigenschaften fpl
rheology Rheologie f, Fließkunde f, Fließlehre f
rheomorphic folds rheomorphe Falten fpl (Fließ-Scherfalten in plastischen Gesteinen wie Salz und Migmatiten)
rheomorphism Rheomorphose f
Rhine Graben Rheintalgraben m
rhizocretion konkretionäre Bildung f um Wurzeln
rhodesite Rhodesit m, $KNaCa_2[H_2Si_8O_{20}] \cdot 5H_2O$

rhodite Rhodit m *(natürliche Au-, Rh-Legierung)*
rhodium Rhodium n, Rh
~ **gold** s. rhodite
rhodizite Rhodizit m, KNaLi$_4$Al$_4$[Be$_3$B$_{10}$O$_{27}$]
rhodochrosite Rhodochrosit m, Manganspat m, Himbeerspat m, MnCO$_3$
rhodolite Rhodolith m *(knollenförmige Kalkbildung durch Algen)*
rhodonite Rhodonit m, Kieselmanganerz n, CaMn$_4$[Si$_5$O$_{15}$]
rhomb Rhombus m
~-**porphyry** Rhombenporphyr m
~ **spar** s. dolomite
rhombic[al] rhombenförmig, rhombisch
~ **dodecahedron** Rhombendodekaeder n
~ **mica** s. phlogopite
rhomboclase Rhomboklas m, FeH[SO$_4$]$_2$·4H$_2$O
rhombododecahedron Rhombendodekaeder n
rhombohedral rhomboedrisch
~ **cleavage** rhomboedrische Spaltbarkeit f
~ **iron ore** s. 1. haematite; 2. siderite
~ **system** rhomboedrisches (trigonales) System n
rhombohedron Rhomboeder n
rhomboid Rhomboid n
~ **ripple marks** rhombenförmige Rippelmarken fpl
rhomboidal rhomboidisch, rautenförmig
Rhuddanian [Stage] Rhuddenium n *(basale Stufe des Llandovery)*
rhumbs Rautenböden mpl
rhums bituminöser Schiefer m *(Schottland)*
rhyacolite s. sanidine
rhyodacite Rhyodazit m
rhyolite Rhyolith m *(Ergußäquivalent aplitgranitischer Magmen)*
rhyotaxitic rhyotaxitisch *(für Fließtextur)*
rhythmic rhythmisch
~ **layering** rhythmische [magmatische] Schichtung f
~ **sedimentation** rhythmische Ablagerung f
rhythmite Rhythmit m *(Sedimenttyp)*
rhythmites feine Wechselschichtung f
ria coast (shore line) Ria[s]küste f
rib 1. Erzader f; 2. Rippe f *(aus härterem Gestein)*
~-**and-furrow** Schrägschichtungsbögen mpl *(bei Sedimentgefügen)*
riband jasper s. ribbon jasper
ribbed 1. gerippt; 2. mit Schiefer durchsetzt
~ **coal seam** Kohlenflöz n mit Schieferzwischenlage
ribbon agate Bandachat m
~ **clay** Bänderton m
~ **gneiss** gebänderter Gneis m
~ **injection** Lageninjektion f *(in s-Flächen)*
~ **jasper** Bandjaspis m *(s.a. chalcedony)*
~ **structure** Lagentextur f, Bändertextur f
ribboned gebändert
rich fündig, edel
~ **clay** fetter Ton m

~ **ore** hochhaltiges Erz n, Reicherz n, Edelerz n
richellite Richellit m, Ca$_3$Fe$_{10}$[(OH,F)$_3$|(PO$_4$)$_2$]$_4$·nH$_2$O
riches of species Artenreichtum m
richetite Richetit m *(Uranmineral)*
Richmondian [Stage] Richmond[ien] n *(Stufe des Cincinnatiens in Nordamerika)*
richmondite Richmondit m, Al[PO$_4$]·4H$_2$O
richterite Richterit m, Na$_2$Ca (Mg, Fe$^"$, Mn, Fe$^{'''}$, Al)$_5$[(OH, F)Si$_4$O$_{11}$]$_2$
rickardite Rickardit m, Cu$_3$Te$_2$
riddam durch Eisenhydroxidschlämme rot gefärbtes Wasser
ride over/to sich schieben über
rider kleines Begleitflöz n; eingeklemmte Scholle f
ridge 1. Hügelkette f, Bergkette f, Gebirgskette f, Höhenrücken m, Höhenzug m, Joch n, Sattel m, Rippe f, Kamm m; 2. Leiste f *(Paläontologie)*
~ **fold** langgestreckter Dom m
~ **line** Sattellinie f
~-**pool complex** Strangkomplex m *(Moor)*
~ **uplift** Sattelbiegung f, Aufsattelung f
ridged ice aufgefaltetes Eis n
~-**up bed** aufgerichtete Schicht f
ridgy kammartig
riebeckite Riebeckit m, Na$_2$Fe$_3^{"}$Fe$^{'''}_2$[(OH, F)|Si$_4$O$_{11}$]$_2$
Riecke's principle Rieckesches Prinzip n
riffle Stromschnelle f
~ **bank (splitter)** Riffelteiler m
rift 1. Rift n, große Horizontalverschiebung f, Spalte f; 2. beste Teilbarkeit n *(in Plutoniten)*; 3. Schnittlinie einer Störungsfläche mit der Oberfläche
~-**block mountain** Horstgebirge n
~ **mountains** Riftgebirge npl, mittelozeanische Gebirgszüge mpl *(beiderseits des Scheitelgrabens)*
~ **trough** Störungsgraben m
~ **valley** tektonischer (zentraler) Graben m, Grabensenke f, medianer Kammgraben m *(innerhalb der mittelozeanischen Schwellen)*
~-**valley lake** Grabensee m
~ **zone** Grabengebiet n, Bruchzone f
rifting Bruchspaltenbildung f
rig Bohranlage f
~ **crew** Bohrmannschaft f
~ **helper** Bohrarbeiter m
~-**hour** Maschinenstunde f
~-**month** Maschinenmonat m
~-**shift** Maschinenschicht f
~ **time** Einsatzzeit f des Bohrgeräts
~-**up and rig-down operations** Umbau m, Montage f und Demontage f
rigging-up crew Montagebrigade f
right-angled stream Querfluß m
~-**hand quartz** Rechtsquarz m
~-**hand tributary** rechter Nebenfluß m
~-**handed crystal** rechtsdrehender Kristall m

rigid starr; [biege]steif
~ **crust** starre Kruste f
~ **lava crust** erhärtete Lavakruste f
~ **masses** starre Massive npl
rigidity Righeit f, Starrheit f; Steifheit f
rill 1. Rinnsal n, Runse f, Rille f; Mondfurche f, Mondgraben m
~ **cast** gefurchter Strömungswulst m
~ **erosion** Rinnenerosion f, Rillenspülung f
~ **mark** Rippelmarke f, Kräuselmarke f, Strandrille f, Rieselmarke f, Wellenfurche f
~ **pattern** Rieselmuster n
~-**stones** Rillensteine mpl (Karrenform)
~-**wash[ing erosion]** Rinnenerosion f, Rillenspülung f
rillet Bächlein n
rim Rand m, Saum m
~ **cement** Hüllzement m (optisch gleichgerichteter Zuwachssaum um Kristalle in Sedimentgefügen)
~ **of the crater** Kraterrand m
~ **syncline** Randsenke f, Ringwanne f, Randmulde f (um Salzstöcke)
rima Kluft f, Riß m; Rima f (Rille auf Mars oder Mond)
rime Rauhreif m
rimmed kettle Moränendepression f mit erhöhten Rändern
rimrock 1. Nebengestein n (Salzdom); 2. goldhaltiges Geröll n
rimstone Kalksinter m an Sinterbeckenrändern
~ **bar** Sinterdamm m
~ **pool** Sinterbecken n
rine pan Eindampfpfanne f zur Salzgewinnung
ring dike Ringintrusion f, Ringgang m
~ **fault** kreisförmige Verwerfung f
~ **fracture** Kreisbruch m
~-**fracture intrusion** s. ~ **dike**
~ **mark** Ringmarke f
~ **ore** Kokardenerz n, Ringelerz n
~ **structure** Ringstruktur f
~ **support** Tragring m
~ **wall** Ringwall m
ringing Widerhall m, Echo n, Hall m (Seismik)
ringwoodite Ringwoodit m (Olivin mit Spinellstruktur)
ringy schwingend, schwingungsartig (Seismik)
rinkite Rinkit m, (Na, Ca, Ce)$_3$(Ti, Ce)[(F, OH, O)$_2$|Si$_2$O$_7$]
rinkolite 1. Rinkolit m (Ce-, Ca-, Sr-, Na-Titanosilikat); 2. s. mosandrite
rinneite Rinneit m, K$_3$Na[FeCl$_6$]
rip/to nachreißen
rip hartes Gestein n
~ **current** Brandungsrückströmung f, Rippströmung f
~ **tide** Gezeitenwirbel m
riparian am Ufer liegend, uferanliegend
~ **lands** Ufergelände n
ripper-scraper method Lösen n von Fels mittels schwerer Reißraupen und anschließendem Schurfladen

ripping Felsaufreißen n mittels Reißhakenkraft
ripple Kräuseln n des Wassers, Kräuselung f
~ **bedding** Rippelschichtung f
~ **cross lamination** Rippelschichtung f, Rippelflaserung f, Kleinrippel-Schrägschichtungs-Flaserung f
~ **drift** Rippelschichtung f
~ **mark** Rippelmarke f, Strandrippel f, Wellenfurche f
~-**marked** gerippelt, gefurcht (Sedimentgefüge)
~ **marking** Rippelmarkenbildung f
~ **scour** gerippelte Erosionsmulde f
~ **trough** Rippeltal n
rippled gerippelt
ripples 1. Rippeln fpl, Rippelungen fpl, Rippelmarken fpl; 2. Kräuselwellen fpl
ripplet kleine Welle f
rippling Rippelmarkenbildung f
ripply wellig, gekräuselt
riprap Steinschüttung f (als Erosionsschutz)
~ **foundation** Gründung f aus Steinschüttung
riprapped slope Steinböschung f
rise/to 1. sich heben; 2. aufgehen
~ **to the surface** ausstreichen, ausbeißen (besonders bei Erzen)
rise 1. Erhebung f, Hebung f, Steigen n; 2. Aufgang m (eines Gestirns)
~ **dike** Verwerfung f ins Hangende
~ **drift** Überhauen n, Aufhauen n
~ **heading** Aushauen n (in der Kohle)
~ **of pressure** Druckanstieg m
riser 1. Verwerfer m (Verwerfungskluft); 2. Leitrohrtour f für die Verbindung Bohrinsel/Meeresboden
rising borehole Hochbohrung f
~ **current** aufsteigende Strömung f
~-**head test** Pumpversuch m (Tagebauentwässerung)
~ **nappe** Springdecke f
~ **solution** aufsteigende Lösung f
~ **tide** steigendes Wasser n
~ **tide wave** Flutwelle f
~ **velocity** Steiggeschwindigkeit f
risörite Risörit m (Varietät von Fergusonit)
Riss [Drift] Riß n, Riß-Eiszeit f, Riß-Kaltzeit f (Pleistozän, Alpen)
~-**Mindel Interval** Riß-Mindel-Interglazial n (Pleistozän, Alpen)
rither Nebengestein n, taubes Gestein n
river Fluß m, Strom m (s.a. stream 1.)
~ **alimentation** Flußspeisung f
~ **arm** Flußarm m
~ **bank** Flußufer n
~-**bar placer** Flußseife f
~ **basin** Flußbecken n; Flußgebiet n, Stromgebiet n, Einzugsgebiet n, Entwässerungsgebiet n
~ **basin forecasting** Einzugsgebietsprognose f
~ **bed** Flußbett n, Strombett n
~ **bed elevation (gradation)** Flußbetterhöhung f

river 298

~ **bed morphology** Flußmorphologie f
~ **beheading** s. ~ capture
~ **bench** Flußterrasse f
~ **bend** Flußbiegung f, Flußknie n, Flußschleife f, Flußkrümmung f
~ **bluff** Steilufer n
~-**borne** flußverfrachtet
~-**borne sediment** Flußsediment n
~ **capture** Flußenthauptung f, Flußanzapfung f, Flußkappung f
~ **changing** Flußverlagerung f
~ **channel** Flußbett n, Strombett n, Fließrinne f
~ **corrasion** Flußkorrasion f
~ **course** Flußlauf m
~ **curve** Flußkrümmung f
~ **dam** Talsperre f
~ **deflection** Flußablenkung f
~ **delta** Flußdelta n
~ **deposit** Flußablagerung f
~ **discharge** Abflußmenge f eines Wasserlaufs
~-**dissolved load** im Flußwasser gelöste Stoffe mpl
~ **diversion** Flußverlegung f, Flußableitung f
~ **diversion by ponding** Flußverlegung f durch Abdämmung
~ **drifts** s. ~ load
~ **elbow** s. ~ bend
~ **erosion** Flußerosion f
~ **flat** Inundationsfläche f, Überflutungsebene f, Talaue f, Flußniederung f
~ **flood plain** Flußaue f
~ **floor** Flußsohle f
~ **fracturing** Wasserfrac-Verfahren n (Schichtaufbrechung)
~ **gauge** Wasserstandsanzeiger m, Pegel m
~ **gold** Seifengold f
~ **gorge** Flußdurchbruch m
~ **gradient** Flußgefälle n
~ **gravel** Flußkies m
~ **head** Flußquelle f, Quellfluß m
~ **ice** Flußeis n
~ **inundation** Flußüberschwemmung f
~ **inversion** Flußumkehr[ung] f
~ **island (islet)** Flußinsel f
~-**laid deposition** Flußablagerung f
~-**laid terrace** Flußterrasse f
~ **levee** Flußdeich m
~ **load** Flußgeschiebe n, Schuttlast f eines Flusses
~ **loop** Flußschlinge f
~-**marsh soil** Auenboden m
~ **meadow** Flußaue f
~ **meander** Flußmäander m, Flußschleife f
~ **mouth** Flußmündung f, Strommündung f
~ **of the plains** Flachlandstrom m
~ **pebble** Flußgeröll n
~ **piracy** s. ~-capture
~ **placer** Flußseife f
~ **plain** Talaue f
~ **pollution** Flußverschmutzung f, Flußverunreinigung f

~ **reach** Flußlauf m
~ **realignment** Flußregulierung f
~ **regimen** Wasserhaushalt m eines Flusses
~ **sand** Flußsand m
~ **shifting** Flußverlegung f
~ **source** Flußquelle f, Quellfluß m
~ **stage** Flußwasserstand m
~ **structural works** Flußbauten mpl
~ **swamp** Flußmorast m
~ **system** Flußsystem n
~ **terrace** Flußterrasse f
~ **training [works]** Flußregulierung f
~ **valley** Flußtal n, Flußniederung f
~ **wall** Flußdamm m
~ **wash** angespülter Flußschutt m
~ **weir** Flußwehr n
~ **widening** Flußausbauchung f
riveret s. rivulet
riverlet Bächlein n, Flüßchen n, Rinnsal n, Gerinne n
riverside Flußufer n
~ **soil** Auboden m
riving seams offene Schichtspalten fpl (im Steinbruch)
rivulet Bach m, Flüßchen n, Bächlein n
rms velocity s. root-mean-square velocity
road bed Straßenunterbau m
~ **stone** Straßen[bau]schotter m, Schotter m
roadway side Streckenstoß m
~ **support** Streckenausbau m
~ **system** Streckennetz n
~ **wall** Streckenstoß m
roar Getöse n, Brausen n (Vulkanismus)
roaring basin Tosbecken n (einer Talsperre)
~ **noise of a blow-out** ohrenbetäubendes Geräusch n eines Ausbruchs (z.B. von Erdöl)
rob/to Raubbau treiben
robble Verwerfung f
robinsonite Robinsonit m, $7PbS \cdot 6Sb_2S_3$
roche s. rotch
~ **mountonnée** Rundhöcker m
rock Gestein n; Felsen m
~ **abrasive property** Abrasivität f
~ **affected by working** verritztes Gebirge n
~ **alteration** Gesteinsumwandlung f
~ **anhydrite** massiger Anhydrit m
~ **arch** Felsentor n
~ **asphalt** Asphaltgestein n, Bergasphalt m, Naturasphalt m, Erdasphalt m
~ **avalanche** Felslawine f, Steinlawine f, Bergsturz m
~ **bar** Felsriegel m, Felsschwelle f
~ **basin** Schalenstein m, Felsschüssel f, Pfannenbildung f, Opferkessel m, Kesselstein m (Erosionsform)
~-**basin lake** Felsbeckensee m, Karsee m
~ **bed** Gesteinsschicht f, Felsuntergrund m
~ **behaviour** Gebirgsverhalten n
~ **bench** Denudationsterrasse f, Brandungsplatte f
~ **bind** Kohlensandstein m, sandiger Schiefer m
~ **bit** Rollenmeißel m

rock

- ~ **bit drilling** Rollenmeißelbohren *n*
- ~ **blanket** söhlige (horizontale) Felsschicht *f*
- ~ **blasting** Gesteinssprengung *f*, Felssprengung *f*
- ~ **bleeding** Wasserabgabefähigkeit *f* des Gesteins
- ~ **block system** Kluftkörperverband *m*
- ~ **bolting** Felsvernagelung *f*, Gebirgsverankerung *f*
- ~ **bonding** Kluftkörperverband *m*
- ~-**bound** von Felsen eingeschlossen
- ~ **breaking** Gesteinszerfall *m*, Zerklüftung *f*
- ~ **breaking by freezing** Gesteinszerfall *m* durch Frost, Frostverwitterung *f*
- ~ **brittleness** Gesteinssprödigkeit *f*
- ~ **burst** [schwerer] Gebirgsschlag *m*, Steinschlag *m*
- ~-**burst properties** Gebirgsschlagverhalten *n*
- ~ **cave** Felsenbetthöhle *f*
- ~ **chips** Bohrklein *n*
- ~ **component** Gesteinsbestandteil *m*, Gesteinskomponente *f*
- ~ **cone** Felskegel *m*
- ~ **constituent** *s.* ~ component
- ~ **core bit** Rollen[kern]krone *f*, Rollenkernbohrer *m*
- ~ **cork** *s.* 1. chrysotile; 2. antigorite
- ~ **creep[ing]** Felskriechen *m*, Gekriech *n*; Gleitfähigkeit *f*
- ~ **crusher** Steinbrecher *m*, Grobzerkleinerungsmaschine *f*
- ~ **crystal** Bergkristall *m*
- ~ **cutting in formation** Felsaushub *m* für das Planum
- ~ **cutting saw** Gesteinssäge *f*
- ~ **dating** radiometrische Gesteinsdatierung *f*
- ~ **debris** Gesteinstrümmer *pl*, Gesteinsschutt *m*, Felsschutt *m*
- ~ **decay** Gesteinsverwitterung *f*
- ~ **deformation** Gebirgsverformung *f*
- ~ **desert** Steinwüste *f*, Felswüste *f*
- ~ **destruction** Gesteinszerstörung *f*
- ~ **disintegration** Lockerung *f* des Gesteinszusammenhalts
- ~ **dredge** Gesteinsdredsche *f* (maritime Erkundung)
- ~ **drift** Gesteinsstrecke *f*
- ~ **drillability** Bohrbarkeit *f* des Gesteins
- ~ **drilling** Bohren *n* im Gestein, Gesteinsbohrung *f*
- ~ **dusting** Gesteinsstaubverfahren *n*
- ~ **elasticity** Gesteinselastizität *f*
- ~ **exposure** Gesteinsaufschluß *m*, Gesteinsausbiß *m*
- ~ **face** Felswand *f*
- ~ **failure** Gesteinsbruch *m*, Felsbruch *m*
- ~ **fall** Bergsturz *m*, Felssturz *m*, Steinschlag *m*, Steinfall *m*
- ~ **fan** Schutthalde *f*
- ~ **fault** Flözvertaubung *f*
- ~ **fill** Steinschüttung *f*
- ~-**fill dam** Steinfülldamm *m*
- ~ **fissure spring** Spaltenquelle *f*
- ~ **fissuring** Gesteinszerklüftung *f*
- ~ **floor** Felsboden *m*, Felssohle *f*
- ~ **flour** Gesteinsmehl *n*, feinster Staubsand *m*, Gletschermilch *f*
- ~ **fluidity** Gesteinsfließfähigkeit *f*
- ~ **folding** Gesteinsfaltung *f*
- ~-**forming** gesteinsbildend
- ~-**forming mineral** gesteinsbildendes Mineral *n*, gesteinsbildender Gemengteil *m*
- ~ **foundation** Gründungsfels *m*
- ~ **fragment** Gesteinsbruchstück *n*
- ~ **fragmentation** Zerkleinerung *f* des Gesteins
- ~ **framework** geologischer Rahmen *m*
- ~ **gas** *s.* natural gas
- ~ **glacier** Blockgletscher *m*, Steingletscher *m*, Schuttgletscher *m*
- ~ **gypsum** massiger Gips *m*
- ~ **hardness** Gesteinshärte *f*
- ~ **hardness category** Kategorie *f* der Gesteinshärte
- ~ **hardness reducer** Härteminderer *m*
- ~-**hound** (*sl*) Geologe *m*
- ~ **identification** Gesteinsbestimmung *f*
- ~ **in place (situ)** anstehendes Gestein *n*
- ~ **incrustation** Gesteinsüberzug *m*
- ~ **inrush** Steinfall *m*
- ~ **interstice** Felsspalt *m*
- ~ **investigation** Gesteinsuntersuchung *f*
- ~ **kernel** Steinkern *m*
- ~ **kindreds** Gesteinsverwandtschaft *f*, Gesteinssippschaft *f*
- ~ **ledge** Felsleiste *f*
- ~ **magma** Gesteinsmagma *n*
- ~ **magnetism** Gesteinsmagnetismus *m*
- ~-**making** *s.* ~-forming
- ~ **mass** Gebirgsmassiv *n*, Gesteinsmassiv *n*
- ~ **masses** Gebirge *n* (im Gegensatz zum Gestein)
- ~ **material** Gesteinsmaterial *n*
- ~ **meal** Steinmehl *n*, Bergmehl *n*
- ~ **mechanics** Gebirgsmechanik *f*, Felsmechanik *f*
- ~ **milk** Gletschermilch *f*, Bergmilch *f*
- ~ **mill** Strudeltopf *m*, Strudelloch *n*
- ~ **noise** Knistergeräusch *n* (im Gebirge)
- ~ **oil** *s.* petroleum
- ~ **ore** anstehendes Erz *n*
- ~ **outcrop** Gesteinsaufschluß *m*, Gesteinsausbiß *m*
- ~ **permeability** Gesteinsdurchlässigkeit *f*, Durchlässigkeit *f* des Gesteins
- ~ **phosphate** Phosphorit *m*, Rohphosphat *n*
- ~ **pile** Haufwerk *n* (Steinbruch)
- ~ **pillar** Felspfeiler *m*
- ~ **plant** Schotterwerk *n*
- ~ **plasticity** Gesteinsplastizität *f*
- ~ **porosity** Gesteinsporosität *f*
- ~ **precipice** Felsabsturz *m*
- ~ **pressure** Gebirgsdruck *m*, Gesteinsdruck *m*, petrostatischer Druck *m*
- ~ **properties** Gesteinseigenschaften *fpl*

rock

- ~ protection Felssicherung f
- ~ quarry Steinbruch m
- ~ reinforcement Felsbewehrung f
- ~ relative humidity relative Feuchtigkeit f [des Gesteins]
- ~ rotting Gesteinszerfall m
- ~ salt Steinsalz n
- ~ sample taker Gesteinsprobe[nent]nahmegerät n
- ~ saw Gesteinssäge f
- ~ scoring Gesteinszerschrammung f
- ~ sealing Felsinjektion f, Kluftinjektion f, Gesteinsauspressung f
- ~ sequence Gesteinsfolge f
- ~ series Gesteinsserie f
- ~ shattering Gesteinszertrümmerung f
- ~ shell Gesteinshülle f
- ~ shelter überhängendes Gebirge n, Halbhöhle f
- ~ sill Felsschwelle f, Felsriegel m
- ~ slide Bergschlipf m, Felsrutschung f, Felssturz m
- ~ slide area Felsrutschgebiet n
- ~ slope Felshang m, Felsböschung f
- ~ soap Bergseife f
- ~ spur Felsvorsprung m
- ~ stability Gesteinsstandfestigkeit f
- ~ stone Wackelstein m
- ~ stratification Gebirgsschichtung f; Gesteinsschichtung f
- ~-stratigraphic unit lithostratigrafische Einheit f
- ~ stratum Gesteinsschicht f
- ~ stream Bergsturzmasse f, Blockstrom m
- ~ strength Gebirgsfestigkeit f; Gesteinswiderstandsfähigkeit f
- ~ succession Gesteinsfolge f
- ~ swelling Quellfähigkeit f
- ~ tank Felskessel m
- ~ temperature Gesteinstemperatur f
- ~ terrace Denudationsterrasse f, Felsterrasse f
- ~ threshold Felsschwelle f, Felsriegel m
- ~ thrust Gebirgsschub m
- ~ tribe Gesteinssippe f
- ~ type Lithotyp m (Kohlentyp der Steinkohle)
- ~ unit s. lithostratigraphic unit
- ~ wall 1. Nebengestein n; 2. Felswand f
- ~ waste Gesteinsabfall m, Steinschutt m, Felstrümmer pl, Steintrümmer pl
- ~ weathering Gesteinsverwitterung f
- ~ weight pressure Überlagerungsdruck m
- ~ wool Gesteinswolle f, Steinwolle f
- ~ wreaths s. stone rings

rockbridgeite Rockbridgit m, $(Fe^{..}, Mn)Fe_4^{...}[(OH)_5|(PO_4)_3]$

rockgrit grober Sandstein m

rockhead s. bedrock

rocking stone Wackelstein m

Rocklandian [Stage] Rockland[ien] n, Rocklandium n (Stufe des Champlainings in Nordamerika)

Rockwell hardness Rockwellhärte f

rockwood braune Varietät von Asbest

rocky felsig, steinig

- ~ beach Felsstrand m
- ~ bottom Felsgrund m
- ~ cape Felskap n
- ~ coast Felsküste f
- ~ crust Gesteinskruste f
- ~ debris soil Felsschuttboden m
- ~ desert Felswüste f
- ~ desert plateau Felswüstenplateau n
- ~ island Felsinsel f
- ~ matter Gangart f
- ~ reef Felsenriff n
- ~ shore Felsufer n

rod Meßlatte f

rodding structure s. mullion structure

roddings boudinierte Quarzausscheidungen fpl

rodingite Rodingit m (Granat-Pyroxen-Gestein)

rodlets s. resin rodlets 1.

rodlike structure faserige Struktur f

roeblingite Roeblingit m, $PbCa_3H_6[SO_4|(SiO_4)_3]$

roemerite Römerit m, $Fe\cdot Fe_2^{...}[SO_4]_4 \cdot 14H_2O$

roentgenite Röntgenit m, $Ca_2Ce_3[F_3|(CO_3)_5]$

roestone Rogenstein m

rognon Felsspitze f (aus einem Gebirgsgletscher herausragend)

roke Erzgang m

roll 1. Faltung f (in einem Flöz); 2. Kippung f, Neigung f (z.B. eines Flugzeugs bzw. Fernerkundungsaufnahmesystems in Flugrichtung)

- ~ along Schießen n in bezug auf einen gemeinsamen Tiefenpunkt (Seismik)
- ~ along switch Spurwahlschalter m (beim seismischen CDP-Verfahren)
- ~ mark Rollmarke f
- ~-up ball Wickelfalte f

rollability s. pivotability

rolled pebbles Bachgeröll n

roller schwerer Brecher m, Sturzwelle f, Strudel m, Woge f

- ~ bit Rollenmeißel m

rolling wellig

- ~ country flachwelliges Hügelland n
- ~ mill Walzenmühle f
- ~-out limit Ausrollgrenze f (nach Atterberg)
- ~ strata Rippelschichten fpl
- ~ upland welliges Hochland n

romeite Roméit m, $(Ca, NaH)Sb_2O_6(O, OH, F)$

roof Firste f, Hangendes n, Dach n, Decke f

- ~-and-wall structure synsedimentäre Gleitstruktur f
- ~ arch Firstgewölbe n
- ~ bar Kappe f (Ausbau)
- ~ bolt Gebirgsanker m, Gesteinsanker m, Ankerbolzen m
- ~-bolt head Ankerkopf m
- ~-bolt plate Ankerplatte f
- ~-bolting Ankerausbau m
- ~ break Reißen n des Hangenden
- ~ control Beherrschung f des Hangenden
- ~ deflection Firstendurchbiegung f

~ **emission** Firstenausgasung *f*
~ **fall** Hereinbrechen *n* (Bruch *m*) des Hangendes, Firstbruch *m (Strebbau)*
~-**fall exploitation** Bruchabbau *m*
~ **foundering** Niederbrechen *n* des Hangenden *(in eine Magmenkammer)*
~ **limb** hangender Schenkel *m (einer Falte)*
~ **movements** Gebirgsbewegungen *fpl*
~ **of drift** Streckenfirste *f*
~ **ore** Firstenerz *n*
~ **pendant** große Dachgesteinsscholle *f (in einem Batholith)*
~ **pillar** Hangendschwebe *f*
~ **pressure** Firstendruck *m*
~ **ripping** Firstennachreißen *n*
~ **rock** Deckgebirge *n*
~ **settlement** Setzen *n* des Gebirges
~ **slate** Dachschiefer *m*
~ **strata** Dachschichten *fpl*
~ **subsidence** Absenkung *f* des Hangenden
~ **support** Firstenausbau *m*
~ **thickness** Mächtigkeit *f* des Hangenden
roofing slab Dachplatte *f*
~ **slate** Dachschiefer *m*
room and pillar caving Pfeilerbruchbau *m*
~ **and pillar method** Kammerpfeilerbau *m*
roomwork Kammerbau *m*
rooseveltite Rooseveltit *m*, α-Bi[AsO$_4$]
root Wurzel *f*
~ **cast** Wurzelstruktur *f*
~ **clay** *s.* underclay
~ **hair** Wurzelhaar *n*
~-**mean-square velocity** [quadratischer] Mittelwert *m* der Geschwindigkeit
~ **penetrability (penetration capability)** Durchdringungsvermögen *n* der Wurzel
~ **region** Wurzelregion *f (der Überschiebungsdecke)*
~ **scar** Narbe *f (Tektonik)*
~ **stock** Wurzelstock *m*
~ **zone** Wurzelzone *f*
rooting Durchwurzelung *f*
rootled bed Wurzelboden *m (unter dem Flöz)*
rootless wurzellos, allochthon
~ **nappe** wurzellose Decke *f*
ropelike tauförmig
~ **lava** *s.* ropy lava
ropiness tauartige Beschaffenheit *f (der Lava)*
ropy flow structure Taufließtextur *f*
~ **lava** Fladenlava *f*, Stricklava *f*, Gekröselava *f*
~ **structure** Flußgefüge *n*, Fluidalgefüge *n*
roquésite Roquésit *m*, CuInS$_2$
rosasite Rosasit *m*, (Zn, Cu)$_2$[(OH)$_2$|CO$_3$]
roscherite Roscherit *m*, (Ca, Mn, Fe)Be[OH|PO$_4$]·2/$_3$H$_2$O
roscoelite Roscoelith *m*, KV$_2$[(OH)$_2$|AlSi$_3$O$_{10}$]
rose diagram Richtungsrose *f*, Kluftrosendarstellung *f*
~ **quartz** Rosenquarz *m*
~ **spar** Rosenspat *m*, Managanspat *m (s.a. rhodochrosite)*
roselite Roselith *m*, α-Ca$_2$Co[AsO$_4$]$_2$·2H$_2$O

rosenbuschite Rosenbuschit *m*, (Ca, Na)$_6$Zr(Ti, Mn, Nb)[(F, O)$_2$|Si$_2$O$_7$]$_2$
rosette structure Kokardenstruktur *f*
rosickyite Rosickyit *m (γ-Schwefel)*
rosieresite Rosieresit *m (Pb-, Cu-haltiger Evansit)*
rosin jack Honigblende *f (gelbe Varietät von Zinkblende)*
Rosiwal analysis Integrationsanalyse *f (in der Petrografie)*
rossite Rossit *m*, Ca[V$_2$O$_6$]·4H$_2$O
rosy quartz Rosenquarz *m*
rot/to faulen
rotary blasthole drilling Rotarysprenglochverfahren *n*
~ **drilling** Rotarybohrverfahren *n*, Rotarybohren *n*, Drehbohren *n*
~ **drilling rig** Rotarybohrgerät *n*
~ **fault** Drehverwerfung *f*
~-**percussion drilling** Drehschlagbohren *n*
~ **reflection** Drehspiegelung *f*
~ **speed** Drehzahl *f (des gesteinszerstörenden Werkzeugs)*
~ **table** Drehtisch *m (bei Bohranlagen)*
rotate/to rotieren
rotating crystal method Drehkristallmethode *f*
~ **speed** Umlaufgeschwindigkeit *f (bei Bohrungen)*
~ **time** reine Bohrzeit *f*
rotation axis Drehachse *f*
~ **speed** Drehzahl *f (bei Bohrungen)*
~ **twin** Rotationszwilling *m*
rotational axis Rotationsachse *f*
~ **sieve** Drehsieb *n*, Trommelsieb *n*
~ **wave** *s.* shear wave 1.
rotatory fault Drehverwerfung *f*
~ **motion (movement)** Drehbewegung *f*
~ **polarization** Drehpolarisation *f*
~ **power** optisches Drehvermögen *n*
~ **reflection** Drehspiegelung *f*
rotch[e] weicher brüchiger Sandstein *m*
Rotliegendes Rotliegendes *n (Fazies, Oberkarbon bis Mittelperm)*
rotten zersetzt, verwittert, morsch, verfault
~ **lode** zersetzter Gang *m*
~ **rock** zersetztes Gestein *n*
rottenstone Tripel *m*, Tripelerde *f*
rotting Zersetzung *f*, Verwitterung *f*, Vermoderung *f*
~ **process** Verwitterungsprozeß *m*
rough rauh
~ **analysis** Rohanalyse *f*
~ **average** annähernder Durchschnitt *m*
~ **diamond** ungeschliffener Diamant *m*, Rohdiamant *m*
~ **drilling** Vorbohren *n*
~ **grinding** Vorschleifen *n*
~-**ground** roh abgeschliffen
~ **lignite** Rohbraunkohle *f*
~ **ore** Derberz *n*
~ **quarry block** Rohblock *m (Natursteinindustrie)*

rough 302

~ **sheets** feste Schichten *fpl*
roughneck *(sl)* Bohrarbeiter *m*
roughness factor for overland flow Reliefeinfluß *m* auf oberirdischen Abfluß
~ **of channel bed** Strombettrelief *n*
~ **of relief** Unebenheit *f* des Reliefs
~ **pattern** Rauhigkeitsfeld *n*, Rauhigkeitsverteilung *f*
roughs sandiger Aufbereitungsrückstand *m* (Cornwall)
roughway *(sl)* Spaltrichtung *f* ohne natürliche Teilbarkeit *(eines Massengesteins)*
round ore *s.* lean ore
~ **trip** Ein- und Ausbau *m*, Bohrmarsch *m (des Gestänges)*
rounded [ab]gerundet
~ **at the edges** kantengerundet
~ **boulders** gerundete Blöcke *mpl*
~ **clints** Rundkarren *pl*
~ **diamonds** gerundete Diamanten *mpl*
roundness Zurundung *f*, Rundung *f*
~ **index** Abrundungskoeffizient *m*
roundstone Rollkiesel *m*
roustabout *(sl)* Bohrarbeiter *m*
route selection Trassierung *f*, Trassenwahl *f*
routing through reservoirs Speicherwegsamkeit *f*
row of craters Kraterreihe *f*
roweite Roweit *m*, CaMn[B$_2$O$_5$]·H$_2$O
rowlandite Rowlandit *m*, (Y, Fe, Ce)$_3$[(F, OH)|(SiO$_4$)$_2$]
rows *s.* roughs
royalty Förderabgabe *f*, Förderzins *m*
rozenite Rozenit *m*, Fe[SO$_4$]·4H$_2$O
rubbish 1. Gangmasse *f*, Abraum *m*, Berge *pl*, Versatzberge *pl*, Haufwerk *n*, taubes Gestein *n*; 2. Industriediamanten *mpl* (Sammelbezeichnung)
~ **dump (heap)** Bergehalde *f*
~ **of an open cut** Abraum *m* eines Tagebaus
~ **pillar** Bergepfeiler *m*
rubble Schutt *m*, taubes Gestein *n*, Geröll *n*, Geschiebe *n*, Abraum *m*, grober Kies *m*, Bruchstein *m*, Schotter *m*, Haufwerk *n*, Trümmergestein *n*
~ **breccia** Geröllbrekzie *f*
~ **drift** Verwitterungsschutt *m*
~ **land** steiniger Boden *m*
~ **ore** Erzmulm *m*
~ **slope** Schutthalde *f*, Gehängeschutt *m*
~ **stone** Bruchstein *m*, Geröll *n*, Rollstein *m*, Geschiebe *n*
rubbles Bruchmassen *fpl*
rubbly soil steiniger Boden *m*
rubefaction Rotfärbung *f*
rubellite Rubellit *m (s.a.* tourmaline)
rubidium Rubidium *n*, Rb
~ **vapour magnetometer** Rubidiumdampfmagnetometer *n*
rubrite Rubrit *m*, MgFe[SO$_4$]$_4$·18H$_2$O
rubstone Wetzstein *m (Gesteinsart)*
ruby Rubin *m (s.a.* corundum)

~ **blende** Rubinblende *f (s.a.* sphalerite)
~ **copper [ore]** *s.* cuprite
~ **of arsenic** *s.* realgar
~ **silver [ore]** *s.* 1. proustite; 2. pyrargyrite
~ **sulphur** *s.* realgar
~ **zinc** 1. rote Zinkblende *f (s.a.* sphalerite); 2. *s.* zincite
ruck Pyritschmitze *f* im Dachschiefer
rud roter Ocker *m*
rudaceous psephitisch
~ **rock** psephitisches Gestein *n*
~ **texture** psephitische Struktur *f*
rudd *s.* rud
ruddle Rötel *m*, Ocker *m*
rudely bedded undeutlich geschichtet
rudimentary rudimentär, verkümmert
rudite *s.* psephite
rudstone korngestütztes Karbonatgestein mit mehr als 10% Komponenten >2 mm
rudyte *s.* psephite
ruffled groove cast gefiederte Rillenmarke *f*
~ **water surface** gekräuselte Wasserfläche *f*
ruffles durch Wasserwirbel erzeugte Rippelmarken *fpl*
rugged uneben, rauh
~ **limestone rocky land** Schrattenfeld *n*, Kalkstein-Karst-Morphologie *f*
ruggedness Rauheit *f*, Unebenheit *f*
ruin agate Trümmerachat *m*
rule of thumb Faustregel *f*
~-**of-thumb** nach Faustregeln durchgeführt
rumbling Rollen *n*, Rumpeln *n*, Rumoren *n (Vulkanismus)*
rumple Runzel *f*
rumpled gerunzelt
run a drift/to einen Stollen treiben
~ **casing** verrohren, auskleiden *(eine Bohrung)*
~ **dry** versiegen *(Brunnen)*
~ **from** streichen von
~ **in** niederbringen, einbauen *(eine Bohrung)*
~ **off** abrinnen, abfließen
run 1. Rinnsal *n*, Gerinne *n*; 2. Analysenreihe *f*, experimenteller Verlauf *m*; 3. *s.* round trip
~ **gravel** Alluvialschotter *m*
~ **of lode** Gangstreichen *n*, Gangrichtung *f*
~ **of mine** Rohfördergut *n*
~-**of-mine coal** Rohkohle *f*, Förderkohle *f*, ungesiebte (grubenfeuchte) Kohle *f*
~-**of-mine ore** Roherz *n*, Fördererz *n*, Gruben[förder]erz *n*
runite Schriftgranit *m*
runlet Bächlein *n*
runnel Flüßchen *n*, Rinnsal *n*
runnels and ridges Schwellen *fpl* und Rinnen *fpl (dem Strand vorgelagert)*
running country (ground, measures) schwimmendes Gebirge *n*
~ **of the drilling string** Einbau *m* des Bohrstrangs
~ **of the filter** Filtereinbau *m*
~ **of water** Wasserabfluß *m*
~ **sand** Schwimmsand *m*, Treibsand *m*, Triebsand *m*, Quicksand *m*

runoff Abfluß *m*, Abflußmenge *f*, Wasserführung *f*, Oberflächenabfluß *m*
~ **coefficient** Abflußfaktor *m*
~ **factor** Abflußbedingung *f*
~ **forecast** Wasser[abfluß]mengenprognose *f*
~ **from rainfall** Regenabflußmenge *f*
~ **hydrograph** Abflußganglinie *f*
~ **modulus** Abflußspende *f*
~ **phenomena** Abflußgeschehen *n (Summe aller Abflußerscheinungen)*
~ **process** Abflußvorgang *m*
~ **rill** Abflußrille *f*
runways Rinnen *fpl*
Rupelian [Stage] Rupel[ium] *n (Stufe des Oligozäns)*
rupes Rupes *f (geologische Furche auf dem Mond)*
rupicolous plants Felspflanzen *fpl*
rupture Ruptur *f*, Bruch *m*, Riß *m*
~ **by separation** Trennbruch *m*
~ **by shearing** Scherbruch *m*
~ **by sliding** Gleitungsbruch *m*
~ **cone** Bruchkegel *m*
~ **curve** Mohrsche Hüllkurve *f*
~ **deformation** Bruchdeformation *f*
~ **load** Bruchlast *f*
ruptured von Sprüngen durchzogen
~ **zone** Bruchzone *f*
rupturing Bruchbildung *f*
rusakovite Rusakovit *m*, $Fe^{3+}_5[(OH)_9|(V,P)O_4)_2]\cdot 3H_2O$
Ruscinian [Stage] Ruscinium *n (kontinentale Stufe des Pliozäns)*
rush in/to hineinströmen
~ **out** ausströmen
rush of water starker Wasserzufluß *m*, Wasserdurchbruch *m*
russelite Russelit *m*, $(Bi_2,W)O_3$
Russian platform Russische Plattform (Tafel) *f*
rust-coloured rostfarben
rustumite Rustumit *m*, $Ca_4[(OH)_2|Si_2O_7]$
rusty rostfleckig, rostig
~ **band** Roststreifen *m*
~ **-brown** rostbraun
~ **-weathering** rostbraun verwitternd
rute schmaler Erztrum *m*
ruthenium Ruthenium *n*, Ru
rutherfordine Rutherfordin *m*, $[UO_2|CO_3]$
rutilant rotstrahlend, rotglänzend
rutile Rutil *m*, TiO_2
ruware flacher Granitdom *m*
Ryazanian [Stage] Ryazan *n*, Ryazan-Stufe *f (basale Stufe der Unterkreide im borealen Reich)*

S

S-chert kieselige Leitgesteinsbank *f*
S-dolostone dolomitische Leitgesteinsbank *f*
S-joint S-Kluft *f*, Längskluft *f (Granittektonik)*
s-plane nicht verstellte s-Fläche *f*

S-shaped sigmoid
s-surface s-Fläche *f*, Einzelelement *n* des sedimentären Flächengefüges
S-tectonite S-Tektonit *m*
S wave Scherungswelle *f*, Transversalwelle *f*, S-Welle *f*
Saalian orogeny saalische Faltungsphase *f*
sabakha, sabkha[t] *s.* sebkha
sabugalite Sabugalit *m*, $(AlH)_{0,5}[UO_2|PO_4]_2 \cdot 10H_2O$
sabulous sandig, sandführend, sandhaltig
saccaroidal zuckerkörnig
~ **texture** zuckerkörnige Struktur *f*
sacklike structure Wollsackabsonderung *f (bei Granit)*
sacrificial table *s.* rock basin
sacrum Sacrum *n*, Kreuzbein *n*
saddle Sattel *m (geomorphologisch)*
~ **axis** Antiklinalachse *f*
~ **back** Sattelscheitel *m*
~ **bend** Sattelscharnier *n*, Antiklinalscharnier *n*
~ **-form** sattelförmig
~ **reef** Sattelreef *n*, Sattelgang *m*, Sattelvererzung *f (Gangfüllung im Faltenscheitel)*
~ **valley** Satteltal *n*
~ **vein** Sattelgang *m*
safe yield zulässige Entnahmemenge *f*, sichere Ausbeute *f*
safety belt Sicherheitsgurt *m*
~ **factor** Sicherheitsfaktor *m*
~ **joint** Sicherheitsverbinder *m*
~ **lamp** Sicherheitslampe *f*
~ **line** Sicherheitsseil *n*
~ **margin** Sicherheitsgrenze *f*
~ **pillar** Sicherheitspfeiler *m*
~ **precautions** Sicherheitsmaßnahmen *fpl*
~ **valve** Sicherheitsventil *n*
~ **zone** Sicherheitszone *f*, Sicherheitsbereich *m*
safflorite Arsenikkobalt *m*, Eisenkobaltkies *m*, Safflorit *m*, Spatiopyrit *m*, $CoAs_2$
sag [downward]/to absacken
sag Achsenmulde *f*, Becken *n*, Depression *f (großtektonische Strukturform)*; Bodensenkung *f*
~ **-and-swell topography** kuppige Glaziallandschaft *f*
~ **fault (structure)** Belastungssetzung *f*, Sakkungsstruktur *f*
sagenite Sagenit *m (nadeliger Rutil im Glimmer)*
sagenitic quartz Quarz *m* mit Rutilnadeln
saggar clay Kapselton *m*
sagged-downward block abgesunkene Scholle *f*
saggar clay Kapselton *m*
sagging Bodensenkung *f*
~ **of the beds** Hakenschlagen *n* der Schichten
sagittal plane zweiter Hauptabschnitt *m (Optik)*
sagre clay *s.* sagger clay
sagvandite Sagvandit *m (metamorphes Gestein)*

Saharan

Saharan basin Saharabecken n
sahlinite Sahlinit m, $Pb_{14}[Cl_4|O_9|(AsO_4)_2]$
Saint Croixan s. Croixian
~ Elmo's fire Elmsfeuer n
Sakmarian [Stage] Sakmara n, Samarien n, Sakmarium n (basale Stufe des Unterperms)
Salair phases of folding Salairische Faltungsphasen fpl (Mittel- und Oberkambrium Zentralasiens)
salar Salzablagerung f in der Wüste
saléeite Saléeit m, $Mg[UO_2|PO_4]_2 \cdot 10H_2O$
salesite Salesit m, $Cu[OH|IO_3]$
salic salisch
salient Vorsprung m
~ angle ausspringender Winkel m
~ feature Hauptmerkmal n
saliferous salzführend, salzhaltig
~ clay Salzton m
~ residual water salinare Reliktlösung f
~ rock Salzgestein n; Salzgebirge n
~ water versalzenes Wasser n
salifiable salzbildend
salification Salzbildung f, Versalzung f
salify/to in ein Salz verwandeln
saligenous salzbildend
salina Saline f, Salzbergwerk n, Salzpfanne f
Salinan [Stage] Salinan n (Stufe des Cayugans)
salinas Salzebenen fpl (in Südamerika)
saline salzartig, salzig, salin
saline Saline f, Salzbergwerk n; Salzquelle f
~ clay soil Salztonboden m
~ crust Salzkruste f
~ deposit Salzablagerung f
~ dome s. salt dome
~ lake Salzsee m
~ licks salzige Ablagerungen fpl
~ manure Düngesalz n
~ precipitate Salzausscheidung f
~ rock Salzgestein n; Salzgebirge n
~ soil Salzboden m
~ spring Salzquelle f, Solquelle f
~ taste Salzgeschmack m
~ vegetation Salzvegetation f
~ water Salinenwasser n, Salzwasser n
salinelle Salse f, Schlammvulkan m
saliniferous s. saliferous
saliniform salzförmig
salinity Salzgehalt m, Salzhaltigkeit f, Salinität f
~ control Kontaminationsschutz m vor Salzwasser
~ of sea water Meerwassersalinität f
~ stratification Schichtung f nach dem Salzgehalt
salinization Versalzung f
salinized water versalzenes Wasser n
salinous salzartig, salzhaltig
salite Salit m (Pyroxenmischkristall)
salitral salzausscheidend (bei Sumpfsenken)
Salmian [Stage] s. Tremadocian
salmoite Salmoit m (Zn-Phosphat)

304

salmonsite Salmonsit m, $(Mn, Fe^{...})_5H_2[PO_4,(OH)_4]_4 \cdot 4H_2O$
salse Salse f, Schlammvulkan m
salt a sample/to eine Probe verfälschen (um Fündigkeit vorzutäuschen)
salt Salz n, Steinsalz n
~ and pepper sand Sand m mit hellen und dunklen Komponenten
~ balance Salzhaushalt m
~-bearing salzhaltig, salzführend
~ bed Salzschicht f, Salzlager n, Salzablagerung f
~ brine Salzlauge f, Salzsole f, Sole f
~ caverns storage Salzkavernenspeicher m
~ coal Salzkohle f (zumeist salzhaltige Braunkohle)
~-containing salzhaltig
~ content Salzgehalt m
~ cornice Salzüberhang m
~ cote Salzgrube f
~ crust Salzkruste f
~ deposit Salzlagerstätte f, Salzvorkommen n
~ desert Salzwüste f, Takyr m
~ dilution Salzauswaschung f
~-dilution method Salzungsversuch m (Tracertest)
~ dome Salzdom m, Salzhorst m, Salzstock m, Salzkuppel f
~-dome prospect vermuteter Salzstock m
~-dome undershooting Unterschießen n eines Salzstocks
~ earth podzol ausgelaugter Alkaliboden m
~ efflorescence 1. Salzausblühung f; 2. Salzausstrich m
~-encrusted mit einer Salzkruste überzogen
~ garden Salzgarten m
~ glacier Salzgletscher m
~ incrustation Salzinkrustation f
~ intrusion Salzintrusion f
~ karst Salzkarst m
~ lake Salzsee m
~ lick Salzlecke f (natürliche)
~-loving salzliebend, halophil
~ marsh Salzsumpf m, Salzwassermarsch f
~ meadow Salzwiese f
~ mine Salzbergwerk n
~ mine storage of gas Gasspeicherung f in einem Salzbergwerk
~ overhang Salzüberhang m
~ pan 1. Meeressaline f, Salzpfanne f, Salzgarten m; 2. harte Salzschicht f
~ pillow Salzkissen n
~ pillow stage Salzkissenstadium n
~ pit Salzgrube f
~ plain Salztonebene f, Salzsteppe f
~ plug Salzstock m, Salzhorst m
~ plugging of well Salzverstopfung f einer Bohrung
~ removal Entsalzung f
~ ridge Salzrücken m, schmaler gestreckter Salzdom m
~ rock Salzgestein n; Salzgebirge n

~ secretion Salzausscheidung f
~-sensitive plant salzempfindliche Pflanze f
~ solubility Salzlöslichkeit f
~ spring Salzquelle f, Solquelle f
~ steppe Salzsteppe f
~ structure Salzstruktur f
~ table Salzhang m, Ablaugungsebene f (bei Salzstöcken)
~ tectonics Salztektonik f
~ water Salzwasser n; Solquelle f
~-water bath Solbad n
~-water disposal Salzwasserbeseitigung f
~-water disposal well Schluckbrunnen m für Salzwasser
~-water intrusion Salzwassereinbruch m, Salzwasserintrusion f
~-water lagoon Salzwasserlagune f
~-water marsh Salzwassersumpf m, Salzmoor n
~-water source Salzwasserquelle f, Solquelle f
~ wedging Salzsprengung f
~ well Solbrunnen m
~ withdrawal basin Salzabwanderungsbecken n
saltation sprungweiser Transport m (Fluß)
~ marks Springmarken fpl
saltbush Salzkraut n
saltern s. salt garden
saltiness Salzgehalt m
salting of soil Versalzung f des Bodens
saltish brackig
saltpeter s. saltpetre
saltpetre Salpeter m, Nitrokalit m, Kalisalpeter m, KNO_3
saltstone halitreiches Gestein n, NaCl-reiches Gestein n
saltworks Saline f, Salzgrube f, Salzwerk n
salty salzhaltig, salzig
~ water Salzwasser n
samarium Samarium n, Sm
samarskite Samarskit m, $(Y, Er, Fe, Mn, Ca, U, Th, Zr)(Nb, Ta)_2(O, OH)_6$
same symmetry/of the symmetriegleich
samiresite s. betafite
Samoisian [Stage] s. Latdorfian
sample/to Probe nehmen (ziehen), bemustern
sample Muster n, Probe f; Stichprobe f (mathematische Statistik)
~ bag Musterbeutel m, Probenbeutel m
~ bottle Probeflasche f
~-collecting techniques Verfahren n (Technik f) der Probenahme
~ coning Kegelteilung f (einer Probe)
~ cutter Probenahmegerät n
~ divider Probenteiler m (Gerät)
~ grabber Probenehmer m (Person)
~ increment Einzelprobe f
~ interval s. ~ period
~ log Spülprobenlog n
~ logger Bohrprobenanzeiger m
~ man Probenehmer m (Person)
~ of oil Bodenprobe f

~ period Abtastintervall n
~ piece Prüfkörper m
~ quartering Probenviertelung f
~ reducing Probenreduktion f (Verringerung des Umfangs einer Probe)
~ section Probenahmegebiet n
~ splitting Probenteilung f
~ taken at random Stichprobe f
~-taking bullet apparatus Geschoßkerner m
sampleite Sampleit m, $CaNaCu_5[Cl|(PO_4)_4] \cdot 5H_2O$
sampler 1. Probenehmer m (Person); 2. Probenahmegerät n
sampling Probenahme f, Bemusterung f; Stichprobenerhebung f (mathematische Statistik)
~ area Sammelgebiet n (Gebiet, aus dem nach Verfahren der statistischen Probenahme Daten gewonnen werden)
~ device Probenahmegerät n
~ error Probenahmefehler m
~ function Abtastfunktion f
~ of cuttings Probenahme f von Bohrklein, Bohrprobe f
~ point Probenstelle f
~ reliability Zuverlässigkeit f der Probenahme
~ strategy Strategie f (Konzept n) der Datensammlung
~ time Zeitdauer f der Datensammlung (Signalintegrationsdauer eines fotoelektrischen oder Mikrowellendetektors)
~ tool Probenahmegerät n
~ well Probebrunnen m
samsonite Samsonit m, $2Ag_2S \cdot MnS \cdot Sb_2S_3$
samum s. simoom
sanbornite Sanbornit m, $Ba_2[Si_4O_{10}]$
sand/to absanden
~ up versanden
sand 1. Sand m; 2. Sandgestein n (Speichergestein für Erdöl), Erdölspeicher m
~ bar längliche Sandbank f, Nehrung f
~ beach Sandstrand m
~-blasted pebble Windkanter m
~ bobbing Schleifen n mit Sand
~ calcite Kalzit m mit Sandeinschluß
~-carrying capacity Sandtragfähigkeit f
~ cay Sandinsel f, Sandinselchen n
~ content Sandgehalt m
~ content set Sandmeßglas n
~ crystal s. ~ calcite
~ cutting Sand[aus]schliff m
~ deposit Sandvorkommen n, Versandung f
~ desert Sandwüste f
~ dressing Absanden n, Absandung f
~ drift 1. Sandtreiben n, Sandwehen n; 2. Flugsand m
~ dune Sanddüne f
~ dust Sandstaub m
~ erosion Sandausscheuerung f
~ filling (Am) Versandung f
~ flat Sandwatt n
~ flood Flugsand m
~ for facing Klebsand m (tonhaltig)

sand

- ~ **gall** s. ~ pipe
- ~ **heath** Sandheide f
- ~ **heaving** Mitfördern n von Sand
- ~ **hill** Sanddüne f
- ~ **line** 1. Sand-Ton-Linie f *(Bohrlochelektrik)*; 2. Schlämmseil n
- ~ **lineation** Sandriefung f
- ~ **of tidal flat** Wattensand m
- ~ **oil fracturing** Sand-Öl-Fracverfahren n *(zum Schichtaufbrechen)*
- ~-**packed model** Sandmodell n
- ~ **pipe** Erdpfeife f, geologische Orgel f, Erdorgel f, Sandröhre f
- ~ **pit** Sandgrube f
- ~ **plain** Sandfeld n
- ~ **quarry** Sandgrube f
- ~ **reef** s. ~ bar
- ~ **reel** Schlämmtrommel f
- ~ **ripples** Sandrippeln fpl
- ~ **roll** synsedimentäre Rollstruktur f
- ~ **scratch** Sandschliff m
- ~ **seams** *(sl)* pegmaplitische Trümer npl *(Steinbruch)*
- ~ **shadow** Sedimentfahne f
- ~ **silting** Versandung f
- ~ **spit** Sandbank f
- ~ **spreading** Absanden n, Absandung f
- ~ **stratum** Sandschicht f
- ~ **streak** Strömungsriefe f, Sandschmitze
- ~ **thickness** Speichermächtigkeit f
- ~ **tube** Blitzröhre f
- ~ **volcano** Sandkegel m, Sandvulkan m
- ~ **wave** Strombank f, Sandrücken m, Sandwelle f, Großrippel f *(in Flußbetten)*
- ~ **working** Sandgrube f
- **sandbag** Glazialsandtasche f *(im Braunkohlenflöz)*
- **sandbank** Untiefe f, Watt n, Sandbank f
- **sanderite** Sanderit m, Mg[SO$_4$]·2H$_2$O
- **sandface** Bohrlochwand f *(im Speicherbereich)*
- **sandflat** Wattsand m
- **sandfracing** Sandfrac-Verfahren n *(zum Schichtaufbrechen)*
- **sanding** 1. Absanden n, Absandung f, 2. Aufsandung f
- ~-**up** Versandung f, Versanden n
- **sandkey** Sandinsel f, Sandinselchen n
- **sandlike** sandartig
- **sandr** s. outwash plain
- **sandrock** s. sandstone
- **sandstone** Sandstein m
- ~ **band** Sandsteinzwischenlage f
- ~-**bearing nodular galenite** Knottensandstein m
- ~ **bed** Sandsteinlage f
- ~ **bound with lime** Sandstein m mit kalkigem Bindemittel
- ~ **dike** Sandsteingang m
- ~ **grit** grobkörniger Sandstein m
- ~ **pipe** gigantischer Belastungswulst m
- ~ **quarry** Sandsteinbruch m
- ~ **vein** Sandsteingang m
- **sandstorm** Sandsturm m
- **sandur** s. outwash plain
- **sandy** sandig, sandführend; sandartig
- ~ **beach** Sandstrand m
- ~ **chalk** sandige Kreide f
- ~ **clay** magerer Ton m, Sandton m
- ~ **clay loam** sandig-toniger Lehm m
- ~ **coarse and medium gravel** sandiger Grob- und Mittelkies m
- ~ **country** Sandgegend f
- ~ **desert** Sandwüste f, Areg m *(arabisch)*
- ~ **gravel** feiner Kies m
- ~ **ground** Sandboden m
- ~ **limestone** Kalksandstein m
- ~ **loess** Sandlöß m
- ~ **marl** Sandmergel m
- ~ **muck** sandiger Humus m
- ~ **mud** sandiger Schlick m
- ~ **mudstone** sandiger Tonstein m
- ~-**pebble desert** Sand-Kies-Wüste f
- ~ **shale** sandiger Schieferton m, Sandschiefer m
- ~ **siltstone** Sand-Siltstein m
- ~ **soil** Sandboden m
- **Sangamon Interglacial Age** Sangamon-Interglazial n *(Pleistozän in Nordamerika, entspricht dem Eem-Interglazial Europas)*
- **Sangamonian** Sangamon n *(Pleistozän in Nordamerika)*
- **sanidine** Sanidin m, K[AlSi$_3$O$_8$]
- **sanidinite** Sanidinit m
- ~ **facies** Sanidinitfazies f
- **sanitary landfill** geordnete Deponie f
- **Sannoisian [Stage]** Sannoisien n *(Stufe des Oligozäns)*
- **Santonian [Stage]** Santon n *(Stufe der Oberkreide)*
- **santorin** Santorinerde f
- **sap/to** untergraben
- **sap** braune Verfärbungszone f an Klüften und Schichtfugen *(Steinbruch)*
- **sapanthracite** Sapropelkohle f im Anthrazitstadium
- **sapanthracon** karbone Sapropelkohle f
- **saponification** Verseifung f
- **saponify/to** verseifen
- **saponite** Saponit m, Seifenstein m, (Mg, Fe)[(OH)$_2$|AlSiO]
- **sapperite** mineralische Zellulose f *(in Braunkohlen und fossilem Holz)*
- **sapphire** Saphir m *(s.a. corundum)*
- ~ **quartz** Saphirquarz m, blauer Quarz m
- **sapphirine** Saphirin m, Mg$_2$Al$_4$[O$_6$|SiO$_4$]
- **sapping** Kliffunterhöhlung f *(in weicheren Schichten)*
- **saprocoll** erhärteter (gallertartiger) Faulschlamm m, Saprokoll n
- **saprodil** tertiäre Sapropelkohle f
- **saprofication** Faulschlammbildung f, Sapropelbildung f
- **saprolite** Rückstandsgestein n in situ

sapromixtite Sapromixtit *m (Sapropelkohle)*
sapropel Sapropel *m (n)*, Faulschlamm *m*
~ **calc** Sediment *n* aus Kalkalgen und Sapropel
~ **clay** Sediment *n* aus Sapropel und Ton
~ **rock** *s.* sapropelite
~ **tar** Sapropelitteer *m*
sapropelic *s.* sapropelitic
sapropelite Sapropelit *m*, Faulschlammgestein *n*
sapropelitic sapropelitisch, fäulnisliebend, saprophil
~ **coal** sapropelitische Kohle *f*
saprophytic saprophytisch
sapropsammite sandiger Sapropelit *m*
saprovitrinite Vitrinit *m* in sapropelitischer Kohle
SAR *s.* synthetic aperture radar
Saracan stone 1. *s.* grayweather; 2. erratischer Sandsteinblock *m*
Saratogan [Stage] Saratogien *n (Stufe des Oberkambriums)*
sarcoline fleischfarben
sarcolite Sarkolith *m*, $(Ca, Na)_8[O_2|(Al(Al, Si)Si_2O_8)_6]$
sarcopside Sarkopsid *m*, $(Fe, Mn,Ca)_3[PO_4]_2$
sard Sard[er] *m*, bräunlicher Karneol *m (s.a. quartz)*
sardachate Sardachat *m*, schwarz und weißer Bandachat *m*
Sardinian phase of folding sardische Faltungsphase *f (Oberkambrium-Tremadoc, Mittelmeergebiet)*
sardonyx Sardonyx *m (s.a. chalcedony)*
Sargassum Sargassotang *m*, Beerentang *m*
sarkinite Sarkinit m, $Mn_2[OH|AsO_4]$
Sarmatian [Stage] Sarmat[ien] *n*, Sarmatium *n (Stufe des Miozäns)*
sarsen *s.* grayweather
~ **stone** erratischer Sandsteinblock *m*
sartorite Sartorit *m*, Bleiarsenglanz *m*, Skleroklas *m*, Arsenomelan *m*, $PbS·As_2S_3$
sassolin, sassolite Sassolin *m*, $B(OH)_3$
satellite 1. Satellit *m*, Trabant *m*; 2. Ganggefolgschaft *f (bei Plutoniten)*
~ **body** Satellitenkörper *m*
~-**borne camera** Satellitenkamera *f*
~ **borne scanner** Satellitenscanner *m (auf einem Satelliten montiertes Linienabtastgerät)*
~-**carrying instruments** Meßsatellit *m*
~ **flood mapping** Kartierung *f* des Überflutungsgebiets mittels Satellitenfernerkundung
~ **imagery** Satellitenaufnahmen *fpl*
~ **monitoring** Satellitenüberwachung *f*
~ **orbit** Flugbahn *f* des Satelliten
~ **system** Satellitensystem *n*
sathrolith *s.* regolith
satin spar (stone) Atlasspat *m*, Atlasstein *m*, Faserkalk *m*, Fasergips *m*
saturable sättigungsfähig
saturate/to 1. sättigen; 2. durchtränken
saturated gesättigt
~ **ground** wassergesättigter Boden *m*

~ **system** gesättigtes System *n*
saturation 1. Sättigung *f*; 2. Durchtränkung *f*
~ **curve** Sättigungskuve *f*
~ **layer** Staunässebereich *m*
~ **pressure** Sättigungsdruck *m*
~ **value** Sättigungsgrad *m*
~ **vapour pressure** Sättigungsdampfdruck *m*
~ **zone** Sättigungszone *f*
Saucesian [Stage] Saucesien *n (marine Stufe, unteres Miozän in Nordamerika)*
Saugamon Interglacial Age Saugamon-Interglazial *n (entspricht dem Riß/Würm-Interglazial)*
saurians Saurier *mpl*
sausage structure *s.* boudinage
saussurite Saussurit *m (Mineralgemenge in zersetztem Plagioklas)*
~-**gabbro** Saussuritgabbro *m*
saussuritization Saussuritisierung *f*
saussuritize/to saussuritisieren
savanna Savanne *f*
~ **forest** Savannenlichtwald *m*
savannah *(Am)* Savanne *f*
saw down/to einsägen *(Fluß)*
saw-toothed core bit Zahnkrone *f*
sawback tief eingeschnittener Gebirgskamm *m* mit Gipfelflur
sawing residue Sägeschmant *m (Gesteinssäge)*
Sawkillian [Stage] Sawkill[ien] *n (Stufe des Ulsters in Nordamerika)*
saxicolous plants Felspflanzen *fpl*
Saxo-Thuringian zone saxothuringische Zone *f*, Saxothuringikum *n*
Saxonian [Stage] Saxon[ien] *n*, Saxonium *n (Stufe des Perms in Mittel- und Westeuropa)*
~ **type of fold structure** saxonischer Faltungstyp *m*
saxonite Saxonit *m (Varietät von Peridotit)*
sborgite Sborgit *m*, $Na[B_5O_6(OH)_4]·3H_2O$
scabble/to bossieren, Bruchsteinflächen glätten
scabbling 1. Bossieren *n*, 2. Gesteinsfragment *n*
~ **hammer** Bossierhammer *m*
scabland features (forms) glaziale Schmelzwasserformen *fpl*
scacchite Scacchit *m*, $MnCl_2$
scad Goldklumpen *m*
scaffold-type structure Gerüststruktur *f (von Tonmineralen)*
scalar skalar
scalariform treppenartig, stufenartig
scale 1. Maßstab *m*; 2. Mineralschuppe *f*, Blättchen *n*; 3. Ruschel *f*, Rutschschuppe *f*, Schuppe *f (Hochscholle einer kleinen Überschiebung)*; 4. Gesteinsschuppe *f*; 5. Kruste *f*, Ablagerung *f*
~ **deposit** Versinterung *f*
~ **magnifying glass** Meßlupe *f*
~ **of airphoto** Bildmaßstab *m (Luftbildgeologie)*
~ **of chart** Kartenmaßstab *m*

scale

~ **of hardness** Härteskala f
~ **of mica** Glimmerblättchen n
~ **of seismic intensity** Erdbebenstärkeskala f
scaled schuppig
scalenohedron Skalenoeder n
scaling Abblättern n, Abblätterung f, schalenförmige Ablösung f
~ **law** Verknüpfungsgesetz n (seismologischer Parameter)
scall lockeres Gestein n
scalloped cirque ausgekerbtes Kar n
~ **surface** löcherige Oberfläche f
scalloping Wellung f (sedimentäre Struktur)
scalped anticline gekappte Antiklinale f
scaly schalig, schuppig
~ **chalk** klüftige Kreide f
~ **structure** Schuppengefüge n
scan line Abtastlinie f, Abtastzeile f
Scandinavian shield Skandinavischer Schild m
scandium Skandium n, Sc
scanner Gerät n für Rasterbildaufnahmen (Geofernerkundung)
scanning electron microscope Rasterelektronenmikroskop n
scapolite Skapolith m (Mischkristall von Mejonit und Marialith)
scapolitization Skapolithisierung f
scar 1. Narbe f (Geotektonik); 2. felsige Anhöhe f; isolierter, hervorstehender Fels m
SCAR = Scientific Committee on Antarctic Research
scarbroite Scarbroit m, $Al(HO)_3$
scarcement stehengebliebenes Gebirgsstück n
scarcely noticeable kaum merklich, sehr leicht (2. Stufe der Erdbebenstärkeskala)
scarcity of lime Kalkarmut f
scares Pyritlamellen fpl der Kohle
scarf Abrißnische f
~ **cloud** Schleierwolke f, Schalwolke f
scarn Skarn m (Kalksilikatfels)
scarp Böschung f, Abhang m, Steilrand m, Steilwand f, Abdachung f, Hangfläche f
~ **face** Steilwand f, Böschung f
scarped abschüssig, steil, abgeböscht
~ **tableland** treppenförmiges Stufenland n
scarplet Absatz m, Stufe f
scarred gekritzt, narbig (durch Eis)
scatter/to [ver]streuen
scatter Streuung f (von Messungen)
~ **diagram** Punktdiagramm n (in der Gefügeanalyse)
scattered fragments Schutt m
scattering Streuung f
~ **coefficient** Streukoeffizient m
scatterometer Streuungsmesser m
scaur steiler Felshang m (Schottland)
scavenger Aasfresser m
scavenging animal Aasfresser m
~ **of the hole** Spülen n des Bohrlochs
scawtite Scawtit m, $Ca_6[Si_3O_9]_2 \cdot CaCO_3 \cdot 2H_2O$
scenery Landschaftsbild n

308

scepterlike growth Szepterwachstum n
SCG = Scientific Committee for Inter-Union Cooperation in Geophysics
schafarzicite Schafarzikit m, $FeSb_2O_4$
schairerite Schairerit m, $Na_3[(F, Cl)|SO_4]$
schallerite Schallerit m, $(Mn, Fe)_8[(OH)_{10}|(Si, As)_6O_{15}]$
schalstein Schalstein m
schapbachite Schapbachit m, α-$AgBiS_2$
schären-type of coast line Schärenküste f
scheelite Scheelit m, $Ca[WO_4]$
scheelitine Stolzit m, Scheelbleierz n, Tungstein m, β-$Pb[WO_4]$
scheererite Scheererit m (Erdwachs)
schefferite Schefferit m (Pyroxenmischkristall)
schematic section schematischer Schnitt m
scherbakovite Scherbakovit m, $(K, Na, Ba)_3(Ti, Nb)_2[Si_3O_7]_2$
schertelite Schertelit m, $(NH_4)_2MgH_2[PO_4]_2 \cdot 4H_2O$
schiller spar Schillerspat m, Bastit m (Pseudomorphose von Serpentin nach Bronzit)
schillerization Irisieren n, Labradorisieren n, Schillern n, Aventurisieren n
schillerize/to irisieren, labradorisieren, schillern, aventurisieren
schirmerite Schirmerit m, $PbS \cdot 2Ag_2S \cdot 2Bi_2S_3$
schist kristalliner Schiefer m (feinschiefriger als Gneis)
schistic schieferartig
~ **rock** schiefriges Gestein n
schistoid schieferartig
schistose schieferig
~ **structure** schieferige Textur f, Schieferung f
schistosity Schieferung f (im engeren Sinne in Glimmerschiefer und Gneis)
~ **fold** s. similar fold
schistous schieferartig, schieferig, schieferhaltig
schlatt Schlatt n, Windausblasungsmulde f
schlich s. slime
schliere Schliere f
schlierenlike flaserig
schlieric schlierig
~ **structure** Schlierentextur f
schluff Schluff m
Schlumberger electrode array Schlumberger-Anordnung f
~ **logs** Schlumberger-Logs npl
Schmidt field balance Schmidtsche Feldwaage f
~ **net** Schmidtsches Netz n
schneebergite Schneebergit m, Romeit m (s.a. romeite)
schoderite Schoderit m, $Al[(P, V)O_4] \cdot 4H_2O$
schoenite Schönit m, $K_2Mg[SO_4]_2 \cdot 6H_2O$
schoepite Schoepit m, $8[UO_2|(OH)_2] \cdot 8H_2O$
schorl Schörl m, schwarzer Turmalin m, Eisenturmalin n, $NaFe_3Al_6[(OH)|(BO_3)_3|Si_6O_{18}]$
~ **rock** Turmalinfels m
~ **schist** Turmalinschiefer m
schorlaceous schörlartig

schorlite s. schorl
schorlomite Schorlomit m (Varietät von Melanit)
schratten formation Schrattenbildung f
schrattenfeld Schrattenfeld n
schrattenkalk Schrattenkalk m
schreibersite Schreibersit m, (Fe,Ni,Co)$_3$P
schroeckingerite Schröckingerit m, NaCa$_3$[UO$_2$|F|SO$_4$|(CO$_3$)$_3$]·10H$_2$O
schroetterite s. allophane
schuchardtite Schuchardtit m (Varietät von Antigorit)
schuetteite Schuetteit m, Hg$_3$[O$_2$|SO$_4$]
schultenite Schultenit m, HPbAsO$_4$
schulzenite Schulzenit m (Cu-haltige Varietät von Heterogenit)
schungite Schungit m (hochinkohlter Anthrazit)
schwartzembergite Schwartzembergit m, Pb$_5$[Cl$_3$O$_3$|JO$_3$]
schwazite Schwazit m, Quecksilberfahlerz n (Hg-haltiger Tetraedrit)
science of mineral deposits Lagerstättenkunde f
~ **of rocks** Gesteinskunde f
~ **of structure** Gefügekunde f
scintillate/to flimmern, szintillieren
scintillation Flimmern n, Szintillation f
~ **counter (detector)** Szintillationszähler m
~ **tube** s. scintillometer
scintillator Szintillator m
scintillometer Szintillometer n
Scirpus peat Schilftorf m
scissions thrust Durchscherungsüberschiebung f
~ **thrust sheet** Abscherungsdecke f
scissors fault s. pivotal fault
~ **window** Scherenfenster n (Tektonik)
scissure Riß m, Spalt m
sclaffery kleinstückig zerfallend (Schottland)
scleroblasts Skleroblasten mpl (Bildungszellen von Knochen, Spiculae u.ä.)
sclerometer Härtemesser m, Sklerometer n
sclerophyll plants Hartlaubgewächse npl
sclerotic plate Knochenplatte f
~ **plate ring** Knochenplattenring m
sclerotinite Sklerotinit m (Kohlenmaceral)
sclerotization Sklerotisation f (Imprägnierung mit Kalksalzen)
sclit, sclutt (sl) Brandschiefer m (Schottland)
scolecite Skolezit m, Ca[Al$_2$Si$_3$O$_{10}$]·3H$_2$O
scolithus sandstone Scolithussandstein m
scoop [out]/to auskolken, ausschürfen
scooping[-out] Ausschürfung f
scopiform besenförmig
SCOR = Scientific Committee on Oceanic Research
scoria Schlacke f, Gesteinsschlacke f (vulkanisch)
~ **cone** Schlackenkegel m
~ **moraine** Pseudomoräne f
scoriaceous schlackenähnlich, schlackenartig

~ **basalt** Schlackenbasalt m
~ **lapilli** Schlackenlapilli pl
~ **sand** Schlackensand m
~ **surface** schaumige Oberfläche f
scoriated schlackig
scorification Schlackenbildung f, Verschlackung f
scorified lava schlackige Lava f
scoriform schlackenähnlich
scorify/to [ver]schlacken
scoring Spalte f, Kerbe f; Auskolken n
scorious verschlackt
scorodite Skorodit m, Knoblaucherz n, Fe[AsO$_4$]·2H$_2$O
scorzalite Scorzalith m, (Fe, Mg)Al$_2$[OH|PO$_4$]$_2$
Scotch topaz gelber Quarz m
Scottish Highlands Schottische Hochlande npl (Gesteinsprovinz)
scour/to abschleifen, ausschürfen, abfegen, [ab]scheuern (Winderosion, Eiserosion)
~ **off** abscheuern
~ **out** auswaschen
scour Ausscheuern n, Tiefenschurf m (im Flußbett)
~ **and fill** kolkförmige Erosion f, kleindimensionale Erosionsrinne f
~ **lineation** Kolkriefen fpl
~ **mark** Fließrille f, Kolkmarke f, Auskolkung f, Strömungsrinne f, Erosionsmarke f
~ **outlet** Grundablaß m
~ **side** Stoßseite f
scouring Abschleifung f, Einschleifen n, Auswaschung f, Auskolkung f, scheuernde Wirkung f (z.B. des Gletschereises)
~ **sand** Auswaschungssand m
scourway Abflußrinne f
scout/to abschürfen
scout (Am) Industriespion m im Erdölgeschäft
scouting 1. Exploration f; 2. Aufschlußbohrung f
scovan lode Zinnerzgang m
scove Stufferz n
scrap Abfall m (Handelsglimmersorte)
scratch/to schrammen, ritzen
scratch Schramme f, Ritz m
~ **hardness** Ritzhärte f
~ **hardness number** Ritzhärtezahl f
~ **hardness tester** Ritzhärteprüfer m
~ **test** Ritzverfahren n
scratched gekritzt (durch Eis)
~ **boulder** gekritztes Geschiebe n
~ **by ice** eisgeschrammt
scratcher Kratzer m
scratches 1. Rutschschrammen fpl; 2. Friktionsstreifen mpl
~ **on the section** Schliffkratzer mpl (Anschliff)
scree Schutthalde f, Geröllhalde f; Felsschutt m, Schutt m, Gesteinsschutt m, Geröll n, Steingeröll n
~ **breccia** Moränenbrekzie f, Schuttbrekzie f
~ **debris** Schutt m
~ **material** Gehängeschutt m

screen

screen/to sieben, schlämmen *(Gold)*
screen Filter *n*
~ **analysis** Siebanalyse *f*
~ **liner** Siebliner *m*, Siebfilterrohr *n*, Liner *m* mit Lochöffnungen
~ **pipe** Schlitzrohr *n (in Brunnen)*
~ **underflow** Siebdurchgang *m*
~ **well** Filterbrunnen *m*
screened ore Scheideerz *n*
screening 1. Siebklassierung *f*, Korngrößentrennung *f*; 2. Schlämmen *n (von Gold)*; 3. Fernhalten *n* von Sand; 4. Einbau *m* einer geschlitzten Rohrtour
~ **device** Scheideanlage *f*
~ **plant** Klassieranlage *f (Erze)*
screw auger Spiralbohrer *m*
~ **axis** Schraubenachse *f*
~ **conveyor** Schneckenförderer *m*
~ **motion** Schraubenbewegung *f*
scrin 1. irreguläre Eisensteinknolle *f (Schottland)*; 2. untergeordnetes Gangtrum *n*
scrub Buschland *n*, Steppe *f (Australien)*
scrubstone *(sl)* Kalksandstein *m*
scry/to schürfen
scud 1. Bö *f*, Windbö *f*; Regenschauer *m*; 2. Pyritzwischenlage *f*, Tonzwischenlage *f*
~ **of wind** Windbö *f*
sculping Aufspaltung *f* von Schiefern
sculpture Skulptur *f (auf Fossilgehäusen)*
sculpturing of rock Bearbeitung *f* des Gesteins
scun Erztrum *n*
Scythian [Stage], Scythic [Stage] Skyth *n (Stufe der alpinen Trias)*
se-fabric Externgefüge *n*
sea 1. Meer *n*, See *f*; 2. Seegang *m*
~ **arch** Brandungstor *n*
~ **area** Meeresgebiet *n*
~ **balls** Pflanzballen *mpl (in marinen Sedimenten)*
~ **basin** Meeresbecken *n*
~ **beach** Meeresstrand *m*
~-**beach placer** Meeresküstenseife *f*
~ **bottom** Meeresgrund *m*, Meeresboden *m*
~ **breeze** auflandiger Wind *m*
~ **butterfly** Pteropode *f*, Flügelschnecke *f*
~ **cave** Brandungshöhle *f*
~ **cavern** Grotte *f*
~ **chasm** Kliffeinschnitt *m (durch Wellenerosion)*
~ **cliff** Küstenkliff *n*
~ **coast** Küste *f*, Strandlinie *f*, Meeresküste *f*, Seeküste *f*
~ **current** Meeresströmung *f*
~ **dike** Seedeich *m*, Meeresdeich *m*
~ **drift** Seeablagerung *f*
~ **fire** Meeresleuchten *n*
~ **floe** schwimmendes Eisfeld *n*
~ **flood** Sturmflut *f*
~-**floor spreading** Spreizbewegung *f (Auseinanderdriften n)* des Meeresbodens
~-**floor well head** Bohrlochabschluß *m* auf dem Meeresboden

~ **foam** Meeresschaum *m*, Gischt *m*
~ **fog** Seenebel *m*, Küstennebel *m*
~ **gate** Meerenge *f*
~ **holm** unbewohnte Insel *f*
~ **ice** Meereis *n*
~ **inlet** Meeresarm *m*
~ **level** Meeresspiegel *m*, Normalnull *n*, NN
~ **level/above** über dem Meeresspiegel
~ **level/below** untermeerisch
~-**level elevation** Höhe *f* über Normalnull
~-**level fluctuation** Meeresspiegelschwankung *f*
~ **lily** Seelilie *f*
~ **limit** Strandlinie *f*
~-**lion guano** Seelöwenguano *m*
~ **mammal** marines Säugetier *n*
~ **mill** Meermühle *f*
~ **mount[ain]** *s.* seamount
~ **mud** Wattboden *m*
~ **sand** Seesand *m*
~ **shore** Meeresufer *n*, Meeresküste *f*, Küste *f*
~ **side** Küste *f*
~ **slide** submarine Gleitung *f*
~ **stack** durch Wellenerosion abgegliederte Felsnadel *f*
~ **surveys** Seedienst *m (Geophysik)*
~ **transgression** Meerestransgression *f*
~ **urchin** Seeigel *m*
~ **wall** Hafendamm *m*, Strandmauer *f*, Deich *m*
~ **water** Meerwasser *n*
~-**water desalination** Meerwasserentsalzung *f*
~ **wax** *s.* maltha
~ **weather service** Seewetterdienst *m*
~-**worn** marin erodiert
seabed Meeresboden *m*
seaboard Seeküste *f*, Wasserkante *f*, Küstenstrich *m*, Meeresküste *f*
seaborne Schiffs...
seaknoll Tiefsee-Erhebung *f (kleiner als sea mount)*
seal up/to abdichten
seal Abdichtung *f*, Barriere *f*; Sperre *f*, Abschluß *m*
~ **capacity** Rückhaltevermögen *n*
sealed joint verschlossene Kluft *f*
~ **liquid** Flüssigkeitseinschluß *m*
sealing membrane Dichtungsschleier *m*, Dichtungswand *f*
~ **rock** Deckschicht *f*
~ **trench** *s.* ~ membrane
~-**up of a hole** Abdichtung *f (eines Bohrlochs)*
seam 1. Flöz *n*, Lage *f*, Lager *n*; 2. Lettenkluft *f*
~ **cut** Flözanschnitt *m*
~ **exit** Schichtenkopf *m*
~ **formation** Flözbildung *f*
~ **formation curve** Flözbildungskurve *f (grafische Darstellung der Bildungsphasen)*
~ **identification** Flözidentifizierung *f*
~ **nodule** *s.* coal apple
~ **of coal** Kohlenflöz *n*

~ **section** Flözprofil *n*
~ **swell** Flözscharung *f*
~ **thickness** Flözmächtigkeit *f*
~ **wave** Flözwelle *f*
seamanite Seamanit *m*, $Mn_3[PO_4|BO_3] \cdot 3H_2O$
seamount Tiefseeberg *m*, Tiefseekuppe *f*, submariner Berg *m*
~ **chain** untermeerische Bergkette *f*
seamy rock 1. flözführendes Gebirge *n*; 2. klüftiges Gestein *n*
seapeak submarine Gipfelkuppe *f*
seaquake Seebeben *n*, submarines Beben *n*
search/to schürfen
search Schürfen *n*, Schurf *m*
~ **for deposits** Lagerstättensuche *f*
searcher Schürfer *m*
searching Schürfen *n*, Schurf *m*, Schürfung *f*
searlesite Searlesit *m*, $NaB[Si_2O_6] \cdot H_2O$
seascarp unterseeischer Abhang (Steilabhang) *m*, unterseeische Abdachung *f*
seaside Meeresküste *f*, Küste *f*
season Jahreszeit *f*
seasonal jahreszeitlich
~ **banding** jahreszeitliche Bänderung *f*
~ **deposit** jahreszeitlich bedingte Ablagerung *f*
~ **lake** periodischer See *m*
~ **runoff** jahreszeitlicher Abfluß *m*
~ **variation** jahreszeitliche Variation *f*
seasonally banded (stratified) clay Bänderton *m* mit Jahresringen
seat Sohle *f*; Liegendes *n*
~ **clay** Liegendton *m*, Unterton *m* (von Kohleflözen)
~ **earth** fossiler Bodenhorizont *m* unter dem Flöz
~ **of generation** Entstehungsort *m*
~ **of settlement** Untergrund *m* des Bauwerks
~ **rock** Liegendes *n* eines Flözes
~ **seal** Liegendsperre *f*, Sohlensperre *f*
~ **stone** *s*. ~ rock
seaweed Tang *m*, Seegras *n*
sebkha Sebkha *f* (aride Ebene aus Ton-, Schluff- oder Sandablagerungen, oft mit Salzinkrustationen)
sebkra *s*. sebkha
second-derivative map Karte *f* der zweiten Ableitung (Seismik)
~**-derivative value** Wert *m* der zweiten Ableitung (Seismik)
~ **order correction** Korrektur *f* zweiter Ordnung (Seismik)
~ **order of branches** Sekundäräste *mpl*
~**-to-last water interlayer** Dreischichttonmineralwasser *n*
secondary cementation Verkittung *f*, sekundäre Zementation *f* (im Sediment)
~ **comminution** Feinzerkleinerung *f*
~ **cone** Nebenkegel *m*
~ **constituent** Nebenbestandteil *m*
~ **cosmic radiation** kosmische Sekundärstrahlung *f*
~ **crater** Nebenkrater *m*

~ **depression** Nebentief *n*
~ **divide** Nebenwasserscheide *f*
~ **downward change** sekundärer Teufenunterschied *m*
~ **electromagnetic field** elektromagnetisches Sekundärfeld *n*
~ **exploitation** Sekundärgewinnung *f*, Zweitgewinnung *f*
~ **fault** sekundäre Verwerfung *f*
~ **halo** sekundärer Dispersionshof *m* (durch Verwitterungsprozesse entstanden)
~ **impact** sekundärer Einschlag *m* (durch Meteoriteneinschlag verursacht)
~ **mountain** Mittelgebirge *n*
~ **oil recovery** sekundäre Ölgewinnung *f*, Sekundärentölung *f*
~ **permeability** Wasserdurchlässigkeit *f* durch Fugen und Spalten
~ **podzolized soil** Sekundärpodsolboden *m*
~ **quartzite** Sekundärquarzit *m*, metasomatischer Quarzit *m*
~ **radiation** Sekundärstrahlung *f*
~ **recovery [method]** Sekundärverfahren *n* (der Ölgewinnung)
~ **stratification** Resedimentationsgefüge *n*; Sekundärschichtung *f*, Umlagerungsschichtung *f*
~ **variation in depth** sekundärer Teufenunterschied *m*
~ **vein** Nebengang *m*
~ **wave** zweiter Vorläufer *m*, sekundäre Welle *f* (Seismik)
secreted sedimentaries Ausscheidungssedimente *npl*
secretion Ausscheidung *f*
sectile schneidbar (mit dem Messer)
section 1. Ausschnitt *m*; 2. Profil *n*
~ **gauge log** Kaliberlog *n*, Kalibermessung *f*
~ **of a valley** Taleinschnitt *m*
secular säkular
~ **inequalities** säkulare Störungen *fpl*
~ **perturbation** säkulare Störung *f*
~ **rise** säkulare Hebung *f*
~ **sinking** säkulare Senkung *f*
~ **variation** Säkularvariation *f*
secure exploitation deepness sichere Abbautiefe *f*
sedd *s*. sudd
sedentary organisms sessile Organismen *mpl*
~ **soil** Sedentärboden *m*, Primärboden *m*
sedge moor Seggenmoor *n*
~ **peat** Seggentorf *m*
sedifluction Sedifluktion *f*, Fließen *n* unverfestigter Sedimente
sediment Sediment[gestein] *n*
~**-bearing** sedimentführend
~ **discharge** Geschiebefracht *f*, Geschiebemenge *f*
~**-infesting organisms** im Sediment wühlende Organismen *mpl*
~ **load** Schwebstoff *m*
~ **particle** Sedimentpartikel *f*

sediment

~ **runoff** Schwebstofffracht *f*
~ **sump** Schlammfang *m (eines Brunnens)*
~ **transport** Sedimenttransport *m*
sedimentary sedimentär
~ **blocks** sedimentäre Klippen *fpl*
~ **boudinage structure** Sedimentboudinage *f (durch Sedifluktion)*
~ **complex** Schichtenkomplex *m*
~ **cover** Sedimentdecke *f*
~ **cycle** Sedimentationszyklus *m*
~ **deposit** sedimentäre Lagerstätte *f*, Trümmerlagerstätte *f*
~ **environment** 1. Ablagerungsmilieu *n*; 2. Sedimentationsraum *m*, Sedimentationsgebiet *n*
~ **exhalative deposit** sedimentär-exhalative Lagerstätte *f*
~ **foreigns** sedimentäre Klippen *fpl*
~ **gneiss** Paragneis *m*
~ **klippe** *s.* olistolith
~ **petrography** Sedimentpetrografie *f*
~ **rock** Sedimentgestein *n*
~ **schist** kristalliner Schiefer *m* sedimentären Ursprungs
~ **tectonics** die Sedimentation beeinflussende tektonische Faktoren
~ **water** Sedimentationswasser *n*
sedimentate/to sedimentieren, ablagern
sedimentation Sedimentation *f*, Sedimentbildung *f*, Ablagerung *f*
~ **basin** Sedimentationsbecken *n*
~ **stage** Sedimentationsetappe *f*
~ **tank** Klärbrunnen *m*
~ **test** Sedimentationsprobe *f*
~ **unit** Sedimentationseinheit *f*
sedimentogenic rock sedimentogenes Gestein *n*
sedimentology Sedimentologie *f*
sediments carried in suspension Flußtrübe *f*
seed Samen *m*
seep/to [durch]sickern, aussickern, einsickern
~ **in** verrieseln
seep 1. Ausschwitzen *n*; 2. natürlicher Austritt *m (Öl, Gas)*
seepage 1. Sickerung *f*, Versickerung *f*, Einsickern *n*, Durchsickerung *f*, Aussickerung *f*; 2. Ölsumpf *m*, Ölausbiß *m*; 3. natürlicher Austritt *m (Öl, Gas)*
~ **distance** Sickerstrecke *f*
~ **face** Sickerfläche *f*
~ **failure** hydraulischer Grundbruch *m*
~ **flow** Sickerströmung *f*, Abfluß *m* durch Aussickerung
~ **force** Sickerwasserdruck *m*
~ **path** Sickerlinie *f*
~ **pressure** Sickerwasserdruck *m*
~ **rate** Sickergeschwindigkeit *f*
~ **refluxion** Laugenrückfluß *m* durch den Porenraum zum Meer *(bei frühdiagenetischer Dolomitbildung)*
~ **runnel** Sickerbach *m*
~ **spring** flächenhafter Grundwasseraustritt *m*

~ **surface** Sickerfläche *f*
~ **through dikes** Kuverwasser *n*
~ **velocity** *s.* Darcy velocity
~ **water** 1. austretendes Sickerwasser *n*; 2. Qualmwasser *n*
seggar clay Kapselton *m*
segment 1. Sektor *m*; 2. Reflexionselement *n*
segregated band Seigerungsstreifen *m*
~ **vein** Segregationsgang *m*
segregation Seigerung *f*, Ausscheidung *f*, Entmischung *f*; Schwereschichtung *f*
~ **due to unmixing** Entmischungssegregation *f*
~ **in magmas** *s.* magmatic differentiation
~ **rate** Phasentrennungsrate *f*
seiche Seiche *f*
seidozerite Seidozerit *m*, $Na_4MnTi(Zr,Ti)[O|(F,OH)|Si_2O_7]_2$
seis *(sl)* Geophon *n*
seism Erdstoß *m*
seismal *s.* seismic
seismic[al] seismisch
~**activity** Erdbebentätigkeit *f*
~ **area** Erdbebengebiet *n*
~ **centre** Erdbebenherd *m*
~ **crew** seismischer Meßtrupp *m*
~ **detector location** seismischer Beobachtungspunkt *m*
~ **district** Erdbebengebiet *n*
~ **effects** seismische Auswirkungen *fpl*
~ **focus** Erdbebenherd *m*
~ **instruments** seismische Instrumente *npl*
~ **intensity** seismische Intensität *f*
~ **investigation** Erdbebenforschung *f*
~ **line** Schütterlinie *f*
~ **logging** seismische Bohrlochmessung *f*
~ **method** seismografische Untersuchungsmethode *f*
~ **observation point** seismischer Beobachtungspunkt *m*
~ **observatory** Erdbebenwarte *f*
~ **origin** Epizentrum *n*
~ **party** seismischer Meßtrupp *m*
~ **prospecting** seismische Erkundung *f*
~ **record** Seismogramm *n*
~ **record in wiggle-trace form** seismische Registrierung *f* in Linienschrift
~ **reflection** seismische Reflexion *f*
~ **reflection method** Reflexionsseismik *f*
~ **refraction** seismische Refraktion *f*
~ **sea wave** seismisch bedingte Flutwelle *f*
~ **shadow zone** seismischer Schatten *m*
~ **shock** Erd[beben]stoß *m*
~ **station** Erdbebenstation *f*
~ **stripping** Stripping *n*, Abdecken *n (seismisches Reduktionsverfahren)*
~ **surveying unit** seismischer Meßtrupp *m*
~ **wave** Erdbebenwelle *f*
~ **wave propagation** Fortpflanzung *f* seismischer Wellen
~ **zone** Schütterzone *f*, Erdbebenzone *f*
seismicity Seismizität *f*
seismics *s.* seismology

seismogram Seismogramm n
seismograph Seismograf m, Erdbebenanzeiger m, Erdbebenschreiber m, Erdbebenmesser m
~ **station** Erdbebenwarte f
seismographic[al] seismisch
~ **prospecting** seismische Erkundung f
seismological seismologisch
~ **science** Erdbebenkunde f
seismologist Seismologe m, Erdbebenforscher m
seismology Seismologie f, Seismik f, Erdbebenkunde f
seismometer Seismometer n, Erdbebenmesser m
~ **spacing** Seismografenabstand m
~ **spread** Seismografenaufstellung f
seismometry Erdbebenmessung f
seismoscope Seismoskop n
seismotectonic seismotektonisch
seismotectonics Seismotektonik f
seladonite Seladonit m (Mineral der Muskovitreihe)
select/to ausklauben, auslesen
selection Klauben n, Klaubarbeit f
~ **of route** Trassierung f, Trassenwahl f
selective diagram Diagramm n eines Kornteilgefüges
~ **evaporation** selektive Verdunstung f
~ **folds** Selektivfalten fpl
~ **fracturing** selektives Fraccen n (zum Schichtaufbrechen)
~ **fusion** selektives Aufschmelzen n
~ **melting** selektives Schmelzen n
~ **replacement** selektive Verdrängung f
~ **weathering** selektive Verwitterung f
seleniferous selenhaltig
selenite Selenit m, Marienglas n, Gips m (s.a. gypsum)
selenium Selen n, Se
selenizone s. slit band
selenocentric selenozentrisch, mondmittelpunktbezogen
selenodesy Mondvermessungskunde f, Selenodäsie f
selenographic selenografisch, mondkundlich
selenography Selenografie f, Mondbeschreibung f
selenolite Selenolith m, SeO$_2$
selenology Selenologie f, Mondkunde f
selenotectonics Mondtektonik f
self-alteration Autometamorphose f
~-**capture** Selbstanzapfung f
~-**faced** glattflächig
~-**faced cleavage plane** glatte Spaltungsebene f
~-**fluxing ore** selbstgehendes Erz n
~-**potential method** Eigenpotentialverfahren n
~-**propelled drilling rig** selbstfahrende Bohranlage f
~-**purification** Selbstreinigung f
~-**recording** selbstregistrierend

~-**recording rain gauge** Schreibregenmesser m
~-**registering** selbstregistrierend
~-**reversal** Selbstumkehrung f (Erdmagnetfeld)
~-**sharpening core bit** selbstschärfende Krone f
~-**sufficiency** Eigenversorgung f (Anteil der Inlandsproduktion an der Bedarfsdeckung)
~-**supply** Selbstversorgung f (mit Wasser)
~-**sustaining** selbsttragend
seligmannite Seligmannit m, 2PbS·Cu$_2$S·As$_2$S$_3$
sellaite Sellait m, MgF$_2$
selliform sattelförmig
selvage 1. Salband n, Lettenbesteg m; 2. Saum m (bei Fossilgehäusen)
semianthracite (Am) Magerkohle f (bis gering inkohlter Anthrazit)
semiaquatic amphibisch
semiarid semiarid
semibog[gy] soil halbsumpfiger Boden m
semiconchoidal halbmuschelig, schwachmuschelig, muschelig bis splitterig
semiconductor counter Halbleiterzähler m
semicrystalline halbkristallinisch
semidesert Halbwüste f, Wüstensteppe f
semidiurnal halbtäglich
semifusinite Semifusinit m (Kohlenmaceral)
semifusite Semifusit m (Kohlenmikrolithotyp)
semilongitudinal fault spießeckige Verwerfung f
semilunar Halbmond...
semiopal Halbopal m
semiopaque matter s. brown matter
semipermeable halbdurchlässig
~ **bed** geringpermeabler Grundwasserleiter m, Geringwasserleiter m
semipodzol Semipodsol m
semipolar halbpolar
semiprecious stone Halbedelstein m
semiprocessed mineral angearbeiteter mineralischer Rohstoff m, mineralisches Halbfertigprodukt n
semisavanna Halbsavanne f
semisteady state quasistationärer Strömungszustand m
semisteep halbsteil
semisubmersible barge Halbtaucher m (schwimmende Bohrplattform)
semiterrestrial semiterrestrisch
semitranslucent matter s. brown matter
semitransverse fault spießeckige Verwerfung f
semitropical subtropisch
semivariogram Semivariogramm n (durch den Wert 2 dividiertes Variogramm)
semivitrinite Semivitrinit m (Kohlenmaceral; stark reflektierender Vitrinit)
semseyite Semseyit m, 9PbS·4Sb$_2$S$_3$
senaite Senait m, (Fe··,Fe···,Mn,Pb)$_2$(Ti, Fe···)$_5$O$_{12}$
senarmontite Senarmontit m, Sb$_2$O$_3$
Senecan [Series] Senecan n (Nordamerika, ent-

spricht dem Adorf einschließlich des höchsten Givets in Europa)
sengierite Sengierit m, $Cu_2[(OH)_2|(UO_2)_2|V_2O_8]\cdot 6H_2O$
senile topography topografische Greisenformen fpl (Topografie am Ende eines Erosionszyklus)
Senonian Senonien n, Senon n im Sinne von D'Orbigny (Oberkreide, Coniac bis Maastricht)
sensator Druckmeßdose f
sense of left-hand screw motion Linksdrehsinn m
~ **of right-hand screw motion** Rechtsdrehsinn m
~ **of rotation** Drehsinn m
sensibility analysis s. sensitivity analysis
sensible heat sensible Wärme f (Wärmeleitung und -konvektion)
sensitive clay strukturempfindlicher Ton m
~ **current-measuring device** sensitiver Strömungsmesser m
~ **element** Meßfühler m
~ **tint** teinte sensible (Rot 1. Ordnung)
sensitivity Empfindlichkeit f
~ **analysis** Sensitivitätsanalyse f, Sensibilitätsanalyse f (bei der Projektbewertung)
sensor calibration Sensoreichung f
separate/to trennen; abscheiden ; aufbereiten
~ **out** sich abscheiden, ausscheiden
separated beaks klaffende Wirbel mpl (bei Fossilschalen)
separating funnel Scheidetrichter m
separation Trennung f; Abscheidung f; Aufbereitung f
~ **fracture** Trennbruch m
~ **of components of stream-flow** s. ~ of flow
~ **of crystals** Kristallabscheidung f
~ **of flow** Abflußseparation f (Trennung A_u/A_o)
~ **plane** Trennungsfläche f
sepiolite Sepiolith m, Meerschaum m, $Mg_4[(OH)_2|Si_6O_{15}]\cdot 2H_2O+4H_2O$
septa Scheidewände fpl, Septen npl (bei Fossilien)
~-**bearing** mit Septen
~-**less** ohne Septen
septal neck Siphonaldüte f (Cephalopoden)
~ **suture** Lobenlinie f
septarian nodule Septarie f
septate/to trennen, spalten (in Septarien)
septentrional nördlich
septic tank Faulbecken n
septicity Fäulnis f
septivalence Siebenwertigkeit f
septivalent siebenwertig
Sequanian Sequanien n (fazielle Entwicklung, oberes Oxford, Schweizer Jura)
sequence Reihenfolge f, Aufeinanderfolge f, Altersfolge f
~ **of bedding** Schichtenfolge f
~ **of crystallization** Kristallisationsfolge f
~ **of formations** Formationsfolge f

~ **of generations** Generationsabfolge f
~ **of strata (stratification)** Schichtenfolge f
sequential erosion nachträgliche Erosion f
~ **forms** Folgeformen fpl (Morphologie)
serac Eisblock m auf zerklüfteten Gletschern, Firnpfeiler m
serandite Serandit m, $(Mn, Ca)_2Na[Si_3O_8OH]$
SERE s. spatial effective resolution element
serendibite Serendibit m, $(Ca, Mg)_5[AlO)_5[BO_3|(SiO_4)_3]$
serial section Serienprofil n
seriate fabric serialkörniges Gefüge n
sericite Serizit m, Kaliglimmer m (s.a. muscovite)
~ **phyllite** Serizitphyllit m
~ **quartzite** Serizitquarzit m
~ **slate** Serizitschiefer m
sericitization Serizitisierung f
sericitize/to serizitisieren
series Serie f (Einheit der biostratigrafischen Skala, im älteren deutschen Schrifttum auch Abteilung)
~ **of blanketing slices** Deckenpaket n, Deckenhäufung f
~ **of mixed crystals** Mischkristallreihe f
~ **of observations** Beobachtungsreihe f
~ **of strata** Schichtkomplex m, Schichtgruppe f, Schichtfolge f, Schichtenreihe f
serir S[s]erir m, Geröllwüste f, Kieswüste f
serozemic soil Grauerde f, Sjerosjom m
serpent kame s. esker
serpentine geschlängelt
serpentine Serpentin m (s.a. 1. antigorite; 2. chrysotile)
~ **asbestos** Serpentinasbest m
~ **marble** s. ophicalcite
~ **rock** s. serpentinite
~ **schist** Serpentinschiefer m
serpentinite Serpentinit m (serpentinisierter Peridotit)
serpentinization Serpentinisierung f
serpentinize/to serpentinisieren
serpierite Serpierit m, $Ca(Cu,Zn)_4[(OH)_3|SO_4]_2\cdot 3H_2O$
serpophite Serpophit m (Varietät von Serpentinit)
Serpuchovian [Stage] Serpuchov-Stufe f (höchstes Unterkarbon, Osteuropa)
serpula reef Serpulariff n
serrate gezackt, zackig, sägeartig
serrated form zackige Form f
Serravalian [Stage] Serravil[ium] n (Stufe des Miozäns)
service contract Dienstleistungsvertrag m (bei Durchführung geologischer Untersuchungsarbeiten)
~ **water** Brauchwasser n, Nutzwasser n, Gebrauchswasser n
~ **well** Hilfsbohrung f
sesquioxide Sesquioxid n
sessile benthos sessiles Benthos n
seston Seston n

shallow

set/to untergehen *(Gestirne)*
~ **casing** verrohren, auskleiden, Rohrfahrt absetzen, Futterrohre setzen
~ **out observation points** vermarken *(eine Strecke)*
~ **up** auslegen, aufstellen
~ **up a map** eine Karte orientieren
set Schrägschichtungseinheit *f*
~ **of joints** Kluftbündel *n*, Hauptkluftschar *f*
~ **of mine** Grubenfeld *n*
~-**up of trend functions** Trendansatz *m (Vorschrift für eine Schar von Trendfunktionen)*
sett Pflasterstein *m*
setting 1. Festwerden *n*; 2. Aufstellung *f (eines Kristalls)*
~ **angle** Verstellwinkel *m*
~ **depth** Einbauteufe *f*
~ **load** Klemmlast *f*, Setzlast *f*
~ **of conductor** Standrohrsetzen *n*
~-**up** Aufbau *m (eines Magnetfelds)*
settle/to 1. [nach]sacken, sich setzen; 2. ablagern; sedimentieren; 3. absenken; 4. absinken
~ **down[ward]** absinken
settled production stabilisierte Produktion *f*
~ **production rate** gleichmäßige Produktionsrate *f*
settlement Setzung *f*
~ **analysis** Setzungsanalyse *f*, Schlämmanalyse *f*
~ **basin** Ablagerungsbecken *n*
~ **measurement** Setzungsmessung *f*
settling 1. Sackung *f*, Nachsacken *n*, Sichsetzen *n*; 2. Ablagerung *f*; 3. Absenken *n*; 4. Absinken *n*
~ **analysis** Setzungsanalyse *f*, Schlämmanalyse *f*
~ **basin** Klärbecken *n*
~ **pond** Absetzteich *m*, Klärbecken *n*
~ **slurry** absetzbare Trübe *f*
~ **speed** 1. Absenkungsgeschwindigkeit *f (Bodenmechanik)*; 2. Absetzgeschwindigkeit *f*, Sinkgeschwindigkeit *f*
~ **tank** Klärbecken *n*
~ **velocity** s. ~ speed
~ **well** Klärbrunnen *m*
sevardy soil Rasenboden *m*
Sevatian [Substage] Sevat[ium] *n (Unterstufe, Obere Trias, Tethys)*
seven-spot network *(Am)* Sieben-Sonden-Anordnung *f*
sewage Abwasser *n*, Abwässer *npl*
~ **engineering** Abwasserwesen *n*, Kanalisationstechnik *f*
~ **gas** Faulgas *n*
~ **water** Rieselwasser *n*, Abwasser *n*
sewer/to entwässern
sewerage Entwässerung *f*
~ **and sewage disposal** Abwasserwesen *n*, Kanalisationstechnik *f*
~ **system** Entwässerungsverfahren *n*
sexivalence Sechswertigkeit *f*

sexivalent sechswertig
sexual dimorphism Sexualdimorphismus *m*, Geschlechtsdimorphismus *m*
seybertite Seybertit *m (s.a. clintonite)*
shab bröckliges schieferiges Gestein *n*
shackanite Shackanit *m (Analcimtrachyt)*
shade/to beschatten
shading Schummerung *f*
shadow cone Schattenkegel *m*
shaft Schacht *m*
~ **boring** Schachtbohren *n*
~ **bottom** Schachtsohle *f*
~ **cross section** Schachtscheibe *f*
~ **drilling** Schachtbohren *n*
~ **head** Schachtausgang *m*
~ **landing** Füllort *n (Erdöl)*
~ **mouth** Schachtmundloch *n*; Rasenbank *f*
~ **prospect** Schürfschacht *m*
~ **safety pillar** Schachtsicherheitspfeiler *m*
~ **tower** Förderturm *m*
shafting Schachtabteufen *n*
shagreen/to chagrinieren
shagreen Chagrin *n*
shake 1. Erdbeben *n*; 2. senkrechter Riß *m*; Dichtklüftungszone *f*; 3. Höhle *f*
~ **table** Schütteltisch *m (Testgerät für Geophone)*
~ **wave** s. shear wave 1.
shaker Schüttelsieb *n*, Rüttelsieb *n*
~ **table** Schwingtisch *m*, Schütteltisch *m*
shakes engständige oberflächennahe Bankungsklüftung *f (in Steinbrüchen)*
shaking Beben *n*, Erschütterung *f*
~ **table** Schwingtisch *m*, Schütteltisch *m*
~ **test** Schüttelprobe *f*
shale Schiefer[ton] *m*, Tonschiefer *m (70–80% Tonminerale, der Rest Silt)*
~ **band** Schiefermittel *n*
~ **break** Schiefertoneinlage *f*, Schiefertonzwischenlage *f*
~ **crescent** Schiefertonschmitze *f*
~ **distillation** Schieferölgewinnung *f*
~ **naphtha** Benzin *n* aus Ölschiefer
~ **oil** Schieferöl *n*
~ **oil factory** Ölschieferwerk *n*
~ **oil industry** Ölschieferindustrie *f*
~-**out** Vertonung *f*
~ **partings** sehr dünne Schiefertoneinlagen *fpl (in Sandsteinen)*
~ **rock** schiefriges Gestein *n*
~ **shaker** Schlammschüttelsieb *n*, Schüttelsieb *n*
~ **tar** Schieferteer *m*
shaley schiefrig *(s.a. shaly)*
shalification Vertonung *f (durch Karbonatauslösung)*
shallow flach, seicht, untief
shallow Untiefe *f*, Furt *f*
~ **boring** flache Bohrung *f*
~-**burial stage** Stadium *n* mit geringmächtiger Sedimentbedeckung
~ **depth** geringe Tiefe *f*

shallow 316

~ **drilling** Flachbohren n (bis 500 m)
~ **foundation** Flachgründung f
~ **hole** Flachbohrung f
~ **karst** Halbkarst m
~ **lake** Seichtwassersee m
~ **moor** Flachmoor n
~ **refraction** flache Refraktion f
~ **sea** Flachsee f
~-**sea deposit** Flachseeablagerung f
~ **water** 1. Flachwasser n, Seichtwasser n; 2. Wattenmeer n
~-**water deposit** Flachseeablagerung f
~-**water facies** Flachwasserfazies f
~-**water surveys** Flachwasservermessung f
~ **well** Flachbohrung f
shallower pool test Erweiterungsbohrung f auf neuem Horizont
shallowing Seichtwerden n (des Ozeans)
shaly argillitisch
~-**bedded** lamellenförmig geschichtet (2 bis 10 mm Lamellendicke)
~ **clay** Schieferton m
~ **clay with coal** kohlehaltiger Schieferton m
~ **coal** tonige (tonig-schiefrige) Kohle f
~ **limestone** Schieferkalk m
~ **marl** Tonmergel m
~ **sand** toniger Sand m
~ **sandstone** Schiefersandstein m
shandite Shandit m, β-$Ni_3Pb_2S_2$
shank s. limb
shap granite porphyrischer Granit mit großen verzwillingten fleischfarbenen Feldspäten
shape factor Formfaktor m (eines Reservoirs)
~ **of particle** Kornform f
~ **of the earth** Erdgestalt f
~ **section** Profil n
shard Vulkanglasscherbe f
~ **cobalt** Scherbenkobalt m (Varietät von Arsen)
shark tooth Haifischzahn m
sharp scharfkantig
~ **crest** Grat m
~ **dip** steiles Einfallen n
~-**edged** scharfkantig
~ **sand** scharfkörniger Sand m
~-**topped crest** Grat m
sharpite Sharpit m, [$UO_2|CO_3$]·H_2O
sharply focussing scharfeinstellend
~ **incised valley** tiefeingeschnittenes Tal n
~ **upturned** steil aufgerichtet
sharpstone Sedimentit m aus eckigen Körnern (<2 mm)
shastaite Shastait m (Dazit)
shastalite Shastalit m (frisches Andesitglas)
shatter/to sich zersplittern (Erzgang)
shatter belt Trümmerzone f
~ **breccia** Reibungsbrekzie f, Dislokationsbrekzie f
~ **clay** zermürbter Ton m
~ **rock** brüchiges Gestein n
~ **zone** Trümmerzone f, Zerrüttungszone f, Mylonitzone f

shattering Zerbröckeln n
shattuckite Shattuckit m (Mineral der Dioptasgruppe)
sheaflike garbenförmig
shear/to abscheren
shear Abscherung f, Scherung f, Schub m
~ **cleavage** s. slip cleavage
~ **drag** Reibungskraft f (von Flüssigkeiten in Bewegung am festen Medium)
~ **fold** Scherfalte f
~ **folding** Scherfaltung f
~ **fracture** s. sliding fracture
~ **joint** Scherkluft f
~ **load** Scherbelastung f
~ **modulus** Schubmodul m, Schermodul m, Lamèsche Konstante f
~ **plane** Scherebene f, Scherfläche f
~ **resistance** Scherfestigkeit f, Scherwiderstand m (eines Gesteinsverbands)
~ **slice** Gleitbrett n (Tektonik)
~ **slide** kleiner Erdrutsch m, Rutschung f
~ **strain** Scherdehnung f
~ **strength** Scherfestigkeit f
~ **stress** Scherbeanspruchung f, Scherspannung f, Schubspannung f
~ **structure** Abscherungstextur f
~ **thrust** Abscherungsüberschiebung f
~ **thrust sheet** Abscherungsdecke f
~ **wave** s. shearing wave
~ **zone** Gangzug m, Staffelbruch m, Scherzone f
~-**zone deposit** Lagerstätte f in einer Scherzone
shearing Abscherung f, Scherung f
~ **displacement** scherende Bewegung f
~ **nappe** Abscherungsdecke f
~-**off thrust** Abscherungsüberschiebung f
~ **resistance** Abscherfestigkeit f
~ **test** Scherversuch m
~-**thrust sheet** Überschiebungsdecke f (tektonisch)
~ **wave** Scherwelle f, Transversalwelle f, S-Welle f
shed coal Kohlenzwischenlage f
shedding Abwerfen n, Abtrennen n
sheen Glanz m (Mineral)
sheep tracks Schafstiegen fpl
sheepback s. roche moutonnée
sheet Lage f, Schicht f (dünn); Absonderungsfläche f
~ **erosion** Schichtfluterosion f, Flächenerosion f
~ **flood** Schichtflut f, flächenhafte Abspülung f
~ **flow** laminares Fließen n, Schichtenströmung f
~ **jointing** bankige Absonderung f
~ **of basalt** Basaltdecke f
~ **of creeping waste** kriechende Schuttdecke f, Wanderschuttdecke f
~ **of drift** (Am) Gleitschicht f
~ **of flint** Feuersteinband n
~ **of ice** Eisscholle f

~ **quarry** Steinbruch *m* mit [vorwiegend] horizontaler Klüftung
~ **sands** *(Am)* Deckensandstein *m*
~ **silicate** Schichtsilikat *n*, Phyllosilikat *n*
~ **structure** 1. bankige Absonderung *f*; 2. Dekkenfaltung *f*
sheeted geschichtet
~ **zone** Gangzug *m*
sheeting 1. Schichtung *f*; 2. Überzug *m*; 3. Abschalung *f*
~ **plane** Schichtfläche *f*
sheetlike plattenartig
sheetwash [flow] Schichtflut *f*
Sheinwoodian [Stage] Sheinwoodium *n (obere Stufe des Wenlock)*
shelf 1. Schelf *m*; 2. Riff *n*, Sandbank *f*; 3. festes Gestein (Gebirge) *n*, Abraum *m (Cornwall)*
~ **break** Schelfabbruch *m (zum Kontinentalabhang)*
~ **channels** Schelfrinnen *fpl*
~ **coast** Schelfküste *f*
~ **deposit** Schelfablagerung *f*
~ **edge** Kontinentalrand *m*
~ **embayment** Schelfbucht *f*
~ **formation** Schelfbildung *f*
~ **ice** Schelfeis *n*
~ **margin** Schelfrand *m*
~ **of a rock** Felsplatte *f*
~ **sea** Schelfmeer *n*
shell 1. Schale *f*, Gehäuse *n*; 2. Muschel *f*
~ **auger** Schappe *f*, Schappenbohrer *m*, Bohrschappe *f*
~ **bank** Schillbank *f*, Muschelbank *f*
~ **breccia** Muschelbrekzie *f*
~ **fragment** Schalenfragment *n*
~-**like** muschelig
~-**like fracture** muscheliger Bruch *m*
~ **limestone** Muschelkalk *m*
~ **marl** Muschelmergel *m*
~ **sandstone** Muschelsandstein *m*
shellfish Schalentier *n*
shelly schalig, muschelig
~ **limestone** Muschelkalk *m*
~ **sand** Muschelsand *m*
~ **sandstone** Muschelsandstein *m*
shelter cave Nischenhöhle *f*
shelterbelt Windschutzstreifen *m*
shelving schräg, abfallend
shelving Abhang *m*
~ **bottom** abfallender Boden *m*
~ **coast** Steilküste *f*
~ **dune** Steildüne *f*
~ **shore** abfallendes Ufer *n*
shelvingness Böschung *f*, Abdachung *f*
Shermanian *s.* Trentonian
sherwoodite Sheerwoodit *m*, $Ca_3[V_8O_{22}] \cdot 15H_2O$
shield Schild *m m (großtektonische Strukturform)*
~ **basalt** Schildbasalt *m*, Flächenbasalt *m (von zahlreichen kleinen Schloten gefördert)*
~-**shaped** schildförmig
~ **volcano** Schildvulkan *m*

shielded deposition verdeckte Ablagerung *f*
shift 1. Verschiebung *f*, Verwerfung *f*, Sprungweite *f*; 2. Schichtbesetzung *f*
~-**day** Schichttag *m*
~ **fault** Seitenverschiebung *f*, Horizontalverschiebung *f*
~-**hour** Schichtstunde *f*
~ **in the earth's axis** absolute Polverschiebung *f*
~ **in the shore line** Strandverschiebung *f*
~ **of level** Niveauänderung *f*
~ **of river course** Flußverlegung *f*
~ **of the fault** Sprungweite *f*
shifting Verwerfung *f*
~ **beach** Treibsandgrund *m*
~ **bed** bewegliche Flußsohle *f*
~ **dune** Wanderdüne *f*
~ **of divides** Verschiebung *f* der Wasserscheiden
~ **of river** Flußverlegung *f*
~ **of the volcanic vent** Schlotverlagerung *f*
~ **rock** schwimmendes Gebirge *n*
~ **sand** Schwimmsand *m*, Treibsand *m*, Triebsand *m*, Fließsand *m*
shifts Schwankungen *fpl*, Oszillationen *fpl*
shindle Dachschiefer *m*
shingle 1. Steingeröll *n*, Geschiebe *n*; Kieselgeröll *n*, grober Kies (Meereskies) *m*; 2. Schuppe *f (tektonisch)*
~ **beach** Kieselstrand *m*
~-**block structure** Schwartenbildung *f*, Serie *f* flacher Überschiebungen
~ **rampart** Geschiebewall *m*
shingling *s.* imbricate structure
shining glänzend
~ **lustre** Hochglanz *m*
shiny glänzend
shipboard gravity meter Seegravimeter *n*
shipping ore verhüttungsfähiges (versandfertiges) Erz *n*, Reicherz *n*
shist *s.* schist
shiver Dachschiefer *m*, Tafelschiefer *m*
shoad Bruchstück *n* vom Ausbiß eines Ganges; Seifenzinn *n*
shoading Oberflächenerkundung *f (auf Zinn)*
shoal Untiefe *f*, Bank *f*, Riff *n*, Furt *f*, Sandbank *f*
~ **of meteors** Meteorschwarm *m*
~ **water deposit** Flachseeablagerung *f*
shoaliness Untiefe *f*
shoaling Versanden *n*
shoaly seicht
shock Stoß *m*
~-**altered rock** Gestein *n* mit Schockwellenmetamorphose
~ **bump** *s.* rock burst
~ **lithification** Verfestigung *f* durch Impaktmetamorphose *(z.B. von Mondstaub zu Mikrobrekzie)*
~ **magnitude** Stoßstärke *f (Seismik)*
~-**melted** durch Schockmetamorphose geschmolzen

shock

- ~ **metamorphism** Impaktmetamorphose f, Schockmetamorphose f
- ~ **wave** Stoßwelle f, Schockwelle f
- **shodar/to** schürfen
- **shode** s. shoad
- **shoding** s. shoading
- **shoestring gully erosion** Rinnenerosion f
- ~ **sand** Sandwalze f, schmale, langgestreckte Sandlinse f, fossiler Strandwall m
- ~ **trap** Shoestring-Falle f
- **shoestrings** Linsenlagerstätte f (Lagerstätte im Bereich fossiler Flußläufe)
- **shonkinite** Shonkinit m (Nephelinsyenit)
- **shoot/to** sprengen, torpedieren
- ~ **locations** Orte einpeilen
- **shoot** Apophyse f, Schießen n (Seismik)
- ~ **of ore** Erzschuß m (steiler Erzfall in einem Gang)
- ~ **of variation** reicher Erzfall m
- **shooting** 1. Schießen n, Sprengen n; 2. Torpedieren n, Aufschießen n (von Horizonten)
- ~ **flow cast** gescharte große Fließmarke f
- ~ **ground** festes Gebirge n, Schußgebirge n
- ~ **of wells** Torpedieren n, Sprengung f im Bohrloch
- ~ **star** Meteor m, Sternschnuppe f
- **shore** Strand m, Ufer n, Küste f, Gestade n (s.a. beach)
- ~ **cliff** Küstenkliff n
- ~ **deposit** Küstenablagerung f, Strandablagerung f
- ~ **development** Uferentwicklung f
- ~ **drift[ing]** Küstenströmung f, Litoralströmung f, Küstenversetzung f, Strandverdriftung f, Wandergeschiebe n
- ~ **dune** Stranddüne f
- ~ **face** Strandstufe f in der Brecherzone
- ~ **face terrace** litorale Aufschüttungsterrasse f
- ~ **gravel** Strandkies m, Strandschotter m
- ~ **ice** Küsteneis n
- ~ **jetty** (Am) Seebuhne f, Strandbuhne f
- ~-**laid sediments** Küstenablagerungen fpl
- ~ **line** Küstenlinie f, Strandlinie f
- ~-**line cycle** mariner (litoraler) Zyklus m
- ~ **line of depression** Senkungsküste f
- ~ **line of elevation** Hebungsküste f
- ~ **line of emergence** aufgetauchte Küste f, Auftauchküste f, Hebungsküste f
- ~ **line of progradation** Anwachsküste f, Anschwemmungsküste f
- ~ **line of retrogradation** Abrasionsküste f
- ~ **line of submergence** untergetauchte Küste f, Untertauchküste f, Senkungsküste f
- ~ **moorland** Marsch f
- ~ **platform** Brandungsterrasse f, Brandungsplatte f, Schorre f
- ~ **pond** Strandsee m
- ~ **profile** Küstenprofil n
- ~ **protection** Küstenschutz m, Küstensicherung f
- ~ **reef** Küstenriff n
- ~ **sediment** Küstensediment n
- ~ **terrace** Strandterrasse f, Küstenterrasse f
- **Shore hardness** Shore-Härte f
- **short-columnar** kurzsäulig
- ~-**path multiple** Kurzwegmultiple f
- ~-**period perturbations** kurzperiodische Störungen fpl
- ~-**range forecast** kurzfristige Vorhersage f
- ~ **shot** Langsamschichtschuß m (Seismik)
- ~ **ton** Kurztonne f (907,185 kg, Einheit der Masse in den USA)
- **shortage of water** Wasserarmut f
- **shortening** Zusammenschub m, Verkürzung f
- **shortest distance between the traces** flache Sprungweite f
- **shortite** Shortit m, $Na_2Ca_2[CO_3]_3$
- **shortwall working** Stoßbau m
- **shoshonite** Shoshonit m (Alkalibasalt)
- **shot** seismische Sprengung f, Schuß m (Seismik)
- ~ **bit** Schrotkrone f
- ~ **boring** Schrotbohren n
- ~ **break** Schußmoment m, Abriß m (Zeitpunkt der Explosion der Sprengstoffladung)
- ~ **copper** in kleinen Stückchen vorkommendes gediegenes Kupfer n
- ~ **delay time** Laufzeitdifferenz f am Schußpunkt (Seismik)
- ~ **depth** Schußtiefe f
- ~ **drilling** Schrotbohren n
- ~ **firing** Sprengarbeit f
- ~ **hole** 1. Sprengloch n, Schuß[bohr]loch n (Seismik); 2. torpedierte Sonde f
- ~-**hole noise** Bohrlochstörungen fpl (Seismik)
- ~ **point** Schußpunkt m
- ~-**point distance** Schußpunktabstand m
- ~-**point gap** Aufstellungslücke f am Sprengpunkt
- ~ **soil** Bohnerzboden m
- **shotcrete** Spritzbeton m, Torkretbeton m
- **shott** Schott m, versalzenes Becken n
- **shotty gold** kleinkörniges Gold n
- **shoulder** Schulter f, Vorsprung m
- **shove** horizontale (söhlige) Schublänge f
- ~-**moraine** s. push moraine
- **shovel dredger** Löffelbagger m
- ~ **sampling** Schaufelprobenahme f
- **shoving** Schub m
- **show steep dips/to** steil einfallen
- **shower** Wolkenbruch m, Platzregen m, Regenschauer m
- ~ **of ash** Aschenregen m
- ~ **of meteorites** Meteorfall m
- **showings** Spuren fpl, Anzeichen npl
- **shredded** bröckelig
- ~ **structure** bröckeliges Gefüge n
- **shrink/to** einschrumpfen
- **shrinkage** Schumpfung f
- ~ **crack** Schrumpfungsriß m
- ~ **factor** Schrumpfungsfaktor m (Erdöl)
- ~ **pore** Schrumpfpore f
- ~ **stoping** Firstenstoßbau m
- ~ **theory** Kontraktionstheorie f, Schrumpfungstheorie f

shrinking Schumpfung f
shrub Strauch m, Busch m
~-coppice dune angeblasener Sedimentwall m (hinter Buschwerk oder Erdhaufen)
~ desert Strauchwüste f
~ steppe Buschsteppe f
shruberry Buschwerk n
shungite Schungit m (sporenhaltiger aschereicher Anthrazit, Onegasee)
shut down temporarily/to vorübergehend einstellen, vorläufig stillegen
~ in a well eine Sonde schließen
shut-down time Stillstandszeit f
~-in bottom-hole pressure Sohlenschließdruck m
~-in pressure Schließdruck m
~-in time of a well Schließdauer f einer Bohrung
~-in well geschlossene Bohrung f, eingeschlossene Sonde f, [ab]geschlossene Sonde f
shutting ground festes Gebirge n
~-in of a well Schließen n einer Bohrung
shuttles senkrecht zum Einfallen gerichtete Risse mpl
si-fabric Intergefüge n
sial Sial n
sialic sialisch
siallitic siallitisch
~ terra rossa Kalkrotlehm m
Siberian platform Sibirische Tafel f
SIBHP s. shut-in bottom-hole pressure
sibirskite Sibirskit m, $Ca_2[B_2O_5] \cdot H_2O$
sibling species Zwillingsarten fpl
sickle-shaped, sicklelike sichelförmig
sicklerite Sicklerit m, $Li_{<1}(Mn,Fe)[PO_4]$
sickness of soil Bodenerschöpfung f
sicula Sicula f (bei Graptolithen)
side-track/to vorbeibohren; ablenken, umgehen (eine Bohrung)
side branch Abzweigung f
~ canal Abflußkanal m
~ canyon Nebencañon m
~ dome s. brachydome
~ elevation Kreuzriß m, Querprofil n
~ entry Abbaustrecke f parallel zu den Schlechten
~-force coefficient Querkraftbeiwert m
~ lap s. overlap
~-leaved nebenblattständig
~ lobes Nebenbereich m
~-looking radar Seitensichtradar n
~ recovery Rohstoffgewinnung f aus geologischen Untersuchungsarbeiten
~ shot Nebenschuß m, Eweiterungsschuß m
~ slope Seitenböschung f
~ stream Nebenfluß m
~ tracking Ablenkung f (einer Bohrung)
~ valley Nebental n
~-veined seitennervig
~ wall core Kern m aus der Bohrlochwand, Seitenkern m
~ wall coring Kernen n aus der Bohrlochwand, seitliche Kernentnahme f
~ wall of a vein Salband n
~ wall sample Probe f aus der Bohrlochwand
sidehill (Am) s. hillside
sidereal siderisch, Stern...
~ day Sterntag m
~ hour Sternstunde f
~ month siderischer Monat m
~ period Umlaufzeit f der Gestirne, siderische Umlaufzeit f
~ system Sternsystem n
~ time Sternzeit f, siderische Zeit f
~ universe Weltall n
~ year Sternjahr n, siderisches Jahr n
siderite 1. Siderit m, Spateisenstein m, Eisenspat m, Sphärosiderit m, $FeCO_3$; 2. Eisenmeteorit m, Meteorstein m; 3. indigoblaue Varietät von Quarz
~ nodule Toneisensteingalle f
~ rock massiger Siderit m
sideritic sideritisch
~ shale Tonschiefer m mit Toneisenstein
siderolite Siderolith m, eisenhaltiger Meteorstein m
sideromelane Sideromelan m (Basaltglas)
sideronatrite Sideronatrit m, $Na_2Fe[OH|(SO_4)_2] \cdot 3H_2O$
siderophile siderophil
siderophyre Siderophyr m (Meteorit)
siderotil Siderotil m, $Fe[SO] \cdot 5H_2O$
sideslip/to seitlich abrutschen
sideslip Seitenabrutsch m
sief Longitudinaldüne f
Siegenian [Stage] Siegen[ien] n, Siegenium n (Stufe des Unterdevons)
siegenite Siegenit m, $(Co, Ni)_3S_4$
Siena [earth] Sienaerde f (Farberde)
sierra Gebirgskette f
sieve analysis Siebanalyse f
~ residue Siebrückstand m
~ texture Siebstruktur f
sift/to absieben, aussieben
~ out aussieben
sifting Sortierung f
siftings Siebfeines n, Abgesiebtes n
sight Sicht f, Blick m (Peilung, Winkel oder festgelegter Meßpunkt)
Sigillaria Sigillarie f
sigloite Sigloit m, $FeAl_2[O|PO_4]_2 \cdot 8H_2O$
sigmoidal fold Sigmoide f, Sigmoidalfalte f
signal correction Signalkorrektur f
~ enhancement Signalverbesserung f (z.B. durch Stapelung)
~-to-noise ratio Signal-Rausch-Verhältnis n; Nutz-Stör-Verhältnis n
signature Signatur f
~ analysis Merkmalanalyse f (z.B. spektrale in der Fernerkundung)
sil gelbe Ockererde f
silcrete Kieselkonglomerat n (Horizont kieseligen Materials, gewöhnlich gebildet durch Silifizierung eines Sediments in warm-ariden und -semiariden Gebieten)

silcrust

silcrust Kieselkruste f
Silesian [Epoch, Series] s. Upper Carboniferous
silex Silex n *(natürliches, feinkristallines Kieselgestein)*
silica Siliziumdioxid n, SiO_2
~ **brick** Quarzkalkziegel m, Silikastein m *(Steine und Erden)*
~ **gel (jelly)** Kieselgel n, Kieselgallerte f
~ **skeleton** Kieselskelett n
silicate Silikat n
~ **cotton** s. mineral wool
~ **of aluminium** Alumosilikat n
~ **of zinc** s. calamine
~ **rock** Silikatgestein n
silicating Verkieseln n, Silifizieren n
silication Verkieselung f, Silifikation f
silicatization s. silicification
siliceous kieselig, silifiziert, siliziumhaltig
~ **concretion** Kieselkonkretion f
~ **deposit** kieselhaltige Ablagerung f
~ **earth** Kieselerde f
~ **residual solution** kieselsäurereiche Restlösung f
~ **residue** silikatischer Rückstand m *(unlöslich)*
~ **schist (shale)** Kieselschiefer m
~-**shelled** kieselschalig
~ **sinter** Kieselsinter m
~ **skeleton** Kieselskelett n
~ **sponge** Kieselschwamm m
silicic kieselsäurereich, SiO_2-reich
~ **acid** Kieselsäure f
siliciclastics Silikaklastika npl
silicification Verkieselung f, Silifizierung f, Silifikation f
silicified verkieselt, silifiziert
~ **forest** versteinerter Wald m
~ **wood** verkieseltes Holz n
silicify/to verkieseln, silifizieren
silicifying *(Am)* Verkieseln n, Silifizieren n
silicinate mit SiO_2 zementiert
silicious s. siliceous
silicium Silizium n, Si
silicomagnesiofluorite Silicomagnesiofluorit m, $H_2Ca_4Mg_3Si_2O_7F_{10}$
silicon Silizium n, Si
silicosis Silikose f
silcrete Krustenbildung auf oder nahe der Oberfläche durch Kieselsäurezementation
silky lustre Seidenglanz m
sill 1. Lagergang m, Massiv n, Stock m, Sill m; 2. Schwelle f
~ **of ore** Erzlager n
~ **of variogram** Maximalwert m des Variogramms, Varianz f unkorrelierter Zuwächse
sillar nicht verschweißte Bimssteinablagerung f
silled basin untermeerisch abgeschnürtes Becken n
sillénite Sillénit m, γ-Bi_2O_3
sillimanite Sillimanit m, Faserkiesel m, Al_2SiO_5
silt [up]/to verschlammen, verlanden

silt 1. Schlamm m, Schlick m; Schluff m, Silt m; 2. Treibsand m; 3. Bohrschmant m; 4. Boden mit mehr als 80% Silt
~-**bearing** schluffhaltig
~ **charge** Schwebstoffbelastung f
~-**covered** schlammbedeckt
~ **fraction** Schluffkorn n
~ **loam** schluffiger Lehm m
~ **loam to silt** leichter Lehm m
~ **of precipitates** Senkstoffablagerung f
~ **pan** harte Schlammschicht f
~ **plain** Schlickebene f
~ **rock** Schluffstein m
~ **sampler** Schwebstoffschöpfer m
~ **sluicing** Schluffauswaschung f
~ **soil** Schlammboden m
siltation Verschlammung f
silted verschlammt
~ **estuary** verschlammtes Mündungsbecken n
~ **river** verschlammter Fluß m
~-**up** aufgeschlickt, verschlammt
silting Anschwemmung f, Verschlammung f, Aufschlickung f, Sedimentierung f, Auflandung f
~ **deposit** Schlammablagerung f
~-**up** Auflandung f, Kolmation f, Aufschwemmung f, Anschwemmung f, Kolmatierung f, Verlandung f, Verschlickung f
siltite s. siltstone
siltstone verfestigter Schluffmergel m; Siltstein m, Schluffstein m
silttil eluvialer Geschiebemergel m
silty schluffartig, schluffhaltig, schlammig
~ **bog** schwarzer Sumpfboden m
~ **clay** schluffiger Ton m
~ **clay loam** schluffig-toniger Lehm m
~ **fine sandstone** schluffiger Feinsandstein m
~ **loam** Schlufflehm m
~ **mud** schluffiger Schlick m
~ **sand** Schlicksand m
~ **slate** schluffiger Tonschiefer m
~ **soil** Staubboden m, Schluffboden m
Silurian Silur[system] n *(chronostratigrafisch)*; Silur n, Silurperiode f *(geochronologisch)*; Silur n, Silurzeit f *(allgemein)*
~ **Age** Silur n, Silurzeit f
~ **Period** Silur n, Silurperiode f
~ **System** Silur[system] n
silver Silber n, Ag
~-**bearing** silberführend, silberhaltig
~ **deposit** Silbererzlagerstätte f
~ **fahlerz** s. tetrahedrite
~ **glance** s. argentite
~ **litharge** Silberglätte f
~ **ore** Silbererz n
~ **sand** weißer Feinsand m
silvery silberartig, silberglänzend, silberfarben, silbern
~ **lustre** Silberglanz m
silvestrite Silvestrit m *(tellurisches Eisennitrid)*
sima Sima n
similar faces gleichwertige Flächen fpl *(von Kristallen)*

~ fold Parallelfalte f *(ohne Mächtigkeitsveränderung in den Schenkeln)*
similigley Pseudogley m
simonellite Simonellit m, $C_{15}H_{20}$
simoom, simoon Sandsturm m
simple cross stratification einfache Schrägschichtung f
~ geosyncline Monogeosynklinale f
~ multiple einfache Multiple f
~ reflection einfache Reflexion f
~ shear einfache (reine) Scherung f
~ split seam in zwei Lager aufgespaltenes Flöz n
simplification (simplified) coast Ausgleichsküste f
simplotite Simplotit m, $CaV_4O_9 \cdot 5H_2O$
simpsonite Simpsonit m, $Ta_3Al_4(O_{13}OH)$
simulation analysis of ground-water flow Modellierung f der Grundwasserdynamik
~ of reservoir Lagerstättenmodellierung f, Speichermodellierung f
simultaneity Gleichzeitigkeit f
simultaneous gleichzeitig, kontemporär
~ cross folding kontemporäre Querfaltung f
~ crystallization gleichzeitige Ausscheidung f
~ drilling Simultanbohren n *(Mehrlochbohren)*
~ events gleichzeitige Ereignisse npl
sinc x Spaltfunktion f *(Fourier-Transformation einer Rechteckwelle)*
sincosite Sincosit m, $Ca[V(OH)_2|PO_4]_2 \cdot 3H_2O$
Sinemurian [Stage] Sinemur[ien] n, Sinemurium n, Lotharingium n *(Stufe des Unteren Juras)*
singing Resonanz f *(Seismogramm)*; Singing n *(Kurzwegmultiple in einer Wasserschicht)*
~ sand tönender Sand m
single-celled animal Einzeller m
~-core barrel Einfachkernrohr n
~ crystal Einkristall n
~-ended spread Stichprofil n *(Seismik)*
~-grain soil strukturloser Boden m
~-grain structure Einzelkornstruktur f *(des Bodens)*
~-group slip [laminares] Gesteinsfließen n
~-lens multiband camera einlinsige Mehrkanalkamera f
~-phase flow Einphasenströmung f
~-point mooring system Einpunktverankerungssystem n *(Boje zur Übergabe von Erdöl/Erdgas an den Tanker)*
~-prism spectrograph Einprismaspektrograf m
~-row shooting Einreihensprengen n
~-shot photoclinometer Single-shot-Gerät n *(Neigungsmeßgerät)*
~ water layer fest gebundenes Porenwasser n *(im Tonmineral)*
~ well Einzelsonde f
singly refractive einfachbrechend
sinhalite Sinhalit m, $MgAl[BO_4]$
Sinian Sinium n *(Jungpräkambrium Chinas)*
sink a well/to eine Bohrung abteufen
~ down absinken
~ shafts Schächte abteufen

sink 1. Schlotte f; 2. Kessel m, Erdfall m, Bodensenke f; 3. Pinge f
~ and float Schwimm- und Sinkaufbereitung f
~ lake Dolinensee m
sinker bar Schwerstange f
sinkhole 1. Doline f, Karsttrichter m, Karstschlot m; Einsturztrichter m, Erdfall m; Flußschwinde f; 2. Saugbrunnen m
~ lake Dolinensee m
sinking Einsturz m
~ area absinkendes Gebiet n
~ coast Senkungsküste f
~ creek steilwandiges Tal n, Cañon m
~ of the borehole Niederbringen n des Bohrlochs
~ of the coast Küstensenkung f
~ of the ground-water level Grundwasserabsenkung f
~ trough Durchteufung f
~ velocity Sinkgeschwindigkeit f
~ work Abteufarbeiten fpl
sinoite Sinoit m, Si_2N_2O *(Meteoritenmineral)*
sinoper s. sinople
sinopite roter Ton m *(aus Anatolien)*
sinople eisenhaltiger Ton m; Eisenkiesel m
sinter Sinter m
~ deposit Sinterablagerung f
~ formation Sinterbildung f
~ incrustation Sinterkruste f
~ terrace Sinterterrasse f
sintered expanded clay Sinterblähton m
sintering Sinterung f
sinuate wellig, gewunden
sinuosity Krümmung f, Windung f
sinuous gewunden
~ flow turbulente Strömung f
sinus Sinus m *(Bucht auf Mars oder Mond)*
sinusoidal fold Sinusfalte f
siphon spring Siphonquelle f
siphonal deposits Siphonalausscheidungen fpl *(Cephalopoden)*
~ duct Ausguß m *(bei Fossilgehäusen)*
siphoneous algae Schlauchalgen fpl
siphuncle Sipho m
sirens Seekühe fpl
sirocco Sc[h]irokko m, Sirokko m
sister group Schwestergruppe f
sitaparite Sitaparit m, Bixbyit m, $(Mn, Fe)_2O_3$
site Baustelle f
~ exploration Bodenuntersuchung f, Untergrundforschung f, Baugrunduntersuchung f
~ of a well Bohr[ansatz]punkt m
~ of deposition Ablagerungsstelle f
~ of works Baustelle f
~ plan Lageplan m, Situationsplan m
~ sketch Situationsskizze f
~ soil anstehender Boden m
situated above darüber befindlich, im Hangenden von
~ below darunter befindlich, im Liegenden von
sixfold sechszählig *(Symmetrieachse)*

size

size/to 1. bereißen, beräumen; 2. klassieren
size analysis Korngrößenanalyse f
~ **analysis by sedimentation** Sedimentationsanalyse f
~ **category** Kornklasse f, Kornfraktion f
~ **category fraction** Kornklassenfraktion f
~ **degradation** Krümelzerbröckelung f
~ **distribution** Körnungsaufbau m, Korngrößenverteilung f
~ **distribution curve** Körnungskennlinie f
~ **distribution fraction** Kornklassenfraktion f
~ **fraction** s. ~ category
~ **grade** Korngrößenklasse f
~ **of coal** Kohlengröße f, Kohlensorte f
~ **of grain (granulation)** Körnung f, Korngröße f
~ **range** Körnungsbereich m, Korngrößenbereich m, Kornspanne f
~ **range index** Korngrößenindex m
sizing Klassierung f nach der Korngröße
~ **plant** Klassieranlage f
sjögrenite Sjögrenit m, $Mg_6Fe_2[(OH)_{16}CO_3] \cdot 4H_2O$
skarn Skarn m
skayler Erosionsrücken *(auf einer Schneefläche senkrecht zur Windrichtung)*
skeletal skelettförmig; bioklastisch; organogendetritisch mit Skelettresten
~ **debris** Skelettfragmente npl
~ **elements** Skelettelemente npl
~ **mineral forms** gestrickte Mineralformen fpl
~ **remains** Skelettreste mpl
~ **soil** Skelettboden m, Gesteinsboden m
~ **strands** Skelettfasern fpl
skeleton Skelett n
~ **crystal** Skelettkristall m
~ **of lime** Kalkskelett n
~ **of silica** Kieselskelett n
~ **soil** Skelettboden m
~ **structure** Skelettstruktur f
skemmatite Skemmatit m *(Gemenge von Psilomelan und Polianit)*
skerry felsig
skerry Schäre f, Felsenriff n
~ **coast** Schärenküste f
sketch map Kartenskizze f
~ **profile** Profilskizze f
skew schief, schräg
skew 1. Gangapophyse f; 2. Verklemmung f *(eines Magnetbands)*
skewness 1. Schiefe f *(von Kornverteilungskurven)*; 2. Asymmetrie f *(von Polarisationsfiguren)*
skiagite Skiagit m, $Fe_3Fe_2[SiO_4]_3$ *(hypothetisches Granatmolekül)*
Skiddavian Slate Skiddaw-Schiefer m *(Gruppe, Tremadoc − unteres Llanvirn)*
skidding friction Gleitreibung f
skin depth Eindringtiefe f
~ **effect** 1. Skineffekt m *(Zone verringerter Permeabilität durch Spülungseinwirkung um ein Bohrloch)*; 2. Skineffekt m, Hauteffekt m, Stromverdrängungseffekt m

~ **impression** Hautabdruck m
skip cast (mark) Hüpfmarke f
sklodowskite Sklodowskit m, $MgH_2[UO_2|SiO_4]_2 \cdot 5H_2O$
skutterudite Skutterudit m, $CoAs_3$
sky wave Raumwelle f, reflektierte Welle f
~-**wave interference** Interferenz f der von der Ionosphäre reflektierten Wellen
skystone Meteorit m
slab Platte f
~ **jointing** plattenförmige Absonderung f
~ **of lithosphere** Lithosphärenplatte f
~ **of rock** Gesteinsplatte f
~ **pahoehoe** Scherbenlava f
~-**shaped** plattenartig
~ **structure** bankförmige (bankige) Absonderung f, Plattentextur f
slabby plattig
slablike plattenartig
slack witterungsempfindlich
~ **coal** Kohlengrus m
slacking of the walls Ablösung f des Gebirges
slag Schlacke f
~ **bomb** Schlackenbombe f
~ **cone** Schlackenkegel m
~ **shingle** Schlackenbruch m *(als Straßenbaumaterial)*
~ **wool** s. mineral wool
slaggy schlackenähnlich
slaglike schlackenähnlich
slaked lime gelöschter Kalk m, $Ca(OH)_2$
slant/to abböschen
~ **down** sich abdachen
slant schräg
slant Neigung f, Einfallen n, Abhang m
~ **drilling** Schrägbohren m
~ **hole** Schrägbohrung f, geneigte Bohrung f
~ **range** schräge Entfernung zwischen dem Bodenobjekt und dem Flugzeug- bzw. Satellitensensor
slanting abschüssig, geneigt
slanting Abböschung f
~ **hole** schräges Bohrloch n
slap s. slack coal
slashes sumpfige Stellen fpl
slate Schiefer m, Dachschiefer m, Tonschiefer m *(schwach metamorphes Schiefergestein)*
~ **bed** Schieferbank f
~ **break** Schiefereinlage f
~ **clay** Schieferton m
~ **flour** Schiefermehl n
~ **mountains** Schiefergebirge n
~ **oil** Schieferöl n
~ **pit** Schiefergrube f
~ **powder** Schiefermehl n
~ **quarry** Schieferbruch m
~ **ribbons** Schichtungsbänderung f, Schichtungsrippelung f *(auf der Fläche senkrecht zur Schichtung)*
~ **rock** Schiefergebirge n
slatelike schieferartig, schieferähnlich
slates Dachschieferplatten fpl
slatiness Transversalschiefrigkeit f

slaty schieferähnlich, schiefrig, geschiefert, schieferartig
~ **cleavage** S_1-Schieferung f, Transversalschieferung f
~-**cleavage fold** s. similar fold
~ **coal** Schieferkohle f, Blätterkohle f
~ **fracture** schiefrige Bruchfläche f
~ **grit** Sandschiefer m
~ **marl** Schiefermergel m
~ **structure** Schiefertextur f
slave station Tochterstation f, Nebenstation f; Wanderstation f (Geoelektrik)
slavikite Slavikit m, $Fe[OH|SO_4] \cdot 8H_2O$
slawn mit Ton ausgefüllte Kluft f
sleck 1. Grubenschlamm m; 2. roter Sandstein m
sledging Grobspalten n (von Bruchsteinen)
sleeper charge vorbesetzte Ladung f (in Schußbohrung einige Tage vorher eingesetzte Sprengstoffladung)
sleet/to graupeln, hageln
sleet Schloße f; Schlack m; (Am) Eiskörnchen n
slenderness ratio Schlankheitsgrad m
slew Moorsenke f, Sumpfwiese f
sliced feldspar kataklasierter (zerbrochener) Feldspat m
slick s. slime
slickenside Gleitfläche f, Harnisch m, Rutschharnisch m, Rutschfläche f, Rutschspiegel m
slickensided clay zerruschelter Ton m
slickensiding Gleitschicht f
slicking Erztrum n
slickolites Stylolithenharnisch m, Nadelharnisch m
slicks s. slickenside
slide/to gleiten
~ **down** heruntergleiten
slide 1. schichtenparallele Verwerfung f; 2. Überschiebungsfläche f; 3. Gleitung f; [subaquatische] Rutschung f; 4. (Am) Geröll n, Geschiebe n; 5. Dünnschliff m
~ **cast** Gleitmarke f
~-**correction excavation** Abtrag m von Rutschungsmassen
~ **furrow** Rutschrinne f
~ **mark** Gleitmarke f, Schleifmarke f
~ **mass** Rutschmasse f
~ **of a bank** Rutschung f einer Böschung
~ **plane** Gleitebene f
~ **rock** Felsschutt m, Gehängeschutt m
~ **slope** Rutschbahn f
sliding-down Hinabgleiten n
~ **erosion** schleichende Erosion f
~ **fracture** Verschiebungsbruch m, Gleitbruch m, Scherbruch m
~ **phenomenon** Rutschvorgang m
~ **plane** Gleitfläche f
~ **rupture** Verschiebungsbruch m
~ **wedge [roof-]bolt** Doppelkeilanker m
slight damage erschreckend (6. Stufe der Erdbebenstärkeskala)

~ **depth** geringe Tiefe f
~ **dip** schwaches Einfallen n
~ **thickness** geringe Mächtigkeit f
slightly folded schwach gefaltet
~ **inclined** schwach einfallend
~ **sandy** schwach sandig
slim hole Kernbohrloch n mit kleinem Durchmesser, Schürfbohrloch n
slime 1. Bohrschmant m, Bohrschlamm m, Bohrschlick m; 2. Erzschlamm m, Erztrübe f; 3. Schweb m
~ **peat** Morast m
~ **pit** Schlammsumpf m
slimy schlammig, schlickig; schleimig, gallertig
~ **sapropel** gallertartiger Faulschlamm m
sline Querkluft f
sling muds Gleitschlick m
slip downward/to heruntergleiten
~ **over** aufgleiten
slip 1. kleiner Erdrutsch m, Rutschung f; 2. flache Sprunghöhe f; 3. Schlechte f; kleine Verwerfung f (Kohlenbergbau); 4. Gestängeabfangkeil m
~ **area** Rutschungsgebiet n
~ **band** Translationslinie f, Translationsstreifen m
~ **bands** Zeilenstruktur f, Gleitlinienstreifung f, Translationsstreifung f, Gleitbänder npl
~ **bedding** Gleitstauchung f, Gleitfaltung f, Rutschfaltung f
~ **block** Gleitpacken m
~ **cleavage** zur Verwerfung gleichlaufende Spaltfläche f
~ **face** 1. Gleitfläche f, Rutschfläche f; 2. Sturzseite f
~ **fault** normale Verwerfung f, Überschiebung f
~ **fibre asbestos** Längsfaserasbest m (Faser parallel zu den Salbändern)
~ **fold** Gleitfalte f
~ **folding** Gleitfaltung f
~ **fracture** Gleitbruch m
~ **line** Gleitlinie f
~-**off slope** Gleithang m
~ **plane** 1. Schubfläche f, Verwerfungsfläche f; 2. Gleitfläche f, Translationsebene f
~ **striae** Harnischrillung f, Gleitstreifung f
~ **surface** Gleitfläche f, Rutschfläche f
~-**things** s. slippy backs
~ **vein** Verwerfungsgang m
slippage Abgleitung f, Gleiten n
~ **phenomenon** Gleiteffekt m, Gleitströmung f
slippery roof unsicheres Hangendes n
~ **soil** rutschender Boden m
slipping Verwurf m
~ **earthwork** rutschender Boden m
~ **mass** abgerutschte Bodenmasse f
~ **of a slope** Abbröckelung f einer Böschung
~ **plane** Gleitfläche f, Rutschfläche f
slippy rissig, voller kleiner Verwerfungen
~ **backs** vertikale Schlechten fpl

slit 324

slit Spalte f
~ **band** Schlitzzone f *(Gastropoden)*
~ **sample** Schlitzprobe f
~ **window** Schlitzfenster n *(Tektonik)*
sloam Toneinlagerung f
slob Moor n, Sumpf m; Schlamm m
slocking stone reiche Erzstufe f
slope [away]/to abfallen
~ **down** verflachen
~ **steeply** steil abböschen
slope Abdachung f, Hang m, Hangneigung f, Senke f; 2. Bremsberg m, tonnlägiger Schacht m
~ **boring** schräge Bohrung f
~ **creep** Gehängekriechen n
~ **current** Böschungsfließen n
~ **cutting** Böschungsverschneidung f
~ **failure** Böschungsrutsch m
~ **gullies** tiefe Rinnen fpl *(im Kontinentalhang)*
~ **lines** Böschungslinien fpl
~ **of a dike** Deichböschung f; Dammböschung f
~ **of a saddle** Sattelflügel m
~ **of cutting (embankment)** Abtragsböschung f
~ **of river** Flußgefälle n
~ **of the river bank** Uferböschung f *(eines Flusses)*
~ **ratio** Böschungsverhältnis n
~ **spring** Hangquelle f
~ **stability** Standfestigkeit f von Böschungen
~ **tectonics** Hangtektonik f
~ **wash** Gehängelehm m
~-**wash alluvium** abgespülter Gehängeschutt m
sloped geneigt; abschüssig
slopeward side Böschungsseite f
sloping abschüssig, schräg, geneigt, abfallend
sloping Abböschung f
sloppy schlammig
slot schmaler senkrechter Durchlaß m
~-**and-wegde [roof-]bolt** Schlitzkeilanker m
slotted liner Liner m mit Schlitzöffnungen
~ **sampling vessel** Schlitzgefäß n *(Probenahme)*
slough off/to ausschlämmen
slough 1. Sumpf m, Morast m, versumpfter Wasserlauf m; 2. Priel m; 3. Wasserrösche f
sloughing Nachfall m *(im Bohrloch)*
~ **formation** nicht standfestes, sich ablösendes Gebirge n
~ **shale** quellender Schieferton m
sloughy sumpfig
slovan *(sl)* 1. Ausgehendes n eines Ganges; 2. Wasserrösche f
slow creeping of wet soil Erdfließen n, Solifluktion f
slowness 1. Slowness f, reziproke Geschwindigkeit f *(Seismologie)*; 2. Laufzeit f pro Längeneinheit *(Bohrlochseismik)*
SLR s. side-looking radar
sludge Schlick m, Schlamm m, Matsch m; Bohrschmant m, Bohrtrübe f

~ **barrel** Sedimentrohr n, Schlammrohr n
~ **cuttings** Bohrschlamm m
~ **gas** Faulgas n
~ **ice** Neueis n
~ **sample** Spülprobe f *(Tiefbohren)*
~ **water** Schlammtrübe f
sludging Schlammrutschung f
sludgy schlammig, matschig
sluffing Ablösung f des Gebirges an der Firste
slug/to pulsierend fließen
slug flow Brecherströmung f
sluggish träge fließend *(Fluß)*
~ **stream** träge fließendes Gewässer n
sluice weir Durchlaßwehr n, Schützenwehr n
sluiceway Grundablaß m
slum[b] *(sl)* Brandschiefer m
Slumberjag s. Schlumberger logs
slump subaquatische (submarine) Rutschung f, Gleitung f
~ **balls** Rutschkörper mpl, Rutschwülste mpl, Gleitblöcke mpl, Sedimentrollen fpl
~ **bedding** Gleitstauchung f, Gleitfaltung f, Rutschfaltung f
~ **fold** synsedimentäre intraformationelle Falte f
~ **mark** Rutschmarke f
~ **of temperature** Temperatursturz m
~ **overfold** Rutschfalte f
~ **sheet** Rutschungsschicht f
slurry Schlamm m, Schlammwasser n, Trübe f
~ **slump** Trübestrom m
slush 1. durchtränkter Schnee m, Schlammeis n; 2. weicher Schlamm m, Trübe f
~ **pit** Schlammgrube f; Wasserloch n *(zur Mischung der Bohrspülung)*
~ **pump** Spülpumpe f
~ **pump delivery** Volumenstrom m *(Fördermenge f)* der Spülpumpe
~ **pump pressure** Spülpumpendruck m
slyne s. cleat
small bubble of gas kleine Gasblase f, Gasbläschen n
~ **circle** Kleinkreis m; Breitenkreis m
~ **fold** Kleinfalte f
~ **globe** Kügelchen n
~ **grain** Körnchen n
~ **hail** Frostgraupeln fpl
~ **hardness** Mikrohärte f
~ **ore** Erzschlich m
~-**scale folding** Kleinfaltung f
~-**scale mining** Bergbau m kleinen Maßstabs, Bergbau m geringerer Förderleistung
~-**scale structures** Kleintektonik f
~-**sized** kleinstückig
~ **thrust outlier** Überschiebungsklippe f
~ **tin** Zinnschlich m
smalls Grubenklein n; Feinerz n; Feinkohle f
smaltine s. smaltite
smaltite Smaltin m, Speiskobalt m, Glanzkobalt m, $CoAs_2$
smaragd s. emerald
smaragdine smaragdfarben

smaragdite Smaragdit *m (aktinolithische Hornblende)*
smearing 1. Registrierung *f* aus der Bewegung; 2. Überdeckung *f (Seismik)*
smectite group *s.* montmorillonite group
smeddum 1. Zwischenmittel *n (Ton oder Schiefer, Schottland)*; 2. feines Pulver *n (beim Sieben)*
smelt/to schmelzen, verhütten
smeltable verhüttungsfähig, verhüttbar
smeltery Schmelzhütte *f*, Hüttenwerk *n*
smelting Schmelzen *n*, Verhüttung *f*
~ **house** Erzhütte *f*
~ **ore** Schmelzerz *n*
smiddam, smiddum, smitham, smithem *s.* smeddum
smithite Smithit *m*, $Ag_2S \cdot As_2S_3$
smithsonite Smithsonit *m*, Zinkspat *m*, Galmei *m*, $ZnCO_3$
smitten *s.* smeddum
smoke cloud Rauchwolke *f*
~ **column** Rauchsäule *f*
~ **hole** Fumarole *f*
~ **wacke** Rau[c]hwacke *f*
smokeless fuel raucharmer Brennstoff *m*
smokestone Rauchtopas *m*, Rauchquarz *m*
smoking crest rauchender Dünendamm *m*
smoky rußig
~ **quartz (topaz)** Rauchquarz *m*, Rauchtopas *m*
smooth 1. sanft, geglättet; 2. [ab]gestumpft
~-**edged** glattrandig
~ **fold** Fließfalte *f*
~ **fracture** glatter Bruch *m*
~-**shelled** glattschalig
smoothed [ab]gestumpft, kantenbestoßen *(bei Geröllen)*
smoothness Glätte *f*, Ebenheit *f (z.B. der Erdoberfläche)*
SMOW Isotopenstandard für Deuterium *(Ozeanwasser)*
smudge coal Kohlenschlamm *m*, Schlammkohle *f*, erdige Kohle *f*
smut erdige Kohle *f*, verwitterter Kohlenausbiß *m*
smuth *s.* smut
smythan *s.* smeddum
S/N *s.* siganl-to-noise ratio
snail Schnecke *f*
snake stone *s.* ammonite
snaking stream Mäanderfluß *m*
snapping dislocation plötzliche Bewegung *f* an einer Störung
snout of glacier Gletscherzunge *f*
snow Schnee *m*
~ **avalanche** Schneelawine *f*
~ **blast** Schneesturm *m*
~-**capped peak** Schneegipfel *m*
~ **cloud** Schneewolke *f*
~ **cornice** Schneewächte *f*, Firnbrücke *f*
~ **cover** Schneedecke *f*
~-**covered** schneebedeckt

~ **creep** Schneegekriech *n*
~ **flurry** Schneegestöber *n*
~-**free** schneefrei
~ **gauge** Schneemesser *m*
~ **glacier** Firngletscher *m*
~ **layer** Schneeschicht *f*
~ **limit (line)** Schneegrenze *f*
~ **of the penitents** Büßerschnee *m*
~ **plateau** Firnfeld *n*
~ **plume** Schneewächte *f*, Firnbrücke *f*
~ **region** Schneegebiet *n*
~ **shower** Schneeschauer *m*
~-**slab avalanche** Schneebrettlawine *f*
~ **squall** Schneegestöber *n*
~ **water** Schmelzwasser *n*
~ **wreath** Schneeanhäufung *f*
SNOW Isotopenstandard für Deuterium *(antarktischer Schnee)*
snowball structure 1. Sandsteinrolle *f (sedimentäre Struktur)*; 2. Schneeballstruktur *f (gedrehtes Interngefüge in Metamorphitmineralen)*
snowbank Schneewehe *f*
snowbreak Schneeschmelze *f*
snowbridge Schneebrücke *f*
snowclad schneebedeckt
snowdrift Schneewehe *f*, Schneeverwehung *f*
~ **site** Schneewächte *f*, Firnbrücke *f*
snowfall Schneefall *m*, Schneemenge *f*
snowfield Schneefeld *n*, Ferner *m*, Firnfeld *n*
snowflake Schneeflocke *f*
snowless schneefrei
snowmelt Schneeschmelze *f*
~ **runoff** Schmelzwasserabfluß *m*
snowslide Schneesturz *m*, Lawine *f*
~ **track** Lawinengasse *f*
snowslip Schneesturz *m*, Lawine *f*
snowstorm Schneesturm *m*
snowy schneebedeckt, schneereich
SNR *s.* signal-to-noise ratio
soak/to durchtränken
~ **in (into)** einsickern, versickern, durchsickern
~ **the salt out** entsalzen
~ **with** [durch]tränken mit
soakage of the rock Durchnässung *f* des Gebirges
soaking Durchtränkung *f*
~-**in** Versickern, Versickerung *f*, Einsickern *n*
soapstone Seifenstein *m*, Speckstein *m*, Steatit *m*, Saponit *m*, Topfstein *m*, $Mg_3[(OH)_2|Si_{11}O_{10}]$
soapy back glatte, lettige Ablösung *f*
~ **clay** fetter Ton *m*
~ **lustre** Fettglanz *m*
sobralite Sobralit *m*, Pyroxmangit *m (s.a. pyroxmangite)*
socket Zahngrube *f (am Schalenschloß von Mollusken, Ostracoden)*
sod Grasnarbe *f*, Grasboden *m*, Rasendecke *f*
~ **podzol** Rasenpodsolboden *m*
soda Soda *f*, Natron *n*, $Na_2CO_3 \cdot 10H_2O$
~ **alum** Natronalaun *m*, $NaAl[SO_4]_2 \cdot 12H_2O$

soda

- ~ **amphibole** Alkalihornblende *f*
- ~ **feldspar** *s.* plagioclase
- ~ **lake** Natronsee *m*
- ~-**lime feldspar** Kalknatronfeldspat *m* (*s.a.* plagioclase)
- ~ **nitre** Natronsalpeter *m*, Chilesalpeter *m*, Nitronatrit *m*, NaNO$_3$
- ~ **soil** Sodaboden *m*

sodalite Sodalith *m*, Na$_8$[Cl$_2$|(AlSiO$_4$)$_6$]
sodded slope Rasenböschung *f*
soddy soil Rasenboden *m*
soddyite Soddyit *m*, (UO$_2$)$_{15}$[(OH)$_{20}$|Si$_6$O$_{17}$]·8H$_2$O
sodic soil natriumhaltiger Boden *m*
sodium Natrium *n*, Na

- ~ **alum** *s.* soda alum
- ~ **chloride** Natriumchlorid *n*, Chlornatrium *n*, Kochsalz *n*, NaCl

sods Ton *m* unter dem Flöz, Liegendton *m*
soehngeite Söhngeit *m*, Ga(OH)$_3$
soft weich *(Gestein)*

- ~ **abrasive** sanft wirkendes Schleifmittel (Poliermittel) *n*
- ~-**bodied invertebrate** Weichtier *n*
- ~ **brown coal** Weichbraunkohle *f*
- ~ **brown-coal stage** Weichbraunkohlenstadium *n* (Inkohlungs- oder Karbonifikationsstadium)
- ~ **clay** plastischer Ton *m*
- ~ **country (ground)** mildes Gebirge *n*
- ~ **hail** Graupeln *fpl*
- ~ **rock** faules Gestein *n*, fauler Fels *m*
- ~ **seat** Fireclaylager *n* unter dem Flöz
- ~ **water** weiches Wasser *n*
- ~ **water marsh** Süßwassermoor *n*

soften water/to Wasser enthärten
softened water enthärtetes Wasser *n*
softener Weichmacher *m*, Enthärtungsmittel *n*
softening Enthärtung *f*

- ~ **of water** Wasserenthärtung *f*
- ~ **plant** Wasserenthärtungsanlage *f*
- ~ **point** Erweichungspunkt *m*

soggy feucht, sumpfig

- ~ **moor** Naßmoor *n*

soil Boden *m*

- ~ **acidity** Bodenazidität *f*
- ~ **aeration** Bodendurchlüftung *f*
- ~ **aggradation** Bodenaufschüttung *f*
- ~ **air** Bodenluft *f*
- ~ **analysis** Bodenanalyse *f*
- ~ **appraisal** Bodentaxonomie *f*
- ~ **array** Bodenstruktur *f*
- ~ **asphalt** *(Am)* Bitumenvermörtelung *f*, bituminöse Bodenvermörtelung *f*
- ~ **association** Bodenassoziation *f*
- ~ **bacteria** Bodenbakterien *fpl*
- ~ **bearing capacity** Tragfähigkeit *f* des Bodens
- ~ **biochemistry** Biochemie *f* des Bodens
- ~ **blowing** Bodenverwehung *f*
- ~ **cement** Bodenbeton *m*, Bodenzement *m*, Zementvermörtelung *f*
- ~ **characteristic** Bodenziffer *f*
- ~ **chemistry** Bodenchemie *f*
- ~-**colloid[al particle]** Bodenkolloid *n*, Bodenquellstoff *m*
- ~ **compaction** [künstliche] Bodenverdichtung *f*, Bodensetzung *f*
- ~ **conditions** Bodenverhältnisse *npl*
- ~ **conservation** Bodenschutz *m*, Bodenerhaltung *f*
- ~ **consolidation** [natürliche] Bodenverdichtung *f*, Eigenverfestigung *f*, Eigensetzung *f*
- ~ **constituents** Bodenbestandteile *mpl*
- ~ **corrosion** Bodenkorrosion *f*
- ~ **cover** Bodendecke *f*
- ~-**cover complex** Bodendeckschicht *f*
- ~ **creep** Bodengekriech *n*
- ~ **crumb** Bodenkrümel *m*, Erdkrümel *m*
- ~ **cultivation** Bodenbearbeitung *f*
- ~ **cut** Bodeneinschnitt *m*
- ~ **degradation** Bodendegradierung *f*
- ~ **densification** [künstliche] Bodenverdichtung *f*
- ~ **density** Bodendichte *f*
- ~ **depth** Gründigkeit *f*
- ~ **development** Bodenbildung *f*
- ~ **dynamics** Bodendynamik *f*
- ~ **engineer** Bodenmechaniker *m*
- ~ **engineering** Erd- und Grundbau *m*
- ~ **erodibility** Erosionsfähigkeit *f* des Bodens
- ~ **erosion** Bodenerosion *f*, Bodenabtragung *f*
- ~ **evaporation** Bodenverdunstung *f*, Bodenausdünstung *f*
- ~ **evaporation pan** Bodenverdunstungsmesser *m*
- ~ **excavation** Bodenausbruch *m*
- ~ **exhaustion** Bodenermüdung *f*, Bodenerschöpfung *f*
- ~ **exploration** Bodenuntersuchung *f*, Untergrundforschung *f*, Baugrunduntersuchung *f*
- ~-**failure investigation** Grundbruchuntersuchung *f*
- ~ **fertility** Bodenfruchtbarkeit *f*
- ~-**fixing** bodenbefestigend
- ~ **flow** Solifluktion *f*, Bodenfließen *n*, Erdfließen *n*, Bodenversetzung *f*
- ~ **flowage** Erdfluß *m*, Bodenfluß *m*
- ~ **formation** Bodenbildung *f*
- ~-**forming** bodenbildend
- ~ **frost** Bodenfrost *m*
- ~ **gas** Bodengas *n*
- ~ **genetics** Bodengenetik *f*
- ~ **horizon** Bodenhorizont *m*
- ~ **humidity** Bodenfeuchtigkeit *f*
- ~ **improvement** Bodenverbesserung *f*
- ~-**improving** bodenverbessernd
- ~ **investigation** Bodenuntersuchung *f*, Untergrundforschung *f*, Baugrunduntersuchung *f*
- ~ **layer** Bodenschicht *f*
- ~ **leaching** Bodenauswaschung *f*, Bodenauslaugung *f*
- ~ **loading** Bodendruck *m*
- ~ **loosening** Lockerung *f* des Bodens
- ~-**making** bodenbildend
- ~ **map** Bodenkarte *f*, Baugrundkarte *f*

~ **mapping** Bodenkartierung f
~ **mechanics** Bodenmechanik f, Baugrundmechanik f, bautechnische Bodenkunde f
~ **mechanics laboratory** Erdbaulabor[atorium] n
~ **microflora** Bodenmikroflora f
~ **moisture** Bodenfeuchtigkeit f
~-**moisture content** Bodenwassergehalt m
~-**moisture gradient** Bodenfeuchtigkeitsgradient m
~-**moisture tension** Bodenwasserspannung f
~ **mortar** Bodenmörtel m
~ **particle** Bodenteilchen n
~ **permeability** Bodendurchlässigkeit f
~ **physics** Bodenphysik f
~ **porosity** Bodenporosität f
~ **profile** Bodenprofil n
~ **property** Bodeneigenschaft f
~-**protecting,** ~-**protective** bodenschützend
~ **research equipment** Bodenuntersuchungsgeräte npl (Geophysik)
~ **respiration** Bodenverdunstung f
~ **sample** Bodenprobe f
~ **science** Bodenkunde f, Bodenlehre f
~ **scientist** Bodenwissenschaftler m
~ **separation in layers** Abschlämmen n des Bodens (bei der mechanischen Bodenanalyse)
~ **series** Bodenschicht f
~ **shifting** Bodenbewegung f
~ **shrinkage** Bodenschrumpfung f
~ **sickness** Bodenmüdigkeit f
~ **skeleton** Bodenskelett n
~ **solidification and sealing** Bodenverfestigung f und -abdichtung f
~ **solution** Bodenwasser n
~ **specimen** Bodenprobe f
~ **stabilization** Stabilisierung (Festigung) f des Untergrunds, Bodenverfestigung f
~ **stabilization with asphaltic bitumen** Bitumenvermörtelung f, bituminöse Bodenvermörtelung f
~ **stabilizer** Bodenstabilisator m
~-**stabilizing** bodenbefestigend
~ **sterilization** Bodensterilisierung f
~ **stratum** Bodenschicht f
~ **stripes** Erdstreifen mpl
~ **structure** Bodenstruktur f
~ **study** s. ~ exploration
~ **subgrade** Erdplanum n, Untergrund m
~ **suction** Bodenwasserspannung f
~ **survey** Bodenaufnahme f
~ **survey chart** Bodenübersichtskarte f
~ **swamping** Bodenversumpfung f
~ **swelling** Bodenquellung f
~ **tank** Lysimeter n
~ **temperature** Bodentemperatur f
~ **test** Bodenprüfung f, Bodenanalyse f
~ **testing** Bodenuntersuchung f
~-**testing laboratory** Erdbaulabor[atorium] n
~ **thin section** Bodendünnschliff m
~ **trafficability** s. trafficability
~ **type** Bodenart f
~-**ulmin** Humus m

~ **water** Bodenwasser n
~-**water bed** Feuchtigkeitszone f des Bodens, Bodenwasserschicht f
~-**water belt** Bodenwasserzone f
~ **waterproofing** Bodenabdichtung f
~ **wetness** Bodenfeuchte f
soils classification Bodenklassifizierung f
~ **laboratory** Erdbaulabor[atorium] n
~ **mapping** Bodenkartierung f
sol Sol n
solar solar, Sonnen..., Solar...
~ **activity period** Sonnentätigkeitsperiode f
~ **atmosphere** Sonnenatmosphäre f
~ **constant** Solarkonstante f
~ **corona** Sonnenhof m, Sonnenkorona f
~ **cosmic radiation** solare kosmische Strahlung f
~ **day** Sonnentag m
~ **disk** Sonnenscheibe f
~ **eclipse** Sonnenfinsternis f
~ **energy** Sonnenenergie f
~ **eruption (flare)** Sonneneruption f
~ **halo** Hof m um die Sonne
~ **magnetism** Sonnenmagnetismus m
~ **power** Sonnenenergie f
~ **prominence** Sonnenprotuberanz f
~ **radiation** Sonnenstrahlung f
~ **spectrum** Sonnenspektrum n
~ **system** Sonnensystem n
~-**terrestrial** solar-terrestrisch
~ **tides** Sonnengezeiten pl
~ **time** Sonnenzeit f
~ **wind** Sonnenwind m
~ **year** Sonnenjahr n
solarimeter Sonnenstrahlungsmesser m
sole 1. Liegendfläche f einer sedimentären Schicht; 2. liegende Hauptstörungsfläche f (z.B. einer Schuppeneinheit)
~ **mark** Schichtflächenmarke f, Schichtflächenerscheinung f, Sohlmarke f
soled facettiert
~ **cobble** glazial abgeschliffener Block m
solenoidal quellenfrei
solfanaria Schwefelgrube f
solfatara Solfatare f
~ **mound** Solfatarenhügel m
solfataric action Solfatarentätigkeit f
~ **vent** Schwefelquelle f
solid 1. fest; 2. anstehend (Kohle, Gestein)
solid Feststoff m
~ **angle** Raumwinkel m
~ **bedrock** gewachsener Fels m, Anstehendes n, anstehendes Gebirge n
~ **bob** [feste] Polierscheibe f
~ **control system** Reinigungssystem m
~ **discharge** 1. Schuttfracht f; 2. Auswürfling m
~ **gob** Bergevollversatz m
~ **load** Schuttlast f
~ **masonry weir** festes gemauertes Wehr n
~ **ore** anstehendes Erz n
~ **ore deposit** Erzstock m, massige Lagerstätte f

solid 328

- ~ **packing** Bergevollversatz *m*
- ~ **product** Auswürfling *m*
- ~ **rock** festes Gebirge *n*, Fels *m*, festes (anstehendes) Gestein *n*
- ~ **solution** Mischkristall *m*
- ~**-state imaging system** Abbildungssystem *n* aus Festkörperdetektoren
- ~ **state reaction** Reaktion *f* im festen Zustand
- ~ **substance volume** Feststoffvolumen *n*

solidification Verfestigung *f*, Erstarrung *f*
- ~ **age** Erstarrungsalter *n*
- ~ **point** Erstarrungspunkt *m*

solidified lava erstarrte Lava *f*
solidify/to fest werden, sich verfestigen, erstarren
solids density Reindichte *f*
solifluction Bodenfließen *n*, Solifluktion *f*, Bodenfluktion *f*, Erdfließen *n*
- ~ **pocket** Solifluktionstasche *f*
- ~ **terrace** Solifluktionsterrasse *f*

solifluxion *s.* solifluction
solitaire Solitär *m*
solitary coral Einzelkoralle *f*
Solnhofen Platy Limestone Solnhofener Plattenkalk *m (Malm im Süddeutschen Becken)*
- ~ **Slates** Solnhofener Schiefer *mpl*

sodic soil solodartiger Boden *m*
solodization Solodierung *f*
solodized soil salziger Boden *m*
solonetzic, solonetzlike solone[t]zartig
solstice Solstitium *n*, Sonnenwende *f*
solstitial Sonnenwend...
- ~ **point** Solstitialpunkt *m*, Sonnenwendepunkt *m*

solubility Löslichkeit *f*
- ~ **product** Löslichkeitsprodukt *n*

soluble löslich
- ~ **in acids** säurelöslich
- ~ **in water** wasserlöslich

solum 1. Ackerkrume *f*; 2. A- und B-Horizont des Bodens
solution Lösung *f*
- ~ **bottom** Hartboden *m*, Hartgrund *m (verkrusteter Sedimentationsgrund)*
- ~ **breccia** Lösungsbrekzie *f*
- ~ **cavity** Lösungshohlraum *m*
- ~ **channels** Karren *pl*
- ~ **facets** Lösungsfacetten *fpl*
- ~ **fissure** Lösungsspalte *f*
- ~ **gas drive** Gasexpansionstrieb *m*
- ~ **gas drive pool** Gasexpansionstrieblager *n*
- ~ **gas-oil ratio** Gas-Öl-Lösungsverhältnis *n (in der Lagerstätte unter Druck)*
- ~ **hollows** Lösungsnäpfe *mpl*
- ~ **mobilization** Lösungsmobilisierung *f*
- ~ **of drying-up** Eindunstungslösung *f*
- ~ **of replacement** Umwandlungslösung *f*
- ~ **opening** Lösungshohlraum *m*
- ~ **pan** flache Auslaugungsdepression *f*
- ~ **pocket** Auslaugungstasche *f*
- ~ **porosity** Lösungsporosität *f*
- ~ **residue** Lösungsrückstand *m*
- ~ **resulting from rock decomposition** Verwitterungslösung *f*
- ~ **ripples** Lösungsrippeln *fpl*
- ~ **sink** Trichterdoline *f*
- ~ **subsidence** Absenkung *f* durch Lösung
- ~ **transfer** Lösungsumsatz *m*

solvent Lösungsmittel *n*
- ~ **action (activity)** Lösungstätigkeit *f*
- ~ **leaching** Laugung *f* mit Lösungsmittel
- ~ **power** Lösungskraft *f*
- ~ **property** Lösungseigenschaft *f*

somal unit lateral auffingernde stratigrafische Einheit *f*
somma crater Sommakrater *m*
- ~ **ring** Sommawall *m*, Ringwall *m*
- ~ **volcano** Sommavulkan *m*, Vulkan *m* mit Ringwall

sommaite Sommait *m (Leuzitmonzonit)*
sonic altimeter Schallhöhenmesser *m*, Echolot *n*
- ~ **depth finder** Echolot *n*
- ~ **drilling** Schallbohren *n*
- ~ **log[ging]** Akustiklog[verfahren] *n*, Schallkernen *n*
- ~ **sounding** Echolotung *f*
- ~ **speed (velocity)** Schallgeschwindigkeit *f*

sonolite Sonolith *m*, $Mn_9[(OH,F)_2|(SiO_4)_4]$
sonomaite Sonomait *m*, $Mg_3Al_2[SO_4]_6 \cdot 33H_2O$
sonoprobe Sonoprobe *f (Sender für Echolotmessungen)*
soot coal *(sl)* Rußkohle *f (fusinit- bzw. fusitreiche Steinkohle)*
sooty chalcocite erdiger Chalkosin *m*
sorotiite Sorotiit *m (Eisen-Stein-Meteorit)*
sort/to sortieren, auslesen, scheiden, klauben
sorted bedding sortierte Schichtung *f*
sorting 1. Sortierung *f*, Auslesen *n*, Scheiden *n*, Klauben *n*; 2. Setzungsklassierung *f* durch flüssige Medien
- ~ **board** *s.* ~ table
- ~ **coefficient** Sortierungskoeffizient *m (z.B. von Korngrößengemischen)*
- ~ **house** Scheidehaus *n*
- ~ **index** Sortierungsgrad *m*
- ~ **of ores** Erzscheidung *f*
- ~ **plant** Scheideanlage *f*
- ~ **table** Sortiertisch *m*, Lesetisch *m*, Klaubetisch *m*
- ~ **unit** Scheideapparat *m*

sound/to 1. schallen, tönen; 2. abklopfen *(Festigkeitsuntersuchung)*; 3. [aus]loten
- ~ **the ground** den Grund abloten

sound 1. Sund *m*, Meerenge *f*, Haff *n*; 2. Schall *m*, Klang *m*; Ton *m*; 3. Sonde *f*
- ~ **coal** unverritzte Kohle *f*
- ~ **intensity** *s.* seismic intensity
- ~ **rock** gesunder Fels *m*, gesundes Gestein *n*
- ~**-stone** Phonolith *m*
- ~ **travel time** Schallaufzeit *f*
- ~ **wave** Schallwelle *f*

sounder *s.* sounding device
sounding Lotung *f*
- ~ **balloon** Ballonsonde *f*

~ device Lotungsanlage f, Lotgerät n, Echolot n
~ graphs Sondierungskurven fpl
~ line Lotungslinie f
~ rocket Höhenrakete f, Raketensonde f
~ rod Peilstange f
~ weight Meßlot n (Grundwasserspiegelmessung)
soundings lotbare Wassertiefen fpl
sour corrosion Korrosion f durch Schwefelgehalt des Erdöls
~ natural gas schwefelwasserstoffhaltiges (saures) Erdgas n
source 1. Quelle f; 2. Ursprung m
~ area Ursprungsgebiet n
~ aspects Bildungsbedingungen fpl, Bildungsmilieu n
~ bed s. ~ rock
~ intensity Anfangsintensität f (Radioisotop)
~ of contamination Verschmutzungsquelle f
~ of discovery Fundort m
~ of energy Energiequelle f
~ of financing Finanzierungsquelle f (für geologische Untersuchungsarbeiten)
~ of heat Wärmequelle f
~ of ore Erzfundort m, Erzlagerstätte f
~ of pollution Verschmutzungsquelle f
~-receiver product Strahlenschema n (Seismik)
~ rock Muttergestein n, Ausgangsgestein n, Speichergestein n (für Erdöl oder Erdgas)
south-polar antarktisch, Südpol...
~ pole Südpol m
South Atlantic fissure südatlantische Spalte f
southern hemisphere südliche Halbkugel f
~ lights Südlicht n
Southern Cross Kreuz n des Südens
souzalite Souzalith m, $(Mg, Fe^{\cdot\cdot})_3(Al, Fe^{\cdot\cdot\cdot})_4[(OH)_3|(PO_4)_2]_2 \cdot 2H_2O$
SP = self potential
spa Mineralquelle f
space Raum m
~-centered lattice raumzentriertes Gitter n
~ exploration Weltraumforschung f
~ geology Raumgeologie f
~ group Raumgruppe f, Kristallklasse f
~ group lattice s. ~ lattice
~ lag Abstand m, räumliche Verschiebung f
~ lattice Raumgitter n (bei Kristallen)
~ probe Raumsonde f, Weltraumsonde f
~ radiation Raumstrahlung f
spacing Abstand m (z.B. zwischen Elektroden einer Bohrlochsonde)
~ of joints Kluftabstand m
spadaite Spadait m (Granat zwischen Spessartin und Andradit)
spall/to abblättern, abbrechen
spall Gesteinsabschlag m (durch Verwitterung abgespaltenes Gesteinsbruchstück)
spalling Abbruch m
span 1. Zeitspanne f; 2. lokale geologische Zeiteinheit f; 3. Spannweite f, Stützweite f; 4. Abstand m (zwischen den Aufnehmern einer Bohrlochsonde)
~ loading Spannweitenbelastung f
spangle of mica Glimmerblättchen n
spangolite Spangolith m, $Cu_6Al[(OH)_{12}|Cl|SO_4] \cdot 3H_2O$
spar 1. Spat m; 2. Spiere f, Rundholz n, Sparren m, Längsholm m, Holm m
sparagmite Sparagmit m
sparite Sparit m (spätiger Kalzit- oder Aragonitzement)
spark spectrum Funkenspektrum n
Sparnacian [Stage]]Sparnacien n (Stufe des Paläozäns)
sparry spätig; spatartig; spathaltig
~ calcite s. sparite
~ gypsum Frauenglas n, Marienglas n, blättriger Gips m
~ iron [ore] s. siderite 1.
~ limestone grobkristalliner Kalkstein m
sparse vegetation spärliche Vegetation f
spartalite Zinkit m, Rotzinkerz n, ZnO
spasmodic activity unregelmäßige Tätigkeit f
spastolite Spastoid n (stark verformtes Ovoid)
spastolitic texture spastolithische Struktur f
spathic spatartig; spätig; spathaltig
~ [iron] ore s. siderite 1.
spathiform spätig
spathose spatförmig
spathous blättrig
spatial Weltraum...
~ effective resolution element effektives geometrisches Auflösungselement n
~ model Raummodell n
~ resolution räumliches (geometrisches) Auflösungsvermögen n (eines Fernerkundungssensors)
spatiopyrite s. safflorite
spatous s. sparry
spatter cone Schweißschlackenkegel m
~ rampart Schlackenwall m
spavin s. seat earth
spear pyrite Speerkies m
special folds Spezialfalten fpl
speciation Artbildung f, Speziation f
species Art f, Spezies f
~ distribution Artenverteilung f
~ formation Artbildung f
~ of stone Gebirgsart f
specific capacity of well 1. Fassungsvermögen n (eines Brunnens); 2. spezifische Ergiebigkeit f
~ conductivity spezifische Leitfähigkeit f (eines wasserführendes Gesteins)
~ discharge s. Darcy velocity
~ electrical conductance spezifische elektrische Leitfähigkeit f
~ factor spezifischer Fakor m
~ gravity spezifisches Gewicht n
~ heat spezifische Wärme f
~ porosity entwässerbarer Porenanteil m, nutzbare Porosität f

specific

- **~ retention** Wasserrückhaltevermögen n, Wasserhaltewert m
- **~ surface** spezifische Oberfläche f (einer Gesteinspartikel)
- **~ susceptibility** spezifische Suszeptibilität f
- **~ symmetry** Eigensymmetrie f
- **~ weight** spezifisches Gewicht n
- **~ yield** Lufthaltewert m
- **~ yield of pore space** grundwassererfüllbarer Hohlraumanteil m
- **specimen** Probe f, Prüfstück n, Handstück n
- **~ gold** sichtbares Freigold n
- **~ of ore** Erzprobe f
- **~ support grid** Objektträgerplättchen n (für Elektronenmikroskope)
- **speckled** gesprenkelt, maserig, gefleckt
- **spectral band** Spektralband n
- **~ efficiency** spektraler Wirkungsgrad m
- **~ emissivity** spektrales Emissionsvermögen n
- **~ measurement** Spektralmessung f
- **~ reflectance** relatives spektrales Reflexionsvermögen n (spektrales Verhältnis der reflektierten zur einfallenden Energie)
- **~ signature** Spektralsignatur f, Spektralmerkmal n (eines Objekts)
- **spectroanalytic** spektralanalytisch
- **spectrographic analysis** Spektralanalyse f
- **spectrohelioscope** Spektrohelioskop n
- **spectrology** Spektralanalyse f
- **spectrometer** Spektrometer n
- **spectroscope** Spektroskop n
- **spectroscopic[al]** spektroskopisch
- **~ analysis** Spektralanalyse f
- **spectroscopy** Spektroskopie f
- **spectrum** Spektrum n
- **~ analysis** Spektralanalyse f
- **specular galena** Bleispiegel m
- **~ gypsum** Frauenglas n, Marienglas n
- **~ haematite, ~ iron [ore]** Glanzeisenerz n, Eisenglanz m (s.a. haematite)
- **~ pitch** Glanzkohle f
- **specularite** Glanzeisenerz n, Eisenglanz m (s.a. haematite)
- **speculative resources** prognostische Vorräte mpl Gruppe Delta 2
- **speed of filtration** Filtergeschwindigkeit f
- **~ of light** Lichtgeschwindigkeit f
- **~ of propagation** Fortpflanzungsgeschwindigkeit f
- **~ of registration** Registriergeschwindigkeit f
- **~ of rotation** Rotationsgeschwindigkeit f
- **spelaeal limestone** Höhlenkalkstein m
- **spelaean** Grotten...
- **spelaeolite** Tropfsteinbildung f, Sintergebilde n
- **spelaeologist** Höhlenforscher m
- **spelaeology** Höhlenkunde f, Speläologie f
- **spelaeothem** Tropfstein m, karbonatische Höhlenablagerung f
- **spelter** Zink n, Rohzink n, unreines Hüttenzink n
- **spencerite** Spencerit m, $Zn_2[OH|PO_4] \cdot 1/2H_2O$

330

- **spend/to** Ausbeute liefern, ergiebig sein
- **spent sulphite liquor** Sulfitablauge f
- **spergenite** Spergenit m (Karbonatgestein mit sortierten Fossilfragmenten)
- **sperrylite** Sperrylith m, $PtAs_2$
- **spessartine, spessartite** Spessartin m, Mangangranat m, $Mn_3Al_2[SiO_4]_3$
- **spewy soil** sumpfiger Boden m
- **sphaerite** sphärolithische Phosphatkonkretion f, Phosphatknolle f, Sphaerit m, Variscit m (s.a. variscite)
- **sphaero...** s. sphero...
- **sphaerolite** s. spherulite
- **sphaerolitic** s. spherulitic
- **sphagnum** Sphagnum n, Sumpfmoos n, Torfmoos n, Weißmoos n
- **~ bog** Hochmoor n
- **sphalerite** Sphalerit m, Zinkblende f, α-ZnS
- **sphene** Sphen m, Titanit m, $CaTi[O|SiO_4]$
- **sphenolith** Sphenolith m, keilförmiger Intrusivkörper m
- **sphere** 1. Himmelskugel f; 2. Sphäre f
- **~ ore** Kokardenerz n, Kugelerz n
- **~ packing** Kugelpackung f (Kristallografie)
- **spherical** achsensymmetrisch, sphärisch; kugelig
- **~ divergence** sphärische Divergenz f (Abnahme der Wellenenergie mit der Entfernung)
- **~ flow** kugelsymmetrische Strömung f
- **spherite** s. sphaerite
- **spherocobaltite** Sphaerokobaltit m, Kobaltspat m, $CoCO_3$
- **spherocrystal** Sphärokristall m
- **spheroid** Sphäroid n, Rotationsellipsoid n
- **spheroidal** sphäroidisch, kugelähnlich
- **~ granite** Kugelgranit m
- **~ jointing** kugelige Absonderungsklüftung f
- **~ parting** kugelschalige Absonderung f
- **~ structure** sphäroidales Gefüge n
- **~ weathering** kugelige Verwitterungsformen fpl, Wollsackverwitterung f
- **spheroidizing property** Ballungsfähigkeit f
- **spherophyric** sphärolithisch, felsosphäritisch
- **spherosiderite** Sphaerosiderit m, Toneisenstein m (s.a. siderite)
- **spherule** Kügelchen n, Tröpfchen n
- **~ texture** sphärolithische Struktur f, sphärolithisches Gefüge n
- **spherulite** Kugelkörperchen n, rundes Kristallkörperchen n, Sphärolith m
- **spherulitic** sphärolithisch
- **~ texture** sphärolithische Struktur f, sphärolithisches Gefüge n
- **spicular chert** Spiculit m (Hornstein aus Kieselschwammresten)
- **spicularite** s. spiculite
- **spicule of ice** Eisnadel f
- **~ ooze** Schwammnadelschlamm m
- **spiculite** poröser Spiculit m
- **spider** Keiltopf m (am Bohrlochkopf)
- **spike** Impuls m
- **spiky** stengelig

spilite Spilit *m*
spilitic spilitisch
spill Ausufern *n*
~-over Überlauf *m*
~-over glacier Überlaufgletscher *m*
~ point Strukturtiefstpunkt *m*, Überlaufpunkt *m* *(Aquifergasspeicher)*
spillage in open sea Auslaufverlust *m* auf dem offenen Meer
spillway Überfall *m*, Überlauf *m* *(einer Talsperre oder eines Gletschers)*
~ tunnel Überlaufstollen *m*, Hochwasserstollen *m*
spilosite Spilosit *m*
Spilsby sandstone Spilsby-Sandstein *m* *(oberjurassisch bis unterkretazischer Sandstein in England)*
spinal [vertebral] column Wirbelsäule *f*
spindle head Dreheinrichtung *f*
~-shaped spindelförmig
~-shaped bomb Spindel *f*, bipolare Bombe *f*
~-type drilling rig Spindelbohrgerät *n*
spindrift 1. Gischt *m*; 2. Sandfahne *f*; Staubfahne *f*; Schneefahne *f*
spine 1. Horn *n*, Felsnadel *f*; 2. Nehrung *f*, Landzunge *f*; 3. Dorn *m* *(bei Fossilgehäusen)*; 4. Stielgang *m*, Schlotgang *m*
spinel Spinell *m*, $MgAl_2O_4$
spinifex structure Spinifex-Gefüge *n*
spinning rope Spillseil *n*
spiracle 1. Lavaschornstein *m*; 2. Blasenröhre *f* *(bei Vulkaniten)*
spiral auger zylindrischer Schneckenbohrer *m*
~ axis Schraubung *f*
~ ball Wickelfalte *f*, Sedimentrolle *f*
~ garnet rotierender Granat *m*
~ nebula Spiralnebel *m*
~ structure Spiralgefüge *n*
spirally coiled spiralig aufgerollt
spire 1. Lavadorn *m*, Felsnadel *f*; 2. Gewinde *n* *(bei Fossilgehäusen)*
spirifer Spirifer *m*
spiroffite Spiroffit *m*, $(Mn, Zn)_2Te_3O_8$
spit spitz zulaufende Sandbank *f*
~-out Folge *f* *(Seismik)*
splash erosion Erosion *f* durch Regen
~ zone Benetzungszone *f*
splays divergierende Störungen *fpl* *(am Ende einer Bruchlinie)*
spliced vein verdrückter und überlappend neu einsetzender Gang *m*
splint coal Durain *m*, Mattkohle *f* *(hauptsächlich aus Duroclarit, Claroduritoder aus Vitrinerit)*
splinter/to splittweise abhauen
splinter of magnesia Magnesiastäbchen *n*
splintery splitterig
~ fracture splitteriger Bruch *m*
split/to spalten
~ along spalten nach
~ off sich verzweigen

split 1. Spalt *m*, Riß *m*, Bruch *m*; 2. Zentralaufstellung *f* *(Seismik)*
~ coal Kohlenflöz *n* mit mächtigen Zwischenmitteln
~ deep shooting, ~ [-dip] spread Zentralaufstellung *f* *(Schußpunkt im Zentrum der Geophonaufstellung)*
splitting 1. Spaltbarkeit *f*, Spaltung *f*; 2. *Platte unter 0,10mm Dicke (Handelsglimmersorte)*
~ by frost Eisklüftigkeit *f*
~ of a lode into branches Gangzertrümerung *f*
spodumene Spodumen *m*, $LiAl[Si_2O_6]$
spoil taubes Gestein *n*, Abraum *m*
~ area Haldenfläche *f*
~ bank (dump) Halde *f*, Abraumkippe *f*, Schutthalde *f*
sponge ice Grundeis *n*
~ iron Eisenschwamm *m*
~ needle Schwammnadel *f*
~ ore Schwammerz *n*
~ reef Spongienriff *n*
~ spicule Schwammnadel *f*
~ spicule ooze Schwammnadelschlamm *m*
Spongiae Spongien *npl*, Schwämme *mpl*
spongiform schwammartig
spongious schwammig
spongoline, spongolite Spongolit *m* *(Sediment aus Schwammresten)*
spongy schwammig, porös
~ structure schwammige Textur *f*
spontaneous combustion (heating) Selbstentzündung *f* *(von Kohlen)*
~ potential Eigenpotential *n*
~ potential curve Eigenpotentialkurve *f*
~ potential logging Eigenpotentialmessung *f*
~ potential method Eigenpotentialmethode *f*
spoon sample Löffelprobe *f*, Sondenprobe *f*
sporadic[al] zerstreut vorkommend
sporangium Sporangium *n*
spore Spore *f*
~ vessel Sporangium *n*, Sporenkapsel *f*
sporinite Sporinit *m* *(Kohlenmaceral)*
sporite Sporit *m* *(Kohlenmikrolithotyp)*
sporoclarite Sporoclarit *m* *(Kohlenmikrolithotyp; sporenreicher Clarit)*
sporodurite Sporodurit *m* *(Kohlenmikrolithotyp; sporenreicher Durit)*
sporulation Sporenbildung *f*
spot activity Sonnenfleckenaktivität *f*
~ checking Stichprobenahme *f*
~ coring Informationskernen *n*
~ sample Stichprobe *f*, Punktprobe *f*
~ strength Punktfestigkeit *f*
spotted fleckig, gefleckt, gesprenkelt
~ schist (shale, slate) Fleckschiefer *m*
spotty fleckig, eingesprengt *(von Mineralen)*
~ vein gesprenkelter Gang *m*
spouting spring kontinuierliche Springquelle *f*, Sprudel *m* *(Quelle)*
~ well Springer *m*, Springquelle *f*, Springsonde *f* *(Erdöl)*

spray

spray 1. Spritzwasser n, Gischt m; 2. Gangapophyse f
spread Aufstellung f, Anordnung f, Verteilung f (z.B. der Geophone)
spreading Spreizbewegung f
~ **coefficient** Streuungsbeiwert m
~ **of the ocean floor** Spreizbewegung f (Auseinanderdriften n) des Meeresbodens
sprig-crystal Bergkristall m
spring 1. Quelle f; 2. Springtide f, Springflut f; 3. hydraulischer Grundbruch m
~ **break of ice** Eisgang m
~ **equinox** Frühlings-Äquinoktium n, Frühlings-Tagundnachtgleiche f
~ **fen** Quellmoor n
~ **flood** Frühjahrshochflut f
~ **gravimeter** Federgravimeter n
~ **of mineral water** Mineralquelle f
~ **pits** Quelltrichter mpl
~ **snow** körniger nasser Schnee m
~ **tide** Springtide f, Springflut f
~ **water** Quellwasser n
~ **well** Quellbrunnen m, Filterbrunnen m
Springeran [Stage] *Stufe des Pennsylvaniens*
springing Kämpferpunkt m
~ **line** Kämpferlinie f
springlet kleine Quelle f
sprinkled gesprenkelt
~-**through** durchsprenkelt
sprinkling eingesprengtes Erz n
spruce ochre brauner (gelber) Ocker m
spud Ansetzen n einer Bohrung
~-**in** Anbohren n
spudder Vorbohrer m; Schlagbohrer m
spudding Ansetzen n einer Bohrung
~-**in** Bohrbeginn m
spur 1. Ausläufer m, Bergvorsprung m; 2. Ast m, Abzweig m eines Ganges
spurrite Spurrit m, Ca$_5$[CO$_3$|(SiO$_4$)$_2$]
squall Bö f
~ **front** Böenfront f
~ **of wind** Windbö f
squally böig, stürmisch
~ **weather** böiges Wetter n
squamiform schuppenförmig
~ **load cast** schuppenförmige Belastungsmarke (Fließmarke) f
squamose structure schuppiges Gefüge n
square-set stoping Blockbau m mit Geviertzimmerung
squat 1. s. slime, mud, mire; 2. kleiner Gangerzkörper m; Erzfall m; Zinnerz n mit Gangart
squeeze off/to abquetschen
~ **out** verdrücken, abpressen, ausquetschen, zerquetschen, auswalzen
squeeze Auspressung f, Wasserdruckversuch m
~ **cementation** Druckzementierung f
~ **cementing operation** Druckzementation f
squeezed fold Quetschfalte f *(Falte mit Materialtransport in die Schenkel)*
~ **middle limb** verdünnter Mittelschenkel m
~-**out middle limb** ausgequetschter Mittelschenkel m
squeezing-out Abpressen n
squiggle Linienschrift f *(Seismik)*
stability Stabilität f; Standsicherheit f, Standfestigkeit f; Widerstandsfähigkeit f
~ **field** Stabilitätsfeld n
stabilization of earthwork Bodenbefestigung f
~ **of flow conditions** Stabilisierung f des Strömungszustands
stabilized platform stabilisierte Plattform f *(auf Schiffen für Messungen der Schwerkraft)*
stabilizing workings Sicherungsarbeiten fpl
stable stabil; standfest; beständig; ungestört *(Lagerung)*
~ **channel** stabiles Flußbett n
~ **continental shelf** stabiler Kontinentalschelf m
~ **equilibrium** stabiles Gleichgewicht n
~ **isotope** stabiles Isotop n
~ **phase** stabile Phase f
~ **relict** stabiles Relikt n
~ **rock** festes Gebirge n
~ **shelf** stabiler Schelf m
staccato injection wiederholte Injektion f
stack 1. Brandungssäule f, Brandungspfeiler m; 2. Stapelung f *(Seismik)*
~ **caves** Fußhöhlen fpl
~ **multiplicity** Stapelgrad m *(Seismik)*
~ **resistance** Übergangswiderstand m der Elektrodenstäbe *(Geoelektrik)*
~ **velocity** Stapelgeschwindigkeit f
stacking of drill pipe stands Abstellen n der Gestängezüge
~ **process** Stapelung f *(Seismik)*
stade Stadium n *(von pleistozänen Eisbewegungen)*
stadia Nivellierinstrument n
stadial moraine Endmoräne f
staff Meßlatte f
~ **gauge** Lattenpegel m, Pegellatte f
stage 1. Stufe f *(Einheit der biostratigrafischen Gliederung)*; 2. Stadium n; 3. drehbarer Objekttisch m
~ **cementing** Stufenzementation f, absatzweises Zementieren n
~ **hydrograph** Wasserstandsganglinie f
~ **micrometer** Objektmikrometer n
~ **of deglaciation** Zwischeneiszeit f, Interglazial n
~ **of detailed prospecting** Stadium n der eingehenden Erkundung
~ **of evolution** Entwicklungsstadium n
~ **of geological prospecting** Stadium n geologischer Untersuchungsarbeiten
~ **of late maturity** Altersstadium n
~ **of maturity** Reifestadium n
~ **of old age** Greisenstadium n
~ **of previous prospecting** Stadium n der Vorerkundung
~ **of youth** Jugendstadium n
~ **working** Tagebau m

stages/by etappenweise
stagnant stagnierend
~ **backwater** stehendes Wasser *n*
~ **basin** abflußloses (geschlossenes) Becken *n*
~ **pool** Tümpel *m*
~ **water** stehendes Gewässer *n*, stagnierendes Wasser *n*, Standwasser *n*, Altwasser *n*
stagnate/to stagnieren
stagnating stagnierend
stagnation layer Staunässebereich *m*
~ **point** Umkehrpunkt *m* *(Grundwasserströmung am Brunnen)*
~ **pressure** Staudruck *m*
stain of oi Ölfleck *m*
stained fleckig, gesprenkelt
stainierite Stainierit *m*, Heterogenit *m*, CoOOH
staining test Anfärbeprobe *f (Mineralprüfung)*
stake out/to abstecken
stake vorübergehende Markierung *f (Seismik)*
~ **resistance** Übergangswiderstand *m* der Elektrodenstäbe *(Geoelektrik)*
stalactic[al] stalaktitisch
stalactiform stalaktitisch, tropfsteinartig
stalactital stalaktitisch
stalactite Stalaktit *m*
~ **cavern** Tropfsteinhöhle *f*
stalactitic[al] stalaktitisch
stalacto stalagmite durch Vereinigung von Stalagmit und Stalaktit entstandene Säule *f*
stalagma stalaktitischer Kalkstein *m*
stalagmeter Stalagmeter *n*, Tropfenmesser *m*
stalagmite Stalagmit *m*
stalagmitic[al] stalagmitartig, stalagmitisch
stalk Stengel *m*
stalked stengelig
stamp mill Pochwerk *n*
stand pipe 1. Standrohr *n (Bohren)*; 2. Steigleitung *f (für Wasser)*
~ **-up formation** festes Gebirge *n*
standard cell Standardzelle *f (nach Eskola)*
~ **condition pressure** Normdruck *m*
~ **electric logging** elektrisches Standardmeßverfahren *n*
~ **for reflectance measurement** Reflexionsstandard *m*
~ **mean ocean water** Normal-Ozeanwasser-Standard *m*
~ **mineral** Standardmineral *n*
~ **section** Standardprofil *n*
~ **specification** Normenvorschrift *f*
~ **stratum** Leithorizont *m*
~ **time** Normalzeit *f*
standing level Ruhewasserspiegel *m*
~ **on end** vertikal, seiger
~ **time** Standdauer *f*
~ **water** stehendes Gewässer *n*
standstill *Zeitdauer, während der keine Spiegelschwankungen des Meeres auftreten*
stannary Zinnbergwerk *n*, Zinngrube *f*
stannic zinnhaltig, Zinn...
stanniferous zinnführend, zinnhaltig

stannite Stannin *m*, Zinnkies *m*, Cu_2FeSnS_4
stannopalladinite Stannopalladinit *m*, Pd_3Sn_2
stannous zinnhaltig, Zinn...
stannum Zinn *n*, Sn *(s.a.* tin)
staple Gesenk *n*, Blindschacht *m*
star Stern *m*
~ **ash** Sternenasche *f*
~ **cloud** Sternwolke *f*
~ **cluster** Sternhaufen *m*
~ **day** Sterntag *m*
~ **map** Sternkarte *f*, Sterntafel *f*
~ **of first magnitude** Stern *m* erster Größe
~ **quartz** Sternquarz *m*
~ **sapphire** Sternsaphir *m (s.a.* corundum)
~ **-shaped** sternförmig
~ **streaming** Sternströme *mpl*
starfish Seestern *m*
staring Nachauftragnehmerschaft *f (für geologische Untersuchungsarbeiten)*
starless sternenlos
starlight *s.* starlit
starlight Sternenlicht *n*
starlike sternartig
starlit sternklar
starred gestirnt
starriness Sternenhelle *f*
starry gestirnt, sternhell, sternartig
start a borehole/to ein Bohrloch ansetzen
~ **a drift** eine Strecke ansetzen
~ **drilling** mit Bohren beginnen
starting place Ursprungsstelle *f*
starved basin ausgehungertes Becken *n (Senkung überwiegt Sedimentation)*
stassfurtite Staßfurtit *m (s.a.* boracite)
state of aggregation Aggregatzustand *m*
~ **of being eroded** Erosionsgrad *m*
~ **of crystallization** Kristallisationszustand *m*, Kristallisationsstadium *n*
~ **of development** Entwicklungsstadium *n*
~ **of flow** Strömungsstadium *n*, Strömungszustand *m*
~ **of fusion** geschmolzener Zustand *m*
~ **of hydration** Hydratationszustand *m*
~ **of inertia** Beharrungszustand *m (beim Pumpversuch)*
~ **of stress** Spannungszustand *m*
~ **of weightlessness** Zustand *m* der Schwerelosigkeit
static bottom-hole pressure statischer Bodendruck *m*
~ **casing pressure** Ringraumruhedruck *m*
~ **correction** statische Korrektur *f*
~ **friction** Haftreibung *f*, Ruhereibung *f*
~ **friction coefficient** Reibungsbeiwert *m* der Ruhe
~ **ground-water resource** Grundwasserlagerstättenvorrat *m*
~ **head** statische Auftriebshöhe (Druckhöhe) *f*
~ **level** Ruhewasserspiegel *m*
~ **load test** statische Belastungsprüfung *f*
~ **metamorphism** statische Metamorphose *f*, Belastungsmetamorphose *f*

static

- ~ **pressure head** statische Druckhöhe f
- ~ **prestrain** statische Vorspannung f
- ~ **tubing pressure** Ruhedruck m im Steigrohr
- **statically indetermined system** statisch unbestimmtes System n (Gebirgsmechanik)
- **station** Station f, Meßpunkt m
- ~ **interval** s. stationary interval
- **stationary** stationär, ruhend
- ~ **drilling rig** stationäre (ortsfeste) Bohranlage f
- ~ **dune** ruhende Düne f
- ~ **interval** Stationsabstand m, Meßpunktabstand m
- ~ **mass** stationäre Masse f
- ~ **time series** stationäre Zeitreihen fpl
- **statistical record** statistische Aufzeichnung f
- **statocysts** Statocysten fpl, Hörbläschen npl
- **statoliths** Statolithen mpl (Gleichgewichtssteine bei Wirbellosen)
- **statuary marble, statue-marble** Bildhauermarmor m, Statuenmarmor m
- **status of preservation** Erhaltungszustand m (z.B. von Fossilien)
- **staurolite** Staurolith m, AlFe$_2$O$_3$(OH)·4Al$_2$[O|SiO$_4$]
- ~-**in isograd** Staurolith-Isograd m (Beginn des Auftretens von Staurolith)
- **staurotide** s. staurolite
- **steady flow** stationäre Strömung f
- ~ **flow of ground water** stationäre Grundwasserströmung f
- ~ **mass** stationäre Masse f
- ~ **pressure decline in the reservoir** stetiger Abfall m des Lagerstättendrucks
- ~ **rain** Landregen m
- ~-**state flow** stationäre Strömung f
- **steam** Dampf m
- ~ **blast** Dampfstrahl m
- ~ **column** Rauchsäule f (eines Vulkans)
- ~ **flooding** Dampffluten n (Sekundärfördermethode für Erdöl und Erdgas)
- ~ **injection process** Dampfflutverfahren n
- **steatite** Steatit m, Speckstein m, Seifenstein m, Saponit m, Topfstein m, dichter Talk m, Mg$_3$[(OH)$_2$|Si$_4$O$_{10}$]
- **steatitic** specksteinartig
- **steel band** Pyritband n in der Kohle
- ~ **jack** Schalenblende f, Zinkblende f, ZnS
- ~ **ore** s. siderite 1.
- **steenstrupine** Steenstrupin m, Na$_2$Ce(Mn, Ta, Fe,...)H$_2$[(Si, P)O$_4$]$_3$
- **steep in lye/to** laugen
- **steep** abschüssig, steil
- ~ **angle reflection** Steilwinkelreflexion f
- ~ **bank** Steilufer n
- ~ **coast** Steilküste f; steiler Abhang m
- ~ **dip** steiles Einfallen n
- ~-**dipping strata** steil einfallende Schichten fpl
- ~ **dune** Steildüne f
- ~ **escarpment** Steilabfall m
- ~ **face** Steilhang m
- ~ **fall** steiler Abfall m
- ~-**limbed fold** Falte f mit steilen Schenkeln
- ~ **saddle** Steilsattel m
- ~ **seam** steiles Flöz n, steil gelagerte Schicht f
- ~-**sided** steil[wandig], steilbegrenzt
- ~ **slope** Steilböschung f, Steilabhang m
- ~-**sloped** steil[wandig]
- ~ **vein** steiler Gang m
- ~-**walled** steil[wandig]
- **steepening of dip** Vergrößerung f des Einfallens
- **steeply inclined strata** steil einfallende Schichten fpl
- ~ **sloping** steil abfallend
- ~ **tilted up,** ~ **upturned** steil aufgerichtet
- **steepness** Abschüssigkeit f, Steilheit f
- **steigerite** Steigerit m, Al[VO$_4$]·3H$_2$O
- **stellar** stellar, sternförmig, Stern..., astral
- ~ **ash** Sternenasche f
- ~ **body** Himmelskörper m
- ~ **coal** s. stellarite
- ~ **constellation** Sternbild n
- ~ **magnetic field** stellares Magnetfeld n
- ~ **matter** Sternmaterie f
- ~ **spectrum** Sternspektrum n
- ~ **time** Sternzeit f
- **stellarite** Stellarit m, Asphalt m (von Nova Scotia)
- **stellate** sternförmig
- ~ **cluster** sternförmiger Haufen m
- **stellated** sternförmig
- ~ **structure** radiales Gefüge n
- **stellerite** Stellerit m (s.a. stilbite)
- **stelliferous** bestirnt
- **stellular** sternchenartig
- **stelznerite** Stelznerit m, Antlerit m (s.a. antlerite)
- **stem** Stamm m (Paläontologie)
- ~ **ossicles** Stielglieder npl
- **stemflow** Niederschlagsmenge, die den Erdboden über die Baumstämme erreicht
- **stemming** Anstauung f, Stauung f (von Wasser)
- **stenohaline** stenohalin
- **stenonite** Stenonit m, Sr$_2$Al[F$_5$|CO$_3$]
- **step** Staffel f, Stufe f, Treppe f, Absatz m (z.B. in Gesteinsschichten und Flözen)
- ~ **fault** Staffelbruch m, Treppenverwerfung f, Terrassenverwerfung f
- ~ **faults hading against the dip** antithetische Staffelverwerfungen fpl
- ~ **faults hading with the dip** synthetische Staffelverwerfungen fpl
- ~ **fold** Flexur f, Monoklinalfalte f
- ~ **function** Sprungfunktion f, Rechteckfunktion f
- **stepanovite** Stepanovit m, NaMgFe$^{\cdots}$[C$_2$O$_4$]$_8$·8–9H$_2$O
- **stepback** Stepback n (Korrektur für Messungen auf See)
- **Stephanian [Stage]** Stefan[ien] n, Stefanium (Stufe des Oberkarbons in Mittel- und Westeuropa)

stephanite Stephanit m, Sprödglaserz n, Schwarzgültigerz n, $5Ag_2S \cdot Sb_2S_3$
step-out Differenz in der Ankunftszeit einer seismischen Reflexion zwischen zwei benachbarten Spuren
~-out well Erweiterungsbohrung f auf bekanntem Horizont
steplike profile stufenförmiger Abhang m
steppe Steppe f
~ **black earth** schwarzer Steppenboden m, Tschernosem m
~ **bleached earth** ausgelaugter Alkaliboden m
~ **covered with low bushes** Zwergstrauchsteppe f
~ **soil** Steppenboden m
~ **zone** Steppenzone f
stepped stufenförmig
~ **bore (hole)** abgesetzte Bohrung f
~ **profile** stufenförmiger Abhang m
stepping stufenförmig
steppization Steppenbildung f
stercorite Stercorit m, $(NH_4)NaH[PO_4] \cdot 4H_2O$
stereobase Stereobasis f (Luftgeologie)
stereographic stereografisch
~ **projection** stereografische Projektion f
stereophotogrammetrical survey stereofotogrammetrische Aufnahme f
stereoscopic interpretation of imagery Stereobildauswertung f
~ **model** Stereomodell n (Luftgeologie)
~ **pair** Stereopaar n (Luftgeologie)
~ **viewing** Stereobetrachtung f
sterile 1. taub, erzfrei; 2. unfruchtbar
~ **mass** taubes Mittel n
sternbergite Sternbergit m, $AgFe_2S_3$
sternum Sternum n, Brustbein n
sterny grobkörnig
sterrettite Sterretit m, $Sc[PO_4] \cdot 2H_2O$
stetefeldite Stetefeldit m, $Ag_{1-2}Sb_{2-1}(O, OH, H_2O)_7$
stevensite s. montmorillonite
stewartite Stewartit m, $MnFe_2[OH|PO_4]_2 \cdot 8H_2O$
stey s. steep
stib s. hitch
stibarsenic Stibarsen m, AsSb
stiberite s. ulexite
stibial antimonartig, Antimon...
stibiated mit Antimonit gemengt
stibiconite Stibiconit m, $SbSb_2O_6OH$
stibine Antimonnickelglanz m (s.a. ullmannite)
stibiodomeykite Stibiodomeykit m, $3CU_3(As, Sb)$
stibioluzonite Stibioluzonit m, Cu_3SbS_4
stibiopalladinite Stibiopalladinit m, Pd_3Sb
stibiotantalite Stibiotantalit m, $Sb(Ta, Nb)O_4$
stibium Antimon n, Sb
stiblite s. stibiconite
stibnite Stibnit m, Antimonglanz m, Antimonit m, Grauspießglanz m, Sb_2S_3
stichtite Stichtit m, $Mg_6Cr_2[(OH)_{16}|CO_3] \cdot 4H_2O$
stick sulphur Stangenschwefel m
stickiness Klebrigkeit f

sticking of ore Hängenbleiben n von Erz (am Nebengestein)
~ **of the pipe** Festwerden n des Rohrs
stickogram diagrams digitalisierte Darstellung f der Impulsformen (Seismik)
sticky klebrig, leimig
~ **clay** klebriger Ton m
~ **formation** drückendes Gebirge n
~ **limit** Klebgrenze f
~ **shale** haftender (klebender, schmieriger) Schieferton m
stictolithic structure Fleckentextur f (bei Magmatit)
stiff breeze steife Brise f
~**-fissured clay** steifer geklüfteter Ton m
~**-plastic** steifplastisch
stiffness Steifigkeit f
~ **coefficient** Steifezahl f, Steifheitsmodul m
stigmarian bed Wurzelboden m
~ **roots** Stigmarien fpl
stilbite Stilbit m, $Ca[Al_2Si_7O_{18}] \cdot 7H_2O$
stilleite Stilleit m, ZnSe
stilling basin (pool, well) Beruhigungsbecken n, Tosbecken n
stillwater Stillwasser n
stillwellite Stillwellit m, $(Ce, La)_3[B_3O_6|Si_3O_9]$
stilpnomelane Stilpnomelan m (Fe-Silikat, Mineral der Hydrobiotit-Vermiculit-Reihe)
stilpnosiderite Eisenpecherz n, Pecheisenerz n, Stilpnosiderit m (amorphes Brauneisen)
stimulate well flow/to die Förderung anregen (bei einer Sonde)
stimulation of well Anregung f der Förderung (einer Sonde)
stink coal Papierkohle f
~ **damp** stinkende Wetter pl (mit H_2S angereichert)
stinking schist Stinkschiefer m
stinkstone Stinkschiefer m; Stinkkalk m
stishovite Stishovit m, SiO_2 tetragonal
stochastics Stochastik f
stock 1. Vorrat m; 2. Halde f; 3. Stock m (magmatisch)
~ **coal** Haldenkohle f
~ **of water** Wasservorrat m
~ **tank oil** entgastes Erdöl n
~**-water well** Anreicherungsbrunnen m
stockpile Vorratshalde f
stockpiled material Haldenmaterial n
stockpiling 1. Haldenschüttung f, Haldenlagerung f; 2. Lagerhaltung f
stockwork Erzkörper m größerer Tiefenerstreckung, Erzstock m
stoichiometric stöchiometrisch
stoichiometry Stöchiometrie f
Stokes equation Stokessches Gesetz n
stokesite Stokesit m, $Ca_2Sn_2[Si_6O_{18}] \cdot 4H_2O$
stolzite Stolzit m, Scheelbleierz n, $PbWO_4$
stomach stone Magenstein m (z.B. in Verbindung mit Sauriern)
stone 1. Gesteinsstück n, Stein m; 2. Halbedelstein m; 3. Toneisenstein m

stone

~ **alum** Steinalaun *m*, Bergalaun *m*
~ **band** Bergemittel *n*
~ **bed** Steinbank *f*
~ **bind** *s.* rock bind
~ **breaker** Grobbrecher *m*, Schotterbrecher *m*
~ **bubble** Lithophyse *f (in Magmatiten)*
~ **chips** Steinsplitter *mpl*
~ **circle** *s.* ~ rings
~ **coal** Anthrazit *m*; Steinkohle *f*
~ **crusher** *s.* ~ breaker
~-**crushing plant** Schotterwerk *n*
~ **desert** Steinwüste *f*, Felswüste *f*
~ **drain** Steindräne *f*
~ **drift** Gesteinsstrecke *f*
~ **dust** Gesteinsstaub *m*
~ **dust barrier,** ~ **duster** Gesteinsstaubsperre *f*
~ **field** Felsenmeer *n*
~ **garland** Steingirlande *f*
~ **grating** Steingitter *n*
~ **grinding** Steinschliff *m*
~ **head** festes Gestein *n*
~ **ice** fossiles Eis *n*
~ **marrow** Steinmark *n (s.a.* nacrite)
~ **meteorite** Steinmeteorit *m*
~ **net** *s.* ~ rings
~ **oil** *s.* petroleum
~ **pit** Steinbruch *m*
~ **pitch** Steinpech *n*, Glaspech *n*
~ **polygon** *s.* ~ rings
~ **polygon soil** Wabenboden *m*, Polygonalboden *m*
~ **quarry** Steinbruch *m*
~ **rings** Polygonalstrukturen *fpl*, Steinringe *mpl (Frostboden)*
~ **river (run)** Bergsturzmasse *f*, Blockstrom *m*
~ **slab correction** Gesteinsplattenkorrektur *f*
~ **strings** Steinbänder *npl*
~ **stripes** Steinstreifen *mpl (Frostboden)*
~ **sweeping** Steinschlag *m*
~ **turf** dichter Torf *m*
~ **wreath** *s.* ~ rings
Stone Age Steinzeit *f*
stonegall Tonkonkretion *f* in Sandstein
stones Bruchgestein *n*
stoneware clay Steinzeugton *m*
stony steinig; steinartig; steinern
~ **cast** Steinkern *m*
~ **desert** Steinwüste *f*, Felswüste *f*
~ **iron meteorite** Lithosiderit *m (Meteorit)*
~ **meteorite** Steinmeteorit *m*
~ **soil** Steinboden *m*
~ **waste** Steinwüste *f*, Felswüste *f*
stool Baumstubben *m*
stop up/to verstopfen
stop-cocking stoßweises Springenlassen *n (einer Ölbohrung)*
stope/to über sich abbrechen *(Magma)*
~ **in** zubruchgehen
~ **overhand** im Firstenbau abbauen
~ **underhand** einen Strossenstoß abbauen
stope Abbauort *n*, Strosse *f*
~ **filling** Bergeversatz *m*

~ **rejection** taubes Gestein *n*
stoping 1. Aufstemmen *n (von Magma);* 2. Strossenbau *m*
~ **ground** erzführendes Gestein *n*
stopping basin Rückhaltebecken *n*, Hochwasserrückhaltebecken *n*
storage Stau *m*, Aufstau *m*, Anstauung *f*, Speicherung *f*
~ **basin** Speicherbecken *n*
~ **capacity** Speicherkapazität *f*, Speichervermögen *n*, Stauraum *m*
~ **coefficient** Speicherkoeffizient *m (Grundwasserleiter)*
~ **cycle** Speicherzyklus *m*
~-**draft curve** Vorratsergänzungskurve *f*
~ **lake** Stausee *m*
~ **method** Speichermethode *f (bei radioaktiver Altersbestimmung)*
~ **properties** Speichereigenschaften *fpl*
~ **reservoir** Stausee *m*; Talsperrenbecken *n*, Rückhaltebecken *n*
storeyed peak plain Gipfelflurtreppe *f*
storing Stapelung *f*
storm orkanartiger Sturm *m (Beaufortskala)*
~ **beach** Hochwasserstrand *m*
~ **centre** Sturmzentrum *n*
~ **cloud** Wetterwolke *f*, Gewitterwolke *f*
~ **precipitation** Platzregen *m*
~ **rainfall** Sturzregen *m*
~ **scud** niedrigziehende Sturmwolke *f*
~ **stone** *(sl)* Donnerkeil *m*, Belemnit *m*
~ **surge** Sturmflut *f*
~-**surge lamination** Sturmflutschichtung *f*
~ **tide** Sturmflut *f*
~ **vortex** Sturmwirbel *m*
~ **water** Regenwasser *n*, Niederschlagswasser *n*
~ **wave** Sturmwelle *f*
stottite Stottit *m*, $FeGe(OH)_6$
stowage Versatz *m*, Bergeversatz *m*
stowing material Versatzgut *n*, Versatzberge *pl*
straddle spread *s.* split spread
straight ungemischt
~-**chain paraffins** geradkettige Paraffine *npl*
~ **channel pattern** Rinnenmuster *n* eines annähernd geradlinig verlaufenden Flusses
~ **circulation** direkte Spülung *f*
~ **coast line** geradlinige Küste *f*
~ **down** lotgerecht, senkrecht
~ **extinction** gerade Auslöschung *f*
~ **hole drilling** Geradbohren *n*
~-**line portion** geradliniger Abschnitt *m (z.B. einer Druckaufbaukurve)*
~ **mineral oil** reines Mineralöl *n*
~ **tusk** gerader Stoßzahn *m*
straighten up/to aufrichten
straightened-up layer aufgerichtete Schicht *f*
strain Strain *m*, Deformation *f*
~ **cleavage** *s.* ~-slip cleavage
~ **drop** Deformationsabfall *m*
~ **ellipsoid** Deformationsellipsoid *n*

stratigraphy

~ **gauge** Dehnungsmesser *m*, Dehnungsmeßstreifen *m*
~ **hardening** Kaltverfestigung *f*
~ **shadows** undulöse Auslöschung *f*
~-**slip cleavage** S₂-Schieferung *f*, Schubklüftung *f*, Runzelschieferung *f*
~ **work** Deformationsarbeit *f*
strainer Filterrohr *n*
strainmeter Strainseismograf *m*
strainometer Dehnungsmesser *m*
strait Straße *f*, Meerenge *f*
strake Schmelzwasserspur *f (auf der Gletscheroberfläche)*
strand Strand *m*
~ **dune** Stranddüne *f*
~ **line** Strandlinie *f*, Uferlinie *f*
~-**line pool** Küstenrifflagerstätte *f (Erdöl)*
~ **plain** Strandebene *f*
strandflat Küstenplattform *f*
strange allochthon, ortsfremd
strangling horizon Würgehorizont *m*, Kryoturbationshorizont *m (Frostboden)*
stranskiite Stranskiit *m*, CuZn₂[AsO₄]₂
strat trap *s*. stratigraphic trap
strata 1. Gebirge *n (im montangeologischen Sinne)*; 2. Schichten *fpl*, Gesteinsschichten *fpl (s.a. stratum)*
~ **bolting** Verankerung *f* des Hangenden, Gebirgsverankerung *f*, Ankerausbau *m*
~-**bound deposit** sedimentäre Schichtlagerstätte *f*
~ **bridge** Gesteinsbrücke *f*
~ **cohesion** Gebirgsfestigkeit *f*
~ **control** Beherrschung *f* des Gebirges, Hangendpflege *f*
~ **displacement** Schichtenverschiebung *f*, Gebirgsverlagerung *f*
~/**in** flözweise
~ **joint** schichtungsparallele Kluft *f*
~ **movement** Gebirgsbewegung *f*
~ **profile** Schichtenprofil *n*
~ **section** Schichtenschnitt *m*
~ **sequence (series)** Schichtenaufbau *m*, Schichtenfolge *f*
~ **spring** Schichtquelle *f*
~ **time** sich aus Schichtdicke und Sedimentationsrate ergebende Zeitdauer *f*
stratal Schichten...
stratascope Strataskop *n*
strath 1. ehemaliger Talboden *m* mit mächtiger Alluvione *(auf Peneplain)*; 2. breites Flußtal *n*
straticulate/to schichten
straticulate in dünnen Schichten geordnet, gebändert
stratification Lagerung *f*, Schichtung *f*
~ **lamina** Schichtblatt *n*
~ **line** Schichtenlage *f*, Schichtenfuge *f*
~ **of the ice** Blaublättertextur *f (eines Gletschers)*
~ **plane** Schicht[ungs]fläche *f*, Ablagerungsfläche *f*

~ **surfaces** Bankungsklüfte *fpl (schichtungsparallele Klüfte in Sedimentgesteinen)*
stratified deposit schichtige Lagerstätte *f*
~ **flow** Schichtenströmung *f*
~ **in thick beds** bankig
~ **rock** Schichtgestein *n*, Sedimentgestein *n*
~ **sampling** differenzierte Probenahme *f (Probenahme aus einer Mischung verschiedener Gesamtheiten mit einer Wichtung jeder der Gesamtheiten)*
~ **structure** schichtiges Gefüge *n*
~ **water** geschichtetes Wasser *n (durch Temperatur und Salinität)*
stratiform 1. schichtenförmig; 2. schichtwolkenförmig
~ **deposit** *s*. strata-bound deposit
stratify/to schichten, [dar]überschichten
stratigrapher Stratigraf *m*
stratigraphic[al] stratigrafisch
~ **age** stratigrafisches Alter *n*
~ **arrangement** Schichtenaufbau *m*
~ **bottom edge** stratigrafische Unterkante *f*
~ **boundary plane** stratigrafische Grenzfläche *f*
~ **break** stratigrafische Unterbrechung *f*, Schichtlücke *f*, Hiatus *m*
~ **classification** stratigrafische Klassifikation *f*
~ **column** Schichtenfolge *f*
~ **condensation** stratigrafische Kondensation *f*
~ **conditions** Lagerungsbedingungen *fpl*
~ **connotation** stratigrafische Begriffsabgrenzung *f*
~ **division** stratigrafische Gliederung *f*
~ **gap** Lücke *f* in der Schichtenfolge, stratigrafische Lücke *f*, Schichtlücke *f*
~ **geologist** Stratigraf *m*
~ **geology** Formationskunde *f*, Stratigrafie *f*
~ **guide lines** stratigrafische Richtlinien *fpl*
~ **hiatus** *s*. ~ gap
~ **interpretation** stratigrafische Auswertung (Deutung) *f*
~ **interval** stratigrafisches Intervall *n (Anzahl von Schichten zwischen zwei Leithorizonten)*
~ **level** *s*. marker 1.
~ **nomenclature** stratigrafische Nomenklatur *f*
~ **range** stratigrafische Verbreitung *f*, geologische Lebensdauer *f (eines Fossils)*
~ **section** Schichtenprofil *n*
~ **separation** stratigrafische Sprunghöhe *f*
~ **sequence (succession)** Schichtenfolge *f*
~ **table** Formationstabelle *f*
~ **terminology** stratigrafische Terminologie *f*
~ **throw** stratigrafische Sprunghöhe *f*
~ **trap** stratigrafische Falle *f*
~ **unconformity** stratigrafische Diskordanz *f*, Erosionsdiskordanz *f*, Emersionsfläche *f*
~ **unit** stratigrafische Einheit *f*
~ **well** Basisbohrung *f*, stratigrafische Bohrung *f*, Parameterbohrung *f*
stratigraphically above im Hangenden
stratigraphy Stratigrafie *f*, Formationskunde *f*

stratocirrus 338

stratocirrus cloud Zirrostratus *m*, Cirrostratus *m*
stratocumulus cloud Stratokumulus *m*, Stratocumulus *m*
stratosphere Stratosphäre *f*
~ **radiation** Stratosphärenstrahlung *f*
stratotype Stratotyp *m*
stratovolcano Stratovulkan *m*, Schichtvulkan *m*
stratum Schicht *f*, Gesteinsschicht *f*, Lage *f* (*s.a.* strata)
~ **length** Schichtlänge *f*
~ **of coal** Kohlenschicht *f*
~ **thickness** Schichtmächtigkeit *f*
~ **water** Schichtwasser *n*
stratus Stratus *m*, Schichtwolke *f*
~ **cloud** Stratuswolke *f*
straw stalactite Federkielstalaktit *m*
stray current Streustrom *m*
~ **earth current** vagabundierender Erdstrom *m*
~ **sand** zufällig auftretende Sandlinse *f*
strays Flugsand *m*
streak/to ädern, streifen
streak 1. Schliere *f*; 2. Streifen *m*, Strich *m* (*eines Minerals*); 3. Erzschnur *f*, Erzader *f*; 4. Schmitze *f*
~ **colour** Strichfarbe *f* (*Porzellantafel*)
~ **lightning** Linienblitz *m*
~ **of coal** Kohleschmitze *f*
~ **of sand** Sandschmitze *f*
~ **plate** Strichplatte *f*
~ **test** Strichprobe *f*
streaked 1. adrig, [band]streifig, gestreift, gemasert, maserig, schlierig; 2. linear-parallel angeordnet
~ **structure** Fluidaltextur *f*, Schlierentextur *f*; Flasertextur *f*
streakiness Streifigkeit *f*
streaking linearparallele Mineralanordnung *f*
streaky *s.* streaked
stream/to 1. strömen; 2. Erz waschen
stream 1. Strom *m*, Fluß *m*, Wasserlauf *m* (*s.a.* river); 2. Strömung *f*; 3. Talgletscher *m*; 4. Lavastrom *m*
~ **bed** Strombett *n*, Flußbett *n*
~ **bed erosion** Auswaschen *n* des Flußbetts
~ **beheading** *s.* ~ capture
~-**borne materials discharge** Sinkstoffgehalt *m*
~-**borne sediment** Flußsediment *n*
~ **capture** Flußenthauptung *f*, Flußanzapfung *f*, Flußkappung *f*
~ **centre line** Flußachse *f*
~ **channel** Flußbett *n*, Strombett *n*, Flußrinne *f*
~ **cut** Flußeinschnitt *m*
~ **debouchure** Flußmündung *f*
~ **discharge** Abflußmenge *f* eines Wasserlaufs
~ **diversion** *s.* river diversion
~ **erosion** Flußerosion *f*
~-**flow control** Abflußregulierung *f*
~-**flow regime** Flußregime *n*
~ **frequency** Abflußschwankung *f*
~ **function** Strömungsfunktion *f*, Stromfunktion *f*

~ **gauging** Wassermengenmessung *f*, Abflußbeobachtung *f* (*des Flußwassers*)
~ **gauging network** Flußpegelnetz *n*
~ **gold** Seifengold *n*
~ **gradient** Stromgefälle *n*
~ **gravel** Flußkies *m*
~ **hydrograph** Strömungsganglinie *f*, Abflußganglinie *f*
~ **ice** Flußeis *n*
~ **inversion** Flußumkehr[ung] *f*
~-**laid sediment** Flußsediment *n*
~ **line** Stromlinie *f*
~ **line flow** laminare Strömung *f*
~ **of lava** Lavastrom *m*
~ **ore** Seifenerz *n*
~ **piracy** *s.* ~ capture
~ **placer** Flußseife *f*
~ **power** Strömungsenergie *f*
~ **rejuvenation** Flußverjüngung *f*
~ **robbery** *s.* ~ capture
~ **spacing** Flußabstand *m*
~ **surface** Stromfläche *f*
~ **system** Stromsystem *n*
~ **tin** Seifenzinn *n*, Zinnseife *f*
~ **transportation** Flußtransport *m*
~-**transported** flußverfrachtet
~ **velocity** 1. Strömungsgeschwindigkeit *f*; 2. Flußgeschwindigkeit *f*
~-**worn** flußzerschnitten (*Tal*)
streamer Streamer *m* (*seeseismischer Kabelbaum*)
streaming 1. Strömung *f*; 2. Seifenerzgewinnung *f*; 3. linearparallele Mineralanordnung *f*; Streckung *f*
~ **potential** Strömungspotential *n*
streamlet Bächlein *n*, Flüßchen *n*, Rinnsal *n*, Gerinne *n*
streamline Stromlinie *f*
streamtube Stromröhre *f*
streamy von Wasserläufen durchzogen
strengite Strengit *m*, $Fe[PO_4] \cdot 2H_2O$
strength behaviour Festigkeitsverhalten *n*
~ **criteria** Festigkeitskriterien *npl*
~ **of a source** Quellenergiebigkeit *f*
~ **of coke** Koksfestigkeit *f*
~ **of rupture** Bruchfestigkeit *f*
~ **of the rock mass** Gebirgsfestigkeit *f*
~ **under peripheral pressure** Manteldruckfestigkeit *f*
stress Spannung *f*, Streß *m*
~ **analysis** Festigkeitsnachweis *m*
~ **calculation** Festigkeitsberechnung *f*
~ **component** Spannungskomponente *f*
~ **concentration** Spannungsanhäufung *f*
~ **condition** Spannungszustand *m*
~ **deviator** Spannungsdeviator *m*
~ **distribution** Spannungsverteilung *f*
~ **drop** Spannungsabfall *m*
~ **field** Spannungsfeld *n*
~ **freezing** Einfrieren *n* des Spannungszustands
~ **gradient** Spannungsgefälle *n*

~ **limit** Bruchgrenze f
~ **minerals** Streßminerale npl
~ **of soil moisture** Bodenwasserspannung f
~ **pattern** Spannungsverteilung f
~ **relaxation** Spannungsrelaxation f
~ **release** Spannungsfreisetzung f
~-**relief blasting** Entspannungssprengen n
~ **reversal** Lastwechsel m
~ **state** Spannungszustand m
~-**strain curve** Last-Dehnungs-Kurve f
~-**strain diagram** Spannungs-Dehnungs-Diagramm n
~-**strain relation** Spannungs-Dehnungs-Beziehung f
~ **tensor** Spannungstensor m
~ **trajectory** Hauptspannungslinie f
stretch section Dämpfungslänge f (Teil des seeseismischen Kabelbaums)
~ **thrust** Extensionsüberschiebung f
stretched-out middle limb ausgequetschter Mittelschenkel m
stretching 1. Zerrung f, Dehnung f, Streckung f, Längung f (von Geröllen, Mineralen, Blasen bei Deformation); 2. Lineation f
~ **fault** Zerrungsbruch m, Trennbruch m
~ **haloes** Streckungshöfe mpl
strewn field of tektites Tektitenstreufeld n
stria 1. Rutschstreifen m, Rutschrille f, Schramme f, Friktionsstreifen m; 2. Fiederstreifen m (bei Zwillingskristallen); 3. Riefe f, Furche f
striate/to kritzen
striate s. striated
striated gestreift, gefurcht, geschrammt, geriffelt, gekritzt
~ **boulder** gekritztes (geschrammtes) Geschiebe n
~ **fracture** streifiger Bruch m
~ **ground** Streifenboden m
~ **gypsum** Federgips m
~ **mica** Strahlenglimmer m
~ **ore** strahliges Erz n
~ **pebbles (rock pavements)** gekritzte Geschiebe npl
~ **soil** Streifenboden m
striation 1. Riefung f, Kritze f, Schramme f (sedimentär); 2. Rutschrillen fpl, Rutschstreifen mpl, Friktionsstreifen mpl (tektonisch)
~ **cast (mark)** Driftstreifung f, Riefenmarke f
striction Einschnürung f
strigovite Strigovit m (Mineral der Chloritgruppe)
strike/to 1. streichen; 2. stoßen auf, finden
~ **gold** auf Gold stoßen
~ **oil** auf Öl stoßen
strike 1. Streichen n, Streichrichtung f; 2. Fund m
~/**across the** quer zum Streichen
~/**along the** streichend, im Streichen
~ **and dip readings** Streich- und Fallmessungen fpl
~ **direction** Streichrichtung f

~ **fault** Längsverwerfung f, streichende Störung f, Seitenverschiebung f
~ **fold** streichende Falte f, Falte f parallel zum Schichtstreichen
~ **joint** Längsspalte f
~ **line** Streichlinie f
~ **of beds** Schichtstreichen n
~/**on the** streichend, im Streichen
~ **shift** Verschiebung f im Streichen
~ **slip** horizontale (söhlige) Schublänge f; streichende Sprunghöhe f
~-**slip fault** Blattverschiebung f, Transversalverschiebung f (Verwerfung mit Verschiebung in Richtung des Verwerfungsstreichens)
~ **valley** subsequentes Tal n, Nachfolgetal n
striking Streichrichtung f
string 1. Erztrum n; 2. Strang m; 3. Bohrlochverrohrung f; 4. Kette f (von Geophonen)
~ **bog** Strangmoor n
~ **of casing** Rohrstrang m
~ **of lakes** Seenkette f
~ **of lost casing** Verrohrung f
~ **ore** Erzschnur f
stringer 1. Trum n, Erzschnur f (Lagerstätten); 2. Äderchen n (in Gesteinen); 3. schallharte dünne Schicht f
~ **lead** Erztrum n; Trümerzone f, Durchtrümerung f
~ **lode** Erzschnur f
~ **of quartz** Quarzäderchen n
~ **zone** mineralisierte Zerrüttungszone f, Trümerzone f, Durchtrümerung f
Stringocephalus Limestone Stringocephalenkalk m (Givet)
stringy faserig
strip/to abräumen, abstreifen, bloßlegen
~ **away (off)** abräumen
strip chart Samplerlog n
~ **coal** Tagebaukohle f
~ **mine** Tagebau m
~ **mining** 1. Gewinnung f mittels Bagger; 2. Tagebau m; Abbauen n vom bloßgelegten Ausbiß; Tagebaugewinnung f
~ **pit** Tagebau m
striped streifig, gestreift
~ **ground** Streifenboden m
~ **jasper [stone]** Bandjaspis m (s.a. chalcedony)
stripped gas entbenziniertes Gas n
~ **illite** degradierter Illit m
~ **peneplain** abgedeckte Rumpfebene f
~ **plain** mit Erosionshärtlingen bedeckte Erosionsfläche f
~ **sheet** Deckgebirgsdecke f
stripper [well] Melksonde f, Stripperbohrung f (Sonde an der Grenze der Wirtschaftlichkeit)
stripping 1. Bloßlegen n, Räumungsarbeit f, Abtragung f; 2. Abraum m
~ **ratio** Abraum-Kohle-Verhältnis n
~ **site** Tagebaufeld n
stromatactis stromataktische Struktur f (in Karbonatgesteinen)

stromatic

stromatic structure stromatische Textur *f*, Lagentextur *f (bei Migmatit)*
stromatolite Stromatolith *m*
stromatolitic stromatolithisch
~ **facies** Stromatolithenfazies *f*
Stromatopora limestone Stromatoporenkalk *m*
Strombolian activity Strombolitätigkeit *f*, Schlakkenwurftätigkeit *f*
stromeyerite Stromeyerit *m*, Silberkupferglanz *m*, $Cu_2S \cdot Ag_2S$
strong 1. [druck]fest; 2. groß, bedeutend *(Gänge)*; 3. aufweckend *(5. Stufe der Erdbebenstärkeskala)*
~-**dipping strata** steil einfallende Schichten *fpl*
~ **gale** Sturm *m*
~ **motion earthquake** Zerstörungsbeben *n*, Erdbeben *n* mit starker Erschütterungswirkung
~ **motion instrument (seismometer)** [unempfindliches] Seismometer *n* im Schüttergebiet
~ **vein** mächtige Ader *f*, mächtiger Gang *m*
~ **wind** steife Brise *f*
stronger magnification stärkere Vergrößerung *f*
strongly arched stark gewölbt
~ **folded** stark gefaltet
~ **magnetic** stark magnetisch
strontianite Strontianit *m*, Strontiumkarbonat *n*, $SrCO_3$
strontium Strontium *n*, Sr
structural strukturell, tektonisch, Bau..., Gefüge...
~ **basin** Einbruchsbecken *n*
~ **bench** topografische Bezeichnung für Schichtenausstrich
~ **change** Gefügeänderung *f*
~ **character** Struktureigenschaft *f*
~ **characteristics** *s.* analytic characteristics
~ **composition** Gefügeaufbau *m*
~ **constituent** Gefügebestandteil *m*
~ **crest** Strukturscheitel *m*
~ **depression** Einbruchsbecken *n*
~ **disconformity** *s.* ~ discordance
~ **discordance** Dislokationsdiskordanz *f*, tektonische Diskordanz *f*, Strukturdiskordanz *f*
~ **drilling well** Strukturbohrung *f*
~ **feature** tektonisches Merkmal *n*
~ **form** Strukturform *f*
~ **geology** 1. tektonische Geologie *f*, Tektonik *f*; 2. allgemeine geologische Strukturlehre *f*
~ **layer** Strukturstockwerk *n*
~ **map** Strukturkarte *f*
~ **material** Baustoff *m*, Baumaterial *n*
~ **petrology** *s.* petrotectonics
~ **plateau** Schichttafelland *n*
~ **stage** Strukturstockwerk *n*
~ **style** Baustil *m (Tektonik)*
~ **surface** Strukturfläche *f*
~ **syncline** tektonische Mulde *f*
~ **terrace** Schichtterrasse *f*, Denudationsterrasse *f*, Verwitterungsterrasse *f*
~ **test hole** *s.* structure hole
~ **trap** strukturelle Falle *f*

340

~ **unconformity** *s.* ~ discordance
~ **valley** tektonisches Tal *n*
structure 1. Gefüge *n (allgemein)*; 2. Textur *f (bei Gesteinen)*
~ **contour map** Streichlinienkarte *f*, Konturenkarte *f*
~ **discovery** Entdeckung (Auffindung) *f* einer Struktur
~ **drilling** Aufschlußbohrung *f*, Strukturbohrung *f*
~ **favourable for the accumulation of petroleum** Fangstruktur *f (für die Ansammlung von Erdöl günstige Struktur)*
~ **ground** Texturboden *m*
~ **hole** geologische Schürfbohrung (Strukturbohrung) *f*, Erkundungsbohrung *f*
~ **map** tektonische Karte *f*
~ **of planes** Flächengefüge *n*
~ **of rock mass** Gebirgsverband *m*
~ **of the subsurface** Struktur *f* des Untergrunds
~ **section** Strukturprofil *n*
~ **well** *s.* ~ hole
structured Struktur...
structureless gefügelos, strukturlos, amorph
struggle for live Kampf *m* ums Dasein
Strunian *s. str. s.* Etroeungt
strunzite Strunzit *m*, $MnFe^{\cdots}[OH|PO_4]_2 \cdot 6H_2O$
strut thrust Kompetenzüberschiebung *f (tektonisch)*
strutting Verbolzung *f*
struvite Struvit *m*, $NH_4Mg[PO_4] \cdot 6H_2O$
stub Stubben *m*
stubborn ore strengflüssiges Erz *n*
stuff mit Gangart verhaftetes Erz *n*
stuffed burrows Stopfbauten *mpl (Ichnologie)*
~ **structure** Stopfgefüge *n (Ichnologie)*
stulm Stollen *m*
stump Neck *m*, Stielgang *m*
~ **horizon** Stubbenhorizont *m (Torf- und Kohlenlagerstätten)*
~ **of tree** Baumstubben *m*
sturdiness Härte *f*, Festigkeit *f*; Standfestigkeit *f*
sturdy kräftig, fest; standfest
stützite Stützit *m*, Ag_5Te_3
Styliolina Limestone Styliolinenkalk *m (Devon)*
stylolite Stylolith *m*
stylolitic stylolithisch
~ **contact** stylolithischer Kontakt *m*
~ **limestone** Nagelkalk *m*, Dütenmergel *m*, Tütenkalk *m*
~ **seam** Drucksutur *f (von Stylolithen)*
~ **structure** Drucksutur *f*, stylolithische Textur *f*, Dütentextur *f*
stylotypite Stylotyp[it] *m*, Tetraedrit *m (s.a.* tetrahedrite)
suanite Suanit *m*, $Mg_2[B_2O_5]$
subaerial subaerisch
~ **agents** Verwitterungskräfte *fpl*
~ **eruption** subaerischer Ausbruch *m*
~ **waste** Verwitterungsschutt *m*

subalpine subalpin
subaluminous rocks Gesteine, in denen $Al_2O_3 \cong Na_2O + K_2O$
subangular kantengerundet
subaquatic eruption Unterwasserausbruch m, subaquatische Eruption f
~ **volcano** Unterwasservulkan m
subaqueous unter Wasser, Unterwasser...
~ **bar** subaquatischer Sandrücken m
~ **deposit** Unterwasserablagerung f
~ **gliding (slumping)** subaquatisches Abgleiten n
~ **soil** Unterwasserboden m
~ **solifluction** s. ~ gliding
~ **spring** Unterwasserquelle f
~ **till** von Eisbergen verschleppter Detritus m
subarea Teilgebiet n
Subatlanticum Subatlantikum n (Holozän)
subbase Druckverteilungsschicht f
subbituminous coal [stage A–C] (Am) Hartbraunkohle f (nach dem Inkohlungsgrad: Glanzbraunkohle, Stufe A–B; Mattbraunkohle, Stufe C)
Subboreal Subboreal n (Holozän)
subcapillary subkapillar
~ **interstice** subkapillarer Hohlraum m
Subcarboniferous s. Lower Carboniferous, Mississippian
subcarrier Zwischenmodulation f (Trägerschwingung, Seismik)
subcooled unterkühlt
subcrop verdeckter [submariner] Ausstrich m (einer Schicht)
subcrustal subkrustal
~ **convection currents** Konvektionsströmungen fpl in der subkrustalen Zone
subcrystalline halbkristallinisch
subcutaneous karst subkutaner Karst m
subdeposit Unterlagerung f
subdivision Unterteilung f
subduction Subduktion f, Verschluckung f (tektonisch)
~ **zone** Subduktionszone f
subdued mountains Rückengebirge n, Mittelgebirge n
~ **relief** geringes Relief n
~ **ridge** flacher Höhenzug m
subeconomic reserves wirtschaftlich nicht [ab]bauwürdige Vorräte mpl
suberinite Suberinit m (Braunkohlenmaceral)
subface [of stratum] Sohlfläche f
subfacies Subfazies f
subfamily Unterfamilie f
subgelisol Niefrostboden m
subgenus Untergattung f
subglacial subglazial
~ **eruption** subglazialer Ausbruch m
~ **stream** subglazialer Bach m
~ **till** unter dem Eis geschlepptes Moränenmaterial n
subgrade Erdplanum n, Untergrund m
~ **excavation** Planumauskofferung f

subgravity verminderte Schwere f, Unterschwere f
subgraywacke Subgrauwacke f
subhedral hypidiomorph
~ **structure** hypidiomorphes Gefüge n
Subhercynian phases of folding subherzynische Faltungsphasen fpl
subirrigation Untergrundbewässerung f
subjacent darunter liegend, tiefer gelegen
~ **bed** Liegendes n, liegende Schicht f
~ **stratum** unterlagernde Schicht f, Liegendschicht f
subject to flooding überschwemmungsbedroht
~ **to frost attack** frostempfindlich
~ **to heavy pressure** druckhaft
~ **to rock bursts** gebirgsschlaggefährdet
subjection to bending Biegebeanspruchung f
~ **to pressure** Druckbeanspruchung f
~ **to tension** Zugbeanspruchung f
subjoint Nebenkluft f
sublabile sandstone Sandstein m mit 80–90% Quarz
sublacustrine sublakustrin
sublevation Erosion f unverfestigter Sedimente
sublevel Zwischensohle f, Teilsohle f, Teilsohlenstrecke f
~ **[space] stoping** Zwischensohlen[bruch]bau m
sublimation Sublimation f
sublittoral nahe der Küste liegend
submarginal moraine Endmoräne f
~ **resources** Vorräte, die erst bei stärkerer Verbesserung der Bedingungen bauwürdig werden
submarine untermeerisch, unterseeisch, submarin
~ **bars** dem Strand vorgelagerte Schwellen fpl und Rinnen fpl
~ **canyons** submarine Cañons mpl (am Kontinentalabhang)
~ **channel** submarine Rinne f
~ **detrital slope** submarine Schutthalde f
~ **earthquake** Seebeben n
~ **erosion** untermeerische Erosion (Abtragung) f
~-**exhalative-sedimentary deposit** submarin-exhalativ-sedimentäre Lagerstätte f
~ **fresh ground water** süßes untermeerisches Grundwasser n
~ **hydrothermal field** submarines Hydrothermalfeld n
~ **landslide** submarine Rutschung f
~ **landslide deposit** durch submarinen Erdrutsch entstandene Lagerstätte f
~ **minerals** ökonomisch interessierende Minerale npl des maritimen Raums
~ **pipeline** untermeerische Rohrleitung f
~ **platform** Unterwasserplattform f
~ **ridge** untermeerischer Rücken m
~ **salty ground water** salinäres untermeerisches Grundwasser n

submarine 342

~ **sill** untermeerische Schwelle f
~ **spring** unterseeische Quelle f
~ **topography** Topografie f des Meeresgrundes
~ **trench** untermeerischer Graben m
~ **valley** submarines Tal n
~ **volcanic earthquake** vulkanisches Seebeben n
~ **volcano** unterseeischer (submariner) Vulkan m
~ **weathering** submarine Verwitterung f, Halmyrolyse f
submature nicht ganz reif
submerge/to überfluten, untertauchen
submerged 1. überschwemmt, versunken; 2. ersoffen *(Grube)*
~ **area** Inundationsgebiet n, Überschwemmungsfläche f
~ **dam** Unterwasserdamm m
~ **forest** versunkener Wald m
~ **reef** Unterwasserriff n
~ **ridge** untermeerischer Rücken m
~ **shore line** Senkungsküste f, untergetauchte Küste f
~ **spring** unterseeische Quelle f
submergence 1. Untertauchen n, Überflutung f, Überschwemmung f; Eintauchtiefe f; 2. Bodensenkung f, Senkung f
~ **of coast** Küstensenkung f
~ **of ground** Bodensenkung f
~ **of surface** Oberflächensenkung f
submergible dam überflutbarer Staudamm m
submerging of outlet Unterwasserentlastung f
submersed submers, untergetaucht
submersible Unterwasser…, Tauch…
~ **barge** versenkbarer Schiffsprahm m *(für Meeresbohrung)*
submersion Eintauchen n, Untertauchen n, Überschwemmung f
submetallic metallartig
~ **lustre (sheen)** metallartiger Glanz m
submicroscopic[al] submikroskopisch
submorphic crater Restkrater m
submountain region Vorgebirge n
~ **water ditch** Wasserrösche f
subnate innerhalb (unterhalb) der Erdkruste gebildet
suboceanic subozeanisch, untermeerisch, submarin
subophitic teilweise ophitisch
suborder Unterordnung f
subordinate cone Nebenkegel m
~ **mineral** Nebenmineral n, Begleitmineral n
~ **nappe** Teildecke f
~ **vent** Nebenschlot m
~ **volcano** Nebenvulkan m
suboutcrop verdecktes Ausstreichen n
subpermafrost water Grundwasser n unter dem Permafrost
subphylum Unterstamm m
subpolar 1. nahe dem Pol gelegen; 2. unter dem Himmelspol gelegen

subpressure Unterdruck m
subrecent eruption subrezenter Ausbruch m
subrosion Subrosion f, Ablaugung f
~ **solution** Ablaugungslösung f
subrounded abgekantet, [halb]gerundet
subsaline brackig
subsample Teilprobe f
subsampling Teilprobenahme f
subsaturated untersättigt
subsaturation unvollkommene Sättigung f
subsea unterseeisch, submarin
~ **christmas tree** Unterwassereruptionskreuz n
~ **completion** Unterwasserkomplettierung f
~ **drilling venture** Meeresbohrung f, Unterwasserbohrung f
~ **equipment** Unterwasserausrüstung f
~ **mineral resources** maritime Mineralreserven fpl
~ **production system** Unterwasserproduktionssystem n
~ **work-over** Aufwältigung f unter der See
subsequent subsequent, nachträglich
~ **cross folding** verschiedenzeitliche Querfaltung f
~ **deposit** epigenetische Lagerstätte f
~ **erosion** späte Erosion f
~ **valley** subsequentes Tal n, Nachfolgetal n
subside/to sich senken, sich setzen, niedergehen
subsided block abgesunkene Scholle f
subsidence Senkung f, Absenkung f, Absinken n, Setzen n; Einbruch m, Grundbruch m
~ **basin** Einsturzbecken n
~ **curve** Senkungskurve f
~ **damage** Bergschaden m
~ **earthquake** Einsturzbeben n
~ **factor** Absenkungsfaktor m
~ **of coast** Küstensenkung f
~ **of ground** Bodensenkung f
~ **of ground-water level** Grundwasserabsenkung f
~ **slope** Schieflage f *(Bodensenkung)*
~ **trough** Senkungswanne f, Senkungstrog m
~ **wave** Senkungswelle f
subsidiary cone Nebenkegel m
~ **fault** Nebenverwerfung f, Begleitverwerfung f
~ **fissure** Nebenspalte f
~ **sheet** Teildecke f
subsiding area Absenkungszone f
~ **water** fallendes Wasser n
subsilicic rock basisches Gestein n
subsoil Unterboden m *(Erdschicht unmittelbar unter der Oberfläche)*; Untergrund m, Baugrund m
~ **consolidation** natürliche Baugrundverdichtung f
~ **drainage** Untergrundentwässerung f
~ **exploration** Baugrunduntersuchung f
~ **water** Grundwasser n
~ **water level** Grundwasserspiegel m

343　　**sud**

~ **water-level contours** Grundwassergleichen *fpl*
~ **water packing** Grundwasserabdichtung *f*
~ **water table** Grundwasserspiegel *m*
subsoiling Untergrundlockerung *f*
subsolar tropisch, zwischen den Wendekreisen
subsolifluction Subsolifluktion *f*, Untergrundfließen *n*
subsolution Subsolution *f*
subspecies Subspezies *f*, Unterart *f*
substage Unterstufe *f*
substitution Substitution *f*, Ersetzung *f*, Verdrängung *f*
substratal lineation Lineation *f* auf der Schichtunterseite *(sedimentär)*
substratum 1. Unterlage *f (von Überschiebungsdecken)*; 2. gewachsener Baugrund *m*; 3. Substrat *n*; 4. Unterschicht *f*, tiefere Schicht *f*
~ **of old rock** Grundgebirge *n*
substructure Unterbau *m*
subsurface unterirdisch, Untergrund…
~ **barrier** unterirdische Barriere *f*
~ **catchment area** unterirdisches Einzugsgebiet *n*
~ **contour** Isobathe *f*, Tiefenlinie *f*
~ **contour map** Isobathenkarte *f*, Tiefenlinienkarte *f*
~ **coverage** Reflektorlänge *f (Seismik)*
~ **discharge** unterirdischer Abfluß *m*
~ **draining** Untergrundentwässerung *f*
~ **drilling** untertägiges Bohren *n*
~ **erosion** Auskolkung *f*, Ausspülung *f*
~ **flow** unterirdischer Wasserlauf *m*
~ **investigation** Bodenuntersuchung *f*, Untergrundforschung *f*, Baugrunduntersuchung *f*
~ **irrigation** unterirdische Bewässerung *f*
~ **line** *s*. ~ contour
~ **map** strukturelle Untergrundkarte *f*
~ **pump** Tiefbohrpumpe *f*
~ **runoff** unterirdischer Abfluß *m*
~ **stratigraphic correlation** Tiefenkorrelierung *f*
~ **structure** Struktur *f* des Untergrunds
~ **water** unterirdisches Wasser *n*, unterirdische Hydrosphäre *f*
~ **water ditch** Wasserrösche *f*
subterminal outflow subterminaler Lavaausfluß *m*
subterranean unterirdisch
~ **cauldron subsidence** unterirdischer Kesselbruch *m*
~ **current** Grundwasserstrom *m*
~ **geometry** Markscheidekunst *f*
~ **irrigation** Untergrundbewässerung *f*, Dränbewässerung *f*
~ **outcrop** verdeckter Ausstrich *m*, maskiertes Ausgehendes *n*
~ **river** Höhlenfluß *m*
~ **rumbling** unterirdische Geräusche *npl (Vulkanismus)*
~ **storage** Untergrundspeicherung *f*

~ **storage of gas** unterirdische Gasspeicherung *f*
~ **stream** unterirdischer Wasserlauf *m*
~ **water** Tiefenwasser *n*; Grundwasser *n*; unterirdisches Wasser *n*, unterirdische Hydrosphäre *f*
~ **water parting** unterirdische Wasserscheide *f*
~ **water system** Grundwasserhaushalt *m*
subterraneous *s*. subterranean
subtidal Sublitoral *n (Bereich zwischen der extremen Niedrigwassermarke und der Untergrenze der photischen Zone)*, „Unterwasserbereich" *m*
subtractive colours process Methode der Erzeugung praktisch aller Farben durch Subtraktion der subtraktiven Primärfarben Blaugrün, Magentarot und Gelb in verschiedenen Anteilen unter Verwendung einer einzelnen weißen Lichtquelle
subtranslucent halbdurchsichtig
subtransparent halbdurchscheinend
subtropic[al] subtropisch
~ **region** subtropische Zone *f*
subtropics Subtropen *pl*
subtype [coal] *(Am)* Kohlenmikrolithotyp *m*
subumbonal am Wirbel *(bei Fossilgehäusen)*
subvariety Unterart *f*, Unterform *f*
Subvariscan foredeep subvariskische Vortiefe *f*
subvitreous shining glasartig glänzend
subvolcanic subvulkanisch
~ **deposit** subvulkanische Lagerstätte *f*
~ **structure** Unterbau *m* des Vulkans
subvolcano Subvulkan *m*
subweathering velocity Geschwindigkeit *f* unterhalb der Langsamschicht (Verwitterungsschicht)
subzone Subzone *f*
success ratio of holes Anteil *m* erfolgreicher Bohrungen
succession Sukzession *f*, Abfolge *f (s.a. suite)*
~ **of beds** Schichtenfolge *f*
~ **of formations** Formationsfolge *f*
~ **of layers** Schichtenfolge *f*
~ **of stages** Stufenfolge *f*
~ **of strata** Schichtenfolge *f*
successive failure fortschreitender Bruch *m*
succinic Bernstein…, sukzinisch
succinite Bernstein *m*, Sukzinit *m*
sucked stone wabenförmiges (hoch poröses) Gestein *n*
sucker-rod-type pump Tiefpumpe *f* mit Gestänge *(Ölförderung)*
sucrosic *s*. saccharoidal
suction Saugvermögen *n*, Saugwirkung *f*; Sog *m*
~ **counter flush drilling** Saugbohrverfahren *n*
~ **dredger** Saugbagger *m*
~ **line** Saugleitung *f*
~ **pipe check valve and screen** Saugkorb *m*
sud bei Überflutung abgelagerter Sand *m*

sudd

sudd Papyrusmoor n; verrottetes Pflanzenmaterial n
sudden beginning deutlicher (scharfer) Einsatz m (Seismik)
~ **downpour** Platzregen m
~ **drawdown** plötzliche Absenkung f
~ **escape of gas** plötzlicher Gasausbruch m
~ **excavation** plötzlicher Ausbruch m (von Gas im Kohlenbergbau)
Sudeten phase of folding sudetische Faltungsphase f
Sudetic phase sudetische Phase f
Suess effect Suess-Effekt m (nach H. Suess)
suevite Suevit m (Brekzie mit Stoßwellenmetamorphose)
suffer depression/to absinken
~ **extinction** aussterben
~ **uplift** gehoben werden
sugary s. saccharoidal
suite Serie f, Folge f (s.a. succession)
~ **of cores** Kernfolge f, Kernsatz m
~ **of formations** Formationsfolge f
sulcus Furche f (in der Skulptur)
sulfur (Am) s. sulphur
sullage Schlammablagerung f, Abwässer npl
sulphate ion Sulfation n
~ **reduction** Sulfatreduktion f
~**-reducing bacteria** sulfatreduzierende Bakterien fpl
sulphite liquor Sulfitablauge f
sulphoborite Sulfoborit m, $Mg_3[SO_4|(BO_2OH)_2] \cdot 4H_2O$
sulphohalite Sulfohalit m, $Na_6[F|Cl|(SO_4)_2]$
sulphophil[e] sulfophil
sulphur Schwefel m, S
~ **bacteria** Schwefelbakterien fpl
~ **balls** Pyritkonkretionen fpl in Kohle
~**-coloured** schwefelgelb
~ **deposit** Schwefellagerstätte f
~ **dome** Schwefeldiapir m
~ **fumes** Schwefeldämpfe mpl
~ **mine** Schwefelgrube f
~**-mud flow** Schwefelschlammstrom m
~ **pit** Schwefelgrube f
~ **smell** Schwefel[wasserstoff]geruch m
~ **spring** Schwefelquelle f
~ **water** Schwefelwasser n
sulphureous schwefelartig; schweflig; schwefelhaltig
~ **flue dust** schwefelhaltiger Flugstaub m
~ **oil** schwefelhaltiges Öl n
~ **spring** Schwefelquelle f
sulphuret of iron Schwefelkies m (s.a. pyrite)
sulphuretted hydrogen Schwefelwasserstoff m, H_2S
~**-hydrogen fumarole** Schwefelwasserstoffumarole f
sulphuric schwefelsauer, Schwefel...
~ **acid** Schwefelsäure f, H_2SO_4
~ **waters** Schwefelwässer npl
sulphurious s. sulphureous

sulphurization Schwefelung f
sultry drückend, schwül
~ **weather** Schwüle f
sulvanite Sulvanit m, Cu_3VS_4
summation method Summationsverfahren n (zur Berechnung der Langsamschichtkorrektur)
summer flood Sommerhochwasser n
~ **lightning** Wetterleuchten n
~ **monsoon** Sommermonsun m
~ **silt** Silt-Sommerlage f (von Warven)
~ **solstice** Sommersolstitium n, Sommersonnenwende f
~ **stratification** Sommerschichtung f
~ **water level** Sommerwasserstand m
summit 1. Bergspitze f, Gipfel m, Gipfelpunkt m; 2. Poleck n (Kristallografie)
~ **altitude** Gipfelhöhe f
~ **area** Gipfelflur f
~ **concordance** Gipfelhöhenkonstanz f
~ **effusion** Gipfelerguß m
~ **eruption** Gipfelausbruch m, Zentralausbruch m
~ **level of a crystal** Ecke f eines Kristalls
~ **overflow** terminaler Lavaausfluß m
~ **plateau** Gipfelplateau n
~ **region (surface)** Gipfelflur f
sump Schachtsumpf m
~ **hole** Erdreservoir n
sun Sonne f
~**-baked** sonnengehärtet
~ **crack** Trockenriß m
~**-cracked** von Trockenrissen durchzogen
~ **elevation angle** Sonnenerhebungswinkel m (Winkel, den die Sonne mit dem Horizont einschließt)
~ **irradiation** Sonnenbestrahlung f
~ **opal** Feueropal m
~**-synchronous satellite** sonnensynchroner Satellit m (überfliegt gleiche Orte stets zur gleichen Ortszeit)
Sundance Formation Sundance-Formation f (oberer Dogger und unterer Malm in Nordamerika)
sunk shaft abgeteufter Schacht m
~ **well** Senkbrunnen m
sunken block Tiefscholle f, abgesunkene Scholle f
~ **caldera** Einbruchskaldera f, Einsturzkaldera f
~ **rocks** unterseeische Felsen mpl
sunless sonnenlos
sunlight Sonnenlicht n, Sonnenschein m
sunny side Sonnenseite f
sunray Sonnenstrahl m
sunrise Sonnenaufgang m
sun's blackout Sonnenfinsternis f
~ **corona** Sonnenkorona f
~ **disk** Sonnenscheibe f
~ **interior** Sonneninneres n
~ **magnetism** Sonnenmagnetismus m
~ **motion** Sonnenbewegung f
sunset Sonnenuntergang m
~ **colours** Abendröte f

sunspot Sonnenfleck *m*
~ **activity** Sonnenfleckenaktivität *f*
~ **cycle** Sonnenfleckenzyklus *m*
~ **group** Sonnenfleckengruppe *f*
~ **number** Sonnenfleckenrelativzahl *f*
~ **period** Sonnenfleckenperiode *f*
sunstone Aventurinfeldspat *m*
sunup Sonnenaufgang *m*
superadded aufgesetzt
superanthracite Graphitanthrazit *m*
supercap sand Scheitellagerstätte *f* über dem Deckgebirge
supercapillary superkapillar
supercompressibility Realgasverhalten *n*
superconducting magnetometer (quantum interference device) Supraleitungsmagnetometer *n*, SQUID *n*
supercooled unterkühlt
supercooling Unterkühlung *f*
supercritical überkritisch
supercrust of earth oberflächlicher Teil *m* der Erdkruste
~ **rock** Oberflächengestein *n*
supercrustal superkrustal
superdeep drilling übertiefes Bohren *n (über 3000 m)*
superface [of stratum] Dachfläche *f*
superficial oberflächlich; oberflächennah
~ **compaction** Oberflächenverdichtung *f*
~ **configuration** Oberflächengestalt *f*
~ **covering** Oberflächendecke *f*
~ **current** Oberstrom *m (des Meeres)*
~ **deposit** oberflächennahe Lagerstätte *f*; Oberflächenablagerung *f*
~ **fold** Oberflächenfalte *f*
~ **folding** Oberflächenfaltung *f*
~ **layer** Deckschicht *f*, überlagernde Schicht *f*, Oberflächenschicht *f*
~ **ooid** Ooid, bei dem der Kern dicker als das angelagerte Gefüge ist
~ **outflow** Oberflächenerguß *m*
~ **rock** Oberflächengestein *n*
~ **water** Oberflächenwasser *n*
superficies Oberfläche *f*, Fläche *f*
superflood *(Am)* Katastrophenhochwasser *n*
superfluent lava flow terminaler Lavaausfluß *m*
supergene deszendent
~ **alterations** deszendente Umbildungen *fpl*
~ **ore** sekundäres Erz *n (Oxydations- und Zementationserz)*
~ **sulphide zone** Zementationszone *f*
~ **water** niedersinkendes Wasser *n*
superglacial postglazial
~ **moraine** Oberflächenmoräne *f*
~ **stream** Schmelzwasserbach *m (Gletscher)*
supergroup Hauptgruppe *f*, Abteilung *f (größte Einheit der lithostratigrafischen Gliederung)*
superheated überhitzt
superimposed [sich] überlagernd, übereinandergelagert, überprägt
~ **bed** überlagernde Schicht *f*

~ **fold** heteroachse Überlagerung *f (einer älteren Falte durch eine jüngere)*
~ **load** aufgebrachte Last *f*, Auflast *f*
~ **mode** Kombination *f* von Darstellungsarten
~ **river** epigenetischer Fluß *m*
~ **stratum** überlagernde Schicht *f*
~ **valley** epigenetisches (aufgesetztes) Tal *n*
superimposition Überlagerung *f*, Überprägung *f*
superincumbent überlagernd, überliegend, darüber gelagert
~ **beds** Hangendschichten *fpl*
~ **pressure of the ground** Firstendruck *m*
superior mirage Sonnenspiegelung *f* nach oben
~ **planet** äußerer Planet *m*
superjacent aufliegend, darüber liegend
~ **stratum** überlagernde Schicht *f*
~ **water** darüberliegendes Wasser *n*
superlunary jenseits des Mondes gelegen
supernova Supernova *f*
superpose/to übereinanderlegen, überlagern
superposed übereinanderliegend
~ **bed** aufliegende Schicht *f*
~ **folding** postume Falte *f*
~ **valley** *s.* superimposed valley
superposition Überlagerung *f*, Auflagerung *f*
~ **of stresses** Spannungsüberlagerung *f*
~ **pattern** Anlagerungsgefüge *n*
~ **principle** Superpositionsprinzip *n*
superprint Überprägung *f*
supersaline hypersalin *(tektonisch)*
supersaturate/to übersättigen
supersaturation Übersättigung *f*
supersonic flow Überschallströmung *f*
~ **sounder** Ultraschallot *n*
supersonics Ultraschall *m*
superstandard refraction übernormale Brechung *f*
superstratum obere Schicht *f*
superstructure Oberbau *m*, Deckgebirge *n*, Überbau *m*
superterranean, superterrene, superterrestrial über der Erde befindlich
supervised classification überwachte Klassifizierung *f*
supplementary pressure Zusatzdruck *m*
~ **pressure zone** Kernzone *f*
~ **twins** Ergänzungszwillinge *mpl*
supply well Versorgungsbrunnen *m*
support Ausbau *m*
~ **film** Trägerfolie *f*
~ **of workings** Instandhaltung *f* der Grubenbaue
~ **pattern** Ausbauschema *n*
~ **pressure** Stützdruck *m*
supporting force Stützkraft *f*
~ **frame** Stützgerüst *n*
~ **of rock** Abstützen *n* des Gesteins
~ **pillar** Stützpfeiler *m*, Strebpfeiler *m*
~ **skeleton** Stützgerüst *n*
supposed coast line vermutete Uferlinie *f*

suppression

suppression Abschwächung f, Unterdrückung f
supracrustal suprakrustal
~ **formation** Deckgebirge n (über dem Grundgebirge)
supragelisol Boden m über dem Pergelisol
supraglacial stream Schmelzwasserbach m (Gletscher)
supramarine eruption übermeerischer Ausbruch m
suprapermafrost [layer] Permafrostboden m, Dauerfrostbodendeckschicht f
~ **water** Grundwasser n oberhalb des Permafrostbodens
supratenuous fold s. bending fold
supratidal Marsch f
supravolcano aufgesetzter Vulkan m
surcharge aufgebrachte Last f, Auflast f
surf Meeresbrandung f, Brandung f
~ **beat** Brandungsschlag m
~ **breccia** Brandungsbrekzie f
~ **ripples** Brandungsrippeln fpl
~**-surge** Brandungswoge f, Brecher m
~ **zone** Brandungszone f
surface Fläche f, Oberfläche f; Tagesoberfläche f; Erdoberfläche f
~**-active agent** oberflächenaktiver Stoff m
~ **bed** Oberflächenschicht f
~ **boundary layer** Oberflächengrenzschicht f
~ **break** Bergschaden m
~ **casing** Standrohr n, Leitrohr n
~ **conditions** Oberflächenbeschaffenheit f
~ **configuration** Oberflächengestaltung f
~ **conservation** Oberflächenkonservierung f
~ **contour [line]** Isohypse f, Höhen[schicht]linie f
~ **crazing** Maronage f, feine Rißbildung f
~ **crusting** Bodenverkrustung f
~ **damage** Bergschaden m
~ **debris** Oberflächenschutt m
~ **density** Flächendichte f
~ **deposit** Oberflächenablagerung f
~ **depression** Oberflächensenkung f (Bergschaden); Pinge f
~ **disintegration** Verwitterung f
~ **drainage** Oberflächenentwässerung f
~ **edge** Ausgehendes n
~ **energy** Oberflächenenergie f (einer Gesteinspartikel)
~ **equipment** Übertageanlage f, Übertageausrüstung f
~ **evaporation** Oberflächenverdunstung f
~ **exposure** Tagesaufschluß m
~ **features** Oberflächenformen fpl
~ **film** dünne Oberflächenschicht f
~ **fitting** Flächenausgleich m
~ **form** Oberflächenform f
~ **formation** Deckschicht f
~ **friction** Oberflächenreibung f
~ **geology** Oberflächengeologie f
~ **grinding** Oberflächenschliff m
~ **ground-water level distance** Sickerstrecke f

~ **hardness** Oberflächenhärte f
~ **humidity** Bodenfeuchte f
~ **installations** Übertageanlagen fpl
~ **irradiation** Oberflächenbestrahlung f
~ **irrigation** Oberflächenbewässerung f
~ **layer** Oberflächenschicht f, Randschicht f, Deckschicht f
~ **level** Rasensohle f
~ **load** Oberflächenbelastung f
~ **mapping** Oberflächenkartierung f
~ **markings** Marken fpl, Skulpturen fpl (Sedimentgefüge)
~ **mining** Tagebau[betrieb] m
~ **moraine** Ober[flächen]moräne f
~ **of bedding** Schichtebene f
~ **of conformity** Kontinuitätsfläche f
~ **of constant slope** Böschungsfläche f
~ **of depression** Depressionsfläche f (Grundwasserabsenkung)
~ **of discontinuity** 1. Diskontinuitätsfläche f, Unstetigkeitsfläche f (Seismik); 2. Aufgleitfläche f
~ **of flow** Durchflußquerschnitt m
~ **of fracture** Bruchfläche f
~ **of instability** Unstetigkeitsfläche f
~ **of junction** Berührungsfläche f
~ **of lamination** Schichtebene f
~ **of section** Schnittfläche f
~ **of separation** Trennungsfläche f
~ **of sliding** Gleitfläche f
~ **of stratification** Schichtebene f
~ **of subsidence** Abgleitfläche f
~ **of subsoil water** Grundwasseroberfläche f
~ **of the ground** Tagesoberfläche f
~ **of unconformity** Diskordanzfläche f
~ **of water** Wasserspiegel m
~ **oil indications** Oberflächenanzeichen npl von Erdöllagerstätten
~ **outcrop[ping]** Ausgehendes n
~ **peat** Fasertorf m, Moostorf m, Wurzeltorf m
~ **plant** Tagesanlage f
~ **pressure** Manteldruck m
~ **removing** Oberflächenabtragung f
~ **retention** Oberflächenwasserbindung f
~ **rock** Oberflächengestein n, Deckgebirge n
~ **roughness** Oberflächenrauhigkeit f, Unebenheit f der Oberfläche
~ **runoff** oberirdischer Abfluß m, Oberflächenabfluß m
~ **scratching test** Ritzhärteprobe f
~**-set bit** oberflächenbesetzte Bohrkrone f
~ **slide** Schliffläche f
~ **slope** Oberflächengefälle n
~ **soil** Bodenkrume f, Mutterboden m
~ **stability** Oberflächenfestigkeit f
~ **strain indicator** Oberflächengeber m
~ **stratum** Deckschicht f
~ **stream** Oberflächenströmung f
~ **string** Leitrohrtour f, erste Rohrfahrt f, Standrohr n
~ **structure** Oberflächenstruktur f, Oberflächenbau m

~-structure map Strukturkarte f der Oberfläche
~ subsidence Bergschaden m
~ temperature Oberflächentemperatur f
~ tension Oberflächenspannung f
~ termination Ausgehendes n
~ thrust Reliefüberschiebung f
~ wash of rain Oberflächenabspülung f *(durch Regen)*
~ water Oberflächenwasser n, Tageswasser n
~ wave Oberflächenwelle f
~ weathering Verwitterung f
~ well Flachbrunnen m
~ wind Bodenwind m
~ winning (workings) Tagebaubetrieb m
surfactant oberflächenaktiver Stoff m
~ muds Spülungen fpl mit oberflächenentspannenden Zusätzen
surficial s. superficial
surficials *(Am)* Zersetzungsprodukte npl von Magmatiten in situ
surfy brandend, Brandungs...
surge/to pulsierend fließen
surge Woge f, Welle f, Sturzsee f
~ tank Wasserschloß n
surplus area Akkumulationsgebiet n
surreitic structure surreitische Textur f, Zerrungstextur f *(bei Migmatiten)*
surrounding rock Nebengestein n, Gesteinsmantel m
sursassite Sursassit m, $Mn_2H_3Al_2[O|OH|SiO_4|Si_2O_7]$
survey/to vermessen, aufnehmen *(Karten)*
~ a mine eine Grube vermessen (aufnehmen)
~ underground markscheiden
survey 1. Vermessung f, Aufnahme f; 2. Übersicht f; 3. Erkundung f *(durch topografische, geologische oder geophysikalische Messungen)*
~ by aerial photographs Luftbildvermessung f
~ map Katasterblatt n
~ measurements markscheiderische Messungen fpl
~ of a country Landesaufnahme f, Geländeaufnahme f
~ party Vermessungstrupp m, Meßtrupp m
~ plan markscheiderische Aufnahme f, Vermessungsplan m
~ plane Vermessungsflugzeug n
~ vessel Vermessungsschiff n
~ with plane table Meßtischaufnahme f
surveying 1. Aufnahme f, Vermessung f; 2. Vermessungskunde f; Markscheidekunde f
~ apparatus Aufnahmegerät n
~ instrument Vermessungsinstrument n
~ of details Detailaufnahme f
~ of underground Markscheiden n, untertägige Vermessung f
~ party Vermessungstrupp m, Meßtrupp m
~ rod Absteckpfahl m, Meßbake f
~ vessel Vermessungsschiff n
surveyor Feldmesser m, Markscheider m

~ of mines Markscheider m
surveyor's table Meßtisch m
survival species überlebende Art f
susceptibility Suszeptibilität f
suspended load Schwebstoffe mpl, Schwebefracht f
~ load discharge Schwebstofführung f
~ load sampler Schwebstoffschöpfer m
~ matter Schwebstoffe mpl, Trübe f
~ solids suspendierte Teilchen npl, Schwebstoffe mpl
~ subsurface water schwebendes Grundwasser n, vadoses (in der Aerationszone schwebendes) Wasser n, Ober[flächen]wasser n
~ water ruhendes Porensaugwasser n
~ well eingestellte Bohrung f
suspensate suspendiertes Sediment n
suspension Suspension f
~ current s. turbidity current
~ load Schwebelast f *(Fluß)*
~ of mine work Einstellung f des Grubenbetriebs
suspensoids suspendierte Stoffe mpl, Schwebstoffe mpl
sussexite Sussexit m, $Mn_2[B_2O_5] \cdot H_2O$
sustained load Dauerlast f
~ runoff regulierter Abfluß m
~ wave gesteuerte (rückgekoppelte) Welle f
~ yield Dauerspende f *(einer Quelle)*
sutural line Lobenlinie f
~ texture verzahnte Struktur f
suture 1. Sutur f; 2. Naht f *(bei Fossilgehäusen)*
~ joint s. stylolite
~ line s. sutural line
~ of the twin plane Zwillingsnaht f
sutured contacts suturierte Kornverzahnung f
svabite Svabit m, $Ca_5[F|(AsO_4)_3]$
svanbergite Svanbergit m, $SrAl_3[(OH)_6|SO_4PO_4]$
Svecofennian folding svekofennische (svekofennidische) Faltung f *(Präkambrium)*
Svecofennides Svekofenniden fpl
swab Swabbkolben m *(Ölförderung)*
swabbing Kolben n, Swabben n *(Ölförderung)*
~ well gekolbte Sonde f
swag Absenkung f der Firste, Senken n des Hangenden
swale Grundmoränentümpel m, Talmulde f, Bodensenke f
swallet 1. Schluckloch n, Schlundloch n, Ponor m; 2. Wassereinbruch m
swallow [hole] Schluckloch n, Schlundloch n, Ponor m, Sickerstelle f, Flußschwinde f
swally s. swelly
swamp Moor n, Sumpf m, Morast m
~ ditch Sickergraben m
~ forest soil Sumpfwaldboden m
~ formation Moorbildung f, Versumpfung f; Torfmoorbildung f
~ meadow Sumpfwiese f
~ ore Sumpferz n, Raseneisenerz n, Ortstein m

swamp

~ vegetation Sumpfvegetation f
swamped moorig, sumpfig, schlammig
swampiness sumpfige Beschaffenheit f
swamping Versumpfung f
swampland Moorland n
swampy morastig, sumpfig
~ **area** Sumpfgebiet n
~ **flat** Sumpfniederung f
~ **land** Moorboden m
~ **soil** Sumpfboden m
~ **tundra soil** Tundramoorboden m
sward Rasen m
swarm Schwarm m
~ **earthquakes** Schwarmbeben npl, Erdbebenschwarm m
~ **of meteors** Meteorschwarm m
swartzite Swartzit m, $CaMg[UO_2|(CO_3)_3] \cdot 12H_2O$
swash mark Spülbogen m, Spülmarke f, Spülsaum m (Sedimentgefüge)
swathwidth Schwadbreite f (Breite des Aufnahmestreifens bei der Luft- und Satellitenfernerkundung)
swaugh im Gang auftretende Lette f
sweating Ausschwitzung f, Durchsickerung f, Wasserabstoßen n
swedenborgite Swedenborgit m, $NaSbBe_4O_7$
sweep/to schwemmen
~ **away** fortschwemmen
sweep 1. Gangtrum n; 2. Sweep m, Gleitsinus m (Signalform des Vibroseis-Verfahrens)
~-out Entölung f, Entgasung f
sweeping Herabwandern n, Fortschreiten n (der Mäander)
sweet corrosion Korrosion f bei geringem Schwefelanteil des Erdöls
~ **natural gas** schwefelwasserstofffreies (süßes) Erdgas n
swell up/to aufquellen
swell 1. Schwelle f, Bodenwelle f, Anhöhe f; 2. Anschwellung f, Verdickung f; 3. lokale Flözverdickung f, Kohlensack m; 4. Sandlinsen (Tonlinsen) fpl im Flöz; 5. langgestreckter, flacher Dom m (großtektonische Strukturform); 6. Dünung f
~ **of water** Stau m, Aufstau m, Anstauung f (von Wasser)
swellable quellbar
swelling Anschwellung f, Quellen n
~ **ground** quellendes Gebirge n
~ **index** Blähzahl f (Steinkohle)
~ **power** Blähungsvermögen n (von Steinkohlen)
~ **pressure** Schwelldruck m
~ **property** Blähungsgrad m, Quellungsvermögen n
~ **rock** plastisches Gebirge n
~-up Quellen n, Aufquellen n
swelly lokale Flözverdickung f, Vertiefung f (im Liegenden eines Kohlenflözes)
swiftly running water schnellfließendes Wasser n
swilley s. swelly

swineback s. horseback
swinestone Anthrakonit m, Stinkstein m, Stinkkalk m
swing moor Schwingmoor n
swinging seitliches Verlegen n (eines Mäanderstreifens)
~ **river** pendelnder Fluß m
swirling water quirlendes (wirbelndes) Wasser n
swivel Spülkopf m (bei Bohrung)
~ **head** Dreheinrichtung f
swollen river angeschwollener Fluß m
sycite feigenförmige Feuersteinknolle f
syenite Syenit m
syenitic syenitisch
syenodiorite Syenodiorit m
sylvanite Sylvanit m, Schrifterz n, $AuAgTe_4$
sylvin[e] s. sylvite
sylvinite Sylvinit m, Hartsalz n
sylvite Sylvin m, KCl
sylvogenic soil Waldboden m
symbiosis Symbiose f, Lebensgemeinschaft f
symmetric[al] about an axis achsensymmetrisch
~ **anticline** aufrechte Antiklinale f
~ **fold** symmetrische (aufrechte) Falte f
symmetrically related crystals gesetzmäßig (symmetrisch) verwachsene Kristalle mpl
~ **ripple marks** symmetrische Rippelmarken fpl
symmetry class Symmetrieklasse f, Kristallklasse f
~ **element** Symmetrieelement n
~ **of crystals** Kristallsymmetrie f
~ **of fabric** Gefügesymmetrie f
symmict structure strukturloses Sedimentblatt n in gradierten Sedimenten
~ **varve** Warve f ohne gradierten Kornaufbau
symmictite verfestigtes Symmicton n
symmicton Symmicton n (unsortiertes nichtkarbonatisches terrigenes Sedimentmaterial)
symon fault Erosionsvertaubung f im Flöz
sympathetic mountain glaciation gleichzeitige Gebirgsvergletscherung f
sympatric im gleichen geografischen Gebiet auftretend
symplectic intergrowth symplektische Durchwachsung f
~ **texture** symplektische Struktur f
symplesite Symplesit m, $Fe_3[AsO_4]_2 \cdot 8H_2O$
symptomatic mineral diagnostisches Mineral n, Indikatormineral n
synadelphite Synadelphit m, $Mn_4[(OH)_5|AsO_4]$
synaeresis Synärese f (kolloidchemischer Vorgang einer subaquatischen Entwässerung)
synantetic mineral synantetisches Mineral n
synantexis deuterische Umwandlung f
synchisite Synchisit m, $CaCe[F|(CO_3)_2]$
synchrogenic rocks gleichaltrige Gesteine npl
synchronal s. synchronous
synchroneity Gleichaltrigkeit f, Zeitäquivalenz f (der Schichten)

synchronous synchron, gleichaltrig
- ~ **deposits** gleichaltrige Ablagerungen *fpl*
- ~ **satellite** Synchronsatellit *m*

synclastic synklastisch
synclinal synklinal, muldenartig
- ~ **axis** Synklinalachse *f*, Muldenachse *f*
- ~ **curve** Synklinale *f*, Mulde *f*
- ~ **depression** Muldeneinsenkung *f*
- ~ **flexure** Flexurgraben *m*
- ~ **fold** Synklinale *f*, Mulde *f*
- ~ **formation** Muldenbildung *f*
- ~ **lake** Muldensee *m*
- ~ **limb** Muldenflügel *m*
- ~ **spring** Muldenquelle *f*
- ~ **turn** Muldenbiegung *f*, Muldenscharnier *n*
- ~ **valley** Synklinaltal *n*

syncline Synklinale *f*, Mulde *f*
- ~ **water** Randwasser *n*, Synklinalwasser *n*

synclinore, synclinorium Synklinorium *n*
syndiagenese Diagenesefrühstadium *n*
syndiagenetic deformation syndiagenetische Deformation *f*
syndromous load cast zusammengesetzte Belastungsmarke *f (Sedimentgefüge)*
syneclise Syneklise *f*
synecology Synökologie *f*
syneresis crack Synäreseriß *m*, Sprung *m* im alternden Gel *(infolge Entwässerung)*
syngenesis Syngenese *f*
syngenetic syngenetisch
- ~ **ore deposit** syngenetische Erzlagerstätte *f*
- ~ **river** syngenetischer Fluß *m*

syngenite Syngenit *m*, $K_2Ca[SO_4]_2 \cdot H_2O$
synkinematic synkinematisch *(s.a. synorogene)*
synodic satellite synodischer Satellit *m*
synoptic synoptisch
- ~ **diagram** synoptisches Diagramm *n*
- ~ **meteorology** synoptische Meteorologie *f*, Übersichtswetterkunde *f*
- ~ **network** synoptisches Netz *n*
- ~ **view** Übersichtsbetrachtung *f*

synorogene, synorogeneous, synorogenic synorogen
- ~ **granite** synorogener (synkinematischer) Granit *m*
- ~ **phase** synorogene magmatische Phase *f*
- ~ **plutonism** synorogener Plutonismus *m*

synsedimentary synsedimentär
syntaxial enlargement von Crinoidenstielgliedern ausgehende Sammelkristallisation *f*
- ~ **rim cementation** von Crinodenstielgliedern ausgehende Zementation *f*

syntaxis Konvergenz *f* im Streichen von Gebirgszügen
syntectonic syntektonisch
syntexis Syntexis *f*, magmatische Assimilation *f*
synthetic aperture radar Radar *n* mit synthetischer Apertur
- ~ **fault** synthetische (rechtfallende) Verwerfung *f*
- ~ **precious stone** synthetischer Edelstein *m*

- ~ **seismogram** synthetisches Seismogramm *n*

syntopogenic am gleichen (ähnlichen) Platz gebildet
syntype Syntypus *m*
sysserskite Sysserskit *m (Iridosmin mit >50% Os)*
syssiderite Silikat-Eisen-Meteorit *m (s.a. siderolite)*
system System *n (Einheit der biostratigrafischen Skala, im älteren deutschen Schrifttum auch Formation)*
- ~ **of cracks** Spaltensystem *n*, Kluftsystem *n*
- ~ **of crystals** Kristallsystem *n*
- ~ **of faults** Bruchsystem *n*
- ~ **of joints** Kluftsystem *n*, Hauptkluftscharen *fpl*
- ~ **of reference** Bezugssystem *n*
- ~ **of rivers and streams** Flußnetz *n*
- ~ **of veins** Gangsystem *n*

systematic geography allgemeine Geografie *f*
- ~ **sampling** systematische Probenahme *f*

systematics Systematik *f (s.a. taxonomy)*
szaibelyite Szaibelyit *m*, Ascharit *m*, $Mg_2[B_2O_5] \cdot H_2O$
szik soil Szik-Boden *m*
szmikite Szmikit *m*, $Mn[SO_4] \cdot H_2O$
szomolnokite Szomolnokit *m*, $Fe[SO_4] \cdot H_2O$

T

T-D = time-depth
T-plane Gleitebene *f (im Kristall)*
T-section T-Profil *n (Dünnschliff parallel zur Schichtung oder Probenoberfläche)*
T-X = time-distance
taaffeite Taaffeit *m*, Al_4MgBeO_8
tabet soil auftauender Boden *m*
tabetification Tabetisolbildung *f*
tabetisol Tabetisol *m (nichtgefrorener Boden zwischen Permafrost und jährlicher Frostzone)*
table drive Drehtischantrieb *m (bei Bohrungen)*
- ~ **mount** *s.* guyot
- ~ **mountain** Tafelgebirge *n*, Tafelberg *m*
- ~ **of strata** Formationstabelle *f*
- ~ **slate** Dachschiefer *m*
- ~ **spar** Tafelspat *m (s.a. wollastonite)*

tableland Tafelland *n*, Hochebene *f*
tablelike tafelartig
- ~ **structure** tafelförmiger Bau *m*

tabling Herdarbeit *f (Aufbereitung)*
tabular tafelig, tafelförmig
- ~ **cross-bedding** tafelige Schrägschichtung *f*, Diagonalschichtung *f*
- ~ **cross stratification** ebenflächig begrenzte Schrägschichtung *f*
- ~ **deposit** plattenförmige Lagerstätte *f*
- ~ **iceberg** Tafeleisberg *m*
- ~ **jointing** *s.* ~ structure
- ~ **spar** *s.* table spar

tabular 350

~ **structure** plattige (bankige) Absonderung f, tafelförmiger Bau m
tachhydrite Tachhydrit m, $CaCl_2 \cdot 2MgCl_2 \cdot 12H_2O$
tachometer Drehzahlmesser m, Tachometer n
tachylite, tachylyte Tachylit m (basaltisches Glas)
Taconian s. Taconic
Taconic takonisch
~ **phase** takonische Faltungsphase f (Grenzbereich Ordovizium/Silur)
taconite Takonit m (Eisenjaspiliterz)
tactite Taktit m, allochemer Kontaktskarn m
tadpole nests Kaulquappennester npl (Interferenzrippeln)
~ **plot** Vektordiagramm n (der Bohrlochneigungsmessung)
taeniolite Taeniolith m, $KLiMg_2[F_2|Si_4O_{10}]$
tafoni-type of weathering Tafoniverwitterung f
Taghanican [Stage] Taghanic[um] n (basale Stufe des Senecans in Nordamerika)
tagilite Tagilit m, $Cu_2[OH|PO_4] \cdot H_2O$
tahitite Tahitit m (Alkalibasalt)
taiga Taiga f
tail 1. Endphase f, Coda f; 2. Schweif m (eines Kometen); 3. Protokoll n, Erläuterung f
~ **buoy** Endboje f (des seismischen Kabelbaums)
~ **production** Endproduktion f
~ **segment** Schwanzsegment n (Paläontologie)
~ **skeleton** Schwanzskelett n (Paläontologie)
~ **water** Stauwasser n, abfließendes Wasser n
tailing 1. Tailing n, Verlängerung f (z.B. der Länge eines seismischen Wellenzugs); 2. s. tailings
~ **dam** Bergehalde f, Bergekippe f
~-**out** Auskeilen n
tailings 1. Überlauf m; 2. Abfallerz n; Abgang m, Berge pl; 3. Halde f
~ **pond** Bergeteich m, Schlammteich m
tailor-made zugeschnitten (z.B. Spülung auf Bohrlochbedingungen)
tailrace Ablaufgraben m, Ablaufkanal m, Unterwasserkanal m
~ **tunnel** Unterwasserstollen m, Ableitungsstollen m
tails s. tailings
tailshield Schwanzschild m (Paläontologie)
tailslide/to nach hinten abrutschen
take a bearing/to peilen
~ **cross bearings** einschneiden
~ **sample** Probe nehmen, bemustern
~ **the bearings of** anvisieren
take-off point Abgangspunkt m (eines Strahls am Refraktor)
taking of samples Probenahme f
takir s. takyr
takyr Salztonbecken n (in Asien)
~ **soil** Takyr-Boden m
takyrlike soil takyrartiger Boden m
talc Talk m, Talkum n, $Mg_3[(OH)_2|Si_4O_{10}]$

~ **schist (slate)** Talkschiefer m
talcite massiger Talk m
talcky talkig
talcoid talkartig
talcose, talcous talkhaltig, talkartig
talcum s. talc
talik s. tabetisol
tallow peat leicht entzündlicher Torf m
talmessite Talmessit m, $Ca_2Mg[AsO_4]_2 \cdot 2H_2O$
talus Schutt m, Schutthalde f, Felsenmeer n, Gesteinsfragment n, Murkegel m
~ **breccia** Schuttbrekzie f
~ **centre** Schüttungszentrum n
~ **cone** Schuttkegel m
~ **creep** Schuttkriechen n
~ **deposits** Hangschuttablagerungen fpl
~ **fan** Schuttfächer m
~ **material** Schutthalde f, Gehängeschutt m
~ **slope** Schutthang m, Schutthalde f
~ **soil** Schuttboden m
~ **spring** Hangschuttquelle f
tamarugite Tamarugit m, $NaAl[SO_4]_2 \cdot 6H_2O$
tamp Verdämmen n (von Schußbohrungen)
tamped concrete Stampfbeton m
tamping 1. Versatz m; 2. Verdämmen n (von Schußbohrungen)
tandem launch Mehrsatellitenstart m
~ **rocket** Tandemrakete f, Zwillingsrakete f
~ **turbodrill** mehrstufige Bohrturbine f
tangeite Tangeit m, $CaCu[OH|VO_4]$
tangential cross-bedding schaufelförmige (bogige) Schrägschichtung f
~ **plane** Berührungsebene f, Tangentialebene f
~ **stress** Tangentialspannung f
~ **thrust** tangentialer Schub m
~ **wave** Scherwelle f
tangentially sliced in Staffelbrüchen abgesunken
tank natürliches Wasserreservoir n
~ **farm** Erdöllager n, Erdöldepot n
tantalite Tantalit m, $(Fe, Mn)(Ta, Nb)_2O_6$
tantalum ore Tantalerz n
tanzanite Tansanit m (blauer Zoisit)
tap water Leitungswasser n
tapalpite Tapalpit m, $3Ag_2(S, Te) \cdot Bi_2(S, Te)_3$
tape weit aushaltendes, dünnes Erzband n
taper/to beschneiden (ein Seismogramm)
~ **out** auskeilen, verschwinden
taper Steigung f (eines Keils)
~ **tap** Spitzfänger m
taphonomy Taphonomie f, Fossilisationskunde f
taphrogenesis Taphrogenese f
taphrogenic movements taphrogene Bewegungen fpl
taphrogeny Taphrogenese f
taping Messung f mit Meßband
tapiolite Tapiolit m, $(Fe, Mn)(Ta, Nb)_2O_6$
tapping 1. Anzapfung f; 2. Wassergewinnung f
~ **of a spring** Quellfassung f

~ of ground water Grundwasserentnahme f, Grundwasserfassung f
tar 1. Teer m; 2. (Am) oft für natürliches halbfestes Erdöl
~ asphalt Teerasphalt m
~ from lignite Braunkohlenteer m
~ from shale schweres Schieferöl n
~ oil Teeröl n
~ pit Asphaltgrube f
~ sand Schwerölsandstein m, Totölsandstein m
taramellite Taramellit m, $Ba_2(Fe, Ti, Fe)_2[(OH)_2|Si_4O_{12}]$
tarapacaite Tarapacait m, $K_2[CrO_4]$
tarbuttite Tarbuttit m, $Zn_2[OH|PO_4]$
target 1. Zielobjekt n; 2. Zielpunkt m, Bohrziel n; 3. Kurvenschar f, Auswertediagramm n
tarless teerfrei
tarn Karsee m
tarnish Anlauffarbe f von Mineralen
tarnished angelaufen, trüb
tarnowitzite Tarnowitzit m, Bleiaragonit m (Mischkristall)
tarry teerartig, teerig
~ gas teerhaltiges Gas n
Tartarian [Stage] Tatar[ium] n, Tatarische Stufe f (Stufe des Oberperms im westlichen Uralvorland)
tasmanite Tasmanit m (Ölschiefer, Algengestein)
tauriscite Tauriscit m, $Fe[SO_4] \cdot 7H_2O$
tautirite Tautirit m (Nephelinmonzonit)
tavistockite Tavistockit m, $Ca_3Al_2[OH|PO_4]_3$
tavorite Tavorit m, $LiFe[OH|PO_4]$
tawmawite Tawmawit m, Chromepidot m (Varietät von Epidot)
taxitic structure taxitische Textur f
taxonomic[al] taxonomisch
~ distance of trend surfaces taxonomischer Abstand m zweier Trendflächen
~ position taxonomische Stellung f
taxonomy Taxonomie f
taylorite Taylorit m, $(K, NH_4)_2[SO_4]$
tchernozem s. chernozem
teallite Teallit m, $PbSnS_2$
tear 1. Zerrung f, Riß m; 2. Gang m, Sprung m (tägliche Veränderung des Nullwerts eines Instruments)
~ fault Blattverschiebung f, transversale Horizontalverschiebung f
~-shaped bomb Tränenbombe f, Lavaträne f, Peleträne f
tearing zone Zerrungsgebiet n
teary ground mildes Nebengestein n, gebräches Gebirge n
technical and economical plan of geological exploration Plan m der geologischen Erkundungsarbeiten, technischer Leistungsplan m
technogeochemistry Technogeochemie f
technosphere Technosphäre f
tectofacies Tektofazies f
tectogene Tektogen n

tectogenesis Tektogenese f
tectonic tektonisch
~ analysis tektonische Analyse f
~ breccia tektonische Brekzie f, Reibungsbrekzie f, Deformationsbrekzie f
~ contact tektonischer Kontakt m, tektonische Grenzfläche f
~ cycle tektonischer Zyklus m
~ denudation tektonische Denudation f
~ earthquake tektonisches Beben n, Dislokationsbeben n
~ flow s. ~ transport
~ form tektonische Form f
~ fracture tektonischer Bruch m
~ framework of sedimentation tektonisch wirksame Elemente npl eines Sedimentationsraums
~ geology Tektonik f
~ level Stockwerkstektonik f (Ampferer u.a.); tektonisches Stockwerk n (Weymann u.a.)
~ movement tektonische Bewegung f
~ overpressure tektonischer Überdruck m (Überlagerung hydrostatischer Spannungen durch gerichtete Spannungen)
~ selection Faziestektonik f
~ stor[e]y tektonisches Stockwerk n
~ termination tektonisches Unterbrechen n
~ transport Richtung f der tektonischen Durchbewegung, tektonischer Transport m, tektonisches Fließen (Gesteinsfließen) n
~ unconformity tektonische Diskordanz f
~ valley tektonisches Tal n
~ window tektonisches (geologisches) Fenster n
tectonically disturbed tektonisch gestört
~ undisturbed tektonisch ungestört
tectonics Tektonik f
tectonism 1. Krusteninstabilität f; 2. tektonische Aktivität f eines regionalen Strukturelements
tectonite Tektonit m
~ fabric Tektonitgefüge n
tectonization Tektonisierung f, tektonische Umarbeitung f
tectonized region tektonisch beeinflußtes Gebiet n
tectonophysics Tektonophysik f
tectonosphere Tektonosphäre f
tectorium Tektorium n (Verdickungsschicht bei Foraminiferen)
tectosilicate Tektosilikat n, Gerüstsilikat n
tectotope Tektotop n
teepleite Teepleit m, $Na_2[Cl|B(OH)_4]$
tegmen Kelchdecke f (bei Crinoiden)
teineite Teineit m, $Cu[TeO_3] \cdot 2H_2O$
tektite Tektit m, Glasmeteorit m
telemagmatic deposit telemagmatische Lagerstätte f
telemeter/to fernmessen
telemetering Fernmessen n, Fernmessung f
telemetric data transfer Datenfernübertragung f

telemetry

telemetry Fernmeßtechnik f
telescope level Nivellierinstrument n mit Fernrohr
~ **mast** ausziehbarer Bohrmast m
telescoped vein teleskopischer Gang m
telescoping Teleskoping n, Übereinanderfolge f mehrerer Paragenesen
teleseism Fernbeben n
telethermal telethermal
telinite Telinit m (Kohlenmaceral)
tellurian s. telluric
telluric tellurisch
~ **current** Erdstrom m
~ **diurnal variation** Tagesvariante f der Erdströme
~ **method** Tellurik f
~ **silver** Tellursilber n, Hessit m, Ag$_2$Te (s.a. hessite)
~ **water** tellurisches Wasser n
tellurics Tellurik f
telluriferous tellurführend, tellurhaltig
tellurine Kieselgur f, Diatomeenerde f, Infusorienerde f
tellurite Tellurit m, Tellurocker m, TeO$_2$
tellurium Tellur n, Te
~ **glance** s. nagyagite
~ **ore** Tellurerz n
telmatic coal facies telmatische Kohlenfazies f
~ **peat** s. reed peat
telocollinite Telocollinit m (Kohlensubmaceral)
telson Telson n, Schwanzstachel m, Schwanzsegment n (der Crustaceen)
Telychian [Stage] Telychium n (höchste Stufe des Llandovery)
temblor (Am) Erdbeben n, Beben n
temperate gemäßigt
~-**arid** gemäßigt-arid
~ **climate** gemäßigtes Klima n
~-**humid** gemäßigt-humid
~ **region (zone)** gemäßigte Zone f
temperature Temperatur f
~ **build-up** Temperaturaufbau m
~ **gradient log** Temperaturgradientenlog n
~ **inversion** Temperaturinversion f
~ **logging** Temperaturmessung f
~ **of intrusion** Intrusionstemperatur f
~ **of the earth** Erdwärme f
~ **range** Temperaturbereich m
~ **rise** Temperaturanstieg m
~ **survey** Temperaturmessung f
~ **variation** Temperaturschwankung f
tempering colour Anlauffarbe f
tempest Gewitter n
tempestite Tempestit m, Sturmflutablagerung f
template 1. Modell n, Diagramm n; 2. Plattformtyp ortsfester Bohrinseln
templet s. template
temporarily abandoned vorübergehend eingestellt, vorläufig stillgelegt
~ **shut-in well** vorübergehend geschlossene Sonde f
~ **suspended** s. ~ abandoned
temporary abandon of a well Konservierung f einer Bohrung
~ **base plate** vorläufige Bodenplatte f (auf dem Meeresboden am Bohrlochabschluß abgesetzte Einrichtung)
~ **casing** vorläufige Verrohrung f
~ **hardness** Bikarbonathärte f (des Wassers)
~ **lake** periodischer See m
~ **solfatara** vergängliche Solfatare f
~ **water** zeitweilig auftretendes Wasser n
tenacious zäh
tenacity Zähigkeit f
tengerite Tengerit m (Y-Karbonat)
tennantite Tennantit m, Arsenfahlerz n, 3Cu$_2$S·As$_2$S$_3$
tenor durchschnittlicher Metallgehalt m (eines Erzes)
tenorite Tenorit m, CuO
tenside Tensid n, oberflächenaktiver Stoff m
tensile crack Trennbruch m
~ **failure** Dehnungsbruch m
~ **shear test** Scherzugversuch m
~ **strength** Zugfestigkeit f
~ **strength of rock mass** Gebirgszugfestigkeit f
~ **strength of soil** Spannkraft f des Bodens
~ **stress** Zugspannung f
~ **test** Zugversuch m
~ **test diagram** s. stress-strain diagram
tension Spannung f, Zug m
~ **crack** Spannungsriß m
~ **device** Tensiometer n
~ **failure** Zugbruch m
~ **fault** Disjunktivbruch m, disjunktive Dislokation f, Abschiebung f, Dehnungsverwerfung f
~ **fracture** Dehnungsriß m
~ **gashes en échelon** Fiederspalten fpl
~ **joint** Zugkluft f, Zerrkluft f, Reißkluft f
~-**leg platform** zugseilverankerte Bohrinsel f
~ **zoning** Spannungszone f
tentacles Tentakel mpl (Paläontologie)
tentaculite schist Tentakulitenschiefer m
tentaculites bed Tentakulitenschicht f
tenuidurite Tenuidurit m (Kohlenmikrolithotyp)
tepetate s. caliche
tephra Tephra f (Vulkanoklastit)
tephrite Tephrit m
tephroite Tephroit m, Mn$_2$[SiO$_4$]
Terebratula bed Terebratelbank f
teretifolious rundblättrig
tergum Tergit n, Tergum n (Arthropoden)
terlinguaite Terlinguait m, 2HgO·Hg$_2$Cl$_2$
terminal endständig, gipfelständig
terminal Ende n, Endpunkt m
~ **deposit** Endablagerung f
~ **moraine** Endmoräne f, Stirnmoräne f
~ **pressure** Enddruck m
~ **resistance** Endwiderstand m, Abschlußwiderstand m
ternary system Dreistoffsystem n

terra rossa Terra rossa f *(roter Residualton auf Kalkstein)*
terrace Terrasse f, Geländestufe f
~ **flight** Terrassentreppe f
~ **slope** Terrassenböschung f
terraced terrassenförmig
~ **flute cast** terrassierter Strömungswulst m
~ **landscape** Stufenlandschaft f
terracette slope Hang m mit Bodenfließmarken
terracettes Erdleisten fpl, Rasenstufen fpl *(Bodenfließen an Hängen)*
terraciform terrassenförmig
terracing Terrassenbildung f, Terrassierung f
terracotta Terrakotta f, Terrakotte f
terrain analysis (appreciation) Geländeauswertung f
~ **correction** Geländekorrektur f
~ **photosurvey** fotografische Geländeaufnahme f
~ **reconnaissance** Geländeerkundung f
~ **sector** Geländeabschnitt m
~ **surface** Geländeoberfläche f
~ **survey** Geländevermessung f
terrane Gebirgsglied n, Formation f, Schichtenfolge f
terranean terran
terraqueous zone wasserführender Teil m *(der Lithosphäre)*
terre verte Grünerde f
terrene Erdoberfläche f
terreous erdig
terrestrial terrestrisch, Erd...
~ **atmosphere** Erdatmosphäre f
~ **ball** Erdkugel f
~ **body** Erdkörper m
~ **coal facies** terrestrische Kohlenfazies f
~ **corrugations** Faltung f der Erdrinde
~ **crust** Erdkruste f
~ **current** Erdstrom m
~ **deposit** kontinentale Ablagerung f
~ **detritus** terrestrische Schuttgesteine npl
~ **electricity** Geoelektrizität f, Erdelektrizität f
~ **equator** Erdäquator m
~ **facies** terrestrische Fazies f, Kontinentalfazies f
~ **formations** terrestrische Bildungen fpl
~ **globe** Erdglobus m
~ **heat** Erdwärme f
~ **latitude** geografische Breite f
~ **longitude** geografische Länge f
~-**magnetic** erdmagnetisch
~-**magnetic field** erdmagnetisches Feld n
~-**magnetic pole** erdmagnetischer Pol m
~ **magnetism** Erdmagnetismus m, Geomagnetismus m
~ **orbit** Erdbahn f
~ **peat** oberhalb des Wasserspiegels gebildeter Torf m
~ **photogrammetry** Erdbildmessung f
~ **pole** Erdpol m
~ **refraction** atmosphärische Brechung f
~ **scintillation** Luftflimmern n

~ **sphere** Erdkugel f
~ **thermodynamics** Thermodynamik f der Erde
~ **water** terrestrisches Wasser n
terrigene s. terrigenous
terrigenous terrigen, vom Kontinent stammend
~ **deposit** terrigene Ablagerung f
~ **detritus** Landschutt m
~ **sediment** terrigene Ablagerung f, terrigenes Sediment n
territorial section Geländeabschnitt m
territory Territorium n, Gebiet n
tertiary oil recovery tertiäre Entölung f
Tertiary Tertiär[system] n *(chronostratigrafisch)*; Tertiär n, Tertiärperiode f *(geochronologisch)*; Tertiär n, Tertiärzeit f *(allgemein)*
~ **Age** Tertiär n, Tertiärzeit f
~ **Period** Tertiär n, Tertiärperiode f
~ **quartzite** Tertiärquarzit m
~ **System** Tertiär[system] n
tertschite Tertschit m, $Ca_2[B_5O_6(OH)_7] \cdot 6\frac{1}{2}H_2O$
teschemacherite Teschemacherit m, NH_4HCO_3
teschenite Teschenit m *(Alkaligestein)*
tessera von Scherzonen begrenzte stabile Struktureinheit f
tesseral tesseral
test 1. Versuch m; Test m; 2. Schale f, Gehäuse n
~ **boring** Versuchsbohrung f, Aufschlußbohrung f
~ **gallery** Versuchsstrecke f
~ **hole** Versuchsbohrloch n, Probebohrung f
~ **line** Testmessung f, Versuchsprofil n
~ **pill** Eichpräparat n, Etalon n
~ **pit** Schürfschacht m, Schürfgraben m
~ **pressure** Prüfdruck m
~ **site** Testplatz m, Versuchsgebiet n, Übungsgebiet n, Prüfgelände n *(z.B. für die Eichung von Fernerkundungssensoren)*
~ **specimen** Prüfkörper m, Probekörper m
~ **well** 1. Schürfbohrung f; 2. Versuchsbrunnen m
tester Prüfgerät n, Probegerät n
tetartohedral tetartoedrisch
tetartohedron Tetartoeder n, Viertelflächner m
tetartosymmetric s. tetartohedral
tethered balloon verankerter Ballon m *(z.B. an einem Halteseil)*
Tethyan geosyncline Tethys f
~ **Realm** tethyales Faunenreich n
Tethys Tethys f
tetradymite Tetradymit m, Tellurwismut n, Bi_2Te_2S
tetragonal tetragonal
~ **soil** Tetragonalboden m
~ **system** tetragonales System n
tetrahedral tetraedrisch
~ **coordination** tetraedrische Koordination f, Viererkoordination f
tetrahedrite Tetraedrit m, Fahlerz n, Antimonfahlerz n, Cu_3SbS_{3-4}
tetrahedron Tetraeder n, Vierflächner m

tetrahexahedron

tetrahexahedron Tetrahexaeder n, Tetrakishexaeder n
tetrakishexahedron s. tetrahexahedron
textinite Textinit m (Braunkohlenmaceral)
textural texturell, gefügemäßig
~ **maturity** strukturelle Reife f, Maturität f (Sedimentgefüge)
texture Textur f; Struktur f (für Gesteine)
~ **goniometer** Texturgoniometer n, Gefügekamera f
thalassic deposit eupelagische Ablagerung f, Hochseeablagerung f
~ **rock** küstenfern gebildetes Sedimentgestein n
thalassocratic sea level Seespiegel m im Maximum einer Transgression
thalassocraton Tiefkraton n
thalassography, thalassology s. oceanography
thalattogenic durch Vertikalbewegungen des Meeresbodens gebildet
thalenite Thalenit m, $Y_2[Si_2O_7]$
thallium Thallium n, Tl
~ **ore** Thalliumerz n
thanatocoenosis Thanatokönose f, Thanatocoenose f, Grabgemeinschaft f
Thanetian [Stage] Thanétien n, Thanet[ium] f (Stufe des Paläozäns)
thaumasite Thaumasit m, $Ca_3H_2[CO_3|SO_4|SiO_4]\cdot 13H_2O$
thaw/to schmelzen, tauen
thaw Tauwetter n, Frostaufgang m
~ **and freeze** Schmelzen n und Wiedergefrieren n
~ **depressions** Thermokarstniederungen fpl
~ **weather** Tauwetter n
thawing layer Auftauschicht f
thecae Theken fpl (bei Graptoliten)
thenardite Thenardit m, $\alpha\text{-}Na_2[SO_4]$
theory of catastrophic destruction Katastrophenlehre f
~ **of continental drift** Theorie f der Kontinentalverschiebungen
~ **of descent** Abstammungslehre f
~ **of fixed beams** Plattentheorie f
~ **of induced cleavage** Theorie f der Vorzerklüftung
theralite Theralith m
therma Therme f
thermal thermisch
~ **analysis** Thermoanalyse f
~ **aureole** Kontaktaureole f
~ **capacity of water** Wärmekapazität f des Wassers
~ **conductibility factor** Wärmeleitzahl f
~ **conductivity** Wärmeleitfähigkeit f
~ **degradation** thermischer Abbau m (Erdöl)
~ **demagnetization** thermische Entmagnetisierung f
~ **diffusivity** Temperaturleitfähigkeit f
~ **drilling** thermisches Bohren n
~ **equator** Wärmeäquator m
~ **equilibrium** thermisches Gleichgewicht n

354

~ **expansion of water** Wärmeausdehnung f des Wassers
~ **fault fissure** Thermenlinie f
~ **field** Thermalfeld n, Wärmefeld n
~ **inertia** thermische Trägheit f, Wärmeträgheit f
~ **infrared** thermisches Infrarot n
~**-infrared scanner** Linienabtaster m im thermischen Infrarotbereich
~ **mapper** Wärmekartiergerät n (Gerät zur bildlichen Darstellung wärmestrahlender Objekte)
~ **metamorphism** Thermometamorphose f, Kontaktmetamorphose f
~ **oil recovery** thermale Entölung f
~ **potential** Wärmepotential n
~ **radiation** Wärmestrahlung f
~ **resistance** thermische Trägheit f
~ **spring** Therme f, Thermalquelle f
~ **spring deposit** Thermalquellenablagerung f
~ **stratification** Wärmeschichtung f
~ **value** Heizwert m
~ **water** Thermalwasser n
~ **water outlet** Thermalwasseraustritt m
thermally altered coals thermisch veränderte Kohlen fpl
~ **metamorphosed coke** Naturkoks m
thermite fossile brennbare Substanz f
thermoaqueous durch heißes Wasser entstanden
thermodynamic potential thermodynamisches Potential n
~ **stability** thermodynamische Stabilität f
thermoelectric thermoelektrisch
thermoelectricity Thermoelektrizität f
thermogravimetry Thermogravimetrie f
thermokarst Thermokarst m
thermolabile in Wärme zersetzbar
thermoluminescence Thermolumineszenz f
thermometamorphism Thermometamorphose f, Kontaktmetamorphose f
thermometer probe Temperaturmeßsonde f
thermonatrite Thermonatrit m, $Na_2CO_3\cdot H_2O$
thermophilic thermophil
thermoremanent magnetization thermoremanenter Magnetismus m
thetomorphic glass thetomorphes Glas n (durch Schockmetamorphose im festen Zustand verglaste Mineralkörner)
thick mächtig
~ **banks/in** dickbankig
~**-bedded** dickbankig
~ **deposit** mächtige Ablagerung f
~ **fog** dichter Nebel m
~**-layered** dickbankig
~ **layers/in** dickbankig
~ **section** Dickschliff m
~**-shaly** dickplattig
~**-shelled mountains** Gebirge npl mit tiefer Wurzelzone
~ **slice** Dickschliff m
~**-stratified** dickbankig

~-walled dickwandig
thicken [up]/to sich auftun, an Mächtigkeit zunehmen
thickening Mächtigkeitszunahme f, Verdickung f (einer Schicht)
thickly s. thick-...
thickness Dicke f, Mächtigkeit f
~ of deposit s. ~ of stratum
~ of layer Mächtigkeit f der Schicht, Schichtdicke f
~ of load s. ~ of stratum
~ of soil Bodenmächtigkeit f
~ of stratum Mächtigkeit f eines Flözes (Ganges, Erzkörpers, Lagers)
~ of the filter cake Dicke f der Filtrationskruste
thief sand saugender (ölabsorbierender) Sand m
thieving horizon schluckender (Spülung aufnehmender) Horizont m
thigh bone s. femur
thill (sl) 1. Strosse f, Sohle f; 2. s. seat earth
thin away/to auskeilen
~ off ausdünnen
~ out auskeilen
thin geringmächtig
~-banded dünngebändert
~ banks/in dünnbankig
~-bedded dünngeschichtet, feingeschichtet
~-foliated dünnblättrig
~-interlayered bedding feine Wechselschichtung f
~-lamellar shaly dünnlamelliert schiefrig
~-laminated dünnblättrig
~-laminated sandstone Blättersandstein m
~ layers/in dünnbankig
~ oil column Erdölsaum m
~ rock section Gesteinsdünnschliff m
~ seam geringmächtiges Flöz n, Schmitze f
~ section Dünnschliff m
~-shaly dünnplattig
~-shelled mountains Deckengebirge n ohne (mit flacher) Wurzelzone
~-skinned dünnschalig
~ slide Dünnschliff m
~-stratified dünnbankig
thinly s. thin-...
thinned-out middle limb ausgequetschter Mittelschenkel m
thinning Verdrückung f, Verdünnung f (einer Schicht)
~ of the limbs Schenkelverdünnung f
~-out Auskeilen n
thirl Querschlag m, Durchhieb m
thixotropic thixotrop
~ hardening Thixotropieeffekt m
thixotropy Thixotropie f, Wechselfestigkeit f
tholeiite Tholeiit m (basaltisches Gestein)
tholoid s. volcanic dome
thomsenolite Thomsenolith m, NaCa[AlF$_6$]·H$_2$O
thomsonite Thomsonit m, NaCa$_2$[Al$_2$(Al,Si)Si$_2$O$_{10}$·6H$_2$O

thoracic legs Thorakalfüße mpl (bei Arthropoden)
~ ring Thoraxring m (bei Trilobiten)
~ somite Thoraxsegment n (bei Trilobiten)
thorax Thorax m, Rumpf m (bei Trilobiten)
thoreaulite Thoreaulith m, Sn[(Ta, Nb)$_2$O$_7$]
thoria Thorerde f
thorianite Thorianit m, ThO$_2$
thoriated thoriumhaltig
thorite Thorit m, Orangit m, ThSiO$_4$
thorium Thor[ium] n, Th
~ ore Thoriumerz n
thorn house Gradiersaline f
thorogummite Thorogummit m, (Th,U)[(SiO$_4$(OH)$_4$]
thorotungstite Thorotungstit m, 2W$_2$O$_3$·H$_2$O+(ThO$_2$,Ce$_2$O$_3$,ZrO$_2$)+H$_2$O
thoroughfare kleiner Kanal m (der eine Landspitze oder Küstenbarriere durchschneidet)
thoroughly crystalline eukristallin, vollkristallinisch
thortveitite Thortveitite m, Sc$_2$[Si$_2$O$_7$]
Thoulet solution Thouletsche Lösung f
thread sehr dünnes Mineralrum n
~-lace scoria s. reticulite
~ of maximum velocity, ~ of the current Stromstrich m
three-D-seismics flächenhafte seismische Aufnahme f, 3-D-Seismik f
~-dimensional räumlich, dreidimensional
~-dimensional coordinates Raumkoordinaten fpl
~-dimensional diagram räumliches Schaubild n
~-dimensional flow räumliche Strömung f
~-dimensional lattice Raumgitter n
~-dimensional state of deformation räumlicher Verformungszustand m
~-dimensional trend Raumtrend m
~-facetted stone Dreikanter m
~-layer structure Dreischichtstruktur f
~-phase flow Dreiphasenströmung f
~-point method Dreipunktverfahren n
threefold coordination Dreierkoordination f
threeling Drilling m (bei Kristallen)
threshold concentration Grenzkonzentration f (Wassermineralisation)
~ pressure Dichtheitsdruck m
~ velocity Grenzgeschwindigkeit f (z.B. für Winderosion)
thribble Gestängezug m aus drei Bohrstangen
throat Öffnung f, Schlund m, Vulkanschlot m, Eruptionskanal m
~ of a volcano Kraterschlund m
throstlebrest (sl) stark mit Gangart verwachsenes Erz n (Derbyshire)
throughfall Niederschlagsmenge, die den Boden direkt über Vegetationslücken erreicht
throughput Förderung f
throw over the dump/to auf Halde stürzen
throw Verwerfung f, Sprung m, vertikale Sprunghöhe f, Verwurf m

throw

~ of fault Sprunghöhe f einer Verwerfung
throwing-up Auswurf m
thrown gestört; verworfen
~-down ins Liegende verworfen
~ side gesunkener Flügel m
thrust 1. Schub m; 2. Vorschubkraft f (bei einer Bohrung)
~ cleavage 1. Überschiebungsschieferung f (Tektonik); 2. Druckschlechten fpl (Kohle)
~ crumple Überschiebungsfalte f
~ far-out delta weit vorgeschobenes Delta n
~ fault Aufschiebung f, inverse Verwerfung f, Konjunktivbruch m
~ fault trap Überschiebungsfalle f
~-faulted überschoben
~ folding Faltenüberschiebung f
~ force Schubkraft f
~ loading Schubbelastung f
~ mass Überschiebungsmasse f
~ of the ground Erddruck m
~-out delta vorgeschobenes Delta n
~ outlier Deckenscholle f
~-over überschoben
~ plane Überschiebungsfläche f
~ sheet Überschiebungsdecke f, Schubdecke f
~ slices abgescherte Schubpakete npl
~ slip flache Schubhöhe f
~ structure Deckenfaltung f
~ wedges abgescherte Schubpakete npl
thrusted blocks aufgeschobene Schollen fpl
thrusting Überschiebung f, Verschiebung f
~ force Schubkraft f
~ movement Überschiebungsbewegung f
thufur s. earth hummocks
thulite Thulit m (Mn-Zoisit und Mn-Epidot)
thumper Schlageinrichtung f (zur Erzeugung seismischer Energie)
thunder/to donnern
thunder Donner m
~ cloud Gewitterwolke f
~ shower Gewitterregen m
~ squall Gewitterbö f
thunderhead Gewitterwolke f, Gewitterwand f
thunderous gewitterschwül
thunderstorm high Gewitterhoch n
thundery gewitterig, gewitterschwül
~ depressions Sommergewitter npl
thuringite Thuringit m, $(Mg, Fe)_3(Fe, Al)_3[(OH)_8|AlSi_3O_{10}]$
thurm 1. kleine Störung f, kleine Verwerfung f; 2. vom Meer überspültes Vorgebirge n
Thurnian Thurnien n (Teil der Präglazialfolge, England, tiefstes Pleistozän)
tidal Gezeiten...
~ area Watt n
~ bedding Gezeitenschichtung f
~ bulge Gezeitenberg m
~ cataclysm Sturmflut f
~ channel Wattrinne f
~ correction Gezeitenkorrektion f
~ current Gezeitenstrom m, Gezeitenströmung f

~ delta Gezeitendelta n
~ effect Tideneffekt m
~ estuary Trichtermündung f (eines Flusses)
~ flat Watt n
~-flat area Wattengebiet n
~ fluctuation Gezeitenschwankung f
~ forces Flutkräfte fpl
~ friction Gezeitenreibung f
~ glacier s. tidewater glacier
~ gravimeter Gezeitengravimeter n
~ inlet Gezeitenpriel m
~ lamination Gezeitenschichtung f
~ marsh Wattboden m, Gezeitenmarsch f
~ mud deposits Gezeitenablagerung f, Schlick m
~ outflow Ebbestrom m
~ outlet Gezeitenpriel m
~ power station Gezeitenkraftwerk n
~ range Fluthöhe f, Tidenhub m
~ river Tidefluß m, Ästuar n
~ scourway Gezeitenkolk m
~ sea Meer n mit Gezeiten
~ silts Wattenschlick m
~ stream Gezeitenstrom m
~ swell Sturmflut f
~ territory Ebbe-und-Flut-Gebiet n
~ wave Flutwelle f, Gezeitenwelle f
~ zone Gezeitensaum m
tide Tide f, Ebbe f und Flut f
~ beach Gezeitenstrand m
~ current Gezeitenstrom m, Gezeitenströmung f
~ gauge Gezeitenpegel m, Flutmesser m
~-land swamps Wattenmeer n
~ mark Niedrigwasserlinie f, Flutgrenze f
~ register Gezeitenpegel m, Flutmesser m
~-swept flat Watt n
tideland Wattenmeer n
tideless gezeitenlos
tidewater glacier ins Meer kalbender Gletscher m
~ stream Gezeitenfluß m
tie Anschlußmessung f, Korrelationsmessung f
~ line Trennlinie f; Konode f
~ point Überlappungspunkt m; Anschlußpunkt m
~ rods Tiefanker mpl
tiemannite Tiemannit m, HgSe
tierra blanca s. caliche
tiers of different structural character Gefügestockwerke npl (tektonisch)
tiff spätiges Mineral n (z.B. Kalzit, Baryt)
Tiffanian [Stage] Tiffanien n (Stufe des Paläozäns)
tiger's-eye Tigerauge n (SiO_2-Pseudomorphose nach Krokydolith)
~ sandstone Tigersandstein m, gestreifter Sandstein m
tight dicht
~ fold Isoklinalfalte f (s.a. closed fold)
~ hole geheime Bohrung f (Bohrung, über die keine Angaben gemacht werden)

~ **pull of the drill pipe** Festfahren *n* des Bohrstrangs
~ **sand** schwer durchlässiger Sand *m*
~ **soil** bindiger harter Boden *m*
tightening Einschnürung *f*, Einklemmung *f*
tightly folded stark gefaltet
tightset geschlossene Kluft *f (Steinbruch)*
tikhonenkovite Tikhonenkovit *m*, (Sr, Ca)[AlF$_4$OH·H$_2$O]
tilasite Tilasit *m*, CaMg[F|AsO$_4$]
tile Dachziegel *m*
~ **earth** kompakter Tonboden *m*
~ **ore** Ziegelerz *n (1. Verwitterungsprodukt von Kupferkies; 2. Dolomit mit Zinnober)*
till Geschiebelehm *m*, Geschiebemergel *m*, Grundmoräne *f*, Moränenschutt *m*
~ **ball** Geschiebeklumpen *m*
~-**covered** grundmoränenbedeckt
~ **layer** Geschiebemergelschicht *f*
~-**plains topography** Grundmoränenlandschaft *f*
~ **sheet** Geschiebelehmdecke *f*
~ **stone** Geschiebeblock *m*
~ **wall** in Gletscherspalten aufgequetschter Geschiebemergel *m*
tilled soil Ackerkrume *f*
tilleyite Tilleyit *m*, Ca$_5$[(CO$_3$)$_2$|Si$_2$O$_7$]
tillite fossiler Blocklehm *m*, Tillit *m (fossile Moräne)*
tilloid geschiebemergelartig
tilt 1. Kippung *f*; 2. *Neigung einer Fernerkundungsplattform, z.B. eines Flugzeugs oder Satelliten, in Flugrichtung*
~-**block basin** durch Blockkippung verursachtes Becken *n*
~ **of the earth's axis** Neigung *f* der Erdachse
tilted geneigt; schräggestellt
~ **block** Kippscholle *f*
~ **fault block** gekippte Scholle *f*
~ **strata** gekippte Schichten *fpl*
tilth 1. Ackerland *n*; 2. bestelltes Land *n*; 3. Bodengare *f*
tilthtop soil Ackerkrume *f*
tilting Schrägstellung *f*
~ **of strata** Schichtenaufrichtung *f*
tiltmeter Neigungsmesser *m*
timber of forest Hochwald *m*
~ **soil** Waldboden *m*
timbered steppe Waldsteppe *f*
~ **upland moor** Waldhochmoor *n*
timberline [obere] Baumgrenze *f*
time after circulation stops Standzeit *f*
~-**average relationship** Zeit-Mittel-Gleichung *f*
~ **belt** *(Am)* Zeitzone *f*
~ **break** Abriß *m (Zeitmarkierung des Schußmoments)*
~ **delay** Zeitverzögerung *f*
~-**depth chart** Karte *f* für die Laufzeit als Funktion der Tiefe
~-**depth curve** T-D-Kurve *f* (1. *Laufzeitkurve*; 2. *grafische Darstellung der Laufzeit als Funktion der Tiefe)*

~ **dilatation** Zeitdilatation *f*
~-**distance curve** Laufzeitkurve *f*
~-**distance graph** 1. Laufzeitkurve *f*; 2. tau-xi-Kurve *f*
~ **domain** Zeitbereich *m*
~ **lead** Kurzzeitgebiet *n*; Zeitverminderung *f*
~ **mark** Zeitmarke *f*
~ **of a drilling cycle** volle Zeit *f* für das Niederbringen einer Bohrung
~ **of a run** Dauer *f* eines Bohrmarsches
~ **of advent** Einsatzzeit *f (Seismik)*
~ **of arrival** Ankunftszeit *f (Seismik)*
~ **of coal formation** Kohlenbildungszeit *f*
~ **of deglaciation** Zwischeneiszeit *f*
~ **of incidence** Einsatzzeit *f (Seismik)*
~ **of origin** Herdzeit *f (Erdbeben)*
~ **of radiation** Strahlungszeit *f (Radioisotop)*
~ **of transit** Laufzeit *f (Seismik)*
~ **on bottom** Bohrzeit *f* auf Sohle
~ **registration** Zeitmarkierung *f*
~-**rock unit** *s.* ~-*stratigraphic unit*
~ **section** Zeitschnitt *m*
~ **series** Zeitreihe *f*
~ **sharing** Simultanbearbeitung *f*
~-**stratigraphic unit** stratigrafische Gliederungseinheit *f (z.B. System, Serie, Stufe)*
~-**subsidence curve** Senkungs-Zeit-Kurve *f*
~ **tie** Zeitabschluß *m*
~ **variation** zeitliche Variation *f*
~ **window** Zeitfenster *n*
~ **zone** Zeitzone *f*
timer lines Zeitmarken *fpl (Seismogramm)*
Timiskaming Timiskaming *n (oberes Altpräkambrium in Nordamerika)*
tin Zinn *n*, Sn
~-**bearing** zinnführend, zinnhaltig
~ **buddle** Zinnwäsche *f*
~ **deposit** Zinnlagerstätte *f*
~ **floor** unregelmäßig verteiltes Zinnerz *n*
~ **gravels** Zinngraupen *fpl*
~ **lode** Zinnerzgang *m*
~ **mine** Zinnbergwerk *n*
~ **mining** Zinnbergbau *m*
~ **ore** *s.* cassiterite
~ **placer** Zinnseife *f*
~ **pyrite** Zinnkies *m*, Stannin *m*, Cu$_2$FeSnS$_4$
~-**smelting plant** Zinnhütte *f*
~ **spar (stone)** *s.* cassiterite
~ **stuff** rohes Zinnerz *n*, Zinnzwitter *m (mit Gangart verwachsenes Zinnerz)*
~-**white cobalt** *s.* smaltite
~-**witts** Zinnkonzentrat *n (noch unrein)*
~ **wood** Holzzinn *n (radialfasriger Zinnstein)*
~ **works** Zinnhütte *f*
~ **yield** Zinnausbringen *n*
tincalconite Tinkalkonit *m*, Na$_2$[B$_4$O$_5$(OH)$_4$]·3H$_2$O
tinder ore *s.* jamesonite
tinguaite Tinguait *m (Alkalisyenit)*
tinker *(sl)* kohlenstoffhaltiger Schiefer *m*
tinning Zinnbergbau *m*
tinny zinnartig, zinnhaltig

tinticite

tinticite Tinticit *m*, $Fe_3[(OH)_3|(PO_4)_2]\cdot 3H_2O$
tinzenite Tinzenit *m*, Axinit *m (s.a.* axinite)
Tioughniogan [Stage] Tioughnioga *n (Stufe, Givet in Nordamerika)*
tip up/to hochkippen, abkippen
tip Halde *f*
tipped gekippt, schräggestellt
tipper 1. Kippe *f*; 2. Wiese-Pfeil *m (Geomagnetik)*
tipping downslope of the outcrops Hakenwerfen *n* der Schichten
~ **movement** Kippbewegung *f*
~ **of the blocks** Schollenabkippung *f*
tirr Abraumdecke *f* im Steinbruchbetrieb *(Schottland)*
titanaugite Titanaugit *m (mit 3–5% TiO_2)*
titanic iron ore *s.* ilmenite
~ **schorl** *s.* rutile
titaniferous titanführend, titanhaltig
titanite Titanit *m*, $CaTi[O|SiO_4]$
titanium Titan *n*, Ti
~ **ore** Titanerz *n*
titanomagnetite Titanomagnetit *m (Mischkristall von Magnetit und Ulvit)*
titanomorphite Titanomorphit *m (Zersetzungsprodukt von Rutil und Ilmenit)*
titanous titanhaltig
Tithonian [Stage] Tithon *n (hangende Stufe des Malms, Tethys)*
T. L. *s.* transmitted light
Toadian Toad[ien] *n (Skyth bis unteres Ladin, Nordamerika)*
toad's eye [tin] Holzzinn *n (radialfasriger Zinnstein)*
toadstone *(sl)* Melaphyr *m*, Basaltporphyr *m*
Toarcian [Stage] Toarc[ien] *n*, Toarcium *n (hangende Stufe des Lias)*
tobermorite Tobermorit *m*, $Ca_5H_2[Si_3O_9]_2\cdot 4H_2O$
toe failure Basisbruch *m*
~-**nail** schaufelförmige Kluft *f*
~ **of a hole** Bohrlochtiefstes *n*
~ **of stope** Feldortsstoß *m*, Ortsbrust *f*
~ **of the bank** Fuß *m* der Bruchwand
~ **of the dam** Dammfuß *m*
~ **set** Sohlblatt *n (Schichtung)*
token kleines Flöz, das ein großes anzeigt
tombolo Inselnehrung *f*, Landspitze *f*, angegliederte Halbinsel *f*; Sandbank *f* zwischen Insel und Festland
Tommotian [Stage] Tommot *n (Stufe, Unterkambrium Sibiriens)*
ton Tonne *f (SI-fremde Einheit der Masse)*
tonalite 1. Tonalit *m*; 2. Quarzdiorit *m*
tongue 1. Keil *m*; 2. Landzunge *f*, Landspitze *f*
~ **of ice** Eiszunge *f*
tonguelike basin Zungenbecken *n*
tonnage of a mine Förderleistung *f* eines Bergwerks
tool joint Gestängezugverbinder *m*
~ **marks** Gegenstandsmarken *fpl (Sedimentgefüge)*
~ **pusher** Oberbohrmeister *m*, Bohrmeister *m*

358

~ **withdrawal** Aufholen *n* des Bohrwerkzeugs
tooth Schloßzahn *m (bei Fossilgehäusen)*
~-**bearing bone** zahntragender Knochen *m*, Dentale *n*
~ **enamel** Zahnschmelz *m*, Dentin *n*
top 1. Oberkante *f (einer geologischen Einheit)*; 2. Scheitel *m (eines Salzstocks)*; 3. Firste *f*, Dach *n*
~-**bottom determination** Geopetalgefüge *n*
~ **coal** oberste Kohlenschicht *f*; Flözoberkate *f (Kohle)*
~ **heading** Firststrecke *f*
~ **layer** oberste Schicht *f*; Oberbank *f (eines Flözes)*
~ **of clouds** Wolkenobergrenze *f*
~ **part** oberster Teil *m*
~ **pressure** Scheiteldruck *m*, Firstendruck *m*
~ **seal** Hangendsperre *f*
~-**set beds** Dachschichten *fpl (bei Deltaschichtung)*
~ **side** Oberkante *f*
~ **slicing** Scheibenbruchbau *m*, abwärts geführter Querbruchbau *m*
~ **soil** Ackerkrume *f*
~ **view** Aufsicht *f (bezogen auf die Projektionsebene)*
~ **wall** Hangendes *n*
~ **water** Hangendwasser *n (bei Erdgas- oder Erdölbohrungen)*
~ **water level** Stauhöhe *f*
topaz Topas *m*, $Al_2[F_2|SiO_4]$
~ **quartz** Zitrin *m (s.a.* quartz)
~ **tock** *s.* topazfels
topazfels Topasfels *m (brekzisiertes Kontaktgestein mit Topas)*
topazite Topasit *m (Ganggestein mit Quarz und Topas)*
topazization Topasbildung *f*
topazolite Topazolith *m*, gelber Granit *m*
topazoseme Topas-Quarz-Turmalin-Gestein *n*
toph, tophin *s.* tophus
tophus Kalktuff *m*
topmost slice obere Abbauscheibe *f*
topographic[al] topografisch
~ **catchment area** oberirdisches Einzugsgebiet *n*
~ **chart** Geländekarte *f*
~ **contour [line]** Isophyse *f*, Höhen[schicht]linie *f*
~ **correction** topografische Reduktion *f (Gravimetrie)*
~ **divide** oberirdische Wasserscheide *f*
~ **drawing** Kartenskizze *f*
~ **drawing board** topografischer Meßtisch *m*
~ **features** Terrainbeschaffenheit *f*
~ **forms** Erdoberflächenformen *fpl*
~ **map** Geländekarte *f*
~ **reconnaissance** Landesaufnahme *f*
~ **relief** topografisches Relief *n*
~ **sketch** Terrainskizze *f*
~ **survey** Geländeaufnahme *f*, Erdvermessung *f*

Tournaisian

~ **unconformity** topografische Diskordanz f
topographically prominent im Gelände hervortretend
topography Topografie f, Oberflächengestaltung f
~ **of the sea bottom** Gestaltung f des Meeresbodens
topotropic analysis Achsenverteilungsanalyse f
topotype Topotypus m *(Fundstück vom Ort des Holotypus)*
topped durch Bohrung angetroffen
topset 1. Schelfaufschüttung f, Ablagerung f auf dem Schelf; 2. Dachschicht f, Deckschicht; Deltaschicht f
~ **beds** obere Schichten fpl von Deltaablagerungen
topsoil Erdkrume f, Ackerkrume f, Bodenkrume f, Mutterboden m, Dammerde f
topspit Deckschutt m, Deckgebirge n
tor Härtling m, Felsburg f, hoher felsiger Hügel m
torbanite Torbanit m *(Bogheadkohle von Torbane Hill, Schottland)*
torbernite Torbernit m, Kupferuranglimmer m, $Cu[UO_2|PO_4]_2 \cdot 10(12-8)H_2O$
torch peat Pollentorf m
tornadic Tornado...
tornado Tornado m, Wirbelsturm m
~ **cloud** Tornadowolke f
~ **vortex** Tornadowirbel m
törnebohmite Törnebohmit m, $(Ce, La, Al)_3[OH|(SiO_4)_2]$
torose wulstig
~ **load cast** wulstige Belastungsmarke f
torpedoing Torpedierung f *(der Verrohrung von Ölbohrungen in Förderhorizonten)*
torque Drehmoment n
~ **failure** Verdrehungsbruch m
~ **loading** Drehbelastung f
Torrejonian [Stage] Torrejonien n *(Wirbeltierstufe des Paläozäns in Nordamerika)*
torrent Gießbach m, Sturzbach m, Wildbach m
~ **control work** Wildbachverbauung f
~ **deposit** Wildbachablagerung f
~-**laid** in schnellfließendem Wasser abgelagert
~ **of lava** Lavastrom m
~ **of melt water** Schmelzwasserstrom m
~ **of mud** Schlammstrom m, Murgang m *(Vulkanismus)*
~ **[of] rain** Platzregen m, Wolkenbruch m
~ **regulation** Wildbachverbauung f
torrential gießbachartig
~ **cross-bedding** Schichtflutkreuzschichtung f
~ **downpour** Regenguß m, Sturzregen m
~ **fan** Murkegel m
~ **mountain stream** s. ~ stream
~ **rain** Wolkenbruch m, Platzregen m
~ **stream** Gießbach m, Sturzbach m, Wildbach m
~ **wash** Murgang m, Murbruch m

torreyite Torreyit m, $(Mg, Zn, Mn)_7[(OH)_{12}|SO_4]\cdot 4H_2O$
torrid zone heiße (tropische) Zone f
Torridonian Sandstone Torridon-Sandstein m
torsion Torsion f, Verdrehung f, Drillung f
~ **balance** Drehwaage f
~ **failure** Torsionsbruch m
~ **fold** Korkenzieherfalte f
~ **modulus** Torsionsmodul m
~ **seismometer** Torsionsseismograf m, Torsionsseismometer n
~ **stress** Torsionsspannung f
torsional stress Torsionsspannung f
torso mountain Restberg m
Tortonian [Stage] Torton[ium] n *(Stufe des Miozäns)*
tortuosity Tortuosität f
total depth Endteufe f
~ **displacement** wahre Schublänge f, flache allgemeine Sprunghöhe f
~ **eclipse** totale Finsternis f
~ **heave** streichende Sprungweite f
~ **intensity** Totalintensität f
~ **lunar eclipse** totale Mondfinsternis f
~ **output** Gesamtausbeute f, Gesamtertrag m
~ **porosity** Gesamtporosität f
~ **radiation** Gesamtstrahlung f, Globalstrahlung f
~ **recovery** Gesamtausbeute f, Gesamtertrag m
~ **reflection** Totalreflexion f
~ **refraction** totale Brechung f
~ **reserve** Gesamtvorrat m
~ **rock sample** Gesamtgesteinsprobe f
~ **soil moisture capacity** Gesamtwasserkapazität f des Bodens
~ **solar eclipse** totale Sonnenfinsternis f
~ **thickness** Gesamtmächtigkeit f
~ **throw** flache Sprunghöhe f
~ **time** Gegenzeit f, Gesamtlaufzeit f
totalizator Totalisator m *(Niederschlagsmesser)*
touchstone Lydit m, schwarzer Kieselschiefer m, Probierstein m
tough zäh; sprödbruchunempfindlich
~ **silt** steifer Schluff m
toughness Zähigkeit f; Sprödbruchunempfindlichkeit f
tour Rohrtour f
~ **report** Bohrbericht m
tourmaline Turmalin m *(komplexes Borosilikat)*
~-**bearing** turmalinführend
~ **granite** Turmalingranit m
~ **rock** s. tourmalite
~ **schist** Turmalinschiefer m
~ **sun** Turmalinsonne f
tourmalinic turmalinartig, turmalinhaltig
tourmalinization Turmalinisierung f
tourmalinize/to turmalinisieren
tourmalite Turmalin-Quarz-Gestein n
Tournaisian [Stage] Tournai n *(Stufe des Unterkarbons)*

tournhouse

tournhouse *(sl)* Gangmasse *f*
tower 1. Turm *m*; 2. *s.* tour
~ karst Turmkarst *m*
towering cloud Wolkenturm *m*
township *(Am)* kartografisch festliegende quadratische Flächen von 6 Meilen Basislänge. *Die Township ist in 36 Sections mit je einer Quadratmeile Flächeninhalt unterteilt. Gesamtfläche = 36 Quadratmeilen = 93,2360 km²*
toxic element toxisches (giftiges) Element *n*
trace a bed/to eine Schicht [an der Oberfläche] verfolgen
trace Spur *f*
~ amount Spurengehalt *m (im Grundwasser)*
~ analysis Spurenuntersuchung *f,* Spuranalyse *f (der tatsächlichen Laufzeiten der Einsätze für jede Spur)*
~ element Oligoelement *n,* Spurenelement *n*
~ fossil Spurenfossil *n (Ichnologie)*
traceable nachweisbar
tracer Tracer *m,* Markierungsstoff *m*
~ element Spurenelement *n*
traces Schnittlinien *fpl,* Kreuzlinien *fpl*
~ of life Lebensspuren *fpl*
~ of natural gas Erdgasspuren *fpl*
~ of oil Ölspuren *fpl*
trachea Trachee *f*
trachyandesite Trachyandesit *m*
trachybasalt Trachybasalt *m*
trachyostracous dickschalig
trachyte Trachyt *m*
~ tuff Trachyttuff *m*
trachytic trachytisch
trachytoidl[al] trachytartig
track Trittsiegel *n (Ichnologie)*
~ level Fördersohle *f*
~ width Feld[es]breite *f*
trackway Fährte *f (Ichnologie)*
traction Bodentransport *m (von Sediment in fließendem Wasser)*
~ load Bodenlast *f,* Schleppast *f,* Geschiebelast *f,* Geschiebefracht *f (eines Flusses)*
tractional load *s.* traction load
tractive force Schleppkraft *f (des Wassers)*
trade [wind] Passat[wind] *m*
~-wind belt Passatgürtel *m*
~-wind current Passatwindströmung *f*
trafficability ingenieurgeologische Verkehrsbelastbarkeit *f,* Begehbarkeit *f (eines Geländes)*
trail Schleifspur *f,* Kriechspur *f,* Gleitspur *f*
~ of the fault Harnischmylonit *m* mit Verschiebungsrichtung *f* und Verwerfung
trailed fault an einer älteren Störung abgelenkte jüngere Störung *f*
trailer Nachbeben *n,* Nachläufer *m*
trailway *s.* trackway
train 1. Spur *f,* Furche *f,* Rinne *f;* 2. Schweif *m,* Meteorschweif *m*
~ of stone Blockstrom *m*
training set *Ensemble genau definierter Bodenobjekte, das zur Eichung von Fernerkundungsdaten verwendet wird*

trajectories of the principal stresses Hauptspannungstrajektorien *fpl*
trajectory Flugbahn *f*
tramble/to waschen *(Erz)*
tranquillity Ruhe *f (eines Vulkans)*
transcurrent fault Blattverschiebung *f,* Seitenverschiebung *f,* transversale Horizontalverschiebung *f*
~ fault system Blattverschiebungssystem *n,* Seitenverschiebungssystem *n*
transducer Geber *m,* Fühler *m;* Übertrager *m*
transference of load Lastübertragung *f*
transform faulting Seitenverschiebung *f* durch Dehnung *(im zentralen Bereich der ozeanischen Rücken)*
transformation Transformation *f,* Feldtransformation *f*
transformational breccia Einsturzbrekzie *f (in Auslaugungsgebieten)*
transformed into peat vertorft
~ wave transformierte Welle *f,* Wechselwelle *f (Seismik)*
transgress/to transgredieren
transgressing transgredierend
~ sea transgredierendes Meer *n*
transgression Transgression *f*
~ sea Transgressionsmeer *n*
transgressive transgressiv
~ overlap transgredierende Lagerung *f*
~ stratum transgredierende Schicht *f*
~ superposition transgressive Lagerung *f*
transient Impuls *m,* Stoß *m*
~ electromagnetic method Feldaufbaumethode *f (elektromagnetisches Verfahren mittels Einschaltströmen)*
~ flow instationäre Strömung *f*
~ pressure behaviour instationärer Druckverlauf *m*
~ response Einschwingvorgang *m (z.B. eines Seismografen);* [integrierte] Impulsantwort *f*
~ wave Einschwingwelle *f (Seismik)*
transit theodolite Theodolit *m (mit geringerer Genauigkeit)*
~ time 1. Laufzeit *f;* Übergangszeit *f,* Übertragszeit *f (Seismik);* 2. Durchgangszeit *f (Astronomie)*
~ time measurement Laufzeitmessung *f*
transition bed Übergangsschicht *f*
~ belt Übergangszone *f*
~ bog Übergangsmoor *n*
~ facies Übergangsfazies *f*
~ regime Übergangsregime *n (zwischen unterem und oberem Fließregime)*
transitional zone Übergangszone *f*
translation Translation *f*
~ banding (gliding striae) Translationsstreifung *f*
~ grating Translationsgitter *n*
~ group Translationsgruppe *f*
~ lattice Translationsgitter *n*
~ plane Translationsfläche *f*
translational, translatory translatorisch

~ **fault** Parallelverwerfung *f*
~ **shift** Parallelverschiebung *f*
translucence, translucency Lichtdurchlässigkeit *f*
translucent durchscheinend, durchsichtig
~ **at [the] edges** kantendurchscheinend
~ **attritus** *(Am)* Attritus *m (im Dünnschliff der Kohlen lichtdurchlässiges organisches Material)*
~ **edges/with** kantendurchscheinend
~ **humic degradation matter** *s.* degradinite
translunar translunar, jenseits des Mondes
transmissibility Transmissibilität *f,* Wasserleitfähigkeit *f,* Durchlässigkeitsvermögen *n,* Profildurchlässigkeit *f*
transmission constant K-Wert *m (Hydrologie)*
~ **electron microscope** Durchstrahlungselektronenmikroskop *n*
~ **rate** vertikale Strömungsrate *f*
transmissivity Durchlässigkeit *f (Permeabilität × Schichtdicke)*
transmittance curve Durchlaßcharakteristik *f,* Transmissionskurve *f*
transmitted light Durchlicht *n*
~ **polarized light** durchfallendes polarisiertes Licht *n*
transmitter 1. Transmitter *m,* Meßwandler *m;* 2. Sender *m*
transparency 1. Durchsichtigkeit *f,* Transparenz *f;* 2. durchfallendes Licht *n,* Durchlicht *n;* 3. Mutterpause *f*
transparent durchsichtig, transparent, durchscheinend
~ **cut** Dünnschliff *m*
~ **on edges** kantendurchscheinend
~ **positive original** Mutterpause *f*
transport Verfrachtung *f*
~ **of detritus** Geschiebeführung *f (eines Flusses)*
~ **of solutes** Beförderung *f* von gelösten Stoffen
transportation Transport *m*
transportational agents Transportkräfte *fpl*
transported soil Absatzboden *m,* Kolluvialboden *m,* sekundärer (allochthoner) Boden *m*
transporting capacity Transportfähigkeit *f*
transposition Umscherung *f*
transuranic (transuranium) elements Transurane *npl*
transversal wave Transversalwelle *f (Seismik)*
transverse transversal
~ **anticline** Quersattel *m*
~ **crevasse** Querspalte *f (eines Gletschers)*
~ **dune** Querdüne *f*
~ **earthquake** Transversalbeben *n*
~ **expansion** Querdehnung[sziffer] *f*
~ **extension** Querdehnung *f*
~ **fault** Querverwerfung *f,* transversale Horizontalverschiebung *f*
~ **fissure** Querspalt *m*
~ **folding** Querfaltung *f*
~ **gallery** Querstrecke *f*

~ **heading** Querschlag *m*
~ **joint** Transversalkluft *f*
~ **lamination** Transversalschieferung *f*
~ **mica** Querglimmer *m*
~ **rift** Querspalte *f*
~ **ripple marks** Transversalrippeln *fpl*
~ **scour mark** transversale Kolkmarke *f*
~ **section** Querprofil *n,* Querschnitt *m*
~ **shear** *s.* ~ thrust
~ **stress** Biegebeanspruchung *f,* Biegespannung *f*
~ **stylolite** Horizontalstylolith *m*
~ **thrust** Horizontalverschiebung *f,* Seitenverschiebung *f,* Blattverschiebung *f*
~ **valley** Durchbruchstal *n*
~ **valley profile** Querprofil *n* eines Tals
~ **wave** Transversalwelle *f*
trap 1. Falle *f (für Öl oder Gas);* 2. *s.* traprock
~-**down** *s.* downthrow
~ **flow** Trappdecke *f*
~ **sandstone** Grauwackensandstein *m*
~-**shotten gneiss** pseudotachylitischer Gneis *m*
~-**up** *s.* upthrow
trapezohedral trapezoedrisch
trapezohedron Trapezoeder *n*
trapezoid Trapezoid *n*
trapezoidal trapezoidförmig
~ **coal (lignite)** Moorkohle *f*
trappean die Eigenschaft von Trapp besitzend
~ **rock** Trappfels *m*
trapped oil akkumuliertes Erdöl *n*
~-**radiation region** Strahlungsgürtel *m (der Erde)*
trappoid trappartig
traprock Trapp *m,* Deckenbasalt *m,* Flutbasalt *m,* Plateaubasalt *m*
trascite Traskit *m,* $Ba_5FeTi[(OH)_4|Si_6O_{18}]$
trash Abraum *m*
~ **line** Spülsaum *m,* Wellenlinie *f*
trass Traß *m,* Tuffstein *m*
travel/to migrieren
travel Migration *f*
~ **of the oil** Ölmigration *f*
~ **time** Laufzeit *f*
~-**time curve** Laufzeitkurve *f*
~ **time of sound** Schallaufzeit *f (Seismik)*
travelled erratisch
travelling dune Wanderdüne *f*
~ **limit angle** dynamischer Grenzwinkel *m*
~ **rig** fahrbare Bohranlage *f*
~ **wave** fortschreitende Welle *f,* Wanderwelle *f*
traverse Traverse *f (1.* Meßlinie; 2. Serie von verbundenen Profilen*)*
travertine Travertin *m,* Kalktravertin *m,* Kalktuff *m*
tray Trog *m,* Waschtrog *m;* Trog *m,* Mulde *f*
treasure box reiches Erznest *n,* Erzfall *m*
treat/to 1. bearbeiten; verarbeiten; 2. aufbereiten, verhütten
treatment 1. Bearbeitung *f;* Verarbeitung *f;* 2. Aufbereitung *f,* Verhüttung *f*

treatment

~ **of water** Wasseraufbereitung f
~ **with silicate** Verkieseln n
trechmannite Trechmannit m, $Ag_2S \cdot As_2S_3$
tree agate Baumachat m (s.a. chalcedony)
~ **fern** Baumfarn m
~ **line** [obere] Baumgrenze f
~ **steppe** Baumsteppe f
~ **stump** Baumstubben m
~ **trunk** Baumstamm m
treeless baumlos
treelike crystal Dendrit m
trellis drainage pattern gitterförmiges Flußnetz n
trellised drainage spalierartiges Entwässerungssystem n
~ **pattern** rostförmige Anordnung f
Tremadoc [Stage] s. Tremadocian
Tremadocian [Stage] Tremadoc n (Stufe des Unterordoviziums)
tremble/to beben
trembling bog Schwingmoor n, Schwingwiese f
~ **of the ground** Bodenerschütterung f
tremolite Tremolit m, $Ca_2Mg_5[(OH, F)|Si_4O_{11}]_2$
tremor Erschütterung f
Trempealeauan [Stage] Trempealeauen n (Stufe im Grenzbereich Kambrium/Ordovizium und Unteres Ordovizium in Nordamerika)
trench 1. Tiefseegraben m; 2. Verschluckungszone f [konvergierender Platten]; 3. Einschnitt m, Graben m, Schürfgraben m
~ **along roads** Straßeneinschnitt m
~ **fault** Graben m, Tiefscholle f
~ **gap** Bewegungsbahn f (Spalte an einer Verschluckungs- oder Subduktionszone)
trenchlike gorge Klamm f
trend/to streichen
trend 1. Streichen n, Streichrichtung f; 2. Trend m (als mathematische Funktion)
~ **analysis** Trendanalyse f
~ **coefficient** Trendkoeffizient m
~ **curve** Trendkurve f
~ **function** Trendfunktion f
~ **hypersurface** Trendhyperfläche f
~ **of beds** Schichtstreichen n
~ **of evolution** Entwicklungsrichtung f
~ **of folding** Faltungsstreichen n
~ **residual** Trendrest m, Restwert m eines Trends (Differenz zwischen Beobachtungsergebnis und Trendfunktion)
~ **surface** Trendfläche f
~-**surface analysis** Trendflächenanalyse f, Flächentrendanalyse f
~-**surface map** Trendflächenkarte f
~-**surface mapping** Trendflächenabbildung f, Trendflächenkonstruktion f
~ **with orthogonal polynomials** Trend m mit orthogonalen Polynomen
Trentonian [Stage] Trenton n (Stufe des Champlainiens in Nordamerika)
trevorite Trevorit m, $NiFeO_4$
triad dreizählige Symmetrieachse f

trial Probe f
~ **borehole** Versuchsbohrloch n
~ **boring** Versuchsbohrung f, Probebohrung f
~ **drilling** s. ~ boring
~ **heading** Untersuchungsstrecke f
~ **pit** Schürfgrube f, Schürfloch n, Schürfschacht m
~ **pumping** Probeabsenkung f (Hydrologie)
triangular overfall Dreiecksüberfall m (Wassermengenmessung)
triangulation Triangulierung f
~ **net** Triangulationsnetz n
~ **station** trigonometrischer Festpunkt m
Triassic triassisch
Triassic Trias f, Triassystem n (chronostratigrafisch); Trias[periode] f (geochronologisch); Trias[zeit] f (allgemein)
~ **Age** Trias[zeit] f
~ **Period** Trias[periode] f
~ **System** Trias f, Triassystem n
triaxial [compression] cell Triaxialgerät n, dreiaxiale Druckzelle f
~ **compression test** dreiaxialer Druckversuch m
~ **loading** Triaxialbelastung f
~ **stress** dreiachsiger Spannungszustand m
~ **test** dreiaxialer Drehversuch m
tributary Zu[bringer]fluß m, Nebenfluß m
~ **canyon** Zweigcañon m, Nebencañon m
~ **glacier** Seitengletscher m
~ **ravine** Nebenschlucht f
tributor Goldgräber m
trichalcite Trichalcit m, $Cu_3[AsO_4] \cdot 5H_2O$
trichroic trichroitisch, pleochroitisch
trichroism Trichroismus m, Pleochroismus m
trickle down[ward]/to herabrinnen, herabtröpfeln
trickling Rinnsal n
~ **water** Tropfwasser n
triclinic triklin[isch]
~ **system** triklines System n
triclinicity Triklinität f
tricone rock bit Dreirollenmeißel m
tridymite Tridymit m, SiO_2
trifted snow Schneeverwehung f
trigger Auslöseimpuls m
~ **bit** Vierrollenmeißel m
~ **pulse** Auslöseimpuls m
triggering Auslösung f (eines Vorgangs)
trigonal trigonal
trigonite Trigonit m, $Pb_3MnH[AsO_3]_3$
trigonometrical point trigonometrischer Punkt m
~ **station** trigonometrische Station f
trihedral triedrisch, dreiflächig
trihedron Trieder n, Dreiflächner m
trilling Drilling m (Kristallverwachsung aus drei Individuen)
trilobate[d], trilobed dreilappig
trilobite Trilobit m
trimacerite Trimacerit m (Kohlenmikrolithotyp, Arten: Duroclarit, Vitrinertoliptit, Clarodurit)

trimerite Trimerit m, $CaMn_2[BeSiO_4]_2$
trimetric system s. orthorhombic system
trimorph[ic] trimorph
trimorphism Trimorphismus m
trimorphous trimorph
Trinidad pitch Trinidadasphalt m
trinkerite Trinkerit m *(fossiles Harz)*
trip Bohrmarsch m
~ **gas** bei Zirkulationsstillstand angesammeltes Gas n
tripestone gewundene Anhydritkonkretion f, Gekrösegips m, Schlangengips m
triphane s. spodumene
triphylite Triphylin m, $Li(Fe, Mn)[PO_4]$
triple point Tripelpunkt m, Dreiphasenpunkt m
triplet Triplet n *(Verfahren mit drei Ablesungen)*
triplite Triplit m, Eisenpecherz n, $(Mn, Fe)_2[F|PO_4]$
triploidite Triploidit m, $(Mn, Fe)_2[OH|PO_4]$
tripoli 1. Tripoli m *(Gestein aus silikatischen Verwitterungsrückständen)*; 2. Tripel m, Tripelerde f, Polierschiefer m
~ **earth (powder)** Tripel m, Tripelerde f
tripolite s. tripoli 1.
trippkeite Trippkeit m, $CuAs_2O_4$
tripton Tripton n *(organischer Detritus)*
tripuhyite Tripuhyit m, $FeSb_2O_6$
triradiate dreistrahlig
tritiated water tritiiertes (tritiumangereichertes) Wasser n
tritium Tritium n
tritomite Tritomit m *(Th-, Ce-, Y-, Ca-Borosilikat)*
triturate/to zerreiben, pulverisieren
trituration Zerreibung f, Pulverisierung f
troctolite Troktolith m, Forellenstein m *(Varietät von Gabbro)*
trögerite Trögerit m, $(H_3O)_2[UO_2|AsO_4]_2 \cdot 6H_2O$
trogtalite Trogtalit m, $CoSe_2$
troilite Troilit m, FeS *(Meteoritenmineral)*
trolleite Trolleit m, $Al_4[OH|PO_4]_3$
trolley trogförmige Schichtendepression f
trolly s. trolley
trommel Waschtrommel f, Sortiertrommel f
Trompeter's zone Trompetersche Zone f
trona Trona m, $Na_3H[CO_3]_2 \cdot 2H_2O$
trondhjemite Trondhjemit m *(granitisches Tiefengestein)*
troostite Troostit m *(Varietät von Willemit)*
tropic tropisch *(s.a. tropical)*
tropic Wendekreis m
~ **of Cancer** Wendekreis m des Krebses
~ **of Capricorn** Wendekreis m des Steinbocks
tropical tropisch
~ **climate** tropisches Klima n, Tropenklima n
~ **cyclone** tropischer Wirbelsturm m
~ **forest** Tropenwald m
~ **forest bog** Tropenwaldmoor n
~ **podzol** tropischer Podsolboden m
~ **primeval forest** tropischer Urwald m

tropics Tropen pl
troposphere Troposphäre f, Wolkenzone f
trouble tektonische Störung f *(allgemein und im Kohlenflöz)*
troubled ground gestörtes Gebirge n
trough 1. Trog m, tektonische Mulde f, Einbruchsbecken n; 2. Tiefdruckrinne f
~ **axis** Trogachse f
~ **core** Muldenkern m
~ **cross stratification** Muldenschichtung f, bogige (schaufelförmige, synklinale) Schrägschichtung f
~ **fault** Verwerfungsgraben m, Grabensenke f, Grabenbruch m, gegensinnig fallendes Störungspaar n
~ **limb** Muldenschenkel m *(einer Falte)*
~ **of a syncline** Muldentiefstes n
~ **of a wave** Wellental m
~-**shaped** muldenartig, trogförmig
~-**shaped valley** s. ~ valley
~ **valley** Trogtal n, Muldental n
troughlike wannenförmig
troutstone Forellenstein m *(s.a. troctolite)*
troy weight Edelmetallgewicht n
trub Kohleschiefer m
truck rig auf schwerem LKW montiertes Bohrgerät n
trudellite Trudellit m, $Al_{10}[OH]_4|Cl_4|SO_4]_3 \cdot 30H_2O$
true-amplitude recovery Wiederherstellung f der wahren Amplitude
~ **anomaly** wahre Anomalie f
~ **azimuth** echter Azimut m
~ **bedding** Normalschichtung f
~ **cleavage** Kristallisationsschieferung f
~ **dip** wahres Einfallen n
~ **fold** s. flexure fold
~ **ground-water velocity** Filtergeschwindigkeit f
~ **lode** s. fissure vein
~ **loess** Primärlöß m
~ **meridian** wahrer Meridian m
~ **north** geografisch Nord
~ **resistivity** wirklicher elektrischer Widerstand m *(z.B. einer Formation)*
~ **thickness** wahre Mächtigkeit f *(einer Schicht)*
~ **top** wahre Oberkante f
~ **vein** s. fissure vein
truffite Lignit m *(mit Trüffelgeruch)*
trumpet-shaped trompetenförmig
truncated 1. abgetragen *(Erosion)*; 2. abgestumpft *(Kristalle)*; 3. fortgeschwemmt, abgeschwemmt, weggespült
~ **fold** Faltenrumpf m
~ **upland** Rumpfgebirge n, Rumpfscholle f
truncation 1. Abtragung f *(Erosion)*; 2. Abstumpfung f *(Kristalle)*; 3. Fortschwemmung f
~ **effect** Abbruchfehler m
~ **trap** Transgressionsfalle f
trunk sheet Stammdecke f
~ **stream** Hauptfluß m
truscottite Truscottit m, Reyerit m, $Ca_2[Si_4O_{10}] \cdot H_2O$

truth

truth radiometer Radiometer n zur Messung der wahren Objektstrahlung
tscheffkinite Tscheffkinit m, Tschevkinit m, $(Ce, La)_2Ti_2[O_4|Si_2O_7]$
tschermakite Tschermakit m, $Ca_2Mg_3(Al, Fe)_2[(OH, F)_2|Al_2Si_6O_{22}]$
Tschermak's molecule s. Ca-Tschermak's molecule
tschermigite Tschermigit m, Ammonalaun m, $NH_4Al[SO_4]_2 \cdot 12H_2O$
tschkalowite Tschkalowit m, $Na_2[BeSi_2O_6]$
tsumebite Tsumebit m, $Pb_2Cu[(OH)_3|PO_4] \cdot 3H_2O$
tsunami Flutwelle f, Springwelle f
tub washing Setzwäsche f (von Erzen)
tubbing support Tübbingausbau m
tube 1. Rohr n, Röhre f; 2. Schlot m
~ **feet** Ambulakralfüße mpl (Echinodermata)
~ **of flow** Stromröhre f
tubelike röhrenartig
tubicolar annelids (worms) Röhrenwürmer mpl
tubing Steigrohr n
~ **string** Fördertour f
tubular röhrenartig
~ **spring** Rundnischenquelle f, Karstquelle f
~ **structure** röhrenförmiges Gefüge n
tubulous röhrenartig
tufa Tuff m (sedimentär)
~ **deposit** Tuffablagerung f
~-**depositing** tuffablagernd
~ **rock** Tuffgestein n
tufaceous tuffartig, tufführend (sedimentären Tuff)
~ **concretion** Kalksinter m, Kalktuff m
~ **earth** Tufferde f
~ **limestone** Kalktuff m
~ **shale** Tuffschiefer m
tuff Tuff m (vulkanisch)
~ **balls** s. accretionary lapilli
~ **cone** vulkanischer Tuffkegel m, Tuffvulkan m
~-**depositing** tuffablagernd
~ **flow** s. ignimbrite
tuffaceous tuffartig, tufführend (vulkanischen Tuff)
tuffisite Tuffisit m (Mischgestein aus Tuff und Nebengesteinsfragmenten)
tuffite Tuffit m
tuffolava Tufflava f
tuffstone verfestigter Tuff m
tugtupite Tugtupit m, $Na_8[Cl_2|(BeAlSi_4O_{12})_2]$
tumbling bay Tosbecken n (einer Tasperre)
tumefy/to anschwellen, sich aufblähen (von Mineralen vor der Lötrohrflamme)
tumescence Aufwölbung f (bei vulkanischer Tätigkeit)
tumid schwellend, blähend
tumidity 1. Schwellung f; 2. Gehäusedicke f (von Fossilien)
tumulose mit kleinen Hügeln besetzt
tumulus Quellkuppe f, Lavadom m
tundra Tundra f

~ **polygons** Tetragonalboden m, Schachbrettboden m
~ **soil** Tundraboden m
tunellite Tunellit m, $Sr[B_6O_9(OH)_2] \cdot 3H_2O$
tungsten Wolfram n, W
~ **carbide button (insert) bit** Warzenmeißel m
~ **ore** Wolframerz n
tungstenic Wolfram...
tungsteniferous wolframhaltig
tungstenite Tungestenit m, WS_2
tungstic ochre s. tungstite
tungstite Tungstit m, Wolframocker m, $WO_2(OH)_2$
tunnel driving Durchstich m eines Tunnels
~ **erosion** unterirdische Erosion f
~ **face** Stollenmundloch n
~ **valley** Flußgewässer n unter dem Eis
tunneldale s. tunnel valley
tunnelling Tunnelbau m
~ **machine** Streckenvortriebsmaschine f
turanite Turanit m, $5CuO \cdot V_2O_5 \cdot 2H_2O$
turbary Torfgewinnungsstätte f, Torfstich m
turbid trübe (bei Kristallen)
turbidite Turbidit m
turbidity Trübung f (von Kristallen)
~ **current (flow)** Suspensionsstrom m, Trübestrom m
turbobit Turbinenmeißel m
turbodrilling Turbinenbohren n
turbulence Turbulenz f, Wirbelbildung f
turbulent turbulent, Wirbel...
~ **boundary layer** turbulente Grenzschicht f
~ **flow** turbulentes Fließen n, Turbulenzströmung f, Wirbelströmung f, Flechtströmung f
turf 1. Grasnarbe f, Rasen m; 2. Rasensode f; 3. Torf m, Torfballen m
~ **bed** Torfschicht f
~-**forming** torfbildend
~ **pit** Torfgrube f
~ **podzol** Moorpodsol m
turfed slope Rasenböschung f
turfy torfartig; torfreich; Torf...
~ **soil** Torfboden m
turkey shoot Vergleichsschießen n, Kontrollschießen n (Seismik)
turkis s. turquois
turmaline s. tourmaline
turn into vapour/to verdampfen, verdunsten
turn Ablenken n (z.B. einer Bohrung)
~ **of the tides** Flutwechsel m
turning angle of a percussion bit Umsetzwinkel m des Meißels
turntable Drehtisch m (bei Bohrungen)
Turolian [Stage] Turolium n (kontinentale Stufe des Pliozäns)
Turonian [Stage] Turon[ien] n, Turonium n (Stufe der Oberkreide)
turquois[e] Türkis m, $CuAl_6[(OH)_2|PO_4]_4 \cdot 4H_2O$
turritiform turmförmig
turtle-structure anticline Schildkrötenstruktur f (Salztektonik)

tusk Stoßzahn *m*
tussock Grasbüschel *n*
Tuvalian [Substage] Tuval *n (Unterstufe, Obere Trias, Tethys)*
tuyamunite *s.* tyuyamunite
twilight Dämmerung *f*, Zwielicht *n*; Abenddämmerung *f*
twilit dämmerig
twin Zwilling *m (Kristall)*
~-axis Zwillingsachse *f*
~ boundary Zwillingsgrenze *f*
~ crater Zwillingskrater *m*
~ crystal Zwillingskristall *m*
~ doline Zwillingsdoline *f*
~ formation Zwillingsbildung *f*
~ gliding Zwillingsgleitung *f*
~ hole Zwillingsbohrung *f*
~ plane Zwillingsfläche *f*, Zwillingsebene *f*
~ star Doppelstern *m*, Zwillingsstern *m*
~ volcano Doppelvulkan *m*
twinkling Flimmern *n (von Sternen)*
twinned verzwillingt
twinning Zwillingsbildung *f*, Verzwilligung *f*
~ lamellae Zwillingslamellen *fpl*
~ lamination due to pressure Druckzwillingslamellierung *f*
~ law Zwillingsgesetz *n*
~ plane Zwillingsfläche *f*, Zwillingsebene *f*
~ position Zwillingsstellung *f*
twist-off 1. Überdrehungsbruch *m*, Torsionsbruch *m*; 2. Gestängebruch *m*
twisted verdreht, gedreht
~ bomb gedrehte Bombe *f*
twister 1. Drehungskristall *m*, Drillingskristall *m*; 2. *(Am)* Tornado *m*
~ crystal Drehungskristall *m*, Drillingskristall *m*
twitch Gangverengung *f*, Gangverdrückung *f*
twith *s.* twitch
two-bell diving system Zwei-Glocken-Tauchsystem *n*
~-dimensional eben, zweidimensional
~-dimensional flow ebene Strömung *f*
~-dimensional trend Flächentrend *m*
~-layered doppelschichtig
~-phase flow Zweiphasenströmung *f*
~ string well Zweistrangfördersonde *f*
~-way multiple Vollwegmultiple *f*
~-way travel time Lotzeit *f*
twofold zweizählig *(Symmetrieachse)*
tychite Tychit *m*, $Na_6Mg_2[SO_4](CO_3)_4$)
type area Typusgebiet *n*
~ form Leitform *f*
~ fossil Leitfossil *n*
~ locality Typuslokalität *f*
~ of coal *(Am)* 1. Mikrolithotyp *m*; 2. Kohlenvarietät *f*; 3. Kohlenart *f (Rang)*
~ ot flow Strömungstyp *m*, Strömungszustand *m*
~ section Stratotyp *m*
~ specimen Typusart *f (Paläontologie)*
typhonic Taifun...

typhoon Taifun *m*
~ track Taifunbahn *f*
typomorphic typomorph
~ mineral Leitmineral *n*
tyrite *s.* fergusonite
tyrolite Tirolit *m*, $Ca_2Cu_9[(OH)_{10}(AsO_4)_4] \cdot 10H_2O$
tyrrellite Tyrrellit *m*, $(Cu, Co, Ni)_3Se_4$
tysonite Tysonit *m*, $(Ce, La)F_3$
tyuyamunite Tyuyamunit *m*, Tujamunit *m*, $Ca[(UO_2)_2|V_2O_8] \cdot 5-8^1/_2H_2O$

U

U-shaped valley Trogtal *n*, U-Tal *n*
uadi trockenes Tal *n*
ubiquitous element durchlaufendes (allgegenwärtiges) Element *n*
~ mineral Durchläufer *m*
udometer Regenmesser *m*
udometric Regenmessungs...
uhligite Uhligit *m*, $Ca(Zr, Ti)_2O_5$ mit Al_2TiO_5
uintahite *s.* gilsonite
Uintan [Stage] Uintan[ien] *n (Wirbeltierstufe des Eozäns in Nordamerika)*
ukrainite Ukrainit *m (Varietät von Monzonit)*
Ulatisian [Stage] Ulatisien *n (marine Stufe des Eozäns in Nordamerika)*
ulexite Ulexit *m*, Boronatrokalzit *m*, $NaCa[B_5O_6(OH)_6] \cdot 5H_2O$
uliginous schlammig, sumpfig, morastig
ullmannite Ullmannit *m*, Antimonnickelglanz *m*, NiSbS
ulmic acid Humussäure *f*
ulmification Vertorfung *f*
ulmin Humusgel *n*
ulminite Ulminit *m (Braunkohlenmaceral)*
ulmite Ulmit *m (Humussäure)*
ulmohumid acid *s.* ulmin
ulmous earth Humuserde *f*
~ substance Huminstoff *m*
Ulsterian [Series] Ulsterien *n (Serie des Devons, Unterdevon in Nordamerika)*
ultimate analysis Elementaranalyse *f*
~ elongation Bruchdehnung *f*
~ load Grenzlast *f*
~ production Gesamtproduktion *f*
~ recovery Gesamtausbeute *f*, Gesamtertrag *m*
~ stage Endstadium *n*
~ strength Bruchfestigkeit *f*
ultrabasic ultrabasisch
~ rock ultrabasisches Gestein *n*
ultrabasite Ultrabasit *m (s.a. diaphorite)*
ultradominant vorwiegend
ultrahaline hypersalin
ultramafic *s.* ultrabasic
ultrametamorphic ultrametamorph
ultrametamorphism Ultrametamorphose *f*
ultramylonite Ultramylonit *m*
ultramylonitic ultramylonitisch
ultrasonic drilling Ultraschallbohren *n*

ultrasonic 366

- ~ **flowmeter** Ultraschallströmungsmesser m
- ~ **impulse transmitter** Ultraschallimpulsgerät n
- ~ **wave** Ultraschallwelle f
- **ultrasonics, ultrasound** Ultraschall m
- **ultraviolet imagery** Ultraviolettaufnahmen fpl (Aufnahmen im ultravioletten Bereich des Spektrums)
- **ultraviolet lamp** Ultraviolettlampe f, UV-Lampe f
- **ulvite** Ulvit m, Fe_2TiO_4
- **umangite** Umangit m, Cu_3Se_2
- **umber** Umbra f (Mn-haltiger Ton)
- **umbilicus** Nabel m
- **umbo** Wirbel m, Schnabel m (von zweischaligen Fossilien)
- **umbra** Schatten m (z.B. Erdschatten, Mondschatten); Kernschatten m; dunkler Teil m eines Sonnenflecks
- **umbral** Schatten...
- **umohoite** Umohoit m, $[UO_2|MoO_4]\cdot 4H_2O$
- **UMP** s. Upper Mantle Project
- **umptekite** Umptekit m
- **unaided eye** unbewaffnetes (bloßes) Auge n
- **unaka** Monadnock m
- **unaltered** unverändert; unverwittert
- ~ **rock** frisches (gesundes) Gestein n
- **unassorted** unklassiert
- **unbedded** ungeschichtet, nicht geschichtet
- **unbiased sampling** Probenahme f ohne systematischen Fehler, unverfälschte Probenahme f
- **unburnable** unbrennbar
- **uncallow** Abraum m, Deckgebirge n
- **uncased hole** unverrohrtes Bohrloch n
- **uncleavable** unspaltbar
- **unclouded** unbewölkt
- **uncohesive** nichtbindig
- **uncoil/to** sich aufrollen (Evolutionsstadium von Ammoniten)
- **uncompacted** unverfestigt
- **unconfined ground water** ungespanntes Grundwasser n, Grundwasser n mit freier Oberfläche
- **unconformability of dip** tektonische Diskordanz f, Winkeldiskordanz f
- ~ **of erosion** Erosionsdiskordanz f
- ~ **of overlap (transgression)** Transgressionsdiskordanz f
- **unconformable** diskordant, ungleichförmig
- ~ **fold** disharmonische Falte f
- **unconformity** Diskordanz f, Ungleichförmigkeit f
- ~ **by erosion** Erosionsdiskordanz f
- ~ **trap** Diskordanzfalle f
- **unconsolidated** unverfestigt
- ~ **deposit** lockeres Gebirge n
- ~ **rock** Lockergestein n, unverfestiges (nichtbindiges) Gestein n
- ~ **strata** Lockergestein n; unverfestigtes (gebräches, loses) Gebirge n
- **uncontaminated sample** unkontaminierte Probe f
- **uncover/to** bloßlegen, freilegen; erschürfen

- **uncovering** Bloßlegung f, Freilegung f; Erschürfen n
- **uncrystalline** amorph.
- **uncrystallized** nicht kristallisiert
- **unctuous** fettig, seifig (Gestein)
- ~ **clay** schwerer (fetter) Ton m
- **undation** Undation f
- ~ **theory** Undationstheorie f
- **undecayed** unverwittert
- **undecomposable** unzersetzbar
- **undecomposed** unverwittert, unzersetzt
- **undeformed** unverformt; ungestört
- **underclay** Wurzelboden m, Basalton m im Flözliegenden
- **undercurrent** Unterströmung f
- **undercut/to** 1. unterschneiden, unterhöhlen, unterspülen; 2. schrämen
- **undercut slope** Unterschneidungshang m, Prallhang m
- **undercutting** 1. Unterschneidung f, Unterhöhlung f, Unterspülung f; 2. Schrämen n
- **underdrainage** Dränung f, Dränage f, Trockenlegung f, Untergrundentwässerung f
- **underfit stream** Kümmerfluß m
- **underflow** Unterströmung f, Tiefenstrom m
- **undergauge hole** verengtes Bohrloch n
- **undergo subsidence/to** absinken
- ~ **uplift** gehoben werden
- **underground** Untergrund..., unter Tage, unterirdisch
- ~ **combustion** In-situ-Verbrennungsprozeß m
- ~ **corrosion** Bodenkorrosion f
- ~ **dam** Untergrundstauwerk n
- ~ **detention time** Aufenthaltsdauer f im Boden (Grundwasser)
- ~ **drainage** unterirdische Entwässerung f
- ~ **drilling** Untertagebohren n
- ~ **flow of liquids** unterirdischer Abfluß m
- ~ **gas storage** Untergrundgasspeicherung f
- ~ **gasification** Untertagevergasung f, Vergasung f in der Lagerstätte
- ~ **hydroelectric plant** Kavernenkraftwerk n
- ~ **lake** Höhlensee m
- ~ **liquefaction** Verflüssigung f unter Tage
- ~ **milling** Untertageaufbereitung f
- ~ **mine drainage** untertägige Grubenentwässerung f
- ~ **mining** Untertagebau m, Tiefbau m
- ~ **operations** Untertagebetrieb m
- ~ **power station** Kavernenkraftwerk n
- ~ **seepage** Sickerströmung f, Grundwasserstromsickerung f
- ~ **stoping** Abbau m unter Tage
- ~ **storage** Untergrundspeicherung f
- ~ **storage chamber** Untergrundspeicher m
- ~ **stream** Höhlengerinne n
- ~ **surveying** Markscheiden n, Grubenaufnahme f
- ~ **surveyor** Markscheider m
- ~ **tapping** unterirdische Anzapfung f
- ~ **vaporization** Untertageverdampfung f

~ water Grundwasser n
~ working Grubenbau m
~ workings Untertagearbeit f, Grubenbaue mpl
underhand stoping Strossenbau m
underlain by unterlagert von, im Liegenden von
underlay lode geneigter Gang m
~ **shaft** tonnlägiger Schacht m im Liegenden eines Ganges
underlayer Unterschicht f
underlie/to unter [etwas] liegen, unterlagern
underlier 1. Sohle f; 2. s. underlay shaft
underlimb liegender Schenkel m (einer Falte)
underlying bed Liegendes n
~ **reservoir** Untergrundspeicher m
~ **rock** anstehendes Gestein n
~ **seam** liegendes Flöz n, Flöz n im Liegenden
~ **stratum** Liegendes n
~ **stratum of the ground water** Grundwassersohlschicht f
undermass Unterbau m
undermine/to unterhöhlen, unterwaschen
underneath ridge geologische Klippe f
underply Zwischenmittel n im unteren Teil eines mächtigen Flözes
underream/to nachbohren, nachräumen, unterschneiden
underreaming Nachbohren n, Nachräumen n, Unterschneiden n
undersaturated untersättigt
~ **rock** untersättigtes Gestein n
undersaturation Untersättigung f
undersea mining maritime Rohstoffgewinnung f, unterseeischer Abbau m
underseam Liegendflöz n
underseepage Sickerströmung f, Grundwasserstromsickerung f
underside Liegendscholle f, tiefer Flügel m
undersize Unterkorn n
undersoil Untergrund m
underthrust überkippt (mehr als 180°)
~ **fault[ing]** Schollenunterschiebung f
~ **sheet** Tauchdecke f
underthrusting Schollenunterschiebung f
undertow Sog m (Brandung)
underwall Liegendes n
underwash/to unterwaschen, unterspülen
underwashing Unterwaschung f, Unterspülung f
underwater completion Unterwasserkomplettierung f
undeveloped unerschlossen
undifferentiated ungespalten
~ **dike rock** aschistes (ungespaltenes) Ganggestein n
undisintegrated unverwittert
undisturbed ungestört
~ **bed** ungestörte Schicht f, ungestörtes Gestein n
~ **soil** Mutterboden m
~ **soil sample** ungestörte Bodenprobe f
~ **stratification** ungestörte Lagerung f

undulating wellig
undulation 1. Welligkeit f; 2. Undulation f (Kristalloptik)
undulatory undulatorisch, wellenförmig
~ **extinction** undulöse (undulierende) Auslöschung f
~ **motion** Wellenbewegung f
undulous s. undulatory
unearth/to ausgraben
unequally lobed s. heterocercal
unessential constituent unwesentlicher Gemengteil m
uneven fracture unebener Bruch m
~-**grained** ungleichmäßig körnig
unexploited field nicht aufgeschlossenes Feld n
unexplored area unaufgeschlossenes Gebiet n
unfaulted ungestört, nicht verworfen
unfilled porosity freie Porosität f
unfixed sand Treibsand m
~ **soil** unverfestigter Boden m
unfossiliferous fossilfrei
unfossilized nicht fossilisiert
unfused ungeschmolzen
ungemachite Ungemachit m, $K_3Na_8Fe[OH|(SO_4)_2]_3 \cdot 9H_2O$
unglaciated nicht vereist (vergletschert)
ungot coal seam unverritztes Kohlenflöz n
ungula Huf m, Ungula f
uniaxial einachsig
~ **crystal** einachsiger Kristall m
uniclinal monoklinal
uniform gleichförmig
~ **dilatancy** gleichförmige Dehnung f
~ **flow** gleichförmige (laminare) Strömung f
~ **miscibility** lückenlose Mischbarkeit f
uniformism 1. Gleichförmigkeit f; 2. Aktualismus m
uniformitarianism Aktualismus m
uniformly bedded gleichmäßig geschichtet
unilateral einseitig
~ **conductance** asymmetrische Leitfähigkeit f
~ **pressure** einseitiger Druck m
uninflammable coal magere Steinkohle f, Magerkohle f
unintentional deviation of the hole Abweichung f des Bohrlochs
~ **unscrewing** ungewolltes Abschrauben n (des Bohrstrangs oder der Futterrohre)
unipolar bomb geschwänzte Bombe f
uniserial uniserial, einreihig
unit cell Elementarzelle f (Kristallphysik)
~ **exploitation** gemeinschaftliche Gewinnung f
~ **hydrograph** Abflußgang m (Abflußschwankung eines Vorfluters)
~ **of vegetation** Vegetationseinheit f
~ **stress** spezifische Spannung f
~ **weight** Raumgewicht n
unitary yield spezifische Förderrate f
univalve einschalig
univalve Einschaler m
univariant univariant (einen Freiheitsgrad besitzend)

universal

universal gas constant allgemeine Gaskonstante f
~ **gravitation** allgemeine Massenanziehung f
~ **stage** Universaldrehtisch m
~ **three-axis stage** dreiachsiger Universaldrehtisch m
~ **time** Weltzeit f, mittlere Greenwichzeit f
universe Universum n, Weltall n
unkindly lode unbauwürdiger Gang m
unleached nicht ausgelaugt
unlevelled nicht söhlig
unlimited depth ewige Teufe f
unlined hole unverrohrte Bohrung f
unloading Entlastung f (durch Erosion)
unmanned diving boat, ~ **submersible** unbemanntes Tauchboot n
unmetamorphosed nicht metamorph
unmixing Entmischung f
~ **texture** Entmischungsstruktur f
unmoved ungestört
unoriented texture richtungslose Struktur f
unpenetrated bed nicht durchspießte Schicht f
unpicked sample unausgesuchte Probe f
unpolarized light unpolarisiertes Licht n
unproductive time unproduktive Zeit f
unprofitable unbauwürdig, nicht [ab]bauwürdig
unproven reserves nicht nachgewiesene Reserven fpl
unrestricted movement Gesteinsdurchbewegung f mit Mineralstreckung in Bewegungsrichtung
unripe peat unreifer Torf m
unsaturated ungesättigt
~ **conductivity** ungesättigte Leitfähigkeit f
~ **infiltration rate** ungesättigte Infiltrationsrate f
unsorted unsortiert
unstable instabil, labil
~ **equilibrium** instabiles Gleichgewicht n
~ **ground** nicht standfestes Gebirge n
~ **phase** instabile Phase f
~ **relict** instabiles Relikt n
~ **shelf** mobiler Schelf m
unsteady-state flow instationäre Strömung f
unstratified schichtungslos, ungeschichtet
~ **rock** Massengestein n
unsupervised classification unüberwachte Klassifizierung f
unsymmetrical fold asymmetrische Falte f
unused well toter Brunnen m
unusual stylolite Horizontalstylolith m
unwasted unverwittert
unwater/to entwässern, trockenlegen
unwatering Entwässerung f, Trockenlegung f
unweathered unverwittert
unwilling to pick nicht tiefenkorrelierbar
unworkable unbauwürdig, nicht [ab]bauwürdig
unworked unverritzt, jungfräulich
~ **area** unverritztes Feld n
~ **coal** anstehende Kohle f

up-... s. up...
uparching Aufwölbung f
~ **fold** Sattelfalte f
~ **of strata** Aufwölbung f von Schichten
upbending fold Gebirgssattel m
upbowing Aufwölbung f
upbuilding Aufschüttung f
upbulge Aufwölbung f
upcast Verwerfung f ins Hangende, Überschiebung f
~ **fault** Aufschiebung f, Überschiebung f
~ **side** gehobener Flügel m
~ **slip** Sprung m (ins Hangende)
upcurrent stromaufwärts
updip 1. entgegengesetzt der Fallrichtung; bergauf; 2. schwebend
updoming Aufwölbung f
upfaulted gehoben (an einer Verwerfung)
upfaulting Aufschieben n
upfold Antiklinale f, Antiklinalfalte f, Gebirgssattel m, Sattelbogen m, Sattel m
upfolding Auffaltung f
upgrade/to anreichern (Erz)
upgrade stromaufwärts
upgrade Steigung f
~**-stream water** Wasser n aus dem Oberlauf des Stroms
upgrading Aufbereiten n
~ **plant** Aufbereitungsanlage f
~ **ratio** Anreicherungsgrad m
upheaval 1. Hebung f; 2. Quellen n der Sohle
~ **phase** Hebungsphase f
upheave/to sich erheben; heben
uphill oben gelegen, ansteigend, bergauf
uphill Erhebung f
uphole geophone Aufzeitgeophon n
~ **shooting** Aufzeitschießen n
~ **stack** vertikale Stapelung f (Seismik)
~ **time** Aufzeit f
~ **velocity** Geschwindigkeit f der Spülung im Ringraum
upland hoch gelegen
upland Hochland n
~ **areas** Oberland n
~ **bog** Hochmoor n
~ **fretting** starke Zerkarung f
~ **grooving** schwache Zerkarung f
~ **plain** Hochebene f
uplands Mittelgebirge npl
upleap gehobener Flügel m
uplift/to herausheben
uplift 1. Hebung f, Heraushebung f; Auftrieb m; 2. Aufrichtung f (der Schichten); Bodenerhebung f, Horst m; 3. Wiederanstieg m (des Grundwasserspiegels)
~ **pressure** Sohlenwasserdruck m (einer Sperrmauer)
uplifted [fault] block gehobene Scholle f, Hochscholle f, Hangendscholle f
~ **peneplain** Rumpfgebirge n, gehobene Rumpffläche f
~ **reef** erhöhtes Riff n

~ shelf erhöhter Schelf *m*
~ wall gehobener Flügel *m*
upper air obere Luftschichten *fpl*, obere Atmosphäre *f*
~ air observation Höhenbeobachtung *f*
~ aquifer Hangendgrundwasserleiter *m*
~ atmosphere obere Atmosphäre *f*, obere Luftschichten *fpl*
~ bed Hangendschicht *f*
~ block gehobene Scholle *f*, Hochscholle *f*, Hangendscholle *f*
~ confining bed Deckschicht *f*
~ course Oberlauf *m* *(eines Flusses)*
~ course of river obere Flußstrecke *f*
~ flow regime oberes Fließregime *n* *(fluviatiler Transport)*
~ layer Deckschicht *f*
~ leaf hangender Teil *m* eines Flözes
~ limb hangender Schenkel *m*
~ mantle oberer Mantel (Erdmantel) *m*
~ reservoir Oberbecken *n*
~ stage hangende Stufe *f*
~ surface Dachfläche *f*
~ till *s.* englacial till
~ wall Hangendes *n*
~ water Hangendwasser *n*
~ yield point obere Streckgrenze *f*
Upper Cambrian [Epoch, Series] Oberkambrium *n*
~ Carboniferous [Epoch, Series] 1. Oberkarbon *n*, Siles[ium] *n* *(in West- und Mitteleuropa Namur A bis einschließlich Stefan)*; 2. Oberkarbon *n* *(in der UdSSR Stefan)*
~ Chalk Obere Schreibkreide *f* *(Cenoman bis Maastricht, England)*
~ Cretaceous [Epoch, Series] Oberkreide *f*
~ Devonian [Epoch, Series] Oberdevon *n*
~ Greensand Formation Oberer Grünsand *m* *(mittleres und oberes Alb, England)*
~ Jurassic [Epoch, Series] Oberer (Weißer) Jura *m*, Malm *m*
~ Mantle Project Projekt *n* zur Erforschung des oberen Erdmantels
~ Ordovician [Epoch, Series] Oberes Ordovizium *n* *(oberstes Caradoc und Ashgill)*
~ Palaeozoic Jungpaläozoikum *n* *(Karbon bis Perm)*
~ Permian [Epoch, Series] Oberperm *n*
~ Triassic [Epoch, Series] Obere Trias *f* *(Karn, Nor und Rhät)*
uppermost bed oberste Schicht *f*
~ stage hangende Stufe *f*
upridging of the beds Schichtenaufrichtung *f*
upright aufrecht, stehend, seiger
~ fold aufrechte Falte *f*
uprising Aufgang *m* *(z.B. der Sonne)*
uprush Auflaufen *n* der Wellen
upsetted moraine Stauchmoräne *f*
upslide Sprung *m*, Verwerfung *f*
~ motion Aufgleiten *n*
~ surface Aufgleitfläche *f*
upslope hangauf[wärts]

~ fog Hangnebel *m*
~ wind Talwind *m*
upstream oberwasserseitig, bergseitig, flußaufwärts
~ cofferdam offener Fangdamm *m*
~ face Wasserseite *f*
~ facing of dam Bergseite *f* der Talsperre
~ facing of weir Bergseite *f* des Wehrkörpers
~ slope Luvhang *m*
~ water line Oberwasserspiegel *m*
upstroke aufwärtsgehender Hub *m* *(bei einer Bohrung)*
upstructure strukturaufwärts
upswelling Aufschwellung *f*
uptake Aufnahme *f*, Absorption *f*
upthrow Überschiebung *f*
~ fault Verwerfung *f* ins Hangende, widersinnige (inverse) Verwerfung *f*, Aufschiebung *f*
~ side hangende Scholle *f*, höher liegende Scholle *f* an einer Verwerfung
upthrown [fault] block gehobene Scholle *f*, Hochscholle *f*
~ side of a fault gehobener Flügel *m* einer Verwerfung (Störung)
upthrust 1. Aufpressung *f*; 2. Überschiebung *f*, Aufschiebung *f*
~ fault Überschiebung *f*, Aufschiebung *f*
upturned aufgerichtet
~ bed aufgerichtete Schicht *f*
~ edges of the strata aufgerichtete Schichtkanten *fpl*
~ strata aufgerichtete Schichten *fpl*
upturning Aufpressung *f*
upward arching (bowing, buckling, doming) Aufwölbung *f*
~ drag Schleppung *f* nach oben
upwarp/to aufwölben
upwarp[ing] Aufwölbung *f*, Beule *f*, Schichtenaufbiegung *f*
upwedging Aufpressung *f*
upwell water Auftriebswasser *n*
upwelling Emporquellen *n*, Aufwallung *f*
~ glowing cloud überquellende Glutwolke *f*
~ water Auftriebswasser *n*
upwind Aufwind *m*
~ side Luvseite *f*
uraconite Uraconit *m* *(teils Zippeit, teils Uranopilit)*
uralborite Uralborit *m*, $CaB_2O_4 \cdot 2H_2O$
Uralian Subprovince Ural-Subprovinz *f* *(Paläobiogeografie, Unterdevon)*
uralite Uralit *m* *(aus Pyroxen entstandener Amphibol)*
~ schist Uralitschiefer *m*
uralitic diabase Uralitdiabas *m*
uralitization Uralitisierung *f*
uralitize/to uralitisieren
uralolite Uralolith *m*, $CaBe_3[OH|PO_4]_2 \cdot 4H_2O$
uramphite Uramphit *m*, $(NH_4)_2[UO_2|PO_4]_2 \cdot xH_2O$
uraniferous uranhaltig
uraninite Uraninit *m*, Uranpecherz *n*, Pechblende *f*, UO_2

uranium   370

uranium Uran n, U
~-bearing uranhaltig
~ content Urangehalt m
~-dated urandatiert
~ decay Uranzerfall m
~ fission Uranspaltung f
~ ore Uranerz n
~ splitting Uranspaltung f
urano-organic ore uranorganisches Erz n
uranocircite Uranocircit m, Ba[UO$_2$|PO$_4$]$_2$·10H$_2$O
uranography Uranografie f, Himmelsbeschreibung f
uranolite Meteorit m
uranology Himmelskunde f
uranometry Uranometrie f, Himmelsmessung f
uranophane Uranophan m, CaH$_2$[UO$_2$|SiO$_4$]$_2$·5H$_2$O
uranopilite Uranopilit m, [6UO$_2$|5(OH)$_2$|SO$_4$]·12H$_2$O
uranoscopy Himmelsbeobachtung f
uranospathite Uranospathit m, Cu[UO$_2$|(As, P)O$_4$]$_2$·12H$_2$O
uranosphaerite Uranosphärit m, [UO$_2$(OH)$_2$|BiOOH]
uranospinite Uranospinit m, Ca[UO$_2$|AsO$_4$]$_2$·10H$_2$O
uranothallite Uranothallit m, Liebigit m, Ca$_2$UO$_2$(CO$_3$)$_3$·10H$_2$O
uranothorite Uranothorit m, (Th, U)[SiO$_4$]
uranotil[e] s. uranophane
uranous uranartig; uranhaltig
urao s. trona
urban urban, städtisch
~ geology Kommunalgeologie f
ureilite Ureilit m (Meteorit)
ureis s. ground ice
urinestone Anthrakonit m (mit Kohle verunreinigter Kalzit)
urry (sl) blauer Ton m
ursilite Ursilit m, (Ca, Mg)$_2$[(UO$_2$)$_2$|Si$_5$O$_{14}$]·9–10H$_2$O
urtite Urtit m
U.S. gal. Erdölfördermaß, 3,7 Liter
usbekite Usbekit m, 3CuO·V$_2$O$_5$·3H$_2$O
used water Abwasser n
useful head nutzbares Gefälle n
~ mineral nutzbares Mineral n
~ mineral deposit nutzbare mineralische Lagerstätte f
~ seam thickness [ab]bauwürdige Flözmächtigkeit f
usefulness Aussagewert m (von Messungen)
useless rock taubes Gestein n
USGS = United States Geological Survey
ussingite Ussingit m, Na$_2$[OH|AlSi$_3$O$_8$]
ustarasite Ustarasit m, PbS·3Bi$_2$S$_3$
utahite Utahit m, Jarosit m (s.a. jarosite)
utilization Nutzbarmachung f
~ of water power Wasserkraftnutzung f
uvala Uvala f, Karstmulde f, Schüsseldoline f

uvanite Uvanit m, [(UO$_2$)$_2$|V$_6$O$_{17}$]·15H$_2$O
uvarovite Uwarowit m, Ca$_3$Cr$_2$(SiO$_4$)$_3$
uvite Uvit m, CaMg$_3$(Al$_5$Mg)[(OH)$_{1+3}$|(BO$_3$)$_3$|Si$_6$O$_{18}$]
uwarowite Uwarowit m, Ca$_3$Cr$_2$(SiO$_4$)$_3$
uzbekite Uzbekit m, Usbekit m, 3CuO·V$_2$O$_5$·3H$_2$O

V

V-ditch V-förmiger Graben m
V-shaped valley Kerbtal n, V-förmiges Tal n, V-Tal n
V-step V-Stufe f (optische Klassifikationsgröße für das Reflexionsvermögen des Vitrinits bei der Kohlenartenanalyse)
vacancy Leerstelle f (im Kristallgitter)
vadose vados
~ spring vadose Quelle f
~ water vadoses Wasser n
~ zone Zone f des Sickerwassers
vaesite Vaesit m, NiS$_2$
vaeyrynenite Väyrynenit m, MnBe[(OH, F)|PO$_4$]
vag getrockneter Torf m
vagabondary currents vagabundierende Ströme mpl
Vaginatum Limestone Vaginatenkalk m (Unteres Ordovizium)
vagrant benthos vagiles Benthos n (Paläontologie)
Valanginian [Stage] Valangin[ien] n, Valanginium n (tiefere Unterkreide)
valence, valency Wertigkeit f
Valentian [Stage] s. Llandoverian
valentinite Antimonblüte f, Valentinit m, Weißspießglanz m, Sb$_2$O$_3$
valid name gültiger Name m (Nomenklaturregeln)
valleriite Valleriit m, CuFeS$_2$
Vallesian [Stage] Vallesium n (kontinentale Stufe des Pliozäns)
valley Tal n
~ blocked-up by drift durch Geschiebe abgeriegeltes Tal n
~ bog Talmoor n
~ bottom Talboden m, Talsohle f
~ breeze Talwind m
~ broadening Talerweiterung f
~ channel Talbett n
~ cut Taleinschnitt m
~ due to folding Faltungstal n
~ encumbered by drift durch Geschiebe abgeriegeltes Tal n
~ fill Talaufschüttung f, Talschutt m, Alluvionen fpl
~ flat[s] Talaue f
~ floor Talboden m, Talsohle f
~ formation Talbildung f
~ formed by melt water Schmelzwassertal n
~ glacier Talgletscher m
~ gravel Talschotter m

vegetable

- **~ head** Quellmulde *f*, Talschluß *m*
- **~ landscape** Tallandschaft *f*
- **~ loam** Tallehm *m*
- **~ meander** Talmäander *m*
- **~ mire** Talmoor *f*
- **~ mouth** Talausgang *m*
- **~ plain** Talaue *f*
- **~ sand** Talsand *m*
- **~ side [slope]** Talhang *m*
- **~ slope** Talhang *m*
- **~ spring** Talquelle *f*
- **~ terrace** Talterrasse *f*
- **~ thrust** Talzuschub *m*
- **~ train** fluvioglaziale Schotter *mpl*
- **~ wall** Talwand *f*
- **~ widening** Talerweiterung *f*

vallis Vallis *f (Tal, Graben auf Mars oder Mond)*
valuable mineral Wertstoffmineral *n*
valuation [technisch-ökonomische] Lagerstätteneinschätzung *f*
valvate schalig *(Paläontologie)*
valve Klappe *f (Paläontologie)*
- **~ auger** Bohrschappe *f*, Bohrlöffel *m*, Ventilschappe *f*, Ventilbohrer *m*

Van Allen belt Van Allenscher Strahlungsgürtel *m*
vanadiferous vanadinhaltig
vanadinite Vanadinit *m*, Vanadinbleierz *n*, $Pb_5[Cl|(VO_4)_3]$
vanadium Vanadin *n*, Vanadium *n*, V
- **~ ore** Vanadinerz *n*

vanadous vanadinartig; vanadinhaltig
vanalite Vanalit *m*, $NaAl_8V_{10}O_{38} \cdot 30H_2O$
vandenbrand[e]ite Vandenbrandeit *m*, $[UO_2|(OH)_2] \cdot Cu(OH)_2O$
vandendriesscheite Vandendriesscheit *m*, $8[UO_2|(OH)_2] \cdot Pb(OH)_2 \cdot 4H_2O$
vanishing point Fluchtpunkt *m*
vanning machine Erzwaschmaschine *f*
vanoxite Vanoxit *m*, $2V_2O_4 \cdot V_2O_5 \cdot 8H_2O$
vanthoffite Vanthoffit *m*, $Na_6Mg[SO_4]_4$
vanuralite Vanuralit *m*, $Al[OH|(UO_2)_2|VO_8] \cdot 8H_2O$
vapor *(Am) s.* vapour
vaporization Verdampfung *f*, Verdunstung *f*
vaporize/to verdampfen, verdunsten
vaporous dampfförmig
- **~ envelope** Dampfhülle *f*
- **~ water** Bodendampfwasser *n*

vapour Dampf *m*
- **~ cloud** Dampfwolke *f*
- **~ column** Dampfsäule *f*
- **~ density** Dampfdichte *f*
- **~ pressure** Dampfdruck *m*, Dampfspannung *f*
- **~ pressure lowering** Dampfdruckerniedrigung *f*
- **~ tension** Dampfdruck *m*, Dampfspannung *f*

variable area recording Flächenschrift *f*
- **~ density recording** Dichteschrift *f*

variance Varianz *f* einer Zufallsvariablen
- **⌐ analysis** Varianzanalyse *f*
- **~ component** Varianzkomponente *f*

variation Variation *f*, Veränderung *f*, Abweichung *f*
- **~ in the earth magnetic field** Änderung *f* des magnetischen Erdfeldes
- **~ of altitude of the pole** Polhöhenschwankung *f*
- **~ of level** Spiegelschwankung *f*
- **~ of precipitation** Niederschlagsschwankung *f*
- **~ of terrestrial magnetism** erdmagnetische Variation *f*
- **~ of the magnetic needle** Abweichung *f* der Magnetnadel, magnetische Mißweisung *f*
- **~ range** Variationsreihe *f*

varied artenreich
- **~ flow** veränderlicher Abfluß *m*

variegated bunt, scheckig
- **~ copper ore** *s.* bornite
- **~ sandstone** bunter Sandstein *m*, Buntsandstein *m*

varietal character Variationsmerkmal *n*
- **~ form** Abart *f*

variety 1. Varietät *f*, Spielart *f*, Abart *f*; 2. Auswahl *f*
variogram Variogramm *n*
variole Sphärolith *m*
variolite Variolit *m*
variolitic structure variolitische Textur *f*
various [lithologisch] bunt, heterogen, zusammengesetzt, wechselnd
Variscan variszisch, variskisch, varistisch (*s.a.* Hercynian)
- **~ folding** variszische Faltung *f*
- **~ Mountains** variszisches Gebirge *n*
- **~ orogen** variszisches Orogen *n*
- **~ trend** variszisches Streichen *n*

Variscian *s.* Variscan
Variscides *s.* Variscan orogen
variscite Variscit *m*, $Al[PO_4] \cdot 2H_2O$
varisize-grained ungleichkörnig
varnish Lack *m*, Wüstenlack *m*
varulite Varulith *m*, $(Na, Ca)_2(Fe, Mn)_3[PO_4]_3$
varve Warve *f*
varved clay dünngeschichteter Ton *m*, Warventon *m*, Bänderton *m*
- **~ slate** metamorpher Warventon *m (in Verbindung mit Tilliten)*

varvity Jahresschichtung *f*, Warvenschichtung *f*
varying lustre Schillerglanz *m*
vascular plants Gefäßpflanzen *fpl*
vaterite Vaterit *m*, $CaCO_3$ hexagonal
vaugnerite Vaugnerit *m (Varietät von Granodiorit)*
vault of heaven, vaulted sky Himmelsgewölbe *n*, Firmament *n*
vauquelinite Vauquelinit *m*, $PbCu[OH|CrO_4|PO_4]$
vauxite Vauxit *m*, $FeAl_2[PO_4]_2 \cdot 7H_2O$
veatchite Veatchit *m*, $Sr[B_3O_4(OH)_2]_2$
vees Lettenbesteg *m* auf Kohleschlechten
vegasite Vegasit *m*, Plumbojarosit *m*, $PbFe_6[(OH)_6|(SO_4)_2]_2$
vegetable pflanzlich

vegetable 372

- ~ **blanket** Pflanzendecke *f*, Vegetationsdecke *f*
- ~ **carpet** Pflanzenwuchs *m*
- ~ **cover** *s.* ~ blanket
- ~ **debris** fossile Pflanzen *fpl* (Pflanzenreste *mpl*)
- ~ **deposit** Pflanzenablagerung *f*
- ~ **discharge** pflanzliche Transpiration *f*
- ~ **earth** *s.* ~ mould
- ~ **eater** Pflanzenfresser *m*
- ~-**eating** pflanzenfressend
- ~ **feeder** Pflanzenfresser *m*
- ~ **kingdom** Pflanzenreich *n*
- ~ **layer** Pflanzendecke *f*, Vegetationsdecke *f*
- ~ **mould** Pflanzenerde *f*, Humus *m*
- ~ **remains** *s.* ~ debris
- ~ **retardance** Abflußverzögerung *f* durch Vegetation *(Hydrologie)*
- ~ **slime** Faulschlamm *m*
- ~ **soil** Ackerkrume *f*

vegetal *s.* vegetable
vegetarian Pflanzenfresser *m*
vegetate/to 1. kristallisieren; 2. ausscheiden, ausschwitzen
vegetation Vegetation *f*

- ~ **cover[ing]** Pflanzendecke *f*, Vegetationsdecke *f*
- ~ **print** Pflanzenabdruck *m*

vegetative cover[ing] Pflanzendecke *f*, Vegetationsdecke *f*
veil cloud Schleierwolke *f*
vein 1. Gesteinsgang *m* (*s.a.* lode); 2. gangartige Erzausscheidung *f*; Trum *n*

- ~ **accompaniment** Ganggefolgschaft *f*
- ~ **bitumen** *s.* asphaltite
- ~ **breccia** Gangbrekzie *f*
- ~ **deposit** Ganglagerstätte *f*
- ~ **filling** Gangfüllung *f*
- ~ **fissure** Gangspalte *f*
- ~ **following bedding planes** Lagergang *m*
- ~/**in** gangförmig
- ~ **infilling** Gangfüllung *f*
- ~ **material** Gangmaterial *n*
- ~ **matter** Gangmasse *f*, Gangkörper *m*
- ~ **of quartz** Quarzgang *m*
- ~ **of spotty character** Gang *m* mit unregelmäßiger eingesprengter Mineralisation
- ~ **ore** Gangerz *n*
- ~ **rock** Ganggestein *n*
- ~ **skirts** Nebengesteinswände *fpl* eines Ganges
- ~ **stone** Ganggestein *n*
- ~ **structure** Ganggefüge *n*
- ~ **stuff** Gangmittel *n*, Gangart *f*; Gangmasse *f* (ohne Erz)
- ~ **system** Gangsystem *n*
- ~ **tin** Bergzinn *n*
- ~ **wall** Salband *n*, Gangwand *f*

veined 1. gangartig; 2. marmoriert, gemasert
- ~ **gneiss** Bändergneis *m*, metatektischer Gneis *m*
- ~ **marble** Adermarmor *m*

veining 1. Gangbildung *f*; 2. Bänderung *f*

veinlet kleiner Gang *m*, Gangtrum *n*
- ~ **of quartz** Quarzäderchen *n*

veinlike gangähnlich
veinstone *s.* vein stone
veinstuff *s.* vein stuff
veiny geadert, adrig
veise Kohlenschlechte *f*
veld[t] baumloses Grasland *n*, Steppe *f* (in Südafrika)
velocity-depth diagram Geschwindigkeits-Tiefen-Diagramm *n*

- ~ **filter** Richtungsfilter *n* (Seismik)
- ~ **log** Geschwindigkeitslog *n*
- ~ **measurement** Geschwindigkeitsmessung *f*
- ~ **meter** Geschwindigkeitsmesser *m* (für Wasserströmung)
- ~ **of current** Strömungsgeschwindigkeit *f*, Fließgeschwindigkeit *f*
- ~ **of diffusion** Diffusionsgeschwindigkeit *f*
- ~ **of flow** Fließgeschwindigkeit *f*, Strömungsgeschwindigkeit *f*
- ~ **of flow in pores** Porengeschwindigkeit *f*
- ~ **of light** Lichtgeschwindigkeit *f*
- ~ **of propagation** Fortpflanzungsgeschwindigkeit *f*, Ausbreitungsgeschwindigkeit *f*
- ~ **of sound** Schallgeschwindigkeit *f*
- ~ **of underground flow** Fließgeschwindigkeit *f* (des Grundwassers)
- ~ **of wave propagation** Fortpflanzungsgeschwindigkeit *f* der Wellen
- ~ **potential of a ground-water flow** Geschwindigkeitspotential *n* einer Grundwasserströmung
- ~ **profile** Geschwindigkeitsprofil *n*
- ~ **survey** Geschwindigkeitsbestimmung *f* (Seismik)
- ~ **through the pores** Porengeschwindigkeit *f*

vena schmales Erztrümchen *n*
Vendian *s.* Wendian
veneered hill mit dünner Geschiebedecke bedeckter Hügel *m*
venite Venit *m* (Migmatitart)
vent Öffnung *f*, Schlot *m*
- ~ **breccia** Vulkanschlotbrekzie *f*
- ~ **in the crater** Krateröffnung *f*

ventifact äolisch bearbeiteter Felsen *m*, Dreikanter *m*, Windkanter *m*
ventilation shaft Wetterschacht *m*
ventral fin Bauchflosse *f*
- ~ **tegmen** ventrale Kelchdecke *f* (bei Crinoiden)
- ~ **valve** Stielklappe *f*, Bauchklappe *f* (bei Brachiopoden)
- ~ **view** Ventralansicht *f* (Paläontologie)

Venturian [Stage] Venturien *n* (marine Stufe, oberes Pliozän bis tiefstes Pleistozän in Nordamerika)
venturine quartz Aventurin *m*
venule kleiner Gang *m*
Venus hair stone Venushaar *n* (Quarz mit eingewachsenen Rutilnadeln)
verde salt *s.* thenardite

Vindobonian

vergency Vergenz f
~ fan Vergenzfächer m
vermicular wurmartig *(bei Mineralen)*
~ rock Gestein n aus fossilen Wurmausscheidungen
vermiculite Vermiculit m, $(Mg, Fe)_3[(Si, Al)_4O_{10}][OH_2]\cdot 4H_2O$
vernadite Vernadit m, $H_2MnO_3 + H_2O$
vernadskite Vernadskyit m *(Antlerit pseudomorph nach Dolerophanit)*
vernal equinox Frühlings-Äquinoktium n, Frühlings-Tagundnachtgleiche f
verplanckite Verplanckit m, $Ba_6Mn_3[(OH)_6|Si_6O_{18}]$
verrucose warzenförmig, knotig
versant Flanke f (Abhang m) eines Gebirgszugs
vertex Zenit m
vertical vertikal, seiger
~ accretion deposit Aufschlickung f *(aus einem Fluß)*
~ aerial photograph Senkrechtaufnahme f *(Luftbild)*
~ beds Kopfgebirge n, seiger stehende Schichten fpl
~ component seismograph Vertikalseismograf m
~ depth Seigerteufe f
~ displacement seigere Sprunghöhe f, Schubhöhe f
~ erosion Tiefenerosion f
~ exaggeration vertikale Überhöhung f
~ extent Tiefenstreckung f, Aushalten n nach der Tiefe *(eines Ganges)*
~ fault Vertikalverwerfung f, Seigersprung m
~ filter well Vertikalfilterbrunnen m
~ gradation of facies Faziesänderung f in der Vertikalen
~ hole vertikale Bohrung f
~ illuminator Opakilluminator m
~ loop method Induktionsverfahren n mit vertikalem Primärkreis
~ magnetometer Vertikalmagnetometer n
~ migration Vertikalmigration f
~ motion seismograph Vertikalseismograf m
~ movement senkrechte Bewegung f
~ ordering vertikale Gliederung f
~ pendulum Vertikalpendel n
~ permeability vertikale Durchlässigkeit f
~ scale exaggerated twice, ~ scale twice vertikal zweimal überhöhter Maßstab m
~ seam stehendes Flöz n
~ section Seigerriß m, Schichtenprofil n
~ seismic profiling seismische Vertikalprofilierung f
~ seismograph Vertikalseismograf m
~ stack vertikale Stapelung f *(Seismik)*
~ throw seigere Sprunghöhe f, Schubhöhe f
~ time Lotzeit f
~ variability map Vertikalvariationskarte f *(Magnetik)*
vertically initiated domal nuée ardente senkrechte Explosionsglutwolke f

very deep hole drilling übertiefe Bohrung f
~ distant earthquake weites Fernbeben n
~ fine sand Mehlsand m *(0,0625–0,125 mm Durchmesser)*
~ fine sandstone Mehlsandstein m
~ low frequency method VLF-Methode f *(elektromagnetisches Erkundungsverfahren)*
~ low grade metamorphism sehr schwache Metamorphose f, Anchimetamorphose f
~ slight sehr leicht *(2. Stufe der Erdbebenstärkeskala)*
vesicle Blase f
vesicular blasig, zellig
~ texture Blasenstruktur f
~ tissue s. coenosteum
vestige Rudiment n
vestigial rudimentär, [zu]rückgebildet
vestry [ab]bauwürdiger Gangteil m
Vesuvian type Vesuvtypus m
vesuvianite Vesuvian m, $Ca_{10}(Mg, Fe)_2Al_4[(OH)_4|(SiO_4)_5|(Si_2O_7)_2]$
vesuvite Vesuvit m *(Varietät von Tephrit)*
veszelyite Veszelyit m, $(Cu, Zn)_3[(OH)_3PO_4]\cdot H_2O$
VHA = Very High Aluminium
vibrate/to erschüttern, schwingen, vibrieren, erbeben
vibrated rock-fill dam gerüttelter Steindamm m
vibrating screen Schüttelsieb n
~-wire strain gauge Schwingsaitendehnungsmesser m
vibration 1. Erschütterung f, Schwingung f, Vibration f, Beben n; 2. Zittern n *(Seismik)*
~ direction Schwingungsrichtung f
~ mark Schwingungsmarke f
vibrator Vibrator m *(seismische Energiequelle)*
vibratory drilling Vibrationsbohren n
~ percussion drilling Vibrationsschlagbohren n
~ rotary drilling Vibrationsrotarybohren n
vibrofrac hydraulische Rißbildung f mittels Druckschwankungen
vibrograph Vibrograf m, Schwingungsschreiber m
vibroseis Vibroseis n *(mit hydraulischem Vibrator als Energiequelle)*
vicarious species vikariierende Art f *(Ökologie)*
viewing equipment Betrachtungsgeräte npl *(z.B. für die Auswertung von Fernerkundungsaufnahmen)*
vigor s. climax
Villafranchian Villafranchien n, Villafranchium n *(Pliozän und unteres Pleistozän in Italien)*
villamaninite Villamaninit m, $(Cu, Ni, Co, Fe)(S, Se)_2$
villiaumite Villiaumit m, NaF
Vindelician mountains vindelizische Schwelle f
Vindobonian [Stage] Vindobonien n *(Stufe des Miozäns)*

violarite 374

violarite Violarit m, FeNi$_2$S$_4$
violent stream Sturzbach m, Wildbach m
virgation Virgation f
Virgatites Beds Virgatitenschichten fpl
Virgilian [Stage] Virgil n (hangende Stufe des Pennsylvaniens in Nordamerika)
virgin unverritzt, jungfräulich
~ **and idle lands** Neu- und Brachland n
~ **bed** unberührte (unverritzte) Schicht f
~ **earth material** jungfräulicher Boden m
~ **field** unverritztes Lagerstättenfeld n
~ **flow** unbeeinflußte (ungestörte) Strömung f
~ **forest** Urwald m
~ **gold** gediegenes Gold n
~ **rock** unverritztes Gebirge n
~ **soil** Rohboden m, Neuland n
viridine Viridin m (Andalusitvarietät)
viridite Viridit m (Chloritmineral)
visceral cavity Viszeralhöhle f, Coeloma n
~ **skeleton** Viszeralskelett n, Visceralcranium n
viscid dickflüssig
viscoelastic flow viskoelastisches Fließen n
viscoplastic viskoplastisch
viscosimeter Viskosimeter n
viscosimetric analysis viskosimetrische Analyse f
viscosity Viskosität f, Zähflüssigkeit f
viscous viskos, zäh[flüssig]
~ **flow** viskoses Fließen n
~ **flow force** viskose Fließkraft f
~ **lava** zähflüssige Lava f
Visean [Stage] Visé n (Stufe des Unterkarbons)
visibility Sichtweite f
visible coal field Ausgehendes n eines Kohlenflözes
~ **horizon** sichtbarer Horizont m
~ **region** sichtbarer Bereich m (des Spektrums)
visibly crystalline phanerokristallin
visual angle optischer Winkel m
~ **inspection** Prüfung f durch Augenschein
~ **interpretation** visuelle Auswertung f (z.B. von Fernerkundungsaufnahmen)
viterbite Viterbit m (Varietät von Leuzitphonolith)
vitiated air faule Wetter pl
vitrain Glanzkohle f (Kohlenlithotyp)
vitreous glasartig
~ **basalt** Basaltglas n
~ **copper** s. chalcocite
~ **lustre** Glasglanz m
~ **silver** s. argentite
vitric tuff Glastuff m
vitrification Frittung f, oberflächliche Anschmelzung f, Sintern n
vitrify/to verglasen, sintern
vitrinertite Vitrinertit m (Kohlenmikrolithotyp)
vitrinertoliptite Vitrinertoliptit m (Kohlenmikrolithotyp)
vitrinite Vitrinit m (Kohlenmaceral)

vitriphyric für Porphyrgefüge mit mikroglasiger Grundmasse
vitrite Vitrit m (Kohlenmikrolithotyp)
vitroclastic vitroklastisch
vitrodetrinite Vitrodetrinit m (Kohlenmaceral)
vitrophyric vitrophyrisch
vivianite Vivianit m, Blaueisenerz n, Fe$_3$·(PO$_4$)$_2$·8H$_2$O
vladimirite Vladimirit m, Ca[AsO$_4$]$_2$·4H$_2$O
vlasovite Vlasovit m, Na$_2$Zr[O|Si$_4$O$_{10}$]
VLF = very low frequency
V.M. s. volatile matter
vogesite Vogesit m (Lamprophyr)
vogle s. vug
voglite Voglit m, Ca$_2$Cu[UO$_2$|(CO$_3$)$_4$]·6H$_2$O
void Pore f, Porenraum m, Hohlraum m
~ **ratio** relativer Porenraum m, Porenziffer f
~ **space** freies Porenvolumen n
~ **water** Porenwasser n
voidage Porosität f
volant fliegend
volatile flüchtig
~ **constituent** flüchtiger Bestandteil m
~ **fluxes** flüchtige Bestandteile mpl [des Magmas]
~ **matter** flüchtige Bestandteile mpl
~ **substance** flüchtiger Bestandteil m
volatiles flüchtige Bestandteile mpl
volatility Flüchtigkeit f
volatilization Verflüchtigung f, Verdunstung f, Verdampfung f
volatilize/to sich verflüchtigen, verdunsten, verdampfen
volborthite Volborthit m, Cu$_3$[VO$_4$]$_2$·3H$_2$O
volcanello kleiner Vulkan m
volcanic vulkanisch
~ **activity** vulkanische Tätigkeit f
~ **arc** Vulkanbogen m; vulkanische Zone f
~ **area** Vulkangebiet n
~ **ash** vulkanische Asche f
~ **belt** Vulkangürtel m
~ **blast** Eruptionswolke f
~ **blowpiping** vulkanischer Gasausbruch m
~ **bomb** vulkanische Bombe f
~ **breccia** vulkanische Brekzie f
~ **butte** Vulkankegel m
~ **cauldron subsidence** vulkanischer Kesselbruch m
~ **chamber** Magmakammer f, Magmaherd m
~ **channel (chimney)** Vulkanschlot m, Eruptionsschlot m
~ **cinder** vulkanische Schlacke f
~ **cloud** Eruptionswolke f
~ **cluster** Vulkangruppe f
~ **coast** Vulkangebirgsküste f
~ **cone** Vulkankegel m
~ **debris** unkonsolidiertes pyroklastisches Material //
~ **dome** Vulkankuppe f
~ **duct** Vulkanschlot m, Eruptionsschlot m
~ **dumpling** Lavaball m
~ **dust** vulkanischer Staub m

~ **earthquake** vulkanisches Erdbeben *n*
~ **edifices** Vulkanbauten *mpl*
~ **ejecta** pyroklastisches Lockerprodukt *n*, Tephra *n*
~ **emanation** Aushauchung *f*, Exhalation *f*
~ **embryo** Vulkanembryo *m*
~ **eruption** Vulkanausbruch *m*
~ **fissure** Vulkanspalte *f*
~ **fissure trough** *s.* ~ rent
~ **flow** Lavastrom *m*
~ **foam** Bimsstein *m*
~ **focus** Vulkanherd *m*
~ **funnel** Vulkanschlot *m*, Eruptionsschlot *m*
~ **glass** Vulkanglas *n*, Gesteinsglas *n*, Obsidian *m*
~ **harbour** natürlicher Hafen *m* in Vulkanruine
~ **head** Vulkankuppe *f*
~ **island** Vulkaninsel *f*
~ **knob** Vulkankuppe *f*
~ **landscape** Vulkanlandschaft *f*
~ **mud flow** *s.* lahar
~ **orifice** Vulkanschlot *m*, Eruptionsschlot *m*
~ **outbreak (outburst)** Vulkanausbruch *m*
~ **phases** vulkanische Phasen *fpl*
~ **pisolites** *s.* accretionary lapilli
~ **plug** Vulkanpfropfen *m*
~ **rent** Eruptionsspalte *f*
~ **ridge** vulkanischer Rücken *m*
~ **rock** Eruptivgestein *n*, Ergußgestein *n*, Vulkanit *m*
~ **rubble** *s.* ~ debris
~ **scoria** vulkanische Schlacke *f*
~ **sink** Einbruchskaldera *f*
~ **skeleton** Vulkanruine *f*
~ **sounds** vulkanische Schallerscheinungen *fpl*
~ **spine** Lavadorn *m*
~ **throat** Vulkanschlot *m*, Eruptionsschlot *m*
~ **thunderstorm** vulkanisches Gewitter *n*
~ **tremors** vulkanische Beben *npl*
~ **tuff** vulkanisches Tuffgestein *n*
~ **vent** Vulkanschlot *m*, Eruptionsschlot *m*
~ **water** vulkanisches Wasser *n*
~ **wreck** Vulkanruine *f*
volcanicity Vulkanismus *m*
volcanics Vulkanite *mpl*
volcanism Vulkanismus *m*
volcanist Vulkanologe *m*
volcano Vulkan *m*
~-**tectonic collapse** vulkanotektonischer Einbruch *m*
~-**tectonic depression** vulkanotektonische Senke *f*
~-**tectonic fracture (rent)** vulkanotektonischer Bruch *m*
~-**tectonic subsidence structure** vulkanotektonische Einsturzform *f*
volcanologist Vulkanologe *m*
volcanology Vulkanologie *f*
Volgian [Stage] Wolga *n*, Wolgastufe *f (hangende Stufe des Malms im Borealen Reich)*
volkovite Volkovit *m*, (Sr, Ca/$_2$[B$_4$O$_5$(OH)$_4$][B$_5$O$_6$(OH)$_4$]$_2$ · 2H$_2$O

voltaite Voltait *m*, K$_2$Fe$_9$[SO$_4$]$_{12}$ · 18H$_2$O
Voltzia Sandstone Voltziensandstein *m*
voltzite Voltzin *m*, Zn(S,As)
volume of ebb Ebbewassermenge *f*
~ **of flood** Flutwassermenge *f*
~ **of the reservoir of a barrage** Stauinhalt *m* einer Talsperre
~ **of water** Wassermenge *f*
~ **of water discharging on ebb tide** Ebbewassermenge *f*
~ **of water entering on flood tide** Flutwassermenge *f*
~ **reduction cracks** Schwundrisse *mpl*
~ **strain** Volumendehnung *f*
~ **weight** Volumengewicht *n*
volumetric method volumetrische Methode *f (Vorratsberechnung von Erdöl, Erdgas)*
~ **reserve estimation** volumetrische Vorratsschätzung *f*
volution Umgang *m*, Windung *f (bei Cephalopodenschalen, s.a. whorl)*
vonsensite Vonsensit *m*, (Fe, Mg)$_2$Fe[O$_2$|BO$_3$]
voog große Druse *f*
vooga hole *s.* vug
vornice-fed glacier Subtyp *von* drift glacier
vortex Strudel *m*
~ **structure** Schlingenbau *m*
vorticity Wirbeligkeit *f*
~ **zone** Wirbelgebiet *n*, Wirbelzone *f*
vou-hole, vough *s.* vug
Vraconnian [Stage] Vraconne *n (Stufe des oberen Albs, Tethys)*
vrbaite Vrbait *m*, Tl$_4$Hg$_3$Sb$_2$As$_8$S$_{20}$
vredenburgite Vredenburgit *m*, (Mn, Fe)$_3$O$_4$
VSP *s.* vertical seismic profiling
vug Druse *f*, Geode *f*; offene Kluft *f*
vuggulated mit Drusen durchsetzt
vuggy drusenreich
~ **lode** drusiger (kavernöser) Gang *m*
~ **opening** Drusenraum *m*
vugh *s.* vug
vugular limestone drusiger Kalkstein *m*
~ **pore space** Lösungshohlraum *m*
~ **porosity** kavernöse Porosität *f*, Kavernosität *f*
vulcanian theory Plutonismus *m*
vulcanism *s.* volcanism
vulcanist Anhänger *m* des Vulkanismus
vulcanite Vulcanit *m*, CuTe
vulcanologist *s.* volcanologist
vulcanology *s.* volcanology
vulpinite Vulpinit *m (Anhydrit für ornamentale Zwecke)*
vysotskite Vysotskit *m*, (Pd, Ni)S

W

W-chert Kieselgesteinsknollen *fpl (als Verwitterungsbildungen)*
W-dolostone Verwitterungsdolomit *m (an alten Landoberflächen)*

W

W-wave Wiederkehrwelle f
Waal[ian] Waal n, Waal-Warmzeit f *(unteres Pleistozän in Nordwesteuropa)*
wacke Wacke f, Grauwacke f
wackestone schlammgestütztes Karbonatgestein mit mehr als 10% Komponenten (Dunham-Klassifikation 1962)
wad Wad m *(kollomorphes Mineralgemenge der Braunsteinfamilie)*
wadd s. watt
wadeite Wadeit m, $K_2Zr[Si_3O_9]$
Wadern Beds Waderner Schichten fpl *(Perm, Westeuropa)*
wadi Wadi n, Trockental n
wagnerite Wagnerit m, $Mg[F(PO_4)]$
wairakite Wairakit m, $Ca[AlSi_2O_6]_2 \cdot 2H_2O$
wairauite Wairauit m, CoFe
walchowite Walchowit m, $(C_{15}H_{26}O)_4$
walkaway Verwitterungsschießen n
walking beam 1. Bohrschwengel m *(Seilbohren)*; 2. Schlagbaum m
wall 1. Wand[ung] f; 2. Nebengestein n; 3. Stoß m
~ **of a well** Bohrlochwand f
~ **rock** Nebengestein n, Salband n
~ **rock alteration** Nebengesteinsumwandlung f
~ **saltpetre** Salpeterausblühung f
~ **scraper** Bohrlochschaber m
wallbound crusts wandständige Krusten fpl
~ **growth** wandständiges Wachstum n
walled plain Wallebene f, Ringgebirge n *(des Mondes)*
walls caving Einsturz m der Bohrlochwandung
walpurgite Walpurgin m, $[(BiO)_4|UO_2|(AsO_4)_2] \cdot 3H_2O$
walstromite Walstromit m, $BaCa_2[Si_3O_9]$
wandering coal absetziges Kohlenflöz n
~ **dune** Wanderdüne f
wane/to 1. abnehmen *(Mond)*; 2. abschmelzen, schrumpfen
waning 1. Abnehmen n *(des Mondes)*; 2. Schrumpfen n
want 1. Auswaschung f, Zwischenmittel n im Flöz *(Erosionswanne)*; 2. lokale Schichtlücke f
wardite Wardit m, $NaAl_3[(OH)_4|PO_4]_2 \cdot 2H_2O$
warm-air front Warmluftfront f
~ **front** Warmfront f
~ **glacier (ice)** nicht gefrorenen Untergrund überfahrender Gletscher m
~ **loess** Löß m aus Wüstenstaub
~ **spring** warme Quelle f
warp downward/to abbiegen
~ **upward** aufwölben
warp Anschwemmung f, Aufschwemmung f, Schlamm m, Schlick m
~ **bed** Schlammschicht f *(Flußtrichter)*
~ **clay** Auenton m
~ **sand** Flußsand m
~ **soil** Auenboden m
warped verbogen, gekrümmt; unregelmäßig geschichtet

~ **stratum** verbogene Schicht f
~ **surface** gekrümmte Fläche f
warping Krustenverbiegung f, weitspannige Aufwölbung f, Beulung f
~ **of beds** Runzelbildung f dünner Schichten *(besonders in Bohrkernen)*
~ **of land** Aufschwemmung f des Bodens
warrant *(sl)* untergelagerter Ton m
warwickite Warwickit m, $(Mg, Fe)_3Ti[O|BO_3]_2$
Wasatchian [Stage] Wasatch[ien] n *(Wirbeltierstufe, oberstes Paläozän und unteres Eozän in Nordamerika)*
wash/to abspülen; schlämmen *(Erz)*
~ **away** fortschwemmen, abschwemmen
~ **down** abspülen; schlämmen *(Erz)*
~ **out** ausschlämmen
~ **over** überbohren, überspülen
wash 1. Wassererosion f, Auswaschung f; 2. Alluvialschutt m, Geröll n
~ **boring** Spülbohren n
~-**boring rig** Spülbohrgerät n
~ **dirt** waschfähige goldführende Gerölle (Lokkersedimente) npl
~ **fault** s. want 1.
~ **fluid** Spülflüssigkeit f
~ **ore** Wascherz n, Seifenerz n
~-**out** Erosionsfurche f, Erosionsrinne f, Wasserrinne f, Priel m, Auskesselung f
~-**over crescents** Aufspülbögen mpl
~-**over fan** Fächer m aus Küstensand
~ **plain** Sanderfläche f
~ **stuff** s. ~ dirt
~ **tub** Gletschertopf m
washable waschbar, naß aufbereitbar
washed dirt Waschberge pl
~ **gravel plain** s. outwash plain
~ **ore slime** Erzschlich m
~-**out hole** Auskesselung f
~-**up material** angeschwemmtes Material n
washing Wassersortierung f *(bei Sedimenten)*
~-**away of soil** Bodenabspülung f
~-**off** Abspülung f
~-**out** Auswaschung f
~ **stuffs** s. wash dirt
wastage 1. geschiebeablagernde Ablation f; 2. Schutt m, Ablationsrückstand m
~ **area** Schwundgebiet n *(Gletscher)*
waste [away]/to abschmelzen
waste Abfall m, Bruch m, Abraum m; Schutt m
~ **area** Alter Mann m
~ **brine** Ablauge f
~-**covered mountains** im Schutt ertrunkenes Gebirge n
~ **gravel soil** Schuttboden m, Schotterboden m
~ **heap** Halde f
~ **heap ore** Haldenerz n
~ **land** Ödland n
~ **material (matter)** Schuttmaterial n
~ **of ice** Eiswüste f
~ **of sand** Sandwüste f

~ **pile** Abraumhalde *f*
~ **plain** Schuttebene *f*
~ **repository** Mülldeponie *f*
~ **rock** Berge *pl*, taubes Gestein *n*
~ **salt** Abraumsalz *n*
~ **slope** Schuttböschung *f*
~ **storage site** Mülldeponie *f*
~ **water** Abwasser *n*
~**-way** Überfall *m*, Überlauf *m (einer Talsperre)*
wasting process zerstörender Vorgang *m*
wastrel Versatzberge *pl*
water out/to verwässern *(Erdöllagerstätten)*
water Wasser *n*
~**-absorbing** hygroskopisch, wasseraufnehmend
~**-absorbing capacity** Wasseraufnahmevermögen *n*, Wasseraufnahmekapazität *f*
~ **action** Wasserwirkung *f*; Wellenschlag *m*
~ **adit** Wasserlösungsstollen *m*
~ **balance** Wasserbilanz *f*
~ **balance equation** Wasserhaushaltsgleichung *f*
~**-base** wasserhaltig
~ **basin** Wasserbecken *n*
~**-bearing** wasserführend; Wasser enthaltend
~**-bearing bed** wasserführende Schicht *f*, Aquifer *m*, Grundwasserleiter *m*
~**-bearing deposit** wasserführende Lagerstätte *f*
~**-bearing formation (horizon)** *s.* ~-bearing bed
~**-bearing layer** wasserspeichernde Schicht *f*
~**-bearing soil bed** wasserführende Bodenschicht *f*
~**-bearing strata** wasserführende Schichten *fpl*, wasserführendes Gebirge *n*
~ **block** Wasserblock *m*
~ **body** Wasserkörper *m*
~**-bogged soil** versumpfter Boden *m*
~**-borne** wasserverfrachtet
~**-borne sediment** Sinkstoff *m*
~ **breaker** Wellenbrecher *m*
~ **budget** Wasserhaushalt *m*
~ **capacity** Wasserkapazität *f (des Bodens)*
~**-carrying** wasserhaltig, wasserführend
~ **catchment** 1. Wassergewinnung *f*; 2. Wasserfassung *f (Anlage)*
~**-charged** wasserdurchtränkt
~ **circulation** Wasserkreislauf *m*
~**-clear** wasserhell *(Edelstein)*
~**-clearing plant** Wasserkläranlage *f*
~ **column** Wassersäule *f*
~ **condition** Wasserbeschaffenheit *f*, Wasserzusammensetzung *f*
~ **conditioning** Wasseraufbereitung *f*
~ **conduct gallery** Wasserüberleitungsstollen *m*
~ **coning** Wasserkegelbildung *f*
~ **conservation** Gewässerschutz *m*
~ **constitution** Wasserbeschaffenheit *f*, Wasserzusammensetzung *f*

water

~ **consumption** Wasserverbrauch *m*
~**-containing capacity** Wasserhaltevermögen *n*, wasserbindende Kraft *f (eines Bodens)*
~ **content** Wassergehalt *m*
~ **control** Wasserbekämpfung *f (Bergbau)*
~ **current** Wasserströmung *f*
~**-current ripples** Wasserströmungsrippeln *fpl*
~ **cushion** Wasserkissen *n*
~ **cut** Wasserförderanteil *m*
~ **cycle** Wasserkreislauf *m*
~ **delivery** Wasserversorgung *f*
~ **demand** Wasserbedarf *f*
~ **development** Wassergewinnung *f*
~ **discharge** Wassermenge *f*
~ **disposal well** Abwasserbohrung *f*
~ **ditch** Wassergraben *m*, Wasserrösche *f*
~ **divide** Wasserscheide *f*
~ **diviner** Wünschelrutengänger *m*
~ **divining** Wassersuche *f* mit der Wünschelrute
~ **drainage** Wasserhaltung *f*, Wasserableitung *f*
~**-drifted** wasserverfrachtet *(s.a.* ~-borne*)*
~ **drive** Wassertrieb *m*
~ **drive pool** Wassertrieblager *n*
~ **drop** Wassertropfen *m*
~ **droplet** Wassertröpfchen *n*
~ **economy** Wasserwirtschaft *f*
~ **encroachment** Vordringen *n* des Randwassers *(im Ölträger)*
~ **engineering** Wasserbau *m*, Hydrotechnik *f*
~ **exploitation** Wassergewinnung *f*
~ **eye** *s.* rock basin
~ **feeder** Wasserzubringer *m*, Wasserzufluß *m*
~ **fill** Wasserfüllung *f*
~ **film** Wasserhülle *f*
~ **flooding** Wasserfluten *n (Sekundärfördermethode für Erdöl und Erdgas)*
~ **formation** wasserführende Schicht *f*
~**-free well** wasserfreie Bohrung *f*
~ **from crevices** Spaltenwasser *n*
~ **gap** durchflossenes Durchbruchstal *n*
~ **gauge** Pegel *m*
~ **ground** wasserführendes Gestein *n*
~ **gun** Watergun *f (seeseismische Energiequelle)*
~ **hardness** Wasserhärte *f*
~ **head** Wassersäule[nhöhe] *f*
~ **hoisting** Wasserhebung *f*
~**-holding capacity** Wasserhaltevermögen *n*, wasserbindende Kraft *f (eines Bodens)*
~**-holding pores** Poren *fpl*; Feinporen *fpl*; Mittelporen *fpl*
~ **hole** Wasserloch *n*
~ **horizon** Wasserhorizont *m*, Wasserleiter *m*
~**-impregnated** wasserdurchtränkt
~ **in unconnected pores** Wasser *n* in abgeschlossenen Poren
~ **incursion** Verwässerung *f*
~ **inflow** Wassereinbruch *m*; Wasserzufluß *m*
~ **influx** Wasserzufluß *m*; Wasserzulauf *m*
~ **inhibition value** Wasseraufnahmevermögen *n*, Sättigungswert *m*

water 378

- ~ injection Wassereinpressen *n*
- ~ inlet Wassereinlaß *m*, Wassereintritt *m*
- ~-input well Wassereinpreßbohrung *f*
- ~ intake Wasseraufnahme *f*, Wassereinlaß *m*
- ~ intrusion Wassereinbruch *m*
- ~-invaded geflutet
- ~ invasion Wassereinbruch *m*
- ~ jet Wasserstrahl *m*
- ~ law Wassergesetz *n*
- ~ layer Wasserleiter *m*, Wasserhorizont *m*
- ~ layering Wasserschichtung *f*
- ~ level Grundwasserspiegel *m*, Wasserspiegel *m*
- ~-level contour line Ganglinie *f* des Wasserstands
- ~-level decrease Spiegelabsenkung *f*
- ~-level gauge (indicator) Wasserstands[an]zeiger *m*, Limnimeter *n*
- ~-level isoline Ganglinie *f* des Wasserstands
- ~ level mark Wasserstandsmarke *f*
- ~-level recorder selbstregistrierender Wasserstands[an]zeiger *m*, Schreibpegel *m*
- ~ line Wasserstandslinie *f*
- ~ loss of mud Wasserabgabe *f* der Spülung
- ~ management Wasserwirtschaft *f*
- ~ mark Wasserstandsmarke *f*
- ~ movement Wasserbewegung *f*
- ~ need Wasserbedarf *m*
- ~ of capillarity Kapillarwasser *n*, Porensaugwasser *n*
- ~ of compaction Kompaktionswasser *n*, ausgepreßtes Wasser *n*
- ~ of constitution Kristallwasser *n*, Konstitutionswasser *n*; Kristallisationswasser *n*, Hydrationswasser *n*, Hydratwasser *n*
- ~ of head gespanntes Grundwasser *n*
- ~ of hydration Hydrationswasser *n*, Hydratwasser *n*; Kristallisationswasser *n*; Kristallwasser *n*, Konstitutionswasser *n*
- ~ of imbibition Bergfeuchtigkeit *f*
- ~-oil displacement Verdrängung *f* des Öls durch Wasser
- ~ opal *s.* hyalite
- ~ outbreak Wasserdurchbruch *m*
- ~ outlet Wasseraustritt *m*, Wasserauslauf *m*
- ~ overflow Wasserüberlauf *m*
- ~ particle Wassertröpfchen *n*, Wassertropfen *m*
- ~ parting Wasserscheide *f*
- ~ percolation Durchsickerung *f* des Wassers
- ~ permeability Wasserdurchlässigkeit *f*, Durchlässigkeit *f* für Wasser
- ~ place Wasserplatz *m*
- ~ pocket Fels[en]tasche *f*
- ~ policy Wasserwirtschaft *f*
- ~ pollution Wasserverunreinigung *f*, Wasserverschmutzung *f*
- ~ pollution control Wasserschutz *m*
- ~ post Pegel *m*
- ~ power Wasserkraft *f*
- ~ pressure Wasserdruck *m*
- ~ pressure test Wasserdurchlässigkeitsprüfung *f*

- ~ procuring dike Wasserfassungsdamm *m*
- ~ pumpage Wasserhebung *f*
- ~ purification Wasserreinigung *f*
- ~-purifying plant Wasserkläranlage *f*
- ~ quality Wasserqualität *f*, Wasserbeschaffenheit *f*
- ~ regime Wasserhaushalt *m*
- ~-repellent hydrophob
- ~ requirement Wasserbedarf *m*
- ~ reserve Wasservorrat *m*
- ~ resistivity elektrischer Widerstand *m* des Formationswassers
- ~ resources Wasservorräte *mpl*
- ~ resources management Wasserwirtschaft *f*
- ~ resources planning Wasservorratsplanung *f*
- ~ resources policy Wasserwirtschaft *f*
- ~ resources project Wasservorratsprojekt *n*
- ~-retaining wasserhaltend
- ~-retaining capacity, ~ retentiveness (rententivity) Wasserrückhaltevermögen *n*, Wasserspeicherungsvermögen *n*
- ~ right Wasserrecht *n*
- ~ rise head Stauhöhe *f*
- ~-rock interaction Wasser-Gestein-Wechselwirkung *f*
- ~-rolled mechanisch beansprucht durch Bewegung im Wasser
- ~ runoff Wasserabfluß *m*
- ~ sample Wasserprobe *f*
- ~ sample-taker Wasserprobe[nent]nahmegerät *n*
- ~ sapphire Wassersaphir *m*, Dichroit *m* (*s.a.* cordierite)
- ~-saturated wassergesättigt
- ~ saturation Wassersättigung *f*
- ~ scarcity Wassermangel *m*, Wasserknappheit *f*
- ~-scoured ausgewaschen
- ~ seepage Einsickern *n* von Wasser
- ~ separation capability Wasserabgabevermögen *n*
- ~ shortage Wassermangel *m*, Wasserknappheit *f*
- ~ shut-off Wasserabsperrung *f*, Wassersperre *f*
- ~ slip wasserführende Kluft (Spalte) *f*
- ~-softening plant Wasserenthärtungsanlage *f*
- ~ spotting around the drilling string Wasserwanne *f*
- ~ spray Wassersprühregen *m*
- ~ spraying Wasserberieselung *f*
- ~ stage forecast Wasserstandsvorhersage *f*
- ~ stage measurement Wasserstandsmessung *f*
- ~ stage recorder Wasserspiegelmesser *m*
- ~ stage regime Wasserstandsverhältnisse *npl*
- ~ storage Wasserspeicherung *f*
- ~ storage basin Staubecken *n*, Sammelbecken *n*
- ~ store Wasserreservoir *n*
- ~ stratum Wasserschicht *f*, wasserführende Schicht *f*
- ~ supply Wasserhaushalt *m*, Wasserversorgung *f*

~ **supply forecast** Wasserhaushaltsprognose f
~ **supply line** Wasserversorgungsleitung f
~ **supply service** Wasserwirtschaft f
~ **surface** Wasseroberfläche f, Wasserspiegel m
~ **surface ascent** Stau m
~ **surface temperature** Temperatur f der Wasseroberfläche
~ **table** 1. Grundwasserspiegel m, Wasserspiegel m, Grundwasseroberfläche f; 2. Randwassergrenze f
~ **table fluctuation** Schwankung f des Wasserspiegels
~ **table gradient** Grundwasserspiegelgefälle n
~ **table isohypse** Grundwasserhöhenlinie f, Isohypse f des Grundwasserspiegels
~ **table slope** Depressionskurve f
~ **table well** Brunnen m mit freiem Grundwasserspiegel
~ **tension** Saugspannung f
~ **treatment** Wasseraufbereitung f
~ **trouble** Wasserschwierigkeiten fpl
~ **tunnel** Wasserstollen m, Wasserrösche f
~ **utilization** Wasserausnutzung f
~ **vapour** Wasserdampf m
~ **vein** wasserführende Spalte f
~ **well** Wasserbrunnen m
~ **whirlpool** Wasserwirbel m
~ **winning** Wassergewinnung f
~ **witching** Wünschelrutenmutung f, Wünschelrutengehen n
~-**worn sand** im Wasser abgerundeter Sand m
~ **yield** Wasserhöffigkeit f, Wasserabgabe f
watercourse 1. Wasserlauf m; 2. Vorfluter m
~ **regulation** Flußregulierung f
waterfall Wasserfall m, Kaskade f
waterfinder Wünschelrutengänger m
waterflooding s. water flooding
watering Bewässerung f
~ **ditch** Berieselungsgraben m
waterlogged wasserdurchtränkt, wassergesättigt
~ **deposit** wasserführende Lagerstätte f
~ **ground** [wasser]gesättigter Boden m, wassergesättigtes Gebirge n
~ **snow** nasser Schnee m
waterlogging Bodenvernässung f
waterproof wasserdicht, wasserundurchlässig
~ **blanket** Dichtungsvorlage f, Dichtungsteppich m, Dichtungsschürze f
~ **stratum** wasserundurchlässige Schicht f
waterproofing membrane Dichtungshaut f, Dichtungsschleier m
waters from glacier melting, ~ from the melting ice Schmelzwässer npl
watershed 1. Einzugsgebiet n; 2. Wasserscheide f
~ **divide** Wasserscheide f
~ **line** *(Am)* Wasserscheide f
waterside Gestade n
~ **face** Wasserseite f
waterspout 1. Trombe f, Wasserhose f; 2. Platzregen m

watertight wasserdicht
~ **diaphragm** Dichtungshaut f, Dichtungsschleier m
~ **facing** Dichtungsschürze f
~ **screen** Dichtungshaut f, Dichtungsschleier m
waterway Wasserstraße f
waterworks Wasseranlage f, Wasserversorgung f, Wasserbau m
watery clay Tonbrei m
~ **mud** Spülflüssigkeit f *(bei einer Bohrung)*
~ **rock** wasserführendes Gebirge n
watt Watt n *(s.a. tidal flat)*
Waucobian [Series] Waucobien n, Georgien n *(Serie, Unterkambrium in Nordamerika)*
wave Welle f, Woge f
~ **action** Wellenschlag m, Wellentätigkeit f
~ **attack** Wellenschlag m
~ **base** Wellenbasis f
~-**built terrace** litorale (submarine) Aufschüttungsterrasse f
~ **crest** Wellenberg m, Wellenkamm m
~-**cut** von den Wellen erodiert
~-**cut bench** s. ~-cut platform
~-**cut chasm** Brandungskluft f
~-**cut notch** Brandungs[hohl]kehle f, Brandungskerbe f
~-**cut platform** Brandungsplattform f, Abrasionsplatte f, Küstenterrasse f, Brandungsplatte f, Schorre f
~-**cut rock bench** s. ~-cut platform
~-**cut scarp** s. sea cliff
~-**cut shelf (terrace)** s. ~-cut platform
~ **energy** Wellenenergie f *(Seismik)*
~ **equation** Wellengleichung f
~ **erosion** Wellenerosion f
~ **flow** Wellenströmung f
~ **front** Wellenfront f
~ **front chart** Wellenfrontdiagramm n *(Seismik)*
~ **height** Wellenhöhe f
~ **impact** Wellenanprall m
~ **length** Wellenlänge f
~ **mark** Spülmarke f
~ **motion** Wellenbewegung f
~ **number filter** Wellenzahlfilter n
~ **of cold** Kältewelle f
~ **of heat** Hitzewelle f
~ **of retrogressive erosion** rückschreitende Erosionswelle f
~ **path** Wellenweg m
~ **pressure** Wellendruck m
~ **propagation** Wellenausbreitung f, Wellenfortpflanzung f
~ **range** Wellenbereich m
~ **ripple marks** Seegangsrippeln fpl
~ **train** Wellenzug m
~ **trough** Wellental n
~ **velocity** Wellengeschwindigkeit f
~-**washed** wellenbespült
~-**worn** wellenzerfressen
~-**worn material** Brandungsschutt m

waved

waved suture wellige (gewellte) Sutur f
wavelet 1. kleine Welle f; 2. Wavelet n (elementarer Wellenzug)
wavelike wellenartig
wavellite Wavellit m, $Al_3[(OH)_3|(PO_4)_2]\cdot 5H_2O$
waves of condensation Verdichtungswellen fpl (Seismik)
~ of distortion Distorsionswellen fpl (Seismik)
waviness Fältelung f, Welligkeit f
wavy wellenartig, wellig
~ bedding wellige Schichtung f
~ extinction undulöse Auslöschung f
~ vein Linsengang m, Lentikulargang m, boudinierter Gang m
wax s. mineral wax
waxwall/to verletten
waxy lustre Wachsglanz m
~ mineral wachsartiges Mineral n
way-up primäre Hangendrichtung f einer Schicht (durch Sedimentationsmerkmale nachgewiesen)
wayboard dünne Trennschicht f (z.B. Schieferlage zwischen Kalkbänken)
waylandite Waylandit m, (Bi, Ca) $Al_3[(OH)_6|(PO_4)_2]$
weak schwach, nur teilweise beobachtet (3. Stufe der Erdbebenstärkeskala)
~ rock witterungsempfindliches (leicht verwitterbares) Gestein n
~ soil weicher Boden m
weakly folded schwach gefaltet
~ reactive reaktionsträge
Weald Clay Wealdenton m, Wälderton m
Wealden Wealden n, Wealdium n (brackisch bis limnisch terrestrische Ausbildung der Unterkreide)
wear/to abtragen, abschleifen, abscheuern
~ away down abtragen
wear Verschleiß m, Abtragung f, Abscheuerung f, Abnutzung f
wearing-away, wearing-down Abtragung f
weather/to verwittern
weather Wetter n
~ chart Wetterkarte f
~ conditions Witterungsverhältnisse npl, Wetterlage f
~ forecast[ing] Wettervorhersage f
~ limit Wetterscheide f
~ map Wetterkarte f
~ modification Wetteränderung f
~ observatory Wetterwarte f
~ parting Wetterscheide f
~ pit s. rock basin
~ prediction Wettervorhersage f
~ report Wetterbericht m, Wetternachrichten fpl
~-resistant wetterbeständig
~ satellite Wettersatellit m
~ service meteorologischer Dienst m, Wetterdienst m
~ shore Windufer n, exponiertes Ufer n
~ side Luvseite f, Wetterseite f

~ stain Bleichung f, Entfärbung f (in der Verwitterungszone)
~ station meteorologische Station f, Wetterwarte f, Wetterdienststelle f, Wetterstation f
weathered abgetragen, verwittert
~-away abgewittert
~ bed s. ~ layer
~ ice verwittertes Eis n
~ layer verwitterte Schicht f, Verwitterungsschicht f
~ material Verwitterungsmaterial n
~ zone Verwitterungszone f
weathering 1. Verwitterung f, Auswitterung f; 2. seismische Langsamschicht f
~ agents Verwitterungskräfte fpl
~-back Seitenverwitterung f (der Talhänge)
~ correction Langsamschichtkorrektur f (Seismik)
~ crust Verwitterungskruste f, Verwitterungsrinde f
~ layer verwitternde Schicht f, Verwitterungsschicht f
~ of rocks Gesteinsverwitterung f
~ process Verwitterungsvorgang m, Verwitterungsprozeß m
~ residues Verwitterungsrückstände mpl
~ to clay Vertonung f
~ to loam Verlehmung f
weberite Weberit m, $Na_2Mg[AlF_7]$
Weber's cavity Weberscher Hohlraum m
~ wave Webersche Welle f
websterite Websterit m (Pyroxenit)
weddellite Weddellit m, $Ca[C_2O_4]\cdot 2H_2O$
wedge asunder/to s. ~ out
~ off abspalten
~ out sich verdrücken, auskeilen
wedge 1. Keil m; 2. Schuppe f (tektonisch)
~ block Keilscholle f
~ edge Ende n einer Schicht in seitlicher Richtung
~ effect Sprengwirkung f (z.B. durch Frost)
~-shaped keilförmig
~-shaped cross-bedding keilförmige Schrägschichtung f
wedgelike keilförmig
wedgework Sprengwirkung f (z.B. durch Frost)
~ of salts Salzsprengung f
wedging-out Auskeilen n
weed (sl) taubes Gestein n
~ killer s. herbicide
weeksite Weeksit m, $K_2[(UO_2)_2|(Si_2O_5)_3]\cdot 4H_2O$
weep drain Sickerdrainage f
~ hole s. weeper
weeper Vorbohrung f zur Entwässerung des Gesteins (vom Stollen aus)
weeping Einsickerung f
~ core [erdöl]ausschwitzender Bohrkern m
~ rock poröses Gestein n mit Wasseraustritten
wegscheiderite Wegscheiderit m, $Na_2CO_3\cdot 3NaHCO_3$
wehrlite 1. Wehrlit m, BiTe; 2. Wehrlit m (Peridotit)

weibullite Weibullit m, $PbS \cdot Bi_2Se_3$
weighboard Lettenkluft f, Besteg m, Lettenbesteg m
weighing board s. weighboard
weight 1. Gewicht n; 2. Setzen n des Gebirges
~ **drop** Gewichtsschlag m, Fallgewicht n
~ **indicator** Bohrdruckmesser m, Gewichtskontrollmesser m *(Bohrtechnik)*
~ **on bit** Bohrdruck m
weighted array Aufstellung f mit Richtungswirkung *(für die Geophone oder Schüsse)*
~ **mud** beschwerte Spülung f
weighting material Beschwerungsmittel n
weightless schwerelos
weightlessness Schwerelosigkeit f
weilite Weilit m, $CaH[AsO_4]$
weinschenkite Weinschenkit m, $(Y, Er)[PO_4] \cdot 2H_2O$
weir Damm m, Fangbuhne f, Wehr n, Stauanlage f, Überfall m
~ **plant** Wehranlage f
weiselbergite Weiselbergit m *(Augitporphyrit)*
weissite Weissit m, Cu_2Te
weisstein Weißstein m, Granulit m
welded zusammengebacken
~ **dike** aplitisch-pegmatitische Gangschlieren mit unscharfen Salbändern
~ **pumice (tuff)** Schmelztuff m, Gluttuff m, Ignimbrit m
well out/to ausfließen, ausströmen *(von Lava)*
~ **up** emporquellen, aufwallen
well 1. Brunnen m, Brunnenbohrung f; 2. Schacht m, Brunnenschacht m; 3. Bohrloch n; Sonde f
~ **axis** Bohrlochachse f
~ **bore** s. well 1.; 3.
~ **bore damage** Bohrlochschädigung f
~ **bore fill-up** Bohrlochauffüllung f
~ **bore storage** Bohrlochspeicherung f
~-**boring plant** Brunnenbohranlage f
~ **cavity** Bohrlochauskesselung f
~ **cementing** Bohrlochzementation f
~ **collecting area** Brunneneinzugsgebiet n
~ **completion** Komplettierung f einer Bohrung, Bohrlochvorbereitung f
~ **construction** Brunnenbau m
~ **control equipment** Sicherheitseinrichtungen fpl am Bohrlochmund
~ **coordinates** Bohrlochkoordinaten fpl
~ **cuttings** Bohrklein n
~ **depth** Bohrlochlänge f
~ **depth in plumb line** Bohrlochteufe f
~ **diameter** Bohrlochdurchmesser m
~-**digger** Brunnengräber m
~ **dip** Bohrlochabweichung f
~ **discharge** Brunnenergiebigkeit f
~-**drill blasting** Tiefbohrlochschießen n
~-**drill hole** Tiefbohrloch n
~ **drilling tools** Brunnenbohrwerkzeuge npl
~ **effluent** Lagerstätteninhalt m *(im Sondenbereich)*

~ **face** Bohrlochsohle f
~ **file** Bohrarchiv n
~ **filter** 1. Brunnenfilter n; 2. Filterrohr n
~ **fire** Sondenbrand m
~ **flowing under back pressure control** gedrosselt fließende Sonde f
~ **for adding water** Anreicherungsbrunnen m
~ **foundation** Brunnengründung f
~ **function** Brunnenfunktion f *(mathematische Fassung von Ergiebigkeit und Fassungsvermögen)*
~ **geochemistry** Bohrlochgeochemie f
~ **gone to water** verwässerte Sonde f
~ **head** Bohrlochkopf m, Mündung f einer Sonde
~-**head assembly** Bohrlochkopfausrüstung f
~ **head pressure** Kopfdruck m
~ **interference** gegenseitige Beeinflussung f von Sonden
~ **life** Lebensdauer f einer Sonde
~ **location** Bohr[ansatz]punkt m
~ **log** 1. Bohrprofil n; 2. Brunnentest m
~ **logging** Bohrlochmessung f, geophysikalisches Bohrlochmeßverfahren n, Bohrlochgeophysik f
~ **loss** Brunenverlust m *(Wassermenge)*
~ **lowering** Brunnenabsenkung f
~ **mouth** Bohrlochmund m
~ **of natural gas** Erdgasquelle f
~ **on the beam** Pumpensonde f
~ **orifice** Brunnenmundloch n
~ **perforating** Perforierung f einer Bohrung
~ **point installation** Grundwasser[ab]senkungsanlage f mit Filterbrunnen
~ **producing by flow** selbstfließende (frei ausfließende) Bohrung f
~ **production** Förderrate f, Ergiebigkeit f der Bohrung; Brunnenergiebigkeit f
~ **productivity** Bohrungsproduktivität f
~ **radius** Brunnenradius m
~ **shaft** Brunnenschacht m
~ **shooting** Bohrlochtorpedierung f
~-**sinker** Brunnengräber m
~ **site** Bohrstelle f
~ **spacing** Bohrlochabstand m
~ **stimulation** Bohrlochstimulierung f, Bohrungsintensivierung f
~ **support** Brunnenausbau m
~ **system** s. ~ point installation
~ **test** Bohrlochtest m, Sondentest m
~ **ties** Korrelation seismischer mit geologischen Daten im Bohrprofil
~ **treatment** Bohrlochbehandlung f
~ **water** Brunnenwasser n
~ **whistle** Brunnenpfeife f *(Meßgerät für den Grundwasserstand)*
~ **yield** Ertrag m einer Sonde
welling-out of lava Ausfließen n von Lava
wellsite Wellsit m *((K, Ca)-reicher Harmotom)*
welt Wulst m, Schwelle f
Wendian Wendium n, Vendium n *(oberster Teil des Kryptozoikums)*

wenkite 382

wenkite Wenkit m, $(Ba, K)_{4,5}(Ca, Na)_{4,5}[(OH)_4(SO_4)_2|Al_9Si_{12}O_{48}]$
Wenlockian [Epoch, Series] Wenlock[ien] n, Wenlockium n (mittleres Silur)
Wenner electrode array Wennersche Elektrodenanordnung f
wenzelite Wenzelit m, Huréaulith m, $(Mn, Fe)_5H_2[PO_4]_4 \cdot 4H_2O$
Wernerian Wernerianer m (Anhänger der Werner-Schule); Neptunist m
wernerite Skapolith m, Wernerit m (s.a. scapolite)
wester/to untergehen
westerlies westliche Winde mpl
westgrenite Westgrenit m, $(Bi, Ca)(Ta, Nb)_2O_6OH$
Westphalian [Stage] Westfal[ien] n, Westfalium n (Stufe des Oberkarbons in Mittel- und Westeuropa)
wet cleaning Naßaufbereitung f, Naßsortierung f
~ **crushing** Naßzerkleinerung f, Naßmahlen n
~ **day** Regentag m
~ **dressing of ores** Naßaufbereitung f von Erzen
~ **firn** nasser Altschnee m
~ **fog** feuchter Nebel m
~ **grinding** Naßmahlen n, Naßschliff m
~ **natural gas** feuchtes Erdgas n, Naßgas n
~ **oil** Naßöl n
~ **process** naßmechanisches Verfahren n
~ **sand** Schwimmsand m
~ **screening** Naßsiebung f
~ **sump** feuchter Ölsumpf m
~ **tropics** [immer] feuchte Tropen pl
~ **washer** Naßreiniger m
~ **washing** Naßreinigung f
~-**weather rill** Regenrille f
~ **year** nasses Jahr n
wettability Benetzbarkeit f
wettable benetzbar
wetting Befeuchten n, Anfeuchten n (einer Gesteinsprobe)
~ **agent** Netzmittel n
~ **front** Benetzungsfront f
~ **property** Benetzungseigenschaft f
~ **water** Haftwasser n
whaleback Drum[lin] m
wharf Landungsbrücke f, Kai m
wheal Grube f, Zeche f (in Cornwall)
wheel ore Rädelerz n, Antimonkupferglanz m (s.a. bournonite)
Wheelerian [Stage] Wheelerien n (marine Stufe, tieferes Pleistozän in Nordamerika)
wheelerite Wheelerit m (fossiles Harz)
wherryite Wherryit m (Varietät von Caledonit)
whet slate Wetzschiefer m
whetstone Wetzstein m
whewellite Whewellit m, $Ca[C_2O_4] \cdot H_2O$
whimstone s. whinstone
whin s. ~-rock
~ **dike** Eruptivgesteinsgang m, Basaltgang m (Schottland)

~ **float** basischer Magmatit m (im Kohlenflöz auftretend)
~ **gaw** schmaler Gang m
~-**rock** 1. Basalt[tuff] m, Dolerit m; 2. sehr hartes Gestein
whinny basaltartig
whinsill basischer Lagergang m
whinstone 1. Handelsbezeichnung für unverwitterte basische Effusivgesteine; 2. s. whinrock
whipstock Ablenkkeil m (bei Bohrungen)
whirl Wirbel m
~-**balls** Wirbelbälle mpl
~ **disturbance** Wirbelstörung f
~-**wind of dust** Staubwirbel m
~ **zone** Aufwirbelungszone f
whirling pillar of dust Staubsäule f
whirlpool Wirbel m, Wasserstrudel m, Strudel[kessel] m
whirlwind Wirbelwind m, Windhose f
whisker Whisker m, Haarkristall m
whistling meteor pfeifender Meteor m
white agate s. chalcedony
~ **alkali** Salzausblühung f auf Alkaliböden
~ **antimony** Weißspießglanzerz n, Weißspießglanz m (s.a. valentinite)
~ **arsenic** s. arsenolite
~ **bole** weißer Bolus m, weiße Boluserde f
~-**burning clay** weißbrennender Ton m
~ **chalk** weiße Kreide f, weißer Kreidekalk m
~ **coal** Wasserkraft f
~ **cobalt** s. cobaltite
~ **copperas** s. goslarite
~ **damp** CO_2-Wetter pl (in Kohlengruben)
~ **feldspar** s. albite
~ **garnet** s. leucite
~ **iron pyrite** s. marcasite
~ **lead ore** s. cerussite
~ **mundic** s. arsenopyrite
~ **nickel** s. chloanthite
~ **noise** weißes Rauschen n
~ **noise level** Störpegel m des weißen Rauschens
~ **paste** weißer, schiefriger Kohlensandstein m
~ **products** Raffinerieprodukte npl, weiße Produkte npl
~ **sapphire** weißer Korund m
~ **smoker** „Whitesmoker" m, „weißer Räucherer" m (Kamin im Meeresboden)
~ **stone** Granulit m, Weißstein m
~ **tellurium** s. sylvanite
~ **vitriol** s. goslarite
~ **ware clay** Steingutton m
whitecap Gischt m, weiße Schaumkrone f
whiting 1. Wassertrübung durch feinverteilten Aragonit; Karbonatwolke in Oberflächenwässern; 2. Schlämmkreide f
whitlockite Whitlockit m, β-$Ca_3[PO_4]_2$
Whitneyan [Stage] Whitneyan n (Wirbeltierstufe, Oligozän in Nordamerika)
whitneyite Whitneyit m, (Cu, As)

whole coal unverritztes Kohlenfeld *n*
~ **rock** Gesamtgestein *n*, Gesamtgesteinsprobe *f*
whorl Umgang *m (bei Fossilgehäusen)*
~ **of spire** spiraliger Umgang *m (bei Fossilgehäusen)*
~ **thickness** Windungsbreite *f (Molluskenschalen)*
whumstone *s.* whinstone
wich Solquelle *f*, Salzquelle *f (keltisch)*
wide angle reflection Weitwinkelreflexion *f*
~-**aperture CDP [stack]** Weitwinkelstapelung *f*
~-**band stack** Breitbandstapelung *f (Seismik)*
~-**bottomed valley** breitsohliges Tal *n*
~-**spaced** in weiten Abständen
widening of a lode Ausbauchung *f* eines Ganges
~ **of the hole** Erweitern *n* des Bohrlochs
~ **of valley** Talerweiterung *f*
Widmannstätten figures Widmannstättensche Figuren *fpl*
width 1. Breite *f*; 2. wahre Gangmächtigkeit *f*
~ **of cut** Feld[es]breite *f*
~ **of outcrop** Ausstrichbreite *f*
~ **of overfall** Überfallbreite *f*
~ **of the channel** Breite *f* der Fahrrinne
wiggle stick Wünschelrute *f*
~ **trace** Linienschriftspur *f (Seismik)*
wightmanite Wightmanit *m*, $Mg_9[(OH)_6|BO_3]\cdot 2H_2O$
wild coal dünne Kohlenflözchen *npl* mit viel Zwischenmitteln
~ **flowing** Erdölausbruch *m*
~ **goose** Gangspur *f (Seismik)*
~ **well** nicht kontrollierbarer Ölspringer *m*, wild eruptierende Sonde *f*
wildcat *(Am)* Aufschlußbohrung *f*, Pilotbohrung *f*, Suchbohrung *f*, Erkundungsbohrung *f (im unbekannten Bereich)*
~ **drilling** Niederbringen *n* von Aufschlußbohrungen
~ **flowing** Erdölausbruch *m*
~ **well** *s.* wildcat
wildcatting Bohren *n* im unbekannten Gebiet
~ **campaign** Suchbohrprogramm *n (mit oder ohne geologische Vorarbeiten)*
wilderness unberührtes Gebiet *n*; Naturschutzgebiet *n*, Landschaftsschutzgebiet *n*
wilkeite Wilkeit *m*, $Ca_5[(F,O)|PO_4SiO_4,SO_4)_3]$
willemite Willemit *m*, $Zn_2[SiO_4]$
wimble scoop Schappenbohrer *m*
wind about/to mäandern
wind Wind *m*
~ **abrasion** Windschliff *m*, Deflation *f*
~ **assortment** Windsichtung *f*
~ **at high altitudes** Höhenwind *m*
~-**blown** windbewegt, äolisch
~-**blown sand** Flugsand *m*, Treibsand *m*
~-**borne** windbewegt, äolisch beansprucht
~-**borne sand** Flugsand *m*, Treibsand *m*
~-**borne sediment** äolisches Sediment *n*, Windsediment *n*

~-**borne soil** Windabsatzboden *m*, windtransportierter Boden *m*
~ **burble** Luftwirbel *m*
~-**carried** windverfrachtet
~-**carved** äolisch erodiert
~-**carved pebble** Windkanter *m*, Dreikanter *m*
~ **carving** *s.* ~ corrasion
~-**channelled surface** windgefurchte Oberfläche *f*
~ **corrasion** Windkorrasion *f*, Windschliff *m*, äolische Erosion *f*
~ **current ripples** Windrippeln *fpl*
~-**cut pebble** Windkanter *m*, Dreikanter *m*
~ **denivellation** Wasserspiegelschwankung *f* durch Winddrift
~ **deposit** äolische Ablagerung *f*
~-**deposited** äolisch abgelagert
~-**deposited sediment** äolisches Sediment *n*
~ **direction** Windrichtung *f*
~ **drift** Windabdrift *f*
~-**drifted** windbewegt
~-**driven sand** Flugsand *m*, Treibsand *m*
~-**eroded** windzerfressen
~ **erosion** Winderosion *f*, Windschliff *m*
~ **force** Windstärke *f*
~ **forest strip** Windschutzstreifen *m*
~-**formed rocks** äolische Gesteine *npl*
~ **gap** trockenes Durchbruchstal *n*
~ **gauge** Windmesser *m*
~-**grooved surface** windgefurchte Oberfläche *f*
~-**laid** windverfrachtet
~-**laid deposit** äolische Ablagerung *f*, Windablagerung *f*
~-**made ripples** Windrippeln *fpl*
~-**measuring device** Windmeßvorrichtung *f*
~-**polished** windgeglättet
~-**polished rock** Windschliff *m (Ergebnis)*
~-**polishing** Windschliff *m (Tätigkeit)*
~ **pressure** Winddruck *m*
~-**ripple marks** Windrippelmarken *fpl*
~-**rippled sand** windgefurchter Sand *m*
~ **ripples** Windrippeln *fpl*, Sandrippeln *fpl*
~ **rose** Windrose *f*
~ **scour** Windauskolkung *f*
~-**shadow drift** Windschattensand *m*
~-**shaped pebble** Windkanter *m*, Dreikanter *m*
~-**slab avalanche** Schneebrettlawine *f*
~ **speed** Windgeschwindigkeit *f*
~ **strength** Windstärke *f*
~ **transport** Windtransport *m*
~-**transported** windverfrachtet
~ **vane** Windfahne *f*
~ **velocity** Windgeschwindigkeit *f*
~-**worn** winderodiert
~-**worn pebble** Windkanter *m*, Dreikanter *m*
windfacetted pebble[s] Kantengeröll *n*, Facettengeschiebe *n*
windfall profit Gewinn *m* aus unverhofft fündigen oder reichen Aufschlüssen
winding Windung *f*
windkanter Windkanter *m*; Dreikanter *m*

window

window tektonisches Fenster n
~ frost Eisblumen fpl
windrow ridges Windreihenkämme mpl
wind's eye Windrichtung f
windward dem Winde ausgesetzt
~ bank windseitiges Ufer n
~ eddy Luvwirbel m
~ side Wetterseite f, Luv f, Windseite f
~ slope windseitiger Abhang m
winebergite Winebergit m, $Al_4[(OH)_{10}|SO_4] \cdot 7H_2O$
wing Schenkel m einer Antiklinale
~ auger Flügelbohrer m
~ venation Flügeladerung f
winged headland Vorgebirge n mit zwei Nehrungsspitzen
winning Aufschließung f, Aufschluß m
~ of the seam Abbau m des Flözes
winnow/to worfeln, sortieren, sichten
winnowed gold durch Windsichtung gewonnenes Goldkonzentrat n
~ sediment ausgesondertes Sediment n
winnowing Windsortierung f (bei Sedimenten)
winter/to überwintern
winter clay Ton-Winterlage f (von Warven)
~ flood Winterhochwasser n
~ monsoon Wintermonsun m
~ solstice Wintersolstitium n, Wintersonnenwende f
~ thunderstorm Wintergewitter n
~ water level Winterwasserstand m
wintry temperature winterliche Temperatur f
winze Gesenk n, Blindschacht m
wire 1. Draht m, Kabel n; 2. Förderseil n (für die Seilbahnförderung)
~-line core barrel Seilkernrohr n
~-line coring Seilkernen n
~-line grab Seilfangspeer m
~-line log Kabelsonde f
~-line logging tool [geophysikalisches] Bohrlochmeßgerät n
~-line spiral fishing tool Seilfangspirale f
~ silver Drahtsilber n, Haarsilber n
~ sounding Drahtlotung f
~-weight gauge Fallot n (Grundwasserspiegelmessung)
wisaksonite Wisaksonit m (metamikter Uranothorit)
Wisconsin [Ice Age] Wisconsin-Eiszeit f (entspricht der Würmeiszeit)
wiserite Wiserit m, $Mn_4[(OH,Cl)_4|B_2O_5]$
withdraw/to rauben (Ausbau)
withdrawal Förderung f (nichteruptiv)
wither away/to versiegen
witherite Witherit m, $BaCO_3$
wittichenite Wittichenit m, $3Cu_2S \cdot Bi_2S_3$
wittite Wittit m, $5PbS \cdot 3Bi_2(S,Se)_3$
wodginite Wodginit m, $(Ta, Nb, Sn, Mn, Fe)_2O_4$
wöhlerite Wöhlerit m, $Ca_2NaZr[(F, OH, O)_2|Si_2O_7]$
wolchonskoite Wolchonskoit m (Mineral der Montmorillonitreihe)

wolfachite Wolfachit m, Ni(As, Sb)S
Wolfcamp Wolfcampanien n (Stufe des Perms in Amerika)
wolfram Wolfram n, W
wolframite Wolframit m, $(Fe, Mn)WO_4$
wollastonite Wollastonit m, $Ca_3[Si_3O_9]$
wollongongite Wollongongit m, Bituminit m (Bogheadkohle)
wölsendorfite Wölsendorfit m, $2[UO_2(OH)_2] \cdot PbO$
Wolstonian Wolstonien n (Pleistozän, Britische Inseln, entspricht etwa der Riß-Eiszeit der Alpen)
wood agate Holzachat m
~ haematite roter Glaskopf m (s.a. haematite)
~ opal Holzopal m (s.a. opal)
~ peat Bruchwaldtorf m, Holztorf m
~ tin Holzzinn n
wooded bewaldet
~ soil Waldboden m
~ steppe Waldsteppe f
~ swamp Waldmoor n
woodhouseite Woodhouseit m, $CaAl_3[(OH)_6|SO_4PO_4]$
woodland Waldgelände n, Waldung f
woodsteppe chernozem Waldsteppentschernosem m
woodstone verkieseltes Holz n
woody holzig, Holz...
~ peat Waldmoorboden m
woodyard interglazialer Waldhorizont m
woolly rhinoceros wollhaariges Nashorn n
woolpack (sl) konkretionäre Kalksteinmasse f (s.a. ballstone)
woolsack Wollsack m (Absonderungsform)
Wordian [Stage] Word n (Stufe des Mittelperms)
work/to abbauen
~ away abtragen
~ by coffins abstrossen
~ through durchörtern
work barge Arbeitsbarke f
~ of deformation Formänderungsarbeit f
~ of erosion Erosionstätigkeit f
~-over Aufwältigung f
~-over operations Aufwältigungsarbeiten fpl
~ sampling Stichprobenahme f
workability 1. Verarbeitbarkeit f, Bearbeitbarkeit f; 2. Abbaufähigkeit f, Bauwürdigkeit f, Abbauwürdigkeit f
workable 1. verarbeitbar, bearbeitbar; 2. abbaufähig, [ab]bauwürdig
~ bed [ab]bauwürdige Schicht f
~ deposit nutzbare Lagerstätte f, [ab]bauwürdiges Vorkommen n
~ ore [ab]bauwürdiges Erz n
~ ore field [ab]bauwürdiges Erzvorkommen n
worked area Verhiebsfläche f
~-out abgebaut, erschöpft
~-out mine erschöpfte Zeche f
~-out seam erschöpftes Flöz n
working Abbau[betrieb] m

~ **deposit** in Abbau befindliche Lagerstätte *f*
~ **face** Abbaustoß *m*, Ortsstoß *m*
~ **level** Abbausohle *f*
~-**out of deposits** Erschöpfung *f* von Lagerstätten
~ **thickness of a seam** Arbeitshöhe *f* im Flöz
world climate program Weltklimaprogramm *n*
~ **quake** Weltbeben *n*
worm auger Schneckenbohrer *m*
~ **castings (excrements)** Wurmausscheidungen *fpl*
~-**shaped** wurmartig *(Mineral)*
worn abgetragen
~-**down** eingeebnet
worthiness of being worked Bauwürdigkeit *f*, Abbauwürdigkeit *f*
worthless vein tauber Gang *m*
worthy of being worked [ab]bauwürdig
wough Nebengestein *n* eines Erzganges *(Schottland)*
wreath of smoke Rauchfahne *f (Vulkanismus)*
wrench off/to abreißen *(Gletscher)*
wrench fault Transversalverschiebung *f*, Blattverschiebung *f*
~ **faulting** Seitenverschiebung *f (z.B. ozeanischer Rücken durch Zerscherung)*
wrinkle Kräuselung *f (s.a.* crenulation 1.)
~ **layer** Runzelschicht *f (Cephalopoden)*
~ **mark** Runzelmarke *f*
~ **ridges** Magmawülste *mpl*, Rippen *fpl (auf dem Mond)*
wrist *s.* carpus
wrong facies complex Scheinfazieskomplex *m*
wulfenite Wulfenit *m*, Gelbbleierz *n*, Pb[MoO$_4$]
Wulff net Wulffsches Netz *n*
Würm [Drift] Würm-Eiszeit *f*, Würm-Kaltzeit *f (Pleistozän, Alpen)*
Würmian [Interstadial] Würm-Interstadial *n (Pleistozän, Alpen)*
wurtzilite Wurtzilit *m (asphaltisches Pyrobitumen)*
wurtzite Wurtzit *m*, Schalenblende *f*, ZnS
wych *s.* wich
wyomingite Wyomingit *m (Ergußgestein)*
wythern Gang *m*

X

x-mas tree Eruptionskreuz *n*
X-ray analysis Röntgenanalyse *f*
X-ray crystal structure Röntgenstruktur *f*
X-ray diffraction analysis Röntgenbeugungsanalyse *f*
X-ray diffraction pattern Röntgenbeugungsdiagramm *n*
X-ray fluorescence spectrometry Röntgenfluoreszenzspektrometrie *f*
X-ray fluorescence spectroscopy Röntgenfluoreszenzspektroskopie *f*
X-ray interference pattern Röntgenbeugungsbild *n*

X-ray target Röntgenstrahlenbild *n*
X-ray texture analysis röntgenografische Gefügeanalyse *f*
X-ray texture goniometer Zählrohr-Texturgoniometer *n*
xanthiosite Xanthiosit *m*, Ni$_3$[AsO$_4$]$_2$
xanthite Xanthit *m (gelber Vesuvian)*
xanthochroite Xanthochroit *m*, CdS
xanthoconite Xanthokon *m*, Ag$_3$AsS$_3$
xanthophyllite Xanthophyllit *m*, Ca(Mg, Al)$_{3-2}$[(OH)$_2$|Al$_2$Si$_2$O$_{10}$]
xanthosiderite *s.* limonite
xenoblast Xenoblast *m*
xenoblastic xenoblastisch
xenocryst Xenocryst *m*, allothigener Kristall *m*, Einsprengling *m*
xenogenous epigenetisch
xenolite *s.* sillimanite
xenolith Xenolith *m*, exogener Einschluß *m*
xenomorphic xenomorph, allotriomorph
~ **crystal** xenomorpher Kristall *m*
xenotime Xenotim *m*, Ytterspat *m*, Y[PO$_4$]
xerophilous xerophil, Trockenheit liebend
xerophytic forest Trockenwald *m*
xonotlite Xonotlit *m*, Ca$_6$[(OH)$_2$|Si$_6$O$_{17}$]
XRF *s.* X-ray fluorescence spectrometry
xylanthrax Holzkohle *f*
xyloid brown coal xylitische Weichbraunkohle *f*
~ **lignite** vitrinitische Hartbraunkohle *f*; xylitische Braunkohle *f*
xylopal Holzopal *m (s.a.* opal)

Y

yardang, yarding Yardan *m (scharfkantiger Rücken zwischen zwei Deflationstälern)*
Yarmouth Yarmouth *n (Pleistozän in Nordamerika)*
Yarmouth [Interglacial Age] Yarmouth-Interglazial *n (entspricht dem Mindel-Riß-Interglazial)*
Yarmouthian *s.* Yarmouth
yavapaiite Yavapaiit *m*, KFe[SO$_4$]$_2$
yaw azimutale Drehung bzw. Abweichung eines Flugzeugs oder eines Fernerkundungsaufnahmesystems von der Flugrichtung
yawing Hin- und Herschwanken *n (einer Magnetnadel)*
Yazoo river Flußsystem *n* mit parallelen Nebenflüssen
11-year-cycle elfjähriger Zyklus *m (der Sonnenfleckentätigkeit)*
yearly discharge jährliche Abflußmenge *f*
~ **rainfall** Jahresregenmenge *f*, jährliche Niederschlagsmenge *f*
yeatmanite Yeatmanit *m*, Mn$_9$Zn$_2$Mg$_4$[O|(OH)$_{14}$|(AsO$_4$)$_2$|(SiO$_4$)$_2$]
yellow arsenic *s.* orpiment
~ **copper ore** *s.* chalcopyrite
~ **copperas** *s.* copiapite

yellow

~ **earth** Ocker *m*
~ **ground** verwitterter Kimberlit *m*
~ **lead ore** *s.* wulfenite
~ **ochre** Berggelb *n*
~ **ore (pyrite)** *s.* chalcopyrite
~ **ratebane** *s.* orpiment
yellowing Gelbwerden *n*, Verlehmung *f*
yenite *s.* ilvaite
yield Ausbeute *f*, Ergiebigkeit *f*, Ertrag *m*
~ **factor** Abflußspende *f*
~ **limit** Fließgrenze *f*
~ **of an aquiferous layer** Grundwasserergiebigkeit *f*
~ **of well** Brunnenergiebigkeit *f*
~ **point** Fließgrenze *f*, Streckgrenze *f*
~ **strength** Fließfestigkeit *f*
~ **stress** *s.* ~ point
~-**time diagram** Weg-Zeit-Diagramm *n (Gebirgsdruck)*
yielding nachgiebig
yieldingness Ausbeute *f*, Ergiebigkeit *f*
Ynezian [Stage] Ynez[ien] *n*, Ynezium *n (marine Stufe, Paläozän in Nordamerika)*
yo-yo-technique Yo-Yo-Verfahren *n (der Seeseismik)*
yoderite Yoderit *m*, (Al, Mg, Fe)$_2$[(O, OH)|SiO$_4$]
yoked basin *s.* zeugogeosyncline
Yoldia Sea Yoldiameer *n*
yosemite 1. Yosemit *m (Gestein der Granitgruppe)*; 2. Spezialform eines Trogtals
yoshimuraite Yoshimurait *m*, (Ba, Sr)$_2$(Mn, Fe, Mg)$_2$(Ti, Fe)[(OH, Cl)$_2$|(S, P, Si)O$_4$|Si$_2$O$_7$]
young stage Jugendstadium *n*
~ **volcanic rock** neovulkanisches Gestein *n*
Younger Tertiary [System] Jungtertiär *n*
younging of strata *s.* facing of strata
Young's modulus [of elasticity] Elastizitätsmodul *m*
youstone *s.* nephrite
youth[ful] stage Jugendstadium *n (bei Erosion)*
youthfully dissected jung zerschnitten
Ypresian [Stage] Ypern *n*, Ypres[ium] *n (Stufe des Eozäns)*
ytterbite *s.* gadolinite
yttria Yttererde *f*
yttrialite Yttrialith *m (Y-Th-Silikat)*
yttric, yttriferous ytterhaltig
yttrium Yttrium *n*, Y
yttrocerite Yttrocerit *m*, Cerfluorit *m*, (Ca, Ce)F$_2$
yttrocrasite Yttrokrasit *m*, YTi$_2$O$_5$OH
yttrofluorite Yttrofluorit *m*, (Ca$_3$, Y$_2$)F$_6$
yttrotantalite Yttrotantalit *m (Y-, Er-, U-, Ca-, Fe-Tantalat)*
yu *s.* nephrite
yugawaralite Yugawaralith *m*, Ca[Al$_2$Si$_5$O$_{14}$]·3H$_2$O
yuh *s.* nephrite
yukonite Yukonit *m*, (Ca$_3$Fe$_2$···)(AsO$_4$)$_2$·2Fe(OH)$_3$·5H$_2$O
yustone *s.* nephrite

Z

Zanclian [Stage] Zanclien *n (Stufe des Pliozäns)*
~/**Tabianian [Stages]** Zanclium/Tabianium *n (basale Stufen des Pliozäns)*
zaratite Zaratit *m*, Ni$_3$[(OH)$_4$|CO$_3$]·4H$_2$O
zavariskite Zavariskit *m*, BiOF
zawn Kaverne *f (Cornwall)*
Zemorrian [Stage] Zemorrien *n (marine Stufe, Oligozän und unterstes Miozän in Nordamerika)*
zenith Zenit *m*
~ **angle** Zenitwinkel *m*
~ **angle of the hole** Zenitwinkel *m* des Bohrlochs
zeolite Zeolith *m (Mineralgruppe locker gebauter Tektosilikate)*
~ **facies** Zeolithfazies *f*
zeolitic zeolithartig; zeolithhaltig
zeolitization Zeolithisierung *f*, Zeolithbildung *f*
zeophyllite Zeophyllith *m*, Ca$_4$[F$_2$|(OH)$_2$|Si$_3$O$_8$]·2H$_2$O
zero drawdown boundary Reichweitenbegrenzung *f*
~ **gauge** Nullpegel *m*
~ **meridian** Nullmeridian *m*
~ **of level** Normalnull *n*, NN
zeta potential Zetapotential *n (Grenzfläche)*
zeugen *s.* earth pillar
zeugogeosyncline Zeugogeosynklinale *f (Parageosynklinale)*
zeunerite Zeunerit *m*, Cu[UO$_2$|AsO$_4$]$_2$·10(16–10)H$_2$O
zigger/to absinken, versickern
zigher kleiner Wasserlauf *m*
zigzag fold Zickzackfalte *f*, Kaskadenfalte *f*
~ **pattern** Zickzackmuster *n*
zinc Zink *n*, Zn
~-**bearing** zinkführend, zinkhaltig
~ **blende** *s.* sphalerite
~ **bloom** *s.* hydrozincite
~ **chat** verwachsenes Zinkerz *n*
~-**containing** zinkführend, zinkhaltig
~ **spar** *s.* smithsonite
~ **spinel** *s.* gahnite
zincaluminite Zinkaluminit *m*, Zn$_3$Al$_3$[(OH)$_{13}$|SO$_4$]·2H$_2$O
zincdibraunite Zinkdibraunit *m*, ZnMn$_2$O$_3$·2H$_2$O
zinciferous zinkführend, zinkhaltig
zincite Zinkit *m*, Rotzinkerz, ZnO
zinckenite Zinckenit *m*, PbS·Sb$_2$S$_3$
zincky zinkartig, Zink…
zinclavendulane Zinklavendulan *m*, (Ca, Na)$_2$(Zn,Cu)$_5$[Cl|(AsO$_4$)·4–5H$_2$O
zincobotryogene Zincobotryogen *m*, (Zn, Mg, Mn, Fe)Fe[OH|(SO$_4$)$_2$]·6,6H$_2$O
zincocopiapite Zincocopiapit *m*, (Zn, Fe, Mn)Fe$_4$[OH|(SO$_4$)$_3$]$_2$·18H$_2$O
zincous zinkartig, Zink…

zincrockbridgeite Zinkrockbridgeit m, $ZnFe_4[(OH)_5|(PO_4)_3]$
zincy s. zincky
zinkenite s. zinckenite
zinkiferous zinkhaltig, zinkführend
zinkosite Zinkosit m, $Zn[SO_4]$
zinky zinkartig, Zink...
zinnwaldite Zinnwaldit m, $KLiFeAl[(F,OH)_2|AlSi_3O_{10}]$
zippeite Zippeit m, Uranblüte f, $[6UO_2|3(OH)_2|3SO_4]\cdot 12H_2O$
zircon ZIrkon m, $Zr[SiO_4]$
zirconium Zirkon n, Zirkonium n, Zr
zirkelite Zirkelit m, $(Ca,Ce,Y,Fe)(Ti,Zr,Th)_3O_7$
zirklerite Zirklerit m, $9FeCl_2\cdot 4AlOOH$
Zlichovian [Stage] Zlichov n, Zlichov-Stufe f *(Stufe des Unterdevons)*
zodiac Tierkreis m, Zodiakus m
~ **light** Tierkreislicht n, Zodiakallicht n
zodiacal figure Sternbildfigur f
~ **light** Tierkreislicht n, Zodiakallicht n
zoic zoisch, fossile Tierüberreste enthaltend
zoisite Zoisit m, $Ca_2Al_3[O|OH|SiO_4|Si_2O_7]$
zonal zonenförmig, Zonen...
~ **arrangement** zonenförmige (zonale) Anordnung f
~ **boundary** Zonengrenze f
~ **structure** zonales Gefüge f
zonality Zonalität f
zonated zonenförmig
zonation Verteilung f auf Zonen
zone Zone f *(kleinste Einheit der biostratigrafischen Skala)*
~ **axis** Zonenachse f
~ **circle** Zonenkreis m
~ **fossil** Zonenfossil n, Leitfossil n
~ **melting** Zonenschmelzverfahren n
~ **of affected overburden** Einwirkungsbereich m
~ **of alteration** Umwandlungszone f
~ **of capillarity** Saugsaum m, Kapillarzone f, Überwasserspiegelzone f, Grundluftzone f
~ **of concrescence** Verwachsungszone f
~ **of continuous subsidence** säkular sich senkender Raum m

~ **of folding** Faltungszone f
~ **of glacier ablation** Zehrgebiet n eines Gletschers
~ **of influence** Beeinflussungsbereich m
~ **of invasion of borehole fluid** Eindringzone f der Bohrlochspülung
~ **of jointing** Ruschelzone f, Kluftschwarm m
~ **of maximum development** Zone f der maximalen Entwicklung *(von Arten)*
~ **of oxidation** Oxydationszone f
~ **of permanent downwarp[ing]** säkular sich senkender Raum m
~ **of reduction** Zementationszone f
~ **of regular subsidence** Zone f gleichmäßiger Absenkung
~ **of sanitary protection** Schutzzone f
~ **of snow supply of the glacier** Nährgebiet n des Gletschers
~ **of stringers** Trümerzone f
~ **of subsidence** Senkungszone f
~ **of transition** Übergangszone f
~ **of weakness** Schwächezone f
~ **of weathering** Verwitterungszone f
~ **succession** Zonenfolge f
~ **time** Zonenzeit f, Ortszeit f
~ **type** Lithotyp m *(Kohlentyp der Steinkohle)*
~ **with clusters of joints** Ruschelzone f, Kluftschwarm m
zoned zonenverteilt
~ **crystal** Zonarkristall m
zoning Zonarstruktur f, Zonalität f, Zonung f
~ **of primary mineralization** primärer Teufenunterschied m *(bei Mineralgängen)*
zonule Teil m einer Subzone *(fossilbelegt)*
zoogenic, zoogenous zoogen
zoogeographic[al] zoogeografisch, tiergeografisch
~ **province** zoogeografische Provinz f
zoogeography Zoogeografie f, Tiergeografie f
zoölite, zoölith tierisches Fossil n, Tierversteinerung f
zooplankton Schwebefauna f, Zooplankton n
zunyite Zunyit m, $Al_{12}[AlO_4|(OH,F)_{18}Cl|Si_5O_{16}]$
zussmanite Zussmanit m, $KFe_{11}(Mg,Mn)_2[OH|(Si_{5.5}Al_{0.5})\cdot O_{14}(OH)_4]$
zwieselite Zwieselit m, $(Fe,Mn)_2[F|PO_4]$